CRITICAL
THEORY
SINCE
PLATO

CRITICAL THEORY
SINCE PLATO

THIRD EDITION

— Edited by —
Hazard Adams
University of Washington

and

Leroy Searle
University of Washington

THOMSON

WADSWORTH

Australia   Canada   Mexico   Singapore   Spain   United Kingdom   United States

THOMSON
WADSWORTH

Critical Theory Since Plato, Third Edition
Hazard Adams/Leroy Searle

Publisher: Michael Rosenberg
Development Editor: Mary Beth Walden
Editorial Production Manager: Michael Burggren
Executive Marketing Manager: Carrie Brandon
Associate Marketing Manager: Joe Piazza
Senior Print Buyer: Mary Beth Hennebury
Photo Manager: Sheri Blaney
Permissions Editor: Karyn Morrison

Compositor/Project Manager: Pre-Press Company, Inc.
Cover Designer: Dutton and Sherman Design
Printer: Malloy Lithographing, Inc.

Cover Image: Alberti, Leon Battista (1402–1472) © Erich Lessing/Art Resource, NY
Facade of Santa Maria Novella, architectural detail. 1458.
Location: S. Maria Novella, Florence, Italy

Printed in the United States of America.
1 2 3 4 5 6 08 07 06 05 04

For more information contact Thomson Wadsworth,
25 Thomson Place, Boston, Massachusetts 02210 USA,
or you can visit our Internet site at http://www.thomson.com

For permission to use material from this text or product,
submit a request online at http://www.thomsonrights.com

Any additional questions about permissions can be
submitted by email to thomsonrights@thomson.com

ISBN: 0-155-05504-6

Library of Congress Control Number: 2004101932

CONTENTS

Preface . . . . *xix*

GENERAL INTRODUCTION 1

PLATO 8
  Ion 10
  from Republic 16
  from Phaedrus 36
  from Sophist 38
  from Philebus 40
  from Cratylus 41

ARISTOTLE 48
  from Physics 49
  from Metaphysics 51
  Poetics 52
  from Rhetoric 69

MARCUS TULLIUS CICERO 74
  from Brutus 75

QUINTUS HORATIUS FLACCUS (HORACE) 78
  Art of Poetry 79

STRABO 86
  from Geography 87

PUBLIUS CORNELIUS TACITUS 90
  from Dialogue on Oratory 91

PSEUDO-LONGINUS 94
On the Sublime 95

PLUTARCH 119
from How The Young Man Should Study Poetry 120

FLAVIUS PHILOSTRATUS 124
from Lives of the Sophists 125

PLOTINUS 127
from Enneads 128

SAINT AUGUSTINE 140
from On Christian Doctrine 141

ANICUS MANLIUS SEVERINUS BOETHIUS 147
from The Consolation of Philosophy 148

SAINT THOMAS AQUINAS 149
from Summa Theologica 150

DANTE ALIGHIERI 153
from The Banquet 154
from Letter to Can Grande Della Scala 154

GIOVANNI BOCCACCIO 157
from Life of Dante 158
from Genealogy of the Gentile Gods 160

JULIUS CAESAR SCALIGER 168
from Poetics 169

LODOVICO CASTELVETRO 176
from The Poetics of Aristotle Translated and Explained . 177

SIR PHILIP SIDNEY 185
  An Apology for Poetry 186

GIORDANO BRUNO 207
  from Concerning the Cause, the Principle, and the One . 208

GIACOPO MAZZONI 215
  from On the Defense of the Comedy of Dante 216

TORQUATO TASSO 226
  from Discourses on the Heroic Poem 227

SIR FRANCIS BACON 234
  from The Advancement of Learning 235
  Preface to the Wisdom of the Ancients 236
  from The New Organon 238

PIERRE CORNEILLE 244
  Of the Three Unities of Action, Time, and Place 245

JOHN DRYDEN 253
  An Essay of Dramatic Poesy 254

JOHN LOCKE 281
  from An Essay Concerning Human Understanding 282

ALEXANDER POPE 297
  An Essay on Criticism 298

JOSEPH ADDISON 307
  On the Pleasures of the Imagination 308

GIAMBATTISTA VICO 313
  from The New Science 314

DAVID HUME 322
Of the Standard of Taste 323

EDMUND BURKE 332
from A Philosophical Inquiry Into the Origin of Our
Ideas of the Sublime and Beautiful 333

EDWARD YOUNG 347
from Conjectures on Original Composition 348

SAMUEL JOHNSON 357
Rambler, Number 4: On Fiction 358
from Rasselas 360
from Preface to Shakespeare 361

HENRY HOME, LORD KAMES 369
from Elements of Criticism: Introduction 370
Chapter XXV 372

GOTTHOLD EPHRAIM LESSING 378
from Laocoön 379

DENIS DIDEROT 383
from The Paradox of Acting 384

SIR JOSHUA REYNOLDS 393
from Discourses on Art 394

IMMANUEL KANT 416
from Critique of Judgment 419

MARY WOLLSTONECRAFT 441
from A Vindication of the Rights of Woman 442

WILLIAM BLAKE 447
   from The Marriage of Heaven and Hell 448
   from Letter to Thomas Butts 448
   from Annotations to Reynolds' *Discourses* 448
   from A Descriptive Catalogue 458
   from A Vision of the Last Judgment 458

FRIEDRICH SCHILLER 460
   from Letters on the Aesthetic Education of Man 461

FRIEDRICH SCHLEGEL 473
   from Critical Fragments (Lyceum Fragments) 474
   from Athenaeum Fragments 477
   from On Incomprehensibility 480

WILLIAM WORDSWORTH 481
   Preface to the Second Edition of Lyrical Ballads 482

SAMUEL TAYLOR COLERIDGE 493
   Shakespeare's Judgment Equal to His Genius 494
   from On the Principles of Genial Criticism 497
   from Biographia Literaria 501
   from Essays on the Principles of Method 508
   from The Statesman's Manual 519
   from On the Constitution of Church and State 519

WILHELM VON HUMBOLDT 523
   from Collected Works 524

JOHN KEATS 534
   from Letter to Benjamin Bailey 535
   from Letter to George and Thomas Keats 536
   from Letter to John Taylor 536
   from Letter to Richard Woodhouse 536

PERCY BYSSHE SHELLEY 537
   A Defense of Poetry 538

GEORG WILHELM FRIEDRICH HEGEL 552
   from The Philosophy of Fine Art 553
   from The Phenomenology of Mind 561

RALPH WALDO EMERSON 566
   from The American Scholar 567
   The Poet 570

EDGAR ALLAN POE 580
   from The Poetic Principle 581

MATTHEW ARNOLD 586
   The Function of Criticism at the Present Time 587
   from The Study of Poetry 599

CHARLES BAUDELAIRE 604
   from The Salon of 1859 604

KARL MARX and FRIEDRICH ENGELS 607
   Manifesto of the Communist Party 608
   from The German Ideology 614
   from A Contribution to the Critique of
      Political Economy 615

WALTER PATER 617
   from Studies in the History of the Renaissance 618

INTRODUCTION: THE MODERN ERA 621

HIPPOLYTE ADOLPHE TAINE 639
  from History of English Literature 640

CHARLES SANDERS PEIRCE 652
  On a New List of Categories (1868) 655
  from Lessons from the History of Philosophy 661
  The First Rule of Reason 666
  from Training in Reasoning 667
  from What Pragmatism Is (1905) 668

WALT WHITMAN 673
  from Democratic Vistas (1871) 674

FRIEDRICH NIETZSCHE 686
  from The Birth of Tragedy from the Spirit of Music 687
  Truth and Falsity in an Ultramoral Sense 692

ÉMILE ZOLA 698
  from The Experimental Novel 699

OSCAR WILDE 711
  The Decay of Lying 712

STÉPHANE MALLARMÉ 726
  The Evolution of Literature 727
  The Book: A Spiritual Instrument 729
  Mystery in Literature 731

GOTTLOB FREGE 734
  On Sense and Meaning 735

SIGMUND FREUD 746
   from Letter to Wilhelm Fleiss, October 15, 1897 747
   from Thirteenth Lecture: Archaic and Infantile
      Features in Dreams 748
   from Lecture Twenty-One: Development of the Libido
      and Sexual Organization 752

LEO TOLSTOY 757
   What Is Art? 758

EDMUND HUSSERL 770
   Investigation I: Expression and Meaning 773

FERDINAND de SAUSSURE 786
   from Course in General Linguistics 787

VIKTOR SHKLOVSKY 796
   Art as Technique 797

T. S. ELIOT 806
   Tradition and the Individual Talent 807

BERTRAND RUSSELL 811
   Descriptions 812

PAUL VALÉRY 818
   Leonardo and the Philosophers 819

LUDWIG WITTGENSTEIN 823
   from Tractatus Logio-Philosophicus 825
   from Philosophical Investigations 836

I. A. RICHARDS 856
   from Principles of Literary Criticism 857
   from Science and Poetry 860
   from Practical Criticism 863

BORIS EICHENBAUM 867
   The Theory of the "Formal Method" 868

VIRGINIA WOOLF 885
   A Room of One's Own 886

WILLIAM EMPSON 894
   from Seven Types of Ambiguity 895

MIKHAIL M. BAKHTIN 912
   from Epic and Novel: Toward a Methodology for
     the Study of the Novel 913

VALENTIN N. VOLOSINOV 926
   Verbal Interaction 926

ANTONIO GRAMSCI 936
   from Prison Notebooks 937

JOHN CROWE RANSOM 953
   Poetry: A Note in Ontology 954

R. P. BLACKMUR 964
   A Critic's Job of Work 965

RUDOLPH CARNAP 978
   The Elimination of Metaphysics Through Logical
     Analysis of Language 980

JACQUES LACAN 990
   The Mirror Stage as Formative of the Function
     of the I as Revealed in Psychoanalytic Experience . . . 991

WALTER BENJAMIN 995
   Theses on the Philosophy of History 996

WILLIAM CARLOS WILLIAMS 1001
   Against the Weather 1002

KENNETH BURKE 1011
   Literature as Equipment for Living 1012

ERNST CASSIRER 1016
   from An Essay on Man 1018

W. K. WIMSATT and MONROE C. BEARDSLEY . . . 1026
   The Intentional Fallacy 1027

CLEANTH BROOKS 1035
   The Heresy of Paraphrase 1036
   Irony as a Principle of Structure 1043

MARTIN HEIDEGGER 1051
   from Letter on Humanism 1053

R. S. CRANE 1071
   The Critical Monism of Cleanth Brooks 1072

M. H. ABRAMS 1087
   from Orientation of Critical Theories 1087

THEODOR W. ADORNO 1101
  Cultural Criticism and Society 1102
  from Negative Dialectics 1110

CLAUDE LÉVI-STRAUSS 1119
  The Structural Study of Myth 1120

ROMAN JAKOBSON 1132
  The Metaphoric and Metonymic Poles 1132

NORTHROP FRYE 1136
  from Anatomy of Criticism 1138

NOAM CHOMSKY 1166
  from A Review of B. F. Skinner's *Verbal Behavior* 1167

JEAN PAUL SARTRE 1175
  I. Marxism and Existentialism 1176

FRANTZ FANON 1187
  On National Culture 1187

JACQUES DERRIDA 1203
  Structure, Sign and Play in the Discourse of
    the Human Sciences 1206
  Meaning and Representation 1215
  from Of Grammatology 1220

HANS ROBERT JAUSS 1237
  from Literary History as a Challenge to Literary Theory   1238

ROLAND BARTHES 1255
  The Death of the Author 1256

MICHEL FOUCAULT 1259
 What Is an Author? 1260
 Truth and Power 1269

THOMAS S. KUHN 1280
 from Postscript—1969 1282

LOUIS ALTHUSSER 1297
 from Ideology and Ideological State Apparatuses 1298

PAUL de MAN 1309
 Criticism and Crisis 1310
 The Resistance to Theory 1317

CLIFFORD GEERTZ 1328
 Thick Description: Toward an Interpretive Theory
  of Culture 1329

MARY LOUISE PRATT 1343
 from Toward a Speech Act Theory of Literary
  Discourse 1344
 from Chapter Three: The Linguistics of Use 1349

RAYMOND WILLIAMS 1356
 from Marxism and Literature, Part III 1357

EDWARD W. SAID 1369
 from Orientalism 1370

ANNETTE KOLODNY 1384
 from Dancing Through the Minefield: Some
  Observations on the Theory, Practice, and Politics
  of a Feminist Literary Criticism 1385

STANLEY FISH 1395
   Is There a Text in This Class? 1396

PIERRE BOURDIEU 1403
   from Language and Symbolic Power 1404

JEAN FRANÇOIS LYOTARD 1417
   Answering the Question: What Is Postmodernism? 1418

BENEDICT ANDERSON 1424
   The Origins of National Consciousness 1424

JÜRGEN HABERMAS 1429
   Excursus on Leveling the Genre Distinction Between
   Philosophy and Literature 1430

GILLES DELEUZE and FÉLIX GUATTARI 1442
   1. Introduction: Rhizome 1443

RICHARD RORTY 1457
   The Contingency of Language 1458

EVE KOSOFSKY SEDGWICK 1469
   from Epistemology of the Closet 1470

STEPHEN J. GREENBLATT 1476
   Resonance and Wonder 1477

JUDITH BUTLER 1489
   Imitation and Gender Insubordination 1490

JOHN GUILLORY 1500
    from Literature after Theory 1500

GAYATRI CHAKRAVORTY SPIVAK 1509
    Teaching for the Times 1510

ERNESTO LACLAU 1525
    Subject of Politics, Politics of the Subject 1526

Index *1535*

Preface

Since the publication of the first edition in 1971, the field of critical theory has expanded dramatically, particularly after the 1960s. This edition, accordingly, has been reshaped throughout, not only to reflect recent work but also to provide a more substantial historical background for it. This third edition of *Critical Theory Since Plato* follows the basic plan of previous editions in offering a general introduction (plus a supplementary introduction to modern criticism—see page 621), with selections prefaced by headnotes and brief bibliographic information, all presented in chronological order. We have avoided the use of thematic or other rubrics that group texts by approach or subject, since each individual selection reflects substantive individual work, by older as well as more recent writers, that may connect with other authors and historical periods in multiple ways. The aim is to present in a single volume, of moderate size, materials for a course of resentative readings in the history of critical theory in Western culture, without privileging any particular scheme of associations.

The special problems of representing contemporary criticism since 1965 are already familiar to scholars, teachers, and students. The issue is not merely the sheer growth of the field itself, in the number of universities that now offer (and in many cases, require) courses in criticism and theory, together with a dramatic increase in professional publications on theoretical subjects in literary and cultural study. Even more important, we believe, are changes in the conception of the field that can be evaluated only by patient historical and philosophical reflection. Some of these problems we addressed in *Critical Theory Since 1965* (Tallahassee: Florida State University Press, 1986), but in this volume our approach has been more comprehensive.

As critical theory has become more diverse, it has also become increasingly divergent in the sense that the special problems of particular areas of study demand separate and extensive treatment that cannot reasonably be satisfied by a general and historical anthology such as this one. Fortunately, very good resources for more extended work on such areas are now readily available. What is required, we believe, is a selection of essential and substantive materials to facilitate a rethinking of the historical shape and trajectory of the expanded field as a whole. Thus, readers will find in this edition amplified resources to examine the rhetorical and pedagogical function of the literary in the ancient world, with sometimes surprising pertinence to contemporary studies of discursive practices, just as they will find throughout a greater diversity of philosophical selections, ancient and modern, and a broad representation of work addressing contemporary themes pertaining to the role of theory and the place of literature in collective cultural life.

In particular, we have been concerned in this edition to take full advantage of historical reflection as a way to put contemporary practices and concerns in an expansive framework. This pertains not only to the addition, for example, of selections from the dialogues of Plato that formerly were not seen as pertinent to the literary, but the representation of other philosophical perspectives from the last one or two centuries where, conversely, the problems usually associated exclusively with the literary have been found to be fundamental for all organized thinking. We have, in this spirit, included new selections by such philosophers and theorists as Charles Sanders Peirce, Edmund Husserl, Gottlob Frege, Bertrand Russell, Ludwig Wittgenstein, Rudolph Carnap, Valentin N. Volosinov, Jean Paul Sartre, Martin Heidegger, Frantz Fanon, Jacques Derrida, Edward W. Said, Gayatri Chakravorty Spivak, Judith Butler, and Ernesto Laclau, among others, that together make clear the shortsightedness of insular and exclusive reliance on only certain traditions of thinking on fundamental topics. Additional material extending the scope of this edition is available on-line at www.textchoice.com.

Two general observations concerning the selections in this anthology bear special mention. The first is that we have been guided in our editorial choices by the conviction that the intellectual problems of the literary, and more generally, the imaginative, are fundamental and not topical. The sense of crisis and controversy that has marked recent criticism is, in this light, partly the result of the discovery that many of our dominant philosophical presuppositions are vulnerable precisely because they have been unable to accommodate the vigorous and dynamic quality of imaginative thinking. The second is that imaginative thinking, so considered, remains one of the greatest practical resources upon which we can draw, as a continuing source of the ongoing discourse of justice that has been particularly prominent in contemporary critical theory.

Finally, we wish to thank our students and colleagues, especially the late Ernst Behler, Robert L. Montgomery, Henry Staten, Raimonda Modiano, Nicholas Halmi, and Gary Handwerk, whose generous conversations and suggestions have been most appreciated.

Hazard Adams
Leroy Searle

GENERAL INTRODUCTION

I

This third edition is a thorough revision of the second. Our choice of selections reflects an effort to represent the main themes in the history of literary criticism and theory in Western culture from Plato to the present and to recognize that this history forms an important part of the comparative history of ideas and cannot be more than partially separated from certain other disciplines. Thus some texts not directly concerned with literature have been included; in a few cases these texts imply hostility to literature. They are important because they helped to generate an apologetic and defensive reaction among critics and poets. An example in the twentieth century is the work of the logical positivists, of Rudolph Carnap and Bertrand Russell, and their relation, for example, to the critical writings of I. A. Richards and, in turn, his curious relation to the American New Critics. But more important is Plato himself; the ambivalence he exhibited toward poetry gave rise to numerous defenses over centuries, some actually citing Plato, even as attackers cited him in their own support. Indeed, much of the long history of the defense of poetry has been expressed in, and captured by, the terms set forth by its attackers, the first and foremost being Plato, whose search for justice in *Republic* led his Socrates to advocate the banishment of poets. The defense of poetry has long sought to overcome the Socratic attack, but too often within the language put in his mouth by Plato. The history of literary criticism and theory has always been intertwined with that of philosophy, sometimes vexing it, sometimes being vexed by it. Although our principal effort has been to reflect the main intellectual paths, we have sought to make an eclectic selection without succumbing to fashions that seem to us not a particularly important part of the history of literary thought. Further, we have tried to make sense of the developments that have given late-twentieth-century criticism the appearance of disorder.

It must be added for clarity's sake that this book's title is meant to refer to *literary* criticism and theory and what has influenced or paralleled it. We do not use the term "critical theory" specifically to designate the social thought of the Frankfurt School of critical theory founded in the 1930s, with which were associated such names as Max Horkheimer and Theodor W. Adorno, though these thinkers contribute to our history. It must be added, too, that we recognize that some late-twentieth-century theorists called in question the notion of literature itself, seeking to break down distinctions between modes of linguistic utterance tacitly accepted for centuries and explicitly argued for earlier in the century. In our view there is a literary art that criticism and theory traditionally addressed. Our concern is to study how that art has been and continues to be thought about, even when the immediate effect has been to call it into question.

We have found ourselves compelled to enlarge significantly not only the selections from Plato and Aristotle to reflect the variety of their views and influences but also the selection of other classical texts, in part to show the relation of rhetorical theory to poetics. Thus Cicero, Strabo, Tacitus, and Plutarch appear here for the first time, as do selections from Plato's *Phaedrus, Sophist,* and *Philebus* and Aristotle's *Metaphysics* and *Rhetoric.* These additions have in turn encouraged us to enlarge the selections from the Renaissance with the addition of Scaliger, as well as additional writings by Mazzoni and Bacon. A reading of these texts enriches significantly one's sense of the movement of literary thought and its considerable range; and it indicates that certain issues recur in different dress.

As in the two previous editions, we have chosen to print the selections roughly in chronological order, resisting organizing them by an allegedly dominant theme. There are many different ways to classify these texts, and to locate them by theme or example of school or movement would tend to make their arguments appear simpler, neater, and less multidimensional than they usually are. An argument can be made that the greatest critics resist classification anyway and even contain in their work irresolvable contradictions that in the end may be the most interesting things about them. In any case, we assume that teachers and students will select texts and make comparisons for themselves and not simply absorb imposed categories. We offer deliberately more than any sane course can or ought to cover. Any syllabus will have to be selective. As a result of our view, discussion of themes, traditions, and fundamental concepts are here restricted to the headnotes, footnotes, an introduction to the modern era, and what follows immediately and briefly below.

II

One way to consider the work of a critic is to note the words that carry most weight in that person's discourse, making sure to recognize that often words change their meanings radically over time and from one critic to another and even within a critic's own career. Indeed, one can often see that a critical quarrel is over who is to establish a word's definition and claim, so to speak, its ownership. One may be reminded here that Kenneth Burke wrote of a "stealing back and forth of symbols" that occurs in many disciplines and cultural situations. The history of Western criticism as we know it begins with such a quarrel—over the word "imitation" *(mimesis).* Plato used it in one sense, Aristotle in quite another, and Horace in still another. It can be said that each claimed the prestige of the word for his way of looking at literature.

Certainly the word was prestigious. It dominated, in one or another of its various senses, literary thought for over two thousand years. Even after that it had brief periods of revival. Its prestige waned when philosophical speculation turned, roughly in the seventeenth century, from ontological concerns, inquiry into the nature of Being, to epistemological ones, that is, inquiry into how we know.

Indeed, if we recognize the radical simplification inevitable in any such effort, we can divide the history of philosophy and of literary thought into four major phases of general emphasis. The first three phases have been the ontological, the epistemological, and the linguistic. The first and by far the longest phase, the ontological, addressing the nature of Being, can be seen at once in Plato's location of Being in the eternal ideas or forms. Aristotle's shifting of the location of Being and his redefinition of ideas also redefined imitation. It comes as no surprise that the ontological interest raised over and over the issue of the status of literary fictions. The question of Being dominated philosophy, and that of verisimilitude dominated literary thought through the Middle Ages and well into the Renaissance.

Then, however, the emphasis shifted to what had come to be regarded as a prior question. One began no longer with the problem of Being but instead that of knowing, the assumption being that it was necessarily the prior question. The classic expressions of the epistemological problem were those of René Descartes and John Locke in the seventeenth century. Descartes's rationalism began with an attempted deduction of the human subject's indubitable knowledge, arriving at what is known as the Cartesian *cogito:* "I think; therefore I am" seemed the fundamental ground. Descartes proceeded from this to deduce further knowledge. Locke's empiricism, following on the experimentalism of Francis Bacon, divided experience into secondary (subjective) qualities and primary (objective) qualities of experience, privileging all that was primary, that is, all that he regarded ascertainable as real through measurement. Knowledge became identical with the results of scientific method. The epistemological age threatened to separate the literary from reality in a new way, or rather reserved the real world for science and tended to drive literature into subjectivity and thence into a kind of solipsism. We place Walter Pater's conclusion to his *Studies in the History of the Renaissance,* notorious in its time, at the end of the first part of this book. It is there because it radically represents the movement into subjectivity generated ultimately by epistemology. A variety of movements had tacitly or explicitly, as in Pater's case, accepted poetic subjectivity, either to exploit it by identifying poetry with the expression of irrational, personal experience or feeling or to overcome it to some extent by at least a partial recapture of objectivity, either of taste (David Hume), of morality (Samuel Johnson), or, later, of experimental method itself (Émile Zola). At the same time, the epistemological phase focused much attention on the mind of the subject. But the mind was also beginning to be objectified and systematically studied, or at least so it began to be hoped. Poetry once again found itself embattled. The epistemological phase, nevertheless, greatly enlivened critical discourse, rescuing it from a vocabulary, grown up around the word *imitation,* that had fairly well exhausted itself. However, until literature could find a theory that would overcome its relegation to subjectivity, it would suffer denigration of its value. Even today it suffers from the popularity of the object-subject opposition.

The rise of aesthetics was, it turned out, one form of defense, particularly Immanuel Kant's effort to establish what he called "subjective universality" in aesthetic response to the beautiful and the sublime. But as is so often the case in philosophy as well as in literary theory, the problem was not so much solved as shelved in favor of a new and fresher one. As the ontological question had given way to the epistemological one, so the epistemological question gave way to the linguistic one. To ask about Being led eventually and perhaps inevitably to ask about how and what we can know. But other questions came to seem even prior to that: Can what we call knowing occur apart from language or other systems of symbols like mathematics? To what extent does language inform us? To what extent are we enclosed within it? For a very long time, with some important exceptions, philosophers considered language a way of expressing and communicating prior experiences and ideas, which it represented (copied, imitated) in words. But as the epistemological phase developed it seemed that the matter was much more complicated, that language, not merely perception, played a constitutive role in the way reality appeared to us. The idea of language as representing or imitating some prior entity now had to vie with the idea that language made these entities or at least established the limits within which these entities existed for us.

The querying of language had begun at least as early as Plato's *Cratylus,* but the great surge of interest occurred in the seventeenth and eighteenth centuries and has never died out, though it has taken a variety of forms that could produce a large and interesting anthology of its own. There were historical (including search for origins), philological, semantic, and semiotic interests, roughly in that historical order. Locke found it necessary in 1690 to devote a part of his *Essay Concerning Human Understanding* to the problem of language, though he clung for the most part to a traditionalist and rather naïve view. Giambattista Vico in *The New Science* (1725), ahead of his time, though in some ways a reactionary, proposed a way of considering language that related its source and fundamental nature to what he called a "poetic logic." The origin of language became a popular topic on which many, including Jean Jacques Rousseau, wrote; but eventually the approach died out as it began to appear that the origin of language was as mysterious as the origin of humanity. Indeed, the two things came to be considered a sort of twin birth (one might add myth to this family), man being characterized as a linguistic or symbol-making animal. Views of this sort, set forth by Wilhelm von Humboldt early in the nineteenth century, and carried into the twentieth by Ernst Cassirer, were echoed in various ideological contexts in the twentieth.

It has always been recognized, of course, that literature is composed of language. From the earliest times poets have been obsessed with language as a medium of their art. The elaborate development of the discipline of rhetoric in the ancient world attests to an interest in the ways language can be employed to specific effects. The Renaissance produced numerous treatises on linguistic devices, especially tropes and prosody. But the new linguistic phase saw language as fundamental to human nature, not just as a human tool. The more recent excursion into language theory known as semiotics or the theory of signs was, however, less interested in these anthropological matters than in analyzing language as if it had a life of its own or was itself a system. The source of this interest was mainly structuralist linguistics, grounded in the work of Ferdinand de Saussure, the terminology of which flooded later twentieth-century theory in America by way of Europe, where structuralist linguistics displayed a relation to Russian Formalist literary theory. In England and in America it met other forces that had emphasized language. I. A. Richards's semantically oriented views had led to his characterization of a poem as a "piece of language," and his student William Empson had studied poems as texts in which linguistic ambiguities abounded. T. S. Eliot had emphasized the objectivity of the poem as a linguistic artifact, although Eliot did not foresee the lengths to which later theorists would take his notions. Richards and Eliot strongly, and in quite different ways, influenced the American New Criticism, sponsored principally by John Crowe Ransom and carried out in theory and practice by such critics as Cleanth Brooks, R. P. Blackmur, Allen Tate, Robert Penn Warren, W. K. Wimsatt, and Monroe C. Beardsley. The New Critics, however, knew virtually nothing of Eastern European literary theory until the arrival and subsequent activity of René Wellek in the United States, and even his views took on their coloring. The terminology of the New Criticism remained derived from the English critics known to it, mainly Samuel Taylor Coleridge and, when it became more philosophical, Kant.

Until sometime in the mid-1960s the New Criticism's academic followers dominated literary study as it was professed in the United States and to some extent in England. The first major and most articulate response to the New Criticism was that by the Canadian critic Northrop Frye in his *Anatomy of Criticism* (1957), perhaps the most impressive single work of criticism in the century, certainly the wittiest, and a very ambitious effort to provide a general theory that would encompass systematically most past literary thought. Frye provided his own phasal history of both literature and criticism, absorbed the New Criticism into one phase, and offered a paradox that identified criticism with both art and science, suggesting that the venerable distinction between the two had to be rethought. Frye's work had some affinities with Structuralism, but without any of its terminology and with strong links to the tradition of English criticism. Mainly, however, it was grounded in Frye's vision of William Blake's notion of art.

Structuralism first came to America principally through Saussure's *Course in General Linguistics,* the writings of Roland Barthes, and Claude Lévi-Strauss's anthropology. It had a very short life in its pure form, for in 1966 at a conference at Johns Hopkins University the French philosopher Jacques Derrida delivered his now famous paper "Structure, Sign, and Play in the Discourse of the Human Sciences." Thus was born Deconstruction, a critique of the structuralist position as grounded in the work of Saussure and Lévi-Strauss. Derrida pointed out inconsistencies in Structuralism having to do with the notion of nature in Lévi-Strauss and origins or centers of meaning in Saussure. A new terminology flooded literary theory.

By this time, rather than the world containing language, language seemed to contain the world. The critic Edward W. Said, desiring to restore the primacy of what he called "worldliness" for a politically and morally active criticism, characterized both Structuralism and Deconstruction as presuming "wall-to-wall language." Barthes had carried the notion of linguistic structure into a variety of areas, so that aspects of the world—myth, sport, fashion, and so forth—seemed to copy the structure of language. It seemed that if there was anything left of imitation, its direction had been reversed. The world as we can know it copied the structure of language.

Structuralism dissolved substance into sets of pure relations. Rather than things, Structuralism was concerned with the relations among things. It was the relation of or, in structuralist terminology, the "difference" between things, that became real, not the things themselves. The model was Saussure's language seen as a system of differences, each linguistic unit definable in terms of its difference from all the other units in the system, not in terms of its relation to an object beyond it. Derrida pointed out that such systems had no center, grounding point, or first word, and that meaning never came to rest in any origin. The search for meaning was allegedly involved in an infinite regress, and interpretation as it had traditionally been understood and practiced was a philosophically impossible activity. Rigorously pursued, it produced irresolvable contradictions or *aporias*.

Deconstruction evolved, in spite of Derrida's deliberate resistance to calling it a method, a critical technique that threatened to dominate the American academy as had the New Criticism, though it was much less popular in Derrida's France. In contrast to the New Criticism, to which it later appeared to have some similarity, Deconstruction emerged not out of previous criticism but out of Derrida's discussions of philosophical texts. It is possible to consider Deconstruction the culmination in theory of the linguistic phase. Later movements, in spite of a continued interest in language, sought to free themselves from what came to be called the "prison house of language."

Reservations about the New Criticism, when it replaced the old philology, literary history, and Marxism then dominant in the academy, had been mainly political, accusing it either of political reaction or of isolation from life in a new form of aestheticism. This accusation was later made against Deconstruction, though, unlike many of the New Critics, Derrida himself could certainly not be identified as a political reactionary or conservative. Still, Deconstruction's emphasis on the final elusiveness of centers or grounds and its theory of difference was anathema to any explicitly ideological or materialistically grounded position. But Deconstruction was not the only linguistically based philosophical theory or, in the eyes of many, even the dominant one. Indeed, in English and American philosophy the continental tradition back to Hegel and through Phenomenology and Deconstruction was either ignored or denigrated. It was especially the work of Ludwig Wittgenstein that influenced philosophers who came to concentrate almost exclusively on the analysis of language. Wittgenstein's influence was quite different from that of Saussure and had its own special history, since Wittgenstein changed his views radically between his first book, *Tractatus Logico-Philosophicus* (1918), and *Philosophical Investigations* (1958). The latter work proved more interesting to literary critics because it moved beyond the antipoetical logical positivism of its predecessor.

III

Although we are now discussing matters to which we give more detailed attention in our introduction to the modern era (below, page 621), it is worthwhile here to complete the brief phasal history on which we embarked. It is fair to say that in the wake of Deconstruction and political events since the 1960s a new phase was reached that might be called the phase of political moralism or, if one objects to the term "moralism," the phase of political and cultural critique. As the twentieth century ended there was still in some quarters a Marxist-derived social criticism. There were the critiques of colonialism and racism. There was the feminist movement, which had taken a variety of turns, generated quarrels within itself, and was often now subsumed under the critique of what is called gender. All of these developments were grounded on a certain set of moral principles connected with theories of power and were activist in the desire to bring about social change. With respect to theories of power the work of Michel Foucault stood out as most influential.

It is an interesting and somewhat depressing fact that as the century moved along most criticism and almost all theoretical literary discourse came to be located in universities and written by people who were not themselves poets, novelists, or dramatists. This was in stark contrast to all earlier centuries, including the earliest part of the twentieth. This development had many causes and some results that changed the scene drastically. Only one of the latter we shall mention here. It was the tendency among many academics to spend less time discussing what at least used to be called "literary" texts and more time debating theories. In earlier ages poets like Dante, Sidney, and

Wordsworth wrote erudite defenses of their own poetic practices that were of general theoretical interest. Many of the earliest New Critics were poets or novelists who ended up teaching in universities. It should be no surprise that programs in creative writing began to flourish at this time, for the New Criticism was in some important respects oriented to a writerly perspective. Today's theorist, though inhabiting English or foreign language departments, may be more interested in, and read more, psychoanalytic or political writing and perhaps even publish more about philosophical or anthropological discourses than literature in the traditional sense. One might observe also that the phases we have discussed above have become progressively shorter. The period of the dominance of imitation was at least two thousand years long, of epistemology maybe three hundred, of linguistics two hundred at most. The huge increase of academic activity today eats up theory almost as fast as it is produced. This is all the more reason for attempting to view it in a historical perspective.

The late twentieth century was, to shift Said's phrase, an age of wall-to-wall theory in whatever it is that literary study became. In his essay "Mixed Genres" (1980) the anthropologist Clifford Geertz discussed this situation as ubiquitous in the "human sciences." The risks of superficiality and perhaps ideological dogmatism became greater, but there was also a new set of interests that stretched from discipline to discipline. It appeared, however, that a new defense of poetry and perhaps of literary criticism itself might have to be mounted in part to respond to the tendency of the phase of political moralism to treat literary texts almost exclusively as documents for social analysis. This came about in a lively though confusing ferment of sociopolitical actions and ideas virtually worldwide. It left literary study in apparent chaos and even from one point of view seemed to be a return to earlier historical interests. The present situation has impelled us to write a second introduction, specifically to the modern era. We hope it will help to make sense of and give some order to the period from about 1870 to the present by suggesting in part that these developments may open the way for interesting new configurations in literary thought.

Plato

---

c.427–c. 347 B.C.

Student of Socrates and founder of the Academy in Athens, Plato is regarded as the first major figure in the history of Western philosophy. Among writers whose works are extant he is the earliest to discuss poetry at any length. Further, he is, as author of dialogues, an accomplished literary figure; and here is a paradox, given the criticism of poets that he puts into the mouth of the fictionalized Socrates in *Republic.* The paradox may be extended, for in numerous places Socrates himself quotes the poets, professes his love for Homer, asserts that true poets are divinely inspired, and tells stories, to which he frequently has recourse when the dialectic stalls itself. Even further, Plato himself writes in a dramatic form, the same form that his Socrates criticizes as imitation. Indeed, it is impossible to imagine Plato if there had not been the poets who preceded him, for he owes so much to them in approach. There is, therefore, a deep irony in Socrates's dismissal of the poets from his ideal commonwealth.

It is Plato who bequeaths to the tradition of literary criticism the concept of imitation or *mimesis,* dominant in literary criticism well into the eighteenth century. Even after that, imitation had periods of revival. In *Republic,* imitation is given two meanings, a broadly philosophical one involving Plato's ontology and epistemology and one pertaining to literary technique, though the two are closely related. Plato has Socrates locate reality in what are called ideas or forms rather than in the world of appearances or phenomena experienced through the senses. He regards objects that we perceive as mere copies of their ideas. It is only our rational power exercised in dialectical search that can advance us toward truth. Nevertheless, Socrates declares in *Phaedrus* that there are various types of divine madness or possession, one of which is that of the true poet. On the other hand, it is difficult if not impossible to determine whether this madness is truly divinely inspired or demonic; and the poet and all artists are imitators, making copies of appearances, thus twice removed from reality. This removal is alleged also to be characteristic of the utterances of sophists and rhetoricians, who are more sinister than poets because they often deliberately delude and gain illicit power over their listeners. In *Republic,* Socrates speaks of acceptable and unacceptable stories and banishes the poets, except those who limit their compositions to hymns or praises of the state; but he allows for the possibility of their return if they can successfully defend themselves either in verse or in prose, thereby setting the stage and the terms for numerous defenses to come.

The second meaning of imitation is the technical one. Socrates speaks in *Republic* of pure imitative form (as in the drama), where the poet has others speak, pure narrative, where the poet speaks always in his own voice, and a mixture of the two (as in epic). In his view, imitation is the most deceptive of these because the author never speaks in his own voice. There is a huge irony here because in no dialogue does Plato ever speak for himself. In *Sophist,* the second form of imitation is described as of two types: icastic and phantastic, the former being imitation with the aim of making a likeness, the latter imitation of imagined things or the making of mere appearances.

Plato's, or at least the fictive Socrates's, view of critics (or the closest thing in Plato to them) appears in *Ion,* where Socrates converses with the successful though obtuse rhapsode Ion, a professional reciter of and commentator on epic poetry, specifically Homer. Socrates would demolish Ion's claim that as a rhapsode he is an expert on Homer's work by asking him whether he is an expert on everything or even anything mentioned in Homer's epics and driving him toward one final absurd claim. Socrates concludes that Ion's powers as a rhapsode must be irrationally inspired. For Socrates (at least in this dialogue), a poem is only the sum of its subject matter or content; he ignores its existence as something in itself, a formal structure. This emphasis and the argument in *Republic* give good reason to regard Plato as the founder of moralistic and didactic criticism, the separation of content from form, and the consequent privileging of the former.

Later Platonists maintained a similar theory of ideas, but many, including Plotinus (below, page 127), sought to defend poetry and fine art as an avenue to a grasp of intellectual beauty. Some found in Plato's own tendency to myth-making the establishment of a tradition of allegorical interpretation in which many works were read as arcane expressions of Platonic ideas. Even a criticism that regards poetry as antirational, as found in certain nineteenth-century critics, often claims support in Socrates's treatment of poetic madness in *Phaedrus.* Even when the critic is avowedly anti-Platonic, as for example John Crowe Ransom (below, page 953), or simply anti-poetic as in Stephen Gosson's *Schoole of Abuse,* which gave rise to a somewhat Platonic answer by Sir Philip Sidney (below, page 185), Plato's influence is present. More recently Plato's treatment of language in *Cratylus* and *Philebus* has caught the attention of poststructuralist theorists.

Among the numerous translations of Plato's works, a standard edition is that of Benjamin Jowett, *The Dialogues of Plato* (first edition, 1871, fourth edition, 1953, edited by others). The twelve-volume (1914–1930) Loeb Classical Library edition has Greek and English facing texts. A more recent collection of translations by many hands is *The Collected Dialogues of Plato,* edited by Edith Hamilton and Huntington Cairns (second printing with corrections, 1963). All standard histories of philosophy, aesthetics, and criticism devote substantial space to Plato. See J. W. H. Atkins, *Literary Criticism in Antiquity,* 2 vols. (1934); G. M. A. Grube, *Plato's Thought* (1935); Rupert C. Lodge, *Plato's Theory of Art* (1953); G. M. A. Grube, *The Greek and Roman Critics* (1965); Rosemary Harriott, *Poetry and Criticism Before Plato* (1969); Gregory Vlastos, ed., *Plato: A Collection of Critical Essays,* 2 vols. (1971); J. Moravczik and P. Temko, eds., *Plato on Beauty, Wisdom, and the Arts* (1982); Julius A. Elias, *Plato's Defense of Poetry* (1984); Gregory Vlastos, *Socrates, Ironist and Moral Philosopher* (1991); D. Thomas Benediktson, *Literature and the Visual Arts in Ancient Greece and Rome* (2000); Julia Annas and Christopher Rowe, eds., *New Perspectives on Plato, Modern and Ancient* (2002); Ruby Blondell, *The Play of Character in Plato's Dialogues* (2002); Gregory Nagy, *Plato's Rhapsody and Homer's Music: The Aesthetics of the Panhellenic Festival in Classical Athens* (2002).

Ion

PERSONS OF THE DIALOGUE:
Socrates, Ion

Socrates   Welcome, Ion. Are you from your native city of Ephesus?

Ion   No, Socrates; but from Epidaurus, where I attended the festival of Asclepius.[1]

Socrates   And do the Epidaurians have contests of rhapsodes at the festival?

Ion   O yes; and of all sorts of musical performers.

Socrates   And were you one of the competitors—and did you succeed?

Ion   I obtained the first prize of all, Socrates.

Socrates   Well done; and I hope that you will do the same for us at the Panathenaea.

Ion   And I will, please heaven.

Socrates   I often envy the profession of a rhapsode, Ion; for you have always to wear fine clothes, and to look as beautiful as you can is a part of your art. Then, again, you are obliged to be continually in the company of many good poets; and especially of Homer,[2] who is the best and most divine of them; and to understand him, and not merely learn his words by rote, is a thing greatly to be envied. And no man can be a rhapsode who does not understand the meaning of the poet. For the rhapsode ought to interpret the mind of the poet to his hearers, but how can he interpret him well unless he knows what he means? All this is greatly to be envied.

Ion   Very true, Socrates; interpretation has certainly been the most laborious part of my art; and I believe myself able to speak about Homer better than any man; and that neither Metrodorus of Lampsacus, nor Stesimbrotus of Thasos, nor Glaucon, nor any one else who ever was, had as good ideas about Homer as I have, or as many.

Socrates   I am glad to hear you say so, Ion; I see that you will not refuse to acquaint me with them.

Ion   Certainly, Socrates; and you really ought to hear how exquisitely I render Homer. I think that the Homeridae should give me a golden crown.[3]

Socrates   I shall take an opportunity of hearing your embellishments of him at some other time. But just now I should like to ask you a question: Does your art extend to Hesiod and Archilochus[4] or to Homer only?

Ion   To Homer only; he is in himself quite enough.

Socrates   Are there any things about which Homer and Hesiod agree?

Ion   Yes; in my opinion there are a good many.

Socrates   And can you interpret better what Homer says, or what Hesiod says, about these matters in which they agree?

Ion   I can interpret them equally well, Socrates, where they agree.

Socrates   But what about matters in which they do not agree?—for example, about divination, of which both Homer and Hesiod have something to say,—

Ion   Very true:

Socrates   Would you or a good prophet be a better interpreter of what these two poets say about divination, not only when they agree, but when they disagree?

Ion   A prophet.

Socrates   And if you were a prophet, would you be able to interpret them when they disagree as well as when they agree?

Ion   Clearly.

Socrates   But how did you come to have this skill about Homer only and not about Hesiod or the other poets? Does not Homer speak the same themes which all other poets handle? Is not war his great argument? And does he not speak of human society and of intercourse of men, good and bad, skilled and unskilled, and of the good conversing with one another and with mankind, and about what happens in heaven and in the world below, and the generations of gods and heroes? Are not these the themes of which Homer sings?

Ion   Very true, Socrates.

Socrates   And do not the other poets sing of the same?

Ion   Yes, Socrates; but not in the same way as Homer.

Socrates   What, in a worse way?

Ion   Yes, in a far worse.

Socrates   And Homer in a better way?

Ion   He is incomparably better.

Socrates   And yet surely, my dear friend Ion, in a discussion about arithmetic, where many people are speaking, and one speaks better than the rest, there is somebody who can judge which of them is the good speaker?

Socrates   And he who judges of the good will be the same as he who judges of the bad speakers?

Ion   The same.

Socrates   And he will be the arithmetician?

Ion   Yes.

Plato's Dialogues: These selections from Plato are reprinted from Benjamin Jowett, tr., *The Dialogues of Plato,* third edition (Oxford: The Clarendon Press, 1892). Ion is regarded as an early dialogue, circa 390 B.C. *Sophist, Philebus,* and *Cratylus* are thought to belong to Plato's middle period. *Republic* was composed in about 373 B.C.

[1] Greek god of healing.
[2] The works attributed to Homer were probably written between 1200 and 800 B.C.
[3] Poets who composed in the style of Homer.

---

[4] Archilochus (fl. 714–676 b.c.), one of the earliest known Ionian Greek poets.

Socrates Well, and in discussions about the whole-someness of food, when many persons are speaking, and one speaks better than the rest, will he who recognizes the better speaker be a different person from him who recognizes the worse, or the same?

Ion Clearly the same.

Socrates And who is he, and what is his name?

Ion The physician.

Socrates And speaking generally, in all discussions in which the subject is the same and many men are speaking, will not he who knows the good know the bad speaker also? For if he does not know the bad, neither will he know the good when the same topic is being discussed.

Ion True.

Socrates Is not the same person skilful in both?

Ion Yes.

Socrates And you say that Homer and the other poets, such as Hesiod and Archilochus, speak of the same things, although not in the same way; but the one speaks well and the other not so well?

Ion Yes; and I am right in saying so.

Socrates And if you knew the good speaker, you would also know the inferior speakers to be inferior?

Ion That is true.

Socrates Then, my dear friend, can I be mistaken in saying that Ion is equally skilled in Homer and in other poets, since he himself acknowledges that the same person will be a good judge of all those who speak of the same things; and that almost all poets do speak of the same things?

Ion Why then, Socrates, do I lose attention and go to sleep and have absolutely no ideas of the least value, when any one speaks of any other poet; but when Homer is mentioned, I wake up at once and am all attention and have plenty to say?

Socrates The reason, my friend, is obvious. No one can fail to see that you speak of Homer without any art or knowledge. If you were able to speak of him by rules of art, you would have been able to speak of all other poets; for poetry is a whole.

Ion Yes.

Socrates And when any one acquires any other art as a whole, the same may be said of them. Would you like me to explain my meaning, Ion?

Ion Yes, indeed, Socrates; I very much wish that you would for I love to hear you wise men talk.

Socrates O that we were wise, Ion, and that you could truly call us so; but you rhapsodes and actors, and the poets whose verses you sing, are wise; whereas I am a common man, who only speaks the truth. For consider what a very commonplace and trivial thing is this which I have said—a thing which any man might say: that when a man has acquired a knowledge of a whole art, the enquiry into good and bad is one and the same. Let us consider this matter; is not the art of painting a whole?

Ion Yes.

Socrates And there are and have been many painters good and bad.

Ion Yes.

Socrates And did you ever know any one who was skilful in pointing out the excellences and defects of Polygnotus the son of Aglaophon but incapable of criticizing other painters; and when the work of any other painter was produced, went to sleep and was at a loss and had no ideas; but when he had to give his opinion about Polygnotus, or whoever the painter might be, and about him only, woke up and was attentive and had plenty to say?

Ion No indeed, I have never known such a person.

Socrates Or did you ever know of any one in sculpture, who was skilful in expounding the merits of Daedalus the son of Metion, or of Epeius the son of Panopeus, or of Theodorus the Samian, or of any individual sculptor; but when the works of sculptors in general were produced, was at a loss and went to sleep and had nothing to say?

Ion No indeed; no more than the other.

Socrates And if I am not mistaken, you never met with any one among flute-players or harp-players or singers to the harp or rhapsodes who was able to discourse of Olympus or Thamyras or Orpheus, or Phemius the rhapsode of Ithaca, but was at a loss when he came to speak of Ion of Ephesus, and had no notion of his merit or defects?

Ion I cannot deny what you say, Socrates. Nevertheless I am conscious in my own self, and the world agrees with me in thinking that I do speak better and have more to say about Homer than any other man. But I do not speak equally well about others—tell me the reason of this.

Socrates I perceive, Ion; and I will proceed to explain to you what I imagine to be the reason of this. The gift which you possess of speaking excellently about Homer is not an art, but, as I was just saying, an inspiration; there is a divinity moving you, like that contained in the stone which Euripides calls a magnet, but which is commonly known as the stone of Heraclea. This stone not only attracts iron rings, but also imparts to them a similar power of attracting other rings; and sometimes you may see a number of pieces of iron and rings suspended from one another so as to form quite a long chain: and all of them derive their power of suspension from the original stone. In like manner the Muse first of all inspires men herself; and from these inspired persons a chain of other persons is suspended, who take the inspiration. For all good poets, epic as well as lyric, compose their beautiful poems not by art, but because they are inspired and possessed. And as the Corybantian[5] revellers when they dance are not in their right mind, so the lyric poets are not in their right mind when they are composing their beautiful strains: but when falling under the power of music and metre they are inspired and possessed; like Bacchic maidens who draw milk and honey from the rivers when they are under the influence of Dionysus[6] but not when they are in their right mind. And the soul of the lyric poet does the same, as they themselves say; for they tell us that they bring songs from honeyed fountains, culling them out of the gardens and dells of the Muses;[7] they, like the bees, winging their way from flower to flower. And this is true. For the poet is a light and winged and holy thing, and there is no invention in him until he has been inspired and is out of his senses, and the mind is no longer in him: when he has not attained to this state, he is powerless and is unable to utter his oracles. Many are the noble words in which poets speak concerning the actions of men; but like yourself when speaking about Homer, they do not speak of them by any rules of art: they are simply inspired to utter that to which the Muse impels them, and that only; and when inspired, one of them will make dithyrambs,[8] another hymns of praise, another choral strains, another epic or iambic verses—and he who is good at one is not good at any other kind of verse: for not by art does the poet sing, but by power divine. Had he learned by rules of art, he would have known how to speak not of one theme only, but of all; and therefore God takes away the minds of poets, and uses them as his ministers, as he also uses diviners and holy prophets, in order that we who hear them may know them to be speaking not of themselves who utter these priceless words in a state of unconsciousness, but that God himself is the speaker, and that through them he is conversing with us. And Tynnichus the Chalcidian affords a striking instance of what I am saying: he wrote nothing that any one would care to remember but the famous paean which is in every one's mouth, one of the finest poems ever written, simply an invention of the Muses, as he himself says. For in this way the God would seem to indicate to us and not allow us to doubt that these beautiful poems are not human, or the work of man, but di-

vine and the work of God; and that the poets are only the interpreters of the Gods by whom they are severally possessed. Was not this the lesson which the God intended to teach when by the mouth of the worst of poets he sang the best of songs? Am I not right, Ion?

Ion   Yes, indeed, Socrates, I feel that you are; for your words touch my soul, and I am persuaded that good poets by a divine inspiration interpret the things of the Gods to us.

Socrates   And you rhapsodists are the interpreters of the poets?

Ion   There again you are right.

Socrates   Then you are the interpreters of interpreters?

Ion   Precisely.

Socrates   I wish you would frankly tell me, Ion, what I am going to ask of you: When you produce the greatest effect upon the audience in the recitation of some striking passage, such as the apparition of Odysseus leaping forth on the floor, recognized by the suitors and casting his arrows at his feet, or the description of Achilles rushing at Hector, or the sorrows of Andromache, Hecuba, or Priam,—are you in your right mind? Are you not carried out of yourself, and does not your soul in an ecstasy seem to be among the persons or places of which you are speaking, whether they are in Ithaca or in Troy or whatever may be the scene of the poem?

Ion   That proof strikes home to me, Socrates. For I must frankly confess that at the tale of pity my eyes are filled with tears, and when I speak of horrors, my hair stands on end and my heart throbs.

Socrates   Well, Ion, and what are we to say of a man who at a sacrifice or festival, when he is dressed in holiday attire, and has golden crowns upon his head, of which nobody has robbed him, appears weeping or panic-stricken in the presence of more than twenty thousand friendly faces, when there is no one despoiling or wronging him;—is he in his right mind or is he not?

Ion   No indeed, Socrates, I must say that, strictly speaking, he is not in his right mind.

Socrates   And are you aware that you produce similar effects on most spectators?

Ion   Only too well; for I look down upon them from the stage, and behold the various emotions of pity, wonder, sternness, stamped upon their countenances when I am speaking: and I am obliged to give my very best attention to them; for if I make them cry I myself shall laugh, and if I make them laugh I myself shall cry when the time of payment arrives.

Socrates   Do you know that the spectator is the last of the rings which, as I am saying, receive the power of the original magnet from one another? The rhapsode like yourself

---

[5] The Corybantes were mystic divinities often associated with the mother-goddesses Rhea and Demeter and worshipped in enthusiastic rituals.

[6] Greek god of wine and natural passions, called Bacchus by the Romans. He is often contrasted with Apollo, who represents intellect and rationality. "Apollonian" and "Dionysiac" were employed by Nietzsche in *The Birth of Tragedy* (below, page 687) to describe two major forces in Greek tragedy. Aphrodite and Eros were respectively goddess and god of love.

[7] The Muses were earliest the goddesses of song and later came to preside over the different types of poetry, the arts, and the sciences.

[8] Dionysiac choral hymns.

and the actor are intermediate links, and the poet himself is the first of them. Through all these the God sways the souls of men in any direction which he pleases, and makes one man hang down from another. Thus there is a vast chain of dancers and masters and undermasters of choruses, who are suspended, as if from the stone, at the side of the rings which hang down from the Muse. And every poet has some Muse from whom he is suspended, and by whom he is said to be possessed, which is nearly the same thing; for he is taken hold of. And from these first rings, which are the poets, depend others, some deriving their inspiration from Orpheus, others from Musaeus;[9] but the greater number are possessed and held by Homer. Of whom, Ion, you are one, and are possessed by Homer; and when any one repeats the words of another poet you go to sleep, and know not what to say; but when any one recites a strain of Homer you wake up in a moment, and your soul leaps within you, and you have plenty to say; for not by art or knowledge about Homer do you say what you say, but by divine inspiration and by possession; just as the Corybantian revellers too have a quick perception of that strain only which is appropriated to the God by whom they are possessed, and have plenty of dances and words for that, but take no heed of any other. And you, Ion, when the name of Homer is mentioned have plenty to say, and have nothing to say of others. You ask, 'Why is this?' The answer is that you praise Homer not by art but by divine inspiration.

Ion   That is good, Socrates; and yet I doubt whether you will ever have eloquence enough to persuade me that I praise Homer only when I am mad and possessed; and if you could hear me speak of him I am sure you would never think this to be the case.

Socrates   I should like very much to hear you, but not until you have answered a question which I have to ask. On what part of Homer do you speak well?—not surely about every part.

Ion   There is no part, Socrates, about which I do not speak well: of that I can assure you.

Socrates   Surely not about things in Homer of which you have no knowledge?

Ion   And what is there in Homer of which I have no knowledge?

Socrates   Why, does not Homer speak in many passages about arts? For example, about driving; if I can only remember the lines I will repeat them.

Ion   I remember, and will repeat them.

Socrates   Tell me then, what Nestor says to Antilochus, his son, where he bids him be careful of the turn at the horse-race in honour of Patroclus.

Ion   'Bend gently,' he says, 'in the polished chariot to the left of them, and urge the horse on the right hand with whip and voice; and slacken the rein. And when you are at the goal, let the left horse draw near, yet so that the nave of the well-wrought wheel may not even seem to touch the extremity, and avoid catching the stone.'[10]

Socrates   Enough. Now, Ion, will the charioteer or the physician be the better judge of the propriety of these lines?

Ion   The charioteer, clearly.

Socrates   And will the reason be that this is his art, or will there be any other reason?

Ion   No, that will be the reason.

Socrates   And every art is appointed by God to have knowledge of a certain work; for that which we know by the art of the pilot we do not know by the art of medicine?

Ion   Certainly not.

Socrates   Nor do we know by the art of the carpenter that which we know by the art of medicine?

Ion   Certainly not.

Socrates   And this is true of all the arts;—that which we know with one art we do not know with the other? But let me ask a prior question: You admit that there are differences of arts?

Ion   Yes.

Socrates   You would argue, as I should, that when one art is of one kind of knowledge and another of another, they are different?

Ion   Yes.

Socrates   Yes, surely; for if the subject of knowledge were the same, there would be no meaning in saying that the arts were different—if they both gave the same knowledge. For example, I know that here are five fingers, and you know the same. And if I were to ask whether I and you became acquainted with this fact by the help of the same art of arithmetic, you would acknowledge that we did.

Ion   Yes.

Socrates   Tell me, then, what I was intending to ask you—whether this holds universally? Must the same art have the same subject of knowledge, and different arts other subjects of knowledge?

Ion   That is my opinion, Socrates.

Socrates   Then he who has no knowledge of a particular art will have no right judgment of the sayings and doings of that art?

Ion   Very true.

Socrates   Then which will be a better judge of the lines which you were reciting from Homer, you or the charioteer?

---

[9] Ancient legendary Greek poets.

[10] [Jowett] *Iliad* XXIII, 335.

Ion   The charioteer.

Socrates   Why, yes, because you are a rhapsode and not a charioteer.

Ion   Yes.

Socrates   And the art of the rhapsode is different from that of the charioteer?

Ion   Yes.

Socrates   And if a different knowledge, then a knowledge of different matters?

Ion   True.

Socrates   You know the passage in which Hecamede, the concubine of Nestor, is described as giving to the wounded Machaon a posset, as he says,

'Made with Pramnian wine; and she grated cheese of goat's milk with a grater of bronze, and at his side placed an onion which gives a relish to drink.'[11]

Now would you say that the art of the rhapsode or the art of medicine was better able to judge of the propriety of these lines?

Ion   The art of medicine.

Socrates   And when Homer says,

'And she descended into the deep like a leaden plummet, which, set in the horn of ox that ranges in the fields, rushes along carrying death among the ravenous fishes,'—[12]

will the art of the fisherman or of the rhapsode be better able to judge whether these lines are rightly expressed or not?

Ion   Clearly, Socrates, the art of the fisherman.

Socrates   Come now, suppose that you were to say to me: 'Since you, Socrates, are able to assign different passages in Homer to their corresponding arts, I wish that you would tell me what are the passages of which the excellence ought to be judged by the prophet and prophetic art'; and you will see how readily and truly I shall answer you. For there are many such passages, particularly in the Odyssey; as, for example, the passage in which Theoclymenus the prophet of the house of Melampus says to the suitors:—

'Wretched men! what is happening to you? Your heads and your faces and your limbs underneath are shrouded in night; and the voice of lamentation bursts forth, and your cheeks are wet

with tears. And the vestibule is full, and the court is full, of ghosts descending into the darkness of Erebus, and the sun has perished out of heaven, and an evil mist is spread abroad.'[13]

And there are many such passages in the Iliad also; as for example in the description of the battle near the rampart, where he says:—

'As they were eager to pass the ditch, there came to them an omen: a soaring eagle, holding back the people on the left, bore a huge bloody dragon in his talons, still living and panting; nor had he yet resigned the strife, for he bent back and smote the bird which carried him on the breast by the neck, and he in pain let him fall from him to the ground into the midst of the multitude. And the eagle, with a cry, was borne afar on the wings of the wind.'[14]

These are the sort of things which I should say that the prophet ought to consider and determine.

Ion   And you are quite right, Socrates, in saying so.

Socrates   Yes, Ion, and you are right also. And as I have selected from the Iliad and Odyssey for you passages which describe the office of the prophet and the physician and the fisherman, do you, who know Homer so much better than I do, Ion, select for me passages which relate to the rhapsode and the rhapsode's art, and which the rhapsode ought to examine and judge of better than other men.

Ion   All passages, I should say, Socrates.[15]

Socrates   Not all, Ion, surely. Have you already forgotten what you were saying? A rhapsode ought to have a better memory.

Ion   Why, what am I forgetting?

Socrates   Do you not remember that you declared the art of the rhapsode to be different from the art of the charioteer?

Ion   Yes, I remember.

Socrates   And you admitted that being different they would have different subjects of knowledge?

Ion   Yes.

Socrates   Then upon your own showing the rhapsode, and the art of the rhapsode, will not know everything?

Ion   I should exclude certain things, Socrates.

Socrates   You mean to say that you would exclude pretty much the subjects of the other arts. As he does not know all of them, which of them will he know?

---

[11] [Jowett] *Iliad* XI, 630, 638.
[12] [Jowett] *Iliad* XXIV, 80.
[13] [Jowett] *Odyssey* XX, 351.
[14] [Jowett] *Iliad* XII, 200.
[15] Had Ion answered, "The poems as itself a thing," he would have fared better.

Ion   He will know what a man and what a woman ought to say and what a freeman and what a slave ought to say, and what a ruler and what a subject.

Socrates   Do you mean that a rhapsode will know better than the pilot what the ruler of a sea-tossed vessel ought to say?

Ion   No; the pilot will know best.

Socrates   Or will the rhapsode know better than the physician what the ruler of a sick man ought to say?

Ion   He will not.

Socrates   But he will know what a slave ought to say?

Ion   Yes.

Socrates   Suppose the slave to be a cowherd; the rhapsode will know better than the cowherd what he ought to say in order to soothe the infuriated cows?

Ion   No, he will not.

Socrates   But he will know what a spinning-woman ought to say about the working of wool?

Ion   No.

Socrates   At any rate he will know what a general ought to say when exhorting his soldiers?

Ion   Yes, that is the sort of thing which the rhapsode will be sure to know.

Socrates   Well, but is the art of the rhapsode the art of the general?

Ion   I am sure that I should know what a general ought to say.

Socrates   Why, yes, Ion, because you may possibly have a knowledge of the art of the general as well as of the rhapsode; and you may also have a knowledge of horsemanship as well as of the lyre: and then you would know when horses were well or ill managed. But suppose I were to ask you: By the help of which art, Ion, do you know whether horses are well managed, by your skill as a horseman or as a performer on the lyre—what would you answer?

Ion   I should reply, by my skill as a horseman.

Socrates   And if you judged of performers on the lyre, you would admit that you judged of them as a performer on the lyre, and not as a horseman?

Ion   Yes.

Socrates   And in judging of the general's art, do you judge of it as a general or a rhapsode?

Ion   To me there appears to be no difference between them.

Socrates   What do you mean? Do you mean to say that the art of the rhapsode and of the general is the same?

Ion   Yes, one and the same.

Socrates   Then he who is a good rhapsode is also a good general?

Ion   Certainly, Socrates.

Socrates   And he who is a good general is also a good rhapsode?

Ion   No; I do not say that.

Socrates   But you do say that he who is a good rhapsode is also a good general.

Ion   Certainly.

Socrates   And you are the best of Hellenic rhapsodes?

Ion   Far the best, Socrates.

Socrates   And are you the best general, Ion?

Ion   To be sure, Socrates; and Homer was my master.

Socrates   But then, Ion, what in the name of goodness can be the reason why you, who are the best of generals as well as the best of rhapsodes in all Hellas, go about as a rhapsode when you might be a general? Do you think that the Hellenes want a rhapsode with his golden crown, and do not want a general?

Ion   Why, Socrates, the reason is, that my countrymen, the Ephesians, are the servants and soldiers of Athens, and do not need a general; and you and Sparta are not likely to have me, for you think that you have enough generals of your own.

Socrates   My good Ion, did you never hear of Apollodorus of Cyzicus?

Ion   Who may he be?

Socrates   One who, though a foreigner, has often been chosen their general by the Athenians: and there is Phanosthenes of Andros and Heraclides of Clazomenae, whom they have also appointed to the command of their armies and to other offices, although aliens, after they had shown their merit. And will they not choose Ion the Ephesian to be their general, and honour him, if he prove himself worthy? Were not the Ephesians originally Athenians, and Ephesus is no mean city? But, indeed, Ion, if you are correct in saying that by art and knowledge you are able to praise Homer, you do not deal fairly with me, and after all your professions of knowing many glorious things about Homer, and promises that you would exhibit them, you are only a deceiver, and so far from exhibiting the art of which you are a master, will not, even after my repeated entreaties, explain to me the nature of it. You have literally as many forms as Proteus;[16] and now you go all manner of ways, twisting and turning, and, like Proteus, become all manner of people at once, and at last slip away from me in the disguise of a general, in order that you may escape exhibiting your Homeric lore. And if you have art, then, as I was saying, in falsifying your promise that you would exhibit

---

[16]Greek sea god who could change his shape at will.

Homer, you are not dealing fairly with me. But if, as I believe, you have no art, but speak all these beautiful words about Homer unconsciously under his inspiring influence, then I acquit you of dishonesty, and shall only say that you are inspired. Which do you prefer to be thought, dishonest or inspired?

Ion   There is a great difference, Socrates, between the two alternatives; and inspiration is by far the nobler.

Socrates   Then, Ion, I shall assume the nobler alternative; and attribute to you in your praises of Homer inspiration, and not art.

Republic
from   on Education
Book II

Persons of the Dialogue:
Socrates, Adeimantus

Come then, and let us pass a leisure hour in story-telling, and our story shall be the education of our heroes.

By all means.

And what shall be their education? Can we find a better than the traditional sort?—and this has two divisions, gymnastic for the body, and music[1] for the soul.

True.

Shall we begin education with music, and go on to gymnastic afterwards?

By all means.

And when you speak of music, do you include literature or not?

I do.

And literature may be either true or false?[2]

Yes.

And the young should be trained in both kinds, and we begin with the false?

I do not understand your meaning, he said.

You know, I said, that we begin by telling children stories which though not wholly destitute of truth, are in the main fictitious; and these stories are told them when they are not of an age to learn gymnastics.

Very true.

That was my meaning when I said that we must teach music before gymnastics.

Quite right, he said.

You know also that the beginning is the most important part of any work, especially in the case of a young and tender thing; for that is the time at which the character is being formed and the desired impression is more readily taken.

Quite true.

And shall we just carelessly allow children to hear any casual tales which may be devised by casual persons, and to receive into their minds ideas for the most part the very opposite of those which we should wish them to have when they are grown up?

We cannot.

Then the first thing will be to establish a censorship of the writers of fiction, and let the censors receive any tale of fiction which is good, and reject the bad; and we will desire mothers and nurses to tell their children the authorised ones only. Let them fashion the mind with such tales, even more fondly than they mould the body with their hands; but most of those which are now in use must be discarded.

Of what tales are you speaking? he said.

You may find a model of the lesser in the greater, I said; for they are necessarily of the same type, and there is the same spirit in both of them.

Very likely, he replied; but I do not as yet know what you would term the greater.

Those, I said, which are narrated by Homer and Hesiod, and the rest of the poets, who have ever been the great story-tellers of mankind.

But which stories do you mean, he said; and what fault do you find with them?

A fault which is most serious, I said; the fault of telling a lie, and, what is more, a bad lie.[3]

But when is this fault committed?

Whenever an erroneous representation is made of the nature of gods and heroes,—as when a painter paints a portrait not having the shadow of a likeness to the original.

---

[1] *Republic* begins as a discussion of justice, set in motion by Thrasymachus's argument that justice is what is to the advantage of the powerful. The argument is opposed by Socrates, who raises the question of the relation of justice to the good and proceeds to develop his notion of the ideal state and the education of those who are to be its guardians. Music, for Socrates, includes poetry principally because by tradition poetry was spoken to music, usually of the lyre.

[2] This discussion dealing with the truth or falsity of poetry and a similar discussion in *Sophist* (below, page 38) begin a tradition in criticism. Defenders of poetry developed various arguments explaining why poetry could contain truth from Plotinus (below, page 127), through Sidney's argument for allegorical truth (below, page 191), to Mazzoni's distinction (page 220), borrowed directly from *Sophist,* between icastic and phantastic imitation, and finally to some modern theories suggesting that poetry provides a special kind of knowledge.

---

[3] Elsewhere in *Republic,* Socrates says that lies on behalf of the preservation of the state are acceptable. Presumably these are not "bad" lies.

Yes, he said, that sort of thing is certainly very blame-able; but what are the stories which you mean?

First of all, I said, there was that greatest of all lies, in high places, which the poet told about Uranus, and which was a bad lie too,—I mean what Hesiod says that Uranus did, and how Cronus retaliated on him.[4] The doings of Cronus, and the sufferings which in turn his son inflicted upon him, even if they were true, ought certainly not to be lightly told to young and thoughtless persons; if possible, they had better be buried in silence. But if there is an absolute necessity for their mention, a chosen few might hear them in a mystery,[5] and they should sacrifice not a common [Eleusinian] pig, but some huge and unprocurable victim; and then the number of the hearers will be very few indeed.

Why, yes, said he, those stories are extremely objectionable.

Yes, Adeimantus, they are stories not to be repeated in our State; the young man should not be told that in committing the worse of crimes he is far from doing anything outrageous; and that even if he chastises his father when he does wrong, in whatever manner, he will only be following the example of the first and greatest among the gods.[6]

I entirely agree with you, he said; in my opinion those stories are quite unfit to be repeated.

Neither, if we mean our future guardians to regard the habit of quarrelling among themselves as of all things the basest, should any word be said to them of the wars in heaven, and of the plots and fightings of the gods against one another, for they are not true. No, we shall never mention the battles of the giants, or let them be embroidered on garments; and we shall be silent about the innumerable other quarrels of gods and heroes with their friends and relatives. If they would only believe us we would tell them that quarrelling is unholy, and that never up to this time has there been any quarrel between citizens; this is what old men and old women should begin by telling children; and when they grow up, the poets also should be told to compose for them in a similar spirit. But the narrative of Hephaestus binding Hera his mother,[7] or how on another occasion Zeus sent him flying for taking her part when she was being beaten,[8] and all the battles of the gods in Homer—these tales must not be admitted into our State, whether they are supposed to have an allegorical meaning or not. For a young person cannot judge what is allegorical and what is literal, anything that he receives into his mind at that age is likely to become indelible and unalterable; and therefore it is most important that the tales which the young first hear should be models of virtuous thoughts.

There you are right, he replied; but if any one asks where are such models to be found and of what tales are you speaking—how shall we answer him?

I said to him, You and I, Adeimantus, at this moment are not poets, but founders of a State: now the founders of a State ought to know the general forms in which poets should cast their tales and the limits which must be observed by them, but to make the tales is not their business.

Very true, he said; but what are these forms of theology which you mean?

Something of this kind, I replied:—God is always to be represented as he truly is, whatever be the sort of poetry, epic, lyric or tragic, in which the representation is given.

Right.

And is he not truly good? and must he not be represented as such?

Certainly.

And no good thing is hurtful?

No, indeed.

And that which is not hurtful hurts not?

Certainly not.

And that which hurts not does no evil?

No.

And can that which does no evil be a cause of evil?

Impossible.

And the good is advantageous?

Yes.

And therefore the cause of well-being?

Yes.

It follows therefore that the good is not the cause of all things, but of the good only?

Assuredly.

Then God, if he be good, is not the author of all things, as the many assert, but he is the cause of a few things only, and not of most things that occur to men. For few are the goods of human life, and many are the evils, and the good is to be attributed to God alone; of the evils the causes are to be sought elsewhere, and not in him.

That appears to me to be most true, he said.

Then we must not listen to Homer or to any other poet who is guilty of the folly of saying that two casks

'Lie at the threshold of Zeus, full of lots, one of good, the other of evil lots,'

---

[4] Uranus confined his children, whom he hated, in Tartarus. He was castrated and dethroned by the Titan Cronus, who later lost his throne to Zeus. This story is told by Hesiod (seventh century B.C.) in his *Theogony* (154, 459).
[5] A religious ritual.
[6] Zeus.
[7] Kept ignorant of his parentage, Hephaestus, son of Zeus and Hera, trapped Hera in a chair until she told him who his parents were.
[8] When Hephaestus took Hera's part in an argument with Zeus, Zeus hurled him from Olympus down to the island of Lemnos. Some writers attribute his lameness to this fall.

and that he to whom Zeus gives a mixture of the two

'Sometimes meets with evil fortune, at other times with good;'

but that he to whom is given the cup of unmingled ill,

'Him wild hunger drives o'er the beauteous earth.'

And again—

'Zeus, who is the dispenser of good and evil to us.'[9]

And if any one asserts that the violation of oaths and treaties, which was really the work of Pandarus,[10] was brought about by Athene and Zeus, or that the strife and contention of the gods was instigated by Themis and Zeus, he shall not have our approval; neither will we allow our young men to hear the words of Aeschylus, that

'God plants guilt among men when he desires utterly to destroy a house.'

And if a poet writes of the sufferings of Niobe—the subject of the tragedy in which these iambic verses occur—or of the house of Pelops, or of the Trojan war or on any similar theme, either we must not permit him to say that these are the works of God, or if they are of God, he must devise some explanation of them such as we are seeking; he must say that God did what was just and right, and they were the better for being punished: but that those who are punished are miserable, and that God is the author of their misery— the poet is not to be permitted to say; though he may say that the wicked are miserable because they require to be punished, and are benefited by receiving punishment from God; but that God being good is the author of evil to any one is to be strenuously denied, and not to be said or sung or heard in verse or prose by any one whether old or young in any well-ordered commonwealth. Such a fiction is suicidal, ruinous, impious.

I agree with you, he replied, and am ready to give my assent to the law.

Let this then be one of our rules and principles concerning the gods, to which our poets and reciters will be expected to conform—that God is not the author of all things, but of good only.

---

[9] [Jowett] *Iliad* XXIV, 527.
[10] [Jowett] *Iliad* II, 69.

That will do, he said.

And what do you think of a second principle? Shall I ask you whether God is a magician, and of a nature to appear insidiously now in one shape, and now in another— sometimes himself changing and passing into many forms, sometimes deceiving us with the resemblance of such transformations; or is he one and the same inmutably fixed in his own proper image?

I cannot answer you, he said, without more thought.

Well, I said; but if we suppose a change in anything, that change must be effected either by the thing itself, or by some other things.

Most certainly.

And things which are at their best are also least liable to be altered or discomposed; for example, when healthiest and strongest, the human frame is least liable to be affected by meats and drinks, and the plant which is in the fullest vigour also suffers least from winds or the heat of the sun or any similar causes.

Of course.

And will not the bravest and wisest soul be least confused or deranged by any external influence?

True.

And the same principle, as I should suppose, applies to all composite things—furniture, houses, garments: when good and well made, they are least altered by time and circumstances.

Very true.

Then everything which is good, whether made by art or nature, or both, is least liable to suffer change from without?

True.

But surely God and the things of God are in every way perfect?

Of course they are.

Then he can hardly be compelled by external influence to take many shapes?

He cannot.

But may he not change and transform himself?

Clearly, he said, that must be the case if he is changed at all.

And will he then change himself for the better and fairer, or for the worse and more unsightly?

If he change at all he can only change for the worse, for we cannot suppose him to be deficient either in virtue or beauty.

Very true, Adeimantus; but then, would any one, whether God or man, desire to make himself worse?

Impossible.

Then it is impossible that God should ever be willing to change; being, as is supposed, the fairest and best that is conceivable, every God remains absolutely and for ever in his own form.

That necessarily follows, he said, in my judgment.

Then, I said, my dear friend, let none of the poets tell us that

'The gods, taking the disguise of strangers
from other lands, walk up and down cities in all
sorts of forms;[11]

and let no one slander Proteus and Thetis,[12] neither let any one, either in tragedy or in any other kind of poetry, introduce Hera disguised in the likeness of a priestess asking an alms

'For the life-giving daughters of Inachus the river of Argos;'

—let us have no more lies of that sort. Neither must we have mothers under the influence of the poets scaring their children with a bad version of these myths—telling how certain gods, as they say, 'Go about by night in the likeness of so many strangers and in divers forms:' but let them take heed lest they make cowards of their children, and at the same time speak blasphemy against the gods.

Heaven forbid, he said.

But although the gods are themselves unchangeable, still by witchcraft and deception they may make us think that they appear in various forms?

Perhaps, he replied.

Well, but can you imagine that God will be willing to lie, whether in word or deed, or to put forth a phantom of himself?

I cannot say, he replied.

Do you not know, I said, that the true lie, if such an expression may be allowed, is hated of gods and men?

What do you mean? he said.

I mean that no one is willingly deceived in that which is the truest and highest part of himself, or about the truest and highest matters; there, above all, he is most afraid of a lie having possession of him.

Still, he said, I do not comprehend you.

The reason is, I replied, that you attribute some profound meaning to my words: but I am only saying that deception, or being deceived or uninformed about the highest realities in the highest part of themselves, which is the soul, and in that part of them to have and to hold the lie, is what mankind least like;—that, I say, is what they utterly detest.

There is nothing more hateful to them.

And, as I was just now remarking, this ignorance in the soul of him who is deceived may be called the true lie; for the lie in words is only a kind of imitation and shadowy image of a previous affection[13] of the soul, not pure unadulterated falsehood. Am I not right?

Perfectly right.

The true lie is hated not only by the gods, but also by men?

Yes.

Whereas the lie in words is in certain cases useful and not harmful; in dealing with enemies—that would be an instance; or again, when those whom we call our friends in a fit of madness or illusion are going to do some harm, then it is useful and is a sort of medicine or preventive; also in the tales of mythology, of which we were just now speaking—because we do not know the truth about ancient times, we make falsehood as much like truth as we can, and to turn it to account.

Very true, he said.

But can any of these reasons apply to God? Can we suppose that he is ignorant of antiquity, and therefore has recourse to invention?

That would be ridiculous, he said.

Then the lying poet has no place in our idea of God?

I should say not.

Or perhaps he may tell a lie because he is afraid of enemies?

That is inconceivable.

But he may have friends who are senseless or mad?

But no mad or senseless person can be a friend of God.

Then no motive can be imagined why God should lie?

None whatever.

Then the superhuman and divine is absolutely incapable of falsehood?

Yes.

Then is God perfectly simple and true both in word and deed; he changes not; he deceives not, either by sign or word, by dream or waking vision.

Your thoughts, he said, are the reflection of my own.

You agree with me then, I said, that this is the second type or form in which we should write and speak about divine things. The gods are not magicians who transform themselves, neither do they deceive mankind in any way.

I grant that.

Then, although we are admirers of Homer, we do not admire the lying dream which Zeus sends to Agamemnon;

---

[11] [Jowett] *Odyssey* XVII, 485.
[12] Thetis was the wife of Peleus, by whom she became the mother of Achilles.

[13] State of being.

neither will we praise the verses of Aeschylus in which Thetis says that Apollo at her nuptials

> 'Was celebrating in song her fair progeny whose days were to be long, and to know no sickness. And when he had spoken of my lot as in all things blessed of heaven he raised a note of triumph and cheered my soul. And I thought that the word of Phoebus,[14] being divine and full of prophecy, would not fail. And now he himself who uttered the strain, he who was present at the banquet, and who said this—he it is who has slain my son.'[15]

These are the kind of sentiments about the gods which will arouse our anger; and he who utters them shall be refused a chorus; neither shall we allow teachers to make use of them in the instruction of the young, meaning, as we do, that our guardians, as far as men can be, should be true worshippers of the gods and like them.

I entirely agree, he said, in these principles, and promise to make them my laws.

from
Book III

PERSONS OF THE DIALOGUE:
Socrates, Adeimantus, Glaucon

Such then, I said, are our principles of theology—some tales are to be told, and others are not to be told to our disciples from their youth upwards, if we mean them to honour the gods and their parents, and to value friendship with one another.

Yes; and I think that our principles are right, he said.

But if they are to be courageous, must they not learn other lessons besides these, and lessons of such a kind as will take away the fear of death? Can any man be courageous who has the fear of death in him?

Certainly not, he said.

And can he be fearless of death, or will he choose death in battle rather than defeat and slavery, who believes the world below to be real and terrible?

Impossible.

Then we must assume a control over the narrators of this class of tales as well as over the others, and beg them not simply to revile, but rather to commend the world below, intimating to them that their descriptions are untrue, and will do harm to our future warriors.

That will be our duty, he said.

Then, I said, we shall have to obliterate many obnoxious passages, beginning with the verses,

> 'I would rather be a serf on the land of a poor and portionless man that rule over all the dead who have come to nought.'[1]

We must also expunge the verse, which tells us how Pluto feared,

> 'Lest the mansions grim and squalid which the gods abhor should be seen both of mortals and immortals.'[2]

And again:—

> 'O heavens! verily in the house of Hades there is soul and ghostly form but no mind at all!'[3]

Again of Tiresias:—

> '[To him even after death did Persephone[4] grant mind,] that he alone should be wise; but the other souls are fitting shades.'[5]

Again:—

> 'The soul flying from the limbs had gone to Hades, lamenting her fate, leaving manhood and youth.'[6]

Again:—

> 'And the soul, with shrilling cry, passed like smoke beneath the earth.'[7]

---

[1][Jowett] *Odyssey* IX, 489.
[2][Jowett] *Iliad* XX, 64.
[3][Jowett] *Iliad* XXIII, 103.
[4]Goddess of the underworld.
[5][Jowett] *Odyssey* X, 495.
[6][Jowett] *Iliad* XVI, 856.
[7][Jowett] *Iliad* XXIII, 100.

---

[14]Apollo as sun god.
[15]This play of Aeschylus (525–456 B.C.) is lost.

And,—

> 'As bats in hollow of mystic cavern, when-
> ever any of them has dropped out of the string and
> falls from the rock, fly shrilling and cling to one
> another, so did they with shrilling cry hold to-
> gether as they moved.'[8]

And we must beg Homer and the other poets not to be angry if we strike out these and similar passages, not because they are unpoetical, or unattractive to the popular ear, but be-cause the greater the poetical charm of them, the less are they meet for the ears of boys and men who are meant to be free, and who should fear slavery more than death.

Undoubtedly.

Also we shall have to reject all the terrible and ap-palling names which describe the world below—Cocytus and Styx, ghosts under the earth, and sapless shades, and any similar words of which the very mention causes a shud-der to pass through the inmost soul of him who hears them. I do not say that these horrible stories may not have a use of some kind; but there is a danger that the nerves of our guardians[9] may be rendered too excitable and effeminate by them.

There is a real danger, he said.

Then we must have no more of them.

True.

Another and a nobler strain must be composed and sung by us.

Clearly.

And shall we proceed to get rid of the weepings and wailings of famous men?

They will go with the rest.

But shall we be right in getting rid of them? Reflect: our principle is that the good man will not consider death terrible to any other good man who is his comrade.

Yes; that is our principle.

And therefore he will not sorrow for his departed friend as though he had suffered anything terrible?

He will not.

Such an one, as we further maintain, is sufficient for himself and his own happiness, and therefore is least in need of other men.

True, he said.

And for this reason the loss of a son or brother, or the deprivation of fortune, is to him of all men least terrible.

Assuredly.

And therefore he will be least likely to lament, and will bear with the greatest equanimity any misfortune of this sort which may befall him.

Yes, he will feel such a misfortune far less than another.

Then we shall be right in getting rid of the lamenta-tions of famous men, and making them over to women (and not even to women who are good for anything), or to men of a baser sort, that those who are being educated by us to be the defenders of their country may scorn to do the like.

That will be very right.

Then we will once more entreat Homer and the other poets not to depict Achilles,[10] who is the son of a goddess, first lying on his side, then on his back, and then on his face; then starting up and sailing in a frenzy along the shores of the barren sea; now taking the sooty ashes in both his hands[11] and pouring them over his head, or weeping and wailing in the various modes which Homer has delineated. Nor should he describe Priam the kinsman of the gods as praying and beseeching,

> 'Rolling in the dirt, calling each man loudly by his
> name.'[12]

Still more earnestly will we beg of him at all events not to introduce the gods lamenting and saying,

> 'Alas! my misery! Alas! that I bore the bravest to my
> sorrow.'[13]

But if he must introduce the gods, at any rate let him not dare so completely to misrepresent the greatest of the gods, as to make him say—

> 'O heavens! with my eyes verily I behold a
> dear friend of mine chased round and round the
> city, and my heart is sorrowful.'[14]

Or again:—

> 'Woe is me that I am fated to have Sarpedon,
> dearest of men to me, subdued at the hands of Pa-
> troclus the son of Menoctius.'[15]

---

[8][Jowett] *Odyssey* XXIV, 6.
[9]They who are trained to become guardians of the state.

---

[10][Jowett] *Iliad* XXIV, 10.
[11][Jowett] *Iliad* XVIII, 23.
[12][Jowett] *Iliad* XXII, 414.
[13][Jowett] *Iliad* XVIII, 54.
[14][Jowett] *Iliad* XXII, 168.
[15][Jowett] *Iliad* XVI, 433.

For if, my sweet Adeimantus, our youth seriously listen to such unworthy representations of the gods, instead of laughing at them as they ought, hardly will any of them deem that he himself, being but a man, can be dishonoured by similar actions; neither will he rebuke any inclination which may arise in his mind to say and do the like. And instead of having any shame or self-control, he will be always whining and lamenting on slight occasions.

Yes, he said, that is most true.

Yes, I replied; but that surely is what ought not to be, as the argument has just proved to us; and by that proof we must abide until it is disproved by a better.

It ought not to be.

Neither ought our guardians to be given to laughter. For a fit of laughter which has been indulged to excess almost always produces a violent reaction.

So I believe.

Then persons of worth, even if only mortal men, must not be represented as overcome by laughter, and still less must such a representation of the gods be allowed.

Still less of the gods, as you say, he replied.

Then we shall not suffer such an expression to be used about the gods as that of Homer when he describes how

'Inextinguishable laughter arose among the blessed gods, when they saw Hephaestus bustling about the mansion.'[16]

On your views, we must not admit them.

On my views, if you like to father them on me;[17] that we must not admit them is certain.

Again, truth should be highly valued; if, as we were saying, a lie is useless to the gods, and useful only as a medicine to men, then the use of such medicines should be restricted to physicians; private individuals have no business with them.

Clearly not, he said.

Then if any one at all is to have the privilege of lying, the rulers of the State should be the persons; and they, in their dealings either with enemies or with their own citizens, may be allowed to lie for the public good. But nobody else should meddle with anything of the kind; and although the rulers have this privilege, for a private man to lie to them in return is to be deemed a more heinous fault than for the patient or the pupil of a gymnasium not to speak the truth about his own bodily illnesses to the physician or to the trainer, or for a sailor not to tell the captain what is happening about the ship and the rest of the crew, and how things are going with himself or his fellow sailors.

Most true, he said.

If, then, the ruler catches anybody beside himself lying in the State,

'Any of the craftsmen, whether he be priest or physician or carpenter,'[18]

he will punish him for introducing a practice which is equally subversive and destructive of ship or State.

Most certainly, he said, if our idea of the State is ever carried out.

In the next place our youth must be temperate?

Certainly.

Are not the chief elements of temperance, speaking generally, obedience to commanders and self-control in sensual pleasures?

True.

Then we shall approve such language as that of Diomede in Homer,

'Friend, sit still and obey my word,'[19]

and the verses which follow,

'The Greeks marched breathing prowess,[20]
. . . . in silent awe of their leaders.'[21]

and other sentiments of the same kind.

We shall.

What of this line,

'O heavy with wine, who hast the eyes of a dog and the heart of a stag,'[22]

and of the words which follow? Would you say that these, or any similar impertinences which private individuals are supposed to address to their rulers, whether in verse or prose, are well or ill spoken?

They are ill spoken.

They may very possibly afford some amusement, but they do not conduce to temperance. And therefore they are likely to do harm to our young men—you would agree with me there?

---

[16][Jowett] *Iliad* I, 599.
[17]"To call me the author of them."
[18]*Odyssey* XVII, 383.
[19][Jowett] *Iliad* IV, 412.
[20][Jowett] *Odyssey* III, 8.
[21][Jowett] *Odyssey* IV, 431.
[22][Jowett] *Odyssey* I, 225.

Yes.

And then, again, to make the wisest of men say that nothing in his opinion is more glorious than

> 'When the tables are full of bread and meat,
> and the cup-bearer carries round wine which he
> draws from the bowl and pours into the cups;'[23]

is it fit or conducive to temperance for a young man to hear such words? Or the verse

> 'The saddest of fates is to die and meet destiny from hunger'?[24]

What would you say again to the tale of Zeus, who, while other gods and men were asleep and he the only person awake, lay devising plans, but forgot them all in a moment through his lust, and was so completely overcome at the sight of Hera that he would not even go into the hut, but wanted to lie with her on the ground, declaring that he had never been in such a state of rapture before, even when they first met one another

> 'Without the knowledge of their parents;'[25]

or that other tale of how Hephaestus, because of similar goings on, cast a chain around Ares and Aphrodite?[26]

Indeed, he said, I am strongly of opinion that they ought not to hear that sort of thing.

But any deeds of endurance which are done or told by famous men, these they ought to see and hear; as, for example, what is said in the verses,

> 'He smote his breast, and thus reproached his heart,
> Endure, my heart; far worse hast thou endured!'[27]

Certainly, he said.

In the next place, we must not let them be receivers of gifts or lovers of money.

Certainly not.

Neither must we sing to them of

'Gifts persuading gods, and persuading reverend kings.'[28]

Neither is Phoenix, the tutor of Achilles, to be approved or deemed to have given his pupil good counsel when he told him that he should take the gifts of the Greeks and assist them,[29] but that without a gift he should not lay aside his anger. Neither will we believe or acknowledge Achilles himself to have been such a lover of money that he took Agamemnon's gifts, or that when he had received payment he restored the dead body of Hector, but that without payment he was unwilling to do so.[30]

Undoubtedly, he said, these are not sentiments which can be approved.

Loving Homer as I do, I hardly like to say that in attributing these feelings to Achilles, or in believing that they are truly attributed to him, he is guilty of downright impiety. As little can I believe the narrative of his insolence to Apollo, where he says,

> 'Thou hast wronged me, O far-darter,[31] most
> abominable of deities. Verily I would be even with
> thee, if I had only the power;'[32]

or his insubordination to the river-god,[33] on whose divinity he is ready to lay hands; or his offering to the dead Patroclus of his own hair,[34] which had been previously dedicated to the other river-god Spercheius, and that he actually performed this vow; or that he dragged Hector round the tomb of Patroclus,[35] and slaughtered the captives at the pyre;[36] of all this I cannot believe that he was guilty, any more than I can allow our citizens to believe that he, the wise Cheiron's pupil, the son of a goddess and of Peleus who was the gentlest of men and third in descent from Zeus, was so disordered in his wits as to be at one time the slave of two seemingly inconsistent passions, meanness, not untainted by avarice, combined with overweening contempt of gods and men.

You are quite right, he replied.

And let us equally refuse to believe, or allow to be repeated, the tale of Theseus son of Poseidon, or of Pirithous son of Zeus, going forth as they did to perpetrate a horrid rape,[37] or of any other hero or son of a god daring to do such

---

[23][Jowett] *Odyssey* IX, 8.
[24][Jowett] *Odyssey* XII, 342.
[25][Jowett] *Iliad* XIV, 281.
[26][Jowett] *Odyssey* VIII, 266.
[27][Jowett] *Odyssey* XX, 17.
[28][Jowett] Quoted by Suidas as attributed to Hesiod.

[29][Jowett] *Iliad* IX, 515.
[30][Jowett] *Iliad* XXIV, 175.
[31]"Far-darter" refers to Apollo, skilled as an archer.
[32][Jowett] *Iliad* XXII, 15sq.
[33][Jowett] *Iliad* XXI, 130, 223sq.
[34][Jowett] *Iliad* XXIII, 151.
[35][Jowett] *Iliad* XXII, 394.
[36][Jowett] *Iliad* XXIII, 175.
[37]Pirithous aided Theseus in carrying off Helen, then a child, to Aphidnae. Theseus then aided Pirithous in an attempt to carry off Persephone from the underworld.

impious and dreadful things as they falsely ascribe to them in our day: and let us further compel the poets to declare either that these acts were not done by them, or that they were not the sons of gods;—both in the same breath they shall not be permitted to affirm. We will not have them, trying to persuade our youth that the gods are the authors of evil, and that heroes are no better than men—sentiments which, as we were saying, are neither pious nor true, for we have already proved that evil cannot come from the gods.

Assuredly not.

And further they are likely to have a bad effect on those who hear them; for everybody will begin to excuse his own vices when he is convinced that similar wickednesses are always being perpetrated by—

'The kindred of the gods, the relatives of
Zeus, whose ancestral altar, the altar of Zeus, is
aloft in air on the peak of Ida,'

and who have

'the blood of deities yet flowing in their veins.'[38]

And therefore let us put an end to such tales, lest they engender laxity of morals among the young.

By all means, he replied.

But now that we are determining what classes of subjects are or are not to be spoken of, let us see whether any have been omitted by us. The manner in which gods and demigods and heroes and the world below should be treated has been already laid down.

Very true.

And what shall we say about men? That is clearly the remaining portion of our subject.

Clearly so.

But we are not in a condition to answer this question at present, my friend.

Why not?

Because, if I am not mistaken, we shall have to say that about men poets and story-tellers are guilty of making the gravest misstatements when they tell us that wicked men are often happy, and the good miserable; and that injustice is profitable when undetected, but that justice is a man's own loss and another's gain—these things we shall forbid them to utter, and command them to sing and say the opposite.

To be sure we shall, he replied.

But if you admit that I am right in this, then I shall maintain that you have implied the principle for which we have been all along contending.

I grant the truth of your inference.

That such things are or are not to be said about men is a question which we cannot determine until we have discovered what justice is, and how naturally advantageous to the possessor, whether he seems to be just or not.

Most true, he said.

Enough of the subjects of poetry: let us now speak of the style; and when this has been considered, both matter and manner will have been completely treated.

I do not understand what you mean, said Adeimantus.

Then I must make you understand; and perhaps I may be more intelligible if I put the matter in this way. You are aware, I suppose, that all mythology and poetry is a narration of events, either past, present, or to come?

Certainly, he replied.

And narration may be either simple narration, or imitation, or a union of the two?[39]

That again, he said, I do not quite understand.

I fear that I must be a ridiculous teacher when I have so much difficulty in making myself apprehended. Like a bad speaker, therefore, I will not take the whole of the subject, but will break a piece off in illustration of my meaning. You know the first lines of the Iliad, in which the poet says that Chryses prayed Agamemnon to release his daughter, and that Agamemnon flew into a passion with him; whereupon Chryses, failing of his object, invoked the anger of the God against the Achaeans. Now as far as these lines,

'And he prayed all the Greeks, but especially
the two sons of Atreus, the chiefs of the people.'

the poet is speaking in his own person; he never leads us to suppose that he is any one else. But in what follows he takes the person of Chryses, and then he does all that he can to make us believe that the speaker is not Homer, but the aged priest himself. And in this double form he has cast the entire narrative of the events which occurred at Troy and in Ithaca and throughout the Odyssey.

Yes.

And a narrative it remains both in the speeches which the poet recites from time to time and in the intermediate passages?

Quite true.

---

[38][Jowett] From the *Niobe* of Aeschylus.

[39]Here Socrates employs "imitation" not in the sense of copying copies of the ideas but to distinguish from straight narration the poet's putting words in the mouth of a character, as in a play.

But when the poet speaks in the person of another, may we not say that he assimilates his style to that of the person who, as he informs you, is going to speak?

Certainly.

And this assimilation of himself to another, either by the use of voice or gesture, is the imitation of the person whose character he assumes?

Of course.

Then in this case the narrative of the poet may be said to proceed by way of imitation?

Very true.

Or, if the poet everywhere appears and never conceals himself, then again the imitation is dropped, and his poetry becomes simple narration. However, in order that I may make my meaning quite clear, and that you may no more say, 'I don't understand,' I will show how the change might be effected. If Homer had said, 'The priest came, having his daughter's ransom in his hands, supplicating the Achaeans, and above all the kings;' and then if instead of speaking in the person of Chryses, he had continued in his own person, the words would have been, not imitation, but simple narration. The passage would have run as follows (I am no poet, and therefore I drop the metre), 'The priest came and prayed the gods on behalf of the Greeks that they might capture Troy and return safely home, but begged that they would give him back his daughter, and take the ransom which he brought, and respect the God. Thus he spoke, and the other Greeks revered the priest and assented. But Agamemnon was wroth, and bade him depart and not come again, lest the staff and chaplets[40] of the God should be of no avail to him—the daughter of Chryses should not be released, he said—she should grow old with him in Argos. And then he told him to go away and not to provoke him, if he intended to get home unscathed. And the old man went away in fear and silence, and, when he had left the camp, he called upon Apollo by his many names, reminding him of everything which he had done pleasing to him, whether in building his temples, or in offering sacrifice, and praying that his good deeds might be returned to him, and that the Achaeans might expiate his tears by the arrows of the god,'—and so on. In this way the whole becomes simple narrative.

I understand, he said.

Or you may suppose the opposite case—that the intermediate passages are omitted, and the dialogue only left.

That also, he said, I understand; you mean, for example, as in tragedy.

---

[40]Wreaths or garlands for the head.

You have conceived my meaning perfectly; and if I mistake not, what you failed to apprehend before is now made clear to you, that poetry and mythology are, in some cases, wholly imitative—instances of this are supplied by tragedy and comedy; there is likewise the opposite style, in which the poet is the only speaker—of this the dithyramb affords the best example; and the combination of both is found in epic, and in several other styles of poetry. Do I take you with me?

Yes, he said; I see now what you meant.

I will ask you to remember also what I began by saying, that we had done with the subject and might proceed to the style.

Yes, I remember.

In saying this, I intended to imply that we must come to an understanding about the mimetic art,—whether the poets, in narrating their stories, are to be allowed by us to imitate, and if so, whether in whole or in part, and if the latter, in what parts; or should all imitation be prohibited?

You mean, I suspect, to ask whether tragedy and comedy shall be admitted into our State?

Yes, I said; but there may be more than this in question: I really do not know as yet, but whither the argument may blow, thither we go.

And go we will, he said.

Then, Adeimantus, let me ask you whether our guardians ought to be imitators; or rather, has not this question been decided by the rule already laid down that one man can only do one thing well, and not many; and that if he attempt many, he will altogether fail of gaining much reputation in any?

Certainly.

And this is equally true of imitation; no one man can imitate many things as well as he would imitate a single one?

He cannot.

Then the same person will hardly be able to play a serious part in life, and at the same time to be an imitator and imitate many other parts as well; for even when two species of imitation are nearly allied, the same persons cannot succeed in both, as, for example, the writers of tragedy and comedy—did you not just now call them imitations?

Yes, I did: and you are right in thinking that the same persons cannot succeed in both.

Any more than they can be rhapsodists and actors at once?

True.

Neither are comic and tragic actors the same; yet all these things are but imitations.

They are so.

And human nature, Adeimantus, appears to have been coined into yet smaller pieces, and to be as incapable of imitating many things well, as of performing well the actions of which the imitations are copies.

Quite true, he replied.

If then we adhere to our original notion and bear in mind that our guardians, setting aside every other business, are to dedicate themselves wholly to the maintenance of freedom in the State, making this their craft, and engaging in no work which does not bear on this end, they ought not to practise or imitate anything else; if they imitate at all, they should imitate from youth upward only those characters which are suitable to their profession—the courageous, temperate, holy, free, and the like; but they should not depict or be skilful at imitating any kind of illiberality or baseness, lest from imitation they should come to be what they imitate. Did you never observe how imitations, beginning in early youth and continuing far into life, at length grow into habits and become a second nature, affecting body, voice, and mind?

Yes, certainly, he said.

Then, I said, we will not allow those for whom we profess a care and of whom we say that they ought to be good men, to imitate a woman, whether young or old, quarrelling with her husband, or striving and vaunting against the gods in conceit of her happiness, or when she is in affliction, or sorrow, or weeping; and certainly not one who is in sickness, love, or labour.

Very right, he said.

Neither must they represent slaves, male or female, performing the offices of slaves?

They must not.

And surely not bad men, whether cowards or any others, who do the reverse of what we have just been prescribing, who scold or mock or revile one another in drink or out of drink, or who in any other manner sin against themselves and their neighbours in word or deed, as the manner of such is. Neither should they be trained to imitate the action or speech of men or women who are mad or bad; for madness, like vice, is to be known but not to be practised or imitated.

Very true, he replied.

Neither may they imitate smiths or other artificers, or oarsmen, or boatswains, or the like?

How can they, he said, when they are not allowed to apply their minds to the callings of any of these?

Nor may they imitate the neighing of horses, the bellowing of bulls, the murmur of rivers and roll of the ocean, thunder, and all that sort of thing?

Nay, he said, if madness be forbidden, neither may they copy the behaviour of madmen.

You mean, I said, if I understand you aright, that there is one sort of narrative style which may be employed by a truly good man when he has anything to say, and that another sort will be used by a man of an opposite character and education.

And which are these two sorts? he asked.

Suppose, I answered, that a just and good man in the course of a narration comes on some saying or action of another good man,—I should imagine that he will like to personate him, and will not be ashamed of this sort of imitation: he will be most ready to play the part of the good man when he is acting firmly and wisely; in a less degree when he is overtaken by illness or love or drink, or has met with any other disaster. But when he comes to a character which is unworthy of him, he will not make a study of that; he will disdain such a person, and will assume his likeness, if at all, for a moment only when he is performing some good action; at other times he will be ashamed to play a part which he has never practised, nor will he like to fashion and frame himself after the baser models; he feels the employment of such an art, unless in jest, to be beneath him, and his mind revolts at it.

So I should expect, he replied.

Then he will adopt a mode of narration such as we have illustrated out of Homer, that is to say, his style will be both imitative and narrative: but there will be very little of the former, and a great deal of the latter. Do you agree?

Certainly, he said; that is the model which such a speaker must necessarily take.

But there is another sort of character who will narrate anything, and, the worse he is, the more unscrupulous he will be; nothing will be too bad for him: and he will be ready to imitate anything, not as a joke, but in right good earnest, and before a large company. As I was just now saying, he will attempt to represent the roll of thunder, the noise of wind and hail, or the creaking of wheels, and pulleys, and the various sounds of flutes, pipes, trumpets, and all sorts of instruments: he will bark like a dog, bleat like a sheep, or crow like a cock; his entire art will consist in imitation of voice and gesture, and there will be very little narration.

That, he said, will be his mode of speaking.

These, then, are the two kinds of style?

Yes.

And you would agree with me in saying that one of them is simple and has but slight changes; and if the harmony and rhythm are also chosen for their simplicity, the result is that the speaker, if he speaks correctly, is always pretty much the same in style, and he will keep within the limits of a single harmony (for the changes are not great), and in like manner he will make use of nearly the same rhythm?

That is quite true, he said.

Whereas the other requires all sorts of harmonies and all sorts of rhythms, if the music and the style are to correspond, because the style has all sorts of changes.

That is also perfectly true, he replied.

And do not the two styles, or the mixture of the two, comprehend all poetry, and every form of expression in words? No one can say anything except in one or other of them or in both together.

They include all, he said.

And shall we receive into our State all the three styles, or one only of the two unmixed styles? or would you include the mixed?

I should prefer only to admit the pure imitator of virtue.

Yes, I said, Adeimantus; but the mixed style is also very charming: and indeed the pantomimic, which is the opposite of the one chosen by you, is the most popular style with children and their attendants, and with the world in general.

I do not deny it.

But I suppose you would argue that such a style is unsuitable to our State, in which human nature is not twofold or manifold, for one man plays one part only?

Yes; quite unsuitable.

And this is the reason why in our State, and in our State only, we shall find a shoemaker to be a shoemaker and not a pilot also, and a husbandman to be a husbandman and not a dicast[41] also, and a soldier a soldier and not a trader also, and the same throughout?

True, he said.

And therefore when any one of these pantomimic gentlemen, who are so clever that they can imitate anything, comes to us, and makes a proposal to exhibit himself and his poetry, we will fall down and worship him as a sweet and holy and wonderful being; but we must also inform him that in our State such as he are not permitted to exist; the law will not allow them. And so when we have anointed him with myrrh, and set a garland of wool upon his head, we shall send him away to another city. For we mean to employ for our souls' health the rougher and severer poet or storyteller, who will imitate the style of the virtuous only, and will follow those models which we prescribed at first when we began the education of our soldiers.

We certainly will, he said, if we have the power.

Then now, my friend, I said, that part of music or literary education which relates to the story or myth may be considered to be finished; for the matter and manner have both been discussed.

I think so too, he said.

Next in order will follow melody and song.

That is obvious.

Every one can see already what we ought to say about them, if we are to be consistent with ourselves.

I fear, said Glaucon, laughing, that the word 'every one' hardly includes me, for I cannot at the moment say what they should be; though I may guess.

At any rate you can tell that a song or ode has three parts—the words, the melody, and the rhythm; that degree of knowledge may presuppose?

Yes, he said; so much as that you may.

And as for the words, there will surely be no difference between words which are and which are not set to music; both will conform to the same laws, and these have been already determined by us?

Yes.

And the melody and rhythm will depend upon the words?

Certainly.

We were saying, when we spoke of the subject-matter, that we had no need of lamentations and strains of sorrow?

True.

And which are the harmonies expressive of sorrow? You are musical, and can tell me.

The harmonies which you mean are the mixed or tenor Lydian, and the full-toned or bass Lydian, and such like.

These then, I said, must be banished; even to women who have a character to maintain they are of no use, and much less to men.

Certainly.

In the next place, drunkenness and softness and indolence are utterly unbecoming the character of our guardians.

Utterly unbecoming.

And which are the soft or drinking harmonies?

The Ionian, he replied, and the Lydian; they are termed 'relaxed.'

Well, and are these of any military use?

Quite the reverse, he replied; and if so the Dorian and the Phrygian are the only ones which you have left.

I answered: Of the harmonies I know nothing, but I want to have one warlike, to sound the note or accent which a brave man utters in the hour of danger and stern resolve, or when his cause is failing, and he is going to wounds or death or is overtaken by some other evil, and at every such crisis meets the blows of fortune with firm step and a determination to endure; and another to be used by him in times of peace and freedom of action, when there is no pressure of necessity, and he is

---

[41]Juror.

seeking to persuade God by prayer, or man by instruction and admonition, or on the other hand, when he is expressing his willingness to yield to persuasion or entreaty or admonition, and which represents him when by prudent conduct he has attained his end, not carried away by his success, but acting moderately and wisely under the circumstances, and acquiescing in the event. These two harmonies I ask you to leave; the strain of necessity and the strain of freedom, the strain of the unfortunate and the strain of the fortunate, the strain of courage, and the strain of temperance; these, I say, leave.

And these, he replied, are the Dorian and Phrygian harmonies of which I was just now speaking.

Then, I said, if these and these only are to be used in our songs and melodies, we shall not want multiplicity of notes or a panharmonic scale?

I suppose not.

Then we shall not maintain the artificers of lyres with three corners and complex scales, or the makers of any other many-stringed curiously-harmonised instruments?

Certainly not.

But what do you say to flute-makers and flute-players? Would you admit them into our State when you reflect that in this composite use of harmony the flute is worse than all the stringed instruments put together; even the panharmonic music is only an imitation of the flute?

Clearly not.

There remain then only the lyre and the harp for use in the city, and the shepherds may have a pipe in the country.

That is surely the conclusion to be drawn from the argument.

The preferring of Apollo and his instruments to Marsyas and his instruments is not at all strange, I said.[42]

Not at all, he replied.

And so, by the dog of Egypt, we have been unconsciously purging the State, which not long ago we termed luxurious.

And we have done wisely, he replied.

Then let us now finish the purgation, I said. Next in order to harmonies, rhythms will naturally follow, and they should be subject to the same rules, for we ought not to seek out complex systems of metre, or metres of every kind, but rather to discover what rhythms are the expressions of a courageous and harmonious life; and when we have found them, we shall adapt the foot and the melody to words having a like spirit, not the words to the foot and melody. To say what these rhythms are will be your duty—you must teach me them, as you have already taught me the harmonies.

But, indeed, he replied, I cannot tell you. I only know that there are some three principles of rhythm out of which metrical systems are framed, just as in sounds there are four notes[43] out of which all the harmonies are composed; that is an observation which I have made. But of what sort of lives they are severally the imitations I am unable to say.

Then, I said, we must take Damon[44] into our counsels; and he will tell us what rhythms are expressive of meanness, or insolence, or fury, or other unworthiness, and what are to be reserved for the expression of opposite feelings. And I think that I have an indistinct recollection of his mentioning a complex Cretic rhythm; also a dactylic or heroic, and he arranged them in some manner which I do not quite understand, making the rhythms equal in the rise and fall of the foot, long and short alternating; and, unless I am mistaken, he spoke of an iambic as well as of a trochaic rhythm, and assigned to them short and long quantities.[45] Also in some cases he appeared to praise or censure the movement of the foot quite as much as the rhythm; or perhaps a combination of the two; for I am not certain what he meant. These matters, however, as I was saying, had better be referred to Damon himself, for the analysis of the subject would be difficult, you know?

Rather so, I should say.

But there is no difficulty in seeing that grace or the absence of grace is an effect of good or bad rhythm.

None at all.

And also that good and bad rhythm naturally assimilate to a good and bad style; and that harmony and discord in like manner follow style; for our principle is that rhythm and harmony are regulated by the words, and not the words by them.

Just so, he said, they should follow the words.

And will not the words and the character of the style depend on the temper of the soul?

Yes.

And everything else on the style?

Yes.

Then beauty of style and harmony and grace and good rhythm depend on simplicity,—I mean the true simplicity of a rightly and nobly ordered mind and character, not that other simplicity which is only an euphemism for folly?[46]

---

[42]In a contest with Apollo, which Marsyas lost, Marsyas played the flute, Apollo the lyre.

[43][Jowett] The four notes of the tetrachord.

[44]A celebrated musician and sophist.

[45][Jowett] Socrates expresses himself carelessly in accordance with his assumed ignorance of the details of the subject. In the first part of the sentence he appears to be speaking of paeonic rhythms which are in the ratio of 1/1; in the second part, of dactylic and anapestic rhythms, which are in the ratio of $1/_2$ or 2/1.

[46]Socrates tends to identify beauty or the beautiful with mathematical proportion.

Very true, he replied.

And if our youth are to do their work in life, must they not make these graces and harmonies their perpetual aim?

They must.

And surely the art of the painter and every other creative and constructive art are full of them,—weaving, embroidery, architecture, and every kind of manufacture; also nature, animal and vegetable,—in all of them there is grace or the absence of grace. And ugliness and discord and inharmonious motion are nearly allied to ill words and ill nature, as grace and harmony are the twin sisters of goodness and virtue and bear their likeness.

That is quite true, he said.

But shall our superintendence go no further, and are the poets only to be required by us to express the image of the good in their works, on pain, if they do anything else, of expulsion from our State? Or is the same control to be extended to other artists, and are they also to be prohibited from exhibiting the opposite forms of vice and intemperance and meanness and indecency in sculpture and building and the other creative arts; and is he who cannot conform to this rule of ours to be prevented from practising his art in our State, lest the taste of our citizens be corrupted by him? We would not have our guardians grow up amid images of moral deformity, as in some noxious pasture, and there browse and feed upon many a baneful herb and flower day by day, little by little, until they silently gather a festering mass of corruption in their own soul. Let our artists rather be those who are gifted to discern the true nature of the beautiful and graceful; then will our youth dwell in a land of health, amid fair sights and sounds, and receive the good in everything; and beauty, the effluence of fair works, shall flow into the eye and ear, like a health-giving breeze from a purer region, and insensibly draw the soul from earliest years into likeness and sympathy with the beauty of reason.

There can be no nobler training than that, he replied.

And therefore, I said, Glaucon, musical training is a more potent instrument than any other, because rhythm and harmony find their way into the inward places of the soul, on which they mightily fasten, imparting grace, and making the soul of him who is rightly educated graceful, or of him who is ill-educated ungraceful; and also because he who has received this true education of the inner being will most shrewdly perceive omissions or faults in art and nature, and with a true taste, while he praises and rejoices over and receives into his soul the good, and becomes noble and good, he will justly blame and hate the bad, now in the days of his youth, even before he is able to know the reason why; and when reason comes he will recognise and salute the friend with whom his education has made him long familiar.

Yes, he said, I quite agree with you in thinking that our youth should be trained in music and on the grounds which you mention.

Just as in learning to read, I said, we were satisfied when we knew the letters of the alphabet, which are very few, in all their recurring sizes and combinations; not slighting them as unimportant whether they occupy a space large or small, but everywhere eager to make them out; and not thinking ourselves perfect in the art of reading until we recognise them wherever they are found:

True—

Or, as we recognise the reflection of letters in the water, or in a mirror, only when we know the letters themselves; the same art and study giving us the knowledge of both:

Exactly—

Even so, as I maintain, neither we nor our guardians, whom we have to educate, can ever become musical until we and they know the essential forms, in all their combinations, and can recognise them and their images wherever they are found, not slighting them either in small things or great, but believing them all to be within the sphere of one art and study.

Most assuredly.

And when a beautiful soul harmonizes with a beautiful form, and the two are cast in one mould, that will be the fairest of sights to him who has an eye to see it?

The fairest indeed.

from
Book X

PERSONS OF THE DIALOGUE:
Socrates, Glaucon

Of the many excellences which I perceive in the order of our State, there is none which upon reflection pleases me better than the rule about poetry.

To what do you refer?

To the rejection of imitative poetry, which certainly ought not to be received; as I see far more clearly now that the parts of the soul have been distinguished.

What do you mean?

Speaking in confidence, for I should not like to have my words repeated to the tragedians and the rest of the imitative tribe—but I do not mind saying to you, that all poetical imitations are ruinous to the understanding of the hearers, and that the knowledge of their true nature is the only antidote to them.

Explain the purport of your remark.

Well, I will tell you, although I have always from my earliest youth had an awe and love of Homer, which even now makes the words falter on my lips, for he is the great captain and teacher of the whole of that charming tragic company; but a man is not to be reverenced more than the truth, and therefore I will speak out.

Very good, he said.

Listen to me then, or rather, answer me.

Put your question.

Can you tell me what imitation[1] is? for I really do not know.

A likely thing, then, that I should know.

Why not? for the duller eye may often see a thing sooner than the keener.

Very true, he said; but in your presence, even if I had any faint notion, I could not muster courage to utter it. Will you enquire yourself?

Well then, shall we begin the enquiry in our usual manner: Whenever a number of individuals have a common name, we assume them to have also a corresponding idea or form:—do you understand me?

I do.

Let us take any common instance; there are beds and tables in the world—plenty of them, are there not?

Yes.

But there are only two ideas or forms of them—one the idea of a bed, the other of a table.

True.

And the maker of either of them makes a bed or he makes a table for our use, in accordance with the idea—that is our way of speaking in this and similar instances—but no artificer makes the ideas themselves: how could he?

Impossible.

And there is another artist,—I should like to know what you would say of him.

Who is he?

One who is the maker of all the works of all other workmen.

What an extraordinary man!

Wait a little, and there will be more reason for your saying so. For this is he who is able to make not only vessels of every kind, but plants and animals, himself and all other things—the earth and heaven, and the things which are in heaven or under the earth; he makes the gods also.

He must be a wizard and no mistake.

Oh! you are incredulous, are you? Do you mean that there is no such maker or creator, or that in one sense there might be a maker of all these things but in another not? Do you see that there is a way in which you could make them all yourself?

What way?

An easy way enough; or rather, there are many ways in which the feat might be quickly and easily accomplished, none quicker than that of turning a mirror round and round—you would soon enough make the sun and the heavens, and the earth and yourself, and other animals and plants, and all the other things of which we were just now speaking, in the mirror.

Yes, he said; but they would be appearances only.

Very good, I said, you are coming to the point now. And the painter too is, as I conceive, just such another—a creator of appearances, is he not?

Of course.

But then I suppose you will say that what he creates is untrue. And yet there is a sense in which the painter also creates a bed?

Yes, he said, but not a real bed.

And what of the maker of the bed? were you not saying that he too makes, not the idea which, according to our view, is the essence of the bed, but only a particular bed?

Yes, I did.

Then if he does not make that which exists he cannot make true existence, but only some semblance of existence; and if any one were to say that the work of the maker of the bed, or of any other workman, has real existence, he could hardly be supposed to be speaking the truth.

At any rate, he replied, philosophers would say that he was not speaking the truth.

No wonder, then, that his work too is an indistinct expression of truth.

No wonder.

Suppose now that by the light of the examples just offered we enquire who this imitator is?

If you please.

Well then, here are three beds: one existing in nature, which is made by God, as I think that we may say—for no one else can be the maker?

No.

There is another which is the work of the carpenter?

Yes.

And the work of the painter is a third?

Yes.

Beds, then, are of three kinds, and there are three artists who superintend them: God, the maker of the bed, and the painter?

---

[1]Socrates speaks of imitative poets, meaning dramatists and those others who do not speak in their own voices. However, in the larger sense of imitation to be developed here, all poets and other kinds of artists are imitators.

Yes, there are three of them.

God, whether from choice or from necessity, made one bed in nature and one only; two or more such ideal beds neither ever have been nor ever will be made by God.

Why is that?

Because even if He had made but two, a third would still appear behind them which both of them would have for their idea, and that would be the ideal bed and not the two others.

Very true, he said.

God knew this, and He desired to be the real maker of a real bed, not a particular maker of a particular bed, and therefore He created a bed which is essentially and by nature one only.

So we believe.

Shall we, then, speak of Him as the natural author or maker of the bed?

Yes, he replied: inasmuch as by the natural process of creation He is the author of this and of all other things.

And what shall we say of the carpenter—is not he also the maker of the bed?

Yes.

But would you call the painter a creator and maker?

Certainly not.

Yet if he is not the maker, what is he in relation to the bed?

I think, he said, that we may fairly designate him as the imitator of that which the others make.

Good, I said; then you call him who is third in the descent from nature an imitator?

Certainly, he said.

And the tragic poet is an imitator, and therefore, like all other imitators, he is thrice removed from the king and from the truth?

That appears to be so.

Then about the imitator we are agreed. And what about the painter?—I would like to know whether he may be thought to imitate that which originally exists in nature, or only the creations of artists?

The latter.

As they are or as they appear? you have still to determine this.

What do you mean?

I mean, that you may look at a bed from different points of view, obliquely or directly or from any other point of view, and the bed will appear different, but there is no difference in reality. And the same of all things.

Yes, he said, the difference is only apparent.

Now let me ask you another question: Which is the art of painting designed to be—an imitation of things as they are, or as they appear—of appearance or of reality?

Of appearance.

Then the imitator, I said, is a long way off the truth, and can do all things because he lightly touches on a small part of them, and that part an image. For example: A painter will paint a cobbler, carpenter, or any other artist, though he knows nothing of their arts; and, if he is a good artist, he may deceive children or simple persons, when he shows them his picture of a carpenter from a distance, and they will fancy that they are looking at a real carpenter.

Certainly.

And whenever any one informs us that he has found a man who knows all the arts, and all things else that anybody knows, and every single thing with a higher degree of accuracy than any other man—whoever tells us this, I think that we can only imagine him to be a simple creature who is likely to have been deceived by some wizard or actor whom he met, and whom he thought all-knowing, because he himself was unable to analyse the nature of knowledge and ignorance and imitation.

Most true.

And so, when we hear persons saying that the tragedians, and Homer, who is at their head, know all the arts and all things human, virtue as well as vice, and divine things too, that the good poet cannot compose well unless he knows his subject, and that he who has not this knowledge can never be a poet, we ought to consider whether here also there may not be a similar illusion. Perhaps they may have come across imitators and been deceived by them; they may not have remembered when they saw their works that these were but imitations thrice removed from the truth, and could easily be made without any knowledge of the truth, because they are appearances only and not realities? Or, after all, they may be in the right, and poets do really know the things about which they seem to the many to speak so well?

The question, he said, should by all means be considered.

Now do you suppose that if a person were able to make the original as well as the image, he would seriously devote himself to the image-making branch? Would he allow imitation to be the ruling principle of his life, as if he had nothing higher in him?

I should say not.

The real artist, who knew what he was imitating, would be interested in realities and not in imitations; and would desire to leave as memorials of himself works many and fair; and, instead of being the author of encomiums, he would prefer to be the theme of them.

Yes, he said, that would be to him a source of much greater honour and profit.

Then, I said, we must put a question to Homer; not about medicine, or any of the arts to which his poems only incidentally refer: we are not going to ask him, or any other poet, whether he has cured patients like Asclepius, or left behind him a school of medicine such as the Asclepiads were, or whether he only talks about medicine and other arts at second-hand; but we have a right to know respecting military tactics, politics, education, which are the chiefest and noblest subjects of his poems, and we may fairly ask him about them. 'Friend Homer,' then we say to him, 'if you are only in the second remove from truth in what you say of virtue, and not in the third—not an image maker or imitator—and if you are able to discern what pursuits make men better or worse in private or public life, tell us what State was ever better governed by your help? The good order of Lacedaemon is due to Lycurgus, and many other cities great and small have been similarly benefited by others; but who says that you have been a good legislator to them and have done them any good? Italy and Sicily boast of Charondas, and there is Solon who is renowned among us; but what city has anything to say about you?' Is there any city which he might name?

I think not, said Glaucon; not even the Homerids themselves pretend that he was a legislator.

Well, but is there any war on record which was carried on successfully by him, or aided by his counsels, when he was alive?

There is not.

Or is there any invention of his, applicable to the arts or to human life, such as Thales the Milesian or Anacharsis the Scythian, and other ingenious men have conceived, which is attributed to him?

There is absolutely nothing of the kind.

But, if Homer never did any public service, was he privately a guide or teacher of any? Had he in his lifetime friends who loved to associate with him, and who handed down to posterity an Homeric way of life, such as was established by Pythagoras who was so greatly beloved for his wisdom, and whose followers are to this day quite celebrated for the order which was named after him?

Nothing of the kind is recorded of him. For surely, Socrates, Creophylus, the companion of Homer, that child of flesh, whose name always makes us laugh, might be more justly ridiculed for his stupidity, if, as is said, Homer was greatly neglected by him and others in his own day when he was alive?

Yes, I replied, that is the tradition. But can you imagine, Glaucon, that if Homer had really been able to educate and improve mankind—if he had possessed knowledge and not been a mere imitator—can you imagine, I say, that he would not have had many followers, and been honoured and loved by them? Protagoras of Abdera, and Prodicus of Ceos, and a host of others, have only to whisper to their contemporaries; 'You will never be able to manage either your own house or your own State until you appoint us to be your ministers of education'—and this ingenious device of theirs has such an effect in making men love them that their companions all but carry them about on their shoulders. And is it conceivable that the contemporaries of Homer, or again of Hesiod, would have allowed either of them to go about as rhapsodists, if they had really been able to make mankind virtuous? Would they not have been as unwilling to part with them as with gold, and have compelled them to stay at home with them? Or, if the master would not stay, then the disciples would have followed him about everywhere, until they had got education enough?

Yes, Socrates, that, I think, is quite true.

Then must we not infer that all these poetical individuals, beginning with Homer, are only imitators; they copy images of virtue and the like, but the truth they never reach? The poet is like a painter who, as we have already observed, will make a likeness of a cobbler though he understands nothing of cobbling; and his picture is good enough for those who know no more than he does, and judge only by colours and figures.

Quite so.

In like manner the poet with his words and phrases may be said to lay on the colours of the several arts, himself understanding their nature only enough to imitate them; and other people, who are as ignorant as he is, and judge only from his words, imagine that if he speaks of cobbling, or of military tactics, or of anything else, in metre and harmony and rhythm, he speaks very well—such is the sweet influence which melody and rhythm by nature have. And I think that you must have observed again and again what a poor appearance the tales of poets make when stripped of the colours which music puts upon them, and recited in simple prose.

Yes, he said.

They are like faces which were never really beautiful, but only blooming, and now the bloom of youth has passed away from them?

Exactly.

Here is another point: The imitator or maker of the image knows nothing of true existence; he knows appearances only. Am I not right?

Yes.

Then let us have a clear understanding, and not be satisfied with half an explanation.

Proceed.

Of the painter we say that he will paint reins, and he will paint a bit?

Yes.

And the worker in leather and brass will make them?

Certainly.

But does the painter know the right form of the bit and reins? Nay, hardly even the workers in brass and leather who make them; only the horseman who knows how to use them—he knows their right form.

Most true.

And may we not say the same of all things?

What?

That there are three arts which are concerned with all things: one which uses, another which makes, a third which imitates them?

Yes.

And the excellence or beauty or truth of every structure, animate or inanimate, and of every action of man, is relative to the use for which nature or the artist has intended them.

True.

Then the user of them must have the greatest experience of them, and he must indicate to the maker the good or bad qualities which develop themselves in use; for example, the flute-player will tell the flute-maker which of his flutes is satisfactory to the performer; we will tell him how he ought to make them, and the other will attend to his instructions?

Of course.

The one knows and therefore speaks with authority about the goodness and badness of flutes, while the other, confiding in him, will do what he is told by him?

True.

The instrument is the same, but about the excellence or badness of it the maker will only attain to a correct belief; and this he will gain from him who knows, by talking to him and being compelled to hear what he has to say, whereas the user will have knowledge?

True.

But will the imitator have either? Will he know from use whether or no his drawing is correct or beautiful? or will he have right opinion from being compelled to associate with another who knows and gives him instructions about what he should draw?

Neither.

Then he will no more have true opinion than he will have knowledge about the goodness or badness of his imitations?

I suppose not.

The imitative artist will be in a brilliant state of intelligence about his own creations?

Nay, very much the reverse.

And still he will go on imitating without knowing what makes a thing good or bad, and may be expected therefore to imitate only that which appears to be good to the ignorant multitude?

Just so.

Thus far then we are pretty well agreed that the imitator has no knowledge worth mentioning of what he imitates. Imitation is only a kind of play or sport, and the tragic poets, whether they write in Iambic or in Heroic verse, are imitators in the highest degree?

Very true.

And now tell me, I conjure you, has not imitation been shown by us to be concerned with that which is thrice removed from the truth?

Certainly.

And what is the faculty in man to which imitation is addressed?

What do you mean?

I will explain: The body which is large when seen near, appears small when seen at a distance?

True.

And the same object appears straight when looked at out of the water, and crooked when in the water; and the concave becomes convex, owing to the illusion about colours to which the sight is liable. Thus every sort of confusion is revealed within us; and this is that weakness of the human mind on which the art of conjuring and of deceiving by light and shadow and other ingenious devices imposes, having an effect upon us like magic.

True.

And the arts of measuring and numbering and weighing come to the rescue of the human understanding—there is the beauty of them—and the apparent greater or less, or more or heavier, no longer have the mastery over us, but give way before calculation and measure and weight?

Most true.

And this, surely, must be the work of the calculating and rational principle in the soul?

To be sure.

And when this principle measures and certifies that some things are equal, or that some are greater or less than others, there occurs an apparent contradiction?

True.

But were we not saying that such a contradiction is impossible—the same faculty cannot have contrary opinions at the same time about the same thing?

Very true.

Then that part of the soul which has an opinion contrary to measure is not the same with that which has an opinion in accordance with measure?

True.

And the better part of the soul is likely to be that which trusts to measure and calculation?

Certainly.

And that which is opposed to them is one of the inferior principles of the soul?

No doubt.

This was the conclusion at which I was seeking to arrive when I said that painting or drawing, and imitation in general, when doing their own proper work, are far removed from truth, and the companions and friends and associates of a principle within us which is equally removed from reason, and that they have no true or healthy aim.

Exactly.

The imitative art is an inferior who marries an inferior, and has inferior offspring.

Very true.

And is this confined to the sight only, or does it extend to the hearing also, relating in fact to what we term poetry?

Probably the same would be true of poetry.

Do not rely, I said, on a probability derived from the analogy of painting; but let us examine further and see whether the faculty with which poetical imitation is concerned is good or bad.

By all means.

We may state the question thus:—Imitation imitates the actions of men, whether voluntary or involuntary, on which, as they imagine, a good or bad result has ensued, and they rejoice or sorrow accordingly. Is there anything more?

No, there is nothing else.

But in all this variety of circumstances is the man at unity with himself—or rather, as in the instance of sight there was confusion and opposition in his opinions about the same things, so here also is there not strife and inconsistency in his life? Though I need hardly raise the question again, for I remember that all this has been already admitted; and the soul has been acknowledged by us to be full of these and ten thousand similar oppositions occurring at the same moment?

And we were right, he said.

Yes, I said, thus far we were right; but there was an omission which must now be supplied.

What was the omission?

Were we not saying that a good man, who has the misfortune to lose his son or anything else which is most dear to him, will bear the loss with more equanimity than another?

Yes.

But will he have no sorrow, or shall we say that although he cannot help sorrowing, he will moderate his sorrow?

The latter, he said, is the truer statement.

Tell me: will he be more likely to struggle and hold out against his sorrow when he is seen by his equals, or when he is alone?

It will make a great difference whether he is seen or not.

When he is by himself he will not mind saying or doing many things which he would be ashamed of any one hearing or seeing him do?

True.

There is a principle of law and reason in him which bids him resist, as well as a feeling of his misfortune which is forcing him to indulge his sorrow?

True.

But when a man is drawn in two opposite directions, to and from the same object, this, as we affirm, necessarily implies two distinct principles in him?

Certainly.

One of them is ready to follow the guidance of the law?

How do you mean?

The law would say that to be patient under suffering is best, and that we should not give way to impatience, as there is no knowing whether such things are good or evil; and nothing is gained by impatience; also, because no human thing is of serious importance, and grief stands in the way of that which at the moment is most required.

What is most required? he asked.

That we should take counsel about what has happened, and when the dice have been thrown order our affairs in the way which reason deems best; not, like children who have had a fall, keeping hold of the part struck and wasting time in setting up a howl, but always accustoming the soul forthwith to apply a remedy, raising up that which is sickly and fallen, banishing the cry of sorrow by the healing art.

Yes, he said, that is the true way of meeting the attacks of fortune.

Yes, I said; and the higher principle is ready to follow this suggestion of reason?

Clearly.

And the other principle, which inclines us to recollection of our troubles and to lamentation, and can never have enough of them, we may call irrational, useless, and cowardly?

Indeed, we may.

And does not the latter—I mean the rebellious principle—furnish a great variety of materials for imitation? Whereas the wise and calm temperament, being always nearly equable, is not easy to imitate or to appreciate when imitated, especially at a public festival when a promiscuous crowd is assembled in a theatre. For the feeling represented is one to which they are strangers.

Certainly.

Then the imitative poet who aims at being popular is not by nature made, nor is his art intended, to please or to affect the rational principle in the soul; but he will prefer the passionate and fitful temper, which is easily imitated?

Clearly.

And now we may fairly take him and place him by the side of the painter, for he is like him in two ways: first, inasmuch as his creations have an inferior degree of truth—in this, I say, he is like him; and he is also like him in being concerned with an inferior part of the soul; and therefore we shall be right in refusing to admit him into a well-ordered State, because he awakens and nourishes and strengthens the feelings and impairs the reason. As in a city when the evil are permitted to have authority and the good are put out of the way, so in the soul of man, as we maintain, the imitative poet implants an evil constitution, for he indulges the irrational nature which has no discernment of greater and less, but thinks the same thing at one time great and at another small—he is a manufacturer of images and is very far removed from the truth.

Exactly.

But we have not yet brought forward the heaviest count in our accusation:—the power which poetry has of harming even the good (and there are very few who are not harmed), is surely an awful thing?

Yes, certainly, if the effect is what you say.

Hear and judge: The best of us, as I conceive, when we listen to a passage of Homer, or one of the tragedians, in which he represents some pitiful hero who is drawling out his sorrows in a long oration, or weeping, and smiting his breast—the best of us, you know, delight in giving way to sympathy, and are in raptures at the excellence of the poet who stirs our feelings most.

Yes, of course I know.

But when any sorrow of our own happens to us, then you may observe that we pride ourselves on the opposite quality—we would fain be quiet and patient; this is the manly part, and the other which delighted us in the recitation is now deemed to be the part of a woman.

Very true, he said.

Now can we be right in praising and admiring another who is doing that which any one of us would abominate and be ashamed of in his own person?

No, he said, that is certainly not reasonable.

Nay, I said, quite reasonable from one point of view.

What point of view?

If you consider, I said, that when in misfortune we feel a natural hunger and desire to relieve our sorrow by weeping and lamentation, and that this feeling which is kept under control in our own calamities is satisfied and delighted by the poets;—the better nature in each of us, not having been sufficiently trained by reason or habit, allows the sympathetic element to break loose because the sorrow is another's; and the spectator fancies that there can be no disgrace to himself in praising and pitying any one who comes telling him what a good man he is, and making a fuss about his troubles; he thinks that the pleasure is a gain, and why should he be supercilious and lose this and the poem too? Few persons ever reflect, as I should imagine, that from the evil of other men something of evil is communicated to themselves. And so the feeling of sorrow which has gathered strength at the sight of the misfortunes of others is with difficulty repressed in our own.

How very true!

And does not the same hold also of the ridiculous? There are jests which you would be ashamed to make yourself, and yet on the comic stage, or indeed in private, when you hear them, you are greatly amused by them, and are not at all disgusted at their unseemliness;—the case of pity is repeated;—there is a principle in human nature which is disposed to raise a laugh, and this which you once restrained by reason, because you were afraid of being thought a buffoon, is now let out again; and having stimulated the risible faculty at the theatre, you are betrayed unconsciously to yourself into playing the comic poet at home.

Quite true, he said.

And the same may be said of lust and anger and all the other affections, of desire and pain and pleasure, which are held to be inseparable from every action—in all of them poetry feeds and waters the passions instead of drying them up; she lets them rule, although they ought to be controlled, if mankind are ever to increase in happiness and virtue.

I cannot deny it.

Therefore, Glaucon, I said, whenever you meet with any of the eulogists of Homer declaring that he has been the educator of Hellas, and that he is profitable for education and for the ordering of human things, and that you should take him up again and again and get to know him and regulate your whole life according to him, we may love and honour those who say these things—they are excellent people, as far as their lights extend; and we are ready to acknowledge that Homer is the greatest of poets and first of tragedy writers; but we must remain firm in our conviction that hymns to the gods and praises of famous men are the only poetry which ought to be admitted into our State. For if you go beyond this and allow the honeyed muse to enter, either in epic or lyric verse, not law and the reason of mankind, which by common consent have ever been deemed best, but pleasure and pain will be the rulers in our State.

That is most true, he said.

And now since we have reverted to the subject of poetry, let this our defence serve to show the reasonableness of our former judgment in sending away out of our State an art having the tendencies which we have described; for reason constrained us. But that she may not impute to us any harshness or want of politeness, let us tell her that there is an ancient quarrel between philosophy and poetry; of which there are many proofs, such as the saying of 'the yelping hound howling at her lord,' or of one 'mighty in the vain talk of fools,' and 'the mob of sages circumventing Zeus,' and the 'subtle thinkers who are beggars after all'; and there are innumerable other signs of ancient enmity between them. Notwithstanding this, let us assure our sweet friend and the sister arts of imitation, that if she will only prove her title to exist in a well-ordered State we shall be delighted to receive her—we are very conscious of her charms; but we may not on that account betray the truth. I dare say, Glaucon, that you are as much charmed by her as I am, especially when she appears in Homer?

Yes, indeed, I am greatly charmed.

Shall I propose, then, that she be allowed to return from exile, but upon this condition only—that she make a defence of herself in lyrical or some other metre?

Certainly.

And we may further grant to those of her defenders who are lovers of poetry and yet not poets the permission to speak in prose on her behalf: let them show not only that she is pleasant but also useful to States and to human life, and we will listen in a kindly spirit; for if this can be proved we shall surely be the gainers—I mean, if there is a use in poetry as well as a delight?

Certainly, he said, we shall be the gainers.

If her defence fails, then, my dear friend, like other persons who are enamoured of something, but put a restraint upon themselves when they think their desires are opposed to their interests, so too must we after the manner of lovers give her up, though not without a struggle. We too are inspired by that love of poetry which the education of noble States has implanted in us, and therefore we would have her appear at her best and truest; but so long as she is unable to make good her defence, this argument of ours shall be a charm to us, which we will repeat to ourselves while we listen to her strains; that we may not fall away into the childish love of her which captivates the many. At all events we are well aware that poetry being such as we have described is not to be regarded seriously as attaining to the truth: and he who listens to her, fearing for the safety of the city which is within him, should be on his guard against her seductions and make our words his law.

Yes, he said, I quite agree with you.

Yes, I said, my dear Glaucon, for great is the issue at stake, greater than appears, whether a man is to be good or bad. And what will any one be profited if under the influence of honour or money or power, aye, or under the excitement of poetry, he neglect justice and virtue?

Yes, he said; I have been convinced by the argument, as I believe that any one else would have been.

from

Phaedrus

PERSONS OF THE DIALOGUE:
Socrates, Phaedrus

The third kind is the madness[1] of those who are possessed by the Muses: which taking hold of a delicate and virgin soul, and there inspiring frenzy, awakens lyrical and all other numbers: with these adorning the myriad actions of ancient heroes for the instruction of posterity. But he who, having no touch of the Muses' madness in his soul, comes to the door and thinks that he will get into the temple by the help of art—he, I say, and his poetry are not admitted: the sane man disappears and is nowhere when he enters into rivalry with the madman.

Socrates   And of madness there were two kinds; one produced by human infirmity, the other was a divine release of the soul from yoke of custom and convention.[2]

Phaedrus   True.

Socrates   The divine madness was subdivided into four kinds, prophetic, initiatory, poetic, erotic, having four gods presiding over them; the first was the inspiration of Apollo, the second that of Dionysus, the third that of the Muses, the fourth that of Aphrodite and Eros. In the description of the last kind of madness, which was also said to be the best, we spoke of the affection of love in a figure, into which we introduced a tolerably credible and possibly true though partly erring myth, which was also a hymn in honour of Love, who is your lord and also mine, Phaedrus, and the guardian of fair children, and to him we sung the hymn in measured and solemn strain.

Phaedrus   I know that I had great pleasure in listening to you.

[1]The types of madness, of which the poetic is the third, are mentioned in the excerpt below.
[2]Discussed earlier in the dialogue.

Socrates Let us take this instance and note how the transition was made from blame to praise.

Phaedrus What do you mean?

Socrates I mean to say that the composition was mostly playful. Yet in these chance fancies of the hour were involved two principles of which we should be too glad to have a clearer description if art could give us one.

Phaedrus What are they?

Socrates First, the comprehension of scattered particulars in one idea; as in our definition of love, which whether true or false certainly gave clearness and consistency to the discourse, the speaker should define his several notions and so make his meaning clear.

Phaedrus What is the other principle, Socrates?

Socrates The second principle is that of division into species according to the natural formation, where the joint is, not breaking any part as a bad carver might. Just as our two discourses, alike assumed, first of all, a single form of unreason; and then, as the body which from being one becomes double and may be divided into a left side and right side, each having parts right and left of the same name—after this manner the speaker proceeded to divide the parts of the left side and did not desist until he found in them an evil or left-handed love which he justly reviled; and the other discourse leading us to the madness which lay on the right side, found another love, also having the same name, but divine, which the speaker held up before us and applauded and affirmed to be the author of the greatest benefits.

Phaedrus Most true.

Socrates I am myself a great lover of these processes of division and generalization; they help me to speak and to think. And if I find any man who is able to see 'a One and Many' in nature,[3] him I follow, and 'walk in his footsteps as if he were a god.' And those who have this art, I have hitherto been in the habit of calling dialecticians; but God knows whether the name is right or not. And I should like to know what name you would give to your or to Lysias'[4] disciples, and whether this may not be that famous art of rhetoric which Thrasymachus and others teach and practise? Skilful speakers they are, and impart their skill to any who is willing to make kings of them and to bring gifts to them.

Socrates At the Egyptian city of Naucratis, there was a famous old god, whose name was Theuth; the bird which is called the Ibis is sacred to him, and he was the inventor of many arts, such as arithmetic and calculation and geometry and astronomy and draughts and dice, but his great discovery was the use of letters. Now in those days the god Thamus was the king of the whole country of Egypt; and he dwelt in that great city of Upper Egypt which the Hellenes call Egyptian Thebes, and the god himself is called by them Ammon. To him came Theuth and showed his inventions, desiring that the other Egyptians might be allowed to have the benefit of them; he enumerated them, and Thamus enquired about their several uses, and praised some of them and censured others, as he approved or disapproved of them. It would take a long time to repeat all that Thamus said to Theuth in praise or blame of the various arts. But when they came to letters, This, said Theuth, will make the Egyptians wiser and give them better memories; it is a specific both for the memory and for the wit. Thamus replied: O most ingenious Theuth, the parent or inventor of an art is not always the best judge of the utility or inutility of his own inventions to the users of them. And in this instance, you who are the father of letters, from a paternal love of your own children have been led to attribute to them a quality which they cannot have; for this discovery of yours will create forgetfulness in the learners' souls, because they will not use their memories; they will trust to the external written characters and not remember of themselves. The specific which you have discovered is an aid not to memory, but to reminiscence, and you give your disciples not truth, but only the semblance of truth; they will be hearers of many things and will have learned nothing; they will appear to be omniscient and will generally know nothing; they will be tiresome company, having the show of wisdom without the reality.[5]

Phaedrus Yes, Socrates, you can easily invent tales of Egypt, or of any other country.

Socrates There was a tradition in the temple of Dodona that oaks first gave prophetic utterances. The men of old, unlike in their simplicity to young philosophy, deemed that if they heard the truth even from 'oak or rock,' it was enough for them; whereas you seem to consider not whether a thing is or is not true, but who the speaker is and from what country the tale comes.

Phaedrus I acknowledge the justice of your rebuke; and I think that the Theban is right in his view about letters.

Socrates He would be a very simple person, and quite a stranger to the oracles of Thamus or Ammon, who should leave in writing or receive in writing any art under

---

[3]On "one and many" see the excerpt from *Philebus* (below, page 40).

[4]This dialogue begins with Phaedrus reading aloud to Socrates Lysias's oration on love, in which he argues that one should accept someone who is not in love with one rather than a lover. Socrates ironically praises the speech, but only as a piece of rhetoric. In connection with this see *Sophist* (below, page 39).

[5]The story of Theuth and Thamus is interesting in the light of modern linguistics, which tends also to privilege speech over writing and Jacques Derrida's (below page 1221ff.) poststructuralist criticism of this.

the idea that the written word would be intelligible or certain; or who deemed that writing was at all better than knowledge and recollection of the same matters?

Phaedrus   That is most true.

Socrates   I cannot help feeling, Phaedrus, that writing is unfortunately like painting; for the creations of the painter have the attitude of life, and yet if you ask them a question they preserve a solemn silence. And the same may be said of speeches. You would imagine that they had intelligence, but if you want to know anything and put a question to one of them, the speaker always gives one unvarying answer. And when they have been once written down they are tumbled about anywhere among those who may or may not understand them, and know not to whom they should reply, to whom not: and, if they are maltreated or abused, they have no parent to protect them; and they cannot protect or defend themselves.

Phaedrus   That again is most true.

Socrates   Is there not another kind of word or speech far better than this, and having far greater power—a son of the same family, but lawfully begotten?

Phaedrus   Whom do you mean, and what is his origin?

Socrates   I mean an intelligent word graven in the soul of the learner, which can defend itself, and knows when to speak and when to be silent.

Phaedrus   You mean the living word of knowledge which has a soul, and of which the written word is properly no more than an image?

Socrates   Yes, of course that is what I mean.

from

Sophist

PERSONS OF THE DIALOGUE:
Theaetetus, Stranger

Stranger   How do the Sophists make young men believe in their supreme and universal wisdom? For if they neither disputed nor were thought to dispute rightly, or being thought to do so were deemed no wiser for their controversial skill, then, to quote your own observation, no one would give them money or be willing to learn their art.[1]

Theaetetus   They certainly would not.

---

[1] Up to this point the dialogue has been concerned with the attempt to make clear what a sophist is, and the sophist has proved difficult to pin down because he appears in many guises. Generally, in the dialogues sophists are identified with rhetoricians, of whom the Stranger (and elsewhere Socrates) is deeply suspicious.

Stranger   But they are willing.

Theaetetus   Yes, they are.

Stranger   Yes, and the reason, as I should imagine, is that they are supposed to have knowledge of those things about which they dispute?

Theaetetus   Certainly.

Stranger   And they dispute about all things?

Theaetetus   True.

Stranger   And therefore, to their disciples, they appear to be all-wise?

Theaetetus   Certainly.

Stranger   But they are not; for that was shown to be impossible.

Theaetetus   Impossible, of course.

Stranger   Then the Sophist has been shown to have a sort of conjectural or apparent knowledge only of all things, which is not the truth?

Theaetetus   Exactly; no better description of him could be given.

Stranger   Let us now take an illustration, which will still more clearly explain his nature.

Theaetetus   What is it?

Stranger   I will tell you, and you shall answer me, giving your very closest attention. Suppose that a person were to profess, not that he could speak or dispute, but that he knew how to make and do all things, by a single art.

Theaetetus   All things?

Stranger   I see that you do not understand the first word that I utter, for you do not understand the meaning of 'all.'

Theaetetus   No, I do not.

Stranger   Under all things, I include you and me, and also animals and trees.

Theaetetus   What do you mean?

Stranger   Suppose a person to say that he will make you and me, and all creatures.

Theaetetus   What would he mean by 'making'? He cannot be a husbandman;—for you said that he is a maker of animals.

Stranger   Yes; and I say that he is also the maker of the sea, and the earth, and the heavens, and the gods, and of all other things; and, further, that he can make them in no time, and sell them for a few pence.

Theaetetus   That must be a jest.

Stranger   And when a man says that he knows all things, and can teach them to another at a small cost, and in a short time, is not that a jest?

Theaetetus   Certainly.

Stranger   And is there any more artistic or graceful form of jest than imitation?

Theaetetus Certainly not; and imitation is a very comprehensive term, which includes under one class the most diverse sorts of things.

Stranger We know, of course, that he who professes by one art to make all things is really a painter, and by the painter's art makes resemblances of real things which have the same name with them; and he can deceive the less intelligent sort of young children, to whom he shows his pictures at a distance, into the belief that he has the absolute power of making whatever he likes.

Theaetetus Certainly.

Stranger And may there not be supposed to be an imitative art of reasoning? Is it not possible to enchant the hearts of young men by words poured through their ears, when they are still at a distance from the truth of facts, by exhibiting to them fictitious arguments, and making them think that they are true, and that the speaker is the wisest of men in all things?

Theaetetus Yes; why should there not be another such art?

Stranger But as time goes on, and their hearers advance in years, and come into closer contact with realities, and have learnt by sad experience to see and feel the truth of things, are not the greater part of them compelled to change many opinions which they formerly entertained, so that the great appears small to them, and the easy difficult, and all their dreamy speculations are overturned by the facts of life?

Theaetetus That is my view, as far as I can judge, although, at my age, I may be one of those who see things at a distance only.

Stranger And the wish of all of us, who are your friends, is and always will be to bring you as near to the truth as we can without the sad reality. And now I should like you to tell me, whether the Sophist is not visibly a magician and imitator of true being; or are we still disposed to think that he may have a true knowledge of the various matters about which he disputes?

Theaetetus But how can he, Stranger? Is there any doubt, after what has been said, that he is to be located in one of the divisions of children's play?

Stranger Then we must place him in the class of magicians and mimics.

Theaetetus Certainly we must.

Stranger And now our business is not to let the animal out, for we have got him in a sort of dialectical net, and there is one thing which he decidedly will not escape.

Theaetetus What is that?

Stranger The inference that he is a juggler.

Theaetetus Precisely my own opinion of him.

Stranger Then, clearly, we ought as soon as possible to divide the image-making art, and go down into the net, and, if the Sophist does not run away from us, to seize him according to orders and deliver him over to reason, who is the lord of the hunt, and proclaim the capture of him; and if he creeps into the recesses of the imitative art, and secretes himself in one of them, to divide again and follow him up until in some sub-section of imitation he is caught. For our method of tackling each and all is one which neither he nor any other creature will ever escape in triumph.

Theaetetus Well said; and let us do as you propose.

Stranger Well, then, pursuing the same analytic method as before, I think that I can discern two divisions of the imitative art, but I am not as yet able to see in which of them the desired form is to be found.[2]

Theaetetus Will you tell me first what are the two divisions of which you are speaking?

Stranger One is the art of likeness-making;—generally a likeness of anything is made by producing a copy which is executed according to the proportions of the original, similar in length and breadth and depth, each thing receiving also its appropriate colour.

Theaetetus Is not this always the aim of imitation?

Stranger Not always; in works either of sculpture or of painting, which are of any magnitude, there is a certain degree of deception; for if artists were to give the true proportions of their fair works, the upper part, which is farther off, would appear to be out of proportion in comparison with the lower, which is nearer; and so they give up the truth in their images and make only the proportions which appear to be beautiful, disregarding the real ones.

Theaetetus Quite true.

Stranger And that which being other is also like, may we not fairly call a likeness or image?

Theaetetus Yes.

Stranger And may we not, as I did just now, call that part of the imitative art which is concerned with making such images the art of likeness-making?

Theaetetus Let that be the name.

Stranger And what shall we call those resemblances of the beautiful, which appear such owing to the unfavourable position of the spectator, whereas if a person had the power of getting a correct view of works of such magnitude, they would appear not even like that to which they

---

[2]Here the Stranger makes an influential distinction between "icastic" and "phantastic" forms of imitation, the first likeness-making and the second the making of things that do not exist. See Sidney (below, page 199); Mazzoni (below, page 220).

profess to be like? May we not call these 'appearances,' since they appear only and are not really like?

Theaetetus Certainly.

Stranger There is a great deal of this kind of thing in painting, and in all imitation.

Theaetetus Of course.

Stranger And may we not fairly call the sort of art, which produces an appearance and not an image, phantastic art?

Theaetetus Most fairly.

Stranger These then are the two kinds of image-making—the art of making likenesses, and phantastic or the art of making appearances?

Theaetetus True.

Stranger I was doubtful before in which of them I should place the Sophist, nor am I even now able to see clearly; verily he is a wonderful and inscrutable creature. And now in the cleverest manner he has got into an impossible place.

Theaetetus Yes, he has.

Stranger Do you speak advisedly, or are you carried away at the moment by the habit of assenting into giving a hasty answer?

Theaetetus May I ask to what you are referring?

Stranger My dear friend, we are engaged in a very difficult speculation—there can be no doubt of that; for how a thing can appear and seem, and not be, or how a man can say a thing which is not true, has always been and still remains a very perplexing question. Can any one say or think that falsehood really exists, and avoid being caught in a contradiction? Indeed, Theaetetus, the task is a difficult one.

Theaetetus Why?

Stranger He who says that falsehood exists has the audacity to assert the being of not-being; for this is implied in the possibility of falsehood. But, my boy, in the days when I was a boy, the great Parmenides protested against this doctrine, and to the end of his life he continued to inculcate the same lesson—always repeating both in verse and out of verse:

'Keep your mind from this way of enquiry, for never will you show that not-being is.'[3]

---

[3]Parmenides (b.c. 515 B.C.), Greek philosopher. Both forms of imitation make things that do not, according to the Stranger, have being. This leads to a discussion of "being" and "not-being" and the puzzle that these words create.

PERSONS OF THE DIALOGUE:
Protarchus, Philebus, Socrates

Socrates When, my boy, the one does not belong to the class of things that are born and perish, as in the instances which we were giving, for in those cases, and when unity is of this concrete nature, there is, as I was saying, a universal consent that no refutation is needed; but when the assertion is made that man is one, or ox is one, or beauty one, or the good one, then the interest which attaches to these and similar unities and the attempt which is made to divide them gives birth to a controversy.[1]

Protarchus Of what nature?

Socrates In the first place, as to whether these unities have a real existence; and then how each individual unity, being always the same, and incapable either of generation or of destruction, but retaining a permanent individuality, can be conceived either as dispersed and multiplied in the infinity of the world of generation, or as still entire and yet divided from itself, which latter would seem to be the greatest impossibility of all, for how can one and the same thing be at the same time in one and in many things? These, Protarchus, are the real difficulties, and this is the one and many to which they relate; they are the source of great perplexity if ill decided, and the right determination of them is very helpful.

Protarchus Then, Socrates, let us begin by clearing up these questions.

Socrates That is what I should wish.

Protarchus And I am sure that all my other friends will be glad to hear them discussed; Philebus, fortunately for us, is not disposed to move, and we had better not stir him up with questions.

Socrates Good; and where shall we begin this great and multifarious battle, in which such various points are at issue? Shall we begin thus?

Protarchus How?

Socrates We say that the one and many become identified by thought, and that now, as in time past, they run about together, in and out of every word which is uttered, and that this union of them will never cease, and is not now beginning, but is, as I believe, an everlasting quality of

---

[1]Socrates has been discussing whether knowledge is one thing or many things and the general question of the one and the many, or oneness and manyness.

thought itself, which never grows old.[2] Any young man, when he first tastes these subtleties, is delighted, and fancies that he has found a treasure of wisdom; in the first enthusiasm of his joy he leaves no stone, or rather no thought unturned, now rolling up the many into the one, and kneading them together, now unfolding and dividing them; he puzzles himself first and above all, and then he proceeds to puzzle his neighbours, whether they are older or younger, or of his own age—that makes no difference; neither father nor mother does he spare; no human being who has ears is safe from him, hardly even his dog, and a barbarian would have no chance of escaping him, if an interpreter could only be found.

from

Cratylus

PERSONS OF THE DIALOGUE:
Socrates, Hermogenes, Cratylus

Socrates   Have we not been saying that the correct name indicates the nature of the thing:—has this proposition been sufficiently proven?[1]

Cratylus   Yes, Socrates, what you say, as I am disposed to think, is quite true.

Socrates   Names, then, are given in order to instruct?

Cratylus   Certainly.

Socrates   And naming is an art, and has artificers?

Cratylus   Yes.

Socrates   And who are they?

Cratylus   The legislators,[2] of whom you spoke at first.

Socrates   And does this art grow up among men like other arts? Let me explain what I mean: of painters, some are better and some worse?

Cratylus   Yes.

Socrates   The better painters execute their works, I mean their figures, better, and the worse execute them worse; and of builders also, the better sort build fairer houses, and the worse build them worse.

Cratylus   True.

Socrates   And among legislators, there are some who do their work better and some worse?

Cratylus   No; there I do not agree with you.

Socrates   Then you do not think that some laws are better and others worse?

Cratylus   No, indeed.

Socrates   Or that one name is better than another?

Cratylus   Certainly not.

Socrates   Then all names are rightly imposed?

Cratylus   Yes, if they are names at all.

Socrates   Well, what do you say to the name of our friend Hermogenes, which was mentioned before:—assuming that he has nothing of the nature of Hermes in him, shall we say that this is a wrong name, or not his name at all?[3]

Cratylus   I should reply that Hermogenes is not his name at all, but only appears to be his, and is really the name of somebody else, who has the nature which corresponds to it.

Socrates   And if a man were to call him Hermogenes, would he not be even speaking falsely? For there may be a doubt whether you can call him Hermogenes, if he is not.

Cratylus   What do you mean?

Socrates   Are you maintaining that falsehood is impossible? For if this is your meaning I should answer, that there have been plenty of liars in all ages.

Cratylus   Why, Socrates, how can a man say that which is not?—say something and yet say nothing? For is not falsehood saying the thing which is not?

Socrates   Your argument, friend, is too subtle for a man of my age. But I should like to know whether you are one of those philosophers who think that falsehood may be spoken but not said?

Cratylus   Neither spoken nor said.

Socrates   Nor uttered nor addressed? For example: If a person, saluting you in a foreign country, were to take your hand and say: 'Hail, Athenian stranger, Hermogenes, son of Smicrion'—these words, whether spoken, said, uttered, or addressed, would have no application to you but only to our friend Hermogenes, or perhaps to nobody at all?

Cratylus   In my opinion, Socrates, the speaker would only be talking nonsense.

Socrates   Well, but that will be quite enough for me, if you will tell me whether the nonsense would be true or false, or partly true and partly false:—which is all that I want to know.

---

[2]Some translations mention sentences or language rather than thought here, explicitly identifying the problem as one of language.

[1]The dialogue has begun with a discussion between Hermogenes and Socrates of names and their appropriateness to what they denote. Socrates has speculated that there were original, primary, or "first" names, from which later "secondary" names were derived.

[2]Early in the dialogue, Socrates and Hermogenes have agreed that the legislator is the giver of names. Shelley uses "legislator" in this sense in a much quoted passage at the end of his *Defense of Poetry* (below, page 551).

---

[3]Early in the dialogue there has been a discussion of what we call proper names.

Cratylus I should say that he would be putting himself in motion to no purpose; and that his words would be an unmeaning sound like the noise of hammering at a brazen pot.

Socrates But let us see, Cratylus, whether we cannot find a meeting-point, for you would admit that the name is not the same with the thing named?

Cratylus I should.

Socrates And would you further acknowledge that the name is an imitation of the thing?

Cratylus Certainly.

Socrates And you would say that pictures are also imitations of things, but in another way?

Cratylus Yes.

Socrates I believe you may be right, but I do not rightly understand you! Please to say, then, whether both sorts of imitation (I mean both pictures or words) are not equally attributable and applicable to the things of which they are the imitation.

Cratylus They are.

Socrates First look at the matter thus: you may attribute the likeness of the man to the man, and of the woman to the woman; and so on?

Cratylus Certainly.

Socrates And conversely you may attribute the likeness of the man to the woman, and of the woman to the man?

Cratylus Very true.

Socrates And are both modes of assigning them right, or only the first?

Cratylus Only the first.

Socrates That is to say, the mode of assignment which attributes to each that which belongs to them and is like them?

Cratylus That is my view.

Socrates Now then, as I am desirous that we being friends should have a good understanding about the argument, let me state my view to you: the first mode of assignment, whether applied to figures or to names, I call right, and when applied to names only, true as well as right; and the other mode of giving and assigning the name which is unlike, I call wrong, and in the case of names, false as well as wrong.

Cratylus That may be true, Socrates, in the case of pictures; they may be wrongly assigned; but not in the case of names—they must be always right.

Socrates Why, what is the difference? May I not go to a man and say to him, 'This is your picture,' showing him his own likeness, or perhaps the likeness of a woman; and when I say 'show,' I mean bring before the sense of sight.

Cratylus Certainly.

Socrates And may I not go to him again, and say, 'This is your name'?—for the name, like the picture, is an imitation. May I not say to him—'This is your name'? and may I not then bring to his sense of hearing the imitation of himself, when I say, 'This is a man;' or of a female of the human species, when I say, 'This is a woman,' as the case may be? Is not all that quite possible?

Cratylus I would fain agree with you, Socrates; and therefore I say, Granted.

Socrates That is very good of you, if I am right, which need hardly be disputed at present. But if I can assign names as well as pictures to objects, the right assignment of them we may call truth, and the wrong assignment of them falsehood. Now if there be such a wrong assignment of names, there may also be a wrong or inappropriate assignment of verbs; and if of names and verbs then of the sentences, which are made up of them. What do you say, Cratylus?

Cratylus I agree; and think that what you say is very true.

Socrates And further, primitive nouns may be compared to pictures, and in pictures you may either give all the appropriate colours and figures, or you may not give them all—some may be wanting; or there may be too many or too much of them—may there not?

Cratylus Very true.

Socrates And he who gives all gives a perfect picture or figure; and he who takes away or adds also gives a picture or figure, but not a good one.

Cratylus Yes.

Socrates In like manner, he who by syllables and letters imitates the nature of things, if he gives all that is appropriate will produce a good image, or in other words a name; but if he subtracts or perhaps adds a little, he will make an image but not a good one; whence I infer that some names are well and others ill made.

Cratylus That is true.

Socrates Then the artist of names may be sometimes good, or he may be bad?

Cratylus Yes.

Socrates And this artist of names is called the legislator?

Cratylus Yes.

Socrates Then like other artists the legislator may be good or he may be bad; it must surely be so if our former admissions hold good?

Cratylus Very true, Socrates; but the case of language, you see, is different; for when by the help of grammar we assign the letters α or β, or any other letters to a certain name, then, if we add, or subtract, or misplace a letter, the name which is written is not only written wrongly, but not written at all; and in any of these cases becomes other than a name.

Socrates   But I doubt whether your view is altogether correct, Cratylus.

Cratylus   How so?

Socrates   I believe that what you say may be true about numbers, which must be just what they are, or not be at all; for example, the number ten at once becomes other than ten if a unit be added or subtracted, and so of any other number: but this does not apply to that which is qualitative or to anything which is represented under an image. I should say rather that the image, if expressing in every point the entire reality, would no longer be an image. Let us suppose the existence of two objects: one of them shall be Cratylus, and the other the image of Cratylus; and we will suppose, further, that some God makes not only a representation such as a painter would make of your outward form and colour, but also creates an inward organization like yours, having the same warmth and softness; and into this infuses motion, and soul, and mind, such as you have, and in a word copies all your qualities, and places them by you in another form; would you say that this was Cratylus and the image of Cratylus, or that there were two Cratyluses?

Cratylus   I should say that there were two Cratyluses.

Socrates   Then you see, my friend, that we must find some other principle of truth in images, and also in names: and not insist that an image is no longer an image when something is added or subtracted. Do you not perceive that images are very far from having qualities which are the exact counterpart of the realities which they represent?

Cratylus   Yes, I see.

Socrates   But then how ridiculous would be the effect of names on things, if they were exactly the same with them! For they would be the doubles of them, and no one would be able to determine which were the names and which were the realities.

Cratylus   Quite true.

Socrates   Then fear not, but have the courage to admit that one name may be correctly and another incorrectly given: and do not insist that the name shall be exactly the same with the thing; but allow the occasional substitution of a wrong letter, and if of a letter also of a noun in a sentence, and if of a noun in a sentence also of a sentence which is not appropriate to the matter, and acknowledge that the thing may be named, and described, so long as the general character of the thing which you are describing is retained; and this, as you will remember, was remarked by Hermogenes

and myself in the particular instance of the names of the letters.

Cratylus   Yes, I remember.

Socrates   Good; and when the general character is preserved, even if some of the proper letters are wanting, still the thing is signified;—well, if all the letters are given; not well, when only a few of them are given. I think that we had better admit this, lest we be punished like travellers in Ægina who wander about the street late at night: and be likewise told by truth herself that we have arrived too late; or if not, you must find out some new notion of correctness of names, and no longer maintain that a name is the expression of a thing in letters or syllables; for if you say both, you will be inconsistent with yourself.

Cratylus   I quite acknowledge, Socrates, what you say to be very reasonable.

Socrates   Then as we are agreed thus far, let us ask ourselves whether a name rightly imposed ought not to have the proper letters.

Cratylus   Yes.

Socrates   And the proper letters are those which are like the things?

Cratylus   Yes.

Socrates   Enough then of names which are rightly given. And in names which are incorrectly given, the greater part may be supposed to be made up of proper and similar letters, or there would be no likeness; but there will be likewise a part which is improper and spoils the beauty and formation of the word: you would admit that?

Cratylus   There would be no use, Socrates, in my quarrelling with you, since I cannot be satisfied that a name which is incorrectly given is a name at all.

Socrates   Do you admit a name to be the representation of a thing?

Cratylus   Yes, I do.

Socrates   But do you not allow that some nouns are primitive, and some derived?

Cratylus   Yes, I do.

Socrates   Then if you admit that primitive or first nouns are representations of things, is there any better way of framing representations than by assimilating them to the objects as much as you can; or do you prefer the notion of Hermogenes and of many others, who say that names are conventional, and have a meaning to those who have agreed about them, and who have previous knowledge of the things intended by them, and that convention is the only principle; and whether you abide by our present convention, or make a new and opposite one, according to which you call small great and great small—that, they would say, makes no difference, if you are only agreed. Which of these two notions do you prefer?

Cratylus Representation by likeness, Socrates, is infinitely better than representation by any chance sign.

Socrates Very good: but if the name is to be like the thing, the letters out of which the first names are composed must also be like things. Returning to the image of the picture, I would ask, How could any one ever compose a picture which would be like anything at all, if there were not pigments in nature which resembled the things imitated, and out of which the picture is composed?

Cratylus Impossible.

Socrates No more could names ever resemble any actually existing thing, unless the original elements of which they are compounded bore some degree of resemblance to the objects of which the names are the imitation: And the original elements are letters?

Cratylus Yes.

Socrates Let me now invite you to consider what Hermogenes and I were saying about sounds. Do you agree with me that the letter φ is expressive of rapidity, motion, and hardness? Were we right or wrong in saying so?

Cratylus I should say that you were right.

Socrates And that λ was expressive of smoothness, and softness, and the like?

Cratylus There again you were right.

Socrates And yet, as you are aware, that which is called by us σχληρότης, is by the Eretrians called σχληρότηρ.

Cratylus Very true.

Socrates But are the letters ρ and σ equivalents; and is there the same significance to them in the termination ρ, which there is to us in σ, or is there no significance to one of us?

Cratylus Nay, surely there is a significance to both of us.

Socrates In as far as they are like, or in as far as they are unlike?

Cratylus In as far as they are like.

Socrates Are they altogether alike?

Cratylus Yes; for the purpose of expressing motion.

Socrates And what do you say of the insertion of the λ? for that is expressive not of hardness but of softness.

Cratylus Why, perhaps the letter λ is wrongly inserted, Socrates, and should be altered into ρ, as you were saying to Hermogenes and in my opinion rightly, when you spoke of adding and subtracting letters upon occasion.

Socrates Good. But still the word is intelligible to both of us; when I say σχληρὸς (hard), you know what I mean.

Cratylus Yes, my dear friend, and the explanation of that is custom.

Socrates And what is custom but convention?[4] I utter a sound which I understand, and you know that I understand the meaning of the sound: this is what you are saying?

Cratylus Yes.

Socrates And if when I speak you know my meaning, there is an indication given by me to you?

Cratylus Yes.

Socrates This indication of my meaning may proceed from unlike as well as from like, for example in the λ of σχληρότης. But if this is true, then you have made a convention with yourself, and the correctness of a name turns out to be convention, since letters which are unlike are indicative equally with those which are like, if they are sanctioned by custom and convention. And even supposing that you distinguish custom from convention ever so much, still you must say that the signification of words is given by custom and not by likeness, for custom may indicate by the unlike as well as by the like. But as we are agreed thus far, Cratylus (for I shall assume that your silence gives consent), then custom and convention must be supposed to contribute to the indication of our thoughts; for suppose we take the instance of number, how can you ever imagine, my good friend, that you will find names resembling every individual number, unless you allow that which you term convention and agreement to have authority in determining the correctness of names? I quite agree with you that words should as far as possible resemble things; but I fear that this dragging in of resemblance, as Hermogenes says, is a shabby thing, which has to be supplemented by the mechanical aid of convention with a view to correctness; for I believe that if we could always, or almost always, use likenesses, which are perfectly appropriate, this would be the most perfect state of language; as the opposite is the most imperfect. But let me ask you, what is the force of names, and what is the use of them?

Cratylus The use of names, Socrates, as I should imagine, is to inform; the simple truth is, that he who knows names knows also the things which are expressed by them.

Socrates I suppose you mean to say, Cratylus, that as the name is, so also is the thing; and that he who knows the one will also know the other, because they are similars, and all similars fall under the same art or science; and therefore you would say that he who knows names will also know things.

Cratylus That is precisely what I mean.

Socrates But let us consider what is the nature of this information about things which, according to you, is given

---

[4]The discussion here may be compared with Saussure's discussion of signifiers (below, page 787).

us by names. Is it the best sort of information? or is there any other? What do you say?

Cratylus I believe that to be both the only and the best sort of information about them; there can be no other.

Socrates But do you believe that in the discovery of them, he who discovers the names discovers also the things; or is this only the method of instruction, and is there some other method of enquiry and discovery.

Cratylus I certainly believe that the methods of enquiry and discovery are of the same nature as instruction.

Socrates Well, but do you not see, Cratylus, that he who follows names in the search after things, and analyses their meaning, is in great danger of being deceived?

Cratylus How so?

Socrates Why clearly he who first gave names gave them according to his conception of the things which they signified—did he not?

Cratylus True.

Socrates And if his conception was erroneous, and he gave names according to his conception, in what position shall we who are his followers find ourselves? Shall we not be deceived by him?

Cratylus But, Socrates, am I not right in thinking that he must surely have known; or else, as I was saying, his names would not be names at all? And you have a clear proof that he has not missed the truth, and the proof is—that he is perfectly consistent. Did you ever observe in speaking that all the words which you utter have a common character and purpose?

Socrates But that, friend Cratylus, is no answer. For if he did begin in error, he may have forced the remainder into agreement with the original error and with himself; there would be nothing strange in this, any more than in geometrical diagrams, which have often a slight and invisible flaw in the first part of the process, and are consistently mistaken in the long deductions which follow. And this is the reason why every man should expend his chief thought and attention on the consideration of his first principles:— are they or are they not rightly laid down? and when he has duly sifted them, all the rest will follow. Now I should be astonished to find that names are really consistent. And here let us revert to our former discussion: Were we not saying that all things are in motion and progress and flux, and that this idea of motion is expressed by names? Do you not conceive that to be the meaning of them?

Cratylus Yes; that is assuredly their meaning, and the true meaning.

Socrates Let us revert to ἐπιστήμη (knowledge), and observe how ambiguous this word is, seeming rather to signify stopping the soul at things than going round with

them; and therefore we should leave the beginning as at present, and not reject the ε, but make an insertion of an ι instead of an ε (not πιστήμη, but ἐπιστήμη). Take another example: βέβαιον (sure) is clearly the expression of station and position, and not of motion. Again, the word ἱστορία (enquiry) bears upon the face of it the stopping (ἱστάναι) of the stream; and the word πιστὸν (faithful) certainly indicates cessation of motion; then, again, μνήμη (memory), as any one may see, expresses rest in the soul, and not motion. Moreover, words such as ἁμαρτία and συμφορὰ, which have a bad sense, viewed in the light of their etymologies will be the same as σύνεσις and ἐπιστήμη and other words which have a good sense (cp. ὁμαρτεῖν, συνιέναι, ἕπεσθαι, συμφέρεσθαι); and much the same may be said of of ἀμαθία and ἀκολασία, for ἀμαθία may be explained as ἡ ἅμα θεῷ ἰόντος πορεία, and ἀκολασία as ἡ ἀκολουθία τοῖς πράγμασιν. Thus the names which in these instances we find to have the worst sense, will turn out to be framed on the same principle as those which have the best. And any one I believe who would take the trouble might find many other examples in which the giver of names indicates, not that things are in motion or progress, but that they are at rest; which is the opposite of motion.

Cratylus Yes, Socrates, but observe; the greater number express motion.

Socrates What of that, Cratylus? Are we to count them like votes? and is correctness of names the voice of the majority? Are we to say of whichever sort there are most, those are the true ones?

Cratylus No; that is not reasonable.

Socrates Certainly not. But let us have done with this question and proceed to another, about which I should like to know whether you think with me. Were we not lately acknowledging that the first givers of names in states, both Hellenic and barbarous, were the legislators, and that the art which gave names was the art of the legislator?

Cratylus Quite true.

Socrates Tell me, then, did the first legislators, who were the givers of the first names, know or not know the things which they named?

Cratylus They must have known, Socrates.

Socrates Why, yes, friend Cratylus, they could hardly have been ignorant.

Cratylus I should say not.

Socrates Let us return to the point from which we digressed. You were saying, if you remember, that he who gave names must have known the things which he named; are you still of that opinion?

Cratylus I am.

Socrates   And would you say that the giver of the first names had also a knowledge of the things which he named?

Cratylus   I should.

Socrates   But how could he have learned or discovered things from names if the primitive names were not yet given? For, if we are correct in our view, the only way of learning and discovering things, is either to discover names for ourselves or to learn them from others.

Cratylus   I think that there is a good deal in what you say, Socrates.

Socrates   But if things are only to be known through names, how can we suppose that the givers of names had knowledge, or were legislators before there were names at all, and therefore before they could have known them?[5]

Cratylus   I believe, Socrates, the true account of the matter to be, that a power more than human gave things their first names, and that the names which are thus given are necessarily their true names.

Socrates   Then how came the giver of the names, if he was an inspired being or God, to contradict himself? For were we not saying just now that he made some names expressive of rest and others of motion? Were we mistaken?

Cratylus   But I suppose one of the two not to be names at all.

Socrates   And which, then, did he make, my good friend; those which are expressive of rest, or those which are expressive of motion? This is a point which, as I said before, cannot be determined by counting them.

Cratylus   No; not in that way, Socrates.

Socrates   But if this is a battle of names, some of them asserting that they are like the truth, others contending that *they* are, how or by what criterion are we to decide between them? For there are no other names to which appeal can be made, but obviously recourse must be had to another standard which, without employing names, will make clear which of the two are right; and this must be a standard which shows the truth of things.

Cratylus   I agree.

Socrates   But if that is true, Cratylus, then I suppose that things may be known without names?

Cratylus   Clearly.

Socrates   But how would you expect to know them? What other way can there be of knowing them, except the true and natural way, through their affinities, when they are akin to each other, and through themselves? For that which

is other and different from them must signify something other and different from them.

Cratylus   What you are saying is, I think, true.

Socrates   Well, but reflect; have we not several times acknowledged that names rightly given are the likenesses and images of the things which they name?

Cratylus   Yes.

Socrates   Let us suppose that to any extent you please you can learn things through the medium of names, and suppose also that you can learn them from the things themselves—which is likely to be the nobler and clearer way; to learn of the image, whether the image and the truth of which the image is the expression have been rightly conceived, or to learn of the truth whether the truth and the image of it have been duly executed?

Cratylus   I should say that we must learn of the truth.

Socrates   How real existence is to be studied or discovered is, I suspect, beyond you and me. But we may admit so much, that the knowledge of things is not to be derived from names. No; they must be studied and investigated in themselves.

Cratylus   Clearly, Socrates.

Socrates   There is another point. I should not like us to be imposed upon by the appearance of such a multitude of names, all tending in the same direction. I myself do not deny that the givers of names did really give them under the idea that all things were in motion and flux; which was their sincere but, I think, mistaken opinion. And having fallen into a kind of whirlpool themselves, they are carried round, and want to drag us in after them. There is a matter, master Cratylus, about which I often dream, and should like to ask your opinion: Tell me, whether there is or is not any absolute beauty or good, or any other absolute existence?

Cratylus   Certainly, Socrates, I think so.

Socrates   Then let us seek the true beauty: not asking whether a face is fair, or anything of that sort, for all such things appear to be in a flux; but let us ask whether the true beauty is not always beautiful.

Cratylus   Certainly.

Socrates   And can we rightly speak of a beauty which is always passing away, and is first this and then that; must not the same thing be born and retire and vanish while the word is in our mouths?

Cratylus   Undoubtedly.

Socrates   Then how can that be a real thing which is never in the same state? for obviously things which are the same cannot change while they remain the same; and if they are always the same and in the same state, and never depart from their original form, they can never change or be moved.

Cratylus   Certainly they cannot.

---

[5]The discussion here verges on the question of origin and suggests infinite regress. See Derrida (below, page 1208ff.), who implies the impossibility of source or origin in his treatment of Claude Lévi-Strauss's anthropology. Derrida finds the same problem in Saussure's concept of a closed linguistic structure.

Socrates Nor yet can they be known by any one; for at the moment that the observer approaches, then they become other and of another nature, so that you cannot get any further in knowing their nature or state, for you cannot know that which has no state.

Cratylus True.

Socrates Nor can we reasonably say, Cratylus, that there is knowledge at all, if everything is in a state of transition and there is nothing abiding; for knowledge too cannot continue to be knowledge unless continuing always to abide and exist. But if the very nature of knowledge changes, at the time when the change occurs there will be no knowledge; and if the transition is always going on, there will always be no knowledge, and, according to this view, there will be no one to know and nothing to be known: but if that which knows and that which is known exist ever, and the beautiful and the good and every other thing also exist, then I do not think that they can resemble a process or flux, as we were just now supposing. Whether there is this eternal nature in things, or whether the truth is what Heracleitus[6] and his followers and many others say, is a question hard to determine; and no man of sense will like to put himself or the education of his mind in the power of names: neither will he so far trust names or the givers of names as to be confident in any knowledge which condemns himself and other existences to an unhealthy state of unreality: he will not believe that all things leak like a pot, or imagine that the world is a man who has a running at the nose. This may be true, Cratylus, but is also very likely to be untrue; and therefore I would not have you be too easily persuaded of it. Reflect well and like a man, and do not easily accept such a doctrine: for you are young and of an age to learn. And when you have found the truth, come and tell me.

Cratylus I will do as you say, though I can assure you, Socrates, that I have been considering the matter already, and the result of a great deal of trouble and consideration is that I incline to Heracleitus.

Socrates Then, another day, my friend, when you come back, you shall give me a lesson; but at present, go into the country, as you are intending, and Hermogenes shall set you on your way.

Cratylus Very good, Socrates; I hope, however, that you will continue to think about these things yourself.[7]

---

[6]Heraclitus held that all things are in flux.

[7]The dialogue ends in uncertainty and ambivalence about what it has accomplished with respect to understanding language.

Aristotle

384–322 B.C.

The first extant and probably the most influential treatise on poetry in the Western world is Aristotle's *Poetics.* Earlier works by him, for example *Physics* and *Metaphysics,* contain important statements about art and nature that bear on literature; and *Rhetoric,* written after *Poetics,* distinguishes rhetoric as a practical art involving "doing" from productive arts, including poetic, that involve "making." Aristotle's *Rhetoric* has had a strong influence on criticism, for many later writers have blurred or obliterated the distinction even to the extent that in some cases poetic seems to have become a branch of rhetoric (or the art of persuasion). That *Poetics* was lost to European thought for many centuries may have contributed to the importance of rhetoric over poetic until the rediscovery of *Poetics* in the Renaissance. From that time, commentaries on *Poetics* abound, the most important of the earliest being Castelvetro's (below, page 177).

Aristotle was a student of Plato, though he came to disagree with his teacher particularly with respect to Plato's doctrine of ideas or forms. In *Poetics,* he approaches literature to some extent as if he were a classical biologist. He intends to classify and categorize systematically the kinds of literary art, beginning with epic and tragic drama. Unfortunately, not all of *Poetics* has survived, and it breaks off before the discussion of comedy. Nevertheless, our sense of Aristotle's method is established. He is the first critic to attempt a systematic discussion of literary genres.

It appears that Aristotle means to answer directly Plato's criticism of the poet as merely an imitator of appearances (phenomena). He disagrees with Plato about where to locate reality. He does not believe that the world of appearances is merely an ephemeral copy of changeless ideas (forms). Indeed, he denies the being of ideas (in Plato's sense) apart from things. He believes that change is a fundamental reality, a process of nature, which is a creative force with a teleological direction. In this respect, the argument of *Poetics* serves an important purpose in Aristotle's philosophy as a whole, since it provides a critical example in which form can be linked to *telos* or purpose directly, providing support for a teleological interpretation of nature. Reality is the process in which a form is manifested from matter by nature. The poet's imitation is an analogy of this process; the poet takes a form from nature and reshapes it in a different matter or medium. This medium, which the form does not inhabit in nature, is the source of each work's inward principle of order and consequently its independence from slavish copying. The poet is thus an imitator and a maker, and imitation is, in fact, a kind of making. In imitation the poet discovers the ultimate form of an action.

This is why, for Aristotle, the plot of a tragedy is of prime importance—over character, thought, diction, song, and spectacle, though these are all elements of tragic drama. The poet makes the meaning of events by making their structure as plot; he does this in a medium, which is principally words. Literary art, along with the fine arts (all the productive arts), is thus an improvement on nature in that the poet has brought to completion what nature, operating with its own principles, is still developing.

These ideas have heavily influenced criticism from the Renaissance to this day. Renaissance critics often sought to blend Aristotle with the dominant Platonism, especially where defense of poetry was the aim, but the two philosophers' disagreement about the location of the ideas always seemed to intervene. Then neoclassical critics, following Castelvetro, extended to extremes what appeared to them to be Aristotle's fixed rules about the so-called unities. Other followers of Aristotle emphasized either his theory of imitation or the analytic procedures exhibited in his discussion of tragedy.

Aristotle's attention to the poem as an object that can be discussed in terms of its formal nature is probably his greatest contribution to literary theory, though his treatment of tragedy as bringing about a catharsis or purgation of pity and fear has been of great interest and much debated.

The standard, complete translation of Aristotle's works is that edited by J. A. Smith and W. D. Ross, *The Works of Aristotle,* 11 vols. (1908–1931). Translations of *Poetics* together with commentaries abound: for example, S. H. Butcher, *Aristotle's Theory of Poetry and Fine Art* (1894); G. F. Else, *Aristotle's Poetics: The Argument* (1957); G. M. A. Grube, *Aristotle on Poetry and Style* (1958); L. Golden and O. B. Hardison, *Aristotle's* Poetics: *A Translation and Commentary for Students of Literature.* See also C. S. Baldwin, *Ancient Rhetoric and Poetic* (1924); W. R. Roberts, *Greek Rhetoric and Literary Theory* (1928); F. L. Lucas, *Tragedy in Relation to Aristotle's* Poetics (1928); J. W. H. Atkins, *Literary Criticism in Antiquity,* 2 vols. (1934); Richard McKeon, "Literary Criticism and the Concept of Imitation in Antiquity" in R. S. Crane, ed., *Critics and Criticism* (1952); Humphry House, *Aristotle's* Poetics (1956); G. Kennedy, *The Art of Persuasion in Greece* (1963); Elder Olson, ed., *Aristotle's* Poetics *and English Literature* (1965); Harvey Goldstein, "Mimesis and Catharsis Reexamined," *Journal of Aesthetics and Art Criticism,* XXIV (1966); Teddy Brunius, *Imagination and Katharsis* (1966); K. V. Erickson, ed., *Aristotle: The Classical Heritage of Rhetoric* (1974); S. Halliwell, *Aristotle's* Poetics (1986); Eugene Garver, *Aristotle's Rhetoric: An Art of Character* (1994); D. J. Farley and A. Nehemas, eds., *Aristotle's* Rhetoric: *Philosophical Essays* (1994).

from

Physics

(Book 2, Chapter 8)

8 We must explain then (1) that Nature belongs to the class of causes which act for the sake of something; (2) about the necessary and its place in physical problems, for all writers ascribe things to this cause, arguing that since the hot and the cold, &c., are of such and such a kind, therefore certain things *necessarily* are and come to be—and if they mention any other cause (one[1] his 'friendship and strife', another[2] his 'mind'), it is only to touch on it, and then goodbye to it.

A difficulty presents itself: why should not nature work, not for the sake of something, nor because it is better so, but just as the sky rains, not in order to make the corn grow, but of necessity? What is drawn up must cool, and what has been cooled must become water and descend, the result of this being that the corn grows. Similarly if a man's

Aristotle's *Physics* was probably an early work, written before *Poetics* and *Rhetoric*. The text is from the translation by R. P. Hardie and R. K. Gaye in W. D. Ross, ed., *The Works of Aristotle,* Vol. II (Oxford at the Clarendon Press, 1930).

[1] [Hardie and Gaye] Empedocles [Greek philosopher, fifth century B.C.]
[2] [Hardie and Gaye] Anaxagoras [Greek philosopher, 500?–428 B.C.]

crop is spoiled on the threshing-floor, the rain did not fall for the sake of this—in order that the crop might be spoiled—but that result just followed. Why then should it not be the same with the parts in nature, e. g. that our teeth should come up *of necessity*—the front teeth sharp, fitted for tearing, the molars broad and useful for grinding down the food—since they did not arise for this end, but it was merely a coincident result; and so with all other parts in which we suppose that there is purpose? Wherever then all the parts came about just what they would have been if they had come to be for an end, such things survived, being organized spontaneously in a fitting way; whereas those which grew otherwise perished and continue to perish, as Empedocles says his 'man-faced ox-progeny' did.

Such are the arguments (and others of the kind) which may cause difficulty on this point. Yet it is impossible that this should be the true view. For teeth and all other natural things either invariably or normally come about in a given way: but of not one of the results of chance or spontaneity is this true. We do not ascribe to chance or mere coincidence the frequency of rain in winter, but frequent rain in summer we do; nor heat in the dog-days, but only if we have it in winter. If then, it is agreed that things are either the result of coincidence or for an end, and these cannot be the result of coincidence or spontaneity, it follows that they must be for an end; and that such things are all due to nature even the champions of the theory which is before us would agree. Therefore action for an end is present in things which come to be and are by nature.

Further, where a series has a completion, all the preceding steps are for the sake of that. Now surely as in intelligent action, so in nature; and as in nature, so it is in each action, if nothing interferes. Now intelligent action is for the sake of an end; therefore the nature of things also is so. Thus if a house, e. g., had been a thing made by nature, it would have been made in the same way as it is now by art[3]; and if things made by nature were made also by art, they would come to be in the same way as by nature. Each step then in the series is for the sake of the next; and generally art partly completes what nature cannot bring to a finish,[4] and partly imitates her. If, therefore, artificial products are for the sake of an end, so clearly also are natural products. The relation of the later to the earlier terms of the series is the same in both.

This is most obvious in the animals other than man: they make things neither by art nor after inquiry or deliberation. Wherefore people discuss whether it is by intelligence or by some other faculty that these creatures work,—spiders, ants, and the like. By gradual advance in this direction we come to see clearly that in plants too that is produced which is conducive to the end—leaves, e. g. grow to provide shade for the fruit. If then it is both by nature and for an end that the swallow makes its nest and the spider its web, and plants grow leaves for the sake of the fruit and send their roots down (not up) for the sake of nourishment, it is plain that this kind of cause is operative in things which come to be and are by nature. And since 'nature' means two things, the matter and the form, of which the latter is the end, and since all the rest is for the sake of the end, the form must be the cause in the sense of 'that for the sake of which'.

Now mistakes come to pass even in the operations of art: the grammarian makes a mistake in writing and the doctor pours out the wrong dose. Hence clearly mistakes are possible in the operations of nature also. If then in art there are cases in which what is rightly produced serves a purpose, and if where mistakes occur there was a purpose in what was attempted, only it was not attained, so must it be also in natural products, and monstrosities will be failures in the purposive effort. Thus in the original combinations the 'ox-progeny' if they failed to reach a determinate end must have arisen through the corruption of some principle corresponding to what is now the seed.

Further, seed must have come into being first, and not straightway the animals: the words 'whole-natured first . . .'[5] must have meant seed.

Again, in plants too we find the relation of means to end, though the degree of organization is less. Were there then in plants also 'olive-headed vine-progeny', like the 'man-headed ox-progeny', or not? An absurd suggestion; yet there must have been, if there were such things among animals.

Moreover, among the seeds anything must have come to be at random. But the person who asserts this entirely does away with 'nature' and what exists 'by nature'. For those things are natural which, by a continuous movement originated from an internal principle, arrive at some completion: the same completion is not reached from every principle; nor any chance completion, but always the tendency in each is towards the same end, if there is no impediment.

---

[3] By "art" Aristotle does not mean just the fine arts and literature, but also the deliberate making of things by human beings—for example, houses, furniture, tools, laws. In *Rhetoric,* Aristotle distinguishes rhetoric as a practical art from poetic as a productive art.

[4] See Wilde (below, page 712).

[5] [Hardie and Gaye] Empedocles, Fragment 62.4.

The end and the means towards it may come about by chance. We say, for instance, that a stranger has come by chance, paid the ransom, and gone away, when he does so as if he had come for that purpose, though it was not for that that he came. This is incidental, for chance is an incidental cause, as I remarked before. But when an event takes place always or for the most part, it is not incidental or by chance. In natural products the sequence is invariable, if there is no impediment.

It is absurd to suppose that purpose is not present because we do not observe the agent deliberating. Art does not deliberate. If the ship-building art were in the wood, it would produce the same results *by nature*. If, therefore, purpose is present in art, it is present also in nature. The best illustration is a doctor doctoring himself: nature is like that.

from

Metaphysics

(Book A (1), Chapters 1–2)

1 All men by nature desire to know. An indication of this is the delight we take in our senses; for even apart from their usefulness they are loved for themselves; and above all others the sense of sight. For not only with a view to action, but even when we are not going to do anything, we prefer seeing (one might say) to everything else. The reason is that this, most of all the senses, makes us know and brings to light many differences between things.

By nature animals are born with the faculty of sensation, and from sensation memory is produced in some of them, though not in others. And therefore the former are more intelligent and apt at learning than those which cannot remember; those which are incapable of hearing sounds are intelligent though they cannot be taught, e. g. the bee, and any other race of animals that may be like it; and those which besides memory have this sense of hearing can be taught.

The animals other than man live by appearances and memories, and have but little of connected experience; but the human race lives also by art and reasonings. Now from memory experience is produced in men; for the several memories of the same thing produce finally the capacity for a single experience. And experience seems pretty much like science and art, but really science and art come to men *through* experience; for 'experience made art', as Polus says,[1] 'but inexperience luck'. Now art arises when from many notions gained by experience one universal judgement about a class of objects is produced. For to have a judgement that when Callias was ill of this disease this did him good, and similarly in the case of Socrates and in many individual cases, is a matter of experience; but to judge that it has done good to all persons of a certain constitution, marked off in one class, when they were ill of this disease, e. g. to phlegmatic or bilious people when burning with fever—this is a matter of art.[2]

With a view to action experience seems in no respect inferior to art, and men of experience succeed even better than those who have theory without experience. (The reason is that experience is knowledge of individuals, art of universals,[3] and actions and productions are all concerned with the individual; for the physician does not cure *man,* except in an incidental way, but Callias or Socrates or some other called by some such individual name, who happens to be a man. If, then, a man has the theory without the experience, and recognizes the universal but does not know the individual included in this, he will often fail to cure; for it is the individual that is to be cured.) But yet we think that *knowledge* and *understanding* belong to art rather than to experience, and we suppose artists to be wiser than men of experience (which implies that Wisdom depends in all cases rather on knowledge); and this because the former know the cause, but the latter do not. For men of experience know that the thing is so, but do not know why, while the others know the 'why' and the cause. Hence we think also that the masterworkers in each craft are more honourable and know in a truer sense and are wiser than the manual workers, because they know the causes of the things that are done (we think the manual workers are like certain lifeless things which act indeed, but act without knowing what they do, as fire burns—but while the lifeless things perform each of their functions by a natural tendency, the labourers perform them through habit); thus we view them as being wiser not in virtue of being able to act, but of having the theory for themselves and knowing the causes. And in general it is a sign of the man who knows and of the man who does not

---

Aristotle's *Metaphysics* was probably begun after *Physics* and before *Poetics,* but it may have been written over a long period of time. The text is from the translation by W. D. Ross in J. A. Smith and W. D. Ross, eds., *The Works of Aristotle,* Vol. VIII (Oxford at the Clarendon Press, 1908).

[1] [Ross] Cf. Plato, *Gorgias,* 448c, 462BC.
[2] That is, the art of medicine or the physician's art.
[3] See Aristotle's distinction between poetry and history in *Poetics* (below, page 57).

know, that the former can teach, and therefore we think art more truly knowledge than experience is; for artists can teach, and men of mere experience cannot.

Again, we do not regard any of the senses as Wisdom; yet surely these give the most authoritative knowledge of particulars. But they do not tell us the 'why' of anything— e.g. why fire is hot; they only say *that* it is hot.

At first he who invented any art whatever that went beyond the common perceptions of man was naturally admired by men, not only because there was something useful in the inventions, but because he was thought wise and superior to the rest. But as more arts were invented, and some were directed to the necessities of life, others to recreation, the inventors of the latter were naturally always regarded as wiser than the inventors of the former, because their branches of knowledge did not aim at utility.[4] Hence when all such inventions were already established, the sciences which do not aim at giving pleasure or at the necessities of life were discovered, and first in the places where men first began to have leisure. This is why the mathematical arts were founded in Egypt; for there the priestly caste was allowed to be at leisure.

We have said in the *Ethics* what the difference is between art and science and the other kindred faculties; but the point of our present discussion is this, that all men suppose what is called Wisdom to deal with the first causes and the principles of things; so that, as has been said before, the man of experience is thought to be wiser than the possessors of any sense-perception whatever, the artist wiser than the men of experience, the master-worker than the mechanic, and the theoretical kinds of knowledge to be more of the nature of Wisdom than the productive. Clearly then Wisdom is knowledge about certain principles and causes.

Poetics

1 Our subject being Poetry, I propose to speak not only of the art in general but also of its species and their respective capacities; of the structure of plot required for a good poem; of the number and nature of the constituent parts of a poem; and

likewise of any other matters in the same line of inquiry. Let us follow the natural order and begin with the primary facts.

Epic poetry and Tragedy, as also Comedy, Dithyrambic poetry,[1] and most flute-playing and lyre-playing, are all, viewed as a whole, modes of imitation. But at the same time they differ from one another in three ways, either by a difference of kind in their means, or by differences in the objects, or in the manner of their imitations.

I. Just as colour and form are used as means by some, who (whether by art or constant practice) imitate and portray many things by their aid, and the voice is used by others; so also in the above-mentioned group of arts, the means with them as a whole are rhythm, language, and harmony— used, however, either singly or in certain combinations. A combination of harmony and rhythm alone is the means in flute-playing and lyre-playing, and any other arts there may be of the same description, e. g. imitative piping. Rhythm alone, without harmony, is the means in the dancer's imitations; for even he, by the rhythms of his attitudes, may represent men's characters, as well as what they do and suffer. There is further an art which imitates by language alone, without harmony, in prose or in verse, and if in verse, either in some one or in a plurality of metres. This form of imitation is to this day without a name. We have no common name for a mime of Sophron or Xenarchus and a Socratic Conversation; and we should still be without one even if the imitation in the two instances were in trimeters or elegiacs or some other kind of verse—though it is the way with people to tack on 'poet' to the name of a metre, and talk of elegiac-poets and epic-poets, thinking that they call them poets not by reason of the imitative nature of their work, but indiscriminately by reason of the metre they write in.[2] Even if a theory of medicine or physical philosophy be put forth in a metrical form, it is usual to describe the writer in this way; Homer and Empedocles, however, have really nothing in common apart from their metre; so that, if the one is to be called a poet, the other should be termed a physicist rather than a poet. We should be in the same position also, if the imitation in these instances were in all the metres, like the *Centaur* (a rhapsody in a medley of all metres) of Chaere-

---

[4]There is a long tradition in which poets and critics defend poetry on grounds not different from these. See, as an extreme example, Wilde on the value of the uselessness of art (below, page 712).

Aristotle's *Poetics* was composed in about 330 B.C. The text is from the translation by Ingram Bywater from W. D. Ross, ed., *The Works of Aristotle,* Vol. XI (Oxford at the Clarendon Press, 1924). The text of *Poetics* is regarded as incomplete and may have included a discussion of comedy.

[1]Early Greek lyric poetry originating in songs sung at festivals of Dionysus.
[2]The matter of whether verse is a definitive element of the poem is discussed by a number of later critics, for example Scaliger (below, page 169), who believes that it is.

mon; and Chaeremon[3] one has to recognize as a poet. So much, then, as to these arts. There are, lastly, certain other arts, which combine all the means enumerated, rhythm, melody, and verse, e. g. Dithyrambic and Nomic poetry,[4] Tragedy and Comedy; with this difference, however, that the three kinds of means are in some of them all employed together, and in others brought in separately, one after the other. These elements of difference in the above arts I term the means of their imitation.

2 II. The objects the imitator represents are actions, with agents who are necessarily either good men or bad—the diversities of human character being nearly always derivative from this primary distinction, since the line between virtue and vice is one dividing the whole of mankind. It follows, therefore, that the agents represented must be either above our own level of goodness, or beneath it, or just such as we are; in the same way as, with the painters, the personages of Polygnotus are better than we are, those of Pauson worse, and those of Dionysius just like ourselves. It is clear that each of the above-mentioned arts will admit of these differences, and that it will become a separate art by representing objects with this point of difference. Even in dancing, flute-playing, and lyre-playing such diversities are possible; and they are also possible in the nameless art that uses language, prose or verse without harmony, as its means; Homer's personages, for instance, are better than we are; Cleophon's are on our own level; and those of Hegemon of Thasos, the first writer of parodies, and Nicochares, the author of the *Diliad,* are beneath it. The same is true of the Dithyramb and the Nome: the personages may be presented in them with the difference exemplified in the . . . of . . . and Argas, and in the Cyclopses of Timotheus and Philoxenus. This difference it is that distinguishes Tragedy and Comedy also; the one would make its personages worse, and the other better, than the men of the present day.

3 III. A third difference in these arts is in the manner in which each kind of object is represented. Given both the same means and the same kind of object for imitation, one may either (1) speak at one moment in narrative and at another in an assumed character, as Homer does; or (2) one may remain the same throughout, without any such change; or (3) the imitators may represent the whole story dramatically, as though they were actually doing the things described.[5]

As we said at the beginning, therefore, the differences in the imitation of these arts come under three heads, their means, their objects, and their manner.

So that as an imitator Sophocles[6] will be on one side akin to Homer, both portraying good men; and on another to Aristophanes, since both present their personages as acting and doing. This in fact, according to some, is the reason for plays being termed dramas, because in a play the personages act the story. Hence too both Tragedy and Comedy are claimed by the Dorians as their discoveries; Comedy by the Megarians—by those in Greece as having arisen when Megara became a democracy, and by the Sicilian Megarians on the ground that the poet Epicharmus was of their country, and a good deal earlier than Chionides and Magnes; even Tragedy also is claimed by certain of the Peloponnesian Dorians. In support of this claim they point to the words 'comedy' and 'drama'. Their word for the outlying hamlets, they say, is *comae,* whereas Athenians call them *demes*—thus assuming that comedians got the name not from their *comoe* or revels, but from their strolling from hamlet to hamlet, lack of appreciation keeping them out of the city. Their word also for 'to act', they say, is *dran,* whereas Athenians use *prattein.*

So much, then, as to the number and nature of the points of difference in the imitation of these arts.

4 It is clear that the general origin of poetry was due to two causes, each of them part of human nature. Imitation is natural to man from childhood, one of his advantages over the lower animals being this, that he is the most imitative creature in the world, and learns at first by imitation. And it is also natural for all to delight in works of imitation. The truth of this second point is shown by experience: though the objects themselves may be painful to see, we delight to view the most realistic representations of them in art, the forms for example of the lowest animals and of dead bodies. The explanation is to be found in a further fact: to be learning something is the greatest of pleasures not only to the philosopher but also to the rest of mankind, however small their capacity for it; the reason of the delight in seeing the picture is that one is at the same time learning—gathering the meaning of things, e. g. that the man there is so-and-so; for if one has not seen the thing before, one's pleasure will not be in the picture as an imitation of it, but will be due to

---

[3] All but fragments of the plays of this fourth-century B.C. Athenian tragic poet have been lost. Of the other works that Aristotle mentions in *Poetics* all but *Iliad* and *Odyssey,* probably composed in the late eighth or early seventh century B.C., many have been completely lost: the plays of Cleophon and Hegemon, the poems of Timotheus and Philoxenus about the Cyclops, the burlesque poem *Margites,* once attributed to Homer, the plays of Agathon, Sophocles's *Lynceus,* Astydamus's *Alcmaeon,* Telegonus's *Wounded Odysseus,* and the plays of Carcinus, Dicaeogenes, and Polydus the Sophist.
[4] A type of Greek poetry written to be sung and accompanied by flute or lyre.

[5] This distinction was made by Plato (above, page 24).
[6] The tragedies of Sophocles (496?–406 B.C.), author of the trilogy on Oedipus, figure strongly in *Poetics* as the proper models for tragedy.

the execution or colouring or some similar cause. Imitation, then, being natural to us—as also the sense of harmony and rhythm, the metres being obviously species of rhythms—it was through their original aptitude, and by a series of improvements for the most part gradual on their first efforts, that they created poetry out of their improvisations.

Poetry, however, soon broke up into two kinds according to the differences of character in the individual poets; for the graver among them would represent noble actions, and those of noble personages; and the meaner sort the actions of the ignoble. The latter class produced invectives at first, just as others did hymns and panegyrics. We know of no such poem by any of the pre-Homeric poets, though there were probably many such writers among them; instances, however, may be found from Homer downwards, e. g. his *Margites,* and the similar poems of others. In this poetry of invective its natural fitness brought an iambic metre into use; hence our present term 'iambic', because it was the metre of their 'iambs' or invectives against one another. The result was that the old poets became some of them writers of heroic and others of iambic verse. Homer's position, however, is peculiar: just as he was in the serious style the poet of poets, standing alone not only through the literary excellence, but also through the dramatic character of his imitations, so too he was the first to outline for us the general forms of Comedy by producing not a dramatic invective, but a dramatic picture of the Ridiculous; his *Margites* in fact stands in the same relation to our comedies as the *Iliad* and *Odyssey* to our tragedies. As soon, however, as Tragedy and Comedy appeared in the field, those naturally drawn to the one line of poetry became writers of comedies instead of iambs, and those naturally drawn to the other, writers of tragedies instead of epics, because these new modes of art were grander and of more esteem than the old.

If it be asked whether Tragedy is now all that it need be in its formative elements, to consider that, and decide it theoretically and in relation to the theatres, is a matter for another inquiry.

It certainly began in improvisations—as did also Comedy; the one originating with the authors of the Dithyramb, the other with those of the phallic songs, which still survive as institutions in many of our cities. And its advance after that was little by little, through their improving on whatever they had before them at each stage. And it was in fact only after a long series of changes that the movement of Tragedy stopped on its attaining to its natural form.[7] (1) The number

of actors was first increased to two by Aeschylus, who curtailed the business of the Chorus, and made the dialogue, or spoken portion, take the leading part in the play. (2) A third actor and scenery were due to Sophocles. (3) Tragedy acquired also its magnitude. Discarding short stories and a ludicrous diction, through its passing out of its satyric stage,[8] it assumed, though only at a late point in its progress, a tone of dignity; and its metre changed then from trochaic to iambic. The reason for their original use of the trochaic tetrameter was that their poetry was satyric and more connected with dancing than it now is. As soon, however, as a spoken part came in, nature herself found the appropriate metre. The iambic, we know, is the most speakable of metres, as is shown by the fact that we very often fall into it in conversation, whereas we rarely talk hexameters, and only when we depart from the speaking tone of voice. (4) Another change was a plurality of episodes or acts. As for the remaining matters, the superadded embellishments and the account of their introduction, these must be taken as said, as it would probably be a long piece of work to go through the details.

5 As for Comedy, it is (as has been observed) an imitation of men worse than the average; worse, however, not as regards any and every sort of fault, but only as regards one particular kind, the Ridiculous, which is a species of the Ugly. The Ridiculous may be defined as a mistake or deformity not productive of pain or harm to others; the mask, for instance, that excites laughter, is something ugly and distorted without causing pain.

Though the successive changes in Tragedy and their authors are not unknown, we cannot say the same of Comedy; its early stages passed unnoticed, because it was not as yet taken up in a serious way. It was only at a late point in its progress that a chorus of comedians was officially granted by the archon[9]; they used to be mere volunteers. It had also already certain definite forms at the time when the record of those termed comic poets begins. Who it was who supplied it with masks, or prologues, or a plurality of actors and the like, has remained unknown. The invented Fable, or Plot, however, originated in Sicily with Epicharmus and Phormis; of Athenian poets Crates was the first to drop the Comedy of invective and frame stories of a general and nonpersonal nature, in other words, Fables or Plots.

Epic poetry, then, has been seen to agree with Tragedy to this extent, that of being an imitation of serious subjects in a grand kind of verse. It differs from it, however, (1) in

---

[7] Here Aristotle adopts a notion of historical development and indicates that tragedy has reached a final stage, though he leaves open the question of whether it is a perfected form.

[8] Plays of Dorian invention, usually burlesques of mythological characters and event. Satyrs formed the chorus.

[9] One of the nine Athenian magistrates.

that it is in one kind of verse and in narrative form[10]; and (2) in its length—which is due to its action having no fixed limit of time, whereas Tragedy endeavours to keep as far as possible within a single circuit of the sun, or something near that.[11] This, I say, is another point of difference between them, though at first the practice in this respect was just the same in tragedies as in epic poems. They differ also (3) in their constituents, some being common to both and others peculiar to Tragedy—hence a judge of good and bad in Tragedy is a judge of that in epic poetry also. All the parts of an epic are included in Tragedy; but those of Tragedy are not all of them to be found in the Epic.

6 Reserving hexameter poetry and Comedy for consideration hereafter,[12] let us proceed now to the discussion of Tragedy; before doing so, however, we must gather up the definition resulting from what has been said. A tragedy, then, is the imitation of an action that is serious and also, as having magnitude, complete in itself; in language with pleasurable accessories, each kind brought in separately in the parts of the work; in a dramatic, not in a narrative form; with incidents arousing pity and fear, wherewith to accomplish its catharsis of such emotions.[13] Here by 'language with pleasurable accessories' I mean that with rhythm and harmony or song superadded; and by 'the kinds separately' I mean that some portions are worked out with verse only, and others in turn with song.

I. As they act the stories, it follows that in the first place the Spectacle (or stage-appearance of the actors) must be some part of the whole; and in the second Melody and Diction, these two being the means of their imitation. Here by 'Diction' I mean merely this, the composition of the verses; and by 'Melody', what is too completely understood to require explanation. But further: the subject represented also is an action; and the action involves agents, who must necessarily have their distinctive qualities both of character and thought, since it is from these that we ascribe certain qualities to their actions. There are in the natural order of things, therefore, two causes, Thought and Character, of their actions, and consequently of their success or failure in their lives. Now the action (that which was done) is represented in the play by the Fable or Plot. The Fable, in our present sense of the term, is simply this, the combination of the incidents, or things done in the story[14]; whereas Character is what makes us ascribe certain moral qualities to the agents; and Thought is shown in all they say when proving a particular point or, it may be, enunciating a general truth. There are six parts consequently of every tragedy, as a whole (that is) of such or such quality, viz. a Fable or Plot, Characters, Diction, Thought, Spectacle, and Melody; two of them arising from the means, one from the manner, and three from the objects of the dramatic imitation; and there is nothing else besides these six. Of these, its formative elements, then, not a few of the dramatists have made due use, as every play, one may say, admits of Spectacle, Character, Fable, Diction, Melody, and Thought.

II. The most important of the six is the combination of the incidents of the story. Tragedy is essentially an imitation not of persons but of action and life, of happiness and misery. All human happiness or misery takes the form of action; the end for which we live is a certain kind of activity, not a quality. Character gives us qualities, but it is in our actions—what we do—that we are happy or the reverse. In a play accordingly they do not act in order to portray the Characters; they include the Characters for the sake of the action. So that it is the action in it, i. e. its Fable or Plot, that is the end and purpose of the tragedy; and the end is everywhere the chief thing. Besides this, a tragedy is impossible without action, but there may be one without Character. The tragedies of most of the moderns are characterless—a defect common among poets of all kinds, and with its counterpart in painting in Zeuxis as compared with Polygnotus; for whereas the latter is strong in character, the work of Zeuxis is devoid of it. And again: one may string together a series of characteristic speeches of the utmost finish as regards Diction and Thought, and yet fail to produce the true tragic effect; but one will have much better success with a tragedy which, however inferior in these respects, has a Plot, a combination of incidents, in it. And again: the most powerful elements of attraction in Tragedy, the Peripeties and Discoveries, are parts of the Plot. A further proof is in the fact that beginners succeed earlier with

---

[10] That is, the narrator speaks directly except, of course, where characters are made by the narrator to speak. Plato called epic a mixed mode for this reason. See above, page 25.

[11] Some Renaissance and Neoclassical critics hardened this observation into the rule of unity of time. See Castelvetro (below, page 176) and Corneille (below, page 244).

[12] This part of *Poetics* is lost, if it ever existed. For an attempt to construct the missing argument see Lane Cooper, *An Aristotelian Theory of Comedy* (1922).

[13] This is Aristotle's famous definition of tragedy. The term *catharsis* has given rise to much dispute. It is variously translated as "purgation" or "purification" or sometimes both and is generally thought to refer to the audience, but some theorists have argued that it refers to the purgation of the tragic hero's guilt.

[14] An alternative reading would be "arrangement of the incidents," which would more clearly distinguish the way the author presents them from their sheer chronological order.

the Diction and Characters than with the construction of a story; and the same may be said of nearly all the early dramatists. We maintain, therefore, that the first essential, the life and soul, so to speak, of Tragedy is the Plot; and that the Characters come second—compare the parallel in painting, where the most beautiful colours laid on without order will not give one the same pleasure as a simple black-and-white sketch of a portrait. We maintain that Tragedy is primarily an imitation of action, and that it is mainly for the sake of the action that it imitates the personal agents. Third comes the element of Thought, i. e. the power of saying whatever can be said, or what is appropriate to the occasion. This is what, in the speeches in Tragedy, falls under the arts of Politics and Rhetoric; for the older poets make their personages discourse like statesmen, and the modern like rhetoricians. One must not confuse it with Character. Character in a play is that which reveals the moral purpose of the agents, i. e. the sort of thing they seek or avoid, where that is not obvious—hence there is no room for Character in a speech on a purely indifferent subject. Thought, on the other hand, is shown in all they say when proving or disproving some particular point, or enunciating some universal proposition. Fourth among the literary elements is the Diction of the personages, i. e., as before explained, the expression of their thoughts in words, which is practically the same thing with verse as with prose. As for the two remaining parts, the Melody is the greatest of the pleasurable accessories of Tragedy. The Spectacle, though an attraction, is the least artistic of all the parts, and has least to do with the art of poetry. The tragic effect is quite possible without a public performance[15] and actors; and besides, the getting-up of the Spectacle is more a matter for the costumier than the poet.

7 Having thus distinguished the parts, let us now consider the proper construction of the Fable or Plot, as that is at once the first and the most important thing in Tragedy. We have laid it down that a tragedy is an imitation of an action that is complete in itself, as a whole of some magnitude; for a whole may be of no magnitude to speak of. Now a whole is that which has beginning, middle, and end. A beginning is that which is not itself necessarily after anything else, and which has naturally something else after it; an end is that which is naturally after something itself, either as its necessary or usual consequent, and with nothing else after it; and

a middle, that which is by nature after one thing and has also another after it. A well-constructed Plot, therefore, cannot either begin or end at any point one likes; beginning and end in it must be of the forms just described. Again: to be beautiful, a living creature, and every whole made up of parts, must not only present a certain order in its arrangement of parts, but also be of a certain definite magnitude. Beauty is a matter of size and order, and therefore impossible either (1) in a very minute creature, since our perception becomes indistinct as it approaches instantaneity; or (2) in a creature of vast size—one, say, 1,000 miles long—as in that case, instead of the object being seen all at once, the unity and wholeness of it is lost to the beholder. Just in the same way, then, as a beautiful whole made up of parts, or a beautiful living creature, must be of some size, but a size to be taken in by the eye, so a story or Plot must be of some length, but of a length to be taken in by the memory.[16] As for the limit of its length, so far as that is relative to public performances and spectators, it does not fall within the theory of poetry. If they had to perform a hundred tragedies, they would be timed by water-clocks, as they are said to have been at one period. The limit, however, set by the actual nature of the thing is this: the longer the story, consistently with its being comprehensible as a whole, the finer it is by reason of its magnitude. As a rough general formula, 'a length which allows of the hero passing by a series of probable or necessary stages from misfortune to happiness, or from happiness to misfortune', may suffice as a limit for the magnitude of the story.

8 The Unity of a Plot does not consist, as some suppose, in its having one man as its subject.[17] An infinity of things befall that one man, some of which it is impossible to reduce to unity; and in like manner there are many actions of one man which cannot be made to form one action. One sees, therefore, the mistake of all the poets who have written a *Heracleid,* a *Theseid,* or similar poems; they suppose that, because Heracles was one man, the story also of Heracles must be one story. Homer, however, evidently understood this point quite well, whether by art or instinct, just in the same way as he excels the rest in every other respect. In

---

[15] It has been argued that Aristotle is more interested in tragedy as read than as seen by an audience.

[16] Theories of the beautiful and sublime in the eighteenth and early nineteenth centuries (Addison, Burke, Kant, Schopenhauer) may be considered with respect to Aristotle's notion of magnitude. See, especially, Kant (below, page 416), as well as Poe (below, page 580), who discusses the attention span of the reader.

[17] Late-eighteenth- and early-nineteenth-century theories emphasizing organicism, self-expression, and subjectivity tend to reverse this view, placing what Aristotle calls character above plot.

writing an *Odyssey,* he did not make the poem cover all that ever befell his hero—it befell him, for instance, to get wounded on Parnassus and also to feign madness at the time of the call to arms, but the two incidents had no necessary or probable connexion with one another—instead of doing that, he took as the subject of the *Odyssey,* as also of the *Iliad,* an action with a Unity of the kind we are describing. The truth is that, just as in the other imitative arts one imitation is always of one thing, so in poetry the story, as an imitation of action, must represent one action, a complete whole, with its several incidents so closely connected that the transposal or withdrawal of any one of them will disjoin and dislocate the whole. For that which makes no perceptible difference by its presence or absence is no real part of the whole.

9 From what we have said it will be seen that the poet's function is to describe, not the thing that has happened, but a kind of thing that might happen, i. e. what is possible as being probable or necessary. The distinction between historian and poet is not in the one writing prose and the other verse— you might put the work of Herodotus into verse, and it would still be a species of history; it consists really in this, that the one describes the thing that has been, and the other a kind of thing that might be. Hence poetry is something more philosophic and of graver import than history, since its statements are of the nature rather of universals, whereas those of history are singulars. By a universal statement I mean one as to what such or such a kind of man will probably or necessarily say or do—which is the aim of poetry, though it affixes proper names to the characters; by a singular statement, one as to what, say, Alcibiades did or had done to him.[18] In Comedy this has become clear by this time; it is only when their plot is already made up of probable incidents that they give it a basis of proper names, choosing for the purpose any names that may occur to them, instead of writing like the old iambic poets about particular persons. In Tragedy, however, they still adhere to the historic names; and for this reason: what convinces is the possible; now whereas we are not yet sure as to the possibility of that which has not happened, that which has happened is manifestly possible, else it would not have come to pass. Nevertheless even in Tragedy there are some plays with but one or two known names in them, the rest being inventions; and there are some without a single known name, e. g. Agathon's *Antheus,* in which both incidents and names are of the poet's invention; and it is no less

delightful on that account. So that one must not aim at a rigid adherence to the traditional stories on which tragedies are based. It would be absurd, in fact, to do so, as even the known stories are only known to a few, though they are a delight none the less to all.

It is evident from the above that the poet must be more the poet of his stories or Plots than of his verses, inasmuch as he is a poet by virtue of the imitative element in his work, and it is actions that he imitates. And if he should come to take a subject from actual history, he is none the less a poet for that; since some historic occurrences may very well be in the probable and possible order of things; and it is in that aspect of them that he is their poet.

Of simple Plots and actions the episodic are the worst. I call a Plot episodic when there is neither probability nor necessity in the sequence of its episodes. Actions of this sort bad poets construct through their own fault, and good ones on account of the players. His work being for public performance, a good poet often stretches out a Plot beyond its capabilities, and is thus obliged to twist the sequence of incident.

Tragedy, however, is an imitation not only of a complete action, but also of incidents arousing pity and fear. Such incidents have the very greatest effect on the mind when they occur unexpectedly and at the same time in consequence of one another; there is more of the marvellous in them then than if they happened of themselves or by mere chance. Even matters of chance seem most marvellous if there is an appearance of design as it were in them; as for instance the statue of Mitys at Argos killed the author of Mitys' death by falling down on him when a looker-on at a public spectacle; for incidents like that we think to be not without a meaning. A Plot, therefore, of this sort is necessarily finer than others.

10 Plots are either simple or complex, since the actions they represent are naturally of this twofold description. The action, proceeding in the way defined, as one continuous whole, I call simple, when the change in the hero's fortunes takes place without Peripety[19] or Discovery; and complex, when it involves one or the other, or both. These should each of them arise out of the structure of the Plot itself, so as to be the consequence, necessary or probable, of the antecedents. There is a great difference between a thing happening *propter hoc* and *post hoc.*[20]

11 A Peripety is the change of the kind described from one state of things within the play to its opposite, and that too in

---

[18] The matter of universals and particulars (in a somewhat different sense from here) became of special importance in the eighteenth century and later. See Johnson (below, page 357), Reynolds (below, page 393), Blake's comments on Reynolds (below, page 448), and Cassirer (below, page 1018).

[19] Reversal of fortune.
[20] "Because of this" and "after this."

the way we are saying, in the probable or necessary sequence of events; as it is for instance in *Oedipus:* here the opposite state of things is produced by the Messenger, who, coming to gladden Oedipus and to remove his fears as to his mother, reveals the secret of his birth. And in *Lynceus:*[21] just as he is being led off for execution, with Danaus at his side to put him to death, the incidents preceding this bring it about that he is saved and Danaus put to death. A Discovery is, as the very word implies, a change from ignorance to knowledge, and thus to either love or hate, in the personages marked for good or evil fortune. The finest form of Discovery is one attended by Peripeties, like that which goes with the Discovery in *Oedipus.* There are no doubt other forms of it; what we have said may happen in a way in reference to inanimate things, even things of a very casual kind; and it is also possible to discover whether some one has done or not done something. But the form most directly connected with the Plot and the action of the piece is the first-mentioned. This, with a Peripety, will arouse either pity or fear—actions of that nature being what Tragedy is assumed to represent; and it will also serve to bring about the happy or unhappy ending. The Discovery, then, being of persons, it may be that of one party only to the other, the latter being already known; or both the parties may have to discover themselves. Iphigenia, for instance, was discovered to Orestes by sending the letter;[22] and another Discovery was required to reveal him to Iphigenia.

Two parts of the Plot, then, Peripety and Discovery, are on matters of this sort. A third part is Suffering; which we may define as an action of a destructive or painful nature, such as murders on the stage, tortures, woundings, and the like. The other two have been already explained.

12 The parts of Tragedy to be treated as formative elements in the whole were mentioned in a previous Chapter. From the point of view, however, of its quantity, i. e. the separate sections into which it is divided, a tragedy has the following parts: Prologue, Episode, Exode, and a choral portion, distinguished into Parode and Stasimon; these two are common to all tragedies, whereas songs from the stage and *Commoe* are only found in some. The Prologue is all that precedes the Parode of the chorus; an Episode all that comes in between two whole choral songs; the Exode all that follows after the last choral song. In the choral portion the Parode is the whole first statement of the chorus; a Stasimon, a song of the chorus without anapaests or trochees; a *Commos,* a lamentation sung by chorus and actor in concert. The parts of Tragedy to be used as formative elements in the whole we have already mentioned; the above are its parts from the point of view of its quantity, or the separate sections into which it is divided.

13 The next points after what we have said above will be these: (1) What is the poet to aim at, and what is he to avoid, in constructing his Plots? and (2) What are the conditions on which the tragic effect depends?

We assume that, for the finest form of Tragedy, the Plot must be not simple but complex; and further, that it must imitate actions arousing fear and pity, since that is the distinctive function of this kind of imitation. It follows, therefore, that there are three forms of Plot to be avoided. (1) A good man must not be seen passing from happiness to misery, or (2) a bad man from misery to happiness. The first situation is not fear-inspiring or piteous, but simply odious to us. The second is the most untragic that can be; it has no one of the requisites of Tragedy; it does not appeal either to the human feeling in us, or to our pity, or to our fears. Nor, on the other hand, should (3) an extremely bad man be seen falling from happiness into misery. Such a story may arouse the human feeling in us, but it will not move us to either pity or fear; pity is occasioned by undeserved misfortune, and fear by that of one like ourselves; so that there will be nothing either piteous or fear-inspiring in the situation. There remains, then, the intermediate kind of personage, a man not pre-eminently virtuous and just, whose misfortune, however, is brought upon him not by vice and depravity but by some error of judgement, of the number of those in the enjoyment of great reputation and prosperity; e.g. Oedipus, Thyestes, and the men of note of similar families. The perfect Plot, accordingly, must have a single, and not (as some tell us) a double issue; the change in the hero's fortunes must be not from misery to happiness, but on the contrary from happiness to misery; and the cause of it must lie not in any depravity, but in some great error on his part; the man himself being either such as we have described, or better, not worse, than that. Fact also confirms our theory. Though the poets began by accepting any tragic story that came to hand, in these days the finest tragedies are always on the story of some few houses, on that of Alcmeon, Oedipus, Orestes, Meleager, Thyestes, Telephus, or any others that may have been involved, as either agents or sufferers, in some deed of horror. The theoretically best tragedy, then, has a Plot of this description. The critics, therefore, are wrong who blame Euripides for taking this line in his tragedies, and giving many of them an unhappy ending. It is, as we have said, the right line to take. The best proof is this: on the stage, and in the public performances, such plays, properly worked out, are seen to be the most truly tragic; and Euripides, even if his

---

[21][Bywater] By Theocritus [third century B.C.].
[22][Bywater] *Iphigenia in Tauris,* 272ff. [by Euripides (c. 485–406 B.C.)].

execution be faulty in every other point, is seen to be nevertheless the most tragic certainly of the dramatists. After this comes the construction of Plot which some rank first, one with a double story (like the *Odyssey*) and an opposite issue for the good and the bad personages. It is ranked as first only through the weakness of the audiences; the poets merely follow their public, writing as its wishes dictate. But the pleasure here is not that of Tragedy. It belongs rather to Comedy, where the bitterest enemies in the piece (e. g. Orestes and Aegisthus) walk off good friends at the end, with no slaying of any one by any one.

14 The tragic fear and pity may be aroused by the Spectacle: but they may also be aroused by the very structure and incidents of the play—which is the better way and shows the better poet. The Plot in fact should be so framed that, even without seeing the things take place, he who simply hears the account of them shall be filled with horror and pity at the incidents; which is just the effect that the mere recital of the story in *Oedipus* would have on one. To produce this same effect by means of the Spectacle is less artistic, and requires extraneous aid. Those, however, who make use of the Spectacle to put before us that which is merely monstrous and not productive of fear, are wholly out of touch with Tragedy; not every kind of pleasure should be required of a tragedy, but only its own proper pleasure.

The tragic pleasure is that of pity and fear, and the poet has to produce it by a work of imitation; it is clear, therefore, that the causes should be included in the incidents of his story. Let us see, then, what kinds of incident strike one as horrible, or rather as piteous. In a deed of this description the parties must necessarily be either friends, or enemies, or indifferent to one another. Now when enemy does it on enemy, there is nothing to move us to pity either in his doing or in his meditating the deed, except so far as the actual pain of the sufferer is concerned; and the same is true when the parties are indifferent to one another. Whenever the tragic deed, however, is done within the family—when murder or the like is done or meditated by brother on brother, by son on father, by mother on son, or son on mother—these are the situations the poet should seek after. The traditional stories, accordingly, must be kept as they are, e. g. the murder of Clytaemnestra by Orestes and of Eriphyle by Alcmeon. At the same time even with these there is something left to the poet himself; it is for him to devise the right way of treating them. Let us explain more clearly what we mean by 'the right way'. The deed of horror may be done by the doer knowingly and consciously, as in the old poets, and in Medea's murder of her children in Euripides. Or he may do it, but in ignorance of his relationship, and discover that afterwards, as does the Oedipus in Sophocles. Here

the deed is outside the play; but it may be within it, like the act of the Alcmeon in Astydamas, or that of the Telegonus in *Ulysses Wounded*.[23] A third possibility is for one meditating some deadly injury to another, in ignorance of his relationship, to make the discovery in time to draw back. These exhaust the possibilities, since the deed must necessarily be either done or not done, and either knowingly or unknowingly.

The worst situation is when the personage is with full knowledge on the point of doing the deed, and leaves it undone. It is odious and also (through the absence of suffering) untragic; hence it is that no one is made to act thus except in some few instances, e. g. Haemon and Creon in *Antigone*.[24] Next after this comes the actual perpetration of the deed meditated. A better situation than that, however, is for the deed to be done in ignorance, and the relationship discovered afterwards, since there is nothing odious in it, and the Discovery will serve to astound us. But the best of all is the last; what we have in *Cresphontes*,[25] for example, where Merope, on the point of slaying her son, recognizes him in time; in *Iphigenia*, where sister and brother are in a like position; and in *Helle*,[26] where the son recognizes his mother, when on the point of giving her up to her enemy.

This will explain why our tragedies are restricted (as we said just now) to such a small number of families. It was accident rather than art that led the poets in quest of subjects to embody this kind of incident in their Plots. They are still obliged, accordingly, to have recourse to the families in which such horrors have occurred.

On the construction of the Plot, and the kind of Plot required for Tragedy, enough has now been said.

15 In the Characters there are four points to aim at. First and foremost, that they shall be good. There will be an element of character in the play, if (as has been observed) what a personage says or does reveals a certain moral purpose; and a good element of character, if the purpose so revealed is good. Such goodness is possible in every type of personage, even in a woman or a slave, though the one is perhaps an inferior, and the other a wholly worthless being. The second point is to make them appropriate. The Character before us may be, say, manly; but it is not appropriate in a female Character to be manly, or clever. The third is to make them like the reality, which is not the same as their being good and appropriate, in our sense of the term. The fourth is to make them consistent and the same throughout; even if inconsistency be part of the man before one for

---

[23] [Bywater] Perhaps by Sophocles.
[24] [Bywater] L. 1231.
[25] [Bywater] By Euripides.
[26] [Bywater] Author unknown.

imitation as presenting that form of character, he should still be consistently inconsistent. We have an instance of baseness of character, not required for the story, in the Menelaus in *Orestes*[27]; of the incongruous and unbefitting in the lamentation of Ulysses in *Scylla,*[28] and in the (clever) speech of Melanippe; and of inconsistency in *Iphigenia at Aulis,*[29] where Iphigenia the suppliant is utterly unlike the later Iphigenia. The right thing, however, is in the Characters just as in the incidents of the play to endeavour always after the necessary or the probable; so that whenever such-and-such a personage says or does such-and-such a thing, it shall be the necessary or probable outcome of his character; and whenever this incident follows on that, it shall be either the necessary or the probable consequence of it. From this one sees (to digress for a moment) that the Dénouement also should arise out of the plot itself, and not depend on a stage-artifice, as in *Medea,* or in the story of the (arrested) departure of the Greeks in the *Iliad.* The artifice must be reserved for matters outside the play—for past events beyond human knowledge, or events yet to come, which require to be foretold or announced; since it is the privilege of the Gods to know everything. There should be nothing improbable among the actual incidents. If it be unavoidable, however, it should be outside the tragedy, like the improbability in the *Oedipus* of Sophocles. But to return to the Characters. As Tragedy is an imitation of personages better than the ordinary man, we in our way should follow the example of good portrait-painters, who reproduce the distinctive features of a man, and at the same time, without losing the likeness, make him handsomer than he is. The poet in like manner, in portraying men quick or slow to anger, or with similar infirmities of character, must know how to represent them as such, and at the same time as good men, as Agathon and Homer have represented Achilles.

All these rules one must keep in mind throughout, and, further, those also for such points of stage-effect as directly depend on the art of the poet, since in these too one may often make mistakes. Enough, however, has been said on the subject in one of our published writings.[30]

16 Discovery in general has been explained already. As for the species of Discovery, the first to be noted is (1) the least artistic form of it, of which the poets make most use through mere lack of invention, Discovery by signs or marks. Of these signs some are congenital, like the 'lance-head which the

Earth-born have on them',[31] or 'stars', such as Carcinus brings in his *Thyestes;* others acquired after birth—these latter being either marks on the body, e. g. scars, or external tokens, like necklaces, or (to take another sort of instance) the ark in the Discovery in *Tyro.*[32] Even these, however, admit of two uses, a better and a worse; the scar of Ulysses is an instance; the Discovery of him through it is made in one way by the nurse[33] and in another by the swineherds.[34] A Discovery using signs as a means of assurance is less artistic, as indeed are all such as imply reflection; whereas one bringing them in all of a sudden, as in the *Bath-story,*[35] is of a better order. Next after these are (2) Discoveries made directly by the poet; which are inartistic for that very reason; e. g. Orestes' Discovery of himself in *Iphigenia:* whereas his sister reveals who she is by the letter,[36] Orestes is made to say himself what the poet rather than the story demands. This, therefore, is not far removed from the first-mentioned fault, since he might have presented certain tokens as well. Another instance is the 'shuttle's voice' in the *Tereus* of Sophocles. (3) A third species is Discovery through memory, from a man's consciousness being awakened by something seen. Thus in *The Cyprioe* of Dicaeogenes, the sight of the picture makes the man burst into tears; and in the *Tale of Alcinous,*[37] hearing the harper Ulysses is reminded of the past and weeps; the Discovery of them being the result. (4) A fourth kind is Discovery through reasoning; e. g. in *The Choephoroe;*[38] 'One like me is here; there is no one like me but Orestes; he, therefore, must be here.' Or that which Polyidus the Sophist suggested for *Iphigenia;* since it was natural for Orestes to reflect: 'My sister was sacrificed, and I am to be sacrificed like her.' Or that in the *Tydeus* of Theodectes: 'I came to find a son, and am to die myself.' Or that in *The Phinidae:* on seeing the place the women inferred their fate, that they were to die there, since they had also been exposed there. (5) There is, too, a composite Discovery arising from bad reasoning on the side of the other party. An instance of it is in *Ulysses the False Messenger:*[39] he said he should know the bow—which he had not seen; but to suppose from that that he would know it again (as though he had once seen it) was bad reasoning. (6) The best of all Discoveries, however, is that arising from the incidents themselves, when

---

[27] By Euripides.
[28] [Bywater] A dithyramb by Timotheus [446–357 B.C.].
[29] [Bywater] Ll1211ff., 1368ff. [by Euripides].
[30] [Bywater] In the lost dialogue *On Poets.*

[31] [Bywater] Authorship unknown.
[32] [Bywater] By Euripides.
[33] [Bywater] *Odyssey* XIX, 386–475.
[34] [Bywater] *Odyssey* XXI, 205–225.
[35] [Bywater] *Odyssey* XIX, 392.
[36] [Bywater] *Iphigenia in Tauris,* 727ff.
[37] [Bywater] *Odyssey* VIII, 521ff. (cf. VIII, 83ff.).
[38] [Bywater] Ll. 168–234.
[39] [Bywater] Authorship [of *Phinidae* and *Ulysses the False Messenger*] unknown.

the great surprise comes about through a probable incident, like that in the *Oedipus* of Sophocles; and also in *Iphigenia;*[40] for it was not improbable that she should wish to have a letter taken home. These last are the only Discoveries independent of the artifice of signs and necklaces. Next after them come Discoveries through reasoning.

17 At the time when he is constructing his Plots, and engaged on the Diction in which they are worked out, the poet should remember (1) to put the actual scenes as far as possible before his eyes. In this way, seeing everything with the vividness of an eye-witness as it were, he will devise what is appropriate, and be least likely to overlook incongruities. This is shown by what was censured in Carcinus, the return of Amphiaraus from the sanctuary; it would have passed unnoticed, if it had not been actually seen by the audience; but on the stage his play failed, the incongruity of the incident offending the spectators. (2) As far as may be, too, the poet should even act his story with the very gestures of his personages. Given the same natural qualifications, he who feels the emotions to be described will be the most convincing; distress and anger, for instance, are portrayed most truthfully by one who is feeling them at the moment. Hence it is that poetry demands a man with a special gift for it, or else one with a touch of madness in him; the former can easily assume the required mood, and the latter may be actually beside himself with emotion. (3) His story, again, whether already made or of his own making, he should first simplify and reduce to a universal form, before proceeding to lengthen it out by the insertion of episodes. The following will show how the universal element in *Iphigenia,* for instance, may be viewed: A certain maiden having been offered in sacrifice, and spirited away from her sacrificers into another land, where the custom was to sacrifice all strangers to the Goddess, she was made there the priestess of this rite. Long after that the brother of the priestess happened to come; the fact, however, of the oracle having for a certain reason bidden him go thither, and his object in going, are outside the Plot of the play. On his coming he was arrested, and about to be sacrificed, when he revealed who he was—either as Euripides puts it, or (as suggested by Polyidus) by the not improbable exclamation, 'So I too am doomed to be sacrificed, as my sister was'; and the disclosure led to his salvation. This done, the next thing, after the proper names have been fixed as a basis for the story, is to work in episodes or accessory incidents. One must mind, however, that the episodes are appropriate,

like the fit of madness[41] in Orestes, which led to his arrest, and the purifying,[42] which brought about his salvation. In plays, then, the episodes are short; in epic poetry they serve to lengthen out the poem. The argument of the *Odyssey* is not a long one. A certain man has been abroad many years; Poseidon is ever on the watch for him, and he is all alone. Matters at home too have come to this, that his substance is being wasted and his son's death plotted by suitors to his wife. Then he arrives there himself after his grievous sufferings; reveals himself, and falls on his enemies; and the end is his salvation and their death. This being all that is proper to the *Odyssey,* everything else in it is episode.

18 (4) There is a further point to be borne in mind. Every tragedy is in part Complication and in part Dénouement; the incidents before the opening scene, and often certain also of those within the play, forming the Complication; and the rest the Dénouement. By Complication I mean all from the beginning of the story to the point just before the change in the hero's fortunes; by Dénouement, all from the beginning of the change to the end. In the *Lynceus* of Theodectes, for instance, the Complication includes, together with the presupposed incidents, the seizure of the child and that in turn of the parents; and the Dénouement all from the indictment for the murder to the end. Now it is right, when one speaks of a tragedy as the same or not the same as another, to do so on the ground before all else of their Plot, i.e. as having the same or not the same Complication and Dénouement. Yet there are many dramatists who, after a good Complication, fail in the Dénouement. But it is necessary for both points of construction to be always duly mastered. (5) There are four distinct species of Tragedy—that being the number of the constituents also that have been mentioned:[43] first, the complex Tragedy, which is all Peripety and Discovery; second, the Tragedy of suffering, e. g. the *Ajaxes* and *Ixions;* third, the Tragedy of character, e. g. *The Phthiotides*[44] and *Peleus.*[45] The fourth constituent is that of 'Spectacle', exemplified in *The Phorcides,*[46] in *Prometheus,*[47] and in all plays with the scene laid in the nether world. The poet's aim, then, should be to combine every element of interest, if possible, or else the more important and the major part of them. This is now especially necessary owing to the unfair criticism to

---

[40] [Bywater] *Iphigenia in Tauris,* 582.

[41] [Bywater] *Iphigenia in Tauris,* 281ff.
[42] [Bywater] *Iphigenia in Tauris,* 1163ff.
[43] [Bywater] This does not agree with anything actually said before.
[44] [Bywater] By Sophocles.
[45] [Bywater] Probably Sophocles's *Peleus* is incorrect.
[46] [Bywater] By Aeschylus [525–456 B.C.].
[47] [Bywater] Probably a satyric drama by Aeschylus.

which the poet is subjected in these days. Just because there have been poets before him strong in the several species of tragedy, the critics now expect the one man to surpass that which was the strong point of each one of his predecessors. (6) One should also remember what has been said more than once, and not write a tragedy on an epic body of incident (i. e. one with a plurality of stories in it), by attempting to dramatize, for instance, the entire story of the *Iliad*. In the epic owing to its scale every part is treated at proper length; with a drama, however, on the same story the result is very disappointing. This is shown by the fact that all who have dramatized the fall of Ilium in its entirety, and not part by part, like Euripides, of the whole of the Niobe story, instead of a portion, like Aeschylus, either fail utterly or have but ill success on the stage; for that and that alone was enough to ruin even a play by Agathon. Yet in their Peripeties, as also in their simple plots, the poets I mean show wonderful skill in aiming at the kind of effect they desire—a tragic situation that arouses the human feeling in one, like the clever villain (e. g. Sisyphus) deceived, or the brave wrongdoer worsted. This is probable, however, only in Agathon's sense, when he speaks of the probability of even improbabilities coming to pass. (7) The Chorus too should be regarded as one of the actors; it should be an integral part of the whole, and take a share in the action—that which it has in Sophocles, rather than in Euripides. With the later poets, however, the songs in a play of theirs have no more to do with the Plot of that than of any other tragedy. Hence it is that they are now singing intercalary pieces, a practice first introduced by Agathon. And yet what real difference is there between singing such intercalary pieces, and attempting to fit in a speech, or even a whole act, from one play into another?

19 The Plot and Characters having been discussed, it remains to consider the Diction and Thought. As for the Thought, we may assume what is said of it in our Art of Rhetoric, as it belongs more properly to that department of inquiry. The Thought of the personages is shown in everything to be effected by their language—in every effort to prove or disprove, to arouse emotion (pity, fear, anger, and the like), or to maximize or minimize things. It is clear, also, that their mental procedure must be on the same lines in their actions likewise, whenever they wish them to arouse pity or horror, or to have a look of importance or probability. The only difference is that with the act the impression has to be made without explanation; whereas with the spoken word it has to be produced by the speaker, and result from his language. What, indeed, would be the good of the speaker, if things appeared in the required light even apart from anything he says?

As regards the Diction, one subject for inquiry under this head is the turns given to the language when spoken; e. g. the difference between command and prayer, simple statement and threat, question and answer, and so forth. The theory of such matters, however, belongs to Elocution and the professors of that art. Whether the poet knows these things or not, his art as a poet is never seriously criticized on that account. What fault can one see in Homer's 'Sing of the wrath, Goddess'?—which Protagoras has criticized as being a command where a prayer was meant, since to bid one do or not do, he tells us, is a command. Let us pass over this, then, as appertaining to another art, and not to that of poetry.

20 The Diction viewed as a whole is made up of the following parts: the Letter (or ultimate element), the Syllable, the Conjunction, the Article, the Noun, the Verb, the Case, and the Speech. (1) The Letter is an indivisible sound of a particular kind, one that may become a factor in an intelligible sound. Indivisible sounds are uttered by the brutes also, but no one of these is a Letter in our sense of the term. These elementary sounds are either vowels, semi-vowels, or mutes. A vowel is a Letter having an audible sound without the addition of another Letter. A semi-vowel, one having an audible sound by the addition of another Letter; e. g. S and R. A mute, one having no sound at all by itself, but becoming audible by an addition, that of one of the Letters which have a sound of some sort of their own; e. g. G and D. The Letters differ in various ways: as produced by different conformations or in different regions of the mouth; as aspirated, not aspirated, or sometimes one and sometimes the other; as long, short, or of variable quantity; and further as having an acute, grave, or intermediate accent. The details of these matters we must leave to the metricians. (2) A Syllable is a non-significant composite sound, made up of a mute and a Letter having a sound (a vowel or semi-vowel); for GR, without an A, is just as much a Syllable as GRA, with an A. The various forms of the Syllable also belong to the theory of metre. (3) A Conjunction is (*a*) a non-significant sound which, when one significant sound is formable out of several, neither hinders nor aids the union, and which, if the Speech thus formed stands by itself (apart from other Speeches), must not be inserted at the beginning of it; e. g., μέυ, δή, τοι, δέ. Or (*b*) a non-significant sound capable of combining two or more significant sounds into one; e. g. ἀμφί, περί, &c. (4) An Article is a non-significant sound marking the beginning, end, or dividing-point of a Speech, its natural place being either at the extremities or in the middle. (5) A Noun or name is a composite significant sound not involving the idea of time, with parts which have no significance by themselves in it. It is to be remembered that in a compound we do not think of the parts as

having a significance by themselves in it. It is to be remembered that in a compound we do not think of the parts as having a significance also by themselves; in the name 'Theodorus', for instance, the δῶρον means nothing to us. (6) A Verb is a composite significant sound involving the idea of time, with parts which (just as in the Noun) have no significance by themselves in it. Whereas the word 'man' or 'white' does not imply *when,* 'walks' and 'has walked,' involve in addition to the idea of walking that of time present or time past. (7) A Case of a Noun or Verb is when the word means 'of' or 'to' a thing, and so forth, or for one or many (e. g. 'man' and 'men'); or it may consist merely in the mode of utterance, e. g. in question, command, &c. 'Walked?' and 'Walk!' are Cases of the verb 'to walk' of this last kind. (8) A Speech is a composite significant sound, some of the parts of which have a certain significance by themselves. It may be observed that a Speech is not always made up of Noun and Verb; it may be without a Verb, like the definition of man; but it will always have some part with a certain significance by itself. In the Speech 'Cleon walks', 'Cleon' is an instance of such a part. A Speech is said to be one in two ways, either as signifying one thing, or as a union of several Speeches made into one by conjunction. Thus the *Illiad* is one Speech by conjunction of several; and the definition of man is one through its signifying one thing.

21 Nouns are of two kinds, either (1) simple, i. e. made up of non-significant parts, like the word γῆ, or (2) double; in the latter case the word may be made up either of a significant and a non-significant part (a distinction which disappears in the compound), or of two significant parts. It is possible also to have triple, quadruple, or higher compounds, like most of our amplified names; e. g. 'Hermocaïcoxanthus' and the like.

Whatever its structure, a Noun must always be either (1) the ordinary word for the thing, or (2) a strange word, or (3) a metaphor, or (4) an ornamental word, or (5) a coined word, or (6) a word lengthened out, or (7) curtailed, or (8) altered in form. By the ordinary word I mean that in general use in a country; and by a strange word, one in use elsewhere. So that the same word may obviously be at once strange and ordinary, though not in reference to the same people; οἴγυνον, for instance, is an ordinary word in Cyprus, and a strange word with us. Metaphor consists in giving the thing a name that belongs to something else; the transference being either from genus to species, or from species to genus, or from species to species, or on grounds of analogy. That from genus to species is exemplified in 'Here stands my ship';[48] for lying at anchor is the 'stand-

ing' of a particular kind of thing. That from species to genus in 'Truly ten thousand good deeds has Ulysses wrought',[49] where 'ten thousand', which is a particular large number, is put in place of the generic 'a large number'. That from species to species in 'Drawing the life with the bronze', and in 'Severing with the enduring bronze',[50] where the poet uses 'draw' in the sense of 'sever' and 'sever' in that of 'draw', both words meaning to 'take away' something. That from analogy is possible whenever there are four terms so related that the second (B) is to the first (A), as the fourth (D) to the third (C); for one may then metaphorically put D in lieu of B, and B in lieu of D. Now and then, too, they qualify the metaphor by adding on to it that to which the word it supplants is relative. Thus a cup (B) is in relation to Dionysus (A) what a shield (D) is to Ares (C). The cup accordingly will be metaphorically described as the 'shield *of Dionysus*' (D + A), and the shield as the 'cup *of Ares*'[51] (B + C). Or to take another instance: As old age (D) is to life (C), so is evening (B) to day (A). One will accordingly describe evening (B) as the 'old age *of the day*' (D + A)—or by the Empedoclean equivalent; and old age (D) as the 'evening'[52] or 'sunset *of life*'[53] (B + C). It may be that some of the terms thus related have no special name of their own, but for all that they will be metaphorically described in just the same way. Thus to cast forth seed-corn is called 'sowing'; but to cast forth its flame, as said of the sun, has no special name. This nameless act (B), however, stands in just the same relation to its object, sunlight (A), as sowing (D) to the seed-corn (C). Hence the expression in the poet, 'sowing around a god-created *flame*'[54] (D + A). There is also another form of qualified metaphor. Having given the thing the alien name, one may by a negative addition deny of it one of the attributes naturally associated with its new name. An instance of this would be to call the shield not the 'cup *of Ares*', as in the former case, but a 'cup *that holds no wine*'. . . . A coined word is a name which, being quite unknown among a people, is given by the poet himself; e. g. (for there are some words that seem to be of this origin) ἔρνυγες for horns, and ἀρητήρ for priest.[55] A word is said to be lengthened out, when it has a short vowel made long, or an extra syllable inserted; e. g. πόληος for πόλεως,

[48][Bywater] *Odyssey* I, 185; XXIV, 308.

[49][Bywater] *Iliad* II, 272.
[50][Bywater] Empedocles [fifth century B.C.].
[51][Bywater] Timotheus.
[52][Bywater] Alexis [fourth century B.C.].
[53][Bywater] Plato, *Laws,* 770A.
[54][Bywater] Authorship unknown.
[55][Bywater] *Iliad* I, 11.

Πηληιάδεω for Πηλείδου. It is said to be curtailed, when it has lost a part; e. g. κρῖ, δῶ, and ὄψ in μία γίνεται ἀμφοτέρων ὄψ.[56] It is an altered word, when part is left as it was and part is of the poet's making; e. g. δεξιτερόν for δεξιόν, in δεξιτερὸν κατὰ μαζόν.[57]

The Nouns themselves (to whatever class they may belong) are either masculines, feminines, or intermediates (neuter). All ending in N, P, Σ, or in the two compounds of this last, Ψ and Ξ, are masculines. All ending in the invariably long vowels, H and Ω, and in A among the vowels that may be long, are feminines. So that there is an equal number of masculine and feminine terminations, as Ψ and Ξ are the same as Σ, and need not be counted. There is no Noun, however, ending in a mute or in either of the two short vowels, E and O. Only three (μέλι, κόμμι, πέπερι) end in I and five in Υ. The intermediates, or neuters, end in the variable vowels or in N, P, Σ.

22 The perfection of Diction is for it to be at once clear and not mean. The clearest indeed is that made up of the ordinary words for things, but it is mean, as is shown by the poetry of Cleophon and Sthenelus. On the other hand the Diction becomes distinguished and non-prosaic by the use of unfamiliar terms, i. e. strange words, metaphors, lengthened forms, and everything that deviates from the ordinary modes of speech.—But a whole statement in such terms will be either a riddle or a barbarism, a riddle, if made up of metaphors, a barbarism, if made up of strange words. The very nature indeed of a riddle is this, to describe a fact in an impossible combination of words (which cannot be done with the real names for things, but can be with their metaphorical substitutes); e.g. 'I saw a man glue brass on another with fire',[58] and the like. The corresponding use of strange words results in a barbarism.—A certain admixture, accordingly, of unfamiliar terms is necessary. These, the strange word, the metaphor, the ornamental equivalent, &c., will save the language from seeming mean and prosaic, while the ordinary words in it will secure the requisite clearness. What helps most, however, to render the Diction at once clear and non-prosaic is the use of the lengthened, curtailed, and altered forms of words. Their deviation from the ordinary words will, by making the language unlike that in general use, give it a non-prosaic appearance; and their having much in common with the words in general use will give

it the quality of clearness. It is not right, then, to condemn these modes of speech, and ridicule the poet for using them, as some have done; e. g. the elder Euclid, who said it was easy to make poetry if one were to be allowed to lengthen the words in the statement itself as much as one likes—a procedure he caricatured by reading Ἐπιχάρην εἶδον Μαραθῶνάδε βαδίζοντα,[59] and οὐχ ἂν γ' ἐράμενοσ τὸν ἐχείνου ἐλλέβορον[60] as verses. A too apparent use of these licenses has certainly a ludicrous effect, but they are not alone in that; the rule of moderation applies to all the constituents of the poetic vocabulary; even with metaphors, strange words, and the rest, the effect will be the same, if one uses them improperly and with a view to provoking laughter. The proper use of them is a very different thing. To realize the difference one should take an epic verse and see how it reads when the normal words are introduced. The same should be done too with the strange word, the metaphor, and the rest; for one has only to put the ordinary words in their place to see the truth of what we are saying. The same iambic, for instance, is found in Aeschylus and Euripides, and as it stands in the former it is a poor line; whereas Euripides, by the change of a single word, the substitution of a strange for what is by usage the ordinary word, has made it seem a fine one. Aeschylus having said in his *Philoctetes*:

φαγέδαινα ἥ μου σάρκας ἐσθίει ποδός[61]

Euripides has merely altered the ἐσθίει here into θοινᾶται. Or suppose

νῦν δέ μ' ἐὼν ὀλίγος τε καὶ οὐτιδανὸς καὶ ἀεικής[62]

to be altered, by the substitution of the ordinary words, into

νῦν δέ μ' ἐὼν μικρός τε καὶ ἀσθενικὸς καὶ ἀειδής.[63]

Or the line

δίφρον ἀεικέλιον καταθεὶς ὀλίγην τε τράπεζαν[64]

---

[56][Bywater] Empedocles.

[57][Bywater] *Iliad* V, 393.

[58][Bywater] *Cleobulina* [by Cratinus, c. 499–422 B.C.]

[59]"I saw Epichares walking toward Marathon."

[60]"I might not be wanting his hellebore."

[61]"The cancer that feeds on my foot's flesh."

[62]"But now one, being meager and of no valor and unimportant." [Bywater] *Odyssey* IX, 515.

[63]"But now one, being small and puny and unsightly."

[64]"Having set forth a lowly seat and a mean table." [Bywater] *Odyssey* XX, 259.

into

$$\delta\acute{\iota}\varphi\rho o\nu \quad \mu o\chi\vartheta\eta\rho\grave{o}\nu \quad \kappa\alpha\tau\alpha\vartheta\epsilon\grave{\iota}\varsigma \quad \mu\iota\kappa\rho\acute{\alpha}\nu \quad \tau\epsilon$$
$$\tau\rho\acute{\alpha}\pi\epsilon\zeta\alpha\nu.^{65}$$

Or ἠόνες βοόωσιν[66] into ἠόνες κράζουσιν.[67] Add to this that Ariphrades used to ridicule the tragedians for introducing expressions unknown in the language of common life, δωμάτων ἄπο (for ἀπὸ δωμάτων), σέθεν, ἐγὼ δέ νιν,[68] Ἀχιλλέως πέρι (for περὶ Ἀχιλλέως), and the like.[69] The mere fact of their not being in ordinary speech gives the Diction a non-prosaic character; but Ariphrades was unaware of that. It is a great thing, indeed, to make a proper use of these poetical forms, as also of compounds and strange words. But the greatest thing by far is to be a master of metaphor. It is the one thing that cannot be learnt from others; and it is also a sign of genius, since a good metaphor implies an intuitive perception of the similarity in dissimilars.

Of the kinds of words we have enumerated it may be observed that compounds are most in place in the dithyramb, strange words in heroic, and metaphors in iambic poetry. Heroic poetry, indeed, may avail itself of them all. But in iambic verse, which models itself as far as possible on the spoken language, only those kinds of words are in place which are allowable also in an oration, i. e. the ordinary word, the metaphor, and the ornamental equivalent.

Let this, then, suffice as an account of Tragedy, the art imitating by means of action on the stage.

23 As for the poetry which merely narrates, or imitates[70] by means of versified language (without action), it is evident that it has several points in common with Tragedy.

I. The construction of its stories should clearly be like that in a drama; they should be based on a single action, one that is a complete whole in itself, with a beginning, middle, and end, so as to enable the work to produce its own proper pleasure with all the organic unity of a living creature. Nor should one suppose that there is anything like them in our usual histories. A history has to deal not with one action, but with one period and all that happened in that to one or more

persons, however disconnected the several events may have been. Just as two events may take place at the same time, e. g. the sea-fight off Salamis and the battle with the Carthaginians in Sicily, without converging to the same end, so too of two consecutive events one may sometimes come after the other with no one end as their common issue. Nevertheless most of our epic poets, one may say, ignore the distinction.

Herein, then, to repeat what we have said before, we have a further proof of Homer's marvellous superiority to the rest. He did not attempt to deal even with the Trojan war in its entirety, though it was a whole with a definite beginning and end—through a feeling apparently that it was too long a story to be taken in in one view, or if not that, too complicated from the variety of incident in it. As it is, he has singled out one section of the whole; many of the other incidents, however, he brings in as episodes, using the Catalogue of the Ships, for instance, and other episodes to relieve the uniformity of his narrative. As for the other epic poets, they treat of one man, or one period; or else of an action which, although one, has a multiplicity of parts in it. This last is what the authors of the *Cypria*[71] and *Little Iliad*[72] have done. And the result is that, whereas the *Iliad* or *Odyssey* supplies materials for only one, or at most two tragedies, the *Cypria* does that for several and the *Little Iliad* for more than eight: for an *Adjudgment of Arms*, a *Philoctetes*, a *Neoptolemus*, a *Eurypylus*, a *Ulysses as Beggar*, a *Laconian Women*, a *Fall of Ilium*, and a *Departure of the Fleet*; as also a *Sinon*, and a *Women of Troy*.

24 II. Besides this, Epic poetry must divide into the same species as Tragedy; it must be either simple or complex, a story of character or one of suffering. Its parts, too, with the exception of Song and Spectacle, must be the same, as it requires Peripeties, Discoveries, and scenes of suffering just like Tragedy. Lastly, the Thought and Diction in it must be good in their way. All these elements appear in Homer first; and he has made due use of them. His two poems are each examples of construction, the *Iliad* simple and a story of suffering, the *Odyssey* complex (there is Discovery throughout it) and a story of character. And they are more than this, since in Diction and Thought too they surpass all other poems.

There is, however, a difference in the Epic as compared with Tragedy, (1) in its length, and (2) in its metre. (1) As to its length, the limit already suggested will suffice: it must be possible for the beginning and end of the work to be taken in in one view—a condition which will be fulfilled if the poem

---

[65]"Having set forth a poor seat and a small table."
[66]"The shores howl." [Bywater] *Iliad* XVII, 265.
[67]"The shores squall."
[68][Bywater] Sophocles, *Oedipus at Colonus*, 986.
[69]The anastrophic use of prepositions, that is, the inversion of customary word order, is uncommon and never occurs in Greek prose.
[70]Here imitation is enlarged beyond the technical use referring only to drama.

---

[71][Bywater] Authorship unknown.
[72][Bywater] Authorship unknown.

be shorter than the old epics, and about as long as the series of tragedies offered for one hearing. For the extension of its length epic poetry has a special advantage, of which it makes large use. In a play one cannot represent an action with a number of parts going on simultaneously; one is limited to the part on the stage and connected with the actors. Whereas in epic poetry the narrative form makes it possible for one to describe a number of simultaneous incidents; and these, if germane to the subject, increase the body of the poem. This then is a gain to the Epic, tending to give it grandeur, and also variety of interest and room for episodes of diverse kinds. Uniformity of incident by the satiety it soon creates is apt to ruin tragedies on the stage. (2) As for its metre, the heroic[73] has been assigned it from experience; were any one to attempt a narrative poem in some one, or in several, of the other metres, the incongruity of the thing would be apparent. The heroic in fact is the gravest and weightiest of metres—which is what makes it more tolerant than the rest of strange words and metaphors, that also being a point in which the narrative form of poetry goes beyond all others. The iambic and trochaic, on the other hand, are metres of movement, the one representing that of life and action, the other that of the dance. Still more unnatural would it appear, if one were to write an epic in a medley of metres, as Chaeremon did.[74] Hence it is that no one has ever written a long story in any but heroic verse; nature herself, as we have said, teaches us to select the metre appropriate to such a story.

Homer, admirable as he is in every other respect, is especially so in this, that he alone among epic poets is not unaware of the part to be played by the poet himself in the poem. The poet should say very little *in propria persona*, as he is no imitator when doing that. Whereas the other poets are perpetually coming forward in person, and say but little, and that only here and there, as imitators, Homer after a brief preface brings in forthwith a man, a woman, or some other Character—no one of them characterless, but each with distinctive characteristics.

The marvellous is certainly required in Tragedy. The Epic, however, affords more opening for the improbable, the chief factor in the marvellous, because in it the agents are not visibly before one. The scene of the pursuit of Hector would be ridiculous on the stage—the Greeks halting instead of pursuing him, and Achilles shaking his head to stop them;[75] but in the poem the absurdity is overlooked. The marvellous, however, is a cause of pleasure, as is shown by the fact that we all tell a story with additions, in the belief that we are doing our hearers a pleasure.

Homer more than any other has taught the rest of us the art of framing lies[76] in the right way. I mean the use of paralogism. Whenever, if A is or happens, a consequent, B, is or happens, men's notion is that, if the B is, the A also is—but that is a false conclusion. Accordingly, if A is untrue, but there is something else, B, that on the assumption of its truth follows as its consequent, the right thing then is to add on the B. Just because we know the truth of the consequent, we are in our own minds led on to the erroneous inference of the truth of the antecedent. Here is an instance, from the *Bath-story* in the *Odyssey*.[77]

A likely impossibility is always preferable to an unconvincing possibility.[78] The story should never be made up of improbable incidents; there should be nothing of the sort in it. If, however, such incidents are unavoidable, they should be outside the piece, like the hero's ignorance in *Oedipus* of the circumstances of Laius' death; not within it, like the report of the Pythian games in *Electra*,[79] or the man's having come to Mysia from Tegea without uttering a word on the way, in *The Mysians*.[80] So that it is ridiculous to say that one's Plot would have been spoilt without them, since it is fundamentally wrong to make up such Plots. If the poet has taken such a Plot, however, and one sees that he might have put it in a more probable form, he is guilty of absurdity as well as a fault of art. Even in the *Odyssey* the improbabilities in the setting-ashore of Ulysses[81] would be clearly intolerable in the hands of an inferior poet. As it is, the poet conceals them, his other excellences veiling their absurdity. Elaborate Diction, however, is required only in places where there is no action, and no Character or Thought to be revealed. Where there is Character or Thought, on the other hand, an over-ornate Diction tends to obscure them.

25 As regards Problems and their Solutions, one may see the number and nature of the assumptions on which they proceed by viewing the matter in the following way. (1) The poet being an imitator just like the painter or other maker of likenesses, he must necessarily in all instances represent things in

---

[73]Dactylic hexameter.
[74][Bywater] *Centaur*, cf. 1447b, 21.
[75][Bywater] *Iliad* XXII, 205.

[76]On later views of the poet as liar see, for example, Sidney (below, page 198) and Wilde (below, page 713).
[77][Bywater] *Odyssey* XIX, 164–260.
[78]On this point one may contrast Aristotle's discourse, which emphasizes the means (medium) and the poetic whole, with Plato's, which emphasizes straightforward imitation. See Mazzoni (below, page 220) on icastic and phantastic imitation.
[79][Bywater] Sophocles, *Electra*, 660ff.
[80][Bywater] Probably by Aeschylus.
[81][Bywater] *Odyssey*, XIII, 116ff.

one or other of three aspects, either as they were or are, or as they are said or thought to be or to have been, or as they ought to be. (2) All this he does in language, with an admixture, it may be, of strange words and metaphors, as also of the various modified forms of words, since the use of these is conceded in poetry. (3) It is to be remembered, too, that there is not the same kind of correctness in poetry as in politics, or indeed any other art. There is, however, within the limits of poetry itself a possibility of two kinds of error, the one directly, the other only accidentally connected with the art. If the poet meant to describe the thing correctly, and failed through lack of power of expression, his art itself is at fault. But if it was through his having meant to describe it in some incorrect way (e. g. to make the horse in movement have both right legs thrown forward) that the technical error (one in a matter of, say, medicine or some other special science), or impossibilities of whatever kind they may be, have got into his description, his error in that case is not in the essentials of the poetic art. These, therefore, must be the premisses of the Solutions in answer to the criticisms involved in the Problems.[82]

I. As to the criticisms relating to the poet's art itself. Any impossibilities there may be in his descriptions of things are faults. But from another point of view they are justifiable, if they serve the end of poetry itself—if (to assume what we have said of that end) they make the effect of either that very portion of the work or some other portion more astounding. The Pursuit of Hector is an instance in point. If, however, the poetic end might have been as well or better attained without sacrifice of technical correctness in such matters, the impossibility is not to be justified, since the description should be, if it can, entirely free from error. One may ask, too, whether the error is in a matter directly or only accidentally connected with the poetic art; since it is a lesser error in an artist not to know, for instance, that the hind has no horns, than to produce an unrecognizable picture of one.

II. If the poet's description be criticized as not true to fact, one may urge perhaps that the object ought to be as described—an answer like that of Sophocles, who said that he drew men as they ought to be, and Euripides as they were. If the description, however, be neither true nor of the thing as it ought to be, the answer must be then, that it is in accordance with opinion. The tales about Gods, for instance, may be as wrong as Xenophanes thinks, neither true nor the better thing to say; but they are certainly in accordance with opinion.[83] Of other statements in poetry one may perhaps say, not that they are better than the truth, but that the fact was so at the time; e. g. the description of the arms: 'their spears stood upright, butt-end upon the ground';[84] for that was the usual way of fixing them then, as it is still with the Illyrians. As for the question whether something said or done in a poem is morally right or not, in dealing with that one should consider not only the intrinsic quality of the actual word or deed, but also the person who says or does it, the person to whom he says or does it, the time, the means, and the motive of the agent—whether he does it to attain a greater good, or to avoid a greater evil.

III. Other criticisms one must meet by considering the language of the poet: (1) by the assumption of a strange word in a passage like οὐρῆας μὲν πρῶτον,[85] where by οὐρῆας Homer may perhaps mean not mules but sentinels. And in saying of Dolon, ὃς ῥ᾿ ἤτοι εἶδος μὲν ἔην χαχός,[86] his meaning may perhaps be, not that Dolon's body was deformed, but that his face was ugly, as εὐειδής is the Cretan word for handsome-faced. So, too, ζωρότερον δὲ κέραιε[87] may mean not 'mix the wine stronger', as though for topers, but 'mix it quicker', (2) Other expressions in Homer may be explained as metaphorical; e. g. in ἄλλοι μέν ῥα θεοί τε καὶ ἀνέρες εὖδον ⟨ἅπαντες⟩ παννύκιοι,[88] as compared with what he tells us at the same time, ἤ τοι ὅτ᾿ ἐς πεδίον τὸ Τρωικὸν ἀθρήσειεν, αὐλῶν συρίγγων †τε ὁμαδόν†,[89] the word ἅπαντες, 'all', is metaphorically put for 'many', since 'all' is a species of 'many'. So also his οἴη δ᾿ ἄμμορος[90] is metaphorical, the best known standing 'alone'. (3) A change, as Hippias of Thasos suggested, in the mode of reading a word will solve the difficulty in δίδομεν δέ οἱ,[91] and in τὸ μὲν οὐ καταπύθεται ὄμβρω.[92] (4) Other difficulties may be solved by another punctuation; e. g. in Empedocles, αἶψα δὲ θνήτ᾿ ἐφύοντο, τὰ πρὶν μάθον ἀθάνατα ζωρά τε πρὶν χέχρητο. Or (5) by the assumption of an equivocal term, as in παρῴχηκεν δὲ πλέω νύξ,[93] where πλέω is equivocal. Or (6) by an appeal to the custom of language. Wine-and-water we call 'wine'; and it

---

[82] This section appears to be a direct response to Plato's theory of imitation.
[83] Xenophanes (sixth century B.C.) said that stories about the gods at least reflected man's opinions about the gods.

[84] [Bywater] *Iliad* X, 152.
[85] [Bywater] *Iliad* I, 50.
[86] [Bywater] *Iliad* X, 316.
[87] [Bywater] *Iliad* IX, 202.
[88] "Now all the gods and men were sleeping through the night." [Bywater] Cf. *Iliad* X, 1; II, 1.
[89] "Often he turned his gaze to the Trojan plain, he marveled at the sound of flutes and pipes." *Iliad* X, 11–13.
[90] "Alone she has no part . . . ." [Bywater] *Iliad* XVIII, 489 = *Odyssey* V, 275.
[91] [Bywater] Cf. Sophocles, *Electra*, 166b 1; *Iliad* II, 15.
[92] [Bywater] *Iliad* XXIII, 327.
[93] [Bywater] *Iliad* X, 251.

is on the same principle that Homer speaks of a κνημὶς νεοτεύκτου κασσιτέροιο,[94] a 'greave of new-wrought *tin*'. A worker in iron we call a 'brazier'; and it is on the same principle that Ganymede is described as the '*wine*-server' of Zeus,[95] though the Gods do not drink wine. This latter, however, may be an instance of metaphor. But whenever also a word seems to imply some contradiction, it is necessary to reflect how many ways there may be of understanding it in the passage in question; e. g. in Homer's τῇ β̌ ἔσχετο χάλκεοσσν ἔγχο[96] one should consider the possible senses of 'was stopped there'—whether by taking it in this sense or in that one will best avoid the fault of which Glaucon speaks: 'They start with some improbable presumption; and having so decreed it themselves, proceed to draw inferences, and censure the poet as though he had actually said whatever they happen to believe, if his statement conflicts with their own notion of things.' This is how Homer's silence about Icarius has been treated. Starting with the notion of his having been a Lacedaemonian, the critics think it strange for Telemachus not to have met him when he went to Lacedaemon. Whereas the fact may have been as the Cephallenians say, that the wife of Ulysses was of a Cephallenian family, and that her father's name was Icadius, not Icarius. So that it is probably a mistake of the critics that has given rise to the Problem.

Speaking generally, one has to justify (1) the Impossible by reference to the requirements of poetry, or to the better, or to opinion. For the purposes of poetry a convincing impossibility is preferable to an unconvincing possibility; and if men such as Zeuxis depicted be impossible, the answer is that it is better they should be like that, as the artist ought to improve on his model. (2) The Improbable one has to justify either by showing it to be in accordance with opinion, or by urging that at times it is not improbable; for there is a probability of things happening also against probability. (3) The contradictions found in the poet's language one should first test as one does an opponent's confutation in a dialectical argument, so as to see whether he means the same thing, in the same relation, and in the same sense, before admitting that he has contradicted either something he has said himself or what a man of sound sense assumes as true. But there is no possible apology for improbability of Plot or depravity of character, when they are not necessary and no use is made of them, like the improbability in the appearance of Aegeus in *Medea*[97] and the baseness of Menelaus in *Orestes*.

The objections, then, of critics start with faults of five kinds: the allegation is always that something is either (1) impossible, (2) improbable, (3) corrupting, (4) contradictory, or (5) against technical correctness. The answers to these objections must be sought under one or other of the above-mentioned heads, which are twelve in number.

26 The question may be raised whether the epic or the tragic is the higher form of imitation. It may be argued that, if the less vulgar is the higher, and the less vulgar is always that which addresses the better public, an art addressing any and every one is of a very vulgar order.[98] It is a belief that their public cannot see the meaning, unless they add something themselves, that causes the perpetual movements of the performers—bad flute-players, for instance, rolling about, if quoit-throwing is to be represented, and pulling at the conductor, if Scylla is the subject of the piece. Tragedy, then, is said to be an art of this order—to be in fact just what the later actors were in the eyes of their predecessors; for Mynniscus used to call Callippides 'the ape', because he thought he so overacted his parts; and a similar view was taken of Pindarus also. All Tragedy, however, is said to stand to the Epic as the newer to the older school of actors. The one, accordingly, is said to address a cultivated audience, which does not need the accompaniment of gesture; the other, an uncultivated one. If, therefore, Tragedy is a vulgar art, it must clearly be lower than the Epic.

The answer to this is twofold. In the first place, one may urge (1) that the censure does not touch the art of the dramatic poet, but only that of his interpreter; for it is quite possible to overdo the gesturing even in an epic recital, as did Sosistratus, and in a singing contest, as did Mnasitheus of Opus. (2) That one should not condemn all movement, unless one means to condemn even the dance, but only that of ignoble people—which is the point of the criticism passed on Callippides and in the present day on others, that their women are not like gentlewomen. (3) That Tragedy may produce its effect even without movement or action in just the same way as Epic poetry; for from the mere reading

---

[94] [Bywater] *Iliad* XXI, 592.

[95] [Bywater] *Iliad* XX, 234.

[96] "The Bronze spear was stopped there." [Bywater] *Iliad* XX, 267.

[97] [Bywater] L. 663.

[98] Aristotle here introduces the problem of literary judgment and, obliquely, the taste of the audience. The theme is strong in eighteenth-century aesthetics. See, for example, Hume (below, page 323) and Kames (below, page 370), where both discuss taste.

of a play its quality may be seen. So that, if it be superior in all other respects, this element of inferiority is no necessary part of it.

In the second place, one must remember (1) that Tragedy has everything that the Epic has (even the epic metre being admissible), together with a not inconsiderable addition in the shape of the Music (a very real factor in the pleasure of the drama) and the Spectacle. (2) That its reality of presentation is felt in the play as read, as well as in the play as acted. (3) That the tragic imitation requires less space for the attainment of its end; which is a great advantage, since the more concentrated effect is more pleasurable than one with a large admixture of time to dilute it—consider the *Oedipus* of Sophocles, for instance, and the effect of expanding it into the number of lines of the *Iliad*. (4) That there is less unity in the imitation of the epic poets, as is proved by the fact that any one work of theirs supplies matter for several tragedies; the result being that, if they take what is really a single story, it seems curt when briefly told, and thin and waterish when on the scale of length usual with their verse. In saying that there is less unity in an epic, I mean an epic made up of a plurality of actions, in the same way as the *Iliad* and *Odyssey* have many such parts, each one of them in itself of some magnitude; yet the structure of the two Homeric poems is as perfect as can be, and the action in them is as nearly as possible one action. If, then, Tragedy is superior in these respects, and also, besides these, in its poetic effect (since the two forms of poetry should give us, not any or every pleasure, but the very special kind we have mentioned), it is clear that, as attaining the poetic effect better than the Epic, it will be the higher form of art.

So much for Tragedy and Epic poetry—for these two arts in general and their species; the number and nature of their constituent parts; the causes of success and failure in them; the Objections of the critics, and the Solutions in answer to them.

makes a man see himself as the possessor of goodness, a thing that every being that has a feeling for it desires to possess: to be loved means to be valued for one's own personal qualities.[1] To be admired is also pleasant, simply because of the honour implied. Flattery and flatterers are pleasant: the flatterer is a man who, you believe, admires and likes you. To do the same thing often is pleasant, since, as we saw, anything habitual is pleasant. And to change is also pleasant: change means an approach to nature, whereas invariable repetition of anything causes the excessive prolongation of a settled condition: therefore, says the poet,

Change is in all things sweet.[2]

That is why what comes to us only at long intervals is pleasant, whether it be a person or a thing; for it is a change from what we had before, and, besides, what comes only at long intervals has the value of rarity. Learning things and wondering at things are also pleasant as a rule; wondering implies the desire of learning, so that the object of wonder is an object of desire; while in learning one is brought into one's natural condition. Conferring and receiving benefits belong to the class of pleasant things; to receive a benefit is to get what one desires; to confer a benefit implies both possession and superiority, both of which are things we try to attain. It is because beneficent acts are pleasant that people find it pleasant to put their neighbours straight again and to supply what they lack. Again, since learning and wondering are pleasant, it follows that such things as acts of imitation must be pleasant—for instance, painting, sculpture, poetry—and every product of skilful imitation; this latter, even if the object imitated is not itself pleasant; for it is not the object itself which here gives delight; the spectator draws inferences ('That is a so-and-so') and thus learns something fresh.[3] Dramatic turns of fortune and hairbreadth escapes from perils are pleasant, because we feel all such things are wonderful.

from

Rhetoric

from
Book I

. . . it is pleasant to love—if you love wine, you certainly find it delightful: and it is pleasant to be loved, for this too

---

Aristotle's *Rhetoric* was apparently written after *Poetics.* The text is from the translation by W. Rhys Roberts in W. D. Ross, ed., *The Works of Aristotle,* Vol. XI (Oxford at the Clarendon Press, 1924).

---

[1] In Book 1 of *Rhetoric,* Aristotle describes rhetoric as the counterpart of dialectic and defines rhetoric as "the faculty of observing in any given case the available means of persuasion." He divides rhetoric into three types: political (deliberative), forensic (legal), and epideictic (ceremonial). He then proceeds to discuss pleasure as " a movement by which the soul as a whole is consciously brought into its normal state of being." He then mentions a number of pleasant things.

[2] [Roberts] Euripides, *Orestes,* 234.

[3] *Poetics,* above, page 52.

And since what is natural is pleasant, and things akin to each other seem natural to each other, therefore all kindred and similar things are usually pleasant to each other; for instance, one man, horse, or young person is pleasant to another man, horse, or young person. Hence the proverbs 'mate delights mate', 'like to like' 'beast knows beast', 'jackdaw to jackdaw', and the rest of them. But since everything like and akin to oneself is pleasant, and since every man is himself more like and akin to himself than any one else is, it follows that all of us must be more or less fond of ourselves. For all this resemblance and kinship is present particularly in the relation of an individual to himself. And because we are all fond of ourselves, it follows that what is our own is pleasant to all of us, as for instance our own deeds and words. That is why we are usually fond of our flatterers, [our lovers,] and honour; also of our children, for our children are our own work. It is also pleasant to complete what is defective, for the whole thing thereupon becomes our own work. And since power over others is very pleasant, it is pleasant to be thought wise, for practical wisdom secures us power over others. (Scientific wisdom is also pleasant, because it is the knowledge of many wonderful things.) Again, since most of us are ambitious, it must be pleasant to disparage our neighbours as well as to have power over them. It is pleasant for a man to spend his time over what he feels he can do best; just as the poet says,

> To that he bends himself,
> To that each day allots most time, wherein
> He is indeed the best part of himself.[4]

Similarly, since amusement and every kind of relaxation and laughter too belong to the class of pleasant things, it follows that ludicrous things are pleasant, whether men, words, or deeds. We have discussed the ludicrous separately in the treatise on the *Art of Poetry*.[5]

So much for the subject of pleasant things: by considering their opposites we can easily see what things are unpleasant.

from
Book III

1 In making a speech one must study three points: first, the means of producing persuasion; second, the style, or language, to be used; third, the proper arrangement of the various parts of the speech. We have already specified the sources of persuasion. We have shown that these are three in number[6]; what they are; and why there are only these three: for we have shown that persuasion must in every case be effected either (1) by working on the emotions of the judges themselves, (2) by giving them the right impression of the speakers' character, or (3) by proving the truth of the statements made. . . .

Our next subject will be the style of expression. For it is not enough to know *what* we ought to say; we must also say it *as* we ought; much help is thus afforded towards producing the right impression of a speech. The first question to receive attention was naturally the one that comes first naturally—how persuasion can be produced from the facts themselves. The second is how to set these facts out in language. A third would be the proper method of delivery; this is a thing that affects the success of a speech greatly; but hitherto the subject has been neglected. Indeed, it was long before it found a way into the arts of tragic drama and epic recitation: at first poets acted[7] their tragedies themselves. It is plain that delivery has just as much to do with oratory as with poetry. (In connexion with poetry, it has been studied by Glaucon of Teos among others.) It is, essentially, a matter of the right management of the voice to express the various emotions—of speaking loudly, softly, or between the two; of high, low, or intermediate pitch; of the various rhythms that suit various subjects. These are the three things—volume of sound, modulation of pitch, and rhythm—that a speaker bears in mind. It is those who *do* bear them in mind who usually win prizes in the dramatic contests; and just as in drama the actors now count for more than the poets, so it is in the contests of public life, owing to the defects of our political institutions. No systematic treatise upon the rules of delivery has yet been composed; indeed, even the study of language made no progress till late in the day. Besides, delivery is—very properly—not regarded as an elevated subject of inquiry. Still, the whole business of rhetoric being concerned with appearances, we must pay attention to the subject of delivery, unworthy though it is, because we cannot do without it. The right thing in speaking really is that we should be satisfied not to annoy our hearers, without trying to delight them: we ought in fairness to fight our case with no help beyond the bare facts: nothing, therefore, should matter except the proof of those facts. Still, as has been already said, other things affect the result considerably, owing to the defects of our

---

[4] [Roberts] Fragment 183N2.
[5] [Roberts] Not found in the *Poetics* as it exists today. Aristotle probably analyzed the causes and conditions of laughter, when treating of Comedy in his lost Second Book.

---

[6] Aristotle lists them again below.
[7] [Roberts] Or, "delivered."

hearers. The arts of language cannot help having a small but real importance, whatever it is we have to expound to others: the way in which a thing is said does affect its intelligibility. Not, however, so much importance as people think. All such arts are fanciful and meant to charm the hearer. Nobody uses fine language when teaching geometry.

When the principles of delivery have been worked out, they will produce the same effect as on the stage. But only very slight attempts to deal with them have been made and by a few people, as by Thrasymachus in his 'Appeals to Pity'. Dramatic ability is a natural gift, and can hardly be systematically taught. The principles of good diction can be so taught, and therefore we have men of ability in this direction too, who win prizes in their turn, as well as those speakers who excel in delivery—speeches of the written or literary kind owe more of their effect to their diction than to their thought.

It was naturally the poets who first set the movement going; for words represent things, and they had also the human voice at their disposal, which of all our organs can best represent other things. Thus the arts of recitation and acting were formed, and others as well. Now it was because poets seemed to win fame through their fine language when their thoughts were simple enough, that the language of oratorical prose at first took a poetical colour, e. g. that of Gorgias.[8] Even now most uneducated people think that poetical language makes the finest discourses. That is not true: the language of prose is distinct from that of poetry. This is shown by the state of things to-day, when even the language of tragedy has altered its character. Just as iambics were adopted, instead of tetrameters, because they are the most prose-like of all metres, so tragedy has given up all those words, not used in ordinary talk, which decorated the early drama and are still used by the writers of hexameter poems. It is therefore ridiculous to imitate a poetical manner which the poets themselves have dropped; and it is now plain that we have not to treat in detail the whole question of style, but may confine ourselves to that part of it which concerns our present subject, rhetoric. The other—the poetical—part of it has been discussed in the treatise on the *Art of Poetry*.[9]

2 We may, then, start from the observations there made, including the definition of style. Style to be good must be clear, as is proved by the fact that speech which fails to convey a plain meaning will fail to do just what speech has to do. It must also be appropriate, avoiding both meanness and undue elevation; poetical language is certainly free from meanness, but it is not appropriate to prose. Clearness is secured by using the words (nouns and verbs alike) that are current and ordinary. Freedom from meanness, and positive adornment too, are secured by using the other words mentioned in the *Art of Poetry*.[10] Such variation from what is usual makes the language appear more stately. People do not feel towards strangers as they do towards their own countrymen, and the same thing is true of their feeling for language. It is therefore well to give to everyday speech an unfamiliar air: people like what strikes them, and are struck by what is out of the way. In verse such effects are common, and there they are fitting: the persons and things there spoken of are comparatively remote from ordinary life. In prose passages they are far less often fitting because the subject-matter is less exalted. Even in poetry, it is not quite appropriate that fine language should be used by a slave or a very young man, or about very trivial subjects: even in poetry the style, to be appropriate, must sometimes be toned down, though at other times heightened. We can now see that a writer must disguise his art and give the impression of speaking naturally and not artificially. Naturalness is persuasive, artificiality is the contrary; for our hearers are prejudiced and think we have some design against them, as if we were mixing their wines for them. It is like the difference between the quality of Theodorus' voice and the voices of all other actors: his really seems to be that of the character who is speaking, theirs do not. We can hide our purpose successfully by taking the single words of our composition from the speech of ordinary life. This is done in poetry by Euripides, who was the first to show the way to his successors.[11]

Language is composed of nouns and verbs. Nouns are of the various kinds considered in the treatise on Poetry.[12] Strange words, compound words, and invented words must be used sparingly and on few occasions: on *what* occasions we shall state later. The reason for this restriction has been already indicated: they depart from what is suitable, in the direction of excess. In the language of prose, besides the regular and proper terms for things, metaphorical terms only can be used with advantage. This we gather from the fact that these two classes of terms, the proper or regular and the metaphorical—these and no others—are used by everybody in conversation. We can now see that a good writer can produce a style that is distinguished without being obtrusive, and is at the same time clear, thus satisfying our definition of good oratorical prose. Words of ambiguous meaning[13] are

---

[8] A well-known rhetorician (c. 480–376 B.C.) fictionalized in Plato's *Gorgias*.
[9] [Roberts] *Poetics,* above, page 52ff.
[10] [Roberts] *Poetics,* above, page 62ff.
[11] [Roberts] Dionysius of Halicarnassus [d. 8 B.C.], *On Literary Composition,* 78n.
[12] [Roberts] *Poetics,* above, page 63.
[13] [Roberts] Homonyms, in the Greek.

chiefly useful to enable the sophist to mislead his hearers. Synonyms are useful to the poet, by which I mean words whose ordinary meaning is the same, e. g. πορεύεσθαι (*advancing*) and βαδίζειν (*proceeding*); these two are ordinary words and have the same meaning.

In the *Art of Poetry*,[14] as we have already said, will be found definitions of these kinds of words; a classification of Metaphors; and mention of the fact that metaphor is of great value both in poetry and in prose. Prose-writers must, however, pay specially careful attention to metaphor, because their other resources are scantier than those of poets. Metaphor, moreover, gives style clearness, charm, and distinction as nothing else can: and it is not a thing whose use can be taught by one man to another. Metaphors, like epithets, must be fitting, which means that they must fairly correspond to the thing signified: failing this, their inappropriateness will be conspicuous: the want of harmony between two things is emphasized by their being placed side by side. It is like having to ask ourselves what dress will suit an old man; certainly not the crimson cloak that suits a young man. And if you wish to pay a compliment, you must take your metaphor from something better in the same line; if to disparage, from something worse. To illustrate my meaning: since opposites are in the same class, you do what I have suggested if you say that a man who begs 'prays', and a man who prays 'begs'; for praying and begging are both varieties of asking. So Iphicrates called Callias a 'mendicant priest' instead of a 'torch-bearer', and Callias replied that Iphicrates must be uninitiated or he would have called him not a 'mendicant priest' but a 'torch-bearer'. Both are religious titles, but one is honourable and the other is not. Again, somebody calls actors 'hangers-on of Dionysus', but they call themselves 'artists': each of these terms is a metaphor, the one intended to throw dirt at the actor, the other to dignify him. And pirates now call themselves 'purveyors'. We can thus call a crime a mistake, or a mistake a crime. We can say that a thief 'took' a thing, or that he 'plundered' his victim. An expression like that of Euripides' Telephus,

King of the oar, on Mysia's coast he landed,[15]

is inappropriate; the word 'king' goes beyond the dignity of the subject, and so the art is *not* concealed. A metaphor may be amiss because the very syllables of the words conveying it fail to indicate sweetness of vocal utterance. Thus Diony-

sius the Brazen in his elegies calls poetry 'Calliope's screech'.[16] Poetry and screeching are both, to be sure, vocal utterances. But the metaphor is bad, because the sounds of 'screeching', unlike those of poetry, are discordant and unmeaning. Further, in using metaphors to give names to nameless things, we must draw them not from remote but from kindred and similar things, so that the kinship is clearly perceived as soon as the words are said. Thus in the celebrated riddle

I marked how a man glued bronze with fire to another man's body,[17]

the process is nameless; but both it and gluing are a kind of application, and that is why the application of the cuppingglass is here called a 'gluing'. Good riddles do, in general, provide us with satisfactory metaphors: for metaphors imply riddles, and therefore a good riddle can furnish a good metaphor. Further, the materials of metaphors must be beautiful; and the beauty, like the ugliness, of all words may as Licymnius says, lie in their sound or in their meaning. Further, there is a third consideration—one that upsets the fallacious argument of the sophist Bryson, that there is no such thing as foul language, because in whatever words you put a given thing your meaning is the same. This is untrue. One term may describe a thing more truly than another, may be more like it, and set it more intimately before our eyes. Besides, two different words will represent a thing in two different lights; so on this ground also one term must be held fairer or fouler than another. For both of two terms will indicate what *is* fair, *or* what *is* foul, but not simply their fairness or their foulness, or if so, at any rate not in an equal degree. The materials of metaphor must be beautiful to the ear, to the understanding, to the eye or some other physical sense. It is better, for instance, to say 'rosy-fingered morn',[18] than 'crimson-fingered' or, worse still, 'redfingered morn'. The epithets that we apply, too, may have a bad and ugly aspect, as when Orestes is called a 'motherslayer'; or a better one, as when he is called his 'father's avenger'.[19] Simonides, when the victor in the mule-race offered him a small fee, refused to write him an ode, because, he said, it was so unpleasant to write odes to half-asses: but on receiving an adequate fee, he wrote

[14][Roberts], *Poetics*, above, page 65.
[15][Roberts] *Telephus*, N, page 583.

[16][Roberts] Dionysius Chalcus [fifth century B.C.], Fragment 7.
[17][Roberts] *Cleobulina*, Fragment 1.
[18][Roberts] *Iliad* I, 477, etc.
[19][Roberts] Euripides, *Orestes*, 1587, 1588.

Hail to you, daughters of storm-footed steeds,[20]

though of course they were daughters of asses too. The same effect is attained by the use of diminutives, which make a bad thing less bad and a good thing less good. Take, for instance, the banter of Aristophanes in the *Babylonians* where he uses 'goldlet' for 'gold', 'cloaklet' for 'cloak', 'scofflet' for 'scoff', and 'plaguelet'. But alike in using epithets and in using diminutives we must be wary and must observe the mean.

---

[20][Roberts] Simonides [Greek poet (c. 556–468? B.C.], Fragment 7.

Marcus Tullius Cicero

106–43 B.C.

Cicero, sometimes popularly called Tully, was in his own time renowned as a politician and orator and is universally regarded as one of the greatest of Latin prose stylists. He composed many works, among the best known being *Orations Against Catiline, Philippics, Against Verres,* and *On the Manilian Law.* His philosophical writings, tending toward Stoicism, are less impressive. He composed three works on the art of oratory. Important documents in the history of rhetoric, they are *De Oratore* (*On the Orator,* 55 B.C.), *Brutus* (early 46 B.C.), and *Orator* (late 46 B.C.). The first of these describes the orator as appropriately also a philosopher. It has been said that the work was designed to resolve the enmity of philosopher to orator declared by Plato's Socrates. *Brutus,* written to Marcus Junius Brutus, later one of the assassins of Julius Caesar, is mainly devoted to the history of oratory. The selection presented below is a digression from that topic. In it, Cicero argues for the inevitability of the agreement between the public and the expert critic over the quality of an oration. This is put in contrast to the judgment of a musical performance or the poetic art, where critical expertise is necessary. *Orator,* best known of the three works, is in the form of a letter to Brutus and is mainly devoted to elocution with very brief attention to the four other accepted aspects of oratory—invention, arrangement, delivery, and memory. While meant to be a general discussion of oratory, *Orator* was also Cicero's defense of his own ornate oratorical style against the so-called Attic group of younger stylists, who opted for plainness and lucidity in the tradition of the Attic writers, including the historians Xenophon and Thucydides. Brutus, though a young friend of Cicero, was one of this group.

Cicero's works are collected in the Loeb Classics Library edition of twenty-eight volumes (1972–). *Brutus* has been edited by A. E. Douglas (1966). Among the vast literature on Cicero, see Aubrey Gwynn, *Roman Education from Cicero to Quintilian* (1926); D. R. Shackleton Bailey, *Cicero* (1972); G. V. Sumner, *The Orators in Cicero's Brutus* (1973); W. K. Lacey, *Cicero and the End of the Roman Republic* (1978); Thomas N. Mitchell, *Cicero: The Ascending Years* (1979); Neal Wood, *Cicero's Social and Political Thought* (1988); Richard Leo Enos, *The Literate Mode of Cicero's Legal Rhetoric* (1988); Elaine Fantham, *Roman Literary Culture: From Cicero to Apuleius* (1996); Jeffrey Walker, *Rhetoric and Poetics in Antiquity* (2000).

from

Brutus

Here Atticus interposed[1]: "What do you mean by saying 'in your judgement and the judgement of the public'? Is it always true that in the approval or disapproval of an orator the judgement of the crowd coincides with the judgement of experts? Or is it not rather true that some orators win the approbation of the multitude, others of those qualified to judge?"

"Your question is a good one, Atticus," I replied, "but you will get an answer from me which perhaps everyone would not accept."

"Why," said Atticus, "should you be concerned for general approbation if only you can win the assent of Brutus here?"

"You are quite right, Atticus," I replied. "This discussion about the reasons for esteeming an orator good or bad I much prefer should win the approval of you and of Brutus, but as for my oratory I should wish it rather to win the approval of the public. The truth is that the orator who is approved by the multitude must inevitably be approved by the expert. What is right or wrong in a man's speaking I shall be able to judge, provided I have the ability and knowledge to judge; but what sort of an orator a man is can only be recognized from what his oratory effects. Now there are three things in my opinion which the orator should effect: instruct his listener, give him pleasure, stir his emotions. By what virtues in the orator each one of these is effected, or from what faults the orator fails to attain the desired effect, or in trying even slips and falls, a master of the art will be able to judge. But whether or not the orator succeeds in conveying to his listeners the emotions which he wishes to convey, can only be judged by the assent of the multitude and the approbation of the people. For that reason, as to the question whether an orator is good or bad, there has never been disagreement between experts and the common people. Can you suppose that, in the lifetime and activity of those whom I have named above, the ranking of orators in the judgement of the people and of experts was not the same? If you had put to any man of the common people this question: 'Who is the greatest orator in our commonwealth?' he might have hesitated as between Antonius or Crassus, or one might have named Antonius, another Crassus. Would no one have expressed a preference to them for Philippus, with all his charm and dignity and wit, whom I, deliberately weighing

such qualities on the scale of theory, have placed next to them? Certainly not; for this is the very mark of supreme oratory, that the supreme orator is recognized by the people. Thus, while Antigenidas the flutist may very well have said to a pupil, whom the public had listened to coldly, 'play for me and for the Muses';[2] I would say rather to our Brutus here, addressing as he does commonly a great audience, 'play for me and for the people, my dear Brutus.' They will recognize the effect, I shall understand the reason for it. When one hears a real orator he believes what is said, thinks it true, assents and approves; the orator's words win conviction. You, sir, critic and expert, what more do you ask? The listening throng is delighted, is carried along by his words, is in a sense bathed deep in delight. What have you here to cavil with? They feel now joy now sorrow, are moved now to laughter now to tears; they show approbation detestation, scorn aversion; they are drawn to pity to shame to regret; are stirred to anger wonder, hope fear; and all these come to pass just as the hearers' minds are played upon by word and thought and action. Again, what need to wait for the verdict of some critic? It is plain that what the multitude approves must win the approval of experts. Take this finally as an illustration of the correctness of popular judgement (wherein I repeat there never was nor is any disagreement between the people and the critic or expert): There have been orators in great number with many varied styles of speaking, but was there ever among them all one who was adjudged preeminent by the verdict of the masses who did not likewise win the approval of the experts? In our fathers' day, for example, was there ever any doubt that, if a man were free to choose his counsel, his choice would fall upon either Antonius or Crassus? There were many others available, and yet, while as between these two one might hesitate, as to selecting the one or the other no one hesitated. Or again, when in my youth Cotta and Hortensius were at the bar, who, if he had freedom of choice, preferred another to either of them?"

"Why," said Brutus at this point, "do you instance others? In your own case have we not often seen the choice of clients, and the judgement of Hortensius himself? When he was associated in cases with you (I know because I was often present in your conferences) the concluding speech, where there was the greatest opportunity for effect, he always left in you."

Cicero's *Brutus* was written early in 46 B.C. The text is from Cicero, *Brutus*, translated by G. L. Hendrickson in the Loeb Classical Library (London: William Heinemann; Cambridge, Mass.: Harvard University Press, 1939).

[1] Persons of the dialogue are Atticus, friend to Cicero and author of *Liber Annalis*, Brutus, and Cicero himself.

[2] This distinction between judgment of the practical art of oratory, or rhetoric, and the productive or fine arts is grounded in the notion that proper judgment of the practical art is based entirely on the success of the desired effect on the populace, while judgment of fine art requires educated expertise and some standard, represented here by the Muses. The distinction is repeated a little later. Later still, a standard for oratory other than public approbation seems to sneak into the argument after all.

"Yes, it is true," I replied; "his kindliness of feeling toward me, I fancy, made him extravagant in doing me honour. What the popular judgement about me is I do not know; but of others I can affirm confidently, that those who in the opinion of the masses were accounted the best speakers are the very ones who have been most approved by trained critics. Demosthenes could never have said what is reported of the famous poet Antimachus. When reading that long and well-known poem of his before an assembled audience, in the very midst of his reading all his listeners left him but Plato: 'I shall go on reading,' he said, 'just the same; for me Plato alone is as good as a hundred thousand.' And quite right; for a poem full of obscure allusions can from its nature only win the approbation of the few; an oration meant for a general public must aim to win the assent of the throng. If Demosthenes on the other hand had held only Plato as his auditor and was deserted by the rest, he could not have uttered a single word. And you, Brutus? Could you have done a thing if the whole assembly, as it did once with Curio, had deserted you?"

"I confess frankly," he replied, "that even in cases where I am only concerned with a bench of judges and not with the people, even so, if I am abandoned by the circle of listeners, I am quite unable to speak."

"Yes," I said, "that is inevitably the case. Thus, for example, if the wind instrument when blown upon does not respond with sound, the musician knows that the instrument must be discarded, and so in like manner the popular ear is for the orator a kind of instrument; if it refuses to accept the breath blown into it, or if, as a horse to the rein, the listener does not respond, there is no use of urging him. There is however this difference, that the crowd sometimes gives its approval to an orator who does not deserve it, but it approves without comparison. When it is pleased by a mediocre or even bad speaker it is content with him; it does not apprehend that there is something better; it approves what is offered, whatever its quality; for even a mediocre orator will hold its attention, if only he amounts to anything at all, since there is nothing that has so potent an effect upon human emotions as well-ordered and embellished speech.

"Thus, for example, what common man listening to Quintus Scaevola in behalf of Marcus Coponius, the case to which I referred before, would have expected, or indeed would have thought it possible, to hear anything more finished or more nicely expressed or in any respect better? It was Scaevola's object to prove that Manius Curius (who had been named as heir in the event that an expected posthumous son should die before said son had reached his majority) could not become heir, because in fact no posthumous son was born. How full and precise he was on testamentary

law, on ancient formulas, on the manner in which the will should have been drawn if Curius were to be recognized as heir even if no son were born; what a snare was set for plain people if the exact wording of the will were ignored, and if intentions were to be determined by guess-work, and if the written words of simple-minded people were to be perverted by the interpretation of clever lawyers. How much he had to say about the authority of his father, who had always upheld the doctrine of strict interpretation, and in general how much concerning observance of the civil law as handed down! In saying all this with mastery and knowledge, and again with his characteristic brevity and compactness, not without ornament and with perfect finish, what man of the people would have expected or thought that anything better could be said?

"Crassus, however, in rebuttal began with a story of a boy's caprice, who while walking along the shore found a thole-pin, and from that chance became infatuated with the idea of building himself a boat to it. He urged that Scaevola in like manner, seizing upon no more than a thole-pin of fact and captious reason, had upon it made out a case of inheritance imposing enough to come before the centumviral court. From this beginning, and following it up with other suggestions of like character, he captivated the ears of all present and diverted their minds from earnest consideration of the case to a mood of pleasantry—one of the three things which I have said it was the function of the orator to effect. Thereupon he urged that the will, the real intention of the testator, was this: that in the event of no son of his surviving to the age of legal competence—no matter whether such a son was never born, or should die before that time—Curius was to be his heir; that most people wrote their wills in this way and that it was valid procedure and always had been valid. With these and many similar arguments he won credence—which is another of the three functions of the orator. He then passed over to general right and equity; defended observance of the manifest will and intention of the testator; pointed out what snares lay in words, not only in wills but elsewhere, if obvious intentions were ignored; what tyrannical power Scaevola was arrogating to himself if no one hereafter should venture to make a will unless in accordance with his idea. Setting forth all this, at once with earnestness and abundant illustration, and with great variety of clever and amusing allusion, he provoked such admiration and won such assent that no opposition seemed possible. This was an example of that function of the orator which in my division was third, but in significance first and greatest. Now that judge of ours, from the ranks of the plain people, who had admired the one speaker when heard by himself, on hearing the other would abandon his first estimate as absurd.

But the trained critic on the other hand, listening to Scaevola, would have recognized at once that his oratory lacked something of richness and resourcefulness. If however when the case was over you had asked both of our judges which of the two orators was superior, you would find beyond a doubt that the judgement of the expert was never at variance with the judgement of the masses.

"Wherein then is the trained critic superior to the untrained? In respect of something which is difficult to explain, and yet highly important; since it is certainly important to know how that, which ought to be effected by eloquence or ought not to fail of effect, is in fact effected or fails of effect. The trained listener also has this advantage over the untrained: that when two or more orators enjoy the favourable esteem of the people, the former is often in position to recognize which style of oratory is best. As for oratory which does not win the approval of the people, it is quite unable to win the approval of the expert either. For just as from the sound of the strings on the harp the skill with which they are struck is readily recognized, so what skill the orator has in playing on the minds of his audience is recog-nized by the emotion produced. Thus the intelligent critic, not by patient sitting and attentive listening, but by a single glance in passing can often form a correct judgement of an orator. He observes one of the judges yawning, talking to a fellow judge, sometimes even gossiping in a group, sending out to learn the time, asking the presiding judge to adjourn the court: he recognizes that in that case there is present no orator whose words can play on the minds of the court, as the hand of the musician plays upon the strings. Again, if in passing he notices that the judges are alert, attentive, and have the appearance whether of learning eagerly about the case in hand and of showing assent by their faces, or of hanging upon the words of the orator, like a bird lured by the trapper's notes, or (most of all) that they are stirred to pity, hate, or some like emotion—all these if he observe only in passing, without hearing a word, yet he will recognize inevitably that an orator is present in that court, and that the proper work of an orator is in process or is already accomplished."

To this exposition they both agreed. . . .

Quintus Horatius Flaccus

(Horace)

65–8 B.C.

The verse-letter of Quintus Horatius Flaccus, popularly known as Horace, to the Piso family is presented here in a prose translation. Horace's work is hardly profound as theoretical criticism, but its apt statements have been many times repeated as authoritative. Certainly the voice of Aristotle is occasionally heard through Horace's urbane phraseology and versification, though we can see Aristotle's views beginning to be turned into received rules of composition. Horace is more interested in the practical question of how the poet may delight and instruct an intelligent reader than he is in defining what a poem is or what literature is. He comments on a wide range of problems of literary composition and offers advice to the prospective writer. Further, his poem, as a poem, has influenced Neoclassical writers such as Boileau-Despreaux and Pope (below, page 297) to emulate it.

"It is asked," Horace remarks, "whether a praiseworthy poem is the product of Nature or of conscious Art." It is a question that persists. Coleridge, for example, deals with it in one of its versions with respect to Shakespeare (below, page 494). Involved in another version is the question of imitation, and here Horace recognizes the importance of copying nature but emphasizes imitation of the methods of earlier authors. This emphasis is echoed frequently by Neoclassical critics, and it is heard in modern versions in T. S. Eliot (below, page 806) and Northrop Frye (below, page 1136), both of whom are deeply concerned with the continuity of literary tradition.

The idea that the poem is like a picture, attributed to Horace through interpretation of his phrase *ut pictura poesis,* is not original with him but goes back at least to the fifth-century B.C. poet Simonides. It has been yanked from its context in *Art of Poetry* and left devoid of qualifications made there. Horace says that poetry is like painting in that some works are best viewed up close, some farther away, some in the shadow, and some in the light. He uses this analogy to emphasize the variety of poetry and the act of reading rather than to refer to the effects of "painting" in words. At the same time, Horace does generally see similarities and tends to think of the poem in spatial figures. One may compare Gotthold Lessing's discussion of the differences between poetry and the plastic arts (below, page 379) to the tenets of those who, thinking they follow Horace, emphasize the similarities.

Horace emphasizes decorum, by which he means the adherence to good taste and the relation of parts to wholes; but his views are not to be confused with Romantic and postromantic organic theories of unity. Though he thinks that the poet may invent if his invention is harmonious, there are definite limits beyond which an author should not step, risking good taste. Neoclassical critics occasionally turned Horace's suggestions into strictures.

A useful standard edition is the Loeb Classics *Satires. Epistles and Ars Poetica,* edited by H. R. Fairclough (1936). See Grant Showerman, *Horace and His Influence* (1922); A. Y. Campbell, *Horace: A New Intepretation* (1924); J. W. H. Atkins, *Literary Criticism in Antiquity,* Vol. II (1934); P. F. Saintonge and others, *Horace: Three Phases of His Influence* (1936); Edouard Frankel, *Horace* (1957); C. O. Brink, *Horace on Poetry* (1963); G. M. A. Grube, *The Greek and Roman Critics* (1965); G. C. Fiske, *Lucilius and Horace: A Study of the Classical Theory of Imitation* (1966); Kenneth J. Reckford, *Horace* (1969); Niall Rudd, ed., *Horace 2000: Essays for the Bimillenium* (1993).

Art of Poetry

If a painter should decide to join the neck of a horse to a human head, and to lay many-colored feathers upon limbs taken from here or there, so that what is a comely woman above ended as a dark, grotesque fish below, could you, my friends, if you were allowed to see it, keep from laughing? Believe me, dear Pisos,[1] a book may be like just such a picture if it portray idle imaginings shaped like the dreams of a sick man, so that neither head nor foot can be properly ascribed to any one shape. You may say, "Painters and Poets have always had an equal privilege of daring to do anything they wish." This is true; as poets, we claim this licence for ourselves, and grant it to others. But we do not carry it so far as to allow that savage animals should be united with tame, serpents with birds, lambs with tigers.

Works with solemn beginnings, which start with great promises, often have one or two purple patches tacked on, in order to catch the eye. For example, there may be a description of Diana's grove and altar, and of "the moving stream that winds through the fair fields," or the River Rhine, or a description of a rainbow. This is not the place for such things. Perhaps you can sketch a cypress tree. But what has that to do with the matter if you have been commissioned to portray a sailor struggling in despair to escape from a shipwreck? A wine-jar may be intended at the start; why, then, from the potter's wheel, does it end up as a pitcher? In short, whatever your work may be, let it at least have simplicity and unity.

Among us poets, most—O father and sons worthy of you—are deceived by a superficial idea of the correct thing to do. I try to be brief, and only end by being obscure. Attempting to be smooth, one simply ends up lacking vigor and fire. Another, in striving for the sublime, may fall into bombast; while still another, by being too cautious and afraid of the storm, creeps along the ground. If one has a single subject, and then tries too eagerly to vary it by any means possible, one is then like a painter who puts a dolphin into a forest, or a wild boar on top of the ocean-waves. Avoiding a fault [in this case attempting to avoid monotony], one may fall into a worse one unless there be real artistic skill.

The humblest craftsman over near the Aemilian school[2] will model fingernails and imitate waving hair in bronze; but the total work will be unhappy because he does not know how to represent it as a unified whole. I should no more wish to be like him, if I desired to compose something, than to be praised for my dark hair and eyes and yet go through life with my nose turned awry. You who write, take a subject equal to your powers, and consider at length how much your shoulders can bear. Neither proper words nor lucid order will be lacking to the writer who chooses a subject within his powers. The excellence and charm of the arrangement, I believe, consists in the ability to say only what needs to be said at the time, deferring or omitting many points for the moment. The author of the long-promised poem must accept and reject as he proceeds. (Ll. 1–45.)

In addition to using taste and care in arranging words, you will express yourself most effectively if you give novelty to a familiar word by means of a skilful setting. If you have to use new terms for out-of-the-way things, you then have a chance to coin words unheard of by the Cethegi, who wear loincloths [and are thus too old-fashioned to

proper places

proper words

Horace's *Art of Poetry,* also known as *Epistle to the Pisos,* was composed in about 20 B.C. The text is from Walter Jackson Bate, ed., *Criticism: The Major Texts* (New York: Harcourt Brace Jovanovich, 1970), translated by the editor.

[1] [Bate] Horace's *Art of Poetry* is in the form of an epistle addressed to the father and two sons of the Piso family.

[2] [Bate] A school for gladiators; the shops of the bronze-workers were located here.

wear tunics]; and you will be allowed the license of doing this if you do it moderately. New and lately coined words will also be accepted if they are drawn from the Greek fountain; but the spring must be tapped sparingly. Why should a Roman refuse this privilege to Virgil and Varius when it was allowed to Caecilius and Plautus? Why should I be grudged the liberty of adding a few words when Cato and Ennius have enriched our native language and brought forth new terms for things?[3] It has always been and always will be allowed to issue words bearing the stamp of the present day.

As the forest changes its leaves at the decline of the year, so, among words, the oldest die; and like all things young, the new ones grow and flourish. We, and all that belongs to us, are destined for death. And this is so whether we build a harbor, channeling the sea into the shelter of the land in order to protect our fleets from the north winds—a kingly work indeed; or whether a marsh, long a waste and passable only by boats, is drained and tilled in order to feed neighboring cities; or whether a river that formerly destroyed crops has been diverted into a better channel. All mortal things shall perish; still less shall the currency and charm of words always endure. Many words that have lapsed in use will be reborn, and many now in high repute will die, if custom wills it, within whose power lie the judgment, rule, and standard of speech. (Ll. 46–72.)

Homer has shown in what meter [dactylic hexameter] the deeds of kings and captains and the sorrows of war may be written. Verses of unequal lengths, paired in couplets,[4] were used for elegies, and later for the sentiments felt when prayers were granted. But it is unknown and still disputed who the writer was who first used these elegiac verses. Anger armed Archilochus[5] with his own verse form, the *iambic*. Both Comedy and Tragedy have adopted this meter as best fitted for dialogue, able to drown out the noise of the audience, and suitable for action. (Ll. 73–82.)

The Muse has granted to the lyre the task of celebrating gods and the children of gods, the champion in boxing, the victorious horse in a race, the desire of lovers, and the carefree pleasure in wine. If I am unable to understand and retain these clear-cut distinctions and poetic genres, why should I be considered a poet? Why, through false shame, should I prefer to be ignorant rather than to know? A subject for Comedy refuses to be written in verse suitable for Tragedy. In a similar way, the banquet of Thyestes could not be related in lines suitable for ordinary life and hence appropriate for Comedy. Let each style keep the place to which it belongs. Yet these are times when even Comedy elevates its style, and an angry Chremes raves with swelling voice. Also, in Tragedy, Telephus and Peleus[6] often give vent to their sorrow in the language of prose when, in poverty and exile, they discard their bombast and *sesquipedalian* words [words a foot and a half long] in order to touch the heart of the spectator with their grief. (Ll. 83–98.)

It is not enough for poems to be beautiful; they must be affecting, and must lead the heart of the hearer as they will. As people's faces smile on those who smile, in a similar way they sympathize with those who weep. If you wish me to weep, you must first feel grief yourself. Only then, O Telephus or Peleus, will your misfortunes affect me. If your words are not appropriate, I shall laugh or go to sleep. Sad words are appropriate to a sorrowful face, furious words are fitting to the angry, gay jests to the merry, serious words to the solemn. For Nature first forms us within to meet all the changes of fortune. She causes us to rejoice or impels us to anger, or burdens us down to the ground with a heavy grief. Afterwards, with the tongue as her interpreter, she expresses the emotions of the heart. If the words of a speaker seem inappropriate to his situation, the Romans, both the aristocracy and the populace, will simply laugh. It will make a great difference whether it is a god who is speaking or a hero, a ripe old man or a youth still in his flower, a wealthy woman or a bustling nurse, a traveling merchant or the tiller of a fertile farm, a Colchian or an Assyrian, one raised in Thebes or in Argos.

Either follow tradition or else make what you invent be consistent. If, in writing, you wish to bring in the famous Achilles, let him be restless, irascible, unyielding, and fierce. Let him refuse to allow any laws to apply to himself; let him place his trust in his sword. Let your Medea be fierce and firm, your Ino sorrowful, your Ixion faithless, your Io a

---

[3][Bate] Lucius Varius Rufus (c. 74–14 B.C.), friend of Virgil and Horace, was author of the tragedy *Thyestes*. Of the earlier writers mentioned by Horace as coining words, Caecilius Statius (died c. 168 B.C.), was a Roman comic poet; and his friend Ennius was noted as a tragic and narrative poet who tried to adapt the Latin language to the Homeric hexameter, and to refine literature and the language according to Greek example. M. Portius Cato (234–149 B.C.) or "Cato the Elder" was the first important Latin prose writer. The plays of Plautus (c. 250–184 B.C.), the Roman comic dramatist, were closely modeled after Greek originals.

[4][Bate] The "elegaic" couplet consisted of a hexameter followed by a pentameter, the shorter second line giving the couplet a melancholy and falling rhythm.

[5][Bate] A remarkable Greek satirist (seventh century B.C.), famous for his bitter and effective realism.

[6][Bate] Chremes was a comic character in Terence [195–159 B.C.]. Peleus was the father of Achilles, and Telephus, the son-in-law of Priam, was wounded and later cured by Achilles.

wanderer, your Orestes despondent.[7] If you try something not yet attempted in the theater, and boldly create a new character, have him remain to the close the sort of person he was when he first appeared, and keep him consistent. It is hard to treat a commonly known subject in an original way. It is better to dramatize the *Iliad* into acts than to offer a subject unknown and unsung. In publicly known matters, you will be able to achieve originality if you do not translate word for word, nor jump into a narrow imitative groove, from which both fear and the rules followed in the given work prevent your escape. (Ll. 99–135.)

Nor should you begin as the Cyclic writer of old began: "I shall sing the fortune of Priam, and the noble war." What will this boaster produce worthy of this mouthing? Mountains will labor, and bring forth a mere mouse. How much more fitting for a writer not to make such an inept claim: "Muse, tell me of the man who, after Troy fell, saw the cities and manners of many people."[8] He does not intend to give you smoke after the first flash, but rather light after the smoke, so that he will set forth in time some notable and striking tales: Antiphates, Scylla, Charybdis, the Cyclops. Nor does he start the tale of Diomed's return with the story of Meleager's death, nor begin the Trojan war by telling of the twin eggs.[9] Instead, he always hastens to the climax, and plunges the listener into the middle of things as though they were already known. He leaves out what he is afraid he cannot make more illustrious with his touch, and he invents, mixing fiction with truth, in such a way that the beginning, middle, and end are all appropriate with each other. (Ll. 136–252.)

Hear what I, and the people with me, expect. If you want an appreciative listener who waits till the close, staying until the singing attendant cries out, "Applaud!"—you must mark the characteristics of each period of life and present what is fitting to the various natures and ages. The boy who has just learned to speak and walk loves to play with his friends, flies into anger, and forgets it quickly, changing every hour. The beardless stripling, now free from his tutor,

delights in horses, dogs, and in the grassy, sunlit field. He is soft as wax in being influenced by evil; he is rude to advisers, slow to provide sensibly for himself, wasteful with money, high-spirited, passionate, but quick to change in his desires. With different interests, the maturer mind of the man seeks wealth and friendship. He serves ambition, and is afraid of doing whatever he might later wish undone. Many evils plague the old man, whether he seeks wealth and then like a miser abstains from using it, or because he is without spirit or courage in all his affairs, slow, greedy for a longer life, petulant, obstinate, or the sort of person who glorifies his own boyhood days and damns the present youth. Old age brings many blessings; it also takes many away. Lest the role of old age be assigned to a youth, or that of grown manhood to a child, we should always emphasize the characteristics appropriate to each age.

Events are either acted out on the stage or else they are narrated. Now the mind is much less stirred by hearing things described than it is by actually seeing them, with one's own eyes, as a spectator. On the other hand, you must not show on the stage itself the kind of thing that should have taken place behind the scenes. In fact, many things must be kept from sight for an actor to tell about later. For example, Medea should not butcher her children in plain view of the audience, nor the wicked Atreus cook human flesh in public.[10] Nor, of course, should Procne be transformed into a bird, nor Cadmus into a serpent. Whatever you try to show me openly in this way simply leaves me unbelieving and rather disgusted.

Let your play, if it is to continue to have appeal and be produced, have five acts, no more nor less. And do not have a god—a *deus ex machina*—intervene unless there is a knot worthy of having such a deliverer to untie it! Nor should there be a fourth actor trying to speak.[11] (Ll. 153–192.)

The Chorus ought to maintain the part and function of an actor with vigor, and not sing anything between the acts that does not advance the action or fit into the plot. It should take the side of the good, give them friendly advice, control the angry, and show affection to those who are afraid to do evil. It should praise moderation in eating, healthful justice and laws, and peace, with the gates of cities lying open. It should respect secrets, and it should implore the gods to

---

[7] [Bate] Because of her husband's desertion of her, Medea (the subject of the tragedy by Euripides) killed her children in order to make her husband suffer. Ino lost one of her children because she angered the goddess Hera. Ixion, who slew his father-in-law after inviting him to a feast, was shunned by men, was rescued by Zeus, proved faithless to him, was then banished to Hades, and as punishment was tied to a perpetually revolving wheel. Io, the mistress of Zeus, was transformed into a heifer, pursued by jealous Hera, Zeus's wife, and forced to wander. Orestes, son of Agamemnon, avenged his mother's killing of his father by slaying her and her consort.

[8] [Bate] The opening of the *Odyssey*.

[9] [Bate] Meleager, an uncle of Diomed, died before Diomed was born. The twin eggs were the offspring of Leda and Zeus, who assumed the form of a swan when with Leda. From one of the eggs came Helen, thus ultimately the Trojan war.

[10] [Bate] Atreus, king of Mycenae, killed the two sons of his brother Thyestes and placed their flesh before their father at a banquet. Procne, the sister of Philomela, was, according to the Latin version of the legend, changed into a swallow. Another ancient legend tells the story of Cadmus, king of Illyria, and his wife Harmonia, who were changed into serpents and carried to the Elysian fields.

[11] [Bate] Compare Aristotle (*Poetics,* Ch. IV) on the number of actors. [above, page 54]

remove good fortune from the arrogant and bring it back to the miserable. (Ll. 193–200.)

At one time, the flute, not decked out in brass as it is now, rivaling the trumpet, but slight, simple, and with few stops, was used to set the tone and accompany the Chorus. With its sound, it filled the benches, which were not yet too crowded, and where—when people gathered—there were few enough so that they could be easily counted, and those were thrifty, virtuous, and honest. But later on, nations that were victorious in war began to widen their boundaries, and longer walls were built around their cities. On feast-days, people were able to give themselves up freely to drinking in the daytime; and then greater licence was given to music and rhythm. For what taste could one expect to find in an ignorant crowd, free from its daily toil, in the peasant mixed with the city-dweller, the low-born with the nobles? Therefore, the flute-player added movement and decoration to his earlier art. He now began to strut across the stage, trailing a robe. New sounds were added to the restrained music of the lyre. A hurried style brought with it a new sort of language; and wise, prophetic sayings were also brought forth to sound like the oracles of Delphi. (Ll. 201–219.)

The poet who first competed in tragic verse for the prize of a wretched goat soon began to bring on to the stage naked, rustic satyrs.[12] Without losing dignity, he introduced coarse jests; for only by the lure and charm of novelty could he hold the sort of spectator who, after the Bacchic rites, was completely drunk and wild. In amusing the audience with the laughter and jests of your satyrs, however, and in passing from grave to gay, it is more fitting to do it in such a way that no god or hero whom you are bringing on the stage, and whom we have been accustomed to see in royal gold and purple, should be allowed to sink down into the low talk of dingy taverns, or, in trying to raise himself, simply clutch at clouds and emptiness. Tragedy scorns any temptation to babble light verses, as a matron who is asked to dance on festal days takes her place among the impudent satyrs with modest shame. If I were writing Satyric plays, O Pisos, I should not, for my part, wish to use only ordinary, unadorned language, I should not wish to get so far away from the language of Tragedy that no one could tell who is speaking—whether it is Davus, or bold Pythias, who

cheated Simo out of a talent, or whether it is Silenus,[13] who guards and serves his divine charge.

For me, the ideal of poetic style is to mould familiar material with such skill that anyone might hope to achieve the same feat. And yet so firmly would the material be ordered and interconnected (and such is the beauty that one may draw out in that way from the familiar) that he would work and sweat in vain to rival it. Therefore, to my mind, when these rustic fauns are introduced on the stage, they should not act as though they had dwelt in the streets and the forum, languishing with adolescent love-verses, or cracking obscene and embarrassing jokes. The knights, and people of any standing or estate, do not enjoy and wish to offer a crown to everything that pleases the sort of people who buy popcorn and candy.[14] (Ll. 220–250.)

A short syllable followed by a long one is called an "iambus." This is a rapid foot. Hence the term "trimeter" was given to straight iambic lines that had as many as six beats.[15] Not long ago, however, since it is a tolerant and accommodating form of meter, it admitted the weighty spondee [two long stresses], in order to allow the line to move with more stately slowness, but still with the provision that the iambic always retain its place at least in the second and fourth feet of the line. In what some like to call the "noble" trimeters of Accius, the iambic foot rarely appears; and also in the pompous lines with which Ennius blessed the stage one sees either hasty or careless work, or else sheer ignorance of the art of poetry. Not all critics can notice faulty meter. Therefore our Roman poets have been granted an indulgence quite undeserved. Is that any excuse for me to run wild and write without restraint? Or, supposing that my faults will be noticed by everyone, should I consider myself safe just because I keep within the limits of whatever is pardoned? I may perhaps escape blame by doing that, but I shall have deserved no praise. As for yourselves, thumb through and study the Greek masterpieces by day and night. But, you will say, our forefathers admired the wit and meter of Plautus! Yes, they admired both with tolerance, not to say stupidity, if you and I are any judges of the difference between coarse and urbane language, or have any ability to detect true rhythm by the ear and the finger. (Ll. 251–274.)

---

[12] [Bate] Horace supposes that the term "tragedy" (that is, "goat-song") arose because the dramas had once been written for the prize of a goat. Actually, the participants were originally dressed in goat skins; hence the origin of the word. Satyric dramas (not to be confused with *satiric*) mark a survival of this custom. Greek tragedies were performed in trilogies; and at their conclusion, as a fourth drama, was presented a *satyric* play, partly serious and partly jesting, in which the chorus consisted of satyrs clothed in goat skins.

[13] [Bate] Not to be confused with Damon and Pythias. Davus, a male slave, and Pythias, a female, who deceived her master, Simo, are typical comic characters in Terence [Publius Terentius Afer, c. 190–159 B.C.], whereas Silenus, the teacher of Bacchus and the merry and wise father of the satyrs, was a philosopher.

[14] [Bate] That is, the Roman equivalent, roasted peas and chestnuts.

[15] [Bate] Because it was sufficiently rapid for two feet to make one metrical unit, a six-foot iambic line would nevertheless be called a "trimeter."

Thespis[16] is said to have been the man who discovered Tragedy—a type of poetry hitherto unknown—and to have carried his plays around on wagons to be sung and acted by players whose faces had been smeared with wine-lees. Later on, Aeschylus, who invented the use of the mask and the tragic robe, had his players act on a stage built of small planks, and taught them to talk in lofty words and move in a stately manner with buskined feet. Then came the Old Comedy, popular with everyone. But its free manner degenerated into an excess of violence that deserved to be restrained. It yielded to regulation, and the Chorus, with its ability to do harm now removed, simply sank into silence, to its own shame. Our own poets have left no style unattempted. Nor is it least to their credit that they have been courageous enough to leave the footsteps of the Greeks and celebrate the deeds of their own nation, whether in Comedy or Tragedy. Rome would be as eminent in literature as it is in valor and arms if its poets, one and all, did not find a laborious use of the file[17] so exasperating. O descendants of Numa Pompilius, condemn a poem that time and labor have not corrected and refined tenfold, down to the very fingernail. (Ll. 275–294.)

Just because Democritus believes that sheer native genius is better than wretched art, and excludes sane poets from Helicon,[18] a good number do not cut their fingernails and beards. They live in solitude and stay away from the baths, since anyone can acquire the distinction and name of a poet if he never entrusts to Licinus, the barber, a head that three Anticyras[19] could not remedy! I suppose I am quite a fool, then, to go and purge myself of bile when the spring comes. Otherwise no one could write better poems! But then, the game would hardly be worth it. So what I shall try to do, therefore, is to serve as a whetstone which, though it cannot itself do any cutting, is able to sharpen steel. Though I myself write nothing worth while, I shall at least teach the duty and office of the poet, instruct him where to get his materials, show what moulds and develops him, what is fitting to him and what is not, where the good can lead him and where the wrong. (Ll. 295–308.)

In all good writing the source and fountain is wisdom. The Socratic writings can offer you the material; and when the subject is grasped, the words will come easily. He who has learned what he owes his nation and his friends, what love is due to a parent, brother, and guest, what is the duty of a senator or a judge, what the role of a general sent to war, will know how to give the appropriate nature to each character. I should counsel one who has learned the art of imitation to turn to life and real manners as his model, and draw from there a living language. Sometimes a play, interspersed with commonplaces and having an appropriate characterization, even though lacking in beauty, power, and art, still gives delight to the people and entertains them more than do verses without matter or mere trifling songs.

To the Greeks, who desired only glory, the Muse gave genius and greatness of style. Our Roman youth, however, learn how to divide the *as*[20] into a hundred parts. "Let the son of Albinus answer: if you take from five-twelfths an ounce, how much is left? You ought to know by now!" "A third of an *as*." "Splendid! *You'll* be able to look after *yourself!* And if you add an ounce, how much is that?" "One half an *as*." When this interest in commercial gain has stained the soul, how can we expect to have poems worthy of being preserved in cedar oil and kept in cypress cases? (Ll. 309–332.)

The aim of the poet is to inform or delight,[21] or to combine together, in what he says, both pleasure and applicability to life. In instructing, be brief in what you say in order that your readers may grasp it quickly and retain it faithfully. Superfluous words simply spill out when the mind is already full. Fiction invented in order to please should remain close to reality. Your play must not demand that the audience believe anything you take a whim to portray. You cannot have a living child snatched from the belly of Lamia[22] after she has devoured him. The elders of Rome censure poetry that lacks instruction; the young aristocrats, on the other hand, scorn austere poetry. He who combines the useful and the pleasing wins out by both instructing and delighting the reader. That is the sort of book that will make money for the publisher, cross the seas, and extend the fame of the author. (Ll. 333–347.)

There are faults, however, that we can willingly forgive. For the string does not always give out the sound that the mind and hand wished. When you desire a flat, it often gives you a sharp. The arrow, too, does not always hit its mark. When the beauties in a poem predominate, I shall not make an issue of a few blemishes that have resulted from carelessness or human frailty. How shall we sum up the

---

[16][Bate] The Greek poet (sixth century B.C.) who first introduced an actor to reply to the chorus.

[17][Bate] The metaphor is drawn from sculpture, the file being used to give a completely smooth finish.

[18][Bate] A mountain sacred to the Muses, where the fountain Hippocrene flowed.

[19][Bate] Anticyra was a town famous for producing hellebore, a drug useful in killing lice and other insects.

[20][Bate] A Roman unit of money that is divisible into twelve "ounces."

[21]This description of the proper aim of the poet is changed from the challenge issued by Socrates (*Republic,* above, page 36), who required proof of both delight *and* teaching from defenders of poetry.

[22][Bate] A witch, in Greek nursery lore, who ate children.

matter, then? As a copyist deserves to be condemned if, after being constantly warned, he keeps on making the same mistake, and as a musician is laughed at if he always falters on the same note, in a similar way I regard the poet that blunders constantly as being like Choerilus,[23] whose two or three good lines cause surprised laughter. I am also irritated whenever the great Homer nods. But then, when a work is long, sleep inevitably creeps over it. Poetry is like painting. One work will please you more if you stand close to it; the other strikes more if you stand farther away. One shows more to advantage when seen in the shadow; another, unafraid of the sharp view of the critic, ought to be viewed in the light.[24] One will please only once; the other, though looked at ten times, will continue to please. (Ll. 347–365.)

You, elder youth of the Piso family, though your judgment has profited from your father's training and though you are sensible in your own right, take this to heart and remember it: only in certain things can mediocrity be tolerated or forgiven. A lawyer, pleading an ordinary suit, may fall short of the eloquent Messalla, and know less than Aulus Cascellius, but he is still respected. But neither gods, men, nor booksellers, tolerate a mediocre poet. At a pleasant banquet, poor music, cheap perfume, and poppy seeds mixed with Sardinian honey, are offensive; the banquet could have done very well without them. And in a similar way, a poem, born and created in order to give the soul delight, if once it falls short of the highest excellence, sinks to the lowest level. If a person cannot play a game, he refrains from trying to handle the weapons used in the Campus Martius; and if he is unfamiliar with the ball, quoit, or hoop, he remains apart lest, with perfectly good reason, the nearby crowd laugh at him. On the other hand, a person will dare to write poetry without knowing how to do it. "Why not?" he thinks. He is a free man, well born, perhaps with a knight's income, and has a good character. But *you,* I am sure, will do or say nothing stupid; you have enough judgment and good sense not to do so. Still, if you ever do write anything, show it first to Maecius the critic, or to your father, or to me. Then put your manuscript back in the closet, and keep it for nine years. One can always destroy what one has not yet published; but a word that is published can never be canceled. (Ll. 366–389.)

While men still dwelt in the woods, Orpheus, the priest and interpreter of the gods, drew them away from slaughtering each other and from foul living. Hence the legend that he tamed tigers and fierce lions. Hence also the story that Amphion, founder of Thebes, moved stones by the sound of his lyre, and led them to go wherever he wished by his supplicating magic. In olden times, this was regarded as wisdom: to mark a line between the public and private rights, the differences between sacred and secular, to prohibit promiscuous living, assign rights to the married, build towns, and engrave laws on wooden tablets. Thus honor and fame came to poets and their verses, as if they were divine. Afterwards, Homer became renowned; and Tyrtaeus[25] with his songs inspired men's hearts to perform warlike deeds. Oracles were delivered in verse, and the conduct of life was taught in them. The favor of kings was solicited in Pierian[26] strains, and festal dramas celebrated the conclusion of great labors. Therefore you do not need to feel ashamed for the Muse, skilled at the lyre, and for Apollo, the god of poetry. (Ll. 391–407.)

It is asked whether a praiseworthy poem is the product of Nature or of conscious Art. For my own part, I do not see the value of study without native ability, nor of genius without training; so completely does each depend on the other and blend with it. The athlete who wishes to reach the longed-for goal has striven and borne much in boyhood, has endured heat and cold, and kept away from women and wine. The flute-player at the Pythian games has learned his lessons and submitted to a teacher. Today people think it enough to say: "I fashion wonderful poems. The devil take the hindmost [as though poetry were a game]. It's not right for me to be left behind, and admit I do not know what I have never really learned."

Like a crier who collects a crowd to buy his wares, a poet, if rich in land or investments, bids his flatterers come to the call of gain. Though he can serve a costly banquet, go surety for a man who is bankrupt, or rescue someone snared in the grim suit-at-law, I should be surprised if, with all his good fortune, he can distinguish between a false and true friend. When you give someone a present, do not then ask him, when he is filled with joy because of your gift, to listen to your verses. For he will simply exclaim: "Beautiful! good! perfect!" He will change color, drop tears from his

---

[23] [Bate] A minor epic poet (fourth century B.C.) who accompanied Alexander the Great on his campaigns. Alexander, who said he would rather have been the Thersites of Homer than the Achilles of Choerilus, offered him a piece of gold for every good verse he wrote, and apparently did not deplete his treasury in doing so.

[24] This is the famous *ut pictura poesis* passage, much referred to and remarked on for centuries, and often taken more literally (rather than analogically) than the context indicates. The sentence in the original Latin reads: *Ut pictura poesis: erit quae, si propius stes, te capeat magis, et quaedam, si longius abstes.* The notion that a poem is like a picture held until the nineteenth century, when poetry began to be likened more often to music.

[25] [Bate] A Greek schoolmaster who composed war songs that were popular with the Spartans.

[26] [Bate] Pieria was the birthplace of the Muses.

friendly eyes, leap up, and stamp the ground. Just as the hired mourners at a funeral lament and do more than those who really grieve, so the insincere admirer seems to be more moved than a true one. We are told that kings, when they wish to see whether a man is worthy of their friendship, test him by getting him drunk. In a similar way, if you write poems, do not be taken in by the spirit of the fox. If you read anything to Quintilius,[27] however, he would say "Correct this or that, please." If after trying it vainly two or three times, you said you could not do better, he would have you cut out the offending lines and take them back to the anvil. If you chose simply to defend the passage rather than improve it, he would waste no more words or effort. And you might then love yourself and your work all alone, without rivals. A good, sensible critic will censure weak lines and condemn harsh ones. He will draw a line through those that are awkward, and will cut off pretentious decorations. He will force you to clarify obscure passages; he will point out doubtful meanings, and mark what ought to be changed. He will prove to be another Aristarchus.[28] He will not say:

---

[27] [Bate] A famous Homeric scholar of Alexandria (second century B.C.).

[28] [Bate] A Greek critic of Alexandria (c. 220–143 B.C.), supposed author of more than eight hundred commentaries, editor of the major Greek poets and tragedians, particularly Homer, and famous in antiquity as the prototype of the severely alert and demanding critic.

"Why should I disagree with my friend about trifles?" For it is trifles of this sort that get the friend into trouble when he has been laughed at and unfavorably received.

As people avoid someone afflicted with the itch, with jaundice, the fits, or insanity, so sensible men stay clear of a mad poet. Children tease him and rash fools follow him. Spewing out verses, he wanders off, with his head held high, like a fowler with his eyes on the black-birds; and if he falls into a well or ditch, he may call out, "Help, fellow citizens!"—but no one cares to help him. If anyone did wish to aid him by letting down a rope, I should say: "How do you know he didn't throw himself down on purpose, and doesn't want to be saved?" And I should tell him how the Sicilian poet, Empedocles, met his end: wishing to be thought an immortal god, he deliberately leapt into the burning crater of Aetna. You must allow poets to have the right and ability to destroy themselves. Saving a man against his will is as bad as murder. He is not doing this for the first time. And if he is pulled out now, he will not become like other people and get over this desire for a famous death. Nor is it clear why he writes verses. Perhaps he defiled the family grave, or disturbed a consecrated spot. He is mad, at any rate; and like a bear that has been strong enough to break the bars of its cage, he frightens away both the learned and the ignorant by reciting his verses. If he catches a victim, he clings to him and reads him to death, like a leech that will not leave the skin until it is filled with blood. (Ll. 408–476.)

Strabo

64 or 63 B.C.–after 21 A.D.

Strabo's *Geography,* in seventeen books, was an effort to discuss the world as it was then known to him. His work followed by about two centuries the first known (but now lost) geographical writings, those of Eratosthenes, of whom Strabo was critical but upon whose writings he substantially depended. Strabo appears to have traveled frequently, but he did not visit many of the more remote places he discusses. Beyond what he tells us about himself and his family we know almost nothing. His historical writings are lost.

Strabo's view of poets, with Homer the model, is that they are wise teachers. In this he opposes Eratosthenes, who regarded them merely as entertainers. But Strabo acknowledges that part of their value is that they teach in an entertaining way, so he offers, at about the same time as Horace (above, page 78), an early version of what was to become a common Renaissance view, responding to Plato, that poetry delights and teaches (for example, Sidney, below, page 186). Strabo's grounds for his view are the poems of Homer, whom he regards as an authority on and teacher of geography. For this Strabo has been much criticized for a naïve assumption about Homer's accuracy. He held that Homer deliberately mixed fact with myth, the latter providing the poetic delight that made learning pleasant. Thus though teaching and delight both define the poem, teaching is more important. Poets were the first wise men, preceding prose writers, who copied poetry in various respects. In Strabo's view myth was not itself allegorical representation of philosophy or history, as some held, though Homer at times employed allegory. Myths were valuable to poets mainly because people, especially children, love tales of things they do not know about. Myths were sanctioned not only by poets but also by the givers of law because they provide "insight into the emotional nature of the reasoning animal" and can evoke both pleasure and fear through their portentiousness.

The standard work of Strabo is *The Geography of Strabo* in the Loeb Classical Library (1917) in Greek and English translation. See Ronald Sime, *Anatolica: Studies in Strabo* (1994); Daniela Dueck, *Strabo of Anasia: A Greek Man of Letters in Augustan Rome* (2000).

from

Geography

3. As I was saying, Eratosthenes[1] contends that the aim of every poet is to entertain, not to instruct. The ancients assert, on the contrary, that poetry is a kind of elementary philosophy, which, taking us in our very boyhood, introduces us to the art of life and instructs us, with pleasure to ourselves, in character, emotions, and actions. And our School[2] goes still further and contends that the wise man alone is a poet. That is the reason why in Greece the various states educate the young, at the very beginning of their education, by means of poetry; not for the mere sake of entertainment, of course, but for the sake of moral discipline. Why, even the musicians, when they give instruction in singing, in lyre-playing, or in flute-playing, lay claim to this virtue, for they maintain that these studies tend to discipline and correct the character. You may hear this contention made not merely by the Pythagoreans, but Aristoxenus[3] also declares the same thing. And Homer, too, has spoken of the bards as disciplinarians in morality, as when he says of the guardian of Clytaemnestra: "Whom the son of Atreus as he went to Troy strictly charged to keep watch over his wife"; and he adds that Aegisthus was unable to prevail over Clytaemnestra until "he carried the bard to a lonely isle and left him there—while as for her, he led her to his house, a willing lady with a willing lover." But, even apart from this, Eratosthenes contradicts himself; for shortly before the pronouncement above-mentioned, and at the very beginning of his treatise on geography, he says that from the earliest times all the poets have been eager to display their knowledge of geography; that Homer, for instance, made a place in his poems for everything that he had learned about the Ethiopians and the inhabitants of Egypt and Libya, and that he has gone into superfluous detail in regard to Greece and the neighbouring countries, speaking of Thisbe as the "haunt of doves," Haliartus as "grassy," Anthedon as "on the uttermost borders," Lilaea as "by the springs of Cephisus"; and he adds that Homer never lets fall an inappropriate epithet. Well then, I ask, is the poet who makes use of these epithets like a person engaged in entertaining, or in instructing? "The latter, of course," you reply; "but while these epithets have been used by him for purposes of instruction, everything beyond the range of observation has been filled, not only by Homer but by others also, with mythical marvels." Eratosthenes, then, should have said that "every poet writes partly for purposes of mere entertainment and partly for instruction"; but his words were "mere entertainment and not instruction." And Eratosthenes gives himself quite unnecessary pains when he asks how it adds to the excellence of the poet for him to be an expert in geography, or in generalship, or in agriculture, or in rhetoric, or in any kind of special knowledge with which some people have wished to invest him. Now the desire to endow Homer with all knowledge might be regarded as characteristic of a man whose zeal exceeds the proper limit, just as would be the case if a man—to use a comparison of Hipparchus[4]— should hang apples and pears, or anything else that it cannot bear, on an Attic "eiresione"[5]; so absurd would it be to endow Homer with all knowledge and with every art. You may be right, Eratosthenes, on that point, but you are wrong when you deny to Homer the possession of vast learning, and go on to declare that poetry is a fable-prating old wife, who has been permitted to "invent" (as you call it) whatever she deems suitable for purposes of entertainment. What, then? Is no contribution made, either, to the excellence of him who hears the poets recited—I again refer to the poet's being an expert in geography, or generalship, or agriculture, or rhetoric, in which subjects one's hearing of poetry naturally invests the poet with special knowledge?

4. Assuredly Homer has attributed all knowledge of this kind, at least, to Odysseus, whom he adorns beyond his fellows with every kind of excellence; for his Odysseus "of many men the towns did see and minds did learn," and he is the man who "is skilled in all the ways of wile and cunning device." Odysseus is continually spoken of as "the sacker of cities" and as the capturer of Troy "by means of his counsels and his persuasiveness and his deceitful arts"; and Diomedes says of him: "But while he cometh with me, even out of burning fire might we both return." More than that, Odysseus prides himself on being a farmer. For instance, with regard to reaping he says: "In the deep grass might the match be, and might I have a crooked scythe, and thou an-

Geography was written sometime between 7 A.D. and 20 A.D. The text from volume one of *The Geography of Strabo* is from the translation from the Greek in eight volumes by Horace Leonard Jones based in part on the unfinished version by John Robert Sitlington Sterret in the Loeb Classical Library (London: William Heinemann; New York: G. P. Putnam's Sons, 1917).

[1] Eratosthenes (c. 276–194 B.C.), mathematician and first known geographer.
[2] Stoicism.
[3] Aritoxenus, grammarian contemporary of Strabo.

[4] Hipparchus of Nicaea (fl. 100 B.C.), astronomer.
[5] [Jones] The "eiresione" was an olive (or laurel) branch adorned with the first fruits of a given land and carried around to the accompaniment of a song of thanksgiving and prayer.

other like it"; and with regard to ploughing: "Then shouldst thou see me, whether or no I would cut a clean furrow unbroken before me." And not only does Homer thus possess wisdom about these matters, but all enlightened men cite the poet as a witness whose words are true, to prove that practical experience of this kind contributes in the highest degree to wisdom.

5. Rhetoric is, to be sure, wisdom applied to discourse; and Odysseus displays this gift throughout the entire Iliad, in the Trial, in the Prayers, and in the Embassy, where Homer says: "But when he uttered his great voice from his chest, and words like unto the snowflakes of winter, then could no mortal man contend with Odysseus." Who, then, can assume that the poet who is capable of introducing other men in the role of orators, or of generals, or in other roles that exhibit the accomplishments of the art of rhetoric, is himself but one of the buffoons or jugglers, capable only of bewitching and flattering his hearer but not of helping him? Nor can we assume that any excellence of a poet whatever is superior to that which enables him to imitate life through the means of speech. How, then, can a man imitate life if he has no experience of life and is a dolt? Of course we do not speak of the excellence of a poet in the same sense as we speak of that of a carpenter or a blacksmith; for their excellence depends upon no inherent nobility and dignity, whereas the excellence of a poet is inseparably associated with the excellence of the man himself, and it is impossible for one to become a good poet unless he has previously become a good man.

6. So, then, to deny the art of rhetoric to Homer is to disregard my position entirely. For what is so much a part of rhetoric as style? And what is so much a part of poetry? And who has surpassed Homer in style? "Assuredly," you answer, "but the style of poetry is different from that of rhetoric." In species, yes; just as in poetry itself the style of tragedy differs from that of comedy, and in prose the style of history differs from that of forensic speech. Well then, would you assert that discourse is not a generic term,[6] either, whose species are metrical discourse and prose discourse? Or, rather, is discourse, in its broadest sense, generic, while rhetorical discourse is not generic, and style is simply an excellence of discourse?—But prose discourse—I mean artistic prose—is, I may say, an imitation of poetic discourse; for poetry, as an art, first came upon the scene and was first to win approval. Then came Cadmus, Pherecydes, Hecataeus, and their followers, with prose

writings in which they imitated the poetic art, abandoning the use of metre but in other respects preserving the qualities of poetry. Then subsequent writers took away, each in his turn, something of these qualities, and brought prose down to its present form, as from a sublime height. In the same way one might say that comedy took its structure from tragedy, but that it also has been degraded—from the sublime height of tragedy to its present "prose-like" style, as it is called. And further, the fact that the ancients used the verb "sing" instead of the verb "tell" bears witness to this very thing, namely, that poetry was the source and origin of style, I mean ornate, or rhetorical, style. For when poetry was recited, it employed the assistance of song; this combination formed melodic discourse, or "ode"; and from "ode" they began to use the terms rhapsody, tragedy, and comedy. Therefore, since "tell" was first used in reference to poetic "style" and since among the ancients this poetic style was accompanied by song, the term "sing" was to them equivalent to the term "tell"; and then after they had misused the former of these two terms by applying it to prose discourse, the misuse passed over to the latter term also. And, furthermore, the very fact that non-metrical discourse was termed "pedestrian" indicates its descent from a height, or from a chariot, to the ground.

7. Nor, indeed, is the statement of Eratosthenes true that Homer speaks only of places that are near by and in Greece; on the contrary, he speaks also of many places that are distant; and when Homer indulges in myths he is at least more accurate than the later writers, since he does not deal wholly in marvels, but for our instruction he also uses allegory,[7] or revises myths, or curries popular favour, and particularly in his story of the wanderings of Odysseus; and Eratosthenes makes many mistakes when he speaks of these wanderings and declares that not only the commentators on Homer but also Homer himself are dealers in nonsense. But it is worth my while to examine these points more in detail.

8. In the first place, I remark that the poets were not alone in sanctioning myths, for long before the poets the states and the lawgivers had sanctioned them as a useful expedient, since they had an insight into the emotional nature of the reasoning animal; for man is eager to learn, and his fondness for tales is a prelude to this quality. It is fondness for tales, then, that induces children to give their attention to narratives and more and more to take part in them. The reason for this is that myth is a new language in them—a language that tells them, not of things as they are, but of a

---

[6]Thus, for Strabo poetry and rhetoric fall under the same genre and the special difference is meter and prose.

[7]Strabo is friendly here to a tradition, not dead even today, that Homer wrote allegorically. See Bacon (below, page 234), who treats Greek mythology generally as allegorical.

different set of things. And what is new is pleasing, and so is what one did not know before; and it is just this that makes men eager to learn. But if you add thereto the marvellous and the portentous, you thereby increase the pleasure, and pleasure acts as a charm to incite to learning. At the beginning we must needs make use of such bait for children, but as the child advances in years we must guide him to the knowledge of facts, when once his intelligence has become strong and no longer needs to be coaxed. Now every illiterate and uneducated man is, in a sense, a child, and, like a child, he is fond of stories; and for that matter, so is the half-educated man, for his reasoning faculty has not been fully developed, and, besides, the mental habits of his childhood persist in him. Now since the portentous is not only pleasing, but fear-inspiring as well, we can employ both kinds of myth for children, and for grown-up people too. In the case of children we employ the pleasing myths to spur them on, and the fear-inspiring myths to deter them; for instance, Lamia[8] is a myth, and so are the Gorgon,[9] and Ephialtes, and Mormolyce.[10] Most of those who live in the cities are incited to emulation by the myths that are pleasing, when they hear the poets narrate mythical deeds of heroism, such as the Labours of Heracles[11] or of Theseus,[12] or hear of honours bestowed by gods, or, indeed, when they see paintings or primitive images or works of sculpture which suggest any similar happy issue of fortune in mythology; but they are deterred from evil courses when, either through descriptions or through typical representations of objects unseen, they learn of divine punishments, terrors, and threats—or even when they merely believe that men have met with such experiences. For in dealing with a crowd of women, at least, or with any promiscuous mob, a philosopher cannot influence them by reason or exhort them to reverence, piety and faith; nay, there is need of religious fear also, and this cannot be aroused without myths and marvels. For thunderbolt, aegis, trident, torches, snakes, thyrsus-lances,—arms of the gods—are myths, and so is the entire ancient theology. But the founders of states gave their sanction to these things as bugbears wherewith to scare the simple-minded. Now since this is the nature of mythology, and since it has come to have its place in the social and civil scheme of life as well as in the history of actual facts, the ancients clung to their system of education for children and applied it up to the age of maturity; and by means of poetry they believed that they could satisfactorily discipline every period of life. But now, after a long time, the writing of history and the present-day philosophy have come to the front. Philosophy, however, is for the few, whereas poetry is more useful to the people at large and can draw full houses—and this is exceptionally true of the poetry of Homer. And the early historians and physicists were also writers of myths.

9. Now inasmuch as Homer referred his myths to the province of education, he was wont to pay considerable attention to the truth. "And he mingled therein" a false element also, giving his sanction to the truth, but using the false to win the favour of the populace and to out-general the masses. "And as when some skilful man overlays gold upon silver," just so was Homer wont to add a mythical element to actual occurrences, thus giving flavour and adornment to his style; but he has the same end in view as the historian or the person who narrates facts. So, for instance, he took the Trojan war, an historical fact, and decked it out with his myths; and he did the same in the case of the wanderings of Odysseus; but to hang an empty story of marvels on something wholly untrue is not Homer's way of doing things. For it occurs to us at once, doubtless, that a man will lie more plausibly if he will mix in some actual truth, just as Polybius says, when he is discussing the wanderings of Odysseus. This is what Homer himself means when he says of Odysseus: "So he told many lies in the likeness of truth;" for Homer does not say "all" but "many" lies; since otherwise they would not have been "in the likeness of truth." Accordingly, he took the foundations of his stories from history.

---

[8] [Jones] A familiar female goblin, devourer of children, in ancient nursery-legends.
[9] A female monster, for example, the Medusa.
[10] [Jones] The giant whose eyes were put out by Apollo and Heracles.
[11] Hercules, mythological figure of prodigious strength.
[12] Mythological hero who slew the Minotaur.

Publius Cornelius Tacitus

c.55–c.117 A.D.

Tacitus is known principally for his *Annals,* which recount the history of Rome from the death of Augustus (14 A.D.) to the death of Nero (68 A.D.). Parts are lost. His *Histories,* written before the *Annals,* dealt with the period 68 A.D. to the death of the tyrannical Domitian in 96 A.D., but much of this work is also lost. We know little of Tacitus beyond what we are told in his own writings.

The *Dialogue on Oratory (De Oratoribus),* a selection of which follows, was possibly written as early as the eighth decade A.D., but it may date as late as 100 A.D. It is written in the style of Cicero's dialogues. It is set in the home of the poet Curiatus Maternus, who had abandoned rhetoric and the law to write tragedies. This decision led eventually to his execution by order of Domitian, who took offense at one or more of them. There are two other participants in the dialogue. They are Marcus Aper, a prominent Roman magistrate and orator, and Vipstanus Messalla, who had been a tribune in Vespasian's army and was one of the authorities Tacitus used in his *Histories.* Messalla does not speak in the selection included here. All three participants are, of course, fictionalized.

The principal subject of the dialogue is the alleged decline of Roman oratory because of contemporary political conditions and failure to study the old orators. Aper defends contemporary practice and criticizes poets, namely Maternus, for withdrawal from society. Maternus responds in defense of poets. Later, in a section not presented below, Messalla enters the discussion on the side of the "ancient" rhetoricians. As a whole, the dialogue presents Tacitus's defense of poetry and of the older rhetoric, for he clearly sides with Maternus and Messalla.

The best known works of Tacitus are his life of Gaius Julius Argricola, the *Histories,* and the *Annals,* the last two being historical works. They are all best consulted in the Loeb Classical Library editions. See Clarence W. Mendell, *Tacitus: The Man and His Works* (1957); Ronald Martin, *Tacitus* (1981); T. J. Luce and A. J. Woodman, eds., *Tacitus and the Tacitean Tradition*; A. J. Woodman, *Tacitus Reviewed* (1998).

from

Dialogue on Oratory

"As for poetry and verse-making, to which Maternus[1] is eager to devote the whole of his life—for that was the starting-point of this talk—they neither bring their author any higher standing nor do they advance his material interests; and the satisfaction they furnish is as short-lived as their fame is empty and profitless. Very likely you will not relish what I am saying, Maternus, or what I intend to state in the course of my argument; but I ask all the same, When an Agamemnon or a Jason talks well in one of your plays, who profits by that? Does any one gain a verdict by it, and feel beholden to you accordingly, as he goes home? Take our friend Saleius,[2] a first-rate poet, or—if that is a more complimentary designation—a most illustrious bard: does any one escort him to his house, or wait on him to pay his respects, or follow in his train? Why surely, if any of his friends or relatives gets into trouble, or even himself, he will hie him to you, Secundus, or to you, Maternus,—not because you are a poet, or with any idea of getting you to write verses in his defence: Bassus has his own home supply of these, and pretty, charming verses they are, though the upshot of them all is that, when he has concocted after long lucubration a single volume in a whole year, working every day and most nights as well, he finds himself obliged to run round into the bargain and beg people to be kind enough to come and form an audience. That too costs him something, for he has to get the loan of a house, to fit up a recitation-hall, to hire chairs, and to distribute programmes. And even supposing his reading is a superlative success, in a day or two all the glory of it passes away, like a plant culled too soon in the blade or the bud, without reaching any real solid fruitage: what he gets out of it is never a friend, never a client, never any lasting gratitude for a service rendered, but only fitful applause, empty compliments, and a satisfaction that is fleeting. We were full of praise the other day for Vespasian's[3] striking and extraordinary generosity in presenting Bassus with five hundred thousand sesterces. And to win for oneself by one's ability the favour of an Emperor is, no doubt, a fine thing; but how much finer is it, if the low state of one's fortune should make it necessary, to pay court to oneself instead, to be one's own good genius, and to make trial of one's own bounty? And there is more. A poet, when he is minded laboriously to produce some creditable composition, has to turn his back on the society of friends and on all the charms of city-life; abandoning every other function, he must retire into the solitude, as poets themselves say, of the woods and the groves.

"Nor is it even the case that a great name and fame, which is the only object they strive for, protesting that it is the one reward of all their toil, falls to the lot of poets as much as of orators: average poets no one knows, and good poets but few. Why, take your public readings, few and far between as they are: when do they get noised abroad throughout the capital, to say nothing of coming to be known in the various provinces? How very seldom it is that, when a stranger arrives in Rome from Spain or Asia Minor, not to mention my own native land of Gaul, he makes inquiry after Saleius Bassus! And if anyone does happen to ask for him, when once he has clapped eyes on the poet, he passes on his way, quite satisfied,—just as if it had been a picture or a statue that he had seen. Now I do not want you to take what I am saying as though I am trying to frighten away from verse composition those who are constitutionally devoid of oratorical talent, if they really can find agreeable entertainment for their spare time in this branch of literature, and gain for themselves a niche in the temple of fame. My belief is that there is something sacred and august about every form and every department of literary expression: I am of the opinion that it is not only your tragic buskin[4] or the sonorous epic that we ought to exalt above the pursuit of non-literary accomplishments, but the charm of lyric poetry as well, and the wanton elegy, the biting iambic, the playful epigram, and in fact all the other forms in which literature finds utterance. My quarrel is with you, Maternus, and it is this: though your natural gifts point upwards to the true pinnacle of eloquence, you prefer to wander in bypaths, and when you could easily reach the top you loiter over comparatively trivial pursuits. If you had been a Greek, a native of a country where it is quite respectable to practise the arts that serve only for pastime, and if heaven had given you the great bodily strength of a Nicostratus,[5] I should protest against allowing your brawny arms, framed for combats in the arena, to be thrown away on the tame sport of hurling the javelin or the discus; and in the same way now I am trying to get you away from the lecture-hall and the stage to the forum and to the real contests of actions-at-law. And all

---

De Oratoribus was probably written between 77 A.D. and 100 A.D. The translation from the Latin is by Sir William Peterson, *The Dialogues of Publius Cornelius Tacitus* in the Loeb Classical Library (London: William Heinemann; New York: G. P. Putnam's Sons, 1925).

[1] M. Aper has been speaking and continues.
[2] Saleius Bassus, Roman epic poet, contemporary of Tacitus.
[3] Vespasian, Roman emperor from 69 to 79 A.D.

---

[4] Leather boot worn by actors.
[5] Argive general of prodigious strength.

the more since you cannot shelter yourself behind the plea which helps out so many, namely, that people are less likely to take umbrage at the professional activity of the poet than at that of the public speaker. Why, your generous temperament is up in a blaze at once, and it is not in defence of a friend that you make yourself objectionable, but, what is more dangerous, in defence of Cato.[6] And the offence you give cannot be held excused by the obligation to render a friendly service, or by loyalty to a client, or by the excitement of an unpremeditated utterance, made off-hand; no, it looks as if of set purpose you had selected that characteristic personality, whose words would have great weight. I know what can be said on the other side: it is this that excites unbounded applause, it is this that in the recitation-room promptly secures great commendation and afterwards becomes the theme of universal remark. Away then with the plea that what you want is peace and quietness, seeing that you deliberately choose an adversary who is so much above you. For us orators let it suffice to play our parts in private and present-day controversies, and if in these it is at times incumbent, in defence of a friend who is in jeopardy, to say what is displeasing to the powers that be, may we win commendation for our loyalty and indulgence for our outspokenness."

Aper's words were, as usual with him, somewhat vehement in their tone, and his face was hard set. When he had finished, Maternus replied blandly, and with a quiet smile: "I was getting ready to make my impeachment of the orators as thoroughgoing as Aper's eulogy had been; for my expectation was that he would turn from that eulogy to disparage poets and lay the pursuit of poesy in the dust. But he quite cleverly disarmed me by yielding the point that verse composition may be indulged in by anyone who would not make a good lawyer. Now while I might possibly accomplish something, though not without effort, as a barrister, yet on the other hand it was by dramatic readings that I took the first step on the path of fame, when in Nero's[7] reign I broke the power of Vatinius,[8] that unconscionable usurper who was desecrating even the sanctity of letters; and any reputation or renown I may possess to-day is due, I fancy, to the fame of my poetry rather than to my speeches. And now I have determined to throw off the yoke of my practice at the bar. The retinue that attends you when you go out of doors, and the crowd of morning callers have no charms for me, any more than the bronze medallions which even against my will have forced their way into my house. So far as I have gone I find in uprightness a readier protection than in eloquence for my personal standing and my peace of mind; and I am not afraid of ever having to address the senate except in the interests of some one else who is in jeopardy.

"As for the woods and the groves and the idea of a quiet life, which came in for such abuse from Aper, so great is the joy they bring me that I count it among the chief advantages of poetry that it is not written amid the bustle of the city, with clients sitting in wait for you at your own front door, or in association with accused persons, shabbily dressed and with tearful faces: no, the poetic soul withdraws into the habitations of purity and innocence, and in these hallowed dwellings finds its delight. Here is the cradle of eloquence, here its holy of holies; this was the form and fashion in which the faculty of utterance first won its way with mortal men, streaming into hearts that were as yet pure and free from any stain of guilt; poetry was the language of the oracles. The gain-getting rhetoric now in vogue, greedy for human blood, is a modern invention, the product of a depraved condition of society. As you said yourself, Aper, it has been devised for use as a weapon of offence. The age of bliss, on the other hand, the golden age, as we poets call it, knew nothing of either accusers or accusations; but it had a rich crop of poets and bards, who instead of defending the evil-doer chanted the praises of those that did well. And to none was greater fame or more exalted rank accorded than to them, first in high heaven itself; for they were the prophets, it was said, of the oracles of the gods, and were present as guests at their banquets; and thereafter at the courts of god-born holy kings, in whose company we never hear of a pleader, but of an Orpheus,[9] a Linus,[10] and, if you care to go further back, Apollo himself. If you think there is too much legend and fiction about all this, you surely will admit, Aper, that Homer has been revered by after ages just as much as Demosthenes,[11] and that the fame of Euripides or Sophocles is not confined to narrower limits than that of Lysias[12] or Ilyperides. And to-day you will find a larger number of critics ready to disparage Cicero's[13] reputation than Virgil's[14]; while there is no published oration of Asinius[15] or

---

[6]Maternus had written *Cato,* which had offended many for its anti-imperial sentiments. Probably the subject was the republican Cato the Younger (95–46 B.C.).

[7]Roman emperor from 54 to 68 A.D.

[8]Hated courtier under Nero.

[9]Legendary Greek poet.

[10]Mythological figure identified with dirges and songs.

[11]Renowned Greek orator (384–322 B.C.).

[12]Greek orator (458–378 B.C.), fictionalized by Plato in *Phaedrus.*

[13]Cicero is regarded as among the "ancients."

[14]Roman author (70–19 B.C.) of *Aeneid* and other famous works.

[15]C. Asinius Pollio (76 B.C.–4 A.D.), Roman orator, poet, and historian.

Messalla[16] so celebrated as the 'Medea' of Ovid[17] or the 'Thyestes' of Varius.[18]

"Nor should I hesitate to contrast the poet's lot in life and his delightful literary companionships with the unrest and anxiety that mark the orator's career. What though in his case a consulship be the crown of all the contests and law-suits he so dearly loves: for my part I would rather have the seclusion in which Virgil lived, tranquil and serene, without forfeiting either the favour of the sainted Augustus, or popularity with the citizens of Rome. This is vouched for by the letters of Augustus, and by the behaviour of the citizens themselves; for on hearing a quotation from Virgil in the course of a theatrical performance, they rose to their feet as one man, and did homage to the poet, who happened to be present at the play, just as they would have done to the Emperor himself. And in our own day too Pomponius Secundus[19] ranks just as high as Domitius Afer,[20] alike in personal standing and in enduring reputation. As for your Crispus[21] and your Marcellus,[22] whom you hold up to me as patterns for imitation, what is there about their boasted condition that we ought to covet? Is it the fear they feel, or the fear they inspire in others? Is it the fact that, besieged as they are from day to day by all sorts of petitions, they set the backs up of those whom they are unable to oblige? Or that, being constrained to curry favour in every direction, they can never show themselves either sufficiently servile to the powers that be, or sufficiently independent to us? And what does this great power of theirs amount to? Why, the Emperor's freedmen often possess as much. As for myself, may the 'sweet Muses,'[23] as Virgil says, bear me away to their holy places where sacred streams do flow, beyond the reach of anxiety and care, and free from the obligation of performing each day some task that goes against the grain. May I no longer have anything to do with the mad racket and the hazards of the forum, or tremble as I try a fall with white-faced Fame. I do not want to be roused from sleep by the clatter of morning callers or by some breathless messenger from the palace; I do not care, in drawing my will, to give a money-pledge for its safe execution through anxiety as to what is to happen afterwards;[24] I wish for no larger estate than I can leave to the heir of my own free choice. Some day or other the last hour will strike also for me, and my prayer is that my effigy may be set up beside my grave, not grim and scowling, but all smiles and garlands, and that no one shall seek to honour my memory either by a motion in the senate or by a petition to the Emperor."

---

[16] Not the Messalla to appear later in the dialogue, but a literary and political figure (59 or 70 B.C.–c. 3 B.C. to 3 A.D.).
[17] A lost play. Ovid (43 B.C.–18 A.D.).
[18] A lost play. Varius, Augustan poet, dates unknown.
[19] Roman poet and consul (fl. 30–50 A.D.).
[20] Roman orator (fl. 25–29 A.D.).
[21] Vibrus Crispus, Roman orator, contemporary of Tacitus.
[22] Probably Eprius Marcellus, orator and older contemporary of Tacitus.

[23] [Peterson] *Georgics* II, 475.
[24] [Peterson] It was recognized under the Empire that the best security a testator could take for the validity of his will was to include the emperor himself in his dispositions, and put him down for a handsome legacy.

Pseudo-Longinus

First Century A.D.

The author of the work popularly known as *On the Sublime* (Peri hupsos) is unknown. For a long time it was attributed to Dionysius Cassius Longinus, a Greek philosopher of the third century A.D. The author's desire is to inquire into how poetic inspiration is best expressed. In doing this, he writes in the tradition of the classical rhetoricians, devoting much space to a description of various rhetorical devices that he deems useful to sublime expression. But he is not interested in persuasion and does not view tropes as merely support for argument. Further, he emphasizes the imitation and emulation of great writers, for the great writers, he argues, were those with great souls. There is, for him, something more to writing than can be conventionally learned. Skill in invention and ordering of the parts of a whole are important, but sublimity "flashing forth at the right moment scatters everything before it like a thunderbolt." This does not mean, however, that the writer or orator should give way to any stray inspiration, for unordered sublimity is ineffective and opposed to the orderliness of nature. There is always the danger of a pompous, false sublimity: "Evil are the swellings, both in body and in diction."

Although the Pseudo-Longinus identifies the effect of sublimity as "transport" and implies that it is beyond definition, he proceeds to mention five elements that help to create elevated language. The first of these is the power of the author, apparently in part innate, to form "great conceptions." The second element he describes simply as "vehement and inspired passion," also perhaps an innate power. The final three can be considered rhetorical features: the due formation of figures, noble diction, and dignified and elevated composition. He values truth and the real over the fabulous, and he argues that grandeur with some faults is preferable to moderate, correct success, because of the importance of "sheer elevation of spirit."

The extant manuscript breaks off shortly after the author has indicated that the decline of democratic government has probably been a reason for the decline in sublimity among writers and orators.

Partly as a result of this work, the sublime came to be of fashionable interest in the eighteenth century. Interest in it went hand in hand with increased interest in the effect of the external objects of nature and art on the perceiving mind. Addison (below, page 307), Burke (below, page 332), Kant (below, page 416), and Schopenhauer each developed notions of the sublime, particularly with respect to the experience of the audience, viewer, or reader. The Pseudo-Longinus, though interested, of course, in rhetorical effect and the moving of audiences, locates and tends to emphasize sublimity in the author and his expression more than in the effect on the audience.

The translation of W. R. Roberts (1899) may be supplemented by the Loeb Classics translation of W. H. Fyfe (1927). See W. H. Atkins, *Literary Criticism in Antiquity*

(1934); T. R. Henn, *Longinus and English Criticism* (1934); S. H. Monk, *The Sublime: A Study of Critical Theories in Eighteenth-Century England* (1935); Jules Brody, *Boileau and Longinus* (1957); G. M. A Grube, *The Greek and Roman Critics* (1965); Demetro St. Martin, *Bibliography of the Essay on the Sublime* (1965).

On the Sublime

I

You will remember, my dear Postumius Terentianus,[1] that when we examined together the treatise of Caecilius[2] on the sublime, we found that it fell below the dignity of the whole subject, while it failed signally to grasp the essential points, and conveyed to its readers but little of that practical help which it should be a writer's principal aim to give. In every systematic treatise two things are required. The first is a statement of the subject; the other, which although second in order ranks higher in importance, is an indication of the methods by which we may attain our end. Now Caecilius seeks to show the nature of the sublime by countless instances as though our ignorance demanded it, but the consideration of the means whereby we may succeed in raising our own capacities to a certain pitch of elevation he has, strangely enough, omitted as unnecessary. 2. However, it may be that the man ought not so much to be blamed for his shortcomings as praised for his happy thought and his enthusiasm. But since you have urged me, in my turn, to write a brief essay on the sublime for your special gratification, let us consider whether the views I have formed contain anything which will be of use to public men. You will yourself, my friend, in accordance with your nature and with what is fitting, join me in appraising each detail with the utmost regard for truth; for he answered well who, when asked in what qualities we resemble the gods, declared that we do so in benevolence and truth. 3. As I am writing to you, my good friend, who are well versed in lit-

erary studies, I feel almost absolved from the necessity of premising at any length that sublimity is a certain distinction and excellence in expression, and that it is from no other source than this that the greatest poets and writers have derived their eminence and gained an immortality of renown. 4. The effect of elevated language upon an audience is not persuasion but transport. At every time and in every way imposing speech, with the spell it throws over us, prevails over that which aims at persuasion and gratification. Our persuasions we can usually control, but the influences of the sublime bring power and irresistible might to bear, and reign supreme over every hearer. Similarly, we see skill in invention, and due order and arrangement of matter, emerging as the hard-won result not of one thing nor of two, but of the whole texture of the composition, whereas sublimity flashing forth at the right moment scatters everything before it like a thunderbolt, and at once displays the power of the orator in all its plenitude. But enough; for these reflections, and others like them, you can, I know well, my dear Terentianus, yourself suggest from your own experience.

II

First of all, we must raise the question whether there is such a thing as an art of the sublime or lofty. Some hold that those are entirely in error who would bring such matters under the precepts of art. A lofty tone, says one, is innate, and does not come by teaching; nature is the only art that can compass it. Works of nature are, they think, made worse and altogether feebler when wizened by the rules of art. 2. But I maintain that this will be found to be otherwise if it be observed that, while nature as a rule is free and independent in matters of passion and elevation, yet is she wont not to act at random and utterly without system. Further, nature is the original and vital underlying principle in all cases, but system can define limits and fitting seasons, and can also contribute the safest rules for use and practice. Moreover, the expression of the sublime is more exposed to danger when it goes its own way without the guidance of knowledge—when it is suffered to be unstable and unballasted—when it is left at the mercy of

---

The oldest known manuscript of *On the Sublime* is of the tenth century and is incomplete. It was first published in 1554 by the Italian critic Robortelli. The text is from W. R. Roberts, tr., *Longinus on the Sublime* (Cambridge, Eng.: Cambridge University Press, 1899). Ellipses indicate lost passages. The sources of Longinus's quotations from other works are identified as fully as possible in the footnotes. Some quotations cannot be traced to a work or even to an author.

[1] Unknown.
[2] Probably Caecilius Calaetinus, Greek rhetorician at Rome in the reign of Augustus (63 B.C.–14 A.D.).

mere momentum and ignorant audacity. It is true that it often needs the spur, but it is also true that it often needs the curb. 3. Demosthenes[3] expresses the view, with regard to human life in general, that good fortune is the greatest of blessings, while good counsel, which occupies the second place, is hardly inferior in importance, since its absence contributes inevitably to the ruin of the former. This we may apply to diction, nature occupying the position of good fortune, art that of good counsel. Most important of all, we must remember that the very fact that there are some elements of expression which are in the hands of nature alone, can be learnt from no other source than art. If, I say, the critic of those who desire to learn were to turn these matters over in his mind, he would no longer, it seems to me, regard the discussion of the subject as superfluous or useless. . . .

III

Quell they the oven's far-flung splendor glow!
Ha, let me but one hearth-abider mark—
One flame-wreath torrentlike I'll whirl on high:
I'll burn the roof, to cinders shrivel it!—
Nay, now my chant is not of noble strain.[4]

Such things are not tragic but pseudotragic—"flame-wreaths," and "belching to the sky," and Boreas represented as a "flute-player," and all the rest of it. They are turbid in expression and confused in imagery rather than the product of intensity, and each one of them, if examined in the light of day, sinks little by little from the terrible into the contemptible. But since even in tragedy, which is in its very nature stately and prone to bombast, tasteless tumidity is unpardonable, still less, I presume, will it harmonize with the narration of fact. 2. And this is the ground on which the phrases of Gorgias of Leontini are ridiculed when he describes Xerxes as the "Zeus of the Persians" and vultures as "living tombs." So is it with some of the expressions of Callisthenes which are not sublime but high-flown, and still more with those of Cleitarchus, for the man is frivolous and blows, as Sophocles has it, "on pigmy hautboys: mouthpiece have they none." Other examples will be found in Amphicrates and Hegesias and Matris, for often when these writers seem to themselves to be inspired they are in no true frenzy but are simply tri-

fling.[5] 3. Altogether, tumidity seems particularly hard to avoid. The explanation is that all who aim at elevation are so anxious to escape the reproach of being weak and dry that they are carried, as by some strange law of nature, into the opposite extreme. They put their trust in the maxim that "failure in a great attempt is at least a noble error."

4. But evil are the swellings, both in the body and in diction, which are inflated and unreal, and threaten us with the reverse of our aim: for nothing, say they, is drier than a man who has the dropsy. While tumidity desires to transcend the limits of the sublime, the defect which is termed puerility is the direct antithesis of elevation, for it is utterly low and mean and in real truth the most ignoble vice of style. What, then, is this puerility? Clearly, a pedant's thoughts, which begin in learned trifling and end in frigidity. Men slip into this kind of error because, while they aim at the uncommon and elaborate and most of all at the attractive, they drift unawares into the tawdry and affected. 5. A third, and closely allied, kind of defect in matters of passion is that which Theodorus used to call "parenthyrsus." By this is meant unseasonable and empty passion, where no passion is required, or immoderate, where moderation is needed. For men are often carried away, as if by intoxication, into displays of emotion which are not caused by the nature of the subject, but are purely personal and wearisome. In consequence they seem to hearers who are in no wise affected to act in an ungainly way. And no wonder: for they are beside themselves, while their hearers are not. But the question of the passions we reserve for separate treatment.

IV

Of the second fault of which we have spoken—frigidity—Timaeus[6] supplies many examples. Timaeus was a writer of considerable general ability, who occasionally showed that he was not incapable of elevation of style. He was learned and ingenious, but very prone to criticize the faults of others while blind to his own. Through his passion for continually starting novel notions, he often fell into the merest childishness. 2. I will set down one or two examples only of his manner, since the greater number have

---

[3] Athenian Greek orator (384–322 B.C.).
[4] From the lost play *Oreithyia* by Aeschylus.

[5] Gorgias, Sicilian Greek rhetorician (c. 480–376 B.C.); Callisthenes, Athenian orator in the reign of Alexander (356–323 B.C.); Cleitarchus, historian in the reign of Alexander; Amphicrates, probably the Athenian sophist and rhetorician (first century B.C.); Hegesias of Magnesia, rhetorician and historian (early third century B.C.); Matris, Greek rhetorician (dates uncertain).
[6] Timaeus, Sicilian historian (c. 356–c. 260 B.C.).

been already appropriated by Caecilius. In the course of a eulogy on Alexander the Great, he describes him as "the man who gained possession of the whole of Asia in fewer years than it took Isocrates[7] to write his *Panegyric* urging war against the Persians." Strange indeed is the comparison of the man of Macedon with the rhetorician. How plain it is, Timaeus, that the Lacedaemonians, thus judged, were far inferior to Isocrates in prowess, for they spent thirty years in the conquest of Messene, whereas he composed his *Panegyric* in ten. 3. Consider again the way in which he speaks of the Athenians who were captured in Sicily. "They were punished because they had acted impiously towards Hermes and mutilated his images, and the infliction of punishment was chiefly due to Hermocrates the son of Hermon, who was descended, in the paternal line, from the outraged god." I am surprised, beloved Terentianus, that he does not write with regard to the despot Dionysius that "Dion and Heracleides deprived him of his sovereignty because he had acted impiously towards Zeus and Heracles." 4. But why speak of Timaeus when even those heroes of literature, Xenophon[8] and Plato, though trained in the school of Socrates, nevertheless sometimes forget themselves for the sake of such paltry pleasantries? Xenophon writes in the *Polity of the Lacedaemonians:* "You would find it harder to hear their voice than that of busts of marble, harder to deflect their gaze than that of statues of bronze; you would deem them more modest than the very maidens in their eyes."[9]

It was worthy of an Amphicrates and not of a Xenophon to call the pupils of our eyes "modest maidens." Good heavens, how strange it is that the pupils of the whole company should be believed to be modest notwithstanding the common saying that the shamelessness of individuals is indicated by nothing so much as the eyes! "Thou sot, that hast the eyes of a dog," as Homer has it.[10] 5. Timaeus, however, has not left even this piece of frigidity to Xenophon, but clutches it as though it were hid treasure. At all events, after saying of Agathocles[11] that he abducted his cousin, who had been given in marriage to another man, from the midst of the nuptial rites, he asks, "Who could have done this had he not had wantons, in place of maidens, in his eyes?" 6. Yes, and Plato (usually so divine) when he means

simply *tablets* says, "They shall write and preserve *cypress* memorials in the temples."[12]

And again, "As touching walls, Megillus, I should hold with Sparta that they be suffered to lie asleep in the earth and not summoned to arise."[13] 7. The expression of Herodotus to the effect that beautiful women are "eye-smarts" is not much better.[14] This, however, may be condoned in some degree since those who use this particular phrase in his narrative are barbarians and in their cups, but not even in the mouths of such characters is it well that an author should suffer, in the judgment of posterity, from an unseemly exhibition of triviality.

V

All these ugly and parasitical growths arise in literature from a single cause, that pursuit of novelty in the expression of ideas which may be regarded as the fashionable craze of the day. Our defects usually spring, for the most part, from the same sources as our good points. Hence, while beauties of expression and touches of sublimity and charming elegances withal, are favorable to effective composition, yet these very things are the elements and foundation, not only of success, but also of the contrary. Something of the kind is true also of variations and hyperboles and the use of the plural number, and we shall show subsequently the dangers to which these seem severally to be exposed. It is necessary now to seek and to suggest means by which we may avoid the defects which attend the steps of the sublime.

VI

The best means would be, my friend, to gain, first of all, clear knowledge and appreciation of the true sublime. The enterprise is, however, an arduous one. For the judgment of style is the last and crowning fruit of long experience. Nonetheless, if I must speak in the way of precept, it is not impossible perhaps to acquire discrimination in these matters by attention to some such hints as those which follow.

VII

You must know, my dear friend, that it is with the sublime as in the common life of man. In life nothing can be

---

[7] Isocrates, Greek orator (436–338 B.C.).
[8] Xenophon, Greek Athenian historian (c. 430–c. 370 B.C.).
[9] [Roberts] III, 5.
[10] [Roberts] *Iliad* I, 225.
[11] *Agathocles*, tyrant of Sicily (361–289 B.C.).
[12] [Roberts] *Laws* V, 741.
[13] [Roberts] *Laws* VI, 778.
[14] Herodotus (c. 484–425 B.C.), Greek historian, *History* V, 18

considered great which it is held great to despise. For instance, riches, honors, distinctions, sovereignties, and all other things which possess in abundance the external trappings of the stage, will not seem, to a man of sense, to be supreme blessings, since the very contempt of them is reckoned good in no small degree, and in any case those who could have them, but are high-souled enough to disdain them, are more admired than those who have them. So also in the case of sublimity in poems and prose writings, we must consider whether some supposed examples have not simply the appearance of elevation with many idle accretions, so that when analyzed they are found to be mere vanity—objects which a noble nature will rather despise than admire. 2. For, as if instinctively, our soul is uplifted by the true sublime; it takes a proud flight, and is filled with joy and vaunting, as though it had itself produced what it has heard. 3. When, therefore, a thing is heard repeatedly by a man of intelligence, who is well-versed in literature, and its effect is not to dispose the soul to high thoughts, and it does not leave in the mind more food for reflection than the words seem to convey, but falls, if examined carefully through and through into disesteem, it cannot rank as true sublimity because it does not survive a first hearing. For that is really great which bears a repeated examination, and which it is difficult or rather impossible to withstand, and the memory of which is strong and hard to efface. 4. In general, consider those examples of sublimity to be fine and genuine which please all and always. For when men of different pursuits, lives ambitions, ages, languages, hold identical views on one and the same subject, then that verdict which results, so to speak, from a concert of discordant elements makes our faith in the object of admiration strong and unassailable.

VIII

There are, it may be said, five principal sources of elevated language. Beneath these five varieties there lies, as though it were a common foundation, the gift of discourse, which is indispensable. First and most important is the power of forming great conceptions, as we have elsewhere explained in our remarks on Xenophon. Secondly, there is vehement and inspired passion. These two components of the sublime are for the most part innate. Those which remain are partly the product of art. The due formation of figures deals with two sorts of figures, first those of thought and secondly those of expression. Next there is noble diction, which in turn comprises choice of words, and use of metaphors, and elaboration of language. The fifth cause of elevation—one

which is the fitting conclusion of all that have preceded it—is dignified and elevated composition. Come now, let us consider what is involved in each of these varieties, with this one remark by way of preface, that Caecilius has omitted some of the five divisions, for example, that of passion. 2. Surely he is quite mistaken if he does so on the ground that these two, sublimity and passion, are a unity, and if it seems to him that they are by nature one and inseparable. For some passions are found which are far removed from sublimity and are of a low order, such as pity, grief and fear; and on the other hand there are many examples of the sublime which are independent of passion, such as the daring words of Homer with regard to the Aloadac[15] to take one out of numberless instances, "Yea, Ossa in fury they strove to upheave on Olympus on high, / With forest-clad Pelion above that thence they might step to the sky."[16] And so of the words which follow with still greater force: "Ay, and the deed had they done."[17] 3. Among the orators, too, eulogies and ceremonial and occasional addresses contain on every side examples of dignity and elevation, but are for the most part void of passion. This is the reason why passionate speakers are the worst eulogists, and why, on the other hand, those who are apt in encomium are the least passionate. 4. If, on the other hand, Caecilius thought that passion never contributes at all to sublimity, and if it was for this reason that he did not deem it worthy of mention, he is altogether deluded. I would affirm with confidence that there is no tone so lofty as that of genuine passion, in its right place, when it bursts out in a wild gust of mad enthusiasm and as it were fills the speaker's words with frenzy.

IX

Now the first of the conditions mentioned, namely elevation of mind, holds the foremost rank among them all. We must, therefore, in this case also, although we have to do rather with an endowment than with an acquirement, nurture our souls (as far as that is possible) to thoughts sublime, and make them always pregnant, so to say, with noble inspiration. 2. In what way, you may ask, is this to be done? Elsewhere I have written as follows: "Sublimity is the echo of a great soul." Hence also a bare idea, by itself and without a spoken word, sometimes excites admiration just because of the greatness of soul implied. Thus the silence of Ajax in the

---

[15]Two mythical sons of Aloeus, son of Poseidon.
[16][Roberts] *Odyssey* XI, 315–316.
[17][Roberts] *Odyssey* XI, 317.

underworld is great and more sublime than words.[18] 3. First, then, it is absolutely necessary to indicate the source of this elevation, namely, that the truly eloquent must be free from low and ignoble thoughts. For it is not possible that men with mean and servile ideas and aims prevailing throughout their lives should produce anything that is admirable and worthy of immortality. Great accents we expect to fall from the lips of those whose thoughts are deep and grave. 4. Thus it is that stately speech comes naturally to the proudest spirits. You will remember the answer of Alexander to Parmenio when he said "For my part I had been well content." . . .

. . . the distance from earth to heaven; and this might well be considered the measure of Homer no less than of strife. 5. How unlike to this the expression which is used of sorrow by Hesiod, if indeed the *Shield* is to be attributed to Hesiod: "Rheum from her nostrils was trickling."[19] The image he has suggested is not terrible but rather loathsome. Contrast the way in which Homer magnifies the higher powers:

And far as a man with his eyes through the sea line haze
    may discern.
On a cliff as he sitteth and gazeth away o'er the wine-dark
    deep,
So far at a bound do the loud-neighing steeds of the death-
    less leap.[20]

He makes the vastness of the world the measure of their leap. The sublimity is so overpowering as naturally to prompt the exclamation that if the divine steeds were to leap thus twice in succession they would pass beyond the confines of the world. 6. How transcendent also are the images in the Battle of the Gods:

Far round wide heaven and Olympus echoed his clarion of
    thunder;
And Hades, king of the realm of shadows, quaked
    thereunder.
And he sprang from his throne, and he cried aloud in the
    dread of his heart
Lest o'er him earth-shaker Poseidon should cleave the
    ground apart,
And revealed to immortals and mortals should stand those
    awful abodes,
Those mansions ghastly and grim, abhorred of the very
    gods.[21]

You see, my friend, how the earth is torn from its foundations, Tartarus[22] itself is laid bare, the whole world is upturned and parted asunder, and all things together—heaven and hell, things mortal and things immortal—share in the conflict and the perils of that battle! 7. But although these things are awe-inspiring, yet from another point of view, if they be not taken allegorically, they are altogether impious, and violate our sense of what is fitting. Homer seems to me, in his legends of wounds suffered by the gods, and of their feuds, reprisals, tears, bonds, and all their manifold passions, to have made, as far as lay within his power, gods of the men concerned in the Siege of Troy, and men of the gods. But whereas we mortals have death as the destined haven of our ills if our lot is miserable, he portrays the gods as immortal not only in nature but also in misfortune. 8. Much superior to the passages respecting the Battle of the Gods are those which represent the divine nature as it really is—pure and great and undefiled; for example, what is said of Poseidon in a passage fully treated by many before ourselves:

Her far-stretching ridges, her forest-trees, quaked in
    dismay,
And her peaks, and the Trojans' towns, and the ships of
    Achaia's array,
Beneath his immortal feet, as onward Poseidon strode.
Then over the surges he drave: leapt sporting before the god
Sea-beasts that uprose all around from the depths, for their
    king they knew,
And for rapture the sea was disparted, and onward the car-
    steeds flew.[23]

9. Similarly, the legislator of the Jews, no ordinary man, having formed and expressed a worthy conception of the might of the Godhead, writes at the very beginning of his laws, "God said,"—what? "Let there be light, and there was light; let there be land, and there was land."[24] 10. Perhaps I shall not seem tedious, my friend, if I bring forward one passage more from Homer—this time with regard to the concerns of *men*—in order to show that he is wont himself to enter into the sublime actions of his heroes. In his poem the battle of the Greeks is suddenly veiled by mist and baffling night. Then Ajax, at his wits' end, cries:

---

[18] [Roberts] *Odyssey* XI, 543.
[19] *Shield of Heracles,* 217, attributed by some to Hesiod (fl. eighth century B.C.).
[20] [Roberts] *Iliad* V, 770–772.
[21] [Roberts] *Iliad* XX, 61–65; XXI, 388.

[22] In *Iliad* the place beneath the earth to which the Titans were banished.
[23] [Roberts] *Iliad* XIII, 18, 19, 27–29; XX, 60.
[24] *Genesis* I, 3.

Zeus, Father, yet save thou Achaia's sons from beneath the
   gloom
And make clear day, and vouchsafe unto us with our eyes to
   see!
So it be but in light, destroy us!²⁵

That is the true attitude of an Ajax. He does not pray for life,
for such a petition would have ill beseemed a hero. But
since in the hopeless darkness he can turn his valor to no noble end, he chafes at his slackness in the fray and craves the
boon of immediate light, resolved to find a death worthy of
his bravery, even though Zeus should fight in the ranks
against him. 11. In truth, Homer in these cases shares the
full inspiration of the combat, and it is neither more nor less
than true of the poet himself that

Mad rageth he as Ares the shaker of spears, or as mad flames
   leap
Wild-wasting from hill unto hill in the folds of a forest deep,
And the foam-froth fringeth his lips.²⁶

He shows, however, in the *Odyssey* (and this further
observation deserves attention on many grounds) that, when
a great genius is declining, the special token of old age is the
love of marvelous tales. 12. It is clear from many indications that the *Odyssey* was his second subject. A special
proof is the fact that he introduces in that poem remnants of
the adventures before Ilium as episodes, so to say, of the
Trojan War. And indeed, he there renders a tribute of mourning and lamentation to his heroes as though he were carrying out a long-cherished purpose. In fact, the *Odyssey* is
simply an epilogue to the *Iliad:*

There lieth Ajax the warrior wight. Achilles is there.
There is Patroclus, whose words had weight as a god he
   were;
There lieth mine own dear son.²⁷

13. It is for the same reason, I suppose, that he has made
the whole structure of the *Iliad,* which was written at the
height of his inspiration, full of action and conflict, while
the *Odyssey* for the most part consists of narrative, as is
characteristic of old age. Accordingly, in the *Odyssey*
Homer may be likened to a sinking sun, whose grandeur

remains without its intensity. He does not in the *Odyssey*
maintain so high a pitch as in those poems of Ilium. His
sublimities are not evenly sustained and free from the liability to sink: there is not the same profusion of accumulated passions, nor the supple and oratorical style, packed
with images drawn from real life. You seem to see henceforth the ebb and flow of greatness, and a fancy roving in
the fabulous and incredible, as though the ocean were
withdrawing into itself and were being laid bare within its
own confines. 14. In saying this I have not forgotten the
tempests in the *Odyssey* and the story of the Cyclops and
the like. If I speak of old age, it is nevertheless the old age
of Homer. The fabulous element, however, prevails
throughout this poem over the real. The object of this digression has been, as I said, to show how easily great natures in their decline are sometimes diverted into absurdity, as in the incident of the wine-skin and of the men
who were fed like swine by Circe ("whining porkers," as
Zoilus²⁸ called them), and of Zeus like a nestling nurtured
by the doves, and of the hero who was without food for ten
days upon the wreck, and of the incredible tale of the slaying of the suitors. For what else can we term these things
than veritable dreams of Zeus? 15. These observations
with regard to the *Odyssey* should be made for another reason—in order that you may know that the genius of great
poets and prose-writers, as their passion declines, finds its
final expression in the delineation of character. For such
are the details which Homer gives, with an eye to characterization, of life in the home of Odysseus; they form as it
were a comedy of manners.

X

Let us next consider whether we can point to anything further that contributes to sublimity of style. Now, there inhere
in all things by nature certain constituents which are part
and parcel of their substance. It must needs be, therefore,
that we shall find one source of the sublime in the systematic selection of the most important elements, and the power
of forming, by their mutual combination, what may be
called one body. The former process attracts the hearer by
the choice of the ideas, the latter by the aggregation of those
chosen. For instance, Sappho²⁹ everywhere chooses the

---

²⁵[Roberts] *Iliad* XVII, 645–647.
²⁶[Roberts] *Iliad* XV, 605–607.
²⁷[Roberts] *Odyssey* III, 109–111.

²⁸Zoilus, grammarian (fourth century B.C.), noted for his attacks on Homer
   and Plato.
²⁹Sappho of Myteline or Lesbos, lyric poet (seventh to sixth century B.C.).

emotions that attend delirious passion from its accompaniments in actual life. Wherein does she demonstrate her supreme excellence? In the skill with which she selects and binds together the most striking and vehement circumstances of passion:

2. Peer of gods he seemeth to me, the blissful
   Man who sits and gazes at thee before him,
   Close beside thee sits, and in silence hears thee Silverly
     speaking.

Laughing love's low laughter. Oh this, this only
Stirs the troubled heart in my breast to tremble!
For should I but see thee a little moment,
   Straight is my voice hushed;

Yea, my tongue is broken, and through and through me
'Neath the flesh impalpable fire runs tingling;
Nothing see mine eyes, and a noise of roaring Waves in
   my ear sounds;

Sweat runs down in rivers, a tremor seizes
All my limbs, and paler than grass in autumn,
Caught by pains of menacing death, I falter, Lost in the
   love-trance.

3. Are you not amazed how at one instant she summons, as though they were all alien from herself and dispersed, soul, body, ears, tongue, eyes, color? Uniting contradictions, she is, at one and the same time, hot and cold, in her senses and out of her mind, for she is either terrified or at the point of death. The effect desired is that not one passion only should be seen in her, but a concourse of the passions. All such things occur in the case of lovers, but it is, as I said, the selection of the most striking of them and their combination into a single whole that has produced the singular excellence of the passage. In the same way Homer, when describing tempests, picks out the most appalling circumstances. 4. The author of the *Arimaspeia* thinks to inspire awe in the following way:

A marvel exceeding great is this withal to my soul—
Men dwell on the water afar from the land, where deep seas
   roll.
Wretches are they, for they reap but a harvest of travail and
   pain,
Their eyes on the stars ever dwell, while their hearts abide
   in the main.
Often, I ween, to the gods are their hands upraised on high,

And with hearts in misery heavenward-lifted in prayer do
   they cry.[30]

It is clear, I imagine, to everybody that there is more elegance than terror in these words. 5. But what says Homer? Let one instance be quoted from among many:

And he burst on them like as a wave swift-rushing beneath
   black clouds,
Heaved huge by the winds, bursts down on a ship, and the
   wild foam shrouds
From the stem to the stern her hull, and the storm-blast's
   terrible breath
Roars in the sail, and the heart of the shipmen shuddereth
In fear, for that scantly upborne are they now
   from the clutches of death.[31]

6. Aratus[32] has attempted to convert this same expression to his own use: "And a slender plank averteth their death." Only, he has made it trivial and neat instead of terrible. Furthermore, he has put bounds to the danger by saying "A plank keeps off death." After all, it *does* keep it off. Homer, however, does not for one moment set a limit to the terror of the scene, but draws a vivid picture of men continually in peril of their lives, and often within an ace of perishing with each successive wave. Moreover, he has in the words ὑπὲκ θανάτοιο, forced into union, by a kind of unnatural compulsion, prepositions not usually compounded. He has thus tortured his line into the similitude of the impending calamity, and by the constriction of the verse has excellently figured the disaster, and almost stamped upon the expression the very form and pressure of the danger, ὑπὲκ θανάτοιο φέρονται.[33] 7. This is true also of Archilochus[34] in his account of the shipwreck, and of Demosthenes in the passage which begins "It was evening," where he describes the bringing of the news.[35] The salient points they selected, one might say, according to merit and massed them together, inserting in the midst nothing frivolous, mean, or trivial. For these faults mar the

---

[30] [Roberts] Once, but no longer attributed to Aristeas, Greek poet (eighth or ninth century B.C.).
[31] [Roberts] *Iliad* XV, 624–628.
[32] Greek poet, fl. c. 270 B.C.
[33] Upec thanatoi pherontai.
[34] Archilochus of Pharos, early Greek poet (fl. 714–676 B.C.).
[35] Demosthenes, Athenian orator (384–322 B.C.), *On the Crown*, 169.

effect of the whole, just as though they introduced chinks or fissures into stately and co-ordered edifices, whose walls are compacted by their reciprocal adjustment.

XI

An allied excellence to those already set forth is that which is termed *amplification*. This figure is employed when the narrative or the course of a forensic argument admits, from section to section, of many starting points and many pauses, and elevated expressions follow, one after the other, in an unbroken succession and in an ascending order. 2. And this may be effected either by way of the rhetorical treatment of commonplaces, or by way of intensification (whether events or arguments are to be strongly presented), or by the orderly arrangement of facts or of passions; indeed, there are innumerable kinds of amplification. Only, the orator must in every case remember that none of these methods by itself, apart from sublimity, forms a complete whole, unless indeed where pity is to be excited or an opponent to be disparaged. In all other cases of amplification, if you take away the sublime, you will remove as it were the soul from the body. For the vigor of the amplification at once loses its intensity and its substance when not resting on a firm basis of the sublime. 3. Clearness, however, demands that we should define concisely how our present precepts differ from the point under consideration a moment ago, namely the marking-out of the most striking conceptions and the unification of them; and wherein, generally, the sublime differs from amplification.

XII

Now the definition given by the writers on rhetoric does not satisfy me. Amplification is, say they, discourse which invests the subject with grandeur. This definition, however, would surely apply in equal measure to sublimity and passion and figurative language, since they too invest the discourse with a certain degree of grandeur. The point of distinction between them seems to me to be that sublimity consists in elevation, while amplification embraces a multitude of details. Consequently, sublimity is often comprised in a single thought, while amplification is universally associated with a certain magnitude and abundance. 2. Amplification (to sum the matter up in a general way) is an aggregation of all the constituent parts and topics of a subject, lending strength to the argument by dwelling upon it, and differing herein from proof that, while the latter demonstrates the matter under investigation. . . .

With his vast riches Plato swells, like some sea, into a greatness which expands on every side. 3. Wherefore it is, I suppose, that the orator in his utterance shows, as one who appeals more to the passions, all the glow of a fiery spirit. Plato, on the other hand, firm-planted in his pride and magnificent stateliness, cannot indeed be accused of coldness, but he has not the same vehemence. 4. And it is in these same respects, my dear friend Terentianus, that it seems to me (supposing always that we Greeks are allowed to have an opinion upon the point) that Cicero differs from Demosthenes in elevated passages. For the latter is characterized by sublimity which is for the most part rugged, Cicero by profusion. Our orator,[36] owing to the fact that in his vehemence—aye, and in his speed, power and intensity—he can as it were consume by fire and carry away all before him, may be compared to a thunderbolt or flash of lightning. Cicero, on the other hand, it seems to me, after the manner of a widespread conflagration, rolls on with all-devouring flames, having within him an ample and hiding store of fire, distributed now at this point now at that, and fed by an unceasing succession. 5. This, however, you[37] will be better able to decide; but the great opportunity of Demosthenes' highpitched elevation comes where intense utterance and vehement passion are in question, and in passages in which the audience is to be utterly enthralled. The profusion of Cicero is in place where the hearer must be flooded with words, for it is appropriate to the treatment of commonplaces, and to perorations for the most part and digressions, and to all descriptive and declamatory passages, and to writings on history and natural science, and to many other departments of literature.

XIII

To return from my digression. Although Plato thus flows on with noiseless stream, he is none the less elevated. You know this because you have read the *Republic* and are familiar with his manner. "Those," says he,

> who are destitute of wisdom and goodness and are ever present at carousals and the like are carried on the downward path, it seems, and wander thus throughout their life. They never look upwards to the truth, nor do they lift their heads, nor enjoy any pure and lasting pleasure, but like cattle they have their eyes ever cast downwards and bent

---

[36]Demosthenes.
[37]You Romans.

upon the ground and upon their feeding-places, and they graze and grow fat and breed, and through their insatiate desire of these delights they kick and butt with horns and hoofs of iron and kill one another in their greed.[38]

2. This writer shows us, if only we were willing to pay him heed, that another way (beyond anything we have mentioned) leads to the sublime. And what, and what manner of way, may that be? It is the imitation and emulation of previous great poets and writers. And let this, my dear friend, be an aim to which we steadfastly apply ourselves. For many men are carried away by the spirit of others as if inspired, just as it is related of the Pythian priestess[39] when she approaches the tripod, where there is a rift in the ground which (they say) exhales divine vapor. By heavenly power thus communicated she is impregnated and straightway delivers oracles in virtue of the afflatus.[40] Similarly from the great natures of the men of old there are borne in upon the souls of those who emulate them (as from sacred caves) what we may describe as effluences, so that even those who seem little likely to be possessed are thereby inspired and succumb to the spell of the others' greatness. 3. Was Herodotus alone a devoted imitator of Homer? No, Stesichorus[41] even before his time, and Archilochus, and above all Plato, who from the great Homeric source drew to himself innumerable tributary streams. And perhaps we should have found it necessary to prove this, point by point, had not Ammonius[42] and his followers selected and recorded the particulars. 4. This proceeding is not plagiarism; it is like taking an impression from beautiful forms or figures or other works of art. And it seems to me that there would not have been so fine a bloom of perfection on Plato's philosophical doctrines, and that he would not in many cases have found his way to poetical subject matter and modes of expression, unless he had with all his heart and mind struggled with Homer for the primacy, entering the lists like a young champion matched against the man whom all admire, and showing perhaps too much love of contention and breaking a lance with him as it were, but de-

riving some profit from the contest none the less. For, as Hesiod says, "This strife is good for mortals."[43] And in truth that struggle for the crown of glory is noble and best deserves the victory in which even to be worsted by one's predecessors brings no discredit.

XIV

Accordingly it is well that we ourselves also, when elaborating anything which requires lofty expression and elevated conception, should shape some idea in our minds as to how perchance Homer would have said this very thing, or how it would have been raised to the sublime by Plato or Demosthenes or by the historian Thucydides. For those personages, presenting themselves to us and inflaming our ardor and as it were illumining our path, will carry our minds in a mysterious way to the high standards of sublimity which are imaged within us. 2. Still more effectual will it be to suggest this question to our thoughts: What sort of hearing would Homer, had he been present, or Demosthenes have given to this or that when said by me, or how would they have been affected by the other? For the ordeal is indeed a severe one, if we presuppose such a tribunal and theater for our own utterances, and imagine that we are undergoing a scrutiny of our writings before these great heroes, acting as judges and witnesses. 3. A greater incentive still will be supplied if you add the question, in what spirit will each succeeding age listen to me who have written thus? But if one shrinks from the very thought of uttering aught that may transcend the term of his own life and time, the conceptions of his mind must necessarily be incomplete, blind, and as it were untimely born, since they are by no means brought to the perfection needed to ensure a futurity of fame.

XV

Images, moreover, contribute greatly, my young friend, to dignity, elevation, and power as a pleader. In this sense some call them mental representations. In a general way the name of *image* or *imagination* is applied to every idea of the mind, in whatever form it presents itself, which gives birth to speech. But at the present day the word is predominantly used in cases where, carried away by enthusiasm and passion, you think you see what you describe, and you place it before the eyes of your hearers.

[38][Roberts] IX, 586
[39]Priestess at Delphi.
[40]Inspiration. Pseudo-Longinus advises a way of imitating great writers different from the way that Horace (above, p. 78) suggests. One should seek to be possessed of their spirit and genius, not merely to copy their techniques. The author considers valuable the inspired state of which Socrates is sometimes suspicious (above, p. 12).
[41]Stesichorus, Sician poet (632–552 B.C.)
[42]Possibly Ammonius of Alexandria (b. 458 B.C.).

[43][Roberts] *Works and Days,* 24.

2. Further, you will be aware of the fact that an image has one purpose with the orators and another with the poets, and that the design of the poetical image is enthrallment, of the rhetorical—vivid description. Both, however, seek to stir the passions and the emotions.

> Mother!—'beseech thee, hark not thou on me
> Yon maidens gory-eyed and snaky-haired!
> Lo there!—lo there!—they are nigh—they leap
>   on me![44]

And: "Ah! she will slay me! whither can I fly?"[45]

In these scenes the poet himself saw Furies, and the image in his mind he almost compelled his audience also to behold. 3. Now, Euripides is most assiduous in giving the utmost tragic effect to these two emotions—fits of love and madness. Herein he succeeds more, perhaps, than in any other respect, although he is daring enough to invade all the other regions of the imagination. Notwithstanding that he is by nature anything but elevated, he forces his own genius, in many passages, to tragic heights, and everywhere in the matter of sublimity it is true of him (to adopt Homer's words) that "the tail of him scourgeth his ribs and his flanks to left and to right,/And he lasheth himself into frenzy, and spurreth him on to the fight."[46]

4. When the Sun hands the reins to Phaethon, he says

> "Thou, driving, trespass not on Libya's sky,
> Whose heat, by dews untempered, else shall split
> Thy car asunder."

And after that,

> "Speed onward toward the Pleiads seven thy course."
> Thus far the boy heard; then he snatched the reins:
> He lashed the flanks of that wing-wafted team;
> Loosed rein; and they through folds of cloudland soared.
> Hard after on a fiery star his sire
> Rode, counseling his son—"Ho! thither drive!
> Hither thy car turn—hither!"

Would you not say that the soul of the writer enters the chariot at the same moment as Phaethon and shares in his dangers and in the rapid flight of his steeds? For it could never have conceived such a picture had it not been borne in

no less swift career on that journey through the heavens. The same is true of the words which Euripides attributes to his Cassandra: "O chariot-loving Trojans." 5. Aeschylus, too, ventures on images of a most heroic stamp. An example will be found in his *Seven Against Thebes,* where he says

> For seven heroes, squadron-captains fierce,
> Over a black-rimmed shield have slain a bull,
> And, dipping in the bull's blood each his hand,
> By Ares and Enyo, and by Panic
> Lover of blood, have sworn.[47]

In mutual fealty they devoted themselves by that joint oath to a relentless doom. Sometimes, however, he introduces ideas that are rough-hewn and uncouth and harsh; and Euripides, when stirred by the spirit of emulation, comes perilously near the same fault, even in spite of his own natural bent. 6. Thus in Aeschylus the palace of Lycurgus at the coming of Dionysus is strangely represented as possessed: "A frenzy thrills the hall; the roofs are bacchant/With ecstasy:" an idea which Euripides has echoed, in other words, it is true, and with some abatement of its crudity, where he says: "The whole mount shared their bacchic ecstasy."[48] 7. Magnificent are the images which Sophocles has conceived of the death of Oedipus, who makes ready his burial amid the portents of the sky.[49] Magnificent, too, is the passage where the Greeks are on the point of sailing away and Achilles appears above his tomb to those who are putting out to sea—a scene which I doubt whether anyone has depicted more vividly than Simonides.[50] But it is impossible to cite all the examples that present themselves. 8. It is no doubt true that those which are found in the poets contain, as I said, a tendency to exaggeration in the way of the fabulous and that they transcend in every way the credible, but in oratorical imagery the best feature is always its reality and truth. Whenever the form of a speech is poetical and fabulous and breaks into every kind of impossibility, such digressions have a strange and alien air. For example, the clever orators forsooth of our day, like the tragedians, see Furies, and—fine fellows that they are—cannot even understand that Orestes when he cries "Unhand me!—of mine Haunting Fiends thou art—/ Dost grip my waist to hurl me into hell!"[51] has these fancies because he is mad. 9. What,

[44][Roberts] Euripides, *Orestes,* 255–257.
[45][Roberts] Euripides, *Iphiginia in Tauris,* 291.
[46][Roberts] *Iliad* XX, 170–171.
[47][Roberts] *Iliad* XX, 42–46.
[48][Roberts] *Bacchae,* 726.
[49][Roberts] *Oedipus at Colonus,* 1586.
[50]Simonides of Ceos, Greek lyric poet (c. 556–468? B.C.).
[51][Roberts] Euripides, *Orestes,* 264.

then, can oratorical imagery effect? Well, it is able in many ways to infuse vehemence and passion into spoken words, while more particularly when it is combined with the argumentative passages it not only persuades the hearer but actually makes him its slave. Here is an example. "Why, if at this very moment," says Demosthenes,

> a loud cry were to be heard in front of the courts, and we were told that the prison-house lies open and the prisoners are in full flight, no one, whether he be old or young, is so heedless as not to lend aid to the utmost of his power; aye, and if anyone came forward and said that yonder stands the man who let them go, the offender would be promptly put to death without a hearing.[52]

10. In the same way, too, Hyperides[53] on being accused, after he had proposed the liberation of the slaves subsequently to the great defeat, said "This proposal was framed, not by the orator, but by the battle of Chaeroneia." The speaker has here at one and the same time followed a train of reasoning and indulged a flight of imagination. He has, therefore, passed the bounds of mere persuasion by the boldness of his conception. 11. By a sort of natural law in all such matters we always attend to whatever possesses superior force; whence it is that we are drawn away from demonstration pure and simple to any startling image within whose dazzling brilliancy the argument lies concealed. And it is not unreasonable that we should be affected in this way, for when two things are brought together, the more powerful always attracts to itself the virtue of the weaker. 12. It will be enough to have said thus much with regard to examples of the sublime in thought, when produced by greatness of soul, imitation, or imagery.

XVI

Here, however, in due order comes the place assigned to figures; for they, if handled in the proper manner, will contribute, as I have said, in no mean degree to sublimity. But since to treat thoroughly of them all at the present moment would be a great, or rather an endless task, we will now, with the object of proving our proposition, run over a few only of those which produce elevation of diction. 2. Demosthenes is bringing forward a reasoned vindication of

his public policy. What was the natural way of treating the subject? It was this. "You were not wrong, you who engaged in the struggle for the freedom of Greece. You have domestic warrant for it. For the warriors of Marathon did no wrong, nor they of Salamis, nor they of Plataea."[54] When, however, as though suddenly inspired by heaven and as it were frenzied by the god of prophecy, he utters his famous oath by the champions of Greece ("assuredly ye did no wrong; I swear it by those who at Marathon stood in the forefront of the danger"), in the public view by this one figure of adjuration, which I here term apostrophe, he deifies his ancestors. He brings home the thought that we ought to swear by those who have thus nobly died as we swear by gods, and he fills the mind of the judges with the high spirit of those who there bore the brunt of the danger, and he has transformed the natural course of the argument into transcendent sublimity and passion and that secure belief which rests upon strange and prodigious oaths. He instills into the minds of his hearers the conviction—which acts as a medicine and an antidote—that they should, uplifted by these eulogies, feel no less proud of the fight against Philip than of the triumph at Marathon and Salamis. By all these means he carries his hearers clean away with him through the employment of a single figure. 3. It is said, indeed, that the germ of the oath is found in Eupolis: "For, by the fight I won at Marathon, / No one shall vex my soul and rue it not." But it is not sublime to swear by a person in any chance way; the sublimity depends upon the place and the manner and the circumstances and the motive. Now in the passage of Eupolis there is nothing but the mere oath, addressed to the Athenians when still prosperous and in no need of comfort. Furthermore, the poet in his oath has not made divinities of the men in order so to create in his hearers a worthy conception of their valor, but he has wandered away from those who stood in the forefront of the danger to an inanimate thing—the fight. In Demosthenes the oath is framed for vanquished men, with the intention that Chaeroneia should no longer appear a failure to the Athenians. He gives them at one and the same time, as I remarked, a demonstration that they have done no wrong, an example, the sure evidence of oaths, a eulogy, an exhortation. 4. And since the orator was likely to be confronted with the objection, "You are speaking of the *defeat* which has attended your administration, and yet you swear by *victories,*" in what follows he consequently measures even individual words, and

---

[52][Roberts] *Against Timocrates*, 208.
[53]Hyperides, Greek orator (?–322 B.C.).

[54][Roberts] *On the Crown*, 208.

chooses them unerringly, showing that even in the revels of the imagination sobriety is required. "Those," he says, "who stood in the forefront of the danger at Marathon, and those who fought by sea at Salamis and Artemisium, and those who stood in the ranks at Plataea." Nowhere does he use the word *conquered,* but at every turn he has evaded any indication of the result, since it was fortunate and the opposite of what happened at Chaeroneia. So he at once rushes forward and carries his hearer off his feet. "All of whom," says he, "were accorded a public burial by the state, Aeschines, and not *the successful only.*"

XVII

I ought not, my dear friend, to omit at this point an observation of my own, which shall be most concisely stated. It is that, by a sort of natural law, figures bring support to the sublime, and on their part derive support in turn from it in a wonderful degree. Where and how, I will explain. The cunning use of figures is peculiarly subject to suspicion, and produces an impression of ambush, plot, fallacy. This is so when the plea is addressed to a judge with absolute powers, and particularly to despots, kings, and leaders in positions of superiority. Such a one at once feels resentment if, like a foolish boy, he is tricked by the paltry figures of the oratorical craftsman. Construing the fallacy into a personal affront, sometimes he becomes quite wild with rage, or if he controls his anger, steels himself utterly against persuasive words. Wherefore a figure is at its best when the very fact that it is a figure escapes attention. 2. Accordingly, sublimity and passion form an antidote and a wonderful help against the mistrust which attends upon the use of figures. The art which craftily employs them lies hid and escapes all future suspicion, when once it has been associated with beauty and sublimity. A sufficient proof is the passage already adduced, "By the men of Marathon I swear." By what means has the orator here concealed the figure? Clearly, by the very excess of light. For just as all dim lights are extinguished in the blaze of the sun, so do the artifices of rhetoric fade from view when bathed in the pervading splendor of sublimity. 3. Something like this happens also in the art of painting. For although light and shade, as depicted in colors, lie side by side upon the same surface, light nevertheless meets the vision first, and not only stands out, but also seems far nearer. So also with the manifestations of passion and the sublime in literature. They lie nearer to our minds through a sort of natural kinship and through their own radiance, and always strike our attention before the figures, whose art they throw into the shade and as it were keep in concealment.

XVIII

But what are we next to say of questions and interrogations? Is it not precisely by the visualizing qualities of these figures that Demosthenes strives to make his speeches far more effective and impressive? "Pray tell me—tell me, you sir— do you wish to go about and inquire of one another, is there any news? Why, what greater news could there be than this, that a Macedonian is subduing Greece? Is Philip dead? No; but he is ill. Dead or ill, what difference to you? Should anything happen to him, you will speedily create another Philip."[55] Again he says, "Let us sail against Macedonia. Where shall we find a landing-place? someone asks. The war itself will discover the weak places in Philip's position."[56] All this, if stated plainly and directly, would have been altogether weaker. As it is, the excitement, and the rapid play of question and answer, and the plan of meeting his own objections as though they were urged by another, have by the help of the figure made the language used not only more elevated but also more convincing. 2. For an exhibition of passion has a greater effect when it seems not to be studied by the speaker himself but to be inspired by the occasion: and questions asked and answered by oneself simulate a natural outburst of passion. For just as those who are interrogated by others experience a sudden excitement and answer the inquiry incisively and with the utmost candor, so the figure of question and answer leads the hearer to suppose that each deliberate thought is struck out and uttered on the spur of the moment, and thus beguiles his reason. We may further quote that passage of Herodotus which is regarded as one of the most elevated: "if thus. . ."

XIX

The words issue forth without connecting links and are poured out as it were, almost outstripping the speaker himself, "Locking their shields," says Xenophon, "they thrust fought slew fell."[57] 2. And so with the words of Eurylochus: "We passed, as thou badst, Odysseus, midst twilight of oaktrees round./ There amidst of the forest-glens a beautiful palace we found."[58] For the lines detached from one another, but nonetheless hurried along, produce the impression of an agitation which interposes obstacles and at the same

---

[55][Roberts] *Philippics* I, 10.
[56][Roberts] *Philippics* I, 44.
[57][Roberts] *Hellenica* IV, 3, 19.
[58][Roberts] *Odyssey* X, 251–252.

time adds impetuosity. This result Homer has produced by the omission of conjunctions.

XX

A powerful effect usually attends the union of figures for a common object, when two or three mingle together as it were in partnership, and contribute a fund of strength, persuasiveness, beauty. Thus, in the speech against Meidias, examples will be found of asyndeton, interwoven with instances of anaphora and diatyposis.[59] "For the smiter can do many things (some of which the sufferer cannot even describe to another) by attitude, by look, by voice."[60] 2. Then, in order that the narrative may not, as it advances, continue in the same groove (for continuance betokens tranquility, while passion—the transport and commotion of the soul—sets order at defiance), straightway he hurries off to other asyndeta and repetitions. "By attitude, by look, by voice, when he acts with insolence, when he acts like an enemy, when he smites with his fists, when he smites you like a slave." By these words the orator produces the same effect as the assailant—he strikes the mind of the judges by the swift succession of blow on blow. 3. Starting from this point again, as suddenly as a gust of wind, he makes another attack. "When smitten with blows of fists," he says, "when smitten upon the cheek. These things stir the blood, these drive men beyond themselves, when unused to insult. No one can, in describing them, convey a notion of the indignity they imply." So he maintains throughout, though with continual variation, the essential character of the repetitions and asyndeta. In this way, with him, order is disorderly, and on the other hand disorder contains a certain element of order.

XXI

Come now, add, if you please, in these cases connecting particles after the fashion of the followers of Isocrates. Furthermore, this fact too must not be overlooked that the smiter may do many things, first by attitude, then by look, then again by the mere voice. You will feel, if you transcribe the passage in this orderly fashion, that the rugged impetuosity of passion, once you make it smooth and equable by adding the copulatives, falls pointless and immediately loses

all its fire. 2. Just as the binding of the limbs of runners deprives them of their power of rapid motion, so also passion, when shackled by connecting links and other appendages, chafes at the restriction, for it loses the freedom of its advance and its rapid emission as though from an engine of war.

XXII

Hyperbata, or inversions, must be placed under the same category. They are departures in the order of expressions or ideas from the natural sequence; and they bear, it may be said, the very stamp and impress of vehement emotion. Just as those who are really moved by anger, or fear, or indignation, or jealousy, or any other emotion (for the passions are many and countless, and none can give their number), at times turn aside, and when they have taken one thing as their subject often leap to another, foisting in the midst some irrelevant matter, and then again wheel round to their original theme, and driven by their vehemence, as by a veering wind, now this way now that with rapid changes, transform their expressions, their thoughts, the order suggested by a natural sequence, into numberless variations of every kind; so also among the best writers it is by means of hyperbaton that imitation approaches the effects of nature. For art is perfect when it seems to be nature, and nature hits the mark when she contains art hidden within her. We may illustrate by the words of Dionysius of Phocaea in Herodotus. "Our fortunes lie on a razor's edge, men of Ionia; for freedom or for bondage, and that the bondage of runaway slaves. Now, therefore, if you choose to submit to hardships, you will have toil for the moment, but you will be able to overcome your foes."[61]

2. Here the natural order would have been: "Men of Ionia, now is the time for you to meet hardships; for our fortunes lie on a razor's edge." But the speaker postpones the words "men of Ionia." He starts at once with the danger of the situation, as though in such imminent peril he had no time at all to address his hearers. Moreover, he inverts the order of ideas. For instead of saying that they ought to endure hardships, which is the real object of his exhortation, he first assigns the reason because of which they ought to endure hardships, in the words "our fortunes lie on a razor's edge." The result is that what he says seems not to be premeditated but to be prompted by the necessities of the moment. 3. In a still higher degree Thucydides is most bold and

---

[59]Asyndeton: the omission of the conjunction connecting clauses in a sentence; anaphora: the repetition of a word or phrase at the beginning of successive clauses; diatyposis: vivid descritpion.
[60][Roberts] Demosthenes, *Against Meidias*, 72.

[61][Roberts] *History* VI, 11.

skillful in disjoining from one another by means of transpositions things that are by nature intimately united and indivisible. Demosthenes is not so masterful as Thucydides, but of all writers he most abounds in this kind of figure, and through his use of hyperbata makes a great impression of vehemence, yes, and of unpremeditated speech, and moreover draws his hearers with him into all the perils of his long inversions. 4. For he will often leave in suspense the thought which he has begun to express, and meanwhile he will heap, into a position seemingly alien and unnatural, one thing upon another parenthetically and from any external source whatsoever, throwing his hearer into alarm lest the whole structure of his words should fall to pieces, and compelling him in anxious sympathy to share the peril of the speaker; and then unexpectedly, after a long interval, he adds the long-awaited conclusion at the right place, namely the end, and produces a far greater effect by this very use, so bold and hazardous, of hyperbaton. Examples may be spared because of their abundance.

XXIII

The figures which are termed polyptota—accumulations, and variations, and climaxes—are excellent weapons of public oratory, as you are aware, and contribute to elegance and to every form of sublimity and passion. Again, how greatly do changes of cases, tenses, persons, numbers, genders, diversify and enliven exposition. 2. Where the use of numbers is concerned, I would point out that style is not adorned only or chiefly by those words which are, as far as their forms go, in the singular but in meaning are, when examined, found to be plural: as in the lines "A countless crowd forthright/Far-ranged along the beaches were clamoring 'Thunny in sight!'" The fact is more worthy of observation that in certain cases the use of the plural (for the singular) falls on the ear with still more imposing effect and impresses us by the very sense of multitude which the number conveys.

3. Such are the words of Oedipus in Sophocles:

> O   nuptials,   nuptials,
> Ye gendered me, and, having gendered, brought
> To light the selfsame seed, and so revealed
> Sires, brothers, sons, in one—all kindred blood!—
> Brides, mothers, wives, in one!—yea, whatso deeds
> Most shameful among humankind are done.[62]

The whole enumeration can be summed up in a single proper name—on the one side Oedipus, on the other Jocasta. Nonetheless, the expansion of the number into the plural helps to pluralize the misfortunes as well. There is a similar instance of multiplication in the line: "Forth Hectors and Sarpedons marching came," and in that passage of Plato concerning the Athenians which we have quoted elsewhere. 4. "For no Pelopes, nor Cadmi, nor Aegypti and Danai, nor the rest of the crowd of born foreigners dwell with us, but ours is the land of pure Greeks, free from foreign admixture," etc.[63] For naturally a theme seems more imposing to the ear when proper names are thus added, one upon the other, in troops. But this must only be done in cases in which the subject admits of amplification or redundancy or exaggeration or passion—one or more of these—since we all know that a richly caparisoned style is extremely pretentious.

XXIV

Further (to take the converse case) particulars which are combined from the plural into the singular are sometimes most elevated in appearance. "Thereafter," says Demosthenes, "all Peloponnesus was at variance."[64] "And when Phrynichus had brought out a play entitled *The Capture of Miletus,* the whole theater burst into tears."[65] For the compression of the number from multiplicity into unity gives more fully the feeling of a single body. 2. In both cases the explanation of the elegance of expression is, I think, the same. Where the words are singular, to make them plural is the mark of unlooked-for passion; and where they are plural, the rounding of a number of things into a fine-sounding singular is surprising owing to the converse change.

XXV

If you introduce things which are past as present and now taking place, you will make your story no longer a narration but an actuality. Xenophon furnishes an illustration. "A man," says he, "has fallen under Cyrus' horse, and being trampled strikes the horse with his sword in the belly. He rears and unseats Cyrus, who falls."[66] This construction is specially characteristic of Thucydides.

---

[62][Roberts] *Oedipus the King,* 1403–1408.

[63][Roberts] *Menexinus,* 245.
[64][Roberts] *On the Crown,* 18.
[65][Roberts] Herodotus, *History* VI, 21.
[66][Roberts] *Cyropaedia* VII, i, 37.

XXVI

In like manner the interchange of persons produces a vivid impression, and often makes the hearer feel that he is moving in the midst of perils: "Thou hadst said that with toil unspent, and all unwasted of limb, / They closed in the grapple of war, so fiercely they rushed to the fray;"[67] and the line of Aratus: "Never in that month launch thou forth amid lashing seas."[68] 2. So also Herodotus: "From the city of Elephantine thou shalt sail upwards, and then shalt come to a level plain; and after crossing this tract, thou shalt embark upon another vessel and sail for two days, and then shalt thou come to a great city whose name is Meroe."[69] Do you observe, my friend, how he leads you in imagination through the region and makes you *see* what you hear? All such cases of direct personal address place the hearer on the very scene of action. 3. So it is when you seem to be speaking, not to all and sundry, but to a single individual: "But Tydeides—thou wouldst not have known him, for whom that hero fought."[70] You will make your hearer more excited and more attentive, and full of active participation, if you keep him on the alert by words addressed to himself.

XXVII

There is further the case in which a writer, when relating something about a person, suddenly breaks off and converts himself into that selfsame person. This species of figure is a kind of outburst of passion:

Then with a far-ringing shout to the Trojans Hector cried,
Bidding them rush on the ships, bidding leave the spoils blood-dyed—
And whomso I mark from the galleys aloof on the farther side,
I will surely devise his death.[71]

The poet assigns the task of narration, as is fit, to himself, but the abrupt threat he suddenly, with no note of warning, attributes to the angered chief. It would have been frigid had he inserted the words, "Hector said so and so." As it is, the swift transition of the narrative has outstripped the swift transitions of the narrator. 2. Accordingly this figure should be used by preference when a sharp crisis does not suffer the writer to tarry, but constrains him to pass at once from one person to another. An example will be found in Hecataeus: "Ceyx treated the matter gravely, and straightway bade the descendants of Heracles depart; for I am not able to succor you. In order, therefore, that ye may not perish yourselves and injure me, get you gone to some other country."[72] 3. Demosthenes in dealing with Aristogeiton has, somewhat differently, employed this variation of person to betoken the quick play of emotion. "And will none of you," he asks, "be found to be stirred by loathing or even by anger at the violent deeds of this vile and shameless fellow, who—you whose license of speech, most abandoned of men, is not confined by barriers nor by doors, which might perchance be opened!"[73] With the sense thus incomplete, he suddenly breaks off and in his anger almost tears asunder a single expression into two persons—"he who, O thou most abandoned!" Thus, although he has turned aside his address and seems to have left Aristogeiton, yet through passion he directs it upon him with far greater force. 4. Similarly with the words of Penelope:

Herald, with what behest art thou come from the suitor-band?
To give to the maids of Odysseus the godlike their command
To forsake their labors, and yonder for them the banquet to lay?
I would that of all their wooing this were the latest day,
That this were the end of your banquets, your uttermost reveling-hour,
Ye that assemble together and all our substance devour,
The wise Telemachus' store, as though ye never had heard,
In the days overpast of your childhood, your fathers' praising word,
How good Odysseus was.[74]

XXVIII

As to whether or no periphrasis[75] contributes to the sublime, no one, I think, will hesitate. For just as in music the so-called accompaniments bring out the charm of the

---

[67][Roberts] *Iliad* XV, 697–698.
[68]Aratus of Soli (fl. 270 B.C.); [Roberts] *Phenomena*, 287.
[69][Roberts] *History* II, 29.
[70][Roberts] *Iliad* V, 85.
[71][Roberts] *Iliad* XV, 346–349.

[72]Hecataeus (c. 550–476 B.C.), Greek historian and geographer.
[73][Roberts] *Against Aristogeiton* I, 27.
[74][Roberts] *Odyssey* IV, 681–689.
[75]Circumlocution.

melody, so also periphrasis often harmonizes with the normal expression and adds greatly to its beauty, especially if it has a quality which is not inflated and dissonant but pleasantly tempered. 2. Plato will furnish an instance in proof at the opening of his funeral oration. "In truth they have gained from us their rightful tribute, in the enjoyment of which they proceed along their destined path, escorted by their country publicly, and privately each by his kinsmen."[76] Death he calls "their destined path," and the tribute of accustomed rites he calls "being escorted publicly by their fatherland." Is it in a slight degree only that he has magnified the conception by the use of these words? Has he not rather, starting with unadorned diction, made it musical, and shed over it like a harmony the melodious rhythm which comes from periphrasis? 3. And Xenophon says, "You regard toil as the guide to a joyous life. You have garnered in your souls the goodliest of all possessions and the fittest for warriors. For you rejoice in praise more than in all else."[77] In using, instead of "you are willing to toil," the words "you deem toil the guide to a joyous life," and in expanding the rest of the sentence in like manner, he has annexed to his eulogy a lofty idea. 4. And so with that inimitable phrase of Herodotus: "The goddess afflicted with an unsexing malady those Scythians who had pillaged the temple."[78]

XXIX

A hazardous business, however, eminently hazardous, is periphrasis, unless it be handled with discrimination; otherwise it speedily falls flat, with its odor of empty talk and its swelling amplitude. This is the reason why Plato (who is always strong in figurative language, and at times unseasonably so) is taunted because in his *Laws* he says that "neither gold nor silver treasure should be allowed to establish itself and abide in the city."[79] The critic says that, if he had been forbidding the possession of cattle, he would obviously have spoken of ovine and bovine treasure.

2. But our parenthetical disquisition with regard to the use of figures as bearing upon the sublime has run to sufficient length, my dear Terentianus; for all these things lend additional passion and animation to style, and passion is as intimately allied with sublimity as sketches of character with entertainment.

XXX

Since, however, it is the case that, in discourse, thought and diction are for the most part developed one through the other, come let us proceed to consider any branches of the subject of diction which have so far been neglected. Now it is, no doubt, superfluous to dilate to those who know it well upon the fact that the choice of proper and striking words wonderfully attracts and enthralls the hearer, and that such a choice is the leading ambition of all orators and writers, since it is the direct agency which ensures the presence in writings, as upon the fairest statues, of the perfection of grandeur, beauty, mellowness, dignity, force, power, and any other high qualities there may be, and breathes into dead things a kind of living voice. All this it is, I say, needless to mention, for beautiful words are in very truth the peculiar light of thought. 2. It may, however, be pointed out that stately language is not to be used everywhere, since to invest petty affairs with great and high-sounding names would seem just like putting a full-sized tragic mask upon an infant boy. But in poetry and . . .

XXXI

. . . full of vigor and racy; and so is Anacreon's[80] line. "That Thracian mare no longer do I heed." In this way, too, that original expression of Theopompus[81] merits praise. Owing to the correspondence between word and thing it seems to me to be highly expressive; and yet Cacilius for some unexplained reason finds fault with it. "Philip," says Theopompus, "had a genius for *stomaching* things." Now a homely expression of this kind is sometimes much more telling than elegant language, for it is understood at once since it is drawn from common life, and the fact that it is familiar makes it only the more convincing. So the words *stomaching things* are used most strikingly of a man who, for the sake of attaining his own ends, patiently and with cheerfulness endures things shameful and vile. 2. So with the words of Herodotus. "Cleomenes," he says, "went mad, and with a small sword cut the flesh of his own body into strips, until he slew himself by making mincemeat of his entire person."[82] And, "Pythes fought on shipboard, until he was utterly hacked to pieces."[83] These phrases graze the very

---

[76][Roberts] *Menixenus,* 236.
[77][Roberts] *Cyropaedia* I, v, 12.
[78][Roberts] *History* I, 105.
[79][Roberts] VII, 801.

[80]Anacreon (c. 560–475 B.C.), Greek lyric poet.
[81]Theopompus (c. 378–300 B.C.), Greek historian.
[82][Roberts] *History* VI, 75.
[83][Roberts] *History* VII, 181.

edge of vulgarity, but they are saved from vulgarity by their expressiveness.

XXXII

Further, with regard to the number of metaphors to be employed, Caecilius seems to assent to the view of those who lay it down that not more than two, or at the most three, should be ranged together in the same passage. Demosthenes is, in fact, the standard in this as in other matters. The proper time for using metaphors is when the passions roll like a torrent and sweep a multitude of them down their resistless flood. 2. "Men," says he,

> who are vile flatterers, who have maimed their own fatherlands each one of them, who have toasted away their liberty first to Philip and now to Alexander, who measure happiness by their belly and their lowest desires, and who have overthrown that liberty and that freedom from despotic mastery which to the Greeks of an earlier time were the rules and standards of good.[84]

Here the orator's wrath against the traitors throws a veil over the number of the tropes. 3. In the same spirit, Aristotle and Theophrastus[85] point out that the following phrases serve to soften bold metaphors—*as if*, and *as if were*, and *if one may so say*, and *if one may venture such an expression*; for the qualifying words mitigate, they say, the audacity of expression. 4. I accept that view, but still for number and boldness of metaphors I maintain, as I said in dealing with figures, that strong and timely passion and noble sublimity are the appropriate palliatives. For it is the nature of the passions, in their vehement rush, to sweep and thrust everything before them, or rather to demand hazardous turns as altogether indispensable. They do not allow the hearer leisure to criticize the number of the metaphors because he is carried away by the fervor of the speaker. 5. Moreover, in the treatment of commonplaces and in descriptions there is nothing so impressive as a number of tropes following close one upon the other. It is by this means that in Xenophon the anatomy of the human tabernacle is magnificently depicted, and still more divinely in Plato. Plato says that its head is a citadel; in the midst, between the head and the breast, is built the neck like some isthmus. The vertebrae, he says, are fixed beneath like pivots. Pleasure is a bait which tempts men to ill,

the tongue the test of taste; the heart is the knot of the veins and the wellspring of the blood that courses round impetuously, and it is stationed in the guard-house of the body. The passages by which the blood races this way and that he names alleys. He says that the gods, contriving succor for the beating of the heart (which takes place when dangers are expected, and when wrath excites it, since it then reaches a fiery heat), have implanted the lungs, which are soft and bloodless and have pores within, to serve as a buffer, in order that the heart may, when its inward wrath boils over, beat against a yielding substance and so escape injury. The seat of the desires he compared to the women's apartments in a house, that of anger to the men's. The spleen he called the napkin of the inward parts, whence it is filled with secretions and grows to a great and festering bulk. After this, the gods canopied the whole with flesh, putting forward the flesh as a defense against injuries from without, as though it were a hair-cushion. The blood he called the fodder of the flesh. "In order to promote nutrition," he continues, "they irrigated the body, cutting conduits as in gardens, in order that, with the body forming a set of tiny channels, the streams of the veins might flow as from a never-failing source." When the end comes, he says that the cables of the soul are loosed like those of a ship, and she is allowed to go free.[86] 6. Examples of a similar nature are to be found in a never-ending series. But those indicated are enough to show that figurative language possesses great natural power, and that metaphors contribute to the sublime; and at the same time that it is impassioned and descriptive passages which rejoice in them to the greatest extent. 7. It is obvious, however, even though I do not dwell upon it, that the use of tropes, like all other beauties of expression, is apt to lead to excess. On this score Plato himself is much criticized, since he is often carried away by a sort of frenzy of words into strong and harsh metaphors and into inflated allegory. "For it is not readily observed," he says, "that a city ought to be mixed like a bowl, in which the mad wine seethes when it has been poured in, though when chastened by another god who is sober, falling thus into noble company, it makes a good and temperate drink."[87] For to call water "a sober god," and mixing "chastening," is—the critics say—the language of a poet, and one who is in truth far from sober. 8. Fastening upon such defects, however, Caecilius ventured, in his writings in praise of Lysias,[88] to make the assertion that Lysias was altogether superior to Plato. In so doing he

---

[84][Roberts] *On the Crown*, 296.
[85]Theophrastus (c. 380–287 B.C.), Greek philosopher.

[86][Roberts] Plato, *Timaeus*, 65–85.
[87][Roberts] *Laws* VI, 773.
[88]Lysias (458–380 B.C.), Greek orator.

gave way to two blind impulses of passion. Loving Lysias better even than himself, he nevertheless hates Plato more perfectly than he loves Lysias. In fact, he is carried away by the spirit of contention, and even his premises are not, as he thought, admitted. For he prefers the orator as faultless and immaculate to Plato as one who has often made mistakes. But the truth is not of this nature, nor anything like it.

XXXIII

Come, now, let us take some writer who is really immaculate and beyond reproach. Is it not worthwhile, on this very point, to raise the general question whether we ought to give the preference, in poems and prose writings, to grandeur with some attendant faults, or to success which is moderate but altogether sound and free from error? Aye, and further, whether a greater number of excellences, or excellences higher in quality, would in literature rightly bear away the palm? For these are inquiries appropriate to a treatise on the sublime, and they imperatively demand a settlement. 2. For my part, I am well aware that lofty genius is far removed from flawlessness; for invariable accuracy incurs the risk of pettiness, and in the sublime, as in great fortunes, there must be something which is overlooked. It may be necessarily the case that low and average natures remain as a rule free from failing and in greater safety because they never run a risk or seek to scale the heights, while great endowments prove insecure because of their very greatness. 3. In the second place, I am not ignorant that it naturally happens that the worse side of human character is always the more easily recognized, and that the memory of errors remains indelible, while that of excellences quickly dies away. 4. I have myself noted not a few errors on the part of Homer and other writers of the greatest distinction, and the slips they have made afford me anything but pleasure. Still I do not term them willful errors, but rather oversights of a random and casual kind, due to neglect and introduced with all the heedlessness of genius. Consequently I do not waver in my view that excellences higher in quality, even if not sustained throughout, should always on a comparison be voted the first place, because of their sheer elevation of spirit if for no other reason. Granted that Apollonius[89] in his *Argonautica* shows himself a poet who does not trip, and that in his pastorals Theocritus is, except in a few externals, most happy, would you not, for all that, choose to be Homer rather than Apollonius? 5. Again: Does Eratosthenes[90] in the *Ergione* (a little poem which is altogether free from flaw) show himself a greater poet than Archilochus with the rich and disorderly abundance which follows in his train and with that outburst of the divine spirit within him which it is difficult to bring under the rules of law? Once more: In lyric poetry would you prefer to be Bacchylides[91] rather than Pindar?[92] And in tragedy to be Ion of Chios[93] rather than—Sophocles? It is true that Bacchylides and Ion are faultless and entirely elegant writers of the polished school, while Pindar and Sophocles, although at times they burn everything before them as it were in their swift career, are often extinguished unaccountably and fail most lamentably. But would anyone in his senses regard all the compositions of Ion put together as an equivalent for the single play of the *Oedipus?*

XXXIV

If successful writing were to be estimated by number of merits and not by the true criterion, thus judged Hyperides would be altogether superior to Demosthenes. For he has a greater variety of accents than Demosthenes and a greater number of excellences, and like the pentathlete he falls just below the top in every branch. In all the contests he has to resign the first place to his rivals, while he maintains that place as against all ordinary persons. 2. Now Hyperides not only imitates all the strong points of Demosthenes with the exception of his composition, but he has embraced in a singular degree the excellences and graces of Lysias as well. For he talks with simplicity, where it is required, and does not adopt like Demosthenes one unvarying tone in all his utterances. He possesses the gift of characterization in a sweet and pleasant form and with a touch of piquancy. There are innumerable signs of wit in him—the most polished raillery, high-bred ease, supple skill in the contests of irony, jests not tasteless or rude after the well-known Attic manner but naturally suggested by the subject, clever ridicule, much comic power, biting satire with well-directed fun, and what may be termed an inimitable charm investing the whole. He is excellently fitted by nature to excite pity; in narrating a fable he is facile, and with his pliant spirit he is also most easily turned towards a digression (as for instance in his rather poetical presentation of the story of Leto), while he has treated his funeral oration in the epideictic[94] vein with probably unequalled success. 3. Demosthenes, on the other hand, is not

---

[89]Apollonius (fl. 222–181 B.C.), Alexandrian poet.
[90]Eratosthenes (276–194 B.C.), Greek scientist, grammarian, and historian.

[91]Baechylides (fl. 460 B.C.), Greek lyric poet.
[92]Pindar (518–438 B.C.), Greek lyric poet.
[93]Ion (fl. 450 B.C.), Greek tragic poet.
[94]Declamatory, either encomium or invective.

an apt delineator of character, he is not facile, he is anything but pliant or epideictic, he is comparatively lacking in the entire list of excellences just given. Where he forces himself to be jocular and pleasant, he does not excite laughter but rather becomes the subject of it, and when he wishes to approach the region of charm, he is all the farther removed from it. If he had attempted to write the short speech about Phryne or about Athenogenes, he would have all the more commended Hyperides to our regard. 4. The good points of the latter, however, many though they be, are wanting in elevation; they are the staid utterances of a sober-hearted man and leave the hearer unmoved, no one feeling terror when he reads Hyperides. But Demosthenes draws—as from a store—excellences allied to the highest sublimity and perfected to the utmost, the tone of lofty speech, living passions, copiousness, readiness, speed (where it is legitimate), and that power and vehemence of his which forbid approach. Having, I say, absorbed bodily within himself these mighty gifts which we may deem heaven-sent (for it would not be right to term them human), he thus with the noble qualities which are his own routs all comers even where the qualities he does not possess are concerned, and overpowers with thunder and with lightning the orators of every age. One could sooner face with unflinching eyes a descending thunderbolt than meet with steady gaze his bursts of passion in their swift succession.

XXXV

But in the case of Plato and Lysias there is, as I said, a further point of difference. For not only in the degree of his excellences, but also in their number, Lysias is much inferior to Plato; and at the same time he surpasses him in his faults still more than he falls below him in his excellences. 2. What fact, then, was before the eyes of those superhuman writers who, aiming at everything that was highest in composition, contemned an all-pervading accuracy? This besides many other things, that Nature has appointed us men to be no base or ignoble animals; but when she ushers us into life and into the vast universe as into some great assembly, to be as it were spectators of the mighty whole and the keenest aspirants for honor, forthwith she implants in our souls the unconquerable love of whatever is elevated and more divine than we. 3. Wherefore not even the entire universe suffices for the thought and contemplation within the reach of the human mind, but our imaginations often pass beyond the bounds of space, and if we survey our life on every side and see how much more it everywhere abounds in what is striking, and great, and beautiful, we shall soon discern the purpose of our birth. 4. This is why, by a sort of natural impulse, we admire not the small streams, useful and pellucid though they be, but the Nile, the Danube or the Rhine, and still more the ocean. Nor do we view the tiny flame of our own kindling (guarded in lasting purity as its light ever is) with greater awe than the celestial fires though they are often shrouded in darkness; nor do we deem it a greater marvel than the craters of Etna, whose eruptions throw up stones from its depths and great masses of rock, and at times pour forth rivers of that pure and unmixed subterranean fire. 5. In all such matters we may say that what is useful or necessary men regard as commonplace, while they reserve their admiration for that which is astounding.

XXXVI

Now as regards the manifestations of the sublime in literature, in which grandeur is never, as it sometimes is in nature, found apart from utility and advantage, it is fitting to observe at once that, though writers of this magnitude are far removed from faultlessness, they nonetheless all rise above what is mortal; that all other qualities prove their possessors to be men, but sublimity raises them near the majesty of God; and that, while immunity from errors relieves from censure, it is grandeur that excites admiration. 2. What need to add thereto that each of these supreme authors often redeems all his failures by a single sublime and happy touch, and (most important of all) that if one were to pick out and mass together the blunders of Homer, Demosthenes, Plato, and all the rest of the greatest writers, they would be found to be a very small part, nay an infinitesimal fraction, of the triumphs which those heroes achieve on every hand? This is the reason why the judgment of all posterity—a verdict which envy itself cannot convict of perversity—has brought and offered those meeds of victory which up to this day it guards intact and seems likely still to preserve, "long as earth's waters shall flow, and her tall trees burgeon and bloom." 3. In reply, however, to the writer who maintains that the faulty *Colossus* is not superior to the *Spearman* of Polycleitus,[95] it is obvious to remark among many other things that in art the utmost exactitude is admired, grandeur in the works of nature; and that it is by nature that man is a being gifted with speech. In statues likeness to man is the quality required; in discourse we demand, as I said, that which transcends the human. 4. Nevertheless—and the counsel about to be given reverts to the beginning of our memoir—since freedom from failings is for the most part

---

[95]Polycleitus (fl. 452–412 B.C.), Greek sculptor.

the successful result of art, and excellence (though it may be unevenly sustained) the result of sublimity, the employment of art is in every way a fitting aid to nature; for it is the conjunction of the two which tends to ensure perfection.

Such are the decisions to which we have felt bound to come with regard to the questions proposed; but let every man cherish the view which pleases him best.

XXXVII

Closely related to metaphors (for we must return to our point) are comparisons and similes, differing only in this respect. . . .

XXXVIII

. . . such hyperboles as: "unless you carry your brains trodden down in your heels."[96] It is necessary, therefore, to know where to fix the limit in each case; for an occasional overshooting of the mark ruins the hyperbole, and such expressions, when strained too much, lose their tension, and sometimes swing round and produce the contrary effect. 2. Isocrates, for example, fell into unaccountable puerility owing to the ambition which made him desire to describe everything with a touch of amplification. The theme of his *Panegyric* is that Athens surpasses Lacedaemon in benefits conferred upon Greece, and yet at the very outset of his speech he uses these words: "Further, language has such capacity that it is possible thereby to debate things lofty and invest things small with grandeur, and to express old things in a new way, and to discourse in ancient fashion about what has newly happened.[97] "Do you then, Isocrates," it may be asked, "mean in that way to interchange the facts of Lacedaemonian and Athenian history?" For in his eulogy of language he has, we may say, published to his hearers a preamble warning them to distrust himself. 3. Perhaps, then, as we said in dealing with figures generally, those hyperboles are best in which the very fact that they are hyperboles escapes attention. This happens when, through stress of strong emotion, they are uttered in connection with some great crisis, as is done by Thucydides in the case of those who perished in Sicily. "The Syracusans," he says, "came down to the water's edge and began the slaughter of those chiefly who were in the river, and the water at once became polluted, but none the less it was swallowed although muddy

and mixed with blood, and to most it was still worth fighting for."[98] That a draught of blood and mud should still be worth fighting for, is rendered credible by the intensity of the emotion at a great crisis. 4. So with the passage in which Herodotus tells of those who fell at Thermopylae. "On this spot," he says, "the barbarians buried them as they defended themselves with daggers—those of them who had daggers still left—and with hands and mouths."[99] Here you may be inclined to protest against the expressions "fight with their very mouths" against men in armor, and "being buried" with darts. At the same time the narrative carries conviction; for the event does not seem to be introduced for the sake of the hyperbole, but the hyperbole to spring naturally from the event. 5. For (as I never cease to say) the deeds and passions which verge on transport are a sufficient lenitive and remedy for every audacity of speech. This is the reason why the quips of comedy, although they may be carried to the extreme of absurdity, are plausible because they are so amusing. For instance, "Smaller his field was than a Spartan letter." For mirth, too, is an emotion, an emotion which has its root in pleasure. 6. Hyperboles are employed in describing things small as well as great, since exaggeration is the common element in both cases. And, in a sense, ridicule is an amplification of the paltriness of things.

XXXIX

The fifth of those elements contributing to the sublime which we mentioned, my excellent friend, at the beginning, still remains to be dealt with, namely the arrangement of the words in a certain order. In regard to this, having already in two treatises sufficiently stated such results as our inquiry could compass, we will add, for the purpose of our present undertaking, only what is absolutely essential, namely the fact that harmonious arrangement is not only a natural source of persuasion and pleasure among men but also a wonderful instrument of lofty utterance and of passion. 2. For does not the flute instill certain emotions into its hearers and as it were make them beside themselves and full of frenzy, and supplying a rhythmical movement constrain the listener to move rhythmically in accordance therewith and to conform himself to the melody, although he may be utterly ignorant of music? Yes, and the tones of the harp, although in themselves they signify nothing at all, often cast a wonderful spell, as you know, over an audience by means of the variations of sounds, by their pulsation against one another, and by their

---

[96][Roberts] *On Halonesus* 45, attributed by some to Demosthenes.
[97][Roberts] 8.

[98][Roberts] *History of the Peloponnesian War,* VII, 84.
[99][Roberts] *History* VII, 225.

mingling in concert. 3. And yet these are mere semblances and spurious copies of persuasion, not (as I have said) genuine activities of human nature. Are we not, then, to hold that composition (being a harmony of that language which is implanted by nature in man and which appeals not to the hearing only but to the soul itself), since it calls forth manifold shapes of words, thoughts, deeds, beauty, melody, all of them born at our birth and growing with our growth, and since by means of the blending and variation of its own tones it seeks to introduce into the minds of those who are present the emotion which affects the speaker and since it always brings the audience to share in it and by the building of phrase upon phrase raises a sublime and harmonious structure: are we not, I say, to hold that harmony by these selfsame means allures us and invariably disposes us to stateliness and dignity and elevation and every emotion which it contains within itself, gaining absolute mastery over our minds? But it is folly to dispute concerning matters which are generally admitted, since experience is proof sufficient. 4. An example of a conception which is usually thought sublime and is really admirable is that which Demosthenes associates with the decree: "This decree caused the danger which then beset the city to pass by just-as a cloud."[100] But it owes its happy sound no less to the harmony than to the thought itself. For the thought is expressed throughout in dactylic rhythms, and these are most noble and productive of sublimity; and therefore it is that they constitute the heroic, the finest meter that we know. For if you derange the words of the sentence and transpose them in whatever way you will, as for example "This decree just-as a cloud caused the danger of the time to pass by"; nay, if you cut off a single syllable only and say "caused to pass by as a cloud," you will perceive to what an extent harmony is in unison with sublimity. For the very words "just-as a cloud" begin with a long rhythm, which consists of four metrical beats; but if one syllable is cut off and we read "as a cloud," we immediately maim the sublimity by the abbreviation. Conversely, if you elongate the word and write "caused to pass by just-as-if a cloud," it means the same thing, but no longer falls with the same effect upon the ear, inasmuch as the abrupt grandeur of the passage loses its energy and tension through the lengthening of the concluding syllables.

XL

Among the chief causes of the sublime in speech, as in the structure of the human body, is the collocation of members,

a single one of which if severed from another possesses in itself nothing remarkable, but all united together make a full and perfect organism. So the constituents of grandeur, when separated from one another, carry with them sublimity in distraction this way and that, but when formed into a body by association and when further encircled in a chain of harmony they become sonorous by their very rotundity; and in periods sublimity is, as it were, a contribution made by a multitude. 2. We have, however, sufficiently shown that many writers and poets who possess no natural sublimity and are perhaps even wanting in elevation have nevertheless, although employing for the most part common and popular words with no striking associations of their own, by merely joining and fitting these together, secured dignity and distinction and the appearance of freedom from meanness. Instances will be furnished by Philistus among others, by Aristophanes in certain passages, by Euripides in most. 3. In the last-mentioned author, Heracles, after the scene in which he slays his children, uses the words: "Full-fraught am I with woes—no space for more."[101] The expression is a most ordinary one, but it has gained elevation through the aptness of the structure of the line. If you shape the sentence in a different way, you will see this plainly, the fact being that Euripides is a poet in virtue of his power of composition rather than of his invention. 4. In the passage which describes Dirce torn away by the bull:

> Whitherso'er he turned
> Swift wheeling round, he haled and hurled withal
> Dame, rock, oak, intershifted ceaselessly.

the conception itself is a fine one, but it has been rendered more forcible by the fact that the harmony is not hurried or carried as it were on rollers, but the words act as buttresses for one another and find support in the pauses, and issue finally in a well-grounded sublimity.

XLI

There is nothing in the sphere of the sublime, that is so lowering as broken and agitated movement of language, such as is characteristic of pyrrhics and trochees and dichorees,[102] which fall altogether to the level of dance music. For all overrhythmical writing is at once felt to be affected and

---

[100][Roberts] *On the Crown*, 188.

[101][Roberts] *Heracles*, 1245.

[102]A pyrrhic is a metrical foot consisting of two short syllables; a trochee, a foot consisting of one long syllable followed by one short syllable. A dichoree consists of two trochees treated as a unit.

finical and wholly lacking in passion owing to the monotony of its superficial polish. 2. And the worst of it all is that, just as petty lays draw their hearer away from the point and compel his attention to themselves, so also overrhythmical style does not communicate the feeling of the words but simply the feeling of the rhythm. Sometimes, indeed, the listeners knowing beforehand the due terminations stamp their feet in time with the speaker, and as in a dance give the right step in anticipation. 3. In like manner those words are destitute of sublimity which lie too close together, and are cut up into short and tiny syllables, and are held together as if with wooden bolts by sheer inequality and ruggedness.

XLII

Further, excessive concision of expression tends to lower the sublime, since grandeur is marred when the thought is brought into too narrow a compass. Let this be understood not of proper compression, but of what is absolutely petty and cut into segments. For concision curtails the sense, but brevity goes straight to the mark. It is plain that, vice versa, prolixities are frigid, for so is everything that resorts to unseasonable length.

XLIII

Triviality of expression is also apt to disfigure sublimity. In Herodotus, for example, the tempest is described with marvelous effect in all its details, but the passage surely contains some words below the dignity of the subject. The following may serve as an instance—"when the sea seethed."[103] The word *seethed* detracts greatly from the sublimity because it is an ill-sounding one. Further, "the wind," he says, "grew fagged," and those who clung to the spars met "an unpleasant end."[104] The expression *grew fagged* is lacking in dignity, being vulgar; and the word *unpleasant* is inappropriate to so great a disaster. 2. Similarly, when Theopompus had dressed out in marvelous fashion the descent of the Persian king upon Egypt, he spoilt the whole by some petty words.

For which of the cities (he says) or which of the tribes in Asia did not send envoys to the Great King? Which of the products of the earth or of the achievements of art was not, in all its beauty or

preciousness, brought as an offering to his presence? Consider the multitude of costly coverlets and mantles, in purple or white or embroidery; the multitude of pavilions of gold furnished with all things useful; the multitude, too, of tapestries and costly couches. Further, gold and silver plate richly wrought, and goblets and mixing bowls, some of which you might have seen set with precious stones, and others finished with care and at great price. In addition to all this, countless myriads of Greek and barbaric weapons, and beasts of burden beyond all reckoning and victims fattened for slaughter, and many bushels of condiments, and many bags and sacks and sheets of papyrus and all other useful things, and an equal number of pieces of salted flesh from all manner of victims, so that the piles of them were so great that those who were approaching from a distance took them to be hills and eminences confronting them.

3. He runs off from the more elevated to the more lowly, whereas he should, on the contrary, have risen higher and higher. With his wonderful description of the whole outfit he mixes bags and condiments and sacks, and conveys the impression of a confectioner's shop! For just as if, in the case of those very adornments, between the golden vessels and the jeweled mixing bowls and the silver plate and the pavilions of pure gold and the goblets, a man were to bring and set in the midst paltry bags and sacks, the proceeding would have been offensive to the eye, so do such words when introduced out of season constitute deformities and as it were blots on the diction.

4. He might have described the scene in broad outline just as he says that hills blocked their way, and with regard to the preparations generally have spoken of "wagons and camels and the multitude of beasts of burden carrying everything that ministers to the luxury and enjoyment of the table," or have used some such expression as "piles of all manner of grain and things which conduce preeminently to good cookery and comfort of body," or if he must necessarily put it in so uncompromising a way, he might have said that "all the dainties of cooks and caterers were there." 5. In lofty passages we ought not to descend to sordid and contemptible language unless constrained by some overpowering necessity, but it is fitting that we should use words worthy of the subject and imitate nature, the artificer of man, for she has not placed in full view our grosser parts or the means of purging our frame, but has hidden them away as far as was possible, and as Xenophon says has put their channels in the remotest background, so as not to sully the

---

[103][Roberts] *History* VII, 188.
[104][Roberts] *History* VII, 191; VIII, 13.

beauty of the entire creature. 6. But enough; there is no need to enumerate, one by one, the things which produce triviality. For since we have previously indicated those qualities which render style noble and lofty, it is evident that their opposites will for the most part make it low and base.

XLIV

It remains however (as I will not hesitate to add, in recognition of your love of knowledge) to clear up, my dear Terentianus, a question which a certain philosopher has recently mooted. "I wonder," he says, "as no doubt do many others, how it happens that in our time there are men who have the gift of persuasion to the utmost extent, and are well fitted for public life, and are keen and ready, and particularly rich in all the charms of language, yet there no longer arise really lofty and transcendent natures unless quite exceptionally. So great and worldwide a dearth of high utterance attends our age." 2. "Can it be," he continued, "that we are to accept the trite explanation that democracy is the kind nursing-mother of genius, and that literary power may be said to share its rise and fall with democracy and democracy alone? For freedom, it is said, has power to feed the imaginations of the lofty-minded and to inspire hope, and where it prevails there spreads abroad the eagerness of mutual rivalry and the emulous pursuit of the foremost place. 3. Moreover, owing to the prizes which are open to all under popular government, the mental excellences of the orator are continually exercised and sharpened, and as it were rubbed bright, and shine forth (as it is natural they should) with all the freedom which inspires the doings of the state. Today," he went on, "we seem in our boyhood to learn the lessons of a righteous servitude, being all but enswathed in its customs and observances, when our thoughts are yet young and tender, and never tasting the fairest and most productive source of eloquence (by which," he added, "I mean freedom), so that we emerge in no other guise than that of sublime flatterers." 4. This is the reason, he maintained, why no slave ever becomes an orator, although all other faculties may belong to menials. In the slave there immediately burst out signs of fettered liberty of speech, of the dungeon as it were, of a man habituated to buffetings. 5. "For the day of slavery," as Homer has it, "takes away half our manhood."[105] "Just as," he proceeded, "the cages (if what I hear is true) in which are kept the pygmies, commonly called *nani,* not only hinder the growth of the creatures confined within them, but actu-

ally attenuate them through the bonds which beset their bodies, so one has aptly termed all servitude (though it be most righteous) the cage of the soul and a public prison-house." 6. I answered him thus: "It is easy, my good sir, and characteristic of human nature, to find fault with the age in which one lives. But consider whether it may not be true that it is not the world's peace that ruins great natures, but far rather this war illimitable which holds our desires in its grasp, aye, and further still those passions which occupy as with troops our present age and utterly harry and plunder it. For the love of money, (a disease from which we all now suffer sorely) and the love of pleasure make us their thralls, or rather, as one may say, drown us body and soul in the depths, the love of riches being a malady which makes men petty, and the love of pleasure one which makes them most ignoble. 7. On reflection I cannot discover how it is possible for us, if we value boundless wealth so highly, or (to speak more truly) deify it, to avoid allowing the entrance into our souls of the evils which are inseparable from it. For vast and unchecked wealth is accompanied, in close conjunction and step for step, as they say, by extravagance, and as soon as the former opens the gates of cities and houses, the latter immediately enters and abides. And when time has passed the pair build nests in the lives of men, as the wise say, and quickly give themselves to the rearing of offspring, and breed ostentation, and vanity, and luxury, no spurious progeny of theirs, but only too legitimate. If these children of wealth are permitted to come to maturity, straightway they beget in the soul inexorable masters—insolence, and lawlessness, and shamelessness. 8. This must necessarily happen, and men will no longer lift up their eyes or have any further regard for fame, but the ruin of such lives will gradually reach its complete consummation and sublimities of soul fade and wither away and become contemptible, when men are lost in admiration of their own mortal parts and omit to exalt that which is immortal. 9. For a man who has once accepted a bribe for a judicial decision cannot be an unbiased and upright judge of what is just and honorable (since to the man who is venal his own interests must seem honorable and just), and the same is true where the entire life of each of us is ordered by bribes, and huntings after the death of others, and the laying of ambushes for legacies, while gain from any and every source we purchase—each one of us—at the price of life itself, being the slaves of pleasure. In an age which is ravaged by plagues so sore, is it possible for us to imagine that there is still left an unbiased and incorruptible judge of works that are great and likely to reach posterity, or is it not rather the case that all are influenced in their decisions by the passion for gain? 10. Nay, it is perhaps better for men like ourselves to be ruled than to

---

[105][Roberts] *Odyssey* XVII, 322.

be free, since our appetites, if let loose without restraint upon our neighbors like beasts from a cage, would set the world on fire with deeds of evil. 11. Summing up, I maintained that among the banes of the natures which our age produces must be reckoned that half-heartedness in which the life of all of us with few exceptions is passed, for we do not labor or exert ourselves except for the sake of praise and pleasure, never for those solid benefits which are a worthy object of our own efforts and the respect of others. 12. But "'tis best to leave these riddles unresolved,"[106] and to proceed to what next presents itself, namely the subject of the passions, about which I previously undertook to write in a separate treatise. These form, as it seems to me, a material part of discourse generally and of the sublime itself. . . .

---

[106][Roberts] Euripides, *Electra,* 379.

Plutarch

c.46–c.120 A.D.

Of Plutarch's life almost nothing is known other than what he tells us in his own writings. He is best known for his immensely popular *Parallel Lives,* in which he writes brief (to us today) biographies of eminent Greeks and parallels each with the life of a Roman. His so-called *Moralia,* written mainly before *Lives,* ranges over many subjects: education, ethics, metaphysics, and philology among them. He was an admirer of Plato for his ethics and was certainly influenced by Aristotle, but his own philosophical work is rather superficial. He wrote vigorously against the Epicureans and the Stoics, although here and there he quotes Epicurus favorably. His long popularity is attested by the many writers through history who have referred to him.

The remarks on poetry in the selection that follows reflect a characteristically balanced attitude. Poetry is a part of ethical training of youth and is a good preparation for later and more important philosophical studies, but it contains the bad as well as the good. All poetry has fable and falsehood in it. Plutarch goes to some lengths to show that in literary works bad statements are often countered by good ones, and youths need to learn to discriminate the good from the bad and not gullibly accept everything they read. They should not approve the false because it pleases aesthetically but instead seek what is "useful and salutary." Nevertheless, Plutarch prefers a poetry of myth and fable over one of merely elaborate meter and diction. The representation of bad things is allowable if appropriate to the "character at hand." Words, which have variable meaning, must be understood in context. Along with this, Plutarch distinguishes between imitating something beautiful (or presumably ugly) and imitating something beautifully.

Plutarch's writings are available in both Greek and English in many volumes in the Loeb Classical Library. See R. H. Barrow, *Plutarch* (1967); C. J. Gianicaris, *Plutarch* (1970); D. A. Russell, *Plutarch* (1973); Judith Mossman, ed., *Plutarch and His Intellectual World: Essays on Plutarch* (1997).

from

How the Young Man Should Study Poetry

If, my dear Marcus Sedatus,[1] it is true, as the poet Philoxenus[2] used to say, that of meats those that are not meat, and of fish those that are not fish, have the best flavour, let us leave the expounding of this matter to those persons of whom Cato[3] said that their palates are more sensitive than their minds. And so of philosophical discourses it is clear to us that those seemingly not at all philosophical, or even serious, are found more enjoyable by the very young, who present themselves at such lectures as willing and submissive hearers. For in perusing not only Aesop's[4] *Fables,* and *Tales from the Poets,* but even the *Abaris* of Heracleides,[5] the *Lycon* of Ariston,[6] and philosophic doctrines about the soul when these are combined with tales from mythology,[7] they get inspiration as well as pleasure. Wherefore we ought not only to keep the young decorous in the pleasures of eating and drinking, but, even more, in connexion with what they hear and read, by using in moderation, as a relish, that which gives pleasure, we should accustom them to seek what is useful and salutary therein.

* * *

In the art of poetry there is much that is pleasant and nourishing for the mind of a youth, but quite as much that is disturbing and misleading, unless in the hearing of it he have proper oversight. For it may be said, as it seems, not only of the land of the Egyptians but also of poetry, that it yields

> Drugs, and some are good when mixed and others baneful[8] to those who cultivate it.

Hidden therein are love and desire and winning converse,
Suasion that steals away the mind of the very wisest.[9]

For the element of deception in it does not gain any hold on utterly witless and foolish persons. This is the ground of Simonides'[10] answer to the man who said to him, "Why are the Thessalians the only people whom you do not deceive?" His answer was, "Oh, they are too ignorant to be deceived by me"; and Gorgias[11] called tragedy a deception wherein he who deceives is more honest than he who does not deceive, and he who is deceived is wiser than he who is not deceived. Shall we then stop the ears of the young, as those of the Ithacans were stopped, with a hard and unyielding wax, and force them to put to sea in the Epicurean[12] boat, and avoid poetry and steer their course clear of it; or rather shall we set them against some upright standard of reason and there bind them fast, guiding and guarding their judgement, that it may not be carried away from the course by pleasure towards that which will do them hurt?

No, not even Lycurgus, the mighty son of Dryas[13]

had sound sense, because, when many became drunk and violent, he went about uprooting the grapevines instead of bringing the springs of water nearer, and thus chastening the "frenzied god," as Plato says, "through correction by another, a sober, god."[14] For the tempering of wine with water removes its harmfulness without depriving it at the same time of its usefulness. So let us not root up or destroy the Muses' vine of poetry, but where the mythical and dramatic part grows all riotous[15] and luxuriant, through pleasure unalloyed, which gives it boldness and obstinacy in seeking acclaim, let us take it in hand and prune it and pinch it back. But where with its grace it approaches a true kind of culture, and the sweet allurement of its language is not fruitless or vacuous, there let us introduce philosophy and blend it with poetry. For as the mandragora, when it grows beside the vine and imparts its influence to the wine, makes this weigh less heavily on those who drink it, so poetry, by taking up its themes from philosophy and blending them with fable, renders the task of learning light and agreeable for the young. Wherefore poetry should not be avoided by those who are

---

The text of "How the Young Man Should Study Poetry," written probably before the *Lives,* is from Plutarch's *Moralia,* Vol. 1, translated from the Greek by Frank Cole Babbitt, The Loeb Classical Library (London: William Heinemann; New York: G. P. Putnam's Sons, 1927).

[1] Known only as a friend to Plutarch.

[2] Of Cythera (435–380 B.C.). Only fragments of his work remain.

[3] M. Porcius Cato (234?–149 B.C.), Roman military and political figure.

[4] None of Aesop's (sixth c. B.C.) are extant, the fables as we know them being spurious.

[5] Heracleides of Pontus, a student of Plato and prolific author.

[6] Peripatetic philosopher, fl. 270–230 B.C.

[7] [Babbitt] Plutarch probably has Plato in mind and is thinking of passages like "The Last Judgment," *Gorgias,* 523 ff.

[8] [Babbitt] *Odyssey* IV, 230.

[9] [Babbitt] *Iliad* XIV, 216.

[10] Greek poet, fl. 625 B.C.

[11] Of Leontini (c. 483–376 B.C.).

[12] Epicurus, Greek philosopher (341–270 B.C.).

[13] [Babbitt] *Iliad* VI, 130.

[14] [Babbitt] *Laws,* 773d.

[15] [Babbitt] Cf. Theophrastus, *De causis plantarum* III, 1.5.

intending to pursue philosophy, but they should use poetry as an introductory exercise in philosophy, by training themselves habitually to seek the profitable in what gives pleasure, and to find satisfaction therein; and if there be nothing profitable, to combat such poetry and be dissatisfied with it. For this is the beginning of education,

> If one begin each task in proper way
> So is it likely will the ending be,[16]

as Sophocles says.

First of all, then, the young man should be introduced into poetry with nothing in his mind so well imprinted, or so ready at hand, as the saying, "Many the lies the poets tell,"[17] some intentionally and some unintentionally; intentionally, because for the purpose of giving pleasure and gratification to the ear (and this is what most people look for in poetry) they feel that the truth is too stern in comparison with fiction. For the truth, because it is what actually happens, does not deviate from its course, even though the end be unpleasant; whereas fiction, being a verbal fabrication, very readily follows a roundabout route, and turns aside from the painful to what is more pleasant. For not metre nor figure of speech nor loftiness of diction nor aptness of metaphor nor unity of composition has so much allurement and charm, as a clever interweaving of fabulous narrative. But, just as in pictures, colour is more stimulating than line-drawing because it is life-like, and creates an illusion, so in poetry falsehood combined with plausibility is more striking, and gives more satisfaction, than the work which is elaborate in metre and diction, but devoid of myth and fiction. This explains why Socrates, being induced by some dreams to take up poetry, since he was not himself a plausible or naturally clever workman in falsehood, inasmuch as he had been the champion of truth all his life, put into verse the fables of Aesop,[18] assuming that there can be no poetic composition which has no addition of falsehood.

* * *

Let us equip the young from the very outset to keep ever sounding in their ears the maxim, that the art of poetry is not greatly concerned with the truth, and that the truth about these matters, even for those who have made it their sole business to search out and understand the verities, is exceed-

ingly hard to track down and hard to get hold of, as they themselves admit; and let these words of Empedocles be constantly in mind:

> Thus no eye of man hath seen nor ear hath heard this,
> Nor can it be comprehended by the mind,[19]

and the words of Xenophanes:

> Never yet was born a man nor ever shall be
> Knowing the truth about the gods and what I say of all things,[20]

and by all means the words of Socrates, in Plato,[21] when he solemnly disavows all acquaintance with these subjects. For young people then will give less heed to the poets, as having some knowledge of these matters, when they see that such questions stagger the philosophers.

We shall steady the young man still more if, at his first entrance into poetry, we give a general description of the poetic art as an imitative art and faculty analogous to painting. And let him not merely be acquainted with the oft-repeated saying that "poetry is articulate painting, and painting is inarticulate poetry,"[22] but let us teach him in addition that when we see a lizard or an ape or the face of Thersites[23] in a picture, we are pleased with it and admire it, not as a beautiful thing, but as a likeness. For by its essential nature the ugly cannot become beautiful; but the imitation, be it concerned with what is base or with what is good, if only it attain to the likeness, is commended. If, on the other hand, it produces a beautiful picture of an ugly body, it fails to give what propriety and probability require. Some painters even depict unnatural acts, as Timomachus painted a picture of Medea slaying her children, and Theon of Orestes slaying his mother, and Parrhasius of the feigned madness of Odysseus, and Chaerephanes of the lewd commerce of women with men.[24] In these matters it is especially necessary that the young man should be trained by being taught that what we commend is not the action which is the subject of the imitation, but the art, in case the subject in hand has been properly imitated. Since, then, poetry also often gives an imitative recital of base deeds,

---

[16]Fragment.
[17][Babbitt] Proverbial; cf. Aristotle, *Metaphysics* I, 2.
[18][Babbitt] Cf. Plato, *Phaedo*, 60a.

[19]Sicilian Greek philosopher (mid fifth century B.C.). Fragment. [Babbitt] The passage is quoted more fully by Sextus Empiricus.
[20](Sixth century B.C.), founder of the Eleatic school of Greek philosophy. Fragment.
[21][Babbitt] Plato, *Phaedo*, 69n.
[22]Probably a quotation from Simonides (fifth century B.C.), Greek lyric poet.
[23]The most ugly and impudent talker among the Greeks at Troy. See *Iliad* II, 212 and elsewhere.
[24]Probably Timotheus, Greek sculptor (fourth century B.C.); Theon of Samos and Chaerephanes (fourth century B.C.), Greek painters.

or of wicked experiences and characters, the young man must not accept as true what is admired and successful therein, nor approve it as beautiful, but should simply commend it as fitting and proper to the character in hand.

* * *

There is a fact, however, which we must recall to the minds of the young not once merely, but over and over again, by pointing out to them that while poetry, inasmuch as it has an imitative basis, employs embellishment and glitter in dealing with the actions and characters that form its groundwork, yet it does not forsake the semblance of truth, since imitation depends upon plausibility for its allurement. This is the reason why the imitation that does not show an utter disregard of the truth brings out, along with the actions, indications of both vice and virtue commingled; as is the case with that of Homer, which emphatically says good-bye to the Stoics, who will have it that nothing base can attach to virtue, and nothing good to vice, but that the ignorant man is quite wrong in all things, while, on the other hand, the man of culture is right in everything. These are the doctrines that we hear in the schools; but in the actions and in the life of most men, according to Euripides,[25]

> The good and bad cannot be kept apart
> But there is some commingling.

But when poetic art is divorced from the truth, then chiefly it employs variety and diversity. For it is the sudden changes that give to its stories the elements of the emotional, the surprising, and the unexpected, and these are attended by very great astonishment and enjoyment; but sameness is unemotional and prosaic. Therefore poets do not represent the same people as always victorious or prosperous or successful in everything; no, not even the gods, when they project themselves into human activities, are represented in the poets' usage as free from emotion or fault, that the perturbing and exciting element in the poetry shall nowhere become idle and dull, for want of danger and struggle.

Now since this is so, let the young man, when we set him to reading poems, not be prepossessed with any such opinions about those good and great names, as, for instance, that the men were wise and honest, consummate kings, and standards of all virtue and uprightness. For he will be greatly injured if he approves everything, and is in a state of wonderment over it, but resents nothing, refusing even to listen or accept the opinion of him who, on the contrary, censures persons that do and say such things as these:

> This I would, O Zeus, Athena, and Apollo,
> That not one escape death of all the Trojans living
> And of the Greeks; but that you and I elude destruction,
> So that we alone may raze Troy's sacred bulwarks,[26]

and

> Saddest of all the sad sounds that I heard was the cry of
>   Cassandra,
> Priam's daughter, whom Clytemnestra craftily planning
> Slew o'er my body,[27]

and

> That I seduce the girl and ensure her hate for my father.
> So I obeyed her and did it,[28]

and

> Father Zeus, none other of the gods is more baleful.[29]

Let the young man, then, not get into the habit of commending anything like this, nor let him be plausible and adroit in making excuses or in contriving some specious quibbles to explain base actions, but rather let him cherish the belief that poetry is an imitation of character and lives, and of men who are not perfect or spotless or unassailable in all respects, but pervaded by emotions, false opinions, and sundry forms of ignorance, who yet through inborn goodness frequently change their ways for the better. For if the young man is so trained, and his understanding so framed, that he feels elation and a sympathetic enthusiasm over noble words and deeds, and an aversion and repugnance for the mean, such training will render his perusal of poetry harmless. But the man who admires everything, and accommodates himself to everything, whose judgement, because of his preconceived opinion, is enthralled by the heroic names, will, like those who copy Plato's stoop or Aristotle's lisp, unwittingly become inclined to conform to much that is base.

* * *

Take these lines of Thespis[30]:

> You see that Zeus is first of gods in this,
> Not using lies or boast or silly laugh;
> With pleasure lie alone is unconcerned.

---

25 [Babbitt] Euripides, *Phoenissae*, 549.

26 [Babbitt] *Iliad* XVI, 97.
27 [Babbitt] *Odyssey* XI, 421.
28 [Babbitt] *Iliad* IX, 452.
29 [Babbitt] *Iliad* III, 365.
30 [Babbitt] Nothing by Thespis has been preserved, although a few lines attributed to him were current.

What difference is there between this and the statement, "for the Divine Being sits throned afar from pleasure and pain," as Plato[31] has put it? Consider what is said by Bacchylides[32]:

> I shall assert that virtue hath the highest fame,
> But wealth with even wretched men is intimate,

and again by Euripides to much the same effect:

> There's naught that I hold
> In a higher esteem
> Than a virtuous life;
> 'Twill ever be joined
> With those that are good.[33]

and

> Why seek vain possessions? Do ye think
> Virtue by wealth to compass?
> Wretched amid your comforts shall ye sit.[34]

Is not this a proof of what the philosophers say regarding wealth and external advantages, that without virtue they are useless and unprofitable for their owners?

This method of conjoining and reconciling such sentiments with the doctrines of philosophers brings the poet's work out of the realm of myth and impersonation, and, moreover, invests with seriousness its helpful sayings. Besides, it opens and stimulates in advance the mind of the youth by the sayings in philosophy. For he comes to it thus not altogether without a foretaste of it, nor without having heard of it, nor indiscriminately stuffed with what he has heard always from his mother and nurse, and, I dare say, from his father and his tutor as well, who all beatify and worship the rich, who shudder at death and pain, who regard virtue without money and repute as quite undesirable and a thing of naught. But when they hear the precepts of the philosophers, which go counter to such opinions, at first astonishment and confusion and amazement take hold of them, since they cannot accept or tolerate any such teaching, unless, just as if they were now to look upon the sun after having been in utter darkness, they have been made accus-

tomed, in a reflected light, as it were, in which the dazzling rays of truth are softened by combining truth with fable, to face facts of this sort without being distressed, and not to try to get away from them.[35] For if they have previously heard or read in poetry such thoughts as these:

> To mourn the babe for th' ills to which he comes;
> But him that's dead, and from his labours rests,
> To bear from home with joy and cheering words,[36]

and

> What needs have mortals save two things alone,
> Demeter's grain and draught from water-jar?[37]

and

> O Tyranny, beloved of barbarous folk,[38]

and

> And mortal men's felicity
> Is gained by such of them as feel least grief,[39]

they are less confused and disquieted upon hearing at the lectures of the philosophers that "Death is nothing to us,"[40] and "The wealth allowed by Nature is definitely limited,"[41] and "Happiness and blessedness do not consist in vast possessions or exalted occupations or offices or authority, but on impassivity, calmness, and a disposition of the soul that sets its limitations to accord with Nature."[42]

Wherefore, both because of these considerations and because of those already adduced, the young man has need of good pilotage in the matter of reading, to the end that, forestalled with schooling rather than prejudice, in a spirit of friendship and goodwill and familiarity, he may be convoyed by poetry into the realm of philosophy.

---

[31] [Babbitt] Plato, *Letters* III, 315c.
[32] [Babbitt] *Bachylides* I, 21.
[33] [Babbitt] Fragment.
[34] [Babbitt] Plutarch, as was his practice . . . seems to have condensed this quotation [a fragment of Euripides].

[35] [Babbitt] The whole passage is reminiscent of Plato, *Republic* VII, cha. 2 (515e).
[36] [Babbitt] Celebrated lines from the *Cresphontes* of Euripides, fragment.
[37] [Babbitt] Euripides, fragment.
[38] [Babbitt] Fragment, author unknown.
[39] [Babbitt] Fragment, author unknown.
[40] [Babbitt] One of Epicurus's "leading principles." Diogenes Laertius X, 139.
[41] [Babbitt] Another of Epicurus's "leading principles." Diogenes Laertius X, 144.
[42] [Babbitt] Also from Epicurus, without much doubt, but not to be found in just this form; cf., however, Diogenes Laertius X, 139, 141, 144.

Flavius Philostratus

c.170–c. 245

Philostratus came from the island of Lemnos, entered the Syrian court circle presided over by the Empress Julia Domna, and later lived in Athens, where he composed his *Lives of the Sophists.* This work is important in providing us with a sense of the significance of the sophists in the intellectual life of the period after Plato and through the earliest Christian centuries. It seems to have been completed sometime between 230 and 238.

The introduction to Book I of *Lives* provides a clear picture of what sophists were and helps us to understand the antipathy of Plato's Socrates toward them. Sophists were influential in many walks of life and particularly in the education of their times. Philostratus contrasts them with philosophers by claiming that philosophers seek knowledge while sophists proceed from assumed knowledge. He contrasts the old and the later new ("second") sophistic, and he emphasizes the importance of rhetorical skill to sophistic success, a skill that includes extemporaneous oratory and improvization on virtually any theme. Thus he recognizes the connection between sophistry and rhetoric that helped to fuel Socrates's suspicion of both, which extended to poetry (above, page 38ff.). One finds later in Mazzoni (below, page 219ff.) an attempt to rehabilitate poetry's identification with sophistic.

Philostratus is also known for his *Life of Apollonius of Tyana,* in which, among other things, he suggests that the mind of someone looking at an object produces an imitation. Thus he seems to say that it is necessary for any theory of art to take into consideration the activity of the beholder.

Philostratus's *Life of Apollonius of Tyana* is translated by F. C. Conybeare (1960). Brief commentary on this work may be found in E. H. Gombrich, *Art and Illusion* (1961) and G. M. A. Grube, *The Greek and Roman Critics* (1965). A later *Lives* was written by Eunopius (346–414), which included, among others, commentary on Plotinus (below, page 127) and Porphyry.

from
Lives of the Sophists

Book I

We must regard the ancient sophistic art as philosophic rhetoric. For it discusses the themes that philosophers treat of, but whereas they, by their method of questioning, set snares for knowledge, and advance step by step as they confirm the minor points of their investigations, but assert that they have still no sure knowledge, the sophist of the old school assumes a knowledge of that whereof he speaks. At any rate, he introduces his speeches with such phrases as "I know," or "I am aware," or "I have long observed," or "For mankind there is nothing fixed and sure." This kind of introduction gives a tone of nobility and self-confidence to a speech and implies a clear grasp of the truth.[1] The method of the philosophers resembles the prophetic art which is controlled by man and was organized by the Egyptians and Chaldeans and, before them, by the Indians, who used to conjecture the truth by the aid of countless stars; the sophistic method resembles the prophetic art of soothsayers and oracles. For indeed one may hear the Pythian oracle say:

I know the number of the sands of the sea and the measure
    thereof.[2]

and

Far-seeing Zeus gives a wooden wall to the Trito-Born,[3]

and

Nero, Orestes, Alcmaeon, matricides,[4]

and many other things of this sort, just like a sophist.

Now ancient sophistic, even when it propounded philosophical themes, used to discuss them diffusely and at length;[5] for it discoursed on courage, it discoursed on justice, on the heroes and gods, and how the universe has been fashioned into its present shape. But the sophistic that followed it, which we must not call "new," for it is old, but rather "second," sketched the types of the poor man and the rich, of princes and tyrants, and handled arguments that are concerned with definite and special themes for which history shows the way. Gorgias of Leontini founded the older type in Thessaly,[6] and Aeschines,[7] son of Atrometus, founded the second, after he had been exiled from political life at Athens and had taken up his abode in Caria and Rhodes; and the followers of Aeschines handled their themes according to the rules of art, while the followers of Gorgias handled theirs as they pleased.

The fountains of extempore eloquence flowed, some say, from Pericles their source, and hence Pericles has won his great reputation as an orator; but others say that it arose with Python of Byzantium, of whom Demosthenes says[8] that he alone of the Athenians was able to check Python's insolent and overpowering flow of words; while yet others say that extempore speaking was an invention of Aeschines; for after he sailed from Rhodes to the court of Mausolus of Caria, he delighted the king by an improvised speech. But my opinion is that Aeschines did indeed improvise more often than any other speaker, when he went on embassies and gave reports of these missions, and when he defended clients in the courts and delivered political harangues; but I think that he left behind him only such speeches as he had composed with care, for fear that he might fall far short of the elaborate speeches of Demosthenes, and that it was Gorgias who founded the art of extempore oratory. For when he appeared in the theatre at Athens he had the courage to say, "Do you propose a theme"; and he was the first to risk this bold announcement, whereby he as good as advertised that he was omniscient and would speak on any subject whatever, trusting to the inspiration of the moment; and I think that this idea occurred to Gorgias for the following reason. Prodicus of Ceos[9] had composed a certain pleasant fable in which Virtue and Vice came to Heracles[10] in the

---

The Lives of the Sophists. The selection here is from Wilmer Cave Wright, tr., *Philostratus and Eunopius, The Lives of the Sophists,* Loeb Classical Library (London: William Heinemann; Cambridge, Mass.: Harvard University Press, 1921).

[1] [Wright] For Plato's criticism by sophistic assurance cf. *Meno,* 70; *Symposium,* 208c; *Theatetus,* 180a.
[2] [Wright] Herodotus i, 147; *Life of Apollonius* vi, 11.
[3] [Wright] i.e., Athene, whose city Athens is protected by the wooden wall of her navy.
[4] [Wright] Seutonius, *Nero* 39; *Life of Apollonius* iv, 38; the enigmatic or bombastic phraseology of the oracles reminds Philostratus of the oracular manner and obscurity of certain sophists.

[5] [Wright] Plato, *Sophist,* 217c.
[6] Gorgias (c. 483–c. 376). [Wright] Plato, *Meno,* 70e.
[7] Aeschines (389–314 B.C.), Greek orator.
[8] [Wright] Demosthenes [385?–322 B.C., Greek statesman and orator], *On the Crown,* 136; the same account is given by Philostratus, *Life of Apollonius* vii, 37. Python came to Athens as the agent of Philip of Macedon.
[9] Prodicus, Greek orator and sophist, contemporary of Socrates.
[10] Heracles (Hercules), heroic figure of Greek myth, famous for his strength.

shape of women, one of them dressed in seductive and many-coloured attire, the other with no care for effect; and to Heracles, who was still young, Vice offered idleness and sensuous pleasures, while Virtue offered squalor and toil on toil. For this story Prodicus wrote a rather long epilogue, and then he toured the cities and gave recitations of the story in public, for hire, and charmed them after the manner of Orpheus and Thamyris.[11] For these recitations he won a great reputation at Thebes and a still greater at Sparta, as one who benefited the young by making this fable widely known. Thereupon Gorgias ridiculed Prodicus for handling a theme that was stale and hackneyed, and he abandoned himself to the inspiration of the moment. Yet he did not fail to arouse envy. There was at Athens a certain Chaerephon, not the one who used to be nicknamed "Boxwood" in Comedy,[12] because he suffered from anaemia due to hard study, but the one I now speak of had insolent manners and made scurrilous jokes; he rallied Gorgias for his ambitious efforts, and said: "Gorgias, why is it that beans blow out my stomach, but do not blow up the fire?"[13] But he was not at all disconcerted by the question and replied: "This I leave for you to investigate; but here is a fact which I have long known, that the earth grows canes[14] for such as you."

The Athenians when they observed the too great cleverness of the sophists, shut them out of the law-courts on the ground that they could defeat a just argument by an unjust, and that they used their power to warp men's judgement. That is the reason why Aeschines[15] and Demosthenes[16] branded each other with the title of sophist, not because it was a disgrace, but because the very word was suspect in the eyes of the jury; for in their career outside the courts they claimed consideration and applause on the very ground that they were sophists. In fact, Demosthenes, if we may believe Aeschines,[17] used to boast to his friends that he had won over the votes of the jury to his own views; while Aeschines at Rhodes[18] would not, I think, have given the first place to a study of which the Rhodians knew nothing before his coming, unless he had already devoted serious attention to it at Athens.

The men of former days applied the name "sophist," not only to orators whose surpassing eloquence won them a brilliant reputation, but also to philosophers who expounded their theories with ease and fluency. Of these latter, then, I must speak first, because, though they were not actually sophists, they seemed to be so, and hence came to be so called.

---

[11] Orpheus, Greek mythological musician and poet; Thamyris, ancient Thracean bard.

[12] Chaerephon, sophist, disciple of Socrates. [Wright] Chaerephon was a favorite butt of comedy and was thus nicknamed on account of his sallow complexion, as one should say "tallow faced." . . . He was also called the "bat."

[13] [Wright] There is a play on the verb, which means both "inflate" and "blow the bellows." The same question is asked in *Athenaeus*, 408; in both passages "fire" seems to mean "the intelligence" as opposed to material appetite. The comic poets satirized the sophists for investigating such questions.

[14] [Wright] The jest lies in the ambiguity of the meaning and also the application here of this word, which is originally "hollow reed," such as that used by Prometheus to steal fire from heaven, but was also the regular word for a rod for chastisement; it has the latter meaning in the *Life of Apollonius of Tyana* viii, 3.

[15] [Wright] E.g., *Against Timarchus,* 170.

[16] [Wright] E.g., *On the Crown,* 276.

[17] [Wright] *Against Timarchus.*

[18] [Wright] Aeschines founded a school of rhetoric at Athens.

Plotinus

205–c. 262

The philosopher Plotinus was a native of Egypt, probably of Roman descent. At age twenty-eight he went to Alexandria to study philosophy; later he was on Gordian III's expedition to the East and escaped when the emperor was assassinated in Mesopotamia. From about 244 he was in Rome, where he founded a school of neoplatonism. His *Enneads* (six sets of nine essays each) were edited and arranged by his pupil Porphyry, who wrote a biography of him. For Plotinus, the world we experience is an "emanation" from the ultimate idea or One, and everything seeks to return to it. The One, sometimes called the First, expresses itself in a triad: the intellectual principle or Being, the reason principle or the higher reasoning soul, and the vegetal lower-acting soul, called sometimes the Third. Plotinus identifies these three in the myth of the relations of Ouranus, Kronos, who succeeded him, and Zeus, who dethroned Kronos. The more beautiful a thing is, the closer it is to the One, which is identified metaphorically with pure light. The further away from the One the more it is imbedded in darkness and matter. Matter is indefinite, unembodied, without magnitude, void, and alien. In its fundamental nature it is utter darkness and has nothing we find in things of sense.

Art, as in Plotinus's example of a sculpture, is the freeing of form or idea from matter, a bringing of the Idea to at least some degree of light. The beauty of the work of art is not in any material object as such or any object imitated but in the Idea or form that the artist imposes on his materials. In this sense, the artist's work is a cleansing that has a purpose similar to that of the ancient Dionysian rites of purification. Indeed, Plotinus seems often to think through myth and its connection to ritual. The Idea comes from or through the artist's mind and is derived from intellect and ultimately from connection with the One: "Phidias wrought the *Zeus* upon no model among things of sense but by apprehending what form Zeus must take if he chose to become manifest to sight." The Idea is imposed on the mass of exterior matter. In this process the indivisible One is exhibited "in diversity."

Plotinus thus departs from the Platonic Socrates's complaint about imitation. He considers the artist a creator of valuable spiritual insight by virtue of his attention to form in contrast to Socrates, who would have us gain insight into the One by rational dialectical search. But art is never, for Plotinus, a perfect incarnation of beauty, which never fully appears, for art always remains to some extent material.

Several poets and critics belonging to the English Romantic movement were influenced by Plotinian attitudes. We find hints of Plotinus in Blake, Wordsworth, Shelley, and Keats; and Coleridge's notion of imagination has some connection.

A standard translation is that by Stephen MacKenna, *The Enneads,* revised by B. S. Page (1956). See W. R. Inge, *The Philosophy of Plotinus* (1918); P. V. Pistorius, *Plotinus and Neoplatonism* (1952); Eugenie de Keyser, *La signification de l'art dans les Enneades de Plotin* (1955); Emile Brehier, *The Philosophy of Plotinus* (1958); John

Bussanich, *The One and Its Relation to Intellect in Plotinus* (1967); Gerard O'Daley, *Plotinus' Philosophy of the Self* (1973); Dominic J. O'Meara, *Plotinus: An Introduction to the Enneads* (1995); Margaret R. Miles, *Plotinus on Body and Beauty* (1999); Sara Rappe, *Reading Neoplatonism* (2000).

from

Enneads

Beauty

1. Beauty addresses itself chiefly to sight; but there is a beauty for the hearing too, as in certain combinations of words and in all kinds of music, for melodies and cadences are beautiful; and minds that lift themselves above the realm of sense to a higher order are aware of beauty in the conduct of life, in actions, in character, in the pursuits of the intellect; and there is the beauty of the virtues. What loftier beauty there may be, yet, our argument will bring to light.

What, then, is it that gives comeliness to material forms and draws the ear to the sweetness perceived in sounds, and what is the secret of the beauty there is in all that derives from Soul?

Is there some One Principle from which all take their grace, or is there a beauty peculiar to the embodied and another for the bodiless? Finally, one or many, what would such a Principle be?

Consider that some things, material shapes for instance, are gracious not by anything inherent but by something communicated, while others are lovely of themselves, as, for example, Virtue.

The same bodies appear sometimes beautiful, sometimes not; so that there is a good deal between being body and being beautiful.

What, then, is this something that shows itself in certain material forms? This is the natural beginning of our inquiry.

What is it that attracts the eyes of those to whom a beautiful object is presented, and calls them, lures them, towards it, and fills them with joy at the sight? If we possess ourselves of this, we have at once a standpoint for the wider survey.

Almost everyone declares that the symmetry of parts towards each other and towards a whole, with, besides, a certain charm of colour, constitutes the beauty recognized by the eye, that in visible things, as indeed in all else, universally, the beautiful thing is essentially symmetrical, patterned.

But think what this means.

Only a compound can be beautiful, never anything devoid of parts; and only a whole; the several parts will have beauty, not in themselves, but only as working together to give a comely total. Yet beauty in an aggregate demands beauty in details: it cannot be constructed out of ugliness; its law must run throughout.

All the loveliness of colour and even the light of the sun, being devoid of parts and so not beautiful by symmetry, must be ruled out of the realm of beauty. And how comes gold to be a beautiful thing? And lightning by night, and the stars, why are these so fair?

In sounds also the simple must be proscribed, though often in a whole noble composition each several tone is delicious in itself.

Again since the one face, constant in symmetry, appears sometimes fair and sometimes not, can we doubt that beauty is something more than symmetry, that symmetry itself owes its beauty to a remoter principle?

Turn to what is attractive in methods of life or in the expression of thought; are we to call in symmetry here? What symmetry is to be found in noble conduct, or excellent laws, in any form of mental pursuit?

What symmetry can there be in points of abstract thought?

The symmetry of being accordant with each other? But there may be accordance or entire identity where there is nothing but ugliness: the proposition that honesty is merely a generous artlessness chimes in the most perfect harmony with the proposition that morality means weakness of will; the accordance is complete.

Then again, all the virtues are a beauty of the Soul, a beauty authentic beyond any of these others; but how does symmetry enter here? The Soul, it is true, is not a simple unity, but still its virtue cannot have the symmetry of size or of number: what standard of measurement could preside over the compromise or the coalescence of the Soul's faculties or purposes?

Plotinus wrote the *Enneads*, of which these selections are a part, in about 260. They were ordered, edited, and published between 300 and 305 by Porphyry, Greek scholar, philosopher, and student of religions. The text is from Stephen MacKenna, tr., *The Enneads*, revised by B. S. Page (London: Faber and Faber, 1956).

Finally, how by this theory would there be beauty in the Intellectual-Principle, essentially the solitary?

2. Let us, then, go back to the source, and indicate at once the Principle that bestows beauty on material things.

Undoubtedly this Principle exists; it is something that is perceived at the first glance, something which the Soul names as from an ancient knowledge and, recognizing, welcomes it, enters into unison with it.

But let the Soul fall in with the Ugly and at once it shrinks within itself, denies the thing, turns away from it, not accordant, resenting it.

Our interpretation is that the Soul—by the very truth of its nature, by its affiliation to the noblest Existents in the hierarchy of Being—when it sees anything of that kin, or any trace of that kinship, thrills with an immediate delight, takes its own to itself, and thus stirs anew to the sense of its nature and of all its affinity.

But, is there any such likeness between the loveliness of this world and the splendours in the Supreme? Such a likeness in the particulars would make the two orders alike: but what is there in common between beauty here and beauty There?

We hold that all the loveliness of this world comes by communion in Ideal-Form.

All shapelessness whose kind admits of pattern and form, as long as it remains outside of Reason and Idea, is ugly by that very isolation from the Divine-Thought. And this is the Absolute Ugly: an ugly thing is something that has not been entirely mastered by pattern, that is by Reason, the Matter not yielding at all points and in all respects to Ideal-Form.

But where the Ideal-Form has entered, it has grouped and co-ordinated what from a diversity of parts was to become a unity: it has rallied confusion into co-operation: it has made the sum one harmonious coherence: for the Idea is a unity and what it moulds must come to unity as far as multiplicity may.

And on what has thus been compacted to unity, Beauty enthrones itself, giving itself to the parts as to the sum: when it lights on some natural unity, a thing of like parts, then it gives itself to that whole. Thus, for an illustration, there is the beauty, conferred by craftsmanship, of all a house with all its parts, and the beauty which some natural quality may give to a single stone.

This, then, is how the material thing becomes beautiful—by communicating in the thought (Reason, Logos) that flows from the Divine.

3. And the Soul includes a faculty peculiarly addressed to Beauty—one incomparably sure in the appreciation of its own, when Soul entire is enlisted to support its judgement.

Or perhaps the Soul itself acts immediately, affirming the Beautiful where it finds something accordant with the Ideal-Form within itself, using this Idea as a canon of accuracy in its decision.

But what accordance is there between the material and that which antedates all Matter?

On what principle does the architect, when he finds the house standing before him correspondent with his inner ideal of a house, pronounce it beautiful? Is it not that the house before him, the stones apart, is the inner idea stamped upon the mass of exterior matter, the indivisible exhibited in diversity?

So with the perceptive faculty: discerning in certain objects the Ideal-Form which has bound and controlled shapeless matter, opposed in nature to Idea, seeing further stamped upon the common shapes some shape excellent above the common, it gathers into unity what still remains fragmentary, catches it up and carries it within, no longer a thing of parts, and presents it to the Ideal-Principle as something concordant and congenial, a natural friend: the joy here is like that of a good man who discerns in a youth the early signs of a virtue consonant with the achieved perfection within his own soul.

The beauty of colour is also the outcome of a unification: it derives from shape, from the conquest of the darkness inherent in Matter by the pouring-in of light, the unembodied, which is a Rational-Principle and an Ideal-Form.

Hence it is that Fire itself is splendid beyond all material bodies, holding the rank of Ideal-Principle to the other elements, making ever upwards, the subtlest and sprightliest of all bodies, as very near to the unembodied; itself alone admitting no other, all the others penetrated by it: for they take warmth but this is never cold; it has colour primally; they receive the Form of colour from it; hence the splendour of its light, the splendour that belongs to the Idea. And all that has resisted and is but uncertainly held by its light remains outside of beauty, as not having absorbed the plenitude of the Form of colour.

And harmonies unheard in sound create the harmonies we hear and wake the Soul to the consciousness of beauty, showing it the one essence in another kind: for the measures of our sensible music are not arbitrary but are determined by the Principle whose labour is to dominate Matter and bring pattern into being.

Thus far of the beauties of the realm of sense, images and shadow-pictures; fugitives that have entered into Matter—to adorn, and to ravish, where they are seen.

4. But there are earlier and loftier beauties than these. In the sense-bound life we are no longer granted to know them,

but the Soul, taking no help from the organs, sees and proclaims them. To the vision of these we must mount, leaving sense to its own low place.

As it is not for those to speak of the graceful forms of the material world who have never seen them or known their grace—men born blind, let us suppose—in the same way those must be silent upon the beauty of noble conduct and of learning and all that order who have never cared for such things, nor may those tell of the splendour of virtue who have never known the face of Justice and of Moral-Wisdom beautiful beyond the beauty of Evening and of Dawn.

Such vision is for those only who see with the Soul's sight—and at the vision, they will rejoice, and awe will fall upon them and a trouble deeper than all the rest could ever stir, for now they are moving in the realm of Truth.

This is the spirit that Beauty must ever induce, wonderment and a delicious trouble, longing and love and a trembling that is all delight. For the unseen all this may be felt as for the seen; and this the Souls feel for it, every Soul in some degree, but those the more deeply that are the more truly apt to this higher love—just as all take delight in the beauty of the body but all are not stung as sharply, and those only that feel the keener wound are known as Lovers.[1]

5. These Lovers, then, lovers of the beauty outside of sense, must be made to declare themselves.

What do you feel in presence of the grace you discern in actions, in manners, in sound morality, in all the works and fruits of virtue, in the beauty of Souls? When you see that you yourselves are beautiful within, what do you feel? What is this Dionysiac[2] exultation that thrills through your being, this straining upwards of all your soul, this longing to break away from the body and live sunken within the veritable self?

These are no other than the emotions of Souls under the spell of love.

But what is it that awakens all this passion? No shape, no colour, no grandeur of mass: all is for a Soul, something whose beauty rests upon no colour, for the moral wisdom the Soul enshrines and all the other hueless splendour of the virtues. It is that you find in yourself, or admire in another, loftiness of spirit; righteousness of life; disciplined purity; courage of the majestic face; gravity, modesty that goes fearless and tranquil and passionless; and, shining down upon all, the light of god-like Intellection.

All these noble qualities are to be reverenced and loved, no doubt, but what entitles them to be called beautiful?

They exist: they manifest themselves to us: anyone that sees them must admit that they have reality of Being; and is not Real-Being really beautiful?

But we have not yet shown by what property in them they have wrought the Soul to loveliness: what is this grace, this splendour as of Light, resting upon all the virtues?

Let us take the contrary, the ugliness of the Soul, and set that against its beauty: to understand, at once, what this ugliness is and how it comes to appear in the Soul will certainly open our way before us.

Let us then suppose an ugly Soul, dissolute, unrighteous: teeming with all the lusts; torn by internal discord; beset by the fears of its cowardice and the envies of its pettiness; thinking, in the little thought it has, only of the perishable and the base; perverse in all its impulses; the friend of unclean pleasures; living the life of abandonment to bodily sensation and delighting in its deformity.

What must we think but that all this shame is something that has gathered about the Soul, some foreign bane outraging it, soiling it, so that, encumbered with all manner of turpitude, it has no longer a clean activity or a clean sensation, but commands only a life smouldering dully under the crust of evil; that, sunk in manifold death, it no longer sees what a Soul should see, may no longer rest in its own being, dragged ever as it is towards the outer, the lower, the dark?

An unclean thing, I dare to say; flickering hither and thither at the call of objects of sense, deeply infected with the taint of body, occupied always in Matter, and absorbing Matter into itself; in its commerce with the Ignoble it has trafficked away for an alien nature its own essential Idea.

If a man has been immersed in filth or daubed with mud, his native comeliness disappears and all that is seen is the foul stuff besmearing him: his ugly condition is due to alien matter that has encrusted him, and if he is to win back his grace it must be his business to scour and purify himself and make himself what he was.

So, we may justly say, a Soul becomes ugly—by something foisted upon it, by sinking itself into the alien, by a fall, a descent into body, into Matter. The dishonour of the Soul is in its ceasing to be clean and apart. Gold is degraded when it is mixed with earthy particles; if these be worked out, the gold is left and is beautiful, isolated from all that is foreign, gold with gold alone. And so the Soul; let it be but cleared of the desires that come by its too intimate converse with the body, emancipated from all the passions, purged of all that embodiment has thrust upon it, withdrawn, a soli-

---

[1] Plotinus recalls here Socrates on love in Plato's *Phaedrus*.
[2] The Greek god known to Romans as Bacchus, identified with fertility rites, often orgiastic, and with the sources of the drama. See Nietzsche (below, page 687).

tary, to itself again—in that moment the ugliness that came only from the alien is stripped away.

6. For, as the ancient teaching was, moral-discipline and courage and every virtue, not even excepting Wisdom itself, all is purification.

Hence the Mysteries[3] with good reason adumbrate the immersion of the unpurified in filth, even in the Nether-World, since the unclean loves filth for its very filthiness, and swine foul of body find their joy in foulness.

What else is Sophrosyny, rightly so-called, but to take no part in the pleasures of the body, to break away from them as unclean and unworthy of the clean? So too, Courage is but being fearless of the death which is but the parting of the Soul from the body, an event which no one can dread whose delight is to be his unmingled self. And Magnanimity is but disregard for the lure of things here. And Wisdom is but the Act of the Intellectual-Principle withdrawn from the lower places and leading the Soul to the Above.

The Soul thus cleansed is all Idea and Reason, wholly free of body, intellective, entirely of that divine order from which the wellspring of Beauty rises and all the race of Beauty.

Hence the Soul heightened to the Intellectual-Principle is beautiful to all its power. For Intellection and all that proceeds from Intellection are the Soul's beauty, a graciousness native to it and not foreign, for only with these is it truly Soul. And it is just to say that in the Soul's becoming a good and beautiful thing is its becoming like to God, for from the Divine comes all the Beauty and all the Good in beings.

We may even say that Beauty *is* the Authentic-Existents and Ugliness is the Principle contrary to Existence: and the Ugly is also the primal evil; therefore its contrary is at once good and beautiful, or is Good and Beauty: and hence the one method will discover to us the Beauty-Good and the Ugliness-Evil.

And Beauty, this Beauty which is also The Good, must be posed as The First: directly deriving from this First is the Intellectual-Principle which is pre-eminently the manifestation of Beauty; through the Intellectual-Principle Soul is beautiful. The beauty in things of a lower order—actions and pursuits for instance—comes by operation of the shaping Soul which is also the author of the beauty found in the world of sense. For the Soul, a divine thing, a fragment as it were of the Primal Beauty, makes beautiful to the fullness of their capacity all things whatsoever that it grasps and moulds.

7. Therefore we must ascend again towards the Good, the desired of every Soul. Anyone that has seen This, knows what I intend when I say that it is beautiful. Even the desire of it is to be desired as a Good. To attain it is for those that will take the upward path, who will set all their forces towards it, who will divest themselves of all that we have put on in our descent: so, to those that approach the Holy Celebrations of the Mysteries, there are appointed purifications and the laying aside of the garments worn before, and the entry in nakedness—until, passing, on the upward way, all that is other than the God, each in the solitude of himself shall behold that solitary-dwelling Existence, the Apart, the Unmingled, the Pure, that from Which all things depend, for Which all look and live and act and know, the Source of Life and of Intellection and of Being.

And one that shall know this vision—with what passion of love shall he not be seized, with what pang of desire, what longing to be molten into one with This, what wondering delight! If he that has never seen this Being must hunger for It as for all his welfare, he that has known must love and reverence It as the very Beauty; he will be flooded with awe and gladness, stricken by a salutary terror; he loves with a veritable love, with sharp desire; all other loves than this he must despise, and disdain all that once seemed fair.

This, indeed, is the mood even of those who, having witnessed the manifestation of Gods or Supernals, can never again feel the old delight in the comeliness of material forms: what then are we to think of one that contemplates Absolute Beauty in Its essential integrity, no accumulation of flesh and matter, no dweller on earth or in the heavens—so perfect Its purity—far above all such things in that they are non-essential, composite, not primal but descending from This?

Beholding this Being—the Choragus of all Existence, the Self-Intent that ever gives forth and never takes—resting, rapt, in the vision and possession of so lofty a loveliness, growing to Its likeness, what Beauty can the Soul yet lack? For This, the Beauty supreme, the absolute, and the primal, fashions Its lovers to Beauty and makes them also worthy of love.

And for This, the sternest and the uttermost combat is set before the Souls; all our labour is for This, lest we be left without part in this noblest vision, which to attain is to be blessed in the blissful sight, which to fail of is to fail utterly.

For not he that has failed of the joy that is in colour or in visible forms, not he that has failed of power or of honours or of kingdom has failed, but only he that has failed of

---

[3]Greek religious rituals often associated with Delphi.

only This, for Whose winning he should renounce kingdoms and command over earth and ocean and sky, if only, spurning the world of sense from beneath his feet, and straining to This, he may see.

8. But what must we do? How lies the path? How come to vision of the inaccessible Beauty, dwelling as if in consecrated precincts, apart from the common ways where all may see, even the profane?

He that has the strength, let him arise and withdraw into himself, foregoing all that is known by the eyes, turning away for ever from the material beauty that once made his joy. When he perceives those shapes of grace that show in body, let him not pursue: he must know them for copies, vestiges, shadows, and hasten away towards That they tell of. For if anyone follow what is like a beautiful shape playing over water—is there not a myth telling in symbol of such a dupe, how he sank into the depths of the current and was swept away to nothingness? So too, one that is held by material beauty and will not break free shall be precipitated, not in body but in Soul, down to the dark depths loathed of the Intellective-Being, where, blind even in the Lower-World, he shall have commerce only with shadows, there as here.

'Let us flee then to the beloved Fatherland': this is the soundest counsel. But what is this flight? How are we to gain the open sea? For Odysseus is surely a parable to us when he commands the flight from the sorceries of Circe or Calypso—not content to linger for all the pleasure offered to his eyes and all the delight of sense filling his days.[4]

The Fatherland to us is There whence we have come, and There is The Father.

What then is our course, what the manner of our flight? This is not a journey for the feet; the feet bring us only from land to land; nor need you think of coach or ship to carry you away; all this order of things you must set aside and refuse to see: you must close the eyes and call instead upon another vision which is to be waked within you, a vision, the birth-right of all, which few turn to use.

9. And this inner vision, what is its operation?

Newly awakened it is all too feeble to bear the ultimate splendour. Therefore the Soul must be trained—to the habit of remarking, first, all noble pursuits, then the works of beauty produced not by the labour of the arts but by the

virtue of men known for their goodness: lastly, you must search the souls of those that have shaped these beautiful forms.

But how are you to see into a virtuous Soul and know its loveliness?

Withdraw into yourself and look. And if you do not find yourself beautiful yet, act as does the creator of a statue that is to be made beautiful: he cuts away here, he smoothes there, he makes this line lighter, this other purer, until a lovely face has grown upon his work. So do you also: cut away all that is excessive, straighten all that is crooked, bring light to all that is overcast, labour to make all one glow of beauty and never cease chiselling your statue, until there shall shine out on you from it the godlike splendour of virtue, until you shall see the perfect goodness surely established in the stainless shrine.

When you know that you have become this perfect work, when you are self-gathered in the purity of your being, nothing now remaining that can shatter that inner unity, nothing from without clinging to the authentic man, when you find yourself wholly true to your essential nature, wholly that only veritable Light which is not measured by space, not narrowed to any circumscribed form nor again diffused as a thing void of term, but ever unmeasurable as something greater than all measure and more than all quantity—when you perceive that you have grown to this, you are now become very vision: now call up all your confidence, strike forward yet a step—you need a guide no longer—strain, and see.

This is the only eye that sees the mighty Beauty. If the eye that adventures the vision be dimmed by vice, impure, or weak, and unable in its cowardly blenching to see the uttermost brightness, then it sees nothing even though another point to what lies plain to sight before it. To any vision must be brought an eye adapted to what is to be seen, and having some likeness to it. Never did eye see the sun unless it had first become sunlike, and never can the Soul have vision of the First Beauty unless itself be beautiful.

Therefore, first let each become godlike and each beautiful who cares to see God and Beauty. So, mounting, the Soul will come first to the Intellectual-Principle and survey all the beautiful Ideas in the Supreme and will avow that this is Beauty, that the Ideas are Beauty. For by their efficacy comes all Beauty else, by the offspring and essence of the Intellectual-Being. What is beyond the Intellectual-Principle we affirm to be the nature of Good radiating Beauty before it. So that, treating the Intellectual-Cosmos as one, the first is the Beautiful: if we make distinction there, the Realm of Ideas constitutes the Beauty of the Intellectual Sphere; and The Good, which lies beyond, is the Fountain at once and

[4]Porphyry (233–c. 305), follower and biographer of Plotinus, wrote a commentary on a part of *Odyssey* that carries out the idea of the work as an allegory.

Principle of Beauty: the Primal Good and the Primal Beauty have the one dwelling-place and, thus, always, Beauty's seat is There.

On the Intellectual Beauty

1. It is a principle with us that one who has attained to the vision of the Intellectual Cosmos and grasped the beauty of the Authentic Intellect will be able also to come to understand the Father and Transcendent of that Divine Being. It concerns us, then, to try to see and say, for ourselves and as far as such matters may be told, how the Beauty of the divine Intellect and of the Intellectual Cosmos may be revealed to contemplation.

Let us go to the realm of magnitudes:—suppose two blocks of stone lying side by side: one is unpatterned, quite untouched by art; the other has been minutely wrought by the craftsman's hands into some statue of god or man, a Grace or a Muse, or if a human being, not a portrait but a creation in which the sculptor's art has concentrated all loveliness.

Now it must be seen that the stone thus brought under the artist's hand to the beauty of form is beautiful not as stone—for so the crude block would be as pleasant—but in virtue of the Form or Idea introduced by the art. This form is not in the material; it is in the designer before ever it enters the stone; and the artificer holds it not by his equipment of eyes and hands but by his participation in his art. The beauty, therefore, exists in a far higher state in the art; for it does not come over integrally into the work; that original beauty is not transferred; what comes over is a derivative and a minor: and even that shows itself upon the statue not integrally and with entire realization of intention but only in so far as it has subdued the resistance of the material.

Art, then, creating in the image of its own nature and content, and working by the Idea or Reason-Principle of the beautiful object it is to produce, must itself be beautiful in a far higher and purer degree since it is the seat and source of that beauty, indwelling in the art, which must naturally be more complete than any comeliness of the external. In the degree in which the beauty is diffused by entering into matter, it is so much the weaker than that concentrated in unity; everything that reaches outwards is the less for it, strength less strong, heat less hot, every power less potent, and so beauty less beautiful.

Then again every prime cause must be, within itself, more powerful than its effect can be: the musical does not derive from an unmusical source but from music; and so the art exhibited in the material work derives from an art yet higher.[1]

Still the arts are not to be slighted on the ground that they create by imitation of natural objects; for, to begin with, these natural objects are themselves imitations; then, we must recognize that they give no bare reproduction of the thing seen but go back to the Reason-Principles from which Nature itself derives, and furthermore, that much of their work is all their own; they are holders of beauty and add where nature is lacking.[2] Thus Pheidias wrought the Zeus upon no model among things of sense but by apprehending what form Zeus must take if he chose to become manifest to sight.[3]

2. But let us leave the arts and consider those works produced by Nature and admitted to be naturally beautiful which the creations of art are charged with imitating, all reasoning life and unreasoning things alike, but especially the consummate among them, where the moulder and maker has subdued the material and given the form he desired. Now what is the beauty here? It has nothing to do with the blood or the menstrual process: either there is also a colour and form apart from all this or there is nothing unless sheer ugliness or (at best) a bare recipient, as it were the mere Matter of beauty.

Whence shone forth the beauty of Helen, battle-sought; or of all those women like in loveliness to Aphrodite; or of Aphrodite herself; or of any human being that has been perfect in beauty; or of any of these gods manifest to sight, or unseen but carrying what would be beauty if we saw?

In all these is it not the Idea, something of that realm but communicated to the produced from within the producer, just as in works of art, we held, it is communicated from the arts to their creations? Now we can surely not believe that, while the made thing and the Idea thus impressed upon Matter are beautiful, yet the Idea not so alloyed but resting still with the creator—the Idea primal, immaterial, firmly a unity—is not Beauty.

If material extension were in itself the ground of beauty, then the creating principle, being without extension, could not be beautiful: but beauty cannot be made to depend upon magnitude since, whether in a large object or a small, the one Idea equally moves and forms the mind by its inherent power. A further indication is that as long as the object

---

[1] As beauty moves outward and downward from the One through the artist to the materials he shapes, it becomes weaker.
[2] Plotinus seems to answer Plato directly here.
[3] The statue called *Olympian Zeus,* known only from descriptions by ancient writers, was among the most famous works of Phidias (c. 500–c. 432 B.C.).

remains outside us we know nothing of it; it affects us by entry; but only as an Idea can it enter through the eyes which are not of scope to take an extended mass: we are, no doubt, simultaneously possessed of the magnitude which, however, we take in not as mass but by an elaboration upon the presented form.[4]

Then again the principle producing the beauty must be, itself, ugly, neutral, or beautiful: ugly, it could not produce the opposite; neutral, why should its product be the one rather than the other? The Nature, then, which creates things so lovely must be itself of a far earlier[5] beauty; we, undisciplined in discernment of the inward, knowing nothing of it, run after the outer, never understanding that it is the inner[6] which stirs us; we are in the case of one who sees his own reflection but not realizing whence it comes goes in pursuit of it.

But that the thing we are pursuing is something different and that the beauty is not in the concrete object is manifest from the beauty there is in matters of study, in conduct and custom; briefly, in soul or mind. And it is precisely here that the greater beauty lies, perceived whenever you look to the wisdom in a man and delight in it, not wasting attention on the face, which may be hideous, but passing all appearance by and catching only at the inner comeliness, the truly personal; if you are still unmoved and cannot acknowledge beauty under such conditions, then looking to your own inner being you will find no beauty to delight you and it will be futile in that state to seek the greater vision, for you will be questing it through the ugly and impure.

This is why such matters are not spoken of to everyone; you, if you are conscious of beauty within, remember.

3. Thus there is in the Nature-Principle itself an Ideal archetype of the beauty that is found in material forms and, of that archetype again, the still more beautiful archetype in Soul, source of that in Nature. In the proficient soul this is brighter and of more advanced loveliness: adorning the soul and bringing to it a light from that greater light which is Beauty primally, its immediate presence sets the soul reflecting upon the quality of this prior, the archetype which has no such entries, and is present nowhere but remains in itself alone, and thus is not even to be called a Reason-Principle but is the creative source of the very first Reason-Principle which is the Beauty to which Soul serves as Matter.[7]

This prior, then, is the Intellectual-Principle,[8] the veritable, abiding and not fluctuant since not taking intellectual quality from outside itself. By what image, thus, can we represent it? We have nowhere to go but to what is less. Only from itself can we take an image of it; that is, there can be no representation of it, except in the sense that we represent gold by some portion of gold—purified, either actually or mentally, if it be impure—insisting at the same time that this is not the total thing gold, but merely the particular gold of a particular parcel. In the same way we learn in this matter from the purified Intellect in ourselves or, if you like, from the gods and the glory of the Intellect in them.

For assuredly all the gods are august and beautiful in a beauty beyond our speech. And what makes them so? Intellect; and especially Intellect operating within them (the divine sun and stars) to visibility. It is not through the loveliness of their corporeal forms: even those that have body are not gods by that beauty; it is in virtue of Intellect that they, too, are gods, and as gods beautiful. They do not veer between wisdom and folly: in the immunity of Intellect unmoving and pure, they are wise always, all-knowing, taking cognizance not of the human but of their own being and of all that lies within the contemplation of Intellect. Those of them whose dwelling is in the heavens are ever in this meditation—what task prevents them?—and from afar they look, too, into that further heaven by a lifting of the head. The gods belonging to that higher Heaven itself, they whose station is upon it and in it, see and know in virtue of their omnipresence to it. For all There[9] is heaven; earth is heaven, and sea heaven; and animal and plant and man; all is the heavenly content of that heaven: and the gods in it, despising neither men nor anything else that is there where all is of the heavenly order, traverse all that country and all space in peace.

4. To 'live at ease' is There; and to these divine beings verity is mother and nurse, existence and sustenance; all that is not of process but of authentic being they see, and themselves in all: for all is transparent, nothing dark, nothing re-

---

[4]This passage is interesting in connection with Aristotle's remark (above, page 56) and later theories of the sublime (for example, Burke, below, page 340, and Kant, below, page 434).

[5]Not temporally earlier in nature but eternal and outside time.

[6]"Inner" refers to that which is closer to the One, "outer" to that beyond spirit in matter.

[7]The movement from beauty to soul to nature-principle to matter is an outward movement away from the One toward greater diversity but less reality. The artist's struggle with matter is an effort to restore it to greater unity with the One by investing it with form. This may be compared to Aristotle's notion of improvement on nature (above, page 48), to Sidney's (below, page 186), and to Wilde's (below, p. 712).

[8]Again, not temporally.

[9]"There" is the condition of pure reality, pure Idea.

sistant; every being is lucid to every other, in breadth and depth; light runs through light. And each of them contains all within itself, and at the same time sees all in every other, so that everywhere there is all, and all is all and each all, and infinite the glory. Each of them is great; the small is great; the sun, There, is all the stars; and every star, again, is all the stars and sun. While some one manner of being is dominant in each, all are mirrored in every other.

Movement There is pure (as self-caused), for the moving principle is not a separate thing to complicate it as it speeds.

So, too, Repose is not troubled, for there is no admixture of the unstable; and the Beauty is all beauty since it is not resident in what is not beautiful. Each There walks upon no alien soil; its place is its essential self; and, as each moves, so to speak, towards what is Above, it is attended by the very ground from which it starts: there is no distinguishing between the Being and the Place; all is Intellect, the Principle and the ground on which it stands, alike. Thus we might think that our visible sky (the ground or place of the stars), lit as it is, produces the light which reaches us from it, though of course this is really produced by the stars (as it were, by the Principles of light alone, not also by the ground as the analogy would require).

In our realm[10] all is part rising from part and nothing can be more than partial; but There each being is an eternal product of a whole and is at once a whole and an individual manifesting as part but, to the keen vision There, known for the whole it is.

The myth of Lynceus seeing into the very deeps of the earth tells us of those eyes in the divine. No weariness overtakes this vision which yet brings no such satiety as would call for its ending; for there never was a void to be filled so that, with the fullness and the attainment of purpose, the sense of sufficiency be induced: nor is there any such incongruity within the divine that one Being There could be repulsive to another: and of course all There are unchangeable. This absence of satisfaction means only a satisfaction leading to no distaste for that which produces it; to see is to look the more, since for them to continue in the contemplation of an infinite self and of infinite objects is but to acquiesce in the bidding of their nature.

Life, pure, is never a burden; how then could there be weariness There where the living is most noble? That very life is wisdom, not a wisdom built up by reasonings but complete from the beginning, suffering no lack which could set it inquiring, a wisdom primal, unborrowed, not some-

thing added to the Being, but its very essence. No wisdom, thus, is greater; this is the authentic knowing, assessor to the divine Intellect as projected into manifestation simultaneously with it; thus, in the symbolic saying, Justice is assessor to Zeus.

(Perfect wisdom:) for all the Principles of this order, dwelling There, are as it were visible images projected from themselves, so that all becomes an object of contemplation to contemplators immeasurably blessed. The greatness and power of the wisdom There we may know from this, that it embraces all the real Beings, and has made all and all follow it, and yet that it is itself those beings, which sprang into being with it, so that all is one and the essence There is wisdom. If we have failed to understand, it is that we have thought of knowledge as a mass of theorems and an accumulation of propositions, though that is false even for our sciences of the sense-realm. But in case this should be questioned, we may leave our own sciences for the present, and deal with the knowing in the Supreme at which Plato glances where he speaks of 'that knowledge which is not a stranger in something strange to it'—though in what sense, he leaves us to examine and declare, if we boast ourselves worthy of the discussion. This is probably our best starting-point.

5. All that comes to be, work of nature or of craft, some wisdom has made: everywhere a wisdom presides at a making.

No doubt the wisdom of the artist may be the guide of the work; it is sufficient explanation of the wisdom exhibited in the arts; but the artist himself goes back, after all, to that wisdom in Nature which is embodied in himself; and this is not a wisdom built up of theorems but one totality, not a wisdom consisting of manifold detail co-ordinated into a unity but rather a unity working out into detail.[11]

Now, if we could think of this as the primal wisdom, we need look no further, since, at that, we have discovered a principle which is neither a derivative nor a 'stranger in something strange to it'. But if we are told that, while this Reason-Principle is in Nature, yet Nature itself is its source, we ask how Nature came to possess it; and, if Nature derived it from some other source, we ask what that other source may be; if, on the contrary, the principle is self-sprung, we need look no further: but if (as we assume) we are referred to the Intellectual-Principle we must make clear whether the Intellectual-Principle engendered the wisdom: if we learn that it did, we ask whence: if from itself, then inevitably it is itself Wisdom.

---

[10] The realm of matter and sense perception.

[11] Plotinus's vision of Plato's one and many.

The true Wisdom, then (found to be identical with the Intellectual-Principle), is Real Being; and Real Being is Wisdom; it is wisdom that gives value to Real Being; and Being is Real in virtue of its origin in wisdom. It follows that all forms of existence not possessing wisdom are, indeed, Beings in right of the wisdom which went to their forming, but, as not in themselves possessing it, are not Real Beings.

We cannot, therefore, think that the divine Beings of that sphere, or the other supremely blessed There, need look to our apparatus of science: all of that realm (the very Beings themselves), all is noble image, such images as we may conceive to lie within the soul of the wise—but There not as inscription but as authentic existence. The ancients had this in mind when they declared the Ideas (Forms) to be Beings, Essentials.

6. Similarly, as it seems to me, the wise of Egypt—whether in precise knowledge or by a prompting of nature—indicated the truth where, in their effort towards philosophical statement, they left aside the writing-forms that take in the detail of words and sentences—those characters that represent sounds and convey the propositions of reasoning—and drew pictures instead, engraving in the temple-inscriptions a separate image for every separate item: thus they exhibited the absence of discursiveness in the Intellectual Realm.

For each manifestation of knowledge and wisdom is a distinct image, an object in itself, an immediate unity, not an aggregate of discursive reasoning and detailed willing. Later from this wisdom in unity there appears, in another form of being, an image, already less compact, which announces the original in terms of discourse and unravels the causes by which things are such that the wonder rises how a generated world can be so excellent.

For, one who knows must declare his wonder that this wisdom, while not itself containing the causes by which Being exists and takes such excellence, yet imparts them to the entities produced according to its canons. This excellence, whose necessity is scarcely or not at all manifest to search, exists, if we could but find it out, before all searching and reasoning.

What I say may be considered in one chief thing, and thence applied to all the particular entities:

7. Consider the universe: we are agreed that its existence and its nature come to it from beyond itself; are we, now, to imagine that its maker first thought it out in detail—the earth, and its necessary situation in the middle; water and, again, its position as lying upon the earth; all the other elements and objects up to the sky in due place and order; living beings with their appropriate forms as we know them, their inner organs and their outer limbs—and that having thus appointed every item beforehand, he then set about the execution?

Such designing was not even possible; how could the plan for a universe come to one that had never looked outward? Nor could he work on material gathered from elsewhere as our craftsmen do, using hands and tools; feet and hands are of the later order.

One way, only, remains: all things must exist in something else; of that prior—since there is no obstacle, all being continuous within the realm of reality—there has suddenly appeared a sign, an image, whether given forth directly or through the ministry of soul or of some phase of soul matters nothing for the moment: thus the entire aggregate of existence springs from the divine world, in greater beauty There because There unmingled but mingled here.

From the beginning to end all is gripped by the Forms of the Intellectual Realm: Matter itself is held by the Ideas of the elements and to these Ideas are added other Ideas and others again, so that it is hard to work down to crude Matter beneath all that sheathing of Idea. Indeed since Matter itself is, in its degree, an Idea—the lowest—all this universe is Idea and there is nothing that is not Idea as the archetype was. And all is made silently, since nothing had part in the making but Being and Idea—a further reason why creation went without toil. The Exemplar was the Idea of an All and so an All must come into being.

Thus nothing stood in the way of the Idea, and even now it dominates, despite all the clash of things: the creation is not hindered on its way even now; it stands firm in virtue of being All. To me, moreover, it seems that if we ourselves were archetypes, Ideas, veritable Being, and the Idea with which we construct here were our veritable Essence, then our creative power, too, would toillessly effect its purpose: as man now stands, he does not produce in his work a true image of himself: become man, he has ceased to be the All; ceasing to be man—we read—'he soars aloft and administers the Cosmos entire'; restored to the All he is maker of the All.

But—to our immediate purpose—it is possible to give a reason why the earth is set in the midst and why it is round and why the ecliptic runs precisely as it does, but, looking to the creating principle, we cannot say that because this was the way therefore things were so planned: we can say only that because the Exemplar is what it is, therefore the things of this world are good; the causing principle, we might put it, reached the conclusion before all formal reasoning and not from any premises, not by sequence or plan but before either, since all of that order is later, all reason, demonstration, persuasion.

Since there is a Source, all the created must spring from it and in accordance with it; and we are rightly told not to go seeking the causes impelling a Source to produce, especially when this is the perfectly sufficient Source and identical with the Term: a Source which is Source and Term must be the All-Unity, complete in itself.

8. This then is Beauty primally: it is entire and omnipresent as an entirety; and therefore in none of its parts or members lacking in beauty; beautiful thus beyond denial. Certainly it cannot be anything (be, for example, Beauty) without being wholly that thing; it can be nothing which it is to possess partially or in which it utterly fails (and therefore it must entirely be Beauty entire).

If this principle were not beautiful, what other could be? Its prior does not deign to be beautiful; that which is the first to manifest itself—Form and object of vision to the intellect—cannot but be lovely to see. It is to indicate this that Plato, drawing on something well within our observation, represents the Creator as approving the work he has achieved: the intention is to make us feel the lovable beauty of the archetype and of the Divine Idea; for to admire a representation is to admire the original upon which it was made.

It is not surprising if we fail to recognize what is passing within us: lovers, and those in general that admire beauty here, do not stay to reflect that it is to be traced, as of course it must be, to the Beauty There. That the admiration of the Demiurge[12] is to be referred to the Ideal Exemplar is deliberately made evident by the rest of the passage: 'He admired; and determined to bring the work into still closer likeness with the Exemplar': he makes us feel the magnificent beauty of the Exemplar by telling us that the Beauty sprung from this world is, itself, a copy from That.

And indeed if the divine did not exist, the transcendently beautiful, in a beauty beyond all thought, what could be lovelier than the things we see? Certainly no reproach can rightly be brought against this world save only that it is not That.

9. Let us, then, make a mental picture of our universe: each member shall remain what it is, distinctly apart; yet all is to form, as far as possible, a complete unity so that whatever comes into view, say the outer orb of the heavens, shall bring immediately with it the vision, on the one plane, of the sun and of all the stars with earth and sea and all living things as if exhibited upon a transparent globe.

Bring this vision actually before your sight, so that there shall be in your mind the gleaming representation of a sphere, a picture holding all the things of the universe moving or in repose or (as in reality) some at rest, some in motion. Keep this sphere before you, and from it imagine another, a sphere stripped of magnitude and of spatial differences; cast out your inborn sense of Matter, taking care not merely to attenuate it: call on God, maker of the sphere whose image you now hold, and pray Him to enter. And may He come bringing His own Universe with all the gods that dwell in it—He who is the one God and all the gods, where each is all, blending into a unity, distinct in powers but all one god in virtue of that one divine power of many facets.

More truly, this is the one God who is all the gods; for, in the coming to be of all those, this, the one, has suffered no diminishing. He and all have one existence, while each again is distinct. It is distinction by state without interval: there is no outward form to set one here and another there and to prevent any from being an entire identity; yet there is no sharing of parts from one to another. Nor is each of those divine wholes a power in fragment, a power totalling to the sum of the measurable segments: the divine is one all-power, reaching out to infinity, powerful to infinity: and so great is God that his very members are infinites. What place can be named to which He does not reach?

Great, too, is this firmament of ours and all the powers constelled within it, but it would be greater still, unspeakably, but that there is inbound in it something of the petty power of body; no doubt the powers of fire and other bodily substances might themselves be thought very great, but in fact, it is through their failure in the true power that we see them burning, destroying, wearing things away, and slaving towards the production of life; they destroy because they are themselves in process of destruction, and they produce because they belong to the realm of the produced.

The power in that other world has merely Being and Beauty of Being. Beauty without Being could not be, nor Being voided of Beauty: abandoned of Beauty, Being loses something of its essence. Being is desirable because it is identical with Beauty; and Beauty is loved because it is Being. How then can we debate which is the cause of the other, where the nature is one? The very figment of Being needs some imposed image of Beauty to make it passable,[13] and even to ensure its existence; it exists to the degree in which it has taken some share in the beauty of Idea; and the more

---

[12] The secondary deity who made the world.

[13] Acceptable.

deeply it has drawn on this, the less imperfect it is, precisely because the nature which is essentially the beautiful has entered into it the more intimately.

10. This is why Zeus, although the oldest of the gods and their sovereign, advances first (in the Phaedrus myth) towards that vision, followed by gods and demigods and such souls as are of strength to see. That Being appears before them from some unseen place and rising loftily over them pours its light upon all things, so that all gleams in its radiance; it upholds some beings, and they see; the lower are dazzled and turn away, unfit to gaze upon that sun, the trouble falling the more heavily on those most remote.

Of those looking upon that Being and its content, and able to see, all take something but not all the same vision always: intently gazing, one sees the fount and principle of Justice, another is filled with the sight of Moral Wisdom, the original of that quality as found, sometimes at least, among men, copied by them in their degree from the divine virtue which, covering all the expanse, so to speak, of the Intellectual Realm is seen, last attainment of all, by those who have known already many splendid visions.

The gods see, each singly and all as one. So, too, the souls; they see all There in right of being sprung, themselves, of that universe and therefore including all from beginning to end and having their existence There if only by that phase which belongs inherently to the Divine, though often too they are There entire, those of them that have not incurred separation.

This vision Zeus takes and it is for such of us, also, as share his love and appropriate our part in the Beauty There, the final object of all seeing, the entire beauty upon all things; for all There sheds radiance, and floods those that have found their way thither so that they too become beautiful; thus it will often happen that men climbing heights where the soil has taken a yellow glow will themselves appear so, borrowing colour from the place on which they move. The colour flowering on that other height we speak of is Beauty; or rather all There is light and beauty, through and through, for the beauty is no mere bloom upon the surface.

To those that do not see entire, the immediate impression is alone taken into account; but those drunken with this wine, filled with the nectar, all their soul penetrated by this beauty, cannot remain mere gazers: no longer is there a spectator outside gazing on an outside spectacle; the clear-eyed hold the vision within themselves, though, for the most part, they have no idea that it is within but look towards it as to something beyond them and see it as an object of vision caught by a direction of the will.

All that one sees as a spectacle is still external; one must bring the vision within and see no longer in that mode of separation but as we know ourselves; thus a man filled with a god—possessed by Apollo or by one of the Muses—need no longer look outside for his vision of the divine being; it is but finding the strength to see divinity within.

11. Similarly any one, unable to see himself, but possessed by that God, has but to bring that divine-within before his consciousness and at once he sees an image of himself, himself lifted to a better beauty: now let him ignore that image, lovely though it is, and sink into a perfect self-identity, no such separation remaining; at once he forms a multiple unity with the God silently present; in the degree of his power and will, the two become one; should he turn back to the former duality, still he is pure and remains very near to the God; he has but to look again and the same presence is there.

This conversion brings gain: at the first stage, that of separation, a man is aware of self; but retreating inwards, he becomes possessor of all; he puts sense away behind him in dread of the separated life and becomes one in the Divine; if he plans to see in separation, he sets himself outside.

The novice must hold himself constantly under some image of the Divine Being and seek in the light of a clear conception; knowing thus, in a deep conviction, whither he is going—into what a sublimity he penetrates—he must give himself forthwith to the inner and, radiant with the Divine Intellections (with which he is now one), be no longer the seer, but, as that place has made him, the seen.

Still, we will be told, one cannot be in beauty and yet fail to see it. The very contrary: to see the divine as something external is to be outside of it; to become it is to be most truly in beauty: since sight deals with the external, there can here be no vision unless in the sense of identification with the object.

And this identification amounts to a self-knowing, a self-consciousness, guarded by the fear of losing the self in the desire of a too wide awareness.

It must be remembered that sensations of the ugly and evil impress us more violently than those of what is agreeable and yet leave less knowledge as the residue of the shock: sickness makes the rougher mark, but health, tranquilly present, explains itself better; it takes the first place, it is the natural thing, it belongs to our being; illness is alien, unnatural, and thus makes itself felt by its very incongruity, while the other conditions are native and we take no notice. Such being our nature, we are most completely aware of ourselves when we are most completely identified with the object of our knowledge.

This is why in that other sphere, when we are deepest in that knowledge by intellection, we are aware of none; we are expecting some impression on sense, which has nothing to report since it has seen nothing and never could in that order see anything. The unbelieving element is sense; it is the other, the Intellectual-Principle, that sees; and if this too doubted, it could not even credit its own existence, for it can never stand away and with bodily eyes apprehend itself as a visible object.

12. We have told how this vision is to be procured, whether by the mode of separation or in identity: now, seen in either way, what does it give to report?

The vision has been of God in travail of a beautiful offspring, God engendering a universe within himself in a painless labour and—rejoiced in what he has brought into being, proud of his children—keeping all closely by Him, for the pleasure He has in his radiance and in theirs.

Of this offspring—all beautiful, but most beautiful those that have remained within—only one has become manifest without; from him (Zeus, sovran over the visible universe), the youngest born, we may gather, as from some image, the greatness of the Father and of the Brothers that remain within the Father's house.

Still the manifested God cannot think that he has come forth in vain from the father; for through him another universe has arisen, beautiful as the image of beauty, and it could not be lawful that Beauty and Being should fail of a beautiful image.

This second Cosmos at every point copies the archetype: it has life and being in copy, and has beauty as springing from that diviner world. In its character of image it holds, too, that divine perpetuity without which it would only at times be truly representative and sometimes fail like a construction of art; for every image whose existence lies in the nature of things must stand during the entire existence of the archetype.

Hence it is false to put an end to the visible sphere as long as the Intellectual endures, or to found it upon a decision taken by its maker at some given moment.

That teaching shirks the penetration of such a making as is here involved: it fails to see that as long as the Supreme is radiant there can be no failing of its sequel but, that exist-ing, all exists. And—since the necessity of conveying our meaning compels such terms—the Supreme has existed for ever and for ever will exist.

13. The God fettered (as in the Kronos[14] Myth) to an unchanging identity leaves the ordering of this universe to his son (to Zeus), for it could not be in his character to neglect his rule within the divine sphere, and, as though sated with the Authentic-Beauty, seek a lordship too recent and too poor for his might. Ignoring this lower world, Kronos (Intellectual-Principle) claims for himself his own father (Ouranos,[15] the Absolute, or One) with all the upward-tending between them: and he counts all that tends to the inferior, beginning from his son (Zeus, the All-Soul), as ranking beneath him. Thus he holds a mid-position determined on the one side by the differentiation implied in the severance from the very highest and, on the other, by that which keeps him apart from the link between himself and the lower: he stands between a greater father and an inferior son. But since that father is too lofty to be thought of under the name of Beauty, the second God remains the primally beautiful.

Soul also has beauty, but is less beautiful than Intellect as being its image and therefore, though beautiful in nature, taking increase of beauty by looking to that original. Since then the All-Soul—to use the more familiar term—since Aphrodite[16] herself is so beautiful, what name can we give to that other? If Soul is so lovely in its own right, of what quality must that prior be? And since its being is derived, what must that power be from which the Soul takes the double beauty, the borrowed and the inherent?

We ourselves possess beauty when we are true to our own being; our ugliness is in going over to another order; our self-knowledge, that is to say, is our beauty; in self-ignorance we are ugly.

Thus beauty is of the Divine and comes Thence only.

Do these considerations suffice to a clear understanding of the Intellectual Sphere or must we make yet another attempt by another road?

---

[14] Kronos, the Titan who ruled before being unseated by Zeus.
[15] Ouranus, who ruled before being dethroned by Kronos.
[16] Aphrodite, Greek goddess of love and beauty.

Saint Augustine

354–430

On Christian Doctrine brings Augustine to the attention of semioticians and literary theorists. Thought about the sign is not new with him, but he formulated a theory of it that gave it particular importance in the tradition of Christian interpretation of Scripture and paved the way for later elaborate theories of allegory, such as those we see in Saint Thomas Aquinas (below, page 149) and Dante (below, page 153). For Augustine, signs are "things used to signify something," and words are things the whole use of which is signification. But if all signs are things, not all things are signs. Here he seems to resist any elaborate construction of a complete theory of "correspondences" such as is found in certain later mystics and symbolist critics like Baudelaire (below, page 604), where all nature is an occult language. A sign is important because it points to something else, and that something is ultimately for Augustine the Trinity of Father, Son, and Holy Ghost. The sign, therefore, is not valuable as pleasurable in itself but rather in its movement of signification toward God. Signs cannot embody God, however, because God is ineffable. When Augustine speaks of enjoyment it is not enjoyment of the aesthetic surface of the sign, but of its ultimate signified. This view leads to concepts of allegory in medieval criticism in which the surface hides, but then yields, a depth of intellectual beauty. Thus Augustine is a predecessor of recent secular valorizations of allegory over symbolism, the former of which implies a difference between sign and signified and the latter of which implies the signified incarnate in the symbol.

Augustine's treatment of a passage from the Song of Solomon in the selection below has been much cited. In it he reads the passage allegorically and admits failure to understand fully why the passage's figurative language gives him more pleasure than a nonfigurative expression of the same idea would. He tentatively ventures that what is discovered with difficulty gives pleasure, this notion being frequently repeated even into Renaissance criticism. The distinction that Augustine draws between the natural and the conventional sign leads in later language theory to the arbitrary nature of the linguistic sign, as in Locke (below, page 281) and Saussure (below, page 786).

Saint Augustine's works (in Latin) are collected in *Opera omnia* (1836–1838). See H. J. Marrou, *Saint Augustin et la fin de la culture antique* (1938); Étienne Gilson, *Introduction à l' étude de saint Augustin* (1939); R. W. Battenhouse et al., *A Companion to the Study of St. Augustine* (1955); Peter Brown, *Augustine of Hippo: A Biography* (1967); Robert A. Markus, ed., *Augustine: A Collection of Critical Essays* (contains B. D. Jackson's "The Theory of Signs in St. Augustine's *De doctrina Christiana*") (1972); Robert E. Meagher, *An Introduction to St. Augustine* (1972); Robert J. O'Connell, *Art and Christian Intelligence in St. Augustine* (1978); Henry Chadwick, *Augustine* (1986); Carol Harrison, *Beauty and Revelation in the Thought of Saint Augustine* (1992); Gary Wills, *Saint Augustine* (1999).

from

On Christian Doctrine

from

Book One

I

1. There are two things necessary to the treatment of the Scriptures: a way of discovering those things which are to be understood, and a way of teaching what we have learned. We shall speak first of discovery and second of teaching. This is a great and arduous work, and since it is difficult to sustain, I fear some temerity in undertaking it. It would be thus indeed if I relied on myself alone, but now while the hope of completing such a work lies in Him from whom I have received much concerning these things in thought, it is not to be feared that He will cease giving me more when I have begun to use what He has already given me. Everything which does not decrease on being given away is not properly owned when it is owned and not given. For He says, "He that hath, to him shall be given."[1] Therefore He will give to those that have, that is, to those benevolently using that which they have received He will increase and heap up what He gives. There were at one time five loaves and at another time seven before they began to be given to the needy;[2] and when this began to be done, baskets and hampers were filled, although thousands of men were fed. Just as the loaves increased when they were broken, the Lord has granted those things necessary to the beginning of this work, and when they begin to be given out they will be multiplied by His inspiration, so that in this task of mine I shall not only suffer no poverty of ideas but shall rejoice in wonderful abundance.

II

2. All doctrine concerns either things or signs, but things are learned by signs. Strictly speaking, I have here called a "thing" that which is not used to signify something else, like wood, stone, cattle, and so on; but not that wood concerning which we read that Moses cast it into bitter waters that their bitterness might be dispelled,[3] nor that stone which Jacob placed at his head,[4] nor that beast which Abraham sacrificed in place of his son.[5] For these are things in such a way that they are also signs of other things.[6] There are other signs whose whole use is in signifying, like words. For no one uses words except for the purpose of signifying something. From this may be understood what we call "signs"; they are things used to signify something. Thus every sign is also a thing, for that which is not a thing is nothing at all; but not every thing is also a sign. And thus in this distinction between things and signs, when we speak of things, we shall so speak that, although some of them may be used to signify something else, this fact shall not disturb the arrangement we have made to speak of things as such first and of signs later. We should bear in mind that now we are to consider what things are, not what they signify beyond themselves.

III

3. Some things are to be enjoyed, others to be used, and there are others which are to be enjoyed and used. Those things which are to be enjoyed make us blessed. Those things which are to be used help and, as it were, sustain us as we move toward blessedness in order that we may gain and cling to those things which make us blessed. If we who enjoy and use things, being placed in the midst of things of both kinds, wish to enjoy those things which should be used, our course will be impeded and sometimes deflected, so that we are retarded in obtaining those things which are to be enjoyed, or even prevented altogether, shackled by an inferior love.

IV

4. To enjoy something is to cling to it with love for its own sake. To use something, however, is to employ it in obtaining that which you love, provided that it is worthy of love. For an illicit use should be called rather a waste or an abuse. Suppose we were wanderers who could not live in blessedness except at home, miserable in our wandering and

---

Saint Augustine's *On Christian Doctrine* was begun in about 396 and completed in 426. The text is from W. D. Robertson, Jr., tr., *On Christian Doctrine* (New York: Macmillan Publishing Co., 1958).

[1] [Robertson] Matt. 13.12.
[2] [Robertson] Matt. 14.17; 215.34.

[3] [Robertson] Exod. 15.25.
[4] [Robertson] Gen. 28.11.
[5] [Robertson] Gen. 22.13.
[6] That is, typological allegory. See Aquinas (below, page 151). [Robertson] According to St. Augustine the "wood" is a sign of the cross. The "stone" and the "beast" represent the human nature of Christ.

desiring to end it and to return to our native country. We would need vehicles for land and sea which could be used to help us to reach our homeland, which is to be enjoyed. But if the amenities of the journey and the motion of the vehicles itself delighted us, and we were led to enjoy those things which we should use, we should not wish to end our journey quickly, and, entangled in a perverse sweetness, we should be alienated from our country, whose sweetness would make us blessed. Thus in this mortal life, wandering from God,[7] if we wish to return to our native country where we can be blessed we should use this world and not enjoy it, so that the "invisible things" of God "being understood by the things that are made"[8] may be seen, that is, so that by means of corporal and temporal things we may comprehend the eternal and spiritual.

V

5. The things which are to be enjoyed are the Father, the Son, and the Holy Spirit, a single Trinity, a certain supreme thing common to all who enjoy it, if, indeed, it is a thing and not rather the cause of all things, or both a thing and a cause. It is not easy to find a name proper to such excellence, unless it is better to say that this Trinity is one God and that "of him, and by him, and in him are all things."[9] Thus there are the Father, the Son, and the Holy Spirit, and each is God, and at the same time all are one God; and each of them is a full substance, and at the same time all are one substance. The Father is neither the Son nor the Holy Spirit; the Son is neither the Father nor the Holy Spirit; the Holy Spirit is neither the Father nor the Son. But the Father is the Father uniquely; the Son is the Son uniquely; and the Holy Spirit is the Holy Spirit uniquely. All three have the same eternity, the same immutability, the same majesty, and the same power. In the Father is unity, in the Son equality, and in the Holy Spirit a concord of unity and equality; and these three qualities are all one because of the Father, all equal because of the Son, and all united because of the Holy Spirit.

VI

6. Have we spoken or announced anything worthy of God? Rather I feel that I have done nothing but wish to speak: if I have spoken, I have not said what I wished to

say. Whence do I know this, except because God is ineffable? If what I said were ineffable, it would not be said. And for this reason God should not be said to be ineffable, for when this is said something is said. And a contradiction in terms is created, since if that is ineffable which cannot be spoken, then that is not ineffable which can be called ineffable. This contradiction is to be passed over in silence rather than resolved verbally. For God, although nothing worthy may be spoken of Him, has accepted the tribute of the human voice and wished us to take joy in praising Him with our words. In this way he is called *Deus*. Although He is not recognized in the noise of these two syllables, all those who know the Latin language, when this sound reaches their ears, are moved to think of a certain most excellent immortal nature.

* * *

XXXV

39. The sum of all we have said since we began to speak of things thus comes to this: it is to be understood that the plenitude and the end of the Law and of all the sacred Scriptures is the love of a Being which is to be enjoyed and of a being that can share that enjoyment with us, since there is no need for a precept that anyone should love himself. That we might know this and have the means to implement it, the whole temporal dispensation was made by divine Providence for our salvation. We should use it, not with an abiding but with a transitory love and delight like that in a road or in vehicles or in other instruments, or, if it may be expressed more accurately, so that we love those things by which we are carried along for the sake of that toward which we are carried.

XXXVI

40. Whoever, therefore, thinks that he understands the divine Scriptures or any part of them so that it does not build the double love of God and of our neighbor does not understand it at all. Whoever finds a lesson there useful to the building of charity, even though he has not said what the author may be shown to have intended in that place, has not been deceived, nor is he lying in any way. Lying involves the will to speak falsely; thus we find many who wish to lie, but no one who wishes to be deceived. Since a man lies knowingly but suffers deception unwittingly, it is obvious that in a given instance a man who is deceived is better than a man who lies, because it is better to suffer iniquity than to perform it. Everyone who lies commits iniquity, and if anyone thinks a lie may sometimes be useful, he must think that

[7][Robertson] Cf. 2 Cor. 5.6 (Vulg.).
[8][Robertson] Rom. 1.20.
[9][Robertson] Rom. 1.36.

iniquity is sometimes useful also. But no one who lies keeps faith concerning that about which he lies. For he wishes that the person to whom he lies should have that faith in him which he does not himself keep when he lies. But every violator of faith is iniquitous. Either iniquity is sometimes useful, which is impossible, or a lie is always useless.

41. But anyone who understands in the Scriptures something other than that intended by them is deceived, although they do not lie. However, as I began to explain, if he is deceived in an interpretation which builds up charity, which is the end of the commandments, he is deceived in the same way as a man who leaves a road by mistake but passes through a field to the same place toward which the road itself leads. But he is to be corrected and shown that it is more useful not to leave the road, lest the habit of deviating force him to take a crossroad or a perverse way.

XXXVII

In asserting rashly that which the author before him did not intend, he may find many other passages which he cannot reconcile with his interpretation. If he acknowledges these to be true and certain, his first interpretation cannot be true, and under these conditions it happens, I know not why, that, loving his own interpretation, he begins to become angrier with the Scriptures than he is with himself. And if he thirsts persistently for the error, he will be overcome by it. "For we walk by faith and not by sight,"[10] and faith will stagger if the authority of the Divine Scriptures wavers. Indeed, if faith staggers, charity itself languishes. And if anyone should fall from faith, it follows that he falls also from charity, for a man cannot love that which he does not believe to exist. On the other hand, a man who both believes and loves, by doing well and by obeying the rules of good customs, may bring it about that he may hope to arrive at that which he loves. Thus there are these three things for which all knowledge and prophecy struggle: faith, hope, and charity.

XXXVIII

42. But the vision we shall see will replace faith, and that blessedness to which we are to come will replace hope; and when these things are falling away, charity will be increased even more. If we love in faith what we have not seen, how much more will we love it when we begin to see it? And if we love in hope what we have not attained, how

much more will we love it when we have attained it? Between temporal and eternal things there is this difference: a temporal thing is loved more before we have it, and it begins to grow worthless when we gain it, for it does not satisfy the soul, whose true and certain rest is eternity; but the eternal is more ardently loved when it is acquired than when it is merely desired. It is possible for no one desiring it to expect it to be more valuable than it actually is so that he may find it less worthy than he expected it to be. However highly anyone approaching it may value it, he will find it more valuable when he attains it.

XXXIX

43. Thus a man supported by faith, hope, and charity, with an unshaken hold upon them, does not need the Scriptures except for the instruction of others. And many live by these three things in solitude without books. Whence in these persons I think the saying is already exemplified, "whether prophecies shall be made void, or tongues shall cease, or knowledge shall be destroyed."[11] In them, as if by instruments of faith, hope, and charity, such an erudition has been erected that, holding fast to that which is perfect, they do not seek that which is only partially so[12]—perfect, that is, in so far as perfection is possible in this life. For in comparison with the life to come, the life of no just and holy man is perfect here. Hence "there remain," he says, "faith, hope, and charity, these three: but the greatest of these is charity."[13] And when anyone shall reach the eternal, two of these having fallen away, charity will remain more certain and more vigorous.

XL

44. Therefore, when anyone knows the end of the commandments to be charity "from a pure heart, and a good conscience, and an unfeigned faith,"[14] and has related all of his understanding of the Divine Scriptures to these three, he may approach the treatment of these books with security. For when he says "charity" he adds "from a pure heart," so that nothing else would be loved except that which should be loved. And he joins with this "a good conscience" for the sake of hope, for he in whom there is the smallest taint of bad conscience despairs of attaining that which he believes

---

[10] [Robertson] 2 Cor. 5.7.

[11] [Robertson] 1 Cor. 13.8.
[12] [Robertson] 1 Cor. 13.10.
[13] [Robertson] 1 Cor. 13.13.
[14] [Robertson] 1 Tim. 1.5.

in and loves. Third, he says "an unfeigned faith." If our faith involves no lie, then we do not love that which is not be loved, and living justly, we hope for that which will in no way deceive our hope.

With this I have said as much as I wished to say concerning faith at the present time, since in other books either by others or by myself much has already been said. Then may this be the limit to this book. In the remainder we shall discuss signs, in so far as God has granted us ability.

from
Book Two

I

1. Just as I began, when I was writing about things, by warning that no one should consider them except as they are, without reference to what they signify beyond themselves, now when I am discussing signs I wish it understood that no one should consider them for what they are but rather for their value as signs which signify something else. A sign is a thing which causes us to think of something beyond the impression the thing itself makes upon the senses. Thus if we see a track, we think of the animal that made the track; if we see smoke, we know that there is a fire which causes it; if we hear the voice of a living being, we attend to the emotion it expresses; and when a trumpet sounds, a soldier should know whether it is necessary to advance or to retreat, or whether the battle demands some other response.

2. Among signs, some are natural and others are conventional. Those are natural which, without any desire or intention of signifying, make us aware of something beyond themselves, like smoke which signifies fire. It does this without any will to signify, for even when smoke appears alone, observation and memory of experience with things bring a recognition of an underlying fire. The track of a passing animal belongs to this class, and the face of one who is wrathful or sad signifies his emotion even when he does not wish to show that he is wrathful or sad, just as other emotions are signified by the expression even when we do not deliberately set out to show them. But it is not proposed here to discuss signs of this type. Since the class formed a division of my subject, I could not disregard it completely, and this notice of it will suffice.

II

3. Conventional signs are those which living creatures show to one another for the purpose of conveying, in so far

as they are able, the motion of their spirits or something which they have sensed or understood. Nor is there any other reason for signifying, or for giving signs, except for bringing forth and transferring to another mind the action of the mind in the person who makes the sign. We propose to consider and to discuss this class of signs in so far as men are concerned with it, for even signs given by God and contained in the Holy Scriptures are of this type also, since they were presented to us by the men who wrote them. Animals also have signs which they use among themselves, by means of which they indicate their appetites. For a cock who finds food makes a sign with his voice to the hen so that she runs to him. And the dove calls his mate with a cry or is called by her in turn, and there are many similar examples which may be adduced. Whether these signs, or the expression or cry of a man in pain, express the motion of the spirit without intention of signifying or are truly shown as signs is not in question here and does not pertain to our discussion, and we remove this division of the subject from this work as superfluous.

III

4. Among the signs by means of which men express their meanings to one another, some pertain to the sense of sight, more to the sense of hearing, and very few to the other senses. For when we nod, we give a sign only to the sight of the person whom we wish by that sign to make a participant in our will. Some signify many things through the motions of their hands, and actors give signs to those who understand with the motions of all their members as if narrating things to their eyes. And banners and military standards visibly indicate the will of the captains. And all of these things are like so many visible words. More signs, as I have said, pertain to the ears, and most of these consist of words. But the trumpet, the flute, and the harp make sounds which are not only pleasing but also significant, although as compared with the number of verbal signs the number of signs of this kind are few. For words have come to be predominant among men for signifying whatever the mind conceives if they wish to communicate it to anyone. However, Our Lord gave a sign with the odor of the ointment with which His feet were anointed;[15] and the taste of the sacrament of His body and blood signified what He wished;[16] and when the woman was healed by touching the hem of His garment,[17] something was signified. Nevertheless, a multi-

---

[15] [Robertson] John 12.3–8. For the "odor of the ointment," see 3. 12. 18.
[16] [Robertson] Matt. 26.28; Luke 22.19–20.
[17] [Robertson] Matt. 9.20–22.

tude of innumerable signs by means of which men express their thoughts is made up of words. And I could express the meaning of all signs of the type here touched upon in words, but I would not be able at all to make the meanings of words clear by these signs.

IV

5. But because vibrations in the air soon pass away and remain no longer than they sound, signs of words have been constructed by means of letters. Thus words are shown to the eyes, not in themselves but through certain signs which stand for them. These signs could not be common to all peoples because of the sin of human dissension which arises when one people seizes the leadership for itself. A sign of this pride is that tower erected in the heavens where impious men deserved that not only their minds but also their voices should be dissonant.[18]

V

6. Thus it happened that even the Sacred Scripture, by which so many maladies of the human will are cured, was set forth in one language, but so that it could be spread conveniently through all the world it was scattered far and wide in the various languages of translators that it might be known for the salvation of peoples who desired to find in it nothing more than the thoughts and desires of those who wrote it and through these the will of God, according to which we believe those writers spoke.

VI

7. But many and varied obscurities and ambiguities deceive those who read casually, understanding one thing instead of another: indeed, in certain places they do not find anything to interpret erroneously, so obscurely are certain sayings covered with a most dense mist. I do not doubt that this situation was provided by God to conquer pride by work and to combat disdain in our minds, to which those things which are easily discovered seem frequently to become worthless. For example, it may be said that there are holy and perfect men with whose lives and customs as an exemplar the Church of Christ is able to destroy all sorts of superstitions in those who come to it and to incorporate them into itself, men of good faith, true servants of God, who putting aside the burden of the world, come to the holy

laver of baptism and ascending thence, conceive through the Holy Spirit and produce the fruit of a twofold love of God and their neighbor. But why is it, I ask, that if anyone says this he delights his hearers less than if he had said the same thing in expounding that place in the Canticle of Canticles where it is said of the Church, as she is being praised as a beautiful woman, "Thy teeth are as flocks of sheep, that are shorn, which come up from the washing, all with twins, and there is none barren among them"?[19] Does one learn anything else besides that which he learns when he hears the same thought expressed in plain words without this similitude? Nevertheless, in a strange way, I contemplate the saints more pleasantly when I envisage them as the teeth of the Church cutting off men from their errors and transferring them to her body after their hardness has been softened as if by being bitten and chewed. I recognize them most pleasantly as shorn sheep having put aside the burdens of the world like so much fleece, and as ascending from the washing, which is baptism, all to create twins, which are the two precepts of love, and I see no one of them sterile of this holy fruit.

8. But why it seems sweeter to me than if no such similitude were offered in the divine books, since the thing perceived is the same, is difficult to say and is a problem for another discussion.[20] For the present, however, no one doubts that things are perceived more readily through similitudes and that what is sought with difficulty is discovered with more pleasure. Those who do not find what they seek directly stated labor in hunger; those who do not seek because they have what they wish at once frequently become indolent in disdain. In either of these situations indifference is an evil. Thus the Holy Spirit has magnificently and wholesomely modulated the Holy Scriptures so that the more open places present themselves to hunger and the more obscure places may deter a disdainful attitude. Hardly anything may be found in these obscure places which is not found plainly said elsewhere.

* * *

VIII

12. But let us turn our attention to the third step which I have decided to treat as the Lord may direct my discourse. He will be the most expert investigator of the Holy Scriptures who has first read all of them and has some knowledge of them, at least through reading them if not through

---

[18][Robertson] Cf. Gen. 11.1–9.

[19][Robertson] Cant. (Song of Sol.) 4.2.
[20]Here Augustine fails to enter into speculation about the power of tropes.

understanding them. That is, he should read those that are said to be canonical. For he may read the others more securely when he has been instructed in the truth of the faith so that they may not preoccupy a weak mind nor, deceiving it with vain lies and fantasies, prejudice it with something contrary to sane understanding. In the matter of canonical Scriptures he should follow the authority of the greater number of catholic Churches, among which are those which have deserved to have apostolic seats and to receive epistles. He will observe this rule concerning canonical Scriptures, that he will prefer those accepted by all catholic Churches to those which some do not accept; among those which are not accepted by all, he should prefer those which are accepted by the largest number of important Churches to those held by a few minor Churches of less authority. If he discovers that some are maintained by the larger number of Churches, others by the Churches of weightiest authority, although this condition is not likely, he should hold them to be of equal value.

* * *

IX

14. In all of these books those fearing God and made meek in piety seek the will of God. And the first rule of this undertaking and labor is, as we have said, to know these books even if they are not understood, at least to read them or to memorize them, or to make them not altogether unfamiliar to us. Then those things which are put openly in them either as precepts for living or as rules for believing are to be studied more diligently and more intelligently, for the more one learns about these things the more capable of understanding he becomes. Among those things which are said

openly in Scripture are to be found all those teachings which involve faith, the mores of living, and that hope and charity which we have discussed in the previous book. Then, having become familiar with the language of the Divine Scriptures, we should turn to those obscure things which must be opened up and explained so that we may take examples from those things that are manifest to illuminate those things which are obscure, bringing principles which are certain to bear on our doubts concerning those things which are uncertain. In this undertaking memory is of great value, for if it fails rules will not be of any use.

X

15. There are two reasons why things written are not understood: they are obscured either by unknown or by ambiguous signs. For signs are either literal or figurative. They are called literal when they are used to designate those things on account of which they were instituted; thus we say *bos* [ox] when we mean an animal of a herd because all men using the Latin language call it by that name just as we do. Figurative signs occur when that thing which we designate by a literal sign is used to signify something else; thus we say "ox" and by that syllable understand the animal which is ordinarily designated by that word, but again by that animal we understand an evangelist, as is signified in the Scripture, according to the interpretation of the Apostle, when it says, "Thou shalt not muzzle the ox that treadeth out the corn."[21]

---

[21] [Robertson] Deut. 25.4. For the apostolic interpretation, see 1 Cor. 9.9; 1 Tim. 5.18.

Anicus Manlius
Severinus Boethius

c.480–524 or 525

Boethius wrote the *Consolation of Philosophy* in prison under sentence of death. A philosopher and Roman statesman under Theodoric, he fell out of favor and was savagely executed. His book became very popular in the Middle Ages and was translated into English by Geoffrey Chaucer. At one time, Boethius set out to translate all of both Plato and Aristotle into Latin, and he hoped eventually to produce a philosophy that transcended their differences. In the end, however, the influence of Plato was stronger. The selection below, from near the beginning of Book I, indicates that the ancient quarrel between philosophy and poetry that Plato's Socrates spoke of (above, page 36) continued into Boethius's time and that Boethius regarded poetry as dangerous because it fed the passions. But Boethius also had religious reasons for his suspicion of the Muses of Poetry. One was that the Muses were pagan; and another was that the arts catered to sensual and earthly interests. In the Christian ascetic view of the time, the arts were considered trivial at best in comparison with theological pursuits. Boethius followed the Church Fathers generally in his suspicion of art.

But there is an odd ambivalence reflected in the makeup of Boethius's book, for it includes thirty-nine poems, all in positions of emphasis, interspersed in a dialogue between Boethius and the Muse of Philosophy. Sometimes these poems are spoken by Philosophy herself. Boethius's attack here is one of the best known after Plato in which the criticism of poetry is balanced to some extent, if not by praise, at least by rhetorical acts that temper the attack itself.

Boethius also wrote dissertations on music and arithmetic, in which one finds traditional classical emphasis on harmony and abstract formal order. Here again the roots of Boethius's aesthetic are Platonic and, through Saint Augustine's *De Musica*, Pythagorean.

A useful abridged version of the *Consolation* is the edition by J. J. Buchanan (1957), which can be compared with the more recent complete Penguin editon translated by V. E. Watts (1969). See H. M. Barrett, *Boethius: Some Aspects of His Times and Work* (1940); Margaret Gibson, ed., *Boethius: His Life, Thought, and Influence* (1981); Henry Chadwick, *Boethius: The Consolations of Music, Logic, Theology, and Philosophy* (1981); Edmund Reiss, *Boethius* (1982); Seth Lever, *Boethius and Dialogue* (1985); Gerard O'Daley, *The Poetry of Boethius* (1991).

from

The Consolation of Philosophy

Book I

Prose I: Philosophy Approaches Boethius: The Form of Her Appearance Is Allegorical

While I was pondering thus in silence and using my pen to set down my tearful complaint, there appeared to me standing overhead a woman whose countenance was full of majesty, whose gleaming eyes surpassed in power of insight those of ordinary mortals, whose color was full of life, and whose strength was still intact though she was so full of years that by no means would it be believed that she was of our times. One could but doubt her varying stature, for at one moment she repressed it to the common measure of man, at another she seemed to touch with her crown the very heavens; and when she raised her head higher it pierced even the sky and baffled the sight of those who would look upon it. Her clothes were wrought of the finest thread by subtle workmanship into an indissoluble material. These she had woven with her own hands, as I learned afterwards from her own disclosure. Their color was somewhat dimmed by the dullness of long neglect, as happens likewise in the case of smoke-grimed death masks. On the border below was woven the symbol Π, on that above was to be read

a Θ.[1] And between the two letters there could be seen degrees by which, as by the rungs of a ladder, ascent might be made from the lower principle to the higher. Yet the hands of certain rough men had torn this garment and had snatched such pieces as they could therefrom. In her right hand she carried books; in her left she brandished a scepter.

When she saw that the Muses of poetry were present by my couch giving words to my lamenting, she was stirred a while; her eyes flashed fiercely as she said: "Who has suffered these seducing mummers[2] to approach this sick man? Never have they nursed his sorrowings with any remedies, but rather fostered them with poisonous sweets. These are they who stifle the fruit-bearing harvest of reason with the barren briars of the passions; they do not free the minds of men from disease but accustom them thereto. I would think it less grievous if your allurements drew away from me some common man like those of the vulgar herd, seeing that in such a one my labors would be harmed not at all. But this man has been nurtured in the lore of Eleatics and Academics.[3] Away with you, sirens, seductive even to perdition, and leave him to my Muses to be cared for and healed!"

Thus rebuked, that band cast a saddened glance upon the ground, confessing their shame in blushes, and passed forth dismally over the threshold.

Boethius wrote *Consolatione Philosophiae* in about 523. The text is from *The Consolation of Philosophy,* edited and abridged by J. J. Buchanan (New York: Frederick Ungar, 1957), pages 1–3. Buchanan's text is based on the W. V. Cooper translation but revised.

---

[1] [Buchanan] Π and Θ are the first letters of the Greek word denoting practical and theoretical, the two divisions of philosophy.

[2] That is, actors, players in a derogatory sense. The drama was opposed by Augustine and the Church generally. Here Boethius suggests that the Muses represent the kind of false copying that Plato's Socrates denigrated and the making of dangerous illusions. In the original Latin, Boethius wrote "scenicas meretriculas," more literally translated as "theatrical wenches" or "wenches of the theater."

[3] Two schools of Greek philosophy. The Eleatics were followers of Xenophanes of Colophon, a sixth-century-B.C. philosopher who lived in Elia. The Academic school of philosophy was founded by Plato, who taught for forty years at the grove called Academy outside of Athens.

Saint Thomas Aquinas

1225–1274

The medieval churchman St. Thomas Aquinas was the greatest of the Scholastic Philosophers, and the system of his *Summa Theologica* was declared in 1879 the offical philosophy of Roman Catholicism. St. Thomas's work was Aristotelian rather than Platonic, seeking the marriage of reason and faith.

The selection from the *Summa* below represents a theory of allegorical interpretation of Scripture that developed early in the Christian era; allegorical interpretation of Homer can be found as early as the sixth century B.C. and was still being practiced in the third century A.D. by Porphyry. Neoplatonic allegorizing can be found throughout the history of interpretive practice. Christian interpretation probably began with the methods of Philo Judaeus, a philosopher of the first century A.D., and by the churchmen Origen, Clement, Jerome, Augustine, and Gregory. The system that St. Thomas sets forth was probably first worked out in the fifth century. It reflects the fundamental idea that the world is itself a symbol subject to interpretation as the work of God. This principle was secularized by nineteenth-century French symbolists like Charles Baudelaire, whose sonnet *Correspondences* nevertheless owes more to the pagan saying, attributed to Hermes Trismegistus, that things below copy things above.

St. Thomas, of course, is interested only in Scripture. However, Dante Alighieri (below, page 154) explicitly extends the principles of interpretation to his own secular (though highly religious) *Commedia* in his letter to Can Grande della Scala and the *Convivio.*

St. Thomas argues that spiritual truths are properly and naturally taught by figures taken from corporeal things and, contrary to Boethius, that for these truths to be veiled is not harmful dissimulation but, with Augustine, the cause of beneficial exercise of the mind. His twofold system of interpretation, involving literal and spiritual levels, is really sixfold, since both have three parts. Under the literal are the historical, the etiological, and the analogical. Under the spiritual are the allegorical, the moral, and the anagogical.

There is plenty of evidence that the Thomistic system has occasionally been imposed arbitrarily on literary works, but it did open up the possibility of discovering multiple meanings in poems. It does not, however, allow for ambiguity in the senses put forward in the twentieth century, principally by William Empson in his *Seven Types of Ambiguity* (below, page 895). The interest in the relationship between signs or symbols and what they signify or denote arose again in the Romantic period, first in discussions of symbolism, later in linguistics. In Northrop Frye's theory of symbols (below, page 1138) the Thomistic terms reappear with secularized though related meanings.

The standard translation of *Summa Theologica* is by the Dominican Fathers (1927). See A. C. Pegis, ed., *The Basic Writings of Saint Thomas Aquinas,* in two volumes

(1945); Leonard Callahan, *A Theory of Esthetic According to the Principles of St. Thomas Aquinas* (1927); Thomas Gilby, *Poetic Experience* (1934, 1967); John Duffy, *A Philosophy of Poetry Based on Thomistic Principles* (1945); T. F. Torrance, "Scientific Hermeneutics According to St. Thomas Aquinas," *Journal of Biblical Studies,* new series XIII (1962), pages 259–89. The 1929 work of Etienne Gilson, *The Philosophy of St. Thomas Aquinas,* has now been translated, as has Umberto Eco's *The Aesthetics of Thomas Aquinas* (1970). See also Armond A. Maurer, *About Beauty: A Thomistic Interpretation* (1983).

from

Summa Theologica

from

The Nature and Domain of Sacred Doctrine

(In Ten Articles)

To place our purpose within definite limits, we must first investigate the nature and domain of sacred doctrine. Concerning this there are ten points of inquiry:—

(I) Whether sacred doctrine is necessary? (2) Whether it is a science?[1] (3) Whether it is one or many? (4) Whether it is speculative or practical? (5) How it is compared with other sciences? (6) Whether it is a wisdom? (7) Whether God is its subject-matter? (8) Whether it is argumentative? (9) Whether it rightly employs metaphors and similes? (10) Whether the Sacred Scripture of this doctrine may be expounded in different senses?

* * *

NINTH ARTICLE
Whether Holy Scripture Should Use Metaphors?

We proceed thus to the Ninth Article:—

Objection 1. It seems that Holy Scripture should not use metaphors. For that which is proper to the lowest sci-

ence seems not to befit this science, which holds the highest place of all. But to proceed by the aid of various similitudes and figures is proper to poetic, the least of all the sciences. Therefore it is not fitting that this science should make use of such similitudes.

Obj. 2. Further, this doctrine seems to be intended to make truth clear. Hence a reward is held out to those who manifest it: *They that explain me shall have life everlasting* (*Ecclus.* xxiv. 31). But by such similitudes truth is obscured. Therefore to put forward divine truths under the likeness of corporeal things does not befit this doctrine.[2]

Obj. 3. Further, the higher creatures are, the nearer they approach to the divine likeness. If therefore any creature be taken to represent God, this representation ought chiefly to be taken from the higher creatures, and not from the lower; yet this is often found in the Scriptures.

On the contrary, It is written (*Osee* xii. 10): *I have multiplied visions, and I have used similitudes by the ministry of the prophets.* But to put forward anything by means of similitudes is to use metaphors. Therefore sacred doctrine may use metaphors.

I answer that, It is befitting Holy Scripture to put forward divine and spiritual truths by means of comparisons with material things. For God provides for everything according to the capacity of its nature. Now it is natural to man to attain to intellectual truths through sensible things, because all our knowledge originates from sense. Hence in Holy Scripture spiritual truths are fittingly taught under the likeness of material things. This is what Dionysius says: *We cannot be enlightened by the divine rays except they be hidden within the covering of many sacred veils.*[3] It is also befitting Holy Scripture, which is proposed to all without distinction of persons—*To the wise and to the unwise I am*

The *Summa Theologica,* of which this selection is a part, was written from 1256 to 1272. The text is from *Introduction to Saint Thomas Aquinas,* edited by Anton Pegis, The Modern Library, a division of Random House. According to Pegis the correct title of the work is *Summa* or *Summa Theologicae.* It may be interpreted to mean the highest or ultimate theology.
[1] "Science" here means a true branch of learning that proceeds by rational principles.

[2] Here the objector is in agreement with the Platonic suspicion of the image.
[3] *Of the Celestial Hierarchy* I, 2. This work is one of a number of theological writings of unknown origin that had great influence on medieval thought. Scholars are now certain that these works, long attributed to Dionysius Areopagiticus, an Athenian convert to Christianity in the first century A.D., were actually written in the fourth or fifth centuries. The author is traditionally called pseudo-Dionysius or the pseudo-Areopagite.

metaphor
aids rather than
inhibits understanding

a debtor (*Rom.* i. 14)—that spiritual truths be expounded by means of figures taken from corporeal things, in order that thereby even the simple who are unable by themselves to grasp intellectual things may be able to understand it.[4]

Reply Obj. 1. Poetry makes use of metaphors to produce a representation, for it is natural to man to be pleased with representations. But sacred doctrine makes use of metaphors as both necessary and useful.

Reply Obj. 2. The ray of divine revelation is not extinguished by the sensible imagery wherewith it is veiled, as Dionysius says;[5] and its truth so far remains that it does not allow the minds of those to whom the revelation has been made, to rest in the likenesses, but raises them to the knowledge of intelligible truths; and through those to whom the revelation has been made others also may receive instruction in these matters. Hence those things that are taught metaphorically in one part of Scripture, in other parts are taught more openly. The very hiding of truth in figures is useful for the exercise of thoughtful minds,[6] and as a defense against the ridicule of the unbelievers, according to the words, *Give not that which is holy to dogs* (*Matt.* vii. 6).

Reply Obj. 3. As Dionysius says,[7] it is more fitting that divine truths should be expounded under the figure of less noble than of nobler bodies; and this for three reasons. First, because thereby men's minds are the better freed from error. For then it is clear that these things are not literal descriptions of divine truths, which might have been open to doubt had they been expressed under the figure of nobler bodies, especially in the case of those who could think of nothing nobler than bodies. Second, because this is more befitting the knowledge of God that we have in this life. For what He is not is clearer to us than what He is. Therefore similitudes drawn from things farthest away from God form within us a truer estimate that God is above whatsoever we may say or think of Him. Third, because thereby divine truths are the better hidden from the unworthy.

TENTH ARTICLE
Whether in Holy Scripture a Word May Have Several Senses?

We proceed thus to the Tenth Article:—

Objection 1. It seems that in Holy Scripture a word cannot have several senses, historical or literal, allegorical, tropological or moral, and anagogical.[8] For many different senses in one text produce confusion and deception and destroy all force of argument.[9] Hence no argument, but only fallacies, can be deduced from a multiplicity of propositions. But Holy Scripture ought to be able to state the truth without any fallacy. Therefore in it there cannot be several senses to a word.

Obj. 2. Further, Augustine says that *the Old Testament has a fourfold division: according to history, etiology, analogy, and allegory.*[10] Now these four seem altogether different from the four divisions mentioned in the first objection. Therefore it does not seem fitting to explain the same word of Holy Scripture according to the four different senses mentioned above.

Obj. 3. Further, besides these senses, there is the parabolical, which is not one of these four.

On the contrary, Gregory says: *Holy Scripture by the manner of its speech transcends every science, because in one and the same sentence, while it describes a fact, it reveals a mystery.*[11]

I answer that, The author of Holy Scripture is God, in Whose power it is to signify His meaning, not by words only (as man also can do), but also by things themselves. So, whereas in every other science things are signified by words, this science has the property that the things signified by the words have themselves also a signification.[12] Therefore that first signification whereby words signify things belongs to the first sense, the historical or literal. That signification whereby things signified by words have themselves also a signification is called the spiritual sense, which is based on the literal, and presupposes it. Now this spiritual sense has a threefold division. For as the Apostle says (*Heb.* x. I) the Old Law is a figure of the New Law,[13] and Dionysius says *the New Law itself is a figure of future glory.*[14] Again, in the New Law, whatever our Head has done is a type of what we ought to do. Therefore, so far as the things of the Old Law signify the things of the New Law, there is the allegorical[15] sense; so far as the things done in Christ, or so far as the things which signify Christ, are signs of what we ought to do, there is the moral sense. But so far as they signify what relates to eternal glory, there is the anagogical sense.[16] Since the literal sense

---

[4] An argument made for poetry by, for example, Sidney (below, page 194).

[5] *Of the Celestial Hierarchy* I, 2. Here appears the notion that the Bible is allegorical, though there will be a suspicion of allegory when it is thought the only harbor of meaning.

[6] This notion appears in St. Augustine (above, page 145) and is frequently used to defend poetry in later ages.

[7] *Of the Celestial Hierarchy* II, 2.

[8] These are the levels on which interpretation is made. See Dante (below, page 154).

[9] See, for example, Locke (below, page 282).

[10] *Of the Value of Belief* III.

[11] *Moralia* XX, 1; Gregory I (Saint Gregory the Great, c. 540–604, pope, 590–604).

[12] See St. Augustine (above, page 144).

[13] The Old and New Testaments respectively.

[14] *Of the Ecclesiastical Hierarchy* Volume 2 (PG 3, 501).

[15] This sense comes to be called the typological, the Old Testament containing "types" that anticipate events in the New.

[16] See Frye's secularization of this system (below, page 1138).

is that which the author intends, and since the author of Holy Scripture is God, Who by one act comprehends all things by His intellect, it is not unfitting, as Augustine says,[17] if, even according to the literal sense, one word in Holy Scripture should have several senses.

Reply Obj. I. The multiplicity of these senses does not produce equivocation or any other kind of multiplicity, seeing that these senses are not multiplied because one word signifies several things, but because the things signified by the words can be themselves signs of other things. Thus in Holy Scripture no confusion results, for all the senses are founded on one—the literal—from which alone can any argument be drawn, and not from those intended allegorically, as Augustine says.[18] Nevertheless, nothing of Holy Scripture perishes because of this, since nothing necessary to faith is contained under the spiritual sense which is not elsewhere put forward clearly by the Scripture in its literal sense.[19]

---

[17] *Confessions* XII, 31.

[18] *Epistles* XCIII, 8.

[19] St. Thomas is careful to preserve the historical meaning of the Bible as the ground for every other meaning. Typological readings preserve the Bible's historical nature, while allegory, in its usual sense, can be a threat to spirit away the historical sense.

Reply Obj. 2. These three—history, etiology, analogy—are grouped under the literal sense. For it is called history, as Augustine expounds,[20] whenever anything is simply related: it is called etiology when its cause is assigned, as when Our Lord gave the reason why Moses allowed the putting away of wives—namely, because of the hardness of men's hearts (*Matt.* xix. 8): it is called analogy whenever the truth of one text of Scripture is shown not to contradict the truth of another. Of these four, allegory alone stands for the three spiritual senses. Thus Hugh of St. Victor includes the anagogical under the allegorical sense, laying down three senses only—the historical, the allegorical and the tropological.[21]

Reply Obj. 3. The parabolical sense is contained in the literal, for by words things are signified properly and figuratively. Nor is the figure itself, but that which is figured, the literal sense. When Scripture speaks of God's arm, the literal sense is not that God has such a member, but only what is signified by this member, namely, operative power. Hence it is plain that nothing false can ever underlie the literal sense of Holy Scripture.

---

[20] *Of the Value of Belief* 3.

[21] Cf. *Of the Sacraments* I, 4; also *Of Scripture and Sacred Writing* 3.

Dante Alighieri

1265–1321

Dante is, of course, best known for his *Commedia,* popularly known in English as *The Divine Comedy.* His twofold scheme of interpretation, which is really fourfold, is clearly similar to that of St. Thomas Aquinas. It is set forth in a letter that dedicates the third part of the *Commedia* to Can Grande della Scala and earlier in *Il Convivio (The Banquet).* These statements have, of course, been of particular interest to students of the *Commedia;* but it is possible that Dante has led readers who apply it rigorously somewhat astray.

We see here a system intended for Scripture applied to secular writing. For Dante and others, the allegorical mode was not merely a matter of artistic cleverness; it was part and parcel of their way of thinking about the world, which was itself considered full of symbolic meaning—like a work of art, we might say today. But for Dante the reverse was the case; the work of art was like the world.

Dante's definition of comedy as the reverse of tragedy, at least with respect to plot, may seem to indicate a rather simplified approach to genres in the light of Aristotle's detailed treatment of tragedy (above, page 52ff.), but it does serve to broaden the scope of the term and free it from narrow association with the merely amusing or farcical.

There are numerous selections of Dante's writings and an enormous scholarly literature. Some significant critical works relevant to the texts below are H. F. Dunbar, *Symbolism in Medieval Thought* (1929); C. S. Singleton, *Dante Studies I, Commedia, Elements of Structure* (1954); P. J. Toynbee, *Dante Alighieri, His Life and Works* (1965); three studies by Erich Auerbach, "Typological Symbolism in Medieval Literature," *Yale French Studies* IX (1952), *Mimesis* (1953), and *Dante, Poet of the Secular World* (1961); Robert Hollander, *Allegory in Dante's Commedia* (1969); Guiseppe Mazzotta, *Dante, Poet of the Desert: History and Allegory in the* Divine Comedy (1979); Michael Caesar, ed., *Dante: The Critical Heritage: 1314?–1870* (1989); Robert Hollander, *Dante's Epistle to Cangrande* (1993); Angelo Mazzocca, *Linguistic Theories in Dante and the Humanists* (1993); Warren Ginsberg, *Dante's Aesthetic of Being* (1999); Dino Bigongiari, *Essays on Dante and Medieval Culture* (2000).

from

The Banquet

I say that, as is affirmed in the first chapter, it is meet for this exposition to be both literal and allegorical.[1] And to make this intelligible, it should be known that writings can be understood and ought to be expounded chiefly in four senses. The first is called literal, and this is that sense which does not go beyond the strict limits of the letter;[2] the second is called allegorical, and this is disguised under the cloak of such stories, and is a truth hidden under a beautiful fiction. Thus Ovid says that Orpheus with his lyre made beasts tame, and trees and stones move towards himself; that is to say that the wise man by the instrument of his voice makes cruel hearts grow mild and humble, and those who have not the life of science and of art move to his will, while they who have no rational life are as it were like stones. And wherefore this disguise was invented by the wise will be shown in the last tractate but one. Theologians indeed do not apprehend this sense in the same fashion as poets;[3] but, inasmuch as my intention is to follow here the custom of poets, I will take the allegorical sense after the manner which poets use.

The third sense is called moral: and this sense is that for which teachers ought as they go through writings intently to watch for their own profit and that of their hearers; as in the Gospel when Christ ascended the Mount to be transfigured, we may be watchful of his taking with himself the three Apostles out of the twelve; whereby morally it may be understood that for the most secret affairs we ought to have few companions.

The fourth sense is called anagogic, that is, above the senses; and this occurs when a writing is spiritually expounded which even in the literal sense by the things signified likewise gives intimation of higher matters belonging to the eternal glory; as can be seen in that song of the prophet which says that, when the people of Israel went up out of Egypt, Judea was made holy and free. And although it be plain that this is true according to the letter, that which

is spiritually understood is not less true, namely, that when the soul issues forth from sin she is made holy and free as mistress of herself.

from

Letter to Can Grande Della Scala

6. . . . if we desire to furnish some introduction to a part of any work, it behooves us to furnish some knowledge of the whole of which it is a part. Wherefore I too, desiring to furnish something by way of introduction to the above-named portion of the *Comedy,*[1] have thought that something concerning the whole work should be premised, that the approach to the part should be the easier and more complete. There are six things then which must be inquired into at the beginning of any work of instruction: to wit, the subject, agent, form, and end, the title of the work, and the branch of philosophy it concerns. And there are three of these wherein this part which I purposed to design for you differs from the whole; to wit, subject, form, and title; whereas in the others it differs not, as is plain on inspection. And so, an inquiry concerning these three must be instituted specially with reference to the work as a whole; and when this has been done the way will be sufficiently clear to the introduction of the part. After that we shall examine the other three, not only with reference to the whole but also with reference to that special part which I am offering to you.

7. To elucidate, then, what we have to say, be it known that the sense of this work is not simple, but on the contrary it may be called polysemous, that is to say, "of more senses than one": for it is one sense which we get through the letter, and another which we get through the thing the letter signifies; and the first is called literal, but the second allegorical or mystic. And this mode of treatment, for its better manifestation, may be considered in this verse: "When Israel came out of Egypt, and the house of Jacob from a people of strange speech. Judea became his sanctification,

---

The Banquet (Il Convivio) was written sometime between 1304 and 1308. The text is from W. W. Jackson, tr., *Dante's Convivio* (Oxford: Clarendon Press, 1909).
[1] See St. Thomas Aquinas (above, page 151).
[2] This corresponds to St. Thomas's historical level, but Dante is writing fiction, so he refers to the "letter" of the text, which expresses the fiction directly and "literally" as a history.
[3] Here Dante seems to be acknowledging the difference between poetic allegory and Biblical typology (St. Thomas's "allegory").

The letter to a friend and patron who lived in Verona was written in about 1318. Some doubt has been cast on Dante's authorship (see Helmut Hatzfield, "Modern Literary Scholarship as Reflected in Dante Criticism," *Comparative Literature* III [1951], page 296), but it is still popularly attributed to him. The text is from P. H. Wicksteed, tr., *Translations of the Later Works of Dante* (London: J. M. Dent & Sons, 1904).
[1] Dante is referring to Part III of *The Divine Comedy,* "Paradiso."

Israel his power."[2] For if we inspect the letter alone the departure of the children of Israel from Egypt in the time of Moses is presented to us; if the allegory, our redemption wrought by Christ; if the moral sense, the conversion of the soul from the grief and misery of sin to the state of grace is presented to us; if the anagogical, the departure of the holy soul from the slavery of this corruption to the liberty of eternal glory is presented to us. And although these mystic senses have each their special denominations, they may all in general be called allegorical, since they differ from the literal and historical; for *allegory* is derived from *alleon,* in Greek, which means the same as the Latin *alienum* or *diversum.*

8. When we understand this we see clearly that the subject round which the alternative senses play must be twofold. And we must therefore consider the subject of this work as literally understood, and then its subject as allegorically intended. The subject of the whole work, then, taken in the literal sense only, is "the state of souls after death," without qualification, for the whole progress of the work hinges on it and about it. Whereas if the work be taken allegorically the subject is "man, as by good or ill deserts, in the exercise of the freedom of his choice, he becomes liable to rewarding or punishing justice."

9. Now the form is twofold, the form of the treatise and the form of the treatment. The form of the treatise is threefold, according to its threefold division. The first division is that by which the whole work is divided into three cantiche;[3] the second that whereby each cantica is divided into cantos; the third, that whereby each canto is divided into lines. The form or method of treatment is poetic, fictive, descriptive, digressive, transumptive; and likewise proceeding by definition, division, proof, refutation, and setting forth of examples.[4]

10. The title of the work is, "Here beginneth the *Comedy* of Dante Alighieri, a Florentine by birth, not by character." To understand which, be it known that *comedy* is derived from *comus,* "a village," and *oda,* which is, "song"; whence comedy is, as it were, "rustic song." So comedy is a certain kind of poetic narration differing from all others. It differs, then, from tragedy in its content, in that tragedy begins admirably and tranquilly, whereas its end or exit is foul and terrible; and it derives its name from *tragus,* which is a "goat" and *oda,* as though to say "goat-song," that is fetid

like a goat, as appears from Seneca in his tragedies; whereas comedy introduces some harsh complication, but brings its matter to a prosperous end, as appears from Terence, in his comedies.[5] And hence certain writers, on introducing themselves, have made it their practice to give the salutation: "I wish you a tragic beginning and a comic end." They likewise differ in their mode of speech, tragedy being exalted and sublime, comedy lax and humble, as Horace has it in his *Poetica,* where he gives comedians leave sometimes to speak like tragedians and conversely:

> Interdum tamen et vocem comaedia tollit,
> Iratusque Chremes tumido delitigat ore;
> Et tragicus plerumque dolet sermone pedestri.[6]

And hence it is evident that the title of the present work is "the *Comedy.*" For if we have respect to its content, at the beginning it is horrible and fetid, for it is hell and in the end it is prosperous, desirable, and gracious, for it is paradise. If we have respect to the method of speech the method is lax and humble, for it is the vernacular speech in which very women communicate. There are also other kinds of poetic narration, as the bucolic song, elegy, satire, and the utterance of prayer, as may also be seen from Horace in his *Poetica.* But concerning them naught need at present be said.

11. There can be no difficulty in assigning the subject of the part I am offering you; for if the subject of the whole, taken literally, is "the state of souls after death," not limited but taken without qualification, it is clear that in this part that same state is the subject, but with a limitation; to wit, "the state of blessed souls after death"; and if the subject of the whole work taken allegorically is "man as by good or ill deserts, in the exercise of the freedom of his choice, he becomes liable to rewarding or punishing justice," it is manifest that the subject in this part is contracted to "man as by good deserts, he becomes liable to rewarding justice."

12. And in like manner the form of the part is clear from the form assigned to the whole; for if the form of the treatise as a whole is threefold, in this part it is twofold only, namely, division of the cantiche and of the cantos. The first division cannot be a part of its special form, since it is itself a part under that first division.

[2]Psalms 114.1–2.
[3]The three parts: "Inferno," "Purgatorio," "Paradiso."
[4]The terms Dante uses are in part taken from the tradition of poetics, in part from that of rhetoric.
[5]Lucius Annaeus Seneca (c. 3 B.C.–c. 65 A.D.), Roman tragic dramatist; Publius Terentius Afer (Terence) (c. 190–c. 159 B.C.), Roman comic dramatist.
[6]"Yet there are times when even Comedy elevates its style, and an angry Chremes raves with swelling voice. Also, in Tragedy [Telephus and Peleus] often give vent to their sorrow in the language of prose." (Bate translation), Horace, *Art of Poetry* (above, page 80).

13. The title of the work is also clear, for if the title of the whole work is "Here beginneth the *Comedy*," and so forth as set out above, the title of this part will be "Here beginneth the third cantica of Dante's *Comedy,* which is entitled Paradise."

14. Having investigated the three things in which the part differs from the whole, we must examine the other three, in which there is no variation from the whole. The agent, then, of the whole and of the part is the man already named, who is seen throughout to be such.

15. The end of the whole and of the part may be manifold, to wit, the proximate and the ultimate, but dropping all subtle investigation, we may say briefly that the end of the whole and of the part is to remove those living in this life from the state of misery and lead them to the state of felicity.

Giovanni Boccaccio

1313–1375

The interpretive methods advocated by St. Thomas Aquinas for divine texts and by Dante Alighieri for secular ones were certainly in Boccaccio's mind when he wrote about the differences between poetry and theology, which he avers lie in subject matter more than in method. Poetry makes fictions, whereas theology always tells the truth directly. Boccaccio defends poetry, however, against those who say that because it lies it is fundamentally immoral. Holding that poetry is allegorical and truthful at hidden levels, though untruthful on the surface (the historical level of St. Thomas and Dante, above, page 151 and page 154), Boccaccio defends the use of allegory in the same way as does St. Thomas (above, page 151): Meaning acquired by toil should ultimately be of more pleasure and better retained. He also indicates that the truth of poetry often comes in the form of a generalization about life and manners expressed in a fiction. Jesus himself uttered parables of this sort. When their subject is the same, poetry and theology are nearly the same.

Boccaccio defends the pagan poets, insisting that they clothe many physical and moral truths in their inventions. His arguments tend to summarize assumptions underlying the whole tradition of interpretation even from pre-Christian times, when Homer and Hesiod were subjected to allegorical interpretation. Boccaccio, like medieval theorists and Renaissance critics, insisted that a hidden moral meaning redeemed poetry's "lies." It took longer for critics to arrive at the idea that there is something that poetry uniquely does, that *truth* in the sense of rationality is perhaps not quite the right word to describe it. Only with a renewed interest in symbolism and theories of language in nineteenth-and twentieth-century critics was there an effort to define the poem's mode of knowledge or truth in terms that avoided recourse to strict rationality on the one hand and mysticism and pure irrationality on the other.

Boccaccio is, of course, best known for his collection of one hundred tales, *The Decameron,* but he also wrote many other works, both fictional and critical.

C. G. Osgood's *Boccaccio on Poetry* (1930, 1956) contains with commentary and introduction the Preface and Books XIV and XV of the *Genealogy of the Gentile Gods.* See also J. R. Smith, *The Earliest Lives of Dante* (1901, 1903); T. C. Chubb, *The Life of Giovanni Boccaccio* (1930); Herbert G. Wright, *Boccacio in England, from Chaucer to Tennyson* (1957); Stavros Deligiorgis, *Narrative Intellection in the* Decameron (1975); Vittore Branca, *Boccaccio: The Man and His Works* (1976); Thomas G. Bergin, *Boccaccio* (1981).

from

Life of Dante

from

Chapter IX

Digression Concerning Poetry

If we apply our minds, and examine it by reason, I think we can easily discover that the ancient poets have followed, so far as is possible for the human mind, the steps of the Holy Spirit, which, as we see in Holy Scripture, revealed to future generations its highest secrets by the mouths of many, making them utter under a veil that which in due time it intended to make known openly through works. Therefore, if we closely examine their writings, we shall see that poets described beneath the mask of certain fictions (to the end that the imitator might not appear different from the thing imitated) that which had been, or which was in their day, or that which they presumed or desired would happen in the future.

Wherefore, although the two forms of writing do not have the same end in view, but only a like method of treatment—whereto my mind is chiefly directed at present—the same praise may be given to both in the words of Gregory,[1] who said of the sacred Scripture what may also be said of poetry, namely, that in the same account it discloses the text and its underlying mystery. Thus at the same moment by the one it disciplines the wise, and by the other it strengthens the foolish. It possesses openly that by virtue of which it may nourish little children, and preserves in secret that whereby it holds rapt in admiration the minds of sublime thinkers. Thus it is like a river, if I may use the figure, wherein the little lamb may wade, and the great elephant freely swim. But let us proceed to the verification of these statements.

Chapter X

On the Difference Between Poetry and Theology

Holy Scripture—which we call theology—sometimes under the form of history, again in the meaning of a vision, now by the signification of a lament, and in many other ways, designs to reveal to us the high mystery of the incarnation of the Divine Word, his life, the circumstances of his death, his victorious resurrection and wonderful ascension, and his other acts, so that, being thus taught, we may attain to that glory which he by his death and resurrection opened to us, after it had been long closed through the sin of the first man. In like manner do poets in their works—which we term poetry—sometimes under fictions of various gods, again by the transformation of men into imaginary forms, and at times by gentle persuasion, reveal to us the causes of things, the effects of virtues and of vices, what we ought to flee and what follow; in order that we may attain by virtuous action the end that they, although they did not rightly know the true God, believed to be our supreme salvation.

Thus the Holy Spirit wished to show by the green bush, wherein Moses saw God like unto a burning flame,[2] the virginity of her that above every other creature is pure, who was to be the habitation and retreat of the Lord of Nature, and yet was not to be contaminated by her conception, nor by the birth of the Word of the Father. In the vision seen by Nebuchadnezzar[3] of the statue of many metals, demolished by a stone which, in turn, was changed into a mountain, the Holy Spirit would declare that all past ages were to be overthrown by the doctrine of Christ, who was and is a living rock, and that the Christian religion, born of this rock, was to become a thing immovable and ever-enduring like the mountains. By the lamentations of Jeremiah it would proclaim the future destruction of Jerusalem.

In like manner our poets, in feigning that Saturn had many children, of whom he devoured all save four, desired to make us perceive merely that Saturn is time, wherein everything is brought forth, and which, even as it produces, also destroys all things and brings them to naught. The four children undevoured by him are first, Jupiter, that is, the element of fire; secondly, Juno, spouse and sister of Jupiter, in other words the air, by means of which fire works its effects here below; thirdly, Neptune, god of the sea, or the element of water; the fourth and last is Pluto, god of hell, that is, the earth, which is lower than any other element.

Similarly, our poets feign that Hercules was transformed from a man into a god, and Lycaon into a wolf. They wished to point the moral that by virtuous action, like

---

Vita di Dante was written in 1364 and first published in 1477. The text is from J. R. Smith, tr., *The Earliest Lives of Dante* (New York: Holt, Rinehart and Winston, 1901).
[1](540?–604), pope from 590 to 604, author of numerous theological works.

[2]Genesis 3.2.
[3]Daniel 2.31–35. In this paragraph Boccaccio performs a typological reading of the Bible, in which the New Testament is prefigured in the Old. See St. Thomas Aquinas (above, page 151).

that of Hercules, man becomes a god by participation in heaven, and that by acting viciously with Lycaon, albeit one seem a man, of a truth he can be said to be that beast which everyone knows through an effect most similar to his defect; even as Lycaon, by reason of his greed and avarice, is represented as changed into a wolf, since these are the characteristics of a wolf. Likewise our poets imagine the beauty of the Elysian Fields, by which I understand the sweetness of paradise; and the obscurity of Dis,[4] which I take to mean the bitterness of hell. This they did that we, attracted by the pleasure of the one and terrified by the suffering of the other, might pursue the virtues that will lead us to Elysium, and flee the vices that would cause us to be ferried over to Dis.

I omit the illumination of these things by more detailed illustration, for—although I should wish to make them as clear as is possible and fitting, since they would be most pleasing and would strengthen my argument—I doubt not that I should be carried much farther than the main subject requires, and further than that I do not wish to go.

Certainly enough has been said to make us understand that theology and poetry agree in their method of treatment. But in their subject matter I say they are not only most diverse, but are even to some extent opposed to each other. For the subject of sacred theology is divine truth, while that of ancient poetry is the men and gods of the pagans. They are opposed, in that theology presupposes nothing unless it be true, while poetry puts forth certain things as true that are surely false, misleading, and contrary to the Christian religion. But certain lackwits rise up against the poets, saying that they have composed evil and indecent fables not consonant with the truth, and that they ought to show their ability and teach their doctrines to mortals in other form than that of fictions; and for this reason I wish to proceed a little further in the present reasoning.

Let these persons, then, consider the visions of Daniel, Isaiah, Ezekiel, and others of the Old Testament, which, described by the divine pen, are revealed by him for whom there is neither beginning nor end. Let them in the New Testament also consider the visions of the Evangelist, which are full of wonderful truth for those who understand them. And if no poetic fable is found that is so far from truth or probability as, in many places on the surface, these appear to be, let it be conceded, on the other hand,

that poets alone have written fables that are not likely to give either pleasure or profit. I might proceed without replying to the censure which they pass on poets because they have made known their teachings in fables or under the guise of fables, for I know that while in this they foolishly blame the poets, they incautiously fall into censuring that Spirit who is no less than the Way, the Truth, and the Life. Yet, notwithstanding, I have in mind to satisfy them somewhat.

It is manifest that everything acquired by labor has more sweetness than that which comes without effort. The obvious truth, since it is quickly and easily seized, delights us and passes into the memory. But in order that, acquired by toil, it should be more pleasing and for that reason the better retained, the poets concealed it under many things that are not, apparently, in accord therewith.[5] They chose fables rather than any other disguise, because the beauties thereof attract those whom neither philosophic demonstrations nor persuasions are able to draw. What shall we say, then, of poets? Shall we hold that they were madmen, as these present lackwits, not knowing whereof they speak, deem them? Certainly they were not. They were rather in their acts men of profound understanding, which is hidden in the fruit, and of an excellent and highly wrought eloquence, which is evident in the bark and leaves. But let us return to the place where we left off.

I say that theology and poetry can be considered as almost one and the same thing when their subject is the same. Indeed I go further, and assert that theology is simply the poetry of God. What is it but poetic fiction to say in one place of Scripture that Christ is a lion and in another a lamb, now that he is a serpent and now a dragon, and in still another place that he is a rock? And he is called by many other names, to repeat all of which would take too long. What else signify the words of the Savior in the Gospel, if not a teaching different from the outward sense, which manner of speaking we term, using a more common word, allegory. It is clear, then, that not only is poetry theology, but also that theology is poetry. And truly if my words, in so great a matter, merit little credence, I shall not be disturbed; at least let Aristotle, a most worthy authority on all great questions, be believed, who affirmed that he found the poets were the first theologians.[6] Let this suffice for this part, and let us turn to show why poets alone among learned men have been granted the honor of the laurel crown.

---

[4] Roman god of the underworld.

[5] An argument employed by St. Thomas Aquinas (above, page 151).
[6] *Metaphysics* III, 4.

from
Genealogy of the Gentile Gods

from
Book XIV

VII. The Definition of Poetry,
Its Origin, and Function[1]

This poetry, which ignorant triflers cast aside, is a sort of fervid and exquisite invention, with fervid expression, in speech or writing, of that which the mind has invented. It proceeds from the bosom of God, and few, I find, are the souls in whom this gift is born; indeed so wonderful a gift it is that true poets have always been the rarest of men. This fervor of poesy is sublime in its effects: it impels the soul to a longing for utterance; it brings forth strange and unheard-of creations of the mind;[2] it arranges these meditations in a fixed order, adorns the whole composition with unusual interweaving of words and thoughts; and thus it veils truth in a fair and fitting garment of fiction.[3] Further, if in any case the invention so requires, it can arm kings, marshal them for war, launch whole fleets from their docks, nay, counterfeit sky, land, sea, adorn young maidens with flowery garlands, portray human character in its various phases, awake the idle, stimulate the dull, restrain the rash, subdue the criminal, and distinguish excellent men with their proper need of praise: these, and many other such, are the effects of poetry. Yet if any man who has received the gift of poetic fervor shall imperfectly fulfill its function here described, he is not, in my opinion, a laudable poet. For, however deeply the poetic impulse stirs the mind to which it is granted, it very rarely accomplishes anything commendable if the instruments by which its concepts are to be wrought out are wanting—I mean, for example, the precepts of grammar and rhetoric, an abundant knowledge of which is opportune. I grant that many a man already writes his mother tongue ad-

mirably, and indeed has performed each of the various duties of poetry as such; yet over and above this, it is necessary to know at least the principles of the other liberal arts, both moral and natural, to possess a strong and abundant vocabulary, to behold the monuments and relics of the ancients, to have in one's memory the histories of the nations, and to be familiar with the geography of various lands, of seas, rivers, and mountains.

Furthermore, places of retirement, the lovely handiwork of nature herself, are favorable to poetry, as well as peace of mind and desire for worldly glory; the ardent period of life also has very often been of great advantage. If these conditions fail, the power of creative genius frequently grows dull and sluggish.

Now since nothing proceeds from this poetic fervor, which sharpens and illumines the powers of the mind, except what is wrought out by art, poetry is generally called an art. Indeed the word *poetry* has not the origin that many carelessly suppose, namely *poio, pois,* which is but Latin *fingo, fingis;* rather it is derived from a very ancient Greek word *poetes,*[4] which means in Latin exquisite discourse (*exquisita locutio*). For the first men who, thus inspired, began to employ an exquisite style of speech, such, for example, as song in an age hitherto unpolished, to render this unheard-of discourse sonorous to their hearers, let it fall in measured periods; and lest by its brevity it fail to please, or, on the other hand, become prolix and tedious, they applied to it the standard of fixed rules, and restrained it within a definite number of feet and syllables. Now the product of this studied method of speech they no longer called by the more general term poesy, but poem. Thus as I said above, the name of the art, as well as its artificial product, is derived from its effect.

Now though I allege that this science of poetry has ever streamed forth from the bosom of God upon souls while even yet in their tenderest years, these enlightened cavilers will perhaps say that they cannot trust my words. To any fair-minded man the fact is valid enough from its constant recurrence. But for these dullards I must cite witnesses to it. If, then, they will read what Cicero, a philosopher rather than a poet, says in his oration delivered before the senate in behalf of Aulus Licinius Archias, perhaps they will come more easily to believe me. He says: "And yet we have it on the highest and most learned authority, that while other arts are matters of science and formula and technique, poetry de-

---

De Genealogiis was written in about 1366. The text is from Charles G. Osgood, tr., *Boccaccio on Poetry* (Princeton: Princeton University Press, 1930).
[1][Osgood] Perhaps the most significant chapter; it embodies most of Boccaccio's ideas about poetry: definition, etymology, elements and conditions of creation, effects and function, and the superiority of poetry to mere rhetoric. In setting these down, Boccaccio has consulted his own experience as a poet as well as traditional criticism, especially as recorded in Petrarch, Dante, Isidore, Macrobius, Augustine, and Cicero.
[2]This idea may go back to Plato's idea of the poet's "possession" and to his concept of "phantastic" imitation in *Sophist* (above, page 39). Note its presence in Sidney (below, page 199). Sidney probably got it from the sixteenth-century Italian critic Minturno.
[3]This suggests an allegorical meaning as the "truth" of the poem.

---

[4][Osgood] Boccaccio's limitations in Greek have allowed him to follow Isidore of Seville (*Etymology* VIII, vii, 2 *De Poeta*)—bad etymology and all—in this whole passage, as did writers before him who knew no Greek.

pends solely upon an inborn faculty, is evoked by a purely mental activity, and is infused with a strange supernal inspiration."

But not to protract this argument, it is now sufficiently clear to reverent men, that poetry is a practical art, springing from God's bosom and deriving its name from its effect, and that it has to do with many high and noble matters that constantly occupy even those who deny its existence. If my opponents ask when and in what circumstances, the answer is plain: the poets would declare with their own lips under whose help and guidance they compose their inventions when, for example, they raise flights of symbolic steps to heaven, or make thick-branching trees spring aloft to the very stars, or go winding about mountains to their summits. Haply, to disparage this art of poetry now unrecognized by them, these men will say that it is rhetoric which the poets employ. Indeed, I will not deny it in part, for rhetoric has also its own inventions. Yet, in truth, among the disguises of fiction rhetoric has no part, for whatever is composed as under a veil, and thus exquisitely wrought, is poetry and poetry alone.[5]

IX. It Is Rather Useful than Damnable to Compose Stories

These fine cattle bellow still further to the effect that poets are tale-mongers, or, to use the lower and more hateful term which they sometimes employ in their resentment—liars. No doubt the ignorant will regard such an imputation as particularly objectionable. But I scorn it. The foul language of some men cannot infect the glorious name of the illustrious. Yet I grieve to see these revilers in a purple rage let themselves loose upon the innocent. If I conceded that poets deal in stories, in that they are composers of fiction, I think I hereby incur no further disgrace than a philosopher would in drawing up a syllogism. For if I show the nature of a fable or story, its various kinds, and which kinds these "liars" employ, I do not think the composers of fiction will appear guilty of so monstrous a crime as these gentlemen maintain. First of all, the word *fable (fabula)* has an honorable origin in the verb *for, faris,* hence "conversation" *(confabulatio),* which means only "talking together" *(collocutio).* This is clearly shown by Luke in his gospel, where he is speaking of the two disciples who went to the village of Emmaus after the Passion. He says: "And they talked together of all these things which had happened. And it came to pass, that,

while they communed together, and reasoned, Jesus himself drew near, and went with them."[6]

Hence, if it is a sin to compose stories, it is a sin to converse, which only the veriest fool would admit. For nature has not granted us the power of speech unless for purposes of conversation, and the exchange of ideas.

But, they may object, nature meant this gift for a useful purpose, not for idle nonsense: and fiction is just that—idle nonsense. True enough, if the poet had intended to compose a mere tale. But I have time and time again proved that the meaning of fiction is far from superficial. Wherefore, some writers have framed this definition of fiction *(fabula):* Fiction is a form of discourse, which, under guise of invention, illustrates or proves an idea: and, as its superficial aspect is removed, the meaning of the author is clear. If, then, sense is revealed from under the veil of fiction, the composition of fiction is not idle nonsense. Of fiction I distinguish four kinds. The first superficially lacks all appearance of truth; for example, when brutes or inanimate things converse. Aesop, an ancient Greek, grave and venerable, was past master in this form; and though it is a common and popular form both in city and country, yet Aristotle, chief of the Peripatetics,[7] and a man of divine intellect, did not scorn to use it in his books. The second kind at times superficially mingles fiction with truth, as when we tell of the daughters of Minyas at their spinning, who, when they spurned the orgies of Bacchus, were turned to bats; or the mates of the sailor Acestes, who for contriving the rape of the boy Bacchus, were turned to fish.[8] This form has been employed from the beginning by the most ancient poets, whose object it has been to clothe in fiction divine and human matters alike: they who have followed the sublimer inventions of the poets have improved upon them; while some of the comic writers have perverted them, caring more for the approval of a licentious public than for honesty. The third kind is more like history than fiction, and famous poets have employed it in a variety of ways. For however much the heroic poets seem to be writing history—as Virgil in his description of Aeneas tossed by the storm, or Homer in his account of Ulysses bound to the mast to escape the lure of the Sirens' song— yet their hidden meaning is far other than appears on the surface. The better of the comic poets. Terence and Plautus, for example, have also employed this form, but they intend naught other than the literal meaning of their lines. Yet by their art they portray varieties of human nature and conversation, incidentally teaching the reader and putting him on

---

[5]Although allegory alone does not distinguish poetry from rhetoric, Boccaccio obviously considers it important.

[6]Luke 24.14–15.
[7]Disciples of Aristotle, who walked about while he was teaching.
[8]Myths recorded in Ovid, *Metamorphoses* III, 582–686; IV, 31–415.

his guard. If the events they describe have not actually taken place, yet since they are common, they could have occurred, or might at some time.[9] My opponents need not be so squeamish—Christ, who is God, used this sort of fiction again and again in his parables!

The fourth kind contains no truth at all, either superficial or hidden, since it consists only of old wives' tales.

Now, if my eminent opponents condemn the first kind of fiction, then they must include the account in Holy Writ describing the conference of the trees of the forest on choosing a king.[10] If the second, then nearly the whole sacred body of the Old Testament will be rejected. God forbid, since the writings of the Old Testament and the writings of the poets seem as it were to keep step with each other, and that too in respect to the method of their composition. For where history is lacking, neither one concerns itself with the superficial possibility, but what the poet calls fable or fiction our theologians have named figure. The truth of this may be seen by fairer judges than my opponents, if they will but weigh in a true scale the outward literary semblance of the visions of Isaiah, Ezekiel, Daniel, and other sacred writers on the one hand, with the outward literary semblance of the fiction of poets on the other. If they find any real discrepancy in their methods, either of implication or exposition, I will accept their condemnation. If they condemn the third form of fiction, it is the same as condemning the form which our Savior Jesus Christ, the Son of God, often used when he was in the flesh, though Holy Writ does not call it *poetry,* but *parable;* some call it *exemplum,* because it is used as such.

I count as naught their condemnation of the fourth form of fiction, since it proceeds from no consistent principle, nor is fortified by the reinforcement of any of the arts, nor carried logically to a conclusion. Fiction of this kind has nothing in common with the works of the poets, though I imagine these objectors think poetry differs from it in no respect.

I now ask whether they are going to call the Holy Spirit, or Christ, the very God, liars, who both in the same Godhead have uttered fictions. I hardly think so, if they are wise. I might show them, your Majesty,[11] if there were time, that difference of names constitutes no objection where methods agree. But they may see for themselves. Fiction, which they scorn because of its mere name, has been the means, as we often read, of quelling minds aroused to a mad rage, and subduing them to their pristine gentleness. Thus,

when the Roman plebs seceded from the senate, they were called back from the sacred mount to the city by Menenius Agrippa, a man of great influence, all by means of a story. By fiction, too, the strength and spirits of great men worn out in the strain of serious crises, have been restored. This appears, not by ancient instance alone, but constantly. One knows of princes who have been deeply engaged in important matters, but after the noble and happy disposal of their affairs of state, obey, as it were, the warning of nature, and revive their spent forces by calling about them such men as will renew their weary minds with diverting stories and conversation. Fiction has, in some cases, sufficed to lift the oppressive weight of adversity and furnish consolation, as appears in Lucius Apuleius; he tells how the highborn maiden Charis, while bewailing her unhappy condition as captive among thieves, was in some degree restored through hearing from an old woman the charming story of Psyche.[12] Through fiction, it is well known, the mind that is slipping into inactivity is recalled to a state of better and more vigorous fruition. Not to mention minor instances, such as my own, I once heard Giacopo Sanseverino, Count of Tricarico and Chiarmonti, say that he had heard his father tell of Robert, son of King Charles—himself in after time the famous King of Jerusalem and Sicily—how as a boy he was so dull that it took the utmost skill and patience of his master to teach him the mere elements of letters. When all his friends were nearly in despair of his doing anything, his master, by the most subtle skill, as it were, lured his mind with the fables of Aesop into so grand a passion for study and knowledge, that in a brief time he not only learned the liberal arts familiar to Italy, but entered with wonderful keenness of mind into the very inner mysteries of sacred philosophy. In short, he made of himself a king whose superior in learning men have not seen since Solomon.

Such then is the power of fiction that it pleases the unlearned by its external appearance, and exercises the minds of the learned with its hidden truth; and thus both are edified and delighted[13] with one and the same perusal. Then let not these disparagers raise their heads to vent their spleen in scornful words, and spew their ignorance upon poets! If they have any sense at all, let them look to their own speciousness before they try to dim the splendor of others with the cloud of their maledictions. Let them see, I pray, how pernicious are their jeers, fit to rouse the laughter only of girls. When they have made themselves clean, let them purify the tales of others, mindful of Christ's commandment to

[9] Reminiscent of Aristotle's idea of plausibility (above, page 66).
[10] Judg. 9.8–15.
[11] The *Genealogy* is dedicated to Hugo IV, king of Cyprus from 1324 to 1358, even though Hugo had died before it was finished.
[12] Apuleius (c. 124–?), *The Golden Ass* IV, 21.
[13] See Horace (above, page 83).

the accusers of the woman taken in adultery, that he who was without sin should cast the first stone.

XIII. Poets Are Not Liars

These enemies of poetry further utter the taunt that poets are liars. This position they try to maintain by the hackneyed objection that poets write lies in their narratives, to wit, that a human being was turned into a stone—a statement in every aspect contrary to the truth. They urge besides that poets lie in asserting that there are many gods, though it is established in all certainly that there is but One—the True and Omnipotent.[14] They add that the greatest Latin poet, Virgil, told the more or less untrue story of Dido,[15] and allege other like instances. I fancy they think their point is already won, and so indeed it would be, were there no one to repel their boorish vociferations with the truth. Yet further discussion seems hardly necessary for I supposed that I had already answered this objection above,[16] where at sufficient length I defined a story, its kinds, what sorts the poets employ, and wherefore.

But if the matter is to be resumed, I insist that, whatever those fellows think, poets are not liars. I had supposed that a lie was a certain very close counterfeit of the truth which served to destroy the true and substitute the false. Augustine mentions eight kinds of lies,[17] of which some are, to be sure, graver than others, yet none, if we employ them consciously, free from sin and the mark of infamy that denotes a liar. If the enemies of poetry will consider fairly the meaning of this definition, they will become aware that their charge of falsehood is without force, since poetic fiction has nothing in common with any variety of falsehood, for it is not a poet's purpose to deceive anybody with his inventions; furthermore, poetic fiction differs from a lie in that in most instances it bears not only no close resemblance to the literal truth, but no resemblance at all; on the contrary, it is quite out of harmony and agreement with the literal truth.

Yet there is one kind of fiction very like the truth, which as I said, is more like history than fiction, and which by most ancient agreement of all peoples has been free from taint of falsehood. This is so in virtue of their consent from of old that anyone who could might use it as an illustration in which the literal truth is not required, nor its opposite forbidden. And if one considers the function of the poet already described, clearly poets are not constrained by this bond to employ literal truth on the surface of their inventions; besides, if the privilege of ranging through every sort of fiction be denied them, their office will altogether resolve itself into naught.

Again: if all my preceding argument should deserve reprobation—and I hardly think it possible—yet this fact remains irrefutable, that no one can in the proper discharge of his duty incur by that act the taint of infamy. If the judge, for example, lawfully visits capital punishment upon malefactors, it is not called homicide. Neither is a soldier who wastes the enemy's fields called a robber. Though a lawyer gives his client advice not wholly just, yet if he breaks not the bounds of the law he does not deserve to be called a falsifier. So also a poet, however he may sacrifice the literal truth in invention, does not incur the ignominy of a liar, since he discharges his very proper function not to deceive, but only by way of invention.

Yet if they will insist that whatever is not literally true, is, however uttered, a lie, I accept it for purposes of argument; if not, I will spend no more energy in demolishing this objection of theirs. Rather I will ask them to tell me what name should be applied to those parts of the Revelation of John the Evangelist—expressed with amazing majesty of inner sense, though often at first glance quite contrary to the truth—in which he has veiled the great mysteries of God. And what will they call John himself? What too will they call the other writers who have employed the same style to the same end? I certainly should not dare answer for them "lies" and "liars," even if I might. Yet I know well they will say what I myself in part am about to say—should anyone ask me—that John and the other prophets were men of absolute truthfulness, a point already conceded. My opponents will add that their writings are not fiction but rather figures, to use the correct term, and their authors are figurative writers. O silly subterfuge! As if I were likely to believe that two things to all appearances exactly alike should gain the power of different effects by mere change or difference of name.

But not to dispute the point, I grant they are figures. Then, let me ask, does the truth which they express lie on their surface? If they wish me to think it does, what else is it but a lie thus to veil the eyes of my understanding, as they also veil the truth beneath? Well then, if these sacred writers must be called liars, though not held such, since indeed they are none, no more are poets to be considered liars who lean with their whole weight upon mere invention.

---

[14] [Osgood] The oft-repeated argument of early apologists, particularly Tertullian, Amobius, Lactantis, and Augustine.

[15] See St. Augustine, *Confessions* I, 13. He makes a criticism of spending time reading poetic fictions, which he considers a waste.

[16] In Chapter 9.

[17] *On Lying*, 14.

Yet without question poets do say in their works that there are many gods, when there is but One. But they should not therefore be charged with falsehood; since they neither believe nor assert it as a fact, but only as a myth or fiction, according to their wont. Who is witless enough to suppose that a man deeply versed in philosophy hasn't any more sense than to accept polytheism? As sensible men we must easily admit that the learned have been most devoted investigators of the truth, and have gone as far as the human mind can explore; thus they know beyond any shadow of doubt that there is but one God. As for poets, their own works clearly show that they have attained to such knowledge. Read Virgil and you will find the prayer: "If any vows, Almighty Jove, can bend Thy will"[18]—an epithet which you will never see applied to another god. The multitude of other gods they looked upon not as gods, but as members or functions of the Divinity; such was Plato's opinion, and we call him a theologian. But to these functions they gave a name in conformity with deity because of their veneration for the particular function in each instance.

But I do not expect these disturbers to hold their peace here. They will cry out the louder that poets have written many lies about this one true God—whom, as I have just said, they recognize—and on that count deserve to be called liars. Of course I do not doubt that pagan poets had an imperfect sense of the true God, and so sometimes wrote of him what was not altogether true—a lie, as their accusers call it. But for all that I think they should hardly be called liars. There are two kinds of liars: first, those who knowingly and willfully lie, whether to injure another person or not, or even to help him. These should not be called merely liars, but, more appropriately, "willful deceivers." The second class are those who have told a falsehood without knowing it. Among these last a further discussion is in order. For in some cases ignorance is neither to be excused nor endured. For example, the law forbids any man privately to hold a citizen prisoner. John Doe has detained Richard Roe, his debtor, and pleads exemption from fine through ignorance of the law; but since such ignorance of the law seems stupid and negligent, it can constitute no defense. Likewise a Christian who is of age should find no protection in ignorance of the articles of faith. On the other hand there are those whose ignorance is excusable, such as boys ignorant of philosophy or a mountaineer ignorant of navigation, or a man congenitally blind who does not know his letters. Such are the pagan poets who, with all their

knowledge of the liberal arts, poetry, and philosophy, could not know the truth of Christianity; for that light of the eternal truth which lighteth every man that cometh into the world had not yet shone forth upon the nations. Not yet had these servants gone throughout all the earth bidding every man to the supper of the Lamb. To the Israelites alone had this gift been granted of knowing the true God aright, and truly worshiping him. But they never invited anyone to share the great feast with them, nor admitted any of the Gentiles at their doors. And if pagan poets wrote not the whole truth concerning the true God, though they thought they did, such ignorance is an acceptable excuse and they ought not to be called liars.

But my opponents will say, that whatever ignorance occasioned the lie, he who told it, is nonetheless a liar. True; but I repeat, they who sinned in pardonable ignorance are not to be damned by the same token as the offenders whose ignorance was crass and negligent; for the law, both in its equity and its austerity, holds them excused, wherefore, they incur not the brand of a lie.

If these disparagers still insist in spite of everything that poets are liars, I accuse the philosophers, Aristotle, Plato, and Socrates of sharing their guilt. Now, I expect, these expert critics will again lift their voices to heaven and cry to the sound of harp and cithera that this objection of theirs has suffered no harm. Fools! Though one small shield be shattered, the whole front does not waver. Let them not exult, but remember how often they have now been belabored and beaten back.

Their objection to Virgil—that no wise man would ever consent to tell the story of Dido—is utterly false. With his profound knowledge of such lore, he was well aware that Dido had really been a woman of exceptionally high character, who would rather die by her own hand than subdue the vow of chastity fixed deep in her heart to a second marriage. But that he might attain the proper effect of his work under the artifice of a poetic disguise, he composed a story in many respects like that of this historic Dido, according to the privilege of poets established by ancient custom. Possibly someone more worthy of a reply than my opponents—perhaps even thou, O Prince—may ask to what purpose this was necessary for Virgil. By way of fitting answer let me then say that his motive was fourfold.

First, that in the same style which he had adopted for the *Aeneid* he might follow the practice of earlier poets, particularly Homer, whom he imitated in this work. For poets are not like historians, who begin their account at some convenient beginning and describe events in the unbroken order of their occurrence to the end. Such, we observe, was Lucan's method, wherefore many think of him rather as a met-

---

[18] *Aeneid* II, 689.

rical historian than a poet.[19] But poets, by a far nobler device, begin their proposed narrative in the midst of the events, or sometimes even near the end; and thus they find excuse for telling preceding events which seem to have been omitted. Thus Homer, in the *Odyssey,* begins, as it were, near the end of Ulysses's wanderings and shows him wrecked upon the Phaeacian shore, then has him tell King Alcinous everything that had happened to him hitherto since he left Troy. Virgil chose the same method in describing Aeneas as a fugitive from the shore of Troy after the city was razed. He found no place so appropriate on which to land him before he reached Italy as the coast of Africa; for at any nearer point he had been sailing continuously among his enemies the Greeks. But since the shore of Africa was at that time still the home of rude and barbarous rustics, he desired to bring his hero to somebody worthy of regard who might receive him and urge him to tell of his own fate and that of the Trojans. Such a one above all he found in Dido, who, to be sure, is supposed to have dwelt there not then, but many generations later, yet Dido he presents as already living, and makes her the hostess of Aeneas; and we read how at her command he told the story of his own troubles and those of his friends.

Virgil's second purpose,[20] concealed within the poetic veil, was to show with what passions human frailty is infested, and the strength with which a steady man subdues them. Having illustrated some of these, he wished particularly to demonstrate the reasons why we are carried away into wanton behavior by the passion of concupiscence; so he introduces Dido, a woman of distinguished family, young, fair, rich, exemplary, famous for her purity, ruler of her city and people, of conspicuous wisdom and eloquence, and, lastly, a widow, and thus from former experience in love, the more easily disposed to that passion. Now all these qualifications are likely to excite the mind of a highborn man, particularly an exile and castaway thrown destitute upon an unknown shore. So he represents in Dido the attracting power of the passion of love, prepared for every opportunity, and in Aeneas one who is readily disposed in that way and at length overcome. But after showing the enticements of lust, he points the way of return to virtue by bringing in Mercury, messenger of the gods, to rebuke Aeneas, and call him back from such indulgence to deeds of glory. By Mer-

cury, Virgil means either remorse, or the reproof of some outspoken friend, either of which rouses us from slumber in the mire of turpitude, and calls us back into the fair and even path to glory. Then we burst the bonds of unholy delight, and, armed with new fortitude, we unfalteringly spurn all seductive flattery, and tears, prayers, and such, and abandon them as naught.

Virgil's third purpose is to extol, through his praise of Aeneas, the *gens Julia* in honor of Octavius; this he does by showing him resolutely and scornfully setting his heel upon the wanton and impure promptings of the flesh and the delights of women.

It is Virgil's fourth purpose to exalt the glory of the name of Rome. This he accomplishes through Dido's execrations at her death; for they imply the wars between Carthage and Rome, and prefigure the triumphs which the Romans gained thereby—a sufficient glorification of the city's name.

Thus it appears that Virgil is not a liar, whatever the unthinking suppose; nor are the others liars who compose in the same manner.

XVII. That Poets Are Merely Apes of the Philosophers

A few of the enemies of poetry who would outdo the rest in their attack say that poets are but apes of the philosophers. I cannot make sure whether such eructation comes from a wish to raise a general laugh, like their cheap jokes among silly girls, or whether it rises from real conviction, or from a mere low and idle desire to ridicule. If the first, then the wise should suffer it to pass, though with some feeling of indignation. For they often see eminent men bantered by the ignorant, who at many a street corner appear disguised as filleted asses, or hogs in their trappings, or in fringed and variegated skins of different beasts; and thus disguised freely utter, with less impropriety, any ribald lampoons they can make up. But if this charge against poets comes from conviction or from desire to ridicule, it is, in either case, both stupid and vicious. The apes' natural and invariable habit (as I remember saying elsewhere) is to imitate as far as they can everything they see, even to the actions of men. Whence these men speciously infer that poets, being imitators, are therefore apes of the philosophers: now this is not so absurd, even if it were true; for philosophers have been for the most part honorable men, and inventors of noble arts. But the ignorant deceive themselves. If they but understood the works of the poets, they would see that, far from being apes, they should be reckoned of the very number of the

---

[19] This point about Marcus Annaeus Lucan (39–65), a Roman epic poet, is later made by Scaliger (below, page 168).

[20] Virgil's "second purpose" seems to correspond to the allegorical and moral levels described by St. Thomas and Dante (above, page 152 and page 154). Boccaccio's explanation follows that of Fulgentius, a Latin grammarian of the sixth century A.D., who described the *Aeneid* as a picture of human life.

philosophers, since they never veil with their inventions anything which is not wholly consonant with philosophy as judged by the opinions of the ancients. And then, too, the pure imitator never sets foot outside his model's track—a fact not observed in poets. For though their destination is the same as that of the philosophers, they do not arrive by the same road. The philosopher, everyone knows, by a process of syllogizing, disproves what he considers false, and in like manner proves his theory, and does all this as obviously as he can. The poet conceives his thought by contemplation, and, wholly without the help of syllogism, veils it as subtly and skillfully as he can under the outward semblance of his invention. The philosopher as a rule employs an unadorned prose style, with something of scorn for literary embellishment. The poet writes in meter, with an artist's most scrupulous care, and in a style distinguished by exquisite charm. It is, furthermore, a philosopher's business to dispute in the lecture room, but a poet's to sing in solitude. With such discrepancy between them, the poet cannot prove to be "the ape of the philosopher." If they called them apes of nature, the epithet might be less irritating, since the poet tries with all his powers to set forth in noble verse the effects, either of nature herself, or of her eternal and unalterable operation. If my opponents care to consider it, they will perceive the forms, habits, discourse, and actions of all animate things, the courses of heaven and the stars, the shattering force of the winds, the roar and crackling of flames, the thunder of the waves, high mountains and shady groves, and rivers in their courses—all these will they find so vividly set forth that the very objects will seem actually present in the tiny letters of the written poem. In this sense, I admit, the poets are apes, and I hold it a task full of honor to attempt with art what nature performs in the fullness of her power. So much upon this point. It would be better for such critics if they would use their best efforts to make us all become apes of Christ, rather than jeer at the labors of poets, which they do not understand. Sometimes people who try to scratch another's itching back feel someone's bloody nails in their own skin—and not so pleasantly either!

from
Book XV

VIII. The Pagan Poets of Mythology Are Theologians

There are certain pietists who, in reading my words, will be moved by holy zeal to charge me with injury to the most sacrosanct Christian religion; for I allege that the pagan poets are theologians—a distinction which Christians grant only to those instructed in sacred literature. These critics I hold in high respect; and I thank them in anticipation for such criticism, for I feel that it implies their concern for my welfare. But the carelessness of their remarks shows clearly the narrow limitations of their reading. If they had read widely, they could not have overlooked that very well-known work on the *City of God,* they might have seen how, in the sixth book, Augustine cites the opinion of the learned Varro, who held that theology is threefold in its divisions—mythical, physical, and civil.[21] It is called mythical, from the Greek *mythicon,* "a myth," and in this kind, as I have already said, is adapted to the use of the comic stage. But this form of literature is reprobate among better poets on account of its obscenity. Physical theology is, as etymology shows, natural and moral, and being commonly thought a very useful thing, it enjoys much esteem. Civil or political theology, sometimes called the theology of state worship, relates to the commonwealth, but through the foul abominations of its ancient ritual, it was repudiated by them of the true faith and the right worship of God. Now of these three, physical theology is found in the great poets since they clothe many a physical and moral truth in their inventions, including within their scope not only the deeds of great men, but matters relating to their gods. And particularly, as they first composed hymns of praise to the gods, and, as I have said, in a poetic guise, presented their great powers and acts, they won the name of theologians even among the primitive pagans. Indeed Aristotle[22] himself avers that they were the first to ponder theology; and though they got their name from no knowledge or lore of the true God, yet at the advent of true theologians they could not lose it, so great was the natural force of the word derived from the theory of any divinity whatsoever. Aware, I suppose, that the title "theologian" once fairly won, cannot be lost, the present-day theologians call themselves

---

[21] [Osgood] *City of God* VI, 5: "Now what are we to say of this proposition of his [Varro's] namely, that there are three kinds of theology, that is, of the account which is given of the gods; and of these, the one is called mythical, the other physical, and the third civil? Did the Latin usage permit, we should call the kind which he has placed first in order 'fabular' *(fabulare),* but let us call it 'fabulous' *(fabulosum),* for 'mythical' is derived from the Greek μιθος, a fable; but that the second should be called 'natural,' the usage of speech now admits; the third he himself has designated in Latin calling it 'civil.' Then he says, 'they call that kind "mythical" which the poets chiefly use; "physical" that which the philosophers use; "civil" that which the people use.'" Augustine condemns the first and third forthwith. For the second, embodying as it does profound if erroneous doctrine about nature and God, he has more respect (VII, 5ff.). On this Boccaccio leans, though one suspects his citation of Augustine as a flourish for effect upon his opponents.

[22] *Metaphysics* II, 4, 12.

professors of sacred theology to distinguish themselves from theologians of mythological cast or any other. Such distinction admits no possible exception as implying an injury to the name of Christianity. Do we not speak of all mortals who have bodies and rational souls as men? Some may be Gentiles, some Israelites, some Agarenes, some Christians, and some so depraved as to deserve the name of gross beasts, not men. Yet we do not wrong our Savior by calling them men, though with his Godhead he is known to have been literally human. No more is there any harm in speaking of the old poets as theologians. Of course, if any one were to call them sacred, the veriest fool would detect the falsehood.

On the other hand there are times, as in this book, when the theology of the ancients will be seen to exhibit what is right and honorable, though in most such cases it should be considered rather physiology or ethology than theology, according as the myths embody the truth concerning physical nature or human. But the old theology can sometimes be employed in the service of catholic truth, if the fashioner of the myths should choose. I have observed this in the case of more than one orthodox poet in whose investiture of fiction the sacred teachings were clothed. Nor let my pious critics be offended to hear the poets sometimes called even sacred theologians. In like manner sacred theologians turn physical when occasion demands; if in no other way, at least they prove themselves physical theologians as well as sacred when they express truth by the fable of the trees choosing a king.

Julius Caesar Scaliger

1484–1558

Scaliger was a philologist, physician, and natural scientist. His *Poetics,* posthumously published, became the source of Aristotelian "rules" for neo-classical writers, at least in northern Europe, but it was meant to be a defense of Virgil and Seneca and went beyond Aristotle in many ways. In the issues it takes up it is representative of its time. Scaliger was influenced by both Aristotle and Horace and by the rhetorical principles of Cicero and Quintilian and thus exemplifies the marriage of rhetoric and poetics that was attempted in Roman criticism and later in the Renaissance. It is rhetoric that tends to dominate Scaliger's approach to literature, and one senses that he may be reducing poetry to oratory. He adopts the Horatian maxim that poetry should delight and teach, but he also emphasizes persuasion. In the end, for him, the poet's moral purpose is paramount.

When Scaliger echoes Aristotle, he often vulgarizes him. This can be seen in the additions he makes to Aristotle's definition of tragedy (above, page 55) and in his own treatment of comedy. He plunges into the discussion begun by Aristotle concerning the difference between poetry and history, generally equating poetry with verse. Sometimes he bases his distinction purely on the medium, sometimes on the subject matter. In the process, he makes statements that are reminiscent of Plato's contrast in *Sophist* (above, page 39) between icastic and phantastic imitation, emphasizing the poet as the god-creator of his work. This idea is later taken up by Sidney (below, page 199), but neither Scaliger nor Sidney is really anticipating a Romantic theory of creative imagination, as in Coleridge (below, page 504). Neither works out of an epistemology not yet invented.

Scaliger, as a scientist of his time, is a classifier and seems almost to regard classification as itself an end, as if, once one decides where to pigeonhole something, that ends the role of criticism.

The only translation into English of Scaliger's *Poetics* is a selection of passages by F. M. Padelford, *Select Translations from Scaliger's* Poetics (1905). See Vernon Hall, Jr., *Life of Julius Caesar Scaliger 1484–1558* (1950). Commentary *passim* on Scaliger can be found in standard histories, including Joel Spingarn, *Literary Criticism in the Renaissance* (1899); Bernard Weinberg, *A History of Literary Criticism in the Italian Renaissance* in two volumes (1961), and Baxter Hathaway's two books, *The Age of Criticism: The Late Renaissance in Italy* (1962) and *Marvels and Commonplaces: Renaissance Italian Literary Criticism* (1968).

from

Poetics

Everything that pertains to mankind may be classed as necessary, useful, or pleasure-giving, and by an inherent characteristic of all these classes the power of speech was implanted in man from the very beginning, or, as time went on, was acquired. Since man's development depended upon learning, he could not do without that agency which was destined to make him the partaker of wisdom. Our speech is, as it were, the postman of the mind, through the services of whom civil gatherings are announced, the arts are cultivated, and the claims of wisdom intercede with men for man. It is of course necessary to secure from others those things which we need, to give orders to have things done, to prohibit, to propose, to dispose, to establish, and to abolish. Such were the functions of early speech.

Then the usefulness and effectiveness of language were increased by rules governing construction, dimensions, as it were, being given to a rude and formless body. Thus arose the established laws of speech. Later, language was adorned and embellished as with raiments, and then it appeared illustrious both in form and in spirit. As to an undefined body the metric science appoints breadth, angles, and length—the masters of harmony also add proportion, the ῥυθμοί[1] of the Greeks—so to an unordered language law first gave the so-called rules. Next, more careful cultivation added knowledge of windings, of valleys and hills, of retreats, of light and shade. To speak figuratively, such cultivation afforded the soldier his necessary armor, the senator his useful toga, or the more elegant citizen his richer pleasure-robe. Not unlike these were the ends which language served, since necessity demanded language in the search of the philosophers after truth, utility dictated its cultivation in statesmanship, and pleasure drew it to the theatre. The language of the philosophers, confined to exact, logical reasoning, was necessarily concise and adapted to the subject-matter. On the other hand, in the forum and the camp less precise expression was permissible, governed by the subject, the place, the time, and the audience, and such speaking was called oratory. The third class contains two species, not very unlike, which in common employ narration, and use much embellishment. They differ, however, in that one professes to record the fixed truth, and employs a simple style of composition, while the other either adds a fictitious element to the truth, or imitates the truth by fiction, of course with more elaboration. While, as we have said, they are both equally narrative in character, the name History came to be applied to the former alone, since, I suppose, it was satisfied merely with that field of writing adapted to setting forth actual events. On the other hand, the latter was called Poetry, or Making, because it narrated not only actual events, but also fictitious events as if they were actual, and represented them as they might be or ought to be. Wherefore the basis of all poetry is imitation.

Imitation, however, is not the end of poetry, but is intermediate to the end. The end is the giving of instruction in pleasurable form,[2] for poetry teaches, and does not simply amuse, as some used to think. Whenever language is used, the purpose, of course, is to acquaint the hearer with a fact or with the thought of the speaker, but because the primitive poetry was sung, its design seemed merely to please; yet underlying the music was that for the sake of which music was provided only as a sauce. In time this rude and pristine invention was enriched by philosophy, which made poetry the medium of its teaching. Let it be further said that when poetry describes military counsels, at one time open and frank, at another crafty—the στρατήγημα[3] of the Greeks—when it tells of tempests, of wars, of routs, of various artifices, all is for one purpose: it imitates that it may teach. So in *The Frogs* of Aristophanes, to the one who asked him, 'What merit in a poet can arouse the greatest admiration for him?' Euripides made a good answer when he replied, 'The ability to impress adroitly upon citizens the need of being better men.' Plato was less happy in the *Ion* in saying that a rhapsodist cannot satisfactorily represent military or nautical doings, because such arts are foreign to him.[4] For the rhapsodist will say nothing worse about such things than the poet has written of them, since, as is very well remarked in the same passage, while the poet is the imitator of things, the rhapsodist is he who acts out the imitation, and according as the poet represents, the rhapsodist can reproduce.

Now is there not one end, and one only, in philosophical exposition, in oratory, and in the drama? Assuredly such is the case. All have one and the same end—persuasion;

Scaliger's *Poetics* was posthumously published in 1561. The text, translated from the Latin, is by F. M. Padelford, *Select Translations from Scaliger's Poetics* (New Haven: Yale University Press, 1905).
[1] Rhythm.

[2] Socrates challenged defenders of poetry to show this to be true (Plato, above, page 36). The notion is expressed in Horace (above, page 80), and Scaliger adopts it, particularly against those early churchmen who would disparage poetry as trivial entertainment.
[3] Strategema, the acts of a general.
[4] See Plato (above, page 15).

for, you see, just as we were saying above, whenever language is used it either expresses a fact or the opinion of the speaker. The end of learning is knowledge, that is, knowledge, of course, interpreted in no narrow sense. An accurate and simple definition of knowledge is as follows: Belief based either upon conclusive evidence, or upon a loose notion. Thus we say, 'I know that Dido committed suicide because Aeneas departed.' Now we do not know any such thing, but this is popularly accepted as the truth. Persuasion, again, means that the hearer accepts the words of the speaker. The soul of persuasion is truth, truth either fixed and absolute, or susceptible of question. Its end is to convince, or to secure the doing of something. Truth, in turn, is agreement between that which is said about a thing and the thing itself.

By no means are we to accept the popular idea that eloquent speaking, rather than persuasion, is the end of oratory, for the arguments of the grammarians on this point are not valid. Clearly, if a man does not persuade, this is due to no fault of the art, but either to the issue, which it is beyond the power of the orator to control, wherefore he does not cease to be an orator, or to some defect of his own, which may either reside in his speaking or in the bad cause which he espouses. In this last case he is either no orator, or else he is a knave.[5]

Eloquent speaking certainly cannot be the end, for obviously it is the means to an end, or a mode of the means. An end is not that which serves another end, but that which all serves, and so one uses eloquence that he may persuade. Moreover, you are not the arbiter of your eloquence, but the judge is, and if he does not think you eloquent, not only is your eloquence fruitless, but it is not eloquence at all.[6] Therefore you may go away frustrated in your purpose, even though you have spoken eloquently. Further, it is not possible that both the defendant and the plaintiff should be equally eloquent; in fact it is necessary that one or the other should lose his cause, or should merit losing it. Therefore he will not be your orator whom you have picked out as eloquent.

Finally, in that treatise entitled Εἰσαγωγικός, attributed to Galen, and in that other work on the science of medicine, the Σύστασις, which is more confidently attributed to him, two kinds of arts are recognized.[7] If Quintilian,[8] by

the way, had run across this idea in Plato, from whom Galen borrowed it, he would have changed his theory about the end of oratory. Two kinds there are, then. Arts of the one kind can attain their ends in and of themselves, such as shoemaking, carpentry, and the like; the others are not thus able, as oratory, medicine, and navigation. The latter arts the Greeks denominate στογαστικαί (conjectural), because, as is stated in the Philebus,[9] they proceed, so to speak, by conjecture, not by fixed principle. Now, for my part, I take a different view. Medicine always cures curable diseases, but the physician does not always do so, because he is embarrassed by many obstacles; wherefore in that case he fails to be a doctor. In fact the physician does not accept an incurable case unless he be careless, or stupid, greedy for fees, or rash. Further, accidents are wont to befall the sick, either through their own instrumentality, or that of their servants, or through some chance happening, as of the atmosphere, the sun, dampness, anger, grief, fear, and the like. Here belong what Hippocrates and other physicians call external agencies—τὰ ἐξωθεν.[10] Indeed, not even nature herself is a perfectly reliable workman, for occasionally she is embarrassed and fails of her end, as when she produces a monstrosity, or brings forth defective bodies.

The orator, then, speaks in the forum that good may be meted to good men, and punishment to evil men; in assemblies and councils that public affairs may be well administered; and in eulogies that we may be won from evil by good example, and may pursue and practice that which is set forth as honest. In this last class, the epideictic,[11] certain invectives are to be included. Other kinds of invectives, however, belong to judicial bodies, such as those uttered in the presence of witnesses; still others to deliberative bodies, as the speeches against Antony and Catiline,[12] and the addresses on consular provinces.

All of these different kinds of speaking have a common end. To be sure, there are those who contend that in judicial proceedings the end is justice; in deliberative proceedings, utility; and in eulogies, honesty; but such are properly rebuked by Quintilian. The ground of the rebuke should be noted rather carefully, for not only do these men reason superficially, but they even contradict themselves. In fact, in another passage they confound utility with honesty. But all that aside, be it observed that utility is the end

---

[5] Scaliger is well aware of the suspicion of rhetoric and sophistry in Plato, and he tries to separate the art of oratory as such from the false practitioners of it.

[6] See Cicero (above, page 74).

[7] Two works of the celebrated Greek physician (129–c. 199).

[8] Marcus Fabius Quintilianus (c. 35–95), influential rhetorician, author of Institutio oratoria.

[9] A dialogue probably of Plato's middle period (above, page 40).

[10] Ta exothen, matters outside the house.

[11] Sometimes called the rhetoric of praise or blame; ceremonial, as it is called by Aristotle, usually without the external purpose of the judicial and deliberative types.

[12] Orations by Cicero.

of all the virtues, wherefore also of justice. And since justice is the righteous payment to a man of that which is his own or its equivalent, justice is the end of deliberative counsels. Justice is even the end of war, for the councils of war—they are very many—are held for the sake of justice. Finally, if the end of man is virtue, honesty is either a state of mind induced by virtue, or it is the soul of virtue. Of every human office, of every act and thought, honesty will be the end.

We must consider even more carefully than did Quintilian the basis for the classification of the different kinds of speaking. That he might simplify the three-fold division, he classified as follows: cases either are subject for judicial investigation, or are outside of it. The latter relate either to the past or to the future. Those relating to the past are epideictic; those of the future, deliberative. But now who does not appreciate that in judicial proceedings the past is involved? Wherefore it is not possible for the latter to form a sub-species of the judicial. So I would have altered the statement as follows: a case is either in the past or in the future; the latter alone prescribes deliberation; the former divides into the forensic, or judicial, and the epideictic. Although that discerning man, the disciple of the first philosopher, classed them as forensic, deliberative, and epideictic, an accused man is never tried or defended without praise or censure either of a person, an event, an act, a word, or a policy, and in like manner never without deliberation. Indeed, it is deliberated whether to convict or to acquit the defendant. So you see that there cannot be species or genera of cases, because no species of one is able to be part of another species.

Finally, it is improper, as some do, to call speeches of a deliberative nature hortatory, for persuasion is the end of all speaking. What else does an orator do than create confidence, and this, to persuade? Quintilian makes an equally bad mistake when he interprets the word ἐπιδεικτικός to mean ostentatious speaking, on the ground that the word usually had this meaning among the Greeks. So far is this from the truth, that the philosophers used it to define the most simple and exact exposition.

Let it be observed, while we are on the subject, that in deliberative and judicial speaking the orator depends upon his audience. Indeed, the accomplishment of that purpose in behalf of which he essays to speak hinges upon the favor of his hearers. Let it be further noted, that in epideictic speaking the case is the opposite of this, inasmuch as the mind of the hearer is surrendered to the speaker. It is, indeed, as if he who adjudges praise were himself relieved from judgment. These points in which we differ from the recognized opinions of the rhetoricians must, from the very nature of my undertaking, be dwelt upon, just as we have dealt more accurately with various other matters. Thus we might say that the translative state could be subsumed under the conjectural,[13] since in both, the fact being conceded, it is a question who is responsible for it. All kinds of speeches have this in common. The orator in the forum debates concerning life, vices, virtues, examining them in the state of quality, and in that in which inquiry is made concerning what is,[14] just as in councils the question is what is to be preferred. But the philosopher and the poet deal with all such matters in the very same spirit, each in his own person or in that of another. As an illustration of the latter mode, Socrates introduces Diotimas or Aspasia, and Plato brings forward Socrates; and the orator in like manner interjects personifications. If he would eulogize a man, he must needs touch upon the story of his life, his family, his nation; and this allies him with the historian. The historian, on his part, frequently adds a characterization, such as we read of Camillus, Scipio, Hannibal, Jugurtha, and Cicero; and, as it were, intersperses his decrees. But it is only poetry which includes everything of this kind, excelling those other arts in this, that while they, as we have said above, represent things just as they are, in some sense like a speaking picture,[15] the poet depicts quite another sort of nature, and a variety of fortunes; in fact, by so doing, he transforms himself almost into a second deity.[16] Of those things which the Maker of all framed, the other sciences are, as it were, overseers; but since poetry fashions images of those things which are not, as well as images more beautiful than life of those things which are, it seems unlike other literary forms, such as history, which confine themselves to actual events, and rather to be another god, and to create. In view of this fact, its common title was furnished it, not by the agreement of men, but by the provident wisdom of nature. I must express my surprise that when the learned Greeks had most happily defined the poet as the *maker,* our ancestors should be so unfair to themselves as to limit the term to candle-makers, for though usage has sanctioned this practice, etymologically it is absurd.[17]

---

[13] [Padelford] For these technical terms see Quintilian, Book 3, Chapter 6, especially section 45ff.

[14] [Padelford] The definitive state.

[15] See Horace (above, page 78).

[16] Sidney seems to have adopted this remark, below, page 188.

[17] [Padelford] Saintsbury, *Hist. of Crit.* 2.71: "This joke requires a little explanation and adaptation to get it into English. The Latin is *miror majores nostros sibi tam iniquos fuisse ut factoris vocem maluerint oleariorum cancellis circumscribere.* In fact *fattojo* and *fattojano,* if not *fattore,* do mean in Italian 'oil-press' and 'oil-presser.'"

* * *

We may make a threefold classification of poets, according to poetical inspiration, age, and subjects.[18] Plato first, and then Aristotle, said that there are diversities of inspiration, for some men are born inspired, while others, born ignorant and rude, and even averse to the art, are seized on by the divine madness, and wrested from their lowliness. It is the work of the gods, who, though divine, use even these as their servants. Thus Plato himself, in the *Ion*, calls such men the interpreters and expounders of the gods.[19] Wherefore the dictum expressed in the *Republic*, which some crude and insensible men would construe to the exclusion of poets from the republic, should be taken less seriously, for though he condemns certain scurrilous passages in the poets, we are not on that account to ignore those other passages which Plato cites times out of mind in support of his own theories. Plato should remark how many impertinent and low stories he himself employs, what filthy thoughts this Greek rogue often forces upon us. Surely the *Symposium*, the *Phaedrus,* and other such monstrous productions, are not worth reading.

The poets invoke the Muses, that the divine madness may imbue them to do their work. Of these divinely possessed ones, two classes are to be recognized. The one class are those to whom the divine power comes from above, with no mental effort on their part except the simple invocation. Hesiod classed himself in this category, and Homer is placed there by universal consent. The other class is aroused by the fumes of unmixed wine, which draws out the instruments of the mind, the spirits themselves, from the material parts of the body. Horace said that Ennius was such a poet, and such we consider Horace himself. Tradition says the same of Alcaeus and Aristophanes. Alcman did not escape such censure, and Sophocles applied it to Aeschylus: 'Wine,' he said, 'not Aeschylus, was the author of his tragedies.'

Again, poets may be divided into three classes, according to the age in which they wrote. First, there was that pristine, crude, and uncultivated age, of which only a vague impression remains. No name survives, unless it be that of Apollo, as the originator of poetry. Then there is the second and venerable period, when religion and the mysteries are first sung. Among the poets of this period are numbered Orpheus, Musaeus, and Linus; Plato includes Olympus also. Of the third period Homer is the founder and parent, and it includes Hesiod and other such writers. If it were not for historical records, one could fancy that Musaeus was later than Homer, for he is more polished and refined. Aelian states that Oroebantius of Troezen, and Dares the Phrygian, flourished before Homer, and that in Homer's time the *Iliad* of Dares was held in esteem. The same author has it that Syager the poet even antedated Musaeus and Orpheus, and that he was the first to write of the Trojan war.

The third classification is according to subject-matter. This the Greeks call ὑποκείμενον;[20] our uncultivated philosophers, most correctly, subject; and the Latin philosophers, somewhat inappositely, argument. Of this class of poets there are as many kinds as there are styles of subjects treated. Yet for the sake of treatment, the poets may be classed under three principal heads. The first is that of the religious poets. Such are Orpheus and Amphion, whose art was so divine that they are believed to have given a soul to inanimate things. The second is that of the philosophical poets, and these again are of two sorts—natural, as Empedocles, Nicander, Aratus, and Lucretius; and moral, including the political, as Solon and Tyrtaeus; the economical, as Hesiod; and the general, as Phocylides, Theognis, and Pythagoras.

Now all that we have been saying may be equally well applied to women authors. They too merit praise. Such authors are Sappho; Corinna, the mistress of Pindar; Hedyle, the mother of the Samian or Athenian poet Hedylus, who excelled in iambic poetry; Megalostrata, whom Alcman loved, and others.

I leave it to the judgment of each one to determine whether or no the poetry of Martius and of the Sibyls should be referred to such categories as the above. My preference is not to do so, for they do not narrate past events, but predict future ones. This part of theology is not simply learning about the gods, but actual utterance of the things disclosed by the gods.

As for our poetry,[21] Gellius is authority for the statement that it was born during the Second Punic War. Let me give his own choice words: 'In the Second Punic War, with winged step the Muse bore herself to the warlike, rugged race of Romulus.'[22] On the other hand, it is commonly re-

---

[18] Scaliger includes in his threefold classification a number of legendary Greek poets: in the classification according to age, those who antedate Homer, and in the classification according to subject matter, Orpheus, Amphion, and the Sibyls. The identity of Martius is unknown. The other Greek poets Scaliger mentions are known to have written between the seventh and first centuries B.C.

[19] See Plato (above, page 12).

[20] Upokeimenon, what lies beneath.

[21] Roman poetry.

[22] A Gellius, *Noctes Atticae* (Attican Nights) XVII, xxi, 45.

ceived that Livius Andronicus wrote his dramas before Naevius, who gave his to the public in the year 519 (A. U. C.).[23]

Now that the poets are enumerated and classified, certain questions may receive attention. Why does Horace question whether or not comedy is poetry? Forsooth, because it is humble, must it be denied the title of poetry? Surely an unfortunate ruling! So far from comedy not being poetry, I would almost consider it the first and truest of all poetry, for comedy employs every kind of invention, and seeks for all kinds of material.

Another question: Was Lucan a poet? Surely he was. As usual, the grammarians deny this, and object that he wrote history. Well now! produce a pure history. Lucan must differ from Livy, and the difference is verse. Verse is the property of the poet. Then who will deny that all epic poets go to history for their subjects? History, sometimes delineated only in semblance, sometimes idealized, and always with changed aspect, is made the basis of poetry. Is not this the practice of Homer? Do we not do this in the tragedies themselves? Such is the practice of Lucan. Instance the image of the country offering itself to Caesar, the spirit called forth from Hades, and other such episodes. Wherefore, indeed, it seems to me that it would be better to give the title of poet to Livy than to deny it to Lucan. For as the tragic poets base their plays upon true events, but adapt the actions and speeches to the characters, so Livy and Thucydides insert orations which were never recognized by those to whom they were attributed. Moreover, although Aristotle exercised this censure so severely that he would refuse the name of poet to versifiers, yet in practice he speaks differently, and says: 'As Empedocles poetically wrote (ἐποίησεν)'; so he even calls Empedocles, who feigned not at all, a poet.[24]

* * *

Tragedy and comedy are of the same genus, and share in common the name drama. Clearly this is not far from the thought that Plato touched upon, but did not elaborate, in the *Symposium*.

The grammarians did some more false teaching about comedy when they said that it was poetry based upon imitation, and consisted in gesticulation and delivery, for surely a comedy is no less a comedy if it be read in silence. Then

gesture is confined to recitation, and not all who read, recite. Moreover, we hear too much about imitation being the end of poetry in general. So our definition would be: Comedy is a dramatic poem, which is filled with intrigue, full of action, happy in its outcome, and written in a popular style.

An inaccurate definition of the Latin comedy described it as 'a plot free from the suggestion of danger, dealing with the life and affairs of the private citizen.' In the first place, this definition covers other, non-dramatic stories, which can be presented in simple narration. In the second place, there is always the suggestion of danger in comedy, although the outcome is invariably tame. What else is danger than the approach or the visitation of imminent danger? Further, there is not only danger in comedy, but violence at the hands of panderers, rivals, lovers, servants, or masters. Thus in the *Asinaria* and *The Ghost* even the masters themselves are ill-treated. Once more, this definition would not admit the official class, wearers of the toga, for they are not private citizens. Finally, the definition would embrace mimes and dramatic satires.

Crates of Athens was the first to write comedy free from the shackles of metre.[25]

Now since comedy and tragedy are of the same genus, it is important to know the extent of the similarity. We will first treat of tragedy in general, and then later we will discuss the characters and actions in comedy and tragedy respectively.

* * *

The definition of tragedy given by Aristotle is as follows: 'Tragedy is an imitation of an action that is illustrious, complete, and of a certain magnitude, in embellished language, the different kinds of embellishments being variously employed in the different parts, and not in the form of narration, but through pity and fear effecting the purgation of such like passions.'[26] I do not wish to attack this definition other than by adding my own: A tragedy is the imitation of the adversity of a distinguished man; it employs the form of action, presents a disastrous *dénouement,* and is expressed in impressive metrical language. Though Aristotle adds harmony and song, they are not, as the philosophers say, of the essence of tragedy; its one and only essential is acting. Then the phrase 'of a certain magnitude' is put in to differentiate the tragedy from the epic, which is sometimes prolix. It is not always so, however, as the work

---

[23] The Roman year 519 is 235 B.C.
[24] Aristotle does not refuse the name of poet to versifiers but asserts that to versify does not mean one has written a poem. See Aristotle (above, page 52).

[25] Greek poet, fifth century B.C. His works except for fragments are lost.
[26] See Aristotle (above, page 55).

of Musaeus[27] illustrates. Further, the mention of 'purgation' is too restrictive, for not every subject produces this effect. 'A certain magnitude', to return to the phrase, means not too long and not too short, for a few verses would not satisfy the expectant public, who are prepared to atone for the disgusting prosiness of many a day by the enjoyment of a few hours. Prolixity, however, is just as bad, when you must say with Plautus: 'My legs ache with sitting, and my eyes with looking.'[28]

* * *

The early orators had only one end in view, to persuade and move their hearers, and their language was correspondingly rude; the poets sought only to please, and they whiled away their leisure simply with alluring songs. In due time, however, orator and poet secured from each other that which they lacked respectively. Isocrates is credited with having first given graceful movement to a hitherto rude diction, though deeper students of the literary monuments award this distinction to Thrasymachus, and add that his diligent efforts were furthered by Gorgias, while the work of Isocrates was to add the finishing touch.[29] As to poetry, on the other hand, it was rendered more thoughtful by being transferred from the country to the town, where plots were added to furnish warning examples, and sentiments to furnish precepts.

Horace most aptly said, 'He carries every vote who mingles the useful with the pleasing,'[30] for poetry bends all its energies to these two ends, to teach and to please. Now to realize these ends one's work must conform to certain principles. In the first place his poem must be deeply conceived, and be unvaryingly self-consistent. Then he must take pains to temper all with variety (varietas), for there is no worse mistake than to glut your hearer before you are done with him. What then are the dishes which would create distaste rather than pleasure? The third poetic quality is found in but few writers, and is what I would term vividness (efficacia); there is also a Greek name for it which will be given in the proper place. By vividness I mean a certain potency and force in thought and language which compels one to be a willing listener. The fourth is winsomeness (suavitas), which tempers the ardency of this last quality, of itself inclined to be harsh. Insight and foresight (prudentia), vari-

ety, vividness, and winsomeness, these, then, are the supreme poetic qualities.

* * *

We have already remarked that for objects of every kind there exists one perfect original to which all the rest can be referred as their norm and standard. In epic poetry, which describes the descent, life, and deeds of heroes, all other kinds of poetry have such a norm, so that to it they turn for their regulative principles. Now our First Book has shown into what species poetry is divided. We shall therefore derive from the sovereignty of the epic the universal controlling rules for the composition of each other kind, according to its distinctive subject-matter and nature. Having thus found the laws common to all, we are to determine the privileges of each, making heroic poetry our point of departure.

After one has determined in a general way the events and characters of a poem, has adjusted them to times and places, and has deduced the sequence of action, there remains the composition according to a well-known principle. The precept of Horace to begin ab ovo is by no means to be followed.[31] Rather let the first rule be, to begin with something grand, cognate with the theme, and intimately related. This rule was observed by Lucan,[32] who, in writing of the Civil War, begins with Caesar's crossing of the Rubicon, because for this act the senate adjudged him an enemy, and compelled him to make war. A second rule: Do not repeat and double on your tracks, lest you become tedious. If the same event is often repeated, it is of necessity intrusively forced upon the attention, which is utterly contrary to the general rules heretofore established. The very thing, therefore, which you are going to take as your principal theme should not be placed first in the narrative, for the mind of the hearer is to be kept in suspense, awaiting that which is to develop. It is obviously a unique and chief virtue to hold the hearer captive. For this reason the greatest of poets so arranged his material that the end of the narrative of Aeneas was in reality the beginning of the action proper: 'Thence me in my wanderings the God has driven to your shores.' From this point the story moves on evenly. To be sure, it is interrupted by novel experiences, but these are constituent parts of it, or closely related. Thus the insertion of the story of Camilla looks to the fact that her death is atoned for by the death of Aruns. The critics have failed to note the nice

[27] Probably the author of Hero and Leander, c. fifth century.
[28] Titus Maccius Plautus (c. 254–c. 184 B.C.), Roman poet and comic playwright.
[29] All those mentioned were celebrated Greek rhetoricians.
[30] Horace (above, page 83).

[31] Horace hardly says this.
[32] Marcus Annaeus Lucanus (39–65), Latin poet, in his Bellum civile.

variation in this passage, for though in this catalogue of warriors he gives the country, parents, and race of many, he only says of Camilla that she was fleet of foot, and the reason is that Diana was to tell the story of her life in a later book. In this instance, Virgil was acting in obvious conformity with the above principle. This principle of arrangement has a most admirable realization in the *Aethiopica* of Heliodorus,[33] a book, I take it, that should be most carefully conned by the epic poet, as furnishing him the best model.

Another principle is that an author should divide his book into chapters in imitation of nature, which subdivides into parts of parts, all so related that they consitute an organic body. But in doing this, you should so assign each part to its proper place that the book shall seem to have shaped itself inevitably, an achievement perfectly realized only by the divine Maro.[34] If one will read the *Aeneid* attentively, he will see that it conforms to this principle. To be sure, the *Georgics* does not, but this exception is due to the nature of the subject-matter.

* * *

Of well-governed conduct there is, as it were, a definite form, which the philosophers call right reason. Is there any form of evil conduct? No, there is not. But in the absence of such form we are either bad or else indifferent. What then does the poet teach? Does he teach actions, which arise from mental states or dispositions, the $\delta\iota\alpha\theta\acute{\epsilon}\sigma\epsilon\iota\varsigma$[35] of the Greeks? Or does he teach us how to become such men that the faculty of doing good is potent, and the principle of avoiding evil conduct is implanted?

Aristotle ruled that since poetry is comparable to that civic institution which leads us to happiness, happiness being nothing other than perfect action, the poet does not lead us to imitate character, but action. Surely he is right; we agree perfectly. But what he adds offers a little more difficulty. He says that there cannot be a tragedy without action, though there may be one without disposition. Under the circumstances, I would here translate $\overset{\text{'}}{\eta}\theta o\varsigma$[36] by 'character,' for he says that the tragic poets of his day usually constructed plots that lacked delineation of character. Thus Zeuxis the painter gave no expression of character in his work, and Polygnotus excelled in character-drawing. But if now $\overset{\text{'}}{\eta}\theta o\varsigma$ means 'an inclination to a certain course of action,' and this is excluded from tragedy, the action will be altogether fortuitous, and wholly dependent on chance. To illustrate: Orestes once committed murder by slaying his mother. Yet here there is no question of character, for it was not a characteristic action. On the other hand, Aegisthus was a murderer in character, and so were Polymnestor, Pylades, Euclio, Pseudolus, Ballio, and Davus. So our inquiry is not as to whether the poet teaches character or action, but as to whether he teaches a mental disposition, or the outward expression of it. Though many things are done contrary to character, they are not done without our being disposed to do them. The result of the inquiry is, then, that the poet teaches mental disposition through action, so that we embrace the good and imitate it in our conduct, and reject the evil and abstain from that. Action, therefore, is a mode of teaching; disposition, that which we are taught. Wherefore action is, as it were, the pattern or medium in a plot, disposition its end. But in civil life action is the end, and disposition its *form*.

If any one thinks that our distinctions are more subtle than the subject warrants, he need not take it to heart; he will find it very easy to leave the whole matter alone.

Aristotle was also illogical in attributing to tragedy alone that which was the common property of poetry, just as when he formulated metrical laws from words and the parts of words, and afterwards ignored those very laws themselves.

---

[33] Writer of the Greek romance in ten books (late fourth century).

[34] Virgil (Publius Virgilius Maro, 70–19 B.C.).

[35] Diathesies, disposition, arrangement, composition.

---

[36] Ethos, character.

Lodovico Castelvetro

(1505–1571)

Castelvetro, known in his time for the breadth of his learning, wrote a commentary on Aristotle that remained the best known and most influential until the end of the eighteenth century even though many disagreed with his interpretation. He begins the following selection from the commentary with the assertion that he is in complete agreement with Aristotle on all points. However, as we read, we discover that there are some significant differences, at least from the way Aristotle is usually interpreted today. Indeed, Castelvetro often uses Aristotle as a beginning for the elaboration of his own views, and in the process he frequently distorts or hardens Aristotle. It is clear early in the selection below, for example, that his meandering comparison of poetry to history goes beyond what Aristotle said or is likely to have thought. It is clear also that he casts a moralistic meaning over Aristotle's psychologistic notion of catharsis. But probably most significant is his attitude toward fiction, especially the unities of action and time. Thus tragedy and epic should be based on historical events (comedy is excepted), and the time represented in a tragedy should not be of more than a day.

Answering Plato and following Horace, Castelvetro requires the poem to delight and teach, as do many of his contemporaries. In his effort to square this requirement with Aristotle's notion of catharsis, he must try to show that catharsis is itself delightful, an "oblique pleasure" connected with our own self-love. Utility and delight are interrelated, and poetry is of particular use because it offers significant events rather than dry abstract persuasion.

Perhaps the most telling, and certainly the most charming, of Castelvetro's illustrations of unity in the detail of plot is the story of Michelangelo restoring the beard to a statue of a rediscovered river god. In telling this story, Castelvetro emphasizes the importance of the relationship among the parts of the work of art to each other and to the whole, and here he comes closer to a truly Aristotelian attitude than do his more rigid discussions of verisimilitude and the unities.

No full translation of Castelvetro's commentary on Aristotle's *Poetics* exists. An edition in Italian was published in 1978. The reader may consult A. H. Gilbert, ed., *Literary Criticism: Plato to Dryden* (1962) and Andrew Bongiorno, ed., *Castelvetro and the Art of Poetry: An Abridged Translation* (1984) for further translated parts. See H. B. Charlton, *Castelvetro's Theory of Poetry* (1913) and R. C. Malzi, *Castelvetro's Annotations to the "Inferno"* (1966). Castelvetro is discussed in the major histories of this period of Italian criticism: Joel E. Spingarn, *A History of Literary Criticism in the Renaissance* (1899); Bernard Weinberg, *A History of Literary Criticism in the Italian Renaissance* in two volumes (1961); Baxter Hathaway, *The Age of Criticism: The Late Renaissance in Italy* (1962).

from

The *Poetics* of Aristotle Translated and Explained

I

. . . Aristotle writes that the sciences and the arts and history are not subjects of poetry. But I, who do not in the least have an opinion different from Aristotle's and think he is entirely correct, believe I can explain the reasons which have led me to hold the same views; which if not altogether identical with Aristotle's, are perhaps not very different. . . . Poetry is a likeness of or resemblance to history. And, since history is divided into two main parts, that is, subject matter and words, so poetry is divided into two main parts which are likewise subject matter and words. But history and poetry differ in these two parts in that history does not have a subject matter provided by the talent of the historian; rather it is prepared for him by the course of worldly events or by the manifest or hidden will of God. The words are provided by the historian, but they are the sort used in reasoning. The subject matter of poetry is discovered and imagined by the talent of the poet, and its words are not the sort used in reasoning, because men are not accustomed to reason in verse. But the words of poetry are composed in measured verse by the working of the poet's genius.

Now the subject matter of poetry ought to be similar to that of history and resemble it, but it should not be identical, because if it were it would no longer be similar or resembling and if it were not similar or resembling, the poet would not have exerted himself at all and would not have shown the sharpness of his talent in discovering it and hence would not deserve praise. And especially he would not deserve that praise by which he is thought to be more divine than human; for he knows how to manage a tale, imagined by himself about things which have never happened, so as to make it no less delightful and no less verisimilar than what occurs through the course of worldly events or the infinite providence of God, either manifest or hidden. Therefore when the poet takes his subject matter from history, that is, from events which have happened, he takes no pains, nor is it clear that he is either a good or a bad

poet, that is, that he does or does not know how to discover things like the truth, and he cannot be praised for making resemblances and thus he is criticized and considered to have little judgment because he has not recognized this. Or else he is thought to possess an evil and deceptive nature if with the covering and colors of poetic language he has tried to dupe his readers or listeners into believing that there is poetic material beneath his words and hence to gain false commendation for it. Logically, therefore, Lucan, Silius Italicus, and Girolamo Fracastoro in his *Joseph* are to be removed from the company of poets and deprived of the glorious title of poetry because in their writings they have treated material already dealt with by historians, it is sufficient that it has already happened and was not thought up by these writers.[1]

From this also it can be understood that the arts and sciences cannot be the subject matter of poetry and cannot with approval be included in poems, because the arts and sciences, having already been considered and understood by reasons which are necessary and verisimilar and by the long experience of philosophers and artists, are in the same position as history and things which have already occurred. The poet who merely embellishes with poetic language the subjects already established and written by others, and about which it can be said that history has already been composed, has no place here in the sense that he can boast of being a poet. Therefore it is not astonishing if those versifiers, Empedocles, Lucretius, Nicander, Serenus, Girolamo Fracastoro in his *Syphilis,* Aratus, Manilius, Giovanni Pontano in his *Urania,* and Virgil in his *Georgics,* are not accepted into the company of poets, for even if they themselves have been the first to discover some science or art, not deriving them from another philosopher or artist, and have revealed their discoveries in verse, they should not thereby be called poets.[2] For if they have discovered some science or art by speculation, they have still discovered something already in existence and bound to continue to exist in the nature of things, something with which that science is concerned or according to which that art is constituted. They will have discharged the office of a good philosopher or a good artist, but not of a good poet, which is by observation to make resemblances of the truth about what happens to men through fortune, and by resemblances to provide delight to the

---

Castelvetro's Poetica *d'Aristotele vulgarizzata et sposta* was published in 1570 and revised in 1576. The text printed here was translated especially for this book by Robert L. Montgomery. Chapter numbers are those of Aristotle's *Poetics.*

---

[1] Marcus Annaeus Lucanus (39–65), Roman poet; Silius Italicus (c. 25–c. 100), Roman poet; Girolamo Fracastoro (1483–1553), Italian physician.
[2] Aristotle raises the question of whether Empedocles (fifth century B.C.) was a poet. See above, page 52. The poets to whom Castelvetro refers wrote discourses in verse on various subjects.

audience, leaving the discovery of the truth derived from natural or accidental things to the philosopher or to the artists who have their own ways of delighting or entertaining which are quite distant from that of the poet.

In addition to this, the subject matter of the arts and sciences, for another reason more evident to common sense, cannot be the subject matter of poetry, inasmuch as poetry has been found solely to delight and recreate; and I say to delight and recreate the minds of the vulgar multitude and common people.[3] They do not understand the reasons, distinctions, or arguments subtle and remote from the practice of common men which philosophers use in investigating the truth of things and artists in practicing their skills. It is not fitting that a listener, when another speaks to him, should be annoyed or displeased, for we are naturally uncommonly irritated when another speaks to us in a way which we cannot understand. Therefore if we concede that the subject matter of the arts and sciences is the subject matter of poetry, we will also concede that either poetry was not discovered to delight or that it was not meant for the common people, but so that it might instruct and that for the sake of those sophisticated in letters and dissertation. This will be acknowledged to be false by what we shall prove as we proceed.

Now because poetry has been found, as I say, to delight and recreate the common people, it ought to have as its subject matter those things which can be understood by the common people and which, when they are understood, make them happy. These are things which happen daily, which are talked about by the people, and which resemble news of the world and history. And for this reason, I affirm, with respect to the subject matter, that poetry is a likeness of or resemblance to history. The subject matter, because it resembles history, not only makes its inventor glorious and makes and constitutes him a poet, but also delights more than an account of things that have really happened. . . . To which may be added versification, by which the poet speaks marvelously and delightfully . . . for example, by being able without unseemliness to raise his voice on the stage so that the people may listen in complete comfort. . . . Because, then, the subject matter of the arts and sciences is not understood by the people, not only should it be avoided and shunned as the universal subject of a poem, but also we must guard against using any part of the arts and sciences in any place in the poem. In this respect Lucan and Dante in

his *Comedy* have especially and unnecessarily erred when they reveal the time of year and the time of day and night by astrology. Neither Homer nor Virgil in the *Aeneid* ever fell into this error. Therefore I cannot but be somewhat amazed at Quintilian who supposes that no one ignorant of the art of astrology or unskilled in philosophy can be a good reader of poetry.[4] . . .

IV

Aristotle did not hold the opinion that poetry was a special gift of the gods, yielded to one man rather than to another, as is the gift of prophecy and similar privileges which do not derive from nature and are not common to all. Doubtless he means, even though he does not state it openly, to challenge the opinion which some have attributed to Plato that poetry is infused in men by divine frenzy.[5] This opinion must have had its origin in the ignorance of the common people, and it flourished and gained favor through the vain-glory of poets for this reason and in this way. Anything which someone else does is highly regarded and admired by those who lack the ability to do it themselves, and because men commonly measure the bodily strength and the skill of others by their own, they consider a miracle and a special gift of God what they cannot obtain by their own natural powers and see that others have obtained. Therefore the first poets were reputed by the ignorant to be filled with the divine spirit and assisted by God. They admired excessively the invention of the fable in the poets' compositions, and also the continuation of many verses by which the fable was revealed, and they were especially admiring when they saw the divine response of Apollo given in such verses, for they thought that through these the gods spoke. Therefore they could not understand that it was possible that the poet could invent a fable so like the truth and so delightful; and after he invented it, they could not see how he could lay it out in verse and in verse so well chosen that such things could not be made by other than human means. . . . This popular belief, though false, was pleasing to poets because it afforded them great praise and they were considered dear to the gods. Therefore they nourished the belief with their consent, and making it seem that things were as they said, they began at the opening of their works to invoke the aid of the Muses and of Apollo, the god who

---

[3]This is the common Renaissance description of poetry's aim, a reply to Plato's challenge (above, page 36) and a repetition of Horace's statement in *Art of Poetry* (above, page 83).

[4]Marcus Fabius Quintilianus (40–c. 118), Roman rhetorician, *Institutes* I, 4.
[5]See Plato, *Ion* (above, page 12); *Phaedrus* (above, page 36).

rules over poetry, and to pretend that they uttered their poems through the mouths of those gods. . . . It is therefore mistaken to attribute to Plato his opinion about the frenzy induced in the poet by the gods, for, as I have said, its origin is in the agreement of poets cultivating their own interest. When Plato mentions it in his books, he is undoubtedly joking, as it is usually his habit to do in similar situations. Thus in the *Phaedrus,* when he says the lover is possessed by madness and wants to prove that not everyone possessed by madness is necessarily in the grasp of an evil spirit, he suggests that it is a benevolent madness which possesses the prophetic women at Delphos and the priests at Dodona, and the Sybil, and other diviners, and poets. But he is not really proving that poets are possessed by any divine madness; rather he is adducing a similar case by an example such as was commonly believed.[6] . . . And he writes jokingly in the *Apology* of Socrates when he says that poets do not understand what they write in their poems when moved by divine madness.[7] This is plain enough, for if he were speaking seriously and believed that poems derived from divine inspiration, why did he exclude them from his republic? . . .

The imitation natural to men is one thing; that required of poetry is another. For the imitation of others which is natural to men and which is in them from childhood, by which they first acquire knowledge, by which all men are disposed more than animals, and as a result of which they are made glad, is nothing other than following the example of others and doing as they do without knowing the reason why. But the imitation required of poetry not only does not follow the examples set by another, nor does it do what others do without knowing the reason why they do so, but it also does something quite different from what is available and proposes instead, so to speak, an example for which it is necessary that the poet know very well the reasons why he does what he does. And he must take time to think and to discern, insofar as he can with certainty, that the imitation required of poetry does not consist, and ought not to consist, in what may be called literal copying, but does consist, or ought to, in what may be called the struggle of the poet and the disposition of fortune or the course of worldly affairs, in finding an accident in human behavior delightful to hear and marvelous. . . .

VI

Because it seemed to Plato that tragedy by the example of tragic characters could injure citizens and debase good customs in them, making them vile, cowardly, and sentimental, he did not wish tragedy to be represented in his republic, for he believed that if the people heard and saw men thought to be valorous doing and saying things which sentimental people do and say, then the frightened and the vile would console themselves and pardon weakness of spirit in themselves, as well as fear and pusillanimity, seeing that they had companions among the great, such as kings. And following such examples they would let themselves improperly be moved by such passion.[8] But Aristotle, so that men would not believe, on the authority of Plato, that he himself, writing about the method of tragedy, had contrived to present it as an art harmful to the citizenry and apt to contaminate their morals, affirmed that tragedy functioned in precisely the opposite way. That is, by its example and by its frequent representation it brings spectators from baseness to magnanimity, from anxiety to security, and from sentimentality to severity, habituating them by repeated usage of things worthy of pity, fear, and baseness to be neither sentimental, nor fearful, nor base; for tragedy by means of the aforesaid passions, terror and pity, purges and expels those same passions from the hearts of men.[9] Now to make clearly understood what Aristotle perhaps wanted to say but uttered darkly and scarcely hinted at, either because, as is often said, his remarks in this book are brief notes for use in a larger work, or because he did not wish openly to censure the opinion of his master Plato, whom he held in some reverence, it is necessary to realize that just as pure wine of a certain quantity, which has had no drop of water mixed in it, has more vigor and spirit than the same amount of wine of equal quality mixed with a large proportion of water, for although it is greater in quantity than the former, by the addition of so much water it becomes watery and loses all its previous vigor and spirit; so the love of fathers for their children is much greater and more fervent and they care for them better when there are few, that is three or two or one, than they would for many, that is a hundred or a thousand or more. Likewise men's pity and fear directed towards a few pitiful and fearful cases are more vigorous and move them more powerfully than if they are scattered among a greater number of events worthy of

---

[6] Castelvetro's argument is not powerful enough to reason away Socrates's words, which attribute poetry and other forms of prophetic utterance and ecstatic behavior to divine inspiration. But see the introduction to Plato, above, page 8.

[7] Plato, *Apology,* 22.

[8] Plato, *Republic* (above, page 21).

[9] This is Castelvetro's moralistic version of Aristotle's catharsis, *Poetics* (above, page 55).

pity and fear. Therefore tragedy which represents to us similar actions and makes us see and hear them more often than
we would see and hear them without it is the cause of pity
and terror being diminished in us because we have to divide
the effect of these passions among so many diverse actions.
We see the proof of this most appreciably during epidemics,
for at the beginning when three or four people begin to die
we find ourselves moved by pity and fear, but then when we
see hundreds and thousands die, the feeling of pity and fear
ceases in us. We know this also by the experience of dangerous skirmishes in which new soldiers are at first terrified by
the booming of the guns and arquebuses[10] and experience
the greatest pity for the dead and wounded, but after they
have been in many battles they stand fast and see before
their eyes companions wounded and dead without feeling
much pity. Perhaps these reasons, although they are quite
powerful, are not so important that because of them the law
forbidding tragedy ought to be annulled, since they are directed elsewhere toward the target Plato aimed at in his prohibition. And so that the way things are may be clear it must
be understood that there are persons who undergo the most
fearful and pitiful experiences, such as those previously
mentioned. These persons are of two sorts, the strong and
the timid, and similarly the actions are of two sorts, the rare
and the frequent, and both have diverse effects according to
the diverse ways in which they occur. Therefore if the persons who suffer are strong and patient, the example of their
suffering and patience affects the souls of others and expels
fear and pity, but if those persons are timid and weak, their
example increases terror and pity in the spectators and confirms them in their fearfulness and weakness. . . . Similarly
if fearful and pitiful actions are rare they move men to terror
and pity more, but if they occur frequently they are less
moving and because of their frequency they can purge terror
and pity from the hearts of mortal men. This occurs for two
reasons: one is that when we witness the occurrence of many
misfortunes which do not involve us, little by little we feel
more secure and convince ourselves that God, who has
watched over us many times in the past, will also protect us
in the future; the other is that those misfortunes which happen frequently and to many people, do not seem so fearful
and as a result do not seem so pitiful, although we may be
sure that they will touch us since we see that so many others
have not been spared. . . . Plato, then, when he forbids
tragedy as inducing fear and pity, forbids it because of the
example of respected persons who exhibit weakness of soul

in adversity, is harmful to the people.[11] If this is so, it is so
because in tragedy as Plato understood it the same type of
character is always introduced. . . .

If the plot is the end of tragedy, and hence of any kind
of poem (for the plot occupies the same place in any kind of
poem as it does in tragedy), then it is final and not accessory
to the morals of the characters but on the contrary their
morals are accessory to the plot. Then their morals do not
occupy the final place and are accessory to the plot, and it
follows that many authors of great renown in letters among
the ancients and moderns, among them Julius Caesar della
Scala, or Scaliger, have gravely erred in supposing that the
intention of good poets, such as Homer and Virgil in their
most famous works, the *Iliad,* the *Odyssey,* and the *Aeneid,*
is to depict and exhibit to the world, let us say, a commander in the most excellent manner possible, or a brave leader
or a wise man, and their natures, and similar nonsense. If
this is true, the moral qualities of characters would not be
used by poets to support the action, as Aristotle says; on the
contrary, the action would be used to exhibit moral qualities.[12] Otherwise, if this material were primary and not
accessory, it could not be poetic subject matter, being naturally the subject of philosophy, treated by many philosophers and especially by Aristotle and Theophrastus.[13]
Therefore, good poets such as Homer and Virgil in their
most famous works, and others like them, have tried to compose a proper fable, according to which the characters and
moral qualities are suited, and thus more appealing, in other
words marvelous and verisimilar. . . .

VIII

Aristotle . . . stubbornly demands that the action which comprises the plot should be one and concern one character
only, and if there are other actions that they support each
other. He adduces no reason or proof for this except the example of the tragic poets and Homer who have adhered to
the single action of a single character in composing the fa-

---

[10] An early gun.

[11] In *Republic* (above, page 21).

[12] Castelvetro refers to Aristotle's claim for the importance of plot, *Poetics*
(above, page 55).

[13] See Aristotle's *Nichomachean Ethics* and Theophrastus's (d. 287 B.C.)
Characters, both influential in neoclassical literary characterization. At this
point one might well weigh Sidney's discussion of "the speaking picture of
poesy" against Castelvetro's priorities. In his *Apology,* Sidney remarks,
"Let but Sophocles bring you Ajax on a stage, killing and whipping sheep
and oxen, thinking them the army of the Greeks, with their chieftans
Agamemnon and Menelaus, and tell me if you have not a more familiar
insight into anger than finding in the schoolmen his genus and difference"
(below, page 192).

ble. But it can be easily seen that in tragedy and comedy the fable has a single action, or two when by one depending on the other they can be thought single, and it has most often a single character rather than one family, not because the fable is unsuited to more than one action, but because the length of time of twelve hours at most and restrictions of place in which the action is represented do not permit a multitude of actions, or even the actions of one family, nor for that matter the whole of one action, if it is somewhat long. And this is the principal and necessary reason why the fable of tragedy and of comedy ought to be one, that is containing the single action of one character, or two thought of as one because of their dependence on each other. This motive of limited time and place could not work so as to restrict Homer to a single action of a single character in the epic, which can narrate not just a single action, but more, and longer, and occurring in diverse lands.

IX

In the plot of tragedy and epic there necessarily occur events which have been reported to have taken place in the life of a particular man, and which are known in a summary way, as, for example, Orestes, accompanied by his friend Pylades and aided by him and by his sister Electra, murdering his mother Clytemnestra. But no one knows particularly or exactly the ways and means he took to accomplish the murder. Now the reason is clear, and so abundantly clear, that it can be demonstrated, for it is proper that the plot of tragedy and epic should accept things which have actually happened and which are common to it and to historical truth. For the plot of these two kinds of poetry should include action not simply human but also magnificent and regal. And if it ought to include regal events, it follows that it includes action that has actually occurred and is certain, and is the action of a king who has existed and is known to have existed, since we are unable to imagine a king who has not existed nor attribute any action to him. And insofar as he existed and is known to have existed, we cannot attribute to him actions which have not occurred. It would be as if we were to say that before the Roman republic was established there was a king of the Romans named Julius and then say that he lay with his daughter, or as if we were to say that Julius Caesar the permanent dictator of the Romans murdered his wife Calpurnia when he discovered her in adultery; for it is not true that any king of the Romans was so named or so committed any such incestuous act, and it is equally untrue that Julius Caesar discovered his wife in adultery and murdered her. Because kings are known through fame and through history, as well as their notable actions, to introduce

new names of kings and to attribute to them new actions is to contradict history and fame and to sin against open truth. This is a much greater sin in the composition of the plot than to sin in verisimilitude. Therefore the plots of all tragedies and all epics are and ought to be composed of events which can be called historical, although for several reasons Aristotle had a different view. . . . But the above-mentioned events ought not to be manifested by history or fame except summarily and in a general way, so that the poet can perform his task and show his skill in discovering the ways and particular means by which these incidents have had their fulfillment. For if these ways and particular means by which these incidents were brought to completion were made clear in other ways, we would not have material suitable for the plot, nor would it be pertinent to the poet, but to the historians. Neither with all this should we allow the opinion that it is easier to compose the plot of a tragedy or an epic than that of a comedy, just because in the plots of those poems the poets does not invent everything on his own, as he does in comedy. . . .

Now to fill in the plot of comedy the poet by his skill finds universal and particular incidents. And because they are completely invented by him, neither events which have occurred nor history has any part. He also supplies names for the characters as it pleases him and can do so without inconvenience and he ought reasonably to do so. He can construct the incident he has chosen in all its parts and accordingly it should deal with a private person about whom, along with the incidents that have happened to him, there is no knowledge, and they will not be passed on to the memory of those in the future either by history or fame. Therefore, someone who makes up new and entire incidents involving private persons and gives them names as it pleases him, cannot be contradicted by history or fame as having reported falsehoods. And if he wishes rational men to think him a poet, that is, an inventor, he ought to invent everything, because, since the private subject matter makes it easy for him, he can invent it. But no one ought to believe that the inventor of the comic plot has license to invent new cities he has imagined, or rivers, or mountains, or kingdoms or customs or laws, or to alter the course of nature, making it snow in summer or putting the harvest in winter, and so on. For it is fitting to follow history and truth, if in constructing his plot he happens to require such things, just as in the same way it is fitting for the poet making a tragic or epic plot. . . . Therefore the possibility that things have happened, which is the subject of poetry and the actuality of what has happened, which is the subject of history, distinguish the former from the latter, and this is the essential difference between the two, and not what some have asserted, that is, that history is distinguished from poetry by its prose and poetry from history by its verse.[14] . . .

It appears that if things which have happened cannot constitute poetry and do not contribute to the constitution of a poem, they ought to contribute to the distinction and diminution of poetry when they are mingled with things which might possibly happen in the future and with things invented by the poet, if we compare actual events with those which might happen in the future mixed with what can really happen in the future. That is, it would seem that the plot of tragedy and epic, when made up of actions which have occurred, and retaining true names (as we have shown plots ought to be formed) would make its author less a poet than the author of a comedy or of the plot of a tragedy in which all the events and names are invented, as is the case with the tragedy of Agathon called *The Flowers*.[15] For if the plot entirely made up of events which have occurred does not allow him to be a poet at all, then the plot made up in part of events which have occurred would to that extent deny him his role as poet and so he would be less a poet than he who is totally the poet because his plot is made up of events entirely invented or events which could happen in the future. Nonetheless it is my judgment that the maker of the tragic and epic taken from history and with real names should not be considered a lesser poet than the maker of a plot in which every event and every name is imaginary. Perhaps instead he ought to be considered greater. For events which have occurred, with which the first sort of poet is concerned in making the plot of epic and tragedy, are not so many nor are they spread out in such a way that they relieve him of the effort of invention, for everyone can imagine similar things without great subtlety of wit. We may suppose something that every man can easily imagine, such as the story in broad outline of a son who murders his mother who has murdered her husband and hounded her son out of the kingdom so she may enjoy her lover. But the difficulty is in finding the means for the son to achieve this murder in a marvelous fashion such as has not occurred previously. This difficulty is greater than that of inventing the general line of plot and the particular ways and means by which it draws to a conclusion, since the general line of the plot invented by the poet is not so fixed or stable that it cannot be altered or changed, if it turns out to be appropriate or if he is unable to make his characters clever or dull or endowed with other qualities, as he judges it to be best according to the ways which occurred to him initially of making a fine plot. Who-

ever takes his plot from events which have occurred cannot do this, since he is held within certain limits from which he is not allowed to escape.

And to show by one example what this difference is, I say that not many years ago during excavations in Rome there was found a marble statue of a large, fine river god whose beard was broken and sparse, and by means of that portion which remained on the chin it was evident that the entire beard, according to proportion, would reach to the navel, even though the point of the beard was seen to rest high on the chest without reaching any further. Everyone marveled at this, and no one was able to imagine what that beard was like when it was intact. Only Michelangelo Buonarroti,[16] a sculptor of most rare skill who was present, stood still for a while, and realizing how things stood, said, "Bring me some clay." It was brought and he formed that part of the beard which was lacking of such a size that it matched the proportions of the rest. And fastening it on he drew it down to the navel. Then tying it up with one knot he showed clearly that the point of the beard he had formed struck the high point of the chest at the same place as the broken beard. Therefore to the great admiration of all those present he showed how the missing beard was made and how it was knotted. And there was no one there who did not judge that Michelangelo for subtlety of wit in having restored that missing beard so remarkably was to be preferred before any other artist in having made an entire beard suitable to his judgment without regard to any of the remaining pieces of the original beard.

XIII

Now whether it is true or false that tragedy can have no other subject matter than what is fearful or pitiable, I will not at the moment discuss. But it does seem that this has not been proven by Aristotle in the things he has said so far, although he does assume that they are proven. But since he has set out to contradict Plato, who said that tragedy is injurious to the people's good morals, he does not wish to approve a kind of tragedy other than that which according to him is advantageous in providing the people with good morals and by means of fear and pity purges those same passions, driving them out of the souls of the people in the manner we have mentioned above. And he is so intent on this matter that he does not avoid contradicting himself and the things he has said previously. Therefore if poetry is established primarily for delight and not for profit, as he has

---

[14]This discussion can be compared to Scaliger's (above, page 173).
[15]Agathon (c. 447–c. 400 B.C.), Greek tragic poet.

[16](1475–1564), Italian sculptor, painter, and poet.

shown, in speaking of the origin of poetry in general, why does he say that in tragedy, which is a kind of poetry, utility is what is principally sought for? Why is not delight principally sought without regard to utility? Either he ought to ignore utility or at least he should not give it so much attention that he rejects all other kinds of tragedy which lack it. He should restrict himself to one single kind of utility, that which effects only the purgation of fear and pity. And even so, if utility is to be considered, other kinds of tragedy can be presented, as for example that which deals with the change of good men from misery to happiness, or of evil men from happiness to misery, so that the people, convinced by the examples proposed, may confirm themselves in the holy belief that God looks after the world and the special providence of his own, defending them and confounding his and their enemies. . . .

XIV

The delight proper to tragedy is that which derives from fear and pity proceeding from the change from happiness to misery due to the error of a person of middling virtue. But someone may ask what sort of delight it is which derives from watching a good man undeservedly forced from happiness to misery, since that ought not rationally to give delight but displeasure. Now I have no doubt that Aristotle meant by the word *pleasure* the purgation and expulsion of fear and pity from the human soul by means of the operation of the same passions, in the fashion which I have already explained above at length. Thus purgation and expulsion, if they proceed as he affirms from those same passions, can quite properly be called *hedone* [ηδονή], that is, pleasure or delight, and strictly speaking it ought to be called utility, for it is health of mind gotten through bitter medicine. Therefore pleasure derived from pity and fear, which is truly pleasure, is that which we have previously called oblique pleasure. And it occurs when, feeling pain from the misery which comes unjustly to another, we recognize that we are good, since injustice displeases us. This recognition is the greatest pleasure for us, by reason of the natural love which we have for ourselves. And added to this pleasure is another which is not in the least trivial, that is, when we see tribulations beyond reason which have come upon others and which might possibly come upon us or upon others like us, we realize tacitly and unconsciously that we are subject to the same fortune and that we cannot trust in the tranquil course of worldly things. This delight is much greater than if another, acting as a teacher and openly presenting the subject, instructs us in the same lesson. For the experience of events which have happened impresses doctrine more in our

minds than the mere voice of the teacher, and we rejoice more in the little which we learn for ourselves than in the greater amount which we learn from others, since we cannot learn from others if we do not confess ourselves to be ignorant of what we learn and obliged to them for what we learn from them. And perhaps the wise man was thinking of such things when he said that it is better to go to the house of mourning than to the house of banqueting.[17]

XVII

It has been concluded that he who knows how to transform himself into an impassioned person is also skilled at representing such a character, that is, he knows without art how to say and do those things which are suited to someone in a state of passion. And not everyone is apt for this, but only those endowed with a good wit, and an impassioned person can be represented not only by this means but also by another, which is to consider carefully what people in a state of passion say and do in such circumstances. This method is not for everyone, but only for the gifted man. It follows, then, that poetry is conceived and practiced by the gifted man and not the madman, as some have said, for the madman is not able to assume various passions, nor is he a careful observer of what impassioned men say and do. But we should be aware of what seems to me to be an error in the text, since the words ἤμανικοῦ ("or of the madman") should be written ου μανικοῦ ("not of the madman"). . . . It is not surprising that *not* should be made *or* by those who have already swallowed that opinion about poetic furor, which was foisted upon minds of men as we have explained above, and which the arguments of Aristotle have refuted. It is true that the reading *or of the madman* can be retained without wandering much from the idea expressed above if we read *or of the madman as rather than of the madman.* . . . That is, Aristotle says that poetry is usually the work of the gifted man rather than of the madman, but because *than* put in the place of *rather than* seems to be more appropriate to verse than to prose, we stand on what we said at first.[18]

XXIV

Now to understand fully what is being discussed, it must be remembered that Aristotle said before that there were two dimensions to tragedy, one accessible to the senses and ex-

---

[17] Ecclesiastes 7.4: "The heart of the wise is in the house of mourning, but the heart of fools is in the house of mirth."
[18] *Poetics* (above, page 52).

ternal and measurable by the clock; the other accessible to the intellect and internal and measurable by the mind and which comprises the movement from misery to happiness or from happiness to misery. The duration which is accessible to the senses and is measured by the clock, cannot last more than one revolution of the sun over the earth for the reasons mentioned above; this duration, which has nothing to do with art according to Aristotle, nevertheless is shaped by and receives its measure from the time of the intellectual di-mension, for the two cannot be diverse in time measurement. For, as we said above, as much length of time is to be taken in representing in tragedy an action moving from misery to happiness or from happiness to misery as would elapse in the actual or imagined occurrence of the action.[19]

---

[19] This passage is representative of a number of commentaries insisting on the so-called unity of time. See Corneille (below, page 245).

Sir Philip Sidney

1554–1586

Sidney's *Apology for Poetry* (in its first version the *Defense of Poetry*) appeared in print only after his death, and his highly esteemed writings, including his sonnets and the *Arcadia* (1590), were known only in manuscript during his lifetime. Sidney served part of his life in the Netherlands as diplomat and soldier. He died in the Battle of Zutphen.

Though Sidney is not an original critic, he is interesting because he provides a broad picture of Renaissance critical attitudes, being acquainted with some of the Italian criticism of his age and apparently well schooled in Plato, Aristotle, and Horace. The *Apology* answers an attack on poetry by Stephen Gosson in his *School of Abuse,* in which Gosson also criticizes "pipers, players, jesters, and such like caterpillars of a commonwealth." Gosson's essay, oddly enough, is dedicated to Sidney. Sidney answers the following complaints, all made by Gosson: first, that poetry is a waste of time, an argument that goes back at least to Tertullian (c. 160–c. 230); second, that it is the "mother of lies," a view implicit in Plato and St. Augustine and of considerable force in the Puritan ethic that Gosson seems to have embraced; third, that it is a "nurse of abuse" and teaches sinfulness; and, finally, that Plato, an important and wise authority, banished the poets from his commonwealth. Against these complaints Sidney avers that in early societies poetry was the main source of education, that it exercised a moral influence on culture, and that the poet was anciently revered by all. He answers Plato's challenge first by picking up Horace's famous statement (above, page 83) that the poet teaches and delights and then arguing that the poet goes beyond nature to offer visions of better things: "Nature never set forth the earth in so rich tapestry as divers poets have done—neither with pleasant rivers, fruitful trees, sweet-smelling flowers, not whatsoever else may make the too much loved earth more lovely. Her world is brazen, the poets only deliver a golden." This passage is rich in its sources. It suggests the Aristotelian idea that the poet brings to completion that which nature is always in the process of completing. It reverses in a Plotinian way Plato's attack on the poet as a copier of copies, suggesting the vision of a higher level of reality.

Sidney seems to repeat Scaliger (above, page 171) when he remarks, "Only the poet, disdaining to be tied to any such subjection, lifted up with the vigor of his own invention, doth grow in effect another nature." The passage has interested modern readers, partly because it seems to anticipate a Romantic concept of the creative imagination, as in Coleridge (below, page 504). That concept, however, is based on an epistemology unknown to Sidney and his time. Rather, he is probably elaborating on remarks made by Scaliger in connection with a contrast between poetry and history.

The *Defense* has been edited by A. S. Cook (1890), the *Apology* by E. S. Shuckburgh (1891), and by J. C. Collins (1907). See J. E. Spingarn, *Literary Criticism in the Renaissance* (1899); Gregory Smith, ed., *Elizabethan Critical Essays* I (1904); M. W.

Wallace, *The Life of Sir Philip Sidney* (1915); K. O. Myrick, *Sir Philip Sidney as a Literary Craftsman* (1935); Forrest Robinson, *The Shape of Things Known: Sidney's* Apology *and Its Philosophical Tradition* (1972); Andrew D. Weiner, *Sir Philip Sidney and the Poetics of Protestantism* (1978); John Webster, ed., *William Temple's Analysis of Sir Philip Sidney's* Apology for Poetry (1984); Katherine Duncan-Jones, *Sir Philip Sidney: Courtier and Poet* (1991). On Stephen Gosson, see William Ringler, *Stephen Gosson: A Biographical and Critical Study* (1942).

An Apology for Poetry

When the right virtuous Edward Wotton and I were at the Emperor's Court together, we gave ourselves to learn horsemanship of John Pietro Pugliano, one that with great commendation had the place of an esquire in his stable. And he, according to the fertileness of the Italian wit, did not only afford us the demonstration of his practice, but sought to enrich our minds with the contemplations there which he thought most precious. But with none I remember mine ears were at any time more loaden, than when (either angered with slow payment, or moved with our learnerlike admiration) he exercised his speech in the praise of his faculty. He said soldiers were the noblest estate of mankind, and horsemen the noblest of soldiers. He said they were the masters of war and ornaments of peace; speedy goers and strong abiders; triumphers both in camps and courts. Nay, to so unbelieved a point he proceeded, as that no earthly thing bred such wonder to a prince as to be a good horseman. Skill of government was but a *pedenteria*[1] in comparison. Then would he add certain praises, by telling what a peerless beast a horse was, the only serviceable courtier without flattery, the beast of most beauty, faithfulness, courage, and such more, that, if I had not been a piece of a logician before I came to him, I think he would have persuaded me to have wished myself a horse. But thus much at least with his no few words he drove into me, that self-love is better than any gilding to make that seem gorgeous wherein ourselves are parties. Wherein, if Pugliano's strong affection and weak arguments will not satisfy you, I will give you a nearer example of myself, who (I know not by what mischance) in these my not old years and idlest times having slipped into the title of a poet, am provoked to say something unto you in the defense of that my unelected vocation, which if I handle with more good will than good reasons, bear with me, since the scholar is to be pardoned that followeth the steps of his master. And yet I must say that, as I have just cause to make a pitiful[2] defense of poor Poetry, which from almost the highest estimation of learning is fallen to be the laughingstock of children, so have I need to bring some more available proofs, since the former is by no man barred of his deserved credit, the silly latter hath had even the names of philosophers used to the defacing of it, with great danger of civil war among the Muses.

And first, truly, to all them that professing learning inveigh against poetry may justly be objected, that they go very near to ungratefulness, to seek to deface that which, in the noblest nations and languages that are known, hath been the first light-giver to ignorance, and first nurse, whose milk by little and little enabled them to feed afterwards of tougher knowledges. And will they now play the hedgehog that, being received into the den, drove out his host, or rather the vipers, that with their birth kill their parents? Let learned Greece in any of her manifold sciences be able to show me one book before Musaeus. Homer, and Hesiod,[3] all three nothing else but poets. Nay, let any history be brought that can say any writers were there before them, if they were not men of the same skill, as Orpheus, Linus,[4] and some other are named, who, having been the first of that country that made pens deliverers of their knowledge to their posterity, may justly challenge to be called their fathers in learning, for not only in time they had this priority (although in itself antiquity be venerable) but went before them, as causes to draw with their charming sweetness the wild untamed wits to an admiration of knowledge, so, as Amphion[5] was said to move stones with his poetry to build Thebes, and Orpheus to be listened to by beasts—indeed stony and

---

Sidney's *Apology for Poetry* was written in 1583 and published posthumously in 1595. There are two versions, the *Apology* and the earlier *Defense of Poetry*. The text here is based on the later version.
[1] Pedantry, or pointless learning.
[2] Pitying.
[3] Musaeus (c. ninth century B.C.), semimythical Greek poet; Homer (c. eighth century B.C.); Hesiod (c. eighth century B.C.).
[4] Mythological ancient Greek poets.
[5] See Horace, *Art of Poetry* (above, page 84).

beastly people.[6] So among the Romans were Livius Andronicus, and Ennius.[7] So in the Italian language the first that made it aspire to be a treasurehouse of science were the poets Dante, Boccaccio, and Petrarch.[8] So in our English were Gower and Chaucer.[9]

After whom, encouraged and delighted with their excellent foregoing, others have followed, to beautify our mother tongue, as well in the same kind as in other arts. This did so notably show itself, that the philosophers of Greece durst not a long time appear to the world but under the masks of poets. So Thales, Empedocles, and Parmenides sang their natural philosophy in verses; so did Pythagoras and Phocylides their moral counsels; so did Tyrtaeus in war matters, and Solon in matters of policy:[10] or rather, they, being poets, did exercise their delightful vein in those points of highest knowledge, which before them lay hid to the world. For that wise Solon was directly a poet it is manifest, having written in verse the notable fable of the Atlantic Island,[11] which was continued by Plato.

And truly, even Plato, whosoever well considereth shall find that in the body of his work, though the inside and strength were philosophy, the skin as it were and beauty depended most of poetry: for all standeth upon dialogues, wherein he feigneth many honest burgesses of Athens to speak of such matters, that, if they had been set on the rack, they would never have confessed them, besides his poetical describing the circumstances of their meetings, as the well ordering of a banquet, the delicacy of a walk, with interlacing mere tales, as Gyges' Ring,[12] and others, which who knoweth not to be flowers of poetry did never walk into Apollo's garden.

And even historiographers (although their lips sound of things done, and verity be written in their foreheads) have been glad to borrow both fashion and perchance weight of poets. So Herodotus[13] entitled his history by the name of the nine Muses; and both he and all the rest that followed him either stole or usurped of poetry their passionate describing of passions, the many particularities of battles, which no man could affirm, or, if that be denied me, long orations put in the mouths of great kings and captains, which it is certain they never pronounced. So that, truly, neither philosopher nor historiographer could at the first have entered into the gates of popular judgments, if they had not taken a great passport of poetry, which in all nations at this day, where learning flourisheth not, is plain to be seen, in all which they have some feeling of poetry. In Turkey, besides their lawgiving divines, they have no other writers but poets. In our neighbor country Ireland, where truly learning goeth very bare, yet are their poets held in a devout reverence. Even among the most barbarous and simple Indians where no writing is, yet have they their poets, who make and sing songs, which they call *areytos,* both of their ancestors' deeds and praises of their gods—a sufficient probability that, if ever learning come among them, it must be by having their hard dull wits softened and sharpened with the sweet delights of poetry. For until they find a pleasure in the exercises of the mind, great promises of much knowledge will little persuade them that know not the fruits of knowledge. In Wales, the true remnant of the ancient Britons, as there are good authorities to show the long time they had poets, which they called bards, so through all the conquests of Romans, Saxons, Danes, and Normans, some of whom did seek to ruin all memory of learning from among them, yet do their poets, even to this day, last; so as it is not more notable in soon beginning than in long continuing. But since the authors of most of our sciences were the Romans, and before them the Greeks, let us a little stand upon their authorities, but even so far as to see what names they have given unto this now scorned skill.

Among the Romans a poet was called *vates,* which is as much as a diviner, foreseer, or prophet, as by his conjoined words *vaticinium* and *vaticinari* is manifest: so heavenly a title did that excellent people bestow upon this heart-ravishing knowledge. And so far were they carried into the admiration thereof, that they thought in the chanceable hitting upon any such verses great foretokens of their following fortunes were placed. Whereupon grew the word of *sortes Virgilianae,* when, by sudden opening Virgil's book, they lighted upon any verse of his making: whereof the histories of the emperors' lives are full, as of Albinus, the governor of our island, who in his childhood met with this verse, *"Arma amens capio nec sat rationis in armis"*;[14]

---

[6] Mythological ancient Greek poets.

[7] Livius Andronicus (third century B.C.), Roman poet; Ennius (239–169 B.C.), Roman poet.

[8] Dante (above, page 153); Boccaccio (above, page 157).

[9] John Gower, (1330?–1408) and Geoffrey Chaucer (c. 1340–1400), Middle English poets.

[10] Rather than dispute whether some of these writers were poets, Sidney tends to blur traditional distinctions that go back to Aristotle (above, page 52) between poetry and other kinds of writing. Thales (636–546 B.C.); Empedocles (fl. c. 460 B.C.); Parmenides (c. 513 B.C.–?); Pythagoras (fl. late sixth century B.C.); Phocylides (560–? B.C.); Tyrtaeus (fl. seventh century B.C.); Solon (c. 639–559 B.C.).

[11] Atlantis.

[12] In *Republic* II, Socrates tells of the descent of Gyges, a shepherd boy, into a chasm in which he finds a ring that can render him invisible.

[13] Each of the nine books of *The Persian Wars* by Herodotus (484?–425? B.C.) was named for a Muse.

[14] "Insane, I take arms, nor is there reason for arms." *Aeneid* II, 314.

and in his age performed it: which, although it were a very vain and godless superstition, as also it was to think that spirits were commanded by such verses—whereupon this word charms, derived of *carmina,* "cometh"—so yet serveth it to show the great reverence those wits were held in. And altogether not without ground, since both the Oracles of Delphos and Sibylla's prophecies were wholly delivered in verses. For that same exquisite observing of number and measure in words, and that high flying liberty of conceit proper to the poet, did seem to have some divine force in it.

And may not I presume a little further, to show the reasonableness of this word *vates,* and say that the holy David's Psalms are a divine poem? If I do, I shall not do it without the testimony of great learned men, both ancient and modern. But even the name Psalms will speak for me, which, being interpreted, is nothing but "songs"; then that it is fully written in meter, as all learned Hebricians agree, although the rules be not yet fully found; lastly and principally, his handling his prophecy, which is merely poetical. For what else is the awaking his musical instruments, the often and free changing of persons, his notable *prosopopeias,*[15] when he maketh you, as it were, see God coming in his majesty, his telling of the beasts' joyfulness, and hills' leaping, but a heavenly poesy, wherein almost he showeth himself a passionate lover of that unspeakable and everlasting beauty to be seen by the eyes of the mind, only cleared by faith? But truly now having named him, I fear me I seem to profane that holy name, applying it to poetry, which is among us thrown down to so ridiculous an estimation. But they that with quiet judgments will look a little deeper into it, shall find the end and working of it such as, being rightly applied, deserveth not to be scourged out of the church of God.

But now, let us see how the Greeks named it, and how they deemed of it. The Greeks called him "a poet," which name hath, as the most excellent, gone through other languages. It cometh of this word *poiein,* which is "to make": wherein, I know not whether by luck or wisdom, we Englishmen have met with the Greeks in calling him a *maker:* which name, how high and incomparable a title it is, I had rather were known by marking the scope of other sciences than by my partial allegation.

There is no art delivered to mankind that hath not the works of nature for his principal object, without which they could not consist, and on which they so depend, as they become actors and players, as it were, of what nature will have set forth. So doth the astronomer look upon the stars, and, by that he seeth, setteth down what order nature hath taken therein. So do the geometrician and arithmetician in their diverse sorts of quantities. So doth the musician in times tell you which by nature agree, which not. The natural philosopher thereon hath his name, and the moral philosopher standeth upon the natural virtues, vices, and passions of man: and "follow nature" (saith he) "therein, and thou shalt not err." The lawyer saith what men have determined; the historian what men have done. The grammarian speaketh only of the rules of speech; and the rhetorician and logician, considering what in nature will soonest prove and persuade, thereon give artificial rules, which still are compassed within the circle of a question according to the proposed matter. The physician weigheth the nature of a man's body, and the nature of things helpful or hurtful unto it. And the metaphysic, though it be in the second and abstract notions, and therefore be counted supernatural, yet doth he indeed build upon the depth of nature. Only the poet, disdaining to be tied to any such subjection, lifted up with the vigor of his own invention, doth grow in effect another nature, in making things either better than nature bringeth forth, or, quite anew, forms such as never were in nature, as the Heroes, Demigods, Cyclopes, Chimeras, Furies, and such like: so as he goeth hand in hand with nature, not enclosed within the narrow warrant of her gifts, but freely ranging only within the zodiac of his own wit.[16]

Nature never set forth the earth in so rich tapestry as divers poets have done—neither with pleasant rivers, fruitful trees, sweet-smelling flowers, nor whatsoever else may make the too much loved earth more lovely. Her world is brazen, the poets only deliver a golden. But let those things alone, and go to man—for whom as the other things are, so it seemeth in him her uttermost cunning is employed—and know whether she have brought forth so true a lover as Theagenes, so constant a friend as Pylades, so valiant a man as Orlando, so right a prince as Xenophon's Cyrus,[17] so excellent a man every way as Virgil's Aeneas. Neither let this be jestingly conceived, because the works of the one be essential, the other in imitation or fiction; for any understanding knoweth the skill of the artificer standeth in that idea or foreconceit of the work, and not in the work itself. And that the poet hath that idea is manifest, by delivering them forth in such excellency as he hath imagined them. Which delivering forth also is not wholly imaginative, as we

---

[15]Personifications.

[16]This passage is perhaps the best known in the *Apology.* It is worth comparision with Scaliger's (above, page 171).

[17]The account of the Persian emperor Cyrus (?–529 B.C.) by Xenophon (c. 430–c. 355 B.C.) in his *Cyropaedia* is mainly fictional.

are wont to say by them that build castles in the air: but so far substantially it worketh, not only to make a Cyrus, which had been but a particular excellency, as nature might have done, but to bestow a Cyrus upon the world, to make many Cyruses, if they will learn aright why and how that maker made him.

Neither let it be deemed too saucy a comparison to balance the highest point of man's wit with the efficacy of nature; but rather give right honor to the heavenly Maker of that maker, who, having made man to his own likeness, set him beyond and over all the works of that second nature: which in nothing he showeth so much as in poetry, when with the force of a divine breath he bringeth things forth far surpassing her doings, with no small argument to the incredulous of that first accursed fall of Adam, since our erected wit maketh us know what perfection is, and yet our infected will keepeth us from reaching unto it. But these arguments will by few be understood, and by fewer granted. Thus much (I hope) will be given me, that the Greeks with some probability of reason gave him the name above all names of learning. Now let us go to a more ordinary opening of him, that the truth may be more palpable: and so I hope, though we get not so unmatched a praise as the etymology of his names will grant, yet his very description, which no man will deny, shall not justly be barred from a principal commendation.

Poesy therefore is an art of imitation, for so Aristotle[18] termeth it in his word *mimesis,* that is to say, a representing, counterfeiting, or figuring forth—to speak metaphorically, a speaking picture; with this end, to teach and delight.[19] Of this have been three several kinds. The chief, both in antiquity and excellency, were they that did imitate the inconceivable excellencies of God. Such were David in his Psalms; Solomon in his Song of Songs, in his Ecclesiastes, and Proverbs; Moses and Deborah in their Hymns; and the writer of Job, which, beside other, the learned Emanuel Tremellius and Franciscus Junius do entitle the poetical part of the Scripture. Against these none will speak that hath the Holy Ghost in due holy reverence.

In this kind, though in a full wrong divinity, were Orpheus, Amphion, Homer in his *Hymns,* and many other, both Greeks and Romans, and this poesy must be used by whosoever will follow St. James's counsel in singing psalms when they are merry, and I know is used with the fruit of comfort by some, when, in sorrowful pangs of their death-

bringing sins, they find the consolation of the never-leaving goodness.

The second kind is of them that deal with matters philosophical: either moral, as Tyrtaeus, Phocylides, and Cato; or natural, as Lucretius and Virgil's *Georgics;* or astronomical, as Manilius and Pontanus; or historical, as Lucan;[20] which who mislike, the fault is in their judgments quite out of taste, and not in the sweet food of sweetly uttered knowledge. But because this second sort is wrapped within the fold of the proposed subject, and takes not the course of his own invention, whether they properly be poets or no let grammarians dispute; and go to the third, indeed right poets, of whom chiefly this question ariseth, betwixt whom and these second is such a kind of difference as betwixt the meaner sort of painters, who counterfeit only such faces as are set before them, and the more excellent, who, having no law but wit, bestow that in colors upon you which is fittest for the eye to see, as the constant though lamenting look of Lucretia, when she punished in herself another's fault.

Wherein he painteth not Lucretia whom he never saw, but painteth the outward beauty of such a virtue. For these third be they which most properly do imitate to teach and delight, and to imitate borrow nothing of what is, hath been, or shall be; but range, only reined with learned discretion, into the divine consideration of what may be, and should be.[21] These be they that, as the first and most noble sort may justly be termed *vates,* so these are waited on in the excellentest languages and best understandings, with the fore-described name of poets; for these indeed do merely make to imitate, and imitate both to delight and teach, and delight to move men to take that goodness in hand, which without delight they would fly as from a stranger, and teach, to make them know that goodness whereunto they are moved: which being the noblest scope to which ever any learning was directed, yet want there not idle tongues to bark at them. These be subdivided into sundry more special denominations. The most notable be the heroic, lyric, tragic, comic, satiric, iambic, elegiac, pastoral, and certain others, some of these being termed according to the matter they deal with, some by the sorts of verses they liked best to write in; for indeed the greatest part of poets have appareled their poetical inventions in that numbrous kind of writing which is called verse—indeed but appareled, verse being but an ornament

---

[18] See Aristotle, *Poetics* (above, page 52).
[19] See Horace, *Art of Poetry* (above, page 83).

[20] Marcus Porcius Cato (95–46 B.C.); Lucretius (94–55 B.C.); Manilius (first century B.C.), Roman poet; Giovanni Pontano (1426–1503), Italian writer; Marcus Annaeus Lucanus (Lucan) (39–65).
[21] See Aristotle, *Poetics* (above, page 57).

and no cause to poetry, since there have been many most excellent poets that never versified, and now swarm many versifiers that need never answer to the name of poets. For Xenophon, who did imitate so excellently as to give us *effigiem iusti imperil*, "the portraiture of a just empire," under name of Cyrus (as Cicero saith of him), made therein an absolute heroical poem.

So did Heliodorus in his sugared invention of that picture of love in *Theagenes and Chariclea*;[22] and yet both these writ in prose: which I speak to show that it is not rhyming and versing that maketh a poet—no more than a long gown maketh an advocate, who though he pleaded in armor should be an advocate and no soldier.[23] But it is that feigning notable images of virtues, vices, or what else, with that delightful teaching, which must be the right describing note to know a poet by, although indeed the senate of poets hath chosen verse as their fittest raiment, meaning, as in matter they passed all in all, so in manner to go beyond them—not speaking (table talk fashion or like men in a dream) words as they chanceably fall from the mouth, but peising[24] each syllable of each word by just proportion according to the dignity of the subject.

Now therefore it shall not be amiss first to weigh this latter sort of poetry by his works, and then by his parts, and, if in neither of these anatomies he be condemnable, I hope we shall obtain a more favorable sentence. This purifying of wit, this enriching of memory, enabling of judgment, and enlarging of conceit, which commonly we call learning, under what name soever it come forth, or to what immediate end soever it be directed, the final end is to lead and draw us to as high a perfection as our degenerate souls, made worse by their clayey lodgings, can be capable of. This, according to the inclination of the man, bred many formed impressions. For some that thought this felicity principally to be gotten by knowledge and no knowledge to be so high and heavenly as acquaintance with the stars, gave themselves to astronomy; others, persuading themselves to be demigods if they knew the causes of things, became natural and supernatural philosophers; some an admirable delight drew to music; and some the certainty of demonstration to the mathematics. But all, one and other, having this scope—to know, and by knowledge to lift up the mind from the dungeon of the body to the enjoying his own divine essence. But when by the balance of experience it was found that the astronomer looking to the stars might fall into a ditch, that the

inquiring philosopher might be blind in himself, and the mathematician might draw forth a straight line with a crooked heart, then, lo, did proof, the overruler of opinions, make manifest that all these are but serving sciences, which, as they have each a private end in themselves, so yet are they all directed to the highest end of the mistress-knowledge, by the Greeks called *architectonike*, which stands (as I think) in the knowledge of a man's self, in the ethic and politic consideration, with the end of well doing and not of well knowing only—even as the saddler's next end is to make a good saddle, but his farther end to serve a nobler faculty, which is horsemanship; so the horseman's to soldiery, and the soldier not only to have the skill, but to perform the practice of a soldier. So that, the ending end of all earthly learning being virtuous action, those skills, that most serve to bring forth that, have a most just title to be princes over all the rest. Wherein we can show the poet's nobleness, by setting him before his other competitors, among whom as principal challengers step forth the moral philosophers, whom, me thinketh, I see coming towards me with a sullen gravity, as though they could not abide vice by daylight, rudely clothed for to witness outwardly their contempt of outward things, with books in their hands against glory, whereto they set their names, sophistically speaking against subtlety, and angry with any man in whom they see the foul fault of anger. These men casting largesse as they go of definitions, divisions, and distinctions, with a scornful interrogative do soberly ask whether it be possible to find any path so ready to lead a man to virtue as that which teacheth what virtue is—and teacheth it not only by delivering forth his very being, his causes, and effects, but also by making known his enemy, vice (which must be destroyed), and his cumbersome servant, passion (which must be mastered), by showing the generalities that containeth it, and the specialities that are derived from it; lastly, by plain setting down, how it extendeth itself out of the limits of a man's own little world to the government of families, and maintaining of public societies.

The historian scarcely giveth leisure to the moralist to say so much, but that he, laden with old mouse-eaten records, authorizing himself (for the most part) upon other histories, whose greatest authorities are built upon the notable foundation of hearsay; having much ado to accord differing writers and to pick truth out of partiality; better acquainted with a thousand years ago than with the present age, and yet better knowing how this world goeth than how his own wit runneth; curious for antiquities and inquisitive of novelties: a wonder to young folks and a tyrant in table talk, denieth, in a great chafe, that any man for teaching of virtue, and virtuous actions, is comparable to him. "I am

---

[22] Heliodorus's (fl. third century B.C.) work was actually called *Aethiopica*.
[23] Sidney here follows Aristotle, *Poetics* (above, page 52).
[24] Giving weight to.

'*lux vitae, temporum magistra, vita memoriae, nuntia vetustatis,*'" &c.[25]

The philosopher (saith he)

teacheth a disputative virtue, but I do an active. His virtue is excellent in the dangerless Academy of Plato, but mine showeth forth her honorable face in the battles of Marathon, Pharsalia, Poitiers, and Agincourt. He teacheth virtue by certain abstract considerations, but I only bid you follow the footing of them that have gone before you. Old-aged experience goeth beyond the fine-witted philosopher, but I give the experience of many ages. Lastly, if he make the song book, I put the learner's hand to the lute; and if he be the guide, I am the light.

Then would he allege you innumerable examples, conferring story by story, how much the wisest senators and princes have been directed by the credit of history, as Brutus, Alphonsus of Aragon, and who not, if need be? At length the long line of their disputation maketh a point in this, that the one giveth the precept, and the other the example.

Now, whom shall we find (since the question standeth for the highest form in the school of learning) to be moderator? Truly, as me seemeth, the poet; and if not a moderator, even the man that ought to carry the title from them both, and much more from all other serving sciences. Therefore compare we the poet with the historian, and with the moral philosopher; and, if he go beyond them both, no other human skill can match him. For as for the Divine, with all reverence it is ever to be excepted, not only for having his scope as far beyond any of these as eternity exceedeth a moment, but even for passing each of these in themselves.

And for the lawyer, though Jus be the daughter of justice, and justice the chief of virtues, yet because he seeketh to make men good rather *formidine poenae* than *virtutis amore,*[26] or, to say righter, doth not endeavor to make men good, but that their evil hurt not others, having no care, so he be a good citizen, how bad a man he be: therefore, as our wickedness maketh him necessary, and necessity maketh him honorable, so is he not in the deepest truth to stand in rank with these who all endeavor to take naughtiness away, and plant goodness even in the secretest cabinet of our souls. And these four are all that any way deal in that consideration of men's manners, which being the supreme knowledge, they that best breed it deserve the best commendation.

The philosopher therefore and the historian are they which would win the goal, the one by precept, the other by example. But both, not having both, do both halt. For the philosopher, setting down with thorny argument the bare rule, is so hard of utterance, and so misty to be conceived, that one that hath no other guide but him shall wade in him till he be old before he shall find sufficient cause to be honest. For his knowledge standeth so upon the abstract and general, that happy is that man who may understand him, and more happy that can apply what he doth understand.

On the other side, the historian, wanting the precept, is so tied, not to what should be but to what is, to the particular truth of things and not to the general reason of things, that his example draweth no necessary consequence, and therefore a less fruitful doctrine.

Now doth the peerless poet perform both: for whatsoever the philosopher saith should be done, he giveth a perfect picture of it in someone by whom he presupposeth it was done; so as he coupleth the general notion with the particular example. A perfect picture I say, for he yieldeth to the powers of the mind an image of that whereof the philosopher bestoweth but a wordish description: which doth neither strike, pierce, nor possess the sight of the soul so much as that other doth.[27]

For as in outward things, to a man that had never seen an elephant or a rhinoceros, who should tell him most exquisitely all their shapes, color, bigness, and particular marks, or of a gorgeous palace the architecture, with declaring the full beauties might well make the hearer able to repeat, as it were by rote, all he had heard, yet should never satisfy his inward conceits with being witness to itself of a true lively knowledge: but the same man, as soon as he might see those beasts well painted, or the house well in model, should straightways grow, without need of any description, to a judicial comprehending of them: so no doubt the philosopher with his learned definition—be it of virtue, vices, matters of public policy or private government—replenisheth the memory with many infallible grounds of wisdom, which, notwithstanding, lie dark before the imaginative and judging power, if they be not illuminated or figured forth by the speaking picture of poesy.

---

[25] "The light of life, the master of the times, the life of memory, the messenger of antiquity." Cicero, *On the Orator* II, ix, 36.

[26] "Through fear of punishment" rather than "through love of virtue."

[27] Sidney's placing poetry midway between the precept of philosophy and the example of history leads to allegorical readings of poems and gives a new meaning to the idea of the poem as a "speaking picture." The original contrast of poetry to philosophy and history is Aristotle's, *Poetics* (above, page 57).

Tully[28] taketh much pains, and many times not without poetical helps, to make us know the force love of our country hath in us. Let us but hear old Anchises speaking in the midst of Troy's flames, or see Ulysses in the fullness of all Calypso's delights bewail his absence from barren and beggarly Ithaca. Anger, the Stoics say, was a short madness: let but Sophocles bring you Ajax on a stage, killing and whipping sheep and oxen, thinking them the army of Greeks, with their chieftains Agamemnon and Menelaus, and tell me if you have not a more familiar insight into anger than finding in the schoolmen his genus and difference. See whether wisdom and temperance in Ulysses and Diomedes, valor in Achilles, friendship in Nisus and Euryalus, even to an ignorant man carry not an apparent shining, and contrarily, the remorse of conscience in Oedipus, the soon repenting pride of Agamemnon, the self-devouring cruelty in his father Atreus, the violence of ambition in the two Theban brothers, the sour-sweetness of revenge in Medea, and, to fall lower, the Terentian Gnatho and our Chaucer's Pandar[29] so expressed that we now use their names to signify their trades; and finally, all virtues, vices, and passions so in their own natural seats laid to the view, that we seem not to hear of them, but clearly to see through them. But even in the most excellent determination of goodness, what philosopher's counsel can so readily direct a prince, as the feigned Cyrus in Xenophon; or a virtuous man in all fortunes, as Aeneas in Virgil; or a whole commonwealth, as the way of Sir Thomas More's *Utopia*?[30] I say the way, because where Sir Thomas More erred, it was the fault of the man and not of the poet, for that way of patterning a commonwealth was most absolute, though he perchance hath not so absolutely performed it. For the question is, whether the feigned image of poesy or the regular instruction of philosophy hath the more force in teaching: wherein if the philosophers have more rightly showed themselves philosophers than the poets have attained to the high top of their profession, as in truth, *"mediocribus esse poetis, / Non dii, non homines, non concessere columnae;"*[31] it is. I say again, not the fault of the art, but that by few men that art can be accomplished.

Certainly, even our Saviour Christ could as well have given the moral commonplaces of uncharitableness and humbleness as the divine narration of Dives and Lazarus; or of disobedience and mercy, as that heavenly discourse of the lost child and the gracious father; but that his through-searching wisdom knew the estate of Dives burning in hell, and of Lazarus being in Abraham's bosom, would more constantly (as it were) inhabit both the memory and judgment. Truly, for myself, meseems I see before my eyes the lost child's disdainful prodigality, turned to envy a swine's dinner: which by the learned divines are thought not historical acts, but instructing parables. For conclusion, I say the philosopher teacheth, but he teacheth obscurely, so as the learned only can understand him; that is to say, he teacheth them that are already taught. But the poet is the food for the tenderest stomachs, the poet is indeed the right popular philosopher, whereof Aesop's tales give good proof: whose pretty allegories, stealing under the formal tales of beasts, make many, more beastly than beasts, begin to hear the sound of virtue from these dumb speakers.

But now may it be alleged that, if this imagining of matters be so fit for the imagination, then must the historian needs surpass, who bringeth you images of true matters, such as indeed were done, and not such as fantastically or falsely may be suggested to have been done. Truly, Aristotle himself, in his discourse of poesy, plainly determineth this question, saying that poetry is *philosophoteron* and *spoudaioteron*, that is to say, it is more philosophical and more studiously serious than history. His reason is, because poesy dealeth with *katholou*, that is to say, with the universal consideration, and the history with *kathekaston*, the particular: "now," saith he, "the universal weighs what is fit to be said or done, either in likelihood or necessity (which the poesy considereth in his imposed names), and the particular only marks whether Alcibiades did, or suffered, this or that."[32] Thus far Aristotle: which reason of his (as all his) is most full of reason. For indeed, if the question were whether it were better to have a particular act truly or falsely set down, there is no doubt which is to be chosen, no more than whether you had rather have Vespasian's picture right as he was, or at the painter's pleasure nothing resembling. But if the question be for your own use and learning, whether it be better to have it set down as it should be, or as it was, then certainly is more doctrinable the feigned Cyrus in Xenophon than the true Cyrus in Justin,[33] and the feigned Aeneas in Virgil than the right Aeneas in Dares Phrygius.[34]

As to a lady that desired to fashion her countenance to the best grace, a painter should more benefit her to portrait a

---

[28] Cicero.

[29] In his *Troilus and Criseyde.*

[30] More (1478–1535), *Utopia.*

[31] "To poets to be second-rate is a privilege which neither men nor gods nor bookstores ever allowed." Horace, *Art of Poetry* (above, page 84).

[32] See Aristotle, *Poetics* (above, page 57).

[33] Justinus (second century). His historical work is based on that of Tragus Pompeius in the time of Augustus.

[34] *Daretis Phrygii de Excido Trojae Historia,* said to be the work of Dares, a priest of Troy, is actually of later composition.

most sweet face, writing Canidia upon it, than to paint Canidia as she was, who, Horace sweareth, was foul and ill favored.

If the poet do his part aright, he will show you in Tantalus, Atreus, and such like, nothing that is not to be shunned; in Cyrus, Aeneas, Ulysses, each thing to be followed; where the historian, bound to tell things as things were, cannot be liberal (without he will be poetical) of a perfect pattern, but, as in Alexander or Scipio himself, show doings, some to be liked, some to be misliked. And then how will you discern what to follow but by your own discretion, which you had without reading Quintus Curtius?[35] And whereas a man may say, though in universal consideration of doctrine the poet prevaileth, yet that the history, in his saying such a thing was done, doth warrant a man more in that he shall follow.

The answer is manifest: that if he stand upon that *was*—as if he should argue, because it rained yesterday, therefore it should rain today—then indeed it hath some advantage to a gross conceit; but if he know an example only informs a conjectured likelihood, and so go by reason, the poet doth so far exceed him, as he is to frame his example to that which is most reasonable, be it in warlike, politic, or private matters; where the historian in his bare *was* hath many times that which we call fortune to overrule the best wisdom. Many times he must tell events whereof he can yield no cause: or, if he do, it must be poetical. For that a feigned example hath as much force to teach as a true example (for as for to move, it is clear, since the feigned may be tuned to the highest key of passion), let us take one example wherein a poet and a historian do concur.

Herodotus and Justin do both testify that Zopyrus, King Darius's faithful servant, seeing his master long resisted by the rebellious Babylonians, feigned himself in extreme disgrace of his king: for verifying of which, he caused his own nose and ears to be cut off, and so flying to the Babylonians, was received, and for his known valor so far credited, that he did find means to deliver them over to Darius. Much like matter doth Livy[36] record of Tarquinius and his son. Xenophon excellently feigneth such another stratagem performed by Abradates in Cyrus's behalf. Now would I fain know, if occasion be presented unto you to serve your prince by such an honest dissimulation, why you do not as well learn it of Xenophon's fiction as of the other's verity—and truly so much the better, as you shall save your nose by

the bargain; for Abradates did not counterfeit so far. So then the best of the historian is subject to the poet; for whatsoever action, or faction, whatsoever counsel, policy, or war stratagem the historian is bound to recite, that may the poet (if he list) with his imitation make his own, beautifying it both for further teaching, and more delighting, as it pleaseth him, having all, from Dante's heaven to his hell, under the authority of his pen. Which if I be asked what poets have done so, as I might well name some, yet say I, and say again, I speak of the art, and not of the artificer.

Now, to that which commonly is attributed to the praise of histories, in respect of the notable learning is gotten by marking the success, as though therein a man should see virtue exalted and vice punished—truly that commendation is peculiar to poetry, and far off from history. For indeed poetry ever setteth virtue so out in her best colors, making Fortune her well-waiting handmaid, that one must needs be enamored of her. Well may you see Ulysses in a storm, and in other hard plights; but they are but exercises of patience and magnanimity, to make them shine the more in the near-following prosperity. And of the contrary part, if evil men come to the stage, they ever go out (as the tragedy writer answered to one that misliked the show of such persons) so manacled as they little animate folks to follow them. But the historian, being captived to the truth of a foolish world, is many times a terror from well doing, and an encouragement to unbridled wickedness.

For see we not valiant Miltiades rot in his fetters: the just Phocion and the accomplished Socrates put to death like traitors; the cruel Severus live prosperously; the excellent Severus miserably murdered; Sylla and Marius dying in their beds; Pompey and Cicero slain then when they would have thought exile a happiness?

See we not virtuous Cato driven to kill himself, and rebel Caesar so advanced that his name yet, after 1,600 years, lasteth in the highest honor? And mark but even Caesar's own words of the forenamed Sylla (who in that only did honestly, to put down his dishonest tyranny). *Literas nescivit,*[37] as if want of learning caused him to do well. He meant it not by poetry, which, not content with earthly plagues, deviseth new punishments in hell for tyrants, nor yet by philosophy, which teacheth *Occidendos esse;*[38] but no doubt by skill in history, for that indeed can afford your Cypselus, Periander, Phalaris, Dionysius, and I know not how many more of the same kennel, that speed well enough in their abominable injustice or usurpation. I conclude,

---

[35] Probably Quintus Curtius Rufus (first century A.D.?), historian of Alexander. His works are lost.
[36] Titus Livius (59 B.C.–17 A.D.), Roman historian.

---

[37] "He was ignorant of literature."
[38] "They are to be put to death."

therefore, that he excelleth history, not only in furnishing the mind with knowledge, but in setting it forward to that which deserveth to be called and accounted good: which setting forward, and moving to well doing, indeed setteth the laurel crown upon the poet as victorious, not only of the historian, but over the philosopher, howsoever in teaching it may be questionable.

For suppose it be granted (that which I suppose with great reason may be denied) that the philosopher, in respect of his methodical proceeding, doth teach more perfectly than the poet, yet do I think that no man is so much *philophilosophos* as to compare the philosopher, in moving, with the poet.

And that moving is of a higher degree than teaching, it may by this appear, that it is well-nigh the cause and the effect of teaching. For who will be taught, if he be not moved with desire to be taught, and what so much good doth that teaching bring forth (I speak still of moral doctrine) as that it moveth one to do that which it doth teach? For, as Aristotle saith, it is not *gnosis* but *praxis*[39] must be the fruit. And how *praxis* cannot be, without being moved to practice, it is no hard matter to consider.

The philosopher showeth you the way, he informeth you of the particularities, as well of the tediousness of the way, as of the pleasant lodging you shall have when your journey is ended, as of the many by-turnings that may divert you from your way. But this is to no man but to him that will read him, and read him with attentive studious painfulness; which constant desire whosoever hath in him, hath already passed half the hardness of the way, and therefore is beholding to the philosopher but for the other half. Nay truly, learned men have learnedly thought that where once reason hath so much overmastered passion as that the mind hath a free desire to do well, the inward light each mind hath in itself is as good as a philosopher's book; seeing in nature we know it is well to do well, and what is well and what is evil, although not in the words of art which philosophers bestow upon us. For out of natural conceit the philosophers drew it; but to be moved to do that which we know, or to be moved with desire to know, *Hoc opus, hic labor est.*[40]

Now therein of all sciences (I speak still of human, and according to the humane conceits) is our poet the monarch. For he doth not only show the way, but giveth so sweet a prospect into the way, as will entice any man to enter into it. Nay, he doth, as if your journey should lie through a fair vineyard, at the first give you a cluster of grapes, that, full

of that taste, you may long to pass further. He beginneth not with obscure definitions, which must blur the margent[41] with interpretations, and load the memory with doubtfulness; but he cometh to you with words set in delightful proportion, either accompanied with, or prepared for, the well-enchanting skill of music; and with a tale forsooth he cometh unto you, with a tale which holdeth children from play, and old men from the chimney corner. And, pretending no more, doth intend the winning of the mind from wickedness to virtue: even as the child is often brought to take most wholesome things by hiding them in such other as have a pleasant taste: which, if one should begin to tell them the nature of aloes or rhubarb they should receive, would sooner take their physic at their ears than at their mouth. So is it in men (most of which are childish in the best things, till they be cradled in their graves): glad they will be to hear the tales of Hercules, Achilles, Cyrus, and Aeneas; and, hearing them, must needs hear the right description of wisdom, valor, and justice; which, if they had been barely, that is to say philosophically, set out, they would swear they be brought to school again.

That imitation whereof poetry is, hath the most conveniency to nature of all other, insomuch that, as Aristotle saith, those things which in themselves are horrible, as cruel battles, unnatural monsters, are made in poetical imitation delightful. Truly, I have known men, that even with reading *Amadis de Gaule*[42] (which God knoweth wanteth much of a perfect poesy) have found their hearts moved to the exercise of courtesy, liberality, and especially courage.

Who readeth Aeneas carrying old Anchises on his back, that wisheth not it were his fortune to perform so excellent an act? Whom do not the words of Turnus move, the tale of Turnus having planted his image in the imagination?—*"Fugientem haec terra videbit? / Usque adeone mori miserum est?"*[43] Where the philosophers, as they scorn to delight, so must they be content little to move, saving wrangling whether virtue be the chief or the only good, whether the contemplative or the active life do excel: which Plato and Boethius well knew, and therefore made Mistress Philosophy very often borrow the masking raiment of Poesy.[44] For even those hardhearted evil men who think virtue a school name, and know no other good but *indulgere genio,*[45] and therefore despise the austere admonitions of the

---

[39]Not "knowledge" but "action."
[40]"This the work, this the labor." *Aeneid* VI, 129.

[41]In Sidney's day, the margins of the page were often used for notes.
[42]Anonymous medieval French romance of chivalry, fourteenth century.
[43]"Will the land see [Turnus] in flight?/ Is it so miserable to die?" *Aeneid* XII, 645–46.
[44]Sidney regards Plato as a poet because he wrote dramatic dialogues, Boethius because he interspersed prose with poetry in the *Consolation of Philosophy.*
[45]"To indulge one's nature."

philosopher, and feel not the inward reason they stand upon, yet will be content to be delighted—which is all the good fellow poet seemeth to promise—and so steal to see the form of goodness, which seen they cannot but love ere themselves be aware, as if they took a medicine of cherries. Infinite proofs of the strange effects of this poetical invention might be alleged; only two shall serve, which are so often remembered as I think all men know them.

The one of Menenius Agrippa,[46] who, when the whole people of Rome had resolutely divided themselves from the Senate, with apparent show of utter ruin, though he were (for that time) an excellent orator, came not among them upon trust of figurative speeches or cunning insinuations, and much less with farfetched maxims of philosophy, which (especially if they were Platonic) they must have learned geometry before they could well have conceived; but forsooth he behaves himself like a homely and familiar poet. He telleth them a tale, that there was a time when all the parts of the body made a mutinous conspiracy against the belly, which they thought devoured the fruits of each other's labor: they concluded they would let so unprofitable a spender starve. In the end, to be short (for the tale is notorious, and as notorious that it was a tale), with punishing the belly they plagued themselves. This applied by him wrought such effect in the people, as I never read that ever words brought forth but then so sudden and so good an alteration; for upon reasonable conditions a perfect reconcilement ensued. The other is of Nathan the Prophet, who, when the holy David had so far forsaken God as to confirm adultery with murder, when he was to do the tenderest office of a friend, in laying his own shame before his eyes, sent by God to call again so chosen a servant, how doth he it but by telling of a man whose beloved lamb was ungratefully taken from his bosom?—the application most divinely true, but the discourse itself feigned. Which made David (I speak of the second and instrumental cause) as in a glass to see his own filthiness, as that heavenly Psalm of Mercy well testifieth.

By these, therefore, examples and reasons, I think it may be manifest that the poet, with that same hand of delight, doth draw the mind more effectually than any other art doth: and so a conclusion not unfitly ensueth, that, as virtue is the most excellent resting place for all worldly learning to make his end of, so poetry, being the most familiar to teach it, and most princely to move towards it, in the most excellent work is the most excellent workman. But I am content

not only to decipher him by his works (although works in commendation or dispraise must ever hold an high authority), but more narrowly will examine his parts: so that, as in a man, though all together may carry a presence full of majesty and beauty, perchance in some one defectious piece we may find a blemish. Now in his parts, kinds, or species (as you list to term them), it is to be noted that some poesies have coupled together two or three kinds, as tragical and comical, whereupon is risen the tragicomical. Some, in the like manner, have mingled prose and verse, as Sannazzaro[47] and Boethius. Some have mingled matters heroical and pastoral. But that cometh all to one in this question, for, if severed they be good, the conjunction cannot be hurtful. Therefore, perchance forgetting some, and leaving some as needless to be remembered, it shall not be amiss in a word to cite the special kinds, to see what faults may be found in the right use of them.

Is it then the pastoral poem which is misliked? For perchance where the hedge is lowest they will soonest leap over. Is the poor pipe disdained, which sometime out of Melibaeus' mouth can show the misery of people under hard lords or ravening soldiers, and again, by Tityrus, what blessedness is derived to them that lie lowest from the goodness of them that sit highest; sometimes, under the pretty tales of wolves and sheep, can include the whole considerations of wrongdoing and patience; sometimes show that contention for trifles can get but a trifling victory; where perchance a man may see that even Alexander and Darius, when they strave who should be cock of this world's dunghill, the benefit they got was that the afterlivers may say, *"Haec memini et victum frustra contendere Thirsin: / Ex illo Coridon, Coridon es tempore nobis"?*[48]

Or is it the lamenting elegiac, which in a kind heart would move rather pity than blame, who bewails with the great philosopher Heraclitus the weakness of mankind and the wretchedness of the world; who surely is to be praised, either for compassionate accompanying just causes of lamentation, or for rightly pointing out how weak be the passions of woefulness? Is it the bitter but wholesome iambic, which rubs the galled mind, in making shame the trumpet of villainy with bold and open crying out against naughtiness? Or the satiric, who *"omne vafer vitium ridenti tangit amico"*;[49] who sportingly never leaveth until he make a man laugh at folly, and, at length ashamed, to laugh at himself,

---

[46] In 494, the consul Menenius is said to have settled a dispute between patricians and plebeians with his tale of the belly and parts of the body.

[47] Jacopo Sannazzaro (1458–1530), Italian author of the prose romance *Arcadia,* lyrics, and Latin writings.

[48] "I remember those things, and that Thyrsus conquered, strove in vain: / From that time Corydon for us is Corydon." Virgil, *Eclogue* VII, 69–70.

[49] "The rogue touches every vice, while he makes his friend laugh." Persius (34–62), *Satires* I, 116–17.

which he cannot avoid, without avoiding the folly; who, while *"circum praecordia ludit,"*[50] giveth us to feel how many headaches a passionate life bringeth us to; how, when all is done, *"est Ulubris animus si nos non deficit aequus?"*[51]

No, perchance it is the comic, whom naughty playmakers and stage-keepers have justly made odious. To the argument of abuse I will answer after. Only thus much now is to be said, that the comedy is an imitation of the common errors of our life, which he representeth in the most ridiculous and scornful sort that may be, so as it is impossible that any beholder can be content to be such a one.

Now, as in geometry the oblique must be known as well as the right, and in arithmetic the odd as well as the even, so in the actions of our life who seeth not the filthiness of evil wanteth a great foil to perceive the beauty of virtue. This doth the comedy handle so in our private and domestical matters, as with hearing it we get as it were an experience, what is to be looked for of a niggardly Demea, of a crafty Davus, of a flattering Gnatho, of a vainglorious Thraso; and not only to know what effects are to be expected, but to know who be such, by the signifying badge given them by the comedian. And little reason hath any man to say that men learn evil by seeing it so set out; since, as I said before, there is no man living but, by the force truth hath in nature, no sooner seeth these men play their parts, but wisheth them in *pistrinum;*[52] although perchance the sack of his own faults lie so behind his back that he seeth not himself dance the same measure; whereto yet nothing can more open his eyes than to find his own actions contemptibly set forth. So that the right use of comedy will (I think) by nobody be blamed, and much less of the high and excellent tragedy, that openeth the greatest wounds, and showeth forth the ulcers that are covered with tissue; that maketh kings fear to be tyrants, and tyrants manifest their tyrannical humors; that, with stirring the affects of admiration and commiseration, teacheth the uncertainty of this world, and upon how weak foundations gilden roofs are builded; that maketh us know, *"Qui sceptra saevus duro imperio regit, / Timet timentes, metus in auctorem redit."*[53]

But how much it can move, Plutarch yieldeth a notable testimony of the abominable tyrant Alexander Pheraeus, from whose eyes a tragedy, well made and represented, drew abundance of tears, who, without all pity, had murdered infinite numbers, and some of his own blood, so as he, that was not ashamed to make matters for tragedies, yet could not resist the sweet violence of a tragedy.

And if it wrought no further good in him, it was that he, in despite of himself, withdrew himself from hearkening to that which might mollify his hardened heart. But it is not the tragedy they do mislike; for it were too absurd to cast out so excellent a representation of whatsoever is most worthy to be learned. Is it the lyric that most displeaseth, who with his turned lyre, and well-accorded voice, giveth praise, the reward of virtue, to virtuous acts, who gives moral precepts, and natural problems, who sometimes raiseth up his voice to the height of the heavens, in singing the lauds of the immortal God? Certainly, I must confess my own barbarousness. I never heard the old song of Percy and Douglas[54] that I found not my heart moved more than with a trumpet; and yet is it sung but by some blind crowder, with no rougher voice than rude style; which, being so evil appareled in the dust and cobwebs of that uncivil age, what would it work, trimmed in the gorgeous eloquence of Pindar?[55] In Hungary I have seen it the manner at all feasts, and other such meetings, to have songs of their ancestors' valor; which that right soldierlike nation think the chiefest kindlers of brave courage. The incomparable Lacedaemonians did not only carry that kind of music ever with them to the field, but even at home, as such songs were made, so were they all content to be the singers of them, when the lusty men were to tell what they did, the old men what they had done, and the young men what they would do. And where a man may say that Pindar many times praiseth highly victories of small moment, matters rather of sport than virtue; as it may be answered, it was the fault of the poet, and not of the poetry, so indeed the chief fault was in the time and custom of the Greeks, who set those toys at so high a price that Philip of Macedon reckoned a horse race won at Olympus among his three fearful felicities. But as the inimitable Pindar often did, so is that kind most capable and most fit to awake the thoughts from the sleep of idleness, to embrace honorable enterprises.

There rests the heroical, whose very name (I think) should daunt all backbiters; for by what conceit can a tongue be directed to speak evil of that which draweth with it no less champions than Achilles, Cyrus, Aeneas, Turnus, Tydeus, and Rinaldo? Who doth not only teach and move to

---

[50]"He plays about the heart."

[51]"Is happiness to be found in Ulubria if balance does not fail us?" Horace, *Epistles* I, xi, 30.

[52]A mill in which slaves were put to work as punishment.

[53]"The savage tyrant who wields his scepter with a heavy hand fears the timid, and fear returns to its author." Seneca (c. 3 B.C.–c. 65 A.D.), *Oedipus,* 705–6.

[54]The ballad of *Chevy Chase,* one of the oldest English ballads.

[55]Pindar (c. 518–c. 438 B.C.), Greek lyric poet.

a truth, but teacheth and moveth to the most high and excellent truth; who maketh magnanimity and justice shine throughout all misty fearfulness and foggy desires; who, if the saying of Plato and Tully be true, that who could see virtue would be wonderfully ravished with the love of her beauty—this man sets her out to make her more lovely in her holiday apparel, to the eye of any that will deign not to disdain until they understand. But if anything be already said in the defense of sweet Poetry, all concurreth to the maintaining the heroical, which is not only a kind, but the best and most accomplished kind of poetry.[56] For as the image of each action stirreth and instructeth the mind, so the lofty image of such worthies most inflameth the mind with desire to be worthy, and informs with counsel how to be worthy. Only let Aeneas be worn in the tablet of your memory, how he governeth himself in the ruin of his country, in the preserving his old father, and carrying away his religious ceremonies, in obeying the god's commandment to leave Dido, though not only all passionate kindness, but even the human consideration of virtuous gratefulness, would have craved other of him; how in storms, how in sports, how in war, how in peace, how a fugitive, how victorious, how besieged, how besieging, how to strangers, how to allies, how to enemies, how to his own; lastly, how in his inward self, and how in his outward government, and I think, in a mind not prejudiced with a prejudicating humor, he will be found in excellency fruitful, yea, even as Horace saith, *"melius Chrysippo et Crantore."*[57]

But truly I imagine it falleth out with these poetwhippers, as with some good women, who often are sick, but in faith they cannot tell where. So the name of poetry is odious to them, but neither his cause nor effects, neither the sum that contains him nor the particularities descending from him, give any fast handle to their carping dispraise.

Since then poetry is of all human learning the most ancient and of most fatherly antiquity, as from whence other learnings have taken their beginnings; since it is so universal that no learned nation doth despise it, nor no barbarous nation is without it; since both Roman and Greek gave divine names unto it, the one of *prophesying,* the other of *making,* and that indeed that name of *making* is fit for him, considering that whereas other arts retain themselves within their subject, and receive, as it were, their being from it, the poet only bringeth his own stuff, and doth not learn a conceit out of a matter, but maketh matter for a conceit; since

neither his description nor his end containeth any evil, the thing described cannot be evil; since his effects be so good as to teach goodness and to delight the learners; since therein (namely in moral doctrine, the chief of all knowledges) he doth not only far pass the historian, but, for instructing, is well-nigh comparable to the philosopher, and, for moving, leaves him behind him; since the Holy Scripture (wherein there is no uncleanness) hath whole parts in it poetical, and that even our Saviour Christ vouchsafed to use the flowers of it; since all his kinds are not only in their united forms but in their severed dissections fully commendable; I think (and think I think rightly) the laurel crown appointed for triumphing captains doth worthily (of all other learnings) honor the poet's triumph. But because we have ears as well as tongues, and that the lightest reasons that may be will seem to weigh greatly, if nothing be put in the counterbalance, let us hear, and, as well as we can, ponder, what objections may be made against this art, which may be worthy either of yielding or answering.

First, truly I note not only in these *mysomousoi,* "poet-haters," but in all that kind of people who seek a praise by dispraising others, that they do prodigally spend a great many wandering words in quips and scoffs, carping and taunting at each thing, which, by stirring the spleen, may stay the brain from a thorough beholding the worthiness of the subject.

Those kind of objections, as they are full of very idle easiness, since there is nothing of so sacred a majesty but that an itching tongue may rub itself upon it, so deserve they no other answer, but, instead of laughing at the jest, to laugh at the jester. We know a playing wit can praise the discretion of an ass, the comfortableness of being in debt, and the jolly commodity of being sick of the plague. So of the contrary side, if we will turn Ovid's[58] verse, *"Ut lateat virtus proximitate mali,"* that "good lie hid in nearness of the evil," Agrippa will be as merry in showing the vanity of science as Erasmus was in commending of folly.[59] Neither shall any man or matter escape some touch of these smiling railers. But for Erasmus and Agrippa, they had another foundation than the superficial part would promise. Marry,[60] these other pleasant faultfinders, who will correct the verb before they understand the noun, and confute others' knowledge before they confirm their own, I would have them only remember

[56] Here Sidney expresses a Renaissance attitude that is contrary to Aristotle, who favored tragedy over epic.
[57] "Better than Chrysippus and Crantor." *Epistles* I, ii, 4.
[58] Publius Ovidus Naso (43 B.C.–18 A.D.), Latin poet.
[59] Sidney is referring to a treatise titled *On the Uncertainty and Vanity of the Sciences and Art* by Henry Cornelius Agrippa (1486–1535), German physician and astrologer, and to the famous satire *The Praise of Folly* by Desiderius Erasmus (1466?–1536), Dutch humanist.
[60] To be sure; indeed.

that scoffing cometh not of wisdom; so as the best title in true English they get with their merriments is to be called good fools, for so have our grave forefathers ever termed that humorous kind of jesters. But that which giveth greatest scope to their scorning humors is rhyming and versing. It is already said (and, as I think, truly said) it is not rhyming and versing that maketh poesy. One may be a poet without versing, and a versifier without poetry. But yet presuppose it were inseparable (as indeed it seemeth Scaliger judgeth) truly it were an inseparable commendation.[61] For if *oratio* next to *ratio*, "speech" next to "reason," be the greatest gift bestowed upon mortality, that cannot be praiseless which doth most polish that blessing of speech; which considers each word, not only (as a man may say) by his forcible quality, but by his best measured quantity, carrying even in themselves a harmony (without, perchance, number, measure, order, proportion be in our time grown odious). But lay aside the just praise it hath, by being the only fit speech for music (music, I say, the most divine striker of the senses), thus much is undoubtedly true, that if reading be foolish without remembering, memory being the only treasurer of knowledge, those words which are fittest for memory are likewise most convenient for knowledge.

Now, that verse far exceedeth prose in the knitting up of the memory, the reason is manifest—the words (besides their delight, which hath a great affinity to memory) being so set as one word cannot be lost but the whole work fails; which accuseth itself, calleth the remembrance back to itself, and so most strongly confirmeth it. Besides, one word so, as it were, begetting another, as, be it in rhyme or measured verse, by the former a man shall have a near guess to the follower: lastly, even they that have taught the art of memory have showed nothing so apt for it as a certain room divided into many places well and thoroughly known. Now, that hath the verse in effect perfectly, every word having his natural seat, which seat must needs make the words remembered. But what needeth more in a thing so known to all men? Who is it that ever was a scholar that doth not carry away some verses of Virgil, Horace, or Cato, which in his youth he learned, and even to his old age serve him for hourly lessons? But the fitness it hath for memory is notably proved by all delivery of arts: wherein for the most part, from grammar to logic, mathematic, physic, and the rest, the rules chiefly necessary to be borne away are compiled in verses. So that, verse being in itself sweet and orderly, and being best for memory, the only handle of knowledge, it must be in jest that any man can speak against it. Now then

go we to the most important imputations laid to the poor poets. For aught I can yet learn, they are these. First, that there being many other more fruitful knowledges, a man might better spend his time in them than in this. Secondly, that it is the mother of lies. Thirdly, that it is the nurse of abuse, infecting us with many pestilent desires, with a siren's sweetness drawing the mind to the serpent's tale of sinful fancy— and herein, especially, comedies give the largest field to ear (as Chaucer saith)—how both in other nations and in ours, before poets did soften us, we were full of courage, given to martial exercises, the pillars of manlike liberty, and not lulled asleep in shady idleness with poets' pastimes. And lastly, and chiefly, they cry out with an open mouth, as if they outshot Robin Hood, that Plato banished them out of his commonwealth.[62] Truly, this is much, if there be much truth in it. First, to the first, that a man might better spend his time is a reason indeed: but it doth (as they say) but *petere principium*:[63] for if it be, as I affirm, that no learning is so good as that which teacheth and moveth to virtue, and that none can both teach and move thereto so much as poetry, then is the conclusion manifest that ink and paper cannot be to a more profitable purpose employed. And certainly, though a man should grant their first assumption, it should follow (methinks) very unwillingly, that good is not good because better is better. But I still and utterly deny that there is sprung out of earth a more fruitful knowledge. To the second therefore, that they should be the principal liars, I answer paradoxically, but truly, I think truly, that of all writers under the sun the poet is the least liar and, though he would, as a poet can scarcely be a liar. The astronomer, with his cousin the geometrician, can hardly escape, when they take upon them to measure the height of the stars.

How often, think you, do the physicians lie, when they aver things good for sickness, which afterwards send Charon a great number of souls drowned in a potion before they come to his ferry? And no less of the rest, which take upon them to affirm. Now, for the poet, he nothing affirms, and therefore never lieth. For, as I take it, to lie is to affirm that to be true which is false; so as the other artists, and especially the historian, affirming many things, can, in the cloudy knowledge of mankind, hardly escape from many lies. But the poet (as I said before) never affirmeth.[64] The poet never maketh any circles about your imagination, to conjure you to believe for true what he writes. He citeth not authorities of other histories, but even for his entry calleth

---

[61] Scaliger identifies poetry with verse (above, page 173).

[62] *Republic* (above, page 27).
[63] "Beg the question."
[64] See Wilde's approach to this issue (below, page 712ff.).

the sweet Muses to inspire into him a good invention; in truth, no laboring to tell you what is, or is not, but what should or should not be. And therefore, though he recount things not true, yet because he telleth them not for true, he lieth not—without we will say that Nathan lied in his speech, before alleged, to David; which as a wicked man durst scarce say, so think I none so simple would say that Aesop lied in the tales of his beasts: for who thinks that Aesop writ it for actually true were well worthy to have his name chronicled among the beasts he writeth of.

What child is there that, coming to a play, and seeing *Thebes* written in great letters upon an old door, doth believe that it is Thebes? If then a man can arrive, at that child's age, to know that the poets' persons and doings are but pictures what should be, and not stories what have been, they will never give the lie to things not affirmatively but allegorically and figuratively written. And therefore, as in history, looking for truth, they go away full fraught with falsehood, so in poesy, looking for fiction, they shall use the narration but as an imaginative ground plot of a profitable invention.

But hereto is replied, that the poets give names to men they write of, which argueth a conceit of an actual truth, and so, not being true, proves a falsehood. And doth the lawyer lie then, when under the names of John a Stile and John a Noakes he puts his case? But that is easily answered. Their naming of men is but to make their picture the more lively, and not to build any history; painting men, they cannot leave men nameless. We see we cannot play at chess but that we must give names to our chessmen; and yet, methinks, he were a very partial champion of truth that would say we lied for giving a piece of wood the reverend title of a bishop. The poet nameth Cyrus or Aeneas no other way than to show what men of their fames, fortunes, and estates should do.

Their third is, how much it abuseth men's wit, training it to wanton sinfulness and lustful love: for indeed that is the principal, if not the only, abuse I can hear alleged. They say the comedies rather teach than reprehend amorous conceits. They say the lyric is larded with passionate sonnets, the elegiac weeps the want of his mistress, and that even to the heroical Cupid hath ambitiously climbed. Alas, Love, I would thou couldst as well defend thyself as thou canst offend others. I would those on whom thou dost attend could either put thee away, or yield good reason why they keep thee. But grant love of beauty to be a beastly fault (although it be very hard, since only man, and no beast, hath that gift to discern beauty); grant that lovely name of Love to deserve all hateful reproaches (although even some of my masters the philosophers spent a good deal of their lamp-oil in setting forth the excellency of it); grant, I say, whatsoever

they will have granted; that not only love, but lust, but vanity, but (if they list) scurrility, possesseth many leaves of the poet's books: yet think I, when this is granted, they will find their sentence may with good manners put the last words foremost, and not say that poetry abuseth man's wit, but that man's wit abuseth poetry.

For I will not deny but that man's wit may make poesy, which should be *eikastike,* which some learned have defined, "figuring forth good things," to be *phantastike,* which doth, contrariwise, infect the fancy with unworthy objects,[65] as the painter, that should give to the eye either some excellent perspective, or some fine picture, fit for building or fortification, or containing in it some notable example, as Abraham sacrificing his son Isaac, Judith killing Holofernes, David fighting with Goliath, may leave those, and please an ill-pleased eye with wanton shows of better hidden matters. But what, shall the abuse of a thing make the right use odious? Nay truly, though I yield that poesy may not only be abused, but that being abused, by the reason of his sweet charming force, it can do more hurt than any other army of words, yet shall it be so far from concluding that the abuse should give reproach to the abused, that contrariwise it is a good reason, that whatsoever, being abused, doth most harm, being rightly used (and upon the right use each thing conceiveth his title), doth most good.

Do we not see the skill of physic (the best rampire to our often-assaulted bodies), being abused, teach poison, the most violent destroyer? Doth not knowledge of law, whose end is to even and right all things, being abused, grow the crooked fosterer of horrible injuries? Doth not (to go to the highest) God's word abused breed heresy, and his name abused become blasphemy? Truly, a needle cannot do much hurt, and as truly (with leave of ladies be it spoken) it cannot do much good. With a sword thou mayest kill thy father, and with a sword thou mayest defend thy prince and country. So that, as in their calling poets the fathers of lies they say nothing, so in this their argument of abuse they prove the commendation.

They allege herewith, that before poets began to be in price our nation hath set their heart's delight upon action, and not upon imagination, rather doing things worthy to be written, than writing things fit to be done. What that beforetime was, I think scarcely Sphinx can tell, since no memory is so ancient that hath the precedence of poetry. And certain it is that, in our plainest homeliness, yet never was the Albion nation without poetry. Marry, this argument, though it

---

[65] This distinction originates in Plato's *Sophist* (above, page 40). It is taken up by Mazzoni (below, page 218).

be leveled against poetry, yet is it indeed a chain-shot against all learning, or bookishness, as they commonly term it. Of such mind were certain Goths, of whom it is written that, having in the spoil of a famous city taken a fair library, one hangman, belike, fit to execute the fruits of their wits, who had murdered a great number of bodies, would have set fire to it. "No," said another very gravely, "take heed what you do, for while they are busy about these toys, we shall with more leisure conquer their countries."

This indeed is the ordinary doctrine of ignorance, and many words sometimes I have heard spent in it: but because this reason is generally against all learning, as well as poetry, or rather, all learning but poetry; because it were too large a digression to handle, or at least too superfluous (since it is manifest that all government of action is to be gotten by knowledge, and knowledge best by gathering many knowledges, which is reading), I only, with Horace, to him that is of that opinion, *"iubeo stultum esse libenter";*[66] for as for poetry itself, it is the freest from this objection. For poetry is the companion of the camps.

I dare undertake, Orlando Furioso, or honest King Arthur, will never displease a soldier: but the quiddity of *ens* and *prima materia*[67] will hardly agree with a corselet. And therefore, as I said in the beginning, even Turks and Tartars are delighted with poets. Homer, a Greek, flourished before Greece flourished. And if to a slight conjecture a conjecture may be opposed, truly it may seem, that, as by him their learned men took almost their first light of knowledge, so their active men received their first motions of courage. Only Alexander's example may serve, who by Plutarch is accounted of such virtue, that fortune was not his guide but his footstool; whose acts speak for him, though Plutarch did not—indeed the Phoenix of warlike princes. This Alexander left his schoolmaster, living Aristotle, behind him, but took dead Homer with him. He put the philosopher Callisthenes to death for his seeming philosophical, indeed mutinous, stubbornness, but the chief thing he ever was heard to wish for was that Homer had been alive. He well found he received more bravery of mind by the pattern of Achilles than by hearing the definition of fortitude: and therefore, if Cato misliked Fulvius for carrying Ennius with him to the field, it may be answered that, if Cato misliked it, the noble Fulvius liked it, or else he had not done it: for it was not the excellent Cato Uticensis (whose authority I would much more have reverenced), but it was the former, in truth a bitter punisher of faults, but else

a man that had never well sacrificed to the Graces. He misliked and cried out upon all Greek learning, and yet, being eighty years old, began to learn it, belike fearing that Pluto understood not Latin. Indeed, the Roman laws allowed no person to be carried to the wars but he that was in the soldier's role, and therefore, though Cato misliked his unmustered person, he misliked not his work. And if he had, Scipio Nasica, judged by common consent the best Roman, loved him. Both the other Scipio brothers, who had by their virtues no less surnames than of Asia and Afric, so loved him that they caused his body to be buried in their sepulcher. So as Cato's authority being but against his person, and that answered with so far greater than himself, is herein of no validity. But now indeed my burden is great; now Plato's name is laid upon me, whom, I must confess, of all philosophers I have ever esteemed most worthy of reverence, and with great reason, since of all philosophers he is the most poetical. Yet if he will defile the fountain out of which his flowing streams have proceeded, let us boldly examine with what reasons he did it. First truly, a man might maliciously object that Plato, being a philosopher, was a natural enemy of poets. For indeed, after the philosophers had picked out of the sweet mysteries of poetry the right discerning true points of knowledge, they forthwith, putting it in method, and making a school art of that which the poets did only teach by a divine delightfulness, beginning to spurn at their guides, like ungrateful 'prentices, were not content to set up shops for themselves, but sought by all means to discredit their masters; which by the force of delight being barred them, the less they could overthrow them, the more they hated them. For indeed, they found for Homer seven cities strove who should have him for their citizen; where many cities banished philosophers as not fit members to live among them. For only repeating certain of Euripides' verses, many Athenians had their lives saved of the Syracusians, when the Athenians themselves thought many philosophers unworthy to live.

Certain poets, as Simonides and Pindarus, had so prevailed with Hiero the First, that of a tyrant they made him a just king; where Plato could do so little with Dionysius, that he himself of a philosopher was made a slave. But who should do thus, I confess, should require the objections made against poets with like cavillation against philosophers; as likewise one should do that should bid one read *Phaedrus* or *Symposium* in Plato, or the discourse of love in Plutarch, and see whether any poet do authorize abominable filthiness, as they do. Again, a man might ask out of what commonwealth Plato did banish them. In sooth, thence where he himself alloweth community of women. So as belike this banishment grew not for effeminate wantonness, since little should poetical sonnets be hurtful when a man might have what woman he listed. But I honor philosophical instructions, and bless the wits which bred them: so as they be not abused, which is likewise stretched to poetry.

St. Paul himself, who yet, for the credit of poets, allegeth twice two poets, and one of them by the name of a prophet, setteth a watchword upon philosophy—indeed upon the abuse. So doth Plato upon the abuse, not upon poetry. Plato found fault that the poets of his time filled the world with wrong opinions of the gods, making light tales of that unspotted essence, and therefore would not have the youth depraved with such opinions. Herein may much be said; let this suffice: the poets did not induce such opinions, but did imitate those opinions already induced. For all the Greek stories can well testify that the very religion of that time stood upon many and many-fashioned gods, not taught so by the poets, but followed according to their nature of imitation. Who list may read in Plutarch the discourses of Isis and Osiris, of the cause why oracles ceased, of the divine providence, and see whether the theology of that nation stood not upon such dreams which the poets indeed superstitiously observed, and truly (since they had not the light of Christ) did much better in it than the philosophers, who, shaking off superstition, brought in atheism. Plato therefore (whose authority I had much rather justly construe than unjustly resist) meant not in general of poets, in those words of which Julius Scaliger saith, *"Qua authoritate barbari quidam atque hispidi abuti velint ad poetas e republica exigendos",*[68] but only meant to drive out those wrong opinions of Deity (whereof now, without further law, Christianity hath taken away all the hurtful belief), perchance (as he thought) nourished by the then esteemed poets. And a man need go no further than to Plato himself to know his meaning: who, in his dialogue called *Ion,* giveth high and rightly divine commendation to poetry. So as Plato, banishing the abuse, not the thing, not banishing it, but giving due honor unto it, shall be our patron and not our adversary. For indeed I had much rather (since truly I may do it) show their mistaking of Plato (under whose lion's skin they would make an asslike braying against poesy) than go about to overthrow his authority; whom, the wiser a man is, the more just cause he shall find to have in admiration; especially since he attributeth unto poesy more than myself do, namely, to be a very inspiring of a divine force, far above man's wit, as in the afore-named dialogue is apparent.[69]

Of the other side, who would show the honors have been by the best sort of judgments granted them, a whole sea of examples would present themselves: Alexanders, Caesars, Scipios, all favorers of poets; Laelius, called the Roman Socrates, himself a poet, so as part of *Heautontimorumenos*[70] in Terence was supposed to be made by him, and even the Greek Socrates, whom Apollo confirmed to be the only wise man, is said to have spent part of his old time in putting Aesop's fables into verses. And therefore, full evil should it become his scholar Plato to put such words in his master's mouth against poets. But what need more? Aristotle writes the *Art of Poesy:* and why, if it should not be written? Plutarch teacheth the use to be gathered of them, and how, if they should not be read? And who reads Plutarch's either history or philosophy, shall find he trimmeth both their garments with guards of poesy. But I list not to defend poesy with the help of her underling historiography. Let it suffice that it is a fit soil for praise to dwell upon; and what dispraise may set upon it, is either easily overcome, or transformed into just commendation. So that, since the excellencies of it may be so easily and so justly confirmed, and the low-creeping objections so soon trodden down; it not being an art of lies, but of true doctrine; not of effeminateness, but of notable stirring of courage; not of abusing man's wit, but of strengthening man's wit; not banished, but honored by Plato; let us rather plant more laurels for to engarland our poets' heads (which honor of being laureate, as besides them only triumphant captains wear, is a sufficient authority to show the price they ought to be had in) than suffer the ill-favoring breath of such wrong-speakers once to blow upon the clear springs of poesy.

But since I have run so long a career in this matter, methinks, before I give my pen a full stop, it shall be but a little more lost time to inquire why England (the mother of excellent minds) should be grown so hard a stepmother to poets, who certainly in wit ought to pass all other, since all only proceedeth from their wit, being indeed makers of themselves, not takers of others. How can I but exclaim, *"Musa, mihi causas memora, quo numine laeso!"*[71] Sweet Poesy, that hath anciently had kings, emperors, senators, great captains, such as, besides a thousand others, David, Adrian, Sophocles, Germanicus, not only to favor poets, but to be poets; and of our nearer times can present for her patrons a Robert, king of Sicily, the great King Francis of

---

[68] "Which authority some crude and insensible men would construe to the exclusion of poets from the republic." Scaliger, *Poetics* (above, page 172).
[69] Sidney somewhat distorts Socrates's position in *Ion* (above, page 12) and tries to turn it to the poets' advantage.

[70] Caius Laelius Sapiens (c. 186–after 120 B.C.), said to have influenced the poet Terence's (195–c. 159 B.C.) *The Self-Tormentor.*
[71] "Muse, relate to me how her divinity was injured." *Aeneid* I, 8.

James of Scotland; such cardinals as Bembus ____; such famous preachers and teachers as Beza and Melancthon; so learned philosophers as Fracastorius and Scaliger; so great orators as Pontanus and Muretus; so piercing wits as George Buchanan; so grave counselors as, besides many, but before all, that Hospital of France, than whom (I think) that realm never brought forth a more accomplished judgment, more firmly builded upon virtue—I say these, with numbers of others, not only to read others' poesies, but to poetize for others' reading—that poesy, thus embraced in all other places, should only find in our time a hard welcome in England, I think the very earth lamenteth it, and therefore decketh our soil with fewer laurels than it was accustomed. For heretofore poets have in England also flourished, and, which is to be noted, even in those times when the trumpet of Mars did sound loudest. And now that an overfaint quietness should seem to strew the house for poets, they are almost in as good reputation as the mountebanks at Venice. Truly even that, as of the one side it giveth great praise to poesy, which like Venus (but to better purpose) hath rather be troubled in the net with Mars than enjoy the homely quiet of Vulcan; so serves it for a piece of a reason why they are less grateful to idle England, which now can scarce endure the pain of a pen. Upon this necessarily followeth, that base men with servile wits undertake it, who think it enough if they can be rewarded of the printer. And so as Epaminondas is said, with the honor of his virtue, to have made an office, by his exercising it, which before was contemptible, to become highly respected, so these, no more but setting their names to it, by their own disgracefulness disgrace the most graceful poesy. For now, as if all the Muses were got with child, to bring forth bastard poets, without any commission they do post over the banks of Helicon, till they make the readers more weary than post-horses, while, in the meantime, they, "queis meliore luto finxit praecordia Titan,"[72] are better content to suppress the outflowing of their wit, than, by publishing them, to be accounted knights of the same order. But I that, before ever I durst aspire unto the dignity, am admitted into the company of the paper-blurrers, do find the very true cause of our wanting estimation is want of desert, taking upon us to be poets in despite of Pallas. Now, wherein we want desert were a thankworthy labor to express: but if I knew, I should have mended myself. But I, as I never desired the title, so have I neglected the means to come by it. Only, overmastered by some thoughts, I yielded an inky tribute unto them. Marry, they that delight in poesy itself should seek to know what they do, and how they do, and, especially, look themselves in an unflattering glass of reason, if they be inclinable unto it. For poesy must not be drawn by the ears; it must be gently led, or rather it must lead; which was partly the cause that made the ancient-learned affirm it was a divine gift, and no human skill; since all other knowledges lie ready for any that hath strength of wit; a poet no industry can make, if his own genius be not carried unto it; and therefore is it an old proverb, Orator fit, poeta nascitur.[73] Yet confess I always that as the fertilest ground must be manured, so must the highest-flying wit have a Daedalus to guide him. That Daedalus, they say, both in this and in other, hath three wings to bear itself up into the air of due commendation: that is, art, imitation, and exercise. But these, neither artificial rules nor imitative patterns, we much cumber ourselves withal. Exercise indeed we do, but that very fore-backwardly: for where we should exercise to know, we exercise as having known: and so is our brain delivered of much matter which never was begotten by knowledge. For, there being two principal parts—matter to be expressed by words and words to express the matter—in neither we use art or imitation rightly. Our matter is quodlibet[74] indeed, though wrongly performing Ovid's verse, "Quicquic conabar dicere, versus erat":[75] never marshaling it into an assured rank, that almost the readers cannot tell where to find themselves.

Chaucer, undoubtedly, did excellently in his Troilus and Cressida; of whom, truly, I know not whether to marvel more, either that he in that misty time could see so clearly, or that we in this clear age walk so stumblingly after him. Yet had he great wants, fit to be forgiven in so reverent antiquity. I account the Mirror of Magistrates[76] meetly furnished of beautiful parts, and in the Earl of Surrey's[77] Lyrics many things tasting of a noble birth, and worthy of a noble mind. The Shepherd's Calendar[78] hath much poetry in his eclogues, indeed worthy the reading, if I be not deceived. That same framing of his style to an old rustic language I dare not allow, since neither Theocritus in Greek, Virgil in Latin, nor Sannazzaro in Italian did affect it. Besides these, do I not remember to have seen but few (to speak boldly) printed, that have poetical sinews in them: for proof whereof, let but most of the verses be put in prose, and then

---

72 "The hearts of whom Titan has formed of finer clay." Juvenal (fl. late first century), Satires XVI, 35.

73 "The orator is made, the poet born."

74 A subtle theological question proposed as an exercise for argument.

75 "Whatever I tried to say, it was verse." Tristia IV, x, 26.

76 The correct title is A Mirror for Magistrates.

77 Henry Howard (c. 1517–1547).

78 By Edmund Spenser (1552?–1599).

ask the meaning; and it will be found that one verse did but beget another, without ordering at the first what should be at the last; which becomes a confused mass of words, with a tingling sound of rhyme, barely accompanied with reason.

Our tragedies and comedies (not without cause cried out against), observing rules neither of honest civility nor of skillful poetry, excepting *Gorboduc*[79] (again, I say, of those that I have seen), which notwithstanding, as it is full of stately speeches and wellsounding phrases, climbing to the height of Seneca's style, and as full of notable morality, which it doth most delightfully teach, and so obtain the very end of poesy, yet in truth it is very defectious in the circumstances, which grieveth me, because it might not remain as an exact model of all tragedies. For it is faulty both in place and time, the two necessary companions of all corporal actions. For where the stage should always represent but one place, and the uttermost time presupposed in it should be, both by Aristotle's precept and common reason, but one day, there is both many days, and many places, inartificially imagined.[80] But if it be so in *Gorboduc,* how much more in all the rest, where you shall have Asia of the one side, and Africa of the other, and so many other underkingdoms, that the player, when he cometh in, must ever begin with telling where he is, or else the tale will not be conceived? Now ye shall have three ladies walk to gather flowers and then we must believe the stage to be a garden. By and by we hear news of shipwreck in the same place, and then we are to blame if we accept it not for a rock.

Upon the back of that comes out a hideous monster, with fire and smoke, and then the miserable beholders are bound to take it for a cave. While in the meantime two armies fly in, represented with four swords and bucklers, and then what hard heart will not receive it for a pitched field? Now, of time they are much more liberal, for ordinary it is that two young princes fall in love. After many traverses, she is got with child, delivered of a fair boy; he is lost, groweth a man, falls in love, and is ready to get another child; and all this in two hours' space: which, how absurd it is in sense, even sense may imagine, and art hath taught, and all ancient examples justified, and, at this day, the ordinary players in Italy will not err in. Yet will some bring in an example of *Eunuchus* in Terence,[81] that containeth matter of two days, yet far short of twenty years. True it is, and so was it to be played in two days, and so fitted to the time it set forth. And though Plautus hath in one place done amiss, let

us hit with him, and not miss with him. But they will say, How then shall we set forth a story, which containeth both many places and many times? And do they not know that a tragedy is tied to the laws of poesy, and not of history; not bound to follow the story, but, having liberty, either to feign a quite new matter, or to frame the history to the most tragical conveniency? Again, many things may be told which cannot be showed, if they know the difference betwixt reporting and representing. As, for example, I may speak (though I am here) of Peru, and in speech digress from that to the description of Calicut; but in action I cannot represent it without Pacolet's horse. And so was the manner the ancients took, by some nuncius[82] to recount things done in former time or other place. Lastly, if they will represent an history, they must not (as Horace saith) begin *ab ovo,*[83] but they must come to the principal point of that one action which they will represent. By example this will be best expressed. I have a story of young Polydorus, delivered for safety's sake, with great riches, by his father Priam to Polymnestor, king of Thrace, in the Trojan war time. He, after some years, hearing the overthrow of Priam, for to make the treasure his own, murdereth the child. The body of the child is taken up by Hecuba. She, the same day, findeth a slight to be revenged most cruelly of the tyrant. Where now would one of our tragedy writers begin, but with the delivery of the child? Then should he sail over into Thrace, and so spend I know not how many years, and travel numbers of places. But where doth Euripides? Even with the finding of the body, leaving the rest to be told by the spirit of Polydorus. This need no further to be enlarged; the dullest wit may conceive it. But besides these gross absurdities, how all their plays be neither right tragedies, nor right comedies, mingling kings and clowns, not because the matter so carrieth it, but thrust in clowns by head and shoulders, to play a part in majestical matters, with neither decency nor discretion, so as neither the admiration and commiseration, nor the right sportfulness, is by their mongrel tragicomedy obtained. I know Apuleius[84] did somewhat so, but that is a thing recounted with space of time, not represented in one moment: and I know the ancients have one or two examples of tragicomedies, as Plautus[85] hath *Amphitrio*. But, if we mark them well, we shall find, that they never, or very daintily, match hornpipes and funerals. So falleth it out that, having indeed no right comedy, in that comical part of our tragedy we have nothing but scurrility, unworthy of any

---

[79] The first Elizabethan blank-verse tragedy (1561).
[80] Here Sidney follows Castelvetro (above, page 184) and others in ascribing a rigid unity of time to Aristotle.
[81] Sidney's mistake. He should refer to *The Self-Tormentor* of Terence.

[82] Messenger.
[83] "From the egg." See Horace, *Art of Poetry* (above, page 81).
[84] Lucius Apuleius (c. 124–?), author of *The Golden Ass.*
[85] Titus Massius Plautus (c. 254–184 B.C.), Roman poet.

chaste ears, or some extreme show of doltishness, indeed fit to lift up a loud laughter, and nothing else: where the whole tract of a comedy should be full of delight, as the tragedy should be still maintained in a well-raised admiration. But our comedians think there is no delight without laughter; which is very wrong, for though laughter may come with delight, yet cometh it not of delight, as though delight should be the cause of laughter; but well may one thing breed both together. Nay, rather in themselves they have, as it were, a kind of contrariety: for delight we scarcely do but in things that have a conveniency to ourselves or to the general nature: laughter almost ever cometh of things most disproportioned to ourselves and nature. Delight hath a joy in it, either permanent or present. Laughter hath only a scornful tickling.

For example, we are ravished with delight to see a fair woman, and yet are far from being moved to laughter. We laugh at deformed creatures, wherein certainly we cannot delight. We delight in good chances, we laugh at mischances; we delight to hear the happiness of our friends, or country, at which he were worthy to be laughed at that would laugh. We shall, contrarily, laugh sometimes to find a matter quite mistaken and go down the hill against the bias, in the mouth of some such men, as for the respect of them one shall be heartily sorry, yet he cannot choose but laugh; and so is rather pained than delighted with laughter. Yet deny I not but that they may go well together. For as in Alexander's picture well set out we delight without laughter, and in twenty mad antics we laugh without delight, so in Hercules, painted with his great beard and furious countenance, in woman's attire, spinning at Omphale's commandment, it breedeth both delight and laughter. For the representing of so strange a power in love procureth delight: and the scornfulness of the action stirreth laughter. But I speak to this purpose, that all the end of the comical part be not upon such scornful matters as stirreth laughter only, but, mixed with it, that delightful teaching which is the end of poesy. And the great fault even in that point of laughter, and forbidden plainly by Aristotle,[86] is that they stir laughter in sinful things, which are rather execrable than ridiculous; or in miserable, which are rather to be pitied than scorned. For what is it to make folks gape at a wretched beggar, or a beggarly clown; or, against the law of hospitality, to jest at strangers, because they speak not English so well as we do? What do we learn, since it is certain *"Nil habet infelix paupertas durius in se, / Quam quod ridiculos homines facit"?*[87] But rather a busy loving

courtier, a heartless threatening Thraso, a self-wise-seeming schoolmaster, an awry-transformed traveler—these if we saw walk in stage names, which we play naturally, therein were delightful laughter, and teaching delightfulness: as in the other, the tragedies of Buchanan do justly bring forth a divine admiration. But I have lavished out too many words of this play matter. I do it because, as they are excelling parts of poesy, so is there none so much used in England, and none can be more pitifully abused; which, like an unmannerly daughter showing a bad education, causeth her mother poesy's honesty to be called in question. Other sorts of poetry almost have we none, but that lyrical kind of songs and sonnets: which, Lord, if he gave us so good minds, how well it might be employed, and with how heavenly fruit, both private and public, in singing the praises of the immortal beauty, the immortal goodness of that God who giveth us hands to write and wits to conceive; of which we might well want words, but never matter; of which we could turn our eyes to nothing, but we should ever have new budding occasions. But truly many of such writings as come under the banner of unresistible love, if I were a mistress, would never persuade me they were in love; so coldly they apply fiery speeches, as men that had rather read lovers' writings, and so caught up certain swelling phrases (which hang together like a man which once told me the wind was at northwest, and by south, because he would be sure to name winds enough), than that in truth they feel those passions, which easily (as I think) may be betrayed by that same forcibleness or *energia*[88] (as the Greeks call it) of the writer. But let this be a sufficient though short note, that we miss the right use of the material point of poesy.

Now, for the outside of it, which is words, or (as I may term it) diction, it is even well worse. So is that honey-flowing matron eloquence appareled, or rather disguised, in a courtesanlike painted affectation: one time with so far-fetched words, they may seem monsters, but must seem strangers, to any poor Englishman; another time, with coursing of a letter, as if they were bound to follow the method of a dictionary; another time, with figures and flowers, extremely winter-starved. But I would this fault were only peculiar to versifiers, and had not as large possession among prose-printers, and (which is to be marveled) among many scholars, and (which is to be pitied) among some preachers. Truly I could wish, if at least I might be so bold

---

[86] Sidney distorts Aristotle here.

[87] "Unhappy poverty has nothing worse in itself than that it makes men ridiculous." Juvenal, *Satires* II, 152–53.

[88] A term used by many Renaissance critics.

to wish in a thing beyond the reach of my capacity, the diligent imitators of Tully and Demosthenes[89] (most worthy to be imitated) did not so much keep Nizolian paper books of their figures and phrases, as by attentive translation (as it were) devour them whole, and make them wholly theirs. For now they cast sugar and spice upon every dish that is served to the table, like those Indians, not content to wear earrings at the fit and natural place of the ears, but they will thrust jewels through their nose and lips, because they will be sure to be fine.

Tully, when he was to drive out Catiline, as it were with a thunderbolt of eloquence, often used that figure of repetition, *"Vivit, Vivit? Imo in Senatum venit,"* &c.[90] Indeed, inflamed with a well-grounded rage, he would have his words (as it were) double out of his mouth, and so do that artificially which we see men do in choler naturally. And we, having noted the grace of those words, hale them in sometime to a familiar epistle, when it were too much choler to be choleric. Now for similitudes in certain printed discourses, I think all herberists, all stories of beasts, fowls, and fishes are rifled up, that they come in multitudes to wait upon any of our conceits; which certainly is as absurd a surfeit to the ears as is possible: for the force of a similitude not being to prove anything to a contrary disputer, but only to explain to a willing hearer; when that is done, the rest is a most tedious prattling, rather overswaying the memory from the purpose whereto they were applied, than any whit informing the judgment, already either satisfied, or by similitudes not to be satisfied. For my part, I do not doubt, when Antonius and Crassus, the great forefathers of Cicero in eloquence, the one (as Cicero testifieth of them) pretended not to know art, the other not to set by it, because with a plain sensibleness they might win credit of popular ears; which credit is the nearest step to persuasion; which persuasion is the chief mark of oratory—I do not doubt (I say) that but they used these knacks very sparingly; which, who doth generally use, any man may see doth dance to his own music; and so be noted by the audience more careful to speak curiously than to speak truly.

Undoubtedly (at least to my opinion undoubtedly) I have found in divers small-learned courtiers a more sound style than in some professors of learning: of which I can guess no other cause, but that the courtier, following that which by practice he findeth fittest to nature, therein (though he know it not) doth according to art, though not by art: where the other, using art to show art, and not to hide art (as in these cases he should do), flieth from nature, and indeed abuseth art.

But what? Methinks I deserve to be pounded for straying from poetry to oratory: but both have such an affinity in this wordish consideration, that I think this digression will make my meaning receive the fuller understanding—which is not to take upon me to teach poets how they should do, but only, finding myself sick among the rest, to show some one or two spots of the common infection grown among the most part of writers: that, acknowledging ourselves somewhat awry, we may bend to the right use both of matter and manner; whereto our language giveth us great occasion, being indeed capable of any excellent exercising of it. I know some will say it is a mingled language. And why not so much the better, taking the best of both the other? Another will say it wanteth grammar. Nay truly, it hath that praise, that it wanteth grammar: for grammar it might have, but it needs it not; being so easy of itself, and so void of those cumbersome differences of cases, genders, moods, and tenses, which I think was a piece of the Tower of Babylon's curse, that a man should be put to school to learn his mother tongue. But for the uttering sweetly and properly the conceits of the mind, which is the end of speech, that hath it equally with any other tongue in the world: and is particularly happy in compositions of two or three words together, near the Greek, far beyond the Latin: which is one of the greatest beauties can be in a language.

Now, of versifying there are two sorts, the one ancient, the other modern: the ancient marked the quantity of each syllable, and according to that framed his verse; the modern observing only number (with some regard of the accent), the chief life of it standeth in that like sounding of the words, which we call rhyme. Whether of these be the most excellent, would bear many speeches. The ancient (no doubt) more fit for music, both words and tune observing quantity, and more fit lively to express divers passions, by the low and lofty sound of the well-weighed syllable. The latter likewise, with his rhyme, striketh a certain music to the ear: and, in fine, since it doth delight, though by another way, it obtains the same purpose: there being in either sweetness, and wanting in neither majesty. Truly the English, before any other vulgar language I know, is fit for both sorts: for, for the ancient, the Italian is so full of vowels that it must ever be cumbered with elisions; the Dutch so, of the other side, with consonants, that they cannot yield the sweet sliding fit for a verse; the French, in his whole language, hath not one word that hath his accent in the last syllable saving two, called *antepenultima;* and little more hath the Spanish; and, therefore, very gracelessly may they use dactyls. The English is subject to none of these defects.

---

[89] Demosthenes (384–322 B.C.), Greek rhetorician and orator.
[90] "He lives. He lives? He even comes into the Senate."

Now, for the rhyme, though we do not observe quantity, yet we observe the accent very precisely: which other languages either cannot do, or will not do so absolutely. That *caesura*, or breathing place in the midst of the verse, neither Italian nor Spanish have, the French, and we, never almost fail of. Lastly, even the very rhyme itself the Italian cannot put in the last syllable, by the French named the "masculine rhyme," but still in the next to the last, which the French call the "female," or the next before that, which the Italians term *sdrucciola*. The example of the former is *buono:suono*, of the *sdrucciola, femina:semina*. The French, of the other side, hath both the male, as *bon:son,* and the female, as *plaise:taise,* but the *sdrucciola* he hath not: where the English hath all three, as *due:true, father:rather, motion:potion,* with much more which might be said, but that I find already the triflingness of this discourse is much too much enlarged. So that since the ever-praiseworthy poesy is full of virtue-breeding delightfulness, and void of no gift that ought to be in the noble name of learning; since the blames laid against it are either false or feeble; since the cause why it is not esteemed in England is the fault of poet-apes, not poets; since, lastly, our tongue is most fit to honor poesy, and to be honored by poesy; I conjure you all that have had the evil luck to read this ink-wasting toy of mine, even in the name of the nine Muses, no more to scorn the sacred mysteries of poesy, no more to laugh at the name of *poets,* as though they were next inheritors to fools, no more to jest at the reverent title of a *rhymer;* but to believe, with Aristotle, that they were the ancient treasurers of the Grecians' divinity; to believe, with Bembus,[91] that they were first bringers-in of all civility; to believe, with Scaliger, that no philosopher's precepts can sooner make you an honest man than the reading of Virgil; to believe, with Clauserus, the translator of Cornutus, that it

pleased the heavenly Deity, by Hesiod and Homer, under the veil of fables, to give us all knowledge, logic, rhetoric, philosophy, natural and moral, and *Quid non?;*[92] to believe, with me, that there are many mysteries contained in poetry, which of purpose were written darkly, least by profane wits it should be abused; to believe, with Landino,[93] that they are so beloved of the gods that whatsoever they write proceeds of a divine fury; lastly, to believe themselves, when they tell you they will make you immortal by their verses.

Thus doing, your name shall flourish in the printers' shops; thus doing, you shall be of kin to many a poetical preface; thus doing, you shall be most fair, most rich, most wise, most all; you shall dwell upon superlatives. Thus doing, though you be *"libertino patre natus,"* you shall suddenly grow *"Herculea proles,"* *"si quid mea carmina possunt."*[94] Thus doing, your soul shall be placed with Dante's Beatrix, or Virgil's Anchises. But if (fie of such a but) you be born so near the dull-making cataract of Nilus that you cannot hear the planetlike music of poetry, if you have so earth-creeping a mind that it cannot lift itself up to look to the sky of poetry, or rather, by a certain rustical disdain, will become such a mome as to be a momus of poetry; then, though I will not wish unto you the ass's ears of Midas, nor to be driven by a poet's verses (as Bubonax was) to hang himself, nor to be rhymed to death, as is said to be done in Ireland; yet thus much curse I must send you, in the behalf of all poets, that while you live, you live in love, and never get favor for lacking skill of a sonnet, and, when you die, your memory die from the earth for want of an epitaph.

---

[91] Pietro Bembo (1470–1547), Italian critic.

[92] "What not?"

[93] Cristoforo Landino wrote a commentary on Homer (1542).

[94] Thus doing, though you be "the son of a freed man," you shall suddenly grow "Herculean offsprings," "if my poems can accomplish anything." Phrases from Horace, Ovid, and Virgil respectively.

Giordano Bruno

1548–1600

In many ways, the Italian philosopher Giordano Bruno, influenced in his thought by the celebrated Platonist Marsilio Ficino (1433–1499), is an ideal representative of contradictory forces in the Renaissance. He was educated as a Dominican friar but was accused of heresy in the 1570s and fled Italy, taking temporary teaching posts at Toulouse, Paris, Wittenberg, and Oxford, where he was the guest of the poet Fulke Greville and possibly Sir Philip Sidney. Bruno viewed the philosophical development of his own time, including the revolutionary work of Nicolaus Copernicus (1473–1543) and his closer contemporary Galileo Galilei (1564–1642) as the opening of a great age of science and philosophy. Like both Copernicus and Galileo, Bruno was severely persecuted by the Inquisition, but his fate was drastically worse, being burned at the stake in Rome when he steadfastly refused to renounce his philosophical and theological views. Bruno's many heresies included the view, espoused in the selection here, that the entire universe is both infinite and animate: God cannot be localized in a spatial heaven but is a spiritual and intellectual principle in all things. In particular he viewed the influence of conventional church authority, which eventually put him to death, as a perversion of wisdom and truth. In one inflammatory work, *The Expulsion of the Triumphant Beast,* he represented the pope and other ecclesiastic authorities as the very evil that needed to be expelled. Among many ironies affecting his later reception and influence is the fact that while he saw himself as part of a scientific revolution, his rejection of empiricism, materialism, and the belief that nature could be understood as merely mechanical operations upon elementary particles or atoms put him on the wrong side of contemporary developments. Thus he has been associated with mystics and pseudoscientific projects such as the alchemists' search for the Philosopher's Stone and belief in the "arts of memory" as possibly allowing the direct assertion of mind over matter. For later thinkers, such as Baruch Spinoza (1632–1677) and the Cambridge Platonists, particularly Ralph Cudworth (1617–1688), and, more dramatically, for thinkers such as Friedrich Jacobi (1743–1819) and Coleridge (below, page 493) in the Romantic era, Bruno appeared as a vital forerunner, a point of resistance to a view of nature as mechanical. His notion of spirit as distributed through nature was crucial not only for early versions of Pantheism, but lent at least analogical support to the development of naturphilosophie, after Johann Gottlieb Fichte (1762–1814), Friedrich Schelling (1775–1854), and Hegel (below, page 552).

There is a complete edition and translation of Bruno's *Della causa, principio, ed uno* (1584) by Robert De Lucca (1998). *The Expulsion of the Triumphant Beast* has been translated by Arthur D. Imerti (1964). See Dorothea Waley Singer, *Giordano Bruno, His Life and Thought* (1950), which includes a translation of Bruno's *On the Infinite Universe and Worlds;* Francis A. Yates, *Giordano Bruno and the Hermetic Tradition* (1964) and *The Art of Memory* (1966); Paul-Henri Michel, *The Cosmology of Giordano Bruno* (1973); Hilary Gatti, *Giordano Bruno and Renaissance Science* (1999).

from

Concerning the Cause, the Principle, and the One

Dixon Then you say, Theophilus, that everything which is not a first principle and a first cause, has such a principle and such a cause?

Theophilus Without doubt and without the least controversy.

Dixon Do you believe, accordingly, that whoever knows the things thus caused and originated must know the ultimate cause and principle?

Theophilus Not easily the proximate cause or the proximate principle; it would be extremely difficult to recognize even the traces of an ultimate cause and creative principle.

Dixon Then how do you think that those things which have a first and a proximate cause and principle can be really known, if their efficient cause (which is one of the things which contribute to the true cognition of things) is hidden?

Theophilus I grant you that it is easy to set forth the theory of proof, but the proof itself is difficult. It is very practicable to set forth the causes, circumstances, and methods of sciences; but afterward our method-makers and analytical scholars can use but awkwardly their *organum,* the principles of their methods, and their arts of arts.

* * *

Theophilus I should say, then, that one should not expect the natural philosopher to make plain all causes and principles; but only the physical, and only the principal and most essential of these. And although these depend upon the first cause and first principle, and can be said to possess such a cause and principle, this is, in any case, not such a necessary relation that from the knowledge of the one the knowledge of the other would follow; and therefore one should not expect that in the same science both should be set forth.

Dixon How is that?

Theophilus Because from the cognition of all dependent things, we are unable to infer other knowledge of first cause and principle, than by the somewhat inefficacious method of traces. All things are, indeed, derived from the Creator's will or goodness, which is the principle of His works, and from which proceeds the universal effect. The same consideration arises in the case of works of art, in so much as he who sees the statue does not see the sculptor; he who sees the portrait of Helen does not see Apelles: but he sees only the result of the work which comes from the merit and genius of Apelles.[1] This work is entirely an effect of the accidents and circumstances of the substance of that man, who, as to his absolute essence, is not in the least known.

Dixon So that to know the universe is like knowing nothing of the being and substance of the first principle, because it is like knowing the accidents of the accidents.

Theophilus Exactly, but I would not have you imagine that I mean that in God himself there are Accidents, or that He could be known, as it were, by His Accidents.

Dixon I do not attribute to you so crude a thought, and I know that it is one thing to say that the things extraneous to the divine nature are accidents, another thing to say that they are His Accidents, and yet another thing to say that they are, *as it were,* His Accidents: By the last way of speaking I believe you mean that they are the effects of the divine activity; but that these effects, in so far as they may be the substance of things, and even the natural substances themselves, in any case are, as it were, the remotest accidents whereby we merely touch an apprehension of the divine supernatural essence.

Theophilus Well said.

Dixon Behold, then, of the divine substance, as well because it is infinite as because it is extremely remote from its effects (while these effects are the furthest boundary of the source of our reasoning faculties), we can know nothing,—unless through the means of traces, as the Platonists say, of remote effects, as the Peripatetic philosophers say, of the dress or outer covering, as say the Cabalists, of the mere shoulders and back, as the Talmudists say,[2] or of the mirror, the shadow, the enigma, as the Apocalyptic writers say.

Theophilus All the more is this the case because we do not see perfectly this universe whose substance and principle are so difficult of comprehension. And thus it follows that with far less ground can we know the first principle and cause through its effect, than Apelles may be known through the statue he has made. For the statue all may see and examine, part by part; but not so the grand and infinite effect of the Divine Power. Therefore our simile should be understood not as a matter of close comparison.

Concerning the Cause, the Principle, and the One. Bruno's work (1584) is here reproduced in part from Benjamin Rand, ed., *Modern Classical Philosophers* (Boston: Houghton Mifflin Co., 1908, 1924, 1936). Translated by Josiah Royce and Katherine Royce.

---

[1] Apelles (fourth century B.C.), Greek painter.
[2] [Royce] Cf. Exodus xxxiii, 18–31.

Dixon   Thus it is, and thus I understand it.

Theophilus   It would be well, then, to abstain from speaking of so lofty a matter.

Dixon   I agree to that, because it suffices, morally and theologically, to know the first principle in so far as higher spirits have revealed it, and divine men have declared it. Beyond this point, not only whatever Law and Theology you will, but also all wise philosophy has held it as a profane and turbulent disposition, to rush into demanding reasons and definitions for such things as are above the sphere of our intelligence.

Theophilus   Very good: but these do not deserve blame so much as those deserve praise who struggle *towards* the knowledge of that cause and principle; who learn its grandeur as much as possible by allowing the eyes of their well-regulated minds to roam amongst yonder magnificent stars,—those luminous bodies which are so many habitable worlds, vast and animate, and are most excellent deities. These seem, and are, countless worlds not unlike that which contains us. It is impossible that these can have their existence of themselves, considering that they are composite and dissoluble (although not for that reason do they deserve annihilation, as has been well said in the Timæus). It is needful that they should know their principle and cause; and consequently with the grandeur of their existence, of their life and of their works, they show and set forth, in infinite space, with innumerable voices the infinite excellence and majesty of their first principle and cause. Leaving then (as you say) those considerations in so far as they are superior to all sense and intellect, we will consider that principle and cause in so far as, in its traces, it either is identical with nature itself, or lies revealed to us in the extent and in the lap of nature. Question me, then, in order, if you wish me to answer you in order.

Dixon   I will do so. But first, since you constantly speak of Cause and Principle, I should like to know whether those are used by you as synonymous words?

Theophilus   No.

Dixon   Then what difference is there between the one and the other term?

Theophilus   I answer that when we speak of God as first principle and first cause, we mean one and the same thing but from different points of view; when we speak of principles and causes in Nature, we speak of different things from different points of view. We speak of God as the first principle inasmuch as all things come only after Him in an ordered rank of *before* and *after,* either, according to their nature, or according to their duration, or according to their value. We call God the first cause, in so far as all things are distinct from Him, as the effect from the efficient, the thing produced from that which produced it. And these two points of view are different, because not everything which comes first and is of more value is the cause of that which comes later and is of less value; and not everything which is the cause is prior to and of more worth than that which is caused, as will be plain to him who reflects carefully.

Dixon   Then tell me, in speaking of natural things, what is the difference between cause and principle?

Theophilus   Although at times the one term is used in place of the other, nevertheless, properly speaking, not everything which is a principle is a cause, because a point is the principle of a line, but it is not the cause of the line; the instant is the principle of temporal activity, the place whence is the principle of the motion, the premises are the principle of the argument, but they are not the cause. Therefore principle is a more general term than cause.

Dixon   Then restricting these two terms to certain special significations, according to the custom of those who reform their terminology, I believe you to mean that Principle is that which intrinsically brings to pass the constitution of things, and which remains in what it has produced. Thus, for instance, matter and form remain in their composite; or again, the elements of which things have been composed, and into which they tend to resolve themselves again, are principles. You call Cause that which operates from without in the production of things, and which has its being outside of the things produced, as is the case with the efficient cause, and the end for which the thing produced is ordained.

Theophilus   Very good.

Dixon   Since, then, we have come to an understanding concerning the difference between those things, I wish you to devote your attention first to the Causes and then to the Principles. And as to the Causes, I desire first to know about the first efficient cause, about the formal cause, which you say is conjoined to the efficient; and, lastly, about the final cause, which is understood to be the power which moves this.

Theophilus   The order of discourse which you propose pleases me much. Now as to the efficient cause: I assert that the universal physical efficient cause is the universal Intellect, which is the first and principal faculty of the world-soul and which is the universal form of the Cosmos.

Dixon   Your thought appears to me to be not only in agreement with that of Empedocles, but more certain, more distinct, and more explicit, and also (in so far as I can see from the above) more profound: yet you will give me pleasure if you will explain the whole more in detail, beginning by informing me just what is that universal intellect.

Theophilus   The universal intellect is the most intimate, real, and essential faculty and effective part of the world-soul. This is one and the same thing which fills the whole, illumines the universe and directs nature to produce the various species as is fitting, and has the same relation to the production of natural things as our intellect to the parallel production of our general ideas.[3] This is called by the Pythagoreans the moving spirit and propelling power of the universe; as saith the poet, "Totamque infusa per artus, mens agitat molem, et toto se corpore miscet."[4] This is called by the Platonic philosophers the world-builder. This builder (they say) proceeds from the higher world (which is, in fact, one) to this world of sense, which is divided into many, and in which not only harmony but also discord reigns, because it is sundered into parts. This intellect, infusing and extending something of its own into matter, restful and moveless in itself, produces all things. By the Magi this intelligence is called most fruitful of seeds, or even the seed-sower, since it is He who impregnates matter with all its forms, and according to the type and condition of these succeeds in shaping, forming, and arranging all in such admirable order, as cannot be attributed to chance, or to any principle which cannot consciously distinguish or arrange. Orpheus calls this Intellect the eye of the world, because it sees all natural objects, both within and without, in order that all things may succeed in producing and maintaining themselves in their proper symmetry, not only intrinsically but also extrinsically. By Empedocles it is called the Distinguisher, since it never wearies of unfolding the confused forms within the breast of matter or of calling forth the birth of one thing from the corruption of another. Plotinus calls it the father and progenitor, because it distributes seeds throughout the field of nature, and is the proximate dispenser of forms. By us this Intellect is called the inner artificer, because it forms and shapes material objects from within, as from within the seed or the root is sent forth and unfolded the trunk, from within the trunk are put forth the branches, from within the branches the finished twigs, and from within the twigs unfurl the buds, and there within are woven like nerves, leaves, flowers and fruits; and inversely, at certain times the sap is recalled from the flowers and fruits to the twigs, from the twigs to the branches, from the branches to the trunk, and from the trunk to the root. Just so it is with animals; its work proceeding from the original seed, and from the centre of the heart, to the external mem-

bers, and from these finally gathering back to the heart the unfolded powers, it behaves as if again knotting together spun-out threads. Now, since we believe that even inanimate works, such as we know how to produce with a certain order, imitatively working on the surface of matter, are not produced without forethought and mind,—as when, cutting and sculpturing a piece of wood, we bring forth the effigy of a horse: how much greater must we believe is that creative intelligence which, from the interior of the germinal matter, brings forth the bones, extends the cartilage, hollows out the arteries, breathes into the pores, weaves the fibres, forms the branching nerves, and with such admirable mastery arranges the whole? I say, how much greater an artificer is He who is not restricted to one sole part of the material world, but operates continually throughout the whole. There are three sorts of intelligence; the divine, which is all things, the mundane which makes all things, and the other kinds of spirits which become everything. For it is needful that between the extremes the means should be found, which is the true efficient cause, not so much extrinsic as even intrinsic, of all natural things.

Dixon I should like to see you distinguish, as you understand them, extrinsic cause and intrinsic cause.

Theophilus I call a cause extrinsic when as an efficient it does not form a part of the things compounded and produced. I call a cause intrinsic in so far as it does not operate around and outside of objects, but in the manner just explained. Hence a cause is extrinsic by being distinct from the substance and essence of its effects, and therefore its existence is not like that of things that are generated and decay, although it embraces such things. A cause is intrinsic with respect to the actuality of its own workings.

* * *

Dixon The aim, and the final cause for which the efficient is working, is the perfection of the universe, which implies that in diverse portions of matter all forms are actually existent. In this end the intellect takes such great pleasure and delight that it never wearies of calling forth all sorts of forms from matter, as it appears that Empedocles also would have it.

Theophilus Very well. Now I add to this that just as this efficient cause is omnipresent in the universe, and is special and particular in the parts and members thereof, just so its form and its purpose.

Dixon Now, enough has been said about causes; let us proceed to the discussion of principles.

Theophilus In order, then, to get at the constitutive principles of things, I will next discuss form. For this is in

---

[3] [Royce] The reference is to a well-known scholastic parallel of the universals present *in things* and the universals present *in our minds* when we form our ideas of natural classes. The universal Intellect is related to the production of natural forms, or species, as our mind is related to the production of our ideas of these species.

[4] [Royce] Infused through the members, mind vitalizes the whole mass and is mingled with the whole body.

some sort the same as the aforesaid efficient cause; since the intelligence which is a power of the world-soul has been called the proximate efficient cause of all natural things.

Dixon But how can the same subject be at once principle and cause of natural things? How can it have the definition of an intrinsic part instead of an extrinsic part?

Theophilus I declare that this is not incongruous, considering that the soul is within the body as the pilot is within the ship. And the pilot, in so far as he shares the motion of the ship, is a part of it. Yet considered in so far as he guides and moves it, he is not regarded as a part, but as a distinct efficient cause. Just so the soul of the universe, in so far as it animates and informs things, is an intrinsic and formal part of that universe. But in so far as it directs and governs, it is not a part, it does not rank as a principle, but as a cause. Aristotle himself grants this, who, nevertheless, denies that the soul has that relation to the body which the steersman has to the ship: yet considering it with regard to that power which thinks and knows, he does not dare to call it a perfection and form of the body; but he considers it as an efficient cause, separate in essence from matter. He says that that is a thing which comes from without, self-existent and separated from the composite.

Dixon I approve what you say, because if that existence separate from the body belongs to the intellectual powers of our minds, and if this intellectual power has the value of an efficient cause, much more should the same be affirmed concerning the Soul of the World. Because Plotinus[5] says, writing against the Gnostics, that the Universal Soul rules the universe with much greater ease than our souls rule our bodies. Besides there is a great difference in the way in which the one and the other rules. The World-Soul, as if unbound, rules the world in such a way that it is not hampered by that which it controls, and does not suffer from, nor with other things. It rises without effort to lofty things. In giving life and perfection to the body, it does not itself take any taint of imperfection from that body; and therefore it is eternally conjoined with the same subject. The human soul is manifestly in quite the contrary condition. Since then, according to your principles, the perfections which exist in our inferior natures, in a far higher degree should be attributed to, and perceived in, superior natures, we ought doubtless to confirm the distinction which you have brought out. But we must recognize this not only in the Soul of the world, but also in every star. For it is the case (as the aforesaid philosopher holds), that they

all have the power of contemplating God, the principles (sources) of all things and the arrangement of all parts of the universe. He does not indeed think that this takes place through memory, reasoning, and consideration; because each of their works is an eternal work, and there is no action which can be new to them, and therefore they do nothing which is not fitting to the whole, perfect, and with a certain and preordained order, and they accomplish all without an act of consideration. Aristotle shows this by using the example of a perfect writer, or zither-player. While in this case nature does not reason or reflect, he does not wish it to be concluded that she works without intelligence and final intention; because exquisite writers and musicians pay less attention to what they are doing, and yet do not blunder like the inexpert and clumsy, who while thinking and attending more, yet accomplish their work less perfectly, and not without blunders.

Theophilus You understand me. Let us now pass on to the more special. It seems to me that they detract from the divine goodness and from the excellence of that great soul and simulacrum of the first principle, who will not understand nor affirm that the world with all its members is animate. How should God be envious of his image, or how should the architect not love his own individual work, of whom Plato says that he takes pleasure in his work because of his own similitude which he admires in it. And truly, what more beautiful than this universe could be presented to the eyes of the Deity? And it being the case that this consists of its parts, to which of these should more be imparted than to the formal principle? I will leave for a better and more particular discourse a thousand natural reasons beyond this topical or logical one.

Dixon I do not care to have you exert yourself in that direction, considering that there is no philosopher of any reputation, even among the Peripatetics, who does not hold that the Universe and its spheres are in some way animated. I should now be glad to know in what manner you hold that this form makes its way into the material of the universe?

Theophilus It joins itself to it in such a manner that corporeal nature, which in itself is not beautiful, in so far as it is capable of it, shares the beauty of the soul, since there is no beauty which does not consist of some figure or form, and no form which has not been produced by a soul.

Dixon I seem to be hearing an entirely new thing. You hold perhaps that not only the form of the Universe, but all forms of natural objects are souls?

Theophilus Yes.

Dixon Have all things, then, souls?

Theophilus Yes.

Dixon But who will grant you this?

---

[5] Plotinus (above, page 127).

Theophilus But who with reason will be able to gainsay it?

Dixon According to common sense, not all things are alive.

Theophilus The commonest sense is not the truest.

Dixon I easily believe that that can be defended. But the fact that a thing can be defended does not suffice to make it true; considering that it also must be proved.

Theophilus That is not difficult. Are there not philosophers who say that the world has a soul?

Dixon There surely are many, and very notable ones.

Theophilus Then why do not the same philosophers say that all the parts of the world have souls?

Dixon They surely do say that, but only concerning the most important parts, and those which are true parts of the world. Since with no less ground they hold that the soul is no less omnipresent throughout the world and in every conceivable part of it, than the souls of living beings perceptible to us are completely present throughout them.

Theophilus Then what things do you think are not true parts of the Universe?

Dixon Those that are not what the Peripatetics call primal bodies, such as the earth, together with the waters and other parts, which, according to your statement, constitute the complete animate organism; or such as the moon, the sun, and other heavenly bodies. Beside these principal animate organisms there are those which are not primary parts of the universe, of which some are said to have a vegetative soul, some a sensitive soul, others an intellectual soul.

Theophilus Yet, if accordingly the soul which is in everything, is also in the parts of everything, why do you not hold that it is in the parts of the parts?

Dixon It may be, but in the parts of the parts of animate things.

Theophilus Now what things are there which are not animate, or are not parts of animate things?

Dixon Does it seem to you that we have so few such things before our eyes? All things which have not life.

Theophilus And what are the things that have not life, at least the vital principle?

Dixon To come to an understanding, do you hold that there may be any things which may not have soul and which may not have the vital principle?

Theophilus That, in fine, is what I hold.

* * *

Theophilus I say, then, that the table as a table is not animate, nor the garments, nor the leather as leather, nor the glass as glass, but as natural things and composites they have within themselves matter and form. Let a thing be even as small and tiny as you will, it has within itself some portion of spiritual substance, which, if it finds a fitting vehicle, unfolds itself so as to become a plant, or an animal, and receives the members of whatsoever body you will, such as is commonly said to be animated, because spirit is found in all things, and there is not the least corpuscle which does not contain within itself some portion that may become living.

* * *

Dixon You show me the seemingly true way in which the opinion of Anaxagoras[6] may be maintained, who held that all things are in all things. For since spirit, or soul, or universal form, exists in all things, all may be produced from all.

Theophilus I do not say seemingly true, but true. For spirit is found in all things, those which are not living creatures are still vitalized, if not according to the perceptible presence of animation and life, yet they are animate according to the principle and, as it were, primal being of animation and life.

* * *

On other occasions I shall be able to discuss more at length the mind, the spirit, the soul, the life, which penetrates all, is in all, and moves all matter, fills the lap of that matter and dominates it rather than is dominated by it. For the spiritual substance cannot be overpowered by the material, but rather embraces it.

Dixon That appears to me to conform not only to the sense of Pythagoras, whose opinion the Poet rehearses when he says,—

> Principio caelum ac terras camposque liquentes,
> Lucentemque globum lunae Titaniaque astra
> Spiritus intus alit, totamque infusa per artus
> Mens agitat molem, totoque se corpore miscet,[7]

but also it conforms to the Theologian who says, "The spirit rules over and fills the earth, and that it is which contains all things." And another, speaking perchance of the dealings of

---

[6] Anaxagoras (500? B.C.–428 B.C.), Greek philosopher and mathematician.
[7] [Royce] In the beginning the sky, the earth and fields of the waters,
    Glistening orb of the moon, and also the radiant sunlight,
    All is inspired with life, and trembling through every member,
    Mind vitalizes the mass, and with the whole body is mingled.
        Virgil's *Aeneid* VI, 724 ff.

form with matter and with potentiality, says that the latter is dominated by actuality and by form.

Theophilus   If then, spirit, mind, life, is found in all things, and in various degrees fills all matter, it must certainly follow, that it is the true actuality, and the true form of all things. The soul of the world, then, is the formal, constitutive principle of the universe, and of that which is contained within it. I say that if life is found in all things, the soul must be the form of all things; that which through everything presides over matter, holds sway over composite things, effects the composition and consistency of their parts. And therefore such form is no less enduring than matter. This I understand to be One in all things.

* * *

While this form thus changes place and circumstance, it is impossible that it should be annulled; because the spiritual substance is not less real than the material. Then only external forms can change and even be annulled, because they are not things, but of things; they are not substances; they are accidents and circumstances.

* * *

Theophilus   We have then an intrinsic principle,—formal, eternal, and subsistent, incomparably better than that which the Sophists have imagined, who play with accidents, ignorant of the substance of things, and who are led to assume corruptible substances because they call chiefly, primarily and principally that substance which results from composition. For the latter is only an accident, containing within itself no stability and truth, and resolves itself into nothing. They call that the true man which results from composition; they call that the true soul which is either the perfection of a living body, or at least a thing which results from a certain sympathy of complexion and members. Therefore, it is not strange that they do so much and so greatly fear death and dissolution; as those for whom ruin of their being is imminent. Against this madness nature cries out with a loud voice, assuring us that neither bodies nor souls should fear death, since both matter and form are absolutely constant principles.

* * *

Dixon   Then you approve, in some sort, the opinion of Anaxagoras who calls the particular forms of Nature latent, and in a sense that of Plato who deduces them from ideas, and in a manner that of Empedocles who makes them proceed from intelligence, and in some sort that of Aristotle who makes them, as it were, issue from the potentiality of matter?

Theophilus   Yes. Because, as we have said, where there is form, there is, in a certain manner, everything. Where there is soul, spirit, life, there is everything, for the creator of ideal forms and varieties is intellect. And even if it does not obtain forms from matter, it nevertheless does not go begging for them outside of matter, because this spirit fills the whole.

Polyhymnius   *Velim scire quo modo forma est anima mundi ubique tola,*[8] if it is indivisible? It must, then, be very big, even of infinite dimensions, if one may call the world infinite.

Gervasius   There is good ground for its being large, as also a preacher at Grandazzo in Sicily said of our Lord: where as a sign that He is present through the whole world, he ordered a crucifix as big as the church, in the similitude of God the Father, who has the Empyrean heavens for a canopy; the starry heavens for his throne, and has such long legs that they reach down to the earth, which serves him for a footstool. To him came a certain peasant, and questioned him thus. Reverend father, now how many ells of cloth would it take to make his breeches? And another said that all the peas and beans of Melazzo and Nicosia would not suffice to fill his stomach. Look to it, then, that this World-soul is not made after such a fashion.

Theophilus   I do not know how to resolve your doubt, Gervasius, but perhaps I can that of Master Polyhymnius. I can, however, to satisfy you both, give you a comparison, because I wish you to carry away some fruits of our reasoning and discourse. Know, then, in brief, that the Soul of the World, and the Divinity are not omnipresent through all and through every part, in the way in which material things could be there: because this is impossible to any sort of body, and to any sort of spirit; but in a manner which is not easy to explain to you if not in this way. You should take notice that if the Soul of the World and the universal form are said to be everywhere, we do not mean *corporeally* and *dimensionally,* because such things cannot be; and just so they cannot be in any part. But they are *spiritually* present in everything—as, for example (perhaps a rough one), you can imagine a voice which is throughout a whole room and in every part of the room; because, through all, it is completely heard: just as these words which I utter are heard completely

---

[8] "I want to know in what way the form is everywhere the whole soul of the world, if it is indivisible."

by all, even were there a thousand present, and my voice, could it reach throughout the whole world, would be everywhere through everything. I tell you then, Master Polyhymnius, that the soul is not indivisible like a point, but in some sort like the voice. And I answer you, Gervasius, that the Divinity is not everywhere in the sense that the God of Grandazzo was in the whole of the chapel, because, although he was present throughout the church, yet all of him was not present everywhere, but his head was in one part, his feet in another, his arms and his chest in yet other parts. But that other is in its entirety in every part, as my voice is heard completely in every part of this room.

Giacopo Mazzoni

(1548–1598)

Mazzoni's *On the Defense of the Comedy of Dante* is the second of his two works on the same subject. The first, by far shorter than the second, was a hasty response, published in 1572, to an attack on Dante by the pseudonymous Ridolfo Castravilla. The work excerpted here was an answer to Belisario Bulgarini's response to Mazzoni's earlier defense. Bulgarini argued for absolute verisimilitude, probability, and unity in poetry, claiming that Dante's work lacked these necessities.

Defending Dante, Mazzoni proposed a threefold definition of poetry, emphasizing that a science or an art is properly characterized not by its subject matter or, in the case of poetry, the object imitated, but rather by the mode of its treatment of the object. By the same token, an art can be treated in more than one way depending on the perspective in which we view it. With respect to poetry there are three of these. In the first perspective, poetry is simply imitation and the making of an "idol" with "no other end in its artifice than to represent and resemble." Such idols (in this perspective) "have no other existence or use except by reason of imitation or in imitation." In this definition the strictly aesthetic aim is the defining element. The idol is particular, credible, and verisimilar, but not necessarily true. What is important is the thing created: "The verisimilitude which is sought by poets is of such a nature that it is feigned by poets according to their own will."

In the second perspective, the poem is seen as a provider of delight, for it is a means of positive cessation of "serious and difficult activities" in recreation, play, or amusement. Such delight can be regarded as "free and independent of any law," or it can be seen as "subject to and regulated by the civil faculty," that is, the principle for understanding the proper organizations and functions of human society. In this, the third perspective, poetry is seen in terms of its social use and value. Thus Mazzoni attempts to preserve a notion of poetry's unique, purposive character while demonstrating its social and ethical role. One cannot quite say that the purposiveness is internal, as it is later characterized by Kant (below, page 416), for the purpose is seen as imitation, but the imitation is freed, to about the same degree as in Aristotle, from canons of truth to an external reality.

In the *Defense*, Mazzoni draws on many classical writers for support, but his views go back to both Plato and Aristotle, just as they did in his effort to reconcile the two in his earlier philosophical work *De Triplico Hominum Vita, Activa Nempe, Contempliva, et Religiosa Methodi Tres* (1576). For example, he adopts Plato's distinction in *Sophist* (above, page 40) between icastic and phantastic imitation as well as Aristotle's preference for the "credible impossible" over the "incredible possible." Like Plato, he identifies poetry with sophistic, but not, as Plato's Socrates does, to denigrate it. He attempts systematic definition in an Aristotelian manner.

Mazzoni's work has never been translated in full into English. A. H. Gilbert, ed., *Literary Criticism: Plato to Dryden* provides a selection. Robert L. Montgomery has translated the Introduction and Summary and provided a critical preface (1983). See Bernard Weinberg, *A History of Literary Criticism in the Italian Renaissance* in two volumes (1961); Baxter Hathaway, *The Age of Criticism: The Late Renaissance in Italy* (1962) and *Marvels and Commonplaces* (1968); Murray Krieger, "Jacopo Mazzoni: Depository of Diverse Critical Traditions or Source of a New One," *Poetic Presence and Illusion* (1979).

from

On the Defense of the Comedy of Dante

from

Introduction and Summary

*   *   *

. . . since it is the division of knowable things and not of things in themselves that divides the sciences, it necessarily follows that the same thing can be treated by different sciences according to different modes of knowing and consideration. Nor should this seem novel to anyone, for Aristotle in different books that contain different arts and sciences has at certain times treated the same thing, but he has always treated it with a different mode of consideration. For example, in the *Rhetoric* he discusses many things that seem appropriate to moral philosophy, and he does the same thing in the *Poetics*. But the manner of treatment is quite different when he treats these things in the *Moral Philosophy* than when he comes to repeat them in the *Poetics* or *Rhetoric*. For in the latter work everything is directed toward the persuasible, in the *Poetics* toward the imitable, and in the *Moral Philosophy* toward (so to speak) that which concerns human happiness. Since therefore the sciences are distinguished by their objects, not insofar as they are things, but insofar as they are knowable, so the arts of whatever things there are, are distinguished not by objects insofar as they are things but by objects insofar as they are (I cannot say it otherwise if I wish to speak accurately) artificiable.

Since on this topic I find no doctrine more copious or sound than that of Plato in the tenth book of the *Republic*,

so, following in his footsteps, I say that there are three types of object and that they have three ways in which they can be devised; as a consequence these constitute three species of arts in the first category. The objects are idea, work, and idol. The idea is the object of the ruling, or we might say, the governing arts. The work is the object of the fabricating arts, and the idol is the object of the imitating arts. Therefore the modes of the objects of the arts, insofar as they are capable of being differently treated by artifice will be three; that is, the observable, the fabricable, the imitable. The arts that only contemplate a thing pertinent to some object are the ruling arts, and they are founded in the idea. Such is the art of horsemanship when it deals with the bridle. For the art of horsemanship does not consist in making the bridle but is concerned only with the idea of how it has to work and prescribes to the bridle maker what he must hold to, to make it work. The arts that make the bridle (which was first conceived by the ruling art) are those that have as object what is called the work. The arts that make what was first conceived by the ruling arts are the fabricating arts and have as object what is called the work, and such is bridlemaking, which makes the work of the bridle and nothing else. The imitating arts have been so named because they deal with the object only insofar as it is imitable; hence Plato said that it has an idol as object, which means the simulacrum or image of some other things.[1]

Since, therefore, the same thing may be treated in different sciences under different modes of the knowable, so also the same thing can be submitted to different arts by different modes of artifice. And we have a clear example in the bridle: it belongs to the art of horsemanship when considered in its idea, to the art of bridlemaking when made as a work, and to painting when imitated as an idol.

But there may arise a doubt of some importance in thus distinguishing the imitative arts from other arts, for it would seem that the fabricating arts also deserve the name of imitation, since each one of these imitates in its work the model of the idea conceived by the ruling art. Thus, for example,

---

Della difesa della Comedia di Dante was first published in 1587. It may be that some parts of the text were brought to completion by Mazzoni's assistant Tucio del Corno. The *Defense* was preceded by the shorter *Discorso in difeso della del divino poeta Dante* (1572). The text of the introduction and summary is from Robert L. Montgomery, tr., *On the Defense of the Comedy of Dante* (Tallahassee: University Presses of Florida, 1983). The section from Book I was translated by Robert L. Montgomery for this edition.

---

[1] See Plato, *Republic* (above, page 31).

the art of bridlemaking forms a bridle exactly in conformity to the idea conceived by horsemanship. Therefore it would seem that the fabricating arts are not very well distinguished from the imitating arts. I respond that (as has already been said) the distinction between arts derives from their objects insofar as they are capable of being devised variously and distinctly. Now the artifice of the work is not only to represent the idea of the ruling art; it also has to serve other ends. And in this way we can say that bridlemaking forms the bridle in accordance with the idea conceived by horsemanship; still, this bridle is not made in order to represent the similitude of the idea, but rather so that it can be used in various ways in managing horses. Hence we see that the artifice of the fabricating arts aims at something other than just representing or resembling; therefore I say that the fabricating arts cannot be called imitative.[2] But those arts that have the idol as object have an object that has no other end in its artifice but to represent and resemble; hence they are called imitative. And just as philosophers have come to call the logical faculty rational, not because it uses reason—for in this sense all the arts and all the faculties are rational—but because it has an object that takes all its being from reason and in reason; so we say that the imitative arts are so named, not because they use imitation—for in this sense all the arts involve more or less some kind of imitation—but because they have objects that have no other being or use except by reason of imitation or in imitation.

This, I believe, is what Plato wished to show in the second book of the *Laws* where he said, "For the rightness of imitation consists, as we were saying, in this, that it is made of such a nature and size that the imitation expresses the nature and size of the object itself."[3] And Proclus, almost at the end of the *Poetic Questions* based on the authority of Plato, says: "Each imitator has as his aim the making of a likeness of an example, whether or not it should please anyone."[4] And the same thing was repeated by Maximus of Tyre, as we will show further on.

It can therefore be concluded that the imitative arts have been so named because they have as objects[5] those things which are good for no other end or no other use than to represent or to resemble; and they are distinguished from the other arts that are not called imitative because their objects are good for other uses or other ends than representation or resemblance alone. In this way, then, the idol is the object of the imitative arts.

* * *

. . . when we previously concluded that the idol is the object of the imitative arts, we did not mean that sort of idol that originates without human artifice, . . . but instead that which does have its origins in our artifice, arising only from our phantasy or our intellect by means of our choice and will, like the idols in painting, sculpture, and so on. I conclude therefore that this species of idol is that which is a suitable object of human imitation and that when Aristotle said at the beginning of the *Poetics* that all the kinds of poetry are imitation,[6] he meant that sort of imitation which has as its object the idol that arises from human artifice in the way we have stated. Rather I will say further that all imitations that arise from human artifice insofar as they are imitations have the idol as object in this manner.

But it would seem that the words of Suidas are contrary to this determination, for he shows himself believing that the idol that derives from human artifice is not an adequate object of the imitative arts, unless the idol is joined to some other different thing that he calls a similitude. Here are his words: "Idols are effigies of things that do not subsist, like tritons, sphinxes, or centaurs. But similitudes are the images of subsistent things, like beasts or men."[7] According to this statement of Suidas we see that there are two imitations. One of them represents the true, as a painter does when he represents with colors the effigy of a known man; and the other represents the caprice of the person who is doing the imitating, just as the painter does when he depicts according to the caprice of his phantasy. We see at the same time that the idol is the object of this second sort of imitation and at the same time that the similitude is the object of the first. Therefore, it is not true that the idol that is born of human artifice is an adequate object of every imitation.

We may respond that this statement of Suidas concerning the idol is too narrow and also in opposition to what other writers have said. Hesychius, uttering other sentiments about the term "idol," speaks as follows: "The idol

---

[2][Montgomery] Those interested in mimetic theory in the Renaissance should consult Baxter Hathaway's *The Age of Criticism: The Late Renaissance in Italy,* especially Part 1.

[3][Montgomery] Plato, *Laws* II, 668. This is the first of Mazzoni's many quotations from Plato. With few exceptions Mazzoni uses Ficino's Latin translation.

[4][Montgomery] Proclus's commentary on Plato is an elaborate Neoplatonic system departing in many ways from Plato's thought. Here and elsewhere Mazzoni seems to be using *Platonis Omnia Opera cum Commentarius Procli in Timaeum & Politica, Thesauro Veteris Philosophae Maximo* (Basle, 1534). For this quotation see page 367.

[5]That is, not objects imitated but the artistic objects made.

[6]See Aristotle, *Poetics* (above, page 52).

[7][Montgomery] Suidas, *TO MEN TIAPON BIBΛION ΣΟΥΔΑ* (Basle, 1544, sig. C2).

is similitude, image, and sign."[8] He shows clearly then with these words that the idol is also taken as a similitude and as an image of something discovered. Ammonius in the *Etymology* and Favorinus in the *Vocabulary* explaining the etymology of the idol have said that it derives "from the verb εἴδω [eido], which means match or resemble,"[9] almost as if it meant that the idol is of things that are apparent but not found and of things that are found, of which it represents the likeness. Let us add to it what Plato left us in writing in the *Sophist* that imitation is of two species, one of which he names the icastic, and it is that which represents things that are really found or at least have been, and the other he called phantastic, of which we have examples in paintings made according to the caprice of the artist. And even he himself says the same thing in the tenth book of the *Republic*, namely that the idol is the object of every imitation. Therefore the idol must also be common to phantastic imitation.[10]

* * *

Now I add that poetry ought to be placed under this imitative art or imitation, as a species under its genus. Therefore, in beginning to define poetry one can say that it is imitation.

* * *

. . . it seems to me that we ought to affirm two conclusions as correct. The first of them is that the false is not always necessarily the subject of poetry. The second is that since the subject of poetry is sometimes true and sometimes false, there is consequently a need to constitute a poetic subject that by itself can be sometimes true and sometimes false. Nor should the authorities cited above move us away from this opinion to that by which it appeared proven that the poetic subject is always the false, since it would be wise to take it in the way that we will explain when we discuss the nature of the poetic subject. Upon investigation I believe that there is no rule more to the point than that which was taught by Aristotle at the beginning of the *Posterior Analytics* for finding the predicate. He named this *per se* and *primo*, that is, when we lay out in sequence all those things that can probably be poetic subjects and then take them one by one and identify their contrary, we are able to see what, by its removal and the introduction of its contrary as a con-

tradiction, is more damaging to poetry. That then will be a major indication of what is a more appropriate and intrinsic subject of poetry than all the others.[11] Therefore, there will be these subjects: the possible and the credible.

Now if we remove the false and in its place put the true, we do not therefore destroy poetry, since we have already said that it can stand together with the true. The same can be said of the possible, for if the impossible is substituted in poetry, it will not therefore come to be corrupted or spoiled, if the impossible is credible. But if we take away the credible and in its place put the incredible, the nature of poetry is totally destroyed. And on the other hand taking the credible and at the same time removing the possible, we still have the poetic subject, as Aristotle has clearly testified in the following words: "As to what belongs to poetry, the credible impossible is more often to be preferred to the incredible and possible."[12] Therefore it ought to be said that among all these there is no more appropriate subject of poetry than the credible. And even more to the point, how much the credible by its very nature includes both the true and the false, for often not only the true but also the false is credible.

* * *

. . . because it has already been decided on the authority of Aristotle that the credible is the subject of the art of the poets, it seems to me that we can draw three conclusions from what has been said. The first of them is that the poet being always concerned with the credible, he must as a necessary consequence treat everything in a fashion suitable to the credible, that is, always making use of singular and sensible means to represent the things he writes about whatever they may be. And even if he treats things pertinent to contemplative doctrine, he must make every effort to represent them by idols and sensible simulacra, which Empedocles did not do. Hence, he was more often termed a physicist than a poet.

* * *

. . . it is not denied to the poet to treat things pertinent to the sciences and the speculative intellect, but he treats them in a

---

[8] [Montgomery] Hesychius, *Hesychii Dictionarium* (Florence, 1520).
[9] [Montgomery] Favorinus, *Magnum ac Per Utile Dictionarium,* page 164.
[10] See Plato, *Sophist* (above, page 40).

[11] [Montgomery] *Posterior Analytics* I, iii–v. "Per se" refers to things that are an essential part of something else: "Thus in the sphere of what is knowable in the absolute sense, attributes which are called *per se* as implying or implied by their subjects, belong to those subjects in virtue of their own nature and necessity." Also, "an attribute only belongs to a subject universally when it can be shown to belong to any chance instance of that subject primarily." (Loeb ed., pages 45–7). The Greek terms for *per se* and *primo* are καθαὺ τό and πρώτου.
[12] See Aristotle, *Poetics* (above, page 66).

credible manner, making idols and poetic images, as Dante, with most marvelous and noble artifice, has certainly done in representing all intellectual nature and the intelligible world itself with idols and images most beautifully to all eyes.

I recall that Plato in the *Phaedrus,* exalting his own invention, wrote just to this point: "But of that place that is beyond the heavens, I do not know that any of the poets has ever treated or is likely to treat it in a manner worthy of the way it is."[13] And so on. But if he had seen Dante's third canticle, he would without any doubt have recognized his own invention as inferior and given the palm to Dante, and consequently to poets for knowing how to make idols and images appropriate to giving to the popular understanding the quality of the supercelestial world. Concerning this I have written at length in the fifth book where I also show with what tact Dante has at times introduced either a philosopher or a theologian to discuss matters pertinent to the contemplative sciences in an understandable fashion, never deviating from the credible. The second conclusion is that, since the poet has the credible as his subject, he ought therefore to oppose credible things to the true and the false, the possible and the impossible, by which I mean that he ought to give more importance to the credible than to any of the others I have enumerated.

Therefore, if it should happen that two things should appear before the poet, one of them false but credible and the other true but incredible or at least not very credible, then the poet must leave the true and follow the credible.

* * *

The third and last conclusion, which is almost a corollary of the previous two, is that poetry, in order to give more importance to the credible than to the true, must be strictly categorized under the rational faculty named by the ancients "sophistic." And for a complete understanding of this truth, which (unless I am mistaken) has until now remained mysterious, it must be understood that the poetic art may be taken in two modes, that is, either according as it is concerned with the laws of the poetic idol, or according as it is concerned with fashioning or forming the poetic idol.

The first mode ought to be called "poetics" and the second "poetry." In the first mode is the ruling art, which uses the idol and is part of the civil faculty, as we will show a little further on. In the second mode is the art that forms and fabricates the idol and is a species of the rational faculty. As I have said, it ought to be included under

sophistic, since it does not care about the true. I am aware that I may have offended the sensibilities of poets by fastening upon an art considered until now virtually divine and the title of sophistic, which has come to be thought repellent and scandalous.[14]

* * *

Now only true philosophy directs the intellect by means of the true and the will by means of the good. Therefore only the sophistic totally contrary to true philosophy misdirects the intellect by means of the false and the will by means of evil. It was this sort of sophistic which was condemned by Plato and Aristotle and all their followers, and apparently Plato wanted to gather under this species of sophistic the poetry of Homer as that which misdirected the intellect by representing false things about the gods and heroes and that which misdirected the will with that variety of imitation and immoderate augmenting of our feelings which were discussed just previously.[15] And therefore one could say that any other poetry like that of Homer would have to be placed under the sophistic condemned by that philosopher, and not only was it banished from Plato's *Republic* but also from that of the Athenians, as Philostratus has written in the following words: "The Athenians, perceiving the eloquence of the sophists, chased them from the courts, on the grounds that they dominated the courts with unjust utterance and had too great a power over the law."[16] Therefore the species of sophistic condemned by the philosopher is that which misdirects the intellect with falsehood and the will with injustice. Under which he also places that sort of poetry which produces the same disorders and which does not really deserve the name of poetry, since it does not form its idols according to the laws of poetic practice or theory, as was plainly discussed a little before.

The second species of sophistic is that which Philostratus called the old sophistic, which indeed sets feigned things before the intellect, yet does not mislead the will, so that it claims in every way to make it conformable to what is just. And that kind of sophistic was never condemned by the ancients. And if, even so, it should appear to someone that it deserves condemnation for misleading the intellect by some falsehood, I say that he should know that the ancient pagan philosophers (being at variance in this matter with the truth

---

[13] Plato, *Phaedrus.*

[14] Mazzoni is, of course, well aware of the influence of Plato's treatment of sophists and rhetoricians, with whom he classed poets.

[15] [Montgomery] *Republic* II, 377–8, and *Protagoras,* 316.

[16] [Montgomery] Philostrastus, *Lives of the Sophists* I, 483. Loeb ed., pages 10–11.

of sacred theology) have praised this misleading of the intellect in certain things, when it is directed to a legitimate end. And in this respect Plato preferred that the magistrate should be able to tell lies to his citizens for the sake of some public good.[17] I pass over the fact that this species of sophistic almost always contains some truth under the skin of a first appearance.

Now I maintain that phantastic poetry regulated by the proper laws belongs to that ancient sophistic, since it also offers feigned things to our intellects in order to regulate the appetite. And often it contains under the outer covering of fiction the truth of many noble concepts.

The third species of sophistic is that which Philostratus called the second sophistic, which does not employ feigned names and events, but rather true names and real actions on which are based discussions appropriate to the rules of justice.

* * *

Under the third species of sophistic we ought in my judgment to place icastic poetry, which represents true actions and persons but always in a credible way. Therefore, on the basis of this entire discussion of sophistic with the fundamentals we have provided, everyone can understand that poetry is a rational faculty and that, among other rational faculties, it ought not to be placed with those that teach the truth, avoiding all other matters, but with those that employ all their power to examine the apparent credible, avoiding the true, and that this was the reason the ancients called it sophistic.

* * *

Therefore, I firmly conclude that poetry is a sophistic art and that through imitation, which is its proper genus, and the credible, which is its subject, and through delight, which is its end, when it is under that genus, and has that subject, and gains that end, it is many times forced to find room for the false.

* * *

And so the credible is the subject of poetry. But because it is also the subject of rhetoric we must necessarily see in what way it can be made to become proper to both poetry

and rhetoric, since we will not fall into the error of those who accept the verisimilar false.

I say therefore that the credible insofar as it is credible is the subject of rhetoric and the credible insofar as it is marvelous is the subject of poetry, for poetry must not only utter credible things but also marvelous things. And for this reason when it can do so credibly, it falsifies human and natural history and passes beyond them to impossible things,... So that, if two things equally credible were offered to the poet, one of them more marvelous than the other, though false, not just impossible, the poet ought to take it and refuse the other.

* * *

But perhaps there is someone who might wonder why the credible marvelous is not found in company with the true. And he might also suppose that what was said before—that poetry sometimes admits the true—is wrong. I respond that sometimes true things are found in poetry which are often more marvelous than the false.

* * *

Therefore let us summarize what has been said on the poetic subject, that it ought to be credible and at the same time marvelous, and then joining this subject to the form already disclosed above, we can now say that *poetry is an imitation made with harmony, rhythm, and verses, singly or together, of things credible and marvelous.*

There remains for the completion of this definition that we find the efficient and final causes of poetry.[18] Now as for the efficient cause, we might dispatch it by saying that it is the human intellect. But this is a cause common to all the other arts, and we only wish to find one that is more appropriate to poetry and that, joined to its end, will reveal the proper origin and legitimate use of poetry.

Therefore in order to lay the foundation for this, I believe there is no surer way than to consider what that art is that discovers the use of poetry, because that, unless I deceive myself, will reveal the origin and end of poetry. I think, then, that the civil faculty[19] is that which discovers

---

[17][Montgomery] *Republic* III, 389 (above, page 22).

[18] Two of the four causes delineated by Aristotle. Efficient cause: that which brings about a change, produces an object; final cause: the purpose of an action.

[19] [Montgomery] By the civil faculty Mazzoni means, roughly speaking, ethics, or the mode of discourse that decides the social relevance of something.

not only the use of poetry but also explains the norm and the rules for the poetic idol. The following consideration presses me toward this belief, namely, that all the natural powers and the arts that are born of human reason are usually directed to contrary objects, as for example medicine, which not only deals with health and healthful potions but also with sickness and poisons. We can say also that the legal profession likewise not only professes to deal with justice but with injustice as well.

Now keeping this in mind, I say that the civil faculty not only professes to understand the justness of human actions but also the justness of the cessation of human actions, a justness that is opposed to the first justness as deprivation is opposed to habit. But because someone might object that the habits of our intellects and the human arts consider only positive contraries, and not privations, I therefore add that a positive contrary and privation are always treated by the same art. As, for example, natural philosophy not only deals with the contrary of movement insofar as it is positive, that is, the contrariety found in movement insofar as it is up or down, but also the contrary of privation, that is between movement and the cessation of movement, in other words, rest. So I say that biology is concerned not only with the contrary differences that produce different species, in which a positive contrariety is understood, but also with contraries of privation, such as life and death. I add (and this is really worth noting) that privation, which has the power of rendering its subject determined or prepared to receive a determined form, at the same time receives its determination and (so to speak) its qualification from the form itself. Concerning this there is the plain and authentic testimony of Simplicius in the commentary on the first book of the *Physics* in these words: "But the privation of anything is in the same genus, for it is determined and qualified by its form. Hence on this point Aristotle says that privation is a certain mode of form."[20] And for this reason privation is considered by the same science that considers form. But the cessation of a process, as will be explained a little further on, must dispose and prepare men so that they are more apt and eager for the process. Therefore the same faculty will provide the rule for the activity and its cessation. And note that I do not take cessation to be total privation or extinction of activity, but only cessation of serious and difficult activities, and so in the word *cessation* we include the activities of play and amusement which we do for recreation and entertainment. So it can be said that the contrariety of function and cessation is not only privation but (as was said above) also positive. It is pri-

vation insofar as the cessation indicates the absence of serious work. It is positive insofar as the cessation of serious work might contain some pleasant activity apt to restore the spirits fatigued by the more important function. This is clearly enough indicated by Aristotle in the tenth book of the *Ethics* and the eighth of the *Politics,* where discussing cessation (which he treats at length in the fifth chapter of the second book), the name is always ἀνάπαυσις and not σχολή to make it clear that he does not take the otium that is the father of all vices as entertainment or the cessation of serious things, but rather some peaceful and gentle activity.[21]

So it appears to me that one can firmly say that in order for cessation to be the opposite of privative and positive activity, it must necessarily be the concern of one art and a single faculty. But the civil faculty is that which considers the rightness of an activity, so it should also consider the rightness of its cessation. Within it, as I have said, are contained all the activities of amusement, that is, those performed in games. Therefore the consideration of the rightness of pleasure will without any doubt be pertinent in some way to the civil faculty and to moral philosophy. But among all games none is found more worthy, more noble, and more central than what the poets' work has made. Therefore the civil faculty takes care to consider principally among the other pleasures the standard and rightness of poetry.

Now, that the ancients believed that poetry was a game is shown in the abovementioned chapter of the second book on the authority of Virgil, Horace, Timocles the comic poet, Plato in the tenth book of the *Republic,* and in the fifth of the *Laws,* and Eusebius of Caesarea in the twelfth book of the *Evangelical Preparations*. To these can be added the authority of Aristotle, who in the seventh book of the *Politics* calls games "the imitations of those things you do seriously." And there is the authority of Plato who in the second book of the *Laws* says of poetic imitation: "Again I call it amusement and play."[22] From all these considerations it seems to me that it can be reasonably said that the civil faculty ought to be divided into two principal parts, one of which is concerned with the laws of activities and is given the general name of politics, that is, the civil law. The other is concerned with the laws of cessation or the laws of recreational activities, and is called poetics. And on this basis I believe that the *Poetics* is the ninth book of the *Politics,* and my view seems to me all the more correct in that I find in

[20] [Montgomery] Simplicius, *In Aristotelis Physicorum Libros Quattuor Priores Commentaria* (Berlin, 1882), pages 233, ll. 25–28.

[21] [Montgomery] *Nichomachean Ethics* X, 3; *Politics* VIII generally concerns education and leisure. The sixth chapter of the second book would seem more to Mazzoni's point than the fifth, which deals with a number of topics ranging from the justice system to political innovation.

[22] [Montgomery] Aristotle, *Politics* VII, 1334a; Plato, *Laws* II, 667.

the eighth book of the *Politics* and at the beginning of the first chapter of the *Poetics* he commences to deal with music, in order to proceed step by step to discuss the recreation of the civil faculty. And so I say that the first seven books of the *Politics* speak of the civil faculty at work and the last two speak of the civil faculty (so to speak) at rest, a state we have just previously called poetics.[23]

Therefore poetics is part of the civil faculty and is what prescribes the standards, the rules, and the laws of the idol in poetry. So in a way it can be said that poetics deals with the idea of the idol and poetry with the making of it. Thus poetics will be in its genus the ruling art, using the idol made by poets to that end we have just previously mentioned. And in its genus poetry will be the fabricating art, the maker of the idol, which is then to be used by poetics and by the civil faculty.

We can therefore add to the previous words concerning the definition of poetry its efficient cause and say: *Poetry is an imitation made with harmony, number, and verses, singly or together, of credible and marvelous things discovered by the civil faculty.*

Up to this point we have disclosed the form, the subject matter, and the making of poetry, so that it remains only to turn our hand to the discussion of its final cause. Ancient and modern writers have raised a great fuss about this, not knowing very well whether they should take usefulness or delight or both, or neither the one nor the other, as the end of poetry. And if I have to confess the truth freely, it seems to me that until now we have walked in darkness in this matter, and especially the moderns, who have not known (unless I am deceived) in any way how to illuminate this dark and intricate path with the light of dialectic, for all that in Plato, in Aristotle, and in other writers are found scattered scintillas of the truth from which they could take light enough. Now in order to recover it for us more easily I believe it will be well to reveal at the first the reason why this subject seems dark and intricate and difficult. For, knowing the difficulty, we are also able to understand that on its solution depends totally the settled and complete doctrine on this matter. So I say that it would surprise a great many, and with reason, if we could find out from writers whether delight or utility is the end of poetry. For if it is true that poetry is an imitative art and

that every imitative art has the idol as its object, and that the idol (as has been proven before) is good for nothing but to represent or resemble, then it seems to me that we have to say that poetry has no other end than to represent or resemble. Therefore, it is unreasonable to inquire whether utility or delight is the end of poetry. I might add that if utility or delight were the end of poetry, it would not be an imitative art.

I demonstrate this as follows: because the imitative arts are different from other arts that are not imitative, that is, because the object of the imitative arts is good for no other use than to represent, the object of the other arts that are not imitative is good for some other use, either useful or pleasing. Therefore, if the object of poetry should have as its end either usefulness or enjoyment, it would follow necessarily that it would be good for something other than to represent, and so poetry would not be an imitative art.

* * *

. . . I say that poetry can be considered in three different modes, that is, as an imitative art, either as enjoyment or amusement simply, or as enjoyment or amusement directed, ruled, and defined by the civil faculty. If it is considered as an imitative art, I say that it has no other end than to represent or resemble correctly. And this is what Plato, Proclus, and Maximus of Tyre meant in the passages cited above. Now it should be understood that (as Aristotle has written in the tenth book of the *Ethics*) delight is an accident proper to some functions, and among them is without doubt most proper to imitation, since it seems in a way joined to it so that no mode of imitation can be found that does not at the same time bring both delight and pleasure.

* * *

Since, therefore, imitation is always linked to delight, so it happens that all those who have attempted to produce games and enjoyment have produced them with some kind of imitation, as I have shown in discussing the ancient game of chess in the sixth chapter of the second book, and I may add here (to provide an example different from those two) the game of primero,[24] in which is represented the image of ochlocracy, that is, that republic in which the common people have the most power. For since in this kind of republic the aristocrats are weak and the common people strong, so

---

[23] [Montgomery] The latter part of Book VII and all of Book VIII discuss liberal education, that is, the education appropriate to a free man. For Aristotle this means not just someone not a slave, but a citizen relieved from compulsion to labor or earn a living by commerce. The civil faculty at rest or leisure thus concerns itself with contemplation and with the study and appreciation of certain kinds of elevated enjoyment such as music and poetry.

[24] [Montgomery] A card game, often called "prime" in Renaissance England.

in the game the cards commonly given the noblest names are of lesser value than the other cards that have the vulgar name of waste paper because of their baseness. Now since imitation itself can be considered as part of the abovementioned game, in this mode it has no other end than to represent the image of ochlocracy and can be deemed a game and amusement, and in such a mode we recognize no other end than delight and pleasure. So I say that poetry can in the same way be thought of as an imitative art and as a game and amusement.

In the first mode it has as its end the correctness of the idol, that is, whether the thing has been imitated in an appropriate way. But in the second mode it contemplates delight and pleasure as its end, and these are joined to a good and perfect imitation. Therefore, I conclude that poetry as an imitative art has the correctness of the idol as its end, but as a thing that should be used for play and amusement and to interrupt some more serious and rigorous business, it here proposes as its end delight born of appropriate imitation. Now this delight that poetry brings us can be looked at in two ways: that is, either as free and independent of any law, or as subject to and regulated by the civil faculty. In the first mode it is the end of that poetry which was classified under the kind of sophistic worthy of blame, because it disordered the appetite with immoderate delight, producing complete rebellion against reason and bringing on damage and loss to a virtuous life.

That was the sort of poetry banished from his republic by Plato, concerning the reason for which Maximus of Tyre has written in his eighth sermon that just as Mithecus, the most excellent cook, was banished by the Spartans, despite the fact that he was greatly esteemed among the other peoples of Greece, only because his art had no other end than to please the taste, which was totally repugnant to the sobriety of the Lacedaemonians;[25] so also did Plato banish poets from his republic as having regard for nothing other than delighting too freely. And Proclus in the *Poetic Questions,* having admitted that this sort of poetry is truly enjoyable, supplies the reasons why it is damaging and harmful to civil life: "I will therefore suggest two reasons why Plato did not accept tragedy and comedy in a proper republic as worthy of the education of the young. One was the variety (as it is called) of the imitations; the other was the unlimited moving of the passions, which he wished to moderate however he could. To this can be added as a third the case of saying any sort of

wickedness in those same genres about gods and heroes."[26] And so on.

If, therefore, one has to reason about the end of this poetry, it can be definitely said that as an imitative art its end is the correctness of the idol, but that as recreation its only end is pleasure.

But if delight is considered insofar as it is regulated and defined by the civil faculty, we will necessarily have to say that it is directed toward the useful and consequently is that species of poetry which was placed under praiseworthy sophistic, that is, under that which orders the appetite and submits it to the reason, and, considered as game, defined by the civil faculty to have usefulness as its end.

* * *

Now without any doubt I think that as regards the end of poetry this is a correct opinion, that is, that perfect poetry regards delight as the cause of the useful. And as proof of my opinion, I am going to make the following discussion a little different from that of Plato.

Therefore I say that perfect poetry is game and is modified by the civil faculty; insofar as it is recreation it has delight as its end, but insofar as it is modified or, so to speak, characterized by moral philosophy, it puts delight first in order to provide a later benefit. And from this it seems to me that the civil faculty has decided that everyone may enjoy the delight that comes from poetry. And it has been so established by Plato in his *Laws* and by other legislators. I say further that the Athenian Republic so valued the delight brought to the people by poets that they were not ashamed to give each year many hundreds of coins to its citizens to buy themselves seats in the theatre where they could more easily hear the comedies and tragedies acted.

* * *

Now it is not likely that the republic would have tried with such cost to the treasury to have the people easily experience the delight given by poetry if they had not at the same time believed that by means of this delight there could be introduced some benefit into the minds of those who would willingly receive it. And if it should seem to anyone that it is necessary to set forth more in detail the mode and type of this benefit, I am pressed, in order to satisfy this desire, to say something briefly.

---

[25] [Montgomery] *Maximus of Tyre, Sermones sive Disputationes* XLI, number 29.

[26] [Montgomery] Proclus, *In Platonis Rem Publicam Commentarii,* ed. Kroll, II, 50–51.

Plato wanted his republic to be composed of three sorts of persons: artisans, soldiers, and magistrates. Proclus added that under the category of artisans Plato included all the lower- and middle-class citizens, and that under the category of magistrates he included all those more powerful people who had the government of the republic in their hands.[27] Now based upon this supposition I say that there are, deriving from the providence of the civil faculty in the city, three principal kinds of poetry—the heroic, the tragic, and the comic, each one of which makes use of delight to benefit all the people; each principally aimed at the benefit of one of those three parts that are, according to Plato, necessary to civil community. And so we say that the heroic poem was principally directed at soldiers, since by means of the virtuous actions of the heroes represented in such poems, they would be as if spurred on by glory driven to imitate it. Tragedy principally looks to the utility and benefit of princes, magistrates, and the powerful and, so as to keep them always under the justice of the laws, represents freely the dreadful and terrible downfall of great persons, which comes almost to be a bridle to restrain and moderate the size of their fortune. Comedy has as its principal intention the benefit of persons of low or moderate estate, and to console them for their modest fortune it usually presents actions that always end happily. And in this way, I think, the civil faculty inclines to the understanding that the humble and popular life is so much more enjoyable and filled with greater contentment than the grand or regal life.

* * *

Since the civil faculty seeks to implant in the minds of humble citizens obedience to their superiors, so that out of desire for novelties they should not be moved to disobedience or rebellion, and so that they should always remain content with their condition, it gave birth to comedy, in which the humble life is shown to be happy, fortunate, and capable of infinite solace. On the other hand, since the more powerful and all those raised to the mastery of others have not had to pay too much attention to their fortune, and consequently have become insupportable and insolent in their rule, the civil faculty wished to create tragedy, which would function as an adequate counterweight to the insolence of prosperous fortune. Hence all those who find themselves in such a condition will be able to extract useful instruction in moderating the pride characteristic of their state. This usefulness of tragedy, I believe, is clearly enough indicated by Dio Chrysostum in these words: "Nor is it anyone poor that the

tragic situation deals with. On the contrary, all tragedies concern the Atreidi, the Agamemnons, and the Oedipuses, who possess a great abundance of gold, silver, fields, and cattle. So they say that the golden fleece was the greatest of all misfortunes.[28] And so on.

Now it seems to me that from what has been said before concerning the utility to be derived from comedy and tragedy, we can conclude that those two kinds of poems are directed by the civil faculty to the extinguishing of sedition and the preservation of peace. And because the civil faculty also has to keep military education in mind, in order that in times of war the republic may be capable of defending itself, it seems to me that it can probably be supposed that for this end the civil faculty created the heroic poem, in which is celebrated the highest strength of the heroes, and especially of those who generously disdain death for the sake of the country, to the end of reminding our soldiers of like examples so that they will consequently be more prone to despise the perils of death for the safety and increase of the public good. And in this way we see that these three species of poetry ruled by the civil faculty, in addition to delight, bring utility and benefit to the republic, instructing in an almost concealed way the three kinds of men, from which (according to Plato) the ideal order of citizens is made up.

* * *

Now to come to the end of this definition, I think it would be well to recapitulate in a brief epilogue what has been said before about the final cause of poetry. I say therefore that since language is always the instrument of the concupiscible power and has enjoyment as its end, but that, nevertheless considered as an instrument of the irascible power, it has as its end the defense of the sensitive soul; and if considered as an instrument of the rational power, its end is language. In the same way poetry is always an imitative art, and insofar as it is such, its end is always to represent the images of things correctly. Nevertheless, considered as a game, its end is delight; and considered as a game modified by the civil faculty, its immediate end is delight, but directed to profit.

On this premise, it seems to me that it can be concluded that poetry is capable of three definitions according as it is looked at in three different ways, that is, either as imitation, or purely as a game, or as a game modified by the civil faculty. In the first mode it can, perhaps, be defined this way: *Poetry is an art made with verse, number, and harmony, singly or together, imitative of the credible mar-*

---

27 [Montgomery] The same, II, 47.

28 [Montgomery] Dio Chrysostom, "In Athens about His Banishment," *Orations* XIII; Loeb ed., Volume II, page 107.

velous, and invented by the human intellect to represent the images of things suitably. In the second mode this other definition would perhaps be appropriate: *Poetry is a game made with verse, number, and harmony, singly or together, imitating the credible marvelous, and invented by the human intellect in order to delight.*

* * *

In the third mode perhaps there is room for this last definition: *Poetry is a game made with verses, number, and harmony, singly or together, imitating the credible marvelous and invented by the civil faculty to delight the people in a useful way.* Of poetry considered in this mode, we have to understand fully all the authorities that attribute to it the end of usefulness by means of delight. In this regard we should attend to the following words of Proclus, in which he talks of poetry more as a kind of learning than as imitation: "Now if it must be an imitation, as we have said, it also has to concern itself with worthy goodness. For I say that all its virtuous deeds, whether or not they are fashioned by imitation, have no more important end than the good."[29]

From these three definitions there necessarily follow four corollaries. The first of these is that poetry taken in the first two modes is neither ruled nor governed by the civil faculty. The second is that only poetry in the third mode is that which is ruled and governed by moral philosophy or the civil faculty. The third is that the poetic that considers the idol in the first mode and that which likewise considers the idol in the second mode of poetry should not in any way be called a part of moral philosophy. The fourth and last corollary is that only the poetic that considers the idol in the third mode of poetry is that which really deserves to be called part of the civil faculty. And each good poet should put together his poems according to the rules of this mode of poetry, as Dante has done better than all the others.

from
Book I

I say, then, that the phantasy is the power of the soul common to dreams and to poetic verisimilitude. But because my opponents do not doubt of what I too believe, that the phantasy is the power upon which the dream is founded (which Aristotle said many times and which has been repeated more often by his followers), it is therefore well to explain that poetic verisimilitude is also based on the same power. The verisimilitude which is sought by the poets is of such a nature that it is feigned by poets according to their own will. Therefore it is necessary that it should be fashioned by that power which has the virtue of forming concepts in accordance with the will. Now this power cannot in any way be intellectual, for the intellectual power is necessary in producing concepts in accordance with the nature of objects. Hence the subtle Scotus in many places in his *Sentences* says that the intellect is a capacity more natural than free. Therefore it is necessary that the power fitted to generate verisimilar concepts dependent upon the will be the power of the phantasy, called by the Latins *imaginative.* And all that we have said was stated first by Aristotle in the second book of *De Anima:*

> It is in our power to imagine not only things which can be, but also those which cannot, such as men with three heads and three bodies, as Geryon in the fables is supposed to have been, and as men with wings, like Zetes and Calais the sons of Boreas, and the Centaurs and Scylla and Charybdis. For in whatever way a painter may depict an animal of any form, so it is possible to create it in the mind. In addition when we think that some formidable and fearful calamity may occur, we immediately dismiss our courage and our whole body trembles, we shake, and we grow pale. . . . But when we build these things in our mind (as when we imagine terrifying earthquakes and the fierce aspects of wild beasts), we are not affected at all, no consternation follows, and just as paintings do not affect us, neither do visions nor those figments which we willfully gather together. From this we can distinguish imagination from opinion and apprehension.[30]

Therefore if I am not mistaken we can clearly see that the phantasy is the proper power of the poetic fable, since it alone is capable of those fictions which we ourselves are able to create. From this it follows necessarily that poetry is composed of feigned and imagined things, because it is based in the phantasy.

---

[29] [Montgomery] Proclus, "Poetic Questions," *In Platonis Rem Publicam Commentarii,* ed. Kroll, II, 67.

[30] [Montgomery] This quotation is not from Aristotle, whose remarks on the imagination are more cursory, but from the commentary of Themistius, philosopher and rhetorician of the fourth century A.D.

Torquato Tasso

1544–1595

Among the greatest of the poets of the Renaissance, Tasso is also well known for his critical writings, especially the discourse in which he defended his own epic practice. The best known of his epics is *Jerusalem Delivered* (completed 1575, published 1581), on the subject of the First Crusade. The *Discorsi del Poema Eroica* was written after *Jerusalem Delivered* was completed and before it was revised and extended into the poem *Jerusalem Conquered.* Tasso was well aware of the major critical issues of his time and the pressures to which poet and critic had to respond. As Cavalchini and Samuel point out in their introduction to their translation of the *Discorsi,* "Tasso took them all into account, reconciling society's demand that poetry should entertain, the Church's demand that poetry should encourage the faith, the humanist's veneration for antiquity, the modernist's self-applause—and managed not to degrade poetry into entertainment, confuse it with propaganda (in the original sense of that term), disparage ancients, medievals, or moderns; he even managed not to be anti-Aristotelian or anti-Platonic."

Indeed, in Book One, Tasso follows an Aristotelian procedure in producing a definition of epic that is somewhat in parallel with and in contrast to Aristotle's definition of tragedy, though it is not stated completely in any one place, but is accumulated as he goes along. The aim of Book One is to set forth a definition as the basis for a general theory of epic. Thus Tasso begins by asking what the *idea* of a heroic poem is by raising the question of poetry in general. Aristotelian imitation is invoked as a common property of all poetry, and poetry's purpose is defined as "to help men by the example of human deeds" and to provide "pleasure directed toward usefulness," usefulness having human virtue as its end.

Tasso places the epic under poetic imitation, employing "imitation" in the broader sense to include narration, while still contrasting it with tragedy with respect to mode of imitation. Rather than purgation, which is the end Aristotle gave to tragedy, epic moves its reader to wonder, though it is not the only genre that does so. It is an "imitation of a nobler action, great and perfect, narrated in the loftiest verse, with the purpose of moving the mind to wonder and thus being useful." At the conclusion of the sixth and last book of the *Discorsi,* Tasso offers a contrast between epic and tragedy that shows wonder to be at the service of human improvement: ". . . if there are two ways of improving us through example, one inciting us to good works by showing the reward of excellence and an almost divine worth, the other frightening us from evil with penalties, the first is the way of epic, the second that of tragedy, which for this reason is less useful and gives less delight."

The standard edition of Tasso's *Discourses* is *Discorsi dell' Arte Poetica e del Poema Eroica,* edited by Luigi Poma (1964). See Bernard Weinberg, *A History of Literary Criticism in the Italian Renaissance* (1961); Maggie Günsberg, *The Epic Rhetoric of Tasso: Theory and Practice* (1988); Lawrence F. Rhu, *The Genesis of Tasso's Narrative Theory* (1993).

from

Discourses on the Heroic Poem

Book One

To begin with then, I say that in all things one must consider the end, as Aristotle declares in his *Topics*. But the end, being single, cannot be found in many particulars. Still, by considering the good in various particular goodnesses, we form the idea of the good, just as Zeuxis formed the idea of the beautiful when he wished to paint Helen in Croton.[1] And this is perhaps the difference between the ideas of natural things in the divine mind and those of artificial things which the human intellect figures to itself: with one the universal exists before, and with the other after the things themselves. The idea of an artistic product is formed after consideration of many things, among which that one is best which most closely approximates to the idea. And since I have to show the idea of the most excellent kind of poem, the heroic, I must not offer only one poem, even the most beautiful, as example, but, collecting the beauties and perfections of many, I must explain how the most perfect and most beautiful can be fashioned.

But first we must find out what the heroic poem is, or rather what its genre is, and then examine the idea, since from the idea, as Aristotle says, again in the *Topics,* one knows if the definition is right. Although in some things this principle does not in fact work well, in the matter of which we are speaking we may certainly consider idea and definition together. Furthermore, if—the arguments being so many—we ought to look at the exemplar, let us turn to the idea itself, since the idea is the true exemplar. Indeed, we may use the complete definition in place of rule and example, as Alexander of Aphrodisias[2] teaches when expounding that same passage in Aristotle. Let us therefore study first what a poem is, or poetry in general, and then we will find the definition of this species—I mean the heroic or epic poem, as it may be called.

Poetry has many species: one is the epic; the others are tragedy, comedy, and songs accompanied by the cithara, bagpipes, reedpipes, or other pastoral instruments. They are all alike in that they imitate. We may therefore affirm that poetry is nothing other than imitation. But painting, sculpture, and other similar arts also imitate; and hence the necessity of clarifying the differences that separate poetry from the other imitative arts. Clearly they do not differ because of the subjects imitated, since the same subject—the Trojan war or the wanderings of Ulysses—may be taken by painter and poet; it is not then a difference in the actions imitated that makes the arts different, but rather that one uses colours and the other words, either with or without meter.

Poetry then is an imitation in verse. But imitation of what? Of human and divine actions, the Stoics said. It follows that those who do not sing human or divine actions are not poets. Thus Homer was not a poet when he described the war between the frogs and the mice,[3] nor Virgil when he described the customs, laws, and wars of the bees.[4] On the other hand, he who describes divine actions is a poet. Thus Empedocles was a poet when he taught how Love and Discord corrupt this perceptible world and generate the intelligible one; and Plato too when he had Timaeus narrate how God the father, calling together the other lesser gods, created the world[5]—or if he was not a complete poet, because he did not use verse, at least he deserves the name by virtue of what he imitated. But if this is so, then, since all the acts of nature are governed by divine providence, whoever describes them would be a poet. Nor do I think epic poets would have excluded from their number Homer, Empedocles, Parmenides, Oppian, or others who borrowed true poets' verse like a cart, as Plutarch says.[6] Perhaps they would have excluded Lucretius, since he denies their ancient notion of πρόνοια,[7] and makes the creation of the world not a divine act but the work of chance. Such acts are not, in Aristotle's opinion, appropriate for poetry. Someone, however, may ask why only divine and human actions are appropriate and not the actions of the elements and other natural forces.

If all actions can be imitated, then the kinds of action being many, the kinds of poem must also be many; and since in this equivocal genre [of action], as Simplicius[8] says in [his commentary on] the *Categories* [of Aristotle], the first species is contemplation, which is the action of the intellect, acts of contemplation can also be imitated by poets.

Discorsi Del Poema Eroica was first published in Naples in 1594. This selection is reprinted from *Discourses on the Heroic Poem* by Torquato Tasso, translated by Mariella Cavalchini and Irene Samuel (Oxford: Oxford University Press, 1973).

[1]Zeuxis (fl. 424–380 B.C.), Greek painter.
[2]Commentator on Aristotle (fl. 200 A.D.).

[3]Long wrongly attributed to Homer. [Cavalchini and Samuel] *Batromyomachia.*
[4][Cavalchini and Samuel] The Fourth Georgic.
[5][Cavalchini and Samuel] *Timaeus,* 41a ff.
[6]Plutarch (above, page 119). [Cavalchini and Samuel] *How to Read the Poets,* 16.
[7]T. Carus Lucretius (94–55 B.C.), Roman poet; pronoia: forethought.
[8]Late Neoplatonic philosopher (sixth century).

Some indeed contend that the subject of Dante's poem is a contemplation because that voyage of his to Hell and Purgatory has no meaning other than the speculations of his mind.[9] Others prefer to call his subject a dream, like the *Trionfi* of Petrarch and the *Amorosa Visione* of Boccaccio. But those who hold this view oppose his subject, even more than Plato opposes imitation itself on the ground that the idea has the first degree of truth, the natural form or thing itself the second degree, and the imitation or image the third.[10] For the imitator who represents not a true action but a dream would be still more imperfect—giving the image of an action still further removed from the truth. Plato's doctrine permits no other conclusion, although Synesius[11] wrote that fables originate in dreams and that a dream may perfectly well be the end, as it is the beginning of a fable.

Now Aristotle, although he maintains that Empedocles is more physicist than poet, does not conclude that he is not a poet at all.[12] And if he is in some sort a poet, the actions of the elements do constitute a subject for poetry, though at the lowest level. Therefore Lucretius and Pontano[13] are poets too, and others who have written in verse about nature. If this definition is correct, poetry ought not to be defined as the imitation of human and divine actions, since that would exclude imitation of the elements and other natural phenomena, and imitations of animals, and thus exclude the work not only of Empedocles, Lucretius, and Oppian[14] but even some of Homer's.

For another thing, it seems to me that no divine action is imitated as such, since, so far as it is divine, it cannot be imitated by any of the means proper to poetry. Still Aristotle writes in the first book of his *Politics* that many represent the lives, appearances, and features of the gods in the semblance of man; and Isocrates said that the poetry of Homer and the first tragedies were worth marvelling at because, having considered the nature of the human mind, they used both forms in an unusual way, he handling the wars and battles of the demigods in fictions, they presenting their fables directly to the eyes.[15] And Marcus Tullius Cicero said that

Homer approximated the human to the divine, *mallem divina ad nos*,[16] meaning that he described the gods as men and human passions as divine, because to speak and to consult are human acts, as getting angry and feeling pity are human passions. Athanasius too—to add a religious writer to so many pagan ones—in his book *Contra Gentiles*[17] stated that the gentiles' god is a mixture of the reasonable and the unreasonable, since his form joins the human and the bestial—as for example the Egyptians' Dog-headed Anubis—and that they even attributed to their gods deeds almost bestial. Hence, if the painter when he portrays Jupiter and Mars, Isis and Osiris, paints nothing but a human or animal form, since he cannot imitate divinity, so too the poet is an imitator not of divine forms and deeds, but mainly or properly of human ones. The difference between the imitator of divine and human things is thus as great as that between ideas proper and what we call images and likenesses. Among ideas too, as Aristotle observes in the first book of his *Metaphysics* (and his commentator Alexander agrees), there is this, or a comparable, difference between the rational and the irrational. It is no wonder, then, if images are similarly formed. But going back to Homer, I say that if he imitates the gods under the almost opposite guise of human forms, deeds, and passions, we may assert that he is an imitator of human actions and of those of the gods in so far as they are human. So too, in his battle of the frogs and mice, he transfers to animals words, feelings, and habits which are proper to men. I would therefore conclude that poetry is nothing but an imitation of human actions, which are properly imitable, and that all others are imitated not in themselves but by accident, and not as principal but as accessory. In this manner it is also possible to imitate the actions not only of animals, such as the battle of the unicorn and the elephant, or of the swan and the eagle, but also of nature, as sea storms, pestilence, floods, fire, earthquakes, and the like.

Furthermore, since, as we have said, every definition should look to the best, in defining poetry we have to set before ourselves an excellent purpose. But the best purpose is to help men by the example of human deeds, since the example of animals cannot be equally useful and that of divine actions is not suited to us. Poetry, therefore, should be directed to this purpose. Poetry, then, is an imitation of human actions, fashioned to teach us how to live. And since every action is performed with some reflection and choice, poetry

---

[9] [Cavalchini and Samuel] Notably the position of Giacomo Mazzoni in his *Difesa della Commedia di Dante* (Cesina, 1587).

[10] Plato, *Republic* (above, page 16).

[11] Synesius (fourth century B.C.), Greek philosopher.

[12] *Poetics* (above, page 52).

[13] Giovanni Pontano (1426–1503), Italian poet and historian.

[14] Appianus (fl. 206), Greek poet.

[15] [Cavalchini and Samuel] See Isocrates (436–338 B.C., Greek orator and rhetorician), *To Nicocles,* 48–9. The passage presents a number of difficulties. We follow Poma's reading *usarono* (for *Usiamo* in the text of 1594—see Poma, p. 300, note to 65, 26), and translate *falsamente* "in fictions" to approximate Tasso's words both to the passage in Isocrates and to his own meaning.

[16] [Cavalchini and Samuel] "The divine rather to us." Cicero, *Tusculan Disputations* I, 26, 65. Cicero in fact writes *divina mallem ad nos*, and Tasso slightly blurs the point of the passage: "Homer . . . attributed human feelings to the gods; I had rather he had attributed *divine feelings* to us."

[17] [Cavalchini and Samuel] 1. 9, 20b ff.

will deal with moral habit and with thought, which the Greeks called διάνοια.[18] And although such imitation affords immense pleasure, one cannot say that the purposes are two, one being pleasure, the other utility, as Horace seems to have suggested in the line,

Poets aim either to benefit, or to amuse,[19]

for one single art cannot have two purposes, one independent of the other. Either it should set aside the benefit of warning and advising, as Isocrates holds, and in accordance with the example of Homer and the tragic poets turn the whole force of its words entirely to delight; or, if it wishes to be useful, it should direct its pleasure to this end. It may be that pleasure directed to usefulness is the end of poetry. That is why we read in Isocrates's second oration[20] that the ancient poets left instructions for life, as a result of which men became better, and in the *Panathenaicus* that poetry deters us from many crimes. That is why no other training is more suitable for the young. Its usefulness, however, is rather to be judged by the art which is the architect of the others: the statesman is the one who ought to consider what poetry and what delight to forbid so that pleasure, which should be like the honey smeared on a cup when one gives medicine to a child, may not affect us like deadly poison or keep our minds idle. The poet then is to set as his purpose not delight—the opinion incidentally of Eratosthenes,[21] which Strabo picked up, defending Homer against accusations—but usefulness, because poetry, as that author, following the view of the ancients, held, is a first philosophy which instructs us from our early years in moral habits and the principles of life. Indeed his followers held that only the poet is wise.

We should at least grant that the end of poetry is not just any enjoyment but only that which is coupled with virtue, since it is utterly unworthy of a good poet to give the pleasure of reading about base and dishonest deeds, but proper to give the pleasure of learning together with virtue. Hence perhaps the purpose of pleasure (as Fracastoro[22] held in his *Dialogue on Poetry*) is not to be scorned; on the contrary, to aim at pleasure is nobler than to aim at profit, since enjoyment is sought for itself, and other things for its sake. In this respect it is like happiness, which is man's goal as

citizen; indeed nothing can be found more like happiness. Besides, it favours virtue since it exalts human nature, as we read in Athenaeus; wherefore those who love enjoyment usually become generous and magnificent. But the useful is not sought for itself but for something else; this is why it is a less noble purpose than pleasure and has less resemblance to the final purpose. Then if the poet as such has this aim, he will not wander far from the mark to which he should address his thoughts as an archer points his arrows. But as a citizen, or at least in so far as his art is subordinate to the queen of the arts, he seeks the sort of profit that is virtuous rather than useful.

Of the two ends, therefore, that the poet sets himself, one pertains to his art, the other to the higher art. But in regarding his own end, he must be careful that he does not through excess fall into the very opposite, for virtuous delights are contrary to vicious ones. They merit no praise at all, therefore, who have described amorous embraces in the fashion of Ariosto[23] depicting Ruggiero with Alcina, or Ricciardetto with Fiordispina. And perhaps Trissino[24] too might better have kept silent about many things when he virtually sets before our eyes the amorous pleasure that the emperor Justinian took in his wife. But he meant to imitate Homer, who feigns that Juno and Jupiter on the summit of Mount Ida were covered by a cloud, an invention that [Bernardo] Tasso charmingly carries over in his *Amadigi*,[25] when he describes the embrace of Mirinda and Alidoro, as though to hint that the rest must be hidden under a cloud of silence. Virgil is decidedly modest about the love-making of Aeneas and Dido, and only briefly mentions what followed the rain sent by Juno:

'To the same cave came Dido and the Trojan chief, etc.'[26]

Thus, as we have said, poetry is an imitation of human actions with the purpose of being useful by pleasing, and the poet is an imitator who could, as many have, use his art to delight without profiting. If he avoids that, he is a good poet, and in this perhaps like the orator, who is judged, as Aristotle held,[27] not only for his skill but for his will, and unlike the dialectician, who is esteemed not for his disposition but for his talent. Occasionally a definition defines not the thing simply, but the thing in its perfection, as Aristotle himself

---

[18] Dianoia. [Cavalchini and Samuel] From Aristotle's *Poetics* VI, 16. Tasso uses *costume* (usually in the plural *costumi*) to translate ηθος and *sentenzia* (elsewhere *sentenza,* the equivalent of Latin *sententia*) to translate διάνοια.
[19] Horace, *Art of Poetry* (above, page 83).
[20] [Cavalchini and Samuel] *To Nicocles,* 43.
[21] Eratosthenes (276–c. 194 B.C.), librarian at Alexandria.
[22] Girolamo Fracastoro (1483–1553), Italian physician.
[23] Ludovico Ariosto (1474–1533), *Orlando Furioso.*
[24] Gian Georgio Trissino (1478–1550).
[25] Bernardo Tasso (1493–1569), father of Torquato. [Cavalchini and Samuel] Canto 34.
[26] [Cavalchini and Samuel] "Speluncam Dido dux et Troianus eandem deveniunt," etc. (*Aeneid* 4, 165–6).
[27] [Cavalchini and Samuel] *Rhetoric* 1, 2, 1356.

says in the *Topics.* To this type belongs the definition of the orator as the man who knows everything worthy of belief on any matter whatever, and overlooks nothing—he is indeed the faultless orator. Perhaps this definition is what moved Strabo, the first to say that the poet's virtue accompanies that of the man, and that no one can be a good poet who is not a good man.[28] Later Quintilian was inspired to define the orator as a good man trained in speaking, disregarding the words of Aristotle, which call him not a good man, but a good orator.[29] I doubt, however, that this definition of Quintilian's deserved the reproach of Cavalcanti,[30] since the perfectly equipped orator could not really be defined otherwise. To be sure, goodness is no part of his skill, but a perfection of his moral nature. But if any objection is to be made, that of Alexander of Aphrodisias[31] is applicable: this kind of definition defines not the whole but the part. And perhaps Quintilian did not mean to apply his definition to all, but only to the perfect orator. Similarly, in the definition of the poet, whoever says that the poet is both a good man and a good imitator of human actions and moral habits, whose purpose is profit with delight, may not be giving a definition that fits all poets; but he does define the most excellent.

Well then, if the poet is an imitator of human actions and habits, poetry will be an imitation of the same things; and if he is a good imitator, his poetry will be good. Some, however, have maintained that the poet is not to regard the goodness of things so much as their beauty. Among them is Navagero, in Fracastoro, where he proves that the poet's aim is to consider the idea of the beautiful, and almost contradicts the view of Aristotle in his *Ethics* that the idea is not practically useful at all. But whatever Aristotle held on that point, and however his Greek commentator explained it, I certainly cannot object to the poet's concentrating on the idea of beauty. Still, if the ideas to which the orator is accustomed to direct his gaze are several, as Hermogenes[32] liked to think, I don't know why the poet must consider only that of beauty, and not the other six as well. But apparently Navagero thought that the form of beauty contains all the others or that the beautiful appears in all of them, in as much as the beautiful is inherent in clarity, grandeur, swiftness, passion, gravity, and truth. And if I am not mistaken, Navagero wanted clarity to be not only clear, but at once clear and beautiful; and so with all the other forms. But since this issue belongs particularly to diction, I shall deal with it when I come to discuss the art of using words.

Now, the opinion of Maximus of Tyre[33] does not seem to me contemptible, that philosophy and poetry are two in name but of a single substance, as light is in respect to the sun. He defines poetry as a philosophy ancient in time, metrical in sound, fictitious in subject. But philosophy, according to him, is a youthful poetry, looser in rhythm, and more open in its arguments. Now my view is that the manner of considering things differentiates one from the other: poetry considers them in as much as they are beautiful, and philosophy in as much as they are good, as the same author elsewhere notes, saying that Homer had to do two things, one pertaining to philosophy, the other to poetry, that there he regarded virtue, here the image of the fable.[34] Poetry then seeks and yearns for beauty and strives to reveal it in two ways: one narration, the other representation, both of which are contained under imitation as their genus. But sometimes it is named from one particular manner of imitation. Those therefore who have defined poetry as a narration of a memorable and possible human action have offered a definition applicable not to all kinds of poetry but only to the epic poem, or the heroic, if we prefer that name; they have excluded tragedy and comedy, unless the term narration involves an ambiguity which they might have cleared up better with the help of Aristotle's authority, as I have occasionally done, and others too more perfectly. We shall say then that narrating is proper to the epic, the name used for those who write of the deeds of heroes, as by Cicero, for example, and Eustathius,[35] the commentator on Homer. And a further difference between epic poetry and tragedy, besides the mode, arises from the difference in the means or instruments employed to imitate; for tragedy, in order to purge the soul, uses rhythm and harmony in addition to verse. Epic and tragedy differ then in two ways: in the means they use to imitate and in their mode of imitating. They agree in one element, the things imitated, since tragedy too, as Aristotle says in the *Problems,* represents the actions of heroes. But

[28] [Cavalchini and Samuel] The *locus classicus* on the poet as a good man appears in Strabo's *Geography* 1, 25. [See above, page 87].

[29] [Cavalchini and Samuel] Tasso may have in mind Quintilian, *Institutes of Oratory* 2, 15, 33–5, and Aristotle, *Rhetoric* 2, 1, 3–7.

[30] Guido Cavalcanti (?–1300), Italian poet and statesman.

[31] Alexander of Aphrodisias (fl. 200), commentator on Aristotle.

[32] Hermogenes (fl. 161–180), Greek rhetorician.

[33] Maximus of Tyre (fl. second century), Greek rhetorician.

[34] [Cavalchini and Samuel] The first reference to Maximus of Tyre is to *Dissertationes* 29, end of 169, where poetry as compared to philosophy is said to be "tempore vetustior, harmonia metrica, argumento fabulosa" [of ancient times, metrical harmony, legendary plot]. The second reference is apparently to 16.95b, where philosophy is compared in this respect with painting, but at the end of the passage Homer is said to have done two things in his books, "quorum alterum ad poësin pertinet, et fabulae speciem habet: alterum ad Philosophiam, et virtutem commendat, veritatem docet" [carry out the art of poetry and retain the form of story as well as to recommend philosophy and virtue and teach truth].

[35] Eutasthius (d. 1198), archbishop of Thessalonica.

from comedy the heroic poem differs in every way since it differs also in the things and persons imitated. Let us put aside tragedy and comedy, as well as the kind of narrative which resembles comedy as the *Iliad* resembles tragedy in that it imitates base things as Homer did in the *Margites,* in imitation of which perhaps our poet created Margut.[36] My chief intention is not to discuss these and other species.

I say that the heroic poem is an imitation of an action noble, great, and perfect, narrated in the loftiest verse, with the aim of giving profit through delight, so that the delight may get us to read more willingly and thus not lose the profit. But all poetry, of course, profits by delighting: tragedy profits by delighting, and so too comedy. Now the end of each ought to be peculiar to it: as the art of making bridles has one aim and that of making halberds another, although both are subordinate to the art of war and directed to the single goal it sets, in the same way tragedy should have one end, comedy another, the epic poem another still—or another effect since the form of each thing is distinguished by its proper effect. Now the effect of tragedy is to purge the soul by terror and compassion, and that of comedy is to move laughter at base things (as Maggi declares in his separate study *De Ridiculis*).[37] From this effect comedy derives its usefulness, since as we laugh at the baseness we see in others, we grow ashamed to commit similar baseness. The epic poem ought therefore to afford its own delight with its own effect—which is perhaps to move wonder, an effect that seems far from peculiar to it, since tragedy too moves wonder, as the words of Isocrates that I have already cited suggest: 'That is why Homer's poetry and those who first conceived of tragic plays are worthy of admiration.'[38] Still we may argue that if wonder arises from novelty, Homer's poetry might seem wonderful, but not tragedy, which dealt many years later with the same subjects, long familiar to everyone throughout Greece—unless perhaps it was the new mode of handling that made what was worn by time and use seem marvellous, as it no longer did in later tragedians. Still many statements in Aristotle's *Poetics* imply that tragedy should move wonder, and particularly this:

> since tragedy represents not only a complete action but also incidents that cause fear and pity, and this happens most of all when the incidents are unexpected and yet one is a consequence of the

other. For in that way the incidents will cause more amazement than if they happened mechanically and accidentally, etc.[39]

Moreover, marvellous events make horror and pity easier to induce. And comedy too moves wonder, baseness alone without wonder being insufficient to make us laugh at things that seem ugly: when the wonder or novelty stops, laughter too stops. All the same, to move wonder fits no kind of poetry so much as epic: so Aristotle[40] teaches, and Homer himself in Hector's flight; for the wonder that almost stuns us as we see one man alone dismaying an entire army with his threats and gestures would be inappropriate to tragedy, yet makes the epic poem marvellous. Nor would the death of Hector or others be appropriate on stage; these, as Philostratus[41] tells in the *Life of Apollonius,* were forbidden by Aeschylus, who indeed won the name 'father of tragedy' because he largely mitigated its crudity. Nor would the metamorphosis of Cadmus into a serpent, which Ovid quite properly narrated, be appropriate to the stage, nor that of Arethusa, or the nymphs transformed into ships[42] in Virgil, or Proteus into the many shapes described in the *Georgics* and earlier in the *Odyssey,* nor that in the circle of thieves of which Dante boasts: 'Let Ovid be silent about Cadmus and Arethusa; for if in his lines he turns him into a serpent and her into a fountain, I do not grudge it to him.'[43] So too with the metamorphosis in Boccaccio of Fileno[44] into a spring, or in Boiardo of the sorcerer into various shapes,[45] or of Ariosto's Astolfo into myrtle.[46] And so too with many other transformations that we read of with wonder in many other poets, ancient and modern. We gladly read in epic about many wonders that might be unsuitable on stage, both because they are proper to epic and because the reader allows many liberties which the spectator forbids. The use of machines is seldom therefore praised in tragedy,[47] while in the epic gods and angels frequently descend from heaven and participate in human actions, giving counsel and help, as

---

[36]The work *Margites* was once attributed to Homer. [Cavalchini and Samuel] Tasso writes *nostri poeti* implying that Margut also appears in works other than Pulci's *Morgante.*

[37]Vincenzo Maggi (d. 1564), Italian critic.

[38][Cavalchini and Samuel] Tasso gives the passage from *To Nicocles,* 48–9, in Italian.

[39]*Poetics* (above, page 57).

[40]*Poetics* (above, page 66).

[41]Flavius Philostratus (above, page 124).

[42][Cavalchini and Samuel] Tasso miswrites *delle ninfe converse in navi* (of the nymphs transformed into ships) for the transformation of the ships into nymphs in *Aeneid* 9, 80–122.

[43][Cavalchini and Samuel]
Taccia di Cadmo d'Aretusa Ovidio;
che se quello in serpente e questa in fonte
converte poetando, io non l'invidio.

[44][Cavalchini and Samuel] *In Filocolo.*

[45][Cavalchini and Samuel] *Orlando Furioso* 6, 20–53.

[46][Cavalchini and Samuel] *Cantos* 5ff.

[47]Aristotle, *Poetics* (above, page 59).

Apollo and Minerva do in the *Iliad* and *Odyssey* of Homer and in the *Ercole* of Giraldl,[48] Venus in Virgil's *Aeneid* and in Bolognetti,[49] and many other gods in these and other poems. So too the angel Michael descends in *Orlando Furioso*[50] and the angel Palladio and Nettunio in the *Italia Liberata*.[51] Thus all these poems seem conceived and brought to a conclusion virtually by providence itself, to which tragedy grants scarcely any role since there it would also cause indignation, which Aristotle did not allow.[52] Giraldi and others, therefore, should not have introduced Nemesis on the stage. Moreover, other kinds of poem move wonder in order to move laughter or compassion or some other emotion. But the epic poet has no other purpose, moves compassion in order to move wonder, and in fact moves it much more powerfully and more often. We shall then say that the epic poem is an imitation of a noble action, great and perfect, narrated in the loftiest verse, with the purpose of moving the mind to wonder and thus being useful.

The epic poem, like any other thing that is a whole, has its components. Its qualitative components are doubtless four: (First is) the fable, which Aristotle defines as the imitation of the action and for its sake of those who perform the action—this part he calls the first principle and soul of the poem. The second is the moral habit of the persons introduced in the fable. The third is thought. The last is diction.[53] But the number of quantitative parts is more doubtful, although they can perhaps be divided into another four thus: in the first part, which corresponds to the prologue of tragedy, the poet proposes, narrates, declares the present state of things, and supplies information about the past, as Homer does in his poems, particularly the *Odyssey;* in the second part, things become disturbed; in the third they begin to unravel; in the fourth they reach their end, their completion, so to speak. And if we wish to use their proper names, they can be called the introduction, the perturbation, the reversal, and the conclusion. Among these I have not counted the episode, although this part is proper to both tragic and epic poems, more in fact to epic, since there its place is not fixed, as the quantitative parts must be. One might also take the quantitative parts as only three: the beginning, the middle, and the end, as Aristotle calls them in defining the whole. But this division is more appropriate to poems whose fable is not involved but simple. The parts of the fable are three. (First is) the reversal, which the Greeks called peripeteia, a change from good to bad fortune or from bad to good; in the heroic poem it is a double change, because some characters pass from prosperity to adversity and others the reverse. Still it ought always to be a change for the better because the happier ending is more suitable to this kind of poem. Pulci, therefore, does not merit much praise for ending with the death of Orlando and other paladins.[54] The second part of the fable is recognition, a passing from ignorance to knowledge of persons once known and later forgotten, whether simple, as that of Ulysses, or mutual, as between Iphigenia and Orestes; and this passage should cause either happiness or misery. The third part is *pathos,* that is a grievous perturbation full of anxieties, such as deaths and wounds and lamentations and complaints, which can move pity; and this part can be seen at the end of the *Iliad.*

Now, having ascertained the nature of this noblest kind of poem and its parts, we may proceed to consider with what art they may be composed, and then judge the definition of the idea. We shall also give some attention to the material, because artificial forms involve consideration of their material. And by the material of poetry I do not mean letters, syllables, words, as Scaliger did, since these may be the materials of both speech and verse; the material of poetry to my mind is properly defined as the subject which it undertakes to treat. As Porphyry[55] says, in all things a certain something is usually present that corresponds proportionally to matter and form; and this is not properly the end, as Scaliger thought, because the matter is never the end, nor are the material and the final cause the same. Rather, the formal and final causes usually go together; as the Latins say, they coincide. The end, therefore, is the form given by the skill of the poet, who, by adding, diminishing, and varying, disposes the matter and gives another aspect to the action and things he deals with.

Here I would make a fresh start in my treatment of the poet's art if I were not faced with an objection Castelvetro makes against Aristotle: that he ought not to have dealt with the poetic before the historic art, since just as history precedes poetry and truth verisimilitude, so the art of setting down the true should be given first, and then that of adorning the verisimilar—which might not be necessary after the first.[56] Such an opinion strikes me as based on two fundamental concepts, one altogether false: that history precedes

---

[48]Giraldi Cinthio (1504–1573), Italian poet and dramatist.
[49]Francesco Bolognetti (c. 1520–c. 1576), Italian poet.
[50][Cavalchini and Samuel] Malagigi in *Orlando Innamorato.*
[51][Cavalchini and Samuel] Canto 14.
[52]*Poetics* (above, page 57).
[53]*Poetics* (above, page 55).

[54][Cavalchini and Samuel] *Morgante* 27, 149–53.
[55]Porphyry (233–305), Neoplatonic Greek philosopher.
[56]Castelvetro (above, page 181).

poetry. For poets are the most ancient of all writers, and historians began to write centuries later; for which reason we ought not to call that art first whose matter was born later. Moreover, if the historian's art allows a place to rhythm, ornament, and figures of speech, who does not know that these were virtually lent to the writer by the poet? Neither the orator nor others who write prose have therefore anything that is not, so to speak, usurped. But if Castelvetro or others should reply that history, although perhaps second in time, comes first in nature in as much as it sets down the true, which precedes its semblance, I would answer that the poet considers the verisimilar only as it is universal, and therefore it was correct to give precedence to the art of writing on the universal. Nor need we argue whether the universal exists before or after particular things; as Aristotle said more than once, it is enough that it is better known. Aristotle did not give instructions for writing history, perhaps because he thought it a simpler matter. If it belongs to the orator, rhetorical precepts are enough; and if it has some things of its own, as Demetrius Phalereus[57] implies (assigning one kind of sentence structure to the historian, another to the orator), this is not enough to justify a distinct and separate art. The same skill can be employed on the true and the verisimilar. In fact when Aristotle says that poetry deals rather with the universal, he implies the function of history, which is to narrate the particular.[58] But this is not imitating, since imitation is by its nature linked not with truth, but with verisimilitude. Historians, then, ought not to imitate; and if the speeches they include are not without imitation, it is usually because the historian does not narrate what was said in the senate or the army, but what is likely to have been said. Indeed the kind of oration appropriate to the historian is the indirect rather than the direct, as Trogus Pompeius[59] thought. In many speeches in the Greek historians Herodotus and Xenophon, and others later, one sees almost a poetic imitation, where the historian, not content with his own territory, seems to trespass on the confines of poetry. But these things, if I may, I shall examine in the proper place, putting on one side of the scale the judgement of Polybius, who both wrote history and taught how it should be written, and of Dionysius of Halicarnassus, who wrote a commentary on Thucydides, and on the other the authority of Thucydides himself and the other two historians named above, as well as Livy and Sallust, the most highly esteemed Latin historians, who, if I am right, imitated the Greeks. This imitation, however, is not the kind we are discussing, nor the kind Fracastoro meant, which is unsuitable to the historian. Thus, given the diversity of writers and their views, it will not seem superfluous to deal with the historian's art. But now I propose to write of the things I have begun.

---

[57]Demetrius (c. 345–283 B.C.), Greek orator and poet. [Cavalchini and Samuel] *On Style* I, 19–21.
[58]*Poetics* (above, page 57).

---

[59]The earlier historian (fl. in the age of Augustus) from whose work Justinus got his material.

Sir Francis Bacon

1561–1626

Sir Francis Bacon, member of Parliament, Queen's Counsel Extraordinary, King's Counsel, Solicitor General, Attorney General, and in 1618 finally Lord Chancellor, was also one of the greatest intellectual figures of his age. His *Essays,* which enjoyed great popularity, and other works (*The Advancement of Learning, The Great Instauration,* and *The New Organon*) have placed him among the important British philosophers. Champion of the experimental method, Bacon gives in *The Advancement of Learning* a new twist to the contrast of poetry to other things. Usually, since Aristotle, the contrast has been to history and philosophy. Bacon, anticipating the distinction between subject and object that comes with empirical method, writes: "[Poesie] doth raise and erect the mind, by submitting the show of things to the desires of the mind, whereas Reason doth buckle and bow the mind unto the nature of things." For Bacon, as for Sidney earlier, poetry seems to present an improvement over the world we live in, since it can express our desires as well as our experience, to which history is tied. In this he anticipates Northrop Frye's dialectic of repugnance and desire as the poles of poetic subject matter. Further, because it submits to the desires of the mind it is involved with morality or a vision of what is good. But Bacon's improved world is the world of desire, not that of Platonic ideas.

Bacon enters into the study of mythology, a significant intellectual interest from his time into the nineteenth century and beyond (though questions about myth changed radically in the twentieth century). Generally, three attitudes toward myth vied for ascendancy. Some held that myths were allegories of religious mysteries, Homer being read in this way by Porphyry. Some, called Euhemerists, after Euhemerus (fl. c. 300 B.C.), held that myths were histories corrupted over time by linguistic change, the twentieth-century poet Robert Graves having revived this tradition. Others thought that myths were stories arising out of primitive experience of nature, as in Vico (below, page 313). Bacon doesn't think of all myths as veiling an allegorical meaning, but he believes that some myths surely must. At the same time he thinks that many myths ingeniously interpreted as allegories were never so intended.

In *The Great Instauration,* part of the preface to which appears below, Bacon champions as his own the method of experimental inquiry into nature. He regards induction as the means of emancipating the mind from the traditional deductive logic of the syllogism, which he holds produces no intellectual progress and provides no release from the "idols or phantoms by which the mind is occupied." Bacon's method is a precursor of modern efforts to make an inductive science of both literature (Zola, below, page 698) and criticism (Taine, below, page 639). The opposing force is modern efforts to distinguish poetry from science, especially among the American New Critics. Perhaps Bacon's most vociferous critic among literary artists was William Blake, who accused him of atheism and declared that his philosophy had "ruined England."

See Fulton H. Anderson, ed., *The New Organon and Related Writings* (1960). A standard edition is that by James Spedding, R. L. Ellis, and D. D. Heath, eds., in three volumes (1870). See C. D. Broad, *The Philosophy of Francis Bacon* (1926); M. W. Bundy, "Bacon's True Opinion of Poetry," *Studies in Philology* XXXII (1930), 244–64; L. C. Knights, "Bacon and the Seventeenth-Century Dissociation of Sensibility," *Scrutiny* XI (1943), 268–85; Karl R. Wallace, *Francis Bacon on Communication and Rhetoric* (1943); F. H. Anderson, *The Philosophy of Francis Bacon* (1948); D. G. James, *The Dream of Learning* (1951); J. L. Harrison, "Bacon's View of Rhetoric, Poetry, and Imagination," *Huntington Library Quarterly* XX (1957), 107–26; Charles Whitney, *Francis Bacon and Modernity* (1986); Robert M. Schuler, *Francis Bacon and Scientific Poetry* (1992); W. A. Sessions, *Francis Bacon Revisited* (1996); Lisa Jardine and Alan Stewart, *Hostage to Fortune: The Troubled Life of Francis Bacon* (1998); Stephen Gaukroger, *Francis Bacon and the Transformation of Early Modern Philosophy* (2001).

from

The Advancement of Learning

Poesy is a part of learning in measure of words for the most part restrained, but in all other points extremely licensed, and doth truly refer to the imagination, which, being not tied to the laws of matter, may at pleasure join that which nature hath severed, and sever that which nature hath joined, and so make unlawful matches and divorces of things: "*Pictoribus atque poetis*, etc."[1] It is taken in two senses in respect of words or matter. In the first sense it is but a character of style, and belongeth to arts of speech, and is not pertinent for the present. In the latter, it is, as hath been said, one of the principal portions of learning, and is nothing else but feigned history, which may be styled as well in prose as in verse.

The use of this feigned history hath been to give some shadow of satisfaction to the mind of man in those points wherein the nature of things doth deny it, the world being in proportion inferior to the soul; by reason whereof there is agreeable to the spirit of man a more ample greatness, a more exact goodness, and a more absolute variety than can be found in the nature of things. Therefore, because the acts or events of true history have not that magnitude which satisfieth the mind of man, poesy feigneth acts and events greater and more heroical; because true history propoundeth the successes and issues of actions not so agreeable to the merits of virtue and vice, therefore poesy feigns them more just in retribution and more according to revealed provi-

dence; because true history representeth actions and events more ordinary and less interchanged, therefore poesy endueth them with more rareness and more unexpected and alternative variations: so as it appeareth that poesy serveth and confereth to magnanimity, morality, and to delectation. And therefore it was ever thought to have some participation of divineness, because it doth raise and erect the mind, by submitting the shows of things to the desires of the mind, whereas reason doth buckle and bow the mind unto the nature of things. And we see that by these insinuations and congruities with man's nature and pleasure, joined also with the agreement and consort it hath with music, it hath had access and estimation in rude times and barbarous regions, where other learning stood excluded.

The division of poesy which is aptest in the propriety thereof (besides those divisions which are common unto it with history, as feigned chronicles, feigned lives, and the appendices of history, as feigned epistles, feigned orations, and the rest) is into poesy narrative, representative, and allusive. The narrative is a mere imitation of history with the excesses before remembered, choosing for subject commonly wars and love, rarely state, and sometimes pleasure or mirth. Representative is as a visible history, and is an image of actions as if they were present, as history is of actions in nature as they are, that is past; allusive, or parabolical, is a narration applied only to express some special purpose or conceit: which latter kind of parabolical wisdom was much more in use in the ancient times, as by the fables of Aesop, and the brief sentences of the seven,[2] and the use of hiero-

---

The Advancement of Learning was first published in 1605. The text is based on the 1605 edition.
[1] "Painters as well as poets." Horace (above, page 79).

[2] There were different lists of the so-called Wise Men of Ancient Greece. They usually included Thales, Solon, Bias, Pittacus, Periander, Chilon, and Cleabolus.

glyphics may appear. And the cause was for that it was then of necessity to express any point of reason which was more sharp or subtle than the vulgar in that manner, because men in those times wanted both variety of examples and subtlety of conceit: and as hieroglyphics were before letters, so parables were before arguments: and nevertheless now and at all times they do retain much life and vigor, because reason cannot be so sensible, nor examples so fit.

But there remaineth yet another use of poesy parabolical opposite to that which we last mentioned; for that tendeth to demonstrate and illustrate that which is taught or delivered, and this other to retire and obscure it: that is, when the secrets and mysteries of religion, policy, or philosophy, are involved in fables or parables. Of this in divine poesy we see the use is authorized. In heathen poesy we see the exposition of fables doth fall out sometimes with great felicity, as in the fable that the giants being overthrown in their way against the gods, the earth their mother in revenge thereof brought forth fame:

> Illam terra parens ira irritata deorem,
> Extremam, ut perhibent, Cueo Enceladoque sororem
> Progenuit:[3]

expounded that when princes and monarchs have suppressed actual and open rebels, then the malignity of people, which is the mother of rebellion, doth bring forth libels and slanders, and taxations of the states, which is of the same kind with rebellion, but more feminine: so in the fable that the rest of the gods having conspired to bind Jupiter, Pallas called Briareus with his hundred hands to his aid, expounded that monarchies need not fear any curbing of their absoluteness by mighty subjects, as long as by wisdom they keep the hearts of the people, who will be sure to come in on their side: so in the fable that Achilles was brought up under Chyron the centaur, who was part a man and part a beast, expounded ingenuously, but corruptly, by Machiavelli[4] that it belongeth to the education and discipline of princes to know as well how to play the part of the lion in violence and the fox in guile, as of the man in virtue and justice. Nevertheless in many the like encounters, I do rather think that the fable was first and the exposition devised than that the moral was first and thereupon the fable framed. For I find it was an ancient vanity in Chrysippus that troubled himself with great contention to fasten the assertions of the

Stoics upon the fictions of the ancient poets: but yet that all the fables and fictions of the poets were but pleasure and not figure, I interpose no opinion.[5] Surely of those poets which are now extant, even Homer himself (notwithstanding he was made a kind of scripture by the later schools of the Grecians) yet I should without any difficulty pronounce, that his fables had no such inwardness in his own meaning: but what they might have, upon a more original tradition, is not easy to affirm, for he was not the inventor of many of them. In this third part of learning which is poesy, I can report no deficience. For being as a plant that cometh of the lust of the earth, without a formal seed, it hath sprung up and spread abroad, more than any other kind: but to ascribe unto it that which is due for the expressing of affections, passions, corruptions and customs, we are beholding to poets more than to the philosophers' works, and for wit and eloquence not much less than to orators' harangues.

Preface to the Wisdom of the Ancients

The most ancient times (except what is preserved of them in the scriptures) are buried in oblivion and silence; to that silence succeeded the fables of the poets; to those fables the written records which have come down to us. Thus between the hidden depths of antiquity and the days of tradition and evidence that followed there is drawn a veil, as it were, of fables, which come in and occupy the middle region that separates what has perished from what survives.

Now I suppose most people will think I am but entertaining myself with a toy, and using much the same kind of licence in expounding the poets' fables which the poets themselves did in inventing them; and it is true that if I had a mind to vary and relieve my severer studies with some such exercise of pleasure for my own or my reader's recreation, I might very fairly indulge in it. But that is not my meaning. Not but that I know very well what pliant stuff fable is made of, how freely it will follow any way you please to draw it, and how easily with a little dexterity and dis-

---

[3] "Angered by the gods, Mother Earth, it is said, gave birth to the last one, sister to Caeus and Enceladus." Virgil, *Aeneid* IV, 178.
[4] Niccolo Machiavelli (1469–1527), Italian writer, author of *The Prince* (1532).

[5] There has been disagreement since Bacon, continuing even today, over whether myths were originally allegories of philosophy or were later interpreted in an allegorical way. Bacon continues to discuss this in the next selection.
De Sapientia Veterum (*The Wisdom of the Ancients*) was first published in 1609. The translation from the Latin is from James Spedding, R. L. Ellis, and D. D. Heath, eds., *The Works of Francis Bacon* (1861–1864).

course of wit meanings which it was never meant to bear may be plausibly put upon it. Neither have I forgotten that there has been old abuse of the thing in practice; that many, wishing only to gain the sanction and reverence of antiquity for doctrines and inventions of their own, have tried to twist the fables of the poets into that sense; and that this is neither a modern vanity nor a rare one, but old of standing and frequent in use; that Chrysippus[1] long ago, interpreting the oldest poets after the manner of an interpreter of dreams, made them out to be Stoics; and that the alchemists more absurdly still have discovered in the pleasant and sportive fictions of the transformation of bodies, allusion to experiments of the furnace. All this I have duly examined and weighed, as well as all the levity and looseness with which people indulge their fancy in the matter of allegories; yet for all this I cannot change my mind. For in the first place, to let the follies and licence of a few detract from the honour of parables in general is not to be allowed, being indeed a boldness savouring of profanity, seeing that religion delights in such veils and shadows; and to take them away would be almost to interdict all communion between divinity and humanity. But passing that and speaking of human wisdom only, I do certainly for my own part (I freely and candidly confess) incline to this opinion, that beneath no small number of the fables of the ancient poets there lay from the very beginning a mystery and an allegory. It may be that my reverence for the primitive time carries me too far, but the truth is that in some of these fables, as well in the very frame and texture of the story as in the propriety of the names by which the persons that figure in it are distinguished, I find a conformity and connexion with the thing signified, so close and so evident that one cannot help believing such a signification to have been designed and meditated from the first, and purposely shadowed out. For who is there so impenetrable and that can so shut his eyes to a plain thing, but when he is told that after the *Giants* were put down *Fame* sprang up as their posthumous sister,[2] he will at once see that it is meant of those murmurs of parties and seditious rumours which always circulate for a time after the suppression of a rebellion? Or again who can hear that the *Giant Typhon* cut off and carried away *Jupiter's* sinews, and that *Mercury* stole them from Typhon and gave them back to Jupiter,[3] without at once perceiving that it relates to successful rebellions, by which kings have their sinews both of money and authority cut off; yet not so but that by fair words and wise edicts the

minds of the subjects may be presently reconciled, and as it were stolen back, and so kings recover their strength? Or who can hear that in that memorable expedition of the gods against the giants[4] the braying of *Silenus's ass* had a principal stroke in putting the giants to flight, and not be sure that the incident was invented in allusion to the vast attempts of rebels, dissipated as they commonly are by empty rumours and vain terrors? Then again there is a conformity and significancy in the very names, which must be clear to everybody. Metis, Jupiter's wife, plainly means counsel; Typhon, swelling; Pan, the universe; Nemesis, revenge; and the like. And what if we find here and there a bit of real history underneath, or some things added only for ornament, or times confounded, or part of one fable transferred to another and a new allegory introduced? Such things could not but occur in stories invented (as these were) by men who both lived in different ages and had different ends, some being more modern, some more ancient, some having in their thoughts natural philosophy, others civil affairs; and therefore they need not trouble us.

But there is yet another sign, and one of no small value, that these fables contain a hidden and involved meaning, which is that some of them are so absurd and stupid upon the face of the narrative taken by itself, that they may be said to give notice from afar and cry out that there is a parable below. For a fable that is probable may be thought to have been composed merely for pleasure, in imitation of history. But when a story is told which could never have entered any man's head either to conceive or relate on its own account, we must presume that it had some further reach. What a fiction (for instance) is that of Jupiter and Metis! Jupiter took Metis to wife: as soon as he saw that she was with child, he ate her up; whereupon he grew to be with child himself, and so brought forth out of his head Pallas in armour![5] Surely I think no man had ever a dream so monstrous and extravagant, and out of all natural ways of thinking.

But the consideration which has most weight with me is this, that few of these fables were invented, as I take it, by those who recited and made them famous—Homer, Hesiod, and the rest. For had they been certainly the production of that age and of those authors by whose report they have come down to us, I should not have thought of looking for anything great or lofty from such a source. But it will appear upon an attentive examination that they are delivered not as new inventions then first published, but as stories already received and believed. And since they are told in different ways by writers nearly contemporaneous, it is easy to

---

[1] Greek stoic philosopher (280–207 B.C.).
[2] Virgil, *Aeneid* IV, 178ff. This and later citations may not actually be Bacon's immediate sources.
[3] Hesiod, *Theogony,* 819ff.

---

[4] Euripides, *Cyclops,* 5ff.
[5] Pindar, *Olympian Odes* VII, 34ff.

see that what all the versions have in common came from ancient tradition, while the parts in which they vary are the additions introduced by the several writers for embellishment—a circumstance which gives them in my eyes a much higher value: for so they must be regarded as neither being the inventions nor belonging to the age of the poets themselves, but as sacred relics and light airs breathing out of better times, that were caught from the traditions of more ancient nations and so received into the flutes and trumpets of the Greeks.

Nevertheless, if any one be determined to believe that the allegorical meaning of the fable was in no case original and genuine, but that always the fable was first and the allegory put in after, I will not press that point; but allowing him to enjoy that gravity of judgment (of the dull and leaden order though it be) which he affects, I will attack him, if indeed he be worth the pains, in another manner upon a fresh ground. Parables have been used in two ways, and (which is strange) for contrary purposes. For they serve to disguise and veil the meaning, and they serve also to clear and throw light upon it. To avoid dispute then, let us give up the former of these uses. Let us suppose that these fables were things without any definite purpose, made only for pleasure. Still there remains the latter use. No force of wit can deprive us of that. Nor is there any man of ordinary learning that will object to the reception of it as a thing grave and sober, and free from all vanity, of prime use to the sciences, and sometimes indispensable: I mean the employment of parables as a method of teaching, whereby inventions that are new and abstruse and remote from vulgar opinions may find an easier passage to the understanding.[6] On this account it was that in the old times, when the inventions and conclusions of human reason (even those that are now trite and vulgar) were as yet new and strange, the world was full of all kinds of fables, and enigmas, and parables, and similitudes: and these were used not as a device for shadowing and concealing the meaning, but as a method of making it understood; the understandings of men being then rude and impatient of all subtleties that did not address themselves to the sense, indeed scarcely capable of them. For as hieroglyphics came before letters, so parables came before arguments. And even now if any one wish to let new light on any subject into men's minds, and that without offence or harshness, he must still go the same way and call in the aid of similitudes.

Upon the whole I conclude with this: the wisdom of the primitive ages was either great or lucky: great, if they knew what they were doing and invented the figure to

shadow the meaning; lucky, if without meaning or intending it they fell upon matter which gives occasion to such worthy contemplations. My own pains, if there be any help in them, I shall think well bestowed either way: I shall be throwing light either upon antiquity or upon nature itself.

That the thing has been attempted by others I am of course aware, but if I may speak what I think freely without mincing it, I must say that the pains which have been hitherto taken that way, though great and laborious, have gone near to deprive the inquiry of all its beauty and worth; while men of no experience in affairs, nor any learning beyond a few commonplaces, have applied the sense of the parables to some generalities and vulgar observations, without attaining their true force, their genuine propriety, or their deeper reach. Here, on the other hand, it will be found (if I mistake not) that though the subjects be old, yet the matter is new; while leaving behind us the open and level parts, we bend our way towards the nobler heights that rise beyond.

from

The New Organon

The Plan of the Great Instauration

The Arguments of the Several Parts

It being part of my design to set everything forth, as far as may be, plainly and perspicuously (for nakedness of the mind is still, as nakedness of the body once was, the companion of innocence and simplicity), let me first explain the order and plan of the work. I distribute it into six parts.

The first part exhibits a summary or general description of the knowledge which the human race at present possesses. For I thought it good to make some pause upon that which is received; that thereby the old may be more easily made perfect and the new more easily approached. And I hold the improvement of that which we have to be as much an object as the acquisition of more. Besides which it will make me the better listened to; for "He that is ignorant (says the proverb) receives not the words of knowledge, unless thou first tell him that which is in his own heart." We will therefore make a coasting voyage along the shores of the arts and sciences received, not without importing into them some useful things by the way.

In laying out the divisions of the sciences, however, I take into account not only things already invented and known, but likewise things omitted which ought to be there.

---

[6]This argument for the use of myths is transferred to the defense of poetry. For example, see Shelley (below, page 538).

For there are found in the intellectual as in the terrestrial globe waste regions as well as cultivated ones. It is no wonder, therefore, if I am sometimes obliged to depart from the ordinary divisions. For in adding to the total you necessarily alter the parts and sections; and the received divisions of the sciences are fitted only to the received sum of them as it stands now.

With regard to those things which I shall mark as omitted, I intend not merely to set down a simple title or a concise argument of that which is wanted. For as often as I have occasion to report anything as deficient, the nature of which is at all obscure, so that men may not perhaps easily understand what I mean or what the work is which I have in my head, I shall always (provided it be a matter of any worth) take care to subjoin either directions for the execution of such work, or else a portion of the work itself executed by myself as a sample of the whole, thus giving assistance in every case either by work or by counsel. For if it were for the sake of my own reputation only and other men's interests were not concerned in it, I would not have any man think that in such cases merely some light and vague notion has crossed my mind, and that the things which I desire and attempt are no better than wishes, when they are in fact things which men may certainly command if they will, and of which I have formed in my own mind a clear and detailed conception. For I do not propose merely to survey these regions in my mind, like an augur taking auspices, but to enter them like a general who means to take possession. So much for the first part of the work.

Having thus coasted past the ancient arts, the next point is to equip the intellect for passing beyond. To the second part, therefore, belongs the doctrine concerning the better and more perfect use of human reason in the inquisition of things, and the true helps of the understanding, that thereby (as far as the condition of mortality and humanity allows) the intellect may be raised and exalted, and made capable of overcoming the difficulties and obscurities of nature. The art which I introduce with this view (which I call "Interpretation of Nature") is a kind of logic, though the difference between it and the ordinary logic is great, indeed, immense. For the ordinary logic professes to contrive and prepare helps and guards for the understanding, as mine does; and in this one point they agree. But mine differs from it in three points especially—viz., in the end aimed at, in the order of demonstration, and in the starting point of the inquiry.

For the end which this science of mine proposes is the invention not of arguments but of arts; not of things in accordance with principles, but of principles themselves; not of probable reasons, but of designations and directions for works. And as the intention is different, so, accordingly, is the

effect; the effect of the one being to overcome an opponent in argument, of the other to command nature in action.

In accordance with this end is also the nature and order of the demonstrations. For in the ordinary logic almost all the work is spent about the syllogism.[1] Of induction, the logicians seem hardly to have taken any serious thought, but they pass it by with a slight notice and hasten on to the formulæ of disputation. I, on the contrary, reject demonstration by syllogism as acting too confusedly and letting nature slip out of its hands. For although no one can doubt that things which agree in a middle term agree with one another (which is a proposition of mathematical certainty), yet it leaves an opening for deception, which is this: the syllogism consists of propositions—propositions of words; and words are the tokens and signs of notions. Now if the very notions of the mind (which are as the soul of words and the basis of the whole structure) be improperly and overhastily abstracted from facts, vague, not sufficiently definite, faulty—in short, in many ways, the whole edifice tumbles. I therefore reject the syllogism, and that not only as regards principles (for to principles the logicians themselves do not apply it) but also as regards middle propositions, which, though obtainable no doubt by the syllogism, are, when so obtained, barren of works, remote from practice, and altogether unavailable for the active department of the sciences. Although, therefore, I leave to the syllogism and these famous and boasted modes of demonstration their jurisdiction over popular arts and such as are matter of opinion (in which department I leave all as it is), yet in dealing with the nature of things I use induction throughout, and that in the minor propositions as well as the major. For I consider induction to be that form of demonstration which upholds the sense, and closes with nature, and comes to the very brink of operation, if it does not actually deal with it.

Hence it follows that the order of demonstration is likewise inverted. For hitherto the proceeding has been to fly at once from the sense and particulars up to the most general propositions, as certain fixed poles for the argument to turn upon, and from these to derive the rest by middle terms—a short way, no doubt, but precipitate and one which will never lead to nature, though it offers an easy and ready way to disputation. Now my plan is to proceed regularly and gradually from one axiom to another, so that the most general are not reached till the last; but then, when you do come to them, you find them to be not empty notions but well defined, and such as nature would really recognize as her first principles, and such as lie at the heart and marrow of things.

---

[1] Bacon is critical here of the tradition of logic that descended from Aristotle (above, page 48).

But the greatest change I introduce is in the form itself of induction and the judgment made thereby. For the induction of which the logicians speak, which proceeds by simple enumeration, is a puerile thing, concludes at hazard, is always liable to be upset by a contradictory instance, takes into account only what is known and ordinary, and leads to no result.

Now what the sciences stand in need of is a form of induction which shall analyze experience and take it to pieces, and by a due process of exclusion and rejection lead to an inevitable conclusion. And if that ordinary mode of judgment practiced by the logicians was so laborious, and found exercise for such great wits, how much more labor must we be prepared to bestow upon this other, which is extracted not merely out of the depths of the mind, but out of the very bowels of nature.

Nor is this all. For I also sink the foundations of the sciences deeper and firmer; and I begin the inquiry nearer the source than men have done heretofore, submitting to examination those things which the common logic takes on trust. For first, the logicians borrow the principles of each science from the science itself; secondly, they hold in reverence the first notions of the mind; and lastly, they receive as conclusive the immediate informations of the sense, when well disposed. Now upon the first point, I hold that true logic ought to enter the several provinces of science armed with a higher authority than belongs to the principles of those sciences themselves, and ought to call those putative principles to account until they are fully established. Then with regard to the first notions of the intellect, there is not one of the impressions taken by the intellect when left to go its own way, but I hold it as suspect and no way established until it has submitted to a new trial and a fresh judgment has been thereupon pronounced. And lastly, the information of the sense itself I sift and examine in many ways. For certain it is that the senses deceive; but then at the same time they supply the means of discovering their own errors; only the errors are here, the means of discovery are to seek.

The sense fails in two ways. Sometimes it gives no information, sometimes it gives false information. For first, there are very many things which escape the sense, even when best disposed and no way obstructed, by reason either of the subtlety of the whole body or the minuteness of the parts, or distance of place, or slowness or else swiftness of motion, or familiarity of the object, or other causes. And again when the sense does apprehend a thing its apprehension is not much to be relied upon. For the testimony and information of the sense has reference always to man, not to the universe; and it is a great error to assert that the sense is the measure of things.

To meet these difficulties, I have sought on all sides diligently and faithfully to provide helps for the sense—substitutes to supply its failures, rectifications to correct its errors; and this I endeavor to accomplish not so much by instruments as by experiments. For the subtlety of experiments is far greater than that of the sense itself, even when assisted by exquisite instruments—such experiments, I mean, as are skillfully and artificially devised for the express purpose of determining the point in question. To the immediate and proper perception of the sense, therefore, I do not give much weight; but I contrive that the office of the sense shall be only to judge of the experiment, and that the experiment itself shall judge of the thing. And thus I conceive that I perform the office of a true priest of the sense (from which all knowledge in nature must be sought, unless men mean to go mad) and a not unskillful interpreter of its oracles; and that while others only profess to uphold and cultivate the sense, I do so in fact. Such then are the provisions I make for finding the genuine light of nature and kindling and bringing it to bear. And they would be sufficient of themselves if the human intellect were even and like a fair sheet of paper with no writing on it. But since the minds of men are strangely possessed and beset so that there is no true and even surface left to reflect the genuine rays of things, it is necessary to seek a remedy for this also.

Now the idols, or phantoms, by which the mind is occupied are either adventitious or innate. The adventitious come into the mind from without—namely, either from the doctrines and sects of philosophers or from perverse rules of demonstration. But the innate are inherent in the very nature of the intellect, which is far more prone to error than the sense is. For let men please themselves as they will in admiring and almost adoring the human mind, this is certain: that as an uneven mirror distorts the rays of objects according to its own figure and section, so the mind, when it receives impressions of objects through the sense, cannot be trusted to report them truly, but in forming its notions mixes up its own nature with the nature of things.

And as the first two kinds of idols are hard to eradicate, so idols of this last kind cannot be eradicated at all. All that can be done is to point them out, so that this insidious action of the mind may be marked and reproved (else as fast as old errors are destroyed new ones will spring up out of the ill complexion of the mind itself, and so we shall have but a change of errors, and not a clearance); and to lay it down once for all as a fixed and established maxim that the intellect is not qualified to judge except by means of induction, and induction in its legitimate form. This doctrine, then, of the expurgation of the intellect to qualify it for dealing with truth is comprised in three refutations: the refutation of the philosophies; the refutation of the demonstrations; and the refutation of the natural human reason. The explanation of which things, and of the true relation between the nature of things and the nature of the mind, is as the strewing and decoration of the bridal chamber of the mind and the universe, the divine goodness assisting, out of which marriage let us hope (and be this the prayer of the bridal song) there may spring helps to man, and a line and race of inventions that may in some degree subdue and overcome the necessities and miseries of humanity. This is the second part of the work.

But I design not only to indicate and mark out the ways, but also to enter them. And therefore the third part of the work embraces the "phenomena of the universe"; that is to say, experience of every kind, and such a natural history as may serve for a foundation to build philosophy upon. For a good method of demonstration or form of interpreting nature may keep the mind from going astray or stumbling, but it is not any excellence of method that can supply it with the material of knowledge. Those, however, who aspire not to guess and divine, but to discover and know, who propose not to devise mimic and fabulous worlds of their own, but to examine and dissect the nature of this very world itself, must go to facts themselves for everything. Nor can the place of this labor and search and world-wide perambulation be supplied by any genius or meditation or argumentation; no, not if all men's wits could meet in one. This, therefore, we must have or the business must be forever abandoned. But up to this day such has been the condition of men in this matter that it is no wonder if nature will not give herself into their hands.

For first, the information of the sense itself, sometimes failing, sometimes false; observation, careless, irregular, and led by chance; tradition, vain, and fed on rumor; practice, slavishly bent upon its work; experiment, blind, stupid, vague, and prematurely broken off; lastly, natural history trivial and poor—all these have contributed to supply the understanding with very bad materials for philosophy and the sciences.

Then an attempt is made to mend the matter by a preposterous subtlety and winnowing of argument. But this comes too late, the case being already past remedy, and is far from setting the business right or sifting away the errors. The only hope, therefore, of any greater increase or progress lies in a reconstruction of the sciences.

Of this reconstruction the foundation must be laid in natural history, and that of a new kind and gathered on a new principle. For it is in vain that you polish the mirror if there are no images to be reflected; and it is as necessary that the intellect should be supplied with fit matter to work upon, as with safeguards to guide its working. But my his-

tory differs from that in use (as my logic does) in many things—in end and office, in mass and composition, in subtlety, in selection also, and setting forth, with a view to the operations which are to follow.

For first, the object of the natural history which I propose is not so much to delight with variety of matter or to help with present use of experiments, as to give light to the discovery of causes and supply a suckling philosophy with its first food. For though it be true that I am principally in pursuit of works and the active department of the sciences, yet I wait for harvest-time and do not attempt to mow the moss or to reap the green corn. For I well know that axioms once rightly discovered will carry whole troops of works along with them, and produce them, not here and there one, but in clusters. And that unseasonable and puerile hurry to snatch by way of earnest at the first works which come within reach, I utterly condemn and reject as an Atalanta's apple that hinders the race.[2] Such then is the office of this natural history of mine.

Next, with regard to the mass and composition of it: I mean it to be a history not only of nature free and at large (when she is left to her own course and does her work her own way)—such as that of the heavenly bodies, meteors, earth and sea, minerals, plants, animals—but much more of nature under constraint and vexed; that is to say, when by art and the hand of man she is forced out of her natural state, and squeezed and moulded. Therefore I set down at length all experiments of the mechanical arts, of the operative part of the liberal arts, of the many crafts which have not yet grown into arts properly so called, so far as I have been able to examine them and as they conduce to the end in view. Nay (to say the plain truth), I do in fact (low and vulgar as men may think it) count more upon this part both for helps and safeguards than upon the other, seeing that the nature of things betrays itself more readily under the vexations of art than in its natural freedom.

Nor do I confine the history to bodies, but I have thought it my duty besides to make a separate history of such virtues as may be considered cardinal in nature. I mean those original passions or desires of matter which constitute the primary elements of nature; such as dense and rare, hot and cold, solid and fluid, heavy and light, and several others.

Then again, to speak of subtlety: I seek out and get together a kind of experiments much subtler and simpler than those which occur accidentally. For I drag into light many things which no one who was not proceeding by a regular

---

[2] In Greek legend, Atalanta agreed to marry only the man who could defeat her in a footrace. One opponent, Hippomanes, dropped three golden apples on the track, and Atalanta paused to pick them up, losing the race.

and certain way to the discovery of causes would have thought of inquiring after, being indeed in themselves of no great use; which shows that they were not sought for on their own account, but having just the same relation to things and works which the letters of the alphabet have to speech and words—which, though in themselves useless, are the elements of which all discourse is made up.

Further, in the selection of the relation and experiments I conceive I have been a more cautious purveyor than those who have hitherto dealt with natural history. For I admit nothing but on the faith of eyes, or at least of careful and severe examination, so that nothing is exaggerated for wonder's sake, but what I state is sound and without mixture of fables or vanity. All received or current falsehoods also (which by strange negligence have been allowed for many ages to prevail and become established) I proscribe and brand by name, that the sciences may be no more troubled with them. For it has been well observed that the fables and superstitions and follies which nurses instill into children do serious injury to their minds; and the same consideration makes me anxious, having the management of the childhood, as it were, of philosophy in its course of natural history, not to let it accustom itself in the beginning to any vanity. Moreover, whenever I come to a new experiment of any subtlety (though it be in my own opinion certain and approved), I nevertheless subjoin a clear account of the manner in which I made it, that men, knowing exactly how each point was made out, may see whether there be any error connected with it and may arouse themselves to devise proofs more trustworthy and exquisite, if such can be found; and finally, I interpose everywhere admonitions and scruples and cautions, with a religious care to eject, repress, and, as it were, exorcise every kind of phantasm.

Lastly, knowing how much the sight of man's mind is distracted by experience and history, and how hard it is at the first (especially for minds either tender or preoccupied) to become familiar with nature, I not unfrequently subjoin observations of my own, being as the first offers inclinations, and, as it were, glances of history toward philosophy, both by way of an assurance to men that they will not be kept forever tossing on the waves of experience, and also that when the time comes for the intellect to begin its work, it may find everything the more ready. By such a natural history, then, as I have described, I conceive that a safe and convenient approach may be made to nature, and matter supplied of good quality and well prepared for the understanding to work upon.

And now that we have surrounded the intellect with faithful helps and guards, and got together with most careful selection a regular army of divine works, it may seem that we have no more to do but to proceed to philosophy itself. And yet in a matter so difficult and doubtful there are still some things which it seems necessary to premise, partly for convenience of explanation, partly for present use.

Of these the first is to set forth examples of inquiry and invention according to my method, exhibited by anticipation in some particular subjects; choosing such subjects as are at once the most noble in themselves among those under inquiry, and most different one from another, that there may be an example in every kind. I do not speak of those examples which are joined to the several precepts and rules by way of illustration (for of these I have given plenty in the second part of the work); but I mean actual types and models, by which the entire process of the mind and the whole fabric and order of invention from the beginning to the end, in certain subjects, and those various and remarkable, should be set, as it were, before the eyes. For I remember that in the mathematics it is easy to follow the demonstration when you have a machine beside you, whereas without that help all appears involved and more subtle than it really is. To examples of this kind—being in fact nothing more than an application of the second part in detail and at large—the fourth part of the work is devoted.

The fifth part is for temporary use only, pending the completion of the rest, like interest payable from time to time until the principal be forthcoming. For I do not make so blindly for the end of my journey as to neglect anything useful that may turn up by the way. And therefore I include in this part such things as I have myself discovered, proved, or added—not, however, according to the true rules and methods of interpretation, but by the ordinary use of the understanding in inquiring and discovering. For besides that I hope my speculations may, in virtue of my continual conversancy with nature, have a value beyond the pretensions of my wit, they will serve in the meantime for wayside inns, in which the mind may rest and refresh itself on its journey to more certain conclusions. Nevertheless I wish it to be understood in the meantime that they are conclusions by which (as not being discovered and proved by the true form of interpretation) I do not at all mean to bind myself. Nor need any one be alarmed at such suspension of judgment in one who maintains not simply that nothing can be known, but only that nothing can be known except in a certain course and way; and yet establishes provisionally certain degrees of assurance for use and relief until the mind shall arrive at a knowledge of causes in which it can rest. For even those schools of philosophy which held the absolute impossibility of knowing anything were not inferior to those which took upon them to pronounce. But then they did not provide helps for the sense and understanding, as I have done, but simply took away all their authority; which is quite a different thing—almost the reverse.

The sixth part of my work (to which the rest is subservient and ministrant) discloses and sets forth that philosophy which by the legitimate, chaste, and severe course of inquiry which I have explained and provided is at length developed and established. The completion, however, of this last part is a thing both above my strength and beyond my hopes. I have made a beginning of the work—a beginning, as I hope, not unimportant: the fortune of the human race will give the issue, such an issue, it may be, as in the present condition of things and men's minds cannot easily be conceived or imagined. For the matter in hand is no mere felicity of speculation, but the real business and fortunes of the human race, and all power of operation. For man is but the servant and interpreter of nature: what he does and what he knows is only what he has observed of nature's order in fact or in thought; beyond this he knows nothing and can do nothing. For the chain of causes cannot by any force be loosed or broken, nor can nature be commanded except by being obeyed. And so those twin objects, human knowledge and human power, do really meet in one; and it is from ignorance of causes that operation fails.

And all depends on keeping the eye steadily fixed upon the facts of nature and so receiving their images simply as they are. For God forbid that we should give out a dream of our own imagination for a pattern of the world; rather may he graciously grant to us to write an apocalypse or true vision of the footsteps of the Creator imprinted on his creatures.

Therefore do thou, O Father, who gavest the visible light as the first fruits of creation, and didst breathe into the face of man the intellectual light as the crown and consummation thereof, guard and protect this work, which coming from thy goodness returneth to thy glory. Thou when thou turnedst to look upon the works which thy hands had made, sawest that all was very good, and didst rest from thy labors. But man, when he turned to look upon the work which his hands had made, saw that all was vanity and vexation of spirit, and could find no rest therein. Wherefore if we labor in thy works with the sweat of our brows, thou wilt make us partakers of thy vision and thy sabbath. Humbly we pray that this mind may be steadfast in us, and that through these our hands, and the hands of others to whom thou shalt give the same spirit, thou wilt vouchsafe to endow the human family with new mercies.

Pierre Corneille

1606–1684

In France and England during the seventeenth and eighteenth centuries there was a tendency to read Aristotle more as a prescriptive critic and less as a descriptive one. There was considerable discussion of the so-called unities of action, time, and place, derived from his *Poetics,* though, as Corneille points out, Aristotle nowhere specifically mentions unity of place. Critics varied considerably in the degrees of rigidity with which they prescribed these unities. Though Corneille is sometimes alleged to have been rigidly prescriptive, a reading of the last of his three discourses, *Of the Three Unities,* reveals the practical attitude of a working playwright. Corneille wrote criticisms, called *Examens,* of his own work, and in the selection below he frequently alludes to his own plays. At the end of his discourse, he indicates that he discovers his own adherence to the unity of place, rigidly defined, in only three of his plays; and he says that he will be indulgent of those dramatists who "may succeed on the stage through some appearance of regularity." He asserts that it is easy for critics to be severe, but let them write a few plays and they might "slacken the rules." Corneille is thus not as committed to exterior canons of judgment as that earlier commentator on the unities, Castelvetro (above, page 176); nor does he approach the dogmatism of the English critics John Dennis and Thomas Rymer. Indeed, his attitude is similar to that of another working playwright, John Dryden (below, page 253), whom he influenced.

Corneille tries to refer rules of dramatic art to common sense and the situation of the audience as well as to Aristotle. He was thinking of how to make effective the sort of play familiar to him. With respect to such plays, the "rules" may make more sense than we are now likely to admit.

Translations of the major plays of Corneille are available in Lacy Lockert, tr., *Chief Plays of Corneille* (1957). For an understanding of Corneille's critical attitudes, see Pierre Legouis, "Corneille and Dryden as Dramatic Critics," *Seventeenth-Century Studies Presented to Sir Herbert Grierson,* (1938), pages 269–78; Robert Mantero, *Corneille critique et son temps: Ogier, Mairet, Scudéry* (1964); Gordon Pocock, *Corneille and Racine: Problems of Tragic Form* (1973); Mitchell Greenberg, *Corneille, Classicism, and the Ruses of Symmetry* (1986); A. Donald Sellstrom, *Corneille, Tasso, and Modern Poetics* (1986); David Clarke, *Pierre Corneille: Poetics and Political Drama Under Louis XIII* (1992); Claire L. Carline, *Pierre Corneille Revisited* (1998).

Of the Three Unities of Action, Time, and Place

The two preceding discourses and the critical examination of the plays which my first two volumes contain have furnished me so many opportunities to explain my thoughts on these matters that there would be little left for me to say if I absolutely forbade myself to repeat.

I hold then, as I have already said, that in comedy, unity of action consists in the unity of plot or the obstacle to the plans of the principal actors, and in tragedy in the unity of peril, whether the hero falls victim to it or escapes. It is not that I claim that several perils cannot be allowed in the latter or several plots or obstacles in the former, provided that one passes necessarily from one to the other; for then escape from the first peril does not make the action complete since the escape leads to another danger; and the resolution of one plot does not put the actors at rest since they are confounded afresh in another. My memory does not furnish me any ancient examples of this multiplicity of perils linked each to each without the destruction of the unity of action; but I have noted independent double action as a defect in *Horace* and in *Théodore,* for it is not necessary that the first kill his sister upon gaining his victory nor that the other give herself up to martyrdom after having escaped prostitution; and if the death of Polyxène and that of Astyanax in Seneca's *Trojan Women* do not produce the same irregularity I am very much mistaken.[1]

In the second place, the term *unity of action* does not mean that tragedy should show only one action on the stage. The one which the poet chooses for his subject must have a beginning, a middle, and an end; and not only are these three parts separate actions which find their conclusion in the principal one, but, moreover, each of them may contain several others with the same subordination. There must be only one complete action, which leaves the mind of the spectator serene;[2] but that action can become complete only through several others which are less perfect and which, by serving as preparation, keep the spectator in a pleasant suspense. This is what must be contrived at the end of each act

in order to give continuity to the action. It is not necessary that we know exactly what the actors are doing in the intervals which separate the acts, nor even that they contribute to the action when they do not appear on the stage; but it is necessary that each act leave us in the expectation of something which is to take place in the following one.

If you asked me what Cléopâtre is doing in *Rodogune* between the time when she leaves her two sons in the second act until she rejoins Antiochus in the fourth, I should be unable to tell you, and I do not feel obliged to account for her; but the end of this second act prepares us to see an amicable effort by the two brothers to rule and to hide Rodogune from the venomous hatred of their mother. The effect of this is seen in the third act, whose ending prepares us again to see another effort by Antiochus to win back these two enemies one after the other and for what Séleucus does in the fourth, which compels that unnatural mother[3] to resolve upon what she tries to accomplish in the fifth, whose outcome we await with suspense.

In *Le Menteur* the actors presumably make use of the whole interval between the third and fourth acts to sleep; their rest, however, does not impede the continuity of the action between those two acts because the third does not contain a complete event. Dorante ends it with his plan to seek ways to win back the trust of Lucrèce, and at the very beginning of the next he appears so as to be able to talk to one of her servants and to her, should she show herself.

When I say that it is not necessary to account for what the actors do when they are not onstage, I do not mean that it is not sometimes very useful to give such an accounting, but only that one is not forced to do it, and that one ought to take the trouble to do so only when what happens behind the scenes is necessary for the understanding of what is to take place before the spectators. Thus I say nothing of what Cléopâtre did between the second and the fourth acts, because during all that time she can have done nothing important as regards the principal action which I am preparing for; but I point out in the very first lines of the fifth act that she has used the interval between these latter two for the killing of Séleucus, because that death is part of the action. This is what leads me to state that the poet is not required to show all the particular actions which bring about the principal one; he must choose to show those which are the most advantageous, whether by the beauty of the spectacle or by the brilliance or violence of the passions they produce, or by some other attraction which is connected with them, and to hide the others behind the scenes while informing the spectator of them by a narration or by some other artistic device;

Corneille's *Of the Three Unities of Action, Time, and Place* was published in 1660. The text, translated by Donald Schier, is from Scott Elledge and Donald Schier, eds., *The Continental Model: Selected French Critical Essays of the Seventeenth Century* (Minneapolis: University of Minnesota Press, 1960).
[1] *Horace* and *Théodore* are plays by Corneille. The unattributed plays mentioned in the following pages are all by Corneille. Lucius Annaeus Seneca (c. 3 B.C.–c. 65 A.D.), Roman playwright and philosopher.
[2] This is Corneille's reading of Aristotle's catharsis (above, page 55).

[3] Cléopâtre.

above all, he must remember that they must all be so closely connected that the last are produced by the preceding and that all have their source in the protasis which ought to conclude the first act. This rule, which I have established in my first discourse, although it is new and contrary to the usage of the ancients, is founded on two passages of Aristotle. Here is the first of them: "There is a great difference," he says, "between events which succeed each other and those which occur because of others."[4] The Moors come into the *Cid* after the death of the Count and not because of the death of the Count; and the fisherman comes into *Don Sanche* after Charles is suspected of being the Prince of Aragon and not because he is suspected of it; thus both are to be criticized. The second passage is even more specific and says precisely "that everything that happens in tragedy must arise necessarily or probably from what has gone before."[5]

The linking of the scenes which unites all the individual actions of each act and of which I have spoken in criticizing *La Suivante* is a great beauty in a poem and one which serves to shape continuity of action through continuity of presentation; but, in the end, it is only a beauty and not a rule. The ancients did not always abide by it although most of their acts have but two or three scenes. This made things much simpler for them than for us, who often put as many as nine or ten scenes into each act. I shall cite only two examples of the scorn with which they treated this principle: one is from Sophocles, in *Ajax,* whose monologue before he kills himself has no connection with the preceding scene; the other is from the third act of Terence's *The Eunuch,* where Antipho's soliloquy has no connection with Chremes and Pythias, who leave the stage when he enters. The scholars of our century, who have taken the ancients for models in the tragedies they have left us, have even more neglected that linking than did the ancients, and one need only glance at the plays of Buchanan, Grotius, and Heinsius, of which I spoke in the discussion of *Polyeucte,* to agree on that point. We have so far accustomed our audiences to this careful linking of scenes that they cannot now witness a detached scene without considering it a defect; the eye and even the ear are outraged by it even before the mind has been able to reflect upon it. The fourth act of *Cinna* falls below the others through this flaw; and what formerly was not a rule has become one now through the assiduousness of our practice.

I have spoken of three sorts of linkings in the discussion of *La Suivante:* I have shown myself averse to those of sound, indulgent to those of sight, favorable to those of presence and speech; but in these latter I have confused two things which ought to be separated. Links of presence and speech both have, no doubt, all the excellence imaginable; but there are links of speech without presence and of presence without speech which do not reach the same level of excellence. An actor who speaks to another from a hiding place without showing himself forms a link of speech without presence which is always effective; but that rarely happens. A man who remains onstage merely to hear what will be said by those whom he sees making their entrance forms a link of presence without speech; this is often clumsy and falls into mere pretense, being contrived more to accede to this new convention which is becoming a precept than for any need dictated by the plot of the play. Thus, in the third act of *Pompée,* Achorée, after having informed Charmion of the reception Caesar gave to the king when he presented to him the head of that hero, remains on the stage where he sees the two of them come together merely to hear what they will say and report it to Cléopâtre. Ammon does the same thing in the fourth act of *Andromède* for the benefit of Phinée, who retires when he sees the king and all his court arriving. Characters who become mute connect rather badly scenes in which they play little part and in which they count for nothing. It is another matter when they hide in order to find out some important secret from those who are speaking and who think they are not overheard, for then the interest which they have in what is being said, added to a reasonable curiosity to find out what they cannot learn in any other way, gives them an important part in the action despite their silence; but in these two examples Ammon and Achorée lend so cold a presence to the scenes they overhear that, to be perfectly frank, whatever feigned reason I give them to serve as pretext for their action, they remain there only to connect the scenes with those that precede, so easily can both plays dispense with what they do.

Although the action of the dramatic poem must have its unity, one must consider both its parts: the complication and the resolution. "The complication is composed," according to Aristotle,

> in part of what has happened offstage before the beginning of the action which is there described, and in part from what happens onstage; the rest belongs to the resolution. The change of fortune forms the separation of these two parts. Everything which precedes it is in the first part, and this change, with what follows it, concerns the other.[6]

---

[4] *Poetics* (above, page 57).
[5] *Poetics* (above, page 57).

[6] *Poetics* (above, page 52).

The complication depends entirely upon the choice and in- dustrious imagination of the poet and no rule can be given for it, except that in it he ought to order all things according to probability or necessity, a point which I have discussed in the second discourse; to this I add one piece of advice, which is that he involve himself as little as possible with things which have happened before the action he is present- ing. Such narrations are annoying, usually because they are not expected, and they disturb the mind of the spectator, who is obliged to burden his memory with what has hap- pened ten or twelve years before in order to understand what he is about to see; but narrations which describe things which happened and take place behind the scenes once the action has started always produce a better effect because they are awaited with some curiosity and are a part of the action which is being shown. One of the reasons why so many illustrious critics favor *Cinna* above anything else I have done is that it contains no narration of the past, the one Cinna makes in describing his plot to Emilie being rather an ornament which tickles the mind of the spectators than a necessary marshaling of the details they must know and im- press upon their memories for the understanding of what is to come. Emilie informs them adequately in the first two scenes that he is conspiring against Augustus in her favor, and if Cinna merely told her that the plotters are ready for the following day he would advance the action just as much as by the hundred lines he uses to tell both what he said to them and the way in which they received his words. There are plots which begin at the very birth of the hero like that of *Héraclius,* but these great efforts of the imagination de- mand an extraordinary attention of the spectator and often keep him from taking a real pleasure in the first perfor- mance, so much do they weary him.

In the resolution I find two things to avoid: the mere change of intention and the machine.[7] Not much skill is re- quired to finish a poem when he who has served as the ob- stacle to the plans of the principal actors for four acts de- sists in the fifth without being constrained to do so by any remarkable event: I have spoken of this in the first dis- course and I shall add nothing to that here. The machine requires no more skill when it is used only to bring down a god who straightens everything out when the actors are un- able to do so. It is thus that Apollo functions in the *Orestes:*[8] this prince and his friend Pylades, accused by Tyndarus and Menelaus of the death of Clytemnestra and condemned after prosecution by them, seize Helen and Hermione; they kill, or think they kill the first, and threaten to do so the same with the other if the sentence pronounced against them is not revoked. To smooth out these difficulties Euripides seeks nothing subtler than to bring Apollo down from heaven, and he, by absolute au- thority, orders that Orestes marry Hermione and Pylades Electra; and lest the death of Helen prove an obstacle to this, it being improbable that Hermione would marry Orestes since he had just killed her mother, Apollo informs them that she is not dead, that he has protected her from their blows and carried her off to heaven at the moment when they thought they were killing her. This use of the machine is entirely irrelevant, being founded in no way on the rest of the play, and makes a faulty resolution. But I find a little too harsh the opinion of Aristotle, who puts on the same level the chariot Medea uses to flee from Corinth after the vengeance she has taken on Creon. It seems to me there is a sufficient basis for this in the fact that she has been made a magician and that actions of hers as far sur- passing natural forces as that one have been mentioned in the play. After what she did for Jason at Colchis and after she had made his father Aeson young again following his return, and after she had attached invisible fire to the gift she gave to Creusa, the flying chariot is not improbable and the poem has no need of other preparation for that ex- traordinary effect. Seneca gives it preparation by this line which Medea speaks to her nurse: *"Tuum quoque ipsa cor- pus hinc mecum aveham;"*[9] and I by this one which she speaks to Aegeus: "I shall follow you tomorrow by a new road." Thus the condemnation of Euripides, who took no precautions, may be just and yet not fall on Seneca or on me; and I have no need to contradict Aristotle in order to justify myself on this point.

From the action I turn to the acts, each of which ought to contain a portion of it, but not so equal a portion that more is not reserved for the last than for the others and less given to the first than to the others. Indeed, in the first act one may do no more than depict the moral nature of the characters and mark off how far they have got in the story which is to be presented. Aristotle does not prescribe the number of the acts; Horace limits it to five;[10] and although he prohibits having fewer, the Spaniards are obstinate enough to stop at three and the Italians often do the same thing. The Greeks used to separate the acts by the chanting of the chorus, and since I think it reasonable to believe that in some of their poems they made it chant more than four

---

[7] *Deus ex machina.* See *Poetics* (above, page 59).
[8] By Euripides (c. 480–406 B.C.), Greek dramatist.
[9] "You, too, poor corpse, I bear away with me." Seneca, *Medea.*
[10] *Art of Poetry* (above, page 81).

times, I should not want to say they never exceeded five. This way of distinguishing the acts was less handy than ours, for either they paid attention to what the chorus was chanting or they did not; if they did, the mind of the spectators was too tense and had no time in which to rest; if they did not, attention was too much dissipated by the length of the chant, and when a new act began, an effort of memory was needed to recall to the imagination what had been witnessed and at what point the action had been interrupted. Our orchestra presents neither of these two inconveniences; the mind of the spectator relaxes while the music is playing and even reflects on what he has seen, to praise it or to find fault with it depending on whether he has been pleased or displeased; and the short time the orchestra is allowed to play leaves his impressions so fresh that when the actors return he does not need to make an effort to recall and resume his attention.

The number of scenes in each act has never been prescribed by rule, but since the whole act must have a certain number of lines which make its length proportionate to that of the others, one may include in it more or fewer scenes depending on whether they are long or short to fill up the time which the whole act is to consume. One ought, if possible, to account for the entrance and exit of each actor; I consider this rule indispensable, especially for the exit, and think there is nothing so clumsy as an actor who leaves the stage merely because he has no more lines to speak.

I should not be so rigorous for the entrances. The audience expects the actor, and although the setting represents the room or the study of whoever is speaking, yet he cannot make his appearance there unless he comes out from behind the tapestry, and it is not always easy to give a reason for what he has just done in town before returning home, since sometimes it is even probable that he has not gone out at all. I have never seen anybody take offense at seeing Emilie begin *Cinna* without saying why she has come to her room; she is presumed to be there before the play begins, and it is only stage necessity which makes her appear from behind the scenes to come there. Thus I should willingly dispense from the rigors of the rule the first scene of each act but not the others, because once an actor is on the stage anyone who enters must have a reason to speak to him or, at least, must profit from the opportunity to do so when it offers. Above all, when an actor enters twice in one act, in comedy or in tragedy, he must either lead one to expect that he will soon return when he leaves the first time, like Horace in the second act and Julie in the third act of *Horace,* or explain on returning why he has come back so soon.

Aristotle wishes the well-made tragedy to be beautiful and capable of pleasing without the aid of actors and quite aside from performance.[11] So that the reader may more easily experience that pleasure, his mind, like that of the spectator, must not be hindered, because the effort he is obliged to make to conceive and to imagine the play for himself lessens the satisfaction which he will get from it. Therefore, I should be of the opinion that the poet ought to take great care to indicate in the margin the less important actions which do not merit being included in the lines, and which might even mar the dignity of the verse if the author lowered himself to express them. The actor easily fills this need on the stage, but in a book one would often be reduced to guessing and sometimes one might even guess wrong, unless one were informed in this way of these little things. I admit that this is not the practice of the ancients; but you must also allow me that because they did not do it they have left us many obscurities in their poems which only masters of dramatic art can explain; even so, I am not sure they succeed as often as they think they do. If we forced ourselves to follow the method of the ancients completely, we should make no distinction between acts and scenes because the Greeks did not. This failure on their part is often the reason that I do not know how many acts there are in their plays, nor whether at the end of an act the player withdraws so as to allow the chorus to chant, or whether he remains onstage without any action while the chorus is chanting, because neither they nor their interpreters have deigned to give us a word of indication in the margin.

We have another special reason for not neglecting that helpful little device as they did: this is that printing puts our plays in the hands of actors who tour the provinces and whom we can thus inform of what they ought to do, for they would do some very odd things if we did not help them by these notes. They would find themselves in great difficulty at the fifth act of plays that end happily, where we bring together all the actors on the stage (a thing which the ancients did not do); they would often say to one what is meant for another, especially when the same actor must speak to three or four people one after the other. When there is a whispered command to make, like Cléopâtre's to Laonice which sends her to seek poison, an aside would be necessary to express this in verse if we were to do without the marginal indications, and that seems to me much more intolerable than the notes, which give us the real and only way, following the opinion of Aristotle, of making the tragedy as beautiful in the reading as in performance, by making it easy for the reader to imagine what the stage presents to the view of the spectators.

[11] *Poetics* (above, page 56).

The rule of the unity of time is founded on this statement of Aristotle "that the tragedy ought to enclose the duration of its action in one journey of the sun or try not to go much beyond it."[12] These words gave rise to a famous dispute as to whether they ought to be understood as meaning a natural day of twenty-four hours or an artificial day of twelve; each of the two opinions has important partisans, and, for myself, I find that there are subjects so difficult to limit to such a short time that not only should I grant the twenty-four full hours but I should make use of the license which the philosopher gives to exceed them a little and should push the total without scruple as far as thirty. There is a legal maxim which says that we should broaden the mercies and narrow the rigors of the law, *odia restringenda, favores ampliandi;*[13] and I find that an author is hampered enough by this constraint which forced some of the ancients to the very edge of the impossible. Euripides, in *The Suppliants,* makes Theseus leave Athens with an army, fight a battle beneath the walls of Thebes, which was ten or twelve leagues away, and return victorious in the following act; and between his departure and the arrival of the messenger who comes to tell the story of his victory, the chorus has only thirty-six lines to speak. That makes good use of such a short time. Aeschylus makes Agamemnon come back from Troy with even greater speed.[14] He had agreed with Clytemnestra, his wife, that as soon as the city was taken he would inform her by signal fires built on the intervening mountains, of which the second would be lighted as soon as the first was seen, the third at the sight of the second, and so on: by this means she was to learn the great news the same night. However, scarcely had she learned it from the signal fires when Agamemnon arrives, whose ship, although battered by a storm, if memory serves, must have traveled as fast as the eye could see the lights. The *Cid* and *Pompée,* where the action is a little precipitate, are far from taking so much license; and if they force ordinary probability in some way, at least they do not go as far as such impossibilities.

Many argue against this rule, which they call tyrannical, and they would be right if it were founded only on the authority of Aristotle: but what should make it acceptable is the fact that common sense supports it. The dramatic poem is an imitation, or rather a portrait of human actions, and it is beyond doubt that portraits gain in excellence in proportion as they resemble the original more closely. A performance lasts two hours and would resemble reality

perfectly if the action it presented required no more for its actual occurrence. Let us then not settle on twelve or twenty-four hours, but let us compress the action of the poem into the shortest possible period, so that the performance may more closely resemble reality and thus be more nearly perfect. Let us give, if that is possible, to the one no more than the two hours which the other fills, I do not think that *Rodogune* requires much more, and perhaps two hours would be enough for *Cinna.* If we cannot confine the action within the two hours, let us take four, six, or ten, but let us not go much beyond twenty-four for fear of falling into lawlessness and of so far reducing the scale of the portrait that it no longer has its proportionate dimensions and is nothing but imperfection.

Most of all, I should like to leave the matter of duration to the imagination of the spectators and never make definite the time the action requires unless the subject needs this precision, but especially not when probability is a little forced, as in the *Cid,* because precision serves only to make the crowded action obvious to the spectator. Even when no violence is done to a poem by the necessity of obeying this rule, why must one state at the beginning that the sun is rising, that it is noon at the third act, and that the sun is setting at the end of the last act? This is only an obtrusive affectation; it is enough to establish the possibility of the thing in the time one gives to it and that one be able to determine the time easily if one wishes to pay attention to it, but without being compelled to concern oneself with the matter. Even in those actions which take no longer than the performance it would be clumsy to point out that a half hour has elapsed between the beginning of one act and the beginning of the next.

I repeat what I have said elsewhere, that when we take a longer time, as, for instance, ten hours, I should prefer that the eight extra be used up in the time between the acts and that each act should have as its share only as much time as performance requires, especially when all scenes are closely linked together. I think, however, that the fifth act, by special privilege, has the right to accelerate time so that the part of the action which it presents may use up more time than is necessary for performance. The reason for this is that the spectator is by then impatient to see the end, and when the outcome depends on actors who are offstage, all the dialogue given to those who are onstage awaiting news of the others drags and action seems to halt. There is no doubt that from the point where Phocas exits in the fifth act of *Héraclius* until Amyntas enters to relate the manner of his death, more time is needed for what happens offstage than for the speaking of the lines in which Héraclius, Martian, and Pulchérie complain of their misfortune. Prusias and Flaminius,

---

[12] *Poetics* (above, page 55).
[13] Corneille has inverted the order; literally, "restrict the odious, amplify the favorable."
[14] *Agamemnon* by Aeschylus (525–456 B.C.), Greek dramatist.

in the fifth act of *Nicomède,* do not have the time they would need to meet at sea, take counsel with each other, and return to the defense of the queen; and the Cid has not enough time to fight a duel with Don Sanche during the conversations of the Infanta with Léonor and of Chimène with Elvire. I was aware of this and yet have had no scruples about this acceleration of which, perhaps, one might find several examples among the ancients, but the laziness of which I have spoken will force me to rest content with this one, which is from the *Andria* of Terence. Simo slips his son Pamphilus into the house of Glycerium in order to get the old man, Crito, to come out and to clear up with him the question of the birth of his mistress, who happens to be the daughter of Chremes. Pamphilus enters the house, speaks to Crito, asks him for the favor and returns with him; and during this exit, this request, and this reentry. Simo and Chremes, who remain onstage, speak only one line each, which could not possibly give Pamphilus more than time enough to ask where Crito is, certainly not enough to talk with him and to explain to him the reasons for which he should reveal what he knows about the birth of the unknown girl.

When the conclusion of the action depends on actors who have not left the stage and about whom no one is awaiting news, as in *Cinna* and *Rodogune,* the fifth act has no need of this privilege because then all the action takes place in plain sight, as does not happen when part of it occurs offstage after the beginning of the act. The other acts do not merit the same freedom. If there is not time enough to bring back an actor who had made his exit, or to indicate what he has done since that exit, the accounting can be postponed to the following act; and the music, which separates the two acts, may use up as much time as is necessary; but in the fifth act no postponement is possible: attention is exhausted and the end must come quickly.

I cannot forget that although we must reduce the whole tragic action to one day, we can nevertheless make known by a narration or in some other more artful way what the hero of the tragedy has been doing for several years, because there are plays in which the crux of the plot lies in an obscurity of birth which must be brought to light, as in *Oedipus.* I shall not say again that the less one burdens oneself with past actions, the more favorable the spectator will be, because of the lesser degree of trouble he is given when everything takes place in the present and no demands are made on his memory except for what he has seen; but I cannot forget that the choice of a day both illustrious and long-awaited is a great ornament to a poem. The opportunity for this does not always present itself, and in all that I have written until now you will find only four of that kind: the day in *Horace* when two nations are to decide

the question of supremacy of empire by a battle; and the ones in *Rodogune, Andromède,* and *Don Sanche.* In *Rodogune* it is a day chosen by two sovereigns for the signature of a treaty of peace between the hostile crowns, for a complete reconciliation of the two rival governments through a marriage, and for the elucidation of a more than twenty-year-old secret concerning the right of succession of one of the twin princes on which the fate of the kingdom depends, as does the outcome of both their loves. The days in *Andromède* and *Don Sanche* are not of lesser importance, but, as I have just said, such opportunities do not often present themselves, and in the rest of my works I have been able to choose days remarkable only for what chance makes happen on them and not by the use to which public arrangements destined them long ago.

As for the unity of place, I find no rule concerning it in either Aristotle or Horace. This is what leads many people to believe that this rule was established only as a consequence of the unity of one day, and leads them to imagine that one can stretch the unity of place to cover the points to which a man may go and return in twenty-four hours. This opinion is a little too free, and if one made an actor travel posthaste, the two sides of the theater might represent Paris and Rouen. I could wish, so that the spectator is not at all disturbed, that what is performed before him in two hours might actually be able to take place in two hours, and that what he is shown in a stage setting which does not change might be limited to a room or a hall depending on a choice made beforehand; but often that is so awkward, if not impossible, that one must necessarily find some way to enlarge the place as also the time of the action. I have shown exact unity of place in *Horace, Polyeucte,* and *Pompée,* but for that it was necessary to present either only one woman, as in *Polyeucte;* or to arrange that the two who are presented are such close friends and have such closely related interests that they can be always together, as in *Horace;* or that they may react as in *Pompée* where the stress of natural curiosity drives Cléopâtre from her apartments in the second act and Cornélie in the fifth; and both enter the great hall of the king's palace in anticipation of the news they are expecting. The same thing is not true of *Rodogune:* Cléopâtre and she have interests which are too divergent to permit them to express their most secret thoughts in the same place. I might say of that play what I have said of *Cinna,* where, in general, everything happens in Rome and, in particular, half of the action takes place in the quarters of Auguste and half of it in Emilie's apartments. Following that arrangement, the first act of this tragedy would be laid in Rodogune's antechamber, the second, in Cléopâtre's apartments, the third, in Rodogune's; but if the fourth act can begin in Rodogune's apartments it cannot finish there, and what Cléopâtre says to her two sons one after the other would be badly out of place there. The fifth act needs a throne room where a great crowd can be gathered. The same problem is found in *Héraclius.* The first act could very well take place in Phocas's quarters, the second, in Léontine's apartments; but if the third begins in Pulchérie's rooms it cannot end there, and it is outside the bounds of probability that Phocas should discuss the death of her brother in Pulchérie's apartments.

The ancients, who made their kings speak in a public square, easily kept a rigorous unity of place in their tragedies. Sophocles, however, did not observe it in his *Ajax,* when the hero leaves the stage to find a lonely place in which to kill himself and does so in full view of the people; this easily leads to the conclusion that the place where he kills himself is not the one he has been seen to leave, since he left it only to choose another.

We do not take the same liberty of drawing kings and princesses from their apartments, and since often the difference and the opposition on the part of those who are lodged in the same palace do not allow them to take others into their confidence or to disclose their secrets in the same room, we must seek some other compromise about unity of place if we want to keep it intact in our poems; otherwise we should have to decide against many plays which we see succeeding brilliantly.

I hold, then, that we ought to seek exact unity as much as possible, but as this unity does not suit every kind of subject, I should be very willing to concede that a whole city has unity of place. Not that I should want the stage to represent the whole city, that would be somewhat too large, but only two or three particular places enclosed within its walls. Thus the scene of *Cinna* does not leave Rome, passing from the apartments of Auguste to the house of Emilie. *Le Menteur* takes place in the Tuileries and in the Place Royale at Paris, and *La Suite* shows us the prison and Mélisse's house at Lyons. The *Cid* increases even more the number of particular places without leaving Seville; and since the close linking of scenes is not observed in that play, the stage in the first act is supposed to represent Chimène's house, the Infante's apartments in the king's palace, and the public square; the second adds to these the king's chamber. No doubt there is some excess in this freedom. In order to rectify in some way this multiplication of places when it is inevitable, I should wish two things done: first, that the scene should never change in a given act but only between the acts, as is done in the first three acts of *Cinna;* the other, that these two places should not need different stage settings and that neither of the two should ever be named, but only the general place which includes them both, as Paris, Rome,

Lyons, Constantinople, and so forth. This would help to deceive the spectator, who, seeing nothing that would indicate the difference in the places, would not notice the change, unless it was maliciously and critically pointed out, a thing which few are capable of doing, most spectators being warmly intent upon the action which they see on the stage. The pleasure they take in it is the reason why they do not seek out its imperfections lest they lose their taste for it; and they admit such an imperfection only when forced, when it is too obvious, as in *Le Menteur* and *La Suite,* where the different settings force them to recognize the multiplicity of places in spite of themselves.

But since people of opposing interests cannot with verisimilitude unfold their secrets in the same place, and since they are sometimes introduced into the same act through the linking of scenes which the unity of place necessarily produces, one must find some means to make it compatible with the contradiction which rigorous probability finds in it, and consider how to preserve the fourth act of *Rodogune,* in both of which I have already pointed out the contradiction which lies in having enemies speak in the same place. Jurists allow legal fictions, and I should like, following their example, to introduce theatrical fictions by which one could establish a theatrical place which would not be Cléopâtre's chamber nor Rodogune's, in the play of that name, nor that of Phocas, of Léontine or of Pulchérie in *Héraclius,* but a room contiguous to all these other apartments to which I should attribute these two privileges: first, that each of those who speaks in it is presumed to enjoy the same secrecy there as if he were in his own room; and second, that whereas in the usual arrangement it is sometimes proper for those who are onstage to go off, in order to speak privately with others in their rooms, these latter might meet the former onstage without shocking convention, so as to preserve both the unity of place and the linking of scenes. Thus Rodogune, in the first act, encounters Laonice, whom she must send for so as to speak with her; and, in the fourth act, Cléopâtre encounters Antiochus on the very spot where he has just moved Rodogune to pity, even though in utter verisimilitude the prince ought to seek out his mother in her own room since she hates the princess too much to speak to him in Rodogune's, which following the first scene, would be the locus of the whole act, if one did not introduce that compromise which I have mentioned into the rigorous unity of place.

Many of my plays will be at fault in the unity of place if this compromise is not accepted, for I shall abide by it always in the future when I am not able to satisfy the ultimate rigor of the rule. I have been able to reduce only three plays,

Horace, Polyeucte, and *Pompée,* to the requirements of the rule. If I am too indulgent with myself as far as the others are concerned, I shall be even more so for those which may succeed on the stage through some appearance of regularity. It is easy for critics to be severe; but if they were to give ten or a dozen plays to the public, they might perhaps slacken the rules more than I do, as soon as they have recognized through experience what constraint their precision brings about and how many beautiful things it banishes from our stage. However that may be, these are my opinions, or if you prefer, my heresies concerning the principal points of the dramatic art, and I do not know how better to make the ancient rules agree with modern pleasures. I do not doubt that one might easily find better ways of doing that, and I shall be ready to accept them when they have been put into practice as successfully as, by common consent, mine have been.

John Dryden

1631–1700

Dryden's *Essay of Dramatic Poesy* provides perhaps the fullest single representation of issues and attitudes in neoclassical criticism. And it is particularly important because it belies one popular view of neoclassical criticism, namely, that it was wholly dogmatic and a slave to its own arbitrary decrees. Dryden is not imprisoned by rules and is able to see many sides of the issues he raises. At the center of his essay lies the classical idea of decorum enunciated by Horace, but decorum is never for Dryden merely obeisance to the prevailing fashion.

The essay, strongly influenced by Corneille and Ben Jonson, is written in the form of a dialogue among four gentlemen: Eugenius, Crites, Lisideius, and Neander. The last, Neander, seems to speak for Dryden himself. First they consider whether the ancients or the moderns wrote better, a quarrel of some popularity later satirized by Jonathan Swift. This question turns into a discussion of the so-called unities of time, place, and action, what they are, and whether they must be observed. Discussion then moves to a relative judgment of the French and English playwrights and whether the traditional genres of tragedy and comedy ought properly to be mixed in a single work, as the English had done. There is finally a consideration of the propriety of writing plays in rhymed verse.

Eugenius argues that the moderns excel the ancients, having profited from the rules that the ancient writers laid down; he remarks in passing that the ancients did not themselves observe the unity of place. Crites, defending the ancients, points out that they invented the principles of dramatic art enunciated by Aristotle and Horace, who established the unities adopted by the French; he observes that the greatest English modern, Ben Jonson, followed the ancients. Crites, who is opposed to rhyme in plays, argues that though the moderns excel in science, the ancient age was the true age of poetry. Lisideius, who defines a play as "a just and lively image of human nature, representing its passions and humors, and the changes of fortune to which it is subject for the delight and instruction of mankind," defends the French playwrights and attacks the English tendency to mix genres. Neander, who has the last word, adopts a position favoring the moderns, respectful of the ancients, critical of too rigid insistence on dramatic laws, and willing to accept rhyme in its proper place.

In Lisideius's definition, which is provisionally accepted by the other three, there are two fundamental theoretical points: drama is an imitation, and its aim is to delight and teach. The essay becomes deeply involved with the problem of imitation when it considers how closely the dramatist must adhere to the unities of time, place, and action. If imitation means that the play must create a direct illusion of "real" life, then the unities must be strictly observed; but if it does not, then the question is perhaps what formal integrity, independent of a sort of naive realism, the playwright ought to be seeking. The principle of decorum in Dryden is associated finally with an idea of formal integrity.

In 1668 Dryden also wrote a "Defense" of his essay, devoted mainly to advocating the use of rhyme. In the course of this essay, he remarks: "Delight is the chief, if not the only, end of poetry: instruction can be admitted but in the second place, for poesy only instructs as it delights." A slippery statement, it nevertheless places Dryden on the side of delight in an old argument.

Dryden's critical works are available in a number of editions. That by W. P. Ker, *Essays by John Dryden* in two volumes (1900), though still useful, has largely been superseded by George Watson's *John Dryden: Of Dramatic Poesy and Other Critical Essays* in two volumes (1962). Commentary on Dryden includes A. M. Ellis, "Horace's Influence on Dryden," *Philological Quarterly* IV (1925), 39–60; L. I. Bredvold, *The Intellectual Milieu of John Dryden* (1934); Hoyt Trowbridge, "The Place of Rules in Dryden's Criticism," *Modern Philology* XLIV (1946–1947), 84–96; F. L. Huntley, *On Dryden's* Essay of Dramatic Poesy (1951); Phillip Harth, *Contexts of Dryden's Thought* (1968); H. James Jensen, *A Glossary of John Dryden's Critical Terms* (1969); Robert D. Hume, *Dryden's Criticism* (1970); Edward Pechter, *Dryden's Classical Theory of Literature* (1975); Michael Werth Gelber, *The Just and the Lively: The Literary Criticism of John Dryden* (1999).

An Essay of Dramatic Poesy

It was that memorable day,[1] in the first summer of the late war, when our navy engaged the Dutch; a day wherein the two most mighty and best appointed fleets which any age had ever seen, disputed the command of the greater half of the globe, the commerce of nations, and the riches of the universe. While these vast floating bodies, on either side, moved against each other in parallel lines, and our countrymen, under the happy conduct of his Royal Highness, went breaking, by little and little, into the line of the enemies; the noise of the cannon from both navies reached our ears about the city, so that all men being alarmed with it, and in a dreadful suspense of the event which we knew was then deciding, everyone went following the sound as his fancy led him; and leaving the town almost empty, some took towards the park, some cross the river, others down it; all seeking the noise in the depth of silence.

Among the rest, it was the fortune of Eugenius, Crites, Lisideius, and Neander,[2] to be in company together; three of them persons whom their wit and quality have made known to all the town; and whom I have chose to hide under these borrowed names, that they may not suffer by so ill a relation as I am going to make of their discourse.

Taking then a barge which a servant of Lisideius has provided for them, they made haste to shoot the bridge, and left behind them that great fall of waters which hindered them from hearing what they desired: after which, having disengaged themselves from many vessels which rode at anchor in the Thames, and almost blocked up the passage towards Greenwich, they ordered the watermen to let fall their oars more gently; and then, everyone favoring his own curiosity with a strict silence, it was not long ere they perceived the air break about them like the noise of distant thunder, or of swallows in a chimney: those little undulations of sound, though almost vanishing before they reached them, yet still seeming to retain somewhat of their first horror, which they had betwixt the fleets. After they had attentively listened till such time as the sound by little and little

---

Dryden's *Essay of Dramatic Poesy* was first published in 1664. A revised edition appeared in 1668. The text is based on the 1668 edition. Dryden often slightly misquotes the Roman writers to whom he refers.

[1] June 3, 1665.

[2] The characters have sometimes been identified as follows: Eugenius: Charles Sackville (1603–1707); Crites: Sir Robert Howard (1626–1698), Dryden's brother-in-law, poet, and dramatist; Lisideius: Sir Charles Sedley (c. 1639–1701), dramatist; Neander: Dryden.

went from them, Eugenius, lifting up his head, and taking notice of it, was the first who congratulated to the rest that happy omen of our nation's victory: adding, "We had but this to desire in confirmation of it, that we might hear no more of that noise, which was now leaving the English coast." When the rest had concurred in the same opinion, Crites, a person of a sharp judgment, and somewhat too delicate a taste in wit, which the world have mistaken in him for ill-nature, said, smiling to us, that if the concernment of this battle had not been so exceeding great, he could scarce have wished the victory at the price he knew he must pay for it, in being subject to the reading and hearing of so many ill verses as he was sure would be made upon it. Adding, that no argument could 'scape some of those eternal rhymers, who watch a battle with more diligence than the ravens and birds of prey; and the worst of them surest to be first in upon the quarry: while the better able either out of modesty writ not at all, or set that due value upon their poems, as to let them be often called for and long expected! "There are some of those impertinent people you speak of," answered Lisideius, "who to my knowledge are already so provided, either way, that they can produce not only a panegyric upon the victory, but, if need be, a funeral elegy on the Duke; and after they have crowned his valor with many laurels, at last deplore the odds under which he fell, concluding that his courage deserved a better destiny." All the company smiled at the conceit of Lisideius; but Crites, more eager than before, began to make particular exceptions against some writers, and said, the public magistrate ought to send betimes to forbid them; and that it concerned the peace and quiet of all honest people, that ill poets should be as well silenced as seditious preachers. "In my opinion," replied Eugenius, "you pursue your point too far; for as to my own particular, I am so great a lover of poesy, that I could wish them all rewarded, who attempt but to do well; at least, I would not have them worse used than Sylla the Dictator did one of their brethren heretofore: *'Quem in concione vidimus,'* says Tully, *'cum ei libellum malus poeta de populo subjecisset, quod epigramma in eum fecisset tantummodo alternis versibus longiusculis, statim ex iis rebus quas tunc vendebat jubere ei praemium tribui, sub ea conditione ne quid postea scriberet.'*[3] "I could wish with all my heart," replied Crites, "that many whom we know were as bountifully thanked upon the same condition—that they would never trouble us

again. For amongst others, I have a mortal apprehension of two poets, whom this victory with the help of both her wings, will never be able to escape." "'Tis easy to guess whom you intend," said Lisideius; "and without naming them, I ask you, if one of them does not perpetually pay us with clenches[4] upon words, and a certain clownish kind of raillery? If now and then he does not offer at a catachresis or Clevelandism,[5] wresting and torturing a word into another meaning: in fine, if he be not one of those whom the French could call *un mauvais bouffon;*[6] one that is so much a well-willer to the satire, that he spares no man; and though he cannot strike a blow to hurt any, yet ought to be punished for the malice of the action, as our witches are justly hanged, because they think themselves so; and suffer deservedly for believing they did mischief, because they meant it." "You have described him," said Crites, "so exactly, that I am afraid to come after you with my other extremity of poetry. He is one of those who, having had some advantage of education and converse, knows better than the other what a poet should be, but puts it into practice more unluckily than any man; his style and matter are everywhere alike: he is the most calm, peaceable writer you ever read: he never disquiets your passions with the least concernment, but still leaves you in as even a temper as he found you; he is a very leveler in poetry: he creeps along with ten little words in every line, and helps out his numbers with *for to,* and *unto* and all the pretty expletives he can find, till he drags them to the end of another line: while the sense is left tired halfway behind it: he doubly starves all his verses, first for want of thought, and then of expression; his poetry neither has wit in it, nor seems to have it; like him in Martial: *'Pauper videri Cinna vult, et est pauper.'*[7]

"He affects plainness, to cover his want of imagination: when he writes the serious way, the highest flight of his fancy is some miserable antithesis, or seeming contradiction; and in the comic he is still reaching at some thin conceit, the ghost of a jest, and that too flies before him, never to be caught; these swallows which we see before us on the Thames are the just resemblance of his wit: you may observe how near the water they stoop, how many proffers they make to dip, and yet how seldom they touch it; and when they do, 'tis but the surface: they skim over it but to catch a gnat, and then mount into the air and leave it."

---

[3] "We note that in an assembly once, when a bad poet handed up from the crowd a small book in which he had composed an epigram about him, only in somewhat long alternating verse, he at once ordered that he be given a reward from among those things that he was selling, on condition that he never again write anything." Cicero, *In Defense of Archius* X, 25.

[4] Plays on words, puns.
[5] Catachresis: an incorrect use of words, usually an outlandish metaphor or "Clevelandism," which refers to the work of John Cleveland (1613–1658), English satiric metaphysical poet.
[6] "A sorry jester."
[7] Marcus Valerius Martialis (c. 40–104), Roman poet: "Cinna wishes to appear poor, and is poor." *Epigrams* VIII, 19.

"Well, gentlemen," said Eugenius, "you may speak your pleasure of these authors; but though I and some few more about the town may give you a peaceable hearing, yet assure yourselves, there are multitudes who would think you malicious and them injured: especially him whom you first described; he is the very withers of the city: they have bought more editions of his works than would serve to lay under all their pies at the Lord Mayor's Christmas. When his famous poem first came out in the year 1660, I have seen them reading it in the midst of 'change time; nay so vehement they were at it, that they lost their bargain by the candles' ends; but what will you say, if he has been received amongst the great ones? I can assure you he is, this day, the envy of a great person who is lord in the art of quibbling; and who does not take it well, that any man should intrude so far into his province." "All I would wish," replied Crites, "is that they who love his writings, may still admire him, and his fellow poet: *'Qui Bavium non odit, &c.,'*[8] is curse sufficient." "And farther," added Lisideius, "I believe there is no man who writes well, but would think himself very hardly dealt with, if their admirers should praise anything of his: *'Nam quos contemnimus, eorum quoque laudes contemnimus.'"*[9] "There are so few who write well in this age," says Crites, "that methinks any praises should be welcome; they neither rise to the dignity of the last age, nor to any of the ancients: and we may cry out of the writers of this time, with more reason than Petronius of his, *'Pace vestra liceat dixisse, primi omnium eloquentiam perdidistis':*[10] you have debauched the true old poetry so far, that nature, which is the soul of it, is not in any of your writings."

"If your quarrel," said Eugenius, "to those who now write, be grounded only on your reverence to antiquity, there is no man more ready to adore those great Greeks and Romans than I am: but on the other side, I cannot think so contemptibly of the age I live in, or so dishonorably of my own country, as not to judge we equal the ancients in most kinds of poesy, and in some surpass them; neither know I any reason why I may not be zealous for the reputation of our age, as we find the ancients themselves in reference to those who lived before them. For you hear your Horace saying, *'Indignor quidquam reprehendi, non quia crasse / Compositum, illepidève putetur, sed quia nuper.'*[11] And after: *'Si meliora dies, ut vina, poemata reddit, / Scire velim, pretium chartis quotus arroget annus?'*[12]

"But I see I am engaging in a wide dispute, where the arguments are not like to reach close on either side; for poesy is of so large an extent, and so many both of the ancients and moderns have done well in all kinds of it, that in citing one against the other, we shall take up more time this evening than each man's occasions will allow him: therefore I would ask Crites to what part of poesy he would confine his arguments, and whether he would defend the general cause of the ancients against the moderns, or oppose any age of the moderns against this of ours?"

Crites, a little while considering upon this demand, told Eugenius he approved his propositions, and if he pleased, he would limit their dispute to dramatic poesy; in which he thought it not difficult to prove, either that the ancients were superior to the moderns, or the last age to this of ours.

Eugenius was somewhat surprised, when he heard Crites make choice of that subject. "For ought I see," said he, "I have undertaken a harder province than I imagined; for though I never judged the plays of the Greek or Roman poets comparable to ours, yet, on the other side, those we now see acted come short of many which were written in the last age: but my comfort is, if we are o'ercome, it will be only by our own countrymen: and if we yield to them in this one part of poesy, we more surpass them in all the other: for in the epic or lyric way, it will be hard for them to show us one such amongst them, as we have many now living, or who lately were so: they can produce nothing so courtly writ, or which expresses so much the conversation of a gentleman, as Sir John Suckling; nothing so even, sweet, and flowing, as Mr. Waller; nothing so majestic, so correct, as Sir John Denham; nothing so elevated, so copious, and full of spirit, as Mr. Cowley;[13] as for the Italian, French, and Spanish plays, I can make it evident, that those who now write surpass them; and that the drama is wholly ours."

All of them were thus far of Eugenius his opinion, that the sweetness of English verse was never understood or practiced by our fathers; even Crites himself did not much oppose it: and every one was willing to acknowledge how much our poesy is improved by the happiness of some writers yet living; who first taught us to mold our thoughts into easy and significant words; to retrench the superfluities of expression, and to make our rhyme so properly a part of the verse, that is should never mislead the sense, but itself be led and governed by it.

---

[8] "Who does not hate Bavius . . . ? Virgil, *Eclogues* III, 90.

[9] "For we despise the praises of those we despise." Petronius (d. c. 66), Roman satirist, *Satyricon.*

[10] "By your leave, let me say you were first to destroy eloquence for all." *Satyricon,* 2.

[11] "I am offended when someone is criticized, not because it is badly composed or thought to lack charm, but because it is recent." *Epistles* II, i, 76.

[12] "If time causes poems to improve like wine, how many years, I would like to know, would it take?" *Epistles* II, i, 34.

---

[13] Suckling (1609–1642), Edmund Waller (1609–1687), Denham (1615–1649), Abraham Cowley (1618–1667), English poets.

Eugenius was going to continue this discourse, when Lisideius told him it was necessary, before they proceeded further, to take a standing measure of their controversy; for how was it possible to be decided who writ the best plays, before we know what a play should be? But, this once agreed on by both parties, each might have recourse to it, either to prove his own advantages, or to discover the failings of his adversary.

He had no sooner said this, but all desired the favor of him to give the definition of a play; and they were the more importunate, because neither Aristotle, nor Horace, nor any other, who writ of that subject, had ever done it.[14]

Lisideius, after some modest denials, at last confessed he had a rude notion of it; indeed, rather a description than a definition; but which served to guide him in his private thoughts, when he was to make a judgment of what others writ: that he conceived a play ought to be, a just and lively image of human nature, representing its passions and humors, and the changes of fortune to which it is subject, for the delight and instruction of mankind.

This definition, though Crites raised a logical objection against it; that it was only *a genere et fine,*[15] and so not altogether perfect; was yet well received by the rest: and after they had given order to the watermen to turn their barge, and row softly, that they might take the cool of the evening in their return, Crites, being desired by the company to begin, spoke on behalf of the ancients, in this manner:

"If confidence presage a victory, Eugenius, in his own opinion, has already triumphed over the ancients: nothing seems more easy to him, than to overcome those whom it is our greatest praise to have imitated well; for we do not only build upon their foundation, but by their models. Dramatic poesy had time enough, reckoning from Thespis (who first invented it) to Aristophanes,[16] to be born, to grow up, and to flourish in maturity. It has been observed of arts and sciences, that in one and the same century they have arrived to a great perfection; and no wonder, since every age has a kind of universal genius, which inclines those that live in it to some particular studies: the work then being pushed on by many hands, must of necessity go forward.

"Is it not evident, in these last hundred years (when the study of philosophy[17] has been the business of all the virtuosi in Christendom), that almost a new nature has been revealed to us? That more errors of the school have been detected, more useful experiments in philosophy have been made, more noble secrets in optics, medicine, anatomy, astronomy, discovered, than in all those credulous and doting ages from Aristotle to us? So true is it, that nothing spreads more fast than science, when rightly and generally cultivated.

"Add to this, the more than common emulation that was in those times of writing well; which though it be found in all ages and all persons that pretend to the same reputation, yet poesy, being then in more esteem than now it is, had greater honors decreed to the professors of it, and consequently the rivalship was more high between them; they had judges ordained to decide their merit, and prizes to reward it; and historians have been diligent to record of Aeschylus, Euripides, Sophocles, Lycophron,[18] and the rest of them, both who they were that vanquished in these wars of the theater, and how often they were crowned: while the Asian kings and Grecian commonwealths scarce afforded them a nobler subject than the unmanly luxuries of a debauched court, or giddy intrigues of a factious city. *'Alit aemulatio ingenia,'* says Paterculus, *'et nunc invidia, nunc admiratio incitationem accendit':* emulation is the spur of wit; and sometimes envy, sometimes admiration, quickens our endeavors.[19]

"But now, since the rewards of honor are taken away, that virtuous emulation is turned into direct malice; yet so slothful, that it contents itself to condemn and cry down others, without attempting to do better: 'tis a reputation too unprofitable, to take the necessary pains for it: yet, wishing they had it is incitement enough to hinder others from it. And this, in short, Eugenius, is the reason why you have now so few good poets, and so many severe judges. Certainly, to imitate the ancients well, much labor and long study is required; which pains, I have already shown our poets would want encouragement to take, if yet they had ability to go through with it. Those ancients have been faithful imitators and wise observers of that nature which is so torn and ill represented in our plays; they have handed down to us a perfect resemblance of her; which we, like ill copiers, neglecting to look on, have rendered monstrous, and disfigured. But, that you may know how much you are indebted to those your masters, and be ashamed to have so ill requited them, I must remember you, that all the rules by which we practice the drama at this day (either such as relate to the justness and symmetry of the plot, or the episodical ornaments, such as descriptions, narrations, and other

---

[14]But see Aristotle's definition of tragedy (above, page 55), though not a general definition of a play.

[15]"By genre and purpose."

[16]Thespis, very early Greek dramatist; Aristophanes (c. 444–c. 380 B.C.), Greek comic dramatist.

[17]The term is used here in the larger sense to denote all branches of learning.

[18]Aeschylus (525–456 B.C.), Euripides (c. 480–406 B.C.), Sophocles (c. 496–406 B.C.), Greek tragic dramatists; Lycophron, Alexandrian grammarian and poet (fl. c. third century B.C.).

[19]Caius Velleius Paterculus (first century), *History of Rome* I, 17.

beauties, which are not essential to the play) were delivered to us from the observations which Aristotle made, of those poets, which either lived before him, or were his contemporaries: we have added nothing of our own, except we have the confidence to say our wit is better; of which none boast in this our age, but such as understand not theirs. Of that book which Aristotle has left us, περὶ τῆς Ποιητικῆς,[20] Horace his *Art of Poetry* is an excellent comment, and, I believe, restores to us that second book of his concerning comedy, which is wanting in him.

"Out of these two have been extracted the famous rules, which the Freneh call *des trois unités*,[21] or, the three unities, which ought to be observed in every regular play; namely, of time, place, and action.

"The unity of time they comprehend in twenty-four hours, the compass of a natural day, or as near as it can be contrived; and the reason of it is obvious to everyone—that the time of the feigned action, or fable of the play, should be proportioned as near as can be to the duration of that time in which it is represented: since therefore, all plays are acted on the theater in a space of time much within the compass of twenty-four hours, that play is to be thought the nearest imitation of nature, whose plot or action is confined within that time; and, by the same rule which concludes this general proportion of time, it follows, that all the parts of it are to be equally subdivided; as namely, that one act take not up the supposed time of half a day, which is out of proportion to the rest; since the other four are then to be straitened within the compass of the remaining half: for it is unnatural that one act, which being spoke or written is not longer than the rest, should be supposed longer by the audience; 'tis therefore the poet's duty, to take care that no act should be imagined to exceed the time in which it is represented on the stage; and that the intervals and inequalities of time be supposed to fall out between the acts.

"This rule of time, how well it has been observed by the ancients, most of their plays will witness; you see them in their tragedies (wherein to follow this rule, is certainly most difficult) from the very beginning of their plays, falling close into that part of the story which they intend for the action or principal object of it, leaving the former part to be delivered by narration: so that they set the audience, as it were, at the post where the race is to be concluded; and, saving them the tedious expectation of seeing the poet set out and ride the beginning of the course, you behold him not till he is in sight of the goal, and just upon you.

"For the second unity, which is that of place, the ancients meant by it, that the scene ought to be continued through the play, in the same place where it was laid in the beginning: for the stage on which it is represented being but one and the same place, it is unnatural to conceive it many; and those far distant from one another. I will not deny but, by the variation of painted scenes, the fancy, which in these cases will contribute to its own deceit, may sometimes imagine it several places, with some appearance of probability; yet it still carries the greater likelihood of truth, if those places be supposed so near each other, as in the same town or city; which may all be comprehended under the larger domination of one place; for a greater distance will bear no proportion to the shortness of time which is allotted in the acting, to pass from one of them to another; for the observation of this, next to the ancients, the French are to be most commended. They tie themselves so strictly to the unity of place, that you never see in any of their plays, a scene changed in the middle of an act: if the act begins in a garden, a street, or chamber, 'tis ended in the same place; and that you may know it to be the same, the stage is so supplied with persons, that it is never empty all the time: he that enters the second, has business with him who was on before; and before the second quits the stage, a third appears who has business with him. This Corneille calls '*la liaison des scènes*,' the continuity or joining of the scenes[22]; and 'tis a good mark of a well-contrived play, when all the persons are known to each other, and every one of them has some affairs with all the rest.

"As for the third unity, which is that of action, the ancients meant no other by it than what the logicians do by their *finis*, the end or scope of any action; that which is the first in intention, and last in execution: now the poet is to aim at one great and complete action, to the carrying on of which all things in his play, even the very obstacles, are to be subservient; and the reason of this is as evident as any of the former.

"For two actions, equally labored and driven on by the writer, would destroy the unity of the poem; it would be no longer one play, but two: not but that there may be many actions in a play, as Ben Jonson has observed in his *Discoveries*;[23] but they must be all subservient to the great one, which our language happily expresses in the name of *underplots*: such as in Terence's[24] *Eunuch* is the difference and reconcilement of Thais and Phaedria, which is not the chief business of the play, but promotes the marriage of Chaerea

---

[20] *Poetics;* the conventional citation is "Περι ποιητκης", "Concerning (the) Poetic art."

[21] Corneille (above, page 245).

[22] Corneille (above, page 246); Castelvetro (above, page 180).

[23] *Discoveries* IV.

[24] Publius Terentius Afer (195–159 B.C.), Roman comic poet.

and Chremes's sister, principally intended by the poet. There ought to be but one action, says Corneille, that is, one complete action which leaves the mind of the audience in a full repose; but this cannot be brought to pass but by many other imperfect actions, which conduce to it, and hold the audience in a delightful suspense of what will be.[25]

"If by these rules (to omit many other drawn from the precepts and practice of the ancients) we should judge our modern plays, 'tis probable that few of them would endure the trial: that which should be the business of a day, takes up in some of them an age; instead of one action, they are the epitomes of a man's life; and for one spot of ground (which the stage should represent) we are sometimes in more countries than the map can show us.

"But if we will allow the ancients to have contrived well, we must acknowledge them to have writ better; questionless we are deprived of a great stock of wit in the loss of Menander among the Greek poets, and of Caecilius, Afranius, and Varius, among the Romans[26]; we may guess at Menander's excellency by the plays of Terence, who translated some of his; and yet wanted so much of him, that he was called by C. Caesar the half-Menander; and of Varius, by the testimonies of Horace, Martial, and Velleius Paterculus. 'Tis probable that these, could they be recovered, would decide the controversy; but so long as Aristophanes in the old comedy, and Plautus[27] in the new are extant, while the tragedies of Euripides, Sophocles, and Seneca, are to be had, I can never see one of those plays which are now written, but it increases my admiration of the ancients. And yet I must acknowledge farther, that to admire them as we ought, we should understand them better than we do. Doubtless many things appear flat to us, whose wit depended on some custom or story, which never came to our knowledge; or perhaps on some criticism in their language, which being so long dead, and only remaining in their books, 'tis not possible they should make us know it perfectly. To read Macrobius, explaining the propriety and elegancy of many words in Virgil,[28] which I had before passed over without consideration, as common things, is enough to assure me that I ought to think the same of Terence; and that in the purity of his style (which Tully so much valued that he ever carried his works about him) there is yet left in him great room for admiration, if I knew but where to place it. In the meantime

I must desire you to take notice, that the greatest man of the last age (Ben Jonson) was willing to give place to them in all things: he was not only a professed imitator of Horace, but a learned plagiary of all the others; you track him everywhere in their snow: if Horace, Lucan, Petronius Arbiter, Seneca, and Juvenal,[29] had their own from him, there are few serious thoughts which are new in him: you will pardon me, therefore, if I presume he loved their fashion, when he wore their clothes. But since I have otherwise a great veneration for him, and you, Eugenius, prefer him above all other poets, I will use no farther argument to you than his example: I will produce Father Ben to you, dressed in all the ornaments and colors of the ancients; you will need no other guide to our party, if you follow him; and whether you consider the bad plays of our age, or regard the good ones of the last, both the best and worst of the modern poets will equally instruct you to esteem the ancients."

Crites had no sooner left speaking, but Eugenius, who had waited with some impatience for it, thus began:

"I have observed in your speech, that the former part of it is convincing as to what the moderns have profited by the rules of the ancients; but in the latter you are careful to conceal how much they have excelled them; we own all the helps we have from them, and want neither veneration nor gratitude while we acknowledge that to overcome them we must make use of the advantages we have received from them: but to these assistances we have joined our own industry; for, had we sat down with a dull imitation of them, we might then have lost somewhat of the old perfection, but never acquired any that was new. We draw not therefore after their lines, but those of nature; and having the life before us, besides the experience of all they knew, it is no wonder if we hit some airs and features which they have missed. I deny not what you urge of arts and sciences, that they have flourished in some ages more than others; but your instance in philosophy makes for me: for if natural causes be more known now than in the time of Aristotle, because more studied, it follows that poesy and other arts may, with the same pains, arrive still nearer to perfection; and, that granted, it will rest for you to prove that they wrought more perfect images of human life than we; which seeing in your discourse you have avoided to make good, it shall now be my task to show you some part of their defects, and some few excellencies of the moderns. And I think there is none among us can imagine I do it enviously, or with purpose to detract from them; for what interest of fame or profit can the living lose

[25]Corneille (above, page 245).
[26]Menander (342–291 B.C.), Greek dramatist; Caecalius Statius (d. 168 B.C.); Afranius (fl. c. 100 B.C.), L. Varius Rufus (first century B.C.), Roman dramatists.
[27]Titus Maccius Plautus (c. 254–184 B.C.), Roman comic poet.
[28]Ambrosius Macrobius (fl. c. 400), Roman grammarian and critic.
[29]Annaeus Seneca (c. early first century B.C.–69 A.D.), Roman philosopher and dramatist; Marcus Annaeus Lucanus (39–65), Roman poet; Decimus Junius Juvenalis (fl. first century), Roman satirist.

by the reputation of the dead? On the other side, it is a great truth which Velleius Paterculus affirms: '*Audita visis libentius laudamus; et praesentia invidia, praeterita admiratione prosequimur; et his nos obrui, illis instrui credimus*':[30] that praise or censure is certainly the most sincere, which unbribed posterity shall give us.

"Be pleased then in the first place to take notice, that the Greek poesy, which Crites has affirmed to have arrived to perfection in the reign of the old comedy, was so far from it, that the distinction of it into acts was not known to them; or if it were, it is yet so darkly delivered to us that we cannot make it out.

"All we know of it is, from the singing of their chorus; and that too is so uncertain, that in some of their plays we have reason to conjecture they sung more than five times. Aristotle indeed divides the integral parts of a play into four. First, the protasis, or entrance, which gives light only to the characters of the persons, and proceeds very little into any part of the action. Secondly, the epitasis, or working up of the plot; where the play grows warmer, the design or action of it is drawing on, and you see something promising that it will come to pass. Thirdly, the catastasis, or counterturn, which destroys that expectation, embroils the action in new difficulties, and leaves you far distant from that hope in which it found you; as you may have observed in a violent stream resisted by a narrow passage—it runs round to an eddy, and carries back the waters with more swiftness than it brought them on. Lastly, the catastrophe, which the Grecians called λύσις,[31] the French *le dénouement*, and we the discovery or unraveling of the plot: there you see all things settling again upon their first foundations; and, the obstacles which hindered the design or action of the play once removed, it ends with that resemblance of truth and nature, that the audience are satisfied with the conduct of it. Thus this great man delivered to us the image of a play; and I must confess it is so lively, that from thence much light has been derived to the forming it more perfectly into acts and scenes: but what poet first limited to five the number of the acts, I know not; only we see it so firmly established in the time of Horace, that he gives it for a rule in comedy; '*Neu brevior quinto, neu sir productior actu.*'[32] So that you see the Grecians cannot be said to have consummated this art; writing rather by entrances, than by acts, and having rather

a general indigested notion of a play, than knowing how and where to bestow the particular graces of it.

"But since the Spaniards at this day allow but three acts, which they call *jornadas,* to a play, and the Italians in many of theirs follow them, when I condemn the ancients, I declare it is not altogether because they have not five acts to every play, but because they have not confined themselves to one certain number: it is building a house without a model; and when they succeeded in such undertakings, they ought to have sacrificed to Fortune, not to the Muses.

"Next, for the plot, which Aristotle called τὸ μῦθος, and often τῶν πραγμάτων σύνθεσις,[33] and from him the Romans *fabula,* it has already been judiciously observed by a late writer, that in their tragedies it was only some tale derived from Thebes or Troy, or at least something that happened in those two ages; which was worn so threadbare by the pens of all the epic poets, and even by tradition itself of the talkative Greeklings, (as Ben Jonson calls them,) that before it came upon the stage, it was already known to all the audience: and the people, so soon as ever they heard the name of Oedipus, knew as well as the poet, that he had killed his father by a mistake, and committed incest with his mother, before the play; that they were now to hear of a great plague, an oracle, and the ghost of Laius: so that they sat with a yawning kind of expectation, till he was to come with his eyes pulled out, and speak a hundred or two of verses in a tragic tone, in complaint of his misfortunes. But one Oedipus, Hercules, or Medea, had been tolerable: poor people, they 'scaped not so good cheap; they had still the *chapon bouille*[34] set before them till their appetites were cloyed with the same dish, and, the novelty being gone, the pleasure vanished; so that one main end of dramatic poesy in its definition, which was to cause delight, was of consequence destroyed.

"In their comedies, the Romans generally borrowed their plots from the Greek poets; and theirs was commonly a little girl stolen or wandered from her parents, brought back unknown to the same city: there got with child by some lewd young fellow, who, by the help of his servant, cheats his father; and when her time comes, to cry '*Juno Lucina, fer opem,*'[35] one or other sees a little box or cabinet which was carried away with her, and so discovers her to her friends, if some god do not prevent it, by coming down in a machine, and take the thanks of it to himself.

"By the plot you may guess much of the characters of the persons. An old father, who would willingly, before he

---

[30] "We praise more gladly things heard than seen; and we accompany envy for the present with admiration for the past; and we believe we are oppressed by the former, instructed by the latter." *History of Rome* II, 92.

[31] "Unraveling"; cf. *Poetics* 1154a.10b.

[32] "Let it be neither shorter nor longer than five acts." Horace (above, page 81).

[33] "The putting together of the actions."

[34] "Boiled capon" or "tasty dish."

[35] "Juno, goddess of births, help."

dies, see his son well married; his debauched son, kind in his nature to his wench, but miserably in want of money; a servant or slave, who has so much wit to strike in with him, and help to dupe his father; a braggadocio captain, a parasite, and a lady of pleasure.

"As for the poor honest maid, whom all the story is built upon, and who ought to be one of the principal actors in the play, she is commonly a mute in it: she has the breeding of the old Elizabeth way, for maids to be seen and not to be heard; and it is enough you know she is willing to be married, when the fifth act requires it.

"These are plots built after the Italian mode of houses; you see through them all at once: the characters are indeed the imitations of nature, but so narrow, as if they had imitated only an eye or an hand, and did not dare to venture on the lines of a face, or the proportion of a body.

"But in how strait a compass soever they have bounded their plots and characters, we will pass it by, if they have regularly pursued them, and perfectly observed those three unities of time, place, and action; the knowledge of which you say is derived to us from them. But in the first place give me leave to tell you, that the unity of place, however it might be practiced by them, was never any of their rules: we neither find it in Aristotle, Horace, or any who have written of it, till in our age the French poets first made it a precept of the stage. The unity of time, even Terence himself (who was the best and most regular of them) has neglected: his *Heautontimorumenos,* or *Self-Punisher,* takes up visibly two days; therefore, says Scaliger, the two first acts concluding the first day were acted overnight; the three last on the ensuing day; and Euripides, in tying himself to one day, has committed an absurdity never to be forgiven him; for in one of his tragedies he has made Theseus go from Athens to Thebes, which was about forty English miles, under the walls of it to give battle, and appear victorious in the next act; and yet, from the time of his departure to the return of the nuntius, who gives the relation of his victory, Aethra and the chorus have but thirty-six verses; that is not for every mile a verse.

"The like error is as evident in Terence his *Eunuch,* when Laches, the old man, enters in a mistake the house of Thais; where, betwixt his exit and the entrance of Pythias, who comes to give an ample relation of the garboils he has raised within, Parmeno, who was left upon the stage, has not above five lines to speak. *'C'est bien employer un temps si court,*[36] says the French poet, who furnished me with one of the observations: and almost all their tragedies will afford us examples of the like nature.

---

[36] "It is well to employ a time so short." Corneille (above, page 249).

"'Tis true, they have kept the continuity, or, as you called it, *'liaison des scènes,'* somewhat better: two do not perpetually come in together, talk, and go out together; and other two succeed them, and do the same throughout the act, which the English call by the name of single scenes; but the reason is, because they have seldom above two or three scenes, properly so-called, in every act; for it is to be accounted a new scene, not every time the stage is empty; but every person who enters, though to others, makes it so; because he introduces a new business. Now the plots of their plays being narrow, and the persons few, one of their acts was written in a less compass than one of our well-wrought scenes; and yet they are often deficient even in this. To go no further than Terence; you find in the *Eunuch* Antipho entering single in the midst of the third act, after Cremes and Pythias were gone off; in the same play you have likewise Dorias beginning the fourth act alone; and after she had made a relation of what was done at the soldier's entertainment (which by the way was very inartificial, because she was presumed to speak directly to the audience, and to acquaint them with what was necessary to be known, but yet should have been so contrived by the poet as to have been told by persons of the drama to one another, and so by them to have come to the knowledge of the people), she quits the stage, and Phaedria enters next, alone likewise: he also gives you an account of himself, and of his returning from the country, in monologue; to which unnatural way of narration Terence is subject in all his plays. In his *Adelphi,* or *Brothers,* Syrus and Demea enter after the scene was broken by the departure of Sostrata, Geta, and Canthara; and indeed you can scarce look into any of his comedies, where you will not presently discover the same interruption.

"But as they have failed both in laying of their plots, and managing of them, swerving from the rules of their own art by misrepresenting nature to us, in which they have ill satisfied one intention of a play, which was delight; so in the instructive part they have erred worse; instead of punishing vice and rewarding virtue, they have often shown a prosperous wickedness, and an unhappy piety: they have set before us a bloody image of revenge in Medea, and given her dragons to convey her safe from punishment: a Priam and Astyanax murdered, and Cassandra ravished, and the lust and murder ending in the victory of him who acted them: in short, there is no indecorum in any of our modern plays, which if I would excuse, I could not shadow with some authority from the ancients.

"And one farther note of them let me leave you: tragedies and comedies were not writ then as they are now, promiscuously, by the same person; but he who found his genius bending to the one, never attempted the other way.

This is so plain, that I need not instance to you, that Aristophanes, Plautus, Terence, never any of them writ a tragedy; Aeschylus, Euripides, Sophocles, and Seneca, never meddled with comedy: the sock and buskin were not worn by the same poet. Having then so much care to excel in one kind, very little is to be pardoned them, if they miscarried in it; and this would lead me to the consideration of their wit, had not Crites given me sufficient warning not to be too bold in my judgment of it; because, the languages being dead, and many of the customs and little accidents on which it depended lost to us, we are not competent judges of it. But though I grant that here and there we may miss the application of a proverb or a custom, yet a thing well said will be wit in all languages; and though it may lose something in the translation, yet to him who reads it in the original, 'tis still the same: he has an idea of its excellency, though it cannot pass from his mind into any other expression or words than those in which he finds it. When Phaedria, in the *Eunuch*, had a command from his mistress to be absent two days, and, encouraging himself to go through with it, said, *'Tandem ego non illa caream, si sit opus, vel totum triduum?'*[37]—Parmeno, to mock the softness of his master, lifting up his hands and eyes, cries out, as it were in admiration, *'Hui! universum triduum!'*[38] the elegancy of which *'universum,'* though it cannot be rendered in our language, yet leaves an impression on our souls: but this happens seldom in him; in Plautus oftener, who is infinitely too bold in his metaphors and coining words, out of which many times his wit is nothing; which questionless was one reason why Horace falls upon him so severely in those verses:

> *Sed proavi nostri Plautinos et numeros et*
> *Laudavere sales, nimium patienter utrumque,*
> *Ne dicam stolidè.*[39]

For Horace himself was cautious to obtrude a new word on his readers, and makes custom and common use the best measure of receiving it into our writings:

> *Multa renascentur quae nunc cecidere, cadentque*
> *Quae nunc sunt in honore vocabula, si volet usus,*
> *Quem penes arbitrium est, et jus, et norma loquendi.*[40]

"The not observing this rule is that which the world has blamed in our satirist, Cleveland: to express a thing hard and unnaturally, is his new way of elocution. 'Tis true, no poet but may sometimes use a catachresis: Virgil does it—*'Mistaque ridenti colocasia fundei acantho'*[41]—in his eclogue of *Pollio;* and in his seventh *Aeneid.*

> *mirantur et undae,*
> *Miratur nemus insuetum fulgentia longe*
> *Scuta virum fluvio pictasque innare carinas.*[42]

And Ovid once so modestly, that he asks leave to do it: *'quem, si verbo audacia detur, / Haud metuam summi dixisse palatia caeli':*[43] calling the court of Jupiter by the name of Augustus his palace; though in another place he is more bold, where he says, *'et longas visent Capitolia pompas.'*[44] But to do this always, and never be able to write a line without it, though it may be admired by some few pedants, will not pass upon those who know that wit is best conveyed to us in the most easy language; and is most to be admired when a great thought comes dressed in words so commonly received, that it is understood by the meanest apprehensions, as the best meat is the most easily digested: but we cannot read a verse of Cleveland's without making a face at it, as if every word were a pill to swallow: he gives us many times a hard nut to break our teeth, without a kernel for our pains. So that there is this difference betwixt his *Satires* and Doctor Donne's; that the one gives us deep thoughts in common language, though rough cadence; the other gives as common thoughts in abstruse words: 'tis true, in some places his wit is independent of his words, as in that of the *Rebel Scot:* 'Had Cain been Scot, God would have changed his doom; / Not forced him wander, but confined him home.'[45]

"'*Si sic omnia dixisset!*'[46] This is wit in all languages: 'tis like Mercury, never to be lost or killed: and so that other—'For beauty, like white powder, makes no noise, / And yet the silent hypocrite destroys.'[47] You see, the last line is highly metaphorical, but it is so soft and gentle, that it does not shock us as we read it.

---

[37] "Shall I not do without her, if it is necessary, even for three whole days?" Terence, *Eunuch* II, i.

[38] "Alas, three whole days." Terence, *Eunuch* II, i.

[39] "But our ancestors lauded both the meters and wit of Plautus, admiring each tolerantly, I shall not say stupidly." Horace (above, page 82).

[40] "Many words will revive that are now out of use, and many which are now esteemed will die out, if custom wills it, in whose power is the decision, both the law and the norms of speech." Horace (above, page 80).

[41] "And the colocasia will bloom, mingled with the laughing acanthus." *Eclogues* IV, 20.

[42] "The woods and waters wonder at the gleam of shields, and painted ships, that stem the stream." *Aeneid* VIII, 91 (Dryden's translation).

[43] Publius Ovidius Naso (43 B.C.–16 A.D.): "If verbal license is granted, I shall not at all fear to call it the palace of the sky." *Metamorphoses* I, 175.

[44] "And the Capitol sees long processions." *Metamorphoses* I, 561.

[45] Cleveland, *Rebel Scot,* 63–4.

[46] "If only he had said it all this way." Juvenal, *Satires* X, 123.

[47] Cleveland, *Rupertismus,* 39–40.

"But, to return from whence I have digressed, to the considerations of the ancients' writing, and their wit; of which by this time you will grant us in some measure to be fit judges. Though I see many excellent thoughts in Seneca, yet he of them who had a genius most proper for the stage, was Ovid; he had a way of writing so fit to stir up a pleasing admiration and concernment, which are the objects of a tragedy, and to show the various movements of a soul combating betwixt two different passions, that, had he lived in our age, or in his own could have writ with our advantages, no man but must have yielded to him; and therefore I am confident the *Medea* is none of his: for, though I esteem it for the gravity and sententiousness of it, which he himself concludes to be suitable to a tragedy—'*Omne genus scripti gravitate tragaedia vincit*'[48]—yet it moves not my soul enough to judge that he, who in the epic way wrote things so near the drama as the story of Myrrha, of Caunus and Biblis, and the rest, should stir up no more concernment where he most endeavored it. The masterpiece of Seneca I hold to be that scene in the *Troades,* where Ulysses is seeking for Astyanax to kill him; there you see the tenderness of a mother so represented in Andromache, that it raises compassion to a high degree in the reader, and bears the nearest resemblance of anything in their tragedies to the excellent scenes of passion in Shakespeare, or in Fletcher[49]: for love scenes, you will find few among them; their tragic poets dealt not with that soft passion, but with lust, cruelty, revenge, ambition, and those bloody actions they produced; which were more capable of raising horror than compassion in an audience: leaving love untouched, whose gentleness would have tempered them, which is the most frequent of all the passions, and which being the private concernment of every person, is soothed by viewing its own image in a public entertainment.

"Among their comedies, we find a scene or two of tenderness, and that where you would least expect it, in Plautus; but to speak generally, their lovers say little, when they see each other, but '*anima mea, vita mea:* ζωή καὶ ψυχή,'[50] as the women in Juvenal's time used to cry out in the fury of their kindness: then indeed to speak sense were an offense. Any sudden gust of passion (as an ecstasy of love in an unexpected meeting) cannot better be expressed than in a word and a sigh, breaking one another. Nature is dumb on such occasions; and to make her speak, would be to represent her unlike herself. But there are a thousand other concernments of lovers, as jealousies, complaints, contrivances, and the like, where not to open their minds at large to each other, were to be wanting to their own love, and to the expectation of the audience, who watch the movements of their minds, as much as the changes of their fortunes. For the imaging of the first is properly the work of a poet; the latter he borrows of the historian."

Eugenius was proceeding in that part of his discourse, when Crites interrupted him. "I see," said he, "Eugenius and I are never like to have this question decided betwixt us; for he maintains the moderns have acquired a new perfection in writing; I can only grant they have altered the mode of it. Homer described his heroes men of great appetites, lovers of beef broiled upon the coals, and good fellows; contrary to the practice of the French romances, whose heroes neither eat, nor drink, nor sleep, for love. Virgil makes Aeneas a bold avower of his own virtues: '*Sum pius Aeneas, fama super aethera notus*';[51] which in the civility of our poets is the character of a fanfaron or Hector: for with us the knight takes occasion to walk out, or sleep, to avoid the vanity of telling his own story, which the trusty squire is ever to perform for him. So in their love scenes, of which Eugenius spoke last, the ancients were more hearty, we more talkative: they writ love as it was then the mode to make it; and I will grant thus much to Eugenius, that perhaps one of their poets, had he lived in our age, '*si foret hoc nostrum fato delapsus in aevum*'[52] (as Horace says of Lucilius), he had altered many things; not that they were not as natural before, but that he might accommodate himself to the age he lived in. Yet in the meantime, we are not to conclude anything rashly against those great men, but preserve to them the dignity of masters, and give that honor to their memories, '*quos Libitina sacravit,*'[53] part of which we expect may be paid to us in future times."

This moderation of Crites, as it was pleasing to all the company, so it put an end to that dispute: which Eugenius, who seemed to have the better of the argument, would urge no farther: but Lisideius, after he had acknowledged himself of Eugenius his opinion concerning the ancients, yet told him, he had forborne, till his discourse were ended, to ask him why he preferred the English plays above those of other nations? and whether we ought not to submit our stage to the exactness of our next neighbors?

"Though," said Eugenius, "I am at all times ready to defend the honor of my country against the French, and to maintain, we are as well able to vanquish them with our pens, as our ancestors have been with their swords; yet, if

---

[48]"Tragedy excels all other kinds of writing in gravity." *Tristia* II, 381.
[49]John Fletcher (1579–1625), English dramatist.
[50]Zoa kai psoxa: "My soul, my life."

[51]"I am the pious Aeneas, famed above the heavens." *Aeneid* I, 378.
[52]"If dropped by fate into our age." Horace, *Satires* I, x, 68.
[53]"Which Libitina has made sacred." Horace, *Epistles* II, i, 49.

you please," added he, looking upon Neander, "I will commit this cause to my friend's management; his opinion of our plays is the same with mine: and besides, there is no reason, that Crites and I, who have now left the stage, should reenter so suddenly upon it; which is against the laws of comedy."

"If the question had been stated," replied Lisideius, "who had writ best, the French or English, forty years ago, I should have been of your opinion, and adjudged the honor to our own nation; but since that time," said he, turning towards Neander, "we have been so long together bad Englishmen, that we had not leisure to be good poets. Beaumont, Fletcher, and Jonson[54] (who were only capable of bringing us to that degree of perfection which we have) were just then leaving the world; as if (in an age of so much horror) wit, and those milder studies of humanity, had no farther business among us. But the Muses, who ever follow peace, went to plant in another country: it was then that the great Cardinal of Richelieu began to take them into his protection; and that, by his encouragement, Corneille, and some other Frenchmen, reformed their theater, which before was as much below ours, as it now surpasses it and the rest of Europe. But because Crites in his discourse for the ancients has prevented me, by touching upon many rules of the stage which the moderns have borrowed from them, I shall only, in short, demand of you, whether you are not convinced that of all nations the French have best observed them? In the unity of time you find them so scrupulous, that it yet remains a dispute among their poets, whether the artificial day of twelve hours, more or less, be not meant by Aristotle, rather than the natural one of twenty-four; and consequently, whether all plays ought not to be reduced into that compass. This I can testify, that in all their dramas writ within these last twenty years and upwards, I have not observed any that have extended the time to thirty hours: in the unity of place they are full as scrupulous; for many of their critics limit it to that very spot of ground where the play is supposed to begin; none of them exceed the compass of the same town or city. The unity of action in all plays is yet more conspicuous; for they do not burden them with underplots, as the English do: which is the reason why many scenes of our tragicomedies carry on a design that is nothing of kin to the main plot; and that we see two distinct webs in a play, like those in ill-wrought stuffs; and two actions, that is, two plays, carried on together, to the confounding of the audience; who, before they are warm in their concernments for one part, are diverted to another; and

by that means espouse the interest of neither. From hence likewise it arises, that the one half of our actors are not known to the other. They keep their distances, as if they were Montagues and Capulets, and seldom begin an acquaintance till the last scene of the fifth act, when they are all to meet upon the stage. There is no theater in the world has anything so absurd as the English tragicomedy; 'tis a drama of our own invention, and the fashion of it is enough to proclaim it so; here a course of mirth, there another of sadness and passion, a third of honor, and fourth a duel: thus, in two hours and a half, we run through all the fits of Bedlam. The French affords you as much variety on the same day, but they do it not so unseasonably, or *mal à propos,* as we: our poets present you the play and the farce together; and our stages still retain somewhat of the original civility of the *Red Bull: 'Alque ursum et pugiles media inter carmina poscunt.'*[55] The end of tragedies or serious plays, says Aristotle, is to beget admiration, compassion, or concernment; but are not mirth and compassion things incompatible? and is it not evident that the poet must of necessity destroy the former by intermingling of the latter? That is, he must ruin the sole end and object of his tragedy, to introduce somewhat that is forced in, and is not of the body of it. Would you not think that physician mad, who, having prescribed a purge, should immediately order you to take restringents upon it?

"But to leave our plays, and return to theirs. I have noted one great advantage they have had in the plotting of their tragedies; that is, they are always grounded upon some known history: according to that of Horace, *'Ex noto fictum carmen sequar',*[56] and in that they have so imitated the ancients, that they have surpassed them. For the ancients, as was observed before, took for the foundation of their plays some poetical fiction, such as under that consideration could move but little concernment in the audience, because they already knew the event of it. But the French goes farther: *'Atque ita mentitur, sic veris falsa remiscet, / Primo ne medium, medio ne discrepet imum.'*[57] He so interweaves truth with probable fiction, that he puts a pleasing fallacy upon us; mends the intrigues of fate, and dispenses with the severity of history, to reward that virtue which has been rendered to us there unfortunate. Sometimes the story has left the success so doubtful, that the writer is free, by the privilege of a poet, to take that which of two or more relations will best suit with his design: as for example, the death of

---

[54]Francis Beaumont (1584–1616), Ben Jonson (1573?–1637), English dramatists.

[55]"In the middle of plays they demand a bear and boxers." Horace, *Epistles* II, i, 185.

[56]"From known stories I shall make a poem." Horace (above, page 82).

[57]"He so lies, so mingles the false with the true, that one cannot distinguish beginning, middle, and end." Horace (above, page 81).

Cyrus, whom Justin and some others report to have perished in the Scythian war, but Xenophon affirms to have died in his bed of extreme old age. Nay more, when the event is past dispute, even then we are willing to be deceived, and the poet, if he contrives it with appearance of truth, has all the audience of his party; at least during the time his play is acting: so naturally we are kind to virtue, when our own interest is not in question, that we take it up as the general concernment of mankind. On the other side, if you consider the historical plays of Shakespeare, they are rather so many chronicles of kings, or the business many times of thirty or forty years, cramped into a representation of two hours and a half; which is not to imitate or paint nature, but rather to draw her in miniature, to take her in little; to look upon her through the wrong end of a perspective, and receive her images not only much less, but infinitely more imperfect than the life: this, instead of making a play delightful, renders it ridiculous: *'Quodcumque ostendis mihi sic, incredulus odi.'*[58] For the spirit of man cannot be satisfied but with truth, or at least verisimility; and a poem is to contain, if not τὰ ἔτυμα, yet ἐτύμοισιν ὁμοῖα,[59] as one of the Greek poets has expressed it.

"Another thing in which the French differ from us and from the Spaniards, is, that they do not embarrass, or cumber themselves with too much plot; they only represent so much of a story as will constitute one whole and great action sufficient for a play; we, who undertake more, do but multiply adventures; which, not being produced from one another, as effects from causes, but barely following, constitute many actions in the drama, and consequently make it many plays.

"But by pursuing close one argument, which is not cloyed with many turns, the French have gained more liberty for verse, in which they write; they have leisure to dwell on a subject which deserves it; and to represent the passions (which we have acknowledged to be the poet's work), without being hurried from one thing to another, as we are in the plays of Calderon,[60] which we have seen lately upon our theaters, under the name of Spanish plots. I have taken notice but of one tragedy of ours, whose plot has the uniformity and unity of design in it, which I have commended in the French; and that is *Rollo*, or rather, under the name of Rollo, the story of Bassianus and Geta in Hero-

dian:[61] there indeed the plot is neither large nor intricate, but just enough to fill the minds of the audience, not to cloy them. Besides, you see it founded upon the truth of history, only the time of the action is not reduceable to the strictness of the rules; and you see in some places a little farce mingled, which is below the dignity of the other parts; and in this all our poets are extremely peccant: even Ben Johnson himself, in *Sejanus* and *Catiline*, has given us this oleo[62] of a play, this unnatural mixture of comedy and tragedy; which to me sounds just as ridiculously as the history of David with the merry humors of Goliath. In *Sejanus* you may take notice of the scene betwixt Livia and the physician, which is a pleasant satire upon the artificial helps of beauty: in *Catiline* you may see the parliament of women; the little envies of them to one another; and all that passes betwixt Curio and Fulvia: scenes admirable in their kind, but of an ill mingle with the rest.

"But I return again to the French writers, who, as I have said, do not burden themselves too much with plot, which has been reproached to them by an ingenious person of our nation as a fault; for, he says, they commonly make but one person considerable in a play; they dwell on him, and his concernments, while the rest of the persons are only subservient to set him off. If he intends this by it, that there is one person in the play who is of greater dignity than the rest, he must tax, not only theirs, but those of the ancients, and which he would be loath to do, the best of ours; for it is impossible but that one person must be more conspicuous in it than any other, and consequently the greatest share in the action must devolve on him. We see it so in the management of all affairs; even in the most equal aristocracy, the balance cannot be so justly poised, but someone will be superior to the rest, either in parts, fortune, interest, or the consideration of some glorious exploit; which will reduce the greatest part of business into his hands.

"But, if he would have us to imagine, that in exalting one character the rest of them are neglected, and that all of them have not some share or other in the action of the play, I desire him to produce any of Corneille's tragedies, wherein every person, like so many servants in a well-governed family, has not some employment, and who is not necessary to the carrying on of the plot, or at least to your understanding it.

"There are indeed some protatic persons[63] in the ancients, whom they make use of in their plays, either to hear

[58] Whatever you thus show me I find incredible and odious." Horace (above, page 81).
[59] Ta etuma etmoisin omoia: "true things" yet "things like the truth." Hesiod, *Theogony*, 27.
[60] Pedro Calderon de la Barca (1600–1681), Spanish poet and dramatist.
[61] Herodianus (first to second century), Greek writer on Roman history.
[62] Hotchpotch or medley.
[63] Characters appearing only in the introductory part of plays.

or give the relation: but the French avoid this with great address, making their narrations only to or by such, who are some way interested in the main design. And now I am speaking of relations, I cannot take a fitter opportunity to add this in favor of the French, that they often use them with better judgment and more *à propos* than the English do. Not that I commend narrations in general—but there are two sorts of them. One, of those things which are antecedent to the play, and are related to make the conduct of it more clear to us. But 'tis a fault to choose such subjects for the stage as will force us on that rock, because we see they are seldom listened to by the audience, and that is many times the ruin of the play; for, being once let pass without attention, the audience can never recover themselves to understand the plot: and indeed it is somewhat unreasonable that they should be put to so much trouble, as that, to comprehend what passes in their sight, they must have recourse to what was done, perhaps, ten or twenty years ago.

"But there is another sort of relations, that is, of things happening in the action of the play, and supposed to be done behind the scenes; and this is many times both convenient and beautiful; for by it the French avoid the tumult which we are subject to in England, by representing duels, battles, and the like: which renders our stage too like the theaters where they fight prizes. For what is more ridiculous than to represent an army with a drum and five men behind it; all which the hero of the other side is to drive in before him; or to see a duel fought, and one slain with two or three thrusts of the foils, which we know are so blunted, that we might give a man an hour to kill another in good earnest with them.

"I have observed that in all our tragedies, the audience cannot forbear laughing when the actors are to die; it is the most comic part of the whole play. All passions may be lively represented on the stage, if to the well-writing of them the actor supplies a good commanded voice, and limbs that move easily; and without stiffness; but there are many actions which can never be imitated to a just height: dying especially is a thing which none but a Roman gladiator could naturally perform on the stage, when he did not imitate or represent, but naturally do it; and therefore it is better to omit the representation of it.

"The words of a good writer, which describe it lively, will make a deeper impression of belief in us than all the actor can persuade us to, when he seems to fall dead before us; as a poet in the description of a beautiful garden, or a meadow, will please our imagination more than the place itself can please our sight. When we see death represented, we are convinced it is but fiction; but when we hear it related, our eyes, the strongest witnesses, are wanting, which might have undeceived us; and we are willing to favor the

sleight, when the poet does not too grossly impose on us. They therefore who imagine these relations would make no concernment in the audience, are deceived, by confounding them with the other, which are of things antecedent to the play: those are made often in cold blood, as I may say, to the audience; but these are armed with our concernments, which were before awakened in the play. What the philosophers say of motion, that, when it is once begun, it continues of itself, and will do so to eternity, without some stop put to it, is clearly true on this occasion: the soul, being already moved with the characters and fortunes of those imaginary persons, continues going of its own accord; and we are no more weary to hear what becomes of them when they are not on the stage, than we are to listen to the news of an absent mistress. But it is objected, that if one part of the play may be related, then why not all? I answer, some parts of the action are more fit to be represented, some to be related. Corneille says judiciously, that the poet is not obliged to expose to view all particular actions which conduce to the principal: he ought to select such of them to be seen, which will appear with the greatest beauty, either by the magnificence of the show, or the vehemence of passions which they produce, or some other charm which they have in them; and let the rest arrive to the audience by narration.[64] 'Tis a great mistake in us to believe the French present no part of the action on the stage; every alteration or crossing of a design, every new-sprung passion, and turn of it, is a part of the action, and much the noblest, except we conceive nothing to be action till they come to blows; as if the painting of the hero's mind were not more properly the poet's work than the strength of his body. Nor does this anything contradict the opinion of Horace, where he tells us, *'Segnius irritant animos demissa per aurem, / Quam quae sunt oculis subjecta fidelibus.'* For he says immediately after,

> *Non tamen intus*
> *Digna geri promes in scenam; multaque tolles*
> *Ex oculis, quae mox narret facundia praesens.*

Among which many he recounts some: *'Nec pueros coram populo Medea trucidet, / Aut in avem Progne mutetur, Cadmus in anguem'; &c.*[65] That is, those actions which by reason of their cruelty will cause aversion in us, or by reason of

---

[64]See Corneille (above, page 245).

[65]"What we hear through the ears stirs the mind less forcibly than what are placed before trustworthy eyes." . . . "Do not bring on the stage much which should be done off of it; keep many things from sight and presently narrate them with eloquence." . . . "Do not let Medea kill her children before the audience, nor change Procne into a bird, Cadmus into a snake." Horace (above, page 81).

their impossibility, unbelief, ought either wholly to be avoided by a poet, or only delivered by narration. To which we may have leave to add such as to avoid tumult (as was before hinted), or to reduce the plot into a more reasonable compass of time, or for defect of beauty in them, are rather to be related than presented to the eye. Examples of all these kinds are frequent, not only among all the ancients, but in the best received of our English poets. We find Ben Jonson using them in his *Magnetic Lady,* where one comes out from dinner, and relates the quarrels and disorders of it, to save the undecent appearance of them on the stage, and to abbreviate the story; and this in express imitation of Terence, who had done the same before him in his *Eunuch,* where Pythias makes the like relation of what had happened within at the soldier's entertainment. The relations likewise of Sejanus's death, and the prodigies before it, are remarkable; the one of which was hid from sight, to avoid the horror and tumult of the representation; the other, to shun the introducing of things impossible to be believed. In that excellent play, *The King and No King,* Fletcher goes yet farther: for the whole unraveling of the plot is done by narration in the fifth act, after the manner of the ancients; and it moves great concernment in the audience, though it be only a relation of what was done many years before the play. I could multiply other instances, but these are sufficient to prove that there is no error in choosing a subject which requires this sort of narrations; in the ill-managing of them, there may.

"But I find I have been too long in this discourse, since the French have many other excellencies not common to us; as that you never see any of their plays end with a conversion, or simple change of will, which is the ordinary way which our poets use to end theirs. It shows little art in the conclusion of a dramatic poem, when they who have hindered the felicity during the four acts, desist from it in the fifth, without some powerful cause to take them off; and though I deny not but such reasons may be found, yet it is a path that is cautiously to be trod, and the poet is to be sure he convinces the audience that the motive is strong enough. As for example, the conversion of the usurer in *The Scornful Lady,* seems to me a little forced; for, being a usurer, which implies a lover of money to the highest degree of covetousness (and such the poet has represented him), the account he gives for the sudden change is, that he has been duped by the wild young fellow; which in reason might render him more wary another time, and make him punish himself with harder fare and coarser clothes, to get it up again: but that he should look on it as a judgment, and so repent, we may expect to hear of in a sermon, but I should never endure it in a play.

"I pass by this; neither will I insist on the care they take, that no person after his first entrance shall ever appear, but the business which brings him upon the stage shall be evident; which, if observed, must needs render all the events in the play more natural: for there you see the probability of every accident, in the cause that produced it; and that which appears chance in the play, will seem so reasonable to you, that you will there find it almost necessary: so that in the exits of the actors you have a clear account of their purpose and design in the next entrance (though, if the scene be well wrought, the event will commonly deceive you), for there is nothing so absurd, says Corneille, as for an actor to leave the stage, only because he has no more to say.[66]

"I should now speak of the beauty of their rhyme, and the just reason I have to prefer that way of writing in tragedies before ours in blank verse; but because it is partly received by us, and therefore not altogether peculiar to them, I will say no more of it in relation to their plays. For our own, I doubt not but it will exceedingly beautify them; and I can see but one reason why it should not generally obtain, that is, because our poets write so ill in it. This indeed may prove a more prevailing argument than all others which are used to destroy it, and therefore I am only troubled when great and judicious poets, and those who are acknowledged such, have writ or spoke against it: as for others, they are to be answered by that one sentence of an ancient author: '*Sed ut primo ad consequendos eos quos priores ducimus, accendimur, ita ubi aut praeteriri, aut aequari eos posse desperavimus, studium cum spe senescit: quod, scilicet, assequi non potest, sequi desinit . . . praeteritoque eo in quo eminere non possumus, aliquid in quo nitamur, conquirimus.*'"[67]

Lisideius concluded in this manner; and Neander, after a little pause, thus answered him:

"I shall grant Lisideius, without much dispute, a great part of what he has urged against us; for I acknowledge that the French contrive their plots more regularly, and observe the laws of comedy, and decorum of the stage (to speak generally), with more exactness than the English. Farther, I deny not but he has taxed us justly in some irregularities of ours, which he has mentioned; yet, after all, I am of opinion that neither our faults nor their virtues are considerable enough to place them above us.

"For the lively imitation of nature being in the definition of a play, those which best fulfill that law ought to be

---

[66] See Corneille (above, page 248).

[67] "But as we are inspired at first to follow those whom we consider leaders, so when we despair of the possibility of excelling or equaling them, our enthusiasm declines with our hope; for, of course, what is not able to attain it ceases to follow . . . that being past in which we are not able to excel, we seek something else for which to strive." Paterculus, *History of Rome* I, 127.

esteemed superior to the others. 'Tis true, those beauties of the French poesy are such as will raise perfection higher where it is, but are not sufficient to give it where it is not: they are indeed the beauties of a statue, but not of a man, because not animated with the soul of poesy, which is imitation of humor and passions: and this Lisideius himself, or any other, however biased to their party, cannot but acknowledge, if he will either compare the humors of our comedies, or the characters of our serious plays, with theirs. He that will look upon theirs which have been written till these last ten years, or thereabouts, will find it a hard matter to pick out two or three passable humors amongst them. Corneille himself, their archpoet, what has he produced except *The Liar,* and you know how it was cried up in France; but when it came upon the English stage, though well translated, and that part of Dorant acted to so much advantage by Mr. Hart as I am confident it never received in its own country, the most favorable to it would not put it in competition with many of Fletcher's or Ben Jonson's. In the rest of Corneille's comedies you have little humor; he tells you himself, his way is, first to show two lovers in good intelligence with each other; in the working up of the play to embroil them by some mistake, and in the latter end to clear it, and reconcile them.

"But of late years Molière, the younger Corneille, Quinault,[68] and some others, have been imitating afar off the quick turns and graces of the English stage. They have mixed their serious plays with mirth, like our tragicomedies, since the death of Cardinal Richelieu; which Lisideius and many others not observing, have commended that in them for a virtue which they themselves no longer practice. Most of their new plays are, like some of ours, derived from the Spanish novels. There is scarce one of them without a veil, and a trusty Diego,[69] who drolls much after the rate of the *Adventures.* But their humors, if I may grace them with that name, are so thin sown, that never above one of them comes up in any play. I dare take upon me to find more variety of them in some one play of Ben Jonson's, than in all theirs together; as he who has seen *The Alchemist, The Silent Woman,* or *Bartholomew Fair,* cannot but acknowledge with me.

"I grant the French have performed what was possible on the groundwork of the Spanish plays; what was pleasant before, they have made regular: but there is not above one good play to be writ on all those plots; they are too much alike to please often; which we need not the experience of our own stage to justify. As for their new way of mingling mirth with serious plot, I do not, with Lisideius, condemn the thing, though I cannot approve their manner of doing it. He tells us, we cannot so speedily recollect ourselves after a scene of great passion and concernment, as to pass to another of mirth and humor, and to enjoy it with any relish: but why should he imagine the soul of man more heavy than his senses? Does not the eye pass from an unpleasant object to a pleasant in a much shorter time than is required to this? And does not the unpleasantness of the first commend the beauty of the latter? The old rule of logic might have convinced him, that contraries, when placed near, set off each other. A continued gravity keeps the spirit too much bent; we must refresh it sometimes, as we bait in a journey, that we may go on with greater ease. A scene of mirth, mixed with tragedy, has the same effect upon us which our music has betwixt the acts; and that we find a relief to us from the best plots and language of the stage, if the discourses have been long. I must therefore have stronger arguments, ere I am convinced that compassion and mirth in the same subject destroy each other; and in the meantime cannot but conclude, to the honor of our nation, that we have invented, increased, and perfected a more pleasant way of writing for the stage, than was ever known to the ancients or moderns of any nation, which is tragicomedy.

"And this leads me to wonder why Lisideius and many others should cry up the barrenness of the French plots, above the variety and copiousness of the English. Their plots are single; they carry on one design, which is pushed forward by all the actors, every scene in the play contributing and moving towards it. Our plays, besides the main design, have underplots or by-concernments, of less considerable persons and intrigues, which are carried on with the motion of the main plot: just as they say the orb of the fixed stars, and those of the planets, though they have motions of their own, are whirled about by the motion of the *primum mobile,* in which they are contained. That similitude expresses much of the English stage; for if contrary motions may be found in nature to agree; if a planet can go east and west at the same time, one way by virtue of his own motion, the other by the force of the first mover, it will not be difficult to imagine how the underplot, which is only different, not contrary to the great design, may naturally be conducted along with it.

"Eugenius has already shown us, from the confession of the French poets, that the unity of action is sufficiently preserved, if all the imperfect actions of the play are conducing to the main design; but when those petty intrigues of a play are so ill ordered, that they have no coherence with

---

[68]Molière (Jean Baptiste Poquelin, 1622–1673), Philippe Quinault (1635–1688), French dramatists.

[69]A comic servant in *The Adventures of Five Hours* (1663) by Samuel Tuke, adapted from a play attributed to Calderon.

the other, I must grant that Lisideius has reason to tax that want of due connection; for coordination in a play is as dangerous and unnatural as in a state. In the meantime he must acknowledge, our variety, if well ordered, will afford a greater pleasure to the audience.

"As for his other argument, that by pursuing one single theme they gain an advantage to express and work up the passions, I wish any example he could bring from them would make it good; for I confess their verses are to me the coldest I have ever read. Neither, indeed, is it possible for them, in the way they take, so to express passion, as that the effects of it should appear in the concernment of an audience, their speeches being so many declamations, which tire us with the length; so that instead of persuading us to grieve for their imaginary heroes, we are concerned for our own trouble, as we are in the tedious visits of bad company; we are in pain till they are gone. When the French stage came to be reformed by Cardinal Richelieu, those long harangues were introduced, to comply with the gravity of a churchman. Look upon the *Cinna* and the *Pompey;* they are not so properly to be called plays, as long discourses of reasons of state; and *Polyeucte* in matters of religion is as solemn as the long stops upon our organs.[70] Since that time it is grown into a custom, and their actors speak by the bourglass, as our parsons do; nay, they account it the grace of their parts, and think themselves disparaged by the poet, if they may not twice or thrice in a play entertain the audience with a speech of an hundred or two hundred lines. I deny not but this may suit well enough with the French; for as we, who are a more sullen people, come to be diverted at our plays, so they, who are of an airy and gay temper, come thither to make themselves more serious: and this I conceive to be one reason why comedy is more pleasing to us, and tragedies to them. But to speak generally: it cannot be denied that short speeches and replies are more apt to move the passions and beget concernment in us, than the other; for it is unnatural for anyone in a gust of passion to speak long together, or for another in the same condition to suffer him, without interruption. Grief and passion are like floods raised in little brooks by a sudden rain; they are quickly up; and if the concernment be poured unexpectedly in upon us, it overflows us: but a long sober shower gives them leisure to run out as they came in, without troubling the ordinary current. As for comedy, repartee is one of its chiefest graces; the greatest pleasure of the audience is a chase of wit, kept up on both sides, and swiftly managed. And this our forefathers, if not we, have had in Fletcher's plays, to a much higher degree of perfection than the French poets can arrive at.

"There is another part of Lisideius his discourse, in which he has rather excused our neighbors, than commended them; that is, for aiming only to make one person considerable in their plays. 'Tis very true what he has urged, that one character in all plays, even without the poet's care, will have advantage of all the others; and that the design of the whole drama will chiefly depend on it. But this hinders not that there may be more shining characters in the play: many persons of a second magnitude, any, some so very near, so almost equal to the first, that greatness may be opposed to greatness, and all the persons be made considerable, not only by their quality, but their action. 'Tis evident that the more the persons are, the greater will be the variety of the plot. If then the parts are managed so regularly, that the beauty of the whole be kept entire, and that the variety become not a perplexed and confused mass of accidents, you will find it infinitely pleasing to be led in a labyrinth of design, where you see some of your way before you, yet discern not the end till you arrive at it. And that all this is practicable, I can produce for examples many of our English plays: as *The Maid's Tragedy, The Alchemist, The Silent Woman:* I was going to have named *The Fox,*[71] but that the unity of design seems not exactly observed in it; for there appear two actions in the play; the first naturally ending with the fourth act; the second forced from it in the fifth: which yet is the less to be condemned in him, because the disguise of Volpone, though it suited not with his character as a crafty or covetous person, agreed well enough with that of a voluptuary; and by it the poet gained the end he aimed at, the punishment of vice, and the reward of virtue, which that disguise produced. So that to judge equally of it, it was an excellent fifth act, but not so naturally proceeding from the former.

"But to leave this, and pass to the latter part of Lisideius his discourse, which concerns relations: I must acknowledge with him, that the French have reason when they hide that part of the action which would occasion too much tumult on the stage, and choose rather to have it made known by narration to the audience. Farther, I think it very convenient, for the reasons he has given, that all incredible actions were removed; but, whether custom has so insinuated itself into our countrymen, or nature has so formed them to fierceness, I know not; but they will scarcely suffer combats and other objects of horror to be taken from them. And indeed, the indecency of tumults is all which can be objected against fighting: for why may not our imagination as well suffer itself to be deluded with the probability of it, as with any other thing in the play? For my part, I can with as

[70] Plays by Corneille.

[71] *The Maid's Tragedy* by Beaumont and Fletcher, the others by Jonson.

great ease persuade myself that the blows which are struck, are given in good earnest, as I can, that they who strike them are kings or princes, or those persons which they represent. For objects of incredibility, I would be satisfied from Lisideius, whether we have any so removed from all appearance of truth, as are those of Corneille's *Andromède;* a play which has been frequented the most of any he has writ. If the Perseus, or the son of an heathen god, the Pegasus, and the monster, were not capable to choke a strong belief, let him blame any representation of ours hereafter. Those indeed were objects of delight; yet the reason is the same as to the probability: for he makes it not a ballet or masque, but a play, which is to resemble truth. But for death, that it ought not to be represented, I have, besides the arguments alleged by Lisideius, the authority of Ben Jonson, who has forborne it in his tragedies; for both the death of Sejanus and Catiline are related: though in the latter I cannot but observe one irregularity of that great poet; he has removed the scene in the same act from Rome to Catiline's army, and from thence again to Rome; and besides, has allowed a very inconsiderable time, after Catiline's speech, for the striking of the battle, and the return of Petreius, who is to relate the event of it to the senate: which I should not animadvert on him, who was otherwise a painful observer of τὸ πρέπον, or the *decorum* of the stage, if he had not used extreme severity in his judgment on the incomparable Shakespeare for the same fault.—To conclude on this subject of relations; if we are to be blamed for showing too much of the action, the French are as faulty for discovering too little of it: a mean betwixt both should be observed by every judicious writer, so as the audience may neither be left unsatisfied by not seeing what is beautiful or shocked by beholding what is either incredible or undecent.

"I hope I have already proved in this discourse, that though we are not altogether so punctual as the French, in observing the laws of comedy, yet our errors are so few, and little, and those things wherein we excel them so considerable, that we ought of right to be preferred before them. But what will Lisideius say, if they themselves acknowledge they are too strictly tied up by those laws, for breaking which he has blamed the English? I will allege Corneille's words, as I find them in the end of his discourse of the three unities: *'Il est facile aux spéculatifs d'être sévères,' &c.;* 'tis easy for speculative persons to judge severely; but if they would produce to public view ten or twelve pieces of this nature, they would perhaps give more latitude to the rules than I have done, when, by experience, they had known how much we are bound up and constrained by them, and how many beauties of the stage they banished from it.[72] To illus-

trate a little what he has said: by their servile observations of the unities of time and place, and integrity of scenes, they have brought on themselves that dearth of plot, and narrowness of imagination, which may be observed in all their plays. How many beautiful accidents might naturally happen in two or three days, which cannot arrive with any probability in the compass of twenty-four hours? There is time to be allowed also for maturity of design, which, amongst great and prudent persons, such as are often represented in tragedy, cannot, with any likelihood of truth, be brought to pass at so short a warning. Farther; by tying themselves strictly to the unity of place, and unbroken scenes, they are forced many times to omit some beauties which cannot be shown where the act began; but might, if the scene were interrupted, and the stage cleared for the persons to enter in another place; and therefore the French poets are often forced upon absurdities; for if the act begins in a chamber, all the persons in the play must have some business or other to come thither, or else they are not to be shown that act; and sometimes their characters are very unfitting to appear there. As, suppose it were the king's bedchamber; yet the meanest man in the tragedy must come and dispatch his business there, rather than in the lobby or courtyard (which is fitter for him), for fear the stage should be cleared, and the scenes broken. Many times they fall by it in a greater inconvenience; for they keep their scenes unbroken, and yet change the place; as in one of their newest plays, where the act begins in the street. There a gentleman is to meet his friend; he sees him with his man, coming out from his father's house; they talk together, and the first goes out: the second, who is a lover, has made an appointment with his mistress; she appears at the window, and then we are to imagine the scene lies under it. This gentleman is called away, and leaves his servant with his mistress; presently her father is heard from within; the young lady is afraid the servingman should be discovered, and thrusts him in through a door, which is supposed to be her closet. After this, the father enters to the daughter, and now the scene is in a house; for he is seeking from one room to another for this poor Philipin, or French Diego, who is heard from within drolling and breaking many a miserable conceit upon his sad condition. In this ridiculous manner the play goes on, the stage being never empty all the while: so that the street, the window, the houses, and the closet, are made to walk about, and the persons to stand still. Now what, I beseech you, is more easy than to write a regular French play, or more difficult than write an irregular English one, like those of Fletcher, or of Shakespeare?

"If they content themselves, as Corneille did, with some flat design, which, like an ill riddle, is found out ere it

---

[72] Above, page 252.

be half proposed, such plots we can make every way regular, as easily as they; but whene'er they endeavor to rise to any quick turns and counterturns of plot, as some of them have attempted, since Corneille's plays have been less in vogue, you see they write as irregularly as we, though they cover it more speciously. Hence the reason is perspicuous, why no French plays, when translated, have, or ever can succeed on the English stage. For, if you consider the plots, our own are fuller of variety; if the writing, ours are more quick and fuller of spirit; and therefore 'tis a strange mistake in those who decry the way of writing plays in verse, as if the English therein imitated the French. We have borrowed nothing from them; our plots are weaved in English looms: we endeavor therein to follow the variety and greatness of characters which are derived to us from Shakespeare and Fletcher; the copiousness and well-knitting of the intrigues we have from Jonson; and for the verse itself we have English precedents of elder date than any of Corneille's plays. Not to name our old comedies before Shakespeare, which were all writ in verse of six feet, or Alexandrines, such as the French now use, I can show in Shakespeare, many scenes of rhyme together, and the like in Ben Jonson's tragedies: in *Catiline* and *Sejanus* sometimes thirty or forty lines, I mean besides the chorus, or the monologues; which, by the way, showed Ben no enemy to this way of writing, especially if you look upon his *Sad Shepherd,* which goes sometimes on rhyme, sometimes on blank verse, like a horse who eases himself on trot and amble. You find him likewise commending Fletcher's pastoral of *The Faithful Shepherdess,* which is for the most part rhyme, though not refined to that purity to which it hath since been brought. And these examples are enough to clear us from a servile imitation of the French.

"But to return from whence I have digressed: I dare boldly affirm these two things of the English drama; first, that we have many plays of ours as regular as any of theirs, and which, besides, have more variety of plot and characters; and secondly, that in most of the irregular plays of Shakespeare or Fletcher (for Ben Jonson's are for the most part regular) there is a more masculine fancy and greater spirit in the writing, than there is in any of the French. I could produce, even in Shakespeare's and Fletcher's works, some plays which are almost exactly formed; as *The Merry Wives of Windsor,* and *The Scornful Lady:* but because (generally speaking) Shakespeare, who writ first, did not perfectly observe the laws of comedy, and Fletcher, who came nearer to perfection, yet through carelessness made many faults; I will take the pattern of a perfect play from Ben Jonson, who was a careful and learned observer of the dramatic laws, and from all his comedies I shall select *The Silent*

Woman; of which I will make a short examen, according to those rules which the French observe."

As Neander was beginning to examine *The Silent Woman,* Eugenius, looking earnestly upon him; "I beseech you, Neander," said he, "gratify the company, and me in particular, so far, as before you speak of the play, to give us a character of the author; and tell us frankly your opinion, whether you do not think all writers, both French and English, ought to give place to him."

"I fear," replied Neander, "that in obeying your commands I shall draw a little envy on myself. Besides, in performing them, it will be first necessary to speak somewhat of Shakespeare and Fletcher, his rivals in poesy; and one of them, in my opinion, at least his equal, perhaps his superior.

"To begin, then, with Shakespeare. He was the man who of all modern, and perhaps ancient poets, had the largest and most comprehensive soul. All the images of nature were still present to him, and he drew them, not laboriously, but luckily; when he describes anything, you more than see it, you feel it too. Those who accuse him to have wanted learning, give him the greater commendation: he was naturally learned; he needed not the spectacles of books to read nature; he looked inwards, and found her there.[73] I cannot say he is everywhere alike; were he so, I should do him injury to compare him with the greatest of mankind. He is many times flat, insipid; his comic wit degenerating into clenches, his serious swelling into bombast. But he is always great, when some great occasion is presented to him; no man can say he ever had a fit subject for his wit, and did not then raise himself as high above the rest of poets, *'Quantum lenta solent inter viburna cupressi.'*[74] The consideration of this made Mr. Hales of Eton say, that there was no subject of which any poet ever writ, but he would produce it much better treated of in Shakespeare; and however others are now generally preferred before him, yet the age wherein he lived, which had contempories with him Fletcher and Jonson, never equaled them to him in their esteem; and in the last king's court, when Ben's reputation was at highest, Sir John Suckling, and with him the greater part of the courtiers, set our Shakespeare far above him.

"Beaumont and Fletcher, of whom I am next to speak, had, with the advantage of Shakespeare's wit, which was their precedent, great natural gifts, improved by study: Beaumont especially being so accurate a judge of plays, that Ben Jonson, while he lived, submitted all his writings to his

---

[73] The notion of Shakespeare as a natural, untutored genius persisted even into the time of Coleridge, who opposed the idea. See Coleridge (below, page 494).

[74] "As cypresses usually do among supple trees." Virgil, *Eclogues* I, 25.

censure, and, 'tis thought, used his judgment in correcting, if not contriving, all his plots. What value he had for him, appears by the verses he writ to him; and therefore I need speak no farther of it. The first play that brought Fletcher and him in esteem was their *Philaster:* for before that, they had written two or three very unsuccessfully, as the like is reported of Ben Jonson, before he writ *Every Man in His Humor.* Their plots were generally more regular than Shakespeare's, especially those which were made before Beaumont's death; and they understood and imitated the conversation of gentlemen much better; whose wild debaucheries, and quickness of wit in repartees, no poet can ever paint as they have done. Humor, which Ben Jonson derived from particular persons, they made it not their business to describe: they represented all the passions very lively, but above all, love. I am apt to believe the English language in them arrived to its highest perfection: what words have since been taken in, are rather superfluous than ornamental. Their plays are now the most pleasant and frequent entertainments of the stage; two of theirs being acted through the year for one of Shakespeare's or Jonson's: the reason is, because there is a certain gaiety in their comedies, and pathos in their more serious plays, which suits generally with all men's humors. Shakespeare's language is likewise a little obsolete, and Ben Jonson's wit comes short of theirs.

"As for Jonson, to whose character I am now arrived, if we look upon him while he was himself (for his last plays were but his dotages), I think him the most learned and judicious writer which any theater ever had. He was a most severe judge of himself, as well as others. One cannot say he wanted wit, but rather that he was frugal of it. In his works you, find little to retrench or alter. Wit, and language, and humor also in some measure, we had before him; but something of art was wanting to the drama, till he came. He managed his strength to more advantage than any who preceded him. You seldom find him making love in any of his scenes, or endeavoring to move the passions; his genius was too sullen and saturnine to do it gracefully, especially when he knew he came after those who had performed both to such a height. Humor was his proper sphere; and in that he delighted most to represent mechanic people. He was deeply conversant in the ancients, both Greek and Latin, and he borrowed boldly from them: there is scarce a poet or historian among the Roman authors of those times whom he has not translated in *Sejanus* and *Catiline.* But he had done his robberies so openly, that one may see he fears not to be taxed by any law. He invades authors like a monarch; and what would be theft in other poets, is only victory in him. With the spoils of these writers he so represents old Rome to us, in its rites, ceremonies, and customs, that if one of

their poets had written either of his tragedies, we had seen less of it than in him. If there was any fault in his language, 'twas that he weaved it too closely and laboriously, in his serious plays: perhaps too, he did a little too much romanize our tongue, leaving the words which he translated almost as much Latin as he found them: wherein, though he learnedly followed the idiom of their language, he did not enough comply with the idiom of ours. If I would compare him with Shakespeare, I must acknowledge him the more correct poet, but Shakespeare the greater wit. Shakespeare was the Homer, or father of our dramatic poets; Jonson was the Virgil, the pattern of elaborate writing; I admire him, but I love Shakespeare. To conclude of him; as he has given us the most correct plays, so in the precepts which he has laid down in his *Discoveries,* we have as many and profitable rules for perfecting the stage, as any wherewith the French can furnish us.

"Having thus spoken of the author, I proceed to the examination of his comedy, *The Silent Woman.*"

Examen of The Silent Woman

"To begin first with the length of the action; it is so far from exceeding the compass of a natural day, that it takes not up an artificial one. 'Tis all included in the limits of three hours and an half, which is no more than is required for the presentment on the stage. A beauty perhaps not much observed; if it had, we should not have looked on the Spanish translation of *Five Hours* with so much wonder. The scene of it is laid in London; the latitude of place is almost as little as you can imagine; for it lies all within the compass of two houses, and after the first act, in one. The continuity of scenes is observed more than in any of our plays, except his own *Fox* and *Alchemist.* They are not broken above twice or thrice at most in the whole comedy; and in the two best of Corneille's plays, the *Cid* and *Cinna,* they are interrupted once apiece. The action of the play is entirely one; the end or aim of which is the settling Morose's estate on Dauphine. The intrigue of it is the greatest and most noble of any pure unmixed comedy in any language; you see in it many persons of various characters and humors, and all delightful: as first, Morose, or an old man, to whom all noise but his own talking is offensive. Some who would be thought critics, say this humor of his is forced: but to remove that objection, we may consider him first to be naturally of a delicate hearing, as many are, to whom all sharp sounds are unpleasant; and secondly, we may attribute much of it to the peevishness of his age, or the wayward authority of an old man in his own house, where he may make himself obeyed; and this the poet seems to allude to in his name Morose. Besides this, I am assured from divers persons, that Ben Jonson was actually acquainted with such a man, one altogether as ridiculous as he is here represented. Others say, it is not enough to find one man of such an humor; it must be common to more, and the more common the more natural. To prove this, they instance in the best of comical characters, Falstaff: there are many men resembling him; old, fat, merry, cowardly, drunken, amorous, vain, and lying. But to convince these people, I need but tell them, that humor is the ridiculous extravagance of conversation, wherein one man differs from all others. If then it be common, or communicated to many, how differs it from other men's? Or what indeed causes it to be ridiculous so much as the singularity of it? As for Falstaff, he is not properly one humor, but a miscellany of humors or images, drawn from so many several men: that wherein he is singular is his wit, or those things he says *praeter expectatum,* unexpected by the audience; his quick evasions, when you imagine him surprised, which, as they are extremely diverting of themselves, so receive a great addition from his person; for the very sight of such an unwieldy old debauched fellow is a comedy alone. And here, having a place so proper for it, I cannot but enlarge somewhat upon this subject of humor into which I am fallen. The ancients had little of it in their comedies; for the τὸ γελοῖον[75] of the old comedy, of which Aristophanes was chief, was not so much to imitate a man, as to make the people laugh at some odd conceit, which had commonly somewhat of unnatural or obscene in it. Thus, when you see Socrates brought upon the stage, you are not to imagine him made ridiculous by the imitation of his actions, but rather by making him perform something very unlike himself; something so childish and absurd, as by comparing it with the gravity of the true Socrates, makes a ridiculous object for the spectators. In their new comedy which succeeded, the poets sought indeed to express the ἦθος,[76] as in their tragedies the πάθος[77] of mankind. But this ἦθος contained only the general characters of men and manners; as old men, lovers, servingmen, courtesans, parasites, and such other persons as we see in their comedies; all which they made alike: that is, one old man or father, one lover, one courtesan, so like another, as if the first of them had begot the rest of every sort: *'Ex homine hunc natum dicas.'*[78] The same custom they observed likewise in their tragedies. As for the French, though they have the word *humeur* among them, yet they have small use of it in their comedies or farces; they being but ill imitations of

the *ridiculum,* or that which stirred up laughter in the old comedy. But among the English 'tis otherwise: where by humor is meant some extravagant habit, passion, or affection, particular (as I said before) to some one person, by the oddness of which, he is immediately distinguished from the rest of men; which being lively and naturally represented, most frequently begets that malicious pleasure in the audience which is testified by laughter; as all things which are deviations from common customs are ever the aptest to produce it: though by the way this laughter is only accidental, as the person represented is fantastic or bizarre; but pleasure is essential to it, as the imitation of what is natural. The description of these humors, drawn from the knowledge and observation of particular persons, was the peculiar genius and talent of Ben Jonson; to whose play I now return.

"Besides Morose, there are at least nine or ten different characters and humors in *The Silent Woman;* all which persons have several concernments of their own, yet are all used by the poet, to the conducting of the main design to perfection. I shall not waste time in commending the writing of this play; but I will give you my opinion, that there is more wit and acuteness of fancy in it than in any of Ben Jonson's. Besides, that he has here described the conversation of gentlemen in the persons of True-Wit, and his friends, with more gaiety, air, and freedom, than in the rest of his comedies. For the contrivance of the plot, 'tis extreme elaborate, and yet withal easy; for the λύσις, or untying of it, 'tis so admirable, that when it is done, no one of the audience would think the poet would have missed it; and yet it was concealed so much before the last scene, that any other way would sooner have entered into your thoughts. But I dare not take upon me to commend the fabric of it, because it is altogether so full of art, that I must unravel every scene in it to commend it as I ought. And this excellent contrivance is still the more to be admired, because 'tis comedy, where the persons are only of common rank, and their business private, not elevated by passions or high concernments, as in serious plays. Here everyone is a proper judge of all he sees, nothing is represented but that with which he daily converses: so that by consequence all faults lie open to discovery, and few are pardonable. 'Tis this which Horace has judiciously observed:

> *Creditur, ex medio quia res arcessit, habere*
> *Sudoris minimum; sed habet comedia tanto*
> *Plus oneris, quanto veniae minus.*[79]

---

[75] To geloion: "ridiculous."
[76] Ethos: "character."
[77] Pathos: "suffering."
[78] "You would say this one was born from that man." Terence, *Eunuch* III, ii, 7.

[79] "It is thought that because it draws its materials from common life comedy requires the least pains, but it is as much more difficult as it has less indulgence." *Epistles* II, 1.

But our poet who was not ignorant of these difficulties, had prevailed himself of all advantages; as he who designs a large leap takes his rise from the highest ground. One of these advantages is that which Corneille has laid down as the greatest which can arrive to any poem, and which he himself could never compass above thrice in all his plays; viz. the making choice of some signal and long-expected day, whereon the action of the play is to depend. This day was that designed by Dauphine for the setting of his uncle's estate upon him; which to compass, he contrives to marry him. That the marriage had been plotted by him long beforehand, is made evident by what he tells True-Wit in the second act, that in one moment he had destroyed what he had been raising many months.

"There is another artifice of the poet, which I cannot here omit, because by the frequent practice of it in his comedies he has left it to us almost as a rule; that is, when he has any character or humor wherein he would show a *coup de maître,* or his highest skill, he recommends it to your observation by a pleasant description of it before the person first appears. Thus, in *Bartholomew Fair* he gives you the pictures of Numps and Cokes, and in this those of Daw, Lafoole, Morose, and the collegiate ladies; all which you hear described before you see them. So that before they come upon the stage, you have a longing expectation of them, which prepares you to receive them favorably; and when they are there, even from their first appearance you are so far acquainted with them, that nothing of their humor is lost to you.

"I will observe yet one thing further of this admirable plot; the business of it rises in every act. The second is greater than the first; the third than the second; and so forward to the fifth. There too you see, till the very last scene, new difficulties arising to obstruct the action of the play; and when the audience is brought into despair that the business can naturally be effected, then, and not before, the discovery is made. But that the poet might entertain you with more variety all this while, he reserves some new characters to show you, which he opens not till the second and third act. In the second Morose, Daw, the Barber, and Otter; in the third the collegiate ladies: all which he moves afterwards in by-walks, or underplots, as diversions to the main design, lest it should grow tedious, though they are still naturally joined with it, and somewhere or other subservient to it. Thus, like a skillful chess-player, by little and little he draws out his men, and makes his pawns of use to his greater persons.

"If this comedy and some others of his were translated into French prose (which would now be no wonder to them, since Molière has lately given them plays out of verse, which have not displeased them), I believe the controversy would soon be decided betwixt the two nations, even making them the judges. But we need not call our heroes to our aid; be it spoken to the honor of the English, our nation can never want in any age such who are able to dispute the empire of wit with any people in the universe. And though the fury of a civil war, and power for twenty years together abandoned to a barbarous race of men, enemies of all good learning, had buried the Muses under the ruins of monarchy; yet, with the restoration of our happiness, we see revived poesy lifting up its head, and already shaking off the rubbish which lay so heavy on it. We have seen since his Majesty's return, many dramatic poems which yield not to those of any foreign nation, and which deserve all laurels but the English. I will set aside flattery and envy: it cannot be denied but we have had some little blemish either in the plot or writing of all those plays which have been made within these seven years (and perhaps there is no nation in the world so quick to discern them, or so difficult to pardon them, as ours): yet if we can persuade ourselves to use the candor of that poet, who, though the most severe of critics, has left us this caution by which to moderate our censures—*'ubi plura nitent in carmine, non ego paucis / Offendar maculis'*[80]—if, in consideration of their many and great beauties, we can wink at some slight and little imperfections, if we, I say, can be thus equal to ourselves, I ask no favor from the French. And if I do not venture upon any particular judgment of our late plays, 'tis out of the consideration which an ancient writer gives me: *'vivorum, ut magna admiratio, ita censura difficilis'.*[81] betwixt the extremes of admiration and malice, 'tis' hard to judge uprightly of the living. Only I think it may be permitted me to say, that as it is no lessening to us to yield to some plays, and those not many, of our own nation in the last age, so can it be no addition to pronounce of our present poets, that they have far surpassed all the ancients, and the modern writers of other countries."

This, my Lord, was the substance of what was then spoke on that occasion; and Lisideius, I think, was going to reply, when he was prevented thus by Crites: "I am confident," said he, "that the most material things that can be said have been already urged on either side; if they have not, I must beg of Lisideius that he will defer his answer till another time: for I confess I have a joint quarrel to you both, because you have concluded, without any reason given for it, that rhyme is proper for the stage. I will not dispute how ancient it hath been among us to write this way; perhaps our

---

[80] "Where many things shine out in a poem, I shall not be offended at little faults." Horace (above, page 83).

[81] "As admiration of the living is great, so censure is difficult." Paterculus, *History of Rome* II, 36.

ancestors knew no better till Shakespeare's time. I will grant it was not altogether left by him, and that Fletcher and Ben Jonson used it frequently in their pastorals, and sometimes in other plays. Farther, I will not argue whether we received it originally from our own countrymen, or from the French for that is an inquiry of as little benefit, as theirs who, in the midst of the great plague, were not so solicitous to provide against it, as to know whether we had it from the malignity of our own air, or by transportation from Holland. I have therefore only to affirm, that it is not allowable in serious plays; for comedies, I find you already concluding with me. To prove this, I might satisfy myself to tell you, how much in vain it is for you to strive against the stream of the people's inclination; the greatest part of which are prepossessed so much with those excellent plays of Shakespeare, Fletcher, and Ben Jonson, which have been written out of rhyme, that except you could bring them such as were written better in it, and those too by persons of equal reputation with them, it will be impossible for you to gain your cause with them, who will still be judges. This it is to which, in fine, all your reasons must submit. The unanimous consent of an audience is so powerful, that even Julius Caesar (as Macrobius reports of him), when he was perpetual dictator, was not able to balance it on the other side. But when Laberius, a Roman knight, at his request contended in the mime with another poet, he was forced to cry out, *'Etiam favente me victus es, Laberi.'*[82] But I will not on this occasion take the advantage of the greater number, but only urge such reasons against rhyme, as I find in the writings of those who have argued for the other way. First then, I am of opinion, that rhyme is unnatural in a play, because dialogue there is presented as the effect of sudden thought: for a play is the imitation of nature; and since no man without premeditation speaks in rhyme, neither ought he to do it on the stage. This hinders not but the fancy may be there elevated to an higher pitch of thought than it is in ordinary discourse; for there is a probability that men of excellent and quick parts may speak noble things extempore: but those thoughts are never fettered with the numbers or sound of verse without study, and therefore it cannot be but unnatural to present the most free way of speaking in that which is the most constrained. For this reason, says Aristotle, 'tis best to write tragedy in that kind of verse which is the least such, or which is nearest prose: and this amongst the ancients was the Iambic, and with us is blank verse, or the measure of verse kept exactly without rhyme.[83] These numbers there-

fore are fittest for a play; the others for a paper of verses, or a poem; blank verse being as much below them, as rhyme is improper for the drama. And if it be objected that neither are blank verses made extempore, yet, as nearest nature, they are still to be preferred. But there are two particular exceptions, which many besides myself have had to verse; by which it will appear yet more plainly how improper it is in plays. And the first of them is grounded on that very reason for which some have commended rhyme: they say, the quickness of repartees in argumentative scenes receives an ornament from verse. Now what is more unreasonable than to imagine that a man should not only light upon the wit, but the rhyme too, upon the sudden? This nicking of him who spoke before both in sound and measure, is so great a happiness, that you must at least suppose the persons of your play to be born poets: *'Arcades omnes, et cantare pares, et respondere parati':*[84] they must have arrived to the degree of *'quicquid conabar dicere'*[85]—to make verses almost whether they will or no. If they are anything below this, it will look rather like the design of two, than the answer of one: it will appear that your actors hold intelligence together; that they perform their tricks like fortune-tellers, by confederacy. The hand of art will be too visible in it, against that maxim of all professions, *'Ars est celare artem,'* that it is the greatest perfection of art to keep itself undiscovered. Nor will it serve you to object, that however you manage it, 'tis still known to be a play; and, consequently, the dialogue of two persons understood to be the labor of one poet. For a play is still an imitation of nature; we know we are to be deceived, and we desire to be so; but no man ever was deceived but with a probability of truth; for who will suffer a gross lie to be fastened on him?[86] Thus we sufficiently understand, that the scenes which represent cities and countries to us are not really such, but only painted on boards and canvas; but shall that excuse the ill painture or designment of them? Nay, rather ought they not to be labored with so much the more diligence and exactness, to help the imagination? Since the mind of man does naturally tend to, and seek after truth; and therefore the nearer anything comes to the imitation of it, the more it pleases.

"Thus, you see, your rhyme is uncapable of expressing the greatest thoughts naturally, and the lowest it cannot with any grace: for what is more unbefitting the majesty of verse, than to call a servant, or bid a door be shut in rhyme? And yet this miserable necessity you are forced upon. But verse,

---

[82]"Even with my favor you are defeated, Laberius." Macrobius, *Saturnalia* II, 7.
[83]*Poetics* (above, page 65).

[84]"All the Arcadians, prepared both to sing together and to respond." Virgil, *Eclogues* VII, 4.
[85]"To say whatever I attempted." Ovid, *Tristia* IV, x, 25.
[86]This view is echoed by Samuel Johnson (below, page 357).

you say, circumscribes a quick and luxuriant fancy, which would extend itself too far on every subject, did not the labor which is required to well-turned and polished rhyme, set bounds to it. Yet this argument, if granted, would only prove that we may write better in verse, but not more naturally. Neither is it able to evince that; for he who wants judgment to confine his fancy in blank verse, may want it as much in rhyme; and he who has it will avoid errors in both kinds. Latin verse was as great a confinement to the imagination of those poets, as rhyme to ours; and yet you had Ovid saying too much on every subject. 'Nescivit,' says Seneca, 'quod bene cessit relinquere':[87] of which he gives you one famous instance in his description of the deluge: 'Omnia pontus erat, deerant quoque litora ponto'; now all was sea, nor had that sea a shore.[88] Thus Ovid's fancy was not limited by verse, and Virgil needed not verse to have bounded his.

"In our own language we see Ben Johnson confining himself to what ought to be said, even in the liberty of blank verse; and yet Corneille, the most judicious of the French poets, is still varying the same sense a hundred ways, and dwelling eternally on the same subject, though confined by rhyme. Some other exceptions I have to verse; but being these I have named are for the most part already public, I conceive it reasonable they should first be answered."

"It concerns me less than any," said Neander (seeing he had ended), "to reply to this discourse; because when I should have proved that verse may be natural in plays, yet I should always be ready to confess, that those which I have written in this kind come short of that perfection which is required. Yet since you are pleased I should undertake this province, I will do it, though with all imaginable respect and deference, both to that person from whom you have borrowed your strongest arguments, and to whose judgment, when I have said all, I finally submit. But before I proceed to answer your objections, I must first remember you, that I exclude all comedy from my defense; and next that I deny not but blank verse may be also used; and content myself only to assert, that in serious plays where the subject and characters are great, and the plot unmixed with mirth, which might allay or divert these concernments which are produced, rhyme is there as natural and more effectual than blank verse.

"And now having laid down this as a foundation, to begin with Crites, I must crave leave to tell him, that some of his arguments against rhyme reach no farther than, from the faults or defects of ill rhyme, to conclude against the use of it in general. May not I conclude against blank verse by the same reason? If the words of some poets who write in it, are either ill chosen, or ill placed, which makes not only rhyme, but all kind of verse in any language unnatural, shall I, for their vicious affectation, condemn those excellent lines of Fletcher, which are written in that kind? Is there any thing in rhyme more constrained than this line in blank verse, *I heaven invoke, and strong resistance make?* where you see both the clauses are placed unnaturally, that is, contrary to the common way of speaking, and that without the excuse of a rhyme to cause it: yet you would think me very ridiculous, if I should accuse the stubbornness of blank verse for this, and not rather the stiffness of the poet. Therefore, Crites, you must either prove that words, though well chosen, and duly placed, yet render not rhyme natural in itself; or that, however natural and easy the rhyme may be, yet it is not proper for a play. If you insist on the former part, I would ask you, what other conditions are required to make rhyme natural in itself, besides an election of apt words, and a right disposing of them? For the due choice of your words expresses your sense naturally, and the due placing them adapts the rhyme to it. If you object that one verse may be made for the sake of another, though both the words and rhyme be apt, I answer, it cannot possibly so fall out; for either there is a dependence of sense betwixt the first line and the second, or there is none; if there be that connection, then in the natural position of the words the latter line must of necessity flow from the former; if there be no dependence, yet still the due ordering of words makes the last line as natural in itself as the other: so that the necessity of a rhyme never forces any but bad or lazy writers to say what they would not otherwise. 'Tis true, there is both care and art required to write in verse. A good poet never concludes upon the first line, till he has sought out such a rhyme as may fit the sense, already prepared to heighten the second: many times the close of the sense falls into the middle of the next verse, or farther off, and he may often prevail himself of the same advantages in English which Virgil had in Latin; he may break off in the hemistich,[89] and begin another line. Indeed, the not observing these two last things, makes plays which are writ in verse so tedious: for though, most commonly, the sense is to be confined to the couplet, yet nothing that does *perpetuo tenore fluere,* run in the same channel, can please always. 'Tis like the murmuring of a stream, which not varying in the fall, causes at first attention, at last drowsiness. Variety of cadences is the best rule; the greatest help to the actors, and refreshment to the audience.

[87]"He did not know how to end when he should have." Ovid, quoted in Seneca, *Controversies* IX, 5.
[88]Ovid, *Metamorphoses* I, 292.
[89]Half a line of verse.

"If then verse may be made natural in itself, how becomes it improper to a play? You say the stage is the representation of nature, and no man in ordinary conversation speaks in rhyme. But you foresaw when you said this, that it might be answered—neither does any man speak in blank verse, or in measure without rhyme. Therefore you concluded, that which is nearest nature is still to be preferred. But you took no notice that rhyme might be made as natural as blank verse, by the well placing of the words, &c. All the difference between them, when they are both correct, is, the sound in one, which the other wants; and if so, the sweetness of it, and all the advantage from it, which are handled in the preface to *The Rival Ladies,*[90] will yet stand good. As for that place of Aristotle, where he says, plays should be writ in that kind of verse which is nearest prose,[91] it makes little for you: blank verse being properly but measured prose. Now measure alone, in any modern language, does not constitute verse; those of the ancients in Greek and Latin consisted in quantity of words, and a determinate number of feet. But when, by the inundation of the Goths and Vandals into Italy, new languages were brought in, and barbarously mingled with the Latin, of which the Italian, Spanish, French, and ours (made out of them and the Teutonic) are dialects, a new way of poesy was practiced; new, I say, in those countries, for in all probability it was that of the conquerors in their own nations. This new way consisted in measure or number of feet, and rhyme; the sweetness of rhyme, and observation of accent, supplying the place of quantity in words, which could neither exactly be observed by those barbarians, who knew not the rules of it, neither was it suitable to their tongues, as it had been to the Greek and Latin. No man is tied in modern poesy to observe any farther rule in the feet of his verse, but that they be dissyllables; whether spondee, trochee, or iambic, it matters not; only he is obliged to rhyme. Neither do the Spanish, French, Italian, or Germans, acknowledge at all, or very rarely, any such kind of poesy as blank verse amongst them. Therefore, at most 'tis but a poetic prose, a *sermo pedestris;* and as such, most fit for comedies, where I acknowledge rhyme to be improper. Farther; as to that quotation of Aristotle, our couplet verses may be rendered as near prose as blank verse itself, by using those advantages I lately named, as breaks in a hemistich, or running the sense into another line, thereby making art and order appear as loose and free as nature: or not tying ourselves to couplets strictly, we may use the benefit of the Pindaric way practiced in *The Siege of Rhodes;*[92]

where the numbers vary, and the rhyme is disposed carelessly, and far from often chiming. Neither is that other advantage of the ancients to be despised, of changing the kind of verse when they please, with the change of the scene, or some new entrance; for they confine not themselves always to iambics, but extend their liberty to all lyric numbers, and sometimes even to hexameter. But I need not go so far to prove that rhyme, as it succeeds to all other offices of Greek and Latin verse, so especially to this of plays, since the custom of all nations at this day confirms it, all the French, Italian, and Spanish tragedies are generally writ in it; and sure the universal consent of the most civilized parts of the world ought in this, as it doth in other customs, to include the rest.

"But perhaps you may tell me, I have proposed such a way to make rhyme natural, and consequently proper to plays, as is unpracticable; and that I shall scarce find six or eight lines together in any play, where the words are so placed and chosen as is required to make it natural. I answer, no poet need constrain himself at all times to it. It is enough he makes it his general rule; for I deny not but sometimes there may be a greatness in placing the words otherwise; and sometimes they may sound better, sometimes also the variety itself is excuse enough. But if, for the most part, the words be placed as they are in the negligence of prose, it is sufficient to denominate the way practicable; for we esteem that to be such, which in the trial oftener succeeds than misses. And thus far you may find the practice made good in many plays: where you do not, remember still, that if you cannot find six natural rhymes together, it will be as hard for you to produce as many lines in blank verse, even among the greatest of our poets, against which I cannot make some reasonable exception.

"And this, Sir, calls to my remembrance the beginning of your discourse, where you told us we should never find the audience favorable to this kind of writing, till we could produce as good plays in rhyme, as Ben Jonson. Fletcher, and Shakespeare, had writ out of it. But it is to raise envy to the living, to compare them with the dead. They are honored, and almost adored by us, as they deserve; neither do I know any so presumptuous of themselves as to contend with them. Yet give me leave to say thus much, without injury to their ashes; that not only we shall never equal them, but they could never equal themselves, were they to rise and write again. We acknowledge them our fathers in wit; but they have ruined their estates themselves before they came to their children's hands. There is scarce a humor, a character, or any kind of plot, which they have not blown upon. All comes sullied or wasted to us: and were they to entertain this age, they could not make so plenteous treatments out of such decayed fortunes. This therefore will be a good argu-

---

[90] By Dryden.
[91] *Poetics* (above, page 52).
[92] By William Davenant (1606–1668).

ment to us, either not to write at all, or to attempt some other way. There is no bays to be expected in their walks: *'tentanda via est, qua me quoque possum tollere humo.'*[93]

"This way of writing in verse they have only left free to us; our age is arrived to a perfection in it, which they never knew; and which (if we may guess by what of theirs we have seen in verse, as *The Faithful Shepherdess,* and *Sad Shepherd*) 'tis probable they never could have reached. For the genius of every age is different; and though ours excel in this, I deny not but that to imitate nature in that perfection which they did in prose, is a greater commendation than to write in verse exactly. As for what you have added, that the people are not generally inclined to like this way; if it were true, it would be no wonder, that betwixt the shaking off an old habit, and the introducing of a new, there should be difficulty. Do we not see them stick to Hopkins' and Sternhold's psalms, and forsake those of David, I mean Sandys his translation of them? If by the people you understand the multitude, the οἱ πολλοί,[94] 'tis no matter what they think; they are sometimes in the right, sometimes in the wrong: their judgment is a mere lottery. *'Est ubi plebs rectè putat, est ubi peccat.'*[95] Horace says it of the vulgar, judging poesy. But if you mean the mixed audience of the populace and the noblesse, I dare confidently affirm that a great part of the latter sort are already favorable to verse; and that no serious plays written since the king's return have been more kindly received by them, than *The Siege of Rhodes,* the *Mustapha, The Indian Queen,* and *Indian Emperor.*[96]

"But I come now to the inference of your first argument. You said the dialogue of plays is presented as the effect of sudden thought, but no man speaks suddenly, or extempore, in rhyme; and you inferred from thence, that rhyme, which you acknowledge to be proper to epic poesy, cannot equally be proper to dramatic, unless we could suppose all men born so much more than poets, that verses should be made in them, not by them.

"It has been formerly urged by you, and confessed by me, that since no man spoke any kind of verse extempore, that which was nearest nature was to be preferred. I answer you, therefore, by distinguishing betwixt what is nearest to the nature of comedy, which is the imitation of common persons and ordinary speaking, and what is nearest the nature of a serious play: this last is indeed the representation

of nature, but 'tis nature wrought up to an higher pitch. The plot, the characters, the wit, the passions, the descriptions, are all exalted above the level of common converse, as high as the imagination of the poet can carry them, with proportion to verisimility. Tragedy, we know, is wont to imagine to us the minds and fortunes of noble persons, and to portray these exactly; heroic rhyme is nearest nature, as being the noblest kind of modern verse. *'Indignatur enim privatis et prope socco / Dignis carminibus narrari coena Thyestae,'*[97] says Horace: and in another place, *'Effutire leves indigna tragaedia versus.'*[98] Blank verse is acknowledged to be too low for a poem, nay more, for a paper of verses; but if too low for an ordinary sonnet, how much more for tragedy, which is by Aristotle, in the dispute betwixt the epic poesy and the dramatic, for many reasons he there alleges, ranked above it?[99]

"But setting this defense aside, your argument is almost as strong against the use of rhyme in poems as in plays; for the epic way is everywhere interlaced with dialogue, or discoursive scenes; and therefore you must either grant rhyme to be improper there, which is contrary to your assertion, or admit it into plays by the same title which you have given it to poems. For though tragedy be justly preferred above the other, yet there is a great affinity between them, as may easily be discovered in that definition of a play which Lisideius gave us. The genus of them is the same, a just and lively image of human nature, in its actions, passions, and traverses of fortune: so is the end, namely, for the delight and benefit of mankind. The characters and persons are still the same viz. the greatest of both sorts; only the manner of acquainting us with those actions, passions, and fortunes, is different. Tragedy performs it viva voce, or by action, in dialogue; wherein it excels the epic poem, which does it chiefly by narration, and therefore is not so lively an image of human nature. However, the agreement betwixt them is such, that if rhyme be proper for one, it must be for the other. Verse, 'tis true, is not the effect of sudden thought; but this hinders not that sudden thought may be represented in verse, since those thoughts are such as must be higher than nature can raise them without premeditation, especially to a continuance of them, even out of verse; and consequently you cannot imagine them to have been sudden either in the poet or in the actors. A play, as I have said, to be like nature, is to be set above it; as statues which are placed

---

[93] "I must find a way by which I can raise myself from the earth." Virgil, *Georgics* III, 8–9.
[94] Oi polloi, or "Hoi polloi," the masses.
[95] "Sometimes the people are right, sometimes not." Horace, *Epistles* II, 63.
[96] *The Mustapha* by David Mallet (1705?–1765); *The Indian Queen* and *The Indian Emperor* were written by Dryden, the former in collaboration with Robert Howard.

[97] "It is improper for the banquet of Thyestes to be told in familiar verses and comic style." Horace (above, page 80).
[98] "It is improper for tragedy to babble forth light verses." Horace (above, page 82).
[99] *Poetics* (above, page 69).

on high are made greater than the life, that they may descend to the sight in their just proportion.

"Perhaps I have insisted too long on this objection; but the clearing of it will make my stay shorter on the rest. You tell us, Crites, that rhyme appears most unnatural in repartees, or short replies: when he who answers, it being presumed he knew not what the other would say, yet makes up that part of the verse which was left incomplete, and supplies both the sound and measure of it. This, you say, looks rather like the confederacy of two, than the answer of one.

"This, I confess, is an objection which is in everyone's mouth, who loves not rhyme: but suppose, I beseech you, the repartee were made only in blank verse, might not part of the same argument be turned against you? For the measure is as often supplied there, as it is in rhyme; the latter half of the hemistich as commonly made up, or a second line subjoined as a reply to the former; which any one leaf in Jonson's plays will sufficiently clear to you. You will often find in the Greek tragedians, and in Seneca, that when a scene grows up into the warmth of repartees, which is the close fighting of it, the latter part of the trimeter is supplied by him who answers; and yet it was never observed as a fault in them by any of the ancient or modern critics. The case is the same in our verse, as it was in theirs; rhyme to us being in lieu of quantity to them. But if no latitude is to be allowed a poet, you take from him not only his license of *'quidlibet audendi,'*[100] but you tie him up in a straiter compass than you would a philosopher. This is indeed *'Musas colere severiores.'*[101] You would have him follow nature, but he must follow her on foot: you have dismounted him from his Pegasus. But you tell us, this supplying the last half of a verse, or adjoining a whole second to the former, looks more like the design of two, than the answer of one. Supposing we acknowledge it: how comes this confederacy to be more displeasing to you, than in a dance which is well contrived? You see there the united design of many persons to make up one figure: after they have separated themselves in many petty divisions, they rejoin one by one into a gross: the confederacy is plain amongst them, for chance could never produce any thing so beautiful; and yet there is nothing in it that shocks your sight. I acknowledge the hand of art appears in repartee, as of necessity it must in all kinds of verse. But there is also the quick and poignant brevity of it (which is an high imitation of nature in those sudden gusts of passion) to mingle with it; and this, joined with the cadency and sweetness of the rhyme, leaves nothing in the soul of the hearer to desire. 'Tis an art which appears; but it appears only like the shadowings of painture, which being to cause the rounding of it, cannot be absent; but while that is considered, they are lost: so while we attend to the other beauties of the matter, the care and labor of the rhyme is carried from us, or at least drowned in its own sweetness, as bees are sometimes buried in their honey. When a poet has found the repartee, the last perfection he can add to it, is to put it into verse. However good the thought may be, however apt the words in which 'tis couched, yet he finds himself at a little unrest, while rhyme is wanting: he cannot leave it till that comes naturally, and then is at ease, and sits down contented.

"From replies, which are the most elevated thoughts of verse, you pass to the most mean ones, those which are common with the lowest of household conversation. In these, you say, the majesty of verse suffers. You instance in the calling of a servant, or commanding a door to be shut, in rhyme. This, Crites, is a good observation of yours, but no argument: for it proves no more but that such thoughts should be waived, as often as may be, by the address of the poet. But suppose they are necessary in the places where he uses them, yet there is no need to put them into rhyme. He may place them in the beginning of a verse, and break it off, as unfit, when so debased, for any other use; or granting the worst, that they require more room than the hemistich will allow, yet still there is a choice to be made of the best words, and least vulgar (provided they be apt) to express such thoughts. Many have blamed rhyme in general, for this fault, when the poet with a little care might have redressed it. But they do it with no more justice, than if English poesy should be made ridiculous for the sake of the water poet's[102] rhymes. Our language is noble, full, and significant; and I know not why he who is master of it may not clothe ordinary things in it as decently as the Latin, if he use the same diligence in his choice of words. *'Delectus verborum origo est eloquentiae.'*[103] It was the saying of Julius Caesar, one so curious in his, that none of them can be changed but for a worse. One would think, *unlock the door,* was a thing as vulgar as could be spoken; and yet Seneca could make it sound high and lofty in his Latin: *'Reserate clusos regii postes laris';* set wide the palace gates.[104]

"But I turn from this exception, both because it happens not above twice or thrice in any play that those vulgar thoughts are used; and then too, were there no other apology to be made, yet the necessity of them, which is alike in all kind of writing, may excuse them. Besides that the great

---

[100] "Trying anything." Horace (above, page 79).
[101] "To worship the severer Muses." Martial, *Epigrams* IX, 12.

[102] John Taylor (1580–1633), English poet and River Thames boatman.
[103] "Choice of words is the origin of eloquence." Cicero, *Brutus* LXXII, 253.
[104] *Phaedra,* 871.

eagerness and precipitation with which they are spoken makes us rather mind the substance than the dress; that for which they are spoken, rather than what is spoke. For they are always the effect of some hasty concernment, and something of consequence depends on them.

"Thus, Crites, I have endeavored to answer your objections; it remains only that I should vindicate an argument for verse, which you have gone about to overthrow. It had formerly been said, that the easiness of blank verse renders the poet too luxuriant, but that the labor of rhyme bounds and circumscribes an overfruitful fancy; the sense there being commonly confined to the couplet, and the words so ordered that the rhyme naturally follows them, not they the rhyme. To this you answered, that it was no argument to the question in hand; for the dispute was not which way a man may write best, but which is most proper for the subject on which he writes.

"First, give me leave, sir, to remember you, that the argument against which you raised this objection, was only secondary: it was built on this hypothesis, that to write in verse was proper for serious plays. Which supposition being granted (as it was briefly made out in that discourse, by showing how verse might be made natural), it asserted, that this way of writing was a help to the poet's judgment, by putting bounds to a wild overflowing fancy. I think, therefore, it will not be hard for me to make good what it was to prove. But you add, that were this let pass, yet he who wants judgment in the liberty of his fancy, may as well show the defect of it when he is confined to verse; for he who has judgment will avoid errors, and he who has it not, will commit them in all kinds of writing.

"This argument, as you have taken it from a most acute person, so I confess it carries much weight in it: but by using the word *judgment* here indefinitely, you seem to have put a fallacy upon us. I grant, he who has judgment, that is, so profound, so strong, so infallible a judgment, that he needs no helps to keep it always poised and upright, will commit no faults either in rhyme or out of it. And on the other extreme, he who has a judgment so weak and crazed that no helps can correct or amend it, shall write scurvily out of rhyme, and worse in it. But the first of these judgments is nowhere to be found, and the latter is not fit to write at all. To speak therefore of judgment as it is in the best poets; they who have the greatest proportion of it, want other helps than from it, within. As for example, you would be loath to say, that he who was endued with a sound judgment had no need of history, geography, or moral philosophy, to write correctly. Judgment is indeed the master workman in a play; but he requires many subordinate hands, many tools to his assistance. And verse I affirm to be one of these; 'tis a rule and line by which he keeps his building compact and even, which otherwise lawless imagination would raise either irregularly or loosely. At least, if the poet commits errors with this help, he would make greater and more without it: 'tis, in short, a slow and painful, but the surest kind of working. Ovid, whom you accuse for luxuriancy in verse, had perhaps been farther guilty of it, had he writ in prose. And for your instance of Ben Jonson, who, you say, writ exactly without the help of rhyme; you are to remember, 'tis only an aid to a luxuriant fancy, which his was not: as he did not want imagination, so none ever said he had much to spare. Neither was verse then refined so much to be an help to that age, as it is to ours. Thus then the second thoughts being usually the best, as receiving the maturest digestion from judgment, and the last and most mature product of those thoughts being artful and labored verse it may well be inferred, that verse is a great help to a luxuriant fancy; and this is what that argument which you opposed was to evince."

Neander was pursuing this discourse so eagerly, that Eugenius had called to him twice or thrice, ere he took notice that the barge stood still, and that they were at the foot of Somerset Stairs, where they had appointed it to land. The company were all sorry to separate so soon, though a great part of the evening was already spent; and stood awhile looking back on the water, which the moonbeams played upon, and made it appear like floating quicksilver: at last they went up through a crowd of French people, who were merrily dancing in the open air, and nothing concerned for the noise of guns which had alarmed the town that afternoon. Walking thence together to the piazza, they parted there; Engenius and Lisideius to some pleasant appointment they had made, and Crites and Neander to their several lodgings.

John Locke

1632–1704

One of the most influential of English philosophers, Locke is best known for his epistemological and political views. As an epistemologist, he was an associationist who saw knowledge as beginning with simple sense perceptions (single "ideas") and combining these into complex abstract ideas. He founded an empiricism based on a hard and fast distinction between the primary qualities of experience, those things that are measurable, and secondary qualities (color, smell, sound, taste, and so forth), which he held to be produced as the result of the impact of the primary qualities on the passively perceiving subject. Thus Locke invented a version of the opposition between the object and the subject. Unlike the subject invented by rationalists like René Descartes (1596–1650), this subject is born with no innate ideas; it is *tabula rasa,* a blank tablet, upon which natural experience writes. As a political philosopher, Locke heavily influenced the writers of the American documents of independence, holding for the equality of all human beings, a "social contract" governed by the natural law of equality, and a government operating by checks and balances.

Of his two major works, *Two Treatises on Civil Government* and *An Essay Concerning Human Understanding,* both published in 1690, the latter has a significant bearing on literary theory. In it, Locke does not speak of literature, in which he seems to have had little interest, but he does set forth as the subject of Book Three a theory of words. For Locke, words are signs of ideas, simple ideas being perceptions, that precede them. Their relation to these ideas is purely arbitrary, though after repeated use they seem natural. Except for proper names, words are general and do not refer to specific objects. Rather, they signify abstract ideas built up from combinations of simple ones. These ideas are the "nominal" essences of genera and species, real essences being hidden and unkown to us. After a discussion of the "imperfection" of words and the sources of misunderstanding to which the use of language is prone, Locke remarks on the difficulties we encounter in the interpretation of ancient authors. Though they may use the same words, the ideas these words may denote can differ widely. Locke's giving the priority to ideas over words leads him in his chapter on the abuse of words to inveigh against figurative language, or tropes, "which insinuate wrong ideas, move the passions, and thereby mislead the judgment." For Locke, rhetoric is the instrument of error and deceit.

The attack on rhetoric is, of course, not new with Locke, for Plato's Socrates raised similar complaints against the rhetoricians and sophists and invented a distrust of poetry that persisted into Locke's time and after. Both regard mathematics as the only really trustworthy language. Locke locates the truth we can know in the abstractions we make from combining simple empirically derived ideas into ever more complex ones. Plato, on the other hand, locates truth in a realm of pure ideas or forms.

Post-eighteenth-century treatment of rhetoric gradually turned Locke's view of tropes inside out. Words came to be seen as having a constitutive role in the making of ideas. The reversal culminates in recent theories, in which all language is inescapably rhetorical (as in de Man, below, page 1309), and in deconstruction generally, where the signified is not a prior idea but other words, which in turn signify other words in an infinite verbal chain where meaning (as pure idea or fixed referent) is infinitely deferred (Derrida, below, page 1203).

Locke's epistemological views are seen grounding those of many later writers, for example, Burke (below, page 332), Johnson (below, page 357), and Reynolds (below, page 393), the last of whom seems to blend Locke's empiricism with Platonic idealism.

Locke's *Philosophical Works* were edited in 1901 by J. A. St. John. See Kenneth MacLean, *John Locke and English Literature of the Eighteenth Century* (1936); Ernest L. Tuveson, *Imagination as a Means of Grace: Locke and the Aesthetics of Romanticism* (1960); John W. Yolton, *Locke and the Compass of Human Understanding* (1970); Herman Perret, *Ideologie et semiologie chez Locke et Condillac* (1975); I. C. Tipton, ed., *Locke on Human Understanding* (1984); John W. Yolton, *Locke: An Introduction* (1985); Kevin L. Cope, *John Locke Revisited* (1999).

from

An Essay Concerning Human Understanding

Book Three

Chapter II

Of the Signification of Words

Sect. 1. *Words are sensible signs necessary for communication.*—Man, though he has great variety of thoughts, and such from which others, as well as himself, might receive profit and delight; yet they are all within his own breast, invisible and hidden from others, nor can of themselves be made to appear. The comfort and advantage of society not being to be had without communication of thoughts, it was necessary that man should find out some external sensible signs, whereby those invisible ideas which his thoughts are made up of, might be made known to others. For this purpose nothing was so fit, either for plenty or quickness, as those articulate sounds, which, with so much ease and variety, he found himself able to make. Thus we may conceive how words which were by nature so well adapted to that purpose, come to be made use of by men, as the signs of their ideas; not by any natural connexion that there is between particular articulate sounds, and certain ideas, for then there would be but one language among all men: but by a voluntary imposition, whereby such a word is made arbitrarily the mark of such an idea. The use then of words is to be sensible marks of ideas; and the ideas they stand for are their proper and immediate signification.

Sect. 2. *Words are the sensible signs of his ideas who uses them.*—The use men have of these marks being either to record their own thoughts for the assistance of their own memory, or, as it were, to bring out their ideas, and lay them before the view of others; words in their primary or immediate signification stand for nothing but the ideas in the mind of him that uses them, how imperfectly soever or carelessly those ideas are collected from the things which they are supposed to represent. When a man speaks to another, it is that he may be understood; and the end of speech is, that those sounds, as marks, may make known his ideas to the hearer. That then which words are the marks of, are the ideas of the speaker: nor can any one apply them as marks immediately to any thing else but the ideas that he himself hath. For this would be to make them signs of his own conceptions, and yet apply them to other ideas; which would be to make them signs, and not signs of his ideas at the same time; and so, in effect, to have no signification at all. Words being voluntary signs, they cannot be voluntary signs imposed by him on things he knows not. That would be to make them signs of nothing, sounds without signification. A man cannot make his words the signs either of qualities in

Locke's *Essay Concerning Human Understanding* was first published in London in 1690.

things, or of conceptions in the mind of another, whereof he has none in his own. Until he has some ideas of his own, he cannot suppose them to correspond with the conceptions of another man; nor can he use any signs for them; for thus they would be the signs of he knows not what, which is, in truth, to be the signs of nothing. But when he represents to himself other men's ideas by some of his own, if he consent to give them the same names that other men do, it is still to his own ideas; to ideas that he has, and not to ideas that he has not.

Sect. 3. This is so necessary in the use of language, that in this respect the knowing and the ignorant, the learned and unlearned, use the words they speak (with any meaning) all alike. They, in every man's mouth, stand for the ideas he has, and which he would express by them. A child having taken notice of nothing in the metal he hears called gold, but the bright shining yellow colour, he applies the word gold only to his own idea of that colour, and nothing else; and therefore calls the same colour in a peacock's tail, gold. Another, that hath better observed, adds to shining yellow great weight; and then the sound gold, when he uses it, stands for a complex idea of a shining yellow, and very weighty substance. Another adds to those qualities, fusibility: and then the word gold signifies to him a body, bright, yellow, fusible, and very heavy. Another adds malleability. Each of these uses equally the word gold, when they have occasion to express the idea which they have applied it to; but it is evident, that each can apply it only to his own idea; nor can he make it stand as a sign of such a complex idea as he has not.

Sect. 4. *Words often secretly referred, first, to the ideas in other men's minds.*—But though words, as they are used by men, can properly and immediately signify nothing but the ideas that are in the mind of the speaker; yet they in their thoughts give them a secret reference to two other things.

First, They suppose their words to be marks of the ideas in the minds also of other men, with whom they communicate: for else they should talk in vain, and could not be understood, if the sounds they applied to one idea were such as by the hearer were applied to another; which is to speak two languages. But in this, men stand not usually to examine whether the idea they and those they discourse with have in their minds be the same: but think it enough that they use the word, as they imagine, in the common acceptation of that language; in which they suppose that the idea they make it a sign of is precisely the same, to which the understanding men of that country apply that name.

Sect. 5. *Secondly, to the reality of things.*—Secondly, Because men would not be thought to talk barely of their own imaginations, but of things as really they are; therefore they often suppose their words to stand also for the reality of things. But this relating more particularly to substances, and their names, as perhaps the former does to simple ideas and modes, we shall speak of these two different ways of applying words more at large, when we come to treat of the names of mixed modes and substances in particular: though give me leave here to say, that it is a perverting the use of words, and brings unavoidable obscurity and confusion into their signification, whenever we make them stand for any thing but those ideas we have in our own minds.

Sect. 6. *Words by use readily excite ideas.*—Concerning words, also, it is farther to be considered: first, that they being immediately the signs of men's ideas; and by that means the instruments whereby men communicate their conceptions, and express to one another those thoughts and imaginations they have within their own breasts; there comes by constant use to be such a connexion between certain sounds and the ideas they stand for, that the names heard almost as readily excite certain ideas, as if the objects themselves, which are apt to produce them, did actually affect the senses. Which is manifestly so in all obvious sensible qualities, and in all substances that frequently and familiarly occur to us.

Sect. 7. *Words often used without signification.*—Secondly, That though the proper and immediate signification of words are ideas in the mind of the speaker, yet because by familiar use from our cradles we come to learn certain articulate sounds very perfectly, and have them readily on our tongues, and always at hand in our memories, but yet are not always careful to examine or settle their significations perfectly; it often happens that men, even when they would apply themselves to an attentive consideration, do set their thoughts more on words than things. Nay, because words are many of them learned before the ideas are known for which they stand; therefore some, not only children, but men, speak several words no otherwise than parrots do, only because they have learned them, and have been accustomed to those sounds. But so far as words are of use and signification, so far is there a constant connexion between the sound and the idea, and a designation that the one stands for the other; without which application of them, they are nothing but so much insignificant noise.

Sect. 8. *Their signification perfectly arbitrary.*—Words, by long and familiar use, as has been said, come to excite in men certain ideas so constantly and readily, that they are apt to suppose a natural connexion between them. But that they signify only men's peculiar ideas, and that by a perfect arbitrary imposition, is evident, in that they often fail to excite in others (even that use the same language) the same ideas we take them to be the signs of; and every man has so inviolable a liberty to make words stand for what ideas he pleases, that no one hath the power to make others have the same ideas in their minds that he has, when they use the same words that he does. And therefore the great Augustus himself, in the possession of that power which ruled the world, acknowledged he could not make a new Latin word; which was as much as to say, that he could not arbitrarily appoint what idea any sound should be a sign of in the mouths and common language of his subjects. It is true, common use, by a tacit consent, appropriates certain sounds to certain ideas in all languages, which so far limits the signification of that sound, that unless a man applies it to the same idea, he does not speak properly: and let me add, that unless a man's words excite the same ideas in the hearer which he makes them stand for in speaking, he does not speak intelligibly. But whatever be the consequence of any man's using of words differently, either from their general meaning, or the particular sense of the person to whom he addresses them, this is certain their signification, in his use of them, is limited to his ideas, and they can be signs of nothing else.

Chapter III

Of General Terms

Sect. 1. *The greatest part of words general.*—All things that exist being particulars, it may perhaps be thought reasonable that words, which ought to be conformed to things, should be so too; I mean in their signification: but yet we find the quite contrary. The far greatest part of words, that make all languages, are general terms; which has not been the effect of neglect or chance, but of reason and necessity.

Sect. 2. *For every particular thing to have a name is impossible.*—First, It is impossible that every particular thing should have a distinct peculiar name. For the signification and use of words, depending on that connexion which the mind makes between its ideas, and the sounds it uses as signs of them, it is necessary, in the application of names to things, that the mind should have distinct ideas of the things, and retain also the particular name that belongs to every one, with its peculiar appropriation to that idea. But it is beyond the power of human capacity to frame and retain distinct ideas of all the particular things we meet with; every bird and beast men saw, every tree and plant that affected the senses could not find a place in the most capacious understanding. If it be looked on as an instance of a prodigious memory, that some generals have been able to call every soldier in their army by his proper name, we may easily find a reason why men have never attempted to give names to each sheep in their flock, or crow that flies over their head; much less to call every leaf of plants, or grain of sand that came in their way, by a peculiar name.

Sect. 3. *And useless.*—Secondly, If it were possible, it would yet be useless; because it would not serve to the chief end of language. Men would in vain heap up names of particular things that would not serve them to communicate their thoughts. Men learn names, and use them in talk with others, only that they may be understood; which is then only done, when by use or consent the sound I make by the organs of speech excites in another man's mind, who hears it, the idea I apply it to in mine, when I speak it. This cannot be done by names applied to particular things, whereof I alone having the ideas in my mind, the names of them could not be significant or intelligible to another who was not acquainted with all those very particular things which had fallen under my notice.

Sect. 4. Thirdly, But yet granting this also feasible (which I think is not), yet a distinct name for every particular thing would not be of any great use for the improvement of knowledge; which, though founded in particular things, enlarges itself by general views; to which things reduced, into sorts under general names, are properly subservient. These, with the names belonging to them, come within some compass, and do not multiply every moment, beyond what either the mind can contain, or use requires: and therefore, in these, men have for the most part stopped; but yet not so as to hinder themselves from distinguishing particular things by appropriated names where convenience demands it. And therefore in their own species, which they have most to do with, and wherein they have often occasion to mention particular persons, they make use of proper names; and their distinct individuals have distinct denominations.

Sect. 5. *What things have proper names.*—Besides persons, countries also, cities, rivers, mountains, and other the like distinctions of place, have usually found peculiar names, and that for the same reason; they being such as men have often an occasion to mark particularly, and, as it were, set before others in their discourses with them. And I doubt not, but if we had reason to mention particular horses, as often as we have to mention particular men we should have proper names for the one as familiar as for the other; and Bucephalus would be a word as much in use as Alexander. And therefore we see that, among jockies, horses have their proper names to be known and distinguished by as commonly as their servants; because, among them, there is often occasion to mention this or that particular horse, when he is out of sight.

Sect. 6. *How general words are made.*—The next thing to be considered is, how general words come to be made. For since all things that exist are only particulars, how come we by general terms, or where find we those general natures they are supposed to stand for? Words become general, by being made the signs of general ideas; and ideas become general, by separating from them the circumstances of time, and place, and any other ideas, that may determine them to this or that particular existence. By this way of abstraction, they are made capable of representing more individuals than one; each of which having in it a conformity to that abstract idea, is (as we call it) of that sort.

Sect. 7. But to deduce this a little more distinctly, it will not perhaps be amiss to trace our notions and names from their beginning, and observe by what degrees we proceed, and by what steps we enlarge our ideas from our first infancy. There is nothing more evident, than that the ideas of the persons children converse with (to instance in them alone) are like the persons themselves, only particular. The ideas of the nurse and the mother are well framed in their minds; and, like pictures of them there, represent only those individuals. The names they first gave to them are confined to these individuals; and the names of nurse and mamma the child uses, determine themselves to those persons. Afterwards, when time and a larger acquaintance have made them observe, that there are a great many other things in the world, that in some common agreements of shape, and several other qualities, resemble their father and mother, and those persons they have been used to, they frame an idea, which they find those many particulars do partake in; and to that they give, with others, the name man for example. And thus they come to have a general name, and a general idea. Wherein they make nothing new, but only leave out the complex idea they had of Peter and James, Mary and Jane, that which is peculiar to each, and retain only what is common to them all.

Sect. 8. By the same way that they come by the general name and idea of man, they easily advance to more general names and notions. For observing that several things that differ from their idea of man, and cannot therefore be comprehended under that name, have yet certain qualities, wherein they agree with man, by retaining only those qualities, and uniting them into one idea, they have again another and more general idea; to which having given a name, they make a term of a more comprehensive extension: which new idea is made, not by any new addition, but only, as before, by leaving out the shape, and some other properties signified by the name man, and retaining only a body, with life, sense, and spontaneous motion, comprehended under the name animal.

Sect. 9. *General natures are nothing but abstract ideas.*—That this is the way whereby men first formed general ideas, and general names to them, I think, is so evident, that there needs no other proof of it, but the considering of a man's self, or others, and the ordinary proceedings of their minds in knowledge: and he that thinks general natures or notions are any thing else but such abstract and partial ideas of more complex ones, taken at first from particular existences, will, I fear, be at a loss where to find them. For let any one reflect, and then tell me, wherein does his idea of man differ from that of Peter and Paul; or his idea of horse from that of Bucephalus,[1] but in the leaving out something that is peculiar to each individual, and retaining so much of those particular complex ideas of several particular existences as they are found to agree in? Of the complex ideas signified by the names man and horse leaving out but those particulars wherein they differ, and retaining only those wherein they agree, and of those making a new distinct complex idea, and giving the name animal to it; one has a more general term, that comprehends with man several other creatures. Leave out of the idea of animal, sense and spontaneous motion; and the remaining complex idea, made up of the remaining simple ones of body, life and nourishment, becomes a more general one, under the more comprehensive term *vivens.* And not to dwell longer upon this particular, so evident in itself, by the same way the mind proceeds to body, substance, and at last to being, thing, and such universal terms, which stand for any of our ideas whatsoever. To conclude, this whole mystery of *genera* and *species,* which make such a noise in the schools, and are with justice so little regarded out of them, is nothing else but abstract ideas, more or less comprehensive, with names annexed to them. In all which this is constant and unvariable, that every more general term stands for such an idea, as is but a part of any of those contained under it.

Sect. 10. *Why the genus is ordinarily made use of in definitions.*—This may show us the reason why, in the defining of words, which is nothing but declaring their significations, we make use of the genus, or next general word that comprehends it. Which is not out of necessity, but only to save the labour of enumerating the several simple ideas, which the next general word or genus stands for; or, perhaps, sometimes the shame of not being able to do it. But though defining by *genus* and *differentia* (I crave leave to use these terms of art, though originally Latin, since they most properly suit those notions they are applied to) I say, though defining by the *genus* be the shortest way, yet I think it may be doubted whether it be the best. This I am sure, it is not the only, and so not absolutely necessary. For

---

[1]Bucephalus, horse of Alexander the Great.

definition being nothing but making another understand by words what idea the term defined stands for, a definition is best made by enumerating those simple ideas that are combined in the signification of the term defined; and if instead of such an enumeration men have accustomed themselves to use the next general term, it has not been out of necessity, or for greater clearness, but for quickness and despatch sake. For, I think, that to one who desired to know what idea the word man stood for, it should be said, that man was a solid extended substance, having life, sense, spontaneous motion, and the faculty of reasoning; I doubt not but the meaning of the term man would be as well understood, and the idea it stands for be at least as clearly made known as when it is defined to be a rational animal: which, by the several definitions of animal, *vivens,* and *corpus,* resolves itself into those enumerated ideas. I have, in explaining the term man, followed here the ordinary definition of the schools: which though, perhaps, not the most exact, yet serves well enough to my present purpose. And one may, in this instance, see what gave occasion to the rule, that a definition must consist of *genus* and *differentia;* and it suffices to show us the little necessity there is of such a rule, or advantage in the strict observing of it. For definitions, as has been said, being only the explaining of one word by several others, so that the meaning or idea it stands for may be certainly known; languages are not always so made according to the rules of logic, that every term can have its signification exactly and clearly expressed by two others. Experience sufficiently satisfies us to the contrary; or else those who have made this rule have done ill, that they have given us so few definitions conformable to it. But of definitions, more in the next chapter.

Sect. 11. *General and universal are creatures of the understanding.*—To return to general words, it is plain by what has been said, that general and universal belong not to the real existence of things; but are the inventions and creatures of the understanding, made by it, for its own use, and concern only signs, whether words or ideas. Words are general, as has been said, when used for signs of general ideas, and so are applicable indifferently to many particular things: and ideas are general, when they are set up as the representatives of many particular things; but universality belongs not to things themselves which are all of them particular in their existence; even those words and ideas which in their signification are general. When therefore we quit particulars, the generals that rest are only creatures, of our own making; their general nature being nothing but the capacity they are put into by the understanding, of signifying or representing many particulars. For the signification they have is nothing but a relation, that by the mind of man is added to them.

Sect. 12. *Abstract ideas are the essences of the genera and species.*—The next thing therefore to be considered is, what kind of signification it is that general words have. For, as it is evident that they do not signify barely one particular thing; for then they would not be general terms, but proper names; so on the other side it is as evident, they do not signify a plurality; for man and men would then signify the same, and the distinction of numbers (as the grammarians call them) would be superfluous and useless. That then which general words signify is a sort of things; and each of them does that by being a sign of an abstract idea in the mind, to which idea, as things existing are found to agree, so they come to be ranked under that name; or, which is all one, be of that sort. Whereby, it is evident that the essences of the sorts, or (if the Latin word pleases better) species of things, are nothing else but these abstract ideas. For the having the essence of any species being that which makes any thing to be of that species, and the conformity to the idea to which the name is annexed being that which gives a right to that name; the having the essence, and the having that conformity, must needs be the same thing; since to be of any species, and to have a right to the name of that species, is all one. As, for example, to be a man, or of the species man, and to have a right to the name man, is the same thing. Again, to be a man or of the species man, and have the essence of a man, is the same thing. Now since nothing can be a man, or have a right to the name man, but what has a conformity to the abstract idea the name man stands for; nor any thing be a man, or have a right to the species man, but what has the essence of that species: it follows that the abstract idea for which the name stands, and the essence of the species is one and the same. From whence it is easy to observe, that the essences of the sorts of things, and consequently the sorting of this, is the workmanship of the understanding, that abstracts and makes those general ideas.

Sect. 13. *They are the workmanship of the understanding, but have their foundation in the similitude of things.*—I would not here be thought to forget, much less to deny, that nature in the production of things makes several of them alike; there is nothing more obvious, especially in the races of animals and all things propagated by seed. But yet, I think, we may say the sorting of them under names is the workmanship of the understanding, taking occasion from the similitude it observes among them to make abstract general ideas, and set them up in the mind, with names annexed to them, as patterns or forms (for in that sense the word form has a very proper signification), to which as particular things existing are found to agree, so they come to be of that species, have that denomination, or are put into that *classis.* For when we say, this is a man, that a horse; this justice, that cruelty; this a watch, that a jack; what do we else but rank things under different specific names, as agreeing to those abstract ideas, of which we have made those names the signs? And what are the essences of those species, set out and marked by names, but those abstract ideas in the mind; which are, as it were, the bonds between particular things that exist, and the names they are to be ranked under? And when general names have any connexion with particular beings, these abstract ideas are the medium that unites them; so that the essences of species, as distinguished and denominated by us, neither are, nor can be any thing, but those precise abstract ideas we have in our minds. And therefore the supposed real essences of substances, if different from our abstract ideas, cannot be the essences of the species we rank things into. For two species may be one as rationally as two different essences be the essence of one species: and I demand what are the alterations may, or may not, be in a horse or lead, without making either of them to be of another species? In determining the species of things by our abstract ideas, this is easy to resolve: but if any one will regulate himself herein by supposed real essences, he will, I suppose, be at a loss; and he will never be able to know when any thing precisely ceases to be of the species of a horse or lead.

Sect. 14. *Each distinct abstract idea is a distinct essence.*—Nor will any one wonder that I say these essences, or abstract ideas (which are the measures of name, and the boundaries of species), are the workmanship of the understanding, who considers, that at least the complex ones are often, in several men, different collections of simple ideas; and therefore that is covetousness to one man, which is not so to another. Nay, even in substances, where their abstract ideas seem to be taken from the things themselves, they are not constantly the same; no, not in that species which is most familiar to us, and with which we have the most intimate acquaintance; it having been more than once doubted, whether the fœtus born of a woman were a man; even so far, as that it hath been debated, whether it were, or were not to be nourished and baptized; which could not be, if the abstract idea or essence, to which the name man belonged, were of nature's making, and were not the uncertain and various collection of simple ideas, which the understanding puts together, and then abstracting it, affixed a name to it. So that in truth every distinct abstract idea is a distinct essence: and the names that stand for such distinct ideas are the names of things essentially different. Thus a circle is as essentially different from an oval, as a sheep from a goat; and rain is as essentially different from snow, as water from earth; the abstract idea which is the essence of one being impossible to be communicated to the other. And thus any two abstract ideas, that in any part vary one

from another, with two distinct names annexed to them, constitute two distinct sorts, or, if you please, species, as essentially different, as any two of the most remote or opposite in the world.

Sect. 15. *Real and nominal essences.*—But since the essences of things are thought by some (and not without reason) to be wholly unknown, it may not be amiss to consider the several significations of the word essence.

First, essence may be taken for the being of any thing, whereby it is what it is. And thus the real internal, but generally, in substances, unknown constitution of things, whereon their discoverable qualities depend, may be called their essence. This is the proper original signification of the word, as is evident from the formation of it; *essentia,* in its primary notation, signifying properly being. And in this sense it is still used, when we speak of the essence of particular things, without giving them any name.

Secondly, the learning and disputes of the schools having been much busied about genus and species, the word essence has almost lost its primary signification; and instead of the real constitution of things, has been almost wholly applied to the artificial constitution of genus and species. It is true, there is ordinarily supposed a real constitution of the sorts of things; and it is past doubt, there must be some real constitution, on which any collection of simple ideas coexisting must depend. But it being evident that things are ranked under names into sorts or species, only as they agree to certain abstract ideas to which we have annexed those names, the essence of each genus or sort comes to be nothing but that abstract idea, which the general or sortal (if I may have leave so to call it from sort, as I do general from genus) name stands for. And this we shall find to be that which the word essence imports in its most familiar use. These two sorts of essences, I suppose, may not unfitly be termed, the one the real, the other the nominal essence.

Sect. 16. *Constant connexion between the name and nominal essence.*—Between the nominal essence and the name there is so near a connexion, that the name of any sort of things cannot be attributed to any particular being but what has this essence, whereby it answers that abstract idea, whereof that name is the sign.

Sect. 17. *Supposition, that species are distinguished by their real essences, useless.*—Concerning the real essences of corporeal substances (to mention these only), there are, if I mistake not, two opinions. The one is of those who, using the word essence for they know not what, suppose a certain number of those essences, according to which all natural things are made, and wherein they do exactly every one of them partake, and so become of this or that species. The other and more rational opinion is, of those who look on all natural things to have a real, but unknown constitution of their insensible parts; from which flow those sensible qualities which serve us to distinguish them one from another, according as we have occasion to rank them into sorts under common denominations. The former of these opinions, which supposes these essences as a certain number of forms or moulds, wherein all natural things that exist are cast and do equally partake, has, I imagine, very much perplexed the knowledge of natural things. The frequent productions of monsters, in all the species of animals, and of changelings and other strange issues of human birth, carry with them difficulties not possible to consist with this hypothesis: since it is as impossible that two things, partaking exactly of the same real essence, should have different properties, as that two figures partaking of the same real essence of a circle should have different properties. But were there no other reason against it, yet the supposition of essences that cannot be known, and the making of them nevertheless to be that which distinguishes the species of things, is so wholly useless and unserviceable to any part of our knowledge, that that alone were sufficient to make us lay it by, and content ourselves with such essences of the sorts or species of things, as come within the reach of our knowledge; which, when seriously considered, will be found, as I have said, to be nothing else but those abstract complex ideas to which we have annexed distinct general names.

Sect. 18. *Real and nominal essence the same in simple ideas and modes, different in substances.*—Essences being thus distinguished into nominal and real, we may farther observe, that in the species of simple ideas and modes, they are always the same, but in substances, always quite different. Thus a figure, including a space between three lines, is the real as well as nominal essence of a triangle; it being not only the abstract idea to which the general name is annexed, but the very *essentia* or being of the thing itself, that foundation from which all its properties flow, and to which they are all inseparably annexed. But it is far otherwise concerning that parcel of matter which makes the ring on my finger, wherein these two essences are apparently different. For it is the real constitution of its insensible parts, on which depend all those properties of colour, weight, fusibility, fixedness, &c. which are to be found in it, which constitution we know not, and so having no particular idea of, have no name that is the sign of it. But yet it is its colour, weight, fusibility, fixedness, &c. which makes it to be gold, or gives it a right to that name, which is therefore its nominal essence; since nothing can be called gold, but what has a conformity of qualities to that abstract complex idea to which that name is annexed. But this distinction of essences belonging par-

ticularly to substances, we shall, when we come to consider their names, have an occasion to treat of more fully.

Sect. 19. *Essences ingenerable and incorruptible.*— That such abstract ideas, with names to them, as we have been speaking of, are essences, may farther appear by what we are told concerning essences, viz. that they are all ingenerable and incorruptible: which cannot be true of the real constitutions of things, which begin and perish with them. All things that exist, besides their author, are all liable to change; especially those things we are acquainted with, and have ranked into bands under distinct names or ensigns. Thus that which was grass to-day is to-morrow the flesh of a sheep, and within a few days after becomes part of a man: in all which, and the like changes, it is evident their real essence, *i. e.* that constitution, whereon the properties of these several things depended, is destroyed, and perishes with them. But essences being taken for ideas, established in the mind, with names annexed to them, they are supposed to remain steadily the same, whatever mutations the particular substances are liable to. For whatever becomes of Alexander and Bucephalus, the ideas to which man and horse are annexed are supposed nevertheless to remain the same; and so the essences of those species are preserved whole and undestroyed, whatever changes happen to any or all of the individuals of those species. By this means, the essence of a species rests safe and entire, without the existence of so much as one individual of that kind. For were there now no circle existing any where in the world (as perhaps that figure exists not any where exactly marked out), yet the idea annexed to that name would not cease to be what it is; nor cease to be as a pattern to determine which of the particular figures we meet with have or have not a right to the name circle, and so to show which of them, by having that essence, was of that species. And though there neither were nor had been in nature such a beast as an unicorn, or such a fish as a mermaid; yet supposing those names to stand for complex abstract ideas, that contained no inconsistency in them, the essence of a mermaid is as intelligible as that of a man; and the idea of an unicorn as certain, steady, and permanent as that of a horse. From what has been said, it is evident, that the doctrine of the immutability of essences proves them to be only abstract ideas; and is founded on the relation established between them and certain sounds as signs of them; and will always be true as long as the same name can have the same signification.

Sect. 20. *Recapitulation.*—To conclude, this is that which in short I would say, viz. that all the great business of *genera* and species, and their essences, amounts to no more but this, that men making abstract ideas, and settling them in their minds with names annexed to them, do thereby enable themselves to consider things, and discourse of them, as it were in bundles, for the easier and readier improvement and communication of their knowledge; which would advance but slowly, were their words and thoughts confined only to particulars.

Chapter IX

Of the Imperfection of Words

Sect. 1. *Words are used for recording and communicating our thoughts.*—From what has been said in the foregoing chapters, it is easy to perceive what imperfection there is in language, and how the very nature of words makes it almost unavoidable for many of them to be doubtful and uncertain in their significations. To examine the perfection or imperfection of words it is necessary first to consider their use and end: for as they are more or less fitted to attain that, so are they more or less perfect. We have, in the former part of this discourse, often upon occasion mentioned a double use of words.

First, one for the recording of our own thoughts.

Secondly, the other for the communicating of our thoughts to others.

Sect. 2. *Any words will serve for recording.*—As to the first of these, for the recording our own thoughts for the help of our own memories, whereby, as it were, we talk to ourselves, any words will serve the turn. For since sounds are voluntary and indifferent signs of any ideas, a man may use what words he pleases, to signify his own ideas to himself; and there will be no imperfection in them, if he constantly use the same sign for the same idea, for then he cannot fail of having his meaning understood, wherein consists the right use and perfection of language.

Sect. 3. *Communication by words civil or philosophical.*—As to communication of words, that too has a double use.

I. Civil.

II. Philosophical.

First, by their civil use, I mean such a communication of thoughts and ideas by words, as may serve for the upholding common conversation and commerce, about the ordinary affairs and conveniences of civil life, in the societies of men one among another.

Secondly, by the philosophical use of words, I mean such a use of them as may serve to convey the precise notions of things, and to express, in general propositions, certain and undoubted truths, which the mind may rest upon, and be satisfied with, in its search after true knowledge. These two uses are very distinct, and a great deal less exact-

ness will serve in the one than in the other, as we shall see in what follows.

Sect. 4. *The imperfection of words in the doubtfulness of their signification.*—The chief end of language in communication being to be understood, words serve not well for that end, neither in civil nor philosophical discourse, when any word does not excite in the hearer the same idea which it stands for in the mind of the speaker. Now since sounds have no natural connexion with our ideas, but have all their signification from the arbitrary imposition of men, the doubtfulness and uncertainty of their siginification, which is the imperfection we here are speaking of, has its cause more in the ideas they stand for, than in any incapacity there is in one sound more than in another, to signify any idea: for in that regard they are all equally perfect.

That then which makes doubtfulness and uncertainty in the signification of some more than other words, is the difference of ideas they stand for.

Sect. 5. *Causes of their imperfection.*—Words having naturally no signification, the idea which each stands for must be learned and retained by those who would exchange thoughts, and hold intelligible discourse with others in any language. But this is hardest to be done where,

First, the ideas they stand for are very complex, and made up of a great number of ideas put together.

Secondly, where the ideas they stand for have no certain connexion in nature; and so no settled standard, any where in nature existing, to rectify and adjust them by.

Thirdly, when the signification of the word is referred to a standard, which standard is not easy to be known.

Fourthly, where the signification of the word, and the real essence of the thing, are not exactly the same.

These are difficulties that attend the signification of several words that are intelligible. Those which are not intelligible at all, such as names standing for any simple ideas, which another has not organs or faculties to attain,—as the names of colours to a blind man, or sounds to a deaf man,—need not here be mentioned.

In all these cases we shall find an imperfection in words, which I shall more at large explain, in their particular application to our several sorts of ideas; for if we examine them, we shall find that the names of mixed modes are most liable to doubtfulness and imperfection, for the two first of these reasons; and the names of substances chiefly for the two latter.

Sect. 6. *The names of mixed modes doubtful.*—First, the names of mixed modes are many of them liable to great uncertainty and obscurity in their signification.

First, because the ideas they stand for are so complex.—I. Because of that great composition these complex ideas are often made up of. To make words serviceable to the end of communication, it is necessary (as has been said) that they excite in the hearer exactly the same idea they stand for in the mind of the speaker. Without this, men fill one another's heads with noise and sounds; but convey not thereby their thoughts, and lay not before one another their ideas, which is the end of discourse and language. But when a word stands for a very complex idea that is compounded and decompounded, it is not easy for men to form and retain that idea so exactly as to make the name in common use stand for the same precise idea, without any the least variation. Hence it comes to pass, that men's names of very compound ideas, such as for the most part are moral words, have seldom, in two different men, the same precise signification; since one man's complex idea seldom agrees with another's, and often differs from his own, from that which he had yesterday, or will have to-morrow.

Sect. 7. *Secondly, because they have no standards.*— II. Because the names of mixed modes, for the most part, want standards in nature, whereby men may rectify and adjust their significations; therefore they are very various and doubtful. They are assemblages of ideas put together at the pleasure of the mind, pursuing its own ends of discourse, and suited to its own notions; whereby it designs not to copy any thing really existing, but to denominate and rank things, as they come to agree with those archetypes or forms it has made. He that first brought the word sham, or wheedle, or banter, in use, put together, as he thought fit, those ideas he made it stand for; and as it is with any new names of modes, that are now brought into any language, so it was with the old ones, when they were first made use of. Names therefore that stand for collections of ideas which the mind makes at pleasure, must needs be of doubtful signification, when such collections are nowhere to be found constantly united in nature, nor any patterns to be shown whereby men may adjust them. What the word murder, or sacrilege, &c. signifies, can never be known from things themselves: there be many of the parts of those complex ideas which are not visible in the action itself; the intention of the mind, or the relation of holy things, which make a part of murder or sacrilege, have no necessary connexion with the outward and visible action of him that commits either: and the pulling the trigger of the gun, with which the murder is committed, and is all the action that perhaps is visible, has no natural connexion with those other ideas that make up the complex one, named murder. They have their union and combination only from the understanding, which unites them under one name: but uniting them without any rule or pattern, it cannot be but that the signification of the name that stands for such voluntary collections should be often various in the minds of dif-

ferent men, who have scarce any standing rule to regulate themselves and their notions by, in such arbitrary ideas.

Sect. 8. *Propriety not a sufficient remedy.*—It is true, common use, that is the rule of propriety, may be supposed here to afford some aid, to settle the signification of language; and it cannot be denied but that in some measure it does. Common use regulates the meaning of words pretty well for common conversation; but nobody having an authority to establish the precise signification of words, nor determine to what ideas any one shall annex them, common use is not sufficient to adjust them to philosophical discourses; there being scarce any name of any very complex idea (to say nothing of others) which in common use has not a great latitude, and which, keeping within the bounds of propriety, may not be made the sign of far different ideas. Besides, the rule and measure of propriety itself being nowhere established, it is often matter of dispute whether this or that way of using a word be propriety of speech or no. From all which it is evident, that the names of such kind of very complex ideas are naturally liable to this imperfection, to be of doubtful and uncertain signification; and even in men that have a mind to understand one another, do not always stand for the same idea in speaker and hearer. Though the names glory and gratitude be the same in every man's mouth through a whole country, yet the complex collective idea, which every one thinks on, or intends by that name, is apparently very different in men using the same language.

Sect. 9. *The way of learning these names contributes also to their doubtfulness.*—The way also wherein the names of mixed modes are ordinarily learned, does not a little contribute to the doubtfulness of their signification. For if we will observe how children learn languages, we shall find that to make them understand what the names of simple ideas, or substances, stand for, people ordinarily show them the thing whereof they would have them have the idea; and then repeat to them the name that stands for it, as white, sweet, milk, sugar, cat, dog. But as for mixed modes, especially the most material of them, moral words, the sounds are usually learned first; and then to know what complex ideas they stand for, they are either beholden to the explication of others, or (which happens for the most part) are left to their own observation and industry; which being little laid out in the search of the true and precise meaning of names, these moral words are in most men's mouths little more than bare sounds; or when they have any, it is for the most part but a very loose and undetermined, and consequently obscure and confused signification. And even those themselves, who have with more attention settled their notions, do yet hardly avoid the inconvenience, to have them stand for complex ideas, different from those which other, even intelligent and studious men, make them the signs of. Where shall one find any, either controversial debate, or familiar discourse, concerning honour, faith, grace, religion, church, &c. wherein it is not easy to observe the different notions men have of them? which is nothing but this, that they are not agreed in the signification of those words, nor have in their minds the same complex ideas which they make them stand for: and so all the contests that follow thereupon are only about the meaning of a sound. And hence we see, that in the interpretation of laws, whether divine or human, there is no end; comments beget comments, and explications make new matter for explications; and of limiting, distinguishing, varying the signification of these moral words, there is no end. These ideas of men's making are, by men still having the same power, multiplied *in infinitum.* Many a man who was pretty well satisfied of the meaning of a text of scripture, or clause in the code, at first reading, has by consulting commentators quite lost the sense of it, and by those elucidations given rise or increase to his doubts, and drawn obscurity upon the place. I say not this, that I think commentaries needless; but to show how uncertain the names of mixed modes naturally are, even in the mouths of those who had both the intention and the faculty of speaking as clearly as language was capable to express their thoughts.

Sect. 10. *Hence unavoidable obscurity in ancient authors.*—What obscurity this has unavoidably brought upon the writings of men, who have lived in remote ages and in different countries, it will be needless to take notice; since the numerous volumes of learned men, employing their thoughts that way, are proofs more than enough to show what attention, study, sagacity, and reasoning are required, to find out the true meaning of ancient authors. But there being no writings we have any great concernment to be very solicitous about the meaning of, but those that contain either truths we are required to believe, or laws we are to obey, and draw inconveniences on us when we mistake or transgress; we may be less anxious about the sense of other authors, who writing but their own opinions, we are under no greater necessity to know them, than they to know ours. Our good or evil depending not on their decrees, we may safely be ignorant of their notions: and therefore, in the reading of them, if they do not use their words with a due clearness and perspicuity, we may lay them aside, and, without any injury done them, resolve thus with ourselves:

"Si non vis intelligi, debes neglegi."[2]

Sect. 11. *Names of substances of doubtful signification.*—If the signification of the names of mixed modes are uncertain, because there be no real standards existing in nature to which those ideas are referred, and by which they may be adjusted, the names of substances are of a doubtful signification, for a contrary reason, viz. because the ideas they stand for are supposed conformable to the reality of things, and are referred to standards made by nature. In our ideas of substances, we have not the liberty, as in mixed modes, to frame what combinations we think fit, to be the characteristical notes to rank and denominate things by. In these we must follow nature, suit our complex ideas to real existences, and regulate the signification of their names by the things themselves, if we will have our names to be the signs of them, and stand for them. Here, it is true, we have patterns to follow, but patterns that will make the signification of their names very uncertain; for names must be of a very unsteady and various meaning, if the ideas they stand for be referred to standards without us, that either cannot be known at all, or can be known but imperfectly and uncertainly.

Sect. 12. *Names of substances referred, first, to real essences that cannot be known.*—The names of substances have, as has been shown, a double reference in their ordinary use.

First, sometimes they are made to stand for, and so their signification is supposed to agree to, the real constitution of things, from which all their properties flow, and in which they all centre. But this real constitution, (or as it is apt to be called) essence, being utterly unknown to us, any sound that is put to stand for it must be very uncertain in its application; and it will be impossible to know what things are, or ought to be, called a horse, or anatomy, when those words are put for real essences that we have no ideas of at all. And therefore, in this supposition, the names of substances being referred to standards that cannot be known, their significations can never be adjusted and established by those standards.

Sect. 13. *Secondly, to coexisting qualities, which are known but imperfectly.*—The simple ideas that are found to coexist in substances being that which their names immediately signify, these, as united in the several sorts of things, are the proper standards to which their names are referred, and by which their significations may be best rectified. But neither will these archetypes so well serve this purpose, as to leave these names without very various and uncertain significations: because these simple ideas that coexist, and are united in the same subject, being very numerous, and having all an equal right to go into the complex specific idea, which the specific name is to stand for; men, though they

---

[2] "If you wish not to be understood, you deserve to be neglected."

propose to themselves the very same subject to consider, yet frame very different ideas about it; and so the name they use for it unavoidably comes to have, in several men, very different significations. The simple qualities which make up the complex ideas, being most of them powers, in relation to changes, which they are apt to make in, or receive from other bodies, are almost infinite. He that shall but observe what a great variety of alterations any one of the baser metals is apt to receive from the different application only of fire: and how much a greater number of changes any of them will receive in the hands of a chemist, by the application of other bodies; will not think it strange that I count the properties of any sort of bodies not easy to be collected, and completely known by the ways of inquiry, which our faculties are capable of. They being therefore at least so many that no man can know the precise and definite number, they are differently discovered by different men, according to their various skill, attention, and ways of handling; who therefore cannot choose but have different ideas of the same substance, and therefore make the signification of its common name very various and uncertain. For the complex ideas of substances being made up of such simple ones as are supposed to coexist in nature, every one has a right to put into his complex ideas those qualities he has found to be united together. For though in the substance of gold one satisfied himself with colour and weight, yet another thinks solubility in aq. regia as necessary to be joined with that colour in his idea of gold as any one does its fusibility; solubility in aq. regia being a quality as constantly joined with its colour and weight, as fusibility, or any other; others put into it ductility or fixedness, &c. as they have been taught by tradition or experience. Who of all these has established the right signification of the word gold? or who shall be the judge to determine? Each has its standard in nature, which he appeals to; and with reason thinks he has the same right to put into his complex idea, signified by the word gold, those qualities which upon trial he has found united, as another, who has not so well examined, has to leave them out; or a third, who has made other trials, has to put in others. For the union in nature of these qualities being the true ground of their union in one complex idea, who can say one of them has more reason to be put in, or left out, than another? From hence it will always unavoidably follow, that the complex ideas of substances, in men using the same name for them, will be very various; and so the significations of those names very uncertain.

Sect. 14. *Thirdly to coexisting qualities which are known but imperfectly.*—Besides, there is scarce any particular thing existing, which, in some of its simple ideas, does not communicate with a greater, and in others a less number

of particular beings: who shall determine, in this case, which are those that are to make up the precise collection that is to be signified by the specific name; or can, with any just authority, prescribe which obvious or common qualities are to be left out; or which more secret, or more particular are to be put into the signification of the name of any substance? All which together seldom or never fail to produce that various and doubtful signification in the names of substances, which causes such uncertainty, disputes, or mistakes, when we come to a philosophical use of them.

Sect. 15. *With this imperfection, they may serve for civil, but not well for philosophical use.*—It is true, as to civil and common conversation, the general names of substances, regulated in their ordinary signification by some obvious qualities, (as by the shape and figure in things of known seminal propagation, and in other substances, for the most part, by colour, joined with some other sensible qualities) do well enough to design the things men would be understood to speak of; and so they usually conceive well enough the substances meant by the word gold, or apple, to distinguish the one from the other. But in philosophical inquiries and debates, where general truths are to be established, and consequences drawn from positions laid down—there the precise signification of the names of substances will be found, not only not to be well established, but also very hard to be so. For example, he that shall make malleableness, or a certain degree of fixedness, a part of his complex idea of gold, may make propositions concerning gold, and draw consequences from them, that will truly and clearly follow from gold, taken in such a signification; but yet such as another man can never be forced to admit, nor be convinced of their truth, who makes not malleableness, or the same degree of fixedness, part of that complex idea, that the name gold, in his use of it, stands for.

Sect. 16. *Instance, liquor.*—This is a natural, and almost unavoidable imperfection in almost all the names of substances, in all languages whatsoever, which men will easily find, when once passing from confused or loose notions, they come to more strict and close inquiries: for then they will be convinced how doubtful and obscure those words are in their signification, which in ordinary use appeared very clear and determined. I was once in a meeting of very learned and ingenious physicians, where by chance there arose a question, whether any liquor passed through the filaments of the nerves. The debate having been managed a good while, by variety of arguments on both sides, I (who had been used to suspect that the greatest parts of disputes were more about the signification of words than a real difference in the conception of things) desired, that before they went any farther on in this dispute, they would first examine, and establish among them, what the word liquor signified. They at first were a little surprised at the proposal; and had they been persons less ingenious, they might perhaps have taken it for a very frivolous or extravagant one; since there was no one there that thought not himself to understand very perfectly what the word liquor stood for; which I think, too, none of the most perplexed names of substances. However, they were pleased to comply with my motion; and, upon examination, found that the signification of that word was not so settled and certain as they had all imagined, but that each of them made it a sign of a different complex idea. This made them believe that the main of their dispute was about the signification of the term; and that they differed very little in their opinions concerning some fluid and subtle matter passing through the conduits of the nerves, though it was not so easy to agree whether it was to be called liquor or no—a thing which, when considered, they thought it not worth the contending about.

Sect. 17. *Instance, gold.*—How much this is the case in the greatest part of disputes that men are engaged so hotly in, I shall perhaps have an occasion in another place to take notice. Let us only here consider a little more exactly the fore-mentioned instance of the word gold, and we shall see how hard it is precisely to determine its signification. I think all agree to make it stand for a body of a certain yellow shining colour; which being the idea to which children have annexed that name, the shining yellow part of a peacock's tail is properly to them gold. Others finding fusibility, joined with that yellow colour in certain parcels of matter, make of that combination a complex idea, to which they give the name gold, to denote a sort of substances; and so exclude from being gold all such yellow shining bodies as by fire will be reduced to ashes; and admit to be of that species, or to be comprehended under that name gold, only such substances, as having that shining yellow colour, will by fire be reduced to fusion, and not to ashes. Another, by the same reason, adds the weight; which being a quality as straightly joined with that colour as its fusibility, he thinks has the same reason to be joined in its idea, and to be signified by its name; and therefore the other made up of body, of such a colour and fusibility, to be imperfect; and so on of all the rest: wherein no one can show a reason why some of the inseparable qualities, that are always united in nature, should be put into the nominal essence, and others left out; or why the word gold, signifying that sort of body the ring on his finger is made of, should determine that sort, rather by its colour, weight, and fusibility, than by its colour, weight and solubility in aq. regia: since the dissolving of it by that liquor is as inseparable from it as the fusion by fire; and they are both of them nothing but the relation which that sub-

stance has to two other bodies, which have a power to operate differently upon it. For by what right is it that fusibility comes to be a part of the essence signified by the word gold, and solubility but a property of it; or why is its colour part of the essence, and its malleableness but a property? That which I mean is this: that these being all but properties depending on its real constitution, and nothing but powers, either active or passive, in reference to other bodies; no one has authority to determine the signification of the word gold (as referred to such a body existing in nature) more to one collection of ideas to be found in that body than to another: whereby the signification of that name must unavoidably be very uncertain; since, as has been said, several people observe several properties in the same substance; and, I think, I may say nobody at all. And therefore we have but very imperfect descriptions of things, and words have very uncertain significations.

Sect. 18. *The names of simple ideas the least doubtful.*—From what has been said, it is easy to observe what has been before remarked, viz. That the names of simple ideas are, of all others, the least liable to mistakes, and that for these reasons. First, because the ideas they stand for, being each but one single perception, are much easier got, and more clearly retained, than the more complex ones; and therefore are not liable to the uncertainty which usually attends those compounded ones of substances and mixed modes, in which the precise number of simple ideas, that make them up, are not easily agreed, and so readily kept in the mind: and secondly, because they are never referred to any other essence, but barely that perception they immediately signify; which reference is that which renders the signification of the names of substances naturally so perplexed, and gives occasion to so many disputes. Men that do not perversely use their words, or on purpose set themselves to cavil, seldom mistake, in any language which they are acquainted with, the use and signification of the names of simple ideas: white and sweet, yellow and bitter, carry a very obvious meaning with them, which every one precisely comprehends, or easily perceives he is ignorant of, and seeks to be informed. But what precise collection of simple ideas modesty or frugality stand for in another's use, is not so certainly known. And however we are apt to think we well enough know what is meant by gold or iron; yet the precise complex idea others make them the signs of, is not so certain; and I believe it is very seldom that, in speaker and hearer, they stand for exactly the same collection: which must needs produce mistakes and disputes, when they are made use of in discourses, wherein men have to do with universal propositions, and would settle in their minds universal truths, and consider the consequences that follow from them.

Sect. 19. *And next to them, simple modes.*—By the same rule, the names of simple modes are, next to those of simple ideas, least liable to doubt and uncertainty, especially those of figure and number, of which men have so clear and distinct ideas. Who ever, that had a mind to understand them, mistook the ordinary meaning of seven, or a triangle? And in general the least compounded ideas in every kind have the least dubious names.

Sect. 20. *The most doubtful are the names of very compounded mixed modes and substances.*—Mixed modes, therefore, that are made up but of a few and obvious simple ideas, have usually names of no very uncertain signification; but the same names of mixed modes, which comprehend a great number of simple ideas, are commonly of a very doubtful and undetermined meaning, as has been shown. The names of substances, being annexed to ideas that are neither the real essences nor exact representations of the patterns they are referred to, are liable yet to greater imperfection and uncertainty, especially when we come to a philosophical use of them.

Sect. 21. *Why this imperfection charged upon words.*—The great disorder that happens in our names of substances, proceeding for the most part from our want of knowledge, and inability to penetrate into their real constitutions, it may probably be wondered, why I charge this as an imperfection rather upon our words than understandings. This exception has so much appearance of justice, that I think myself obliged to give a reason why I have followed this method. I must confess, then, that when I first began this discourse of the understanding, and a good while after, I had not the least thought that any consideration of words was at all necessary to it. But when, having passed over the original and composition of our ideas, I began to examine the extent and certainty of our knowledge, I found it had so near a connexion with words, that, unless their force and manner of signification were first well observed, there could be very little said clearly and pertinently concerning knowledge; which being conversant about truth, had constantly to do with propositions; and though it terminated in things, yet it was for the most part so much by the intervention of words, that they seemed scarce separable from our general knowledge. At least, they interpose themselves so much between our understandings and the truth, which it would contemplate and apprehend, that, like the medium through which visible objects pass, their obscurity and disorder do not seldom cast a mist before our eyes, and impose upon our understandings. If we consider, in the fallacies men put upon themselves as well as others, and the mistakes in men's disputes and notions, how great a part is owing to words, and their uncertain or mistaken significations—we

shall have reason to think this no small obstacle in the way to knowledge; which, I conclude, we are the more carefully to be warned of, because it has been so far from being taken notice of as an inconvenience, that the arts of improving it have been made the business of men's study, and obtained the reputation of learning and subtility, as we shall see in the following chapter. But I am apt to imagine, that were the imperfections of language, as the instruments of knowledge, more thoroughly weighed, a great many of the controversies that make such a noise in the world, would of themselves cease; and the way to knowledge, and perhaps peace, too, lie a great deal opener than it does.

Sect. 22. *This should teach us moderation, in imposing our own sense of old authors.*—Sure I am, that the signification of words, in all languages, depending very much on the thoughts, notions, and ideas of him that uses them, must unavoidably be of great uncertainty to men of the same language and country. This is so evident in the Greek authors, that he that shall peruse their writings, will find in almost every one of them a distinct language, though the same words. But when to this natural difficulty in every country there shall be added different countries and remote ages, wherein the speakers and writers had very different notions, tempers, customs, ornaments, and figures of speech, &c. every one of which influenced the signification of their words then, though to us now they are lost and unknown; it would become us to be charitable one to another in our interpretations or misunderstanding of those ancient writings; which, though of great concernment to be understood, are liable to the unavoidable difficulties of speech, which (if we except the names of simple ideas, and some very obvious things) is not capable, without a constant defining the terms, of conveying the sense and intention of the speaker, without any manner of doubt and uncertainty to the hearer. And in discourses of religion, law, and morality, as they are matters of the highest concernment, so there will be the greatest difficulty.

Sect. 23. The volumes of interpreters and commentators on the old and new Testaments are but too manifest proofs of this. Though every thing said in the text be infallibly true, yet the reader may be, nay cannot choose but be, very fallible in the understanding of it. Nor is to be wondered, that the will of God, when clothed in words, should be liable to that doubt and uncertainty which unavoidably attends that sort of conveyance; when even his Son, whilst clothed in flesh, was subject to all the frailties and inconveniences of human nature, sin excepted: and we ought to magnify his goodness, that he hath spread before all the world such legible characters of his works and providence, and given all mankind so sufficient a light of reason, that they to whom this written word never came, could not (whenever they set themselves to search) either doubt of the being of a God, or of the obedience due to him. Since then the precepts of natural religion are plain, and very intelligible to all mankind, and seldom come to be controverted; and other revealed truths, which are conveyed to us by books and languages, are liable to the common and natural obscurities and difficulties incident to words; methinks it would become us to be more careful and diligent in observing the former, and less magisterial, positive, and imperious in imposing our own sense and interpretations of the latter.

Chapter X

Of the Abuse of Words

Sect. 23. To conclude this consideration of the imperfection, and the abuse of language; the ends of language in our discourse with others, being chiefly these three: First, to make known one man's thoughts or ideas to another. Secondly, to do it with as much ease and quickness, as is possible; and thirdly, thereby to convey the knowledge of things. Language is either abused, or deficient, when it fails in any of these three.

First, words fail in the first of these ends, and lay not open one man's ideas to another's view. First, when men have names in their mouths without any determined ideas in their minds, whereof they are the signs: or secondly, when they apply the common received names of any language to ideas, to which the common use of that language does not apply them: or thirdly, when they apply them very unsteadily, making them stand now for one, and by and by for another idea.

Sect. 24. Secondly, men fail of conveying their thoughts, with all the quickness and ease that may be, when they have complex ideas, without having distinct names for them. This is sometimes the fault of language itself, which has not in it a sound yet applied to such a signification: and sometimes the fault of the man, who has not yet learned the name for that idea he would show another.

Sect. 25. Thirdly, there is no knowledge of things conveyed by man's words, when their ideas agree not to the reality of things. Though it be a defect, that has its original in our ideas, which are not so conformable to the nature of things, as attention, study, and application might make them: Yet it fails not to extend itself to our words too, when we use them as signs of real beings, which never yet had any reality or existence.

Sect. 26. First, he that hath words of any language, without distinct ideas in his mind, to which he applies them, does, so far as he uses them in discourse, only make a noise without any sense or signification; and how learned soever he may seem by the use of hard words, or learned terms, is not much more advanced thereby in knowledge, than he would be in learning, who had nothing in his study but the bare titles of books, without possessing the contents of them. For all such words however put into discourse, according to the right construction of grammatical rules, or the harmony of well turned periods, do yet amount to nothing but bare sounds, and nothing else.

Sect. 27. Secondly, he that has complex ideas, without particular names for them, would be in no better case than a bookseller, who had in his warehouse volumes that lay there unbound, and without titles; which he could therefore make known to others only by showing the loose sheets, and communicating them only by tale. This man is hindered in his discourse for want of words to communicate his complex ideas, which he is therefore forced to make known by an enumeration of the simple ones that compose them; and so is fain often to use twenty words to express what another man signifies in one.

Sect. 28. Thirdly, he that puts not constantly the same sign for the same idea, but uses the same words sometimes in one, and sometimes in another signification, ought to pass in the schools and conversation for as fair a man as he does in the market and exchange, who sells several things under the same name.

Sect. 29. Fourthly, he that applies the words of any language to ideas different from those to which the common use of that country applies them, however his own understanding may be filled with truth and light, will not by such words be able to convey much of it to others, without defining his terms. For however the sounds are such as are familiarly known, and easily enter the ears of those who are accustomed to them; yet standing for other ideas than those they usually are annexed to, and are wont to excite in the mind or the hearers, they cannot make known the thoughts of him who thus uses them.

Sect. 30. Fifthly, he that imagined to himself substances such as never have been, and filled his head with ideas which have not any correspondence with the real nature of things, to which yet he gives settled and defined names, may fill his discourse, and perhaps another man's head, with the fantastical imaginations of his own brain, but will be very far from advancing thereby one jot in real and true knowledge.

Sect. 31. He that hath names without ideas, wants meaning in his words, and speaks only empty sounds. He that hath complex ideas without names for them, wants liberty and despatch in his expressions, and is necessitated to use periphrases. He that uses his words loosely and unsteadily, will either be not minded, or not understood. He that applies his names to ideas different from their common use, wants propriety in his language, and speaks gibberish. And he that hath the ideas of substances disagreeing with the real existence of things, so far wants the materials of true knowledge in his understanding, and hath instead thereof chimeras.

Sect. 32. *How in substances.*—In our notions concerning substances, we are liable to all the former inconveniences: v. g. 1. He that uses the word tarantula, without having any imagination or idea what it stands for, pronounces a good word; but so long means nothing at all by it. 2. He that in a new discovered country shall see several sorts of animals and vegetables, unknown to him before, may have as true ideas of them as of a horse or a stag; but can speak of them only by a description, till he shall either take the names the natives call them by, or give them names himself. 3. He that uses the word body sometimes for pure extension, and sometimes for extension and solidity together, will talk very fallaciously. 4. He that gives the name horse to that idea which common usage calls mule, talks improperly, and will not be understood. 5. He that thinks the name centaur stands for some real being, imposes on himself, and mistakes words for things.

Sect. 33. *How in modes and relations.*—In modes and relations generally we are liable only to the four first of these inconveniences; viz. 1. I may have in my memory the names of modes, as gratitude or charity, and yet not have any precise ideas annexed in my thoughts to those names. 2. I may have ideas, and not know the names that belong to them; v. g. I may have the idea of a man's drinking till his colour and humour be altered, till his tongue trips, and his eyes look red, and his feet fail him; and yet not know that it is to be called drunkenness. 3. I may have the ideas of virtues or vices, and names also, but apply them amiss: v. g. when I apply the name frugality to that idea which others call and signify by this sound, covetousness. 4. I may use any of those names with inconstancy. 5. But, in modes and relations I cannot have ideas disagreeing to the existence of things: for modes being complex ideas made by the mind at pleasure; and relation being but by way of considering or comparing two things together, and so also an idea of my own making; these ideas can scarce be found to disagree with any thing existing, since they are not in the mind as the copies of things regularly made by nature, nor as properties inseparably flowing from the internal constitution or essence of any substance; but as it were patterns lodged in my memory, with names annexed to them, to denominate actions and relations by, as they come to exist. But the mistake is commonly in my giving a wrong name to my conceptions; and so using words in a different sense from other people, I am not understood, but am thought to have wrong ideas of them, when I give wrong names to them. Only if I put in my ideas of mixed modes or relations any inconsistent ideas together, I fill my head also with chimeras; since such ideas, if well examined, cannot so much exist in the mind, much less any real being ever be denominated from them.

Sect. 34. *Figurative speech also an abuse of language.*—Sixthly, since wit and fancy find easier entertainment in the world than dry truth and real knowledge, figurative speeches and allusion in language will hardly be admitted as an imperfection or abuse of it. I confess, in discourses where we seek rather pleasure and delight than information and improvement, such ornaments as are borrowed from them can scarce pass for faults. But yet if we would speak of things as they are, we must allow that all the art of rhetoric, besides order and clearness, all the artificial and figurative application of words eloquence hath invented, are for nothing else but to insinuate wrong ideas, move the passions, and thereby mislead the judgment, and so indeed are perfect cheats; and, therefore, however laudable or allowable oratory may render them in harangues and popular addresses, they are certainly, in all discourses that pretend to inform or instruct, wholly to be avoided; and where truth and knowledge are concerned, cannot but be thought a great fault, either of the language or person that makes use of them. What, and how various they are, will be superfluous here to take notice; the books of rhetoric which abound in the world will instruct those who want to be informed: only I can not but observe how little the preservation and improvement of truth and knowledge is the care and concern of mankind; since the arts of fallacy are endowed and preferred. It is evident how much men love to deceive and be deceived, since rhetoric, that powerful instrument of error and deceit, has its established professors, is publicly taught, and has always been had in great reputation: and, I doubt not, but it will be thought great boldness, if not brutality in me, to have said thus much against it. Eloquence, like the fair sex, has too prevailing beauties in it to suffer itself ever to be spoken against. And it is in vain to find fault with those arts of deceiving wherein men find pleasure to be deceived.

Alexander Pope

1688–1744

Thoroughly neoclassical in its premises, the *Essay on Criticism* follows in the tradition of Horace and Boileau. Pope's approach differs from that of the two previous poets, however, in that his advice is mainly for critics and secondarily for poets. Nevertheless he must establish the principles of sound artistic practice. The basic rule of art for Pope is to "follow nature." Nature he sees in an Aristotelian way as a process. This fundamental form of reality is the proper object of imitation. As for rules, they are but "nature methodized"; the form of nature is nature's own self-made restraint. But the poet can transgress the rules if the basic aim of poetry is achieved. In these remarks Pope comes near to expressing an idea of the sublime. Clearly the poet must have a strong sense of literary tradition in order to make intelligent judgments, and the critic must have it too. Pope, in lines that have since become famous, notes Virgil's discovery that to imitate Homer is also to imitate nature.

Most important, the critic should avoid pride; he should try to sense and share the spirit in which his author wrote. Pope goes beyond this precept to remind critics that the author cannot accomplish more than he intends. This argument raises problems that have been of interest to the modern critical mind: the question of the usefulness of knowing a poet's intention, which is disputed by Wimsatt and Beardsley (below, page 1027) and the relationship between intuition and expression, which Croce discusses in his *Aesthetic*. Certainly what Pope recommends to the critic is superior to the varieties of critical narrowness that he draws up for censure: blind invocation of rules, judgment on a part in isolation from the whole, total emphasis on conceits, imagery, or prosody. He is equally critical of slavery to fashion and to personal whim, and he insists on the critic's having the qualities of honesty, modesty, and courage. The critics whom he selects for his admiration indicate his stance: Aristotle, Horace, Dionysius of Halicarnassus, Petronius Arbiter, Quintilian, Longinus, Erasmus, Vida (who wrote an "Art of Poetry"), and finally Boileau. The Earl of Roscommon, a Restoration writer who translated Horace, and William Walsh, a minor poet and friend of Pope's, are also praised. It is clear that at age twenty-one the prodigious Pope takes up, with this poem, defense of the classical tradition.

The standard edition of Pope is the Twickenham edition of the *Works,* edited by John Butt (in six volumes, 1939–1967). See also Joseph Warton, *An Essay on the Genius and Writings of Pope* (in two volumes, 1756, 1782); Austin Warren, *Pope as Critic and Humanist* (1929); E. N. Hooker, "Pope on Wit: The *Essay on Criticism,*" *Hudson Review,* II (1950), 84–100; William Empson, " 'Wit' in the *Essay on Criticism,*" *Hudson Review,* II (1950), 559–77; Arthur Fenner, Jr., "The Unity of Pope's *Essay on Criticism,*" *Philological Quarterly,* XXXIX (1960), 435–56; Bertrand A. Goldgar, ed., *Literary Criticism of Alexander Pope* (1965); Maynard Mack, *Alexander Pope: A Life* (1985); Wallace Jackson and R. Paul Yoder, eds., *Critical Essays on Alexander Pope* (1993).

An Essay on Criticism

—*Si quid novisti rectius istis,
Candidus imperti; si non, bis utere mecum.*[1]

HORACE

Part I

'Tis hard to say, if greater want of skill
Appear in writing or in judging ill;
But, of the two, less dang'rous is th' offense
To tire our patience, than mislead our sense:
Some few in that, but numbers err in this,
Ten censure wrong for one who writes amiss;
A fool might once himself alone expose;
Now one in verse makes many more in prose.
　　'Tis with our judgments as our watches, none
Go just alike, yet each believes his own.　　　　　　10
In poets as true genius is but rare,
True taste as seldom is the critic's share;
Both must alike from heav'n derive their light,
These born to judge, as well as those to write.
Let such teach others who themselves excel,
And censure freely, who have written well.
Authors are partial to their wit,[2] 'tis true,
But are not critics to their judgment too?
　　Yet, if we look more closely, we shall find
Most have the seeds of judgment in their mind.　　20
Nature affords at least a glimm'ring light;
The lines, though touched but faintly, are drawn right:
But as the slightest sketch, if justly traced
Is by ill-coloring but the more disgraced,
So by false learning is good sense defaced:
Some are bewildered in the maze of schools,[3]
And some made coxcombs nature meant but fools:
In search of wit,[4] these lose their common sense,
And then turn critics in their own defense:
Each burns alike, who can, or cannot write,　　　　30
Or with a rival's, or a eunuch's spite.
All fools have still[5] an itching to deride,
And fain would be upon the laughing side.

If Maevius[6] scribble in Apollo's spite,
There are who judge still worse than he can write.
　　Some have at first for wits,[7] then poets passed,
Turned critics next, and proved plain fools at last.
Some neither can for wits nor critics pass,
As heavy mules are neither horse nor ass.
Those half-learned witlings, num'rous in our isle,　　40
As half-formed insects on the banks of Nile,[8]
Unfinished things, one knows not what to call,
Their generation's so equivocal;
To tell[9] them would a hundred tongues require,
Or one vain wit's, that might a hundred tire.
　　But you who seek to give and merit fame,
And justly bear a critic's noble name,
Be sure yourself and your own reach to know,
How far your genius, taste, and learning go;
Launch not beyond your depth, but be discreet,　　50
And mark that point where sense and dullness meet.
　　Nature to all things fixed the limits fit,
And wisely curbed proud man's pretending wit.
As on the land while here the ocean gains,
In other parts it leaves wide sandy plains;
Thus in the soul while memory prevails,
The solid pow'r of understanding fails;
Where beams of warm imagination play,
The memory's soft figures melt away.
One science only will one genius fit;　　　　　　　60
So vast is art, so narrow human wit:
Not only bounded to peculiar arts,
But oft' in those confined to single parts.
Like kings we lose the conquest gained before,
By vain ambition still to make them more:
Each might his sev'ral province well command,
Would all but stoop to what they understand.
　　First follow nature, and your judgment frame
By her just standard, which is still[10] the same:
Unerring nature! still divinely bright,　　　　　　70
One clear, unchanged, and universal light,
Life, force, and beauty, must to all impart,
At once the source, and end, and test of art.
Art from that fund each just supply provides;
Works without show, and without pomp presides:[11]
In some fair body thus th' informing soul

Pope's *Essay on Criticism* was first published in 1711. It may have been composed as early as 1707.
[1] "If you know of any maxims superior to these, let me know of them; if not, make use of these as I do." *Epistles* I, vi.
[2] The genius of their own writing.
[3] School of criticism.
[4] Genius, intellect.
[5] Always.
[6] A contemporary of Horace regarded as a poetaster, also known as Bavius.
[7] Geniuses.
[8] It was once thought, though not with any certainty, that insects were formed by the sun on the Nile's banks.
[9] Count.
[10] Always.
[11] See Horace, *Art of Poetry* (above, page 79).

With spirits feeds, with vigor fills the whole;
Each motion guides, and ev'ry nerve sustains,
Itself unseen, but in th' effects remains.
Some, to whom heav'n in wit has been profuse,
Want as much more, to turn it to its use;
For wit and judgment often are at strife,
Though meant each other's aid, like man and wife.
'Tis more to guide, than spur the Muse's steed;
Restrain his fury, then provoke his speed:
The winged courser, like a gen'rous[12] horse,
Shows most true mettle when you check his course.

    Those rules of old discovered, not devised,
Are nature still, but nature methodized:
Nature, like liberty, is but restrained   90
By the same laws which first herself ordained.

    Hear how learned Greece her useful rules indites,
When to repress, and when indulge our flights:
High on Parnassus' top her sons she showed,
And pointed out those arduous paths they trod;
Held from afar, aloft, th' immortal prize,
And urged the rest by equal steps to rise,
Just precepts thus from great examples giv'n,
She drew from them what they derived from heav'n;
The gen'rous critic fanned the poet's fire,   100
And taught the world with reason to admire.
Then criticism the Muse's handmaid proved,
To dress her charms, and make her more beloved:
But following wits from that intention strayed;
Who could not win the mistress, wooed the maid;
Against the poets their own arms they turned,
Sure to hate most the men from whom they learned.
So modern 'pothecaries, taught the art
By doctors' bills[13] to play the doctor's part,
Bold in the practice of mistaken rules,   110
Prescribe, apply, and call their masters fools.
Some on the leaves of ancient authors prey;
Nor time nor moths e'er spoiled so much as they:
Some dryly plain, without invention's aid,
Write dull receipts how poems may be made;
These leave the sense, their learning to display,
And those explain the meaning quite away.

    You then whose judgment the right course would steer,
Know well each ancient's proper character;
His fable,[14] subject, scope[15] in ev'ry page;   120
Religion, country, genius of his age:

Without all these at once before your eyes,
Cavil you may, but never criticize.
Be Homer's works your study and delight,
Read them by day, and meditate by night;
Thence form your judgment, thence your maxims bring,
And trace the Muses upward to their spring.
Still with itself compared, his text peruse;
And let your comment be the Mantuan Muse.[16]

    When first young Maro[17] in his boundless mind
A work t' outlast immortal Rome designed,   130
Perhaps he seemed above the critic's law,
And but from nature's fountain scorned to draw:
But when t' examine every part he came,
Nature and Homer were, he found, the same.
Convinced, amazed, he checks the bold design,
And rules as strict his labored work confine
As if the Stagyrite[18] o'erlooked each line.
Learn hence for ancient rules a just esteem;
To copy nature is to copy them.   140

    Some beauties yet no precept can declare,[19]
For there's a happiness as well as care.
Music resembles poetry; in each
Are nameless graces which no methods teach,
And which a master hand alone can reach.
If, where the rules not far enough extend,
(Since rules were made but to promote their end)
Some lucky license answer to the full
Th' intent proposed, that license is a rule.
Thus Pegasus, a nearer way to take,   150
May boldly deviate from the common track.
Great wits sometimes may gloriously offend,
And rise to faults true critics dare not mend;
From vulgar bounds with brave disorder part,
And snatch a grace beyond the reach of art,
Which, without passing through the judgment, gains
The heart, and all its end at once attains.
In prospects thus some objects please our eyes,
Which out of nature's common order rise,
The shapeless rock, or hanging precipice.   160
But though the ancients thus their rules invade,
(As kings dispense with laws themselves have made)
Moderns, beware! or if you must offend
Against the precept, ne'er transgress its end;

---

[12] Spirited, noble.
[13] Prescriptions.
[14] Plot.
[15] Aim.

---

[16] Virgil was born at Mantua.
[17] Virgil (Publius Virgilius Maro, 70–19 B.C.).
[18] Aristotle, born at Stagira.
[19] Explain.

Let it be seldom, and compelled by need;
And have, at least, their precedent to plead;
The critic else proceeds without remorse,
Seizes your fame, and puts his laws in force.
    I know there are, to whose presumptuous thoughts
Those freer beauties, ev'n in them, seem faults.   170
Some figures monstrous and misshaped appear,
Considered singly, or beheld too near,
Which, but proportioned to their light,[20] or place,
Due distance reconciles to form and grace.
A prudent chief not always must display
His pow'rs in equal ranks, and fair array,
But with th' occasion and the place comply,
Conceal his force, nay, seem sometimes to fly.
Those oft' are stratagems which errors seem,
Nor is it Homer nods but we that dream.[21]   180
    Still green with bays each ancient altar stands,
Above the reach of sacrilegious hands;
Secure from flames, from envy's fiercer rage,
Destructive war, and all-involving age.
See, from each clime, the learned their incense bring;
Hear, in all tongues consenting paeans ring!
In praise so just let ev'ry voice be joined,
And fill the gen'ral chorus of mankind.
Hail, bards triumphant! Born in happier days;
Immortal heirs of universal praise!
Whose honors with increase of ages grow,   190
As streams roll down, enlarging as they flow;
Nations unborn your mighty names shall sound,
And worlds applaud, that must not yet be found!
O may some spark of your celestial fire,
The last, the meanest of your sons inspire
(That on weak wings, from far, pursues your flights;
Glows while he reads, but trembles as he writes)
To teach vain wits a science little known,
T' admire superior sense, and doubt their own!   200

Part II

Of all the causes which conspire to blind
Man's erring judgment, and misguide the mind,
What the weak head with strongest bias rules,
Is pride, the never-failing vice of fools.

Whatever nature has in worth denied,
She gives in large recruits of needful pride;
For as in bodies, thus in souls, we find
What wants in blood and spirits, swelled with wind:
Pride, where wit fails, steps in to our defense,
And fills up all the mighty void of sense: 210
If once right reason drives that cloud away,
Truth breaks upon us with resistless day.
Trust not yourself; but, your defects to know,
Make use of ev'ry friend—and ev'ry foe.
    A little learning is a dang'rous thing;
Drink deep, or taste not the Pierian spring:[22]
There shallow draughts intoxicate the brain,
And drinking largely sobers us again.
Fired at first sight with what the Muse imparts,
In fearless youth we tempt the heights of arts,   220
While from the bounded level of our mind,
Short views we take, nor see the lengths behind;
But more advanced, behold with strange surprise,
New distant scenes of endless science rise!
So pleased at first the tow'ring Alps we try,
Mount o'er the vales, and seem to tread the sky,
Th' eternal snows appear already past,
And the first clouds and mountains seem the last:
But those attained, we tremble to survey
The growing labors of the lengthened way;   230
Th' increasing prospect tires our wand'ring eyes,
Hills peep o'er hills, and Alps on Alps arise!
    A perfect judge will read each work of wit
With the same spirit that its author writ;
Survey the whole, nor seek slight faults to find
Where nature moves, and rapture warms the mind;
Nor lose for that malignant dull delight,
The gen'rous pleasure to be charmed with wit.
But in such lays as neither ebb nor flow,
Correctly cold, and regularly low,   240
That, shunning faults, one quiet tenor keep,
We cannot blame indeed—but we may sleep.
In wit, as nature, what affects our hearts
Is not th' exactness of peculiar parts;
'Tis not a lip, or eye, we beauty call,
But the joint force and full result of all.
Thus when we view some well-proportioned dome,
(The world's just wonder,[23] and ev'n thine, O Rome![24])
No single parts unequally surprise,

---

[20] Pope here refers to the famous *ut pictura poeisis* passage in Horace (above, page 84), where Horace observes that some paintings are better viewed close up, some farther away. Transposed to a discussion of literature, "light" means something like "context."

[21] The allusion to Horace continues. Horace remarks that Homer's art occasionally fails (above, page 84). Pope suggests that it is the reader, not Homer, who "nods."

---

[22] Pieria is by legend the birthplace of the Muses.

[23] The sky.

[24] The dome of St. Peter's in Rome.

All comes united to th' admiring eyes;   250
No monstrous height, or breadth, or length, appear;
The whole at once is bold, and regular.

    Whoever thinks a faultless piece to see,
Thinks what ne'er was, nor is, nor e'er shall be.
In ev'ry work regard the writer's end,
Since none can compass more than they intend;[25]
And if the means be just, the conduct true,
Applause, in spite of trivial faults, is due.
As men of breeding, sometimes men of wit,
T' avoid great errors, must the less commit;   260
Neglect the rules each verbal critic[26] lays,
For not to know some trifles is a praise.
Most critics, fond of some subservient art,
Still make the whole depend upon a part:
They talk of principles, but notions prize,
And all to one loved folly sacrifice.

    Once on a time, La Mancha's knight,[27] they say,
A certain bard encount'ring on the way,
Discoursed in terms as just, with looks as sage,
As e'er could Dennis,[28] of the Grecian stage;   270
Concluding all were desp'rate sots and fools,
Who durst depart from Aristotle's rules.
Our author, happy in a judge so nice,
Produced his play, and begged the knight's advice;
Made him observe the subject, and the plot,
The manners, passions, unities;[29] what not?
All which, exact to rule, were brought about,
Were but a combat in the lists left out.

    "What! leave the combat out?" exclaims the knight.
"Yes, or we must renounce the Stagyrite."   280
"Not so, by heav'n!" (he answers in a rage)
"Knights, squires, and steeds, must enter on the stage."
"So vast a throng, the stage can ne'er contain."
"Then build a new, or act it in a plain."

    Thus critics of less judgment than caprice,
Curious,[30] not knowing, not exact[31] but nice,[32]
Form short ideas, and offend in arts
(As most in manners) by a love to parts.

    Some to conceit alone their taste confine,
And glitt'ring thoughts struck out at ev'ry line;   290

Pleased with a work where nothing's just or fit;
One glaring chaos and wild heap of wit.
Poets, like painters, thus unskilled to trace
The naked nature, and the living grace,
With golds and jewels cover ev'ry part,
And hide with ornaments their want of art.
True wit is nature to advantage dressed;
What oft' was thought, but ne'er so well expressed;
Something, whose truth convinced at sight we find,
That gives us back the image of our mind.   300
As shades more sweetly recommend the light,
So modest plainness set off sprightly wit:
For works may have more wit than does them good,
As bodies perish through excess of blood.

    Others for language all their care express,
And value books, as women men, for dress:
Their praise is still—the style is excellent;
The sense, they humbly take upon content.[33]
Words are like leaves, and where they most abound,
Much fruit of sense beneath is rarely found.   310
False eloquence, like the prismatic glass,
Its gaudy colors spreads on ev'ry place;
The face of nature we no more survey,
All glares alike, without distinction gay;
But true expression, like th' unchanging sun,
Clears and improves whate'er it shines upon,
It gilds all objects, but it alters none.
Expression is the dress of thought, and still
Appears more decent,[34] as more suitable:
A vile conceit in pompous words expressed   320
Is like a clown in regal purple dressed:
For diff'rent styles with diff'rent subjects sort,
As several garbs with country, town, and court.
Some by old words to fame have made pretense,
Ancients in praise, mere moderns in their sense;
Such labored nothings, in so strange a style,
Amaze th' unlearned, and make the learned smile.
Unlucky, as Fungoso[35] in the play,
These sparks with awkward vanity display
What the fine gentleman wore yesterday;   330
And but so mimic ancient wits at best,
As apes our grandsires, in their doublets dressed.
In words, as fashions, the same rule will hold;
Alike fantastic, if too new, or old:
Be not the first by whom the new are tried,
Nor yet the last to lay the old aside.

---

[25] The notion of authorial intention is problematized in twentieth-century criticism. See especially Wimsatt and Beardsley (below, page 1027).
[26] A critic concerned with the finer points of language.
[27] Don Quixote.
[28] John Dennis (1657–1734), English critic.
[29] See, for example, Castelvetro (above, page 184).
[30] Fastidious.
[31] Sound.
[32] Punctilious.

---

[33] On faith.
[34] Attractive.
[35] A character in Ben Jonson's *Every Man Out of His Humour* (1599).

But most by numbers judge a poet's song,
And smooth or rough, with them, is right or wrong:
In the bright Muse, though thousand charms conspire,
Her voice is all these tuneful fools admire;   340
Who haunt Parnassus but to please their ear,
Not mend their minds; as some to church repair
Not for the doctrine, but the music there.
These equal syllables alone require,
Though oft' the ear the open vowels tire;
While expletives their feeble aid do join,
And ten low[36] words oft' creep in one dull line:
While they ring round the same unvaried chimes,
With sure returns of still expected rhymes;
Where'er you find "the cooling western breeze,"   350
In the next line, it "whispers through the trees":
If crystal streams "with pleasing murmurs creep,"
The reader's threatened (not in vain) with "sleep":
Then, at the last and only couplet, fraught
With some unmeaning thing they call a thought,
A needless Alexandrine[37] ends the song,
That, like a wounded snake, drags its slow length along.
Leave such to tune their own dull rhymes, and know
What's roundly smooth, or languishingly slow;
And praise the easy vigor of a line   360
Where Denham's strength and Waller's sweetness join.[38]
True ease in writing comes from art, not chance,
As those move easiest who have learned to dance.
'Tis not enough no harshness gives offense;
The sound must seem an echo to the sense.
Soft is the strain when zephyr gently blows,
And the smooth stream in smoother numbers flows;
But when loud surges lash the sounding shore,
The hoarse, rough verse should like the torrent roar:
When Ajax strives some rock's vast weight to throw,
The line too labors, and the words move slow: 370
Not so when swift Camilla[39] scours the plain,
Flies o'er th' unbending corn, and skims along the main.
Hear how Timotheus'[40] varied lays surprise,
And bid alternate passions fall and rise,
While at each change, the son of Libyan Jove[41]
Now burns with glory, and then melts with love;
Now his fierce eyes with sparkling fury glow,

Now sighs steal out, and tears begin to flow:
Persians and Greeks like turns of nature[42] found,
And the world's victor stood subdued by sound!   380
The pow'r of music all our hearts allow,
And what Timotheus was, is Dryden now.
      Avoid extremes, and shun the fault of such
Who still are pleased too little or too much.
At ev'ry trifle scorn to take offense,
That always shews great pride, or little sense:
Those heads, as stomachs, are not sure the best
Which nauseate all, and nothing can digest.
Yet let not each gay turn thy rapture move;   390
For fools admire, but men of sense approve:
As things seem large which we through mists descry,
Dullness is ever apt to magnify.
      Some foreign writers, some our own despise;
The ancients only, or the moderns prize.[43]
Thus wit, like faith, by each man is applied
To one small sect, and all are damned beside.
Meanly they seek the blessing to confine,
And force that sun but on a part to shine,
Which not alone the southern wit sublimes,[44]   400
But ripens spirits in cold northern climes;
Which, from the first has shone on ages past,
Enlights the present, and shall warm the last;
Though each may feel increases and decays,
And see now clearer and now darker days;
Regard not then if wit be old or new,
But blame the false, and value still the true.
      Some ne'er advance a judgment of their own
But catch the spreading notion of the town;
They reason and conclude by precedent,   410
And own stale nonsense which they ne'er invent.
Some judge of authors' names, not works, and then
Nor praise nor blame the writings, but the men.
Of all this servile herd, the worst is he
That in proud dullness joins with quality;[45]
A constant critic at the great man's board,
To fetch and carry nonsense for my lord.
What woeful stuff this madrigal would be,
In some starved hackney sonneteer, or me!
But let a lord once own the happy lines,   420
How the wit brightens! How the style refines!

---

[36] Commonplace.
[37] A line of iambic hexameter.
[38] John Denham (1615–1669), Edmund Waller (1607–1687), English poets.
[39] An Amazon in the *Aeneid*.
[40] Alleged to be a court musician much admired by Alexander the Great.
[41] "The son of Libyan Jove" refers to Alexander the Great.

---

[42] Similar changes of feeling.
[43] Pope alludes to the arguments over who were superior, the ancients or the moderns, that occurred mainly in the seventeenth century. See, for example, Dryden (above, page 256).
[44] Elevates.
[45] People of high class or rank.

Before his sacred name flies ev'ry fault,
And each exalted stanza teems with thought!

    The vulgar thus through imitation err,
As oft the learned by being singular;
So much they scorn the crowd, that if the throng
By chance go right, they purposely go wrong:
So schismatics[46] the plain believers quit,
And are but damned for having too much wit.
Some praise at morning what they blame at night,
But always think the last opinion right.   430
A Muse by these is like a mistress used,
This hour she's idolized, the next abused;
While their weak heads, like towns unfortified,
'Twixt sense and nonsense daily change their side.
Ask them the cause; they're wiser still they say;
And still tomorrow's wiser than today.
We think our fathers fools, so wise we grow;
Our wiser sons, no doubt, will think us so.
Once school-divines[47] this zealous isle o'erspread;   440
Who knew most sentences, was deepest read:
Faith, gospel, all, seemed made to be disputed,
And none had sense enough to be confuted.
Scotists and Thomists,[48] now in peace remain,
Amidst their kindred cobwebs in Duck Lane.[49]
If faith itself has diff'rent dresses worn,
What wonder modes in wit should take their turn?
Oft' leaving what is natural and fit,
The current folly proves[50] the ready wit;
And authors think their reputation safe,   450
Which lives as long as fools are pleased to laugh.

    Some, valuing those of their own side or mind,
Still make themselves the measure of mankind:
Fondly[51] we think we honor merit then,
When we but praise ourselves in other men.
Parties in wit attend on those of state,
And public faction doubles private hate.
Pride, malice, folly, against Dryden rose,
In various shapes of parsons, critics, beaus;
But sense survived when merry jests were past;   460
For rising merit will buoy up at last.
Might he return, and bless once more our eyes,

New Blackmores and new Milbourns[52] must arise:
Nay, should great Homer lift his awful head,
Zoilus[53] again would start up from the dead.
Envy will merit, as its shade, pursue;
But like a shadow, proves the substance true:
For envied wit, like Sol eclipsed, makes known
Th' opposing body's grossness, not its own.
When first that sun too pow'rful beams displays,   470
It draws up vapors which obscure its rays;
But ev'n those clouds at last adorn its way,
Reflect new glories, and augment the day.

    Be thou the first true merit to befriend;
His praise is lost, who stays till all commend.
Short is the date, alas! of modern rhymes,
And 'tis but just to let them live betimes.
No longer now that golden age appears,
When patriarch wits survived a thousand years;
Now length of fame (our second life) is lost,   480
And bare threescore is all ev'n that can boast;
Our sons their fathers' failing language see,
And such as Chaucer is, shall Dryden be.
So when the faithful pencil has designed
Some bright idea of the master's mind,
Where a new world leaps out at his command,
And ready nature waits upon his hand;
When the ripe colors soften and unite,
And sweetly melt into just shade and light;
When mellowing years their full perfection give,   490
And each bold figure just begins to live,
The treach'rous colors the fair art betray,
And all the bright creation fades away!

    Unhappy wit, like most mistaken things,
Atones not for that envy which it brings;
In youth alone its empty praise we boast,
But soon the short-lived vanity is lost;
Like some fair flow'r the early spring supplies,
That gaily blooms, but ev'n in blooming dies.
What is this wit, which must our cares employ?   500
The owner's wife, that other men enjoy;
Then most our trouble still when most admired,
And still the more we give, the more required;
Whose fame with pains we guard, but lose with ease,
Sure some to vex, but never all to please;
'Tis what the vicious fear, the virtuous shun,
By fools 'tis hated, and by knaves undone!

---

[46] Members of a dissenting religious faction.
[47] Theologians.
[48] Followers of the theologians Duns Scotus (1265?–1308?) and St. Thomas Aquinas (1215?–1274).
[49] A London street where books were sold.
[50] Offers an opportunity to.
[51] Foolishly.

---

[52] Sir Richard Blackmore (1650–1729), English writer; Luke Milbourne (1649–1720), English clergyman.
[53] A severe critic of Homer (fourth century B.C.).

If wit so much from ign'rance undergo,
Ah, let not learning too commence its foe!
Of old, those met rewards who could excel,   510
And such were praised who but endeavored well:
Though triumphs were to gen'rals only due,
Crowns were reserved to grace the soldiers too.
Now, they who reach Parnassus' lofty crown,
Employ their pains to spurn some others down
And while self-love each jealous writer rules,
Contending wits become the sport of fools;
But still the worst with most regret commend,
For each ill author is as bad a friend.
To what base ends, and by what abject ways,   520
Are mortals urged through sacred[54] lust of praise!
Ah, ne'er so dire a thirst of glory boast,
Nor in the critic let the man be lost.
Good nature and good sense must ever join;
To err is human, to forgive, divine.

    But if in noble minds some dregs remain
Not yet purged off, of spleen and sour disdain,
Discharge that rage on more provoking crimes,
Nor fear a dearth in these flagitious times.
No pardon vile obscenity should find,   530
Though wit and art conspire to move your mind;
But dullness with obscenity must prove
As shameful sure as impotence in love.
In the fat age of pleasure, wealth, and ease,
Sprung the rank weed, and thrived with large increase:
When love was all an easy monarch's[55] care;
Seldom at council, never in a war,
Jilts[56] ruled the state, and statesmen farces writ;
Nay, wits had pensions, and young lords had wit;
The fair sat panting at a courtier's play,   540
And not a mask[57] went unimproved away;
The modest fan was lifted up no more,
And virgins smiled at what they blushed before.
The foll'wing license of a foreign reign[58]
Did all the dregs of bold Socinus[59] drain;
Then unbelieving priests reformed the nation,
And taught more pleasant methods of salvation;
Where heaven's free subjects might their rights dispute,
Lest God himself should seem too absolute:
Pulpits their sacred satire learned to spare,   550

And vice admired[60] to find a flatt'rer there!
Encouraged thus, wit's Titans braved the skies,
And the press groaned with licensed blasphemies.
These monsters, critics! with your darts engage,
Here point your thunder, and exhaust your rage!
Yet shun their fault, who, scandalously nice,
Will needs mistake an author into vice:
All seems infected that th' infected spy,
As all looks yellow to the jaundiced eye.

Part III

Learn then what morals critics ought to show,   560
For 'tis but half a judge's task, to know.
'Tis not enough, taste, judgment, learning, join;
In all you speak, let truth and candor shine,
That not alone what to your sense is due
All may allow, but seek your friendship too.

    Be silent always when you doubt your sense,
And speak, though sure, with seeming diffidence:
Some positive, persisting fops we know,
Who, if once wrong, will needs be always so;
But you with pleasure own your errors past,   570
And make each day a critique on the last.

    'Tis not enough your counsel still be true;
Blunt truths more mischief than nice falsehoods do;
Men must be taught as if you taught them not,
And things unknown proposed as things forgot.
Without good breeding truth is disapproved;
That only makes superior sense beloved.

    Be niggards of advice on no pretense,
For the worst avarice is that of sense.
With mean complaisance ne'er betray your trust,   580
Nor be so civil as to prove unjust.
Fear not the anger of the wise to raise;
Those best can bear reproof, who merit praise.

    'Twere well might critics still this freedom take,
But Appius[61] reddens at each word you speak,
And stares, tremendous, with a threat'ning eye,
Like some fierce tyrant in old tapestry.
Fear most to tax an honorable fool,
Whose right it is uncensured, to be dull:
Such, without wit, are poets when they please,   590
As without learning they can take degrees.[62]

---

[54] Accursed.
[55] Charles II of England (1630–1685).
[56] Mistresses.
[57] A woman wearing a mask, a fashion of the day.
[58] William III (1650–1702) came from the Netherlands.
[59] Faustus Socinus (1539–1604), heretical European theologian.

---

[60] Marveled.
[61] John Dennis, known for irritability as a critic, was author of the play *Appius and Virginia.*
[62] A reference to the privileges given nobles at the universities.

Leave dang'rous truths to unsuccessful satires,
And flattery to fulsome dedicators,
Whom, when they praise, the world believes no more,
Than when they promise to give scribbling o'er.
'Tis best sometimes your censure to restrain,
And charitably let the dull be vain;
Your silence there is better than your spite,
For who can rail so long as they can write?
Still humming on, their drowsy course they keep,   600
And lashed so long, like tops, are lashed asleep.
False steps but help them to renew the race,
As, after stumbling, jades will mend their pace.
What crowds of these, impenitently bold,
In sounds and jingling syllables grown old.
Still run on poets in a raging vein,
Ev'n to the dregs and squeezing of the brain,
Strain out the last dull droppings of their sense,
And rhyme with all the rage of impotence.
    Such shameless bards we have; and yet, 'tis true,
There are as mad, abandoned critics too.   611
The bookful blockhead, ignorantly read,
With loads of learned lumber in his head,
With his own tongue still edifies his ears,
And always list'ning to himself appears:
All books he reads, and all he reads assails,
From Dryden's *Fables* down to Durfey's *Tales*.[63]
With him most authors steal their works, or buy;
Garth did not write his own *Dispensary*.[64]
Name a new play, and he's the poet's friend,   620
Nay, showed his faults—but when would poets mend?
No place so sacred from such fops is barred,
Nor is Paul's church more safe than Paul's churchyard:[65]
Nay, fly to altars, there they'll talk you dead;
For fools rush in where angels fear to tread.
Distrustful sense with modest caution speaks,
It still looks home, and short excursions makes;
But rattling nonsense in full volleys breaks,
And never shocked, and never turned aside,
Bursts out, resistless, with a thund'ring tide.   630
    But where's the man, who counsel can bestow,
Still pleased to teach, and yet not proud to know?
Unbiased, or by favor, or by spite.
Not dully prepossessed, nor blindly right;
Though learned, well-bred and though well-bred, sincere;

Modestly bold, and humanly severe;
Who to a friend his faults can freely show,
And gladly praise the merit of a foe?
Blessed with a taste exact, yet unconfined;
A knowledge both of books and humankind;   640
Gen'rous converse; a soul exempt from pride;
And love to praise, with reason on his side?
    Such once were critics; such the happy few
Athens and Rome in better ages knew.
The mighty Stagyrite first left the shore,
Spread all his sails, and durst the deeps explore;
He steered securely, and discovered far,
Led by the light of the Maeonian star.[66]
Poets, a race long unconfined and free,
Still fond and proud of savage liberty,   650
Received his[67] laws, and stood convinced 'twas fit,
Who conquered nature, should preside o'er wit.
    Horace still charms with graceful negligence,
And without method talks us into sense;
Will, like a friend, familiarly convey
The truest notions in the easiest way.
He, who supreme in judgment, as in wit,
Might boldly censure, as he boldly writ,
Yet judged with coolness, though he sung with fire;
His precepts teach but what his works inspire.   660
Our critics take a contrary extreme,
They judge with fury, but they write with phlegm:
Nor suffers Horace more in wrong translations
By wits, than critics in as wrong quotations.
    See Dionysius[68] Homer's thoughts refine,
And call new beauties forth from ev'ry line!
    Fancy and art in gay Petronius[69] please,
The scholar's learning, with the courtier's ease.
    In grave Quintilian's[70] copious work, we find
The justest rules, and clearest method joined.   670
Thus useful arms in magazines we place,
All ranged in order, and disposed with grace;
But less to please the eye, than arm the hand,
Still fit for use, and ready at command.
    Thee, bold Longinus![71] All the Nine inspire,
And bless their critic with a poet's fire:
An ardent judge, who, zealous in his trust,

---

[63] Thomas D'Urfey (1653–1723), English songwriter and dramatist, published his *Tales* in 1704.
[64] Samuel Garth (1661–1719), poet and physician, published *The Dispensary* in 1699.
[65] Place of booksellers.

[66] Homer.
[67] Aristotle's.
[68] Dionysius of Halicarnassus (first century B.C.), Greek rhetorician, historian, and critic.
[69] Petronius (d. 66), Roman satirist.
[70] Marcus Fabius Quintilianus (c. 40–118), Roman rhetorician.
[71] Longinus. See Pseudo-Longinus (above, page 94).

With warmth gives sentence, yet is always just;
Whose own example strengthens all his laws;
And is himself that great sublime he draws.

    Thus long succeeding critics justly reigned,
License repressed, and useful laws ordained.
Learning and Rome alike in empire grew,
And arts still followed where her eagles flew;
From the same foes, at last, both felt their doom,
And the same age saw learning fall, and Rome.
With tyranny, then superstition joined,
As that the body, this enslaved the mind;
Much was believed, but little understood,
And to be dull was construed to be good;   690
A second deluge learning thus o'er-run,
And the monks finished what the Goths begun.

    At length Erasmus,[72] that great injured name,
(The glory of the priesthood, and the shame!)
Stemmed the wild torrent of a barb'rous age,
And drove those holy vandals off the stage.

    But see! Each Muse, in Leo's[73] golden days;
Starts from her trance, and trims her withered bays;
Rome's ancient genius, o'er its ruins spread,
Shakes off the dust, and rears his rev'rend head.   700
Then sculpture and her sister arts revive;
Stones leaped to form, and rocks began to live;
With sweeter notes each rising temple rung;
A Raphael painted, and a Vida[74] sung.
Immortal Vida: on whose honored brow
The poet's bays and critic's ivy grow:
Cremona now shall ever boast thy name,
As next in place to Mantua, next in fame!

    But soon by impious arms from Latium[75] chased,
Their ancient bounds the banished Muses passed: 710
Thence arts o'er all the northern world advance,
But critic learning flourished most in France;

The rules a nation, born to serve, obeys;
And Boileau[76] still in right of Horace sways.
But we, brave Britons, foreign laws, despised,   680
And kept unconquered, and uncivilized;
Fierce for the liberties of wit, and bold,
We still defied the Romans, as of old.
Yet some there were, among the sounder few
Of those who less presumed, and better knew,   720
Who durst assert the juster ancient cause,
And here restored wit's fundamental laws.
Such was the Muse, whose rules and practice tell
"Nature's chief masterpiece is writing well."[77]
Such was Roscommon,[78] not more learned than good,
With manners gen'rous as his noble blood;
To him the wit of Greece and Rome was known,
And ev'ry author's merit, but his own.
Such late was Walsh[79]—the Muse's judge and friend,
Who justly knew to blame or to commend;   730
To failings mild, but zealous for desert;
The clearest head, and the sincerest heart.
Thus humble praise, lamented shade! Receive;
This praise at least a grateful Muse may give:
The Muse, whose early voice you taught to sing,
Prescribed her heights, and pruned[80] her tender wing,
(Her guide now lost) no more attempts to rise,
But in low numbers[81] short excursions tries;
Content, if hence th' unlearned their wants may view,
The learned reflect on what before they knew: 740
Careless of censure, nor too fond of fame;
Still pleased to praise, yet not afraid to blame;
Averse alike to flatter, or offend;
Not free from faults, nor yet too vain to mend.

---

[72] Desiderius Ersamus (1467–1536), Dutch humanist.
[73] Leo X (1475–1521), pope from 1513 to 1521.
[74] Raphael Santi (1483–1520), Italian painter; Mareo Girolamo Vida (c. 1490–1566), Italian Latin poet, who wrote an "Art of Poetry."
[75] Italy.

[76] Nicolas Boileau-Despréaux (1636–1711), French critic and poet.
[77] John Sheffield, Duke of Buckinghamn (1648–1721) wrote in verse *An Essay Upon Poetry* (1682).
[78] Wentworth Dillon, fourth Earl of Roscommon (1633?–1685), English poet.
[79] William Walsh (1663–1708), English poet, recently deceased friend of Pope's.
[80] Preened.
[81] Verses.

Joseph Addison

1672–1719

In his essays on the pleasures of the imagination, Addison is concerned with the effect of the work on the reader and thus deals with questions that in the eighteenth century came to be classified under the term "aesthetics." The matter he treats is considered later in the century by Burke (below, page 332), Hume (below, page 322), Kant (below, page 416), and others. Addison goes beyond those many predecessors who argue that literature properly delights and teaches to discuss what he calls the "primary" and "secondary" pleasures of the imagination. Although he uses terms employed earlier by Locke (above, page 281) and later, but differently, by Coleridge, his meanings for them, though derived from Locke, are his own. The primary pleasures are those resulting from our immediate experience or "ideas" of objects; the secondary pleasures arise from our experience of ideas of such objects when the objects are not actually present to perception but are represented to us. Pleasures of the imagination are not as "refined" as those of the understanding, since the imagination does not inquire into causes, but they are more obvious and easier to acquire.

Addison does not proceed in his thinking quite to an idea of an "aesthetic emotion" or "aesthetic distance," as do Kant and later theorists; but he does point out that it is possible for something disagreeable in life to be presented agreeably in description. His explanation of this agreeability is not, however, very convincing: he thinks that we are pleased in the face of a disagreeable, terrifying, or pitiful representation because we are not directly affected by it and thus need not fear it. We are happy with our good fortune.

Like a number of critics going back to Aristotle, Addison believes that art improves on nature and direct experience. Adopting Locke's concept of the association of ideas, he argues that the imagination compares ideas previously derived from direct experience with ideas derived from art. Those from nature often suffer by comparison. He admits that he cannot really explain why we should obtain so much pleasure from these comparisons or from the act of comparison implicit in mimicry. He concludes with a passage reminiscent of Sidney's remark (above, page 188) that the poet goes beyond nature to deliver a "golden" world, but Addison is talking only about the pleasure this affords, not some greater neoplatonic reality. Addison cannot answer many of the questions he addresses, and they raise important concerns for theorists for at least one hundred years after his discussion of them.

The definitive edition of *The Spectator* is that of D. F. Bond (in five volumes, 1965). G. A. Aitken edited both *The Spectator* (in eight volumes, 1898) and *The Tatler* (in four volumes, 1898–1899). See C. D. Thorpe, "Addison and Hutchinson on the Imagination," *English Literary History* II (1935), 215–34; Martin Kallich, "The Association of Ideas: Hobbes, Locke, and Addison," *English Literary History* XII (1945), 290–315; C. D. Thorpe, "Addison's Contribution to Criticism," *The Seventeenth Century: Studies by R. F. Jones and Others* (1951), 316–29; L. A. Eliasoff, *The Cultural Milieu of Addison's*

Literary Criticism (1963); David A. Hansen, "Addison on Ornament and Poetic Style," *Studies in Criticism and Aesthetics, 1660–1800,* Howard Anderson and John S. Shea, eds. (1967); E. and D. Bloom, eds., *Addison and Steele: The Critical Heritage* (1980); Robert M. Otten, *Joseph Addison* (1982); Robert L. Montgomery, *Terms of Response* (1992); Charles A. Knight, *Joseph Addison and Richard Steele: A Reference Guide, 1730–1991* (1994); Shaun Irlam, *Elations: The Poetics of Enthusiasm in Eighteenth-Century Britain* (1999).

On the Pleasures of the Imagination

The Spectator

Number 411

June 21, 1712

Avia Pieridum peragro loca, nullius ante
Trita solo; juvat integros accedere fonteis;
Atque haurire:[1]

LUCRETIUS

Our sight is the most perfect and most delightful of all our senses. It fills the mind with the largest variety of ideas, converses with its objects at the greatest distance, and continues the longest in action without being tired or satiated with its proper enjoyments. The sense of feeling can indeed give us a notion of extension, shape, and all other ideas that enter at the eye, except colors; but at the same time it is very much straitened and confined in its operations, to the number, bulk, and distance of its particular objects. Our sight seems designed to supply all these defects, and may be considered as a more delicate and diffusive kind of touch, that spreads itself over an infinite multitude of bodies, comprehends the largest figures, and brings into our reach some of the most remote parts of the universe.

It is this sense which furnishes the imagination with its ideas; so that by the pleasures of the imagination or fancy (which I shall use promiscuously) I here mean such as arise from visible objects, either when we have them actually in our view, or when we call up their ideas into our minds by paintings, statues, descriptions, or any the like occasion. We cannot indeed have a single image in the fancy that did not make its first entrance through the sight; but we have the power of retaining, altering and compounding those images, which we have once received, into all the varieties of picture and vision that are most agreeable to the imagination; for by this faculty a man in a dungeon is capable of entertaining himself with scenes and landskips more beautiful than any that can be found in the whole compass of nature.

There are few words in the English language which are employed in a more loose and uncircumscribed sense than those of the *fancy* and the *imagination.*[2] I therefore thought it necessary to fix and determine the notion of these two words, as I intend to make use of them in the thread of my following speculations, that the reader may conceive rightly what is the subject which I proceed upon. I must therefore desire to remember, that by the pleasures of the imagination, I mean only such pleasures as arise originally from sight, and that I divide these pleasures into two kinds: my design being first of all to discourse of those primary pleasures of the imagination, which entirely proceed from such objects as are before our eyes; and in the next place to speak of those secondary pleasures of the imagination which flow from the ideas of visible objects, when the objects are not actually before the eye, but are called up into our memories, or formed into agreeable visions of things that are either absent or fictitious.[3]

The pleasures of the imagination, taken in their full extent, are not so gross as those of sense, nor so refined as those of the understanding. The last are, indeed, more preferable, because they are founded on some new knowledge or im-

---

These three essays on the pleasures of the imagination appeared in three issues of *The Spectator* in 1712.
[1] "I travel through the untrodden pages of the Muses, where no one has gone before; it is a delight to approach fresh springs, and to drink." Titus Lucretius Carus (94–55 B.C.), *On the Nature of Things* I, 926–8.

[2] Like most thinkers of the time, Addison does not distinguish imagination from fancy as Coleridge later does (below, page 504).
[3] Addison's use of "primary" and "secondary" loosely recalls Locke's use of the terms to mean objective and subjective qualities of experience (above, page 281), but Addison has adapted them to his own use, as did Coleridge later in a different way based on different epistemological assumptions (below, page 501).

provement in the mind of man; yet it must be confessed, that those of the imagination are as great and as transporting as the other. A beautiful prospect delights the soul, as much as a demonstration; and a description in Homer has charmed more readers than a chapter in Aristotle. Besides the pleasures of the imagination have this advantage, above those of the understanding, that they are more obvious, and more easy to be acquired. It is but opening the eye, and the scene enters. The colors paint themselves on the fancy, with very little attention of thought or application of mind in the beholder. We are struck, we know not how, with the symmetry of anything we see, and immediately assent to the beauty of an object, without inquiring into the particular causes and occasions of it.

A man of a polite imagination is let into a great many pleasures, that the vulgar are not capable of receiving. He can converse with a picture, and find an agreeable companion in a statue. He meets with a secret refreshment in a description, and often feels a greater satisfaction in the prospect of fields and meadows, than another does in the possession. It gives him, indeed, a kind of property in everything he sees, and makes the most rude uncultivated parts of nature administer to his pleasures: so that he looks upon the world, as it were, in another light, and discovers in it a multitude of charms, that conceal themselves from the generality of mankind.

There are, indeed, but very few who know how to be idle and innocent, or have a relish of any pleasures that are not criminal; every diversion they take is at the expense of some one virtue or another, and their very first step out of business is into vice or folly. A man should endeavor, therefore, to make the sphere of his innocent pleasures as wide as possible, that he may retire into them with safety, and find in them such a satisfaction as a wise man would not blush to take. Of this nature are those of the imagination, which do not require such a bent of thought as is necessary to our more serious employments, nor at the same time, suffer the mind to sink into that negligence and remissness, which are apt to accompany our more sensual delights, but, like a gentle exercise to the faculties, awaken them from sloth and idleness, without putting them upon any labor or difficulty.

We might here add, that the pleasures of the fancy are more conducive to health, than those of the understanding, which are worked out by dint of thinking, and attended with too violent a labor of the brain. Delightful scenes, whether in nature, painting, or poetry, have a kindly influence on the body, as well as the mind, and not only serve to clear and brighten the imagination, but are able to disperse grief and melancholy, and to set the animal spirits in pleasing and agreeable motions. For this reason Sir Francis Bacon,[4] in his

essay upon health, has not thought it improper to prescribe to his reader a poem or a prospect, where he particularly dissuades him from knotty and subtle disquisitions, and advises him to pursue studies that fill the mind with splendid and illustrious objects, as histories, fables, and contemplations of nature.

I have in this paper, by way of introduction, settled the notion of those pleasures of the imagination which are the subject of my present undertaking, and endeavored, by several considerations, to recommend to my reader the pursuit of those pleasures. I shall, in my next paper, examine the several sources from whence these pleasures are derived.

The Spectator

Number 416

June 27, 1712

Quatenus hoc simile est oculis, quod mente videmus.[5]

LUCRETIUS

I at first divided the pleasures of the imagination, into such as arise from objects that are actually before our eyes, or that once entered in at our eyes, and are afterwards called up into the mind, either barely by its own operations, or on occasion of something without us, as statues or descriptions. We have already considered the first division, and shall therefore enter on the other, which, for distinction sake, I have called the secondary pleasures of the imagination. When I say the ideas we receive from statues, descriptions, or such like occasions, are the same that were once actually in our view, it must not be understood that we had once seen the very place, action, or person which are carved or described. It is sufficient, that we have seen places, persons, or actions in general, which bear a resemblance, or at least some remote analogy with what we find represented. Since it is in the power of the imagination, when it is once stocked with particular ideas, to enlarge, compound, and vary them at her own pleasure.[6]

Among the different kinds of representation, statuary is the most natural, and shews us something *likest* the object that is represented. To make use of a common instance, let one who is born blind take an image in his hands, and trace out with his fingers the different furrows and impressions of

---

[4] Bacon (above, page 234).

[5] "How similar is what we see with our minds to what we see with our eyes." Slightly misquoted from Lucretius, *On the Nature of Things* IV, 750–51.
[6] Here Addison has expressed Locke's notion that we combine the simple ideas of experience to make complex ones.

the chisel, and he will easily conceive how the shape of a man, or beast, may be represented by it; but should he draw his hand over a picture, where all is smooth and uniform, he would never be able to imagine how the several prominencies and depressions of a human body could be shewn on a plain piece of canvas, that has in it no unevenness or irregularity. Description runs yet further from the things it represents than painting; for a picture bears a real resemblance to its original, which letters and syllables are wholly void of Colors speak all languages, but words are understood only by such a people or nation. For this reason, though men's necessities quickly put them on finding out speech, writing is probably of a later invention than painting; particularly we are told, that in America when the Spaniards first arrived there, expresses were sent to the Emperor of Mexico in paint, and the news of his country delineated by the strokes of a pencil, which was a more natural way than that of writing, though at the same time much more imperfect, because it is impossible to draw the little connections of speech, or to give the picture of a conjunction or an adverb. It would be yet more strange to represent visible objects by sounds that have no ideas annexed to them, and to make something like description in music. Yet it is certain, there may be confused, imperfect notions of this nature raised in the imagination by an artificial composition of notes; and we find that great masters in the art are able, sometimes to set their hearers in the heat and hurry of a battle, to overcast their minds with melancholy scenes and apprehensions of deaths and funerals, or to lull them into pleasing dreams of groves and Elysiums.

In all these instances, this secondary pleasure of the imagination proceeds from that action of the mind, which compares the ideas arising from the original objects, with the ideas we receive from the statue, picture, description, or sound that represents them. It is impossible for us to give the necessary reason, why this operation of the mind is attended with so much pleasure, as I have before observed on the same occasion; but we find a great variety of entertainments derived from this single principle: for it is this that not only gives us a relish of statuary, painting and description, but makes us delight in all the actions and arts of mimicry. It is this that makes the several kinds of wit pleasant, which consists, as I have formerly shewn, in the affinity of ideas: And we may add, it is this also that raises the little satisfaction we sometimes find in the different sorts of false wit; whether it consist in the affinity of letters, as an anagram, acrostic; or of syllables, as in doggerel rhymes, echoes; or of words, as in puns, quibbles; or of a whole sentence or poem, to wings, and altars. The final cause, probably, of annexing pleasure to this operation of the mind, was to quicken and encourage us in our searches after truth, since the distinguishing one thing from another, and the right discerning betwixt our ideas, depends wholly upon our comparing them together, and observing the congruity or disagreement that appears among the several works of nature.

But I shall here confine myself to those pleasures of the imagination, which proceed from ideas raised by *words,* because most of the observations that agree with descriptions are equally applicable to painting and statuary.

Words, when well chosen, have so great a force in them, that a description often gives us more lively ideas than the sight of things themselves. The reader finds a scene drawn in stronger colors, and painted more to the life in his imagination, by the help of words, than by an actual survey of the scene which they describe. In this case the poet seems to get the better of nature; he takes, indeed, the landskip after her, but gives it more vigorous touches, heightens its beauty, and so enlivens the whole piece, that the images which flow from the objects themselves appear weak and faint, in comparison of those that come from the expressions.[7] The reason, probably, may be, because in the survey of any object, we have only so much of it painted on the imagination, as comes in at the eye; but in its description, the poet gives us as free a view of it as he pleases, and discovers to us several parts, that either we did not attend to, or that lay out of our sight when we first beheld it. As we look on any object, our idea of it is, perhaps, made up of two or three simple ideas; but when the poet represents it, he may either give us a more complex idea of it, or only raise in us such ideas as are most apt to affect the imagination.[8]

It may be here worth our while to examine, how it comes to pass that several readers, who are all acquainted with the same language, and know the meaning of the words they read, should nevertheless have a different relish of the same descriptions. We find one transported with a passage, which another runs over with coldness and indifference, or finding the representation extremely natural, where another can perceive nothing of likeness and conformity. This different taste must proceed either from the perfection of imagination in one more than in another, or from the different ideas that several readers affix to the same words. For, to have a true relish, and form a right judgment of a description, a man should be born with a good imagination, and must have well weighed the force and energy that lie in the several words of a language, so as to be able to distinguish

---

[7] The idea of the poet's improvement on nature can be traced from Aristotle (above, page 48), through Plotinus (above, page 133), to Sidney (above, page 188), and thence to Wilde (below, page 712).

[8] Addison treats ideas as does Locke (above, page 281).

which are most significant and expressive of their proper ideas, and what additional strength and beauty they are capable of receiving from conjunction with others. The fancy must be warm, to retain the print of those images it hath received from outward objects; and the judgment discerning, to know what expressions are most proper to clothe and adorn them to the best advantage. A man who is deficient in either of these respects, though he may receive the general notion of a description, can never see distinctly all its particular beauties: as a person with a weak sight may have the confused prospect of a place that lies before him, without entering into its several parts, or discerning the variety of its colors in their full glory and perfection.

The Spectator

Number 418

June 30, 1712

. . . Ferat et rubus asper amomum.[9]

VIRGIL

The pleasures of these secondary views of the imagination, are of a wider and more universal nature than those it has when joined with sight; for not only what is great, strange or beautiful, but anything that is disagreeable when looked upon, pleases us in an apt description. Here, therefore, we must inquire after a new principle of pleasure, which is nothing else but the action of the mind, which *compares* the ideas that arise from words, with the ideas that arise from the objects themselves; and why this operation of the mind is attended with so much pleasure, we have before considered. For this reason therefore, the description of a dunghill is pleasing to the imagination, if the image be represented to our minds by suitable expressions; though, perhaps, this may be more properly called the pleasure of the understanding than of the fancy, because we are not so much delighted with the image that is contained in the description, as with the aptness of the description to excite the image.

But if the description of what is little, common or deformed, be acceptable to the imagination, the description of what is great, surprising or beautiful, is much more so; because here we are not only delighted with *comparing* the representation with the original, but are highly pleased with the original itself. Most readers, I believe, are more charmed

with Milton's description of paradise, than of hell; they are both, perhaps, equally perfect in their kind, but in the one the brimstone and sulphur are not so refreshing to the imagination, as the beds of flowers and the wilderness of sweets in the other.

There is yet another circumstance which recommends a description more than all the rest, and that is, if it represents to us such objects as are apt to raise a secret ferment in the mind of the reader, and to work, with violence, upon his passions. For, in this case, we are at once warmed and enlightened, so that the pleasure becomes more universal, and is several ways qualified to entertain us. Thus, in painting, it is pleasant to look on the picture of any face, where the resemblance is hit, but the pleasure increases, if it be the picture of a face that is beautiful, and is still greater if the beauty be softened with an air of melancholy or sorrow. The two leading passions which the more serious parts of poetry endeavor to stir up in us, are terror and pity. And here, by the way, one would wonder how it comes to pass, that such passions as are very unpleasant at all other times, are very agreeable when excited by proper descriptions. It is not strange, that we should take delight in such passages as are apt to produce hope, joy, admiration, love, or the like emotions in us, because they never rise in the mind without an inward pleasure which attends them. But how comes it to pass, that we should take delight in being terrified or dejected by a description, when we find so much uneasiness in the fear or grief which we receive from any other occasion?

If we consider, therefore, the nature of this pleasure, we shall find that it does not arise so properly from the description of what is terrible, as from the reflection we make on ourselves at the time of reading it. When we look on such hideous objects, we are not a little pleased to think we are in no danger of them. We consider them at the same time, as dreadful and harmless; so that the more frightful appearance they make, the greater is the pleasure we receive from the sense of our own safety. In short, we look upon the terrors of a description with the same curiosity and satisfaction that we survey a dead monster.

Informe cadaver
Protrahitur, nequeunt expleri corda tuendo
Terribiles oculos: vultum, villosaque setis
Pectora semiferi, atque extinctos faucibus ignes.[10]

VIRGIL

---

[9] "Rough bramble bears balsam." *Eclogues* VI, 3–4.

[10] "The hideous cadaver is dragged along; their hearts cannot be satisfied gazing on the terrible eyes, the countenance, and the shaggy hair of the chest of the half-wild creature and the extinct fire from his throat." *Aeneid* VIII, 264.

It is for the same reason that we are delighted with the reflecting upon dangers that are past, or in looking on a precipice at a distance, which would fill us with a different kind of horror, if we saw it hanging over our heads.

In the like manner, when we read of torments, wounds, deaths, and the like dismal accidents, our pleasure does not flow so properly from the grief which such melancholy descriptions give us, as from the secret comparison which we make between ourselves and the person who suffers. Such representations teach us to set a just value upon our own condition, and make us prize our good fortune, which exempts us from the like calamities.[11] This is, however, such a kind of pleasure as we are not capable of receiving, when we see a person actually lying under the tortures that we meet with in a description; because, in this case, the object presses too close upon our senses, and bears so hard upon us, that it does not give us time or leisure to reflect on ourselves. Our thoughts are so intent upon the miseries of the sufferer, that we cannot turn them upon our own happiness. Whereas, on the contrary, we consider the misfortunes we read in history or poetry, either as past, or as fictitious, so that the reflection upon ourselves rises in us insensibly, and overbears the sorrow we conceive for the sufferings of the afflicted.

But because the mind of man requires something more perfect in matter, than what it finds there, and can never meet with any sight in nature which sufficiently answers its highest ideas of pleasantness; or, in other words, because the imagination can fancy to itself things more great, strange, or beautiful, than the eye ever saw, and is still sensible of some defect in what it has seen; on this account it is the part of a poet to humor the imagination in its own notions, by mending and perfecting nature where he describes a reality, and by adding greater beauties than are put together in nature, where he describes a fiction.[12]

He is not obliged to attend her in the slow advances which she makes from one season to another, or to observe her conduct in the successive production of plants and flowers. He may draw into his description all the beauties of the spring and autumn, and make the whole year contribute something to render it the more agreeable. His rose trees, woodbines and jessamines may flower together, and his beds be covered at the same time with lilies, violets, and amaranths. His soil is not restrained to any particular set of plants, but is proper either for oaks or myrtles, and adapts itself to the products of every climate. Oranges may grow wild in it; myrrh may be met with in every hedge, and if he thinks it proper to have a grove of spices, he can quickly command sun enough to raise it. If all this will not furnish out an agreeable scene, he can make several new species of flowers, with richer scents and higher colors than any that grow in the gardens of nature. His consorts of birds may be as full and harmonious, and his woods as thick and gloomy as he pleases. He is at no more expense in the long vista, than a short one, and can as easily throw his cascades from a precipice of half a mile high, as from one of twenty yards. He has his choice of the winds, and can turn the course of his rivers in all the variety of meanders, that are most delightful to the reader's imagination. In a word, he has the modeling of nature in his own hands, and may give her what charms he pleases, provided he does not reform her too much, and run into absurdities, by endeavoring to excel.

---

[11] This is a not unusual explanation in the time and may be contrasted with Aristotle's notion of catharsis (above, page 55) and later ones of the sublime, especially Kant's (below, page 419).

[12] For Addison, the poet's improvement on nature is to provide pleasure and is apparently not involved in an Aristotelian completion of nature or a Platonic movement to a higher reality.

Giambattista Vico

1668–1774

Vico argued in his *New Science* that the first science should be that of mythology, that is, research into the real source and meaning of myths. He offered the view that after the flood of Noah human beings divided into two groups, the Hebrews and the Gentiles. The latter, whom he calls the Gentes, spread out over the world and, having lost the original language given directly to Adam, had to invent their own languages. They were savage "giants" living lone bestial lives in the great forests of the earth. Their first words and their first myth (language and myth were simultaneously created) related to a sky-god invented out of fear. Their languages, composed at first of mute signs, reflected a common "mental language" and experience and were naturally metaphorical. These giants, incapable of rational abstraction, employed what Vico calls a "poetic metaphysics" and a "poetic logic," giving "the things they wondered at substantial being after their own ideas."

Vico finds the origins of the poetic in the primitive imagination, offering a concept of "sympathetic nature" that anticipates later Romantic thought, the work of some modern anthropologists, and a number of critics in the mid-twentieth century who employed the terms "myth" and "ritual." He exerted a considerable influence on the anthropological philosophy of Ernst Cassirer (below, page 1016) and on Northrop Frye (below, page 1136).

Vico gives a new twist to Aristotle's conception of the "credible impossibility" (above, page 66) in poetry, seeing it as the result of primitive wonder and imaginative power. He values highly Homer and the most ancient poets as creators of culture. The philosophers built up systems of abstract thought from the poets' imaginative creations. (In connection with this, see Blake, below, page 448.) Thus Vico is one of the earliest theorists to base his notion of the importance of art on the principle that abstract thought emerges from iconic expression or mythical thinking. As a consequence, Vico reverses the usual rationalistic treatment of poetic tropes as deviations from the norms of language. Tropes are the first and "necessary modes of expression." His view may be contrasted to that of Locke (above, page 296) and is a precursor of Herbert Read's *Icon and Idea* (1955), in which the iconic sign is seen as a predecessor of the abstract idea.

As an interpreter of ancient myths, Vico differs from Platonists like Porphyry, Henry Reynolds (author of *Mythomystes* [c.1632]), and Thomas Taylor, Porphyry's early-nineteenth-century translator. These writers viewed myths as allegories of prior mystical or philosophical concepts. Myths were, for Vico, "true narrations" in the languages of tropes, not translatable into abstract concepts.

The New Science of Giambattista Vico, translated by T. G. Bergin and M. H. Fisch (1968) is a revised translation of the third edition. Bergin and Fisch have also translated *The Autobiography of Giambattista Viso* (1944). See Benedetto Croce, *The Philosophy of Giambattista Vico* (1913); H. P. Adams, *The Life and Writings of Giambattista Vico*

(1935); A. A. Grimaldi, *The Universal Humanity of Giambattista Vico* (1958); G. Tagliocazzo and H. White, eds., *Giambattista Vico: An International Symposium* (1969); Leon Pompa, *Vico: A Study of the New Science* (1975); Isaiah Berlin, *Vico and Herder* (1976); Donald Philip Verene, *Vico's Science of Imagination* (1981); Mark Lilla, *G. B. Vico: The Making of an Anti-Modern* (1983); Gino Bedani, *Vico Revisited* (1989); Guiseppe Mazzotta, *The New Map of the World: The Poetic Philosophy of Giambattista Vico* (1999). See also the journal *New Vico Studies,* founded in 1981.

from

The New Science

Premising such reflections on the vain opinion of their own antiquity held by these gentile nations and above all by the Egyptians,[1] we should begin our study of gentile learning [*tutto lo scibile gentilesco*] by scientifically ascertaining this important starting point—where and when that learning had its first beginnings in the world—and by adducing human reasons thereby in support of Christian faith [*tutto il credibile cristiano*], which takes its start from the fact that the first people of the world were the Hebrews, whose prince was Adam, created by the true God at the time of the creation of the world. It follows that the first science to be learned should be mythology or the interpretation of fables; for, as we shall see, all the histories of the gentiles have their beginnings in fables, which were the first histories of the gentile nations.[2] By such a method the beginnings of the sciences as well as of the nations are to be discovered, for they sprang from the nations and from no other source. It will be shown throughout this work that they had their beginnings in the public needs or utilities of the peoples and that they were later perfected as acute individuals applied their reflection to them. This is the proper starting point for universal history, which all scholars say is defective in its beginnings.

* * *

We have said above in the Axioms[3] that all the histories of the gentile nations have had fabulous beginnings, that

among the Greeks (who have given us all we know of gentile antiquity) the first sages were the theological poets,[4] and that the nature of everything born or made betrays the crudeness of its origin. It is thus and not otherwise that we must conceive the origins of poetic wisdom. And as for the great and sovereign esteem in which it has been handed down to us, this has its origin in the two conceits, that of nations and that of scholars, and it springs even more from the latter than from the former. For just as Manetho, the Egyptian high priest, translated all the fabulous history of Egypt into a sublime natural theology, so the Greek philosophers translated theirs into philosophy.[5] And they did so not merely for the reason that the histories as they had come down to both alike were most unseemingly, but for the following five reasons as well.

The first was reverence for religion, for the gentile nations were everywhere founded by fables on religion. The second was the grand effect thence derived, namely this civil world, so wisely ordered that it could only be the effect of a superhuman wisdom. The third was the occasions which, as we shall see, these fables, assisted by the veneration of religion and the credit of such great wisdom, gave the philosophers for instituting research and for meditating lofty things in philosophy. The fourth was the ease with which they were thus enabled, as we shall also show farther on, to explain their sublime philosophical meditations by means of the expressions happily left them by the poets. The fifth and last, which is the sum of them all, is the confirmation of their own meditations which the philosophers derived from the authority of religion and the wisdom of the poets. Of these five reasons, the first two and the last contain the praises of the divine wisdom which ordained this world of nations, and the witness the philosophers bore to it even

---

Vico's *Principii d'una scienza nuovo* was first published in 1725. The text is from Thomas Goddard Bergin and Max Harold Fisch, trs., *The New Science of Giambattista Viso: Revised Translation of the Third Edition* (1744) (Ithaca: Cornell University Press, 1968).

[1] Vico argues that the Egyptians were not as ancient a people as supposed.

[2] Vico does not mean "nation" in the modern sense associated with place, but rather a people banded together through origin, language, or institutions.

[3] Vico begins his book with a series of axioms that he later develops.

---

[4] Among whom would be Homer and Hesiod, though there would have been earlier, primitive ones now lost. They were "theological" because gentile religion, myth, and poetry had a common beginning and originated in religious experience, the first myth being that of Jove.

[5] See Blake (below, page 448) for his version of this history.

in their errors. The third and fourth are deceptions permitted by divine providence, that thence there might arise philosophers to understand and recognize it for what it truly is, an attribute of the true God.

Throughout this book it will be shown that as much as the poets had first sensed in the way of vulgar wisdom, the philosophers later understood in the way of esoteric wisdom; so that the former may be said to have been the sense and the latter the intellect of the human race. What Aristotle said of the individual man is therefore true of the race in general: *"Nihil est in intellectu quin prius fuerit in sensu."*[6] That is, the human mind does not understand anything of which it has had no previous impression (which our modern metaphysicians call *occasion*) from the senses. Now the mind uses the intellect when, from something it senses, it gathers something which does not fall under the senses; and this is the proper meaning of the Latin verb *intelligere*.

Now, before discussing poetic wisdom, it is necessary for us to see what wisdom in general is. Wisdom is the faculty which commands all the disciplines by which we acquire all the sciences and arts that make up humanity. Plato defines wisdom as "the perfecter of man."[7] Man, in his proper being as man, consists of mind and spirit, or, if we prefer, of intellect and will. It is the function of wisdom to fulfill both these parts in man, the second by way of the first, to the end that by a mind illuminated by knowledge of the highest institutions, the spirit may be led to choose the best. The highest institutions in this universe are those turned toward and conversant with God; the best are those which look to the good of all mankind. The former are called divine institutions, the latter human. True wisdom, then, should teach the knowledge of divine institutions in order to conduct human institutions to the highest good. We believe that this was the plan upon which Marcus Terentius Varro,[8] who earned the title "most learned of the Romans," erected his great work, [*The Antiquities*] *Of Divine and Human Institutions,* of which the injustice of time has unhappily bereft us. We shall treat of these institutions in the present book so far as the weakness of our education and the meagerness of our erudition permit.

Wisdom among the gentiles began with the Muse, defined by Homer in a golden passage of the *Odyssey* as "knowledge of good and evil,"[9] and later called divination. It was on the natural prohibition of this practice, as something naturally denied to man, that God founded the true re-

ligion of the Hebrews, from which our Christian religion arose. The Muse must thus have been properly at first the science of divining by auspices,[10] and this was the vulgar wisdom of all nations, of which we shall have more to say presently. It consisted in contemplating God under the attribute of his providence, so that from *divinari*[11] his essence came to be called divinity. We shall see presently that the theological poets, who certainly founded the humanity of Greece, were versed in this wisdom, and this explains why the Latins called the judicial astrologers "professors of wisdom." Wisdom was later attributed to men renowned for useful counsels given to mankind, as in the case of the Seven Sages of Greece. The attribution was then extended to men who for the good of peoples and nations wisely ordered and governed commonwealths. Still later the word *wisdom* came to mean knowledge of natural divine things; that is, metaphysics, called for that reason divine science, which, seeking knowledge of man's mind in God, and recognizing God as the source of all truth, must recognize him as the regulator of all good. So that metaphysics must essentially work for the good of the human race, whose preservation depends on the universal belief in a provident divinity. It is perhaps for having demonstrated this providence that Plato deserved to be called divine; and that which denies to God this great attribute must be called stupidity rather than wisdom. Finally among the Hebrews, and thence among us Christians, wisdom was called the science of eternal things revealed by God; a science which, among the Tuscans, considered as knowledge of the true good and true evil, perhaps owed to that fact the first name they gave it, "science in divinity."

We must therefore distinguish more truly than Varro did the three kinds of theology. First, poetic theology, that of the theological poets, which was the civil theology of all the gentile nations. Second, natural theology, that of the metaphysicians. Third, our Christian theology, a mixture of civil and natural with the loftiest revealed theology; all three united in the contemplation of divine providence. (Our third kind takes the place of Varro's poetic theology, which among the gentiles was the same as civil theology, though he distinguished it from both civil and natural theology because, sharing the vulgar common error that the fables contained high mysteries of sublime philosophy, he believed it to be a mixture of the two.) Divine providence has so conducted human institutions that, starting from the poetic theology which regulated them by certain sensible signs

---

[6] *On the Soul*, 432. Vico uses the Latin translation.
[7] *Alcibiades* I, 124.
[8] Marcus Terentius Varro (116–28 B.C.), Roman scholar.
[9] XIII, 63.

[10] Omens.
[11] To divine, to prophesy.

believed to be divine counsels sent to man by the gods, and by means of the natural theology which demonstrates providence by eternal reasons which do not fall under the senses, the nations were disposed to receive revealed theology in virtue of a supernatural faith, superior not only to the senses but to human reason itself.

But because metaphysics is the sublime science which distributes their determinate subject matters to all the so-called subaltern sciences; and because the wisdom of the ancients was that of the theological poets, who without doubt were the first sages of the gentile world; and because the origins of all things must by nature have been crude: for all these reasons we must trace beginnings of poetic wisdom to a crude metaphysics. From this, as from a trunk, there branch out from one limb logic, morals, economics, and politics, all poetic; and from another, physics, the mother of cosmography and astronomy, the latter of which gives their certainty to its two daughters, chronology and geography—all likewise poetic. We shall show clearly and distinctly how the founders of gentile humanity by means of their natural theology (or metaphysics) imagined the gods; how by means of their logic they invented languages; by morals, created heroes; by economics, founded families, and by politics, cities; by their physics, established the beginnings of things as all divine; by the particular physics of man, in a certain sense created themselves; by their cosmography, fashioned for themselves a universe entirely of gods; by astronomy, carried the planets and constellations from earth to heaven; by chronology, gave a beginning to [measured] times; and how by geography the Greeks, for example, described the [whole] world within their own Greece.

Thus our science comes to be at once a history of the ideas, the customs, and the deeds of mankind. From these three we shall derive the principles of the history of human nature, which we shall show to be the principles of universal history, which principles it seems hitherto to have lacked.

* * *

From these first men, stupid, insensate, and horrible beasts, all the philosophers and philologians should have begun their investigations of the wisdom of the ancient gentiles; that is, from the giants in the proper sense in which we have just taken them. (Father Boulduc[12] in his *De ecclesia ante Legem* says the scriptural names of the giants signify "pious, venerable and illustrious men"; but this can be understood only of the noble giants who by divination founded the gentile religions and gave the giants its name.) And they should have begun with metaphysics, which seeks its proof not in the external world but within the modifications of the mind of him who meditates it. For since this world of nations has certainly been made by men, it is within these modifications that its principles should have been sought. And human nature, so far as it is like that of animals, carries with it this property, that the senses are its sole way of knowing things.

Hence poetic wisdom, the first wisdom of the gentile world, must have begun with a metaphysic not rational and abstract like that of learned men now, but felt and imagined as that of these first men must have been, who, without power of ratiocination, were all robust sense and vigorous imagination. This metaphysics was their poetry, a faculty born with them (for they were furnished by nature with these senses and imaginations); born of their ignorance of causes, for ignorance, the mother of wonder, made everything wonderful to men who were ignorant of everything. Their poetry was at first divine, because, as we saw in the passage from Lactantius,[13] they imagined the causes of the things they felt and wondered at to be gods. (This is now confirmed by the American Indians, who call gods all the things that surpass their small understanding. We may add the ancient Germans dwelling about the Arctic Ocean, of whom Tacitus[14] tells that they spoke of hearing the sun pass at night from west to east through the sea, and affirmed that they saw the gods. These very rude and simple nations help us to a much better understanding of the founders of the gentile world with whom we are now concerned.) At the same time they gave the things they wondered at substantial being after their own ideas, just as children do, whom we see take inanimate things in their hands and play with them and talk to them as though they were living persons.

In such fashion the first men of the gentile nations, children of nascent mankind, created things according to their own ideas. But this creation was infinitely different from that of God. For God, in his purest intelligence, knows things, and, by knowing them, creates them; but they, in their robust ignorance, did it by virtue of a wholly corporeal imagination. And because it was quite corporeal, they did it with marvelous sublimity; a sublimity such and so great that

---

[12] Jacques Boulduc (c. 1580–1650).

[13] [Vico] That is a golden passage in Lactantius Fermianus (*Divine Institutions* I, 15) where he considers the origins of idolatry, saying: "Rude men at first called them [the king and his family] gods either for their wonderful excellence (wonderful it seemed to men still rude and simple), or, as commonly happens, in admiration of present power, or on account of the benefits by which they had been brought to humanity.

[14] On Tacitus see above, page 90.

it excessively perturbed the very persons who by imagining did the creating, for which they were called *poets,* which is Greek for *creators.* Now this is the threefold labor of great poetry: (1) to invent sublime fables suited to the popular understanding, (2) to perturb to excess, with a view to the end proposed: (3) to teach the vulgar to act virtuously, as the poets have taught themselves; as will presently be shown.[15] Of this nature of human institutions it remained an eternal property, expressed in a noble phrase of Tacitus, that frightened men vainly "no sooner imagine than they believe" (*fingunt simul creduntque*).

Of such natures must have been the first founders of gentile humanity when at last the sky fearfully rolled with thunder and flashed with lightning, as could not but follow from the bursting upon the air for the first time of an impression so violent. As we have postulated, this occurred a hundred years after the flood in Mesopotamia and two hundred years after it throughout the rest of the world; for it took that much time to reduce the earth to such a state that, dry of the moisture of the universal flood, it could send up dry exhalations or matter igniting in the air to produce lightning. Thereupon a few giants, who must have been the most robust, and who were dispersed through the forest on the mountain heights where the strongest beasts have their dens, were frightened and astonished by the great effect whose cause they did not know, and raised their eyes and became aware of the sky. And because in such a case the nature of the human mind leads it to attribute its own nature to the effect, and because in that state their nature was that of men all robust bodily strength, who expressed their very violent passions by shouting and grumbling, they pictured the sky to themselves as a great animated body, which in that aspect they called Jove, the first god of the so-called greater gentes,[16] who meant to tell them something by the hiss of his bolts and the clap of his thunder. And thus they began to exercise that natural curiosity which is the daughter of ignorance and the mother of knowledge, and which, opening the mind of man, gives birth to wonder. This characteristic still persists in the vulgar, who, when they see a comet or sundog or some other extraordinary thing in nature, and particularly in the countenance of the sky, at once turn curious and anxiously inquire what it means. When they wonder at the prodigious effects of the magnet on iron, even in this age of minds enlightened and instructed by philosophy, they come out with this: that the magnet has an occult sympathy for the iron; and they make of all nature a vast animate body which feels passions and effects.

But the nature of our civilized minds is so detached from the senses, even in the vulgar, by abstractions corresponding to all the abstract terms our languages abound in, and so refined by the art of writing, and as it were spiritualized by the use of numbers, because even the vulgar know how to count and reckon, that it is naturally beyond our power to form the vast image of this mistress called Sympathetic Nature. Men shape the phrase with their lips but have nothing in their minds; for what they have in mind is falsehood, which is nothing; and their imagination no longer avails to form a vast false image. It is equally beyond our power to enter into the vast imagination of those first men, whose minds were not in the least abstract, refined, or spiritualized, because they were entirely immersed in the senses, buffeted by the passions, buried in the body. That is why we said above that we can scarcely understand, still less imagine, how those first men thought who founded gentile humanity.

In this fashion the first theological poets created the first divine fable, the greatest they ever created: that of Jove, king and father of men and gods, in the act of hurling the lightning bolt; an image so popular, disturbing, and instructive that its creators themselves believed in it, and feared, revered, and worshiped it in frightful religions. And by that trait of the human mind noticed by Tacitus whatever these men saw, imagined, or even made or did themselves they believed to be Jove; and to all of the universe that came within their scope, and to all its parts, they gave the being of animate substance. This is the civil history of the expression "All things are full of Jove" (*Iovis omnia plena*)[17] by which Plato later understood the ether which penetrates and fills everything.[18] But for the theological poets Jove was no higher than the mountain peaks. The first men, who spoke by signs, naturally believed that lightning bolts and thunderclaps were signs made to them by Jove; whence from *nuo,* "to make a sign," came *numen,* "the divine will," by an idea more than sublime and worthy to express the divine majesty. They believed that Jove commanded by signs, that such signs were real words, and that nature was the language of Jove. The science of this language the gentiles universally believed to be divination, which by the Greeks was called theology, meaning the science of the language of the gods. Thus Jove acquired the fearful kingdom of the lightning and became the king of men and gods; and he acquired the two titles, that of best (*optimus*) in the sense of strongest (*fortissimus*) (as by a reverse process *fortis* meant in early Latin what *bonus* did in late), and that of greatest (*maximus*) from

---

[15] Vico connects contemporary poetry with the ancient theological poets, though, as we shall see, there has been a profound change in consciousness.
[16] "Nations," in Vico's sense (footnote 2).

[17] Virgil, *Eclogues* III, 60.
[18] *Cratylus,* 412.

his vast body, the sky itself. From the first great benefit he conferred on mankind by not destroying it with his bolts, he received the title *Soter,* or savior. (This is the first of three principles we have taken for our science.) And for having put an end to the feral wandering of these few giants, so that they became the princes of the gentes, he received the epithet *Stator,* stayer or establisher. The Latin philologians explain this epithet too narrowly from Jove, invoked by Romulus, having stopped the Romans in their flight from the battle with the Sabines.

Thus the many Joves the philologians wonder at are so many physical histories preserved for us by the fables, which prove the universality of the flood. For every gentile nation had its Jove, and the Egyptians had the conceit to say that their Jove Ammon was the most ancient of them all.

Thus in accordance with what has been said about the principles of the poetic characters, Jove was born naturally in poetry as a divine character or imaginative universal, to which everything having to do with the auspices was referred by all the ancient gentile nations, which must therefore all have been poetic by nature. Their poetic wisdom began with this poetic metaphysics, which contemplated God by the attribute of his providence; and they were called theological poets, or sages who understood the language of the gods expressed in the auspices of Jove; and were properly called divine in the sense of diviners, from *divinari,* "to divine or predict." Their science was called Muse, defined by Homer as the knowledge of good and evil; that is, divination, on the prohibition of which God ordained his true religion for Adam. Because they were versed in this mystic theology, the Greek poets, who explained the divine mysteries of the auspices and oracles, were called *mystae,* which Horace learnedly renders "interpreters of the gods."[19] Every gentile nation had its own sibyl versed in this science, and we find mention of twelve of them. Sibyls and oracles are the most ancient institutions of the gentile world.

All the things here discussed agree with that golden passage of Eusebius [i.e., Lactantius] on the origins of idolatry: that the first people, simple and rough, invented the gods "from terror of present power." Thus it was fear which created gods in the world; not fear awakened in men by other men, but fear awakened in men by themselves. Along with this origin of idolatry is demonstrated likewise the origin of divination, which was brought into the world at the same birth. The origins of these two were followed by that of the sacrifices made to procure or rightly understand the auspices.

That such was the origin of poetry is finally confirmed by this eternal property of it: that its proper material is the credible impossibility.[20] It is impossible that bodies should be minds, yet it was believed that the thundering sky was Jove. And nothing is dearer to poets than singing the marvels wrought by sorceresses by means of incantations. All this is to be explained by a hidden sense the nations have of the omnipotence of God. From this sense springs another by which all peoples are naturally led to do infinite honors to divinity. In this manner the poets founded religions among the gentiles.

All that has been so far said here upsets all the theories of the origin of poetry from Plato and Aristotle down to Patrizzi,[21] Scaliger, and Castelvetro. For it has been shown that it was deficiency of human reasoning power that gave rise to poetry so sublime that the philosophies which came afterward, the arts of poetry and of criticism, have produced none equal or better and have even prevented its production. Hence it is Homer's privilege to be, of all the sublime, that is, the heroic poets, the first in the order of merit as well as in that of age. This discovery of the origins of poetry does away with the opinion of the matchless wisdom of the ancients, so ardently sought after from Plato to Bacon's *De sapientia veterum.*[22] For the wisdom of the ancients was the vulgar wisdom of the lawgivers who founded the human race, not the esoteric wisdom of great and rare philosophers. Whence it will be found, as it has been in the case of Jove, that all the mystic meanings of lofty philosophy attributed by the learned to the Greek fables and the Egyptian hieroglyphics are as impertinent as the historical meanings they both must have had are natural.

* * *

That which is metaphysics insofar as it contemplates things in all the forms of their being, is logic insofar as it considers things in all the forms by which they may be signified. Accordingly, as poetry has been considered by us above as a poetic metaphysics in which the theological poets imagined bodies to be for the most part divine substances, so now that same poetry is considered as poetic logic, by which it signifies them.

Logic comes from *logos,* whose first and proper meaning was *fabula,* "fable," carried over into Italian as *favella,*

---

[19] Above, page 80.

[20] The origin of the phrase is in Aristotle (above, page 66). See also Mazzoni (above, page 218).

[21] Francisco Patrizzi (or Patrizi (1529–1597), Italian philosopher, poet, and critic.

[22] See Bacon (above, page 236).

"speech." In Greek the fable was also called *mythos,* "myth," whence comes the Latin *mutus,* "mute." For speech was born in mute times as mental [or sign] language, which Strabo[23] in a golden passage says existed before vocal or articulate [language]; whence *logos* means both "word" and "idea." It was fitting that the matter should be so ordered by divine providence in religious times, for it is an eternal property of religions that they attach more importance to meditation than to speech. Thus the first language in the first mute times of the nations must have begun with signs, whether gestures or physical objects, which had natural relations to the ideas [to be expressed]. For this reason *logos,* or "word," meant also "deed" to the Hebrews and "thing" to the Greeks, as Thomas Gataker observes in his *De instrumenti stylo.*[24] Similarly, *mythos* came to be defined for us as *vera narratio,* or "true speech," the natural speech which first Plato and then Iamblichus said had been spoken in the world at one time. But this was mere conjecture on their part, and Plato's effort to recover this speech in the *Cratylus* was therefore vain, and he was criticized for it by Aristotle and Galen. For that first language, spoken by the theological poets, was not a language in accord with the nature of things it dealt with (as must have been the sacred language invented by Adam, to whom God granted divine onomathesia, the giving of names to things according to the nature of each), but was a fantastic speech making use of physical substances endowed with life and most of them imagined to be divine.

This is the way in which the theological poets apprehended Jove, Cybele or Berecynthia, and Neptune, for example, and, at first mutely pointing, explained them as substances of the sky, the earth, and the sea, which they imagined to be animate divinities and were therefore true to their senses in believing them to be gods. By means of these three divinities, in accordance with what we have said above concerning poetic characters, they explained everything appertaining to the sky, the earth, and the sea. And similarly by means of the other divinities they signified the other kinds of things appertaining to each, denoting all flowers, for instance, by Flora, and all fruits by Pomona. We nowadays reverse this practice in respect of spiritual things, such as the faculties of the human mind, the passions, virtues, vices, sciences, and arts; for the most part the ideas we form of them are so many feminine personifications, to which we refer all the causes, properties, and effects that severally appertain to them. For when we wish to give utterance to our understanding of spiritual things, we must seek aid from our imagination to explain them and, like painters, form human images of them. But these theological poets, unable to make use of the understanding, did the opposite and more sublime thing: they attributed senses and passions, as we saw not long since, to bodies, and to bodies as vast as sky, sea, and earth. Later, as these vast imaginations shrank and the power of abstraction grew, the personifications were reduced to diminutive signs. Metonymy drew a cloak of learning over the prevailing ignorance of these origins of human institutions, which have remained buried until now. Jove becomes so small and light that he is flown about by an eagle. Neptune rides the waves in a fragile chariot. And Cybele rides seated on a lion.[25]

Thus the mythologies, as their name indicates, must have been the proper languages of the fables; the fables being imaginative class concepts, as we have shown, the mythologies must have been the allegories corresponding to them. Allegory is defined as *diversiloquium* insofar as, by identity not of proportion but (to speak scholastically) of predicability, allegories signify the diverse species or the diverse individuals comprised under these genera. So that they must have a univocal signification connoting a quality common to all their species and individuals (as Achilles connotes an idea of valor common to all strong men, or Ulysses an idea of prudence common to all wise men); such that these allegories must be the etymologies of the poetic languages, which would make their origins all univocal, whereas those of the vulgar languages are more often analogical. We also have the definition of the word *etymology* itself as meaning *veriloquium,* just as fable was defined as *vera narratio.*

All the first tropes are corollaries of this poetic logic. The most luminous and therefore the most necessary and frequent is metaphor. It is most praised when it gives sense and passion to insensate things, in accordance with the metaphysics above discussed, by which the first poets attributed to bodies the being of animate substances, with capacities measured by their own, namely sense and passion, and in this way made fables of them. Thus every metaphor so formed is a fable in brief. This gives a basis for judging the time when metaphors made their appearance in the languages. All the metaphors conveyed by likenesses taken from bodies to signify the operations of abstract minds must date from times when philosophies were taking shape. The proof of this is that in every language the terms needed for the refined arts and recondite sciences are of rustic origin.

---

[23] Strabo (above, page 86).

[24] A dissertation on the style of the New Testament by Thomas Gataker (1574–1654), English clergyman and critic.

[25] This passage anticipates later Romantic distinctions between allegory and symbolism, though Vico does not use "allegory" in the later sense. See, for example, Coleridge (below, page 519).

It is noteworthy that in all languages the greater part of the expressions relating to inanimate things are formed by metaphor from the human body and from the human senses and passions. Thus, head for top or beginning; the brow and shoulders of a hill; the eyes of needles and of potatoes; mouth for any opening; the lip of a cup or pitcher; the teeth of a rake, a saw, a comb; the beard of wheat; the tongue of a shoe; the gorge of a river; a neck of land; an arm of the sea; the hands of a clock; heart for center (the Latins used *umbilicus,* navel, in this sense); the belly of a sail; foot for end or bottom; the flesh of fruits; a vein of rock or mineral; the blood of grapes for wine; the bowels of the earth.[26] Heaven or the sea smiles; the wind whistles; the waves murmur; a body groans under a great weight. The farmers of Latium[27] used to say fields were thirsty, bore fruit, were swollen with grain; and our rustics speak of plants making love, vines going mad, resinous trees weeping. Innumerable other examples could be collected from all languages. All of which is a consequence of our axiom that man in his ignorance makes himself the rule of the universe, for in the examples cited he has made of himself an entire world. So that, as rational metaphysics teaches that man becomes all things by understanding them (*homo intelligendo fit omnia*), this imaginative metaphysics shows that man becomes all things by *not* understanding them (*homo non intelligendo fit omnia*); and perhaps the latter proposition is truer than the former, for when man understands he extends his mind and takes in the things, but when he does not understand he makes the things out of himself and becomes them by transforming himself into them.

In such a logic, sprung from such a metaphysics, the first poets had to give names to things from the most particular and the most sensible ideas. Such ideas are the sources, respectively, of synecdoche and metonymy. Metonymy of agent for act resulted from the fact that names for agents were commoner than names for acts. Metonymy of subject for form and accident was due to inability to abstract forms and qualities from subjects. Certainly metonymy of cause for effect produced in each case a little fable, in which the cause was imagined as a woman clothed with her effects: ugly Poverty, sad Old Age, pale Death.

Synecdoche developed into metaphor as particulars were elevated into universals or parts united with the other parts together with which they make up their wholes. Thus the term *mortals* was originally and properly applied only to men, as the only beings whose mortality there was any occasion to notice. The use of *head* for man or person, so frequent in vulgar Latin, was due to the fact that in the forests only the head of a man could be seen from a distance. The word *man* itself is abstract, comprehending as in a philosophic genius the body and all its parts, the mind and all its faculties, the spirit and all its dispositions. In the same way, *tignum* and *culmen,* "log" and "top," came to be used with entire propriety when thatching was the practice for rafter and thatch; and later, with the adornment of cities, they signified all the materials and trim of a building. Again, *tectum,* "roof," came to mean a whole house because in the first times a covering sufficed for a house. Similarly, *puppis,* "poop," for a ship, because it was the highest part and therefore the first to be seen by those on shore; as in the returned barbarian times a ship was called a sail. Similarly, *mucro,* "point," for sword, because the latter is an abstract word and as in a genus comprehends pummel, hilt, edge, and point; and it was the point they felt which aroused their fear. Similarly, the material for the formed whole, as *iron* for sword, because they did not know how to abstract the form from the material. That bit of synecdoche and metonymy, *Tertia messis erat* ("It was the third harvest"), was doubtless born of a natural necessity, for it took more than a thousand years for the astronomical term *year* to rise among the nations; and even now the Florentine peasantry say, "We have reaped so many times," when they mean "so many years." And that knot of two synecdoches and a metonymy, *Post aliquot, mea regna videns, mirabor, aristas?* ("After a few harvests shall I wonder at seeing my kingdoms?"),[28] betrays only too well the poverty of expression of the first rustic times, in which the phrase "so many ears of wheat"—even more particular than harvests—was used for "so many years." And because of the excessive poverty of the expression, the grammarians have assumed an excess of art behind it.

Irony certainly could not have begun until the period of reflection, because it is fashioned of falsehood by dint of a reflection which wears the mask of truth.[29] Here emerges a great principle of human institutions, confirming the origin of poetry disclosed in this work: that since the first men of the gentile world had the simplicity of children, who are truthful by nature, the first fables could not feign anything false; they must therefore have been, as they have been defined above, true narrations.

From all this it follows that all the tropes (and they are all reducible to the four types above discussed), which have

---

[26] [Bergin and Fisch] Several of Vico's examples for which there are no common English parallels are here omitted, and substitutions are made for several others.

[27] Italy.

[28] Virgil, *Eclogues* I, 69.

[29] In other words, human beings had to develop the abstract concept of the false before irony was possible.

hitherto been considered ingenious inventions of writers, were necessary modes of expression of all the first poetic nations, and had originally their full native propriety. But these expressions of the first nations later became figurative when, with the further development of the human mind, words were invented which signified abstract forms or genera comprising their species or relating parts with their wholes. And here begins the overthrow of two common errors of the grammarians: that prose speech is proper speech, and poetic speech improper; and that prose speech came first and afterward speech in verse.

Poetic monsters and metamorphoses arose from a necessity of this first humane nature, its inability to abstract forms or properties from subjects. By their logic they had to put subjects together in order to put their forms together, or to destroy a subject in order to separate its primary form from the contrary form which had been imposed upon it. Such a putting together of ideas created the poetic monsters. In Roman law, as Antoine Favre observes in his *Iurisprudentiae papinianeae scientia,*[30] children born of prostitutes are called monsters because they have the nature of men together with the bestial characteristic of having been born of vagabond or uncertain unions. And it was as being monsters of this sort, we shall find, that children born of noble women without benefit of solemn nuptials were commanded by the Law of the Twelve Tables to be thrown into the Tiber.

The distinguishing of ideas produced metamorphoses. Among other examples preserved by ancient jurispudence is the heroic Latin phrase *fundum fieri,* "to become ground of," used in place of *auctorem fieri,* to become author of, to authorize, to ratify; the explanation being that, as the ground supports the farm or soil and that which is sown, planted, or built thereon, so the ratifier supports an act which without his ratification would fail; and he does this by quitting the form of a being moving at will, which he is, and taking on the contrary form of a stable thing.

* * *

The philosophers and philologians should all have begun to treat of the origins of languages and letters from the following principles. (1) That the first men of the gentile world conceived ideas of things by imaginative characters of animate and mute substances. (2) That they expressed themselves by means of gestures or physical objects which had natural relations with the ideas; for example, three ears of grain, or acting as if swinging a scythe three times, to signify three years. (3) That they thus expressed themselves by a language with natural significations. (Plato and Iamblichus[31] said such a language had once been spoken in the world; it must have been the most ancient language of Atlantis, which scholars would have us believe expressed ideas by the nature of the things, that is, by their natural properties.) It is because the philosophers and philologians have treated separately these two things which are naturally conjoined [—the origins of languages and letters—] that the inquiry into the origins of letters has proved so difficult for them—as difficult as that into the origins of languages, with which they have been either not at all or very little concerned.

---

[30] Antoine Favre, late-sixteenth-century lawyer and writer.

[31] Iamblichus (d. c. 330), neoplatonic philosopher.

David Hume

1711–1776

Hume's literary essays continue the emphasis on the psychology of the reader and audience that we find in Addison (above, page 307) and Hume's contemporary Burke (below, page 332). Rigorously empirical, Hume calls in question most of the assumptions of classical rationalist philosophy. But then he must worry over the problem of subjectivity implicit in the empiricist Locke's distinction (above, page 281) between primary and secondary qualities of experience. Although he is fully cognizant of the immense difficulties of arriving at a standard of taste, his essay *Of the Standard of Taste* is very critical of subjective relativism. There are, for him, principles of art based on the experience of what has pleased, not on what is true or false. In order to discover these principles, the critic must have recourse to the "common sentiments of human nature." But there are countless variables; a reader's sentiments are affected by time, place, and situation. Therefore, Hume seems to propose a certain state of mind as the source of the standard of taste. It is not then a matter of calling for a majority vote. In order for a reader's vote to count, so to speak, he must exhibit "a perfect serenity of mind, a recollection of thought, a due attention to the object," a "delicacy of imagination," lack of prejudice, and freedom from slavish love of current or local fashion. Furthermore, to exercise judgment in this state of mind requires practice. Hasty judgments are likely to be wrong or at least superficial. Thus it is clear that to live up to a standard of taste, as Hume describes it, is a tall order. In much of all this Hume anticipates Kant's effort (below, page 420) to establish a notion of aesthetic disinterest, and indeed Kant was a careful reader of Hume.

After making it seem virtually impossible ever to discover a person of adequate delicacy in the proper state of mind, and thus an adequate standard, Hume points out that indeed it seems in practice more possible than we would suppose. Terence and Virgil have stood the test of time, while philosophers and their theories have been subject to endless disputes. Thus human beings, in his view, are collectively more capable of consistent exercise of taste than of reason. These issues are taken up a few years later by Kames (below, page 369).

Hume's antireligious, or at least anti-Christian, views come out in his criticism of violence in religious art and of religious bigotry appealed to by certain playwrights.

Useful texts of Hume are *The Essays, Moral, Political, and Literary,* edited by T. H. Green and T. H. Grose (in four volumes, 1874–1875), *Essential Works of David Hume,* edited by Ralph Cohen (1965), and *Four Dissertations,* introduction by John Immerwahr (1993). See J. F. Doering, "Hume and the Theory of Tragedy," *PMLA* LI (1937), 1130–44; N. K. Smith, *The Philosophy of David Hume* (1941); Martin Kallich, "The Associationist Criticism of Francis Hutcheson and David Hume," *Studies in Philology* XVIII (1946), 644–67; Teddy Brunius, *David Hume on Criticism* (1952); E. C. Mossner, *The Life of David Hume* (1954); A. J. Ayer, *Hume* (1980); John Mullan,

Sentiment and Sociability: The Language of Feeling in the Eighteenth Century (1988);
M. A. Box, *The Suasive Art of David Hume* (1990); John V. Price, *David Hume* (1991);
Terence Penelhum, *David Hume: An Introduction to His Philosophical System* (1992).

Of the Standard of Taste

The great variety of taste, as well as of opinion, which prevails in the world, is too obvious not to have fallen under everyone's observation. Men of the most confined knowledge are able to remark a difference of taste in the narrow circle of their acquaintance, even where the persons have been educated under the same government, and have early imbibed the same prejudices. But those who can enlarge their view to contemplate distant nations and remote ages, are still more surprised at the great inconsistence and contrariety. We are apt to call barbarous whatever departs widely from our own taste and apprehension: but soon find the epithet of reproach retorted on us. And the highest arrogance and self-conceit is at last startled, on observing an equal assurance on all sides, and scruples, amidst such a contest of sentiment, to pronounce positively in its own favor.

As this variety of taste is obvious to the most careless inquirer; so will it be found, on examination, to be still greater in reality than in appearance. The sentiments of men often differ with regard to beauty and deformity of all kinds, even while their general discourse is the same. There are certain terms in every language, which import blame, and others praise; and all men, who use the same tongue, must agree in their application of them. Every voice is united in applauding elegance, propriety, simplicity, spirit in writing; and in blaming fustian, affectation, coldness, and a false brilliancy: but when critics come to particulars, this seeming unanimity vanishes; and it is found, that they had affixed a very different meaning to their expressions. In all matters of opinion and science, the case is opposite: The difference among men is there oftener found to lie in generals than in particulars; and to be less in reality than in appearance. An explanation of the terms commonly ends the controversy; and the disputants are surprised to find, that they had been quarreling, while at bottom they agreed in their judgment.

Those who found morality on sentiment, more than on reason, are inclined to comprehend ethics under the former

observation, and to maintain, that, in all questions, which regard conduct and manners, the difference among men is really greater than at first sight it appears. It is indeed obvious that writers of all nations and all ages concur in applauding justice, humanity, magnanimity, prudence, veracity; and in blaming the opposite qualities. Even poets and other authors, whose compositions are chiefly calculated to please the imagination, are yet found, from Homer down to Fénelon,[1] to inculcate the same moral precepts, and to bestow their applause and blame on the same virtues and vices. This great unanimity is usually ascribed to the influence of plain reason; which, in all these cases, maintains similar sentiments in all men, and prevents those controversies, to which the abstract sciences are so much exposed. So far as the unanimity is real, this account may be admitted as satisfactory: but we must also allow that some part of the seeming harmony in morals may be accounted for from the very nature of language. The word *virtue,* with its equivalent in every tongue, implies praise; as that of *vice* does blame: And no one, without the most obvious and grossest impropriety, could affix reproach to a term, which in general acceptation is understood in a good sense; or bestow applause, where the idiom requires disapprobation. Homer's general precepts, where he delivers any such, will never be controverted; but it is obvious, that, when he draws particular pictures of manners, and represents heroism in Achilles and prudence in Ulysses, he intermixes a much greater degree of ferocity in the former, and of cunning and fraud in the latter, than Fénelon would admit of. The sage Ulysses in the Greek poet seems to delight in lies and fictions, and often employs them without any necessity or even advantage: But his more scrupulous son, in the French epic writer, exposes himself to the most imminent perils, rather than depart from the most exact line of truth and veracity.

The admirers and followers of the Alcoran[2] insist on the excellent moral precepts interspersed throughout that wild and absurd performance. But it is to be supposed, that the Arabic words, which correspond to the English, equity,

---

Of the Standard of Taste was first published as part of Hume's *Four Dissertations* in 1757.

[1] Francois Fénelon (1651–1715), French churchman and writer.
[2] The Koran, sacred book of the Muslims.

justice, temperance, meekness, charity, were such as, from the constant use of that tongue, must always be taken in a good sense; and it would have argued the greatest ignorance, not of morals, but of language, to have mentioned them with any epithets, besides those of applause and approbation. But would we know, whether the pretended prophet had really attained a just sentiment of morals? Let us attend to his narration; and we shall soon find, that he bestows praise on such instances of treachery, inhumanity, cruelty, revenge, bigotry, as are utterly incompatible with civilized society. No steady rule of right seems there to be attained to; and every action is blamed or praised, so far only as it is beneficial or hurtful to the true believers.

The merit of delivering true general precepts in ethics is indeed very small. Whoever recommends any moral virtues, really does no more than is implied in the terms themselves. That people, who invented the word *charity,* and used it in a good sense, inculcated more clearly and much more efficaciously, the precept, "be charitable," than any pretended legislator or prophet, who should insert such a maxim in his writings. Of all expressions, those, which, together with their other meaning, imply a degree either of blame or approbation, are the least liable to be perverted or mistaken.

It is natural for us to seek a standard of taste; a rule by which the various sentiments of men may be reconciled; at least, a decision afforded, confirming one sentiment, and condemning another.

There is a species of philosophy, which cuts off all hopes of success in such an attempt, and represents the impossibility of ever attaining any standard of taste. The difference, it is said, is very wide between judgment and sentiment. All sentiment is right; because sentiment has a reference to nothing beyond itself, and is always real, wherever a man is conscious of it. But all determinations of the understanding are not right; because they have a reference to something beyond themselves, to wit, real matter of fact; and are not always conformable to that standard. Among a thousand different opinions which different men may entertain of the same subject, there is one, and but one, that is just and true; and the only difficulty is to fix and ascertain it. On the contrary, a thousand different sentiments, excited by the same object, are all right: because no sentiment represents what is really in the object. It only marks a certain conformity or relation between the object and the organs or faculties of the mind; and if that conformity did not really exist, the sentiment could never possibly have being. Beauty is no quality in things themselves: it exists merely in the mind which contemplates them; and each mind perceives a different beauty. One person may

even perceive deformity, where another is sensible of beauty; and every individual ought to acquiesce in his own sentiment, without pretending to regulate those of others. To seek the real beauty, or real deformity, is as fruitless an inquiry, as to pretend to ascertain the real sweet or real bitter. According to the disposition of the organs, the same object may be both sweet and bitter; and the proverb has justly determined it to be fruitless to dispute concerning tastes. It is very natural, and even quite necessary, to extend this axiom to mental, as well as bodily taste; and thus common sense, which is so often at variance with philosophy, especially with the skeptical kind, is found, in one instance at least, to agree to pronouncing the same decision.

But though this axiom, by passing into a proverb, seems to have attained the sanction of common sense; there is certainly a species of common sense which opposes it, at least serves to modify and restrain it. Whoever would assert an equality of genius and elegance between Ogilby[3] and Milton, or Bunyan and Addison,[4] would be thought to defend no less an extravagance, than if he had maintained a molehill to be as high as Tenerife,[5] or a pond as extensive as the ocean. Though there may be found persons, who give the preference to the former authors, no one pays attention to such a taste; and we pronounce without scruple the sentiment of these pretended critics to be absurd and ridiculous. The principle of the natural equality of tastes is then totally forgot, and while we admit it on some occassions, where the objects seem near an equality, it appears an extravagant paradox, or rather a palpable absurdity, where objects so disproportioned are compared together.

It is evident that none of the rules of composition are fixed by reasoning *a priori,* or can be esteemed abstract conclusions of the understanding, from comparing those habitudes and relations of ideas, which are eternal and immutable. Their foundation is the same with that of all the practical sciences, experience; nor are they anything but general observations, concerning what has been universally found to please in all countries and in all ages. Many of the beauties of poetry and even of eloquence are founded on falsehood and fiction, on hyperboles, metaphors, and an abuse or perversion of terms from their natural meaning. To check the sallies of the imagination, and to reduce every expression to geometrical truth and exactness, would be the most contrary to the laws of criticism; because it would pro-

---

[3] John Ogilby (1600–1656), English poet, translator, and printer.
[4] John Bunyan (1628–1688), author of *Pilgrim's Progress;* Addison (above, page 307).
[5] A mountain in the Canary Islands.

duce a work, which, by universal experience, has been found the most insipid and disagreeable. But though poetry can never submit to exact truth, it must be confined by rules of art, discovered to the author either by genius or observation. If some negligent or irregular writers have pleased, they have not pleased by their transgressions of rule or order, but in spite of these transgressions: They have possessed other beauties, which were conformable to just criticism; and the force of these beauties has been able to overpower censure, and give the mind a satisfaction superior to the disgust arising from the blemishes. Ariosto[6] pleases; but not by his monstrous and improbable fictions, by his bizarre mixture of the serious and comic styles, by the want of coherence in his stories, or by the continual interruptions of his narration. He charms by the force and clearness of his expression, by the readiness and variety of his inventions, and by his natural pictures of the passions, especially those of the gay and amorous kind: And however his faults may diminish our satisfaction, they are not able entirely to destroy it. Did our pleasure really arise from those parts of his poem, which we denominate faults, this would be no objection to criticism in general: It would only be an objection to those particular rules of criticism, which would establish such circumstances to be faults, and would represent them as universally blameable. If they are found to please, they cannot be faults; let the pleasure, which they produce, be ever so unexpected and unaccountable.

But though all the general rules of art are founded only on experience and on the observation of the common sentiments of human nature, we must not imagine, that, on every occasion, the feelings of men will be conformable to these rules. Those finer emotions of the mind are of a very tender and delicate nature, and require the concurrence of many favorable circumstances to make them play with facility and exactness, according to their general and established principles. The least exterior hindrance to such small springs, or the least internal disorder, disturbs their motion, and confounds the operation of the whole machine. When we would make an experiment of this nature, and would try the force of any beauty or deformity, we must choose with care a proper time and place, and bring the fancy to a suitable situation and disposition. A perfect serenity of mind, a recollection of thought, a due attention to the object; if any of these circumstances be wanting, our experiment will be fallacious, and we shall be unable to judge of the catholic and universal beauty. The relation, which nature has placed between the form and the sentiment, will at least be more

obscure; and it will require greater accuracy to trace and discern it. We shall be able to ascertain its influence not so much from the operation of each particular beauty, as from the durable admiration, which attends those works, that have survived all the caprices of mode and fashion, all the mistakes of ignorance and envy.

The same Homer, who pleased at Athens and Rome two thousand years ago, is still admired at Paris and at London. All the changes of climate, government, religion, and language, have not been able to obscure his glory. Authority or prejudice may give a temporary vogue to a bad poet or orator; but his reputation will never be durable or general. When his compositions are examined by posterity or by foreigners, the enchantment is dissipated, and his faults appear in their true colors. On the contrary, a real genius, the longer his works endure, and the more wide they are spread, the more sincere is the admiration which he meets with. Envy and jealousy have too much place in a narrow circle; and even familiar acquaintance with his person may diminish the applause due to his performances: but when these obstructions are removed, the beauties, which are naturally fitted to excite agreeable sentiments, immediately display their energy; and while the world endures, they maintain their authority over the minds of men.

It appears then, that, amidst all the variety and caprice of taste, there are certain general principles of approbation or blame, whose influence a careful eye may trace in all operations of the mind. Some particular forms or qualities, from the original structures of the internal fabric, are calculated to please, and others displease; and if they fail of their effect in any particular instance, it is from some apparent defect or imperfection in the organ. A man in a fever would not insist on his palate as able to decide concerning flavors; nor would one, affected with the jaundice, pretend to give a verdict with regard to colors. In each creature, there is a sound and defective state; and the former alone can be supposed to afford us a true standard of taste and sentiment. If, in the sound state of the organ, there be an entire or a considerable uniformity of sentiment among men, we may thence derive an idea of the perfect beauty; in like manner as the appearance of objects in daylight, to the eye of a man in health, is denominated their true and real color, even while color is allowed to be merely a phantasm of the senses.

Many and frequent are the defects in the internal organs which prevent or weaken the influence of those general principles, on which depends our sentiment of beauty or deformity. Though some objects, by the structure of the mind, be naturally calculated to give pleasure, it is not to be expected, that in every individual the pleasure will be equally felt. Particular incidents and situations occur, which either

---

[6]Lodovico Ariosto (1474–1533), Italian poet, author of *Orlando Furioso*.

throw a false light on the objects, or hinder the true from conveying to the imagination the proper sentiment and perception.

One obvious cause, why many feel not the proper sentiment of beauty, is the want of that delicacy of imagination, which is requisite to convey a sensibility of those finer emotions. This delicacy everyone pretends to: everyone talks of it; and would reduce every kind of taste or sentiment to its standard. But as our intention in this essay is to mingle some light of the understanding with the feeling of sentiment, it will be proper to give a more accurate definition of delicacy, than has hitherto been attempted. And not to draw our philosophy from too profound a source, we shall have recourse to a noted story in *Don Quixote.*

"It is with good reason," says Sancho to the squire with the great nose, "that I pretend to have a judgment in wine: this is a quality hereditary in our family. Two of my kinsmen were once called to give their opinion of a hogshead, which was supposed to be excellent, being old and of a good vintage. One of them tastes it; considers it; and after mature reflection pronounces the wine to be good, were it not for a small taste of leather, which he perceived in it. The other, after using the same precautions, gives also his verdict in favor of the wine; but with the reserve of a taste of iron, which he could easily distinguish. You cannot imagine how much they were both ridiculed for their judgment. But who laughed in the end? On emptying the hogshead, there was found at the bottom, an old key with a leathern thong tied to it."

The great resemblance between mental and bodily taste will easily teach us to apply this story. Though it be certain that beauty and deformity, more than sweet and bitter, are not qualities in objects, but belong entirely to the sentiment, internal or external; it must be allowed, that there are certain qualities in objects, which are fitted by nature to produce those particular feelings.[7] Now as these qualities may be found in a small degree, or may be mixed and confounded with each other, it often happens, that the taste is not affected with such minute qualities, or is not able to distinguish all the particular flavors, amidst the disorder, in which they are presented. Where the organs are so fine, as to allow nothing to escape them; and at the same time so exact as to perceive every ingredient in the composition: this we call delicacy of taste, where we employ these terms in the literal or metaphorical sense. Here then the general rules of beauty are of use; being drawn from established models, and from the observation of what pleases or displeases,

when presented singly and in a high degree: and if the same qualities, in a continued composition and in a smaller degree, affect not the organs with a sensible delight or uneasiness, we exclude the person from all pretensions to this delicacy. To produce these general rules or avowed patterns of composition is like finding the key with the leathern thong; which justified the verdict of Sancho's kinsmen, and confounded those pretended judges who had condemned them. Though the hogshead had never been emptied, the taste of the one was still equally delicate, and that of the other equally dull and languid: but it would have been more difficult to have proved the superiority of the former, to the conviction of every bystander. In like manner, though the beauties of writing had never been methodized, or reduced to general principles; though no excellent models had ever been acknowledged; the different degrees of taste would still have subsisted, and the judgment of one man been preferable to that of another; but it would not have been so easy to silence the bad critic, who might always insist upon his particular sentiment, and refuse to submit to his antagonist. But when we show him an avowed principle of art; when we illustrate this principle by examples, whose operation, from his own particular taste, he acknowledges to be conformable to the principle; when we prove, that the same principle may be applied to the present case, where he did not perceive or feel its influence: he must conclude, upon the whole, that the fault lies in himself, and that he wants the delicacy, which is requisite to make him sensible of every beauty and every blemish, in any composition or discourse.

It is acknowledged to be the perfection of every sense or faculty, to perceive with exactness its most minute objects, and allow nothing to escape its notice and observation. The smaller the objects are, which become sensible to the eye, the finer is that organ, and the more elaborate its make and composition. A good palate is not tried by strong flavors; but by a mixture of small ingredients, where we are still sensible of each part, notwithstanding its minuteness and its confusion with the rest. In like manner, a quick and acute perception of beauty and deformity must be the perfection of our mental taste; nor can a man be satisfied with himself while he suspects, that any excellence or blemish in a discourse has passed him unobserved. In this case, the perfection of the man, and the perfection of the sense or feeling, are found to be united. A very delicate palate, on many occasions, may be a great inconvenience both to a man himself and to his friends: but a delicate taste of wit or beauty must always be a desirable quality; because it is the source of all the finest and most innocent enjoyments, of which human nature is susceptible. In this decision the sentiments of

---

[7]Hume here follows Locke's distinction between primary and secondary qualities of experience. See above, page 281.

all mankind are agreed. Wherever you can ascertain a delicacy of taste, it is sure to meet with approbation; and the best way of ascertaining it is to appeal to those models and principles, which have been established by the uniform consent and experience of nations and ages.

But though there be naturally a wide difference in point of delicacy between one person and another, nothing tends further to increase and improve this talent, than practice in a particular art, and the frequent survey or contemplation of a particular species of beauty. When objects of any kind are first presented to the eye or imagination, the sentiment, which attends them, is obscure and confused; and the mind is, in a great measure, incapable of pronouncing concerning their merits or defects. The taste cannot perceive the several excellences of the performance; much less distinguish the particular character of each excellency, and ascertain its quality and degree. If it pronounce the whole in general to be beautiful or deformed, it is the utmost that can be expected; and even this judgment, a person, so unpracticed, will be apt to deliver with great hesitation and reserve. But allow him to acquire experience in those objects, his feeling becomes more exact and nice: he not only perceives the beauties and defects of each part, but marks the distinguishing species of each quality, and assigns it suitable praise or blame. A clear and distinct sentiment attends him through the whole survey of the objects; and he discerns that very degree and kind of approbation or displeasure, which each part is naturally fitted to produce. The mist dissipates, which seemed formerly to hang over the object: the organ acquires greater perfection in its operations: and can pronounce, without danger of mistake, concerning the merits of every performance. In a word, the same address and dexterity, which practice gives to the execution of any work, is also acquired by the same means, in the judging of it.

So advantageous is practice to the discernment of beauty, that, before we can give judgment on any work of importance, it will even be requisite, that that very individual performance be more than once perused by us, and be surveyed in different lights with attention and deliberation. There is a flutter or hurry of thought which attends the first perusal of any piece, and which confounds the genuine sentiment of beauty. The relation of the parts is not discerned: the true characters of style are little distinguished: the several perfections and defects seem wrapped up in a species of confusion, and present themselves indistinctly to the imagination. Not to mention, that there is a species of beauty, which, as it is florid and superficial, pleases at first; but being found incompatible with a just expression either of reason or passion, soon palls upon the taste, and is then rejected with disdain, at least rated at much lower value.

It is impossible to continue in the practice of contemplating any order of beauty, without being frequently obliged to form comparisons between the several species and degrees of excellence, and estimating their proportion to each other. A man, who has had no opportunity of comparing the different kinds of beauty, is indeed totally unqualified to pronounce an opinion with regard to any object presented to him. By comparison alone we fix the epithets of praise or blame, and learn how to assign the due degree of each. The coarsest daubing contains a certain luster of colors and exactness of imitation, which are so far beauties, and would affect the mind of a peasant or Indian with the highest admiration. The most vulgar ballads are not entirely destitute of harmony or nature; and none but a person, familiarized to superior beauties, would pronounce their numbers harsh, or narration uninteresting. A great inferiority of beauty gives pain to a person conversant in the highest excellence of the kind, and is for that reason pronounced a deformity: as the most finished object, with which we are acquainted, is naturally supposed to have reached the pinnacle of perfection, and to be entitled to the highest applause. One accustomed to see, and examine, and weigh the several performances, admired in different ages and nations, can only rate the merits of a work exhibited to his view, and assign its proper rank among the productions of genius.

But to enable a critic the more fully to execute this undertaking, he must preserve his mind free from all prejudice, and allow nothing to enter into his consideration, but the very object which is submitted to his examination. We may observe, that every work of art, in order to produce its due effect on the mind, must be surveyed in a certain point of view, and cannot be fully relished by persons, whose situation, real or imaginary, is not conformable to that which is required by the performance.[8] An orator addresses himself to a particular audience, and must have a regard to their particular genius, interest, opinions, passions, and prejudices; otherwise he hopes in vain to govern their resolutions, and inflame their affections. Should they even have entertained some prepossessions against him, however unreasonable, he must not overlook this disadvantage; but, before he enters upon the subject, must endeavor to conciliate their affection, and acquire their good graces. A critic of a different age or nation, who should peruse this discourse, must have all these circumstances in his eye, and must place himself in the same situation as the audience, in order to form a true judgment of the oration. In like manner, when any work is addressed to

---

[8] Hume here begins to anticipate Kant's notion of aesthetic disinterest (below, page 420).

the public, though I should have a friendship or enmity with the author, I must depart from this situation; and considering myself as a man in general, forget, if possible, my individual being and my peculiar circumstances. A person influenced by prejudice, complies not with this condition; but obstinately maintains his natural position, without placing himself in that point of view, which the performance supposes. If the work be addressed to persons of a different age or nation, he makes no allowance for their peculiar views and prejudices; but full of the manners of his own age and country, rashly condemns what seemed admirable in the eyes of those for whom alone the discourse was calculated. If the work be executed for the public, he never sufficiently enlarges his comprehension, or forgets his interest as a friend or enemy, as a rival or commentator. By this means, his sentiments are perverted; nor have the same beauties and blemishes the same influence upon him, as if he had imposed a proper violence on his imagination, and had forgotten himself for a moment. So far his taste evidently departs from the true standard; and of consequence loses all credit and authority.

It is well known, that in all questions, submitted to the understanding, prejudice is destructive of sound judgment, and perverts all operations of the intellectual faculties: it is no less contrary to good taste; nor has it less influence to corrupt our sentiment of beauty. It belongs to good sense to check its influence in both cases; and in this respect, as well as in many others, reason, if not an essential part of taste, is at least requisite to the operations of this latter faculty. In all the nobler productions of genius, there is a mutual relation and correspondence of parts; nor can either the beauties or blemishes be perceived by him, whose thought is not capacious enough to comprehend all those parts, and compare them with each other, in order to perceive the consistence and uniformity of the whole. Every work of art has also a certain end or purpose, for which it is calculated; and is to be deemed more or less perfect, as it is more or less fitted to attain this end. The object of eloquence is to persuade, of history to instruct, of poetry to please by means of the passions and the imagination.[9] These ends we must carry constantly in our view, when we peruse any performance; and we must be able to judge how far the means employed are adapted to their respective purposes. Besides every kind of composition, even the most poetical, is nothing but a chain of propositions and reasonings; not always, indeed, the justest and

most exact, but still plausible and specious, however disguised by the coloring of the imagination. The persons introduced in tragedy and epic poetry, must be represented as reasoning, and thinking, and concluding, and acting, suitably to their character and circumstances; and without judgment, as well as taste and invention, a poet can never hope to succeed in so delicate an undertaking. Not to mention, that the same excellence of faculties which contributes to the improvement of reason, the same clearness of conception, the same exactness of distinction, the same vivacity of apprehension, are essential to the operations of true taste, and are its infallible concomitants. It seldom, or never happens, that a man of sense, who has experience in any art, cannot judge of its beauty; and it is no less rare to meet with a man who has a just taste without a sound understanding.

Thus, though the principles of taste be universal, and, nearly, if not entirely the same in all men; yet few are qualified to give judgment on any work of art, or establish their own sentiment as the standard of beauty. The organs of internal sensation are seldom so perfect as to allow the general principles their full play, and produce a feeling correspondent to those principles. They either labor under some defect, or are vitiated by some disorder; and by that means, excite a sentiment, which may be pronounced erroneous. When the critic has no delicacy, he judges without any distinction, and is only affected by the grosser and more palpable qualities of the object: the finer touches pass unnoticed and disregarded. Where he is not aided by practice, his verdict is attended with confusion and hesitation. Where no comparison has been employed, the most frivolous beauties, such as rather merit the name of defects, are the objects of his admiration. Where he lies under the influence of prejudice, all his natural sentiments are perverted. Where good sense is wanting, he is not qualified to discern the beauties of design and reasoning, which are the highest and most excellent. Under some or other of these imperfections, the generality of men labor; and hence a true judge in the finer arts is observed, even during the most polished ages, to be so rare a character: strong sense, united to delicate sentiment, improved by practice, perfected by comparison, and cleared of all prejudice, can alone entitle critics to this valuable character; and the joint verdict of such, wherever they are to be found, is the true standard of taste and beauty.

But where are such critics to be found? By what marks are they to be known? How distinguish them from pretenders? These questions are embarrassing; and seem to throw us back into the same uncertainty, from which, during the course of this essay, we have endeavored to extricate ourselves.

---

[9] Hume's identification of poetry with pleasure and not instruction departs from the Horatian notion (above, page 83) that poets should teach and delight, echoed by many critics of Hume's time. The elimination of instruction raises interesting problems that Hume addresses later in the essay.

But if we consider the matter aright, these are questions of fact, not of sentiment. Whether any particular person be endowed with good sense and a delicate imagination, free from prejudice, may often be the subject of dispute, and be liable to great discussion and inquiry: But that such a character is valuable and estimable will be agreed in by all mankind. Where these doubts occur, men can do no more than in other disputable questions, which are submitted to the understanding: they must produce the best arguments, that their invention suggests to them; they must acknowledge a true and decisive standard to exist somewhere, to wit, real existence and matter of fact; and they must have indulgence to such as differ from them in their appeals to this standard. It is sufficient for our present purpose, if we have proved, that the taste of all individuals is not upon an equal footing, and that some men in general, however difficult to be particularly pitched upon, will be acknowledged by universal sentiment to have a preference above others.

But in reality the difficulty of finding, even in particulars, the standard of taste, is not so great as it is represented. Though in speculation, we may readily avow a certain criterion in science and deny it in sentiment, the matter is found in practice to be much more hard to ascertain in the former case than in the latter. Theories of abstract philosophy, systems of profound theology, have prevailed during one age: in a successive period, these have been universally exploded: their absurdity has been detected: other theories and systems have supplied their place, which again gave place to their successors: and nothing has been experienced more liable to the revolutions of chance and fashion than these pretended decisions of science. The case is not the same with beauties of eloquence and poetry. Just expressions of passion and nature are sure, after a little time, to gain public applause, which they maintain forever. Aristotle, and Plato, and Epicurus, and Descartes,[10] may successively yield to each other: but Terence and Virgil[11] maintain a universal, undisputed empire over the minds of men. The abstract philosophy of Cicero[12] has lost its credit: the vehemence of his oratory is still the object of our admiration.

Though men of delicate taste be rare, they are easily to be distinguished in society, by the soundness of their understanding and the superiority of their faculties above the rest of mankind. The ascendant, which they acquire, gives a prevalence to that lively approbation, with which they receive any productions of genius, and renders it generally predominant. Many men, when left to themselves, have but a faint and dubious perception of beauty, who yet are capable of relishing any fine stroke, which is pointed out to them. Every convert to the admiration of the real poet or orator is the cause of some new conversion. And though prejudices may prevail for a time, they never unite in celebrating any rival to the true genius, but yield at last to the force of nature and just sentiment. Thus, though a civilized nation may easily be mistaken in the choice of their admired philosopher, they never have been found long to err, in their affection for a favorite epic or tragic author.

But notwithstanding all our endeavors to fix a standard of taste, and reconcile the discordant apprehensions of men, there still remain two sources of variation, which are not sufficient indeed to confound all the boundaries of beauty and deformity, but will often serve to produce a difference in the degrees of our approbation or blame. The one is the different humors of particular men; the other, the particular manners and opinions of our age and country. The general principles of taste are uniform in human nature: where men vary in their judgments, some defect or perversion in the faculties may commonly be remarked; proceeding either from prejudice, from want of practice, or want of delicacy; and there is just reason for approving one taste, and condemning another. But where there is such a diversity in the internal frame or external situation as is entirely blameless on both sides, and leaves no room to give one the preference above the other; in that case a certain degree of diversity in judgment is unavoidable, and we seek in vain for a standard, by which we can reconcile the contrary sentiments.

A young man, whose passions are warm, will be more sensibly touched with amorous and tender images, than a man more advanced in years, who takes pleasure in wise, philosophical reflections concerning the conduct of life and moderation of the passions. At twenty, Ovid may be the favorite author; Horace at forty; and perhaps Tacitus at fifty.[13] Vainly would we, in such cases, endeavor to enter into the sentiments of others, and divest ourselves of those propensities, which are natural to us. We choose our favorite author as we do our friend, from a conformity of humor and disposition. Mirth or passion, sentiment or reflection; whichever of these most predominates in our temper, it gives us a peculiar sympathy with the writer who resembles us.

One person is more pleased with the sublime; another with the tender; a third with raillery. One has a strong sensibility to blemishes, and is extremely studious of correctness:

---

[10] Epicurus (341–270 B.C.), Greek philosopher; René Descartes (1596–1650), French philosopher.

[11] Publius Terentius Afer (c. 185–c. 159 B.C.), Roman comic dramatist; Virgil (70–19 B.C.), Roman poet.

[12] Cicero, see above, page 74.

[13] Publius Ovidius Naso (43 B.C.–17 A.D.), Roman poet; Horace (above, page 78); Tacitus (above, page 90).

another has a more lively feeling of beauties, and pardons twenty absurdities and defects for one elevated or pathetic stroke. The ear of this man is entirely turned toward conciseness and energy; that man is delighted with a copious, rich, and harmonious expression. Simplicity is affected by one; ornament by another. Comedy, tragedy, satire, odes, have each its partisans, who prefer that particular species of writing to all others. It is plainly an error in a critic, to confine his approbation to one species or style of writing, and condemn all the rest. But it is almost impossible not to feel a predilection for that which suits our particular turn and disposition. Such preferences are innocent and unavoidable, and can never reasonably be the object of dispute, because there is no standard, by which they can be decided.

For a like reason, we are more pleased, in the course of our reading, with pictures and characters, that resemble objects which are found in our own age or country, than with those which describe a different set of customs. It is not without some effort, that we reconcile ourselves to the simplicity of ancient manners, and behold princesses carrying water from the spring, and kings and heroes dressing their own victuals. We may allow in general, that the representation of such manners is no fault in the author, nor deformity in the piece; but we are not so sensibly touched with them. For this reason, comedy is not easily transferred from one age or nation to another. A Frenchman or Englishman is not pleased with the *Andria* of Terence, or *Clitia* of Machiavel;[14] where the fine lady, upon whom all the play turns, never once appears to the spectators, but is always kept behind the scenes, suitably to the reserved humor of the ancient Greeks and modern Italians. A man of learning and reflection can make allowance for these peculiarities of manners; but a common audience can never divest themselves so far of their usual ideas and sentiments, as to relish pictures which in no wise resemble them.

But here there occurs a reflection, which may, perhaps, be useful in examining the celebrated controversy concerning ancient and modern learning;[15] where we often find the one side excusing any seeming absurdity in the ancients from the manners of the age, and the other refusing to admit this excuse, or at least, admitting it only as an apology for the author, not for the performance. In my opinion, the proper boundaries in this subject have seldom been fixed between the contending parties. Where any innocent peculiarities of manners are represented, such as those above mentioned, they ought certainly to be admitted; and a man, who is shocked with them, gives an evident proof of false delicacy and refinement. The poet's monument more durable than brass must fall to the ground like common brick or clay, were men to make no allowance for the continual revolutions of manners and customs, and would admit of nothing but what was suitable to the prevailing fashion. Must we throw aside the pictures of our ancestors, because of their ruffs and farthingales? But where the ideas of morality and decency alter from one age to another, and where vicious manners are described, without being marked with the proper characters of blame and disapprobation; this must be allowed to disfigure the poem, and to be a real deformity. I cannot, nor is it proper I should, enter into such sentiments; and however I may excuse the poet, on account of the manners of his age, I never can relish the composition. The want of humanity and of decency, so conspicuous in the characters drawn by several of the ancient poets, even sometimes by Homer and the Greek tragedians, diminishes considerably the merit of their noble performances, and gives modern authors an advantage over them. We are not interested in the fortunes and sentiments of such rough heroes: we are displeased to find the limits of vice and virtue so much confounded: and whatever indulgence we may give to the writer on account of his prejudices, we cannot prevail on ourselves to enter into his sentiments, or bear an affection to characters, which we plainly discover to be blamable.

The case is not the same with moral principles, as with speculative opinions of any kind. These are in continual flux and revolution. The son embraces a different system from the father. Nay, there scarcely is any man, who can boast of great constance and uniformity in this particular. Whatever speculative errors may be found in the polite writings of any age or country, they detract but little from the value of those compositions. There needs but a certain turn of thought or imagination to make us enter into all the opinions, which then prevailed, and relish the sentiments or conclusions derived from them. But a very violent effort is requisite to change our judgment of manners, and excite sentiments of approbation or blame, love or hatred, different from those to which the mind from long custom has been familiarized. And where a man is confident of the rectitude of that moral standard, by which he judges, he is justly jealous of it, and will not pervert the sentiments of his heart for a moment, in complaisance to any writer whatsoever.

Of all speculative errors, those, which regard religion, are the most excusable in compositions of genius; nor is it ever permitted to judge of the civility or wisdom of any people, or even of single persons, by the grossness or refinement of their theological principles. The same good sense, that di-

---

[14] Niccolo de Bernardo Machiavelli (1469–1527), better known as a historian and political writer.
[15] See especially Dryden (above, page 254ff.).

rects men in the ordinary occurrences of life, is not harkened to in religious matters, which are supposed to be placed altogether above the cognizance of human reason. On this account, all the absurdities of the pagan system of theology must be overlooked by every critic, who would pretend to form a just notion of ancient poetry; and our posterity, in their turn, must have the same indulgence to their forefathers. No religious principles can ever be imputed as a fault to any poet, while they remain merely principles, and take no such strong possession of his heart, as to lay him under the imputation of bigotry or superstition. Where that happens, they confound the sentiments of morality, and alter the natural boundaries of vice and virtue. They are therefore eternal blemishes, according to the principle above mentioned; nor are the prejudices and false opinions of the age sufficient to justify them.

It is essential to the Roman Catholic religion to inspire a violent hatred of every other worship, and to represent all pagans, Mahometans, and heretics as the objects of divine wrath and vengeance. Such sentiments, though they are in reality very blamable, are considered as virtues by the zealots of that communion, and are represented in their tragedies and epic poems as a kind of divine heroism. This bigotry has disfigured two very fine tragedies of the French theater, *Polyeucte* and *Athalie*,[16] where an intemperate zeal for particular modes of worship is set off with all the pomp imaginable, and forms the predominant character of the heroes. "What is this," says the sublime Joad to Josabet, finding her in discourse with Mathan, the priest of Baal, "does the daughter of David speak to this traitor? Are you not afraid, lest the earth should open and pour forth flames to devour you both? Or lest these holy walls should fall and crush you together? What is his purpose? Why comes that enemy of God hither to poison the air, which we breathe, with his horrid presence?" Such sentiments are received with great applause on the theater of Paris; but at London the spectators would be full as much pleased to hear Achilles tell Agamemnon, that he was a dog in his forehead, and a deer in his heart, or Jupiter threaten Juno with a sound drubbing, if she will not be quiet.

Religious principles are also a blemish in any polite composition, when they rise up to superstition, and intrude themselves into every sentiment, however remote from any connection with religion. It is no excuse for the poet, that the customs of his country had burthened life with so many religious ceremonies and observances, that no part of it was exempt from that yoke. It must forever be ridiculous in Petrarch to compare his mistress Laura, to Jesus Christ. Nor is it less ridiculous in that agreeable libertine, Boccace,[17] very seriously to give thanks to God Almighty and the ladies, for their assistance in defending him against his enemies.

---

[16] *Polyeucte* by Pierre Corneille (above, page 244); *Athalie* by Jean Racine (1639–1699), French dramatist.

[17] Giovanni Boccaccio (above, page 157).

Edmund Burke

1729–1797

Edmund Burke is perhaps best known for his *Reflections on the Revolution in France* (1790), in which he is strongly critical of the revolution, and for his political career; but the *Philosophical Inquiry into the Origin of Our Ideas of the Sublime and Beautiful,* written when Burke was in his twenties, has an important place in the history of critical discourse. Burke's premises, like Addison's (above, page 307) in his essays on the pleasures of the imagination, are those of the empirical tradition of John Locke (above, page 281). He assumes that all our knowledge comes via sense experience and that we combine the simple ideas of sense into more complex ones.

For Burke, "imagination," which he calls "a sort of creative power" (what Coleridge later calls the "fancy") operates in two ways: by "representing at pleasure the images of things in the order and manner in which they were received by the senses" and by "combining those images in a new manner, and according to a different order." Thus the imagination can never produce anything "absolutely new"; it can at the most combine and reorder basic sense perceptions.

Burke's acknowledgement, like Aristotle's (above, page 53), that we take pleasure in resemblances shows his concern with the problem of imitation. He is wary of Plato's criticism of the artist as a servile copier and suggests that the painter's failure to please the shoemaker in his representation of a shoe "was no impeachment to the taste of the painter; it only showed some want of knowledge in the art of making shoes." In raising this issue, Burke is concerned primarily with the problem of taste and whether there is a single standard, a logic of taste (see his contemporary Hume on this issue, [above, page 322]). He admits that the painter and the shoemaker differ in knowledge but insists that they share something too: "the pleasure arising from a natural object, so far as each perceives it justly imitated; the satisfaction in seeing an agreeable figure; the sympathy proceeding from a striking and affecting incident." He thinks that agreements on judgments of taste are more common to men than the results of reason, though there are differences in the degree to which men possess sensibility. Burke also believes that taste improves as judgment improves through increased knowledge, attention, and exercise. He finds taste and judgment intertwined in all human activity.

The body of Burke's treatise is concerned with the ideas of the sublime and the beautiful. Here he is clearly in the debt of the Pseudo-Longinus, but his fundamental orientation is different. Longinus writes of ways of achieving sublimity in a literary work. Burke proceeds from the subjective aesthetic experience of the reader to a discussion of what causes a response that may be described as sublime:

> Whatever is fitted in any sort to excite the ideas of pain and danger, that is to say, whatever is in any sort terrible, or is conversant about terrible objects, or operates in a manner analogous to terror, is a source of the sublime; that is, it is productive of the strongest emotion which the mind is capable of feeling.

Burke on the subject of language is again Lockeian, but his emphasis is not Locke's on the danger and misuse of words but rather on the power of the poetic use of words to affect the sensibility. He points out that this power does not necessarily arise from images raised in the mind of the reader, a common notion that is many years later attacked by I. A. Richards.

The standard edition of *A Philosophical Inquiry into the Origin of Our Ideas of the Sublime and Beautiful* is that edited with a long introduction by J. T. Boulton (1958). The six-volume edition of the *Works* edited by William Willis (1936) may also be consulted. See T. M. Moore, *The Background of Burke's Theory of the Sublime* (1938); Samuel H. Monk, *The Sublime* (1938); Dixon Wecter, "Burke's Theory Concerning Words, Images, and Emotions," *PMLA* LV (1940), 167–81; Walter J. Hipple, Jr., *The Beautiful, the Sublime, and the Picturesque in Eighteenth-Century British Aesthetic Theory* (1957); Gerald Chapman, *Edmund Burke: The Practical Imagination* (1967); George W. Fasel, *Edmund Burke* (1983); Stanley Ayling, *Edmund Burke: His Life and Opinions* (1988); Tom Furniss, *Edmund Burke's Aesthetic Ideology: Language, Gender, and Political Economy in Revolution* (1993).

from

A Philosophical Inquiry Into the Origin of Our Ideas of the Sublime and Beautiful

Introduction On Taste

On a superficial view we may seem to differ very widely from each other in our reasonings, and no less in our pleasures; but, notwithstanding this difference, which I think to be rather apparent than real, it is probable that the standard both of reason and taste is the same in all human creatures. For if there were not some principles of judgment as well as of sentiment common to all mankind, no hold could possibly be taken either on their reason or their passions, sufficient to maintain the ordinary correspondence of life.[1] It appears indeed to be generally acknowledged, that with regard to truth and falsehood there is something fixed. We find people in their disputes continually appealing to certain tests and standards, which are allowed on all sides, and are supposed to be established in our common nature. But there is not the same obvious concurrence in any uniform or settled principles which relate to taste. It is even commonly supposed that this delicate and aerial faculty, which seems too volatile to endure even the chains of a definition, cannot be properly tried by any test, nor regulated by any standard. There is so continual a call for the exercise of the reasoning faculty; and it is so much strengthened by perpetual contention, that certain maxims of right reason seem to be tacitly settled amongst the most ignorant. The learned have improved on this rude science, and reduced those maxims into a system. If taste has not been so happily cultivated, it was not that the subject was barren, but that the laborers were few or negligent; for to say the truth, there are not the same interesting motives to impel us to fix the one, which urge us to ascertain the other. And, after all, if men differ in their opinions concerning such matters, their difference is not attended with the same important consequences; else I make no doubt but that the logic of taste, if I may be allowed the expression, might very possibly be as well digested, and we might come to discuss matters of this nature with as much certainty, as those which seem more immediately within the province of mere reason. And, indeed, it is very necessary, at the entrance into such an inquiry as our present, to make this point as clear as possible; for if taste has no fixed principles, if the imagination is not affected according to some invariable and certain laws, our labor is likely to be employed to very little purpose; as it must be judged a useless, if not an absurd undertaking, to lay down rules for caprice, and to set up for a legislator of whims and fancies.

A Philosophical Inquiry Into the Origin of Our Ideas of the Sublime and Beautiful was first published in 1757; a revised edition appeared in 1759. The text is based on the 1759 edition.
[1] Compare Hume, *Of the Standard of Taste* (above, page 323), published in the same year.

The term *taste,* like all other figurative terms, is not extremely accurate; the thing which we understand by it is far from a simple and determinate idea in the minds of most men, and it is therefore liable to uncertainty and confusion. I have no great opinion of a definition, the celebrated remedy for the cure of this disorder. For, when we define, we seem in danger of circumscribing nature within the bounds of our own notions, which we often take up by hazard or embrace on trust, or form out of a limited and partial consideration of the object before us, instead of extending our ideas to take in all that nature comprehends, according to her manner of combining. We are limited in our inquiry by the strict laws to which we have submitted at our setting out. *"Circa vilem patulumque morabimur orbem, / Unde pudor proferre pedem vetat aut operis lex."*[2]

A definition may be very exact, and yet go but a very little way towards informing us of the nature of the thing defined; but let the virtue of a definition be what it will, in the order of things, it seems rather to follow than to precede our inquiry, of which it ought to be considered as the result. It must be acknowledged that the methods of disquisition and teaching may be sometimes different, and on very good reason undoubtedly; but, for my part, I am convinced that the method of teaching which approaches most nearly to the method of investigation is incomparably the best; since, not content with serving up a few barren and lifeless truths, it leads to the stock on which they grew;[3] it tends to set the reader himself in the track of invention, and to direct him into those paths in which the author has made his own discoveries, if he should be so happy as to have made any that are valuable.

But to cut off all pretense for caviling, I mean by the word *taste,* no more than that faculty or those faculties of the mind, which are affected with, or which form a judgment of, the works of imagination and the elegant arts. This is, I think, the most general idea of that word, and what is the least connected with any particular theory. And my point in this inquiry is, to find whether there are any principles, on which the imagination is affected, so common to all, so grounded and certain, as to supply the means of reasoning satisfactorily about them. And such principles of taste I fancy there are; however paradoxical it may seem to those, who on a superficial view imagine that there is so great a diversity of tastes, both in kind and degree, that nothing can be more indeterminate.

All the natural powers in man, which I know, that are conversant about external objects, are the senses; the imagination; and the judgment. And first with regard to the senses. We do and we must suppose, that as the conformation of their organs are nearly or altogether the same in all men, so the manner of perceiving external objects is in all men the same, or with little difference. We are satisfied that what appears to be light to one eye, appears light to another; that what seems sweet to one palate, is sweet to another; that what is dark and bitter to this man, is likewise dark and bitter to that; and we conclude in the same manner of great and little, hard and soft, hot and cold, rough and smooth; and indeed of all the natural qualities and affections of bodies. If we suffer ourselves to imagine, that their senses present to different men different images of things, this skeptical proceeding will make every sort of reasoning on every subject vain and frivolous, even that skeptical reasoning itself which had persuaded us to entertain a doubt concerning the agreement of our perceptions. But as there will be little doubt that bodies present similar images to the whole species, it must necessarily be allowed, that the pleasures and the pains which every object excites in one man, it must raise in all mankind, whilst it operates naturally, simply, and by its proper powers only; for if we deny this, we must imagine that the same cause, operating in the same manner, and on subjects of the same kind, will produce different effects; which would be highly absurd. Let us first consider this point in the sense of taste, and the rather as the faculty in question has taken its name from that sense. All men are agreed to call vinegar sour, honey sweet, and aloes bitter; and as they are all agreed in finding these qualities in those objects, they do not in the least differ concerning their effects with regard to pleasure and pain. They all concur in calling sweetness pleasant, and sourness and bitterness unpleasant. Here there is no diversity in their sentiments; and that there is not, appears fully from the consent of all men in the metaphors which are taken from the sense of taste. A sour temper, bitter expressions, bitter curses, a bitter fate, are terms well and strongly understood by all. And we are altogether as well understood when we say, a sweet disposition, a sweet person, a sweet condition and the like. It is confessed, that custom and some other causes have made many deviations from the natural pleasures or pains which belong to these several tastes; but then the power of distinguishing between the natural and the acquired relish remains to the very last. A man frequently comes to prefer the taste of tobacco to that of sugar, and the flavor of vinegar to that of milk; but this makes no confusion in tastes, whilst he is sensible that the tobacco and vinegar are not sweet, and whilst he knows that habit alone has reconciled his palate to

[2] "We shall linger with the low and open world, from which modesty and the law of work prevent our feet from moving." Horace (above, page 79), but misquoted.
[3] Here Burke follows the empiricism of Bacon (above, page 234) and Locke (above, page 281).

these alien pleasures. Even with such a person we may speak, and with sufficient precision, concerning tastes. But should any man be found who declares, that to him tobacco has a taste like sugar, and that he cannot distinguish between milk and vinegar; or that tobacco and vinegar are sweet, milk bitter, and sugar sour; we immediately conclude that the organs of this man are out of order, and that his palate is utterly vitiated. We are as far from conferring with such a person upon tastes, as from reasoning concerning the relations of quantity with one who should deny that all the parts together were equal to the whole. We do not call a man of this kind wrong in his notions, but absolutely mad. Exceptions of this sort, in either way, do not at all impeach our general rule, nor make us conclude that men have various principles concerning the relations of quantity or the taste of things. So that when it is said, taste cannot be disputed, it can only mean, that no one can strictly answer what pleasure or pain some particular man may find from the taste of some particular thing. This indeed cannot be disputed; but we may dispute, and with sufficient clearness too, concerning the things which are naturally pleasing or disagreeable to the sense. But when we talk of any peculiar or acquired relish, then we must know the habits, the prejudices, or the distempers of this particular man, and we must draw our conclusion from those.

This agreement of mankind is not confined to the taste solely. The principle of pleasure derived from sight is the same in all. Light is more pleasing than darkness. Summer, when the earth is clad in green, when the heavens are serene and bright, is more agreeable than winter, when everything makes a different appearance. I never remember that anything beautiful, whether a man, a beast, a bird, or a plant, was ever shown, though it were to a hundred people, that they did not all immediately agree that it was beautiful, though some might have thought that it fell short of their expectation, or that other things were still finer. I believe no man thinks a goose to be more beautiful than a swan, or imagines that what they call a Friesland hen excels a peacock. It must be observed too, that the pleasures of the sight are not near so complicated, and confused, and altered by unnatural habits and associations, as the pleasures of the taste are; because the pleasures of the sight more commonly acquiesce in themselves; and are not so often altered by considerations which are independent of the sight itself. But things do not spontaneously present themselves to the palate as they do to the sight; they are generally applied to it, either as food or as medicine; and from the qualities which they possess for nutritive or medicinal purposes they often form the palate by degrees, and by force of these associations. Thus opium is pleasing to Turks, on account of the agree-

able delirium it produces. Tobacco is the delight of Dutchmen, as it diffuses a torpor and pleasing stupefaction. Fermented spirits please our common people, because they banish care, and all consideration of future or present evils. All of these, together with tea and coffee, and some other things, have passed from the apothecary's shop to our tables, and were taken for health long before they were thought of for pleasure. The effect of the drug has made us use it frequently; and frequent use, combined with the agreeable effect, has made the taste itself at last agreeable. But this does not in the least perplex our reasoning; because we distinguish to the last the acquired from the natural relish. In describing the taste of an unknown fruit, you would scarcely say that it had a sweet and pleasant flavor like tobacco, opium, or garlic, although you spoke to those who were in the constant use of these drugs, and had great pleasure in them. There is in all men a sufficient remembrance of the original natural causes of pleasure, to enable them to bring all things offered to their senses to that standard, and to regulate their feelings and opinions by it. Suppose one who had so vitiated his palate as to take more pleasure in the taste of opium than in that of butter or honey, to be presented with a bolus of squills; there is hardly any doubt but that he would prefer the butter or honey to this nauseous morsel, or to any other bitter drug to which he had not been accustomed; which proves that his palate was naturally like that of other men in all things, that it is still like the palate of other men in many things, and only vitiated in some particular points. For in judging of any new thing, even of a taste similar to that which he had been formed by habit to like, he finds his palate affected in the natural manner, and on the common principles. Thus the pleasure of all the senses, of the sight, and even of the taste, that most ambiguous of the senses, is the same in all, high and low, learned and unlearned.

Besides the ideas, with their annexed pains and pleasures, which are presented by the sense; the mind of man possesses a sort of creative power of its own; either in representing at pleasure the images of things in the order and manner in which they were received by the senses, or in combining those images in a new manner, and according to a different order. This power is called imagination;[4] and to this belongs whatever is called wit, fancy, invention, and the like. But it must be observed, that this power of the imagination is incapable of producing anything absolutely new; it can only vary the disposition of those ideas which it has

---

[4] The notion of combination corresponds to Locke's notion of complex ideas (above, page 285). Coleridge's definition of imagination (below, page 504) provides a contrast.

received from the senses. Now the imagination is the most extensive province of pleasure and pain, as it is the region of our fears and our hopes, and of all our passions that are connected with them; and whatever is calculated to affect the imagination with these commanding ideas, by force of any original natural impression, must have the same power pretty equally over all men. For since the imagination is only the representation of the senses, it can only be pleased or displeased with the images, from the same principle on which the sense is pleased or displeased with the realities; and consequently there must be just as close an agreement in the imaginations as in the senses of men. A little attention will convince us that this must of necessity be the case.

But in the imagination, besides the pain or pleasure arising from the properties of the natural object, a pleasure is perceived from the resemblance which the imitation has to the original: the imagination, I conceive, can have no pleasure but what results from one or other of these causes. And these causes operate pretty uniformly upon all men, because they operate by principles in nature, and which are not derived from any particular habits or advantages. Mr. Locke very justly and finely observes of wit, that it is chiefly conversant in tracing resemblances; he remarks, at the same time, that the business of judgment is rather in finding differences.[5] It may perhaps appear, on this supposition, that there is no material distinction between the wit and the judgment, as they both seem to result from different operations of the same faculty of comparing. But in reality, whether they are or are not dependent on the same power of the mind, they differ so very materially in many respects, that a perfect union of wit and judgment is one of the rarest things in the world. When two distinct objects are unlike to each other, it is only what we expect; things are in their common way; and therefore they make no impression on the imagination: but when two distinct objects have a resemblance, we are struck, we attend to them, and we are pleased. The mind of man has naturally a far greater alacrity and satisfaction in tracing resemblances than in searching for differences: because by making resemblances we produce new images; we unite, we create, we enlarge our stock; but in making distinctions we offer no food at all to the imagination; the task itself is more severe and irksome, and what pleasure we derive from it is something of a negative and indirect nature. A piece of news is told me in the morning; this, merely as a piece of news, as a fact added to my stock, gives me some pleasure. In the evening I find there was nothing in it. What do I gain by this, but the dissatisfaction to find that I had been imposed upon? Hence it is that men are much more naturally inclined to belief than to incredulity. And it is upon this principle, that the most ignorant and barbarous nations have frequently excelled in similitudes, comparisons, metaphors, and allegories, who have been weak and backward in distinguishing and sorting their ideas. And it is for a reason of this kind, that Homer and the oriental writers, though very fond of similitudes, and though they often strike out such as are truly admirable, seldom take care to have them exact; that is, they are taken with the general resemblance, they paint it strongly, and they take no notice of the difference which may be found between the things compared.

Now as the pleasure of resemblance is that which principally flatters the imagination, all men are nearly equal in this point, as far as their knowledge of the things represented or compared extends. The principle of this knowledge is very much accidental, as it depends upon experience and observation, and not on the strength or weakness of any natural faculty; and it is from this difference in knowledge, that what we commonly, though with no great exactness, call a difference in taste proceeds. A man to whom sculpture is new, sees a barber's block, or some ordinary piece of statuary; he is immediately struck and pleased, because he sees something like a human figure; and, entirely taken up with this likeness, he does not at all attend to its defects. No person, I believe, at the first time of seeing a piece of imitation ever did. Some time after, we suppose that this novice lights upon a more artificial work of the same nature; he now begins to look with contempt on what he admired at first; not that he admired it even then for its unlikeness to a man, but for that general though inaccurate resemblance which it bore to the human figure. What he admired at different times in these so different figures, is strictly the same; and though his knowledge is improved, his taste is not altered. Hitherto his mistake was from a want of knowledge in art, and this arose from his inexperience; but he may be still deficient from a want of knowledge in nature. For it is possible that the man in question may stop here, and that the masterpiece of a great hand may please him no more than the middling performance of a vulgar artist; and this not for want of better or higher relish, but because all men do not observe with sufficient accuracy on the human figure to enable them to judge properly of an imitation of it. And that the critical taste does not depend upon a superior principle in men, but upon superior knowledge, may appear from several instances. The story of the ancient painter and the shoemaker is very well known. The shoemaker set the painter right with regard to some mistakes he had made in the shoe of one of his figures, which the painter, who had not made such

---

[5] See Locke (above, page 281), a not uncommon notion at the time.

accurate observations on shoes, and was content with a general resemblance, had never observed. But this was no impeachment to the taste of the painter; it only showed some want of knowledge in the art of making shoes.[6] Let us imagine, that an anatomist had come into the painter's working room. His piece is in general well done, the figure in question in a good attitude, and the parts well adjusted to their various movements; yet the anatomist, critical in his art, may observe the swell of some muscle not quite just in the peculiar action of the figure. Here the anatomist observes what the painter had not observed; and he passes by what the shoemaker had remarked. But a want of the last critical knowledge in anatomy no more reflected on the natural good taste of the painter, or of any common observer of his piece, than the want of an exact knowledge in the formation of a shoe. A fine piece of a decollated head of St. John the Baptist was shown to a Turkish emperor: he praised many things, but he observed one defect: he observed that the skin did not shrink from the wounded part of the neck. The sultan on this occasion, though his observation was very just, discovered no more natural taste than the painter who executed this piece, or than a thousand European connoisseurs, who probably would have made the same observation. His Turkish majesty had indeed been well acquainted with that terrible spectacle, which the others could only have represented in their imagination. On the subject of their dislike there is a difference between all these people, arising from the different kinds and degrees of their knowledge; but there is something in common to the painter, the shoemaker, the anatomist, and the Turkish emperor, the pleasure arising from a natural object, so far as each perceives it justly imitated; the satisfaction in seeing an agreeable figure; the sympathy proceeding from a striking and affecting incident. So far as taste is natural, it is nearly common to all.

In poetry, and other pieces of imagination, the same parity may be observed. It is true, that one man is charmed with *Don Belianis,*[7] and reads Virgil coldly; whilst another is transported with the *Aeneid,* and leaves *Don Belianis* to children. These two men seem to have a taste very different from each other; but in fact they differ very little. In both these pieces, which inspire such opposite sentiments, a tale exciting admiration is told; both are full of action, both are passionate; in both are voyages, battles, triumphs, and continual changes of fortune. The admirer of *Don Belianis* perhaps does not understand the refined language of the *Aeneid,* who, if it was degraded into the style of the *Pilgrim's Progress,* might feel it in all its energy, on the same principle which made him an admirer of *Don Belianis.*

In his favorite author he is not shocked with the continual breaches of probability, the confusion of times, the offenses against manners, the trampling upon geography; for he knows nothing of geography and chronology, and he has never examined the grounds of probability. He perhaps reads of a shipwreck on the coast of Bohemia; wholly taken up with so interesting an event, and only solicitous for the fate of his hero, he is not in the least troubled at this extravagant blunder. For why should he be shocked at a shipwreck on the coast of Bohemia, who does not know but that Bohemia may be an island in the Atlantic Ocean? And after all, what reflection is this on the natural good taste of the person here supposed?[8]

So far then as taste belongs to the imagination, its principle is the same in all men; there is no difference in the manner of their being affected, nor in the causes of the affection; but in the degree there is a difference, which arises from two causes principally; either from a greater degree of natural sensibility, or from a closer and longer attention to the object. To illustrate this by the procedure of the senses, in which the same difference is found, let us suppose a very smooth marble table to be set before two men; they both perceive it to be smooth, and they are both pleased with it because of this quality. So far they agree. But suppose another, and after that another table, the latter still smoother than the former, to be set before them. It is now very probable that these men, who are so agreed upon what is smooth, and in the pleasure from thence, will disagree when they come to settle which table has the advantage in point of polish. Here is indeed the great difference between tastes, when men come to compare the excess or diminution of things which are judged by degree and not by measure. Nor is it easy, when such a difference arises, to settle the point, if the excess or diminution be not glaring. If we differ in opinion about two quantities, we can recourse to a common measure, which may decide the question with the utmost exactness; and this, I take it, is what gives mathematical knowledge a greater certainty than any other. But in things whose excess is not judged by greater or smaller, as smoothness and roughness, hardness and softness, darkness and light, the shades of colors, all these are very easily distinguished when the difference is any way considerable, but not when it is minute, for want of some common measures, which perhaps may never come to be discovered. In these nice

---

[6] Pliny (the Elder, c. 23–79), *Natural History* XXV, 84–5. Burke's use seems a criticism of Plato's complaint against the poet as imitator (above, page 25ff.).

[7] *The Famous and Delectable History of Don Belianus of Greece* (1673), an anonymous chapbook.

[8] This apparently refers to Shakespeare's *A Winter's Tale* III, iii, 2.

cases, supposing the acuteness of the sense equal, the greater attention and habit in such things will have the advantage. In the question about the tables, the marble-polisher will unquestionably determine the most accurately. But notwithstanding this want of a common measure for settling many disputes relative to the senses, and their representative the imagination, we find that the principles are the same in all, and that there is no disagreement until we come to examine into the preeminence or difference of things, which brings us within the province of the judgment.

So long as we are conversant with the sensible qualities of things, hardly any more than the imagination seems concerned; little more also than the imagination seems concerned when the passions are represented, because by the force of natural sympathy they are felt in all men without any recourse to reasoning, and their justness recognized in every breast. Love, grief, fear, anger, joy, all these passions have, in their turns, affected every mind; and they do not affect it in an arbitrary or casual manner, but upon certain, natural, and uniform principles. But as many of the works of imagination are not confined to the representation of sensible objects, nor to efforts upon the passions, but extend themselves to the manners, the characters, the actions, and designs of men, their relations, their virtues and vices, they come within the province of the judgment, which is improved by attention, and by the habit of reasoning. All these make a very considerable part of what are considered as the objects of taste; and Horace sends us to the schools of philosophy and the world for our instruction in them.[9] Whatever certainty is to be acquired in morality and the science of life; just the same degree of certainty have we in what relates to them in works of imitation. Indeed it is for the most part in our skill in manners, and in the observances of time and place, and of decency in general, which is only to be learned in those schools to which Horace recommends us, that what is called taste, by way of distinction, consists: and which is in reality no other than a more refined judgment. On the whole, it appears to me, that what is called taste, in its most general acceptation, is not a simple idea, but is partly made up of a perception of the primary pleasures of sense, of the secondary pleasures of the imagination, and of the conclusions of the reasoning faculty, concerning the various relations of these, and concerning the human passions, manners, and actions. All this is requisite to form taste, and the groundwork of all these is the same in the human mind; for as the senses are the great originals of all our ideas, and consequently of all our pleasures, if they are not uncertain

and arbitrary, the whole groundwork of taste is common to all, and therefore there is a sufficient foundation for a conclusive reasoning on these matters.

Whilst we consider taste merely according to its nature and species, we shall find its principles entirely uniform; but the degree in which these principles prevail, in the several individuals of mankind, is altogether as different as the principles themselves are similar. For sensibility and judgment, which are the qualities that compose what we commonly call a *taste,* vary exceedingly in various people. From a defect in the former of these qualities arises a want of taste; a weakness in the latter constitutes a wrong or a bad one. There are some men formed with feelings so blunt, with tempers so cold and phlegmatic, that they can hardly be said to be awake during the whole course of their lives. Upon such persons the most striking objects make but a faint and obscure impression. There are others so continually in the agitation of gross and merely sensual pleasures, or so occupied in the low drudgery of avarice, or so heated in the chase of honors and distinction, that their minds, which had been used continually to the storms of these violent and tempestuous passions, can hardly be put in motion by the delicate and refined play of the imagination. These men, though from a different cause, become as stupid and insensible as the former; but whenever either of these happen to be struck with any natural elegance or greatness, or with these qualities in any work of art, they are moved upon the same principle.

The cause of a wrong taste is a defect of judgment. And this may arise from a natural weakness of understanding (in whatever the strength of that faculty may consist), or, which is much more commonly the case, it may arise from a want of a proper and well-directed exercise, which alone can make it strong and ready. Besides, that ignorance, inattention, prejudice, rashness, levity, obstinacy, in short, all those passions, and all those vices, which pervert the judgment in other matters, prejudice it no less in this its more refined and elegant province. These causes produce different opinions upon everything which is an object of the understanding, without inducing us to suppose that there are no settled principles of reason. And indeed, on the whole, one may observe, that there is rather less difference upon matters of taste among mankind, than upon most of those which depend upon the naked reason; and that men are far better agreed on the excellence of a description in Virgil, than on the truth or falsehood of a theory of Aristotle.

A rectitude of judgment in the arts, which may be called a good taste, does in a great measure depend upon sensibility; because if the mind has no bent to the pleasures of the imagination, it will never apply itself sufficiently to

---

[9]Horace (above, page 83).

works of that species to acquire a competent knowledge of them. But though a degree of sensibility is requisite to form a good judgment, yet a good judgment does not necessarily arise from a quick sensibility to pleasure; it frequently happens that a very poor judge, merely by force of a greater complexional sensibility, is more affected by a very poor piece, than the best judge by the most perfect; for as everything new, extraordinary, grand, or passionate, is well calculated to affect such a person, and that the faults do not affect him, his pleasure is more pure and unmixed; and as it is merely a pleasure of the imagination, it is much higher than any which is derived from a rectitude of judgment; the judgment is for the greater part employed in throwing stumbling blocks in the way of the imagination, in dissipating the scenes of its enchantment, and in tying us down to the disagreeable yoke of our reason; for almost the only pleasure that men have in judging better than others, consists in a sort of conscious pride and superiority, which arises from thinking rightly; but then this is an indirect pleasure, a pleasure which does not immediately result from the object which is under contemplation. In the morning of our days, when the senses are unworn and tender, when the whole man is awake in every part, and the gloss of novelty fresh upon all the objects that surround us, how lively at that time are our sensations, but how false and inaccurate the judgments we form of things! I despair of ever receiving the same degree of pleasure from the most excellent performances of genius, which I felt at that age from pieces which my present judgment regards as trifling and contemptible. Every trivial cause of pleasure is apt to affect the man of too sanguine a complexion: his appetite is too keen to suffer his taste to be delicate; and he is in all respects what Ovid says of himself in love, *"Molle meum levibus cor est violabile telis, / Et semper causa est, cur ego semper amem."*[10] One of this character can never be a refined judge; never what the comic poet calls *"elegans formarum spectator."*[11] The excellence and force of a composition must always be imperfectly estimated from its effect on the minds of any, except we know the temper and character of those minds. The most powerful effects of poetry and music have been displayed, and perhaps are still displayed, where these arts are but in a very low and imperfect state. The rude hearer is affected by the principles which operate in these arts even in their rudest condition; and he is not skillful enough to perceive the defects. But as the arts advance toward their perfection, the science of criticism advances with equal pace, and the pleasure of judges is frequently interrupted by the faults which are discovered in the most finished compositions.

Before I leave this subject, I cannot help taking notice of an opinion which many persons entertain, as if the taste were a separate faculty of the mind, and distinct from the judgment and imagination; a species of instinct, by which we are struck naturally, and at first glance, without any previous reasoning, with the excellences or the defects of a composition. So far as the imagination and the passions are concerned, I believe it true, that the reason is little consulted; but where disposition, where decorum, where congruity are concerned, in short, wherever the best taste differs from the worst, I am convinced that the understanding operates, and nothing else; and its operation is in reality far from being always sudden, or, when it is sudden, it is often far from being right. Men of the best taste by consideration come frequently to change these early and precipitate judgments, which the mind, from its aversion to neutrality and doubt loves to form on the spot. It is known that the taste (whatever it is) is improved exactly as we improve our judgment, by extending our knowledge, by a steady attention to our object, and by frequent exercise. They who have not taken these methods, if their taste decides quickly, it is always uncertainly; and their quickness is owing to their presumption and rashness, and not to any sudden irradiation, that in a moment dispels all darkness from their minds. But they who have cultivated that species of knowledge which makes the object of taste, by degrees and habitually attain not only a soundness but a readiness of judgment, as men do by the same methods on all other occasions. At first they are obliged to spell, but at last they read with ease and with celerity; but this celerity of its operations is no proof that the taste is a distinct faculty. Nobody, I believe, has attended the course of a discussion which turned upon matters within the sphere of mere naked reason, but must have observed the extreme readiness with which the whole process of the argument is carried on, the grounds discovered, the objections raised and answered, and the conclusions drawn from premises, with a quickness altogether as great as the taste can be supposed to work with; and yet where nothing but plain reason either is or can be suspected to operate. To multiply principles for every different appearance is useless, and unphilosophical too in a high degree.

This matter might be pursued much farther; but it is not the extent of the subject which must prescribe our bounds, for what subject does not branch out to infinity? It is the nature of our particular scheme, and the single point of view in which we consider it, which ought to put a stop to our researches.

---

[10] "My soft heart is vulnerable to light darts, and there is always a reason why I am always in love." *Heroides* XV, 79–80, but misquoted.

[11] "A refined observer of forms." Terence, *Eunuch,* 566.

Part One

Section VII

Of the Sublime

Whatever is fitted in any sort to excite the ideas of pain, and danger, that is to say, whatever is in any sort terrible, or is conversant about terrible objects, or operates in a manner analogous to terror, is a source of the sublime; that is, it is productive of the strongest emotion which the mind is capable of feeling. I say the strongest emotion, because I am satisfied the ideas of pain are much more powerful than those which enter on the part of pleasure. Without all doubt, the torments which we may be made to suffer, are much greater in their effect on the body and mind, than any pleasures which the most learned voluptuary could suggest, or than the liveliest imagination, and the most sound and exquisitely sensible body could enjoy. Nay I am in great doubt, whether any man could be found who would earn a life of the most perfect satisfaction, at the price of ending it in the torments, which justice inflicted in a few hours on the late unfortunate regicide in France.[12] But as pain is stronger in its operation than pleasure, so death is in general a much more affecting idea than pain; because there are very few pains, however exquisite, which are not preferred to death; nay, what generally makes pain itself, if I may say so, more painful, is, that it is considered as an emissary of this king of terrors. When danger or pain press too nearly, they are incapable of giving any delight, and are simply terrible; but at certain distances, and with certain modifications, they may be, and they are delightful, as we every day experience.[13] The cause of this I shall endeavor to investigate hereafter.

Section X

Of Beauty

The passion which belongs to generation, merely as such, is lust only; this is evident in brutes, whose passions are more unmixed, and which pursue their purposes more directly than ours. The only distinction they observe with regard to their mates, is that of sex. It is true, that they stick severally to their own species in preference to all others. But this preference, I imagine, does not arise from any sense of beauty which they find in their species, as Mr. Addison supposes,[14] but from a law of some other kind to which they are subject; and this we may fairly conclude, from their apparent want of choice amongst those objects to which the barriers of their species have confined them. But man, who is a creature adapted to a greater variety and intricacy of relation, connects with the general passion, the idea of some social qualities, which direct and heighten the appetite which he has in common with all other animals; and as he is not designed like them to live at large, it is fit that he should have something to create a preference, and fix his choice, and this in general should be some sensible quality; as no other can so quickly, so powerfully, or so surely produce its effect. The object therefore of this mixed passion which we call love, is the beauty of the sex. Men are carried to the sex in general, as it is the sex, and by the common law of nature; but they are attached to particulars by personal beauty. I call beauty a social quality; for where women and men, and not only they, but when other animals give us a sense of joy and pleasure in beholding them (and there are many that do so), they inspire us with sentiments of tenderness and affection towards their persons; we like to have them near us, and we enter willingly into a kind of relation with them, unless we should have strong reasons to the contrary. But to what end, in many cases, this was designed, I am unable to discover; for I see no greater reason for a connection between man and several animals who are attired in so engaging a manner, than between him and some others who entirely want this attraction, or possess it in a far weaker degree. But it is probable, that providence did not make even this distinction, but with a view to some great end, though we cannot perceive distinctly what it is, as his wisdom is not our wisdom, nor our ways his ways.

Part Three

Section XXVII

The Sublime and Beautiful Compared

On closing this general view of beauty, it naturally occurs, that we should compare it with the sublime; and in this comparison there appears a remarkable contrast. For sublime objects are vast in their dimensions, beautiful ones comparatively small; beauty should be smooth, and polished; the great, rugged and negligent; beauty should shun the right line, yet deviate from it insensibly; the great in many cases loves the right line, and when it deviates, it often makes a strong deviation; beauty should not be obscure; the great ought to be dark and gloomy; beauty should be light and delicate; the

---

[12]Robert Damiens (1714–1757), who attempted to murder Louis XV of France and was tortured to death.
[13]This is a matter that Addison tried to deal with (above, page 311).
[14]In *The Spectator*, No. 413.

great ought to be solid, and even massive. They are indeed ideas of a very different nature, one being founded on pain, the other on pleasure; and however they may vary afterwards from the direct nature of their causes, yet these causes keep up an eternal distinction between them, a distinction never to be forgotten by any whose business it is to affect the passions. In the infinite variety of natural combinations we must expect to find the qualities of things the most remote imaginable from each other united in the same object. We must expect also to find combinations of the same kind in the works of art. But when we consider the power of an object upon our passions, we must know that when anything is intended to affect the mind by the force of some predominant property, the affection produced is like to be the more uniform and perfect, if all the other properties or qualities of the object be of the same nature, and tending to the same design as the principal; "If black, and white blend, soften, and unite, / A thousand ways, are there no black and white?"[15] If the qualities of the sublime and beautiful are sometimes united, does this prove, that they are the same, does it prove, that they are any way allied, does it prove even that they are not opposite and contradictory? Black and white may soften, may blend, but they are not therefore the same. Nor when they are so softened and blended with each other, or with different colors, is the power of black as black, or of white as white, so strong as when each stands uniform and distinguished.

Part Five

Section I

Of Words

Natural objects affect us, by the laws of that connection, which Providence has established between certain motions and configurations of bodies, and certain consequent feelings in our minds. Painting affects in the same manner, but with the superadded pleasure of imitation. Architecture affects by the laws of nature, and the law of reason; from which latter result the rules of proportion, which make a work to be praised or censured, in the whole or in some part, when the end for which it was designed is or is not properly answered. But as to words; they seem to me to affect us in a manner very different from that in which we are affected by natural objects, or by painting or architecture; yet words have as considerable a share in exciting ideas of beauty and of the sublime as any of those, and sometimes a much

greater than any of them; therefore an enquiry into the manner by which they excite such emotions is far from being unnecessary in a discourse of this kind.

Section II

The Common Effect of Poetry, Not by Raising Ideas of Things

The common notion of the power of poetry and eloquence, as well as that of words in ordinary conversation, is; that they affect the mind by raising in it ideas of those things for which custom has appointed them to stand. To examine the truth of this notion, it may be requisite to observe that words may be divided into three sorts.[16] The first are such as represent many simple ideas *united by nature* to form some one determinate composition, as man, horse, tree, castle, &c. These I call *aggregate words.* The second, are they that stand for one simple idea of such compositions and no more; as red, blue, round, square, and the like. These I call *simple abstract* words. The third, are those, which are formed by an union, an *arbitrary* union of both the others, and of the various relations between them, in greater or lesser degrees of complexity; as virtue, honour, persuasion, magistrate, and the like. These I call *compounded abstract* words. Words, I am sensible, are capable of being classed into more curious distinctions; but these seem to be natural, and enough for our purpose; and they are disposed in that order in which they are commonly taught, and in which the mind gets the ideas they are substituted for. I shall begin with the third sort of words; compound abstracts, such as virtue, honour, persuasion, docility. Of these I am convinced, that whatever power they may have on the passions, they do not derive it from any representation raised in the mind of the things for which they stand. As compositions, they are not real essences, and hardly cause, I think, any real ideas. No body, I believe, immediately on hearing the sounds, virtue, liberty, or honour, conceives any precise notion of the particular modes of action and thinking, together with the mixt and simple ideas, and the several relations of them for which these words are substituted; neither has he any general idea, compounded of them; for if he had, then some of those particular ones, though indistinct perhaps, and confused, might come soon to be perceived. But this, I take it, is hardly ever the case. For put yourself upon analysing one of these words, and you must reduce it from one set of general words to another, and then into the simple

---

[15] Alexander Pope, *Essay on Man* II, 213–4, but misquoted.

[16] The threefold classification is similar to Locke's (above, page 282).

abstracts and aggregates, in a much longer series than may be at first imagined, before any real idea emerges to light, before you come to discover any thing like the first principles of such compositions; and when you have made such a discovery of the original ideas, the effect of the composition is utterly lost. A train of thinking of this sort, is much too long to be pursued in the ordinary ways of conversation, nor is it at all necessary that it should. Such words are in reality but mere sounds; but they are sounds, which being used on particular occasions, wherein we receive some good, or suffer some evil, or see others affected with good or evil; or which we hear applied to other interesting things or events; and being applied in such a variety of cases that we know readily by habit to what things they belong, they produce in the mind, whenever they are afterwards mentioned, effects similar to those of their occasions. The sounds being often used without reference to any particular occasion, and carrying still their first impressions, they at last utterly lose their connection with the particular occasions that gave rise to them; yet the sound without any annexed notion continues to operate as before.

Section III

General Words Before Ideas

Mr Locke has somewhere observed with his usual sagacity, that most general words, those belonging to virtue and vice, good and evil, especially, are taught before the particular modes of action to which they belong are presented to the mind; and with them, the love of the one, and the abhorrence of the other; for the minds of children are so ductile, that a nurse, or any person about a child, by seeming pleased or displeased with any thing, or even any word, may give the disposition of the child a similar turn.[17] When afterwards, the several occurrences in life come to be applied to these words; and that which is pleasant often appears under the name of evil; and what is disagreeable to nature is called good and virtuous; a strange confusion of ideas and affections arises in the minds of many; and an appearance of no small contradiction between their notions and their actions. There are many, who love virtue, and who detest vice, and this not from hypocrisy or affection, who notwithstanding very frequently act ill and wickedly in particulars without the least remorse; because these particular occasions never came into view, when the passions on the side of virtue were so warmly affected by certain words

heated originally by the breath of others; and for this reason, it is hard to repeat certain sets of words, though owned by themselves unoperative, without being in some degree affected, especially if a warm and affecting tone of voice accompanies them, as suppose,

Wise, valiant, generous, good and great.

These words, by having no application, ought to be unoperative; but when words commonly sacred to great occasions are used, we are affected by them even without the occasions. When words which have been generally so applied are put together without any rational view, or in such a manner that they do not rightly agree with each other, the stile is called bombast. And it requires in several cases much good sense and experience to be guarded against the force of such language; for when propriety is neglected, a greater number of these affecting words may be taken into the service, and a greater variety may be indulged in combining them.

Section IV

The Effect of Words

If words have all their possible extent of power, three effects arise in the mind of the hearer. The first is, the *sound;* the second, the *picture,* or representation of the thing signified by the sound; the third is, the *affection* of the soul produced by one or by both of the foregoing. *Compounded abstract words,* of which we have been speaking, (honour, justice, liberty, and the like,) produce the first and the last of these effects, but not the second. *Simple abstracts,* are used to signify some one simple idea without much adverting to others which may chance to attend it, as blue, green, hot, cold, and the like; these are capable of affecting all three of the purposes of words; as the *aggregate* words, man, castle, horse, &c. are in a yet higher degree. But I am of opinion, that the most general effect even of these words, does not arise from their forming pictures of the several things they would represent in the imagination; because on a very diligent examination of my own mind, and getting others to consider theirs, I do not find that once in twenty times any such picture is formed, and when it is, there is most commonly a particular effort of the imagination for that purpose.[18] But

---

[17]Locke, *Essay* III, v, 15; ix, 9.

[18]This notion is similar to that of I. A. Richards in his *Practical Criticism* (1929), where he observes that many readers do not form pictures in their minds when reading poems and this does not seem to affect their judgment or appreciation.

the aggregate words operate as I said of the compound abstracts, not by presenting any image to the mind, but by having from use the same effect on being mentioned, that their original has when it is seen. Suppose we were to read a passage to this effect. "The river Danube rises in a moist and mountainous soil in the heart of Germany, where winding to and fro it waters several principalities, until turning into Austria and leaving the walls of Vienna it passes into Hungary; there with a vast flood augmented by the Saave and the Drave it quits Christendom, and rolling through the barbarous countries which border on Tartary, it enters by many mouths into the Black sea." In this description many things are mentioned, as mountains, rivers, cities, the sea, &c. But let anybody examine himself, and see whether he has had impressed on his imagination any pictures of a river, mountain, watery soil, Germany, &c. Indeed it is impossible, in the rapidity and quick succession of words in conversation, to have ideas both of the sound of the word, and of the thing represented; besides, some words expressing real essences, are so mixed with others of a general and nominal import, that it is impracticable to jump from sense to thought, from particulars to generals, from things to words, in such a manner as to answer the purposes of life; nor is it necessary that we should.

Section V

Examples that Words May Affect Without Raising Images

I find it very hard to persuade several that their passions are affected by words from whence they have no ideas; and yet harder to convince them, that in the ordinary course of conversation we are sufficiently understood without raising any images of the things concerning which we speak. It seems to be an odd subject of dispute with any man, whether he has ideas in his mind or not. Of this at first view, every man, in his own forum, ought to judge without appeal. But strange as it may appear, we are often at a loss to know what ideas we have of things, or whether we have any ideas at all upon some subjects. It even requires a good deal of attention to be thoroughly satisfied on this head. Since I wrote these papers I found two very striking instances of the possibility there is, that a man may hear words without having any idea of the things which they represent, and yet afterwards be capable of returning them to others, combined in a new way, and with great propriety, energy and instruction. The first instance, is that of Mr. Blacklock, a poet blind from his birth. Few men blessed with the most perfect sight can describe

visual objects with more spirit and justness than this blind man; which cannot possibly be attributed to his having a clearer conception of the things he describes than is common to other persons. Mr. Spence, in an elegant preface which he has written to the works of this poet, reasons very ingeniously, and I imagine for the most part very rightly upon the cause of this extraordinary phenomenon; but I cannot altogether agree with him, that some improprieties in language and thought which occur in these poems have arisen from the blind poet's imperfect conception of visual objects, since such improprieties, and much greater, may be found in writers even of an higher class than Mr. Blacklock, and who, notwithstanding, possessed the faculty of seeing in its full perfection.[19] Here is a poet doubtless as much affected by his own descriptions as any that reads them can be; and yet he is affected with this strong enthusiasm by things of which he neither has, nor can possibly have any idea further than that of a bare sound; and why may not those who read his works be affected in the same manner that he was, with as little of any real ideas of the things described? The second instance is of Mr. Saunderson, professor of mathematics in the university of Cambridge. This learned man had acquired great knowledge in natural philosophy, in astronomy, and whatever sciences depend upon mathematical skill. What was the most extraordinary, and the most to my purpose, he gave excellent lectures upon light and colours; and this man taught others the theory of those ideas which they had, and which he himself undoubtedly had not.[20] But it is probable, that the words red, blue, green, answered to him as well as the ideas of the colours themselves; for the ideas of greater or lesser degrees of refrangibility being applied to these words, and the blind man being instructed in what other respects they were found to agree or to disagree, it was as easy for him to reason upon the words as if he had been fully master of the ideas. Indeed it must be owned he could make no new discoveries in the way of experiment. He did nothing but what we do every day in common discourse. When I wrote this last sentence, and used the words *every day* and *common discourse,* I had no images in my mind of any succession of time; nor of men in conference with each other; nor do I imagine that the reader will have any such ideas on reading it. Neither when I spoke of red, blue, and green, as well as of refrangibility;

---

[19]Thomas Blalock (1721–1791), author of *Poems* (1746), was blinded at the age of six months. Burke refers to Joseph Spence's *Account of the Life, Character, and Poems of Mr. Blalock* (1754).
[20]Nicholas Saunderson (1682–1739), professor of mathematics at Cambridge, had lost his eyesight early in life. He published *Elements of Algebra* in 1740.

had I these several colours, or the rays of light passing into a different medium, and there diverted from their course, painted before me in the way of images. I know very well that the mind possesses a faculty of raising such images at pleasure; but then an act of the will is necessary to this; and in ordinary conversation or reading it is very rarely that any image at all is excited in the mind. If I say, "I shall go to Italy next summer," I am well understood. Yet I believe no body has by this painted in his imagination the exact figure of the speaker passing by land or by water, or both; sometimes on horseback, sometimes in a carriage; with all the particulars of the journey. Still less has he any idea of Italy, the country to which I proposed to go; or of the greenness of the fields, the ripening of the fruits, and the warmth of the air, with the change to this from a different season, which are the ideas for which the word *summer* is substituted; but least of all has he any image from the word *next;* for this word stands for the idea of many summers, with the exclusion of all but one: and surely the man who says *next summer,* has no images of such a succession, and such an exclusion. In short, it is not only of those ideas which are commonly called abstract, and of which no image at all *can* be formed, but even of particular real beings, that we converse without having any idea of them excited in the imagination; as will certainly appear on a diligent examination of our own minds. Indeed so little does poetry depend for its effect on the power of raising sensible images, that I am convinced it would lose a very considerable part of its energy, if this were the necessary result of all description. Because that union of affecting words which is the most powerful of all poetical instruments, would frequently lose its force along with its propriety and consistency, if the sensible images were always excited. There is not perhaps in the whole Eneid a more grand and laboured passage, than the description of Vulcan's cavern in Etna, and the works that are there carried on. Virgil dwells particularly on the formation of the thunder which he describes unfinished under the hammers of the Cyclops. But what are the principles of this extraordinary composition?

> *Tres imbris torti radios, tres nubis aquosae*
> *Addiderant; rutili tres ignis et alitis austri;*
> *Fulgores nunc terrificos, sonitumque, metumque*
> *Miscebant operi, flammisque sequacibus iras.*[21]

This seems to me admirably sublime; yet if we attend coolly to the kind of sensible image which a combination of ideas of this sort must form, the chimeras of madmen cannot appear more wild and absurd than such a picture. *"Three rays of twisted showers, three of watery clouds, three of fire, and three of the winged south wind; then mixed they in the work terrific lightnings, and sound, and fear, and anger, with pursuing flames."* This strange composition is formed into a gross body; it is hammered by the Cyclops, it is in part polished, and partly continues rough. The truth is, if poetry gives us a noble assemblage of words, corresponding to many noble ideas, which are connected by circumstances of time or place, or related to each other as cause and effect, or associated in any natural way, they may be moulded together in any form, and perfectly answer their end. The picturesque connection is not demanded; because no real picture is formed; nor is the effect of the description at all the less upon this account. What is said of Helen by Priam and the old men of his council, is generally thought to give us the highest possible idea of that fatal beauty.

> οὐ νέμεσις Τρῶας καὶ ἐϋκνήμιδας ᾿Αχαιοὺς
> τοιῆδ᾽ ἀμφὶ γυναικὶ πολὺν χρόνον ἄλγεα πάσχειν·
> αἰνῶς ἀθανάτῃσι θεῆς εἰς ὦπα ἔοικεν.[22]

> *They cry'd, no wonder such celestial charms*
> *For nine long years have set the world in arms;*
> *What winning graces! what majestic mien!*
> *She moves a goddess, and she looks a queen.*   POPE.

Here is not one word said of the particulars of her beauty; nothing which can in the least help us to any precise idea of her person; but yet we are much more touched by this manner of mentioning her than by these long and laboured descriptions of Helen, whether handed down by tradition, or formed by fancy, which are to be met with in some authors. I am sure it affects me much more than the minute description which Spenser has given of Belphebe;[23] though I own that there are parts in that description, as there are in all the descriptions of that excellent writer, extremely fine and poetical. The terrible picture which Lucretius has drawn of religion, in order to display the magnanimity of his philosophical hero in opposing her, is thought to be designed with great boldness and spirit.

> *Humana ante oculos fœdè cum vita jaceret,*
> *In terris, oppressa gravi sub religione,*
> *Quæ caput e caeli regionibus ostendebat*
> *Horribili desuper visu mortalibus instans;*

---

[21]*Aeneid* VIII, 429–32.

[22]*Iliad* III, 156–8.
[23]Edmund Spenser (1552?–1599), *The Faerie Queene* II, iii, 21–31.

Primus Graius homo mortales tollere contra
Est oculos ausus.———[24]

What idea do you derive from so excellent a picture? none at all most certainly; neither has the poet said a single word which might in the least serve to mark a single limb or feature of the phantom, which he intended to represent in all the horrors imagination can conceive. In reality poetry and rhetoric do not succeed in exact description so well as painting does; their business is to affect rather by sympathy than imitation; to display rather the effect of things on the mind of the speaker, or of others, than to present a clear idea of the things themselves. This is their most extensive province, and that in which they succeed the best.

Section VI

Poetry Not Strictly an Imitative Art

Hence we may observe that poetry, taken in its most general sense, cannot with strict propriety be called an art of imitation. It is indeed an imitation so far as it describes the manners and passions of men which their words can express; where *animi motus effert interprete lingua.*[25] There it is strictly imitation; and all merely *dramatic* poetry is of this sort. But *descriptive* poetry operates chiefly by *substitution;* by the means of sounds, which by custom have the effect of realities. Nothing is an imitation further than as it resembles some other thing; and words undoubtedly have no sort of resemblance to the ideas for which they stand.

Section VII

How Words Influence the Passions

Now, as words affect, not by any original power, but by representation, it might be supposed, that their influence over the passions should be but light; yet it is quite otherwise; for we find by experience that eloquence and poetry are as capable, nay indeed much more capable of making deep and lively impressions than any other arts, and even than nature itself in very many cases. And this arises chiefly from these three causes. First, that we take an extraordinary part in the passions of others, and that we are easily affected and brought into sympathy by any tokens which are shewn of them; and there are no tokens which can express all the circumstances of most passions so fully as words; so that if a person speaks upon any subject, he can not only convey the subject to you, but likewise the manner in which he is himself affected by it. Certain it is, that the influence of most things on our passions is not so much from the things themselves, as from our opinions concerning them; and these again depend very much on the opinions of other men, conveyable for the most part by words only. Secondly; there are many things of a very affecting nature, which can seldom occur in the reality, but the words which represent them often do; and thus they have an opportunity of making a deep impression and taking root in the mind, whilst the idea of the reality was transient; and to some perhaps never really occurred in any shape, to whom it is notwithstanding very affecting, as war, death, famine, &c. Besides, many ideas have never been at all presented to the senses of any men but by words, as God, angels, devils, heaven and hell, all of which have however a great influence over the passions. Thirdly; by words we have it in our power to make such *combinations* as we cannot possibly do otherwise. By this power of combining we are able, by the addition of well-chosen circumstances, to give a new life and force to the simple object. In painting we may represent any fine figure we please; but we never can give it those enlivening touches which it may receive from words. To represent an angel in a picture, you can only draw a beautiful young man winged; but what painting can furnish out any thing so grand as the addition of one word, "the angel of the *Lord?*" It is true, I have here no clear idea, but these words affect the mind more than the sensible image did, which is all I contend for. A picture of Priam dragged to the altar's foot, and there murdered, if it were well executed would undoubtedly be very moving; but there are very aggravating circumstances which it could never represent.

Sanguine faedantem quos ipse sacraverat *ignes.*[26]

As a further instance, let us consider those lines of Milton, where he describes the travels of the fallen angels through their dismal habitation,

---

[24] Lucretius (Titus Lucretius Carus, c. 99–c. 55 B.C.), *On the Nature of Things* I, 62–7, but misquoted. "Whilst human kind/Throughout the lands lay miserably crushed/Before all eyes beneath Religion—who/Would show her head along the region skies,/Glowering on mortals with her hideous face—/A Greek it was who first opposing dared/Raise mortal eyes that terror to withstand." Leonard translation.

[25] Horace, *Art of Poetry* (above, page 80).

[26] Virgil, *Aeneid* II, 502.

————*O'er many a dark and dreary vale*
They pass'd, and many a region dolorous;
O'er many a frozen, many a fiery Alp;
Rock, caves, lakes, fens, bogs, dens and shades of death,
A universe of death.[27]

Here is displayed the force of union in

Rocks, caves, lakes, dens, bogs, fens and shades;

which yet would lose the greatest part of their effect, if they were not the

Rocks, caves, lakes, dens, bogs, fens and shades————
————*of* Death.

This idea or this affection caused by a word, which nothing but a word could annex to the others, raises a very great degree of the sublime; and this sublime is raised yet higher by what follows, a *"universe of Death."* Here are again two ideas not presentable but by language; and an union of them great and amazing beyond conception; if they may properly be called ideas which present no distinct image to the mind;—but still it will be difficult to conceive how words can move the passions which belong to real objects, without representing these objects clearly. This is difficult to us, because we do not sufficiently distinguish, in our observations upon language, between a clear expression, and a strong expression. These are frequently confounded with each other, though they are in reality extremely different. The former regards the understanding; the latter belongs to the passions. The one describes a thing as it is; the other describes it as it is felt. Now, as there is a moving tone of voice, an impassioned countenance, an agitated gesture, which affect independently of the things about which they are exerted, so there are words, and certain dispositions of words, which being peculiarly devoted to passionate subjects, and always used by those who are under the influence of any passion; they touch and move us more than those which far more clearly and distinctly express the subject matter. We yield to sympathy, what we refuse to descrip-

tion. The truth is, all verbal description, merely as naked description, though never so exact, conveys so poor and insufficient an idea of the thing described, that it could scarcely have the smallest effect, if the speaker did not call in to his aid those modes of speech that mark a strong and lively feeling in himself. Then, by the contagion of our passions, we catch a fire already kindled in another, which probably might never have been struck out by the object described. Words, by strongly conveying the passions, by those means which we have already mentioned, fully compensate for their weakness in other respects. It may be observed that very polished languages, and such as are praised for their superior clearness and perspicuity, are generally deficient in strength. The French language has that perfection, and that defect. Whereas the oriental tongues, and in general the languages of most unpolished people, have a great force and energy of expression; and this is but natural. Uncultivated people are but ordinary observers of things, and not critical in distinguishing them; but, for that reason, they admire more, and are more affected with what they see, and therefore express themselves in a warmer and more passionate manner. If the affection be well conveyed, it will work its effect without any clear idea; often without any idea at all of the thing which has originally given rise to it.

It might be expected from the fertility of the subject, that I should consider poetry as it regards the sublime and beautiful more at large; but it must be observed that in this light it has been often and well handled already. It was not my design to enter into the criticism of the sublime and beautiful in any art, but to attempt to lay down such principles as may tend to ascertain, to distinguish, and to form a sort of standard for them; which purposes I thought might be best effected by an enquiry into the properties of such things in nature as raise love and astonishment in us; and by shewing in what manner they operated to produce these passions. Words were only so far to be considered, as to shew upon what principle they were capable of being the representatives of these natural things, and by what powers they were able to affect us often as strongly as the things they represent, and sometimes much more strongly.

[27] *Paradise Lost* II, 618–22.

Edward Young

1683–1765

The poet Edward Young is probably best known for his poem *Night Thoughts,* in nine "nights," but his *Conjectures on Original Composition* is a classic of its kind. In it Young foreshadows two tendencies that flowered later in Romanticism. First, he turns from interest in the relation of poem to reader to that between author and poem. This is particularly evident in Young's advice to critics: know thyself and reverence thyself, and his emphasis on personal genius. Second, he turns from concerns with rules and conventions to interest in originality. His emphasis is on what later comes to be called the artist's subjectivity. An example of how these views are reflected in Young's essay is his criticism of imitation, by which he means, as did Horace (above, page 78), imitation of preceding authors, mainly the ancients. If imitation is to remain a fundamental critical notion, its proper object must not be a predecessor's work but his "taste" and, as in Pseudo-Longinus (above, page 103), his "spirit." Young's aim is to change the main preoccupations of criticism as it has been practiced by the neoclassicists, and to emphasize the uniqueness of personal genius and the element of poetry that is "beyond prose reason." He does not distinguish poetry from prose by an analysis of language; he does not have a theory of language adequate to that task. Rather, he evokes the elements alleged to be properly characteristic of a good author.

It is not surprising that Young embroils himself in the old controversy about the ancients and moderns. Although he argues that the ancients excelled the moderns, he does not believe that a modern who is equal or even superior to the ancients is an impossibility. Slavish adherence to the ways of the ancients (his negative version of imitation) has suppressed innate genius and diminished the modern capacity for greatness. But genius, nevertheless, can appear at any time. This is not to say that one should be ignorant of the classics. They are properly part of one's education.

Young also foreshadows Romanticism in his use of metaphors of organicism and natural growth when he describes original composition: "The mind of a man of genius is a fertile and pleasant field. . . . An original may be said to be of a vegetable nature; it rises spontaneously from the vital root of genius. It grows, it is not made."

The *Poetical Works* of Young were edited in two volumes by John Mitford (1844). *Conjectures on Original Composition in a Letter to the Author of* Sir Charles Grandison has been edited by E. J. Morley (1981). See H. C. Shelley, *The Life and Letters of Edward Young* (1914); Isabel St. John Bliss, *Edward Young* (1969); Joel Weinsheimer, *Imitation* (1984).

from

Conjectures on Original Composition

In a Letter to the Author of

Sir Charles Grandison

Dear Sir,

We confess the follies of youth without a blush; not so, those of age. However, keep me a little in countenance, by considering, that age wants amusements more, though it can justify them less, than the preceding periods of life. How you may relish the pastime here sent you, I know not. It is miscellaneous in its nature, somewhat licentious in its conduct; and, perhaps, not overimportant in its end. However, I have endeavored to make some amends, by digressing into subjects more important, and more suitable to my season of life. A serious thought standing single among many of a lighter nature, will sometimes strike the careless wanderer after amusement only, with useful awe: as monumental marbles scattered in a wide pleasure-garden (and such there are) will call to recollection those who would never have sought it in a churchyard-walk of mournful yews.

To one such monument I may conduct you, in which is a hidden luster, like the sepulchral lamps of old; but not like those will this be extinguished, but shine the brighter for being produced, after so long concealment, into open day.

You remember that your worthy patron, and our common friend, put some questions on the serious drama, at the same time when he desired our sentiments on original, and on moral composition. Though I despair of breaking through the frozen obstructions of age, and care's incumbent cloud, into that flow of thought, and brightness of expression, which subjects so polite require; yet will I hazard some conjectures on them.

I begin with original composition; and the more willingly, as it seems an original subject to me, who have seen nothing hitherto written on it: but, first, a few thoughts on composition in general. Some are of opinion, that its growth, at present, is too luxuriant; and that the press is

overcharged. Overcharged, I think, it could never be, if none were admitted, but such as brought their imprimatur from sound understanding, and the public good. Wit, indeed, however brilliant, should not be permitted to gaze self-enamored on its useless charms, in that fountain of fame (if so I may call the press), if beauty is all that it has to boast; but, like the first Brutus,[1] it should sacrifice its most darling offspring to the sacred interests of virtue, and real service of mankind.

This restriction allowed, the more composition the better. To men of letters, and leisure, it is not only a noble amusement, but a sweet refuge; it improves their parts, and promotes their peace: It opens a back door out of the bustle of this busy, and idle world, into a delicious garden of moral and intellectual fruits and flowers; the key of which is denied to the rest of mankind. When stung with idle anxieties, or teased with fruitless impertinence, or yawning over insipid diversions, then we perceive the blessing of a lettered recess. With what a gust do we retire to our disinterested, and immortal friends in our closet, and find our minds, when applied to some favorite theme, as naturally, and as easily quieted, and refreshed, as a peevish child (and peevish children are we all till we fall asleep) when laid to the breast? Our happiness no longer lives on charity; nor bids fair for a fall, by leaning on that most precarious, and thorny pillow, another's pleasure, for our repose. How independent of the world is he, who can daily find new acquaintance, that at once entertain, and improve him, in the little world, the minute but fruitful creation, of his own mind?

These advantages composition affords us, whether we write ourselves, or in more humble amusement peruse the works of others. While we bustle through the thronged walks of public life, it gives us a respite, at least, from care; a pleasing pause of refreshing recollection. If the country is our choice, or fate, there it rescues us from sloth and sensuality, which, like obscene vermin, are apt gradually to creep unperceived into the delightful bowers of our retirement, and to poison all its sweets. Conscious guilt robs the rose of its scent, the lily of its luster; and makes an Eden a deflowered, and dismal scene.

Moreover, if we consider life's endless evils, what can be more prudent, than to provide for consolation under them? A consolation under them the wisest of men have found in the pleasures of the pen. Witness, among many more, Thucydides, Xenophon, Tully, Ovid, Seneca, Pliny the younger, who says *"In uxoris infirmitate, et amicorum periculo, aut morte turbatus, ad studia, unicum doloris*

Conjectures on Original Composition was first published in 1759. The author of the novel *Sir Charles Grandison* (1753) was Young's friend Samuel Richardson, who suggested the essay and helped him revise it for publication.

---

[1]Lucius Junius Brutus (sixth to fifth centuries B.C.), the first Roman consul, is said to have put his two sons to death for their participation in a conspiracy.

levamentum, confugio."[2] And why not add to these their modern equals, Chaucer, Raleigh, Bacon, Milton, Clarendon,[3] under the same shield, unwounded by misfortune, and nobly smiling in distress?

Composition was a cordial to these under the frowns of fortune; but evils there are, which her smiles cannot prevent, or cure. Among these are the languors of old age. If those are held honorable, who in a hand benumbed by time have grasped the just sword in defense of their country; shall they be less esteemed, whose unsteady pen vibrates to the last in the cause of religion, of virtue, of learning? Both these are happy in this, that by fixing their attention on objects most important, they escape numberless little anxieties, and that *tedium vitae*[4] which often hangs so heavy on its evening hours. May not this insinuate some apology for my spilling ink, and spoiling paper, so late in life?

But there are, who write with vigor, and success, to the world's delight, and their own renown. These are the glorious fruits where genius prevails. The mind of a man of genius is a fertile and pleasant field, pleasant as Elysium, and fertile as Tempe;[5] it enjoys a perpetual spring. Of that spring, originals are the fairest flowers: imitations are of quicker growth, but fainter bloom. Imitations are of two kinds; one of nature, one of authors: the first we call originals, and confine the term imitation to the second. I shall not enter into the curious inquiry of what is, or is not, strictly speaking, original, content with what all must allow, that some compositions are more so than others; and the more they are so, I say, the better. Originals are, and ought to be, great favorites, for they are great benefactors; they extend the republic of letters, and add a new province to its dominion: imitators only give us a sort of duplicates of what we had, possibly much better, before; increasing the mere drug of books, while all that makes them valuable, knowledge and genius, are at a stand. The pen of an original writer, like Armida's wand,[6] out of a barren waste calls a blooming spring: out of that blooming spring an imitator is a transplanter of laurels, which sometimes die on removal, always languish in a foreign soil.

But suppose an imitator to be most excellent (and such there are), yet still he but nobly builds on another's foundation; his debt is, at least, equal to his glory; which therefore, on the balance, cannot be very great. On the contrary, an original, though but indifferent (its originality being set aside), yet has something to boast; it is something to say with him in Horace, *"Meo sum pauper in aere";*[7] and to share ambition with no less than Caesar, who declared he had rather be the first in a village, than the second at Rome.

Still farther: an imitator shares his crown, if he has one, with the chosen object of his imitation; an original enjoys an undivided applause. An original may be said to be of a vegetable nature; it rises spontaneously from the vital root of genius;[8] it grows, it is not made: imitations are often a sort of manufacture wrought up by those mechanics, art, and labor, out of preexistent materials not their own.

Again: we read imitation with somewhat of his languor, who listens to a twice-told tale: our spirits rouse at an original; that is a perfect stranger, and all throng to learn what news from a foreign land: And though it comes, like an Indian prince, adorned with feathers only, having little of weight; yet of our attention it will rob the more solid, if not equally new: Thus every telescope is lifted at a new-discovered star; it makes a hundred astronomers in a moment, and denies equal notice to the sun. But if an original, by being as excellent, as new, adds admiration to surprise, then are we at the writer's mercy; on the strong wing of his imagination, we are snatched from Britain to Italy, from climate to climate, from pleasure to pleasure; we have no home, no thought, of our own; till the magician drops his pen: and then falling down into ourselves, we awake to flat realities, lamenting the change, like the beggar who dreamt himself a prince.

It is with thoughts, as it is with words; and with both, as with men; they may grow old, and die. Words tarnished, by passing through the mouths of the vulgar, are laid aside as inelegant, and obsolete. So thoughts, when become too common, should lose their currency; and we should send new metal to the mint, that is, new meaning to the press. The division of tongues at Babel did not more effectually debar men from making themselves a name (as the Scripture speaks) than the too great concurrence, or union of tongues will do forever. We may as well grow good by another's virtue, or fat by another's food, as famous by another's thought. The world will pay its debt of praise but once; and instead of applauding, explode a second demand, as a cheat.

---

[2] Thucydides (c. 457–c. 401 B.C.) and Xenophon (c. 430–c. 359 B.C.), Greek historians; Tully (Cicero, see above, p. 74); Lucius Annaeus Seneca (c. 3 B.C.–c. 65 A.D.), Roman philosopher and dramatist; Caius Plinius Secundus (62?–c. 113), Roman orator and statesman: "With my wife ill, and my friends in danger, and troubled by death, I flee to studies, the single comfort of sorrow." *Epistles* VIII, 19.

[3] Geoffrey Chaucer (1340?–1400), Sir Walter Raleigh (1552–1618), Sir Francis Bacon (above, page 234), John Milton (1608–1674), Edward Hyde, Earl of Clarendon (1609–1674), all English literary men.

[4] "Tedium of life."

[5] Elysium, in Greek myth the place of virtuous souls after death; Tempe, valley in Greece sacred to Apollo.

[6] Arminda is a character in Torquato Tasso's *Gerusalemme Liberato.*

---

[7] "I am poor in my property," that is, poor but not in debt. *Epistles* II, ii, 12.

[8] For a discussion of later organic metaphors for the imagination, see M. H. Abrams, *The Mirror and the Lamp: Romantic Theory and the Critical Tradition* (1953), esp. 201 ff.

If it is said, that most of the Latin classics, and all the Greek, except perhaps, Homer, Pindar, and Anacreon,[9] are in the number of imitators, yet receive our highest applause; our answer is, that they though not real, are accidental originals; the works they imitated, few excepted, are lost: they, on their father's decease, enter as lawful heirs, on their estates in fame: the fathers of our copyists are still in possession; and secured in it, in spite of Goths, and flames by the perpetuating power of the press. Very late must a modern imitator's fame arrive, if it waits for their decease.

An original enters early on reputation: fame, fond of new glories, sounds her trumpet in triumph at its birth; and yet how few are awakened by it into the noble ambition of like attempts? Ambition is sometimes no vice in life; it is always a virtue in composition. High in the towering Alps is the fountain of the Po; high in fame, and in antiquity, is the fountain of an imitator's undertaking; but the river, and the imitation, humbly creep along the vale. So few are our originals, that, if all other books were to be burnt, the lettered world would resemble some metropolis in flames where a few incombustible buildings, a fortress, temple, or tower, lift their heads, in melancholy grandeur, amid the mighty ruin. Compared with this conflagration, old Omar lighted up but a small bonfire, when he heated the baths of the barbarians, for eight months together, with the famed Alexandrian library's inestimable spoils, that no profane book might obstruct the triumphant progress of his holy Alcoran[10] round the globe.

But why are originals so few? Not because the writer's harvest is over, the great reapers of antiquity having left nothing to be gleaned after them; nor because the human mind's teeming time is past, or because it is incapable of putting forth unprecedented births; but because illustrious examples engross, prejudice, and intimidate. They engross our attention, and so prevent a due inspection of ourselves; they prejudice our judgment in favor of their abilities, and so lessen the sense of our own; and they intimidate us with the splendor of their renown, and thus under diffidence bury our strength. Nature's impossibilities, and those of diffidence lie wide asunder.

Let it not be suspected, that I would weakly insinuate anything in favor of the moderns, as compared with ancient authors: no, I am lamenting their great inferiority. But I think it is no necessary inferiority; that it is not from divine destination, but from some cause far beneath the moon: I think that human souls, through all periods, are equal; that

due care, and exertion, would set us nearer our immortal predecessors than we are at present; and he who questions and confutes this, will show abilities not a little tending toward a proof of that equality, which he denies.

After all, the first ancients had no merit in being originals: they could not be imitators. Modern writers have a choice to make; and therefore have a merit in their power. They may soar in the regions of liberty, or move in the soft fetters of easy imitation; and imitation has as many plausible reasons to urge, as pleasure has to offer to Hercules. Hercules made the choice of a hero, and so became immortal.

Yet let no assertors of classic excellence imagine, that I deny the tribute it so well deserves. He that admires not ancient authors, betrays a secret he would conceal, and tells the world, that he does not understand them. Let us be as far from neglecting, as from copying, their admirable compositions; sacred be their rights, and inviolable their fame. Let our understanding feed on theirs; they afford the noblest nourishment; but let them nourish, not annihilate, our own. When we read, let our imagination kindle at their charms; when we write, let our judgment shut them out of our thoughts; treat even Homer himself as his royal admirer was treated by the cynic; bid him stand aside, nor shade our composition from the beams of our own genius; for nothing original can rise, nothing immortal, can ripen, in any other sun.

Must we then, you say, not imitate ancient authors? Imitate them, by all means; but imitate aright. He that imitates the divine *Iliad,* does not imitate Homer; but he who takes the same method, which Homer took, for arriving at a capacity of accomplishing a work so great. Tread in his steps to the sole fountain of immortality; drink where he drank, at the true Helicon, that is, at the breast of nature: imitate; but imitate not the composition, but the man. For may not this paradox pass into a maxim? viz. "The less we copy the renowned ancients, we shall resemble them the more."[11]

But possibly you may reply that you must either imitate Homer, or depart from nature.[12] Not so: for suppose you was to change place, in time, with Homer; then, if you write naturally, you might as well charge Homer with an imitation of you. Can you be said to imitate Homer for writing so, as you would have written, if Homer had never been? As far as a regard to nature, and sound sense, will permit a departure from your great predecessors; so far, ambitiously, depart from them; the farther from them in similitude, the nearer

---

[11] For a later version of this idea, see Eliot, *Tradition and the Individual Talent* (below, page 807).

[12] Young seems to recall here Pope's remark in *An Essay on Criticism* (above, page 299) that Virgil discovered that the imitation of Homer and of nature were the same.

---

[9] Pindar (522?–443 B.C.) and Anacreon (572?–488 B.C.), Greek lyric poets.
[10] The Koran, Muslim sacred book.

are you to them in excellence; you rise by it into an original; become a noble collateral, not a humble descendant from them. Let us build our compositions with the spirit, and in the taste, of the ancients; but not with their materials: thus will they resemble the structures of Pericles at Athens, which Plutarch[13] commends for having had an air of antiquity as soon as they were built. All eminence, and distinction, lies out of the beaten road; excursion, and deviation, are necessary to find it; and the more remote your path from the highway, the more reputable; if, like poor Gulliver (of whom anon) you fall not into a ditch, in your way to glory.

What glory to come near, what glory to reach, what glory (presumptuous thought!) to surpass, our predecessors? And is that then in nature absolutely impossible? Or is it not, rather, contrary to nature to fail in it? Nature herself sets the ladder, all wanting is our ambition to climb. For by the bounty of nature we are as strong as our predecessors; and by the favor of time (which is but another round in nature's scale) we stand on higher ground. As to the first, were they more than men? Or are we less? Are not our minds cast in the same mold with those before the flood? The flood affected matter; mind escaped. As to the second; though we are moderns, the world is an ancient; more ancient far, than when they, whom we most admire, filled it with their fame. Have we not their beauties, as stars, to guide; their defects, as rocks, to be shunned; the judgment of ages on both, as a chart to conduct, and a sure helm to steer us in our passage to greater perfection than theirs? And shall we be stopped in our rival pretensions to fame by this just reproof? *"Stat contra, dicitque tibi tua pagina, fur es."*[14] It is by a sort of noble contagion, from a general familiarity with their writings, and not by any particular sordid theft, that we can be the better for those who went before us. Hope we, from plagiarism, any dominion in literature; as that of Rome arose from a nest of thieves?

Rome was a powerful ally to many states; ancient authors are our powerful allies; but we must take heed, that they do not succor, till they enslave, after the manner of Rome. Too formidable an idea of their superiority, like a specter, would fright us out of a proper use of our wits; and dwarf our understanding, by making a giant of theirs. Too great awe for them lays genius under restraint, and denies it that free scope, that full elbowroom, which is requisite for striking its most masterly strokes. Genius is a masterworkman, learning is but an instrument; and an instrument, though most valuable, yet not always indispensable. Heaven will not admit of a partner in the accomplishment of some

favorite spirits; but rejecting all human means, assumes the whole glory to itself. Have not some, though not famed for erudition, so written, as almost to persuade us, that they shone brighter, and soared higher, for escaping the boasted aid of that proud ally?

Nor is it strange; for what, for the most part, mean we by genius, but the power of accomplishing great things without the means generally reputed necessary to that end? A genius differs from a good understanding, as a magician from a good architect; that raises his structure by means invisible; this by the skillful use of common tools. Hence genius has ever been supposed to partake of something divine. *Nemo unquam vir magnus fuit, sine aliquo afflatu divino.*[15]

Learning, destitute of this superior aid, is fond, and proud, of what has cost it much pains; is a great lover of rules, and boaster of famed examples: as beauties less perfect, who owe half their charms to cautious art, learning inveighs against natural unstudied graces, and small harmless inaccuracies, and sets rigid bounds to that liberty, to which genius often owes its supreme glory; but the no-genius its frequent ruin. For unprescribed beauties, and unexampled excellence, which are characteristics of genius, lie without the pale of learning's authorities, and laws; which pale, genius must leap to come at them: but by that leap, if genius is wanting, we break our necks; we lose that little credit, which possibly we might have enjoyed before. For rules, like crutches, are a needful aid to the lame, though an impediment to the strong. A Homer casts them away; and like his Achilles, *"Jura negat sibi nata, nihil non arrogat,"*[16] by native force of mind. There is something in poetry beyond prose-reason; there are mysteries in it not to be explained, but admired; which render mere prose-men infidels to their divinity. And here pardon a second paradox; viz. "Genius often then deserves most to be praised, when it is most sure to be condemned; that is, when its excellence, from mounting high, to weak eyes is quite out of sight."

If I might speak farther of learning, and genius, I would compare genius to virtue, and learning to riches. As riches are most wanted where there is least virtue; so learning where there is least genius. As virtue without much riches can give happiness, so genius without much learning can give renown. As it is said in Terence, *"Pecuniam negligere interdum maximum est lucrum";*[17] so to neglect of learning, genius sometimes owes its greater glory. Genius, therefore, leaves but the second place, among men of letters, to the

---

[13] Plutarch (above, page 119), known principally for his biographical writings.

[14] "Your page stands against you and says to you that you are a thief." Martial (Marcus Valerius Martialis, c. 40–c. 104), *Epigrams* I, lv, 12.

[15] "No one was ever a great man without some divine inspiration."

[16] "He says that the laws are not created for him, and he claims everything [for himself]." Horace (above, page 79).

[17] Terence (Publius Terentius Afer, c. 185–c. 159 B.C.): "To neglect money is sometimes the greatest gain." *Adelphi*, 215–6.

learned. It is their merit, and ambition, to fling light on the works of genius, and point out its charms. We most justly reverence their informing radius for that favor; but we must much more admire the radiant stars pointed out by them.

A star of the first magnitude among the moderns was Shakespeare; among the ancients, Pindar; who (as Vossius[18] tells us) boasted of his no-learning, calling himself the eagle, for his flight above it. And such genii as these may, indeed, have much reliance on their own native powers. For genius may be compared to the natural strength of the body; learning to the super induced accouterments of arms: if the first is equal to the proposed exploit, the latter rather encumbers, than assists; rather retards, than promotes, the victory. *"Sacer nobis inest Deus,"*[19] says Seneca. With regard to the moral world, conscience, with regard to the intellectual, genius, is that god within. Genius can set us right in composition, without the rules of the learned; as conscience sets us right in life, without the laws of the land; this, singly, can make us good, as men: that, singly, as writers, can, sometimes, make us great.

I say, sometimes, because there is a genius, which stands in need of learning to make it shine. Of genius there are two species, an earlier, and a later; or call them infantine, and adult. An adult genius comes out of nature's hand, as Pallas out of Jove's head, at full growth, and mature: Shakespeare's genius was of this kind; on the contrary, Swift stumbled at the threshold, and set out for distinction on feeble knees: his was an infantine genius; a genius, which, like other infants, must be nursed, and educated, or it will come to naught: Learning is its nurse, and tutor; but this nurse may overlay with an indigested load, which smothers common sense; and this tutor may mislead, with pedantic prejudice, which vitiates the best understanding: as too great admirers of the fathers of the church have sometimes set up their authority against the true sense of Scripture; so too great admirers of the classical fathers have sometimes set up their authority, or example, against reason. *"Neve minor, neu sit quinto productior actu fabula."*[20] So says Horace, so says ancient example. But reason has not subscribed. I know but one book that can justify our implicit acquiescence in it: and (by the way) on that book a noble disdain of undue deference to prior opinion has lately cast, and is still casting, a new and inestimable light.

But, superstition for our predecessors set aside, the classics are forever our rightful and revered masters in composition; and our understandings bow before them: but when? When a master is wanted; which, sometimes, as I have shown, is not the case. Some are pupils of nature only, nor go farther to school: from such we reap often a double advantage; they not only rival the reputation of the great ancient authors, but also reduce the number of mean ones among the moderns. For when they enter on subjects which have been in former hands, such is their superiority, that, like a tenth wave, they overwhelm, and bury in oblivion all that went before: and thus not only enrich and adorn, but remove a load, and lessen the labor, of the lettered world.

"But," you say, "since originals can arise from genius only, and since genius is so very rare, it is scarce worthwhile to labor a point so much, from which we can reasonably expect so little." To show that genius is not so very rare as you imagine, I shall point out strong instances of it, in a far distant quarter from that mentioned above. The minds of the schoolmen were almost as much cloistered as their bodies; they had but little learning, and few books; yet may the most learned be struck with some astonishment at their so singular natural sagacity, and most exquisite edge of thought. Who would expect to find Pindar and Scotus, Shakespeare and Aquinas, of the same party?[21] Both equally shew an original, unindebted, energy; the *vigor igneus,* and *caelestis origo,*[22] burns in both; and leaves us in doubt whether genius is more evident in the sublime flights and beauteous flowers of poetry, or in the profound penetrations, and marvelously keen and minute distinctions, called the thorns of the schools. There might have been more able consuls called from the plow, than ever arrived at that honor: Many a genius, probably, there has been, which could neither write, nor read. So that genius, that supreme luster of literature, is less rare than you conceive.

By the praise of genius we detract not from learning; we detract not from the value of gold, by saying that diamond has greater still. He who disregards learning, shows that he wants its aid; and he that overvalues it, shows that its aid has done him harm. Overvalued indeed it cannot be, if genius, as to composition, is valued more. Learning we thank, genius we revere; that gives us pleasure, this gives us rapture; that informs, this inspires; and is itself inspired; for genius is from heaven, learning from man: this sets us above the low, and illiterate; that, above the learned, and polite. Learning is borrowed knowledge; genius is knowledge innate, and quite our own. Therefore, as Bacon observes, it may take a nobler name, and be called wisdom;[23] in which sense of wisdom, some are born wise.

---

[18] Gerhardus Johannes Vossius (1577–1649), Dutch humanist.
[19] "Sacred is the god dwelling in us."
[20] "The play should be neither shorter nor longer than five acts." Horace, *Art of Poetry* (above, page 81).

[21] John Duns Scotus (d. 1308), Irish or Scottish philosopher.
[22] "Glowing energy" and "heavenly origin."
[23] From *The Advancement of Learning.*

But here a caution is necessary against the most fatal of errors in those automaths, those self-taught philosophers of our age, who set up genius, and often, mere fancied genius, not only above human learning, but divine truth. I have called genius wisdom; but let it be remembered, that in the most renowned ages of the most refined heathen wisdom (and theirs is not Christian) "the world by wisdom knew not God, and it pleased God by the foolishness of preaching to save those that believed."[24] In the fairyland of fancy, genius may wander wild; there it has a creative power, and may reign arbitrarily over its own empire of chimeras. The wide field of nature also lies open before it, where it may range unconfined, make what discoveries it can, and sport with its infinite objects uncontrolled, as far as visible nature extends, painting them as wantonly as it will: but what painter of the most unbounded and exalted genius can give us the true portrait of a seraph? He can give us only what by his own or others' eyes, has been seen; though that indeed infinitely compounded, raised, burlesqued, dishonored, or adorned: in like manner, who can give us divine truth unrevealed? Much less should any presume to set aside divine truth when revealed, as incongruous to their own sagacities—is this too serious for my subject? I shall be more so before I close.

Having put in a caveat against the most fatal of errors, from the too great indulgence of genius, return we now to that too great suppression of it, which is detrimental to composition; and endeavor to rescue the writer, as well as the man. I have said, that some are born wise; but they, like those that are born rich, by neglecting the cultivation and produce of their own possessions, and by running in debt, may be beggared at last; and lose their reputations, as younger brothers' estates, not by being born with less abilities than the rich heir, but at too late an hour.

Many a great man has been lost to himself, and the public, purely because great ones were born before him. Hermias,[25] in his collections on Homer's blindness, says, that Homer requesting the gods to grant him a sight of Achilles, that hero rose, but in armor so bright, that it struck Homer blind with the blaze. Let not the blaze of even Homer's Muse darken us to the discernment of our own powers; which may possibly set us above the rank of imitators; who, though most excellent, and even immortal (as some of them are) yet still but *dii minorum gentium*,[26] nor can expect the largest share of incense, the greatest profusion of praise, on their secondary altars.

But farther still: a spirit of imitation hath many ill effects; I shall confine myself to three. First, it deprives the liberal and politer arts of an advantage which the mechanic enjoy: In these, men are ever endeavoring to go beyond their predecessors; in the former, to follow them. And since copies surpass not their originals, as streams rise not higher than their spring, rarely so high; hence, while arts mechanic are in perpetual progress, and increase, the liberal are in retrogradation, and decay. These resemble pyramids, are broad at bottom, but lessen exceedingly as they rise; those resemble rivers which, from a small fountainhead, are spreading ever wider and wider, as they run. Hence it is evident, that different portions of understanding are not (as some imagine) allotted to different periods of time; for we see, in the same period, understanding rising in one set of artists, and declining in another. Therefore nature stands absolved, and our inferiority in composition must be charged on ourselves.

Nay, so far are we from complying with a necessity, which nature lays us under, that, secondly, by a spirit of imitation we counteract nature, and thwart her design. She brings us into the world all originals: no two faces, no two minds, are just alike; but all bear nature's evident mark of separation on them. Born originals, how comes it to pass that we die copies? That meddling ape imitation, as soon as we come to years of indiscretion (so let me speak), snatches the pen, and blots out nature's mark of separation, cancels her kind intention, destroys all mental individuality; the lettered world no longer consists of singulars, it is a medley, a mass; and a hundred books, at bottom, are but one. Why are monkeys such masters of mimicry? Why receive they such a talent at imitation? Is it not as the Spartan slaves received a license for ebriety;[27] that their betters might be ashamed of it?

The third fault to be found with a spirit of imitation is, that with great incongruity it makes us poor, and proud: makes us think little, and write much; gives us huge folios, which are little better than more reputable cushions to promote our repose. Have not some sevenfold volumes put us in mind of Ovid's sevenfold channels of the Nile at the conflagration? *"Ostia septem / Pulverulenta vacant septem sine flumine valles."*[28] Such leaden labors are like Lycurgus's iron money, which was so much less in value than in bulk, that it required barns for strongboxes, and a yoke to draw five hundred pounds.[29]

---

[24] Corinthians 1.21.
[25] Hermias: probably the poet Hermaias, contemporary of Alexander the Great (fourth century B.C.).
[26] "Gods of lesser classes."

[27] Drunkenness.
[28] "Its seven mouths dusty and empty, seven valleys without streams," Ovid (Publius Ovidius Naso, 43 B.C.–18 A.D.), *Metamorphoses* II, 255–6.
[29] According to false tradition, Lycurgus, the Spartan law-giver (ninth century B.C.?), abolished gold and silver currency and substituted iron.

But notwithstanding these disadvantages of imitation, imitation must be the lot (and often an honorable lot it is) of most writers. If there is a famine of invention in the land, like Joseph's brethren, we must travel far for food; we must visit the remote, and rich, ancients; but an inventive genius may safely stay at home; that, like the widow's curse,[30] is divinely replenished from within; and affords us a miraculous delight. Whether our own genius be such, or not, we diligently should inquire; that we may not go abegging with gold in our purse. For there is a mine in man, which must be deeply dug ere we can conjecture its contents. Another often sees that in us, which we see not ourselves; and may there not be that in us which is unseen by both? That there may, chance often discovers, either by a luckily chosen theme, or a mighty premium, or an absolute necessity of exertion, or a noble stroke of emulation from another's glory; as that on Thucydides from hearing Herodotus repeat part of his history at the Olympic games: had there been no Herodotus, there might have been no Thucydides,[31] and the world's admiration might have begun at Livy for excellence in that province of the pen. Demosthenes had the same stimulation on hearing Callistratus; or Tully[32] might have been the first of consummate renown at the bar.

Quite clear of the dispute concerning ancient and modern learning, we speak not of performance, but powers. The modern powers are equal to those before them; modern performance in general is deplorably short. How great are the names just mentioned? Yet who will dare affirm, that as great may not rise up in some future, or even in the present age? Reasons there are why talents may not appear, none why they may not exist, as much in one period as another. An evocation of vegetable fruits depends on rain, air, and sun; an evocation of the fruits of genius no less depends on externals. What a marvelous crop bore it in Greece, and Rome? And what a marvelous sunshine did it there enjoy? What encouragement from the nature of their governments, and the spirit of their people? Virgil and Horace owed their divine talents to heaven; their immortal works, to men; thank Maecenas and Augustus for them. Had it not been for these, the genius of those poets had lain buried in their ashes. Athens expended on her theater, painting, sculpture, and architecture, a tax levied for the support of a war. Caesar dropped his papers when Tully spoke; and Philip trembled at the voice of Demosthenes: and has there arisen but one Tully, one Demosthenes, in so long a course of years? The powerful eloquence of them both in one stream, should never bear me down into the melancholy persuasion, that several have not been born, though they have not emerged. The sun as much exists in a cloudy day, as in a clear; it is outward, accidental circumstances that with regard to genius either in nation, or age, *"Collectas fugat nubes, solemque reducit."*[33] As great, perhaps, greater than those mentioned (presumptuous as it may sound) may, possibly, arise; for who hath fathomed the mind of man? Its bounds are as unknown, as those of the creation; since the birth of which, perhaps, not one has so far exerted, as not to leave his possibilities beyond his attainments, his powers beyond his exploits. Forming our judgments altogether by what has been done, without knowing, or at all inquiring, what possibly might have been done, we naturally enough fall into too mean an opinion of the human mind. If a sketch of the divine *Iliad* before Homer wrote, had been given to mankind, by some superior being, or otherwise, its execution would, probably, have appeared beyond the power of man. Now, to surpass it, we think impossible. As the first of these opinions would evidently have been a mistake, why may not the second be so too? Both are founded on the same bottom; on our ignorance of the possible dimensions of the mind of man.

Nor are we only ignorant of the dimensions of the human mind in general, but even of our own. That a man may be scarce less ignorant of his own powers, than an oyster of its pearl, or a rock of its diamond; that he may possess dormant, unsuspected abilities, till awakened by loud calls, or stung up by striking emergencies, is evident from the sudden eruption of some men, out of perfect obscurity, into public admiration, on the strong impulse of some animating occasion; not more to the world's great surprise, than their own. Few authors of distinction but have experienced something of this nature, at the first beamings of their yet unsuspected genius on their hitherto dark composition: the writer starts at it, as at a lucid meteor in the night; is much suprised; can scarce believe it true. During his happy confusion, it may be said to him, as to Eve at the lake, "What there thou seest, fair creature, is thyself."[34] Genius, in this view, is like a dear friend in our company under disguise; who, while we are lamenting his absence, drops his mask, striking us, at once, with equal surprise and joy. This sensation, which I speak of in a writer, might favor, and so promote, the fable of poetic inspiration; a poet of a strong imagination, and stronger vanity, on feeling it, might

---

[30]1 Kings 17.16.
[31]Thucydides (c. 457–c. 401 B.C.), Herodotus (484?–425? B.C.), Greek historians. The story is almost certainly spurious.
[32]Livy (Titus Livius, 59 B.C.–17 A.D.), Roman historian; Demosthenes (c. 384–332 B.C.) and Callistratus (fourth century B.C.), Greek orators and rhetoricians; Tully (Cicero, see above, p. 74).

[33]"Drives away the gathered clouds and brings back the sun." *Aeneid* I, 143.
[34]John Milton, *Paradise Lost* IV, 468.

naturally enough realize the world's mere compliment, and think himself truly inspired. Which is not improbable; for enthusiasts of all kinds do no less.

Since it is plain that men may be strangers to their own abilities; and by thinking meanly of them without just cause, may possibly lose a name, perhaps a name immortal; I would find some means to prevent these evils. Whatever promotes virtue, promotes something more, and carries its good influence beyond the moral man: to prevent these evils, I borrow two golden rules from ethics, which are no less golden in composition, than in life. 1. Know thyself; 2dly, Reverence thyself: I design to repay ethics in a future letter, by two rules from rhetoric for its service.

1st. Know thyself. Of ourselves it may be said, as Martial says of a bad neighbor, *"Nil tam prope, proculque nobis."*[35] Therefore dive deep into thy bosom; learn the depth, extent, bias, and full forte of thy mind; contract full intimacy with the stranger within thee; excite and cherish every spark of intellectual light and heat, however smothered under former negligence, or scattered through the dull, dark mass of common thoughts; and collecting them into a body, let thy genius rise (if a genius thou hast) as the sun from chaos; and if I should then say, like an Indian, worship it, (though too bold) yet should I say little more than my second rule enjoins, (viz.) reverence thyself.

That is, let not great examples, or authorities, browbeat thy reason into too great a diffidence of thyself: thyself so reverence, as to prefer the native growth of thy own mind to the richest import from abroad; such borrowed riches make us poor. The man who thus reverences himself, will soon find the world's reverence to follow his own. His works will stand distinguished; his the sole property of them; which property alone can confer the noble title of an author; that is, of one who (to speak accurately) thinks, and composes; while other invaders of the press, how voluminous, and learned soever, (with due respect be it spoken) only read, and write.

This is the difference between those two luminaries in literature, the well-accomplished scholar, and the divinely-inspired enthusiast; the first is, as the bright morning star; the second, as the rising sun. The writer who neglects those two rules above will never stand alone; he makes one of a group, and thinks in wretched unanimity with the throng: incumbered with the notions of others, and impoverished by their abundance, he conceives not the least embryo of new thought; opens not the least vista through the gloom of ordi-

nary writers, into the bright walks of rare imagination, and singular design; while the true genius is crossing all public roads into fresh untrodden ground; he, up to the knees in antiquity, is treading the sacred footsteps of great examples, with the blind veneration of a bigot saluting the papal toe; comfortably hoping full absolution for the sins of his own understanding, from the powerful charm of touching his idol's infallibility.

Such meanness of mind, such prostration of our own powers, proceeds from too great admiration of others. Admiration has, generally, a degree of two very bad ingredients in it; of ignorance, and of fear; and does mischief in composition, and in life. Proud as the world is, there is more superiority in it given, than assumed: and its grandees of all kinds owe more of their elevation to the littleness of others' minds, than to the greatness of their own. Were not prostrate spirits their voluntary pedestals, the figure they make among mankind would not stand so high. Imitators and translators are somewhat of the pedestal kind, and sometimes rather raise their original's reputation, by showing him to be by them inimitable, than their own. Homer has been translated into most languages; Aelian[36] tells us, that the Indians, (hopeful tutors!) have taught him to speak their tongue. What expect we from them? Not Homer's Achilles, but something, which, like Patroclus, assumes his name, and, at its peril, appears in his stead; nor expect we Homer's Ulysses, gloriously bursting out of his cloud into royal grandeur, but an Ulysses under disguise, and a beggar to the last. Such is that inimitable father of poetry, and oracle of all the wise, whom Lycurgus transcribed; and for an annual public recital of whose works Solon enacted a law;[37] that it is much to be feared, that his so numerous translations are but as the published testimonials of so many nations, and ages, that this author so divine is untranslated still.

But here, *"Cynthius aurem / Vellit,"*[38] and demands justice for his favorite, and ours. Great things he has done; but he might have done greater. What a fall is it from Homer's numbers, free as air, lofty and harmonious as the spheres, into childish shackles, and tinkling sounds! But, in his fall, he is still great—

> Nor appears
> Less than archangel ruined, and the excess
> Of glory obscured.[39]

---

[35] "Nothing so near, yet so far from us," *Epigrams* I, lxxxvi, 10.

[36] Claudius Aelianus (fl. second century), Roman rhetorician.
[37] Solon (c. 639–c. 559 B.C.), Athenian legislator.
[38] "Apollo plucks my ear." Virgil, *Eclogues* VI, 3–4.
[39] Milton, *Paradise Lost* I, 592–4.

Had Milton never wrote, Pope had been less to blame: But when in Milton's genius, Homer, as it were, personally rose to forbid Britons doing him that ignoble wrong; it is less pardonable, by that effeminate decoration, to put Achilles in petticoats a second time: how much nobler had it been, if his numbers had rolled on in full flow, through the various modulations of masculine melody, into those grandeurs of solemn sound, which are indispensably demanded by the native dignity of heroic song? How much nobler, if he had resisted the temptation of that gothic demon, which modern poesy tasting, became mortal? O how unlike the deathless, divine harmony of three great names (how justly joined), of Milton, Greece, and Rome? His verse, but for this little speck of mortality, in its extreme parts, as his hero had in his heel; like him, had been invulnerable, and immortal. But, unfortunately, that was undipped in Helicon; as this, in Styx. Harmony as well as eloquence is essential to poesy; and a murder of his music is putting half Homer to death. *Blank* is a term of diminution; what we mean by blank verse, is, verse unfallen, uncursed; verse reclaimed, reinthroned in the true language of the gods; who never thundered nor suffered their Homer to thunder, in rhyme, and therefore, I beg you, my friend, to crown it with some nobler term; nor let the greatness of the thing lie under the defamation of such a name.

But supposing Pope's *Iliad* to have been perfect in its kind; yet it is a translation still; which differs as much from an original, as the moon from the sun. *"—Phoeben alieno jusserat igne / Impleri, solemque suo."*[40] But as nothing is more easy than to write originally wrong; originals are not here recommended, but under the strong guard of my first rule—know thyself. Lucian,[41] who was an original, neglected not this rule, if we may judge by his reply to one who took some freedom with him. He was at first, an apprentice to a statuary; and when he was reflected on as such, by being called Prometheus, he replied, "I am indeed the inventor of new work, the model of which I owe to none; and, if I do not execute it well, I deserve to be torn by twelve vultures, instead of one."

---

[40]"He had ordered Phoebe to shine with another's light, the sun with its own." Claudian (Claudius Claudianus, d. c. 408), *Against Rufinus* I, 9–10.

[41]Lucianus (c. 125–d. after 180), Greek prose writer.

Samuel Johnson

1709–1784

Johnson is among the last neoclassical critics and is one of the most influential. He fares less well as a consistent theorist than as a practical critic of penetrating insights. The selections below reveal some of his fundamental assumptions. Two of the most important are his grounding of critical judgment on morality and his idea that poets should represent general nature rather than particular experiences. Both of these premises raise interesting problems from the point of view of later critics—for example, most of the Romantics—who tended to judge moralistic criticism as too narrow and held that the poet should express the particular. Yet later critics could not dismiss Johnson, for even if his theory seemed to them inadequate, they had to acknowledge the power of his many insights into particular works.

Johnson's realistic attitude resists the "wild strain of imagination" that led to pastoral conventions and the machinery of imaginary giants, knights, and castles. He was one of the first to judge James Macpherson's allegedly ancient Celtic poems attributed to Ossian. Yet his realism is in the end secondary to his moral concerns. For him the realistic writer runs a greater moral risk than concocters of unlikely romances, since the latter's tales are so improbable as not to be believed in the first place. Contemporary realistic writers, Johnson observed, because they come closer to truth, must also come closer to the morally right in what they present. It is obviously difficult to resolve in a single criticism the desire for realism with an insistence that wickedness either not be represented at all or get its just deserts.

The question of whether poets represent general nature or particular experience is one that has intrigued critics for a long time. Johnson's preference for general nature was endorsed by Sir Joshua Reynolds (below, page 394), attacked by Blake (below, page 449), and worried over by a number of Romantic critics. The key passage in Imlac's discourse on poetry in Johnson's novel *Rasselas* is the remark, "The business of the poet . . . is to examine, not the individual, but the species: to remark general properties and large appearances: he does not number the streaks of the tulip. . . ." When Johnson mentions the "species" he is not referring to some Platonic universal idea but something more like a generalization from sense experience. The nature Johnson's poet properly imitates is what may be abstracted from numerous particular experiences and found to be common to all the objects of a class. Thus, in the wake of the empiricism of thinkers like Bacon (above, page 234) and Locke (above, page 281), the neoclassical object of art shifts from Platonic universals to the generalized abstraction. The opposing view is, for example, that of Goethe in his conversations with Eckermann: "It was, in short, not in my line, as a poet, to strive to embody anything *abstract*."

Johnson's *Preface to Shakespeare* expresses the fundamental notions mentioned above and also deals with a number of other matters. He treats the traditional division of drama into tragedy and comedy as inadequate to deal with Shakespeare. He has little patience with the long quarrel in literary criticism between those who preferred the ancients and those who preferred the moderns, and he believes that poetry properly delights and teaches, the latter by moral example.

Sir John Hawkins's fifteen-volume edition of Johnson's works (1787–1789) was long the standard collection. It was followed by the Yale edition, edited by A. T. Hazen and others (1958 ff.). Standard editions of Johnson's critical works include *Lives of the English Poets,* edited by G. B. Hill (1905), and *Johnson on Shakespeare,* edited by Walter Raleigh (1908). See W. R. Keast, "The Theoretical Foundations of Johnson's Criticism" in R. S. Crane, ed., *Critics and Criticism* (1952); J. H. Hagstrum, *Samuel Johnson's Literary Criticism* (1952); Allen Tate, "Johnson on the Metaphysical Poets," *The Forlorn Demon* (1953), 112–30; W. J. Bate, *The Achievement of Samuel Johnson* (1955); Martin Kallich, "Samuel Johnson's Principles of Criticism and Imlac's 'Dissertation Upon Poetry,'" *Journal of Aesthetics and Art Criticism* XXV (1966), 71–82; James Boulton, ed., *Johnson: The Critical Heritage* (1971); Leopold Damrosch, *The Uses of Johnson's Criticism* (1976); Joel Weinsheimer, *Imitation* (1984); Nicholas Hudson, *Samuel Johnson and Eighteenth-Century Thought* (1988); Edward Tomarken, *Samuel Johnson on Shakespeare* (1991); Thomas M. Woodman, *A Preface to Samuel Johnson* (1983); Charles H. Hinnant, *"Steel for the Mind": Samuel Johnson and Critical Discourse* (1994).

Rambler, Number 4:
On Fiction

Simul et jucunda et idonea dicere Vitae.[1]

HORACE

And join both profit and delight in one.

CREECH[2]

The works of fiction, with which the present generation seems more particularly delighted, are such as exhibit life in its true state, diversified only by accidents that daily happen in the world, and influenced by passions and qualities which are really to be found in conversing with mankind.

This kind of writing may be termed not improperly the comedy of romance, and is to be conducted nearly by the rules of comic poetry. Its province is to bring about natural events by easy means, and to keep up curiosity without the help of wonder: it is therefore precluded from the machines and expedients of the heroic romance, and can neither employ giants to snatch away a lady from the nuptial rites, nor knights to bring her back from captivity; it can neither bewilder its personages in deserts, nor lodge them in imaginary castles.

I remember a remark made by Scaliger upon Pontanus,[3] that all his writings are filled with the same images; and that if you take from him his lilies and his roses, his satyrs and his dryads, he will have nothing left that can be called poetry. In like manner, almost all the fictions of the last age will vanish, if you deprive them of a hermit and a wood, a battle and a shipwreck.

Why this wild strain of imagination found reception so long, in polite and learned ages, it is not easy to conceive; but we cannot wonder that, while readers could be procured, the authors were willing to continue it: for when a man had by practice gained some fluency of language, he had no further care than to retire to his closet, let loose his invention, and heat his mind with incredibilities; a book was thus

---

Johnson's essay on fiction, *Rambler, Number Four,* appeared on Saturday, March 31, 1750.
[1] "To speak of life both agreeably and appropriately," *Art of Poetry,* 334 (above, page 83).
[2] Thomas Creech (1659–1700), English translator.

[3] In Scaliger's *Poetics* V, 4. Giovanno Pontanus (1426–1503), Italian writer.

produced without fear of criticism, without the toil of study, without knowledge of nature, or acquaintance with life.

The task of our present writers is very different; it requires, together with that learning which is to be gained from books, that experience which can never be attained by solitary diligence, but must arise from general converse, and accurate observation of the living world. Their performances have, as Horace expresses it, *"plus oneris quantum veniae minus,"* little indulgence, and therefore more difficulty.[4] They are engaged in portraits of which everyone knows the original, and can detect any deviation from exactness of resemblance. Other writings are safe, except from the malice of learning, but these are in danger from every common reader, as the slipper ill executed was censured by a shoemaker who happened to stop in his way at the Venus of Apelles.[5]

But the fear of not being approved as just copiers of human manners, is not the most important concern that an author of this sort ought to have before him. These books are written chiefly to the young, the ignorant, and the idle, to whom they serve as lectures of conduct, and introductions into life. They are the entertainment of minds unfurnished with ideas, and therefore easily susceptible of impressions; not fixed by principles, and therefore easily following the current of fancy; not informed by experience, and consequently open to every false suggestion and partial account.

That the highest degree of reverence should be paid to youth, and that nothing indecent should be suffered to approach their eyes or ears are precepts extorted by sense and virtue from an ancient writer, by no means eminent for chastity of thought.[6] The same kind, though not the same degree of caution, is required to everything which is laid before them, to secure them from unjust prejudices, perverse opinions, and incongruous combinations of images.

In the romances formerly written, every transaction and sentiment was so remote from all that passes among men, that the reader was in very little danger of making any applications to himself; the virtues and crimes were equally beyond his sphere of activity; and he amused himself with heroes and with traitors, deliverers and persecutors, as with beings of another species, whose actions were regulated upon motives of their own, and who had neither faults nor excellencies in common with himself.

But when an adventurer is leveled with the rest of the world, and acts in such scenes of the universal drama, as may be the lot of any other man; young spectators fix their eyes upon him with closer attention, and hope by observing his behavior and success to regulate their own practices, when they shall be engaged in the like part.

For this reason these familiar histories may perhaps be made of greater use than the solemnities of professed morality, and convey the knowledge of vice and virtue with more efficacy than axioms and definitions. But if the power of example is so great, as to take possession of the memory by a kind of violence, and produce effects almost without the intervention of the will, care ought to be taken that, when the choice is unrestrained, the best examples only should be exhibited; and that which is likely to operate so strongly, should not be mischievous or uncertain in its effects.

The chief advantage which these fictions have over real life is, that their authors are at liberty, though not to invent, yet to select objects, and to cull from the mass of mankind, those individuals upon which the attention ought most to be employed; as a diamond, though it cannot be made, may be polished by art, and placed in such a situation, as to display that luster which before was buried among common stones.

It is justly considered as the greatest excellency of art, to imitate nature; but it is necessary to distinguish those parts of nature, which are most proper for imitation: greater care is still required in representing life, which is so often discolored by passion, or deformed by wickedness. If the world be promiscuously described, I cannot see of what use it can be to read the account; or why it may not be as safe to turn the eye immediately upon mankind, as upon a mirror which shows all that presents itself without discrimination.

It is therefore not a sufficient vindication of a character, that it is drawn as it appears, for many characters ought never to be drawn; nor of a narrative, that the train of events is agreeable to observation and experience, for that observation which is called knowledge of the world, will be found much more frequently to make men cunning than good. The purpose of these writings is surely not only to show mankind, but to provide that they may be seen hereafter with less hazard; to teach the means of avoiding the snares which are laid by treachery for innocence, without infusing any wish for that superiority with which the betrayer flatters his vanity; to give the power of counteracting fraud, without the temptation to practice it; to initiate youth by mock encounters in the art of necessary defense, and to increase prudence without impairing virtue.

Many writers, for the sake of following nature, so mingle good and bad qualities in their principal personages, that they are both equally conspicuous; and as we accompany

---

[4] *Epistles* II, i, 170.
[5] See Burke (above, page 336). The story is from Pliny's *Natural History* XXXV, 84–5.
[6] Juvenal (Decimus Junius Juvenalis, first to second century), *Satires* XIV.

them through their adventures with delight, and are led by degrees to interest ourselves in their favor, we lose the abhorrence of their faults, because they do not hinder our pleasure, or, perhaps, regard them with some kindness for being united with so much merit.

There have been men indeed splendidly wicked, whose endowments threw a brightness on their crimes, and whom scarce any villainy made perfectly detestable, because they never could be wholly divested of their excellencies; but such have been in all ages the great corrupters of the world, and their resemblance ought no more to be preserved, than the art of murdering without pain.

Some have advanced, without due attention to the consequences of this notion, that certain virtues have their correspondent faults; and therefore that to exhibit either apart is to deviate from probability. Thus men are observed by Swift to be "grateful in the same degree as they are resentful."[7] This principle, with others of the same kind, supposes man to act from a brute impulse, and pursue a certain degree of inclination, without any choice of the object; for, otherwise, though it should be allowed that gratitude and resentment arise from the same constitution of the passions, it follows not that they will be equally indulged when reason is consulted; yet unless that consequence be admitted, this sagacious maxim becomes an empty sound, without any relation to practice or to life.

Nor is it evident, that even the first motions to these effects are always in the same proportion. For pride, which produces quickness of resentment, will obstruct gratitude, by unwillingness to admit that inferiority which obligation implies; and it is very unlikely, that he who cannot think he receives a favor will acknowledge or repay it.

It is of the utmost importance to mankind, that positions of this tendency should be laid open and confuted; for while men consider good and evil as springing from the same root, they will spare the one for the sake of the other, and in judging, if not of others at least of themselves, will be apt to estimate their virtues by their vices. To this fatal error all those will contribute, who confound the colors of right and wrong, and instead of helping to settle their boundaries, mix them with so much art, that no common mind is able to disunite them.

In narratives, where historical veracity has no place, I cannot discover why there should not be exhibited the most perfect idea of virtue; of virtue not angelical nor above probability, for what we cannot credit we shall never imitate, but the highest and purest that humanity can reach,

which, exercised in such trials as the various revolutions of things shall bring upon it, may, by conquering some calamities, and enduring others, teach us what we may hope, and what we can perform. Vice, for vice is necessary to be shewn, should always disgust; nor should the graces of gaiety, or the dignity of courage, be so united with it, as to reconcile it to the mind. Wherever it appears, it should raise hatred by the malignity of its practices, and contempt by the meanness of its stratagems; for while it is supported by either parts or spirit, it will be seldom heartily abhorred. The Roman tyrant was content to be hated, if he was but feared; and there are thousands of the readers of romances willing to be thought wicked, if they may be allowed to be wits. It is therefore to be steadily inculcated, that virtue is the highest proof of understanding, and the only solid basis of greatness; and that vice is the natural consequence of narrow thoughts, that it begins in mistake, and ends in ignominy.

from

Rasselas

Chapter X

Imlac's History Continued. A Dissertation Upon Poetry

"Wherever I went, I found that poetry was considered as the highest learning, and regarded with a veneration somewhat approaching to that which man would pay to the angelic nature.[1] And it yet fills me with wonder, that, in almost all countries, the most ancient poets are considered as the best: whether it be that every other kind of knowledge is an acquisition gradually attained, and poetry is a gift conferred at once; or that the first poetry of every nation surprised them as a novelty, and retained the credit by consent which it received by accident at first: or whether, as the province of poetry is to describe nature and passion, which are always the same, the first writers took possession of the most striking objects for description, and the most probable occurrences for fiction, and left nothing to those that followed them, but transcription of the same events, new combinations of the same images. Whatever be the reason, it is commonly observed that the early writers are in possession of nature, and

---

[7] Jonathan Swift (1667–1745), Anglo-Irish writer.

The History of Rasselas, Prince of Abyssinia was first published in 1759.
[1] Speaking to Prince Rasselas is the poet Imlac.

their followers of art: that the first excel in strength and invention, and the latter in elegance and refinement.

"I was desirous to add my name to this illustrious fraternity. I read all the poets of Persia and Arabia, and was able to repeat by memory the volumes that are suspended in the mosque of Mecca. But I soon found that no man was ever great by imitation. My desire of excellence impelled me to transfer my attention to nature and to life. Nature was to be my subject, and men to be my auditors: I could never describe what I had not seen: I could not hope to move those with delight or terror, whose interests and opinions I did not understand.

"Being now resolved to be a poet, I saw everything with a new purpose; my sphere of attention was suddenly magnified: no kind of knowledge was to be overlooked. I ranged mountains and deserts for images and resemblances, and pictured upon my mind every tree of the forest and flower of the valley. I observed with equal care the crags of the rock and the pinnacles of the palace. Sometimes I wandered along the mazes of the rivulet, and sometimes watched the changes of the summer clouds. To a poet nothing can be useless. Whatever is beautiful, and whatever is dreadful, must be familiar to his imagination: he must be conversant with all that is awfully vast or elegantly little. The plants of the garden, the animals of the wood, the minerals of the earth, and meteors of the sky, must all concur to store his mind with inexhaustible variety: for every idea is useful for the enforcement or decoration of moral or religious truth; and he, who knows most, will have most power of diversifying his scenes, and of gratifying his reader with remote allusions and unexpected instruction.

"All the appearances of nature I was therefore careful to study, and every country which I have surveyed has contributed something to my poetical powers."

"In so wide a survey," said the prince, "you must surely have left much unobserved. I have lived, till now, within the circuit of these mountains, and yet cannot walk abroad without the sight of something which I had never beheld before, or never heeded."

"The business of a poet," said Imlac, "is to examine, not the individual, but the species; to remark general properties and large appearances: he does not number the streaks of the tulip, or describe the different shades in the verdure of the forest. He is to exhibit in his portraits of nature such prominent and striking features, as recall the original to every mind; and must neglect the minuter discriminations,[2] which one may have remarked, and another have neglected,

for those characteristics which are alike obvious to vigilance and carelessness.

"But the knowledge of nature is only half the task of a poet; he must be acquainted likewise with all the modes of life. His character requires that he estimate the happiness and misery of every condition; observe the power of all the passions in all their combinations, and trace the changes of the human mind as they are modified by various institutions and accidental influences of climate or custom, from the sprightliness of infancy to the despondence of decrepitude. He must divest himself of the prejudices of his age or country; he must consider right and wrong in their abstracted and invariable state; he must disregard present laws and opinions, and rise to general and transcendental truths, which will always be the same: he must therefore content himself with the slow progress of his name; contemn the applause of his own time, and commit his claims to the justice of posterity. He must write as the interpreter of nature, and the legislator of mankind, and consider himself as presiding over the thoughts and manners of future generations; as a being superior to time and place.

"His labor is not yet at an end: he must know many languages and many sciences; and, that his style may be worthy of his thoughts, must, by incessant practice, familiarize to himself every delicacy of speech and grace of harmony."

from

Preface to *Shakespeare*

That praises are without reason lavished on the dead, and that the honors due only to excellence are paid to antiquity, is a complaint likely to be always continued by those, who, being able to add nothing to truth, hope for eminence from the heresies of paradox; or those, who, being forced by disappointment upon consolatory expedients, are willing to hope from posterity what the present age refuses, and flatter themselves that the regard which is yet denied by envy, will be at last bestowed by time.

Antiquity, like every other quality that attracts the notice of mankind, has undoubtedly votaries that reverence it, not from reason, but from prejudice. Some seem to admire indiscriminately whatever has been long preserved, without considering that time has sometimes cooperated with chance; all perhaps are more willing to honor past than present

[2] On "minute discriminations" see also Reynolds (below, page 394) and Blake (below, page 449).

Johnson's *Preface to Shakespeare* was first published in 1765 in his eight-volume edition of Shakespeare's plays. The text printed here comprises the first part of the essay.

excellence; and the mind contemplates genius through the shades of age, as the eye surveys the sun through artificial opacity. The great contention of criticism is to find the faults of the moderns, and the beauties of the ancients. While an author is yet living we estimate his powers by his worst performance, and when he is dead, we rate them by his best.

To works, however, of which the excellence is not absolute and definite, but gradual and comparative; to works not raised upon principles demonstrative and scientific, but appealing wholly to observation and experience, no other test can be applied than length of duration and continuance of esteem. What mankind have long possessed they have often examined and compared; and if they persist to value the possession, it is because frequent comparisons have confirmed opinion in its favor. As among the works of nature no man can properly call a river deep, or a mountain high, without the knowledge of many mountains, and many rivers; so in the productions of genius, nothing can be styled excellent till it has been compared with other works of the same kind. Demonstration immediately displays its power, and has nothing to hope or fear from the flux of years; but works tentative and experimental must be estimated by their proportion to the general and collective ability of man, as it is discovered in a long succession of endeavors. Of the first building that was raised, it might be with certainty determined that it was round or square; but whether it was spacious or lofty must have been referred to time. The Pythagorean scale of numbers was at once discovered to be perfect; but the poems of Homer we yet know not to transcend the common limits of human intelligence, but by remarking, that nation after nation, and century after century, has been able to do little more than transpose his incidents, new-name his characters, and paraphrase his sentiments.

The reverence due to writings that have long subsisted arise therefore not from any credulous confidence in the superior wisdom of past ages, or gloomy persuasion of the degeneracy of mankind, but is the consequence of acknowledged and indubitable positions, that what has been longest known has been most considered, and what is most considered is best understood.

The poet, of whose works I have undertaken the revision,[1] may now begin to assume the dignity of an ancient, and claim the privilege of established fame and prescriptive veneration. He has long outlived his century, the term commonly fixed as the test of literary merit.[2] Whatever advantages he might once derive from personal allusions, local customs, or temporary opinions, have for many years been lost; and every topic of merriment, or motive of sorrow, which the modes of artificial life afforded him, now only obscure the scenes which they once illuminated. The effects of favor and competition are at an end; the tradition of his friendships and his enmities has perished; his works support no opinion with arguments, nor supply any faction with invectives; they can neither indulge vanity nor gratify malignity; but are read without any other reason than the desire of pleasure, and are therefore praised only as pleasure is obtained; yet, thus unassisted by interest or passion, they have passed through variations of taste and changes of manners, and, as they devolved from one generation to another, have received new honors at every transmission.

But because human judgment, though it be gradually gaining upon certainty, never becomes infallible; and approbation, though long continued, may yet be only the approbation of prejudice or fashion; it is proper to inquire, by what peculiarities of excellence Shakespeare has gained and kept the favor of his countrymen.

Nothing can please many, and please long, but just representations of general nature. Particular manners, can be known to few, and therefore few only can judge how nearly they are copied. The irregular combinations of fanciful invention may delight awhile, by that novelty of which the common satiety of life sends us all in quest; but the pleasures of sudden wonder are soon exhausted, and the mind can only repose on the stability of truth.

Shakespeare is above all writers, at least above all modern writers, the poet of nature; the poet that holds up to his readers a faithful mirror of manners and of life. His characters are not modified by the customs of particular places, unpracticed by the rest of the world; by the peculiarities of studies or professions, which can operate but upon small numbers; or by the accidents of transient fashions or temporary opinions: they are the genuine progeny of common humanity, such as the world will always supply, and observation will always find. His persons act and speak by the influence of those general passions and principles by which all minds are agitated, and the whole system of life is continued in motion. In the writings of other poets a character is too often an individual; in those of Shakespeare it is commonly a species.

It is from this wide extension of design that so much instruction is derived. It is this which fills the plays of Shakespeare with practical axioms and domestic wisdom. It was said of Euripides,[3] that every verse was a precept; and

---

[1] Criticism and editing.
[2] Here Johnson deliberately revises what is meant by "ancients" in the old controversy about the ancients and the moderns.

[3] Euripides (c. 480–c. 406 B.C.), Greek tragic dramatist. The allusion is to Cicero, *Epistles* XVI, 8.

it may be said of Shakespeare, that from his works may be collected a system of civil and economical prudence. Yet his real power is not shewn in the splendor of particular passages, but by the progress of his fable, and the tenor of his dialogue; and he that tries to recommend him by select quotations, will succeed like the pedant in Hierocles;[4] who, when he offered his house to sale, carried a brick in his pocket as a specimen.

It will not easily be imagined how much Shakespeare excels in accommodating his sentiments to real life, but by comparing him with other authors. It was observed of the ancient schools of declamation, that the more diligently they were frequented, the more was the student disqualified for the world, because he found nothing there which he should ever meet in any other place. The same remark may be applied to every stage but that of Shakespeare. The theater, when it is under any other direction, is peopled by such characters as were never seen, conversing in a language which was never heard, upon topics which will never rise in the commerce of mankind. But the dialogue of this author is often so evidently determined by the incident which produces it, and is pursued with so much ease and simplicity, that it seems scarcely to claim the merit of fiction, but to have been gleaned by diligent selection out of common conversation, and common occurrences.

Upon every other stage the universal agent is love, by whose power all good and evil is distributed, and every action quickened or retarded. To bring a lover, a lady and a rival into the fable; to entangle them in contradictory obligations, perplex them with oppositions of interest, and harass them with violence of desires inconsistent with each other; to make them meet in rapture and part in agony; to fill their mouths with hyperbolical joy and outrageous sorrow; to distress them as nothing human ever was delivered; is the business of a modern dramatist. For this probability is violated, life is misrepresented, and language is depraved. But love is only one of many passions; and as it has no great influence upon the sum of life, it has little operation in the dramas of a poet, who caught his ideas from the living world, and exhibited only what he saw before him. He knew, that any other passion, as it was regular or exorbitant, was a cause of happiness or calamity.

Characters thus ample and general were not easily discriminated and preserved, yet perhaps no poet ever kept his personages more distinct from each other. I will not say with Pope,[5] that every speech may be assigned to the proper speaker, because many speeches there are which have nothing characteristical; but perhaps, though some may be equally adapted to every person, it will be difficult to find any that can be properly transferred from the present possessor to another claimant. The choice is right, when there is reason for choice.

Other dramatists can only gain attention by hyperbolical or aggravated characters, by fabulous and unexampled excellence or depravity, as the writers of barbarous romances invigorated the reader by a giant and a dwarf; and he that should form his expectations of human affairs from the play, or from the tale, would be equally deceived. Shakespeare has no heroes; his scenes are occupied only by men, who act and speak as the reader thinks that he should himself have spoken or acted on the same occasion: Even where the agency is supernatural the dialogue is level with life. Other writers disguise the most natural passions and most frequent incidents; so that he who contemplates them in the book will not know them in the world: Shakespeare approximates the remote, and familiarizes the wonderful; the event which he represents will not happen, but if it were possible, its effects would probably be such as he has assigned; and it may be said, that he has not only shewn human nature as it acts in real exigencies, but as it would be found in trials, to which it cannot be exposed.

This therefore is the praise of Shakespeare, that his drama is the mirror of life; that he who has 'mazed his imagination, in following the phantoms which other writers raise up before him, may here be cured of his delirious ecstasies, by reading human sentiments in human language, by scenes from which a hermit may estimate the transactions of the world, and a confessor predict the progress of the passions.

His adherence to general nature has exposed him to the censure of critics, who form their judgments upon narrow principles. Dennis and Rymer[6] think his Romans not sufficiently Roman; and Voltaire[7] censures his kings as not completely royal. Dennis is offended, that Menenius, a senator of Rome, should play the buffoon, and Voltaire perhaps thinks decency violated when the Danish usurper is represented as a drunkard. But Shakespeare always makes nature predominate over accident; and if he preserves the essential character, is not very careful of distinctions superinduced and adventitious. His story requires Romans or kings, but he

---

[4] *Hierocles Commentarius in Aurea Carmina,* once but no longer ascribed to the neoplatonist Hierocles (fifth century A.D.).
[5] In Pope's *Preface to Shakespeare.*

[6] John Dennis (1657–1734), English critic, author of *An Essay on the Genius and Writings of Shakespeare* (1712); Thomas Rymer (1641–1713), English critic who called *Othello* "a bloody farce without salt or savour" in his *A Short View of Tragedy* (1692).
[7] Francois Marie Arouet de Voltaire (1694–1778), *Letters Concerning the English Nation* (1733).

thinks only on men. He knew that Rome, like every other city, had men of all dispositions; and wanting a buffoon, he went into the senate house for that which the senate house would certainly have afforded him. He was inclined to shew a usurper and a murderer not only odious but despicable, he therefore added drunkenness to his other qualities, knowing that kings love wine like other men, and that wine exerts its natural power upon kings. These are the petty cavils of petty minds; a poet overlooks the casual distinction of country and condition, as a painter, satisfied with the figure, neglects the drapery.

The censure which he has incurred by mixing comic and tragic scenes, as it extends to all his works, deserves more consideration. Let the fact be first stated, and then examined.

Shakespeare's plays are not in the rigorous and critical sense either tragedies or comedies, but compositions of a distinct kind; exhibiting the real state of sublunary nature, which partakes of good and evil, joy and sorrow, mingled with endless variety of proportion and innumerable modes of combination: and expressing the course of the world, in which the loss of one is the gain of another; in which, at the same time, the reveler is hasting to his wine, and the mourner burying his friend; in which the malignity of one is sometimes defeated by the frolic of another; and many mischiefs and many benefits are done and hindered without design.

Out of this chaos of mingled purposes and casualties the ancient poets, according to the laws which custom had prescribed, selected, some the crimes of men, and some their absurdities; some the momentous vicissitudes of life, and some the lighter occurrences; some the terrors of distress, and some the gaieties of prosperity. Thus rose the two modes of imitation, known by the names of tragedy and comedy, compositions intended to promote different ends by contrary means, and considered as so little allied, that I do not recollect among the Greeks or Romans a single writer who attempted both.

Shakespeare has united the powers of exciting laughter and sorrow not only in one mind, but in one composition. Almost all his plays are divided between serious and ludicrous characters, and, in the successive evolutions of the design, sometimes produce seriousness and sorrow, and sometimes levity and laughter.

That this is a practice contrary to the rules of criticism will be readily allowed; but there is always an appeal open from criticism to nature. The end of writing is to instruct; the end of poetry is to instruct by pleasing. That the mingled drama may convey all the instruction of tragedy or comedy cannot be denied, because it includes both in its alterations of exhibition and approaches nearer than either to the appearance of life, by shewing how great machinations and slender designs may promote or obviate one another, and the high and the low cooperate in the general system by unavoidable concatenation.

It is objected, that by this change of scenes the passions are interrupted in their progression, and that the principal event, being not advanced by a due graduation of preparatory incidents, wants at last the power to move, which constitutes the perfection of dramatic poetry. This reasoning is so specious, that it is received as true even by those who in daily experience feel it to be false. The interchanges of mingled scenes seldom fail to produce the intended vicissitudes of passion. Fiction cannot move so much, but that the attention may be easily transferred; and though it must be allowed that pleasing melancholy be sometimes interrupted by unwelcome levity, yet let it be considered likewise, that melancholy is often not pleasing, and that the disturbance of one man may be the relief of another; that different auditors have different habitudes; and that, upon the whole, all pleasure consists in variety.

The players, who in their edition divided our author's works into comedies, histories, and tragedies, seem not to have distinguished the three kinds by any very exact or definite ideas.

An action which ended happily to the principal persons, however serious or distressful through its intermediate incidents, in their opinion, constituted a comedy. This idea of a comedy continued long amongst us; and plays were written, which, by changing the catastrophe, were tragedies today, and comedies tomorrow.

Tragedy was not in those times a poem of more general dignity or elevation than comedy; it required only a calamitous conclusion, with which the common criticism of that age was satisfied, whatever lighter pleasure it afforded in its progress.

History was a series of actions, with no other than chronological succession, independent on each other, and without any tendency to introduce or regulate the conclusion. It is not always very nicely distinguished from tragedy. There is not much nearer approach to unity of action in the tragedy of *Antony and Cleopatra,* than in the history of *Richard the Second.* But a history might be continued through many plays; as it had no plan, it had no limits.

Through all these denominations of the drama, Shakespeare's mode of composition is the same; an interchange of seriousness and merriment, by which the mind is softened at one time, and exhilarated at another. But whatever be his purpose, whether to gladden or depress, or to conduct the story, without vehemence or emotion, through tracts of easy and familiar dialogue, he never fails to attain his purpose; as he commands us, we laugh or mourn, or sit silent with quiet expectation, in tranquility without indifference.

When Shakespeare's plan is understood, most of the criticisms of Rymer and Voltaire vanish away. The play of *Hamlet* is opened, without impropriety, by two sentinels; Iago bellows at Brabantio's window, without injury to the scheme of the play, though in terms which a modern audience would not easily endure; the character of Polonius is seasonable and useful; and the gravediggers themselves may be heard with applause.

Shakespeare engaged in dramatic poetry with the world open before him; the rules of the ancients were yet known to few; but public judgment was unformed; he had no example of such fame as might force him upon imitation, nor critics of such authority as might restrain his extravagance: He therefore indulged his natural disposition, and his disposition, as Rymer has remarked, led him to comedy. In tragedy he often writes, with great appearance of toil and study, what is written at last with little felicity; but in his comic scenes, he seems to produce without labor what no labor can improve. In tragedy he is always struggling after some occasion to be comic; but in comedy he seems to repose, or to luxuriate, as in a mode of thinking congenial to his nature. In his tragic scenes there is always something wanting, but his comedy often surpasses expectation or desire. His comedy pleases by the thoughts and the language, and his tragedy for the greater part by incident and action. His tragedy seems to be skill, his comedy to be instinct.

The force of his comic scenes has suffered little diminution from the changes made by a century and a half, in manners or in words. As his personages act upon principles arising from genuine passion, very little modified by particular forms, their pleasures and vexations are communicable to all times and to all places; they are natural, and therefore durable; the adventitious peculiarities of personal habits, are only superficial dies,[8] bright and pleasing for a little while, yet soon fading to a dim tinct, without any remains of former luster; but the discriminations of true passion are the colors of nature; they pervade the whole mass, and can only perish with the body that exhibits them. The accidental compositions of heterogeneous modes are dissolved by the chance which combined them; but the uniform simplicity of primitive qualities neither admits increase, nor suffers decay. The sand heaped by one flood is scattered by another, but the rock always continues in its place. The stream of time, which is continually washing the dissoluble fabrics of other poets, passes without injury by the adamant of Shakespeare.

---

[8] Dyes.

If there be, what I believe there is, in every nation, a style which never becomes obsolete, a certain mode of phraseology so consonant and congenial to the analogy and principles of its respective language as to remain settled and unaltered; this style is probably to be sought in the common intercourse of life, among those who speak only be understood, without ambition of elegance. The polite are always catching modish innovations, and the learned depart from established forms of speech, in hope of finding or making better; those who wish for distinction forsake the vulgar, when the vulgar is right; but there is a conversation above grossness and below refinement, where propriety resides, and where this poet seems to have gathered his comic dialogue. He is therefore more agreeable to the ears of the present age than any other author equally remote, and among his other excellencies deserves to be studied as one of the original masters of our language.

These observations are to be considered not as unexceptionably constant, but as containing general and predominant truth. Shakespeare's familiar dialogue is affirmed to be smooth and clear, yet not wholly without ruggedness or difficulty; as a country may be eminently fruitful, though it has spots unfit for cultivation: His characters are praised as natural, though their sentiments are sometimes forced, and their actions improbable; as the earth upon the whole is spherical, though its surface is varied with protuberances and cavities.

Shakespeare with his excellencies has likewise faults, and faults sufficient to obscure and overwhelm any other merit. I shall shew them in the proportion in which they appear to me, without envious malignity or superstitious veneration. No question can be more innocently discussed than a dead poet's pretensions to renown; and little regard is due to that bigotry which sets candor higher than truth.

His first defect is that to which may be imputed most of the evil in books or in men. He sacrifices virtue to convenience, and is so much more careful to please than to instruct, that he seems to write without any moral purpose. From his writings indeed a system of social duty may be selected, for he that thinks reasonably must think morally; but his precepts and axioms drop casually from him; he makes no just distribution of good or evil, nor is always careful to shew in the virtuous a disapprobation of the wicked; he carries his persons indifferently through right and wrong, and at the close dismisses them without further care, and leaves their examples to operate by chance. This fault the barbarity of his age cannot extenuate; for it is always a writer's duty to make the world better, and justice is a virtue independent on time or place.

The plots are often so loosely formed, that a very slight consideration may improve them, and so carelessly pursued, that he seems not always fully to comprehend his own design. He omits opportunities of instructing or delighting which the train of his story seems to force upon him, and apparently rejects those exhibitions which would be more affecting, for the sake of those which are more easy.

It may be observed, that in many of his plays the latter part is evidently neglected. When he found himself near the end of his work, and, in view of his reward, he shortened the labor to snatch the profit. He therefore remits his efforts where he should most vigorously exert them, and his catastrophe is improbably produced or imperfectly represented.

He had no regard to distinction of time or place, but gives to one age or nation, without scruple, the customs, institutions, and opinions of another, at the expense not only of likelihood, but of possibility. These faults Pope has endeavored, with more zeal than judgment, to transfer to his imagined interpolators. We need not wonder to find Hector quoting Aristotle, when we see the loves of Theseus and Hippolyta combined with the gothic mythology of fairies. Shakespeare, indeed, was not the only violator of chronology, for in the same age Sidney, who wanted not the advantages of learning, has, in his, *Arcadia,* confounded the pastoral with the feudal times the days of innocence, quiet and security, with those of turbulence, violence, and adventure.

In his comic scenes he is seldom very successful, when he engages his characters in reciprocations of smartness and contests of sarcasm; their jests are commonly gross, and their pleasantry licentious; neither his gentlemen nor his ladies have much delicacy, nor are sufficiently distinguished from his clowns by any appearance of refined manners. Whether he represented the real conversation of his time is not easy to determine; the reign of Elizabeth is commonly supposed to have been a time of stateliness, formality and reserve; yet perhaps the relaxations of that severity were not very elegant. There must, however, have been always some modes of gaiety preferable to others, and a writer ought to choose the best.

In tragedy his performance seems constantly to be worse, as his labor is more. The effusions of passion which exigence forces out are for the most part striking and energetic; but whenever he solicits his invention, or strains his faculties, the offspring of his throes is tumor, meanness, tediousness, and obscurity.

In narration he affects a disproportionate pomp of diction, and a wearisome train of circumlocution, and tells the incident imperfectly in many words, which might have been more plainly delivered in few. Narration in dramatic poetry is naturally tedious, as it is inactive, and obstructs the progress of the action; it should therefore always be rapid, and enlivened by frequent interruption. Shakespeare found it an encumbrance, and instead of lightening it by brevity, endeavored to recommend it by dignity and splendor.

His declamations or set speeches are commonly cold and weak, for his power was the power of nature; when he endeavored, like other tragic writers, to catch opportunities of amplification, and instead of inquiring what the occasion demanded, to show how much his stores of knowledge could supply, he seldom escapes without the pity or resentment of his reader.

It is incident to him to be now and then entangled with an unwieldly sentiment, which he cannot well express, and will not reject; he struggles with it awhile, and if it continues stubborn, comprises it in words such as occur, and leaves it to be disentangled and evolved by those who have more leisure to bestow upon it.

Not that always where the language is intricate the thought is subtle, or the image always great where the line is bulky; the equality of words to things is very often neglected, and trivial sentiments and vulgar ideas disappoint the attention, to which they are recommended by sonorous epithets and swelling figures.

But the admirers of this great poet have never less reason to indulge their hopes of supreme excellence, than when he seems fully resolved to sink them in dejection, and mollify them with tender emotions by the fall of greatness, the danger of innocence, or the crosses of love. He is not long soft and pathetic without some idle conceit, or contemptible equivocation. He no sooner begins to move, than he counteracts himself; and terror and pity, as they are rising in the mind, are checked and blasted by sudden frigidity.

A quibble is to Shakespeare, what luminous vapors are to the traveler; he follows it at all adventures; it is sure to lead him out of his way, and sure to engulf him in the mire. It has some malignant power over his mind, and its fascinations are irresistible. Whatever be the dignity or profundity of his disquisition, whether he be enlarging knowledge or exalting affection, whether he be amusing attention with incidents, or enchaining it in suspense, let but a quibble spring up before him, and he leaves his work unfinished. A quibble is the golden apple for which he will always turn aside from his career, or stoop from his elevation. A quibble, poor and barren as it is, gave him such delight, that he was content to purchase it, by the sacrifice of reason, propriety and truth. A quibble was to him the fatal Cleopatra for which he lost the world, and was content to lose it.

It will be thought strange, that, in enumerating the defects of this writer, I have not yet mentioned his neglect of the unities; his violation of those laws which have been instituted and established by the joint authority of poets and critics.

For his other deviations from the art of writing I resign him to critical justice, without making any other demand in his favor, than that which must be indulged to all human excellence: that his virtues be rated with his failings: but, from the censure which this irregularity may bring upon him, I shall, with due reverence to that learning which I must oppose, adventure to try how I can defend him.

His histories, being neither tragedies nor comedies, are not subject to any of their laws; nothing more is necessary to all the praise which they expect, than that the changes of action be so prepared as to be understood, that the incidents be various and affecting, and the characters consistent, natural, and distinct. No other unity is intended, and therefore none is to be sought.

In his other works he has well enough preserved the unity of action. He has not, indeed, an intrigue regularly perplexed and regularly unraveled: he does not endeavor to hide his design only to discover it, for this is seldom the order of real events, and Shakespeare is the poet of nature: But his plan has commonly what Aristotle requires, a beginning, a middle, and an end;[9] one event is concatenated with another, and the conclusion follows by easy consequence. There are perhaps some incidents that might be spared, as in other poets there is much talk that only fills up time upon the stage; but the general system makes gradual advances, and the end of the play is the end of expectation.

To the unities of time and place he has shewn no regard; and perhaps a nearer view of the principles on which they stand will diminish their value, and withdraw from them the veneration which, from the time of Corneille,[10] they have very generally received, by discovering that they have given more trouble to the poet, than pleasure to the auditor.

The necessity of observing the unities of time and place arises from the supposed necessity of making the drama credible. The critics hold it impossible, that an action of months or years can be possibly believed to pass in three hours; or that the spectator can suppose himself to sit in the theater, while ambassadors go and return between distant kings, while armies are levied and towns besieged, while an exile wanders and returns, or till he whom they saw courting his mistress, shall lament the untimely fall of his son. The mind revolts from evident falsehood, and fiction loses its force when it departs from the resemblance of reality.

From the narrow limitation of time necessarily arises the contraction of place. The spectator, who knows that he saw the first act at Alexandria, cannot suppose that he sees the next at Rome, at a distance to which not the dragons of Medea could, in so short a time, have transported him; he knows with certainty that he has not changed his place, and he knows that place cannot change itself; that what was a house cannot become a plain; that what was Thebes can never be Persepolis.

Such is the triumphant language with which a critic exults over the misery of an irregular poet, and exults commonly without resistance or reply. It is time therefore to tell him by the authority of Shakespeare, that he assumes, as an unquestionable principle, a position, which, while his breath is forming it into words, his understanding pronounces to be false. It is false, that any representation is mistaken for reality; that any dramatic fable in its materiality was ever credible, or, for a single moment, was ever credited.

The objection arising from the impossibility of passing the first hour at Alexandria, and the next at Rome, supposes, that when the play opens, the spectator really imagines himself at Alexandria, and believes that his walk to the theater has been a voyage to Egypt, and that he lives in the days of Antony and Cleopatra. Surely he that imagines this may imagine more. He that can take the stage at one time for the palace of the Ptolemies, may take it in half an hour for the promontory of Actium. Delusion, if delusion be admitted, has no certain limitation; if the spectator can be once persuaded, that his old acquaintance are Alexander and Caesar, that a room illuminated with candles is the plain of Pharsalia, or the bank of Granicus, he is in a state of elevation above the reach of reason, or of truth, and from the heights of empyrean poetry, may despise the circumscriptions of terrestrial nature. There is no reason why a mind thus wandering in ecstasy should count the clock, or why an hour should not be a century in that calenture of the brains that can make the stage a field.

The truth is, that the spectators are always in their senses, and know, from the first act to the last, that the stage is only a stage, and that the players are only players. They came to hear a certain number of lines recited with just gesture and elegant modulation. The lines relate to some action, and an action must be in some place; but the different actions that complete a story may be in places very remote from each other; and where is the absurdity of allowing that space to represent first Athens, and then Sicily, which was always known to be neither Sicily nor Athens, but a modern theater?

By supposition, as place is introduced, time may be extended; the time required by the fable elapses for the most part between the acts; for, of so much of the action as is represented, the real and poetical duration is the same. If, in the first act, preparations for war against Mithridates are represented to be made in Rome, the event of the war may, without absurdity, be represented, in the catastrophe, as happening in Pontus; we know that there is neither war, nor preparation for war; we know that we are neither in Rome nor Pontus; that neither Mithridates nor Lucullus are before us. The drama exhibits successive imitations of successive actions; and why may not the second imitation represent an

---

[9] *Poetics* (above, page 56).
[10] See Corneille (above, page 244).

action that happened years after the first, if it be so connected with it, that nothing but time can be supposed to intervene? Time is, of all modes of existence, most obsequious to the imagination; a lapse of years is as easily conceived as a passage of hours. In contemplation we easily contract the time of real actions, and therefore willingly permit it to be contracted when we only see their imitation.

It will be asked, how the drama moves, if it is not credited. It is credited with all the credit due to a drama. It is credited, whenever it moves, as a just picture of a real original; as representing to the auditor what he would himself feel, if he were to do or suffer what is there feigned to be suffered or to be done. The reflection that strikes the heart is not, that the evils before us are real evils, but that they are evils to which we ourselves may be exposed. If there be any fallacy, it is not that we fancy the players, but that we fancy ourselves unhappy for a moment; but we rather lament the possibility than suppose the presence of misery, as a mother weeps over her babe, when she remembers that death may take it from her. The delight of tragedy proceeds from our consciousness of fiction; if we thought murders and treasons real, they would please no more.

Imitations produce pain or pleasure, not because they are mistaken for realities, but because they bring realities to mind. When the imagination is recreated by a painted landscape, the trees are not supposed capable to give us shade, or the fountains coolness; but we consider how we should be pleased with such fountains playing beside us, and such woods waving over us. We are agitated in reading the history of Henry the Fifth, yet no man takes his book for the field of Agincourt. A dramatic exhibition is a book recited with concomitants that increase or diminish its effect. Familiar comedy is often more powerful in the theater, than in the page; imperial tragedy is always less. The humor of Petruchio may be heightened by grimace; but what voice or what gesture can hope to add dignity or force to the soliloquy of Cato?

A play read, affects the mind like a play acted. It is therefore evident, that the action is not supposed to be real; and it follows, that between the acts a longer or shorter time may be allowed to pass, and that no more account of space or duration is to be taken by the auditor of a drama, than by the reader of a narrative, before whom may pass in an hour the life of a hero, or the revolutions of an empire.

Whether Shakespeare knew the unities, and rejected them by design, or deviated from them by happy ignorance, it is, I think, impossible to decide, and useless to inquire. We may reasonably suppose, that, when he rose to notice, he did not want the counsels and admonitions of scholars and critics, and that he at last deliberately persisted in a practice, which he might have begun by chance. As nothing is essen-

tial to the fable, but unity of action, and as the unities of time and place arise evidently from false assumptions, and, by circumscribing the extent of the drama, lessen its variety, I cannot think it much to be lamented, that they were not known by him, or not observed: nor, if such another poet could arise, should I very vehemently reproach him, that his first act passed at Venice, and his next in Cyprus. Such violations of rules merely positive, become the comprehensive genius of Shakespeare, and such censures are suitable to the minute and slender criticism of Voltaire:

> *Non usque adeo permiscuit imis*
> *Longus summa dies, ut non, si voce Metelli*
> *Serventur leges, malint a Caesare tolli.*[11]

Yet when I speak thus slightly of dramatic rules, I cannot but recollect how much wit and learning may be produced against me; before such authorities I am afraid to stand, not that I think the present question one of those that are to be decided by mere authority, but because it is to be suspected, that these precepts have not been so easily received but for better reasons than I have yet been able to find. The result of my inquiries, in which it would be ludicrous to boast of impartiality, is, that the unities of time and place are not essential to a just drama, that though they may sometimes conduce to pleasure, they are always to be sacrificed to the nobler beauties of variety and instruction; and that a play, written with nice observation of critical rules, is to be contemplated as an elaborate curiosity, as the product of superfluous and ostentatious art, by which is shewn, rather what is possible, than what is necessary.

He that, without diminution of any other excellence, shall preserve all the unities unbroken, deserves the like applause with the architect, who shall display all the orders of architecture in a citadel, without any deduction from its strength; but the principal beauty of a citadel is to exclude the enemy; and the greatest graces of a play, are to copy nature and instruct life.

Perhaps what I have here not dogmatically but deliberately written, may recall the principles of the drama to a new examination. I am almost frightened at my own temerity; and when I estimate the fame and the strength of those that maintain the contrary opinion, am ready to sink down in reverential silence; as Aeneas withdrew from the defense of Troy, when he saw Neptune shaking the wall, and Juno heading the besiegers.

---

[11] "A long time has not so confused the highest and lowest that the laws made by Metellus may not wish to be overthrown by Caesar." Lucan (Marcus Annaeus Lucanus, 39–65), *Pharsalia* III, 138–40.

Henry Home, Lord Kames

1696–1782

Kames, a distinguished Scottish judge, historian, and man of letters, wrote one of the most ambitious works of aesthetic criticism of the eighteenth century, *Elements of Criticism* (1762, enlarged 1763), though he is probably best known for his *Essays on the Principles of Morality and Natural Religion* (1751). The two are related, for in Kames's thought taste leads to morality and morality and taste are governed by common principles. Kames can be seen to proceed from Addison (above, page 307) on the pleasures of the imagination in holding that works of art are occasions for mental processes in the viewer or reader. For Kames, true judgments of taste are immediate, based in feeling, and properly disinterested, being uniform, arising out of a common human nature. There are, nevertheless, in actual practice varying expressions of taste as the result of different human situations including social and economic classes. Human feelings are mental, not merely existent in the organs of sense.

Kames divides the pleasures into a hierarchy of three. At the top are the pleasures of intellect. In the middle are the pleasures of eye and ear (including art). At the bottom are the pleasures of the other senses, which Kames calls "organic," pleasures of momentary sensual gratification subject to satiety. The intellectual pleasures are or can be accompanied by stress that is not present in the pleasures of eye and ear. All of the "genuine rules of criticism" are derived from universal human feelings, which establish the universal laws of taste, but these can be and are dimmed in most people. Thus the judgments of taste of only a few people are trustworthy. The notion of a universal standard is hardly acceptable to a modern anthropological view that emphasizes and honors ethnic and social diversity, which parallels the notion of difference that became emphasized in linguistics after Saussure (below, page 786).

The selection below is profitably compared with those from Hume (above, page 322) on the standard of taste and Kant (below, page 419) on aesthetic disinterest.

See Walter J. Hipple, *The Beautiful, the Sublime, and the Picturesque in Eighteenth-Century British Aesthetic Theory* (1957); Arthur E. McGuinness, *Henry Home, Lord Kames* (1970); William Christian Lehmann, *Henry Home, Lord Kames, and the Scottish Enlightenment* (1971); Ian Simpson Ross, *Lord Kames and the Scotland of His Day* (1972); Robert L. Montgomery, *Terms of Response* (1992).

from

Elements of Criticism: Introduction

The five senses agree in the following particular, that nothing external is perceived till it first make an impression upon the organ of sense; the impression, for example, made upon the hand by a stone, upon the palate by sugar, and upon the nostrils by a rose. But there is a difference as to our consciousness of that impression. In touching, tasting, and smelling, we are conscious of that impression. Not so in seeing and hearing. When I behold a tree, I am not sensible of the impression made upon my eye; nor of the impression made upon my ear, when I listen to a song. This difference in the manner of perception, distinguishes remarkably hearing and seeing from the other senses; and distinguishes still more remarkably the feelings of the former from those of the latter. A feeling pleasant or painful cannot exist but in the mind; and yet because in tasting, touching, and smelling, we are conscious of the impression made upon the organ, we naturally place there also, the pleasant or painful feeling caused by that impression. And because such feelings seem to be placed externally at the organ of sense, we, for that reason, conceive them to be merely corporeal. We have a different apprehension of the pleasant and painful feelings derived from seeing and hearing. Being insensible here of the organic impression, we are not misled to assign a wrong place to these feelings; and therefore we naturally place them in the mind, where they really exist. Upon that account, they are conceived to be more refined and spiritual, than what are derived from tasting, touching, and smelling.

The pleasures of the eye and ear being thus elevated above those of the other external senses, acquire so much dignity as to make them a laudable entertainment. They are not, however, set upon a level with those that are purely intellectual; being not less inferior in dignity to intellectual pleasures, than superior to the organic or corporeal. They indeed resemble the latter, being like them produced by external objects: but they also resemble the former, being like them produced without any sensible organic impression. Their mixt nature and middle place betwixt organic and intellectual pleasures, qualify them to associate with either. Beauty heightens all the organic feelings, as well as those that are intellectual. Harmony, though it aspires to inflame devotion, disdains not to improve the relish of a banquet.

The pleasures of the eye and ear have other valuable properties beside those of dignity and elevation. Being sweet and moderately exhilerating, they are in their tone equally distant from the turbulence of passion, and languor of inaction; and by that tone are perfectly well qualified, not only to revive the spirits when sunk by sensual gratification, but also to relax them when overstrained in any violent pursuit. Here is a remedy provided for many distresses. And to be convinced of its salutary effects, it will be sufficient to run over the following particulars. Organic pleasures have naturally a short duration: when continued too long, or indulged to excess, they lose their relish, and beget satiety and disgust. To relieve us from that uneasiness, nothing can be more happily contrived than the exhilerating pleasures of the eye and ear, which take place imperceptibly, without much varying the tone of mind. On the other hand, any intense exercise of the intellectual powers, becomes painful by overstraining the mind. Cessation from such exercise gives not instant relief: it is necessary that the void be filled with some amusement, gently relaxing the spirits.[1] Organic pleasure, which hath no relish but while we are in vigour, is ill qualified for that office: but the finer pleasures of sense, which occupy without exhausting the mind, are excellently well qualified to restore its usual tone after severe application to study or business, as well as after satiety from sensual gratification.

Our first perceptions are of external objects, and our first attachments are to them. Organic pleasures take the lead. But the mind, gradually ripening, relisheth more and more the pleasures of the eye and ear; which approach the purely mental, without exhausting the spirits; and exceed the purely sensual, without danger of satiety. The pleasures of the eye and ear have accordingly a natural aptitude to attract us from the immoderate gratification of sensual appetite. For the mind, once accustomed to enjoy a variety of external objects without being conscious of the organic impression, is prepared for enjoying internal objects where there cannot be an organic impression. Thus the author of nature, by qualifying the human mind for a succession of enjoyments from the lowest to the highest, leads it by gentle steps from the most groveling corporeal pleasures, for which solely it is fitted in the beginning of life, to those refined and sublime pleasures which are suited to its maturity.

This succession, however, is not governed by unavoidable necessity. The God of nature offers it to us, in order to advance our happiness; and it is sufficient, that he hath enabled us to complete the succession. Nor has he made our

---

Kames's *Elements of Criticism* was published in three volumes in 1762 and again (enlarged) in 1763. The text is from the 1762 edition.

[1] [Kames] Du Bos judiciously observes that silence doth not tend to calm an agitated mind; but that soft and slow music hath a fine effect.

talk disagreeable or difficult. On the contrary, the transition is sweet and easy, from corporeal pleasures to the more refined pleasures of sense; and not less so, from these to the exalted pleasures of morality and religion. We stand therefore engaged in honour, as well as interest, to second the purposes of nature, by cultivating the pleasures of the eye and ear, those especially that require extraordinary culture,[2] such as are inspired by poetry, painting, sculpture, music, gardening, and architecture. This chiefly is the duty of the opulent, who have leisure to improve their minds and their feelings. The fine arts are contrived to give pleasure to the eye and the ear, disregarding the inferior senses. A taste for these arts is a plant that grows naturally in many soils; but, without culture, scarce to perfection in any soil. It is susceptible of much refinement; and is, by proper care, greatly improved. In this respect, a taste in the fine arts goes hand in hand with the moral sense, to which indeed it is nearly allied. Both of them discover what is right and what is wrong. Fashion, temper, and education, have an influence upon both, to vitiate them, or to preserve them pure and untainted. Neither of them are arbitrary or local. They are rooted in human nature, and are governed by principles common to all men. The principles of morality belong not to the present undertaking. But as to the principles of the fine arts, they are evolved, by studying the sensitive part of human nature, and by learning what objects are naturally agreeable, and what are naturally disagreeable. The man who aspires to be a critic in these arts, must pierce still deeper. He must clearly perceive what objects are lofty, what low, what are proper or improper, what are manly, and what are mean or trivial. Hence a foundation for judging of taste, and for reasoning upon it. Where it is conformable to principles, we can pronounce with certainty, that it is correct; otherwise, that it is incorrect, and perhaps whimsical. Thus the fine arts, like morals, become a rational science; and, like morals, may be cultivated to a high degree of refinement.

Manifold are the advantages of criticism, when thus studied as a rational science. In the first place, a thorough acquaintance with the principles of the fine arts, redoubles the entertainment these arts afford. To the man who resigns himself entirely to sentiment or feeling, without interposing any sort of judgment, poetry, music, painting, are mere pastime. In the prime of life, indeed, they are delightful, being supported by the force of novelty, and the heat of imagination. But they lose their relish gradually with their novelty; and are generally neglected in the maturity of life, which disposes to more serious and more important occupations. To those who deal in criticism as a regular science, governed by just principles, and giving scope to judgment as well as to fancy, the fine arts are a favourite entertainment; and in old age maintain that relish which they produce in the morning of life.[3]

In the next place, a philosophic inquiry into the principles of the fine arts, inures the reflecting mind to the most enticing sort of logic. Reasoning upon subjects so agreeable tends to a habit; and a habit, strengthening the reasoning faculties, prepares the mind for entering into subjects more difficult and abstract. To have, in this respect, a just conception of the importance of criticism, we need but reflect upon the common method of education; which, after some years spent in acquiring languages, hurries us, without the least preparatory discipline, into the most profound philosophy. A more effectual method to alienate the tender mind from abstract science, is beyond the reach of invention. With respect to such speculations, the bulk of our youth contract a sort of hobgoblin terror, which is seldom, if ever, subdued. Those who apply to the arts, are trained in a very different manner. They are led, step by step, from the easier parts of the operation, to what are more difficult; and are not permitted to make a new motion, till they be perfected in those which regularly precede it. The science of criticism appears then to be an intermediate link, finely qualified for connecting the different parts of education into a regular chain. This science furnisheth an inviting opportunity to exercise the judgement: we delight to reason upon subjects that are equally pleasant and familiar: we proceed gradually from the simpler to the more involved cases: and in a due course of discipline, custom, which improves all our faculties, bestows acuteness upon those of reason, sufficient to unravel all the intricacies of philosophy.

Nor ought it to be overlooked, that the reasonings employed upon the fine arts are of the same kind with those which regulate our conduct. Mathematical and metaphysical reasonings have no tendency to improve social intercourse: nor are they applicable to the common affairs of life. But a just taste in the fine arts, derived from rational principles, is a fine preparation for acting in the social state with dignity and propriety.

---

[2][Kames] A taste for natural objects is born with us in perfection. To relish a fine countenance, a rich landscape, or a vivid colour, culture is unnecessary. The observation holds equally in natural sounds, such as the singing of birds, or the murmuring of a brook. Nature here, the artificer of the object as well as of the percipient, hath suited them to each other with great accuracy. But of a poem, a cantata, a picture, and other artificial productions, a true relish is not commonly attained without study and practice.

---

[3][Kames] "Though logic may subsist without rhetoric or poetry, yet so necessary to these last is a sound and correct logic, that without it, they are no better than warbling trifles." Hermes, page 6. [By James Harris, *A Philosophical Inquiry Concerning Universal Grammar* (1751)].

The science of criticism tends to improve the heart not less than the understanding. I observe, in the first place, that it hath a fine effect in moderating the selfish affections. A just taste in the fine arts, by sweetening and harmonizing the temper, is a strong antidote to the turbulence of passion and violence of pursuit. Elegance of taste procures to a man so much enjoyment at home, or easily within reach, that in order to be occupied, he is, in youth, under no temptation to precipitate into hunting, gaming, drinking; nor, in middle age, to deliver himself over to ambition; nor, in old age, to avarice. Pride, a disgustful selfish passion, exerts itself without control, when accompanied with a bad taste. A man of this stamp, upon whom the most striking beauty makes but a faint impression, feels no joy but in gratifying his ruling passion by the discovery of errors and blemishes. Pride, on the other hand, finds in the constitution no enemy more formidable than a delicate and discerning taste. The man upon whom nature and culture have bestowed this blessing, feels great delight in the virtuous dispositions and actions of others. He loves to cherish them, and to publish them to the world. Faults and failings, it is true, are to him not less obvious: but these he avoids, or removes out of sight, because they give him pain. In a word, there may be other passions, which, for a season, disturb the peace of society more than pride: but no other passion is so unwearied an antagonist to the sweets of social intercourse. Pride, tending assiduously to its gratification, puts a man perpetually in opposition to others; and disposes him more to relish bad than good qualities, even in a bosom-friend. How different that disposition of mind, where every virtue in a companion or neighbour, is, by refinement of taste, set in its strongest light; and defects or blemishes, natural to all, are suppressed, or kept out of view?

In the next place, delicacy of taste tends not less to invigorate the social affections, than to moderate those that are selfish. To be convinced of this tendency, we need only reflect, that delicacy of taste necessarily heightens our sensibility of pain and pleasure, and of course our sympathy, which is the capital branch of every social passion. Sympathy in particular invites a communication of joys and sorrows, hopes and fears. Such exercise, soothing and satisfactory in itself, is productive necessarily of mutual good-will and affection.

One other advantage of criticism is reserved to the last place, being of all the most important, that it is a great support to morality. I insist on it with entire satisfaction, that no occupation attaches a man more to his duty than that of cultivating a taste in the fine arts. A just relish of what is beautiful, proper, elegant, and ornamental, in writing or painting, in architecture or gardening, is a fine preparation for dis-

cerning what is beautiful, just, elegant, or magnanimous, in character and behaviour. To the man who has acquired a taste so acute and accomplished, every action, wrong or improper, must be highly disgustful. If, in any instance, the overbearing power of passion sway him from his duty, he returns to it upon the first reflection, with redoubled resolution never to be swayed a second time. He has now an additional motive to virtue, a conviction derived from experience, that happiness depends on regularity and order, and that a disregard to justice or propriety never fails to be punished with shame and remorse.[4]

* * *

Chapter XXV

Standard of Taste

That there is no disputing about "taste", meaning taste in its most extensive sense, is a saying so generally received as to have become a proverb. One thing indeed is evident, that if the proverb hold true with respect to any one external sense, it must hold true with respect to all. If the pleasures of the palate disdain a comparative trial and reject all criticism, the pleasures of touch, of smell, of sound, and even of sight, must be equally privileged. At this rate, a man is not within the reach of censure, even where, insensible to beauty, grandeur, or elegance, he prefers the Saracen's head upon a sign-post before the best tablature of Raphael,[5] or a rude Gothic tower before the finest Grecian building: nor where he prefers the smell of a rotten carcass before that of the most odoriferous flower: nor jarring discords before the most exquisite harmony.

But we must not stop here. If the pleasures of external sense be exempted from criticism, why not every one of our pleasures, from whatever source derived? If taste in the proper sense of the word cannot be disputed, there is as little room for disputing it in its figurative sense. The proverb accordingly comprehends both; and in that large sense may be resolved into the following general proposition, That

---

[4] [Kames] Genius is allied to a warm and inflammable constitution, delicacy of taste to calmness and sedateness. Hence it is common to find genius in one who is a prey to every passion; which can scarce happen with respect to delicacy of taste. Upon a man possessed of this blessing, the moral duties, as well as the fine arts, make a deep impression, so as to counterbalance every irregular desire. And even supposing a strong temptation, it can take no fast hold of a calm and sedate temper.
[5] Raffaello Santi (1483–1520), Italian painter.

with respect to the sensitive part of our nature, by which some objects are agreeable some disagreeable, there is not such a thing as a *good* or *bad,* a *right* or *wrong;* that every man's taste is to himself an ultimate standard without appeal; and consequently that there is no ground of censure against any one, if such a one there be, who prefers Blackmore[6] before Homer, selfishness before benevolence, or cowardice before magnanimity.

The proverb in the foregoing instances, is indeed carried very far. It seems difficult, however, to sap its foundation, or with success to attack it from any quarter. For in comparing the various tastes of individuals, it is not obvious what standard must be appealed to. Is not every man equally a judge of what is agreeable or disagreeable to himself? Doth it not seem odd, and perhaps absurd, that a man *ought not* to be pleased when he is, or that he *ought* to be pleased when he is not?

This reasoning may perplex, but, in contradiction to sense and feeling, will never afford conviction. A man of taste must necessarily feel the reasoning to be false, however unqualified to detect the fallacy. At the same time, though no man of taste will subscribe to the proverb as holding true in every case, no man will venture to affirm that it holds true in no case. Subjects there are undoubtedly, that we may like or dislike indifferently, without any imputation upon our taste. Were a philosopher to make a scale for human pleasures with many divisions, in order that the value of each pleasure may be denoted by the place it occupies, he would not think of making divisions without end, but would rank together many pleasures arising perhaps from different objects, either as being equally valuable, or differing so imperceptibly as to make a separation unnecessary. Nature hath taken this course, so far as appears to the generality of mankind. There may be subdivisions without end; but we are only sensible of the grosser divisions, comprehending each of them many pleasures of various kinds. To these the proverb is applicable in the strictest sense; for with respect to pleasures of the same rank, what ground can there be for preferring one before another? If a preference in fact be given by any individual, it cannot be taste, but custom, imitation, or some peculiarity of mind.

Nature in her scale of pleasures, has been sparing of divisions: she hath wisely and benevolently filled every division with many pleasures; in order that individuals may be contented with their own lot, without envying the happiness of others: many hands must be employ'd to procure us the conveniencies of life; and it is necessary that the different branches of business, whether more or less agreeable, be filled with hands. A taste too nice and delicate, would obstruct this plan; for it would crowd some employments, leaving others, not less useful, totally neglected. In our present condition, happy it is, that the plurality are not delicate in their choice. They fall in readily with the occupations, pleasures, food, and company, that fortune throws in their way; and if at first there be any displeasing circumstance, custom soon makes it easy.

The proverb will be admitted so far as it regards the particulars now explained. But when apply'd in general to every subject of taste, the difficulties to be encountered are insuperable. What shall we say, in particular, as to the difficulty that arises from human nature itself? Do we not talk of a good and a bad taste? of a right and a wrong taste? and upon that supposition, do we not, with great confidence, censure writers, painters, architects, and every one who deals in the fine arts? Are such criticisms absurd and void of foundation? Have the foregoing expressions, familiar in all languages and among all people, no sort of meaning? This can hardly be: what is universal must have a foundation in nature. If we can reach this foundation, the standard of taste will no longer be a secret.

All living creatures are by nature distributed into classes; the individuals of each, however diversified by slighter differences, having a wonderful uniformity in their capital parts internal and external. Each class is distinguishable from others by an external form; and not less distinguishable by an internal constitution, manifested by certain powers, feelings, desires, and actions, peculiar to the individuals of each class. Thus each class may be conceived to have a common nature, which, in framing the individuals belonging to the class, is taken for a model or standard.

Independent altogether of experience, men have a sense or conviction of a common nature or standard, not only in their own species, but in every species of animals. And hence it is a matter of wonder, to find any individual deviating from the common nature of the species, whether in its internal or external construction: a child born with an aversion to its mother's milk, is a matter of wonder, not less than if born without a mouth, or with more than one.[7]

With respect to this common nature or standard, we are so constituted as to conceive it to be *perfect* or *right;* and consequently that individuals *ought* to be made conformable to it. Every remarkable deviation accordingly from the

---

[6]Sir Richard Blackmore (1654–1729), English physician and writer, author of four epics.

[7][Kames] See *Essays on Morality and Natural Religion,* part I, essay 2, chapter i.

standard, makes an impression upon us of imperfection, irregularity, or disorder: it is disagreeable and raises in us a painful emotion: monstrous births, exciting the curiosity of a philosopher, fail not at the same time to excite aversion in a high degree.

Lastly, we have a conviction, that the common nature of man is invariable not less than universal: we conceive that it hath no relation to time nor to place; but that it will be the same hereafter as at present, and as it was in time past; the same among all nations and in all corners of the earth. Nor are we deceived: giving allowance for the difference of culture and gradual refinement of manners, the fact corresponds to our conviction.

This conviction of a common nature or standard, and of its perfection, is the foundation of morality; and accounts clearly for that remarkable conception we have, of a right and a wrong taste in morals. It accounts not less clearly for the conception we have of a right and a wrong taste in the fine arts. A person who rejects objects generally agreeable, and delights in objects generally disagreeable, is condemned as a monster: we disapprove his taste as bad or wrong; and we have a clear conception that he deviates from the common standard. If man were so framed as not to have any notion of a common standard, the proverb mentioned in the beginning would hold universally, not only in the fine arts but in morals: upon that supposition, the taste of every man, with respect to both, would to himself be an ultimate standard. But the conviction of a common standard being made a part of our nature, we intuitively conceive a taste to be right or good if conformable to the common standard, and wrong or bad if disconformable.

No particular concerning human nature is more universal, than the uneasiness a man feels when in matters of importance his opinions are rejected by others. Why should difference in opinion create uneasiness, more than difference in stature, in countenance, or in dress? The sense of a common standard is the only principle that can explain this mystery. Every man, generally speaking, taking it for granted that his opinions agree with the common sense of mankind, is therefore disgusted with those of a contrary opinion, not as differing from him, but as differing from the common standard. Hence in all disputes, we find the parties, each of them equally, appealing constantly to the common sense of mankind as the ultimate rule or standard. Were it not for this standard, of which the conviction is universal, I cannot discover the slightest foundation for rancor or animosity when persons differ in essential points more than in points purely indifferent. With respect to the latter, which are not supposed to be regulated by any standard, individuals are permitted to think for themselves with impunity. The

same liberty is not indulged with respect to the former: for what reason, other than that the standard by which these are regulated, ought, as we judge, to produce an uniformity of opinion in all men? In a word, to this sense of a common standard must be wholly attributed the pleasure we take in those who espouse the same principles and opinions with ourselves, as well as the aversion we have at those who differ from us. In matters left indifferent by the standard, we find nothing of the same pleasure or pain. A bookish man, unless sway'd by convenience, relisheth not the contemplative more than the active part of mankind: his friends and companions are chosen indifferently out of either class. A painter consorts with a poet or musician, as readily as with those of his own art; and one is not the more agreeable to me for loving beef, as I do, nor the less agreeable for preferring mutton.

I have said, that my disgust is raised, not by differing from me, but by differing from what I judge to be the common standard. This point, being of importance, ought to be firmly established. Men, it is true, are prone to flatter themselves, by taking it for granted, that their opinions and their taste are in all respects agreeable to the common standard. But there may be exceptions, and experience shows there are some. There are instances without number, of persons who cling to the grosser amusements of gaming, eating, drinking, without having any relish for more elegant pleasures, such, for example, as are afforded by the fine arts. Yet these very persons, talking the same language with the rest of mankind, pronounce in favour of the more elegant pleasures: they invariably approve those who have a more refined taste, and are ashamed of their own as low and sensual. It is in vain to think of giving a reason for this singular impartiality against self, other than the authority of the common standard. Every individual of the human species, the most groveling not excepted, hath a natural sense of the dignity of human nature.[8] Hence every man is esteemed and respected in proportion to the dignity of his character, sentiments, and actions. And from the instances now given we discover, that the sense of the dignity of human nature is so vigorous, as even to prevail over self-partiality, and to make us despise our own taste compared with the more elevated taste of others.

In our sense of a common standard and in the pleasure individuals give us by their conformity to it, a curious final cause is discovered. An uniformity of taste and sentiment in matters of importance, forms an intimate connection among individuals, and is a great blessing in the social state. With respect to morals in particular, unhappy it would be for

---

[8] [Kames] See chapter ii.

mankind did not this uniformity prevail: it is necessary that the actions of all men be uniform with respect to right and wrong; and in order to uniformity of action, it is necessary that all men think the same way in these particulars: if they differ through any irregular bias, the common sense of mankind is appealed to as the rule; and it is the province of judges, in matters especially of equity, to apply that rule. The same uniformity, it is yielded, is not so strictly necessary in other matters of taste: men, though connected in general as members of the same state, are, by birth, office, or occupation, separated and distinguished into different classes; and are thereby qualified for different amusements: variety of taste, so far, is no obstruction to the general connection. But with respect to the more capital pleasures, such as are best enjoy'd in common, uniformity of taste is necessary for two great ends, first to connect individuals the more intimately in the social life, and next to advance these pleasures to their highest perfection. With respect to the first, if instead of a common taste, every man had a taste peculiar to himself, leading him to place his happiness upon things indifferent or perhaps disagreeable to others, these capital pleasures could not be enjoy'd in common: every man would pursue his own happiness by flying from others; and instead of a natural tendency to union, remarkable in the human species, union would be our aversion: man would not be a consistent being: his interest would lead him to society, and his taste would draw him from it. The other end will be best explained by entering upon particulars. Uniformity of taste gives opportunity for sumptuous and elegant buildings, for fine gardens, and extensive embellishments, which please universally. Works of this nature could never have reached any degree of perfection, had every man a taste peculiar to himself: there could not be any suitable reward, either of profit or honour, to encourage men of genius to labour in such works. The same uniformity of taste is equally necessary to perfect the arts of music, sculpture, and painting; and to support the expense they require after they are brought to perfection. Nature is in every particular consistent with herself. We are formed by nature to have a high relish for the fine arts, which are a great source of happiness, and extremely friendly to virtue. We are, at the same time, formed with an uniformity of taste, to furnish proper objects for this high relish: if uniformity of taste did not prevail, the fine arts could never have made any figure.

Thus, upon a sense common to the species, is erected a standard of taste, which without hesitation is apply'd to the taste of every individual. This standard, ascertaining what actions are right what wrong, what proper what improper, hath enabled moralists to establish rules for our conduct from which no person is allowed to swerve. We have the same standard for ascertaining in all the fine arts, what is beautiful or ugly, high or low, proper or improper, proportioned or disproportioned. And here, as in morals, we justly condemn every taste that swerves from what is thus ascertained by the common standard.

The discovery of a rule or standard for trying the taste of individuals in the fine arts as well as in morals, is a considerable advance, but completes not our journey. We have a great way yet to travel. It is made out that there is a standard: but it is not made out, by what means we shall prevent mistaking a false standard for that of nature. If from opinion and practice we endeavour to ascertain the standard of nature, we are betray'd into endless perplexities. Viewing this matter historically, nothing appears more various and more wavering than taste in the fine arts. If we judge by numbers, the Gothic taste of architecture will be preferred before that of Greece; and the Chinese taste probably before both. It would be endless, to recount the various tastes of gardening that have prevailed in different ages, and still prevail in different countries. Despising the modest colouring of nature, women of fashion in France daub their cheeks with a red powder. Nay, the unnatural swelling in the neck, a disease peculiar to the inhabitants of the Alps, is relished by that people. But we ought not to be discouraged by such untoward instances. For do we not find the like contradictions with respect to morals? was it not once held lawful, for a man to expose his infant children, and, when grown up, to sell them for slaves? was it not held equally lawful, to punish children for the crime of their parents? was not the murder of an enemy in cold blood an universal practice? what stronger instance can be given, than the abominable practice of human sacrifices, not less impious than immoral? Such aberrations from the rules of morality, prove only, that men, originally savage and brutish, acquire not rationality or any delicacy of taste, till they be long disciplined in society. To ascertain the rules of morality, we appeal not to the common sense of savages, but of men in their more perfect state: and we make the same appeal, in forming the rules that ought to govern the fine arts. In neither can we safely rely on a local or transitory taste; but on what is the most universal and the most lasting among polite nations.

In this very manner, a standard for morals has been established with a good deal of accuracy; and so well fitted for practice, that in the hand of able judges it is daily apply'd with general satisfaction. The standard of taste in the fine arts, is not yet brought to such perfection. And there is an obvious reason for its slower progress. The sense of a right and a wrong in action, is conspicuous in the breast of every individual, almost without exception. The sense of a right and a wrong in the fine arts, is more faint and wavering: it is by nature a tender plant, requiring much culture to bring it to maturity: in a barren soil it cannot live; and in any soil, without cultivation, it is weak and sickly. I talk chiefly with relation to its more refined objects: for some objects make such lively impressions of beauty, grandeur, and proportion, as without exception to command the general taste. There appears to me great contrivance, in distinguishing thus the moral sense from a taste in the fine arts. The former, as a rule of conduct and as a law we ought to obey, must be clear and authoritative. The latter is not intitled to the same authority, since it contributes to our pleasure and amusement only. Were it more strong and lively, it would usurp upon our duty, and call off the attention from matters of greater moment. Were it more clear and authoritative, it would banish all difference of taste: a refined taste would not form a character, nor be intitled to esteem. This would put an end to rivalship, and consequently to all improvement.

But to return to our subject. However languid and cloudy the common sense of mankind may be with respect to the fine arts, it is yet the only standard in these as well as in morals. And when the matter is attentively considered, this standard will be found less imperfect than it appears to be at first sight. In gathering the common sense of mankind upon morals, we may safely consult every individual. But with respect to the fine arts, our method must be different: a wary choice is necessary; for to collect votes indifferently, will certainly mislead us: those who depend for food on bodily labour, are totally void of taste; of such a taste at least as can be of use in the fine arts. This consideration bars the greater part of mankind; and of the remaining part, many have their taste corrupted to such a degree as to unqualify them altogether for voting. The common sense of mankind must then be confined to the few that fall not under these exceptions. But as such selection seems to throw matters again into uncertainty, we must be more explicit upon this branch of our subject.

Nothing tends more than voluptuousness to corrupt the whole internal frame, and to vitiate our taste, not only in the fine arts, but even in morals. It never fails, in course of time, to extinguish all the sympathetic affections, and to bring on a beastly selfishness which leaves nothing of man but the shape. About excluding persons of this stamp there will be no dispute. Let us next bring under trial, the opulent whose chief pleasure is expense. Riches, coveted by most men for the sake of superiority and to command respect, are generally bestow'd upon costly furniture, numerous attendants, a princely dwelling, every thing superb and gorgeous, to amaze and humble all beholders. Simplicity, elegance, propriety, and every thing natural, sweet, or amiable, are despised or neglected; for these are not at the command of riches, and make no figure in the public eye. In a word, nothing is relished, but what serves to gratify pride, by an imagined exaltation of the possessor above those he reckons the vulgar. Such a tenor of life contracts the heart and makes every principle give way to self-interest. Benevolence and public spirit, with all their refined emotions, are little felt and less regarded. And if these be excluded, there can be no place for the faint and delicate emotions of the fine arts.

The exclusion of classes so many and various, reduces within a narrow compass those who are qualified to be judges in the fine arts. Many circumstances are necessary to form a judge of this sort: there must be a good natural taste: this taste must be improved by education, reflection, and experience: it must be preserved alive, by a regular course of life, by using the goods of fortune with moderation, and by following the dictates of improved nature which gives welcome to every rational pleasure without deviating into excess. This is the tenor of life which of all contributes the most to refinement of taste; and the same tenor of life contributes the most to happiness in general.

If there appear much uncertainty in a standard that requires so painful and intricate a selection, we may possibly be reconciled to it by the following consideration, That, with respect to the fine arts, there is less difference of taste than is commonly imagined. Nature hath marked all her works with indelible characters of high or low, plain or elegant, strong or weak. These, if at all perceived, are seldom misapprehended by any taste; and the same marks are equally perceptible in works of art. A defective taste is incurable; and it hurts none but the possessor, because it carries no authority to impose upon others. I know not if there be such a thing as a taste naturally bad or wrong; a taste, for example, that prefers a groveling pleasure before one that is high and elegant. Groveling pleasures are never preferred: they are only made welcome by those who know no better. Differences about objects of taste, it is true, are endless: but they generally concern trifles, or possibly matters of equal rank where the preference may be given either way with impunity. If, on any occasion, the dispute go deeper and persons differ where they ought not, a depraved taste will readily be discovered on one or other side, occasioned by imitation, custom, or corrupted manners, such as are described above.

If, after all that is said, the standard of taste be thought not yet sufficiently ascertained, there is still one resource in which I put great confidence. What I have in view, are the principles that constitute the sensitive part of our nature. By means of these principles, common to all men, a wonderful uniformity is preserved among the emotions and feelings of different individuals; the same object making upon every person the same impression; the same in kind, at least, if not in degree. There have been aberrations, as above observed, from these principles; but soon or late they always prevail, by restoring the wanderers to the right track. The uniformity of taste here accounted for, is the very thing that in other words is termed the common sense of mankind. And this discovery leads us to means for ascertaining the common sense of mankind or the standard of taste, more unerringly than the selection above insisted on. Every doubt with relation to this standard, occasioned by the practice of different nations and different times, may be cleared by applying to the principles that ought to govern the taste of every individual. In a word, a thorough acquaintance with these principles will enable us to form the standard of taste; and to lay a foundation for this valuable branch of knowledge, is the declared purpose of the present undertaking.

Gotthold Ephraim Lessing

1729–1781

In his important work on Greek art, published in 1755, Johann Winckelmann ana-lyzed the famous statue of Laocoön and his children struggling with two serpents. Winckelmann was interested in the representation of Laocoon's attitude and wondered specifically why his mouth was not open to express his agony. He concluded that Greek ideals of restraint forbade it. This discussion served as an impetus for Lessing, who claims that to have the mouth open would be indecorous; the moment caught in the sculpture is properly that before the cry, for to depict the moment of the cry itself would create disgust and distress rather than pity.

Lessing objects to the "mania for description" in poetry and allegory in painting and sculpture. He argues that the artist must recognize certain "restraints on expression" generated by the limitations of the medium. He goes on to formulate fundamental dif-ferences between sculpture and painting and poetry. In his view, sculpture and painting have no temporal dimension, whereas poetry can present actions in time: sculpture and painting can imitate actions, "but only by way of indication, and through the means of bodies." Poetry can paint bodies, "but only by way of indication, and through the means of actions." Thus in poetry there is a considerable "frugality in the description of bodily objects." Lessing seeks to demonstrate this by discussion of Homer's way of describing objects. Other differences that Lessing notes are that the plastic and pictorial artists find execution more difficult, the poets invention, and that the artists cannot effectively pre-sent the invisible, while poets can. Further, the act of reading makes impossible the syn-thesis of a description in words where illusion is the aim. Lessing argues that this is be-cause the words must be read in a temporal order.

There had been a long tradition of criticism tending to blur the differences between the various media of art. The idea of the poem as a "speaking picture" is attributed to the Greek poet Simonides (c. 556–468? B.C.) and was given added force by readers of Horace's phrase *ut pictura poeisis* (as in painting, so in poetry [above, page 84]), though the Horatian phrase was taken out of context and as a result misread. The movement gained strength in eighteenth-century interest in the so-called "sister arts." Lessing did not succeded in making his distinctions among the arts reign supreme, though he did in-fluence numerous later critics, including Schiller in his *On Naive and Sentimental Po-etry* (1795–1796), to draw a distinction between spatial and temporal arts.

Lessing's analysis implies that art is fundamentally mimetic. Modern art raises new questions about the relation of temporal movement to static representation. Neverthe-less, Lessing's argument, though sometimes rigid, does emphasize the fact that each medium has particular limitations and possibilities.

Numerous translations of *Laocoön* exist. The most useful are by E. C. Beasley (1853), Ellen Frothingham (1873), Sir Robert Phillimore (1874), Albert Hamann

(1892), L. E. Upcott (1895), and E. A. McCormick (1962). *Selected Prose Works,* translated by E. C. Beasley and Hellen Zimmern (1879), contains selections from Lessing's *Hamburg Dramaturgy* (1767–1768). See W. G. Howard, "Burke Among the Forerunners of Lessing," *PMLA* XXII (1907), 608–32; Irving Babbitt, *The New Laocoön* (1910); J. G. Robertson, *Lessing's Dramatic Theory* (1939); F. O. Nolte, *Lessing's* Laocoön (1940); Max Kommeril, *Lessing und Aristoteles* (1940); Peter Heller, *Dialectics and Nihilism* (1966); V. A. Rudowski, "Action as the Essence of Poetry: A Revaluation of Lessing's Argument," *PMLA* LXXXII (1967), 333–41; David E. Welberg, *Lessing's* Laocoön: *Semiotics and Aesthetics in the Age of Reason* (1984); Robert Scott Leventhal, *The Discipline of Interpretation: Lessing, Herder, Schlegel, and Hermeneutics in Germany, 1750–1800* (1994).

from

Laocoön

Chapter XVI

But I will try to consider the matter upon first principles. I reason in this way. If it be true that painting, in its imitations, makes use of entirely different means and signs from those which poetry employs; the former employing figures and colors in space, the latter articulate sounds in time—if, incontestably, signs must have a proper relation to the thing signified, then coexistent signs can only express objects which are coexistent, or the parts of which coexist, but signs which are successive can only express objects which are in succession, or the parts of which succeed one another in time. Objects which coexist, or the parts of which coexist, are termed bodies. It follows that bodies, with their visible properties, are the proper objects of painting. Objects which succeed, or the parts of which succeed to each other, are called generally actions. It follows that actions are the proper object of poetry.[1]

But all bodies do not exist only in space, but also in time. They have continued duration, and in every moment of their duration may assume a different appearance and stand in a different relation. Each of these momentary appearances and relations is the effect of a preceding, and the cause of a subsequent action, and so presents us, as it were, a center of action. It follows that painting can imitate actions, but only by way of indication, and through the means of bodies.

On the other hand, actions cannot subsist by themselves, but must be dependent on certain beings. Insofar, now, as these beings are bodies, or may be regarded as such, poetry also paints bodies, but only by way of indication, and through the means of actions.

Painting, with regard to compositions in which the objects are coexistent, can only avail itself of one moment of action, and must therefore choose that which is the most pregnant, and by which what has gone before and what is to follow will be most intelligible.

And even thus poetry, in her progressive imitations, can only make use of one single property of bodies, and must therefore choose that one which conveys to us the most sensible idea of the form of the body, from that point of view for which it employs it.

From this is derived the rule of the unity of picturesque epithets, and of frugality in the description of bodily objects.

I should put little confidence in this dry chain of argument did I not find it fully confirmed by the practice of Homer, or rather, I should say, if the practice of Homer had not introduced me to it. Upon these principles only the great manner of the Greek can be defined, and explained, and the sentence which it deserves be passed on the directly opposite manner of so many modern poets who wish to rival the painter in a performance in which they must necessarily be surpassed by him. I find that Homer paints nothing but progressive actions, and paints all bodies and individual things only on account of their relation to these actions, and generally with a single trait. What wonder is it, then, that the painter, where Homer has painted, finds little or nothing for himself to do, and that his harvest is only to be gathered where history brings together a multitude of beautiful bod-

---

Laocoön was first published in 1766. The text is from the translation by Sir Robert Phillimore (1874).
[1] Here Lessing follows Aristotle's *Poetics* (above, page 53).

ies, in beautiful attitudes, within a space favorable to art, while the poet himself may paint as little as he pleases these bodies, these attitudes, and this space? Let anyone go through the whole series of paintings, piece by piece, which Caylus[2] has taken from him, and he will find a confirmation of this remark.

Here I leave the Count, who would make the color-grinding stone of the painter the touchstone of the poet, in order that I may throw a greater light upon the manner of Homer.

I say that Homer usually makes use of one trait. A ship is to him at one time a dark ship, at another a hollow ship, at another a swift ship, at the most a well-rowed black ship. He goes no farther in the painting of a ship but the navigation, the departure, the arrival of the ship; out of these he makes a detailed picture, a picture out of which the painter must make five or six separate pictures if he wishes to place it entirely upon his canvas.

If particular circumstances compel Homer to fix our attention for a longer time upon one individual corporeal object, he nevertheless produces no picture which the painter can imitate with his pencil; but he knows how to use numberless expedients of art, so as to place this single object in a successive series of moments, and for the last of which the painter is obliged to wait, in order that he may show us completely formed that object, the gradual formation of which we have seen in the poet. For example, when Homer wishes to show us the chariot of Juno, he makes Hebe put together every piece of it before our eyes. We see the spokes and the axletrees, and the driving-seat, the pole, the traces, and the straps, not brought together as a whole, but as they are separately put together by the hands of Hebe. Upon the wheels alone the poet lavishes more than one trait, and he shows us the eight brazen spokes, the golden fellies, the tires of bronze, the silver naves—each individual separate thing. One might almost say, that because there were more wheels than one, therefore he was obliged to spend much more time on their description than the putting on of each particular part would in reality have required.

Ἥβη δ' ἀμφ ὀχέεσσι θοῶς βάλε καμπύλα κύκλα,
Χάλκεα, ὀκτάκνημα, σιδηρέῳ ἄξονι ἀμφίς.
Τῶν ἤτοι χρυσέη ἴτυς ἄφθιτος, ἀντὰρ ὑπερθεν
Χάλκε' ἐπίσσωτρα, προσαρηρότα, θαῦμα ἰδέσθαι.
Πλῆμναι δ' ἀργύρου εἰσὶ περίδρομοι ἀμφοτέρωθεν.
Δίφρος δὲ χρυσέοισι καὶ ἀργυρέοισιν ἱμᾶσιν
Ἐντέταται. δοιαὶ δὲ περίδρομοι ἀντυγές εἰσιν.
Τοῦ δ' ἐξ ἀργύρεος ῥυμὸς πέλεν. αὐτὰρ ἐπ' ἄκρω

Δῆσε χρύσειον καλόν ζυγὸν, ἐν, δὲ λέπαδνα
Κάλ' ἔβαλε χρύσει'. . .[3]

Does Homer wish to show us how Agamemnon was clad? Then the king must put on his whole clothing piece by piece before our eyes—the soft undergarment, the great mantle, the beautiful sandals, the sword—and then he is ready, and grasps the scepter. We see the raiment in which the poet paints the act of his being clothed; another would have painted the clothes in detail down to the smallest fringe, and we shall have seen nothing of the action of putting on the raiment.

Μαλακὸν δ' ἔνδυνε χιτῶνα,
Καλὸν, νηγάνεον. περὶ δὲ μέγα βάλλετο φᾶρος.
Ποσσὶ δ' ὑπὸ λιπαροῖσιν ἐδήσατο καλὰ πέδιλα.
Ἀμφὶ δ' ἄρ' ὤμοισιν βάλετο ξίφος ἀργυρόηλον,
Είλετο δὲ σκῆπτρον πατρώϊον, ἄφθιτον αἰεί.[4]

And as to that scepter which here is only described as ancestral and immortal, as in another place one like it is described only as χρυσείοις ἤλοισι πεπαρμένον, garnished with golden bosses, when I say we are to have a more complete and more accurate picture of this mighty scepter, what is it that Homer does? Does he paint for us, besides the golden bosses, the wood of which it is made, and the carved head? Yes, it would have been so in a description of heraldic art, in order that in future time it might be possible to make one exactly like it. And I am certain that many a modern poet would have given such an heraldic description, with the simple and honest notion that he himself was really painting because a painter could imitate him. But did Homer trouble himself with considering how far he should leave the painter behind him? Instead of a description he gives us the history of the scepter: first we see it as worked by Vulcan; next it glitters in the hand of Jupiter; then it proclaims the dignity

---

[2] Anne Claude, Comte de Caylus, *Tableaux tires de* l'Illiade, *de* l'Odysée *de Homere et de* l'Enéide *de Virgile* (1754–1758).

[3] [Phillimore] "Her golden-bridled steeds/Then Saturn's daughter brought abroad; and Hebe, she proceeds/To address her chariot instantly; she gives it—either wheel/Beamed with eight spokes of sounding brass; the axletree was steel,/The fell'ff's incorruptible gold, their upper brands of brass,/Their matter most unvalued, their work of wondrous grace./The naves in which the spokes were driven, were all with silver bound;/The chariot's seat, two hoops of gold and silver strengthened round;/Edged with a gold and silver fringe; the beam that looked before,/Was massy silver; on whose top, geres all of gold it wore,/And golden poitrils." *Iliad,* 722–31 (Chapman's translation).

[4] [Phillimore] "The dream gone, his voice still murmured/About the king's ears: who sat up, put him in his bed/His silken inner weed; fair, new, and then in haste arose;/Cast on his ample mantle, tied to his soft feet fair shoes;/His silver-hilted sword he hung about his shoulders, took his father's scepter never stained; which then abroad he shook." *Iliad,* 42–6 (Chapman's translation).

of Mercury; then it becomes the commander staff of the warrior Pelops; and then it is the pastoral staff of the peaceful Atreus.

> Σκῆπτρον ἔχων, τὸ μὲν ''Ηφαιστος κάμε τεύχων,
> ''Ηφαιστος μὲν δῶκε Διϊ Κρωνίωνι ἄνακτι.
> Αὐτὰρ ἄρα Ζεὺς δῶκε διακτόρῳ Ἀργειφόντῃ.
> Ἑρμείας δὲ ἄναξ δῶκεν Πέλοπι πληξίππῳ.
> Αὐτὰρ ὁ αὖτε Πλοψ δῶκ' Ἀτρέϊ, ποιμένι λαῶν.
> Ἀτρεὺς δὲ θνῄσκων ἔλιπεν πολύαρνι Θυέστῃ.
> Αὐτὰρ ὁ αὖτε Θυέστ' Ἀγαμέμνονι λεῖπε φορῆναι.
> Πολλῇσιν νήσοισι καὶ Ἀργεϊ παντὶ ἀνάσσειν.[5]

And thus, at last, I am better acquainted with this scepter than if a painter had placed it before my eyes, or a second Vulcan delivered it into my hand. I should not be surprised to find that one of the ancient expositors of Homer had admired this passage, as containing the most perfect allegory of the origin, the progress, the establishment, and finally of the hereditary character of kingly authority among men. I should smile, indeed, if I were to read that Vulcan, who wrought the scepter, represented fire, that thing which is most indispensable to the support of man, that relief of our necessities which had induced the first mortals to subject themselves to the rule of a single person; that the first king was a son of Time (Ζεὺς Κρωνίων), a venerable old man, who wished to share his power with an eloquent clever man, with a Mercury (διακτόρῳ Ἀργειφόντῃ), or entirely to give it up to him; that the wise orator, at a time when the young state was threatened by foreign foes, had delivered up his supreme authority to the bravest warrior (Πέλοπι πληξίππῳ); that the brave warrior, after he had subdued the enemy and secured the state, had found means to transfer it to his son, who, as a peace loving ruler, as a beneficent pastor of his people, had made them acquainted with good living and abundance (ποιμὴν λαῶν), whereby he had paved the way after his death for the wealthiest of his relations (πολύρνι Θυέστῃ); so that what hitherto confidence had bestowed and merit had considered rather as a burthen than a dignity, should now be obtained by presents and bribes, and secured forever to the family, like any other acquired property. I should smile, but I should notwithstanding be confirmed in my esteem for the poet to whom so much could be attributed.

But this lies out of my path, and I consider the history of the scepter merely as an artifice to induce us to contemplate for a while an individual thing without introducing us to a frigid description of its separate parts. Also, when Achilles swears by his scepter to avenge the contumely with which Agamemnon has treated him, Homer gives us the history of this scepter. We see it green and flourishing on the mountain, the steel severs it from the trunk, strips off its leaves and bark, and makes it a fitting instrument to signify, in the hands of the judges of the people, their divine dignity.

> Καὶ μὰ τόδε σκῆπτρον, τὸ μὲν οὔποτε φύλλα καὶ ὄζους
> φύσει, ἐπειδὴ πρῶτα τομὴν ἐν ὄρεσσι λέλοιπεν,
> Οὐδ' ἀναθηλήσει. περι γάρ ῥά ἑ χαλκὸς ἔλεψεν
> φύλλα τε καὶ φλοιόν. νῦν αὐτέ μιν υἷες Ἀχαιῶν
> Ἐν παλάμῃς φορέουσι δικασπόλοι. οἵτε θέμιστας
> Πρὸς Διὸς εἰρύαται.[6]

It was not so much the object of Homer to paint two scepters of different materials and forms, as to make a clear and plain representation to us of the difference of power of which these scepters were the emblems. The former, a work by Vulcan; the latter cut on the mountain by an unknown hand: the former, the ancient possession of a noble house; the latter destined for the strongest hand: the former in the hand of a monarch stretched over many islands and over the whole of Argos; the latter borne by one chosen out of the midst of the Greeks, to whom, with others, the administration of the laws was confided. This was really the distance at which Agamemnon and Achilles stood from each other; a distance which Achilles himself, in spite of all his blind wrath, could not do otherwise than confess.

But not only on those occasions when Homer combines with his descriptions of this kind ulterior objects, but also when he only desires to show us the picture, he will disperse, as it were, the picture in a kind of history of the object, in order that the different parts of it, which in nature we

---

[5][Phillimore] "Then stood divine Atrides up, and set his hand compressed/His scepter, th'elaborate work of fiery Mulciber:/Who gave it to Saturnian Jove; Jove to his messenger;/His messenger, Argicides, to Pelops, skilled in horse; Pelops to Atreus, chief of men: he dying, gave it course/To prince Thyestes, rich in herds; Thyestes to the hand/Of Agamemnon rendered it, and with it the command/Of many isles, and Argos all." *Iliad,* 101–08 (Chapman's translation).

[6][Phillimore] "Yet I vow, and by a great oath swear,/Even by this scepter, that as this never again shall bear/Green leaves or branches, no increase with any growth his size;/Nor did since first it left the hills, and had his faculties/And ornaments bereft with iron; which now to other end/Judges of Greece bear, and their laws, received from Jove, defend." *Iliad,* 234–9 (Chapman's translation).

see combined together, may in his picture as naturally seem to follow upon each other, and to keep true step with the flow of his narrative. For example, he wishes to paint for us the bow of Pandarus: a bow of horn, of such-and-such a length, well-polished, and tipped at both ends with beaten gold. What does he do? Does he give us a dry enumeration of all its properties, one after the other? No such thing: that would be to give an account of a bow, to enumerate its qualities; but not to paint one. He begins with the chase of the wild goat, out of whose horns the bow is made. Pandarus had lain in wait for him in the rocks, and had slain him: the horns were of extraordinary size, and on that account he destined them for a bow. They are brought to the workshop; the artist unites, polishes, decorates them. And so, as I have said, we see the gradual formation by the poet of that which we can only see in a completed form in the work of the painter.

> Τόξον ἐύξοον, ἰζάλον αιγὸς
> Ἀγρίου, ὅν ρά ποτ' αὐτὸς, ὑπὸ στρένοιο τυχήσας,
> Πέτρης ἐκβαίνοντα δεδεγμένος ἐν προδοκῇσιν,

Βεβλήκει πρὸς στῆθος. ὁδ' ὕπτιος ἔμπεσε πέτρη.
Τοῦ κέρα ἐκ κεφαλῆς ἑκκαιδεκάδωρα πεφύκει,
Καὶ τα μὲν ασσκήσ κεροξόος ἤραρε τέκτων,
Πᾶν δ'εὖ λειήνας, χρυσέην ἐπέθηκε κορώνην.[7]

I should never have done if I were to transcribe all the instances of this kind. They will occur in multitudes to him who really knows his Homer.

---

[7][Phillimore] "Who instantly drew forth a bow most admirably made/Of th'antler of a jumping goat, bred in a steep upland,/Which archerlike (as long before he took his hidden stand/The doomed one skipping from a rock) into the breast he smote,/And headlong felled him from his cliff. The forehead of the goat/Held out a wondrous goodly palm, that sixteen branches brought,/Of all of which (joined) an useful bow a skillful bowyer wrought./Which poked and polished both the ends he hid with horns of gold." *Iliad*, 105–11 (Chapman's translation).

Denis Diderot

1713–1784

Diderot was one of the great figures of the Enlightenment. Famous principally for the enormously influential Encyclopedia of twenty-eight volumes, published under his editorship in collaboration with Jean d'Alembert, he was also the author of philosophical works, satires, novels, and plays. Diderot's essay *Paradoxe sur le comédien,* written in the form of a dialogue, ruptures the usual theoretical compact between poet, actor, work, and audience that declares that what the poet experiences and writes about and the actor acts is authentically felt and that this is what, conveyed to an audience, moves it. In a dialogue that in manner and to a considerable degree in thought anticipates Oscar Wilde's attack on the truth of imitation, Diderot attacks the notion of sentiment as sincerely conveyed by an actor. Diderot insists, contrary, incidentally, to statements in earlier works he had written, that the actor must have in himself an "unmoved disinterested onlooker" in order to move an audience. To play from the heart is to be subject to waves of feeling and to risk the destruction of unity. To imitate nature is not to *be* natural. It must be the audience that feels, not the actor, who must sedulously imitate feeling. Thus imitation is clearly identified with artifice: "What, then is truth for stage purposes? It is the conforming of action, diction, face, voice, movement, and gesture, to an ideal type invented by the poet, and frequently enhanced by the player."

Although Diderot does not dwell long on the poet's role, he does make clear that poetic composition begins when sensibility is dulled. He is advocating a sort of psychical distance that Keats later characterized as "negative capability" and for which even Wordsworth, the champion of feeling, kept a place in his notion that poetic emotion is an "emotion recollected in tranquillity." Clearly Diderot is attacking the sort of emotional excess that can occur in a cult of sensibility. At the same time he opposes those notions of the "falsity" of acting common in puritanical opposition to the theater by insisting on the integrity of artistry, even though the picture he draws of the typical actor is quite unflattering.

William Archer's answer to Diderot, written in 1888, is published with Diderot's essay in the book from which this selection is reprinted. See among recent work on Diderot, David Funt, *Diderot and the Esthetics of the Enlightenment* (1968); Lester G. Crocker, *Diderot's Chaotic Order* (1974); Otis Fellows, *Diderot* (1977); Merle L. Perkins, *Diderot and the Time-Space Continuum* (1982); Geoffrey Bremner, *Order and Chance: The Pattern of Diderot's Thought* (1983); Peter France, *Diderot* (1983); Jay Caplan, *Framed Narratives: Diderot's Genealogy of the Beholder* (1985); James Creech, *Diderot: Thresholds of Representation* (1986); Derek F. Connon, *Innovation and Renewal: A Study of the Theatrical Works of Diderot* (1989); Robert L. Montgomery, *Terms of Response* (1992).

from

The Paradox of Acting

It is Nature who bestows personal gifts—appearance, voice, judgment, tact. It is the study of the great models, the knowledge of the human heart, the habit of society, earnest work, experience, close acquaintance with the boards, which perfect Nature's gifts. The actor who is merely a mimic can count upon being always tolerable; his playing will call neither for praise nor for blame.

The Second   Or else for nothing but blame.

The First   Granted. The actor who goes by Nature alone is often detestable, sometimes excellent. But in whatever line, beware of a level mediocrity. No matter how harshly a beginner is treated, one may easily foretell his future success. It is only the incapables who are stifled by cries of 'Off! off!' How should Nature without Art make a great actor when nothing happens on the stage exactly as it happens in nature, and when dramatic poems are all composed after a fixed system of principles? And how can a part be played in the same way by two different actors when, even with the clearest, the most precise, the most forceful of writers, words are no more, and never can be more, than symbols, indicating a thought, a feeling, or an idea; symbols which need action, gesture, intonation, expression, and a whole context of circumstance, to give them their full significance? When you have heard these words—

> 'Que fait là votre main?'
> 'Je tâte votre habit, l'étoffe en est moelleuse'
> ['Your hand—what does it there?'
> 'It feels your robe; 'tis soft and pleasant to the touch']

what do you know of their meaning? Nothing. Weigh well what follows, and remember how often and how easily it happens that two speakers may use the same words to express entirely different thoughts and matters. The instance I am going to cite is a very singular one; it is the very work of your friend that we have been discussing. Ask a French actor what he thinks of it; he will tell you that every word of it is true. Ask an English actor, and he will swear that, '*By God,* there's not a sentence to change! It is the very gospel of the stage!' However, since there is nothing in common

between the way of writing comedy and tragedy in England, and the way of writing stage poems in France; since, according to Garrick[1] himself, an actor who will play you a scene of Shakespeare to perfection is ignorant of the first principles of declamation needed for Racine;[2] since, entwined by Racine's musical lines as if by so many serpents whose folds compress his head, his feet, his hands, his legs, and his arms, he would, in attempting these lines, lose all liberty of action; it follows obviously that the French and the English actors, entirely at one as to the soundness of our author's principles, are yet at variance, and that the technical terms of the stage are so broad and so vague that men of judgment, and of diametrically opposite views, yet find in them the light of conviction. Now hold closer than ever to your maxim, '*Avoid explanation if what you want is a mutual understanding.*'[3]

The Second   You think that in every work, and especially in this, there are two distinct meanings, both expressed in the same terms, one understood in London, the other in Paris?

The First   Yes; and that these terms express so clearly the two meanings that your friend himself has fallen into a trap. In associating the names of English with those of French actors, applying to both the same precepts, giving to both the same praise and the same reproofs, he has doubtless imagined that what he said of the one set was equally true of the other.

The Second   According to this, never before was author so wrong-headed.

The First   I am sorry to admit that this is so, since he uses the same words to express one thing at the Crossroads of Bussy and another thing at Drury Lane. Of course I may be wrong. But the important point on which your author and I are entirely at variance concerns the qualities above all necessary to a great actor. In my view he must have a deal of judgment. He must have in himself an unmoved and disinterested onlooker. He must have, consequently, penetration and no sensibility; the art of mimicking everything, or, which comes to the same thing, the same aptitude for every sort of character and part.

The Second   No sensibility?

The First   None. I have not yet arranged my ideas logically, and you must let me tell them to you as they come to me, with the same want of order that marks your friend's book. If the actor were full, really full, of feeling, how could

---

Diderot's *Paradoxe sur le comédien* was written in the 1770s and revised in 1778, but it was not published until 1830. These excerpts are from *The Paradox of Acting* (Hill and Wang, a division of Farrar, Srauss and Giroux, Inc., 1957). The translation is by Walter Herries Pollock.

[1] David Garrick (1717–1779), English actor.
[2] Jean Racine (1639–1699), French dramatist.
[3] [Pollock] This was a favorite aphorism of Grimm, to whom the first sketch of the *Paradoxe* was addressed.

he play the same part twice running with the same spirit and success? Full of fire at the first performance, he would be worn out and cold as marble at the third. But take it that he is an attentive mimic and thoughtful disciple of Nature, then the first time he comes on the stage as Augustus, Cinna, Orosmanes, Agamemnon, or Mahomet, faithful copying of himself and the effects he has arrived at, and constantly observing human nature, will so prevail that his acting, far from losing in force, will gather strength with the new observations he will make from time to time. He will increase or moderate his effects, and you will be more and more pleased with him. If he is himself while he is playing, how is he to stop being himself? If he wants to stop being himself, how is he to catch just the point where he is to stay his hand?

What confirms me in this view is the unequal acting of players who play from the heart. From them you must expect no unity. Their playing is alternately strong and feeble, fiery and cold, dull and sublime. To-morrow they will miss the point they have excelled in to-day; and to make up for it will excel in some passage where last time they failed. On the other hand, the actor who plays from thought, from study of human nature, from constant imitation of some ideal type, from imagination, from memory, will be one and the same at all performances, will be always at his best mark; he has considered, combined, learnt and arranged the whole thing in his head; his diction is neither monotonous nor dissonant. His passion has a definite course—it has bursts, and it has reactions; it has a beginning, a middle, and an end. The accents are the same, the positions are the same, the movements are the same; if there is any difference between two performances, the latter is generally the better. He will be invariable; a looking-glass, as it were, ready to reflect realities, and to reflect them ever with the same precision, the same strength, and the same truth. Like the poet he will dip for ever into the inexhaustible treasure-house of Nature, instead of coming very soon to an end of his own poor resources.

What acting was ever more perfect than Clairon's?[4] Think over this, study it; and you will find that at the sixth performance of a given part she has every detail of her acting by heart, just as much as every word of her part. Doubtless she has imagined a type, and to conform to this type has been her first thought; doubtless she has chosen for her purpose the highest, the greatest, the most perfect type her imagination could compass. This type, however, which she has borrowed from history, or created as who should create

some vast spectre in her own mind, is not herself. Were it indeed bounded by her own dimensions, how paltry, how feeble would be her playing! When, by dint of hard work, she has got as near as she can to this idea, the thing is done; to preserve the same nearness is a mere matter of memory and practice. If you were with her while she studied her part how many times you would cry out, *That is right!* and how many times she would answer, *You are wrong!*

Just so a friend of Le Quesnoy's[5] once cried, catching him by the arm. 'Stop! you will make it worse by bettering it—you will spoil the whole thing!, 'What I have done,' replied the artist, panting with exertion, 'you have seen; what I have got hold of and what I mean to carry out to the very end you cannot see.'

I have no doubt that Clairon goes through just the same struggles as Le Quesnoy in her first attempts at a part; but once the struggle is over, once she has reached the height she has given to her spectre, she has herself well in hand, she repeats her efforts without emotion. As it will happen in dreams, her head touches the clouds, her hands stretch to grasp the horizon on both sides; she is the informing soul of a huge figure, which is her outward casing, and in which her efforts have enclosed her. As she lies careless and still on a sofa with folded arms and closed eyes she can, following her memory's dream, hear herself, see herself, judge herself, and judge also the effects she will produce. In such a vision she has a double personality; that of the little Clairon and of the great Agrippina.

The Second   According to you the likest thing to an actor, whether on the boards or at his private studies, is a group of children who play at ghosts in a graveyard at dead of night, armed with a white sheet on the end of a broomstick, and fending forth from its shelter hollow groans to frighten wayfarers.

The First   Just so, indeed. Now with Dumesnil[6] it is a different matter: she is not like Clairon. She comes on the stage without knowing what she is going to say; half the time she does not know what she is saying: but she has one sublime moment. And pray, why should the actor be different from the poet, the painter, the orator, the musician? It is not in the stress of the first burst that characteristic traits come out; it is in moments of stillness and self-command; in moments entirely unexpected. Who can tell whence these traits have their being? They are a sort of inspiration. They come when the man of genius is hovering between nature

---

[4]Mlle. Clairon (1723–1803), French actress.

[5][Pollock] This is a mistake of Diderot's. The person referred to is Duquesnoy, the Belgian sculptor.
[6]Mlle. Dumesnil (1713–1804), French actress.

and his sketch of it, and keeping a watchful eye on both. The beauty of inspiration, the chance hits of which his work is full, and of which the sudden appearance startles himself, have an importance, a success, a sureness very different from that belonging to the first fling. Cool reflection must bring the fury of enthusiasm to its bearings.

The extravagant creature who loses his self-control has no hold on us; this is gained by the man who is self-controlled. The great poets, especially the great dramatic poets, keep a keen watch on what is going on, both in the physical and the moral world.

The Second   The two are the same.

The First   They dart on everything which strikes their imagination; they make, as it were, a collection of such things. And from these collections, made all unconsciously, issue the grandest achievements of their work.

Your fiery, extravagant, sensitive fellow, is for ever on the boards; he acts the play, but he gets nothing out of it. It is in him that the man of genius finds his model. Great poets, great actors, and, I may add, all great copyists of Nature, in whatever art, beings gifted with fine imagination, with broad judgment, with exquisite tact, with a sure touch of taste, are the least sensitive of all creatures. They are too apt for too many things, too busy with observing, considering, and reproducing, to have their inmost hearts affected with any liveliness. To me such an one always has his portfolio spread before him and his pencil in his fingers.

It is we who feel; it is they who watch, study, and give us the result. And then . . . well, why should I not say it? Sensibility is by no means the distinguishing mark of a great genius. He will have, let us say, an abstract love of justice, but he will not be moved to temper it with mercy. It is the head, not the heart, which works in and for him. Let some unforeseen opportunity arise, the man of sensibility will lose it; he will never be a great king, a great minister, a great commander, a great advocate, a great physician. Fill the front of a theatre with tearful creatures, but I will none of them on the boards. Think of women, again. They are miles beyond us in sensibility; there is no sort of comparison between their passion and ours. But as much as we are below them in action, so much are they below us in imitation. If a man who is really manly drops a tear, it touches us more nearly than a storm of weeping from a woman. In the great play, the play of the world, the play to which I am constantly recurring, the stage is held by the fiery souls, and the pit is filled with men of genius. The actors are in other words madmen; the spectators, whose business it is to paint their madness, are sages. And it is they who discern with a ready eye the absurdity of the motley crowd, who reproduce it for you, and who make you laugh both at the unhappy models who have bored you to death and at yourself. It is they who watch you, and who give you the mirth-moving picture of the tiresome wretch and of your own anguish in his clutches.

You may prove this to demonstration, and a great actor will decline to acknowledge it; it is his own secret. A middling actor or a novice is sure to contradict you flatly; and of some others it may be said that they believe they feel, just as it has been said of some pious people that they believe they believe; and that without faith in the one case and without sensibility in the other there is no health.

This is all very well, you may reply; but what of these touching and sorrowful accents that are drawn from the very depth of a mother's heart and that shake her whole being? Are these not the result of true feeling? are these not the very inspiration of despair? Most certainly not. The proof is that they are all planned; that they are part of a system of declamation; that, raised or lowered by the twentieth part of a quarter of a tone, they would ring false; that they are in subjection to a law of unity; that, as in harmony, they are arranged in chords and in discords; that laborious study is needed to give them completeness; that they are the elements necessary to the solving of a given problem; that, to hit the right mark once, they have been practised a hundred times; and that, despite all this practice, they are yet found wanting. Look you, before he cries *'Zaïre vous pleurez,'* or *'Vous y serez ma fille,'* the actor has listened over and over again to his own voice. At the very moment when he touches your heart he is listening to his own voice; his talent depends not, as you think, upon feeling, but upon rendering so exactly the outward signs of feeling, that you fall into the trap. He has rehearsed to himself every note of his passion. He has learnt before a mirror every particle of his depair. He knows exactly when he must produce his handkerchief and shed tears; and you will see him weep at the word, at the syllable, he has chosen, not a second sooner or later. The broken voice, the half-uttered words, the stifled or prolonged notes of agony, the trembling limbs, the faintings, the bursts of fury—all this is pure mimicry, lessons carefully learned, the grimacing of sorrow, the magnificent aping which the actor remembers long after his first study of it, of which he was perfectly conscious when he first put it before the public, and which leaves him, luckily for the poet, the spectator, and himself, a full freedom of mind. Like other gymnastics, it taxes only his bodily strength. He puts off the sock or the buskin; his voice is gone; he is tired; he changes his dress, or he goes to bed; and he feels neither trouble, nor sorrow, nor depression, nor weariness of soul. All these emotions he has given to you. The actor is tired, you are unhappy; he has had exertion without feeling, you feeling without exertion. Were it otherwise the player's lot would be the most wretched on earth: but he is not the person he represents; he plays it, and plays it so well that you think he is the person; the deception is all on your side; he knows well enough that he is not the person.

For diverse modes of feeling arranged in concert to obtain the greatest effect, scored orchestrally, played *piano* and played *forte*, harmonised to make an individual effect—all that to me is food for laughter. I hold to my point, and I tell you this: 'Extreme sensibility makes middling actors; middling sensibility makes the ruck of bad actors; in complete absence of sensibility is the possibility of a sublime actor.' The player's tears come from his brain, the sensitive being's from his heart; the sensitive being's soul gives unmeasured trouble to his brain: the player's brain gives sometimes a touch of trouble to his soul: he weeps as might weep an unbelieving priest preaching of the Passion; as a seducer might weep at the feet of a woman whom he does not love, but on whom he would impose; like a beggar in the street or at the door of a church—a beggar who substitutes insult for vain appeal; or like a courtesan who has no heart, and who abandons herself in your arms.

Have you ever thought on the difference between the tears raised by a tragedy of real life and those raised by a touching narrative? You hear a fine piece of recitation; by little and little your thoughts are involved, your heart is touched, and your tears flow. With the tragedy of real life the thing, the feeling and the effect, are all one; your heart is reached at once, you utter a cry, your head swims, and the tears flow. These tears come of a sudden, the others by degrees. And here is the superiority of a true effect of nature over a well-planned scene. It does at one stroke what the scene leads up to by degrees, but it is far more difficult to reproduce its effect; one incident ill given would shatter it. Accents are more easily mimicked than actions, but actions go straighter to the mark. This is the basis of a canon to which I believe there is not exception. If you would avoid coldness you must complete your effect by action and not by talk.

So, then, have you no objection to make? Ah! I see! You give a recitation in a drawing-room; your feelings are stirred; your voice fails you; you burst into tears. You have, as you say, felt, and felt deeply. Quite so; but had you made up your mind to that? Not at all. Yet you were carried away, you surprised and touched your hearers, you made a great hit. All this is true enough. But now transfer your easy tone, your simple expression, your everyday bearing, to the stage, and, I assure you, you will be paltry and weak. You may cry to your heart's content, and the audience will only laugh. It will be the tragedy outside a booth at a fair. Do you suppose

that the dialogue of Corneille, of Racine, of Voltaire,[7] or, let me add, of Shakespeare, can be given with your ordinary voice and with your fireside tone? No; not a bit more than you would tell a fireside story with the open-mouthed emphasis fit for the boards.

The Second Perhaps Racine and Corneille, great names as they are, did nothing of account.

The First Oh, blasphemy! Who could dare to say it? Who to endorse it? The merest word Corneille wrote cannot be given in everyday tone.

But, to go back, it must have happened to you a hundred times that at the end of your recitation, in the very midst of the agitation and emotion you have caused in your drawingroom audience, a fresh guest has entered, and wanted to hear your again. You find it impossible, you are weary to the soul. Sensibility, fire, tears, all have left you. Why does not the actor feel the same exhaustion? Because there is a world of difference between the interests excited by a flattering tale and by your fellow-man's misfortune. Are you Cinna? Have you ever been Cleopatra, Merope, Agrippina? Are these same personages on the stage ever historical personages? Not at all. They are the vain images of poetry. No, nor even that. They are the phantoms fashioned from this or that poet's special fantasy. They are well enough on the stage, these hippogriffs, so to call them, with their actions, their bearing, their intonations. They would make but a sorry figure in history; they would raise laughter in society. People would whisper to each other, 'Is this fellow mad? Where in the world does this Don Quixote come from? Who is the inventor of all this stuff? In what world do people talk like this?'

The Second And why are they not intolerable on the stage?

The First Because there is such a thing as stage convention. As old a writer as Æschylus[8] laid this down as a formula—it is a protocol three thousand years old.

The Second And will this protocol go on much longer?

The First That I cannot tell you. All I know is that one gets further away from it as one gets nearer to one's own time and country. Find me a situation closer to that of Agamemnon in the first scene of *Iphigenia*[9] than that of *Henri IV;* when, beset by fears only too well founded, he said to those around him, 'They will kill me; there is noth-

---

[7]Corneille (above, page 244). Francois Marie Arouet de Voltaire (1694–1778), French writer.
[8]Aeschylus (525–456 B.C.), Greek tragic dramatist.
[9]By Racine.

ing surer; they will kill me!' Suppose that great man, that superb and hapless monarch, troubled in the night-watches with this deadly presentiment, got up and knocked at the door of Sully, his minister and friend—is there, think you, a poet foolish enough to make Henri say—

'Oui, c'est Henri, s'est ton roi qui t'éveille;
Viens, reconnais la voix qui frappe ton oreille?'
(Ay, it is Agamemnon [Henri], 'tis thy King
That wakes thee; his the voice that strikes thine ear.)

Or to make Sully reply—

'C'est vous-même, seigneur? Quel important besoin
Vous a faît devancer l'aurore de si loin?
A peine un faible jour vous éclaire et me guide,
Vos yeux seuls et les miens sont ouverts . . .'
[Is't thou indeed, my lord? What grave concern
Has made thee leave thy couch before the dawn?
A feeble light scarce lets me see thy face,
No eyes but ours are open yet in Aulis . . . .][10]

The Second   Perhaps Agamemnon really talked like that.

The First   No more than Henri IV did. Homer talks like that; Racine talks like that; poetry talks like that; and this pompous language can only be used by unfamiliar personages, spoken from poetical lips, with a poetical tone. Reflect a little as to what, in the language of the theatre, is *being true*. It is showing things as they are in nature? Certainly not. Were it so the true would be the commonplace. What, then, is truth for stage purposes? It is the conforming of action, diction, face, voice, movement, and gesture, to an ideal type invented by the poet, and frequently enhanced by the player. That is the strange part of it. This type not only influences the tone, it alerts the actor's very walk and bearing. And hence it is that the player in private and the player on the boards are two personages, so different that one can scarce recognise the player in private. The first time I saw Mlle. Clairon in her own house I exclaimed, by a natural impulse, 'Ah, mademoiselle, I thought you were at least a head taller!'

An unhappy, a really unhappy woman, may weep and fail to touch you; worse than that, some trivial disfigurement in her may incline you to laughter; the accent which is apt to her is to your ears dissonant and vexatious; a movement which is habitual to her makes her grief show ignobly and sulkily to you; almost all the violent passions lend themselves to grimaces which a tasteless artist will copy but too faithfully, and which a great actor will avoid. In the very whirlwind of passion we would have a man preserve his manly dignity. And what is the effect of this heroic effort? To give relief and temperance to sorrow. We would have this heroine fall with a becoming grace, that hero die like a gladiator of old in the midst of the arena to the applause of the circus, with a noble grace, with a fine and picturesque attitude. And who will execute this design of ours? The athlete who is mastered by pain, shattered by his own sensibility, or the athlete who is trained, who has self-control, who, as he breathes his last sigh, remembers the lessons of the gymnasium? Neither the gladiator of old nor the great actor dies as people die in their beds; it is for them to show us another sort of death, a death to move us: and the critical spectator will feel that the bare truth, the unadorned fact, would seem despicable and out of harmony with the poetry of the rest.

Not, mark you, that Nature unadorned has not her moments of sublimity; but I fancy that if there is any one sure to give and preserve their sublimity it is the man who can feel it with his passion and his genius, and reproduce it with complete self-possession.

I will not, however, deny that there is a kind of acquired or factitious sensibility; but if you would like to know what I think about it, I hold it to be nearly as dangerous as natural sensibility. By little and little it leads the actor into mannerism and monotony. It is an element opposed to the variety of a great actor's functions. He must often strip it from him; and it is only a head of iron which can make such a self-abnegation. Besides, it is far better for the ease and success of his study, for the catholicity of his talent and the perfection of his playing, that there should be no need of this strange parting of self from self. Its extreme difficulty, confining each actor to one single line, leads perforce to a numerous company, where every part is ill played; unless, indeed, the natural order of things is reversed, and the pieces are made for the actors. To my thinking the actors, on the contrary, ought to be made for the pieces.

The Second   But if a crowd of people collected in the street by some catastrophe begin of a sudden, and each in his own way, and without any concert, to exhibit a natural sensibility, they will give you a magnificent show, and display you a thousand types, valuable for sculpture, music, and poetry.

The First   True enough. But will this show compare with one which is the result of a pre-arranged plan, with the harmony which the artist will put into it when he transfers it from the public way to his stage or canvas? If you say it

---

[10]The lines are from speeches by Agamemnon amd Arcas in Racine's *Iphigénie* with "Henri" substituted for Agamemnon.

will, then I shall make you this answer: What is this boasted magic of art if it only consists in spoiling what both nature and chance have done better than art? Do you deny that one can improve on nature? Have you never, by way of praising a woman, said she is as lovely as one of Raphael's[11] Madonnas? Have you never cried, on seeing a fine landscape, 'It's as good as a description in a novel'? Again, you are talking to me of a reality. I am talking to you of an imitation. You are talking to me of a passing moment in Nature. I am talking to you of a work of Art, planned and composed—a work which is built up by degrees, and which lasts. Take now each of these actors; change the scene in the street as you do on the boards, and show me your personages left successively to themselves, two by two or three by three. Leave them to their own swing; make them full masters of their actions; and you will see what a monstrous discord will result. You will get over this by making them rehearse together. Quite so. And then good-bye to their natural sensibility; and so much the better.

A play is like any well-managed association, in which each individual sacrifices himself for the general good and effect. And who will best take the measure of the sacrifice? The enthusiast or the fanatic? Certainly not. In society, the man of judgment; on the stage, the actor whose wits are always about him. Your scene in the street has the same relation to a scene on the stage that a band of savages has to a company of civilised men.

Now is the time to talk to you of the disastrous influence which a middling associate has on a first-rate player. This player's conception is admirable; but he has to give up his ideal type in order to come down to the level of the poor wretch who is playing with him. Then he says farewell to his study and his taste. As happens with talks in the street or at the fireside, the principal speaker lowers his tone to that of his companion. Or if you would like another illustration, take that of whist, where you lose a deal of your own skill if you cannot rely on your partner. More than this, Clairon will tell you, if you ask her, that Le Kain[12] would maliciously make her play badly or inadequately, and that she would avenge herself by getting him hissed. What, then, are two players who mutually support each other? Two personages whose types are, in due proportion, either equal, or else in them the subordination demanded by the circumstances, as laid down by the poet, is observed. But for this there would be an excess, either of strength or of weakness; and such a want of harmony as this is avoided more frequently by the strong descending to the weak than by its raising the weak

to its own level. And pray, do you know the reason of the numberless rehearsals that go on? They are to strike the balance between the different talents of the actors, so as to establish a general unity in the playing. When the vanity of an individual interferes with this balance the result is to injure the effect and to spoil your enjoyment; for it is seldom that the excellence of one actor can atone for the mediocrity, which it brings into relief, of his companions. I have known a great actor suffer from his temperament in this way. The stupid public said he was extravagant, instead of discerning that his associate was inadequate.

Come, you are a poet; you have a piece for the stage; and I leave you to choose between actors with the soundest judgments and the coolest heads and actors of sensibility. But before you make up your mind let me ask you one question. What is the time of life for a great actor? The age when one is full of fire, when the blood boils in the veins, when the slightest check troubles one to the soul, when the wit blazes at the veriest spark? I fancy not. The man whom Nature stamps an actor does not reach his topmost height until he has had a long experience, until the fury of the passions is subdued, until the head is cool and the heart under control. The best wine is harsh and crude in its fermenting. It is by long lying in the cask that it grows generous. Cicero, Seneca, and Plutarch,[13] I take to represent the three ages of composition in men. Cicero is often but a blaze of straw, pretty to look at; Seneca a fire of vine-branches, hurtful to look at; but when I stir old Plutarch's ashes I come upon the great coals of a fire that gives me a gentle warmth.

* * *

Is it at the moment when you have just lost your friend or your adored one that you set to work at a poem on your loss? No! ill for him who at such a moment takes pleasure in his talent. It is when the storm of sorrow is over, when the extreme of sensibility is dulled, when the event is far behind us, when the soul is calm, that one remembers one's eclipsed happiness, that one is capable of appreciating one's loss, that memory and imagination unite, one to retrace the other to accentuate, the delights of a past time: then it is that one regains self-possession and expression. One writes of one's falling tears, but they do not fall while one is hunting a strong epithet that always escapes one; one writes of one's falling tears, but they do not fall while one is employed in polishing one's verse; or if the tears do flow the pen drops from the hand: one falls to feeling, and one ceases writing.

---

[11]Raphael Santi (1483–1520), Italian painter.
[12]Le Kain (Henri Louis Cain, 1728–1778), French actor.

[13]Cicero (above, page 74); Marcus Annaeus Seneca (d. 38), Roman philosopher and dramatist.

Again, it is with intense pleasure as with intense pain—both are dumb. A tender-hearted and sensitive man sees again a friend he has missed during a long absence; the friend makes an unexpected reappearance, and the other's heart is touched; he rushes to him, he embraces him, he would speak, but cannot: he stammers and trips over his words; he says he knows not what, he does not hear the answer: if he could see that the delight is not mutual, how hurt he would be! Judge, this picture being true, how untrue are the stage meetings, where both friends are so full of intelligence and self-control. What could I not say to you of the insipid and eloquent disputes as to who is to die, or rather who is not to die, but that this text, on which I should enlarge for ever, would take us far from our subject? Enough has been said for men of true and fine taste; what I could add would teach nothing to the rest. Now, who is come to the rescue of these absurdities so common on the stage? The actor? and what actor?

The circumstances in which sensibility is as hurtful in society as on the stage are a thousand to one. Take two lovers, both of whom have their declaration to make. Who will come out of it best? Not I, I promise you. I remember that I approached the beloved object with fear and trembling; my heart beat, my ideas grew confused, my voice failed me, I mangled all I said; I cried *yes* for *no;* I made a thousand blunders; I was illimitably inept; I was absurd from top to toe, and the more I saw it, the more absurd I became. Meanwhile, under my very eyes, a gay rival, light-hearted and agreeable, master of himself, pleased with himself, losing no opportunity for the finest flattery, made himself entertaining and agreeable, enjoyed himself; he implored the touch of a hand which was at once given him, he sometimes caught it without asking leave, he kissed it once and again. I the while, alone in a corner, avoiding a sight which irritated me, stifling in my sighs, cracking my fingers with grasping my wrists, plunged in melancholy, covered with a cold sweat, I could neither show nor conceal my vexation. People say of love that it robs witty men of their wit, and gives it to those who had none before: in other words, makes some people sensitive and stupid, others cold and adventurous.

The man of sensibility obeys the impulse of Nature, and gives nothing more or less than the cry of his very heart; the moment he moderates or strengthens this cry he is no longer himself, he is an actor.

The great actor watches appearances; the man of sensibility is his model; he thinks over him, and discovers by after-reflection what it will be best to add or cut away. And so from mere argument he goes to action.

* * *

Is there such a thing as artificial sensibility? Consider, sensibility, whether acquired or inborn, is not in place in all characters. What, then, is the quality acquired which makes an actor great in *l'Avare, le Joueur, le Flatteur, le Grondeur, le Médecin malgré lui* (the least sensitive or moral personage yet devised by a poet), *le Bourgeois Gentilhomme, la Malade Imaginaire, la Cœur Imaginaire*[14]—in Nero, in Mithridates, in Atreus, in Phocas, in Sertorius, and in a host of other characters, tragic and comic, where sensibility is diametrically opposed to the spirit of the part? It is the faculty of knowing and imitating all natures. Believe me, we need not multiply causes when one cause accounts for all appearances.

Sometimes the poet feels more deeply than the actor; sometimes, and perhaps oftener, the actor's conception is stronger than the poet's; and there is nothing truer than Voltaire's exclamation, when he heard Clairon in a piece of his, *'Did I really write that?'* Does Clairon know more about it than Voltaire? Anyhow, at that moment the ideal type in the speaking of the part went well beyond the poet's ideal type in the writing of it. But this ideal type was not Clairon. Where, then, lay her talent? In imagining a mighty shape, and in copying it with genius. She imitated the movement, the action, the gesture, the whole embodiment of a being far greater than herself. She had learnt that Æschines, repeating a speech of Demosthenes,[15] could never reproduce 'the roar of the brute.' He said to his disciples, 'If this touches you, or nearly, what would have been the effect *si audivissetis bestiam mugientem* [had you heard the roaring beast]?' The poet had engendered the monster, Clairon made it roar.

It would be a strange abuse of language to give the name of sensibility to this faculty of reproducing all natures, even ferocious natures. Sensibility, according to the only acceptation yet given of the term, is, as it seems to me, that disposition which accompanies organic weakness, which follows on easy affection of the diaphragm, on vivacity of imagination, on delicacy of nerves, which inclines one to being compassionate, to being horrified, to admiration, to fear, to being upset, to tears, to faintings, to rescues, to flights, to exclamations, to loss of self-control, to being contemptuous, disdainful, to having no clear notion of what is true, good, and fine, to being unjust, to going mad. Multiply souls of sensibility, and you will multiply in the same proportion good and bad actions of every kind, extravagant praise and extravagant blame.

* * *

---

[14] Plays by Molière.
[15] Aeschines (389–314 B.C.), Demonsthenes (384?–322 B.C.), Athenian orators.

The Second   A great actor's soul is formed of the subtle element with which a certain philosopher filled space, an element neither cold nor hot, heavy nor light, which affects no definite shape, and capable of assuming all, keeps none.

The First   A great actor is neither a pianoforte, nor a harp, nor a spinnet, nor a violin, nor a violoncello; he has no key peculiar to him; he takes the key and the tone fit for his part of the score, and he can take up any. I put a high value on the talent of a great actor; he is a rare being—as rare as, and perhaps greater than, a poet.

He who in society makes it his object, and unluckily has the skill, to please every one, is nothing, has nothing that belongs to him, nothing to distinguish him, to delight some and weary others. He is always talking, and always talking well; he is an adulator by profession, he is a great courtier, he is a great actor.

The Second   A great courtier, accustomed since he first drew breath to play the part of a most ingenious puppet,[16] takes every kind of shape at the pull of the string in his master's hands.

The First   A great actor is also a most ingenious puppet, and his strings are held by the poet, who at each line indicates the true form he must take.

The Second   So then a courtier, an actor, who can take only one form, however beautiful, however attractive it may be, are a couple of wretched pasteboard figures?

The First   I have no thought of calumniating a profession I like and esteem—I mean, the actor's. I should be in despair if a misunderstanding of my observations cast a shade of contempt on men of a rare talent and a true usefulness, on the scourges of absurdity and vice, on the most eloquent preachers of honesty and virtue, on the rod which the man of genius wields to chastise knaves and fools. But look around you, and you will see that people of never-failing gaiety have neither great faults nor great merits; that as a rule people who lay themselves out to be agreeable are frivolous people, without any sound principle; and that those who, like certain persons who mix in our society, have no character, excel in playing all.

Has not the actor a father, a mother, a wife, children, brothers, sisters, acquaintances, friends, a mistress? If he were endowed with that exquisite sensibility which people regard as the thing principally needed for his profession, harrassed and struck like us with an infinity of troubles in quick succession, which sometimes wither and sometimes tear our hearts, how many days would he have left to devote to our amusement? Mighty few. The Groom of the Chambers would vainly interpose his sovereignty, the actor's state would often make him answer, 'My lord, I cannot laugh today,' or, 'It is over cares other than Agamemnon's that I would weep.' It is not known, however, that the troubles of life, common to actors as to us, and far more opposed to the free exercise of their calling, often interrupt them.

In society, unless they are buffoons, I find them polished, caustic, and cold; proud, light of behavior, spendthrifts, self-interested; struck rather by our absurdities than touched by our misfortunes; masters of themselves at the spectacle of an untoward incident or the recital of a pathetic story; isolated, vagabonds, at the command of the great; little conduct, no friends, scarce any of those holy and tender ties which associate us in the pains and pleasures of another, who in turn shares our own. I have often seen an actor laugh off the stage; I do not remember to have ever seen one weep. What do they, then, with this sensibility that they arrogate and that people grant them? Do they leave it on the stage at their exit, to take it up again at their next entrance?

What makes them slip on the sock or the buskin? Want of education, poverty, a libertine spirit. The stage is a resource, never a choice. Never did actor become so from love of virtue, from desire to be useful in the world, or to serve his country of family; never from any of the honourable motives which might incline a right mind, a feeling heart, a sensitive soul, to so fine a profession.

I myself, in my young days, hesitated between the Sorbonne and the stage. In the bitterest depth of winter I used to go and recite aloud parts in Molière and in Corneille in the solitary alleys of the Luxembourg. What was my project? To gain applause? Perhaps. To mix on intimate terms with actresses whom I found charming, and who I knew were not straitlaced? Certainly. I know not what I would not have done to please Gaussin,[17] who was then making her first appearance, and was beauty itself; or Dangeville,[18] who on the stage was so full of charm.

It has been said that actors have no character, because in playing all characters they lose that which Nature gave them, and they become false just as the doctor, the surgeon, and the butcher, become hardened. I fancy that here cause is confounded with effect, and that they are fit to play all characters because they have none.

* * *

---

[16] [Pollock] *Pantin,* a figure cut out in card with strings attached. I have used the word *puppet* to avoid roundabout expression.

[17] Mlle. Gaussin, French actress contemporary of Diderot.
[18] Mlle. Dangeville (1714–1796), French actress.

'My friend, there are three types—Nature's man, the poet's man, the actor's man. Nature's is less great than the poet's, the poet's less great than the great actor's, which is the most exalted of all. This last climbs on the shoulders of the one before him and shuts himself up inside a great basket-work figure of which he is the soul. He moves this figure so as to terrify even the poet, who no longer recognises himself; and he terrifies us, as you have very well put it, just as children frighten each other by tucking up their little skirts and putting them over their heads, shaking themselves about, and imitating as best they can the croaking lugubrious accents of the spectre that they counterfeit. Have you not seen engravings of children's sports? Have you not observed an urchin coming forward under a hideous old man's mask, which hides him from head to foot? Behind this mask he laughs at his little companions, who fly in terror before him. This urchin is the true symbol of the actor; his comrades are the symbol of the audience. If the actor has but middling sensibility, and if that is his only merit, will you not call him a middling man? Take care, for this is another trap I am laying for you. And if he is endowed with extreme sensibility what will come of it?— What will come of it? That he will either play no more, or play ludicrously ill; yes, ludicrously; and to prove it you can see the same thing in me when you like. If I have a recital of some pathos to give, a strange trouble arises in my heart and head; my tongue trips, my voice changes, my ideas wander, my speech hangs fire. I babble; I perceive it; tears course down my cheeks; I am silent. But with this I make an effect— in private life; on the stage I should be hooted.

Why?

Because people come not to see tears, but to hear speeches that draw tears; because this truth of nature is out of tune with the truth of convention. Let me explain myself: I mean that neither the dramatic system, nor the action, nor the poet's speeches, would fit themselves to my stifled, broken, sobbing declamation. You see that it is not allowable to imitate Nature, even at her best, or Truth too closely; there are limits within which we must restrict ourselves.

Sir Joshua Reynolds

1723–1792

In 1768, under the sponsorship of George III, a number of English painters organized the Royal Academy of Art. A charter member and the Academy's first president, Joshua Reynolds delivered the first of his fifteen discourses at the official opening of the Academy in 1769. Of the three discourses printed below, the third was delivered in 1770, the seventh in 1776, and the thirteenth in 1786. Each discourse was an address given to students entering the Academy.

Although the *Discourses* concern painting, they are of interest to the student of literary theory and criticism because they express so clearly a number of notions implicit in eighteenth-century attitudes toward art in general, including literature. In *Discourse III* Reynolds argues that the artist seeks to represent not "singular forms, local customs, particularities, and details," but the "central form" of the object. This "central form" sometimes appears to Reynolds as a sort of Platonic idea, but usually it is, as in Johnson (above, page 357), a generalization from the particularities of sense data, or, as Reynolds puts it, "the abstract of the various individual forms belonging to that class." The young artist becomes skilled by observing, selecting, digesting, methodizing, and comparing observations. Yet, at the same time, art receives its value from its approximation to an ideal beauty, and this sounds more like the neoplatonist Plotinus (above, page 127) than the empiricist Locke (above, page 281).

Reynolds was clearly influenced by the tradition of empirical philosophy and the theory of association of ideas, and argues from the Lockeian notion that we build up complex ideas by comparing and combining simple perceptions of sense into more complex wholes. His argument defending the generalized abstraction in art comes under attack in William Blake's marginalia to the *Discourses* (below, page 449), where Blake defends the work of art as a minute particularity. The trend from Romanticism to Modernism tends to follow Blake's line rather than Reynolds's, though the line is tangled in controversy at times. One problem the controversy raises is whether there is ultimately a logic of art that allows a particularity or a concretion in some way to be a universal (in the sense in which Vico [above, page 318] speaks of "imaginative universals") without its metamorphosing into a generalization and thus losing its claim to immediacy.

The *Discourses* were written and delivered over a number of years, and one can detect a fashionable change of emphasis by reading consecutively the three reprinted here. *Discourse VII,* though more flexible than *Discourse III* in its treatment of imitation, reflects the attitudes of the empiricists, particularly those of Burke (above, page 332). *Discourse XIII,* delivered sixteen years after *Discourse III,* departs from a rigidly rationalistic attitude toward creativity and taste, proposing a concept of intuition and adopting a more flexible attitude toward imitation.

Editions of the *Discourses* include those of E. G. Johnson (1891), Roger Fry (1905), Louis Dimier (1909), R. R. Wark (1959), and H. W. Beechey, the last in the two-volume collection of Reynolds's *Literary Works* (1835). See F. W. Hilles, *The Literary Career of Sir Joshua Reynolds* (1936); Scott Elledge, "The Background and Development in English Criticism of the Theories of Generality and Particularity," *PMLA* LXII (1947), 142–82; Ellis Waterhouse, *Reynolds* (1973); Richard Wendorf, *Sir Joshua Reynolds: The Painter in Society* (1996).

from

Discourses on Art

Discourse III

Gentlemen,

It is not easy to speak with propriety to so many students of different ages and different degrees of advancement. The mind requires nourishment adapted to its growth; and what may have promoted our earlier efforts might retard us in our nearer approaches to perfection.

The first endeavors of a young painter, as I have remarked in a former discourse, must be employed in the attainment of mechanical dexterity, and confined to the mere imitation of the object before him. Those who have advanced beyond the rudiments, may, perhaps, find advantage in reflecting on the advice which I have likewise given them, when I recommended the diligent study of the works of our great predecessors; but I at the same time endeavored to guard them against an implicit submission to the authority of any one master however excellent: or by a strict imitation of his manner, precluding themselves from the abundance and variety of nature. I will now add that nature herself is not to be too closely copied. There are excellencies in the art of painting beyond what is commonly called the imitation of nature: and these excellencies I wish to point out. The students who, having passed through the initiatory exercises, are more advanced in the art, and who, sure of their hand, have leisure to exert their understanding, must now be told, that a mere copier of nature can never produce anything great; can never raise and enlarge the conceptions, or warm the heart of the spectator.

The wish of the genuine painter must be more extensive: instead of endeavoring to amuse mankind with the minute neatness of his imitations, he must endeavor to improve them by the grandeur of his ideas; instead of seeking praise by deceiving the superficial sense of the spectator, he must strive for fame by captivating the imagination.

The principle now laid down, that the perfection of this art does not consist in mere imitation, is far from being new or singular. It is, indeed, supported by the general opinion of the enlightened part of mankind. The poets, orators, and rhetoricians of antiquity are continually enforcing this position: that all the arts receive their perfection from an ideal beauty, superior to what is to be found in individual nature. They are ever referring to the practice of the painters and sculptors of their times, particularly Phidias[1] (the favorite artist of antiquity), to illustrate their assertions. As if they could not sufficiently express their admiration of his genius by what they knew, they have recourse to poetical enthusiasm.[2] They call it inspiration; a gift from heaven. The artist is supposed to have ascended the celestial regions, to furnish his mind with this perfect idea of beauty. "He," says Proclus,

> who takes for his model such forms as nature produces, and confines himself to an exact imitation of them, will never attain to what is perfectly beautiful. For the works of nature are full of disproportion, and fall very short of the true standard of beauty. So that Phidias, when he formed his Jupiter, did not copy any object ever presented to his sight; but contemplated only that image which he had conceived in his mind from Homer's description.[3]

And thus Cicero, speaking of the same Phidias: "Neither did this artist," says he,

> when he carved the image of Jupiter or Minerva, set before him any one human figure, as a pattern, which he was to copy; but having a more perfect idea of beauty fixed in his mind, this he steadily contemplated, and to the imitation of this all his skill and labor were directed.[4]

Reynolds's *Discourses on Art* were first published together in 1797 in an edition edited by Edmond Malone, though all had been published individually before then. The text is based on Malone's third edition (1801).

[1] Phidias (c. 490–c. 417 B.C.), Athenian sculptor.
[2] On enthusiasm as a religious movement see Ronald Knox, *Enthusiasm* (1950).
[3] Proclus (412–485), neoplatonic philosopher, *On Plato's* Timaeus II.
[4] Cicero (above, page 74), *On Oratory* II, 9.

The moderns are not less convinced than the ancients of this superior power existing in the art; nor less sensible of its effects. Every language has adopted terms expressive of this excellence. The *gusto grande* of the Italians, the *beau idéal* of the French, and the *great style,* and *taste* among the English, are but different appellations of the same thing. It is this intellectual dignity, they say, that ennobles the painter's art; that lays the line between him and the mere mechanic; and produces those great effects in an instant, which eloquence and poetry, by slow and repeated efforts, are scarcely able to attain.

Such is the warmth with which both the ancients and moderns speak of this divine principle of the art; but, as I have formerly observed, enthusiastic admiration seldom promotes knowledge. Though a student by such praise may have his attention roused, and a desire excited of running in this great career, yet it is possible that what has been said to excite, may only serve to deter him. He examines his own mind, and perceives there nothing of that divine inspiration with which, he is told, so many others have been favored. He never traveled to heaven to gather new ideas; and he finds himself possessed of no other qualifications than what mere common observation and a plain understanding can confer. Thus he becomes gloomy amidst the splendor of figurative declamation, and thinks it hopeless to pursue an object which he supposes out of reach of human industry.

But on this, as upon many other occasions, we ought to distinguish how much is to be given to enthusiasm, and how much to reason. We ought to allow for, and we ought to commend, that strength of vivid expression which is necessary to convey, in its full force, the highest sense of the most complete effect of art; taking care at the same time, not to lose in terms of vague admiration, that solidity and truth of principle, upon which alone we can reason, and may be enabled to practice.

It is not easy to define in which this great style consists; nor to describe, by words, the proper means of acquiring it, if the mind of the student should be at all capable of such an acquisition. Could we teach taste or genius by rules, they would be no longer taste and genius. But though there neither are, nor can be, any precise invariable rules for the exercise, or the acquisition, of these great qualities, yet we may truly say that they always operate in proportion to our attention in observing the works of nature, to our skill in selecting, and to our care in digesting, methodizing, and comparing our observations. There are many beauties in our art that seem, at first, to lie without the reach of precept, and yet may easily be reduced to practical principles. Experience is all in all; but it is not everyone who profits by experience; and most people err, not so much from want of capacity to find their object, as from not knowing what object to pursue. This great ideal perfection and beauty are not to be sought in the heavens, but upon the earth. They are about us, and upon every side of us. But the power of discovering what is deformed in nature, or in other words, what is particular and uncommon, can be acquired only by experience; and the whole beauty and grandeur of the arts consists, in my opinion, in being able to get above all singular forms, local customs, particularities, and details of every kind.

All the objects which are exhibited to our view by nature, upon close examination will be found to have their blemishes and defects. The most beautiful forms have something about them like weakness, minuteness, or imperfection. But it is not every eye that perceives these blemishes. It must be an eye long used to the contemplation and comparison of these forms; and which, by a long habit of observing what any set of objects of the same kind have in common, has acquired the power of discerning what each wants in particular. This long laborious comparison should be the first study of the painter who aims at the greatest style. By this means, he acquires a just idea of beautiful forms; he corrects nature by herself, her imperfect state by her more perfect. His eye being enabled to distinguish the accidental deficiencies, excrescences, and deformities of things, from their general figures, he makes out an abstract idea of their forms more perfect than any one original; and, what may seem a paradox, he learns to design naturally by drawing his figures unlike to any one object. This idea of the perfect state of nature, which the artist calls the ideal beauty, is the great leading principle, by which works of genius are conducted. By this Phidias acquired his fame. He wrought upon a sober principle, what has so much excited the enthusiasm of the world; and by this method you, who have courage to tread the same path, may acquire equal reputation.

This is the idea which has acquired, and which seems to have a right to, the epithet of *divine;* as it may be said to preside, like a supreme judge, over all the productions of nature; appearing to be possessed of the will and intention of the Creator, as far as they regard the external form of living beings. When a man once possesses his idea in its perfection, there is no danger but that he will be sufficiently warmed by it himself, and be able to warm and ravish everyone else.

Thus it is from a reiterated experience, and a close comparison of the objects in nature, that an artist becomes possessed of the idea of that central form, if I may so express it, from which every deviation is deformity. But the investigation of this form, I grant, is painful, and I know but of one method of shortening the road; this is, by a careful study of the works of the ancient sculptors; who, being indefatigable in the school of nature, have left models of that perfect form behind them, which an artist would prefer as supremely beautiful, who had spent his whole life in that single contemplation. But if industry carried them thus far, may not you also hope for the same reward from the same labor? We have the same school opened to us that was opened to them; for nature denies her instructions to none who desire to become her pupils.

This laborious investigation, I am aware, must appear superfluous to those who think everything is to be done by felicity, and the powers of native genius. Even the great Bacon treats with ridicule the idea of confining proportion to rules, or of producing beauty by selection. "A man cannot tell," says he, "whether Apelles or Albert Dürer were the more trifler: whereof the one would make a personage by geometrical proportions: the other, by taking the best parts out of divers faces, to make one excellent . . . The painter," he adds, "must do it by a kind of felicity . . . and not by rule."[5]

It is not safe to question any opinion of so great a writer, and so profound a thinker, as undoubtedly Bacon was. But he studies brevity to excess; and therefore his meaning is sometimes doubtful. If he means that beauty has nothing to do with rule, he is mistaken. There is a rule, obtained out of general nature, to contradict which is to fall into deformity. Whenever anything is done beyond this rule, it is in virtue of some other rule which is followed along with it, but which does not contradict it. Everything which is wrought with certainty is wrought upon some principle. If it is not, it cannot be repeated. If by felicity is meant anything of chance or hazard, or something born with a man, and not earned, I cannot agree with this great philosopher. Every object which pleases must give us pleasure upon some certain principles; but as the objects of pleasure are almost infinite, so their principles vary without end, and every man finds them out, not by felicity or successful hazard, but by care and sagacity.

To the principle I have laid down, that the idea of beauty in each species of beings is an invariable one, it may be objected that in every particular species there are various central forms, which are separate and distinct from each other, and yet are undeniably beautiful; that in the human figure, for instance, the beauty of *Hercules* is one, of the *Gladiator* another, of the *Apollo* another; which makes so many different ideas of beauty.[6]

It is true, indeed, that these figures are each perfect in their kind, though of different characters and proportions; but still none of them is the representation of an individual, but of a class. And as there is one general form, which, as I have said, belongs to the human kind at large, so in each of these classes there is one common idea and central form, which is the abstract of the various individual forms belonging to that class. Thus, though the forms of childhood and age differ exceedingly, there is a common form in childhood, and a common form in age, which is the more perfect as it is more remote from all peculiarities. But I must add further, that though the most perfect forms of each of the general divisions of the human figure are ideal, and superior to any individual form of that class; yet the highest perfection of the human figure is not to be found in any one of them. It is not in the *Hercules,* nor in the *Gladiator,* nor in the *Apollo;* but in that form which is taken from all, and which partakes equally of the activity of the *Gladiator,* of the delicacy of the *Apollo,* and of the muscular strength of the *Hercules.* For perfect beauty in any species must combine all the characters which are beautiful in that species. It cannot consist in any one to the exclusion of the rest: no one, therefore, must be predominant, that no one may be deficient.

The knowledge of these different characters, and the power of separating and distinguishing them, are undoubtedly necessary to the painter, who is to vary his compositions with figures of various forms and proportions, though he is never to lose sight of the general idea of perfection in each kind.

There is, likewise, a kind of symmetry, or proportion, which may properly be said to belong to deformity. A figure lean or corpulent, tall or short, though deviating from beauty, may still have a certain union of the various parts, which may contribute to make them on the whole not unpleasing.

When the artist has by diligent attention acquired a clear and distinct idea of beauty and symmetry; when he has reduced the variety of nature to the abstract idea; his next task will be to become acquainted with the genuine habits of nature, as distinguished from those of fashion. For in the same manner, and on the same principles, as he has acquired the knowledge of the real forms of nature, distinct from accidental deformity, he must endeavor to separate simple chaste nature from those adventitious, those affected and forced airs or actions with which she is loaded by modern education.

---

[5] Sir Francis Bacon (above, page 234), *Essay XLIII: Of Beauty;* Appelles (fourth century B.C.), Greek painter; Albrecht Dürer (1471–1528), German painter and engraver.

[6] Reynolds is referring to three famous ancient Greek sculptures, now named *The Farnese Hercules, The Borghese Warrior,* and *The Apollo Belvedere.*

Perhaps I cannot better explain what I mean, than by reminding you of what was taught us by the professor of anatomy, in respect to the natural position and movement of the feet. He observed, that the fashion of turning them outwards was contrary to the intent of nature, as might be seen from the structure of the bones, and from the weakness that proceeded from that manner of standing. To this we may add the erect position of the head, the projection of the chest, the walking with straight knees, and many such actions, which we know to be merely the result of fashion, and what nature never warranted, as we are sure that we have been taught them when children.

I have mentioned but a few of those instances, in which vanity or caprice have contrived to distort and disfigure the human form: your own recollection will add to these a thousand more of ill-understood methods, which have been practiced to disguise nature among our dancing-masters, hairdressers, and tailors, in their various schools of deformity.[7]

However the mechanic and ornamental arts may sacrifice to fashion, she must be entirely excluded from the art of painting; the painter must never mistake this capricious changeling for the genuine offspring of nature; he must divest himself of all prejudices in favor of his age or country; he must disregard all local and temporary ornaments, and look only on those general habits which are everywhere and always the same, he addresses his works to the people of every country and every age, he calls upon posterity to be his spectators, and says with Zeuxis, *"in aeternitatem pingo."*[8]

The neglect of separating modern fashions from the habits of nature leads to that ridiculous style which has been practiced by some painters, who have given to Grecian heroes the airs and graces practiced in the court of Louis the Fourteenth; an absurdity almost as great as it would have been to have dressed them after the fashion of that court.

To avoid this error, however, and to retain the true simplicity of nature, is a task more difficult than at first sight it may appear. The prejudices in favor of the fashions and customs that we have been used to, and which are justly called a second nature, make it too often difficult to distinguish that which is natural, from that which is the result of education; they frequently even give a predilection in favor of the artificial mode; and almost everyone is apt to be guided by those local prejudices, who has not chastised his mind and regulated the instability of his affections by the eternal invariable idea of nature.

Here then, as before, we must have recourse to the ancients as instructors. It is from a careful study of their works that you will be enabled to attain to the real simplicity of nature; they will suggest many observations which would probably escape you, if your study were confined to nature alone. And, indeed, I cannot help suspecting that in this instance the ancients had an easier task than the moderns. They had, probably, little or nothing to unlearn, as their manners were nearly approaching to this desirable simplicity; while the modern artist, before he can see the truth of things, is obliged to remove a veil, with which the fashion of the times has thought proper to cover her.

Having gone thus far in our investigation of the great style in painting; if we now should suppose that the artist has found the true idea of beauty, which enables him to give his works a correct and perfect design; if we should suppose also, that he has acquired a knowledge of the unadulterated habits of nature, which gives him simplicity; the rest of his task is, perhaps, less than is generally imagined. Beauty and simplicity have so great a share in the composition of a great style, that he who has acquired them has little else to learn. It must not, indeed, be forgotten, that there is a nobleness of conception, which goes beyond anything in the mere exhibition even of perfect form; there is an art of animating and dignifying the figures with intellectual grandeur, of impressing the appearance of philosophic wisdom or heroic virtue. This can only be acquired by him that enlarges the sphere of his understanding by a variety of knowledge, and warms his imagination with the best productions of ancient and modern poetry.

A hand thus exercised, and a mind thus instructed, will bring the art to a higher degree of excellence than, perhaps, it has hitherto attained in this country. Such a student will disdain the humbler walks of painting, which, however profitable, can never assure him a permanent reputation. He will leave the meaner artist servilely to suppose that those are the best pictures, which are most likely to deceive the spectator. He will permit the lower painter, like the florist or collector of shells to exhibit the minute discriminations, which distinguish one object of the same species from another; while he, like the philosopher, will consider nature in the abstract, and represent in every one of his figures the character of its species.

If deceiving the eye were the only business of the art, there is no doubt, but the minute painter would be more apt to succeed: but it is not the eye, it is the mind, which the painter of genius desires to address; nor will he waste a moment upon those smaller objects, which only serve to catch the sense, to divide the attention, and to counteract his great design of speaking to the heart.

---

[7][Malone] "Those," says Quintilian [Marcus Fabianus Quintilianus, 40–c. 118, Roman rhetorician], "who are taken with the outward show of things, think that there is more beauty in persons who are trimmed, curled, and painted, than uncorrupt nature can give; as if beauty were merely the effect of corruption of manners."

[8]Zeuxis (fl. 424–380 B.C.), Greek painter. "I paint for eternity."

This is the ambition which I wish to excite in your minds, and the object I have had in my view, throughout this discourse, is that one great idea, which gives to painting its true dignity, which entitles it to the name of a liberal art, and ranks it as a sister of poetry.

It may possibly have happened to many young students, whose application was sufficient to overcome all difficulties, and whose minds were capable of embracing the most extensive views, that they have, by a wrong direction originally given, spent their lives in the meaner walks of painting, without ever knowing there was a nobler to pursue. Albert Dürer, as Vasari[9] has justly remarked, would, probably, have been one of the first painters of his age (and he lived in an era of great artists), had he been initiated into those great principles of the art, which were so well understood and practiced by his contemporaries in Italy. But unluckily having never seen or heard of any other manner, he, without doubt, considered his own as perfect.

As for the various departments of painting, which do not presume to make such high pretensions, they are many. None of them are without their merit, though none enter into competition with this universal presiding idea of the art. The painters who have applied themselves more particularly to low and vulgar characters, and who express with precision the various shades of passion, as they are exhibited by vulgar minds (such as we see in the works of Hogarth),[10] deserve great praise; but as their genius has been employed on low and confined subjects, the praise which we give must be as limited as its object. The merrymaking or quarreling of the boors of Teniers; the same sort of productions of Brouwer, or Ostade,[11] are excellent in their kind; and the excellence and its praise will be in proportion as, in those limited subjects and peculiar forms, they introduce more or less of the expression of those passions as they appear in general and more enlarged nature. This principle may be applied to the battlepieces of Bourgognone, the French gallantries of Watteau, and even beyond the exhibition of animal life, to the landscapes of Claude Lorraine, and the seaviews of Vandervelde.[12] All these painters have, in general, the same right, in different degrees, to the name of a painter, which a satirist, an epigrammatist, a sonneteer, a writer of pastorals, or descriptive poetry, has to that of a poet.

In the same rank, and perhaps of not so great merit, is the cold painter of portraits. But this correct and just imitation of his object has its merits. Even the painter of still life, whose highest ambition is to give a minute representation of every part of those low objects which he sets before him, deserves the praise in proportion to his attainment; because no part of this excellent art, so much the ornament of polished life, is destitute of value and use. These, however, are by no means the views to which the mind of the student ought to be primarily directed. Having begun by aiming at better things, if from particular inclination, or from the taste of the time and place he lives in, or from necessity, or from failure in the highest attempts, he is obliged to descend lower, he will bring into the lower sphere of art a grandeur of composition and character that will raise and ennoble his works far above their natural rank.

A man is not weak, though he may not be able to wield the club of Hercules; nor does a man always practice that which he esteems the best; but does that which he can best do. In moderate attempts, there are many walks open to the artist. But as the idea of beauty is of necessity but one, so there can be but one great mode of painting, the leading principle of which I have endeavored to explain.

I should be sorry, if what is here recommended, should be at all understood to countenance a careless or indetermined manner of painting. For though the painter is to overlook the accidental discriminations of nature, he is to exhibit distinctly, and with precision, the general forms of things. A firm and determined outline is one of the characteristics of the great style in painting; and let me add, that he who possesses the knowledge of the exact form which every part of nature ought to have, will be fond of expressing that knowledge with correctness and precision in all his works.

To conclude; I have endeavored to reduce the idea of beauty to general principles; and I had the pleasure to observe that the professor of painting proceeded in the same method, when he showed you that the artifice of contrast was founded but on one principle. I am convinced that this is the only means of advancing science; of clearing the mind from a confused heap of contradictory observations, that do but perplex and puzzle the student when he compares them, or misguide him if he gives himself up to their authority; bringing them under one general head, can alone give rest and satisfaction to an inquisitive mind.

---

[9]Giorgio Vasari (1511–1574), author of biographies of artists.
[10]William Hogarth (1697–1764), English painter and engraver.
[11]David Teniers, the Younger (1610–1690), and Adriaen Brouwer (c. 1605–1638), both Flemish painters; Adriaen Van Ostade (1610–1685), Dutch painter.
[12]Jean-Antoine Watteau (1684–1721), French painter; Claude Lorraine (1600–1682), French painter; probably Willem Van de Velde, the Younger (1633–1707), Dutch painter.

Discourse VII

Gentlemen,

It has been my uniform endeavor, since I first addressed you from this place, to impress you strongly with one ruling idea. I wished you to be persuaded, that success in your art depends almost entirely on your own industry; but the industry which I principally recommended, is not the industry of the hands, but of the mind.

As our art is not a divine gift, so neither is it a mechanical trade. Its foundations are laid in solid science: and practice, though essential to perfection, can never attain that to which it aims, unless it works under the direction of principle.

Some writers upon art carry this point too far, and suppose that such a body of universal and profound learning is requisite, that the very enumeration of its kinds is enough to frighten a beginner. Vitruvius,[13] after going through the many accomplishments of nature, and the many acquirements of learning, necessary to an architect, proceeds with great gravity to assert, that he ought to be well skilled in the civil law; that he may not be cheated in the title of the ground he builds on. But without such exaggeration, we may go so far as to assert, that a painter stands in need of more knowledge than is to be picked off his palette, or collected by looking on his model, whether it be in life or in picture. He can never be a great artist, who is grossly illiterate.

Every man whose business is description, ought to be tolerably conversant with the poets, in some language or other; that he may imbibe a poetical spirit, and enlarge his stock of ideas. He ought to acquire a habit of comparing and digesting his notions. He ought not to be wholly unacquainted with that part of philosophy which gives an insight into human nature, and relates to the manners, characters, passions, and affections. He ought to know something concerning the mind, as well as a great deal concerning the body of man. For this purpose, it is not necessary that he should go into such a compass of reading, as must, by distracting his attention, disqualify him for the practical part of his profession, and makes him sink the performer in the critic. Reading, if it can be made the favorite recreation of his leisure hours, will improve and enlarge his mind, without retarding his actual industry. What such partial and desultory reading cannot afford, may be supplied by the conversation of learned and ingenious men, which is the best of all substitutes for those who have not the means or opportunities of deep study. There are many such men in this age; and they will be pleased with communicating their ideas to artists, when they see them curious and docile, if they are treated with that respect and deference which is so justly their due. Into such society, young artists, if they make it the point of their ambition, will by degrees be admitted. There, without formal teaching, they will insensibly come to feel and reason like those they live with, and find a rational and systematic taste imperceptibly formed in their minds, which they will know how to reduce to a standard, by applying general truth to their own purposes, better perhaps than those to whom they owed the original sentiment.

Of these studies, and this conversation, the desired and legitimate offspring is a power of distinguishing right from wrong; which power applied to works of art, is denominated *taste*. Let me then, without further introduction, enter upon an examination, whether taste be so far beyond our reach, as to be unattainable by care; or be so very vague and capricious, that no care ought to be employed about it.

It has been the fate of arts to be enveloped in mysterious and incomprehensible language, as if it was thought necessary that even the terms should correspond to the idea entertained of the instability and uncertainty of the rules which they expressed.

To speak of genius and taste, as in any way connected with reason or common sense, would be, in the opinion of some towering talkers, to speak like a man who possessed neither; who had never felt that enthusiasm, or, to use their own inflated language, was never warmed by that Promethean fire, which animates the canvas and vivifies the marble.

If, in order to be intelligible, I appear to degrade art by bringing her down from her visionary situation in the clouds, it is only to give her a more solid mansion upon the earth. It is necessary that at some time or other we should see things as they really are, and not impose on ourselves by that false magnitude with which objects appear when viewed indistinctly as through a mist.

We will allow a poet to express his meaning, when his meaning is not well known to himself, with a certain degree of obscurity, as it is one source of the sublime. But when, in plain prose, we gravely talk of courting the Muse in shady bowers; waiting the call and inspiration of Genius, finding out where he inhabits, and where he is to be invoked with the greatest success; of attending to times and seasons when the imagination shoots with the greatest vigor, whether at the summer solstice or the vernal equinox; sagaciously observing how much the wild freedom and liberty of imagination is cramped by attention to established rules; and how this same imagination begins to grow dim in advanced age, smothered and deadened by too much judgment; when we talk such language, or entertain such sentiments as these, we generally rest contented with mere words, or at best entertain notions not only groundless, but pernicious.

If all this means, what it is very possible was originally intended only to be meant, that in order to cultivate an art, a man secludes himself from the commerce of the world, and

---

[13]Marcus Vitruvius Pollio (first century), author of *On Architecture*.

retires into the country at particular seasons; or that at one time of the year his body is in better health, and consequently his mind fitter for the business of hard thinking than at another time; or that the mind may be fatigued and grow confused by long and unremitted application; this I can understand. I can likewise believe, that a man eminent when young for possessing poetical imagination, may, from having taken another road, so neglect its cultivation, as to shew less of its powers in his latter life. But I am persuaded, that scarce a poet is to be found from Homer down to Dryden,[14] who preserved a sound mind in a sound body, and continued practicing his profession to the very last, whose latter works are not as replete with the fire of imagination, as those which were produced in his more youthful days.

To understand literally these metaphors or ideas expressed in poetical language, seems to be equally absurd as to conclude, that because painters sometimes represent poets writing from the dictates of a little winged boy or genius, that this same genius did really inform him in a whisper what he was to write; and that he is himself but a mere machine, unconscious of the operations of his own mind.

Opinions generally received and floating in the world, whether true or false, we naturally adopt and make our own; they may be considered as a kind of inheritance to which we succeed and are tenants for life, and which we leave to our posterity very nearly in the condition in which we received it; it not being much in any one man's power either to impair or improve it. The greatest part of these opinions, like current coin in its circulation, we are used to take without weighing or examining; but by this inevitable inattention many adulterated pieces are received, which, when we seriously estimate our wealth, we must throw away. So the collector of popular opinions, when he embodies his knowledge, and forms a system, must separate those which are true from those which are only plausible. But it becomes more peculiarly a duty to the professors of art not to let any opinions relating to *that* art pass unexamined. The caution and circumspection required in such examination we shall presently have an opportunity of explaining.

Genius and taste, in their common acceptation, appear to be very nearly related; the difference lies only in this, that genius has superadded to it a habit of power of execution: or we may say, that taste, when this power is added, changes its name, and is called genius. They both, in the popular opinion, pretend to an entire exemption from the restraint of rules. It is supposed that their powers are intuitive; that under the name of genius great works are produced, and under the name of taste an exact judgment is given, without our knowing why, and without our being under the least obligation to reason, precept, or experience.

One can scarce state these opinions without exposing their absurdity; yet they are constantly in the mouths of men, and particularly of artists. They who have thought seriously on this subject, do not carry the point so far; yet I am persuaded, that even among those few who may be called thinkers, the prevalent opinion allows less than it ought to the powers of reason; and considers the principles of taste, which give all their authority to the rules of art, as more fluctuating, and as having less solid foundations, than we shall find, upon examination, they really have.

The common saying, that "tastes are not to be disputed," owes its influence, and its general reception, to the same error which leads us to imagine this faculty of too high an original to submit to the authority of an earthly tribunal. It likewise corresponds with the notions of those who consider it as a mere phantom of the imagination, so devoid of substance as to elude all criticism.[15]

We often appear to differ in sentiments from each other, merely from the inaccuracy of terms, as we are not obliged to speak always with critical exactness. Something of this too may arise from want of words in the language in which we speak, to express the more nice discriminations which a deep investigation discovers. A great deal however of this difference vanishes, when each opinion is tolerably explained and understood by constancy and precision in the use of terms.

We apply the term *taste* to that act of the mind by which we like or dislike, whatever be the subject. Our judgment upon an airy nothing, a fancy which has no foundation, is called by the same name which we give to our determination concerning those truths which refer to the most general and most unalterable principles of human nature; to the works which are only to be produced by the greatest efforts of the human understanding. However inconvenient this may be, we are obliged to take words as we find them; all we can do is to distinguish the things to which they are applied.

We may let pass those things which are at once subjects of taste and sense, and which having as much certainty as the senses themselves, give no occasion to inquiry or dispute. The natural appetite or taste of the human mind is for truth; whether that truth results from the real agreement or equality of original ideas among themselves; from the

---

[14]Dryden (above, page 253).

[15]Reynolds's concern is with the taste of the painter. See Burke (above, page 332); Hume (above, page 322); Kant (below, page 416), for discussions of the viewer's or reader's taste.

agreement of the representation of any object with the thing represented; or from the correspondence of the several parts of any arrangement with each other. It is the very same taste which relishes a demonstration in geometry, that is pleased with the resemblance of a picture to an original, and touched with the harmony of music.

All these have unalterable and fixed foundations in nature, and are therefore equally investigated by reason, and known by study; some with more, some with less clearness, but all exactly in the same way. A picture that is unlike, is false. Disproportionate ordonnance of parts is not right; because it cannot be true, until it ceases to be a contradiction to assert, that the parts have no relation to the whole. Coloring is true when it is naturally adapted to the eye, from brightness, from softness, from harmony, from resemblance; because these agree with their object, nature, and therefore are true; as true as mathematical demonstration; but known to be true only to those who study these things.

But beside real, there is also apparent truth, or opinion, or prejudice. With regard to real truth, when it is known, the taste which conforms to it, is, and must be, uniform. With regard to the second sort of truth, which may be called truth upon sufferance, or truth by courtesy, it is not fixed, but variable. However, whilst these opinions and prejudices, on which it is founded, continue, they operate as truth; and the art whose office it is to please the mind, as well as instruct it, must direct itself according to opinion, or it will not attain its end.

In proportion as these prejudices are known to be generally diffused, or long received, the taste which conforms to them approaches nearer to certainty, and to a sort of resemblance to real science, even where opinions are found to be no better than prejudices. And since they deserve, on account of their duration and extent, to be considered as really true, they become capable of no small degree of stability and determination by their permanent and uniform nature.

As these prejudices become more narrow, more local, more transitory, this secondary taste becomes more and more fantastical; recedes from real science; is less to be approved by reason, and less followed in practice; though in no case perhaps to be wholly neglected, where it does not stand, as it sometimes does, in direct defiance of the most respectable opinions received amongst mankind.

Having laid down these positions, I shall proceed with less method, because less will serve, to explain and apply them.

We will take it for granted, that reason is something invariable and fixed in the nature of things; and without endeavoring to go back to an account of first principles, which forever will elude our search, we will conclude, that whatever goes under the name of taste, which we can fairly bring under the dominion of reason, must be considered as equally exempt from change. If therefore, in the course of this inquiry, we can shew that there are rules for the conduct of the artist which are fixed and invariable, it follows of course, that the art of the connoisseur, or, in other words, taste, has likewise invariable principles.

Of the judgment which we make on the works of art, and the preference that we give to one class of art over another, if a reason be demanded, the question is perhaps evaded by answering. I judge from my taste; but it does not follow that a better answer cannot be given, though, for common gazers, this may be sufficient. Every man is not obliged to investigate the causes of his approbation or dislike.

The arts would lie open forever to caprice and casualty, if those who are to judge of their excellencies had no settled principles by which they are to regulate their decisions, and the merit or defect of performances were to be determined by unguided fancy. And indeed we may venture to assert, that whatever speculative knowledge is necessary to the artist, is equally and indispensably necessary to the connoisseur.

The first idea that occurs in the consideration of what is fixed in art, or in taste, is that presiding principle of which I have so frequently spoken in former discourses—the general idea of nature. The beginning, the middle, and the end of everything that is valuable in taste, is comprised in the knowledge of what is truly nature; for whatever notions are not conformable to those of nature, or universal opinion, must be considered as more or less capricious.

My notion of nature comprehends not only the forms which nature produces, but also the nature and internal fabric and organization, as I may call it, of the human mind and imagination. The terms *beauty,* or *nature,* which are general ideas, are but different modes of expressing the same thing, whether we apply these terms to statues, poetry, or picture. Deformity is not nature, but an accidental deviation from her accustomed practice. This general idea therefore ought to be called *nature,* and nothing else, correctly speaking, has a right to that name. But we are so far from speaking, in common conversation, with any such accuracy, that, on the contrary, when we criticize Rembrandt[16] and other Dutch painters, who introduced into their historical pictures exact representations of individual objects with all their imperfections, we say—though it is not in a good taste, yet it is nature.

---

[16] Rembrandt Harmenszoon Van Rijn (1606–1669), Dutch painter and etcher.

This misapplication of terms must be very often perplexing to the young student. Is not art, he may say, an imitation of nature? Must he not therefore who imitates her with the greatest fidelity, be the best artist? By this mode of reasoning Rembrandt has a higher place than Raphael.[17] But a very little reflection will serve to shew us that these particularities cannot be nature: for how can that be the nature of man, in which no two individuals are the same?

It plainly appears, that as a work is conducted under the influence of general ideas, or partial, it is principally to be considered as the effect of a good or a bad taste.

As beauty therefore does not consist in taking what lies immediately before you, so neither, in our pursuit of taste, are those opinions which we first received and adopted, the best choice, or the most natural to the mind and imagination. In the infancy of our knowledge we seize with greediness the good that is within our reach; it is by after-consideration, and in consequence of discipline, that we refuse the present for a greater good at a distance. The nobility or elevation of all arts, like the excellency of virtue itself, consists in adopting this enlarged and comprehensive idea; and all criticism built upon the more confined view of what is natural, may properly be called shallow criticism, rather than false: its defect is, that the truth is not sufficiently extensive.

It has sometimes happened, that some of the greatest men in our art have been betrayed into errors by this confined mode of reasoning. Poussin,[18] who, upon the whole, may be produced as an artist strictly attentive to the most enlarged and extensive ideas of nature, from not having settled principles on this point, has in one instance at least, I think, deserted truth for prejudice. He is said to have vindicated the conduct of Julio Romano[19] for his inattention to the masses of light and shade, or grouping the figures in *The Battle of Constantine,* as if designedly neglected, the better to correspond with the hurry and confusion of a battle. Poussin's own conduct in many of his pictures, makes us more easily give credit to this report. That it was too much his own practice, *The Sacrifice to Silenus,* and *The Triumph of Bacchus and Ariadne,* may be produced as instances; but this principle is still more apparent, and may be said to be even more ostentatiously displayed in his *Perseus* and *Medusa's Head.*

This is undoubtedly a subject of great bustle and tumult, and that the first effect of the picture may correspond to the subject, every principle of composition is violated; there is no principal figure, no principal light, no groups;

everything is dispersed, and in such a state of confusion that the eye finds no repose anywhere. In consequence of the forbidding appearance, I remember turning from it with disgust, and should not have looked a second time, if I had not been called back to a closer inspection. I then indeed found, what we may expect always to find in the works of Poussin, correct drawing, forcible expression, and just character; in short all the excellencies which so much distinguish the works of this learned painter.

This conduct of Poussin I hold to be entirely improper to imitate. A picture should please at first sight, and appear to invite the spectator's attention: if on the contrary the general effect offends the eye, a second view is not always sought, whatever more substantial and intrinsic merit it may possess.

Perhaps no apology ought to be received for offenses committed against the vehicle (whether it be the organ of seeing, or of hearing,) by which our pleasures are conveyed to the mind. We must take care that the eye be not perplexed and distracted by a confusion of equal parts, or equal lights, or offended by an unharmonious mixture of colors, as we should guard against offending the ear by unharmonious sounds. We may venture to be more confident of the truth of this observation, since we find that Shakespeare, on a parallel occasion, has made Hamlet recommend to the players a precept of the same kind—never to offend the ear by harsh sounds: "In the very torrent, tempest, and whirlwind of your passion," says he, "you must acquire and beget a temperance that may give it smoothness." And yet, at the same time, he very justly observes, "The end of playing, both at the first, and now, was and is, to hold, as 'twere, the mirror up to nature."[20] No one can deny, that violent passions will naturally emit harsh and disagreeable tones: yet this great poet and critic thought that this imitation of nature would cost too much, if purchased at the expense of disagreeable sensations, or, as he expresses it of "splitting the ear." The poet and actor, as well as the painter of genius who is well acquainted with all the variety and sources of pleasure in the mind and imagination, has little regard or attention to common nature, or creeping after common sense. By overleaping those narrow bounds, he more effectually seizes the whole mind, and more powerfully accomplishes his purpose. This success is ignorantly imagined to proceed from inattention to all rules, and a defiance of reason and judgment; whereas it is in truth acting according to the best rules and the justest reason.

He who thinks nature, in the narrow sense of the word, is alone to be followed, will produce but a scanty entertainment

---

[17] Raphael Santi (1483–1520), Italian painter.
[18] Nicolas Poussin (1594–1665), French painter.
[19] Giulio Romano (c. 1492–1546), Italian painter.

---

[20] *Hamlet* III, ii, 6–8, 22–4.

for the imagination: everything is to be done with which it is natural for the mind to be pleased, whether it proceeds from simplicity or variety, uniformity or irregularity; whether the scenes are familiar or exotic; rude and wild, or enriched and cultivated; for it is natural for the mind to be pleased with all these in their turn. In short, whatever pleases has in it what is analogous to the mind, and is therefore, in the highest and best sense of the word, natural.

It is the sense of nature or truth which ought more particularly to be cultivated by the professors of art; and it may be observed, that many wise and learned men, who have accustomed their minds to admit nothing for truth but what can be proved by mathematical demonstration, have seldom any relish for those arts which address themselves to the fancy, the rectitude and truth of which is known by another kind of proof: and we may add, that the acquisition of this knowledge requires as much circumspection and sagacity, as is necessary to attain those truths which are more capable of demonstration. Reason must ultimately determine our choice on every occasion; but this reason may still be exerted ineffectually by applying to taste principles which, though right as far as they go, yet do not reach the object. No man, for instance, can deny, that it seems at first view very reasonable, that a statue which is to carry down to posterity the resemblance of an individual, should be dressed in the fashion of the times, in the dress which he himself wore: this would certainly be true, if the dress were part of the man; but after a time, the dress is only an amusement for an antiquarian; and if it obstructs the general design of the piece, it is to be disregarded by the artist. Common sense must here give way to a higher sense. In the naked form, and in the disposition of the drapery, the difference between one artist and another is principally seen. But if he is compelled to exhibit the modern dress, the naked form is entirely hid, and the drapery is already disposed by the skill of the tailor. Were a Phidias to obey such absurd commands, he would please no more than an ordinary sculptor, since, in the inferior parts of every art, the learned and the ignorant are nearly upon a level.

These were probably among the reasons that induced the sculptor of that wonderful figure of Laocoön[21] to exhibit him naked, notwithstanding he was surprised in the act of sacrificing to Apollo, and consequently ought to have been shewn in his sacerdotal habits, if those greater reasons had not preponderated. Art is not yet in so high estimation with us, as to obtain so great a sacrifice as the ancients made, especially the Grecians; who suffered themselves to be represented naked, whether they were generals, lawgivers, or kings.

Under this head of balancing and choosing the greater reason, or of two evils taking the least, we may consider the conduct of Rubens[22] in the Luxembourg gallery, where he has mixed allegorical figures with representations of real personages, which must be acknowledged to be a fault; yet, if the artist considered himself as engaged to furnish this gallery with a rich, various, and splendid ornament, this could not be done, at least in an equal degree, without peopling the air and water with these allegorical figures: he therefore accomplished all that he purposed. In this case all lesser considerations, which tend to obstruct the great end of the work, must yield and give way.

The variety which portraits and modern dresses, mixed with allegorical figures, produce, is not to be slightly given up upon a punctilio of reason, when that reason deprives the art in a manner of its very existence. It must always be remembered that the business of a great painter, is to produce a great picture, he must therefore take especial care not to be cajoled by specious arguments out of his materials.

What has been so often said to the disadvantage of allegorical poetry—that it is tedious, and uninteresting—cannot with the same propriety be applied to painting, where the interest is of a different kind. If allegorical painting produces a greater variety of ideal beauty, a richer, a more various and delightful composition, and gives to the artist a greater opportunity of exhibiting his skill, all the interest he wishes for is accomplished: such a picture not only attracts, but fixes the attention.

If it be objected that Rubens judged ill at first in thinking it necessary to make his work so very ornamental, this puts the question upon new ground. It was his peculiar style; he could paint in no other; and he was selected for that work, probably, because it was his style. Nobody will dispute but some of the best of the Roman or Bolognian schools would have produced a more learned and more noble work.

This leads us to another important province of taste, that of weighing the value of the different classes of the art, and of estimating them accordingly.

All arts have means within them of applying themselves with success both to the intellectual and sensitive part of our natures. It cannot be disputed, supposing both these means put in practice with equal abilities, to which we ought to give the preference; to him who represents the heroic arts and

---

[21] An important Hellenistic sculpture that depicts the Trojan priest of Apollo, Laocoön, and his two sons being attacked by two great serpents. Lessing (above, page 378) uses the sculpture as a central example in his *Laocoön,* though it is not mentioned in the selection above.

[22] Peter Paul Rubens (1577–1640), Flemish painter.

more dignified passions of man, or to him who, by the help of meretricious ornaments, however elegant and graceful, captivates the sensuality, as it may be called, of our taste. Thus the Roman and Bolognian schools are reasonably preferred to the Venetian, Flemish, or Dutch schools, as they address themselves to our best and noblest faculties.

Well-turned periods in eloquence, or harmony of numbers in poetry, which are in those arts what coloring is in painting, however highly we may esteem them, can never be considered as of equal importance with the art of unfolding truths that are useful to mankind, and which make us better or wiser. Nor can those works which remind us of the poverty and meanness of our nature, be considered as of equal rank with what excites ideas of grandeur, or raises and dignifies humanity; or, in the words of a late poet, which makes the beholder "learn to venerate himself as man."[23]

It is reason and good sense therefore which ranks and estimates every art, and every part of that art, according to its importance, from the painter of animated, down to inanimated nature. We will not allow a man, who shall prefer the inferior style, to say it is his taste; taste here has nothing, or at least ought to have nothing to do with the question. He wants not taste, but sense, and soundness of judgment.

Indeed perfection in an inferior style may be reasonably preferred to mediocrity in the highest walks of art. A landskip of Claude Lorrain may be preferred to a history by Luca Giordano;[24] but hence appears the necessity of the connoisseur's knowing in what consists the excellency of each class, in order to judge how near it approaches to perfection.

Even in works of the same kind, as in history-painting, which is composed of various parts, excellence of an inferior species, carried to a very high degree, will make a work very valuable, and in some measure compensate for the absence of the higher kinds of merit. It is the duty of the connoisseur to know and esteem, as much as it may deserve, every part of painting: he will not then think even Bassano[25] unworthy of his notice; who, though totally devoid of expression, sense, grace, or elegance, may be esteemed on account of his admirable taste of colors, which, in his best works, are little inferior to those of Titian.[26]

Since I have mentioned Bassano, we must do him likewise the justice to acknowledge, that though he did not aspire to the dignity of expressing the characters and passions of men, yet, with respect to facility and truth in his manner of touching animals of all kinds, and giving them what painters call "their character," few have ever excelled him.

To Bassano we may add Paul Veronese and Tintoret,[27] for their entire inattention to what is justly thought the most essential part of our art, the expression of the passions. Notwithstanding these glaring deficiencies, we justly esteem their works; but it must be remembered, that they do not please from those defects, but from their great excellencies of another kind, and in spite of such transgressions. These excellencies too, as far as they go, are founded in the truth of general nature; they tell the truth, though not the whole truth.

By these considerations, which can never be too frequently impressed, may be obviated two errors which I observed to have been, formerly at least, the most prevalent, and to be most injurious to artists; that of thinking taste and genius to have nothing to do with reason, and that of taking particular living objects for nature.

I shall now say something on that part of taste, which, as I have hinted to you before, does not belong so much to the external form of things, but is addressed to the mind, and depends on its original frame, or, to use the expression, the organization of the soul; I mean the imagination and the passions. The principles of these are as invariable as the former, and are to be known and reasoned upon in the same manner, by an appeal to common sense deciding upon the common feelings of mankind. This sense, and these feelings appear to me of equal authority, and equally conclusive. Now this appeal implies a general uniformity and agreement in the minds of men. It would be else an idle and vain endeavor to establish rules of art; it would be pursuing a phantom to attempt to move affections with which we were entirely unacquainted. We have no reason to suspect there is a greater difference between our minds than between our forms; of which, though there are no two alike, yet there is a general similitude that goes through the whole race of mankind; and those who have cultivated their taste can distinguish what is beautiful or deformed, or, in other words, what agrees with or deviates from the general idea of nature, in one case, as well as in the other.

The internal fabric of our minds, as well as the external form of our bodies, being nearly uniform; it seems then to follow of course, that as the imagination is incapable of producing anything originally of itself, and can only vary and combine those ideas with which it is furnished by means of the senses, there will be necessarily an agreement in the imaginations as in the senses of men.[28] There being this agreement, it follows, that in all cases, in our lightest

[23] Oliver Goldsmith (1728–1774), Anglo-Irish writer, *The Traveller,* 334.
[24] Luca Giordano (1632–1705), Italian painter.
[25] Jacopo Bassano (1510–1592), Venetian painter.
[26] Titian (Tiziano Vecelli, c. 1477–1576), Venetian painter.
[27] Paolo Veroneze (1528–1588) and Tintoretto (Jacopo Robusti, 1518–1594), Italian painters.
[28] See Burke (above, page 335).

amusements, as well as in our most serious actions and engagements of life, we must regulate our affections of every kind by that of others. The well-disciplined mind acknowledges this authority, and submits its own opinion to the public voice. It is from knowing what are the general feelings and passions of mankind, that we acquire a true idea of what imagination is; though it appears as if we had nothing to do but to consult our own particular sensations, and these were sufficient to ensure us from all error and mistake.

A knowledge of the disposition and character of the human mind can be acquired only by experience: a great deal will be learned, I admit, by a habit of examining what passes in our bosoms, what are our own motives of action, and of what kind of sentiments we are conscious on any occasion. We may suppose an uniformity, and conclude that the same effect will be produced by the same cause in the minds of others. This examination will contribute to suggest to us matters of inquiry; but we can never be sure that our own sensations are true and right, till they are confirmed by more extensive observation. One man opposing another determines nothing; but a general union of minds, like a general combination of the forces of all mankind, makes a strength that is irresistible. In fact, as he who does not know himself does not know others, so it may be said with equal truth, that he who does not know others, knows himself but very imperfectly.

A man who thinks he is guarding himself against prejudices by resisting the authority of others, leaves open every avenue to singularity, vanity, self-conceit, obstinacy, and many other vices, all tending to warp the judgment, and prevent the natural operation of his faculties. This submission to others is a deference which we owe, and indeed are forced involuntarily to pay. In fact, we never are satisfied with our opinions, whatever we may pretend, till they are ratified and confirmed by the suffrages of the rest of mankind. We dispute and wrangle forever; we endeavor to get men to come to us, when we do not go to them.

He therefore who is acquainted with the works which have pleased different ages and different countries, and has formed his opinion on them, has more materials, and more means of knowing what is analogous to the mind of man, than he who is conversant only with the works of his own age or country. What has pleased, and continues to please, is likely to please again: hence are derived the rules of art, and on this immovable foundation they must ever stand.

This search and study of the history of the mind ought not to be confined to one art only. It is by the analogy that one art bears to another, that many things are ascertained, which either were but faintly seen, or, perhaps, would not have been discovered at all, if the inventor had not received the first hints from the practices of a sister art on a similar occasion. The frequent allusions which every man who treats of any art is obliged to make to others in order to illustrate and confirm his principles, sufficiently shew their near connection and inseparable relation.

All arts having the same general end, which is to please; and addressing themselves to the same faculties through the medium of the senses; it follows that their rules and principles must have as great affinity as the different materials and the different organs or vehicles by which they pass to the mind, will permit them to retain.

We may therefore conclude, that the real substance, as it may be called, of what goes under the name of taste, is fixed and established in the nature of things; that there are certain and regular causes by which the imagination and passions of men are affected; and that the knowledge of these causes is acquired by a laborious and diligent investigation of nature, and by the same slow progress as wisdom or knowledge of every kind, however instantaneous its operations may appear, when thus acquired.

It has been often observed, that the good and virtuous man alone can acquire this true or just relish even of works of art. This opinion will not appear entirely without foundation, when we consider that the same habit of mind which is acquired by our search after truth in the more serious duties of life, is only transferred to the pursuit of lighter amusements. The same disposition, the same desire to find something steady, substantial, and durable, on which the mind can lean as it were, and rest with safety, actuates us in both cases. The subject only is changed. We pursue the same method in our search after the idea of beauty and perfection in each; of virtue, by looking forwards beyond ourselves to society, and to the whole; of arts, by extending our views in the same manner to all ages and all times.

Every art, like our own, has in its composition fluctuating as well as fixed principles. It is an attentive inquiry into their difference that will enable us to determine how far we are influenced by custom and habit, and what is fixed in the nature of things.

To distinguish how much has solid foundation, we may have recourse to the same proof by which some hold that wit ought to be tried; whether it preserves itself when translated. That wit is false, which can subsist only in one language; and that picture which pleases only one age or one nation, owes its reception to some local or accidental association of ideas.

We may apply this to every custom and habit of life. Thus the general principles of urbanity, politeness, or civility, have been ever the same in all nations; but the mode in which they are dressed, is continually varying. The general idea of shewing respect is by making yourself less; but the manner, whether by bowing the body, kneeling, prostration, pulling off the upper part of our dress, or taking away the lower, is a matter of custom.

Thus in regard to ornaments, it would be unjust to conclude that because they were at first arbitrarily contrived, they are therefore undeserving of our attention; on the contrary, he who neglects the cultivation of those ornaments, acts contrary to nature and reason. As life would be imperfect without its highest ornaments, the arts, so these arts themselves would be imperfect without their ornaments. Though we by no means ought to rank these with positive and substantial beauties, yet it must be allowed that a knowledge of both is essentially requisite towards forming a complete, whole, and perfect taste. It is in reality from the ornaments that arts receive their peculiar character and complexion; we may add, that in them we find the characteristical mark of a national taste; as by throwing up a feather in the air, we know which way the wind blows, better than by a more heavy matter.

The striking distinction between the works of the Roman, Bolognian, and Venetian schools, consists more in that general effect which is produced by colors, than in the more profound excellencies of the art; at least it is from thence that each is distinguished and known at first sight. Thus it is the ornaments, rather than the proportions of architecture, which at the first glance distinguish the different orders from each other; the Doric is known by its triglyphs, the Ionic by its volutes, and the Corinthian by its acanthus.[29]

What distinguishes oratory from a cold narration, is a more liberal, though chaste, use of those ornaments which go under the name of figurative and metaphorical expressions; and poetry distinguishes itself from oratory by words and expressions still more ardent and glowing. What separates and distinguishes poetry, is more particularly the ornament of verse: it is this which gives it its character, and is an essential without which it cannot exist. Custom has appropriated different meter to different kinds of composition, in which the world is not perfectly agreed. In England the dispute is not yet settled, which is to be preferred, rhyme or blank verse. But however we disagree about what these metrical ornaments shall be, that some meter is essentially necessary, is universally acknowledged.

In poetry or eloquence, to determine how far figurative or metaphorical language may proceed, and when it begins to be affectation or beside the truth, must be determined by taste; though this taste, we must never forget, is regulated and formed by the presiding feelings of mankind, by those works which have approved themselves to all times and all persons. Thus, though eloquence has undoubtedly an essential and intrinsic excellence, and immovable principles common to all languages, founded in the nature of our passions and affections; yet it has its ornaments and modes of address, which are merely arbitrary. What is approved in the eastern nations, as grand and majestic, would be considered by the Greeks and Romans as turgid and inflated; and they, in return, would be thought by the Orientals to express themselves in a cold and insipid manner.

We may add likewise to the credit of ornaments, that it is by their means that art itself accomplishes its purpose. Fresnoy calls coloring, which is one of the chief ornaments of painting, "lena sororis,"[30] that which procures lovers and admirers to the more valuable excellencies of the art.

It appears to be the same right turn of mind which enables a man to acquire the truth, or the idea of what is right, in the ornaments, as in the more stable principles of art. It has still the same center of perfection, though it is the center of a smaller circle.

To illustrate this by the fashion of dress, in which there is allowed to be a good or bad taste. The component parts of dress are continually changing from great to little, from short to long; but the general form still remains: it is still the same general dress which is comparatively fixed, though on a very slender foundation; but it is on this which fashion must rest. He who invents with the most success, or dresses in the best taste, would probably, from the same sagacity employed to greater purposes, have discovered equal skill, or have formed the same correct taste, in the highest labors of art.

I have mentioned taste in dress, which is certainly one of the lowest subjects to which this word is applied; yet, as I have before observed, there is a right even here, however narrow its foundation respecting the fashion of any particular nation. But we have still more slender means of determining, to which of the different customs of different ages or countries we ought to give the preference, since they seem to be all equally removed from nature. If a European, when he has cut off his beard, and put false hair on his head, or bound up his own hair in regular hard knots, as unlike nature as he can possibly make it; and after having rendered them immovable by the help of the fat of hogs, has covered the whole with flour, laid on by a machine with the utmost regularity; if, when thus attired he issues forth, and meets a Cherokee Indian, who has bestowed as much time at his toilet, and laid on with equal

[29] All are types of Greek columns.

[30] Charles Alphonse Dufresnay (1611–1668), French painter and writer. "Gentle sisters."

care and attention his yellow and red ocher on particular parts of his forehead or cheeks; as he judges most becoming; whoever of these two despises the other for his attention to the fashion of his country, whichever first feels himself provoked to laugh, is the barbarian.

All these fashions are very innocent; neither worth disquisition, nor any endeavor to alter them; as the change would, in all probability, be equally distant from nature. The only circumstances against which indignation may reasonably be moved, is where the operation is painful or destructive of health, such as some of the practices at Otaheite,[31] and the strait lacing of the English ladies; of the last of which practices, how destructive it must be to health and long life, the professor of anatomy took an opportunity of proving a few days since in this Academy.

It is in dress as in things of greater consequence. Fashions originate from those only who have the high and powerful advantages of rank, birth and fortune. Many of the ornaments of art, those at least for which no reason can be given, are transmitted to us, are adopted, and acquire their consequence from the company in which we have been used to see them. As Greece and Rome are the fountains from whence have flowed all kinds of excellence, to that veneration which they have a right to claim for the pleasure and knowledge which they have afforded us, we voluntarily add our approbation of every ornament and every custom that belonged to them, even to the fashion of their dress. For it may be observed that, not satisfied with them in their own place, we make no difficulty of dressing statues of modern heroes or senators in the fashion of the Roman armor or peaceful robe; we go so far as hardly to bear a statue in any other drapery.

The figures of the great men of those nations have come down to us in sculpture. In sculpture remain almost all the excellent specimens of ancient art. We have so far associated personal dignity to the persons thus represented, and the truth of art to their manner of representation, that it is not in our power any longer to separate them. This is not so in painting; because having no excellent ancient portraits, that connection was never formed. Indeed we could no more venture to paint a general officer in a Roman military habit, than we could make a statue in the present uniform. But since we have no ancient portraits, to shew how ready we are to adopt those kind of prejudices, we make the best authority among the moderns serve the same purpose. The great variety of excellent portraits with which Van Dyck[32] has enriched this nation, we are not content to admire for their real excellence, but extend our approbation even to the dress which happened to be the fashion of that age. We all very well remember how common it was a few years ago for portraits to be drawn in this fantastic dress, and this custom is not yet entirely laid aside. By this means it must be acknowledged very ordinary pictures acquired something of the air and effect of the works of Van Dyck, and appeared therefore at first sight to be better pictures than they really were; they appeared so, however, to those only who had the means of making this association; and when made, it was irresistible. But this association is nature, and refers to that secondary truth that comes from conformity to general prejudice and opinion; it is therefore not merely fantastical. Besides the prejudice which we have in favor of ancient dresses, there may be likewise other reasons for the effect which they produce; among which we may justly rank the simplicity of them, consisting of little more than one single piece of drapery, without those whimsical capricious forms by which all other dresses are embarrassed.

Thus, though it is from the prejudices we have in favor of the ancients, who have taught us architecture, that we have adopted likewise their ornaments; and though we are satisfied that neither nature nor reason are the foundation of those beauties which we imagine we see in that art, yet if anyone, persuaded of this truth, should therefore invent new orders of equal beauty, which we will suppose to be possible, they would not please; nor ought he to complain, since the old has that great advantage of having custom and prejudice on its side. In this case we leave what has every prejudice in its favor, to take that which will have no advantage over what we have left, but novelty; which soon destroys itself, and at any rate is but a weak antagonist against custom.

Ancient ornaments, having the right of possession, ought not to be removed, unless to make room for that which not only has higher pretensions, but such pretensions as will balance the evil and confusion which innovation always brings with it.

To this we may add, that even the durability of the materials will often contribute to give a superiority to one object over another. Ornaments in buildings, with which taste is principally concerned, are composed of materials which last longer than those of which dress is composed; the former therefore make higher pretensions to our favor and prejudice.

Some attention is surely due to what we can no more get rid of than we can go out of ourselves. We are creatures of prejudice; we neither can nor ought to eradicate it; we must only regulate it by reason; which kind of regulation is indeed little more than obliging the lesser, the local and temporary prejudices, to give way to those which are more durable and lasting.

---

[31] Tahiti.
[32] Anthony Van Dyke (1599–1641), Flemish painter who spent part of his career in England.

He therefore who in his practice of portrait-painting wishes to dignify his subject, which we will suppose to be a lady, will not paint her in the modern dress, the familiarity of which alone is sufficient to destroy all dignity. He takes care that his work shall correspond to those ideas and that imagination which he knows will regulate the judgment of others; and therefore dresses his figure something with the general air of the antique for the sake of dignity, and preserves something of the modern for the sake of likeness. By this conduct his works correspond with those prejudices which we have in favor of what we continually see; and the relish of the antique simplicity corresponds with what we may call the more learned and scientific prejudice.

There was a statue made not long since of Voltaire,[33] which the sculptor, not having that respect for the prejudices of mankind which he ought to have had, made entirely naked, and as meager and emaciated as the original is said to be. The consequence was what might have been expected; it remained in the sculptor's shop, though it was intended as a public ornament and a public honor to Voltaire, for it was procured at the expense of his contemporary wits and admirers.

Whoever would reform a nation, supposing a bad taste to prevail in it, will not accomplish his purpose by going directly against the stream of their prejudices. Men's minds must be prepared to receive what is new to them. Reformation is a work of time. A national taste, however, wrong it may be, cannot be totally changed at once; we must yield a little to the prepossession which has taken hold on the mind, and we may then bring people to adopt what would offend them, if endeavored to be introduced by violence. When Battista Franco was employed, in conjunction with Titian, Paul Veronese and Tintoret,[34] to adorn the library of St. Mark, his work, Vasari says, gave less satisfaction than any of the others: the dry manner of the Roman school was very ill calculated to please eyes that had been accustomed to the luxuriancy, splendor, and richness of Venetian coloring. Had the Romans been the judges of this work, probably the determination would have been just contrary; for in the more noble parts of the art, Battista Franco was perhaps not inferior to any of his rivals.

Gentlemen,

It has been the main scope and principal end of this discourse to demonstrate the reality of a standard in taste, as well as in corporeal beauty; that a false or depraved taste is a thing as well known, as easily discovered, as anything that is deformed, misshapen, or wrong, in our form or outward make; and that this knowledge is derived from the uniformity of sentiments among mankind, from whence proceeds the knowledge of what are the general habits of nature; the result of which is an idea of perfect beauty.

If what has been advanced be true, that beside this beauty or truth, which is formed on the uniform, eternal and immutable laws of nature, and which of necessity can be but one; that beside this one immutable verity there are likewise what we have called apparent or secondary truths, proceeding from local and temporary prejudices, fancies, fashions, or accidental connection of ideas; if it appears that these last have still their foundation, however slender, in the original fabric of our minds; it follows that all these truths or beauties deserve and require the attention of the artist, in proportion to their stability or duration, or as their influence is more or less extensive. And let me add, that as they ought not to pass their just bounds, so neither do they, in a well-regulated taste, at all prevent or weaken the influence of those general principles, which alone can give to art its true and permanent dignity.

To form this just taste is undoubtedly in your own power; but it is to reason and philosophy that you must have recourse; from them you must borrow the balance by which is to be weighed and estimated the value of every pretension that intrudes itself on your notice.

The general objection which is made to the introduction of philosophy into the regions of taste, is, that it checks and restrains the flights of the imagination, and gives that timidity which an overcarefulness not to err or act contrary to reason is likely to produce. It is not so. Fear is neither reason nor philosophy. The true spirit of philosophy, by giving knowledge, gives a manly confidence, and substitutes rational firmness in the place of vain presumption. A man of real taste is always a man of judgment in other respects; and those inventions which either disdain or shrink from reason, are generally, I fear, more like the dreams of a distempered brain than the exalted enthusiasm of a sound and true genius. In the midst of the highest flights of fancy or imagination, reason ought to preside from first to last, though I admit her more powerful operation is upon reflection.

Let me add, that some of the greatest names of antiquity, and those who have most distinguished themselves in works in genius and imagination, were equally eminent for their critical skill. Plato, Aristotle, Cicero, and Horace;[35] and among the moderns, Boileau, Corneille, Pope, and

---

[33]Francois Marie Arouet de Voltaire (1694–1778), French writer.
[34]Battista Franco (1510–1580).

---

[35]See above, page 8, page 48, page 74, and page 78, respectively.

Dryden,[36] are at least instances of genius not being destroyed by attention or subjection to rules and science. I should hope therefore, that the natural consequence of what has been said, would be, to excite in you a desire of knowing the principles and conduct of the great masters of our art, and respect and veneration for them when known.

Discourse XIII

Gentlemen,

To discover beauties, or to point out faults, in the works of celebrated masters, and to compare the conduct of one artist with another, is certainly no mean or inconsiderable part of criticism; but this is still no more than to know the art through the artist. This test of investigation must have two capital defects; it must be narrow, and it must be uncertain. To enlarge the boundaries of the art of painting, as well as to fix its principles, it will be necessary, that, that art, and those principles should be considered in their correspondence with the principles of the other arts, which like this, address themselves primarily and principally to the imagination. When those connected and kindred principles are brought together to be compared, another comparison will grow out of this; that is, the comparison of them all with those of human nature, from whence arts derive the materials upon which they are to produce their effects.

When this comparison of art with art, and of all arts with the nature of man, is once made with success, our guiding lines are as well ascertained and established, as they can be in matters of this description.

This, as it is the highest style of criticism, is at the same time the soundest; for it refers to the eternal and immutable nature of things.

You are not to imagine that I mean to open to you at large, or to recommend to your research, the whole of this vast field of science. It is certainly much above my faculties to reach it; and though it may not be above yours, to comprehend it fully, if it were fully and properly brought before you, yet perhaps the most perfect criticism requires habits of speculation and abstraction, not very consistent with the employment which ought to occupy, and the habits of mind which ought to prevail in a practical artist. I only point out to you these things, that when you do criticize (as all who work on a plan, will criticize more or less), your criticism may be built on the foundation of true principles; and that though you may not always travel a great way, the way that you do travel may be the right road.

I observe, as a fundamental ground, common to all the arts with which we have any concern in this discourse, that they address themselves only to two faculties of the mind, its imagination and its sensibility.

All theories which attempt to direct or control the art, upon any principles falsely called rational, which we form to ourselves upon a supposition of what ought in reason to be the end or means of art, independent of the known first effect produced by objects on the imagination, must be false and delusive. For though it may appear bold to say it, the imagination is here the residence of truth. If the imagination be affected, the conclusion is fairly drawn; if it be not affected, the reasoning is erroneous, because the end is not obtained; the effect itself being the test, and the only test, of the truth and efficacy of the means.

There is in the commerce of life, as in art, a sagacity which is far from being contradictory to right reason, and is superior to any occasional exercise of that faculty, which supersedes it; and does not wait for the slow progress of deduction, but goes at once, by what appears a kind of intuition, to the conclusion. A man endowed with this faculty, feels and acknowledges the truth, though it is not always in his power, perhaps, to give a reason for it; because he cannot recollect and bring before him all the materials that gave birth to his opinion; for very many and very intricate considerations may unite to form the principle, even of small and minute parts, involved in, or dependent on, a great system of things: though these in process of time are forgotten, the right impression still remains fixed in his mind.

This impression is the result of the accumulated experience of our whole life, and has been collected, we do not always know how, or when. But this mass of collective observation, however acquired, ought to prevail over that reason, which however powerfully exerted on any particular occasion, will probably comprehend but a partial view of the subject; and our conduct in life as well as in the arts, is, or ought to be, generally governed by this habitual reason: it is our happiness that we are enabled to draw out on such funds. If we were obliged to enter into a theoretical deliberation on every occasion, before we act, life would be at a stand, and art would be impracticable.

It appears to me therefore, that our first thoughts, that is, the effect which any thing produces on our minds on its first appearance, is never to be forgotten; and it demands for that reason, because it is the first, to be laid up with care. If this be not done, the artist may happen to impose on himself by partial reasoning; by a cold consideration of those animated thoughts which proceed, not perhaps from caprice or rashness (as he may afterwards conceit) but from the fullness of his mind, enriched with the copious stores of all the

---

[36]Nicolas Bolieau-Despréaux (1636–1711), French poet and critic; see above, page 244, page 297, and page 253, respectively.

various inventions which he had ever seen, or had ever passed in his mind. These ideas are infused into his design, without any conscious effort; but if he be not on his guard, he may reconsider and correct them, till the whole matter is reduced to a commonplace invention.

This is sometimes the effect of what I mean to caution you against; that is to say, an unfounded distrust of the imagination and feeling, in favor of narrow, partial, confined, argumentative theories; and of principles that seem to apply to the design in hand; without considering those general impressions on the fancy in which real principles of sound reason, and of much more weight and importance, are involved, and, as it were, lie hid, under the appearance of a sort of vulgar sentiment.

Reason, without doubt, must ultimately determine everything; at this minute it is required to inform us when that very reason is to give way to feeling.

Though I have often spoke of that mean conception of our art which confines it to mere imitation, I must add, that it may be narrowed to such a mere matter of experiment, as to exclude from it the application of science, which alone gives dignity and compass to any art. But to find proper foundations for science is neither to narrow or to vulgarize it; and this is sufficiently exemplified in the success of experimental philosophy. It is the false system of reasoning, grounded on a partial view of things, against which I would most earnestly guard you. And I do it the rather, because those narrow theories, so coincident with the poorest and most miserable practice, and which are adopted to give it countenance, have not had their origin in the poorest minds, but in the mistakes, or possibly in the mistaken interpretations, of great and commanding authorities. We are not therefore in this case misled by feeling, but by false speculation.

When such a man as Plato speaks of painting as only an imitative art, and that our pleasure proceeds from observing and acknowledging the truth of the imitation, I think he misleads us by a partial theory.[37] It is in this poor, partial, and so far, false, view of the art, that Cardinal Bembo[38] has chosen to distinguish even Raphael himself, whom our enthusiasm honors with the name of divine. The same sentiment is adopted by Pope in his epitaph on Sir Godfrey Kneller,[39] and he turns the panegyric solely on imitation, as it is a sort of deception.

I shall not think my time misemployed, if by any means I may contribute to confirm your opinion of what ought to be the object of your pursuit; because, though the best critics must always have exploded this strange idea, yet I know that there is a disposition towards a perpetual recurrence to it, on account of its simplicity and superficial plausibility. For this reason I shall beg leave to lay before you a few thoughts on this subject; to throw out some hints that may lead your minds to an opinion (which I take to be the truth), that painting is not only to be considered as an imitation, operating by deception, but that it is, and ought to be, in many points of view, and strictly speaking, no imitation at all of external nature. Perhaps it ought to be as far removed from the vulgar idea of imitation, as the refined civilized state in which we live, is removed from a gross state of nature; and those who have not cultivated their imaginations, which the majority of mankind certainly have not, may be said, in regard to arts, to continue in this state of nature. Such men will always prefer imitation to that excellence which is addressed to another faculty that they do not possess; but these are not the persons to whom a painter is to look, any more than a judge of morals and manners ought to refer controverted points upon those subjects to the opinions of people taken from the banks of the Ohio, or from New Holland.

It is the lowest style only of arts, whether of painting, poetry, or music, that may be said, in the vulgar sense, to be naturally pleasing. The higher efforts of those arts, we know by experience, do not affect minds wholly uncultivated. This refined taste is the consequence of education and habit; we are born only with a capacity of entertaining this refinement, as we are born with a disposition to receive and obey all the rules and regulations of society; and so far it may be said to be natural to us, and no further.

What has been said, may shew the artist how necessary it is, when he looks about him for the advice and criticism of his friends, to make some distinction of the character, taste, experience, and observation in this art, of those, from whom it is received. An ignorant uneducated man may, like Apelles' critic, be a competent judge of the truth of the representation of a sandal;[40] or to go somewhat higher, like Molière's[41] old woman, may decide upon what is nature, in regard to comic humor; but a critic in the higher style of art, ought to possess the same refined taste, which directed the artist in his work.

To illustrate this principle by a comparison with other arts, I shall now produce some instances to shew, that they,

[37] *Republic* (above, page 31).
[38] Pietro Bembo (1470–1547), author and churchman.
[39] Sir Godfrey Kneller (1646–1723), English painter. Reynolds narrowly reads lines from Pope as praising imitation: ". . . whose art of Nature, and whose pictures thought"; "Living, great Nature fear'd he might outvie/Her works. . . ."
[40] Burke (above, page 336), and Johnson (above, page 359).
[41] Molière (Jean Baptiste Poquelin, 1622–1673), French dramatist.

as well as our own art, renounce the narrow idea of nature, and the narrow theories derived from that mistaken principle, and apply to that reason only which informs us not what imitation is, a natural representation of a given object, but what it is natural for the imagination to be delighted with. And perhaps there is no better way of acquiring this knowledge, than by this kind of analogy: each art will corroborate and mutually reflect the truth on the other. Such a kind of juxtaposition may likewise have this use, that whilst the artist is amusing himself in the contemplation of other arts, he may habitually transfer the principles of those arts to that which he professes; which ought to be always present to his mind, and to which everything is to be referred.

So far is art from being derived from, or having any immediate intercourse with, particular nature as its model, that there are many arts that set out with a professed deviation from it.

This is certainly not so exactly true in regard to painting and sculpture. Our elements are laid in gross common nature, an exact imitation of what is before us: but when we advance to the higher state, we consider this power of imitation, though first in the order of acquisition, as by no means in the scale of perfection.

Poetry addresses itself to the same faculties and the same dispositions as painting, though by different means. The object of both is to accommodate itself to all the natural propensities and inclinations of the mind. The very existence of poetry depends on the license it assumes of deviating from actual nature, in order to gratify natural propensities by other means, which are found by experience full as capable of affording such gratification. It sets out with a language in the highest degree artificial, a construction of measured words, such as never is, nor ever was used by man. Let this measure be what it may, whether hexameter or any other meter used in Latin or Greek—or rhyme, or blank verse varied with pauses and accents, in modern languages—they are all equally removed from nature, and equally a violation of common speech. When this artificial mode has been established as the vehicle of sentiment, there is another principle in the human mind, to which the work must be referred, which still renders it more artificial, carries it still further from common nature, and deviates only to render it more perfect. That principle is the sense of congruity, coherence, and consistency, which is a real existing principle in man; and it must be gratified. Therefore having once adopted a style and a measure not found in common discourse, it is required that the sentiments also should be in the same proportion elevated above common nature, from the necessity of there being an agreement of the parts among themselves, that one uniform whole may be produced.

To correspond therefore with this general system of deviation from nature, the manner in which poetry is offered to the ear, the tone in which it is recited, should be as far removed from the tone of conversation, as the words of which that poetry is composed. This naturally suggests the idea of modulating the voice by art, which I suppose may be considered as accomplished to the highest degree of excellence in the recitative of the Italian opera; as we may conjecture it was in the chorus that attended the ancient drama. And though the most violent passions, the highest distress, even death itself, are expressed in singing or recitative, I would not admit as sound criticism the condemnation of such exhibitions on account of their being unnatural.

If it is natural for our senses, and our imaginations, to be delighted with singing, with instrumental music, with poetry, and with graceful action, taken separately; (none of them being in the vulgar sense natural, even in that separate state); it is conformable to experience, and therefore agreeable to reason as connected with and referred to experience, that we should also be delighted with this union of music, poetry, and graceful action, joined to every circumstance of pomp and magnificence calculated to strike the senses of the spectator. Shall reason stand in the way, and tell us we ought not to like what we know we do like, and prevent us from feeling the full effect of this complicated exertion of art? This is what I would understand by poets and painters being allowed to dare everything; for what can be more daring, than accomplishing the purpose and end of art, by a complication of means, none of which have their archetypes in actual nature?

So far therefore is servile imitation from being necessary, that whatever is familiar, or in any way reminds us of what we see and hear every day, perhaps does not belong to the higher provinces of art, either in poetry or painting. The mind is to be transported, as Shakespeare expresses it, "beyond the ignorant present,"[42] to ages past. Another and a higher order of beings is supposed; and to those beings everything which is introduced into the work must correspond. Of this conduct, under these circumstances, the Roman and Florentine schools afford sufficient examples. Their style by this means is raised and elevated above all others, and by the same means the compass of art itself is enlarged.

We often see grave and great subjects attempted by artists of another school; who, though excellent in the lower class of art, proceeding on the principles which regulate that class, and not recollecting, or not knowing, that they were to

---

[42]*Macbeth* I, v: 54–5.

address themselves to another faculty of the mind, have become perfectly ridiculous.

The picture which I have at present in my thoughts is a sacrifice of Iphigenia, painted by Jan Steen,[43] a painter of whom I have formerly had occasion to speak with the highest approbation; and even in this picture, the subject of which is by no means adapted to his genius, there is nature and expression; but it is such expression, and the countenances are so familiar, and consequently so vulgar, and the whole accompanied with such finery of silks and velvet, that one would be almost tempted to doubt, whether the artist did not purposely intend to burlesque his subject.

Instances of the same kind we frequently see in poetry. Parts of Hobbes's[44] translation of Homer are remembered and repeated merely for the familiarity and meanness of their phraseology, so ill corresponding with the ideas which ought to have been expressed, and, as I conceive, with the style of the original.

We may proceed in the same manner through the comparatively inferior branches of art. There are in works of that class, the same distinction of a higher and a lower style; and they take their rank and degree in proportion as the artist departs more, or less, from common nature, and makes it an object of his attention to strike the imagination of the spectator by ways belonging specially to art—unobserved and untaught out of the school of its practice.

If our judgments are to be directed by narrow, vulgar, untaught or rather ill-taught reason, we must prefer a portrait by Denner[45] or any other high finisher, to those of Titian or Van Dyck; and a landskip of Vanderhyde[46] to those of Titian or Rubens; for they are certainly more exact representations of nature.

If we suppose a view of nature represented with all the truth of the camera obscura,[47] and the same scene represented by a great artist, how little and mean will the one appear in comparison of the other, where no superiority is supposed from the choice of the subject. The scene shall be the same, the difference only will be in the manner in which it is presented to the eye. With what additional superiority then will the same artist appear when he has the power of selecting his materials, as well as elevating his style? Like Nicolas Poussin, he transports us to the environs of ancient Rome, with all the objects which a literary education makes so precious and interesting to man: or, like Sebastian Bour-

don,[48] he leads us to the dark antiquity of the pyramids of Egypt; or, like Claude Lorrain, he conducts us to the tranquility of Arcadian scenes and fairyland.

Like the history-painter, a painter of landskips in this style and with this conduct, sends the imagination back into antiquity; and, like the poet, he makes the elements sympathize with his subject: whether the clouds roll in volumes like those of Titian or Salvator Rosa,[49] or, like those of Claude, are gilded with the setting sun; whether the mountains have sudden and bold projections, or are gently sloped; whether the branches of his trees shoot out abruptly in right angles from their trunks, or follow each other with only a gentle inclination. All these circumstances contribute to the general character of the work, whether it be of the elegant, or of the more sublime kind. If we add to this the powerful materials of lightness and darkness, over which the artist has complete dominion, to vary and dispose them as he pleases; to diminish, or increase them as will best suit his purpose, and correspond to the general idea of his work: a landskip thus conducted, under the influence of a poetical mind, will have the same superiority over the more ordinary and common views, as Milton's *Allegro* and *Penseroso* have over a cold prosaic narration or description; and such a picture would make a more forcible impression on the mind than the real scenes, were they presented before us.

If we look abroad to other arts, we may observe the same distinction, the same division into two classes, each of them acting under the influence of two different principles, in which the one follows nature, the other varies it, and sometimes departs from it.

The theater, which is said "to hold the mirror up to nature," comprehends both those ideas. The lower kind of comedy, or farce, like the inferior style of painting, the more naturally it is represented, the better; but the higher appears to me to aim no more at imitation, so far as it belongs to anything like deception, or to expect that the spectators should think that the events there represented are really passing before them, than Raphael in his cartoons, or Poussin in his sacraments, expected it to be believed, even for a moment, that what they exhibited were real figures.

For want of this distinction, the world is filled with false criticism. Raphael is praised for naturalness and deception, which he certainly has not accomplished, and as certainly never intended; and our late great actor Garrick, has been as ignorantly praised by his friend Fielding;[50] who

[43]Jan Steen (1626–1679), Dutch painter.
[44]Thomas Hobbes (1588–1679), English philosopher.
[45]Balthasar Denner (1685–1749), German painter.
[46]Jan van der Heyden (1637–1712), English painter.
[47]A dark enclosure or box that produces an image on a mirror.

[48]Sebastien Bourdon (1616–1671), French painter.
[49]Salvator Rosa (1615–1673), Italian painter.
[50]David Garrick (1717–1779), English actor; Henry Fielding (1707–1754), English novelist.

doubtless imagined he had hit upon an ingenious device, by introducing in one of his novels (otherwise a work of the highest merit), an ignorant man, mistaking Garrick's representation of a scene in Hamlet, for reality. A very little reflection will convince us, that there is no one circumstance in the whole scene that is of the nature of deception. The merit and excellence of Shakespeare and of Garrick, when they were engaged in such scenes, is of a different and much higher kind. But what adds to the falsity of this intended compliment, is, that the best stage representation appears even more unnatural to a person of such a character, who is supposed never to have seen a play before, than it does to those who have had a habit of allowing for those necessary deviations from nature which the art requires.[51]

In theatric representation, great allowances must always be made for the place in which the exhibition is represented; for the surrounding company, the lighted candles, the scenes visibly shifted in your sight; and the language of blank verse, so different from common English; which merely as English must appear surprising in the mouths of Hamlet, and all the court and natives of Denmark. These allowances are made; but their being made puts an end to all manner of deception: and further; we know that the more low, illiterate, and vulgar any person is, the less he will be disposed to make these allowances, and of course to be deceived by any imitation; the things in which the trespass against nature and common probability is made in favor of the theater, being quite within the sphere of such uninformed men.

Though I have no intention of entering into all the circumstances of unnaturalness in theatrical representations, I must observe, that even the expression of violent passion, is not always the most excellent in proportion as it is the most natural: so great terror and such disagreeable sensations may be communicated to the audience, that the balance may be destroyed by which pleasure is preserved, and holds its predominancy in the mind: violent distortion of action, harsh screamings of the voice, however great the occasion, or however natural on such occasion, are therefore not admissible in the theatric art. Many of these allowed deviations from nature arise from the necessity which there is, that everything should be raised and enlarged beyond its natural state; that the full effect may come home to the spectator, which otherwise would be lost in the comparatively extensive space of the theater. Hence the deliberate and stately step, the studied grace of action, which seems to enlarge the dimensions of the actor, and alone to fill the stage.

All this unnaturalness, though right and proper in its place, would appear affected and ridiculous in a private room; *quid enim deformius, quam scenam in vitam transferre?*[52]

And here I must observe, and I believe it may be considered as a general rule, that no art can be engrafted with success on another art. For though they all profess the same origin, and to proceed from the same stock, yet each has its own peculiar modes both of imitating nature, and of deviating from it, each for the accomplishment of its own particular purpose. These deviations, more especially, will not bear transplantation to another soil.

If a painter should endeavor to copy the theatrical pomp and parade of dress and attitude, instead of that simplicity, which is not a greater beauty in life, than it is in painting, we should condemn such pictures as painted in the meanest style.

So also gardening, as far as gardening is an art, or entitled to that appellation, is a deviation from nature; for if the true taste consists, as many hold, in banishing every appearance of art, or any traces of the footsteps of man, it would then be no longer a garden. Even though we define it, "Nature to advantage dressed,"[53] and in some sense it is such, and much more beautiful and commodious for the recreation of man; it is however, when so dressed, no longer a subject for the pencil of a landskip-painter, as all landskip-painters know, who love to have recourse to nature herself, and to dress her according to the principles of their own art; which are far different from those of gardening, even when conducted according to the most approved principles, and such as a landskip-painter himself would adopt in the disposition of his own grounds, for his own private satisfaction.

I have brought together as many instances as appear necessary, to make out the several points which I wished to suggest to your consideration in this discourse; that your own thoughts may lead you further in the use that may be made of the analogy of the arts, and of the restraint which a full understanding of the diversity of many of their principles ought to impose on the employment of that analogy.

The great end of all those arts is, to make an impression on the imagination and the feeling. The imitation of nature frequently does this. Sometimes it fails, and something else succeeds. I think therefore the true test of all the arts, is not solely whether the production is a true copy of nature, but whether it answers the end of art, which is to produce a pleasing effect upon the mind.

---

[51] Johnson (above, page 367).

[52] "For what is more disgraceful than translating what belongs on the stage into life." For another view, see Wilde (below page 713).
[53] Pope, *Essay on Criticism* (above, page 298).

It remains only to speak a few words of architecture, which does not come under the denomination of an imitative art. It applies itself, like music (and I believe we may add poetry) directly to the imagination, without the intervention of any kind of imitation.

There is in architecture, as in painting, an inferior branch of art, in which the imagination appears to have no concern. It does not however acquire the name of a polite and liberal art, from its usefulness, or administering to our wants or necessities, but from some higher principle: we are sure that in the hands of a man of genius it is capable of inspiring sentiment, and of filling the mind with great and sublime ideas.

It may be worth the attention of artists, to consider what materials are in their hands, that may contribute to this end; and whether this art has it not in its power to address itself to the imagination with effect, by more ways than are generally employed by architects.

To pass over the effect produced by that general symmetry and proportion, by which the eye is delighted, as the ear is with music, architecture certainly possesses many principles in common with poetry and painting. Among those which may be reckoned as the first, is, that of affecting the imagination by means of association of ideas. Thus, for instance, as we have naturally a veneration for antiquity, whatever building brings to our remembrance ancient customs and manners, such as the castles of the barons of ancient chivalry, is sure to give this delight. Hence it is that "towers and battlements"[54] are so often selected by the painter and the poet, to make a part of the composition of their ideal landskip; and it is from hence in a great degree, that in the buildings of Vanbrugh,[55] who was a poet as well as an architect, there is a greater display of imagination, than we shall find perhaps in any other; and this is the ground of the effect which we feel in many of his works, notwithstanding the faults with which many of them are justly charged. For this purpose, Vanbrugh appears to have had recourse to some principles of the Gothic architecture; which, not so ancient as the Grecian, is more so to our imagination, with which the artist is more concerned than with absolute truth.

The barbaric splendor of those Asiatic buildings, which are now publishing by a member of this Academy, may possibly, in the same manner, furnish an architect, not with models to copy, but with hints of composition and general effect, which would not otherwise have occurred.

It is, I know, a delicate and hazardous thing (and as such I have already pointed it out), to carry the principles of one art to another, or even to reconcile in one object the various modes of the same art, when they proceed on different principles. The sound rules of the Grecian architecture are not to be lightly sacrificed. A deviation from them, or even an addition to them, is like a deviation or addition to, or from, the rules of other arts, fit only for a great master, who is thoroughly conversant in the nature of man, as well as all combinations in his own art.

It may not be amiss for the architect to take advantage sometimes of that to which I am sure the painter ought always to have his eyes open, I mean the use of accidents; to follow when they lead, and to improve them, rather than always to trust to a regular plan. It often happens that additions have been made to houses, at various times, for use or pleasure. As such buildings depart from regularity, they now and then acquire something of scenery by this accident, which I should think might not unsuccessfully be adopted by an architect, in an original plan, if it does not too much interfere with convenience. Variety and intricacy is a beauty and excellence in every other of the arts which address the imagination; and why not in architecture?

The forms and turnings of the streets of London, and other old towns, are produced by accident, without any original plan or design; but they are not always the less pleasant to the walker or spectator, on that account. On the contrary, if the city had been built on the regular plan of Sir Christopher Wren,[56] the effect might have been, as we know it is in some new parts of the town, rather unpleasing; the uniformity might have produced weariness, and a slight degree of disgust.

I can pretend to no skill in the detail of architecture. I judge now of the art, merely as a painter. When I speak of Vanbrugh, I mean to speak of him in the language of our art. To speak then of Vanbrugh in the language of a painter, he had originality of invention, he understood light and shadow, and had great skill in composition. To support his principal object, he produced his second and third groups or masses; he perfectly understood in his art what is the most difficult in ours, the conduct of the background, by which the design and invention is set off to the greatest advantage. What the background is in painting, in architecture is the real ground on which the building is erected; and no architect took greater care than he that his work should not appear crude and hard: that is, it did not abruptly start out of the ground without expectation or preparation.

This is a tribute, which a painter owes to an architect who composed like a painter; and was defrauded of the due

---

[54]John Milton (1608–1674), *L'Allegro*, 77.
[55]Sir John Vanbrugh (1664–1726), English architect and dramatist.
[56]Sir Christopher Wren (1632–1723), English architect and astronomer.

reward of his merit by the wits of his time, who did not understand the principles of composition in poetry better than he; and who knew little, or nothing, of what he understood perfectly, the general ruling principles of architecture and painting. His fate was that of the great Perrault;[57] both were the objects of the petulant sarcasms of factious men of letters; and both have left some of the fairest ornaments which to this day decorate their several countries; the façade of the Louvre, Blenheim, and castle Howard.

Upon the whole, it seems to me, that the object and intention of all the arts is to supply the natural imperfection of things, and often to gratify the mind by realizing and embodying what never existed but in the imagination.

It is allowed on all hands, that facts, and events, however they may bind the historian, have no dominion over the poet or the painter. With us, history is made to bend and conform to this great idea of art. And why? Because these arts, in their highest province, are not addressed to the gross senses, but to the desires of the mind, to that spark of divinity which we have within, impatient of being circumscribed and pent up by the world which is about us. Just so much as our art has of this, just so much of dignity, I had almost said of divinity, it exhibits; and those of our artists who possessed this mark of distinction in the highest degree, acquired from thence the glorious appellation of divine.

---

[57] Claude Perrault (1613–1688), French architect.

Immanuel Kant

1724–1804

Kant's three famous critiques, those of *Pure Reason, Practical Reason,* and *Judgment,* are expressions of his critical philosophy, based on the transcendental employment of our cognitive faculties. By "transcendental" Kant does not imply transcendence of the phenomenal world, as in Plato, but rather an account of all knowledge that is occupied not so much with objects as with the mode of our knowledge insofar as this mode of knowledge is possible *a priori.* Kant's critical project, which he described as a "Copernican Revolution in Philosophy," thereby hinges on the discovery or deduction of universal concepts that govern the operation of the faculties of reason, understanding, and judgment.

Writing after the *Critique of Pure Reason,* Kant remarked that he had been "awakened from his dogmatic slumbers" by the skepticism of David Hume, which called into question even the idea of cause and effect. Kant's "critical" turn, accordingly, consists in asking the radical question of how it is possible for us to have knowledge of any kind instead of debating any particular claims to knowledge. While this makes Kant notoriously difficult to read since he is endeavoring to explicate not things we think about but the concepts without which we could not think at all, the language of his own arguments necessarily relies on the very concepts he would explain. Kant, however, did not develop any sustained theory of language, nor any theory of symbolic mediation, both problems taken up in various ways by his subsequent followers and critics, notably, von Humboldt (below, page 523) and Cassirer (below, page 1016) on the continent, and Coleridge (below, page 493), and C. S. Peirce (below, page 652) in England and America.

His *Critique of Judgment* as the third and final component of the Critical Philosophy has always presented unusual problems. Read thematically, it can be taken as primarily a discourse on the aesthetic and more particularly, on the concepts of the beautiful and the sublime. In the context of the other critiques, however, *Critique of Judgment* both draws upon and complicates the epistemological position he expounded in the *Critique of Pure Reason.* There he proposed the existence of the "manifold of sensation," the raw data that is then collected and synthesized through the creative power of the sensibility. The sensibility abstracts from the manifold, formulating the world intellectually according to time and space, the *a priori* forms of "inner" and "outer" sense. Kant argues that we can never know directly "things in themselves"; all we perceive are appearances, intelligible to us only as they conform to our ideas of time and space. At a higher level, further removed from direct sensation, the understanding comes into play and schematizes our sensible experience according to logical "categories"—unity, plurality, totality, substance, causation, and so on. These categories are the *a priori* concepts of the understanding, not derived or inferred from experience but the very concepts without which experience itself would be unintelligible to us. Just as the sensibility is limited by the forms of space and time, the understanding cannot think outside of the categories, even though it is the faculty of knowledge par excellence. The faculty of Reason stands in need of a critique because it is inherently prone to claim knowledge concerning God, Freedom, and Immortality (the "Ideas of Reason") that cannot be established or determined but inevitably leads to contradictions or antinomies. The role of Reason, therefore, is not to produce knowledge but to regulate and guide the Understanding toward its fullest and most unified employment.

Judgment for Kant is the power of cognitive decision, or "thinking the particular as contained under the universal," but his problem is to ascertain first if there is an *a priori* concept or principle for judgment itself, and secondly to determine what it is. Kant separates judgments into two kinds, the "determinant," applying to instances in which the universal is given and the task is to determine if the particular fits under it; and the "reflective," applying to cases where the particular is given for which a universal (if there is one) is to be found. This simple distinction, however, has the potential to severely disturb the edifice of Kant's Critical Philosophy, since it shifts the focus away from the determinant judgment (where Understanding legislates) to the reflective judgment, where discovery, invention, or creation take precedence—subjects that are accorded only the most rudimentary treatment in the *Critique of Pure Reason*. The dominant topics of the third critique, the aesthetic and the teleological judgment, are both reflective, not determinant.

From this point of view, the problems of the beautiful and the sublime, the natural focus of literary and aesthetic commentary, divide quite sharply from Kant's problem, which is to find in our own constitution the ground for an *a priori* principle that is legislative for the faculty of judgment itself. His solution lies in the concept of purposiveness, whether it pertains to human productions (the aesthetic) or the productions of nature (the teleological).

When Kant treats aesthetic purposiveness somewhat paradoxically as purpose without purpose, what is at stake is the idea that any concept of an object which contains, as Kant puts it, "the ground of the actuality of the object," identifies a purpose. That is, we conceive of objects by considering how they are created or made, positing an intelligence or understanding compatible with our own, and only then do we think that we understand the object in question. He therefore defines the "*purposiveness* of [the] form" as "the agreement of a thing with that constitution of things which is only possible according to purposes."[1] Here, Kant returns without comment to the classical problem in Aristotle of *telos* or "final cause," but locates it as an *a priori* principle of judgment, not a property or observable characteristic of things, be they natural or artificial. We understand just what we can bring into agreement with the idea of a world of intentional creation.

When Kant turns to aesthetic judgments, he identifies two kinds, those of the beautiful and those of the sublime. Neither type can be called objective or logical. Both are subjective, but Kant declares that a true aesthetic judgment has subjective universality; that is, one makes it only if one is willing honestly to think that others should also make it. Feelings of sheer pleasure and pain are distinguished from aesthetic judgments, for the former are subjective and individual (some people may like beets, some may not), while the latter, though subjective, are universal. Such judgments Kant characterizes as "disinterested" because they are not referable to one's own feelings of pleasure, pain, prejudice, or personal interest.

Kant argues that in order to find an object beautiful we need therefore not have a concept of how by some idealized standard it is to be used or ought to be used. To make

---

[1] *Critique of Judgment,* J. H. Bernard, trans., p. 17.

that kind of judgment is to refer the object to how well it measures up to some preconceived and therefore external ideal or purpose and thus to make a judgment other than aesthetic. Instead, as he indicates in section 9 of the "Analytic of the Beautiful," our attention should attend to how something is *made,* since the pleasure of the aesthetic judgment follows and does not precede the judgment itself. Therefore each aesthetic judgment is by necessity singular. One can declare a certain rose to be beautiful, but to say that all roses are beautiful is to make a determinative judgment or logical generalization based on what has been a series of singular aesthetic ones.

Clearly the notion of accuracy implied by the Platonic idea of imitation is, for Kant, irrelevant to aesthetic judgment; and the notion of the external idea of beauty that Plato proposes is self-contradictory. All neoclassical external canons of beauty are likewise not aesthetic judgments. Thus Kant's aesthetic theory is perhaps a more radical departure from the tradition of the theory of art and literature than even his epistemology is for philosophy.

In Kant's theorizing we can observe a shift of the problem of the subjective from the situation worried about by the followers of Locke (for example, Hume, above, page 322) toward concern with the internality of the work of art itself. Subjectivity is not abandoned, but the concept of subjective universality and disinterest turns consideration of aesthetic experience toward concern with the work's internal purpose rather than any external purposes it may be put to fulfilling. Even though Kant ultimately refers all experience of art back to the viewer, listener, or reader, he insists that we must talk about the work's beauty *as if* that beauty is determinable independent of us and *as if* the work is an object apart from us with its own being. This being is exactly what Plato's Ion (above, page 10) failed to assert against Socrates's relentless questioning.

The sublime differs from the beautiful. There are two forms of it, the mathematical and the dynamical. The former is concerned with size, the latter with power. The beautiful implies form and boundary, while the sublime implies either infinite size or overwhelming power, that which is "absolutely great." To our imagination, the sublime object is formless and beyond cognition. We take pleasure in the sublime experience even as we recognize our fear, because we see in the experience that we possess a faculty of mind that surpasses all sense. Thus what we really experience as sublime in such situations is our own sublimity or boundlessness of soul. The sublime does not lead to the disinterested contemplative feeling of the beautiful. Rather, it produces depth of feeling that yet also is free of sheer pain and pleasure, though it must overcome the former before experiencing the latter. Thus the sublime object can finally also be regarded as possessing internal purposiveness and our response to it ultimate disinterest.

Critique of Judgment is without question the most influential work of aesthetic theory ever written. It has generated many followers; most of those with other views on the subject have found it necessary to argue with Kant. In modern criticism, Kantian tendencies may be observed in the New Criticism in America, represented below by Ransom (page 953) and Brooks (page 1035).

Among the most useful translations of Kant's works are *Critique of Judgment,* translated by J. H. Bernard, second edition, revised (1951); *Prolegomena to Any Future Metaphysics,* translated by Paul Carus (1902); *Critique of Pure Reason,* translated by Norman Kemp Smith, revised edition (1933); *Critique of Practical Reason,* translated by Lewis W.

Beck (1949); and *Observations on the Feelings of the Beautiful and Sublime,* translated by J. T. Goldthwaite (1960). A new uniform edition under the general editorship of Paul Guyer, however, is in progress from Cambridge University Press. Among the great number of studies of Kant, some of the most useful are Norman Kemp Smith, *A Commentary on Kant's* Critique of Pure Reason, second edition, revised (1929); René Wellek, *Immanuel Kant in England* (1931); H. N. Lee, "Kant's Theory of Aesthetics," P. F. Strawson, *The Bounds of Sense: An Essay on Kant's Critique of Pure Reason* (1966); Jonathan Bennett, *Kant's Analytic* (1966), and *Kant's Dialectic* (1974); Ted Cohen and Paul Guyer, eds., *Essays in Kant's Aesthetics* (1982); Gary Banham, *Kant and the Ends of Aesthetics* (2000); Rodolphe Gauché, *The Idea of Form: Rethinking Kant's Aesthetics* (2003).

from
Critique of Judgment

from
Introduction

IV. Of Judgment as a Faculty Legislating a Priori

Judgment in general is the faculty of thinking the particular as contained under the universal. If the universal (the rule, the principle, the law) be given, the judgment which subsumes the particular under it (even if, as transcendental judgment, it furnishes, *a priori,* the conditions in conformity with which subsumption under that universal is alone possible) is *determinant.* But if only the particular be given for which the universal has to be found, the judgment is merely *reflective.*

The determinant judgment only subsumes under universal transcendental laws given by the understanding; the law is marked out for it, *a priori,* and it has therefore no need to seek a law for itself in order to be able to subordinate the particular in nature to the universal. But the forms of nature are so manifold, and there are so many modifications of the universal transcendental natural concepts left undetermined by the laws given, *a priori,* by the pure understanding—because these only concern the possibility of a nature in general (as an object of sense)—that there must be laws for these [forms] also. These, as empirical, may be contingent from the point of view of *our* understanding; and yet, if they are to be called laws (as the concept of a nature requires), they must be regarded as necessary in virtue of a principle of the unity of the manifold, though it be unknown to us. The reflective judgment, which is obliged to ascend from the particular in nature to the universal, requires on that account a principle that it cannot borrow from experience, because its function is to establish the unity of all empirical principles under higher ones, and hence to establish the possibility of their systematic subordination. Such a transcendental principle, then, the reflective judgment can only give as a law from and to itself. It cannot derive it from outside (because then it would be the determinant judgment); nor can it prescribe it to nature, because reflection upon the laws of nature adjusts itself by nature, and not nature by the conditions according to which we attempt to arrive at a concept of it which is quite contingent in respect of nature.

This principle can be no other than the following: As universal laws of nature have their ground in our understanding, which prescribes them to nature (although only according to the universal concept of it as nature), so particular empirical laws, in respect of what is in them left undetermined by these universal laws, must be considered in accordance with such a unity as they would have if an understanding (although not our understanding) had furnished them to our cognitive faculties, so as to make possible a system of experience according to particular laws of nature. Not as if, in this way, such an understanding must be assumed as actual (for it is only our reflective judgment to which this idea serves as a principle—for reflecting, not for determining); but this faculty thus gives a law only to itself, and not to nature.

Now the concept of an object, so far as it contains the ground of the actuality of this object, is the *purpose;* and the agreement of a thing with that constitution of things which is only possible according to purposes is called the *purposiveness* of its form. Thus the principle of judgment, in respect of the form of things of nature under empirical laws generally, is the *purposiveness of nature* in its variety. That is, nature is represented by means of this concept as if an understanding contained the ground of the unity of the variety of its empirical laws.

Kant's *Kritik der Urteilskraft* was first published in 1790. The text is from the second edition, revised, of the translation by J. H. Bernard (New York: Hafner Publishing Co., Inc., 1951).

The purposiveness of nature is therefore a particular concept, *a priori,* which has its origin solely in the reflective judgment. For we cannot ascribe to natural products anything like a reference of nature in them to purposes; we can only use this concept to reflect upon such products in respect of the connection of phenomena which is given in them according to empirical laws. This concept is also quite different from practical purposiveness (in human art or in morals), though it is certainly thought according to the analogy of these last.

* * *

First Book

Analytic of the Beautiful

First Moment

Of the Judgment of Taste,[1] According to Quality

I. The Judgment of Taste Is Aesthetical

In order to distinguish whether anything is beautiful or not, we refer the representation, not by the understanding to the object for cognition, but by the imagination (perhaps in conjunction with the understanding) to the subject and its feeling of pleasure or pain. The judgment of taste[2] is therefore not a judgment of cognition, and is consequently not logical but aesthetical, by which we understand that whose determining ground can be *no other than subjective.* Every reference of representations, even that of sensations, may be objective (and then it signifies the real [element] of an empirical representation), save only the reference to the feeling of pleasure and pain, by which nothing in the object is signified, but through which there is a feeling in the subject as it is affected by the representation.

To apprehend a regular, purposive building by means of one's cognitive faculty (whether in a clear or a confused

way of representation) is something quite different from being conscious of this representation as connected with the sensation of satisfaction. Here the representation is altogether referred to the subject and to its feeling of life, under the name of the feeling of pleasure or pain. This establishes a quite separate faculty of distinction and of judgment, adding nothing to cognition, but only comparing the given representation in the subject with the whole faculty of representations, of which the mind is conscious in the feeling of its state. Given representations in a judgment can be empirical (consequently, aesthetical); but the judgment which is formed by means of them is logical, provided they are referred in the judgment to the object. Conversely, if the given representations are rational, but are referred in a judgment simply to the subject (to its feeling), the judgment is so far always aesthetical.

II. The Satisfaction Which Determines the Judgment of Taste Is Disinterested

The satisfaction which we combine with the representation of the existence of an object is called "interest." Such satisfaction always has reference to the faculty of desire, either as its determining ground or as necessarily connected with its determining ground. Now when the question is if a thing is beautiful, we do not want to know whether anything depends or can depend on the existence of the thing, either for myself or for anyone else, but how we judge it by mere observation (intuition or reflection). If anyone asks me if I find that palace beautiful which I see before me, I may answer: I do not like things of that kind which are made merely to be stared at. Or I can answer like that Iroquois sachem, who was pleased in Paris by nothing more than by the cook shops. Or again, after the manner of Rousseau,[3] I may rebuke the vanity of the great who waste the sweat of the people on such superfluous things. In fine, I could easily convince myself that if I found myself on an uninhabited island without the hope of ever again coming among men, and could conjure up just such a splendid building by my mere wish, I should not even give myself the trouble if I had a sufficiently comfortable hut. This may all be admitted and approved, but we are not now talking of this. We wish only to know if this mere representation of the object is accompanied in me with satisfaction, however indifferent I may be as regards the existence of the object of this representation. We easily see that, in saying it is *beautiful* and in showing that I have taste, I am concerned, not with that in which I

---

[1] [Kant] The definition of "taste" which is laid down here is that it is the faculty of judging of the beautiful. But the analysis of the judgments of taste must show what is required in order to call an object beautiful. The moments to which this judgment has regard in its reflection I have sought in accordance with the guidance of the logical functions of judgment (for in a judgment of taste a reference to the understanding is always involved). I have considered the moment of quality first because the aesthetical judgment upon the beautiful first pays attention to it.

[2] A significant predecessor on the question of taste is Hume (above, page 322).

[3] Jean Jacques Rousseau (1712–1778), French philosopher.

depend on the existence of the object, but with that which I make out of this representation in myself. Everyone must admit that a judgment about beauty, in which the least interest mingles, is very partial and is not a pure judgment of taste. We must not be in the least prejudiced in favor of the existence of the things, but be quite indifferent in this respect, in order to play the judge in things of taste.

We cannot, however, better elucidate this proposition, which is of capital importance, than by contrasting the pure disinterested[4] satisfaction in judgments of taste with that which is bound up with an interest, especially if we can at the same time be certain that there are no other kinds of interest than those which are to be now specified.

IV. The Satisfaction in the Good Is Bound Up with Interest

Whatever by means of reason pleases through the mere concept is *good.* That which pleases only as a means we call *good for something* (the useful), but that which pleases for itself is *good in itself.* In both there is always involved the concept of a purpose, and consequently the relation of reason to the (at least possible) volition, and thus a satisfaction in the *presence* of an object or an action, i.e. some kind of interest.

In order to find anything good, I must always know what sort of a thing the object ought to be, i.e. I must have a concept of it. But there is no need of this to find a thing beautiful. Flowers, free delineations, outlines intertwined with one another without design and called conventional foliage, have no meaning, depend on no definite concept, and yet they please. The satisfaction in the beautiful must depend on the reflection upon an object, leading to any concept (however indefinite), and it is thus distinguished from the pleasant, which rests entirely upon sensation.

* * *

V. Comparison of the Three Specifically Different Kinds of Satisfaction

The pleasant and the good have both a reference to the faculty of desire, and they bring with them, the former a satisfaction pathologically conditioned (by impulses, stimuli), the latter a pure practical satisfaction which is determined not merely by the representation of the object but also by the represented connection of the subject with the existence of the object. It is not merely the object that pleases, but also its existence. On the other hand, the judgment of taste is merely *contemplative;* i.e., it is a judgment which, indifferent as regards the existence of an object, compares its character with the feeling of pleasure and pain. But this contemplation itself is not directed to concepts; for the judgment of taste is not a cognitive judgment (either theoretical or practical), and thus is not *based* on concepts, nor has its concepts as its *purpose.*

The pleasant, the beautiful, and the good designate then three different relations of representations to the feeling of pleasure and pain, in reference to which we distinguish from one another objects or methods of representing them. And the expressions corresponding to each, by which we mark our complacency in them, are not the same. That which *gratifies* a man is called *pleasant:* that which merely *pleases* him is *beautiful;* that which is *esteemed* or *approved* by him, i.e. that to which he accords an objective worth, is *good.* Pleasantness concerns irrational animals also, but beauty only concerns men, i.e. animal, but still rational, beings—not merely qua rational (e.g. spirits), but qua animal also—and the good concerns every rational being in general. This is a proposition which can only be completely established and explained in the sequel. We may say that, of all these three kinds of satisfaction, that of taste in the beautiful is alone a disinterested and *free* satisfaction; for no interest, either of sense or of reason, here forces our assent. Hence we may say of satisfaction that it is related in the three aforesaid cases to *inclination,* to *favor,* or to *respect.* Now *favor* is the only free satisfaction. An object of inclination and one that is proposed to our desire by a law of reason leave us no freedom in forming for ourselves anywhere an object of pleasure. All interest presupposes or generates a want, and, as the determining ground of assent, it leaves the judgment about the object no longer free.

As regards the interest of inclination in the case of the pleasant, everyone says that hunger is the best sauce, and everything that is eatable is relished by people with a healthy appetite; and thus a satisfaction of this sort shows no choice directed by taste. It is only when the want is appeased that we can distinguish which of many men has or has not taste. In the same way there may be manners (conduct) without virtue, politeness without good will, decorum without modesty, etc. For where the moral law speaks there is no longer, objectively, a free choice as regards what is to be done; and to display taste in its fulfillment (or in judging

---

[4] [Kant] A judgment upon an object of satisfaction may be quite *disinterested,* but yet very *interesting,* that is, not based upon an interest, but bringing an interest with it; of this kind are all pure moral judgments. Judgments of taste, however, do not in themselves establish any interest. Only in society is it *interesting* to have taste; the reason of this will be shown in the sequel. (Another way of considering this in part is to say that to be disinterested is not to be uninterested. Indeed disinterest implies a certain interest.)

of another's fulfillment of it) is something quite different from manifesting the moral attitude of thought. For this involves a command and generates a want, while moral taste only plays with the objects of satisfaction, without attaching itself to one of them.

Explanation of the Beautiful Resulting from the First Moment

Taste is the faculty of judging of an object or a method of representing it by an *entirely disinterested* satisfaction or dissatisfaction. The object of such satisfaction is called *beautiful.*[5]

Second Moment

Of the Judgment of Taste, According to Quantity

VI. The Beautiful Is That Which Apart from Concepts Is Represented as the Object of a Universal Satisfaction

This explanation of the beautiful can be derived from the preceding explanation of it as the object of an entirely disinterested satisfaction. For the fact of which everyone is conscious, that the satisfaction is for him quite disinterested, implies in his judgment a ground of satisfaction for all men. For since it does not rest on any inclination of the subject (nor upon any other premeditated interest), but since the person who judges feels himself quite *free* as regards the satisfaction which he attaches to the object, he cannot find the ground of this satisfaction in any private conditions connected with his own subject, and hence it must be regarded as grounded on what he can presuppose in every other person. Consequently he must believe that he has reason for attributing a similar satisfaction to everyone. He will therefore speak of the beautiful as if beauty were a characteristic of the object and the judgment logical (constituting a cognition of the object by means of concepts of it), although it is only aesthetical and involves merely a reference of the representation of the object to the subject. For it has this similarity

to a logical judgment that we can presuppose its validity for all men. But this universality cannot arise from concepts; for from concepts there is no transition to the feeling of pleasure or pain (except in pure practical laws, which bring an interest with them such as is not bound up with the pure judgment of taste). Consequently the judgment of taste, accompanied with the consciousness of separation from all interest, must claim validity for every man, without this universality depending on objects. That is, there must be bound up with it a title to subjective universality.

VII. Comparison of the Beautiful with the Pleasant and the Good by Means of the Above Characteristic

As regards the pleasant, everyone is content that his judgment, which he bases upon private feeling and by which he says of an object that it pleases him, should be limited merely to his own person. Thus he is quite contented that if he says, "Canary wine is pleasant," another man may correct his expression and remind him that he ought to say, "It is pleasant *to me.*" And this is the case not only as regards the taste of the tongue, the palate, and the throat, but for whatever is pleasant to anyone's eyes and ears. To one, violet color is soft and lovely; to another, it is washed-out and dead. One man likes the tone of wind instruments, another that of strings. To strive here with the design of reproving as incorrect another man's judgment which is different from our own, as if the judgments were logically opposed, would be folly. As regards the pleasant, therefore, the fundamental proposition is valid: *everyone has his own taste* (the taste of sense).

The case is quite different with the beautiful. It would (on the contrary) be laughable if a man who imagined anything to his own taste thought to justify himself by saying: "This object (the house we see, the coat that person wears, the concert we hear, the poem submitted to our judgment) is beautiful *for me.*" For he must not call it *beautiful* if it merely pleases him. Many things may have for him charm and pleasantness—no one troubles himself at that—but if he gives out anything as beautiful, he supposes in others the same satisfaction; he judges not merely for himself, but for everyone, and speaks of beauty as if it were a property of things. Hence he says "the *thing* is beautiful"; and he does not count on the agreement of others with this his judgment of satisfaction, because he has found this agreement several times before, but he *demands* it of them. He blames them if they judge otherwise and he denies them taste, which he nevertheless requires from them. Here, then, we cannot say that each man has his own particular taste. For this would be as much as to say that there is no taste whatever, i.e. no aesthetical judgment which can make a rightful claim upon everyone's assent.

At the same time we find as regards the pleasant that there is an agreement among men in their judgments upon it in regard to which we deny taste to some and attribute it to others, by this not meaning one of our organic senses, but a faculty of judging in respect of the pleasant generally. Thus we say of a man who knows how to entertain his guests with pleasures (of enjoyment for all the senses), so that they are all pleased, "he has taste." But here the universality is only taken comparatively; and there emerge rules which are only *general* (like all empirical ones), and not *universal,* which latter the judgment of taste upon the beautiful undertakes or lays claim to. It is a judgment in reference to sociability, so far as this rests on empirical rules. In respect of the good it is true that judgments make rightful claim to validity for everyone; but the good is represented only *by means of a concept* as the object of a universal satisfaction, which is the case neither with the pleasant nor with the beautiful.

*   *   *

VIII. The Universality of the Satisfaction Is Represented in a Judgment of Taste Only as Subjective

This particular determination of the universality of an aesthetical judgment, which is to be met with in a judgment of taste, is noteworthy, not indeed for the logician, but for the transcendental philosopher. It requires no small trouble to discover its origin, but we thus detect a property of our cognitive faculty which without this analysis would remain unknown.

First, we must be fully convinced of the fact that in a judgment of taste (about the beautiful) the satisfaction in the object is imputed to *everyone,* without being based on a concept (for then it would be the good). Further, this claim to universal validity so essentially belongs to a judgment by which we describe anything as *beautiful* that, if this were not thought in it, it would never come into our thoughts to use the expression at all, but everything which pleases without a concept would be counted as pleasant. In respect of the latter, everyone has his own opinion; and no one assumes in another agreement with his judgment of taste, which is always the case in a judgment of taste about beauty. I may call the first the taste of sense, the second the taste of reflection, so far as the first lays down mere private judgments and the second judgments supposed to be generally valid (public), but in both cases aesthetical (not practical) judgments about an object merely in respect of the relation of its representation to the feeling of pleasure and pain. Now here is something strange. As regards the taste of sense, not only does experience show that its judgment (of pleasure or pain connected with anything) is not valid universally, but everyone is content not to impute agreement with it to others (although actually there is often found a very extended concurrence in these judgments). On the other hand, the taste of reflection has its claim to the universal validity of its judgments (about the beautiful) rejected often enough, as experience teaches, although it may find it possible (as it actually does) to represent judgments which can demand this universal agreement. In fact it imputes this to everyone for each of its judgments of taste, without the persons that judge disputing as to the possibility of such a claim, although in particular cases they cannot agree as to the correct application of this faculty.

Here we must, in the first place, remark that a universality which does not rest on concepts of objects (not even on empirical ones) is not logical but aesthetical; i.e. it involves no objective quantity of the judgment, but only that which is subjective. For this I use the expression *general validity,* which signifies the validity of the reference of a representation, not to the cognitive faculty, but to the feeling of pleasure and pain for every subject. (We can avail ourselves also of the same expression for the logical quantity of the judgment, if only we prefix "objective" to "universal validity," to distinguish it from that which is merely subjective and aesthetical.)

A judgment with *objective universal validity* is also always valid subjectively; i.e. if the judgment holds for everything contained under a given concept, it holds also for everyone who represents an object by means of this concept. But from a *subjective universal validity,* i.e. aesthetical and resting on no concept, we cannot infer that which is logical because that kind of judgment does not extend to the object. But, therefore, the aesthetical universality which is ascribed to a judgment must be of a particular kind, because it does not unite the predicate of beauty with the concept of the object, considered in its whole logical sphere, and yet extends it to the whole sphere of judging persons.

In respect of logical quantity, all judgments of taste are *singular* judgments. For because I must refer the object immediately to my feeling of pleasure and pain, and that not by means of concepts, they cannot have the quantity of objective generally valid judgments. Nevertheless, if the singular representation of the object of the judgment of taste, in accordance with the conditions determining the latter, were transformed by comparison into a concept, a logically universal judgment could result therefrom. E.g., I describe by a judgment of taste the rose that I see as beautiful. But the judgment which results from the comparison of several singular judgments, "Roses in general are beautiful," is no longer described simply as aesthetical, but as a logical judgment based on an aesthetical one. Again the judgment, "The rose is pleasant" (to use) is, although aesthetical and singular, not a judgment of taste but of sense. It is distinguished from the former by the fact that the judgment of taste carries with it an *aesthetic quantity* of universality, i.e. of validity for everyone, which cannot be found in a judgment about the pleasant. It is only judgments about the good which, although they also determine satisfaction in an object, have logical and not merely aesthetical universality, for they are valid of the object as cognitive of it, and thus are valid for everyone.

If we judge objects merely according to concepts, then all representation of beauty is lost. Thus there can be no rule according to which anyone is to be forced to recognize anything as beautiful. We cannot press [upon others] by the aid of any reasons or fundamental propositions our judgment that a coat, a house, or a flower is beautiful. People wish to submit the object to their own eyes, as if the satisfaction in it depended on sensation; and yet, if we then call the object beautiful, we believe that we speak with a universal voice, and we claim the assent of everyone, although on the contrary all private sensation can only decide for the observer himself and his satisfaction.

We may see now that in the judgment of taste nothing is postulated but such a *universal voice,* in respect of the satisfaction without the intervention of concepts, and thus the *possibility* of an aesthetical judgment that can, at the same time, be regarded as valid for everyone. The judgment of taste itself does not *postulate* the agreement of everyone (for that can only be done by a logically universal judgment because it can adduce reasons); it only *imputes* this agreement to everyone, as a case of the rule in respect of which it expects, not confirmation by concepts, but assent from others. The universal voice is, therefore, only an idea (we do not yet inquire upon what it rests). It may be uncertain whether or not the man who believes that he is laying down a judgment of taste is, as a matter of fact, judging in conformity with that idea; but that he refers his judgment thereto, and consequently that it is intended to be a judgment of taste, he announces by the expression "beauty." He can be quite certain of this for himself by the mere consciousness of the separating off everything belonging to the pleasant and the good from the satisfaction which is left; and this is all for which he promises himself the agreement of everyone—a claim which would be justifiable under these conditions, provided only he did not often make mistakes, and thus lay down an erroneous judgment of taste.

IX. Investigation of the Question Whether in the Judgment of Taste the Feeling of Pleasure Precedes or Follows the Judging of the Object

The solution of this question is the key to the critique of taste, and so is worthy of all attention.

If the pleasure in the given object precedes, and it is only its universal communicability that is to be acknowledged in the judgment of taste about the representation of the object, there would be a contradiction. For such pleasure would be nothing different from the mere pleasantness in the sensation, and so in accordance with its nature could have only private validity, because it is immediately dependent on the representation through which the object *is given*.

Hence it is the universal capability of communication of the mental state in the given representation which, as the subjective condition of the judgment of taste, must be fundamental and must have the pleasure in the object as its consequent. But nothing can be universally communicated except cognition and representation, so far as it belongs to cognition. For it is only thus that this latter can be objective, and only through this has it a universal point of reference, with which the representative power of everyone is compelled to harmonize. If the determining ground of our judgment as to this universal communicability of the representation is to be merely subjective, i.e. is conceived independently of any concept of the object, it can be nothing else than the state of mind, which is to be met with in the relation of our representative powers to each other, so far as they refer a given representation to *cognition in general*.

The cognitive powers, which are involved by this representation, are here in free play, because no definite concept limits them to a definite rule of cognition. Hence the state of mind in this representation must be a feeling of the free play of the representative powers in a given representation with reference to a cognition in general. Now a representation by which an object is given that is to become a cognition in general requires *imagination* for the gathering together the manifold of intuition, and *understanding* for the unity of the concept uniting the representations. This state of *free play* of the cognitive faculties in a representation by which an object is given must be universally communicable, because cognition, as the determination of the object with which given representations (in whatever subject) are to agree, is the only kind of representation which is valid for everyone.

The subjective universal communicability of the mode of representation in a judgment of taste, since it is to be possible without presupposing a definite concept, can refer to nothing else than the state of mind in the free play of the imagination and the understanding (so far as they agree with each other, as is requisite for *cognition in general*). We are conscious that this subjective relation, suitable for cognition in general, must be valid for everyone, and thus must be universally communicable, just as if it were a definite cognition, resting always on that relation as its subjective condition.

This merely subjective (aesthetical) judging of the object, or of the representation by which it is given, precedes the pleasure in the same and is the ground of this pleasure in the harmony of the cognitive faculties; but on that universality of the subjective conditions for judging of objects is alone based the universal subjective validity of the satisfaction bound up by us with the representation of the object that we call beautiful.

That the power of communicating one's state of mind, even though only in respect of the cognitive faculties, carries a pleasure with it, this we can easily show from the natural propension of man toward sociability (empirical and psychological). But this is not enough for our design. The pleasure that we feel is, in a judgment of taste, necessarily imputed by us to everyone else, as if, when we call a thing beautiful, it is to be regarded as a characteristic of the object which is determined in it according to concepts, though beauty, without a reference to the feeling of the subject, is nothing by itself. But we must reserve the examination of this question until we have answered that other—if and how aesthetical judgments are possible *a priori*.

We now occupy ourselves with the easier question, in what way we are conscious of a mutual subjective harmony of the cognitive powers with one another in the judgment of taste—is it aesthetically by mere internal sense and sensation, or is it intellectually by the consciousness of our designed activity, by which we bring them into play?

If the given representation which occasions the judgment of taste were a concept uniting understanding and imagination in the judging of the object, into a cognition of the object, the consciousness of this relation would be intellectual (as in the objective schematism of the judgment of which the *Critique*[6] treats). But then the judgment would not be laid down in reference to pleasure and pain, and consequently would not be a judgment of taste. But the judgment of taste, independently of concepts, determines the object in respect of satisfaction and of the predicate of beauty. Therefore that subjective unity of relation can only make itself known by means of sensation. The excitement of both faculties (imagination and understanding) to indeterminate but yet, through the stimulus of the given sensation, harmonious activity, viz. that which belongs to cognition in general, is the sensation whose universal communicability is postulated by the judgment of taste. An objective relation can only be thought, but yet, so far as it is subjective according to its conditions, can be felt in its effect on the mind; and, of a relation based on no concept (like the relation

of the representative powers to a cognitive faculty in general), no other consciousness is possible than that through the sensation of the effect, which consists in the more lively play of both mental powers (the imagination and the understanding) when animated by mutual agreement. A representation which, as individual and apart from comparison with others, yet has an agreement with the conditions of universality which it is the business of the understanding to supply, brings the cognitive faculties into that proportionate accord which we require for all cognition, and so regard as holding for everyone who is determined to judge by means of understanding and sense in combination (i.e. for every man).

Explanation of the Beautiful Resulting from the Second Moment

The *beautiful* is that which pleases universally without requiring a concept.

Third Moment

Of Judgments of Taste, According to the Relation of the Purposes Which Are Brought Into Consideration in Them

* * *

XI. The Judgment of Taste Has Nothing at Its Basis but the Form of the Purposiveness of an Object (or of Its Mode of Representation)

Every purpose, if it be regarded as a ground of satisfaction, always carries with it an interest—as the determining ground of the judgment—about the object of pleasure. Therefore no subjective purpose can lie at the basis of the judgment of taste. But also the judgment of taste can be determined by no representation of an objective purpose, i.e. of the possibility of the object itself in accordance with principles of purposive combination, and consequently by no concept of the good, because it is an aesthetical and not a cognitive judgment. It therefore has to do with no *concept* of the character and internal or external possibility of the object by means of this or that cause, but merely with the relation of the representative powers to one another, so far as they are determined by a representation.

Now this relation in the determination of an object as beautiful is bound up with the feeling of pleasure, which is

---

[6] [Bernard] *Critique of Rure Reason,* "Analytic," Book II, Chapter 1.

declared by the judgment of taste to be valid for everyone; hence a pleasantness merely accompanying the representation can as little contain the determining ground of the judgment as the representation of the perfection of the object and the concept of the good can. Therefore it can be nothing else than the subjective purposiveness in the representation of an object without any purpose (either objective or subjective), and thus it is the mere form of purposiveness in the representation by which an object is *given* to us, so far as we are conscious of it, which constitutes the satisfaction that we without a concept judge to be universally communicable; and, consequently, this is the determining ground of the judgment of taste.

* * *

XIII. The Pure Judgment of Taste Is Independent of Charm and Emotion

Every interest spoils the judgment of taste and takes from its impartiality, especially if the purposiveness is not, as with the interest of reason, placed before the feeling of pleasure but grounded on it. This last always happens in an aesthetical judgment upon anything, so far as it gratifies or grieves us. Hence judgments so affected can lay no claim at all to a universally valid satisfaction, or at least so much the less claim, in proportion as there are sensations of this sort among the determining grounds of taste. That taste is always barbaric which needs a mixture of *charms* and *emotions* in order that there may be satisfaction, and still more so if it make these the measure of its assent.

Nevertheless charms are often not only taken account of in the case of beauty (which properly speaking ought merely to be concerned with form) as contributory to the aesthetical universal satisfaction, but they are passed off as in themselves beauties; and thus the matter of satisfaction is substituted for the form. This misconception, however, which like so many others, has something true at its basis, may be removed by a careful determination of these concepts.

A judgment of taste on which charm and emotion have no influence (although they may be bound up with the satisfaction in the beautiful)—which therefore has as its determining ground merely the purposiveness of the form—is a *pure judgment of taste.*

XIV. Elucidation by Means of Examples

Aesthetical judgments can be divided just like theoretical (logical) judgments into empirical and pure. The first assert pleasantness or unpleasantness; the second assert the beauty of an object or of the manner of representing it. The former are judgments of sense (material aesthetical judgments); the latter as formal are alone strictly judgments of taste.

A judgment of taste is therefore pure only so far as no merely empirical satisfaction is mingled with its determining ground. But this always happens if charm or emotion have any share in the judgment by which anything is to be described as beautiful.

Now here many objections present themselves which, fallaciously, put forward charm not merely as a necessary ingredient of beauty, but as alone sufficient to justify a thing's being called beautiful. A mere color, e.g. the green of a grass plot, a mere tone (as distinguished from sound and noise), like that of a violin, are by most people described as beautiful in themselves, although both seem to have at their basis merely the matter of representations, viz. simply sensation, and therefore only deserve to be called pleasant. But we must at the same time remark that the sensations of colors and of tone have a right to be regarded as beautiful only in so far as they are *pure.* This is a determination which concerns their form and is the only element of these representations which admits with certainty of universal communicability; for we cannot assume that the quality of sensations is the same in all subjects, and we can hardly say that the pleasantness of one color or the tone of one musical instrument is judged preferable to that of another in the same way by everyone.

If we assume with Euler[7] that colors are isochronous vibrations *(pulsus)* of the ether, as sounds are of the air in a state of disturbance, and—what is the most important—that the mind not only perceives by sense the effect of these in exciting the organ, but also perceives by reflection the regular play of impressions (and thus the form of the combination of different representations)—which I very much doubt—then colors and tone cannot be reckoned as mere sensations, but as the formal determination of the unity of a manifold of sensations, and thus as beauties.

But "pure" in a simple mode of sensation means that its uniformity is troubled and interrupted by no foreign sensation, and it belongs merely to the form; because here we can abstract from the quality of that mode of sensation (abstract from the colors and tone, if any, which it represents). Hence all simple colors, so far as they are pure, are regarded as beautiful; composite colors have not this advantage because, as they are not simple, we have no standard for judging whether they should be called pure or not.

---

[7]Leonhard Euler (1707–1783), Swiss mathematician and physicist.

But as regards the beauty attributed to the object on account of its form, to suppose it to be capable of augmentation through the charm of the object is a common error and one very prejudicial to genuine, uncorrupted, well-founded taste. We can doubtless add these charms to beauty, in order to interest the mind by the representation of the object, apart from the bare satisfaction received, and thus they may serve as a recommendation of taste and its cultivation, especially when it is yet crude and unexercised. But they actually do injury to the judgment of taste if they draw attention to themselves as the grounds for judging of beauty. So far are they from adding to beauty that they must only be admitted by indulgence as aliens, and provided always that they do not disturb the beautiful form in cases when taste is yet weak and unexercised.

In painting, sculpture, and in all the formative arts—in architecture and horticulture, so far as they are beautiful arts—the *delineation* is the essential thing; and here it is not what gratifies in sensation but what pleases by means of its form that is fundamental for taste. The colors which light up the sketch belong to the charm; they may indeed enliven the object for sensation, but they cannot make it worthy of contemplation and beautiful. In most cases they are rather limited by the requirements of the beautiful form, and even where charm is permissible it is ennobled solely by this.

Every form of the objects of sense (both of external sense and also mediately of internal) is either *figure* or *play*. In the latter case it is either play of figures (in space, viz. pantomime and dancing) or the mere play of sensations (in time). The *charm* of colors or of the pleasant tones of an instrument may be added, but the *delineation* in the first case and the composition in the second constitute the proper object of the pure judgment of taste. To say that the purity of colors and of tones, or their variety and contrast, seem to add to beauty does not mean that they supply a homogeneous addition to our satisfaction in the form because they are pleasant in themselves; but they do so because they make the form more exactly, definitely, and completely, intuitible, and besides, by their charm excite the representation, while they awaken and fix our attention on the object itself.

Even what we call "ornaments" *[parerga]*, i.e. those things which do not belong to the complete representation of the object internally as elements, but only externally as complements, and which augment the satisfaction of taste, do so only by their forms; as, for example, the frames of pictures or the draperies of statues or the colonnades of palaces. But if the ornament does not itself consist in beautiful form, and if it is used as a golden frame is used, merely to recommend the painting by its *charm,* it is then called *finery* and injures genuine beauty.

Emotion, that is, a sensation in which pleasantness is produced by means of a momentary checking and a consequent more powerful outflow of the vital force, does not belong at all to beauty. But sublimity [with which the feeling of emotion is bound up] requires a different standard of judgment from that which is at the foundation of taste; and thus a pure judgment of taste has for its determining ground neither charm nor emotion—in a word, no sensation as the material of aesthetical judgment.

XV. The Judgment of Taste Is Quite Independent of the Concept of Perfection

Objective purposiveness can only be cognized by means of the reference of the manifold to a definite purpose, and therefore only through a concept. From this alone it is plain that the beautiful, the judging of which has at its basis a merely formal purposiveness, i.e. a purposiveness without purpose, is quite independent of the concept of the good, because the latter presupposes an objective purposiveness, i.e. the reference of the object to a definite purpose.

Objective purposiveness is either external, i.e. the *utility,* or internal, i.e. the *perfection* of the object. That the satisfaction in an object, on account of which we call it beautiful, cannot rest on the representation of its utility is sufficiently obvious from the two preceding sections; because in that case it would not be an immediate satisfaction in the object, which is the essential condition of a judgment about beauty. But objective internal purposiveness, i.e. perfection, comes nearer to the predicate of beauty; and it has been regarded by celebrated philosophers[8] as the same as beauty, with the proviso, *if it is thought in a confused way.* It is of the greatest importance in a critique of taste to decide whether beauty can thus actually be resolved into the concept of perfection.

To judge of objective purposiveness we always need, not only the concept of a purpose, but (if that purposiveness is not to be external utility but internal) the concept of an internal purpose which shall contain the ground of the internal possibility of the object. Now as a purpose in general is that whose *concept* can be regarded as the ground of the possibility of the object itself; so, in order to represent objective purposiveness in a thing, the concept of *what sort of thing it is to be* must come first. The agreement of the manifold in it with this concept (which furnishes the rule for

---

[8][Bernard] Kant probably refers here to [Alexander] Baumgarten (1714–1762), who was the first writer to give the name of aesthetics to the philosophy of taste. He defined beauty as "perfection apprehended through the senses." Kant is said to have used as a textbook at lectures a work by Meier, a pupil of Baumgarten's, on the subject.

combining the manifold) is the *qualitative perfection* of the thing. Quite different from this is *quantitative* perfection, the completeness of a thing after its kind, which is a mere concept of magnitude (of totality).[9] In this *what the thing ought to be* is conceived as already determined, and it is only asked if it has *all* its requisites. The formal element in the representation of a thing, i.e. the agreement of the manifold with a unity (it being undetermined what this ought to be), gives to cognition no objective purposiveness whatever. For since abstraction is made of this unity as *purpose* (what the thing ought to be), nothing remains but the subjective purposeness of the representations in the mind of the intuiting subject. And this, although it furnishes a certain purposiveness of the representative state of the subject, and so a facility of apprehending a given form by the imagination, yet furnishes no perfection of an object, since the object is not here conceived by means of the concept of a purpose. For example, if in a forest I come across a plot of sward around which trees stand in a circle and do not then represent to myself a purpose, viz that it is intended to serve for country dances, not the least concept of perfection is furnished by the mere form. But to represent to oneself a formal *objective* purposiveness without purpose, i.e. the mere form of a *perfection* (without any matter and without the *concept* of that with which it is accordant, even if it were merely the idea of conformity to law in general), is a veritable contradiction.

Now the judgment of taste is an aesthetical judgment, i.e. such as rests on subjective grounds, the determining ground of which cannot be a concept, and consequently cannot be the concept of a definite purpose. Therefore by means of beauty, regarded as a formal subjective purposiveness, there is in no way thought a perfection of the object, as a purposiveness alleged to be formal but which is yet objective. And thus to distinguish between the concepts of the beautiful and the good as if they were only different in logical form, the first being a confused, the second a clear concept of perfection, but identical in content and origin, is quite fallacious. For then there would be no *specific* difference between them, but a judgment of taste would be as much a cognitive judgment as the judgment by which a thing is described as good; just as when the ordinary man says that fraud is unjust he bases his judgment on confused grounds, while the philosopher bases it on clear grounds, but both on identical principles of reason. I have already, however, said that an aesthetical judgment is unique of its kind and gives absolutely no cognition (not even a confused cognition) of the object; this is only supplied by a logical judgment. On the contrary, it simply refers the representation, by which an object is given, to the subject, and brings to our notice no characteristic of the object, but only the purposive form in the determination of the representative powers which are occupying themselves therewith. The judgment is called aesthetical just because its determining ground is not a concept, but the feeling (of internal sense) of that harmony in the play of the mental powers, so far as it can be felt in sensation. On the other hand, if we wish to call confused concepts and the objective judgment based on them aesthetical, we will have an understanding judging sensibly or a sense representing its objects by means of concepts both of which are contradictory. The faculty of concepts, be they confused or clear, is the understanding; and although understanding has to do with the judgment of taste as an aesthetical judgment (as it has with all judgments), yet it has to do with it, not as a faculty by which an object is cognized, but as the faculty which determines the judgment and its representation (without any concept) in accordance with its relation to the subject and the subject's internal feeling, in so far as this judgment may be possible in accordance with a universal rule.

XVI. The Judgment of Taste, by Which an Object Is Declared to Be Beautiful Under the Condition of a Definite Concept, Is Not Pure

There are two kinds of beauty: free beauty (*pulchritudo vaga),* or merely dependent beauty (*pulchritudo adhaerens).* The first presupposes no concept of what the object ought to be; the second does presuppose such a concept and the perfection of the object in accordance therewith. The first is called the (self-subsistent) beauty of this or that thing; the second, as dependent upon a concept (conditioned beauty), is ascribed to objects which come under the concept of a particular purpose.

Flowers are free natural beauties. Hardly anyone but a botanist knows what sort of a thing a flower ought to be; and even he, though recognizing in the flower the reproductive organ of the plant, pays no regard to this natural purpose if he is passing judgment on the flower by taste. There is, then, at the basis of this judgment no perfection of any kind, no internal purposiveness, to which the collection of the manifold is referred. Many birds (such as the parrot, the hummingbird, the bird of paradise) and many sea shells are

---

[9][Bernard] Cf. Preface to the *Metaphysical Elements of Ethics,* p. v: "The word *perfection* is liable to many misconceptions. It is sometimes understood as a concept belonging to transcendental philosophy; viz. the concept of the *totality* of the manifold, which, taken together, constitutes a thing; sometimes, again, it is understood as belonging to teleology, so that it signifies the agreement of the characteristics of a thing with a *purpose.* Perfection in the former sense might be called *quantitative* (material), in the latter *qualitative* (formal) perfection.

beauties, in themselves, which do not belong to any object determined in respect of its purpose by concepts, but please freely and in themselves. So also delineations *à la grecque,* foliage for borders or wall papers, mean nothing in themselves; they represent nothing—no object under a definite concept—and are free beauties. We can refer to the same class what are called in music fantasies (i.e. pieces without any theme), and in fact all music without words.

In the judging of a free beauty (according to the mere form), the judgment of taste is pure. There is presupposed no concept of any purpose which the manifold of the given object is to serve, and which therefore is to be represented in it. By such a concept the freedom of the imagination which disports itself in the contemplation of the figure would be only limited.

But human beauty (i.e. of a man, a woman, or a child), the beauty of a horse, or a building (be it church, palace, arsenal, or summer house), presupposes a concept of the purpose which determines what the thing is to be, and consequently a concept of its perfection; it is therefore adherent beauty. Now as the combination of the pleasant (in sensation) with beauty, which properly is only concerned with form, is a hindrance to the purity of the judgment of taste, so also is its purity injured by the combination with beauty of the good (viz. that manifold which is good for the thing itself in accordance with its purpose).

We could add much to a building which would immediately please the eye if only it were not to be a church. We could adorn a figure with all kinds of spirals and light but regular lines, as the New Zealanders do with their tattooing, if only it were not the figure of a human being. And again this could have much finer features and a more pleasing and gentle cast of countenance provided it were not intended to represent a man, much less a warrior.

Now the satisfaction in the manifold of a thing in reference to the internal purpose which determines its possibility is a satisfaction grounded on a concept; but the satisfaction in beauty is such as presupposes no concept, but is immediately bound up with the representation through which the object is given (not through which it is thought). If now the judgment of taste in respect of the beauty of a thing is made dependent on the purpose in its manifold, like a judgment of reason, and thus limited, it is no longer a free and pure judgment of taste.

It is true that taste gains by this combination of aesthetical with intellectual satisfaction, inasmuch as it becomes fixed; and though it is not universal, yet in respect to certain purposively determined objects it becomes possible to prescribe rules for it. These, however, are not rules of taste, but merely rules for the unification of taste with reason, i.e. of the beautiful with the good, by which the former becomes

available as an instrument of design in respect of the latter. Thus the tone of mind which is self-maintaining and of subjective universal validity is subordinated to the way of thinking which can be maintained only by painful resolve, but is of objective universal validity. Properly speaking, however, perfection gains nothing by beauty, or beauty by perfection; but when we compare the representation by which an object is given to us with the object (as regards what it ought to be) by means of a concept, we cannot avoid considering along with it the sensation in the subject. And thus when both states of mind are in harmony our *whole faculty* of representative power gains.

A judgment of taste, then, in respect of an object with a definite internal purpose, can only be pure if either the person judging has no concept of this purpose or else abstracts from it in his judgment. Such a person, although forming an accurate judgment of taste in judging of the object as free beauty, would yet by another who considers the beauty in it only as a dependent attribute (who looks to the purpose of the object) be blamed and accused of false taste, although both are right in their own way—the one in reference to what he has before his eyes, the other in reference to what he has in his thought. By means of this distinction we can settle many disputes about beauty between judges of taste, by showing that the one is speaking of free, the other of dependent, beauty—that the first is making a pure, the second an applied, judgment of taste.

XVII. Of the Ideal of Beauty

There can be no objective rule of taste which shall determine by means of concepts what is beautiful. For every judgment from this source is aesthetical; i.e. the feeling of the subject, and not a concept of the object, is its determining ground. To seek for a principle of taste which shall furnish, by means of definite concepts, a universal criterion of the beautiful is fruitless trouble, because what is sought is impossible and self-contradictory. The universal communicability of sensation (satisfaction or dissatisfaction) without the aid of a concept—the agreement, as far as is possible, of all times and peoples as regards this feeling in the representation of certain objects—this is the empirical criterion, although weak and hardly sufficing for probability, of the derivation of a taste, thus confirmed by examples, from the deep-lying general grounds of agreement in judging of the forms under which objects are given.

Hence we consider some products of taste as *exemplary*. Not that taste can be acquired by imitating others, for it must be an original faculty. He who imitates a model shows no doubt, in so far as he attains to it, skill; but only shows taste in so far as he can judge of this model itself.[10] It follows from hence that the highest model, the archetype of taste, is a mere idea, which everyone must produce in himself and according to which he must judge every object of taste, every example of judgment by taste, and even the taste of everyone. *Idea* properly means a rational concept, and *ideal* the representation of an individual being, regarded as adequate to an idea.[11] Hence that archetype of taste, which certainly rests on the indeterminate idea that reason has of a maximum, but which cannot be represented by concepts but only in an individual presentation, is better called the ideal of the beautiful. Although we are not in possession of this, we yet strive to produce it in ourselves. But it can only be an ideal of the imagination, because it rests on a presentation and not on concepts, and the imagination is the faculty of presentation. How do we arrive at such an ideal of beauty? A priori, or empirically? Moreover, what species of the beautiful is susceptible of an ideal?

First, it is well to remark that the beauty for which an ideal is to be sought cannot be *vague* beauty, but is *fixed* by a concept of objective purposiveness; and thus it cannot appertain to the object of a quite pure judgment of taste, but to that of a judgment of taste which is in part intellectual. That is, in whatever grounds of judgment an ideal is to be found, an idea of reason in accordance with definite concepts must lie at its basis, which determines a priori the purpose on which the internal possibility of the object rests. An ideal of beautiful flowers, of a beautiful piece of furniture, of a beautiful view, is inconceivable. But neither can an ideal be represented of a beauty dependent on definite purposes, e.g. of a beautiful dwelling house, a beautiful tree, a beautiful garden, etc.; presumably because their purpose is not sufficiently determined and fixed by the concept, and thus the purposiveness is nearly as free as in the case of *vague* beauty. The only being which has the purpose of its existence in itself is *man,* who can determine his purposes by reason; or, where he must receive them from external perception, yet can compare them with essential and universal purposes and can judge this their accordance aesthetically. This *man* is, then, alone of all objects in the world, susceptible of an ideal of *beauty,* as it is only *humanity* in his person, as an intelligence, that is susceptible of the ideal of *perfection.*

But there are here two elements. *First,* there is the aesthetical *normal idea,* which is an individual intuition (of the imagination), representing the standard of our judgment upon man as a thing belonging to a particular animal species. *Secondly,* there is the *rational idea* which makes the purposes of humanity, so far as they cannot be sensibly represented the principle for judging of a figure through which, as their phenomenal effect, those purposes are revealed. The normal idea of the figure of an animal of a particular race must take its elements from experience. But the greatest purposiveness in the construction of the figure that would be available for the universal standard of aesthetical judgment upon each individual of this species—the image which is as it were designedly at the basis of nature's technique, to which only the whole race and not any isolated individual is adequate—this lies merely in the idea of the judging subject. And this, with its proportions as an aesthetical idea, can be completely presented *in concreto* in a model. In order to make intelligible in some measure (for who can extract her whole secret from nature?) how this comes to pass, we shall attempt a psychological explanation.

We must remark that, in a way quite incomprehensible by us, the imagination cannot only recall on occasion the signs for concepts long past, but can also reproduce the image of the figure of the object out of an unspeakable number of objects of different kinds or even of the same kind. Further, if the mind is concerned with comparisons, the imagination can, in all probability, actually, though unconsciously, let one image glide into another; and thus, by the concurrence of several of the same kind, come by an average, which serves as the common measure of all. Everyone has seen a thousand full-grown men. Now if you wish to judge of their normal size, estimating it by means of comparison, the imagination (as I think) allows a great number of images (perhaps the whole thousand) to fall on one another. If I am allowed to apply here the analogy of optical presentation, it is in the space where most of them are combined and inside the contour, where the place is illuminated with the most vivid colors, that the *average size* is cognizable, which, both in height and breadth, is equally far removed from the extreme bounds of the greatest and smallest stature. And this is the stature of a beautiful man. (We could arrive at the same thing mechanically by adding together all thousand magnitudes, heights, breadths, and thicknesses, and dividing the sum by a thousand. But the imagination does this by means of a dynamical effect, which arises from the various impressions of such figures on the organ of internal sense.) If now, in a similar way, for this average man we seek the average head, for this head the average nose, etc., such figure is at the basis of the normal idea in the country where the comparison is instituted. Thus necessarily under these empirical conditions a Negro

---

[10] [Kant] Models of taste as regards the arts of speech must be composed in a dead and learned language. The first in order that they may not suffer that change which inevitably comes over living languages, in which noble expressions become flat, common ones antiquated, and newly created ones have only a short circulation. The second because learned languages have a grammar which is subject to no wanton change of fashion, but the rules of which are preserved unchanged.

[11] [Bernard] This distinction between an *idea* and an *ideal,* as also the further contrast between ideals of the reason and ideals of the imagination, had already been given by Kant in the *Critique of Pure Reason,* "Dialectic," Book II, Chapter 3, Section 1.

must have a different normal idea of the beauty of the human figure from a white man, a Chinaman a different normal idea from a European, etc. And the same is the case with the model of a beautiful horse or dog (of a certain breed). This *normal idea* is not derived from proportions gotten from experience [and regarded] *as definite rules,* but in accordance with it rules for judging become in the first instance possible. It is the image for the whole race, which floats among all the variously different intuitions of individuals, which nature takes as archetype in her productions of the same species, but which appears not to be fully reached in an individual case. It is by no means the whole *archetype of beauty* in the race, but only the form constituting the indispensable condition of all beauty, and thus merely *correctness* in the mental presentation of the race. It is, like the celebrated *Doryphorus* of Polycletus,[12] the *rule* (Myron's *Cow*[13] might also be used thus for its kind). It can therefore contain nothing specifically characteristic, for otherwise it would not be the *normal idea* for the race. Its presentation pleases, not by its beauty, but merely because it contradicts no condition, under which alone a thing of this kind can be beautiful. The presentation is merely correct.[14]

We must yet distinguish the *normal idea* of the beautiful from the *ideal,* which latter, on grounds already alleged, we can only expect in the *human* figure. In this the ideal consists in the expression of the *moral,* without which the object would not please universally and thus positively (not merely negatively in an accurate presentation). The visible expression of moral ideas that rule men inwardly can indeed only be gotten from experience; but to make its connection with all which our reason unites with the morally good in the idea of the highest purposiveness—goodness of heart, purity, strength, peace, etc.—visible as it were in bodily manifestation (as the effect of that which is internal) requires a union of pure ideas of reason with great imagina-

tive power even in him who wishes to judge of it, still more in him who wishes to present it. The correctness of such an ideal of beauty is shown by its permitting no sensible charm to mingle with the satisfaction in the object, and yet allowing us to take a great interest therein. This shows that a judgment in accordance with such a standard can never be purely aesthetical, and that a judgment in accordance with an ideal of beauty is not a mere judgment of taste.

Explanation of the Beautiful Derived from This Third Moment

Beauty is the form of the *purposiveness* of an object, so far as this is perceived in it *without any representation of a purpose.*[15]

Fourth Moment

Of the Judgment of Taste, According to the Modality of the Satisfaction in the Object

XVIII. What the Modality in a Judgment of Taste Is

I can say of every representation that it is at least *possible* that (as a cognition) it should be bound up with a pleasure. Of a representation that I call *pleasant* I say that it *actually* excites pleasure in me. But the *beautiful* we think as having a *necessary* reference to satisfaction. Now this necessity is of a peculiar kind. It is not a theoretical objective necessity, in which case it would be cognized *a priori* that everyone *will feel* this satisfaction in the object called beautiful by me. It is not a practical necessity, in which case, by concepts of a pure rational will serving as a rule for freely acting beings, the satisfaction is the necessary result of an objective law and only indicates that we absolutely (without any further design) ought to act in a certain way. But the necessity which is thought in an aesthetical judgment can only be called exemplary, i.e. a necessity of the assent of *all* to a judgment which is regarded as the example of a universal rule that we cannot state. Since an aesthetical judgment is

---

[12] [Bernard] Polycletus of Argos flourished about 430 B.C. His statue of the *Spearbearer* (Doryphorus) afterward became known as the *Canon,* because in it the artist was supposed to have embodied a perfect representation of the ideal of the human figure.

[13] [Bernard] This was a celebrated statue executed by Myron, a Greek sculptor contemporary with Polycletus.

[14] [Kant] It will be found that a perfectly regular countenance, such as a painter might wish to have for a model, ordinarily tells us nothing because it contains nothing characteristic, and therefore rather expresses the idea of the race than the specific traits of a person. The exaggeration of a characteristic of this kind, that is, such as does violence to the normal idea (the purposiveness of the race) is called *caricature.* Experience also shows that these quite regular countenances commonly indicate internally only a mediocre man, presumably (if it may be assumed that external nature expresses the proportion of internal) because, if no mental disposition exceeds that proportion which is requisite in order to constitute a man free from faults, nothing can be expected of what is called *genius,* in which nature seems to depart from the ordinary relations of mental powers on behalf of some special one.

[15] [Kant] It might be objected to this explanation that there are things in which we see a purposive form without cognizing any purpose in them, like the stone implements often gotten from old sepulchral tumuli with a hole in them, as if for a handle. These, although they plainly indicate by their shape a purposiveness of which we do not know the purpose, are nevertheless not described as beautiful. But if we regard a thing as a work of art, that is enough to make us admit that its shape has reference to some design and definite purpose. And hence there is no immediate satisfaction in the contemplation of it. On the other hand a flower, for instance a tulip, is regarded as beautiful because in perceiving it we find a certain purposiveness which, in our judgment, is referred to no purpose at all.

not an objective cognitive judgment, this necessity cannot be derived from definite concepts and is therefore not apodictic. Still less can it be inferred from the universality of experience (of a complete agreement of judgments as to the beauty of a certain object). For not only would experience hardly furnish sufficiently numerous vouchers for this, but also, on empirical judgments, we can base no concept of the necessity of these judgments.

XIX. The Subjective Necessity, Which We Ascribe to the Judgment of Taste, Is Conditioned

The judgment of taste requires the agreement of everyone, and he who describes anything as beautiful claims that everyone *ought* to give his approval to the object in question and also describe it as beautiful. The *ought* in the aesthetical judgment is therefore pronounced in accordance with all the data which are required for judging, and yet is only conditioned. We ask for the agreement of everyone else, because we have for it a ground that is common to all; and we could count on this agreement, provided we were always sure that the case was correctly subsumed under that ground as rule of assent.

XX. The Condition of Necessity Which a Judgment of Taste Asserts I the Idea of a Common Sense

If judgments of taste (like cognitive judgments) had a definite objective principle, then the person who lays them down in accordance with this latter would claim an unconditioned necessity for his judgment. If they were devoid of all principle, like those of the mere taste of sense, we would not allow them in thought any necessity whatever. Hence they must have a subjective principle which determines what pleases or displeases only by feeling and not by concepts, but yet with universal validity. But such a principle could only be regarded as a *common sense,* which is essentially different from common understanding which people sometimes call common sense *(sensus communis);* for the latter does not judge by feeling but always by concepts, although ordinarily only as by obscurely represented principles.

Hence it is only under the presupposition that there is a common sense (by which we do not understand an external sense, but the effect resulting from the free play of our cognitive powers)—it is only under this presupposition, I say, that the judgment of taste can be laid down.

XXI. Have We Ground for Presupposing a Common Sense?

Cognitions and judgments must, along with the conviction that accompanies them, admit of universal communicability; for otherwise there would be no harmony between them and the object, and they would be collectively a mere subjective play of the representative powers, exactly as scepticism desires. But if cognitions are to admit of communicability, so must also the state of mind—i.e. the accordance of the cognitive powers with a cognition generally and that proportion of them which is suitable for a representation (by which an object is given to us) in order that a cognition may be made out of it—admit of universal communicability. For without this as the subjective condition of cognition, cognition as an effect could not arise. This actually always takes place when a given object by means of sense excites the imagination to collect the manifold, and the imagination in its turn excites the understanding to bring about a unity of this collective process in concepts. But this accordance of the cognitive powers has a different proportion according to the variety of the objects which are given. However, it must be such that this internal relation, by which one mental faculty is excited by another, shall be generally the most beneficial for both faculties in respect of cognition (of given objects); and this accordance can only be determined by feeling (not according to concepts). Since now this accordance itself must admit of universal communicability, and consequently also our feeling of it (in a given representation), and since the universal communicability of a feeling presupposes a common sense, we have grounds for assuming this latter. And this common sense is assumed without relying on psychological observations, but simply as the necessary condition of the universal communicability of our knowledge, which is presupposed in every logic and in every principle of knowledge that is not sceptical.

XXII. The Necessity of the Universal Agreement That Is Thought in a Judgment of Taste Is a Subjective Necessity, Which Is Represented as Objective Under the Presupposition of a Common Sense

In all judgments by which we describe anything as beautiful, we allow no one to be of another opinion, without, however, grounding our judgment on concepts, but only on our feeling, which we therefore place at its basis, not as a private, but as a common feeling. Now this common sense cannot be grounded on experience, for it aims at justifying judgments which contain an *ought.* It does not say that everyone *will* agree with my judgment, but that he *ought.* And so common sense, as an example of whose judgment I here put forward my judgment of taste and on account of which I attribute to the latter an *exemplary* validity, is a mere ideal norm, under the supposition of which I have a right to make into a rule for everyone a judgment that accords therewith, as well as the satisfaction in an object expressed in such judgment. For the principle which concerns the agreement of different judging persons, although only subjective, is yet assumed as subjectively universal (an idea necessary for everyone), and thus can claim universal assent (as if it were objective) provided we are sure that we have correctly subsumed [the particulars] under it.

This indeterminate norm of a common sense is actually presupposed by us, as is shown by our claim to lay down judgments of taste. Whether there is in fact such a common sense, as a constitutive principle of the possibility of experience, or whether a yet higher principle of reason makes it only into a regulative principle for producing in us a common sense for higher purposes; whether, therefore, taste is an original and natural faculty or only the idea of an artificial one yet to be acquired, so that a judgment of taste with its assumption of a universal assent in fact is only a requirement of reason for producing such harmony of sentiment; whether the ought, i.e. the objective necessity of the confluence of the feeling of any one man with that of every other, only signifies the possibility of arriving at this accord, and the judgment of taste only affords an example of the application of this principle—these questions we have neither the wish nor the power to investigate as yet; we have now only to resolve the faculty of taste into its elements in order to unite them at last in the idea of a common sense.

Explanation of the Beautiful Resulting from the Fourth Moment

The *beautiful* is that which without any concept is cognized as the object of a *necessary* satisfaction.

* * *

from Second Book

Analytic of the Sublime

XXIII. Transition from the Faculty Which Judges of the Beautiful to That Which Judges of the Sublime

The beautiful and the sublime[16] agree in this that both please in themselves. Further, neither presupposes a judgment of

sense nor a judgment logically determined, but a judgment of reflection. Consequently the satisfaction belonging to them does not depend on a sensation, as in the case of the pleasant, nor on a definite concept, as in the case of the good; but it is nevertheless referred to concepts, although indeterminate ones. And so the satisfaction is connected with the mere presentation of the object or with the faculty of presentation, so that in the case of a given intuition this faculty or the imagination is considered as in agreement with the *faculty of concepts* of understanding or reason, regarded as promoting these latter. Hence both kinds of judgments are *singular,* and yet announce themselves as universally valid for every subject; although they lay claim merely to the feeling of pleasure, and not to any cognition of the object.

But there are also remarkable differences between the two. The beautiful in nature is connected with the form of the object, which consists in having definite boundaries. The sublime, on the other hand, is to be found in a formless object, so far as in it or by occasion of it *boundlessness* is represented, and yet its totality is also present to thought. Thus the beautiful seems to be regarded as the presentation of an indefinite concept of understanding, the sublime as that of a like concept of reason. There the satisfaction in the one case is bound up with the representation of *quality,* in the other with that of *quantity.* And the latter satisfaction is quite different in kind from the former, for this [the beautiful] directly brings with it a feeling of the furtherance of life, and thus is compatible with charms and with the play of the imagination. But the other the feeling of the sublime is a pleasure that arises only indirectly; viz. it is produced by the feeling of a momentary checking of the vital powers and a consequent stronger outflow of them, so that it seems to be regarded as emotion—not play, but earnest in the exercise of the imagination. Hence it is incompatible with physical charm; and as the mind is not merely attracted by the object but is ever being alternately repelled, the satisfaction in the sublime does not so much involve the positive pleasure as admiration or respect, which rather deserves to be called negative pleasure.

But the inner and most important distinction between the sublime and beautiful is, certainly, as follows. (Here, as we are entitled to do, we only bring under consideration in the first instance the sublime in natural objects, for the sublime of art is always limited by the conditions of agreement with nature.) Natural beauty (which is independent) brings with it a purposiveness in its form by which the object seems to be, as it were, preadapted to our judgment, and thus constitutes in itself an object of satisfaction. On the other hand, that which excites in us, without any reasoning about it, but in the mere apprehension of it, the feeling of the sublime may appear, as regards its form, to violate purpose in respect of the judgment, to be unsuited to our pre-

---

[16]Kant had read Burke on the sublime and beautiful (above, page 333), and strove to go beyond Burke's relatively simplistic views, especially of the sublime.

sentative faculty, and as it were to do violence to the imagination; and yet it is judged to be only the more sublime.

Now we may see from this that, in general, we express ourselves incorrectly if we call any *object of nature* sublime, although we can quite correctly call many objects of nature beautiful. For how can that be marked by an expression of approval which is apprehended in itself as being a violation of purpose? All that we can say is that the object is fit for the presentation of a sublimity which can be found in the mind, for no sensible form can contain the sublime properly so-called. This concerns only ideas of the reason which, although no adequate presentation is possible for them, by this inadequateness that admits of sensible presentation are aroused and summoned into the mind. Thus the wide ocean, disturbed by the storm, cannot be called sublime. Its aspect is horrible; and the mind must be already filled with manifold ideas if it is to be determined by such an intuition to a feeling itself sublime, as it is incited to abandon sensibility and to busy itself with ideas that involve higher purposiveness.

Independent natural beauty discovers to us a technique of nature which represents it as a system in accordance with laws, the principle of which we do not find in the whole of our faculty of understanding. That principle is the principle of purposiveness, in respect of the use of our judgment in regard to phenomena, which requires that these must not be judged as merely belonging to nature in its purposeless mechanism, but also as belonging to something analogous to art. It therefore actually extends, not indeed our cognition of natural objects, but our concept of nature, which is now not regarded as mere mechanism but as art. This leads to profound investigations as to the possibility of such a form. But in what we are accustomed to call sublime there is nothing at all that leads to particular objective principles and forms of nature corresponding to them; so far from it that, for the most part, nature excites the ideas of the sublime in its chaos or in its wildest and most irregular disorder and desolation, provided size and might are perceived. Hence, we see that the concept of the sublime is not nearly so important or rich in consequences as the concept of the beautiful; and that, in general, it displays nothing purposive in nature itself, but only in that possible use of our intuitions of it by which there is produced in us a feeling of a purposiveness quite independent of nature. We must seek a ground external to ourselves for the beautiful of nature, but seek it for the sublime merely in ourselves and in our attitude of thought, which introduces sublimity into the representation of nature. This is a very needful preliminary remark, which quite separates the ideas of the sublime from that of a purposiveness of *nature* and makes the theory of the sublime a mere appendix to the aesthetical judging of that purposive-

ness, because by means of it no particular form is represented in nature, but there is only developed a purposive use which the imagination makes of its representation.

XXIV. Of the Divisions of an Investigation into the Feeling of the Sublime

* * *

But the analysis of the sublime involves a division not needed in the case of the beautiful, viz. a division into the *mathematically* and the *dynamically sublime.*

For the feeling of the sublime brings with it as its characteristic feature a *movement* of the mind bound up with the judging of the object, while in the case of the beautiful taste presupposes and maintains the mind in *restful* contemplation. Now this movement ought to be judged as subjectively purposive (because the sublime pleases us), and thus it is referred through the imagination either to the *faculty of cognition* or *of desire.* In either reference the purposiveness of the given representation ought to be judged only in respect of this *faculty* (without purpose or interest), but in the first case it is ascribed to the object as a *mathematical* determination of the imagination, in the second as *dynamical.* And hence we have this twofold way of representing the sublime.

A. Of the Mathematically Sublime

XXV. Explanation of the Term Sublime

We call that *sublime* which is *absolutely great.* But to be great and to be a great something are quite different concepts (*magnitudo* and *quantitas*). In like manner to say simply *(simpliciter)* that anything is *great* is quite different from saying that it is *absolutely great (absolute, non comparative magnum).* The latter is *what is great beyond all comparison.* What now is meant by the expression that anything is great or small or of medium size? It is not a pure concept of understanding that is thus signified; still less is it an intuition of sense; and just as little is it a concept of reason, because it brings with it no principle of cognition. It must therefore be a concept of judgment or derived from one, and a subjective purposiveness of the representation in reference to the judgment must lie at its basis. That anything is a magnitude *(quantum)* may be cognized from the thing itself, without any comparison of it with other things, viz. if there is a multiplicity of the homogeneous constituting one thing. But to cognize *how great* it is always requires some other magnitude as a measure. But because the judging of magnitude depends, not merely on multiplicity (number), but also on the magnitude of the unit (the measure), and since, to judge of the magnitude of this latter again requires another as measure with which it may be compared, we see that the determination of the magnitude of phenomena can supply no absolute concept whatever of magnitude, but only a comparative one.

If now I say simply that anything is great, it appears that I have no comparison in view, at least none with an objective measure, because it is thus not determined at all how great the object is. But although the standard of comparison is merely subjective, yet the judgment nonetheless claims universal assent; "this man is beautiful" and "he is tall" are judgments, not limited merely to the judging subject, but, like theoretical judgments, demanding the assent of everyone.

In a judgment by which anything is designated simply as great, it is not merely meant that the object has a magnitude, but that this magnitude is superior to that of many other objects of the same kind, without, however, any exact determination of this superiority. Thus there is always at the basis of our judgment a standard which we assume as the same for everyone; this, however, is not available for any logical (mathematically definite) judging of magnitude, but only for aesthetical judging of the same, because it is a merely subjective standard lying at the basis of the reflective judgment upon magnitude. It may be empirical, as, e.g., the average size of the men known to us, of animals of a certain kind, trees, houses, mountains, etc. Or it may be a standard given a priori which, through the defects of the judging subject, is limited by the subjective conditions of presentation *in concreto,* as, e.g., in the practical sphere, the greatness of a certain virtue or of the public liberty and justice in a country, or, in the theoretical sphere, the greatness of the accuracy or the inaccuracy of an observation or measurement that has been made, etc.

Here it is remarkable that, although we have no interest whatever in an object—i.e. its existence is indifferent to us—yet its mere size, even if it is considered as formless, may bring a satisfaction with it that is universally communicable and that consequently involves the consciousness of a subjective purposiveness in the use of our cognitive faculty. This is not indeed a satisfaction in the object (because it may be formless), as in the case of the beautiful, in which the reflective judgment finds itself purposively determined in reference to cognition in general, but a satisfaction in the extension of the imagination by itself.

If (under the above limitation) we say simply of an object "it is great," this is no mathematically definite judgment, but a mere judgment of reflection upon the representation of it, which is subjectively purposive for a certain use of our cognitive powers in the estimation of magnitude; and we always then bind up with the representation a kind of re-

spect, as also a kind of contempt, for what we simply call "small." Further, the judging of things as great or small extends to everything, even to all their characteristics; thus we describe beauty as great or small. The reason of this is to be sought in the fact that whatever we present in intuition according to the precept of the judgment (and thus represent aesthetically) is always a phenomenon, and thus a quantum.

But if we call anything, not only great, but absolutely great in every point of view (great beyond all comparison), i.e. sublime, we soon see that it is not permissible to seek for an adequate standard of this outside itself, but merely in itself. It is a magnitude which is like itself alone. It follows hence that the sublime is not to be sought in the things of nature, but only in our ideas; but in which of them it lies must be reserved for the "Deduction."

The foregoing explanation can be thus expressed: *the sublime is that in comparison with which everything else is small.* Here we easily see that nothing can be given in nature, however great it is judged by us to be, which could not, if considered in another relation, be reduced to the infinitely small; and conversely there is nothing so small which does not admit of extension by our imagination to the greatness of a world if compared with still smaller standards. Telescopes have furnished us with abundant material for making the first remark, microscopes for the second. Nothing, therefore, which can be an object of the senses is, considered on this basis, to be called sublime. But because there is in our imagination a striving toward infinite progress and in our reason a claim for absolute totality, regarded as a real idea, therefore this very inadequateness for that idea in our faculty for estimating the magnitude of things of sense excites in us the feeling of a supersensible faculty. And it is not the object of sense, but the use which the judgment naturally makes of certain objects on behalf of this latter feeling that is absolutely great, and in comparison every other use is small. Consequently it is the state of mind produced by a certain representation with which the reflective judgment is occupied, and not the object, that is to be called sublime.

We can therefore append to the preceding formulas explaining the sublime this other: *the sublime is that, the mere ability to think which shows a faculty of the mind surpassing every standard of sense.*

XXVI. Of That Estimation of the Magnitude of Natural Things Which Is Requisite for the Idea of the Sublime

* * *

Nature is . . . sublime in those of its phenomena whose intuition brings with it the idea of its infinity. This last can only

come by the inadequacy of the greatest effort of our imagination to estimate the magnitude of an object. But now, in mathematical estimation of magnitude, the imagination is equal to
providing a sufficient measure for every object, because the
numerical concepts of the understanding, by means of progression, can make any measure adequate to any given magnitude. Therefore it must be the *aesthetical* estimation of
magnitude in which the effort toward comprehension surpasses the power of the imagination. Here it is felt that we can
comprehend in a whole of intuition the progressive apprehension, and at the same time we perceive the inadequacy of this
faculty, unbounded in its progress, for grasping and using any
fundamental measure available for the estimation of magnitude with the easiest application of the understanding. Now
the proper unchangeable fundamental measure of nature is its
absolute whole, which, regarding nature as a phenomenon,
would be infinity comprehended. But since this fundamental
measure is a self-contradictory concept (on account of the impossibility of the absolute totality of an endless progress), that
magnitude of a natural object on which the imagination fruitlessly spends its whole faculty of comprehension must carry
our concept of nature to a supersensible substrate (which lies
at its basis and also at the basis of our faculty of thought). As
this, however, is great beyond all standards of sense, it makes
us judge as *sublime,* not so much the object, as our own state
of mind in the estimation of it.

Therefore, just as the aesthetical judgment in judging
the beautiful refers the imagination in its free play to the *understanding,* in order to harmonize it with the *concepts* of
the latter in general (without any determination of them), so
does the same faculty, when judging a thing as sublime, refer itself to the *reason,* in order that it may subjectively be
in accordance with its *ideas* (no matter what they are)—i.e.
that it may produce a state of mind conformable to them and
compatible with that brought about by the influence of definite (practical) ideas upon feeling.

We hence see also that true sublimity must be sought
only in the mind of the subject judging, not in the natural
object the judgment upon which occasions this state. Who
would call sublime, e.g., shapeless mountain masses piled
in wild disorder upon one another with their pyramids of
ice, or the gloomy, raging sea? But the mind feels itself
raised in its own judgment if, while contemplating them
without any reference to their form, and abandoning itself to
the imagination and to the reason—which, although placed
in combination with the imagination without any definite
purpose, merely extends it—it yet finds the whole power of
the imagination inadequate to its ideas.

Examples of the mathematically sublime of nature in
mere intuition are all the cases in which we are given, not so
much a larger numerical concept, as a large unit for the mea-

sure of the imagination (for shortening the numerical series).
A tree, the height of which we estimate with reference to the
height of a man, at all events gives a standard for a mountain;
if this were a mile high, it would serve as unit for the number
expressive of the earth's diameter, so that the latter might be
made intuitible. The earth's diameter would supply a unit for
the known planetary system; this again for the Milky Way;
and the immeasurable number of Milky Way systems called
nebulae, which presumably constitute a system of the same
kind among themselves, lets us expect no bounds here. Now
the sublime in the aesthetical judging of an immeasurable
whole like this lies, not so much in the greatness of the number of units, as in the fact that in our progress we ever arrive
at yet greater units. To this the systematic division of the universe contributes, which represents every magnitude in nature
as small in its turn, and represents our imagination with its
entire freedom from bounds, and with it nature, as a mere
nothing in comparison with the ideas of reason if it is sought
to furnish a presentation which shall be adequate to them.

XXVII. Of the Quality of the Satisfaction in Our Judgments upon the Sublime

The feeling of our incapacity to attain to an idea *which is a
law for us* is *respect.* Now the idea of the comprehension of
every phenomenon that can be given us in the intuition of a
whole is an idea prescribed to us by a law of reason, which
recognizes no other measure, definite, valid for everyone,
and invariable, than the absolute whole. But our imagination, even in its greatest efforts, in respect of that comprehension which we expect from it of a given object in a
whole of intuition (and thus with reference to the presentation of the idea of reason) exhibits its own limits and inadequacy, although at the same time it shows that its destination
is to make itself adequate to this idea regarded as a law.
Therefore the feeling of the sublime in nature is respect for
our own destination, which, by a certain subreption, we attribute to an object of nature (conversion of respect for the
idea of humanity in our own subject into respect for the object). This makes intuitively evident the superiority of the
rational determination of our cognitive faculties to the greatest faculty of our sensibility.

The feeling of the sublime is therefore a feeling of pain
arising from the want of accordance between the aesthetical
estimation of magnitude formed by the imagination and the
estimation of the same formed by reason. There is at the
same time a pleasure thus excited, arising from the correspondence with rational ideas of this very judgment of the
inadequacy of our greatest faculty of sense, insofar as it is a
law for us to strive after these ideas. In fact it is for us a law
(of reason) and belongs to our destination to estimate as

small, in comparison with ideas of reason, everything which nature, regarded as an object of sense, contains that is great for us; and that which arouses in us the feeling of this supersensible destination agrees with that law. Now the greatest effort of the imagination in the presentation of the unit for the estimation of magnitude indicates a reference to something *absolutely great,* and consequently a reference to the law of reason, which bids us take this alone as our highest measure of magnitude. Therefore the inner perception of the inadequacy of all sensible standards for rational estimation of magnitude indicates a correspondence with rational laws; it involves a pain, which arouses in us the feeling of our supersensible destination, according to which it is purposive and therefore pleasurable to find every standard of sensibility inadequate to the ideas of understanding.

The mind feels itself *moved* in the representation of the sublime in nature, while in aesthetical judgments about the beautiful it is in *restful* contemplation. This movement may (especially in its beginnings) be compared to a vibration, i.e. to a quickly alternating attraction toward, and repulsion from, the same object. The transcendent (toward which the imagination is impelled in its apprehension of intuition) is for the imagination like an abyss in which it fears to lose itself; but for the rational idea of the supersensible it is not transcendent, but in conformity with law to bring about such an effort of the imagination, and consequently here there is the same amount of attraction as there was of repulsion for the mere sensibility. But the judgment itself always remains in this case only aesthetical, because, without having any determinate concept of the object at its basis, it merely represents the subjective play of the mental powers (imagination and reason) as harmonious through their very contrast. For just as imagination and *understanding,* in judging of the beautiful, generate a subjective purposiveness of the mental powers by means of their harmony, so [in this case] imagination and *reason* do so by means of their conflict. That is, they bring about a feeling that we possess pure self-subsistent reason, or a faculty for the estimation of magnitude, whose superiority can be made intuitively evident only by the inadequacy of that faculty (imagination) which is itself unbounded in the presentation of magnitudes (of sensible objects).

* * *

B. Of the Dynamically Sublime in Nature

XXVIII. Of Nature Regarded as Might

Might is that which is superior to great hindrances. It is called *dominion* if it is superior to the resistance of that which itself possesses might. Nature, considered in an aes-

thetical judgment as might that has no dominion over us, is *dynamically sublime.*

If nature is to be judged by us as dynamically sublime, it must be represented as exciting fear (although it is not true conversely that every object which excites fear is regarded in our aesthetical judgment as sublime). For in aesthetical judgments (without the aid of concepts) superiority to hindrances can only be judged according to the greatness of the resistance. Now that which we are driven to resist is an evil and, if we do not find our faculties a match for it, is an object of fear. Hence nature can be regarded by the aesthetical judgment as might, and consequently as dynamically sublime, only so far as it is considered an object of fear.

But we can regard an object as *fearful* without being afraid *of* it, viz. if we judge of it in such a way that we merely *think* a case in which we would wish to resist it and yet in which all resistance would be altogether vain. Thus the virtuous man fears God without being afraid of him, because to wish to resist him and his commandments he thinks is a case that he need not apprehend. But in every such case that he thinks as not impossible, he cognizes him as fearful.

He who fears can form no judgment about the sublime in nature, just as he who is seduced by inclination and appetite can form no judgment about the beautiful. The former flies from the sight of an object which inspires him with awe, and it is impossible to find satisfaction in a terror that is seriously felt. Hence the pleasurableness arising from the cessation of an uneasiness is *a state of joy.* But this, on account of the deliverance from danger which is involved, is a state of joy when conjoined with the resolve that we shall no more be exposed to the danger; we cannot willingly look back upon our sensations of danger; much less seek the occasion for them again.

Bold, overhanging, and, as it were, threatening rocks; clouds piled up in the sky, moving with lightning flashes and thunder peals; volcanoes in all their violence of destruction; hurricanes with their track of devastation; the boundless ocean in a state of tumult; the lofty waterfall of a mighty river, and such like—these exhibit our faculty of resistance as insignificantly small in comparison with their might. But the sight of them is the more attractive, the more fearful it is, provided only that we are in security; and we willingly call these objects sublime, because they raise the energies of the soul above their accustomed height and discover in us a faculty of resistance of a quite different kind, which gives us courage to measure ourselves against the apparent almightiness of nature.

Now, in the immensity of nature and in the insufficiency of our faculties to take in a standard proportionate to the aesthetical estimation of the magnitude of its *realm,* we find our own limitation, although at the same time in our rational faculty we find a different, nonsensuous standard, which has that infinity itself under it as a unity, in comparison with which everything in nature is small, and thus in our mind we find a superiority to nature even in its immensity. And so also the irresistibility of its might, while making us recognize our own physical impotence, considered as beings of nature, discloses to us a faculty of judging independently of and a superiority over nature, on which is based a kind of self-preservation entirely different from that which can be attacked and brought into danger by external nature. Thus humanity in our person remains unhumiliated, though the individual might have to submit to this dominion. In this way nature is not judged to be sublime in our aesthetical judgments in so far as it excites fear, but because it calls up that power in us (which is not nature) of regarding as small the things about which we are solicitous (goods, health, and life), and of regarding its might (to which we are no doubt subjected in respect of these things) as nevertheless without any dominion over us and our personality to which we must bow where our highest fundamental propositions, and their assertion or abandonment, are concerned. Therefore nature is here called sublime merely because it elevates the imagination to a presentation of those cases in which the mind can make felt the proper sublimity of its destination, in comparison with nature itself.

* * *

Sublimity . . . does not reside in anything of nature, but only in our mind, insofar as we can become conscious that we are superior to nature within, and therefore also to nature without us (so far as it influences us). Everything that excites this feeling in us, e.g. the *might* of nature which calls forth our forces, is called then (although improperly) sublime. Only by supposing this idea in ourselves and in reference to it are we capable of attaining to the idea of the sublimity of that Being which produces respect in us, not merely by the might that it displays in nature, but rather by means of the faculty which resides in us of judging it fearlessly and of regarding our destination as sublime in respect of it.

XLIX. Of the Faculties of the Mind That Constitute Genius

We say of certain products of which we expect that they should at least in part appear as beautiful art, they are without *spirit*,[17]

although we find nothing to blame in them on the score of taste. A poem may be very neat and elegant, but without spirit. A history may be exact and well arranged, but without spirit. A festal discourse may be solid and at the same time elaborate, but without spirit. Conversation is often not devoid of entertainment, but it is without spirit; even of a woman we say that she is pretty, an agreeable talker, and courteous, but without spirit. What then do we mean by *spirit?*

Spirit, in an aesthetical sense, is the name given to the animating principle of the mind. But that by means of which this principle animates the soul, the material which it applies to that purpose, is what puts the mental powers purposively into swing, i.e. into such a play as maintains itself and strengthens the mental powers in their exercise.

Now I maintain that this principle is no other than the faculty of presenting *aesthetical ideas*. And by an *aesthetical idea* I understand that representation of the imagination which occasions much thought, without however any definite thought, i.e., any *concept,* being capable of being adequate to it; it consequently cannot be completely compassed and made intelligible by language. We easily see that it is the counterpart (pendant) of a *rational idea,* which conversely is a concept to which no *intuition* (or representation of the imagination) can be adequate.[18]

The imagination (as a productive faculty of cognition) is very powerful in creating another nature, as it were, out of the material that actual nature gives it. We entertain ourselves with it when experience becomes too commonplace, and by it we remold experience, always indeed in accordance with analogical laws, but yet also in accordance with principles which occupy a higher place in reason (laws, too, which are just as natural to us as those by which understanding comprehends empirical nature). Thus we feel our freedom from the law of association (which attaches to the empirical employment of imagination), so that the material supplied to us by nature in accordance with this law can be worked up into something different which surpasses nature.

Such representations of the imagination we may call *ideas,* partly because they at least strive after something which lies beyond the bounds of experience and so seek to approximate to a presentation of concepts of reason (intellectual ideas), thus giving to the latter the appearance of

---

[17] [Bernard] In English we would rather say "without soul," but I prefer to translate *Geist* consistently by "spirit," to avoid the confusion of it with *Seele*.[1]

[18] This is a key paragraph. The aesthetical idea as described here gives a philosophical basis for the attack on paraphrase of poems in the New Criticism. See Brooks (below, page 1036).

objective reality, but especially because no concept can be fully adequate to them as internal intuitions. The poet ventures to realize to sense, rational ideas of invisible beings, the kingdom of the blessed, hell, eternity, creation, etc.; or even if he deals with things of which there are examples in experience—e.g. death, envy and all vices, also love, fame, and the like—he tries, by means of imagination, which emulates the play of reason in its quest after a maximum, to go beyond the limits of experience and to present them to sense with a completeness of which there is no example in nature. This is properly speaking the art of the poet, in which the faculty of aesthetical ideas can manifest itself in its entire strength. But this faculty, considered in itself, is properly only a talent (of the imagination).

If now we place under a concept a representation of the imagination belonging to its presentation, but which occasions in itself more thought than can ever be comprehended in a definite concept and which consequently aesthetically enlarges the concept itself in an unbounded fashion, the imagination is here creative, and it brings the faculty of intellectual ideas (the reason) into movement; i.e. by a representation more thought (which indeed belongs to the concept of the object) is occasioned than can in it be grasped or made clear.

Those forms which do not constitute the presentation of a given concept itself but only, as approximate representations of the imagination, express the consequences bound up with it and its relationship to other concepts, are called (aesthetical) *attributes* of an object whose concept as a rational idea cannot be adequately presented. Thus Jupiter's eagle with the lightning in its claws is an attribute of the mighty king of heaven, as the peacock is of his magnificent queen. They do not, like *logical attributes,* represent what lies in our concepts of the sublimity and majesty of creation, but something different, which gives occasion to the imagination to spread itself over a number of kindred representations that arouse more thought than can be expressed in a concept determined by words. They furnish an *aesthetical idea,* which for that rational idea takes the place of logical presentation; and thus, as their proper office, they enliven the mind by opening out to it the prospect into an illimitable field of kindred representations. But beautiful art does this not only in the case of painting or sculpture (in which the term "attribute" is commonly employed); poetry and rhetoric also get the spirit that animates their works simply from the aesthetical attributes of the object, which accompany the logical and stimulate the imagination, so that it thinks more by their aid, although in an undeveloped way, than could be comprehended in a concept and therefore in a definite form of words. For the sake of brevity, I must limit myself to a few examples only.

When the great King in one of his poems expresses himself as follows:

Oui, finissons sans trouble et mourons sans regrets,
En laissant l'univers comblé de nos bienfaits.
Ainsi l'astre du jour au bout de sa carrière,
Répand sur l'horizon une douce lumière;
Et les derniers rayons qu'il darde dans les airs,
Sont les derniers soupirs qu'il donne à l'univers;[19]

he quickens his rational idea of a cosmopolitan disposition at the end of life by an attribute which the imagination (in remembering all the pleasures of a beautiful summer day that are recalled at its close by a serene evening) associates with that representation, and which excites a number of sensations and secondary representations for which no expression is found. On the other hand, an intellectual concept may serve conversely as an attribute for a representation of sense, and so can quicken this latter by means of the idea of the supersensible, but only by the aesthetical element, that subjectively attaches to the concept of the latter, being here employed. Thus, for example, a certain poet says, in his description of a beautiful morning: "The sun arose / As calm from virtue springs." The consciousness of virtue, if we substitute it in our thoughts for a virtuous man, diffuses in the mind a multitude of sublime and restful feelings, and a boundless prospect of a joyful future, to which no expression that is measured by a definite concept completely attains.[20]

In a word, the aesthetical idea is a representation of the imagination associated with a given concept, which is bound up with such a multiplicity of partial representations in its free employment that for it no expression marking a definite concept can be found; and such a representation, therefore, adds to a concept much ineffable thought, the feeling of which quickens the cognitive faculties, and with language, which is the mere letter, binds up spirit also.

---

[19] "Yes, let us end without disorder and die without regrets, / Leaving the universe filled with our blessings. / Thus the day star at the end of its course, / Sheds on the horizon a gentle light; / And the last rays that it beams into the air, / Are the last sighs that it gives to the universe." [Bernard] Barni quotes these lines as occurring in one of Frederick the Great's French poems: "Epître au maréchal Keith, sur les vaines terreurs de la mort et les frayeurs d'une autre vie"; but I have not been able to verify his reference. Kant here translates them into German.

[20] [Kant] Perhaps nothing more sublime was ever said and no sublimer thought ever expressed than the famous inscription on the Temple of Isis (Mother nature): "I am all that is and that was and that shall be, and no mortal has lifted my veil." Segner availed himself of this idea in a *suggestive* vignette prefixed to his *Natural Philosophy,* in order to inspire beforehand the pupil whom he was about to lead into that temple with a holy awe, which should dispose his mind to serious attention.

* * *

LIII. Comparison of the Respective Aesthetical Worth of the Beautiful Arts

Of all the arts *poetry* (which owes its origin almost entirely to genius and will least be guided by precept or example) maintains the first rank. It expands the mind by setting the imagination at liberty and by offering, within the limits of a given concept, amid the unbounded variety of possible forms accordant therewith, that which unites the presentment of this concept with a wealth of thought to which no verbal expression is completely adequate, and so rising aesthetically to ideas. It strengthens the mind by making it feel its faculty—free, spontaneous, and independent of natural determination—of considering and judging nature as a phenomenon in accordance with aspects which it does not present in experience either for sense or understanding, and therefore of using it on behalf of, and as a sort of schema for, the supersensible. It plays with illusion, which it produces at pleasure, but without deceiving by it; for it declares its exercise to be mere play, which however can be purposively used by the understanding. Rhetoric, insofar as this means the art of persuasion, i.e. of deceiving by a beautiful show *(ars oratoria),* and not mere elegance of speech (eloquence and style), is a dialectic which borrows from poetry only so much as is needful to win minds to the side of the orator before they have formed a judgment and to deprive them of their freedom; it cannot therefore be recommended either for the law courts or for the pulpit. For if we are dealing with civil law, with the rights of individual persons, or with lasting instruction and determination of people's minds to an accurate knowledge and a conscientious observance of their duty, it is unworthy of so important a business to allow a trace of any luxuriance of wit and imagination to appear, and still less any trace of the art of talking people over and of captivating them for the advantage of any chance person. For although this art may sometimes be directed to legiti-

mate and praiseworthy designs, it becomes objectionable when in this way maxims and dispositions are spoiled in a subjective point of view, though the action may objectively be lawful. It is not enough to do what is right; we should practice it solely on the ground that it is right. Again, the mere concept of this species of matters of human concern, when clear and combined with a lively presentation of it in examples, without any offense against the rules of euphony of speech or propriety of expression, has by itself for ideas of reason (which collectively constitute eloquence) sufficient influence upon human minds; so that it is not needful to add the machinery of persuasion, which, since it can be used equally well to beautify or to hide vice and error, cannot quite lull the secret suspicion that one is being artfully overreached. In poetry everything proceeds with honesty and candor. It declares itself to be a mere entertaining play of the imagination, which wishes to proceed as regards form in harmony with the laws of the understanding; and it does not desire to steal upon and ensnare the understanding by the aid of sensible presentation.[21]

---

[21] [Kant] I must admit that a beautiful poem has always given me a pure gratification, while the reading of the best discourse, whether of a Roman orator or of a modern parliamentary speaker or of a preacher, has always been mingled with an unpleasant feeling of disapprobation of a treacherous art which means to move men in important matters like machines to a judgment that must lose all weight for them on quiet reflection. Readiness and accuracy in speaking (which taken together constitute rhetoric) belong to beautiful art, but the art of the orator *(ars oratoria),* the art of availing oneself of the weaknesses of men for one's own designs (whether these be well meant or even actually good does not matter), is worthy of no *respect.* Again, this art only reached its highest point, both at Athens and at Rome, at a time when the state was hastening to its ruin and true patriotic sentiment had disappeared. The man who, along with a clear insight into things, has in his power a wealth of pure speech, and who with a fruitful imagination capable of presenting his ideas unites a lively sympathy with what is truly good, is *vir bonus dicendi peritus,* the orator without art but of great impressiveness, as Cicero has it, though he may not always be true to this ideal. [Here Kant draws a distinction between poetry and oratory, in contrast to Plato's identification of both with sophistry (above, page 8).]

Mary Wollstonecraft

1759–1797

Mary Wollstonecraft's *A Vindication of the Rights of Woman* (1792) well deserves its rank as the first great feminist work. It is her most famous work, but not her first or last. She had already published fiction when in 1790 she answered Edmund Burke's *Reflections on the Revolution in France* with her *A Vindication of the Rights of Man* before Thomas Paine wrote his *Rights of Man* (1791–1792). Having associated with Dissenters who supported the French Revolution, she was outraged at Burke's attack and in turn opposed British identification of security of property with liberty, arguing for the breakup of large estates and going on to propose numerous reforms, both economic and social. The book made her well known.

In *A Vindication of the Rights of Woman* she went beyond her Dissenter friends, whose views remained strictly patriarchal. Written in about six weeks, the book was insufficiently revised but nevertheless achieves an effective tone. In general, the fundamental principles enunciated are that the mind does not know sex and that, as Claire Tomalin has remarked ". . . society is wasting its assets if it retains women in the role of convenient domestic slaves and alluring mistresses, denies them economic independence and encourages them to be docile and attentive to their looks to the exclusion of all else."

Chapter Six, below, of *Vindication* follows a long chapter that discusses a number of writers' attitudes toward female character and education. Wollstonecraft accepts the common theory of the association of ideas set forth in David Hartley's *Observations of Man* (1749) and employed by David Hume in his *Enquiry Concerning Human Understanding*. Her emphasis on the importance of impressions leads her in Chapter Thirteen, Part Two, to attack the sentimental novels of her time for their pernicious influences on women's intellectual development.

Mary Wollstonecraft's works include *Thoughts on the Education of Daughters* (1787); *Original Stories* (1788); *A Vindication of the Rights of Man* (1790); *A Vindication of the Rights of Woman* (1792); *A Historical and Moral View of the Origin and Progress of the French Revolution* (1794); *Letters Written during a Short Residence in Sweden, Norway and Denmark* (1796); and *Posthumous Works* (ed. Godwin, 1798). See Emma Rauschenbusch-Clough, *A Study of Mary Wollstonecraft and the Rights of Woman* (1898); Virgina Woolf, "Mary Wollstonecraft," *The Second Common Reader* (1932); Margaret George, *One Woman's Situation* (1970); Eleanor Flexner, *Mary Wollstonecraft* (1972); Claire Tomalin, *The Life and Death of Mary Wollstonecraft* (1974); Alan Cumming, *Mary Wollstonecraft and Eighteenth Century Theorists* (1980); Jennifer Lorch, *Mary Wollstonecraft: The Making of a Radical Feminist* (1990); Harriet Divine Jump, *Mary Wollstonecraft: Writer* (1994); Eileen Janes Yeo, *Mary Wollstonecraft and Two Hundred Years of Feminisms* (1997); Janet M. Todd, *Mary Wollstonecraft: A Revolutionary Life* (2000); Ashley Tauchert, *Mary Wollstonecraft and the Accent of the Feminine* (2002); Barbara Taylor, *Mary Wollstonecraft and the Feminist Imagination* (2003).

from

A Vindication of the Rights of Woman

Chapter VI

*The Effect Which an Early Association of Ideas
Has upon the Character*

Educated in the enervating style recommended by the writers on whom I have been animadverting; and not having a chance, from their subordinate state in society, to recover their lost ground, is it surprising that women everywhere appear a defect in nature? Is it surprising, when we consider what a determinate effect an early association of ideas has on the character, that they neglect their understandings, and turn all their attention to their persons?

The great advantages which naturally result from storing the mind with knowledge, are obvious from the following considerations. The association of our ideas is either habitual or instantaneous; and the latter mode seems rather to depend on the original temperature of the mind than on the will. When the ideas, and matters of fact, are once taken in, they lie by for use, till some fortuitous circumstance makes the information dart into the mind with illustrative force, that has been received at very different periods of our lives. Like the lightning's flash are many recollections; one idea assimilating and explaining another, with astonishing rapidity. I do not now allude to that quick perception of truth, which is so intuitive that it baffles research, and makes us at a loss to determine whether it is reminiscence or ratiocination, lost sight of in its celerity, that opens the dark cloud. Over those instantaneous associations we have little power; for when the mind is once enlarged by excursive flights, or profound reflection, the raw materials will, in some degree, arrange themselves. The understanding, it is true, may keep us from going out of drawing when we group our thoughts, or transcribe from the imagination the warm sketches of fancy; but the animal spirits, the individual character, give the colouring.

Over this subtile electric fluid,[1] how little power do we possess, and over it how little power can reason obtain! These fine intractable spirits appear to be the essence of genius, and beaming in its eagle eye, produce in the most eminent degree the happy energy of associating thoughts that surprise, delight, and instruct. These are the glowing minds that concentrate pictures for their fellow-creatures; forcing them to view with interest the objects reflected from the impassioned imagination, which they passed over in nature.

I must be allowed to explain myself. The generality of people cannot see or feel poetically, they want fancy, and therefore fly from solitude in search of sensible objects; but when an author lends them his eyes they can see as he saw, and be amused by images they could not select, though lying before them.

Education thus only supplies the man of genius with knowledge to give variety and contrast to his associations; but there is an habitual association of ideas, that grows 'with our growth,'[2] which has a great effect on the moral character of mankind; and by which a turn is given to the mind that commonly remains throughout life. So ductile is the understanding, and yet so stubborn, that the associations which depend on adventitious circumstances, during the period that the body takes to arrive at maturity, can seldom be disentangled by reason. One idea calls up another, its old associate, and memory, faithful to the first impressions, particularly when the intellectual powers are not employed to cool our sensations, retraces them with mechanical exactness.

This habitual slavery, to first impressions, has a more baneful effect on the female than the male character, because business and other dry employments of the understanding, tend to deaden the feelings and break associations that do violence to reason. But females, who are made women of when they are mere children, and brought back to childhood when they ought to leave the go-cart forever, have not sufficient strength of mind to efface the superinductions of art that have smothered nature.

Every thing that they see or hear serves to fix impressions, call forth emotions, and associate ideas, that give a sexual character to the mind. False notions of beauty and

---

[1] [Wollstonecraft] I have sometimes, when inclined to laugh at materialists, asked whether, as the most powerful effects in nature are apparently produced by fluids, the magnetic, &c. the passions might not be fine volatile fluids that embraced humanity, keeping the more refractory elementary parts together—or whether they were simply a liquid fire that pervaded the more sluggish materials, giving them life and heat? [Reference is to the views of Newton and the Associationists who posited a pervasive fluid that carried vibrations to the perceiver.]

[2] Alexander Pope, *Essay on Man* II, 136.

A Vindication of the Rights of Woman was first published in London in 1792. It was followed in the same year by the second edition, which is the basis for the text printed here.

delicacy stop the growth of their limbs and produce a sickly soreness, rather than delicacy of organs; and thus weakened by being employed in unfolding instead of examining the first associations, forced on them by every surrounding object, how can they attain the vigour necessary to enable them to throw off their factitious character?—where find strength to recur to reason and rise superior to a system of oppression, that blasts the fair promises of spring? This cruel association of ideas, which every thing conspires to twist into all their habits of thinking, or, to speak with more precision, of feeling, receives new force when they begin to act a little for themselves; for they then perceive that it is only through their address to excite emotions in men, that pleasure and power are to be obtained. Besides, the books professedly written for their instruction, which make the first impression on their minds, all inculcate the same opinions. Educated then in worse than Egyptian bondage, it is unreasonable, as well as cruel, to upbraid them with faults that can scarcely be avoided, unless a degree of native vigour be supposed, that falls to the lot of very few amongst mankind.

For instance, the severest sarcasms have been levelled against the sex, and they have been ridiculed for repeating 'a set of phrases learnt by rote,'[3] when nothing could be more natural, considering the education they receive, and that their 'highest praise is to obey, unargued'[4]—the will of man. If they be not allowed to have reason sufficient to govern their own conduct—why, all they learn—must be learned by rote! And when all their ingenuity is called forth to adjust their dress, 'a passion for a scarlet coat,'[5] is so natural, that it never surprised me; and, allowing Pope's summary of their character to be just, 'that every woman is at heart a rake,'[6] why should they be bitterly censured for seeking a congenial mind, and preferring a rake to a man of sense?

Rakes know how to work on their sensibility, whilst the modest merit of reasonable men has, of course, less effect on their feelings, and they cannot reach the heart by the way of the understanding, because they have few sentiments in common.

It seems a little absurd to expect women to be more reasonable than men in their *likings,* and still to deny them the uncontrouled use of reason. When do men *fall-in-love* with sense? When do they, with their superior powers and advantages, turn from the person to the mind? And how can they then expect women, who are only taught to observe be-

haviour, and acquire manners rather than morals, to despise what they have been all their lives labouring to attain? Where are they suddenly to find judgment enough to weigh patiently the sense of an awkward virtuous man, when his manners, of which they are made critical judges, are rebuffing, and his conversation cold and dull, because it does not consist of pretty repartees, or well turned compliments? In order to admire or esteem any thing for a continuance, we must, at least, have our curiosity excited by knowing, in some degree, what we admire; for we are unable to estimate the value of qualities and virtues above our comprehension. Such a respect, when it is felt, may be very sublime; and the confused consciousness of humility may render the dependent creature an interesting object, in some points of view; but human love must have grosser ingredients; and the person very naturally will come in for its share—and, an ample share it mostly has!

Love is, in a great degree, an arbitrary passion, and will reign, like some other stalking mischiefs, by its own authority, without deigning to reason; and it may also be easily distinguished from esteem, the foundation of friendship, because it is often excited by evanescent beauties and graces, though, to give an energy to the sentiment, something more solid must deepen their impression and set the imagination to work, to make the most fair—the first good.

Common passions are excited by common qualities.— Men look for beauty and the simper of good-humoured docility: women are captivated by easy manners; a gentleman-like man seldom fails to please them, and their thirsty ears eagerly drink the insinuating nothings of politeness, whilst they turn from the unintelligible sounds of the charmer—reason, charm he never so wisely. With respect to superficial accomplishments, the rake certainly has the advantage; and of these females can form an opinion, for it is their own ground. Rendered gay and giddy by the whole tenor of their lives, the very aspect of wisdom, or the severe graces of virtue, must have a lugubrious appearance to them; and produce a kind of restraint from which they and love, sportive child, naturally revolt. Without taste, excepting of the lighter kind, for taste is the offspring of judgment, how can they discover that true beauty and grace must arise from the play of the mind? and how can they be expected to relish in a lover what they do not, or very imperfectly, possess themselves? The sympathy that unites hearts, and invites to confidence, in them is so very faint, that it cannot take fire, and thus mount to passion. No, I repeat it, the love cherished by such minds, must have grosser fewel!

The inference is obvious; till women are led to exercise their understandings, they should not be satirized for their attachment to rakes; or even for being rakes at heart, when it

[3] Jonathan Swift, "The Furniture of a Woman's Mind."
[4] John Milton, *Paradise Lost* IV, 636–8.
[5] Swift, *op. cit.*
[6] Pope, *Moral Essays* II, 215–6.

appears to be the inevitable consequence of their education. They who live to please—must find their enjoyments, their happiness, in pleasure! It is a trite, yet true remark, that we never do any thing well, unless we love it for its own sake.

Supposing, however, for a moment, that women were, in some future revolution of time, to become, what I sincerely wish them to be, even love would acquire more serious dignity, and be purified in its own fires; and virtue giving true delicacy to their affections, they would turn with disgust from a rake. Reasoning then, as well as feeling, the only province of woman, at present, they might easily guard against exterior graces, and quickly learn to despise the sensibility that had been excited and hackneyed in the ways of women, whose trade was vice; and allurements, wanton airs. They would recollect that the flame, one must use appropriated expressions, which they wished to light up, had been exhausted by lust, and that the sated appetite, losing all relish for pure and simple pleasures, could only be roused by licentious arts or variety. What satisfaction could a woman of delicacy promise herself in a union with such a man, when the very artlessness of her affection might appear insipid? Thus does Dryden describe the situation,

———'Where love is duty, on the female side,
'On theirs mere sensual gust, and sought with
     surly pride.'[7]

But one grand truth women have yet to learn, though much it imports them to act accordingly. In the choice of a husband, they should not be led astray by the qualities of a lover—for a lover the husband, even supposing him to be wise and virtuous, cannot long remain.

Were women more rationally educated, could they take a more comprehensive view of things, they would be contented to love but once in their lives; and after marriage calmly let passion subside into friendship—into that tender intimacy, which is the best refuge from care; yet is built on such pure, still affections, that idle jealousies would not be allowed to disturb the discharge of the sober duties of life, or to engross the thoughts that ought to be otherwise employed. This is a state in which many men live; but few, very few women. And the difference may easily be accounted for, without recurring to a sexual character. Men, for whom we are told women were made, have too much occupied the thoughts of women; and this association has so entangled love with all their motives of action; and, to harp a little on an old string, having been solely employed either to prepare

themselves to excite love, or actually putting their lessons in practice, they cannot live without love. But, when a sense of duty, or fear of shame, obliges them to restrain this pampered desire of pleasing beyond certain lengths, too far for delicacy, it is true, though far from criminality, they obstinately determine to love, I speak of the passion, their husbands to the end of the chapter—and then acting the part which they foolishly exacted from their lovers, they become abject woers, and fond slaves.

Men of wit and fancy are often rakes; and fancy is the food of love. Such men will inspire passion. Half the sex, in its present infantine state, would pine for a Lovelace;[8] a man so witty, so graceful, and so valiant; and can they *deserve* blame for acting according to principles so constantly inculcated? They want a lover, and protector; and behold him kneeling before them—bravery prostrate to beauty! The virtues of a husband are thus thrown by love into the background, and gay hopes, or lively emotions, banish reflection till the day of reckoning comes; and come it surely will, to turn the sprightly lover into a surly suspicious tyrant, who contemptuously insults the very weakness he fostered. Or, supposing the rake reformed, he cannot quickly get rid of old habits. When a man of abilities is first carried away by his passions, it is necessary that sentiment and taste varnish the enormities of vice, and give a zest to brutal indulgences; but when the gloss of novelty is worn off, and pleasure palls upon the sense, lasciviousness becomes barefaced, and enjoyment only the desperate effort of weakness flying from reflection as from a legion of devils. Oh! virtue, thou art not an empty name! All that life can give—thou givest!

If much comfort cannot be expected from the friendship of a reformed rake of superiour abilities, what is the consequence when he lacketh sense, as well as principles? Verily misery, in its most hideous shape. When the habits of weak people are consolidated by time, a reformation is barely possible; and actually makes the beings miserable who have not sufficient mind to be amused by innocent pleasure; like the tradesman who retires from the hurry of business, nature presents to them only a universal blank; and the restless thoughts prey on the damped spirits.[9] Their reformation, as well as his retirement, actually makes them

---

[7] John Dryden, *Palamon and Arcite* III, 231–2.

[8] A character in Samuel Richardson's *Clarissa*.

[9] [Wollstonecraft] I have frequently seen this exemplified in women whose beauty could no longer be repaired. They have retired from the noisy scenes of dissipation; but, unless they become methodists, the solitude of the select society of their family connections of acquaintance, has presented only a fearful void; consequently, nervous complaints, and all the vapourish train of idleness, rendered them quite useless, and far more unhappy, than when they joined the giddy throng.

wretched because it deprives them of all employment, by quenching the hopes and fears that set in motion their sluggish minds.

If such be the force of habit; if such be the bondage of folly, how carefully ought we to guard the mind from storing up vicious associations; and equally careful should we be to cultivate the understanding, to save the poor wight from the weak dependent state of even harmless ignorance. For it is the right use of reason alone which makes us independent of every thing—excepting the unclouded Reason— 'Whose service is perfect freedom.'

Chapter XIII

Some Instances of the Folly Which the Ignorance of Women Generates; with Concluding Reflections on the Moral Improvement That a Revolution in Female Manners Might Naturally Be Expected to Produce

There are many follies, in some degree, peculiar to women: sins against reason of commission as well as of omission; but all flowing from ignorance or prejudice, I shall only point out such as appear to be particularly injurious to their moral character. And in animadverting on them, I wish especially to prove, that the weakness of mind and body, which men have endeavoured, impelled by various motives, to perpetuate, prevents their discharging the peculiar duty of their sex: for when weakness of body will not permit them to suckle their children, and weakness of mind makes them spoil their tempers—is woman in a natural state?

* * *

Section II

Another instance of that feminine weakness of character, often produced by a confined education, is a romantic twist of the mind, which has been very properly termed *sentimental*.

Women subjected by ignorance to their sensations, and only taught to look for happiness in love, refine on sensual feelings, and adopt metaphysical notions respecting that passion, which lead them shamefully to neglect the duties of life, and frequently in the midst of these sublime refinements they plump into actual vice.

These are the women who are amused by the reveries of the stupid novelists, who, knowing little of human nature, work up stale tales, and describe meretricious scenes, all re-

tailed in a sentimental jargon, which equally tend to corrupt the taste, and draw the heart aside from its daily duties. I do not mention the understanding, because never having been exercised, its slumbering energies rest inactive, like the lurking particles of fire which are supposed universally to pervade matter.

Females, in fact, denied all political privileges, and not allowed, as married women, excepting in criminal cases, a civil existence, have their attention naturally drawn from the interest of the whole community to that of the minute parts, though the private duty of any member of society must be very imperfectly performed when not connected with the general good. The mighty business of female life is to please, and restrained from entering into more important concerns by political and civil oppression, sentiments become events, and reflection deepens what it should, and would have effaced, if the understanding had been allowed to take a wider range.

But, confined to trifling employments, they naturally imbibe opinions which the only kind of reading calculated to interest an innocent frivolous mind, inspires. Unable to grasp any thing great, is it surprising that they find the reading of history a very dry task, and disquisitions addressed to the understanding intolerably tedious, and almost unintelligible? Thus are they necessarily dependent on the novelist for amusement. Yet, when I exclaim against novels, I mean when contrasted with those works which exercise the understanding and regulate the imagination.—For any kind of reading I think better than leaving a blank still a blank, because the mind must receive a degree of enlargement and obtain a little strength by a slight exertion of its thinking powers; besides, even the productions that are only addressed to the imagination, raise the reader a little above the gross gratification of appetites, to which the mind has not given a shade of delicacy.

This observation is the result of experience; for I have known several notable women, and one in particular, who was a very good woman—as good as such a narrow mind would allow her to be, who took care that her daughters (three in number) should never see a novel. As she was a woman of fortune and fashion, they had various masters to attend them, and a sort of menial governess to watch their footsteps. From their masters they learned how tables, chairs, &c. were called in French and Italian; but as the few books thrown in their way were far above their capacities, or devotional, they neither acquired ideas nor sentiments, and passed their time, when not compelled to repeat *words,* in dressing, quarrelling with each other, or conversing with their maids by stealth, till they were brought into company as marriageable.

Their mother, a widow, was busy in the mean time in keeping up her connections, as she termed a numerous acquaintance, lest her girls should want a proper introduction into the great world. And these young ladies, with minds vulgar in every sense of the word, and spoiled tempers, entered life puffed up with notions of their own consequence, and looking down with contempt on those who could not vie with them in dress and parade.

With respect to love, nature, or their nurses, had taken care to teach them the physical meaning of the word; and, as they had few topics of conversation, and fewer refinements of sentiment, they expressed their gross wishes not in very delicate phrases, when they spoke freely, talking of matrimony.

Could these girls have been injured by the perusal of novels? I almost forgot a shade in the character of one of them; she affected a simplicity bordering on folly, and with a simper would utter the most immodest remarks and questions, the full meaning of which she had learned whilst secluded from the world, and afraid to speak in her mother's presence, who governed with a high hand: they were all educated, as she prided herself, in a most exemplary manner; and read their chapters and psalms before breakfast, never touching a silly novel.

This is only one instance; but I recollect many other women who, not led by degrees to proper studies, and not permitted to choose for themselves, have indeed been overgrown children; or have obtained, by mixing in the world, a little of what is termed common sense: that is, a distinct manner of seeing common occurrences, as they stand detached: but what deserves the name of intellect, the power of gaining general or abstract ideas, or even intermediate ones, was out of the question. Their minds were quiescent, and when they were not roused by sensible objects and employments of that kind, they were low-spirited, would cry, or go to sleep.

When, therefore, I advise my sex not to read such flimsy works, it is to induce them to read something superiour; for I coincide in opinion with a sagacious man, who, having a daughter and niece under his care, pursued a very different plan with each.

The niece, who had considerable abilities, had, before she was left to his guardianship, been indulged in desultory reading. Her he endeavoured to lead, and did lead to history and moral essays; but his daughter, whom a fond weak mother had indulged, and who consequently was averse to every thing like application, he allowed to read novels: and used to justify his conduct by saying that if she ever attained a relish for reading them, he should have some foundation to work upon; and that erroneous opinions were better than none at all.

In fact the female mind has been so totally neglected, that knowledge was only to be acquired from this muddy source, till from reading novels some women of superiour talents learned to despise them.

The best method, I believe, that can be adopted to correct a fondness for novels is to ridicule them: not indiscriminately, for then it would have little effect; but, if a judicious person, with some turn for humour, would read several to a young girl, and point out both by tones, and apt comparisons with pathetic incidents and heroic characters in history, how foolishly and ridiculously they caricatured human nature, just opinions might be substituted instead of romantic sentiments.

In one respect, however, the majority of both sexes resemble, and equally shew a want of taste and modesty. Ignorant women, forced to be chaste to preserve their reputation, allow their imagination to revel in the unnatural and meretricious scenes sketched by the novel writers of the day, slighting as insipid the sober dignity and matron graces of history,[10] whilst men carry the same vitiated taste into life, and fly for amusement to the wanton, from the unsophisticated charms of virtue, and the grave respectability of sense.

Besides, the reading of novels makes women, and particularly ladies of fashion, very fond of using strong expressions and superlatives in conversation: and, though the dissipated artificial life which they lead prevents their cherishing any strong legitimate passion, the language of passion in affected tones slips for ever from their glib tongues, and every trifle produces those phosphoric bursts which only mimick in the dark the flame of passion.

---

[10] [Wollstonecraft] I am not alluding to that superiority of mind which leads to the creation of ideal beauty, when he, surveyed with a penetrating eye, appears a tragi-comedy, in which little can be seen to satisfy the heart without the help of fancy.

William Blake

1757–1627

Although Blake's recent reputation and influence have been considerable, his poetry and other writings were virtually unknown in his day. His reputation then was almost entirely as an engraver. He anticipated the interests of a number of Romantic critics who did not know of his work. In *The Marriage of Heaven and Hell* there is a highly condensed myth of the dissociation of reason and imagination similar to Schiller's in his *Letters on the Aesthetic Education of Man* (below, page 461), though Blake pushes the dissociation farther back in time. His notion of the ancient poets as the makers of language has something in common with Vico's (above, page 317). In his discussion of his painting of Chaucer's Canterbury pilgrims there is a germ of a theory of literary archetypes that influenced the work of Northrop Frye (below, page 1136). This interest, which is closely tied to an interest in myth, is developed in a description he wrote of his painting, now lost, called *The Ancient Britons.* The artist's attention to "minute particulars" is the foundation of his argument with Sir Joshua Reynolds in his often severe annotations to Reynolds's *Discourses* (above, page 394).

Blake's distinction between "vision" (which he sometimes calls "allegory addressed to the intellectual powers") and allegory addressed to the "corporeal understanding" arises from his violent distaste for generalized abstraction as the aim of art and is roughly allied to Romantic distinctions between symbolism and allegory. Most of Blake's criticism is immediately concerned with painting, but it is not improper to apply it generally to literature. His own long poems, *The Four Zoas, Milton,* and *Jerusalem,* carry into practice, indeed include a vision of, the artistic activity he advocates in his prose.

Blake raises numerous other issues connected to those already mentioned. He anticipates to some extent Benedetto Croce's argument that intuition and expression are the same and goes even further toward the view that the creative act is unified: "Invention depends altogether upon execution and organization." He objects strenuously to the empiricist notion in Locke (above, page 281), Burke (above, page 335), and Reynolds that we create only by recombining the simple ideas of sense data into new arrangements. This sort of activity he attributes scornfully to the "daughters of memory," identifying "memory" with the mechanical combination of simple ideas. He believes that man does not come into the world a *tabula rasa.* For him, the opinions of Locke, Burke, and Reynolds lead to allegory addressed to the corporeal understanding, the generalized abstractions that disregard particular experience: "What is general nature? Is there such a thing? Strictly speaking, all knowledge is particular." Blake's idea of universality proceeds from identifying microcosm with macrocosm on the principle of synecdoche, a sophistication of what Vico called "poetic logic" (above, page 319) and Cassirer later (below, page 1016) called "mythical thinking."

The standard edition of Blake's writings is *The Complete Poetry and Prose of William Blake,* edited by David V. Erdman, revised edition (1982). The fullest biography is that of G. E. Bentley, Jr., *Stranger from Paradise* (2001). See Northrop Frye, *Fearful Symmetry* (1947) and his "Blake's Treatment of the Archetype," *English Institute Essays* (1950); David V. Erdman, *Blake: Prophet Against Empire* (1954); W. J. T. Mitchell, *Blake's Composite Art* (1978); Morris Eaves, *Blake's Theory of Art* (1982); Nelson Hilton, *Literal Imagination: Blake's Vision of Words* (1983); Robert N. Essick, *William Blake and the Language of Adam* (1989); Hazard Adams, ed., *Critical Essays on William Blake* (1991); Morris Eaves, ed., *The Cambridge Companion to William Blake* (2003).

from

The Marriage of Heaven and Hell

The ancient poets animated all sensible objects with gods or geniuses, calling them by the names and adorning them with the properties of woods, rivers, mountains, lakes, cities, nations, and whatever their enlarged and numerous senses could perceive.

And particularly they studied the genius of each city and country, placing it under its mental deity.

Till a system was formed, which some took advantage of, and enslaved the vulgar by attempting to realize or abstract the mental deities from their objects: thus began priesthood;

Choosing forms of worship from poetic tales.[1]

And at length they pronounced that the gods had ordered such things.

Thus men forgot that all deities reside in the human breast.

from

Letter to Thomas Butts[1]

Allegory addressed to the intellectual powers, while it is altogether hidden from the corporeal understanding, is my def-

inition of the most sublime poetry; it is also somewhat in the same manner defined by Plato.

from

Annotations to Reynolds' *Discourses*

Malone's Account of Reynolds' Life and Writings

Page III

[Blake] Invention depends altogether upon execution or organization; as that is right or wrong so is the invention perfect or imperfect. Whoever is set to undermine the execution of art is set to destroy art. Michelangelo's[1] art depends on Michelangelo's execution altogether.

Page XVI

[Reynolds] I proceeded to copy some of those excellent works. I viewed them again and again. . . . In a short time a new taste and new perceptions began to dawn on me. . . . The truth is, that if these works had really been what I expected, they would have contained beauties superficial and alluring, but by no means such as would have enti-

---

The Marriage of Heaven and Hell was composed and engraved sometime between 1790 and 1793. The excerpt is from Plate 11.
[1] This condensed history of human culture can be compared to Vico's treatment of the development of the culture of the "gentes" (above, page 314) and Schiller's discussion of the dissociation of the intuitive from the speculative (below, page 461).
[1] Thomas Butts (c. 1757–1844 or 1846), patron to Blake. See G. E. Bentley, Jr., "Thomas Butts, White Collar Maecinas," *PMLA* LXXI, 5 (December 1956).

Blake's annotations to Reynolds's *Discourses* were made around 1808 in a copy of *The Works of Sir Joshua Reynolds,* second edition (in three volumes, 1798), edited by Edmond Malone. Blake annotated Malone's introduction and the first eight discourses. The complete texts of *Discourse III* and *Discourse IV* appear above, page 394.
[1] Michelangelo Buonarroti (1475–1564), Italian painter, sculptor, and poet.

tled them to the great reputation which they have so long and so justly obtained.

All this concession is to prove that genius is acquired, as follows in the next page.

Page XVII

I am now clearly of opinion, that a relish for the higher excellencies of art is an acquired taste, which no man ever possessed without long cultivation, and great labor . . . we are often ashamed of our apparent dullness; as if it were to be expected that our minds, like tinder, should instantly catch fire from the divine spark of Raphael's genius.

A mock.

Page XIX

How incapable of producing anything of their own, those are, who have spent most of their time in making finished copies, is an observation well known to all who are conversant with our art.

Finished? What does he mean? Niggling without the correct and definite outline? If he means that copying correctly is a hindrance, he is a liar, for that is the only school to the language of art.

Page XCVIII

But this disposition to abstractions, to generalizing and classification, is the great glory of the human mind.

To generalize is to be an idiot. To particularize is the alone distinction of merit. General knowledges are those knowledges that idiots possess.

Discourse I

Page 14

But young men have not only this frivolous ambition of being thought masters of execution, incit-

ing them on one hand, but also their natural sloth tempting them on the other.

Execution is the chariot of genius.

Discourse II

Page 32

How incapable those are of producing anything of their own, who have spent much of their time in making finished copies, is well known to all who are conversant with our art.

This is most false, for no one can ever design till he has learned the language of art by making many finished copies both of nature and art and of whatever comes in his way from earliest childhood. The difference between a bad artist and a good one is: the bad artist seems to copy a great deal. The good one really does copy a great deal.

Page 33

The great use in copying, if it be at all useful, should seem to be in learning to color; yet even coloring will never be perfectly attained by servilely copying the model before you.

Contemptible: Servile copying is the great merit of copying.

Page 34

Following these rules, and using these precautions, when you have clearly and distinctly learned in what good coloring consists, you cannot do better than have recourse to nature herself, who is always at hand, and in comparison of whose true splendor the best colored pictures are but faint and feeble.

Nonsense: Every eye sees differently. As the eye, such the object.

Page 35

Instead of copying the touches of those great masters, copy only their conceptions. . . . Labor to invent on their general principles and way of thinking. . . . how a Michelangelo or Raphael[2] would have treated this subject.

General principles again: Unless you consult particulars you cannot even know or see Michelangelo or Raphael or anything else.

But as mere enthusiasm will carry you but a little way. . . .

Mere enthusiasm is the all in all! Bacon's philosophy has ruined England. Bacon is only Epicurus over again.[3]

Page 37

Few have been taught to any purpose who have not been their own teachers.

True.

Page 40

A facility of drawing, like that of playing upon a musical instrument, cannot be acquired but by an infinite number of acts.

True.

Page 48

The well-grounded painter . . . is contented that all shall be as great as himself who have undergone the same fatigue. . . .

The man who asserts that there is no such thing as softness in art, and that everything in art is definite and determinate, has not been told this by practice, but by inspiration and vision, because vision is determinate and perfect, and he copies that without fatigue, everything being definite and determinate. Softness is produced alone by comparative strength and weakness in the marking out of the forms. I say these principles could never be found out by the study of nature without con- or innate science.

Discourse III

Page 50

A work of genius is a work "not to be obtained by the invocation of memory and her siren daughters, but by devout prayer to that eternal spirit, who can enrich with all utterance and knowledge and sends out his seraphim with the hallowed fire of his altar to touch and purify the lips of whom he pleases."

MILTON

The following discourse is particularly interesting to blockheads, as it endeavors to prove that there is no such thing as inspiration and that any man of a plain understanding may by thieving from others become a Michelangelo.

Page 52

The wish of the genuine painter must be more extensive: instead of endeavoring to amuse mankind with the minute neatness of his imitations, he must endeavor to improve them by the grandeur of his ideas.

Without minute neatness of execution the sublime cannot exist! Grandeur of ideas is founded on precision of ideas.

Page 54

The moderns are not less convinced than the ancients of this superior power existing in the art; nor less sensible of its effects.

I wish that this was true.

Page 55

Such is the warmth with which both the ancients and moderns speak of this divine principle of the art;

And such is the coldness with which Reynolds speaks! And such is his enmity.

. . . enthusiastic admiration seldom promotes knowledge.

---

[2]Raphael Santi (1483–1520), Italian painter.
[3]Sir Francis Bacon (above, page 234). Epicurus (341–270 B.C.), Greek philosopher, founder of Epicureanism.

Enthusiastic admiration is the first principle of knowledge and its last. Now he begins to degrade, to deny and to mock.

> . . . He examines his own mind, and perceives there nothing of that divine inspiration, with which, he is told, so many others have been favored.

The man who on examining his own mind finds nothing of inspiration ought not dare to be an artist; he is a fool and a cunning knave suited to the purposes of evil demons.

Page 56

> He never traveled to heaven to gather new ideas; and he finds himself possessed of no other qualifications than what mere common observation and a plain understanding can confer.

The man who never in his mind and thoughts traveled to heaven is no artist.

Artists who are above a plain understanding are mocked and destroyed by this president of fools.

> But on this, as upon many other occasions, we ought to distinguish how much is to be given to enthusiasm, and how much to reason . . . taking care . . . not to lose . . . that solidity and truth of principle, upon which alone we can reason, and may be enabled to practice.

It is evident that Reynolds wished none but fools to be in the arts and in order to this, he calls all others vague enthusiasts or madmen.

What has reasoning to do with the art of painting?

Page 57

> . . . most people err, not so much from want of capacity to find their object, as from not knowing what object to pursue.

The man who does not know what object to pursue is an idiot.

> This great ideal perfection and beauty are not to be sought in the heavens, but upon the earth.

A lie!

> They are about us, and upon every side of us.

A lie!

> But the power of discovering what is deformed in nature, or in other words, what is particular and uncommon, can be acquired only by experience;

A lie!

Page 58

> . . . and the whole beauty of the art consists, in my opinion, in being able to get above all singular forms, local customs, particularities, and details of every kind.

A folly! Singular and particular detail is the foundation of the sublime.

> All the objects which are exhibited to our view by nature, upon close examination will be found to have their blemishes and defects. The most beautiful forms have something about them like weakness, minuteness, or imperfection.

Minuteness is their whole beauty.

> This idea of the perfect state of nature, which the artist calls the ideal beauty, is the great leading principle by which works of genius are conducted.

Knowledge of ideal beauty is not to be acquired. It is born with us. Innate ideas are in every man, born with him; they are truly himself. The man who says that we have no innate ideas must be a fool and knave, having no conscience or innate science.

Page 60

> Thus it is from a reiterated experience and a close comparison of the objects in nature, that an artist becomes possessed of the idea of that central form . . . from which every deviation is deformity.

One central form composed of all other forms being granted, it does not therefore follow that all other forms are deformity.

All forms are perfect in the poet's mind, but these are not abstracted nor compounded from nature, but are from imagination.

Page 61

Even the great Bacon treats with ridicule the idea of confusing proportion to rules, or, of producing beauty by selection.

The great Bacon he is called—I call him the little Bacon—says that everything must be done by experiment; his first principle is unbelief, and yet here he says that art must be produced without such method. He is like Sir Joshua, full of self-contradiction and knavery.

There is a rule, obtained out of general nature, to contradict which is to fall into deformity.

What is general nature? Is there such a thing? What is general knowledge? Is there such a thing? Strictly speaking, all knowledge is particular.

Page 62

To the principle I have laid down, that the idea of beauty in each species of beings is an invariable one, it may be objected, that in every particular species there are various central forms, which are separate and distinct from each other, and yet are each undeniably beautiful.

Here he loses sight of a central form and gets into many central forms.

Page 63

It is true, indeed, that these figures are each perfect in their kind, though of different characters and proportions; but still none of them is the representation of an individual, but of a class.

Every class is individual.[4]

Thus, though the forms of childhood and age differ exceedingly, there is a common form in childhood, and a common form in age, which is the more perfect, as it is more remote from all peculiarities.

There is no end to the follies of this man. Childhood and age are equally belonging to every class.

. . . though the most perfect forms of each of the general divisions of the human figure are ideal and superior to any individual form of that class, yet the highest perfection of the human figure is not to be found in any one of them. It is not in the *Hercules,* nor in the *Gladiator,* nor in the *Apollo.* . . .

Here he comes again to his central form.

Page 64

There is, likewise, a kind of symmetry, or proportion, which may properly be said to belong to deformity. A figure lean or corpulent, tall or short, though deviating from beauty, may still have a certain union of the various parts.

The symmetry of deformity is a pretty foolery. Can any man who thinks talk so? Leanness or fatness is not deformity, but Reynolds thought character itself extravagance and deformity. Age and youth are not classes, but properties of each class; so are leanness and fatness.

Page 65

When the artist has by diligent attention acquired a clear and distinct idea of beauty and symmetry; when he has reduced the variety of nature to the abstract idea. . . .

What folly!

Page 67

. . . [the painter] must divest himself of all prejudices in favor of his age or country; he must disregard all local and temporary ornaments, and look only on those general habits, which are everywhere and always the same.

---

[4]Here Blake seems to adopt a view like that which Vico attributes to his primitive "giants" and their "poetic logic," above, page 319.

Generalizing in everything, the man would soon be a fool, but a cunning fool.

Page 71

Albert Dürer, as Vasari[5] has justly remarked, would, probably, have been one of the first painters of his age . . . had he been initiated into those great principles of the art, which were so well understood and practiced by his contemporaries in Italy.

What does this mean, "would have been one of the first painters of his age"? Albert Dürer is, not would have been. Besides, let them look at Gothic figures and Gothic buildings and not talk of Dark Ages or of any age. Ages are all equal. But genius is always above the age.

Page 74

I should be sorry, if what is here recommended, should be at all understood to countenance a careless or indetermined manner of painting. For though the painter is to overlook the accidental discriminations of nature, he is to exhibit distinctly, and with precision, the general forms of things.

Here he is for determinate and yet for indeterminate. Distinct general form cannot exist. Distinctness is particular, not general.

Page 75

A firm and determined outline is one of the characteristics of the great style in painting; and let me add, that he who possesses the knowledge of the exact form which every part of nature ought to have, will be fond of expressing that knowledge with correctness and precision in all his works.

A noble sentence! Here is a sentence, which overthrows all his book.

To conclude; I have endeavored to reduce the idea of beauty to general principles. . . .

---

[5] Albrecht Dürer (1471–1528), German painter and engraver; Giorgio Vasari (1511–1574), biographer of artists.

. . . Bacon's philosophy makes both statesmen and artists fools and knaves.

Discourse IV

Page 78

The two following discourses are particularly calculated for the setting ignorant and vulgar artists as models of execution in art. Let him who will, follow such advice. I will not. I know that the man's execution is as his conception and no better.

Page 79

The value and rank of every art is in proportion to the mental labor employed in it, or the mental pleasure produced by it.

Why does he not always allow this?

Page 80

I have formerly observed that perfect form is produced by leaving out particularities, and retaining only general ideas. . . .

General ideas again!

Invention in painting does not imply the invention of the subject; for that is commonly supplied by the poet or historian.

All but names of persons and places is invention both in poetry and painting.

Page 82

. . . the usual and most dangerous error is on the side of minuteness, and therefore I think caution most necessary where most have failed.

Here is nonsense.

Page 83

The general idea constitutes real excellence. All smaller things, however perfect in their way, are to be sacrificed without mercy to the greater.

Sacrifice the parts, what becomes of the whole?

> Even in portraits, the grace, and, we may add, the likeness, consists more in taking the general air, than in observing the exact similitude of every feature.

How ignorant!

Page 86

> A painter of portraits retains the individual likeness; a painter of history shows the man by showing his actions.

If he does not show the man as well as the action, he is a poor artist.

Page 106

> A history painter paints man in general; a portrait painter, a particular man, and consequently a defective model.

A history painter paints the hero, and not man in general, but most minutely in particular.

Page 111

> The errors of genius ... are pardonable, and none even of the more exalted painters are wholly free of them. ...

Genius has no error; it is ignorance that is error.

Pages 117–18

> If you mean to preserve the most perfect beauty in its most perfect state, you cannot express the passions, all of which produce distortion and deformity, more or less, in the most beautiful faces.

What nonsense!
    Passion and expression is beauty itself. The face that is incapable of passion and expression is deformity itself. Let it be painted and patched and praised and advertised forever, it will only be admired by fools.

Page 119

> We can easily, like the ancients, suppose a Jupiter to be possessed of all those powers and perfections which the subordinate deities were endowed with separately. Yet, when they employed their art to represent him, they confined his character to majesty alone.

False: the ancients were chiefly attentive to complicated and minute discrimination of character; it is the whole of art.

Page 120

> [Pliny wrongfully] observes ... in a statue ... three different characters.

Reynolds cannot bear expression.

Discourse VI

Page 154

> We may venture to say, that as art shall advance. ...

If art was progressive we should have had Michelangelos and Raphaels to succeed and to improve upon each other. But it is not so. Genius dies with its possessor and comes not again till another is born with it.[6]

Page 155

> It must of necessity be, that even works of genius, like every other effect, as they must have their cause, must likewise have their rules.

Identities or things are neither cause nor effect. They are eternal.

---

[6]Elsewhere Blake wrote, "To suppose that art can go beyond the finest specimens of art that are now in the world, is not knowing what art is; it is being blind to the gift of the spirit." The attack on art as progressive is shared by most citics after Blake. It is part of an attempt to distinguish art from science. In Blake and the Romantics it begins with the close identification of the individual artist with his work.

Page 157

. . . our minds should be habituated to the contemplation of excellence; and that, far from being contented to make such habits the discipline of our youth only, we should to the last moment of our lives, continue a settled intercourse with all the true examples of grandeur. Their inventions are not only the food of our infancy, but the substance which supplies the fullest maturity of our vigor.

Reynolds thinks that man learns all that he knows. I say on the contrary that man brings all that he has or can have into the world with him. Man is born like a garden ready planted and sown. This world is too poor to produce one seed.

Page 180

Men who although thus bound down by the almost invincible powers of early habits, have still exerted extraordinary abilities within their narrow and confined circle; and have, from the natural vigor of their mind, given a very interesting expression and force and energy to their works.

He who can be bound down is no genius. Genius cannot be bound; it may be rendered indignant and outrageous. "Oppression makes the wise man mad" (Solomon).

Discourse VII

Page 188

The purpose of the following discourse is to prove that taste and genius are not of heavenly origin and that all who have supposed that they are so are to be considered as weak-headed fanatics.

The obligations Reynolds has laid on bad artists of all classes will at all times make them his admirers, but most especially for this discourse, in which it is proved that the stupid are born with faculties equal to other men, only they have not cultivated them because they thought it not worth the trouble.

Page 194

We will allow a poet to express his meaning, when his meaning is not well known to himself, with a certain degree of obscurity, as it is one source of the sublime.

Obscurity is neither the source of the sublime nor of anything else.

But when, in plain prose, we gravely talk of courting the muse in shady bowers; waiting the call and inspiration of Genius . . . sagaciously observing how much the wild freedom and liberty of imagination is cramped by attention to established rules . . . we generally rest contented with mere words, or at best entertain notions not only groundless but pernicious.

The ancients and the wisest of the moderns were of the opinion that Reynolds condemns and laughs at.

Page 195

. . . scarce a poet is to be found . . . who preserved a sound mind in a sound body, and continued practicing his profession to the very last, whose latter works are not as replete with the fire of imagination, as those which were produced in his more youthful days.

As replete, but not more replete.

To understand literally these metaphors or ideas expressed in poetical language, seems to be equally absurd as to conclude . . .

The ancients did not mean to impose when they affirmed their belief in vision and revelation. Plato was in earnest: Milton was in earnest. They believed that God did visit man really and truly and not as Reynolds pretends.

Page 196

. . . that because painters sometimes represent poets writing from the dictates of a little winged boy or genius, that this same genius really did inform him in a whisper what he was to write; and that he is himself but a mere machine, unconscious of the operations of his own mind.

How very anxious Reynolds is to disprove and condemn spiritual perception!

Page 197

It is supposed that their poems are intuitive, that under the name of genius great works are produced, and under the name of taste an exact judgment given, without our knowing why, and without our being under the least obligation to reason, precept, or experience.

Who ever said this?

* * *

Page 198

. . . I am persuaded, that even among those few who may be called thinkers, the prevalent opinion allows less than it ought to the powers of reason. . . .

The artifice of the Epicurean philosophers is to call all other opinions unsolid and unsubstantial than those which are derived from earth.

We often appear to differ in sentiments from each other, merely from the inaccuracy of terms.

It is not in terms that Reynolds and I disagree. Two contrary opinions can never by any language be made alike. I say, taste and genius are not teachable or acquirable, but are born with us. Reynolds says the contrary.

Page 199

. . . we are obliged to take words as we find them; all we can do is to distinguish the things to which they are applied.

This is false; the fault is not in words, but in things. Locke's opinions of words and their fallaciousness are artful opinions and fallacious also.[7]

Page 200

It is the very same taste which relishes a demonstration in geometry, that is pleased with the re-

semblance of a picture to an original, and touched with the harmony of music.

Demonstration, similitude and harmony are objects of reasoning. Invention, identity and melody are objects of intuition.

Page 201

Coloring is true when it is naturally adapted to the eye, from brightness, from softness, from harmony, from resemblance; because these agree with their object, nature, and therefore are true; as true as mathematical demonstration. . . .

God forbid that truth should be confined to mathematical demonstration!

But beside real, there is also apparent truth, or opinion, or prejudice. With regard to real truth, when it is known, the taste which conforms to it, is, and must be, uniform.

He who does not know truth at sight is unworthy of her notice.

In proportion as these prejudices are known to be generally diffused, or long received, the taste which conforms to them approaches nearer to certainty, and to a sort of resemblance to real science, even where opinions are found to be no better than prejudices.

Here is a great deal to do to prove that all truth is prejudice, for all that is valuable in knowledge is superior to demonstrative science, such as is weighed or measured.

Page 202

As these prejudices become more narrow, more local, more transitory, this secondary taste becomes more and more fantastical. . . .

And so he thinks he has proved that genius and inspiration are all a hum.

* * *

We will take it for granted, that reason is something invariable and fixed in the nature of things. . . .

---

[7] See Locke (above, page 289).

Reason, or a ratio of all we have known, is not the same it shall be when we know more; he therefore takes a falsehood for granted to set out with.

Page 203

. . . we will conclude, that whatever goes under the name of taste, which we can fairly bring under the dominion of reason, must be considered as equally exempt from change.

Now this is supreme fooling.

The arts would lie open forever to caprice and casualty, if those who are to judge of their excellencies had no settled principles by which they are to regulate their decisions. . . .

He may as well say that if man does not lay down settled principles, the sun will not rise in the morning.

Page 204

My notion of nature comprehends not only the forms which nature produces, but also the nature and internal fabric and organization, as I may call it, of the human mind and imagination.

Here is a plain confession that he thinks mind and imagination not to be above the mortal and perishing nature. Such is the end of Epicurean or Newtonian philosophy; it is atheism.

Page 208

This [Poussin's[8] painting of Perseus with Medusa's head] is undoubtedly a subject of great bustle and tumult, and that the first effect of the picture may correspond to the subject, every principle of composition is violated; there is no principal figure, no principal light, no groups. . . . I remember turning from it with disgust. . . .

Reynolds's eye could not bear characteristic coloring or light and shade.

This conduct of Poussin I hold to be entirely improper to imitate. A picture should please at first sight. . . .

Please whom? Some men cannot see a picture except in a dark corner.

Page 209

No one can deny, that violent passions will naturally emit harsh and disagreeable tones. . . .

Violent passions emit the real, good and perfect tones.

Page 214

If it be objected that Rubens[9] judged ill at first in thinking it necessary to make his work so very ornamental, this puts the question upon new ground.

Here it is called ornamental that the Roman and Bolognian schools may be insinuated not to be ornamental.

Page 215

Nobody will dispute but some of the best of the Roman or Bolognian schools would have produced a more learned and more noble work.

Learned and noble is ornamental.

This leads us to another important province of taste, that of weighing the value of the different classes of the art, and of estimating them accordingly.

A fool's balance is no criterion because, though it goes down on the heaviest side, we ought to look what he puts into it.

Page 232

If a European, when he has cut off his beard, and put false hair on his head, or bound up his own natural hair in regular hard knots, as unlike nature as he can possible make it . . . meets a Cherokee Indian, who has . . . laid on with equal care and attention his yellow and red ocher on particular parts of his forehead and cheeks . . . whoever of these two despises the other for this attention to

---

[8] Nicolas Poussin (1594–1665), French painter.

[9] Peter Paul Rubens (1574–1640), Flemish painter.

the fashion of his country, whichever first feels himself provoked to laugh, is the barbarian.

Excellent!

Page 242

In the midst of the highest flights of fancy or imagination, reason ought to preside from first to last. . . .

If this is true, it is a devilish foolish thing to be an artist.

Discourse VIII

Page 244

Burke's *Treatise on the Sublime and Beautiful*[10] is founded on the opinions of Newton and Locke; on this treatise Reynolds has grounded many of his assertions in all his discourses. I read Burke's treatise when very young; at the same time I read Locke on human understanding and Bacon's *Advancement of Learning,*[11] on every one of these books I wrote my opinions, and on looking them over find that my notes on Reynolds in this book are exactly similar. I felt the same contempt and abhorrence then that I do now. They mock inspiration and vision. Inspiration and vision was then, and now is, and I hope will always remain, my element, my eternal dwelling place; how can I then hear it condemned without returning scorn for scorn?

from
A Descriptive Catalogue

from
The Canterbury Pilgrims[1]

The characters of Chaucer's pilgrims are the characters which compose all ages and nations: as one age falls, another rises, different to mortal sight, but to immortals only

the same; for we see the same characters repeated again and again, in animals, vegetables, minerals, and in men; nothing new occurs in identical existence; accident ever varies, substance can never suffer change nor decay.

Of Chaucer's characters, as described in his *Canterbury Tales,* some of the names or titles are altered by time, but the characters themselves forever remain unaltered, and consequently they are the physiognomies or lineaments of universal human life, beyond which nature never steps. Names alter; things never alter. I have known multitudes of those who would have been monks in the age of monkery, who in this deistical age are deists. As Newton numbered the stars, and as Linneus numbered the plants, so Chaucer numbered the classes of men.

from
A Vision of the Last Judgment

The Last Judgment will be when all those are cast away who trouble religion with questions concerning good and evil or eating of the tree of those knowledges or reasonings which hinder the vision of God, turning all into a consuming fire. When imagination, art and science and all intellectual gifts, all the gifts of the Holy Ghost, are looked upon as of no use and only contention remains to man, then the Last Judgment begins, and its vision is seen by the imaginative eye of everyone according to the situation he holds.

The Last Judgment is not fable or allegory, but vision.[1] Fable or allegory are a totally distinct and inferior kind of poetry. Vision or imagination is a representation of what eternally exists, really and unchangeably. Fable or allegory is formed by the daughters of memory. Imagination is surrounded by the daughters of inspiration, who in the aggregate are called Jerusalem. Fable is allegory, but what critics call the fable is vision itself. The Hebrew Bible and the Gospel of Jesus are not allegory, but eternal vision or imagination of all that exists. Note here that fable or allegory is seldom without some vision. *Pilgrim's Progress*[2] is full of it, the Greek poets

---

[10] Above, page 333. Blake attacks particularly Burke's adoption of the theory of the association of ideas.
[11] See above, page 282, and above, page 235.
Blake's *Descriptive Catalogue* was printed for an exhibition of sixteen of his paintings in London in 1809.
[1] Blake executed a painting and engraving of the procession of pilgrims in Geoffrey Chaucer's (c. 1340–1400) *Canterbury Tales* and discusses it at length in the catalogue for his exhibit of 1809.

A Vision of the Last Judgment, Blake's description of his painting *The Last Judgment,* now lost (though there are other last judgments by Blake), was written in 1910 in a manuscript notebook, known for some time as the Rossetti Manuscript.
[1] Compare this with the definition in the letter to Thomas Butts (above, page 448). The language is different, but the thought is the same.
[2] *The Pilgrim's Progress from This World to That Which Is to Come* by John Bunyan (1628–1688).

the same; but allegory and vision ought to be known as two distinct things, and so called for the sake of eternal life. Plato has made Socrates say that poets and prophets do not know or understand what they write or utter; this is a most pernicious falsehood. If they do not, pray, is an inferior kind to be called knowing? Plato confutes himself.

The Last Judgment is one of these stupendous visions. I have represented it as I saw it; to different people it appears differently as everything else does; for though on earth things seem permanent, they are less permanent than a shadow, as we all know too well.

The nature of visionary fancy, or imagination, is very little known, and the eternal nature and permanence of its ever-existent images is considered as less permanent than the things of vegetative and generative nature; yet the oak dies as well as the lettuce, but its eternal image and individuality never dies, but renews by its seed; just so the imaginative image returns by the seed of contemplative thought; the writings of the prophets illustrate these conceptions of the visionary fancy by their various sublime and divine images as seen in the worlds of vision.

Friedrich Schiller

1759–1805

Early in his *Letters on the Aesthetic Education of Man* Schiller proposes his own form of what came to be called, in T. S. Eliot's phrase, the "dissociation of sensibility" (below, page 806). Eliot located the bifurcation of man's sensibility into sense and intellect sometime in the seventeenth century. Schiller places it much earlier. Civilization itself brought about a division in man; the intuitive and the speculative understanding withdrew from each other in defensive hostility; imagination and abstraction stood opposed. The division was fully established by the rise of the state and man's subservence to it.

Schiller's aesthetic speculations express the belief that there is a means by which man can regain his freedom from division, and that the means is art, taken in a very broad sense. Schiller is thus interested in determining the nature of art by explaining its value, indeed its use. But he would eschew the word "use," for it implies utilitarian concerns. He is Kantian, but he goes beyond Kant to formulate his own dialectic. Man possesses two fundamental drives, the sensuous drive *(Stofftrieb)* and the formal drive *(Formtrieb)*. The former is characterized by the domination of sensation and change: "Man in this state is nothing but a unit of quantity, an occupied moment of time." The formal drive, on the other hand, annuls time and change "in its quest for the abstract, eternal, and absolute." From it emerge laws.

These drives demand reconciliation or transcendence in a higher drive, which Schiller calls the play-drive *(Spieltrieb)* and which he associates with art. In play it should be possible for man to "combine the greatest fullness of existence with the highest autonomy and freedom." Play, as in Kant's connection of play with art, is in Schiller nothing trivial. It is the expression of man's fullest nature in aesthetic experience, the healing of division. Schiller describes it much as Kant describes aesthetic "disinterest" and "purposiveness without purpose" (above, page 419). In play the mind is free and self-contained, dominated neither by "sense" nor by "form." By identifying the experiencing of art with freedom Schiller makes huge claims for its cultural value. "Man is more than a match for any of nature's terrors once he knows how to give it form and convert it into an object of his contemplation." Schiller's theory of play thus goes beyond Mazzoni's notion of recreation (above, page 216) and tends to make an ethical principle out of the Kantian aesthetic.

Schiller's most famous theoretical work in addition to the *Letters* is the essay *On Naive and Sentimental Poetry* (1795–1796), in which he speculates on the differences between early and later, more sophisticated poetry in Western culture. The essay represents a concern with the problem of art's relation to the state of culture at a given time. Schiller sought to defend the reflective or "sentimental" poetry of his age in light of a new cultural situation.

Schiller's criticism and writings on aesthetics are in *The Works of Schiller,* edited by N. H. Dole (1902). *Letters on the Aesthetic Education of Man* have been translated by Reginald Snell (1954) and by E. M. Wilkinson and L. A. Willoughby (1967).

Schiller's essays have been edited by Walter Handerer and Daniel O. Dahlstrom (1993). See Victor Basch, *La Poetique de Schiller* (1911); E. C. Welm, *The Philosophy of Schiller in Its Historical Relations* (1912); Frederic Ewen, *The Prestige of Schiller in England 1788–1859* (1932); George Lukacs, "Schiller's Theorie der modernen Literatur," *Goethe und seine Zeit* (1947); Wilham Witte, *Schiller* (1949); Eva Schaper, "Friedrich Schiller: Adventures of a Kantian," *British Journal of Aesthetics* IV (1964), 348–62; Emil Staiger, *Friedrich Schiller* (1967); Ronald Duncan Miller, *Schiller and the Ideal of Freedom* (1970); John Simons, *Friedrich Schiller* (1981); Leonard P. Wassell, *The Philosophical Background of Friedrich Schiller's Aesthetics of Living Form* (1982); Philip J. Kain, *Schiller, Hegel, and Marx* (1982); Lesley Sharpe, *Friedrich Schiller: Drama, Thought, and Politics* (1991); Constantin Behler, *Nostalgic Teleology: Friedrich Schiller and the Schemata of Aesthetic Humanism* (1995).

Letters on the Aesthetic Education of Man

from
Sixth Letter

Closer attention to the character of our age will . . . reveal an astonishing contrast between contemporary forms of humanity and earlier ones, especially the Greek. The reputation for culture and refinement, on which we otherwise rightly pride ourselves *vis-à-vis* humanity in its merely natural state, can avail us nothing against the natural humanity of the Greeks. For they were wedded to all the delights of art and all the dignity of wisdom, without however, like us, falling a prey to their seduction. The Greeks put us to shame not only by a simplicity to which our age is a stranger; they are at the same time our rivals, indeed often our models, in those very excellences with which we are wont to console ourselves for the unnaturalness of our manners. In fullness of form no less than of content, at once philosophic and creative, sensitive and energetic, the Greeks combined the first youth of imagination with the manhood of reason in a glorious manifestation of humanity.

At that first fair awakening of the powers of the mind, sense and intellect did not as yet rule over strictly separate domains; for no dissension had as yet provoked them into hostile partition and mutual demarcation of their frontiers. Poetry had not as yet coquetted with wit, nor speculation prostituted itself to sophistry. Both of them could, when

need arose, exchange functions, since each in its own fashion paid honor to truth. However high the mind might soar, it always drew matter lovingly along with it; and however fine and sharp the distinctions it might make, it never proceeded to mutilate. It did indeed divide human nature into its several aspects, and project these in magnified form into the divinities of its glorious pantheon; but not by tearing it to pieces; rather by combining its aspects in different proportions, for in no single one of their deities was humanity in its entirety ever lacking. How different with us moderns! With us too the image of the human species is projected in magnified form into separate individuals—but as fragments, not in different combinations, with the result that one has to go the rounds from one individual to another in order to be able to piece together a complete image of the species. With us, one might almost be tempted to assert, the various faculties appear as separate in practice as they are distinguished by the psychologist in theory, and we see not merely individuals, but whole classes of men, developing but one part of their potentialities, while of the rest, as in stunted growths, only vestigial traces remain.

I do not underrate the advantages which the human race today, considered as a whole and weighed in the balance of intellect, can boast in the face of what is best in the ancient world. But it has to take up the challenge in serried ranks, and let whole measure itself against whole. What individual modern could sally forth and engage, man against man, with an individual Athenian for the prize of humanity?

Whence this disadvantage among individuals when the species as a whole is at such an advantage? Why was the individual Greek qualified to be the representative of his age, and why can no single modern venture as much? Because it was from all-unifying nature that the former, and from the all-dividing intellect that the latter, received their respective forms.

Schiller's *Briefe über die ästhetische Erziehung des Menschen* was first published in 1795. The text is from *On the Aesthetic Education of Man in a Series of Letters,* edited and translated by E. M. Wilkinson and L. A. Willoughby (Oxford: The Clarendon Press, 1967).

It was civilization itself which inflicted this wound upon modern man. Once the increase of empirical knowledge, and more exact modes of thought, made sharper divisions between the sciences inevitable, and once the increasingly complex machinery of state necessitated a more rigorous separation of ranks and occupations, then the inner unity of human nature was severed too, and a disastrous conflict set its harmonious powers at variance. The intuitive and the speculative understanding now withdrew in hostility to take up positions in their respective fields, whose frontiers they now began to guard with jealous mistrust; and with this confining of our activity to a particular sphere we have given ourselves a master within, who not infrequently ends by suppressing the rest of our potentialities. While in the one a riotous imagination ravages the hard-won fruits of the intellect, in another the spirit of abstraction stifles the fire at which the heart should have warmed itself and the imagination been kindled.

This disorganization, which was first started within man by civilization and learning, was made complete and universal by the new spirit of government. It was scarcely to be expected that the simple organization of the early republics should have survived the simplicity of early manners and conditions; but instead of rising to a higher form of organic existence it degenerated into a crude and clumsy mechanism. That polypoid character of the Greek states, in which every individual enjoyed an independent existence but could, when need arose, grow into the whole organism, now made way for an ingenious clockwork, in which, out of the piecing together of innumerable but lifeless parts, a mechanical kind of collective life ensued. State and church, law and customs, were now torn asunder; enjoyment was divorced from labor, the means from the end, the effort from the reward. Everlastingly chained to a single little fragment of the whole, man himself develops into nothing but a fragment; everlastingly in his ear the monotonous sound of the wheel that he turns, he never develops the harmony of his being, and instead of putting the stamp of humanity upon his own nature, he becomes nothing more than the imprint of his occupation or of his specialized knowledge. But even that meager, fragmentary participation, by which individual members of the state are still linked to the whole, does not depend upon forms which they spontaneously prescribe for themselves (for how could one entrust to their freedom of action a mechanism so intricate and so fearful of light and enlightenment?); it is dictated to them with meticulous exactitude by means of a formulary which inhibits all freedom of thought. The dead letter takes the place of living understanding, and a good memory is a safer guide than imagination and feeling.

Twelfth Letter

Towards the accomplishment of this twofold task—of giving reality to the necessity within, and subjecting to the law of necessity of reality without—we are impelled by two opposing forces which, since they drive us to the realization of their object, may aptly be termed drives. The first of these, which I will call the sensuous drive, proceeds from the physical existence of man, or his sensuous nature. Its business is to set him within the limits of time, and to turn him into matter—not to provide him with matter, since that, of course, would presuppose a free activity of the person capable of receiving such matter, and distinguishing it from the self as from that which persists. By matter in this context we understand nothing more than change, or reality which occupies time. Consequently this drive demands that there shall be change, that time shall have a content. This state, which is nothing but time occupied by content, is called sensation, and it is through this alone that physical existence makes itself known.

Since everything that exists in time exists as a succession, the very fact of something existing at all means that everything else is excluded. When we strike a note on an instrument, only this single note, of all those it is capable of emitting, is actually realized; when man is sensible of the present, the whole infinitude of his possible determinations is confined to this single mode of his being. Wherever, therefore, this drive functions exclusively, we inevitably find the highest degree of limitation. Man in this state is nothing but a unit of quantity, an occupied moment of time—or rather, he is not at all, for his personality is suspended as long as he is ruled by sensation, and swept along by the flux of time.[1]

The domain of this drive embraces the whole extent of man's finite being. And since form is never made manifest except in some material, nor the absolute except through the medium of limitation, it is indeed to this sensuous drive that

---

[1] [Schiller] For this condition of self-loss under the dominion of feeling linguistic usage has the very appropriate expression: to be beside oneself, i.e., to be outside of one's own self. Although this turn of phrase is only used when sensation is intensified into passion, and the condition becomes more marked by being prolonged, it can nevertheless be said that everyone is beside himself as long as he does nothing but feel. To return from this condition to self-possession is termed, equally aptly: to be oneself again, i.e., to return into one's own self, to restore one's person. Of someone who has fainted, by contrast, we do not say that he is beside himself, but that he is away from himself, i.e., he has been rapt away from his self, whereas in the former case he is merely not in his self. Consequently, someone who has come out of a faint has merely come to himself, which state is perfectly compatible with being beside oneself.

the whole of man's phenomenal existence is ultimately tied. But although it is this drive alone which awakens and develops the potentialities of man, it is also this drive alone which makes their complete fulfillment impossible. With indestructible chains it binds the ever-soaring spirit to the world of sense, and summons abstraction from its most unfettered excursions into the infinite back to the limitations of the present. Thought may indeed escape it for the moment, and a firm will triumphantly resist its demands; but suppressed nature soon resumes her rights, and presses for reality of existence, for some content to our knowing and some purpose for our doing.

The second of the two drives, which we may call the formal drive, proceeds from the absolute existence of man, or from his rational nature, and is intent on giving him the freedom to bring harmony into the diversity of his manifestations, and to affirm his person among all his changes of condition. Since this person, being an absolute and indivisible unity, can never be at variance with itself, since we are to all eternity we ourselves) that drive which insists on affirming the personality can never demand anything but that which is binding upon it to all eternity; hence it decides forever as it decides for this moment, and commands for this moment what it commands forever. Consequently it embraces the whole sequence of time, which is as much as to say: it annuls time and annuls change. It wants the real to be necessary and eternal, and the eternal and the necessary to be real. In other words, it insists on truth and on the right.

If the first drive only furnishes cases, this second one gives laws—laws for every judgment, where it is a question of knowledge, laws for every will, where it is a question of action. Whether it is a case of knowing an object, i.e., of attributing objective validity to a condition of our subject, or of acting upon knowledge, i.e., of making an objective principle the determining motive of our condition—in both cases we wrest this our condition from the jurisdiction of time, and endow it with reality for all men and all times, that is with universality and necessity. Feeling can only say: this is true for this individual and at this moment, and another moment, another individual can come along and revoke assertions made thus under the impact of momentary sensation. But once thought pronounces: that is, it decides forever and aye, and the validity of its verdict is guaranteed by the personality itself, which defies all change. Inclination can only say: this is good for you as an individual and for your present need; but your individuality and your present need will be swept away by change, and what you now so ardently desire will one day become the object of your aversion. But once the moral feeling

says: this shall be, it decides forever and aye—once you confess truth because it is truth, and practice justice because it is justice, then you have made an individual case into a law for all cases, and treated one moment of your life as if it were eternity.

Where, then, the formal drive holds sway, and the pure object acts within us, we experience the greatest enlargement of being: all limitations disappear, and from the mere unit of quantity to which the poverty of his senses reduced him, man has raised himself to a unity of ideas embracing the whole realm of phenomena. During this operation we are no longer in time; time, with its whole never-ending succession, is in us. We are no longer individuals; we are species. The judgment of all minds is expressed through our own, the choice of all hearts is represented by our action.

Thirteenth Letter

At first sight nothing could seem more diametrically opposed than the tendencies of these two drives, the one pressing for change, the other for changelessness. And yet it is these two drives which, between them, exhaust our concept of humanity, and make a third fundamental drive which might possibly reconcile the two a completely unthinkable concept. How, then, are we to restore the unity of human nature which seems to be utterly destroyed by this primary and radical opposition?

It is true that their tendencies do indeed conflict with each other, but—and this is the point to note—not in the same objectives, and things which never make contact cannot collide. The sensuous drive does indeed demand change; but it does not demand the extension of this to the person and its domain, does not demand a change of principles. The formal drive insists on unity and persistence—but it does not require the condition to be stabilized as well as the person, does not require identity of sensation. The two are, therefore, not by nature opposed; and if they nevertheless seem to be so, it is because they have become opposed through a wanton transgression of nature, through mistaking their nature and function, and confusing their spheres of operation.[2] To watch over

---

[2] [Schiller] Once you postulate a primary, and therefore necessary, antagonism between these two drives, there is, of course, no other means of maintaining unity in man than by unconditionally subordinating the sensuous drive to the rational. From this, however, only uniformity can result, never harmony, and man goes on forever being divided. Subordination there must, of course, be; but it must be reciprocal. For even though it is true that limitation can never be the source of the absolute, and hence freedom never be dependent upon time, it is no less certain that the absolute can of itself never be the source of limitation, or a condition in time be dependent upon freedom. Both principles are, therefore, at once subordinated to each other and coordinated with each

these, and secure for each of these two drives its proper frontiers, is the task of culture, which is, therefore, in duty bound to do justice to both drives equally: not simply to maintain the rational against the sensuous, but the sensuous against the rational too. Hence its business is twofold: first, to preserve the life of sense against the encroachments of freedom; and second, to secure the personality against the forces of sensation. The former it achieves by developing our capacity for feeling, the latter by developing our capacity for reason.

Since the world is extension in time, i.e., change, the perfection of that faculty which connects man with the world will have to consist in maximum changeability and maximum extensity. Since the person is persistence within change, the perfection of that faculty which is to oppose change will have to be maximum autonomy and maximum intensity. The more facets his receptivity develops, the more labile it is, and the more surface it presents to phenomena, so much more world does man apprehend, and all the more potentialities does he develop in himself. The more power and depth the personality achieves, and the more freedom reason attains, so much more world does man comprehend, and all the more form does he create outside of himself. His education will therefore consist, firstly, in procuring for the receptive faculty the most manifold contracts with the world, and, within the purview of feeling, intensifying passivity to the utmost; secondly, in securing for the determining faculty the highest degree of independence from the receptive, and, within the purview of reason, intensifying activity to the utmost. Where both these aptitudes are conjoined, man will combine the greatest fullness of existence with the highest autonomy and freedom, and instead of losing himself to the world, will rather draw the latter into himself in all its infinitude of phenomena, and subject it to the unity of his reason.

---

other, that is to say, they stand in reciprocal relation to one another: without form no matter, and without matter no form. (This concept of reciprocal action, and its fundamental importance, is admirably set forth in Fichte's *Fundaments of the Theory of Knowledge*, Leipzig, 1794.) How things stand with the person in the realm of ideas we frankly do not know; but that it can never become manifest in the realm of time without taking on matter, of that we are certain. In this realm, therefore, matter will have some say, and not merely in a role subordinate to form, but also coordinate with it and independently of it. Necessary as it may be, therefore, that feeling should have no say in the realm of reason, it is no less necessary that reason should not presume to have a say in the realm of feeling. Just by assigning to each of them its own sphere, we are by that very fact excluding the other from it, and setting bounds to each, bounds which can only be transgressed at the risk of detriment to both.

In the transcendental method of philosophizing, where everything depends on clearing form of content, and obtaining necessity in its pure state, free of all admixture with the contingent, one easily falls into thinking of material things as nothing but an obstacle, and of imagining that our sensuous nature, just because it happens to be a hindrance in this operation, must of necessity be in conflict with reason. Such a way of thinking is, it is true, wholly alien to the spirit of the Kantian system, but it may very well be found in the letter of it.

But man can turn these relations upside down, and thus miss his destiny in two different ways. He can transfer the intensity required by the active function to the passive, let his sensuous drive encroach upon the formal, and make the receptive faculty do the work of the determining one. Or he can assign to the active function that extensity which is proper to the passive, let the formal drive encroach upon the sensuous, and substitute the determining faculty for the receptive one. In the first case he will never be himself; in the second he will never be anything else; and for that very reason, therefore, he will in both cases be neither the one nor the other, consequently—a nonentity.[3]

---

[3] [Schiller] The pernicious effect, upon both thought and action, of an undue surrender to our sensual nature will be evident to all. Not quite so evident, although just as common, and no less important, is the nefarious influence exerted upon our knowledge and upon our conduct by a preponderance of rationality. Permit me therefore to recall, from the great number of relevant instances, just two which may serve to throw light upon the damage caused when the functions of thought and will encroach upon those of intuition and feeling.

One of the chief reasons why our natural sciences make such slow progress is obviously the universal, and almost uncontrollable, propensity to teleological judgments, in which, once they are used constitutively, the determining faculty is substituted for the receptive. However strong and however varied the impact made upon our organs by nature, all her manifold variety is then entirely lost upon us, because we are seeking nothing in her but what we have put into her; because, instead of letting her come in upon us, we are thrusting ourselves out upon her with all the impatient anticipations of our reason. If, then, in the course of centuries, it should happen that a man tries to approach her with his sense-organs untroubled, innocent and wide open, and, thanks to this, should chance upon a multitude of phenomena which we, with our tendency to prejudge the issue, have overlooked, then we are mightily astonished that so many eyes in such broad daylight should have noticed nothing. This premature hankering after harmony before we have even got together the individual sounds which are to go to its making, this violent usurping of authority by ratiocination in a field where its right to give orders is by no means unconditional, is the reason why so many thinking minds fail to have any fruitful effect upon the advancement of science; and it would be difficult to say which has done more harm to the progress of knowledge: a sense-faculty unamenable to form, or a reasoning faculty which will not stay for a content.

It would be no less difficult to determine which does more to impede the practice of brotherly love: the violence of our passions, which disturbs it, or the rigidity of our principles, which chills it—the egotism of our senses or the egotism of our reason. If we are to become compassionate, helpful, effective human beings, feeling and character must unite, even as wide-open senses must combine with vigor of intellect if we are to acquire experience. How can we, however laudable our precepts, how can we be just, kindly, and human towards others, if we lack the power of receiving into ourselves, faithfully and truly, natures unlike ours, of feeling our way into the situation of others, of making other people's feelings our own? But in the education we receive, no less than in that we give ourselves, this power gets repressed in exactly the measure that we seek to break the force of passions, and strengthen character by means of principles. Since it costs effort to remain true to one's principles when feeling is easily stirred, we take the easier way out and try to make character secure by blunting feeling; for it is, of course, infinitely easier to have peace and quiet from an adversary you have disarmed than to master a spirited and active foe. And this, for the most part, is the cooperation that is meant when people speak of forming character; and that, even in the best sense of the word, where it implies the cultivation of the inner, and not merely of the outer, man. A man so formed will, without doubt, be immune from the danger of being crude nature or of appearing as such; but he will at the same

For if the sensuous drive becomes the determining one, that is to say, if the senses assume the role of legislator and the world suppresses the person, then the world ceases to be an object precisely to the extent that it becomes a force. From the moment that man is merely a content of time, he ceases to exist, and has in consequence no content either. With his personality his condition, too, is annulled, because these two concepts are reciprocally related—because change demands a principle of permanence, and finite reality an infinite reality. If, on the other hand, the formal drive becomes receptive, that is to say, if thought forestalls feeling and the person supplants the world, then the person ceases to be autonomous force and subject precisely to the extent that it forces its way into the place of the object—because, in order to become manifest, the principle of permanence requires change, and absolute reality has need of limitation. From the moment that man is only form, he ceases to have a form; the annulling of his condition, consequently, involves that of his person too. In a single word, only inasmuch as he is autonomous, is there reality outside him and is he receptive to it; and only inasmuch as he is receptive, is there reality within him and is he a thinking force.

Both drives, therefore, need to have limits set to them and, inasmuch as they can be thought of as energies, need to be relaxed; the sense-drive so that it does not encroach upon the domain of law, the formal drive so that it does not encroach on that of feeling. But the relaxing of the sense-drive must in no wise be the result of physical impotence or blunted feeling, which never merits anything but contempt. It must be an act of free choice, an activity of the person which, by its intensity, moderates that of the senses and, by mastering impressions, robs them of their depth only in order to give them increased surface. It is character which must set bounds to temperament, for it is only to profit the mind that sense may go short. In the same way the relaxing of the formal drive must not be the result of spiritual impotence or flabbiness of thought or will; for this would only degrade man. It must, if it is to be at all praiseworthy, spring

from abundance of feeling and sensation. Sense herself must, with triumphant power, remain mistress of her own domain, and resist the violence which the mind, by its usurping tactics, would fain inflict upon her. In a single word: Personality must keep the sensuous drive within its proper bounds, and receptivity, or nature, must do the same with the formal drive.

Fourteenth Letter

We have now been led to the notion of a reciprocal action between the two drives, reciprocal action of such a kind that the activity of the one both gives rise to, and sets limits to, the activity of the other, and in which each in itself achieves its highest manifestation precisely by reason of the other being active.

Such reciprocal relation between the two drives is, admittedly, but a task enjoined upon us by reason, a problem which man is only capable of solving completely in the perfect consummation of his existence. It is, in the most precise sense of the word, the idea of his human nature, hence something infinite, to which in the course of time he can approximate ever more closely, but without ever being able to reach it. "He is not to strive for form at the cost of reality, nor for reality at the cost of form; rather is he to seek absolute being by means of a determinate being, and a determinate being by means of infinite being. He is to set up a world over against himself because he is person, and he is to be person because a world stands over against him. He is to feel because he is conscious of himself, and be conscious of himself because he feels."—That he does actually conform to this idea, that he is consequently, in the fullest sense of the word, a human being, is never brought home to him as long as he satisfies only one of these two drives to the exclusion of the other, or only satisfies them one after the other. For as long as he only feels, his person, or his absolute existence, remains a mystery to him; and as long as he only thinks, his existence in time, or his condition, does likewise. Should there, however, be cases in which he were to have this two-fold experience simultaneously, in which he were to be at once conscious of his freedom and sensible of his existence, were, at one and the same time, to feel himself matter and come to know himself as mind, then he would in such cases, and in such cases only, have a complete intuition of his human nature, and the object which afforded him this vision would become for him a symbol of his accomplished destiny and, in consequence (since that is only to be attained in the totality of time), serve him as a manifestation of the infinite.

---

time be armored by principle against all natural feeling, and be equally inaccessible to the claims of humanity from without as he is to those of humanity from within.

It is a most pernicious abuse of the ideal of perfection, to apply it in all its rigor, either in our judgments of other people, or in those cases where we have to act on their behalf. The former leads to sentimental idealism; the latter to hardness and coldness of heart. We certainly make our duty to society uncommonly easy for ourselves by mentally substituting for the actual man who claims our help the ideal man who could in all probability help himself. Severity with oneself combined with leniency towards others is a sign of the truly excellent character. But mostly the man who is lenient to others will also be lenient with himself; and he who is severe with himself will be the same with others. To be lenient to oneself and severe towards others is the most contemptible character of all.

Assuming that cases of this sort could actually occur in experience, they would awaken in him a new drive which, precisely because the other two drives cooperate within it, would be opposed to each of them considered separately and could justifiably count as a new drive. The sense-drive demands that there shall be change and that time shall have a content; the form-drive demands that time shall be annulled and that there shall be no change. That drive, therefore, in which both the others work in concert (permit me for the time being, until I have justified the term, to call it the play-drive), the play-drive, therefore, would be directed towards annulling time within time, reconciling becoming with absolute being and change with identity.

The sense-drive wants to be determined, wants to receive its object; the form-drive wants itself to determine, wants to bring forth its object. The play-drive, therefore, will endeavor so to receive as if it had itself brought forth, and so to bring forth as the intuitive sense aspires to receive.

The sense-drive excludes from its subject all autonomy and freedom; the form-drive excludes from its subject all dependence, all passivity. Exclusion of freedom, however, implies physical necessity, exclusion of passivity moral necessity. Both drives, therefore, exert constraint upon the psyche; the former through the laws of nature, the latter through the laws of reason. The play-drive, in consequence, as the one in which both the others act in concert, will exert upon the psyche at once a moral and a physical constraint; it will, therefore, since it annuls all contingency, annul all constraint too, and set man free both physically and morally. When we embrace with passion someone who deserves our contempt, we are painfully aware of the compulsion of nature. When we feel hostile towards another who compels our esteem, we are painfully aware of the compulsion of reason. But once he has at the same time engaged our affection and won our esteem, then both the compulsion of feeling and the compulsion of reason disappear and we begin to love him, i.e., we begin to play with both our affection and our esteem.

Since, moreover, the sense-drive exerts a physical, the form-drive a moral constraint, the first will leave our formal, the second our material disposition at the mercy of the contingent; that is to say, it is a matter of chance whether our happiness will coincide with our perfection or our perfection with our happiness. The play-drive, in consequence, in which both work in concert, will make our formal as well as our material disposition, our perfection as well as our happiness, contingent. It will therefore, just because it makes both contingent and because with all constraint all contingency too disappears, abolish contingency in both, and, as a result, introduce form into matter and reality into form. To

the extent that it deprives feelings and passions of their dynamic power, it will bring them into harmony with the ideas of reason; and to the extent that it deprives the laws of reason of their moral compulsion, it will reconcile them with the interests of the senses.

Fifteenth Letter

I am drawing ever nearer the goal towards which I have been leading you by a not exactly encouraging path. If you will consent to follow me a few steps further along it, horizons all the wider will unfold and a pleasing prospect perhaps requite you for the labor of the journey.

The object of the sense-drive, expressed in a general concept, we call life, in the widest sense of this term: a concept designating all material being and all that is immediately present to the senses. The object of the form-drive, expressed in a general concept, we call form, both in the figurative and in the literal sense of this word: a concept which includes all the formal qualities of things and all the relations of these to our thinking faculties. The object of the play-drive, represented in a general schema, may therefore be called living form: a concept serving to designate all the aesthetic qualities of phenomena and, in a word, what in the widest sense of the term we call beauty.

According to this explanation, if such it be, the term beauty is neither extended to cover the whole realm of living things nor is it merely confined to this realm. A block of marble, though it is and remains lifeless, can nevertheless, thanks to the architect or the sculptor, become living form; and a human being, though he may live and have form, is far from being on that account a living form. In order to be so, his form would have to be life, and his life form. As long as we merely think about his form, it is lifeless, a mere abstraction; as long as we merely feel his life, it is formless, a mere impression. Only when his form lives in our feeling and his life takes on form in our understanding, does he become living form; and this will always be the case whenever we adjudge him beautiful.

But because we know how to specify the elements which when combined produce beauty, this does not mean that its genesis has as yet in any way been explained; for that would require us to understand the actual manner of their combining, and this, like all reciprocal action between finite and infinite, remains forever inaccessible to our probing. Reason, on transcendental grounds, makes the following demand: Let there be a bond of union between the form-drive and the material drive; that is to say, let there be a play-drive, since only the union of reality with form, contingency with necessity, passivity with freedom, makes the concept of human nature complete. Reason must make this demand because it is reason—because it is its nature to insist on perfection and on the abolition of all limitation, and because any exclusive activity on the part of either the one drive or the other leaves human nature incomplete and gives rise to some limitation within it. Consequently, as soon as reason utters the pronouncement: Let humanity exist, it has by that very pronouncement also promulgated the law: Let there be beauty. Experience can provide an answer to the question whether there is such a thing as beauty, and we shall know the answer once experience has taught us whether there is such a thing as humanity. But how there can be beauty, and how humanity is possible, neither reason nor experience can tell us.

Man, as we know, is neither exclusively matter nor exclusively mind. Beauty, as the consummation of his humanity, can therefore be neither exclusively life nor exclusively form. Not mere life, as acute observers, adhering too closely to the testimony of experience, have maintained, and to which the taste of our age would fain degrade it; not mere form, as it has been adjudged by philosophers whose speculations led them too far away from experience, or by artists who, philosophizing on beauty, let themselves be too exclusively guided by the needs of their craft.[4] It is the object common to both drives, that is to say, the object of the play-drive. This term is fully justified by linguistic usage, which is wont to designate as *play* everything which is neither subjectively nor objectively contingent, and yet imposes no kind of constraint either from within or from without. Since, in contemplation of the beautiful, the psyche finds itself in a happy medium between the realm of law and the sphere of physical exigency, it is, precisely because it is divided between the two, removed from the constraint of the one as of the other. The material drive, like the formal drive, is wholly earnest in its demands; for, in the sphere of knowledge, the former is concerned with the reality, the latter with the necessity of things; while in the sphere of action, the first is directed towards the preservation of life, the second towards the maintenance of dignity: both, therefore, towards truth and towards perfection. But life be-

comes of less consequence once human dignity enters in, and duty ceases to be a constraint once inclination exerts its pull; similarly our psyche accepts the reality of things, or material truth, with greater freedom and serenity once this latter encounters formal truth, or the law of necessity, and no longer feels constrained by abstraction once this can be accompanied by the immediacy of intuition. In a word: By entering into association with ideas all reality loses its earnestness because it then becomes of small account; and by coinciding with feeling necessity divests itself of its earnestness because it then becomes of light weight.

But, you may long have been tempted to object, is beauty not degraded by being made to consist of mere play and reduced to the level of those frivolous things which have always borne this name? Does it not belie the rational concept as well as the dignity of beauty—which is, after all, here being considered as an instrument of culture—if we limit it to mere play? And does it not belie the empirical concept of play—a concept which is, after all, entirely compatible with the exclusion of all taste—if we limit it merely to beauty?

But how can we speak of mere play, when we know that it is precisely play and play alone, which of all man's states and conditions is the one which makes him whole and unfolds both sides of his nature at once? What you, according to your idea of the matter, call limitation, I, according to mine—which I have justified by proof—call expansion. I, therefore, would prefer to put it exactly the opposite way round and say: the agreeable, the good, the perfect, with these man is merely in earnest; but with beauty he plays. True, we must not think here of the various forms of play which are in vogue in actual life, and are usually directed to very material objects. But then in actual life we should also seek in vain for the kind of beauty with which we are here concerned. The beauty we find in actual existence is precisely what the play-drive we find in actual existence deserves; but with the ideal of beauty that is set up by reason, an ideal of the play-drive, too, is enjoined upon man, which he must keep before his eyes in all his forms of play.

We shall not go far wrong when trying to discover a man's ideal of beauty if we inquire how he satisfies his play-drive. If at the Olympic Games the peoples of Greece delighted in the bloodless combats of strength, speed, and agility, and in the nobler rivalry of talents, and if the Roman people regaled themselves with the death throes of a vanquished gladiator or of his Libyan opponent, we can, from this single trait, understand why we have to seek the ideal forms of a Venus, a Juno, an Apollo, not in Rome, but in

---

[4][Schiller] Burke, in his *Philosophical Inquiry into the Origin of Our Ideas of the Sublime and the Beautiful* [above, page 333], makes beauty into mere life. As far as I know, every adherent of dogmatic philosophy, who has ever confessed his belief on this subject, makes it into mere form: among artists, Raphael Mengs, in his *Reflection on Taste in Painting,* not to speak of others. In this, as in everything else, critical philosophy has opened up the way whereby empiricism can be led back to principles, and speculation back to experience.

Greece.[5] Reason, however, declares: The beautiful is to be neither mere life, nor mere form, but living form, i.e., beauty; for it imposes upon man the double law of absolute formality and absolute reality. Consequently reason also makes the pronouncement: With beauty man shall only play, and it is with beauty only that he shall play.

For, to mince matters no longer, man only plays when he is in the fullest sense of the word a human being, and he is only fully a human being when he plays. This proposition, which at the moment may sound like a paradox, will take on both weight and depth of meaning once we have got as far as applying it to the twofold earnestness of duty and of destiny. It will, I promise you, prove capable of bearing the whole edifice of the art of the beautiful, and of the still more difficult art of living. But it is, after all, only in philosophy that the proposition is unexpected; it was long ago alive and operative in the art and in the feeling of the Greeks, the most distinguished exponents of both; only they transferred to Olympus what was meant to be realized on earth. Guided by the truth of that same proposition, they banished from the brow of the blessed gods all the earnestness and effort which furrow the cheeks of mortals, no less than the empty pleasures which preserve the smoothness of a vacuous face; freed those ever-contented beings from the bonds inseparable from every purpose, every duty, every care, and made idleness and indifferency the enviable portion of divinity—merely a more human name for the freest, most sublime state of being. Both the material constraint of natural laws and the spiritual constraint of moral laws were resolved in their higher concept of necessity, which embraced both worlds at once; and it was only out of the perfect union of those two necessities that for them true freedom could proceed. Inspired by this spirit, the Greeks effaced from the features of their ideal physiognomy, together with inclination, every trace of volition too; or rather they made both indiscernible, for they knew how to fuse them in the most intimate union. It is not grace, nor is it yet dignity, which speaks to us from the superb countenance of a Juno Ludovisi; it is neither the one nor the other because it is both at once. While the woman-god demands our veneration, the godlike woman kindles our love; but even as we abandon ourselves in ecstasy to her heavenly grace, her celestial self-sufficiency makes us recoil in terror. The whole figure reposes and dwells in itself, a creation completely self-contained, and, as if existing beyond space, neither yielding nor resisting; here is no force to contend with force, no frailty where temporality might break in. Irresistibly moved and drawn by those former qualities, kept at a distance by these latter, we find ourselves at one and the same time in a state of utter repose and supreme agitation, and there results that wondrous stirring of the heart for which mind has no concept nor speech any name.

Twenty-First Letter

There is, as I observed at the beginning of the last letter, a twofold condition of determinability and a twofold condition of determination. I can now clarify this statement.

The psyche may be said to be determinable simply because it is not determined at all; but it is also determinable inasmuch as it is determined in a way which does not exclude anything, i.e., when the determination it undergoes is of a kind which does not involve limitation. The former is mere indetermination (it is without limits, because it is without reality); the latter is aesthetic determinability (it has limits, because it embraces all reality).

And the psyche may be said to be determined inasmuch as it is limited at all; but it is also determined inasmuch as it limits itself, by virtue of its own absolute power. It finds itself in the first of these two states whenever it feels; in the second, whenever it thinks. What thought is in respect of determination, therefore, the aesthetic disposition is in respect of determinability; the former is limitation by virtue of the infinite force within it, the latter is negation by virtue of the infinite abundance within it. Even as sensation and thought have one single point of contact—viz. that in both states the psyche is determined, and man is something, either individual or person, to the exclusion of all else—but in all other respects are poles apart: so, in like manner, aesthetic determinability has one single point of contact with mere indetermination—viz., that both exclude any determinate mode of existence—while in all other respects they are to each other as nothing is to everything, hence, utterly and entirely different. If, therefore, the latter—indetermination through sheer absence of determination—was thought of as an empty infinity, then aesthetic freedom of determination, which is its counterpart in reality, must be regarded as an infinity filled with content: an idea which accords completely with the results of the foregoing inquiry.

In the aesthetic state, then, man is naught, if we are thinking of any particular result rather than of the totality of

---

[5][Schiller] If (to confine ourselves to the modern world) we compare horse racing in London, bullfights in Madrid, *spectacles* in the Paris of former days, the gondola races in Venice, animal baiting in Vienna, and the gay attractive life of the Corso in Rome, it will not be difficult to determine the different nuances of taste among these different peoples. However, there is far less uniformity among the amusements of the common people in these different countries than there is among those of the refined classes in those same countries, a fact which it is easy to account for.

his powers, and considering the absence in him of any specific determination. Hence we must allow that those people are entirely right who declare beauty, and the mood it induces in us, to be completely indifferent and unfruitful as regards either knowledge or character. They are entirely right; for beauty produces no particular result whatsoever, neither for the understanding nor for the will. It accomplishes no particular purpose, neither intellectual nor moral; it discovers no individual truth, helps us to perform no individual duty and is, in short, as unfitted to provide a firm basis for character as to enlighten the understanding. By means of aesthetic culture, therefore, the personal worth of a man, or his dignity, inasmuch as this can depend solely upon himself, remains completely indeterminate; and nothing more is achieved by it than that he is henceforth enabled by the grace of nature to make of himself what he will—that the freedom to be what he ought to be is completely restored to him.

But precisely thereby something infinite is achieved. For as soon as we recall that it was precisely of this freedom that he was deprived by the one-sided constraint of nature in the field of sensation and by the exclusive authority of reason in the realm of thought, then we are bound to consider the power which is restored to him in the aesthetic mode as the highest of all bounties, as the gift of humanity itself. True, he possesses this humanity *in potentia* before every determinate condition into which he can conceivably enter. But he loses it in practice with every determinate condition into which he does enter. And if he is to pass into a condition of an opposite nature, this humanity must be restored to him each time anew through the life of the aesthetic.[6]

It is, then, not just poetic license but philosophical truth when we call beauty our second creatress. For although it only offers us the possibility of becoming human beings, and for the rest leaves it to our own free will to decide how far we wish to make this a reality, it does in this resemble our first creatress, nature, which likewise conferred upon us nothing more than the power of becoming human, leaving the use and practice of that power to our own free will and decision.

---

[6][Schiller] Admittedly the rapidity with which certain types pass from sensation to thought or decision scarcely—if indeed at all—allows them to become aware of the aesthetic mode through which they must in that time necessarily pass. Such natures cannot for any length of time tolerate the state of indetermination, but press impatiently for some result which in the state of aesthetic limitlessness they cannot find. In others, by contrast, who find enjoyment more in the feeling of total capacity than in any single action, the aesthetic state tends to spread itself over a much wider area. Much as the former dread emptiness, just as little are the latter capable of tolerating limitation. I need scarcely say that the former are born for detail and subordinate occupations, the latter, provided they combine this capacity with a sense of reality, destined for wholeness and for great roles.

Twenty-Second Letter

If, then, in one respect the aesthetic mode of the psyche is to be regarded as naught—once, that is, we have an eye to particular and definite effects—it is in another respect to be looked upon as a state of supreme reality, once we have due regard to the absence of all limitation and to the sum total of the powers which are conjointly active within it. One cannot, then, say that those people are wrong either who declare the aesthetic state to be the most fruitful of all in respect of knowledge and morality. They are entirely right; for a disposition of the psyche which contains within it the whole of human nature, must necessarily contain within it *in potentia* every individual manifestation of it too; and a disposition of the psyche which removes all limitations from the totality of human nature must necessarily remove them from every individual manifestation of it as well. Precisely on this account, because it takes under its protection no single one of man's faculties to the exclusion of the others, it favors each and all of them without distinction; and it favors no single one more than another for the simple reason that it is the ground of possibility of them all. Every other way of exercising its functions endows the psyche with some special aptitude—but only at the cost of some special limitation; the aesthetic alone leads to the absence of all limitation. Every other state into which we can enter refers us back to a preceding one, and requires for its termination a subsequent one; the aesthetic alone is a whole in itself, since it comprises within itself all the conditions of both its origin and its continuance. Here alone do we feel reft out of time, and our human nature expresses itself with a purity and integrity, as though it had as yet suffered no impairment through the intervention of external forces.

That which flatters our senses in immediate sensation exposes our susceptible and labile psyche to every impression—but only by rendering us proportionately less fitted for exertion. That which tenses our intellectual powers and invites them to form abstract concepts, strengthens our mind for every sort of resistance—but only by hardening it and depriving us of sensibility in proportion as it fosters greater independence of action. Precisely because of this, the one no less than the other must lead to exhaustion, since material cannot for long dispense with shaping power, nor power with material to be shaped. If, by contrast, we have surrendered to the enjoyment of genuine beauty, we are at such a moment master in equal degree of our passive and of our active powers, and we shall with equal ease turn to seriousness or to play, to repose or to movement, to compliance or to resistance, to the discussions of abstract thought or to the direct contemplation of phenomena.

This lofty equanimity and freedom of the spirit, combined with power and vigor, is the mood in which a genuine work of art should release us, and there is no more certain touchstone of true aesthetic excellence. If, after enjoyment of this kind, we find ourselves disposed to prefer some one particular mode of feeling or action, but unfitted or disinclined for another, this may serve as infallible proof that we have not had a purely aesthetic experience—whether the cause lies in the object or in our own response or, as is almost always the case, in both at once.

Since in actuality no purely aesthetic effect is ever to be met with (for man can never escape his dependence upon conditioning forces), the excellence of a work of art can never consist in anything more than a high approximation to that ideal of aesthetic purity; and whatever the degree of freedom to which it may have been sublimated, we shall still leave it in a particular mood and with some definite bias. The more general the mood and the less limited the bias produced in us by any particular art, or by any particular product of the same, then the nobler that art and the more excellent that product will be. One can test this by considering works from different arts and different works from the same art. We leave a beautiful piece of music with our feeling excited, a beautiful poem with our imagination quickened, a beautiful sculpture or building with our understanding awakened. But should anyone invite us, immediately after a sublime musical experience, to abstract thought; or employ us, immediately after a sublime poetic experience, in some routine business of everyday life; or try, immediately after the contemplation of beautiful paintings or sculptures, to inflame our imagination or surprise our feeling— he would certainly be choosing the wrong moment. The reason for this is that even the most ethereal music has, by virtue of its material, an even greater affinity with the senses than true aesthetic freedom really allows; that even the most successful poem partakes more of the arbitrary and casual play of the imagination, as the medium through which it works, than the inner lawfulness of the truly beautiful really permits; that even the most excellent sculpture—the most excellent, perhaps, most of all—does, by virtue of its conceptual precision, border upon the austerity of science. Nevertheless, the greater the degree of excellence attained by a work in any of these three arts, the more these particular affinities will disappear; and it is an inevitable and natural consequence of their approach to perfection that the various arts, without any displacement of their objective frontiers, tend to become ever more like each other in their effect upon the psyche. Music, at its most sublime, must become sheer form and affect us with the serene power of antiquity. The plastic arts, at their most perfect, must become music

and move us by the immediacy of their sensuous presence. Poetry, when most fully developed, must grip us powerfully as music does, but at the same time, like the plastic arts, surround us with serene clarity. This, precisely, is the mark of perfect style in each and every art: that it is able to remove the specific limitations of the art in question without thereby destroying its specific qualities, and through a wise use of its individual peculiarities, is able to confer upon it a more general character.[7]

And it is not just the limitations inherent in the specific character of a particular art that the artist must seek to overcome through his handling of it; it is also the limitations inherent in the particular subject matter he is treating. In a truly successful work of art the contents should effect nothing, the form everything; for only through the form is the whole man affected, through the subject matter, by contrast, only one or other of his functions. Subject matter, then, however sublime and all-embracing it may be, always has a limiting effect upon the spirit, and it is only from form that true aesthetic freedom can be looked for. Herein, then, resides the real secret of the master in any art: that he can make his form consume his material; and the more pretentious, the more seductive this material is in itself, the more it seeks to impose itself upon us, the more highhandedly it thrusts itself forward with effects of its own, or the more the beholder is inclined to get directly involved with it, then the more triumphant the art which forces it back and asserts its own kind of dominion over him. The psyche of the listener or spectator must remain completely free and inviolate; it must go forth from the magic circle of the artist pure and perfect as it came from the hands of the Creator. The most frivolous theme must be so treated that it leaves us ready to proceed directly from it to some matter of the utmost import; the most serious material must be so treated that we remain capable of exchanging it forthwith for the lightest play. Arts which affect the passions, such as tragedy, do not invalidate this: in the first place, they are not entirely free arts since they are enlisted in the service of a particular aim (that of pathos); and in the second, no true connoisseur of art will deny that works even of this class are the more perfect, the more they respect the freedom of the spirit even amid the most violent storms of passion. There does indeed exist a fine art of passion; but a fine passionate art is a contradiction in terms; for the unfailing effect of beauty is freedom from passion. No less self-contradictory is the notion of a fine art which teaches (didactic) or improves (moral);

---

[7] Here Schiller recognizes the differences among the arts (see Lessing, *Laocoön,* page 379), but finds those differences transcended in reception.

for nothing is more at variance with the concept of beauty than the notion of giving the psyche any definite bias.[8]

But it is by no means always a proof of formlessness in the work of art itself if it makes its effect solely through its contents; this may just as often be evidence of a lack of form in him who judges it. If he is either too tensed or too relaxed, if he is used to apprehending either exclusively with the intellect or exclusively with the senses, he will, even in the case of the most successfully realized whole, attend only to the parts, and in the presence of the most beauteous form respond only to the matter. Receptive only to the raw material, he has first to destroy the aesthetic organization of a work before he can take pleasure in it, and laboriously scratch away until he has uncovered all those individual details which the master, with infinite skill, had caused to disappear in the harmony of the whole. The interest he takes in it is quite simply either a moral or a material interest; but what precisely it ought to be, namely aesthetic, that it certainly is not.[9] Such readers will enjoy a serious and moving poem as though it were a sermon, a naive or humorous one as though it were an intoxicating drink. And if they were sufficiently lacking in taste to demand edification of a tragedy or an epic—and were it about the Messiah himself—they will certainly not fail to take exception to a poem in the manner of Anacreon or Catullus.[10]

from
Twenty-Fifth Letter

From being a slave of nature, which he remains as long as he merely feels it, man becomes its lawgiver from the moment he begins to think it. That which hitherto merely dominated him as force, now stands before his eyes as object. Whatsoever is object for him has no power over him; for in order to be object at all, it must be subjected to the power that is his. To the extent that he imparts form to matter, and for precisely as long as he imparts it, he is immune to its effects; for spirit cannot be injured by anything except that which robs it of its freedom, and man gives evidence of his freedom precisely by giving form to that which is formless. Only where sheer mass, ponderous and inchoate, holds sway, its murky contours shifting within uncertain bound-

aries, can fear find its seat; man is more than a match for any of nature's terrors once he knows how to give it form and convert it into an object of his contemplation. Once he begins to assert his independence in the face of nature as phenomenon, then he also asserts his dignity *vis-à-vis* nature as force, and with noble freedom rises in revolt against his ancient gods. Now they cast off those ghastly masks which were the anguish of his childhood and surprise him with his own image by revealing themselves as projections of his own mind. The monstrous divinity of the Oriental, which rules the world with the blind strength of a beast of prey, shrinks in the imagination of the Greeks into the friendly contours of a human being. The empire of the Titans falls, and infinite force is tamed by infinite form.

But whilst I was merely seeking a way out from the material world and a transition to the world of spirit, my imagination has run away with me and carried me into the very heart of this latter. Beauty, which is what we were out to seek, already lies behind us; we have o'erleapt it completely in passing from mere life directly to pure form and the pure object. But a sudden leap of this kind is contrary to human nature, and in order to keep step with this latter we shall have to turn back once more to the world of sense.

Beauty is, admittedly, the work of free contemplation, and with it we do indeed enter upon the world of ideas—but, it should be emphasized, without therefore leaving behind the world of sense, as is the case when we proceed to knowledge of truth. Truth is the pure product of abstracting from everything which is material and contingent; it is object, pure and unadulterated, in which none of the limitations of the subject may persist, pure autonomous activity without any admixture of passivity. True, even from the highest abstractions, there is a way back to sense; for thought affects our inner life of feeling, and the perception of logical and moral unity passes over into a feeling of sensuous congruence. But when we take such delight in intellectual knowledge, we distinguish very exactly between our perception and our feeling, and look upon the latter as something incidental, which could well be absent without the knowledge therefore ceasing to be knowledge or truth being any the less true. But it would be a vain undertaking to try to clear our perception of beauty of these connections with feeling—which is why it will not do to think of the one as the effect of the other, but is imperative to consider each as being, at the same time and reciprocally, both effect and cause. In the pleasure we take in knowledge we distinguish without difficulty the transition from activity to passivity, and are clearly aware that the first is over when the latter begins. In the delight we take in beauty, by contrast, no such succession of activity and passivity can be

---

[8]Schiller's aesthetic is concerned with the reader, as is Kant's, but it seeks to overcome the traditional Horatian assumption that the effect of art (if it is on this basis that we are to define art) is properly discussed in terms of its ability to delight and to teach.

[9]The argument here is clearly Kantian. See above, page 416.

[10]Anacreon (fl. c. 521 B.C.), Greek lyric poet; Caius Valerius Catullus (84?–54? B.C.), Roman lyric poet.

discerned; reflection is here so completely interfused with feeling that we imagine that the form is directly apprehended by sense. Beauty, then, is indeed an object for us, because reflection is the condition of our having any sensation of it; but it is at the same time a state of the perceiving subject, because feeling is a condition of our having any perception of it. Thus beauty is indeed form, because we contemplate it; but it is at the same time life, because we feel it. In a word: it is at once a state of our being and an activity we perform.

And just because it is both these things at once, beauty provides us with triumphant proof that passivity by no means excludes activity, nor matter form, nor limitation infinity—that, in consequence, the moral freedom of man is by no means abrogated through his inevitable dependence upon physical things. Beauty is proof of this and, I must add, she alone can furnish such proof. For since in the enjoyment of truth, or logical unity, feeling is not inevitably and of necessity one with thought, but merely follows incidentally upon it, truth can only offer us proof that sensuousness can follow upon rationality, or vice versa; but not that both exist together, nor that they reciprocally work upon each other, nor that they are absolutely and of necessity to be united. On the contrary, from the fact that feeling is excluded as long as we are thinking, and thinking excluded as long as we are feeling, the incompatibility of our two natures would have to be inferred; and, indeed, analytical

philosophers are unable to adduce any better proof that pure reason can in practice be realized in human kind than that this is in fact enjoined upon them. But since in the enjoyment of beauty, or aesthetic unity, an actual union and interchange between matter and form, passivity and activity, momentarily takes place, the compatibility of our two natures, the practicability of the infinite being realized in the finite, hence the possibility of sublimest humanity, is thereby actually proven.

We need, then, no longer feel at a loss for a way which might lead us from our dependence upon sense towards moral freedom, since beauty offers us an instance of the latter being perfectly compatible with the former, an instance of man not needing to flee matter in order to manifest himself as spirit. But if he is already free while still in association with sense, as the fact of beauty teaches, and if freedom is something absolute and supra-sensual, as the very notion of freedom necessarily implies, then there can no longer be any question of how he is to succeed in raising himself from the limited to the absolute, or of how, in his thinking and willing, he is to offer resistance to the life of sense, since this has already happened in beauty. There can, in a single word, no longer be any question of how he is to pass from beauty to truth, since this latter is potentially contained in the former, but only a question of how he is to clear a way for himself from common reality to aesthetic reality, from mere life-serving feelings to feelings of beauty.

Friedrich Schlegel

1772–1829

Friedrich Schlegel was perhaps the leading theorist of German romanticism. Together with his brother August Wilhelm, he edited the important periodical *Athenaeum* from 1798 to 1800. In *Athenaeum* the brothers, with Friedrich Schleiermacher and the poet Novalis (Friedrich von Hardenberg), published a series of fragments, the most important of which were written by Friedrich Schlegel. These, which ranged widely over a variety of thoughts—literary, moral, philosophical, and political—were preceded by the *Lyceum Fragments,* written entirely by Friedrich. These fragments appeared in the *Lyceum der schonen Kunste* (1797) and were widely regarded as the initial expression of Romanticism. A selection appears here under the title *Critical Fragments.* Although the fragments take up many matters, including questions about classicism, perhaps the most important is the attention given to the concepts of wit and irony. The former term is elevated to great heights, for wit is clearly identified with genius and inventive power; yet this can be seen only by a reading of several fragments with their cumulative effect.

Irony is perhaps more important, though always involved dialectically with wit. The section of the essay "On Incomprehensibility" reprinted here is really a commentary or enlargement on two *Lyceum Fragments,* numbers 48 and 108, which are quoted in full in the essay. It is irony that "opposes" wit, always, when successful, intruding a skeptical perspective, in which the writer overcomes the finite limits of his own creativity. Thus the skeptical aspect of irony is actually seen as enabling an advance to a higher level, which, however, reveals human limitation in that the object of knowledge or intellectual desire remains infinite and unattainable. Thus irony can be characterized as both a "divine breath" (42) and a "transcendental buffonery," rising above its own art, virtue, or genius, even as it remains on earth.

Schlegel's critical writings are collected in six volumes by Ernst Behler and Hans Eichner in Friedrich Schlegel, *Kritische Schriften and Fragmente* (1988). Ernst Behler, ed., *Friedrich Schlegel in Zelbstzeugnissen und Bilddocumenten* (1966) documents and discusses Schlegel's life. See Hans Eichner, *Friedrich Schlegel* (1970) for biography, also his *Charakteristiken und Kritiken I (1796–1801)* (1967) for a study of Schlegel's critical theory. See also Benno von Wiese, *Friedrich Schlegel* (1927) and Hans Eichner, "Friedrich Schlegel's Theory of Romantic Poetry," *PMLA* 71 (1956), 1018–41; Victor Lange, "Friedrich Schlegel's Literary Criticism," *Comparative Literature* 7, Fall 1955, 289–305; René Wellek, *A History of Modern Criticism,* 1750–1950 (1955); and Ernst Behler and Roman Struc, eds. and trans., *Dialogue on Poetry and Literary Aphorisms* (1968); Margaret Stoljar, *Athenaeum: A Critical Commentary* (1973); Gary J. Handwerk, *Irony and Ethics in Narrative: From Schlegel to Lacan* (1985); Marike Finlay, *The Romantic Irony of Semiotics: Friedrich Schlegel and the Crisis of Representation* (1988); J. Hillis Miller, "Friedrich Schlegel and the Anti-Ekphrastic Tradition," *Revenge of the Aesthetic,* ed. Michael Clark (2000).

from

Critical Fragments (Lyceum Fragments)

7. My essay on the study of Greek poetry is a mannered prose hymn to the objective quality in poetry. The worst thing about it, it seems to me, is the complete lack of necessary irony; and the best, the confident assumption that poetry is infinitely valuable—as if that were a settled thing.

8. A good preface must be at once the square root and the square of its book.

9. Wit is absolute social feeling, or fragmentary genius.

12. One of two things is usually lacking in the so-called Philosophy of Art: either philosophy or art.

14. In poetry too every whole can be a part and every part really a whole.

18. Novels have a habit of concluding in the same way that the Lord's Prayer begins: with the kingdom of heaven on earth.

20. A classical text must never be entirely comprehensible. But those who are cultivated and who cultivate themselves must always want to learn more from it.

21. Just as a child is only a thing which wants to become a human being, so a poem is only a product of nature which wants to become a work of art.

23. Every good poem must be wholly intentional and wholly instinctive. That is how it becomes ideal.

25. The two main principles of the so-called historical criticism are the Postulate of Vulgarity and the Axiom of the Average. The Postulate of Vulgarity: everything great, good, and beautiful is improbable because it is extraordinary and, at the very least, suspicious. The Axiom of the Average: as we and our surroundings are, so must it have been always and everywhere, because that, after all, is so very natural.

26. Novels are the Socratic dialogues of our time. And this free form has become the refuge of common sense in its flight from pedantry.

27. The critic is a reader who ruminates. Therefore he ought to have more than one stomach.

28. Feeling (for a particular art, science, person, etc.) is divided spirit, is self-restriction: hence a result of self-creation and self-destruction.

30. In modern tragedy, fate is sometimes replaced by God the Father, more often by the devil himself. How is it that this hasn't yet inspired some scholar to formulate a theory of the diabolic genre?

36. Whoever hasn't yet arrived at the clear realization that there might be a greatness existing entirely outside his own sphere and for which he might have absolutely no feeling; whoever hasn't at least felt obscure intimations concerning the approximate location of this greatness in the geography of the human spirit: that person either has no genius in his own sphere, or else he hasn't been educated yet to the niveau of the classic.

37. In order to write well about something, one shouldn't be interested in it any longer. To express an idea with due circumspection, one must have relegated it wholly to one's past; one must no longer be preoccupied with it. As long as the artist is in the process of discovery and inspiration, he is in a state which, as far as communication is concerned, is at the very least intolerant.[1] He wants to blurt out everything, which is a fault of young geniuses or a legitimate prejudice of old bunglers. And so he fails to recognize the value and the dignity of self-restriction, which is after all, for the artist as well as the man, the first and the last, the most necessary and the highest duty. Most necessary because wherever one does not restrict oneself, one is restricted by the world; and that makes one a slave. The highest because one can only restrict oneself at those points and places where one possesses infinite power, self-creation, and self-destruction. Even a friendly conversation which cannot be broken off at any moment, completely arbitrarily, has something intolerant about it. But a writer who can and does talk himself out, who keeps nothing back for himself, and likes to tell everything he knows, is to be pitied. There are only three mistakes to guard against. First: What appears to be unlimited free will, and consequently seems and should seem to be irrational or supra-rational, nonetheless must still at bottom be simply necessary and rational; otherwise the whim becomes willful, becomes intolerant, and self-restriction turns into self-destruction. Second: Don't be in too much of a hurry for self-restriction, but first give rein to self-creation, invention, and inspiration, until you're ready. Third: Don't exaggerate self-restriction.

40. In the sense in which it has been defined and used in Germany, aesthetic is a word which notoriously reveals an equally perfect ignorance of the thing and of the language. Why is it still used?

---

[1] This view is only one of many that appears in Romanticism concerning the relation of writer to his art. These include various theories of self-expression, but also a notion of authorial disinterest in, for example, Keats (below, page 536). Such views seem to be the writerly parallel to readerly aesthetic "disinterest" in Kant (above, page 420).

The *Critical Fragments* first appeared in the *Lyceum* in 1797. They are reprinted in part from Peter Firchow, tr., *Friedrich Schlegel's* Lucinde *and the Fragments* (Minneapolis: University of Minnesota Press, 1971).

48. Irony is the form of paradox. Paradox is everything simultaneously good and great.

51. To use wit as an instrument for revenge is as shameful as using art as a means for titillating the senses.

52. Instead of description, one occasionally gets in poems a rubric announcing that here something or other should really have been described, but the artist was prevented from doing so and most humbly begs to be excused.

53. In respect to their unity, most modern poems are allegories (mysteries, moralities) or novellas (adventures, intrigues), or a mixture or dilution of these.

54. There are writers who drink the absolute like water; and books in which even the dogs refer to the infinite.

55. A really free and cultivated person ought to be able to attune himself at will to being philosophical or philological, critical or poetical, historical or rhetorical, ancient or modern: quite arbitrarily, just as one tunes an instrument, at any time and to any degree.

56. Wit is logical sociability.

57. If some mystical art lovers who think of every criticism as a dissection and every dissection as a destruction of pleasure were to think logically, then "wow" would be the best criticism of the greatest work of art. To be sure, there are critiques which say nothing more, but only take much longer to say it.

58. Just as mankind prefers a great to a just action, so too the artist wants to ennoble and instruct.

59. Chamfort's pet idea that wit is a substitute for an impossible happiness—a small percentage, as it were, of the unpaid debt on the greatest good for which a bankrupt nature must settle—is not much better than Shaftesbury's[2] idea that wit is the touchstone of truth, or the more vulgar prejudice that moral ennoblement is the highest end of the fine arts. Wit is its own end like virtue, like love and art. This brilliant man felt, so it seems, the infinite value of wit, and since French philosophy is inadequate for an understanding of this, he sought instinctively to join what was best in him to what is first and best in that philosophy. And as a maxim, the thought that the wise man must confront fate always *en état d'épigramme* is beautiful and truly cynical.

60. All the classical poetical genres have now become ridiculous in their rigid purity.

61. Strictly understood, the concept of a scientific poem is quite as absurd as that of a poetical science.

62. We already have so many theories about poetical genres. Why have we no concept of poetical genre? Perhaps then we would have to make do with a single theory of poetical genres.

63. Not art and works of art make the artist, but feeling and inspiration and impulse.

64. There should be a new *Laokoön*[3] to determine the limits of music and philosophy. For a proper appreciation of a number of literary works we still need a theory of grammatical music.

65. Poetry is republican speech: a speech which is its own law and end unto itself, and in which all the parts are free citizens and have the right to vote.[4]

67. In England, wit is at least a profession if not an art. There everything becomes craftsmanlike, and in that island even the *roués* are pedants. So too their *wits:* they introduce an absolute willfulness—whose illusion gives to wit its romantic and piquant quality—into reality and so manage to live wittily. Hence their talent for folly. They die for their principles.

70. People who write books and imagine that their readers are the public and that they must educate it soon arrive at the point not only of despising their so-called public but of hating it. Which leads absolutely nowhere.

73. What is lost in average, good, or even first-rate translations is precisely the best part.

78. Many of the very best novels are compendia, encyclopedias of the whole spiritual life of a brilliant individual. Works which have this quality, even if they are cast in a completely different mold—like *Nathan*[5]—thereby take on a novelistic hue. And every human being who is cultivated and who cultivates himself contains a novel within himself. But it isn't necessary for him to express it and write it out.

80. I'm disappointed in not finding in Kant's family tree of basic concepts the category "almost," a category that has surely accomplished, and spoiled, as much in the world and in literature as any other. In the mind of natural skeptics it colors all other concepts and perceptions.

84. From what the moderns aim at, we learn what poetry should become; from what the ancients have done, what it has to be.

85. Every honest author writes for nobody or everybody. Whoever writes for some particular group does not deserve to be read.

86. The function of criticism, people say, is to educate one's readers! Whoever wants to be educated, let him educate himself. This is rude: but it can't be helped.

---

[2] [Firchow] Anthony Ashley Cooper, Third Earl of Shaftesbury (1671–1713), English moral philosopher and one of the shaping spirits of the eighteenth century.

[3] *Laocoön* by Lessing (above, page 378).

[4] A similar remark is made by Ransom (below, page 953).

[5] Lessing's play, *Nathan de Weise* (1779).

89. Isn't it unnecessary to write more than one novel, unless the artist has become a new man? It's obvious that frequently all the novels of a particular author belong together and in a sense make up only one novel.

90. Wit is an explosion of confined spirit.

91. The ancients are not the Jews, Christians, or English of poetry. They are not an arbitrarily chosen artistic people of God; nor do they have the only true saving aesthetic faith; nor do they have a monopoly on poetry.

93. In the ancients we see the perfected letter of all poetry; in the moderns we see its growing spirit.[6]

96. A good riddle should be witty; otherwise nothing remains once the answer has been found. And there's a charm in having a witty idea which is enigmatic to the point of needing to be solved: only its meaning should be immediately and completely clear as soon as it's been hit upon.

98. The following are universally valid and fundamental laws of written communication: (1) one should have something to communicate; (2) one should have somebody to whom one wants to communicate it; (3) one should really be able to communicate it and share it with somebody, not simply express oneself. Otherwise it would be wiser to keep silent.

99. Whoever isn't completely new himself judges the new as if it were old; and the old seems ever new until one grows old oneself.

100. The poetry of one writer is termed philosophical, of another philological, of a third, rhetorical, etc. But what then is poetical poetry?

103. Many works that are praised for the beauty of their coherence have less unity than a motley heap of ideas simply animated by the ghost of a spirit and aiming at a single purpose. What really holds the latter together is that free and equal fellowship in which, so the wise men assure us, the citizens of the perfect state will live at some future date; it's that unqualifiedly sociable spirit which, as the beau monde maintains, is now to be found only in what is so strangely and almost childishly called the great world. On the other hand, many a work of art whose coherence is never questioned is, as the artist knows quite well himself, not a complete work but a fragment, or one or more fragments, a mass, a plan. But so powerful is the instinct for unity in mankind that the author himself will often bring something to a kind of completion which simply can't be made a whole or a unit; often quite imaginatively and yet completely unnaturally. The worst thing about it is that whatever is draped about the solid, really existent fragments in the attempt to mug up a semblance of unity consists largely of dyed rags. And if these are touched up cleverly and deceptively, and tastefully displayed, then that's all the worse. For then he deceives even the exceptional reader at first, who has a deep feeling for what little real goodness and beauty is still to be found here and there in life and letters. That reader is then forced to make a critical judgment to get at the right perception of it! And no matter how quickly the dissociation takes place, still the first fresh impression is lost.

107. The ancients are masters of poetical abstraction; the moderns are better at poetical speculation.

108. Socratic irony is the only involuntary and yet completely deliberate dissimulation. It is equally impossible to feign it or divulge it. To a person who hasn't got it, it will remain a riddle even after it is openly confessed. It is meant to deceive no one except those who consider it a deception and who either take pleasure in the delightful roguery of making fools of the whole world or else become angry when they get an inkling they themselves might be included. In this sort of irony, everything should be playful and serious, guilelessly open and deeply hidden. It originates in the union of *savoir vivre* and scientific spirit, in the conjunction of a perfectly instinctive and a perfectly conscious philosophy. It contains and arouses a feeling of indissoluble antagonism between the absolute and the relative, between the impossibility and the necessity of complete communication. It is the freest of all licenses, for by its means one transcends oneself; and yet it is also the most lawful, for it is absolutely necessary. It is a very good sign when the harmonious bores are at a loss about how they should react to this continuous self-parody, when they fluctuate endlessly between belief and disbelief until they get dizzy and take what is meant as a joke seriously and what is meant seriously as a joke. For Lessing irony is instict; for Hemsterhuis[7] it is classical study; for Hülsen[8] it arises out of the philosophy of philosophy and surpasses these others by far.

109. Gentle wit, or wit without a barb, is a privilege of poetry which prose can't encroach upon: for only by means of the sharpest focus on a single point can the individual idea gain a kind of wholeness.

112. The analytic writer observes the reader as he is; and accordingly he makes his calculations and sets up his machines in order to make the proper impression on him. The synthetic writer constructs and creates a reader as he should be; he doesn't imagine him calm and dead, but alive

---

[6]Schlegel seems to mediate here between ancients and moderns and between the idea of progress in the arts and the generally modern view (see, for example, Blake, above, page 454) that art does not improve.

[7]François Hemsterhuis (1721–1790), Dutch philosopher.

[8][Firchow] August Ludwig Hülsen (1765–1810), German philosopher, friend of Fichte and the Schlegel brothers.

and critical. He allows whatever he has created to take shape gradually before the reader's eyes, or else he tempts him to discover it himself. He doesn't try to make any particular impression on him, but enters with him into the sacred relationship of deepest symphilosophy or sympoetry.

115. The whole history of modern poetry is a running commentary on the following brief philosophical text: all art should become science and all science art: poetry and philosophy should be made one.

117. Poetry can only be criticized by way of poetry. A critical judgment of an artistic production has no civil rights in the realm of art if it isn't itself a work of art, either in its substance, as a representation of a necessary impression in the state of becoming, or in the beauty of its form and open tone, like that of the old Roman satires.

118. Isn't everything that is capable of becoming shopworn already twisted or trite to begin with?

121. The simplest and most immediate questions, like Should we criticize Shakespeare's works as art or as nature? and Are epic and tragedy essentially different or not? and Should art deceive or merely seem to do so? are all questions that can't be answered without the deepest consideration and the most erudite history of art.

123. It is thoughtless and immodest presumption to want to learn something about art from philosophy. There are many who start out that way as if they hope to find something new there, since philosophy, after all, can't and shouldn't be able to do more than order the given artistic experiences and the existing artistic principles into a science, and raise the appreciation of art, extend it with the help of a thoroughly learned history of art, and create here as well that logical mood which unites absolute tolerance with absolute rigor.

from
Athenaeum Fragments

12. It has been said of many monarchs that they would have been admirable citizens; only as kings were they failures. Can we say the same of the Bible? Is it also just an admirable everyday book whose only fault is that it should have become the Bible?

The *Athenaeum Fragments* first appeared in the *Athenaeum* from 1798 to 1800. They are reprinted in part from Peter Firchow, tr., *Friedrich Schlegel's Lucinde and the Fragments* (Minneapolis: University of Minnesota Press, 1971).

68. The only true lover of art is the man who can renounce some of his wishes entirely whenever he finds others completely fulfilled, who can rigorously evaluate even what he loves most, who will, if necessary, submit to explanations, and has a sense for the history of art.

71. People always talk about how an analysis of the beauty of a work of art supposedly disturbs the pleasure of the art lover. Well, the real lover just won't let himself be disturbed!

116. Romantic poetry is a progressive, universal poetry. Its aim isn't merely to reunite all the separate species of poetry and put poetry in touch with philosophy and rhetoric. It tries to and should mix and fuse poetry and prose, inspiration and criticism, the poetry of art and the poetry of nature; and make poetry lively and sociable, and life and society poetical; poeticize wit and fill and saturate the forms of art with every kind of good, solid matter for instruction, and animate them with the pulsations of humor. It embraces everything that is purely poetic, from the greatest systems of art, containing within themselves still further systems, to the sigh, the kiss that the poetizing child breathes forth in artless song. It can so lose itself in what it describes that one might believe it exists only to characterize poetical individuals of all sorts; and yet there still is no form so fit for expressing the entire spirit of an author: so that many artists who started out to write only a novel ended up by providing us with a portrait of themselves. It alone can become, like the epic, a mirror of the whole circumambient world, an image of the age. And it can also—more than any other form—hover at the midpoint between the portrayed and the portrayer, free of all real and ideal self-interest, on the wings of poetic reflection, and can raise that reflection again and again to a higher power, can multiply it in an endless succession of mirrors. It is capable of the highest and most variegated refinement, not only from within outwards, but also from without inwards; capable in that it organizes—for everything that seeks a wholeness in its effects—the parts along similar lines, so that it opens up a perspective upon an infinitely increasing classicism. Romantic poetry is in the arts what wit is in philosophy, and what society and sociability, friendship and love are in life. Other kinds of poetry are finished and are now capable of being fully analyzed. The romantic kind of poetry is still in the state of becoming; that, in fact, is its real essence: that it should forever be becoming and never be perfected. It can be exhausted by no theory and only a divinatory criticism would dare try to characterize its ideal. It alone is infinite, just as it alone is free; and it recognizes as its first commandment that the will of the poet can tolerate no law above itself. The romantic kind of poetry is the only one that is

more than a kind, that is, as it were, poetry itself: for in a certain sense all poetry is or should be romantic.

121. An idea is a concept perfected to the point of irony, an absolute synthesis of absolute antitheses, the continual self-creating interchange of two conflicting thoughts. An ideal is at once idea and fact. If ideals don't have as much individuality for the thinker as the gods of antiquity do for the artist, then any concern with ideas is no more than a boring and laborious game of dice with hollow phrases, or, in the manner of the Chinese bronzes, a brooding contemplation of one's own nose. Nothing is more wretched and contemptible than this sentimental speculation without any object. But one shouldn't call this mysticism, since this beautiful old word is so very useful and indispensable for absolute philosophy, from whose perspective the spirit regards everything as a mystery and a wonder, while from other points of view it would appear theoretically and practically normal. Speculation *en detail* is as rare as abstraction *en gros,* and yet it is these that beget the whole substance of scientific wit, these that are the principles of higher criticism, the highest rungs of spiritual cultivation. The great practical abstraction is what makes the ancients—among whom this was an instinct—actually ancients. In vain did individuals express the ideal of their species completely, if the species themselves, strictly and sharply isolated, weren't freely surrendered, as it were, to their originality. But to transport oneself arbitrarily now into this, now into that sphere, as if into another world, not merely with one's reason and imagination, but with one's whole soul; to freely relinquish first one and then another part of one's being, and confine oneself entirely to a third; to seek and find now in this, now in that individual the be-all and end-all of existence, and intentionally forget everyone else: of this only a mind is capable that contains within itself simultaneously a plurality of minds and a whole system of persons, and in whose inner being the universe which, as they say, should germinate in every monad, has grown to fullness and maturity.

123. Isn't poetry the noblest and worthiest of the arts for this, among other reasons: that in it alone drama becomes possible?

139. From the romantic point of view, even the vagaries of poetry have their value as raw materials and preliminaries for universality, even when they're eccentric and monstrous, provided they have some saving grace, provided they are original.

252. A real aesthetic theory of poetry would begin with the absolute antithesis of the eternally unbridgeable gulf between art and raw beauty. It would describe their struggle and conclude with the perfect harmony of artistic and natural poetry. This is to be found only among the ancients and would in itself constitute nothing but a more elevated history of the spirit of classical poetry. But a philosophy of poetry as such would begin with the independence of beauty, with the proposition that beauty is and should be distinct from truth and morality, and that it has the same rights as these: something that—for those who are able to understand it at all—follows from the proposition I = I. It would waver between the union and the division of philosophy and poetry, between poetry and practice, poetry as such and the genres and kinds of poetry; and it would conclude with their complete union. Its beginning would provide the principles of pure poetics; its middle the theory of the particular, characteristically modern types of poetry: the didactic, the musical, the rhetorical in a higher sense, etc. The keystone would be a philosophy of the novel, the rough outlines of which are contained in Plato's political theory. Of course, to the ephemeral, unenthusiastic dilettantes, who are ignorant of the best poets of all types, this kind of poetics would seem very much like a book of trigonometry to a child who just wants to draw pictures. Only a man who knows or possesses a subject can make use of the philosophy of that subject; only he will be able to understand what that philosophy means and what it's attempting to do. But philosophy can't inoculate someone with experience and sense, or pull them out of a hat—and it shouldn't want to do so. To those who knew it already, philosophy of course brings nothing new; but only through it does it become knowledge and thereby assume a new form.

255. The more poetry becomes science, the more it also becomes art. If poetry is to become art, if the artist is to have a thorough understanding and knowledge of his ends and means, his difficulties and his subjects, then the poet will have to philosophize about his art. If he is to be more than a mere contriver and artisan, if he is to be an expert in his field and understand his fellow citizens in the kingdom of art, then he will have to become a philologist as well.

256. The basic error of sophistic aesthetics is to consider beauty merely as something given, as a psychological phenomenon. Of course, beauty isn't simply the empty thought of something that should be created, but at the same time the thing itself, one of the human spirit's original ways of acting: not simply a necessary fiction, but also a fact, that is, an eternally transcendental one.

304. Philosophy too is the result of two conflicting forces—of poetry and practice. Where these interpenetrate completely and fuse into one, there philosophy comes into being; and when philosophy disintegrates, it becomes mythology or else returns to life. The wisdom of the Greeks was created out of poetry and law. The most sublime philosophy, some few surmise, may once again turn to poetry; and

it is in fact a common occurrence that ordinary people only begin to philosophize according to their own lights after they've stopped living. It seems to me that Schelling's[1] real vocation is to describe better this chemical process of philosophizing, to isolate, wherever possible, its dynamic laws and to separate philosophy—which always must organize and disorganize itself anew—into its living, fundamental forces, and trace these back to their origins. On the other hand, his polemics, particularly his literary critique of philosophy, seem to me to represent a false tendency; and his gift for universality is probably still not sufficiently developed to be able to discover in the philosophy of physics what it seeks.

305. Intention taken to the point of irony and accompanied by the arbitrary illusion of its self-destruction is quite as naive as instinct taken to the point of irony. Just as the naive plays with the contradictions between theory and practice, so the grotesque plays with the wonderful permutations of form and matter, loves the illusion of the random and the strange and, as it were, coquettes with infinite arbitrariness. Humor deals with being and nonbeing, and its true essence is reflection. Hence its closeness to the elegy and to everything transcendental; and hence its arrogance and its bent for the mysticism of wit. Just as genius is necessary to naiveté, so too an earnest, pure beauty is a requisite of humor. Most of all humor likes to hover about the gently and clearly flowing rhapsodies of philosophy or poetry, and abhors cumbersome masses and disconnected parts.

324. All genres are good, says Voltaire,[2] except the one that's boring. But what is the boring genre? It may be bigger than all the rest, and many paths may lead to it. But the shortest probably is when a work itself is unsure of its own proper genre. Did Voltaire never follow this path?

325. Just as Simonides[3] called poetry a talking picture, and painting a mute poem, so might one say that history is philosophy in the state of becoming, and philosophy completed history. But Apollo, who neither speaks nor keeps silent but intimates, no longer is worshipped; and wherever a Muse shows herself, people immediately want to carry her off to be cross-examined. How perversely even Lessing[4] treats this clever Greek's beautiful insight, who perhaps had no opportunity to think of "descriptive poetry,"[5] and who would have considered it quite unnecessary to remember that poetry is spiritual music also, since it would never have occurred to him that the two arts could be separated.

365. Mathematics is, as it were, sensual logic. It relates to philosophy as the material arts, music and sculpture, relate to poetry.

372. In the works of the greatest poets there often breathes the spirit of a different art. Might not this be the case with painters too? Doesn't Michelangelo in a certain sense paint like a sculptor, Raphael like an architect, Correggio like a musician? And surely they aren't for this reason lesser painters than Titian, who was only a painter.[6]

434. Should poetry simply be divided up? Or should it remain one and indivisible? Or fluctuate between division and union? Most of the ways of conceiving a poetical world are still as primitive and childish as the old pre-Copernican ideas of astronomy. The usual classifications of poetry are mere dead pedantry designed for people with limited vision. Whatever somebody is capable of producing, or whatever happens to be in fashion, is the stationary earth at the center of all things. But in the universe of poetry nothing stands still, everything is developing and changing and moving harmoniously; and even the comets obey invariable laws of motion. But until the course of these heavenly bodies can be calculated and their return predicted, the true world system of poetry won't have been discovered.

450. Rousseau's[7] polemic against poetry is really only a bad imitation of Plato. Plato is more against poets than he is against poetry;[8] he thought of philosophy as the most daring dithyramb and the most monodic music. Epicurus[9] is the real enemy of art, for he wants to root out imagination and retain sense only. Spinoza[10] might be viewed as the enemy of poetry in quite a different way: because he demonstrates how far one can get with philosophy and morality unaided by poetry, and because it is very much in the spirit of his system not to isolate poetry.

451. Universality is the successive satiation of all forms and substances. Universality can attain harmony only through the conjunction of poetry and philosophy; and even the greatest, most universal works of isolated poetry and philosophy seem to lack this final synthesis. They come to a stop, still imperfect but close to the goal of harmony. The

---

[1] Friedrich Wilhelm Joseph von Schelling (1775–1854), German philosopher.
[2] François Marie Arouet de Voltaire (1694–1778), French philosopher.
[3] Simonides of Ceos (c. 556–468? B.C.), Greek lyric poet, whose statement influenced critics for centuries.
[4] Schlegel is referring to Lessing's *Laocoön* (above, page 379).
[5] [Firchow] English in the original.

[6] Michelangelo Buonarroti (1475–1564), Raphael Santi (1483–1520), Correggio (Antonio Allegri, 1494–1534), Titian (Tiziano Vecellio, c. 1490–1576), Italian painters.
[7] Jean Jacques Rousseau (1712–1778), French philosopher.
[8] An argument can perhaps be made for this view, since Plato refers to poems with apparent favor frequently in his writings.
[9] Epicurus (341–270 B.C.), Greek philosopher, founder of Epicureanism, which regarded pleasure as the highest good.
[10] Baruch Spinoza (1632–1677), Dutch philosopher.

life of the Universal Spirit is an unbroken chain of inner revolutions; all individuals—that is, all original and eternal
ones—live in him. He is a genuine polytheist and bears
within himself all Olympus.

from

On Incomprehensibility

In order to facilitate a survey of the whole system of irony,
we would like to mention here a few of the choicest kinds.
The first and most distinguished of all is coarse irony. It is
to be found in the real nature of things and is one of the
most widespread of substances; it is properly at home in the
history of mankind. Next there is fine or delicate irony; then
extra-fine. Scaramouche[1] employs the last type when he
seems to be talking amicably and earnestly with someone
when really he is only waiting for the chance to give him—
while preserving the social amenities—a kick in the behind.
This kind of irony is also to be found in poets, as well as
straightforward irony, a type that flourishes most purely and
originally in old gardens where wonderfully lovely grottoes
lure the sensitive friend of nature into their cool wombs only
to be-splash him plentifully from all sides with water and
thereby wipe him clean of delicacy. Further, dramatic irony;
that is, when an author has written three acts, then unexpectedly turns into another man and now has to write the last
two acts. Double irony, when two lines of irony run parallel
side-by-side without disturbing each other: one for the
gallery, the other for the boxes, though a few little sparks
may also manage to get behind the scenes. Finally, there is

the irony of irony. Generally speaking, the most fundamental irony of irony probably is that even it becomes tiresome
if we are always being confronted with it. But what we want
this irony to mean in the first place is something that happens in more ways than one. For example, if one speaks of
irony without using it, as I have just done; if one speaks of
irony ironically without in the process being aware of having fallen into a far more noticeable irony; if one can't
disentangle oneself from irony anymore, as seems to be
happening in this essay on incomprehensibility; if irony
turns into a mannerism and becomes, as it were, ironical
about the author; if one has promised to be ironical for some
useless book without first having checked one's supply and
then having to produce it against one's will, like an actor
full of aches and pains; and if irony runs wild and can't be
controlled any longer.

   What gods will rescue us from all these ironies? The
only solution is to find an irony that might be able to swallow
up all these big and little ironies and leave no trace of them at
all. I must confess that at precisely this moment I feel that
mine has a real urge to do just that. But even this would only
be a short-term solution. I fear that if I understand correctly
what destiny seems to be hinting at, then soon there will arise
a new generation of little ironies: for truly the stars augur the
fantastic. And even if it should happen that everything were
to be peaceful for a long period of time, one still would not be
able to put any faith in this seeming calm. Irony is something
one simply cannot play games with. It can have incredibly
long-lasting aftereffects. I have a suspicion that some of the
most conscious artists of earlier times are still carrying on
ironically, hundreds of years after their deaths, with their
most faithful followers and admirers. Shakespeare has so infinitely many depths, subterfuges, and intentions. Shouldn't he
also, then, have had the intention of concealing insidious
traps in his works to catch the cleverest artists of posterity, to
deceive them and make them believe before they realize what
they're doing that they are somewhat like Shakespeare themselves? Surely, he must be in this respect as in so many others
much more full of intentions than people usually think.

On Incomprehensibility was first published in the *Athenaeum* in 1800. It is
reprinted here in part from Peter Firchow, tr., *Friedrich Schlegel's* Lucinde
and the Fragments (Minneapolis: University of Minnesota Press, 1971).

[1] A type-character of Italian *commedia dell'arte* of the sixteenth and seventeenth centuries.

William Wordsworth

1770–1850

Wordsworth's Preface to the second edition of *Lyrical Ballads,* a major expression of the spirit of English Romanticism, shifts emphasis from the relationship between poem and reader to that between poet and poem. This is not to say that Wordsworth abandons concern for his reader. Far from it: He is deeply interested in the moral purpose and effect of his work. He considers the poet a teacher not of concepts as in the traditional notion of delight and teaching but of immediate intuitions of nature. Nevertheless, he defines the poem primarily in terms of its author's creative activity. He approaches the idea of a poem by first discussing the idea of a poet: "a man speaking to men: a man, it is true, endowed with more lively sensibility, more enthusiasm and tenderness, who has a greater knowledge of human nature, and a more comprehensive soul, than are supposed to be common among mankind." He goes on to describe the poet as one who is able to be affected more than others by imagining things not immediately present to his perception.

Wordsworth then describes the poem as a result of these powers and activities. It is a "spontaneous overflow of powerful feelings; it takes its origin from emotion recollected in tranquility." Both parts of this statement are important, the second qualifying the first: Wordsworth makes clear that the poem does not simply rush forth at the moment of experience, whatever that might be. Memory and contemplation come into play in its composition. Nevertheless, the emphasis is on the importance of feeling.

This emphasis is present also in Wordsworth's description of the poem's aim: In a poem "the feeling therein developed gives importance to the action and situation, and not the action and situation to the feeling." His view contrasts with Aristotle's raising up of plot over characterization (above, page 55). He seems to have made secondary the Aristotelian concept of the poem as an imitation of an action. The poem is the expression of feeling by means of action. This attitude, apparent in germinal form during the eighteenth century in the work of Young (above, page 347) and in the surge of interest in Longinus (above, page 94), distinguishes between feeling, which allegedly unifies, and the analytic powers, which allegedly dissect and break up experience. Feeling becomes the real basis of imagination, which becomes the power to grasp nature in its totality and to order one's experience.

The Preface is well known for the theory of poetic diction that Wordsworth polemically offers in it. He attacks the popular style of his time, accusing it of employing a "gaudy and inane phraseology" that veils nature rather than revealing its spirit. This argument is partly an outgrowth of Wordsworth's own preference for rural over urban life. It is also part of the revived interest in "ancient" British poetry set in motion in part by Bishop Percy's *Reliques of Ancient English Poetry* (1765), which revived traditional ballads. In Wordsworth's view, simple, concrete language expresses a close relationship to "the permanent forms of nature," which he associates with rural life and rural speech. The hackneyed verbal conventions of eighteenth-century poetry he associates with urban artificiality. Coleridge criticized this theory effectively, though not totally fairly, in his *Biographia Literaria.*

The literary criticism of Wordsworth has been collected by N. C. Smith (1905). Also useful is M. L. Peacock, Jr., *Critical Opinions of William Wordsworth* (1950). The standard edition of the *Poetical Works* is that of Ernest de Selincourt and Helen Darbishire (in four volumes, 1941–1947). See also G. McL. Harper, *William Wordsworth: His Life, Works, and Influence* (in two volumes, 1916); M. L. Barstow, *Wordsworth's Theory of Poetic Diction* (1917); Arthur Beatty, *William Wordsworth: His Doctrine and Art in Their Historical Relations* (1922); D. G. James, *Scepticism and Poetry* (1937); C. D. Thorpe, "The Imagination: Coleridge versus Wordsworth," *Philological Quarterly* XVIII (1939), 1–18; R. D. Havens, *The Mind of a Poet* (1941); John Jones, *The Egotistical Sublime: A History of Wordsworth's Imagination* (1954); E. D. Hirsch, Jr., *Wordsworth and Schelling* (1960); G. H. Hartman, *Wordsworth's Poetry, 1787–1814* (1964); W. J. B. Owen, *Wordsworth as Critic* (1969); James A. W. Heffernan, *Wordsworth's Theory of Poetry* (1969); Geoffrey Durrant, *Wordsworth and the Great System* (1970); Albert O. Wlecke, *Wordsworth and the Sublime* (1973); Frances Ferguson, *Wordsworth: Language as Counter-Spirit* (1977); Theresa M. Kelley, *Wordsworth's Revisionary Aesthetics* (1988); Don N. Bialostosky, *Wordsworth: Dialogics and the Practice of Criticism* (1992); Richard Bourke, *Romantic Discourse and Political Modernity* (1993).

Preface to the Second Edition of *Lyrical Ballads*

The first volume of these poems has already been submitted to general perusal. It was published, as an experiment, which, I hoped, might be of some use to ascertain how far, by fitting to metrical arrangement a selection of the real language of men in a state of vivid sensation, that sort of pleasure and that quantity of pleasure may be imparted, which a poet may rationally endeavor to impart.

I had formed no very inaccurate estimate of the probable effect of those poems: I flattered myself that they who should be pleased with them would read them with more than common pleasure: and, on the other hand, I was well aware, that by those who should dislike them they would be read with more than common dislike. The result has differed from my expectation in this only, that a greater number have been pleased than I ventured to hope I should please.

Several of my friends are anxious for the success of these poems, from a belief that, if the views with which they are composed were indeed realized, a class of poetry would be produced, well adapted to interest mankind permanently, and not unimportant in the quality, and in the multiplicity of its moral relations: and on this account they have advised me to prefix a systematic defense of the theory upon which the poems were written. But I was unwilling to undertake the task, knowing that on this occasion the reader would look coldly upon my arguments, since I might be suspected of having been principally influenced by the selfish and foolish hope of *reasoning* him into an approbation of these particular poems: and I was still more unwilling to undertake the task, because, adequately to display the opinions, and fully to enforce the arguments, would require a space wholly disproportionate to a preface. For, to treat the subject with the clearness and coherence of which it is susceptible, it would be necessary to give a full account of the present state of the public taste in this country, and to determine how far this taste is healthy or depraved; which, again, could not be determined without pointing out in what manner language and the human mind act and react on each other, and without retracing the revolutions, not of literature alone, but likewise of society itself. I have therefore altogether declined to enter regularly upon this defense; yet I am sensible

The Preface to the second edition of *Lyrical Ballads* was first published in 1800. Wordsworth subsequently revised it, and the final version appeared in the edition of his poems published in 1849–1850. The text follows that version.

that there would be something like impropriety in abruptly obtruding upon the public, without a few words of introduction, poems so materially different from those upon which general approbation is at present bestowed.

It is supposed, that by the act of writing in verse an author makes a formal engagement that he will gratify certain known habits of association; that he not only thus apprises the reader that certain classes of ideas and expressions will be found in his book, but that others will be carefully excluded. This exponent or symbol held forth by metrical language must in different eras of literature have excited very different expectations: for example, in the age of Catullus, Terence, and Lucretius, and that of Statius or Claudian; and in our own country, in the age of Shakespeare and Beaumont and Fletcher, and that of Donne and Cowley, or Dryden, or Pope.[1] I will not take upon me to determine the exact import of the promise which, by the act of writing in verse, an author in the present day makes to his reader: but it will undoubtedly appear to many persons that I have not fulfilled the terms of an engagement thus voluntarily contracted. They who have been accustomed to the gaudiness and inane phraseology of many modern writers, if they persist in reading this book to its conclusion, will, no doubt, frequently have to struggle with feelings of strangeness and awkwardness: they will look round for poetry, and will be induced to inquire by what species of courtesy these attempts can be permitted to assume that title. I hope therefore the reader will not censure me for attempting to state what I have proposed to myself to perform; and also (as far as the limits of a preface will permit) to explain some of the chief reasons which have determined me in the choice of my purpose: that at least he may be spared any unpleasant feeling of disappointment, and that I myself may be protected from one of the most dishonorable accusations which can be brought against an author; namely, that of an indolence which prevents him from endeavoring to ascertain what is his duty, or, when his duty is ascertained, prevents him from performing it.

The principal object, then, proposed in these poems was to choose incidents and situations from common life, and to relate or describe them, throughout, as far as was possible, in a selection of language really used by men, and, at the same time, to throw over them a certain coloring of imagination, whereby ordinary things should be presented to the mind in an unusual aspect; and further, and above all, to make these incidents and situations interesting by tracing in them, truly though not ostentatiously, the primary laws of our nature: chiefly, as far as regards the manner in which we associate ideas in a state of excitement. Humble and rustic life was generally chosen, because, in that condition, the essential passions of the heart find a better soil in which they can attain their maturity, are less under restraint, and speak a plainer and more emphatic language; because in that condition of life our elementary feelings coexist in a state of greater simplicity, and, consequently, may be more accurately contemplated, and more forcibly communicated; because the manners of rural life germinate from those elementary feelings, and, from the necessary character of rural occupations, are more easily comprehended, and are more durable; and, lastly, because in that condition the passions of men are incorporated with the beautiful and permanent forms of nature. The language, too, of these men has been adopted (purified indeed from what appears to be its real defects, from all lasting and rational causes of dislike or disgust) because such men hourly communicate with the best objects from which the best part of language is originally derived; and because, from their rank in society and the sameness and narrow circle of their intercourse, being less under the influence of social vanity, they convey their feelings and notions in simple and unelaborated expressions. Accordingly, such a language, arising out of repeated experience and regular feelings, is a more permanent, and a far more philosophical language than that which is frequently substituted for it by poets, who think that they are conferring honor upon themselves and their art, in proportion as they separate themselves from the sympathies of men, and indulge in arbitrary and capricious habits of expression, in order to furnish food for fickle tastes, and fickle appetites, of their own creation.[2]

I cannot, however, be insensible to the present outcry against the triviality and meanness, both of thought and language, which some of my contemporaries have occasionally introduced into their metrical compositions; and I acknowledge that this defect, where it exists, is more dishonorable to the writer's own character than false refinement or arbitrary innovation, though I should contend at the same time it is far less pernicious in the sum of its consequences. From such verses the poems in these volumes will be found distinguished at least by one mark of difference, that each of them has a worthy *purpose*. Not that I always began to write with a distinct purpose formally conceived; but habits of

---

[1]Caius Valerius Catullus (84–54 B.C.), Publius Terence Afer (c. 185–c. 159 B.C.), Titus Lucretius Carus (c. 99–c. 55 B.C.), Publius Popinius Statius (c. 40–c. 96), Claudius Claudianus (d. 408), all Roman writers; William Shakespeare (1565–1616), Francis Beaumont (1584–1616), John Fletcher (1579–1625), all English dramatists; John Donne (1571–1631), Abraham Cowley (1618–1667), English poets; John Dryden (above, page 253), Alexander Pope (above, page 297).

[2][Wordsworth] It is worthwhile here to observe that the affecting parts of Chaucer are almost always expressed in language pure and universally intelligible even to this day.

meditation have, I trust, so prompted and regulated my feelings, that my descriptions of such objects as strongly excite those feelings will be found to carry along with them a *purpose*. If this opinion be erroneous, I can have little right to the name of a poet. For all good poetry is the spontaneous overflow of powerful feelings: and though this be true, poems to which any value can be attached were never produced on any variety of subjects but by a man who, being possessed of more than usual organic sensibility, had also thought long and deeply. For our continued influxes of feeling are modified and directed by our thoughts, which are indeed the representatives of all our past feelings; and, as by contemplating the relation of these general representatives to each other, we discover what is really important to men, so, by the repetition and continence of this act, our feelings will be connected with important subjects, till at length, if we be originally possessed of much sensibility, such habits of mind will be produced that, by obeying blindly and mechanically the impulses of those habits, we shall describe objects, and utter sentiments, of such a nature, and in such connection with each other, that the understanding of the reader must necessarily be in some degree enlightened, and his affections strengthened and purified.

It has been said that each of these poems has a purpose. Another circumstance must be mentioned which distinguishes these poems from the popular poetry of the day; it is this, that the feeling therein developed gives importance to the action and situation, and not the action and situation to the feeling.[3]

A sense of false modesty shall not prevent me from asserting that the reader's attention is pointed to this mark of distinction, far less for the sake of these particular poems than from the general importance of the subject. The subject is indeed important! For the human mind is capable of being excited without the application of gross and violent stimulants; and he must have a very faint perception of its beauty and dignity who does know know this, and who does not further know that one being is elevated above another in proportion as he possesses this capability. It has therefore appeared to me that to endeavor to produce or enlarge this capability is one of the best services in which, at any period, a writer can be engaged; but this service, excellent at all times, is especially so at the present day. For a multitude of causes, unknown to former times, are now acting with a combined force to blunt the discriminating powers of the mind, and, unfitting it for all voluntary exertion, to reduce it to a state of almost savage torpor. The most effective of these causes are the great national events which are daily taking place,[4] and the increasing accumulation of men in cities, where the uniformity of their occupations produces a craving for extraordinary incident, which the rapid communication of intelligence hourly gratifies. To this tendency of life and manners the literature and theatrical exhibitions of the country have conformed themselves. The invaluable works of our elder writers, I had almost said the works of Shakespeare and Milton, are driven into neglect by frantic novels,[5] sickly and stupid German tragedies, and deluges of idle and extravagant stories in verse.—When I think upon this degrading thirst after outrageous stimulation, I am almost ashamed to have spoken of the feeble endeavor made in these volumes to counteract it; and, reflecting upon the magnitude of the general evil, I should be oppressed with no dishonorable melancholy, had I not a deep impression of certain inherent and indestructible qualities of the human mind, and likewise of certain powers in the great and permanent objects that act upon it, which are equally inherent and indestructible; and were there not added to this impression a belief that the time is approaching when the evil will be systematically opposed, by men of greater powers, and with far more distinguished success.

Having dwelt thus long on the subjects and aim of these poems, I shall request the reader's permission to apprise him of a few circumstances relating to their *style,* in order, among other reasons, that he may not censure me for not having performed what I never attempted. The reader will find that personifications of abstract ideas rarely occur in these volumes, and are utterly rejected, as an ordinary device to elevate the style, and raise it above prose.[6] My purpose was to imitate, and, as far as possible, to adopt the very language of men; and assuredly such personifications do not make any natural or regular part of that language. They are, indeed, a figure of speech occasionally prompted by passion, and I have made use of them as such; but have endeavored utterly to reject them as a mechanical device of style, or as a family language which writers in meter seem to lay claim to by prescription. I have wished to keep the reader in the company of flesh and blood, persuaded that by so doing I shall interest him. Others who pursue a different track will interest him likewise; I do not interfere with their claim, but wish to prefer a claim of my own. There will also be found in these volumes little of what is usually called poetic diction; as much pains has been taken to avoid it as is ordi-

---

[3] In contrast to Aristotle (above, page 55), Wordsworth does not place action (plot) first in importance.

[4] Among these, the war with France.

[5] Wordsworth refers to the popular "gothic" novels of the time.

[6] Here Wordsworth is allied with other writers of the time who denigrate what they call allegory.

narily taken to produce it; this has been done for the reason already alleged, to bring my language near to the language of men; and further, because the pleasure which I have proposed to myself to impart is of a kind very different from that which is supposed by many persons to be the proper object of poetry. Without being culpably particular, I do not know how to give my reader a more exact notion of the style in which it was my wish and intention to write, than by informing him that I have at all times endeavored to look steadily at my subject; consequently there is, I hope, in these poems little falsehood of description, and my ideas are expressed in language fitted to their respective importance. Something must have been gained by this practice, as it is friendly to one property of all good poetry, namely, good sense: but it has necessarily cut me off from a large portion of phrases and figures of speech which from father to son have long been regarded as the common inheritance of poets. I have also thought it expedient to restrict myself still further, having abstained from the use of many expressions, in themselves proper and beautiful, but which have been foolishly repeated by bad poets, till such feelings of disgust are connected with them as it is scarcely possible by any art of association to overpower.

If in a poem there should be found a series of lines, or even a single line, in which the language, though naturally arranged, and according to the strict laws of meter, does not differ from that of prose, there is a numerous class of critics, who, when they stumble upon these prosaisms, as they call them, imagine that they have made a notable discovery, and exult over the poet as over a man ignorant of his own profession. Now these men would establish a canon of criticism which the reader will conclude he must utterly reject, if he wishes to be pleased with these volumes. And it would be a most easy task to prove to him that not only the language of a large portion of every good poem, even of the most elevated character, must necessarily, except with reference to the meter, in no respect differ from that of good prose, but likewise that some of the most interesting parts of the best poems will be found to be strictly the language of prose when prose is well written. The truth of this assertion might be demonstrated by innumerable passages from almost all the poetical writings, even of Milton himself. To illustrate the subject in a general manner, I will here adduce a short composition of Gray, who was at the head of those who, by their reasonings, have attempted to widen the space of separation betwixt prose and metrical composition, and was more than any other man curiously elaborate in the structure of his own poetic diction.

In vain to me the smiling mornings shine,
And reddening Phoebus lifts his golden fire:

The birds in vain their amorous descant join,
Or cheerful fields resume their green attire.
These ears, alas! for other notes repine;
A different object do these eyes require;
My lonely anguish melts no heart but mine;
And in my breast the imperfect joys expire;
Yet morning smiles the busy race to cheer,
And new-born pleasure brings to happier men;
The fields to all their wonted tribute bear;
To warm their little loves the birds complain.
I fruitless mourn to him that cannot hear,
And weep the more because I weep in vain.[7]

It will easily be perceived, that the only part of this sonnet which is of any value is the lines printed in italics; it is equally obvious that, except in the rhyme, and in the use of the single word *fruitless* for fruitlessly, which is so far a defect, the language of these lines does in no respect differ from that of prose.

By the foregoing quotation it has been shown that the language of prose may yet be well adapted to poetry; and it was previously asserted that a large portion of the language of every good poem can in no respect differ from that of good prose. We will go further. It may be safely affirmed that there neither is, nor can be, any *essential* difference between the language of prose and metrical composition. We are fond of tracing the resemblance between poetry and painting, and, accordingly, we call them sisters:[8] but where shall we find bonds of connection sufficiently strict to typify the affinity betwixt metrical and prose composition? They both speak by and to the same organs: the bodies in which both of them are clothed may be said to be of the same substance, their affections are kindred, and almost identical, not necessarily differing even in degree; poetry[9] sheds no tears "such as angels weep," but natural and human tears; she can boast of no celestial ichor that distinguishes her vital juices from those of prose; the same human blood circulates through the veins of them both.

If it be affirmed that rhyme and metrical arrangement of themselves constitute a distinction which overturns what

---

[7] Thomas Gray (1716–1771), *Sonnet on the Death of Mr. Richard West.*
[8] The term "sister arts" was widely used in the eighteenth century to denote the relations among the arts of poetry, painting, sculpture, and music.
[9] [Wordsworth] I here use the word *poetry* (though against my own judgment) as opposed to the word *prose,* and synonymous with metrical composition. But much confusion has been introduced into criticism by this contradiction of poetry and prose, instead of the more philosophical one of poetry and matter of fact, or science. The only strict antithesis to prose is meter; nor is this, in truth, a strict antithesis, because lines and passages of meter so naturally occur in writing prose, that it would be scarcely possible to avoid them, even were it desirable.

has just been said on the strict affinity of metrical language with that of prose, and paves the way for other artificial distinctions which the mind voluntarily admits, I answer that the language of such poetry as is here recommended is, as far as is possible, a selection of the language really spoken by men; that this selection, wherever it is made with true taste and feeling, will of itself form a distinction far greater than would at first be imagined, and will entirely separate the composition from the vulgarity and meanness of ordinary life; and, if meter be superadded thereto, I believe that a dissimilitude will be produced altogether sufficient for the gratification of a rational mind. What other distinction would we have? Whence is it to come? And where is it to exist? Not, surely, where the poet speaks through the mouths of his characters: it cannot be necessary here, either for elevation of style, or any of its supposed ornaments: for, if the poet's subject be judiciously chosen, it will naturally, and upon fit occasion, lead him to passions the language of which, if selected truly and judiciously, must necessarily be dignified and variegated, and alive with metaphors and figures. I forbear to speak of an incongruity which would shock the intelligent reader, should the poet interweave any foreign splendor of his own with that which the passion naturally suggests: it is sufficient to say that such addition is unnecessary. And surely it is more probable that those passages which with propriety abound with metaphors and figures will have their due effect, if, upon other occasions where the passions are of a milder character, the style also be subdued and temperate.

But as the pleasure which I hope to give by the poems now presented to the reader must depend entirely on just notions upon this subject, and as it is in itself of high importance to our taste and moral feelings, I cannot content myself with these detached remarks. And if, in what I am about to say, it shall appear to some that my labor is unnecessary, and that I am like a man fighting a battle without enemies, such persons may be reminded that, whatever be the language outwardly holden by men, a practical faith in the opinions which I am wishing to establish is almost unknown. If my conclusions are admitted, and carried as far as they must be carried if admitted at all, our judgments concerning the works of the greatest poets both ancient and modern will be far different from what they are at present, both when we praise, and when we censure; and our moral feelings influencing and influenced by these judgments will, I believe, be corrected and purified.

Taking up the subject, then, upon general grounds, let me ask, what is meant by the word *poet*? What is a poet? To whom does he address himself? And what language is to be expected from him?—He is a man speaking to men; a man,

it is true, endowed with more lively sensibility, more enthusiasm and tenderness, who has a greater knowledge of human nature, and a more comprehensive soul, than are supposed to be common among mankind; a man pleased with his own passions and volitions, and who rejoices more than other men in the spirit of life that is in him; delighting to contemplate similar volitions and passions as manifested in the goings-on of the universe, and habitually impelled to create them where he does not find them. To these qualities he has added a disposition to be affected more than other men by absent things as if they were present; an ability of conjuring up in himself passions which are indeed far from being the same as those produced by real events, yet (especially in those parts of the general sympathy which are pleasing and delightful) do more nearly resemble the passions produced by real events than anything which, from the motions of their own minds merely, other men are accustomed to feel in themselves—whence, and from practice, he has acquired a greater readiness and power in expressing what he thinks and feels, and especially those thoughts and feelings which, by his own choice, or from the structure of his own mind, arise in him without immediate external excitement.

But whatever portion of this faculty we may suppose even the greatest poet to possess, there cannot be a doubt that the language which it will suggest to him must often, in liveliness and truth, fall short of that which is uttered by men in real life under the actual pressure of those passions, certain shadows of which the poet thus produces, or feels to be produced, in himself.

However exalted a notion we would wish to cherish of the character of a poet, it is obvious that while he describes and imitates passions, his employment is in some degree mechanical, compared with the freedom and power of real and substantial action and suffering. So that it will be the wish of the poet to bring his feelings near to those of the persons whose feelings he describes,—nay, for short spaces of time, perhaps, to let himself slip into an entire delusion, and even confound and identify his own feelings with theirs; modifying only the language which is thus suggested to him by a consideration that he describes for a particular purpose, that of giving pleasure. Here, then, he will apply the principle of selection which has been already insisted upon. He will depend upon this for removing what would otherwise be painful or disgusting in the passion; he will feel that there is no necessity to trick out or to elevate nature; and, the more industriously he applies this principle, the deeper will be his faith that no words which *his* fancy or imagination can suggest will be to be compared with those which are the emanations of reality and truth.

But it may be said by those who do not object to the general spirit of these remarks, that, as it is impossible for the poet to produce upon all occasions language as exquisitely fitted for the passion as that which the real passion itself suggests, it is proper that he should consider himself as in the situation of a translator, who does not scruple to substitute excellencies of another kind for those which are unattainable by him, and endeavors occasionally to surpass his original, in order to make some amends for the general inferiority to which he feels that he must submit. But this would be to encourage idleness and unmanly despair. Further, it is the language of men who speak of what they do not understand: who talk of poetry as of a matter of amusement and idle pleasure; who will converse with us as gravely about a *taste* for poetry, as they express it, as if it were a thing as indifferent as a taste for rope dancing, or Frontiniac or Sherry. Aristotle, I have been told, has said that poetry is the most philosophic of all writing:[10] it is so: its object is truth, not individual and local, but general,[11] and operative; not standing upon external testimony, but carried alive into the heart by passion; truth which is its own testimony, which gives competence and confidence to the tribunal to which it appeals, and receives them from the same tribunal. Poetry is the image of man and nature. The obstacles which stand in the way of the fidelity of the biographer and historian, and of their consequent utility, are incalculably greater than those which are to be encountered by the poet who comprehends the dignity of his art. The poet writes under one restriction only, namely, the necessity of giving immediate pleasure to a human being possessed of that information which may be expected from him, not as a lawyer, a physician, a mariner, an astronomer, or a natural philosopher, but as a man. Except this one restriction, there is no object standing between the poet and the image of things; between this, and the biographer and historian, there are a thousand.

Nor let this necessity of producing immediate pleasure be considered as a degradation of the poet's art. It is far otherwise. It is an acknowledgment of the beauty of the universe, an acknowledgment the more sincere, because not formal, but indirect; it is a task light and easy to him who looks at the world in the spirit of love: further, it is a homage paid to the native and naked dignity of man, to the grand elementary principle of pleasure, by which he knows, and feels, and lives, and moves. We have no sympathy but what is propagated by pleasure: I would not be misunderstood; but wherever we sympathize with pain, it will be found that the sympathy is produced and carried on by subtle combinations with pleasure. We have no knowledge, that is, no general principles drawn from the contemplation of particular facts, but what has been built up by pleasure, and exists in us by pleasure alone. The man of science, the chemist and mathematician, whatever difficulties and disgusts they may have had to struggle with, know and feel this. However painful may be the objects with which the anatomist's knowledge is connected, he feels that his knowledge is pleasure; and where he has no pleasure he has no knowledge. What then does the poet? He considers man and the objects that surround him as acting and reacting upon each other, so as to produce an infinite complexity of pain and pleasure; he considers man in his own nature and in his ordinary life as contemplating this with a certain quantity of immediate knowledge, with certain convictions, intuitions, and deductions, which from habit acquire the quality of intuitions; he considers him as looking upon this complex scene of ideas and sensations, and finding everywhere objects that immediately excite in him sympathies which, from the necessities of his nature, are accompanied by an overbalance of enjoyment.

To this knowledge which all men carry about with them, and to these sympathies in which, without any other discipline than that of our daily life, we are fitted to take delight, the poet principally directs his attention. He considers man and nature as essentially adapted to each other, and the mind of man as naturally the mirror of the fairest and most interesting properties of nature. And thus the poet, prompted by this feeling of pleasure, which accompanies him through the whole course of his studies, converses with general nature, with affections akin to those which, through labor and length of time, the man of science has raised up in himself, by conversing with those particular parts of nature which are the objects of his studies. The knowledge both of the poet and the man of science is pleasure; but the knowledge of the one cleaves to us as a necessary part of our existence, our natural and unalienable inheritance; the other is a personal and individual acquisition, slow to come to us, and by no habitual and direct sympathy connecting us with our fellow beings. The man of science seeks truth as a remote and unknown benefactor; he cherishes and loves it in his solitude: the poet, singing a song in which all human beings join with him, rejoices in the presence of truth as our visible friend and hourly companion. Poetry is the breath and finer spirit of all knowledge; it is the impassioned expression which is in the countenance of all science. Emphatically may it be said of the poet, as Shakespeare hath said of man, "that he looks before and after." He is the rock of defense

---

[10] Aristotle (*Poetics,* above, page 57) says that poetry is more philosophical than history on the ground that history addresses particulars and poetry universals.

[11] Wordsworth's use of "general" here rather than "universal" indicates the influence of Locke's empiricism (above, page 281).

for human nature; an upholder and preserver, carrying everywhere with him relationship and love. In spite of difference of soil and climate, of language and manners, of laws and customs; in spite of things silently gone out of mind, and things violently destroyed; the poet binds together by passion and knowledge the vast empire of human society, as it is spread over the whole earth, and over all time. The objects of the poet's thoughts are everywhere; though the eyes and senses of man are, it is true, his favorite guides, yet he will follow wheresoever he can find an atmosphere of sensation in which to move his wings. Poetry is the first and last of all knowledge—it is as immortal as the heart of man. If the labors of men of science should ever create any material revolution, direct or indirect, in our condition, and in the impressions which we habitually receive, the poet will sleep then no more than at present; he will be ready to follow the steps of the man of science, not only in those general indirect effects, but he will be at his side, carrying sensation into the midst of the objects of the science itself. The remotest discoveries of the chemist, the botanist, or mineralogist, will be as proper objects of the poet's art as any upon which it can be employed, if the time should ever come when these things shall be familiar to us, and the relations under which they are contemplated by the followers of these respective sciences shall be manifestly and palpably material to us as enjoying and suffering beings. If the time should ever come when what is now called science, thus familiarized to men, shall be ready to put on, as it were, a form of flesh and blood, the poet will lend his divine spirit to aid the transfiguration, and will welcome the being thus produced, as a dear and genuine inmate of the household of man.—It is not, then, to be supposed that anyone who holds that sublime notion of poetry which I have attempted to convey, will break in upon the sanctity and truth of his pictures by transitory and accidental ornaments, and endeavor to excite admiration of himself by arts the necessity of which must manifestly depend upon the assumed meanness of his subject.[12]

What has been thus far said applies to poetry in general, but especially to those parts of composition where the poet speaks through the mouths of his characters; and upon this point it appears to authorize the conclusion that there are few persons of good sense who would not allow that the dramatic parts of composition are defective, in proportion as they deviate from the real language of nature, and are colored by a diction of the poet's own, either peculiar to him as an individual poet or belonging simply to poets in general; to a body of men who, from the circumstance of their compositions being in meter, it is expected will employ a particular language.

It is not, then, in the dramatic parts of composition that we look for this distinction of language; but still it may be proper and necessary where the poet speaks to us in his own person and character. To this I answer by referring the reader to the description before given of a poet. Among the qualities there enumerated as principally conducing to form a poet, is implied nothing differing in kind from other men, but only in degree. The sum of what was said is, that the poet is chiefly distinguished from other men by a greater promptness to think and feel without immediate external excitement, and a greater power in expressing such thoughts and feelings as are produced in him in that manner. But these passions and thoughts and feelings are the general passions and thoughts and feelings of men. And with what are they connected? Undoubtedly with our moral sentiments and animal sensations, and with the causes which excite these; with the operations of the elements, and the appearances of the visible universe; with storm and sunshine, with the revolutions of the seasons, with cold and heat, with loss of friends and kindred, with injuries and resentments, gratitude and hope, with fear and sorrow. These, and the like, are the sensations and objects which the poet describes, as they are the sensations of other men, and the objects which interest them. The poet thinks and feels in the spirit of human passions. How, then, can his language differ in any material degree from that of all other men who feel vividly and see clearly? It might be *proved* that it is impossible. But supposing that this were not the case, the poet might then be allowed to use a peculiar language when expressing his feelings for his own gratification, or that of men like himself. But poets do not write for poets alone, but for men. Unless, therefore, we are advocates for that admiration which subsists upon ignorance, and that pleasure which arises from hearing what we do not understand, the poet must descend from this supposed height; and, in order to excite rational sympathy, he must express himself as other men express themselves. To this it may be added that while he is only selecting from the real language of men, or, which amounts to the same thing, composing accurately in the spirit of such selection, he is treading upon safe ground, and we know what we are to expect from him. Our feelings are the same with respect to meter; for, as it may be proper to remind the reader, the distinction of meter is regular and uniform, and not, like that which is produced by what is usually called *poetic diction*, arbitrary, and subject to infinite caprices

---

[12]In this long paragraph, the old classical contrast of poetry with history and philosophy is replaced by the modern contrast of poetry to science, which dominates criticism into the middle of the twentieth century. It expresses a new anxiety about poetry's cultural position.

upon which no calculation whatever can be made. In the one case, the reader is utterly at the mercy of the poet, respecting what imagery or diction he may choose to connect with the passion; whereas in the other, the meter obeys certain laws, to which the poet and reader both willingly submit because they are certain, and because no interference is made by them with the passion, but such as the concurring testimony of ages has shown to heighten and improve the pleasure which coexists with it.

It will now be proper to answer an obvious question, namely, why, professing these opinions, have I written in verse? To this, in addition to such answer as is included in what has been already said, I reply, in the first place, because, however I may have restricted myself, there is still left open to me what confessedly constitutes the most valuable object of all writing, whether in prose or verse—the great and universal passions of men, the most general and interesting of their occupations, and the entire world of nature before me—to supply endless combinations of forms and imagery. Now, supposing for a moment that whatever is interesting in these objects may be as vividly described in prose, why should I be condemned for attempting to superadd to such description the charm which, by the consent of all nations, is acknowledged to exist in metrical language? To this, by such as are yet unconvinced, it may be answered that a very small part of the pleasure given by poetry depends upon the meter, and that it is injudicious to write in meter, unless it be accompanied with the other artificial distinctions of style with which meter is usually accompanied, and that, by such deviation, more will be lost from the shock which will thereby be given to the reader's associations than will be counterbalanced by any pleasure which he can derive from the general power of numbers. In answer to those who still contend for the necessity of accompanying meter with certain appropriate colors of style in order to the accomplishment of its appropriate end, and who also, in my opinion, greatly underrate the power of meter in itself, it might, perhaps, as far as relates to these volumes, have been almost sufficient to observe that poems are extant, written upon more humble subjects, and in a still more naked and simple style, which have continued to give pleasure from generation to generation. Now if nakedness and simplicity be a defect, the fact here mentioned affords a strong presumption that poems somewhat less naked and simple are capable of affording pleasure at the present day; and what I wished *chiefly* to attempt, at present, was to justify myself for having written under the impression of this belief.

But various causes might be pointed out why, when the style is manly, and the subject of some importance, words metrically arranged will long continue to impart such a pleasure to mankind as he who proves the extent of that pleasure will be desirous to impart. The end of poetry is to produce excitement in coexistence with an overbalance of pleasure; but, by the supposition, excitement is an unusual and irregular state of the mind; ideas and feelings do not, in that state, succeed each other in accustomed order. If the words, however, by which this excitement is produced be in themselves powerful, or the images and feelings have an undue proportion of pain connected with them, there is some danger that the excitement may be carried beyond its proper bounds. Now the copresence of something regular, something to which the mind has been accustomed in various moods and in a less excited state, cannot but have great efficacy in tempering and restraining the passion by an intertexture of ordinary feeling, and of feeling not strictly and necessarily connected with the passion. This is unquestionably true; and hence, though the opinion will at first appear paradoxical, from the tendency of meter to divest language, in a certain degree, of its reality, and thus to throw a sort of half-consciousness of unsubstantial existence over the whole composition, there can be little doubt but that more pathetic situations and sentiments, that is, those which have a greater proportion of pain connected with them, may be endured in metrical composition, especially in rhyme, than in prose. The meter of the old ballads is very artless, yet they contain many passages which would illustrate this opinion; and, I hope, if the following poems be attentively perused, similar instances will be found in them. This opinion may be further illustrated by appealing to the reader's own experience of the reluctance with which he comes to the reperusal of the distressful parts of *Clarissa Harlowe,* or *The Gamester,*[13] while Shakespeare's writings, in the most pathetic scenes, never act upon us, as pathetic, beyond the bounds of pleasure—an effect which, in a much greater degree than might at first be imagined, is to be ascribed to small but continual and regular impulses of pleasurable surprise from the metrical arrangement.—On the other hand (what it must be allowed will much more frequently happen) if the poet's words should be incommensurate with the passion, and inadequate to raise the reader to a height of desirable excitement, then (unless the poet's choice of his meter has been grossly injudicious) in the feelings of pleasure which the reader has been accustomed to connect with meter in general, and in the feeling, whether cheerful or melancholy, which he has been accustomed to connect with that particular movement of meter, there will be found

---

[13] *Clarissa Harlowe* by Samuel Richardson (1689–1761); *The Gamester* by Edward Moore (1712–1757).

something which will greatly contribute to impart passion to the words, and to effect the complex end which the poet proposes to himself.

If I had undertaken a *systematic* defense of the theory here maintained, it would have been my duty to develop the various causes upon which the pleasure received from metrical language depends. Among the chief of these causes is to be reckoned a principle which must be well known to those who have made any of the arts the object of accurate reflection; namely, the pleasure which the mind derives from the perception of similitude in dissimilitude. This principle is the great spring of the activity of our minds, and their chief feeder. From this principle the direction of the sexual appetite, and all the passions connected with it, take their origin: it is the life of our ordinary conversation; and upon the accuracy with which similitude are perceived, depend our taste and our moral feelings. It would not be a useless employment to apply this principle to the consideration of meter, and to show that meter is hence enabled to afford much pleasure, and to point out in what manner that pleasure is produced. But my limits will not permit me to enter upon this subject, and I must content myself with a general summary.

I have said that poetry is the spontaneous overflow of powerful feelings: it takes its origin from emotion recollected in tranquility: the emotion is contemplated till, by a species of reaction, the tranquility gradually disappears, and an emotion, kindred to that which was before the subject of contemplation, is gradually produced, and does itself actually exist in the mind. In this mood successful composition generally begins, and in a mood similar to this it is carried on; but the emotion, of whatever kind, and in whatever degree, from various causes, is qualified by various pleasures, so that in describing any passions whatsoever, which are voluntarily described, the mind will, upon the whole, be in a state of enjoyment. If nature be thus cautious to preserve in a state of enjoyment a being so employed, the poet ought to profit by the lesson held forth to him, and ought especially to take care that, whatever passions he communicates to his reader, those passions, if his reader's mind be sound and vigorous, should always be accompanied with an overbalance of pleasure. Now the music of harmonious metrical language, the sense of difficulty overcome, and the blind association of pleasure which has been previously received from works of rhyme or meter of the same or similar construction, an indistinct perception perpetually renewed of language closely resembling that of real life, and yet, in the circumstance of meter, differing from it so widely—all these imperceptibly make up a complex feeling of delight, which is of the most important use in tempering the painful feeling always found intermingled with powerful descriptions of the deeper passion. This effect is always produced in pathetic and impassioned poetry; while in lighter compositions the ease and gracefulness with which the poet manages his numbers are themselves confessedly a principal source of the gratification of the reader. All that it is *necessary* to say, however, upon this subject, may be effected by affirming, what few persons will deny, that of two descriptions, either of passions, manners, or characters each of them equally well executed, the one in prose and the other in verse, the verse will be read a hundred times where the prose is read once.

Having thus explained a few of my reasons for writing in verse, and why I have chosen subjects from common life, and endeavored to bring my language near to the real language of men, if I have been too minute in pleading my own cause, I have at the same time been treating a subject of general interest; and for this reason a few words shall be added with reference solely to these particular poems, and to some defects which will probably be found in them. I am sensible that my associations must have sometimes been particular instead of general, and that, consequently, giving to things a false importance, I may have sometimes written upon unworthy subjects; but I am less apprehensive on this account, than that my language may frequently have suffered from those arbitrary connections of feelings and ideas with particular words and phrases, from which no man can altogether protect himself. Hence I have no doubt that, in some instances, feelings, even of the ludicrous, may be given to my readers by expressions which appeared to me tender and pathetic. Such faulty expressions, were I convinced they were faulty at present, and that they must necessarily continue to be so, I would willingly take all reasonable pains to correct. But it is dangerous to make these alterations on the simple authority of a few individuals, or even of certain classes of men; for where the understanding of an author is not convinced, or his feelings altered, this cannot be done without great injury to himself: for his own feelings are his stay and support; and, if he set them aside in one instance, he may be induced to repeat this act till his mind shall lose all confidence in itself, and become utterly debilitated. To this it may he added that the critic ought never to forget that he is himself exposed to the same errors as the poet, and perhaps in a much greater degree: for there can be no presumption in saying of most readers that it is not probable they will be so well acquainted with the various stages of meaning through which words have passed, or with the fickleness or stability of the relations of particular ideas to each other; and, above all, since they are so much less interested in the subject, they may decide lightly and carelessly.

Long as the reader has been detained, I hope he will permit me to caution him against a mode of false criticism which has been applied to poetry, in which the language closely resembles that of life and nature. Such verses have been triumphed over in parodies, of which Dr. Johnson's stanza is a fair specimen:

> I put my hat upon my head
> And walked into the Strand,
> And there I met another man
> Whose hat was in his hand.

Immediately under these lines let us place one of the most justly admired stanzas of the *Babes in the Woods.*[14]

> These pretty babes with hand in hand
> Went wandering up and down;
> But never more they saw the man
> Approaching from the town.

In both those stanzas the words, and the order of the words in no respect differ from the most unimpassioned conversation. There are words in both, for example, *the Strand* and *the town,* connected with none but the most familiar ideas; yet the one stanza we admit as admirable, and the other as a fair example of the superlatively contemptible. Whence arises this difference? Not from the meter, not from the language, not from the order of the words; but the *matter* expressed in Dr. Johnson's stanza is contemptible. The proper method of treating trivial and simple verses to which Dr. Johnson's stanza would be a fair parallelism, is not to say, this is a bad kind of poetry, or, this is not poetry; but, this wants sense; it is neither interesting in itself, nor can *lead* to anything interesting; the images neither originate in that sane state of feeling which arises out of thought, nor can excite thought or feeling in the reader. This is the only sensible manner of dealing with such verses. Why trouble yourself about the species till you have previously decided upon the genus? Why take pains to prove that an ape is not a Newton, when it is self-evident that he is not a man?

One request I must make of my reader, which is, that in judging these poems he would decide by his own feelings genuinely, and not by reflection upon what will probably be the judgment of others. How common is it to hear a person say, I myself do not object to this style of composition, or this or that expression, but to such and such classes of people it will appear mean or ludicrous! This mode of criticism,

so destructive of all sound unadulterated judgment, is almost universal: let the reader then abide, independently, by his own feelings, and, if he finds himself affected, let him not suffer such conjectures to interfere with his pleasure.

If an author, by any single composition, has impressed us with respect for his talents, it is useful to consider this as affording a presumption that on other occasions, where we have been displeased, he nevertheless may not have written ill or absurdly; and further, to give him so much credit for this one composition as may induce us to review what has displeased us with more care than we should otherwise have bestowed upon it. This is not only an act of justice, but, in our decisions upon poetry especially, may conduce in a high degree to the improvement of our own taste; for an *accurate* taste in poetry, and in all the other arts, as Sir Joshua Reynolds has observed, is an *acquired* talent, which can only be produced by thought and a long-continued inter-course with the best models of composition.[15] This is mentioned, not with so ridiculous a purpose as to prevent the most inexperienced reader from judging for himself (I have already said that I wish him to judge for himself), but merely to temper the rashness of decision, and to suggest that, if poetry be a subject on which much time has not been bestowed, the judgment may be erroneous; and that, in many cases, it necessarily will be so.

Nothing would, I know, have so effectually contributed to further the end which I have in view, as to have shown of what kind the pleasure is, and how that pleasure is produced, which is confessedly produced by metrical composition essentially different from that which I have here endeavored to recommend: for the reader will say that he has been pleased by such composition, and what more can be done for him? The power of any art is limited; and he will suspect that, if it be proposed to furnish him with new friends, that can be only upon condition of his abandoning his old friends. Besides, as I have said, the reader is himself conscious of the pleasure which he has received from such composition, composition to which he has peculiarly attached the endearing name of poetry; and all men feel an habitual gratitude, and something of an honorable bigotry, for the objects which have long continued to please them: we not only wish to be pleased, but to be pleased in that particular way in which we have been accustomed to be pleased. There is in these feelings enough to resist a host of arguments; and I should be the less able to combat them successfully, as I am willing to allow that, in order entirely to enjoy the poetry which I am recommending, it would be necessary

---

[14] An anonymous ballad.

[15] See *Discourse VII* (above, page 398ff.).

to give up much of what is ordinarily enjoyed. But, would my limits have permitted me to point out how this pleasure is produced, many obstacles might have been removed, and the reader assisted in perceiving that the powers of language are not so limited as he may suppose; and that it is possible for poetry to give other enjoyments, of a purer, more lasting, and more exquisite nature. This part of the subject has not been altogether neglected, but it has not been so much my present aim to prove that the interest excited by some other kinds of poetry is less vivid, and less worthy of the nobler powers of the mind, as to offer reasons for presuming that, if my purpose were fulfilled, a species of poetry would be produced which is genuine poetry, in its nature well adapted to interest mankind permanently, and likewise important in the multiplicity and quality of its moral relations.

From what has been said, and from a perusal of the poems, the reader will be able clearly to perceive the object which I had in view: he will determine how far it has been attained; and, what is a much more important question, whether it will be worth attaining: and upon the decision of these two questions will test my claim to the approbation of the public.

Samuel Taylor Coleridge

1772–1834

For literary criticism in English the influence of Coleridge has been massive and multifaceted, but since the publication of *The Collected Works of Samuel Taylor Coleridge* (1969–) under the general editorship of Kathleen Coburn, one might risk saying that Coleridge's exemplary visibility in literary studies has obscured his remarkable influence in other areas. For his contemporaries and immediate descendants, including such figures as John Stuart Mill and diverse members of the "Apostle's Club" at Cambridge (from John Sterling to James Clerk Maxwell), Coleridge's influence was pervasive. As Sterling said in a letter to J. C. Hare, "To Coleridge I owe education. He taught me to believe that an empirical philosophy is none, that Faith is the highest Reason, that all criticism, whether of literature, laws, or manners, is blind, without the power of discerning the organic unity of the object."[1] As one of the great auto-didacts of all time, however, Coleridge presents many difficulties, as his ambitions to articulate a complete and comprehensive "dynamical philosophy" consistently failed to find a satisfactory publishable form. As a close but critical reader of Kant, Schelling, and Fichte (from all of whom he borrowed extensively), Coleridge was influential in introducing critical and transcendental philosophy to an English audience, as well as shaping early-nineteenth-century English thought on problems of science and method.

The selections here include Coleridge's indispensable work on Shakespeare and a portion of his essay "On the Principles of Genial Criticism," as well as his celebrated definitions of Primary and Secondary Imagination and Fancy, but greater emphasis is given to his speculative work from *Biographia Literaria, The Friend, The Statesman's Manual,* and *On the Constitution of Church and State.* In these works, we see Coleridge vigorously engaged in the effort to articulate a philosophical position in which creativity is not an anomaly but a fundamental principle. Though he borrowed (and stole) from virtually everything he read, from Plato to Ralph Cudworth, to Schelling and Fichte, his work is distinguished by subtle but significant deviations from the forms of idealism characteristic of his German contemporaries. Coleridge in his later years focused increasingly on two troublesome areas: the theological idea of the trinity, and the theoretical practice of natural science. In his remarkable "Essays on Method" from *The Friend* (1809) (reprinted in the 1818 *Encyclopedia Metropolitana* and later acknowledged by Charles Sanders Peirce for their influence upon "all Europe" and as an "improvement" upon Kant),[2] Coleridge develops his view of method as inherently dynamic and progressive, with illustrations of the essential importance of unifying ideas in scientific research (with striking similarities to Thomas Kuhn's later idea of the scientific "paradigm") that identify "central experiments" or "protophenomena" that in a certain sense first *create* scientific facts *as facts.*

---

[1] Quoted from *On the Constitution of Church and State,* lxii.
[2] Peirce, *Collected Papers,* A. W. Burks, ed., 1958.

Coleridge's Trinitarian speculations, though seemingly far removed in topic, share the same conviction that an *Idea* is not simply a representation of an object, but a "living power" that brings the possible into actuality, whether in philosophy, science, religion, politics, or poetry. As these selections suggest, Coleridge's consistent attestation concerning the systematic character of his thought has a good deal more credibility than has usually been granted. Learning how to read him is, accordingly, an ongoing critical project.

The new edition of Coleridge's works edited by Kathleen Coburn, begun in 1969, is nearing completion. It includes several volumes of Coleridge's notebooks and his marginalia to other authors. Some works, however, are still only available in W. G. T. Shedd's seven-volume edition of 1889 and other miscellaneous publications. For general questions and bibliographic information, see *The Cambridge Companion to Coleridge,* edited by Lucy Newlyn (2002), and *Samuel Taylor Coleridge: An Annotated Bibliography of Criticism and Scholarship,* edited by Richard and Josephine Haven and Maurianne Adams (1976–1996). Recent biographies include Rosemary Ashton, *The Life of Samuel Taylor Coleridge: A Critical Biography* (1996), and Richard Holmes's three biographical volumes: *Coleridge* (1982), *Coleridge: Early Visions* (1989), and *Coleridge: Darker Reflections* (1998). See also J. H. Muirhead, *Coleridge as Philosopher* (1930); René Wellek, *Immanuel Kant in England* (1939); Herbert Read, *Coleridge as Critic* (1948); Gordon McKenzie, *Organic Unity in Coleridge's Theory of Imagination* (1957); James R. Jackson, *Method and Imagination in Coleridge's Criticism* (1969); Thomas McFarland, *Coleridge and the Pantheist Tradition* (1969); Owen Barfield, *What Coleridge Thought* (1971); Kathleen Coburn, ed., *Inquiring Spirit: A New Presentation of Coleridge* (1979); Raimonda Modiano, *Coleridge and the Concept of Nature* (1985); James C. McKusick, *Coleridge's Philosophy of Language* (1986); Nigel Leask, *The Politics of Imagination in Coleridge's Thought* (1988); Deirdre Coleman, *Coleridge and The Friend (1809–1810)* (1988); Gerald McNiece, *The Knowledge That Endures: Coleridge, German Philosophy and the Logic of Romantic Thought* (1991); Tim Fulford, *Coleridge's Figurative Language* (1991); Mary Anne Perkins, *Coleridge's Philosophy: Logos as a Unifying Principle* (1994); Douglas Hedley, *Coleridge, Philosophy and Religion: Aids to Reflection and the Mirror of the Spirit* (2000); Nicholas Rowe, ed., *Samuel Taylor Coleridge and the Sciences of Life* (2001); Michael John Kooy, *Coleridge, Schiller, and Aesthetic Education* (2002); Tim Milnes, *Knowledge and Indifference in English Romantic Prose* (2003).

Shakespeare's Judgment Equal to His Genius

Thus, then, Shakespeare appears, from his *Venus and Adonis* and *Rape of Lucrece* alone, apart from all his great works, to have possessed all the conditions of the true poet.[1] Let me now proceed to destroy, as far as may be in my power, the popular notion that he was a great dramatist by mere instinct, that he grew immortal in his own despite, and sank below men of second- or third-rate power when he attempted aught beside the drama—even as bees construct

---

Coleridge's lecture "Shakespeare's Judgment Equal to His Genius" was first published in 1836 but was possibly delivered as early as 1808.

[1]Coleridge had discussed *Venus and Adonis* and *The Rape of Lucrece* in an earlier lecture, *Shakespeare as a Poet Generally.*

their cells and manufacture their honey to admirable perfection; but would in vain attempt to build a nest. Now this mode of reconciling a compelled sense of inferiority with a feeling of pride began in a few pedants, who, having read that Sophocles was the great model of tragedy, and Aristotle the infallible dictator of its rules, and finding that the *Lear, Hamlet, Othello,* and other masterpieces were neither in imitation of Sophocles nor in obedience to Aristotle—and, not having (with one or two exceptions) the courage to affirm, that the delight which their country received from generation to generation, in defiance of the alterations of circumstances and habits, was wholly groundless—took upon them, as a happy medium and refuge, to talk of Shakespeare as a sort of beautiful *lusus naturae,*[2] a delightful monster, wild, indeed, and without taste or judgment, but like the inspired idiots so much venerated in the East, uttering, amid the strangest follies, the sublimest truths. In nine places out of ten in which I find his awful name mentioned, it is with some epithet of "wild," "irregular," "pure child of nature," etc. If all this be true, we must submit to it; though to a thinking mind it cannot but be painful to find any excellence, merely human, thrown out of all human analogy, and thereby leaving us neither rules for intilation, nor motives to imitate; but, if false, it is a dangerous falsehood; for it affords a refuge to secret self-conceit, enables a vain man at once to escape his reader's indignation by general swollen panegyrics, and merely by his *ipse dixit*[3] to treat as contemptible what he has not intellect enough to comprehend, or soul to feel, without assigning any reason, or referring his opinion to any demonstrative principle; thus leaving Shakespeare as a sort of grand lama, adored indeed, and his very excrements prized as relics, but with no authority or real influence. I grieve that every late voluminous edition of his works would enable me to substantiate the present charge with a variety of facts, one-tenth of which would of themselves exhaust the time allotted to me. Every critic, who has or has not made a collection of black letter books—in itself a useful and respectable amusement—puts on the seven-league boots of self-opinion, and strides at once from an illustrator into a supreme judge, and blind and deaf, fills his three-ounce phial at the waters of Niagara; and determines positively the greatness of the cataract to be neither more nor less than his three-ounce phial has been able to receive.

I think this a very serious subject. It is my earnest desire—my passionate endeavor—to enforce at various times and by various arguments and instances the close and reciprocal connection of just taste with pure morality. Without

that acquaintance with the heart of man, or that docility and childlike gladness to be made acquainted with it, which those only can have, who dare look at their own hearts—and that with a steadiness which religion only has the power of reconciling with sincere humility; without this, and the modesty produced by it. I am deeply convinced that no man, however wide his erudition, however patient his antiquarian researches, can possibly understand, or be worthy of understanding, the writings of Shakespeare.

Assuredly, that criticism of Shakespeare will alone be genial which is reverential. The Englishman, who without reverence, a proud and affectionate reverence, can utter the name of William Shakespeare, stands disqualified for the office of critic. He wants one at least of the very senses, the language of which he is to employ, and will discourse, at best, but as a blind man, while the whole harmonious creation of light and shade with all its subtle interchange of deepening and dissolving colors rises in silence to the silent fiat of the uprising Apollo. However inferior in ability I may be to some who have followed me, I own I am proud that I was the first in time who publicly demonstrated to the full extent of the position, that the supposed irregularity and extravagancies of Shakespeare were the mere dreams of a pedantry that arraigned the eagle because it had not the dimensions of the swan. In all the successive courses of lectures delivered by me, since my first attempt at the Royal Institution, it has been, and it still remains, my object, to prove that in all points from the most important to the most minute, the judgment of Shakespeare is commensurate with his genius, nay, that his genius reveals itself in his judgment, as in its most exalted form. And the more gladly do I recur to this subject from the clear conviction, that to judge aright, and with distinct consciousness of the grounds of our judgment, concerning the works of Shakespeare, implies the power and the means of judging rightly of all other works of intellect, those of abstract science alone excepted.

It is a painful truth that not only individuals, but even whole nations, are ofttimes so enslaved to the habits of their education and immediate circumstances, as not to judge disinterestedly even on those subjects, the very pleasure arising from which consists in its disinterestedness, namely, on subjects of taste and polite literature. Instead of deciding concerning their own modes and customs by any rule of reason, nothing appears rational, becoming, or beautiful to them, but what coincides with the peculiarities of their education. In this narrow circle, individuals may attain to exquisite discrimination, as the French critics have done in their own literature; but a true critic can no more be such without placing himself on some central point, from which he may command the whole, that is, some general rule,

---

[2] "Sport of nature."
[3] Literally, "He himself said it."

which, founded in reason, or the faculties common to all men, must therefore apply to each, than an astronomer can explain the movements of the solar system without taking his stand in the sun. And let me remark, that this will not tend to produce despotism, but, on the contrary, true tolerance, in the critic. He will, indeed, require, as the spirit and substance of a work, something true in human nature itself, and independent of all circumstances; but in the mode of applying it, he will estimate genius and judgment according to the felicity with which the imperishable soul of intellect shall have adapted itself to the age, the place, and the existing manners. The error he will expose lies in reversing this, and holding up the mere circumstances as perpetual, to the utter neglect of the power which can alone animate them. For art cannot exist without, or apart from, nature; and what has man of his own to give to his fellowman, but his own thoughts and feelings, and his observations so far as they are modified by his own thoughts or feelings?

Let me, then, once more submit this question to minds emancipated alike from national, or party, or sectarian prejudice. Are the plays of Shakespeare works of rude uncultivated genius, in which the splendor of the parts compensates, if aught can compensate, for the barbarous shapelessness and irregularity of the whole? Or is the form equally admirable with the matter, and the judgment of the great poet not less deserving our wonder than his genius? Or, again, to repeat the question in other words: Is Shakespeare a great dramatic poet on account only of those beauties and excellencies which he possesses in common with the ancients, but with diminished claims to our love and honor to the full extent of his differences from them? Or are these very differences additional proofs of poetic wisdom, at once results and symbols of living power as contrasted with lifeless mechanism—of free and rival originality as contradistinguished from servile imitation, or, more accurately, a blind copying of effects, instead of a true imitation of the essential principles? Imagine not that I am about to oppose genius to rules. No! The comparative value of these rules is the very cause to be tried. The spirit of poetry, like all other living powers, must of necessity circumscribe itself by rules, were it only to unite power with beauty. It must embody in order to reveal itself; but a living body is of necessity an organized one; and what is organization but the connection of parts in and for a whole, so that each part is at once end and means? This is the discovery of criticism; it is a necessity of the human mind; and all nations have felt and obeyed it, in the invention of meter, and measured sounds, as the vehicle and *involucrum*[4] of poetry, itself a fellow-growth from the same life, even as the bark is to the tree!

No work of true genius dares want its appropriate form, neither indeed is there any danger of this. As it must not, so genius cannot, be lawless: for it is even this that constitutes it genius—the power of acting creatively under laws of its own origination. How then comes it that not only single *Zoili,*[5] but whole nations have combined in unhesitating condemnation of our great dramatist, as a sort of African nature, rich in beautiful monsters, as a wild heath where islands of fertility look the greener from the surrounding waste, where the loveliest plants now shine out among unsightly weeds, and now are choked by their parasitic growth, so intertwined that we cannot disentangle the weed without snapping the flower? In this statement I have had no reference to the vulgar abuse of Voltaire, save as far as his charges are coincident with the decisions of Shakespeare's own commentators and (so they would tell you) almost idolatrous admirers. The true ground of the mistake lies in the confounding mechanical regularity with organic form. The form is mechanic, when on any given material we impress a predetermined form, not necessarily arising out of the properties of the material; as when to a mass of wet clay we give whatever shape we wish it to retain when hardened. The organic form, on the other hand, is innate; it shapes, as it develops, itself from within, and the fullness of its development is one and the same with the perfection of its outward form. Such as the life is, such is the form. Nature, the prime genial artist, inexhaustible in diverse powers, is equally inexhaustible in forms, each exterior is the physiognomy of the being within its true image reflected and thrown out from the concave mirror: and even such is the appropriate excellence of her chosen poet, of our own Shakespeare, himself a nature humanized, a genial understanding, directing self-consciously a power and an implicit wisdom deeper even than our consciousness.

I greatly dislike beauties and selections in general; but as proof postive of his unrivaled excellence, I should like to try Shakespeare by this criterion. Make out your amplest catalogue of all the human faculties, as reason or the moral law, the will, the feeling of the coincidence of the two (a feeling *sui generis et demonstratio demonstrationun*[6]) called the conscience, the understanding, or prudence, wit, fancy, imagination, judgment, and then of the objects on which these are to be employed, as the beauties, the terrors, and the seeming caprices of nature, the capabilities, that is, the actual and the ideal, of the human mind, conceived as an

---

[4] Wrapper or envelope; clothing.

[5] Zolius was a critic of Homer.

[6] "Of its own kind (unique) and self-demonstrative."

individual or as a social being, as in innocence or in guilt, in a play-paradise or in a war field of temptation; and then compare with Shakespeare under each of these heads all or any of the writers in prose and verse that have ever lived! Who, that is competent to judge, doubts the result? And ask your own hearts, ask your own commonsense to conceive the possibility of this man being—I say not, the drunken savage of that wretched sciolist,[7] whom Frenchmen, to their shame, have honored before their elder and better worthies—but the anomalous, the wild, the irregular, genius of our daily criticism! What! Are we to have miracles in sport?—Or, I speak reverently, does God choose idiots by whom to convey divine truths to man?

On the Principles of Genial Criticism

from
Essay Third

I proceed to my promised and more amusing task, that of establishing, illustrating, and exemplifying the distinct powers of the different modes of pleasure excited by the works of nature or of human genius with their exponent and appropriable terms. . . .

Agreeable

We use this word in two senses; in the first for whatever agrees with our nature, for that which is congruous with the primary constitution of our senses. Thus green is naturally agreeable to the eye. In this sense the word expresses, at least involves, a preestablished harmony between the organs and their appointed objects. In the second sense, we convey by the word *agreeable,* that the thing has by force of habit (thence called a second nature) been made to agree with us; or that it has become agreeable to us by its recalling to our minds some one or more things that were dear and pleasing to us; or lastly, on account of some after pleasure or advantage, of which it has been the constant cause or occasion. Thus by force of custom men *make* the taste of tobacco,[1] which was at first hateful to the palate, agreeable to them; thus too, as our Shake-

speare observes, "Things base and vile, holding no quality, / Love can transpose to form and dignity—"[2] the crutch that had supported a revered parent, after the first anguish of regret, becomes agreeable to the affectionate child; and I once knew a very sensible and accomplished Dutch gentleman, who, spite of his own sense of the ludicrous nature of the feeling, was more delighted by the first grand concert of frogs he heard in this country, than he had been by Catalina singing in the compositions of Cimarosa.[3] The last clause needs no illustrations, as it comprises all the objects that are agreeable to us, only because they are the means by which we gratify our smell, touch, palate, and mere bodily feeling.

Beautiful

The beautiful, contemplated in its essentials, that is, in *kind* and not in *degree,* is that in which the *many,* still seen as many, becomes one. Take a familiar instance, one of a thousand. The frost on a windowpane has by accident crystallized into a striking resemblance of a tree or a seaweed. With what pleasure we trace the parts, and their relations to each other, and to the whole! Here is the stalk or trunk, and here the branches or sprays—sometimes even the buds or flowers. Nor will our pleasure be less, should the caprice of the crystallization represent some object disagreeable to us, provided only we can see or fancy the component parts each in relation to each, and all forming a whole. A lady would see an admirably painted tiger with pleasure, and at once pronounce it beautiful—nay, an owl, a frog, or a toad, who would have shrieked or shuddered at the sight of the things themselves. So far is the beautiful from depending wholly on association, that it is frequently produced by the mere removal of associations.[4] Many a sincere convert to the beauty of various insects, as of the dragonfly, the fangless snake, *&c.,* has natural history made, by exploding the terror or aversion that had been connected with them.

The most general definition of beauty, therefore, is— that I may fulfill my threat of plaguing my readers with hard words—multeity in unity. Now it will be always found, that whatever is the definition of the *kind,* independent of degree, becomes likewise the definition of the highest degree of that kind. An old coach wheel lies in the coachmaker's yard, disfigured with tar and dirt (I purposely take the most

[7]From *sciolus,* "smatterer."
On the Principles of Genial Criticism Concerning the Fine Arts was first published in 1814 in a Bristol periodical.
[1]Burke (above, page 334).

[2]*Midsummer Night's Dream, I.i.* 232–3. Coleridge, however, substitutes *quality* for *quantity.*
[3]Domenico Cimarosa (1749–1801), Italian composer, a favorite of Coleridge's.
[4]Here Coleridge nearly suggests what would later becalled psychical distance.

trivial instances)—if I turn away my attention from these, and regard the *figure* abstractly, "still," I might say to my companion, "there is beauty in that wheel, and you yourself would not only admit, but would feel it, had you never seen a wheel before. See how the rays proceed from the center to the circumferences, and how many different images are distinctly comprehended at one glance, as forming one whole, and each part in some harmonious relation to each and to all." But imagine the polished golden wheel of the chariot of the sun, as the poets have described it: then the figure, and the real thing so figured, exactly coincide. There is nothing heterogeneous, nothing to abstract from: by its perfect smoothness and circularity in width, each part is (if I may borrow a metaphor from a sister sense) as perfect a melody, as the whole is a complete harmony. This, we should say, is beautiful throughout. Of all "the many," which I actually see, each and all are really reconciled into unity: while the effulgence from the whole coincides with, and seems to represent, the effluence of delight from my own mind in the intuition of it.

It seems evident then, first, that beauty is harmony, and subsists only in composition, and secondly, that the first species of the agreeable can alone be a component part of the beautiful, that namely which is naturally consonant with our senses by the preestablished harmony between nature and the human mind; and thirdly, that even of this species, those objects only can be admitted (according to rule the first) which belong to the eye and ear, because they alone are susceptible of distinction of parts. Should an Englishman gazing on a mass of cloud rich with the rays of the rising sun exclaim, even without distinction of, or reference to its form, or its relation to other objects, "How beautiful!" I should have no quarrel with him. First, because by the law of association there is in all visual beholdings at least an indistinct subsumption of form and relation; and, secondly, because even in the coincidence between the sight and the object there is an approximation to the reduction of the many into one. But who, that heard a Frenchman call the flavor of a leg of mutton a beautiful taste would not immediately recognize him for a Frenchman, even though there should be neither grimace or characteristic nasal twang? The result, then, of the whole is that the shapely (i.e. *formosus*) joined with the naturally agreeable, constitutes what, speaking accurately, we mean by the word *beautiful* (i.e. *pulcher*).

But we are conscious of faculties far superior to the highest impressions of sense; we have life and free will.— What then will be the result, when the beautiful, arising from regular form, is so modified by the perception of life and spontaneous action, as that the latter only shall be the object of our conscious *perception,* while the former merely acts, and yet does effectively act, on our feelings? With pride and pleasure I reply by referring my reader to the group in Mr. Allston's[5] grand picture of the *Dead Man Reviving from the Touch of the Bones of the Prophet Elisha,* beginning with the slave at the head of the reviving body, then proceeding to the daughter clasping her swooning mother; to the mother, the wife of the reviving man; then to the soldier behind who supports her; to the two figures eagerly conversing: and lastly, to the exquisitely graceful girl who is bending downward, and whose hand nearly touches the thumb of the slave! You will find, what you had not suspected, that you have here before you a circular group. But by what variety of life, motion, and passion is all the stiffness, that would result from an obvious regular figure swallowed up, and the figure of the group as much concealed by the action and passion, as the skeleton, which gives the form of the human body, is hidden by the flesh and its endless outlines!

In Raphael's admirable *Galatea*[6] (the print of which is doubtless familiar to most of my readers) the circle is perceived at first sight; but with what multiplicity of rays and chords within the area of the circular group, with what elevations and depressions of the circumference, with what an endless variety and sportive wildness in the component figure, and in the junctions of the figures, is the balance, the perfect reconciliation, effected between these two conflicting principles of the free life, and of the confining form! How entirely is the stiffness that would have resulted from the obvious regularity of the latter, *fused* and (if I may hazard so bold a metaphor) almost *volatilized* by the interpenetration and electrical flashes of the former.

But I shall recur to this consummate work for more specific illustrations hereafter: and have indeed in some measure offended already against the laws of method, by anticipating materials which rather belong to a more advanced stage of the disquisition. It is time to recapitulate, as briefly as possible, the arguments already advanced, and having summed up the result, to leave behind me this, the only portion of these essays, which, as far as the subject itself is concerned, will demand any *effort* of attention from a reflecting and intelligent reader. And let me be permitted to remind him, that the distinctions, which it is my object to

---

[5]Washington Allston (1779–1843), American painter and a friend of Coleridge's. The three essays in *On the Principles of Genial Criticism* were written in order to draw attention to an exhibition of Allston's works.
[6]Galatea was the name of the statue created by Pygmalion, brought to life by Venus in answer to Pygmalion's prayer. Raphael's fresco is in the Villa Farnesina in Rome.

prove and elucidate, have not merely a foundation in nature and the noblest faculties of the human mind, but are likewise the very groundwork, nay, an indispensable condition, of all *rational* inquiry concerning the arts. For it is self-evident, that whatever may be judged of differently by different persons, in the very same degree of moral and intellectual cultivation, extolled by one and condemned by another, without any error being assignable to either, can never be an object of general principles: and vice versa, that whatever can be brought to the test of general principles presupposes a distinct origin from these pleasures and tastes, which, for the wisest purposes, are made to depend on local and transitory fashions, accidental associations, and the peculiarities of individual temperament: to all which the philosopher, equally with the well-bred man of the world, applies the old adage, *de gustibus non est disputandum.*[7] Be it, however, observed that *de gustibus* is by no means the same as *de gustu,* nor will it escape the scholar's recollection, that taste, in its metaphorical use, was first adopted by the Romans, and unknown to the less luxurious Greeks, who designed this faculty, sometimes by the word αἴαθηοις and sometimes by φιλοκαλία[8]—ἀνδρῶν τῶν καο' ἡμᾶς φιλοκαλώτατος γεγονώς—i.e. "endowed by nature with the most exquisite taste of any man of our age," says Porphyry of his friend, Castricius. Still, this metaphor, borrowed from the pregustatores of the old Roman banquets, is singularly happy and appropriate. In the palate, the perception of the object and its qualities is involved in the *sensation,* in the mental taste it is involved in the *sense.* We have a *sensation* of sweetness, in a healthy palate, from honey; a *sense* of beauty, in an uncorrupted taste, from the view of the rising or setting sun.

Recapitulation

Principle the First

That which has become, or which has been *made* agreeable to us, from causes not contained in its own nature, or in its original conformity to the human organs and faculties; that which is not pleasing for its own sake, but by connection or association with some other thing, separate or separable from it, is neither beautiful, nor capable of being a component part of beauty: though it may greatly increase the sum

of our pleasure, when it does not interfere with the beauty of the object, nay, even when it detracts from it. A moss rose, with a sprig of myrtle and jasmine, is not more *beautiful* from having been plucked from the garden, or presented to us by the hand of the woman we love, but is abundantly more delightful. The total pleasure received from one of Mr. Bird's finest pictures may, without any impeachment of our taste, be the greater from his having introduced into it the portrait of one of our friends, or from our pride in him as our townsman, or from our knowledge of his personal qualities; but the amiable artist would rightly consider it a coarse compliment, were it affirmed, that the *beauty* of the piece, or its merit as a work of genius, was the more perfect on this account. I am conscious that I look with a stronger and more pleasurable emotion at Mr. Allston's large landscape, in the spirit of Swiss scenery, from its having been the occasion of my first acquaintance with him in Rome. This may or may not be a compliment to *him;* but the true compliment to the picture was made by a lady of high rank and cultivated taste, who declared, in my hearing, that she never stood before that landscape without seeming to feel the breeze blow out of it upon her. But the most striking instance is afforded by the portrait of a departed or absent friend or parent; which is endeared to us, and more delightful, from some awkward position of the limbs, which had defied the contrivances of art to render it picturesque, but which was the characteristic habit of the original.

Principle the Second

That which is naturally agreeable and consonant to human nature, so that the exceptions may be attributed to disease or defect; that, the pleasure from which is contained in the immediate impression; cannot, indeed, with strict propriety, be called beautiful, exclusive of its relations, but one among the component parts of beauty, in whatever instance it is susceptible of existing as a part of whole. This, of course, excludes the mere objects of the taste, smell, and feeling, though the sensation from these, especially from the latter when organized into touch, may secretly, and without our consciousness, enrich and vivify the perceptions and images of the eye and ear; which alone are true organs of sense, their sensations in a healthy or uninjured state being too faint to be noticed by the mind. We may, indeed, in common conversation, call purple a beautiful color, or the tone of a single note on an excellent pianoforte a beautiful tone; but if we were questioned, we should agree that a rich or delightful color, a rich, or sweet, or clear tone; would have been more appropriate—and this with less hesitation in the latter

---

[7] "There is no disputing tastes."
[8] That is, *"aesthesis,"* perception by the senses; and *"philokalia,"* love of the beautiful. The philosopher Porphyry (ca. 234–305 A.D.) is best known as the biographer of Plotinus.

instance than in the former, because the single tone is more manifestly of the nature of a *sensation,* while color is the medium which seems to blend sensation and perception, so as to hide, as it were, the former in the latter; the direct opposite of which takes place in the lower senses of feeling, smell, and taste. (In strictness, there is even in these an ascending scale. The smell is less sensual and more sentient than mere feeling, the taste than the smell, and the eye than the ear: but between the ear and the taste exists the chasm or break, which divides the beautiful and the elements of beauty from the merely agreeable.) When I reflect on the manner in which smoothness, richness of sound, &c., enter into the formation of the beautiful, I am induced to suspect that they act negatively rather than positively. Something there must be to realize the form, something in and by which the *forma informans*[9] reveals itself: and these, less than any that could be substituted, and in the least possible degree, distract the attention, in the least possible degree obscure the idea, of which they (composed into outline and surface) are the symbol. An illustrative hint may be taken from a pure crystal, as compared with an opaque, semiopaque or clouded mass, on the one hand, and with a perfectly transparent body, such as the air, on the other. The crystal is lost in the light, which yet it contains, embodies, and gives a shape to; but which passes shapeless through the air, and, in the ruder body, is either quenched or dissipated.

Principle the Third

The safest definition, then, of beauty, as well as the oldest, is that of Pythagoras: the reduction of many to one—or, as finely expressed by the sublime disciple of Ammonius,[10] τὸ ἄμερες ὄν, ἐν πολλοῖξ φανταζόμενον,[11] of which the following may be offered as both paraphrase and corollary. *The sense of beauty subsists in simultaneous intuition of the relation of parts, each to each, and of all to a whole: exciting an immediate and absolute complacency, without intervenence, therefore, of any interest, sensual or intellectual.* The beautiful is thus at once distinguished both from the aggreable, which is beneath it, and from the good, which is above it: for both these have an interest necessarily attached to them: both act on the will, and excite a desire for the actual existence of the image or idea contemplated: while the sense of beauty rests gratified in the mere contemplation or intu-

ition, regardless whether it be a fictitious Apollo, or a real Antinous.[12]

The Mystics meant the same, when they define beauty as the subjection of matter to spirit so as to be transformed into a symbol, in and through which the spirit reveals itself; and declare *that* the *most* beautiful, where the most obstacles to a full manifestation have been most perfectly overcome.

* * *

Scholium

We have sufficiently distinguished the beautiful from the agreeable, by the sure criterion, that, when we find an object agreeable, the *sensation* of pleasure always precedes the judgment, and is its determining cause. We *find* it agreeable. But when we declare an object beautiful, the contemplation or intuition of its beauty precedes the *feeling* of complacency, in order of nature at least: nay, in great depression of spirits may even exist without sensibly producing it.

A grief without a pang, void, dark, and drear!
A stifled, drowsy, unimpassioned grief,
    That finds no natural outlet, no relief
      In word, or sigh, or tear!
O dearest lady! in this heartless mood,
To other thoughts by yon sweet throstle wooed!
All this long eve, so balmy and serene,
Have I been gazing at the western sky.[13]

Now the least reflection convinces us that our sensations, whether of pleasure or of pain, are the incommunicable parts of our nature; such as can be reduced to no universal rule; and in which therefore we have no right to expect that others should agree with us, or to blame them for disagreement. That the Greenlander prefers train oil to olive oil, and even to wine, we explain at once by our knowledge of the climate and productions to which he has been habituated. Were the man as enlightened as Plato, his palate would still find that most agreeable to which it had been most accustomed. But when the Iroquois sachem, after having been led to the most perfect specimens of architecture in Paris, said that he saw nothing so beautiful as the cook's shops,[14] we attribute this without hesitation to savagery of intellect, and infer with certainty that the

---

[9] "Shaping form."
[10] The "disciple" in question is Plotinus; Ammonius (also the teacher of Origen) was an Alexandrian philosopher who left no written works.
[11] "The one [which] makes itself manifest in the many." Coleridge expands the idea into an illustration of his principle of organic form.
[12] Antinous was the favorite and lover of the emperor Hadrian, who erected temples and monuments (even a city, Antinoopolis) to him in many places throughout the Roman empire.
[13] From stanza 2 of Coleridge's *Dejection: An Ode.*
[14] Kant used the same example in his *Critique of Judgment,* page 420.

sense of the beautiful was either altogether dormant in his mind, or at best very imperfect. The beautiful, therefore, not originating in the sensations, must belong to the intellect: and therefore we *declare* an object beautiful, and feel an inward right to *expect* that others should coincide with us. But we feel no right to *demand* it: and this leads us to that, which hitherto we have barely touched upon, and which we shall now attempt to illustrate more fully, namely, to the distinction of the beautiful from the good.

Let us suppose Milton in company with some stern and prejudiced Puritan, contemplating the front of York Cathedral, and at length expressing his admiration of its beauty. We will suppose it too at that time of his life, when his religious opinions, feelings, and prejudices most nearly coincided with those of the rigid antiprelatists. P.: Beauty; I am sure, it is not the beauty of holiness. M.: True; but yet it is beautiful. P.: It delights not me. What is it good for? Is it of any use but to be stared at? M.: Perhaps not! But still it is beautiful. P.: But call to mind the pride and wanton vanity of those cruel shavelings, that wasted the labor and substance of so many thousand poor creatures in the erection of this haughty pile. M.: I do. But still it is very beautiful. P.: Think how many score of places of worship, incomparably better suited both for prayer and preaching, and how many faithful ministers might have been maintained, to the blessing of tens of thousands, to them and their children's children, with the treasures lavished on this worthless mass of stone and cement. M.: Too true! But nevertheless it is *very* beautiful. P.: And it is not merely useless; but it feeds the pride of the prelates, and keeps alive the popish and carnal spirit among the people. M.: Even so! And I presume not to question the wisdom, nor detract from the pious zeal, of the first reformers of Scotland, who for these reasons destroyed so many fabrics, scarce inferior in beauty to this now before our eyes. But I did not call it *good,* nor have I told thee, brother! that if this were leveled with the ground, and existed only in the works of the modeler or engraver, that I should desire to reconstruct it. The good consists in the congruity of a thing with the laws of the reason and the nature of the will, and in its fitness to determine the latter to actualize the former: and it is always discursive. The beautiful arises from the perceived harmony of an object, whether sight or sound, with the inborn and constitutive rules of the judgment and imagination: and it is always intuitive. As light to the eye, even such is beauty to the mind, which cannot but have complacency in whatever is perceived as preconfigured to its living faculties. Hence the Greeks called a beautiful object καλόν quasi καλοῦν, i.e. *calling on* the soul, which receives instantly, and welcomes it as something connatural.

Biographia Literaria

from
Chapter 12

A Chapter of requests and premonitions concerning the perusal or omission of the chapter that follows

In the perusal of philosophical works I have been greatly benefited by a resolve, which, in the antithetic form and with the allowed quaintness of an adage or maxim, I have been accustomed to word thus: *"until you understand a writer's ignorance, presume yourself ignorant of his understanding."*[1] This *golden rule* of mine does, I own, resemble those of Pythagoras in its obscurity rather than in its depth. If however the reader will permit me to be my own Hierocles,[2] I trust, that he will find its meaning fully explained by the following instances. I have now before me a treatise of a religious fanatic, full of dreams and supernatural *experiences*.[3] I see clearly the writer's grounds, and their hollowness. I have a complete insight into the causes, which through the medium of his body had acted on his mind; and by application of received and ascertained laws I can satisfactorily explain to my own reason all the strange incidents, which the writer records of himself. And this I can do without suspecting him of any intentional falsehood. As when in broad day-light a man tracks the steps of a traveller, who had lost his way in a fog or by treacherous moonshine, even so, and with the same tranquil sense of certainty, can I follow the traces of this bewildered visionary. I UNDERSTAND HIS IGNORANCE.

On the other hand, I have been re-perusing with the best energies of my mind the Timæus of PLATO. Whatever I comprehend, impresses me with a reverential sense of the author's genius; but there is a considerable portion of the work, to which I can attach no consistent meaning. In other treatises of the same philosopher intended for the average comprehensions of men, I have been delighted with the masterly good sense, with the perspicuity of the language, and the aptness of the inductions. I recollect likewise, that

---

Biographia Literaria was written in 1815 but published in 1817. Excerpts reprinted from James Engell and W. Jackson Bate, eds., *Biographia Literaria* (1983).
[1] Coleridge first expressed this maxim in 1801, in *Collected Notebooks I,* 928 f. 27.
[2] Alexandrian philosophical commentator, fl. 430 A.D.
[3] Coleridge may be referring here to Immanuel Swedenborg, who characteristically reports his visions as "Memorable Experiences." For details, see Engell and Bate, eds., *Biographia Literaria,* 232.

numerous passages in this author, which I thoroughly comprehend, were formerly no less unintelligible to me, than the passages now in question. It would, I am aware, be quite *fashionable* to dismiss them at once as Platonic Jargon. But this I cannot do with satisfaction to my own mind, because I have sought in vain for causes adequate to the solution of the assumed inconsistency. I have no insight into the possibility of a man so eminently wise, using words with such half-meanings to himself, as must perforce pass into no-meaning to his readers. When in addition to the motives thus suggested by my own reason, I bring into distinct remembrance the number and the series of great men, who after long and zealous study of these works had joined in honoring the name of PLATO with epithets, that almost transcend humanity, I feel, that a contemptuous verdict on my part might argue want of modesty, but would hardly be received by the judicious, as evidence of superior penetration. Therefore, utterly baffled in all my attempts to understand the ignorance of Plato, I CONCLUDE MYSELF IGNORANT OF HIS UNDERSTANDING.

In lieu of the various requests which the anxiety of authorship addresses to the unknown reader, I advance but this one; that he will either pass over the following chapter altogether, or read the whole connectedly.[4]

* * *

The postulate of philosophy and at the same time the test of philosophic capacity, is no other than the heaven-descended KNOW THYSELF! (*E cælo descendit, Γνῶθι σεαυτόν*).[5] And this at once practically and speculatively. For as philosophy is neither a science of the reason or understanding only, nor merely a science of morals, but the science of BEING alto-

gether, its primary ground can be neither merely speculative or merely practical, but both in one. All knowledge rests on the coincidence of an object with a subject.[6] (My readers have been warned in a former chapter that for their convenience as well as the writer's, the term, subject, is used by me in its scholastic sense as equivalent to mind or sentient being, and as the necessary correlative of object or *quicquid objicitur menti*.[7]) For we can *know* that only which is true: and the truth is universally placed in the coincidence of the thought with the thing, of the representation with the object represented.

Now the sum of all that is merely OBJECTIVE, we will henceforth call NATURE, confining the term to its passive and material sense, as comprising all the phænomena by which its existence is made known to us. On the other hand the sum of all that is SUBJECTIVE, we may comprehend in the name of the SELF or INTELLIGENCE. Both conceptions are in necessary antithesis. Intelligence is conceived of as exclusively representative, nature as exclusively represented; the one as conscious, the other as without consciousness. Now in all acts of positive knowledge there is required a reciprocal concurrence of both, namely of the conscious being, and of that which is in itself unconscious. Our problem is to explain this concurrence, its possibility and its necessity.

During the act of knowledge itself, the objective and subjective are so instantly united, that we cannot determine to which of the two the priority belongs. There is here no first, and no second; both are coinstantaneous and one. While I am attempting to explain this intimate coalition, I must suppose it dissolved. I must necessarily set out from the one, to which therefore I give hypothetical antecedence, in order to arrive at the other. But as there are but two factors or elements in the problem, subject and object, and as it is left indeterminate from which of them I should commence, there are two cases equally possible.

1. EITHER THE OBJECTIVE IS TAKEN AS THE FIRST, AND THEN WE HAVE TO ACCOUNT FOR THE SUPERVENTION OF THE SUBJECTIVE, WHICH COALESCES WITH IT.

The notion of the subjective is not contained in the notion of the objective. On the contrary they mutually exclude each other. The subjective therefore must supervene to the objective. The conception of nature does not apparently in-

---

[4] We acknowledge the acute irony of breaking this excerpt exactly here, particularly since what follows is a long controversial philosophical discussion, deeply indebted to Schelling's *System of Transcendental Idealism* but drawing also on Kant and Fichte. In Coleridge's many attempts to clarify both his concurrence and his divergence from his contemporaries, this discussion provides a useful outline, though as Coleridge himself recognized, it was not the definitive statement to which he aspired. Particularly in Chapter 13, Coleridge recognized that the pathway upon which he embarked here (largely Schelling's) did *not* lead to his own desired destination, a philosophical account of the imagination. Accordingly, he interrupts his argument by the device of a letter (not included here) that vividly expresses his own dissatisfaction with this line of argument as leading to "the cave of Trophonius" (the architect of the temple to Apollo) where, according to legend, people seeking prophetic enlightenment were dragged down into the depths and subjected to confusing noises and sights before receiving it. See in this connection Coleridge's fuller development of these issues in "Essays on the Principles of Method" from *The Friend*, as well as appendices to *The Statesman's Manual* and *On the Constitution of Church and State* (below, page 508 and page 519).
[5] Adapted from Juvenal 11.27: "It descended from heaven, *Know thyself.*" This motto was inscribed over the temple of the oracle at Delphi.

[6] Coleridge's main source for the following discussion is Schelling's *System of Transcendental Idealism,* sections 1–8, with occasional sentences from other works and numerous alterations, additions, and clarifications. We refer the reader to the extensive notes and citations in Engell and Bate, eds., *Biographia Literaria.*
[7] "Whatever is thrown before (presented to) the mind."

volve the co-presence of an intelligence making an ideal duplicate of it, i.e. representing it. This desk for instance would (according to our natural notions) be, though there should exist no sentient being to look at it. This then is the problem of natural philosophy. It assumes the objective or unconscious nature as the first, and has therefore to explain how intelligence can supervene to it, or how itself can grow into intelligence. If it should appear, that all enlightened naturalists without having distinctly proposed the problem to themselves have yet constantly moved in the line of its solution, it must afford a strong presumption that the problem itself is founded in nature. For if all knowledge has as it were two poles reciprocally required and presupposed, all sciences must proceed from the one or the other, and must tend toward the opposite as far as the equatorial point in which both are reconciled and become identical. The necessary tendence therefore of all natural philosophy is from nature to intelligence; and this, and no other, is the true ground and occasion of the instinctive striving to introduce theory into our views of natural phænomena. The highest perfection of natural philosophy would consist in the perfect spiritualization of all the laws of nature into laws of intuition and intellect. The phænomena *(the material)* must wholly disappear, and the laws alone *(the formal)* must remain. Thence it comes, that in nature itself the more the principle of law breaks forth, the more does the *husk* drop off, the phænomena themselves become more spiritual and at length cease altogether in our consciousness. The optical phænomena are but a geometry, the lines of which are drawn by light, and the materiality of this light itself has already become matter of doubt. In the appearances of magnetism all trace of matter is lost, and of the phænomena of gravitation, which not a few among the most illustrious Newtonians have declared no otherwise comprehensible than as an immediate spiritual influence, there remains nothing but its law, the execution of which on a vast scale is the mechanism of the heavenly motions. The theory of natural philosophy would then be completed, when all nature was demonstrated to be identical in essence with that, which in its highest known power exists in man as intelligence and self-consciousness; when the heavens and the earth shall declare not only the power of their maker, but the glory and the presence of their God, even as he appeared to the great prophet during the vision of the mount in the skirts of his divinity.[8]

This may suffice to show, that even natural science, which commences with the material phænomenon as the reality and substance of things existing, does yet by the necessity of theorising unconsciously, and as it were instinctively, end in nature as an intelligence; and by this tendency the science of nature becomes finally natural philosophy, the one of the two poles of fundamental science.

2. OR THE SUBJECTIVE IS TAKEN AS THE FIRST, AND THE PROBLEM THEN IS, HOW THERE SUPERVENES TO IT A COINCIDENT OBJECTIVE.

In the pursuit of these sciences, our success in each, depends on an austere and faithful adherence to its own principles with a careful separation and exclusion of those, which appertain to the opposite science. As the natural philosopher, who directs his views to the objective, avoids above all things the intermixture of the subjective in his knowledge, as for instance, arbitrary suppositions or rather sufficions, occult qualities, spiritual agents, and the substitution of final for efficient causes; so on the other hand, the transcendental or intelligential philosopher is equally anxious to preclude all interpolation of the objective into the subjective principles of his science, as for instance the assumption of impresses or configurations in the brain, correspondent to miniature pictures on the retina painted by rays of light from supposed originals, which are not the immediate and real objects of vision, but deductions from it for the purposes of explanation. This purification of the mind is effected by an absolute and scientific scepticism to which the mind voluntarily determines itself for the specific purpose of future certainty. Des Cartes who (in his meditations) himself first, at least of the moderns, gave a beautiful example of this voluntary doubt, this self-determined indetermination, happily expresses its utter difference from the scepticism of vanity or irreligion: Nec tamen in eo scepticos imitabar, qui dubitant tantum ut dubitent, et preter incertitudinem ipsam nihil quærunt. Nam contra totus in eo eram ut aliquid certi reperirem. DES CARTES, *de Methodo.*[9] Nor is it less distinct in its motives and final aim, than in its proper objects, which are not as in ordinary scepticism the prejudices of education and circumstance, but those original and innate prejudices which nature herself has planted in all men, and which to all but the philosopher are the first principles of knowledge, and the final test of truth.

Now these essential prejudices are all reducible to the one fundamental presumption, THAT THERE EXIST THINGS

---

[8]Cf. Ps. 19.1; Exod. 24.12–18. In this paragraph and the next, Coleridge is very close to *Naturphilosophie* following Fichte, Schelling, and Steffans; cf. Modiano, *Coleridge and the Concept of Nature.* But see his considerably more sophisticated position on this issue in the "Essays on the Principles of Method" (below, page 508).

---

[9]Descartes, *Discourse on Method,* iii, 29: "In this I did not wish to imitate the skeptics, who doubted only for the sake of doubting and intended to remain always irresolute; on the contrary, my whole purpose was to achieve greater certainty. . . ."

WITHOUT US. As this on the one hand originates, neither in grounds or arguments, and yet on the other hand remains proof against all attempts to remove it by grounds or arguments *(naturam furca expellas tamen usque redibit)*[10] on the one hand lays claim to IMMEDIATE certainty as a position at once indemonstrable and irresistible, and yet on the other hand, inasmuch as it refers to something essentially different from ourselves, nay even in opposition to ourselves, leaves it inconceivable how it could possibly become a part of our immediate consciousness; (in other words how that, which ex hypothesi is and continues to be extrinsic and alien to our being, should become a modification of our being) the philosopher therefore compels himself to treat this faith as nothing more than a prejudice, innate indeed and connatural, but still a prejudice.

The other position, which not only claims but necessitates the admission of its immediate certainty, equally for the scientific reason of the philosopher as for the common sense of mankind at large, namely, I AM, cannot so properly be intitled a prejudice. It is groundless indeed; but then in the very idea it precludes all ground, and separated from the immediate consciousness loses its whole sense and import. It is groundless; but only because it is itself the ground of all other certainty. Now the apparent contradiction, that the former position, namely, the existence of things without us, which from its nature cannot be immediately certain should be received as blindly and as independently of all grounds as the existence of our own being, the transcendental philosopher can solve only by the supposition, that the former is unconsciously involved in the latter; that it is not only coherent but identical, and one and the same thing with our own immediate self-consciousness. To demonstrate this identity is the office and object of his philosophy.

If it be said, that this is Idealism, let it be remembered that it is only so far idealism, as it is at the same time, and on that very account, the truest and most binding realism. For wherein does the realism of mankind properly consist? In the assertion that there exists a something without them, what, or how, or where they know not, which occasions the objects of their perception? Oh no! This is neither connatural or universal. It is what a few have taught and learnt in the schools, and which the many repeat without asking themselves concerning their own meaning. The realism common to all mankind is far elder and lies infinitely deeper than this hypothetical explanation of the origin of our perceptions, an explanation skimmed from the mere surface of mechanical philosophy. It is the table itself, which the man of common sense believes himself to see, not the phantom of a table, from which he may argumentatively deduce the reality of a table, which he does not see. If to destroy the reality of all, that we actually behold, be idealism, what can be more egregiously so, than the system of modern metaphysics, which banishes us to a land of shadows, surrounds us with apparitions, and distinguishes truth from illusion only by the majority of those who dream the same dream?[1] "*I* asserted that the world was mad," exclaimed poor Lee, "and the world said, that I was mad, and confound them, they outvoted me."[11]

It is to the true and original realism, that I would direct the attention. This believes and requires neither more nor less, than that the object which it beholds or presents to itself, is the real and very object. In this sense, however much we may strive against it, we are all collectively born idealists, and therefore and only therefore are we at the same time realists. But of this the philosophers of the schools know nothing, or despise the faith as the prejudice of the ignorant vulgar, because they live and move in a crowd of phrases and notions from which human nature has long ago vanished. Oh, ye that reverence yourselves, and walk humbly with the divinity in your own hearts, ye are worthy of a better philosophy! Let the dead bury the dead,[12] but do you preserve your human nature, the depth of which was never yet fathomed by a philosophy made up of notions and mere logical entities.

* * *

from
Chapter 13

The IMAGINATION then I consider either as primary, or secondary.[13] The primary IMAGINATION I hold to be the living Power and prime Agent of all human Perception, and as a repetition in the finite mind of the eternal act of creation in the infinite I AM. The secondary I consider as an echo of the former, co-existing with the conscious will, yet still as identical with the primary in the *kind* of its agency, and differing only in *degree,* and in the *mode* of its operation. It dissolves, diffuses, dissipates, in order to re-create; or where this

[10] Horace, *Epistles* 1.10.24: "You may drive nature out with a pitchfork but she will return."

[11] The reference is to the Restoration dramatist, Nathaniel Lee (c. 1653–1692), confined at Bedlam (1684–1689). While many remarks of Lee were published in others' writings, this particular one has not been traced.
[12] Cf. Mic. 6.8: ". . . walk humbly with thy God. . ." Cf. Matt. 8.12; Luke 9.60: "Let the dead bury the dead."
[13] As noted above, this celebrated definition of Imagination, primary and secondary, and Fancy appears in Chapter 13 after Coleridge abruptly breaks off his philosophical argument begun in Chapter 12.

process is rendered impossible, yet still at all events it struggles to idealize and to unify. It is essentially *vital*, even as all objects (*as* objects) are essentially fixed and dead.

FANCY, on the contrary, has no other counters to play with, but fixities and definites. The Fancy is indeed no other than a mode of Memory emancipated from the order of time and space; and blended with, and modified by that empirical phenomenon of the will, which we express by the word CHOICE. But equally with the ordinary memory it must receive all its materials ready made from the law of association.

from
Chapter 14

Occasion of the Lyrical Ballads, and the objects originally proposed—Preface to the second edition— The ensuing controversy, its causes and acrimony— Philosophic definitions of a poem and poetry with scholia

During the first year that Mr. Wordsworth and I were neighbours,[14] our conversations turned frequently on the two cardinal points of poetry, the power of exciting the sympathy of the reader by a faithful adherence to the truth of nature, and the power of giving the interest of novelty by the modifying colours of imagination. The sudden charm, which accidents of light and shade, which moon-light or sun-set diffused over a known and familiar landscape, appeared to represent the practicability of combining both. These are the poetry of nature. The thought suggested itself (to which of us I do not recollect) that a series of poems might be composed of two sorts. In the one, the incidents and agents were to be, in part at least, supernatural; and the excellence aimed at was to consist in the interesting of the affections by the dramatic truth of such emotions, as would naturally accompany such situations, supposing them real. And real in *this* sense they have been to every human being who, from whatever source of delusion, has at any time believed himself under supernatural agency. For the second class, subjects were to be chosen from ordinary life; the characters and incidents were to be such, as will be found in every village and its vicinity, where there is a meditative and feeling mind to seek after them, or to notice them, when they present themselves.

In this idea originated the plan of the "Lyrical Ballads," in which it was agreed, that my endeavours should be di-

rected to persons and characters supernatural, or at least romantic; yet so as to transfer from our inward nature a human interest and a semblance of truth sufficient to procure for these shadows of imagination that willing suspension of disbelief for the moment, which constitutes poetic faith. Mr. Wordsworth, on the other hand, was to propose to himself as his object, to give the charm of novelty to things of every day, and to excite a feeling analogous to the supernatural, by awakening the mind's attention from the lethargy of custom, and directing it to the loveliness and the wonders of the world before us; an inexhaustible treasure, but for which in consequence of the film of familiarity[15] and selfish solicitude we have eyes, yet see not, ears that hear not, and hearts that neither feel nor understand.[16]

With this view I wrote the "Ancient Mariner," and was preparing among other poems, the "Dark Ladie," and the "Christabel," in which I should have more nearly realized my ideal, than I had done in my first attempt.[17] But Mr. Wordsworth's industry had proved so much more successful, and the number of his poems so much greater, that my compositions, instead of forming a balance, appeared rather an interpolation of heterogeneous matter. Mr. Wordsworth added two or three poems written in his own character, in the impassioned, lofty, and sustained diction, which is characteristic of his genius.[18] In this form the "Lyrical Ballads" were published; and were presented by him, as an *experiment,* whether subjects, which from their nature rejected the usual ornaments and extra-colloquial style of poems in general, might not be so managed in the language of ordinary life as to produce the pleasurable interest, which it is the peculiar business of poetry to impart. To the second edition he added a preface of considerable length; in which notwithstanding some passages of apparently a contrary import, he was understood to contend for the extension of this style to poetry of all kinds, and to reject as vicious and indefensible all phrases and forms of style that were not included in what he (unfortunately, I think, adopting an equivocal expression) called the language of *real* life.[19] From this preface, prefixed to poems in which it was impossible to deny the presence of original genius, however mistaken its direction might be

---

[14] 1797–1798, while Wordsworth lived at Alfoxden House and Coleridge at Nether Stowey.

[15] Shelley appropriated this metaphor in his "Defense of Poetry" (below, page 542).

[16] Cf. Jer. 5.21; Isa. 6.10.

[17] "Christabel" was at that time unfinished, and was not published until 1816.

[18] That is, "Lines Composed above Tintern Abbey," and one or two including "Lines Written at a Small Distance from My House," "Lines Written in Early Spring," "Expostulation and Reply," and "The Tables Turned."

[19] Wordsworth's phrase was actually, ". . . a selection of the real language of men in a state of vivid sensation . . ." See above, page 482.

deemed, arose the whole long continued controversy. For from the conjunction of perceived power with supposed heresy I explain the inveteracy and in some instances, I grieve to say, the acrimonious passions, with which the controversy has been conducted by the assailants.[20]

Had Mr. Wordsworth's poems been the silly, the childish things, which they were for a long time described as being; had they been really distinguished from the compositions of other poets merely by meanness of language and inanity of thought; had they indeed contained nothing more than what is found in the parodies and pretended imitations of them; they must have sunk at once, a dead weight, into the slough of oblivion, and have dragged the preface along with them. But year after year increased the number of Mr. Wordsworth's admirers. They were found too not in the lower classes of the reading public, but chiefly among young men of strong sensibility and meditative minds; and their admiration (inflamed perhaps in some degree by opposition) was distinguished by its intensity, I might almost say, by its *religious* fervour. These facts, and the intellectual energy of the author, which was more or less consciously felt, where it was outwardly and even boisterously denied, meeting with sentiments of aversion to his opinions, and of alarm at their consequences, produced an eddy of criticism, which would of itself have borne up the poems by the violence, with which it whirled them round and round. With many parts of this preface in the sense attributed to them and which the words undoubtedly seem to authorise, I never concurred; but on the contrary objected to them as erroneous in principle, and as contradictory (in appearance at least) both to other parts of the same preface, and to the author's own practice in the greater number of the poems themselves. Mr. Wordsworth in his recent collection has, I find, degraded this prefatory disquisition to the end of his second volume,[21] to be read or not at the reader's choice. But he has not, as far as I can discover, announced any change in his poetic creed. At all events, considering it as the source of a controversy, in which I have been honored more, than I deserve, by the frequent conjunction of my name with his, I think it expedient to declare once for all, in what points I coincide with his opinions, and in what points I altogether differ. But in order to render myself intelligible I must previously, in as few words as possible, explain my

ideas, first, of a POEM; and secondly, of POETRY itself, in *kind,* and in *essence.*

The office of philosophical *disquisition* consists in just *distinction;* while it is the priviledge of the philosopher to preserve himself constantly aware, that distinction is not division. In order to obtain adequate notions of any truth, we must intellectually separate its distinguishable parts; and this is the technical *process* of philosophy. But having so done, we must then restore them in our conceptions to the unity, in which they actually co-exist; and this is the *result* of philosophy. A poem contains the same elements as a prose composition; the difference therefore must consist in a different combination of them, in consequence of a different object proposed. According to the difference of the object will be the difference of the combination. It is possible, that the object may be merely to facilitate the recollection of any given facts or observations by artificial arrangement; and the composition will be a poem, merely because it is distinguished from prose by metre, or by rhyme, or by both conjointly. In this, the lowest sense, a man might attribute the name of a poem to the well known enumeration of the days in the several months;

> Thirty days hath September,
> April, June, and November, &c.

and others of the same class and purpose. And as a particular pleasure is found in anticipating the recurrence of sounds and quantities, all compositions that have this charm superadded, whatever be their contents, *may* be entitled poems.

So much for the superficial *form.* A difference of object and contents supplies an additional ground of distinction. The immediate purpose may be the communication of truths; either of truth absolute and demonstrable, as in works of science; or of facts experienced and recorded, as in history. Pleasure, and that of the highest and most permanent kind, may *result* from the *attainment* of the end; but it is not itself the immediate end. In other works the communication of pleasure may be the immediate purpose; and though truth, either moral or intellectual, ought to be the *ultimate* end, yet this will distinguish the character of the author, not the class to which the work belongs. Blest indeed is that state of society, in which the immediate purpose would be baffled by the perversion of the proper ultimate end; in which no charm of diction or imagery could exempt the Bathyllus even of an Anacreon, or the Alexis of Virgil,[22] from disgust and aversion!

---

[20] Coleridge's primary reference is to attacks in the *Edinburgh Review* by Francis Jeffrey, from 1802 to 1814–1815.

[21] Cf. *Poems by William Wordsworth: Including Lyrical Ballads, and the Miscellaneous Pieces of the Author, with Additional Poems, a New Preface, and a Supplementary Essay,* in two volumes, 1815.

---

[22] Bathyllus of Samos, a youth loved by Anacreon; Ode 29 (17). Alexis is the youth loved by Corydon in Virgil's *Eclogue 2.*

But the communication of pleasure may be the immediate object of a work not metrically composed; and that object may have been in a high degree attained, as in novels and romances. Would then the mere superaddition of metre, with or without rhyme, entitle *these* to the name of poems? The answer is, that nothing can permanently please, which does not contain in itself the reason why it is so, and not otherwise. If metre be superadded, all other parts must be made consonant with it. They must be such, as to justify the perpetual and distinct attention to each part, which an exact correspondent recurrence of accent and sound are calculated to excite. The final definition then, so deduced, may be thus worded. A poem is that species of composition, which is opposed to works of science, by proposing for its *immediate* object pleasure, not truth; and from all other species (having *this* object in common with it) it is discriminated by proposing to itself such delight from the *whole,* as is compatible with a distinct gratification from each component *part.*

Controversy is not seldom excited in consequence of the disputants attaching each a different meaning to the same word; and in few instances has this been more striking, than in disputes concerning the present subject. If a man chooses to call every composition a poem, which is rhyme, or measure, or both, I must leave his opinion uncontroverted. The distinction is at least competent to characterize the writer's intention. If it were subjoined, that the whole is likewise entertaining or affecting, as a tale, or as a series of interesting reflections, I of course admit this as another fit ingredient of a poem, and an additional merit. But if the definition sought for be that of a *legitimate* poem, I answer, it must be one, the parts of which mutually support and explain each other; all in their proportion harmonizing with, and supporting the purpose and known influences of metrical arrangement. The philosophic critics of all ages coincide with the ultimate judgement of all countries, in equally denying the praises of a just poem, on the one hand, to a series of striking lines or distichs, each of which absorbing the whole attention of the reader to itself disjoins it from its context, and makes it a separate whole, instead of an harmonizing part; and on the other hand, to an unsustained composition, from which the reader collects rapidly the general result unattracted by the component parts. The reader should be carried forward, not merely or chiefly by the mechanical impulse of curiosity, or by a restless desire to arrive at the final solution; but by the pleasureable activity of mind excited by the attractions of the journey itself. Like the motion of a serpent, which the Egyptians made the emblem of intellectual power; or like the path of sound through the air; at every step he pauses and half recedes, and from the retrogressive movement collects the force which again carries him onward. Precipitandus est *liber* spiritus, says Petronius Arbiter most happily.[23] The epithet, *liber,* here balances the preceding verb; and it is not easy to conceive more meaning condensed in fewer words.

But if this should be admitted as a satisfactory character of a poem, we have still to seek for a definition of poetry. The writings of PLATO, and Bishop TAYLOR, and the Theoria Sacra of BURNET,[24] furnish undeniable proofs that poetry of the highest kind may exist without metre, and even without the contradistinguishing objects of a poem. The first chapter of Isaiah (indeed a very large proportion of the whole book) is poetry in the most emphatic sense; yet it would be not less irrational than strange to assert, that pleasure, and not truth, was the immediate object of the prophet. In short, whatever *specific* import we attach to the word, poetry, there will be found involved in it, as a necessary consequence, that a poem of any length neither can be, or ought to be, all poetry.[25] Yet if an harmonious whole is to be produced, the remaining parts must be preserved *in keeping* with the poetry; and this can be no otherwise effected than by such a studied selection and artificial arrangement, as will partake of *one,* though not a *peculiar,* property of poetry. And this again can be no other than the property of exciting a more continuous and equal attention, than the language of prose aims at, whether colloquial or written.

My own conclusions on the nature of poetry, in the strictest use of the word, have been in part anticipated in the preceding disquisition on the fancy and imagination. What is poetry? is so nearly the same question with, what is a poet? that the answer to the one is involved in the solution of the other. For it is a distinction resulting from the poetic genius itself, which sustains and modifies the images, thoughts, and emotions of the poet's own mind. The poet, described in *ideal* perfection, brings the whole soul of man into activity, with the subordination of its faculties to each other, according to their relative worth and dignity. He diffuses a tone, and spirit of unity, that blends, and (as it were) *fuses,* each into each, by that synthetic and magical power, to which we have exclusively appropriated the name of imagination. This power, first put in action by the will and understanding, and retained under their irremissive, though

---

[23] "The *free* spirit must be hurried forward" from *Satyricon* 118, by Petronius Arbiter, Roman consul during the reign of Nero.

[24] Jeremy Taylor (1613–1667), Anglican clergyman and writer; Thomas Burnet (1635–1715), author of *Sacred Theory of the Earth* (1684–1689).

[25] See Edgar Allan Poe's elaboration of this point in "The Poetic Principle" (below, page 581).

gentle and unnoticed, controul *(laxis effertur habenis)*[26] reveals itself in the balance or reconciliation of opposite or
discordant qualities:[27] of sameness, with difference; of the
general, with the concrete; the idea, with the image; the individual, with the representative; the sense of novelty and
freshness, with old and familiar objects; a more than usual
state of emotion, with more than usual order; judgement
ever awake and steady self-possession, with enthusiasm and
feeling profound or vehement; and while it blends and harmonizes the natural and the artificial, still subordinates art
to nature; the manner to the matter; and our admiration of
the poet to our sympathy with the poetry. "Doubtless," as Sir
John Davies observes of the soul (and his words may with
slight alteration be applied, and even more appropriately to
the poetic IMAGINATION.)

> Doubtless this could not be, but that she turns
> Bodies to spirit by sublimation strange,
> As fire converts to fire the things it burns,
> As we our food into our nature change.
>
> From their gross matter she abstracts their forms,
> And draws a kind of quintessence from things;
> Which to her proper nature she transforms
> To bear them light, on her celestial wings.
>
> Thus does she, when from individual states
> She doth abstract the universal kinds;
> Which then re-clothed in divers names and fates
> Steal access through our senses to our minds.[28]

Finally, GOOD SENSE is the BODY of poetic genius,
FANCY its DRAPERY, MOTION its LIFE, and IMAGINATION the
SOUL that is every where, and in each; and forms all into one
graceful and intelligent whole.

Essays on the Principles of Method

from
Essay IV[1]

What is that which first strikes us, and strikes us at once, in
a man of education? And which, among educated men, so
instantly distinguishes the man of superior mind, that (as
was observed with eminent propriety of the late Edmund
Burke) "we cannot stand under the same arch-way during a
shower of rain, *without finding him out?*"[2] Not the weight or
novelty of his remarks; not any unusual interest of facts
communicated by him; for we may suppose both the one
and the other precluded by the shortness of our intercourse,
and the triviality of the subjects. The difference will be impressed and felt, though the conversation should be confined
to the state of the weather or the pavement. Still less will it
arise from any peculiarity in his words and phrases. For if
he be, as we now assume, a *well*-educated man as well as a
man of superior powers, he will not fail to follow the golden
rule of Julius Cæsar, *Insolens verbum, tanquam scopulum,
evitare.*[3] Unless where new things necessitate new terms, he
will avoid an unusual word as a rock. It must have been
among the earliest lessons of his youth, that the breach of
this precept, at all times hazardous, becomes ridiculous in
the topics of ordinary conversation. There remains but one
other point of distinction possible; and this must be, and in
fact is, the true cause of the impression made on us. It is the
unpremeditated and evidently habitual *arrangement* of his
words, grounded on the habit of foreseeing, in each integral
part, or (more plainly) in every sentence, the whole that he
then intends to communicate. However irregular and desultory his talk, there is *method* in the fragments.

Listen, on the other hand, to an ignorant man, though
perhaps shrewd and able in his particular calling; whether
he be describing or relating. We immediately perceive, that
his memory alone is called into action; and that the objects
and events recur in the narration in the same order, and with

---

[26] "Carried on with slackened reins," quoted from Petrarch, *Epistola Barbato Sulmonensi,* ln. 39.

[27] For many of the New Critics, this idea was adopted as essential to the character of poetry. See especially Cleanth Brooks, below page 1037.

[28] Sir John Davies (1570–1626), from *Nosce Teipsum: Of the Soule of Man and the Immortalitie Thereof* (1599), though Coleridge is quoting the lines as he had transcribed (and partly rewritten) them in his own notebook entry of 1811 (*Notebooks* III, 4112; see *The Notebooks of Samuel Taylor Coleridge,* Kathleen Coburn, ed.). Davies's third stanza originally read: "This does she, when from things particular / She doth abstract the universall kinds, / Which bodilesse and immateriall are, / And can be lodg'd but onely in our minds."

"Essays on the Principles of Method" from *The Friend* (1818). Reprinted here from Barbara E. Rooke, ed., *The Friend* (Princeton: Princeton University Press, 1969).

[1] A shorter version of these essays was published earlier in January 1818, as "Essay on Method" in the *Encyclopedia Metropolitana.*

[2] This remark is from Samuel Johnson, quoted (without attribution). See *Boswell's Life of Johnson,* edited by G. Birbeck Hill and L. F. Powell (Oxford, 1934–1950) IV, 275.

[3] Coleridge abbreviates and freely translates in the next sentence the report of Aulus Gellius in *Noctes Atticae* 1.10.4. See also *Biographia Literaria,* I 6, for another use of this passage.

the same accompaniments, however accidental or impertinent, as they had first occurred to the narrator. The necessity of taking breath, the efforts of recollection, and the abrupt rectification of its failures, produce all his pauses; and with exception of the *"and then,"* the *"and there,"* and the still less significant, *"and so,"* they constitute likewise all his connections.

* * *

The difference between the products of a well-disciplined and those of an uncultivated understanding, in relation to what we will now venture to call the *Science of Method,* is often and admirably exhibited by our great Dramatist. We scarcely need refer our readers to the Clown's evidence, in the first scene of the second act of "Measure for Measure," or the Nurse in "Romeo and Juliet." But not to leave the position, without an instance to illustrate it, we will take the "easy-yielding" Mrs. Quickley's relation of the circumstances of Sir John Falstaff's debt to her.

Falstaff What is the gross sum that I owe thee?
Mrs. Quickley Marry, if thou wert an honest man, thyself and the money too. Thou didst swear to me upon a parcel-gilt goblet, sitting in my dolphin chamber, at the round table, by a sea-coal fire, on Wednesday in Whitsun week, when the prince broke thy head for likening his father to a singing-man in Windsor—thou didst swear to me then, as I was washing thy wound, to marry me and make me my lady thy wife. Canst thou deny it? Did not goodwife Keech, the butcher's wife, come in then and call me gossip Quickley?—coming into borrow a mess of vinegar: telling us she had a good dish of prawns—whereby thou didst desire to eat some—whereby I told thee they were ill for a green wound, &c. &c. &c.[4]

And this, be it observed, is so far from being carried beyond the bounds of a fair imitation, that "the poor soul's" thoughts and sentences are more closely interlinked than the truth of nature would have required, but that the connections and sequence, which the habit of Method can alone give, have in this instance a substitute in the fusion of passion. For the absence of Method, which characterizes the uneducated, is occasioned by an habitual submission of the understanding to mere events and images as such, and independent of any power in the mind to classify or appropriate them. The general accompaniments of time and place are the only relations which persons of this class appear to regard in their statements. As this constitutes *their* leading feature, the contrary excellence, as distinguishing the well-educated man, must be referred to the contrary habit. METHOD, therefore, becomes natural to the mind which has been accustomed to contemplate not *things* only, or for their own sake alone, but likewise and chiefly the *relations* of things, either their relations to each other, or to the observer, or to the state and apprehension of the hearers. To enumerate and analyze these relations, with the conditions under which alone they are discoverable, is to teach the science of Method.

The enviable results of this science, when knowledge has been ripened into those habits which at once secure and evince its possession, can scarcely be exhibited more forcibly as well as more pleasingly, than by contrasting with the former extract from Shakspeare the narration given by Hamlet to Horatio of the occurrences during his proposed transportation to England, and the events that interrupted his voyage.

HAMLET Sir, in my heart there was a kind of fighting
That would not let me sleep: methought I lay
Worse than the mutines in the bilboes. Rashly,
And prais'd be rashness for it—*Let us know,*
Our indiscretion sometimes serves us well,
When our deep plots do fall: and that should teach us,
There's a divinity that shapes our ends,
Rough-hew them how we will.
HORATIO That is most certain.
HAMLET Up from my cabin,
My sea-gown scarf'd about me, in the dark
Grop'd I to find out them; had my desire;
Finger'd their pocket; and, in fine, withdrew
To my own room again: making so bold,
My fears forgetting manners, to unseal
Their grand commission; where *I* found, Horatio,
A royal knavery—an exact command,
Larded with many several sorts of reasons,
Importing Denmark's health, and England's too,
With, ho! such bugs and goblins in *my* life,
That on the supervize, no leisure bated,
No, not to stay the grinding of the axe,
My head should be struck off!
HORATIO Is't possible?
HAMLET Here's the commission.—Read it at more
  leisure.[5]

Here the events, with the circumstances of time and place, are all stated with equal compression and rapidity, not one introduced which could have been omitted without

[4] Shakespeare, *Henry IV, part II,* II, i, 80–93.

[5] *Hamlet* V, ii, 4–26, with variations.

injury to the intelligibility of the whole process. If any tendency is discoverable, as far as the mere facts are in question, it is the tendency to omission: and, accordingly, the reader will observe, that the attention of the narrator is called back to one material circumstance, which he was hurrying by, by a direct question from the friend to whom the story is communicated, "HOW WAS THIS SEALED?" But by a trait which is indeed peculiarly characteristic of Hamlet's mind, ever disposed to generalize, and meditative to excess (but which, with due abatement and reduction, is distinctive of every powerful and methodizing intellect), all the digressions and enlargements consist of reflections, truths, and principles of general and permanent interest, either directly expressed or disguised in playful satire.

I sat me down;
Devis'd a new commission; wrote it fair.
I once did hold it, as our statists do,
A baseness to write fair, and laboured much
How to forget that learning; but, sir, now
It did me yeoman's service. Wilt thou know
The effect of what I wrote?
HORATIO   Aye, good my lord.
HAMLET   An earnest conjuration from the king,
As England was his faithful tributary;
As love between them, like the palm, might flourish;
As peace should still her wheaten garland wear,
And many such like As's of great charge—
That on the view and knowing of these contents
He should the bearers put to sudden death,
No shriving time allowed.
HORATIO   How was this sealed?
HAMLET   Why, even in that was heaven ordinant.
I had my father's signet in my purse,
Which was the model of that Danish seal:
Folded the writ up in the form of the other;
Subscribed it; gave't the impression; placed it safely,
The changeling never known. Now, the next day
Was our sea-fight; and what to this was sequent,
Thou knowest already.
HORATIO   So Guildenstern and Rosencrantz go to't?
HAMLET   Why, man, they did make love to this employment.
They are not near my conscience: their defeat
Doth by their own insinuation grow.
'Tis dangerous when the baser nature comes
Between the pass and fell incensed points
Of mighty opposites.[6]

---

[6] *Hamlet* V, ii, 31–62, omitting lines 42 and 44.

It would, perhaps, be sufficient to remark of the preceding passage, in connection with the humorous specimen of narration,

Fermenting o'er with frothy circumstance,[7]

in Henry IV.; that if overlooking the different value of the *matter* in each, we considered the *form* alone, we should find both *immethodical;* Hamlet from the excess, Mrs. Quickley from the want, of reflection and generalization; and that Method, therefore, must result from the due mean or balance between our passive impressions and the mind's own re-action on the same. (Whether this re-action do not suppose or imply a primary act positively *originating* in the mind itself, and prior to the object in order of nature, though co-instantaneous in its manifestation, will be hereafter discussed.) But we had a further purpose in thus contrasting these extracts from our "myriad-minded Bard," (μυριονοῦς ἄνηρ.)[8] We wished to bring forward, each for itself, these two elements of Method, or (to adopt an arithmetical term) its two main *factors*.

Instances of the want of generalization are of no rare occurrence in real life: and the narrations of Shakspeare's Hostess and the Tapster,[9] differ from those of the ignorant and unthinking in general, by their superior humor, the poet's own gift and infusion, not by their want of Method, which is not greater than we often meet with in that class, of which they are the dramatic representatives. Instances of the opposite fault, arising from the excess of generalization and reflection in minds of the opposite class, will, like the minds themselves, occur less frequently in the course of our own personal experience. Yet they will not have been wanting to our readers, nor will they have passed unobserved, though the great poet himself (ὁ τὴν ἑαυτοῦ ψυχὴν ὡσεί ὕλην τινα ἀσώματον μορφαῖς ποικιλαῖς μορφώσας)[10] has more conveniently supplied the illustrations. To complete, therefore, the purpose aforementioned, that of presenting each of the two components as separately as possible, we chose an instance in which, by the surplus of its own activity, Hamlet's mind disturbs the arrangement, of which that very activity had been the cause and impulse.

---

[7] The source has not been identified.
[8] "Myriad-minded man"; cf. William Cave, *Scriptorum ecclesiasticorum historia literaria* (1688), and *Notebooks* I, 1070.
[9] That is, Mistress Quickly (see above); and Pompey the clown in *Measure for Measure* II, i.
[10] "He that moulded his own soul, as some incorporeal material, into various forms." Coleridge's translation from Themistius, *Paraphrase of Aristotle on the Soul*, 3.8.

Thus exuberance of mind, on the one hand, interferes with the *forms* of Method; but sterility of mind, on the other, wanting the spring and impulse to mental action, is wholly destructive of Method itself. For in attending too exclusively to the relations which the past or passing events and objects bear to general truth, and the moods of his own Thought, the most intelligent man is sometimes in danger of overlooking that other relation, in which they are likewise to be placed to the apprehension and sympathies of his hearers. His discourse appears like soliloquy intermixed with dialogue. But the uneducated and unreflecting talker overlooks *all* mental relations, both logical and psychological; and consequently precludes all Method, that is not purely accidental. Hence the nearer the things and incidents in time and place, the more distant, disjointed, and impertinent to each other, and to any common purpose, will they appear in his narration: and this from the want of a *staple,* or *starting-post,* in the narrator himself; from the absence of *the leading Thought,* which, borrowing a phrase from the nomenclature of legislation, we may not inaptly call the INITIATIVE. On the contrary, where the habit of Method is present and effective, things the most remote and diverse in time, place, and outward circumstance, are brought into mental contiguity and succession, the more striking as the less expected. But while we would impress the necessity of this habit, the illustrations adduced give proof that in undue preponderance, and when the prerogative of the mind is stretched into despotism, the discourse may degenerate into the grotesque or the fantastical.

* * *

We have seen that from the confluence of innumerable impressions in each moment of time the mere passive memory must needs tend to confusion—a rule, the seeming exceptions to which (the thunder-bursts in Lear, for instance) are really confirmations of its truth. For, in many instances, the predominance of some mighty Passion takes the place of the guiding Thought, and the result presents the method of Nature, rather than the habit of the Individual. For Thought, Imagination (and we may add, Passion), are, in their very essence, the first, connective, the latter co-adunative: and it has been shown, that if the excess lead to Method misapplied, and to connections of the moment, the absence, or marked deficiency, either precludes Method altogether, both form and substance: or (as the following extract will exemplify) retains the outward form only.

My liege and madam! to expostulate
What majesty should be, what duty is,
Why day is day, night night, and time is time,

Were nothing but to waste night, day and time.
Therefore—since brevity is the soul of wit,
And tediousness the limbs and outward flourishes,
I will be brief. Your noble son is mad:
Mad call I it—for to define true madness,
What is't, but to be nothing else but mad!
But let that go.
QUEEN   *More matter with less art.*
POLONIUS   *Madam! I swear, I use no art at all.*
That he is mad, tis true: tis true, tis pity:
And pity tis, tis true (a foolish figure!
But farewell it, for I will use no art.)
Mad let us grant him then! and now remains,
That we find out the cause of this effect,
Or rather say the cause of this defect:
For this effect defective comes by cause.
Thus it remains, and the remainder thus
Perpend![11]

Does not the irresistible sense of the ludicrous in this flourish of the soul-surviving body of old Polonius's intellect, not less than in the endless confirmations and most undeniable matters of fact, of Tapster Pompey or "the hostess of the tavern" prove to our feelings, even before the word is found which presents the truth to our understandings, that confusion and formality are but the opposite poles of the same null-point?

It is Shakspeare's peculiar excellence, that throughout the whole of his splendid picture gallery (the reader will excuse the confest inadequacy of this metaphor), we find individuality every where, mere portrait no where. In all his various characters, we still feel ourselves communing with the same human nature, which is every where present as the vegetable sap in the branches, sprays, leaves, buds, blossoms, and fruits, their shapes, tastes, and odours. Speaking of the effect, i.e. his works themselves, we may define the excellence of *their* method as consisting in that just proportion, that union and interpenetration of the universal and the particular, which must ever pervade all works of decided genius and true science. For Method implies a *progressive transition,* and it is the meaning of the word in the original language. The Greek Μεθοδος, is literally *a way,* or *path of Transit.* Thus we extol the Elements of Euclid, or Socrates' discourse with the slave in the Menon,[12] as *methodical,* a term which no one who holds himself bound to think or speak correctly, would apply to the alphabetical order or arrangement of a common

---

[11] *Hamlet* II, ii, 86–105.
[12] Cf. Plato, *Meno* 82b–85b.

dictionary. But as, without continuous transition, there can be no Method, so without a pre-conception there can be no transition with continuity. The term, Method, cannot therefore, otherwise than by abuse, be applied to a mere dead arrangement, containing in itself no principle of progression.

from
Essay V

It has been observed, in a preceding page, that the RELATIONS of objects are prime *materials* of Method, and that the contemplation of relations is the indispensible condition of thinking methodically. It becomes necessary therefore to add, that there are two kinds of relation, in which objects of mind may be contemplated. The first is that of LAW, which, in its absolute perfection, is conceivable only of the Supreme Being, whose creative IDEA not only appoints to each thing its *position,* but in that position, and in consequence of that position, gives it its qualities, yea, it gives its very existence, as *that particular* thing.[13] Yet in whatever science the relation of the parts to each other and to the whole is predetermined by a truth originating in the *mind,* and not abstracted or generalized from observation of the parts, there we affirm the presence of a *law,* if we are speaking of the physical sciences, as of Astronomy for instance; or the presence of fundamental *ideas,* if our discourse be upon those sciences, the truths of which, as truths absolute, not merely have an independent *origin* in the mind, but continue to exist in and for the mind alone. Such, for instance, is Geometry, and such are the ideas of a perfect circle, of asymptots, &c.[14]

We have thus assigned the first place in the science of Method to LAW; and first of the first, to *Law,* as the absolute *kind* which comprehending in itself the substance of every possible degree precludes from its conception all degree, not by generalization but by its own plenitude. As such, therefore, and as the sufficient cause of the reality correspondent thereto, we contemplate it as exclusively an attribute of the Supreme Being, inseparable from the idea of God: adding, however, that from the contemplation of law in this, its only perfect form, must be derived all true insight into all other grounds and principles necessary to Method, as the science

common to all sciences, which in each τυγχάνει ὄν ἄλλο αὐτῆς τῆς ἐπιστήμης.[15] Alienated from this (intuition shall we call it? or stedfast faith?) ingenious men may produce schemes, conducive to the peculiar purposes of particular sciences, but no scientific system.

* * *

The grand problem, the solution of which forms, according to Plato, the final object and distinctive character of philosophy, is this: *for all that exists conditionally* (i.e. the existence of which is inconceivable except under the condition of its dependency on some other as its antecedent) *to find a ground that is unconditional and absolute, and thereby to reduce the aggregate of human knowledge to a system.* For the relation common to all being known, the appropriate orbit of each becomes discoverable, together with its peculiar relations to its concentrics in the common sphere of subordination. Thus the centrality of the sun having been established, and the law of the distances of the planets from the sun having been determined, we possess the means of calculating the distance of each from the other. But as all objects of sense are in continual flux, and as the notices of them by the senses must, as far as they are true notices, change with them, while scientific principles (or laws) are no otherwise principles of science than as they are permanent and always the same, the latter were appropriated to the pure reason, either as its products or as* implanted in it. And now the remarkable fact forces itself on our attention, viz. that the material world is found to obey the same laws as had been deduced independently from the reason: and that the masses act by a force, which cannot be conceived to result from the component parts, known or imaginable. In the phænomena of magnetism, electricity, galvanism, and in chemistry generally, the mind is led instinctively, as it were, to regard the working powers as conducted, transmitted, or accumulated by the sensible bodies, and not as inherent. This fact has, at all times, been the strong hold alike of the materialists and of the spiritualists, equally solvable by the two contrary hypotheses, and

---

[13]It should especially be noted here that Coleridge's use of "Law" is here quite distinct from the sense of the term that is associated with a rule: the *law* of a particular thing is its nature; it is, in brief, *itself,* regarded as the principle of its own reality. See below Coleridge's discussion of "Idea" in *On the Constitution of Church and State* (page 519).

[14]In Coleridge's notes in two copies (A and D), he warns against the error of forgetting that the terms Idea and Law are, as he uses them, always correlative, and that in the case of geometry, the appropriate term is not *Idea* but *Theorem.*

[15]Coleridge's translation: "May prove to be something more than the mere aggregate of the knowledges in any particular science." The passage in question, which Coleridge uses as an epigraph to Essay VII, is a composite drawn from Tenneman's *History of Philosophy* II, 242–3, conflating two passages drawn from Plato's *Republic,* 476a–d, and *Charmides,* 166a.

*Which of these two doctrines was Plato's own opinion, it is hard to say. In many passages of his works, the latter (i.e. the doctrine of innate, or rather of connate, ideas) *seems* to be it; but from the character and avowed purpose of these works, as addressed to a promiscuous public, and therefore preparatory and for the discipline of the mind rather than directly doctrinal, it is not improbable that Plato chose it as the more popular representation, and as belonging to the poetic drapery of his Philosophemata.

fairly solved by neither. In the clear and masterly† review of the elder philosophies, which must be ranked among the most splendid proofs of judgment no less than of genius, and more expressly in the critique on the atomic or corpuscular doctrine of Democritus and his followers, as the one extreme, and that of the pure rationalism of Zeno and the Eleatic school as the other,[18] Plato has proved incontrovertibly, that in both alike the basis is too narrow to support the superstructure; that the grounds of both are false or disputable; and that, if these were conceded, yet neither the one nor the other is adequate to the solution of the problem: viz. what is the ground of the co-incidence between reason and experience? Or between the laws of matter and the ideas of the pure intellect? The only answer which Plato deemed the question capable of receiving, compels the reason to pass out of itself and seek the ground of this agreement in a supersensual essence, which being at once the *ideal* of the reason and the cause of the material world, is the pre-establisher of the harmony in and between both. Religion therefore is the ultimate aim of philosophy, in consequence of which philosophy itself becomes the supplement of the sciences, both as the convergence of all to the common end, namely, wisdom; and as supplying the copula, which modified in each in the comprehension of its parts to one whole, is in its principles common to all, as integral parts of one system. And this is METHOD, itself a distinct science, the immediate offspring of philosophy, and the link or

mordant[19] by which philosophy becomes scientific and the sciences philosophical.

from
Essay VI

Ἀπάντων ζητοῦντες λόγον ἔξωθεν, ἀναιροῦσι λόγον.
THEOPH. *in Met.*

Seeking the reason of all things from without, they preclude reason.

The second relation is that of THEORY, in which the existing forms and qualities of objects, discovered by observation or experiment, suggest a given arrangement of many under one point of view: and this not merely or principally in order to facilitate the remembrance, recollection, or communication of the same; but for the purposes of understanding, and in most instances of controlling, them. In other words, all THEORY supposes the general idea of cause and effect. The scientific arts of Medicine, Chemistry, and of Physiology in general, are examples of a method hitherto founded on this second sort of relation.

Between these two lies the Method in the FINE ARTS,[20] which belongs indeed to this second or external relation, because the effect and position of the parts is always more or less influenced by the knowledge and experience of their previous qualities; but which nevertheless constitute a link connecting the second form of relation with the first. For in all, that truly merits the name of *Poetry* in its most comprehensive sense, there is a necessary predominance of the Ideas (i.e. of that which originates in the artist himself), and a comparative indifference of the materials. A true musical taste is soon dissatisfied with the Harmonica, or any similar instrument of glass or steel, because the *body* of the sound (as the Italians phrase it), or that effect which is derived

---

†I can conceive no better remedy for the overweening self-complacency of modern philosophy, than the annulment of its pretended originality. The attempt has been made by Dutens,[16] but he failed in it by flying to the opposite extreme. When he should have confined himself to the philosophies, he extended his attack to the sciences and even to the main discoveries of later times: and thus instead of vindicating the ancients, he became the calumniator of the moderns: as far at least as detraction is calumny. It is my intention to give a course of lectures[17] in the course of the present season, comprizing the origin, and progress, the fates and fortunes of philosophy, from Pythagoras to Locke, with the lives and succession of the philosophers in each sect: tracing the progress of speculative science chiefly in relation to the gradual development of the human mind, but without omitting the favorable or inauspicious influence of circumstances and the accidents of individual genius....

[16] Louis Dutens (1730–1812); member of the Royal Society and editor of Leibnitz *Opera Omnia* (1768). The work to which Coleridge refers is *Recherches sur l'origine des découvertes attribuées aux modernes* (1766, 1769).

[17] Coleridge's Philosophical Lectures were delivered in December 1814 and March 1819.

[18] Democritus (c. 460–370 B.C.), Greek philosopher who systematized the thought of his teacher, Leucippus (fl. fifth century B.C., at Miletus), concerning the constitution of reality, composed of the Void and an infinite number of Atoms from which the physical universe is constructed. Zeno of Elea (c. 495–370 B.C.), student of Parmenides (born c. 515 B.C.), the founder and leader of the "Eleatic School." Parmenides argued that all reality is comprised in "the One," and that one should never assert the existence of that which is not. Aristotle credits Zeno with the invention of dialectic, but he is best known for his celebrated paradoxes concerning movement (for example, Achilles and the Tortoise) and the one.

[19] Coleridge derives this sense from the *mordant* as a substance that enables dye to bond more permanently to fabric. This passage is cited in the OED.

[20] It is important to note here that Coleridge is placing Method in the Fine Arts "between" the *relations* respectively of *Law* and *Theory,* but associating it with the latter as an "external relation." The point of this distinction is that a theory is an arrangement of forms and qualities of objects "under one point of view" and as such should not be confused with any putative law of nature. A theory is, rather, a presentation that facilitates the cognition of the *Idea,* not a specification of the *Law.* As the relations in question pertain to *Ideas,* a theory is hypothetical and/or provisional in the sense that it allows one to state or see explanatory (that is, causal) relations perspicuously. Thus Coleridge does not presume any fundamental difference between poetry and science, but rather a difference in their materials and their ends or purposes.

from the *materials,* encroaches too far on the effect from the *proportions* of the notes, or that which is *given* to Music by the mind. To prove the high value as well as the superior dignity of the first relation; and to evince, that on this alone a *perfect* Method can be grounded, and that the Methods attainable by the second are at best but approximations to the first, or tentative exercises in the hope of discovering it, form the first object of the present disquisition.

These truths we have (as the most pleasing and popular mode of introducing the subject) hitherto illustrated from Shakspeare. But the same truths, namely the necessity of a mental Initiative to all Method, as well as a careful attention to the conduct of the mind in the exercise of Method itself, may be equally, and here perhaps more characteristically, proved from the most familiar of the Sciences. We may draw our elucidation even from those which are at present fashionable among us: from Botany or from Chemistry. In the lowest attempt at a methodical arrangement of the former science, that of artificial classification for the preparatory purpose of a nomenclature, some *antecedent* must have been contributed by the mind itself; some *purpose* must be in view; or some question at least must have been proposed to nature, grounded, as all questions are, upon *some* idea[21] of the answer. As for instance, the assumption,

That two great sexes animate the world.[22]

For no man can confidently conceive a fact to be *universally* true who does not with equal confidence anticipate its *necessity,* and who does not believe that necessity to be demonstrable by an insight into its nature, whenever and wherever such insight can be obtained. We acknowledge, we reverence the obligations of Botany to Linnæus,[23] who, adopting from Bartholinus[24] and others the sexuality of plants, grounded thereon a scheme of classific and distinctive marks, by which one man's experience may be communicated to others, and the objects safely reasoned on while ab-

sent, and recognized as soon as and wherever they are met with. He invented a universal character for the language of Botany chargeable with no greater imperfections than are to be found in the alphabets of every particular language. As for the study of the ancients, so of the works of nature, an accidence and a dictionary are the first and indispensable requisites: and to the illustrious Swede, Botany is indebted for both. But neither was the central idea of vegetation itself, by the light of which we might have seen the collateral relations of the vegetable to the inorganic and to the animal world; nor the constitutive nature and inner necessity of sex itself, revealed to Linnæus.[25]* Hence, as in all other cases where the master-light is missing, so in this: the reflective mind avoids

---

[25] For this important footnote, Coleridge draws upon Kant's *Metaphysical Foundations of a Science of Nature* (1786).

* The word Nature has been used in two senses, viz. actively and passively; energetic (= forma formans), and material (= forma formata). In the first (the sense in which the word is used in the text) it signifies the inward principle of whatever is requisite for the reality of a thing, as *existent:* while the *essence,* or essential property, signifies the inner principle of all that appertains to the *possibility* of a thing. Hence, in accurate language, we say the *essence* of a mathematical circle or other geometrical figure, not the *nature:* because in the conception of forms purely geometrical there is no expression or implication of their real existence. In the second, or material sense, of the word Nature, we mean by it the sum total of all things, as far as they are objects of our senses, and consequently of possible experience— the aggregate of phænomena, whether existing for our outward senses, or for our inner sense. The doctrine concerning material nature would therefore (the word Physiology being both ambiguous in itself, and already otherwise appropriated) be more properly entitled Phænomenology, distinguished into its two grand divisions, Somatology and Psychology. The doctrine concerning energetic nature is comprised in the science of Dynamics: the union of which with Phænomenology, and the alliance of both with the sciences of the Possible, or of the Conceivable, viz. Logic and Mathematics, constitute Natural Philosophy.

Having thus explained the term Nature, we now more especially entreat the reader's attention to the sense, in which here, and every where through this Essay, we use the word Idea. We assert, that the very impulse to universalize any phænomenon involves the prior assumption of some efficient law in nature, which in a thousand different forms is evermore one and the same; entire in each, yet comprehending all; and incapable of being abstracted or generalized from any number of phænomena, because it is itself presupposed in each and all as their common ground and condition: and because every definition of a genus is the adequate definition of the lowest species alone, while the efficient law must contain the ground of all in all. It is *attributed,* never *derived.* The utmost we ever venture to say is, that the falling of an apple *suggested* the law of gravitation to Sir I. Newton. Now a law and an idea are correlative terms, and differ only as object and subject, as being and truth.

Such is the doctrine of the Novum Organum of Lord Bacon, agreeing (as we shall more largely show in the text)[26] in all essential points with the true doctrine of Plato, the apparent differences being for the greater part occasioned by the Grecian sage having applied his principles chiefly to the investigation of the mind, and the method of evolving its powers, and the English philosopher to the development of nature. That our great countryman speaks too often detractingly of the divine philosopher must be explained, partly by the tone given to thinking minds by the Reformation, the founders and fathers of which saw in the Aristotelians, or schoolmen, the antagonists of Protestantism, and in the Italian Platonists the despisers and secret enemies of Christianity itself; and partly, by his having formed his notions of Plato's doctrines from the absurdities and phantasms of his misinterpreters, rather than from an unprejudiced study of the original works.

---

[21] In one copy (H), Coleridge substitutes here "pre-conception" for "idea."

[22] Milton, *Paradise Lost* VII, 788. The original passage reads:

> . . . and other Suns perhaps
> With thir attendant Moons thou wilt descrie
> Communicating Male and Femal Light,
> Which two great Sexes animate the World,
> Stor'd in each Orb perhaps with some that live.

[23] Carolus Linnaeus (1707–1778), Swedish botanist, author of *Genera pantarum* (1737) that based the classification of plant species on observable sexual characteristics. Erasmus Darwin (1731–1802), the grandfather of Charles Darwin and Francis Galton, was instrumental in popularizing the Linnaean "sexual system" in England.

[24] Kaspar Bartholin or Berthelsen (1585–1629), Danish physician and theologian.

Scylla only to lose itself on Charybdis.[27] If we adhere to the general notion of sex, as abstracted from the more obvious modes and forms in which the sexual relation manifests itself, we soon meet with whole classes of plants to which it is found inapplicable. If arbitrarily, we give it indefinite extension, it is dissipated into the barren truism, that all specific products suppose specific *means* of production. Thus a growth and a birth are distinguished by the mere verbal definition, that the latter is a whole in itself, the former not: and when we would apply even this to nature, we are baffled by objects (the flower polypus, &c. &c.) in which each is the other. All that can be done by the most patient and active industry, by the widest and most continuous researches; all that the amplest survey of the vegetable realm, brought under immediate contemplation by the most stupendous collections of species and varieties, can suggest; all that minutest dissection and exactest chemical analysis, can unfold; all that varied experiment and the position of plants and of their component parts in every conceivable relation to light, heat, (and whatever else we distinguish as imponderable substances) to earth, air, water, to the supposed constituents of air and water, separate and in all proportions—in short all that chemical agents and re-agents can disclose or adduce;—all these have been brought, as conscripts, into the field, with the completest accoutrement, in the best discipline, under the ablest commanders. Yet after all that was affected by Linnæus himself, not to mention the labours of Cæsalpinus, Ray, Gesner, Tournefort, and the other heroes who preceded the general adoption of the sexual system, as the basis of artificial arrangement—after all the successive toils and enterprizes of HEDWIG, JUSSIEU, MIRBEL, SMITH, KNIGHT, ELLIS,[28] &c. &c.—what is BOTANY at this present hour? Little more than an enormous nomenclature; a huge catalogue, *bien arrange,*[29] yearly and monthly augmented, in various editions, each with its own scheme of technical memory and its own conveniences of reference! . . . The terms system, method, science, are mere improprieties of courtesy, when applied to a mass enlarging by endless appositions, but without a nerve that oscillates, or a pulse that throbs, in sign of *growth* or inward sympathy. . . .

So long back as the first appearance of Dr. Darwin's Phytonomia,[30] the writer, then in earliest manhood, presumed to hazard the opinion, that the physiological botanists were hunting in a false direction; and sought for analogy where they should have looked for antithesis. He saw, or thought he saw, that the harmony between the vegetable and animal world, was not a harmony of resemblance, but of contrast; and their relation to each other that of corresponding opposites. They seemed to him (whose mind had been formed by observation, unaided, but at the same time unenthralled, by partial experiment) as two streams from the same fountain indeed, but flowing the one due west, and the other direct east; and that consequently, the resemblance would be as the proximity, greatest in the first and rudimental products of vegetable and animal organization.[31] Whereas, according to the received notion, the highest and most perfect vegetable, and the lowest and rudest animal forms, ought to have seemed the links of the two systems, which is contrary to fact. Since that time, the same idea has dawned in the minds of philosophers capable of demonstrating its objective truth by induction of facts in an unbroken series of correspondences in nature. From these men, or from minds enkindled by their labours, we hope hereafter to receive it, or rather the yet higher idea to which it refers us, matured into *laws* of organic nature; and thence to have one other splendid proof, that with the knowledge of LAW alone dwell Power and Prophecy, decisive Experiment, and, lastly, a scientific method, that dissipating with its earliest rays the gnomes of hypothesis and the mists of theory may, within a single generation, open out on the philosophic Seer discoveries that had baffled the gigantic, but blind and guideless industry of ages.

Such, too, is the case with the assumed indecomponible substances of the LABORATORY. They are the symbols of elementary powers, and the exponents of a law, which, as the root of all these powers, the chemical philosopher, whatever his theory may be, is instinctively labouring to extract.[32] This

---

[26] In Essay VIII, not included here. The position expressed here of a deep affinity between Bacon and Plato, while it goes very much against the appearance in Bacon's text of severe criticism of the ancients, but especially Plato and Aristotle, is grounded on Coleridge's view that the methodical investigation of the mind is cognate with the methodical investigation of nature.

[27] Scylla and Charybdis are the two complementary hazards that Odysseus must escape in Homer's *Odyssey*. Scylla is usually depicted as a creature with 12 feet and 6 heads, devouring any creature in reach; while Charybdis drinks in and spews out the ocean water, as in a whirlpool.

[28] Andreas Caesalpinus (1519–1603), Italian botanist; John Ray (c. 1627–1705), English naturalist; Konrad von Gesner (1516–1704), Swiss zoologist; Joseph Pitton de Tournefort (1656–1708), French botanist; Johann Hedwig (1730–1799), German botanist; Antoine Laurent de Jussieu (1748–1836), French biologist; Charles François Brisseau de Mirbel (1776–1854), French botanist; Sir James Edward Smith (1759–1828), English botanist; Thomas Andrew Knight (1759–1838), English horticulturist; John Ellis (c. 1710–1776), English naturalist.

[29] "Well arranged."

[30] Coleridge evidently has in mind here Erasmus Darwin's *Zoonomia* (1794–1796), not his *Phytologia* (1800).

[31] Coleridge is here expressing one of his most characteristic ideas of the expression of polar opposites of one power. See his *Theory of Life* (1848), 71, and his use of the same idea in the discussion of electricity and magenetism in Essay VII (below, page 516).

[32] Coleridge is arguing against the finality of a strict atomism, treating evidently indivisible atoms as symbols or exponents of a dynamic law. Cf. Ralph Cudworth's (1617–1686) massive neoplatonic argument against ancient and modern atomism in his *True Intellectual System of the Universe* (1678), which Coleridge had read and commented on in his notebooks as early as 1795–1796. See *Notebooks* I, 200–05. The interest of Coleridge's argument is that he does not, as did Cudworth, reject atomism as leading inevitably to atheism, but transformed it to show the belief in atoms as ultimate is an error of method.

instinct, again, is itself but the form, in which the idea, the mental Correlative of the law, first announces its incipient germination in his own mind: and hence proceeds the striving after unity of principle through all the diversity of forms, with a feeling resembling that which accompanies our endeavors to recollect a forgotten name; when we seem at once to have and not to have it; which the memory feels but cannot find. Thus, as "the lunatic, the lover, and the poet,"[33] suggest each other to Shakspeare's Theseus, as soon as his thoughts present him the ONE FORM, of which they are but varieties; so water and flame, the diamond, the charcoal, and the mantling champagne, with its ebullient sparkles, are convoked and fraternized by the theory of the chemist. This is, in truth, the first charm of chemistry, and the secret of the almost universal interest excited by its discoveries. The serious complacency which is afforded by the sense of truth, utility, permanence, and progression, blends with and ennobles the exhilarating surprise and the pleasurable sting of curiosity, which accompany the propounding and the solving of an Enigma. It is the sense of a principle of connection given by the mind, and sanctioned by the correspondency of nature. Hence the strong hold which in all ages chemistry has had on the imagination. If in SHAKSPEARE we find nature idealized into poetry, through the creative power of a profound yet observant meditation, so through the meditative observation of a DAVY, a WOOLLASTON, or a HATCHETT,[34]

> By some connatural force,
> Powerful at greatest distance to unite
> With secret amity things of like kind,[35]

we find poetry, as it were, substantiated and realized in nature: yea, nature itself disclosed to us, GEMINAM *istam naturam, quæ fit et facit, et creat et creatur,*[36] as at once the poet and the poem!

from Essay VII

From Shakspeare to Plato, from the philosophic poet to the poetic philosopher, the transition is easy, and the road is crowded with illustrations of our present subject. For of Plato's works, the larger and more valuable portion have all one common end, which comprehends and shines through the particular purpose of each several dialogue; and this is to establish the sources, to evolve the principles, and exemplify the art of METHOD. This is the clue, without which it would be difficult to exculpate the noblest productions of the divine philosopher from the charge of being tortuous and labyrinthine in their progress, and unsatisfactory in their ostensible results. The latter indeed appear not seldom to have been drawn for the purpose of starting a new problem, rather than that of solving the one proposed as the subject of the previous discussion. But with the clear insight that the purpose of the writer is not so much to establish any particular truth, as to remove the obstacles, the continuance of which is preclusive of all truth; the whole scheme assumes a different aspect, and justifies itself in all its dimensions. We see, that to open anew a well of springing water, not to cleanse the stagnant tank, or fill, bucket by bucket, the leaden cistern; that the EDUCATION of the intellect, by awakening the principle and *method* of self-development, was his proposed object, not any specific information that can be *conveyed into it* from without: not to assist in storing the passive mind with the various sorts of knowledge most in request, as if the human soul were a mere repository or banqueting-room, but to place it in such relations of circumstances as should gradually excite the germinal power that craves no knowledge but what it can take up into itself, what it can appropriate, and re-produce in fruits of its own. To shape, to dye, to paint over, and to mechanize the mind, he resigned, as their proper trade, to the sophists, against whom he waged open and unremitting war. For the ancients, as well as the moderns, had their machinery for the extemporaneous mintage of intellects, by means of which, *off-hand,* as it were, the scholar was enabled *to make a figure* on any and all subjects, on any and all occasions.

* * *

In fine, as improgressive arrangement is not Method, so neither is a mere mode or set fashion of doing a thing. Are further facts required? We appeal to the notorious fact that ZoOLOGY, soon after the commencement of the latter half of the last century, was falling abroad, weighed down and crushed, as it were, by the inordinate number and manifoldness of facts and phænomena apparently separate, without evincing the least promise of systematizing itself by any inward combination, any vital interdependence of its parts. JOHN HUNTER,[37] who appeared at times almost a stranger to

---

[33] *Midsummer Night's Dream* V, i, 7.
[34] Sir Humphrey Davy (1778–1829), distinguished British chemist at the Royal Institution (a friend of Coleridge's); William Hyde Wollaston (1766–1828), influential British physicist and metallurgist; Charles Hatchett (c. 1765–1847), British manufacturer and chemist, discoverer of Niobium (his term, Columbium).
[35] *Paradise Lost* IX, 246–8. Original reads "or some connatural force, . . ."
[36] The source is John Scotus Erigena, *De divisione naturae* 1.13 (1681). Coleridge modified the original, which reads *"gemina natura, quae fit et facit, et creat et creatur":* "the divine nature, which made and is making, both creates and is created."

[37] John Hunter (1728–1793), British surgeon and medical experimentalist; see also Coleridge's *Theory of Life* (1848), dedicated to Hunter.

the grand conception, which yet never ceased to work in him as his genius and governing spirit, rose at length in the horizon of physiology and comparative anatomy. In his printed works, the one directing thought seems evermore to flit before him, twice or thrice only to have been seized, and after a momentary detention to have been again let go: as if the words of the charm had been incomplete, and it had appeared at its own will only to mock its calling. At length, in the astonishing preparations for his museum, he constructed it for the scientific apprehension out of the unspoken alphabet of nature. Yet notwithstanding the imperfection in the annunciation of the idea, how exhilarating have been the results! We dare appeal to ABERNETHY,* to EVERARD HOME, to HATCHETT,[38] whose communication to Sir Everard on the egg and its analogies, in a recent paper of the latter (itself of high excellence) in the Philosophical Transactions, we point out as being, in the proper sense of the term, the development of a FACT in the history of physiology, and to which we refer as exhibiting a luminous instance of what we mean by the discovery of a *central phænomenon*. To these we appeal, whether whatever is grandest in the views of CUVIER be not either a reflection of this light or a continuation of its rays, well and wisely directed through fit media to its appropriate object.*

We have seen that a previous act and conception of the mind is indispensible even to the mere semblances of Method: that neither fashion, mode, nor orderly arrangement can be produced without a prior purpose, and "a pre-cogitation *ad intentionem ejus quod quæritur,*"[39] though this purpose may have been itself excited, and this "pre-cogitation" itself abstracted from the perceived likenesses and differences of the objects to be arranged. But it has likewise been shown, that fashion, mode, ordonnance, are not Method, inasmuch as all Method supposes A PRINCIPLE OF UNITY WITH PROGRESSION; in other words, progres-

sive transition without breach of continuity. But such a principle, it has been proved, can never in the sciences of experiment or in those of observation be adequately supplied by a theory built on generalization. For what shall determine the mind to abstract and generalize one common point rather than another? and within what limits, from what number of individual objects, shall the generalization be made? The theory must still require a prior theory for its own legitimate construction. With the mathematician the definition *makes* the object,[40] and pre-establishes the terms which, and which alone, can occur in the after-reasoning. . . .

A mathematical *theoria seu contemplatio*[41] may therefore be perfect. For the mathematician can be certain, that he has contemplated *all* that appertains to his proposition. The celebrated EULER,[42] treating on some point respecting arches, makes this curious remark, "All experience is in contradiction to this; sed potius fidendum est analysi; *i.e.* but this is no reason for doubting the analysis." The words *sound* paradoxical; but in truth mean no more than this, that the properties of *space* are not less certainly the properties of space because they can never be entirely transferred to material bodies. But in physics, that is, in all the sciences which have for their objects the things of nature, and not the *entia rationis*[43]—more philosophically, intellectual acts and the products of those acts, existing exclusively in and for the intellect itself—the definition must follow, and not precede the reasoning. It is representative not constitutive, and is indeed little more than an abbreviature of the preceding observation, and the deductions therefrom. But as the observation, though aided by experiment, is necessarily limited and imperfect, the definition must be equally so. The history of theories, and the frequency of their subversion by the discovery of a single new fact, supply the best illustrations of this truth.*

As little can a true scientific method be grounded on an hypothesis, unless where the hypothesis is an exponential image or picture-language of an *idea* which is contained in

---

*Since the first delivery of this sheet, Mr. Abernethy has realized this anticipation, dictated solely by the writer's wishes, and at that time justified only by his general admiration of Mr. A.'s talents and principles; but composed without the least knowledge that he was then actually engaged in proving the assertion here hazarded, at large and in detail. See his eminent "Physiological Lectures," lately published in one volume octavo.

[38] John Abernathy (1764–1831), a surgeon and student of John Hunter; Coleridge's note below refers to his *Physiological Lectures* (1817); Everard Home (1756–1832), another surgeon and student of Hunter; Charles Hatchett, see note 34 above.

*Nor should it be wholly unnoticed, that Cuvier, who, we understand, was not born in France, and is not of unmixed French extraction, had prepared himself for his illustrious labors (as we learn from a reference in the first chapter of his great work, and should have concluded from the general style of thinking, though the language betrays suppression, as of one who doubted the sympathy of his readers or audience) in a very different school of methodology and philosophy than Paris could have afforded.

[39] "To the investigation of the point at issue"; unknown source.

[40] Coleridge is elaborating a point from Vico (quoted from Jacobi), in *De antiquissima italorum sapientia* (1710); cf. Barbara Rooke, *The Friend* I, 476, n. 1.

[41] "Philosophical speculation or survey."

[42] Leonhart Euler (1707–1783), Swiss mathematician and physicist. The comment has not been located.

[43] "Entities of reason" or "intelligible realities."

*The following extract from a most respectable scientific Journal contains an exposition of the impossibility of a perfect *Theory* in Physics, the more striking because it is directly against the purpose and intention of the writer. We content ourselves with one question, What if Kepler, what if Newton in his investigations concerning the Tides, had held themselves bound to this canon, and instead of propounding a law, had employed themselves exclusively in collecting materials for a *Theory?*

"The magnetic influence has long been known to have a variation which is constantly changing; but that change is so slow, and at the same time so different in various (*different?*) parts of the world, that it would be in vain

it more or less clearly; or the symbol of an undiscovered law, like the characters of unknown quantities in algebra, for the purpose of submitting the phænomena to a scientific calculus. In all other instances, it is itself a real or supposed phænomenon, and therefore a part of the problem which it is to solve. It may be among the foundation-stones of the edifice, but can never be the *ground.*

But in experimental philosophy, it may be said how much do we not owe to accident? Doubtless: but let it not be forgotten, that if the discoveries so made stop there; if they do not excite some master IDEA; if they do not lead to some LAW (in whatever dress of theory or hypotheses the fashions and prejudices of the time may disguise or disfigure it): the discoveries may remain for ages limited in their uses, insecure and unproductive. How many centuries, we might have said millennia, have passed, since the first accidental discovery of the attraction and repulsion of light bodies by rubbed amber, &c. Compare the interval with the progress made within less than a century, after the discovery of the phænomena that led immediately to a THEORY of electricity. That here as in many other instances, the theory was supported by insecure hypotheses; that by one theorist two heterogeneous fluids are assumed, the vitreous and the resinous; by another, a plus and minus of the same fluid; that a third considers it a mere modification of light; while a fourth composes the electrical aura of oxygen, hydrogen, and caloric: this does but place the truth we have been evolving in a stronger and clearer light. For abstract from all these suppositions, or rather imaginations, that which is common to, and involved in them all; and we shall have neither notional fluid or fluids, nor chemical compounds, nor elementary matter,—but the idea of *two—opposite—forces,* tending to rest by equilibrium. These are the sole factors of the calculus, alike in all the theories. These give the *law,* and in it the *method,* both of arranging the phænomena and of substantiating appearances into facts of science; with a success proportionate to the clearness or confusedness of the insight into the law. For this reason, we anticipate the greatest improvements in the *method,* the nearest approaches to a *system* of electricity from these philosophers, who have presented the law most purely, and the correlative idea as an idea: those, namely, who, since the year 1798,[46] in the true spirit of experimental dynamics, rejecting the imagination of any material substrate, simple or compound, contemplate in the phænomena of electricity the operation of a law which reigns through all nature, the law of POLARITY, or the manifestation of one power by opposite forces: who trace in these appearances, as the most obvious and striking of its innumerable forms, the agency of the positive and negative poles of a power essential to all material construction; the second, namely, of the three primary principles, for which the beautiful and most appropriate symbols are given by the mind in the three ideal dimensions of space.

The time is, perhaps, nigh at hand, when the same comparison between the results of two unequal periods; the interval between the knowledge of a fact, and that from the discovery of the law, will be applicable to the sister science of magnetism. But how great the contrast between magnetism and electricity, at the present moment! From remotest antiquity, the attraction of iron by the magnet was known and noticed; but, century after century, it remained the undisturbed property of poets and orators. The fact of the magnet and the fable of the phœnix stood on the same scale of utility. In the thirteenth century, or perhaps earlier, the polarity of the magnet, and its communicability to iron, were discovered; and soon suggested a purpose so grand and important, that it may well be deemed the proudest trophy ever raised by accident*

---

to seek for the means of reducing it to established rules, until all its local and particular circumstances are clearly ascertained and recorded by accurate observations made in various parts of the globe. The necessity and importance of such observations are now pretty generally understood, and they have been actually carrying on for some years past; but these *(and by parity of reason the incomparably greater number that remain to be made)* must be collected, collated, proved, and afterwards brought together into one focus before ever a foundation can be formed upon which any thing like a sound and stable *Theory* can be constituted for the explanation of such changes." *Journal of Science and the Arts,* No. vii. p. 103.[44]

An intelligent friend, on reading the words "into one focus," observed: But what and where is the *lens?* I however fully agree with the writer. All this and much more must have been atchieved before "a sound and stable Theory" could be "constituted"—which even then (except as far as it might occasion the discovery of a law) might possibly *explain* (*ex plicis plana reddere*),[45] but never *account for,* the facts in question. But the most satisfactory comment on these and similar assertions would be afforded by a *matter of fact* history of the rise and progress, the accelerating and retarding momenta, of science in the civilized world.

[44] The article cited is a review of William Bain's *An Essay on the Variations of the Compass* (1817).

[45] The expression is ambiguous, meaning either "to make plain the obscure" (reading "*ex placis*" as *explicatis*) or "to make plain the obvious" (reading it as *explicitis*).

[46] Coleridge is evidently referring to the work of Alessandro Volta (1745–1827) that led to the development of the electrical battery, from 1794 to 1800. Crucial for Coleridge's conjecture here is the confirmation provided in 1831 by the discovery of Michael Faraday (1791–1867) that a magnet, moved through a coil of wire, produced an electrical current, leading later to the expansion of electromagnetic theory by James Clerk Maxwell (1831–1879) to include light. It is of special interest that Maxwell, as an undergraduate at Cambridge, wrote several essays while a member of the "Apostle's Club" (a group with historical links to Coleridge) on the subject of scientific method with intriguing similarities to Coleridge's argument here. See Lewis Campbell and William Garnett, *The Life of James Clerk Maxwell* (1882).

*If accident it were: if the compass did not obscurely travel to us from the remotest east: if its existence there does not point to an age and a race, to which scholars of highest rank in the world of letters, Sir W. Jones, Bailly, Schlegel[47] have attached faith! That it was known before the æra generally assumed for its invention, and not spoken of as a novelty, has been proved by Mr. Southey and others.[48]

in the service of mankind—the invention of the compass. But it led to no idea, to no law, and consequently to no Method: though a variety of phænomena, as startling as they are mysterious, have forced on us a presentiment of its intimate connection with all the great agencies of nature; of a revelation, in ciphers, the key to which is still wanting. We can recall no incident of human history that impresses the imagination more deeply than the moment when Columbus,* on an unknown ocean, first perceived one of these startling facts, the change of the magnetic needle!

In what shall we seek the cause of this contrast between the rapid progress of electricity and the stationary condition of magnetism? As many theories, as many hypotheses, have been advanced in the latter science as in the former. But the theories and fictions of the electricians contained an *idea,* and all the same idea, which has necessarily led to METHOD; implicit indeed, and only regulative hitherto, but which requires little more than the dismission of the imagery to become constitutive like the ideas of the geometrician. On the contrary, the assumptions of the magnetists (as for instance, the hypothesis that the planet itself is one vast magnet, or that an immense magnet is concealed within it; or that of a concentric globe within the earth, revolving on its own independent axis) are but repetitions of the same fact or phænomenon looked at through a magnifying glass; the *reiteration* of the problem, not its solution. The naturalist, who cannot or will not see, that one fact is often worth a thousand, as including them all in itself, and that it first *makes* all the others *facts;* who has not the head to comprehend, the soul to reverence, a *central* experiment or observation[49] (what the Greeks would perhaps have called a *protophænomon*); will never receive an auspicious answer from the oracle of nature.

---

[47] All writers on the ancient Orient: Sir William Jones (1746–1794); Jean Sylvain Bailly (1736–1793); and K. W. F. von Schlegel (1772–1829).

[48] Robert Southey, *Omniana* I, 210, quotes a passage from Alfonso X the Wise from the thirteenth century, mentioning the mariner's needle.

* It cannot be deemed alien from the purposes of this disquisition, if we are anxious to attract the attention of our readers to the importance of speculative meditation, even for the *wordly* interests of mankind; and to that concurrence of nature and historic event with the great revolutionary movements of individual genlus, of which so many instances occur in the study of History—how nature (why should we hesitate in saying, that which in nature itself is more than nature?) seems to come forward in order to meet, to aid, and to reward every idea excited by a contemplation of her methods in the spirit of filial care, and with the humility of love!

[49] See in this context Thomas Kuhn's account of "scientific paradigms" as exemplary scientific achievements that order and propel the problem-solving activity of "normal science" in "Postscript–1969" (below, page 1282).

from

The Statesman's Manual

. . . It is among the miseries of the present age that it recognizes no medium between *Literal* and *Metaphorical.* Faith is either to be buried in the dead letter, or its name and honors usurped by a counterfeit product of the mechanical understanding, which in the blindness of self-complacency confounds SYMBOLS with ALLEGORIES. Now an Allegory is but a translation of abstract notions into a picture-language which is itself nothing but an abstraction from objects of the senses; the principal being more worthless even than its phantom proxy, both alike unsubstantial, and the former shapeless to boot. On the other hand a Symbol (ὁ ἔστιν ἀει ταυτηγόρικον)[1] is characterized by a translucence of the Special in the Individual or of the General in the Especial or of the Universal in the General. Above all by the translucence of the Eternal through and in the Temporal. It always partakes of the Reality which it renders intelligible; and while it enunciates the whole, abides itself as a living part in that Unity, of which it is the representative.

from

On the Constitution of Church and State

. . . By an *idea,* I mean, (in this instance) that conception of a thing, which is not abstracted from any particular state, form, or mode, in which the thing may happen to exist at this or at that time; nor yet generalized from any number or succession of such forms or modes; but which is given by the knowledge of *its ultimate aim.*[1]

The Statesman's Manual first appeared in 1816. Reprinted from R. J. White, ed., *Lay Sermons* (1972), page 31.

[1] "Which is always tautegorical." The OED credits Coleridge with coining "tautegorical" (a term highly praised by Schelling and Benjamin Jowett), citing *Aids to Reflection* (1825): "The base of Symbols and symbolical expressions; the nature of which is always *tautegorical* (that is, expressing the same subject but with a difference) in contradistinction from metaphors and similitudes, that are always *alle*gorical (that is, expressing a different subject but with a resemblance)."

On the Constitution of Church and State was first published in 1829. Reprinted here from *On the Constitution of Church and State,* edited by John Colmer (Princeton: Princeton University Press, 1976).

[1] In the paragraphs preceding this sentence, Coleridge's focus has been specifically upon the Idea of a constitution and its relation to a National Church and its difference from the "Church of Christ." The discussion to follow, however, pertains to a much broader range of issues.

Only one observation I must be allowed to add, that this knowledge, or sense, may very well exist, aye, and powerfully influence a man's thoughts and actions, without his being distinctly conscious of the same, much more without his being competent to express it in definite words. This, indeed, is one of the points which distinguish *ideas* from *conceptions,* both terms being used in their strict and proper significations. The latter, *i.e.* a conception, *consists* in a conscious act of the understanding, bringing any given object or impression into the same class with any number of other objects, or impressions, by means of some character or characters common to them all. *Concipimus,* id est, capimus hoc *cum* illo,[2]—we take hold of both at once, we *comprehend* a thing, when we have learnt to comprise it in a known *class.* On the other hand, it is the privilege of the few to possess an idea: of the generality of men, it might be more truly affirmed, that they are possessed by it.

What is here said, will, I hope, suffice as a popular explanation. For some of my readers, however, the following definition may not, perhaps, be useless or unacceptable. That which, contemplated *objectively* (*i.e.* as existing *externally* to the mind), we call a LAW; the same contemplated *subjectively* (*i.e.* as existing in a subject or mind), is an idea. Hence Plato often names ideas laws; and Lord Bacon, the British Plato, describes the Laws of the material universe as the Ideas in nature. Quod in naturâ *naturatâ* LEX, in naturâ *naturante* IDEA dicitur.[3] By way of illustration take the following. Every reader of Rousseau, or of Hume's Essays, will understand me when I refer to the Original Social Contract, assumed by Rousseau, and by other and wiser men before him, as the basis of all legitimate government.[4] Now, if this be taken as the assertion of an historical fact, or as the application of a conception, generalized from ordinary compacts between man and man, or nation and nation, to an actual occurrence in the first ages of the world; namely, the formation of the first contract, in which men covenanted with each other to associate, or in which a multitude entered into a compact with a few, the one to be governed and the other to govern, under certain declared conditions; I shall run little hazard at this time of day, in declaring the pretended fact a pure fiction, and the conception of such a fact an idle fancy. It is at once false and foolish.* For what if an original contract had actually been entered into, and formally recorded? Still I cannot see what addition of moral force would be gained by the fact. The same sense of moral obligation which binds us to keep it, must have pre-existed in the same force and in relation to the same duties, impelling our ancestors to make it. For what could it do more than bind the contracting parties to act for the general good, according to their best lights and opportunities? It is evident, that no specific scheme or constitution can derive any other claim to our reverence, than that which the presumption of its necessity or fitness for the general good shall give it; and which claim of course ceases, or rather is reversed, as soon as this general presumption of its utility has given place to as general a conviction of the contrary. It is true, indeed, that from duties anterior to the formation of the contract; because they arise out of the very constitution of our humanity, which supposes the social state—it is true, that in order to a rightful removal of the institution, or law, thus agreed on, it is required that the conviction of its inexpediency shall be as general, as the presumption of its fitness was at the time of its establishment. This, the first of the two great paramount interests of the social state demands, namely, that of permanence; but to attribute more than this to any fundamental articles, passed into law by any assemblage of individuals, is an injustice to their successors, and a high offence against the other great interest of the social state, namely,—its progressive improvement. The conception, therefore, of an original contract, is, we repeat, incapable of historic proof as a fact, and it is senseless as a theory.

But if instead of the *conception* or *theory* of an original social contract, you say the *idea* of an ever-originating social contract, this is so certain and so indispensable, that it constitutes the whole ground of the difference between subject and serf, between a commonwealth and a slave-plantation. And this, again, is evolved out of the yet higher idea of *person,* in contra-distinction from *thing*—all social law and justice being grounded on the principle, that a person can never, but by his own fault, become a thing, or, without grievous wrong, be treated as such: and the distinction consisting in this, that a thing may be used altogether and merely as the *means* to an end; but the person must always be included in the *end:* his interest must form a part of the object, a *means*

---

[2] "We *conceive,* that is, we take this *with* that."

[3] "What is called LAW in *created* nature is called IDEA in *creative* nature." Cf. "Essays on the Principles of Method" (above, page 508) and *The Friend* I, 491–2.

[4] Cf. especially *The Social Contract* (1762) by Jean Jacques Rousseau (1712–1778). Coleridge does not mention here the other two principal theorists of the social contract, Thomas Hobbes (1588–1679) and John Locke (1632–1704), both influences on David Hume (1711–1776). Cf. Hume's *A Concise and Genuine Account of the Dispute Between Mr. Hume and Mr. Rousseau* (1766).

*I am not indeed certain, that some operatical farce, under the name of a Social Contract or Compact, might not have been acted by the Illuminati and Constitution-manufacturers, at the close of the eighteenth century,[5] a period which how far it deserved the name, so complacently affixed to it by the contemporaries of "this *enlightened* age," may be doubted. That it was an age of *Enlighteners,* no man will deny.

[5] Coleridge is evidently referring to Adam Weishaupt (1748–1830), founder of the Order of the Illuminated; and Joseph Emmanuel Sieyès (1748–1836). See John Colmer, ed., *Church and State,* 14 n. 2 for additional information.

to which, he, by consent, *i.e.* by his own act, makes himself. We plant a tree, and we fell it; we breed the sheep, and we shear or we kill it; in both cases wholly as means to *our* ends. For trees and animals are *things*. The wood-cutter and the hind are likewise employed as *means,* but on agreement, and that too an agreement of reciprocal advantage, which includes them as well as their employer in the *end*. For they are *persons*.[6] And the government, under which the contrary takes place, is not worthy to be called a STATE, if, as in the kingdom of Dahomey,[7] it be unprogressive; or only by anticipation, where, as in Russia, it is in advance to a better and more *man-worthy* order of things. Now, notwithstanding the late wonderful spread of learning through the community, and though the schoolmaster and the lecturer are abroad, the hind and the woodman may, very conceivably, pass from cradle to coffin, without having once contemplated this idea, so as to be conscious of the same. And there would be even an improbability in the supposition that they possessed the power of presenting this Idea to the minds of others, or even to their own thoughts, verbally as a distinct proposition. But no man, who has ever listened to laborers of this rank, in any alehouse, over the Saturday night's jug of beer, discussing the injustice of the present rate of wages, and the iniquity of their being paid in part out of the parish poor-rates,[8] will doubt for a moment that they are fully possessed by the idea.

In close, though not perhaps obvious connection, with this, is the idea of moral freedom, as the ground of our proper responsibility. Speak to a young Liberal, fresh from Edinburgh or Hackney or the Hospitals, of Free-will, as implied in Free-agency, he will perhaps confess to you with a smile, that he is a Necessitarian,—[9]proceed to assure you that the liberty

of the will is an impossible conception, *a contradiction in terms,** and finish by recommending you to read Jonathan Edwards, or Dr. Crombie, or as it may happen, he may declare the will itself a mere delusion, a non-entity, and ask you if you have read Mr. Lawrence's Lecture.[10] Converse on the same subject with a plain, single-minded, yet reflecting neighbour, and he may probably say (as St. Augustin had said long before him, in reply to the question, What is Time?) I know it well enough when you do not ask me.[12] But alike with both the supposed parties, the self-complacent student, just as certainly as with your less positive neighbour—attend to their actions, their feelings, and even to their words: and you will be in ill luck, if ten minutes pass without affording you full and satisfactory proof, that the *idea* of man's moral freedom possesses and modifies their whole practical being, in all they say, in all they feel, in all they do and are done to: even as the spirit of life, which is contained in no vessel, because it permeates all.

Just so is it with the *constitution. Ask any of our politicians what is meant by the constitution, and it is ten to one that he will give you a false explanation, *ex. gr.* that it is the body of our laws, or that it is the Bill of Rights; or perhaps, if he have read Tom Payne,[13] he may tell you, that we have not yet got one; and yet not an hour may have elapsed, since you heard the same individual denouncing, and possibly with good reason, this or that code of laws, the excise and revenue laws, or those for including pheasants, or those for excluding Catholics, as altogether unconstitutional: and such and such

---

[6]Cf. *The Friend* I, 189–90; and Kant, *The Foundation of the Metaphysics of Morals,* tr., Lewis White Beck (Library of Liberal Arts, 1959), 46: "Now, I say, man and, in general, every rational being exists as an end in himself and not merely as a means to be arbitrarily used by this or that will."

[7]For Coleridge and his contemporaries, the case of Dahomey, notorious both for its role in the slave trade and for the practice of human sacrifice, was a topic of great interest and concern. Cf. Archibald Dalzel's *History of Dahomey* (1793), and Raimonda Modiano, "Unremembered Sights of Violence: The Scandal of Dahomey's Rites of Human Sacrifice in the Abolition of the Slave Trade in England" in *The Poetics of Memory,* edited by Thomas Wägenbaur (1998).

[8]Coleridge is referring to the decision of local magistrates at Speenhamland, Berkshire, to institute a system of supplements for poor workers, subsequently adopted over much of England. The Speenhamland system was attacked from both sides for its effects in making the poor dependent on the parish, just as it encouraged employers to lower wages and to raise rents. See especially Karl Polanyi's *The Great Transformation* (1944), which provides an incisive critique of the effects of Speenhamland on the creation of a wage system and the development of capitalism.

[9]A doctrine of determinism that denies the freedom of the will. Coleridge was himself influenced in this way by the associationism of David Hartley (1705–1757).

*See AIDS TO REFLECTION, p. 226; where this is shewn to be one of the distinguishing characters of *ideas,* and marks at once the difference between an *idea* (a *truth-power* of the reason) and a conception of the understanding; viz. that the former, as expressed in words, is always, and necessarily, a *contradiction in terms*.[11]

[10]Jonathan Edwards (1703–1758), American divine and philosopher, briefly president of Princeton University, author of *A Careful and Strict Enquiry into that Freedom of the Will* . . . (1754); Alexander Crombie (1762–1840), *An Essay on Philosophic Necessity* (1793); William Lawrence (1783–1867), British surgeon who attacked the vitalist theories of John Hunter in *On the Physiology, Zoology, and Natural History of Man* (1819).

[11]The precise language in *Aids to Reflection* (1825) differs: a truth affirmed by Reason "can come forth out of the moulds of the Understanding only in the disguise of two contradictory conceptions, each of which is partially true, and the conjunction of both conceptions becomes the representative or *expression* (the *exponent*) of a truth *beyond* conception and inexpressible."

[12]Paraphrased from St. Augustine (354–430), *Confessions* 11.14.

*I do not say, with the idea: for the constitution itself is an IDEA. This will sound like a paradox or a sneer to those with whom an Idea is but another word for a *fancy,* a something unreal; but not to those who in the ideas contemplate the most real of all realities, and of all operative powers the most *actual*.

[13]I.e., Thomas Paine (1737–1809), author of revolutionary pamphlets and tracts, including *Common Sense* (1776), the *Crisis* papers (1776–1783), and *Rights of Man* (1791).

acts of parliament as gross outrages on the constitution. Mr. Peel, who is rather remarkable for groundless and unlucky concessions, owned that the present Bill[14] breaks in on the constitution of 1688: and, A.D. 1689, a very imposing minority of the then House of Lords, with a decisive majority in the Lower House of Convocation, denounced the constitution of 1688, as breaking in on the English Constitution.

But a Constitution is an idea arising out of the idea of a state; and because our whole history from Alfred onward demonstrates the continued influence of such an idea, or ultimate aim, on the minds of our fore-fathers, in their charac-

---

[14]No small part of the impetus to publish *On the Constitution of Church and State* was the raging controversy over the Catholic Emancipation Bill (enacted in 1829), effectively reversing restrictions and exclusion of Catholics, dating from the 1680s. See G. I. T. Machin, *The Catholic Question in English Politics, 1820–1830* (1964).

ters and functions as public men; alike in what they resisted and in what they claimed; in the institutions and forms of polity which they established, and with regard to those, against which they more or less successfully contended; and because the result has been a progressive, though not always a direct, or equable advance in the gradual realization of the idea; and that it is actually, though even because it is an *idea* it cannot be *adequately,* represented in a correspondent scheme of means really existing; we speak, and have a right to speak, of the idea itself, as actually existing, *i.e.,* as a *principle,* existing in the only way in which a principle can exist—in the minds and consciences of the persons, whose duties it prescribes, and whose rights it determines. In the same sense that the sciences of arithmetic and of geometry, that mind, that life itself, have reality; the constitution has real existence, and does not the less exist in reality, because it both *is,* and *exists as,* an IDEA.

Wilhelm von Humboldt

1767–1835

A Prussian career diplomat and minister of state for thirty-four years (though out of favor for part of that time and eventually summarily dismissed for advanced opinions), von Humboldt was a voluminus writer on many subjects, his collected works amounting to seventeen volumes. He wrote on language in general, certain languages in particular, literature, aesthetics, psychology, and women. He translated the *Agamemnon* of Aeschylus. He was also the author of 1,183 sonnets and a number of narrative poems, all best forgotten. It is in those writings where he extends the Kantian notion of human constitutive powers into the domain of language that he comes down to us as a major thinker, spanning the shift from epistemological to linguistic concerns.

Few of his writings were published in his lifetime. His more famous brother Alexander (1769–1859), an explorer much interested in languages, brought back to Wilhelm information about languages he had come to know about. Wilhelm employed Alexander's information both in his detailed study of the Kavi language of Java, *Kawiwerk,* posthumously published in three volumes, and in his more philosophically oriented studies in linguistics. He wrote on Chinese, Basque, and Mexican, on differences in human linguistic structures, on various periods of linguistic development, and on national linguistic characteristics. For von Humboldt, man is man only through language; language is his defining attribute: "Just as no concept is possible without language, so no object is possible without it for the psyche, since even external ones receive their intrinsic substance only through language." He belongs in a line of thinkers about language from Vico (above, page 313) to Cassirer (below, page 1016), who was clearly influenced by him.

The selections that follow come from a variety of his works. Numbers following each selection refer to volume and page of the *Gesammelte Schriften*.

In addition to *Humanist Without Portfolio* (1963), an anthology of von Humboldt's writings with an interesting introduction by Marian Cowan, his *Linguistic Variability and Intellectual Development* is available in English translation by G. C. Buck and F. A. Raven, as well as *On Language: The Diversity of Human Structure and Its Influence on the Mental Development of Mankind,* translated by Peter Heath. *Gesammelte Schriften* in seventeen volumes was published from 1903 to 1935. See Roger Langham Brown, *Wilhelm von Humboldt's Conception of Linguistic Relativity* (1967); Kurt Muller-Vollmmer, *Poesie und Einbildungskraft* (1967); Richey A. Novak, *Wilhelm von Humboldt as a Literary Critic* (1972); Martin L. Manchester, *The Philosophical Foundations of Humboldt's Linguistic Doctrines* (1985).

from

Collected Works

from
The Eighteenth Century (1796–1797)

All words designating moral qualities can accord only to a certain degree, never wholly, with the things which they designate. Like all words, in fact, they express only concepts, with their relatively firm and definite boundaries, since the things for which the words stand, due to the indissoluble interrelationship of all parts of the moral universe, flow over one into the other without any boundaries that can be noted. Language helps us out of this embarrassment by subjecting the usage of a word to the dicta of practiced feeling, rather than bothering about exact logical definition. Therefore all such words operate in a double sphere: a logical one, bordered by the defined concept which they designate, and a practical one, determined by custom and usage. The true difference between these two spheres ought to rest on the difference which always exists between the concept of an object produced by reason and the image of it formed by sensation and feeling. These, since we sense and feel more, and more subtly than we think, never coincide. The factual difference, however, in most languages rests much more on accident and prejudice. One need only compare the extent of actual usage with the extent of the best and subtlest definitions of such words as "wit," for example, or "delicacy" or "rapture," to convince oneself that one is frequently much greater and just as frequently much smaller than the other.

That is why the beginner in any language expresses himself so unidiomatically without actually making mistakes; that is why the number of synonyms always decreases with the degree of linguistic development; and that is why the linguist always recognizes more of the latter than does the finest, most cultivated author. Now if a word is newly formed, or its meaning freshly defined, then it occupies at first only the logical sphere which coincides with the concept for which it was meant. It therefore presents itself only to our understanding, leaving our imagination and our feelings untouched. . . . This is why neologisms, made in great numbers and intentionally, are advisable only in the completely speculative or technical sciences where only pure rational concepts are dealt with, not real things, or where it suffices to differentiate things by certain singled-out characteristics alone. But in the field of prac-

tical philosophy, where everything depends on not merely thinking the moral objects given in experience but on representing them in their total natural endowment, one must avail oneself of the help of neologisms much more sparingly and cautiously. Else one runs the danger of taking all the spirit and all the fruitfulness out of one's line of reasoning. [II, 73–75]

from
Essay on Aesthetics (1797–1798)

The realm of imagination is directly opposed to the realm of reality, and equally opposed is the character of whatever belongs to one of these realms to anything within the other. Part and parcel of the concept of reality is the segregation of each individual phenomenon; none stands in causal relationship to any other. . . . As soon as one walks over to the realm of possibilities, on the other hand, nothing exists except in a state of dependency upon everything else. Everything, in fact, which cannot be thought of as other than in a condition of inner interaction *is ideal* in the simplest and strictest sense of the word. For it is wholly opposed to reality. [II, 128]

However incomprehensible the art process, however certainly there is something which the artist himself does not understand and the critic can never utter, this much is known: the artist begins by transforming something real into an image. But he soon finds out that this cannot be done except by a sort of living communication, by somehow letting an electric spark of his imagination leap over to the imagination of others, and this not directly but through the mediation of an object into which he breathes his own living soul.

This is the only way open to the artist. And without in any way wanting it, but just by fulfilling his calling and leaving the execution of his task to his imagination, he lifts nature over the boundaries of reality and leads her into the land of ideas, recreating her individuals as ideals. [II, 132]

The concept of ideality, as being something which lies above reality, is reminiscent of the rule that art is imitation of nature, a rule which for a long time we have commanded the artist to follow. It has even been considered a good definition of art itself. It does contain the two main concepts of art, namely reality (here called nature) and imitation (that which does not permit a total identity with its model). But it contains a vagueness or looseness which can be avoided only by the realization (hitherto not often felt) that the essence of art does not lie in the nature of its objects but in the mood of the imagination. . . . Since the artist makes nature (by which we mean everything that can have reality for

These selections from the *Gesammelte Schriften* of von Humboldt are reprinted from Marian Cowan, ed. and tr., *Humanist Without Portfolio: An Anthology of the Writings of Wilhelm von Humboldt* (Detroit: Wayne State University Press, 1963).

us) into an object of the imagination, we may call art *the objectification of nature by the imagination.* [II, 132 f.][1]

If we survey the path that a poet (and every artist) takes, we are overwhelmed by the realization with what a simple aim he starts and what incomprehensible heights he reaches as he executes that aim.

He starts by turning a real object, almost playfully, into an imaginative one, and ends with the greatest and most difficult task which gives to human beings their ultimate meaning: to relate himself intimately to the whole external world and this to him; to accept the world at first like a foreign object but then, in his own fashion and with the organs at his individual disposal, to return it to itself, free and organized.

For all the materials of his observation are organized by him into an ideal form for the imagination. The world around him appears to him like a completely individual, living, harmonious, nowhere restricted or dependent, self-sufficient totality of manifold forms. Thus has he transferred his own inmost and best nature to it, turning it into a creation with which he can then completely sympathize. [II, 142]

from
Catium and Hellas (1806)

The least advantageous influence on any sort of interesting treatment of linguistic studies is exerted by the narrow notion that language originated as a convention and that words are nothing but signs for things or concepts which are independent of them.[2] This view up to a point is certainly correct but beyond this point it is deadly because as soon as it begins to predominate it kills all mental activity and exiles all life. To it we owe the constantly reiterated commonplaces that linguistic study is necessary only for external purposes or for the discipline of as yet unpracticed mentalities; that the best method for learning a language is the one that leads most quickly to the mechanical, automatic understanding and use of it; that any language, if one only knows it well, is about as useful as any other; that it would be best if all nations could agree on the use of a single one—and whatever other prejudices of this sort there are.

A more careful examination demonstrates precisely the opposite of all these notions.

Naturally, a word is a sign insofar as it is used to stand

for a thing or a concept, but in its particular past development and its particular effectiveness it is a particular and independent creature—an individual. The sum of all words—language—is a universe which lies midway between the external, phenomenal one and our own inwardly active one. Naturally it is based upon convention, insofar as all the members of a linguistic group understand one another, but the individual words were first formed out of the natural feeling of the speaker and understood by the similar natural feeling of the hearer. Hence, linguistic study teaches, in addition to the use of a particular language, the analogical relation between man and the world in general, and each individual nation in particular, which is expressed by language. And since the spirit which constantly reveals itself in the world can never be exhaustively known through any given number of views or opinions, but is always discovered to contain something new, it would be far better to multiply the languages on earth as many times as the number of earth's inhabitants might permit. [III, 167 f.]

As little as a word is an image of the thing which it designates, so little is it a mere intimation that this thing is supposed to be thought by reason or represented in imagination. It is differentiated from an image by the possibility inherent in it and in us to imagine the thing according to the most various points of view and in the most various ways; it is different from a mere intimation in that it has its own definite, sensuous form. If you utter the word *Wolke* (cloud) you neither think of its definition nor do you see a single definite image of the natural phenomenon. All its different concepts and images, all the sensations and feelings which have been joined to its perception, everything—finally—which is related in some fashion to it, within us or without us: all these may represent themselves to the mind simultaneously and yet run no danger of confusion because the single sound of the word fastens and secures them. But the sound does even more: it brings back sometimes this, sometimes that association and if, as in the case of *Wolke,* the associative material is rich in itself (*Woge* billow, *Welle* wave, *wälzen* rolling, *Wind* wind, *wehen* blowing, *Wald* woods, etc.) then the sound of the word attunes the soul in a manner befitting the object, partly through itself, partly through recollection and associative analogies. Thus a word reveals itself as an individual with a nature of its own which bears resemblance to an object of art in that, with a sensuous form borrowed from nature, it makes possible an idea which is beyond all nature. Here however the resemblance stops, since the differences leap to the eye. For this idea which lies beyond all nature is precisely that which alone renders the objects in the world capable of being used as materials for thinking and feeling. It is the lack

---

[1] This passage blends a Romantic emphasis on feeling with a Kantian emphasis on the constitutive powers of the mind, suggesting that in certain respects the two notions influence each other.

[2] The statement opposes Locke's view (above, page 282).

of definition of objects which ever and again provides new transitions to other objects (since that which is each time represented or imagined need neither be completely filled in as to detail, nor preserved); the lack of definition without which the independent action of thought would be impossible—and the sensuous vividness which is a result of the spiritual energy that is expended when a language is used. Thinking never treats of an object as isolated and never uses the sum total of its reality. It always skims off its surface relationships, conditions, points of view, and combines these. But a word is by no means merely an empty substratum into which certain details may be placed, but it is a sensuous form which by its incisive simplicity spontaneously indicates that the expressed object, too, should be represented only according to the needs of thought, and, by its origin in an independent psychic act, reorders the merely perceptive psychic capacities back into their boundaries. Moreover, by its capacity for change and its analogic relationship to other linguistic elements, it prepares the connectedness which thinking tries to find out in the world and bring out in its own products. (Finally, by its transitoriness it bids us tarry at no point but hurry on to whatever end itself and all the other words are tending.) In all these respects, the kind of sensuous form a word has . . . is in no way a matter of indifference, and it may be justly asserted that even when words of different languages designate the same, completely sensuous, object, they are by no means perfect synonyms. Whoever utters *hippos, equus,* or *Pferd,* by no means says completely the same thing three times. [III, 169 f.]

from

Introduction to General Linguistics (1810–1811)

Every language sets certain limits to the spirit of those who speak it; it assumes a certain direction and, by doing so, excludes many others. [VII, 621]

from

Announcement of an Essay on the Language and Nation of the Basques (1812)

Language everywhere mediates, first between infinite and finite nature, then between one individual and another. Simultaneously and through the same act it makes union possible and itself originates from it. The whole of its nature never lies in singularity but must always simultaneously be guessed or intuited from otherness. But neither can it be fully explained from oneness and otherness together; it simply is (like everything in the presence of which true mediation occurs) something individuated, unique, incomprehensible. It is something which is given by the idea of union, of the reconciliation of what for us and our way of thinking must always be opposites, and it is a something which is given only in this connection. Linguistic study—which must, in order to avoid becoming chimerical, always begin with the totally dry, pedantic, in fact mechanical analysis of the corporeal, constructible elements of language—thus leads to the depths of humanity. Only one must free oneself of the notions that language can be separated from that which it designates as, for example, the name of a person from the person, and that it is a product of reflection and agreement, an agreed-upon code, as it were, or in fact that it is any work of man at all (in the common sense in which one takes that phrase), not to mention the work of some individual. A true, inexplicable miracle, it breaks loose from the mouth of a nation, and—no less marvellous, though seen by us every day with indifference—it breaks daily through the gurgle of any baby. It is the brightest trace and the surest proof of the fact (leaving out for the moment the celestial relatives of mankind) that man does not possess an absolute, segregated individuality, that "I" and "Thou" are not merely interrelated but—if one could go back to the point of their separation—truly identical concepts, and that there exist, therefore, only concentric circles of individuality, beginning with the weak, frail single person who is in need of support and widening out to the primordial trunk of humanity itself. Otherwise all understanding would be impossible into all eternity. [III, 296–97]

from

On Comparative Linguistics (1820)

Language, I am fully convinced, must be looked upon as being an immediate given in mankind. Taken as a work of man's reason, undertaken in clarity of consciousness, it is wholly inexplicable. Nor does it help to supply man with millennia upon millennia for the "invention" of language. Language could not be invented or come upon if its archetype were not already present in the human mind. For man to understand but a single word truly, not as a mere sensuous stimulus (such as an animal understands a command or the sound of the whip) but as an articulated sound designating a concept, all language, in all its connections, must already lie prepared within him. There are no single, separate facts of language. Each of its elements announces itself as part of a whole. As natural as the supposition of the gradual development of languages is, yet the "invention" of language could only happen all at once. Man is man only through language: to invent language, he would have to be man already. As soon as one imagines that it happened gradually . . . , that by means of a bit more invented language, man became more human, and being more human, thus was enabled to invent a little more language, one fails to recognize the indivisibility of human consciousness and human speech, and the nature of the intellectual act which is necessary to comprehend but a single word, but which then suffices to comprehend all of language.

Naturally this does not mean that one is to think of language as a given that is complete and finished, for then one could not comprehend how a man could understand or use any single given language. It necessarily grows out of an individual, gradually growing up with him, but in such a way that its organization does not lie, like an inert mass, in the dark of a man's soul till it is brought forth, but instead that its laws condition the functions of thought. Thus the very first word gives the hint of and presupposes the whole rest of the language. If one seeks an analogy for this—and there is really nothing comparable to it in the whole realm of the mind—one might remember the natural instincts of animals and call language an intellectual instinct of the mind. [IV, 14 f.]

Thinking is not merely dependent on language in general but, up to a certain degree, on each specific language. People have wished, to be sure, to replace the words of the various languages by universally valid signs, as lines, numbers and algebraic symbols serve in mathematics. But only a tiny part of that which is thinkable can be designated that way, because such symbols by their very nature fit only those concepts which can be produced by mere synthetic construction or are otherwise formed by rationality alone. But where the raw materials of inner perception and sensation are to be imprinted with conceptualization, everything depends on the individual way of looking at things of an individual human being whose language is an inseparable part of him. All attempts to cancel out the many unique signs for eye and ear and replace them with a few general ones are but methods of abbreviated translation. It would be folly and delusion to imagine that such methods might transport one beyond the circumscribed limits of one's own language—not to mention all language. Of course a central point at which languages might meet may be sought for, and even found, and it is necessary when doing comparative studies of language (grammatical as well as lexical) to keep one's

eye directed toward such a center. For . . . there is a number of things which can be determined and defined a priori and hence separated from all conditionalities of a given language. But on the other hand, there is a far greater number of concepts, and grammatical peculiarities as well, which are woven so indissolubly into the individuality of their language that they can neither be held by a thread of inner perception as hovering above all languages, nor translated from one language into another. A most significant part of the content of each language stands in a relation of such undoubted dependency on it that its specific utterance cannot be a matter of no consequence. [IV, 21 ff.]

The mutual interdependence of thought and word illuminates clearly the truth that languages are not really means for representing already known truths but are rather instruments for discovering previously unrecognized ones.[3] The differences between languages are not those of sounds and signs but those of differing world views. Herein is contained the reason for and the final aim of all linguistic study. The sum of the knowable, that soil which the human spirit must till, lies between all the languages and independent of them, at their center. But man cannot approach this purely objective realm other than through his own modes of cognition and feeling, in other words: subjectively. Just where study and research touch the highest and deepest point, just there does the mechanical, logical use of reason—whatever in us can most easily be separated from our uniqueness as individual human beings—find itself at the end of its rope. From here on we need a process of inner perception and creation. And all that we can plainly know about this is its result, namely, that objective truth always rises from the entire energy of subjective individuality. [IV. 27]

In no two languages do we find completely equivalent words designating incorporeal objects: we find words whose meaning is related, to be sure, but none whose is the same. . . . An extremely interesting demonstration of this might be given in connection with *psyche, anima, âme, alma, Seele, soul*, etc. . . . . Such comparison can usually be made only between languages that have a literature. To make such studies would demand profound absorption in each language considered, and yet all language is so rich and fruitful in its eternal youthfulness, its eternal mobility, that the true sense, the sum total of all the connotations of such a word taken as a totality, could never be defined or completed, never be designated in all its grandeur. Time subtracts from it, changes it, adds to it;

---

[3] Humboldt here foreshadows Cassirer's views (below, page 1016).

words grow richer or poorer in content; they are construed sometimes sharply, sometimes loosely. In language, the creative archetypal energies of humanity are active—that deep reservoir of capacity in us whose existence and nature, can neither be understood nor denied. [IV, 248 f.]

from
On the National Characteristics of Languages (1822)

Man thinks, feels, and lives within language alone and must be formed by it, in order—to mention only one aspect—to understand art, which by no means acts through language. But he senses and knows that language is only a means for him; that there is an invisible realm outside it in which he seeks to feel at home and that it is for this reason that he needs the aid of language. The most commonplace observation and the profoundest thought, both lament the inadequacy of language. Both look upon that other realm as a distant country toward which only language leads—and *it* never really. All higher forms of speech are a wrestling with this thought, in which sometimes our power, sometimes our longing, is more keenly felt. [IV, 432]

from
Basic Characteristics of Linguistic Types (1824–1826)

In the nature of tone as such lies the true individuality of each language. Whatever one may do or try to do in order to describe the peculiarity of a language, all one succeeds in defining ever more closely is the genre to which it belongs. As *this* language, however, and no other, it expresses itself only before the listening ear. Although the alphabet of the whole human race is enclosed by certain not even very wide limits, each people with a language of their own have their own tonal system which excludes certain tones altogether, demonstrates strong preference for others, uses different ones to designate different classes of concepts, treats tone combinations in certain ways, etc. One may compare this with the various screeches and tonal varieties of the various animal species. [V, 379]

No one when he uses a word has in mind exactly the same thing that another has, and the difference, however tiny, sends its tremors throughout language, if one may compare language with the most volatile element. With each thought, each feeling, this difference returns, thanks to the element of unvarying identity in individuality, and finally forms a mass of elements which singly went unnoticed. All understanding, therefore, is always at the same time a misunderstanding—this being a truth which it is most useful to know in practical life—and all agreement of feelings and thoughts is at the same time a means for growing apart. [V, 396]

from
On the Episode from the *Mahabharata* Known as the *Bhagavad-Gita II* (1826)

Linguistic usage in everyday life must of course be different from linguistic usage in inward life, representing ideas and feelings, since the speaker in either case partakes of a wholly different mood. For the sharper and purer a thought hovers before his mind, the less it can be endured if the form of speech in which it will be cast is inappropriate. This is the origin of prose—and one should not call everything prose which is not verse. For their fields diverge only where careful attention is given to the form of presentation. The only true view of prose is that it is derived from poetry which always comes first when any language is treated as an art form.[4] For rhythm is the lifeblood of prose as well, and it is not even free of meter, being rather an extension of the narrowly binding meter of poetry. The characteristic difference between poetry and prose, however, is that prose declares by its form that it wishes to accompany and serve thought. Poetry cannot do without at least appearing to control thought or actually bringing it forth. [V, 343]

from
On the Differences in Human Linguistic Structure (1830–1835)

In thinking, a subjective activity forms itself an object. For no type of imaginative representation may be considered a merely receptive apperception of an already existent object.[5] The activity of the senses must be synthetically joined with the inner action of the spirit. From their connection the imaginative representation tears itself loose, becomes objective in

---

[4] This statement agrees with Vico's (above, page 321) and, later, Frye's (below, page 1136).
[5] Here von Humboldt reveals most clearly his neokantian views.

relation to the subjective energy, and then returns to it, having first been perceived in its new, objective form. For this process language is indispensable. For while the spiritual endeavor expresses itself through the lips, its products return through the very ears of the speaker. The representation is therefore truly transformed into actual objectivity without therefore being withdrawn from subjectivity. Only language can accomplish this, and without this constant transformation and retransformation in which language plays the decisive part even in silence, no conceptualization and therefore no true thinking is possible. Without reference, therefore, to the communication between persons, the act of speaking is a necessary condition of thinking even in a single individual in complete solitude. So far as actual reality is concerned, of course, language develops only socially and man understands himself only by having tested the understandability of his words on others. For the objectivity is intensified when the word which one has formed oneself re-echoes from someone else's mouth. And yet nothing is robbed from the simultaneous subjectivity because every human being feels humanly allied to other human beings; it is, in fact, likewise intensified since the representation now transformed into language no longer belongs exclusively to a single subject. By being imparted to others, it joins the collectivity of the entire human race, of which each individual carries a single modification which longs for the wholeness which can only come through the others. The greater and more varied the social operations on language, the more it gains, other conditions being equal. What makes language necessary in the simple act of thought production, is repeated over and over in man's spiritual life; social communication through language affords man conviction and stimulation. The thinking function requires something like itself and yet separated from itself. It is kindled by the sameness; the separateness gives it a touchstone for the validity of its inner products. Although the epistemological ground for truth, for absolute permanence, can only lie within the human being, his spiritual efforts to attain it are ever accompanied by the danger of delusion. Immediately feeling as he does only his ephemerality and his limitations, man must actually look upon this epistemological ground as something lying outside himself. And one of the most powerful means for drawing near it, for measuring its distance from himself, is social communion with others. All speech, beginning with the simplest, is a relating of that which is separately sensed and felt to the common nature of mankind.

It is no different so far as understanding is concerned. It is present in the psyche only by its own activity. Understanding and speaking are but different operations of the same linguistic capacity. Communal speech is never to be compared with the handing on of a given material. The materials of speech must be developed by the intrinsic capacity of listener as well as speaker; what the listener receives is only the stimulus that attunes him harmoniously to the other. It is very natural for human beings to give out immediately with what they have just heard. Thus the whole of language lies within each human being, which only means that each of us contains a striving, regulated by a definitely modified capacity, which both stimulates and restricts, gradually to produce the entire language, as inner or outer demands dictate, and to understand it as it is produced by others.

Understanding as we have just discussed it, however, could not rest upon inner spontaneous activity, and communal speaking would have to be something other than merely mutual awakening of the linguistic capacity of the listeners, if human nature did not lie in the diversity of its individuals, split off from the basic unity of nature, as they are. The comprehension of words is something quite different from the understanding of unarticulated sounds, and comprises a great deal more than the mere mutual evocation of sounds and the objects they signify. Words, to be sure, may also be taken as indivisible wholes, just as in writing one sometimes recognizes the sense of a word group without as yet being certain of its alphabetical composition. It is possible that the child's psyche operates like that when it first begins to understand. But just as not merely the sensory understanding which we share with animals but also the specific human linguistic capacity is stimulated (and it is far more probable that even in an infant there is no moment when this does not hold true, in however small a degree), so the word, too, is perceived as articulated. Now that which is added to the mere evocation of a word's significance by the articulation is that it presents it directly through its form as part of an infinite whole—that of a language. For it is a language that gives us the possibility, even if we know only individual words of it, to form from its elements a truly unlimited number of other words, in accordance with feelings and rules which define them, and thereby to create a relationship among concepts. But our psyche would lack all comprehension of this artful mechanism, it would comprehend articulation no better than a blind man color, if it did not contain an intrinsic capacity to realize that latent possibility. For language simply cannot be looked upon as though it were a collection of materials lying visible and gradually communicable before us, but must be considered forever in process, where the laws of generation are constant but the extent and in a sense even the kind of product remain wholly indefinite. When infants learn to speak, the process cannot be described in terms of the simple addition of words of vocabulary, their retention in memory, and the subsequent attempts at repetitive babbling, but only as a growth of the child's linguistic capacity, judged by age and practice. What has been heard does more than merely communicate itself; it imparts skill to understand more easily what hasn't yet been heard; it casts sudden light upon what was heard long ago but not understood at the time; it sharpens the urge and the capacity to draw more and more of what is heard into memory and to let less and less of it roll by as mere sound. Progress in linguistic capacity is therefore not measurable in even advances, as is progress in—say—vocabulary learning . . . but is constantly intensified and stepped up by the mutual interaction of the material and the child's ability to handle it. A further proof that children do not mechanically learn their native language but undergo a development of linguistic capacity is afforded by the fact that all children, in the most different imaginable circumstances of life, learn to speak within a fairly narrow and definite time span, just as they develop all their main capacities at certain definite growth stages. But how could the listener master the spoken word just by the developmental process of a separate isolated capacity growing in him if there did not underlie speaker and listener alike the same nature, merely divided into mutually corresponding individuality, so that a signal as subtle but as profoundly rooted in nature as is articulated sound is sufficient to stimulate both and mediate a harmony between them!

An objection to this argument might be found by pointing out that if children are transplanted before they learn their native tongue, they develop their linguistic capacity in the foreign one. This undeniable fact, it might be said, clearly shows that language is the mere reproduction of what is heard, depending entirely on social intercourse without consideration of the unity or diversity of the people involved. In the first place, however, it has by no means been determined by exact tests that the inclination toward such children's native speech did not have to be overcome at some cost to the finest nuances of skill in the adopted language. But even disregarding this possibility, the most natural explanation is simply that human beings are everywhere human and the development of linguistic capacity may therefore take place with the aid of any given individual. That doesn't mean that it comes any less from the individual's innate nature; only, since it always needs outer stimulus as well, it must become analogous to whatever stimulus it receives. This it can do, since all human languages are interrelated in some sense. Nonetheless the binding force of closely related origins is plain enough to behold in the division of nations. Nor is it difficult to understand, since national origins are so predominantly powerful in their effect on individuality, and the various languages so intimately related with these origins. If language were not truly connected through its origins in the depths of human nature with even the physical hereditary processes, how then could

one's native tongue have so much power and intimacy for the ear of the uneducated and educated alike, that after a long separation from it it greets one like the sound of magic and creates deep yearning for itself during one's separation from it? This obviously is not a matter of the spiritual content of any language, of its expressed thoughts or feelings, but of the most inexplicable and individual element in it: the sound. When we hear the sound of our native tongue it is as though we heard a part of our self.

And even when we consider the products of language, the notion that it consists but of the designation of perceived objects is not confirmed. With this function alone, the profound and full contents of language can never be exhausted. Just as no concept is possible without language, so no object is possible without it for the psyche, since even external ones receive their intrinsic substance only through language. But the entire method of subjective perception of objects goes necessarily into the development and use of language. For words are born of the subjective perceptions of objects; they are not a copy of the object itself but of the image of it produced in the psyche by its perception. And since subjectivity is unavoidably mingled with all objective perception, one may—quite independently of language—look upon each human individuality as a singular unique standpoint for a world-view. But it becomes far more so through language, since words when confronted with psyche turn themselves into objects, an intrinsic significance being added to them, and thus produce a new characteristic quality. This, being one which characterizes the sound of speech, presents thoroughgoing analogies within a language, and since the language of a given nation is already characterized by a similar subjectivity, each language therefore contains a characteristic world-view. As individual sound mediates between object and person, so the whole of language mediates between human beings and the internal and external nature that affects them. Man surrounds himself by a world of sounds in order to take into himself the world of objects and operate on them. What I am here saying outdistances in no way the simple truth. Man lives with objects mainly, in fact exclusively, since feeling and acting depend on his mental images, as language turns them over to him. The same act which enables him to spin language out of himself enables him to spin himself into language, and each language draws a circle around the people to whom it adheres which it is possible for the individual to escape only by stepping into a different one. The learning of a foreign language should therefore mean the gaining of a new standpoint toward one's world-view, and it does this in fact to a considerable degree, because each language contains the entire conceptual web and mental images of a part of humanity. If it is not always purely felt as such, the reason is only that one so frequently projects one's own world-view, in fact one's own speech habits, onto a foreign language.

One must not think of even the earliest origins of language being limited to a sparse number of words, as one frequently does if one thinks of language not originating in free human sociality, but rather as limited to acts of mutual assistance—a point of view facilitated by the reduction of early humanity to an imaginary status of "children of nature." These notions are among the most erroneous views one could possibly form regarding language. Man is not as helpless as all that, and besides, inarticulated sounds would suffice for the purpose of mere mutual aid in trouble. Language is human even in its very beginnings, and extends broadly without special purposes to all objects of random sensory perception or inner operation. Even (and especially in fact) the languages of so-called savages, who after all should be fairly close to a state of nature as we think of the phrase, show a fullness and diversity of expression which far exceeds simple needs. Words well up from the breast of their own free will, without need or intention, and there doubtless never was a wild wandering horde in any of the earth's desolate places which did not already have its songs. For man, as an animal species, is a singing creature, though one who joins thoughts to the tones.

But language does not merely transplant an undefined number of material elements from nature into the psyche. It also acquaints it with the aspects of form which come to us from the whole complex. Nature unfolds before us a bright many-colored diversity, rich with configurations affecting all our senses, and irradiated by a luminous clarity. Our power of reflection discovers in this richness a regularity or conformity to law which suits our spirit form. Quite apart from the corporeal existence of things there clings to their outlines a magic haze of outward beauty, as though it were made for man's sake alone, in which the conformity to law is wedded to the sensory material in a way which moves and overwhelms us but which we cannot explain. All these things we find again in the analogical echoes of language, for language can represent the state of affairs as we find it. For by entering the world of sound with the aid of language, we do not leave the real world that surrounds us. The conformity to law found in nature is related to that found in linguistic structure, and by stimulating man to perform his loftiest, most human activities, it furthers his understanding of the formal impression that nature makes, since it too cannot be considered other than a development of spiritual energies, however inexplicable. Through the rhythmic and musical form inherent in related sounds, language—affecting yet another human field—heightens the impression of

natural beauty in man, but even independent of this, affects the psyche's mood by just the accents of speech.

Language, being the mass of its products, is different from whatever fragment is spoken at a given time. And before we leave this chapter we must tarry awhile at that difference. A language as a whole contains everything transformed by it into sounds. But just as the materials of thought and the infinitude of its connections can never be exhausted, neither can the number of things to be designated and related by language. A language therefore consists of not only its already formed elements but above all of a methodology for continuing the spiritual labor for which it designates the orbits and the forms. The firmly composed elements form a certain kind of dead mass of language, but this mass carries the living germ of never-ending definability. At each given point and in each given epoch, therefore, language just like nature appears to man as an inexhaustible reservoir, in contrast to all he has already thought and known, a reservoir in which his spirit may still discover the unknown, and his inward sensation may still become aware of things not felt this way before. Each time language is used by a truly original and great genius, that is what happens. And the human race needs for the inspiration of its constantly advancing intellectual efforts and the unfolding of its spiritual lifestuff, the ever open vista beyond what has already been achieved, the assurance that the infinite entanglements yet remaining may gradually be dissolved. But language contains a dark unrevealed depth, as well, and a depth which reaches in two directions. For backwards as well as forwards, it flows out of (or into) an unknown wealth of materials which may be recognized only up to a point and then vanishes from view, leaving the feeling of unfathomable mystery. Language has this infinity, with neither end nor beginning except for a very brief past, in common, so far as our view is concerned, with the whole existence of the human race. But we feel and intuit in language plainly and vividly how even the remote past is related to the feeling of the present, since it has passed through the human sensations of former generations and has retained their living breath. But these same generations are nationally and familially related to us in the same sounds of their native tongue which becomes the expression of our own feelings.

This double aspect of language, partly firm and partly fluid, produces a unique relationship between it and the generations that speak it. They produce within it a depository of words and a system of rules by which it grows in the course of the centuries into an independent power. Our attention was earlier focused on the fact that a thought taken up by language becomes an object for the psyche and thus exerts an effect upon it from the outside. But we have been looking at this object mainly as it has developed from the subject, at the effect, in other words, as emanating from that upon which it reacts. Now we must also look at the process from the opposite point of view, according to which language is truly a foreign object, its effect actually emanating from something quite other than that upon which it reacts. For language must necessarily belong to a twosome and at the same time it is truly the property of the entire human race. Since in writing, too, it holds out slumbering thought to be awakened by the spirit, it builds for itself a unique existence which can only attain validity in any given act of thought, but which in its totality is nonetheless independent of thought. The two contradictory views here suggested—that language is both extrinsic to the psyche and a part of it, that it is both independent from it and dependent on it—pertain to it in reality and make out the individuality of its nature. Nor must we seek to solve the contradiction by saying that language is in part extrinsic and independent, and in part neither. For language is objective and independent to precisely the same degree that it is subjective and dependent. For it has no abiding place anywhere, not even in writing; what we called its dead part must always be newly generated in thought; it must always transfer itself alive into speech or understanding, in other words become wholly transferred to the subject. But this same act of regeneration is what makes it also into an object. To be sure, it experiences the entire operative influence of the human individual, but this same operative influence is bound by what it is and has been. The true solution of the paradox lies in the unity of human nature. Whatever originates with what is one and the same with myself, dissolves the concepts of object and subject, of dependence and independence. Language is mine because I produce it as I do. And because the reason I produce it as I do lies in the speaking and having spoken of all the generations of men, insofar as uninterrupted linguistic communication reaches, it is the language itself that gives me my restrictions. But that which restricts and confines me came into language by human nature of which I am a part, and whatever is strange in language for me is therefore strange only for my individual momentary nature, not for my original, true nature as a human being. [VII, 13–64]

* * *

There are two phenomena of language in which [all the individual aspects of the mutual influences of the character and the language of nations] not only most decisively coincide, but which so reveal the influence of their wholeness that all concepts of particularity disappear from them. These are poetry and prose. We must call them phenomena of lan-

guage, since even the original structure of a language tends to direct it to one or the other, or, where its form is truly a great one, to the proportionate development of both, and since they in turn react back upon the structure of the language. Truly, however, they are first of all the developmental track of intellectuality itself and must, when its structure is not deficient and its orbit not disturbed, necessarily unwind themselves along it. Poetry and prose therefore require most careful study, not only in relation to each other, but particularly in connection with their relative time of origin.

If we look at both from their most concrete as well as their most ideal side simultaneously, we see that they take separate paths to attain similar goals. For both move from reality toward something which does not belong to reality. Poetry conceives of reality in its sensuous phenomenality, as it is externally and internally perceived by us, but it is unperturbed about whatever makes reality be what it is. In fact poetry specifically rejects anything of a reasoning or causal character. It relates the sensuous phenomena in creative imagination, and guides us through them to a view of an artistically ideal wholeness. Prose looks precisely for the roots of reality which connect it to existence in all the vast network of its connections. It then intellectually combines facts with facts and concepts with concepts, striving for an objective connection of them all within an idea. The difference between poetry and prose as just outlined is drawn only as it expresses itself in their true essence, to be sure. If one looks only at any given piece of poetry or prose as it is actually found in a given language . . . one finds that the inner direction here called prose may be executed in metrical or rhythmic language and that of poetry in unmetrical and arhythmic language, but only at some cost to both. For prose expressed in poetic form has neither the character of poetry nor wholly that of prose, and likewise with poetry disguised as prose.[6] Poetic contents perforce bring about poetic garments, and there are many instances of poets who, feeling this power, have completed in verse something they began in prose.

What both poetry and prose have in common—to return now to their intrinsic nature—is the tension and the comprehensiveness of soul that is necessitated by full penetration of reality coupled with attainment of an ideal relationship of infinite variety, plus the ability to recollect the mind to a consistent pursuit of a once decided upon path. Yet this too must be rightly understood to mean that such a path never excludes its opposite within the spiritual economy of a nation and its language, but actually furthers it as

---

[6]This statement recalls earlier discussions going back to Aristotle (above, page 52) on just what the true natures of poetry and prose are. See also Vico (above, page 321).

well as itself. Both, the mood of poetry and that of prose, must complement each other to form the communal spirit which permits men to sink their roots deep into reality, keeping always in mind that the deeper the roots, the more joyous the towering into a freer element. The poetry of a people has not reached its summit until by its variety and its free flexibility it announces the possibility of an equivalent development of prose. Since the human spirit, as we conceive of it in strength and freedom, needs to attain both configurations, we know one by the other, just as we can tell from a fragment of sculpture that it once was part of a grouping.

Prose however may be used in another sense as well. It can stop at the mere presentation of facts and at totally external purposes. It may be used for the mere communication of things, rather than the awakening of ideas and feelings. In such a case it does not depart from ordinary speech and never reaches the true heights of what we have been calling prose. Prose in this wider sense then cannot be considered a developmental track of intellectuality; its references are not to form but to matter alone. But wherever prose pursues its higher path it needs, just like poetry, certain special means for reaching deeply into the human psyche. It has to raise itself to that ennobled form of speech of which alone we may speak if we wish to consider it the true mate of poetry. Prose in this intrinsic sense demands a comprehension of its object which requires all the combined capacities of the total psychic constitution. This means a treatment of the object which shows it as radiating toward all the receptive subjects upon which it works. Discriminating rationality is not active by itself; all the other powers of mind aid it, thus forming the point of view properly known as "spirited," "inspired." In such a union of powers, the spirit carries in addition to its work upon a given object, the imprint of its mood over into

speech. Language, elevated by the verve of thought, shows forth its advantages but subordinates them to purposes of the whole spirit. It is the moral feeling-life that imparts itself to the language; the soul that shines through the style. In a manner wholly individual and peculiar to itself, there reveals itself in prose, through the subordination and the dialectic of its sentences, the logical eurythmy which corresponds to thought development. This is the internal command which ordinary speech obeys when it becomes elevated by a special purpose. If an author yields too far to it, he produces a mixture of poetry and rhetoric prose. But in "spirited," "inspired" prose, all the details here listed singly act together, thereby sketching out the whole living birth of a thought, the whole process of spirit's wrestling with an object. Wherever permitted, the thought shapes up like a free spontaneous inspiration and performs in the realm of truth what spontaneous beauty performs in the realm of poetry.

From all this we may see that poetry and prose are conditioned by similar general demands. In both there must be an inward and spontaneous verve which lifts and carries the spirit. Man in his whole individuatedness must move with his thought toward both outer and inner world and, understanding particulars, leave to them that form which relates them to the whole. In their directions, however, and their means for achieving their effects, poetry and prose are different and can really never be mingled. In reference to language we should particularly note that poetry's true nature is inseparable from that of music,[7] whereas prose entrusts itself to language alone. [VII, 193 ff.]

---

[7] The identification of poetry with music tends at this time to replace the identification of poetry with painting that flourished from Simonides (c. 556–468? B.C.) through the eighteenth century.

John Keats

1795–1821

Many of Keats's letters are remarkable for their wealth of speculation, sometimes derivative of others, packed into a few sentences. Keats thinks of beauty as providing a form of knowledge that cannot be gained by means of "consecutive reasoning." He makes a similar distinction when he opposes the "life of sensations" to that of "thought." His position is not, however, that of a sensualist. He sees thought as the abstracting mode of distancing and dehumanizing objects. The life of sensations he associates with empathetic experience: "If a sparrow come before my window I take part in its existence and pick about the gravel." Poetry, he argues, breaks down the boundaries erected by "thought," which always divides experience into subject and object. Yet this view does not preclude Keats's associating the experience of art with "speculation," on which the imagination is free to act. Like Kant (above, page 420) and Coleridge (above, page 497), he writes as if he distinguishes the beautiful from the agreeable and disagreeable: "The excellence of every art is its intensity, capable of making all disagreeables vanish." *King Lear* is his example. If you have unpleasantness in art there must be a "momentous depth of speculation excited, in which to bury its repulsiveness." The notion of intensity is a forerunner of New Critical emphasis on poetic language.

Since the poem's mode of truth is beauty, the poem cannot be a vehicle only of consecutive reasoning or dogma. The poet must possess "negative capability." He must be able to remain in "uncertainties, mysteries, doubts, without any irritable reaching after fact and reason." Thus Keats offers a writerly version of the disinterest that Kant requires of the reader or viewer (above, page 420). The poet's mode of knowledge is therefore not discursive. Belief becomes a word irrelevant to criticism because it is associated with discursive thought, not beauty. One of the reasons the poet is or must be freed from belief, in this sense of the term, is that a poem grows like a plant: "If poetry comes not as naturally as the leaves to a tree it had better not come at all." The poem's integrity is internal, not externally imposed by some code of belief. The metaphor by which this idea is expressed is the characteristically Romantic one of organicism.

Keats's complete works are available in the edition by H. Buxton Forman (in five volumes, 1900–1901). The letters have been edited by Forman, revised edition (1952), and by Hyder E. Rollins (in two volumes, 1958). See C. D. Thorpe, *The Mind of John Keats* (1926); C. L. Finney, *The Evolution of Keats's Poetry* (1936); W. J. Bate, *Negative Capability* (1939); J. R. Caldwell, *John Keats's Fancy* (1945); Earl Wasserman, *The Finer Tone* (1953); W. J. Bate, *John Keats* (1963); Walter Evert, *Aesthetics and Myth in the Poetry of John Keats* (1965); Douglas Bush, *John Keats* (1966); Stuart M. Sperry, *Keats the Poet* (1973); Stuart Ende, *Keats and the Sublime* (1976); Ronald Sharp, *Keats, Skepticism, and the Religion of Beauty* (1979); Nicholas Rowe, *John Keats and the Culture of Dissent* (1997).

from

Letter to Benjamin Bailey[1]

November 22, 1817

I am certain of nothing but of the holiness of the heart's affections and the truth of imagination—What the imagination seizes as beauty must be truth[2]—whether it existed before or not—for I have the same idea of all our passions as of love they are all in their sublime, creative of essential beauty—in a word, you may know my favorite speculation by my first book and the little song I sent in my last—which is a representation from the fancy of the probable mode of operating in these matters—The imagination may be compared to Adam's dream[3]—he awoke and found it truth. I am the more zealous in this affair, because I have never yet been able to perceive how any thing can be known for truth by consecutive reasoning—and yet it must be—Can it be that even the greatest philosopher ever arrived at his goal without putting aside numerous objections—However it may be, O for a life of sensations rather than of thoughts! It is "a vision in the form of youth" a shadow of reality to come—and this consideration has further convinced me for it has come as auxiliary to another favorite speculation of mine, that we shall enjoy ourselves hereafter by having what we called happiness on earth repeated in a finer tone and so repeated—And yet such a fate can only befall those who delight in sensation rather than hunger as you do after truth—Adam's dream will do here and seems to be a conviction that imagination and its empyreal reflection is the same as human life and its spiritual repetition. But as I was saying—the simple imaginative mind may have its rewards in the repetition of its own silent working coming continually on the spirit with a fine suddenness—to compare great things with small—have you never by being surprised with an old melody—in a delicious place—by a delicious voice, felt over again your very speculations and surmises at the time it first operated on your soul—do you not remember forming to yourself the singer's face more beautiful than it was possible and yet with the elevation of the moment you did not think so—even then you were mounted on the wings of imagination so high—that the prototype must be hereafter—that delicious face you will see—What a time! I am continually running away from the subject—sure this cannot be exactly the case with a complex mind—one that is imaginative and at the same time careful of its fruits—who would exist partly on sensation partly on thought—to whom it is necessary that years should bring the philosophic mind—such a one I consider yours and therefore it is necessary to your eternal happiness that you not only drink this old wine of heaven which I shall call the redigestion of our most ethereal musings on earth; but also increase in knowledge and know all things. I am glad to hear you are in a fair way for Easter—you will soon get through your unpleasant reading and then!—but the world is full of troubles and I have not much reason to think myself pestered with many—I think Jane or Marianne[4] has a better opinion of me than I deserve—for really and truly I do not think my brother's illness connected with mine—you know more of the real cause than they do—nor have I any chance of being racked as you have been—you perhaps at one time thought there was such a thing as worldly happiness to be arrived at, at certain periods of time marked out—you have of necessity from your disposition been thus led away—I scarcely remember counting upon any happiness—I look not for it if it be not in the present hour—nothing startles me beyond the moment. The setting sun will always set me to rights—or if a sparrow come before my window I take part in its existence and pick about the gravel. The first thing that strikes me on hearing a misfortune having befalled another is this, "Well it cannot be helped. He will have the pleasure of trying the resources of his spirit." And I beg now, my dear Bailey, that hereafter should you observe anything cold in me not to put it to the account of heartlessness but abstraction—for I assure you I sometimes feel not the influence of a passion or affection during a whole week—and so long this sometimes continues I begin to suspect myself and the genuineness of my feelings at other times—thinking them a few barren tragedy tears.

Keats's letters have been published in several editions, the most complete and trustworthy of which is that by Hyder E. Rollins. The text is reprinted from Hyder E. Rollins, ed, *The Letters of John Keats, 1814–1821,* Vol. I (Cambridge, Mass.: Harvard University Press, 1958).

[1] Rev. Benjamin Bailey (1791–1853), influential friend to Keats.

[2] This statement recalls the final lines of *Ode on a Grecian Urn:* "Beauty is truth, truth beauty, that is all/Ye know on earth, and all ye need to know."

[3] Gen. II.21–23.

[4] Sisters to J. H. Reynolds (1794–1852), minor poet and friend of Keats.

from
Letter to George and Thomas Keats[5]

December 21, 1817

I spent Friday evening with Wells[6] and went next morning to see *Death on the Pale Horse*. It is a wonderful picture, when West's[7] age is considered; but there is nothing to be intense upon; no women one feels mad to kiss, no face swelling into reality. The excellence of every art is its intensity, capable of making all disagreeables evaporate, from their being in close relationship with beauty and truth—Examine *King Lear* and you will find this exemplified throughout; but in this picture we have unpleasantness without any momentous depth of speculation excited, in which to bury its repulsiveness. . . . I had not a dispute but a disquisition with Dilke,[8] on various subjects; several things dovetailed in my mind, and at once it struck me what quality went to form a man of achievement especially in literature and which Shakespeare possessed so enormously—I mean *negative capability,* that is when a man is capable of being in uncertainties, mysteries, doubts, without any irritable reaching after fact and reason—Coleridge, for instance, would let go by a fine isolated verisimilitude caught from the penetralium of mystery, from being incapable of remaining content with half-knowledge. This pursued through volumes would perhaps take us not further than this, that with a great poet the sense of beauty overcomes every other consideration, or rather obliterates all consideration.

from
Letter to John Taylor[9]

February 27, 1818

In poetry I have a few axioms, and you will see how far I am from their center. First, I think poetry should surprise by a fine excess and not by singularity—it should strike the reader as a wording of his own highest thoughts and appear almost a remembrance—Second, its touches of beauty should never be halfway thereby making the reader breathless instead of content: the rise, the progress, the setting of imagery should like the sun come natural to him—shine over him and set soberly although in magnificence, leaving him in the luxury of twilight—but it is easier to think what poetry should be than to write it—and this leads me on to another axiom. That if poetry comes not as naturally as the leaves to a tree it had better not come at all.

from
Letter to Richard Woodhouse[10]

October 27, 1818

As to the poetical Character itself (I mean that sort of which, if I am any thing, I am a Member; that sort distinguished from the wordsworthian or egotistical sublime; which is a thing per se and stands alone) it is not itself—it has no self—it is every thing and nothing—It has no character—it enjoys light and shade; it lives in gusto, be it foul or fair, high or low, rich or poor, mean or elevated—It has as much delight in conceiving an Iago as an Imogen.[11] What shocks the virtous philosopher, delights the camelion Poet. It does no harm from its relish of the dark side of things any more than from its taste for the bright one: because they both end in speculation. A Poet is the most unpoetical of any thing in existence; because he has no Identity—he is continually in for[12]— and filling some other Body—The Sun, the Moon, the Sea and Men and Women who are creatures of impulse are poetical and have about them an unchangeable attribute—the poet has none; no identity—he is certainly the most unpoetical of all God's Creatures. If then he has no self, and if I am a Poet, where is the Wonder that I should say I would write no more? Might I not at that very instant have been cogitating on the Characters of Saturn and Ops? It is a wretched thing to confess; but is a very fact that not one word I ever utter can be taken for granted as an opinion growing out of my identical nature—how can it, when I have no nature?

---

[5] George (1797–1841) and Thomas (1799–1818), brothers of Keats's.
[6] Charles Jeremiah Wells (c. 1800–1879), friend of Keats's.
[7] Benjamin West (1738–1820), American painter, who lived in London for most of his career.
[8] Charles Wentworth Dilke (1789–1864), civil servant, friend of Keats's.
[9] John Taylor, English publisher, firm of Taylor and Hessey.

[10] Richard Woodhouse (1788–1834), lawyer and advisor to the publishers Taylor and Hessey.
[11] Iago, character in Shakespeare's *Othello;* Imogen, character in Shakespeare's *Cymbeline.*
[12] Perhaps short for "informing."

Percy Bysshe Shelley

1792–1822

Written in answer to Thomas Love Peacock's satirical attack on poetry, Shelley's *Defense of Poetry* makes perhaps greater claims for the poet than anyone else has dared. But for Shelley poetry is more than metrical language. It is the expression of imaginative thought that may appear in many verbal forms. Beginning with a distinction between synthesis and analysis, which he identifies with imagination and reason respectively, Shelley proceeds to attribute to the products of the imagination, which is for him fundamentally poetical, immense spiritual and cultural powers. Shelley does not acknowledge Peacock's argument, which implies a much narrower view of what poetry is, that the range of poetry is progressively diminished by the enlargement of the domain of reason. Shelley maintains that the poet refurbishes language, which would otherwise fall into decay and, as a result, bring about cultural decadence. As a creator of new linguistic possibilities the poet "legislates" and "prophesies": he helps remake the world by reconstructing the principal form through which we see it. To express this, Shelley employs an organic metaphor, characteristically Romantic: the poet's "thoughts are the germs of the flower and the fruit of latest time." Poetry sows the "seeds of social revolution." Because in a sense it is always new, poetry "purges from our inward sight the film of familiarity which obscures from us the wonder of our being. . . . It creates anew the universe." Like Peacock, Shelley presents a cyclical view of the history of poetry, but it lacks Peacock's notion of decline. In his view, the poetic spirit remains in its periodic rebirth a source of insight into universal ideas.

To describe the relation of man's mind to nature, Shelley employs a metaphor familiar to readers of other Romantics, that of the wind harp, or Aeolian lyre. But the lyre is more passive in its relation to the wind than is man's subject in relation to nature's object, and Shelley avers that man produces not merely melody from his experience but "harmony, by an internal adjustment of the sounds or motions thus excited to the impressions which excite them." To describe the act of poetic creation Shelley, like Keats (above, page 536), employs an organic simile, which he combines with an image similar to that of the Aeolian lyre; "The mind in creation is as a fading coal, which some invisible influence, like an inconstant wind, awakens to transitory brightness; this power arises from within, like the color of a flower which fades and changes as it is developed. . . ." Shelley adds to this the notion that what the poet imagines is never fully expressed in the poem, for when composition begins the idea is already fading. This view is frequently implied in Shelley's time. It conflicts with Blake's (above, page 448) and that of some later writers, who think of the poem as a created vision, not an expression of a prior one.

There has been much discussion of the extent to which Shelley is a Platonist. He disagrees, of course, with Plato's Socrates about poets, but he seems to accept the notion of the Platonic idea and is perhaps close to Plotinus in remarks like the one in which he declares that the poet "participates in the eternal, the infinite, and the one."

* * *

Shelley's complete works have been edited in ten volumes by Roger Ingpen and W. E. Peek (1927). John Shawcross has edited Shelley's *Literary and Philosophical Criticism* (1909). See M. T. Solve, *Shelley: His Theory of Poetry* (1927); Floyd Stovall, *Desire and Restraint in Shelley* (1931); B. P. Kurtz, *The Pursuit of Death* (1933); C. H. Grabo, *The Magic Plant* (1936); N. I. White, *Shelley* (1940); Carlos Baker, *Shelley's Major Poetry* (1948); J. A. Notopoulos, *The Platonism of Shelley* (1949); C. E. Pulos, *The Deep Truth: A Study of Shelley's Skepticism* (1954); Peter Butter, *Shelley's Idols of the Cave* (1954); Earle J. Schulze, *Shelley's Theory of Poetry* (1966); John W. Wright, *Shelley's Myth of Metaphor* (1970); Earl Wasserman, *Shelley: A Critical Reading* (1971); Richard Holmes, *Shelley: The Pursuit* (1974); Michael Scrivener, *Radical Shelley* (1982); Donald H. Reiman, *Percy Bysshe Shelley* (1990).

A Defense of Poetry

According to one mode of regarding those two classes of mental action, which are called reason and imagination, the former may be considered as mind contemplating the relations borne by one thought to another, however produced; and the latter, as mind acting upon those thoughts so as to color them with its own light, and composing from them, as from elements, other thoughts, each containing within itself the principle of its own integrity. The one is the τὸ ποιεῖν,[1] or the principle of synthesis, and has for its objects those forms which are common to universal nature and existence itself; the other is the τὸ λογιζεῖν,[2] or principle of analysis, and its action regards the relations of things, simply as relations; considering thoughts, not in their integral unity, but as the algebraical representations which conduct to certain general results. Reason is the enumeration of quantities already known; imagination is the perception of the value of those quantities, both separately and as a whole. Reason respects the differences, and imagination the similitudes of things. Reason is to the imagination as the instrument to the agent, as the body to the spirit, as the shadow to the substance.

Poetry, in a general sense, may be defined to be "the expression of the imagination": and poetry is connate with the origin of man. Man is an instrument over which a series of external and internal impressions are driven, like the alternations of an ever-changing wind over an Aeolian lyre, which move it by their motion to ever-changing melody. But there is a principle within the human being, and perhaps within all sentient beings, which acts otherwise than in the lyre, and produces not melody alone, but harmony, by an internal adjustment of the sounds or motions thus excited to the impressions which excite them. It is as if the lyre could accommodate its chords to the motions of that which strikes them, in a determined proportion of sound; even as the musician can accommodate his voice to the sound of the lyre.[3] A child at play by itself will express its delight by its voice and motions; and every inflection of tone and every gesture will bear exact relation to a corresponding antitype in the pleasurable impressions which awakened it; it will be the reflected image of that impression; and as the lyre trembles and sounds after the wind has died away, so the child seeks, by prolonging in its voice and motions the duration of the effect, to prolong also a consciousness of the cause. In relation to the objects which delight a child, these expressions are what poetry is to higher objects. The savage (for the savage is to ages what the child is to years) expresses the emotions produced in him by surrounding objects in a similar manner; and language and gesture, together with plastic or pictorial imitation, become the image of the combined effect of those objects, and of his apprehension of them. Man in society, with all his passions and his pleasures, next becomes the object of the passions and pleasures of man; an additional class of emotions produces an augmented treasure of expressions; and language, gesture, and the imitative arts, become at once the representation and the medium, the pencil and the picture, the chisel and the statue, the chord and the harmony. The social sympathies, or those laws from which, as from its elements, society results, begin to develop themselves from the moment that two human beings coexist; the future is contained within the present, as the plant within the seed; and equality, diversity, unity, contrast,

---

Shelley's *Defense of Poetry* was written in 1821 but not published until 1840.
[1] "Making."
[2] "Reasoning."

[3] On the Aeolian lyre see M. H. Abrams, "The Correspondent Breeze" in his (ed.) *English Romantic Poets* (1960), 37–54.

mutual dependence, become the principles alone capable of affording the motives according to which the will of a social being is determined to action, inasmuch as he is social; and constitute pleasure in sensation, virtue in sentiment, beauty in art, truth in reasoning, and love in the intercourse of kind. Hence men, even in the infancy of society, observe a certain order in their words and actions, distinct from that of the objects and the impressions represented by them, all expression being subject to the laws of that from which it proceeds. But let us dismiss those more general considerations which might involve an inquiry into the principles of society itself, and restrict our view to the manner in which the imagination is expressed upon its forms.

In the youth of the world, men dance and sing and imitate natural objects, observing in these actions, as in all others, a certain rhythm or order. And, although all men observe a similar, they observe not the same order, in the motions of the dance, in the melody of the song, in the combinations of language, in the series of their imitations of natural objects. For there is a certain order or rhythm belonging to each of these classes of mimetic representation, from which the hearer and the spectator receive an intenser and purer pleasure than from any other: the sense of an approximation to this order has been called taste by modern writers. Every man in the infancy of art observes an order which approximates more or less closely to that from which this highest delight results: but the diversity is not sufficiently marked, as that its gradations should be sensible, except in those instances where the predominance of this faculty of approximation to the beautiful (for so we may be permitted to name the relation between this highest pleasure and its cause) is very great. Those in whom it exists in excess are poets, in the most universal sense of the word; and the pleasure resulting from the manner in which they express the influence of society or nature upon their own minds, communicates itself to others, and gathers a sort of reduplication from that community. Their language is vitally metaphorical; that is, it marks the before unapprehended relations of things and perpetuates their apprehension, until the words which represent them become, through time, signs for portions or classes of thoughts instead of pictures of integral thoughts; and then if no new poets should arise to create afresh the associations which have been thus disorganized, language will be dead to all the nobler purposes of human intercourse. These similitudes or relations are finely said by Lord Bacon to be "the same footsteps of nature impressed upon the various subjects of the world";[4] and he considers the faculty which perceives them as the storehouse of axioms common to all knowledge. In the infancy of society every author is necessarily a poet, because language itself is poetry; and to be a poet is to apprehend the true and the beautiful, in a word, the good which exists in the relation, subsisting, first between existence and perception, and secondly between perception and expression. Every original language near to its source is in itself the chaos of a cyclic poem: the copiousness of lexicography and the distinctions of grammar are the works of a later age, and are merely the catalogue and the form of the creations of poetry.

But poets, or those who imagine and express this indestructible order, are not only the authors of language and of music, of the dance, and architecture, and statuary, and painting; they are the institutors of laws, and the founders of civil society, and the inventors of the arts of life, and the teachers, who draw into a certain propinquity with the beautiful and the true, that partial apprehension of the agencies of the invisible world which is called religion. Hence all original religions are allegorical, or susceptible of allegory, and, like Janus, have a double face of false and true. Poets, according to the circumstances of the age and nation in which they appeared, were called, in the earlier epochs of the world, legislators, or prophets: a poet essentially comprises and unites both these characters. For he not only beholds intensely the present as it is, and discovers those laws according to which present things ought to be ordered, but he beholds the future in the present, and his thoughts are the germs of the flower and the fruit of latest time. Not that I assert poets to be prophets in the gross sense of the word, or that they can foretell the form as surely as they foreknow the spirit of events: such is the pretense of superstition, which would make poetry an attribute of prophecy, rather than prophecy an attribute of poetry.[5] A poet participates in the eternal, the infinite, and the one; as far as relates to his conceptions, time and place and number are not. The grammatical forms which express the moods of time, and the difference of persons, and the distinction of place, are convertible with respect to the highest poetry without injuring it as poetry: and the choruses of Aeschylus, and the book of Job, and Dante's "Paradise," would afford, more than any other writings, examples of this fact, if the limits of this essay did not forbid citation.[6] The creation of sculpture, painting, and music, are illustrations still more decisive.

Language, color, form, and religious and civil habits of action, are all the instruments and materials of poetry; they

---

[4] Bacon (above, page 234), *On the Development of the Sciences* III, i.

[5] Compare Sidney (above, page 187); cf. Plato's *Cratylus* (above, page 45).
[6] Aeschylus (525–456 B.C.), Greek tragic dramatist; Dante (above, page 153).

may be called poetry by that figure of speech which considers the effect as a synonym of the cause. But poetry in a more restricted sense expresses those arrangements of language, and especially metrical language, which are created by that imperial faculty, whose throne is curtained within the invisible nature of man. And this springs from the nature itself of language, which is a more direct representation of the actions and passions of our internal being, and is susceptible of more various and delicate combinations, than color, form, or motion, and is more plastic and obedient to the control of that faculty of which it is the creation. For language is arbitrarily produced by the imagination, and has relation to thoughts alone; but all other materials, instruments, and conditions of art, have relations among each other, which limit and interpose between conception and expression. The former is as a mirror which reflects, the latter as a cloud which enfeebles, the light of which both are mediums of communications. Hence the fame of sculptors, painters, and musicians, although the intrinsic powers of the great masters of these arts may yield in no degree to that of those who have employed language as the hieroglyphic of their thoughts, has never equaled that of poets in the restricted sense of the term; as two performers of equal skill will produce unequal effects from a guitar and a harp. The fame of legislators and founders of religions, so long as their institutions last, alone seems to exceed that of poets in the restricted sense; but it can scarcely be a question, whether, if we deduct the celebrity which their flattery of the gross opinions of the vulgar usually conciliates, together with that which belonged to them in their higher character of poets, any excess will remain.

We have thus circumscribed the word *poetry* within the limits of that art which is the most familiar and the most perfect expression of the faculty itself. It is necessary, however, to make the circle still narrower, and to determine the distinction between measured and unmeasured language; for the popular division into prose and verse is inadmissible in accurate philosophy.[7]

Sounds as well as thoughts have relation both between each other and towards that which they represent, and a perception of the order of those relations has always been found connected with a perception of the order of the relations of thoughts. Hence the language of poets have ever affected a certain uniform and harmonious recurrence of sound, without which it were not poetry, and which is scarcely less indispensable to the communication of its influence, than the words themselves, without reference to

that peculiar order. Hence the vanity of translation; it were as wise to cast a violet into a crucible that you might discover the formal principle of its color and odor, as seek to transfuse from one language into another the creations of a poet. The plant must spring again from its seed, or it will bear no flower—and this is the burthen of the curse of Babel.[8]

An observation of the regular mode of the recurrence of harmony in the language of poetical minds, together with its relation to music, produced meter, or a certain system of traditional forms of harmony and language. Yet it is by no means essential that a poet should accommodate his language to this traditional form, so that the harmony, which is its spirit, be observed. The practice is indeed convenient and popular, and to be preferred, especially in such composition as includes much action: but every great poet must inevitably innovate upon the example of his predecessors in the exact structure of his peculiar versification. The distinction between poets and prose writers is a vulgar error. The distinction between philosophers and poets has been anticipated. Plato was essentially a poet—the truth and splendor of his imagery, and the melody of his language, are the most intense that it is possible to conceive.[9] He rejected the measure of the epic, dramatic, and lyrical forms, because he sought to kindle a harmony in thoughts divested of shape and action, and he forbore to invent any regular plan of rhythm which would include, under determinate forms, the varied pauses of his style. Cicero[10] sought to imitate the cadence of his periods, but with little success. Lord Bacon was a poet.[11] His language has a sweet and majestic rhythm, which satisfies the sense, no less than the almost superhuman wisdom of his philosophy satisfies the intellect; it is a strain which distends, and then bursts the circumference of the hearer's mind, and pours itself forth together with it into the universal element with which it has perpetual sympathy. All the authors of revolutions in opinion are not only necessary poets as they are inventors, nor even as their words unveil the permanent analogy of things by images which participate in the life of truth; but as their periods are harmonious and rhythmical, and contain in themselves the elements of verse; being the echo of the eternal music. Nor are those supreme poets, who have employed traditional

---

[7] Shelley joins Aristotle (above, page 52) and many subsequent critics on this point.

[8] Gen. 11.1–9: Noah's descendants originally spoke one language, but they were punished for the arrogance of building the Tower of Babel and became unintelligible to each other.

[9] Shelley seems to imply that Plato is a dramatic poet who does not write metrically.

[10] Cicero (above, page 74).

[11] [Shelley] See *The String of the Labyrinth* and the essay on death particularly.

forms of rhythm on account of the form and action of their subjects, less capable of perceiving and teaching the truth of things, than those who have omitted that form. Shakespeare, Dante, and Milton (to confine ourselves to modern writers) are philosophers of the very loftiest power.

A poem is the very image of life expressed in its eternal truth. There is this difference between a story and a poem, that a story is a catalogue of detached facts, which have no other connection than time, place, circumstance, cause and effect; the other is the creation of actions according to the unchangeable forms of human nature, as existing in the mind of the creator, which is itself the image of all other minds. The one is partial, and applies only to a definite period of time, and a certain combination of events which can never again recur; the other is universal, and contains within itself the germ of a relation to whatever motives or actions have place in the possible varieties of human nature.[12] Time, which destroys the beauty and the use of the story of particular facts, stripped of the poetry which should invest them, augments that of poetry, and forever develops new and wonderful applications of the eternal truth which it contains. Hence epitomes have been called the moths of just history; they eat out the poetry of it. A story of particular facts is as a mirror which obscures and distorts that which should be beautiful: poetry is a mirror which makes beautiful that which is distorted.

The parts of a composition may be poetical, without the composition as a whole being a poem. A single sentence may be considered as a whole, though it may be found in the midst of a series of unassimilated portions; a single word even may be a spark of inextinguishable thought. And thus all the great historians, Herodotus, Plutarch, Livy,[13] were poets; and although the plan of these writers, especially that of Livy, restrained them from developing this faculty in its highest degree, they made copious and ample amends for their subjection, by filling all the interstices of their subjects with living images.

Having determined what is poetry, and who are poets, let us proceed to estimate its effects upon society.

Poetry is ever accompanied with pleasure: all spirits on which it falls open themselves to receive the wisdom which is mingled with its delight.[14] In the infancy of the world, neither poets themselves nor their auditors are fully aware of the excellence of poetry: for it acts in a divine and unapprehended

manner, beyond and above consciousness; and it is reserved for future generations to contemplate and measure the mighty cause and effect in all the strength and splendor of their union. Even in modern times, no living poet ever arrived at the fullness of his fame; the jury which sits in judgment upon a poet, belonging as he does to all time, must be composed of his peers: it must be impaneled by time from the selectest of the wise of many generations. A poet is a nightingale, who sits in darkness and sings to cheer its own solitude with sweet sounds; his auditors are as men entranced by the melody of an unseen musician, who feel that they are moved and softened, yet know not whence or why. The poems of Homer and his contemporaries were the delight of infant Greece; they were the elements of that social system which is the column upon which all succeeding civilization has reposed. Homer embodied the ideal perfection of his age in human character; nor can we doubt that those who read his verses were awakened to an ambition of becoming like to Achilles, Hector, and Ulysses: the truth and beauty of friendship, patriotism, and persevering devotion to an object, were unveiled to the depths in these immortal creations: the sentiments of the auditors must have been refined and enlarged by a sympathy with such great and lovely impersonations, until from admiring they imitated, and from imitation they identified themselves with the objects of their admiration. Nor let it be objected, that these characters are remote from moral perfection, and that they are by no means to be considered as edifying patterns for general imitation. Every epoch, under names more or less specious, has deified its peculiar errors; revenge is the naked idol of the worship of a semibarbarous age; and self-deceit is the veiled image of unknown evil, before which luxury and satiety lie prostrate. But a poet considers the vices of his contemporaries as a temporary dress in which his creations must be arrayed, and which cover without concealing the eternal proportions of their beauty. An epic or dramatic personage is understood to wear them around his soul, as he may the ancient armor or the modern uniform around his body; whilst it is easy to conceive a dress more graceful than either. The beauty of the internal nature cannot be so far concealed by its accidental vesture, but that the spirit of its form shall communicate itself to the very disguise, and indicate the shape it hides from the manner in which it is worn. A majestic form and graceful motions will express themselves through the most barbarous and tasteless costume. Few poets of the highest class have chosen to exhibit the beauty of their conceptions in its naked truth and splendor; and it is doubtful whether the alloy of costume, habit, &c., be not necessary to temper this planetary music for mortal ears.

The whole objection, however, of the immorality of poetry rests upon a misconception of the manner in which

---

[12]See Aristotle (above, page 57).
[13]Herodotus (484?–425? B.C.); Plutarch (above, page 119); Titus Livius (59 B.C.–17 A.D.).
[14]Shelley adopts the old Horatian description (above, page 83) that answers Socrates's challenge (above, page 36).

poetry acts to produce the moral improvement of man. Ethical science arranges the elements which poetry has created, and propounds schemes and proposes examples of civil and domestic life: nor is it for want of admirable doctrines that men hate, and despise, and censure, and deceive, and subjugate one another. But poetry acts in another and diviner manner. It awakens and enlarges the mind itself by rendering it the receptacle of a thousand unapprehended combinations of thought. Poetry lifts the veil from the hidden beauty of the world, and makes familiar objects be as if they were not familiar; it reproduces all that it represents, and the impersonations clothed in its Elysian light stand thenceforward in the minds of those who have once contemplated them as memorials of that gentle and exalted content which extends itself over all thoughts and actions with which it coexists. The great secret of morals is love; or a going out of our own nature, and an identification of ourselves with the beautiful which exists in thought, action, or person, not our own. A man, to be greatly good, must imagine intensely and comprehensively; he must put himself in the place of another and of many others; the pains and pleasures of his species must become his own. The great instrument of moral good is the imagination; and poetry administers to the effect by acting upon the cause. Poetry enlarges the circumference of the imagination by replenishing it with thoughts of ever new delight, which have the power of attracting and assimilating to their own nature all other thoughts, and which form new intervals and interstices whose void forever craves fresh food. Poetry strengthens the faculty which is the organ of the moral nature of man, in the same manner as exercise strengthens a limb. A poet therefore would do ill to embody his own conceptions of right and wrong, which are usually those of his place and time, in his poetical creations, which participate in neither. By this assumption of the inferior office of interpreting the effect, in which perhaps after all he might acquit himself but imperfectly, he would resign a glory in a participation in the cause. There was little danger that Homer, or any of the eternal poets, should have so far misunderstood themselves as to have abdicated this throne of their widest dominion. Those in whom the poetical faculty, though great, is less intense, as Euripides, Lucan, Tasso, Spenser,[15] have frequently affected a moral aim, and the effect of their poetry is diminished in exact proportion to the degree in which they compel us to advert to this purpose.

Homer and the cyclic poets were followed at a certain interval by the dramatic and lyrical poets of Athens, who flourished contemporaneously with all that is most perfect in the kindred expressions of the poetical faculty; architecture, painting, music, the dance, sculpture, philosophy, and, we may add, the forms of civil life. For although the scheme of Athenian society was deformed by many imperfections which the poetry existing in chivalry and Christianity has erased from the habits and institutions of modern Europe; yet never at any other period has so much energy, beauty, and virtue, been developed; never was blind strength and stubborn form so disciplined and rendered subject to the will of man, or that will less repugnant to the dictates of the beautiful and the true, as during the century which preceded the death of Socrates.[16] Of no other epoch in the history of our species have we records and fragments stamped so visibly with the image of the divinity in man. But it is poetry alone, in form, in action, and in language, which has rendered this epoch memorable above all others, and the storehouse of examples to everlasting time. For written poetry existed at that epoch simultaneously with the other arts, and it is an idle inquiry to demand which gave and which received the light, which all, as from a common focus, have scattered over the darkest periods of succeeding time. We know no more of cause and effect than a constant conjunction of events: poetry is ever found to coexist with whatever other arts contribute to the happiness and perfection of man. I appeal to what has already been established to distinguish between the cause and the effect.

It was at the period here adverted to, that the drama had its birth; and however a succeeding writer may have equaled or surpassed those few great specimens of the Athenian drama which have been preserved to us, it is indisputable that the art itself never was understood or practiced according to the true philosophy of it, as at Athens. For the Athenians employed language, action, music, painting, the dance, and religious institutions, to produce a common effect in the representation of the highest idealisms of passion and of power; each division in the art was made perfect in its kind by artists of the most consummate skill, and was disciplined into a beautiful proportion and unity one towards the other. On the modern stage a few only of the elements capable of expressing the image of the poet's conception are employed at once. We have tragedy without music and dancing; and music and dancing without the highest impersonations of which they are the fit accompaniment, and both without religion and solemnity. Religious institution has indeed been usually banished from the stage. Our system of divesting the actor's face of a mask, on which the many expressions appropriated to his dramatic character might be molded into

---

[15]Euripides (485–406 B.C.), Greek tragic dramatist; Marcus Annaeus Lucanus (39–65), Latin poet; Tasso (above, page 226); Edmund Spenser (1552?–1599), English poet.

[16]Socrates was forced to commit suicide in 399 B.C.

one permanent and unchanging expression, is favorable only to a partial and inharmonious effect; it is fit for nothing but a monologue, where all the attention may be directed to some great master of ideal mimicry. The modern practice of blending comedy with tragedy, though liable to great abuse in point of practice, is undoubtedly an extension of the dramatic circle; but the comedy should be as in *King Lear,* universal, ideal, and sublime. It is perhaps the intervention of this principle which determines the balance in favor of *King Lear* against the *Oedipus Tyrannus* or the *Agamemnon;*[17] or, if you will, the trilogies with which they are connected; unless the intense power of the choral poetry, especially that of the latter, should be considered as restoring the equilibrium. *King Lear,* if it can sustain this comparison, may be judged to be the most perfect specimen of the dramatic art existing in the world; in spite of the narrow conditions to which the poet was subjected by the ignorance of the philosophy of the drama which has prevailed in modern Europe. Calderón, in his religious *autos,*[18] has attempted to fulfill some of the high conditions of dramatic representation neglected by Shakespeare; such as the establishing a relation between the drama and religion, and the accommodating them to music and dancing; but he omits the observation of conditions still more important, and more is lost than gained by the substitution of the rigidly defined and ever-repeated idealisms of a distorted superstition for the living impersonations of the truth of human passion.

But I digress. The connection of scenic exhibitions with the improvement or corruption of the manners of men, has been universally recognized: in other words, the presence or absence of poetry in its most perfect and universal form, has been found to be connected with good and evil in conduct or habit. The corruption which has been imputed to the drama as an effect, begins, when the poetry employed in its constitution ends: I appeal to the history of manners whether the periods of the growth of the one and the decline of the other have not corresponded with an exactness equal to any example of moral cause and effect.

The drama at Athens, or wheresoever else it may have approached to its perfection, ever coexisted with the moral and intellectual greatness of the age. The tragedies of the Athenian poets are as mirrors in which the spectator beholds himself, under a thin disguise of circumstance, stripped of all but that ideal perfection and energy which everyone feels to be the internal type of all that he loves, admires, and would become. The imagination is enlarged by a sympathy with pains and passions so mighty, that they distend in their conception the capacity of that by which they are conceived; the good affections are strengthened by pity, indignation, terror, and sorrow; and an exalted calm is prolonged from the satiety of this high exercise of them into the tumult of familiar life: even crime is disarmed of half its horror and all its contagion by being represented as the fatal consequence of the unfathomable agencies of nature; error is thus divested of its willfulness; men can no longer cherish it as the creation of their choice. In a drama of the highest order there is little food for censure or hatred; it teaches rather self-knowledge and self-respect. Neither the eye nor the mind can see itself, unless reflected upon that which it resembles. The drama, so long as it continues to express poetry, is as a prismatic and many-sided mirror, which collects the brightest rays of human nature and divides and reproduces them from the simplicity of their elementary forms, and touches them with majesty and beauty, and multiplies all that it reflects, and endows it with the power of propagating its like wherever it may fall.

But in periods of the decay of social life, the drama sympathizes with that decay. Tragedy becomes a cold imitation of the forms of the great masterpieces of antiquity, divested of all harmonious accompaniment of the kindred arts; and often the very form misunderstood, or a weak attempt to teach certain doctrines, which the writer considers as moral truths; and which are usually no more than specious flatteries of some gross vice or weakness, with which the author, in common with his auditors, are infected. Hence what has been called the classical and domestic drama. Addison's *Cato*[19] is a specimen of the one; and would it were not superfluous to cite examples of the other! To such purposes poetry cannot be made subservient. Poetry is a sword of lightning, ever unsheathed, which consumes the scabbard that would contain it. And thus we observe that all dramatic writings of this nature are unimaginative in a singular degree; they affect sentiment and passion, which, divested of imagination, are other names for caprice and appetite. The period in our own history of the grossest degradation of the drama is the reign of Charles II,[20] when all forms in which poetry had been accustomed to be expressed became hymns to the triumph of kingly power over liberty and virtue. Milton[21] stood alone illuminating an age unworthy of him. At such periods the calculating principle pervades all the forms of dramatic exhibition, and poetry ceases to be expressed

---

[17] By Shakespeare, Sophocles, and Aeschylus respectively.
[18] Pedro Calderón de la Barca (1600–1681), Spanish dramatist. Autos are one-act sacramental plays.

[19] Addison (above, page 307).
[20] Charles II of England reigned from 1660 to 1685, known as the Restoration period.
[21] John Milton (1608–1674), English poet.

upon them. Comedy loses its ideal universality: wit succeeds to humor; we laugh from self-complacency and triumph, instead of pleasure; malignity, sarcasm, and contempt, succeed to sympathetic merriment; we hardly laugh, but we smile. Obscenity, which is ever blasphemy against the divine beauty in life, becomes, from a very veil which it assumes, more active if less disgusting: it is a monster for which the corruption of society forever brings forth new food, which it devours in secret.

The drama being that form under which a greater number of modes of expression of poetry are susceptible of being combined than any other, the connection of poetry and social good is more observable in the drama than in whatever other form. And it is indisputable that the highest perfection of human society has ever corresponded with the highest dramatic excellence; and that the corruption or the extinction of the drama in a nation where it has once flourished, is a mark of a corruption of manners, and an extinction of the energies which sustain the soul of social life. But, as Machiavelli[22] says of political institutions, that life may be preserved and renewed, if men should arise capable of bringing back the drama to its principles. And this is true with respect to poetry in its most extended sense: all language, institution and form, require not only to be produced but to be sustained: the office and character of a poet participates in the divine nature as regards providence, no less than as regards creation.

Civil war, the spoils of Asia, and the fatal predominance first of the Macedonian, and then of the Roman arms, were so many symbols of the extinction or suspension of the creative faculty in Greece. The bucolic writers, who found patronage under the lettered tyrants of Sicily and Egypt, were the latest representatives of its most glorious reign. Their poetry is intensely melodious; like the odor of the tuberose, it overcomes and sickens the spirit with excess of sweetness; whilst the poetry of the preceding age was as a meadow-gale of June, which mingles the fragrance of all the flowers of the field, and adds a quickening and harmonizing spirit of its own, which endows the sense with a power of sustaining its extreme delight. The bucolic and erotic delicacy in written poetry is correlative with that softness in statuary, music, and the kindred arts, and even in manners and institutions, which distinguished the epoch to which I now refer. Nor is it the poetical faculty itself, or any misapplication of it, to which this want of harmony is to be imputed. An equal sensibility to the influence of the senses and the affections is to be found in the writings of Homer and

Sophocles: the former, especially, has clothed sensual and pathetic images with irresistible attractions. Their superiority over these succeeding writers consists in the presence of those thoughts which belong to the inner faculties of our nature, not in the absence of those which are connected with the external: their incomparable perfection consists in a harmony of the union of all. It is not what the erotic poets have, but what they have not, in which their imperfection consists. It is not inasmuch as they were poets, but inasmuch as they were not poets, that they can be considered with any plausibility as connected with the corruption of their age. Had that corruption availed so as to extinguish in them the sensibility to pleasure, passion, and natural scenery, which is imputed to them as an imperfection, the last triumph of evil would have been achieved. For the end of social corruption is to destroy all sensibility to pleasure; and therefore it is corruption. It begins at the imagination and the intellect as at the core, and distributes itself thence as a paralyzing venom, through the affections into the very appetites, until all become a torpid mass in which hardly sense survives. At the approach of such a period, poetry ever addresses itself to those faculties which are the last to be destroyed, and its voice is heard, like the footsteps of Astraea,[23] departing from the world. Poetry ever communicates all the pleasure which men are capable of receiving: it is ever still the light of life; the source of whatever of beautiful or generous or true can have place in an evil time. It will readily be confessed that those among the luxurious citizens of Syracuse and Alexandria, who were delighted with the poems of Theocritus,[24] were less cold, cruel, and sensual than the remnant of their tribe. But corruption must utterly have destroyed the fabric of human society before poetry can ever cease. The sacred links of that chain have never been entirely disjoined, which descending through the minds of many men is attached to those great minds, whence as from a magnet the invisible effluence is sent forth, which at once connects, animates, and sustains the life of all. It is the faculty which contains within itself the seeds at once of its own and of social renovation. And let us not circumscribe the effects of the bucolic and erotic poetry within the limits of the sensibility of those to whom it was addressed. They may have perceived the beauty of those immortal compositions, simply as fragments and isolated portions: those who are more finely organized, or born in a happier age, may recognize them as episodes to that great poem, which all poets, like the cooperating thoughts of one great mind, have built up since the beginning of the world.

---

[22] Niccolò Machiavelli (1469–1527), Italian political philosopher.

[23] Goddess of Justice, who fled earth in the age of brass.
[24] Theocritus (fl. c. 270 B.C.), Greek pastoral poet.

The same revolutions within a narrower sphere had place in ancient Rome; but the actions and forms of its social life never seem to have been perfectly saturated with the poetical element. The Romans appear to have considered the Greeks as the selectest treasuries of the selectest forms of manners and of nature, and to have abstained from creating in measured language, sculpture, music, or architecture, anything which might bear a particular relation to their own condition, whilst it should bear a general one to the universal constitution of the world. But we judge from partial evidence, and we judge perhaps partially. Ennius, Varro, Pacuvius, and Accius,[25] all great poets, have been lost. Lucretius is in the highest, and Virgil in a very high sense, a creator.[26] The chosen delicacy of expressions of the latter, are as a mist of light which conceal from us the intense and exceeding truth of his conceptions of nature. Livy is instinct with poetry. Yet Horace, Catullus, Ovid, and generally the other great writers of the Virgilian age, saw man and nature in the mirror of Greece.[27] The institutions also, and the religion, of Rome were less poetical than those of Greece, as the shadow is less vivid than the substance. Hence poetry in Rome, seemed to follow, rather than accompany, the perfection of political and domestic society. The true poetry of Rome lived in its institutions; for whatever of beautiful, true, and majestic, they contained, could have sprung only from the faculty which creates the order in which they consist. The life of Camillus, the death of Regulus; the expectation of the senators, in their godlike state, of the victorious Gauls; the refusal of the republic to make peace with Hannibal, after the battle of Cannae, were not the consequences of a refined calculation of the probable personal advantage to result from such a rhythm and order in the shows of life, to those who were at once the poets and the actors of these immortal dramas. The imagination beholding the beauty of this order, created it out of itself according to its own idea; the consequence was empire, and the reward everlasting fame. These things are not the less poetry, *"quia carent vate sacro."*[28] They are the episodes of that cyclic poem written by time upon the memories of men. The past, like an inspired rhapsodist, fills the theatre of everlasting generations with their harmony.

At length the ancient system of religion and manners had fulfilled the circle of its evolutions. And the world would have fallen into utter anarchy and darkness, but that there were found poets among the authors of the Christian and chivalric systems of manners and religion, who created forms of opinion and action never before conceived; which, copied into the imaginations of men, become as generals to the bewildered armies of their thoughts. It is foreign to the present purpose to touch upon the evil produced by these systems: except that we protest, on the ground of the principles already established, that no portion of it can be attributed to the poetry they contain.

It is probable that the poetry of Moses, Job, David, Solomon, and Isaiah, had produced a great effect upon the mind of Jesus and his disciples. The scattered fragments preserved to us by the biographers of this extraordinary person, are all instinct with the most vivid poetry. But his doctrines seem to have been quickly distorted. At a certain period after the prevalence of a system of opinions founded upon those promulgated by him, the three forms into which Plato had distributed the faculties of mind underwent a sort of apotheosis, and became the object of the worship of the civilized world. Here it is to be confessed that "Light seems to thicken," and

> The crow makes wing to the rooky wood,
> Good things of day begin to droop and drowse,
> And night's black agents to their preys do rouse.[29]

But mark how beautiful an order has sprung from the dust and blood of this fierce chaos! How the world, as from a resurrection, balancing itself on the golden wings of knowledge and of hope, has reassumed its yet unwearied flight into the heaven of time. Listen to the music, unheard by outward ears, which is as a ceaseless and invisible wind, nourishing its everlasting course with strength and swiftness.

The poetry in the doctrines of Jesus Christ, and the mythology and institutions of the Celtic[30] conquerors of the Roman Empire, outlived the darkness and the convulsions connected with their growth and victory, and blended themselves in a new fabric of manners and opinion. It is an error to impute the ignorance of the Dark Ages to the Christian doctrines or the predominance of the Celtic nations. Whatever of evil their agencies may have contained sprang from the extinction of the poetical principle, connected with the progress of despotism and superstition. Men, from causes

---

[25] Quintus Ennius (239–169? B.C.) Latin poet; Marcus Terentius Varro (116–21? B.C.), Roman writer; Marcus Pacuvius (c. 220–130 B.C.), Roman tragic dramatist; Lucius Accius (170–?), Roman tragic dramatist.

[26] Titus Lucretius Carus (c. 99–c. 55 B.C.), Roman poet; Virgil (70–19 B.C.), Roman poet.

[27] Horace (above, page 78), Caius Valerius Catullus (84?–54? B.C.), Publius Ovidus Naso (43 B.C.–18 A.D.), all Roman poets.

[28] "Because they lack the divine prophet." Horace, *Odes* IV, ix, but misquoted.

[29] Shakespeare, *Macbeth* III, ii, 50–53.

[30] Shelley must mean Germanic.

too intricate to be here discussed, had become insensible and selfish: their own will had become feeble, and yet they were its slaves, and thence the slaves of the will of others: lust, fear, avarice, cruelty, and fraud, characterized a race amongst whom no one was to be found capable of *creating* in form, language, or institution. The moral anomalies of such a state of society are not justly to be charged upon any class of events immediately connected with them, and those events are most entitled to our approbation which could dissolve it most expeditiously. It is unfortunate for those who cannot distinguish words from thoughts, that many of these anomalies have been incorporated into our popular religion.

It was not until the eleventh century that the effects of the poetry of the Christian and chivalric systems began to manifest themselves. The principle of equality had been discovered and applied by Plato in his *Republic,* as the theoretical rule of the mode in which the materials of pleasure and of power produced by the common skill and labor of human beings, ought to be distributed among them. The limitations of this rule were asserted by him to be determined only by the sensibility of each, or the utility to result to all. Plato, following the doctrines of Timaeus and Pythagoras,[31] taught also a moral and intellectual system of doctrine, comprehending at once the past, the present, and the future condition of man. Jesus Christ divulged the sacred and eternal truths contained in these views to mankind, and Christianity, in its abstract purity, became the exoteric expression of the esoteric doctrines of the poetry and wisdom of antiquity. The incorporation of the Celtic nations with the exhausted population of the south, impressed upon it the figure of the poetry existing in their mythology and institutions. The result was a sum of the action and reaction of all the causes included in it; for it may be assumed as a maxim that no nation or religion can supersede any other without incorporating into itself a portion of that which it supersedes. The abolition of personal and domestic slavery, and the emancipation of women from a great part of the degrading restraints of antiquity, were among the consequences of these events.

The abolition of personal slavery is the basis of the highest political hope that it can enter into the mind of man to conceive. The freedom of women produced the poetry of sexual love. Love became a religion, the idols of whose worship were ever present. It was as if the statues of Apollo and the Muses had been endowed with life and motion, and had walked forth among their worshippers; so that earth became peopled by the inhabitants of a diviner world. The familiar appearance and proceedings of life became wonderful and

heavenly, and a paradise was created as out of the wrecks of Eden. And as this creation itself is poetry, so its creators were poets; and language was the instrument of their art: *"Galeotto fù il libro, e chi lo scrisse."*[32] The Provençal trouveurs, or inventors, preceded Petrarch,[33] whose verses are as spells, which unseal the inmost enchanted fountains of the delight which is in the grief of love. It is impossible to feel them without becoming a portion of that beauty which we contemplate: it were superfluous to explain how the gentleness and the elevation of mind connected with these sacred emotions can render men more amiable, more generous and wise, and lift them out of the dull vapors of the little world of self. Dante understood the secret things of love even more than Petrarch. His *Vita Nuova* is an inexhaustible fountain of purity of sentiment and language: it is the idealized history of that period, and those intervals of his life which were dedicated to love. His apotheosis of Beatrice in Paradise, and the gradations of his own love and her loveliness, by which as by steps he feigns himself to have ascended to the throne of the Supreme Cause, is the most glorious imagination of modern poetry. The acutest critics have justly reversed the judgment of the vulgar, and the order of the great acts of the *Divina Commedia,* in the measure of the admiration which they accord to the "Hell," "Purgatory," and "Paradise." The latter is a perpetual hymn of everlasting love. Love, which found a worthy poet in Plato alone of all the ancients, has been celebrated by a chorus of the greatest writers of the renovated world; and the music has penetrated the caverns of society, and its echoes still drown the dissonance of arms and superstition. At successive intervals, Ariosto, Tasso, Shakespeare, Spenser, Calderon, Rousseau,[34] and the great writers of our own age, have celebrated the dominion of love, planting as it were trophies in the human mind of that sublimest victory over sensuality and force. The true relation borne to each other by the sexes into which humankind is distributed, has become less misunderstood; and if the error which confounded diversity with inequality of the powers of the two sexes has been partially recognized in the opinions and institutions of modern Europe, we owe this great benefit to the worship of which chivalry was the law, and poets the prophets.

The poetry of Dante may be considered as the bridge thrown over the stream of time, which unites the modern and ancient world. The distorted notions of invisible things which Dante and his rival Milton have idealized, are merely the mask and the mantle in which these great poets walk through

---

[31] Plato (above, page 8); Timaeus (fl. 400? B.C.), Greek philosopher; Pythagoras (c. 582–c. 507 B.C.), Greek philosopher.

[32] "Galleot was the book, and he who wrote it." Dante, *The Divine Comedy,* "Inferno" V, 137.

[33] Francesco Petrarca (1304–1374), Italian poet.

[34] Ludovico Ariosto (1474–1533), Italian poet; Tasso (above, page 226); Jean Jacques Rousseau (1712–1778), French philosopher.

eternity enveloped and disguised. It is a difficult question to determine how far they were conscious of the distinction which must have subsisted in their minds between their own creeds and that of the people. Dante at least appears to wish to mark the full extent of it by placing Riphaeus, whom Virgil calls *"justissimus unus,"*[35] in Paradise, and observing a most heretical caprice in his distribution of rewards and punishments.[36] And Milton's poem contains within itself a philosophical refutation of that system, of which, by a strange and natural antithesis, it has been a chief popular support. Nothing can exceed the energy and magnificence of the character of Satan as expressed in *Paradise Lost.* It is a mistake to suppose that he could ever have been intended for the popular personification of evil. Implacable hate, patient cunning, and a sleepless refinement of device to inflict the extremest anguish on an enemy, these things are evil; and, although venial in a slave, are not to be forgiven in a tyrant; although redeemed by much that ennobles his defeat in one subdued, are marked by all that dishonors his conquest in the victor. Milton's Devil as a moral being is as far superior to his God, as one who perseveres in some purpose which he has conceived to be excellent in spite of adversity and torture, is to one who in the cold security of undoubted triumph inflicts the most horrible revenge upon his enemy, not from any mistaken notion of inducing him to repent of a perseverance in enmity, but with the alleged design of exasperating him to deserve new torments. Milton has so far violated the popular creed (if this shall be judged to be a violation) as to have alleged no superiority of moral virtue to his god over his devil.[37] And this bold neglect of a direct moral purpose is the most decisive proof of the supremacy of Milton's genius. He mingled as it were the elements of human nature as colors upon a single pallet, and arranged them in the composition of his great picture according to the laws of epic truth; that is, according to the laws of that principle by which a series of actions of the external universe and of intelligent and ethical beings is calculated to excite the sympathy of succeeding generations of mankind. The *Divina Commedia* and *Paradise Lost* have conferred upon modern mythology a systematic form: and when change and time shall have added one more superstition to the mass of those which have arisen and decayed upon the earth, commentators will be learnedly employed in elucidating the religion of ancestral Europe, only not utterly forgotten because it will have been stamped with the eternity of genius.

Homer was the first and Dante the second epic poet: that is, the second poet, the series of whose creations bore a defined and intelligible relation to the knowledge and sentiment and religion of the age in which he lived, and of the ages which followed it: developing itself in correspondence with their development. For Lucretius had limed the wings of his swift spirit in the dregs of the sensible world; and Virgil, with a modesty that ill became his genius, had affected the fame of an imitator, even whilst he created anew all that he copied; and none among the flock of mock birds, though their notes were sweet, Apollonius Rhodius, Quintus Calaber Smyrnaeus, Nonnus, Lucan, Statius, or Claudian,[38] have sought even to fulfill a single condition of epic truth. Milton was the third epic poet. For if the title of epic in its highest sense be refused to the *Aeneid,* still less can it be conceded to the *Orlando Furioso,* the *Gerusalemme Liberata,* the *Lusiad,* or the *Faerie Queene.*[39]

Dante and Milton were both deeply penetrated with the ancient religion of the civilized world; and its spirit exists in their poetry probably in the same proportion as its forms survived in the unreformed worship of modern Europe. The one preceded and the other followed the Reformation at almost equal intervals. Dante was the first religious reformer, and Luther[40] surpassed him rather in the rudeness and acrimony, than in the boldness of his censures of papal usurpation. Dante was the first awakener of entranced Europe; he created a language, in itself music and persuasion, out of a chaos of inharmonious barbarisms. He was the congregator of those great spirits who presided over the resurrection of learning; the Lucifer of that starry flock which in the thirteenth century shone forth from republican Italy, as from a heaven, into the darkness of the benighted world. His very words are instinct with spirit; each is as a spark, a burning atom of inextinguishable thought; and many yet lie covered in the ashes of their birth, and pregnant with a lightning which has yet found no conductor. All high poetry is infinite; it is as the first acorn, which contained all oaks potentially. Veil after veil may be undrawn, and the inmost naked beauty of the meaning never exposed. A great poem is a fountain forever overflowing with the waters of wisdom and delight; and after one person and one age has exhausted all its divine effluence which their peculiar relations enable them to share, another and yet another succeeds, and new relations are ever developed, the source of an unforseen and an unconceived delight.

---

[35]"The most just one." *Aeneid* II, 426–27.
[36]Riphaeus was a pagan, but Dante put him in Paradise.
[37]Shelley's is the most radical and notorious Romantic reading of Milton's Satan as a heroic figure.
[38]Apollonius Rhodius (fl. third century B.C.), Alexandrian and Rhodian epic poet; Quintus Calabar Smyrnaeus (fourth century A.D.), Greek epic poet; Nonnus (fifth century), Greek poet; Publius Papinius Statius (c. 40–c. 96), Latin poet; Claudius Claudianus (d. 408), Latin poet.
[39]By Virgil, Ariosto, Tasso, Camoens, and Spenser, respectively.
[40]Martin Luther (1481–1546), German Protestant Reformation leader.

The age immediately succeeding to that of Dante, Petrarch, and Boccaccio,[41] was characterized by a revival of painting, sculpture, and architecture. Chaucer caught the sacred inspiration, and the superstructure of English literature is based upon the materials of Italian invention.

But let us not be betrayed from a defense into a critical history of poetry and its influence on society. Be it enough to have pointed out the effects of poets, in the large and true sense of the word, upon their own and all succeeding times.

But poets have been challenged to resign the civic crown of reasoners and mechanists, on another plea. It is admitted that the exercise of the imagination is most delightful, but it is alleged that that of reason is more useful. Let us examine, as the grounds of this distinction, what is here meant by utility. Pleasure or good, in a general sense, is that which the consciousness of a sensitive and intelligent being seeks, and in which, when found, it acquiesces. There are two kinds of pleasure, one durable, universal and permanent; the other transitory and particular. Utility may either express the means of producing the former or the latter. In the former sense, whatever strengthens and purifies the affections, enlarges the imagination, and adds spirit to sense, is useful. But a narrower meaning may be assigned to the word utility, confining it to express that which banishes the importunity of the wants of our animal nature, the surrounding men with security of life, the dispersing the grosser delusions of superstition, and the conciliating such a degree of mutual forbearance among men as may consist with the motives of personal advantage.

Undoubtedly the promoters of utility, in this limited sense, have their appointed office in society. They follow the footsteps of poets, and copy the sketches of their creations into the book of common life. They make space, and give time. Their exertions are of the highest value, so long as they confine their administration of the concerns of the inferior powers of our nature within the limits due to the superior ones. But whilst the skeptic destroys gross superstitions, let him spare to deface, as some of the French writers have defaced, the eternal truths charactered upon the imaginations of men. Whilst the mechanist abridges, and the political economist combines labor, let them beware that their speculations, for want of correspondence with those first principles which belong to the imagination, do not tend, as they have in modern England, to exasperate at once the extremes of luxury and of want. They have exemplified the saying, "To him that hath, more shall be given; and from him that hath not, the little that he hath shall be taken away." The rich have become richer, and the poor have become poorer; and the vessel of the state is driven between the Scylla and Charybdis of anarchy and despotism. Such are the effects which must ever flow from an unmitigated exercise of the calculating faculty.

It is difficult to define pleasure in its highest sense; the definition involving a number of apparent paradoxes. For, from an inexplicable defect of harmony in the constitution of human nature, the pain of the inferior is frequently connected with the pleasures of the superior portions of our being. Sorrow, terror, anguish, despair itself, are often the chosen expressions of an approximation to the highest good. Our sympathy in tragic fiction depends on this principle; tragedy delights by affording a shadow of the pleasure which exists in pain. This is the source also of the melancholy which is inseparable from the sweetest melody. The pleasure that is in sorrow is sweeter than the pleasure of pleasure itself. And hence the saying, "It is better to go to the house of mourning, than to the house of mirth."[42] Not that this highest species of pleasure is necessarily linked with pain. The delight of love and friendship, the ecstasy of the admiration of nature, the joy of the perception and still more of the creation of poetry, is often wholly unalloyed.

The production and assurance of pleasure in this highest sense is true utility. Those who produce and preserve this pleasure are poets or poetical philosophers.

The exertions of Locke, Hume, Gibbon, Voltaire, Rousseau,[43] and their disciples, in favor of oppressed and deluded humanity, are entitled to the gratitude of mankind. Yet it is easy to calculate the degree of moral and intellectual improvement which the world would have exhibited, had they never lived. A little more nonsense would have been talked for a century or two; and perhaps a few more men, women, and children, burn as heretics. We might not at this moment have been congratulating each other on the abolition of the Inquisition in Spain. But it exceeds all imagination to conceive what would have been the moral condition of the world if neither Dante, Petrarch, Boccaccio, Chaucer, Shakespeare, Calderon, Lord Bacon, nor Milton, had ever existed; if Raphael and Michelangelo[44] had never been born; if the Hebrew poetry had never been translated; if a revival of the study of Greek literature had never taken place; if no monuments of ancient sculpture had been handed down to us; and if the poetry of the religion of the ancient world had been extinguished together with its belief.

---

[41]Boccaccio (above, page 157).

[42]Suggests Eccles. 7.2.

[43]Locke (above, page 281); Hume (above, page 322); Edward Gibbon (1737–1794), English historian; Francois Marie Arouet de Voltaire (1694–1778), French philosopher.

[44]Geoffrey Chaucer (c. 1340–1400), English poet; Raphael Santi (1483–1520) and Michelangelo Buonaroti (1475–1564), Italian painters.

The human mind could never, except by the intervention of these excitements, have been awakened to the invention of the grosser sciences, and that application of analytical reasoning to the aberrations of society, which it is now attempted to exalt over the direct expression of the inventive and creative faculty itself.

We have more moral, political and historical wisdom, than we know how to reduce into practice; we have more scientific and economical knowledge than can be accommodated to the just distribution of the produce which it multiplies. The poetry in these systems of thought, is concealed by the accumulation of facts and calculating processes. There is no want of knowledge respecting what is wisest and best in morals, government, and political economy, or at least what is wiser and better than what men now practice and endure. But we let *"I dare not* wait upon *I would,* like the poor cat in the adage."[45] We want the creative faculty to imagine that which we know; we want the generous impulse to act that which we imagine; we want the poetry of life: our calculations have outrun conception; we have eaten more than we can digest. The cultivation of those sciences which have enlarged the limits of the empire of man over the external world, has, for want of the poetical faculty, proportionally circumscribed those of the internal world; and man, having enslaved the elements, remains himself a slave. To what but a cultivation of the mechanical arts in a degree disproportioned to the presence of the creative faculty, which is the basis of all knowledge, is to be attributed the abuse of all invention for abridging and combining labor, to the exasperation of the inequality of mankind? From what other cause has it arisen that the discoveries which should have lightened, have added a weight to the curse imposed on Adam? Poetry and the principle of self of which money is the visible incarnation, are the God and Mammon of the world.

The functions of the poetical faculty are twofold; by one it creates new materials of knowledge and power and pleasure; by the other it engenders in the mind a desire to reproduce and arrange them according to a certain rhythm and order which may be called the beautiful and the good. The cultivation of poetry is never more to be desired than at periods when, from an excess of the selfish and calculating principle, the accumulation of the materials of external life exceed the quantity of the power of assimilating them to the internal laws of human nature. The body has then become too unwieldy for that which animates it.

Poetry is indeed something divine. It is at once the center and circumference of knowledge; it is that which comprehends all science, and that to which all science must be referred. It is at the same time the root and blossom of all other systems of thought; it is that from which all spring, and that which adorns all; and that which, if blighted, denies the fruit and the seed, and withholds from the barren world the nourishment and the succession of the scions of the tree of life. It is the perfect and consummate surface and bloom of all things; it is as the odor and the color of the rose to the texture of the elements which compose it, as the form and splendor of unfaded beauty to the secrets of anatomy and corruption. What were virtue, love, patriotism, friendship—what were the scenery of this beautiful universe which we inhabit; what were our consolations on this side of the grave—and what were our aspirations beyond it, if poetry did not ascend to bring light and fire from those eternal regions where the owl-winged faculty of calculation dare not ever soar? Poetry is not like reasoning, a power to be exerted according to the determination of the will. A man cannot say, "I will compose poetry." The greatest poet even cannot say it; for the mind in creation is as a fading coal, which some invisible influence, like an inconstant wind, awakens to transitory brightness; this power arises from within, like the color of a flower which fades and changes as it is developed, and the conscious portions of our natures are unprophetic either of its approach or its departure. Could this influence be durable in its original purity and force, it is impossible to predict the greatness of the results; but when composition begins, inspiration is already on the decline, and the most glorious poetry that has ever been communicated to the world is probably a feeble shadow of the original conceptions of the poet.[46] I appeal to the greatest poets of the present day, whether it is not an error to assert that the finest passages of poetry are produced by labor and study. The toil and the delay recommended by critics, can be justly interpreted to mean no more than a careful observation of the inspired moments, and an artificial connection of the spaces between their suggestions, by the intertexture of conventional expressions; a necessity only imposed by the limitedness of the poetical faculty itself; for Milton conceived the *Paradise Lost* as a whole before he executed it in portions. We have his own authority also for the Muse having "dictated" to him the "unpremeditated song."[47] And let this be an answer to those who would allege the fifty-six various readings of the first line of the *Orlando Furioso.*[48] Compositions so produced are to poetry what mosaic is to painting. This instinct and intuition of the poetical faculty is still more

---

[45] Shakespeare, *Macbeth* I, vii, 44–45.

[46] For Shelley, in contrast to Blake (above, page 448), the conception is not in the execution but prior to its always lesser approximation.

[47] *Paradise Lost* IX, 23–24.

[48] By Ariosto.

observable in the plastic and pictorial arts; a great statue or picture grows under the power of the artist as a child in the mother's womb; and the very mind which directs the hands in formation is incapable of accounting to itself for the origin, the gradations, or the media of the process.

Poetry is the record of the best and happiest moments of the happiest and best minds. We are aware of evanescent visitations of thought and feeling, sometimes associated with place or person, sometimes regarding our own mind alone, and always arising unforeseen and departing unbidden, but elevating and delightful beyond all expression: so that even in the desire and regret they leave, there cannot but be pleasure, participating as it does in the nature of its object. It is as it were the interpenetration of a diviner nature through our own; but its footsteps are like those of a wind over the sea, which the morning calm erases, and whose traces remain only, as on the wrinkled sand which paves it. These and corresponding conditions of being are experienced principally by those of the most delicate sensibility and the most enlarged imagination; and the state of mind produced by them is at war with every base desire. The enthusiasm of virtue, love, patriotism, and friendship, is essentially linked with such emotions; and whilst they last, self appears as what it is, an atom to a universe. Poets are not only subject to these experiences as spirits of the most refined organization, but they can color all that they combine with the evanescent hues of this ethereal world; a word, a trait in the representation of a scene or a passion, will touch the enchanted chord, and reanimate, in those who have ever experienced these emotions, the sleeping, the cold, the buried image of the past. Poetry thus makes immortal all that is best and most beautiful in the world; it arrests the vanishing apparitions which haunt the interlunations of life, and veiling them, or in language or in form, sends them forth among mankind, bearing sweet news of kindred joy to those with whom their sisters abide—abide, because there is no portal of expression from the caverns of the spirit which they inhabit into the universe of things. Poetry redeems from decay the visitations of the divinity in man.

Poetry turns all things to loveliness; it exalts the beauty of that which is most beautiful, and it adds beauty to that which is most deformed; it marries exultation and horror, grief and pleasure, eternity and change; it subdues to union under its light yoke, all irreconcilable things. It transmutes all that it touches, and every form moving within the radiance of its presence is changed by wondrous sympathy to an incarnation of the spirit which it breathes: its secret alchemy turns to potable gold the poisonous waters which flow from death through life; it strips the evil of familiarity from the world, and lays bare the naked and sleeping beauty, which is the spirit of its forms.

All things exist as they are perceived; at least in relation to the percipient. "The mind is its own place, and of itself can make a heaven of hell, a hell of heaven."[49] But poetry defeats the curse which binds us to be subjected to the accident of surrounding impressions. And whether it spreads its own figured curtain, or withdraws life's dark veil from before the scene of things, it equally creates for us a being within our being. It makes us the inhabitants of a world to which the familiar world is a chaos. It reproduces the common universe of which we are portions and percipients, and it purges from our inward sight the film of familiarity which obscures from us the wonder of our being. It compels us to feel that which we perceive, and to imagine that which we know. It creates anew the universe, after it has been annihilated in our minds by the recurrence of impressions blunted by reiteration. It justifies the bold and true words of Tasso: *"Non merita nome di creatore, se non Iddio ed il poeta."*[50]

A poet, as he is the author to others of the highest wisdom, pleasure, virtue and glory, so he ought personally to be the happiest, the best, the wisest, and the most illustrious of men. As to his glory, let time be challenged to declare whether the fame of any other institutor of human life be comparable to that of a poet. That he is the wisest, the happiest, and the best, inasmuch as he is a poet, is equally incontrovertible: the greatest poets have been men of the most spotless virtue, of the most consummate prudence, and, if we would look into the interior of their lives, the most fortunate of men: and the exceptions, as they regard those who possessed the poetic faculty in a high yet inferior degree, will be found on consideration to confine rather than destroy the rule. Let us for a moment stoop to the arbitration of popular breath, and usurping and uniting in our own persons the incompatible characters of accuser, witness, judge, and executioner, let us decide without trial, testimony, or form, that certain motives of those who are "there sitting where we dare not soar,"[51] are reprehensible. Let us assume that Homer was a drunkard, that Virgil was a flatterer, that Horace was a coward, that Tasso was a madman, that Lord Bacon was a peculator, that Raphael was a libertine, that Spenser was a poet laureate. It is inconsistent with this division of our subject to cite living poets, but posterity has done ample justice to the great names now referred to. Their errors have been weighed and found to have been dust in the balance; if their sins "were as scarlet, they are now white as

---

[49] *Paradise Lost* I, 254–55.
[50] "No one deserves the name of creator except God and the poet." *Discourses on the Heroic Poem,* but misquoted.
[51] *Paradise Lost* IV, 829.

snow":[52] they have been washed in the blood of the mediator and redeemer, time. Observe in what a ludicrous chaos the imputations of real or fictitious crime have been confused in the contemporary calumnies against poetry and poets; consider how little is as it appears—or appears, as it is; look to your own motives, and judge not, lest ye be judged.

Poetry, as has been said, differs in this respect from logic, that it is not subject to the control of the active powers of the mind, and that its birth and recurrence have no necessary connection with the consciousness or will. It is presumptuous to determine that these are the necessary conditions of all mental causation, when mental effects are experienced insusceptible of being referred to them. The frequent recurrence of the poetical power, it is obvious to suppose, may produce in the mind a habit of order and harmony correlative with its own nature and with its effects upon other minds. But in the intervals of inspiration, and they may be frequent without being durable, a poet becomes a man, and is abandoned to the sudden reflex of the influences under which others habitually live. But as he is more delicately organized than other men, and sensible to pain and pleasure, both his own and that of others, in a degree unknown to them, he will avoid the one and pursue the other with an ardor proportioned to this difference. And he renders himself obnoxious to calumny, when he neglects to observe the circumstances under which these objects of universal pursuit and flight have disguised themselves in one another's garments.

But there is nothing necessarily evil in this error, and thus cruelty, envy, revenge, avarice, and the passions purely evil, have never formed any portion of the popular imputations on the lives of poets.

I have thought it most favorable to the cause of truth to set down these remarks according to the order in which they were suggested to my mind, by a consideration of the subject itself, instead of observing the formality of a polemical reply; but if the view which they contain be just, they will be found to involve a refutation of the arguers against poetry, so far at least as regards the first division of the subject. I can readily conjecture what should have moved the gall of some learned and intelligent writers who quarrel with certain versifiers; I, like them, confess myself unwilling to be stunned by the Theseids of the hoarse Codri of the day. Bavius and Maevius[53] undoubtedly are, as they ever were, insuf-

ferable persons. But it belongs to a philosophical critic to distinguish rather than confound.

The first part of these remarks has related to poetry in its elements and principles; and it has been shown, as well as the narrow limits assigned them would permit, that what is called poetry in a restricted sense, has a common source with all other forms of order and of beauty, according to which the materials of human life are susceptible of being arranged, and which is poetry in a universal sense.

The second part[54] will have for its object an application of these principles to the present state of the cultivation of poetry, and a defense of the attempt to idealize the modern forms of manners and opinions, and compel them into a subordination to the imaginative and creative faculty. For the literature of England, an energetic development of which has ever preceded or accompanied a great and free development of the national will, has arisen as it were from a new birth. In spite of the low-thoughted envy which would undervalue contemporary merit, our own will be a memorable age in intellectual achievements, and we live among such philosophers and poets as surpass beyond comparison any who have appeared since the last national struggle for civil and religious liberty. The most unfailing herald, companion, and follower of the awakening of a great people to work a beneficial change in opinion or institution, is poetry. At such periods there is an accumulation of the power of communicating and receiving intense and impassioned conceptions respecting man and nature. The persons in whom this power resides may often, as far as regards many portions of their nature, have little apparent correspondence with that spirit of good of which they are the ministers. But even whilst they deny and abjure they are yet compelled to serve, the power which is seated on the throne of their own soul. It is impossible to read the compositions of the most celebrated writers of the present day without being startled with the electric life which burns within their words. They measure the circumference and sound the depths of human nature with a comprehensive and all-penetrating spirit, and they are themselves perhaps the most sincerely astonished at its manifestations; for it is less their spirit than the spirit of the age. Poets are the hierophants of an unapprehended inspiration; the mirrors of the gigantic shadows which futurity casts upon the present; the words which express what they understand not; the trumpets which sing to battle, and feel not what they inspire; the influence which is moved not, but moves. Poets are the unacknowledged legislators of the world.

---

[52] Suggests Isa. 1.18.
[53] Theseids: Poems on the exploits of Theseus. Codri: Poets who are like a badly thought of poet who is supposed to have written a tragedy about Theseus, but it is likely that he never actually existed. Bavius and Mavius were poetasters who attacked the poetry of their contemporaries Horace and Virgil.

[54] Never written.

Georg Wilhelm Friedrich Hegel

1770–1831

Hegel's aesthetic forms an integral part of his organic philosophy. The idea of the absolute or spirit is the all-inclusive infinite whole, an organic unity in which every part is dependent on and definable in terms of every other part and of the whole itself. Man is part of this whole, and a concrete definition of man must be made in its terms. Crucial to this philosophical scheme is Hegel's conception of dialectic, elaborated in his *Phenomenology of Mind*, tracing the moments of progression from subject (Spirit) to substance. In Hegel's treatment, dialectic proceeds, thesis to antithesis to synthesis, by the process of *sublation* (*auf heben*) in which each thesis is cancelled, lifted up, and preserved, from pure subjectivity to the "absolute standpoint" of spirit as substance.

In the selection below from *The Philosophy of Fine Art,* Hegel insists that art must be treated not in terms of its use "as a mere pastime in the service of pleasure and entertainment" or in terms of any other ulterior purpose; instead it must be considered a mode, like religion and philosophy, through which the idea is made available to consciousness. It is one of the modes by which absolute spirit comes to consciousness of itself. Art presents its matter in sensuous forms. The beautiful in art is the idea carried into concrete form. There are fundamentally three kinds of art—symbolic, classical, and romantic. Hegel explains the first two with more clarity than he does the third. By "symbolic" art Hegel means something very much like what many Romantic critics call allegory. It is an art in which objects represented are made to have arbitrary meanings. In "classical" art there is a much more appropriate relationship between idea and embodiment. For example, the human form in classical art is, according to Hegel, a natural shape appropriate to a representation of the mind. In classical art form and content are merged.

"Romantic art" makes the "inward life of reason . . . the medium and determinate existence of its content." This kind of art transcends itself, so to speak, and canons of appropriateness invoked with respect to symbolic and classical art are cast aside. Art becomes its own domain, the release of Spirit into art itself, not merely into objects represented in art.

Hegel goes on to associate architecture with symbolic art and sculpture with classical art. Romantic art is realized by painting, music, and poetry in ascending order of freedom. In this series of definitions, one observes Hegel making his judgments on the basis of the distance each art is able to traverse in escape from matter, mass, and spatialization. In these terms, painting is more ideal than sculpture, which is more ideal than architecture. Music is more ideal than painting, for in music objects are not represented and a temporal order alone exists. The medium of poetry—words—is most free. Its sensuousness is created by the mind, not by the materials of the art.

In the later parts of his work Hegel considers various sorts of poetry and develops a theory of tragedy. Despite the attention he lavishes on art, however, he does not consider it the highest manifestation of the Idea. It is limited by its media and finally proves less satisfactory to man than religion or philosophy. For many recent critics and theorists, interest in Hegel has centered more on his *Phenomenology* than his aesthetic theory, as the expression of a totalizing system that in seeking a "universal standpoint" becomes particularly problematic in the practical domain of social and intellectual life. Included here is a crucial chapter, "Lordship and Bondage," from the *Phenomenology*.

Hegel's *The Philosophy of Fine Art* has been translated in four volumes by F. P. B. Osmaston (1920). See also *The Introduction to Hegel's Philosophy of Fine Art,* translated by Bernard Bosanquet (1886), also translated by T. M. Knox (1975). Bosanquet's translation was reprinted and edited by Michael Inwood (1993). See A. C. Bradley, "Hegel's Theory of Tragedy" in his *Oxford Lectures on Poetry* (1910); W. T. Stace, *The Philosophy of Hegel* (1924); Israel Knox, *The Aesthetic Theories of Kant, Hegel, and Schopenhauer* (1936); Jack Kaminsky, *Hegel on Art: An Interpretation of Hegel's Aesthetics* (1962); Alexandre Kojeve, *Introduction to the Reading of Hegel* (tr. 1969); Jean Hippolyte, *Genesis and Structure of Hegel's Phenomenology of Spirit* (tr. 1974); Stephen Bungay, *Beauty and Truth: A Study of Hegel's Aesthetics* (1984); Robert Wicks, *Hegel's Theory of Aesthetic Judgment* (1994); Paul Redding, *Hegel's Hermeneutics* (1996); William Meker, ed., *Hegel and Aesthetics* (2000); Allen Speight, *Hegel, Literature, and the Problem of Agency* (2001).

The Philosophy of Fine Art
from
Introduction

First, as to the worthiness of art to form the object of scientific inquiry, it is no doubt the case that art can be utilized as a mere pastime in the service of pleasure and entertainment, either in the embellishment of our surroundings, the imprinting of a delight-giving surface to the external conditions of life, or the emphasis placed by decoration on other objects. In these respects it is unquestionably no independent or free art, but an art subservient to certain objects. The kind of art, however, which we ourselves propose to examine is one which is free in its aim and its means. That art in general can serve other objects, and even be merely a pastime, is a relation which it possesses in common with thought itself. From one point of view thought likewise, as science subservient to other ends, can be used in just the same way for finite purposes and means as they chance to crop up, and as such serviceable faculty of science is not self-determined, but determined by something alien to it. But, further, as distinct from such subservience to particular objects, science is raised of its own essential resources in free independence to truth, and exclusively united with its own aims in discovering the true fulfillment in that truth.

Fine art is not art in the true sense of the term until it is also thus free, and its highest function is only then satisfied when it has established itself in a sphere which it shares with religion and philosophy, becoming thereby merely one mode and form through which the divine, the profoundest interests of mankind, and spiritual truths of widest range, are brought home to consciousness and expressed. It is in works of art that nations have deposited the richest intuitions and ideas they possess; and not infrequently fine art supplies a key of interpretation to the wisdom and religion of peoples; in the case of many it is the only one.[1]

The manuscript notes for Hegel's lectures on aesthetics were posthumously published in 1835. The lectures were first given in 1820, and revised in 1823, 1826, and 1829. The text is from *The Philosophy of Fine Art* by Georg Wilhelm Friedrich Hegel, translated by F. P. B. Osmaston (1920).

---

[1]Hegel goes on to elaborate the parallel between art, philosophy, and religion as ideally penetration into the profundity of a supersensuous world.

* * *

It has already been stated that the content of art is the idea, and the form of its display the configuration of the sensuous or plastic image. It is further the function of art to mediate these two aspects under the reconciled mode of free totality. The first determinant implied by this is the demand that the content, which has to secure artistic representation, shall disclose an essential capacity for such display. If this is not so all that we possess is a defective combination. A content that, independently, is ill adapted to plastic form and external presentment is compelled to accept this form, or a matter that is of itself prosaic in its character is driven to make the best it can of a mode of presentation which is antagonistic to its nature.

The second requirement, which is deducible from the first, is the demand that the content of art should be nothing essentially abstract. This does not mean, however, that it should be merely concrete in the sense that the sensuous object is such in its contrast to all that is spiritual and the content of thought, regarding these as the essentially simple and abstract. Everything that possesses truth for spirit, no less than as part of nature, is essentially concrete, and, despite its universality, possesses both ideality[2] and particularity essentially within it. When we state, for example, of God that he is simply One, the Supreme Being as such, we have thereby merely given utterance to a lifeless abstraction of the irrational understanding. Such a God, as he is thus not conceived in his concrete truth, can supply no content for art, least of all plastic art. Consequently neither the Jews nor the Turks have been able to represent their God, who is not even an abstraction of the understanding in the above sense, under the positive mode in which Christians have represented him. For in Christianity God is conceived in his truth, and as such essentially concrete, as personality, as the subjective focus of conscious life or, more accurately defined, as spirit.

* * *

Inasmuch, however, as it is the function of art to represent the idea to immediate vision in sensuous shape and not in the form of thought and pure spirituality in the strict sense, and inasmuch as the value and intrinsic worth of this presentment consists in the correspondence and unity of the two aspects, that is the idea and its sensuous shape, the supreme level and excellence of art and the reality, which is truly consonant with its notion, will depend upon the degree of intimacy and union with which idea and configuration

appear together in elaborated fusion. The higher truth consequently is spiritual content which has received the shape adequate to the conception of its essence; and this it is which supplies the principle of division for the philosophy of art. For before the mind can attain to the true notion of its absolute essence; it is constrained to traverse a series of stages rooted in this very notional concept; and to this course of stages which it unfolds to itself, corresponds a coalescent series, immediately related therewith, of the plastic types of art, under the configuration whereof mind as art spirit presents to itself the consciousness of itself.[3]

This evolution within the art spirit has further itself two sides in virtue of its intrinsic nature. First, that is to say, the development is itself a spiritual and universal one; in other words there are the definite and comprehensive views of the world[4] in their series of gradations which give artistic embodiment to the specific but widely embracing consciousness of nature, man, and God. Secondly, this ideal or universal art development has to provide for itself immediate existence and sensuous configuration, and the definite modes of this art actualization in the sensuous medium are themselves a totality of necessary distinctions in the realm of art—that is to say, they are the particular types of art. No doubt the types of artistic configuration on the one hand are, in respect to their spirituality, of a general character, and not restricted to any one material, and the sensuous existence is similarly itself of varied multiplicity of medium. Inasmuch, however, as this material potentially possesses, precisely as the mind or spirit does, the idea for its inward soul or significance, it follows that a definite sensuous involves with itself a closer relation and secret bond of association with the spiritual distinctions and specific types of artistic embodiment.[5]

Relatively to these points of view our philosophy will be divided into three fundamental parts.

First, we have a general part. It has for its content and object the universal idea of fine art, conceived here as the

[2][Osmaston] *Subjectivität,* that is, the ideality of consciousness or thought.

[3][Osmaston] That is to say, presents itself to conscious grasp of itself as such art spirit (*als künstlerischer*).
[4][Osmaston] The two evolutions here alluded to are (1) that of a particular way of regarding nature, man, and God in a particular age and nation such as the Egyptian, Greek, and Christian viewed in express relation to art; (2) the several arts—sculpture, music, poetry, and so forth each on their own foundation and viewed relatively to the former evolution.
[5][Osmaston] The point, of course, is that the different media of the several arts are inherently, and in virtue of the fact that we have not here mere matter as opposed to that which is intellectual rather than sensuous, but matter in which the notional concept is already essentially present or pregnant (sound is, for instance, more ideal than the spatial matter of architecture), adapted to the particular arts in which they serve as the medium of expression.

ideal, together with the more elaborated relation under which it is placed respectively to nature and human artistic production.

Secondly, we have evolved from the notional concept of the beauty of art a particular part, insofar as the essential distinctions, which this idea contains in itself, are unfolded in a graduated series of particular modes of configuration.

Thirdly, there results a final part which has to consider the particularized content of fine art itself. It consists in the advance of art to the sensuous realization of its shapes and its consummation in a system of the several arts and their genera and species.

2. In respect to the first and second of these divisions it is important to recollect, in order to make all that follows intelligible, that the idea, viewed as the beautiful in art, is not the idea in the strict sense, that is as a metaphysical logic apprehends it as the absolute. It is rather the idea as carried into concrete form in the direction of express realization, and as having entered into immediate and adequate unity with such reality. For the idea as such, although it is both potentially and explicitly true, is only truth in its universality and not as yet presented in objective embodiment.

* * *

3. But inasmuch as in this way the idea is concrete unity, this unity can only enter the artistic consciousness by the expansion and further mediation of the particular aspects of the idea; and it is through this evolution that the beauty of art receives a totality of particular stages and forms. Therefore, after we have considered fine art in its essence and on its own account, we must see how the beautiful in its entirety breaks up into particular determinations. This gives, as our second part, the doctrine of the types of art. The origin of these types is to be found in the varied ways under which the idea is conceived as the content of art; it is by this means that a distinction in the mode of form under which it manifests itself is conditioned. These types are therefore simply the different modes of relation which obtain between the idea and its configuration, relations which emanate from the idea itself, and thereby present us with the general basis of division for this sphere. For the principle of division must always be found in the notional concept, the particularization and division of which it is.

We have here to consider three relations of the idea to its external process of configuration.

a. First, the origin of artistic creation proceeds from the idea when, being itself still involved in defective definition and obscurity, or in vicious and untrue determinacy, it becomes embodied in the shapes of art. As indeterminate it does not as yet possess in itself that individuality which the

ideal demands. Its abstract character and one-sidedness leaves its objective presentment still defective and contingent. Consequently this first type of art is rather a mere search after plastic configuration than a power of genuine representation. The idea has not as yet found the formative principle within itself, and therefore still continues to be the mere effort and strain to find it. We may in general terms describe this form as the *symbolic* type of art. The abstract idea possesses in it its external shape outside itself in the purely material substance of nature, from which the shaping process proceeds, and to which in its expression it is entirely yoked. Natural objects are thus in the first instance left just as they are, while, at the same time the substantive idea is imposed upon them as their significance, so that their function is henceforth to express the same, and they claim to be interpreted, as though the idea itself was present in them. A rationale of this is to be found in the fact that the external objects of reality do essentially possess an aspect in which they are qualified to express a universal import. But as a completely adequate coalescence is not yet possible, all that can be the outcome of such a relation is an abstract attribute, as when a lion is understood to symbolize strength.

On the other hand this abstractness of the relation makes present to consciousness no less markedly how the idea stands relatively to natural phenomena as an alien; and albeit it expatiates in all these shapes, having no other means of expression among all that is real, and seeks after itself in their unrest and defects of genuine proportion, yet for all that it finds them inadequate to meet its needs. It consequently exaggerates natural shapes and the phenomena of nature in every degree of indefinite and limitless extension; it flounders about in them like a drunkard, and seethes and ferments, doing violence to their truth with the distorted growth of unnatural shapes, and strives vainly by the contrast, hugeness, and splendor of the forms accepted to exalt the phenomena to the plain of the idea. For the idea is here still more or less indeterminate, and unadaptable, while the objects of nature are wholly definite in their shape.

Hence, on account of the incompatibility of the two sides of ideality and objective form to one another, the relation of the idea to the other becomes a negative one. The former, being in its nature ideal, is unsatisfied with such an embodiment, and posits itself as its inward or ideally universal substance under a relation of sublimity over and above all this inadequate superfluity of natural form. In virtue of this sublimity the natural phenomena, of course, and the human form and event are accepted and left simply as they are, but at the same time, recognized as unequal to their significance, which is exalted far above all earthly content.

These features constitute in general terms the character of the primitive artistic pantheism of the East, which, on the one hand, charges the meanest objects with the significance of the absolute idea, or, on the other, compels natural form, by doing violence to its structure, to express its world ideas. And, in consequence, it becomes bizarre, grotesque, and deficient in taste, or turns the infinite but abstract freedom of the substantive idea contemptuously against all phenomenal existence as alike nugatory and evanescent. By such means the significance cannot be completely presented in the expression, and despite all straining and endeavor the final inadequacy of plastic configuration to idea remains insuperable. Such may be accepted as the first type of art—symbolic art with its yearning, its fermentation, its mystery, and sublimity.

b. In the second type of art, which we propose to call *classical,* the twofold defect of symbolic art is annulled. Now the symbolic configuration is imperfect, because, first, the idea here only enters into consciousness in abstract determinacy or indeterminateness: and, secondly, by reason of the fact that the coalescence of import with embodiment can only throughout remain defective, and in its turn also wholly abstract. The classical art type solves both these difficulties. It is, in fact, the free and adequate embodiment of the idea in the shape which, according to its notional concept, is uniquely appropriate to the idea itself. The idea is consequently able to unite in free and completely assonant concord with it. For this reason the classical type of art is the first to present us with the creation and vision of the complete ideal, and to establish the same as realized fact.

The conformability, however, of notion and reality in the classical type ought not to be taken in the purely formal sense of the coalescence of a content with its external form, any more than this was possible in the case of the ideal. Otherwise every copy from nature, and every kind of portrait, every landscape, flower, scene, and so forth, which form the aim of the presentment, would at once become classical in virtue of the fact of the agreement it offers between such content and form. In classical art, on the contrary, the characteristic feature of the content consists in this, that it is itself concrete idea, and as such the concrete spiritual; for it is only that which pertains to spirit which is veritable ideality.[6] To secure such a content we must find out that in nature which on its own account is that which is essentially and explicitly appropriate to the spiritual. It must be the original notion itself,[7] which has invented the form for concrete spir-

ituality, and now the subjective notion—in the present case the spirit of art—has merely discovered it, and made it, as an existence possessed of natural shape, concordant with free and individual spirituality. Such a configuration, which the idea essentially possesses as spiritual, and indeed as individually determinate spirituality, when it must perforce appear as a temporal phenomenon, is the human form. Personification and anthropomorphism have frequently been abused as a degradation of the spiritual. But art, insofar as its function is to bring to vision the spiritual in sensuous guise, must advance to such anthropomorphism, inasmuch as spirit is only adequately presented to perception in its bodily presence. The transmigration of souls in this respect an abstract conception,[8] and physiology ought to make it one of its fundamental principles, that life has necessarily, in the course of its evolution, to proceed to the human form, for the reason that it is alone the visible phenomenon adequate to the expression of intelligence.

The human bodily form, then, is employed in the classical type of art not as purely sensuous existence, but exclusively as the existence and natural shape appropriate to mind. It has therefore to be relieved of all the defective excrescences which adhere to it in its purely physical aspect, and from the contingent finiteness of its phenomenal appearance. The external shape must in this way be purified in order to express in itself the content adequate for such a purpose; and, furthermore, along with this, that the coalescence of import and embodiment may be complete, the spirituality which constitutes the content must be of such a character that is it completely able to express itself in the natural form of man, without projecting beyond the limits of such expression within the sensuous and purely physical sphere of existence. Under such a condition spirit is at the same time defined as particular, the spirit or mind of man, not as simply absolute and eternal. In this latter case it is only capable of asserting and expressing itself as intellectual being.[9]

Out of this latter distinction arises, in its turn, the defect which brings about the dissolution of the classical type of art, and makes the demand for a third and higher form, namely the *romantic* type.

c. The romantic type of art annuls the completed union of the idea and its reality, and occurs, if on a higher plane, to the difference and opposition of both sides, which remained unovercome in symbolic art. The classical type of

---

[6][Osmaston] *Das wahrhaft Innere.* That is, the inward of the truth of conscious life.

[7][Osmaston] Means apparently the notion in its absolute sense.

[8][Osmaston] Because it represents spirit as independent of an appropriate bodily form.

[9][Osmaston] What appears to be denoted by *Geistigkeit* is the generic term of intelligence—that activity of conscious life which does not necessarily make us think of a single individual—the common nature of all spirit.

art no doubt attained the highest excellence of which the sensuous embodiment of art is capable. The defect, such as it is, is due to the effect which obtains in art itself throughout, the limitations of its entire province, that is to say. The limitation consists in this, that art in general and, agreeably to its fundamental idea, accepts for its object spirit, the notion of which is infinite concrete universality, under the guise of sensuously concrete form. In the classical type it sets up the perfected coalescence of spiritual and sensuous existence as adequate conformation of both. As a matter of fact, however, in this fusion mind itself is not represented agreeably to its true notional concept. Mind is the infinite subjectivity of the idea, which as absolute inwardness,[10] is not capable of freely expanding in its entire independence, so long as it remains within the mold of the bodily shape, fused therein as in the existence wholly congenial to it.

To escape from such a condition the romantic type of art once more cancels that inseparable unity of the classical type, by securing a content which passes beyond the classical stage and its mode of expression. This content, if we may recall familiar ideas—is coincident with what Christianity affirms to be true of God as spirit, in contrast to the Greek faith in gods which forms the essential and most fitting content of classical art. In Greek art the concrete ideal substance is potentially, but not as fully realized, the unity of the human and divine nature; a unity which for the very reason that it is purely immediate and not wholly explicit, is manifested without defect under an immediate and sensuous mode. The Greek god is the object of naive intuition and sensuous imagination. His shape is therefore the bodily form of man. The sphere of his power and his being is individual and individually limited; and in his opposition to the individual person[11] is an essence and a power with whom the inward life of soul[12] is merely potentially in unity, but does not itself possess this unity as inward subjective knowledge. The higher stage is the knowledge of this implied unity, which in its latency the classical art type receives as its content and is able to perfectly represent in bodily shape. This elevation of mere potentiality into self-conscious knowledge constitutes an enormous difference. It is nothing less than the infinite difference which, for example, separates man generally from the animal creation. Man is animal; but even in his animal functions he is not restricted within the potential sphere as the animal is, but becomes conscious of them, learns to understand them, and raises them—as, for instance, the process of digestion—into self-conscious science. By this means man dissolves the boundaries of his merely potential immediacy; in virtue of the very fact that he knows himself to be animal he ceases to be merely animal, and as mind is endowed with self-knowledge.

If, then, in this way the unity of the human and divine nature, which in the previous stage was potential, is raised out of this immediate into a self-conscious unity, it follows that the genuine medium for the reality of this content is no longer the sensuous and immediate existence of what is spiritual, that is, the physical body of man, but the self-aware inner life of soul itself. Now it is Christianity—for the reason that it presents to mind God as spirit, and not as the particular individual spirit, but as absolute in spirit and in truth—which steps back from the sensuousness of imagination into the inward life of reason, and makes this rather than bodily form the medium and determinate existence of its content. So also, the unity of the human and divine nature is a conscious unity exclusively capable of realization by means of spiritual knowledge, and in spirit. The new content secured thereby is consequently not indefeasibly bound up with the sensuous presentation, as the mode completely adequate, but is rather delivered from this immediate existence, which has to be hypostatized as a negative factor, overcome and reflected buck into the spiritual unity. In this way romantic art must be regarded as art transcending itself, albeit within the boundary of its own province, and in the form of art itself.

We may therefore briefly summarize our conclusion that in this third stage the object of art consists in the free and concrete presence of spiritual activity, whose vocation it is to appear as such a presence or activity for the inner world of conscious intelligence. In consonance with such an object art cannot merely work for sensuous perception. It must deliver itself to the inward life, which coalesces with its object simply as though this were none other than itself, in other words, to the intimacy of soul, to the heart, the emotional life, which as the medium of spirit itself essentially strives after freedom and seeks and possesses its reconciliation only in the inner chamber of spirit. It is this inward or ideal world which constitutes the content of the romantic sphere: it will therefore necessarily discover its representation as such inner idea or feeling, and in the show or appearance of the same. The world of the soul and intelligence celebrates its triumph over the external world, and, actually in the medium of that outer world, makes that victory to appear, by reason of which the sensuous appearance sinks into worthlessness.

---

[10][Osmaston] By *Innerlichkeit,* which might also be rendered as pure ideality, what is signified is that in a mental state there are no parts outside of each other.

[11][Osmaston] *Subjectikt,* that is, the individual ego of self-consciousness.

[12][Osmaston] *Das subjektive Innere,* literally, the subjective inner state.

On the other hand, this type of art, like every other, needs an external vehicle of expression. As already stated, the spiritual content has here withdrawn from the external world and its immediate unity into its own world. The sensuous externality of form is consequently accepted and represented, as in the symbolic type, as unessential and transient; furthermore the subjective finite spirit and volition is treated in a similar way; a treatment which even includes the idiosyncrasies or caprice of individuals, character, action, or the particular features of incident and plot. The aspect of external existence is committed to contingency and handed over to the adventurous action of imagination, whose caprice is just as able to reflect the facts given as they are, as it can change the shapes of the external world into a medley of its own invention and distort them to mere caricature. For this external element has no longer its notion and significance in its own essential province, as in classical art. It is now discovered in the emotional realm, and this is manifested in the medium of that realm itself rather than in the external and its form of reality, and is able to secure or to recover again the condition of reconciliation with itself in every accident, in all the chance circumstance that falls into independent shape, in all misfortune and sorrow, nay, in crime itself.

Hence it comes about that the characteristics of symbolic art, its indifference, incompatibility and severance of idea from configurative expression, are here reproduced once more, if with essential difference. And this difference consists in the fact that in romantic art the idea, whose defectiveness, in the case of the symbol, brought with it the defect of external form, has to display itself as spirit and in the medium of soul life as essentially self-complete. And it is to complete fundamentally this higher perfection that it withdraws itself from the external element. It can, in short, seek and consummate its true reality and manifestation nowhere but in its own domain.

This we may take to be in general terms the character of the symbolic, classical, and romantic types of art, which in fact constitute the three relations of the idea to its embodiment in the realm of human art. They consist in the aspiration after, the attainment and transcendency of the ideal, viewed as the true concrete notion of beauty.

* * *

Each general type discovers its determinate character in one determinate external material or medium, in which its adequate presentation is secured under the manner it prescribes. But, from another point of view, these types of art, inasmuch as their definition is nonetheless consistent with the fact of the universality of their typical import, break through the boundaries of their specific realization in some definite art species, and achieve an existence in other arts no less, although their position in such is of subordinate importance. For this reason, albeit the particular arts belong specifically to one of these general art types respectively, the adequate external embodiment whereof they severally constitute, yet this does not prevent them, each after its own mode of external configuration, from representing the totality of these art types.[13] To summarize, then, in this third principal division we are dealing with the beauty of art, as it unveils itself in a world of realized beauty by means of the arts and their creations. The content of this world is the beautiful, and the true beautiful, as we have seen, is spiritual being in concrete form, the ideal; or apprehended with still more intimacy it is the absolute mind and truth itself. This region of divine truth artistically presented to sensuous vision and emotion forms the center of the entire world of art. It is the independent, free and divine image,[14] which has completely appropriated the externality of form and medium, and now wears them simply as the means of its self-manifestation. Inasmuch, however, as the beautiful is unfolded here as objective reality, and in this process is differentiated into particular aspects and phases, this center posits its extremes, as realized in their peculiar actuality, in antithetical relation to itself. Thus one of these extremes consists of an objectivity as yet devoid of mind, which we may call the natural environment of God. Here the external element, when it receives form, remains as it was, and does not possess its spiritual aim and content in itself, but in another.[15] The other extreme is the divine as inward, something known, as the manifold particularized subjective existence of deity. It is the truth as operative and vital in sense, soul, and intelligence of particular persons, which does not persist as poured forth into its mold of external shape, but returns into the inward life of individuals. The divine is under such a mode at once distinguishable from its pure manifestation as Godhead, and passes itself thereby into the variety of particularization which belongs to every kind of particular subjective knowledge, feeling, perception, and emotion. In the analogous province of religion with which art, at its highest elevation, is immediately connected, we conceive the same distinction as follows. First, we imagine the natural life on earth in its finitude as standing on one side; but then, secondly, the human consciousness accepts

---

[13][Osmaston] Thus poetry is primarily a Romantic art, but in the epic it is affiliated with the objective character of classical art, or we may say that there is a romantic and classical type of architecture, though the art is primarily symbolic.

[14][Osmaston] *Gestalt.* "Plastic power" is perhaps a better translation.

[15][Osmaston] He means that in architecture the building is merely a shrine or environment of the image of the god.

God for its object, in which the distinction between objectivity and subjectivity falls away; then, finally, we advance from God as such to the devotion of the community, that is to God as he is alive and present in the subjective consciousness. These three fundamental modifications present themselves in the world of art in independent evolution.

a. The first of the particular arts with which, according to their fundamental principle, we have to start is architecture considered as a fine art. Its function consists in so elaborating the external material of inorganic nature that the same becomes intimately connected with spirit as an artistic and external environment. Its medium is matter itself as an external object, a heavy mass that is subject to mechanical laws; and its forms persist as the forms of inorganic nature coordinated with the relations of the abstract understanding such as symmetry and so forth. In this material and in these forms the ideal is incapable of realization as concrete spirituality, and the reality thus presented remains confronting the idea as an external fabric with which it enters into no fusion, or has only entered so far as to establish an abstract relation. And it is in consequence of this that the fundamental type of the art of building is that of symbolism. Architecture is in fact the first pioneer on the highway toward the adequate realization of Godhead. In this service it is put to severe labor with objective nature, that it may disengage it by its effort from the confused growth of finitude and the distortions of contingency. By this means it levels a space for the God, informs his external environment, and builds him his temple, as a fit place for the concentration of spirit, and its direction to the absolute objects of intelligent life. It raises an enclosure for the congregation of those assembled, as a defense against the threatening of the tempest, against rain, the hurricane, and savage animals. It in short reveals the will thus to assemble, and although under an external relation, yet in agreement with the principles of art. A significance such as this it can to a greater or less extent import into its material and its forms, in proportion as the determinate content of its fabric, which is the object of its operations and effort, is more or less significant, is more concrete or more abstract, more profound in penetrating its own essential depth, or more obscure and superficial. Indeed architecture may in this respect proceed so far in the execution of such a purpose as to create an adequate artistic existence for such an ideal content in its very forms and material. In doing so, however, it has already passed beyond its peculiar province and is diverted into the stage immediately above it of sculpture. For the boundary of sculpture lies precisely in this that it retains the spiritual as an inward being which persists in direct contrast to the external embodiment of architecture. It can consequently merely point to that which is absorbed in soul life as to something external to itself.

b. Nevertheless, as above explained, the external and inorganic world is purified by architecture, it is coordinated under symmetrical laws, and made cognate with mind, and as a result the temple of God, the house of his community, stands before us. Into this temple, in the second place, the God himself enters in the lightning-flash of individuality which smites its way into the inert mass, permeating the same with its presence. In other words the infinite[16] and no longer purely symmetrical form belonging to intelligence brings as it were to a focus and informs the shape in which it is most at home. This is the task of sculpture. Insofar as in it the inward life of spirit, to which the art of architecture can merely point away to, makes its dwelling within the sensuous shape and its external material, and to the extent that these two sides come into plastic communion with one another in such a manner that neither is predominant, sculpture receives as its fundamental type the classical art form.

For this reason the sensuous element on its own account admits of no expression here which is not affected by spiritual affinities,[17] just as, conversely, sculpture can reproduce with completeness no spiritual content, which does not maintain throughout adequate presentation to perception in bodily form. What sculpture, in short, has to do is to make the presence of spirit stand before us in its bodily shape and in immediate union therewith at rest and in blessedness; and this form has to be made vital by means of the content of spiritual individuality. The external sensuous material is consequently no longer elaborated either in conformity with its mechanical quality alone, as a mass of weight, nor in shapes of the inorganic world simply, nor in entire indifference to color, etc. It is carried into the ideal forms of the human figure, and, we may add, in the completeness of all three spatial dimensions. In other words and relatively to such a process we must maintain for sculpture that in it the inward or ideal content of spirit are first revealed in their eternal repose and essential self-stability. To such repose and unity with itself there can only correspond that external shape which itself persists in such unity and repose. And this condition is satisfied by configuration viewed in its abstract spatiality.[18] The spirit which sculpture represents is that which is essentially sound, not broken up in the play of chance conceits and passions; and for this reason its exter-

---

[16] [Osmaston] Infinite, of course, in the concrete sense of rounded in itself, as the circle, or, still more, the living organism.

[17] [Osmaston] Literally, "which is not also that of the spiritual sphere."

[18] [Osmaston] That is, an object limited only in space.

nal form also is not dissolved in the manifold variety of appearance, but exhibits itself under this one presentment only as the abstraction of space in the totality of its dimensions.

Assuming, then, that the art of architecture has executed its temple, and the hand of sculpture has placed therein the image of the god, we have in the third place to assume the community of the faithful as confronting the god thus presented to vision in the wide chambers of his dwelling place. Now this community is the spiritual reflection into its own world of that sensuous presence, the subjective and inward animating life of soul, in its union with which both for the artistic content and the external material which manifests it, the determining principle may be identified with particularization in varied shapes and qualities, individualization and the life of soul[19] which they imply. The downright and solid fact of unity the god possesses in sculpture breaks up into the multiplicity of a world of particular souls,[20] whose union is no longer sensuous but wholly ideal.

Here for the first time God himself is revealed as veritably spirit—viz., the spirit revealed in his community. Here at last he is seen apprehended as this moving to and fro, as this alternation between his own essential unity and his realization in the knowledge of individual persons and that separation which it involves, as also in the universal spiritual being[21] and union of the many. In such a community God is disengaged from the abstraction of his unfolded self-seclusion and self-identity, no less than from the immediate absorption in bodily shape, in which he is presented by sculpture. He is, in a word, lifted into the actual sphere of spiritual existence and knowledge, into the reflected appearance, whose manifestation is essentially inward and the life of heart and soul. Thereby the higher content is now the nature of spirit, and that in its ultimate or absolute shape. But at the same time the separation to which we have alluded displays this as particular spiritual being, a specific emotional life. Moreover, for the reason that the main thing here is not the untroubled repose of the God in himself,[22] but his manifestation simply, the Being which is for another, self-revealment in fact, it follows that, on the plane we have now reached, all the varied content of human subjectivity in its vital movement and activity, whether viewed as passion, action, or event, or more generally the wide realm of human feeling, volition and its discontinuance, become one and all for their own sake objects of artistic representation.

* * *

The arts, which are lifted into a higher strain of ideality, abandoning as they do the symbolism of architecture and the classical ideal of sculpture, accept their predominant type from the romantic art form; and these are the arts most fitted to express its mode of configuration. They are, however, a totality of arts, because the romantic type is itself essentially the most concrete.

c. The articulation of this third sphere of the particular arts may be fixed as follows:

(1) The first art which comes next to sculpture is that of painting. It avails itself for a medium of its content and the plastic configuration of the same of visibility as such, to the extent that it is differentiated in its own nature, in other words is defined in the continuity of color. No doubt the material of architecture and sculpture is likewise both visible and colored. It is, however, not, as in painting, visibility in its pure nature, not the essentially simple light, which by its differentiating of itself in its opposition to darkness, and in association with that darkness gives rise to color.[23] This quality of visibility made essentially ideal[24] and treated as such no longer either requires, as in architecture, the abstractly mechanical qualities of mass as appropriate to materials of weight, nor, as is the case with sculpture, the complete dimensuration of spatial condition, even when concentrated into organic forms. The visibility and the making apparent, which belong to painting, possess differences of quality under a more ideal mode—that is, in the specific varieties of color—which liberates art from the objective totality of spatial condition, by being limited to a plane surface.

(2) The second art which continues the further realization of the romantic type and forms a distinct contrast to painting is that of music. Its medium, albeit still sensuous, yet proceeds into still profounder subjectivity and particularization. We have here, too, the deliberate treatment of the sensuous medium as ideal, and it consists in the negation and idealization into the isolated unity of a single point,[25]

---

[19]*Subjektivität.* The particularization in romantic art implies the presence of an ideal element imported by the soul of the artist, which appeals directly to the soul in its emotional life. Compare a picture by an Italian master with a Greek statue.

[20][Osmaston] Literally, "a multiplicity of isolated examples of inwardness."

[21][Osmaston] That is, in the life shared by all as one community actuated by a common purpose.

[22][Osmaston] As in sculpture.

[23][Osmaston] Reference, of course, to Hegel's unfortunate acceptance of Goethe's theory of color.

[24][Osmaston] The color of art is not merely ideal as applied to only two dimensions of space, but also is "subjective" in the artistic treatment of it under a definite "scheme." It is not clear whether Hegel alludes also to this; apparently not, though it is the most important feature. In fact, even assuming his theory of light to be correct, it is difficult entirely to follow his distinction between the appearance of color on a flat or a round surface. As natural color the one would be as ideal as the other. Only regarded as a composition would painting present distinction.

[25][Osmaston] The parts of a chord are not in space, but are ideally cognized. Hegel describes this by saying that music idealizes space and concentrates it to a point. It would perhaps be more intelligible to say that it transmutes the positive effects of a material substance in motion into the positive and more ideal condition of time. The point which is continually negated is at least *qua* music the point, or rather, moment, of a temporal process.

the indifferent external collocation of space,[26] whose complete appearance is retained by painting and deliberately feigned in its completeness. This isolated point, viewed as this process of negation, is an essentially concrete and active process of cancellation within the determinate substance of the material medium, viewed, that is, as motion and vibration of the material object within itself and in its relation to itself. Such an inchoate ideality of matter, which no longer appears under the form of space, but as temporal ideality,[27] is sound or tone. We have here the sensuous set down as negated, and its abstract visibility converted into audibility. In other words sound liberates the ideal content from its fetters in the material substance. This earliest[28] secured inwardness of matter and impregnation of it with soul life supplies the medium for the intimacy and soul of spirit—itself as yet indefinite—permitting, as it does, the echo and reverberation of man's emotional world through its entire range of feelings and passions. In this way music forms the center of the romantic arts, just as sculpture represents the midway point of arrest between architecture and the arts of the romantic subjectivity. Thus, too, it forms the point of transition between the abstract, spatial sensuousness of painting and the abstract spirituality of poetry. Music carries within itself, like architecture, and in contrast to the emotional world simply and its inward self-seclusion, a relation of quantity conformable to the principles of the understanding and their modes of coordinated configuration.[29]

(3) We must look for our third and most spiritual type of artistic presentation among the romantic arts in that of poetry. The supreme characteristic of poetry consists in the power with which it brings into vassalage of the mind and its conceptions the sensuous element from which music and painting began to liberate art. For sound, the only remaining external material retained by poetry, is in it no longer the feeling of the sonorous itself, but is a mere sign without independent significance. And it is, moreover, a sign of idea which has become essentially concrete, and not merely[30] of indefinite feeling and its subtle modes and gradations. And this is how sound develops into the word, as essentially articulate voice, whose intention it is to indicate ideas and

thoughts. The purely negative moment to which music advanced now asserts itself as the wholly concrete point, the point which is mind itself, the self-conscious individual, which produces from itself the infinite expansion of its ideas and unites the same with the temporal condition of sound. Yet this sensuous element, which was still in music immediately united to emotion, is in poetry separated from the content of consciousness. Mind, in short, here determines this content for its own sake and apart from all else into the content of idea; to express such idea it no doubt avails itself; of sound, but employs it merely as a sign without independent worth or substance. . . . Poetry is, in short, the universal art of the mind, which has become essentially free, and which is not fettered in its realization to an externally sensuous material, but which is creatively active in the space and time belonging to the inner world of ideas and emotion. Yet it is precisely in this its highest phase, that art terminates, by transcending itself: it is just here that it deserts the medium of a harmonious presentation of mind in sensuous shape and passes from the poetry of imaginative idea into the prose of thought.

* * *

To sum up, then, what the particular arts realize in particular works of art, are according to their fundamental conception, simply the universal types which constitute the self-unfolding idea of beauty. It is as the external realization of this idea that the wide pantheon of art is being raised; and the architect and builder thereof is the spirit of beauty as it gradually comes to self-cognition, and to complete which the history of the world will require its evolution of centuries.

from

The Phenomenology of Mind

Independence and Dependence of Self-Consciousness: Lordship and Bondage

Self-consciousness exists in itself and for itself, in that, and by the fact that it exists for another self-consciousness; that is to say, it *is* only by being acknowledged or "recognized."

---

[26][Osmaston] By the indifferent externality of space is signified the fact that the parts of space, though external to each other, are not qualitatively distinguishable.

[27][Osmaston] Succession in time is "more ideal" than coexistence in space because it exists only as continuity in a conscious subject.

[28][Osmaston] Painting no doubt introduces ideal elements into the artistic composition of color, but the color still remains the appearance of a material thing or superficies.

[29][Osmaston] That is to say, music or harmony is based on a solid conformity to law on the part of its tones, in their conjunction and succession, their structure and resolution.

[30][Osmaston] As in painting.

"Independence and Dependence of Self-Consciousness: Lordship and Bondage" is reprinted from G. W. F. Hegel, *The Phenomenology of Mind* (1807), translation by J. B. Baillie (1910).

The conception of this its unity in its duplication, of infinitude realizing itself in self-consciousness, has many sides to it and encloses within it elements of varied significance. Thus its moments must on the one hand be strictly kept apart in detailed distinctiveness, and, on the other, in this distinction must, at the same time, also be taken as not distinguished, or must always be accepted and understood in their opposite sense. This double meaning of what is distinguished lies in the nature of self-consciousness: of its being infinite, or directly the opposite of the determinateness in which it is fixed. The detailed exposition of the notion of this spiritual unity in its duplication will bring before us the process of Recognition.

Self-consciousness has before it another self-consciousness; it has come outside itself. This has a double significance. First it has lost its own self, since it finds itself as an *other* being; secondly, it has thereby sublated that other, for it does not regard the other as essentially real, but sees its own self in the other.

It must cancel this its other. To do so is the sublation of that first double meaning, and is therefore a second double meaning. First, it must set itself to sublate the other independent being, in order thereby to become certain of itself as true being, secondly, it thereupon proceeds to sublate its own self, for this other is itself.

This sublation in a double sense of its otherness in a double sense is at the same time a return in a double sense into its self. For, firstly, through sublation, it gets back itself, because it becomes one with itself again through the cancelling of *its* otherness; but secondly, it likewise gives otherness back again to the other self-consciousness, for it was aware of being in the other, it cancels this its own being in the other and thus lets the other again go free.

This process of self-consciousness in relation to another self-consciousness has in this manner been represented as the action of one alone. But this action on the part of the one has itself the double significance of being at once its own action and the action of that other as well. For the other is likewise independent, shut up within itself, and there is nothing in it which is not there through itself. The first does not have the object before it only in the passive form characteristic primarily of the object of desire, but as an object existing independently for itself, over which therefore it has no power to do anything for its own behalf, if that object does not *per se* do what the first does to it. The process then is absolutely the double process of both self-consciousnesses. Each sees the other do the same as itself; each itself does what it demands on the part of the other, and for that reason does what it does, only so far as the other does the same. Action from one side only would be useless, because what is to happen can only be brought about by means of both.

The action has then a *double entente* not only in the sense that it is an act done to itself as well as to the other, but also in the sense that the act *simpliciter is* the act of the one as well as of the other regardless of their distinction.

In this movement we see the process repeated which came before us as the play of forces; in the present case, however, it is found in consciousness. What in the former had effect only for us [contemplating experience], holds here for the terms themselves. The middle term is self-consciousness which breaks itself up into the extremes; and each extreme is this interchange of its own determinateness, and complete transition into the opposite. While *qua* consciousness, it no doubt comes outside itself, still, in being outside itself, it is at the same time restrained within itself, it exists for itself, and its self-externalization is for consciousness. *Consciousness* finds that it immediately is and is not another consciousness, as also that this other is for itself only when it cancels itself as existing for itself, and has self-existence only in the self-existence of the other. Each is the mediating term to the other, through which each mediates and unites itself with itself; and each is to itself and to the other an immediate self existing reality, which, at the same time, exists thus for itself only through this mediation. They recognize themselves as mutually recognizing one another.

This pure conception of recognition, of duplication of self-consciousness within its unity, we must now consider in the way its process appears for self-consciousness. It will, in the first place, present the aspect of the disparity of the two, or the break-up of the middle term into the extremes, which, *qua* extremes, are opposed to one another, and of which one is merely recognized, while the other only recognizes.

Self-consciousness is primarily simple existence for self, self-identity by exclusion of every other from itself. It takes its essential nature and absolute object to be Ego; and in this immediacy, in this bare fact of its self-existence, it is individual. That which for it is other stands as unessential object, as object with the impress and character of negation. But the other is also a self-consciousness; an individual makes its appearance in antithesis to an individual. Appearing thus in their immediacy, they are for each other in the manner of ordinary objects. They are independent individual forms, modes of Consciousness that have not risen above the bare level of life (for the existent object here has been determined as life). They are, moreover, forms of consciousness which have not yet accomplished for one another the process of absolute abstraction, of uprooting all immediate existence, and of being merely the bare, negative fact of self-identical consciousness; or, in other words, have not yet revealed themselves to each other as existing purely for themselves, i.e., as self-consciousness. Each is indeed certain of its own self, but not of the other, and hence its own certainty of itself is still without truth. For its truth would be merely that its own individual existence for itself would be shown to it to be an independent object, or, which is the same thing, that the object would be exhibited as this pure certainty of itself. By the notion of recognition, however, this is not possible, except in the form that as the other is for it, so it is for the other; each in its self through its own action and again through the action of the other achieves this pure abstraction of existence for self.

The presentation of itself, however, as pure abstraction of self-consciousness consists in showing itself as a pure negation of its objective form, or in showing that it is fettered to no determinate existence, that it is not bound at all by the particularity everywhere characteristic of existence as such, and is *not* tied up with life. The process of bringing all this out involves a twofold action—action on the part of the other and action on the part of itself. In so far as it is the other's action, each aims at the destruction and death of the other. But in this there is implicated also the second kind of action, self-activity; for the former implies that it risks its own life. The relation of both self-consciousnesses is in this way so constituted that they prove themselves and each other through a life-and-death struggle. They must enter into this struggle, for they must bring their certainty of themselves, the certainty of being for themselves, to the level of objective truth, and make this a fact both in the case of the other and in their own case as well. And it is solely by risking life that freedom is obtained; only thus is it tried and proved that the essential nature of self-consciousness is not bare existence, is not the merely immediate form in which it at first makes its appearance, is not its mere absorption in the expanse of life. Rather it is thereby guaranteed that there is nothing present but what might be taken as a vanishing moment—that self-consciousness is merely pure self-existence, being-for-self. The individual, who has not staked his life, may, no doubt, be recognized as a Person; but he has not attained the truth of this recognition as an independent self-consciousness. In the same way each must aim at the death of the other, as it risks its own life thereby; for that other is to it of no more worth than itself the other's reality is presented to the former as an external other, as outside itself; it must cancel that externality. The other is a purely existent consciousness and entangled in manifold ways; it must view its otherness as pure existence for itself or as absolute negation.

This trial by death, however, cancels both the truth which was to result from it, and therewith the certainty of self altogether. For just as life is the natural "position" of consciousness, independence without absolute negativity, so death is the natural "negation" of consciousness, negation without independence, which thus remains without the requisite significance of actual recognition. Through death, doubtless, there has arisen the certainty that both did stake their life, and held it lightly both in their own case and in the case of the other; but that is not for those who underwent this struggle. They cancel their consciousness which had its place in this alien element of natural existence; in other words, they cancel themselves and are sublated as terms or extremes seeking to have existence on their own account. But along with this there vanishes from the play of change the essential moment, viz. that of breaking up into extremes with opposite characteristics; and the middle term collapses into a lifeless unity which is broken up into lifeless extremes, merely existent and not opposed. And the two do not mutually give and receive one another back from each other through consciousness; they let one another go quite indifferently, like things. Their act is abstract negation, not the negation characteristic of consciousness, which cancels in such a way that it preserves and maintains what is sublated, and thereby survives its being sublated.

In this experience self-consciousness becomes aware that *life* is as essential to it as pure self-consciousness. In immediate self-consciousness the simple ego is absolute object, which, however, is for us or in itself absolute mediation, and has as its essential moment substantial and solid independence. The dissolution of that simple unity is the result of the first experience; through this there is posited a pure self-consciousness, and a consciousness which is not purely for itself, but for another, i.e. as an existent consciousness, consciousness in the form and shape of thinghood. Both moments are essential, since, in the first instance, they are unlike and opposed, and their reflexion into unity has not yet come to light, they stand as two opposed forms or modes of consciousness. The one is independent, and its essential nature is to be for itself; the other is dependent, and its essence is life or existence for another. The former is the Master, or Lord, the latter the Bondsman.

The master is the consciousness that exists *for itself;* but no longer merely the general notion of existence for self. Rather, it is a consciousness existing on its own account which is mediated with itself through an other consciousness, i.e. through an other whose very nature implies that it is bound up with an independent being or with thinghood in general. The master brings himself into relation to both these moments, to a thing as such, the object of desire, and to the consciousness whose essential character is thinghood. And since the master, is (a) qua notion of self-consciousness, an immediate relation of self-existence, but (b) is now moreover at the same time mediation, or a being-for-self which is for itself only through an other—he [the master] stands in relation (a) immediately to both (b) mediately to each through the other. The master relates himself to the bondsman mediately through independent existence, for that is precisely what keeps the bondsman in thrall; it is his chain, from which he could not in the struggle get away, and for that reason lie proved himself to be dependent, to have his independence in the shape of thinghood. The master, however, is the power controlling this state of existence, for he has shown in the struggle that he holds it to be merely something negative. Since he is the power dominating existence, while this existence again is the power controlling the other [the bondsman], the master holds, par consequence, this other in subordination. In the same way the master relates himself to the thing mediately through the bondsman. The bondsman being a self-consciousness in the broad sense, also takes up a negative attitude to things and cancels them; but the thing is, at the same time, independent for him and, in consequence, he cannot, with all his negating, get so far as to annihilate it outright and be done with it; that is to say, he merely works on it. To the master, on the other hand, by means of this mediating process, belongs the immediate relation, in the sense of the pure negation of it, in other words he gets the enjoyment. What mere desire did not attain, he now succeeds in attaining, viz. to have done with the thing, and find satisfaction in enjoyment. Desire alone did not get the length of this, because of the independence of the thing. The master, however, who has interposed the bondsman between it and himself, thereby relates himself merely to the dependence of the thing, and enjoys it without qualification and without reserve. The aspect of its independence he leaves to the bondsman, who labours upon it.

In these two moments, the master gets his recognition through an other consciousness, for in them the latter affirms itself as unessential, both by working upon the thing, and, on the other hand, by the fact of being dependent on a determinate existence; in neither case can this other get the mastery over existence, and succeed in absolutely negating it. We have thus here this moment of recognition, viz. that the other consciousness cancels itself as self-existent, and, ipso facto, itself does what the first does to it. In the same way we have the other moment, that this action on the part of the second is the action proper of the first; for what is done by the bondsman is properly an action on the part of the master. The latter exists only for himself, that is his essential nature; he is the negative power without qualifica-

tion, a power to which the thing is naught. And he is thus the absolutely essential act in this situation, while the bondsman is not so, he is an unessential activity. But for recognition proper there is needed the moment that what the master does to the other he should also do to himself, and what the bondsman does to himself, he should do to the other also. On that account a form of recognition has arisen that is one sided and unequal.

In all this, the unessential consciousness is, for the master, the object which embodies the truth of his certainty of himself. But it is evident that this object does not correspond to its notion; for, just where the master has effectively achieved lordship, he really finds that something has come about quite different from an independent consciousness. It is not an independent, but rather a dependent consciousness that he has achieved. He is thus not assured of self-existence as his truth; he finds that his truth is rather the unessential consciousness, and the fortuitous unessential action of that consciousness.

The truth of the independent consciousness is accordingly the consciousness of the bondsman. This doubtless appears in the first instance outside itself, and not as the truth of self-consciousness. But just as lordship showed its essential nature to be the reverse of what it wants to be, so, too, bondage will, when completed, pass into the opposite of what it immediately is: being a consciousness repressed within itself, it will enter into itself, and change round into real and true independence.

We have seen what bondage is only in relation to lordship. But it is a self-consciousness, and we have now to consider what it is, in this regard, in and for itself. In the first instance, the master is taken to be the essential reality for the state of bondage; hence, for it, the truth is the independent consciousness existing for itself, although this truth is not taken yet as inherent in bondage itself. Still, it does in fact contain within itself this truth of pure negativity and self-existence, because it has experienced this reality within it. For this consciousness was not in peril and fear for this element or that, nor for this or that moment of time, it was afraid for its entire being; it felt the fear of death, the sovereign master. It has been in that experience melted to its inmost soul, has trembled throughout its every fibre, and all that was fixed and steadfast has quaked within it. This complete perturbation of its entire substance, this absolute dissolution of all its stability into fluent continuity, is, however, the simple, ultimate nature of self-consciousness, absolute negativity, pure self-referent existence, which consequently is involved in this type of consciousness. This moment of pure self-existence is moreover a fact for it; for in the master it finds this as its object. Further, this bondsman's consciousness is not only this total dissolution in a general way; in serving and toiling the bondsman actually carries this out. By serving he cancels in every particular aspect his dependence on and attachment to natural existence, and by his work removes this existence away.

The feeling of absolute power, however, realized both in general and in the particular form of service, is only dissolution implicitly; and albeit the fear of the lord is the beginning of wisdom, consciousness is not therein aware of being self-existent. Through work and labour, however, this consciousness of the bondsman comes to itself. In the moment which corresponds to desire in the case of the master's consciousness, the aspect of the non-essential relation to the thing seemed to fall to the lot of the servant, since the thing there retained its independence. Desire has reserved to itself the pure negating of the object and thereby unalloyed feeling of self. This satisfaction, however, just for that reason is itself only a state of evanescence, for it lacks objectivity or subsistence. Labour, on the other hand, is desire restrained and checked, evanescence delayed and postponed; in other words, labour shapes and fashions the thing. The negative relation to the object passes into the form of the object, into something that is permanent and remains; because it is just for the labourer that the object has independence. This negative mediating agency, this activity giving shape and form, is at the same time the individual existence, the pure self-existence of that consciousness, which now in the work it does is externalized and passes into the condition of permanence. The consciousness that toils and serves accordingly attains by this means the direct apprehension of that independent being as its self.

But again, shaping or forming the object has not only the positive significance that the bondsman becomes thereby aware of himself as factually and objectively self-existent; this type of consciousness has also a negative import, in contrast with its moment, the element of fear. For in shaping the thing it only becomes aware of its own proper negativity, existence on its own account, as an object, through the fact that it cancels the actual form confronting it. But this objective negative element is precisely alien, external reality, before which it trembled. Now, however, it destroys this extraneous alien negative, affirms and sets itself

up as a negative in the element of permanence, and thereby becomes for itself a self-existent being. In the master, the bondsman feels self-existence to be something external, an objective fact; in fear self-existence is present within himself; in fashioning the thing, self-existence comes to be felt explicitly as his own proper being, and he attains the consciousness that he himself exists in its own right and on its own account (*an und für sich*). By the fact that the form is objectified, it does not become something other than the consciousness moulding the thing through work; for just that form is his pure self existence, which therein becomes truly realized. Thus precisely in labour where there seemed to be merely some outsider's mind and ideas involved, the bondsman becomes aware, through this re-discovery of himself by himself, of having and being a "mind of his own."

For this reflexion of self into self the two moments, fear and service in general, as also that of formative activity, are necessary: and at the same time both must exist in a universal manner. Without the discipline of service and obedience, fear remains formal and does not spread over the whole known reality of existence. Without the formative activity shaping the thing, fear remains inward and mute, and consciousness does not become objective for itself. Should consciousness shape and form the thing without the initial state of absolute fear, then it has a merely vain and futile "mind of its own"; for its form or negativity is not negativity *per se*, and hence its formative activity cannot furnish the consciousness of itself as essentially real. If it has endured not absolute fear, but merely some slight anxiety, the negative reality has remained external to it, its substance has not been through and through infected thereby. Since the entire content of its natural consciousness has not tottered and shaken, it is still inherently a determinate mode of being; having a "mind of its own" (*der eigene Sinn*) is simply stubbornness (*Eigensinn*), a type of freedom which does not get beyond the attitude of bondage. As little as the pure form can become its essential nature, so little is that form, considered as extending over particulars, a universal formative activity, an absolute notion; it is rather a piece of cleverness which has mastery within a certain range, but not over the universal power nor over the entire objective reality.

Ralph Waldo Emerson

1803–1882

Emerson's well-known oration *The American Scholar* touches on three of his most important themes under the subject of education: nature, books, and action, in that order of importance. Throughout he draws a distinction between "man thinking" and man parroting "other men's thinking." In the section on books below, he considers both their proper use and their abuse. Education from books is second to that from nature and requires the exercise of the "active soul" of the reader lest the reader sink into passive acceptance and obeisance to "accepted dogmas," thus surrendering individuality.

In his essay *The Poet,* Emerson provides a compendium of Romantic ideas about poetry, though in *The American Scholar* he is critical of romanticism as he knows it. The poet acts out the human need for expression; the poet is the namer; the poet liberates us by means of invention. Language is poetic in origin. As in Vico (above, page 318) every word was originally a poem (Vico called the original word a myth), and ordinary language is thus "fossil poetry"; imagination involves sympathetic identification with all things, "the intellect being where and what it sees"; the country is ranged against the city; nature is itself a symbolic language.

According to Emerson, half of the reality of man is what he expresses, and ideally every man should be able to "report in conversation what has befallen him"; but language tends to wear itself out in clichés (see Shelley, above, page 539). Every thought eventually becomes a sort of prison. It is the poet who forges a refurbishment of language and provides the renewed possibility of mental liberation. In this view, poetic language would seem to constitute and reconstitute the real.

Emerson does not seem to have any theory of the poem as a whole; thought for him is prior to form; the poem is a transcendental thought. But his remarks about the "fluxional" nature of symbols and his criticism of symbols with fixed, univocal meanings are suggestive.

Since Emerson speaks of the poem as expressive of sympathetic identification, his notion of the poetic symbol seems to imply that it partakes of the reality it expresses, that it reaches out to blend with nature, a vehicle of secular communion. In this matter he contributes to a discussion of symbolism that engaged Goethe, Coleridge (above, page 519), Carlyle, Baudelaire, and many others.

Many collections of Emerson's writings are available, but see *Collected Works,* edited by Robert E. Spiller, et al. (1971–). See F. O. Matthiessen, *American Renaissance* (1941); R. L. Rusk, *The Life of Ralph Waldo Emerson* (1949); Sherman Paul, *Emerson's Angle of Vision* (1952); S. E. Whicher, *Freedom and Fate* (1953); Charles Feidelson, *Symbolism and American Literature* (1953); Jeffrey L. Duncan, *The Power and Form of Emerson's Thought* (1973); David D. Porter, *Emerson and Literary Change* (1978); B. L. Packer, *Emerson's Fall* (1982); David Van Leer, *Emerson's Epistemology* (1986); John Michael, *Emerson and Skepticism* (1988); Lawrence

Buell, ed., *Ralph Waldo Emerson: A Collection of Critical Essays* (1993); T. S. McMillin, *Our Preposterous Use of Literature: Emerson and the Nature of Reading* (2000); Peter S. Field, *Ralph Waldo Emerson: The Making of a Democratic Intellectual* (2002); Lawrence Buell, *Emerson* (2003).

from

The American Scholar

[Emerson has just discussed the primary importance of the education of the scholar offered by nature.]

II. The next great influence into the spirit of the scholar, is, the mind of the Past,—in whatever form, whether of literature, of art, of institutions, that mind is inscribed. Books are the best type of the influence of the past, and perhaps we shall get at the truth,—learn the amount of this influence more conveniently,—by considering their value alone.

The theory of books is noble. The scholar of the first age received into him the world around; brooded thereon; gave it the new arrangement of his own mind, and uttered it again. It came into him, life; it went out from him, truth. It came to him, short-lived actions; it went out from him, immortal thoughts. It came to him, business; it went from him, poetry. It was dead fact; now, it is quick thought. It can stand, and it can go. It now endures, it now flies, it now inspires. Precisely in proportion to the depth of mind from which it issued, so high does it soar, so long does it sing.

Or, I might say, it depends on how far the process had gone, of transmuting life into truth. In proportion to the completeness of the distillation, so will the purity and imperishableness of the product be. But none is quite perfect. As no air-pump can by any means make a perfect vacuum, so neither can any artist entirely exclude the conventional, the local, the perishable from his book, or write a book of pure thought, that shall be as efficient, in all respects, to a remote posterity, as to cotemporaries, or rather to the second age. Each age, it is found, must write its own books; or rather, each generation for the next succeeding. The books of an older period will not fit this.

Yet hence arises a grave mischief. The sacredness which attaches to the act of creation,—the act of thought,—is transferred to the record. The poet chanting, was felt to be a divine man: henceforth the chant is divine also. The writer was a just and wise spirit: henceforward it is settled, the

book is perfect; as love of the hero corrupts into worship of his statue. Instantly, the book becomes noxious: the guide is a tyrant. The sluggish and perverted mind of the multitude, slow to open to the incursions of Reason, having once so opened, having once received this book, stands upon it, and makes an outcry, if it is disparaged. Colleges are built on it. Books are written on it by thinkers, not by Man Thinking; by men of talent, that is, who start wrong, who set out from accepted dogmas, not from their own sight of principles. Meek young men grow up in libraries, believing it their duty to accept the views, which Cicero, which Locke, which Bacon,[1] have given, forgetful that Cicero, Locke, and Bacon were only young men in libraries, when they wrote these books.

Hence, instead of Man Thinking, we have the bookworm. Hence, the book-learned class, who value books, as such; not as related to nature and the human constitution, but as making a sort of Third Estate with the world and the soul. Hence, the restores of readings, the emendators, the bibliomaniacs of all degrees.

Books are the best of things, well used; abused, among the worst. What is the right use? What is the one end, which all means go to effect? They are for nothing but to inspire. I had better never see a book, than to be warped by its attraction clean out of my own orbit, and made a satellite instead of a system. The one thing in the world, of value, is the active soul. This every man is entitled to; this every man contains within him, although, in almost all men, obstructed, and as yet unborn. The soul active sees absolute truth; and utters truth, or creates. In this action, it is genius; not the privilege of here and there a favorite, but the sound estate of every man. In its essence, it is progressive. The book, the college, the school of art, the institution of any kind, stop with some past utterance of genius. This is good, say they,—let us hold by this. They pin me down. They look backward and not forward. But genius looks forward: the eyes of man are set in his forehead, not in his hindhead: man hopes: genius creates. Whatever talents may be, if the man create not, the pure efflux of the Deity is not his;—cinders and smoke there may be, but not yet flame. There are

---

Emerson's *The American Scholar* was delivered before the Phi Beta Kappa Society at Cambridge, Mass., on August 31, 1837.

[1]Cicero (above, page 74), Locke (above, page 281), Bacon (above, page 234).

creative manners, there are creative actions, and creative words; manners, actions, words, that is, indicative of no custom or authority, but springing spontaneous from the mind's own sense of good and fair.

On the other part, instead of being its own seer, let it receive from another mind its truth, though it were in torrents of light, without periods of solitude, inquest, and self-recovery, and a fatal disservice is done. Genius is always sufficiently the enemy of genius by over influence. The literature of every nation bear me witness. The English dramatic poets have Shakspearized now for two hundred years.

Undoubtedly there is a right way of reading, so it be sternly subordinated. Man Thinking must not be subdued by his instruments. Books are for the scholar's idle times. When he can read God directly, the hour is too precious to be wasted in other men's transcripts of their readings. But when the intervals of darkness come, as come they must,— when the sun is hid, and the stars withdraw their shining,— we repair to the lamps which were kindled by their ray, to guide our steps to the East again, where the dawn is. We hear, that we may speak. The Arabian proverb says, "A fig tree, looking on a fig tree, becometh fruitful."

It is remarkable, the character of the pleasure we derive from the best books. They impress us with the conviction, that one nature wrote and the same reads. We read the verses of one of the great English poets, of Chaucer, of Marvell, of Dryden,[2] with the most modern joy,—with a pleasure, I mean, which is in great part caused by the abstraction of all *time* from their verses. There is some awe mixed with the joy of our surprise, when this poet, who lived in some past world, two or three hundred years ago, says that which lies close to my own soul, that which I also had wellnigh thought and said. But for the evidence thence afforded to the philosophical doctrine of the identity of all minds, we should suppose some preëstablished harmony, some foresight of souls that were to be, and some preparation of stores for their future wants, like the fact observed in insects, who lay up food before death for the young grub they shall never see.

I would not be hurried by any love of system, by any exaggeration of instincts, to underrate the Book. We all know, that, as the human body can be nourished on any food, though it were boiled grass and the broth of shoes, so the human mind can be fed by any knowledge. And great and heroic men have existed, who had almost no other information than by the printed page. I only would say, that it needs a strong head to bear that diet. One must be an inventor to read well. As the proverb says, "He that would bring

home the wealth of the Indies, must carry out the wealth of the Indies." There is then creative reading as well as creative writing. When the mind is braced by labor and invention, the page of whatever book we read becomes luminous with manifold allusion. Every sentence is doubly significant, and the sense of our author is as broad as the world. We then see, what is always true, that, as the seer's hour of vision is short and rare among heavy days and months, so is its record, perchance, the least part of his volume. The discerning will read, in his Plato or Shakspeare, only that least part,—only the authentic utterances of the oracle;—all the rest he rejects, were it never so many times Plato's and Shakspeare's.

Of course, there is a portion of reading quite indispensable to a wise man. History and exact science he must learn by laborious reading. Colleges, in like manner, have their indispensable office,—to teach elements. But they can only highly serve us, when they aim not to drill, but to create; when they gather from far every ray of various genius to their hospitable halls, and, by the concentrated fires, set the hearts of their youth on flame. Thought and knowledge are natures in which apparatus and pretension avail nothing. Gowns, and pecuniary foundations, though of towns of gold, can never countervail the least sentence or syllable of wit. Forget this, and our American colleges will recede in their public importance, whilst they grow richer every year.

* * *

[Emerson proceeds here to discuss action, which for the scholar is "subordinate," but "essential."]

I have now spoken of the education of the scholar by nature, by books, and by action. It remains to say somewhat of his duties.

They are such as become Man Thinking. They may all be comprised in self-trust. The office of the scholar is to cheer, to raise, and to guide men by showing them facts amidst appearances. He plies the slow, unhonored, and unpaid task of observation. Flamsteed and Herschel,[3] in their glazed observatories, may catalogue the stars with the praise of all men, and, the results being splendid and useful, honor is sure. But he, in his private observatory, cataloguing obscure and nebulous stars of the human mind, which as yet no man has thought of as such,—watching days and months, sometimes, for a few facts; correcting still his old records;—must relinquish display and immediate fame. In the long period of his preparation, he must betray often an ignorance and shiftlessness in popular arts, incurring the

---

[2]Geoffrey Chaucer (1340?–1400), Andrew Marvell (1621–1678), Dryden (above, page 253), English poets.

[3]John Flamsteed (1646–1719) and John F. W. Herschel (1738–1822), English astronomers.

disdain of the able who shoulder him aside. Long he must stammer in his speech; often forego the living for the dead. Worse yet, he must accept,—how often! poverty and solitude. For the ease and pleasure of treading the old road, accepting the fashions, the education, the religion of society, he takes the cross of making his own, and, of course, the self-accusation, the faint heart, the frequent uncertainty and loss of time, which are the nettles and tangling vines in the way of the self-relying and self-directed; and the state of virtual hostility in which he seems to stand to society, and especially to educated society. For all this loss and scorn, what offset? He is to find consolation in exercising the highest functions of human nature. He is one, who raises himself from private considerations, and breathes and lives on public and illustrious thoughts. He is the world's eye. He is the world's heart. He is to resist the vulgar prosperity that retrogrades ever to barbarism, by preserving and communicating heroic sentiments, noble biographies, melodious verse, and the conclusions of history. Whatsoever oracles the human heart, in all emergencies, in all solemn hours, has uttered as its commentary on the world of actions,—these he shall receive and impart. And whatsoever new verdict Reason from her inviolable seat pronounces on the passing men and events of to-day,—this he shall hear and promulgate.

These being his functions, it becomes him to feel all confidence in himself, and to defer never to the popular cry. He and he only knows the world. The world of any moment is the merest appearance. Some great decorum, some fetish of a government, some ephemeral trade, or war, or man, is cried up by half mankind and cried down by the other half, as if all depended on this particular up or down. The odds are that the whole question is not worth the poorest thought which the scholar has lost in listening to the controversy. Let him not quit his belief that a popgun is a popgun, though the ancient and honorable of the earth affirm it to be the crack of doom. In silence, in steadiness, in severe abstraction, let him hold by himself; add observation to observation, patient of neglect, patient of reproach; and bide his own time,—happy enough, if he can satisfy himself alone, that this day he has seen something truly. Success treads on every right step. For the instinct is sure, that prompts him to tell his brother what he thinks. He then learns, that in going down into the secrets of his own mind, he has descended into the secrets of all minds. He learns that he who has mastered any law in his private thoughts, is master to that extent of all men whose language he speaks, and of all into whose language his own can be translated. The poet, in utter solitude remembering his spontaneous thoughts and recording them, is found to have recorded that, which men in crowded cities find true for them also. The orator distrusts at first the

fitness of his frank confessions,—his want of knowledge of the persons he addresses,—until he finds that he is the complement of his hearers;—that they drink his words because he fulfills for them their own nature; the deeper he dives into his privatest, secretest presentiment, to his wonder he finds, this is the most acceptable, most public, and universally true. The people delight in it; the better part of every man feels, This is my music; this is myself.

* * *

I read with joy some of the auspicious signs of the coming days, as they glimmer already through poetry and art, through philosophy and science, through church and state.

One of these signs is the fact, that the same movement which effected the elevation of what was called the lowest class in the state, assumed in literature a very marked and as benign an aspect. Instead of the sublime and beautiful; the near, the low, the common, was explored and poetized. That, which had been negligently trodden under foot by those who were harnessing and provisioning themselves for long journeys into far countries, is suddenly found to be richer than all foreign parts. The literature of the poor, the feelings of the child, the philosophy of the street, the meaning of household life, are the topics of the time. It is a great stride. It is a sign,—is it not? of new vigor, when the extremities are made active, when currents of warm life run into the hands and the feet. I ask not for the great, the remote, the romantic; what is doing in Italy or Arabia; what is Greek art, or Provençal minstrelsy; I embrace the common, I explore and sit at the feet of the familiar, the low. Give me insight into to-day, and you may have the antique and future worlds. What would we really know the meaning of? The meal in the firkin; the milk in the pan; the ballad in the street; the news of the boat; the glance of the eye; the form and the gait of the body;—show me the ultimate reason of these matters; show me the sublime presence of the highest spiritual cause lurking, as always it does lurk, in these suburbs and extremities of nature; let me see every trifle bristling with the polarity that ranges it instantly on an eternal law; and the shop, the plough, and the leger, referred to the like cause by which light undulates and poets sing;—and the world lies no longer a dull miscellany and lumber-room, but has form and order; there is no trifle; there is no puzzle; but one design unites and animates the farthest pinnacle and the lowest trench.

* * *

Another sign of our times, also marked by an analogous political movement, is, the new importance given to the single person. Every thing that tends to insulate the individual,—to surround him with barriers of natural respect, so that each man shall feel the world is his, and man shall treat with man as a sovereign state with a sovereign state;—tends to true union as well as greatness. "I learned," said the melancholy Pestalozzi,[4] "that no man in God's wide earth is either willing or able to help any other man." Help must come from the bosom alone. The scholar is that man who must take up into himself all the ability of the time, all the contributions of the past, all the hopes of the future. He must be an university of knowledges. If there be one lesson more than another, which should pierce his ear, it is, The world is nothing, the man is all; in yourself is the law of all nature, and you know not yet how a globule of sap ascends; in yourself slumbers the whole of Reason; it is for you to know all, it is for you to dare all.

* * *

The Poet

A moody child and wildly wise
Pursued the game with joyful eyes,
Which chose, like meteors, their way,
And rived the dark with private ray:
They overleapt the horizon's edge,
Searched with Apollo's privilege;
Through man, and woman, and sea, and star
Saw the dance of nature forward far;
Through worlds, and races, and terms, and times
Saw musical order, and pairing rhymes.[1]

* * *

Olympian bards who sung
Divine ideas below,
Which always find us young,
And always keep us so.[2]

Those who are esteemed umpires of taste are often persons who have acquired some knowledge of admired pictures or sculptures, and have an inclination for whatever is elegant; but if you inquire whether they are beautiful souls, and whether their own acts are like fair pictures, you learn that they are selfish and sensual. Their cultivation is local, as if you should rub a log of dry wood in one spot to produce fire, all the rest remaining cold. Their knowledge of the fine arts is some study of rules and particulars, or some limited judgment of color or form, which is exercised for amusement or for show. It is a proof of the shallowness of the doctrine of beauty as it lies in the minds of our amateurs, that men seem to have lost the perception of the instant dependence of form upon soul. There is no doctrine of forms in our philosophy. We were put into our bodies, as fire is put into a pan to be carried about; but there is no accurate adjustment between the spirit and the organ, much less is the latter the germination of the former. So in regard to other forms, the intellectual men do not believe in any essential dependence of the material world on thought and volition. Theologians think it a pretty air-castle to talk of the spiritual meaning of a ship or a cloud, of a city or a contract, but they prefer to come again to the solid ground of historical evidence; and even the poets are contented with a civil and conformed manner of living, and to write poems from the fancy, at a safe distance from their own experience. But the highest minds of the world have never ceased to explore the double meaning, or shall I say the quadruple or the centuple or much more manifold meaning, of every sensuous fact; Orpheus, Empedocles, Heraclitus, Plato, Plutarch, Dante, Swedenborg,[3] and the masters of sculpture, picture and poetry. For we are not pans and barrows, nor even porters of the fire and torch-bearers, but children of the fire, made of it, and only the same divinity transmuted and at two or three removes, when we know least about it. And this hidden truth, that the fountains whence all this river of time and its creatures floweth are intrinsically ideal and beautiful, draws us to the consideration of the nature and functions of the poet, or the man of beauty; to the means and materials he uses, and to the general aspect of the art in the present time.

The breadth of the problem is great, for the poet is representative. He stands among partial men for the complete man, and apprises us not of his wealth, but of the common wealth. The young man reveres men of genius, because, to speak truly, they are more himself than he is. They receive of the soul as he also receives, but they more. Nature enhances her beauty, to the eye of loving men, from their belief that the poet is beholding her shows at the same time.

[4]Johann Heinrich Pestalozzi (1746–1827), Swiss educational reformer.

The Poet was written in 1842–1843 and first published in 1844.
[1]Lines by Emerson, revised from his poem *The Poet*.
[2]Emerson, *Ode to Beauty*, 60–63.

[3]Orpheus, legendary ancient Greek poet; Empedocles (c. 495–c. 435 B.C.), Greek philosopher; Heraclitus (c. 535–c. 475 B.C.), Greek philosopher; Plato (above, page 8); Plutarch (above, page 119); Dante (above, page 153); Emanuel Swedenborg (1688–1772), Swedish scientist and mystical theologian.

He is isolated among his contemporaries by truth and by his art, but with this consolation in his pursuits, that they will draw all men sooner or later. For all men live by truth and stand in need of expression. In love, in art, in avarice, in politics, in labor, in games, we study to utter our painful secret. The man is only half himself, the other half is his expression.[4]

Notwithstanding this necessity to be published, adequate expression is rare. I know not how it is that we need an interpreter, but the great majority of men seem to be minors, who have not yet come into possession of their own, or mutes, who cannot report the conversation they have had with nature. There is no man who does not anticipate a super-sensual utility in the sun and stars, earth and water. These stand and wait to render him a peculiar service. But there is some obstruction or some excess of phlegm in our constitution, which does not suffer them to yield the due effect. Too feeble fall the impressions of nature on us to make us artists. Every touch should thrill. Every man should be so much an artist that he could report in conversation what had befallen him. Yet, in our experience, the rays or appulses have sufficient force to arrive at the senses, but not enough to reach the quick and compel the reproduction of themselves in speech. The poet is the person in whom these powers are in balance, the man without impediment, who sees and handles that which others dream of, traverses the whole scale of experience, and is representative of man, in virtue of being the largest power to receive and to impart.

For the universe has three children, born at one time, which reappear under different names in every system of thought, whether they be called cause, operation and effect; or, more poetically, Jove, Pluto, Neptune; or, theologically, the Father, the Spirit and the Son; but which we will call here the Knower, the Doer and the Sayer. These stand respectively for the love of truth, for the love of good, and for the love of beauty. These three are equal. Each is that which he is, essentially, so that he cannot be surmounted or analyzed, and each of these three has the power of the others latent in him and his own, patent.

The poet is the sayer, the namer, and represents beauty. He is a sovereign, and stands on the center. For the world is not painted or adorned, but is from the beginning beautiful; and God has not made some beautiful things, but beauty is the creator of the universe. Therefore the poet is not any permissive potentate, but is emperor in his own right. Criticism is infested with a cant of materialism, which assumes that manual skill and activity is the first merit of all men, and disparages such as say and do not, overlooking the fact that some men, namely poets, are natural sayers, sent into the world to the end of expression, and confounds them with those whose province is action but who quit it to imitate the sayers. But Homer's words are as costly and admirable to Homer as Agamemnon's victories are to Agamemnon. The poet does not wait for the hero or the sage, but, as they act and think primarily, so he writes primarily what will and must be spoken, reckoning the others, though primaries also, yet, in respect to him, secondaries and servants; as sitters or models in the studio of a painter, or as assistants who bring building materials to an architect.

For poetry was all written before time was, and whenever we are so finely organized that we can penetrate into that region where the air is music, we hear those primal warblings and attempt to write them down, but we lose ever and anon a world or a verse and substitute something of our own, and thus miswrite the poem. The men of more delicate ear write down these cadences more faithfully, and these transcripts, though imperfect, become the songs of the nations. For nature is as truly beautiful as it is good, or as it is reasonable, and must as much appear as it must be done, or be known. Words and deeds are quite indifferent modes of the divine energy. Words are also actions, and actions are a kind of words.

The sign and credentials of the poet are that he announces that which no man foretold. He is the true and only doctor;[5] he knows and tells; he is the only teller of news, for he was present and privy to the appearance which he describes. He is a beholder of ideas and an utterer of the necessary and causal. For we do not speak now of men of poetical talents, or of industry and skill in meter, but of the true poet. I took part in a conversation the other day concerning a recent writer of lyrics, a man of subtle mind, whose head appeared to be a music box of delicate tunes and rhythms, and whose skill and command of language we could not sufficiently praise. But when the question arose whether he was not only a lyrist but a poet, we were obliged to confess that he is plainly a contemporary, not an eternal man. He does not stand out of our low limitations, like a Chimborazo[6] under the line, running up from a torrid base through all the climates of the globe, with belts of the herbage of every latitude on its high and mottled sides; but this genius is the landscape garden of a modern house, adorned with fountains and statues, with well-bred men and women

[4]The close identification of poem and poet is a common Romantic notion (see, for example, Wordsworth [above, page 486] and Coleridge [above, page 507]). Indeed, it is a Romantic invention.

[5]Teacher.
[6]Andean volcanic mountain.

standing and sitting in the walks and terraces. We hear, through all the varied music, the ground tone of conventional life. Our poets are men of talents who sing, and not the children of music. The argument is secondary, the finish of the verses is primary.

For it is not meters, but a meter-making argument that makes a poem—a thought so passionate and alive that like the spirit of a plant or an animal it has an architecture of its own, and adorns nature with a new thing. The thought and the form are equal in the order of time, but in the order of genesis the thought is prior to the form.[7] The poet has a new thought; he has a whole new experience to unfold; he will tell us how it was with him, and all men will be the richer in his fortune. For the experience of each new age requires a new confession, and the world seems always waiting for its poet. I remember when I was young how much I was moved one morning by tidings that genius had appeared in a youth who sat near me at table. He had left his work and gone rambling none knew whither, and had written hundreds of lines, but could not tell whether that which was in him was therein told; he could tell nothing but that all was changed—man, beast, heaven, earth and sea. How gladly we listened! How credulous! Society seemed to be compromised. We sat in the aurora of a sunrise which was to put out all the stars. Boston seemed to be at twice the distance it had the night before, or was much farther than that. Rome—what was Rome? Plutarch and Shakespeare were in the yellow leaf, and Homer no more should be heard of. It is much to know that poetry has been written this very day, under this very roof, by your side. What! That wonderful spirit has not expired! These stony moments are still sparkling and animated! I had fancied that the oracles were all silent, and nature had spent her fires; and behold! all night, from every pore, these fine auroras have been streaming. Everyone has some interest in the advent of the poet, and no one knows how much it may concern him. We know that the secret of the world is profound, but who or what shall be our interpreter, we know not. A mountain ramble, a new style of face, a new person, may put the key into our hands. Of course the value of genius to us is in the veracity of its report. Talent may frolic and juggle; genius realizes and adds. Mankind in good earnest have availed so far in understanding themselves and their work, that the foremost watchman on the peak announces his news. It is the truest word ever spoken, and the phrase will be the fittest, most musical, and the unerring voice of the world for that time.

All that we call sacred history attests that the birth of a poet is the principal event in chronology. Man, never so often deceived, still watches for the arrival of a brother who can hold him steady to a truth until he has made it his own. With what joy I begin to read a poem which I confide in as an inspiration! And now my chains are to be broken; I shall mount above these clouds and opaque airs in which I live— opaque, though they seem transparent—and from the heaven of truth I shall see and comprehend my relations. That will reconcile me to life and renovate nature, to see trifles animated by a tendency, and to know what I am doing. Life will no more be a noise; now I shall see men and women, and know the signs by which they may be discerned from fools and satans. This day shall be better than my birthday: then I became an animal; now I am invited into the science of the real. Such is the hope, but the fruition is postponed. Oftener it falls that this winged man, who will carry me into the heaven, whirls me into mists, then leaps and frisks about with me as it were from cloud to cloud, still affirming that he is bound heavenward; and I, being myself a novice, am slow in perceiving that he does not know the way into the heavens, and is merely bent that I should admire his skill to rise like a fowl or a flying fish, a little way from the ground or the water; but the all-piercing, all-feeding and ocular air of heaven that man shall never inhabit. I tumble down again soon into my old nooks, and lead the life of exaggerations as before, and have lost my faith in the possibility of any guide who can lead me thither where I would be.

But, leaving these victims of vanity, let us, with new hope, observe how nature, by worthier impulses, has insured the poet's fidelity to his office of announcement and affirming, namely by the beauty of things, which becomes a new and higher beauty when expressed. Nature offers all her creatures to him as a picture language. Being used as a type, a second wonderful value appears in the object, far better than its old value; and the carpenter's stretched cord, if you hold your ear close enough, is musical in the breeze. "Things more excellent than every image," says Iamblichus, "are expressed through images."[8] Things admit of being used as symbols because nature is a symbol, in the whole, and in every part. Every line we can draw in the sand has expression; and there is no body without its spirit or genius. All form is an effect of character; all condition, of the quality of the life; all harmony, of health; and for this reason a perception of beauty should be

---

[7] Emerson agrees with Shelley (above, page 549) on this point and not with Blake (above, page 448) and but partially with Benedetto Croce (*Aesthetic*, 1900), who identified intuition with expression but added the notion of externalization of the intuition-expression in the material form of the artwork.

[8] Iamblichus, (third to fourth century), neoplatonic philosopher.

sympathetic, or proper only to the good. The beautiful rests on the foundations of the necessary. The soul makes the body, as the wise Spenser teaches:

> So every spirit, as it is more pure,
> And hath in it the more of heavenly light,
> So it the fairer body doth procure
> To habit in, and it more fairly dight,
> With cheerful grace and amiable sight.
> For, of the soul, the body form doth take,
> For soul is form, and doth the body make.[9]

Here we find ourselves suddenly not in a critical speculation but in a holy place, and should go very warily and reverently. We stand before the secret of the world, there where being passes into appearance and unity into variety.

The universe is the externization of the soul. Wherever the life is, that bursts into appearance around it. Our science is sensual, and therefore superficial. The earth and the heavenly bodies, physics and chemistry, we sensually treat, as if they were self-existent; but these are the retinue of that being we have. "The mighty heaven," said Proclus, "exhibits, in its transfigurations, clear images of the splendor of intellectual perceptions; being moved in conjunction with the unapparent periods of intellectual natures."[10] Therefore science always goes abreast with the just elevation of the man, keeping step with religion and metaphysics; or the state of science is an index of our self-knowledge. Since everything in nature answers to a moral power, if any phenomenon remains brute and dark it is because the corresponding faculty in the observer is not yet active.

No wonder then, if these waters be so deep, that we hover over them with a religious regard. The beauty of the fable proves the importance of the sense; to the poet, and to all others; or, if you please, every man is so far a poet as to be susceptible of these enchantments of nature; for all men have the thoughts whereof the universe is the celebration. I find that the fascination resides in the symbol. Who loves nature? Who does not? Is it only poets, and men of leisure and cultivation, who live with her? No; but also hunters, farmers, grooms and butchers, though they express their affection in their choice of life and not in their choice of words. The writer wonders what the coachman or the hunter values in riding, in horses and dogs. It is not superficial qualities. When you talk with him he holds these at as slight a rate as you. His worship is sympathetic; he has no definitions, but he is commanded in nature by the living power which he feels to be there present. No imitation or playing of these things would content him; he loves the earnest of the north wind, of rain, of stone and wood and iron. A beauty not explicable is dearer than a beauty which we can see to the end of. It is nature the symbol, nature certifying the supernatural, body overflowed by life which he worships with coarse but sincere rites.

The inwardness and mystery of this attachment drive men of every class to the use of emblems. The schools of poets and philosophers are not more intoxicated with their symbols than the populace with theirs. In our political parties, compute the power of badges and emblems. See the great ball which they roll from Baltimore to Bunker Hill! In the political processions, Lowell goes in a loom, and Lynn in a shoe, and Salem in a ship. Witness the cider barrel, the log cabin, the hickory stick, the palmetto, and all the cognizances of party. See the power of national emblems. Some stars, lilies, leopards, a crescent, a lion, an eagle, or other figure which came into credit God knows how, on an old rag of bunting, blowing in the wind on a fort at the ends of the earth, shall make the blood tingle under the rudest or the most conventional exterior. The people fancy they hate poetry, and they are all poets and mystics!

Beyond this universality of the symbolic language, we are apprised of the divineness of this superior use of things, whereby the world is a temple whose walls are covered with emblems, pictures and commandments of the Deity—in this, that there is no fact in nature which does not carry the whole sense of nature; and the distinctions which we make in events and in affairs, of low and high, honest and base, disappear when nature is used as a symbol.[11] Thought makes everything fit for use. The vocabulary of an omniscient man would embrace words and images excluded from polite conversation. What would be base, or even obscene, to the obscene, becomes illustrious, spoken in a new connection of thought. The piety of the Hebrew prophets purges their grossness. The circumcision is an example of the power of poetry to raise the low and offensive. Small and mean things serve as well as great symbols. The meaner the type by which a law is expressed, the more pungent it is, and the more lasting in the memories of men; just as we choose the smallest box or case in which any needful utensil can be carried. Bare lists of words are found suggestive to an imaginative and excited mind, as it is related of Lord Chatham that he was accustomed to read in Bailey's Dictionary when he was preparing

---

[9] *A Hymn in Honor of Beauty* XIX, 127–34.
[10] Proclus (410?–485), neoplatonic philosopher.

[11] Compare Baudelaire's sonnet *Correspondences*.

to speak in Parliament.[12] The poorest experience is rich enough for all the purposes of expressing thought. Why covet a knowledge of new facts? Day and night, house and garden, a few books, a few actions, serve us as well as would all trades and all spectacles. We are far from having exhausted the significance of the few symbols we use. We can come to use them yet with a terrible simplicity. It does not need that a poem should be long. Every word was once a poem.[13] Every new relation is a new word. Also we use defects and deformities to a sacred purpose, so expressing our sense that the evils of the world are such only to the evil eye. In the old mythology, mythologists observe, defects are ascribed to divine natures, as lameness to Vulcan, blindness to Cupid, and the like—to signify exuberances.

For as it is dislocation and detachment from the life of God that makes things ugly, the poet, who reattaches things to nature and the whole—reattaching even artificial things and violation of nature, to nature, by a deeper insight—disposes very easily of the most disagreeable facts. Readers of poetry see the factory village and the railway, and fancy that the poetry of the landscape is broken up by these; for these works of art are not yet consecrated in their reading; but the poet sees them fall within the great order not less than the beehive or the spider's geometrical web. Nature adopts them very fast into her vital circles, and the gliding train of cars she loves like her own. Besides, in a centered mind, it signifies nothing how many mechanical inventions you exhibit. Though you add millions, and never so surprising, the fact of mechanics has not gained a grain's weight. The spiritual fact remains unalterable, by many or by few particulars; as no mountain is of any appreciable height to break the curve of the sphere. A shrewd country boy goes to the city for the first time, and the complacent citizen is not satisfied with his little wonder. It is not that he does not see all the fine houses and know that he never saw such before, but he disposes of them as easily as the poet finds place for the railway. The chief value of the new fact is to enhance the great and constant fact of life, which can dwarf any and every circumstance, and to which the belt of wampum and the commerce of America are alike.

The world being thus put under the mind for verb and noun, the poet is he who can articulate it. For though life is great, and fascinates and absorbs; and though all men are intelligent of the symbols through which it is named; yet they cannot originally use them. We are symbols and inhabit symbols; workmen, work, and tools, words and things, birth and death, all are emblems; but we sympathize with the symbols, and being infatuated with the economical uses of things, we do not know that they are thoughts. The poet, by an ulterior intellectual perception, gives them a power which makes their old use forgotten, and puts eyes and a tongue into every dumb and inanimate object. He perceives the independence of the thought on the symbol, the stability of the thought, the accidency and fugacity of the symbol. As the eyes of Lynceus were said to see through the earth, so the poet turns the world to glass, and shows us all things in their right series and procession. For through that better perception he stands one step nearer to things, and sees the flowing or metamorphosis; perceives that thought is multiform; that within the form of every creature is a force impelling it to ascend into a higher form; and following with his eyes the life, uses the forms which express that life, and so his speech flows with the flowing of nature. All the facts of the animal economy, sex, nutriment, gestation, birth, growth, are symbols of the passage of the world into the soul of man, to suffer there a change and reappear a new and higher fact. He uses forms according to the life, and not according to the form. This is true science. The poet alone knows astronomy, chemistry, vegetation and animation, for he does not stop at these facts, but employs them as signs. He knows why the plain or meadow of space was strown with these flowers we call suns and moons and stars; why the great deep is adorned with animals, with men, and gods; for in every word he speaks he rides on them as the horses of thought.

By virtue of this science the poet is the namer or language-maker, naming things sometimes after their appearance, sometimes after their essence, and giving to every one its own name and not another's, thereby rejoicing the intellect, which delights in detachment or boundary. The poets made all the words, and therefore language is the archives of history, and, if we must say it, a sort of tomb of the Muses. For though the origin of most of our words is forgotten, each word was at first a stroke of genius, and obtained currency because for the moment it symbolized the world to the first speaker and to the hearer. The etymologist finds the deadest word to have been once a brilliant picture. Language is fossil poetry. As the limestone of the continent consists of infinite masses of the shells of animalcules, so language is made up of images or tropes, which now, in their secondary use, have long ceased to remind us of their poetic origin.[14] But the poet names the thing because he sees it, or comes one step nearer to it than any other. This expression or naming is not art, but a second nature, grown out of the first, as a leaf out of a tree. What we call nature

---

[12] William Pitt, first Earl of Chatham (1708–1778). Nathan Bailey published two dictionaries (1721, 1730).

[13] Compare Vico (above, page 317).

[14] Compare Shelley (above, page 539).

is a certain self-regulated motion or change; and nature does all things by her own hands, and does not leave another to baptize her but baptizes herself; and this through the metamorphosis again. I remember that a certain poet described it to me thus: "Genius is the activity which repairs the decays of things, whether wholly or partly of a material and finite kind. Nature, through all her kingdoms, insures herself. Nobody cares for planting the poor fungus; so she shakes down from the gills of one agaric countless spores, any one of which, being preserved, transmits new billions of spores tomorrow or next day. The new agaric of this hour has a chance which the old one had not. This atom of seed is thrown into a new place, not subject to the accidents which destroyed its parent two rods off. She makes a man; and having brought him to ripe age, she will no longer run the risk of losing this wonder at a blow, but she detaches from him a new self, that the kind may be safe from accidents to which the individual is exposed. So when the soul of the poet has come to ripeness of thought, she detaches and sends away from it its poems or songs—a fearless, sleepless, deathless progeny, which is not exposed to the accidents of the weary kingdom of time; a fearless, vivacious offspring, clad with wings (such was the virtue of the soul out of which they came) which carry them fast and far, and infix them irrecoverably into the hearts of men. These wings are the beauty of the poet's soul. The songs, thus flying immortal from their mortal parent, are pursued by clamorous flights of censures, which swarm in far greater numbers and threaten to devour them; but these last are not winged. At the end of a very short leap they fall plump down and rot, having received from the souls out of which they came no beautiful wings. But the melodies of the poet ascend and leap and pierce into the deeps of infinite time."

So far the bard taught me, using his freer speech. But nature has a higher end, in the production of new individuals, than security, namely *ascension,* or the passage of the soul into higher forms. I knew in my younger days the sculptor who made the statue of the youth which stands in the public garden. He was, as I remember, unable to tell directly what made him happy or unhappy, but by wonderful indirections he could tell. He rose one day, according to his habit, before the dawn, and saw the morning break, grand as the eternity out of which it came, and for many days after, he strove to express this tranquility, and lo! His chisel had fashioned out of marble the form of a beautiful youth, Phosphorus, whose aspect is such that it is said all persons who look on it become silent. The poet also resigns himself to his mood, and that thought which agitated him is expressed, but *alter idem,*[15] in

a manner totally new. The expression is organic, or the new type which things themselves take when liberated. As, in the sun, objects paint their images on the retina of the eye, so they, sharing the aspiration of the whole universe, tend to paint a far more delicate copy of their essence in his mind. Like the metamorphosis of things into higher organic forms is their change into melodies. Over everything stands its demon or soul, and, as the form of the thing is reflected by the eye, so the soul of the thing is reflected by a melody. The sea, the mountain ridge, Niagara, and every flowerbed, preexist, or superexist, in precantations, which sail like odors in the air, and when any man goes by with an ear sufficiently fine, he overhears them and endeavors to write down the notes without diluting or depraving them. And herein is the legitimation of criticism, in the mind's faith that the poems are a corrupt version of some text in nature with which they ought to be made to tally. A rhyme in one of our sonnets should not be less pleasing than the iterated nodes of a seashell, or the resembling difference of a group of flowers. The pairing of the birds is an idyl, not tedious as our idyls are; a tempest is a rough ode, without falsehood or rant; a summer, with its harvest sown, reaped and stored, is an epic song, subordinating how many admirably executed parts. Why should not the symmetry and truth that modulate these, glide into our spirits, and we participate the invention of nature?

This insight, which expresses itself by what is called imagination, is a very high sort of seeing, which does not come by study, but by the intellect being where and what it sees; by sharing the path or circuit of things through forms, and so making them translucid to others. The path of things is silent. Will they suffer a speaker to go with them? A spy they will not suffer; a lover, a poet, is the transcendency of their own nature—him they will suffer. The condition of true naming, on the poet's part, is his resigning himself to the divine aura which breathes through forms, and accompanying that.

It is a secret which every intellectual man quickly learns, that beyond the energy of his possessed and conscious intellect he is capable of a new energy (as of an intellect doubled on itself), by abandonment to the nature of things; that beside his privacy of power as an individual man, there is a great public power on which he can draw, by unlocking, at all risks, his human doors, and suffering the ethereal tides to roll and circulate through him; then he is caught up into the life of the universe, his speech is thunder, his thought is law, and his words are universally intelligible as the plants and animals. The poet knows that he speaks adequately then only when he speaks somewhat wildly, or "with the flower of the mind"; not with the intellect used as an organ, but with the intellect released from all service and

---

[15]"Same and different."

suffered to take its direction from its celestial life, or as the ancients were wont to express themselves, not with intellect alone but with the intellect inebriated by nectar. As the traveler who has lost his way throws his reins on his horse's neck and trusts to the instinct of the animal to find his road, so must we do with the divine animal who carries us through this world. For if in any manner we can stimulate this instinct, new passages are opened for us into nature; the mind flows into and through things hardest and highest, and the metamorphosis is possible.

This is the reason why bards love wine, mead, narcotics, coffee, tea, opium, the fumes of sandalwood and tobacco, or whatever other procurers of animal exhilaration. All men avail themselves of such means as they can, to add this extraordinary power to their normal powers; and to this end they prize conversation, music, pictures, sculpture, dancing, theaters, traveling, war, mobs, fires, gaming, politics, or love, or science, or animal intoxication—which are several coarser or finer quasi-mechanical substitutes for the true nectar, which is the ravishment of the intellect by coming nearer to the fact. These are auxiliaries to the centrifugal tendency of a man, to his passage out into free space, and they help him to escape the custody of that body in which he is pent up, and of that jail-yard of individual relations in which he is enclosed. Hence a great number of such as were professionally expressers of beauty, as painters, poets, musicians and actors, have been more than others wont to lead a life of pleasure and indulgence; all but the few who received the true nectar; and, as it was a spurious mode attaining freedom, as it was an emancipation not into the heavens but into the freedom of baser places, they were punished for that advantage they won, by a dissipation and deterioration. But never can any advantage be taken of nature by a trick. The spirit of the world, the great calm presence of the Creator, comes not forth to the sorceries of opium or of wine. The sublime vision comes to the pure and simple soul in a clean and chaste body. That is not an inspiration, which we owe to narcotics, but some counterfeit excitement and fury. Milton says that the lyric poet may drink wine and live generously, but the epic poet, he who shall sing of the gods and their descent unto men, must drink water out of a wooden bowl. For poetry is not "devil's wine," but God's wine. It is with this as it is with toys. We fill the hands and nurseries of our children with all manner of dolls, drums and horses; withdrawing their eyes from the plain face and sufficing objects of nature, the sun and moon, the animals, the water and stones, which should be their toys. So the poet's habit of living should be set on a key so low that the common influences should delight him. His cheerfulness should be the gift of the sunlight; the air should suffice for his inspiration, and he should be tipsy with water. That spirit which suffices quiet hearts, which seems to come forth to such from every dry knoll of sere grass, from every pine stump and half-imbedded stone on which the dull March sun shines, comes forth to the poor and hungry, and such as are of simple taste. If thou fill thy brain with Boston and New York, with fashion and covetousness, and wilt stimulate thy jaded senses with wine and French coffee, thou shalt find no radiance of wisdom in the lonely waste of the pine woods.

If the imagination intoxicates the poet, it is not inactive in other men. The metamorphosis excites in the beholder an emotion of joy. The use of symbols has a certain power of emancipation and exhilaration for all men. We seem to be touched by a wand which makes us dance and run about happily like children. We are like persons who come out of a cave or cellar into the open air. This is the effect on us of tropes, fables, oracles and all poetic forms. Poets are thus liberating gods. Men have really got a new sense, and found within their world another world, or nest of worlds; for, the metamorphosis once seen, we divine that it does not stop. I will not now consider how much this makes the charm of algebra and the mathematics, which also have their tropes, but it is felt in every definition; as when Aristotle defines *space* to be an immovable vessel in which things are contained; or when Plato defines a *line* to be a flowing point; or *figure* to be a bound of solid; and many the like. What a joyful sense of freedom we have when Vitruvius announces the old opinion of artists that no architect can build any house well who does not know something of anatomy.[16] When Socrates, in *Charmides,* tells us that the soul is cured of its maladies by certain incantations, and that these incantations are beautiful reasons, from which temperance is generated in souls; when Plato calls the world an animal, and Timaeus affirms that the plants also are animals; or affirms a man to be a heavenly tree, growing with his root, which is his head, upward; and, as George Chapman, following him, writes, "So in our tree of man, whose nervy root / Springs in his top";[17] when Orpheus speaks of hoariness as "that white flower which marks extreme old age"; when Proclus calls the universe the statue of the intellect; when Chaucer, in his praise of "gentilesse," compares good blood in mean condition to fire, which, though carried to the darkest house betwixt this and the mount of Caucasus, will yet hold its natural office and burn as bright as if twenty thousand men did it behold; when John saw, in the Apocalypse, the ruin of the world

[16] Marcus Vitruvius Pollio (first century), Roman writer on architecture.
[17] George Chapman (1559?–1634), Epistle Dedicatory to his translation of *Iliad,* 132–33.

through evil, and the stars fall from heaven as the fig tree casteth her untimely fruit; when Aesop reports the whole catalogue of common daily relations through the masquerade of birds and beasts; we take the cheerful hint of the immortality of our essence and its versatile habit and escapes, as when the gypsies say of themselves "it is in vain to hang them, they cannot die."

The poets are thus liberating gods. The ancient British bards had for the title of their order, "Those who are free throughout the world." They are free, and they make free. An imaginative book renders us much more service at first, by stimulating us through its tropes, than afterward when we arrive at the precise sense of the author. I think nothing is of any value in books excepting the transcendental and extraordinary. If a man is inflamed and carried away by his thought, to that degree that he forgets the authors and the public and heeds only this one dream which holds him like an insanity, let me read his paper, and you may have all the arguments and histories and criticism. All the value which attaches to Pythagoras, Paracelsus, Cornelius Agrippa, Cardan, Kepler, Swedenborg, Schelling, Oken, or any other who introduces questionable facts into his cosmogony, as angels, devils, magic, astrology, palmistry, mesmerism, and so on, is the certificate we have of departure from routine, and that here is a new witness.[18] That also is the best success in conversation, the magic of liberty, which puts the world like a ball in our hands. How cheap even the liberty then seems; how mean to study, when an emotion communicates to the intellect the power to sap and upheave nature; how great the perspective! Nations, times, systems, enter and disappear like threads in tapestry of large figure and many colors; dream delivers us to dream, and while the drunkenness lasts we will sell our bed, our philosophy, our religion, in our opulence.

There is good reason why we should prize this liberation. The fate of the poor shepherd, who, blinded and lost in the snowstorm, perishes in a drift within a few feet of his cottage door, is an emblem of the state of man. On the brink of the waters of life and truth, we are miserably dying. The inaccessibleness of every thought but that we are in, is wonderful. What if you come near to it, you are as remote when you are nearest as when you are farthest. Every thought is also a prison; every heaven is also a prison. Therefore we

love the poet, the inventor, who in any form, whether in an ode or in an action or in looks and behavior, has yielded us a new thought. He unlocks our chains and admits us to a new scene.

This emancipation is dear to all men, and the power to impart it, as it must come from greater depth and scope of thought, is a measure of intellect. Therefore all books of the imagination endure, all which ascend to that truth that the writer sees nature beneath him, and uses it as his exponent. Every verse or sentence possessing this virtue will take care of its own immortality. The religions of the world are the ejaculations of a few imaginative men.

But the quality of the imagination is to flow, and not to freeze. The poet did not stop at the color or the form, but read their meaning; neither may he rest in this meaning, but he makes the same objects exponents of his new thought. Here is the difference betwixt the poet and the mystic, that the last nails a symbol to one sense, which was a true sense for a moment, but soon becomes old and false. For all symbols are fluxional; all language is vehicular and transitive, and is good, as ferries and horses are, for conveyance, not as farms and houses are, for homestead. Mysticism consists is the mistake of an accidental and individual symbol for an universal one. The morning redness happens to be the favorite meteor to the eyes of Jacob Behmen,[19] and comes to stand to him for truth and faith; and, he believes, should stand for the same realities to every reader. But the first reader prefers as naturally the symbol of a mother and child, or a gardener and his bulb, or a jeweler polishing a gem. Either of these, or of a myriad more, are equally good to the person to whom they are significant. Only they must be held lightly, and be very willingly translated into the equivalent terms which others use. And the mystic must be steadily told, all that you say is just as true without the tedious use of that symbol as with it. Let us have a little algebra, instead of this trite rhetoric—universal signs, instead of these village symbols—and we shall both be gainers. The history of hierarchies seems to show that all religious error consisted in making the symbol too stark and solid, and was at last nothing but an excess of the organ of language.

Swedenborg, of all men in the recent ages, stands eminently for the translator of nature into thought. I do not know the man in history to whom things stood so uniformly for words. Before him the metamorphosis continually plays. Everything on which his eye rests, obeys the impulses of moral nature. The figs become grapes whilst he eats them. When some of his angels affirmed a truth, the laurel twig

[18] Pythagoras (c. 582–c. 507 B.C.), Greek philosopher; Paracelsus (Theophrastus Bombastus von Hohenheim, 1493?–1541), Swiss physician and alchemist; Cornelius Agrippa (1486–1535), physician known for his occultist writings; Jerome Cardan (1501–1576?), French occultist; Johannes Kepler (1571–1630), German astronomer; Friedrich Wilhelm Joseph Schelling (1775–1854), German philosopher; Lorenz Oken (1779–1851), German philosopher.

[19] Usually spelled Jacob Boehme (1575–1624), German religious mystic.

which they held blossomed in their hands. The noise which at a distance appeared like gnashing and thumping, on coming nearer was found to be the voice of disputants. The men in one of his visions, seen in heavenly light, appeared like dragons, and seemed in darkness; but to each other they appeared as men, and when the light from heaven shone into their cabin, they complained of the darkness, and were compelled to shut the window that they might see.

There was this perception in him which makes the poet or seer an object of awe and terror, namely that the same man or society of men may wear one aspect to themselves and their companions, and a different aspect to higher intelligences. Certain priests, whom he describes as conversing very learnedly together, appeared to the children who were at some distance, like dead horses; and many the like misappearances. And instantly the mind inquires whether these fishes under the bridge, yonder oxen in the pasture, those dogs in the yard, are immutably fishes, oxen and dogs, or only so appear to me, and perchance to themselves appear upright men; and whether I appear as a man to all eyes. The Brahmins[20] and Pythagoras propounded the same question, and if any poet has witnessed the transformation he doubtless found it in harmony with various experiences. We have all seen changes as considerable in wheat and caterpillars. He is the poet and shall draw us with love and terror, who sees through the flowing vest the firm nature, and can declare it.

I look in vain for the poet whom I describe. We do not with sufficient plainness or sufficient profoundness address ourselves to life, nor dare we chant our own times and social circumstance. If we filled the day with bravery, we should not shrink from celebrating it. Time and nature yield us many gifts, but not yet the timely man, the new religion, the reconciler, whom all things await. Dante's praise is that he dared to write his autobiography in colossal cipher, or into universality. We have yet had no genius in America, with tyrannous eye, which knew the value of our incomparable materials, and saw, in the barbarism and materialism of the times, another carnival of the same gods whose picture he so much admires in Homer; then in the Middle Age; then in Calvinism. Banks and tariffs, the newspaper and caucus, Methodism and Unitarianism, are flat and dull to dull people, but rest on the same foundations of wonder as the town of Troy and the temple of Delphi, and are as swiftly passing away. Our log-rolling, our stumps and their politics, our fisheries, our Negroes and Indians, our boats and our repudiations, the wrath of rogues and the pusillanimity of honest men, the northern trade, the southern plant-

ing, the western clearing, Oregon and Texas, are yet unsung. Yet America is a poem in our eyes; its ample geography dazzles the imagination, and it will not wait long for meters. If I have not found that excellent combination of gifts in my countrymen which I seek, neither could I aid myself to fix the idea of the poet by reading now and then in Chalmers's collection of five centuries of English poets. These are wits more than poets, though there have been poets among them. But when we adhere to the ideal of the poet, we have our difficulties even with Milton and Homer. Milton is too literary, and Homer too literal and historical.

But I am not wise enough for a national criticism, and must use the old largeness a little longer, to discharge my errand from the Muse to the poet concerning his art.

Art is the path of the creator to his work. The paths or methods are ideal and eternal, though few men ever see them; not the artist himself for years, or for a lifetime, unless he come into the conditions. The painter, the sculptor, the composer, the epic rhapsodist, the orator, all partake one desire, namely to express themselves symmetrically and abundantly, not dwarfishly and fragmentarily. They found or put themselves in certain conditions, as, the painter and sculptor before some impressive human figures; the orator into the assembly of the people; and the others in such scenes as each has found exciting to his intellect; and each presently feels the new desire. He hears a voice, he sees a beckoning. Then he is apprised, with wonder, what herds of demons hem him in. He can no more rest; he says, with the old painter, "By God it is in me and must go forth of me." He pursues a beauty, half seen, which flies before him. The poet pours out verses in every solitude. Most of the things he says are conventional, no doubt; but by and by he says something which is original and beautiful. That charms him. He would say nothing else but such things. In our way of talking we say "That is yours, this is mine"; but the poet knows well that it is not his; that it is as strange and beautiful to him as to you; he would fain hear the like eloquence at length. Once having tasted this immortal ichor, he cannot have enough of it, and as an admirable creative power exists in these intellections, it is of the last importance that these things get spoken. What a little of all we know is said! What drops of all the sea of our science are baled up! And by what accident it is that these are exposed, when so many secrets sleep in nature! Hence the necessity of speech and song; hence these throbs and heart-beatings in the orator, at the door of the assembly, to the end namely that thought may be ejaculated as logos, or word.

Doubt not, O poet, but persist. Say "It is in me, and shall out." Stand there, balked and dumb, stuttering and stammering, hissed and hooted, stand and strive, until at

---

[20] Hindu priests.

last rage draw out of thee that dream power which every night shows thee is thine own; a power transcending all limit and privacy, and by virtue of which a man is the conductor of the whole river of electricity. Nothing walks, or creeps, or grows, or exists, which must not in turn arise and walk before him as exponent of his meaning. Comes he to that power, his genius is no longer exhaustible. All the creatures by pairs and by tribes pour into his mind as into a Noah's ark, to come forth again to people a new world. This is like the stock of air for our respiration or for the combustion of our fireplace; not a measure of gallons, but the entire atmosphere if wanted. And therefore the rich poets, as Homer, Chaucer, Shakespeare, and Raphael,[21] have obviously no limits to their works except the limits of their lifetime, and resemble a mirror carried through the street, ready to render an image of every created thing.

O poet! A new nobility is conferred in groves and pastures, and not in castles or by the sword blade any longer. The conditions are hard, but equal. Thou shalt leave the world, and know the Muse only. Thou shalt not know any longer the times, customs, graces, politics, or opinions of men, but shalt take all from the Muse. For the time of towns is tolled from the world by funereal chimes, but in nature the universal hours are counted by succeeding tribes of animals and plants, and by growth of joy on joy. God wills also that thou abdicate a manifold and duplex life, and that thou be content that others speak for thee. Others shall be thy gentlemen and shall represent all courtesy and worldly life for thee; others shall do the great and resounding actions also. Thou shalt lie close hid with nature, and canst not be afforded to the Capitol or the Exchange. The world is full of renunciations and apprenticeships, and this is thine; thou must pass for a fool and a churl for a long season. This is the screen and sheath in which Pan has protected his well-beloved flower, and thou shalt be known only to thine own, and they shall console thee with tenderest love. And thou shalt not be able to rehearse the names of thy friends in thy verse, for an old shame before the holy ideal. And this is the reward; that the ideal shall be real to thee, and the impressions of the actual world shall fall like summer rain, copious, but not troublesome to thy invulnerable essence. Thou shalt have the whole land for thy park and manor, the sea for thy bath and navigation, without tax and without envy; the woods and the rivers thou shalt own, and thou shalt possess that wherein others are only tenants and boarders. Thou true landlord! Sealord! Airlord! Wherever snow falls or water flows or birds fly, wherever day and night meet in twilight, wherever the blue heaven is hung by clouds or sown with stars, wherever are forms with transparent boundaries, wherever are outlets into celestial space, wherever is danger, and awe, and love, there is beauty, plenteous as rain, shed for thee, and though thou shouldst walk the world over, thou shalt not be able to find a condition inopportune or ignoble.

[21] The inclusion of the Italian painter Raphael Santi (1483–1520) in a group of poets reflects the typically Romantic notion that poetry is something other than artifice, that it resides in the spirit of the poet.

Edgar Allan Poe

1809–1849

Poe's essay *The Poetic Principle* is interesting as an example of a certain kind of Romantic extremism as well as an example of renewed interest in the response of the reader. The remark that a long poem is a "flat contradiction in terms" goes far beyond Coleridge's earlier assertion (above, page 507) that a long poem need not be all poetry. In both cases poetry becomes a quality inherent in some writing, and perhaps inherent in nature or experience. It is not identical to a poem. Coleridge's use of "poetry" and "poem" is, however, more precise than Poe's, who leaves us confused about just what he means. We can conclude that for Poe, as for most Romantic sensibilities, the lyric was the model poem. Poe seems to have been prescient when he asserted that no long poem would again be popular.

Poe's judgment on the long poem is made purely in terms of what he conceives the reader's attention span to be. The value of a work depends wholly on the emotional effect, which is limited by the short staying power of the reader. He finds that Book II of Milton's *Paradise Lost* is no good if one has just waded through Book I, but is quite good if one omits Book I and begins with Book II. Hope of an objective judgment of taste, as discussed, for example, by Hume (above, page 323) and Kames (above, page 372), seems to be denied here. In another essay, *The Philosophy of Composition,* written three or four years before *The Poetic Principle,* Poe makes the same points and insists that the poet should begin his composition with a consideration of the effect of the work. He should limit the length of his poem, make it "universally appreciable," and convey a particular tone. Poe opts for sadness, which he considers the "most legitimate of all tones." In this he reveals an extreme form of Romantic taste.

In *The Poetic Principle* Poe also takes the Romantic distinction between poem and discursive statement to an extreme. He attacks the "didactic heresy," by which he means the tendency to think of a poem in terms of its message or discursive content. In this he foreshadows the notion of "heresy of paraphrase" offered by Cleanth Brooks (below, page 1036). For Poe, the poem exists only "for the poem's sake." But when Poe tries to discuss the value of poetry or a poem, he seems unequipped to go beyond remarks about "supernal beauty" and definitions of the poem as the "rhythmical creation of beauty." Still, he presents an example of certain Romantic legacies, and his theories were impressive enough to have influenced Charles Baudelaire, whose critical intelligence was more sophisticated.

Poe's complete works have been edited by J. A. Harrison (in seventeen volumes, 1902); his literary criticism has been edited by R. L. Hough (1965). See also C. H. Sisson, ed., *Poe's Poems and Essays on Poetry* (1995). For commentary that includes discussion of Poe as a literary critic, see Margaret Alterton, *Origins of Poe's Critical Theory* (1925); Floyd Stovall, "Poe's Debt to Coleridge," *Texas Studies in English* X (1930), 70–127; A. H. Quinn, *Edgar Allan Poe: A Critical Biography* (1941); E. H. Davidson,

Poe: A Critical Study (1957); Emerson R. Marks, "Poe as Literary Theorist: A Reappraisal," *American Literature* XXXIII (1961), 296–306; E. W. Parks, *Edgar Allan Poe as a Literary Critic* (1964); Robert D. Jacobs, *Poe: Journalist and Critic* (1969); Arthur Hobson Quinn, *Edgar Allan Poe: A Critical Biography* (1998).

from

The Poetic Principle

In speaking of the poetic principle, I have no design to be either thorough or profound. While discussing, very much at random, the essentiality of what we call poetry, my principal purpose will be to cite for consideration some few of those minor English or American poems which best suit my own taste, or which, upon my own fancy, have left the most definite impression. By "minor poems" I mean, of course, poems of little length. And here, in the beginning, permit me to say a few words in regard to a somewhat peculiar principle, which, whether rightfully or wrongly, has always had its influence in my own critical estimate of the poem. I hold that a long poem does not exist. I maintain that the phrase, *a long poem,* is simply a flat contradiction in terms.

I need scarcely observe that a poem deserves its title only inasmuch as it excites, by elevating the soul. The value of the poem is in the ratio of this elevating excitement. But all excitements are, through a psychal necessity, transient. That degree of excitement which would entitle a poem to be so called at all cannot be sustained throughout a composition of any great length. After the lapse of half an hour, at the very utmost, it flags—fails—a revulsion ensues—and then the poem is, in effect, and in fact, no longer such.

There are, no doubt, many who have found difficulty in reconciling the critical dictum that the *Paradise Lost* is to be devoutly admired throughout, with the absolute impossibility of maintaining for it, during perusal, the amount of enthusiasm which that critical dictum would demand. This great work, in fact, is to be regarded as poetical, only when, losing sight of that vital requisite in all works of art, unity, we view it merely as a series of minor poems. If, to preserve its unity—its totality of effect or impression—we read it (as would be necessary) at a single sitting, the result is but a constant alternation of excitement and depression. After a passage of what we feel to be true poetry, there follows, inevitably, a passage of platitude which no critical prejudg-

ment can force us to admire; but if, upon completing the work, we read it again omitting the first book—that is to say, commencing with the second—we shall be surprised at now finding that admirable which we before condemned—that damnable which we had previously so much admired. It follows from all this that the ultimate, aggregate, or absolute effect of even the best epic under the sun, is a nullity—and this is precisely the fact.

In regard to the *Iliad,* we have, if not positive proof, at least very good reason, for believing it intended as a series of lyrics; but, granting the epic intention, I can say only that the work is based in an imperfect sense of art. The modern epic is, of the supposititious ancient model, but an inconsiderate and blindfold imitation. But the day of these artistic anomalies is over. If, at any time, any very long poem were popular in reality, which I doubt, it is at least clear that no very long poem will ever be popular again.

That the extent of a poetical work is, *ceteris paribus,*[1] the measure of its merit, seems undoubtedly, when we thus state it, a proposition sufficiently absurd—yet we are indebted for it to the quarterly reviews. Surely there can be nothing in mere size, abstractly considered—there can be nothing in mere bulk, so far as a volume is concerned, which has so continuously elicited admiration from these saturnine pamphlets! A mountain, to be sure, by the mere sentiment of physical magnitude which it conveys, does impress us with a sense of the sublime—but no man is impressed after this fashion by the material grandeur of even *The Columbiad.*[2] Even the quarterlies have not instructed us to be so impressed by it. As yet, they have not insisted on our estimating Lamartine by the cubic foot, or Pollok[3] by the pound—but what else are we to infer from their continued prating about "sustained effort"? If, by "sustained effort," any little gentleman has accomplished an epic, let us frankly commend him for the effort—if this indeed be a thing commendable—but let us forbear praising the epic on the effort's account. It is to be hoped that common sense, in the time to come, will prefer deciding upon a work of art,

---

Poe's *The Poetic Principle* was delivered as a lecture several times in 1848 and 1849. It was published posthumously in 1850.

[1] "Other things equal."
[2] *The Columbiad* by Joel Barlow (1754–1812), American poet.
[3] Alphonse Marie Louis de Lamartine (1790–1869), French poet; Robert Pollok (1798–1827), Scottish poet.

rather by the impression it makes, by the effect it produces, than by the time it took to impress the effect or by the amount of "sustained effort" which had been found necessary in effecting the impression. The fact is, that perseverance is one thing, and genius quite another—nor can all the quarterlies in Christendom confound them. By and by, this proposition, with many which I have been just urging, will be received as self-evident. In the meantime, by being generally condemned as falsities, they will not be essentially damaged as truths.

On the other hand, it is clear that a poem may be improperly brief. Undue brevity degenerates into mere epigrammatism. A very short poem, while now and then producing a brilliant or vivid, never produces a profound or enduring effect. There must be the steady pressing down of the stamp upon the wax. Béranger[4] has wrought innumerable things, pungent and spirit-stirring; but, in general, they have been too imponderous to stamp themselves deeply into the public attention; and thus, as so many feathers of fancy, have been blown aloft only to be whistled down the wind.

A remarkable instance of the effect of undue brevity in depressing a poem—in keeping it out of the popular view— is afforded by the following exquisite little serenade:

> I arise from dreams of thee
>> In the first sweet sleep of night,
> When the winds are breathing low,
>> And the stars are shining bright;
> I arise from dreams of thee,
>> And a spirit in my feet
> Hath led me—who knows how?
>> To thy chamber-window, sweet!
>
> The wandering airs, they faint
>> On the dark, the silent stream;
> The champak odors fail
>> Like sweet thoughts in a dream;
> The nightingale's complaint,
>> It dies upon her heart,
> As I must die on thine,
>> Oh, beloved as thou art!
>
> Oh, lift me from the grass!
>> I die! I faint! I fail!
> Let thy love in kisses rain
>> On my lips and eyelids pale.
> My cheek is cold and white, alas!
>> My heart beats loud and fast:

> Oh! Press it close to thine again,
>> Where it will break at last![5]

Very few, perhaps, are familiar with these lines—yet no less a poet than Shelley is their author. Their warm, yet delicate and ethereal imagination will be appreciated by all—but by none so thoroughly as by him who has himself arisen from sweet dreams of one beloved to bathe in the aromatic air of a southern midsummer night.

One of the finest poems by Willis—the very best in my opinion, which he has ever written—has, no doubt, through this same defect of undue brevity, been kept back from its proper position, not less in the critical than in the popular view.

> The shadows lay along Broadway,
>> 'Twas near the twilight tide,
> And slowly there a lady fair
>> Was walking in her pride.
> Alone walked she; but, viewlessly,
>> Walked spirits at her side.
>
> Peace charmed the street beneath her feet
>> And honor charmed the air;
> And all astir looked kind on her,
>> And called her good as fair,
> For all God ever gave to her
>> She kept with chary care.
>
> She kept with care her beauties rare
>> From lovers warm and true,
> For her heart was cold to all but gold,
>> And the rich came not to woo—
> But honored well are charms to sell
>> If priests the selling do.
>
> Now walking there was one more fair—
>> A slight girl, lily pale;
> And she had unseen company
>> To make the spirit quail:
> 'Twixt want and scorn she walked forlorn,
>> And nothing could avail.
>
> No mercy now can clear her brow
>> For this world's peace to pray;

---

[4] Pierre Jean de Béranger (1780–1857), French songwriter.

[5] Percy Bysshe Shelley, *The Indian Serenade*. For a dissenting view see Robert Penn Warren's *Pure and Impure Poetry* (1943, reprinted in Warren's *Selected Essays*, 1958), which makes a negative judgment on the poem characteristic of the New Criticism.

> For, as love's wild prayer dissolved in air,
>   Her woman's heart gave way!
> But the sin forgiven by Christ in heaven
>   By man is cursed away![6]

In this composition we find it difficult to recognize the Willis who has written so many mere "verses of society." The lines are not only richly ideal, but full of energy; while they breathe an earnestness—an evident sincerity of sentiment—for which we look in vain throughout all the other works of this author.

While the epic mania—while the idea that, to merit in poetry, prolixity is indispensable—has, for some years past, been gradually dying out of the public mind, by mere dint of its own absurdity, we find it succeeded by a heresy too palpably false to be long tolerated, but one which, in the brief period it has already endured, may be said to have accomplished more in the corruption of our poetical literature than all its other enemies combined. I allude to the heresy of "the didactic." It has been assumed, tacitly and avowedly, directly and indirectly, that the ultimate object of all poetry is truth. Every poem, it is said, should inculcate a moral; and by this moral is the poetical merit of the work to be adjudged. We Americans, especially, have patronized this happy idea; and we Bostonians, very especially, have developed it in full. We have taken it into our heads that to write a poem simply for the poem's sake,[7] and to acknowledge such to have been our design, would be to confess ourselves radically wanting in the true poetic dignity and force: but the simple fact is, that, would we but permit ourselves to look into our own souls, we should immediately there discover that under the sun there neither exists not can exist any work more thoroughly dignified—more supremely noble than this very poem—this poem per se—this poem which is a poem and nothing more—this poem written solely for the poem's sake.

With as deep a reverence for the true as ever inspired the bosom of man, I would, nevertheless, limit, in some measure, its modes of inculcation. I would limit to enforce them. I would not enfeeble them by dissipation. The demands of truth are severe. She has no sympathy with the myrtles. All that which is so indispensable in song, is precisely all that with which she has nothing whatever to do. It is but making her a flaunting paradox, to wreathe her in gems and flowers. In enforcing a truth, we need severity rather than efflorescence of language. We must be simple, precise, terse. We must be cool, calm, unimpassioned. In a word, we must be in that mood which, as nearly as possible, is the exact converse of the poetical. He must be blind, indeed, who does not perceive the radical and chasmal differences between the truthful and the poetical modes of inculcation. He must be theory-mad beyond redemption who, in spite of these differences, shall still persist in attempting to reconcile the obstinate oils and waters of poetry and truth.

Dividing the world of mind into its three most obvious distinctions, we have the pure intellect, taste, and the moral sense. I place taste in the middle, because it is just this position which in the mind it occupies. It holds intimate relations with either extreme; but from the moral sense is separated by so faint a difference that Aristotle has not hesitated to place some of its operations among the virtues themselves.[8] Nevertheless, we find the offices of the trio marked with a sufficient distinction. Just as the intellect concerns itself with truth, so taste informs us of the beautiful, while the moral sense is regardful of duty. Of this latter, while conscience teaches the obligation, and reason the expediency, taste contents herself with displaying the charms: waging war upon vice solely on the ground of her deformity—her disproportion, her animosity to the fitting, to the appropriate, to the harmonious—in a word, to beauty.

An immortal instinct, deep within the spirit of man, is thus, plainly, a sense of the beautiful. This it is which administers to his delight in the manifold forms, and sounds, and odors, and sentiments amid which he exists. And just as the lily is repeated in the lake, or the eyes of Amaryllis in the mirror, so is the mere oral or written repetition of these forms, and sounds, and colors, and odors, and sentiments, a duplicate source of delight. But this mere repetition is not poetry. He who shall simply sing, with however glowing enthusiasm, or with however vivid a truth of description, of the sights, and sounds, and odors, and colors, and sentiments, which greet him in common with all mankind—he, I say, has yet failed to prove his divine title. There is still a something in the distance which he has been unable to attain. We have still a thirst unquenchable, to allay which he has not shown us the crystal springs. This thirst belongs to the immortality of man. It is at once a consequence and an indication of his perennial existence. It is the desire of the moth for the star. It is no mere appreciation of the beauty before us—but a wild effort to reach the beauty above. Inspired by an ecstatic prescience of the glories beyond the grave, we

---

[6] Nathaniel Parker Willis (1806–1867), American writer, *Unseen Spirits.*

[7] This phrase foreshadows a late-nineteenth-century phrase "art for art's sake" made famous by, among others, Oscar Wilde (below, page 711). See also the essay *Poetry for Poetry's Sake* by A. C. Bradley (delivered as a lecture in 1901) in his *Oxford Lectures on Poetry* (1910).

[8] Aristotle (above, page 48).

struggle, by multiform combinations among the things and thoughts of time, to attain a portion of that loveliness whose very elements, perhaps, appertain to eternity alone. And thus when by poetry—or when by music, the most entrancing of the poetic moods—we find ourselves melted into tears—not as the Abbaté Gravina[9] supposes—through excess of pleasure, but through a certain, petulant, impatient sorrow at our inability to grasp now, wholly, here on earth, at once and forever, those divine and rapturous joys, of which through the poem, or through the music, we attain to but brief and indeterminate glimpses.

The struggle to apprehend the supernal loveliness—this struggle, on the part of souls fittingly constituted—has given to the world all that which it (the world) has ever been enabled at once to understand and to feel as poetic.

The poetic sentiment, of course, may develop itself in various modes—in painting, in sculpture, in architecture, in the dance—very especially in music—and very peculiarly, and with a wide field, in the composition of the landscape garden. Our present theme, however, has regard only to its manifestation in words. And here let me speak briefly on the topic of rhythm. Contenting myself with the certainty that music, in its various modes of meter, rhythm, and rhyme, is of so vast a moment in poetry as never to be wisely rejected—is so vitally important an adjunct, that he is simply silly who declines its assistance—I will not now pause to maintain its absolute essentiality. It is in music, perhaps, that the soul most nearly attains the great end for which, when inspired by the poetic sentiment, it struggles—the creation of supernal beauty. It may be, indeed, that here this sublime end is, now and then, attained in fact. We are often made to feel, with a shivering delight, that from an earthly harp are stricken notes which cannot have been unfamiliar to the angels. And thus there can be little doubt that in the union of poetry with music in its popular sense, we shall find the widest field for the poetic development. The old bards and minnesingers had advantages which we do not possess—and Thomas Moore,[10] singing his own songs, was, in the most legitimate manner, perfecting them as poems.

To recapitulate, then: I would define, in brief, the poetry of words as the rhythmical creation of beauty. Its sole arbiter is taste. With the intellect or with the conscience, it has only collateral relations. Unless incidentally, it has no concern whatever either with duty or with truth.

A few words, however, in explanation. That pleasure which is at once the most pure, the most elevating, and the most intense, is derived, I maintain, from the contemplation of the beautiful. In the contemplation of beauty we alone find it possible to attain that pleasurable elevation, or excitement, of the soul, which we recognize as the poetic sentiment, and which is so easily distinguished from truth, which is the satisfaction of the reason, or from passion, which is the excitement of the heart. I make beauty, therefore—using the word as inclusive of the sublime—I make beauty the province of the poem, simply because it is an obvious rule of art that effects should be made to spring as directly as possible from their causes—no one as yet having been weak enough to deny that the peculiar elevation in question is at least most readily attainable in the poem. It by no means follows, however, that the incitements of passion, or the precepts of duty, or even the lessons of truth, may not be introduced into a poem, and with advantage; for they may subserve, incidentally, in various ways, the general purposes of the work—but the true artist will always contrive to tone them down in proper subjection to that beauty which is the atmosphere and the real essence of the poem.

* * *

[Poe proceeds to present and comment briefly on a number of early-nineteenth-century lyric poems.]

Thus, although in a very cursory and imperfect manner, I have endeavored to convey to you my conception of the poetic principle. It has been my purpose to suggest that, while this principle itself is, strictly and simply, the human aspiration for supernal beauty, the manifestation of the principle is always found in an elevating excitement of the soul—quite independent of that passion which is the intoxication of the heart—or of that truth which is the satisfaction of the reason. For, in regard to passion, alas! Its tendency is to degrade, rather than to elevate the soul. Love, on the contrary—love, the true, the divine Eros—the Uranian, as distinguished from the Dionaean Venus[11]—is unquestionably the purest and truest of all poetical themes. And in regard to truth—if, to be sure, through the attainment of a truth, we are led to perceive a harmony where none was apparent before, we experience, at once, the true poetical effect—but this effect is referable to the harmony alone, and not in the least degree to the truth which merely served to render the harmony manifest.

We shall reach, however, more immediately a distinct conception of what the true poetry is, by mere reference to

---

[9]Giancincenzi Gravina (1664–1718), *Della ragion poetica.*
[10]Thomas Moore (1779–1852), Irish poet.

[11]Uranian and Dionaean Venuses represent spiritual and earthly love respectively.

a few of the simple elements which induce in the poet himself the true poetical effect. He recognizes the ambrosia which nourishes his soul, in the bright orbs that shine in heaven—in the volutes of the flower—in the clustering of low shrubberies—in the waving of the grain fields—in the slanting of tall, eastern trees—in the blue distance of mountains—in the grouping of clouds—in the twinkling of half-hidden brooks—in the gleaming of silver rivers—in the repose of sequestered lakes—in the star-mirroring depths of lonely wells. He perceives it in the songs of birds—in the harp of Aeolus—in the sighing of the night wind—in the repining voice of the forest—in the surf that complaints to the shore—in the fresh breath of the woods—in the scent of the violet—in the voluptuous perfume of the hyacinth—in the suggestive odor that comes to him, at eventide, from far-distant, undiscovered islands, over dim oceans, illimitable and unexplored. He owns it in all noble thoughts—in all unworldly motives—in all holy impulses—in all chivalrous, generous, and self-sacrificing deeds. He feels it in the beauty of woman—in the grace of her step—in the luster of her eye—in the melody of her voice—in her soft laughter—in her sigh—in the harmony of the rustling of her robes. He deeply feels it in her winning endearments—in her burning enthusiasms—in her gentle charities—in her meek and devotional endurances —but above all—ah, far above all—he kneels to it—he worships it in the faith, in the purity, in the strength, in the altogether divine majesty—of her love.

Matthew Arnold

1822–1888

Arnold's *The Function of Criticism at the Present Time* (1864) is one of the most influential essays of his day. Here he treats literary criticism as an important branch of a general cultural criticism. In all branches of knowledge the aim of the critical power is the same: "to see the object as in itself it really is." This requires freeing oneself from polemics, refusing to "remain in a sphere where alone narrow and relative conceptions have any worth and validity." Arnold remarks that this is the difficult and indirect path, but it is the only possible one, for criticism must be "disinterested."

In advocating disinterested criticism, Arnold is censuring what he regards as the parochialism of English critics, their ignorance of European intellectual life, their special brand of "Philistinism." The disinterest that he preaches has some relationship to the idea of aesthetic disinterest in Kant's analysis of the reader's response to the work of art (above, page 420). However, Arnold's disinterest is principally an ethical principle based on the rational power rather than an aesthetic one. Arnold is by no means suggesting a withdrawal from effective social criticism but instead insisting on measured, intelligent, and often necessarily indirect critical activity.

Though he rejected a number of Victorian ideas or fashions, Arnold was quite influential in his own time. In an age marked by the emergence of historical criticism, he argues in *The Study of Poetry* against historical judgments on poems. He also rejects what he calls "personal judgments" on grounds similar to those later set forth by I. A. Richards (below, page 856). But when he comes to the question of what sort of critical judgment ought to be made he is in difficulty. He knows that poetry is not simply document or material for generating subjective emotion. But to discuss its value analytically, Arnold believes, is impossible; the value of a poem must simply be recognized. He is fond of terms like "poetic truth" and "high seriousness" (in his view Chaucer, for example, lacks the latter). His method in *The Study of Poetry* is not to attempt definition of such terms but instead to offer poetic examples of them—"touchstones." These touchstones can be as short as a single line. Like several of his Romantic predecessors, Arnold thinks, in this essay, not so much of the quality of a poem as a whole as he does of the presence of an undefinable poetic quality somewhere in a poem. There is no discursively expressible standard for these touchstones, and the catch-all evaluative term "high seriousness" is not explained. A liberally educated reader is apparently supposed to sense the presence of high seriousness. Sound critical judgments are made by educated people, not by those who make a mindless application of principle or method.

Following Arnold, one might at first think criticism doomed to become (1) purely descriptive or (2) purely expressive, pointing to, but not discussing, specimens of high seriousness. But this view misses Arnold's point that one must finally depend on the developed taste and erudition of the critic. In the 1864 essay, where Arnold speaks of "judging" as the critic's business, he points out that it must be "judgment which almost insensibly forms itself in a fair and clear mind, along with fresh knowledge." It is by "communicating fresh knowledge," not mere information, and not by laying down laws and judgments that the critic performs his most useful task. Arnold thus seeks to avoid both criticism that is really scholarship ancillary to the poem and subjective impressionism that is really poetic writing about poems—the approach advocated, for example, by the French critic and novelist Anatole France (1844–1924), who was consistent with himself when he wrote, "To be quite frank, the critic ought to say 'Gentlemen, I am going to talk about myself on the subject of Shakespeare, or Racine, or Pascal, or Goethe—subjects that offer me a beautiful opportunity.'"

Arnold is an interesting figure in the history of the problem of value judgments. He is also important for his development of the argument that the power of true judgment is cultivated and the sensibility enlarged through a liberal education in which the reading of poetry plays an important role. Echoes of Arnold are frequent in later criticism—in the writings, for example, of I. A. Richards (below, page 856), T. S. Eliot (below, page 806), and Northrop Frye (below, page 1136).

The fifteen-volume edition of Arnold's works (1903–1904) was followed by his *Complete Prose Works,* edited by R. H. Super (1960 ff.). See Lionel Trilling *Matthew Arnold* (1939); E. K. Brown, *Arnold: A Study in Conflict* (1948); David Perkins, "Arnold and the Function of Literature," *English Literary History* XVIII (1951), 287–309; J. S. Eells, *The Touchstones of Matthew Arnold* (1955); William Robbins, *The Ethical Idealism of Matthew Arnold* (1959); D. G. James, *Matthew Arnold and the Decline of English Romanticism* (1961); William A. Madden, *Matthew Arnold: A Study of the Aesthetic Temperament in Victorian England* (1967); Park Honan, *Matthew Arnold: A Life* (1981); Joseph Carroll, *The Cultural Theory of Matthew Arnold* (1982); Stefan Collini, *Arnold* (1988); Mary W. Schneider, *Poetry in the Age of Democracy: The Criticism of Matthew Arnold* (1989); Laurence W. Mazzeno, *Matthew Arnold: The Critical Legacy* (1999).

The Function of Criticism at the Present Time

Many objections have been made to a proposition which, in some remarks of mine on translating Homer, I ventured to put forth; a proposition about criticism and its importance at the present day. I said: "Of the literature of France and Germany, as of the intellect of Europe in general, the main ef-

fort, for now many years, has been a critical effort; the endeavor, in all branches of knowledge, theology, philosophy, history, art, science, to see the object as in itself it really is." I added, that owing to the operation in English literature of certain causes, "almost the last thing for which one would come to English literature is just that very thing which now Europe most desires—criticism"; and that the power and value of English literature was thereby impaired. More than one rejoinder declared that the importance I here assigned to criticism was excessive, and asserted the inherent superiority of the creative effort of the human spirit over its critical effort. And the other day, having been led by a

Arnold's *The Function of Criticism at the Present Time* was first published in 1864.

Mr. Shairp's excellent notice of Wordsworth[1] to turn again to his biography, I found, in the words of this great man, whom I, for one, must always listen to with the profoundest respect, a sentence passed on the critic's business, which seems to justify every possible disparagement of it. Wordsworth says in one of his letters: "The writers in these publications [the reviews], while they prosecute their inglorious employment, cannot be supposed to be in a state of mind very favorable for being effected by the finer influences of a thing so pure as genuine poetry."[2] And a trustworthy reporter of his conversation quotes a more elaborate judgment to the some effect:

> Wordsworth holds the critical power very low, infinitely lower than the inventive; and he said today that if the quantity of time consumed in writing critiques on the works of others were given to original composition, of whatever kind it might be, it would be much better employed; it would make a man find out sooner his own level, and it would do infinitely less mischief. A false or malicious criticism may be much injury to the minds of others, a stupid invention, either in prose or verse, is quite harmless.[3]

It is almost too much to expect of poor human nature, that a man capable of producing some effect in one line of literature, should, for the greater good of society, voluntarily doom himself to impotence and obscurity in another. Still less is this to be expected from men addicted to the composition of the "false or malicious criticism" of which Wordsworth speaks. However, everybody would admit that a false or malicious criticism had better never have been written. Everybody, too, would be willing to admit, as a general proposition, that the critical faculty is lower than the inventive. But is it true that criticism is really, in itself, a baneful and injurious employment; is it true that all time given to writing critiques on the works of others would be much better employed if it were given to original composition, of whatever kind this may be? Is it true that Johnson had better have gone on producing more *Irenes* instead of writing his *Lives of the Poets;*[4] nay, is it certain that Wordsworth himself was better employed in making his *Ecclesiastical Sonnets* than when he made his celebrated Preface, so full of criticism, and criticism of the works of others? Wordsworth was himself a great critic, and it is to be sincerely regretted that he has not left us more criticism; Goethe was one of the greatest of critics, and we may sincerely congratulate ourselves that he has left us so much criticism. Without wasting time over the exaggeration which Wordsworth's judgment on criticism clearly contains, or over an attempt to trace the causes—not difficult, I think, to be traced—which may have led Wordsworth to this exaggeration, a critic may with advantage seize an occasion for trying his own conscience, and for asking himself of what real service at any given moment the practice of criticism either is or may be made to his own mind and spirit, and to the minds and spirits of others.

The critical power is of lower rank than the creative. True; but in assenting to this proposition, one or two things are to be kept in mind. It is undeniable that the exercise of a creative power, that a free creative activity, is the highest function of man; it is proved to be so by man's finding in it his true happiness. But it is undeniable, also, that men may have the sense of exercising this free creative activity in other ways than in producing great works of literature or art; if it were not so, all but a very few men would be shut out from the true happiness of all men. They may have it in well-doing, they may have it in learning, they may have it even in criticizing. This is one thing to be kept in mind. Another is, that the exercise of the creative power in the production of great works of literature or art, however high this exercise of it may rank, is not at all epochs and under all conditions possible; and that therefore labor may be vainly spent in attempting it, which might with more fruit be used in preparing for it, in rendering it possible. This creative power works with elements, with materials; what if it has not those materials, those elements, ready for its use? In that case it must surely wait till they are ready. Now, in literature—I will limit myself to literature, for it is about literature that the question arises—the elements with which the creative power works are ideas; the best ideas on every matter which literature touches, current at the time. At any rate we may lay it down as certain that in modern literature no manifestation of the creative power not working

---

[1] J. C. Shairp, Scots critic, wrote "Wordsworth: The Man and Poet," *North British Review* XLI (1864). [Arnold] I cannot help thinking that a practice, common in England during the last century, and still followed in France, of printing a notice of this kind—a notice by a competent critic—to serve as an introduction to an eminent author's work, might be revived among us with advantage. To introduce all succeeding editions of Wordsworth, Mr. Shairp's notice might, it seems to me, excellently serve; it is written from the point of view of an admirer, nay, of a disciple, and that is right; but then the disciple must be also, as in this case he is, a critic, a man of letters, not, as too often happens, some relation or friend with no qualification for his task except affection for his author.

[2] Letter to Bernard Barton (1816) in Christopher Wordsworth, *Memoirs of William Wordsworth* II (1851), 51.

[3] W. Knight, *Life of Wordsworth* III, 438 (1889 edition).

[4] 1781.

with these can be very important or fruitful. And I say *current* at the time, not merely accessible at the time; for creative literary genius does not principally show itself in discovering new ideas, that is rather the business of the philosopher. The grand work of literary genius is a work of synthesis and exposition, not of analysis and discovery; its gift lies in the faculty of being happily inspired by a certain intellectual and spiritual atmosphere, by a certain order of ideas, when it finds itself in them; of dealing divinely with these ideas, presenting them in the most effective and attractive combinations,—making beautiful works with them, in short. But it must have the atmosphere, it must find itself amidst the order of ideas, in order to work freely; and these it is not so easy to command. This is why great creative epochs in literature are so rare, this is why there is so much that is unsatisfactory in the productions of many men of real genius; because, for the creation of a masterwork of literature two powers must concur, the power of the man and the power of the moment, and the man is not enough without the moment; the creative power has, for its happy exercise, appointed elements, and those elements are not in its own control.

Nay, they are more within the control of the critical power. It is the business of the critical power, as I said in the words already quoted, "in all branches of knowledge, theology, philosophy, history, art, science, to see the object as in itself it really is." Thus it tends, at last, to make an intellectual situation of which the creative power can profitably avail itself. It tends to establish an order of ideas, if not absolutely true, yet true by comparison with that which it displaces; to make the best ideas prevail. Presently these new ideas reach society, the touch of truth is the touch of life, and there is a stir and growth everywhere; out of this stir and growth come the creative epochs of literature.

Or, to narrow our range, and quit these considerations of the general march of genius and of society—considerations which are apt to become too abstract and impalpable—everyone can see that a poet, for instance, ought to know life and the world before dealing with them in poetry; and life and the world being in modern times very complex things, the creation of a modern poet, to be worth much, implies a great critical effort behind it; else it must be a comparatively poor, barren, and short-lived affair. This is why Byron's poetry had so little endurance in it, and Goethe's so much, both Byron and Goethe had a great productive power, but Goethe's was nourished by a great critical effort providing the true materials for it, and Byron's was not; Goethe knew life and the world, the poet's necesssary subjects, much more comprehensively and thoroughly than Byron. He knew a great deal more of them, and he knew them much more as they really are.

It has long seemed to me that the burst of creative activity in our literature, through the first quarter of this century, had about it in fact something premature; and that from this cause its productions are doomed, most of them, in spite of the sanguine hopes which accompanied and do still accompany them to prove hardly more lasting than the productions of far less splendid epochs. And this prematureness comes from its having proceeded without having its proper data, without sufficient materials to work with. In other words, the English poetry of the first quarter of this century, with plenty of energy, plenty of creative force, did not know enough. This makes Byron so empty of matter, Shelley[5] so incoherent, Wordsworth even, profound as he is, yet so wanting in completeness and variety. Wordsworth cared little for books, and disparaged Goethe. I admire Wordsworth, as he is, so much that I cannot wish him different; and it is vain, no doubt, to imagine such a man different from what he is, to suppose that he *could* have been different. But surely the one thing wanting to make Wordsworth an even greater poet than he is—his thought richer, and his influence of wider application—was that he should have read more books, among them, no doubt, those of that Goethe whom he disparaged without reading him.

But to speak of books and reading may easily lead to a misunderstanding here. It was not really books and reading that lacked to our poetry at this epoch; Shelley had plenty of reading, Coleridge[6] had immense reading. Pindar[7] and Sophocles—as we all say so glibly, and often with so little discernment of the real import of what we are saying—had not many books; Shakespeare was no deep reader. True; but in the Greece of Pindar and Sophocles, in the England of Shakespeare, the poet lived in a current of ideas in the highest degree animating and nourishing to the creative power; society was, in the fullest measure, permeated by fresh thought, intelligent and alive. And this state of things is the true basis for the creative power's exercise, in this it finds its data, its materials, truly ready for its hand; all the books and reading in the world are only valuable as they are helps to this. Even when this does not actually exist, books and reading may enable a man to construct a kind of semblance of it in his own mind, a world of knowledge and intelligence in which he may live and work. This is by no means an equivalent to the artist for the nationally diffused life and thought of the epochs of Sophocles or Shakespeare; but besides that

---

[5] George Gordon, Lord Byron (1788–1824), and Shelley (above, page 537), English poets.
[6] Coleridge (above, page 493).
[7] Pindar (518?–c.448 B.C.), Greek lyric poet.

it may be a means of preparation for such epochs, it does really constitute, if many share in it, a quickening and sustaining atmosphere of great value. Such an atmosphere the many-sided learning and the long and widely combined critical effort of Germany formed for Goethe, when he lived and worked. There was no national glow of life and thought there as in the Athens of Pericles or the England of Elizabeth.[8] That was the poet's weakness. But there was a sort of equivalent for it in the complete culture and unfettered thinking of a large body of Germans. That was his strength. In the England of the first quarter of this century there was neither a national glow of life and thought, such as we had in the age of Elizabeth, nor yet a culture and a force of learning and criticism such as were to be found in Germany. Therefore the creative power of poetry wanted, for success in the highest sense, materials and a basis; a thorough interpretation of the world was necessarily denied to it.

At first sight it seems strange that out of the immense stir of the French Revolution and its age should not have come a crop of works of genius equal to that which came out of the stir of the great productive time of Greece, or out of that of the Renaissance, with its powerful episode the Reformation. But the truth is that the stir of the French Revolution took a character which essentially distinguished it from such movements as these. These were, in the main, disinterestedly intellectual and spiritual movements; movements in which the human spirit looked for its satisfaction in itself and in the increased play of its own activity. The French Revolution took a political, practical character. The movement, which went on in France under the old regime from 1700 to 1789, was far more really akin than that of the Revolution itself to the movement of the Renaissance; the France of Voltaire and Rousseau[9] told far more powerfully upon the mind of Europe than the France of the Revolution. Goethe reproached this last expressly with having "thrown quiet culture back." Nay, and the true key to how much in our Byron, even in our Wordsworth, is this!—that they had their source in a great movement of feeling, not in a great movement of mind. The French Revolution, however—that object of so much blind love and so much blind hatred—found undoubtedly its motive power in the intelligence of men, and not in their practical sense; this is what distinguishes it from the English Revolution of Charles the First's time.[10] This is what makes it a more spiritual event than our

Revolution, an event of much more powerful and worldwide interest, though practically less successful; it appeals to an order of ideas which are universal, certain, permanent. 1789 asked of a thing, is it rational? 1642 asked of a thing, is it legal? Or, when it went furthest, is it according to conscience? This is the English fashion, a fashion to be treated, within its own sphere, with the highest respect; for its success, within its own sphere, has been prodigious. But what is law in one place is not law in another; what is law here today is not law even here tomorrow; and as for conscience, what is binding on one man's conscience is not binding on another's: The old woman who threw her stool at the head of the surpliced minister in St. Giles' Church at Edinburgh[11] obeyed an impulse to which millions of the human race may be permitted to remain strangers. But the prescriptions of reason are absolute, unchanging, of universal validity; "to count by tens is the easiest way of counting"—that is a proposition of which everyone, from here to the Antipodes, feels the force; at least I should say so if we did not live in a country where it is not impossible that any morning we may find a letter in the *Times* declaring that a decimal coinage is an absurdity. That a whole nation should have been penetrated with an enthusiasm for pure reason, and with an ardent zeal for making its prescriptions triumph, is a very remarkable thing, when we consider how little of mind, or anything so worthy and quickening as mind, comes into the motives which alone, in general, impel great masses of men. In spite of the extravagant direction given to this enthusiasm, in spite of the crimes and follies in which it lost itself, the French Revolution derives from the force, truth, and universality of the ideas which it took for its law, and from the passion with which it could inspire a multitude for these ideas, a unique and still living power; it is—it will probably long remain— the greatest, the most animating event in history. And as no sincere passion for the things of the mind, even though it turn out in many respects an unfortunate passion, is ever quite thrown away and quite barren of good. France has reaped from hers one fruit—the natural and legitimate fruit though not precisely the grand fruit she expected: she is the country in Europe where *the people* is most alive.

But the mania for giving an immediate political and practical application to all these fine ideas of the reason was fatal. Here an Englishman is in his element: on this theme we can all go on for hours. And all we are in the habit of saying on it has undoubtedly a great deal of truth. Ideas cannot be too much prized in and for themselves, cannot be too much lived with; but to transport them abruptly into the

---

[8] Pericles (c. 495–429 B.C.), Athenian statesman; Queen Elizabeth I reigned from 1558 to 1603.

[9] Francois Marie Arouet de Voltaire (1694–1778), Jean Jacques Rousseau (1712–1778), French philosophers.

[10] Charles I reigned from 1625 to 1649.

---

[11] In 1637 there was an effort at St. Giles's to read the new service prescribed by Charles I for Scotland.

world of politics, and practice, violently to revolutionize this world to their bidding—that is quite another thing. There is the world of ideas and there is the world of practice; the French are often for suppressing the one and the English the other; but neither is to be suppressed. A member of the House of Commons said to me the other day: "That a thing is an anomaly, I consider to be no objection to it whatever." I venture to think he was wrong; that a thing is an anomaly *is* an objection to it, but absolutely and in the sphere of ideas: it is not necessarily, under such-and-such circumstances, or at such-and-such a moment, an objection to it in the sphere of politics and practice. Joubert has said beautifully: *"C'est la force et le droit qui règlent toutes choses dans le monde; la force en attendant le droit."* (Force and right are the governors of this world; force till right is ready.)[12] "Force till right is ready"; and till right is ready, force, the existing order of things, is justified, is the legitimate ruler. But right is something moral, and implies inward recognition, free assent of the will; we are not ready for right—"right," so far as we are concerned, "is not ready,"— until we have attained this sense of seeing it and willing it. The way in which for us it may change and transform force, the existing order of things, and become, in its turn, the legitimate ruler of the world, should depend on the way in which, when our time comes, we see it and will it. Therefore for other people enamored of their own newly discerned right, to attempt to impose it upon us as ours, and violently to substitute their right for our force, is an act of tyranny, and to be resisted. It sets at naught the second great half of our maxim, "force till right is ready." This was the grand error of the French Revolution; and its movement of ideas, by quitting the intellectual sphere and rushing furiously into the political sphere, ran, indeed, a prodigious and memorable course, but produced no such intellectual fruit as the movement of ideas of the Renaissance, and created, in opposition to itself, what I may call an epoch of concentration. The great force of that epoch of concentration was England; and the great voice of that epoch of concentration was Burke. It is the fashion to treat Burke's writings on the French Revolution[13] as superannuated and conquered by the event; as the eloquent but unphilosophical tirades of bigotry and prejudice. I will not deny that they are often disfigured by the violence and passion of the moment, and that in some directions Burke's view was bounded, and his observation therefore at fault. But on the whole, and for those who can make the needful corrections, what distinguishes these writings is their profound, permanent, fruitful, philosophical truth. They contain the true philosophy of an epoch of concentration, dissipate the heavy atmosphere which its own nature is apt to engender round it, and make its resistance rational instead of mechanical.

But Burke is so great because, almost alone in England, he brings thought to bear upon politics, he saturates politics with thought. It is his accident that his ideas were at the service of an epoch of concentration, not of an epoch of expansion; it is his characteristic that he so lived by ideas, and had such a source of them welling up within him, that he could float even an epoch of concentration and English Tory politics with them. It does not hurt him that Dr. Price and the Liberals were enraged with him; it does not even hurt him that George the Third and the Tories were enchanted with him.[14] His greatness is that he lived in a world which neither English Liberalism nor English Toryism is apt to enter;—the world of ideas, not the world of catchwords and party habits. So far is it from being really true of him that he "to party gave up what was meant for mankind," that at the very end of his fierce struggle with the French Revolution after all his invectives against its false pretensions, hollowness, and madness, with his sincere conviction of its mischievousness, he can close a memorandum on the best means of combating it, some of the last pages he ever wrote—the *Thoughts on French Affairs,* in December 1791—with these striking words:

> The evil is stated, in my opinion, as it exists. The remedy must be where power, wisdom, and information, I hope, are more united with good intentions than they can be with me. I have done with this subject, I believe, forever. It has given me many anxious moments for the last two years. *If a great change is to be made in human affairs, the minds of men will be fitted to it; the general opinions and feelings will draw that way. Every fear, every hope will forward it; and then they who persist in opposing this mighty current in human affairs, will appear rather to resist the decrees of Providence itself, than the mere designs of men. They will not be resolute and firm, but perverse and obstinate.*

That return of Burke upon himself has always seemed to me one of the finest things in English literature, or indeed in any literature. That is what I call living by ideas: when one

---

[12]Joseph Joubert (1754–1824), *Pensees* I, 178 (1869 edition).
[13]Edmund Burke (above, page 332).

[14]Richard Price (1723–1791), English dissenting clergyman; George III reigned from 1760 to 1820.

side of a question has long had your earnest support, when all your feelings are engaged, when you hear all around you no language but one, when your party talks this language like a steam engine and can imagine no other—still to be able to think, still to be irresistibly carried, if so it be, by the current of thought to the opposite side of the question, and, like Balaam,[15] to be unable to speak anything but what the Lord has put in your mouth. I know nothing more striking, and I must add that I know nothing more un-English.

For the Englishman in general is like my friend the Member of Parliament, and believes, pointblank, that for a thing to be an anomaly is absolutely no objection to it whatever. He is like the Lord Auckland of Burke's day, who, in a memorandum on the French Revolution, talks of "certain miscreants, assuming the name of philosophers, who have presumed themselves capable of establishing a new system of society."[16] The Englishman has been called a political animal, and he values what is political and practical so much that ideas easily becomes objects of dislike in his eyes, and thinkers "miscreants," because ideas and thinkers have rashly meddled with politics and practice. This would be all very well if the dislike and neglect confined themselves to ideas transported out of their own sphere, and meddling rashly with practice; but they are inevitably extended to ideas as such, and to the whole life of intelligence; practice is everything, a free play of the mind is nothing. The notion of the free play of the mind upon all subjects being a pleasure in itself, being an object of desire, being an essential provider of elements without which a nation's spirit, whatever compensations it may have for them, must, in the long run, die of inanition, hardly enters into an Englishman's thoughts. It is noticeable that the word *curiosity,* which in other languages is used in a good sense, to mean, as a high and fine quality of man's nature, just this disinterested love of a free play of the mind on all subjects, for its own sake—it is noticeable, I say, that this word has in our language no sense of the kind, no sense but a rather bad and disparaging one. But criticism, real criticism is essentially the exercise of this very quality. It obeys an instinct prompting it to try to know the best that is known and thought in the world, irrespectively of practice, politics, and everything of the kind; and to value knowledge and thought as they approach this best, without the intrusion of any other considerations whatever. This is an instinct for which there is, I think, little original sympathy in the practical English nature, and what there was of it has undergone a long benumbing period of blight and

suppression in the epoch of concentration which followed the French Revolution.

But epochs of concentration cannot well endure forever; epochs of expansion, in the due course of things, follow them. Such an epoch of expansion seems to be opening in this country. In the first place all danger of a hostile forcible pressure of foreign ideas upon our practice has long disappeared; like the traveler in the fable, therefore, we begin to wear our cloak a little more loosely. Then, with a long peace the ideas of Europe steal gradually and amicably in, and mingle, though in infinitesimally small quantities at a time, with our own notions. Then, too, in spite of all that is said about the absorbing and brutalizing influence of our passionate material progress, it seems to me indisputable that this progress is likely, though not certain, to lead in the end to an apparition of intellectual life; and that man, after he has made himself perfectly comfortable and has now to determine what to do with himself next, may begin to remember that he has a mind, and that the mind may be made the source of great pleasure. I grant it is mainly the privilege of faith, at present, to discern this end to our railways, our business, and our fortune-making; but we shall see if, here as elsewhere, faith is not in the end the true prophet. Our ease, our traveling, and our unbounded liberty to hold just as hard and securely as we please to the practice to which our notions have given birth, all tend to beget an inclination to deal a little more freely with these notions themselves, to canvass them a little, to penetrate a little into their real nature. Flutterings of curiosity, in the foreign sense of the word, appear amongst us, and it is in these that criticism must look to find its account. Criticism first; a time of true creative activity, perhaps—which, as I have said, must inevitably be preceded amongst us by a time of criticism—hereafter, when criticism has done its work.

It is of the last importance that English criticism should clearly discern what rule for its course, in order to avail itself of the field now opening to it, and to produce fruit for the future, it ought to take. The rule may be summed up in one word—*disinterestedness.*[17] And how is criticism to show disinterestedness? By keeping aloof from what is called "the practical view of things"; by resolutely following the law of its own nature, which is to be a free play of the mind on all subjects which it touches. By steadily refusing to lend itself to any of those ulterior, political, practical considerations about ideas, which plenty of people will be sure to attach to them, which perhaps ought often to be attached to them, which in this country at any rate are certain

---

[15]Numbers 22–24.
[16]Lord Auckland (William Eden, 1744–1814).

[17]Compare Kant (above, page 420).

to be attached to them quite sufficiently, but which criticism has really nothing to do with. Its business is, as I have said, simply to know the best that is known and thought in the world, and by in its turn making this known, to create a current of true and fresh ideas. Its business is to do this with inflexible honesty, with due ability; but its business is to do no more, and to leave alone all questions of practical consequences and applications, questions which will never fail to have due prominence given to them. Else criticism, besides being really false to its own nature, merely continues in the old rut which it has hitherto followed in this country, and will certainly miss the chance now given to it. For what is at present the bane of criticism in this country? It is that practical considerations cling to it and stifle it. It subserves interests not its own. Our organs of criticism are organs of men and parties having practical ends to serve, and with them those practical ends are the first thing and the play of mind the second; so much play of mind as is compatible with the prosecution of those practical ends is all that is wanted. An organ like the *Revue des Deux Mondes,* having for its main function to understand and utter the best that is known and thought in the world, existing, it may be said, as just an organ for a free play of the mind, we have not. But we have the *Edinburgh Review,* existing as an organ of the old Whigs, and for as much play of the mind as may suit its being that; we have the *Quarterly Review,* existing as an organ of the Tories, and for as much play of mind as may suit its being that; we have the *British Quarterly Review,* existing as an organ of the political Dissenters, and for as much play of mind as may suit its being that; we have the *Times,* existing as an organ of the common, satisfied, well-to-do Englishman, and for as much play of mind as may suit its being that. And so on through all the various factions, political and religious, of our society; every faction has, as such, its organs of criticism, but the notion of combining all factions in the common pleasure of a free disinterested play of mind meets with no favor. Directly this play of mind wants to have more scope, and to forget the pressure of practical considerations a little, it is checked, it is made to feel the chain. We saw this the other day in the extinction, so much to be regretted, of the *Home and Foreign Review.* Perhaps in no organ of criticism in this country was there so much knowledge, so much play of mind; but these could not save it. The *Dublin Review* subordinates play of mind to the practical business of English and Irish Catholicism, and lives. It must needs be that men should act in sects and parties, that each of these sects and parties should have its organ, and should make this organ subserve the interests of its action; but it would be well, too, that there should be a criticism, not the minister of these interests, not their enemy but ab-

solutely and entirely independent of them. No other criticism will ever attain any real authority or make any real ways towards its end—the creating a current of true and fresh ideas.

It is because criticism has so little kept in the pure intellectual sphere, has so little detached itself from practice, has been so directly polemical and controversial, that it has so ill accomplished, in this country, its best spiritual work; which is to keep man from a self-satisfaction which is retarding and vulgarizing, to lead him towards perfection, by making his mind dwell upon what is excellent in itself, and the absolute beauty and fitness of things. A polemical practical criticism makes men blind even to the ideal imperfection of their practice, makes them willingly assert its ideal perfection, in order the better to secure it against attack: and clearly this is narrowing and baneful for them. If they were reassured on the practical side, speculative considerations of ideal perfection they might be brought to entertain, and their spiritual horizon would thus gradually widen. Sir Charles Adderley[18] says to the Warwickshire farmers:

> Talk of the improvement of breed! Why, the race we ourselves represent, the men and women, the old Anglo-Saxon race, are the best breed in the whole world. . . . The absence of a too enervating climate, too unclouded skies, and a too luxurious nature, has produced so vigorous a race of people and has rendered us so superior to all the world.

Mr. Roebuck[19] says to the Sheffield cutlers:

> I look around me and ask what is the state of England? Is not property safe? Is not every man able to say what he likes? Can you not walk from one end of England to the other in perfect security? I ask you whether, the world over or in past history, there is anything like it? Nothing. I pray that our unrivaled happiness may last.

Now obviously there is a peril for poor human nature in words and thoughts of such exuberant self-satisfaction, until we find ourselves safe in the streets of the celestial city. *"Das wenige verschwindet leicht dem Blicke / Der vorwärts sieht, wie viel noch übrig bleibt"* says Goethe; "the little that is done seems nothing when we look forward and see how much we have yet to do."[20] Clearly this is a better line

---

[18] Sir Charles Adderley, Conservative statesman, active 1858–1868.
[19] Liberal Member of Parliament for Sheffield.
[20] *Iphigenia in Tauris* i, ii, 91–92.

of reflection for weak humanity, so long as it remains on this earthly field of labor and trial.

But neither Sir Charles Adderley nor Mr. Roebuck is by nature inaccessible to considerations of this sort. They only lose sight of them owing to the controversial life we all lead, and the practical form which all speculation takes with us. They have in view opponents whose aim is not ideal, but practical; and in their zeal to uphold their own practice against these innovators, they go so far as even to attribute to this practice an ideal perfection. Somebody has been wanting to introduce a six-pound franchise, or to abolish church rates, or to collect agricultural statistics by force, or to diminish local self-government. How natural, in reply to such proposals, very likely improper or ill timed, to go a little beyond the mark and to say stoutly, "Such a race of people as we stand, so superior to all the world! The old Anglo-Saxon race, the best breed in the whole world! I pray that our unrivaled happiness may last! I ask you whether, the world over or in past history, there is anything like it?" And so long as criticism answers this dithyramb by insisting that the old Anglo-Saxon race would be still more superior to all others if it had no church rates, or that our unrivaled happiness would last yet longer with a six-pound franchise, so long will the strain, "the best breed in the whole world!" swell louder and louder, everything ideal and refining will be lost out of sight, and both the assailed and their critics will remain in a sphere, to say the truth, perfectly unvital, a sphere in which spiritual progression is impossible. But let criticism leave church rates and the franchise alone, and in the most candid spirit, without a single lurking thought of practical innovation, confront with our dithyramb this paragraph on which I stumbled in a newspaper immediately after reading Mr. Roebuck: "A shocking child murder has just been committed at Nottingham. A girl named Wragg left the workhouse there on Saturday morning with her young illegitimate child. The child was soon afterwards found dead on Mapperly Hills, having been strangled. Wragg is in custody."

Nothing but that; but, in juxtaposition with the absolute eulogies of Sir Charles Adderley and Mr. Roebuck, how eloquent, how suggestive are those few lines! "Our old Anglo-Saxon breed, the best in the whole world!" How much that is harsh and ill favored there is in this best! *Wragg!* If we are to talk of ideal perfection of "the best in the whole world," has any one reflected what a touch of grossness in our race, what an original shortcoming in the more delicate spiritual perceptions, is shown by the natural growth amongst us of such hideous names—Higginbottom, Stiggins, Bugg! In Ionia and Attica they were luckier in this respect than "the best race in the world"; by the Ilissus there was no Wragg, poor thing! And "our unrivaled happi-

ness"—what an element of grimness, bareness, and hideousness mixes with it and blurs it; the workhouse, the dismal Mapperly Hills—how dismal those who have seen them will remember—the gloom, the smoke, the cold, the strangled illegitimate child! "I ask you whether, the world over or in past history, there is anything like it?" Perhaps not, one is inclined to answer; but at any rate, in that case, the world is very much to be pitied. And the final touch—short, bleak and inhuman: "Wragg is in custody." The sex lost in the confusion of our unrivaled happiness; or (shall I say?) the superfluous Christian name lopped off by the straightforward vigor of our old Anglo-Saxon breed! There is profit for the spirit in such contrasts as this; criticism serves the cause of perfection by establishing them. By eluding sterile conflict, by refusing to remain in the sphere where alone narrow and relative conceptions have any worth and validity, criticism may diminish its momentary importance, but only in this way has it a chance of gaining admittance for those wider and and more perfect conceptions to which all its duty is really owed. Mr. Roebuck will have a poor opinion of an adversary who replies to his defiant songs of triumph only by murmuring under his breath, "Wragg is in custody"; but in no other way will these songs of triumph be induced gradually to moderate themselves, to get rid of what in them is excessive and offensive, and to fall into a softer and truer key.

It will be said that it is a very subtle and indirect action which I am thus prescribing for criticism, and that, by embracing in this manner the Indian virtue of detachment and abandoning the sphere of practical life, it condemns itself to a slow and obscure work. Slow and obscure it may be, but it is the only proper work of criticis. The mass of mankind will never have any ardent zeal for seeing things as they are; very inadequate ideas will always satisfy them. On these inadequate ideas reposes, and must repose, the general practice of the world. That is as much as saying that whoever sets himself to see things as they are will find himself one of a very small circle; but it is only by this small circle resolutely doing its own work that adequate ideas will ever get current at all. The rush and roar of practical life will always have a dizzying and attracting effect upon the most collected spectator, and tend to draw him into its vortex; most of all will this be the case where that life is so powerful as it is in England. But it is only by remaining collected, and refusing to lend himself to the point of view of the practical man, that the critic can do the practical man any service; and it is only by the greatest sincerity in pursuing his own course, and by at last convincing even the practical man of his sincerity, that he can escape misunderstandings which perpetually threaten him.

For the practical man is not apt for fine distinctions, and yet in these distinctions truth and the highest culture greatly find their account. But it is not easy to lead a practical man—unless you reassure him as to your practical intentions, you have no chance of leading him—to see a thing which he has always been used to look at from one side only, which he greatly values, and which, looked at from that side, quite deserves, perhaps, all the prizing and admiring which he bestows upon it—that this thing, looked at from another side, may appear must less beneficent and beautiful, and yet retain all its claims to our practical allegiance. Where shall we find language innocent enough, how shall we make the spotless purity of our intentions evident enough, to enable us to say to the political Englishman that the British Constitution itself, which, seen from the practical side, looks such a magnificent organ of progress and virtue, seen from the speculative side—with its compromises, its love of facts, its horror of theory, its studied avoidance of clear thoughts—that, seen from this side, our august Constitution sometimes looks—forgive me, shade of Lord Somers!21—a colossal machine for the manufacture of Philistines? How is Cobbett22 to say this and not be misunderstood, blackened as he is with the smoke of a lifelong conflict in the field of political practice? How is Mr. Carlyle23 to say it and not be misunderstood, after his furious raid into this field with his *Latter-day Pamphlets?* How is Mr. Ruskin,24 after his pugnacious political economy? I say, the critic must keep out of the region of immediate practice in the political, social, humanitarian sphere, if he wants to make a beginning for that more free speculative treatment of things, which may perhaps one day make its benefits felt even in this sphere, but in a natural and thence irresistible manner.

Do what he will, however, the critic will still remain exposed to frequent misunderstandings, and nowhere so much as in this country. For here people are particularly indisposed even to comprehend that without this free disinterested treatment of things, truth and the highest culture are out of the question. So immersed are they in practical life, so accustomed to take all their notions from this life and its processes, that they are apt to think that truth and culture themselves can be reached by the processes of this life, and that it is an impertinent singularity to think of reaching them in any other. "We are all *terrae filli*,"25 cries their eloquent

advocate; "all Philistines together. Away with the notion of proceeding by any other course than the course dear to the Philistines; let us have a social movement, let us organize and combine a party to pursue truth and new thought, let us call it 'the liberal party,' and let us all stick to each other, and back each other up. Let us have no nonsense about independent criticism, and intellectual delicacy, and the few and the many. Don't let us trouble ourselves about foreign thought; we shall invent the whole thing for ourselves as we go along. If one of us speaks well, applaud him; if one of us speaks ill, applaud him too: we are all in the same movement, we are all liberals, we are all in pursuit of truth." In this way the pursuit of truth becomes really a social, practical, pleasurable affair, almost requiring a chairman, a secretary, and advertisements; with the excitement of an occasional scandal, with a little resistance to give the happy sense of difficulty overcome; but, in general, plenty of bustle and very little thought. To act is so easy, as Goethe says: to think is so hard! It is true that the critic has many temptations to go with the stream, to make one of the party movement, one of these *terrae filli*; it seems ungracious to refuse to be a *terrae filius,* when so many excellent people are; but the critic's duty is to refuse, or, if resistance is vain, at least to cry with Obermann: *"Périssons en résistant."*26

How serious a matter it is to try and resist, I had ample opportunity of experiencing when I ventured some time ago to criticize the celebrated first volume of Bishop Colenso.27 The echoes of the storm which was then raised I still, from time to time, hear grumbling around me. That storm arose out of a misunderstanding almost inevitable. It is a result of no little culture to attain to a clear perception that science and religion are two wholly different things. The multitude will forever confuse them; but happily that is of no great real importance, for while the multitude imagines itself to live by its false science, it does really live by its true religion. Dr. Colenso, however, in his first volume did all he

---

21 Lord Somers (1650–1716), champion of the English constitution of 1688.
22 William Cobbett (1762–1835), British journalist and reformer.
23 Thomas Carlyle, English writer (1795–1881).
24 John Ruskin (1819–1900), English critic and social theorist.
25 "Sons of earth."

26 "Let us perish resisting." Etienne Povert de Senancour (1770–1846), *Obermann.*
27 Arnold thought superficial *Pentateuch and Book of Joshua Critically Examined* (1863) by John William Colenso (d. 1883), Bishop of Natal. He criticized the book in "The Bishop and the Philosopher," *Macmillan's Magazine* (January 1863). [Arnold] So sincere is my dislike to all personal attack and controversy, that I abstain from reprinting, and this distance of time from the occasion which called them forth, the essays in which I criticized Dr. Colenso's book; I feel bound, however, after all that has passed, to make here a final declaration of my sincere impenitence for having published them. Nay, I cannot forbear repeating yet once more, for his benefit and that of his readers, this sentence from my original remarks upon him: "There is truth of science and truth of religion: truth of science does not become truth of religion till it is made religious." And I will add: Let us have all the science there is from the men of science, from the men of religion, let us have religion.

could to strengthen the confusion,[28] and to make it dangerous. He did this with the best intentions, I freely admit, and
with the most candid ignorance that this was the natural effect of what he was doing; but, says Joubert, "Ignorance,
which in matters of morals extenuates the crime, is itself, in
intellectual matters, a crime of the first order."[29] I criticized
Bishop Colenso's speculative confusion. Immediately there
was a cry raised: "What is this? Here is a liberal attacking a
liberal. Do not you belong to the movement? Are not you a
friend of truth? Is not Bishop Colenso in pursuit of truth?
Then speak with proper respect of his book. Dr. Stanley[30] is
another friend of truth, and you speak with proper respect of
his book; why make these invidious differences? Both
books are excellent, admirable, liberal; Bishop Colenso's
perhaps the most so, because it is the boldest, and will have
the best practical consequences for the liberal cause. Do you
want to encourage to the attack of a brother liberal his, and
your, and our implacable enemies, the *Church and State Review* or the *Record*—the High Church rhinoceros and the
Evangelical hyena? Be silent, therefore; or rather speak,
speak as loud as ever you can! And go into ecstasies over
the eighty and odd pigeons."

But criticism cannot follow this coarse and indiscriminate method. It is unfortunately possible for a man in pursuit
of truth to write a book which reposes upon a false conception. Even the practical consequences of a book are to genuine criticism no recommendation of it, if the book is, in the
highest sense, blundering. I see that a lady[31] who herself, too,
is in pursuit of truth, and who writes with great ability, but a
little too much, perhaps, under the influence of the practical
spirit of the English liberal movement, classes Bishop
Colenso's book and M. Renan's[32] together, in her survey of
the religious state of Europe, as facts of the same order,
works, both of them, of "great importance"; "great ability,
power, and skill"; Bishop Colenso's, perhaps, the most powerful; at least, Miss Cobbe gives special expression to her
gratitude that to Bishop Colenso "has been given the strength
to grasp, and the courage to teach, truths of such deep import." In the same way, more than one popular writer has
compared him to Luther. Now it is just this kind of false esti-

mate which the critical spirit is, it seems to me, bound to resist. It is really the strongest possible proof of the low ebb at
which, in England, the critical spirit is, that while the critical
hit in the religious literature of Germany is Dr. Strauss's
book,[33] in that of France M. Renan's book, of Bishop
Colenso is the critical hit in the religious literature of England. Bishop Colenso's book reposes on a total misconception of the essential element of the religious problem, as that
problem is now presented for solution. To criticism, therefore, which seeks to have the best that is known and thought
on this problem, it is, however well meant, of no importance
whatever. M. Renan's book attempts a new synthesis of the
elements furnished to us by the four gospels. It attempts, in
my opinion, a synthesis, perhaps premature, perhaps impossible, certainly not successful. Up to the present time, at any
rate, we must acquiesce in Fleury's sentence on such recast-
ings of the Gospel story: "*Quiconque s'imagine la pouvoir
mieux écrire, ne l'entend pas.*"[34] M. Renan had himself
passed by anticipation a like sentence on his own work, when
he said: "If a new presentation of the character of Jesus were
offered to me, I would not have it; its very clearness would
be, in my opinion, the best proof of its insufficiency." His
friends may with perfect justice rejoin that at the sight of the
Holy Land, and of the actual scene of the Gospel story, all the
current of M. Renan's thoughts may have naturally changed,
and a new casting of that story irresistibly suggested itself to
him; and that this is just a case for applying Cicero's maxim:
Change of mind is not inconsistency—"*nemo doctus unquam mutationem consilii inconstantiam dixit esse.*"[35] Nevertheless, for criticism, M. Renan's first thought must still be
the truer one, as long as his new casting so fails more fully to
commend itself, more fully (to use Coleridge's happy phrase
about the Bible[36]) to *find* us. Still M. Renan's attempt is, for
criticism, of the most real interest and importance, since,
with all its difficulty, a fresh synthesis of the New Testament
data—not a making war on them, in Voltaire's fashion, not a
leaving them out of mind, in the world's fashion, but the
putting a new construction upon them, the taking them from
under the old, traditional, conventional point of view and
placing them under a new one—is the very essence of the religious problem, as now presented: and only by efforts in this
direction can it receive a solution.

Again, in the same spirit in which she judges Bishop
Colenso, Miss Cobbe, like so many earnest liberals of our

---

[28] [Arnold] It has been said I make it "a crime against literary criticism and
the higher culture to attempt to inform the ignorant." Need I point out that
the ignorant are not informed by being confirmed in a confusion?
[29] *Pensees* I, 311.
[30] Arthur Penrhyn Stanley. Arnold had compared his *The Bible: Its Form and
Substance* (1863) favorably to Colenso's.
[31] Frances Power Cobbe (b. 1822), writer and lecturer. Arnold is referring to
her *Broken Lights* (1864).
[32] Ernest Renan (1823–1892), French historian and philologist, *The Life of
Jesus* (1835).

[33] David Friedrich Strauss (1808–1874), German theologian, *Life of Jesus*
(1835).
[34] "Whoever imagines that he can write it better, does not understand it."
[35] Cicero (above, page 74), *Letters to Atticus* XV, 7: "No learned man has
said it is inconsistent to change his mind."
[36] In his *Confessions of an Inquiring Spirit* (posthumously published, 1840).

practical race, both here and in America, herself sets vigorously about a positive reconstruction of religion, about making a religion of the future out of hand, or at least setting about making it. We must not rest, she and they are always thinking and saying, in negative criticism, we must be creative and constructive; hence we have such works as her recent *Religious Duty,* and works still more considerable, perhaps, by others, which will be in everyone's mind. These works often have much ability; they often spring out of sincere convictions, and a sincere wish to do good; and they sometimes, perhaps, do good. Their fault is (if I may be permitted to say so) one which they have in common with the British College of Health, in the New Road. Everyone knows the British College of Health; it is that building with the lion and the statue of the Goddess Hygeia before it; at least I am sure about the lion, though I am not absolutely certain about the Goddess Hygeia. This building does credit, perhaps, to the resources of Dr. Morrison and his disciples; but it falls a good deal short of one's idea of what a British College of Health ought to be. In England, where we hate public interference and love individual enterprise, we have a whole crop of places like the British College of Health; the grand name without the grand thing. Unluckily, creditable to individual enterprise as they are, they tend to impair our taste by making us forget what more grandiose, noble, or beautiful character properly belongs to a public institution. The same may be said of the religions of the future of Miss Cobbe and others. Creditable, like the British College of Health, to the resources of their authors, they yet tend to make us forget what more grandiose, noble, or beautiful character properly belongs to religious constructions. The historic religions, with all their faults, have had this; it certainly belongs to the religious sentiment, when it truly flowers, to have this; and we impoverish our spirit if we allow a religion of the future without it. What then is the duty of criticism here? To take the practical point of view, to applaud the liberal movement and all its works—its New Road religions of the future into the bargain—for their general utility's sake? By no means; but to be perpetually dissatisfied with these works, while they perpetually fall short of a high and perfect ideal.

For criticism, these are elementary laws; but they never can be popular, and in this country they have been very little followed, and one meets with immense obstacles in following them. That is a reason for asserting them again and again. Criticism must maintain its independence of the practical spirit and its aims. Even with well-meant efforts of the practical spirit it must express dissatisfaction, if in the sphere of the ideal they seem impoverishing and limiting. It must not hurry on to the goal because of its practical importance. It must be patient, and know how to wait; and flexible, and know how to attach itself to things and how to withdraw from them. It must be apt to study and praise elements that for the fullness of spiritual perfection are wanted, even though they belong to a power which in the practical sphere may be maleficent. It must be apt to discern the spiritual shortcomings or illusions of powers that in the practical sphere may be beneficent. And this without any notion of favoring or injuring, in the practical sphere, one power or the other; without any notion of playing off, in this sphere, one power against the other. When one looks, for instance, at the English divorce court—an institution which perhaps has its practical conveniences, but which in the ideal sphere is so hideous; an institution which neither makes divorce impossible nor makes it decent, which allows a man to get rid of his wife, or a wife of her husband, but makes them drag one another first, for the public edification, through a mire of unutterable infamy—when one looks at this charming institution, I say, with its crowded trials, its newspaper reports, and its money compensations, this institution in which the gross unregenerate British Philistine has indeed stamped an image of himself—one may be permitted to find the marriage theory of Catholicism refreshing and elevating. Or when Protestantism, in virtue of its supposed rational and intellectual origin, gives the law to criticism too magisterially, criticism may and must remind it that its pretensions, in this respect, are illusive and do it harm; that the Reformation was a moral rather than an intellectual event; that Luther's theory of grace no more exactly reflects the mind of the spirit than Bossuet's philosophy of history reflects it;[37] and that there is no more antecedent probability of the Bishop of Durham's stock of ideas being agreeable to perfect reason than of Pope Pius the Ninth's. But criticism will not on that account forget the achievements of Protestantism in the practical and moral sphere; nor that, even in the intellectual sphere, Protestantism,. though in a blind and stumbling manner, carried forward the Renaissance, while Catholicism threw itself violently across its path.

I lately heard a man of thought and energy contrasting the want of ardor and movement which he now found amongst young men in this country with what he remembered in his own youth, twenty years ago. "What reformers we were then!" he exclaimed; "what a zeal we had! How we canvassed every institution in Church and State, and

---

[37] In his *Discourse on Universal History* (1681) Jacques Benigne Bossuet (1627–1704) explains history as divinely guided to the benefit of Catholicism.

were prepared to remodel them all on first principles!" He was inclined to regret, as a spiritual flagging, the lull which he saw. I am disposed rather to regard it as a pause in which the turn to a new mode of spiritual progress is being accomplished. Everything was long seen, by the young and ardent amongst us, in inseparable connection with politics and practical life. We have pretty well exhausted the benefits of seeing things in this connection, we have got all that can be got by so seeing them. Let us try a more disinterested mode of seeing them; let us betake ourselves more to the serener life of the mind and spirit. This life, too, may have its excesses and dangers; but they are not for us at present. Let us think of quietly enlarging our stock of true and fresh ideas, and not, as soon as we get an idea or half an idea, be running out with it into the street, and trying to make it rule there. Our ideas will, in the end, shape the world all the better for maturing a little. Perhaps in fifty years' time it will in the English House of Commons be an objection to an institution that it is an anomaly, and my friend the Member of Parliament will shudder in his grave. But let us in the meanwhile rather endeavor that in twenty years' time it may, in English literature, be an objection to a proposition that it is absurd. That will be a change so vast, that the imagination almost fails to grasp it. *"Ab integro saeclorum nascitur ordo."*[38]

If I have insisted so much on the course which criticism must take where politics and religion are concerned, it is because, where these burning matters are in question, it is most likely to go astray. I have wished, above all, to insist on the attitude which criticism should adopt towards things in general; on its right tone and temper of mind. But then comes another question as to the subject matter which literary criticism should most seek. Here, in general, its course is determined for it by the idea which is the law of its being; the idea of a disinterested endeavor to learn and propagate the best that is known and thought in the world, and thus to establish a current of fresh and true ideas. By the very nature of things, as England is not all the world, much of the best that is known and thought in the world cannot be of English growth, must be foreign; by the nature of things, again, it is just this that we are least likely to know, while English thought is streaming in upon us from all sides, and takes excellent care that we shall not be ignorant of its existence. The English critic of literature, therefore, must dwell much on foreign thought, and with particular heed on any part of it, which, while significant and fruitful in itself, is for any reason specially likely to escape him. Again, judging is often spoken of as the critic's one business, and so in some sense it is; but the judgment which almost insensibly forms itself in a fair and clear mind, along with fresh knowledge, is the valuable one; and thus knowledge, and ever fresh knowledge, must be the critic's great concern for himself. And it is by communicating fresh knowledge, and letting his own judgment pass along with it—but insensibly, and in the second place, not the first, as a sort of companion and clue, not as an abstract lawgiver—that the critic will generally do most good to his readers. Sometimes, no doubt, for the sake of establishing an author's place in literature, and his relation to a central standard (and if this is not done, how are we to get at our "best in the world"?) criticism may have to deal with a subject matter so familiar that fresh knowledge is out of the question, and then it must be all judgment; an enunciation and detailed application of principles. Here the great safeguard is never to let oneself become abstract, always to retain an intimate and lively consciousness of the truth of what one is saying, and, the moment this fails us, to be sure that something is wrong. Still, under all circumstances, this mere judgment and application of principles is, in itself, not the most satisfactory work to the critic; like mathematics, it is tautological, and cannot well give us, like fresh learning, the sense of creative activity.

But stop, someone will say; all this talk is of no practical use to us whatever; this criticism of yours is not what we have in our minds when we speak of criticism; when we speak of critics and criticism, we mean critics and criticism of the current English literature of the day; when you offer to tell criticism its function, it is to this criticism that we expect you to address yourself. I am sorry for it, for I am afraid I must disappoint these expectations. I am bound by my own definition of criticism: "a disinterested endeavor to learn and propagate the best that is known and thought in the world." How much of current English literature comes into this "best that is known and thought in the world"? Not very much I fear; certainly less, at this moment, than of the current literature of France or Germany. Well, then, am I to alter my definition of criticism, in order to meet the requirements of a number of practicing English critics, who, after all, are free in their choice of a business? That would be making criticism lend itself just to one of those alien practical considerations, which, I have said, are so fatal to it. One may say, indeed, to those who have to deal with the mass—so much better disregarded—of current English literature, that they may at all events endeavor, in dealing with this, to try it, so far as they can, by the standard of the best that is known and thought in the world; one may say, that to get anywhere near this standard, every critic should try and

---

[38] "Order is born from the renewal of generations." Virgil, *Eclogues* IV, 5.

possess one great literature, at least, besides his own; and the more unlike his own, the better. But, after all, the criticism I am really concerned with—the criticism which alone can much help us for the future, the criticism which, throughout Europe, is at the present day meant, when so much stress is laid on the importance of criticism and the critical spirit—is a criticism which regards Europe as being, for intellectual and spiritual purposes, one great confederation, bound to a joint action and working to a common result; and whose members have, for their proper outfit, a knowledge of Greek, Roman, and Eastern antiquity, and of one another. Special, local, and temporary advantages being put out of account, that modern nation will in the intellectual and spiritual sphere make most progress, which most thoroughly carries out this program. And what is that but saying that we too, all of us, as individuals, the more thoroughly we carry it out, shall make the more progress?

There is so much inviting us! What are we to take? What will nourish us in growth towards perfection? That is the question which, with the immense field of life and of literature lying before him, the critic has to answer; for himself first, and afterwards for others. In this idea of the critic's business the essays brought together in the following pages have had their origin; in this idea, widely different as are their subjects, they have, perhaps, their unity.

I conclude with what I said at the beginning: to have the sense of creative activity is the great happiness and the great proof of being alive, and it is not denied to criticism to have it; but then criticism must be sincere, simple, flexible, ardent, ever widening its knowledge. Then it may have, in no contemptible measure, a joyful sense of creative activity; a sense which a man of insight and conscience will prefer to what he might derive from a poor, starved, fragmentary, inadequate creation. And at some epochs no other creation is possible.

Still, in full measure, the sense of creative activity belongs only to genuine creation; in literature we must never forget that. But what true man of letters ever can forget it? It is no such common matter for a gifted nature to come into possession of a current of true and living ideas, and to produce amidst the inspiration of them, that we are likely to underrate it. The epochs of Aeschylus and Shakespeare make us feel their preeminence. In an epoch like those is, no doubt, the true life of literature; there is the promised land, towards which criticism can only beckon. That promised land it will not be ours to enter, and we shall die in the wilderness: but to have desired to enter it, to have saluted it from afar, is already, perhaps, the best distinction among contemporaries; it will certainly be the best title to esteem with posterity.

from

The Study of Poetry

The future of poetry is immense, because in poetry, where it is worthy of its high destinies, our race, as time goes on, will find an ever surer and surer stay. There is not a creed which is not shaken, not an accredited dogma which is not shown to be questionable, not a received tradition which does not threaten to dissolve. Our religion has materialized itself in the fact, in the supposed fact; it has attached its emotion to the fact, and now the fact is failing it. But for poetry the idea is everything; the rest is a world of illusion, of divine illusion. Poetry attaches its emotion to the idea; the idea *is* the fact. The strongest part of our religion today is its unconscious poetry.[1]

Let me be permitted to quote these words of my own, as uttering the thought which should, in my opinion, go with us and govern us in all our study of poetry. In the present work it is the course of one great contributory stream to the world river of poetry that we are invited to follow. We are here invited to trace the stream of English poetry. But whether we set ourselves, as here, to follow only one of the several streams that make the mighty river of poetry, or whether we seek to know them all, our governing thought should be the same. We should conceive of poetry worthily, and more highly than it has been the custom to conceive of it. We should conceive of it as capable of higher uses, and called to higher destinies, than those which in general men have assigned to it hitherto. More and more mankind will discover that we have to turn to poetry to interpret life for us, to console us, to sustain us. Without poetry, our science will appear incomplete; and most of what now passes with us for religion and philosophy will be replaced by poetry. Science, I say, will appear incomplete without it. For finely and truly does Wordsworth call poetry "the impassioned expression which is in the countenance of all science"; and what is a countenance without its expression? Again, Wordsworth finely and truly calls poetry "the breath and finer spirit of all knowledge";[2] our religion, parading evidences such as those on which the popular mind relies now; our philosophy, pluming

---

Arnold's *Study of Poetry* was first published in 1880. The selection reprinted here represents approximately the first half of the essay.
[1] Introduction to *The Hundred Greatest Men.*
[2] Preface to the second edition of *Lyrical Ballads* (above, page 487).

itself on its reasonings about causation and finite and infinite being; what are they but the shadows and dreams and false shows of knowledge? The day will come when we shall wonder at ourselves for having trusted to them, for having taken them seriously; and the more we perceive their hollowness, the more we shall prize "the breath and finer spirit of knowledge" offered to us by poetry.

But if we conceive thus highly of the destinies of poetry, we must also set our standard for poetry high, since poetry, to be capable of fulfilling such high destinies, must be poetry of a high order of excellence. We must accustom ourselves to a high standard and to a strict judgment. Sainte-Beuve relates that Napoleon one day said, when somebody was spoken of in his presence as a charlatan: "Charlatan as much as you please; but where is there *not* charlatanism?" "Yes," answers Sainte-Beuve,[3] "in politics, in the art of governing mankind, that is perhaps true. But in the order of thought, in art, the glory, the eternal honor is that charlatanism shall find no entrance; herein lies the inviolableness of that noble portion of man's being." It is admirably said, and let us hold fast to it. In poetry, which is thought and art in one, it is the glory, the eternal honor, that charlatanism shall find no entrance; that this noble sphere be kept inviolate and inviolable. Charlatanism is for confusing or obliterating the distinctions between excellent and inferior, sound and unsound or only half-sound, true and untrue or only half-true. It is charlatanism, conscious or unconscious, whenever we confuse or obliterate these. And in poetry, more than anywhere else, it is unpermissible to confuse or obliterate them. For in poetry the distinction between excellent and inferior, sound and unsound or only half-sound, true and untrue or only half-true, is of paramount importance. It is of paramount importance because of the high destinies of poetry. In poetry, as in criticism of life under the conditions fixed for such a criticism by the laws of poetic truth and poetic beauty, the spirit of our race will find, we have said, as time goes on and as other helps fails, its consolation and stay. But the consolation and stay will be of power in proportion to the power of the criticism of life. And the criticism of life will be of power in proportion as the poetry conveying it is excellent rather than inferior, sound rather than unsound or half-sound, true rather than untrue or half-true.

The best poetry is what we want; the best poetry will be found to have a power of forming, sustaining, and delighting us, as nothing else can. A clearer, deeper sense of the best in poetry, and of the strength and joy to be drawn from it, is the most precious benefit which we can gather from a poetical collection such as the present. And yet in the very nature and conduct of such a collection there is inevitably something which tends to obscure in us the consciousness of what our benefit should be, and to distract us from the pursuit of it. We should therefore steadily set it before our minds at the outset, and should compel ourselves to revert constantly to the thought of it as we proceed.

Yes; constantly in reading poetry, a sense for the best, the really excellent, and of the strength and joy to be drawn from it, should be present in our minds and should govern our estimate of what we read. But this real estimate, the only true one, is liable to be superseded, if we are not watchful, by two other kinds of estimate, the historic estimate and the personal estimate, both of which are fallacious. A poet or a poem may count to us historically, they may count to us on grounds personal to ourselves, and they may count to us really. They may count to us historically. The course of development of a nation's language, thought, and poetry, is profoundly interesting; and by regarding a poet's work as a stage in this course of development we may easily bring ourselves to make it of more importance as poetry than in itself it really is, we may come to use a language of quite exaggerated praise in criticizing it; in short, to overrate it. So arises in our poetic judgments the fallacy caused by the estimate which we may call historic. Then, again, a poet or poem may count to us on grounds personal to ourselves. Our personal affinities, likings and circumstances, have great power to sway our estimate of this or that poet's work, and to make us attach more importance to it as poetry than in itself it really possesses, because to us it is, or has been, of high importance. Here also we overrate the object of our interest, and apply to it a language of praise which is quite exaggerated. And thus we get the source of a second fallacy in our poetic judgments—the fallacy caused by an estimate which we may call personal.

Both fallacies are natural. It is evident how naturally the study of the history and development of poetry may incline a man to pause over reputations and works once conspicuous but now obscure, and to quarrel with a careless public for skipping, in obedience to mere tradition and habit, from one famous name or work in its national poetry to another, ignorant of what it misses, and of the reason for keeping what it keeps, and of the whole process of growth in its poetry. The French have become diligent students of their own early poetry, which they long neglected; the study makes many of them dissatisfied with their so-called classical poetry, the court-tragedy of the seventeenth century, a poetry which Pellisson long ago reproached with its want of the true poetic stamp, with its *politesse stérile et rampante*,[4] but which

---

[3]Charles Augustin Sainte-Beuve (1804–1869), French critic.

[4]"Sterile and servile politeness."

nevertheless has reigned in France as absolutely as if it had been the perfection of classical poetry indeed. The dissatisfaction is natural; yet a lively and accomplished critic, M. Charles d'Héricault, the editor of Clément Marot,[5] goes too far when he says that "the cloud of glory playing round a classic is a mist as dangerous to the future of a literature as it is intolerable for the purpose of history." "It hinders," he goes on,

it hinders us from seeing more than one single point, the culminating and exceptional point; the summary, fictitious and arbitrary, of a thought and of a work. It substitutes a halo for a physiognomy, it puts a statue where there was once a man, and hiding from us all trace of the labor, the attempts, the weaknesses, the failures, it claims not study but veneration; it does not show us how the thing is done, it imposes upon us a model. Above all, for the historian this creation of classic personages is inadmissible; for it withdraws the poet from his time, from his proper life, it breaks historical relationships, it blinds criticism by conventional admiration, and renders the investigation of literary origins unacceptable. It gives us a human personage no longer but a God seated immovable amidst his perfect work, like Jupiter on Olympus; and hardly will it be possible for the young student to whom such work is exhibited at such a distance from him, to believe that it did not issue ready-made from that divine head.

All this is brilliantly and tellingly said, but we must plead for a distinction. Everything depends on the reality of a poet's classic character. If he is a dubious classic, let us sift him; if he is a false classic, let us explode him. But if he is a real classic, if his work belongs to the class of the very best (for this is the true and right meaning of the word *classic, classical*), then the great thing for us is to feel and enjoy his work as deeply as ever we can, and to appreciate the wide difference between it and all work which has not the same high character. This is what is salutary, this is what is formative; this is the great benefit to be got from the study of poetry. Everything which interferes with it, which hinders it, is injurious. True, we must read our classic with open eyes, and not with eyes blinded with superstition; we must perceive when his work comes short, when it drops out of the class of the very best, and we must rate it, in such cases, at its proper value. But the use of this negative criticism is

not in itself, it is entirely in its enabling us to have a clearer sense and a deeper enjoyment of what is truly excellent. To trace the labor, the attempts, the weaknesses, the failures of a genuine classic, to acquaint oneself with his time and his life and his historical relationships, is mere literary dilettantism unless it has that clear sense and deeper enjoyment for its end. It may be said that the more we know about a classic the better we shall enjoy him; and, if we lived as long as Methuselah and had all of us heads of perfect clearness and wills of perfect steadfastness, this might be true in fact as it is plausible in theory. But the case here is much the same as the case with the Greek and Latin studies of our schoolboys. The elaborate philological groundwork which we require them to lay is in theory an admirable preparation for appreciating the Greek and Latin authors worthily. The more thoroughly we lay the groundwork, the better we shall be able, it may be said, to enjoy the authors. True, if time were not so short, and schoolboys' wits not so soon tired and their power of attention exhausted; only, as it is, the elaborate philological preparation goes on, but the authors are little known and less enjoyed. So with the investigator of "historic origins" in poetry. He ought to enjoy the true classic all the better for his investigations; he often is distracted from the enjoyment of the best, and with the less good he overbusies himself, and is prone to overrate it in proportion to the trouble which it has cost him.

The idea of tracing historic origins and historical relationships cannot be absent from a compilation like the present. And naturally the poets to be exhibited in it will be assigned to those persons for exhibition who are known to prize them highly, rather than to those who have no special inclination towards them. Moreover, the very occupation with an author, and the business of exhibiting him, disposes us to affirm and amplify his importance. In the present work, therefore, we are sure of frequent temptation to adopt the historic estimate, or the personal estimate, and to forget the real estimate; which latter, nevertheless, we must employ if we are to make poetry yield us its full benefit. So high is that benefit, the benefit of clearly feeling and of deeply enjoying the really excellent, the truly classic in poetry, that we do well, I say, to set it fixedly before our minds as our object in studying poets and poetry, and to make the desire of attaining it the one principle to which, as the *Imitation* says, whatever we may read or come to know, we always return. *"Cum multa legeris et cognoveris, ad unum semper oportet redire principium."*[6]

---

[5]Charles d'Hericault (1823–1899), French scholar; Clement Marot (1496?–1544), French poet.

[6]"With much reading and learning one must always return to the one principle." Thomas a Kempis (1379?–1471), German monk, *The Imitation of Christ*.

The historic estimate is likely in especial to affect our judgment and our language when we are dealing with ancient poets; the personal estimate when we are dealing with poets our contemporaries, or at any rate modern. The exaggerations due to the historic estimate are not in themselves, perhaps, of very much gravity. Their report hardly enters the general ear; probably they do not always impose even on the literary men who adopt them. But they lead to a dangerous abuse of language. So we hear Caedmon, amongst our own poets, compared to Milton.[7] I have already noticed the enthusiasm of one accomplished French critic for "historic origins." Another eminent French critic, M. Vitet, comments upon that famous document of the early poetry of his nation, the *Chanson de Roland*. It is indeed a most interesting document. The *joculator* or *jongleur Taillefer,* who was with William the Conqueror's army at Hastings, marched before the Norman troops, so said the tradition, singing "of Charlemagne and of Roland and of Oliver, and of the vassals who died at Roncevaux"; and it is suggested that in the *Chanson de Roland* by one Turoldus or Théroulde, a poem preserved in a manuscript of the twelfth century in the Bodleian Library at Oxford, we have certainly the matter, perhaps even some of the words, of the chant which Taillefer sang. The poem has vigor and freshness; it is not without pathos. But M. Vitet is not satisfied with seeing in it a document of some poetic value, and of very high historic and linguistic value; he sees in it a grand and beautiful work, a monument of epic genius. In its general design he finds the grandiose conception, in its details he finds the constant union of simplicity with greatness, which are the marks, he truly says, of the genuine epic, and distinguish it from the artificial epic of literary ages. One thinks of Homer; this is the sort of praise which is given to Homer, and justly given. Higher praise there cannot well be, and it is the praise due to epic poetry of the highest order only, and to no other. Let us try, then, the *Chanson de Roland* at its best. Roland, mortally wounded, lay himself down under a pine tree, with his face turned towards Spain and the enemy—

> De plusurs choses à remembrer li prist,
> De tantes teres cume li bers cunquist,
> De dulce France, des humes de sun lign,
> De Carlemagne sun seignor ki l'nurrit.[8]

That is primitive work, I repeat, with an undeniable poetic quality of its own. It deserves such praise, and such praise is sufficient for it. But now turn to Homer—Ὣς φάτο. τοὺς δ' ἤδη κατέχεν φυσίζοος αἶα / ἐν Λακεδαίμονι αὖδι, φίλη ἐν πατρίδι γαίῃ.[9] We are here in another world, another order of poetry altogether; here is rightly due such supreme praise as that which M. Vitet gives to the *Chanson de Roland.* If our words are to have any meaning, if our judgments are to have any solidity, we must not heap that supreme praise upon poetry of an order immeasurably inferior.

Indeed there can be no more useful help for discovering what poetry belongs to the class of the truly excellent, and can therefore do us most good, than to have always in one's mind lines and expressions of the great masters, and to apply them as a touchstone to other poetry. Of course we are not to require this other poetry to resemble them; it may be very dissimilar. But if we have any tact we shall find them, when we have lodged them well in our minds, an infallible touchstone for detecting the presence or absence of high poetic quality, and also the degree of this quality, in all other poetry which we may place beside them. Short passages, even single lines, will serve our turn quite sufficiently. Take the two lines which I have just quoted from Homer, the poet's comment on Helen's mention of her brothers; or take his

> Ἀ δειλώ, τί σφῶϊ δόμεν Πηληῖ ἄνακτι
> Θνητῷ; ὑμεῖς δ' ἐστὸν ἀγήρω τ' ἀθανάτω τε.
> ἦ ἵνα δυστήνοισι μετ' ἀνδράσιν ἄλγε' ἔχητον;[10]

the address of Zeus to the horses of Peleus; or take finally his Καὶ σέ, γέρον, τὸ πρὶν μὲν ἀκούομεν ὄλβιον εἶναι,[11] the words of Achilles to Priam, a suppliant before him. Take that incomparable line and a half of Dante, Ugolino's tremendous words—*"Io no piangeva; sì dentro impietrai. / Piangevan elli . . ."*[12] take the lovely words of Beatrice to Virgil—

> Io son fatta da Dio, sua mercè, tale,
> Che la vostra miseria non mi tange,
> Nè fiamma d'esto incendio non m'assale . . .[13]

---

[7] Caedmon (fl. 630) and John Milton (1608–1674), English poets.

[8] [Arnold] "Then began he to call many things to remembrance—all the lands which his valor conquered and pleasant France, and the men of his lineage, and Charlemagne his liege lord who nourished him." *Chanson de Roland* III, 939–42.

[9] [Arnold] "So said she, they long since in earth's soft arms were reposing there in their own dear land, their fatherland, Lacadaemon." *Iliad* III, 243–44 (translated by Dr. Hawtrey).

[10] [Arnold] "Ah, unhappy pair, why gave we you to King Peleus, to a mortal? But ye are without old age, and immortal. Was it that with men born to misery ye might have sorrow?" *Iliad* XXIV, 543.

[11] [Arnold] "And you, too, old man, were, as we have heard, happy in former days." *Iliad* XXIV, 543.

[12] [Arnold] "I wailed not, so of stone grew I within. They wailed." *The Divine Comedy,* "Inferno" XXXIII, 39–40.

[13] [Arnold] "Of such sort hath God, thanked be his mercy, made me, that your misery toucheth me not, neither doth the flame of this fire strike me." *The Divine Comedy,* "Inferno" II, 91–93.

take the simple, but perfect, single line—*"In la sua volontade è nostra pace."*[14] Take of Shakespeare a line or two of Henry the Fourth's expostulation with sleep—

> Wilt thou upon the high and giddy mast
> Seal up the ship-boy's eyes, and rock his brains
> In cradle of the rude imperious surge . . .[15]

and take, as well, Hamlet's dying request to Horatio—

> If thou didst ever hold me in thy heart,
> Absent thee from felicity awhile,
> And in this harsh world draw thy breath in pain
> To tell my story . . .[16]

Take of Milton that Miltonic passage:

> Darkened so, yet shone
> Above them all the archangel; but his face
> Deep scars of thunder had intrenched, and care
> Sat on his faded cheek . . .[17]

add two such lines as "And courage never to submit or yield / And what is else not to be overcome . . ."[18] and finish with the exquisite close to the loss of Proserpine, the loss ". . . which cost Ceres all that pain / To seek her through the world."[19] These few lines, if we have tact and can use them, are enough even of themselves to keep clear and sound our judgments about poetry, to save us from fallacious estimates of it, to conduct us to a real estimate.

The specimens I have quoted differ widely from one another, but they have in common this: the possession of the very highest poetical quality. If we are thoroughly penetrated by their power, we shall find that we have acquired a sense enabling us, whatever poetry may be laid before us, to feel the degree in which a high poetical quality is present or wanting there. Critics give themselves great labor to draw out what in the abstract constitutes the characters of a high quality of poetry. It is much better simply to have recourse to concrete examples; to take specimens of poetry of the high, the very highest quality, and to say: The characters of a high quality of poetry are what is expressed *there*. They are far better recognized by being felt in the verse of the master, than by being perused in the prose of the critic. Nevertheless if we are urgently pressed to give some critical account of them, we may safely, perhaps, venture on laying down, not indeed how and why the characters arise, but where and in what they arise. They are in the matter and substance of the poetry, and they are in its manner and style. Both of these, the substance and matter on the one hand, the style and manner on the other, have a mark, an accent, of high beauty, worth, and power. But if we are asked to define this mark and accent in the abstract, our answer must be: No, for we should thereby be darkening the question, not clearing it. The mark and accent are as given by the substance and matter of that poetry, by the style and manner of that poetry, and of all other poetry which is akin to it in quality.

Only one thing we may add as to the substance and matter of poetry, guiding ourselves by Aristotle's profound observation that the superiority of poetry over history consists in its possessing a higher truth and a higher seriousness (ψιλοσοψώτερον καὶ σπουδαιότερον).[20] Let us add, therefore, to what we have said, this: that the substance and matter of the best poetry acquire their special character from possessing, in an eminent degree, truth and seriousness. We may add yet further, what is in itself evident, that to the style and manner of the best poetry their special character, their accent, is given by their diction, and, even yet more, by their movement. And though we distinguish between the two characters, the two accents, of superiority, yet they are nevertheless vitally connected one with the other. The superior character of truth and seriousness, in the matter and substance of the best poetry, is inseparable from the superiority of diction and movement marking its style and manner. The two superiorities are closely related, and are in steadfast proportion one to the other. So far as high poetic truth and seriousness are wanting to a poet's matter and substance, so far also, we may be sure, will a high poetic stamp of diction and movement be wanting to his style and manner. In proportion as this high stamp of diction and movement, again, is absent from a poet's style and manner, we shall find, also, that high poetic truth and seriousness are absent from his substance and matter.[21]

[14][Arnold] "In his will is our peace." *The Divine Comedy*, "Paradise" III, 85.
[15][Arnold] *II Henry IV* III, i, 18–20.
[16][Arnold] *Hamlet* V, ii, 357–60.
[17][Arnold] *Paradise Lost* I, 599–602.
[18][Arnold] *Paradise Lost* I, 108–9.
[19][Arnold] *Paradise Lost* IV, 271–72.

[20]This is not quite what Aristotle said (above, page 57).
[21]In the rest of the essay Arnold proceeds, with the principles already enunciated in view, to "follow rapidly from the commencement the course of our English poetry."

Charles Baudelaire

1821–1867

The French poet Baudelaire was an art critic of considerable power. The selections below from *The Salon of 1859* have to do with painting, but the ideas are applicable to literary works as well. For Baudelaire the imagination is the "queen of faculties." He thinks of it as a truly creative power. Though nature is full of potential meaning that generates a sort of occult wonder (see his famous sonnet *Correspondences*), it is but a dictionary that must be used to construct our experience. The imagination must shape what nature makes available to it.

Baudelaire's view is post-Kantian and post-Romantic. Nature is a sort of manifold of sensation, in Kant's terms, that is given significance by the power of human beings. When nature is thought of as a dictionary—a mere source of the basic elements of a work of art—copying nature is at best a trivial undertaking; man must breathe his own life into his experience and his art.

An early symbolist, Baudelaire displays a criticism that has definite intellectual links with the discussion of symbols by Coleridge and Carlyle and with Emerson's view of the relationship of poetry to nature. His work precedes Mallarme's remark that "all earthly existence must ultimately be contained in a book."

Baudelaire's literary criticism is available in *Baudelaire as a Literary Critic,* translated and edited by L. B. Hyslop and F. E. Hyslop (1964), and *The Mirror of Art: Critical Studies by Baudelaire,* translated and edited by Jonathan Mayne (1956). For commentary consult Marcel Raymond, *From Baudelaire to Surrealism* (1930); Andre Ferran, *L'Esthetique de Baudelaire* (1933); Margaret Gilman, *Baudelaire the Critic* (1943); Martin Turnell, *Baudelaire: A Study of His Poetry* (1953); Enid Starkie, *Baudelaire* (1957); Alfred E. Carter, *Charles Baudelaire* (1977); Rosemary Lloyd, *Baudelaire's Literary Criticism* (1981); Timothy B. Raser, *A Poetics of Art Criticism: The Case of Baudelaire* (1988); Lois Boe Hyslop, *Baudelaire Revisited* (1992); David Carrier, *High Art: Baudelaire and the Origins of Modernist Painting* (1996).

The Salon of 1859

from
Part III

The Queen of Faculties

In recent years we have heard it said in a thousand different ways: "Copy nature; copy only nature. There is no greater delight, no finer triumph, than an excellent copy of nature." And this doctrine, so inimical to art, was alleged to apply not only to painting but to all the arts, even to the novel, even to poetry. To these doctrinaires so satisfied with nature, an imaginative man would certainly have had the right to answer: "I consider it useless and tiresome to portray things as they are, because nothing that exist satisfies me. Nature is ugly, and I prefer the monsters of my imagination to the triteness of actuality." It would have been more philosophical, however, to ask these dogmatists, first whether they are really certain of the existence of external nature,[1] or in case

Baudelaire's *Salon de 1859* appeared in 1859. The text is from *Baudelaire as a Literary Critic,* translated and edited by Lois Boe Hyslop and Francis E. Hyslop, Jr., (University Park: The Pennsylvania State University Press, 1964).

[1]George Berkeley (1685–1753), Anglo-Irish philosopher, and his epistemological idealism seem to be the source of this question.

this question seemed too well calculated to please their caustic humor, whether they are quite certain of knowing *all nature,* all that is contained in nature. A "yes" would have been the most boastful and the most absurd of answers. If I have correctly understood these strange and degrading divagations, the doctrine meant, at least I am doing it the honor of believing that it meant: "The artist, the true artist, the true poet, should paint only in accordance with what he sees and what he feels. He should be *really* true to his own nature. He should avoid, like death itself, borrowing the eyes and emotions of another man, however great that man may be; for in that case his productions would be lies, so far as he is concerned, and not *realities.*" But if the pedants of whom I am speaking (there is pedantry even in what is contemptible) and who have representatives everywhere—since this theory flatters impotence and indolence alike—if these pedants did not wish the matter to be understood in this way, let us simply believe that they meant: "We have no imagination, and we decree that no one shall have any."

How mysterious is this queen of faculties! It affects all the other faculties; it rouses them, it sends them into combat. Sometimes it resembles them to the point of confusion, and yet it is always very much itself, and the persons who are not stirred by it are easily recognizable by an indefinable curse which withers their productions like the fig tree of the Gospel.

It is analysis, it is synthesis; and yet men who excel in analysis and who are fairly apt in summarizing may lack imagination. It is that, and it is not altogether that. It is sensitivity, and yet there are very sensitive persons, too sensitive perhaps, who are devoid of it. It is imagination that has taught man the moral meaning of color, of outline, of sound, and of perfume. In the beginning of the world it created analogy and metaphor. It decomposes all creation, and from the materials, accumulated and arranged according to rules whose origin is found only in the depths of the soul, it creates a new world, it produces the sensation of the new.[2] Since it has created the world (this can really be said, I believe, even in a religious sense), it is only right that it should govern it. What do people say about a warrior without imagination? That he may make an excellent soldier, but that if he is put in command of armies, he will make no conquests. The case is like that of a poet or a novelist who might take the command of his faculties away from his imagination to give it, for example, to his knowledge of the language or to his observation of facts. What is said of a diplomat without imagination? That he may know all about the history of treaties and alliances in the past, but that he will not sense the treaties and alliances that may evolve in the future. Of a scholar without imagination? That he has learned everything that could be learned from what he was taught, but that he will not discover laws that have not yet been conceived. Imagination is the queen of truth, and the possible is one of the provinces of truth. It has a definite relationship with the infinite.

Without it, all the faculties, however sound or keen they may be, are seemingly nonexistent, whereas the weakness of certain secondary faculties, when excited by a vigorous imagination, is a secondary misfortune. None of the faculties can do without it, and it can even replace some of the others. Imagination often guesses, boldly and simply, what the secondary faculties seek and find only after successive trials of several methods unadapted to the nature of things. Lastly, it plays a powerful role even in morality; for if I may be so bold as to ask—what is virtue without imagination? You might as well speak of virtue without pity, virtue without heaven; it is something hard, cruel, sterilizing, which in certain countries has become bigotry and in certain others, Protestantism.

from

Part IV

The Rule of the Imagination

Yesterday evening, after having sent you the last pages of my letter, in which I had written, not without a certain diffidence: "Since imagination has created the world, it governs it." I was scanning *The Night Side of Nature*[3] and I came across these lines which I am quoting solely because they are a paraphrase justifying the line that was worrying me:

> By *imagination,* I do not simply mean to convey the common notion implied by that much abused word, which is only *fancy,* but the *constructive* imagination, which is a much higher function, and which, inasmuch as man is made in the likeness of God, bears a distant relation to that sublime power by which the Creator projects, creates, and upholds his universe.

---

[2] The statement about decomposition of creation suggests Coleridge's definition of imagination (above, page 504).

[3] By Catherine Crowe (1848), clearly influenced by Coleridge's distinction between imagination and fancy. On Crowe see G. T. Clapton, "Baudelaire and Catherine Crowe," *Modern Language Review* XXV, 3 (1930), 286–305.

I am not at all ashamed but, on the contrary, very happy to be in agreement with the excellent Mrs. Crowe, in whom I have always admired the capacity for belief which is as fully developed in her as is the capacity for distrust in many others.

I was saying that long ago I had heard a man,[4] truly scholarly and profoundly learned in his art, express the most comprehensive and yet the most simple ideas on this subject. When I met him for the first time, I had no experience other than that which comes from an overwhelming love and no other reasoning save instinct. It is true that this love and this instinct were fairly keen, for from my earliest youth, my eyes, filled with paintings or engravings, could never be satiated, and I think that worlds could come to an end, *impavidum ferient,*[5] before I would become an iconoclast. Evidently he wanted to be very kind and obliging, for at first we talked of commonplaces, that is to say, of the most comprehensive and the most profound questions— about nature, for example. "Nature is only a dictionary," he would often say. To properly understand the full meaning implied in this statement, one should keep in mind the many ordinary uses of the dictionary. In it one seeks the meaning of words, the genealogy of words, the etymology of words; in short, one extracts from it all the elements that compose a sentence and a narrative. But no one has ever considered the dictionary as a composition in the poetic sense of the word. Painters who obey their imagination seek in their dictionary the elements which suit their conception; yet, in adapting these elements with a certain art, they give them an altogether new physiognomy. Those who lack imagination copy the dictionary. The result is a very great fault, the fault of banality, which is especially true of those painters whose speciality brings them into closer contact with exterior nature—landscape painters, for example, who generally consider it a triumph not to show their personality. Through too much looking, they forget to feel and to think. . . .

I have no fear that anyone will find it absurd to suppose that the same education is applicable to a host of different individuals. For it is evident that systems of rhetoric and prosody are not arbitrarily invented tyrannies, but rather a collection of rules required by the very nature of the spiritual being. And systems of prosody and rhetoric have never kept originality from showing itself clearly. The contrary— namely, that they have aided the development of originality—would be infinitely more true.

To be brief, I am obliged to omit numerous corollaries resulting from my principal formula, in which is contained, so to speak, the entire formulary of the true aesthetic, and which may be expressed thus: The whole visible universe is but a storehouse of images and signs[6] to which imagination will give a relative place and value; it is a sort of food which the imagination must digest and transform. All the powers of the human soul must be subordinated to the imagination, which commandeers them all at one and the same time. Just as knowing the dictionary well does not necessarily imply a knowledge of the art of composition, and just as the art of composition does not itself imply a universal imagination, so a good painter may not be a great painter. But a great painter is inevitably a good painter, because a universal imagination includes the understanding of all means of expression and the desire to master them.

---

[4] The French painter Eugene Delacroix (1799–1863).
[5] "They smash him undismayed," Horace, *Odes* III, iii, 8.

[6] Compare Baudelaire's sonnet *Correspondences.*

Karl Marx

1818–1883

◇ ◇ ◇

Friedrich Engels

1820–1895

Karl Marx and Friedrich Engels, from very different backgrounds, met and began their lifelong collaboration in association with the "Young Hegelians" in Berlin, following Bruno Bauer and others. Marx, a university student, and Engels, a young military officer with notable talent as a journalist (and later, a businessman), were drawn first to the systematic presentation of Hegel's conception of dialectic by the Young Hegelians as a historical process of change, through conflict, that afforded a rational basis for opposition to authoritarian and repressive government. Engels became an adherent of communism, as espoused by Moses Hess, and followed radical causes even after he relocated to Manchester, England, in 1842 to take a position in his family's cotton business. In the same year, Marx became a regular contributor, and later editor, of the *Rheinische Zeitung* in Cologne, publishing numerous editorials on social and economic matters. After active work with radical causes in Paris, Marx moved to London, his residence until his death. From the late 1840s on, the collaborations of Marx and Engels transformed the world of radical politics, particularly after the publication of the *Communist Manifesto* in 1848. The theoretical and practical work of both men also led to a mode and method of political and economic analysis that fused moral, political, and economic analysis in an explicitly materialist framework that remains a critical resource for thinking and writing in virtually all disciplines of the humanities and social sciences. Not only did Marx and Engels have a doctrinal influence on critics and writers, they provided a basis for a broad movement that considered literature a sociological phenomenon, making literature analyzable as a symptom of social situations.

The position of Marx and Engels is that social being determines consciousness and not vice versa. Art, an expression of consciousness, is thus also determined by social being and is therefore usually characterized by struggle in which the class differences and conflicts within society are fought out. Their work comes in the wake of Romanticism's growing interest in the function of the poet in society (as for example in Shelley [above, page 537]). With the growth of positivistic, scientifically oriented philosophies and disciplines in anthropology, sociology, and psychology, interest increased in literature as historical or sociological document. In this context, Marxist writers have frequently placed very heavy emphasis upon Marxism as a form of "scientific" analysis, but it is particularly clear today that much of its vitality as a continuing tradition of analysis depends on its attention to ethical and practical issues of social justice, fusing moral, philosophical, and political questions in a continuing dialectical debate. In the United States and England, Marxist criticism flourished in the 1930s, with a corresponding vogue in Europe continuing through the sixties and later. In Europe, the tradition of dialectical analysis, following Marx and Engels, however, has had a much more central place in intellectual life, reflected now in a wide variety of orientations and positions in criticism, widely disseminated through the work of such thinkers as Sartre (below, page 1175), Althusser (below, page 1297), and Raymond Williams (below, page 1356), and visible in much work in feminist and gender theory, deconstruction, postcolonial studies, and the New Historicism.

For further reading, see Karl Marx and Frederick Engels, *Collected Works* in forty-nine volumes (1975). A valuable collection is *Literature and Art by Karl Marx and Friedrich Engels: Selections from Their Writings* (1947). Among the many studies of Marx and books exhibiting or commenting on a Marxist approach the following may be mentioned: Nikolai Bukharin, *Problems of Soviet Literature* (n. d.); Leon Trotsky, *Literature and Revolution* (1924); G. V. Plekhanov, *Art and Society* (1937); Christopher Caudwell, *Illusion and Reality* (1937) and *Studies in a Dying Culture* (1938); Ralph Fox, *The Novel and The People (1937);* Mikhail Lifshitz, *The Philosophy of Art of Karl Marx* (1938); Georg Lukács, *The Meaning of Contemporary Realism* (1958); Peter Demetz, *Marx, Engels, and die Dichter* (1959); Ernst Fischer, *The Necessity of Art: A Marxist Approach* (1963); Louis Althusser, *For Marx* (1969); Fredric Jameson, *Marxism and Form* (1971) and *The Political Unconscious: Narrative as a Socially Symbolic Act* (1981); Terry Eagleton, *Marxism and Literary Criticism* (1976) and *Literary Theory: An Introduction* (1983); Herbert Marcuse, *The Aesthetic Dimension: Toward a Critique of Marxist Aesthetics* (tr. 1978); Leonard Jackson, *The Dematerialization of Karl Marx: Literature and Marxist Theory* (1994).

Manifesto of the Communist Party

A spectre is haunting Europe—the spectre of Communism. All the powers of old Europe have entered into a holy alliance to exorcise this spectre: Pope and Czar, Metternich and Guizot, French Radicals and German police-spies.

Where is the party in opposition that has not been decried as communistic by its opponents in power? Where

The *Manifesto of the Communisty Party* (commonly cited as "The Communist Manifesto") was first published in London in 1848. Reprinted here in the authorized English translation, copyright 1948 by International Publishers.

the Opposition that has not hurled back the branding reproach of Communism, against the more advanced opposition parties, as well as against its reactionary adversaries?

Two things result from this fact:

I. Communism is already acknowledged by all European powers to be itself a power.

II. It is high time that Communists should openly, in the face of the whole world, publish their views, their aims, their tendencies, and meet this nursery tale of the spectre of Communism with a manifesto of the party itself.

To this end, Communists of various nationalities have assembled in London, and sketched the following manifesto, to be published in the English, French, German, Italian, Flemish and Danish languages.

I

Bourgeois and Proletarians[1]

The history of all hitherto existing society[2] is the history of class struggles.

Freeman and slave, patrician and plebeian, lord and serf, guildmaster[3] and journeyman, in a word, oppressor and oppressed, stood in constant opposition to one another, carried on an uninterrupted, now hidden, now open fight, a fight that each time ended, either in a revolutionary reconstitution of society at large, or in the common ruin of the contending classes.

In the earlier epochs of history, we find almost everywhere a complicated arrangement of society into various orders, a manifold gradation of social rank. In ancient Rome we have patricians, knights, plebeians, slaves; in the Middle Ages, feudal lords, vassals, guild-masters, journeymen, apprentices, serfs; in almost all of these classes, again, subordinate gradations.

The modern bourgeois society that has sprouted from the ruins of feudal society, has not done away with class antagonisms. It has but established new classes, new conditions of oppression, new forms of struggle in place of the old ones.

Our epoch, the epoch of the bourgeoisie, possesses, however, this distinctive feature: It has simplified the class antagonisms. Society as a whole is more and more splitting up into two great hostile camps, into two great classes directly facing each other—bourgeoisie and proletariat.

From the serfs of the Middle Ages sprang the chartered burghers[4] of the earliest towns. From these burgesses the first elements of the bourgeoisie were developed.

The discovery of America, the rounding of the Cape, opened up fresh ground for the rising bourgeoisie. The East-Indian and Chinese markets, the colonisation of America, trade with the colonies, the increase in the means of exchange and in commodities generally, gave to commerce, to navigation, to industry, an impulse never before known, and thereby, to the revolutionary element in the tottering feudal society, a rapid development.

The feudal system of industry, in which industrial production was monopolised by closed guilds,[5] now no longer sufficed for the growing wants of the new markets. The manufacturing system took its place. The guild-masters were pushed aside by the manufacturing middle class; division of labour between the different corporate guilds vanished in the face of division of labour in each single workshop.

Meantime the markets kept ever growing, the demand ever rising. Even manufacture no longer sufficed. Thereupon, steam and machinery revolutionised industrial production. The place of manufacture was taken by the giant, modern industry, the place of the industrial middle class, by industrial millionaires—the leaders of whole industrial armies, the modern bourgeois.

Modern industry has established the world market, for which the discovery of America paved the way. This market has given an immense development to commerce, to navigation, to communication by land. This development has, in its turn, reacted on the extension of industry; and in proportion as industry, commerce, navigation, railways extended, in the same proportion the bourgeoisie developed, increased its capital, and pushed into the background every class handed down from the Middle Ages.

We see, therefore, how the modern bourgeoisie is itself the product of a long course of development, of a series of revolutions in the modes of production and of exchange.

Each step in the development of the bourgeoisie was accompanied by a corresponding political advance of that class. An oppressed class under the sway of the feudal nobility, it became an armed and self-governing association in

(The notes below include the annotations of Engels and the International Publishers editor, from the 1948 edition of the Authorized English Translation. The source of the notes is indicated.)

[1] [Engels] By bourgeoisie is meant the class of modern capitalists, owners of the means of social production and employers of wage-labour; by proletariat, the class of modern wage-labourers who, having no means of production of their own, are reduced to selling their labour power in order to live.

[2] [Engels] That is, all *written* history. In 1837, the prehistory of society, the social organisation existing previous to recorded history, was all but unknown. Since then Haxthausen [August von, 1792–1866] discovered common ownership of land in Russia, Maurer [Georg Ludwig von] proved it to be the social foundation from which all Teutonic races started in history, and, by and by, village communities were found to be, or to have been, the primitive form of society everywhere from India to Ireland. The inner organisation of this primitive communistic society was laid bare, in its typical form, by Morgan's [Lewis H., 1818–1881] crowning discovery of the true nature of the *gens* and its relation to the *tribe*. With the dissolution of these primaeval communities, society begins to be differentiated into separate and finally antagonistic classes. I have attempted to retrace this process of dissolution in *The Origin of the Family, Private Property and the State*.

[3] [Engels] Guild-master, that is a full member of a guild, a master within, not a head of a guild. [(Eds.) See Hegel, above, page 552.]

[4] [International Publishers Ed.] Chartered burghers were freemen who had been admitted to the privileges of a chartered borough thus possessing full political rights.

[5] [International Publishers Ed.] Craft guilds, made up of exclusive and privileged groups of artisans were, during the feudal period, granted monopoly rights to markets by municipal authorities. The guilds imposed minute regulations on their members controlling such matters as working hours, wages, prices, tools and the hiring of workers.

the medieval commune;[6] here independent urban republic (as in Italy and Germany), there taxable "third estate" of the monarchy (as in France); afterwards, in the period of manufacture proper, serving either the semi-feudal or the absolute monarchy as a counterpoise against the nobility, and, in fact, corner-stone of the great monarchies in general—the bourgeoisie has at last, since the establishment of modern industry and of the world market, conquered for itself, in the modern representative state, exclusive political sway. The executive of the modern state is but a committee for managing the common affairs of the whole bourgeoisie.

The bourgeoisie has played a most revolutionary rôle in history.

The bourgeoisie, wherever it has got the upper hand, has put an end to all feudal, patriarchal, idyllic relations. It has pitilessly torn asunder the motley feudal ties that bound man to his "natural superiors," and has left no other bond between man and man than naked self-interest, than callous "cash payment." It has drowned the most heavenly ecstasies of religious fervour, of chivalrous enthusiasm, of philistine sentimentalism, in the icy water of egotistical calculation. It has resolved personal worth into exchange value, and in place of the numberless indefeasible chartered freedoms, has set up that single, unconscionable freedom—Free Trade. In one word, for exploitation, veiled by religious and political illusions, it has substituted naked, shameless, direct, brutal exploitation.

The bourgeoisie has stripped of its halo every occupation hitherto honoured and looked up to with reverent awe. It has converted the physician, the lawyer, the priest, the poet, the man of science, into its paid wage-labourers.

The bourgeoisie has torn away from the family its sentimental veil, and has reduced the family relation to a mere money relation.

The bourgeoisie has disclosed how it came to pass that the brutal display of vigour in the Middle Ages, which reactionaries so much admire, found its fitting complement in the most slothful indolence. It has been the first to show what man's activity can bring about. It has accomplished wonders far surpassing Egyptian pyramids, Roman aqueducts, and Gothic cathedrals; it has conducted expeditions that put in the shade all former migrations of nations and crusades.

The bourgeoisie cannot exist without constantly revolutionising the instruments of production, and thereby the

relations of production, and with them the whole relations of society. Conservation of the old modes of production in unaltered form, was, on the contrary, the first condition of existence for all earlier industrial classes. Constant revolutionising of production, uninterrupted disturbance of all social conditions, everlasting uncertainty and agitation distinguish the bourgeois epoch from all earlier ones. All fixed, fast-frozen relations, with their train of ancient and venerable prejudices and opinions, are swept away, all new-formed ones become antiquated before they can ossify. All that is solid melts into air, all that is holy is profaned, and man is at last compelled to face with sober senses his real conditions of life and his relations with his kind.

The need of a constantly expanding market for its products chases the bourgeoisie over the whole surface of the globe. It must nestle everywhere, settle everywhere, establish connections everywhere.

The bourgeoisie has through its exploitation of the world market given a cosmopolitan character to production and consumption in every country. To the great chagrin of reactionaries, it has drawn from under the feet of industry the national ground on which it stood. All old-established national industries have been destroyed or are daily being destroyed. They are dislodged by new industries, whose introduction becomes a life and death question for all civilised nations, by industries that no longer work up indigenous raw material, but raw material drawn from the remotest zones; industries whose products are consumed, not only at home, but in every quarter of the globe. In place of the old wants, satisfied by the production of the country, we find new wants, requiring for their satisfaction the products of distant lands and climes. In place of the old local and national seclusion and self-sufficiency, we have intercourse in every direction, universal inter-dependence of nations. And as in material, so also in intellectual production. The intellectual creations of individual nations become common property. National one-sidedness and narrow-mindedness become more and more impossible, and from the numerous national and local literatures there arises a world literature.

The bourgeoisie, by the rapid improvement of all instruments of production, by the immensely facilitated means of communication, draws all nations, even the most barbarian, into civilization. The cheap prices of its commodities are the heavy artillery with which it batters down all Chinese walls, with which it forces the barbarians' intensely obstinate hatred of foreigners to capitulate. It compels all nations, on pain of extinction, to adopt the bourgeois mode of production; it compels them to introduce what it calls civilisation into their midst, *i.e.,* to become bourgeois themselves. In a word, it creates a world after its own image.

---

[6][Engels] "Commune" was the name taken in France by the nascent towns even before they had conquered from their feudal lords and masters local self-government and political rights as the "Third Estate." Generally speaking, for the economic development of the bourgeoisie, England is here taken as the typical country, for its political development, France.

The bourgeoisie has subjected the country to the rule of the towns. It has created enormous cities, has greatly increased the urban population as compared with the rural, and has thus rescued a considerable part of the population from the idiocy of rural life. Just as it has made the country dependent on the towns, so it has made barbarian and semi-barbarian countries dependent on the civilised ones, nations of peasants on nations of bourgeois, the East on the West.

More and more the bourgeoisie keeps doing away with the scattered state of the population, of the means of production, and of property. It has agglomerated population, centralised means of production, and has concentrated property in a few hands. The necessary consequence of this was political centralisation. Independent, or but loosely connected provinces, with separate interests, laws, governments and systems of taxation, became lumped together into one nation, with one government, one code of laws, one national class interest, one frontier and one customs tariff.

The bourgeoisie, during its rule of scarce one hundred years, has created more massive and more colossal productive forces than have all preceding generations together. Subjection of nature's forces to man, machinery, application of chemistry to industry and agriculture, steam-navigation, railways, electric telegraphs, clearing of whole continents for cultivation, canalisation of rivers, whole populations conjured out of the ground—what earlier century had even a presentiment that such productive forces slumbered in the lap of social labour?

We see then that the means of production and of exchange, which served as the foundation for the growth of the bourgeoisie, were generated in feudal society. At a certain stage in the development of these means of production and of exchange, the conditions under which feudal society produced and exchanged, the feudal organisation of agriculture and manufacturing industry, in a word, the feudal relations of property became no longer compatible with the already developed productive forces; they became so many fetters. They had to be burst asunder; they were burst asunder.

Into their place stepped free competition, accompanied by a social and political constitution adapted to it, and by the economic and political sway of the bourgeois class.

A similar movement is going on before our own eyes. Modern bourgeois society with its relations of production, of exchange and of property, a society that has conjured up such gigantic means of production and of exchange, is like the sorcerer who is no longer able to control the powers of the nether world whom he has called up by his spells. For many a decade past the history of industry and commerce is but the history of the revolt of modern productive forces against modern conditions of production, against the prop-

erty relations that are the conditions for the existence of the bourgeoisie and of its rule. It is enough to mention the commercial crises that by their periodical return put the existence of the entire bourgeois society on trial, each time more threateningly. In these crises a great part not only of the existing products, but also of the previously created productive forces, are periodically destroyed. In these crises there breaks out an epidemic that, in all earlier epochs, would have seemed an absurdity—the epidemic of overproduction. Society suddenly finds itself put back into a state of momentary barbarism; it appears as if a famine, a universal war of devastation had cut off the supply of every means of subsistence; industry and commerce seem to be destroyed. And why? Because there is too much civilisation, too much means of subsistence, too much industry, too much commerce. The productive forces at the disposal of society no longer tend to further the development of the conditions of bourgeois property; on the contrary, they have become too powerful for these conditions, by which they are fettered, and no sooner do they overcome these fetters than they bring disorder into the whole of bourgeois society, endanger the existence of bourgeois property. The conditions of bourgeois society are too narrow to comprise the wealth created by them. And how does the bourgeoisie get over these crises? On the one hand by enforced destruction of a mass of productive forces; on the other, by the conquest of new markets, and by the more thorough exploitation of the old ones. That is to say, by paving the way for more extensive and more destructive crises, and by diminishing the means whereby crises are prevented.

The weapons with which the bourgeoisie felled feudalism to the ground are now turned against the bourgeoisie itself.

But not only has the bourgeoisie forged the weapons that bring death to itself; it has also called into existence the men who are to wield those weapons—the modern working class—the proletarians.

In proportion as the bourgeoisie, *i.e.,* capital, is developed, in the same proportion is the proletariat, the modern working class, developed—a class of labourers, who live only so long as they find work, and who find work only so long as their labour increases capital. These labourers, who must sell themselves piecemeal, are a commodity, like every other article of commerce, and are consequently exposed to all the vicissitudes of competition, to all the fluctuations of the market.

Owing to the extensive use of machinery and to division of labour, the work of the proletarians has lost all individual character, and, consequently, all charm for the workman. He becomes an appendage of the machine, and it is only the most simple, most monotonous, and most easily acquired knack, that is required of him. Hence, the cost of production of a workman is restricted, almost entirely, to the means of subsistence that he requires for his maintenance, and for the propagation of his race. But the price of a commodity, and therefore also of labour, is equal to its cost of production. In proportion, therefore, as the repulsiveness of the work increases, the wage decreases. Nay more, in proportion as the use of machinery and division of labour increases, in the same proportion the burden of toil also increases, whether by prolongation of the working hours, by increase of the work exacted in a given time, or by increased speed of the machinery, etc.

Modern industry has converted the little workshop of the patriarchal master into the great factory of the industrial capitalist. Masses of labourers, crowded into the factory, are organised like soldiers. As privates of the industrial army they are placed under the command of a perfect hierarchy of officers and sergeants. Not only are they slaves of the bourgeois class, and of the bourgeois state; they are daily and hourly enslaved by the machine, by the over-looker, and, above all, by the individual bourgeois manufacturer himself. The more openly this despotism proclaims gain to be its end and aim, the more petty, the more hateful and the more embittering it is.

The less the skill and exertion of strength implied in manual labour, in other words, the more modern industry develops, the more is the labour of men superseded by that of women. Differences of age and sex have no longer any distinctive social validity for the working class. All are instruments of labour, more or less expensive to use, according to their age and sex.

No sooner has the labourer received his wages in cash, for the moment escaping exploitation by the manufacturer, than he is set upon by the other portions of the bourgeoisie, the landlord, the shopkeeper, the pawnbroker, etc.

The lower strata of the middle class—the small tradespeople, shopkeepers, and retired tradesmen generally, the handicraftsmen and peasants—all these sink gradually into the proletariat, partly because their diminutive capital does not suffice for the scale on which modern industry is carried on, and is swamped in the competition with the large capitalists, partly because their specialised skill is rendered worthless by new methods of production. Thus the proletariat is recruited from all classes of the population.

The proletariat goes through various stages of development. With its birth begins its struggle with the bourgeoisie. At first the contest is carried on by individual labourers, then by the work people of a factory, then by the operatives of one trade, in one locality, against the individual bourgeois

who directly exploits them. They direct their attacks not against the bourgeois conditions of production, but against the instruments of production themselves; they destroy imported wares that compete with their labour, they smash machinery to pieces, they set factories ablaze, they seek to restore by force the vanished status of the workman of the Middle Ages.

At this stage the labourers still form an incoherent mass scattered over the whole country, and broken up by their mutual competition. If anywhere they unite to form more compact bodies, this is not yet the consequence of their own active union, but of the union of the bourgeoisie, which class, in order to attain its own political ends, is compelled to set the whole proletariat in motion, and is moreover still able to do so for a time. At this stage, therefore, the proletarians do not fight their enemies, but the enemies of their enemies, the remnants of absolute monarchy, the landowners, the non-industrial bourgeois, the petty bourgeoisie. Thus the whole historical movement is concentrated in the hands of the bourgeoisie; every victory so obtained is a victory for the bourgeoisie.

But with the development of industry the proletariat not only increases in number; it becomes concentrated in greater masses, its strength grows, and it feels that strength more. The various interests and conditions of life within the ranks of the proletariat are more and more equalised, in proportion as machinery obliterates all distinctions of labour and nearly everywhere reduces wages to the same low level. The growing competition among the bourgeois, and the resulting commercial crises, make the wages of the workers ever more fluctuating. The unceasing improvement of machinery, ever more rapidly developing, makes their livelihood more and more precarious; the collisions between individual workmen and individual bourgeois take more and more the character of collisions between two classes. Thereupon the workers begin to form combinations (trade unions) against the bourgeoisie; they club together in order to keep up the rate of wages; they found permanent associations in order to make provision beforehand for these occasional revolts. Here and there the contest breaks out into riots.

Now and then the workers are victorious, but only for a time. The real fruit of their battles lies, not in the immediate result, but in the ever expanding union of the workers. This union is furthered by the improved means of communication which are created by modern industry, and which place the workers of different localities in contact with one another. It was just this contact that was needed to centralise the numerous local struggles, all of the same character, into one national struggle between classes. But every class struggle is a political struggle. And that union, to attain which the burghers of the Middle Ages, with their miserable highways, required centuries, the modern proletarians, thanks to railways, achieve in a few years.

This organisation of the proletarians into a class, and consequently into a political party, is continually being upset again by the competition between the workers themselves. But it ever rises up again, stronger, firmer, mightier. It compels legislative recognition of particular interests of the workers, by taking advantage of the divisions among the bourgeoisie itself. Thus the ten-hour bill[7] in England was carried.

Altogether, collisions between the classes of the old society further the course of development of the proletariat in many ways. The bourgeoisie finds itself involved in a constant battle. At first with the aristocracy; later on, with those portions of the bourgeoisie itself whose interests have become antagonistic to the progress of industry; at all times with the bourgeoisie of foreign countries. In all these battles it sees itself compelled to appeal to the proletariat, to ask for its help, and thus, to drag it into the political arena. The bourgeoisie itself, therefore, supplies the proletariat with its own elements of political and general education, in other words, it furnishes the proletariat with weapons for fighting the bourgeoisie.

Further, as we have already seen, entire sections of the ruling classes are, by the advance of industry; precipitated into the proletariat, or are at least threatened in their conditions of existence. These also supply the proletariat with fresh elements of enlightenment and progress.

Finally, in times when the class struggle nears the decisive hour, the process of dissolution going on within the ruling class, in fact within the whole range of old society, assumes such a violent, glaring character, that a small section of the ruling class cuts itself adrift, and joins the revolutionary class, the class that holds the future in its hands. Just as, therefore, at an earlier period, a section of the nobility went over to the bourgeoisie, so now a portion of the bourgeoisie goes over to the proletariat, and in particular, a portion of the bourgeois ideologists, who have raised themselves to the level of comprehending theoretically the historical movement as a whole.

Of all the classes that stand face to face with the bourgeoisie today, the proletariat alone is a really revolutionary class. The other classes decay and finally disappear in the face of modern industry; the proletariat is its special and essential product.

[7] [International Publishers Ed.] The ten-hour bill, for which the English workers had been fighting for 30 years, was made a law in 1847.

The lower middle class, the small manufacturer, the shopkeeper, the artisan, the peasant, all these fight against the bourgeoisie, to save from extinction their existence as fractions of the middle class. They are therefore not revolutionary, but conservative. Nay more, they are reactionary, for they try to roll back the wheel of history. If by chance they are revolutionary, they are so only in view of their impending transfer into the proletariat; they thus defend not their present, but their future interests; they desert their own standpoint to adopt that of the proletariat.

The "dangerous class," the social scum *(Lumpenproletariat),* that passively rotting mass thrown off by the lowest layers of old society, may, here and there, be swept into the movement by a proletarian revolution; its conditions of life, however, prepare it far more for the part of a bribed tool of reactionary intrigue.

The social conditions of the old society no longer exist for the proletariat. The proletarian is without property; his relation to his wife and children has no longer anything in common with bourgeois family relations; modern industrial labour, modern subjection to capital, the same in England as in France, in America as in Germany, has stripped him of every trace of national character. Law, morality, religion, are to him so many bourgeois prejudices, behind which lurk in ambush just as many bourgeois interests.

All the preceding classes that got the upper hand, sought to fortify their already acquired status by subjecting society at large to their conditions of appropriation. The proletarians cannot become masters of the productive forces of society, except by abolishing their own previous mode of appropriation, and thereby also every other previous mode of appropriation. They have nothing of their own to secure and to fortify; their mission is to destroy all previous securities for, and insurances of, individual property.

All previous historical movements were movements of minorities, or in the interest of minorities. The proletarian movement is the self-conscious, independent movement of the immense majority, in the interest of the immense majority. The proletariat, the lowest stratum of our present society, cannot stir, cannot raise itself up, without the whole superincumbent strata of official society being sprung into the air.

Though not in substance, yet in form, the struggle of the proletariat with the bourgeoisie is at first a national struggle. The proletariat of each country must, of course, first of all settle matters with its own bourgeoisie.

In depicting the most general phases of the development of the proletariat, we traced the more or less veiled civil war, raging within existing society, up to the point where that war breaks out into open revolution, and where the violent overthrow of the bourgeoisie lays the foundation for the sway of the proletariat.

Hitherto, every form of society has been based, as we have already seen, on the antagonism of oppressing and oppressed classes. But in order to oppress a class, certain conditions must be assured to it under which it can, at least, continue its slavish existence. The serf, in the period of serfdom, raised himself to membership in the commune, just as the petty bourgeois, under the yoke of feudal absolutism, managed to develop into a bourgeois. The modern labourer, on the contrary, instead of rising with the progress of industry, sinks deeper and deeper below the conditions of existence of his own class. He becomes a pauper, and pauperism develops more rapidly than population and wealth. And here it becomes evident, that the bourgeoisie is unfit any longer to be the ruling class in society, and to impose its conditions of existence upon society as an over-riding law. It is unfit to rule because it is incompetent to assure an existence to its slave within his slavery, because it cannot help letting him sink into such a state, that it has to feed him, instead of being fed by him. Society can no longer live under this bourgeoisie, in other words, its existence is no longer compatible with society.

The essential condition for the existence and sway of the bourgeois class, is the formation and augmentation of capital; the condition for capital is wage-labour. Wage-labour rests exclusively on competition between the labourers. The advance of industry, whose involuntary promoter is the bourgeoisie, replaces the isolation of the labourers, due to competition, by their revolutionary combination, due to association. The development of modern industry, therefore, cuts from under its feet the very foundation on which the bourgeoisie produces and appropriates products. What the bourgeoisie therefore produces, above all, are its own grave-diggers. Its fall and the victory of the proletariat are equally inevitable.

from

The German Ideology

The production of ideas, of conceptions, of consciousness, is at first directly interwoven with the material activity and the material intercourse of men, the language of real life. Con-

Die Deutsche Ideologie by Karl Marx and Friedrich Engels was written in 1846 but not published until 1932. Marx's *Zur Kritik der politischen Ökonomie* was published in 1849. Both translated excerpts are from *Literature and Art, by Karl Marx and Friedrich Engels: Selections from Their Writings* (New York: International Publishers, Inc., 1947).

ceiving, thinking, the mental intercourse of men, appear at this stage as the direct efflux of their material behavior. The same applies to mental production as expressed in the language of the politics, laws, morality, religion, metaphysics of a people. Men are the producers of their conceptions, ideas, etc.—real, active men, as they are conditioned by a definite development of their productive forces and of the intercourse corresponding to these, up to its furthest forms. Consciousness can never be anything else than conscious existence, and the existence of men is their actual life process. If in all ideology men and their circumstances appear upside down as in a camera obscura, this phenomenon arises just as much from their historical life process as the inversion of objects on the retina does from their physical life process.

In direct contrast to German philosophy which descends from heaven to earth, here we ascend from earth to heaven. That is to say, we do not set out from what men say, imagine, conceive, nor from men as narrated, thought of, imagined, conceived, in order to arrive at men in the flesh. We set out from real, active men, and on the basis of their real life process we demonstrate the development of the ideological reflexes and echoes of this life process. The phantoms formed in the human brain are also, necessarily, sublimates of their material life process, which is empirically verifiable and bound to material premises. Morality, religion, metaphysics, all the rest of ideology and their corresponding forms of consciousness, thus no longer retain the semblance of independence. They have no history, no development; but men, developing their material production and their material intercourse, alter, along with this their real existence, their thinking and the products of their thinking. Life is not determined by consciousness, but consciousness by life. In the first method of approach the starting point is consciousness taken as the living individual; in the second it is the real living individuals themselves, as they are in actual life, and consciousness is considered solely as *their* consciousness.

This method of approach is not devoid of premises. It starts out from the real premises and does not abandon them for a moment. Its premises are men, not in any fantastic isolation or abstract definition, but in their actual, empirically perceptible process of development under definite conditions. As soon as this active life process is described, history ceases to be a collection of dead facts as it is with the empiricists (themselves still abstract), or an imagined activity of imagined subjects, as with the idealists.

Where speculation ends—in real life—there real, positive science begins: the representation of the practical activity, of the practical process of development of men. Empty talk about consciousness ceases, and real knowledge has to take its place. When reality is depicted, philosophy as an independent branch of activity loses its medium of existence. At the best its place can only be taken by a summing-up of the most general results, abstractions which arise from the observation of the historical development of men. Viewed apart from real history, these abstractions have in themselves no value whatsoever. They can only serve to facilitate the arrangement of historical material, to indicate the sequence of its separate strata. But they by no means afford a recipe or schema, as does philosophy, for neatly trimming the epochs of history. On the contrary, our difficulties begin only when we set about the observation and the arrangement—the real depiction—of our historical material, whether of a past epoch or of the present. The removal of these difficulties is governed by premises which it is quite impossible to state here, but which only the study of the actual life process and the activity of the individuals of each epoch will make evident.

from

A Contribution to the Critique of Political Economy

It is well known that certain periods of highest development of art stand in no direct connection with the general development of society, nor with the material basis and the skeleton structure of its organization. Witness the example of the Greeks as compared with the modern nations or even Shakespeare. As regards certain forms of art, as, e.g., the epos, it is admitted that they can never be produced in the world-epoch-making form as soon as art as such comes into existence; in other words, that in the domain of art certain important forms of it are possible only at a low stage of its development. If that be true of the mutual relations of different forms of art within the domain of art itself, it is far less surprising that the same is true of the relation of art as a whole to the general development of society. The difficulty lies only in the general formulation of these contradictions. No sooner are they specified than they are explained. Let us take for instance the relation of Greek art and of that of Shakespeare's time to our own. It is a well-known fact that Greek mythology was not only the arsenal of Greek art, but also the very ground from which it had sprung. Is the view of nature and of social relations which shaped Greek imagination and Greek [art] possible in the age of automatic machinery, and railways, and locomotives, and electric telegraphs? Where does Vulcan come in as against Roberts

& Co.; Jupiter, as against the lightning rod; and Hermes, as against the Credit Mobilier? All mythology masters and dominates and shapes the forces of nature in and through the imagination; hence it disappears as soon as man gains mastery over the forces of nature. What becomes of the goddess Fame side by side with Printing House Square? Greek art presupposes the existence of Greek mythology, i.e., that nature and even the form of society are wrought up in popular fancy in an unconsciously artistic fashion. That is its material. Not, however, any mythology taken at random, nor any accidental, unconsciously artistic elaboration of nature (including under the latter all objects; hence also society). Egyptian mythology could never be the soil or womb which would give birth to Greek art. But in any event there had to be a mythology. In no event could Greek art originate in a society which excludes any mythological explanation of nature, any mythological attitude towards it and which requires from the artist an imagination free from mythology.

Looking at it from another side: Is Achilles possible side by side with powder and lead? Or is the *Iliad* at all compatible with the printing press and steam press? Do not singing and reciting and the Muses necessarily go out of existence with the appearance of the printer's bar, and do not, therefore, disappear, the prerequisites of epic poetry?

But the difficulty is not in grasping the idea that Greek art and epos are bound up with certain forms of social development. It rather lies in understanding why they still constitute with us a source of aesthetic enjoyment and in certain respects prevail as the standard and model beyond attainment.

A man cannot become a child again unless he becomes childish. But does he not enjoy the artless ways of the child and must he not strive to reproduce its truth on a higher plane? Is not the character of every epoch revived perfectly true to nature in child nature? Why should the social childhood of mankind, where it had obtained its most beautiful development, not exert an eternal charm as an age that will never return? There are ill-bred children and precocious children. Many of the ancient nations belong to the latter class. The Greeks were normal children. The charm their art has for us does not conflict with the primitive character of the social order from which it had sprung. It is rather the product of the latter, and is rather due to the fact that the unripe social conditions under which the art arose and under which alone it could appear could never return.

* * *

In the social production which men carry on they enter into definite relations that are indispensable and independent of their will; these relations of production correspond to a definite stage of development of their material forces of production. The sum total of these relations of production constitutes the economic structure of society—the real foundation, on which rises a legal and political superstructure and to which correspond definite forms of social consciousness. The mode of production in material life determines the social, political, and intellectual life processes in general. It is not the consciousness of men that determines their being, but, on the contrary, their social being that determines their consciousness. At a certain stage of their development, the material forces of production in society come in conflict with the existing relations of production, or—what is but a legal expression for the same thing—with the property relations within which they have been at work before. From forms of development of the forces of production these relations turn into their fetters. Then begins an epoch of social revolution. With the change of the economic foundation the entire immense superstructure is more or less rapidly transformed. In considering such transformations a distinction should always be made between the material transformation of the economic conditions of production which can be determined with the precision of natural science, and the legal, political, religious, aesthetic, or philosophic—in short, ideological—forms in which men become conscious of this conflict and fight it out. Just as our opinion of an individual is not based on what he thinks of himself, so can we not judge of such a period of transformation by its own consciousness; on the contrary this consciousness must be explained rather from the contradictions of material life, from the existing conflict between the social forces of production and the relations of production. No social order ever disappears before all the productive forces for which there is room in it have been developed; and new higher relations of production never appear before the material conditions of their existence have matured in the womb of the old society itself. Therefore, mankind always sets itself only such tasks as it can solve; since, looking at the matter more closely, we will always find that the task itself arises only when the material conditions necessary for its solution already exist or are at least in the process of formation. In broad outlines we can designate the Asiatic, the ancient, the feudal, and the modern bourgeois modes of production as so many epochs in the progress of the economic formation of society. The bourgeois relations of production are the last antagonistic form of the social process of production—antagonistic not in the sense of individual antagonism, but of one arising from the social conditions of life of the individuals; at the same time the productive forces developing in the womb of bourgeois society create the material conditions for the solution of that antagonism. This social formation constitutes, therefore, the closing chapter of the prehistoric stage of human society.

Walter Pater

1839–1894

Often considered the father of aestheticism, Pater set forth the principles of impressionistic criticism in his *Studies in the History of the Renaissance.* A study of his Romantic forebears shows that his more extreme ideas clearly came out of their critical and epistemological positions. So powerful was the influence of his ideas that for a time Pater suppressed the famous Conclusion to his book, which he felt had been misinterpreted as an invitation to irresponsible hedonism. Pater himself advocated a fastidious decorum.

Pater mistrusts abstractions and finds definitions of beauty no basis for aesthetic theories. All aesthetic judgments must finally be referred to the reader's receptivity, his taste. The critic's worth depends on the refinement of his temperament, since objective standards of aesthetic judgment are abstract and useless. For Pater, criticism itself becomes a work of art, and he is justly known for his own impressionistic style of criticism, best and most extremely exemplified by his description of Leonardo da Vinci's *Mona Lisa,* which reads in part as follows: "She is older than the rocks among which she sits; like the vampire, she has been dead many times, and learned the secrets of the grave; and has been a diver in deep seas, and keeps their fallen day about her; and trafficked for strange webs with Eastern merchants, and, as Leda, was the mother of Helen of Troy, and as Saint Anne, the mother of Mary; and all this has been to her but as the sound of lyres and flutes, and lives only in the delicacy with which it has moulded the changing lineaments, and tinged the eyelids and the hands."

Earlier Romantic reservations about abstract thought and general nature, along with Romantic praise of immediate, personal, particular experience and of the sense of time lived rather than time measured, culminate in Pater's solipsistic remarks in the Conclusion of his book: "Experience, already reduced to a swarm ["a group" in 1888] of impressions is ringed round for each of us by that thick wall of personality through which no real voice has ever pierced on its way to us, or from us to that which we can only conjecture to be without." The Romantic hope for empathetic identity with natural objects and other beings is dismissed here, and there remains the gesture of personal style that can easily be thought of as a mask. Pater's view, though more morose, is akin to that of Anatole France, quoted in the headnote to Matthew Arnold (above, page 587).

Heir to the subject–object problem passed on to him by philosophers, Pater carries response to the problem to its extreme. Rejecting the materialists, he also rejects total dependence on rational understanding to give us what knowledge we can have. Expressive of his time, he emphasizes the fleeting temporality of all experience.

The standard text of Pater's work is the ten-volume edition published in 1910. Commentary includes Thomas Wright, *The Life of Walter Pater* (in two volumes, 1907); A. J. Farmer, *Walter Pater as a Critic of English Literature* (1931); T. S. Eliot, "Arnold and Pater," in his *Selected Essays 1917–1932* (1932); Arthur Symons, *A Study of Walter Pater* (1932); R. C. Child, *The Aesthetic of Walter Pater* (1940); Anthony Ward, *Walter*

Pater: The Idea in Nature (1967); Richmond Crinkley, *Walter Pater: Humanist* (1970); William E. Buckler, *Walter Pater: The Critic as Artist of Ideas* (1987); Paul Barolsky, *Walter Pater's Renaissance* (1987); Wolfgang Iser, *Walter Pater: The Aesthetic Moment* (tr. 1987); Denis Donoghue, *Walter Pater, Lover of Strange Souls* (1995); Walter Shuter, *Rereading Walter Pater* (1997).

Studies in the History of the Renaissance

from
Preface

Many attempts have been made by writers on art and poetry to define beauty in the abstract, to express it in the most general terms, to find a universal formula for it. The value of such attempts has most often been in the suggestive and penetrating things said by the way. Such discussions help us very little to enjoy what has been well done in art or poetry, to discriminate between what is more and what is less excellent in them, or to use words like *beauty, excellence, art, poetry,* with more meaning than they would otherwise have. Beauty, like all other qualities presented to human experience, is relative; and the definition of it becomes unmeaning and useless in proportion to its abstractness. To define beauty not in the most abstract, but in the most concrete terms possible, not to find a universal formula for it, but the formula which expresses most adequately this or that special manifestation of it, is the aim of the true student of aesthetics.

"To see the object as in itself it really is,"[1] has been justly said to be the aim of all true criticism whatever; and in aesthetic criticism the first step towards seeing one's object as it really is, is to know one's own impression as it really is, to discriminate it, to realize it distinctly. The objects with which aesthetic criticism deals, music, poetry, artistic and accomplished forms of human life, are indeed receptacles of so many powers or forces; they possess, like natural elements, so many virtues or qualities. What is this song or picture, this engaging personality presented in life or in a book, to me? What effect does it really produce on me? Does it give me pleasure? and if so, what sort or degree of pleasure? How is my nature modified by its presence and under its influence? The answers to these questions are the original facts with which the aesthetic critic has to do; and, as in the study of light, of morals, of number, one must realize such primary data for oneself or not at all. And he who experiences these impressions strongly, and drives directly at the analysis and discrimination of them, need not trouble himself with the abstract question what beauty is in itself, or its exact relation to truth or experience—metaphysical questions, as unprofitable as metaphysical questions elsewhere. He may pass them all by as being, answerable or not, of no interest to him.

The aesthetic critic, then, regards all the objects with which he has to do, all works of art and the fairer forms of nature and human life, as powers or forces, producing pleasurable sensations, each of a more or less peculiar and unique kind. This influence he feels and wishes to explain, analyzing it, and reducing it to its elements. To him, the picture, the landscape, the engaging personality in life or in a book, *La Gioconda,*[2] the hills of Carrara, Pico of Mirandola,[3] are valuable for their virtues, as we say in speaking of a herb, a wine, a gem; for the property each has of affecting one with a special, unique impression of pleasure. Education grows in proportion as one's susceptibility to these impressions increases in depth and variety. And the function of the aesthetic critic is to distinguish, analyze, and separate from its adjuncts, the virtue by which a picture, a landscape, a fair personality in life or in a book, produces this special impression of beauty or pleasure, to indicate what the source of that impression is, and under what conditions it is experienced. His end is reached when he has disengaged that virtue, and noted it, as a chemist notes some natural element, for himself and others; and the rule for those who would reach this end is stated with great exactness in the words of a recent critic of Sainte-Beuve: *"De se borner à connaître de près les belles choses, et à s'en nourrir en exquis amateurs, en humanistes accomplis."*[4]

Pater's *Studies in the History of the Renaissance,* in a later edition called simply *The Renaissance,* was first published in 1873. Pater omitted the Conclusion, after an outcry against it, in the second edition of 1877, but restored it with a few slight changes in 1888. The text is from the 1873 edition.
[1] See Arnold, *The Function of Criticism* (above, page 594).

[2] The Mona Lisa by Leonardo da Vinci (1452–1519).
[3] Giovanni, Count Pico della Mirandola (1463–1494), Italian humanist, to whom Pater devoted Chapter II.
[4] Charles Augustin Sainte-Beuve (1804–1869), French critic. [Pater] "To limit themselves to know lovely things near at hand, and to nourish themselves upon them, like refined conoisseurs, like accomplished humanists."

What is important, then, is not that the critic should possess a correct abstract definition of beauty for the intellect, but a certain kind of temperament, the power of being deeply moved by the presence of beautiful objects. He will remember always that beauty exists in many forms. To him all periods, types, schools of taste, are in themselves equal. In all ages there have been some excellent workmen and some excellent work done. The question he asks is always, In whom did the stir, the genius, the sentiment of the period find itself? Who was the receptacle of its refinement, its elevation, its taste? "The ages are all equal," says William Blake, "but genius is always above its age."[5]

Often it will require great nicety to disengage this virtue from the commoner elements with which it may be found in combination. Few artists, not Goethe or Byron[6] even, work quite cleanly, casting off all debris, and leaving us only what the heat of their imagination has wholly fused and transformed. Take for instance the writings of Wordsworth.[7] The heat of his genius, entering into the substance of his work, has crystalized a part, but only a part, of it; and in that great mass of verse there is much which might well be forgotten. But scattered up and down it, sometimes fusing and transforming entire compositions, like the stanzas on *Resolution and Independence* and the ode on the *Recollections of Childhood,* sometimes, as if at random, turning a fine crystal here and there, in a matter it does not wholly search through and transform, we trace the action of his unique incommunicable faculty, that strange mystical sense of a life in natural things, and of man's life as a part of nature, drawing strength and color and character from local influences, from the hills and streams and natural sights and sounds. Well! That is the *virtue,* the active principle in Wordsworth's poetry; and then the function of the critic of Wordsworth is to trace that active principle, to disengage it, to mark the degree in which it penetrates his verse.

Conclusion

Λέγει που ‘Ηράχλειτος ὅτι πάντα χωρεῖ καὶ οὐδὲν μένει.[8]

PLATO

To regard all things and principles of things as inconstant modes or fashions has more and more become the tendency of modern thought. Let us begin with that which is without—our physical life. Fix upon it in one of its more exquisite intervals, the moment, for instance, of delicious recoil from the flood of water in summer heat. What is the whole physical life in that moment but a combination of natural elements to which science gives their names? But these elements, phosphorus and lime and delicate fibers, are present not in the human body alone: we detect them in places most remote from it. Our physical life is a perpetual motion of them—the passage of the blood, the wasting and repairing of the lenses of the eye, the modification of the tissues of the brain by every ray of light and sound—processes which science reduces to simpler and more elementary forces. Like the elements of which we are composed, the action of these forces extends beyond us; it rusts iron and ripens corn. Far out on every side of us these elements are broadcast, driven by many forces; and birth and gesture and death and the springing of violets from the grave are but a few out of ten thousand resulting combinations. That clear perpetual outline of face and limb is but an image of ours under which we group them—a design in a web, the actual threads of which pass out beyond it. This at least of flame-like our life has, that it is but the concurrence, renewed from moment to moment, of forces parting sooner or later on their ways.

Or if we begin with the inward world of thought and feeling, the whirlpool is still more rapid, the flame more eager and devouring. There it is no longer the gradual darkening of the eye and fading of color from the wall—the movement of the shore side, where the water flows down indeed, though in apparent rest—but the race of the midstream, a drift of momentary acts of sight and passion and thought. At first sight experience seems to bury us under a flood of external objects, pressing upon us with a sharp importunate reality, calling us out of ourselves in a thousand forms of action. But when reflection begins to act upon those objects they are dissipated under its influence; the cohesive force is suspended like a trick of magic; each object is loosed into a group of impressions—color, odor, texture—in the mind of the observer. And if we continue to dwell on this world, not of objects in the solidity with which language invests them, but of impressions unstable, flickering, inconsistent, which burn and are extinguished with our consciousness of them, it contracts still further; the whole scope of observation is dwarfed to the narrow chamber of the individual mind. Experience, already reduced to a swarm of impressions, is ringed round for each one of us by that thick wall of personality through which no real voice has ever pierced on its way to us, or from us to that which we can only conjecture to be without. Every one of those

---

[5] See Blake (above, page 447).
[6] Johann Wolfgang von Goethe (1749–1832), German writer; George Gordon, Lord Byron (1788–1824), English poet.
[7] See Wordsworth (above, page 481).
[8] [Pater] "Somewhere Heraclitus says that everything changes and nothing remains." *Cratylus.*

impressions is the impression of the individual in his isolation, each mind keeping as a solitary prisoner its own dream of a world.[9]

Analysis goes a step further still, and tells us that those impressions of the individual to which, for each one of us, experience dwindles down, are in perpetual flight; that each of them is limited by time, and that as time is infinitely divisible, each of them is infinitely divisible also; all that is actual in it being a single moment, gone while we try to apprehend it, of which it may ever be more truly said that it has ceased to be than that it is. To such a tremulous wisp constantly reforming itself on the stream, to a single sharp impression, with a sense in it, a relic more or less fleeting, of such moments gone by, what is real in our life fines itself down. It is with the movement, the passage and dissolution of impressions, images, sensations, that analysis leaves off—that continual vanishing away, that strange perpetual weaving and unweaving of ourselves.

"*Philosophiren,*" says Novalis, "*ist dephlegmatisiren, vivificiren.*"[10] The service of philosophy, and of religion and culture as well, to the human spirit, is to startle it into a sharp and eager observation. Every moment some form grows perfect in hand or face; some tone on the hills or sea is choicer than the rest; some mood of passion or insight or intellectual excitement is irresistibly real and attractive for us—for that moment only. Not the fruit of experience, but experience itself is the end. A counted number of pulses only is given to us of a variegated, dramatic life. How may we see in them all that is to be seen in them by the finest senses? How can we pass most swiftly from point to point, and be present always at the focus where the greatest number of vital forces unite in their purest energy?

To burn always with this hard gemlike flame, to maintain this ecstasy, is success in life. Failure is to form habits; for habit is relative to a stereotyped world; meantime it is only the roughness of the eye that makes any two persons, things, situations, seem alike. While all melts under our feet, we may well catch at any exquisite passion, or any contribution to knowledge that seems, by a lifted horizon, to set the spirit free for a moment, or any stirring of the senses, strange dyes, strange flowers, and curious odors, or work of the artist's hands, or the face of one's friend. Not to discriminate every moment some passionate attitude in those about us, and in the brilliance of their gifts some tragic dividing of

forces on their ways is, on this short day of frost and sun, to sleep before evening. With this sense of the splendor of our experience and of its awful brevity, gathering all we are into one desperate effort to see and touch, we shall hardly have time to make theories about the things we see and touch. What we have to do is to be forever curiously testing new opinions and courting new impressions, never acquiescing in a facile orthodoxy of Comte or of Hegel,[11] or of our own. Theories, religious or philosophical ideas, as points of view, instruments of criticism, may help us to gather up what might otherwise pass unregarded by us. *La philosophie, c'est la microscope de la pensée.*[12] The theory, or idea, or system, which requires of us the sacrifice of any part of this experience, in consideration of some interest into which we cannot enter, or some abstract morality we have not identified with ourselves, or what is only conventional, has no real claim upon us.

One of the most beautiful places in the writings of Rousseau[13] is that in the sixth book of the *Confessions,* where he describes the awakening in him of the literary sense. An undefinable taint of death had always clung about him, and now in early manhood he believed himself stricken by mortal disease. He asked himself how he might make as much as possible of the interval that remained; and he was not biased by anything in his previous life when he decided that it must be by intellectual excitement, which he found in the clear, fresh writings of Voltaire.[14] Well, we are all *condamnés,* as Victor Hugo says: "*les hommes sont tous condamnés à mort avec des sursis indéfinis*":[15] we have an interval, and then our place knows us no more. Some spend this interval in listlessness, some in high passions, the wisest in art and song. For our one chance is in expanding that interval, in getting as many pulsations as possible into the given time. High passions give one this quickened sense of life, ecstasy and sorrow of love, political or religious enthusiasm, or the "enthusiasm of humanity." Only, be sure it is passion, that it does yield you this fruit of a quickened, multiplied consciousness. Of this wisdom, the poetic passion, the desire of beauty, the love of art for art's sake has most; for art comes to you professing frankly to give nothing but the highest quality to your moments as they pass, and simply for those moments' sake.

---

[9]This solipsistic passage and Pater's description of the Mona Lisa are the best known in his work.

[10]Novalis (Friedrich von Hardenberg, 1772–1801), German poet, "To philosophize is dephlegmatizing, vivifying."

[11]Auguste Comte (1798–1857), French positivistic philosopher; Hegel (above, page 552).

[12]"Philosophy is the microscope of thought."

[13]Jean Jacques Rousseau (1712–1778), French philosopher.

[14]Francois Marie Arouet de Voltaire (1694–1778), French philosopher.

[15]Victor Hugo (1802–1885), French writer, "Men are all condemned to death with indefinite delays."

INTRODUCTION:
THE MODERN ERA

    In the long history of philosophical and aesthetic speculation upon which this volume draws, developments from the later nineteenth century appear as both a culmination and a departure. What is striking in both respects is that modernism in virtually all of its manifestations has had the effect of calling into question the terms in which the prior history of thought about literature, the arts, and philosophy have been represented. It is not that the problems which surface especially in the twentieth century are new. The issue is the sometimes confusing process by which unexpected links and reconfigurations of problems come to light, often requiring a reconception of disciplinary—and interdisciplinary—histories.

    In the specific case of literary criticism, one widely rehearsed version of its history, articulated most clearly by Murray Krieger, is the emergence of modern literary criticism as an academic specialty, the culmination of what Krieger has characterized as an *apologetic* tradition. It was driven by the attempt to defend poetry from its many and varied detractors, responding to Plato's notorious decision in *Republic* to have Socrates exile the poets from the ideal state.[1] This is a narrative that tends to be repetitive in the sense that no defense of poetry, no *apologia* for it, can be final or bring any guarantee that in the next generation (or even the next decade) some new attack against poetry will not emerge. More important, however, the apologetic tradition encourages the assumption that a definitive defense of poetry ought to be realized in a comprehensive theory of poetry as a specific subject of study. Whether it is Aristotle, apparently answering in his *Poetics* the charges of Plato, or later writers, from Dante and Boccaccio to Mazzoni and Sidney, or from Shelley to Frye, the defense of poetry has appeared to depend upon *argument:* if the attacker only understood what poetry *really* is and why it matters, the case would be closed and poetry would be vindicated, once and for all. Yet no argument has yet proved so powerful or compelling as to be genuinely decisive.

    Though the point is clear only in hindsight (if at all), the assumption that there should be some ultimate and therefore decisive argument is contained from the start in the philosophical principles or concepts that shaped the original Socratic attack. The immediate response, that is to say, is likely to be not only apologetic but defensive, thereby granting to the opponent more than may be warranted. While there are cases (such as

---

[1] See Krieger, *The New Apologists for Poetry* (1956); *Theory of Criticism: A Tradition and Its System* (1976); and *The Institution of Theory* (1994).

Shelley's reply to Peacock, or Sidney's response to Gosson) where many details of the exchange are ironic, defenses of poetry are commonly directed, as it were, over the head of a specific detractor to a general audience, borrowing both the concepts and the rhetoric of theoretical discourse that may be fundamentally incompatible with poetry. The deeper problem is less some alleged defect in poetry than a radical insufficiency in the idea of theory itself. A little later, we will examine this matter in more detail, but it will suffice for the moment to recall that the idea of an intellectual theory of *anything* emerges from the very line of argument in Plato's *Republic* that excludes poetry—and the exclusion assumes that "truth" is simple, universal, and accessible to intellectual intuition. After Aristotle's *Poetics,* the subject of poetry is restored at least to the status of being discussable—but only within the framework of a theory of *Eidos* or Form that locates the truth or essence of things in some discernible invariance of form, whether it be an oak tree, a ship, or tragedy. That framework, for Aristotle as for us, is directly traceable to Plato, and is so pervasively incorporated into our ordinary modes of thinking that it effectively disappears as something obvious, something that goes without saying.

In this sense, the apologetic tradition since Aristotle has seemed to pursue a theory of poetry as its end, without necessarily taking up the question of whether or not the fault may lie less with poetry than with a conception of theory that assumes such a formal and timeless framework for truth—a conception congenial to the common understanding, but one that has often been reduced to paradox in the face of genuine novelties or the incontrovertible historical evidence that notions of truth change.[2] We have tended to assume that "truth" can only be empirically or logically discovered, and by necessity always was and always will be True. In this sense, statements valorized as true are distinguished from bare assertions of faith because they can be consistently identified as always being the case. Such truths as the fact that acorns always turn into oaks (but never pine trees), or that the specific relation for acceleration due to gravity is the same for all objects, serve as paradigmatic instances of theoretical propositions because they offer both an explanation and a basis for predictions, evidently grounded in the nature of things.

But what should a theory in criticism do, and what would it be a theory *of?* If a theory takes poetry, or more broadly, imaginative production, as its object, then the closure sought by traditional theorizing evidently does not fit. Poems are *not* among the natural kinds, like oak trees, nor are we interested in them because of their physical properties, as we are with boats. They matter to us because of their effects on thought and feeling, and there is no guarantee that anyone could distinguish a poem from random strings of graphical marks just by looking at it. Poems as such are recognizable only as they are *read* and *interpreted.* Taking poems as mental or ideal objects, however, would involve a contemporary critic in arguments hinging on a kind of Idealism most likely to be treated as either an anachronism or merely a gesture. But in any case, poems are deliberate constructions that we assume, in principle, to be intelligible and readable, just as they are also constructions that *address us,* frequently in immediate and practical ways, as in the celebrated line that concludes Rilke's "Archaic Torso of Apollo": "There is no place that does not see you. You must change your life."

---

[2] Consider, for example, Wittgenstein's incisive remark in *On Certainty* (1969) on the verb, "to know," which seems to imply a guarantee of certainty: "One always forgets the expression 'I thought I knew,'" p. 3.

In this sense, the preponderance of arguments in criticism taken as theoretical are in fact resolutely practical, having to do with judgments and complex relations pertaining obviously to persons and societies, more than to ascertainable and repeatable states of affairs as one would expect in the natural sciences. Moreover, the judgments and relations in question are *not* guaranteed by any direct accuracy in the depiction of events, but only by their intelligibility. If we view the twentieth century from the vantage of its closing decades, the most striking feature of criticism in this regard is the emergence and rapid rise of theory as a designation for a kind of discursive practice that seeks to situate literary works and other cultural products and artifacts within the social field and, to greater or lesser degrees, to examine them in a generally political (or moralistic) way. Unlike theory in other disciplines, recent theory in criticism appears not to have a definite object (even as it constitutes as a "text" any virtual object that can be talked about relative to some theme in discourse) but is instead an apparently unfolding analysis of a set of questions pertaining to such issues as representation, social justice, systems of value, cultural history, and highly charged contemporary topics such as race, gender, and class.

One among many reasons that recent theory in criticism has been controversial is that it thereby tends on the one hand to go very much against the grain of poetics in the apologetic vein, where recent literary criticism, far from defending poetry against its detractors, seems to take on the role of attacking poetry for its multifaceted complicity in the politics of privilege. But on the other, it also goes against the grain of traditional philosophical models of theorizing by substituting a politicized rhetoric for formal logic, and taking the disclosure of the illegitimate or unjust use of power as a more important issue than formulating propositions held to be incontrovertibly true. The resulting quarrels have been hot and difficult (as the habit of calling them "culture wars" suggests), since they are embedded within the crisis-ridden cultural-political reality of our times, where views about particular social issues have served as a kind of moral litmus test for right thinking—including vitriolic attacks on that very notion as an inherently dogmatic insistence on what has come to be called "political correctness."

But the larger (and older) question remains intellectual and philosophical, pertaining quite specifically to poetry as a paradigmatic product of human intelligence and imagination. From beginning to end, the twentieth century has confirmed the venerable point, sometimes ironically through the pursuit of purportedly "scientific" programs, that poetry is not a subject that lies still for patient observation upon a laboratory table. So what *does* poetry have to do with theory? If we understand that term as it is used in science to cover well-formulated and highly verified principles of explanation and prediction, the answer is, evidently, "Not much." At the other extreme, what does theory as a politically inflected practice of social critique have to do with poetry, considered as a richly exemplified practice and an art, a *techné,* and not simply the reflection of a particular ideology? To a convinced advocate of the apologetic tradition the answer might also be, "Not much." But that would be to ignore the most deeply embedded themes and preoccupations of poetry as a *subject matter* that have, after all, called forth the kind of politically inflected theory so prominent in recent years. To read Shakespeare as if his plays were not profoundly engaged with questions concerning the actual politics of kingship, or to strip away morality from Milton in *Paradise Lost* as if it were a mere rhetorical decoration would be to egregiously miss the point, as both John Crowe

Ransom and Robert Penn Warren observed over half a century ago. Poetry is not pure, and its vital complexity lies precisely in the fact that it speaks from and to a human world where all realities are multifaceted.[3]

The specific selections and the approach in this revised edition of *Critical Theory Since Plato* reflect an effort to articulate these issues more thoroughly and thoughtfully. It will be plain from perusing the table of contents that this edition does not simply carry on the generally aesthetic focus of the apologetic tradition, just as it obviously remains committed to the cultural and intellectual history that various defenses of poetry have *made*. So too, it will be clear that we have not attempted to create a comprehensive smorgasbord of currently practiced "approaches" to literary study and criticism. In an earlier companion volume, *Critical Theory Since 1965,* we took the step of broadening the horizon of what ought to be included in the study of "criticism" by adding an appendix that published, for the first time, a broad collection of materials that before 1965 would not have been seen as germane to literary study, but had definitely become so in the emergence of theory after the 1960s, including such figures as Saussure, Wittgenstein, Husserl, Horkheimer, Benjamin, and Lacan, to mention only a few. We believe that subsequent developments certainly justify having taken a broader than usual view of the field.

In this volume, for both theoretical and practical reasons, we are taking a more determined step in the same direction. On the practical side, literary study has virtually exploded (in more than one sense) since mid-century, with the remarkable institutional consolidation of the New Criticism in the 1950s followed by a larger international advocacy for Structuralism—and the equally remarkable and rapid implosion of both after 1965, in successive waves of postmodernist, postformalist, poststructurualist critiques that threatened for many decades to make crisis a permanent state of affairs.[4] What has emerged from this sustained ferment is a proliferation of orientations, practices, and approaches to the study of literature and culture, in the aggregate lumped together as theory, that seems to defy any obvious or cogent taxonomy. The emergence of deconstruction, feminism, postcolonial studies, studies of race, class and ethnicity, new historicism and cultural studies following Foucault, Raymond Williams, and others, queer studies, science studies, and so on, presents for the would-be anthologist what we have concluded is an impossible problem. The "field" is so various and fractured that only by an ill-advised indulgence of the fallacy of mimetic form could anyone hope to "represent" the field—and the result would be as various and fractured as the field itself appears to be, to say nothing of producing a volume so massive and unmanageable that it would be more a burden than a service to students and teachers alike.

Read symptomatically, however, this proliferation of sometimes warring factions and incommensurable approaches does have a much deeper coherence that we make bold to think indicates that we are entering a new epoch that is no longer well served by

---

[3] See, in this context, Robert Penn Warren's "Pure and Impure Poetry" (1943); reprinted in *New and Selected Essays* (1989).

[4] The irony in this case is particularly acute since "Structuralism" in certain fields, such as linguistics, had long been a dominant model, though severely challenged by the early work of Noam Chomsky (below, page 1166) from the late 1950s, whereas structuralism in literary criticism was just being introduced, at the very time deconstruction, following the work of Jacques Derrida, was calling it into fundamental question. Thus, Jacques Ehrmann's influential volume, *Structuralism,* from *Yale French Studies,* first appeared in 1966—the same year as the Johns Hopkins conference on "The Languages of Criticism and the Sciences of Man." Trade publication of both *Structuralism* and *The Structuralist Controversy* was delayed until 1970. In a certain sense, the story was over before it was barely begun.

many of the models and methods that have shaped prior practice. Accordingly, we have not tried merely to "represent" ways of doing criticism (including, in current terms, cultural studies), but have taken a broader view of the problems that poetry has always presented, in the belief that a review of them will show with some precision why it is that no conventional idea of theory, from Plato to yesterday, has had much success with imaginative and creative thinking in *any* form. The self-complicating nature of this possibility is, we believe, now very well known, as it leads into the thickets of such dense paradoxes and deeply layered ironies that even the most intent and focused critics may be led step by step to the point of exasperation with literature precisely because it resolutely *refuses* to conform to the conventional political or philosophical wisdom of the moment. The now familiar complication is our intellectual desire for some conclusion, *any* conclusion, even it if is the embrace of paradox or contradiction as if it were unavoidable or necessary, or the suggestion by the late Paul de Man that the only truth about language is that it always lies, or that the only truth about poetry is that it cannot be read.[5]

Though it is not possible in the scope of this mid-volume introduction to present a very full argument, we must at least outline here how this revised edition presents a reconception of the history of modern criticism. The now commonplace observation that of all the scientists who have ever lived, something more than 90 percent of them are working today evidently also applies to literary scholars and critics, working in university literature and language departments. This is an institutional fact of enormous significance, as it reflects a cultural and political triumph, in the North Atlantic nations at any rate, in establishing systems of schools that are integrated at every level with government, business, and local communities. Over a decade ago, Evan Watkins pointed out that it had long since become virtually impossible for a person to graduate from any school in the United States, from elementary to postgraduate, without taking an English class.[6] If we bear this point in mind, the very impressive consolidation of Anglo-American New Criticism in the 1950s can be seen as a curricular and practical triumph, shaping not only a particular pedagogy that drew immediately on common speculative propositions overwhelmingly concerned with the activity of reading and interpretation, but leading to ambitious projects to rewrite (or write for the first time) the history of criticism as a single enterprise,[7] now, finally, properly housed in English and affiliated literature and language departments. To put the matter simply, the dominant twentieth-century reply to Plato has not been a definitive argument but a pervasive revision of the college catalogue.

It is in this context that the force of the apologetic tradition is most evident; since earlier discussions of theory were concerned with articulating an explanatory account of what a poem (or more generally a literary work) actually was, the compelling motive was to *place* poetry, in terms of its intellectual, moral, and social purposes. The arguments that prevailed, accordingly, were those that could be readily translated into pedagogical, curricular, and professional practices that created a transmissible institution for education, as is most clearly evident in the practice of the New Critics. Far from being

---

[5] See especially, "The Resistance to Theory" (below, page 1317).
[6] *Work Time: English Departments and the Circulation of Cultural Value* (1989).
[7] See especially W. K. Wimsatt and Cleanth Brooks's *Literary Criticism: A Short History* (1959).

"apologetic" in the colloquial sense, moreover, speculative critics from René Wellek to Roman Jakobsen, or Roland Barthes to Northrop Frye, explored the form, language, and structure of poetry as a systematic cultural project of imagining a human world that could be studied with methodological precision and sophistication, much as a physicist might study nature—despite the fact that appeals to this similarity, starting with Aristotle's treatment of the *form* of tragedy as something emerging from nature like an oak tree or a fish, seem wrong, even obviously wrong, from the start. Poetry has to be composed and *instituted,* by actual persons in real, historical societies, even if it appears obvious to poet and critic alike that the work itself comes from our deepest nature. The overwhelming problem is the nature of generative change that we now recognize pertains as much to our sense of the world of nature as it does to the domain of constructed human artifacts.

The overwhelming irony, moreover, is that the massive institutional success of modern literary criticism depends only in contingent ways on the status of any particular speculative or theoretical claims about literature. In simpler terms, the modern success of the apologetic tradition was not at all the attainment of a philosophically coherent and compelling theory, but the institution of a set of course requirements and pedagogical practices that, in effect, shaped the qualitative dimension of being a good citizen of a particular state, and more particularly, established an implicit ideal for the educated or cultured citizen. The peculiar dimension of such complex practices, as arguments, is that they elicit assent without necessarily disclosing the *reasons* for assenting.

The moment of modern, twentieth-century theory is already *post*modern in the sense that it comes into focus only *after* the modernizing work reflected in the institutional reality of schools, curricula, teaching methods, and professional organizations has already been done, with the deep and pervasive assent and support of specific national cultures and governments. Here too, theory follows practice, not just in the context of discourse about literary texts, but extending to the institutional rationale for teaching them at all. From this point of view, one of the primary accomplishments of the philosophers, poets, and critics of the late eighteenth and early nineteenth centuries was the invention of literary history, articulated in the humanists' vision of the wisdom of the ancients and an idealized vision of literature as a profoundly civilizing instrument, continued into the modern era as an extensive technology, even an industry, of the production of *texts* progressively and powerfully linking the literary history of particular languages and peoples to narratives of national glorification and sometimes, of parochial aggrandizement.[8] That is not to deny that a sense of professional probity may provide strong resistance to this kind of ideological narrowing, along with a more inclusive version of what literary education entails, but it cannot be taken for granted in the face of pressure to justify educational pursuits at every level in the terms of a localized view of the world. From the idea of a classical literary curriculum conceived as monuments of an extended civilization has followed a tendency for texts that have made it into the required curriculum to be singled out or justified in the light of displaced narratives concerning what it means to be truly English, or American, or French, and so on, thereby

---

[8] See, for example, Coleridge's extensive discussion of national traits and character in *The Friend* I, 419–23. Since mid-century, moreover, this issue has been thoroughly debated as an issue of ideology and hegemony, especially by such thinkers as Althusser (below, page 1297) and Ernesto Laclau (below, page 1525).

connecting the idea of the artistic "masterpiece" to a much more localized and opinion-ated pride in the "native" language and the nation state—an orientation that is all the more obvious in the fact that departments of "literature" are still relatively rare, but *English, French, Russian, German, Spanish* departments, and so on, are the rule. In these cases, moreover, attention to literature was not necessarily to be taken for granted, since in many instances, it was the teaching of the language that was foregrounded, on philo-logical and linguistic grounds, as the foundation for appreciation and admiration of na-tional literary monuments. In this respect, the steady shift of attention in recent years from the literary text as a privileged (national) object to the critical examination of the social and historical field carries on the work of literary history into the seemingly an-tagonistic practice of cultural studies, to complicate and criticize, if not to undo, the ide-ological link between the literary text and the reality of what has been taken to be coer-cive social and political power.

Initially, this perspective on the problem can afford some protection against over-simplifying the issues, but only if we bear in mind that the radical implications of imag-inative literature cannot be contained by such means, since the ideals in question depend, as even so severe a sociological critic as Pierre Bourdieu acknowledges, upon the practice of an art in which intellectual autonomy and profound discoveries concern-ing human experience are the very substance of its claim to serious regard.[9] This kind of counter-critique, presuming that just because literature, as received or taught, can in-deed be drafted into the service of bourgeois ambition or class consciousness it is there-fore illegitimate, may be motivated by a particular position on issues of class conflict or social resentment, but it provides no explanation at all for how imaginative literature ac-tually does command willing assent, without coercion. In this respect, the value of dis-interestedness that Kant associated with the aesthetic judgment survives even the most concerted assaults on the idea of the aesthetic as an apparent instrument of privilege. But the main point is that seeking social distinction by means of an art is still a particu-lar *use* that may be made of it, whether it involves praising a poem by Tennyson or a narrative by Kipling as representing the epitome of proper English character or behav-ior, or as an appalling manifestation of colonial and imperialistic myopia. In either case, the radical potential of the poem as itself an instrument of thought, discovery, and criti-cal redirection simply cannot be equated with the history of literary reception or with any particular set of accepted practices precisely because what it formulates as expres-sion depends fundamentally on the principle of literary interpretation: there is no auto-matic read-out of meaning without engaging what T. S. Eliot, in *Four Quartets,* charac-terized as "the intolerable wrestle with words and meanings."[10] The generic intuition that separates, say, a poem from a treatise on topology, is that the meaning of the former is never uniquely determined by its correspondence with a particular set of indepen-dently verifiable facts or exact coordinates: poetry places itself in the middle of an ex-acting linguistic mediation that demands of us a reflective and speculative response.

The rise of theory and its seemingly inexorable movement in the direction of a politically inflected cultural studies appears in this light less a movement away from

---

[9] See his *Rules of Art: Genesis and Structure of the Literary Field* (1995); cf. Bourdieu (below, page 1403).
[10] "East Coker," II, ll. 20–21.

literature than it is a transforming continuation of the work of *literary history,* which since the time of Marx and Taine has *always* taken its primary cues from events and circumstances in the social and political field, as reflected most obviously in the fact that the markers of literary periodization are almost invariably drawn from such events as the ascension or death of monarchs, the starting or concluding of wars, the emergence of revolutions and riots, the rise and fall of political parties and administrations, and so on. While it is altogether too easy to take this as a true reflection of literature as a practice that follows the movements of society, it is more directly a reflection of the social reality of *criticism,* as itself an institutionalized practice.[11]

The idea of a "return to literature" is wide of the mark since literary study, particularly the literary historical form in which it has been overwhelmingly institutionalized, routinely teaches literature by holding it, as it were, at arm's length, suspicious of any critical practice thought to be ahistorical, while giving preference to a scholarly focus on its social and political context, its sources and influences, and so on, even as it provides a justification for teaching literature directly or indirectly as part of the training (or indoctrination) of citizens. It is ironic that the apologetic tradition has in fact done what Plato did in his *Republic* but not what he demanded of the defenders of poetry: instead of developing a philosophically credible counter-theory, literary study has focused its attention on the idea and the construction of the modern Republic as both the nation-state and what Wlad Godzich has characterized as the "culture of literacy."[12] The modern guardians of the Republic, in this light, have taken up their duties from the outset not only by learning to read and write, but by a respectful acquaintance with the great literary and philosophical classics of their own civilization. To put it crudely, prospective guardians of the common good don't go anywhere without taking English 101, just as it is generally taken for granted that a deeper literacy is not merely a supplement to right thinking and good citizenship but a the virtual condition of both.

What is all the more interesting is that the institutional creation of a formal and academic literary culture, even though it has always felt embattled and vulnerable, shows its importance not in terms of its economic exchange value, but precisely because, even though it may be co-opted or even corrupted, it is *not offered for sale.* Rather, it operates with a public concern for cultural legitimation and justifies itself in and through reasoned argument that depends implicitly on standards of justice, intellectual honesty, and with a critical irony, disinterestedness, even when arguments are mounted from a partisan standpoint. The irony is just that in arguing, for example, for the inclusion of literary works by women or members of ethnic minorities, the argument presupposes that such a move *is* right and just, and that any fair-minded person would decide in favor, for example, of expanding the curriculum—and in fact, that has been the response. But the overall result is a profound sense of dialectical tension since the study of literature and the study of the culture that allows it to be created are jointly implicated in both asserting and calling into question the values that the culture may take for granted. For this reason, the recognition of contradictions and inconsistencies is not

---

[11] See in this context Sandor Goodheart's brilliant assessment in *Sacrificing Commentary: Reading the End of Literature* (1996) of the tendency of critical commentary to miss the radical implications of great literary accomplishments, systematically substituting the simpler *sources* of literary works for what their authors actually do with them, for example, treating the general myth of Oedipus as if it contained the meaning of Sophocles's play, *Oedipus Tyrannus.*

[12] See especially *The Culture of Literacy* (1994).

a matter to be treated lightly, for they touch upon a deeply embedded network of justifications that are rarely made entirely explicit but are nevertheless real and consequential
as grounds for assent to common values. Moreover, assent is not a crisp matter, like
counting votes: it is, on the contrary, carried out institutionally and incrementally.

Thus in suggesting we have been living through an era of recurrent, even chronic
crisis, we are also suggesting that it was no mere coincidence that the shattering of a for-
malist/structuralist paradigm in the 1960s appeared both as an intellectual impasse, an
aporia, to use Aristotle's term for getting stuck, and as a gathering revolution in the field
of cultural politics. On the one hand, the reliance on conceptions of form and structure
was by no means just a modern methodological preference or a literary strategem, but
the very cornerstone of Platonic and Aristotelian metaphysics, making any challenge to
formalism a potential passage from a familiar sense of order to an apparent field of
chaos. In this connection, challenges to literary formalism do not stop with logical or
evidential objections because they are already implicated in assumptions about the cultural legitimacy of political and ethical principles, such as the idea of individual rights,
the value of freedom, or the importance of justice as an essential component of a common literary heritage. Accordingly, the decades of recurrent crisis from the sixties well
into the nineties carried intimations of something apocalyptic, as challenging familiar
academic logic makes direct use of the very values that logic had helped to create,
turned back upon themselves. Because such connections between a literary heritage and
social values may appear to us as direct intuitions, drawn not from common sense but
from what Kant called the "common understanding," literary arguments can move
rapidly to endorse or embrace potentially revolutionary movements, from Third World
wars of liberation in Asia, Africa, and Latin America, to profound concerns worldwide
for issues of social justice and civil rights as proper to literary criticism. The treacherous difficulty is that such values, taken as intuitive or obvious, can thereby be severed
from the actual processes by which they are inculcated, particularly through the acquisition of an advanced and sophisticated literacy. Justice, for example, which Plato presumed to be a transcendent and eternal Idea, was first formulated not by philosophers
like Socrates but poets like Homer and Sophocles, and it persists in civil society not because it is available to us by some *a priori* intellectual intution, but only as it is restored
imaginatively and reaffirmed by reasoning.

The link that has been pursued in literary studies between social questions and the
structure of knowledge has had a tendency to superheat the sense of outrage and alarm
on all sides of the debate, leading to such absurd charges as that highly verified and established scientific principles are merely the results of social construction by the
governing classes—sometimes, with immediately tragic results, as in the espousal of
such arguments concerning the HIV virus and its connection to AIDS in South Africa
impeding both treatment and education concerning this epidemic[13]—and the equally
absurd contention that the raising of such questions is purely a political move by
"tenured radicals" or partisans on the lunatic fringe. The view we have taken here, once
more, is that these debates, no matter how annoying or alarming they may be, are essential to a process of cultural legitimation that has always been linked to literature, not as

---

[13] See *New York Review of Books* (2002) series on AIDS in Africa, especially the reluctant response of Tdao Mbeke to accept
as compelling scientific evidence concerning the connection between AIDS and the HIV virus.

something under indictment, but as an indispensable imaginative process of reflection and discovery that by its very nature cannot be effectively confined within the scope of any current ideology.

The chief philosophical difficulty for literary speculation is that its primary traditions have taken shape in criticism as an extension of modes of dialectical argument that promise far more than they can deliver. If we begin from Aristotle's distinctly unflattering definition of dialectic as nothing like the inflated universal or "scientific" method of Hegel and Marx, but simply as that mode of argument that proceeds from commonplaces—what people already believe, what they are thought to believe, what the "best" believe, and so on—it is clear why dialectical argument is always inescapably problematic.[14] Whereas Plato had valorized dialectic in the *Phaedrus* as enabling thought itself (266b-c)—even though he himself invariably has recourse to stories when his arguments run into trouble—Aristotle saw more accurately that dialectic never did and never *could* arrive at unambiguous demonstrations because it was inherently bound by what participants already thought they knew. On that score, no invocation of Plato's doctrine of *anamnesis* or learning as recollection would ever suffice to expunge errors or eliminate paradoxes and contradictions already embedded in the common understanding.

It is beyond any serious question that in this light, the apologetic tradition in literary criticism has always been—and remains, even in its currently more contentious and accusatory mode—dialectical to the core. The appropriate conclusion to draw, however, is that to be dialectical means to be in the profoundest sense *untheoretical*—a point we believe applies with no diminished force to current theory—and therefore remains, in all essential respects, entirely within the range of arguments that start and end with commonplaces. For precisely this reason, there is no point at which one cannot continue the examination of the rhetoric of any dialectical argument to make significant and typically distressing discoveries concerning the web of elements that are already and always embedded in the actual beliefs people may happen to hold. What thereby tends to escape notice is the very process by which such beliefs are established and communicated at the outset, including the very language within which such beliefs are framed. In making such an argument, we do not mean to suggest that criticism ought to become, in some way, a science, but that the framework of beliefs and assumptions that have been dominant in the great traditions of literary criticism and philosophy alike are undergoing significant changes that will transform the questions we ask.

Similar conclusions have been reached, though usually in very different terms, as one field after another in the twentieth century has taken the "linguistic turn," in the reflective and critical examination of the nature of language as a mediating instrumentality.[15] The very vividness of the form in which this problem emerged in literary study, however, has had a tendency to block the recognition of its generality. The appearance of deconstruction at what was imagined to be the triumphant ascension of structuralism, for example, seemed a very specific crisis pertaining mainly to literary critics and scholars.

---

[14] See *Topics* and *Sophistical Refutations*. It is germane in this context that Kant followed Aristotle in characterizing dialectic as a "logic of illusion."

[15] Though the phrase itself appears to have originated with Gustav Bergmann, the move it designates is unmistakable with such figures as Peirce, Frege, Wittgenstein, Russell, Carnap, Schlick, I. A. Richards and C.K. Ogden, Saussure, and others. See Richard Rorty, ed., *The Linguistic Turn: Essays in Philosophical Method* (Chicago: University of Chicago Press, 1967; 1992).

This overlooks, with what we take to be unfortunate consequences, the senses in which the admittedly dramatic "moment" of deconstruction in the mid-1960s, was a repetition and reflection of earlier episodes in the history of science, the formalization of symbolic logic and the development of analytical philosophy, all of which led to the disclosure of profound paradoxes lying at the heart of Western philosophy and metaphysics.[16]

In this light, what some may regard as the most unexpected selections in this volume, from such thinkers as Frege, Wittgenstein, Bertrand Russell, and Rudolph Carnap, are here because they show a sometimes astonishing similarity of argument on questions concerning language and representation as we find later in such critics and philosophers as Paul de Man or Jacques Derrida. In continuing along the path we took in *Critical Theory Since 1965,* we think the benefit of seeing philosophers who may have been regarded even as enemies facing the same problems along the sinuous path of the "linguistic turn" may serve as something more than a corrective of perspective concerning academic and field-specific antagonisms. It is, in this light, significant that Richard Rorty's influential anthology, *The Linguistic Turn: Essays in Philosophical Method* (1967), marked for analytical philosophy, with scarcely any mention whatsoever of literary studies, the kind of turning point manifest for literary study in Richard Macksey and Eugenio Donato's *The Structuralist Controversy* (1967), itself with scarcely a mention of analytical philosophy.[17]

If as we are inclined to think, we may be at the threshold of a new era in critical thought, it is evident that a more balanced and productive concourse between literary study and philosophy is necessary, as both fields share a profoundly intertwined history and a common lineage traceable back to Plato's *Republic,* the source not only of his severe strictures against poetry in Book Ten, but also his first full elaboration of his theory of *eidos* or Form in Books Six and Seven. The immediate difficulty is that there is, at present, no convenient way for literary critics and philosophers particularly in the English-speaking world, to carry out such conversations, when the two fields more resemble two bundles of splinters than two branches of the same historical tree, where philosophy no more appears as a unified or coherent field than does literary criticism.

For many reasons, perhaps the most important and problematic figure in this connection is Jacques Derrida, who came to the attention of literary scholars and critics primarily through his rhetorically dramatic and ingenious demonstrations that it is all but impossible ever to explain the idea of structure without already invoking it, thereby calling into question a considerable string of concepts, from "representation" to "meaning." While early on this provided a way to problematize radically the critical expectation that close attention to poetic form and structure would disclose the meaning of a poem as the direct product of a precise, possibly *sui generis* verbal artifact, it presented a more intractable problem itself, not dissimilar to the notorious problems of verification in the modern history of logical positivism, or to the problems Plato faced 2,400 years earlier

---

[16] It should be noted, moreover, that, as Rorty's anthology makes evident, the "linguistic turn" in analytical philosophy provoked very much the same kind of surprised and localized reaction among professional philosophers. See especially work by Rudolph Carnap (below, page 978).

[17] We note and register, however, our dissent from Rorty's later suggestion in his 1992 retrospective postscript, "Twenty-five Years After," that the "linguistic turn" was just "one more tempest in an academic teapot," a gesture with all the appearance of a no-longer "thirty-three-year-old philosopher" trying perhaps to convince himself that collective failures to solve the problem are equally unimportant.

in his *Parmenides* and *Sophist.* In all instances, the critical discovery is that signification turns out to be an infinite chain of differences with no definitive termination in a positive term.

For the New Critics, the idea of literary form had seemed to anchor claims about interpretation as capable of providing truth and value that could not be attained in any other way than by the nuanced use of metaphor, but in practice had not only degenerated into what Robert Scholes once encapsulated in the image of "a clever graduate student 'interpreting' the daylights out of a poem before thirty stupified freshmen"[18] but had broken out into surprisingly inept but nevertheless spirited quarrels over the determinacy or indeterminacy of interpretation.[19]

The case against Structuralism was in some ways more stunning, particularly because of the philosophical analyses by Jacques Derrida, beginning with his brilliant critique of Edmund Husserl in *Speech and Phenomenon,* but with a little more flash in his "Structure, Sign and Play," which by our incomplete survey appears to be the most widely anthologized critical essay of the last fifty years, matched only by T. S. Eliot's "Tradition and the Individual Talent" of 1919. It is in this case that a disquieting feature of Anglo-American speculative criticism becomes obvious: its pervasive, even appalling lack of cogent philosophical support or argument. No small part of the reason is that academic philosophy, in both the United States and the United Kingdom, had followed different but largely parallel trajectories to refocus the mission of philosophy as immediately tied to the clarification of scientific theory (following Russell, Carnap, and other analytical philosophers) or the clarification of logic, language, and concepts (following Wittgenstein, Quine, Austin, and other philosophers attending particularly to language). In both cases, the traditional subjects of aesthetics and ethics were sometimes very frankly and openly relegated to the philosopher's idle time, or treated institutionally as academic classes to assign to faculty members and graduate students who were not up to the demands of "real" logical analysis or the philosophy of science.

The more or less open enmity between faculty in English departments and philosophy departments meant, among other things, that the ordinary curriculum of professional training in literature throughout most of the twentieth century did not include *any* formal study of philosophy—and vice versa. Thus, for example, when Cleanth Brooks, in his very influential book, *The Well-Wrought Urn,* came to the end of his lucid essays on texts and, as it were, discovered the need for philosophical support, he turned to Suzanne Langer for logic and Wilbur Urban for ethics. While both are thinkers of interest, their own interests and orientation appear far removed from the prevailing patterns among their philosophical contemporaries. The problem, of course, is that the prevailing discussion in academic philosophy was uncongenial if not positively hostile to the idea that poetry presented any genuine problems for philosophy. What is entirely missing among Anglo-American critics attending to problems of poetic language and form is any acknowledgment (except in the deeply ironic case of R. S. Crane at Chicago)[20] that the dominant tendency in Anglo-American philosophy had foregrounded the im-

---

[18] 1975 MLA convention forum address, Semiotics and Literature.

[19] See especially E. D. Hirsch, *Validity in Interpretation* (1967), and Jonathan Culler, "Beyond Interpretation" in *The Pursuit of Signs* (1981).

[20] The irony in this case is that Crane is virtually alone in citing Rudolph Carnap's classic essay "Empiricism, Semantics, and Ontology" as support for his idea of critical pluralism. For a brief account, see Leroy Searle, "The New Criticism" in *The Johns Hopkins Guide to Criticism and Theory.*

portance of both topics even more strikingly. The difference, following Carnap's claim from the 1930s, was that only statements that could be confirmed by empirical reference had any cognitive content, leaving statements in poetry and metaphysics as expressive but essentially "meaningless."

The appearance on the scene of such a thinker as Derrida had a perhaps exaggerated impact precisely because he was writing and thinking from within a European academic context where this kind of virtual divorce between literary and philosophical education might have seemed strange if not positively barbaric. By the same token, however, the introduction of contemporary continental philosophical practice by way of literary criticism only made the divide between continental and Anglo-American analytical philosophy appear all the more stark—while doing very little to heal the deep rift between literary critics and philosophers in Anglo-American universities.[21] For an American trained philosopher, for example, the study of Hegel would perhaps have appeared a waste of time and the tradition of Hegelian idealism itself a kind of bad joke, whereas a French or German trained philosopher would find such a dismissive attitude incomprehensible. The point here is that the divide between literary and philosophical education in Anglo-American universities around mid-century had already been played out in philosophy itself. In the continental tradition, following Husserl, Heidegger, Kojéve, and Sartre, for example, professional discourse had long since diverged from a tradition of logical analysis and the philosophy of science following Frege, Wittgenstein, Carnap, and other members of the Vienna Circle that exerted a much more pronounced influence on Anglo-American traditions. Conversely, analytic philosophy since Frege, Russell, and the early Wittgenstein, had largely abandoned the sweeping post-Hegelian dialectical projects from Husserl to Heidegger and Sartre as unproductive.

In the training of American literary critics, on the other hand, philosophy of any description hardly appeared in the curriculum at all. Accordingly, the appeal of continental philosophy was surely enhanced by the fact that it was not so overtly hostile to literary study as local analytical philosophy. Thus, as a new generation of American literary critics pursued their interests in continental philosophy, it was frequently at the expense of any engagement with the kind of rigorous analysis of logic and science at which Anglo-American philosophy excelled.

It would be the continuation of a grave mistake to assume that this was no loss, for it has had the effect of insulating and marginalizing a good deal of the speculative thinking in literary study and the humanities from what is, by any account, one of the most massively important intellectual adventures of the twentieth century, the developments in natural science and technology. This has not meant that thinkers in the humanities have therefore relinquished their congenial, almost hereditary role as critics where science and technology are concerned, but such criticism has been pursued in many cases with an embarrassing ignorance of what scientists and their philosophical advocates have thought science was about, together with the propounding of arguments that would earn one a failing grade in any elementary course on logical reasoning. This has

---

[21] Typical of these problems was a high degree of uncertainty, when analytically oriented philosophy departments conceded the possible value of hiring someone to teach "continental" philosophy found themselves at a loss because all the candidates seemed in their eyes to be vaguely (if not blatantly) fraudulent. A similar but more focused and notorious case arose in England in the 1990s, when Jacques Derrida was proposed as a recipient of an honorary degree from Oxford, only to have the nomination met with vitriolic opposition and contempt.

been manifest not merely in the "bad writing" contests staged every year by such journals as *Philosophy and Literature,* or in such mischievous episodes as the now notorious Alan Sokal affair, where an obviously fraudulent essay, adapting the rhetoric and the terms of fashionable postmodern criticism to the problem of "quantum gravity" was submitted to a critical journal for the explicit purpose of showing quite effectively that where scientific arguments were concerned, the purveyors of such criticism could not tell, as Hamlet puts it, "a hawk from a handsaw" no matter the quarter from which the wind were blowing.[22] The deeper problem is that the relation of science to criticism has been more or less systematically distorted. The commonplace from C. P. Snow that scientists and humanists occupy "two cultures" prevails not because it reflects some fundamental or necessary truth but because there has been no mediating critical discourse to clarify what is, after all, a common matrix of problems that are all set within one common culture of advanced study and inquiry.

In this section of this anthology, accordingly, we have tried to provide not only a representative sampling of crucial arguments that are a continuation of the apologetic tradition, and essays that have exerted a profound shaping effect on the development of contemporary academic institutions in literary study, but a number of pivotal essays and selections that suggest a provisional outline or survey of problems that have occupied many other disciplines over the past century. On the one hand, we have included a number of essays concerning logic, language, and metaphysics, all with an important bearing on thinking about problems of meaning and interpretation. In the same vein, we have included some selections that may, at least initially, strike the reader as very challenging indeed, because they take up, in various ways, what we believe is a core metaphysical problem concerning the very idea of truth, not as something that can be grasped directly by intellectual intuition but must, on the contrary, be constructed.

While this idea may already be reasonably well domesticated, the forms of reasoning by which to pursue a conception of reality as *not* fixed and determined in advance, but open to novelty, to evolution, and to what Charles Sanders Peirce characterized as "habit-taking," are by no means yet settled or familiar. One speculative claim we would wish to introduce is that the very reason imaginative literature has been problematic in Western philosophy lies in a dominant theory of reason that has proved systematically prone to contradictions and paradoxes especially in the effort to explain dynamic, changing systems. It follows that Plato's original charge against poetry reflects less on some fault to be guarded against in works of the poets than on a fundamental insufficiency in the primary traditions of Western metaphysics that posits as necessary and sufficient an impoverished binary conception of reality, whether it takes as paradigmatic *form* and *matter,* or *subject* and *object.*

The view that truth can be understood as a direct representation of "objective" realities fundamentally misrepresents the logical complexity of mediation, and tends to trade upon a correspondingly inadequate dogma concerning the nature of reasoning. Literature, in this light, should not be viewed merely as an object about which to reason, but rather as a primary form of reasoning in its own right, a system of civilizing media-

---

[22] For a comprehensive review of this case, including a republication of Sokal's original essay, "Transgressing the Boundaries: Toward a Transformative Hermeneutics of Quantum Gravity" (1996), see *The Sokal Hoax: The Sham that Shook the Academy,* ed. by Jeffrey Kittay and the Editors of *Lingua Franca* (Lincoln, Neb.: The University of Nebraska Press, 2000).

tion by which commonplace opinion makes its first genuine moves toward self-conscious reflective thought.[23]

In the plan of this revised edition, we are staking a great deal on this conjecture, since if it is sound, the history of criticism since the late nineteenth century looks very different indeed. Instead of an accelerating proliferation of approaches, theories, schools, ideologies, and agendas, both intellectual and political, having less and less common ground, one can see this process as the symptom of a much more coherent set of problems that can be traced in virtually all disciplines and fields. At the outset, the overriding issue in theoretical terms is the problem of symbolic mediation that accompanies any expression, assertion, or claim. Whether the point of departure is Plato or Descartes, Hume or Kant, the project of reason has assumed on the one hand a fully determinable structure in the universe and on the other, specific mental powers that enable (or circumscribe) our knowledge. It is within the framework of these problematic assumptions that the "linguistic turn" is important, not because it provides any resolution for older oppositions or immediate answers to ancient questions, but precisely because it changes the questions. From Coleridge's overly ambitious and ill-fated project to construct a "Logosophia" or "Dynamical Philosophy" that rejected the dialectical illusions of Hegel and other "Doctors of the Absolute," or Charles Sanders Peirce's equally ambitious and ill-fated project to develop his "Pragmaticism" along interestingly similar lines as a post-Kantian critical realism, the turn to the language and, more broadly, to the logic of mediation, has been and remains irresistible.

We have endeavored, accordingly, to focus attention on different traditions from the late nineteenth through the twentieth century by selecting essays and excerpts that can function as a schematic overview of developments that we believe are relevant to the current state of critical theory, by acknowledging explicitly the need for a broader and more encompassing perspective. The problem outlined above of divergences between literary criticism and philosophy are equally evident in other areas as well. In the formal study of language, for example, contemporary literary criticism has been remarkably fixated on the early work of Ferdinand de Saussure, in large measure because other critics and philosophers (such as Barthes, Derrida, Foucault, and de Man) have turned their attention there. But Saussure's account of language, for all its historical importance, is scarcely a model for theorizing about language, or even, for that matter, about the linguistic sign. What is missing is any sense of what happened to "structuralism" in subsequent linguistic theory, following Bloomfield, Whorf and Sapir, and especially Chomsky. The point of interest here is not that one will find any satisfactory general theory of language, whether in Saussure or any subsequent linguist, since the persistent frustration of just such a search is an intrinsic part of the broad intellectual and cultural climate that pervades the Humanities and Social Sciences. It is, moreover, an additional point of interest that any attempt to formulate a theory of language that leaves the poetic out of account is fundamentally flawed by that fact alone.

---

[23] For a further exposition of this idea, see Leroy F. Searle, "The Conscience of the King: Oedipus, Hamlet, and the Problem of Reading" *Comparative Literature* 49 (1997). See also Eric Havelock's *Preface to Plato* (Cambridge, Mass.: Harvard University Press, 1963) and *The Literate Revolution in Greece and Its Cultural Consequence* (Princeton: Princeton University Press, 1982), for very suggestive illustrations of the antiquity of this point of view as a shaping force in the development of literate traditions.

We take it as already sufficiently clear that any coherent theory of poetry would require other theories—of language, of persons, of societies, of history, and some intelligible account of value—that are not to be found by turning to contemporary linguistics, psychology, anthropology, history, or philosophy, since all of these areas of intellectual concern find their theorizing activities in just the same plight as literary criticism. In looking for essential argument in many fields, however, it is not merely our intent to make this an interdisciplinary anthology, but rather to foreground sets of problems that seem to us to be fundamental. Taken together, these problems, beleaguering many different disciplines, show a significant pattern of convergence not toward a comprehensive theory in the old sense, but what amounts to a metaphysical change, affecting our conceptions of reality and thereby changing our understanding of what theories are for and what they ought to do.

Virtually all twentieth-century disciplines have experienced something like the "linguistic turn," in large measure a turning away from the prevailing account of representation that treats a word as if it were in some way a "picture" of a thing (or, following early Wittgenstein, a fact or state of affairs) always presumed to exist prior to the representation. But every attempt to establish this seemingly obvious principle has led to paradoxes and contradictions—and not merely by defect of logical cleverness or acuity of mind. What is still required is a much subtler theory of mediation, not the pseudojouissance of looking at language and finding, gleefully, paradox and aporias everywhere. We should not minimize the difficulty of moving beyond what have now become predictable insights concerning indeterminacy or the insufficiency of traditional "essentialist" modes of thought, but neither should the necessity of doing so be ignored. Some among the entries included here do point in this direction, particularly selections from Charles Sanders Peirce, who formulated the problem as a link between logic and metaphysics, based on his own intense critique of Kant, as early as 1867. Peirce's approach to semiotics (a word he was among the first to use) is in this respect dramatically different from semiology following Saussure, since it departs in a fundamental way from the binary opposition between signifier and signified to present a much fuller and more coherent account of mediation, not as a barrier to the determination of meaning, but as a fundamental process. While there is no question that this way of thinking is not well domesticated, it at least suggests that in examining problems of representation, we should note that the classic model in which a word represents a preexisting concept or thing is a theory of language that has never yet failed to fail, arguably because it is radically inadequate to account for the processes by which our thinking, as well as nature itself, unfolds and develops.

In the same vein, it is the unfolding of disciplinary and institutional lines of inquiry that we have tried to sample, not necessarily because they are connected directly to literature, but because they have initiated inquiry and speculation that continues to influence our collective thinking. The picture we wish to sketch is of the possibility of a genuinely philosophical poetics, a possibility that depends fundamentally on changing (as we manifestly *are* changing) our notions of what *philosophy* and *poetics* might be. The selections here begin with Taine, whose work can be taken as the beginning of the modern writing of literary history. They continue with Peirce and Walt Whitman, who bring together the two metathemes that have served provisionally to organize our work on this project. The first, as already indicated, is the problem of mediation, leading to a pervasive and problematic repetition of the "linguistic turn," in the dramatically uneven exploration of problems of representation, meaning, and metaphysics. The second, however, is more directly social and practical, since it takes up such problems as the relation between imagination and identity, and between power and politics, within a larger critical discourse of justice.

In the first context, we add our efforts to the many attempts, all so far disappointing, to frame discussions between literary criticism and philosophy that reflect the complexity of the problems of representation and meaning, and their bearing upon issues of metaphysics, or what Aristotle called "first philosophy." The immediate problem is the notorious fractiousness of groups of literary critics who violently disagree with each other, mirrored almost exactly by groups of philosophers who do the same. In both cases, the heat of the disagreement reflects a reliance on principles held to be self-evident or already established or on *a priori* claims that impede and complicate understanding. In such areas as the study of metaphor, for example, the long-standing distrust of it has obscured the fact that metaphor is not an aberration but an indispensable instrument of all thought, all predication, without which even the elementary principle of symbolic substitution in mathematics would be unthinkable. Similarly, the prejudice that if an expression is fictional it is therefore necessarily false merely blocks a more attentive consideration of how it is that our hypotheses shape mental experience—including the complex process by which a *fact* is ever recognized and acknowledged *as such.*

In the second context the problems are perhaps more difficult, if that is possible, than aiming for a more informative and intelligent conversation between long-divided and -fractured disciplines. The practical questions, political and moral, that are involved in the fraught process of cultural legitimation need exactly the same kind of patience and intellectual care, an attentiveness made all the more difficult because the questions affect us all directly. Once again it is instructive to return to the masterpiece of Plato's middle period, the *Republic,* where the decision to exile the poets was covered, as by an alibi, under the charge that they were untruthful as well as irrational, framing the monumental discussion of the idea of justice that starts and ends with the vexatious poets. But the argument of *Republic* reflects an even more fundamental problem of trying to reason about moral and political matters without prejudice. In Plato's case, moreover, his insistence upon a simple idea of truth as the guarantor for proper argument, long after he had left behind the artifice of speaking through Socrates, obscures the fact that his own reasoning about moral and political matters was already shaped, at every turn, by the very poets he called into question. If anything, the passions of the last half century have made this problem even more difficult, as the fierce search for villains and oppressors neglects the sobering principle enunciated by William Blake that we "become what we behold." The logical commonplace that one cannot argue from "IS" to "OUGHT" is itself an artifact of a theory of reality and a corresponding theory of reasoning that has always neglected the subtle complexities of imagination as a fundamental power of the mind, and no mere faculty for one's idle time or the production of merely pleasant artifacts, just as it is not a direct pipeline to the muses or the divine that does not require critical reflection.

The most contentious debates in recent criticism are themselves a continuation of a long and difficult discourse of justice, in which such questions as identity, politics, and power are precisely the issues that imaginative art has always addressed in its own ways.

The task before us is to learn more explicitly and fully how imagination and reason can be allies.

The critical dimension of this task lies in discerning, first of all, how the specific themes and issues in contemporary debates can be understood as a continuation of the history from which they have arisen. Just as imaginative literature is a primary form of reasoning, a critical response to it is part of an essential dialogue by which public discourse is shaped and our common, civic understanding is forged. In the current climate, the emergence of cultural studies is the continuation of a long historical trajectory, punctuated by essential discussions of aesthetics and poetic form, by which practical questions are shaped, generally by dialectical means, to ask specifically what is right, what is tolerable, what is good. But at the same time, the serious risk is that the very values invoked in arguing on behalf of individual rights, for social justice, for the fair and equal treatment of racial and other minorities, can themselves be taken for granted as already established. The role of imaginative literature in this context is that it recognizes the fragility of such ideas as justice, and the intimate negotiations by which ideas take hold, person by person, in the concrete exploration of human consequences that can be seen perhaps only in imagination. It follows that any departure from engagement with imaginative texts puts at risk the very values that animate criticism by threatening to turn those values into dogmatic formulas.

We are mindful that the current sense of institutional malaise, reflected in a host of books and essays asking, in various ways, what has happened to the humanities, presents the same dilemma on a larger scale. When colleagues represent each other as enemies, everyone loses. But if, in the present, we recognize the slow and patient historical rhythms by which literature, criticism, and philosophy all develop, there is reason to be confident that the continuing enterprise of critical theory, since Plato, is alive and well.

Hippolyte Adolphe Taine

1828–1893

During the latter half of the nineteenth century there was an attempt to relate scientific method to literary creation and criticism. The analogy between literary creation and experimental method, which can be seen to have followed out of Bacon (above, page 234), was roughly developed in Zola's *Experimental Novel* (below, page 699). An application of something like scientific method was brought into literary criticism in Taine's well-known and influential *History of English Literature,* in which he treats literature not in respect to the psychology of the audience or its reflection of the outer world but as documents for the analysis of an age and a people. Taine begins by arguing that we seek in literature an insight into the inner life of the author. We recognize in this remark vestiges of a central concern of much Romantic criticism. But Taine goes on to suggest that biographical knowledge is only a step to the greater end of understanding a whole people and their moral condition. The end to which literature is to be put is a total historical vision, and this vision will be the result of a scientific process. Taine's view is consistently materialistic and deterministic: "Vice and virtue are products, like vitriol and sugar."

Taine views literature less as a force acting on thought and society than as the result of natural and social factors—race, surroundings, and epoch. It is a class of events regulated by general laws yet to be discovered, pieces of evidence that will contribute to a total view of man.

Yet there is another Taine who does not wish to reduce literature to the rank of just any sort of document: "A great poem, a fine novel, the confessions of a superior man, are more instructive than a heap of historians and their histories." The reason is that literature offers us "the psychology of a soul, frequently of an age, now and then of a race." One might ask how literature can be more valuable than history if its purpose is to serve as documents for historians. This sort of question was asked increasingly in the latter half of the nineteenth century, and the questioning culminated in the attacks on historical criticism made by the New Critics in the first half of the twentieth century. But historical criticism, never really absent as practice, returns in a new guise later on.

The standard translation from the French of Taine's *History of English Literature* is by Henri van Laun (1871). Taine's *Lectures on Art* have been translated by John Durand (1877). An important study is Paul Neve, *La Philosophie de Taine* (1908). See Irving Babbitt, *Masters of Modern French Criticism* (1912); A. A. Eustice, *Hippolyte Taine and the Classical Genius* (1951); S. J. Kahn, *Science and Aesthetic Judgment: A Study in Taine's Critical Method* (1953); H. H. Clark, *The Influence of Science on American Literary Criticism 1860–1910 Including the Vogue of Taine* (1956); Leo Weinstein, *Taine* (1972).

from
History of English Literature

Introduction

The historian might place himself for a certain time, during several centuries or amongst a certain people, in the midst of the spirit of humanity. He might study, describe, relate all the events, the changes, the revolutions which took place in the inner man; and when he had reached the end, he would possess a history of the civilization of the nation and the period he selected.

FRANÇOIS GUIZOT[1]

History has been revolutionized, within a hundred years in Germany, within sixty years in France, and that by the study of their literatures.

It was perceived that a work of literature is not a mere play of imagination, a solitary caprice of a heated brain, but a transcript of contemporary manners, a type of a certain kind of mind. It was concluded that one might retrace, from the monuments of literature, the style of man's feelings and thoughts for centuries back. The attempt was made, and it succeeded.

Pondering on these modes of feeling and thought, men decided that in them were embalmed facts of the highest kind. They saw that these facts bore reference to the most important occurrences, that they explained and were explained by them, that it was necessary thenceforth to give them a rank, and a most important rank, in history. This rank they have received, and from that moment history has undergone a complete change: in its subject matter, its system, its machinery, the appreciation of laws and of causes. It is this change, as it has happened and must still happen, that we shall here endeavor to exhibit.

I

What is your first remark on turning over the great, stiff leaves of a folio, the yellow sheets of a manuscript—a poem, a code of laws, a declaration of faith? This, you say, was not created alone. It is but a mold, like a fossil shell, an imprint, like one of those shapes embossed in stone by an animal which lived and perished. Under the shell there was an animal, and behind the document there was a man. Why do you study the shell, except to represent to yourself the animal? So do you study the document only in order to know the man. The shell and the document are lifeless wrecks, valuable only as a clue to the entire and living existence. We must reach back to this existence, endeavor to recreate it. It is a mistake to study the document, as if it were isolated. This were to treat things like a simple pedant, to fall into the error of the bibliomaniac. Behind all, we have neither mythology nor languages, but only men, who arrange words and imagery according to the necessities of their organs and the original bent of their intellects. A dogma is nothing in itself; look at the people who have made it—a portrait, for instance, of the sixteenth century, the stern and energetic face of an English archbishop or martyr. Nothing exists except through some individual man; it is this individual with whom we must become acquainted. When we have established the parentage of dogmas, or the classification of poems, or the progress of constitutions, or the modification of idioms, we have only cleared the soil: genuine history is brought into existence only when the historian begins to unravel, across the lapse of time, the living man, toiling, impassioned, entrenched in his customs, with his voice and features, his gestures and his dress, distinct and complete as he from whom we have just parted in the street. Let us endeavor, then, to annihilate as far as possible this great interval of time, which prevents us from seeing man with our eyes, with the eyes of our head. What have we under the fair glazed pages of a modern poem? A modern poet, who has studied and traveled, a man like Alfred de Musset, Victor Hugo, Lamartine, or Heine,[2] in a black coat and gloves, welcomed by the ladies, and making every evening his fifty bows and his score of bon mots in society, reading the papers in the morning, lodging as a rule on the second floor; not over gay, because he has nerves, and especially because, in this dense democracy where we choke one another, the discredit of the dignities of office has exaggerated his pretensions while increasing his importance, and because the refinement of his feelings in general disposes him somewhat to believe himself a deity. This is what we take note of under modern meditations or sonnets. Even so, under a tragedy of the seventeenth century we have a poet, like Racine[3] for instance, elegant, staid, a courtier, a fine speaker, with a majestic wig and ribboned shoes, at heart a

---

Taine's *Histoire de la littérature anglaise* was published between 1863 and 1867. The text is from the translation by Henry van Laun (1871).
[1] François Pierre Guillaume Guizot (1787–1874), French statesman and historian, *Civilization in Europe.*

[2] Musset (1810–1857), Hugo (1802–1885), Alphonse Marie Louis de Lamartine (1790–1869), all French writers; Heinrich Heine (1797–1856), German poet.
[3] Jean Racine (1639–1699), French dramatist.

royalist and a Christian, "having received the grace of God not to blush in any company, kings nor Gospelers"; clever at entertaining the prince, and rendering for him into good French the "old French of Amyot"; very respectful to the great, always "knowing his place"; as assiduous and reserved at Marly as at Versailles, amidst the regular pleasures of a polished and fastidious nature, amidst the salutations, graces, airs, and fopperies of the braided lords, who rose early in the morning to obtain the promise of being appointed to some office in case of the death of the present holder, and amongst charming ladies who count their genealogies on their fingers in order to obtain the right of sitting down in the presence of the king or queen. On that head consult St. Simon and the engravings of Pérelle, as for the present age you have consulted Balzac and the watercolors of Eugène Lami.[4] Similarly, when we read a Greek tragedy, our first care should be to realize to ourselves the Greeks, that is, the men who live half naked, in the gymnasia, or in the public squares, under a glowing sky, face to face with the most noble landscapes, bent on making their bodies nimble and strong, on conversing, discussing, voting, carrying on patriotic piracies, but for the rest lazy and temperate, with three urns for their furniture, two anchovies in a jar of oil for their food, waited on by slaves, so as to give them leisure to cultivate their understanding and exercise their limbs, with no desire beyond that of having the most beautiful town, the most beautiful processions, the most beautiful ideas, the most beautiful men. On this subject, a statue such as the *Meleager,* or the *Theseus* of the Parthenon, or still more, the sight of the Mediterranean, blue and lustrous as a silken tunic, and islands arising from it like masses of marble, and added to these, twenty select phrases from Plato and Aristophanes, will teach you much more than a multitude of dissertations and commentaries. And so again, in order to understand an Indian Purāna, begin by imagining to yourself the father of a family, who, "having seen a son on his son's knees," retires, according to the law, into solitude, with an ax and a pitcher, under a banana tree, by the riverside, talks no more, adds fast to fast, dwells naked between four fires, and under a fifth, the terrible sun, devouring and renewing without end all living things; who step by step, for weeks at a time, fixes his imagination upon the feet of Brahma, next upon his knee, next upon his thigh, next upon his navel, and so on, until, beneath the strain of this intense meditation, hallucinations begin to appear, until all the forms of existence, mingled and transformed the one with the other, quaver before a sight dazzled and giddy, until the motionless man, catching in his breath, with fixed gaze, beholds the universe vanishing like a smoke beyond the universal and void Being into which he aspires to be absorbed. To this end a voyage to India would be the best instructor; or for want of better, the accounts of travelers, books of geography, botany, ethnology, will serve their turn. In each case the search must be the same. A language, a legislation, a catechism, is never more than an abstract thing: the complete thing is the man who acts, the man corporeal and visible, who eats, walks, fights, labors. Leave on one side the theory and the mechanism of constitutions, religions and their systems, and try to see men in their workshops, in their offices, in their fields, with their sky and earth, their houses, their dress, cultivations, meals, as you do when, landing in England or Italy, you remark faces and motions, roads and inns, a citizen taking his walk, a workman drinking. Our great care should be to supply as much as possible the want of present, personal, direct, and sensible observation which we can no longer practice; for it is the only means of knowing men. Let us make the past present: in order to judge of a thing, it must be before us; there is no experience in respect of what is absent. Doubtless this reconstruction is always incomplete; it can produce only incomplete judgments; but to that we must resign ourselves. It is better to have an imperfect knowledge than a futile or false one; and there is no other means of acquainting ourselves approximately with the events of other days, than to *see* approximately the men of other days.

This is the first step in history: it was made in Europe at the new birth of imagination, toward the close of the last century, by Lessing, Walter Scott; a little later in France, by Chateaubriand, Augustin Thierry, Michelet, and others.[5] And now for the second step.

II

When you consider with your eyes the visible man, what do you look for? The man invisible. The words which enter your ears, the gestures, the motions of his head, the clothes he wears, visible acts and deeds of every kind, are expressions merely; somewhat is revealed beneath them, and that is a soul. An inner man is concealed beneath the outer man; the second does but reveal the first. You look at his house,

---

[4]Louis de Rouvroy, Duke de Saint-Simon (1675–1755), French courtier and memoirist; Nicolas Perelle, seventeenth-century French painter; Honoré de Balzac (1799–1850), French novelist; Éugene Lami (nineteenth-century stage designer).

[5]Lessing (above, page 378); Scott (1771–1832), Scottish novelist; François René, Viscount de Chateaubriand (1768–1848), French writer; Augustin Thierry (1795–1856), French historian; Jules Michelet (1798–1874), French historian.

furniture, dress; and that in order to discover in them the marks of his habits and tastes, the degree of his refinement or rusticity, his extravagance or his economy, his stupidity or his cunning. You listen to his conversation, and you note the inflections of his voice, the changes in his attitudes; and that in order to judge of his intensity, his self-forgetfulness or his gaiety, his energy or his constraint. You consider his writings, his artistic productions, his business transactions or political ventures; and that in order to measure the scope and limits of his intelligence, his inventiveness, his coolness, to find out the order, the description, the general force of his ideas, the mode in which he thinks and resolves. All these externals are but avenues converging to a center; you enter them simply in order to reach that center; and that center is the genuine man. I mean that mass of faculties and feelings which are produced by the inner man. We have reached a new world, which is infinite, because every action which we see involves an infinite association of reasonings, emotions, sensations new and old, which have served to bring it to light, and which, like great rocks deep-seated in the ground, find in it their end and their level. This underworld is a new subject matter, proper to the historian. If his critical education suffice, he can lay bare, under every detail of architecture, every stroke in a picture, every phrase in a writing, the special sensation whence detail, stroke, or phrase had issue; he is present at the drama which was enacted in the soul of artist or writer; the choice of a word, the brevity or length of a sentence, the nature of a metaphor, the accent of a verse, the development of an argument—everything is a symbol to him; while his eyes read the text, his soul and mind pursue the continuous development and the ever changing succession of the emotions and conceptions out of which the text has sprung: in short, he unveils a psychology. If you would observe this operation, consider the originator and model of contemporary culture, Goethe, who, before writing *Iphigenia*,[6] employed day after day in designing the most finished statues, and who at last, his eyes filled with the noble forms of ancient scenery, his mind penetrated by the harmonious loveliness of antique life, succeeded in reproducing so exactly in himself the peculiarities of the Greek imagination, that he gives us almost the twin sister of the *Antigone* of Sophocles, and the goddesses of Phidias.[7] This precise and proved interpretation of past sensations has given to history, in our days, a second birth; hardly anything of the sort was known to the preceding century. They thought men of every race and century were all but identical; the Greek, the barbarian, the Hindu, the man of the Restoration, and the man of the eighteenth century, as if they had been turned out of a common mold; and all in conformity to a certain abstract conception, which served for the whole human race. They knew man, but not men; they had not penetrated to the soul; they had not seen the infinite diversity and marvelous complexity of souls; they did not know that the moral constitution of a people or an age is as particular and distinct as the physical structure of a family of plants or an order of animals. Nowadays, history, like zoology, has found its anatomy; and whatever the branch of history to which you devote yourself, philology, linguistic lore, mythology, it is by these means you must strive to produce new fruit. Amid so many writers who, since the time of Herder, Otfried Müller,[8] and Goethe, have continued and still improve this great method, let the reader consider only two historians and two works, Carlyle's *Cromwell*, and Sainte-Beuve's *Port Royal*:[9] he will see with what justice, exactness, depth of insight, one may discover a soul beneath its actions and its works; how behind the old general in place of a vulgar, hypocritical schemer, we recover a man travailing with the troubling reveries of a melancholic imagination, but with definite instincts and faculties, English to the core, strange and incomprehensible to one who has not studies the climate and the race; how, with about a hundred meager letters and a score of mutilated speeches, one may follow him from his farm and team, to the general's tent and to the Protector's[10] throne, in his transmutation and development, in his pricks of conscience and his political conclusions, until the machinery of his mind and actions becomes visible, and the inner tragedy, ever changing and renewed, which exercised this great, darkling soul, passes, like one of Shakespeare's, through the soul of the looker on. He will see (in the other case) how, behind the squabbles of the monastery, or the contumacies of nuns, one may find a great province of human psychology; how about fifty characters, that had been buried under the uniformity of a circumspect narrative, reappear in the light of day, each with its own specialty and its countless diversities; how, beneath theological disquisitions and monotonous sermons, one can unearth the beatings of ever living hearts, the convulsions and apathies of monastic life, the unforeseen reassertions and wavy turmoil of nature, the inroads of surrounding worldliness, the intermittent victories of grace, with such a variety of over-

---

[6] Johann Wolfgang von Goethe (1749–1832), *Iphigenie auf Tauris* (1787).
[7] Sophocles (c. 496–406 B.C.), Greek tragic dramatist; Phidias (c. 500–c. 432 B.C.), Greek sculptor.

[8] Johann Gottfried von Herder (1744–1803), German philosopher and critic; Karl Otfried Müller (1797–1840), German archaeologist.
[9] Thomas Carlyle (1795–1881), English writer; Charles Augustin Sainte-Beuve (1804–1869), French critic.
[10] Oliver Cromwell (1599–1658) ruled England from 1649 to 1658, as Lord Protector from 1653.

cloudings, that the most exhaustive description and the most elastic style can hardly gather the inexhaustible harvest, which the critic has caused to spring up on this abandoned field. And so it is throughout. Germany, with its genius so pliant, so liberal, so apt for transformation, so well calculated to reproduce the most remote and anomalous conditions of human thought; England, with its intellect so precise, so well calculated to grapple closely with moral questions, to render them exact by figures, weights and measures, geography, statistics, by quotation and by common sense; France, with her Parisian culture, with her drawing room manners, with her untiring analysis of characters and actions, her irony so ready to hit upon a weakness, her finesse so practiced in the discrimination of shades of thought—all have worked the same soil, and one begins to understand that there is no region of history where it is not imperative to till this deep level, if one would see a serviceable harvest rise between the furrows.

This is the second step; we are in a fair way to its completion. It is the proper work of the contemporary critic. No one has done it so justly and grandly as Sainte-Beuve; in this respect we are all his pupils; his method renews, in our days, in books, and even in newspapers, every kind of literary, of philosophical and religious criticism. From it we must set out in order to begin the further development. I have more than once endeavored to indicate this development; there is here, in my mind, a new path open to history, and I will try to describe it more in detail.

III

When you have observed and noted in man one, two, three, then a multitude of sensations, does this suffice, or does your knowledge appear complete? Is a book of observations a psychology? It is no psychology, and here as elsewhere the search for causes must come after the collection of facts. No matter if the facts be physical or moral, they all have their causes; there is a cause for ambition, for courage, for truth, as there is for digestion, for muscular movement, for animal heat. Vice and virtue are products, like vitriol and sugar; and every complex phenomenon has its springs from other more simple phenomena on which it hangs. Let us then seek the simple phenomena for moral qualities, as we seek them for physical qualities; and let us take the first fact that presents itself: for example, religious music, that of a Protestant church. There is an inner cause which has turned the spirit of the faithful toward these grave and monotonous melodies, a cause broader than its effect; I mean the general idea of the true, external worship which man owes to God. It is this which has modeled the architecture of the temple, thrown

down the statues, removed the pictures, destroyed the ornaments, curtailed the ceremonies, shut up the worshipers in high pews, which prevent them from seeing anything, and regulated the thousand details of decoration, posture, and the general surroundings. This itself comes from another more general cause, the idea of human conduct in all its comprehensiveness, internal and external, prayers, actions, dispositions of every kind by which man is kept face to face with God; it is this which has enthroned doctrine and grace, lowered the clergy, transformed the sacraments, suppressed various practices, and changed religion from a discipline to a morality. This second idea in its turn depends upon a third still more general, that of moral perfection, such as is met with in the perfect God, the unerring judge, the stern watcher of souls, before whom every soul is sinful, worthy of punishment, incapable of virtue or salvation, except by the crisis of conscience which He provokes, and the renewal of heart which He produces. That is the master idea, which consists in erecting duty into an absolute king of human life, and in prostrating all ideal models before a moral model. Here we track the root of man; for to explain this conception it is necessary to consider race itself, that is, the German, the Northman, the structure of his character and intelligence, his general processes of thought and feeling, the sluggishness and coldness of sensation which prevent his falling easily and headlong under the sway of pleasure, the bluntness of his taste, the irregularity and revolutions of his conception, which arrest in him the birth of fair dispositions and harmonious forms, the disdain of appearances, the desire of truth, the attachment to bare and abstract ideas, which develop in him conscience, at the expense of all else. There the search is at an end; we have arrived at a primitive disposition, at a trait proper to all sensations, to all the conceptions of a century or a race, at a particularity inseparable from all the motions of his intellect and his heart. Here lie the grand causes, for they are the universal and permanent causes, present at every moment and in every case, everywhere and always acting, indestructible, and in the end infallibly supreme, since the accidents which thwart them, being limited and partial, end by yielding to the dull and incessant repetition of their force; in such a manner that the general structure of things, and the grand features of events, are their work; and religions, philosophies, poetries, industries, the framework of society and of families, are in fact only the imprints stamped by their seal.

IV

There is then a system in human sentiments and ideas; and this system has for its motive power certain general traits, certain marks of the intellect and the heart common to men of one race, age, or country. As in mineralogy the crystals, however diverse, spring from certain simply physical forms, so in history, civilizations, however diverse, are derived from certain simple spiritual forms. The one are explained by a primitive geometrical element, as the others are by a primitive psychological element. In order to master the classification of mineralogical systems, we must first consider a regular and general solid, its sides and angles, and observe in this the numberless transformations of which it is capable. So, if you would realize the system of historical varieties, consider first a human soul generally, with its two or three fundamental faculties, and in this compendium you will perceive the principal forms which it can present. After all, this kind of ideal picture, geometrical as well as psychological, is hardly complex, and one speedily sees the limits of the outline in which civilizations, like crystals, are constrained to exist.

What do we find, at first sight, in man? Images or representations of things, something, that is, which floats within him, exists for a time, is effaced, and returns again, after he has been looking upon a tree, an animal, any sensible object. This is the subject matter, the development whereof is double, either speculative or practical, according as the representations resolve themselves into a general conception or an active resolution. Here we have the whole of man in an abridgment; and in this limited circle human diversities meet, sometimes in the womb of the primordial matter, sometimes in the twofold primordial development. However minute in their elements, they are enormous in the aggregate, and the least alteration in the factors produces vast alteration in the results. According as the representation is clear and as it were cut out by machinery or confused and faintly defined, according as it embraces a great or small number of the marks of the object, according as it is violent and accompanied by impulses, or quiet and surrounded by calm, all the operations and processes of the human machine are transformed. So, again, according as the ulterior development of the representation varies, the whole human development varies. If the general conception in which it results is a mere dry notation (in Chinese fashion), language becomes a sort of algebra, religion and poetry dwindle, philosophy is reduced to a kind of moral and practical common sense, science to a collection of formulas, classifications, utilitarian mnemonics, and the whole intellect takes a positive bent. If, on the contrary, the general representation in which the conception results is a poetical and figurative creation, a living symbol, as among the Aryan races, language becomes a sort of cloudy and colored word-stage, in which every word is a person, poetry and religion assume a magnificent and inextinguishable grandeur, metaphysics are widely and subtly developed, without regard to positive applications; the whole intellect, in spite of the inevitable deviations and shortcomings of its effort, is smitten with the beautiful and the sublime, and conceives an ideal capable by its nobleness and its harmony of rallying round it the tenderness and enthusiasm of the human race. If, again, the general conception in which the representation results is poetical but not precise; if man arrives at it not by a continuous process, but by a quick intuition; if the original operation is not a regular development, but a violent explosion—then, as with the Semitic races, metaphysics are absent, religion conceives God only as a king solitary and devouring, science cannot grow, the intellect is too rigid and complete to reproduce the delicate operations of nature, poetry can give birth only to vehement and grandiose exclamations, language cannot unfold the web of argument and of eloquence, man is reduced to a lyric enthusiasm, an unchecked passion, a fanatical and constrained action. In this interval between the particular representation and the universal conception are found the germs of the greatest human differences. Some races, as the classical, pass from the first to the second by a graduated scale of ideas, regularly arranged, and general by degrees; others, as the Germanic, traverse the same ground by leaps, without uniformity, after vague and prolonged groping. Some, like the Romans and English, halt at the first steps; others, like the Hindus and Germans, mount to the last. If, again, after considering the passage from the representation to the idea, we consider that from the representation to the resolution, we find elementary differences of the like importance and the like order, according as the impression is sharp, as in southern climates, or dull, as in northern; according as it results in instant action, as among barbarians, or slowly, as in civilized nations; as it is capable or not of growth, inequality, persistence, and connections. The whole network of human passions, the chances of peace and public security, the sources of toil and action, spring from hence. Other primordial differences there are: their issues embrace an entire civilization; and we may compare them to those algebraical formulas which, in a narrow limit, contain in advance the whole curve of which they form the law. Not that this law is always developed to its issue; there are perturbing forces; but when it is so, it is not that the law was false, but that its action was impeded. New elements become mingled with the old; great forces from without counteract the primitive. The race emigrates, like the Aryan, and the change of climate has altered in its case the whole economy, intelligence, and organization of society. The people has been conquered, like the Saxon nation, and a new political structure has imposed on its customs, capacities, and inclinations which it had not. The nation has installed itself in the midst of a conquered people, downtrodden and threatening, like the ancient Spartans; and the necessity of living like troops in the field has violently distorted in an unique direction the whole moral and social constitution. In each case, the mechanism of human history is the same. One continually finds, as the original mainspring, some very general disposition of mind and soul, innate and appended by nature to the race, or acquired and produced by some circumstance acting upon the race. These mainsprings, once admitted, produce their effect gradually: I mean that after some centuries they bring the nation into a new condition, religious, literary, social, economic; a new condition which, combined with their renewed effort, produces another condition, sometimes good, sometimes bad, sometimes slowly, sometimes quickly, and so forth; so that we may regard the whole progress of each distinct civilization as the effect of a permanent force which, at every stage, varies its operation by modifying the circumstances of its action.

V

Three different sources contribute to produce this elementary moral state—the race, the surroundings, and the epoch. What we call the *race* are the innate and hereditary dispositions which man brings with him to the light, and which, as a rule, are united with the marked differences in the temperament and structure of the body. They vary with various peoples. There is a natural variety of men, as of oxen and horses, some brave and intelligent, some timid and dependent, some capable of superior conceptions and creations, some reduced to rudimentary ideas and inventions, some more specially fitted to special works, and gifted more richly with particular instincts, as we meet with species of dogs better favored than others—these for hunting, these for fighting, these for the chase, these again for house dogs or shepherds' dogs. We have here a distinct force—so distinct, that amidst the vast deviations which the other two motive forces produce in him, one can recognize it still; and a race, like the old Aryans, scattered from the Ganges as far as the Hebrides, settled in every clime, spread over every grade of civilization, transformed by thirty centuries of revolutions, nevertheless manifests in its tongues, religions, literatures, philosophies, the community of blood and of intellect which to this day binds its offshoots together. Different as they are, their parentage is not obliterated; barbarism, culture and grafting, differences of sky and soil, fortunes good and bad, have labored in vain: the great marks of the original model have remained, and we find again the two or three principal

lineaments of the primitive imprint underneath the secondary imprints which time has stamped above them. There is nothing astonishing in this extraordinary tenacity. Although the vastness of the distance lets us but half perceive—and by a doubtful light—the origin of species,[11] the events of history sufficiently illumine the events anterior to history, to explain the almost immovable steadfastness of the primordial marks. When we meet with them, fifteen, twenty, thirty centuries before our era, in an Aryan, an Egyptian, a Chinese, they represent the work of several myriads of centuries. For as soon as an animal begins to exist, it has to reconcile itself with its surroundings; it breathes after a new fashion, renews itself, is differently affected according to the new changes in air, food, temperature. Different climate and situation bring it various needs, and consequently a different course of actions; and this, again, a different set of habits; and still again, a different set of aptitudes and instincts. Man, forced to accommodate himself to circumstances, contracts a temperament and a character corresponding to them; and his character, like his temperament, is so much more stable, as the external impression is made upon him by more numerous repetitions, and is transmitted to his progeny by a more ancient descent. So that at any moment we may consider the character of a people as an abridgment of all its preceding actions and sensations; that is, as a quantity and as a weight, not infinite,[12] since everything in nature is finite, but disproportioned to the rest, and almost impossible to lift, since every moment of an almost infinite past has contributed to increase it, and because, in order to raise the scale, one must place in the opposite scale a still greater number of actions and sensations. Such is the first and richest source of these master faculties from which historical events take their rise; and one sees at the outset, that if it be powerful, it is because this is no simple spring, but a kind of lake, a deep reservoir wherein other springs have, for a multitude of centuries, discharged their several streams.

Having thus outlined the interior structure of a race, we must consider the surroundings in which it exists. For man is not alone in the world: nature surrounds him, and his fellow men surround him; accidental and secondary tendencies come to place themselves on his primitive tendencies, and physical or social circumstances disturb or confirm the character committed to their charge. In course of time the climate has had its effect. Though we can follow but obscurely the Aryan peoples from their common fatherland to their final

---

[11] [Taine] Darwin, *The Origin of Species.* Prosper Lucas, *De l'hérédité [On Heredity].*
[12] [Taine] Spinoza, *Ethics,* Part IV. Axiom.

countries, we can yet assert that the profound differences which are manifest between the German races on the one side, and the Greek and Latin on the other arise for the most part from the difference between the countries in which they are settled: some in cold moist lands, deep in black marshy forests or on the shores of a wild ocean, caged in by melancholy or violent sensations, prone to drunkenness and gluttony, bent on a fighting, blood-spilling life; others, again, within a lovely landscape, on a bright and laughing seacoast, enticed to navigation and commerce, exempt from gross cravings of the stomach, inclined from the beginning to social ways, to a settled organization of the state, to feelings and dispositions such as develop the art of oratory, the talent for enjoyment, the inventions of science, letters, arts. Sometimes the state policy has been at work, as in the two Italian civilizations: the first wholly turned to action, conquest, government, legislation, by the original site of its city of refuge, by its borderland emporium, by an armed aristocracy, who, by inviting and drilling the strangers and the conquered, presently set face to face two hostile armies, having no escape from its internal discords and its greedy instincts but in systematic warfare; the other, shut out from unity and any great political ambition by the stability of its municipal character, the cosmopolitan condition of its pope, and the military intervention of neighboring nations, directed the whole of its magnificent, harmonious bent towards the worship of pleasure and beauty. Sometimes the social conditions have impressed their mark, as eighteen centuries ago by Christianity, and twenty-five centuries ago by Buddhism, when around the Mediterranean, as in Hindustan, the extreme results of Aryan conquest and civilization induced an intolerable oppression, the subjugation of the individual, utter despair, a curse upon the world, with the development of metaphysics and myth, so that man in this dungeon of misery, feeling his heart softened, begot the idea of abnegation, charity, tender love, gentleness, humility, brotherly love—there, in a notion of universal nothingness, here under the fatherhood of God. Look around you upon the regulating instincts and faculties implanted in a race—in short, the mood of intelligence in which it thinks and acts at the present time: you will discover most often the work of some one of these prolonged situations, these surrounding circumstances, persistent and gigantic pressures, brought to bear upon an aggregation of men who, singly and together, from generation to generation, are continually molded and modeled by their action; in Spain, an eight-century crusade against the Mussulmans, protracted even beyond and until the exhaustion of the nation by the expulsion of the Moors, the spoliation of the Jews, the establishment of the Inquisition, the Catholic wars; in England, a political establishment of eight centuries, which keeps a man erect and respectful, in in-

dependence and obedience, and accustoms him to strive unitedly, under the authority of the law; in France, a Latin organization, which, imposed first upon docile barbarians, then shattered in the universal crash, is reformed from within under a lurking conspiracy of the national instinct, is developed under hereditary kings, ends in a sort of egality republic, centralized, administrative, under dynasties exposed to revolution. These are the most efficacious of the visible causes which mold the primitive man: they are to nations what education, career, condition, abode, are to individuals; and they seem to comprehend everything, since they comprehend all external powers which shape human matter, and by which the external acts on the internal.

There is yet a third rank of causes; for, with the forces within and without, there is the work which they have already produced together, and this work itself contributes to produce that which follows. Beside the permanent impulse and the given surroundings, there is the acquired momentum. When the national character and surrounding circumstances operate, it is not upon a *tabula rasa*,[13] but on a ground on which marks are already impressed. According as one takes the ground at one moment or another, the imprint is different; and this is the cause that the total effect is different. Consider, for instance, two epochs of a literature or an art—French tragedy under Corneille and under Voltaire, the Greek drama under Aeschylus and under Euripides, Italian painting under da Vinci and under Guido.[14] Truly, at either of these two extreme points the general idea has not changed; it is always the same human type which is its subject of representation or painting; the mold of verse, the structure of the drama, the form of body has endured. But among several differences there is this, that the one artist is the precursor, the other the successor; the first has no model, the second has; the first sees objects face to face, the second sees them through the first; that many great branches of art are lost, many details are perfected, that simplicity and grandeur of impression have diminished, pleasing and refined forms have increased—in short, that the first work has outlived the second. So it is with a people as with a plant; the same sap, under the same temperature, and in the same soil, produces, at different steps of its progressive development, different formations, buds, flowers, fruits, seed vessels, in such a manner that the one which follows has always

---

[13] Blank tablet.
[14] Corneille (above, page 244); François Marie Arouet de Voltaire (1694–1778), French philosopher; Aeschylus (525–456 B.C.) and Euripides (c. 485–406 B.C.), Greek tragic dramatists; Leonardo da Vinci (1452–1519), Italian artist and scientist; Guido Reni (1575–1642), Italian painter and engraver.

the first for its condition, and grows from its death. And if now you consider no longer a brief epoch, as our own time, but one of those wide intervals which embrace one or more centuries, like the Middle Ages, or our last classic age, the conclusion will be similar. A certain dominant ideas has had sway; men, for two, for five hundred years, have taken to themselves a certain ideal model of man: in the Middle Ages, the knight and the monk; in our classic age, the courtier, the man who speaks well. This creative and universal idea is displayed over the whole field of action and thought; and after covering the world with its works, involuntarily systematic, it has faded, it has died away, and lo, a new idea springs up, destined to a like domination, and the like number of creations. And here remember that the second depends in part upon the first, and that the first, uniting its effect with those of national genius and surrounding circumstances, imposes on each new creation its bent and direction. The great historical currents are formed after this law—the long dominations of one intellectual pattern, or a master idea, such as the period of spontaneous creations called the Renaissance, or the period of oratorical models called the Classical Age, or the series of mystical compositions called the Alexandrian and Christian eras, or the series of mythological efflorescences which we meet with in the infancy of the German people, of the Indian and the Greek. Here as elsewhere we have but a mechanical problem; the total effect is a result, depending entirely on the magnitude and direction of the producing causes. The only difference which separates these moral problems from physical ones is, that the magnitude and direction cannot be valued or computed in the first as in the second. If a need or a faculty is a quantity, capable of degrees, like a pressure or a weight, this quantity is not measurable like the pressure or the weight. We cannot define it in an exact or approximative formula; we cannot have more, or give more, in respect of it, than a literary impression; we are limited to marking and quoting the salient points by which it is manifested, and which indicate approximately and roughly the part of the scale which is its position. But though the means of notation are not the same in the moral and physical sciences, yet as in both the matter is the same, equally made up of forces, magnitudes, and directions, we may say that in both the final result is produced after the same method. It is great or small, as the fundamental forces are great or small and act more or less exactly in the same sense, according as the distinct effects of race, circumstance, and epoch combine to add the one to the other, or to annul one another. Thus are explained the long impotences and the brilliant triumphs which make their appearance irregularly and without visible cause in the life of a people; they are caused by internal concords or contrarieties. There was such a concord when in the seventeenth century the sociable character and the conversational aptitude, innate in France, encountered the drawing room manners and the epoch of oratorical analysis; when in the nineteenth century the profound and elastic genius of Germany encountered the age of philosophical compositions and of cosmopolitan criticism. There was such a contrariety when in the seventeenth century the rude and lonely English genius tried blunderingly to adopt a novel politeness; when in the sixteenth century the lucid and prosaic French spirit tried vainly to cradle a living poetry. That hidden concord of creative forces produced the finished urbanity and the noble and regular literature under Louis XIV and Bossuet, the grand metaphysics and broad critical sympathy of Hegel and Goethe.[15] That hidden contrariety of creative forces produced the imperfect literature, the scandalous comedy, the abortive drama under Dryden and Wycherley,[16] the vile Greek importations, the groping elaborate efforts, the scant half-graces under Ronsard and the Pleiad.[17] So much we can say with confidence, that the unknown creations towards which the current of the centuries conducts us, will be raised up and regulated altogether by the three primordial forces; that if these forces could be measured and computed, one might deduce from them as from a formula the specialties of future civilization; and that if, in spite of the evident crudeness of our notations, and the fundamental inexactness of our measures, we try now to form some idea of our general destiny, it is upon an examination of these forces that we must ground our prophecy. For in enumerating them, we traverse the complete circle of the agencies; and when we have considered race, circumstance, and epoch, which are the internal mainsprings, the external pressure, and the acquired momentum, we have exhausted not only the whole of the actual cause, but also the whole of the possible causes of motive.

VI

It remains for us to examine how these causes, when applied to a nation or an age, produce their results. As a rivulet falling from a height spreads its streams, according to the depth of the descent, stage after stage, until it reaches the lowest level of the soil, so the disposition of intellect or soul impressed on

---

[15] Louis XIV of France reigned from 1638 to 1715; Jacques Benigne Bossuet (1627–1704), French prelate.

[16] Dryden (above, page 253); William Wycherley (1640?–1716), English comic dramatist.

[17] Pierre de Ronsard (1524?–1585), French poet, leader of the Pleiad, a group of poets advocating writing in French rather than Latin.

a people by race, circumstance, or epoch, spreads in different proportions and by regular descents, down the diverse orders of facts which make up its civilization.[18] If we arrange the map of a country, starting from the watershed, we find that below this common point the streams are divided into five or six principal basins, then each of these into several secondary basins, and so on, until the whole country with its thousand details is included in the ramifications of this network. So, if we arrange the psychological map of the events and sensations of a human civilization, we find first of all five or six well-defined provinces—religion, art, philosophy, the state, the family, the industries; then in each of these provinces natural departments; and in each of these, smaller territories, until we arrive at the numberless details of life such as may be observed within and around us every day. If now we examine and compare these diverse groups of facts, we find first of all that they are made up of parts, and that all have parts in common. Let us take first the three chief works of human intelligence—religion, art, philosophy. What is a philosophy but a conception of nature and its primordial causes, under the form of abstractions and formularies? What is there at the bottom of a religion or of an art but a conception of this same nature and of these same causes, under form of symbols more or less concise, and personages more or less marked; with this difference, that in the first we believe that they exist, in the second we believe that they do not exist? Let the reader consider a few of the great creations of the intelligence in India, Scandinavia, Persia, Rome, Greece, and he will see that, throughout, art is a kind of philosophy made sensible, religion a poem taken for true, philosophy an art and a religion dried up, and reduced to simple ideas. There is therefore, at the core of each of these three groups, a common element, the conception of the world and its principles; and if they differ among themselves, it is because each combines with the common, a distinct element: now the power of abstraction, again the power to personify and to believe, and finally the power to personify and not believe. Let us now take the two chief works of human association, the family and the state. What forms the state but a sentiment of obedience, by which the many unite under the authority of a chief? And what forms the family but the sentiment of obedience, by which wife and children act under the direction of a father and husband? The family is a natural state, primitive and restrained, as the state is an artificial family, ulterior and expanded; and amongst the

differences arising from the number, origin, and condition of its members, we discover in the small society as in the great, a like disposition of the fundamental intelligence which assimilates and unites them. Now suppose that this element receives from circumstance, race, or epoch certain special marks, it is clear that all the groups into which it enters, will be modified proportionately. If the sentiment of obedience is merely fear,[19] you will find, as in most Oriental states, a brutal despotism, exaggerated punishment, oppression of the subject, servility of manners, insecurity of property, an impoverished production, the slavery of women, and the customs of the harem. If the sentiment of obedience has its root in the instinct of order, sociality, and honor, you will find, as in France, a perfect military organization, a fine administrative hierarchy, a want of public spirit with occasional jerks of patriotism, ready docility of the subject with a revolutionary impatience, the cringing courtier with the counter-efforts of the genuine man, the refined sympathy between conversation and society on the one hand, and the worry at the fireside and among the family on the other, the equality of the married with the incompleteness of the married state, under the necessary constraint of the law. If, again, the sentiment of obedience has its root in the instinct of subordination and the idea of duty, you will find, as among the Germans, security and happiness in the household, a solid basis of domestic life, a tardy and incomplete development of society, an innate respect for established dignities, a superstitious reverence for the past, the keeping up of social inequalities, natural and habitual regard for the law. So in a race, according as the aptitude for general ideas varies, religion, art, and philosophy vary. If man is naturally inclined to the widest universal conceptions, and apt to disturb them at the same time by the nervous delicacy of his oversensitive organization, you will find, as in India, an astonishing abundance of gigantic religious creations, a glowing outgrowth of vast and transparent epic poems, a strange tangle of subtle and imaginative philosophies, all so well interwoven, and so penetrated with a common essence, as to be instantly recognized, by their breadth, their coloring, and their want of order, as the products of the same climate and the same intelligence. If, on the other hand, a man naturally staid and balanced in mind limits of his own accord the scope of his ideas, in order the better to define their form, you will find, as in Greece, a theology of artists and tale-tellers; distinctive gods, soon considered distinct from things, and transformed, almost at the outset, into recognized personages; the sentiment of universal unity all but effaced,

---

[18] [Taine] For this scale of coordinate effects consult Renan, *Langues Sémetiques [General History of the Semitic Languages]*, Chapter 1; Mommsen, *Comparison Between Greek and Roman Civilizations*, third edition, Vol. I, Chapter 2; and Tocqueville, *Consequences of Democracy in America*, Vol. III.

---

[19] [Taine] Montesquieu, *Esprit des lois, principes des trois gouvernements [The Spirit of Laws]*.

and barely preserved in the vague notion of destiny; a philosophy rather close and delicate than grand and systematic, confined to a lofty metaphysics,[20] but incomparable for logic, sophistry, and morals; poetry and arts superior for clearness, spirit, scope, truth, and beauty to all that have ever been known. If, once more, man, reduced to narrow conceptions, and deprived of all speculative refinement, is at the same time altogether absorbed and straitened by practical occupations, you will find, as in Rome, rudimentary deities, mere hollow names, serving to designate the trivial details of agriculture, generation, household concerns, etiqueties in fact of marriage, of the farm, producing a mythology, a philosophy, a poetry, either worth nothing or borrowed. Here, as elsewhere, the law of mutual dependence[21] comes into play. A civilization forms a body, and its parts are connected with each other like the parts of an organic body. As in an animal, instincts, teeth, limbs, osseous structure, muscular envelope, are mutually connected, so that a change in one produces a corresponding change in the rest, and a clever naturalist can by a process of reasoning reconstruct out of a few fragments almost the whole body; even so in a civilization, religion, philosophy, the organization of the family, literature, the arts, make up a system in which every local change induces a general change, so that an experienced historian, studying some particular part of it, sees in advance and half predicts the character of the rest. There is nothing vague in this interdependence. In the living body the regulator is, first, its tendency to manifest a certain primary type; then its necessity for organs whereby to satisfy its wants, and for harmony with itself in order that it may live. In a civilization, the regulator is the presence, in every great human creation, of a productive element, present also in other surrounding creations—to wit, some faculty, aptitude, disposition, effective and discernible, which, being possessed of its proper character, introduces it into all the operations in which it assists, and, according to its variations, causes all the works in which it cooperates to vary also.

VII

At this point we can obtain a glimpse of the principal features of human transformations, and begin to search for the general laws which regulate, not events only, but classes of events, not such and such religion or literature, but a group of literatures or religions. If, for instance, it were admitted that a religion is a metaphysical poem, accompanied by a belief; and remarking at the same time that there are certain epochs, races, and circumstances in which belief, the poetical and metaphysical faculty, are combined with an unwanted vigor; if we consider that Christianity and Buddhism were produced at periods of grand productions, and amid such miseries as raised up the fanatics of the Cévennes; if we recognize, on the other hand, that primitive religions are born at the awakening of human reason, during the richest blossoming of human imagination, at a time of the fairest artlessness and the greatest credulity; if we consider, also, that Mohammedanism appeared with the dawning of poetic prose, and the conception of national unity, amongst a people destitute of science, at a period of sudden development of the intellect, we might then conclude that a religion is born, declines, is reformed and transformed according as circumstances confirm and combine with more or less exactitude and force its three generative instincts; and we should understand why it is endemic in India, amidst imaginative, philosophic, eminently fanatic brains; why it blossomed forth so strangely and grandly in the Middle Ages, amidst an oppressive organization, new tongues and literatures; why it was aroused in the sixteenth century with a new character and heroic enthusiasm, amid universal regeneration, and during the awakening of the German races; why it breaks out into eccentric sects amid the rude American democracy, and under the bureaucratic Russian despotism; why, in fine, it is spread, at the present day, over Europe in such different dimensions and such various characteristics, according to the differences of race and civilization. And so for every kind of human production—for literature, music, the fine arts, philosophy, science, statecraft, industries, and the rest. Each of these has for its direct cause a moral disposition, or a combination of moral dispositions: the cause given, they appear; the cause withdrawn, they vanish: the weakness or intensity of the cause measures their weakness or intensity. They are bound up with their causes, as a physical phenomenon with its condition, as the dew with the fall of the variable temperature, as dilatation with heat. There are such dualities in the moral as in the physical world, as rigorously bound together, and as universally extended in the one as in the other. Whatever in the one case produces, alters, suppresses the first term, produces, alters, suppresses the second as a necessary consequence. Whatever lowers the temperature, deposits the dew. Whatever develops credulity side by side with poetical thoughts, engenders religion. Thus phenomena have been

---

[20][Taine] The Alexandrian philosophy had its birth from the West. The metaphysical notions of Aristotle are isolated; moreover, with him as with Plato, they are but a sketch. By way of contrast consider the systematic vigor of Plotinus, Proclus, Schelling, and Hegel, or the admirable boldness of Brahminica and Buddhist speculation.

[21][Taine] I have endeavored on several occasions to give expression to this law notably in the Preface to *Essais de critique et d'histoire [Critical and Historical Essays]*.

produced; thus they will be produced. As soon as we know the sufficient and necessary condition of one of these vast occurrences, our understanding grasps the future as well as the past. We can say with confidence in what circumstances it will reappear, foresee without rashness many portions of its future history, and sketch with care some features of its ulterior development.

VIII

History is now upon, or perhaps almost upon this footing, that it must proceed after such a method of research. The question propounded nowadays is of this kind. Given a literature, philosophy, society, art, group of arts, what is the moral condition which produced it? What the conditions of race, epoch, circumstance, the most fitted to produce this moral condition? There is a distinct moral condition for each of these formations, and for each of their branches; one for art in general, one for each kind of art—for architecture, painting, sculpture, music, poetry; each has its special germ in the wide field of human psychology; each has its law, and it is by virtue of this law that we see it raised, by chance, as it seems, wholly alone, amid the miscarriage of its neighbors, like painting in Flanders and Holland in the seventeenth century, poetry in England in the sixteenth, music in Germany in the eighteenth. At this moment, and in these countries, the conditions have been fulfilled for one art, not for others, and a single branch has budded in the general barrenness. For these rules of human growth must history search; with the special psychology of each special formation it must occupy itself; the finished picture of these characteristic conditions it must now labor to compose. No task is more delicate or more difficult; Montesquieu[22] tried it, but in his time history was too new to admit of his success; they had not yet even a suspicion of the road necessary to be traveled, and hardly now do we begin to catch sight of it. Just as in its elements astronomy is a mechanical and physiology a chemical problem, so history in its elements is a psychological problem. There is a particular inner system of impressions and operations which makes an artist, a believer, a musician, a painter, a wanderer, a man of society; and of each the affiliation, the depth, the independence of ideas and emotions, are different: each has its moral history and its special structure, with some governing disposition and some dominant feature. To explain each, it would be necessary to write a chapter of esoteric

analysis, and barely yet has such a method been rudely sketched. One man alone, Stendhal,[23] with a singular bent of mind and a singular education, has undertaken it, and to this day the majority of readers find his books paradoxical and obscure: his talent and his ideas were premature; his admirable divinations were not understood, any more than his profound sayings thrown out cursorily, or the astonishing justness of his perception and of his logic. It was not perceived that, under the exterior of a conversationalist and a man of the world, he explained the most complicated of esoteric mechanisms; that he laid his finger on the mainsprings; that he introduced into the history of the heart scientific processes, the art of notation, decomposition, deduction; that he first marked the fundamental causes of nationality, climate, temperament; in short, that he treated of sentiments as they should be treated—in the manner of the naturalist, namely, and of the natural philosopher, who constructs classifications and weighs forces. For this very reason he was considered dry and eccentric: he remained solitary, writing novels, voyages, notes, for which he sought and obtained a score of readers. And yet we find in his books at the present day essays the most suitable to open the path which I have endeavored to describe. No one has better taught us how to open our eyes and see, to see first the men that surround us and the life that is present, then the ancient and authentic documents, to read between the black and white lines of the pages, to recognize under the old impression, under the scribbling of a text, the precise sentiment, the movement of ideas, the state of mind in which they were written. In his writings, in Sainte-Beuve, in the German critics, the reader will see all the wealth that may be drawn from a literary work: when the work is rich, and one knows how to interpret it, we find there the psychology of a soul, frequently of an age, now and then of a race. In this light, a great poem, a fine novel, the confessions of a superior man, are more instructive than a heap of historians with their histories. I would give fifty volumes of charters and a hundred volumes of state papers for the memoirs of Cellini, the epistles of St. Paul, the table-talk of Luther, or the comedies of Aristophanes.[24] In this consists the importance of literary works: they are instructive because they are beautiful; their utility grows with their perfection; and if they furnish documents, it is because they are monuments. The more a book represents visible sentiments, the more it is a work of literature; for the proper office of literature is to take note of sentiments. The more a

---

[22] Charles Louis de Secondat, Baron de la Brède Montesquieu (1689–1755), French political philosopher.

[23] Stendhal (Marie Henri Beyle, 1783–1842), French novelist.
[24] Aristophanes (c. 448–after 388 B.C.), Greek comic dramatist.

book represents important sentiments, the higher is its place in literature; for it is by representing the mode of being of a whole nation and a whole age, that a writer rallies round him the sympathies of an entire age and an entire nation. This is why, amid the writings which set before our eyes the sentiments of preceding generations, a literature, and notably a grand literature, is incomparably the best. It resembles that admirable apparatus of extraordinary sensibility, by which physicians disentangle and measure the most recondite and delicate changes of a body. Constitutions, religions, do not approach it in importance; the articles of a code and of a catechism only show us the spirit roughly and without delicacy. If there are any writings in which politics and dogma are full of life, it is in the eloquent discourses of the pulpit and the tribune, memoirs, unrestrained confessions; and all this belongs to literature: so that, in addition to itself, it has all the advantage of other works. It is then chiefly by the study of literatures that one may construct a moral history, and advance toward the knowledge of psychological laws, from which events spring.

I am about to write the history of a literature, and to seek in it for the psychology of a people: if I have chosen this one in particular, it is not without a reason. I had to find a people with a grand and complete literature, and this is rare: there are few nations who have, during their whole existence, really thought and written. Among the ancients, the Latin literature is worth nothing at the outset, then borrowed and imitative.

Among the moderns, German literature is almost wanting for two centuries.[25] Italian literature and Spanish literature end at the middle of the seventeenth century. Only ancient Greece, modern France and England, offer a complete series of great significant monuments. I have chosen England, because being yet alive, and subject to direct examination, it may be better studied than a destroyed civilization, of which we retain but the scraps, and because, being different from France, it has in the eyes of a Frenchman a more distinct character. Besides, there is a peculiarity in this civilization, that apart from its spontaneous development, it presents a forced deviation, it has suffered the last and most effectual of all conquests, and that the three grounds whence it has sprung, race, climate, the Norman invasion, may be observed in its remains with perfect exactness; so well, that we may examine in this history the two most powerful moving springs of human transformation, natural bent and constraining force, and we may examine them without uncertainty or gap, in a series of authentic and unmutilated memorials. I have endeavored to define these primary springs, to exhibit their gradual effects, to explain how they have ended by bringing to light great political, religious, and literary works, and by developing the recondite mechanism whereby the Saxon barbarian has been transformed into the Englishman of today.

---

[25] [Taine] From 1550–1750.

Charles Sanders Peirce

1839–1914

Charles Sanders Peirce (pronounced "purse") has long been recognized as one of the principal figures in the history of modern symbolic logic, the first American pragmatist, and the principal originator of semiotics. In all of these capacities, however, Peirce has been a problematic figure, in part because his philosophical position is exceptionally demanding, but also because he did not, in his lifetime, complete a comprehensive book that provides a continuous exposition of his thought. Peirce was an incisive historian of logic and metaphysics and one among the earliest American scientists to receive international recognition. In addition to more than 40,000 pages of published books, articles, reviews, and encyclopedia entries, Peirce left a massive collection of unpublished papers still in the process of being edited and published. Peirce's philosophical work was profoundly shaped early on by his intensive critical study of Kant (above, page 416), which led him to the study of medieval realism, especially the writing of Duns Scotus.

Early scholarship on Peirce was understandably slow to grasp either the centrality of Peirce's concern with logic as semiotic or the scope of the implications he drew from it, particularly in his sustained and sometimes sinuous following out of the links between logical reasoning and metaphysics. As Duns Scotus had recognized, the result of a theory of reality that could not account for what he had termed "formal universals" but assumed that reality was encompassed by such terms as Being and Substance, or Form and Matter, was that we could neither account for our ability to make valid generalizations nor prevent philosophical arguments from hopeless entanglements with paradox. Peirce's approach to this problem, explored in precise detail in the first selection here, "On a New List of Categories," was not to seek out or deduce, following Kant, *a priori* principles that are legislative for our conceptions, but to examine what conceptions were indispensable for making even the simplest predications (as in his example, "The stove is black").

The difficulty that readers frequently have in reading Peirce's philosophical essays (like Kant's critiques) sometimes flows from the very simplicity of what he aims to do—a point that may well recall William Blake's (above, page 447) aphorism concerning the gulf that separates the simple from the insipid. Recognizing that Kant's greatest limitation may well have been the absence of any comprehensive theory of symbolic mediation, Peirce keeps attention strictly focused on the task of discerning how the concepts with which we think depend upon other concepts, without making the assumption that we could intuitively recognize which among our conceptions are primary or primitive. "On a New List of Categories" is both an extension of Kant's deduction of his Categories, a return to Aristotle's (above, page 48) first attempt to formulate categories as predicates, and a brilliant breaking of new ground in both method and result. Peirce's account need not be confusing, so long as one recognizes that Peirce's three categories, later reduced to *First, Second,* and *Third,* provide a way to locate the ground of a conception, the scope of its correlation with other instances, and the mediating representation (or "interpretant") that allows us to acknowledge a dimension of reality that is neither matter nor form but a distinct relation as a mode of reality not reducible to either. The schema Peirce introduces in "On a New List of Categories" also makes it possible, in principle, to accommodate both the infinite extensibility of any signifier without falling into recursive paradoxes and contradictions, while keeping open a pathway back to the primary evidence from which any conception was formed.

This latter point is crucial for Peirce's insistence on thinking of philosophy and logic as the essentially communal and collective work of inquiry. Peirce does not rely upon a traditional and dialectical conception of truth as a putative agreement of a representation with its object (a sure formula to precipitate paradoxes), but locates it in the concrete result of inquiry and argument that resolves doubt and fixes belief. The expectation that such a process would end absolutely entirely misses the point of how reasoning and inquiry both unfold as continuous processes. Historically, Peirce located his own work not simply in relation to his contemporaries, but to the historical problems of nominalism and realism, seeing the emergence of an ethos of scientific inquiry as working against the nominalism prevalent since Descartes, and toward a new critical realism.

The other selections reprinted here include writings on the history of philosophy, originally assembled from manuscript sources by the editors of *Collected Papers,* and selected material drawn from essays and courses of lectures, illustrating his own version of pragmatism, obviously quite distinct from the more familiar work of his friend William James and his one-time student, John Dewey. Indeed, one of the principal difficulties in the general reception of Peirce's thought has been a tendency to identify him with a development of ideas original with him that, in their more popular form, are frequently contrary to his own thought, both in reference to pragmatism and to questions of semiotics, where the sharp differences between Peirce and James and Dewey on the one hand, and between Peirce and Saussure (below, page 786) on the other are frequently overlooked or ignored.[1]

Recognition of Peirce as a major philosophical innovator has been relatively slow, despite the obviousness of his genius, but a growing body of recent work, along with a major project to publish his writings in a chronological edition, discussed below, has contributed to a steady increase of interest in and understanding of his work.

The long standard published collection of Peirce's work in eight volumes, *Collected Papers* (1931–1960), edited by Charles Hartshorne and Paul Weiss, vol. 7–8 edited by A. W. Burks, is gradually being replaced by a more ambitious and professionally edited chronological edition, *The Collected Writings of Charles Sanders*

---

[1]The conflation of Dewey, James, and Peirce as indifferently "pragmatists," ignoring Peirce's deliberate coinage of a term he characterized as "ugly enough to keep it safe from kidnappers" (*Collected Papers* 2.414), *pragmaticism,* is a habit of long standing, reflected, for example, in the work of Richard Rorty and Richard Poirier, just as is the tendency to critique pragmatism for its instrumentalism as if it were a general fault, articulated by Horkheimer, Adorno, and Habermas. On the tendency to minimize the difference between Peirce and Saussure, see especially Paul de Man, "The Resistance to Theory" (below, page 1317) and Jonathan Culler's *The Pursuit of Signs: Semiotics, Literature and Deconstruction* (1981).

Peirce (1982–) edited by Max Frisch, Christian Kloesel, Nathan Houser, and others. An electronic edition of *Collected Papers,* edited by John Deely (with an excellent introduction) was released by Past Masters in 1994. For students working with manuscript materials, Richard Robin's *Annotated Catalogue of the Papers of Charles S. Peirce* (1967), with supplements online, is essential. See also Web sites at the Institute for the Study of Pragmaticism at Texas Tech University, originated by Kenneth Ketner, and especially Joseph Ransdell's "Arisbe" portal. Other editions of particular manuscripts, published as study editions, and specialized collections, have included: Kenneth L. Ketner and James E. Cook, eds., *Charles Sanders Peirce: Contributions to the Nation* (1975); Carolyn Eisele, ed., *The New Elements of Mathematics* (in four volumes, 1976); Charles S. Hartwick, ed., *Semiotics and Significs: The Correspondence Between Charles S. Peirce and Lady Victoria Welby* (1977); Carolyn Eisele, ed., *Historical Perspectives on Peirce's Logic of Science: A History of Science* (1985); James Hoopes, ed., *Peirce on Signs: Writings of Semiotics* (1991); Kenneth L. Ketner, ed., *Reasoning and the Nature of Things: The Cambridge Conference Lectures of 1898* (1992); and Patricia Ann Turrisi, ed., *Pragmatism as a Principle and Method of Right Thinking* (1997). For Peirce studies, anthologies have been especially important and are still useful. Notable is Nathan Houser, Christian Kloesel, et al., eds., *The Essential Peirce* (in two volumes, 1992); Morris R. Cohen, ed., *Chance, Love, and Logic: Philosophical Essays by the Late Charles S. Peirce* (1923; 1992); Justus Buchler, ed., *Philosophical Writings of Peirce* (1955); Editors of the Liberal Arts Press, *Essays in the Philosophy of Science* (1957); and Philip P. Wiener, ed., *Values in a Universe of Change: Selected Writings of Charles Sanders Peirce* (1958). Biographical studies of Peirce include Joseph Brent's *Charles Sanders Peirce* (1998); and Kenneth L. Ketner's unconventional narrative, derived from Peirce's papers, *His Glassy Essence: An Autobiography of Charles Sanders Peirce* (1998). For a brief overview of Peirce, see Leroy F. Searle, "Charles Sanders Peirce" in *The Johns Hopkins Guide to Literary Theory and Criticism* (1994). The scholarly response to Peirce is extensive, though the evolving state of accessible materials is sometimes a liability, particularly in earlier studies by Thomas Goudge (1950), Manley Thompson (1953), and Murray Murphey (1961). Still essential is John F. Boler, *Charles Sanders Peirce and Scholastic Realism: A Study of Peirce's Relation to John Duns Scotus* (1962). Since the publication of Karl-Otto Apel's, *Charles S. Peirce: From Pragmatism to Pragmaticism* (1981), the distinctiveness of Peirce's philosophy has been increasingly apparent. See also Peter Skagestad, *The Road of Inquiry: Charles Peirce's Pragmatic Realism* (1981); Christopher Hookway, *Peirce* (1985); Robert Corrington, *An Introduction to C. S. Peirce* (1993); Kelly Parker, *The Continuity of Peirce's Thought* (1998); Andrew Reynolds, *Peirce's Scientific Metaphysics: The Philosophy of Chance, Law, and Evolution* (2002). Students with an interest in Peirce's graphic system of logic or "existential graphs" should begin with Don D. Roberts's pioneering study, *The Existential Graphs of C. S. Peirce* (1973). See also John Sowa, *Conceptual Structures: Information Processing in Mind and Machine* (1984) and subsequent publications, for an influential adaptation of Peirce for artificial-intelligence applications; Jay Zeeman, "Peirce's Graphs" and Peter Ohrstrom, "C. S. Peirce and the Quest for Gamma Graphs" in Dickson Lukose, et al., eds., *Conceptual Structures: Fulfilling Peirce's Dream* (1997), and Sun-Joo Shin, *The Iconic Logic of Peirce's Graphs* (2002).

On a New List of Categories (1868)

545. This paper is based upon the theory already established,[1] that the function of conceptions is to reduce the manifold of sensuous impressions to unity and that the validity of a conception consists in the impossibility of reducing the content of consciousness to unity without the introduction of it.

546. This theory gives rise to a conception of gradation among those conceptions which are universal. For one such conception may unite the manifold of sense and yet another may be required to unite the conception and the manifold to which it is applied; and so on.

547. That universal conception which is nearest to sense is that of *the present, in general.* This is a conception, because it is universal.[2] But as the act of attention has no connotation at all, but is the pure denotative power of the mind, that is to say, the power which directs the mind to an object, in contradistinction to the power of thinking any predicate of that object—so the conception of *what is present in general,* which is nothing but the general recognition of what is contained in attention, has no connotation, and therefore no proper unity. This conception of the present in general, of IT in general, is rendered in philosophical language by the word "substance" in one of its meanings. Before any comparison or discrimination can be made between what is present, what is present must have been recognized as such, as *it,* and subsequently the metaphysical parts which are recognized by abstraction are attributed to this *it,* but the *it* cannot itself be made a predicate. This *it* is thus neither predicated of a subject, nor in a subject, and accordingly is identical with the conception of substance.[3]

548. The unity to which the understanding reduces impressions is the unity of a proposition. This unity consists in the connection of the predicate with the subject; and, therefore, that which is implied in the copula, or the conception of *being,* is that which completes the work of conceptions of reducing the manifold to unity. The copula (or rather the verb which is copula in one of its senses) means either *actually is* or *would be,* as in the two propositions, "There *is* no griffin," and "A griffin *is* a winged quadruped."[4] The conception of *being* contains only that junction of predicate to subject wherein these two verbs agree. The conception of being, therefore, plainly has no content.

If we say "The stove is black," the stove is the *substance,* from which its blackness has not been differentiated, and the *is,* while it leaves the substance just as it was seen, explains its confusedness, by the application to it of blackness as a predicate.

Though being does not affect the subject, it implies an indefinite determinability of the predicate.[5] For if one could know the copula and predicate of any proposition, as ". . . is a tailed-man," he would know the predicate to be applicable to something supposable, at least. Accordingly, we have propositions whose subjects are entirely indefinite, as "There is a beautiful ellipse," where the subject is merely *something actual* or *potential;* but we have no propositions whose predicate is entirely indeterminate, for it would be quite senseless to say, "*A* has the common characters of all things," inasmuch as there are no such common characters.

"On a New List of Categories" was first published in *Proceedings of the American Academy of Arts and Sciences* 7 (1867), 287–98, reprinted in *Collected Papers* (Cambridge, Mass.: Harvard University Press, 1931), I, 545–59 and *Writings* 2, 49–59. Paragraph numbers from *Collected Papers* have been retained for convenience of reference.

[1] Peirce refers to Kant's argument in *The Critique of Pure Reason,* Transcendental Analytic, especially Book I, Analytic of Concepts. Peirce's seemingly matter-of-fact statement is in actuality a remarkably concise interpretation of Kant's aim in the deduction of the categories from the table of judgments. The passage in Kant that is closest in sense to Peirce's claim here is Kant's assertion, in distinguishing between sensible intuition dependent upon the presence of its object and concepts dependent upon their function: "By 'function' I mean the unity of the act of bringing various representations under one common representation. Concepts are based on the spontaneity of thought, sensible intuitions on the receptivity of impressions. Now the only use which the understanding can make of these concepts is to judge by means of them. Since no representation, save what is in an intuition, is in immediate relation to an object, no concept is ever related to an object immediately, but to some other representation of it, be that other representation an intuition, or itself a concept. Judgment is therefore the mediate knowledge of an object, that is, the representation of a representation of it. In every judgment there is a concept which holds of many representations, and among them of a given representation that is immediately related to an object." *The Critique of Pure Reason* B 93, p. 105. (Kemp Smith translation.)

[2] Here, Peirce goes beyond Kant's analysis by treating the present in general as a concept and not as the effect of the *a priori* unity of the apperception. Peirce evidently recognized that without this move, that there would be no way to distinguish between intuitions and concepts, just as it frees him, among other things, from the necessity of analyzing the problematic notion of the unity of the apperception; without this concept, there could be no specific content of consciousness.

[3] Peirce adopts the language of Arisotle's *Categories,* chapter V: 2a:11–13: "Substance in the truest and strictest, the primary sense of that term, is that which is neither asserted of nor can be found in a subject."

[4] By thus identifying the "is" of *being* with the function of the copula in a proposition, Peirce avoids altogether the problem of empirical content that has, since Parmenides, led philosophers to assert a fundamental difference between the factual and the hypothetical (including the fictional). The issue here is not that one cannot tell the difference, only that it is never in itself a genuine problem. For Peirce, the conception of *being* is only its function of joining subject to predicate. Compare the difference of approach between Peirce here and Bertrand Russell in his theory of descriptions (below, page 812).

[5] That is, if one predicate can be established, others could be, potentially without end. By this formulation, Peirce at once anticipates the process of signification as open-ended without making the error of assuming that an infinite chain of signifiers implies a state of indeterminacy.

Thus substance and being are the beginning and end of all conception. Substance is inapplicable to a predicate, and being is equally so to a subject.[6]

549. The terms "precision"[7] and "abstraction," which were formerly applied to every kind of separation, are now limited, not merely to mental separation, but to that which arises from *attention to* one element and *neglect of* the other. Exclusive attention consists in a definite conception or *supposition* of one part of an object, without any supposition of the other. Abstraction or precision ought to be carefully distinguished from two other modes of mental separation, which may be termed *discrimination* and *dissociation*. Discrimination has to do merely with the senses of terms, and only draws a distinction in meaning. Dissociation is that separation which, in the absence of a constant association, is permitted by the law of association of images. It is the consciousness of one thing, without the necessary simultaneous consciousness of the other. Abstraction or precision, therefore, supposes a greater separation than discrimination, but a less separation than dissociation. Thus I can discriminate red from blue, space from color, and color from space, but not red from color. I can prescind red from blue, and space from color (as is manifest from the fact that I actually believe there is an uncolored space between my face and the wall); but I cannot prescind color from space, nor red from color. I can dissociate red from blue, but not space from color, color from space, nor red from color.[8]

Precision is not a reciprocal process. It is frequently the case, that, while A cannot be prescinded from B, B can be prescinded from A. This circumstance is accounted for as follows. Elementary conceptions only arise upon the occasion of experience; that is, they are produced for the first time according to a general law, the condition of which is the existence of certain impressions. Now if a conception does not reduce the impressions upon which it follows to unity, it is a mere arbitrary addition to these latter; and elementary conceptions do not arise thus arbitrarily. But if the impressions could be definitely comprehended without the conception, this latter would not reduce them to unity. Hence, the impressions (or more immediate conceptions) cannot be definitely conceived or attended to, to the neglect of an elementary conception which reduces them to unity. On the other hand, when such a conception has once been obtained, there is, in general, no reason why the premisses which have oc-

---

[6]This distinction is fundamental for Peirce's sense that a scrupulous attention to logic leads to radical metaphysical clarifications—in this instance, by pointing out, without polemic, that much traditional metaphysical speculation is without content because it begins and ends by attempting either to conceive of predicates as if they could be conceived to be substances, or of subjects, as if they could be the focus of discourse concerning being—without recognizing (Scotus is an exception) the problem as an insufficiency pervading Western metaphysics. See Carnap (below, page 980), who makes a similar point by highly polemical, empirical, and ultimately self-contradictory means; and Heidegger (below, page 1051) whose preoccupation with the question of *Being* leads to a counterproductive and ultimately mystifying dismissal of technical logic.

[7][Peirce, added after publication] *Precision*. (1) A high degree of approximation, only attainable by the thorough application of the most refined methods of science.

(2) Its earlier meaning, still more or less used by logicians, is derived from a meaning given to *praecisio* by Scotus and other scholastics: the act of supposing (whether with consciousness of fiction or not) something about one element of a percept, upon which the thought dwells, without paying any regard to other elements. Precision implies more than mere discrimination, which relates merely to the essence of a term. Thus I can, by an act of discrimination, separate color from extension; but I cannot do so by precision, since I cannot suppose that in any possible universe color (not color-sensation, but color as a quality of an object) exists without extension. So with *triangularity* and *trilaterality*. On the other hand, precision implies much less than dissociation, which, indeed, is not a term of logic, but of psychology. It is doubtful whether a person who is not devoid of the sense of sight can separate space from color by dissociation, or, at any rate, not without great difficulty; but he can, and, indeed, does do so, by *precision*, if he thinks a vacuum is uncolored. So it is, likewise, with space and tridimensionality.

Some writers called every description of *abstraction* by the name *precision*, dividing precision into the real and the mental, and the latter into the negative and the positive; but the better usage named these abstraction divided into *real* and *intentional*, and the latter into *negative* (in which character from which abstraction is made is imagined to be *deniable* of the subject prescinded) and into *precisive abstraction* or *precision*, where the subject prescinded is supposed (in some hypothetical state of things) without any supposition, whether affirmative or negative, in respect to the character abstracted. Hence, the *brocard: abstrahentium non est mendacium* [abstraction is not falsehood] (generally enunciated in connection with the *De Anima*, III, VII, 7). Scotus (in II *Physic.*, *Expositio* 20 *textus* 18) says: *"Et si aliquis dicat, quod Mathematici tunc faciunt mendacium: quia considerant ista, quasi essent abstracta a motu, et materia; quia tamen sunt coniuncta materiae. Respondet, quod non faciunt mendacium: quia Mathematicus non considerat, utrum id, de quo demonstrat suas passiones, sit coniunctum materiae, vel abstractum a materia."* This is not the place to treat of the many interesting logical, as well as psychological, discussions which have taken place concerning precision, which is one of the subjects which the scholastics treated in a comparatively modern way, although it leads directly to the question of nominalism and realism. It may, however, be mentioned that Scotus in many places draws a certain distinction variously designated by him and his followers (its nature and application is perhaps made as clear as anywhere in the *Opus Oxon.* III, xxii. *qu. unica, "Utrum Christus fuerit homo in triduo,"* i.e. between the crucifixion and the resurrection), which the Thomists mostly dispute. There is some account of the matter in Chauvinus, *Lexicon* (2d ed.), under *"Praecisio" ... Dictionary of Philosophy and Psychology*, vol. 2, pp. 323–4, Macmillan Co., New York, edition of 1911.

[8]In an earlier draft of this essay (cf. *Writings* 2) Peirce provided the following very useful table, depicting the distinctions in this paragraph in graphical form:

	Blue w/o Red	Space w/o Color	Color w/o Space	Red w/o Color
Discrimination:	0	0	0	X
Precision:	0	0	X	X
Dissociation:	0	X	X	X

0 = what it is possible to think
X = what it is NOT possible to think

casioned it should not be neglected, and therefore the explaining conception may frequently be prescinded from the more immediate ones and from the impressions.

550. The facts now collected afford the basis for a systematic method of searching out whatever universal elementary conceptions there may be intermediate between the manifold of substance and the unity of being. It has been shown that the occasion of the introduction of a universal elementary conception is either the reduction of the manifold of substance to unity, or else the conjunction to substance of another conception. And it has further been shown that the elements conjoined cannot be supposed without the conception, whereas the conception can generally be supposed without these elements. Now, empirical psychology discovers the occasion of the introduction of a conception, and we have only to ascertain what conception already lies in the data which is united to that of substance by the first conception, but which cannot be supposed without this first conception, to have the next conception in order in passing from being to substance.

It may be noticed that, throughout this process, *introspection* is not resorted to. Nothing is assumed respecting the subjective elements of consciousness which cannot be securely inferred from the objective elements.

551. The conception of *being* arises upon the formation of a proposition. A proposition always has, besides a term to express the substance, another to express the quality of that substance; and the function of the conception of being is to unite the quality to the substance. Quality, therefore, in its very widest sense, is the first conception in order in passing from being to substance.

Quality seems at first sight to be given in the impression. Such results of introspection are untrustworthy. A proposition asserts the applicability of a mediate conception to a more immediate one. Since this is asserted, the more mediate conception is clearly regarded independently of this circumstance, for otherwise the two conceptions would not be distinguished, but one would be thought through the other, without this latter being an object of thought, at all. The mediate conception, then, in order to be *asserted* to be applicable to the other, must first be considered without regard to this circumstance, and taken immediately. But, taken immediately, it transcends what is given (the more immediate conception), and its applicability to the latter is hypothetical. Take, for example, the proposition, "This stove is black." Here the conception of *this stove* is the more immediate, that of black the more mediate, which latter, to be predicated of the former, must be discriminated from it and considered *in itself*, not as applied to an object, but simply as embodying a quality, *blackness*. Now this *blackness* is a

pure species or abstraction, and its application to this stove is entirely hypothetical.[9] The same thing is meant by "the stove is black," as by "there is blackness in the stove." *Embodying blackness* is the equivalent of *black*.[10] The proof is this. These conceptions are applied indifferently to precisely the same facts. If, therefore, they were different, the one which was first applied would fulfil every function of the other; so that one of them would be superfluous. Now a superfluous conception is an arbitrary fiction, whereas elementary conceptions arise only upon the requirement of experience; so that a superfluous elementary conception is impossible. Moreover, the conception of a pure abstraction is indispensable, because we cannot comprehend an agreement of two things, except as an agreement in some respect, and this respect is such a pure abstraction as blackness. Such a pure abstraction, reference to which constitutes a *quality* or general attribute, may be termed a *ground*.

Reference to a ground cannot be prescinded from being, but being can be prescinded from it.[11]

552. Empirical psychology has established the fact that we can know a quality only by means of its contrast with or similarity to another.[12] By contrast and agreement a thing is referred to a correlate, if this term may be used in a wider sense than usual. The occasion of the introduction of the conception of reference to a ground is the reference to a correlate, and this is, therefore, the next conception in order.

Reference to a correlate cannot be prescinded from reference to a ground; but reference to a ground may be prescinded from reference to a correlate.

553. The occasion of reference to a correlate is obviously by comparison. This act has not been sufficiently studied by the psychologists, and it will, therefore, be

---

[9] While this paragraph requires very close attention, Peirce's point is simple: the substance (the stove) is the more immediate in experience, but since the proposition "The stove is black" does unify the contents of consciousness (is apprehended as meaningful), the assertion that the predicate does belong to the substance implies that the predicate, the quality, is *first*, in any theory of reality sufficient to permit such simple and seemingly mundane assertions. But there is no need then to posit something like a Platonic Idea of blackness, as if it were *eidos* (form), or *ousia* (substance). It is what it is, a pure abstraction, without reference to anything else, and what is given in intuition is a specific sensation or feeling. But our sense of reality absolutely depends on such pure abstractions: if anything is real, they must be.

[10] [Peirce] This agrees with the author of *De Generibus et Speciebus, Ouvrages Inedits d'Abélard* (Paris, 1836), p. 528. (*Of Genus and Species, Unedited Works of Abelard;* author unidentified.)

[11] This is the first of three similar principles, in an ascending hierarchy. In this case, being can be thought alone, but reference to a ground cannot be thought without also thinking being.

[12] Kloesel and Houser note Peirce's comment on this statement in MS 785: "It may be doubted whether it was philosophical to rest this matter on empirical psychology. The question is extremely difficult." (*Writings* 2, 94).

necessary to adduce some examples to show in what it consists.[13] Suppose we wish to compare the letters p and b. We may imagine one of them to be turned over on the line of writing as an axis, then laid upon the other, and finally to become transparent so that the other can be seen through it. In this way we shall form a new image which mediates between the images of the two letters, inasmuch as it represents one of them to be (when turned over) the likeness of the other. Again, suppose we think of a murderer as being in relation to a murdered person; in this case we conceive the act of the murder, and in this conception it is represented that corresponding to every murderer (as well as to every murder) there is a murdered person; and thus we resort again to a mediating representation which represents the relate as standing for a correlate with which the mediating representation is itself in relation. Again, suppose we look up the word *homme* in a French dictionary; we shall find opposite to it the word *man,* which, so placed, represents *homme* as representing the same two-legged creature which *man* itself represents. By a further accumulation of instances, it would be found that every comparison requires, besides the related thing, the ground, and the correlate, also a *mediating representation which represents the relate to be a representation of the same correlate which this mediating representation itself represents.* Such a mediating representation may be termed an *interpretant,* because it fulfils the office of an interpreter, who says that a foreigner says the same thing which he himself says. The term representation is here to be understood in a very extended sense, which can be explained by instances better than by a definition.[14] In this sense, a word represents a thing to the conception in the mind of the hearer, a portrait represents the person for

whom it is intended to the conception of recognition, a weathercock represents the direction of the wind to the conception of him who understands it, a barrister represents his client to the judge and jury whom he influences.

Every reference to a correlate, then, conjoins to the substance the conception of a reference to an interpretant; and this is, therefore, the next conception in order in passing from being to substance.

Reference to an interpretant cannot be prescinded from reference to a correlate; but the latter can be prescinded from the former.

554. Reference to an interpretant is rendered possible and justified by that which renders possible and justifies comparison. But that is clearly the diversity of impressions. If we had but one impression, it would not require to be reduced to unity, and would therefore not need to be thought of as referred to an interpretant, and the conception of reference to an interpretant would not arise. But since there is a manifold of impressions, we have a feeling of complication or confusion, which leads us to differentiate this impression from that, and then, having been differentiated, they require to be brought to unity. Now they are not brought to unity until we conceive them together as being ours, that is, until we refer them to a conception as their interpretant. Thus, the reference to an interpretant arises upon the holding together of diverse impressions, and therefore it does not join a conception to the substance, as the other two references do, but unites directly the manifold of the substance itself. It is, therefore, the last conception in order in passing from being to substance.

555. The five conceptions thus obtained, for reasons which will be sufficiently obvious, may be termed categories. That is,

Being

Quality (reference to a ground)
Relation (reference to a correlate)
Representation (reference to an interpretant)

[13] The examples Peirce offers below all look forward to the introduction of his third category, the *"interpretant,"* thereby passing perhaps too quickly over the second, the reference to a correlate, which consists in the comparison of one instance (for example, the color of the stove) with another (for example, the color of my shoes). The same (with the same psychological difficulty) applies to the comparison of one instance of the color of the stove (say, on Tuesday) and another, on another day or at a different time, thereby involving memory. In either case, or rather, in both, the comparison is still crucial since it is what gives occasion for the introduction of the conception of the interpretant.

[14] This notoriously difficult concept, as in the case of Thomas Kuhn's use of the term "paradigm" (see below, page 1282), is not only understood in an extended sense, it cannot be (given what Peirce has already argued) understood without examples, since the mediating representation is emphatically *not* the concept as signified, linked to the acoustic image as signifier in Saussure (below, page 787). Hence Peirce's confusing definition, placing the mediating representation between *relate* and *correlate* as an assertion: what the relate represents is the same as what the correlate represents. Note that Peirce thereby carefully avoids saying what it is, since it depends upon a reference to *specific* correlates.

This also confers upon this conception the possibility of indefinite extension, just as the identification of one predicate opens the possibility of indefinite predictability. The "meaning" of an interpretant, that is, can grow and develop without losing its identity or integrity, so long as it can be traced back to the correlates which occasioned and propelled it. In a later essay, "The Law of Mind" (*Collected Papers* 6, 106–63), Peirce articulates the principle in these terms: "Logical analysis applied to mental phenomena shows that there is but one law of mind, namely, that ideas tend to spread continuously and to affect others which stand to them in a peculiar relation of affectability. In this spreading they lose intensity and become welded with other ideas."

Substance

The three intermediate conceptions may be termed accidents.[15]

556. This passage from the many to the one is numerical. The conception of a *third* is that of an object which is so related to two others, that one of these must be related to the other in the same way in which the third is related to that other. Now this coincides with the conception of an interpretant. An other is plainly equivalent to a *correlate*. The conception of second differs from that of other, in implying the possibility of a third. In the same way, the conception of *self* implies the possibility of an *other*. The *ground* is the self abstracted from the concreteness which implies the possibility of an other.

557. Since no one of the categories can be prescinded from those above it, the list of supposable objects which they afford is,

What is

Quale (that which refers to a ground)
Relate (that which refers to ground and correlate)
Representamen (that which refers to ground, correlate, and interpretant)

It

558. A quality may have a special determination which prevents its being prescinded from reference to a correlate. Hence there are two kinds of relation.

First. That of relates whose reference to a ground is a prescindible or internal quality.

Second. That of relates whose reference to a ground is an unprescindible or relative quality.

In the former case, the relation is a mere *concurrence* of the correlates in one character, and the relate and correlate are not distinguished. In the latter case the correlate is set over against the relate, and there is in some sense an *opposition*.

Relates of the first kind are brought into relation simply by their agreement. But mere disagreement (unrecognized) does not constitute relation, and therefore relates of the second kind are only brought into relation by correspondence in fact.

A reference to a ground may also be such that it cannot be prescinded from a reference to an interpretant. In this case it may be termed an *imputed* quality. If the reference of a relate to its ground can be prescinded from reference to an interpretant, its relation to its correlate is a mere concurrence or community in the possession of a quality, and therefore the reference to a correlate can be prescinded from reference to an interpretant. It follows that there are three kinds of representations.

First. Those whose relation to their objects is a mere community in some quality, and these representations may be termed *likenesses*.[16]

Second. Those whose relation to their objects consists in a correspondence in fact, and these may be termed *indices* or *signs*.[17]

Third. Those the ground of whose relation to their objects is an imputed character, which are the same as general signs, and these may be termed *symbols*.

559. I shall now show how the three conceptions of reference to a ground, reference to an object, and reference to an interpretant are the fundamental ones of at least one universal science, that of logic. Logic is said to treat of second intentions as applied to first.[18] It would lead me too far away from the matter in hand to discuss the truth of this statement; I shall simply adopt it as one which seems to me to afford a good definition of the subject-genus of this science. Now, second intentions are the objects of the understanding considered as representations, and the first intentions to which they apply are the objects of those representations. The objects of the understanding, considered as representations, are symbols, that is, signs which are at least potentially general. But the rules of logic hold good of any symbols, of those which are written or spoken as well as of those which are thought. They have no immediate application to likenesses or indices, because no arguments can be constructed of these alone, but do apply to all symbols. All symbols, indeed, are in one sense relative to the understanding, but only in the sense in which also all things are relative to the understanding. On this account, therefore, the relation to the understanding need not be expressed in the definition of the sphere of logic, since it determines no

---

[15] In later work, Peirce simplified this schema to three categories, *First, Second, Third,* generally following the outlines of the discussion below. For its basis in the triad, *ground, object, interpretant,* cf. *Collected Papers* 2.227–29; for a fuller exposition of the categories, cf. *Collected Papers* 1.300–53. See also "What Pragmatism Is," (below, page 668).

[16] [*CP* eds.] In later writings called "icons."

[17] [*CP* eds.] In later writings an index is always taken to be but one of many kinds of signs; a sign being understood in some sense similar to that given in 540.

[18] [*CP* eds.] See Peirce's definition in the *Century Dictionary* (1889) Intention 8; also Albertus Magnus, *Meta.* I, 1, 1, and Th. Aquinas, *Meta.* IV, 4, f. 43 v. A.

limitation of that sphere. But a distinction can be made between concepts which are supposed to have no existence except so far as they are actually present to the understanding, and external symbols which still retain their character of symbols so long as they are only *capable* of being understood. And as the rules of logic apply to these latter as much as to the former (and though only through the former, yet this character, since it belongs to all things, is no limitation), it follows that logic has for its subject-genus all symbols and not merely concepts.[19] We come, therefore, to this, that logic treats of the reference of symbols in general to their objects. In this view it is one of a trivium of conceivable sciences. The first would treat of the formal conditions of symbols having meaning, that is of the reference of symbols in general to their grounds or imputed characters, and this might be called formal grammar;[20] the second, logic,[21] would treat of the formal conditions of the truth of symbols; and the third would treat of the formal conditions of the force of symbols, or their power of appealing to a mind, that is, of their reference in general to interpretants, and this might be called formal rhetoric.[22]

There would be a general division of symbols, common to all these sciences; namely, into,

1. Symbols which directly determine only their *grounds* or imputed qualities, and are thus but sums of marks or *terms;*

2. Symbols which also independently determine their *objects* by means of other term or terms, and thus, expressing their own objective validity, become capable of truth or falsehood, that is, are *propositions;* and,

3. Symbols which also independently determine their *interpretants,* and thus the minds to which they appeal, by premissing a proposition or propositions which such a mind is to admit. These are *arguments.*

And it is remarkable that, among all the definitions of the proposition, for example, as the *oratio indicativa,*[23] as the subsumption of an object under a concept, as the expression of the relation of two concepts, and as the indication of the mutable ground of appearance, there is, perhaps, not one in which the conception of reference to an object or correlate is not the important one. In the same way, the conception of reference to an interpretant or third, is always prominent in the definitions of argument.

In a proposition, the term which separately indicates the object of the symbol is termed the subject, and that which indicates the ground is termed the predicate. The objects indicated by the subject (which are always potentially a plurality—at least, of phases or appearances) are therefore stated by the proposition to be related to one another on the ground of the character indicated by the predicate. Now this relation may be either a concurrence or an opposition. Propositions of concurrence are those which are usually considered in logic; but I have shown in a paper upon the classification of arguments[24] that it is also necessary to consider separately propositions of opposition, if we are to take account of such arguments as the following:

Whatever is the half of anything is less than that of which it is the half:

A is half of B;
A is less than B.

The subject of such a proposition is separated into two terms, a "subject nominative" and an "object accusative."

In an argument, the premises form a representation of the conclusion, because they indicate the interpretant of the argument, or representation representing it to represent its object. The premises may afford a likeness, index, or symbol of the conclusion. In deductive argument, the conclusion is represented by the premises as by a general sign under which it is contained. In hypotheses, something like the conclusion is proved, that is, the premises form a likeness of the conclusion. Take, for example, the following argument:

M is, for instance, PI, PII, PIII, and PIV;
S is PI, PII, PIII, and PIV:
∴ S is M.

Here the first premiss amounts to this, that "PI, PII, PIII, and PIV" is a likeness of M, and thus the premises are or represent a likeness of the conclusion. That it is different with induction another example will show.

SI, SII, SIII, and SIV are taken as samples of the collection M;
SI, SII, SIII, and SIV are P:
∴ All M is P.

---

[19] [Peirce] Herbart says *"Unsre sämmtlichen Gedanken lassen sich von zwei Seiten betrachten; theils als Thätigkeiten unseres Geistes, theils in Hinsicht dessen, was durch sie gedacht wird. In letzterer Beziehung heissen sie Begreffe, weches Wort, indem es das Begriffene bezeichnet, zu abstrahiren gebietet von der Art und Weise, wie wir den Gedanken empfangen, produzieren, oder reproduzieren mögen."* [All of our thoughts may be regarded from two viewpoints, partly as activities of our mind, partly as what is thought through them. In the latter, we call them concepts, the term signifying that what is thought is abstracted from the mode and manner in which we may receive, produce, or reproduce the thought.] From Johann Friedrich Herbart, *Lehrbuch zur Einleitung in die Philosophie* (vol. I of *Sämmtliche Werke* [Leipzig, 1850]). But the whole difference between a concept and an external sign lies in these respects which logic ought, according to Herbart, to abstract from.
[20] [*CP* eds.] Later called Speculative Grammar or Stechiology.
[21] [*CP* eds.] Later called Critical Logic or Critic.
[22] [*CP* eds.] Later called Speculative Rhetoric or Methodeutic.
[23] "Indicative speech."
[24] [*CP* eds.] See *Collected Papers* vol. 2, bk. III, ch. 2.

Hence the first premiss amounts to saying that "SI, SII, SIII, and SIV" is an index of M. Hence the premisses are an index of the conclusion.

The other divisions of terms, propositions, and arguments arise from the distinction of extension and comprehension. I propose to treat this subject in a subsequent paper.[25] But I will so far anticipate that as to say that there is, first, the direct reference of a symbol to its objects, or its denotation; second, the reference of the symbol to its ground, through its object, that is, its reference to the common characters of its objects, or its connotation; and third, its reference to its interpretants through its object, that is, its reference to all the synthetical propositions in which its objects in common are subject or predicate, and this I term the information it embodies. And as every addition to what it denotes, or to what it connotes, is effected by means of a distinct proposition of this kind, it follows that the extension and comprehension of a term are in an inverse relation, as long as the information remains the same, and that every increase of information is accompanied by an increase of one or other of these two quantities. It may be observed that extension and comprehension are very often taken in other senses in which this last proposition is not true.

This is an imperfect view of the application which the conceptions which, according to our analysis, are the most fundamental ones find in the sphere of logic. It is believed, however, that it is sufficient to show that at least something may be usefully suggested by considering this science in this light.

Lessons from the History of Philosophy

§1. Nominalism [1903][1]

15. Very early in my studies of logic, before I had really been devoting myself to it more than four or five years, it became quite manifest to me that this science was in a bad condition, entirely unworthy of the general state of intellectual development of our age; and in consequence of this, every other branch of philosophy except ethics—for it was already clear that psychology was a special science and no part of philosophy—was in a similar disgraceful state. About that time—say the date of [Henry L.] Mansel's *Prolegomena Logica* [1851]—Logic touched bottom. There was no room for it to become more degraded. It had been sinking steadily, and relatively to the advance of physical science, by no means slowly from the time of the revival of learning—say from the date of the last fall of Constantinople [1453]. One important addition to the subject had been made early in the eighteenth century, the Doctrine of Chances. But this had not come from the professed logicians, who knew nothing about it. Whewell, it is true, had been doing some fine work; but it was not of a fundamental character. De Morgan and Boole[2] had laid the foundations for modern exact logic, but they can hardly be said to have begun the erection of the edifice itself. Under these circumstances, I naturally opened the dusty folios of the scholastic doctors. Thought generally was, of course, in a somewhat low condition under the Plantagenets.[3] You can appraise it very well by the impression that Dante, Chaucer, Marco Polo, Froissart, and the great cathedrals make upon us. But [their] logic, relatively to the general condition of thought, was marvellously exact and critical. They can tell us nothing concerning methods of reasoning since their own reasoning was puerile; but their analyses of thought and their discussions of all those questions of logic that almost trench upon metaphysics are very instructive as well as very good discipline in that subtle kind of thinking that is required in logic.

16. In the days of which I am speaking, the age of Robert of Lincoln, Roger Bacon, St. Thomas Aquinas, and Duns Scotus, the question of nominalism and realism was regarded as definitively and conclusively settled in favor of realism. You know what the question was. It was whether laws and general types are figments of the mind or are real. If this be understood to mean whether there really are any laws and types, it is strictly speaking a question of metaphysics and not of logic. But as a first step toward its solution, it is proper to ask whether, granting that our common-sense beliefs are true, the analysis of the meaning of those beliefs shows that, according to those beliefs, laws and

---

[25] "Upon Logical Comprehension and Extension" *Writings* 2, 70–86.
"Lessons from the History of Philosophy" is a collection of comments written at diverse times, but assembled by the original editors of *Collected Papers* at the start of the first volume. From *Collected Papers* 1.15–42. The final entry added here is from A GUESS AT THE RIDDLE consisting of notes and manuscripts for an uncompleted, unpublished book, composed c. 1890. All passages are reprinted from *Collected Papers* (Cambridge, Mass.: Harvard University Press, 1931). For convenience of reference, paragraph numbers from *Collected Papers* have been retained.
[1] From the "Lowell Lectures of 1903," Lecture IIIa.

[2] William Whewell (1794–1866), British philosopher, historian, and philosopher of science; Augustus de Morgan (1806–1871), British logician and mathematician; George Boole (1816–1864), self-taught English mathematician, inventor of binary or Boolean algebra, appointed Professor of Mathematics at Queen's College in Ireland in 1849.
[3] Royal house in England, 1154 to 1485, also called the House of Anjou or the Anjevin dynasty, representing both the houses of Lancaster and York (cf. "War of the Roses"), producing fourteen kings from Henry I to Richard III.

types are objective or subjective. This is a question of logic rather than of metaphysics—and as soon as this is answered the reply to the other question immediately follows after.

17. Notwithstanding a great outburst of nominalism in the fourteenth century which was connected with politics, the nominalists being generally opposed to the excessive powers of the pope and in favor of civil government, a connection that lent to the philosophical doctrine a factitious following, the Scotists, who were realists, were in most places the predominant party, and retained possession of the universities. At the revival of learning they stubbornly opposed the new studies; and thus the word Duns, the proper name of their master, came to mean an adversary of learning.[4] The word originally further implied that the person so called was a master of subtle thought with which the humanists were unable to cope. But in another generation the disputations by which that power of thought was kept in training had lost their liveliness; and the consequence was that Scotism died out when the strong Scotists died. It was a mere change of fashion.

18. The humanists were weak thinkers. Some of them no doubt might have been trained to be strong thinkers; but they had no severe training in thought. All their energies went to writing a classical language and an artistic style of expression. They went to the ancients for their philosophy; and mostly took up the three easiest of the ancient sects of philosophy, Epicureanism, Stoicism, and Scepticism. Epicureanism was a doctrine extremely like that of John Stuart Mill. The Epicureans alone of the later ancient schools believed in inductive reasoning, which they grounded upon the uniformity of nature, although they made the uniformity of nature to consist in somewhat different characters from those Stuart Mill emphasizes. Like Mill, the Epicureans were extreme nominalists. The Stoics advocated the flattest materialism, which nobody any longer has any need of doing since the new invention of Monism enables a man to be perfectly materialist in substance, and as idealistic as he likes in words. Of course the Stoics could not but be nominalists. They took no stock in inductive reasoning. They held it to be a transparent fallacy. The Sceptics of the Renaissance were something like the agnostics of the generation now passing away, except that they went much further. Our agnostics contented themselves with declaring everything beyond ordinary generalizations of experience to be unknowable, while the Sceptics did not think any scientific knowledge of any description to be possible. If you turn over the pages, for example, of Cornelius Agrippa's book *De* [*incertitudine et*] *vanitate scientiarum* [*et artium*] [1531], you will find he takes up every science in succession,

arithmetic, geometry, mechanics, optics, and after examination pronounces each to be altogether beyond the power of the human mind. Of course, therefore, as far as they believed in anything at all, the Sceptics were nominalists.

19. In short, there was a tidal wave of nominalism. Descartes was a nominalist. Locke and all his following, Berkeley, Hartley, Hume, and even Reid, were nominalists. Leibniz was an extreme nominalist, and Rémusat [C. F. M.?] who has lately made an attempt to repair the edifice of Leibnizian monadology, does so by cutting away every part which leans at all toward realism. Kant was a nominalist; although his philosophy would have been rendered compacter, more consistent, and stronger if its author had taken up realism, as he certainly would have done if he had read Scotus. Hegel was a nominalist of realistic yearnings. I might continue the list much further. Thus, in one word, all modern philosophy of every sect has been nominalistic.

20. In a long notice of Frazer's *Berkeley,* in the *North American Review* for October 1871,[5] I declared for realism. I have since very carefully and thoroughly revised my philosophical opinions more than half a dozen times, and have modified them more or less on most topics; but I have never been able to think differently on that question of nominalism and realism. In that paper I acknowledged that the tendency of science has been toward nominalism; but the late Dr. Francis Ellingwood Abbot in the very remarkable introduction to his book entitled *"Scientific Theism"* [1885], showed on the contrary, quite conclusively, that science has always been at heart realistic, and always must be so; and upon comparing his writings with mine, it is easily seen that these features of nominalism which I pointed out in science are merely superficial and transient.

21. The heart of the dispute lies in this. The modern philosophers—one and all, unless Schelling[6] be an exception—recognize but one mode of being, the being of an individual thing or fact, the being which consists in the object's crowding out a place for itself in the universe, so to speak, and reacting by brute force of fact, against all other things. I call that existence.

22. Aristotle, on the other hand, whose system, like all the greatest systems, was evolutionary, recognized besides an embryonic kind of being, like the being of a tree in its seed, or like the being of a future contingent event, depending on how a man shall decide to act. In a few passages Aristotle seems to have a dim aperçue of a third mode of being in the entelechy.[7] The embryonic being for Aristotle was

---

[4]That is, "Dunce."

[5]In *Writings* 2, 462–87.
[6]Friedrich Schelling (1775–1854), Post-Kantian German philosopher.
[7]The realized expression of a potential.

the being he called matter, which is alike in all things, and which in the course of its development took on form. Form is an element having a different mode of being. The whole philosophy of the scholastic doctors is an attempt to mould this doctrine of Aristotle into harmony with christian truth. This harmony the different doctors attempted to bring about in different ways. But all the realists agree in reversing the order of Aristotle's evolution by making the form come first, and the individuation of that form come later. Thus, they too recognized two modes of being; but they were not the two modes of being of Aristotle.

23. My view is that there are three modes of being. I hold that we can directly observe them in elements of whatever is at any time before the mind in any way. They are the being of positive qualitative possibility, the being of actual fact, and the being of law that will govern facts in the future.

24. Let us begin with considering actuality, and try to make out just what it consists in. If I ask you what the actuality of an event consists in, you will tell me that it consists in its happening then and there. The specifications then and there involve all its relations to other existents. The actuality of the event seems to lie in its relations to the universe of existents. A court may issue injunctions and judgments against me and I not care a snap of my finger for them. I may think them idle vapor. But when I feel the sheriff's hand on my shoulder, I shall begin to have a sense of actuality. Actuality is something brute. There is no reason in it. I instance putting your shoulder against a door and trying to force it open against an unseen, silent, and unknown resistance. We have a two-sided consciousness of effort and resistance, which seems to me to come tolerably near to a pure sense of actuality. On the whole, I think we have here a mode of being of one thing which consists in how a second object is. I call that Secondness.

25. Besides this, there are two modes of being that I call Firstness and Thirdness. Firstness is the mode of being which consists in its subject's being positively such as it is regardless of aught else. That can only be a possibility. For as long as things do not act upon one another there is no sense or meaning in saying that they have any being, unless it be that they are such in themselves that they may perhaps come into relation with others. The mode of being a redness, before anything in the universe was yet red, was nevertheless a positive qualitative possibility. And redness in itself, even if it be embodied, is something positive and sui generis. That I call Firstness. We naturally attribute Firstness to outward objects, that is we suppose they have capacities in themselves which may or may not be already actualized, which may or may not ever be actualized, although we

can know nothing of such possibilities [except] so far as they are actualized.

26. Now for Thirdness. Five minutes of our waking life will hardly pass without our making some kind of prediction; and in the majority of cases these predictions are fulfilled in the event. Yet a prediction is essentially of a general nature, and cannot ever be completely fulfilled. To say that a prediction has a decided tendency to be fulfilled, is to say that the future events are in a measure really governed by a law. If a pair of dice turns up sixes five times running, that is a mere uniformity. The dice might happen fortuitously to turn up sixes a thousand times running. But that would not afford the slightest security for a prediction that they would turn up sixes the next time. If the prediction has a tendency to be fulfilled, it must be that future events have a tendency to conform to a general rule. "Oh," but say the nominalists, "this general rule is nothing but a mere word or couple of words!" I reply, "Nobody ever dreamed of denying that what is general is of the nature of a general sign; but the question is whether future events will conform to it or not. If they will, your adjective 'mere' seems to be ill-placed." A rule to which future events have a tendency to conform is ipso facto an important thing, an important element in the happening of those events. This mode of being which consists, mind my word if you please, the mode of being which consists in the fact that future facts of Secondness will take on a determinate general character, I call a Thirdness.

§2. Conceptualism [1909][8]

27. Many philosophers call their variety of nominalism, "conceptualism"; but it is essentially the same thing; and their not seeing that it is so is but another example of that loose and slapdash style of thinking that has made it possible for them to remain nominalists. Their calling their "conceptualism" a middle term between realism and nominalism is itself an example in the very matter to which nominalism relates. For while the question between nominalism and realism is, in its nature, susceptible of but two answers: yes and no, they make an idle and irrelevant point which had been thoroughly considered by all the great realists; and instead of drawing a valid distinction, as they suppose, only repeat the very same confusion of thought which made them nominalists. The question was whether all properties, laws of nature, and predicates of more than an actually existent

---

[8][*CP* ed.] From "Essays on Meaning," June 1909.

subject are, without exception, mere figments or not.[9] The conceptualists seek to wedge in a third position conflicting with the principle of excluded middle. They say, "Those universals are real, indeed; but they are only real thoughts." So much may be said of the philosopher's stone. To give that answer constitutes a man a nominalist. Are the laws of nature, and that property of gold by which it will yield the purple of Cassius,[10] no more real than the philosopher's stone? No, the conceptualists admit that there is a difference; but they say that the laws of nature and the properties of chemical species are results of thinking. The great realists had brought out all the truth there is in that much more distinctly long before modern conceptualism appeared in the world. They showed that the general is not capable of full actualization in the world of action and reaction but is of the nature of what is thought, but that our thinking only apprehends and does not create thought, and that that thought may and does as much govern outward things as it does our thinking. But those realists did not fall into any confusion between the real fact of having a dream and the illusory object dreamed. The conceptualist doctrine is an undisputed truism about thinking, while the question between nominalists and realists relates to thoughts, that is, to the objects which thinking enables us to know.

* * *

§4. Kant and His Refutation of Idealism[11]

35. Kant's whole philosophy turns upon his logic. He gives the name of logic to the greater part of his *Critic of the Pure Reason,* and it is a result of the great fault of his logical theory that he does not extend that name to the whole work. This greatest fault was at the same [time] the greatest merit of his doctrine: it lay in his sharp discrimination of the intuitive and the discursive processes of the mind. The distinction itself is not only familiar to everybody but it had long played a part in philosophy. Nevertheless, it is on such obvious distinctions that the greater systems have been founded, and [Kant] saw far more clearly than any predecessor had done the whole philosophical import of this distinction. This was what emancipated him from Leibnizianism, and at the same time turned him against sensationalism. It was also what enabled him to see that no general description of existence is possible, which is perhaps the most valuable proposition that the *Critic* contains. But he drew too hard a line between the operations of observation and of ratiocination. He allows himself to fall into the habit of thinking that the latter only begins after the former is complete; and wholly fails to see that even the simplest syllogistic conclusion can only be drawn by observing the relations of the terms in the premises and conclusion. His doctrine of the schemata can only have been an afterthought, an addition to his system after it was substantially complete. For if the schemata had been considered early enough, they would have overgrown his whole work.

36. Kant's refutation of idealism in the second edition of the *Critic of the Pure Reason* has been often held to be inconsistent with his main position or even to be knowingly sophistical. It appears to me to be one of the numerous passages in that work which betray an elaborated and vigorous analysis, marred in the exposition by the attempt to state the argument more abstractly and demonstratively than the thought would warrant.

In "Note 1,"[12] Kant says that his argument beats idealism at its own game. How is that? The idealist says that all that we know immediately, that is, otherwise than inferentially, is what is present in the mind; and things out of the mind are not so present. The whole idealist position turns upon this conception of the present.

37. The idealistic argument turns upon the assumption that certain things are absolutely "present," namely what we have in mind at the moment, and that nothing else can be immediately, that is, otherwise than inferentially known. When this is once granted, the idealist has no difficulty in showing that that external existence which we cannot know immediately we cannot know, at all. Some of the arguments used for this purpose are of little value, because they only

---

[9][Peirce] It must not be imagined that any notable realist of the thirteenth or fourteenth century took the ground that any "universal" was what we in English should call a "thing," as it seems that, in an earlier age, some realists and some nominalists, too, had done; though perhaps it is not quite certain that they did so, their writings being lost. Their very definition of a "universal" admits that it is of the same generic nature as a word, namely, is: *"Quod natum optum est praedicari de pluribus."* ["That which is intended to be predicated of many things"] Neither was it their doctrine that any "universal" itself is real. They might, indeed, some of them, think so; but their realism did not consist in that opinion, but in holding that what the word signifies, in contradistinction to what it can be truly said of, is real. Anybody may happen to opine that "the" is a real English word; but that will not constitute him a realist. But if he thinks that, whether the word "hard" itself be real or not, the property, the character, the predicate, hardness, is not invented by men, as the word is, but is really and truly in the hard things and is one in them all, as a description of habit, disposition, or behavior, then he is a realist.

[10] A pigment formed of certain salts of gold, used to paint porcelain. Named after A. Cassius, seventeenth-century German physician.

[11][CP eds.] 35 is an unpublished, uncompleted review of T. K. Abbott's translation of Kant's *Introduction to Logic,* etc. Longmans Green & Co., 1885. 37–38 is "Notes on the Question of the Existence of an External World." c. 1890. 36 and 39 are from fragmentary alternative mss. of that same date.

[12]Cf. *Critique of Pure Reason* [Kemp Smith trans.], Transcendental Analytic, page 245.

go to show that our knowledge of an external world is fallible; now there is a world of difference between fallible knowledge and no knowledge. However, I think it would have to be admitted as a matter of logic that if we have no immediate perception of a non-ego, we can have no reason to admit the supposition of an existence so contrary to all experience as that would in that case be.

38. But what evidence is there that we can immediately know only what is "present" to the mind? The idealists generally treat this as self-evident; but, as Clifford[13] jestingly says, "it is evident" is a phrase which only means "we do not know how to prove." The proposition that we can immediately perceive only what is present seems to me parallel to that other vulgar prejudice that "a thing cannot act where it is not." An opinion which can only defend itself by such a sounding phrase is pretty sure to be wrong. That a thing cannot act where it is not is plainly an induction from ordinary experience, which shows no forces except such as act through the resistance of materials, with the exception of gravity which, owing to its being the same for all bodies, does not appear in ordinary experience like a force. But further experience shows that attractions and repulsions are the universal types of forces. A thing may be said to be wherever it acts; but the notion that a particle is absolutely present in one part of space and absolutely absent from all the rest of space is devoid of all foundation. In like manner, the idea that we can immediately perceive only what is present seems to be founded on our ordinary experience that we cannot recall and reexamine the events of yesterday nor know otherwise than by inference what is to happen tomorrow. Obviously, then, the first move toward beating idealism at its own game is to remark that we apprehend our own ideas only as flowing in time, and since neither the future nor the past, however near they may be, is present, there is as much difficulty in conceiving our perception of what passes within us as in conceiving external perception. If so, replies the idealist, instead of giving up idealism we must go still further to nihilism. Kant does not notice this retort; but it is clear from his footnote that he would have said: Not so; for it is impossible we should so much as think we think in time unless we do think in time; or rather, dismissing blind impossibility, the mere imagination of time is a clear perception of the past. Hamilton[14] stupidly objects to Reid's[15] phrase "immediate memory"; but an immediate, intuitive

consciousness of time clearly exists wherever time exists. But once grant immediate knowledge in time, and what becomes of the idealist theory that we immediately know only the present? For the present can contain no time.

39. But Kant does not pursue this line of thought along the straight road to its natural result; because he is a sort of idealist himself. Namely, though not idealistic as to the substance of things, he is partially so in regard to their accidents. Accordingly, he introduces his distinction of the variable and the persistent *(beharrlich),* and seeks to show that the only way we can apprehend our own flow of ideas, binding them together as a connected flow, is by attaching them to an immediately perceived persistent externality. He refuses to inquire how that immediate external consciousness is possible, though such an inquiry might have probed the foundations of his system.

§5. Hegelism[16]

40. The critical logicians have been much affiliated to the theological seminaries. About the thinking that goes on in laboratories they have known nothing. Now the seminarists and religionists generally have at all times and places set their faces against the idea of continuous growth. That disposition of intellect is the most catholic element of religion. Religious truth having been once defined is never to be altered in the most minute particular; and theology being held as queen of the sciences, the religionists have bitterly fought by fire and tortures all great advances in the true sciences; and if there be no true continuous growth in men's ideas where else in the world should it be looked for? Thence, we find this folk setting up hard lines of demarcation, or great gulfs, contrary to all observation, between good men and bad, between the wise and foolish, between the spirit and the flesh, between all the different kinds of objects, between one quantity and the next. So shut up are they in this conception of the world that when the seminarist Hegel discovered that the universe is everywhere permeated with continuous growth (for that, and nothing else, is the "Secret of Hegel") it was supposed to be an entirely new idea, a century and a half after the differential calculus had been in working order.

41. Hegel, while regarding scientific men with disdain, has for his chief topic the importance of continuity, which was the very idea the mathematicians and physicists had been chiefly engaged in following out for three centuries. This made Hegel's work less correct and excellent in itself than it might have been; and at the same time hid its

---

[13] William Clifford [1845–1879], English mathematician and philosopher. Exact source not traced.

[14] [*CP* eds.] Sir William Hamilton's *Discussions on Philosophy and Literature,* ch. 2, p. 55. What Hamilton objects to is "immediate knowledge of the past" as a definition of memory.

[15] Thomas Reid (1710–1796), Scottish philosopher, principal figure in the development of the philosophy of common sense.

[16] [*CP* eds.] 40 and 41–2 are from separate unidentified fragments, c. 1892.

true mode of affinity with the scientific thought into which the life of the race had been chiefly laid up. It was a misfortune for Hegelism, a misfortune for "philosophy," and a misfortune (in lesser degree) for science.

42. My philosophy resuscitates Hegel, though in a strange costume.

from
A Guess at the Riddle (c. 1890)[17]

3.368 . . . My whole method will be found to be in profound contrast with that of Hegel; I reject his philosophy in toto. Nevertheless, I have a certain sympathy with it, and fancy that if its author had only noticed a very few circumstances he would himself have been led to revolutionize his system. One of these is the double division or dichotomy of the second idea of the triad. He has usually overlooked external Secondness, altogether. In other words, he has committed the trifling oversight of forgetting that there is a real world with real actions and reactions. Rather a serious oversight that. Then Hegel had the misfortune to be unusually deficient in mathematics. He shows this in the very elementary character of his reasoning. Worse still, while the whole burden of his song is that philosophers have neglected to take Thirdness into account, which is true enough of the theological kind, with whom alone he was acquainted (for I do not call it acquaintance to look into a book without comprehending it), he unfortunately did not know, what it would have been of the utmost consequence for him to know, that the mathematical analysts had in great measure escaped this great fault, and that the thorough-going pursuit of the ideas and methods of the differential calculus would be sure to cure it altogether. Hegel's dialectical method is only a feeble and rudimentary application of the principles of the calculus to metaphysics. Finally Hegel's plan of evolving everything out of the abstractest conception by a dialectical procedure, though far from being so absurd as the experientialists think, but on the contrary representing one of the indispensable parts of the course of science, overlooks the weakness of individual man, who wants the strength to wield such a weapon as that.

The First Rule of Reason

135. Upon this first, and in one sense this sole, rule of reason, that in order to learn you must desire to learn, and in so desiring not be satisfied with what you already incline to think, there follows one corollary which itself deserves to be inscribed upon every wall of the city of philosophy:

Do not block the way of inquiry.

136. Although it is better to be methodical in our investigations, and to consider the economics of research, yet there is no positive sin against logic in trying any theory which may come into our heads, so long as it is adopted in such a sense as to permit the investigation to go on unimpeded and undiscouraged. On the other hand, to set up a philosophy which barricades the road of further advance toward the truth is the one unpardonable offence in reasoning, as it is also the one to which metaphysicians have in all ages shown themselves the most addicted.

Let me call your attention to four familiar shapes in which this venomous error assails our knowledge:

137. The first is the shape of absolute assertion. That we can be sure of nothing in science is an ancient truth. The Academy taught it. Yet science has been infested with overconfident assertion, especially on the part of the third-rate and fourth-rate men, who have been more concerned with teaching than with learning, at all times. No doubt some of the geometries still teach as a self-evident truth the proposition that if two straight lines in one plane meet a third straight line so as to make the sum of the internal angles on one side less than two right angles those two lines will meet on that side if sufficiently prolonged. Euclid, whose logic was more careful, only reckoned this proposition as a Postulate, or arbitrary Hypothesis. Yet even he places among his axioms the proposition that a part is less than its whole, and falls into several conflicts with our most modern geometry in consequence. But why need we stop to consider cases where some subtilty of thought is required to see that the assertion is not warranted when every book which applies philosophy to the conduct of life lays down as positive certainty propositions which it is quite as easy to doubt as to believe?

---

[17]From *Collected Papers* 3.368. [*CP* eds.] c. 1890. One of the drafts of this work is headed: "Notes for a Book, to be entitled 'A Guess at the Riddle,' with a Vignette of the Sphynx below the Title." This caption is followed by the remark, "And this book, if ever written, as it soon will be if I am in a situation to do it, will be one of the births of time."

"The First Rule of Reason" is from a series of lectures presented in Cambridge, Massachusetts, in (1898). For a reconstructed text of all the lectures, edited by Kenneth Laine Ketner, see *Reasoning and the Logic of Things* (Cambridge, Mass.: Harvard University Press, 1992). The text reprinted here is from *Collected Papers* (1931), vol. 1, #135–140.

138. The second bar which philosophers often set up across the roadway of inquiry lies in maintaining that this, that, and the other never can be known. When Auguste Comte was pressed to specify any matter of positive fact to the knowledge of which no man could by any possibility attain, he instanced the knowledge of the chemical composition of the fixed stars; and you may see his answer set down in the *Philosophie positive*.[1] But the ink was scarcely dry upon the printed page before the spectroscope was discovered and that which he had deemed absolutely unknowable was well on the way of getting ascertained. It is easy enough to mention a question the answer to which is not known to me today. But to aver that that answer will not be known tomorrow is somewhat risky; for oftentimes it is precisely the least expected truth which is turned up under the ploughshare of research. And when it comes to positive assertion that the truth never will be found out, that, in the light of the history of our time, seems to me more hazardous than the venture of Andrée.[2]

139. The third philosophical stratagem for cutting off inquiry consists in maintaining that this, that, or the other element of science is basic, ultimate, independent of aught else, and utterly inexplicable—not so much from any defect in our knowing as because there is nothing beneath it to know. The only type of reasoning by which such a conclusion could possibly be reached is retroduction. Now nothing justifies a retroductive inference except its affording an explanation of the facts. It is, however, no explanation at all of a fact to pronounce it inexplicable. That, therefore, is a conclusion which no reasoning can ever justify or excuse.

140. The last philosophical obstacle to the advance of knowledge which I intend to mention is the holding that this or that law or truth has found its last and perfect formulation—and especially that the ordinary and usual course of nature never can be broken through. "Stones do not fall from heaven," said Laplace,[3] although they had been falling upon inhabited ground every day from the earliest times. But there is no kind of inference which can lend the slightest probability to any such absolute denial of an unusual phenomenon.

[1] [Peirce] 19me leçon. Auguste Compte (1798–1857), French philosopher; founder of sociology and philosophical Positivism.
[2] [*CP* eds.] In 1897 Salomon August Andrée attempted to fly over the polar regions in a balloon. He died in the attempt.
[3] Pierre-Simon de Laplace (1749–1827), French mathematician and astronomer.

from

Training in Reasoning

Since the vogue in this country of the Herbartian pedagogy,[1] . . . the old ideas which used to cluster about the phrase *Liberal Education* have become scattered. One of those ideas was that the matter of instruction in the common education was of less concern than the training of men's powers. The pedagogists of today sneer at this as an antiquated and crude conception. But for my part I continue to believe that the welfare of the commonwealth depends far less on the assent of all the citizens to any definite propositions—such, we will say, as the doctrine of the independence of the executive, legislative, and judiciary functions, which, after all are easily made handles for bosses, than it does in the power of recognizing the sort of thought and the sort of methods in which it will be well for the government and public opinion to put their trust. In the last analysis it comes to this, that the very focus and centre of common education should be placed in the art of thinking, *ad omnium methodorum principia viam habens* [which contains a path to the principles of all methods]. I do not know why a man should not devote himself to the training of his reasoning powers with as much assiduity as to corporal athletics.

There [are] a good many books that bear upon the subject. . . . But neither reading books nor working exercises—whether they be trivial or serious—will suffice to develop the reasoning powers. An analytical method of procedure is requisite which shall perfect one by one our performance of the different mental operations that enter into the business of inquiry. Now the mental operations concerned in reasoning are three. The first is Observation; the second is Experimentation; and the third is Habituation.

Observation consists of two parts which though theoretically they have much in common yet practically are of almost contrary natures. The first is a sort of subconscious induction, by which upon repeatedly reviewing an object of perception a certain element of it acquires great associational potency—that is, has a magnified tendency to call

From "Training in Reasoning" is from Peirce's 1898 Cambridge Lectures, reprinted here from *Reasoning and the Logic of Things,* edited by Kenneth Laine Ketner with an Introduction by Hillary Putnam and Kenneth Laine Ketner (Cambridge, Mass.: Harvard University Press, 1992).

[1] Johann Friedrich Herbart (1776–1841), German philosopher and educator, proposing that education could be a science, based on applied psychology. After some vogue in the United States, where it tended to become a rigid formalism, it was later supplanted by ideas of "progressive education," particularly as championed by John Dewey.

up other ideas. For example, I cast my eyes let us say upon an impressionist marine picture, one of those things in which the wet pastels are affixed in blotches nearly as large as the end of your little finger. It has a very disagreeable look and seems very meaningless. But as I gaze upon it I detect myself sniffing the salt-air and holding up my cheek to the sea breeze. That subconscious element of observation is I am strongly inclined to think the very most important of all the constituents of practical reasoning. The other part of observation consists in moulding in the upper consciousness a more or less skeletonized idea until it is felt to respond to [the] object of observation. This last element is quite indispensable if one is trying to form a theory of the object in hand, or even to describe it in words; but it goes a long way toward breaking down, denying, and pooh-poohing away, all the fineness of the subconscious observation. It is, therefore, a great art to be able to suppress it and put it into its proper place in cases where it attempts impertinent intermeddling. Do not allow yourself to be imposed upon by the egotism and conceit of the upper consciousness.

Observation may also be divided into three nearly independent genera according to the different natures of the elements observed. Namely, it may be directed to the qualities of objects or to experiential facts of relation, or to the relations between the parts of an image one's own phantasy has created. These are all observations, composed of the two elements I have mentioned. Nevertheless, they are so far different that in training one kind you do not necessarily strengthen either of the others in any sensible measure. It consequently becomes necessary to train each of these three modes of observation separately.

The qualities which we observe may, in the first place, be sensible qualities, colors, sounds, sizes, shapes, etc. Or, in the second place, they may be secondary, or emotional, qualities, such as the esthetic qualities. A training in discrimination of sensible qualities will affect the power of discriminating emotional qualities in no inconsiderable measure, and *vice versa*. Thirdly, there is observational discrimination of mental states, which in my experience has been found associated with sense discrimination much more frequently than I should have anticipated that it would be.

All these powers are most important in reasoning; and I need hardly say that just as a person who has not frequented a gymnasium or its equivalent can in a single month amazingly bring up the strength of a given set of muscles by means of systematic exercise, so a person whose powers of observational discrimination have been neglected can by analogous exercises attain results quite as surprising.

from

What Pragmatism Is (1905)

* * *

411. The writer of this article has been led by much experience to believe that every physicist, and every chemist, and, in short, every master in any department of experimental science, has had his mind moulded by his life in the laboratory to a degree that is little suspected. . . .

412. That laboratory life did not prevent the writer (who here and in what follows simply exemplifies the experimentalist type) from becoming interested in methods of thinking; and when he came to read metaphysics, although much of it seemed to him loosely reasoned and determined by accidental prepossessions, yet in the writings of some philosophers, especially Kant, Berkeley, and Spinoza, he sometimes came upon strains of thought that recalled the ways of thinking of the laboratory, so that he felt he might trust to them; all of which has been true of other laboratory-men.

Endeavoring, as a man of that type naturally would, to formulate what he so approved, he framed the theory that a **conception,** that is, the rational purport of a word or other expression, lies exclusively in its conceivable bearing upon the conduct of life; so that, since obviously nothing that might not result from experiment can have any direct bearing upon conduct, if one can define accurately all the conceivable experimental phenomena which the affirmation or denial of a concept could imply, one will have therein a complete definition of the concept, and **there is absolutely nothing more in it.**[1] For this doctrine he invented the name **pragmatism.** Some of his friends wished him to call it **practicism** or **practicalism** (perhaps on the ground that {*praktikos*} is better Greek than {*pragmatikos*}. But for one who had learned philosophy out of Kant, as the writer, along with nineteen out of every twenty experimentalists who have turned to philosophy, had done, and who still thought in Kantian terms most readily, *praktisch* and *pragmatisch* were as far apart as the two poles, the former belonging in a region of thought where no mind of the experimentalist type can ever make sure of solid ground under his feet, the latter expressing relation to some definite human purpose. Now

From "What Pragmatism Is" was first published in *The Monist,* vol. 15, 161–81 (1905). Reprinted from *Collected Papers* (Cambridge, Mass.: Harvard University Press, 1921), 5.411–27.
[1] This is commonly known as the "pragmatist maxim."

quite the most striking feature of the new theory was its recognition of an inseparable connection between rational cognition and rational purpose; and that consideration it was which determined the preference for the name pragmatism.

* * *

§3. Pragmaticism

414. After awaiting in vain, for a good many years, some particularly opportune conjuncture of circumstances that might serve to recommend his notions of the ethics of terminology, the writer has now, at last, dragged them in over head and shoulders, on an occasion when he has no specific proposal to offer nor any feeling but satisfaction at the course usage has run without any canons or resolutions of a congress. His word "pragmatism" has gained general recognition in a generalized sense that seems to argue power of growth and vitality. The famed psychologist, James, first took it up,[2] seeing that his "radical empiricism" substantially answered to the writer's definition of pragmatism, albeit with a certain difference in the point of view. Next, the admirably clear and brilliant thinker, Mr. Ferdinand C.S. Schiller, casting about for a more attractive name for the "anthropomorphism" of his *Riddle of the Sphinx,* lit, in that most remarkable paper of his on *Axioms as Postulates,*[3] upon the same designation "pragmatism," which in its original sense was in generic agreement with his own doctrine, for which he has since found the more appropriate specification "humanism," while he still retains "pragmatism" in a somewhat wider sense. So far all went happily. But at present, the word begins to be met with occasionally in the literary journals, where it gets abused in the merciless way that words have to expect when they fall into literary clutches. . . . So then, the writer, finding his bantling "pragmatism" so promoted, feels that it is time to kiss his child good-by and relinquish it to its higher destiny; while to serve the precise purpose of expressing the original definition, he begs to announce the birth of the word "pragmaticism," which is ugly enough to be safe from kidnappers.[4]

---

[2][Peirce] See his [William James's] *Pragmatism,* p. 47.

[3]Ferdinand C. S. Schiller (1864–1937), British philosopher; see his *Personal Idealism* (1902), ed. by H. Sturt, p. 63.

[4][Peirce] To show how recent the general use of the word "pragmatism" is, the writer may mention that, to the best of his belief, he never used it in copy for the press before today, except by particular request, in *Baldwin's Dictionary.* [See 1–4.] Toward the end of 1890, when this part of the *Century Dictionary* appeared, he did not deem that the word had sufficient status to appear in that work. [But see 13n.] But he has used it continually in philosophical conversation since, perhaps, the mid-seventies.

415. Much as the writer has gained from the perusal of what other pragmatists have written, he still thinks there is a decisive advantage in his original conception of the doctrine. From this original form every truth that follows from any of the other forms can be deduced, while some errors can be avoided into which other pragmatists have fallen. The original view appears, too, to be a more compact and unitary conception than the others. But its capital merit, in the writer's eyes, is that it more readily connects itself with a critical proof of its truth. . . .

416. The bare definition of pragmaticism could convey no satisfactory comprehension of it to the most apprehensive of minds, but requires the commentary to be given below. Moreover, this definition takes no notice of one or two other doctrines without the previous acceptance (or virtual acceptance) of which pragmaticism itself would be a nullity. They are included as a part of the pragmatism of Schiller, but the present writer prefers not to mingle different propositions. The preliminary propositions had better be stated forthwith.

The difficulty in doing this is that no formal list of them has ever been made. They might all be included under the vague maxim, "Dismiss make-believes." Philosophers of very diverse stripes propose that philosophy shall take its start from one or another state of mind in which no man, least of all a beginner in philosophy, actually is. One proposes that you shall begin by doubting everything, and says that there is only one thing that you cannot doubt, as if doubting were "as easy as lying." Another proposes that we should begin by observing "the first impressions of sense," forgetting that our very percepts are the results of cognitive elaboration.[5] But in truth, there is but one state of mind from which you can "set out," namely, the very state of mind in which you actually find yourself at the time you do "set out"—a state in which you are laden with an immense mass of cognition already formed, of which you cannot divest yourself if you would; and who knows whether, if you could, you would not have made all knowledge impossible to yourself? Do you call it doubting to write down on a piece of paper that you doubt? If so, doubt has nothing to do with any serious business. But do not make believe; if pedantry has not eaten all the reality out of you, recognize, as you must, that there is much that you do not doubt, in the least. Now that which you do not at all doubt, you must and do regard as infallible, absolute truth. Here breaks in Mr. Make Believe: "What! Do you mean to say that one is to believe what is not true, or that what a man does not doubt is ipso facto true?" No, but unless he can make a thing white and black at once, he has to regard what he does not doubt as absolutely true. Now you, *per hypothesiu,* are that man.

---

[5]Peirce is alluding to René Descartes and John Locke (above, page 281). See his "Concerning Certain Faculties Claimed for Man" and "The Fixation of Belief" in *The Essential Peirce,* vol. 1.

"But you tell me there are scores of things I do not doubt. I really cannot persuade myself that there is not some one of them about which I am mistaken." You are adducing one of your make-believe facts, which, even if it were established, would only go to show that doubt has a *limen,* that is, is only called into being by a certain finite stimulus. You only puzzle yourself by talking of this metaphysical "truth" and metaphysical "falsity," that you know nothing about. All you have any dealings with are your doubts and beliefs,[6] with the course of life that forces new beliefs upon you and gives you power to doubt old beliefs. If your terms "truth" and "falsity" are taken in such senses as to be definable in terms of doubt and belief and the course of experience (as for example they would be, if you were to define the "truth" as that to a belief in which belief would tend if it were to tend indefinitely toward absolute fixity), well and good: in that case, you are only talking about doubt and belief. But if by truth and falsity you mean something not definable in terms of doubt and belief in any way, then you are talking of entities of whose existence you can know nothing, and which Ockham's razor would clean shave off. Your problems would be greatly simplified, if, instead of saying that you want to know the "Truth," you were simply to say that you want to attain a state of belief unassailable by doubt.

417. Belief is not a momentary mode of consciousness; it is a habit of mind essentially enduring for some time, and mostly (at least) unconscious; and like other habits, it is (until it meets with some surprise that begins its dissolution) perfectly self-satisfied. Doubt is of an altogether contrary genus. It is not a habit, but the privation of a habit. Now a privation of a habit, in order to be anything at all, must be a condition of erratic activity that in some way must get superseded by a habit.

418. Among the things which the reader, as a rational person, does not doubt, is that he not merely has habits, but also can exert a measure of self-control over his future actions; which means, however, not that he can impart to them any arbitrarily assignable character, but, on the contrary, that a process of self-preparation will tend to impart to action (when the occasion for it shall arise), one fixed character, which is indicated and perhaps roughly measured by the absence (or slightness) of the feeling of self-reproach, which subsequent reflection will induce. Now, this subsequent reflection is part of the self-preparation for action on the next occasion. Consequently, there is a tendency, as

action is repeated again and again, for the action to approximate indefinitely toward the perfection of that fixed character, which would be marked by entire absence of self-reproach. The more closely this is approached, the less room for self-control there will be; and where no self-control is possible there will be no self-reproach.

419. These phenomena seem to be the fundamental characteristics which distinguish a rational being. Blame, in every case, appears to be a modification, often accomplished by a transference, or "projection," of the primary feeling of self-reproach. Accordingly, we never blame anybody for what had been beyond his power of previous self-control. Now, thinking is a species of conduct which is largely subject to self-control. In all their features (which there is no room to describe here), logical self-control is a perfect mirror of ethical self-control—unless it be rather a species under that genus. In accordance with this, what you cannot in the least help believing is not, justly speaking, wrong belief. In other words, for you it is the absolute truth. True, it is conceivable that what you cannot help believing today, you might find you thoroughly disbelieve tomorrow. But then there is a certain distinction between things you "cannot" do, merely in the sense that nothing stimulates you to the great effort and endeavors that would be required, and things you cannot do because in their own nature they are insusceptible of being put into practice. In every stage of your excogitations, there is something of which you can only say, "I cannot think otherwise," and your experientially based hypothesis is that the impossibility is of the second kind.

420. There is no reason why "thought," in what has just been said, should be taken in that narrow sense in which silence and darkness are favorable to thought. It should rather be understood as covering all rational life, so that an experiment shall be an operation of thought. Of course, that ultimate state of habit to which the action of self-control ultimately tends, where no room is left for further self-control, is, in the case of thought, the state of fixed belief, or perfect knowledge.

421. Two things here are all-important to assure oneself of and to remember. The first is that a person is not absolutely an individual. His thoughts are what he is "saying to himself," that is, is saying to that other self that is just coming into life in the flow of time. When one reasons, it is that critical self that one is trying to persuade; and all thought whatsoever is a sign, and is mostly of the nature of language. The second thing to remember is that the man's circle of society (however widely or narrowly this phrase may be understood), is a sort of loosely compacted person, in some respects of higher rank than the person of an indi-

[6][Peirce] It is necessary to say that "belief" is throughout used merely as the name of the contrary to doubt, without regard to grades of certainty nor to the nature of the proposition held for true, i.e., "believed."

vidual organism. It is these two things alone that render it possible for you—but only in the abstract, and in a Pickwickian sense[7]—to distinguish between absolute truth and what you do not doubt.

422. Let us now hasten to the exposition of pragmaticism itself. Here it will be convenient to imagine that somebody to whom the doctrine is new, but of rather preternatural perspicacity, asks questions of a pragmaticist. Everything that might give a dramatic illusion must be stripped off, so that the result will be a sort of cross between a dialogue and a catechism, but a good deal liker the latter—something rather painfully reminiscent of Mangnall's *Historical Questions*.[8]

Questioner: I am astounded at your definition of your pragmatism, because only last year I was assured by a person above all suspicion of warping the truth—himself a pragmatist—that your doctrine precisely was "that a conception is to be tested by its practical effects." You must surely, then, have entirely changed your definition very recently.

Pragmatist: If you will turn to Vols. VI and VII of the *Revue Philosophique,* or to the *Popular Science Monthly* for November 1877 and January 1878 [Papers No. IV and V], you will be able to judge for yourself whether the interpretation you mention was not then clearly excluded. The exact wording of the English enunciation, (changing only the first person into the second), was: "Consider what effects that might conceivably have practical bearing you conceive the object of your conception to have. Then your conception of those effects is the WHOLE of your conception of the object."[9]

Questioner: Well, what reason have you for asserting that this is so?

Pragmatist: That is what I specially desire to tell you. But the question had better be postponed until you clearly understand what those reasons profess to prove.

423. *Questioner:* What, then, is the *raison d'être* of the doctrine? What advantage is expected from it?

Pragmatist: It will serve to show that almost every proposition of ontological metaphysics is either meaningless gibberish[10]—one word being defined by other words, and they by still others, without any real conception ever being reached—or else is downright absurd; so that all such rubbish being swept away, what will remain of philosophy will be a series of problems capable of investigation by the observa-

tional methods of the true sciences—the truth about which can be reached without those interminable misunderstandings and disputes which have made the highest of the positive sciences a mere amusement for idle intellects, a sort of chess—idle pleasure its purpose, and reading out of a book its method. In this regard, pragmaticism is a species of prope-positivism. But what distinguishes it from other species is, first, its retention of a purified philosophy; secondly, its full acceptance of the main body of our instinctive beliefs; and thirdly, its strenuous insistence upon the truth of scholastic realism (or a close approximation to that, well-stated by the late Dr. Francis Ellingwood Abbot[11] in the Introduction to his *Scientific Theism*). So, instead of merely jeering at metaphysics, like other prope-positivists, whether by long drawn-out parodies or otherwise, the pragmaticist extracts from it a precious essence, which will serve to give life and light to cosmology and physics. At the same time, the moral applications of the doctrine are positive and potent; and there are many other uses of it not easily classed. On another occasion, instances may be given to show that it really has these effects.

424. *Questioner:* I hardly need to be convinced that your doctrine would wipe out metaphysics. Is it not as obvious that it must wipe out every proposition of science and everything that bears on the conduct of life? For you say that the only meaning that, for you, any assertion bears is that a certain experiment has resulted in a certain way: Nothing else but an experiment enters into the meaning. Tell me, then, how can an experiment, in itself, reveal anything more than that something once happened to an individual object and that subsequently some other individual event occurred?

Pragmatist: That question is, indeed, to the purpose—the purpose being to correct any misapprehensions of pragmaticism. You speak of an experiment in itself, emphasising "in itself." You evidently think of each experiment as isolated from every other. It has not, for example, occurred to you, one might venture to surmise, that every connected series of experiments constitutes a single collective experiment. What are the essential ingredients of an experiment? First, of course, an experimenter of flesh and blood. Secondly, a verifiable hypothesis. This is a proposition[12]

---

[7] An expression meant in an idiosyncratic or unusual way, after Mr. Pickwick, in Charles Dickens's *The Pickwick Papers* (1837).
[8] Peirce is most likely referring to *Historical Questions from the Bible, with Answers. Written for the Mendip Schools* (1798).
[9] Cf. *Collected Papers* 5.402.
[10] Cf. Carnap (below, page 978).

[11] Francis Ellingwood Abbot (1836–1903), American philosopher and Doctor of Divinity from Harvard; associated with Free Religionist movement, and forced to leave his Unitarian ministry in Dover, New Hampshire.
[12] [Peirce] The writer, like most English logicians, invariably uses the word proposition not as the Germans define their equivalent, Satz, as the language-expression of a judgment *(Urtheil),* but as that which is related to any assertion, whether mental and self-addressed or outwardly expressed, just as any possibility is related to its actualisation. The difficulty of the, at best, difficult problem of the essential nature of a Proposition has been increased, for the Germans, by their *Urtheil,* confounding, under one designation, the mental assertion with the assertible [cf. *Collected Papers* 2.315].

relating to the universe environing the experimenter, or to some well-known part of it and affirming or denying of this only some experimental possibility or impossibility. The third indispensable ingredient is a sincere doubt in the experimenter's mind as to the truth of that hypothesis.

Passing over several ingredients on which we need not dwell, the purpose, the plan, and the resolve, we come to the act of choice by which the experimenter singles out certain identifiable objects to be operated upon. The next is the external (or quasi-external) ACT by which he modifies those objects. Next, comes the subsequent reaction of the world upon the experimenter in a perception; and finally, his recognition of the teaching of the experiment. While the two chief parts of the event itself are the action and the reaction, yet the unity of essence of the experiment lies in its purpose and plan, the ingredients passed over in the enumeration.

425. Another thing: in representing the pragmaticist as making rational meaning to consist in an experiment (which you speak of as an event in the past), you strikingly fail to catch his attitude of mind. Indeed, it is not in an experiment, but in experimental phenomena, that rational meaning is said to consist. When an experimentalist speaks of a phenomenon, such as "Hall's phenomenon,"[13] "Zeemann's phenomenon"[14] and its modification, "Michelson's phenomenon,"[15] or "the chessboard phenomenon," he does not mean any particular event that did happen to somebody in the dead past, but what surely will happen to everybody in the living future who shall fulfill certain conditions. The phenomenon consists in the fact that when an experimentalist shall come to act according to a certain scheme that he has in mind, then will something else happen, and shatter

the doubts of sceptics, like the celestial fire upon the altar of Elijah.

426. And do not overlook the fact that the pragmaticist maxim says nothing of single experiments or of single experimental phenomena (for what is conditionally true in futuro can hardly be singular), but only speaks of general kinds of experimental phenomena. Its adherent does not shrink from speaking of general objects as real, since whatever is true represents a real. Now the laws of nature are true.

427. The rational meaning of every proposition lies in the future. How so? The meaning of a proposition is itself a proposition. Indeed, it is no other than the very proposition of which it is the meaning: it is a translation of it. But of the myriads of forms into which a proposition may be translated, what is that one which is to be called its very meaning? It is, according to the pragmaticist, that form in which the proposition becomes applicable to human conduct, not in these or those special circumstances, nor when one entertains this or that special design, but that form which is most directly applicable to self-control under every situation, and to every purpose. This is why he locates the meaning in future time; for future conduct is the only conduct that is subject to self-control. But in order that that form of the proposition which is to be taken as its meaning should be applicable to every situation and to every purpose upon which the proposition has any bearing, it must be simply the general description of all the experimental phenomena which the assertion of the proposition virtually predicts. For an experimental phenomenon is the fact asserted by the proposition that action of a certain description will have a certain kind of experimental result; and experimental results are the only results that can affect human conduct. No doubt, some unchanging idea may come to influence a man more than it had done; but only because some experience equivalent to an experiment has brought its truth home to him more intimately than before. Whenever a man acts purposively, he acts under a belief in some experimental phenomenon. Consequently, the sum of the experimental phenomena that a proposition implies makes up its entire bearing upon human conduct. Your question, then, of how a pragmaticist can attribute any meaning to any assertion other than that of a single occurrence is substantially answered. . . .

---

[13] The "Hall effect," discovered in 1879 by Edwin Herbert Hall, American physicist, designates the development of a transverse electrical field in a solid conductor when exposed to a magnetic field perpendicular to the current flow.

[14] Or the "Zeeman effect," named after Pieter Zeeman (1865–1943), awarded the Nobel Prize for physics in 1902 with Hendrik A. Lorentz. The Zeeman effect was the discovery that each of the lines of the spectrum of emitted light subjected to a magnetic field split into several lines of slightly different frequency.

[15] Refers to experiments with the interferometer, developed by Albert A. Michelson (1852–1931), for measuring the speed of light; cf. the Michelson-Morley experiment in 1887, proving that there was no movement of the earth relative to the celestial ether—hence proving that there was no ether.

Walt Whitman

1819–1892

Walt Whitman, though known almost exclusively for his poetry, began his career as a journalist with a strong interest in political reporting and cultural commentary. *Democratic Vistas* is his longest prose work, arguing vigorously for a pervasive connection between literature, primarily poetry, and the shaping of the character of individuals and their culture. Drawing inspiration from the great writers of the Romantic era, but especially from Ralph Waldo Emerson, Whitman, like Shelley, argues for a social, cultural, and political role for the poet as not just the "unacknowledged legislator" of mankind, but as the essential formative influence for shaping the future of democracy. While Hippolyte Taine (above, page 639) argues that the literary history of a nation reflects its character, Whitman, in a somewhat prophetic mode, argues that poetry is what *builds* the character of a civilization.

Like his poetry in *Leaves of Grass,* which expanded under the same title year after year, *Democratic Vistas* is an unconventional essay that lays out and elaborates upon three fundamental and connected points. The first is that the emergence of Democracy, not just as a political theory but as a cultural ideal, derives from the principle that the individual is, as he puts it, "a law, or series of laws unto himself," and must be taught to be self-governing. Drawing from Emerson's principle of self-reliance, and echoing Kant's essay, "What Is Enlightenment?" which defines that concept as the struggle to reach a state of true self-governance and autonomy, Whitman's doctrine of "personalism" posits that the modern age, the natural successor to feudalism, has no choice but to focus on the identity and potential of individuals, without discrimination, as the ultimate source of political legitimacy. The second point is that all of the arts, but especially poetry, are the primary training ground for self-discovery and growth, which must be attended to with more scrupulous attention than the two other conditions of democracy he identifies: the distrubution of economic wealth, and the legislative provision of a free and universal franchise. The role of poetry, for Whitman, lies in the cultural work of attempting to find unity in the midst of what he terms "irreconcilable interiors." The third point is that the reading of poetry is too important to be left as the leisure activity of what he sharply characterizes as "supercilious infidels" but should be, on the contrary, "a gymnast's struggle" to construe the hints and framework provided by poetic expression. As he puts it, "Not the book needs so much to be the complete thing, but the reader of the book does. That were to make a nation of supple and athletic minds, well-train'd, intuitive, used to depend on themselves and not on a few coteries of writers."

For this volume, *Democratic Vistas* has been considerably shortened by the removal of much material that focuses on particular observations about American cultural and political life in the aftermath of the Civil War. It is notable that despite Whitman's own urging that this essay, *Leaves of Grass,* and especially "Song of Myself" were his most important works, *Democratic Vistas* has frequently been left out of literary anthologies and editions of Whitman, perhaps because of its somewhat desultory style and thematic expansiveness. In the context of modern literary criticism and theory, however, Whitman's argument provides a very provocative link between the theorizing of Romantic writers such as Blake, Schiller, Coleridge, Shelley, and Emerson, and later movements in literary study that, in a practical vein, set about to create the schools and the pedagogy to teach poetry to all students, even when the teachers may not have been particularly sympathetic to Whitman.

The most convenient collected edition of Whitman's poetry and prose is *Walt Whitman: Complete Poetry and Collected Prose* (New York: The Library of America, 1982). For general guidance in the study of Whitman, the revised edition of Gay Wilson Allen's *The New Walt Whitman Handbook* (1975; reissued, 1986) is still extremely valuable. See also E. Fred Carlisle, *The Uncertain Self: Whitman's Drama of Identity* (1973); Paul Zweig, *Walt Whitman: The Making of the Poet* (1984); Betsy Erkkila, *Whitman the Political Poet* (1989); M. Jimmie Killingsworth, *Whitman's Poetry of the Body: Sexuality, Politics, and the Text* (1989); Ezra Greenspan, *Walt Whitman and the American Reader* (1990), and *The Cambridge Companion to Walt Whitman* (1995); Roger Asselineau, *The Evolution of Walt Whitman* (1999); Mark Maslan, *Whitman Possessed: Poetry, Sexuality, and Popular Authority* (2001); Ed Folsom, ed., *Whitman East and West: New Contexts for Reading Whitman* (2002).

Democratic Vistas (1871)

As the greatest lessons of Nature through the universe are perhaps the lessons of variety and freedom, the same present the greatest lessons also in New World politics and progress. If a man were ask'd, for instance, the distinctive points contrasting modern European and American political and other life with the old Asiatic cultus, as lingering-bequeath'd yet in China and Turkey, he might find the amount of them in John Stuart Mill's profound essay on Liberty[1] in the future, where he demands two main constituents, or sub-strata, for a truly grand nationality—1st, a large variety of character—and 2d, full play for human nature to expand itself in numberless and even conflicting directions. . . .

For our New World I consider far less important for what it has done, or what it is, than for results to come. Sole among nationalities, these States have assumed the task to put in forms of lasting power and practicality . . . the theory of development and perfection by voluntary standards, and self-reliance. Who else, indeed, except the United States, in history, so far, have accepted in unwitting faith, . . . [to] stand, act upon, and go security for, these things? . . .

I will not gloss over the appalling dangers of universal suffrage in the United States. In fact, it is to admit and face these dangers I am writing. To him or her within whose thought rages the battle, advancing, retreating, between democracy's convictions, aspirations, and the people's crudeness, vice, caprices, I mainly write this essay. I shall use the words America and democracy as convertible terms. Not an ordinary one is the issue. The United States are destined either to surmount the gorgeous history of feudalism, or else prove the most tremendous failure of time. . . .

I say that democracy can never prove itself beyond cavil, until it founds and luxuriantly grows its own forms of art, poems, schools, theology, displacing all that exists, or that has been produced anywhere in the past, under opposite influences. It is curious to me that while so many voices, pens, minds, in the press, lecture-rooms, in our Congress, &c., are discussing intellectual topics, pecuniary dangers, legislative problems, the suffrage, tariff and labor questions, and the various business and benevolent needs of America, with propositions, remedies, often worth deep attention, there is one need, a hiatus the profoundest, that no eye seems to perceive, no

---

Democratic Vistas was completed in 1870, was first published in 1871, and was included in Whitman's *Complete Prose Works* (1892). The original essay includes prose written at several different times. This selection indicates with ellipses where material has been removed. For a convenient full edition see Walt Whitman, *Complete Poetry and Collected Prose* (New York: Library of America, 1982). Whitman's spelling has been retained.

[1]John Stuart Mill (1806–1873), English philosopher and writer, author of *On Liberty* (1859).

voice to state. Our fundamental want to-day in the United States, with closest, amplest reference to present conditions, and to the future, is of a class, and the clear idea of a class, of native authors, literatures, far different, far higher in grade than any yet known, sacerdotal, modern, fit to cope with our occasions, lands, permeating the whole mass of American mentality, taste, belief, breathing into it a new breath of life. . . .

View'd, to-day, from a point of view sufficiently overarching, the problem of humanity all over the civilized world is social and religious, and is to be finally met and treated by literature. The priest departs, the divine literatus comes. Never was anything more wanted than, to-day, and here in the States, the poet of the modern is wanted, or the great literatus of the modern. At all times, perhaps, the central point in any nation, and that whence it is itself really sway'd the most, and whence it sways others, is its national literature, specially its archetypal poems. Above all previous lands, a great original literature is surely to become the justification and reliance, (in some respects the sole reliance,) of American democracy.

Few are aware how the great literature penetrates all, gives hue to all, shapes aggregates and individuals, and, after subtle ways, with irresistible power, constructs, sustains, demolishes at will. Why tower, in reminiscence, above all the nations of the earth, two special lands, petty in themselves, yet inexpressibly gigantic, beautiful, columnar? Immortal Judah lives, and Greece immortal lives, in a couple of poems.

Nearer than this. It is not generally realized, but it is true, as the genius of Greece, and all the sociology, personality, politics and religion of those wonderful states, resided in their literature or esthetics, that what was afterwards the main support of European chivalry, the feudal, ecclesiastical, dynastic world over there—forming its osseous structure, holding it together for hundreds, thousands of years, preserving its flesh and bloom, giving it form, decision, rounding it out, and so saturating it in the conscious and unconscious blood, breed, belief, and intuitions of men, that it still prevails powerful to this day, in defiance of the mighty changes of time—was its literature, permeating to the very marrow, especially that major part, its enchanting songs, ballads, and poems. . . .

In short, as, though it may not be realized, it is strictly true, that a few first-class poets, philosophs, and authors, have substantially settled and given status to the entire religion, education, law, sociology, &c., of the hitherto civilized world, by tinging and often creating the atmospheres out of which they have arisen, such also must stamp, and more than ever stamp, the interior and real democratic construction of this American continent, to-day, and days to come. . . . [I]n the civilization of to-day it is undeniable that, over all the arts, literature dominates, serves beyond

all—shapes the character of church and school—or, at any rate, is capable of doing so. Including the literature of science, its scope is indeed unparallel'd.

* * *

For my part, I would alarm and caution even the political and business reader, and to the utmost extent, against the prevailing delusion that the establishment of free political institutions, and plentiful intellectual smartness, with general good order, physical plenty, industry, &c., (desirable and precious advantages as they all are,) do, of themselves, determine and yield to our experiment of democracy the fruitage of success. With such advantages at present fully, or almost fully, possess'd—the Union just issued, victorious, from the struggle with the only foes it need ever fear, (namely, those within itself, the interior ones,) and with unprecedented materialistic advancement—society, in these States, is canker'd, crude, superstitious, and rotten. Political, or law-made society is, and private, or voluntary society, is also. In any vigor, the element of the moral conscience, the most important, the verteber to State or man, seems to me either entirely lacking, or seriously enfeebled or ungrown. . . . In vain have we annex'd Texas, California, Alaska, and reach north for Canada and south for Cuba. It is as if we were somehow being endow'd with a vast and more and more thoroughly-appointed body, and then left with little or no soul.

* * *

First, let us see what we can make out of a brief, general, sentimental consideration of political democracy, and whence it has arisen, with regard to some of its current features, as an aggregate, and as the basic structure of our future literature and authorship. We shall, it is true, quickly and continually find the origin-idea of the singleness of man, individualism, asserting itself, and cropping forth, even from the opposite ideas. But the mass, or lump character, for imperative reasons, is to be ever carefully weigh'd, borne in mind, and provided for. Only from it, and from its proper regulation and potency, comes the other, comes the chance of individualism. The two are contradictory, but our task is to reconcile them.[2]

---

[2][Whitman] The question hinted here is one which time only can answer. Must not the virtue of modern Individualism, continually enlarging, usurping all, seriously affect, perhaps keep down entirely, in America, the like of the ancient virtue of Patriotism, the fervid and absorbing love of general country? I have no doubt myself that the two will merge, and will mutually profit and brace each other, and that from them a greater product, a third, will arise. But I feel that at present they and their oppositions form a serious problem and paradox in the United States.

The political history of the past may be summ'd up as having grown out of what underlies the words, order, safety, caste, and especially out of the need of some prompt deciding authority, and of cohesion at all cost. Leaping time, we come to the period within the memory of people now living, when, as from some lair where they had slumber'd long, accumulating wrath, sprang up and are yet active, (1790, and on even to the present, 1870,) those noisy eructations, destructive iconoclasms, a fierce sense of wrongs, amid which moves the form, well known in modern history, in the old world, stain'd with much blood, and mark'd by savage reactionary clamors and demands. These bear, mostly, as on one inclosing point of need.

For after the rest is said . . . it remains to bring forward and modify everything else with the idea of that Something a man is, (last precious consolation of the drudging poor,) standing apart from all else, divine in his own right, and a woman in hers, sole and untouchable by any canons of authority, or any rule derived from precedent, state-safety, the acts of legislatures, or even from what is called religion, modesty, or art. . . . This idea of perfect individualism it is indeed that deepest tinges and gives character to the idea of the aggregate. For it is mainly or altogether to serve independent separatism that we favor a strong generalization, consolidation. As it is to give the best vitality and freedom to the rights of the States, (every bit as important as the right of nationality, the union,) that we insist on the identity of the Union at all hazards.

The purpose of democracy—supplanting old belief in the necessary absoluteness of establish'd dynastic rulership, temporal, ecclesiastical, and scholastic, as furnishing the only security against chaos, crime, and ignorance—is, . . . to illustrate, at all hazards, this doctrine or theory that man, properly train'd in sanest, highest freedom, may and must become a law, and series of laws, unto himself, surrounding and providing for, not only his own personal control, but all his relations to other individuals, and to the State; and that, while other theories, as in the past histories of nations, have proved wise enough, and indispensable perhaps for their conditions, this, as matters now stand in our civilized world, is the only scheme worth working from, as warranting results like those of Nature's laws, reliable, when once establish'd, to carry on themselves. . . .

As to the political section of Democracy, which introduces and breaks ground for further and vaster sections, few probably are the minds, even in these republican States, that fully comprehend the aptness of that phrase, "THE GOVERNMENT OF THE PEOPLE, BY THE PEOPLE, FOR THE PEOPLE," which we inherit from the lips of Abraham Lincoln; a formula whose verbal shape is homely wit, but

whose scope includes both the totality and all minutiae of the lesson.

The People! Like our huge earth itself, which, to ordinary scansion, is full of vulgar contradictions and offence, man, viewed in the lump, displeases, and is a constant puzzle and affront to the merely educated classes. The rare, cosmical, artist-mind, lit with the Infinite, alone confronts his manifold and oceanic qualities—but taste, intelligence and culture, (so-called,) have been against the masses, and remain so. There is plenty of glamour about the most damnable crimes and hoggish meannesses, special and general, of the feudal and dynastic world over there, with its personnel of lords and queens and courts, so well-dress'd and so handsome. But the People are ungrammatical, untidy, and their sins gaunt and ill-bred.

Literature, strictly consider'd, has never recognized the People, and, whatever may be said, does not today. Speaking generally, the tendencies of literature, as hitherto pursued, have been to make mostly critical and querulous men. It seems as if, so far, there were some natural repugnance between a literary and professional life, and the rude rank spirit of the democracies. There is, in later literature, a treatment of benevolence, a charity business, rife enough it is true; but I know nothing more rare, even in this country, than a fit scientific estimate and reverent appreciation of the People—of their measureless wealth of latent power and capacity, their vast, artistic contrasts of lights and shades—with, in America, their entire reliability in emergencies, and a certain breadth of historic grandeur, of peace or war, far surpassing all the vaunted samples of book-heroes, or any *haut-ton* coteries, in all the records of the world.

* * *

I myself see clearly enough the crude, defective streaks in all the strata of the common people; the specimens and vast collections of the ignorant, the credulous, the unfit and uncouth, the incapable, and the very low and poor. The eminent person just mention'd sneeringly asks whether we expect to elevate and improve a nation's politics by absorbing such morbid collections and qualities therein.[3] The point is a formidable one, and there will doubtless always be num-

[3]Whitman refers to Thomas Carlyle (1795–1881), English writer, specifically, his essay, "Shooting Niagara." Carlyle was extremely skeptical of the value of democracy (as compared with what he and Whitman characterize as feudalism) and was particularly ascerbic on the subject of the American Civil War.

bers of solid and reflective citizens who will never get over it. Our answer is general, and is involved in the scope and letter of this essay. We believe the ulterior object of political and all other government, . . . to be . . . not merely to rule, to repress disorder, &c., but to develop, to open up to cultivation, to encourage the possibilities of all beneficent and manly outcroppage, and of that aspiration for independence, and the pride and self-respect latent in all characters. . . .

I say the mission of government, henceforth, in civilized lands, is not repression alone, and not authority alone, not even of law, nor by that favorite standard of the eminent writer, the rule of the best men, the born heroes and captains of the race, (as if such ever, or one time out of a hundred, get into the big places, elective or dynastic)—but higher than the highest arbitrary rule, to train communities through all their grades, beginning with individuals and ending there again, to rule themselves. . . .

. . . For it is not that democracy is of exhaustive account, in itself. Perhaps, indeed, it is, (like Nature,) of no account in itself. It is that, as we see, it is the best, . . . trainer, for the million, not for grand material personalities only, but for immortal souls. To be a voter with the rest is not so much; and this, like every institute, will have its imperfections. But to become an enfranchised man, and now, impediments removed, to stand and start without humiliation, and equal with the rest; to commence, or have the road clear'd to commence, the grand experiment of development, whose end, (perhaps requiring several generations,) may be the forming of a full-grown man or woman—that is something. . . .

We do not, (at any rate I do not,) put it either on the ground that the People, the masses, even the best of them, are, in their latent or exhibited qualities, essentially sensible and good—nor on the ground of their rights; but that good or bad, rights or no rights, the democratic formula is the only safe and preservative one for coming times. We endow the masses with the suffrage for their own sake, no doubt; then, perhaps still more, from another point of view, for community's sake. Leaving the rest to the sentimentalists, we present freedom as sufficient in its scientific aspect, cold as ice, reasoning, deductive, clear and passionless as crystal.

Democracy too is law, and of the strictest, amplest kind. Many suppose, (and often in its own ranks the error,) that it means a throwing aside of law, and running riot. But, briefly, it is the superior law, not alone that of physical force, the body, which, adding to, it supersedes with that of the spirit. . . . Nor is the esthetic point, always an important one, without fascination for highest aiming souls. The common ambition strains for elevations, to become some privileged exclusive. The master sees greatness and health in being part of the mass; nothing will do as well as common

ground. Would you have in yourself the divine, vast, general law? Then merge yourself in it.

And, topping democracy, this most alluring record, that it alone can bind, and ever seeks to bind, all nations, all men, of however various and distant lands, into a brotherhood, a family. It is the old, yet ever-modern dream of earth, out of her eldest and her youngest, her fond philosophers and poets. Not that half only, individualism, which isolates. There is another half, which is adhesiveness or love, that fuses, ties and aggregates, making the races comrades, and fraternizing all. Both are to be vitalized by religion, (sole worthiest elevator of man or State,) breathing into the proud, material tissues, the breath of life. For I say at the core of democracy, finally, is the religious element. All the religions, old and new, are there. Nor may the scheme step forth, clothed in resplendent beauty and command, till these, bearing the best, the latest fruit, the spiritual, shall fully appear.

A portion of our pages we might indite with reference toward Europe, especially the British part of it, more than our own land, perhaps not absolutely needed for the home reader. But the whole question hangs together, and fastens and links all peoples. The liberalist of to-day has this advantage over antique or medieval times, that his doctrine seeks not only to individualize but to universalize. The great word Solidarity has arisen. Of all dangers to a nation, as things exist in our day, there can be no greater one than having certain portions of the people set off from the rest by a line drawn—they not privileged as others, but degraded, humiliated, made of no account. . . .

And, truly, whatever may be said in the way of abstract argument, for or against the theory of a wider democratizing of institutions in any civilized country, much trouble might well be saved to all European lands by recognizing this palpable fact, (for a palpable fact it is,) that some form of such democratizing is about the only resource now left. That, or chronic dissatisfaction continued, mutterings which grow annually louder and louder, till, in due course, and pretty swiftly in most cases, the inevitable crisis, crash, dynastic ruin. Anything worthy to be call'd statesmanship in the Old World, . . . does not debate to-day whether to hold on, attempting to lean back and monarchize, or to look forward and democratize—but how, and in what degree and part, most prudently to democratize.

* * *

The true gravitation-hold of liberalism in the United States will be a more universal ownership of property, general homesteads, general comfort—a vast, intertwining reticulation of wealth. As the human frame, or, indeed, any object in this manifold universe, is best kept together by the simple miracle of its own cohesion, and the necessity, exercise and profit thereof, so a great and varied nationality, occupying millions of square miles, were firmest held and knit by the principle of the safety and endurance of the aggregate of its middling property owners. So that, from another point of view, ungracious as it may sound, and a paradox after what we have been saying, democracy looks with suspicious, ill-satisfied eye upon the very poor, the ignorant, and on those out of business. She asks for men and women with occupations, well-off, owners of houses and acres, and with cash in the bank—and with some cravings for literature, too; and must have them, and hastens to make them. Luckily, the seed is already well-sown, and has taken ineradicable root. . . .

Political democracy, as it exists and practically works in America, with all its threatening evils, supplies a training-school for making first-class men. It is life's gymnasium, not of good only, but of all. We try often, though we fall back often. A brave delight, fit for freedom's athletes, fills these arenas, and fully satisfies, out of the action in them, irrespective of success. Whatever we do not attain, we at any rate attain the experiences of the fight, the hardening of the strong campaign, and throb with currents of attempt at least. Time is ample. Let the victors come after us. Not for nothing does evil play its part among us. Judging from the main portions of the history of the world, so far, justice is always in jeopardy, peace walks amid hourly pitfalls, and of slavery, misery, meanness, the craft of tyrants and the credulity of the populace, in some of their protean forms, no voice can at any time say, They are not. The clouds break a little, and the sun shines out—but soon and certain the lowering darkness falls again, as if to last forever. Yet is there an immortal courage and prophecy in every sane soul that cannot, must not, under any circumstances, capitulate. *Vive*, the attack—the perennial assault! *Vive*, the unpopular cause—the spirit that audaciously aims—the never-abandon'd efforts, pursued the same amid opposing proofs and precedents.

Once, before the war, (Alas! I dare not say how many times the mood has come!) I, too, was fill'd with doubt and gloom. A foreigner, an acute and good man, had impressively said to me, that day—putting in form, indeed, my own observations: "I have travel'd much in the United States, and watch'd their politicians, and listen'd to the speeches of the candidates, and read the journals, and gone into the public houses, and heard the unguarded talk of men. And I have found your vaunted America honeycomb'd from top to toe with infidelism, even to itself and its own pro-

gramme. I have mark'd the brazen hell-faces of secession and slavery gazing defiantly from all the windows and doorways. I have everywhere found, primarily, thieves and scalliwags arranging the nominations to offices, and sometimes filling the offices themselves. I have found the north just as full of bad stuff as the south. Of the holders of public office in the Nation or the States or their municipalities, I have found that not one in a hundred has been chosen by any spontaneous selection of the outsiders, the people, but all have been nominated and put through by little or large caucuses of the politicians, and have got in by corrupt rings and electioneering, not capacity or desert. I have noticed how the millions of sturdy farmers and mechanics are thus the helpless supplejacks of comparatively few politicians. And I have noticed more and more, the alarming spectacle of parties usurping the government, and openly and shamelessly wielding it for party purposes."

Sad, serious, deep truths. Yet are there other, still deeper, amply confronting, dominating truths. Over those politicians and great and little rings, and over all their insolence and wiles, and over the powerfulest parties, looms a power, too sluggish may-be, but ever holding decisions and decrees in hand, ready, with stern process, to execute them as soon as plainly needed—and at times, indeed, summarily crushing to atoms the mightiest parties, even in the hour of their pride.

In saner hours far different are the amounts of these things from what, at first sight, they appear. Though it is no doubt important who is elected governor, mayor, or legislator, (and full of dismay when incompetent or vile ones get elected, as they sometimes do,) there are other, quieter contingencies, infinitely more important. Shams, &c., will always be the show, like ocean's scum; enough, if waters deep and clear make up the rest. Enough, that while the piled embroider'd shoddy gaud and fraud spreads to the superficial eye, the hidden warp and weft are genuine, and will wear forever. Enough, in short, that the race, the land which could raise such as the late rebellion, could also put it down.

The average man of a land at last only is important. He, in these States, remains immortal owner and boss, deriving good uses, somehow, out of any sort of servant in office, even the basest; (certain universal requisites, and their settled regularity and protection, being first secured,) a nation like ours, in a sort of geological formation state, trying continually new experiments, choosing new delegations, is not served by the best men only, but sometimes more by those that provoke it—by the combats they arouse. Thus national rage, fury, discussion, &c., better than content. Thus, also, the warning signals, invaluable for after times.

* * *

Then still the thought returns, (like the thread-passage in overtures,) giving the key and echo to these pages. When I pass to and fro, different latitudes, different seasons, beholding the crowds of the great cities, New York, Boston, Philadelphia, Cincinnati, Chicago, St. Louis, San Francisco, New Orleans, Baltimore—when I mix with these interminable swarms of alert, turbulent, good-natured, independent citizens, mechanics, clerks, young persons—at the idea of this mass of men, so fresh and free, so loving and so proud, a singular awe falls upon me. I feel, with dejection and amazement, that among our geniuses and talented writers or speakers, few or none have yet really spoken to this people, created a single image-making work for them, or absorb'd the central spirit and the idiosyncrasies which are theirs—and which, thus, in highest ranges, so far remain entirely uncelebrated, unexpress'd.

Dominion strong is the body's; dominion stronger is the mind's. What has fill'd, and fills to-day our intellect, our fancy, furnishing the standards therein, is yet foreign. The great poems, Shakspere included, are poisonous to the idea of the pride and dignity of the common people, the lifeblood of democracy. The models of our literature, as we get it from other lands, ultramarine, have had their birth in courts, and bask'd and grown in castle sunshine; all smells of princes' favors. Of workers of a certain sort, we have, indeed, plenty, contributing after their kind; many elegant, many learn'd, all complacent. But touch'd by the national test, or tried by the standards of democratic personality, they wither to ashes. I say I have not seen a single writer, artist, lecturer, or what not, that has confronted the voiceless but ever erect and active, pervading, underlying will and typic aspiration of the land, in a spirit kindred to itself. Do you call those genteel little creatures American poets? Do you term that perpetual, pistareen, paste-pot work, American art, American drama, taste, verse? I think I hear, echoed as from some mountain-top afar in the west, the scornful laugh of the Genius of these States.

Democracy, in silence, biding its time, ponders its own ideals, not of literature and art only—not of men only, but of women. The idea of the women of America, (extricated from this daze, this fossil and unhealthy air which hangs about the word lady,) develop'd, raised to become the robust equals, workers, and, it may be, even practical and political deciders with the men—greater than man, we may admit, through their divine maternity, always their towering, emblematical attribute—but great, at any rate, as man, in all departments; or, rather, capable of being so, soon as they realize it, and can bring themselves to give up

toys and fictions, and launch forth, as men do, amid real, independent, stormy life.

Then, as towards our thought's finalè, (and, in that, overarching the true scholar's lesson,) we have to say there can be no complete or epical presentation of democracy in the aggregate, or anything like it, at this day, because its doctrines will only be effectually incarnated in any one branch, when, in all, their spirit is at the root and centre. Far, far, indeed, stretch, in distance, our Vistas! How much is still to be disentangled, freed! How long it takes to make this American world see that it is, in itself, the final authority and reliance!

* * *

I submit, therefore, that the fruition of democracy, . . . resides altogether in the future. As, under any profound and comprehensive view of the gorgeous-composite feudal world, we see in it, through the long ages and cycles of ages, the results of a deep, integral, human and divine principle, or fountain, from which issued laws, ecclesia, manners, institutes, costumes, personalities, poems, (hitherto unequall'd,) faithfully partaking of their source, and indeed only arising either to betoken it, or to furnish parts of that varied-flowing display, whose centre was one and absolute—so, long ages hence, shall the due historian or critic make at least an equal retrospect, an equal history for the democratic principle. It too must be adorn'd, credited with its results—then, when it, with imperial power, through amplest time, has dominated mankind—has been the source and test of all the moral, esthetic, social, political, and religious expressions and institutes of the civilized world—has begotten them in spirit and in form, and has carried them to its own unprecedented heights—has had, (it is possible,) monastics and ascetics, more numerous, more devout than the monks and priests of all previous creeds—has sway'd the ages with a breadth and rectitude tallying Nature's own—has fashion'd, systematized, and triumphantly finish'd and carried out, in its own interest, and with unparallel'd success, a new earth and a new man.

* * *

We have frequently printed the word Democracy. Yet I cannot too often repeat that it is a word the real gist of which still sleeps, quite unawaken'd, notwithstanding the resonance and the many angry tempests out of which its syllables have come, from pen or tongue. It is a great word, whose history, I suppose, remains unwritten, because that history has yet to be enacted. It is, in some sort, younger brother of another great and often-used word, Nature, whose history also waits unwritten. As I perceive, the tendencies of our day, in the States, (and I entirely respect them,) are toward those vast and sweeping movements, influences, moral and physical, of humanity, now and always current over the planet, on the scale of the impulses of the elements. Then it is also good to reduce the whole matter to the consideration of a single self, a man, a woman, on permanent grounds. Even for the treatment of the universal, in politics, metaphysics, or anything, sooner or later we come down to one single, solitary soul.

There is, in sanest hours, a consciousness, a thought that rises, independent, lifted out from all else, calm, like the stars, shining eternal. This is the thought of identity—yours for you, whoever you are, as mine for me. Miracle of miracles, beyond statement, most spiritual and vaguest of earth's dreams, yet hardest basic fact, and only entrance to all facts. In such devout hours, in the midst of the significant wonders of heaven and earth, (significant only because of the Me in the centre,) creeds, conventions, fall away and become of no account before this simple idea. Under the luminousness of real vision, it alone takes possession, takes value. Like the shadowy dwarf in the fable, once liberated and look'd upon, it expands over the whole earth, and spreads to the roof of heaven. The quality of BEING, in the object's self, according to its own central idea and purpose, and of growing therefrom and thereto—not criticism by other standards, and adjustments thereto—is the lesson of Nature. True, the full man wisely gathers, culls, absorbs; but if, engaged disproportionately in that, he slights or overlays the precious idiocrasy and special nativity and intention that he is, the man's self, the main thing, is a failure, however wide his general cultivation. Thus, in our times, refinement and delicatesse are not only attended to sufficiently, but threaten to eat us up, like a cancer. Already, the democratic genius watches, ill-pleased, these tendencies. Provision for a little healthy rudeness, savage virtue, justification of what one has in one's self, whatever it is, is demanded. Negative qualities, even deficiencies, would be a relief. Singleness and normal simplicity and separation, amid this more and more complex, more and more artificialized state of society—how pensively we yearn for them! how we would welcome their return!

* * *

America has yet morally and artistically originated nothing. She seems singularly unaware that the models of persons, books, manners, &c., appropriate for former conditions and for European lands, are but exiles and exotics here. No current of her life, as shown on the surfaces of what is au-

thoritatively called her society, accepts or runs into social or esthetic democracy; but all the currents set squarely against it. Never, in the Old World, was thoroughly upholster'd exterior appearance and show, mental and other, built entirely on the idea of caste, and on the sufficiency of mere outside acquisition—never were glibness, verbal intellect, more the test, the emulation—more loftily elevated as head and sample—than they are on the surface of our republican States this day. The writers of a time hint the mottoes of its gods. The word of the modern, say these voices, is the word Culture. We find ourselves abruptly in close quarters with the enemy. This word Culture, or what it has come to represent, involves, by contrast, our whole theme, and has been, indeed, the spur, urging us to engagement. Certain questions arise. As now taught, accepted and carried out, are not the processes of culture rapidly creating a class of supercilious infidels, who believe in nothing? Shall a man lose himself in countless masses of adjustments, and be so shaped with reference to this, that, and the other, that the simply good and healthy and brave parts of him are reduced and clipp'd away, like the bordering of box in a garden? You can cultivate corn and roses and orchards—but who shall cultivate the mountain peaks, the ocean, and the tumbling gorgeousness of the clouds? Lastly—is the readily-given reply that culture only seeks to help, systematize, and put in attitude, the elements of fertility and power, a conclusive reply? I do not so much object to the name, or word, but I should certainly insist, for the purposes of these States, on a radical change of category, in the distribution of precedence. I should demand a programme of culture, drawn out, not for a single class alone, or for the parlors or lecture-rooms, but with an eye to practical life, the west, the working-men, the facts of farms and jack-planes and engineers, and of the broad range of the women also of the middle and working strata, and with reference to the perfect equality of women, and of a grand and powerful motherhood. I should demand of this programme or theory a scope generous enough to include the widest human area. It must have for its spinal meaning the formation of a typical personality of character, eligible to the uses of the high average of men—and not restricted by conditions ineligible to the masses. The best culture will always be that of the manly and courageous instincts, and loving perceptions, and of self-respect—aiming to form, over this continent, an idiocrasy of universalism, which, true child of America, will bring joy to its mother, returning to her in her own spirit, recruiting myriads of offspring, able, natural, perceptive, tolerant, devout believers in her, America, and with some definite instinct why and for what she has arisen, most vast, most formidable of historic births, and is, now and here, with wonderful step, journeying through Time.

The problem, as it seems to me, presented to the New World, is, under permanent law and order, and after preserving cohesion, (ensemble-Individuality,) at all hazards, to vitalize man's free play of special Personalism, recognizing in it something that calls ever more to be consider'd, fed, and adopted as the substratum for the best that belongs to us, (government indeed is for it,) including the new esthetics of our future.

*   *   *

What, however, do we more definitely mean by New World literature? Are we not doing well enough here already? Are not the United States this day busily using, working, more printer's type, more presses, than any other country? uttering and absorbing more publications than any other? Do not our publishers fatten quicker and deeper? (helping themselves, under shelter of a delusive and sneaking law, or rather absence of law, to most of their forage, poetical, pictorial, historical, romantic, even comic, without money and without price—and fiercely resisting the timidest proposal to pay for it.) Many will come under this delusion—but my purpose is to dispel it. I say that a nation may hold and circulate rivers and oceans of very readable print, journals, magazines, novels, library-books, "poetry," &c.—such as the States to-day possess and circulate—of unquestionable aid and value—hundreds of new volumes annually composed and brought out here, respectable enough, indeed unsurpass'd in smartness and erudition—with further hundreds, or rather millions, (as by free forage or theft aforemention'd,) also thrown into the market—and yet, all the while, the said nation, land, strictly speaking, may possess no literature at all.

Repeating our inquiry, what, then, do we mean by real literature? especially the democratic literature of the future? Hard questions to meet. The clues are inferential, and turn us to the past. At best, we can only offer suggestions, comparisons, circuits.

It must still be reiterated, as, for the purpose of these memoranda, the deep lesson of history and time, that all else in the contributions of a nation or age, through its politics, materials, heroic personalities, military eclat, &c., remains crude, and defers, in any close and thorough-going estimate, until vitalized by national, original archetypes in literature. They only put the nation in form, finally tell anything—prove, complete anything—perpetuate anything. Without doubt, some of the richest and most powerful and populous communities of the antique world, and some of the grandest personalities and events, have, to after and present times, left themselves entirely unbequeath'd. Doubtless, greater than any that have come down to us, were among those lands, heroisms, persons, that have not come down to us at all, even by name, date, or location. Others have arrived safely, as from voyages over wide, century-stretching seas. The little ships, the miracles that have buoy'd them, and by incredible chances safely convey'd them, (or the best of them, their meaning and essence,) over long wastes, darkness, lethargy, ignorance, &c., have been a few inscriptions—a few immortal compositions, small in size, yet compassing what measureless values of reminiscence, contemporary portraitures, manners, idioms and beliefs, with deepest inference, hint and thought, to tie and touch forever the old, new body, and the old, new soul! These! and still these! bearing the freight so dear—dearer than pride—dearer than love. All the best experience of humanity, folded, saved, freighted to us here. Some of these tiny ships we call Old and New Testament, Homer, Eschylus, Plato, Juvenal, &c. Precious minims! I think, if we were forced to choose, rather than have you, and the likes of you, and what belongs to, and has grown of you, blotted out and gone, we could better afford, appalling as that would be, to lose all actual ships, this day fasten'd by wharf, or floating on wave, and see them, with all their cargoes, scuttled and sent to the bottom.

Gather'd by geniuses of city, race or age, and put by them in highest of art's forms, namely, the literary form, the peculiar combinations and the outshows of that city, age, or race, its particular modes of the universal attributes and passions, its faiths, heroes, lovers and gods, wars, traditions, struggles, crimes, emotions, joys, (or the subtle spirit of these,) having been pass'd on to us to illumine our own selfhood, and its experiences—what they supply, indispensable and highest, if taken away, nothing else in all the world's boundless storehouses could make up to us, or ever again return.

For us, along the great highways of time, those monuments stand—those forms of majesty and beauty. For us those beacons burn through all the nights. Unknown Egyptians, graving hieroglyphs; Hindus, with hymn and apothegm and endless epic; Hebrew prophet, with spirituality, as in flashes of lightning, conscience like red-hot iron, plaintive songs and screams of vengeance for tyrannies and enslavement; Christ, with bent head, brooding love and peace, like a dove; Greek, creating eternal shapes of physical and esthetic proportion; Roman, lord of satire, the sword, and the codex;—of the figures, some far off and veil'd, others nearer and visible; Dante, stalking with lean form, nothing but fibre, not a grain of superfluous flesh; Angelo, and the great painters, architects, musicians; rich Shakspere, luxuriant as the sun, artist and singer of feudalism in its sunset, with all the gorgeous colors, owner thereof, and using them at will; and so to such as German Kant and Hegel, where they, though near us, leaping over the ages, sit again, impassive, imperturbable, like the Egyptian gods. Of these, and the like of these, is it too much, indeed, to return to our favorite figure, and view them as orbs and systems of orbs, moving in free paths in the spaces of that other heaven, the kosmic intellect, the soul?

Ye powerful and resplendent ones! ye were, in your atmospheres, grown not for America, but rather for her foes, the feudal and the old—while our genius is democratic and modern. Yet could ye, indeed, but breathe your breath of life into our New World's nostrils—not to enslave us, as now, but, for our needs, to breed a spirit like your own—perhaps, (dare we to say it?) to dominate, even destroy, what you yourselves have left! On your plane, and no less, but even higher and wider, must we mete and measure for to-day and here. I demand races of orbic bards, with unconditional uncompromising sway. Come forth, sweet democratic despots of the west!

By points like these we, in reflection, token what we mean by any land's or people's genuine literature. And thus compared and tested, judging amid the influence of loftiest products only, what do our current copious fields of print, covering in manifold forms, the United States, better, for an analogy, present, than, as in certain regions of the sea, those spreading, undulating masses of squid, through which the whale swimming, with head half out, feeds?

Not but that doubtless our current so-called literature, (like an endless supply of small coin,) performs a certain service, and may-be, too, the service needed for the time, (the preparation-service, as children learn to spell). Everybody reads, and truly nearly everybody writes, either books, or for the magazines or journals. The matter has magnitude, too, after a sort. But is it really advancing? or, has it advanced for a long while? There is something impressive about the huge editions of the dailies and weeklies, the mountain stacks of white paper piled in the press-vaults, and the proud, crashing, ten-cylinder presses, which I can stand and watch any time by the half hour. Then, (though the States in the field of imagination present not a single first-class work, not a single great literatus,) the main objects, to amuse, to titillate, to pass away time, to circulate the news, and rumors of news, to rhyme and read rhyme, are yet attain'd, and on a scale of infinity. To-day, in books, in the rivalry of writers, especially novelists, success, (so-call'd,) is for him or her who strikes the mean flat average, the sensational appetite for stimulus, incident, persiflage, &c., and depicts, to the common calibre, sensual, exterior life. To such, or the luckiest of them, as we see, the audiences are

limitless and profitable; but they cease presently. While this day, or any day, to workmen portraying interior or spiritual life, the audiences were limited, and often laggard—but they last forever.

Compared with the past, our modern science soars, and our journals serve—but ideal and even ordinary romantic literature, does not, I think, substantially advance. Behold the prolific brood of the contemporary novel, magazine-tale, theatre-play, &c. The same endless thread of tangled and superlative love-story, inherited, apparently from the Amadises and Palmerins of the 13th, 14th, and 15th centuries over there in Europe. The costumes and associations brought down to date, the seasoning hotter and more varied, the dragons and ogres left out—but the thing, I should say, has not advanced—is just as sensational, just as strain'd—remains about the same, nor more, nor less.

What is the reason our time, our lands, that we see no fresh local courage, sanity, of our own—the Mississippi, stalwart Western men, real mental and physical facts, Southerners, &c., in the body of our literature? especially the poetic part of it. But always, instead, a parcel of dandies and ennuyees, dapper little gentlemen from abroad, who flood us with their thin sentiment of parlors, parasols, piano-songs, tinkling rhymes, the five-hundredth importation—or whimpering and crying about something, chasing one aborted conceit after another, and forever occupied in dyspeptic amours with dyspeptic women. While, current and novel, the grandest events and revolutions, and stormiest passions of history, are crossing to-day with unparallel'd rapidity and magnificence over the stages of our own and all the continents, offering new materials, opening new vistas, with largest needs, inviting the daring launching forth of conceptions in literature, inspired by them, soaring in highest regions, serving art in its highest, (which is only the other name for serving God, and serving humanity,) where is the man of letters, where is the book, with any nobler aim than to follow in the old track, repeat what has been said before—and, as its utmost triumph, sell well, and be erudite or elegant?

Mark the roads, the processes, through which these States have arrived, standing easy, henceforth ever-equal, ever-compact, in their range to-day. European adventures? the most antique? Asiatic or African? old history—miracles—romances? Rather, our own unquestion'd facts. They hasten, incredible, blazing bright as fire. From the deeds and days of Columbus down to the present, and including the present—and especially the late Secession war—when I con them, I feel, every leaf, like stopping to see if I have not made a mistake, and fall'n on the splendid figments of some dream. But it is no dream. We stand, live, move, in the huge flow of our age's materialism—in its spirituality. We have had founded for us the most positive of lands. The founders have pass'd to other spheres—but what are these terrible duties they have left us?

* * *

Present literature, while magnificently fulfilling certain popular demands, with plenteous knowledge and verbal smartness, is profoundly sophisticated, insane, and its very joy is morbid. It needs tally and express Nature, and the spirit of Nature, and to know and obey the standards. I say the question of Nature, largely consider'd, involves the questions of the esthetic, the emotional, and the religious—and involves happiness. A fitly born and bred race, growing up in right conditions of out-door as much as in-door harmony, activity and development, would probably, from and in those conditions, find it enough merely to live—and would, in their relations to the sky, air, water, trees, &c., and to the countless common shows, and in the fact of life itself, discover and achieve happiness—with Being suffused night and day by wholesome extasy, surpassing all the pleasures that wealth, amusement, and even gratified intellect, erudition, or the sense of art, can give.

In the prophetic literature of these States (the reader of my speculations will miss their principal stress unless he allows well for the point that a new Literature, perhaps a new Metaphysics, certainly a new Poetry, are to be, in my opinion, the only sure and worthy supports and expressions of the American Democracy,) Nature, true Nature, and the true idea of Nature, long absent, must, above all, become fully restored, enlarged, and must furnish the pervading atmosphere to poems, and the test of all high literary and esthetic compositions. I do not mean the smooth walks, trimm'd hedges, poseys and nightingales of the English poets, but the whole orb, with its geologic history, the kosmos, carrying fire and snow, that rolls through the illimitable areas, light as a feather, though weighing billions of tons. Furthermore, as by what we now partially call Nature is intended, at most, only what is entertainable by the physical conscience, the sense of matter, and of good animal health—on these it must be distinctly accumulated, incorporated, that man, comprehending these, has, in towering superaddition, the moral and spiritual consciences, indicating his destination beyond the ostensible, the mortal.

To the heights of such estimate of Nature indeed ascending, we proceed to make observations for our Vistas, breathing rarest air. What is I believe called Idealism seems to me to suggest, (guarding against extravagance, and ever modified even by its opposite,) the course of inquiry and

desert of favor for our New World metaphysics, their foundation of and in literature, giving hue to all.*

* * *

I hail with joy the oceanic, variegated, intense practical energy, the demand for facts, even the business materialism of the current age, our States. But wo to the age or land in which these things, movements, stopping at themselves, do not tend to ideas. As fuel to flame, and flame to the heavens, so must wealth, science, materialism—even this democracy of which we make so much—unerringly feed the highest mind, the soul. Infinitude the flight: fathomless the mystery. Man, so diminutive, dilates beyond the sensible universe, competes with, outcopes space and time, meditating even one

*The culmination and fruit of literary artistic expression, and its final fields of pleasure for the human soul, are in metaphysics, including the mysteries of the spiritual world, the soul itself, and the question of the immortal continuation of our identity. In all ages, the mind of man has brought up here—and always will. Here, at least, of whatever race or era, we stand on common ground. Applause, too, is unanimous, antique or modern. Those authors who work well in this field—though their reward, instead of a handsome percentage, or royalty, may be but simply the laurel-crown of the victors in the great Olympic games—will be dearest to humanity, and their works, however esthetically defective, will be treasur'd forever. The altitude of literature and poetry has always been religion—and always will be. The Indian Vedas, the Nackas of Zoroaster, the Talmud of the Jews, the Old Testament, the Gospel of Christ and his disciples, Plato's works, the Koran of Mohammed, the Edda of Snorro, and so on toward our own day, to Swedenborg, and to the invaluable contributions of Leibnitz, Kant and Hegel—these, with such poems only in which, (while singing well of persons and events, of the passions of man, and the shows of the material universe,) the religious tone, the consciousness of mystery, the recognition of the future, of the unknown, of Deity over and under all, and of the divine purpose, are never absent, but indirectly give tone to all—exhibit literature's real heights and elevations, towering up like the great mountains of the earth.

Standing on this ground—the last, the highest, only permanent ground—and sternly criticising, from it, all works, either of the literary, or any art, we have peremptorily to dismiss every pretensive production, however fine its esthetic or intellectual points, which violates or ignores, or even does not celebrate, the central divine idea of All, suffusing universe, of eternal trains of purpose, in the development, by however slow degrees, of the physical, moral, and spiritual kosmos. I say he has studied, meditated to no profit, whatever may be his mere erudition, who has not absorb'd this simple consciousness and faith. It is not entirely new—but it is for Democracy to elaborate it, and look to build upon and expand from it, with uncompromising reliance. Above the doors of teaching the inscription is to appear, Though little or nothing can be absolutely known, perceiv'd, except from a point of view which is evanescent, yet we know at least one permanency, that Time and Space, in the will of God, furnish successive chains, completions of material births and beginnings, solve all discrepancies, fears and doubts, and eventually fulfil happiness—and that the prophecy of those births, namely spiritual results, throws the true arch over all teaching, all science. The local considerations of sin, disease, deformity, ignorance, death, &c., and their measurement by the superficial mind, and ordinary legislation and theology, are to be met by science, boldly accepting, promulging this faith, and planting the seeds of superber laws—of the explication of the physical universe through the spiritual—and clearing the way for a religion, sweet and unimpugnable alike to little child or great savan.*

great idea. Thus, and thus only, does a human being, his spirit, ascend above, and justify, objective Nature, which, probably nothing in itself, is incredibly and divinely serviceable, indispensable, real, here. And as the purport of objective Nature is doubtless folded, hidden, somewhere here—as somewhere here is what this globe and its manifold forms, and the light of day, and night's darkness, and life itself, with all its experiences, are for—it is here the great literature, especially verse, must get its inspiration and throbbing blood. Then may we attain to a poetry worthy the immortal soul of man, and which, while absorbing materials, and, in their own sense, the shows of Nature, will, above all, have, both directly and indirectly, a freeing, fluidizing, expanding, religious character, exulting with science, fructifying the moral elements, and stimulating aspirations, and meditations on the unknown.

The process, so far, is indirect and peculiar, and though it may be suggested, cannot be defined. Observing, rapport, and with intuition, the shows and forms presented by Nature, the sensuous luxuriance, the beautiful in living men and women, the actual play of passions, in history and life—and, above all, from those developments either in Nature or human personality in which power, (dearest of all to the sense of the artist,) transacts itself—out of these, and seizing what is in them, the poet, the esthetic worker in any field, by the divine magic of his genius, projects them, their analogies, by curious removes, indirections, in literature and art. (No useless attempt to repeat the material creation, by daguerreotyping the exact likeness by mortal mental means.) This is the image-making faculty, coping with material creation, and rivaling, almost triumphing over it. This alone, when all the other parts of a specimen of literature or art are ready and waiting, can breathe into it the breath of life, and endow it with identity.

"The true question to ask," says the librarian of Congress in a paper read before the Social Science Convention at New York, October, 1869, "The true question to ask respecting a book, is, has it help'd any human soul?" This is the hint, statement, not only of the great literatus, his book, but of every great artist. It may be that all works of art are to be first tried by their art qualities, their image-forming talent, and their dramatic, pictorial, plot-constructing, euphonious and other talents. Then, whenever claiming to be first-class works, they are to be strictly and sternly tried by their foundation in, and radiation, in the highest sense, and always indirectly, of the ethic principles, and eligibility to free, arouse, dilate.

As, within the purposes of the Kosmos, and vivifying all meteorology, and all the congeries of the mineral, vegetable and animal worlds—all the physical growth and development of man, and all the history of the race in politics, religions, wars, &c., there is a moral purpose, a visible or invisible intention, certainly underlying all—its results and proof needing to be patiently waited for—needing intuition, faith, idiosyncrasy, to its realization, which many, and especially the intellectual, do not have—so in the product, or congeries of the product, of the greatest literatus. This is the last, profoundest measure and test of a first-class literary or esthetic achievement, and when understood and put in force must fain, I say, lead to works, books, nobler than any hitherto known. Lo! Nature, (the only complete, actual poem,) existing calmly in the divine scheme, containing all, content, careless of the criticisms of a day, or these endless and wordy chatterers. And lo! to the consciousness of the soul, the permanent identity, the thought, the something, before which the magnitude even of democracy, art, literature, &c., dwindles, becomes partial, measurable—something that fully satisfies, (which those do not.) That something is the All, and the idea of All, with the accompanying idea of eternity, and of itself, the soul, buoyant, indestructible, sailing space forever, visiting every region, as a ship the sea. And again lo! the pulsations in all matter, all spirit, throbbing forever—the eternal beats, eternal systole and diastole of life in things—wherefrom I feel and know that death is not the ending, as was thought, but rather the real beginning—and that nothing ever is or can be lost, nor ever die, nor soul, nor matter.

* * *

Yet I have dream'd, merged in that hidden-tangled problem of our fate, whose long unraveling stretches mysteriously through time—dream'd out, portray'd, hinted already—a little or a larger band—a band of brave and true, unprecedented yet—arm'd and equipt at every point—the members separated, it may be, by different dates and States, or south, or north, or east, or west—Pacific, Atlantic, Southern, Canadian—a year, a century here, and other centuries there—but always one, compact in soul, conscience-conserving, God-inculcating, inspired achievers, not only in literature, the greatest art, but achievers in all art—a new, undying order, dynasty, from age to age transmitted—a band, a class, at least as fit to cope with current years, our dangers, needs, as those who, for their times, so long, so well, in armor or in cowl, upheld and made illustrious, that far-back feudal, priestly world. To offset chivalry, indeed, those vanish'd countless knights, old altars, abbeys, priests, ages and strings of ages, a knightlier and more sacred cause to-day demands, and shall supply, in a New World, to larger, grander work, more than the counterpart and tally of them.

Arrived now, definitely, at an apex for these Vistas, I confess that the promulgation and belief in such a class or institution—a new and greater literatus order—its possibility, (nay certainty,) underlies these entire speculations—and that the rest, the other parts, as superstructures, are all founded upon it. It really seems to me the condition, not only of our future national and democratic development, but of our perpetuation. In the highly artificial and materialistic bases of modern civilization, with the corresponding arrangements and methods of living, the force-infusion of intellect alone, the depraving influences of riches just as much as poverty, the absence of all high ideals in character—with the long series of tendencies, shapings, which few are strong enough to resist, and which now seem, with steam-engine speed, to be everywhere turning out the generations of humanity like uniform iron castings—all of which, as compared with the feudal ages, we can yet do nothing better than accept, make the best of, and even welcome, upon the whole, for their oceanic practical grandeur, and their restless wholesale kneading of the masses—I say of all this tremendous and dominant play of solely materialistic bearings upon current life in the United States, with the results as already seen, accumulating, and reaching far into the future, that they must either be confronted and met by at least an equally subtle and tremendous force-infusion for purposes of spiritualization, for the pure conscience, for genuine esthetics, and for absolute and primal manliness and womanliness—or else our modern civilization, with all its improvements, is in vain, and we are on the road to a destiny, a status, equivalent, in its real world, to that of the fabled damned.

Prospecting thus the coming unsped days, and that new order in them—marking the endless train of exercise, development, unwind, in nation as in man, which life is for—we see, fore-indicated, amid these prospects and hopes, new law-forces of spoken and written language—not merely the pedagogue-forms, correct, regular, familiar with precedents, made for matters of outside propriety, fine words, thoughts definitely told out—but a language fann'd by the breath of Nature, which leaps overhead, cares mostly for impetus and effects, and for what it plants and invigorates to grow—tallies life and character, and seldomer tells a thing than suggests or necessitates it. In fact, a new theory of literary composition for imaginative works of the very first class, and especially for highest poems, is the sole course open to these States. Books are to be call'd for, and supplied, on the assumption that the process of reading is not a half sleep, but, in highest sense, an exercise, a gymnast's struggle; that the reader is to do something for himself, must be on the alert, must himself or herself construct indeed the poem, argument, history, metaphysical essay—the text furnishing the hints, the clue, the start or frame-work. Not the book needs so much to be the complete thing, but the reader of the book does. That were to make a nation of supple and athletic minds, well-train'd, intuitive, used to depend on themselves, and not on a few coteries of writers.

Investigating here, we see, not that it is a little thing we have, in having the bequeath'd libraries, countless shelves of volumes, records, &c.; yet how serious the danger, depending entirely on them, of the bloodless vein, the nerveless arm, the false application, at second or third hand. We see that the real interest of this people of ours in the theology, history, poetry, politics, and personal models of the past, (the British islands, for instance, and indeed all the past,) is not necessarily to mould ourselves or our literature upon them, but to attain fuller, more definite comparisons, warnings, and the insight to ourselves, our own present, and our own far grander, different, future history, religion, social customs, &c. We see that almost everything that has been written, sung, or stated, of old, with reference to humanity under the feudal and oriental institutes, religions, and for other lands, needs to be re-written, re-sung, re-stated, in terms consistent with the institution of these States, and to come in range and obedient uniformity with them.

We see, as in the universes of the material kosmos, after meteorological, vegetable, and animal cycles, man at last arises, born through them, to prove them, concentrate them, to turn upon them with wonder and love—to command them, adorn them, and carry them upward into superior realms—so, out of the series of the preceding social and political universes, now arise these States. We see that while many were supposing things established and completed, really the grandest things always remain; and discover that the work of the New World is not ended, but only fairly begun.

We see our land, America, her literature, esthetics, &c., as, substantially, the getting in form, or effusement and statement, of deepest basic elements and loftiest final meanings, of history and man—and the portrayal, (under the eternal laws and conditions of beauty,) of our own physiognomy, the subjective tie and expression of the objective, as from our own combination, continuation, and points of view—and the deposit and record of the national mentality, character, appeals, heroism, wars, and even liberties—where these, and all, culminate in native literary and artistic formulation, to be perpetuated; and not having which native, first-class formulation, she will flounder about, and her other, however imposing, eminent greatness, prove merely a passing gleam; but truly having which, she will understand herself, live nobly, nobly contribute, emanate, and, swinging, poised safely on herself, illumin'd and illuming, become a full-form'd world, and divine Mother not only of material but spiritual worlds, in ceaseless succession through time—the main thing being the average, the bodily, the concrete, the democratic, the popular, on which all the superstructures of the future are to permanently rest.

Friedrich Nietzsche

1844–1900

The role of Nietzsche in the history of criticism and theory was much enlarged by the recent perception of him as one of the first real deconstructionists. Thus Jacques Derrida (below, page 1203) saw him as a thinker whose critique of Western metaphysics his own work extends. In *Truth and Falsity in an Ultramoral Sense,* Nietzsche questions the relation of language to truth. What comes under his gaze is the tendency of language always toward abstraction and away from the individual and real, and finally into the threat of rational fixity. The ghost of Kant (above, page 416) is often present here: Things in themselves cannot be known as such. Space and time are the spectacles we cannot remove. But in Nietzsche the theme is not perception as such but the intervention of language, which produces abstract illusions (Platonic ideas, generalizations) that hide the truth of things. From this questioning of language come Nietzsche's questioning of reason and his distinction between what he called the Dionysiac and the Apollonian, set forth in *The Birth of Tragedy from the Spirit of Music.* Appearing one year before *Truth and Falsity,* it was inspired partly by Richard Wagner, although Nietzsche later denounced him. The two terms distinguish the primitive from the rational and, in Nietzsche's view, the potentially unhealthy. As Greek tragedy developed, one impulse came to balance the other, Dionysiac ecstasy being ordered by Apollonian form and repose. Music, an attempt to give form to the world of spirit, strives toward symbolic expression of that Dionysiac wisdom characteristic of tragedy, but in modern life the tragic view has been suppressed in scientific optimism. It may be that it will not reappear until "science [has] at last been pushed to its limits." Every culture that has lost the Dionysiac mythmaking spirit "has lost, by the same token, its natural, healthy creativity." Nietzsche sees Dionysiac art and mythmaking as performing the disruption of the fixity toward which language in its Apollonian phase tends.

Nietzsche's view of art can be profitably contrasted to Zola's scientistic plan for the novel (below, page 699), and an interesting comparison can be made to Cassirer's somewhat more optimistic theory of symbolic forms (below, page 1018).

Nietzsche's complete works in translation are available in the eighteen-volume edition of 1909–1914 edited by Oscar Levy. An edition of Nietzsche in English is partly published. See Erich Heller, *The Disinherited Mind* (1952); Arthur Danto, *Nietzsche as Philosopher* (1965); Karl Jaspers, *Nietzsche* (1965); Joan Stambaugh, *Nietzsche's Thought of the Eternal Return* (1972); Gilles Deleuze, *Nietzsche and Philosophy* (1973, tr. 1983); D. B. Allen, ed., *The New Nietzsche* (1977); D. F. Kull and D. Wood, eds., *Exceedingly Nietzsche* (1988); Ronald Hayman, *Nietzsche: A Critical Life* (1980); Ernst Behler, *Derrida-Nietzsche, Nietzsche-Derrida* (1988); Erich Heller, *The Importance of Nietzsche* (1988); Henry Staten, *Nietzsche's Voice* (1990); A. J. Hoover, *Friedrich Nietzsche: His Life and Thought* (1994); Robert C. Holub, *Friedrich Nietzsche* (1995).

from

The Birth of Tragedy from the Spirit of Music

I

Much will have been gained for aesthetics once we have succeeded in apprehending directly—rather than merely *ascertaining*—that art owes its continuous evolution to the Apollonian-Dionysiac duality, even as the propagation of the species depends on the duality of the sexes, their constant conflicts and periodic acts of reconciliation. I have borrowed my adjectives from the Greeks, who developed their mystical doctrines of art through plausible *embodiments,* not through purely conceptual means. It is by those two art-sponsoring deities, Apollo and Dionysos,[1] that we are made to recognize the tremendous split, as regards both origins and objectives, between the plastic, Apollonian arts and the nonvisual art of music inspired by Dionysos. The two creative tendencies developed alongside one another, usually in fierce opposition, each by its taunts forcing the other to more energetic production, both perpetuating in a discordant concord that agon[2] which the term *art* but feebly denominates: until at last, by the thaumaturgy[3] of a Hellenic act of will, the pair accepted the yoke of marriage and, in this condition, begot Attic[4] tragedy, which exhibits the salient features of both parents.

To reach a closer understanding of both these tendencies, let us begin by viewing them as the separate art realms of *dream* and *intoxication,* two physiological phenomena standing toward one another in much the same relationship as the Apollonian and Dionysiac. It was in a dream, according to Lucretius,[5] that the marvelous gods and goddesses first presented themselves to the minds of men. That great sculptor, Phidias,[6] beheld in a dream the entrancing bodies of more-than-human beings, and likewise, if anyone had asked the Greek poets about the mystery of poetic creation, they too would have referred him to dreams and instructed him much as Hans Sachs instructs us in *Die Meistersinger:*

> My friend, it is the poet's work
> Dreams to interpret and to mark.
> Believe me that man's true conceit
> In a dream becomes complete:
> All poetry we ever read
> Is but true dreams interpreted.[7]

The fair illusion of the dream sphere, in the production of which every man proves himself an accomplished artist, is a precondition not only of all plastic art, but even, as we shall see presently, of a wide range of poetry. Here we enjoy an immediate apprehension of form, all shapes speak to us directly, nothing seems indifferent or redundant. Despite the high intensity with which these dream realities exist for us, we still have a residual sensation that they are illusions; at least such has been my experience—and the frequency, not to say normality, of the experience is borne out in many passages of the poets. Men of philosophical disposition are known for their constant premonition that our everyday reality, too, is an illusion, hiding another, totally different kind of reality. It was Schopenhauer[8] who considered the ability to view at certain times all men and things as mere phantoms or dream images to be the true mark of philosophic talent. The person who is responsive to the stimuli of art behaves toward the reality of dream much the way the philosopher behaves toward the reality of existence: he observes exactly and enjoys his observations, for it is by these images that he interprets life, by these processes that he rehearses it. Nor is it by pleasant images only that such plausible connections are made: the whole divine comedy of life, including its somber aspects, its sudden balkings, impish accidents, anxious expectations, moves past him, not quite like a shadow play—for it is he himself, after all, who lives and suffers through these scenes—yet never without giving a fleeting sense of illusion; and I imagine that many persons have reassured themselves amidst the perils of dream by calling out, "It is a dream! I want it to go on." I have even heard of people spinning out the causality of one and the same dream over three or more successive nights. All these facts clearly bear witness that our innermost being, the common substratum of humanity, experiences dreams with deep delight and a sense of real necessity. This deep

---

Nietzsche's *Die Geburt der Tragödie* was first published in 1872. The text is from *The Birth of Tragedy and the Genealogy of Morals,* translated by Francis Golffing (Doubleday & Co., 1956).

[1]Greek gods of beauty and wine respectively.
[2]Conflict of characters in drama.
[3]Magic or miracle.
[4]Greek.
[5]Titus Lucretius Carus (c. 99–c. 55 B.C.), Roman poet.
[6]Phidias (c. 500–c. 432 B.C.), Greek sculptor.

---

[7]Richard Wagner (1813–1883), German composer, *Die Meistersinger von Nürnberg* III, i, 99–104.
[8]Arthur Schopenhauer (1788–1860), German philosopher.

and happy sense of the necessity of dream experiences was expressed by the Greeks in the image of Apollo. Apollo is at once the god of all plastic powers and the soothsaying god. He who is etymologically the *lucent* one, the god of light, reigns also over the fair illusion of our inner world of fantasy. The perfection of these conditions in contrast to our imperfectly understood waking reality, as well as our profound awareness of nature's healing powers during the interval of sleep and dream, furnishes a symbolic analogue to the soothsaying faculty and quite generally to the arts, which make life possible and worth living. But the image of Apollo must incorporate that thin line which the dream image may not cross, under penalty of becoming pathological, of imposing itself on us as crass reality: a discreet limitation, a freedom from all extravagant urges, the sapient tranquility of the plastic god. His eye must be sunlike, in keeping with his origin. Even at those moments when he is angry and ill-tempered there lies upon him the consecration of fair illusion. In an eccentric way one might say of Apollo what Schopenhauer says, in the first part of *The World as Will and Idea,* of man caught in the veil of Maya:[9] "Even as on an immense, raging sea, assailed by huge wave crests, a man sits in a little rowboat trusting his frail craft, so, amidst the furious torments of this world, the individual sits tranquilly, supported by the *principium individuationis*[10] and relying on it." One might say that the unshakable confidence in that principle has received its most magnificent expression in Apollo, and that Apollo himself may be regarded as the marvelous divine image of the *principium individuationis,* whose looks and gestures radiate the full delight, wisdom, and beauty of "illusion."

In the same context Schopenhauer has described for us the tremendous awe which seizes man when he suddenly begins to doubt the cognitive modes of experience, in other words, when in a given instance the law of causation seems to suspend itself. If we add to this awe the glorious transport which arises in man, even from the very depths of nature, at the shattering of the *principium individuationis,* then we are in a position to apprehend the essence of Dionysiac rapture, whose closest analogy is furnished by physical intoxication. Dionysiac stirrings arise either through the influence of those narcotic potions of which all primitive races speak in their hymns, or through the powerful approach of spring, which penetrates with joy the whole frame of nature. So stirred, the individual forgets himself completely. It is the same Dionysiac power which in medieval Germany drove ever-increasing crowds of people singing and dancing from place to place; we recognize in these St. John's and St. Vitus' dancers the bacchic choruses of the Greeks, who had their precursors in Asia Minor and as far back as Babylon and the orgiastic Sacaea.[11] There are people who, either from lack of experience or out of sheer stupidity, turn away from such phenomena, and, strong in the sense of their own sanity, label them either mockingly or pityingly "endemic diseases." These benighted souls have no idea how cadaverous and ghostly their "sanity" appears as the intense throng of Dionysiac revelers sweeps past them.

Not only does the bond between man and man come to be forged once more by the magic of the Dionysiac rite, but nature itself, long alienated or subjugated, rises again to celebrate the reconciliation with her prodigal son, man. The earth offers its gifts voluntarily, and the savage beasts of mountain and desert approach in peace. The chariot of Dionysos is bedecked with flowers and garlands; panthers and tigers stride beneath his yoke. If one were to convert Beethoven's *Päen to Joy*[12] into a painting, and refuse to curb the imagination when that multitude prostrates itself reverently in the dust, one might form some apprehension of Dionysiac ritual. Now the slave emerges as a freeman; all the rigid, hostile walls which either necessity or despotism has erected between men are shattered. Now that the gospel of universal harmony is sounded, each individual becomes not only reconciled to his fellow but actually at one with him—as though the veils of Maya had been torn apart and there remained only shreds floating before the vision of mystical oneness. Man now expresses himself through song and dance as the member of a higher community; he has forgotten how to walk, how to speak, and is on the brink of taking wing as he dances. Each of his gestures betokens enchantment; through him sounds a supernatural power, the same power which makes the animals speak and the earth render up milk and honey. He feels himself to be godlike and strides with the same elation and ecstasy as the gods he has seen in his dreams. No longer the *artist,* he has himself become a *work of art:* the productive power of the whole universe is now manifest in his transport, to the glorious satisfaction of the primordial One. The finest clay, the most precious marble—man—is here kneaded and hewn, and the chisel blows of the Dionysiac world artist are accompanied by the cry of the Eleusinian mystagogues:[13] "Do you fall on your knees, multitudes, do you divine your creator?"

---

[9]Hindu goddess representing illusion.
[10]Undivided or ultimate principle.
[11]Ancient Babylonian festival, culminating in the death of a surrogate king.
[12]Ludwig von Beethoven (1770–1827), German composer.
[13]The mysteries of Eleusis were secret religious rites practiced in Greece at Eleusis in the spring to honor the goddesses of vegetation and death.

II

So far we have examined the Apollonian and Dionysiac states as the product of formative forces arising directly from nature without the mediation of the human artist. At this stage artistic urges are satisfied directly, on the one hand through the imagery of dreams, whose perfection is quite independent of the intellectual rank, the artistic development of the individual; on the other hand, through an ecstatic reality which once again takes no account of the individual and may even destroy him, or else redeem him through a mystical experience of the collective. In relation to these immediate creative conditions of nature every artist must appear as "imitator," either as the Apollonian dream artist or the Dionysiac ecstatic artist, or, finally (as in Greek tragedy, for example) as dream and ecstatic artist in one. We might picture to ourselves how the last of these, in a state of Dionysiac intoxication and mystical self-abrogation, wandering apart from the reveling throng, sinks upon the ground, and how there is then revealed to him his own condition—complete oneness with the essence of the universe—in a dream similitude.

Having set down these general premises and distinctions, we now turn to the Greeks in order to realize to what degree the formative forces of nature were developed in them. Such an inquiry will enable us to assess properly the relation of the Greek artist to his prototypes or, to use Aristotle's expression, his "imitation of nature."[14] Of the dreams the Greeks dreamed it is not possible to speak with any certainty, despite the extant dream literature and the large number of dream anecdotes. But considering the incredible accuracy of their eyes, their keen and unabashed delight in colors, one can hardly be wrong in assuming that their dreams too showed a strict consequence of lines and contours, hues and groupings, a progression of scenes similar to their best bas-reliefs. The perfection of these dream scenes might almost tempt us to consider the dreaming Greek as a Homer and Homer as a dreaming Greek; which would be as though the modern man were to compare himself in his dreaming to Shakespeare.

Yet there is another point about which we do not have to conjecture at all; I mean the profound gap separating the Dionysiac Greeks from the Dionysiac barbarians. Throughout the range of ancient civilization (leaving the newer civilizations out of account for the moment) we find evidence of Dionysiac celebrations which stand to the Greek type in much the same relation as the bearded satyr, whose name

and attributes are derived from the he-goat, stands to the god Dionysos. The central concern of such celebrations was, almost universally, a complete sexual promiscuity overriding every form of established tribal law; all the savage urges of the mind were unleashed on those occasions until they reached that paroxysm of lust and cruelty which has always struck me as the "witches' cauldron" par excellence. It would appear that the Greeks were for a while quite immune from these feverish excesses which must have reached them by every known land or sea route. What kept Greece safe was the proud, imposing image of Apollo, who in holding up the head of the Gorgon[15] to those brutal and grotesque Dionysiac forces subdued them. Doric art has immortalized Apollo's majestic rejection of all license. But resistance became difficult, even impossible as soon as similar urges began to break forth from the deep substratum of Hellenism itself. Soon the function of the Delphic god[16] developed into something quite different and much more limited: all he could hope to accomplish now was to wrest the destructive weapon, by a timely gesture of pacification, from his opponent's hand. That act of pacification represents the most important event in the history of Greek ritual; every department of life now shows symptoms of a revolutionary change. The two great antagonists have been reconciled. Each feels obliged henceforth to keep to his bounds, each will honor the other by the bestowal of periodic gifts, while the cleavage remains fundamentally the same. And yet, if we examine what happened to the Dionysiac powers under the pressure of that treaty we notice a great difference: in the place of the Babylonian Sacaea, with their throwback of men to the condition of apes and tigers, we now see entirely new rites celebrated: rites of universal redemption, of glorious transfiguration. Only now has it become possible to speak of nature's celebrating an *aesthetic* triumph; only now has the abrogation of the *principium individuationis* become an aesthetic event. That terrible witches' brew concocted of lust and cruelty has lost all power under the new conditions. Yet the peculiar blending of emotions in the heart of the Dionysiac reveler—his ambiguity if you will—seems still to hark back (as the medicinal drug harks back to the deadly poison) to the days when the infliction of pain was experienced as joy while a sense of supreme triumph elicited cries of anguish from the heart. For now in every exuberant joy there is heard an undertone of terror, or else a wistful lament over an irrecoverable loss. It is as though in these Greek festivals a sentimental trait of nature were coming to the fore, as though nature were

---

[14] See Aristotle, *Poetics* (above, page 53).

[15] One of three sisters who when looked upon turned the beholder to stone.
[16] Apollo, whose oracle was at Delphi.

bemoaning the fact of her fragmentation, her decomposition into separate individuals. The chants and gestures of these revelers, so ambiguous in their motivation, represented an absolute *novum*[17] in the world of the Homeric Greeks; their Dionysiac music, in especial, spread abroad terror and a deep shudder. It is true: music had long been familiar to the Greeks as an Apollonian art, as a regular beat like that of waves lapping the shore, a plastic rhythm expressly developed for the portrayal of Apollonian conditions. Apollo's music was a Doric architecture of sound—of barely hinted sounds such as are proper to the cithara. Those very elements which characterize Dionysiac music and, after it, music quite generally: the heart-shaking power of tone, the uniform stream of melody, the incomparable resources of harmony—all those elements had been carefully kept at a distance as being inconsonant with the Apollonian norm. In the Dionysiac dithyramb[18] man is incited to strain his symbolic faculties to the utmost; something quite unheard of is now clamoring to be heard: the desire to tear asunder the veil of Maya, to sink back into the original oneness of nature; the desire to express the very essence of nature symbolically. Thus an entirely new set of symbols springs into being. First, all the symbols pertaining to physical features: mouth, face, the spoken word, the dance movement which coordinates the limbs and bends them to its rhythm. Then suddenly all the rest of the symbolic forces—music and rhythm as such, dynamics, harmony—assert themselves with great energy. In order to comprehend this total emancipation of all the symbolic powers one must have reached the same measure of inner freedom those powers themselves were making manifest; which is to say that the votary of Dionysos could not be understood except by his own kind. It is not difficult to imagine the awed surprise with which the Apollonian Greek must have looked on him. And that surprise would be further increased as the latter realized, with a shudder, that all this was not so alien to him after all, that his Apollonian consciousness was but a thin veil hiding from him the whole Dionysiac realm.

XVII

. . . The struggle of the spirit of music to become manifest in image and myth—a struggle that grew in intensity from the beginnings of lyric poetry to the flowering of Attic tragedy—came to a sudden halt and disappeared, as it were, from the Hellenic scene. Yet the Dionysiac world view born of this struggle managed to survive in the mysteries, and

even in its strangest metamorphoses and debasements did not cease to attract thoughtful minds. Who knows whether that conception will not once again rise as art from its mystical depths?

What concerns us here is the question whether those powers to whose influence Greek tragedy succumbed will maintain their ascendancy permanently, thereby blocking for good the renascence of tragedy and the tragic world view. The fact that the dialectical drive toward knowledge and scientific optimism has succeeded in turning tragedy from its course suggests that there may be an eternal conflict between the theoretical and the tragic world view, in which case tragedy could be reborn only when science had at last been pushed to its limits and, faced with those limits, been forced to renounce its claim to universal validity. For the new hypothetical tragedy the music-practicing Socrates might be a fitting symbol.

If we remember the immediate consequences of the restless and inquisitive spirit of science, it can come as no surprise to us that it destroyed myth and, by the same token, displaced poetry from its native soil and rendered it homeless. If we are right in crediting music with the power to revive myth, then we must look for science in those places where it actively opposes the mythopoeic power of music. It did so in the later Attic dithyramb, whose music no longer expressed the innermost being, or will itself, but only reproduced the phenomenon in a mediate, conceptualized form. Truly musical minds turned away from that degenerate kind of music with the same distaste they felt for the anti-artistic tendencies of Socrates. Aristophanes' sure instinct was doubtless right when he lumped together Socrates, the Euripidean drama, and the music of the new dithyrambic poets, castigating them indifferently as symptoms of a degenerate culture.[19] In the new dithyramb, music is degraded to the imitative portrayal of phenomena, such as battles or storms at sea, and thereby robbed of all its mythopoeic power. For we are not in a condition to yield ourselves to the mythic force when music simply tries to beguile us with external analogies between some natural event and certain rhythmical and acoustical combinations, when our reason is called upon to satisfy itself in the recognition of such analogies. Truly Dionysiac music offers us a universal mirror of the world will: every particular incident refracted in that mirror is enlarged into the image of a permanent truth. Conversely, the tone pictures of the new dithyramb strip every such concrete incident at once of its mythic implications. Music here has become a paltry replica of the phenomenon

---

[17] "New thing."
[18] A wild choric hymn.

[19] Aristophanes (c. 448–after 388 B.C.) satirized Socrates in *The Clouds*. Euripides (c. 485–406 B.C.), Greek tragic dramatist.

and for that very reason infinitely poorer than the phenomenon itself. And the poverty of the replica further reduces the phenomenon to our consciousness. A battle, thus imitated, becomes a mere sequence of marches, trumpet calls and the like, and our imagination is stopped at the level of such superficialities. Tone painting, then, is in every respect at the opposite pole from the mythopoeic power of true music: it further reduces the phenomenon, while Dionysiac music makes every single phenomenon comprehensive and significant. The anti-Dionysiac spirit won a mighty victory when it estranged music from itself and made it a slave to appearances. Euripides, who, albeit in a higher sense, must be called an absolutely unmusical temperament, was for that very reason a passionate partisan of the new dithyramb and used its entire stock-in-trade with a freebooter's prodigality.

We see a different aspect of this anti-Dionysiac, antimythic trend in the increased emphasis on character portrayal and psychological subtlety from Sophocles[20] onward. Character must no longer be broadened so as to become a permanent type, but on the contrary must be so finely individualized, by means of shading and nuances and the strict delineation of every trait, that the spectator ceases to be aware of myth at all and comes to focus on the amazing lifelikeness of the characters and the artist's power of imitation. Here, once again, we see the victory of the particular over the general and the pleasure taken in, as it were, anatomical drawing. We breathe the air of a world of theory, in which scientific knowledge is more revered than the artistic reflection of a universal norm. The cult of the characteristic trait develops apace: Sophocles still paints whole characters and lays myth under contribution in order to render them more fully; Euripides concentrates on large single character traits, projected into violent passions; the new Attic comedy gives us masks, each with a single expression: frivolous old men, hoodwinked panders, roguish slaves, in endless repetition. Where is now the mythopoeic spirit? All that remains to music is to excite jaded nerves or call up memory images, as in tone painting. For the former, the text hardly matters any longer. Already in Euripides things get out of control as soon as his characters or his chorus begin to sing, and heaven only knows what his impudent followers may have been guilty of.

Yet the modish anti-Dionysiac spirit shows itself most clearly in the dénouements of the new plays. In the older tragedy one could feel at the end the metaphysical solace, without which it is impossible to imagine our taking pleasure in tragedy. Most purely, perhaps, in *Oedipus at Colonus*[21] we hear those harmonious sounds of reconciliation from another world. But, once the genius of music has departed from tragedy, tragedy is dead, for what, henceforth, is to furnish that metaphysical solace? The new dramatists tried to resolve the tragic dissonance in terrestrial terms: after having been sufficiently buffeted by fate, the hero was compensated in the end by a distinguished marriage and divine honors. He thus resembled a gladiator, who might perchance be set free after he had taken his beating and was covered with wounds. The place of metaphysical solace was now taken by the *deus ex machina*.[22] I do not mean to assert that the tragic spirit was everywhere quite eradicated by the anti-Dionysiac onset; but we do know that it was forced to flee from the realm of art and take refuge in the limbo of aberrant secret rites. Meanwhile, there raged over the entire surface of the Hellenic world the pestilence of that counterfeit "Greek serenity" of which I spoke earlier: a senescent and unproductive affirmation of this life, in utter contrast to the marvelous naiveté of the older Greeks—flower of an Apollonian culture blossoming over a somber abyss, in token of the victory of the Greek will over suffering, and of the wisdom of suffering. The other variety of Greek cheerfulness—the Alexandrian—shows at its best in the man of theory; it exhibits the same characteristics that I have just derived from the general anti-Dionysiac ascendant. It opposes Dionysiac wisdom and art; tries to dissolve the power of myth; puts in place of a metaphysical comfort a terrestrial consonance and a special *deus ex machina*—the god of engines and crucibles: forces of nature put in the service of a higher form of egotism. It believes that the world can be corrected through knowledge and that life should be guided by science; that it is actually in a position to confine man within the narrow circle of soluble tasks, where he can say cheerfully to life: "I want you. You are worth knowing."

XXIII

If one wants to try whether he is such a spectator or whether he belongs, rather, to the community of Socratic men, he may ask himself honestly with what emotion he responds to the miracle on the stage; whether he feels that his historical sense, trained to look everywhere for strict psychological causation, has been outraged, whether he admits the miracle as a phenomenon that seems natural to child minds but rather remote from himself, or whether he has some different sort of response. Depending on what answer he makes,

---

[20] Sophocles (c. 496–406 B.C.), Greek tragic dramatist.

[21] By Sophocles.

[22] "God from the machine," coincidence employed to carry out the plot, deplored by Aristotle (above, page 59).

he will be able to tell whether he has any understanding at all of myth, which, being a concentrated image of the world, an emblem of appearance, cannot dispense with the miracle. The chances are that almost every one of us, upon close examination, will have to admit that he is able to approach the once-living reality of myth only by means of intellectual constructs. Yet every culture that has lost myth has lost, by the same token, its natural, healthy creativity. Only a horizon ringed about with myths can unify a culture. The forces of imagination and of Apollonian dream are saved only by myth from indiscriminate rambling. The images of myth must be the demonic guardians, ubiquitous but unnoticed, presiding over the growth of the child's mind and interpreting to the mature man his life and struggles. Nor does the commonwealth know any more potent unwritten law than that mythic foundation which guarantees its union with religion and its basis in mythic conceptions. Over against this, let us consider abstract man stripped of myth, abstract education, abstract mores, abstract laws, abstract government; the random vagaries of the artistic imagination unchanneled by any native myth; a culture without any fixed and consecrated place of origin, condemned to exhaust all possibilities and feed miserably and parasitically on every culture under the sun. Here we have our present age, the result of a Socratism bent on the extermination of myth. Man today, stripped of myth, stands famished among all his pasts and must dig frantically for roots, be it among the most remote antiquities. What does our great historical hunger signify, our clutching about us of countless other cultures, our consuming desire for knowledge, if not the loss of myth, of a mythic home, the mythic womb? Let us ask ourselves whether our feverish and frightening agitation is anything but the greedy grasping for food of a hungry man. And who would care to offer further nourishment to a culture which, no matter how much it consumes, remains insatiable and which converts the strongest and most wholesome food into "history" and "criticism"?

Truth and Falsity in an Ultramoral Sense

In some remote corner of the universe, effused into innumerable solar systems, there was once a star upon which clever animals invented cognition. It was the haughtiest,

Ueber Wahrheit und Luge im aussermoralischen Sinne (1873) is from *Early Greek Philosophy and Other Essays,* which constitutes Volume II of the *Complete Works of Friedrich Nietzsche* (in eighteen volumes, 1909–1924), edited by Oscar Levy. The translation is by Maximilian A. Mügge.

most mendacious moment in the history of this world, but yet only a moment. After Nature had taken breath awhile, the star congealed and the clever animals had to die.— Someone might write a fable after this style, and yet he would not have illustrated sufficiently, how wretched, shadowlike, transitory, purposeless, and fanciful the human intellect appears in Nature. There were eternities during which this intellect did not exist, and when it has once more passed away, there will be nothing to show that it has existed. For this intellect is not concerned with any further mission transcending the sphere of human life. No, it is purely human and none but its owner and procreator regards it so pathetically as to suppose that the world revolves around it. If, however, we and the gnat could understand each other, we should learn that even the gnat swims through the air with the same pathos, and feels within itself the flying center of the world. Nothing in Nature is so bad or so insignificant that it will not, at the smallest puff of that force cognition, immediately swell up like a balloon, and just as a mere porter wants to have his admirer, so the very proudest man, the philosopher, imagines he sees from all sides the eyes of the universe telescopically directed upon his actions and thoughts.

It is remarkable that this is accomplished by the intellect, which after all has been given to the most unfortunate, the most delicate, the most transient beings only as an expedient, in order to detain them for a moment in existence, from which without that extra gift they would have every cause to flee as swiftly as Lessing's son.[1] That haughtiness connected with cognition and sensation, spreading blinding fogs before the eyes and over the senses of men, deceives itself therefore as to the value of existence owing to the fact that it bears within itself the most flattering evaluation of cognition. Its most general effect is deception, but even its most particular effects have something of deception in their nature.

The intellect, as a means for the preservation of the individual, develops its chief power in dissimulation; for it is by dissimulation that the feebler and less robust individuals preserve themselves, since it has been denied them to fight the battle of existence with horns or the sharp teeth of beasts of prey. In man this art of dissimulation reaches its acme of perfection: in him deception, flattery, falsehood and fraud,

---

[1] [Mügge] The German poet, Lessing [above, page 378], had been married for just a little over one year to Eva König. A son was born and died the same day, and the mother's life was despaired of. In a letter to his friend Esschenberg the poet wrote: ". . . and I lost him so unwillingly, this son! For he had so much understanding! Do not suppose that the few hours of fatherhood have made me an ape of a father! I know what I say. Was it not understanding, that they had to drag him into the world with a pair of forceps? that he so soon suspected the evil of this world? Was it not understanding, that he seized the first opportunity to get away from it? . . ." Eva König died a week later.

slander, display, pretentiousness, disguise, cloaking convention, and acting to others and to himself, in short, the continual fluttering to and fro around the *one* flame—
Vanity: all these things are so much the rule, and the law,
that few things are more incomprehensible than the way in
which an honest and pure impulse to truth could have arisen
among men. They are deeply immersed in illusions and
dream fancies; their eyes glance only over the surface of
things and see "forms"; their sensation nowhere leads to
truth, but contents itself with receiving stimuli and, so to
say, with playing hide-and-seek on the back of things. In addition to that, at night man allows his dreams to lie to him a
whole lifetime long, without his moral sense ever trying to
prevent them; whereas men are said to exist who by the exercise of a strong will have overcome the habit of snoring.
What indeed *does* man know about himself? Oh! that he
could but once see himself complete, placed as it were in an
illuminated glass case! Does not nature keep secret from
him most things, even about his body, e.g., the convolutions
of the intestines, the quick flow of the blood currents, the intricate vibrations of the fibers, so as to banish and lock him
up in proud, delusive knowledge? Nature threw away the
key; and woe to the fateful curiosity which might be able for
a moment to look out and down through a crevice in the
chamber of consciousness and discover that man, indifferent to his own ignorance, is resting on the pitiless, the
greedy, the insatiable, the murderous, and, as it were, hanging in dreams on the back of a tiger. Whence, in the wide
world, with this state of affairs, arises the impulse to truth?

As far as the individual tries to preserve himself
against other individuals, in the natural state of things he
uses the intellect in most cases only for dissimulation; since,
however, man both from necessity and boredom wants to
exist socially and gregariously, he must needs make peace
and at least endeavor to cause the greatest *bellum omnium
contra omnes*[2] to disappear from his world. This first conclusion of peace brings with it a something which looks like
the first step toward the attainment of that enigmatical bent
for truth. For that which henceforth is to be "truth" is now
fixed; that is to say, a uniformly valid and binding designation of things is invented and the legislature of language
also gives the first laws of truth: since here, for the first time,
originates the contrast between truth and falsity. The liar
uses the valid designations, the words, in order to make the
unreal appear as real, e.g., he says "I am rich," whereas the
right designation for his state would be "poor." He abuses
the fixed conventions by convenient substitution or even inversion of terms. If he does this in a selfish and moreover
harmful fashion, society will no longer trust him but will

even exclude him. In this way men avoid not so much being
defrauded, but being injured by fraud. At bottom, at this
juncture, too, they hate not deception, but the evil, hostile
consequences of certain species of deception. And it is in a
similarly limited sense only that man desires truth: he cov-
ets the agreeable, life-preserving consequences of truth; he
is indifferent toward pure, ineffective knowledge; he is even
inimical toward truths which possibly might prove harmful
or destroying. And, moreover, what after all are those conventions of language? Are they possibly products of knowledge, of the love of truth; do the designations and the things
coincide? Is language the adequate expression of all
realities?

Only by means of forgetfulness can man ever arrive at
imagining that he possesses "truth" in that degree just indicated. If he does not mean to content himself with truth in
the shape of tautology, that is, with empty husks, he will always obtain illusions instead of truth. What is a word? The
expression of a nerve stimulus in sounds. But to infer a
cause outside us from the nerve stimulus is already the
result of a wrong and unjustifiable application of the proposition of causality. How should we dare, if truth with the
genesis of language, if the point of view of certainty with
the designations had alone been decisive; how indeed
should we dare to say: the stone is hard; as if "hard" was
known to us otherwise, and not merely as an entirely subjective stimulus! We divide things according to genders; we
designate the tree as masculine,[3] the plant as feminine:[4]
what arbitrary metaphors! How far-flown beyond the canon
of certainty! We speak of a "serpent";[5] the designation fits
nothing but the sinuosity, and could therefore also appertain
to the worm. What arbitrary demarcations! What one-sided
preferences given sometimes to this, sometimes to that quality of a thing! The different languages placed side by side
show that with words truth or adequate expression matters little: for otherwise there would not be so many languages. The
"Thing-in-itself" (it is just this which would be the pure ineffective truth) is also quite incomprehensible to the creator of
language and not worth making any great endeavor to obtain.
He designates only the relations of things to men and for their
expression he calls to his help the most daring metaphors. A
nerve stimulus, first transformed into a percept! First
metaphor! The percept again copied into a sound! Second
metaphor! And each time he leaps completely out of one
sphere right into the midst of an entirely different one. One
can imagine a man who is quite deaf and has never had a sensation of tone and of music; just as this man will possibly

---

[2] "War of all against all."

[3] [Mügge] In German *the tree—der Baum*—is masculine.
[4] [Mügge] In German *the plant—die Phlanze*—is feminine.
[5] [Mügge] Cf. the German *die Schlange* and *schlingen*, the English *serpent* from the Latin *serpere*.

marvel at Chladni's[6] sound figures in the sand, will discover their cause in the vibrations of the string, and will then proclaim that now he knows what man calls "tone"; even so does it happen to us all with language. When we talk about trees, colors, snow, and flowers, we believe we know something about the things themselves, and yet we only possess metaphors of the things, and these metaphors do not in the least correspond to the original essentials. Just as the sound shows itself as a sad figure, in the same way the enigmatical *x* of the Thing-in-itself is seen first as nerve stimulus, then as percept, and finally as sound.[7] At any rate the genesis of language did not therefore proceed on logical lines, and the whole material in which and with which the man of truth, the investigator, the philosopher works and builds, originates, if not from Nephelococcygia, cloudland, at any rate not from the essence of things.

Let us especially think about the formation of ideas. Every word becomes at once an idea not by having, as might presume, to serve as a reminder for the original experience happening but once and absolutely individualized, to which experience such word owes its origin, no, but by having simultaneously to fit innumerable, more or less similar (which really means never equal, therefore altogether unequal) cases. Every idea originates through equating the unequal. As certainly as no one leaf is exactly similar to any other, so certain is it that the idea "leaf" has been formed through an arbitrary omission of these individual differences, through a forgetting of the differentiating qualities, and this idea now awakens the notion that in nature there is, besides the leaves, a something called *the* "leaf," perhaps a primal form according to which all leaves were woven, drawn, accurately measured, colored, crinkled, painted, but by unskilled hands, so that no copy had turned out correct and trustworthy as a true copy of the primal form. We call a man "honest"; we ask, why has he acted so honestly today? Our customary answer runs, "On account of his honesty." *The* Honesty! That means again: the "leaf" is the cause of the leaves. We really and truly do not know anything at all about an essential quality which might be called *the* honesty, but we do know about numerous individualized; and therefore unequal actions, which we equate by omission of the unequal, and now designate as honest actions; finally out of them we formulate a *qualitas occulta* with the name "Honesty."[8]

The disregarding of the individual and real furnishes us with the idea, as it likewise also gives us the form; whereas nature knows of no forms and ideas, and therefore knows no species but only an *x*, to us inaccessible and indefinable. For our antithesis of individual and species is anthropomorphic too and does not come from the essence of things, although on the other hand we do not dare to say that it does not correspond to it; for that would be a dogmatic assertion and as such just as undemonstrable as its contrary.

What therefore is truth? A mobile army of metaphors, metonymies, anthropomorphisms: in short a sum of human relations which became poetically and rhetorically intensified, metamorphosed, adorned, and after long usage seems to a nation fixed, canonic, and binding; truths are illusions of which one has forgotten that they *are* illusions; worn-out metaphors which have become powerless to affect the senses; coins which have their obverse effaced and now are no longer of account as coins but merely as metal. Still we do not yet know whence the impulse to truth comes, for up to now we have heard only about the obligation which society imposes in order to exist: to be truthful, that is, to use the usual metaphors, therefore expressed morally: we have heard only about the obligation to lie according to a fixed convention, to lie gregariously in a style binding for all. Now man, of course, forgets that matters are going thus with him; he therefore lies in that fashion pointed out unconsciously and according to habits of centuries' standing—and by *this very unconsciousness,* by this very forgetting, he arrives at a sense for truth. Through this feeling of being obliged to designate one thing as "red," another as "cold," a third one as "dumb," awakes a moral emotion relating to truth. Out of the antithesis "liar" whom nobody trusts, whom all exclude, man demonstrates to himself the venerableness, reliability, usefulness of truth. Now as a *"rational"* being he submits his actions to the sway of abstractions; he no longer suffers himself to be carried away by sudden impressions, by sensations, he first generalizes all these impressions into paler, cooler ideas, in order to attach to them the ship of his life and actions. Everything which makes man stand out in bold relief against the animal depends on this faculty of volatilizing the concrete metaphors into a schema, and therefore resolving a perception into an idea. For within the range of those schemata a something becomes possible that never could succeed under the first perceptual impressions: to build up a pyramidal order with castes and grades, to create a new world of laws, privileges, suborders, delimitations, which now stands opposite the other perceptual world of first impressions and assumes the appearance of being the more fixed, general, known, human of the two and therefore the regulating and imperative one.

---

[6]Ernst Florenz Friedrich Chladni (1756–1827), German physicist. Chladni figures were designs formed in sand and put on plates that were then made to vibrate.
[7]Nietzsche here adopts Kant's notion of the unknowable thing in itself.
[8]"Occult quality."

Whereas every metaphor of perception is individual and without its equal and therefore knows how to escape all attempts to classify it, the great edifice of ideas shows the rigid regularity of a Roman columbarium and in logic breathes forth the sterness and coolness which we find in mathematics. He who has been breathed upon by this coolness will scarcely believe that the idea, too, bony and hexahedral and permutable as a die, remains, however, only as the *residuum of a metaphor,* and that the illusion of the artistic metamorphosis of a nerve stimulus into percepts is, if not the mother, then the grandmother of every idea. Now in this game of dice, "Truth" means to use every die as it is designated; to count its points carefully, to form exact classifications, and never to violate the order of castes and the sequences of rank. Just as the Romans and Etruscans for their benefit cut up the sky by means of strong mathematical lines and banned a god as it were into a *templum,* into a space limited in this fashion, so every nation has above its head such a sky of ideas divided up mathematically, and it understands the demand for truth to mean that every conceptual god is to be looked for only in *his* own sphere. One may here well admire man, who succeeded in piling up an infinitely complex dome of ideas on a movable foundation and as it were on running water, as a powerful genius of architecture. Of course in order to obtain hold on such a foundation it must be as an edifice piled up out of cobwebs, so fragile as to be carried away by the waves, so firm as not to be blown asunder by every wind. In this way man as an architectural genius rises high above the bee; she builds with wax, which she brings together out of nature; he with the much more delicate material of ideas, which he must first manufacture within himself. He is very much to be admired here—but not on account of his impulse for truth, his bent for pure cognition of things. If somebody hides a thing behind a bush, seeks it again and finds it in the self same place, then there is not much to boast of, respecting this seeking and finding: thus, however, matters stand with the seeking and finding of "truth" within the realm of reason. If I make the definition of the mammal and then declare after inspecting a camel, "Behold a mammal," then no doubt a truth is brought to light thereby, but it is of very limited value, I mean it is anthropomorphic through and through, and does not contain one single point which is "true-in-itself," real, and universally valid, apart from man. The seeker after such truths seeks at the bottom only the metamorphosis of the world in man; he strives for an understanding of the world as a humanlike thing and by his battling gains at best the feeling of an assimilation. Similarly, as the astrologer contemplated the stars in the service of men and in connection with their happiness and unhappiness, such a

seeker contemplates the whole world as related to man, as the infinitely protracted echo of an original sound: man; as the multiplied copy of the one archetype: man. His procedure is to apply man as the measure of all things, whereby he starts from the error of believing that he has these things immediately before him as pure objects. He therefore forgets that the original metaphors of perception *are* metaphors, and takes them for the things themselves.

Only by forgetting that primitive world of metaphors, only by the congelation and coagulation of an original mass of similes and percepts pouring forth as a fiery liquid out of the primal faculty of human fancy, only by the invincible faith, that *this* sun, *this* window, *this* table is a truth in itself: in short only by the fact that man forgets himself as subject, and what is more as an *artistically creating* subject, only by all this does he live with some repose, safety, and consequence. If he were able to get out of the prison walls of this faith, even for an instant only, his "self-consciousness" would be destroyed at once. Already it costs him some trouble to admit to himself that the insect and the bird perceive a world different from his own, and that the question, which of the two world-perceptions is more accurate, is quite a senseless one, since to decide this question it would be necessary to apply the standard of *right perception,* i.e., to apply a standard which *does not exist.* On the whole it seems to me that the "right perception"—which would mean the adequate expression of an object in the subject—is a nonentity full of contradictions: for between two utterly different spheres, as between subject and object, there is no causality, no accuracy, no expression, but at the utmost an *aesthetical* relation, I mean a suggestive metamorphosis, a stammering translation into quite a distinct foreign language, for which purpose, however, there is needed at any rate an intermediate sphere, an intermediate force, freely composing and freely inventing. The word "phenomenon" contains many seductions, and on that account I avoid it as much as possible, for it is not true that the essence of things appears in the empiric world. A painter who had no hands and wanted to express the picture distinctly present to his mind by the agency of song would still reveal much more with this permutation of spheres than the empiric world reveals about the essence of things. The very relation of a nerve stimulus to the produced percept is in itself no necessary one; but if the same percept has been reproduced millions of times and has been the inheritance of many successive generations of man, and in the end appears each time to all mankind as the result of the same cause, then it attains finally for man the same importance as if it were *the* unique, necessary percept and as if that relation between the original nerve stimulus and the percept produced were a close relation of causality: just as a dream eternally repeated would be perceived and judged as though real. But the congelation and coagulation of a metaphor does not at all guarantee the necessity and exclusive justification of that metaphor.

Surely every human being who is at home with such contemplations has felt a deep distrust against any idealism of that kind, as often as he has distinctly convinced himself of the eternal rigidity, omnipresence, and infallibility of nature's laws: he has arrived at the conclusion that as far as we can penetrate the heights of the telescopic and the depths of the microscopic world, everything is quite secure, complete, infinite, determined, and continuous. Science will have to dig in these shafts eternally and successfully and all things found are sure to have to harmonize and not to contradict one another. How little does this resemble a product of fancy, for if it were one it would necessarily betray somewhere its nature of appearance and unreality. Against this it may be objected in the first place that if each of us had for himself a different sensibility, if we ourselves were only able to perceive sometimes as a bird, sometimes as a worm, sometimes as a plant, or if one of us saw the same stimulus as red, another as blue, if a third person even perceived it as a tone, then nobody would talk of such an orderliness of nature, but would conceive of her only as an extremely subjective structure. Secondly, what is, for us in general, a law of nature? It is not known in itself but only in its effects, that is to say, in its relations to other laws of nature, which again are known to us only as sums of relations. Therefore all these relations refer only one to another and are absolutely incomprehensible to us in their essence; only that which we add: time, space, i.e., relations of sequence and numbers, are really known to us in them. Everything wonderful, however, that we marvel at in the laws of nature, everything that demands an explanation and might seduce us into distrusting idealism, lies really and solely in the mathematical rigor and inviolability of the conceptions of time and space. These, however, we produce within ourselves and throw them forth with that necessity with which the spider spins; since we are compelled to conceive all things under these forms only,[9] then it is no longer wonderful that in all things we actually conceive none but these forms: for they all must bear within themselves the laws of number, and this very idea of number is the most marvelous in all things. All obedience to law which impresses us so forcibly in the orbits of stars and in chemical processes coincides at the bottom with those qualities which we ourselves attach to those things, so that it is we who thereby make the impression upon ourselves. Whence it clearly follows that the artistic formation of metaphors with which every sensation in us begins already presupposes those forms, and is therefore only consummated within them; only out of the persistency of these primal forms the possibility explains itself, how afterward out of the metaphors themselves a structure of ideas could again be compiled. For the latter is an imitation of the relations of time, space, and number in the realm of metaphors.

2

As we saw, it is *language* which has worked originally at the construction of ideas; in later times it is *science*. Just as the bee works at the same time at the cells and fills them with honey, thus science works irresistibly at that great columbarium of ideas, the cemetery of perceptions: builds ever newer and higher storeys; supports, purifies, renews the old cells; and endeavors above all to fill that gigantic framework and to arrange within it the whole of the empiric world, i.e., the anthropomorphic world. And as the man of action binds his life to reason and its ideas, in order to avoid being swept away and losing himself, so the seeker after truth builds his hut close to the towering edifice of science in order to collaborate with it and to find protection. And he needs protection. For there are awful powers which continually press upon him, and which hold out against the "truth" of science "truths" fashioned in quite another way, bearing devices of the most heterogeneous character.

That impulse toward the formation of metaphors, that fundamental impulse of man, which we cannot reason away for one moment—for thereby we should reason away man himself—is in truth not defeated nor even subdued by the fact that out of its evaporated products, the ideas, a regular and rigid new world has been built as a stronghold for it. This impulse seeks for itself a new realm of action and another river-bed, and finds it in *Mythos* and more generally in *Art*. This impulse constantly confuses the rubrics and cells of the ideas by putting up new figures of speech, metaphors, metonymies; it constantly shows its passionate longing for shaping the existing world of waking man as motley, irregular, inconsequently incoherent, attractive, and eternally new as the world of dreams is. For indeed, waking man per se is only clear about his being awake through the rigid and orderly woof of ideas, and it is for this very reason that he sometimes comes to believe that he was dreaming when that woof of ideas has for a moment been torn by Art. Pascal[10] is quite right when he asserts that if the same dream came to us every night, we should be just as much occupied by it as by the things which we see every day; to quote his words,

---

[9] Kant's time and space, pure forms in which all our experience is cast.

[10] Blaise Pascal (1623–1662), French philosopher.

"If an artisan were certain that he would dream every night for fully twelve hours that he was a king, I believe that he would be just as happy as a king who dreams every night for twelve hours that he is an artisan." The wideawake day of a people mystically excitable, let us say of the earlier Greeks, is in fact through the continually working wonder, which the mythos presupposes, more akin to the dream than to the day of the thinker sobered by silence. If every tree may at some time talk as a nymph, or a god under the disguise of a bull carry away virgins, if the goddess Athena herself be suddenly seen as, with a beautiful team, she drives, accompanied by Pisistratus, through the markets of Athens—and every honest Athenian did believe this—at any moment, as in a dream, everything is possible; and all nature swarms around man as if she were nothing but the masquerade of the gods, who found it a huge joke to deceive man by assuming all possible forms.

Man himself, however, has an invincible tendency to let himself be deceived, and he is like one enchanted with happiness when the rhapsodist narrates to him epic romances in such a way that they appear real or when the actor on the stage makes the king appear more kingly than reality shows him. Intellect, that master of dissimulation, is free and dismissed from his service as slave, so long as It is able to deceive without *injuring,* and then It celebrates Its Saturnalia.[11] Never is It richer, prouder, more luxuriant, more skillful and daring; with a creator's delight It throws metaphors into confusion, shifts the boundary stones of the abstractions, so that, for instance, It designates the stream as the mobile way which carries man to that place whither he would otherwise go. Now It has thrown off Its shoulders the emblem of servitude. Usually with gloomy officiousness It endeavors to point out the way to a poor individual coveting existence, and It fares forth for plunder and booty like a servant for his master, but now It Itself has become a master and may wipe from Its countenance the expression of indigence. Whatever It now does, compared with Its former doings, bears within itself dissimulation, just as Its former doings bore the character of distortion. It copies human life, but takes it for a good thing and seems to rest quite satisfied with it. That enormous framework and hoarding of ideas, by clinging to which needy man saves himself through life, is to the freed intellect only a scaffolding and a toy for Its most daring feats, and when It smashes it to pieces, throws it into confusion, and then puts it together ironically, pairing the strangest, separating the nearest items, then It manifests that It has no use for those makeshifts of misery, and that It is now no longer led by ideas but by intuitions. From these in-

tuitions no regular road leads into the land of the spectral schemata, the abstractions; for them the word is not made, when man sees them he is dumb, or speaks in forbidden metaphors and in unheard-of combinations of ideas, in order to correspond creatively with the impression of the powerful present intuition at least by destroying and jeering at the old barriers of ideas.

There are ages, when the rational and the intuitive man stand side by side, the one full of fear of the intuition, the other full of scorn for the abstraction; the latter just as irrational as the former is inartistic. Both desire to rule over life; the one by knowing how to meet the most important needs with foresight, prudence, regularity; the other as an "overjoyous" hero by ignoring those needs and taking that life only as real which simulates appearance and beauty. Whenever intuitive man, as for instance in the earlier history of Greece, brandishes his weapons more powerfully and victoriously than his opponent, there under favorable conditions, a culture can develop and art can establish her rule over life. That dissembling, that denying of neediness, that splendor of metaphorical notions and especially that directness of dissimulation accompany all utterances of such a life. Neither the house of man, nor his way of walking, nor his clothing, nor his earthen jug suggest that necessity invented them; it seems as if they all were intended as the expressions of a sublime happiness, an olympic cloudlessness, and, as it were, a playing at seriousness. Whereas the man guided by ideas and abstractions only wards off misfortune by means of them, without even enforcing for himself happiness out of the abstractions; whereas he strives after the greatest possible freedom from pains, the intuitive man dwelling in the midst of culture has from his intuitions a harvest: besides the warding off of evil, he attains a continuous inpouring of enlightenment, enlivenment, and redemption. Of course when he *does* suffer, he suffers more: and he even suffers more frequently since he cannot learn from experience, but again and again falls into the same ditch into which he has fallen before. In suffering he is just as irrational as in happiness; he cries aloud and finds no consolation. How different matters are in the same misfortune with the Stoic, taught by experience and ruling himself by ideas! He who otherwise only looks for uprightness, truth, freedom from deceptions and shelter from ensnaring and sudden attack, in his misfortune performs the masterpiece of dissimulation, just as the other did in his happiness; he shows no twitching mobile human face but, as it were, a mask with dignified, harmonious features; he does not cry out and does not even alter his voice; when a heavy thundercloud bursts upon him, he wraps himself up in his cloak and with slow and measured step walks away from beneath it.

---

[11] Wild revelry.

Émile Zola

1840–1902

In an age of the rapid advance of science it was perhaps inevitable that many critics would perceive an opposition between poetry and science. It was likely also that some literary critics would seek to draw an analogy between artistic and scientific procedures, and that there would be various sorts of reactions against Romanticism and philosophical idealism, which had held the stage for many years. We see both of these latter attitudes in the French novelist Zola's *The Experimental Novel*. Unlike the Romantics, who distinguished literary from scientific practice, Zola sees the artist adopting the experimental method recommended by Claude Bernard (1813–1878) in his *Introduction à l'étude de la médecine expérimentale*. Zola argues that the experimental novelist is neither a mere copyist of nature nor a photographer: "The idea of experiment carries with it the idea of modification." The novelist can use his "genius," but under control of experiment. The Romanticist dwelt "in the unknown for the pleasure of being there." The experimentalist voyages into the unknown to make it known. The "nonsense and folly" of Romantic lyricism will be diminished, and literature, it appears, will become what today we would call material for the social scientist. Though Zola used the term "experimental" to describe what he was trying to do, the term that is used most often to describe the type of novel he wrote is "naturalistic."

Zola rode the current of positivism and accepted the notion of material progress that accompanied it. His view raises, among other things, the problem of the value of the literature of the past. Since the science of the past has no specific current scientific value, presumably (to extend Zola's analogy), perhaps past literature has no value today. Zola cannot completely accept this; he suggests that ancient poems will survive because of their "beauty," but that sort of virtue is really for him quaint and archaic. Physiological man has replaced metaphysical man. Analytical procedures are the rule. Yet, by introducing that vague term "beauty" at the very end of his essay, Zola seems to admit the limitations of his own position if it were extended to a general theory.

A useful group of translations is *The Experimental Novel and Other Essays* by B. M. Sherman (1893). See F. Doucet, *L'Esthetique de Zola et son application a la critique* (1923); Matthew Josephson, *Zola and His Time* (1928); W. H. Root, *German Criticism of Zola 1875–1893* (1931); Edward Stone, *What Was Naturalism?* (1958); Philip D. Walker, *Émile Zola* (1969); Frederick Hemmings, *Life and Times of Émile Zola* (1977); Joanna Richardson, *Zola* (1978); David Baguley, ed., *Critical Essays on Émile Zola* (1986); Alan Schom, *Émile Zola: A Bourgeois Rebel* (1987); Jean Max Guieu and Alison Hilton, eds., *Émile Zola and the Arts* (1988); Anita Brookner, "Zola: Art for Life's Sake" in her *Romanticism and Its Discontents* (2000).

from

The Experimental Novel

In my literary essays I have often spoken of the application of the experimental method to the novel and to the drama. The return to nature, the naturalistic evolution which marks the century, drives little by little all the manifestation of human intelligence into the same scientific path. Only the idea of a literature governed by science is doubtless a surprise, until explained with precision and understood. It seems to me necessary, then, to say briefly and to the point what I understand by the experimental novel.

I really only need to adapt, for the experimental method has been established with strength and marvelous clearness by Claude Bernard in his *Introduction à l'étude de la médecine expérimentale.*[1] This work, by a savant whose authority is unquestioned, will serve me as a solid foundation. I shall here find the whole question treated, and I shall restrict myself to irrefutable arguments and to giving the quotations which may seem necessary to me. This will then be but a compiling of texts, as I intend on all points to entrench myself behind Claude Bernard. It will often be but necessary for me to replace the word *doctor* by the word *novelist,* to make my meaning clear and to give it the rigidity of a scientific truth.

What determined my choice, and made me choose *L'Introduction* as my basis, was the fact that medicine, in the eyes of a great number of people, is still an art, as is the novel. Claude Bernard all his life was searching and battling to put medicine in a scientific path. In his struggle we see the first feeble attempts of a science to disengage itself little by little from empiricism,[2] and to gain a foothold in the realm of truth, by means of the experimental method. Claude Bernard demonstrates that this method, followed in the study of inanimate bodies in chemistry and in physics, should be also used in the study of living bodies, in physiology and medicine. I am going to try and prove for my part that if the experimental method leads to the knowledge of physical life, it should also lead to the knowledge of the passionate and intellectual life. It is but a question of degree in the same path which runs from chemistry to physiology, then from physiology to anthropology and to sociology. The experimental novel is the goal.

To be more clear, I think it would be better to give a brief résumé of *L'Introduction* before I commence. The applications which I shall make of the texts will be better understood if the plan of the work and the matters treated are explained.

Claude Bernard, after having declared that medicine enters the scientific path, with physiology as its foundation, and by means of the experimental method, first explains the differences which exist between the sciences of observation and the sciences of experiment. He concludes, finally, that experiment is but provoked observation. All experimental reasoning is based on doubt, for the experimentalist should have no preconceived idea, in the face of nature, and should always retain his liberty of thought. He simply accepts the phenomena which are produced, when they are proved.

In the second part he reaches his true subject and shows that the spontaneity of living bodies is not opposed to the employment of experiment. The difference is simply that an inanimate body possesses merely the ordinary, external environment, while the essence of the higher organism is set in an internal and perfected environment endowed with constant physicochemical properties exactly like the external environment; hence there is an absolute determinism in the existing conditions of natural phenomena; for the living as for the inanimate bodies. He calls determinism the cause which determines the appearance of these phenomena. This nearest cause, as it is called, is nothing more than the physical and material condition of the existence or manifestation of the phenomena. The end of all experimental method, the boundary of all scientific research, is then identical for living and for inanimate bodies; it consists in finding the relations which unite a phenomenon of any kind to its nearest cause, or, in other words, in determining the conditions necessary for the manifestation of this phenomenon. Experimental science has no necessity to worry itself about the "why" of things; it simply explains the "how."

After having explained the experimental considerations common to living beings and to inanimate, Claude Bernard passes to the experimental considerations which belong specially to living beings. The great and only difference is this, that there is presented to our consideration, in the organism of living beings, a harmonious group of phenomena. He then treats of practical experiments on living beings, of vivisection, of the preparatory anatomical conditions, of the choice of animals, of the use of calculation in the study of phenomena, and lastly of the physiologist's laboratory.

Finally, in the last part of *L'Introduction,* he gives some examples of physiological experimental investigations in

---

Le Roman expérimentale was first published in 1880. The text is from the translation by B. M. Sherman (1893).

[1] *Introduction to the Study of Experimental Medicine.*

[2] [Sherman] Zola uses *empiricism* in this essay in the sense of *haphazard observation* in contrast with a scientific experiment undertaken to prove a certain truth.

support of the ideas which he has formulated. He then furnishes some examples of experimental criticism in physiology. In the end he indicates the philosophical obstacles which the experimental doctor encounters. He puts in the first rank the false application of physiology to medicine, the scientific ignorance as well as certain illusions of the medical mind. Further, he concludes by saying that empirical medicine and experimental medicine, not being incompatible, ought, on the contrary, to be inseparable one from the other. His last sentence is that experimental medicine adheres to no medical doctrine nor any philosophical system.

This is, very broadly, the skeleton of *L'Introduction* stripped of its flesh. I hope that this rapid exposé will be sufficient to fill up the gaps which my manner of proceeding is bound to produce; for, naturally, I shall cite from the work only such passages as are necessary to define and comment upon the experimental novel. I repeat that I use this treatise merely as a solid foundation on which to build, but a foundation very rich in arguments and proofs of all kinds. Experimental medicine, which but lisps as yet, can alone give us an exact idea of experimental literature, which, being still unhatched, is not even lisping.

I

The first question which presents itself is this: Is experiment possible in literature, in which up to the present time observation alone has been employed?

Claude Bernard discusses observation and experiment at great length. There exists, in the first place, a very clear line of demarcation, as follows:

> The name of *observer* is given to him who applies the simple or complex process of investigation in the study of phenomena which he does not vary, and which he gathers, consequently, as nature offers them to him; the name of *experimentalist* is given to him who employs the simple and complex process of investigation to vary or modify, for an end of some kind, the natural phenomena, and to make them appear under circumstances and conditions in which they are not presented by nature.

For instance, astronomy is a science of observation, because you cannot conceive of an astronomer acting upon the stars; while chemistry is an experimental science, as the chemist acts upon nature and modifies it. This, according to Claude Bernard, is the only true and important distinction which separates the observer from the experimentalist.

* * *

To determine how much observation and experimenting there can be in the naturalistic novel, I only need to quote the following passages:

> The observer relates purely and simply the phenomena which he has under his eyes. . . . He should be the photographer of phenomena, his observation should be an exact representation of nature. . . . He listens to nature and he writes under its dictation. But once the fact is ascertained and the phenomenon observed, an idea or hypothesis comes into his mind, reason intervenes, and the experimentalist comes forward to interpret the phenomenon. The experimentalist is a man who, in pursuance of a more or less probable, but anticipated, explanation of observed phenomena, institutes an experiment in such a way that, according to all probability, it will furnish a result which will serve to confirm the hypothesis or preconceived idea. The moment that the result of the experiment manifests itself, the experimentalist finds himself face to face with a true observation which he has called forth, and which he must ascertain, as all observation, without any preconceived idea. The experimentalist should then disappear, or rather transform himself instantly into the observer, and it is not until after he has ascertained the absolute results of the experiment, like that of an ordinary observation, that his mind comes back to reasoning, comparing, and judging whether the experimental hypothesis is verified or invalidated by these same results.

The mechanism is all there. It is a little complicated, it is true, and Claude Bernard is led on to say:

> When all this passes into the brain of a savant who has given himself up to the study of a science as complicated as medicine still is, then there is such an entanglement between the result of observation and what belongs to experiment that it will be impossible and, besides, useless to try to analyze, in their inextricable *mélange,* each of these terms.

In one word, it might be said that observation "indicates" and that experiment "teaches."

Now, to return to the novel, we can easily see that the novelist is equally an observer and an experimentalist. The observer in him gives the fact as he has observed them, suggests the point of departure, displays the solid earth on which his characters are to tread and the phenomena to develop. Then the experimentalist appears and introduces an experiment, that is to say, sets his characters going in a certain story so as to show that the succession of facts will be such as the requirements of the determinism of the phenomena under examination call for. Here it is nearly always an experiment *"pour voir,"*[3] as Claude Bernard calls it. The novelist starts out in search of a truth. I will take as an example the character of the Baron Hulot, in *Cousine Bette,* by Balzac.[4] The general fact observed by Balzac is the ravages that the amorous temperament of a man makes in his home, in his family, and in society. As soon as he has chosen his subject he starts from known facts; then he makes his experiment, and exposes Hulot to a series of trials, placing him amid certain surroundings in order to exhibit how the complicated machinery of his passions works. It is then evident that there is not only observation there, but that there is also experiment; as Balzac does not remain satisfied with photographing the facts collected by him, but interferes in a direct way to place his character in certain conditions, and of these he remains the master. The problem is to know what such a passion, acting in such a surrounding and under such circumstances, would produce from the point of view of an individual and of society; and an experimental novel, *Cousine Bette,* for example, is simply the report of the experiment that the novelist conducts before the eyes of the public. In fact, the whole operation consists in taking facts in nature, then in studying the mechanism of these facts, acting upon them, by the modification of circumstances and surroundings, without deviating from the laws of nature. Finally, you possess knowledge of the man, scientific knowledge of him, in both his individual and social relations.

Doubtless we are still far from certainties in chemistry and even physiology. Nor do we know any more the reagents which decompose the passions, rendering them susceptible of analysis. Often, in this essay, I shall recall in similar fashion this fact, that the experimental novel is still younger than experimental medicine, and the latter is but just born. But I do not intend to exhibit the acquired results, I simply desire to clearly expose a method. If the experimental novelist is still groping in the most obscure and complex of all the sciences, this does not prevent this science from existing. It is undeniable that the naturalistic novel, such as we understand it today, is a real experiment that a novelist makes on man by the help of observation.

---

[3] "In order to see."
[4] Honoré de Balzac (1799–1850), French novelist.

* * *

But see what splendid clearness breaks forth when this conception of the application of the experimental method to the novel is adequately grasped and is carried out with all the scientific rigor which the matter permits today. A contemptible reproach which they heap upon us naturalistic writers is the desire to be solely photographers. We have in vain declared that we admit the necessity of an artist's possessing an individual temperament and a personal expression; they continue to reply to us with these imbecile arguments, about the impossibility of being strictly true, about the necessity of arranging facts to produce a work of art of any kind. Well, with the application of the experimental method to the novel that quarrel dies out. The idea of experiment carries with it the idea of modification. We start, indeed, from the true facts, which are our indestructible basis; but to show the mechanism of these facts it is necessary for us to produce and direct the phenomena; this is our share of invention, here is the genius in the book. Thus without having recourse to the questions of form and of style, which I shall examine later, I maintain even at this point that we must modify nature, without departing from nature, when we employ the experimental method in our novels. If we bear in mind this definition, that "observation indicates and experiment teaches," we can even now claim for our books this great lesson of experiment.

* * *

I sum up this first part by repeating that the naturalistic novelists observe and experiment, and that all their work is the offspring of the doubt which seizes them in the presence of truths little known and phenomena unexplained, until an experimental idea rudely awakens their genius some day, and urges them to make an experiment, to analyze facts, and to master them.

II

. . . In the last century a more exact application of the experimental method creates physics and chemistry, which then are freed from the irrational and supernatural. Men discover that there are fixed laws, thanks to analysis, and make themselves masters of phenomena. Then a new point is gained. Living beings, in which the vitalists still admitted a mysterious influence, are in their turn brought under and reduced to the general mechanism of matter. Science proves that the existing conditions of all phenomena are the same in living beings as in inanimate; and from that time on physiology assumes little by little the certainty of chemistry and medicine. But are we going to stop there? Evidently not. When it has been proved that the body of a man is a machine, whose machinery can be taken apart and put together again at the will of the experimenter, then we can pass to the passionate and intellectual acts of man. Then we shall enter into the domain which up to the present has belonged to physiology and literature; it will be the decisive conquest by science of the hypotheses of philosophers and writers. We have experimental chemistry and medicine; we shall have an experimental physiology, and later on an experimental novel. It is an inevitable evolution, the goal of which it is easy to see today. All things hang together; it is necessary to start from the determinism of inanimate bodies in order to arrive at the determinism of living beings; and since savants like Claude Bernard demonstrate now that fixed laws govern the human body, we can easily proclaim, without fear of being mistaken, the hour in which the laws of thought and passion will be formulated in their turn. A like determinism will govern the stones of the roadway and the brain of man.

* * *

Now, science enters into the domain of us novelists, who are today the analyzers of man, in his individual and social relations. We are continuing, by our observations and experiments, the work of the physiologist, who has continued that of the physicist and the chemist. We are making use, in a certain way, of scientific psychology to complete scientific physiology; and to finish the series we have only to bring into our studies of nature and man the decisive tool of the experimental method. In one word, we should operate on the characters, the passions, on the human and social data, in the same way that the chemist and the physicist operate on inanimate beings, and as the physiologist operates on living beings. Determinism dominates everything. It is scientific investigation, it is experimental reasoning, which combats one by one the hypotheses of the idealists, and which replaces purely imaginary novels by novels of observation and experiment.

I certainly do not intend at this point to formulate laws. In the actual condition of the science of man the obscurity and confusion are still too great to risk the slightest synthesis. All that can be said is that there is an absolute determinism for all human phenomena. From that on investigation is a duty. We have the method; we should go forward, even if a whole lifetime of effort ends but in the conquest of a small particle of the truth. Look at physiology: Claude

Bernard made grand discoveries, and he died protesting that he knew nothing, or nearly nothing. In each page he confesses the difficulties of his task. "In the phenomenal relations," he says,

> such as nature offers them to us, there always reigns a complexity more or less great. In this respect the complexity of mineral phenomena is much less great than that of living phenomena; this is why the sciences restricted to inanimate bodies have been able to formulate themselves more quickly. In living beings the phenomena are of enormous complexity, and the greater mobility of living organisms renders them more difficult to grasp and to define.

What can be said, then, of the difficulties to be encountered by the experimental novel, which adds to physiology its studies upon the most delicate and complex organs, which deals with the highest manifestations of man as an individual and a social member? Evidently analysis becomes more complicated here. Therefore, if the physiologist is but drawing up his principles today, it is natural that the experimental novelist should be only taking his first steps: we foresee it as a sure consequence of the scientific evolution of the century; but it is impossible to base it on certain laws. Since Claude Bernard speaks of "the restricted and precarious truths of biological science," we can freely admit that the truths of the science of man, from the standpoint of his intellectual and passionate mechanism, are more restricted and precarious still. We are lisping yet, we are the last comers, but that should be only one incentive the more to push us forward to more exact studies; now that we possess the tool, the experimental method, our goal is very plain—to know the determinism of phenomena and to make ourselves master of these phenomena.

Without daring, as I say, to formulate laws, I consider that the question of heredity has a great influence in the intellectual and passionate manifestations of man. I also attach considerable importance to the surroundings.[5] I ought to touch upon Darwin's[6] theories; but this is only a general study of the experimental method as applied to the novel, and I should lose myself were I to enter into details. I will only say a word on the subject of surroundings. We have just seen the great importance given by Claude Bernard to the study of those interorganic conditions which must be

---

[5] Taine (above, page 645).
[6] Charles Darwin's (1809–1882) *Origin of Species* had been published in 1859.

taken into account if we wish to find the determinism of phenomena in living beings. Well, then! In the study of a family, of a group of living beings, I think that the social condition is of equal importance. Someday the physiologist will explain to us the mechanism of the thoughts and the passions; we shall know how the individual machinery of each man works; how he thinks, how he loves, how he goes from reason to passion and folly; but these phenomena, resulting as they do from the mechanism of the organs, acting under the influence of an interior condition, are not produced in isolation or in the bare void. Man is not alone; he lives in society, in a social condition; and consequently, for us novelists, this social condition unceasingly modifies the phenomena. Indeed our great study is just there, in the reciprocal effect of society on the individual and the individual on society. For the physiologist, the exterior and interior conditions are purely chemical and physical, and this aids him in finding the laws which govern them easily. We are not yet able to prove that the social condition is also physical and chemical. It is that certainly, or rather it is the variable product of a group of living beings, who themselves are absolutely submissive to the physical and chemical laws which govern alike living beings and inanimate. From this we shall see that we can act upon the social conditions, in acting upon the phenomena of which we have made ourselves master in man. And this is what constitutes the experimental novel: to possess a knowledge of the mechanism of the phenomena inherent in man, to show the machinery of his intellectual and sensory manifestations, under the influences of heredity and environment, such as physiology shall give them to us, and then finally to exhibit man living in social conditions produced by himself, which he modifies daily, and in the heart of which he himself experiences a continual transformation. Thus, then, we lean on physiology; we take man from the hands of the physiologist solely, in order to continue the solution of the problem, and to solve scientifically the question of how men behave when they are in society.

These general ideas will be sufficient to guide us today. Later on, when science is farther advanced, when the experimental novel has brought forth decisive results, some critic will explain more precisely what I have but indicated today.

* * *

I have reached this point: the experimental novel is a consequence of the scientific evolution of the century; it continues and completes physiology, which itself leans for support on chemistry and medicine; it substitutes for the study of the abstract and the metaphysical man the study of the natural man, governed by physical and chemical laws, and modified by the influences of his surroundings; it is in one word the literature of our scientific age, as the classical and Romantic literature corresponded to a scholastic and theological age. Now I will pass to the great question of the application of all this, and of its justification.

III

. . . This, then, is the end, this is the purpose in physiology and in experimental medicine: to make oneself master of life in order to be able to direct it. Let us suppose that science advances and that the conquest of the unknown is finally completed; the scientific age which Claude Bernard saw in his dreams will then be realized. When that time comes the doctor will be the master of maladies; he will cure without fail; his influence upon the human body will conduce to the welfare and strength of the species. We shall enter upon a century in which man, grown more powerful, will make use of nature and will utilize its laws to produce upon the earth the greatest possible amount of justice and freedom. There is no nobler, higher, nor grander end. Here is our role as intelligent beings: to penetrate to the wherefore of things, to become superior to these things, and to reduce them to a condition of subservient machinery.

Well, this dream of the physiologist and the experimental doctor is also that of the novelist, who employs the experimental method in his study of man as a simple individual and as a social animal. Their object is ours; we also desire to master certain phenomena of an intellectual and personal order, to be able to direct them. We are, in a word, experimental moralists, showing by experiment in what way a passion acts in a certain social condition. The day in which we gain control of the mechanism of this passion we can treat it and reduce it, or at least make it as inoffensive as possible. And in this consists the practical utility and high morality of our naturalistic works, which experiment on man, and which dissect piece by piece this human machinery in order to set it going through the influence of the environment. When things have advanced further, when we are in possession of the different laws, it will only be necessary to work upon the individuals and the surroundings if we wish to find the best social condition. In this way we shall construct a practical sociology, and our work will be a help to political and economical sciences. I do not know, I repeat, of a more noble work, nor of a grander application. To be the master of good and evil, to regulate life, to regulate society, to solve in time all the problems of socialism, above all, to give justice a solid foundation by solving through experiment the questions of criminality—is not this being the most useful and the most moral workers in the human workshop?

Let us compare, for one instant, the work of the idealistic novelists to ours; and here this word idealistic refers to writers who cast aside observation and experiment, and base their works on the supernatural and the irrational, who admit, in a word, the power of mysterious forces outside of the determinism of the phenomena. Claude Bernard shall reply to this for me:

What distinguishes experimental reasoning from scholastic is the fecundity of the one and the sterility of the other. It is precisely the scholastic, who believes he has absolute certitude, who attains to no results. This is easily understood, since by his belief in an absolute principle he puts himself outside of nature, in which everything is relative. It is, on the contrary, the experimenter, who is always in doubt, who does not think he possesses absolute certainty about anything, who succeeds in mastering the phenomena which surround him, and in increasing his power over nature.

By and by I shall return to this question of the ideal, which is in truth but the question of indeterminism. Claude Bernard says truly: "The intellectual conquest of man consists in diminishing and driving back indeterminism, and so, gradually, by the aid of the experimental method, gaining ground for determinism." We experimental novelists have the same task; our work is to go from the known to the unknown, to make ourselves masters of nature; while the idealistic novelists deliberately remain in the unknown, through all sorts of religious and philosophical prejudices, under the astounding pretense that the unknown is nobler and more beautiful than the known. If our work, often cruel, if our terrible pictures needed justification, I should find, indeed, with Claude Bernard this argument conclusive:

You will never reach really fruitful and luminous generalization on the phenomena of life until you have experimented yourself and stirred up in the hospital, the amphitheater, and the laboratory the fetid or palpitating sources of life. If it were necessary for me to give a comparison which would explain my sentiments on the science of life, I should say that it is a superb salon, flooded with light, which you can only reach by passing through a long and nauseating kitchen.

I insist upon the word which I have employed, that of experimental novelists as applied to naturalistic novelists. One page of *L'Introduction* struck me as being very forcible, that in which the author speaks of the vital "circulus."

The muscular and nervous organs preserve the activity of the organs which make the blood; but the blood, in its turn, nourishes the organs which produce it. There is in this a social or organic solidarity, which keeps up a perpetual movement, until the derangement or cessation of the action of a necessary and vital element has broken the equilibrium or brought about some trouble or stoppage in the play of the animal machinery. The problem of the experimentalist doctor consists in finding the cause of any organic disarrangement, that is to say, in seizing the initial phenomenon. We shall see how a dislocation of the organism, or a disarrangement the most complex in appearance, can be traced to a simple initial cause, which calls forth immediately the most complex effects.

All that is necessary here is to change the words experimental doctor to experimental novelist, and this passage is exactly applicable to our naturalistic literature. The social circulus is identical with the vital circulus; in society, as in human beings, a solidarity exists which unites the different members and the different organisms in such a way that if one organ becomes rotten many others are tainted and a very complicated disease results. Hence, in our novels, when we experiment on a dangerous wound which poisons society, we proceed in the same way as the experimentalist doctor; we try to find the simple initial cause in order to reach the complex causes of which the action is the result. Go back once more to the example of Baron Hulot in *Cousine Bette*. See the final result, the dénouement of the novel: an entire family is destroyed, all sorts of secondary dramas are produced, under the action of Hulot's amorous temperament. It is there, in this temperament, that the initial cause is found. One member, Hulot, becomes rotten, and immediately all around him are tainted, the social circulus is interrupted, the health of that society is compromised. What emphasis Balzac lays on the character of Baron Hulot; with what scrupulous care he analyzes him! The experiment deals with him chiefly, because its object is to master the symptoms of this passion in order to govern it. Suppose that Hulot is cured, or at least restrained and rendered inoffensive, immediately the drama ceases to have any longer any *raison d'être;*[7] the equilibrium, or more truly the health, of the social body is again established. Thus the naturalistic novelists are really experimental moralists.

And I reach thus the great reproach with which they think to crush the naturalistic novelists, by treating them as fatalists. How many times have they wished to prove to us that as soon as we did not accept free will, that as soon as man was no more to us than a living machine, acting under the influence of heredity and surroundings, we should fall into gross fatalism, we should debase humanity to the rank of a troop marching under the baton of destiny. It is necessary to define our terms: we are not fatalists, we are determinists, which is not at all the same thing. Claude Bernard explains the two terms very plainly:

> We have given the name of determinism to the nearest or determining cause of phenomena. We never act upon the essence of phenomena in nature, but only on their determinism, and by this very fact, that we act upon it, determinism differs from fatalism, upon which we could not act at all. Fatalism assumes that the appearance of any phenomenon is necessary apart from its conditions, while determinism is just the conditions, essential for the appearance of any phenomenon, and such appearance is never forced. Once the search for the determinism of phenomena is placed as a fundamental principle of the experimental method, there is no longer either materialism, or spiritualism, or inanimate matter, or living matter; there remain but phenomena of which it is necessary to determine the conditions, that is to say, the circumstances which play, by their proximity to these phenomena, the role of nearest cause.

This is decisive. All we do is to apply this method in our novels, and we are the determinists who experimentally try to determine the condition of the phenomena, without departing in our investigations from the laws of nature. As Claude Bernard very truly says, the moment that we can act, and that we do act, on the determining cause of phenomena—by modifying their surroundings, for example—we cease to be fatalists.

Here you have, then, the moral purpose of the experimental novelist clearly defined. I have often said that we do not have to draw a conclusion from our works; and this means that our works carry their conclusion with them. An experimentalist has no need to conclude, because, in truth, experiment concludes for him.[8] A hundred times, if necessary, he will repeat the experiment before the public; he will explain it; but he need neither become indignant nor approve of it personally; such is the truth, such is the way phenomena work; it is for society to produce or not to produce these phenomena, according as the result is useful or dangerous. You cannot imagine, as I have said elsewhere, a savant being provoked with azote because azote is dangerous to life; he suppresses azote when it is harmful, and not otherwise. As our power is not the same as that of a savant, as we are experimentalists without being practitioners, we ought to content ourselves with searching out the determinism of social phenomena, and leaving to legislators and to men of affairs the care of controlling sooner or later these phenomena in such a way as to develop the good and reject the bad, from the point of view of their utility to man.

In our role as experimental moralists we show the mechanism of the useful and the useless, we disengage the determinism of the human and social phenomena so that, in their turn, the legislators can one day dominate and control these phenomena. In a word, we are working with the whole country toward that great object, the conquest of nature and the increase of man's power a hundredfold. Compare with ours the work of the idealistic writers, who rely upon the irrational and the supernatural, and whose every flight upward is followed by a deeper fall into metaphysical chaos. We are the ones who possess strength and morality.

IV

. . . If Claude Bernard confesses that the complexity of its phenomena will prevent medicine, for a long time yet, from arriving at a scientific state, what shall we say of the experimental novel, in which the phenomena are much more complicated still? But this does not prevent the novel from entering upon the scientific pathway, obedient to the general evolution of the century.

Moreover, Claude Bernard himself has indicated the evolutions of the human mind. "The human mind," he says,

> at various periods of its progress has passed successively through feeling, reason, and experiment.

---

[7] "Reason for being."

[8] This is an experimentalist or materialist view of the impersonal relation of author to work. An impersonal view was also developed apart from experimentalism and materialism in the twentieth century by Eliot (below, page 806) and subsequently the New Critics in opposition to Romantic emphasis on the work as an expression of the artist.

First, feeling alone, dominating reason, created the truths of faith, that is to say, theology. Reason, or philosophy, becoming afterward the mistress, brought forth scholasticism. Finally, experiment, that is to say, the study of natural phenomena, taught man that the truths of the exterior world were to be found formulated, in the first place, neither in reason nor in feeling. These last are, indeed, our indispensable guides, but to obtain the truth it is necessary to descend into the objective reality of things, where they lie concealed under their phenomenal form. Thus it is that in the natural progress of things the experimental method appears, which sums up the whole, and which supports itself successfully on the three branches of this immovable tripod: feeling, reason, and experiment. In the search after truth by means of this method, feeling has always the initiative; it engenders the idea a priori or intuition; reason, or the reasoning power, immediately develops the idea and deduces its logical consequences. But if feeling must be guided by the light of reason, reason in its turn must be guided by experiment.

I have given this passage entire, as it is of the greatest importance. It shows clearly the role that the personality of the novelist should play, apart from the style. Since feeling is the starting point of the experimental method, since reason subsequently intervenes to end in experiment, and to be controlled by it, the genius of the experimentalist dominates everything, and this is what has made the experimental method, so inert in other hands, such a powerful tool in the hands of Claude Bernard. I have said the word: method is but the tool; it is the workman, it is the idea, which he brings, which makes the chef-d'oeuvre. I have already quoted these lines: "It is a particular feeling, a *quid proprium*,[9] which constitutes the originality, the invention, or the genius of each one." This, then, is the part taken by genius in the experimental novel. As Claude Bernard says again: "The idea is the seed; the method is the soil which furnishes the conditions for developing and prospering it, and bringing forth its best fruits, according to nature." Thus everything is reduced to a question of method. If you are content to remain in the a priori idea, and enjoy your own feelings without finding any basis for it in reason or any verification in experiment, you are a poet; you venture upon

hypotheses which you cannot prove; you are struggling vainly in a painful indeterminism, and in a way that is often injurious. Listen to these lines of *L'Introduction:*

> Man is naturally a metaphysician and proud; he believes that the idealistic creations of his brain, which coincide with his feelings, represent the reality. Thus it follows that the experimental method is not innate and natural to man, for it is only after having wandered for a long time among theological and scholastical discussions that he ends by recognizing the sterility of his efforts in this path. Man then perceives that he cannot dictate laws to nature, because he does not possess in himself the knowledge and the criterion of exterior things; he realizes that in order to arrive at the truth he must, on the contrary, study the natural laws and submit his ideas, if not his reason, to experiment, that is to say, to the criterion of facts.

What becomes of the genius of the experimental novelist? The genius, the idea a priori, remains, only it is controlled by experiment. The experiment naturally cannot destroy his genius; on the contrary, it confirms it. To take the case of a poet, for example: To show he has genius is it necessary that his feeling, his idea, a priori, should be false? Evidently not, for the genius of a man will be so much the greater when experiment has proved the truth of his personal idea. Our age of lyricism, our Romantic disease, was alone capable of measuring a man's genius by the quantity of nonsense and folly which he put in circulation.[10] I conclude by saying that in our scientific century experiment must prove genius.

This is the drift of our quarrel with the idealistic writers. They always start out from an irrational source of some kind, such as a revelation, a tradition, or conventional authority. As Claude Bernard declares: "We must admit nothing occult; there are but phenomena and the conditions of phenomena." We naturalistic novelists submit each fact to the test of observation and experiment, while the idealistic writers admit mysterious elements which escape analysis, and therefore remain in the unknown, outside of the influence of the laws governing nature. This question of the

---

[10]That Romanticism was diseased had been declared by Goethe, though Schiller claimed that Goethe was himself a Romantic. The notion was revived in the early part of the twentieth century by Irving Babbitt in his *Rousseau and Romanticism* (1919) and T. E. Hulme in his *Speculations* (written 1913–1914, published 1924), where he called Romanticism "spilt religion." Both writers influenced T. S. Eliot and the antiromanticism of the New Critics.

ideal, from the scientific point of view, reduces itself to a question of indeterminate or determinate. All that we do not know, all that escapes us still, that is truly the ideal, and the aim of our human efforts is each day to reduce the ideal, to conquer truth from the unknown. We are all idealists, if we mean by this that we busy ourselves with the ideal. But I dub those idealists who take refuge in the unknown for the pleasure of being there, who have a taste but for the most risky hypotheses, who disdain to submit them to the test of experiment under the pretext that the truth is in themselves and not in the things. These writers, I repeat, accomplish a vain and harmful task, while the observer and the experimentalist are the only ones who work for the strength and happiness of man, making him more and more the master of nature. There is neither nobility, nor dignity, nor beauty, nor morality in not knowing, in lying, in pretending that you are greater according as you advance in error and confusion. The only great and moral works are those of truth.

What we alone must accept is what I will call the stimulus of the ideal. Certainly our science is very limited as yet, beside the enormous mass of things of which we are ignorant. This great unknown which surrounds us ought to inspire us with the desire to pierce it, to explain it by means of scientific methods. And this does not refer only to scientific men; all the manifestations of human intelligence are connected together, all our efforts have their birth in the need we feel of making ourselves masters of the truth.

* * *

V

... I have already repeated twenty times that naturalism is not a personal fantasy, but that it is the intellectual movement of the century. Perhaps they will believe Claude Bernard, who speaks with greater authority on this subject than I can lay claim to; he declares that:

> The revolution which the experimental method has caused in science consists mainly in the substitution of a scientific criterion for a personal authority. It is the characteristic of the experimental method to depend only on itself, as it carries within itself its criterion, which is experiment. It recognizes no authority but that of facts, and it frees itself from personal authority.

Consequently, it no longer admits the authority of any theory either.

> The idea should always remain independent; it must be enchained neither by scientific, nor philosophical, nor religious beliefs. Man must be strong and free in the manifestation of his ideas, must follow his instinct, and not dwell upon the puerile fears of the contradiction of any theories ... he must modify theory by adapting it to nature, and not nature by adapting it to theory.

From this there results an incomparable breadth.

> The experimental method is the scientific method which proclaims the liberty of thought. It not only throws off the philosophical and theological yoke, but it no longer admits scientific personal authority. This is not said from pride or boastfulness. The experimentalist, on the contrary, shows his humility in denying personal authority, for he doubts his own knowledge, and he submits the authority of men to that of experiment and the laws which govern nature.

This is why I have said so many times that naturalism is not a school, as it is not embodied in the genius of one man, nor in the ravings of a group of men, as was Romanticism; that it consists simply in the application of the experimental method to the study of nature and of man. Hence it is nothing but a vast movement, a march forward in which everyone is a workman, according to his genius. All theories are admitted, and the theory which carries the most weight is the one which explains the most. There does not appear to me to be a literary or scientific path larger or more direct. Everyone, the great and the small, moves freely, working and investigating together, each one in his own specialty, and recognizing no other authority than that of facts proved by experiment. Therefore in naturalism there could be neither innovators nor leaders; there are simply workmen, some more skillful than others.

... I have said that in the experimental novel it is best for us to hold to the strictly scientific point of view if we wish to base our studies on solid ground; not to go out from the "how," not to attach ourselves to the "why." However, it is very certain that we cannot always escape this need of our intelligence, this restless curiosity which makes us desire to know the essence of things. I think that it is best for us to accept the philosophical system, which adapts itself the best to the actual condition of the sciences, but simply from a speculative point of view. For example, transformism is actually the most rational system, and is the one which is based most directly upon our knowledge of nature. Behind a science, behind a manifestation of any kind of the human intelligence, there always lies more or less clearly what Claude Bernard calls a philosophical system. To this system it is not well to attach oneself devotedly, but to hold tenaciously to the facts, free to modify the system if the facts call for it. But the system exists nonetheless, and it exists so much the more as science is less advanced and less firm. For us naturalistic novelists, who are still in the lisping stage, hypothesis is fatal. By and by I will take up the role of hypothesis in literature.

Nevertheless, if in practice Claude Bernard thrusts aside philosophical system, he recognizes the necessity of philosophy.

> From a scientific point of view, philosophy represents the eternal desire of the human reason after knowledge of the unknown. Hence philosophers always confine themselves to questions that are in dispute, and to those lofty regions that lie beyond the boundaries of science. In this way they communicate to science a certain inspiration which animates and ennobles it. They strengthen the mind—developing it by an intellectual gymnastics—at the same time that they ever carry it toward the never-completed solution of great problems. Thus they keep up a cult of the unknown, and quicken the sacred fire of investigation, which ought never to be extinguished in the heart of a savant.

This passage is very fine, but the philosophers have never been told in better terms that their hypotheses are pure poetry. Claude Bernard evidently looks upon the philosophers, among whom he believes he has a great many friends, as musicians often gifted with genius, whose music encourages the savants while they work and inspires the sacred fire of their great discoveries. But the philosophers, left to themselves, will sing forever and never discover a single truth.

I have neglected until now the question of form in the naturalistic novel, because it is precisely there that individuality shows in literature. Not only is a writer's genius to be found in the feeling and in the idea a priori but also in the form and style. But the question of method and the question of rhetoric are distinct from each other. And by naturalism, I say again, is meant the experimental method, the introduction of observation and experiment into literature. Rhetoric, for the moment, has no place here. Let us first fix upon the method, on which there should be agreement, and after that accept all the different styles in letters which may be produced, looking upon them as the expressions of the literary temperament of the writers.

If you wish my true opinion upon this subject, it is this: that today an exaggerated importance is given to form. I have a great deal to say on this subject, but it would carry me beyond the limits of this essay. In reality, I think that the form of expression depends upon the method: that language is only one kind of logic and its construction natural and scientific. He who writes the best will not be the one who gallops madly among hypotheses, but the one who walks straight ahead in the midst of truths. We are actually rotten with lyricism; we are very much mistaken when we think that the characteristic of a good style is a sublime confusion with just a dash of madness added; in reality, the excellence of a style depends upon its logic and clearness.

Claude Bernard considers that philosophers are really musicians who play a sort of *Marseillaise* made up of hypotheses, and swell the hearts of the savants as they rush to attack the unknown; and he has much the same idea of artists and writers. I have remarked that a great many of the most intelligent savants, jealous of the scientific certainty which they enjoy, would very willingly confine literature to the ideal. They themselves seem to feel the need of taking little recreations in the world of lies after the fatigue of their exact labors, and they are fond of amusing themselves with the most daring hypotheses, and with fictions which they know perfectly well to be false and ridiculous. Claude Bernard was right when he said: "Literary and artistic productions will never grow old in the sense that they are the expressions of sentiments as unchangeable as human nature." In fact, form is sufficient to immortalize a work; the spectacle of a powerful individuality reproducing nature in superb language will interest all ages; only the works of a savant, from this same point of view, will be read always, for the reason that the thought of a great savant who knows how to write is much more interesting than that of a poet. However far astray the savant may be in his hypothesis, he still remains the equal of the poet, who is certain to have been equally mistaken. The point to be emphasized is this, that our domain is not limited to the expression of sentiments as unchangeable as human nature because it is essential also to exhibit the working of these sentiments.

We have not exhausted our matter when we have depicted anger, avarice, and love; all nature and all of man belong to us, not only in their phenomena, but in the causes of these phenomena. I well know that this is an immense field, the entrance to which they would willingly have refused us; but we have broken down the barriers and have entered it in triumph. This is why I do not accept the following words of Claude Bernard: "In art and letters personality dominates everything. There one is dealing with a spontaneous creation of the mind that has nothing in common with the verification of natural phenomena, in which our minds can create nothing." I have here detected one of our most illustrious savants sharing in the attempt to refuse to letters the entrée to the scientific field. I do not know what letters he refers to in this definition of a literary work: "A spontaneous creation of the mind that has nothing in common with the verification of natural phenomena." Doubtless he has lyrical poetry in his mind, for he never could have written that phrase had he understood the experimental novel as shown in the works of Balzac and Stendhal.[11] I can only repeat what I have said before, that apart from the matter of form and style, the experimental novelist is only one special kind of savant, who makes use of the tools of all other savants, observation and analysis. Our field is the same as the physiologist's, only that it is greater. We operate, like him, on man; and Claude Bernard recognizes this fact himself, that the cerebral phenomena can be determined the same as other phenomena. It is true that Claude Bernard can tell us that we are lost in hypotheses; but to conclude from this that we shall never arrive at the truth sits very badly on him, as he has struggled all his life to make a science of medicine, which the great majority of his contemporaries look upon as an art.

Let us clearly define now what is meant by an experimental novelist. Claude Bernard gives the following definition of an artist: "What is an artist? He is a man who realizes in a work of art an idea or a sentiment which is personal to him." I absolutely reject this definition. On this basis if I represented a man as walking on his head, I should have made a work of art, if such happened to be my personal sentiments. But in that case I should be a fool and nothing else. So one must add that the personal feeling of the artist is always subject to the higher law of truth and nature. We now come to the question of hypothesis. The artist starts out from the same point as the savant; he places himself before nature, has an idea a priori, and works according to this idea. Here alone he separates himself from the savant, if he carries out his idea to the end without verifying its truth by the means of observation and experiment. Those who make use of experiment might well be called experimental artists; but then people will tell us that they are no longer artists, since such people regard art as the burden of personal error which the artist has put into his study of nature. I contend that the personality of the writer should only appear in the idea a priori and in the form, not in the infatuation for the false. I see no objection, besides, to its showing in the hypothesis, but it is necessary to clearly understand what you mean by these words.

It has often been said that writers ought to open the way for savants. This is true, for we have seen in *L'Introduction* that hypothesis and empiricism precede and prepare for the scientific state which is established finally by the experimental method. Man commenced by venturing certain explanations of phenomena, the poets gave expression to their emotions, and the savants ended by mastering hypotheses and fixing the truth; Claude Bernard always assigns the role of pioneers to the philosophers. It is a very noble role, and today it is the writers who should assume it and who should endeavor to fill it worthily. Only let it be well understood that each time that a truth is established by the savants the writers should immediately abandon their hypothesis to adopt this truth; otherwise they will remain deliberately in error without benefiting anyone. It is thus that science, as it advances, furnishes to us writers a solid ground upon which we should lean for support, to better enable us to shoot into new hypotheses. In a word, every phenomenon, once clearly determined, destroys the hypothesis which it replaces, and it is then necessary to transport your hypothesis one step further into the new unknown which arises. I will take a very simple example in order to make myself better understood: it has been proved that the earth revolves around the sun; what would you think of a poet who should adopt the old belief that the sun revolves around the earth? Evidently the poet, if he wishes to risk a personal explanation of any fact, should choose a fact whose cause is not already known. This, then, illustrates the position hypothesis should occupy for experimental novelists; we must accept determined facts, and not attempt to risk about them our personal sentiments, which would be ridiculous, building throughout on the territory that science has conquered; then before the unknown, but only then, exercising our intuition and suggesting the way to science, free to make mistakes, happy if we produce any data toward the solution of the problem. Here I stand at Claude Bernard's practical program, who is forced to accept empiricism as a necessary forerunner. In our experimental novel we can easily risk a few hypotheses on the question of heredity and surroundings, after having respected all that science knows today about the matter. We can prepare the ways, we can furnish the results of observation, human data which may prove very useful. A great lyrical poet has written lately that our century is a century of prophets. Yes, if you wish it; only let it be well understood that these prophets rely neither upon the irrational nor the supernatural. If the prophets thought best to bring up again the most elementary notions, to serve up nature with a strange religious and philosophical sauce, to hold fast to the metaphysical man, to confound and obscure everything, the prophets, notwithstanding their genius in the matter of style,

---

would never be anything but great gooses ignorant whether they would get wet if they jumped into the water. In our scientific age it is a very delicate thing to be a prophet, as we no longer believe in the truths of revelation, and in order to be able to foresee the unknown we must begin by studying the known.

The conclusion to which I wish to come is this: If I were to define the experimental novel I should not say, as Claude Bernard says, that a literary work lies entirely in the personal feeling, for the reason that in my opinion the personal feeling is but the first impulse. Later nature, being there, makes itself felt, or at least that part of nature of which science has given us the secret, and about which we have no longer any right to romance. The experimental novelist is therefore the one who accepts proven facts, who points out in man and in society the mechanism of the phenomena over which science is mistress, and who does not interpose his personal sentiments, except in the phenomena whose determinism is not yet settled, and who tries to test, as much as he can, this personal sentiment, this idea a priori, by observation and experiment.

I cannot understand how our naturalistic literature can mean anything else. I have only spoken of the experimental novel, but I am fairly convinced that the same method, after having triumphed in history and in criticism, will triumph everywhere, on the stage and in poetry even. It is an inevitable evolution. Literature, in spite of all that can be said, does not depend merely upon the author; it is influenced by the nature it depicts and by the man whom it studies. Now if the savants change their ideas of nature, if they find the true mechanism of life, they force us to follow them, to precede them even, so as to play our role in the new hypotheses. The metaphysical man is dead; our whole territory is transformed by the advent of the physiological man. No doubt "Achilles' Anger," "Dido's Love,"[12] will last forever on account of their beauty; but today we feel the necessity of analyzing anger and love, of discovering exactly how such passions work in the human being. This view of the matter is a new one; we have become experimentalists instead of philosophers. In short, everything is summed up in this great fact: the experimental method in letters, as in the sciences, is in the way to explain the natural phenomena, both individual and social, of which metaphysics, until now, has given only irrational and supernatural explanations.

---

[12]Reference to themes in *Iliad* and *Odyssey* respectively.

Oscar Wilde

1854–1900

Wilde's writings are now taken much more seriosuly than they were for decades after his death. Perhaps the Arnoldian desire for high seriousness conflicted with Wilde's way of putting things, which, was witty and often impertinent. Beneath the transvaluations of *The Decay of Lying,* which, along with *The Critic as Artist,* is his most famous piece of criticism, lie significant theoretical implications. Wilde recognized that the theory of imitation had undergone a crucial change. The trend since Kant (above, page 416) and Coleridge (above, page 493) had been to emphasize art's power to *make,* less to *copy.* Art came to be seen as affecting our perception of the world. Wilde proceeds farther; he argues that life and nature imitate art more than art imitates life and nature. His fictional critic Vivian comically blames the fogs of London on certain painters of the nineteenth century. The exaggeration is made to show that we view the world in frameworks that we have been taught. Art, in the restricted sense of fine art, may not be responsible for as much of our world as Vivian claims, but when it is seen to include the popular arts, such as television and advertising, it certainly does affect the way we experience things. No doubt the fine arts help to build up the sense of a more complex and intense world than do the popular arts. Much in modern philosophy, psychology, and sociology reflects this Wildean idea.

Wilde has Vivian take another Kantian idea to an extreme. Vivian argues against usefulness as an element of the art object. Kant did not assert that art objects cannot be useful; instead he held that to judge an art object with respect to its use is not to make an aesthetic judgment. Vivian argues more radically that the art object should have no use. He associates use with verbal content—that is, something that can be abstracted from the work and judged true or false by some process of verification or recourse to an *a priori* set of moral values. He also associates the concept of use with materialistic and utilitarian attitudes. According to Vivian truth in art (actually "lies") is a matter only of style. In this argument we see a return to the Romantic effort to distinguish poetry from discursive argumentation and scientific procedures. Earlier, Sidney (above, page 198) remarked that the poet does not lie because he never affirms. Vivian is not content with that, still less with arguments defending art because it leads us to some Platonic idea. He sees art as a formative force in culture. Why does Vivian speak of art as lying? Because he recognizes the dominance in his time of scientific and discursive modes of structuring our reality, and he wishes to attack this dominance—in his view a terrible imbalance—by the shocking ironic inversion of normal terminology. If only naturalism and science bring truth, then art brings lies, and Vivian chooses lies.

It is to be noticed that, like Plato, Wilde writes a dialogue. This is consistent with his view that the critic is an artist. In the dialogue *The Critic as Artist* Wilde has his character Gilbert say, "Man is least himself when he talks in his own person. Give him a mask and he will tell you the truth."

Hesketh Pearson has edited Wilde's complete work (1936) and his essays (1950). Wilde's criticism is also available in *The Artist as Critic: Critical Writings of Oscar Wilde,* edited by Richard Ellmann (1969). See Arthur Symons, *A Study of Oscar Wilde* (1930); William Gaunt, *The Aesthetic Adventure* (1945); George Woodcock, *The Paradox of Oscar Wilde* (1949); St. John Ervine, *Oscar Wilde* (1952); Kevin Sullivan, *Oscar Wilde* (1972); Ronald Ericksen, *Oscar Wilde* (1972); Christopher Nassaar, *Into the Demon Universe* (1974); Richard Ellmann, *Oscar Wilde* (1988); Regenia Gagnier, ed., *Critical Essays on Oscar Wilde* (1991); Patricia Flanagan Behrendt, *Oscar Wilde: Eros and Aesthetics* (1991); Guy Willoughby, *Art and Christhood: The Aesthetics of Oscar Wilde* (1993); Anne Varty, *A Preface to Oscar Wilde* (1998); Boris Bashford, *Oscar Wilde: The Critic of Humanism* (1999).

The Decay of Lying

Cyril (Coming in through the open window from the terrace.) My dear Vivian, don't coop yourself up all day in the library. It is a perfectly lovely afternoon. The air is exquisite. There is a mist upon the woods, like the purple bloom upon a plum. Let us go and lie on the grass, and smoke cigarettes, and enjoy nature.

Vivian[1]　Enjoy nature! I am glad to say that I have entirely lost that faculty. People tell us that art makes us love nature more than we loved her before; that it reveals her secrets to us; and that after a careful study of Corot and Constable[2] we see things in her that had escaped our observation. My own experience is that the more we study art, the less we care for nature. What art really reveals to us is nature's lack of design, her curious crudities, her extraordinary monotony, her absolutely unfinished condition. Nature has good intentions, of course, but, as Aristotle once said, she cannot carry them out.[3] When I look at a landscape I cannot help seeing all its defects. It is fortunate for us, however, that nature is so imperfect, as otherwise we should have had no art at all. Art is our spirited protest, our gallant attempt to teach nature her proper place. As for the infinite variety of nature, that is a pure myth. It is not to be found in nature herself. It resides in the imagination, or fancy, or cultivated blindness of the man who looks at her.

Cyril　Well, you need not look at the landscape. You can lie on the grass and smoke and talk.

Vivian　But nature is so uncomfortable. Grass is hard and lumpy and damp, and full of dreadful black insects.

Why, even Morris'[4] poorest workman could make you a more comfortable seat than the whole of nature can. Nature pales before the furniture of "the street which from Oxford has borrowed its name," as the poet you love so much once vilely phrased it. I don't complain. If nature had been comfortable, mankind would never have invented architecture, and I prefer houses to the open air. In a house we all feel of the proper proportions. Everything is subordinated to us, fashioned for our use and our pleasure. Egotism itself, which is so necessary to a proper sense of human dignity, is entirely the result of indoor life. Out of doors one becomes abstract and impersonal. One's individuality absolutely leaves one. And then nature is so indifferent, so unappreciative. Whenever I am walking in the park here I always feel that I am no more to her than the cattle that browse on the slope, or the burdock that blooms in the ditch. Nothing is more evident than that nature hates mind. Thinking is the most unhealthy thing in the world, and people die of it just as they die of any other disease. Fortunately, in England, at any rate, thought is not catching. Our splendid physique as a people is entirely due to our national stupidity. I only hope we shall be able to keep this great historic bulwark of our happiness for many years to come; but I am afraid that we are beginning to be overeducated; at least, everybody who is incapable of learning has taken to teaching—that is really what our enthusiasm for education has come to. In the meantime, you had better go back to your wearisome uncomfortable nature, and leave me to correct my proofs.

Cyril　Writing an article! That is not very consistent after what you have just said.

Vivian　Who wants to be consistent? The dullard and the doctrinaire, the tedious people who carry out their principles to the bitter end of action, to the *reductio ad*

The Decay of Lying was first published in 1889.
[1] Vivian and Cyril were the names of Wilde's two sons.
[2] Jean Baptiste Camille Corot (1796–1875), French landscape painter; John Constable (1776–1837), English landscape painter.
[3] *Poetics* (above, page 48).

[4] William Morris (1834–1896), English writer and designer.

absurdum of practice. Not I. Like Emerson,[5] I write over the door of my library the word *whim*. Besides, my article is really a most salutary and valuable warning. If it is attended to, there may be a new Renaissance of art.

Cyril What is the subject?

Vivian I intend to call it *The Decay of Lying: A Protest.*

Cyril Lying! I should have thought that our politicians kept up that habit.

Vivian I assure you that they do not. They never rise beyond the level of misrepresentation, and actually condescend to prove, to discuss, to argue. How different from the temper of the true liar, with his frank, fearless statements, his superb irresponsibility, his healthy, natural disdain of proof of any kind! After all, what is a fine lie? Simply that which is its own evidence. If a man is sufficiently unimaginative to produce evidence in support of a lie, he might just as well speak the truth at once. No, the politicians won't do. Something may, perhaps, be urged on behalf of the bar. The mantle of the sophist has fallen on its members. Their feigned ardors and unreal rhetoric are delightful. They can make the worse appear the better cause, as though they were fresh from Leontine[6] schools, and have been known to wrest from reluctant juries triumphant verdicts of acquittal for their clients, even when those clients, as often happens, were clearly unmistakably innocent. But they are briefed by the prosaic, and are not ashamed to appeal to precedent. In spite of their endeavors, the truth will out. Newspapers, even, have degenerated. They may now be absolutely relied upon. One feels it as one wades through their columns. It is always the unreadable that occurs. I am afraid that there is not much to be said in favor of either the lawyer or the journalist. Besides, what I am pleading for is lying in art. Shall I read you what I have written? It might do you a great deal of good.

Cyril Certainly, if you give me a cigarette. Thanks. By the way, what magazine do you intend it for?

Vivian For the *Retrospective Review*. I think I told you that the elect had revived it.

Cyril Whom do you mean by "the elect"?

Vivian Oh, The Tired Hedonists, of course. It is a club to which I belong. We are supposed to wear faded roses in our buttonholes when we meet, and to have a sort of cult for Domitian.[7] I am afraid you are not eligible. You are too fond of simple pleasures.

Cyril I should be blackballed on the ground of ani-

mal spirits, I suppose?

Vivian Probably. Besides, you are a little too old. We don't admit anybody who is of the usual age.

Cyril Well, I should fancy you are all a good deal bored with each other.

Vivian We are. That is one of the objects of the club. Now, if you promise not to interrupt too often, I will read you my article.

Cyril You will find me all attention.

Vivian (*Reading in a very clear, musical voice.*) "The Decay of Lying: A Protest.* One of the chief causes that can be assigned for the curiously commonplace character of most of the literature of our age is undoubtedly the decay of lying as an art, a science, and a social pleasure. The ancient historians gave us delightful fiction in the form of fact; the modern novelist presents us with dull facts under the guise of fiction. The blue book is rapidly becoming his ideal both for method and manner. He has his tedious *document humain,* his miserable little *coin de la creation,*[8] into which he peers with his microscope. He is to be found at the Librairie Nationale, or at the British Museum, shamelessly reading up his subject. He has not even the courage of other people's ideas, but insists on going directly to life for everything, and ultimately, between encyclopedias and personal experience, he comes to the ground, having drawn his types from the family circle or from the weekly washerwoman, and having acquired an amount of useful information from which never, even in his most meditative moments, can he thoroughly free himself.

"The loss that results to literature in general from this false ideal of our time can hardly be overestimated. People have a careless way of talking about a 'born liar,' just as they talk about a 'born poet.' But in both cases they are wrong. Lying and poetry are arts—arts, as Plato saw, not unconnected with each other[9]—and they require the most careful study, the most disinterested devotion. Indeed, they have their technique, just as the more material arts of painting and sculpture have, their subtle secrets of form and color, their craft mysteries, their deliberate artistic methods. As one knows the poet by his fine music, so one can recognize the liar by his rich rhythmic utterance, and in neither case will the casual inspiration of the moment suffice. Here, as elsewhere, practice must precede perfection. But in modern days while the fashion of writing poetry has become far too common, and should, if possible, be discouraged, the fashion of lying has almost fallen in disrepute. Many a young man starts in life with a natural gift for exaggeration which, if nurtured in congenial and sympathetic surroundings, or

---

[5] Emerson (above, page 566).

[6] Gorgias (c. 485–c. 380 B.C.), Greek sophist and teacher of rhetoric, was from Leontini.

[7] Domitian (51–96), Roman emperor (81–96).

---

[8] "Corner of creation."

[9] *Republic* (above, page 19), but Plato saw lying as a fault.

by the imitation of the best models, might grow into something really great and wonderful. But, as a rule, he comes to nothing. He either falls into careless habits of accuracy—"

Cyril   My dear fellow!

Vivian   Please don't interrupt in the middle of a sentence. "He either falls into careless habits of accuracy, or takes to frequenting the society of the aged and the well-informed. Both things are equally fatal to his imagination, as indeed they would be fatal to the imagination of anybody, and in a short time he develops a morbid and unhealthy faculty of truth-telling, begins to verify all statements made in his presence, has no hesitation in contradicting people who are much younger than himself, and often ends by writing novels which are so like life that no one can possibly believe in their probability. This is no isolated instance that we are giving. It is simply one example out of many; and if something cannot be done to check, or at least to modify, our monstrous worship of facts, art will become sterile, and beauty will pass away from the land.

"Even Mr. Robert Louis Stevenson,[10] that delightful master of delicate and fanciful prose, is tainted with this modern vice, for we know positively no other name for it. There is such a thing as robbing a story of its reality by trying to make it too true, and *The Black Arrow* is so inartistic as not to contain a single anachronism to boast of, while the transformation of Dr. Jekyll reads dangerously like an experiment out of the *Lancet*.[11] As for Mr. Rider Haggard,[12] who really has, or had once, the makings of a perfectly magnificent liar, he is now so afraid of being suspected of genius that when he does tell us anything marvelous, he feels bound to invent a personal reminiscence, and to put it into a footnote as a kind of cowardly corroboration. Nor are our other novelists much better. Mr. Henry James[13] writes fiction as if it were a painful duty, and wastes upon mean motives and imperceptible 'points of view' his neat literary style, his felicitous phrases, his swift and caustic satire. Mr. Hall Caine,[14] it is true, aims at the grandiose, but then he writes at the top of his voice. He is so loud that one cannot hear what he says. Mr. James Payn[15] is an adept in the art of concealing what is not worth finding. He hunts down the obvious with the enthusiasm of a shortsighted detective. As one turns over the pages, the suspense of the author becomes unbearable. The horses of Mr. William Black's[16]

phaeton do not soar towards the sun. They merely frighten the sky at evening into violent chromolithographic effects. On seeing them approach, the peasants take refuge in dialect. Mrs. Oliphant[17] prattles pleasantly about curates, lawn-tennis parties, domesticity, and other wearisome things. Mr. Marion Crawford[18] has immolated himself upon the altar of local color. He is like the lady in the French comedy who talks about *le beau ciel d'Italie*.[19] Besides, he has fallen into a bad habit of uttering moral platitudes. He is always telling us that to be good is to be good, and that to be bad is to be wicked. At times he is almost edifying. *Robert Elsemere* is, of course, a masterpiece—a masterpiece of the *genre ennuyeux,*[20] the one form of literature that the English people seem to thoroughly enjoy. A thoughtful young friend of ours once told us that it reminded him of the sort of conversation that goes on at a meat tea in the house of a serious Nonconformist family, and we can quite believe it. Indeed it is only in England that such a book could be produced. England is the home of lost ideas. As for that great and daily increasing school of novelists for whom the sun always rises in the East End, the only thing that can be said about them is that they find life crude, and leave it raw.

"In France, though nothing so deliberately tedious as *Robert Elsemere* has been produced, things are not much better. M. Guy de Maupassant,[21] with his keen mordant irony and his hard vivid style, strips life of the few poor rags that still cover her, and shows us foul sore and festering wounds. He writes lurid little tragedies in which everybody is ridiculous; bitter comedies at which one cannot laugh for very tears. M. Zola, true to the lofty principle that he lays down in one of his *pronunciamientos* on literature, '*L'homme de génie n'a jamais d'esprit,*'[22] is determined to show that, if he has not got genius, he can at least be dull. And how well he succeeds! He is not without power. Indeed at times, as in *Germinal,* there is something almost epic in his work. But his work is entirely wrong from beginning to end, and wrong not on the ground of morals, but on the ground of art. From any ethical standpoint it is just what it should be. The author is perfectly truthful and describes things exactly as they happen. What more can any moralist desire? We have no sympathy at all with the moral indignation of our time against M. Zola. It is simply the indignation of Tartuffe[23] on being exposed. But from the standpoint of

---

[10]Robert Louis Stevenson (1850–1894), Scottish novelist.

[11]*The Lancet,* English medical journal.

[12]Henry Rider Haggard (1869–1925), English novelist.

[13]Henry James (1843–1916), American novelist who lived in England.

[14]Thomas Henry Hall Caine (1853–1931), English novelist and dramatist.

[15]James Payn (1830–1898), English writer.

[16]William Black (1841–1898), Scottish novelist.

[17]Margaret Oliphant (1828–1897), English novelist.

[18]Francis Marion Crawford (1854–1909), English novelist.

[19]"The beautiful sky of Italy."

[20]"Tiresome sort."

[21]Guy de Maupassant (1850–1893), French writer.

[22]Zola (above, page 698). "The man of genius never has spirit."

[23]In Molière's (1622–1673) play *Tartuffe.*

art, what can be said in favor of the author of *L'Assommoir, Nana,* and *Pot-Bouille?* Nothing. Mr. Ruskin[24] once described the characters in George Eliot's[25] novels as being like the sweepings of a Pentonville omnibus, but M. Zola's characters are much worse. They have their dreary vices, and their drearier virtues. The record of their lives is absolutely without interest. Who cares what happens to them? In literature we require distinction, charm, beauty, and imaginative power. We don't want to be harrowed and disgusted with an account of the doings of the lower orders. M. Daudet[26] is better. He has wit, a light touch, and an amusing style. But he has lately committed literary suicide. Nobody can possibly care for Delobelle with his *'Il fault lutter pour l'art,'*[27] or for Valmajour with his eternal refrain about the nightingale, or for the poet in *Jack* with his *'mots cruels,'*[28] now that we have learned from *Vingt ans de ma vie littéraire*[29] that these characters were taken directly from life. To us they seem to have suddenly lost all their vitality, all the few qualities they ever possessed. The only real people are the people who never existed, and if a novelist is base enough to go to life for his personages he should at least pretend that they are creations, and not boast of them as copies. The justification of a character in a novel is not that other persons are what they are, but that the author is what he is. Otherwise the novel is not a work of art. As for M. Paul Bourget, the master of the *roman psychologique,*[30] he commits the error of imagining that the men and women of modern life are capable of being infinitely analyzed for an innumerable series of chapters. In point of fact, what is interesting about people in good society—and M. Bourget rarely moves out of the Faubourg St. Germain, except to come to London—is the mask that each one of them wears, not the reality that lies behind the mask. It is a humiliating confession, but we are all of us made out of the same stuff. In Falstaff there is something of Hamlet, in Hamlet there is not a little of Falstaff. The fat knight has his moods of melancholy, and the young prince his moments of coarse humor. Where we differ from each other is purely in accidentals: in personal appearance, tricks of habit, and the like. The more one analyzes people, the more all reasons for analysis disappear. Sooner or later one comes to that dreadful universal thing called human nature. Indeed, as anyone who has ever worked among the poor

knows only too well, the brotherhood of man is no mere poet's dream, it is a most depressing and humiliating reality; and if a writer insists upon analyzing the upper classes, he might just as well write of match-girls and costermongers at once." However, my dear Cyril, I will not detain you any further just here. I quite admit that modern novels have many good points. All I insist on is that, as a class, they are quite unreadable.

Cyril That is certainly a very grave qualification, but I must say that I think you are rather unfair in some of your strictures. I like *The Deemster,* and *The Daughter of Heth,* and *Le Disciple,* and *Mr. Isaacs,* and as for *Robert Elsemere,*[31] I am quite devoted to it. Not that I can look upon it as a serious work. As a statement of the problems that confront the earnest Christian it is ridiculous and antiquated. It is simply Arnold's *Literature and Dogma*[32] with the literature left out. It is as much behind the age as Paley's *Evidences,* or Colenso's[33] method of Biblical exegesis. Nor could anything be less impressive than the unfortunate hero gravely heralding a dawn that rose long ago, and so completely missing its true significance that he proposes to carry on the business of the old firm under the new name. On the other hand, it contains several clever caricatures, and a heap of delightful quotations, and Green's philosophy very plentifully sugars the somewhat bitter pill of the author's fiction. I also cannot help expressing my surprise that you have said nothing about the two novelists whom you are always reading, Balzac and George Meredith.[34] Surely they are realists, both of them?

Vivian Ah! Meredith! Who can define him? His style is chaos illumined by flashes of lightning. As a writer he has mastered everything except language: as a novelist he can do everything, except tell a story: as an artist he is everything, except articulate. Somebody in Shakespeare—Touchstone, I think—talks about a man who is always breaking his shins over his own wit, and it seems to me that this might serve as a basis for a criticism of Meredith's method. But whatever he is, he is not a realist. Or, rather, I would say that he is a child of realism who is not on speaking terms with his father. By deliberate choice he has made himself a romanticist. He has refused to bow the knee to Baal, and after all, even if the man's fine spirit did not revolt against the noisy assertions of realism, his style would be quite sufficient of itself to keep life at a respectful distance. By its

---

[24] John Ruskin (1819–1900), English literary and art critic.

[25] George Eliot (Mary Ann Evans, 1819–1880), English novelist.

[26] Alphonse Daudet (1840–1897), French novelist.

[27] "One must struggle for art."

[28] "Cruel words."

[29] *Twenty Years of My Literary Life.*

[30] Paul Bourget (1852–1935), French novelist; "psychological novel."

[31] *The Deemster* by Caine; *The Daughter of Heth* by Black; *Le Disciple* by Bourget; *Mr. Isaacs* by Crawford.

[32] Arnold (above, page 586).

[33] William Paley (1743–1805), English theologian; John William Colenso (d. 1883), Bishop of Natal, criticized by Arnold (above, page 595).

[34] T. H. Green (1836–1882), English philosopher and disciple of Coleridge; Honoré de Balzac (1799–1850), French novelist; George Meredith (1828–1909), English novelist.

means he has planted round his garden a hedge full of thorns, and red with wonderful roses. As for Balzac, he was a most remarkable combination of the artistic temperament with the scientific spirit. The latter he bequeathed to his disciples: the former was entirely his own. The difference between such a book as M. Zola's[35] *L'Assommoir* and Balzac's *Illusions Perdues* is the difference between unimaginative realism and imaginative reality. "All Balzac's characters," said Baudelaire, "are gifted with the same ardor of life that animated himself. All his fictions are as deeply colored as dreams. Each mind is a weapon loaded to the muzzle with will. The very scullions have genius."[36] A steady course of Balzac reduces our living friends to shadows, and our acquaintances to the shadows of shades. His characters have a kind of fervent fiery-colored existence. They dominate us, and defy skepticism. One of the greatest tragedies of my life is the death of Lucien de Rubempré. It is a grief from which I have never been able to completely rid myself. It haunts me in my moments of pleasure. I remember it when I laugh. But Balzac is no more a realist than Holbein[37] was. He created life, he did not copy it. I admit, however, that he set far too high a value on modernity of form, and that, consequently, there is no book of his that, as an artistic masterpiece, can rank with *Salammbô* or *Esmond,* or *The Cloister and the Hearth,* or the *Vicomte de Bragelonne.*[38]

Cyril Do you object to modernity of form, then?

Vivian Yes. It is a huge price to pay for a very poor result. Pure modernity of form is always somewhat vulgarizing. It cannot help being so. The public imagine that, because they are interested in their immediate surroundings, art should be interested in them also, and should take them as her subject matter. But the mere fact that they are interested in these things makes them unsuitable subjects for art. The only beautiful things, as somebody once said, are the things that do not concern us. As long as a thing is useful or necessary to us, or affects us in any way, either for pain or for pleasure, or appeals strongly to our sympathies, or is a vital part of the environment in which we live, it is outside the proper sphere of art.[39] To art's subject matter we should be more or less indifferent. We should, at any rate, have no preferences, no prejudices, no partisan feelings of any kind. It is exactly because Hecuba is nothing to us that her sorrows are such an admirable motive for tragedy. I do not know anything in the whole history of literature sadder than the artistic career of Charles Reade. He wrote one beautiful book. *The Cloister and the Hearth,* a book as much above *Romola* as *Romola* is above *Daniel Deronda,*[40] and wasted the rest of his life in a foolish attempt to be modern, to draw public attention to the state of our convict prisons, and the management of our private lunatic asylums. Charles Dickens was depressing enough in all conscience when he tried to arouse our sympathy for the victims of the poor-law administration; but Charles Reade, an artist, a scholar, a man with a true sense of beauty, raging and roaring over the abuses of contemporary life like a common pampheteer or a sensational journalist, is really a sight for the angels to weep over. Believe me, my dear Cyril, modernity of form and modernity of subject matter are entirely and absolutely wrong. We have mistaken the common livery of the age for the vesture of the Muses, and spend our days in the sordid streets and hideous suburbs of our vile cities when we should be out on the hillside with Apollo. Certainly we are a degraded race, and have sold our birthright for a mess of facts.

Cyril There is something in what you say, and there is no doubt that whatever amusement we may find in reading a purely modern novel, we have rarely any artistic pleasure in rereading it. And this is perhaps the best rough test of what is literature and what is not. If one cannot enjoy reading a book over and over again, there is no use reading it at all. But what do you say about the return to life and nature? This is the panacea that is always being recommended to us.

Vivian I will read you what I say on that subject. The passage comes later on in the article, but I may as well give it to you now: "The popular cry of our time is 'Let us return to life and nature; they will recreate art for us, and send the red blood coursing through her veins; they will show her feet with swiftness and make her hand strong.' But, alas! we are mistaken in our amiable and well-meaning efforts. Nature is always behind the age. And as for life, she is the solvent that breaks up art, the enemy that lays waste her house."

Cyril What do you mean by saying that nature is always behind the age?

Vivian Well, perhaps that is rather cryptic. What I mean is this. If we take nature to mean natural simple

---

[35]Zola (above, page 698).

[36]Baudelaire (above, page 604). From his essay *Theophile Gautier.*

[37]Rubempré: character in Balzac's *A Harlot's Progress*; Hans Holbein (1460–1524), German painter.

[38]*Salammbô* by Flaubert; *Henry Esmond* by William Makepeace Thackeray (1811–1863), English novelist; *The Cloister and the Hearth* by Charles Reade (1814–1884), English novelist; *Vicomte de Bragelonne* by Alexandre Dumas (1807–1870), French novelist.

[39]Here Wilde goes beyond Kant to limit art objects to uselessness in contrast to Kant's view that an object viewed aesthetically must not be considered with respect to its use.

[40]Both by George Eliot.

instinct as opposed to self-conscious culture, the work produced under this influence is always old-fashioned, antiquated, and out of date. One touch of nature may make the whole world kin, but two touches of nature will destroy any work of art. If, on the other hand, we regard nature as the collection of phenomena external to man, people only discover in her what they bring to her. She has no suggestions of her own. Wordsworth[41] went to the lakes, but he was never a lake poet. He found in stones the sermons he had already hidden there. He went moralizing about the district, but his good work was produced when he returned, not to nature but to poetry. Poetry gave him *Laodamia,* and the fine sonnets, and the great ode, such as it is. Nature gave him *Martha Ray* and *Peter Bell,* and the address to Mr. Wilkinson's spade.

Cyril   I think that view might be questioned. I am rather inclined to believe in the "impulse from a vernal wood,"[42] though, of course, the artistic value of such an impulse depends entirely on the kind of temperament that receives it, so that the return to nature would come to mean simply the advance to a great personality. You would agree with that, I fancy. However, proceed with your article.

Vivian   (*Reading.*) "Art begins with abstract decoration, with purely imaginative and pleasurable work dealing with what is unreal and nonexistent. This is the first stage. Then life becomes fascinated with this new wonder, and asks to be admitted into the charmed circle. Art takes life as part of her rough material, recreates it, and refashions it in fresh forms, is absolutely indifferent to fact, invents, imagines, dreams, and keeps between herself and reality the impenetrable barrier of beautiful style, of decorative or ideal treatment. The third stage is when life gets the upper hand, and drives art out into the wilderness. This is the true decadence, and it is from this that we are now suffering.

"Take the case of the English drama. At first in the hands of the monks dramatic art was abstract, decorative, and mythological. Then she enlisted life in her service, and using some of life's external forms, she created an entirely new race of beings, whose sorrows were more terrible than any sorrow man has ever felt, whose joys were keener than lover's joys, who had the rage of the Titans and the calm of the gods, who had monstrous and marvelous sins, monstrous and marvelous virtues. To them she gave a language different from that of actual use, a language full of resonant music and sweet rhythm, made stately by solemn cadence, or made delicate by fanciful rhyme, jeweled with wonderful words, and enriched with lofty diction. She clothed her children in strange raiment and gave them masks, and at her bidding the antique world rose from its marble tomb. A new Caesar stalked through the streets of risen Rome, and with purple sail and flute-led oars another Cleopatra passed up the river to Antioch. Old myth and legend and dream took shape and substance. History was entirely rewritten, and there was hardly one of the dramatists who did not recognize that the object of art is not simple truth but complex beauty. In this they were perfectly right. Art itself is really a form of exaggeration; and selection, which is the very spirit of art, is nothing more than an intensified mode of overemphasis.

"But life soon shattered the perfection of the form. Even in Shakespeare we can see the beginning of the end. It shows itself by the gradual breaking up of the blank verse in the later plays, by the predominance given to prose, and by the overimportance assigned to characterization. The passages in Shakespeare—and they are many—where the language is uncouth, vulgar, exaggerated, fantastic, obscene even, are entirely due to life calling for an echo of her own voice, and rejecting the intervention of beautiful style, through which alone should life be suffered to find expression. Shakespeare is not by any means a flawless artist. He is too fond of going directly to life, and borrowing life's natural utterance. He forgets that when art surrenders her imaginative medium she surrenders everything. Goethe says, somewhere—'*In der Beschränkung zeigt sich erst der Meister.*' 'It is in working within limits that the master reveals himself'—and the limitation, the very condition of any art is style. However, we need not linger any longer over Shakespeare's realism. *The Tempest* is the most perfect of palinodes. All that we desired to point out was, that the magnificent work of the Elizabethan and Jacobean artists contained within itself the seeds of its own dissolution, and that, if it drew some of its strength from using life as a rough material, it drew all its weakness from using life as an artistic method. As the inevitable result of this substitution of an imitative for a creative medium, this surrender of an imaginative form, we have the modern English melodrama. The characters in these plays talk on the stage exactly as they would talk off it; they have neither aspirations nor aspirates; they are taken directly from life and reproduce its vulgarity down to the smallest detail; they present the gait, manner, costume, and accent of real people; they would pass unnoticed in a third-class railway carriage. And yet how wearisome the plays are! They do not succeed in producing even that impression of reality at which they aim, and which is their only reason for existing. As a method, realism is a complete failure.

---

[41] Wordsworth (above, page 481).
[42] Wordsworth, *The Tables Turned.*

"What is true about the drama and the novel is no less true about those arts that we call the decorative arts. The whole history of these arts in Europe is the record of the struggle between Orientalism, with its frank rejection of imitation, its love of artistic convention, its dislike to the actual representation of any object in nature, and our own imitative spirit. Wherever the former has been paramount, as in Byzantium, Sicily, and Spain, by actual contact, or in the rest of Europe by the influence of the Crusades, we have had beautiful and imaginative work in which the visible things of life are transmuted into artistic conventions, and the things that life has not are invented and fashioned for her delight. But wherever we have returned to life and nature, our work has always become vulgar, common, and uninteresting. Modern tapestry, with its aerial effects, its elaborate perspective, its broad expanses of waste sky, its faithful and laborious realism, has no beauty whatsoever. The pictorial glass of Germany is absolutely detestable. We are beginning to weave possible carpets in England, but only because we have returned to the method and spirit of the East. Our rugs and carpets of twenty years ago, with their solemn depressing truths, their inane worship of nature, their sordid reproductions of visible objects, have become, even to the Philistine, a source of laughter. A cultured Mahomedan once remarked to us, 'You Christians are so occupied in misinterpreting the fourth commandment that you have never thought of making an artistic application of the second.' He was perfectly right, and the whole truth of the matter is this: the proper school to learn art in is not life but art."

And now let me read you a passage which seems to me to settle the question very completely: "It was not always thus. We need not say anything about the poets, for they, with the unfortunate exception of Mr. Wordsworth, have been really faithful to their high mission, and are universally recognized as being absolutely unreliable. But in the works of Herodotus,[43] who, in spite of the shallow and ungenerous attempts of modern sciolists to verify his history, may justly be called the Father of Lies; in the published speeches of Cicero and the biographies of Suetonius; in Tacitus at his best; in Pliny's *Natural History;* in Hanno's *Periplus;* in all the early chronicles; in the lives of the saints; in Froissart and Sir Thomas Malory; in the travels of Marco Polo; in Olaus Magnus, and Aldrovandus, and Conrad Lycosthenes, with his magnificent *Prodigiorum et Ostentorum Chronicon;* in the autobiography of Benvenuto Cellini; in the memoirs of Casanova; in Defoe's *History of the Plague;* in Boswell's *Life of Johnson;* in Napoleon's dispatches, and in the works of our own Carlyle, whose *French Revolution* is

one of the most fascinating historical novels ever written, facts are either kept in their proper subordinate position, or else entirely excluded on the general ground of dullness.[44] Now, everything is changed. Facts are not merely finding a footing place in history, but they are usurping the domain of fancy, and have invaded the kingdom of romance. Their chilling touch is over everything. They are vulgarizing mankind. The crude commercialism of America, its materializing spirit, its indifference to the poetical side of things, and its lack of imagination and of high unattainable ideals, are entirely due to that country having adopted for its national hero a man, who, according to his own confession, was incapable of telling a lie, and it is not too much to say that the story of George Washington and the cherry tree has done more harm, and in a shorter space of time, than any other moral tale in the whole of literature."

Cyril My dear boy!

Vivian I assure you it is the case, and the amusing part of the whole thing is that the story of the cherry tree is an absolute myth. However, you must not think that I am too despondent about the artistic future either of America or of our own country. Listen to this: "That some change will take place before this century has drawn to its close we have no doubt whatsoever. Bored by the tedious and improving conversation of those who have neither the wit to exaggerate nor the genius to romance, tired of the intelligent person whose reminiscences are always based upon memory, whose statements are invariably limited by probability, and who is at any time liable to be corroborated by the merest Philistine who happens to be present, society sooner or later must return to its lost leader, the cultured and fascinating liar. Who he was who first, without ever having gone out to the rude chase, told the wondering cavemen at sunset how he had dragged the megatherium from the purple darkness of its jasper cave, or slain the mammoth in single combat and brought back its gilded tusks, we cannot tell, and not one of our modern anthropologists, for all their much-boasted science, has had the ordinary courage to tell us. Whatever was his name or race, he certainly was the true

---

[43]Herodotus (c. 484–c. 425 B.C.), Greek historian.

[44]Cicero (above, page 74); Suetonius (fl. 100), Roman historian; Tacitus (above, page 90); Pliny the Elder (23–79), Roman naturalist; Hanno (fifth century B.C.), Carthaginian navigator; Jean Froissart (c. 1337–1410), Flemisth chronicler; Sir Thomas Malory (fl. 1469), English author of *Morte d'Arthur;* Marco Polo (1254–1323), Venetian traveler in China; Olaus Magnus (1490–1557), Bishop of Uppsala; Aldrovandus (Ulisse Aldovandri, 1522–1607), Italian naturalist; Conrad Lycosthenes (1518–1561), German humanist; Giacomo Casanova (1725–1798), Italian writer; Daniel Defoe (1661?–1731), English writer; James Boswell (1740–1795), Scottish biographer of Johnson (above, page 357); Napoleon Bonaparte (1769–1821), French emperor; Thomas Carlyle (1795–1881), English writer.

founder of social intercourse. For the aim of the liar is simply to charm, to delight, to give pleasure. He is the very basis of civilized society, and without him a dinner party, even at the mansions of the great, is as dull as a lecture at the Royal Society, or a debate at the Incorporated Authors, or one of Mr. Burnand's farcical comedies.[45]

"Nor will he be welcomed by society alone. Art, breaking from the prison-house of realism, will run to greet him, and will kiss his false, beautiful lips, knowing that he alone is in possession of the great secret of all her manifestations, the secret that truth is entirely and absolutely a matter of style; while life—poor, probable, uninteresting human life—tired of repeating herself for the benefit of Mr. Herbert Spencer,[46] scientific historians, and the compilers of statistics in general, will follow meekly after him, and try to reproduce, in her own simple and untutored way, some of the marvels of which he talks.

"No doubt there will always be critics who, like a certain writer in the *Saturday Review,* will gravely censure the teller of fairy tales for his defective knowledge of natural history, who will measure imaginative work by their own lack of any imaginative faculty, and will hold up their ink-stained hands in horror if some honest gentleman, who has never been farther than the yew trees of his own garden, pens a fascinating book of travels like Sir John Mandeville, or, like great Raleigh,[47] writes a whole history of the world, without knowing anything whatsoever about the past. To excuse themselves they will try and shelter under the shield of him who made Prospero the magician, and gave him Caliban and Ariel as his servants, who heard the Tritons blowing their horns round the coral reefs of the Enchanted Isle, and the fairies singing to each other in a wood near Athens, who led the phantom kings in dim procession across the misty Scottish heath, and hid Hecate in a cave with the weird sisters. They will call upon Shakespeare—they always do—and will quote that hackneyed passage about art holding the mirror up to nature, forgetting that this unfortunate aphorism is deliberately said by Hamlet in order to convince the bystanders of his absolute insanity in all art matters."

Cyril   Ahem! Another cigarette, please.

Vivian   My dear fellow, whatever you may say, it is merely a dramatic utterance, and no more represents Shakespeare's real views upon art than the speeches of Iago represent his real views upon morals. But let me get to the end of the passage: "Art finds her own perfection within, and not outside of, herself. She is not to be judged by any external standard of resemblance. She is a veil, rather than a mirror. She has flowers that no forests know of, birds that no woodland possesses. She makes and unmakes many worlds, and can draw the moon from heaven with a scarlet thread. Hers are the 'forms more real than living man,' and hers the great archetypes of which things that have existence are but unfinished copies. Nature has, in her eyes, no laws, no uniformity. She can work miracles at her will, and when she calls monsters from the deep they come. She can bid the almond tree blossom in winter, and send the snow upon the ripe cornfield. At her word the frost lays its silver finger on the burning mouth of June, and the winged lions creep out from the hollows of the Lydian hills. The dryads peer from the thicket as she passes by, and the brown fauns smile strangely at her when she comes near them. She has hawk-faced gods that worship her, and the centaurs gallop at her side."

Cyril   I like that. I can see it. Is that the end?

Vivian   No. There is one more passage, but it is purely practical. It simply suggests some methods by which we could revive this lost art of lying.

Cyril   Well, before you read it to me, I should like to ask you a question. What do you mean by saying that life, "poor, probable, uninteresting human life," will try to reproduce the marvels of art? I can quite understand your objection to art being treated as a mirror. You think it would reduce genius to the position of a cracked looking glass. But you don't mean to say that you seriously believe that life imitates art, that life in fact is the mirror, and art the reality?

Vivian   Certainly I do. Paradox though it may seem—and paradoxes are always dangerous things—it is nonetheless true that life imitates art far more than art imitates life. We have all seen in our own day in England how a certain curious and fascinating type of beauty, invented and emphasized by two imaginative painters, has so influenced life that whenever one goes to a private view or to an artistic salon one sees, here the mystic eyes of Rossetti's[48] dream, the long ivory throat, the strange square-cut jaw, the loosened shadowy hair that he so ardently loved, there the sweet maidenhood of *The Golden Stair,* the blossom-like mouth and weary loveliness of the *Laus Amoris,* the passion-pale face of Andromeda, the thin hands and lithe beauty of the Vivien in *Merlin's Dream.* And it has always been so. A great artist invents a type, and life tries to copy it, to reproduce it in a popular form, like an enterprising publisher.

---

[45] F. C. Burnand, nineteenth-century Cambridge dramatist, later editor of *Punch.*
[46] Herbert Spencer (1820–1903), English philosopher.
[47] Mandeville (fl. fourteenth century), *The Voyage of Sir John Mandeville, Knight* (c. 1357); Sir Walter Raleigh, also spelled Ralegh (1554?–1618), *The History of the World* (1614).

[48] Dante Gabriel Rossetti (1828–1882), English poet and painter.

Neither Holbein nor Van Dyck[49] found in England what they have given us. They brought their types with them, and life with her keen imitative faculty set herself to supply the master with models. The Greeks, with their quick artistic instinct, understood this, and set in the bride's chamber the statue of Hermes or of Apollo, that she might bear children as lovely as the works of art that she looked at in her rapture or her pain. They knew that life gains from art not merely spirituality, depth of thought and feeling, soul-turmoil or soul-peace, but that she can form herself on the very lines and colors of art, and can reproduce the dignity of Phidias as well as the grace of Praxiteles.[50] Hence came their objection to realism. They disliked it on purely social grounds. They felt that it inevitably makes people ugly, and they were perfectly right. We try to improve the conditions of the race by means of good air, free sunlight, wholesome water, and hideous bare buildings for the better housing of the lower orders. But these things merely produce health, they do not produce beauty. For this, art is required, and the true disciples of the great artist are not his studio imitators, but those who become like his works of art, be they plastic as in Greek days, or pictorial as in modern times; in a word, life is art's best, art's only pupil.

As it is with the visible arts, so it is with literature. The most obvious and the vulgarest form in which this is shown is in the case of the silly boys who, after reading the adventures of Jack Sheppard or Dick Turpin,[51] pillage the stalls of unfortunate apple-women, break into sweetshops at night, and alarm old gentlemen who are returning home from the city by leaping out on them in suburban lanes, with black masks and unloaded revolvers. This interesting phenomenon, which always occurs after the appearance of a new edition of either of the books I have alluded to, is usually attributed to the influence of literature on the imagination. But this is a mistake. The imagination is essentially creative and always seeks for a new form. The boy burglar is simply the inevitable result of life's imitative instinct. He is fact, occupied as fact usually is, with trying to reproduce fiction, and what we see in him is repeated on an extended scale throughout the whole of life. Schopenhauer[52] has analyzed the pessimism that characterizes modern thought, but Hamlet invented it. The world has become sad because a puppet was once melancholy. The nihilist, that strange martyr who has no faith, who goes to the stake without enthusiasm, and

dies for what he does not believe in, is a purely literary product. He was invented by Turgenev, and completed by Dostoevski.[53] Robespierre came out of the pages of Rousseau[54] as surely as the People's Palace rose out of the debris of a novel. Literature always anticipates life. It does not copy it, but molds it to its purpose. The nineteenth century, as we know it, is largely an invention of Balzac. Our Luciens de Rubempré, our Rastignacs, and de Marsays made their first appearance on the stage of the *Comédie Humaine*. We are merely carrying out, with footnotes and unnecessary additions, the whim or fancy or creative vision of a great novelist. I once asked a lady, who knew Thackeray intimately, whether he had had any model for Becky Sharp.[55] She told me that Becky was an invention, but that the idea of the character had been partly suggested by a governess who lived in the neighborhood of Kensington Square, and was the companion of a very selfish and rich old woman. I inquired what became of the governess, and she replied, that, oddly enough, some years after the appearance of *Vanity Fair,* she ran away with the nephew of the lady with whom she was living, and for a short time made a great splash in society, quite in Mrs. Rawdon Crawley's[56] style, and entirely by Mrs. Rawdon Crawley's methods. Ultimately she came to grief, disappeared to the Continent, and used to be occasionally seen at Monte Carlo and other gambling places. The noble gentleman from whom the same great sentimentalist drew Colonel Newcome died, a few months after *The Newcomes* had reached a fourth edition, with the word *Adsum* on his lips. Shortly after Mr. Stevenson published his curious psychological story of transformation,[57] a friend of mine, called Mr. Hyde, was in the north of London, and being anxious to get to a railway station, took what he thought would be a short cut, lost his way, and found himself in a network of mean, evil-looking streets. Feeling rather nervous, he began to walk extremely fast, when suddenly out of an archway ran a child right between his legs. It fell on the pavement, he tripped over it, and trampled upon it. Being of course very much frightened and a little hurt, it began to scream, and in a few seconds the whole street was full of rough people who came pouring out of the houses like ants. They surrounded him and asked him his name. He was just about to give it when he suddenly remembered the opening incident in Mr. Stevenson's story. He

---

[49] Anthony Van Dyke (1599–1645), Flemish painter.
[50] Phidias (c. 500–c.432 B.C.) and Praxiteles (c. 370–c. 340 B.C.), both Greek sculptors.
[51] Jack Sheppard (1702–1724) and Dick Turpin (1706–1739), both English criminals.
[52] Arnold Schopenhauer (1788–1860), German philosopher.

[53] Ivan Sergeyevich Turgenev (1818–1883) and Fyodor Mikhailovich Dostoevski (1821–1881), both Russian novelists.
[54] Maximilian Robespierre (1758–1794), French revolutionary; Jean Jacques Rousseau (1712–1778), French philosopher.
[55] Becky Sharp, main character of Thackeray's *Vanity Fair.*
[56] Becky Sharp's married name.
[57] *Dr. Jekyll and Mr. Hyde.*

was so filled with horror at having realized in his own person that terrible and well-written scene, and at having done accidentally, though in fact, what the Mr. Hyde of fiction had done with deliberate intent, that he ran away as hard as he could go. He was, however, very closely followed, and finally he took refuge in a surgery, the door of which happened to be open, where he explained to a young assistant, who happened to be there, exactly what had occurred. The humanitarian crowd were induced to go away on his giving them a small sum of money, and as soon as the coast was clear he left. As he passed out, the name on the brass doorplate of the surgery caught his eye. It was Jekyll. At least it should have been.

Here the imitation, as far as it went, was of course accidental. In the following case the imitation was self-conscious: In the year 1879, just after I had left Oxford, I met at a reception at the house of one of the foreign ministers a woman of very curious exotic beauty. We became great friends, and were constantly together. And yet what interested me most in her was not her beauty, but her character, her entire vagueness of character. She seemed to have no personality at all, but simply the possibility of many types. Sometimes she would give herself up entirely to art, turn her drawing room into a studio, and spend two or three days a week at picture galleries or museums. Then she would take to attending race meetings, wear the most horsey clothes, and talk about nothing but betting. She abandoned religion for mesmerism, mesmerism for politics, and politics for the melodramatic excitements of philanthropy. In fact, she was a kind of Proteus, and as much a failure in all her transformations as was that wondrous sea god when Odysseus laid hold of him. One day a serial began in one of the French magazines. At that time I used to read serial stories, and I well remember the shock of surprise I felt when I came to the description of the heroine. She was so like my friend that I brought her the magazine, and she recognized herself in it immediately, and seemed fascinated by the resemblance. I should tell you, by the way, that the story was translated from some dead Russian writer, so that the author had not taken his type from my friend. Well, to put the matter briefly, some months afterwards I was in Venice, and finding the magazine in the reading room of the hotel, I took it up casually to see what had become of the heroine. It was a most piteous tale, as the girl had ended by running away with a man absolutely inferior to her, not merely in social station, but in character and intellect also. I wrote to my friend that evening about my views on John Bellini, and the admirable ices at Florio's, and the artistic value of gondolas, but added a postscript to the effect that her double in the story had behaved in a very silly manner. I don't know why

I added that, but I remember I had a sort of dread over me that she might do the same thing. Before my letter had reached her, she had run away with a man who deserted her in six months. I saw her in 1884 in Paris, where she was living with her mother, and I asked her whether the story had had anything to do with her action. She told me that she had felt an absolutely irresistible impulse to follow the heroine step by step in her strange and fatal progress, and that it was with a feeling of real terror that she had looked forward to the last few chapters of the story. When they appeared, it seemed to her that she was compelled to reproduce them in life, and she did so. It was a most clear example of this imitative instinct of which I was speaking, and an extremely tragic one.

However, I do not wish to dwell any further upon individual instances. Personal experience is a most vicious and limited circle. All that I desire to point out is the general principle that life imitates art far more than art imitates life, and I feel sure that if you think seriously about it you will find that it is true. Life holds the mirror up to art, and either reproduces some strange type imagined by painter or sculptor, or realizes in fact what has been dreamed in fiction. Scientifically speaking, the basis of life—the energy of life, as Aristotle would call it[58]—is simply the desire for expression, and art is always presenting various forms through which this expression can be attained. Life seizes on them and uses them, even if they be to her own hurt. Young men have committed suicide because Rolla did so, have died by their own hand because by his own hand Werther died. Think of what we owe to the imitation of Christ, of what we owe to the imitation of Caesar.

Cyril The theory is certainly a very curious one, but to make it complete you must show that nature, no less than life, is an imitation of art. Are you prepared to prove that?

Vivian My dear fellow, I am prepared to prove anything.

Cyril Nature follows the landscape painter then, and takes her effects from him?

Vivian Certainly. Where, if not from the Impressionists, do we get those wonderful brown fogs that come creeping down our streets, blurring the gas lamps and changing the houses into monstrous shadows? To whom, if not to them and their master, do we owe the lovely silver mists that brood over our river, and turn to faint forms of fading grace, curved bridge and swaying barge? The extraordinary change that has taken place in the climate of London during the last ten years is entirely due to this particular school of art. You

---

[58] "Energeia" in Aristotle, a rather free translation by Vivian.

smile. Consider the matter from a scientific or a metaphysical point of view, and you will find that I am right. For what is nature? Nature is no great mother who has borne us. She is our creation. It is in our brain that she quickens to life. Things are because we see them, and what we see, and how we see it, depends on the arts that have influenced us. To look at a thing is very different from seeing a thing. One does not see anything until one sees its beauty. Then, and then only, does it come into existence. At present, people see fogs, not because there are fogs, but because poets and painters have taught them the mysterious loveliness of such effects. There may have been fogs for centuries in London. I dare say there were. But no one saw them, and so we do not know anything about them. They did not exist till art had invented them. Now, it must be admitted, fogs are carried to excess. They have become the mere mannerism of a clique, and the exaggerated realism of their method gives dull people bronchitis. Where the cultured catch an effect, the uncultured catch cold. And so, let us be humane, and invite art to turn her wonderful eyes elsewhere. She has done so already, indeed. That white quivering sunlight that one sees now in France, with its strange blotches of mauve, and its restless violet shadows, is her latest fancy, and, on the whole, nature reproduces it quite admirably. Where she used to give us Corots and Daubignys, she gives us now exquisite Monets and entrancing Pisarros.[59] Indeed, there are moments, rare, it is true, but still to be observed from time to time, when nature becomes absolutely modern. Of course she is not always to be relied upon. The fact is that she is in this unfortunate position: art creates an incomparable and unique effect, and, having done so, passes on to other things. Nature, upon the other hand, forgetting that imitation can be made the sincerest form of insult, keeps on repeating this effect until we all become absolutely wearied of it. Nobody of any real culture, for instance, ever talks nowadays about the beauty of a sunset. Sunsets are quite old-fashioned. They belong to the time when Turner[60] was the last note in art. To admire them is a distinct sign of provincialism of temperament. Upon the other hand they go on. Yesterday evening Mrs. Arundel insisted on my going to the window, and looking at the glorious sky, as she called it. Of course I had to look at it. She is one of those absurdly pretty Philistines, to whom one can deny nothing. And what was it? It was simply a very second-rate Turner, a Turner of a bad period, with all the painter's worst faults exaggerated and overemphasized. Of course, I am quite ready to admit that life very

often commits the same error. She produces her false Renés and her sham Vautrins, just as nature gives us, on one day a doubtful Cuyp, and on another a more than questionable Rousseau. Still, nature irritates one more when she does things of that kind. It seems so stupid, so obvious, so unnecessary. A false Vautrin might be delightful. A doubtful Cuyp is unbearable. However, I don't want to be too hard on nature. I wish the Channel, especially at Hastings, did not look quite so often like a Henry Moore,[61] gray pearl with yellow lights, but then, when art is more varied, nature will, no doubt, be more varied also. That she imitates art, I don't think even her worst enemy would deny now. It is the one thing that keeps her in touch with civilized man. But have I proved my theory to your satisfaction?

Cyril   You have proved it to my dissatisfaction, which is better. But even admitting this strange imitative instinct in life and nature, surely you would acknowledge that art expresses the temper of its age, the spirit of its time, the moral and social conditions that surround it, and under whose influence it is produced.

Vivian   Certainly not! Art never expresses anything but itself. This is the principle of my new aesthetics; and it is this, more than that vital connection between form and substance, on which Mr. Pater dwells,[62] that makes music the type of all the arts. Of course, nations and individuals, with that healthy natural vanity which is the secret of existence, are always under the impression that it is of them that the Muses are talking, always trying to find in the calm dignity of imaginative art some mirror of their own turbid passions, always forgetting that the singer of life is not Apollo, but Marsyas.[63] Remote from reality, and with her eyes turned away from the shadows of the cave, art reveals her own perfection, and the wondering crowd that watches the opening of the marvelous, many-petaled rose fancies that it is its own history that is being told to it, its own spirit that is finding expression in a new form. But it is not so. The highest art rejects the burden of the human spirit, and gains more from a new medium or a fresh material than she does from any enthusiasm for art, or from any great awakening of the human consciousness. She develops purely on her own lines. She is not symbolic of any age. It is the ages that are her symbols.

---

[59] Claude Monet (1840–1926), Charles Francois Daubigny (1817–1878), Camille Pissarro (1830–1903), all French painters.
[60] Joseph Mallord William Turner (1775–1851), English painter.

[61] Henry Moore (1831–1895), English painter.
[62] Pater (above, page 617): "All art aspires to the condition of music. For while in all other kinds of art it is possible to distinguish the matter from the form, and the understanding can always make this distinction, yet it is the constant effort of art to obliterate it." *Studies in the History of the Renaissance.*
[63] A mythological figure connected with Greek music. He challenged Apollo to a musical contest, lost, and was punished for his presumption.

Even those who hold that art is representative of time and place and people, cannot help admitting that the more imitative an art is, the less it represents to us the spirit of its age. The evil faces of the Roman emperors look out at us from the foul porphyry and spotted jasper in which the realistic artists of the day delighted to work, and we fancy that in those cruel lips and heavy sensual jaws we can find the secret of the ruin of the empire. But it was not so. The vices of Tiberius[64] could not destroy that supreme civilization, any more than the virtues of the Antonines[65] could save it. It fell for other, for less interesting reasons. The sibyls and prophets of the Sistine may indeed serve to interpret for some that new birth of the emancipated spirit that we call the Renaissance; but what do the drunken boots and crawling peasants of Dutch art tell us about the great soul of Holland? The more abstract, the more ideal an art is, the more it reveals to us the temper of its age. If we wish to understand a nation by means of its art, let us look at its architecture or its music.

Cyril   I quite agree with you there. The spirit of an age may be best expressed in the abstract ideal arts, for the spirit itself is abstract and ideal. Upon the other hand, for the visible aspect of an age, for its look, as the phrase goes, we must, of course, go to the arts of imitation.

Vivian   I don't think so. After all, what the imitative arts really give us are merely the various styles of particular artists, or of certain schools of artists. Surely you don't imagine that the people of the Middle Ages bore any resemblance at all to the figures on medieval stained glass, or in medieval stone and wood carving, or on medieval metalwork, or tapestries, or illuminated manuscripts. They were probably very ordinary-looking people, with nothing grotesque, or remarkable, or fantastic in their appearance. The Middle Ages, as we know them in art, are simply a definite form of style, and there is no reason at all why an artist with this style should not be produced in the nineteenth century. No great artist ever sees things as they really are. If he did, he would cease to be an artist. Take an example from our own day. I know that you are fond of Japanese things. Now, do you really imagine that the Japanese people, as they are presented to us in art, have any existence? If you do, you have never understood Japanese art at all. The Japanese people are the deliberate self-conscious creation of certain individual artists. If you set a picture by Hokusai, or Hokkei,[66] or any of the great native painters, beside a real Japanese gentleman or lady, you will see that there is not the

slightest resemblance between them. The actual people who live in Japan are not unlike the general run of English people; that is to say, they are extremely commonplace, and have nothing curious or extraordinary about them. In fact the whole of Japan is a pure invention. There is no such country, there are no such people. One of our most charming painters went recently to the Land of the Chrysanthemum in the foolish hope of seeing the Japanese. All he saw, all he had the chance of painting, were a few lanterns and some fans. He was quite unable to discover the inhabitants, as his delightful exhibition at Messrs. Dowdeswell's Gallery showed only too well. He did not know that the Japanese people are, as I have said, simply a mode of style, an exquisite fancy of art. And so, if you desire to see a Japanese effect, you will not behave like a tourist and go to Tokyo. On the contrary, you will stay at home, and steep yourself in the work of certain Japanese artists, and then, when you have absorbed the spirit of their style, and caught their imaginative manner of vision, you will go some afternoon and sit in the park or stroll down Piccadilly, and if you cannot see an absolutely Japanese effect there, you will not see it anywhere. Or, to return again to the past, take as another instance the ancient Greeks. Do you think that Greek art ever tells us what the Greek people were like? Do you believe that the Athenian women were like the stately dignified figures of the Parthenon frieze, or like those marvelous goddesses who sat in the triangular pediments of the same building? If you judge from the art, they certainly were so. But read an authority, like Aristophanes,[67] for instance. You will find that the Athenian ladies laced tightly, wore highheeled shoes, dyed their hair yellow, painted and rouged their faces, and were exactly like any silly fashionable or fallen creature of our own day. The fact is that we look back on the ages entirely through the medium of art, and art, very fortunately, has never once told us the truth.

Cyril   But modern portraits by English painters, what of them? Surely they are like the people they pretend to represent?

Vivian   Quite so. They are so like them that a hundred years from now no one will believe in them. The only portraits in which one believes are portraits where there is very little of the sitter and a very great deal of the artist. Holbein's drawings of the men and women of his time impress us with a sense of their absolute reality. But this is simply because Holbein compelled life to accept his conditions, to restrain itself within his limitations, to reproduce his type, and to appear as he wished it to appear. It is style that makes

---

[64] Tiberius (942 B.C.–37 A.D.), Roman emperor (14–37).

[65] Antonines, seven Roman emperors of the second century.

[66] Hokusai (1766–1849) and Hokkei (1780–1850), Japanese artists.

[67] Aristophanes (450–388 B.C.), Greek comic dramatist.

us believe in a thing—nothing but style. Most of our modern portrait painters are doomed to absolute oblivion. They never paint what they see. They paint what the public sees, and the public never sees anything.

Cyril   Well, after that, I think I should like to hear the end of your article.

Vivian   With pleasure. Whether it will do any good, I really cannot say. Ours is certainly the dullest and most prosaic century possible. Why, even sleep has played us false, and has closed up the gates of ivory, and opened the gates of horn.[68] The dreams of the great middle classes of the country, as recorded in Mr. Myers's[69] two bulky volumes on the subject, and in the *Transactions of the Psychical Society,* are the most depressing things that I have ever read. There is not even a fine nightmare among them. They are commonplace, sordid, and tedious. As for the church, I cannot conceive anything better for the culture of a country than the presence in it of a body of men whose duty it is to believe in the supernatural, to perform daily miracles, and to keep alive that mythopoeic faculty which is so essential for the imagination. But in the English church a man succeeds, not through his capacity for belief, but through his capacity for disbelief. Ours is the only church where the skeptic stands at the altar, and where St. Thomas is regarded as the ideal apostle. Many a worthy clergyman, who passes his life in admirable works of kindly charity, lives and dies unnoticed and unknown; but it is sufficient for some shallow, uneducated passman out of either university to get up in his pulpit and express his doubts about Noah's ark, or Balaam's ass, or Jonah and the whale, for half of London to flock to hear him, and to sit openmouthed in rapt admiration at his superb intellect. The growth of common sense in the English church is a thing very much to be regretted. It is really a degrading concession to a low form of realism. It is silly, too. It springs from an entire ignorance of psychology. Man can believe the impossible, but man can never believe the improbable. However, I must read the end of my article: "What we have to do, what at any rate it is our duty to do, is to revive this old art of lying. Much, of course, may be done, in the way of educating the public, by amateurs in the domestic circle, at literary lunches, and at afternoon teas. But this is merely the light and graceful side of lying, such as was probably heard at Cretan dinner parties. There are many other forms. Lying for the sake of gaining some immediate personal advantage, for instance—lying with a moral purpose, as it is usually called—though of late it has been rather looked down upon, was extremely popular with the antique world. Athena laughs when Odysseus tells her 'his words of sly devising,' as Mr. William Morris phrases it, and the glory of mendacity illumines the pale brow of the stainless hero of Euripidean[70] tragedy, and sets among the noble women of the past the young bride of one of Horace's[71] most exquisite odes. Later on, what at first had been merely a natural instinct was elevated into a self-conscious science. Elaborate rules were laid down for the guidance of mankind, and an important school of literature grew up round the subject. Indeed, when one remembers the excellent philosophical treatise of Sanchez[72] on the whole question, one cannot help regretting that no one has ever thought of publishing a cheap and condensed edition of the works of that great casuist. A short primer, *When to Lie and How,* if brought out in an attractive and not too expensive a form, would, no doubt, command a large sale, and would prove of real practical service to many earnest and deep-thinking people. Lying for the sake of the improvement of the young, which is the basis of home education, still lingers amongst us, and its advantages are so admirably set forth in the early books of Plato's *Republic*[73] that it is unnecessary to dwell upon them here. It is a mode of lying for which all good mothers have peculiar capabilities, but it is capable of still further development, and has been sadly overlooked by the school board. Lying for the sake of a monthly salary is, of course, well known in Fleet Street, and the profession of a political leader-writer is not without its advantages. But it is said to be a somewhat dull occupation, and it certainly does not lead to much beyond a kind of ostentatious obscurity. The only form of lying that is absolutely beyond reproach is lying for its own sake, and the highest development of this is, as we have already pointed out, lying in art. Just as those who do not love Plato more than truth cannot pass beyond the threshold of the academe, so those who do not love beauty more than truth never know the inmost shrine of art. The solid, stolid British intellect lies in the desert sands like the sphinx in Flaubert's marvelous tale, and fantasy, *La Chimère,* dances round it, and calls to it with her false, flute-toned voice. It may not hear her now, but surely some day, when we are all bored to death with the commonplace character of modern fiction, it will hearken to her and try to borrow her wings.

"And when that day dawns, or sunset reddens, how joyous we shall all be! Facts will be regarded as discreditable,

---

[68] In Greek mythology the gate of horn and the ivory gate are the gates through which dreams come forth from the realm of sleep. Dreams passing through the gate of horn are true.

[69] Frederick William Henry Myers (1843–1901), English essayist and poet.

[70] Euripides (c. 480–c. 406 B.C.), Greek tragic dramatist.

[71] Horace (above, page 78).

[72] Francisco Sanchez (c. 1550–c. 1623), Spanish philosopher.

[73] Vivian refers ironically to Plato's branding of poets as liars in *Republic* (above, page 19).

truth will be found mourning over her fetters, and romance, with her temper of wonder, will return to the land. The very aspect of the world will change to our startled eyes. Out of the sea will rise Behemoth and Leviathan, and sail round the high-pooped galleys, as they do on the delightful maps of those ages when books on geography were actually readable. Dragons will wander about the waste places, and the phoenix will soar from her nest of fire into the air. We shall lay our hands upon the basilisk, and see the jewel in the toad's head. Champing his gilded oats, the hippogriff will stand in our stalls, and over our heads will float the bluebird, singing of beautiful and impossible things, of things that are lovely and that never happen, of things that are not and that should be. But before this comes to pass, we must cultivate the lost art of lying."

Cyril Then we must certainly cultivate it at once. But in order to avoid making any error, I want you to tell me briefly the doctrines of the new aesthetics.

Vivian Briefly, then, they are these. Art never expresses anything but itself. It has an independent life, just as thought has, and develops purely on its own lines. It is not necessarily realistic in an age of realism, nor spiritual in an age of faith. So far from being the creation of its time, it is usually in direct opposition to it, and the only history that it preserves for us is the history of its own progress. Sometimes it returns upon its footsteps, and revives some antique form, as happened in the archaistic movement of late Greek art, and in the pre-Raphaelite movement of our own day. At other times it entirely anticipates its age, and produces in one century work that it takes another century to understand, to appreciate, and to enjoy. In no case does it reproduce its age. To pass from the art of a time to the time itself is the great mistake that all historians commit.

The second doctrine is this. All bad art comes from returning to life and nature, and elevating them into ideals. Life and nature may sometimes be used as a part of art's rough material, but before they are of any real service to art they must be translated into artistic conventions. The moment art surrenders its imaginative medium it surrenders everything. As a method, realism is a complete failure, and the two things that every artist should avoid are modernity of form and modernity of subject matter. To us, who live in the nineteenth century, any century is a suitable subject for art except our own. The only beautiful things are the things that do not concern us. It is, to have the pleasure of quoting myself, exactly because Hecuba is nothing to us that her sorrows are so suitable a motive for a tragedy. Besides, it is only the modern that ever becomes old-fashioned. M. Zola sits down to give us a picture of the Second Empire. Who care for the Second Empire now? It is out of date. Life goes faster than realism, but romanticism is always in front of life.

The third doctrine is that life imitates art far more than art imitates life. This results not merely from life's imitative instinct, but from the fact that the self-conscious aim of life is to find expression, and that art offers it certain beautiful forms through which it may realize that energy. It is a theory that has never been put forward before, but it is extremely fruitful, and throws an entirely new light upon the history of art.

It follows, as a corollary from this, that external natures also imitates art. The only effects that she can show us are effects that we have already seen through poetry, or in paintings. This is the secret of nature's charm, as well as the explanation of nature's weakness.

The final revelation is that lying, the telling of beautiful untrue things, is the proper aim of art. But of this I think have spoken at sufficient length. And now let us go out on the terrace, where "droops the milk-white peacock like a ghost," while the evening star "washes the dusk with silver." At twilight nature becomes a wonderfully suggestive effect, and is not without loveliness, though perhaps its chief use is to illustrate quotations from the poets. Come! We have talked long enough.

Stéphane Mallarmé

1842–1898

"It will be said, I suppose, that I am attempting to flabbergast the mob with a lofty statement. This is true." Mallarmé's remark, tinged wiith irony, is replete with scorn. He has been accused of preciosity, snobbishness, and obscurantism. There is something as elusive about his critical prose as about his poetry. Perhaps it is because he sees the poet as constantly testing the possibilities, indeed the limits, of language. He hates the newspaper; he loves the book. For him, poetry lies in "the *contemplation* of things, in the image emanating from the reveries which things arouse in us." Poetry does not *name,* it *suggests.* From the common point of view, therefore, that of the "mob," poetry is obscure, enigmatic, and indirect rather than direct in its treatment of things. It is not surprising that for Mallarmé the true sister art of poetry is music.

Stylistic hauteur is one way in which Mallarmé dramatizes his break with both Romantic expressivism and traditional didacticism. Nor is literature for him imitation. Reality is in the poem itself. It may "exist on a piece of paper": "All earthly existence must ultimately be contained in a book." The poet, then, is not expressing himself, teaching the reader, or copying nature, but rather searching out and capturing an elusive reality in words, perhaps *making* reality in words. Though Mallarmé sometimes suggests that the poet is trying, though always failing, to capture Platonic ideas, he also seems to say that the poem organizes reality for us by means of the obscurity of its own nondiscursive aspects. This view represents a characteristic of French symbolist theory that is a precursor of the idea of the independent nature of the poem in much early-twentieth-century criticism.

Mallarmé's complete works are available in French (1945). For an English translation of a selection of Mallarmé's critical writings see *Mallarmé: Selected Prose, Essays, and Letters,* translated by Bradford Cook (1956). See Hayse Cooperman, *The Aesthetics of Mallarmé* (1933); Guy Delfal, *L'Ésthetique de Stéphane Mallarmé* (1951), especially pages 161–84; Wallace Fowlie, *Mallarmé* (1953); Warren Ramsey, "A View of Mallarmé's Poetics," *Romantic Review* XLVI (1955), 178–91; Guy Michaud, *Mallarmé* (tr. 1965); Thomas A. Williams, *Mallarmé and the Language of Symbolism* (1970); Paula Gilbert Lewis, *The Aesthetic of Mallarmé in Relation to His Public* (1976); Judy Karvis, *The Prose of Mallarmé* (1976); Malcolm Bowie, *Mallarmé and the Art of Being Difficult* (1978); Louis Wirth Marvick, *Mallarmé and the Sublime* (1986); Gordon Millan, *A Throw of the Dice: The Life of Stéphane Mallarmé* (1994); Roger Pearson, *Unfolding Mallarmé* (1996); Robert Greer Cohn, ed., *Mallarmé in the Twentieth Century* (1998); Mary Ann Caws, ed., *Mallarmé in Prose* (2001).

The Evolution of Literature

"We are now witnessing a spectacle," he told me, "which is truly extraordinary, unique in the history of poetry: every poet is going off by himself with his own flute, and playing the songs he pleases. For the first time since the beginning of poetry, poets have stopped singing bass. Hitherto, as you know, if they wished to be accompanied, they had to be content with the great organ of official meter. Well, it was simply overplayed and they got tired of it! I am sure that when the great Hugo died,[1] he was convinced that he had buried all poetry for the next century; and yet Paul Verlaine[2] had already written *Sagesse*. We can forgive Hugo his illusion, when we remember all the miracles he produced; he was simply forgetting the eternal instinct, the perpetual and unavoidable growth of the lyrical. But the essential and undeniable point is this: that in a society without stability, without unity, there can be no stable or definitive art. From that incompletely organized society—which also explains the restlessness of certain minds—the unexplained need for individuality was born. The literary manifestations of today are a direct reflection of that need.

"A more immediate explanation of recent innovations is this: it has finally been understood that the old verse form was *not* the absolute, unique, and changeless form, but just one way to be sure of writing good verse. We say to children: 'Don't steal, and you'll be honest.' That is true, but it is not everything. Is it possible to write poetry without reference to time-honored precepts? Poets have answered this question affirmatively, and I believe that they are right. Poetry is everywhere in language, so long as there is rhythm—everywhere except on posters and the back page of the newspaper. In the genre we call *prose*, there are verses—sometimes admirable verses—of all sorts of rhythms. Actually, there is no such thing as prose: there is the alphabet, and then there are verses which are more or less closely knit, more or less diffuse. So long as there is stylistic effort, there is versification.

"I said a minute ago that today's poetry is, in the main, the result of the poets' boredom with official verse. Even the partisans of official verse share this boredom. Isn't it rather abnormal that, when we open a book of poetry, we should be sure of finding uniform and conventional rhythms throughout? And yet, all the while, the writer hopes to arouse our interest in the essential variety of human feelings! Where is the inspiration in all this! Where is the unforeseen! How tiresome it all is! Official verse must be used only in crisis moments of the soul. Modern poets have understood this. With a fine sense of the delicate and the sparing, they hover around the official Alexandrine,[3] approach it with unusual timidity, almost with fear; and rather than use it as their principle or as a point of departure, they suddenly conjure it up, and with it they crown their poem or period!

"Moreover, the same transformation has taken place in music. Instead of the very clearly delineated melodies of the past, we have an infinity of broken melodies which enrich the poetic texture, and we no longer have the impression of strong cadence."

"Is that how the scission was effected?" I asked.

"Why, yes. The Parnassians[4] were fond of a very formal prosody which has its own beauty, and they failed to realize that the modern poets were simply complementing their work; this also had the advantage of creating a sort of interregnum for the noble Alexandrine which had been at bay, crying for mercy. What we have to realize is that the most recent poetical writings do not tend to suppress the official verse; they tend rather to let a little more air into the poem, to create a kind of fluidity or mobility between long-winded verses, which has heretofore been lacking. In an orchestra, for example, you may suddenly hear very fine bursts of sound from the basses; but you know perfectly well that if there were nothing but that, you would soon have enough of it. Young poets space these bursts so that they will occur only when a total effect is to be produced. In this way, the Alexandrine (which was invented by nobody, but rather poured forth spontaneously from the instrument of language) will get out of its present finicky, sedentary state, and henceforth it will be freer, more sudden, more refreshed. Its value will lie exclusively in its use during the soul's most serious times. And future volumes of poetry will be traversed by a majestic first verse which scatters in its wake an infinity of motifs originating in the individual's sensibility.

"So there has been scission because both sides have been unaware that their points of view are reconcilable rather than mutually destructive. On the one hand, the

---

The Evolution of Literature is a report of an interview of Mallarmé by Jules Huret that appeared in *Echo de Paris* in 1891. *The Book: A Spiritual Instrument* was first published in *La Revue Blanche* in 1895. *Mystery in Literature* was first published in *La Revue Blanche* in 1896. The text of all three is from *Mallarmé: Selected Prose, Poems, and Letters* translated by Bradford Cook (Baltimore: The Johns Hopkins Press, 1956).
[1] Victor Marie Hugo (1802–1885), French writer.
[2] Paul Verlaine (1844–1896), French poet.

[3] Alexandrine: iambic hexameter, commonly used by neoclassical French poets.
[4] Parnassians: a group of post-Romantic, pre-symbolist nineteenth-century French poets, named for a mountain sacred to Apollo.

Parnassians have, in effect, been perfectly obedient servants of verse, and have sacrificed their personalities. The young poets, on the other hand, have anchored their instinct in a variety of modes, as if there were no precedent; actually, all they are doing is reducing here and there the stiffness of the Parnassian structures; and it seems to me that the two points of view are complementary.

"Despite all this, I still believe, personally, that, with the miraculous knowledge of verse and with the superb instinct for rhythmic pause which such masters as Banville[5] possess, the Alexandrine can be infinitely varied and can reproduce all possible shades of human passion. Banville's *Forgeron,* for example, has a number of Alexandrines which seem interminable, yet others which are unbelievably concise.

"But, after all, it was a good thing to give our perfect and traditional poetic instrument a little rest. It had been overworked."

"So much for form," I said. "What about content?"

"As far as content is concerned," he answered, "I feel that the young poets are nearer than the Parnassians to the poetical ideal. The latter still treat their subjects as the old philosophers and orators did: that is, they present things directly, whereas I think that they should be presented allusively. Poetry lies in the *contemplation* of things, in the image emanating from the reveries which things arouse in us. The Parnassians take something in its entirety and simply exhibit it; in so doing, they fall short of mystery; they fail to give our minds that exquisite joy which consists of believing that we are creating something. To *name* an object is largely to destroy poetic enjoyment, which comes from gradual divination. The ideal is to *suggest* the object. It is the perfect use of this mystery which constitutes symbol. An object must be gradually evoked in order to show a state of soul; or else, choose an object and from it elicit a state of soul by means of a series of decodings."

"Now," I said, "we are coming to the big objection I was going to make: obscurity!"

"Yes, it is a dangerous thing," he replied, "regardless of whether it results from the reader's inadequacy or from the poet's. But if you avoid the work it involves, you are cheating. If a person of mediocre intelligence and insufficient literary experience happens to open an obscure book and insists on enjoying it, something is wrong; there has simply been a misunderstanding. There must always be enigma in poetry. The purpose of literature—the *only* purpose—is to *evoke* things."

"Was it you, sir," I asked, "who created the new movement in poetry?"

"I detest 'schools,'" he replied, "and anything resembling schools. The professional attitude toward literature is repugnant to me. Literature is entirely an individual matter. As far as I am concerned, a poet today, in the midst of this society which refuses to let him live, is a man who seeks out solitude in order to sculpture his own tomb. The reason I appear to be the leader of a school, is, first of all, that I have always taken an interest in the ideas of young poets; and second, because of my sincerity in recognizing the originality of what the latest writers have contributed. In reality, I am a hermit. I believe that poetry should be for the supreme pomp and circumstance of a constituted society in which glory should have its place. Most people seem to have forgotten glory. In our time the poet can only go on strike against society, and turn his back on all the contaminated ways and means that are offered him. For anything that is offered him is necessarily inferior to his ideal and to his secret labor."

I then asked Mallarmé what Verlaine's position would be in the history of this poetic movement.

"He was the first to react against the impeccable and impassible Parnassian attitudes. His fluid verse and certain of his intentional dissonances were already evident in *Sagesse.* Later on, around 1875, all the Parnassians (except for a few friends such as Mendès, Dierx, and Cladel)[6] shrieked with horror at my *Afternoon of a Faun,* and, all together, they threw it out. For I *was* trying, actually, to make a sort of running pianistic commentary upon the fully preserved and dignified Alexandrine—a sort of musical accompaniment which the poet composes himself, so that the official verse will appear only on the really important occasions. But the father, the real father of all the young poets is Verlaine, the magnificent Verlaine. The attitude of the man is just as noble as the attitude of the writer. For it is the only possible attitude at a time when all poets are outlaws. Think of absorbing all the grief that he has—and with his pride and his tremendous pluck!"

"What do you think of the end of naturalism?"

"Up to now, writers have entertained the childish belief that if they could just choose a certain number of precious stones, for example, and put the names on paper, they would be *making* precious stones. Now, really! That is impossible, no matter how well it is done. Poetry consists of *creation:* we must delve into our souls for states and gleams of such perfect purity, so perfectly sung and illuminated, that they will truly be the jewels of man. When we do that, we have symbol, we have creation, and the word *poetry* has its full meaning. This, in short, is the only possible human creation.

---

[5]Theodore Faullain de Banville (1823–1891), French poet.

[6]Catulle Mendès (1841–1909), Leon Dierx (1838–1912), Leon Cladel (1838–1912), all French poets.

And if, in fact, the precious stones we wear do *not* show a state of soul, they are improperly worn. Take women, for example, external thieves that they are. . . .

"And just think," he added, chuckling, "the marvelous thing about jewelry stores is that, occasionally, we learn from the chief of police that what the woman wore improperly was something she didn't know the secret meaning of—something, therefore, which didn't belong to her.

"But to get back to naturalism. It seems to me that when we use that word, we mean the work of Émile Zola;[7] and when he has finished his work, the name will disappear. I have great admiration for Zola. Actually, what he does is not so much literature as evocative art. He depends as little as possible on literary means. True, he uses words, but that is all. Everything else is based on his marvelous sense of organization and has immediate repercussions in the mind of the mob. His talent is truly powerful; consider his tremendous feeling for life, his mob movements, that texture in Nana's skin that every one of us has touched; and he paints it all with prodigious colors. It really is an admirably organized piece of work. But literature is more of an intellectual thing than that. Things already exist, we don't have to create them; we simply have to see their relationships. It is the threads of those relationships which go to make up poetry and music."

"Are you acquainted with the psychological novel?"

"Slightly. After the great works of Flaubert, the Goncourt brothers,[8] and Zola—which are, in a sense, poems—novelists seem to be going back to the old eighteenth-century French taste which was much more humble and modest, consisting, as it did, not of a pictorial presentation of the outer form of things but rather of a dissection of the motives of the human soul. But there is the same difference between that and poetry as there is between a corset and a beautiful throat."

Before leaving, I asked Mallarmé for the names of those who seemed to him to represent the modern evolution in poetry.

"The young poets," he answered, "who seem to me to have done truly masterful work—that is, original work, completely divorced from the past—are: Morice, Moréas (a delightful poet), and, above all, the man who has given poetry the biggest boost, Henri de Régnier.[9] Like de Vigny,[10] he lives apart, at some distance from here, in retreat and

silence. I greatly respect and admire him. His latest work, *Poémes anciens et romanesques,* is a pure masterpiece.

"So you can see," he said, shaking hands with me, "that, in the final analysis, all earthly existence must ultimately be contained in a book."

The Book: A Spiritual Instrument

I am the author of a statement to which there have been varying reactions, including praise and blame, and which I shall make again in the present article. Briefly, it is this: all earthly existence must ultimately be contained in a book.[1]

It terrifies me to think of the qualities (among them genius, certainly) which the author of such a work will have to possess. I am one of the unpossessed. We will let that pass and imagine that it bears no author's name. What, then, will the work itself be? I answer: a hymn, all harmony and joy; an immaculate grouping of universal relationships come together for some miraculous and glittering occasion. Man's duty is to observe with the eyes of the divinity; for if his connection with that divinity is to be made clear, it can be expressed only by the pages of the open book in front of him.

Seated on a garden bench where a recent book is lying, I like to watch a passing gust half open it and breathe life into many of its outer aspects, which are so obvious that no one in the history of literature has ever thought about them. I shall have the chance to do so now, if I can get rid of my overpowering newspaper. I push it aside: it flies about and lands near some roses as if to hush their proud and feverish whispering; finally, it unfolds around them. I will leave it there along with the silent whispering of the flowers. I formally propose now to examine the differences between this rag and the book, which is supreme. The newspaper is the sea; literature flows into it at will.

Now then—

The foldings of a book, in comparison with the large-sized, open newspaper, have an almost religious significance. But an even greater significance lies in their thickness when they are piled together; for then they form a tomb in miniature for our souls.

Every discovery made by printers has hitherto been absorbed in the most elementary fashion by the newspaper, and can be summed up in the word: *press.* The result has been simply a plain sheet of paper upon which a flow of

---

[7]Émile Zola (above page 698). Mallarmé was wrong about the disappearance of naturalism, which lasted somewhat longer.
[8]Gustave Flaubert (1821–1880), Edmond Goncourt (1822–1896), and Jules Goncourt (1830–1870), French novelists.
[9]Charles Morice (1861–1919), Jean Moréas (1856–1910), Henri de Régnier (1864–1936), all symbolist poets.
[10]Alfred Vigny (1799–1863), French writer.

---

[1]Last sentence of the previous selection.

words is printed in the most unrefined manner. The immediacy of this system (which preceded the production of books) has undeniable advantages for the writer; with its endless line of posters and proof sheets it makes for improvisation. We have, in other words, a "daily paper." But who, then, can make the gradual discovery of the meaning of this format, or even of a sort of popular fairyland charm about it? Then again, the leader, which is the most important part, makes its great free way through a thousand obstacles and finally reaches a state of disinterestedness. But what is the result of this victory? It overthrows the advertisement (which is original slavery) and, as if it were itself the powered printing press, drives it far back beyond intervening articles onto the fourth page and leaves it there in a mass of incoherent and inarticulate cries. A noble spectacle, without question. After this, what else can the newspaper possibly need in order to overthrow the *book* (even though at the bottom—or rather at its foundation, i.e., the *feuilleton*[2]—it resembles the other in its pagination, thus generally regulating the columns)? It will need nothing, in fact; or practically nothing, if the book delays as it is now doing and carelessly continues to be a drain for it. And since even the book's format is useless, of what avail is that extraordinary addition of foldings (like wings in repose, ready to fly forth again) which constitute its rhythm and the chief reason for the secret contained in its pages? Of what avail the priceless silence living there, and evocative symbols following in its wake, to delight the mind which literature has totally delivered?

Yes, were it not for folding of the paper and the depths thereby established, that darkness scattered about in the forms of black characters could not rise and issue forth in gleams of mystery from the page to which we are about to turn.

The newspaper with its full sheet on display makes improper use of printing—that is, it makes good packing paper. Of course, the obvious and vulgar advantage of it, as everybody knows, lies in its mass production and circulation. But the advantage is secondary to a miracle, in the highest sense of the word: words led back to their origin, which is the twenty-four letters of the alphabet, so gifted with infinity that they will finally consecrate language. Everything is caught up in their endless variations and then rises out of them in the form of the principle. Thus typography becomes a rite.

The book, which is a total expansion of the letter, must find its mobility in the letter; and in its spaciousness must establish some nameless system of relationships which will embrace and strengthen fiction.

There is nothing fortuitous in all this, even though ideas may seem to be slaves of chance. The system guarantees them. Therefore we must pay no attention to the book industry with its materialistic considerations. The making of a book, with respect to its flowering totality, begins with the first sentence. From time immemorial the poet has knowingly placed his verse in the sonnet which he writes upon our minds or upon pure space. We, in turn, will misunderstand the true meaning of this book and the miracle inherent in its structure, if we do not knowingly imagine that a given motif has been properly placed at a certain height on the page, according to its own or to the book's distribution of light. Let us have no more of those successive, incessant, back and forth motions of our eyes, traveling from one line to the next and beginning all over again. Otherwise we will miss that ecstasy in which we become immortal for a brief hour, free of all reality, and raise our obsessions to the level of creation. If we do not actively create in this way (as we would music on the keyboard, turning the pages of a score), we would do better to shut our eyes and dream. I am not asking for any servile obedience. For, on the contrary, each of us has within him that lightninglike initiative which can link the scattered notes together.

Thus, in reading, a lonely, quiet concert is given for our minds, and they in turn, less noisily, reach its meaning. All our mental faculties will be present in this symphonic exaltation; but, unlike music, they will be rarefied, for they partake of thought. Poetry, accompanied by the idea, is perfect music, and cannot be anything else.[3]

Now, returning to the case at hand and to the question of books which are read in the ordinary way, I raise my knife in protest, like the cook chopping off chickens' heads.

The virginal foldings of the book are unfortunately exposed to the kind of sacrifice which caused the crimson-edged tomes of ancient times to bleed. I meant that they invite the paper-knife, which stakes our claims to possession of the book. Yet our consciousness alone gives us a far more intimate possession than such a barbarian symbol; for it joins the book now here, now there, varies its melodies, guesses its riddles, and even recreates it unaided. The folds will have a mark which remains intact and invites us to open or close the pages according to the author's desires. There can be only blindness and discourtesy in so murderous and self-destructive an attempt to destroy the fragile, inviolable book. The newspaper holds the advantage here, for it is not exposed to such treatment. But it is nonetheless an

---

[2]The part of a page of a journal or newspaper, usually across the bottom, devoted to literary articles, light fiction, and so forth.

[3]By Mallarmé's time music has thoroughly replaced painting as the art regarded as closest to poetry.

annoying influence; for upon the book—upon the divine and intricate organism required by literature—it inflicts the monotonousness of its eternally unbearable columns, which are merely strung down the pages by hundreds.

"But," I hear someone say, "how can this situation be changed?" I shall take space here to answer this question in detail; for the work of art—which is unique or should be—must provide illustrations. A tremendous burst of greatness, of thought, or of emotion, contained in a sentence printed in large type, with one gradually descending line to a page, should keep the reader breathless throughout the book and summon forth his powers of excitement. Around this would be smaller groups of secondary importance, commenting on the main sentence or derived from it, like a scattering of ornaments.

It will be said, I suppose, that I am attempting to flabbergast the mob with a lofty statement. That is true. But several of my close friends must have noticed that there are connections between this and their own instinct for arranging their writings in an unusual and ornamental fashion, halfway between verse and prose. Shall I be explicit? All right, then, just to maintain that reputation for clarity so avidly pursued by our make-everything-clear-and-easy era. Let us suppose that a given writer reveals one of his ideas in theoretical fashion and, quite possibly, in useless fashion, since he is ahead of his time. He well knows that such revelations, touching as they do on literature, should be brought out in the open. And yet he hesitates to divulge too brusquely things which do not exist; and thus, in his modesty, and to the mob's amazement, he veils them over.

It is because of those daydreams we have before we resume our reading in a garden that our attention strays to a white butterfly flitting here and there, then disappearing; but also leaving behind it the same slight touch of sharpness and frankness with which I have presented these ideas, and flying incessantly back and forth before the people, who stand amazed.

Mystery in Literature

Any affirmations I make here, no matter how justified, are naturally going to be cannon fodder for the jokers in the mob.

Every work of art, apart from its inner treasure, should provide some sort of outward—or even indifferent—meaning through its words. A certain deference should be shown the people: for, after all, they *are* lending out their language, and the work is going to turn it to some unexpected account. It is just as well to keep idlers away; they are glad to see that

the work does not apply to them—such, at least, is their first impression.

Each to his own way and no hard feelings.

And yet somehow there is a disquieting gleam from the depths of the work, hardly distinguishable from its outward show. The clever idlers become suspicious and tell us to stop; for in their considered opinion the meaning of the work is unintelligible.

Heaven help the poor slandered poet who happens to be involved! He will be crushed beneath an immense and rather silly joke. It has always been so; and now, more than ever before, the unanimous and excessive pestilence rages.

There is certainly something occult in men's hearts; I am convinced that there is something abstruse, something closed and hidden in the mob. For whenever she sniffs out the idea that obscurity may be a *reality;* that it may exist, for example, on a piece of paper, in a piece of writing (heaven forbid, of course, that it should exist within itself!), she rises up in a hurricane fury and, with thunders and lightnings, blames the darkness on anything but herself.

Her credulousness finds satisfaction in the corresponding agitations of her fellow citizens; she jumps to extremes. So that whatever that dark fiend from hell (i.e., the poet) may write henceforth, she will shake her head (quite unaware that she herself is the enigma) and, with a whisk of her skirt, assert: "I don't get it!"—even if the poor poet has simply stated that he is blowing his nose.

Obedient as he is to his inborn rhythmical sense, the poet naturally finds a lack of proportion between the storm's cause and effect.

Those fellow citizens, it seems to him, are wrong; following their avowed intention, they plunge their pens within a nightless well and lay only the useless, minimum foundation of intelligibility. Granted that the poet does this too—but that is not all he does. It is hardly discreet of them to rouse the mob to such a fury—the mob, remember! is the vessel of genius—and to pour forth pellmell the monumental stupidity of man.

And all this for a matter of no importance.

They play the game without rules and for useless stakes; they force our lady and patron saint[1] to reveal her dehiscence, her lacuna, her misunderstanding of special dreams which constitute the common measure of all things.

I know for a fact that they are the ones who rush on stage and parade around in humiliating fashion. For to base their arguments on obscurity, to say that they "don't get it" and that if they "don't get it" nobody will, means that they refuse to discriminate from the very outset.

---

[1] The Muse.

The scandal is typical, and it continues to be irrelevant.

It has to do with an undertaking which is of no literary importance—

Their undertaking—

Which consists of revealing only the monotonous outward aspects of the world, as newsboys do. Admittedly, they are struggling beneath the pressure of the moment; but in that situation it is clearly improper to write at all, save to spread banality abroad. What they fail to spread is the priceless mist that floats about the secret abyss of every human thought. All that is vulgar which receives no more than the stamp of immediacy. And although I hesitate to use an image to "put them in their place" personally, nevertheless the crudity of these bores is such that they give us, I would say, not a labyrinth lit by flowers and beckoning to our leisure, but a road lined with headaches and vertical plaster images of man's interminable blindness, with no hidden fountains or greenery bending above them, but only green bottle bottoms and bristling broken glass.

Even the advertisers shy away from it all.

Now, let us imagine a steady brilliance which, even when intermittent, does not seem to be merely momentary.

Music came along and put an end to that kind of work.

For at some point in the composition, a motif breaks through the musical veils of our imagination and frees itself of their unceasing immobility, which is alternately compacted or dissolved through conscious art.

Such is the ordinary way.

Or else the composition can begin with a triumphant burst of sound too sudden to last; then the surprise dies away in a group of hesitating notes which its echo has liberated.

Then again, there is the reverse order: the hesitations are folded darkly together and rumor forth a particular obsession of the mind; they are crowded and massed together; and then out of them arises an ultimate and essential brilliance.

Such is the twin, intellectual fashion found particularly in symphonies which, in turn, found it in the repertory of nature and of the sky.

Yes, I know; mystery is said to be music's domain. But the written word also lays claim to it.

Yes, the supreme and heart-rending musical moments are born of fleeting arabesques, and their bursting is more true, more central, more brilliant than any reasoning. When we consider their matchless efficacy, we feel unable to translate them into any language save that of the listener's ideas. Their contact with our spirit is direct and fitting; we feel somehow that words would be discordant and unwelcome.

And yet the written word, which is the ideal in noiseless flight from earth, regains its rights as it stands beneath that fall of virginal sounds. Both music and lyric call for the previous discarding of the spoken word, of course, in order to prevent mere talking.

In a single surge of opposites, the one descends, the other flies away, and yet the same silken veils follow in the wake of both.

Let me pause now and quietly add this parenthesis. It has always been my purpose that stylistic coloring should be neutral: neither should it be darkened in a dive nor brightly shimmer or splash; nor subject to the alternative, which is rules.

What sure guide is there to intelligibility in the midst of these contrasts? What guarantee?

Syntax.

I do not mean simply such spontaneous twists as are inherent in the facility of conversation, even though they are essential to oratory. The French language in particular is elegant when it appears in negligee. As history will show, this is one of the original French characteristics, one of the nation's truly exquisite natures. But our literature goes beyond this "fashion"; it does not consist merely of correspondence and memoirs. It has its quick high flutterings as well; and when these are on the wing, the writer can observe how extraordinarily well the limpid structure of the language receives the primitive thunderbolts of logic. The sentence may seem to stammer at first, hold back in a knot of incidental bits; then it multiplies, takes on order, and rises up in a noble harmony, wavering all the while in its knowing transpositions.

For those who may be surprised and angered by the broad application of my words, I shall describe the revels of this language.

Words rise up unaided and in ecstasy; many a facet reveals its infinite rarity and is precious to our mind. For our mind is the center of this hesitancy and oscillation; it sees the words not in their usual order, but in projection (like the walls of a cave), so long as that mobility which is their principle lives on, that part of speech which is not spoken. Then quickly, before they die away, they all exchange their brilliancies from afar; or they may touch, and steal a furtive glance.

The argument that a certain indispensable and pedestrian clarity may be lacking here and there is a matter for grammarians. And even if the poor reader were to misread these words continually, his understanding of the slush which makes up the current literary fashion is not much better, and so there is hardly any need to distinguish him from the truly malicious. For he too speaks angrily and insultingly of obscurity. Yet why does he not consider literature's common stock and speak angrily and insultingly of *its* incoherence, its drivel, its plagiarism (not to mention any other deterrent or special accusation); or, again, he might well speak of its platitudes, with particular reference to those who are the first to cry "obscurity!" in order to avoid taxing the public's brains.

To answer these threats, I shall simply observe that several of my contemporaries don't know how to read.

The newspaper, yes; they can read that; it has the advantage of not interrupting the day's routine.

Reading—

Is an exercise—

We must bend our independent minds, page by page, to the blank space which begins each one; we must forget the title, for it is too resounding. Then, in the tiniest and most scattered stopping points upon the page, when the lines of chance have been vanquished word by word, the blanks unfailingly return; before, they were gratuitous; now they are essential; and now at last it is clear that nothing lies beyond; now silence is genuine and just.

It is a virgin space, face to face with the lucidity of our matching vision, divided of itself, in solitude, into halves of whiteness; and each of these is lawful bride at the wedding of the idea.

Thus the invisible air, or song, beneath the words leads our divining eye from word to music; and thus, like a motif, invisibly it inscribes its fleuron and pendant there.

Gottlob Frege

1848–1925

Frege's essay "On Sense and Meaning" (1892) takes up a fundamental philosophical problem pertaining to both epistemology and differentiations in semantic matters. The essay was crucial for the development of philosophical analysis and logical positivism, reflected here in the work of Bertrand Russell (below, page 811), Ludwig Wittgenstein (below, page 823), and Rudolph Carnap (below, page 978). But it also expands analysis from mathematics and formal logic to language, which became the principal interest, and often obsession, of diverse twentieth-century philosophers and literary critics.

Frege's terms "sense" (*Sinn*) and "meaning" (*Bedeutung*) require brief discussion here. Frege's *Bedeutung* was earlier translated as "reference" because of the systematic importance he gives to "meaning" as a cognitive relation to a designatable object. In the case of a=b, (if true) it is assumed that *a* and *b* are both names for the same object, say the number 1; their "equality" implies they have the same "meaning." In the case of the planet Venus, the expressions "morning star" and "evening star" have each a different sense but the same meaning: Venus. While this permits Frege to identify meaning with the "truth value" of expressions (a point of importance for Wittgenstein), it also opens up the puzzle, later to vex logical positivism, of meaningful statements (e. g., "the least rapidly convergent series") that seem to refer to something that evidently cannot be designated. Frege acknowledges that sense is related to both "thought" and "idea," which may vary from person to person without being merely subjective or arbitrary, but this by no means solves the puzzle. Instead, it opens up Frege's analysis to problems concerning the abstract, the hypothetical—and the literary—in ways that are particularly intriguing today.

In Frege's terms, "Odysseus" does have sense, but does it have a meaning? To anyone who thought a statement about Odysseus either true or false, the name would have to have meaning; but whether true or false, a sentence about Odysseus would have sense. In the case of an actor and part, mentioned by Frege in a footnote, it appears that a statement having truth-value offstage is only a thought (has sense) in a play. We might go on to ask whether John Gielgud playing Hamlet and the character Hamlet have the same sense, let alone the same meaning. Frege recognizes a problem here, but he avoids it, calling both "representations," but representations of what? Frege holds that to ask for the truth-value of a statement in, say, a play would "cause us to abandon aesthetic delight for an attitude of scientific investigation," which is, in effect, a move to cordon off the aesthetic without considering its implications for knowledge. The problem is ancient: Sidney (above, page 198) could treat the anomalous status of literary fictions, neither true nor false, as a form of moral teaching by way of figures. Not Frege.

It is therefore ironic that Frege's concerns led directly to paradoxes over the ontological status of things with sense but no meaning—such as logical sets in Russell, "pseudo-statements" in Richards and Carnap, or the theoretical "entities" in Carnap's later work that come to seem very much like literary fictions.

Works by Frege translated into English include *The Foundations of Arithmetic* (1953), *The Basic Laws of Arithmetic* (1964), and *Translations from the Philosophical Writings of Gottlob Frege* (1960). See E. D. Klemke, ed., *Essays on Frege* (1968). On a related subject see Saul Kripke, *Naming and Necessity* (1980).

On Sense and Meaning

Equality[1] gives rise to challenging questions which are not altogether easy to answer. Is it a relation? A relation between objects, or between names or signs of objects? In my *Begriffsschrift*[2] I assumed the latter. The reasons which seem to favour this are the following: $a = a$ and $a = b$ are obviously statements of differing cognitive value; $a = a$ holds *a priori* and, according to Kant,[3] is to be labelled analytic, while statements of the form $a = b$ often contain very valuable extensions of our knowledge and cannot always be established *a priori*. The discovery that the rising sun is not new every morning, but always the same, was one of the most fertile astronomical discoveries. Even to-day the reidentification of a small planet or a comet is not always a matter of course. Now if we were to regard equality as a relation between that which the names '*a*' and '*b*' designate, it would seem that $a = b$ could not differ from $a = a$ (i.e., provided $a = b$ is true). A relation would thereby be expressed of a thing to itself, and indeed one in which each thing stands to itself but to no other thing. What we apparently want to state by $a = b$ is that the signs or names '*a*' and '*b*' designate the same thing, so that those signs themselves would be under discussion; a relation between them would be asserted. But this relation would hold between the names or signs only in so far as they named or designated something. It would be mediated by the connexion of each of the two signs with the same designated thing. But this is arbitrary. Nobody can be forbidden to use any arbitrarily producible event or object as a sign for something. In that case the sentence $a = b$ would no longer refer to the subject matter but only to its mode of designation; we would express no proper knowledge by its means. But in many cases this is just what we want to do. If the sign '*a*' is distinguished from the sign '*b*' only as an object (here, by means of its shape), not as a sign (i.e., not by the manner in which it des-

ignates something), the cognitive value of $a = a$ becomes essentially equal to that of $a = b$, provided $a = b$ is true. A difference can arise only if the difference between the signs corresponds to a difference in the mode of presentation of the thing designated. Let *a*, *b*, *c* be the lines connecting the vertices of a triangle with the midpoints of the opposite sides. The point of intersection of *a* and *b* is then the same as the point of intersection of *b* and *c*. So we have different designations for the same point, and these names ('point of intersection of *a* and *b*,' 'point of intersection of *b* and *c*') likewise indicate the mode of presentation; and hence the statement contains actual knowledge.

It is natural, now, to think of there being connected with a sign (name, combination of words, written mark), besides that which the sign designates, which may be called the meaning of the sign, also what I should like to call the *sense* of the sign, wherein the mode of presentation is contained. In our example, accordingly, the meaning of the expressions 'the point of intersection of *a* and *b*' and 'the point of intersection of *b* and *c*' would be the same, but not their sense. The meaning of 'evening star' would be the same as that of 'morning star,' but not the sense.

It is clear from the context that by sign and name I have here understood any designation figuring as a proper name, which thus has as its meaning a definite object (this word taken in the widest range), but not a concept or a relation, which shall be discussed further in another article.[4] The designation of a single object can also consist of several words or other signs. For brevity, let every such designation be called a proper name.

The sense of a proper name is grasped by everybody who is sufficiently familiar with the language or totality of designations to which it belongs;[5] but this serves to illuminate

---

"On Sense and Meaning" was first published in 1892. This translation by Max Black is reprinted from Peter Geach and Max Black, eds., *Translations from the Philosophical Writings of Gottlob Frege,* third edition, 1980.

[1] [Frege] I use this word in the sense of identity and understand "$a = b$" to have the sense of "*a* is the same as *b*" or "*a* and *b* coincide."

[2] [Black] The reference is to Frege's *Begriffsschrift, eine der arithmetischen nachgebildete Formelsprache des reinen Denkens* (Halle, 1879).

[3] Kant (above, page 416).

---

[4] [Black] See his "Ueber Begriff und Gegenstand" (*Vierteljahrsschrift für wissenschaftliche Philosophie* XVI [1892], 192–205) in *Translations*, pages 42–55.

[5] [Frege] In the case of an actual proper name such as "Aristotle" opinions as to the sense may differ. It might, for instance, be taken to be the following: the pupil of Plato and teacher of Alexander the Great. Anybody who does this will attach another sense to the sentence "Aristotle was born in Stagira" than will a man who takes as the sense of the name: the teacher of Alexander the Great who was born in Stagira. So long as the thing meant remains the same, such variations of sense may be tolerated, although they are to be avoided in the theoretical structure of a demonstrative science and ought not to occur in a perfect language.

only a single aspect of the thing meant, supposing it to have one. Comprehensive knowledge of the thing meant would require us to be able to say immediately whether any given sense attaches to it. To such knowledge we never attain.

The regular connexion between a sign, its sense, and what it means is of such a kind that to the sign there corresponds a definite sense and to that in turn a definite thing meant, while to a given thing meant (an object) there does not belong only a single sign. The same sense has different expressions in different languages or even in the same language. To be sure, exceptions to this regular behavior occur. To every expression belonging to a complete totality of signs, there should certainly correspond a definite sense; but natural languages often do not satisfy this condition, and one must be content if the same word has the same sense in the same context. It may perhaps be granted that every grammatically well-formed expression figuring as a proper name always has a sense. But this is not to say that to the sense there also corresponds a thing meant. The words 'the celestial body most distant from the Earth' have a sense, but it is very doubtful if there is also a thing they mean. The expression 'the least rapidly convergent series' has a sense but demonstrably there is nothing it means, since for every given convergent series, another convergent, but less rapidly convergent, series can be found. In grasping a sense, one is not certainly assured of meaning anything.

If words are used in the ordinary way, what one intends to speak of is what they mean. It can also happen, however, that one wishes to talk about the words themselves or their sense. This happens, for instance, when the words of another are quoted. One's own words then first designate words of the other speaker, and only the latter have their usual meaning. We then have signs of signs. In writing, the words are in this case enclosed in quotation marks. Accordingly, a word standing between quotation marks must not be taken as having its ordinary meaning.

In order to speak of the sense of an expression 'A' one may simply use the phrase 'the sense of the expression "A" '. In indirect speech one talks about the sense, e.g., of another person's remarks. It is quite clear that in this way of speaking words do not have their customary meaning but designate what is usually their sense. In order to have a short expression, we will say: In indirect speech, words are used *indirectly* or have their *indirect* meaning. We distinguish accordingly the *customary* from the *indirect* meaning of a word; and its *customary* sense from its *indirect* sense. The indirect meaning of a word is accordingly its customary sense. Such exceptions must always be borne in mind if the mode of connexion between sign, sense, and meaning in particular cases is to be correctly understood.

The meaning and sense of a sign are to be distinguished from the associated idea. If what a sign means is an object perceivable by the senses, my idea of it is an internal image,[6] arising from memories of sense impressions which I have had and acts, both internal and external, which I have performed. Such an idea is often imbued with feeling; the clarity of its separate parts varies and oscillates. The same sense is not always connected, even in the same man, with the same idea. The idea is subjective: one man's idea is not that of another. There result, as a matter of course, a variety of differences in the ideas associated with the same sense. A painter, a horseman, and a zoologist will probably connect different ideas with the name 'Bucephalus.'[7] This constitutes an essential distinction between the idea and sign's sense, which may be the common property of many people, and so is not a part of a mode of the individual mind. For one can hardly deny that mankind has a common store of thoughts which is transmitted from one generation to another.[8]

In the light of this, one need have no scruples in speaking simply of *the* sense, whereas in the case of an idea one must, strictly speaking, add whom it belongs to and at what time. It might perhaps be said: Just as one man connects this idea, and another that idea, with the same word, so also one man can associate this sense and another that sense. But there still remains a difference in the mode of connexion. They are not prevented from grasping the same sense; but they cannot have the same idea. *Si duo idem faciunt, non est idem.* If two persons picture the same thing, each still has his own idea. It is indeed sometimes possible to establish differences in the ideas, or even in the sensations, of different men; but an exact comparison is not possible, because we cannot have both ideas together in the same consciousness.

The meaning of a proper name is the object itself which we designate by using it; the idea which we have in that case is wholly subjective; in between lies the sense, which is indeed no longer subjective like the idea, but is yet not the object itself. The following analogy will perhaps clarify these relationships. Somebody observes the Moon through a telescope. I compare the Moon itself to the meaning; it is the object of the observation, mediated by the real

---

[6] [Frege] We may include with ideas direct experiences: here, sense-impressions and acts themselves take the place of the traces which they have left in the mind. The distinction is unimportant for our purpose, especially since memories of sense-impressions and acts go along with such impressions and acts themselves to complete the perpetual image. One may on the other hand understand direct experience as including any object in so far as it is sensibly perceptible or spatial.

[7] Alexander the Great's horse.

[8] [Frege] Hence it is inadvisable to use the word "idea" to designate something so basically different.

image projected by the object glass in the interior of the telescope, and by the retinal image of the observer. The former I compare to the sense, the latter is like the idea or experience. The optical image in the telescope is indeed one-sided and dependent upon the standpoint of observation; but it is still objective, inasmuch as it can be used by several observers. At any rate it could be arranged for several to use it simultaneously. But each one would have his own retinal image. On account of the diverse shapes of the observers' eyes, even a geometrical congruence could hardly be achieved, and an actual coincidence would be out of the question. This analogy might be developed still further, by assuming A's retinal image made visible to B; or A might also see his own retinal image in a mirror. In this way we might perhaps show how an idea can itself be taken as an object, but as such is not for the observer what it directly is for the person having the idea. But to pursue this would take us too far afield.

We can now recognize three levels of difference between words, expressions, or whole sentences. The difference may concern at most the ideas, or the sense but not the meaning, or, finally, the meaning as well. With respect to the first level, it is to be noted that, on account of the uncertain connexion of ideas with words, a difference may hold for one person, which another does not find. The difference between a translation and the original text should properly not overstep the first level. To the possible difference here belong also the colouring and shading which poetic eloquence seeks to give to the sense. Such colouring and shading are not objective, and must be evoked by each hearer or reader according to the hints of the poet or the speaker. Without some affinity in human ideas art would certainly be impossible; but it can never be exactly determined how far the intentions of the poet are realized.

In what follows there will be no further discussion of ideas and experiences; they have been mentioned here only to ensure that the idea aroused in the hearer by a word shall not be confused with its sense or its meaning.

To make short and exact expressions possible, let the following phraseology be established:

A proper name (word, sign, sign combination, expression) *expresses* its sense, *means* or *designates* its meaning. By employing a sign we express its sense and designate its meaning.

Idealists or sceptics will perhaps long since have objected: 'You talk, without further ado, of the Moon as an object; but how do you know that the name "the Moon" has any meaning? How do you know that anything whatsoever has a meaning?' I reply that when we say 'the Moon,' we do not intend to speak of our idea of the Moon, nor are we satisfied with the sense alone, but we presuppose a meaning. To assume that in the sentence 'The Moon is smaller than the Earth' the idea of the Moon is in question, would be flatly to misunderstand the sense. If this is what the speaker wanted, he would use the phrase 'my idea of the Moon.' Now we can of course be mistaken in the presupposition, and such mistakes have indeed occurred. But the question whether the presupposition is perhaps always mistaken need not be answered here; in order to justify mention of that which a sign means it is enough, at first, to point our intention in speaking or thinking. (We must then add the reservation: provided such a meaning exists.)

So far we have considered the sense and meaning only of such expressions, words, or signs as we have called proper names. We now inquire concerning the sense and meaning of an entire assertoric sentence. Such a sentence contains a thought.[9] Is this thought, now, to be regarded as its sense or its meaning? Let us assume for the time being that the sentence does mean something. If we now replace one word of the sentence by another having the same meaning, but a different sense, this can have no effect upon the meaning of the sentence. Yet we can see that in such a case the thought changes; since, e.g., the thought in the sentence 'The morning star is a body illuminated by the Sun' differs from that in the sentence 'The evening star is a body illuminated by the Sun.' Anybody who did not know that the evening star is the morning star might hold the one thought to be true, the other false. The thought, accordingly, cannot be what is meant by the sentence, but must rather be considered as its sense. What is the position now with regard to the meaning? Have we a right even to inquire about it? Is it possible that a sentence as a whole has only a sense, but no meaning? At any rate, one might expect that such sentences occur, just as there are parts of sentences having sense but no meaning. And sentences which contain proper names without meaning will be of this kind. The sentence 'Odysseus was set ashore at Ithaca while sound asleep' obviously has a sense. But since it is doubtful whether the name 'Odysseus,' occurring therein, means anything, it is also doubtful whether the whole sentence does. Yet it is certain, nevertheless, that anyone who seriously took the sentence to be true or false would ascribe to the name 'Odysseus' a meaning, not merely a sense; for it is of what the name means that the predicate is affirmed or denied. Whoever does not admit the name has meaning can neither apply nor withhold the predicate. But in that case it would

---

[9] [Frege] By a thought I understand not the subjective performance of thinking but its objective content, which is capable of being the common property of several thinkers.

be superfluous to advance to what the name means; one could be satisfied with the sense, if one wanted to go no further than the thought. If it were a question only of the sense of the sentence, the thought, it would be needless to bother with what is meant by a part of the sentence; only the sense, not the meaning, of the part is relevant to the sense of the whole sentence. The thought remains the same whether 'Odysseus' means something or not. The fact that we concern ourselves at all about what is meant by a part of the sentence indicates that we generally recognize and expect a meaning for the sentence itself. The thought loses value for us as soon as we recognize that the meaning of one of its parts is missing. We are therefore justified in not being satisfied with the sense of a sentence, and in inquiring also as to its meaning. But now why do we want every proper name to have not only a sense, but also a meaning? Why is the thought not enough for us? Because, and to the extent that, we are concerned with its truth-value. This is not always the case. In hearing an epic poem, for instance, apart from the euphony of the language we are interested only in the sense of the sentences and the images and feelings thereby aroused. The question of truth would cause us to abandon aesthetic delight for an attitude of scientific investigation. Hence it is a matter of no concern to us whether the name 'Odysseus,' for instance, has meaning, so long as we accept the poem as a work of art.[10] It is the striving for truth that drives us always to advance from the sense to the thing meant.

We have seen that the meaning of a sentence may always be sought, whenever the meaning of its components is involved; and that this is the case when and only when we are inquiring after the truth-value.

We are therefore driven into accepting the *truth-value* of a sentence as constituting what it means. By the truth-value of a sentence I understand the circumstance that it is true or false. There are no further truth-values. For brevity I call the one the True, the other the False. Every assertoric sentence concerned with what its words mean is therefore to be regarded as a proper name, and its meaning, if it has one, is either the True or the False. These two objects are recognized, if only implicitly, by everybody who judges something to be true—and so even by a sceptic. The designation of the truth-values as objects may appear to be an arbitrary fancy or perhaps a mere play upon words, from which no profound consequences could be drawn. What I am calling

an object can be more exactly discussed only in connexion with concept and relation. I will reserve this for another article.[11] But so much should already be clear, that in every judgment,[12] no matter how trivial, the step from the level of thoughts to the level of meaning (the objective) has already been taken.

One might be tempted to regard the relation of the thought to the True not as that of sense to meaning, but rather as that of subject to predicate. One can, indeed, say: 'The thought that 5 is a prime number is true.' But closer examination shows that nothing more has been said than in the simple sentence '5 is a prime number.' The truth claim arises in each case from the form of the assertoric sentence, and when the latter lacks its usual force, e.g., in the mouth of an actor upon the stage, even the sentence 'The thought that 5 is a prime number is true' contains only a thought, and indeed the same thought as the simple '5 is a prime number.' It follows that the relation of the thought to the True may not be compared with that of subject to predicate.

Subject and predicate (understood in the logical sense) are just elements of thought; they stand on the same level for knowledge. By combining subject and predicate, one reaches only a thought, never passes from sense to meaning, never from a thought to its truth-value. One moves at the same level but never advances from one level to the next. A truth-value cannot be a part of a thought, any more than, say, the Sun can, for it is not a sense but an object.

If our supposition that the meaning of a sentence is its truth-value is correct, the latter must remain unchanged when a part of the sentence is replaced by an expression with the same meaning. And this is in fact the case. Leibniz gives the definition: '*Eadem sunt, quae sibi mutuo substitui possunt, salva veritate.*' If we are dealing with sentences for which the meaning of their component parts is at all relevant, then what feature except the truth-value can be found that belongs to such sentences quite generally and remains unchanged by substitutions of the kind just mentioned?

If now the truth-value of a sentence is its meaning, then on the one hand all true sentences have the same meaning and so, on the other hand, do all false sentences. From this we see that in the meaning of the sentence all that is specific is obliterated. We can never be concerned only with the meaning of a sentence; but again the mere

---

[10] [Frege] It would be desirable to have a special term for signs having only sense. If we name them, say, representations, the words of the actors on the stage would be representations; indeed the actor himself would be a representation.

[11] [Black] See his "Ueber Begriff und Gegenstand" (1892), in *Translations,* pages 42–45. [See Note 4 above.]

[12] [Frege] A judgment, for me, is not the mere grasping of a thought, but the admission of its truth.

thought alone yields no knowledge, but only the thought together with its meaning, i.e. its truth-value. Judgments can be regarded as advances from a thought to a truth-value. Naturally this cannot be a definition. Judgment is something quite peculiar and incomparable. One might also say that judgments are distinctions of parts within truth-values. Such distinction occurs by a return to the thought. To every sense attaching to a truth-value would correspond its own manner of analysis. However, I have here used the word 'part' in a special sense. I have in fact transferred the relation between the parts and the whole of the sentence to its meaning, by calling the meaning of a word part of the meaning of the sentence, if the word itself is a part of the sentence. This way of speaking can certainly be attacked, because the total meaning and one part of it do not suffice to determine the remainder, and because the word 'part' is already used of bodies in another sense. A special term would need to be invented.

The supposition that the truth-value of a sentence is what it means shall now be put to further test. We have found that the truth-value of a sentence remains unchanged when an expression is replaced by another with the same meaning: but we have not yet considered the case in which the expression to be replaced is itself a sentence. Now if our view is correct, the truth-value of a sentence containing another as part must remain unchanged when the part is replaced by another sentence having the same truth-value. Exceptions are to be expected when the whole sentence or its part is direct or indirect quotation; for in such cases as we have seen, the words do not have their customary meaning. In direct quotation, a sentence designates another sentence, and in indirect speech a thought.

We are thus led to consider subordinate sentences or clauses. These occur as parts of a sentence complex, which is, from the logical standpoint, likewise a sentence—a main sentence. But here we meet the question whether it is also true of the subordinate sentence that its meaning is a truth-value. Of indirect speech we already know the opposite. Grammarians view the subordinate clauses as representatives of parts of sentences and divide them accordingly into noun clauses, adjective clauses, adverbial clauses. This might generate the supposition that the meaning of a subordinate clause was not a truth-value but rather of the same kind as the meaning of a noun or adjective or adverb—in short, of a part of a sentence, whose sense was not a thought but only a part of a thought. Only a more thorough investigation can clarify the issue. In so doing, we shall not follow the grammatical categories strictly, but rather group together what is logically of the same kind. Let us first search for cases in which the sense of the subordinate clause, as we have just supposed, is nor an independent thought.

The case of an abstract[13] noun clause, introduced by 'that,' includes the case of indirect quotation, in which we have seen the words to have their indirect meaning, coincident with what is customarily their sense. In this case, then, the subordinate clause has for its meaning a thought, not a truth-value; as sense not a thought, but the sense of the words 'the thought that (etc.),' which is only a part of the thought in the entire complex sentence. This happens after 'say,' 'hear,' 'be of the opinion,' 'be convinced,' 'conclude,' and similar words.[14] There is a different, and indeed somewhat complicated, situation after words like 'perceive,' 'know,' 'fancy,' which are to be considered later.

That in the cases of the first kind the meaning of the subordinate clause is in fact the thought can also be recognized by seeing that it is indifferent to the truth of the whole whether the subordinate clause is true or false. Let us compare, for instance, the two sentences 'Copernicus believed that the planetary orbits are circles' and 'Copernicus believed that the apparent motion of the sun is produced by the real motion of the Earth.' One subordinate clause can be substituted for the other without harm to the truth. The main clause and the subordinate clause together have as their sense only a single thought, and the truth of the whole includes neither the truth nor the untruth of the subordinate clause. In such cases it is not permissible to replace one expression in the subordinate clause by another having the same customary meaning, but only by one having the same indirect meaning, i.e. the same customary sense. Somebody might conclude: The meaning of a sentence is not its truth-value, for in that case it could always be replaced by another sentence of the same truth-value. But this proves too much; one might just as well claim that the meaning of 'morning star' is not Venus, since one may not always say 'Venus' in place of 'morning star.' One has the right to conclude only that the meaning of a sentence is not *always* its truth-value, and that 'morning star' does not always mean the planet Venus, viz, when the word has its indirect meaning. An exception of such a kind occurs in the subordinate clause just considered which has a thought as its meaning.

If one says 'It seems that . . .' one means 'It seems to me that . . .' or 'I think that . . .' We therefore have the same case

---

[13] [Black] Frege probably means clauses grammatically replaceable by an abstract noun-phrase; for example, "Smith denies *that dragons exist*"— "Smith denies *the existence of dragons*"; or again in this context after "denies," "that Brown is wise" is replaceable by "the wisdom of Brown."

[14] [Frege] in *"A lied in saying he had seen B,"* the subordinate clause designates a thought which is said (1) to have been asserted by *A* (2) while *A* was convinced of its falsity.

again. The situation is similar in the case of expressions such as 'to be pleased,' 'to regret,' 'to approve,' 'to blame,' 'to hope,' 'to fear.' If, toward the end of the battle of Waterloo,[15] Wellington was glad that the Prussians were coming, the basis for his joy was a conviction. Had he been deceived, he would have been no less pleased so long as his illusion lasted; and before he became so convinced he could not have been pleased that the Prussians were coming—even though in fact they might have been already approaching.

Just as a conviction or a belief is the ground of a feeling, it can, as in inference, also be the ground of a conviction. In the sentence: 'Columbus inferred from the roundness of the Earth that he could reach India by travelling towards the west,' we have as the meanings of the parts two thoughts, that the Earth is round, and that Columbus by travelling to the west could reach India. All that is relevant here is that Columbus was convinced of both, and that the one conviction was a ground for the other. Whether the Earth is really round and Columbus could really reach India by travelling west, as he thought, is immaterial to the truth of our sentence; but it is not immaterial whether we replace 'the Earth' by 'the planet which is accompanied by a moon whose diameter is greater than the fourth part of its own.' Here also we have the indirect meaning of the words.

Adverbial final clauses beginning 'in order that' also belong here; for obviously the purpose is a thought; therefore: indirect meaning for the words, subjunctive mood.

A subordinate clause with 'that' after 'command,' 'ask,' 'forbid,' would appear in direct speech as an imperative. Such a sentence has no meaning but only a sense. A command, a request, are indeed not thoughts, but they stand on the same level as thoughts. Hence in subordinate clauses depending upon 'command,' 'ask,' etc., words have their indirect meaning. The meaning of such a clause is therefore not a truth-value but a command, a request, and so forth.

The case is similar for the dependent question in phrases such as 'doubt whether,' 'not to know what.' It is easy to see that here also the words are to be taken to have their indirect meaning. Dependent clauses expressing questions and beginning with 'who,' 'what,' 'where,' 'when,' 'how,' 'by what means,' etc., seem at times to approximate very closely to adverbial clauses in which words have their customary meanings. These cases are distinguished linguistically [in German] by the mood of the verb. With the subjunctive, we have a dependent question and indirect

meanings of the words, so that a proper name cannot in general be replaced by another name of the same object.

In the cases so far considered the words of the subordinate clauses had their indirect meaning, and this made it clear that the meaning of the subordinate clause itself was indirect, i.e., not a truth-value but a thought, a command, a request, a question. The subordinate clause could be regarded as a noun, indeed one could say: as a proper name of that thought, that command, etc., which it represented in the context of the sentence structure.

We now come to other subordinate clauses, in which the words do have their customary meaning without however a thought occurring as sense and a truth-value as meaning. How this is possible is best made clear by examples.

Whoever discovered the elliptic form of the planetary orbits died in misery.

If the sense of the subordinate clause were here a thought, it would have to be possible to express it also in a separate sentence. But it does not work, because the grammatical subject 'whoever' has no independent sense and only mediates the relation with the consequent clause 'died in misery.' For this reason the sense of the subordinate clause is not a complete thought, and what it means is Kepler, not a truth value. One might object that the sense of the whole does contain a thought as part, viz. that there was somebody who first discovered the elliptic form of the planetary orbits; for whoever takes the whole to be true cannot deny this part. This is undoubtedly so; but only because otherwise the dependent clause 'whoever discovered the elliptic form of the planetary orbits' would have nothing to mean. If anything is asserted there is always an obvious presupposition that the simple or compound proper names used have meaning. If therefore one asserts 'Kepler died in misery,' there is a presupposition that the name 'Kepler' designates something; but it does not follow that the sense of the sentence 'Kepler died in misery' contains the thought that the name 'Kepler' designates something. If this were the case the negation would have to run not

Kepler did not die in misery

but

Kepler did not die in misery, or the name 'Kepler' has no reference.

That the name 'Kepler' designates something is just as much a presupposition for the assertion

Kepler died in misery

as for the contrary assertion. Now languages have the fault of containing expressions which fail to designate an object (although their grammatical form seems to qualify them for that purpose) because the truth of some sentence is a prerequisite. Thus it depends on the truth of the sentence:

There was someone who discovered the elliptic form of the planetary orbits

whether the subordinate clause

Whoever discovered the elliptic form of the planetary orbits.

really designates an object, or only seems to do so while in fact there is nothing for it to mean. And thus it may appear as if our subordinate clause contained as a part of its sense the thought that there was somebody who discovered the elliptic form of the planetary orbits. If this were right the negation would run:

Either whoever discovered the elliptic form of the planetary orbits did not die in misery or there was nobody who discovered the elliptic form of the planetary orbits.

This arises from an imperfection of language, from which even the symbolic language of mathematical analysis is not altogether free; even there combinations of symbols can occur that seem to mean something but (at least so far) do not mean anything, e.g. divergent infinite series. This can be avoided, e.g., by means of the special stipulation that divergent infinite series shall mean the number 0. A logically perfect language (*Begriffsschrift*) should satisfy the conditions, that every expression grammatically well constructed as a proper name out of signs already introduced shall in fact designate an object, and that no new sign shall be introduced as a proper name without being secured a meaning. The logic books contain warnings against logical mistakes arising from the ambiguity of expressions. I regard as no less pertinent a warning against apparent proper names without any meaning. The history of mathematics supplies errors which have arisen in this way. This lends itself to

demagogic abuse as easily as ambiguity—perhaps more easily. 'The will of the people' can serve as an example; for it is easy to establish that there is at any rate no generally accepted meaning for this expression. It is therefore by no means unimportant to eliminate the source of these mistakes, at least in science, once and for all. Then such objections as the one discussed above would become impossible, because it could never depend upon the truth of a thought whether a proper name had meaning.

With the consideration of these noun clauses may be coupled that of types of adjective and adverbial clauses which are logically in close relation to them.

Adjective clauses also serve to construct compound proper names, though, unlike noun clauses, they are not sufficient by themselves for this purpose. These adjective clauses are to be regarded as equivalent to adjectives. Instead of 'the square root of 4 which is smaller than 0,' one can also say 'the negative square root of 4.' We have here the case of a compound proper name constructed from the expression for a concept with the help of the singular definite article. This is at any rate permissible if the concept applies to one and only one single object.[16]

Expressions for concepts can be so constructed that marks of a concept are given by adjective clauses as, in our example, by the clause 'which is smaller than 0.' It is evident that such an adjective clause cannot have a thought as sense or a truth-value as meaning, any more than the noun clause could. Its sense, which can also in many cases be expressed by a single adjective, is only a part of a thought. Here, as in the case of the noun clause, there is no independent subject and therefore no possibility of reproducing the sense of the subordinate clause in an independent sentence.

Places, instants, stretches of time, logically considered, are objects; hence the linguistic designation of a definite place, a definite instant, or a stretch of time is to be regarded as a proper name. Now adverbial clauses of place and time can be used to construct such a proper name in much the same way as we have seen noun and adjective clauses can. In the same way, expressions for concepts that apply to places, etc., can be constructed. It is to be noted here also that the sense of these subordinate clauses cannot be reproduced in an independent sentence, since an essential component, viz. the determination of place or time,

---

[16] [Frege] In accordance with what was said before, an expression of the kind in question must actually always be assured of meaning, by means of a special stipulation, for example, by the convention that it shall count as meaning 0 when the concept applies to no object or to more than one. [In this context, see Russell (below, page 811).]

is missing and is just indicated by a relative pronoun or a conjunction.[17]

In conditional clauses, also, there most often recognizably occurs an indefinite indicator, with a correlative indicator in the dependent clause. (We have already seen this occur in noun, adjective, and adverbial clauses.) In so far as each indicator relates to the other, both clauses together form a connected whole, which as a rule expresses only a single thought. In the sentence

> If a number is less than 1 and greater than 0,
> its square is less than 1 and greater than 0

the component in question is 'a number' in the antecedent clause and 'its' in the consequent clause. It is by means of this very indefiniteness that the sense acquires the generality expected of a law. It is this which is responsible for the fact that the antecedent clause alone has no complete thought as its sense and in combination with the consequent clause expresses one and only one thought, whose parts are no longer thoughts. It is, in general, incorrect to say that in the hypothetical judgment two judgments are put in reciprocal relationship. If this or something similar is said, the word 'judgment' is used in the same sense as I have connected with the word 'thought,' so that I would use the formulation: 'A hypothetical thought establishes a reciprocal relationship between two thoughts.' This could be true only if an indefinite indicator is absent;[18] but in such a case there would also be no generality.

If an instant of time is to be indefinitely indicated in both the antecedent and the consequent clause, this is often achieved merely by using the present tense of the verb, which in such a case however does not indicate the temporal present. This grammatical form is then the indefinite indicator in the main and subordinate clauses. An example of this is: 'When the Sun is in the tropic of Cancer, the longest day in the northern hemisphere occurs.' Here, also, it is impossible to express the sense of the subordinate clause in a full sentence, because this sense is not a complete thought. If we say: 'The Sun is in the tropic of Cancer,' this would refer to our present time and thereby change the sense. Neither is the sense of the main clause a thought; only the whole, composed of main and subordinate clauses, has such a sense. It may be added that several common components may be indefinitely indicated in the antecedent and consequent clauses.

It is clear that noun clauses with 'who' or 'what' and adverbial clauses with 'where,' 'when,' 'wherever,' 'whenever' are often to be interpreted as having the sense of antecedent clauses, e.g. 'who touches pitch, defiles himself.'

Adjective clauses can also take the place of conditional clauses. Thus the sense of the sentence previously used can be given in the form 'The square of a number which is less than 1 and greater than 0 is less than 1 and greater than 0.'

The situation is quite different if the common component of the two clauses is designated by a proper name. In the sentence:

> Napoleon, who recognized the danger to his right flank, himself led his guards against the enemy position

two thoughts are expressed:

> 1. Napoleon recognized the danger to his right flank
> 2. Napoleon himself led his guards against the enemy position.

When and where this happened is to be fixed only by the context, but is nevertheless to be taken as definitely determined thereby. If the entire sentence is uttered as an assertion, we thereby simultaneously assert both component sentences. If one of the parts is false, the whole is false. Here we have the case that the subordinate clause by itself has a complete thought as sense (if we complete it by indication of place and time). The meaning of the subordinate clause is accordingly a truth-value. We can therefore expect that it may be replaced, without harm to the truth-value of the whole, by a sentence having the same truth-value. This is indeed the case; but it is to be noticed that for purely grammatical reasons, its subject must be 'Napoleon,' for only

---

[17] [Frege] In the case of these sentences, various interpretations are easily possible. The sense of the sentence, "After Schleswig-Holstein was separated from Denmark, Prussia and Austria quarreled" can be rendered "After the separation of Schleswig-Holstein from Denmark, Prussia and Austria quarreled." In this version, it is surely sufficiently clear that the sense is not to be taken as having as a part the thought that Schleswig-Holstein was once separated from Denmark, but that this is the necessary presupposition in order for the expression "after the separation of Schleswig-Holstein from Denmark" to have any meaning at all. To be sure, our sentence can also be interpreted as saying that Schleswig-Holstein was once separated from Denmark. We then have a case which is to be considered later. In order to understand the difference more clearly, let us project ourselves into the mind of a Chinese who, having little knowledge of European history, believes it to be false that Schleswig-Holstein was ever separated from Denmark. He will take our sentence, in the first version, to be neither true nor false, but will deny it to have any meaning, on the ground that its subordinate clause lacks a meaning. This clause would only apparently determine a time. If he interpreted our sentence in the second way, however, he would find a thought expressed in it which he would take to be false, beside a part which would be without meaning for him.

[18] [Frege] At times there is no linguistically explicit indicator and one must be read off from the entire context.

then can it be brought into the form of an adjective clause attaching to 'Napoleon.' But if the demand that it be expressed in this form is waived, and the connexion shown by 'and,' this restriction disappears.

Subsidiary clauses beginning with 'although' also express complete thoughts. This conjunction actually has no sense and does not change the sense of the clause but only illuminates it in a peculiar fashion.[19] We could indeed replace the concessive clause without harm to the truth of the whole by another of the same truth-value; but the light in which the clause is placed by the conjunction might then easily appear unsuitable, as if a song with a sad subject were to be sung in a lively fashion.

In the last cases the truth of the whole included the truth of the component clauses. The case is different if an antecedent clause expresses a complete thought by containing, in place of an indefinite indicator, a proper name or something which is to be regarded as equivalent. In the sentence

If the Sun has already risen, the sky is very cloudy

the time is the present, that is to say, definite. And the place is also to be thought of as definite. Here it can be said that a relation between the truth-values of antecedent and consequent clauses has been asserted, viz., that the case does not occur in which the antecedent means the True and the consequent the False. Accordingly, our sentence is true if the Sun has not yet risen, whether the sky is very cloudy or not, and also if the Sun has risen and the sky is very cloudy. Since only truth-values are here in question, each component clause can be replaced by another of the same truth-value without changing the truth-value of the whole. To be sure, the light in which the subject then appears would usually be unsuitable; the thought might easily seem distorted; but this has nothing to do with its truth-value. One must always observe that there are overtones of subsidiary thoughts, which are however not explicitly expressed and therefore should not be reckoned in the sense. Hence, also, no account need be taken of their truth-values.[20]

The simple cases have now been discussed. Let us review what we have learned.

The subordinate clause usually has for its sense not a thought, but only a part of one, and consequently no truth-

value is being meant. The reason for this is either that the words in the subordinate clause have indirect meaning, so that the meaning, not the sense, of the subordinate clause is a thought; or else that, on account of the presence of an indefinite indicator, the subordinate clause is incomplete and expresses a thought only when combined with the main clause. It may happen, however, that the sense of the subsidiary clause is a complete thought, in which case it can be replaced by another of the same truth-value without harm to the truth of the whole—provided there are no grammatical obstacles.

An examination of all the subordinate clauses which one may encounter will soon provide some which do not fit well into these categories. The reason, so far as I can see, is that these subordinate clauses have no such simple sense. Almost always, it seems, we connect with the main thoughts expressed by us subsidiary thoughts which, although not expressed, are associated with our words, in accordance with psychological laws, by the hearer. And since the subsidiary thought appears to be connected with our words on its own account, almost like the main thought itself, we want it also to be expressed. The sense of the sentence is thereby enriched, and it may well happen that we have more simple thoughts than clauses. In many cases the sentence must be understood in this way, in others it may be doubtful whether the subsidiary thought belongs to the sense of the sentence or only accompanies it.[21] One might perhaps find that the sentence

Napoleon, who recognized the danger to his right flank, himself led his guards against the enemy position

expresses not only the two thoughts shown above, but also the thought that the knowledge of the danger was the reason why he led the guards against the enemy position. One may in fact doubt whether this thought is just slightly suggested or really expressed. Let the question be considered whether our sentence is false if Napoleon's decision had already been made before he recognized the danger. If our sentence could be true in spite of this, the subsidiary thought should not be understood as part of the sense. One would probably decide in favour of this. The alternative would make for a quite complicated situation: We would have more simple thoughts than clauses. If the sentence

Napoleon recognized the danger to his right flank

---

[19] [Frege] Similarly in the case of "but," "yet."
[20] [Frege] The thought of our sentence might also be expressed thus: "Either the Sun has not risen yet or the sky is very cloudy"—which shows how this kind of sentence connexion is to be understood.

[21] [Frege] This may be important for the question whether an assertion is a lie, or an oath a perjury.

were now to be replaced by another having the same truth value, e.g.

Napoleon was already more than 45 years old

not only would our first thought be changed, but also our third one. Hence the truth-value of the latter might change—viz. if his age was not the reason for the decision to lead the guards against the enemy. This shows why clauses of equal truth-value cannot always be substituted for one another in such cases. The clause expresses more through its connexion with another than it does in isolation.

Let us now consider cases where this regularly happens. In the sentence:

Bebel fancies that the return of Alsace-Lorraine would appease France's desire for revenge

two thoughts are expressed, which are not however shown by means of antecedent and consequent clauses, viz.:

(1) Bebel believes that the return of Alsace-Lorraine would appease France's desire for revenge
(2) the return of Alsace-Lorraine would not appease France's desire for revenge.

In the expression of the first thought, the words of the subordinate clause have their indirect meaning, while the same words have their customary meaning in the expression of the second thought. This shows that the subordinate clause in our original complex sentence is to be taken twice over, with different meanings: once for a thought, once for a truth-value. Since the truth-value is not the total meaning of the subordinate clause, we cannot simply replace the latter by another of equal truth-value. Similar considerations apply to expressions such as 'know,' 'discover,' 'it is known that.'

By means of a subordinate causal clause and the associated main clause we express several thoughts, which however do not correspond separately to the original clauses. In the sentence: 'Because ice is less dense than water, it floats on water' we have

(1) Ice is less dense than water;
(2) If anything is less dense than water, it floats on water;
(3) Ice floats on water.

The third thought, however, need not be explicitly introduced, since it is contained in the remaining two. On the other hand, neither the first and third nor the second and third combined would furnish the sense of our sentence. It can now be seen that our subordinate clause

because ice is less dense than water

expresses our first thought, as well as a part of our second. This is how it comes to pass that our subsidiary clause cannot be simply replaced by another of equal truth-value; for this would alter our second thought and thereby might well alter its truth-value.

The situation is similar in the sentence

If iron were less dense than water, it would float on water.

Here we have the two thoughts that iron is not less dense than water, and that something floats on water if it is less dense than water. The subsidiary clause again expresses one thought and a part of the other.

If we interpret the sentence already considered

After Schleswig-Holstein was separated from Denmark, Prussia and Austria quarrelled

in such a way that it expresses the thought that Schleswig-Holstein was once separated from Denmark, we have first this thought, and secondly the thought that, at a time more closely determined by the subordinate clause, Prussia and Austria quarrelled. Here also the subordinate clause expresses not only one thought but also a part of another. Therefore it may not in general be replaced by another of the same truth-value.

It is hard to exhaust all the possibilities given by language; but I hope to have brought to light at least the essential reasons why a subordinate clause may not always be replaced by another of equal truth-value without harm to the truth of the whole sentence structure. These reasons arise:

(1) when the subordinate clause does not have a truth-value as its meaning, inasmuch as it expresses only a part of a thought;
(2) when the subordinate clause does have a truth-value as its meaning but is not restricted to so doing, inasmuch as its sense includes one thought and part of another.

The first case arises:

(a) for words having indirect meaning

(b) if a part of the sentence is only an indefinite indicator instead of a proper name.

In the second case, the subsidiary clause may have to be taken twice over, viz, once in its customary meaning, and the other time in indirect meaning; or the sense of a part of the subordinate clause may likewise be a component of another thought, which, taken together with the thought directly expressed by the subordinate clause, makes up the sense of the whole sentence.

It follows with sufficient probability from the foregoing that the cases where a subordinate clause is not replaceable by another of the same value cannot be brought in disproof of our view that a truth-value is the meaning of a sentence that has a thought as its sense.

Let us return to our starting point.

When we found '$a = a$' and '$a = b$' to have different cognitive values, the explanation is that for the purpose of knowledge, the sense of the sentence, viz., the thought expressed by it, is no less relevant than its meaning, i.e. its truth-value. If now $a = b$, then indeed what is meant by 'b' is the same as what is meant by 'a,' and hence the truth-value of '$a = b$' is the same as that of '$a = a$.' In spite of this, the sense of 'b' may differ from that of 'a,' and thereby the thought expressed in '$a = b$' differs from that of $a = a$.' In that case the two sentences do not have the same cognitive value. If we understand by 'judgment' the advance from the thought to its truth-value, as in the present paper, we can also say that the judgments are different.

Sigmund Freud

1856–1939

Trained as a neurologist, Sigmund Freud pursued the nascent field of psychiatry to become the chief architect and theorist of psychoanalysis. Throughout a turbulent career, which transformed modern thinking about human nature, Freud developed a complex theory of human psychology and sexuality that traced adult mental aberrations and neuroses to early childhood experiences and the more or less systematic repression of the inherently sexual nature of human psychic energy. From his earliest speculations to his more mature theories, a crucial element was the interpretation of dreams as the manifest expression of latent psychic content that may be oblique, disguised, or otherwise represented symbolically, as distressing, anxiety producing, or too painful to confront directly. His practice, relying upon case studies and doctor-patient analytical sessions, produced almost from the very beginning, dramatic narratives and sometimes shocking revelations, that were often followed by sharp critiques and allegations (which continued throughout his career)—having, ironically, the effect of confirming to Freud the essential correctness of his insights and methodology as they provided an explanation for attacks against him.

Central to Freud's theory of the psyche was his use of the figure of Oedipus and what came to be popularly known as the "Oedipus Complex" as a powerful and provocative model for explaining the emergence of the adult ego and the articulation of a dynamic tripartite psychological structure of the Id, the Ego, and the Superego, subject to a more general distinction between the unconscious and the conscious mind. The work of analysis depended upon the supposition that much that happens in mental life is not conscious, hypothetically because of the repression of traumatic events, and must be brought, for the purposes of therapy, to consciousness. What is particularly striking in retrospect is the extraordinary reliance in Freud's theorizing upon literary models, particularly Shakespeare and Sophocles (but not limited to these two), using literary narratives as a way to illuminate or recognize characteristic symptoms discerned in practice. The ambiguity that has fueled a great deal of recent debate is the "scientific" status of Freud's discoveries and proposed principles of explanation. Are the stories upon which Freud relied for the terms of his own theory the source, or just additional evidence for the perspicuity of Freud's analytical insights? The two selections are reprinted here, the first from an early letter to Fleiss, which offers the first glimpse of Freud's more mature theory; and the second, from *A General Introduction to Psychoanalysis,* which explores in detail the structure and the ramifications of the Oedipal complex.

The primary and critical literature on Freud and the Psychoanalytic movement (including later theorists such as C. G. Jung, Jacques Lacan, Karen Horney, Abram Maslow, and others) is vast and complex. The basic writings of Freud himself are available in many collections, but the current standard edition is James Strachey, ed., *The Edition of the Complete Psychological Works of Sigmund Freud* (in twenty-four volumes, 1966–1974). See also, his *Collected Papers* (in five volumes, 1924–1950) and Freud's *Autobiography,* tr. by James Strachey (1935). For readers with a clinical interest in Freud, *Abstracts of The Standard Edition of the Complete Psychological Works of Sigmund Freud,* edited by Carrie Lee Rothgeb (1971; 1975) is essential. Major recent studies include: Stephen A. Mitchell and Margaret J. Black, *Freud and Beyond: A History of Modern Psychoanalytic Thought* (1995); Todd Dufresne, ed., *Returns of the "French Freud": Freud, Lacan, and Beyond* (1997); Jacques Derrida, *Resistances of Psychoanalysis* (1998); Laura Marcus, ed., *Sigmund Freud's Interpretation of Dreams: New Interdisciplinary Essays* (1999); Leonard Jackson, *Literature, Psychoanalysis, and the New Sciences of Mind* (2000); Edward Said, *Freud and the Non-European* (2003).

from

Letter to Wilhelm Fleiss, October 15, 1897

. . . My self-analysis is in fact the most essential thing I have at present and promises to become of the greatest value to me if it reaches its end. In the middle of it, it suddenly ceased for three days, during which I had the feeling of being tied up inside (which patients complain of so much), and I was really disconsolate until I found that these same three days (twenty-eight days ago) were the bearers of identical somatic phenomena. Actually only two bad days with a remission in between. From this one should draw the conclusion that the female period is not conducive to work. Punctually on the fourth day, it started again. Naturally, the pause also had another determinant—the resistance to something surprisingly new. Since then I have been once again intensely preoccupied [with it], mentally fresh, though afflicted with all sorts of minor disturbances that come from the content of the analysis.

My practice, uncannily, still leaves me a great deal of free time. The whole thing is all the more valuable for my purposes, since I have succeeded in finding a few real points of reference for the story. I asked my mother whether she still remembered the nurse. "Of course," she said, "an elderly person, very clever, she was always carrying you off to some church; when you returned home you preached and told us all about God Almighty. During my confinement with Anna (two and a half years younger), it was discovered that she was a thief, and all the shiny new kreuzers and zehners[1] and

all the toys that had been given to you were found in her possession. Your brother Philipp himself fetched the policeman; she then was given ten months in prison." Now look at how this confirms the conclusions of my dream interpretation. It was easy for me to explain the only possible mistake. I wrote to you that she induced me to steal zehners and give them to her. In truth, the dream meant that she stole them herself. For the dream picture was a memory of my taking money from the mother of a doctor—that is, wrongfully. The correct interpretation is: I = she, and the mother of the doctor equals my mother. So far was I from knowing she was a thief that I made a wrong interpretation.

I also inquired about the doctor we had had in Freiberg because one dream concentrated a good deal of resentment on him. In the analysis of the dream figure behind which he was concealed, I also thought of a Professor von Kraus, my history teacher in high school. He did not seem to fit in at all, because my relationship with him was indifferent or even comfortable. My mother then told me that the doctor in my childhood had only one eye, and of all my teachers Professor Kraus was the only one with the same defect! The conclusive force of these coincidences might be weakened by the objection that on some occasion in my later childhood, I had heard that the nurse was a thief and then apparently had forgotten it until it finally emerged in the dream. I myself believe that that is so. But I have another, entirely irrefutable and amusing proof. I said to myself that if the old woman disappeared from my life so suddenly, it must be possible to demonstrate the impression this made on me. Where is it then? Thereupon a scene occurred to me which in the course of twenty-five years has occasionally emerged in my conscious memory without my understanding it. My mother was nowhere to be found; I was crying in despair. My brother Philipp (twenty years older than I) unlocked a wardrobe [*Kasten*] for me, and when I did not find my mother inside it either, I cried even more until, slender and beautiful, she came in through the door. What can this mean? Why did my brother unlock the wardrobe for me,

Freud's Letter to Wilhelm Fleiss, October 15, 1897, is reprinted from *The Complete Letters of Sigmund Freud to Wilhelm Fleiss, 1887–1904,* edited and translated by Jeffrey M. Masson (Cambridge, Mass.: Harvard University Press, 1985), 269–73.

[1] *Kreuzer* and *zehner* are designations of coins.

knowing that my mother was not in it and that thereby he could not calm me down? Now I suddenly understand it. I had asked him to do it. When I missed my mother, I was afraid she had vanished from me, just as the old woman had a short time before. So I must have heard that the old woman had been locked up and therefore must have believed that my mother had been locked up too—or rather, had been "boxed up" [*eingekastelt*]—for my brother Philipp, who is now sixty-three years old, to this very day is still fond of using such puns. The fact that I turned to him in particular proves that I was well aware of his share in the disappearance of the nurse.

Since then I have got much further, but have not yet reached my real point of rest. It is so difficult and would carry us so far afield to communicate what I have not yet finished that I hope you will excuse me from it and content yourself with the knowledge of those elements that are certain. If the analysis fulfills what I expect of it, I shall work on it systematically and then put it before you. So far I have found nothing completely new, [just] all the complications to which I have become accustomed. It is by no means easy. Being totally honest with oneself is a good exercise. A single idea of general value dawned on me. I have found, in my own case too, [the phenomenon of] being in love with my mother and jealous of my father, and I now consider it a universal event in early childhood, even if not so early as in children who have been made hysterical. (Similar to the invention of parentage [family romance][2] in paranoia-heroes, founders of religion). If this is so, we can understand the gripping power of *Oedipus Rex,* in spite of all the objections that reason raises against the presupposition of fate; and we can understand why the later "drama of fate" was bound to fail so miserably. Our feelings rise against any arbitrary individual compulsion, such as is presupposed in *Die Ahnfrau*[3] and the like; but the Greek legend seizes upon a compulsion which everyone recognizes because he senses its existence within himself. Everyone in the audience was once a budding Oedipus in fantasy and each recoils in horror from the dream fulfillment here transplanted into reality, with the full quantity of repression which separates his infantile state from his present one.

Fleetingly the thought passed through my head that the same thing might be at the bottom of *Hamlet* as well. I am not thinking of Shakespeare's conscious intention, but be-

lieve, rather, that a real event stimulated the poet in his representation, in that his unconscious understood the unconscious of his hero. How does Hamlet the hysteric justify his words, "Thus conscience does make cowards of us all?" How does he explain his irresolution in avenging his father by the murder of his uncle—the same man who sends his courtiers to their death without a scruple and who is positively precipitate in murdering Laertes? How better than through the torment he suffers from the obscure memory that he himself had contemplated the same deed against his father out of passion for his mother, and—"use every man after his desert, and who should 'scape whipping?'" His conscience is his unconscious sense of guilt. And is not his sexual alienation in his conversation with Ophelia typically hysterical? And his rejection of the instinct that seeks to beget children? And, finally, his transferral of the deed from his own father to Ophelia's? And does he not in the end, in the same marvelous way as my hysterical patients, bring down punishment on himself by suffering the same fate as his father of being poisoned by the same rival?

I have kept my interest focused so exclusively on the analysis that I have not yet even attempted to try out, instead of my hypothesis that in every instance repression starts from the feminine aspect and is directed against the male one, the opposite hypothesis proposed by you. I shall, however, tackle it sometime. Unfortunately, I barely participate in your work and progress. In this one respect I am better off than you are. What I can tell you about mental frontiers [*Seelenende*] of this world finds in you an understanding critic, and what you can tell me about its celestial frontiers [*Sternenende*] evokes only unproductive amazement in me.

from

Thirteenth Lecture: Archaic and Infantile Features in Dreams

[In the early pages of this lecture, Freud returns to his hypothesis concerning the "dream-work," that under the influence of censorship, the "latent content" is translated into another form. The manifest content in the dream may there-

---

[2] This refers to Freud's designation for the common fantasy of a child that he or she is really the offspring of other parents, typically more noble and attractive.

[3] *Die Anfrau* (The Ancesstress) is a tragedy by Austrian author Franz Grillparzer (1791–1872), published in 1817. The play could be taken as a "tragedy of fate" *(Schicksalsdrama),* in the sense Freud here suggests, though Grillparzer's characters are ultimately responsible for their own fates.

FROM THIRTEENTH LECTURE: ARCHAIC AND INFANTILE FEATURES IN DREAMS, which was first presented in a series of lectures in Vienna, 1915–1917; first published in 1920, revised edition, 1935. Reprinted from *A General Introduction to Psychoanalysis,* authorized English translation of the revised edition by Joan Riviere (New York: Liveright Publishing Corporation, 1935).

fore belong to phases in intellectual development long since outgrown. This Freud designates as the *"archaic"* or *"regressive"* expression of the dream-work, and the task of dream interpretation for the analyst thus arises from what he calls "the peculiar *amnesia of childhood*" in which much of early childhood is forgotten, conjoined with the peculiar survival of selected concrete images or *"screen-memories."* The particular phenomenon to which he turns attention is the manifestation of apparent death wishes in dreams.]

* * *

Let us keep to the death-wishes, which we shall certainly find mostly derived from the unbounded egoism of the dreamer. Wishes of this sort are very often found to be the underlying agents of dreams. Whenever anyone gets in our way in life— and how often must this happen when our relations to one another are so complicated!—a dream is immediately prepared to make away with that person, even if it be father, mother, brother or sister, husband or wife. It appeared to us amazing that such wickedness should be innate in humanity, and certainly we were not inclined to admit without further evidence that this result of our interpretation of dreams was correct. But, when once we had seen that the origin of wishes of this sort must be looked for in the past, we had little difficulty in finding the period in the past of the individual in which there is nothing strange in such egoism and such wishes, even when directed against the nearest and dearest. A child in his earliest years (which later are veiled in oblivion) is just the person who frequently displays such egoism in boldest relief; invariably, unmistakable tendencies of this kind, or, more accurately, surviving traces of them, are plainly visible in him. For a child loves himself first and only later learns to love others and to sacrifice something of his own ego to them. Even the people whom he seems to love from the outset are loved in the first instance because he needs them and cannot do without them—again therefore, from motives of egoism. Only later does the impulse of love detach itself from egoism: it is a literal fact that the child learns how to love through his own egoism.

In this connection it will be instructive to compare a child's attitude towards his brothers and sisters with his attitude towards his parents. The little child does not necessarily love his brothers and sisters, and often he is quite frank about it. It is unquestionable that in them he sees and hates his rivals, and it is well known how commonly this attitude persists without interruption for many years, till the child reaches maturity and even later. Of course it often gives place to a more tender feeling, or perhaps we should say it is

overlaid by this, but the hostile attitude seems very generally to be the earlier. We can most easily observe it in children of two and a half to four years old when a new baby arrives, which generally meets with a very unfriendly reception; remarks such as "I don't like it. The stork is to take it away again" are very common. Subsequently every opportunity is seized to disparage the new-comer; attempts are even made to injure it and actual attacks upon it are by no means unheard-of. If the difference in age is less, by the time the child's mental activity is more fully developed the rival is already in existence and he adapts himself to the situation; if on the other hand there is a greater difference between their ages, the new baby may rouse certain kindly feelings from the first, as an object of interest, a sort of living doll; and when there is as much as eight years or more between them, especially if the elder child is a girl, protective, motherly impulses may at once come into play. But, speaking honestly, when we find a wish for the death of a brother or a sister latent in a dream we need seldom be puzzled, for we find its origin in early childhood without much trouble, or, indeed, quite often in the later years when they still lived together.

There is probably no nursery without violent conflicts between the inhabitants, actuated by rivalry for the love of the parents, competition for possessions shared by them all, even for the actual space in the room they occupy. Such hostility is directed against older as well as younger brothers and sisters. I think it was Bernard Shaw[4] who said: "If there is anyone whom a young English lady hates more than her mother it is her elder sister." Now there is something in this dictum which jars upon us; it is hard enough to bring ourselves to understand hatred and rivalry between brothers and sisters, but how can feelings of hate force themselves into the relation between mother and daughter, parents and children?

This relationship is no doubt a more-favourable one, also from the children's point of view; and this too is what our expectations require: we find it far more offensive for love to be lacking between parents and children than between brothers and sisters. We have, so to speak, sanctified the former love while allowing the latter to remain profane. Yet everyday observation may show us how frequently the sentiments entertained towards each other by parents and grown-up children fall short of the ideal set up by society, and how much hostility lies smouldering, ready to burst into flame if it were not stifled by considerations of filial or parental duty and by other, tender impulses. The motives for this hostility are well known, and we recognize a tendency for those of the same sex to become alienated, daughter

---

[4] George Bernard Shaw (1856–1950), Irish dramatist and writer.

from mother and father from son. The daughter sees in her mother the authority which imposes limits to her will, whose task it is to bring her to that renunciation of sexual freedom which society demands; in certain cases, too, the mother is still a rival, who objects to being set aside. The same thing is repeated still more blatantly between father and son. To the son the father is the embodiment of the social compulsion to which he so unwillingly submits, the person who stands in the way of his following his own will, of his early sexual pleasures and, when there is family property, of his enjoyment of it. When a throne is involved this impatience for the death of the father may approach tragic intensity. The relation between father and daughter or mother and son would seem less liable to disaster; the latter relation furnishes the purest examples of unchanging tenderness, undisturbed by any egoistic consideration.

Why, you ask, do I speak of things so banal and so well known to everybody? Because there exists an unmistakable tendency in people's minds to deny the significance of these things in real life and to pretend that the social ideal is much more frequently realized than it actually is. But it is better that psychology should tell the truth than that it should be left to cynics to do so. This general denial is only applied to real life, it is true; for fiction and drama are free to make use of the motives laid bare when these ideals are rudely disturbed.

There is nothing to wonder at therefore if the dreams of a great number of people bring to light the wish for the removal of their parents, especially of the parent whose sex is the same as the dreamer's. We may assume that the wish exists in waking life as well, sometimes even in consciousness if it can disguise itself behind another motive, as the dreamer in our third example disguised his real thought by pity for his father's useless suffering. It is but rarely that hostility reigns alone,—far more often it yields to more tender feelings which finally suppress it, when it has to wait in abeyance till a dream shows it, as it were, in isolation. That which the dream shows in a form magnified by this very isolation resumes its true proportions when our interpretation has assigned to it its proper place in relation to the rest of the dreamer's life. (H. Sachs.)[5] But we also find this death-wish where there is no basis for it in real life and where the adult would never have to confess to entertaining it in his waking life. The reason for this is that the deepest and most common motive for estrangement, especially between parent and child of the same sex, came into play in the earliest years of childhood.

I refer to that rivalry of affections in which sexual elements are plainly emphasized. The son, when quite a little child, already begins to develop a peculiar tenderness towards his mother, whom he looks upon as his own property, regarding his father in the light of a rival who disputes this sole possession of his; similarly the little daughter sees in her mother someone who disturbs her tender relation to her father and occupies a place which she feels she herself could very well fill. Observation shows us how far back these sentiments date, sentiments which we describe by the term *Oedipus complex,* because in the Oedipus myth the two extreme forms of the wishes arising from the situation of the son—the wish to kill the father and to marry the mother—are realized in an only slightly modified form. I do not assert that the Oedipus complex exhausts all the possible relations which may exist between parents and children; these relations may well be a great deal more complicated. Again, this complex may be more or less strongly developed, or it may even become inverted, but it is a regular and very important factor in the mental life of the child; we are more in danger of underestimating than of overestimating its influence and that of the developments which may follow from it. Moreover, the parents themselves frequently stimulate the children to react with an Oedipus complex, for parents are often guided in their preferences by the difference in sex of their children, so that the father favours the daughter and the mother the son; or else, where conjugal love has grown cold, the child may be taken as a substitute for the love-object which has ceased to attract.

It cannot be said that the world has shown great gratitude to psychoanalytic research for the discovery of the Oedipus complex; on the contrary, the idea has excited the most violent opposition in grown-up people; and those who omitted to join in denying the existence of sentiments so universally reprehended and tabooed have later made up for this by proffering interpretations so wide of the mark as to rob the complex of its value. My own unchanged conviction is that there is nothing in it to deny or to gloss over. We ought to reconcile ourselves to facts in which the Greek myth itself saw the hand of inexorable destiny. Again, it is interesting to find that the Oedipus complex, repudiated in actual life and relegated to fiction, has there come to its own. O. Rank[6] in a careful study of this theme has shown how this very complex has supplied dramatic poetry with an abundance of motives in countless variations, modifications, and disguises, in short, subject to just the distortion familiar

---

[5]Hanns Sachs (1881–1947), Austrian psychoanalyst and editor, with Otto Rank, of *Imago,* one of the premier journals of the psychoanalytic movement, from 1912 to 1937.

[6]Otto Rank (1884–1939), Austrian psychoanalyst. Freud refers to *Inzest Motiv in Dichtung und Sage (The Incest Theme in Literature and Legend,* translation published 1992).

to us in the work of the dream-censorship. So we may look for the Oedipus complex even in those dreamers who have been fortunate enough to escape conflicts with their parents in later life; and closely connected with this we shall find what is termed the *castration complex,* the reaction to that intimidation in the field of sex or to that restraint of early infantile sexual activity which is ascribed to the father.

What we have already ascertained has guided us to the study of the child's mental life, and we may now hope to find in a similar way an explanation of the source of the other kind of prohibited wishes in dreams, i.e. the excessive sexual desires. We are impelled therefore to study the development of the sexual life of the child, and here from various sources we learn the following facts. In the first place, it is an untenable fallacy to suppose that the child has no sexual life and to assume that sexuality first makes its appearance at puberty, when the genital organs come to maturity. On the contrary he has from the very beginning a sexual life rich in content, thought it differs in many points from that which later is regarded as normal. What in adult life are termed "perversions" depart from the normal in the following respects: (1) in a disregard for the barriers of species (the gulf between man and beast), (2) in the insensibility to barriers imposed by disgust, (3) in the transgression of the incest-barrier (the prohibition against seeking sexual gratification with close blood-relations), (4) in homosexuality and, (5) in the transferring of the part played by the genital organs to other organs and different areas of the body. All these barriers are not in existence from the outset, but are only gradually built up in the course of development and education. The little child is free from them: he does not perceive any immense gulf between man and beast, the arrogance with which man separates himself from the other animals only dawns in him at a later period. He shows at the beginning of life no disgust for excrement, but only learns this feeling slowly under the influence of education; he attaches no particular importance to the difference between the sexes, in fact he thinks that both have the same formation of the genital organs; he directs his earliest sexual desires and his curiosity to those, nearest to him or to those, who for other reasons are specially beloved—his parents, brothers and sisters or nurses; and finally we see in him a characteristic which manifests itself again later at the height of some love-relationship—namely, he does not look for gratification in the sexual organs only, but discovers that many other parts of the body possess the same sort of sensibility and can yield analogous pleasurable sensations, playing thereby the part of genital organs. The child may be said then to be *polymorphously perverse,* and even if mere traces of all these impulses are found in him; this is due on the one hand to their

lesser intensity as compared with that which they assume in later life and, on the other hand, to the fact that education immediately and energetically suppresses all sexual manifestations in the child. This suppression may be said to be embodied in a theory; for grown-up people endeavour to over look some of these manifestations, and, by misinterpretation, to rob others of their sexual nature, until in the end the whole thing can be altogether denied. It is often the same people who first inveigh against the sexual "naughtiness" of children in the nursery and then sit down to their writing-tables to defend the sexual purity of the same children. When they are left to themselves or when they are seduced children often display perverse sexual activity to a really remarkable extent. Of course grown-up people are right in not taking this too seriously and in regarding it, as they say, as "childish tricks" and "play," for the child cannot be judged either by a moral or legal code as if he were mature and fully responsible; nevertheless these things do exist, and they have their significance both as evidence of innate constitutional tendencies and inasmuch much as they cause and foster later developments: they give us an insight into the child's sexual life and so into that of humanity as a whole. If then we find all these perverse wishes behind the distortions of our dreams, it only means that dreams in *this respect also* have regressed completely to the infantile condition.

Amongst these forbidden wishes special prominence must still be given to the incestuous desires, i.e. those directed towards sexual intercourse with parents or brothers and sisters. You know in what abhorrence human society holds, or at least professes to hold, such intercourse, and what emphasis is laid upon the prohibitions of it. The most preposterous attempts have been made to account for this horror of incest: some people have assumed that it is a provision of nature for the preservation of the species, manifesting itself in the mind by these prohibitions because in-breeding would result in racial degeneration; others have asserted that propinquity from early childhood has deflected sexual desire from the persons concerned. In both these cases, however, the avoidance of incest would have been automatically secured and we should be at a loss to understand the necessity for stern prohibitions, which would seem rather to point to a strong desire. Psychoanalytic investigations have shown beyond the possibility of doubt, that an *incestuous love-choice* is in fact the first and the regular one, and that it is only later that any opposition is manifested towards it, the causes of which are not to be sought in the psychology of the individual.

Let us sum up the results which our excursions into child psychology have brought to the understanding of dreams. We have learnt not only that the material of the forgotten childish experiences is accessible to the dream, but also that the child's mental life, with all its peculiarities, its egoism, its incestuous object-choice, persists in it and therefore in the unconscious, and that our dreams take us back every night to this infantile stage. This corroborates the belief that *the Unconscious is the infantile mental life,* and, with this, the objectionable impression that so much evil lurks in human nature grows somewhat less. For this terrible evil is simply what is original, primitive and infantile in mental life, what we find in operation in the child, but in part overlook in him because it is on so small a scale, and in part do not take greatly to heart because we do not demand a high ethical standard in a child. By regressing to this infantile stage our dreams appear to have brought the evil in us to light, but the appearance is deceptive, though we have let ourselves be dismayed by it; we are not so evil as the interpretation of our dreams would lead us to suppose.

If the evil impulses of our dreams are merely infantile, a reversion to the beginnings of our ethical development, the dream simply making us children again in thought and feeling, it is surely not reasonable to be ashamed of these evil dreams. But the reasoning faculty is only part of our mental life; there is much in it besides which is not reasonable, and so it happens that, although it is unreasonable, we nevertheless are ashamed of such dreams. We subject them to the dream-censorship and are ashamed and indignant when one of these wishes by way of exception penetrates our consciousness in a form so undisguised that we cannot fail to recognize it; yes, we even at times feel just as much ashamed of a distorted dream as if we really understood it. Just think of the outraged comment of the respectable elderly lady upon her dream about "love service," although it was not interpreted to her. So the problem is not yet solved, and it is still possible that if we pursue this question of the evil in dreams we may arrive at another conclusion and another estimate of human nature.

Our whole enquiry has led to two results which, however, merely indicate the beginning of new problems and new doubts. In the first place: the regression in dreams is one not only of form but of substance. Not only does it translate our thoughts into a primitive form of expression, but it also reawakens the peculiarities of our primitive mental life—the old supremacy of the ego, the initial impulses of our sexual life, even restores to us our old intellectual possession if we may conceive of symbolism in this way. And secondly: all these old infantile characteristics, which were once dominant and solely dominant, must to-day be accounted to the unconscious and must alter and extend our views about it. "Unconscious" is no longer a term for what is temporarily latent: the unconscious is a special realm, with its own desires and modes of expression and peculiar mental mechanisms not elsewhere operative. Yet the latent dream-thoughts disclosed by our interpretation do not belong to this realm; rather they correspond to the kind of thoughts we have in waking life also. And yet they are unconscious: how is the paradox to be resolved? We begin to realize that here we must discriminate. Something which has its origin in our conscious life and shares its characteristics—we call it the "residue" from the previous day—meets together with something from the realm of the unconscious in the formation of a dream, and it is between these two regions that the dream-work is accomplished. The influence of the unconscious impinging upon this residue probably constitutes the condition for regression. This is the deepest insight into the nature of dreams possible to us until we have explored further fields in the mind; but soon it will be time to give another name to the unconscious character of the latent dream-thoughts, in order to distinguish it from that unconscious material which has its origin in the province of the infantile.

We can of course also ask: What is it that forces our mental activity during sleep to such regression? Why cannot the mental stimuli that disturb sleep be dealt with without it? And if on account of the dream-censorship the mental activity has to disguise itself in the old, and now incomprehensible, form of expression, what is the object of re-animating the old impulses, desires and characteristics, now surmounted, what, in short, is the use of *regression in substance* as well as in *form?* The only satisfactory answer would be that this is the one possible way in which dreams can be formed, that, dynamically considered, the relief from the stimulus giving rise to the dream cannot otherwise be accomplished. But this is an answer for which, at present, we have no justification.

from

Lecture Twenty-One: Development of the Libido and Sexual Organization

[Freud begins this lecture with a return to the subject of perversions and its importance for his theory of sexuality, with particular emphasis upon infantile sexuality, espe-

FROM TWENTY-FIRST LECTURE: DEVELOPMENT OF THE LIBIDO AND SEXUAL ORGANIZATION, which was first given in a series of lectures in Vienna, 1915–1917, and first published in 1920, revised edition, 1935. Reprinted from *A General Introduction to Psychoanalysis,* authorized English translation of the revised edition by Joan Riviere (New York: Liveright Publishing Corporation, 1935).

cially as children seek "gratification in the genital organs." He introduces the idea of a *"latency period"* that may be absent, but usually appears from about the sixth to the eighth year, though the period of "greatest interest" for *"libido-development"* comes earlier, usually before the third year. The rapid development of the libido in early childhood carries forward, from an early *"oral* phase" to a period of *"genital organization"* which subordinates the *"libido-function"* to *"the primacy of the genital zone."*]

* * *

To-day we will follow up another aspect of this development—namely, the relation of the sexual component-impulses to an *object;* or, rather, we will take a fleeting glimpse over this development so that we may spend more time upon a comparatively late result of it. Certain of the component-impulses of the sexual instinct have an object from the very beginning and hold fast to it: such are the impulses to mastery (sadism), to gazing (skoptophilia) and curiosity. Others, more plainly connected with particular erotogenic areas in the body, only have an object in the beginning, so long as they are still dependent upon the non-sexual functions, and give it up when they become detached from these later. Thus the first object of the oral component of the sexual instinct is the mother's breast which satisfies the infant's need for nutrition. In the act of sucking for its own sake the erotic component, also gratified in sucking for nutrition, makes itself independent, gives up the object in an external person, and replaces it by a part of the child's own person. The oral impulse becomes *auto-erotic,* as the anal and other erotogenic impulses are from the beginning. Further development has, to put it as concisely as possible, two aims: first, to renounce auto-erotism, to give up again the object found in the child's own body in exchange again for an external one; and secondly, to combine the various objects of the separate impulses and replace them by one single one. This naturally can only be done if the single object is again itself complete, with a body like that of the subject; nor can it be accomplished without some part of the auto-erotic impulse-excitations being abandoned as useless.

The processes by which an object is found are rather involved, and have not so far received comprehensive exposition. For our purposes, it may be emphasized that, when the process has reached a certain point in the years of childhood before the latency period, the object adopted proves almost identical with the first object of the oral pleasure impulse, adopted by reason of the child's dependent relationship to it; it is, namely, the mother, although not the mother's breast. We call the mother the first *love*-object. We

speak of 'love' when we lay the accent upon the mental side of the sexual impulses and disregard, or wish to forget for a moment, the demands of the fundamental physical or 'sensual' side of the impulses. At about the time when the mother becomes the love-object, the mental operation of repression has already begun in the child and has withdrawn from him the knowledge of some part of his sexual aims. Now with this choice of the mother as love-object is connected all that which, under the name of 'the Oedipus complex,' has become of such great importance in the psychoanalytic explanation of the neuroses and which has had a perhaps equally important share in causing the opposition against psychoanalysis.

Here is a little incident which occurred during the present war.[7] One of the staunch adherents of psychoanalysis was stationed in his medical capacity on the German front in Poland; he attracted the attention of his colleagues by the fact that he occasionally effected an unexpected influence upon a patient. On being questioned, he admitted that he worked with psychoanalytic methods and with readiness agreed to impart his knowledge to his colleagues. So every evening the medical men of the corps, his colleagues and superiors, met to be initiated into the mysteries of psychoanalysis. For a time all went well; but when he had introduced his audience to the Oedipus complex a superior officer rose and announced that he did not believe this, it was the behaviour of a cad for the lecturer to relate such things to brave men, fathers of families who were fighting for their country, and he forbade the continuation of the lectures. This was the end; the analyst got himself transferred to another part of the front. In my opinion however, it is a bad outlook if a victory for German arms depends upon an 'organization' of science such as this, and German science will not prosper under any such organization.

Now you will be impatiently waiting to hear what this terrible Oedipus complex comprises. The name tells you: you all know the Greek myth of King Oedipus; whose destiny it was to slay his father and to wed his mother, who did all in his power to avoid the fate prophesied by the oracle, and who in self-punishment blinded himself when he discovered that in ignorance he had committed both these crimes. I trust that many of you have yourselves experienced the profound effect of the tragic drama fashioned by Sophocles from this story. The Attic poet's work portrays the gradual discovery of the deed of Oedipus, long since accomplished, and brings it slowly to light by skilfully prolonged enquiry, constantly fed by new evidence; it has thus

---

[7]That is, World War I.

a certain resemblance to the course of a psychoanalysis. In the dialogue the deluded mother-wife, Jocasta, resists the continuation of the enquiry; she points out that many people in their dreams have mated with their mothers, but that dreams are of no account. To us dreams are of much account, especially typical dreams which occur in many people; we have no doubt that the dream Jocasta speaks of is intimately related to the shocking and terrible story of the myth.

It is surprising that Sophocles' tragedy does not call forth indignant remonstrance in its audience; this reaction would be much better justified in them than it was in the blunt army doctor. For at bottom it is an immoral play; it sets aside the individual's responsibility to social law, and displays divine forces ordaining the crime and rendering powerless the moral instincts of the human being which would guard him against the crime. It would be easy to believe that an accusation against destiny and the gods was intended in the story of the myth; in the hands of the critical Euripides, at variance with the gods, it would probably have become such an accusation. But with the reverent Sophocles there is no question of such an intention; the pious subtlety which declares it the highest morality to bow to the will of the gods, even when they ordain a crime, helps him out of the difficulty. I do not believe that this moral is one of the virtues of the drama, but neither does it detract from its effect; it leaves the hearer indifferent; he does not react to this, but to the secret meaning and content of the myth itself. He reacts as though by self-analysis he had detected the Oedipus complex in himself, and had recognized the will of the gods and the oracle as glorified disguises of his own unconscious; as though he remembered in himself the wish to do away with his father and in his place to wed his mother, and must abhor the thought. The poet's words seem to him to mean: "In vain do you deny that you are accountable, in vain do you proclaim how you have striven against these evil designs. You are guilty, nevertheless; for you could not stifle them; they still survive unconsciously in you." And psychological truth is contained in this; even though man has repressed his evil desires into his Unconscious and would then gladly say to himself that he is no longer answerable for them, he is yet compelled to feel his responsibility in the form of a sense of guilt for which he can discern no foundation.

There is no possible doubt that one of the most important sources of the sense of guilt which so often torments neurotic people is to be found in the Oedipus complex. More than this: in 1913, under the title of *Totem and Tabu,* I published a study of the earliest forms of religion and morality in which I expressed a suspicion that perhaps the sense of guilt of man kind as a whole, which is the ultimate source of religion and morality, was acquired in the beginnings of history through the Oedipus complex. I should much like to tell you more of this, but I had better not; it is difficult to leave this subject when once one begins upon it, and we must return to individual psychology.

Now what does direct observation of children, at the period of object-choice before the latency period, show us in regard to the Oedipus complex? Well, it is easy to see that the little man wants his mother all to himself, finds his father in the way, becomes restive when the latter takes upon himself to caress her, and shows his satisfaction when the father goes away or is absent. He often expresses his feelings directly in words and promises his mother to marry her; this may not seem much in comparison with the deeds of Oedipus, but it is enough in fact; the kernel of each is the same. Observation is often rendered puzzling by the circumstance that the same child on other occasions at this period will display great affection for the father; but such contrasting—or, better, *ambivalent*—states of feeling, which in adults would lead to conflicts, can be tolerated alongside one another in the child for a long time, just as later on they dwell together permanently in the unconscious. One might try to object that the little boy's behaviour is due to egoistic motives and does not justify the conception of an erotic complex; the mother looks after all the child's needs and consequently it is to the child's interest that she should trouble herself about no one else. This too is quite correct; but it is soon clear that in this, as in similar dependent situations, egoistic interests only provide the occasion on which the erotic impulses seize. When the little boy shows the most open sexual curiosity about his mother, wants to sleep with her at night, insists on being in the room while she is dressing, or even attempts physical acts of seduction, as the mother so often observes and laughingly relates, the erotic nature of this attachment to her is established without a doubt. Moreover, it should not be forgotten that a mother looks after a little daughter's needs in the same way without producing this effect; and that often enough a father eagerly vies with her in trouble for the boy without succeeding in winning the same importance in his eyes as the mother. In short, the factor of sex preference is not to be eliminated from the situation by any criticisms. From the point of view of the boy's egoistic interests it would merely be foolish if he did not tolerate two people in his service rather than only one of them.

As you see, I have only described the relationship of a boy to his father and mother; things proceed in just the same way, with the necessary reversal, in little girls. The loving devotion to the father, the need to do away with the superfluous mother and to take her place, the early display of coquetry and the arts of later womanhood, make up a particularly charming picture in a little girl, and may cause us to forget its seriousness and the grave consequences which may later result from this situation. Let us not fail to add that frequently the parents themselves exert a decisive influence upon the awakening of the Oedipus complex in a child, by themselves following the sex attraction where there is more than one child; the father in an unmistakable manner prefers his little daughter with marks of tenderness, and the mother, the son; but even this factor does not seriously impugn the spontaneous nature of the infantile Oedipus complex. When other children appear, the Oedipus complex expands and becomes a family complex. Reinforced anew by the injury resulting to the egoistic interests, it actuates a feeling of aversion towards these new arrivals and an unhesitating wish to get rid of them again. These feelings of hatred are as a rule much more often openly expressed than those connected with the parental complex. If such a wish is fulfilled and after a short time death removes the unwanted addition to the family, later analysis can show what a significant event this death is for the child, although it does not necessarily remain in memory. Forced into the second place by the birth of another child and for the first time almost entirely parted from the mother, the child finds it very hard to forgive her for this exclusion of him; feelings which in adults we should describe as profound embitterment are roused in him, and often become the ground-work of a lasting estrangement. That sexual curiosity and all its consequences is usually connected with these experiences has already been mentioned. As these new brothers and sisters grow up the child's attitude to them undergoes the most important transformations. A boy may take his sister as love-object in place of his faithless mother; where there are several brothers to win the favour of a little sister hostile rivalry, of great importance in after life, shows itself already in the nursery. A little girl takes an older brother as a substitute for the father who no longer treats her with the same tenderness as in her earliest years; or she takes a little sister as a substitute for the child that she vainly wished for from her father.

So much and a great deal more of a similar kind is shown by direct observation of children, and by consideration of clear memories of childhood, uninfluenced by any analysis. Among other things you will infer from this that a child's position in the sequence of brothers and sisters is of very great significance for the course of his later life, a factor to be considered in every biography. What is even more important, however, is that in the face of these enlightening considerations, so easily to be obtained, you will hardly recall without smiling the scientific theories accounting for the prohibition of incest. What has not been invented for this purposes! We are told that sexual attraction is diverted from the members of the opposite sex in one family owing to their living together from early childhood; or that a biological tendency against inbreeding has a mental equivalent in the horror of incests! Whereby it is entirely overlooked that no such rigorous prohibitions in law and custom would be required if any trustworthy natural barriers against the temptation to incest existed. The opposite is the truth. The first choice of object in mankind is regularly an incestuous one, directed to the mother and sister of men, and the most stringent prohibitions are required to prevent this sustained infantile tendency from being carried into effect. In the savage and primitive peoples surviving to-day the incest prohibitions are a great deal stricter than with us; Theodor Reik[8] has recently shown in a brilliant work that the meaning of the savage rites of puberty which represent re-birth is the loosening of the boy's incestuous attachment to the mother and his reconciliation with the father.

Mythology will show you that incest, ostensibly so much abhorred by men, is permitted to their gods without a thought; and from ancient history you may learn that incestuous marriage with a sister was prescribed as a sacred duty for kings (the Pharaohs of Egypt and the Incas of Peru); it was therefore in the nature of a privilege denied to the common herd.

Incest with the mother is one of the crimes of Oedipus and parricide the other. Incidentally, these are the two great offences condemned by totemism, the first social-religious institution of mankind. Now let us turn from the direct observation of children to the analytic investigation of adults who have become neurotic; what does analysis yield in further knowledge of the Oedipus complex? Well, this is soon told. The complex is revealed just as the myth relates it; it will be seen that every one of these neurotics was himself an Oedipus or, what amounts to the same thing, has become a Hamlet in his reaction to the complex. To be sure, the analytic picture of the Oedipus complex is an enlarged and accentuated edition of the infantile sketch; the hatred of the father and the death-wishes against him are no longer vague hints, the affection for the mother declares itself with the aim of possessing her as a woman. Are we really to accredit such grossness and intensity of the feelings to the tender age of childhood; or does the analysis deceive us by introducing another factor? It is not difficult to find one. Every time anyone describes anything past, even if he be a historian, we have to take into account all that he unintentionally imports into that past period

---

[8]Theodor Reik (1888–1969), Austrian psychologist who emigrated to the United States in 1938.

from present and intermediate times, thereby falsifying it. With the neurotic it is even doubtful whether this retroversion is altogether unintentional; we shall hear later on that there are motives for it and we must explore the whole subject of the 'retrogressive phantasy-making' which goes back to the remote past. We soon discover, too, that the hatred against the father has been strengthened by a number of motives arising in later periods and other relationships in life, and that the sexual desires towards the mother have been moulded into forms which would have been as yet foreign to the child. But it would be a vain attempt if we endeavoured to explain the whole of the Oedipus complex by 'retrogressive phantasy-making,' and by motives originating in later periods of life. The infantile nucleus, with more or less of the accretions to it, remains intact, as is confirmed by direct observation of children. The clinical fact which confronts us behind the form of the Oedipus complex as established by analysis now becomes of the greatest practical importance. We learn that at the time of puberty, when the sexual instinct first asserts its demands in full strength, the old familiar incestuous objects are taken up again and again invested by the libido. The infantile object-choice was but a feeble venture in play, as it were, but it laid down the direction for the object-choice of puberty. At this time a very intense flow of feeling towards the Oedipus complex or in reaction to it comes into force; since their mental antecedents have become intolerable, however, these feelings must remain for the most part outside consciousness. From the time of puberty onward the human individual must devote himself to the great task of *freeing himself from the parents;* and only after this detachment is accomplished can he cease to be a child and so become a member of the social community. For a son, the task consists in releasing his libidinal desires from his mother, in order to employ them in the quest of an external love-object in reality; and in reconciling himself with his father if he has remained antagonistic to him, or in freeing himself from his domination if, in the reaction to the infantile revolt, he has lapsed into subservience to him. These tasks are laid down for every man; it is noteworthy how seldom they are carried through ideally, that is, how seldom they are solved in a manner psychologically as well as socially satisfactory. In neurotics, however, this detachment from the parents is not accomplished at all; the son remains all his life in subjection to his father, and incapable of transferring his libido to a new sexual object. In the reversed relationship the daughter's fate may be the same. In this sense the Oedipus complex is justifiably regarded as the kernel of the neuroses.

You will imagine how incompletely I am sketching a large number of the connections bound up with the Oedipus complex which practically and theoretically are of great importance. I shall not go into the variations and possible inversions of it at all. Of its less immediate effects I should like to allude to one only, which proves it to have influenced literary production in a far-reaching manner. Otto Rank has shown in a very valuable work that dramatists throughout the ages have drawn their material principally from the Oedipus and incest complex and its variations and masked forms.[9] It should also be remarked that long before the time of psychoanalysis the two criminal offences of Oedipus were recognized as the true expressions of unbridled instinct. Among the works of the Encyclopaedist Diderot[10] you will find the famous dialogue, *Le neveu de Rameau,* which was translated into German by no less a person than Goethe. There you may read these remarkable words: *Si le petit sauvage était abandonné à lui-même, qu'il conserva toute son inbecillité et qu'il réunit au peu de raison de l'enfant au berceau la violence des passions de l'homme de trente ans, il tordrait le cou à son pére et coucherait avec sa mère.*[11]

There is yet one thing more which I cannot pass over. The mother-wife of Oedipus must not remind us of dreams in vain. Do you still remember the results of our dream-analyses, how so often the dream-forming wishes proved perverse and incestuous in their nature, or betrayed an unsuspected enmity to near and beloved relatives? We then left the source of these evil strivings of feeling unexplained. Now you can answer this question yourselves. They are dispositions of the libido, and investments of objects by libido, belonging to early infancy and long since given up in conscious life, but which at night prove to be still present and in a certain sense capable of activity. But, since all men and not only neurotic persons have perverse, incestuous, and murderous dreams of this kind, we may infer that those who are normal to-day have also made the passage through the perversions and the object-investments of the Oedipus complex; and that this is the path of normal development; only that neurotics show in a magnified and exaggerated form what we also find revealed in the dream-analyses of normal people. And this is one of the reasons why we chose the study of dreams to lead up to that of neurotic symptoms.

---

[9] Cf. Note 6 above.

[10] Denis Diderot (above, page 383); *Rameau's Nephew* was first published in 1762.

[11] If the little savage were left to himself, preserving all of his imbecility, and joined the small reason of the infant in the cradle to the violence of the passions of a man of thirty years of age, he would wring his father's neck and sleep with his mother.

Leo Tolstoy

1828–1910

For Tolstoy, art properly corresponds to the "religious view of life by the people among whom it arose." It follows that every people generates an art appropriate to itself. At least this was true until "church-Christianity," which Tolstoy thought had become debased in its institutional practices, ceased to be the maker of a truly religious view. Loss of belief by the upper classes changed art and made sheer enjoyment its only professed end. The result was false art, and Tolstoy is relentless in his rejection of it. He advocates, against this faithlessness, an art expressive of what he regards as the central message of Christianity—"that Christian principle of universal union which forms the religious perception of our time." Two kinds of art that meet this standard are, first, an art that expresses "feelings flowing from a perception of our sonship to God and of the brotherhood of Man," and, second, expression of "feelings of merriment, of pity, of cheerfulness, of tranquillity. . . ." Both generate a sense of brotherhood in the recipients.

True art, for Tolstoy, is communication and sharing of feelings between men. Its characteristics are (1) the individuality of the feeling, (2) clarity, and (3) (and foremost) sincerity. Tolstoy does not say explicitly how we are to know a work is sincere. Presumably if it conveys a sense of brotherhood its sincerity is proved, but one could, it seems, be sincerely immoral. There is also the question of whether a work of art is valuable if we have already experienced and assimilated a feeling of brotherhood. Presumably this repetition in different circumstances would be valuable as moral reinforcement.

Tolstoy pits himself against the current of theories of art of his time. He rejects all theories of beauty, aesthetic enjoyment, and the like. They are all reducible to either the mystical-transcendental or the hedonistic. The former he regards as absurd, the latter inadequate and decadent. Any art appealing only to the initiate, such as that apparently advocated by Mallarmé and the symbolists, or to a certain class is anathema because it separates people from each other. Tolstoy's attack on Beethoven, especially his *Ninth Symphony,* partly on this ground, is only one of several he makes against well-known and usually revered works.

In sum, Tolstoy judges a work solely on whether it has or has not been an instrument of human progress and contributes to the consequent diminishment of cruelty.

The standard translation is that by Aylmer Maude, *What Is Art? and Essays on Art* (1930). Maude is also editor of *Tolstoy on Art and Its Critics* (1924). See H. W. Garrod, *Tolstoi's Theory of Art* (1935); Isaiah Berlin, *The Hedgehog and the Fox* (1953); R. F. Christian, *Tolstoy: A Critical Introduction* (1969); Edward Crankshaw, *Tolstoy: The Making of a Novelist* (1974); Henry Gifford, *Tolstoy* (1982).

What Is Art?
from
Chapter IV

To the question, what is this art to which is offered up the labor of millions, the very lives of men, and even morality itself? we have extracted replies from the existing aesthetics which all amount to this, that the aim of art is beauty, that beauty is recognized by the enjoyment it gives, and that artistic enjoyment is a good and important thing, because it is enjoyment. In a word, that enjoyment is good because it is enjoyment. Thus what is considered the definition of art is no definition at all, but only a shuffle to justify existing art. Therefore, however strange it may seem to say so, in spite of the mountains of books written about art, no exact definition of art has been constructed. And the reason of this is that the conception of art has been based on the conception of beauty.

Chapter V

What is art if we put aside the conception of beauty, which confuses the whole matter? The latest and most comprehensible definitions of art, apart from the conception of beauty, are the following: (1) *a* Art is an activity arising even in the animal kingdom, and springing from sexual desire and the propensity to play (Schiller, Darwin, Spencer), and *b* accompanied by a pleasurable excitement of the nervous system (Grant Allen).[1] This is the physiological-evolutionary definition. (2) Art is the external manifestation, by means of lines, colors, movements, sounds, or words, of emotions felt by man (Véron). This is the experimental definition. According to the very latest definition (Sully), (3) art is "the production of some permanent object or passing action which is fitted not only to supply an active enjoyment to the producer, but to convey a pleasurable impression to a number of spectators or listeners, quite apart from any personal advantage to be derived from it."[2]

Notwithstanding the superiority of these definitions to the metaphysical definitions which depended on the conception of beauty, they are yet far from exact. The first, the physiological-evolutionary definition, (1) *a*, is inexact, because instead of speaking about the artistic activity itself, which is the real matter in hand, it treats of the derivation of art. The modification of it, *b*, based on the physiological effects on the human organism, is inexact because within the limits of such definition many other human activities can be included, as has occurred in the neoaesthetic theories which reckon as art the preparation of handsome clothes, pleasant scents, and even of victuals.

The experimental definition, (2), which makes art consist in the expression of emotions, is inexact because a man may express his emotions by means of lines, colors, sounds, or words and yet may not act on others by such expression—and then the manifestation of his emotions is not art.

The third definition (that of Sully) is inexact because in the production of objects or actions affording pleasure to the producer and a pleasant emotion to the spectators or hearers apart from personal advantage, may be included the showing of conjuring tricks or gymnastic exercises, and other activities which are not art. And further, many things the production of which does not afford pleasure to the producer and the sensation received from which is unpleasant, such as gloomy, heart-rending scenes in a poetic description or a play, may nevertheless be undoubted works of art.

The inaccuracy of all these definitions arises from the fact that in them all (as also in the metaphysical definitions) the object considered is the pleasure art may give, and not the purpose it may serve in the life of man and of humanity.

In order to define art correctly it is necessary first of all to cease to consider it as a means to pleasure, and to consider it as one of the conditions of human life. Viewing it in this way we cannot fail to observe that art is one of the means of intercourse between man and man.

Every work of art causes the receiver to enter into a certain kind of relationship both with him who produced or is producing the art, and with all those who, simultaneously, previously, or subsequently, receive the same artistic impression.

Speech transmitting the thoughts and experiences of men serves as a means of union among them, and art serves a similar purpose. The peculiarity of this latter means of intercourse, distinguishing it from intercourse by means of words, consists in this, that whereas by words a man transmits his thoughts to another, by art he transmits his feelings.

The activity of art is based on the fact that a man receiving through his sense of hearing or sight another man's expression of feeling, is capable of experiencing the emotion which moved the man who expressed it. To take the simplest example: one man laughs, and another who hears becomes merry, or a man weeps, and another who hears feels sorrow. A man is excited or irritated, and another man seeing him is brought to a similar state of mind. By his

---

Tolstoy's *What Is Art?* was first published in 1898. The selection is from *What Is Art? and Essays on Art,* translated by Aylmer Maude (London: Oxford University Press, 1930).

[1] Schiller (above, page 460); Charles Darwin (1809–1882), English naturalist; Herbert Spencer (1820–1903), English philosopher; Grant Allen (1848–1899), English naturalist.

[2] René Sully-Prudhomme (1839–1907), French poet.

movements or by the sounds of his voice a man expresses courage and determination or sadness and calmness, and this state of mind passes on to others. A man suffers, manifesting his sufferings by groans and spasms, and this suffering transmits itself to other people; a man expresses his feelings of admiration, devotion, fear, respect, or love, to certain objects, persons, or phenomena, and others are infected by the same feelings of admiration, devotion, fear, respect, or love, to the same objects, persons, or phenomena.

And it is on this capacity of man to receive another man's expression of feeling and to experience those feelings himself, that the activity of art is based.

If a man infects another or others directly, immediately, by his appearance or by the sounds he gives vent to at the very time he experiences the feeling; if he causes another man to yawn when he himself cannot help yawning, or to laugh or cry when he himself is obliged to laugh or cry, or to suffer when he himself is suffering—that does not amount to art.

Art begins when one person with the object of joining another or others to himself in one and the same feeling, expresses that feeling by certain external indications. To take the simplest example: a boy having experienced, let us say, fear on encountering a wolf, relates that encounter, and in order to evoke in others the feeling he has experienced, describes himself, his condition before the encounter, the surroundings, the wood, his own lightheartedness, and then the wolf's appearance, its movements, the distance between himself and the wolf, and so forth. All this, if only the boy when telling the story again experiences the feelings he had lived through, and infects the hearers and compels them to feel what he had experienced—is art. Even if the boy had not seen a wolf but had frequently been afraid of one, and if wishing to evoke in others the fear he had felt, he invented an encounter with a wolf and recounted it so as to make his hearers share the feelings he experienced when he feared the wolf, that also would be art. And just in the same way it is art if a man, having experienced either the fear of suffering or the attraction of enjoyment (whether in reality or in imagination), expresses these feelings on canvas or in marble so that others are infected by them. And it is also art if a man feels, or imagines to himself, feelings of delight, gladness, sorrow, despair, courage, or despondency, and the transition from one to another of these feelings, and expresses them by sounds so that the hearers are infected by them and experience them as they were experienced by the composer.

The feelings with which the artist infects others may be most various—very strong or very weak, very important or very insignificant, very bad or very good: feelings of love of one's country, self-devotion and submission to fate or to God expressed in a drama, raptures of lovers described in a novel, feelings of voluptuousness expressed in a picture, courage expressed in a triumphal march, merriment evoked by a dance, humor evoked by a funny story, the feeling of quietness transmitted by an evening landscape or by a lullaby, or the feeling of admiration evoked by a beautiful arabesque—it is all art.

If only the spectators or auditors are infected by the feelings which the author has felt, it is art.

To evoke in oneself a feeling one has once experienced and having evoked it in oneself then by means of movements, lines, colors, sounds, or forms expressed in words, so to transmit that feeling that others experience the same feeling—this is the activity of art.

Art is a human activity consisting in this, that one man consciously by means of certain external signs, hands on to others feelings he has lived through, and that others are infected by these feelings and also experience them.

Art is not, as the metaphysicians say, the manifestation of some mysterious idea of beauty or God; it is not, as the aesthetic physiologists say, a game in which man lets off his excess of stored-up energy; it is not the expression of man's emotions by external signs; it is not the production of pleasing objects; and, above all, it is not pleasure; but it is a means of union among men joining them together in the same feelings, and indispensable for the life and progress towards well-being of individuals and of humanity.

As every man, thanks to man's capacity to express thoughts by words, may know all that has been done for him in the realms of thought by all humanity before his day, and can in the present, thanks to this capacity to understand the thoughts of others, become a sharer in their activity and also himself hand on to his contemporaries and descendants the thoughts he has assimilated from others as well as those that have arisen in himself; so, thanks to man's capacity to be infected with the feelings of others by means of art, all that is being lived through by his contemporaries is accessible to him, as well as the feelings experienced by men thousands of years ago, and he has also the possibility of transmitting his own feelings to others.

If people lacked the capacity to receive the thoughts conceived by men who preceded them and to pass on to others their own thoughts, men would be like wild beasts, or like Kasper Hauser.[3]

And if men lacked this other capacity of being infected by art, people might be almost more savage still, and above all more separated from, and more hostile to, one another.

---

[3][Tolstoy] "The foundling of Nuremberg," found in the marketplace of that town on May 23, 1828, apparently some sixteen years old. He spoke little and was almost totally ignorant even of common objects. He subsequently explained that he had been brought up in confinement underground and visited by only one man, whom he saw but seldom.

And therefore the activity of art is a most important one, as important as the activity of speech itself and as generally diffused.

As speech does not act on us only in sermons, orations, or books, but in all those remarks by which we interchange thoughts and experiences with one another, so also art in the wide sense of the word permeates our whole life, but it is only to some of its manifestations that we apply the term in the limited sense of the word.

We are accustomed to understand art to be only what we hear and see in theaters, concerts, and exhibitions; together with buildings, statues, poems, and novels. . . . But all this is but the smallest part of the art by which we communicate with one another in life. All human life is filled with works of art of every kind—from cradle song, jest, mimicry, the ornamentation of houses, dress, and utensils, to church services, buildings, monuments, and triumphal processions. It is all artistic activity. So that by art, in the limited sense of the word, we do not mean all human activity transmitting feelings but only that part which we for some reason select from it and to which we attach special importance.

This special importance has always been given by men to that part of this activity which transmits feelings flowing from their religious perception, and this small part they have specifically called art, attaching to it the full meaning of the word.

That was how men of old—Socrates, Plato, and Aristotle—looked on art.[4] Thus did the Hebrew prophets and the ancient Christians regard art. Thus it was, and still is, understood by the Mohammedans, and thus it still is understood by religious folk among our own peasantry.

Some teachers of mankind—such as Plato in his *Republic,* and people like the primitive Christians, the strict Mohammedans, and the Buddhists—have gone so far as to repudiate all art.

People viewing art in this way (in contradiction to the prevalent view of today which regards any art as good if only it affords pleasure) held and hold that art (as contrasted with speech, which need not be listened to) is so highly dangerous in its power to infect people against their wills, that mankind will lose far less by banishing all art than by tolerating each and every art.

Evidently such people were wrong in repudiating all art, for they denied what cannot be denied—one of the indispensable means of communication without which mankind could not exist. But not less wrong are the people of civilized European society of our class and day in favoring any art if it but serves beauty, that is, gives people pleasure.

Formerly people feared lest among works of art there might chance to be some causing corruption, and they prohibited art altogether. Now they only fear lest they should be deprived of any enjoyment art can afford, and they patronize any art. And I think the last error is much grosser than the first and that its consequences are far more harmful.

Chapter VI

But how could it happen that that very art which in ancient times was merely tolerated (if tolerated at all), should have come in our times to be invariably considered a good thing if only it affords pleasure?

It has resulted from the following causes. The estimation of the value of art (or rather, of the feelings it transmits) depends on men's perception of the meaning of life; depends on what they hold to be the good and the evil of life. And what is good and what is evil is defined by what are termed religions.

Humanity unceasingly moves forward from a lower, more partial and obscure understanding of life to one more general and more lucid. And in this as in every movement there are leaders—those who have understood the meaning of life more clearly than others—and of these advanced men there is always one who has in his words and by his life expressed this meaning more clearly, lucidly, and strongly, than others. This man's expression of the meaning of life, together with those superstitions, traditions, and ceremonies, which usually form round the memory of such a man, is what is called a religion. Religions are the exponents of the highest comprehension of life accessible to the best and foremost men at a given time in a given society—a comprehension towards which all the rest of that society must inevitably and irresistibly advance. And therefore religions alone have always served, and still serve, as bases for the valuation of human sentiments. If feelings bring men nearer the ideal their religion indicates, if they are in harmony with it and do not contradict it, they are good; if they estrange men from it and oppose it they are bad.

If the religion places the meaning of life in worshipping one God and fulfilling what is regarded as his will, as was the case among the Jews, then the feelings flowing from love of that God and of his law, when successfully transmitted through the art of poetry, by the prophets, by the Psalms, or by the epic of the book of Genesis, are good, high art. All opposing that, as for instance the transmission of feelings of devotion to strange gods, or of feel-

---

[4]Plato (above, page 16); Aristotle (above, page 52).

ings incompatible with the law of God, would be considered bad art. Or if, as was the case among the Greeks, the religion places the meaning of life in earthly happiness, in beauty and in strength, then art successfully transmitting the joy and energy of life would be considered good art, but art transmitting feelings of effeminacy or despondency would be bad art. If the meaning of life is seen in the well-being of one's nation, or in honoring one's ancestors and continuing the mode of life led by them, as was the case among the Romans and the Chinese respectively, then art transmitting feelings of joy at the sacrifice of one's personal well-being for the common weal, or at the exaltation of one's ancestors and the maintenance of their traditions, would be considered good art; but art expressing feelings contrary to these would be regarded as bad. If the meaning of life is seen in freeing oneself from the yoke of animalism, as is the case among the Buddhists, then art successfully transmitting feelings that elevate the soul and humble the flesh will be good art, and all that transmits feelings strengthening the bodily passions will be bad art.

In every age and in every human society there exists a religious sense of what is good and what is bad common to that whole society, and it is this religious conception that decides the value of the feelings transmitted by art. Therefore among all nations art which transmitted feelings considered to be good by the general religious sense was recognized as being good and was encouraged, but art which transmitted feelings considered bad by this general religious sense was recognized as being bad and was rejected. All the rest of the immense field of art by means of which people communicate one with another was not esteemed at all and was only noticed when it ran counter to the religious conception of its age, and then merely to be repudiated. Thus it was among all nations—Greeks, Jews, Indians, Egyptians, and Chinese—and so it was when Christianity appeared.

The Christianity of the first centuries recognized as productions of good art only legends, lives of saints, sermons, prayers, and hymn-singing, evoking love of Christ, emotion at his life, desire to follow his example, renunciation of worldly life, humility, and the love of others; all productions transmitting feelings of personal enjoyment they considered to be bad, and therefore rejected; for instance, tolerating plastic representations only when they were symbolical, they rejected all the pagan sculptures.

This was so among the Christians of the first centuries, who accepted Christ's teaching if not quite in its true form at least not in the perverted, paganized form in which it was subsequently held.

But besides this Christianity, from the time of the wholesale conversion of nations by order of the authorities, as in the days of Constantine, Charlemagne, and Vladímir,[5] there appeared another, a church-Christianity, which was nearer to paganism than to Christ's teaching. And in accord with its own teaching, this church-Christianity estimated quite otherwise the feelings of people and the productions of art which transmitted those feelings.

This church-Christianity not only did not acknowledge the fundamental and essential positions of true Christianity—the immediate relationship of each man to the Father, the consequent brotherhood and equality of all men, and the substitution of humility and love in place of any kind of violence—but on the contrary, having set up a heavenly hierarchy similar to the pagan mythology, and having introduced the worship of Christ, of the Virgin, of angels, of apostles, of saints, and of martyrs, and not only of these divinities themselves but also of their images, it made blind faith in the church and in its ordinances the essential point of its teaching.

However foreign this teaching may have been to true Christianity, however degraded, not only in comparison with true Christianity but even with the conception of life of Romans such as Julian[6] and others, for all that it was to the barbarians who accepted it, a higher doctrine than their former adoration of gods, heroes, and good and bad spirits. And therefore this teaching was a religion to them, and on the basis of this religion the art of that time was assessed. And art transmitting pious adoration of the Virgin, Jesus, the saints, and the angels, a blind faith in and submission to the church, fear of torments, and hope of blessedness in a life beyond the grave, was considered good, while all art opposed to this was held to be bad.

The teaching on the basis of which this art arose was a perversion of Christ's teaching, but the art which sprang up on this perverted teaching was for all that a true art, since it corresponded to the religious view of life held by the people among whom it arose.

The artists of the Middle Ages, vitalized by the same source of feeling—religion—as the mass of the people, and transmitting in architecture, sculpture, painting, music, poetry, or drama, the feelings and states of mind they experienced, were true artists; and their activity, founded on the highest conceptions accessible to their age and common to the entire people—though for our times a mean art—was nevertheless a true one, shared by the whole community.

---

[5]Constantine I (c. 280–337), first Christian emperor of Rome; Charlemagne (742–814), establisher of the Holy Roman Empire; Vladímir I (c. 956–1015), czar of Russia.
[6]Julian the Apostate (331–363), emperor of Rome.

And this was the state of things until in the upper, rich, more educated, classes of European society doubt arose as to the truth of the understanding of life which was expressed by church-Christianity. When after the Crusades and the maximum development of papal power and its abuses, people of the rich classes became acquainted with the wisdom of the classics, and saw on the one hand the reasonable lucidity of the teaching of the ancient sages, and on the other hand the incompatibility of the church doctrine with the teaching of Christ, it became impossible for them to continue to believe the church teaching.

If in externals they still kept to the forms of church teaching, they could no longer believe in it, and held to it only by inertia and to influence the masses, who continued to believe blindly in church doctrine and whom the upper classes for their own advantage considered it necessary to encourage in those beliefs.

So that a time came when church-Christianity ceased to be the general religious doctrine of all Christian people: some—the masses—continued blindly to believe in it, but the upper classes—those in whose hands lay the power and wealth, and therefore the leisure to produce art and the means to stimulate it—ceased to believe that teaching.

In regard to religion the upper circles of the Middle Ages found themselves in the position educated Romans were in before Christianity arose, that is, they no longer believed in the religion of the masses but had no beliefs to put in place of the worn-out church doctrine which for them had lost its meaning.

There was only this difference, that whereas for the Romans who lost faith in their emperor gods and household gods it was impossible to extract anything further from all the complex mythology they had borrowed from conquered nations, and it was consequently necessary to find a completely new conception of life, the people of the Middle Ages when they doubted the truth of the church teaching had no need to seek a fresh one. That Christian teaching which they professed in a perverted form as church doctrine, had mapped out the path of human progress so far ahead that they needed only to rid themselves of those perversions which hid the teaching announced by Christ and to adopt its real meaning—if not completely, at least in a greater degree than the church had done. And this was partially accomplished not only in the reformations of Wyclif, Huss, Luther, and Calvin,[7] but by the whole current of nonchurch Christianity represented in earlier times by the Paulicians and the Bogomilites, and afterwards by the

Waldenses and other nonchurch Christians, who were called heretics.[8] But this could be, and was, done chiefly by poor people—who did not rule. A few of the rich and strong, such as Francis of Assisi[9] and others, accepted the Christian teaching in its full significance even though it undermined their privileged positions. But most people of the upper classes (though in the depth of their souls they had lost faith in the church teaching) could not or would not act thus, because the essence of that Christian view of life which stood ready to be adopted when once they rejected the church faith, was a teaching of the brotherhood (and therefore the equality) of man, and this condemned the privileges by which they lived, in which they had grown up and been educated, and to which they were accustomed. Not in the depth of their hearts believing in the church teaching—which had outlived its age and had no longer any true meaning for them—and not being strong enough to accept true Christianity, men of these rich, governing classes—popes, kings, dukes, and all the great ones of the earth—were left without any religion, with but the external forms of one, which they supported as being profitable and even necessary for themselves since these forms maintained a teaching which justified the privileges they made use of. In reality these people believed in nothing, just as the Romans of the first centuries of our era believed in nothing. But at the same time they were the people who had the power and the wealth, and they were the people who rewarded art and directed it.

And it should be remarked that it was just among these people that there grew up an art esteemed not according to its success in expressing men's religious feelings, but in proportion to its beauty—in other words, according to the enjoyment it gave.

No longer able to believe in the church religion whose falsehood they had detected, and incapable of accepting true Christian teaching which denounced their whole manner of life, these rich and powerful people, stranded with no religious conception of life, involuntarily returned to the pagan view of things which places life's meaning in personal enjoyment. And then took place among the upper classes what is called the Renaissance of science and art, which was really not only a denial of every religion, but also an assertion that religion is unnecessary.

The church doctrine is so coherent a system that it cannot be altered or corrected without destroying it altogether. As soon as doubt arose with regard to the infallibility of the pope (and this doubt was then in the minds of all educated people), doubt inevitably followed as to the truth of tradi-

---

[7] John Wycliffe (c. 1320–1384), John Huss (c. 1369–1415), Martin Luther (1483–1546), John Calvin (1509–1564), all Christian religious reformers.

[8] French Puritan dissenters from Catholicism (c. 1170).
[9] Saint Francis (1182–1226), founder of the Franciscan order.

tion. But doubt as to the truth of tradition is fatal not only to popery and Catholicism but also to the whole church creed with all its dogmas: the divinity of Christ, the resurrection, and the Trinity; and it destroys the authority of the Scriptures, since they were considered to be inspired only because the tradition of the church so decided.

So that the majority of the highest classes of that age, even the popes and the ecclesiastics, really believed in nothing at all. In the church doctrine these people did not believe, for they saw its insolvency; but neither could they follow Francis of Assisi, Peter of Chelczic,[10] and most of the heretics, in acknowledging the moral, social teaching of Christ, for that teaching undermined their social position. So these people remained without any religious view of life; and having none, they could have no standard whereby to estimate what was good and what was bad art, except that of personal enjoyment. And having acknowledged their criterion of what was good to be pleasure, that is beauty, these people of the upper classes of European society went back in their comprehension of art to the gross conception of the primitive Greeks, which Plato had already condemned. And conformably to this understanding of life a theory of art was formulated.

Chapter XV

Art in our society has become so perverted that not only has bad art come to be considered good, but even the very perception of what art really is has been lost. In order to be able to speak about the art of our society it is, therefore, first of all necessary to distinguish art from counterfeit art.

There is one indubitable sign distinguishing real art from its counterfeit—namely, the infectiousness of art. If a man without exercising effort and without altering his standpoint, on reading, hearing, or seeing another man's work experiences a mental condition which unites him with that man and with others who are also affected by that work, then the object evoking that condition is a work of art. And however poetic, realistic, striking, or interesting, a work may be, it is not a work of art if it does not evoke that feeling (quite distinct from all other feelings) of joy and of spiritual union with another (the author) and with others (those who are also infected by it).

It is true that this indication is an *internal* one and that there are people who, having forgotten what the action of real art is, expect something else from art (in our society the

great majority are in this state), and that therefore such people may mistake for this aesthetic feeling the feeling of diversion and a certain excitement which they receive from counterfeits of art. But though it is impossible to undeceive these people, just as it may be impossible to convince a man suffering from color blindness that green is not red, yet for all that, this indication remains perfectly definite to those whose feeling for art is neither perverted nor atrophied, and it clearly distinguishes the feeling produced by art from all other feelings.

The chief peculiarity of this feeling is that the recipient of a truly artistic impression is so united to the artist that he feels as if the work were his own and not someone else's— as if what it expresses were just what he had long been wishing to express. A real work of art destroys in the consciousness of the recipient the separation between himself and the artist, and not that alone, but also between himself and all whose minds receive this work of art. In this freeing of our personality from its separation and isolation, in this uniting of it with others, lies the chief characteristic and the great attractive force of art.

If a man is infected by the author's condition of soul, if he feels this emotion and this union with others, then the object which has effected this is art; but if there be no such infection, if there be not this union with the author and with others who are moved by the same work—then it is not art. And not only is infection a sure sign of art, but the degree of infectiousness is also the sole measure of excellence in art.

The stronger the infection the better is the art, as art, speaking of it now apart from its subject matter—that is, not considering the value of the feelings it transmits.

And the degree of the infectiousness of art depends on three conditions: (1) On the greater or lesser individuality of the feeling transmitted; (2) on the greater or lesser clearness with which the feeling is transmitted; (3) on the sincerity of the artist, that is, on the greater or lesser force with which the artist himself feels the emotion he transmits.

The more individual the feeling transmitted the more strongly does it act on the recipient; the more individual the state of soul into which he is transferred the more pleasure does the recipient obtain and therefore the more readily and strongly does he join in it.

Clearness of expression assists infection because the recipient who mingles in consciousness with the author is the better satisfied the more clearly that feeling is transmitted which, as it seems to him, he has long known and felt and for which he has only now found expression.

But most of all is the degree of infectiousness of art increased by the degree of sincerity in the artist. As soon as the spectator, hearer, or reader, feels that the artist is

---

[10]Petr Chelcický (c. 1390–c. 1460), Czech reformer, whose followers founded the Moravians.

infected by his own production and writes, sings, or plays, for himself, and not merely to act on others, this mental condition of the artist infects the recipient; and, on the contrary, as soon as the spectator, reader, or hearer, feels that the author is not writing, singing, or playing, for his own satisfaction—does not himself feel what he wishes to express, but is doing it for him, the recipient—resistance immediately springs up, and the most individual and the newest feelings and the cleverest technique not only fail to produce any infection but actually repel.

I have mentioned three conditions of contagion in art, but they may all be summed up into one, the last, sincerity; that is, that the artist should be impelled by an inner need to express his feeling. That condition includes the first; for if the artist is sincere he will express the feeling as he experienced it. And as each man is different from everyone else, his feeling will be individual for everyone else; and the more individual it is—the more the artist has drawn it from the depths of his nature—the more sympathetic and sincere will it be. And this same sincerity will impel the artist to find clear expression for the feeling which he wishes to transmit.

Therefore this third condition—sincerity—is the most important of the three. It is always complied with in peasant art, and this explains why such art always acts so powerfully; but it is a condition almost entirely absent from our upper-class art, which is continually produced by artists actuated by personal aims of covetousness or vanity.

Such are the three conditions which divide art from its counterfeits, and which also decide the quality of every work of art considered apart from its subject matter.

The absence of any one of these conditions excludes a work from the category of art and relegates it to that of art's counterfeits. If the work does not transmit the artist's peculiarity of feeling and is therefore not individual, if it is unintelligibly expressed, or if it has not proceeded from the author's inner need for expression—it is not a work of art. If all these conditions are present even in the smallest degree, then the work even if a weak one is yet a work of art.

The presence in various degrees of these three conditions: individuality, clearness, and sincerity, decides the merit of a work of art as art, apart from subject matter. All works of art take order of merit according to the degree in which they fulfill the first, the second, and the third, of these conditions. In one the individuality of the feeling transmitted may predominate; in another, clearness of expression; in a third, sincerity; while a fourth may have sincerity and individuality but be deficient in clearness; a fifth, individuality and clearness, but less sincerity; and so forth, in all possible degrees and combinations.

Thus is art divided from what is not art, and thus is the quality of art, as art, decided, independently of its subject matter, that is to say, apart from whether the feelings it transmits are good or bad.

But how are we to define good and bad art with reference to its content or subject matter?

from

Chapter XVI

How in the subject matter of art are we to decide what is good and what is bad?

Art like speech is a means of communication and therefore of progress, that is, of the movement of humanity forward towards perfection. Speech renders accessible to men of the latest generations all the knowledge discovered by the experience and reflection both of preceding generations and of the best and foremost men of their own times; art renders accessible to men of the latest generations all the feelings experienced by their predecessors and also those felt by their best and foremost contemporaries. And as the evolution of knowledge proceeds by truer and more necessary knowledge dislodging and replacing what was mistaken and unnecessary, so the evolution of feeling proceeds by means of art—feelings less kind and less necessary for the well-being of mankind being replaced by others kinder and more needful for that end. That is the purpose of art. And speaking now of the feelings which are its subject matter, the more art fulfills that purpose the better the art, and the less it fulfills it the worse the art.

The appraisement of feelings (that is, the recognition of one or other set of feelings as more or less good, more or less necessary for the well-being of mankind) is effected by the religious perception of the age.

In every period of history and in every human society there exists an understanding of the meaning of life, which represents the highest level to which men of that society have attained—an understanding indicating the highest good at which that society aims. This understanding is the religious perception of the given time and society. And this religious perception is always clearly expressed by a few advanced men and more or less vividly perceived by members of the society generally. Such a religious perception and its corresponding expression always exists in every society. If it appears to us that there is no religious perception in our society, this is not because there really is none, but only because we do not wish to see it. And we often wish not to see it because it exposes the fact that our life is inconsistent with that religious perception.

Religious perception in a society is like the direction of a flowing river. If the river flows at all it must have a direction. If a society lives, there must be a religious perception indicating the direction in which, more or less consciously, all its members tend.

And so there always has been, and is, a religious perception in every society. And it is by the standard of this religious perception that the feelings transmitted by art have always been appraised. It has always been only on the basis of this religious perception of their age, that men have chosen from amid the endlessly varied spheres of art that art which transmitted feelings making religious perception operative in actual life. And such art has always been highly valued and encouraged, while art transmitting feelings already outlived, flowing from the antiquated religious perceptions of a former age, has always been condemned and despised. All the rest of art transmitting those most diverse feelings by means of which people commune with one another was not condemned and was tolerated if only it did not transmit feelings contrary to religious perception. Thus for instance among the Greeks, art transmitting feelings of beauty, strength, and courage (Hesiod, Homer, Phidias)[11] was chosen, approved, and encouraged, while art transmitting feelings of rude sensuality, despondency, and effeminacy, was condemned and despised. Among the Jews, art transmitting feelings of devotion and submission to the God of the Hebrews and to his will (the epic of Genesis, the prophets, the Psalms) was chosen and encouraged, while art transmitting feelings of idolatry (the golden calf) was condemned and despised. All the rest of art—stories, songs, dances, ornamentation of houses, of utensils, and of clothes—which was not contrary to religious perception, was neither distinguished nor discussed. Thus as regards its subject matter has art always and everywhere been appraised and thus it should be appraised, for this attitude towards art proceeds from the fundamental characteristics of human nature, and those characteristics do not change.

I know that according to an opinion current in our times religion is a superstition humanity has outgrown, and it is therefore assumed that no such thing exists as a religious perception common to us all by which art in our time can be appraised. I know that this is the opinion current in the pseudocultured circles of today. People who do not acknowledge Christianity in its true meaning because it undermines their social privileges, and who therefore invent all kinds of philosophic and aesthetic theories to hide from themselves the meaninglessness and wrongfulness of their lives, cannot think otherwise. These people intentionally, or sometimes unintentionally, confuse the notion of a religious cult with the notion of religious perception, and think that by denying the cult they get rid of the perception. But even the very attacks on religion and the attempts to establish an idea of life contrary to the religious perception of our times, most clearly demonstrate the existence of a religious perception condemning the lives that are not in harmony with it.

If humanity progresses, that is, moves forward, there must inevitably be a guide to the direction of that movement. And religions have always furnished that guide. All history shows that the progress of humanity is accomplished no otherwise than under the guidance of religion. But if the race cannot progress without the guidance of religion—and progress is always going on, and consequently goes on also in our own times—then there must be a religion of our times. So that whether it pleases or displeases the so-called cultured people of today, they must admit the existence of religion—not of a religious cult, Catholic, Protestant, or another, but of religious perception—which even in our times is the guide always present where there is any progress. And if a religious perception exists amongst us, then the feelings dealt with by our art should be appraised on the basis of that religious perception; and as has been the case always and everywhere, art transmitting feelings flowing from the religious perception of our time should be chosen from amid all the indifferent art, should be acknowledged, highly valued, and encouraged, while art running counter to that perception should be condemned and despised, and all the remaining, indifferent art should neither be distinguished nor encouraged.

The religious perception of our time in its widest and most practical application is the consciousness that our well-being, both material and spiritual, individual and collective, temporal and eternal, lies in the growth of brotherhood among men—in their loving harmony with one another. This perception is not only expressed by Christ and all the best men of past ages, it is not only repeated in most varied forms and from most diverse sides by the best men of our times, but it already serves as a clue to all the complex labor of humanity, consisting as this labor does on the one hand in the destruction of physical and moral obstacles to the union of men, and on the other hand in establishing the principles common to all men which can and should unite them in one universal brotherhood. And it is on the basis of this perception that we should appraise all the phenomena of our life and among the rest our art also: choosing from all its realms and highly prizing and encouraging whatever transmits feelings flowing from this religious perception,

---

[11] Hesiod (eighth century B.C.), Homer (eighth century B.C.), Greek poets; Phidias (fifth century B.C.), Greek sculptor.

rejecting whatever is contrary to it, and not attributing to the rest of art an importance that does not properly belong to it.

The chief mistake made by people of the upper classes at the time of the so-called Renaissance—a mistake we still perpetuate—was not that they ceased to value and attach importance to religious art (people of that period could not attach importance to it because, like our own upper classes, they could not believe in what the majority considered to be religion), but their mistake was that they set up in place of the religious art that was lacking, an insignificant art which aimed merely at giving pleasure, that is, they began to choose, to value, and to encourage, in place of religious art, something which in any case did not deserve such esteem and encouragement.

One of the fathers of the church said that the great evil is not that men do not know God, but that they have set up instead of God, that which is not God. So also with art. The great misfortune of the people of the upper classes of our time is not so much that they are without a religious art as that, instead of a supreme religious art chosen from all the rest as being specially important and valuable, they have chosen a most insignificant and, usually, harmful art, which aims at pleasing certain people and which therefore, if only by its exclusive nature, stands in contradiction to that Christian principle of universal union which forms the religious perception of our time. Instead of religious art, an empty and often vicious art is set up, and this hides from men's notice the need of that true religious art which should be present in life to improve it.

It is true that art which satisfies the demands of the religious perception of our time is quite unlike former art, but notwithstanding this dissimilarity, to a man who does not intentionally hide the truth from himself, what forms the religious art of our age is very clear and definite. In former times when the highest religious perception united only some people (who even if they formed a large society were yet but one society among others—Jews, or Athenian or Roman citizens), the feelings transmitted by the art of that time flowed from a desire for the might, greatness, glory, and prosperity of that society, and the heroes of art might be people who contributed to that prosperity by strength, by craft, by fraud, or by cruelty (Ulysses, Jacob, David, Samson, Hercules, and all the heroes). But the religious perception of our times does not select any one society of men; on the contrary it demands the union of all—absolutely of all people without exception—and above every other virtue it sets brotherly love of all men. And therefore the feelings transmitted by the art of our time not only cannot coincide with the feelings transmitted by former art, but must run counter to them.

Christian, truly Christian, art has been so long in establishing itself, and has not yet established itself, just because the Christian religious perception was not one of those small steps by which humanity advances regularly, but was an enormous revolution which, if it has not already altered, must inevitably alter the entire conception of life of mankind, and consequently the whole internal organization of that life. It is true that the life of humanity, like that of an individual, moves regularly; but in that regular movement come, as it were, turning points which sharply divide the preceding from the subsequent life. Christianity was such a turning point; such at least it must appear to us who live by the Christian perception of life. Christian perception gave another, a new direction to all human feelings, and therefore completely altered both the content and the significance of art. The Greeks could make use of Persian art and the Romans could use Greek art, or, similarly, the Jews could use Egyptian art—the fundamental ideals were one and the same. Now the ideal was the greatness and prosperity of the Persians, now the greatness and prosperity of the Greeks, now that of the Romans. The same art was transferred to other conditions and served new nations. But the Christian ideal changed and reversed everything, so that, as the Gospel puts it, "That which was exalted among men has become an abomination in the sight of God."[12] The ideal is no longer the greatness of Pharaoh or of a Roman emperor, not the beauty of a Greek nor the wealth of Phoenicia, but humility, purity, compassion, love. The hero is no longer Dives, but Lazarus the beggar; not Mary Magdalene in the day of her beauty but in the day of her repentance; not those who acquire wealth but those who have abandoned it; not those who dwell in palaces but those who dwell in catacombs and huts; not those who rule over others, but those who acknowledge no authority but God's. And the greatest work of art is no longer a cathedral of victory with statues of conquerors, but the representation of a human soul so transformed by love that a man who is tormented and murdered, yet pities and loves his persecutors.

And the change is so great that men of the Christian world find it difficult to resist the inertia of the heathen art to which they have been accustomed all their lives. The subject matter of Christian religious art is so new to them, so unlike the subject matter of former art, that it seems to them as though Christian art were a denial of art, and they cling desperately to the old art. But this old art, having no longer in our day any source in religious perception, has lost its meaning, and we shall have to abandon it whether we wish to or not.

---

[12]Luke 16.15.

The essence of the Christian perception consists in the recognition by every man of his sonship to God and of the consequent union of men with God and with one another, as is said in the Gospel (John 17:21[13]). Therefore the subject matter of Christian art is of a kind that feeling can unite men with God and with another.

The expression *unite men with God and with one another* may seem obscure to people accustomed to the misuse of these words that is so customary, but the words have a perfectly clear meaning nevertheless. They indicate that the Christian union of man (in contradiction to the partial, exclusive, union of only certain men) is that which unites all without exception.

Art, all art, has this characteristic, that it unites people. Every art causes those to whom the artist's feeling is transmitted to unite in soul with the artist and also with all who receive the same impression. But non-Christian art, while uniting some people, makes that very union a cause of separation between these united people and others; so that union of this kind is often a source not merely of division but even of enmity towards others. Such is all patriotic art, with its anthems, poems, and monuments; such is all church art, that is, the art of certain cults, with their images, statues, processions, and other local ceremonies. Such art is belated and non-Christian, uniting the people of one cult only to separate them yet more sharply from the members of other cults, and even to place them in relations of hostility to one another. Christian art is such only as tends to unite all without exception, either by evoking in them the perception that each man and all men stand in a like relation towards God and towards their neighbor, or by evoking in them identical feelings, which may even be the very simplest, provided that they are not repugnant to Christianity and are natural to everyone without exception.

Good Christian art of our time may be unintelligible to people because of imperfections in its form or because men are inattentive to it, but it must be such that all men can experience the feelings it transmits. It must be the art not of some one group of people, or of one class, or of one nationality, or of one religious cult; that is, it must not transmit feelings accessible only to a man educated in a certain way, or only to an aristocrat, or a merchant, or only to a Russian, or a native of Japan, or a Roman Catholic, or a Buddhist, and so on, but it must transmit feelings accessible to everyone. Only art of this kind can in our time be acknowledged to be good art, worthy of being chosen out from all the rest of art and encouraged.

---

[13] [Maude] "That they may all be one; even as thou, father, art in me and I in thee, that they may also be in us."

Christian art, that is, the art of our time, should be catholic in the original meaning of the word, that is, universal, and therefore it should unite all men. And only two kinds of feeling unite all men: first, feelings flowing from a perception of our sonship to God and of the brotherhood of man; and next, the simple feelings of common life accessible to everyone without exception—such as feelings of merriment, of pity, of cheerfulness, of tranquility, and so forth. Only these two kinds of feelings can now supply material for art good in its subject matter.

And the action of these two kinds of art apparently so dissimilar, is one and the same. The feelings flowing from the perception of our sonship to God and the brotherhood of man—such as a feeling of sureness in truth, devotion to the will of God, self-sacrifice, respect for and love of man—evoked by Christian religious perception; and the simplest feelings, such as a softened or a merry mood caused by a song or an amusing jest intelligible to everyone, or by a touching story, or a drawing, or a little doll: both alike produce one and the same effect—the loving union of man with man. Sometimes people who are together, if not hostile to one another, are at least estranged in mood and feeling, till perhaps a story, a performance, a picture, or even a building, but oftenest of all music, unites them all as by an electric flash, and in place of their former isolation or even enmity they are conscious of union and mutual love. Each is glad that another feels what he feels; glad of the communion established not only between him and all present, but also with all now living who will yet share the same impression; and, more than that, he feels the mysterious gladness of a communion which, reaching beyond the grave, unites us with all men of the past who have been moved by the same feelings and with all men of the future who will yet be touched by them. And this effect is produced both by religious art which transmits feelings of love of God and one's neighbor, and by universal art transmitting the very simplest feelings common to all men.

The art of our time should be appraised differently from former art chiefly in this, that the art of our time, that is, Christian art (basing itself on a religious perception which demands the union of man), excludes from the domain of art good in its subject matter, everything transmitting exclusive feelings which do not unite men but divide them. It relegates such work to the category of art that is bad in its subject matter; while on the other hand it includes in the category of art that is good in subject matter a section not formerly admitted as deserving of selection and respect, namely, universal art transmitting even the most trifling and simple feelings if only they are accessible to all men without exception, and therefore unite them. Such art cannot but

768 ◇ LEO TOLSTOY

be esteemed good in our time, for it attains the end which Christianity, the religious perception of our time, sets before humanity.

Christian art either evokes in men feelings which through love of God and of one's neighbor draw them to closer and ever closer union and make them ready for, and capable of, such union; or evokes in them feelings which show them that they are already united in the joys and sorrows of life. And therefore the Christian art of our time can be and is of two kinds: first, art transmitting feelings flowing from a religious perception of man's position in the world in relation to God and to his neighbor—religious art in the limited meaning of the term; and secondly, art transmitting the simplest feelings of common life, but such always as are accessible to all men in the whole world—the art of common life—the art of the people—universal art. Only these two kinds of art can be considered good art in our time.

*   *   *

In the arts of painting and sculpture, all pictures and statues in so-called genre style, representations of animals, landscapes, and caricatures with subjects comprehensible to everyone, and also all kinds of ornaments, are universal in subject matter. Such productions in painting and sculpture are very numerous (for instance, china dolls), but for the most part such objects (for instance, ornaments of all kinds) are either not considered to be art or are considered to be art of a low quality. In reality all such objects if only they transmit a true feeling experienced by the artist and comprehensible to everyone (however insignificant it may seem to us to be), are works of real, good, Christian art.

I fear it will here be urged against me that having denied that the conception of beauty can supply a standard for works of art, I contradict myself by acknowledging ornaments to be works of good art. The reproach is unjust, for the subject matter of all kinds of ornamentation consists not in the beauty but in the feeling (of admiration at, and delight in, the combination of lines and colors) which the artist has experienced and with which he infects the spectator. Art remains what it was and what it must be: nothing but the infection by one man of another or of others with the feelings experienced by the artist. Among these feelings is the feeling of delight at what pleases the sight. Objects pleasing the sight may be such as please a small or a large number of people, or such as please all men—and ornaments for the most part are of the latter kind. A landscape representing a very unusual view, or a genre picture of a special subject, may not please everyone, but ornaments, from Yakútsk or-

naments to Greek ones, are intelligible to everyone and evoke a similar feeling of admiration in all, and therefore this despised kind of art should in Christian society be esteemed far above exceptional, pretentious pictures and sculptures.

So that in relation to feelings conveyed, there are only two kinds of good Christian art, all the rest of art not comprised in these two divisions should be acknowledged to be bad art, deserving not to be encouraged but to be driven out, denied, and despised, as being art not uniting but dividing people. Such in literary art are all novels and poems which transmit ecclesiastical or patriotic feelings, and also exclusive feelings pertaining only to the class of the idle rich: such as aristocratic honor, satiety, spleen, pessimism, and refined and vicious feelings, flowing from sex-love—quite incomprehensible to the great majority of mankind.

In painting we must similarly place in the class of bad art all ecclesiastical, patriotic, and exclusive pictures; all pictures representing the amusements and allurements of a rich and idle life; all so-called symbolic pictures in which the very meaning of the symbol is comprehensible only to those of a certain circle; and above all pictures with voluptuous subjects—all that odious female nudity which fills all the exhibitions and galleries. And to this class belongs almost all the chamber and opera music of our times—beginning especially with Beethoven (Schumann, Berlioz, Liszt, Wagner)[14]—by its subject matter devoted to the expression of feelings accessible only to people who have developed in themselves an unhealthy nervous irritation evoked by this exclusive, artificial, and complex music.

"What! the *Ninth Symphony* not a good work of art!" I hear exclaimed by indignant voices.

And I reply: Most certainly it is not. All that I have written I have written with the sole purpose of finding a clear and reasonable criterion by which to judge the merits of works of art. And this criterion, coinciding with the indications of plain and sane sense, indubitably shows me that that symphony of Beethoven's is not a good work of art. Of course to people educated in the worship of certain productions and of their authors, to people whose taste has been perverted just by being educated in such a worship, the acknowledgment that such a celebrated work is bad, is amazing and strange. But how are we to escape the indications of reason and common sense?

Beethoven's *Ninth Symphony* is considered a great work of art. To verify its claim to be such I must first ask myself whether this work transmits the highest religious

---

[14] All nineteenth-century German composers.

feeling? I reply in the negative, since music in itself cannot transmit those feelings; and therefore I ask myself next: Since this work does not belong to the highest kind of religious art, has it the other characteristic of the good art of our time—the quality of uniting all men in one common feeling—does it rank as Christian universal art? And again I have no option but to reply in the negative; for not only do I not see how the feelings transmitted by this work could unite people not specially trained to submit themselves to its complex hypnotism, but I am unable to imagine to myself a crowd of normal people who could understand anything of this long, confused, and artificial production, except short snatches which are lost in a sea of what is incomprehensible. And therefore, whether I like it or not, I am compelled to conclude that this work belongs to the rank of bad art. It is curious to note in this connection, that attached to the end of this very symphony is a poem of Schiller's which (though somewhat obscurely) expresses this very thought, namely, that feeling (Schiller speaks only of the feeling of gladness) unites people and evokes love in them. But though this poem is sung at the end of the symphony, the music does not accord with the thought expressed in the verses; for the music is exclusive and does not unite all men, but unites only a few, dividing them off from the rest of mankind.

Edmund Husserl

1859–1938

Though Edmund Husserl is most frequently cited as the principal originator of Phenomenology, that identification has, in many ways, obscured his pivotal importance for the unfolding of twentieth-century intellectual history. In the context of this anthology, and for theory in the humanities, Husserl, particularly in his work before he turned his attention to Phenomenology, appears conspicuously at the crossroads of virtually every major subsequent movement—and not coincidentally, counts among his students both Martin Heidegger and Rudolph Carnap. His earliest major work, *The Philosophy of Arithmetic* (1891), set forth a view of mathematical theory that drew significantly upon psychology—a decision that drew the very sharp and powerful criticism of Gottlob Frege (above, page 734) whose *Foundations of Arithmetic* was published almost a decade earlier, in 1884. It is worth remarking that Frege himself had encountered stinging criticism from the mathematician Georg Cantor (1845–1918), and remained convinced that Cantor had not understood his work. Frege's own review of Husserl could arguably be characterized in a similar way, though the point of difference between Frege's strict formalism and Husserl's reliance on conscious intuition was much more sharp—just as the effect of Frege's aggressively polemical review was evidently much more unsettling. Husserl, however, proceeded with a determination but with serious doubts as to the possibility of reformulating the appraisal of psychology as an empirical pursuit without giving up the philosophical attention to the direct experience of intentional consciousness, a concern he shared in common with his teacher, Franz Brentano (1838–1917). What was at stake, for Husserl, was the fundamental question of whether or not, given the prodigious advances of a formalist view of mathematics and logic, it was still possible to incorporate into the study of these crucial subjects the richness of the actual experience of thinking and the subtlety of insight as the very life of conscious experience that evidently could not be reduced to formal rules. This concern remained the hallmark of Husserl's work throughout his long career.

It was in his remarkable *Logical Investigations* (1900–1901; second edition, 1913) that Husserl carried out what is increasingly regarded as his most important and interesting work. In the "Prolegomena to Pure Logic," itself almost a separate book introducing *Logical Investigations,* Husserl begins with his clear and insistent recognition that the subject could not be fruitfully pursued without a critical account of the work of British empiricist philosophers, especially John Stuart Mill and David Hume, but that stopping there would compromise the objective of understanding logic as a theory of science without reducing it to a merely sterile formalism. Husserl urged instead a "thoroughgoing *division of labour*" between formal mathematics and philosophy, though treating formal mathematics as a "special science" with a crucial, though more limited technical aim in formulating rules and facilitating scientific prediction. Philosophical investigation, on the other hand, aims to clarify "the essence of a thing, an event, a cause," but especially "that wonderful affinity which this essence has with essence of thought, which enables it to be thought, with the essence of knowledge, which makes it knowable, with meanings which make it capable of being meant. . . ."[1]

From this point of view, *Logical Investigations* provided Husserl with the point of departure for the later development of Phenomenology, but it was first of all, one of the earliest and most important texts for the increasingly pervasive "linguistic turn" in subsequent philosophy and criticism. Here too, Husserl differed quite sharply from Frege, whose *Sense and Meaning* (above, page 735) had appeared in 1892 (and which Husserl mentions in the selection reprinted here), though objecting forcefully that allowing questions of reference (and thereby empirical verifiability) to preempt the field of the study of meaning would impose a crippling burden upon the philosophical examination of conscious insight, which clearly ranges much more freely than Frege's model would allow. Since Frege, however, was primarily concerned in that essay with the logical problem of equality, the connection between his work and Husserl's, in this particular, is not widely discussed. What is particularly interesting, however, is how many developments Husserl anticipated, including a mild prediction of trouble ahead for strict formalism—which came, for Frege, in 1902, with Bertrand Russell's devastating detection of an unsolvable contradiction in Frege's *Begriffsschrift* and the logical system developed from it, now popularly known as "Russell's Paradox" (below, page 811)—but also an anticipation of Wittgenstein's "picture theory of meaning" as well as a striking critique of its insufficiency that corresponds quite well with Wittgenstein's own later development of the idea of the "language game."[2] In a similar way, Husserl's work on signs predates Saussure (below, page 786) and Ogden and Richards in *The Meaning of Meaning* (1923), just as it has certain resemblances to the less well known work of Peirce (above, page 652) whose own version of phenomenology Peirce called "Phanerscopy."[3]

The great difficulty in forming, in retrospect, an apposite view of Husserl is exacerbated by his own increasing commitment to a more and more stringently rationalist and Cartesian development of Phenomenology, which, as J. R. Findlay wryly notes, runs the risk of transforming "his brilliant, original analysis of consciousness into one of those ordinary subjectivisms that comfort the shattered ego by assuring it, quite baselessly, that in some secret manner it has manufactured its own shattering world."[4] In one respect, his pursuit of the project of Phenomenology, as a movement, seems to have had the effect of making it less and less possible for anyone else to follow it, but the brilliant analysis of consciousness to which Findlay alludes has been an enormously powerful influence, discernible in figures as disparate as Jean Paul Sartre (below, page 1175), his student, Martin Heidegger (below, page 1051), and two generations of phenomenological thinkers such as Maurice Merleau-Ponty (1908–1961), Gaston Bachelard (1884–1962), Georges Poulet (1902–1991), Paul Ricoeur (b. 1913), Emmanuel Lévinas (1906–1995), Paul de Man (below, page 1309), and Jacques Derrida (below, page 1203). In this respect, Husserl is all the more important, even when his influence is mediated or

---

[1] See *Logical Investigations* I, 245.

[2] See, for example, *Investigations* I, 305, where Husserl employs the same metaphor, though more directly to mathematical operations.

[3] Cf. *Collected Papers* 3.284: "Phaneroscopy is the description of the phaneron; and by the phaneron I mean the collective total of all that is in any way or in any sense present to the mind, quite regardless of whether it corresponds to any real thing or not. If you ask present when, and to whose mind, I reply that I leave these questions unanswered, never having entertained a doubt that those features of the phaneron that I have found in my mind are present at all times and to all minds."

[4] Translator's Introduction, *Logical Investigations* I, 10.

submerged, for mid-century literary criticism, more or less desperately starved for philosophical reflection, but finding analytical philosophy not well suited to literary and cultural investigations. Husserl was not just the originator of a movement, but the source of a style that seemed, on the face of it, far more congenial to the kind of subtle and supple explorations of meaning that literary texts demand. He is also, in a more deeply ironic way, a major source of a counter-style in deconstruction, evinced in the penetrating and lithe critique of Husserl (particularly the Husserl of *Logical Investigations*) by Jacques Derrida (a portion of which is reprinted below, page 1215).

It remains to say that Husserl, from a Jewish background but who converted in the late 1880s to an evangelical Lutheran church, enjoyed through most of his long career the respect and admiration of an ever-growing group of philosophers and thinkers. After his appointment to the University of Freiburg in 1916, his international reputation continued to grow, but in the years after his retirement in 1928, he was humiliated by exclusion from the university after Hitler's rise to power in 1933, an exclusion made all the more bitter later in being enforced by his former student who succeeded him in his chair as professor of philosophy, Martin Heidegger.

An edition of Husserl's works in English translation is in progress, *Works,* vol. 1–9 (1980–2001), and the *Edmund Husserl Bibliography,* compiled by Steven Spileers, was published in 1998. Husserl's major works include: *The Philosophy of Arithmetic* (1891); *Logical Investigations* (1900, 1913; trans. 1970); *Cartesian Meditations: An Introduction to Phenomenology* (1929; trans. 1960); *Ideas: General Introduction to Pure Phenomenology* [Volume 1 of *Ideen zu einer reinen Phänomenologie und phänomenologischen Philosophie*] (trans. 1931); *The Idea of Phenomenology* (1907; trans. 1964); *Phenomenology and the Crisis of Philosophy* (1936, trans. 1965); and *The Phenomenology of Internal Time-Consciousness,* ed. Martin Heidegger (trans. 1964). Important critical studies include: Paul Ricoeur, *Husserl: An Analysis of His Phenomenology* (1967), and *A Key to Ideas I* (1996); Maurice Natanson, *Edmund Husserl: Philosopher of Infinite Tasks* (1973); Jacques Derrida, *Speech and Phenomena and Other Essays on Husserl's Theory of Signs* (1967; trans. 1973) and *The Problem of Genesis in Husserl's Philosophy* (2003); Barry Smith and David W. Smith, eds., *The Cambridge Companion to Husserl* (1995).

from

Investigation I: Expression and Meaning

Chapter One

Essential Distinctions

§1 An ambiguity in the term 'sign'

The terms 'expression' and 'sign' are often treated as synonyms, but it will not be amiss to point out that they do not always coincide in application in common usage. Every sign is a sign for something, but not every sign has 'meaning', a 'sense' that the sign 'expresses'. In many cases it is not even true that a sign 'stands for' that of which we may say it is a sign. And even where this can be said, one has to observe that 'standing for' will not count as the 'meaning' which characterizes the expression. For signs in the sense of indications (notes, marks etc.) *do not express* anything, unless they happen to fulfil a significant as well as an indicative function. If, as one unwillingly does, one limits oneself to expressions employed in living discourse, the notion of an indication seems to apply more widely than that of an expression, but this does not mean that its content is the genus of which an expression is the species. To mean is *not a particular way of being a sign in the sense of indicating something.* It has a narrower application only because meaning—in communicative speech—is always bound up with such an indicative relation, and this in its turn leads to a wider concept, since meaning is also capable of occuring without such a connection. *Expressions* function meaningfully even in *isolated mental life, where they no longer serve to indicate anything.* The two notions of sign do not therefore really stand in the relation of more extensive genus to narrower species.

The whole matter requires more thorough discussion.

§2 The essence of indication

Of the two concepts connected with the word 'sign', we shall first deal with that of an *indication*. The relation that here obtains we shall call the *indicative relation*. In this sense a brand is the sign of a slave, a flag the sign of a na-

tion. Here all marks belong, as characteristic qualities suited to help us in recognizing the objects to which they attach.

But the concept of an indication extends more widely than that of a mark. We say the Martian canals are signs of the existence of intelligent beings on Mars, that fossil vertebrae are signs of the existence of prediluvian animals etc. Signs to aid memory, such as the much-used knot in a handkerchief, memorials etc., also have their place here. If suitable things, events or their properties are deliberately produced to serve as such indications, one calls them 'signs' whether they exercise this function or not. Only in the case of indications deliberately and artificially brought about, does one speak of standing for, and that both in respect of the action which produces the marking (the branding or chalking etc.), and in the sense of the indication itself, i.e. taken in its relation to the object it stands for or that it is to signify.

These distinctions and others like them do not deprive the concept of indication of its essential unity. A thing is only properly an indication if and where it in fact serves to indicate something to some thinking being. If we wish to seize the pervasively common element here present we must refer back to such cases of 'live' functioning. In these we discover as a common circumstance the fact that certain objects or states of affairs *of whose reality someone has actual knowledge* indicate to him *the reality of certain other objects or states of affairs,* in the sense that *his belief in the reality of the one is experienced* (though not at all evidently) *as motivating a belief or surmise in the reality of the other.* This relation of 'motivation' represents a *descriptive unity* among our acts of judgement in which indicating and indicated states of affairs become constituted for the thinker. This descriptive unity is not to be conceived as a mere form-quality founded upon our acts of judgement, for it is in their unity that the essence of indication lies. More lucidly put: the 'motivational' unity of our acts of judgement has itself the character of a unity of judgement; before it as a whole an objective correlate, a unitary state of affairs, parades itself, is meant in such a judgement, appears to be in and for that judgement. Plainly such a state of affairs amounts to just this: that certain things *may* or *must* exist, *since* other things have been given. This 'since', taken as expressing an objective connection, is the objective correlate of 'motivation' taken as a descriptively peculiar way of combining acts of judgement into a single act of judgement.

§3 Two senses of 'demonstration' (Hinweis und Beweis)

We have sketched the phenomenological situation so generally that what we have said applies as much to the

From *Investigation I: Expression and Meaning* was first published in 1900, in *Logische Untersuchungen.* Reprinted from *Logical Investigations,* translated by J. N. Findlay, from the Second German Edition (1913). (London: Routledge & Kegan Paul, 1970), Volume I, pages 269–311.

'demonstration' of genuine inference and proof, as to the 'demonstration' of indication. These two notions should, however, be kept apart. Their distinctness has already been suggested by our stress on the *lack of insight* in indications. In cases where the existence of one state of affairs is evidently inferred from that of another, we do not in fact speak of the latter as an indication or sign of the former, and, conversely, we only speak of demonstration in the strict logical sense in the case of an inference which is or could be informed by insight. Much, no doubt, that is propounded as demonstrative or, in the simplest case, as syllogistically cogent, is devoid of insight and may even be false. But to propound it is at least to make the claim that a relation of consequence could be seen to hold. This is bound up with the fact that there is an objective syllogism or proof, or an objective relationship between ground and consequent, which corresponds to our subjective acts of inferring and proving. These ideal unities are not the experiences of judging in question, but their ideal 'contents', the propositions they involve. The premisses prove the conclusion no matter who may affirm the premisses and the conclusion, or the unity that both form. An ideal rule is here revealed which extends its sway beyond the judgements here and now united by 'motivation'; in supra-empirical generality it comprehends as such all judgements having a like content, all judgements, even, having a like form. Such regularity makes itself subjectively known to us when we conduct proofs with insight, while the precise rule is made known to us through ideative reflection on the contents of the judgements experienced together in the actual context of 'motivation', in the actual inference and proof. These contents are the propositions involved.

In the case of an indication there is no question of all this. Here insight and (to put the matter objectively) knowledge regarding the ideal connections among the contents of the judgements concerned, is quite excluded. When one says that the state of affairs A indicates the state of affairs B, that the existence of the one points to that of the other, one may confidently be expecting to find B true, but one's mode of speech implies no objectively necessary connections between A and B, nothing into which one could have insight. The contents of one's judgements are not here related as premisses are to a conclusion. At times no doubt we do speak of 'indications' even in cases where there is an objective relation of entailment (a mediate one, in fact). A mathematician may make use (so he says) of the fact that an algebraic equation is of uneven order as a sign that it has at least one real root. To be more exact, we are here only concerned with the possibility that someone who fails to carry out and see the cogency of the relevant thought-chain, may make use of a statement about an equation's uneven order as an immediate, blind motive for asserting the equa-

tion to have some necessarily connected property which he needs for his mathematical purposes. In such situations, where certain states of affairs readily serve to indicate others which are, in themselves, their consequences, they do not function in thought as logical grounds of the latter, but work through connections which previous actual demonstration, or blind learning on authority, has established among our convictions, whether as actual mental states or as dispositions for such. Nothing is of course altered in all this by the possible presence of an accompanying merely habitual knowledge of an objectively present rational connection.

If an indication (or the connection of 'motivation' in which such a soi-disant objective relation makes its appearance) is without essential relation to a necessary connection, the question arises whether it may not claim to be essentially related to a connection of probability. Where one thing indicates another, where belief in the one's existence furnishes one with an empirical motive or ground—not necessary but contingent—for belief in the existence of the other, must the motivating belief not furnish a *ground of probability* for the belief it motivates? This is not the place for a close discussion of this pressing question. We need only observe that the question may correctly be answered in the affirmative in so far as such empirical 'motivations' all fall under an ideal jurisdiction in virtue of which they may be spoken of as 'justified' or 'unjustified', or, objectively expressed, in which they may be spoken of as real, i.e. valid, motivations which lead to a probability or perhaps to an empirical certainty, or *per contra,* as merely apparent, i.e. invalid, motivations, which do not lead to such a probability. One may, e.g., cite the controversy as to whether volcanic phenomena do or do not indicate that the earth's interior is molten, and so on. One thing is sure, that to talk of an indication is not to presuppose a definite relation to considerations of probability. Usually such talk relates not to mere surmises but to assured judgements. The ideal jurisdiction to which we have here accorded authority must first demand, therefore, that we should scale down our confident judgements to modest surmises.

I shall here observe, further, that we cannot avoid talking about 'motivation' in a general sense which covers strict demonstration as much as empirical indication. Here in fact we have a quite undeniable phenomenological affinity, obvious enough to register itself in ordinary discourse. We commonly speak of reasoning and inference, not merely in the sense of logic, but in a sense connected with empirical indications. This affinity plainly extends more widely: it covers the field of emotional, and, in particular, of volitional phenomena, to which talk of 'motives' was at first alone confined. Here too 'because' has a part to play, covering as wide a linguistic territory as does the most general sense of 'motivation'. I cannot therefore approve of Meinong's censure of Brentano's terminology, which I have here adopted.[1] But I entirely agree with him that in perceiving something as 'motivated' we are not at all perceiving it as caused.

§4 Digression on the associative origin of indication

The mental facts in which the notion of indication has its 'origin', i.e. in which it can be abstractively apprehended, belong to the wider group of facts which fall under the historical rubric of the 'association of ideas'. Under this rubric we do not merely have those facts which concern the 'accompaniment' and 'reactivation' of ideas stated in the laws of association, but the further facts in which association operates creatively, and produces peculiar descriptive characters and forms of unity.[2] Association does not merely restore contents to consciousness, and then leave it to them to combine with the contents there present, as the essence or generic nature of either may necessarily prescribe. It cannot indeed disturb such unified patterns as depend solely on our mental contents, e.g. the unity of visual contents in the visual field. But it can create additional phenomenological characters and unities which do not have their necessary, law-determined ground in the experienced contents themselves, nor in the generic forms of their abstract aspects.[3] If *A* summons *B* into consciousness, we are not merely simultaneously or successively conscious of both *A* and *B*, but we usually *feel* their connection forcing itself upon us, a connection in which the one points to the other and seems to belong to it. To turn mere coexistence into mutual pertinence, or, more precisely, to build cases of the former into intentional unities of things which seem mutually pertinent, is the constant result of associative functioning. All unity of experience, all empirical unity, whether of a thing, an event or of the order and relation of things, becomes a phenomenal

unity through the felt mutual belongingness of the sides and parts that can be made to stand out as units in the apparent object before us. That one thing points to another, in definite arrangement and connection, is itself apparent to us. The single item itself, in these various forward and backward references, is no mere experienced content, but an apparent object (or part, property etc., of the same) that appears only in so far as experience *(Erfahrung)* endows contents with a new phenomenological *character,* so that they no longer count separately, but help to present an object different from themselves. In this field of facts the fact of indication also has its place, in virtue whereof an object or state of affairs not merely recalls another, and so points to it, but also provides evidence for the latter, fosters the presumption that it likewise exists, and makes us immediately feel this in the manner described above.

§5 Expressions as meaningful signs. Setting aside of a sense of 'expression' not relevant for our purpose

From indicative signs we distinguish *meaningful* signs, i.e. *expressions.* We thereby employ the term 'expression' restrictively: we exclude much that ordinary speech would call an 'expression' from its range of application. There are other cases in which we have thus to do violence to usage, where concepts for which only ambiguous terms exist call for a fixed terminology. We shall lay down, for provisional intelligibility, that each instance or part of *speech,* as also each sign that is essentially of the same sort, shall count as an expression, whether or not such speech is actually uttered, or addressed with communicative intent to any persons or not. Such a definition excludes facial expression and the various gestures which involuntarily accompany speech without communicative intent, or those in which a man's mental states achieve understandable 'expression' for his environment, without the added help of speech. Such 'utterances' are not expressions in the sense in which a case of speech is an expression, they are not phenomenally one with the experiences made manifest in them in the consciousness of the man who manifests them, as is the case with speech. In such manifestations one man communicates nothing to another: their utterance involves no intent to put certain 'thoughts' on record expressively, whether for the man himself, in his solitary state, or for others. Such 'expressions', in short, have properly speaking, *no meaning.* It is not to the point that another person may interpret our involuntary manifestations, e.g. our 'expressive movements', and that he may thereby become deeply acquainted with our inner thoughts and emotions. They 'mean' something to him

---

[1] [Husserl] A. V. Meinong, *Göttinger gel. Anz.* (1892), p. 446. [A. Alexius von Handschuchsheim Meinong (1853–1920), German philosopher and psychologist.]

[2] [Husserl] To use personification and to talk of association as 'creating' something, and to employ other similar figurative expressions in common use, is too convenient to be abandoned. Important as a scientifically exact but circumlocutory description of the relevant facts may be, ready understanding absolutely requires that we talk figuratively wherever ultimate exactness is not needed.

[3] [Husserl] I talk above of 'experienced contents', not of meant, apparent objects or events. Everything that really helps to constitute the individual, 'experiencing' consciousness is an experienced content. What it perceives, remembers, inwardly presents etc., is a meant or intentional object. This point will be further discussed in Investigation V.

in so far as he interprets them, but even for him they are without meaning in the special sense in which verbal signs have meaning: they only mean in the sense of indicating.

In the treatment which follows these distinctions must be raised to complete conceptual clarity.

§6 Questions as to the phenomenological and intentional distinctions which pertain to expressions as such

It is usual to distinguish two things in regard to every expression: 1. The expression physically regarded (the sensible sign, the articulate sound-complex, the written sign on paper etc.); 2. A certain sequence of mental states, associatively linked with the expression, which make it be the expression of something. These mental states are generally called the 'sense' or the 'meaning' of the expression, this being taken to be in accord with what these words ordinarily mean. But we shall see this notion to be mistaken, and that a mere distinction between physical signs and sense-giving experiences is by no means enough, and not at all enough for logical purposes.

The points here made have long been observed in the special case of names. We distinguish, in the case of each name, between what it 'shows forth' (i.e. mental states) and what it means. And again between what it means (the sense or 'content' of its naming presentation) and what it names (the object of that presentation). We shall need similar distinctions in the case of all expression, and shall have to explore their nature precisely. Such distinctions have led to our distinction between the notions of 'expression' and 'indication', which is not in conflict with the fact that an expression in living speech also functions as an indication, a point soon to come up for discussion. To these distinctions other important ones will be added which will concern the relations between meaning and the intuition which illustrates meaning and on occasion renders it evident. Only by paying heed to these relations, can the concept of meaning be clearly delimited, and can the fundamental opposition between the symbolic and the epistemological function of meanings be worked out.

§7 Expressions as they function in communication

Expressions were originally framed to fulfil a communicative function: let us, accordingly, first study expressions in this function, so that we may be able to work out their essential logical distinctions. The articulate sound-complex, the written sign etc., first becomes a spoken word or communicative bit of speech, when a speaker produces it with the intention of 'expressing himself about something' through its means; he must endow it with a sense in certain acts of mind, a sense he desires to share with his auditors. Such sharing becomes a possibility if the auditor also understands the speaker's intention. He does this inasmuch as he takes the speaker to be a person, who is not merely uttering sounds but *speaking to him*, who is accompanying those sounds with certain sense-giving acts, which the sounds reveal to the hearer, or whose sense they seek to communicate to him. What first makes mental commerce possible, and turns connected speech into discourse, lies in the correlation among the corresponding physical and mental experiences of communicating persons which is effected by the physical side of speech. Speaking and hearing, intimation of mental states through speaking and reception thereof in hearing, are mutually correlated.

If one surveys these interconnections, one sees at once that all expressions in *communicative* speech function as *indications*. They serve the hearer as signs of the 'thoughts' of the speaker, i.e. of his sense-giving inner experiences, as well as of the other inner experiences which are part of his communicative intention. This function of verbal expressions we shall call their *intimating function*. The content of such intimation consists in the inner experiences intimated. The sense of the predicate 'intimated' can be understood more narrowly or more widely. The *narrower* sense we may restrict to *acts which impart sense,* while the *wider* sense will cover *all* acts that a hearer may introject into a speaker on the basis of what he says (possibly because he tells us of such acts). If, e.g., we state a wish, our judgement concerning that wish is what we intimate in the narrower sense of the word, whereas the wish itself is intimated in the wider sense. The same holds of an ordinary statement of perception, which the hearer forthwith takes to belong to some actual perception. The act of perception is there intimated in the wider sense, the judgement built upon it in the narrower sense. We at once see that ordinary speech permits us to call an experience which is intimated an experience which is *expressed.*

To understand an intimation is not to have conceptual knowledge of it, not to judge in the sense of asserting anything about it: it consists simply in the fact that the hearer *intuitively* takes the speaker to be a person who is expressing this or that, or as we certainly can say, *perceives* him as such. When I listen to someone, I perceive him as a speaker, I hear him recounting, demonstrating, doubting, wishing etc. The hearer perceives the intimation in the same sense in which he perceives the intimating person—even though the mental phenomena which make him a person cannot fall, for what they are, in the intuitive grasp of another. Common speech credits us with percepts even of other people's inner experiences; we 'see' their anger, their pain etc. Such talk is quite correct, as long as, e.g., we allow outward bodily things likewise to count as perceived, and as long as, in general the notion of perception is not restricted to the adequate, the strictly intuitive percept. If the essential mark of perception lies in the intuitive persuasion that a thing or event is itself before us for our grasping—such a persuasion is possible, and in the main mass of cases actual, without verbalized, conceptual apprehension—then the receipt of such an intimation is the mere perceiving of it. The essential distinction just touched on is of course present here. The hearer perceives the speaker as manifesting certain inner experiences, and to that extent he also perceives these experiences themselves: he does not, however, himself experience them, he has not an 'inner' but an 'outer' percept of them. Here we have the big difference between the real grasp of what is inadequate intuition, and the putative grasp of what is on a basis of inadequate, though intuitive, presentation. In the former case we have to do with an experienced, in the latter case with a presumed being, to which no truth corresponds at all. Mutual understanding demands a certain correlation among the mental acts mutually unfolded in intimation and in the receipt of such intimation, but not at all their exact resemblance.

§8 Expressions in solitary life

So far we have considered expressions as used in communication, which last depends essentially on the fact that they operate indicatively. But expressions also play a great part in uncommunicated, interior mental life. This change in function plainly has nothing to do with whatever makes an expression an expression. Expressions continue to have meanings as they had before, and the same meanings as in dialogue. A word only ceases to be a word when our interest stops at its sensory contour, when it becomes a mere sound-pattern. But when we live in the understanding of a word, it expresses something and the same thing, whether we address it to anyone or not.

It seems clear, therefore, that an expression's meaning, and whatever else pertains to it essentially, cannot coincide with its feats of intimation. Or shall we say that, even in solitary mental life, one still uses expressions to intimate something, though not to a second person? Shall one say that in soliloquy one speaks to oneself, and employs words as signs, i.e. as indications, of one's own inner experiences? I cannot think such a view acceptable. Words function as signs here as they do everywhere else: everywhere they can be said to point to something. But if we reflect on the relation of expression

to meaning, and to this end break up our complex, intimately unified experience of the sense-filled expression, into the two factors of word and sense, the word comes before us as intrinsically indifferent, whereas the sense seems the thing aimed at by the verbal sign and meant by its means: the expression seems to direct interest away from itself towards its sense, and to point to the latter. But this pointing is not an indication in the sense previously discussed. The existence of the sign neither 'motivates' the existence of the meaning, nor, properly expressed, our belief in the meaning's existence. What we are to use as an indication, must be perceived by us as existent. This holds also of expressions used in communication, but not for expressions used in soliloquy, where we are in general content with imagined rather than with actual words. In imagination a spoken or printed word floats before us, though in reality it has no existence. We should not, however, confuse imaginative presentations, and the image-contents they rest on, with their imagined objects. The imagined verbal sound, or the imagined printed word, does not exist, only its imaginative presentation does so. The difference is the difference between imagined centaurs and the imagination of such beings. The word's nonexistence neither disturbs nor interests us, since it leaves the word's expressive function unaffected. Where it *does* make a difference is where intimation is linked with meaning. Here thought must not be merely expressed as meaning, but must be communicated and intimated. We can only do the latter where we actually speak and hear.

One of course speaks, in a certain sense, even in soliloquy, and it is certainly possible to think of oneself as speaking, and even as speaking to oneself, as, e.g., when someone says to himself: 'You have gone wrong, you can't go on like that.' But in the genuine sense of communication, there is no speech in such cases, nor does one tell oneself anything: one merely conceives of oneself as speaking and communicating. In a monologue words can perform no function of indicating the existence of mental acts, since such indication would there be quite purposeless. For the acts in question are themselves experienced by us at that very moment.

§9 Phenomenological distinctions between the phenomena of physical expression and the sense-giving and sense-fulfilling act

If we now turn from experiences specially concerned with intimation, and consider expressions in respect of distinctions that pertain to them equally whether they occur in dialogue or soliloquy, two things seem to be left over: the expressions themselves, and what they express as their meaning or sense. Several relations are, however, intertwined at this point, and talk about 'meaning', or about 'what is expressed', is correspondingly ambiguous. If we seek a foothold in pure description, the concrete phenomenon of the sense-informed expression breaks up, on the one hand, into the *physical phenomenon* forming the physical side of the expression, and, on the other hand, into the *acts* which give it *meaning* and possibly also *intuitive fulness,* in which its relation to an expressed object is constituted. In virtue of such acts, the expression is more than a merely sounded word. It *means* something, and in so far as it means something, it relates to what is objective. This objective somewhat can either be actually present through accompanying intuitions, or may at least appear in representation, e.g. in a mental image, and where this happens the relation to an object is realized. Alternatively this need not occur: the expression functions significantly, it remains more than mere sound of words, but it lacks any basic intuition that will give it its object. The relation of expression to object is now unrealized as being confined to a mere meaning-intention. A *name,* e.g., names its object whatever the circumstances, in so far as it *means* that object. But if the object is not intuitively before one, and so not before one as a named or meant object, mere meaning is all there is to it. If the originally *empty* meaning-intention is now fulfilled, the relation to an object is realized, the naming becomes an actual, conscious relation between name and object named.

Let us take our stand on this fundamental distinction between meaning-intentions void of intuition and those which are intuitively fulfilled: if we leave aside the sensuous acts in which the expression, *qua* mere sound of words, makes its appearance, we shall have to distinguish between two acts or sets of acts. We shall, on the one hand, have acts essential to the expression if it is to be an expression at all, i.e. a verbal sound infused with sense. These acts we shall call the *meaning-conferring acts* or the *meaning-intentions.* But we shall, on the other hand, have acts, not essential to the expression as such, which stand to it in the logically basic relation of *fulfilling* (confirming, illustrating) it more or less adequately, and so actualizing its relation to its object. These acts, which become fused with the meaning-conferring acts in the unity of knowledge or fulfilment, we call the *meaning-fulfilling* acts. The briefer expression 'meaning-fulfilment' can only be used in cases where there is no risk of the ready confusion with the *whole* experience in which a meaning-intention finds fulfilment in its correlated intuition. In the realized relation of the expression to

its objective correlate,[4] the sense-informed expression becomes one with the act of meaning-fulfilment. The sounded word is first made one with the meaning-intention, and this in its turn is made one (as intentions in general are made one with their fulfilments) with its corresponding meaning-fulfilment. The word 'expression' is normally understood—wherever, that is, we do not speak of a 'mere' expression—as the *sense-informed* expression. One should not, therefore, properly say (as one often does) that an expression *expresses its meaning* (its intention). One might more properly adopt the alternative way of speaking according to which the *fulfilling act* appears as *the act expressed by the complete expression:* we may, e.g., say that a statement 'gives expression' to an act of perceiving or imagining. We need not here point out that both meaning-conferring and meaning-fulfilling acts have a part to play in intimation in the case of communicative discourse. The former in fact constitute the inmost core of intimation. To make them known to the hearer is the prime aim of our communicative intention, for only in so far as the hearer attributes them to the speaker will he understand the latter.

§10 The phenomenological unity of these acts

The above distinguished acts involving the expression's appearance, on the one hand, and the meaning-intention and possible meaning-fulfilment, on the other, do not constitute a mere aggregate of simultaneously given items in consciousness. They rather form an intimately fused unity of peculiar character. Everyone's personal experience bears witness to the differing weight of the two constituents, which reflects the asymmetry of the relation between an expression and the object which (through its meaning) it expresses or names. Both are 'lived through', the presentation of the word and the sense-giving act: but, while we experience the former, we do not live *in* such a presentation at all, but solely in enacting its sense, its meaning. And in so far as we do this, and yield ourselves to enacting the meaning-intention and its further fulfilment, our whole interest centres upon the object intended in our intention, and named by its means. (These two ways of speaking have in fact the same meaning.) The function of a word (or rather of an intuitive word-presentation) is to awaken a sense-conferring

---

[4] [Husserl] I often make use of the vaguer expression 'objective correlate' *(Gegenständlichkeit)* since we are here never limited to objects in the narrower sense, but have also to do with states of affairs, properties, and non-independent forms etc., whether real or categorial.

act in ourselves, to point to what is intended, or perhaps given intuitive fulfilment in this act, and to guide our interest exclusively in this direction.

Such pointing is not to be described as the mere objective fact of a regular diversion of interest from one thing to another. The fact that two presented objects *A* and *B* are so linked by some secret psychological coordination that the presentation of *A* regularly arouses the presentation of *B,* and that interest is thereby shifted from *A* to *B*—such a fact does not make *A* the expression of the presentation of *B*. To be an expression is rather a descriptive aspect of the *experienced unity* of sign and thing signified.

What is involved in the descriptive difference between the physical sign-phenomenon and the meaning-intention which makes it into an expression, becomes most clear when we turn our attention to the sign *qua* sign, e.g. to the printed word as such. If we do this, we have an external percept (or external intuitive idea) just like any other, whose object loses its verbal character. If this object again functions as a word, its presentation is wholly altered in character. The word (*qua* external singular) remains intuitively present, maintains its appearance, but we no longer intend it, it no longer properly is the object of our 'mental activity.' Our interest, our intention, our thought—mere synonyms if taken in sufficiently wide senses—point exclusively to the thing meant in the sense-giving act. This means, phenomenologically speaking, that the intuitive presentation, in which the physical world-phenomenon is constituted, undergoes an essential phenomenal modification when its object begins to count as an *expression.* While what constitutes the object's appearing remains unchanged, the intentional character of the experience alters. There is constituted (without need of a fulfilling or illustrative intuition) an act of meaning which finds support in the verbal presentation's intuitive content, but which differs in essence from the intuitive intention directed upon the word itself. With this act, the new acts or act-complexes that we call 'fulfilling' acts or act-complexes are often peculiarly blended, acts whose object coincides with the object meant in the meaning, or named through this meaning.

In our next chapter we shall have to conduct additional researches into the question as to whether the 'meaning-intention', which on our view characteristically marks off an expression from empty 'sound of words' consists in the mere association of mental imagery of the intended object with the sounded words, or at least necessarily involves such an act of fancy, or whether, on the other hand, mental imagery lies outside of the essence of an expression, and rather performs a fulfilling role, even if only of a partial, indirect or provisional character. In order not to blur the main outlines of our thought, we shall not here enter more deeply

into phenomenological questions. In this whole investigation, we need only do as much phenomenology as is required to establish essential, primary distinctions.

The provisional description so far given will have shown how complex is the correct description of a phenomenological situation. Such complexity appears inevitable once we clearly see that all objects and relations among objects only are what they are for us, through acts of thought essentially different from them, in which they become present to us, in which they stand before us as unitary items that we *mean.* Where not the phenomenological, but the naïvely objective interest dominates, where we live in intentional acts without reflecting upon them, all talk of course becomes plain sailing and clear and devoid of circumlocution. One then, in our case, simply speaks of 'expression' and of 'what is expressed', of name and thing named, of the steering of attention from one to the other etc. But where the phenomenological interest dominates, we endure the hardship of having to describe phenomenological relationships which we may have experienced on countless occasions, but of which we were not normally conscious as objects, and we have also to do our describing with expressions framed to deal with objects whose appearance lies in the sphere of our normal interests.

§11 The ideal distinctions between (1) expression and meaning as ideal unities

We have so far considered 'the well-understood expression' as a concrete experience. Instead of considering its two types of factor, the phenomenal expression and the sense-conferring or sense-fulfilling experience, we wish to consider what is, in a certain fashion, given 'in' these: the expression itself, its sense and its objective correlate. We turn therefore from the real relation of acts to the ideal relation of their objects or contents. A subjective treatment yields to one that is objective. The ideality of the relationship between expression and meaning is at once plain in regard to both its sides, inasmuch as, when we ask for the meaning of an expression, e.g. 'quadratic remainder', we are naturally not referring to the sound-pattern uttered here and now, the vanishing noise that can never recur identically: we mean the expression *in specie.* 'Quadratic remainder' is the same expression by whomsoever uttered. The same holds of talk about the expression's meaning, which naturally does not refer to some meaning-conferring experience.

Every example shows that an essential distinction must here be drawn.

If I sincerely say—we shall always presume sincerity— 'The three perpendiculars of a triangle intersect in a point', this is of course based on the fact that I judge so. If someone hears me and understands my assertion, he likewise knows this fact; he 'apperceives' me as someone who judges thus. But is the judging here *intimated* the meaning of my assertion, is it what my assertion asserts, and in that sense expresses? Plainly not. It would hardly occur to anyone, if asked as to the sense or meaning of my assertion, to revert to my judgement as an inner experience. Everyone would rather reply by saying: What this assertion asserts is *the same* whoever may assert it, and on whatever occasion or in whatever circumstances he may assert it, and what it asserts is precisely this, *that the three perpendiculars of a triangle intersect in a point,* no more and no less. One therefore repeats what is in essence 'the same' assertion, and one repeats it because it is the one, uniquely adequate way of expressing the same thing, i.e. its meaning. In this selfsame meaning, of whose identity we are conscious whenever we repeat the statement, nothing at all about judging or about one who judges is discoverable. We thought we were sure that a state of affairs held or obtained objectively, and what, we were sure of we expressed by way of a declarative sentence. The state of affairs is what it is whether we assert that it obtains or not. It is intrinsically an item, a unity, which is capable of so obtaining or holding. But such an obtaining is what appeared before us, and we set it forth as it appeared before us: we said 'So the matter is'. Naturally we could not have done this, we could not have made the assertion, if the matter had not so appeared before us, if, in other words, we had not so judged. This forms part of an assertion as a psychological fact, it is involved in its intimation. But only in such intimation; for while what is intimated consists in inner experiences, what we assert in the judgement involves nothing subjective. My act of judging is a transient experience: it arises and passes away. But what my assertion asserts, the content *that the three perpendiculars of a triangle intersect in a point,* neither arises nor passes away. It is an identity in the strict sense, one and the same geometrical truth.

It is the same in the case of all assertions, even if what they assert is false and absurd. Even in such cases we distinguish their ideal content from the transient acts or affirming and asserting it: it is the meaning of the assertion, a unity in plurality. We continue to recognize its identity of intention in evident acts of reflection: we do not arbitrarily attribute it to our assertions, but discover it in them.

If 'possibility' or 'truth' is lacking, an assertion's intention can only be carried out symbolically: it cannot derive any 'fulness' from intuition or from the categorial functions performed on the latter, in which 'fulness' its value for knowledge consists. It then lacks, as one says, a 'true', a 'genuine' meaning. Later we shall look more closely into this distinction between intending and fulfilling meaning. To characterize the various acts in which the relevant ideal unities are constituted, and to throw light on the essence of their actual 'coincidence' in knowledge, will call for difficult, comprehensive studies. It is plain, however, that each assertion, whether representing an exercise of knowledge or not—whether or not, i.e., it fulfils or can fulfil its intention in corresponding intuitions, and the formative acts involved in these—involves a thought, in which thought, as its unified specific character, its meaning is constituted.

It is this ideal unity men have in mind when they say that 'the' judgement is the meaning of 'the' declarative sentence. Only the fundamental ambiguity of the word 'judgement' at once tends to confuse the evidently grasped ideal unity with the real act of judging, to confuse what the assertion intimates with what it asserts.

What we have here said of complete assertions readily applies also to actual or possible parts of assertions. If I judge *If the sum of the angles in a triangle does not equal two right angles, the axiom of parallels does not hold,* the hypothetical antecedent is no assertion, for I do not say that such an inequation holds. None the less it says something, and what it says is once more quite different from what it intimates. What it says is not my mental act of hypothetical presumption, though I must of course have performed this in order to speak sincerely as I do. But it is rather the case that, when this subjective act is intimated, something objective and ideal is brought to expression: the hypothesis whose conceptual content can appear as the same intentional unity in many possible thought-experiences, and which evidently stands before us in its unity and identity in the objectively-ideal treatment characteristic of all thinking.

The same holds of the other parts of our statements, even of such as do not have the form of propositions.

§12 Continuation: the objective correlate of an expression

Talk of *what an expression expresses* has, in the discussion so far, several essentially different meanings. It relates, *on the one hand,* to intimation in general, and especially in that connection to sense-giving acts, at times also to sense-fulfilling acts (if these are present at all). In an assertion, e.g., we express our judgement (we intimate it), but we also express percepts and other sense-fulfilling acts which illustrate our assertion's meaning. *On the other hand,* such talk relates to the 'contents' of such acts, and primarily to the meanings, which are often enough said to be 'expressed'.

It is doubtful whether the examples analysed, in our last section, would suffice even to lend provisional intelligibility to the notion of meaning, if one could not forthwith introduce a new sense of 'expression' for purposes of comparison. The terms 'meaning', 'content', 'state of affairs' and all similar terms harbour such powerful equivocations that our intention, even if expressed most carefully, still can promote misunderstanding. The third sense of 'being expressed', which we must now discuss, concerns the *objective correlate* meant by a meaning and expressed by its means.

Each expression not merely says something, but says it *of* something: it not only has a meaning, but refers to certain *objects*. This relation sometimes holds in the plural for one and the same expression. But the object never coincides with the meaning. Both, of course, only pertain to an expression in virtue of the mental acts which give it sense. And, if we distinguish between 'content' and object in respect of such 'presentations', one's distinction means the same as the distinction between what is meant or said, on the one hand, and what is spoken of, by means of the expression, on the other.

The necessity of distinguishing between meaning (content) and object becomes clear when a comparison of examples shows us that several expressions may have the same meaning but different objects, and again that they may have different meaning but the same object. There is of course also the possibility of their differing in both respects and agreeing in both. The last occurs in the cases of synonymous expression, e.g. the corresponding expressions in different languages which mean and name the same thing ('London', 'Londres'; 'zwei', 'deux', 'duo' etc.).

Names offer the plainest examples of the separation of meaning from the relation to objects, this relation being in their case usually spoken of as 'naming'. Two names can differ in meaning but can name the same object, e.g. 'the victor at Jena'—'the vanquished at Waterloo'; 'the equilateral triangle'—'the equiangular triangle'. The meaning expressed in our pairs of names is plainly different, though the same object is meant in each case. The same applies to names whose indefiniteness gives them an 'extension'. The expressions 'an equilateral triangle' and 'an equiangular triangle' have the same objective reference, the same range of possible application.

It can happen, conversely, that two expressions have the same meaning but a different objective reference. The expression 'a horse' has the same meaning in whatever context it occurs. But if on one occasion we say 'Bucephalus is a horse', and on another 'That cart-horse is a horse', there has been a plain change in our sense-giving presentation in passing from the one statement to the other. The expression 'a horse' employs the same meaning to present Bucephalus on one occasion and the cart-horse on the other. It is thus with all general names, i.e. names with an 'extension'. 'One' is a name whose meaning never differs, but one should not, for that reason, identify the various 'ones' which occur in a sum: they all mean the same, but they differ in objective reference.

The case of proper names is different, whether they name individual or general objects. A word like 'Socrates' can only name different things by meaning different things, i.e. by becoming *equivocal*. Wherever the word has *one* meaning, it also names *one* object. The same holds of expressions like 'the number two', 'redness' etc. We therefore distinguish equivocal names that have *many meanings* from general or class-names that have *many values*.

The same holds of other types of expression, though in their case talk of objective reference involves certain difficulties in virtue of its manifoldness. If we consider, e.g., statements of the form '*S* is *P*' we generally regard the subject of the statement as the object about which the statement is made. Another view is, however, possible, which treats the *whole* state of affairs which corresponds to the statement as an analogue of the object a name names, and distinguishes this from the object's meaning. If this is done one can quote as examples pairs of sentences such as '*a* is bigger than *b*'—'*b* is smaller than *a*', which plainly say different things. They are not merely grammatically but also 'cogitatively' different, i.e. different in meaning-content. But they express the same state of affairs: the same 'matter' is predicatively apprehended and asserted in two different ways. Whether we define talk of the 'object' of a statement in one sense or the other—each has its own claims—statements are in either case possible which differ in meaning while referring to the same object.

§13 *Connection between meaning and objective reference*

Our examples entitle us to regard the distinction between an expression's meaning and its power to direct itself as a name to this or that objective correlate—and of course the distinction between meaning and object itself—as well-established. It is clear for the rest that the sides to be distinguished in each expression are closely connected: an expression only refers to an objective correlate *because* it means something, it can be rightly said to signify or name the object *through* its meaning. An act of meaning is the determinate manner in which we refer to our object of the moment, though this mode of significant reference and the meaning itself can change while the objective reference remains fixed.

A more profound phenomenological clarification of this relation can be reached only by research into the way expressions and their meaning-intentions function in knowledge. This would show that talk about *two distinguishable sides* to each expression, should not be taken seriously, that the essence of an expression lies solely in its meaning. But the same intuition (as we shall show later) can offer fulfillment of different expressions: it can be categorically apprehended in varying ways and synthetically linked with other intuitions. Expressions and their meaning-intentions do not take their measure, in contexts of thought and knowledge, from mere intuition—I mean phenomena of external or internal sensibility—but from the varying intellectual forms through which intuited objects first become intelligibly determined, mutually related objects. And so expressions, even when they function outside of knowledge, must, as symbolic intentions, point to categorically *formed* unities. Different meanings may therefore pertain to the same intuitions regarded in differing categorical fashion, and may therefore also pertain to the same object. But where a whole range of objects corresponds to a single meaning, this meaning's own essence must be *indeterminate:* it must permit a sphere of possible fulfilment.

These indications may suffice for the moment. They must guard in advance against the error of seriously thinking that sense-giving acts have two distinct sides, one which gives them their meaning, while the other gives them their determinate direction to objects.[5]

§14 Content as object, content as fulfilling sense and content as sense or meaning simpliciter

Relational talk of 'intimation', 'meaning' and 'object' belongs *essentially* to every expression. Every expression intimates something, means something and names or otherwise designates something. In each case, talk of 'expression' is equivocal. As said above, relation to an actually given objective correlate, which fulfils the meaning-intention, is *not* essential to an expression. If this last important case is also taken into consideration, we note that there are two things that can be said to be expressed in the realized relation to the object. We have, on the one hand, the *object itself,* and the object as meant in this or that manner. On the other hand, and more properly, we have the object's ideal correlate in the acts of meaning-fulfilment which constitute it, *the fulfilling sense.* Wherever the meaning-intention is fulfilled in a corresponding intuition, i.e. wherever the expression actually serves to

name a given object, there the object is constituted as one 'given' in certain acts, and, to the extent that our expression really measures up to the intuitive data, as given *in the same manner* in which the expression *means* it. In this unity of coincidence between meaning and meaning-fulfilment, the essence of the meaning-fulfilment corresponds with, and is correlative, to the essence of meaning: the essence of the meaning-fulfilment is the *fulfilling* sense of the expression, or, as one may also call it, the sense expressed by the expression. One says, e.g., that a statement of perception expresses a perception, but also that it expresses the *content* of a perception. We distinguish, in a perceptual statement, as in every statement, between *content* and *object;* by the 'content' we understand the self-identical meaning that the hearer can grasp even if he is not a percipient. We must draw the same distinction in the case of fulfilling acts, in the case, therefore, of perceptions and their categorial formations. Through these acts the objective correlate of our act of meaning stands before us intuitively as the very object we mean. We must, I say, distinguish again, in such fulfilling acts, between their *content,* the meaning-element, as it were, in the categorially formed percept, and the *object* perceived. In the unity of fulfilment, the fulfilling content coincides with the intending content, so that, in our experience of this unity of coincidence, the object, at once intended and 'given', stands before us, not as two objects, but as *one* alone. The ideal conception of the act which *confers* meaning yields us the Idea of the *intending meaning,* just as the ideal conception of the correlative essence of the act which *fulfils* meaning, yields the *fulfilling meaning,* likewise *qua* Idea. This is the *identical content* which, in perception, pertains to the totality of possible acts of perception which intended the same object perceptually, and intend it actually as the same object. This content is therefore the ideal correlate of this *single* object, which may, for the rest, be completely imaginary.

The manifold ambiguities in talk about what an expression expresses, or about an *expressed content,* may therefore be so ordered that one distinguishes between a content in a *subjective,* and a content in an *objective* sense. In the latter respect we must distinguish between:

> The content as intending sense, or as sense, *meaning simpliciter,* the content as fulfilling sense, and the content as object.

§15 The equivocations in talk of meaning and meaninglessness connected with these distinctions

The application of the terms 'meaning' and 'sense', not merely to the content of the meaning-intention inseparable

[5] [Husserl] Cf. with this Twardowski's assumption of a 'presentative activity moving in two directions' in his work *Zur Lehre vom Inhalt und Gegenstand der Vorstellungen* (Vienna, 1894), p. 14. [Kasimir Twardowski (1866–1938), Russian-German psychologist and philosopher.]

from the expression, but also to the content of the meaning-fulfilment, engenders a most unwelcome ambiguity. It is clear from previous indications, where we dealt with the fact of fulfilment, that the acts on either side, in which intending and fulfilling sense are constituted, need not be the same. What tempts us to transfer the same terms from intention to fulfilment, is the peculiar way in which the unity of fulfilment is a unity of identification or coincidence: the equivocation which one hoped a modifying adjective might render innocuous, can scarcely be avoided. We shall continue, of course, to understand by 'meaning' *simpliciter* the meaning which, as the identical element in our intention, is essential to the expressions as such.

'Meaning' is further used by us as synonymous with 'sense'. It is agreeable to have parallel, interchangeable terms in the case of this concept, particularly since the sense of the term 'meaning' is itself to be investigated. A further consideration is our ingrained tendency to use the two words as synonymous, a circumstance which makes it seem rather a dubious step if their meanings are differentiated, and if (as G. Frege has proposed)[6] we use one for meaning in our sense, and the other for the objects expressed. To this we may add that both terms are exposed to the same equivocations, which we distinguished above in connection with the term 'expression', and to many more besides, and that this is so both in scientific and in ordinary speech. Logical clarity is much impaired by the manner in which the sense or meaning of an expression is, often in the same thought-sequence, now looked upon as the acts intimated by it, now as its ideal sense, now as the objective correlate that it expresses. Since fixed terminological landmarks are lacking, the concepts themselves run confusedly into one another.

Fundamental confusions arise from these facts. General and equivocal names are, e.g., repeatedly lumped together, since both can be predicatively referred to a plurality of objects. Lacking fixed concepts, men did not know how to distinguish the *multiple senses* of the equivocal names from the *multiple values* of the general ones. Here we also meet with the frequent unclearness as to the true essence of the difference between collective and general names. For, where collective meanings are fulfilled, we intuit a plurality of items: fulfilment is articulated into a plurality of individual intuitions, and so, if intention and fulfilment are not kept apart, it may well seem that the collective expression in question has many meanings.

It is more important for us to set forth precisely the most detrimental equivocations in talk which concerns

meaning and *sense,* on the one hand, or *meaningless* or *senseless* expressions, on the other. If we separate the blurred concepts, the following list emerges:

1. It is part of the notion of an expression to have a meaning: this precisely differentiates an expression from the other signs mentioned above. A meaningless expression is, therefore, properly speaking, no expression at all: it is at best something that claims or seems to be an expression, though, more closely considered, it is not one at all. Here belong articulate, word-like sound-patterns such as 'Abracadabra', and also combinations of genuine expressions to which no unified meaning corresponds, though their outer form seems to pretend to such a meaning, e.g. 'Green is or'.

2. In meaning, a relation to an object is constituted. To use an expression significantly, and to refer expressively to an object (to form a presentation of it), are one and the same. It makes no difference whether the object exists or is fictitious or even impossible. But if one gives a very rigorous interpretation to the proposition that an expression, in so far as it has meaning, relates to an object, i.e. in a sense which involves the existence of the object, then an expression has *meaning* when an object corresponding to it exists, and it is *meaningless* when no such object exists. Meanings are often spoken of as signifying the *objects* meant, a usage that can scarcely be maintained consistently, as it springs from a confusion with the genuine concept of meaning.

3. If the meaning is identified with the objective correlate of an expression, a name like 'golden mountain' is meaningless. Here men generally distinguish objectlessness from meaninglessness. As opposed to this, men tend to use the word 'senseless' of expressions infected with contradiction and obvious incompatibilities, e.g. 'round square', or to deny them meaning by some equivalent phrase. Sigwart,[7] e.g., says that a self-contradictory formula such as 'square circle' expresses no concept we can think, but that it uses words to set up an insoluble task. The existential proposition 'There is no square circle', on his view denies the possibility of connecting a concept with these words, and by a concept he expressly wants us to understand (if we get him right) the 'general meaning of a word', which is just what we mean by it. Erdmann[8] has similar opinions in regard to the instance 'A square circle is frivolous'. We should, in consistency, have to apply the word 'senseless', not merely to expressions immediately

[6][Husserl] G. Frege, *Über Sinn und Bedeutung, Zeitschr. f. Philos. u. philos. Kritik,* vol. 100, p. 25. (See Frege, above, page 734).

[7][Husserl] *Die Impersonalien,* p. 62. [Christoph Sigwart (1830–1904), German philosopher.]
[8][Husserl] *Logik,* I, p. 235. [Benno Erdmann (1851–1921), German philosopher.]

absurd, but to those whose absurdity is mediate, i.e. the countless expressions shown by mathematicians, in lengthy indirect demonstrations, to be objectless *a priori*. We should likewise have to deny that concepts like *regular dec-ahedron* etc., are concepts at all.

Marty raises the following objection to the thinkers just mentioned. 'If the words are senseless, how could we understand the question as to whether such things exist, so as to answer it negatively? Even to reject such an existence, we must, it is plain, somehow form a presentation of such contradictory material'[9] . . . 'If such absurdities are called senseless, this can only mean that they have no rational sense'.[10] These objections are clinching, in so far as these thinkers' statements suggest that they are confusing the true meaninglessness mentioned above under 1, with another quite different meaninglessness, i.e. *the a priori impossibility of a fulfilling sense*. An expression has meaning in this sense if a possible fulfilment, i.e. the possibility of a unified intuitive illustration, corresponds to its intention. This possibility is plainly meant ideally. It concerns no contingent acts of expression or fulfilment, but their ideal contents: meaning as an ideal unity, here to be called 'intending meaning', on the one hand, and fulfilling meaning, standing to it in a certain relation of precise adequacy, on the other. We apprehend this ideal relation by ideative abstraction based on an act of unified fulfilment. In the contrary case we apprehend the real impossibility of meaning-fulfilment through an experience of the incompatibility of the partial meanings in the intended unity of fulfilment.

The phenomenological clarification of these relationships calls for long, difficult analyses, as will appear in a later investigation.

4. If we ask what an expression means, we naturally recur to cases where it actually contributes to knowledge, or, what is the same, where its meaning-intention is intuitively fulfilled. In this manner the 'notional presentation', i.e. the meaning-intention, gains clarity, it shows itself up as 'correct', as 'really' capable of execution. The draft it makes on intuition is as it were cashed. Since in the unity of fulfilment the act of intention coincides with the fulfilling act, and fuses with it in the most intimate fashion—if indeed there is any difference left over here at all—it readily seems as if the expression first got its meaning here, as if it drew meaning

from the act of fulfilment. The tendency therefore arises to treat the *fulfilling intuitions*—categorially formative acts are here in general passed over—as meanings. But fulfilment is often imperfect—we shall have to devote closer study to all such possibilities—and expressions often go with remotely relevant, only partially illustrative intuitions, if with any at all. Since the phenomenological differences of these cases have not been closely considered, men have come to locate the significance of expressions, even of such as could make no claim to adequate fulfilment, in accompaniments of intuitive imagery. This naturally led to a total denial of meaning to absurd expressions.

The new concept of meaning therefore originates in a confusion of meaning with fulfilling intuition. On this conception, an expression has meaning if and only if its intention—we should say its 'meaning-intention'—is in fact fulfilled, even if only in a partial, distant and improper manner. The understanding of the expression must be given life through certain 'ideas of meaning' (it is commonly said), i.e. by certain *illustrative* images.

The final refutation of highly attractive, opposed notions is an important task which requires lengthy discussions. These we shall postpone to the next chapter, and here go on enumerating different concepts of meaning.

§16 Continuation: meaning and connotation

Another equivocation in our talk about meaninglessness was introduced by John Stuart Mill, and again rests on a new, fifth concept of meaning. He locates the essence of the meaning of names in their connotation, and therefore treats non-connotative names as meaningless. (Sometimes he says, more carefully but less clearly, that they are meaningless in the 'proper' or 'strict' sense.) It is well-known that by 'connotative names' Mill understands such as designate a subject and imply an attribute, by 'non-connotative names' such as designate a subject without (as it is here more clearly put) indicating an attribute as attaching to it.[11] Proper names are non-connotative and so too are names of attributes (e.g. 'whiteness'). Mill compares proper names to the distinctive chalk-marks which the robber, in the well-known tale from the *Arabian Nights*, made on the house.[12] And he goes on to say: 'When we impose a proper name, we perform an operation in some degree analogous

[9] [Husserl] A. Marty, 'Über subjektlose Sätze und das Verhältnis der Grammatik zur Logik und Psychologie', Art. VI, *Vierteljahrschrift f. wiss. Phil.* xix, 80 *f.* [Anton Marty (1847–1914), German philologist and philosopher.]
[10] [Husserl] Ibid. p. 81 note. Cf. Art. V, Vol. xviii, p. 464.

[11] [Husserl] *Logic*, Book I, ch. 2, § 5. [John Stuart Mill (1806–1873), English philosopher, logician and writer. Husserl refers to Mill's *A System of Logic* (1843, 1872).]
[12] [Husserl] *System of Logic*, Book I, ch. 2, § 5.

to what the robber intended in chalking the house. We put a mark, not indeed upon the object itself, but upon the idea of the object. A proper name is but an unmeaning mark which we connect in our minds with the idea of the object, in order that whenever the mark meets our eyes or occurs to our thoughts, we may think of that individual object . . . When we predicate of anything its proper name; when we say, pointing to a man, this is Brown or Smith, or pointing to a city, this is York, we do not, merely by so doing, convey to the reader any information about them, except that those are their names . . . It is otherwise when objects are spoken of by connotative names. When we say, "The town is built of marble", we give the hearer what may be entirely new information, and this merely by the signification of the many-worded connotative name "built of marble". Such names . . . are not mere marks, but more, that is to say significant marks; and the connotation is what constitutes their significance.'[13]

If we set our own analyses alongside of these utterances of Mill's, we cannot help seeing that he confuses distinctions that should in principle be kept apart. Above all, he blurs the distinction between indicating and expressing. The chalk-mark of the robber is a mere indication, while a proper name is an expression.

Like every expression a proper name functions as an indication, i.e. in its intimating role. Here there is a real analogy with the robber's chalk-mark. If the robber sees the chalk-mark he knows: This is the house I must rob. If I hear a proper name uttered, the corresponding presentation is aroused in me, and I know: This is the presentation the speaker is framing in his mind, and that he likewise wishes to arouse in mine. A name, however, has an additional expressiveness to which the intimating function is merely auxiliary. A man's presentation is not of primary importance: we are not concerned to direct interest to it but to the *object* it presents, to what it *refers to* and therefore *names,* and to set this before us as such. In a statement it makes its first appearance as the object about which something is asserted, in a wish-sentence as the object about which something is wished etc. Only in order to perform this task will a proper name, like any other name, become an element in complex, unified expressions, in statements, wish-sentences and the like. But in its relation to its *object* the proper name is not an index. This is at once clear when we reflect on the fact that it is of the essence of an index to point to a fact, an existence, whereas the object named need not be taken to exist at all. When Mill extending his

analogy, holds a proper name to be associated with the idea of the person it names in essentially the same manner as the chalk-mark is associated with the house, but *at once* adds that the point of the association is that we may *think* of the individual object whenever the sign meets our eye or enters our thought, his addition cracks the analogy wide asunder.

Mill correctly stresses the difference between names that are a means towards 'knowing' an object and names which are not, but neither this distinction, nor the equivalent distinction between connotative and non-connotative names, has anything to do with the distinction between the meaningful and the meaningless. The first-mentioned pair of differences are in fact not merely logically equivalent but identical. The difference is simply one of attributive and non-attributive names: to mediate the 'knowledge' of a thing and to mediate its attributes mean exactly the same. It is, no doubt, important, whether a name means a thing directly or only by way of the attributes that pertain to it. But this is a difference within the unitary genus Expression, just as the very important, parallel difference between nominal meanings (or logical 'presentations') which are attributive and those which are not attributive, is a difference within the unitary genus Meaning.

Mill *after a fashion* 'feels' the difference in question by being at times obliged to speak of a meaning of proper names in a sense contrasting with the 'strict' and 'proper' sense ascribed to the meaning of connotative names. He would have done better had he introduced a wholly new sense of meaning (though not, we may say, one to be recommended). The way, at least, in which the distinguished logician brings in his valuable distinction between connotative and non-connotative names has done much to confuse the quite different distinctions we have here been discussing.

One must note, further, that Mill's distinction between what a name *denotes* and what it *connotes* must not be confused with the merely cognate distinction between what a name *names* and what it *means*. This confusion is greatly aided by Mill's exposition.

How important all these distinctions are, and how little it helps to treat them with superficial contempt as being 'merely grammatical', will be shown in further investigations. These will make plain, we hope, that if one blurs the straightforward distinctions we have proposed, we cannot hope for a trustworthy elaboration of the concepts of Presentation and Judgement, in the sense relevant to logic.

---

[13] [Husserl] Op. cit., Book I, ch. 2, § 5.

Ferdinand de Saussure

1857–1913

Saussure is usually regarded as the founder of structuralist linguistics. His posthumously published *Course in General Linguistics* (1913) is a reconstruction by students of his lectures at the University of Geneva in the years 1906–1911. Saussure did not leave even notes for these lectures, so what we have are the students' notes. This has caused some criticism by linguists, at least one of them declaring the *Course* to be written by the Pseudo-Saussure.

Though not concerned with literary texts or with theory, the *Course* has been enormously influential and stands as one of the most important documents for the recent period in which speculation about language has been very important for criticism and theory. Saussure's treatment of the linguistic sign as composed of "signifier" and "signified" and his characterization of language as a system of differences (each word being identified by its difference from the other words in the system) flow through the work of structural and poststructural theorists. His emphasis on the arbitrary nature of the sign, though the idea is as old as Plato's *Cratylus* (above, page 41), is also important, for he develops it systematically beyond his predecessors' thoughts, including a future science, "semiology," not to be confused with "semiotics" proposed by C.S. Peirce (above, page 652).

Saussure's structuralism is the result of his effort to make a science of linguistics. Just as no science wants actual objects in or animals walking through its system, so did Saussure want no objects in his. As a result, the objects that the words are said to denote are (with some inconsistency criticized by others) banished, and the linguistic sign is "diacritical," a combination of signifier and signified. The latter is the concept, the former the so-called sound-image. The relation of sign to object (its denotation or reference) is "arbitrary"; so is the relation of signifier to signified. With the object banished, language can be considered a system with its own internally generated set of rules.

Saussure also drew a distinction between diachronic (historical) and synchronic (structural) linguistics; opting for the latter, he reduced the role of the traditional notions of influence and change in linguistic study. In a Saussurean structure, each word is a unit regarded entirely in terms of its difference from other words in the system. Thus there is a sense in which what we might call the spaces between words take precedence over the words as such. The system can be regarded as one composed of negative relations rather than positive substances.

Of particular interest to literary critics is also Saussure's distinction between *langue* and *parole*. *Langue* is the system of a language as a whole; *parole* is a particular usage within it. In structuralist literary criticism, a literary text is, by analogy, a *parole*.

The *Course*'s influence has been extended into anthropology (principally by Claude Lévi-Strauss [below, page 1119]) and into philosophy by Jacques Derrida (below, page 1203), who puts it, however, under critical scrutiny, particularly with respect to Saussure's emphasis on speech rather than writing. Also, in deconstruction Saussure's closed system is seen as actually infinitely open, since there is nothing to call a halt to a chain of differential relations. Thus analysis of Saussure's system has been one of the forces leading to poststructuralism.

Saussure published little in his lifetime, mainly essays on fairly specialized linguistic subjects. The *Course in General Linguistics* (1913) appeared in English translation in 1959. Saussure's writings in French are found in *Recueil de publications scientifique de F. de Saussure* (1922). Jean Starobinski has presented Saussure's strange *Anagrammes* in *Les Mots sous les mots* (1971), translated as *Words upon Words* (1979). See Rulon S. Wells, "De Saussure's System of Linguistics," *Word* 3 (1947); the introduction by Manuel Mourette-Lema to *A Geneva Reader in Linguistics,* R. Goedel, ed. (1969); Jonathan Culler, *Ferdinand de Saussure* (1976); Roy Harris, *Reading Saussure* (1986) and his *Language, Saussure, and Wittgenstein* (1988); Robert M. Strozier, *Saussure, Derrida, and the Metaphysics of Subjectivity* (1988); Francoise Gadet, *Saussure and Contemporary Culture* (tr. 1989); David Holdcroft, *Saussure: Signs, System, and Arbitrariness* (1991).

from

Course in General Linguistics

Part One

General Principles

Chapter I

Nature of the Linguistic Sign

1. *Sign, Signified, Signifier*

Some people regard language, when reduced to its elements, as a naming-process only—a list of words, each corresponding to the thing that it names. For example:

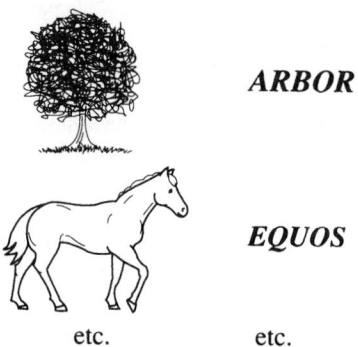

ARBOR

EQUOS

etc.   etc.

_____

Course de linguistque generale was published in France in 1913. The selection here is from *Course in General Linguistics* translated by Wade Baskins (New York: The Philosophical Library, 1959).

This conception is open to criticism at several points. It assumes that ready-made ideas exist before words; it does not tell us whether a name is vocal or psychological in nature (*arbor,* for instance, can be considered from either viewpoint); finally, it lets us assume that the linking of a name and a thing is a very simple operation—an assumption that is anything but true. But this rather naive approach can bring us near the truth by showing us that the linguistic unit is a double entity, one formed by the associating of two terms.

We have seen in considering the speaking-circuit that both terms involved in the linguistic sign are psychological and are united in the brain by an associative bond. This point must be emphasized.

The linguistic sign unites, not a thing and a name, but a concept and a sound-image. The latter is not the material sound, a purely physical thing, but the psychological imprint of the sound, the impression that it makes on our senses. The sound-image is sensory, and if I happen to call it "material," it is only in that sense, and by way of opposing it to the other term of the association, the concept, which is generally more abstract.

The psychological character of our sound-images becomes apparent when we observe our own speech. Without moving our lips or tongue, we can talk to ourselves or recite mentally a selection of verse. Because we regard the words of our language as sound-images, we must avoid speaking of the "phonemes" that make up the words. This term, which suggests vocal activity, is applicable to the spoken word only, to the realization of the inner image in discourse. We can avoid that misunderstanding by speaking of the *sounds* and *syllables* of a word provided we remember that the names refer to the sound-image.

The linguistic sign is then a two-sided psychological entity that can be represented by the drawing:

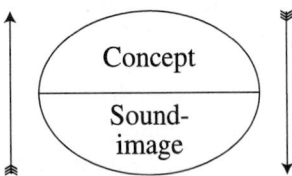

The two elements are intimately united, and each recalls the other. Whether we try to find the meaning of the Latin word *arbor* or the word that Latin uses to designate the concept "tree," it is clear that only the associations sanctioned by that language appear to us to conform to reality, and we disregard whatever others might be imagined.

Our definition of the linguistic sign poses an important question of terminology. I call the combination of a concept and a sound-image a *sign,* but in current usage the term generally designates only a sound-image, a word, for example (*arbor,* etc.). One tends to forget that *arbor* is called a sign only because it carries the concept "tree," with the result that the idea of the sensory part implies the idea of the whole.

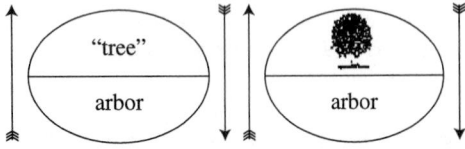

Ambiguity would disappear if the three notions involved here were designated by three names, each suggesting and opposing the others. I propose to retain the word *sign* [*signe*] to designate the whole and to replace *concept* and *sound-image* respectively by *signified* [*signifié*] and *signifier* [*signifiant*]; the last two terms have the advantage of indicating the opposition that separates them from each other and from the whole of which they are parts. As regards *sign,* if I am satisfied with it, this is simply because I do not know of any word to replace it, the ordinary language suggesting no other.

The linguistic sign, as defined, has two primordial characteristics. In enunciating them I am also positing the basic principles of any study of this type.

2. *Principle I: The Arbitrary Nature of the Sign*

The bond between the signifier and the signified is arbitrary. Since I mean by sign the whole that results from the associating of the signifier with the signified, I can simply say: *the linguistic sign is arbitrary.*

The idea of "sister" is not linked by any inner relationship to the succession of sounds *s-ö-r* which serves as its signifier in French; that it could be represented equally by just any other sequence is proved by differences among languages and by the very existence of different languages: the signified "ox" has as its signifier *b-ö-f* on one side of the border and *o-k-s (Ochs)* on the other.

No one disputes the principle of the arbitrary nature of the sign, but it is often easier to discover a truth than to assign to it its proper place. Principle I dominates all the linguistics of language; its consequences are numberless. It is true that not all of them are equally obvious at first glance; only after many detours does one discover them, and with them the primordial importance of the principle.

One remark in passing: when semiology becomes organized as a science, the question will arise whether or not it properly includes modes of expression based on completely natural signs, such as pantomime. Supposing that the new science welcomes them, its main concern will still be the whole group of systems grounded on the arbitrariness of the sign. In fact, every means of expression used in society is based, in principle, on collective behavior or—what amounts to the same thing—on convention. Polite formulas, for instance, though often imbued with a certain natural expressiveness (as in the case of a Chinese who greets his emperor by bowing down to the ground nine times), are nonetheless fixed by rule; it is this rule and not the intrinsic value of the gestures that obliges one to use them. Signs that are wholly arbitrary realize better than the others the ideal of the semiological process; that is why language, the most complex and universal of all systems of expression, is also the most characteristic; in this sense linguistics can become the master-pattern for all branches of semiology although language is only one particular semiological system.

The word *symbol* has been used to designate the linguistic sign, or more specifically, what is here called the signifier. Principle I in particular weighs against the use of this term. One characteristic of the symbol is that it is never wholly arbitrary; it is not empty, for there is the rudiment of a natural bond between the signifier and the signified. The symbol of justice, a pair of scales, could not be replaced by just any other symbol, such as a chariot.

The word *arbitrary* also calls for comment. The term should not imply that the choice of the signifier is left entirely to the speaker (we shall see below that the individual does not have the power to change a sign in any way once it has become established in the linguistic community); I mean that it is unmotivated, i.e. arbitrary in that it actually has no natural connection with the signified.

In concluding let us consider two objections that might be raised to the establishment of Principle I:

1) *Onomatopoeia* might be used to prove that the choice of the signifier is not always arbitrary. But onomatopoeic formations are never organic elements of a linguistic system. Besides, their number is much smaller than is generally supposed. Words like French *fouet* 'whip' or *glas* 'knell' may strike certain ears with suggestive sonority, but to see that they have not always had this property we need only examine their Latin forms (*fouet* is derived from *fāgus* 'beech-tree,' *glas* from *classicum* 'sound of a trumpet'). The quality of their present sounds, or rather the quality that is attributed to them, is a fortuitous result of phonetic evolution.

As for authentic onomatopoeic words (e.g. *glug-glug, tick-tock,* etc.), not only are they limited in number, but also they are chosen somewhat arbitrarily, for they are only approximate and more or less conventional imitations of certain sounds (cf. English *bow-bow* and French *ouaoua*). In addition, once these words have been introduced into the language, they are to a certain extent subjected to the same evolution—phonetic, morphological, etc.—that other words undergo (cf. *pigeon,* ultimately from Vulgar Latin *pīpiō,* derived in turn from an onomatopoeic formation): obvious proof that they lose something of their original character in order to assume that of the linguistic sign in general, which is unmotivated.

2) *Interjections,* closely related to onomatopoeia, can be attacked on the same grounds and come no closer to refuting our thesis. One is tempted to see in them spontaneous expressions of reality dictated, so to speak, by natural forces. But for most interjections we can show that there is no fixed bond between their signified and their signifier. We need only compare two languages on this point to see how much such expressions differ from one language to the next (e.g. the English equivalent of French *aïe!* is *ouch!*). We know, moreover, that many interjections were once words with specific meanings (cf. French *diable!* 'darn!' *mordieu!* 'golly!' from *mort Dieu* 'God's death.' etc.).

Onomatopoeic formations and interjections are of secondary importance, and their symbolic origin is in part open to dispute.

3. *Principle II: The Linear Nature of the Signifier*

The signifier, being auditory, is unfolded solely in time from which it gets the following characteristics; (a) it represents a span, and (b) the span is measurable in a single dimension; it is a line.

While Principle II is obvious, apparently linguists have always neglected to state it, doubtless because they found it too simple; nevertheless, it is fundamental, and its consequences are incalculable. Its importance equals that of Principle I: the whole mechanism of language depends upon it. In contrast to visual signifiers (nautical signals, etc.) which can offer simultaneous groupings in several dimensions, auditory signifiers have at their command only the dimension of time. Their elements are presented in succession; they form a chain. This feature becomes readily apparent when they are represented in writing and the spatial line of graphic marks is substituted for succession in time.

Sometimes the linear nature of the signifier is not obvious. When I accent a syllable, for instance, it seems that I am concentrating more than one significant element on the same point. But this is an illusion; the syllable and its accent constitute only one phonational act. There is no duality within the act but only different oppositions to what precedes and what follows.

Chapter IV

Linguistic Value

1. *Language as Organized Thought Coupled with Sound*

To prove that language is only a system of pure values, it is enough to consider the two elements involved in its functioning: ideas and sounds.

Psychologically our thought—apart from its expression in words—is only a shapeless and indistinct mass. Philosophers and linguists have always agreed in recognizing that without the help of signs we would be unable to make a clear-cut, consistent distinction between two ideas. Without language, thought is a vague, uncharted nebula.[1] There are no pre-existing ideas, and nothing is distinct before the appearance of language.

Against the floating realm of thought, would sounds by themselves yield predelimited entities? No more so than ideas. Phonic substance is neither more fixed nor more rigid than thought; it is not a mold into which thought must of necessity fit but a plastic substance divided in turn into distinct parts to furnish the signifiers needed by thought. The linguistic fact can therefore be pictured in its totality—i.e.

---

[1]The question of what comes first, thought or expression, has its own history and can be traced, for example, from Locke (above, page 281), through Benedetto Croce's *Aesthetic* (1900), to Cassirer's *Philosophy of Symbolic Forms* and his *An Essay on Man* (below, page 1018). But see also Peirce (above, page 652).

language—as a series of contiguous subdivisions marked off on both the indefinite plane of jumbled ideas *(A)* and the equally vague plane of sounds *(B)*. The following diagram gives a rough idea of it:

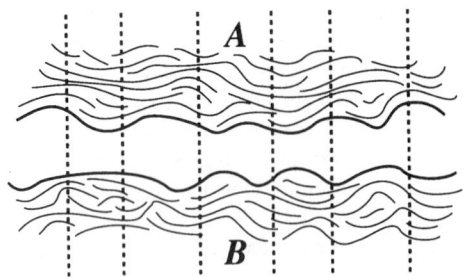

The characteristic role of language with respect to thought is not to create a material phonic means for expressing ideas but to serve as a link between thought and sound, under conditions that of necessity bring about the reciprocal delimitations of units. Thought, chaotic by nature, has to become ordered in the process of its decomposition. Neither are thoughts given material form nor are sounds transformed into mental entities; the somewhat mysterious fact is rather that "thought-sound" implies division, and that language works out its units while taking shape between two shapeless masses. Visualize the air in contact with a sheet of water; if the atmospheric pressure changes, the surface of the water will be broken up into a series of divisions, waves; the waves resemble the union or coupling of thought with phonic substance.

Language might be called the domain of articulations, using the word as it was defined earlier. Each linguistic term is a member, an *articulus* in which an idea is fixed in a sound and a sound becomes the sign of an idea.

Language can also be compared with a sheet of paper: thought is the front and the sound the back; one cannot cut the front without cutting the back at the same time; likewise in language, one can neither divide sound from thought nor thought from sound; the division could be accomplished only abstractedly, and the result would be either pure psychology or pure phonology.

Linguistics then works in the borderland where the elements of sound and thought combine; *their combination produces a form, not a substance.*

These views give a better understanding of what was said before about the arbitrariness of signs. Not only are the two domains that are linked by the linguistic fact shapeless and confused, but the choice of a given slice of sound to name a given idea is completely arbitrary. If this were not

true, the notion of value would be compromised, for it would include an externally imposed element. But actually values remain entirely relative, and that is why the bond between the sound and the idea is radically arbitrary.

The arbitrary nature of the sign explains in turn why the social fact alone can create a linguistic system. The community is necessary if values that owe their existence solely to usage and general acceptance are to be set up; by himself the individual is incapable of fixing a single value.

In addition, the idea of value, as defined, shows that to consider a term as simply the union of a certain sound with a certain concept is grossly misleading. To define it in this way would isolate the term from its system; it would mean assuming that one can start from the terms and construct the system by adding them together when, on the contrary, it is from the interdependent whole that one must start and through analysis obtain its elements.

To develop this thesis, we shall study value successively from the viewpoint of the signified or concept (Section 2), the signifier (Section 3), and the complete sign (Section 4).

Being unable to seize the concrete entities or units of language directly, we shall work with words. While the word does not conform exactly to the definition of the linguistic unit, it at least bears a rough resemblance to the unit and has the advantage of being concrete; consequently, we shall use words as specimens equivalent to real terms in a synchronic system, and the principles that we evolve with respect to words will be valid for entities in general.

2. *Linguistic Value from a Conceptual Viewpoint*

When we speak of the value of a word, we generally think first of its property of standing for an idea, and this is in fact one side of linguistic value. But if this is true, how does *value* differ from *signification?* Might the two words be synonyms? I think not, although it is easy to confuse them, since the confusion results not so much from their similarity as from the subtlety of the distinction that they mark.

From a conceptual viewpoint, value is doubtless one element in signification, and it is difficult to see how signification can be dependent upon value and still be distinct from it. But we must clear up the issue or risk reducing language to a simple naming-process.

Let us first take signification as it is generally understood and as it was pictured previously. As the arrows in the drawing show, it is only the counterpart of the sound-image. Everything that occurs concerns only the sound-image and the concept when we look upon the word as independent and self-contained.

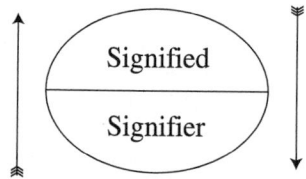

But here is the paradox: on the one hand the concept seems to be the counterpart of the sound-image, and on the other hand the sign itself is in turn the counterpart of the other signs of language.

Language is a system of interdependent terms in which the value of each term results solely from the simultaneous presence of the others, as in the diagram:

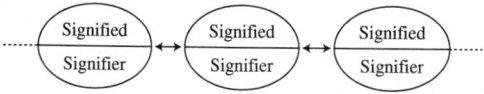

How, then, can value be confused with signification, i.e. the counterpart of the sound-image? It seems impossible to liken the relations represented here by horizontal arrows to those represented above by vertical arrows. Putting it another way—and again taking up the example of the sheet of paper that is cut in two—it is clear that the observable relation between the different pieces A, B, C, D, etc. is distinct from the relation between the front and back of the same piece as in A/A′, B/B′, etc.

To resolve the issue, let us observe from the outset that even outside language all values are apparently governed by the same paradoxical principle. They are always composed:

(1) of a *dissimilar* thing that can be *exchanged* for the thing of which the value is to be determined; and

(2) of *similar* things that can be *compared* with the thing of which the value is to be determined.

Both factors are necessary for the existence of a value. To determine what a five-franc piece is worth one must therefore know: (1) that it can be exchanged for a fixed quantity of a different thing, e.g. bread; and (2) that it can be compared with a similar value of the same system, e.g. a one-franc piece, or with coins of another system (a dollar, etc.). In the same way a word can be exchanged for something dissimilar, an idea; besides, it can be compared with something of the same nature, another word. Its value is therefore not fixed so long as one simply states that it can be "exchanged" for a given concept, i.e. that it has this or that signification: one must also compare it with similar values, with other words that stand in opposition to it. Its content is really fixed only by the concurrence of everything that ex-

ists outside it. Being part of a system, it is endowed not only with a signification but also and especially with a value, and this is something quite different.

A few examples will show clearly that this is true. Modern French *mouton* can have the same signification as English *sheep* but not the same value, and this for several reasons, particularly because in speaking of a piece of meat ready to be served on the table. English uses *mutton* and not *sheep*. The difference in value between *sheep* and *mouton* is due to the fact that *sheep* has beside it a second term while the French word does not.

Within the same language, all words used to express related ideas limit each other reciprocally; synonyms like French *redouter* 'dread,' *craindre* 'fear,' and *avoir peur* 'be afraid' have value only through their opposition: if *redouter* did not exist, all its content would go to its competitors. Conversely, some words are enriched through contact with others: e.g. the new element introduced in *décrépit* (un vieillard *décrépit*) results from the coexistence of *décrépi* (un mur *décrépi*). The value of just any term is accordingly determined by its environment; it is impossible to fix even the value of the word signifying "sun" without first considering its surroundings: in some languages it is not possible to say "sit in the *sun*."

Everything said about words applies to any term of language, e.g. to grammatical entities. The value of a French plural does not coincide with that of a Sanskrit plural even though their signification is usually identical; Sanskrit has three numbers instead of two (*my eyes, my ears, my arms, my legs,* etc. are dual); it would be wrong to attribute the same value to the plural in Sanskrit and in French; its value clearly depends on what is outside and around it.

If words stood for pre-existing concepts, they would all have exact equivalents in meaning from one language to the next; but this is not true. French uses *louer (une maison)* 'let (a house)' indifferently to mean both "pay for" and "receive payment for," whereas German uses two words, *mieten* and *vernieten;* there is obviously no exact correspondence of values. The German verbs *schätzen* and *urteilen* share a number of significations, but that correspondence does not hold at several points.

Inflection offers some particularly striking examples. Distinctions of time, which are so familiar to us, are unknown in certain languages. Hebrew does not recognize even the fundamental distinctions between the past, present, and future. Proto-Germanic has no special form for the future; to say that the future is expressed by the present is wrong, for the value of the present is not the same in Germanic as in languages that have a future along with the present. The Slavic languages regularly single out two aspects of the verb: the perfective represents action as a point, complete in its totality; the imperfective represents it as taking place, and on the line of time. The categories are difficult for a Frenchman to understand, for they are unknown in French; if they were predetermined, this would not be true. Instead of pre-existing ideas then, we find in all the foregoing examples *values* emanating from the system. When they are said to correspond to concepts, it is understood that the concepts are purely differential and defined not by their positive content but negatively by their relations with the other terms of the system. Their most precise characteristic is in being what the others are not.

Now the real interpretation of the diagram of the signal becomes apparent. Thus

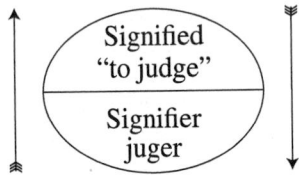

means that in French the concept "to judge" is linked to the sound-image *juger:* in short, it symbolizes signification. But it is quite clear that initially the concept is nothing, that is only a value determined by its relations with other similar values, and that without them the signification would not exist. If I state simply that a word signifies something when I have in mind the associating of a sound-image with a concept, I am making a statement that may suggest what actually happens, but by no means am I expressing the linguistic fact in its essence and fullness.

3. *Linguistic Value from a Material Viewpoint*

The conceptual side of value is made up solely of relations and differences with respect to the other terms of language, and the same can be said of its material side. The important thing in the word is not the sound alone but the phonic differences that make it possible to distinguish this word from all others, for differences carry signification.

This may seem surprising, but how indeed could the reverse be possible? Since one vocal image is no better suited than the next for what it is commissioned to express, it is evident, even *a priori,* that a segment of language can never in the final analysis be based on anything except its noncoincidence with the rest. *Arbitrary* and *differential* are two correlative qualities.

The alteration of linguistic signs clearly illustrates this. It is precisely because the terms *a* and *b* as such are radically incapable of reaching the level of consciousness—one is always conscious of only the *a/b* difference—that each

term is free to change according to laws that are unrelated to its signifying function. No positive sign characterizes the genitive plural in Czech *žen;* still the two forms *žena: žen* function as well as the earlier forms *žena: ženb; žen* has value only because it is different.

Here is another example that shows even more clearly the systematic role of phonic differences: in Greek, *éphēn* is an imperfect and *éstēn* an aorist although both words are formed in the same way; the first belongs to the system of the present indicative of *phēmí* 'I say,' whereas there is no present *stēmi;* now it is precisely the relation *phēmí: éphēn* that corresponds to the relation between the present and the imperfect (cf. *deíknūmi: edeíknūn,* etc.). Signs function, then, not through their intrinsic value but through their relative position.

In addition, it is impossible for sound alone, a material element, to belong to language. It is only a secondary thing, substance to be put to use. All our conventional values have the characteristic of not being confused with the tangible element which supports them. For instance, it is not the metal in a piece of money that fixes its value. A coin nominally worth five francs may contain less than half its worth of silver. Its value will vary according to the amount stamped upon it and according to its use inside or outside a political boundary. This is even more true of the linguistic signifier, which is not phonic but incorporeal—constituted not by its material substance but by the differences that separate its sound-image from all others.

The foregoing principle is so basic that it applies to all the material elements of language, including phonemes. Every language forms its words on the basis of a system of sonorous elements, each element being a clearly delimited unit and one of a fixed number of units. Phonemes are characterized not, as one might think, by their own positive quality but simply by the fact that they are distinct. Phonemes are above all else opposing, relative, and negative entities.

Proof of this is the latitude that speakers have between points of convergence in the pronunciation of distinct sounds. In French, for instance, general use of a dorsal *r* does not prevent many speakers from using a tongue-tip trill; language is not in the least disturbed by it; language requires only that the sound be different and not, as one might imagine, that it have an invariable quality. I can even pronounce the French *r* like German *ch* in *Bach, doch,* etc., but in German I could not use *r* instead of *ch,* for German gives recognition to both elements and must keep them apart. Similarly, in Russian there is no latitude for *t* in the direction of *t'* (palatalized *t*), for the result would be the confusing of two sounds differentiated by the language (cf. *gov-*

orit' 'speak' and *goverit* 'he speaks'), but more freedom may be taken with respect to *th* (aspirated *t*) since this sound does not figure in the Russian system of phonemes.

Since an identical state of affairs is observable in writing, another system of signs, we shall use writing to draw some comparisons that will clarify the whole issue. In fact:

1) The signs used in writing are arbitrary; there is no connection, for example, between the letter *t* and the sound that it designates.

2) The value of letters is purely negative and differential. The same person can write *t,* for instance, in different ways: The only requirement is that the sign for *t* not be confused in his script with the signs used for *l, d,* etc.

3) Values in writing function only through reciprocal opposition within a fixed system that consists of a set number of letters. This third characteristic, though not identical to the second, is closely related to it, for both depend on the first. Since the graphic sign is arbitrary, its form matters little or rather matters only within the limitations imposed by the system.

4) The means by which the sign is produced is completely unimportant, for it does not affect the system (this also follows from characteristic 1). Whether I make the letters in white or black, raised or engraved, with pen or chisel—all this is of no importance with respect to their signification.

4. *The Sign Considered in Its Totality*

Everything that has been said up to this point boils down to this: in language there are only differences. Even more important: a difference generally implies positive terms between which the difference is set up; but in language there are only differences *without positive terms.* Whether we take the signified or the signifier, language has neither ideas nor sounds that existed before the linguistic system, but only conceptual and phonic differences that have issued from the system. The idea or phonic substance that a sign contains is of less importance than the other signs that surround it. Proof of this is that the value of a term may be modified without either its meaning or its sound being affected, solely because a neighboring term has been modified.

But the statement that everything in language is negative is true only if the signified and the signifier are considered separately; when we consider the sign in its totality, we have something that is positive in its own class. A linguistic system is a series of differences of sound combined with a series of differences of ideas; but the pairing of a certain number of acoustical signs with as many cuts made from the mass of thought engenders a system of values; and this system serves as the effective link between the phonic and psy-chological elements within each sign. Although both the signified and the signifier are purely differential and negative when considered separately, their combination is a positive fact; it is even the sole type of facts that language has, for maintaining the parallelism between the two classes of differences is the distinctive function of the linguistic institution.

Certain diachronic facts are typical in this respect. Take the countless instances where alteration of the signifier occasions a conceptual change and where it is obvious that the sum of the ideas distinguished corresponds in principle to the sum of the distinctive signs. When two words are confused through phonetic alteration (e.g. French *décrépit* from *dēcrepitus* and *décrépi* from *crispus*), the ideas that they express will also tend to become confused if only they have something in common. Or a word may have different forms (cf. *chaise* 'chair' and *chaire* 'desk'). Any nascent difference will tend invariably to become significant but without always succeeding or being successful on the first trial. Conversely, any conceptual difference perceived by the mind seeks to find expression through a distinct signifier, and two ideas that are no longer distinct in the mind tend to merge into the same signifier.

When we compare signs—positive terms—with each other, we can no longer speak of difference; the expression would not be fitting, for it applies only to the comparing of two sound-images, e.g. *father* and *mother,* or two ideas, e.g. the idea "father" and the idea "mother"; two signs, each having a signified and signifier, are not different but only distinct. Between them there is only *opposition.* The entire mechanism of language, with which we shall be concerned later, is based on oppositions of this kind and of the phonic and conceptual differences that they imply.

What is true of value is true also of the unit. A unit is a segment of the spoken chain that corresponds to a certain concept; both are by nature purely differential.

Applied to units, the principle of differentiation can be stated in this way: *the characteristics of the unit blend with the unit itself.* In language, as in any semiological system, whatever distinguishes one sign from the others constitutes it. Difference makes character just as it makes value and the unit.

Another rather paradoxical consequence of the same principle is this: in the last analysis what is commonly referred to as a "grammatical fact" fits the definition of the unit, for it always expresses an opposition of terms; it differs only in that the opposition is particularly significant (e.g. the formation of German plurals of the type *Nacht: Nächte*). Each term present in the grammatical fact (the singular without umlaut or final *e* in opposition to the plural with umlaut and *-e*) consists of the interplay of a number of oppositions within the system. When isolated, neither *Nacht* nor *Nächte* is anything: thus everything is opposition. Putting it another way, the *Nacht: Nächte* relation can be expressed by an algebraic formula *a/b* in which *a* and *b* are not simple terms but result from a set of relations. Language, in a manner of speaking, is a type of algebra consisting solely of complex terms. Some of its oppositions are more significant than others; but units and grammatical facts are only different names for designating diverse aspects of the same general fact: the functioning of linguistic oppositions. This statement is so true that we might very well approach the problem of units by starting from grammatical facts. Taking an opposition like *Nacht: Nächte,* we might ask what are the units involved in it. Are they only the two words, the whole series of similar words, *a* and *ä,* or all singulars and plurals, etc.?

Units and grammatical facts would not be confused if linguistic signs were made up of something besides differences. But language being what it is, we shall find nothing simple in it regardless of our approach; everywhere and always there is the same complex equilibrium of terms that mutually condition each other. Putting it another way, *language is a form and not a substance.* This truth could not be overstressed, for all the mistakes in our terminology, all our incorrect ways of naming things that pertain to language, stem from the involuntary supposition that the linguistic phenomenon must have substance.

Chapter V

Syntagmatic and Associative Relations

1. *Definitions*

In a language-state everything is based on relations. How do they function?

Relations and differences between linguistic terms fall into two distinct groups, each of which generates a certain class of values. The opposition between the two classes gives a better understanding of the nature of each class. They correspond to two forms of our mental activity, both indispensable to the life of language.

In discourse, on the one hand, words acquire relations based on the linear nature of language because they are chained together. This rules out the possibility of pronouncing two elements simultaneously. The elements are arranged in sequence on the chain of speaking. Combinations supported by linearity are *syntagms.* The syntagm is always composed of two or more consecutive units (e.g. French *re-*

lire 're-read,' *contre tous* 'against everyone,' *la vie humaine* 'human life.' *Dieu est bon* 'God is good,' *s'il fait beau temps, nous sortirons* 'if the weather is nice, we'll go out,' etc.). In the syntagm a term acquires its value only because it stands in opposition to everything that precedes or follows it, or to both.

Outside discourse, on the other hand, words acquire relations of a different kind. Those that have something in common are associated in the memory, resulting in groups marked by diverse relations. For instance, the French word *enseignement* 'teaching' will unconsciously call to mind a host of other words (*enseigner* 'teach,' *renseigner* 'acquaint,' etc.; or *armement* 'armament,' *changement* 'amendment,' etc.; or *éducation* 'education,' *apprentissage* 'apprenticeship,' etc.). All those words are related in some way.

We see that the co-ordinations formed outside discourse differ strikingly from those formed inside discourse. Those formed outside discourse are not supported by linearity. Their seat is in the brain; they are a part of the inner storehouse that makes up the language of each speaker. They are *associative relations.*

The syntagmatic relation is *in praesentia.* It is based on two or more terms that occur in an effective series. Against this, the associative relation unites terms *in absentia* in a potential mnemonic series.

From the associative and syntagmatic viewpoint a linguistic unit is like a fixed part of a building, e.g. a column. On the one hand, the column has a certain relation to the architrave that it supports; the arrangement of the two units in space suggests the syntagmatic relation. On the other hand, if the column is Doric, it suggests a mental comparison of this style with others (Ionic, Corinthian, etc.) although none of these elements is present in space: the relation is associative.

Each of the two classes of co-ordination calls for some specific remarks.

2. *Syntagmatic Relations*

The examples have already indicated that the notion of syntagm applies not only to words but to groups of words, to complex units of all lengths and types (compounds, derivatives, phrases, whole sentences).

It is not enough to consider the relation that ties together the different parts of syntagms (e.g. French *contre* 'against' and *tous* 'everyone' in *contre tous, contre* and *maître* 'master' in *contremaître* 'foreman'), one must also bear in mind the relation that links the whole to its parts (e.g. *contre tous* in opposition on the one hand to *contre* and on the other *tous,* or *contremaître* in opposition to *contre* and *maître*).

An objection might be raised at this point. The sentence is the ideal type of syntagm. But it belongs to speaking, not to language. Does it follow that the syntagm belongs to speaking? I do not think so. Speaking is characterized by freedom of combinations; one must therefore ask whether or not all syntagms are equally free.

It is obvious from the first that many expressions belong to language. These are the pat phrases in which any change is prohibited by usage, even if we can single out their meaningful elements (cf. *à quoi bon?* 'what's the use?' *allons donc!* 'nonsense!'). The same is true, though to a lesser degree, of expressions like *prendre la mouche* 'take offense easily,' *forcer la main à quelqu'un* 'force someone's hand,' *rompre une lance* 'break a lance,' or even *avoir mal* (*à la tête,* etc.) 'have (a headache, etc.),' *à force de (soins,* etc.) 'by dint of (care, etc.),' *que vous en semble?* 'how do you feel about it?' *pas n'est besoin de . . .* 'there's no need for . . .' etc., which are characterized by peculiarities of signification or syntax. These idiomatic twists cannot be improvised; they are furnished by tradition. There are also words which, while lending themselves perfectly to analysis, are characterized by some morphological anomaly that is kept solely by dint of usage (cf. *difficulté* 'difficulty' beside *facilité* 'facility,' etc., and *mourrai* '[I] shall die' beside *dormirai* '[I] shall sleep').

There are further proofs. To language rather than to speaking belong the syntagmatic types that are built upon regular forms. Indeed, since there is nothing abstract in language, the types exist only if language has registered a sufficient number of specimens. When a word like *indécorable* arises in speaking, its appearance supposes a fixed type, and this type is in turn possible only through remembrance of a sufficient number of similar words belonging to language (*impardonable* 'unpardonable,' *intolérable* 'intolerable,' *infatigable* 'indefatigable,' etc.). Exactly the same is true of sentences and groups of words built upon regular patterns. Combinations like *la terre tourne* 'the world turns,' *que vous dit-il?* 'what does he say to you?' etc. correspond to general types that are in turn supported in the language by concrete remembrances.

But we must realize that in the syntagm there is no clear-cut boundary between the language fact, which is a sign of collective usage, and the fact that belongs to speaking and depends on individual freedom. In a great number of instances it is hard to class a combination of units because both forces have combined in producing it, and they have combined in indeterminable proportions.

3. Associative Relations

Mental association creates other groups besides those based on the comparing of terms that have something in common; through its grasp of the nature of the relations that bind the terms together, the mind creates as many associative se-

ries as there are diverse relations. For instance, in *enseignement* 'teaching,' *enseigner* 'teach,' *enseignons* '(we) teach,' etc., one element, the radical, is common to every term; the same word may occur in a different series formed around another common element, the suffix (cf. *enseignement, armement, changement,* etc.); or the association may spring from the analogy of the concepts signified (*enseignement, instruction, apprentissage, éducation,* etc.); or again, simply from the similarity of the sound-images (e.g. *enseignement* and *justement* 'precisely'). Thus there is at times a double similarity of meaning and form, at times similarity only of form or of meaning. A word can always evoke everything that can be associated with it in one way or another.

Whereas a syntagm immediately suggests an order of succession and a fixed number of elements, terms in an associative family occur neither in fixed numbers nor in a definite order. If we associate *painful, delightful, frightful,* etc. we are unable to predict the number of words that the memory will suggest or the order in which they will appear. A particular word is like the center of a constellation; it is the point of convergence of an indefinite number of coordinated terms.

But of the two characteristics of the associative series—indeterminate order and indefinite number—only the first can always be verified; the second may fail to meet the test. This happens in the case of inflectional paradigms, which are typical of associative groupings. Latin *dominus, domini, dominō,* etc. is obviously an associative group formed around a common element, the noun theme *domin-,* but the series

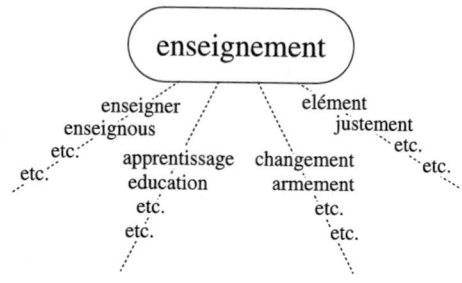

is not indefinite as in the case of *enseignement, changement,* etc.; the number of cases is definite. Against this, the words have no fixed order of succession, and it is by a purely arbitrary act that the grammarian groups them in one way rather than in another; in the mind of speakers the nominative case is by no means the first one in the declension, and the order in which terms are called depends on circumstances.

Victor Shklovsky

1893–1984

A principal notion offered by the Russian Formalist movement early in the twentieth century was that of "defamiliarization." In Shklovsky's essay below the term plays the major role. Defamiliarization is described as a device to destroy habitual or "automatic" perception, as Boris Eichenbaum (below, page 867) later characterized it. Shklovsky presents the notion as part of an attack on the theories of Alexander Potebnya and of the Russian Symbolist movement in general. In place of emphasis on symbols and images as the fundamental defining elements of poetry—"thinking in images"—Shklovsky and the Formalists would study "phonetic and lexical structure" as well as the "characteristic distribution of words . . . the characteristic thought structures compounded from words." The shift led to the Structuralist movement and developments in linguistics associated with the Prague School. All of the structures that Shklovsky mentions create defamiliarization in poetry, the result of which is the experience of new satisfactions and perspectives. Poetry is described as "difficult, roughened, impeded language"; it is "attenuated, tortuous speech"; obviously it is "formed" speech. Even rhythm is seen according to this notion, and the result is a reversal of our usual assumptions about poetic technique.

Shklovsky was a founder of the OPOYAZ group in Russia, which flourished until it came under sharp and repressive attack by the Soviet state. Shklovsky was harshly criticized by Leon Trotsky in his *Literature and Revolution* (1924). The movement was subsequently defended by one of its founders Boris Eichenbaum in his essay "The Theory of the 'Formal Method'" (below, page 868), where Shklovsky's essay is discussed. Shklovsky himself retreated from theorizing in print under Communist rule and engaged in other literary and cinematic activities; finally, he was reconciled with the government.

Shklovsky's writings were collected and published in a single edition in Moscow in 1973–1974 by Khudozh' Lit'ra. His book on Trotsky was translated into English in 1978. See Victor Erlich, *Russian Formalism: History-Doctrine* (rev. ed. 1964); Mikhail M. Bakhtin [P. N. Medvedev], *The Formal Method in Literary Scholarship* (tr. 1978). See also bibliographical material in the selection from Eichenbaum (below, page 867). The Formalist movement is put in the context of Russian literary criticism by R. H. Stacy, *Russian Literary Criticism: A Short History* (1974).

Art as Technique

"Art is thinking in images." This maxim, which even high school students parrot, is nevertheless the starting point for the erudite philologist who is beginning to put together some kind of systematic literary theory. The idea, originated in part by Potebnya, has spread. "Without imagery there is no art, and in particular no poetry," Potebnya writes.[1] And elsewhere, "Poetry, as well as prose, is first and foremost a special way of thinking and knowing."[2]

Poetry is a special way of thinking; it is, precisely, a way of thinking in images, a way which permits what is generally called "economy of mental effort," a way which makes for "a sensation of the relative ease of the process." Aesthetic feeling is the reaction to this economy. This is how the academician Ovsyaniko-Kulikovsky,[3] who undoubtedly read the works of Potebnya attentively, almost certainly understood and faithfully summarized the ideas of his teacher. Potebnya and his numerous disciples consider poetry a special kind of thinking—thinking by means of images; they feel that the purpose of imagery is to help channel various objects and activities into groups and to clarify the unknown by means of the known. Or, as Potebnya wrote:

> The relationship of the image to what is being clarified is that: (a) the image is the fixed predicate of that which undergoes change—the unchanging means of attracting what is perceived as changeable. . . . (b) the image is far clearer and simpler than what it clarifies.[4]

In other words:

> Since the purpose of imagery is to remind us, by approximation, of those meanings for which the image stands, and since, apart from this, imagery is unnecessary for thought, we must be more familiar with the image than with what it clarifies.[5]

It would be instructive to try to apply this principle to Tyutchev's comparison of summer lightning to deaf and dumb demons or to Gogol's comparison of the sky to the garment of God.[6]

"Without imagery there is no art"—"Art is thinking in images." These maxims have led to far-fetched interpretations of individual works of art. Attempts have been made to evaluate even music, architecture, and lyric poetry as imagistic thought. After a quarter of a century of such attempts Ovsyaniko-Kulikovsky finally had to assign lyric poetry, architecture, and music to a special category of imageless art and to define them as lyric arts appealing directly to the emotions. And thus he admitted an enormous area of art which is not a mode of thought. A part of this area, lyric poetry (narrowly considered), is quite like the visual arts; it is also verbal. But, much more important, visual art passes quite imperceptibly into nonvisual art; yet our perceptions of both are similar.

Nevertheless, the definition "Art is thinking in images," which means (I omit the usual middle terms of the argument) that art is the making of symbols, has survived the downfall of the theory which supported it. It survives chiefly in the wake of Symbolism, especially among the theorists of the Symbolist movement.

Many still believe, then, that thinking in images—thinking, in specific scenes of "roads and landscape" and "furrows and boundaries"[7]—is the chief characteristic of poetry. Consequently, they should have expected the history of "imagistic art," as they call it, to consist of a history of changes in imagery. But we find that images change little; from century to century, from nation to nation, from poet to poet, they flow on without changing. Images belong to no one: they are "the Lord's." The more you understand an age, the more convinced you become that the images a given poet used and which you thought his own were taken almost unchanged from another poet. The works of poets are classified or grouped according to the new techniques that poets discover and share, and according to their arrangement and development of the resources of language; poets are much more concerned with arranging images than with creating them. Images are given to poets; the ability to remember them is far more important than the ability to create them.

Shklovsky's *Art as Technique* first appeared in 1917. It is reprinted here from *Russian Formalist Criticism: Four Essays,* translated by Lee T. Lemon and Marion J. Reis (Lincoln: University of Nebraska Press, 1965).

[1] Alexander Potebnya (1835–1891), Russian philologist influenced by Wilhelm von Humboldt. [Shklovsky] Alexander Potebnya, *Iz zapisok po teorii slovesnosti* [*Notes on the Theory of Language*] (Kharkov, 1905), page 83.

[2] [Shklovsky] Ibid., page 97.

[3] [Lemon and Reis] Dimitry Ovsyaniko-Kulikovsky (1835–1920), a leading Russian scholar, was an early contributor to Marxist periodicals and a literary conservative, antagonistic towards the deliberately meaningless poems of the Futurists.

[4] [Shklovsky] Potebnya, *Iz zapisok po teorii slovesnosti,* page 314.

[5] [Shklovsky] Ibid., page 291.

[6] [Lemon and Reis] Fyodor Tyutchev (1803–1873), a poet, and Nicholas Gogol (1809–1852), master of prose fiction and satire, are mentioned here because their bold use of imagery cannot be accounted for by Potebnya's theory. Shklovsky is arguing that writers frequently gain their effects by comparing the commonplace to the exceptional rather than vice versa.

[7] [Lemon and Reis] This is an allusion to Vyacheslav Ivanov's *Borozdy i mezhi* [*Furrows and Boundaries*] (Moscow, 1916), a major statement of symbolist theory.

Imagistic thought does not, in any case, include all the aspects of art nor even all the aspects of verbal art. A change in imagery is not essential to the development of poetry. We know that frequently an expression is thought to be poetic, to be created for aesthetic pleasure, although actually it was created without such intent—e.g., Annensky's opinion that the Slavic languages are especially poetic and Andrey Bely's ecstasy over the technique of placing adjectives after nouns, a technique used by eighteenth-century Russian poets.[8] Bely joyfully accepts the technique as something artistic, or more exactly, as intended, if we consider intention as art. Actually, this reversal of the usual adjective-noun order is a peculiarity of the language (which had been influenced by Church Slavonic). Thus a work may be (1) intended as prosaic and accepted as poetic, or (2) intended as poetic and accepted as prosaic. This suggests that the artistry attributed to a given work results from the way we perceive it. By "works of art," in the narrow sense, we mean works created by special techniques designed to make the works as obviously artistic as possible.

Potebnya's conclusion, which can be formulated "poetry equals imagery," gave rise to the whole theory that "imagery equals symbolism," that the image may serve as the invariable predicate of various subjects. (This conclusion, because it expressed ideas similar to the theories of the Symbolists, intrigued some of their leading representatives—Andrey Bely, Merezhkovsky[9] and his "eternal companions" and, in fact, formed the basis of the theory of Symbolism.) The conclusion stems partly from the fact that Potebnya did not distinguish between the language of poetry and the language of prose. Consequently, he ignored the fact that there are two aspects of imagery: imagery as a practical means of thinking, as a means of placing objects within categories; and imagery as poetic, as a means of reinforcing an impression. I shall clarify with an example. I want to attract the attention of a young child who is eating bread and butter and getting the butter on her fingers. I call, "Hey, butterfingers!" This is a figure of speech, a clearly prosaic trope. Now a different example. The child is playing with my glasses and drops them. I call, "Hey butterfingers!"[10] This figure of speech is a poetic trope. (In the first example, "butterfingers" is metonymic; in the second, metaphoric—but this is not what I want to stress.)

Poetic imagery is a means of creating the strongest possible impression. As a method it is, depending upon its purpose, neither more nor less effective than other poetic techniques; it is neither more nor less effective than ordinary or negative parallelism, comparison, repetition, balanced structure, hyperbole, the commonly accepted rhetorical figures, and all those methods which emphasize the emotional effect of an expression (including words or even articulated sounds).[11] But poetic imagery only externally resembles either the stock imagery of fables and ballads or thinking in images—e.g., the example in Ovsyaniko-Kulikovsky's *Language and Art* in which a little girl calls a ball a little watermelon. Poetic imagery is but one of the devices of poetic language. Prose imagery is a means of abstraction: a little watermelon instead of a lampshade, or a little watermelon instead of a head, is only the abstraction of one of the object's characteristics, that of roundness. It is no different from saying that the head and the melon are both round. This is what is meant, but it has nothing to do with poetry.

The law of the economy of creative effort is also generally accepted. [Herbert] Spencer wrote:

> On seeking for some clue to the law underlying these current maxims, we may see shadowed forth in many of them, the importance of economizing the reader's or the hearer's attention. To so present ideas that they may be apprehended with the least possible mental effort, is the desideratum towards which most of the rules above quoted point. . . . Hence, carrying out the metaphor that language is the vehicle of thought, there seems reason to think that in all cases the friction and inertia of the vehicle deduct from its efficiency; and that in composition, the chief, if not the sole thing to be done, is to reduce this friction and inertia to the smallest possible amount.[12]

And R[ichard] Avenarius:

> If a soul possess inexhaustible strength, then, of

---

[8] Imokenty Feodorovich Annensky (1855–1909) and Andrew Bely (Boris Nikolayevich Bugayev, 1880–1934), Russian symbolist writers.

[9] Dmitri Sergeyevich Merezhkovsky (1865–1941).

[10] [Lemon and Reis] The Russian text involves a play on the word for "hat," colloquial for "clod," "duffer," etc.

[11] [Lemon and Reis] Shklovsky is here doing two things of major theoretical importance: (1) he argues that different techniques serve a single function and that (2) no single technique is all important. The second permits the formalists to be concerned with any and all literary devices; the first permits them to discuss the devices from a single consistent theoretical position.

[12] [Shklovsky] Herbert Spencer, *The Philosophy of Style* (Humboldt Library, vol. 34, New York, 1882), 2–3. [Lemon and Reis] Shklovsky's quoted reference, in Russian, preserves the idea of the original but shortens it.

course, it would be indifferent to how much might be spent from this inexhaustible source; only the necessarily expended time would be important. But since its forces are limited, one is led to expect that the soul hastens to carry out the apperceptive process as expediently as possible—that is, with comparatively the least expenditure of energy, and, hence, with comparatively the best result.[13]

Petrazhitsky, with only one reference to the general law of mental effort, rejects [William] James's theory of the physical basis of emotion, a theory which contradicts his own.[14] Even Alexander Veselovsky acknowledged the principle of the economy of creative effort, a theory especially appealing in the study of rhythm, and agreed with Spencer: "A satisfactory style is precisely that style which delivers the greatest amount of thought in the fewest words."[15] And Andrey Bely, despite the fact that in his better pages he gave numerous examples of "roughened" rhythm and (particularly in the examples from Baratynsky) showed the difficulties inherent in poetic epithets, also thought it necessary to speak of the law of the economy of creative effort in his book[16]—a heroic effort to create a theory of art based on unverified facts from antiquated sources, on his vast knowledge of the techniques of poetic creativity, and on Krayevich's high school physics text.

These ideas about the economy of energy, as well as about the law and aim of creativity, are perhaps true in their application to "practical" language; they were, however, extended to poetic language. Hence they do not distinguish properly between the laws of practical language and the laws of poetic language. The fact that Japanese poetry has sounds not found in conversational Japanese was hardly the first factual indication of the differences between poetic and everyday language. Leo Jakubinsky has observed that the law of the dissimilation of liquid sounds does not apply to poetic language.[17] This suggested to him that poetic language tolerated the admission of hard-to-pronounce conglomerations of similar sounds. In his article, one of the first examples of scientific criticism, he indicates inductively, the contrast (I shall

say more about this point later) between the laws of poetic language and the laws of practical language.[18]

We must, then, speak about the laws of expenditure and economy in poetic language not on the basis of an analogy with prose, but on the basis of the laws of poetic language.

If we start to examine the general laws of perception, we see that as perception becomes habitual, it becomes automatic. Thus, for example, all of our habits retreat into the area of the unconsciously automatic; if one remembers the sensations of holding a pen or of speaking in a foreign language for the first time and compares that with his feeling at performing the action for the ten thousandth time, he will agree with us. Such habituation explains the principles by which, in ordinary speech, we leave phrases unfinished and words half expressed. In this process, ideally realized in algebra, things are replaced by symbols. Complete words are not expressed in rapid speech; their initial sounds are barely perceived. Alexander Pogodin offers the example of a boy considering the sentence "The Swiss mountains are beautiful" in the form of a series of letters: *T, S, m, a, b.*[19]

This characteristic of thought not only suggests the method of algebra, but even prompts the choice of symbols (letters, especially initial letters). By this "algebraic" method of thought we apprehend objects only as shapes with imprecise extensions; we do not see them in their entirety but rather recognize them by their main characteristics. We see the object as though it were enveloped in a sack. We know what it is by its configuration, but we see only its silhouette. The object, perceived thus in the manner of prose perception, fades and does not leave even a first impression; ultimately even the essence of what it was is forgotten. Such perception explains why we fail to hear the prose word in its entirety (see Leo Jakubinsky's article[20]) and, hence, why (along with other slips of the tongue) we fail to pronounce it. The process of "algebrization," the over-automatization of an object, permits the greatest economy of perceptive effort. Either objects are assigned only one proper feature—a number, for example—or else they function as though by formula and do not even appear in cognition:

I was cleaning a room and, meandering about, approached the divan and couldn't remember whether or not I had dusted it. Since these

---

[13]Richard Avenarius (1843–1896), German philosopher.

[14]Leo Petrazhitsky (1867–1931), Russian critic and poet; William James (1842–1910), American philosopher and psychologist.

[15]Alexander Veselovsky (1838–1906), Russian literary scholar.

[16][Lemon and Reis] The Russian *zatrudyonny* means "made difficult." The suggestion is that poems with "easy" or smooth rhythms slip by unnoticed; poems that are difficult or "roughened" force the reader to attend to them. In *Symvolizm* probably.

[17][Shklovsky] Leo Jakubinsky, "O zvukakh poeticheskova yazyka" ["On the Sounds of Poetry"], *Sborniki* I (1916), 38.

[18][Shklovsky] Leo Jakubinsky, "Skopleniyi odinakovykh plavnykh v prakticheseskom I poeticheskom yazykakh" ["The Accumulation of Identical Liquids in Practical and Poetic Language"], *Sborniki* II (1917), 13–21.

[19][Shklovsky] Alexander Pogodoin, *Yazyk, kak tvorchestvo* [*Language as Art*], (Kharkov, 1913), 42. [Lemon and Reis] The original sentence was in French, "Les montaignes de la Suisse sont belles," with the appropriate initials.

[20][Shklovsky] Jakubinsky, *Sborniki* I (1916).

movements are habitual and unconscious, I could not remember and felt that it was impossible to remember—so that if I had dusted it and forgot—that is, had acted unconsciously, then it was the same as if I had not. If some conscious person had been watching, then the fact could be established. If, however, no one was looking, or looking on unconsciously, if the whole complex lives of many people go on unconsciously, then such lives are as if they had never been.[21]

And so life is reckoned as nothing. Habitualization devours works, clothes, furniture, one's wife, and the fear of war. "If the whole complex lives of many people go on unconsciously, then such lives are as if they had never been." And art exists that one may recover the sensation of life; it exists to make one feel things, to make the stone *stony*. The purpose of art is to impart the sensation of things as they are perceived and not as they are known. The technique of art is to make objects "unfamiliar," to make forms difficult, to increase the difficulty and length of perception because the process of perception is an aesthetic end in itself and must be prolonged. *Art is a way of experiencing the artfulness of an object; the object is not important.*

The range of poetic (artistic) work extends from the sensory to the cognitive, from poetry to prose, from the concrete to the abstract: from Cervantes's Don Quixote—scholastic and poor nobleman, half consciously bearing his humiliation in the court of the duke—to the broad but empty Don Quixote of Turgenev; from Charlemagne to the name "king" [in Russian "Charles" and "king" obviously derive from the same root, *korol*][22] The meaning of a work broadens to the extent that artfulness and artistry diminish; thus a fable symbolizes more than a poem, and a proverb more than a fable. Consequently, the least self-contradictory part of Potebnya's theory is his treatment of the fable, which, from his point of view, he investigated thoroughly. But since his theory did not provide for "expressive" works of art, he could not finish his book. As we know, *Notes on the Theory of Literature* was published in 1905, thirteen years after Potebnya's death. Potebnya himself completed only the section on the fable.[23]

After we see an object several times, we begin to recognize it. The object is in front of us and we know about it, but we do not see it[24]—hence we cannot say anything significant about it. Art removes objects from the automatism of perception in several ways. Here I want to illustrate a way used repeatedly by Leo Tolstoy,[25] that writer who, for Merezhkovsky at least, seems to present things as if he himself saw them, saw them in their entirety, and did not alter them.

Tolstoy makes the familiar seem strange by not naming the familiar object. He describes an object as if he were seeing it for the first time, an event as if it were happening for the first time. In describing something he avoids the accepted names of its parts and instead names corresponding parts of other objects. For example, in "Shame" Tolstoy "defamiliarizes" the idea of flogging in this way: "to strip people who have broken the law, to hurl them to the floor, and to rap on their bottoms with switches," and, after a few lines, "to lash about on the naked buttocks." Then he remarks:

> Just why precisely this stupid, savage means of causing pain and not any other—why not prick the shoulders or any part of the body with needles, squeeze the hands or the feet in a vise, or anything like that?

I apologize for this harsh example, but it is typical of Tolstoy's way of pricking the conscience. The familiar act of flogging is made unfamiliar both by the description and by the proposal to change its form without changing its nature. Tolstoy uses this technique of "defamiliarization" constantly. The narrator of "Kholstomer," for example, is a horse, and it is the horse's point of view (rather than a person's) that makes the content of the story seem unfamiliar. Here is how the horse regards the institution of private property:

> I understood well what they said about whipping and Christianity. But then I was absolutely in the dark. What's the meaning of "his own," "his colt"? From these phrases I saw that people thought there was some sort of connection between me and the stable. At the time I simply could not understand the connection. Only much later, when they separated me from the other horses, did I begin to understand. But even then I simply could not see what it meant when they called me "man's property." The words "my horse" referred to me, a living horse, and seemed as strange to me as the words "my land," "my air," "my water."

---

[21] [Shklovsky] Leo Tolstoy's *Diary*, entry dated February 29, 1897. [Lemon and Reis] The date is transcribed incorrectly; it should read March 1, 1897.

[22] Miguel de Cervantes Saavedra (1547–1616), Spanish novelist; Ivan Sergeyevich Turgenev (1818–1883), Russian novelist.

[23] [Shklovsky] Alexander Potebnya, *Iz lektsy po teorii slovesnoti* [*Lectures on the Theory of Language*] (Kharkov, 1914).

[24] [Shklovsky] Victor Shklovsky, *Voskresheniye slova* [*The Resurrection of the Word*] (Petersburg, 1914).

[25] Leo Tolstoy (above, page 757).

But the words make a strong impression on me I thought about them constantly, and only after the most diverse experiences with people did I understand, finally, what they meant. They meant this: In life people are guided by words, not by deeds. It's not so much that they love the possibility of doing or not doing something as it is the possibility of speaking with words, agreed on among themselves, about various topics. Such are the words "my" and "mine," which they apply to different things, creatures, objects, and even to land, people, and horses. They agree that only one may say "mine" about this, that, or the other thing. And the one who says "mine" about the greatest number of things is, according to the game which they've agreed to among themselves, the one they consider the most happy. I don't know the point of all this, but it's true. For a long time I tried to explain it to myself in terms of some kind of real gain, but I had to reject that explanation because it was wrong. Many of those, for instance, who called me their own never rode on me—although others did. And so with those who fed me. Then again, the coachman, the veterinarians, and the outsiders in general treated me kindly, yet those who called me their own did not. In due time, having widened the scope of my observations, I satisfied myself that the notion "my," not only in relation to us horses, has no other basis than a narrow human instinct which is called a sense of or right to private property. A man says "this house is mine" and never lives in it; he only worries about its construction and upkeep. A merchant says "my shop," "my dry goods shop," for instance, and does not even wear clothes made from the better cloth he keeps in his own shop.

There are people who call a tract of land their own, but they never set eyes on it and never take a stroll on it. There are people who call others their own, yet never see them. And the whole relationship between them is that the so-called "owners" treat the others unjustly.

There are people who call women their own, or their "wives," but their women live with other men. And people strive not for the good in life, but for goods they can call their own.

I am now convinced that this is the essential difference between people and ourselves. And therefore, not even considering the other ways in which we are superior, but considering just this one virtue, we can bravely claim to stand higher than men on the ladder of living creatures. The ac-

tions of men, at least those with whom I have had dealings, are guided by *words*—ours, by deeds.

The horse is killed before the end of the story, but the manner of the narrative, its technique, does not change:

Much later they put Serpukhovsky's body, which had experienced the world, which had eaten and drunk, into the ground. They could profitably send neither his hide, nor his flesh, nor his bones anywhere.

But since his dead body, which had gone about in the world for twenty years, was a great burden to everyone, its burial was only a superfluous embarrassment for the people. For a long time no one had needed him; for a long time he had been a burden on all. But nevertheless, the dead who buried the dead found it necessary to dress this bloated body, which immediately began to rot, in a good uniform and good boots; to lay it in a good new coffin with new tassels at the four corners, then to place this new coffin in another of lead and ship it to Moscow; there to exhume ancient bones and at just that spot, to hide this putrefying body, swarming with maggots, in its new uniform and clean boots, and to cover it over completely with dirt.

Thus we see that at the end of the story Tolstoy continues to use the technique even though the motivation for it [the reason for its use] is gone.

In *War and Peace* Tolstoy uses the same technique in describing whole battles as if battles were something new. These descriptions are too long to quote; it would be necessary to extract a considerable part of the four-volume novel. But Tolstoy uses the same method in describing the drawing room and the theater:

The middle of the stage consisted of flat boards, by the sides stood painted pictures representing trees, and at the back a linen cloth was stretched down to the floor boards. Maidens in red bodices and white skirts sat on the middle of the stage. One, very fat, in a white silk dress, sat apart on a narrow bench to which a green pasteboard box was glued from behind. They were all singing something. When they had finished, the maiden in white approached the prompter's box. A man in silk with tight-fitting pants on his fat legs approached her with a plume and began to sing and spread his arms in dismay. The man in the tight pants finished his song alone; then the girl sang. After that both remained silent as the music resounded; and the man, obviously wanting to begin singing his part with her again, began to run his fingers over the hand of the girl in the white dress. They finished their song together, and everyone in the theater began to clap and shout. But the men and women on stage, who represented lovers, start to bow, smiling and raising their hands.

In the second act there were pictures representing monuments and openings in the linen cloth representing the moonlight, and they raised lamp shades on a frame. As the musicians started to play the bass horn and counter-bass, a large number of people in black mantles poured onto the stage from right and left. The people, with something like daggers in their hands, started to wave their arms. Then still more people came running out and began to drag away the maiden who had been wearing a white dress but who now wore one of sky blue. They did not drag her off immediately, but sang with her for a long time before dragging her away. Three times they struck on something metallic behind the side scenes, and everyone got down on his knees and began to chant a prayer. Several times all of this activity was interrupted by enthusiastic shouts from the spectators.

The third act is described:

> . . . But suddenly a storm blew up. Chromatic scales and chords of diminished sevenths were heard in the orchestra. Everyone ran about and again they dragged one of the bystanders behind the scenes as the curtain fell.

In the fourth act, "There was some sort of devil who sang, waving his hands, until the boards were moved out from under him and he dropped down."[26]

In *Resurrection* Tolstoy describes the city and the court in the same way; he uses a similar technique in "Kreutzer Sonata" when he describes marriage—"Why, if people have an affinity of souls, must they sleep together?" But he did not defamiliarize only those things he sneered at:

> Pierre stood up from his new comrades and made his way between the campfires to the other side of the road where, it seemed, the captive soldiers were held. He wanted to talk with them. The French sentry stopped him on the road and ordered him to return. Pierre did so, but not to the campfire, not to his comrades, but to an abandoned, unharnessed carriage. On the ground, near the wheel of the carriage, he sat cross-legged in the Turkish fashion, and lowered his head. He sat motionless for a long time, thinking. More than an hour passed. No one disturbed him. Suddenly he burst out laughing with his robust, good natured laugh—so loudly that the men near him looked around, surprised at his conspicuously strange laughter.
>
> "Ha, ha, ha," laughed Pierre. And he began to talk to himself. "The soldier didn't allow me to pass. They caught me, barred me. Me—me—my immortal soul. Ha, ha, ha," he laughed with tears starting in his eyes.
>
> Pierre glanced at the sky, into the depths of the departing, playing stars. "And all this is mine, all this is in me, and all this is I," thought Pierre. "And all this they caught and put in a planked enclosure." He smiled and went off to his comrades to lie down to sleep.[27]

Anyone who knows Tolstoy can find several hundred such passages in his work. His method of seeing things out of their normal context is also apparent in his last works. Tolstoy described the dogmas and rituals he attacked as if they were unfamiliar, substituting everyday meanings for the customarily religious meanings of the words common in church ritual. Many persons were painfully wounded; they considered it blasphemy to present as strange and monstrous what they accepted as sacred. Their reaction was due chiefly to the technique through which Tolstoy perceived and reported his environment. And after turning to what he had long avoided, Tolstoy found that his perceptions had unsettled his faith.

The technique of defamiliarization is not Tolstoy's alone. I cited Tolstoy because his work is generally known.

Now, having explained the nature of this technique, let us try to determine the approximate limits of its application. I personally feel that defamiliarization is found almost everywhere form is found. In other words, the difference between Potebnya's point of view and ours is this: An image is not a permanent referent for those mutable complexities of life which are revealed through it; its purpose is not to make us perceive meaning, but to create a special perception of the object—*it creates a "vision" of the object instead of serving as a means for knowing it.*

---

[26][Lemon and Reis] The Tolstoy and Gogol translations are ours. The passage occurs in Vol. II, Part 8, Chap. 9 of the edition of *War and Peace* published in Boston by the Dana Estes Co. in 1904–1912.

---

[27][Lemon and Reis] Leo Tolstoy, *War and Peace*, IV, Art. 13, Chap. 14.

The purpose of imagery in erotic art can be studied even more accurately; an erotic object is usually presented as if it were seen for the first time. Gogol, in "Christmas Eve," provides the following example:

> Here he approached her more closely, coughed, smiled at her, touched her plump, bare arm with his fingers, and expressed himself in a way that showed both his cunning and his conceit.
>
> "And what is this you have, magnificent Solokha?" and having said this, he jumped back a little.
>
> "What? An arm, Osip Nikiforovich!" she answered.
>
> "Hmm, an arm! *He, he, he!*" said the secretary cordially, satisfied with his beginning. He wandered about the room.
>
> "And what is this you have, dearest Solokha?" he said in the same way, having approached her again and grasped her lightly by the neck, and in the very same way he jumped back.
>
> "As if you don't see, Osip Nikiforovich!" answered Solokha, "a neck, and on my neck a necklace."
>
> "Hmm! On the neck a necklace! *He, he, he!*" and the secretary again wandered about the room, rubbing his hands.
>
> "And what is this you have, incomparable Solokha?" . . . It is not known to what the secretary would stretch his longer fingers now.

And Knut Hamsun[28] has the following in *Hunger:* "Two white prodigies appeared from beneath her blouse."

Erotic subjects may also be presented figuratively with the obvious purpose of leading us away from their "recognition." Hence sexual organs are referred to in terms of lock and key,[29] or quilting tools,[30] or bow and arrow, or rings and marlinspikes, as in the legend of Stavyor, in which a married man does not recognize his wife, who is disguised as a warrior. She proposes a riddle:

> "Remember, Stavyor, do you recall
> How we little ones walked to and fro in the street?
> You and I together sometimes played with a
> marlinspike—
> You had a silver marlinspike.

> But I had a gilded ring?
> I found myself at it just now and then,
> But you fell in with it ever and always."
> Says Stavyor, son of Godinovich,
> "What! I didn't play with you at marlinspikes!"
> Then Vasilisa Mikulichna: "So he says.
> Do you remember, Stavyor, do you recall,
> Now must you know, you and I together learned to
> read and write;
> Mine was an ink-well of silver,
> And yours a pen of gold?
> But I just moistened it a little now and then,
> And I just moistened it ever and always."[31]

In a different version of the legend we find a key to the riddle:

> Here the formidable envoy Vasilyushka
> Raised her skirts to the very navel,
> And then the young Stavyor, son of Godinovich,
> Recognized her gilded ring. . . .[32]

But defamiliarization is not only a technique of the erotic riddle—a technique of euphemism—it is also the basis and point of all riddles. Every riddle pretends to show its subject either by words which specify or describe it but which, during the telling, do not seem applicable (the type: "black and white and 'red'—read—all over") or by means of odd but imitative sounds ("'Twas brillig, and the slithy toves / Did gyre and gimble in the wabe").[33]

Even erotic images not intended as riddles are defamiliarized ("boobies," "tarts," "piece," etc.). In popular imagery there is generally something equivalent to "trampling the grass" and "breaking the guelder-rose." The technique of defamiliarization is absolutely clear in the widespread image—a motif of erotic affectation—in which a bear and other wild beasts (or a devil, with a different reason for non-recognition) do not recognize a man.[34]

---

28 Knut Hamsun (1859–1952), Norwegian novelist.
29 [Shklovsky] [Dimitry] Savodnikov, *Zagadki russkova naroda* [*Riddles of the Russian People*] (St. Petersburg, 1901), Nos. 102–7.
30 [Shklovsky], Ibid., Nos. 588–91.

31 [Shklovsky] A. E. Gruzinsky, ed., *Pesni, sobrannye P[avel] N. Rybnikovym* [*Songs Collected by P. N. Rybnikov*] (Moscow, 1909–1910, No. 30).
32 [Shklovsky] Ibid., No. 171.
33 From Lewis Carroll's *Jabberwocky.* [Lemon and Reis] We have supplied familiar English examples in place of Shklovsky's word-play. Shklovsky is saying that we create words with no referents or with ambiguous referents in order to force attention to the objects represented by the similar-sounding words. By making the reader go through the extra step on interpreting the nonsense word, the writer prevents an automatic response. A toad is a toad, but "tove" forces one to pause and think about the beast.
34 [Shklovsky] E. R. Romanov, "Besstrashny barin" *Velikorusskiye skazki* (Zapiski Imperskovo Russkovo Geograficheskovo Obschestva XLII, No. 52). Belorussky sbornik, "Spravyadlivy soldat" ["The Intrepid Gentleman," *Great Russian Tales* (Notes of the Imperial Russian Geographical Society, XLII, No. 52). White Russian Anthology, "The Upright Soldier (1886–1912)].

The lack of recognition in the following tale is quite typical:

> A peasant was plowing a field with a piebald mare. A bear approached him and asked, "Uncle, what's made this mare piebald for you?"
>
> "I did the piebalding myself."
>
> "But how?"
>
> "Let me, and I'll do the same for you."
>
> The bear agreed. The peasant tied his feet together with a rope, took the ploughshare from the two-wheeled plough, heated it on the fire, and applied it to his flanks. He made the bear piebald by scorching his fur down to the hide with the hot ploughshare. The man untied the bear, which went off and lay down under a tree.
>
> A magpie flew at the peasant to pick at the meat on his shirt. He caught her and broke one of her legs. The magpie flew off to perch in the same tree under which the bear was lying. Then, after the magpie, a horsefly landed on the mare, sat down, and began to bite. The peasant caught the fly, took a stick, shoved it up its rear, and let it go. The fly went to the tree where the bear and the magpie were. There all three sat.
>
> The peasant's wife came to bring his dinner to the field. The man and his wife finished their dinner in the fresh air, and he began to wrestle with her on the ground.
>
> The bear saw this and said to the magpie and the fly, "Holy priests! The peasant wants to piebald someone again."
>
> The magpie said, "No, he wants to break someone's legs."
>
> The fly said, "No, he wants to shove a stick up someone's rump."[35]

The similarity of technique here and in Tolstoy's "Kholstomer," is, I think, obvious.

Quite often in literature the sexual act itself is defamiliarized; for example, the *Decameron*[36] refers to "scraping out a barrel," "catching nightingales," "gay wool-beating work" (the last is not developed in the plot). Defamiliarization is often used in describing the sexual organs.

A whole series of plots is based on such a lack of recognition; for example, in Afanasyev's[37] *Intimate Tales*

the entire story of "The Shy Mistress" is based on the fact that an object is not called by its proper name—or, in other words, on a game of nonrecognition. So too in Onchukov's[38] "Spotted Petticoats," tale no. 525, and also in "The Bear and the Hare" from *Intimate Tales,* in which the bear and the hare make a "wound."

Such constructions as "the pestle and the mortar," or "Old Nick and the infernal regions" *(Decameron),* are also examples of the technique of defamiliarization. And in my article on plot construction I write about defamiliarization in psychological parallelism. Here, then, I repeat that the perception of disharmony in a harmonious context is important in parallelism. The purpose of parallelism, like the general purpose of imagery, is to transfer the usual perception of an object into the sphere of a new perception—that is, to make a unique semantic modification.

In studying poetic speech in its phonetic and lexical structure as well as in its characteristic distribution of words and in the characteristic thought structures compounded from the words, we find everywhere the artistic trademark—that is, we find material obviously created to remove the automatism of perception; the author's purpose is to create the vision which results from that deautomatized perception. A work is created "artistically" so that its perception is impeded and the greatest possible effect is produced through the slowness of the perception. As a result of this lingering, the object is perceived not in its extension in space, but, so to speak, in its continuity. Thus "poetic language" gives satisfaction. According to Aristotle, poetic language must appear strange and wonderful;[39] and, in fact, it is often actually foreign: the Sumerian used by the Assyrians, the Latin of Europe during the Middle Ages, the Arabisms of the Persians, the Old Bulgarian of Russian literature, or the elevated, almost literary language of folk songs. The common archaisms of poetic language, the intricacy of the sweet new style [*dolce stil nuovo*],[40] the obscure style of the language of Arnaut Daniel[41] with the "roughened" [*harte*] forms *which make pronunciation difficult*—these are used in much the same way. Leo Jakubinsky has demonstrated the principle of phonetic "roughening" of poetic language in the particular case of the repetition of identical sounds. The language of poetry is, then, a difficult, roughened, impeded language. In a few

---

[35] [Shklovsky] D[mitry] S. Zelenin, *Velikorusskiyi skazki Permskoy gubernii* [*Great Russian Tales of the Permian Province* (St. Petersburg, 1913)], No. 70.

[36] By Giovanni Boccaccio (above, page 157).

[37] Alexander Afanazyev (1826–1871), Russian writer.

[38] Nikolai Eugenevich Onchukov (1872–1942), Russian writer.

[39] Aristotle speaks of the use of unusual words (above, page 64), but he warns against a strange diction. He thinks an element of the marvelous is necessary to tragedy (above, page 57).

[40] [Lemon and Reis] Dante, *Purgatorio,* 24:56. Dante refers to the new lyric style of his contemporaries.

[41] Arnaut Daniel (fl. 1189), French troubador.

special instances the language of poetry approximates the language of prose, but this does not violate the principle of "roughened" form.

> Her sister was called Tatyana.
> For the first time we shall
> Wilfully brighten the delicate
> Pages of a novel with such a name.

wrote Pushkin.[42] The usual poetic language of Pushkin's contemporaries was the elegant style of Derzhavin;[43] but Pushkin's style, because it seemed trivial then, was unexpectedly difficult for them. We should remember the consternation of Pushkin's contemporaries over the vulgarity of his expressions. He used the popular language as a special device for prolonging attention, just as his contemporaries generally used Russian words in their usually French speech (see Tolstoy's examples in *War and Peace*).

Just now a still more characteristic phenomenon is under way. Russian literary language, which was originally foreign to Russia, has so permeated the language of the people that it has blended with their conversation. On the other hand, literature has now begun to show a tendency towards the use of dialects (Remizov, Klyuyev, Essenin, and others,[44] so unequal in talent and so alike in language, are intentionally provincial) and of barbarisms (which gave rise to the Severyanin group[45]). And currently Maxim Gorky is changing his diction from the old literary language to the new literary colloquialism of Leskov.[46] Ordinary speech and literary language have thereby changed places (see the work of Vyacheslav Ivanov[47] and many others). And finally, a strong tendency, led by Khlebnikov,[48] to create a new and properly poetic language has emerged. In the light of these developments we can define poetry as *attenuated, tortuous* speech. Poetic speech is *formed speech*. Prose is ordinary speech—economical, easy, proper, the goddess of prose [*dea prosae*] is a goddess of the accurate, facile type, of the "direct" expression of a child. I shall discuss roughened form

and retardation as the general *law* of art at greater length in an article on plot construction.[49]

Nevertheless, the position of those who urge the idea of economy of artistic energy as something which exists in and even distinguishes poetic language seems, at first glance, tenable for the problem of rhythm. Spencer's description of rhythm would seem to be absolutely incontestable:

> Just as the body in receiving a series of varying concussions, must keep the muscles ready to meet the most violent of them, as not knowing when such may come: so, the mind in receiving unarranged articulations, must keep its perspectives active enough to recognize the least easily caught sounds. And as, if the concussions recur in definite order, the body may husband its forces by adjusting the resistance needful for each concussion; so, if the syllables be rhythmically arranged, the mind may economize its energies by anticipating the attention required for each syllable.[50]

This apparently conclusive observation suffers from the common fallacy, the confusion of the laws of poetic and prosaic language. In *The Philosophy of Style* Spencer failed utterly to distinguish between them. But rhythm may have two functions. The rhythm of prose, or of a work song like "Dubinushka," permits the members of the work crew to do their necessary "groaning together" and also eases the work by making it automatic. And, in fact, it is easier to march with music than without it, and to march during an animated conversation is even easier, for the walking is done unconsciously. Thus the rhythm of prose is an important automatizing element; the rhythm of poetry is not. There is "order" in art, yet not a single column of a Greek temple stands exactly in its proper order; poetic rhythm is similarly disordered rhythm. Attempts to systematize the irregularities have been made, and such attempts are part of the current problem in the theory of rhythm. It is obvious that the systematization will not work, for in reality the problem is not one of complicating the rhythm but of disordering the rhythm—a disordering which cannot be predicted. Should the disordering of rhythm become a convention, it would be ineffective as a device for the roughening of language. But I will not discuss rhythm in more detail since I intend to write a book about it.[51]

---

[42] Alexander Sergeyevich Pushkin (1799–1837), Russian poet.

[43] Gavril Romanovich Derzhavin (1743–1816), Russian writer

[44] [Lemon and Reis] Alexy Remizov (1877–1957) is best known as a novelist and satirist; Nicholas Klyuyev (1885–1937) and Sergey Essenin (1895–1925) were "peasant poets." All three were noted for their faithful reproduction of Russian dialects and colloquial language.

[45] [Lemon and Reis] A group noted for its opulent and sensuous verse style.

[46] [Lemon and Reis] Nicholas Leskov (1835–1895), novelist and short story writer, helped popularize the *skaz,* or yarn, and hence, because of the part dialect peculiarities play in the *skaz,* also altered Russian literary language.

[47] Vyacheslav Ivanov (1866–1949), Russian symbolist poet.

[48] Velimir Khlebnikov (1885–1922), Russian Futurist poet and critic.

[49] [Lemon and Reis] Shklovsky is probably referring to his *Razvyortyvaniye syuzheta* [*Plot Development*] (Petrograd, 1921).

[50] [Lemon and Reis] Spencer, page 169. Again the Russian text is shortened from Spencer's original.

[51] [Lemon and Reis] We have been unable to discover the book Shklovsky promised.

T. S. Eliot

1888–1965

T. S. Eliot was probably the most influential poet and critic of the first half of the twentieth century. He was born in St. Louis and educated at Harvard, where he came under the influence of Irving Babbitt, who was highly critical of Romanticism (see especially his *Rousseau and Romanticism* [1919]). Eliot was also acquainted with the self-proclaimed classicist T. E. Hulme, who in his *Speculations* (written in 1913–1914, posthumously published in 1924) called Romanticism "spilt religion" and warned against poetry that "flies away into the circumambient gas." These views Eliot tempered somewhat later in life, but his tastes remained generally "classicist." Indeed, in 1928 he characterized himself as "classical in literature, royalist in politics, Anglo-Catholic in religion." But Eliot's classicism might better be called traditionalism. His raising up of John Donne and the seventeenth-century metaphysical poets is connected with his earliest views, and his essays on them and on Renaissance drama exercised a major influence on the American New Criticism.

In the well-known essay *Tradition and the Individual Talent* (1917) Eliot attacks certain emphases in Romanticism: the cult of originality and the idea that a poem is primarily an expression of the poet's personality. Eliot argues that a great poem always implies its relation to the works of previous poets and artists and that a poet must develop a sense of the presentness as well as the pastness of the past. For Eliot, the poet expresses not a personality but a medium, and it is his concern for the medium that is reflected in those influenced by him. For Eliot, poetry is not a "turning loose of emotion but an escape from emotion." Some commentators have accused Eliot, on the basis of such remarks, of antipoetical coldness. Eliot's point, however, is more like the one Keats made with his term "negative capability" (above, page 536).

Eliot refers in a later essay, *The Frontiers of Criticism* (1956), to "a few of [his] notorious phrases which have had a truly embarrassing success in the world." One of these is surely the "objective correlative," offered in his essay *Hamlet and His Problems* (1919). He describes it as "a set of objects, a situation, a chain of events which shall be the formula for that *particular* emotion" which is the poem's (not the author's) intent. Eliot's argument in the essay is that there is no such thing in *Hamlet,* for the main character is "dominated by an emotion which is inexpressible, because it is in excess of the facts as they appear." Eliot's later view warns against explanations of a poem based on inquiry into origins, while resisting the idea that a poem has just one correct interpretation. We particularly recommend *The Frontiers of Criticism* for Eliot's very cogent reflections on the rise of academic criticism, taking a broader view, but urging that readers ask "when is criticism not literary criticism but something else?"

Eliot's critical works include *The Sacred Wood* (1920), *The Uses of Poetry and the Use of Criticism* (1933), *After Strange Gods* (1934), *Essays Ancient and Modern* (1936), *Christianity and Culture* (1940), *Selected Essays* (rev. ed., 1950), and *On Poetry and Poets* (1957). See F. O. Matthiessen, *The Achievement of T. S. Eliot* (rev. ed., 1947);

Leonard Ungar, ed., *T. S. Eliot: A Selected Critique* (1948); Victor Brombert, *The Criticism of T. S. Eliot* (1949); Sean Lucy, *T. S. Eliot and the Idea of Tradition* (1960); Lewis Freed, *T. S. Eliot: Aesthetics and History* (1962); Northrop Frye, *T. S. Eliot* (1963); Roger Kojecky, *T. S. Eliot's Social Criticism* (1971); Allen Austin, *T. S. Eliot: The Literary and Social Criticism* (1971); Allan Mowbray, *T. S. Eliot's Impersonal Theory of Poetry* (1974); Lewis Freed, *T. S. Eliot: The Critic as Philosopher* (1979); Brian Lee, *Theory and Personality* (1979); Edward Lobb, *T. S. Eliot and the Romantic Critical Tradition* (1981); Gregory Jay, *T. S. Eliot and the Poetics of Literary History* (1983); Harold F. Brooks, *T. S. Eliot as Literary Critic* (1987); Richard Shusterman, *T. S. Eliot and the Philosophy of Criticism* (1988); Tony Sharpe, *T. S. Eliot: A Literary Life* (1995); Kenneth Asher, *T. S. Eliot and Ideology* (1995); Craig Raine, *In Defence of T. S. Eliot* (2000).

Tradition and the Individual Talent

I

In English writing we seldom speak of tradition, though we occasionally apply its name in deploring its absence. We cannot refer to "the tradition" or to "a tradition"; at most, we employ the adjective in saying that the poetry of so-and-so is "traditional" or even "too traditional." Seldom, perhaps, does the word appear except in a phrase of censure. If otherwise, it is vaguely approbative, with the implication, as to the work approved, of some pleasing archaeological reconstruction. You can hardly make the word agreeable to English ears without this comfortable reference to the reassuring science of archaeology.

Certainly the word is not likely to appear in our appreciations of living or dead writers. Every nation, every race, has not only its own creative, but its own critical turn of mind; and is even more oblivious of the shortcomings and limitations of its critical habits than of those of its creative genius. We know, or think we know, from the enormous mass of critical writing that has appeared in the French language the critical method or habit of the French; we only conclude (we are such unconscious people) that the French are "more critical" than we, and sometimes even plume ourselves a little with the fact, as if the French were the less spontaneous. Perhaps they are; but we might remind ourselves that criticism is as inevitable as breathing, and that we should be none the worse for articulating what passes in our minds when we read a book and feel an emotion about

it, for criticizing our own minds in their work of criticism. One of the facts that might come to light in this process is our tendency to insist, when we praise a poet, upon those aspects of his work in which he least resembles anyone else. In these aspects or parts of his work we pretend to find what is individual, what is the peculiar essence of the man. We dwell with satisfaction upon the poet's difference from his predecessors, especially his immediate predecessors; we endeavor to find something that can be isolated in order to be enjoyed. Whereas if we approach a poet without this prejudice we shall often find that not only the best, but the most individual parts of his work may be those in which the dead poets, his ancestors, assert their immortality most vigorously. And I do not mean the impressionable period of adolescence, but the period of full maturity.

Yet if the only form of tradition, of handing down, consisted in following the ways of the immediate generation before us in a blind or timid adherence to its successes, "tradition" should positively be discouraged. We have seen many such simple currents soon lost in the sand; and novelty is better than repetition. Tradition is a matter of much wider significance. It cannot be inherited, and if you want it you must obtain it by great labor. It involves, in the first place, the historical sense, which we may call nearly indispensable to anyone who would continue to be a poet beyond his twenty-fifth year; and the historical sense involves a perception, not only of the pastness of the past, but of its presence; the historical sense compels a man to write not merely with his own generation in his bones, but with a feeling that the whole of the literature of Europe from Homer and within it the whole of the literature of his own country has a simultaneous existence and composes a simultaneous order. This historical sense, which is a sense of the timeless as well as of the temporal and of the timeless and of the temporal together, is what makes a writer traditional. And it

Tradition and the Individual Talent was first published in 1917. The text is from Eliot's *Selected Essays 1917–1932* (1932).

is at the same time what makes a writer most acutely conscious of his place in time, of his own contemporaneity.

No poet, no artist of any art, has his complete meaning alone. His significance, his appreciation is the appreciation of his relation to the dead poets and artists. You cannot value him alone; you must set him, for contrast and comparison, among the dead. I mean this as a principle of aesthetic, not merely historical, criticism. The necessity that he shall conform, that he shall cohere, is not one-sided; what happens when a new work of art is created is something that happens simultaneously to all the works of art which preceded it. The existing monuments form an ideal order among themselves, which is modified by the introduction of the new (the really new) work of art among them. The existing order is complete before the new work arrives; for order to persist after the supervention of novelty, the *whole* existing order must be, if ever so slightly, altered; and so the relations, proportions, values of each work of art toward the whole are readjusted; and this is conformity between the old and the new. Whoever has approved this idea of order, of the form of European, of English literature will not find it preposterous that the past should be altered by the present as much as the present is directed by the past. And the poet who is aware of this will be aware of great difficulties and responsibilities.

In a peculiar sense he will be aware also that he must inevitably be judged by the standards of the past. I say judged, not amputated, by them; not judged to be as good as, or worse or better than, the dead; and certainly not judged by the canons of dead critics. It is a judgment, a comparison, in which two things are measured by each other. To conform merely would be for the new work not really to conform at all; it would not be new, and would therefore not be a work of art. And we do not quite say that the new is more valuable because it fits in; but its fitting in is a test of its value—a test, it is true, which can only be slowly and cautiously applied, for we are none of us infallible judges of conformity. We say: It appears to conform, and is perhaps individual, or it appears individual, and may conform; but we are hardly likely to find that it is one and not the other.

To proceed to a more intelligible exposition of the relation of the poet to the past: he can neither take the past as a lump, an indiscriminate bolus, nor can he form himself wholly on one or two private admirations, nor can he form himself wholly upon one preferred period. The first course is inadmissible, the second is an important experience of youth, and the third is a pleasant and highly desirable supplement. The poet must be very conscious of the main current, which does not at all flow invariably through the most distinguished reputations. He must be quite aware of the obvious fact that art never improves,[1] but that the material of art is never quite the same. He must be aware that the mind of Europe—the mind of his own country—a mind which he learns in time to be much more important than his own private mind—is a mind which changes, and that this change is a development which abandons nothing en route, which does not superannuate either Shakespeare, or Homer, or the rock drawing of the Magdalenian draftsmen. That this development, refinement perhaps, complication certainly, is not, from the point of view of the artist, any improvement. Perhaps not even an improvement from the point of view of the psychologist or not to the extent which we imagine; perhaps only in the end based upon a complication in economics and machinery. But the difference between the present and the past is that the conscious present is an awareness of the past in a way and to an extent which the past's awareness of itself cannot show.

Someone said: "The dead writers are remote from us because we *know* so much more than they did." Precisely, and they are that which we know.

I am alive to a usual objection to what is clearly part of my program for the métier of poetry. The objection is that the doctrine requires a ridiculous amount of erudition (pedantry), a claim which can be rejected by appeal to the lives of poets in any pantheon. It will even be affirmed that much learning deadens or perverts poetic sensibility. While, however, we persist in believing that a poet ought to know as much as will not encroach upon his necessary receptivity and necessary laziness, it is not desirable to confine knowledge to whatever can be put into a useful shape for examinations, drawing rooms, or the still more pretentious modes of publicity. Some can absorb knowledge, the more tardy must sweat for it. Shakespeare acquired more essential history from Plutarch[2] than most men could from the whole British Museum. What is to be insisted upon is that the poet must develop or procure the consciousness of the past and that he should continue to develop this consciousness throughout his career.

What happens is a continual surrender of himself as he is at the moment to something which is more valuable. The progress of an artist is a continual self-sacrifice, a continual extinction of personality.

There remains to define this process of depersonalization and its relation to the sense of tradition. It is in this depersonalization that art may be said to approach the condition of science. I, therefore, invite you to consider, as a suggestive analogy, the action which takes place when a bit

[1] Blake (above, page 454).
[2] Plutarch (above, page 119).

of finely filiated platinum is introduced into a chamber containing oxygen and sulfur dioxide.

II

Honest criticism and sensitive appreciation are directed not upon the poet but upon the poetry. If we attend to the confused cries of the newspaper critics and the susurrus[3] of popular repetition that follows, we shall hear the names of poets in great numbers; if we seek not blue-book knowledge but the enjoyment of poetry, and ask for a poem, we shall seldom find it. I have tried to point out the importance of the relation of the poem to other poems by other authors, and suggested the conception of poetry as a living whole of all the poetry that has ever been written. The other aspect of this impersonal theory of poetry is the relation of the poem to its author. And I hinted, by an analogy, that the mind of the mature poet differs from that of the immature one not precisely in any valuation of "personality," not being necessarily more interesting, or having "more to say," but rather by being a more finely perfected medium in which special, or very varied, feelings are at liberty to enter into new combinations.

The analogy was that of the catalyst. When the two gases previously mentioned are mixed in the presence of a filament of platinum, they form sulfurous acid. This combination takes place only if the platinum is present; nevertheless the newly formed acid contains no trace of platinum, and the platinum itself is apparently unaffected; has remained inert, neutral, and unchanged. The mind of the poet is the shred of platinum. It may partly or exclusively operate upon the experience of the man himself; but, the more perfect the artist, the more completely separate in him will be the man who suffers and the mind which creates; the more perfectly will the mind digest and transmute the passions which are its material.

The experience, you will notice, the elements which enter the presence of the transforming catalyst, are of two kinds: emotions and feelings. The effect of a work of art upon the person who enjoys it is an experience different in kind from any experience not of art. It may be formed out of one emotion, or may be a combination of several; and various feelings, inhering for the writer in particular words or phrases or images, may be added to compose the final result. Or great poetry may be made without the direct use of any emotion whatever: composed out of feelings solely. Canto XV of the *Inferno* (Brunetto Latini) is a working up of the emotion evident in the situation; but the effect, though single as that of

any work of art, is obtained by considerable complexity of detail. The last quatrain gives an image, a feeling attaching to an image, which "came," which did not develop simply out of what precedes, but which was probably in suspension in the poet's mind until the proper combination arrived for it to add itself to. The poet's mind is in fact a receptacle for seizing and storing up numberless feelings, phrases, images, which remain there until all the particles which can unite to form a new compound are present together.

If you compare several representative passages of the greatest poetry you see how great is the variety of types of combination, and also how completely any semiethical criterion of "sublimity" misses the mark. For it is not the "greatness," the intensity, of the emotions, the components, but the intensity of the artistic process, the pressure, so to speak, under which the fusion takes place, that counts. The episode of Paolo and Francesca employs a definite emotion, but the intensity of the poetry is something quite different from whatever intensity in the supposed experience it may give the impression of. It is no more intense, furthermore, than Canto XXVI, the voyage of Ulysses, which has not the direct dependence upon an emotion. Great variety is possible in the process of transmutation of emotion: the murder of Agamemnon, or the agony of Othello, gives an artistic effect apparently closer to a possible original than the scenes from Dante. In the *Agamemnon,* the artistic emotion approximates to the emotion of an actual spectator; in *Othello* to the emotion of the protagonist himself. But the difference between art and the event is always absolute; the combination which is the murder of Agamemnon is probably as complex as that which is the voyage of Ulysses. In either case there has been a fusion of elements. The ode of Keats contains a number of feelings which have nothing particular to do with the nightingale, but which the nightingale, partly, perhaps, because of its attractive name, and partly because of its reputation, served to bring together.

The point of view which I am struggling to attack is perhaps related to the metaphysical theory of the substantial unity of the soul: for my meaning is, that the poet has, not a "personality" to express, but a particular medium, which is only a medium and not a personality, in which impressions and experiences combine in peculiar and unexpected ways. Impressions and experiences which are important for the man may take no place in the poetry, and those which become important in the poetry may play quite a negligible part in the man, the personality.

I will quote a passage which is unfamiliar enough to be regarded with fresh attention in the light—or darkness—of these observations:

---

[3] "Muttering."

And now methinks I could e'en chide myself
For doting on her beauty, though her death
Shall be revenged after no common action.
Does the silkworm expend her yellow labors
For thee? For thee does she undo herself?
Are lordships sold to maintain ladyships
For the poor benefit of a bewildering minute?
Why does yon fellow falsify highways,
And put his life between the judge's lips,
To refine such a thing—keeps horse and men
To beat their valors for her? . . .[4]

In this passage (as is evident if it is taken in its context) there is a combination of positive and negative emotions: an intensely strong attraction toward beauty and an equally intense fascination by the ugliness which is contrasted with it and which destroys it. This balance of contrasted emotion is in the dramatic situation to which the speech is pertinent, but that situation alone is inadequate to it. This is, so to speak, the structural emotion, provided by the drama. But the whole effect, the dominant tone, is due to the fact that a number of floating feelings, having an affinity to this emotion by no means superficially evident, have combined with it to give us a new art emotion.

It is not in his personal emotions, the emotions provoked by particular events in his life, that the poet is in any way remarkable or interesting. His particular emotions may be simple, or crude, or flat. The emotion in his poetry will be a very complex thing, but not with the complexity of the emotions of people who have very complex or unusual emotions in life. One error, in fact, of eccentricity in poetry is to seek for new human emotions to express; and in this search for novelty in the wrong place it discovers the perverse. The business of the poet is not to find new emotions, but to use the ordinary ones and, in working them up into poetry, to express feelings which are not in actual emotions at all. And emotions which he has never experienced will serve his turn as well as those familiar to him. Consequently, we must believe that "emotion recollected in tranquility"[5] is an inexact formula. For it is neither emotion, nor recollection, nor, without distortion of meaning, tranquility. It is a concentration, and a new thing resulting from the concentration, of a very great number of experiences which to the practical and active person would not seem to be experiences at all; it is a concentration which does not happen consciously or of deliberation. These experiences are not "recollected," and they finally unite in an atmosphere which is "tranquil" only in that it is a passive attending upon the event. Of course this is not quite the whole story. There is a great deal, in the writing of poetry, which must be conscious and deliberate. In fact, the bad poet is usually unconscious where he ought to be conscious, and conscious where he ought to be unconscious. Both errors tend to make him "personal." Poetry is not a turning loose of emotion, but an escape from emotion; it is not the expression of personality, but an escape from personality. But, of course, only those who have personality and emotions know what it means to want to escape from these things.

III

ὁ δὲ νοῦς ἴσως Θειότερον τι καὶ ἀπαθές ἐστιν.[6]

This essay proposes to halt at the frontier of metaphysics or mysticism, and confine itself to such practical conclusions as can be applied by the responsible person interested in poetry. To divert interest from the poet to the poetry is a laudable aim: for it would conduce to a juster estimation of actual poetry, good and bad. There are many people who appreciate the expression of sincere emotion in verse, and there is a smaller number of people who can appreciate technical excellence. But very few know when there is an expression of *significant* emotion, emotion which has its life in the poem and not in the history of the poet. The emotion of art is impersonal. And the poet cannot reach his impersonality without surrendering himself wholly to the work to be done. And he is not likely to know what is to be done unless he lives in what is not merely the present, but the present moment of the past, unless he is conscious; not of what is dead, but of what is already living.

---

[4]Cyril Tourneur (early seventeenth century), *The Revenger's Tragedy* III, ix
[5]Wordsworth (above, page 490).

[6]"The mind may be too divine and therefore unmoved."

Bertrand Russell

1872–1970

Bertrand Russell, later the third Earl Russell, was educated at Cambridge, where he was invited to become a member of "The Apostles," an exclusive society dating from the decade following Coleridge's death. He distinguished himself in taking first-class honors in mathematics in 1893, and, a year later, a first-class degree in moral philosophy. Together with G. E. Moore, Russell embraced empiricism and, in a rejection of idealism, focused his attention on developing the analytical means to ensure the highest degree of attainable certainty in philosophical (and scientific) statements. In 1903, he published his first major work, *Principles of Mathematics,* which served as the basis for perhaps his most influential work, in collaboration with Alfred North Whitehead, *Principia Mathematica* (1910–1913). Borrowing the title of Sir Isaac Newton's great work, Russell and Whitehead set out to develop a logical formalism for deriving mathematics from elementary logical principles. The current conventions for representing expressions in symbolic logic are ultimately derived (though with many modifications and improvements) from the work of Russell and Whitehead.

Russell's own philosophical position developed as the search for a philosophical language with a correlative precision. In *Introduction to Mathematical Philosophy* (1919), from which the selection reprinted here is drawn (and which Russell wrote while in prison for his pacifist activities), Russell laid out the groundwork for his theory of logical atomism, subsequently developed by Ludwig Wittgenstein (below, page 823), on the principle that ambiguities and uncertainties in statements could be radically clarified by substituting definite descriptions for names, so as to assure that such nonsensical statements as "The present king of France is bald" could be excluded, on the grounds that since there is no "present king of France," the assertion that he is bald would have no meaning. Russell's undertaking, closely related to the analysis of Gottlob Frege (above, page 734), was the beginning of a strictly logical, and generally empiricist or positivist orientation in philosophy that enjoyed a long period of prominence (if not dominance) in English and North American universities. The developmental trajectory of this project (with which Russell himself lost patience later on) foregrounded two essential principles: first, the stringent clarification of language, so as to eliminate ambiguities and what appeared to be bogus ontological problems; and second, to bring formal logic to bear upon philosophical statements so as to facilitate their evaluation by means of reference or empirical verification. In just this spirit, Russell had located and pointed out to Gottlob Frege a contradiction in Frege's own attempt to develop a strict logical formalism, now known as "Russell's Paradox," that stems from positing a set of sets, for example *V*, consisting of all sets not members of themselves, such that asking the logical status of the set *V* (that is, is it, or is it not a member of itself) produces an inescapable paradox or antinomy. The early work of Ludwig Wittgenstein, *Tractatus-Logico-Philosophicus* (another borrowed title, from Spinoza), advanced this work by formalizing truth functions in "truth tables," to establish logical equality between statements sharing the same truth value. In the chapter reprinted here, however, Russell's main concern remains the problem of definite descriptions, with an engaging and witty style that facilitates the introduction of a degree of technical precision previously very rare in philosophical writing. Russell was awarded the Nobel Prize for Literature in 1950.

In addition to books mentioned above, Russell's philosophical, political, and autobiographical writings include: *The Practice and Theory of Bolshevism* (1920); *The Analysis of Mind* (1921); *Why I Am Not a Christian* (1927); *The Analysis of Matter* (1927); *Marriage and Morals* (1929); *The Scientific Outlook* (1931); *History of Western Philosophy* (1945); and *Human Knowledge: Its Scope and Limits* (1948). See also his influential and popular *The Problems of Philosophy* (1946). Critical and biographical studies include: Alan Wood, *The Passionate Sceptic* (1957); Ronald W. Clark, *Bertrand Russell and His World* (1981); D. F. Pears, *Bertrand Russell and the British Tradition in Philosophy,* second edition (1972); Paul Arthur Schilpp, ed., *The Philosophy of Bertrand Russell,* fifth edition (1974; 1989); Paul Grimley Kuntz, *Bertrand Russell* (1986); Alejandro R. Garciadiego, *Bertrand Russell and the Origins of Set-Theoretic 'Paradoxes'* (1992); Philip Ironside, *The Social and Political Thought of Bertrand Russell: The Development of an Aristotcratic Liberalism* (1996); Ray Monk and Anthony Palmer, eds., *Bertrand Russell and the Origins of Analytical Philosophy* (1996); A. D. Irvine, ed., *Bertrand Russell: Critical Assessments* (in four volumes, 1999).

Descriptions

We dealt in the preceding chapter with the words *all* and *some;* in this chapter we shall consider the word *the* in the singular, and in the next chapter we shall consider the word *the* in the plural. It may be thought excessive to devote two chapters to one word, but to the philosophical mathematician it is a word of very great importance: like Browning's Grammarian with the enclitic δε, I would give the doctrine of this word if I were "dead from the waist down" and not merely in a prison.[1]

We have already had occasion to mention "descriptive functions," *i.e.* such expressions as "the father of *x*" or "the sine of *x*." These are to be defined by first defining "descriptions."

A "description" may be of two sorts, definite and indefinite (or ambiguous). An indefinite description is a phrase of the form "a so-and-so," and a definite description is a phrase of the form "the so-and-so" (in the singular). Let us begin with the former.

"Who did you meet?" "I met a man." "That is a very indefinite description." We are therefore not departing from usage in our terminology. Our question is: What do I really assert when I assert "I met a man"? Let us assume, for the moment, that my assertion is true, and that in fact I met Jones. It is clear that what I assert is *not* "I met Jones." I may say "I met a man, but it was not Jones"; in that case, though I lie, I do not contradict myself, as I should do if when I say I met a man I really mean that I met Jones. It is clear also that the person to whom I am speaking can understand what I say, even if he is a foreigner and has never heard of Jones.

But we may go further: not only Jones, but no actual man, enters into my statement. This becomes obvious when the statement is false, since then there is no more reason why Jones should be supposed to enter into the proposition than why anyone else should. Indeed the statement would remain significant, though it could not possibly be true, even if there were no man at all. "I met a unicorn" or "I met a sea-serpent" is a perfectly significant assertion, if we know what it would be to be a unicorn or a sea-serpent, *i.e.* what is the definition of these fabulous monsters. Thus it is only what

DESCRIPTIONS is Chapter XVI from *Introduction to Mathematical Philosophy* (London: G. Allen & Unwin, Ltd., 1919).
[1]Robert Browning (1812–1889), English poet. The reference is to "A Grammarian's Funeral Shortly After the Revival of Learning," where the grammarian "Gave us the doctrine of the enclitic *de* / Dead from the waist down." Russell wrote the first draft of *Introduction to Mathematical Philosophy* while imprisoned for his pacifist activities.

we may call the *concept* that enters into the proposition. In the case of "unicorn," for example, there is only the concept: there is not also, somewhere among the shades, something unreal which may be called "a unicorn." Therefore, since it is significant (though false) to say "I met a unicorn," it is clear that this proposition, rightly analysed, does not contain a constituent "a unicorn," though it does contain the concept "unicorn."

The question of "unreality," which confronts us at this point, is a very important one. Misled by grammar, the great majority of those logicians who have dealt with this question have dealt with it on mistaken lines. They have regarded grammatical form as a surer guide in analysis than, in fact, it is. And they have not known what differences in grammatical form are important. "I met Jones" and "I met a man" would count traditionally as propositions of the same form, but in actual fact they are of quite different forms: the first names an actual person, Jones; while the second involves a propositional function, and becomes, when made explicit: "The function 'I met x and x is human' is sometimes true." (It will be remembered that we adopted the convention of using "sometimes" as not implying more than once.) This proposition is obviously not of the form "I met x," which accounts for the existence of the proposition "I met a unicorn" in spite of the fact that there is no such thing as "a unicorn."

For want of the apparatus of propositional functions, many logicians have been driven to the conclusion that there are unreal objects. It is argued, *e.g.* by Meinong,[2] that we can speak about "the golden mountain," "the round square," and so on; we can make true propositions of which these are the subjects; hence they must have some kind of logical being, since otherwise the propositions in which they occur would be meaningless. In such theories, it seems to me, there is a failure of that feeling for reality which ought to be preserved even in the most abstract studies. Logic, I should maintain, must no more admit a unicorn than zoology can; for logic is concerned with the real world just as truly as zoology, though with its more abstract and general features. To say that unicorns have an existence in heraldry, or in literature, or in imagination, is a most pitiful and paltry evasion. What exists in heraldry is not an animal, made of flesh and blood, moving and breathing of its own initiative. What exists is a picture, or a description in words. Similarly, to

maintain that Hamlet, for example, exists in his own world, namely, in the world of Shakespeare's imagination, just as truly as (say) Napoleon existed in the ordinary world, is to say something deliberately confusing, or else confused to a degree which is scarcely credible. There is only one world, the "real" world: Shakespeare's imagination is part of it, and the thoughts that he had in writing Hamlet are real. So are the thoughts that we have in reading the play. But it is of the very essence of fiction that only the thoughts, feelings, etc., in Shakespeare and his readers are real, and that there is not, in addition to them, an objective Hamlet. When you have taken account of all the feelings roused by Napoleon in writers and readers of history, you have not touched the actual man; but in the case of Hamlet you have come to the end of him. If no one thought about Hamlet, there would be nothing left of him; if no one had thought about Napoleon, he would have soon seen to it that some one did. The sense of reality is vital in logic, and whoever juggles with it by pretending that Hamlet has another kind of reality is doing a disservice to thought. A robust sense of reality is very necessary in framing a correct analysis of propositions about unicorns, golden mountains, round squares, and other such pseudo-objects.

In obedience to the feeling of reality, we shall insist that, in the analysis of propositions, nothing "unreal" is to be admitted. But, after all, if there *is* nothing unreal, how, it may be asked, *could* we admit anything unreal? The reply is that, in dealing with propositions, we are dealing in the first instance with symbols, and if we attribute significance to groups of symbols which have no significance, we shall fall into the error of admitting unrealities, in the only sense in which this is possible, namely, as objects described. In the proposition "I met a unicorn," the whole four words together make a significant proposition, and the word "unicorn" by itself is significant, in just the same sense as the word "man." But the *two* words "a unicorn" do not form a subordinate group having a meaning of its own. Thus if we falsely attribute meaning to these two words, we find ourselves saddled with "a unicorn," and with the problem how there can be such a thing in a world where there are no unicorns. "A unicorn" is an indefinite description which describes nothing. It is not an indefinite description which describes something unreal. Such a proposition as "x is unreal" only has meaning when "x" is a description, definite or indefinite; in that case the proposition will be true if "x" is a description which describes nothing. But whether the description "x" describes something or describes nothing, it is in any case not a constituent of the proposition in which it occurs; like "a unicorn" just now, it is not a subordinate group having a meaning of its own. All this results from the

[2] Alexius Meinong (1853–1920), Austrian philosopher, a student of Franz Brentano. Meinong's claim is that talk of objects (such as the "golden mountain" that does not exist) can be true in the sense that they designate concepts. Russell refers here to Meinong's *Untersuchungen zur Gegenstandstheorie und Psychologie* (1904; *Investigations of Object-Theory and Psychology*).

fact that, when *"x"* is a description, *"x* is unreal" or *"x* does not exist" is not nonsense, but is always significant and sometimes true.

We may now proceed to define generally the meaning of propositions which contain ambiguous descriptions. Suppose we wish to make some statement about "a so-and-so," where "so-and-so's" are those objects that have a certain property ϕ, *i.e.* those objects x for which the propositional function ϕx is true. (*E.g.* if we take "a man" as our instance of "a so-and-so," ϕx will be "*x* is human.") Let us now wish to assert the property ψ of "a so-and-so," *i.e.* we wish to assert that "a so-and-so" has that property which x has when ψx is true. (*E.g.* in the case of "I met a man," ψx will be "I met *x*.") Now the proposition that "a so-and-so" has the property ψ is *not* a proposition of the form "ψx." If it were, "a so-and-so" would have to be identical with x for a suitable x; and although (in a sense) this may be true in some cases, it is certainly not true in such a case as "a unicorn." It is just this fact, that the statement that a so-and-so has the property ψ is not of the form ψx, which makes it possible for "a so-and-so" to be, in a certain clearly definable sense, "unreal." The definition is as follows:—

> The statement that "an object having the property ϕ has the property ψ"

means:

> "The joint assertion of ϕx and ψx is not always false."

So far as logic goes, this is the same proposition as might be expressed by "some ϕ's are ψ's"; but rhetorically there is a difference, because in the one case there is a suggestion of singularity, and in the other case of plurality. This, however, is not the important point. The important point is that, when rightly analysed, propositions verbally about "a so-and-so" are found to contain no constituent represented by this phrase. And that is why such propositions can be significant even when there is no such thing as a so-and-so.

The definition of *existence,* as applied to ambiguous descriptions, results from what was said at the end of the preceding chapter. We say that "men exist" or "a man exists" if the propositional function "*x* is human" is sometimes true; and generally "a so-and-so" exists if "*x* is so-and-so" is sometimes true. We may put this in other language. The proposition "Socrates is a man" is no doubt *equivalent* to "Socrates is human," but it is not the very same proposition. The *is* of "Socrates is human" expresses the relation of subject and predicate; the *is* of "Socrates is a man" expresses identity. It is a disgrace to the human race that it has chosen to employ the same word "is" for these two entirely different ideas—a disgrace which a symbolic logical language of course remedies. The identity in "Socrates is a man" is identity between an object named (accepting "Socrates" as a name, subject to qualifications explained later) and an object ambiguously described. An object ambiguously described will "exist" when at least one such proposition is true, *i.e.* when there is at least one true proposition of the form "*x* is a so-and-so," where *"x"* is a name. It is characteristic of ambiguous (as opposed to definite) descriptions that there may be any number of true propositions of the above form—Socrates is a man, Plato is a man, etc. Thus "a man exists" follows from Socrates, or Plato, or anyone else. With definite descriptions, on the other hand, the corresponding form of proposition, namely, "*x* is the so-and-so" (where *"x"* is a name), can only be true for one value of x at most. This brings us to the subject of definite descriptions, which are to be defined in a way analogous to that employed for ambiguous descriptions, but rather more complicated.[3]

We come now to the main subject of the present chapter, namely, the definition of the word *the* (in the singular). One very important point about the definition of "a so-and-so" applies equally to "the so-and-so"; the definition to be sought is a definition of propositions in which this phrase occurs, not a definition of the phrase itself in isolation. In the case of "a so-and-so," this is fairly obvious: no one could suppose that "a man" was a definite object, which could be defined by itself. Socrates is a man, Plato is a man, Aristotle is a man, but we cannot infer that "a man" means the same as "Socrates" means and also the same as "Plato" means and also the same as "Aristotle" means, since these three names have different meanings. Nevertheless, when we have enumerated all the men in the world, there is nothing left of which we can say, "This is a man, and not only so, but it is *the* 'a man,' the quintessential entity that is just an indefinite man without being anybody in particular." It is of course quite clear that whatever there is in the world is definite: if it is a man it is one definite man and not any other. Thus there cannot be such an entity as "a man" to be found in the world, as opposed to

---

[3]This is an understatement in light of subsequent developments of this theme in virtually all varieties of logical empiricism and positivism, since it set the stage for protracted, and finally, indeterminate debates concerning the status of abstract entities, and the logical and evidential handling of verification claims. See the starkly different view of C.S. Peirce (above page 652), and the effort of Rudolph Carnap (below, page 978) to ward off the consequences of Russell's extreme claim here.

specific men. And accordingly it is natural that we do not define "a man" itself, but only the propositions in which it occurs.

In the case of "the so-and-so" this is equally true, though at first sight less obvious. We may demonstrate that this must be the case, by a consideration of the difference between a *name* and a *definite description.* Take the proposition, "Scott is the author of *Waverley.*"[4] We have here a name, "Scott," and a description, "the author of *Waverley,*" which are asserted to apply to the same person. The distinction between a name and all other symbols may be explained as follows:—

A name is a simple symbol whose meaning is something that can only occur as subject, *i.e.* something of the kind that, in Chapter XIII, we defined as an "individual" or a "particular." And a "simple" symbol is one which has no parts that are symbols. Thus "Scott" is a simple symbol, because, though it has parts (namely, separate letters), these parts are not symbols. On the other hand, "the author of *Waverley*" is not a simple symbol, because the separate words that compose the phrase are parts which are symbols. If, as may be the case, whatever *seems* to be an "individual" is really capable of further analysis, we shall have to content ourselves with what may be called "relative individuals," which will be terms that, throughout the context in question, are never analysed and never occur otherwise than as subjects. And in that case we shall have correspondingly to content ourselves with "relative names." From the standpoint of our present problem, namely, the definition of descriptions, this problem, whether these are absolute names or only relative names, may be ignored, since it concerns different stages in the hierarchy of "types," whereas we have to compare such couples as "Scott" and "the author of *Waverley,*" which both apply to the same object, and do not raise the problem of types. We may, therefore, for the moment, treat names as capable of being absolute; nothing that we shall have to say will depend upon this assumption, but the wording may be a little shortened by it.

We have, then, two things to compare: (1) a *name,* which is a simple symbol, directly designating an individual which is its meaning, and having this meaning in its own right, independently of the meanings of all other words; (2) a *description,* which consists of several words, whose meanings are already fixed, and from which results whatever is to be taken as the "meaning" of the description.

A proposition containing a description is not identical with what that proposition becomes when a name is substituted, even if the name names the same object as the description describes. "Scott is the author of *Waverley*" is obviously a different proposition from "Scott is Scott": the first is a fact in literary history, the second a trivial truism. And if we put anyone other than Scott in place of "the author of *Waverley,*" our proposition would become false, and would therefore certainly no longer be the same proposition. But, it may be said, our proposition is essentially of the same form as (say) "Scott is Sir Walter," in which two names are said to apply to the same person. The reply is that, if "Scott is Sir Walter" really means "the person named 'Scott' is the person named 'Sir Walter,'" then the names are being used as descriptions: *i.e.* the individual, instead of being named, is being described as the person having that name. This is a way in which names are frequently used in practice, and there will, as a rule, be nothing in the phraseology to show whether they are being used in this way or *as* names. When a name is used directly, merely to indicate what we are speaking about, it is no part of the *fact* asserted, or of the falsehood if our assertion happens to be false: it is merely part of the symbolism by which we express our thought. What we want to express is something which might (for example) be translated into a foreign language; it is something for which the actual words are a vehicle, but of which they are no part. On the other hand, when we make a proposition about "the person called 'Scott,'" the actual name "Scott" enters into what we are asserting, and not merely into the language used in making the assertion. Our proposition will now be a different one if we substitute "the person called 'Sir Walter.'" But so long as we are using names *as* names, whether we say "Scott" or whether we say "Sir Walter" is as irrelevant to what we are asserting as whether we speak English or French. Thus so long as names are used *as* names, "Scott is Sir Walter" is the same trivial proposition as "Scott is Scott." This completes the proof that "Scott is the author of *Waverley*" is not the same proposition as results from substituting a name for "the author of *Waverley,*" no matter what name may be substituted.

When we use a variable, and speak of a propositional function, ϕx say, the process of applying general statements about x to particular cases will consist in substituting a name for the letter "x," assuming that ϕ is a function which has individuals for its arguments. Suppose, for example, that ϕx is "always true"; let it be, say the "law of identity," $x = x$. Then we may substitute for "x" any name we choose, and we shall obtain a true proposition. Assuming for the moment that "Socrates," "Plato," and "Aristotle" are names (a very rash assumption), we can infer from the law of identity

---

[4]Sir Walter Scott (1771–1832), Scottish novelist and poet. His novel, *Waverley,* a story of the Jacobite rebellion of 1745, completed in 1814, was an immediate and enduring success.

that Socrates is Socrates, Plato is Plato, and Aristotle is Aristotle. But we shall commit a fallacy if we attempt to infer, without further premisses, that the author of *Waverley* is the author of *Waverley*. This results from what we have just proved, that, if we substitute a name for "the author of *Waverley*" in a proposition, the proposition we obtain is a different one. That is to say, applying the result to our present case: If "*x*" is a name, "*x=x*" is not the same proposition as "the author of *Waverley* is the author of *Waverley*," no matter what name "*x*" may be. Thus from the fact that all propositions of the form "*x=x*" are true we cannot infer, without more ado, that the author of *Waverley* is the author of *Waverley*. In fact, propositions of the form "the so-and-so is the so-and-so" are not always true: it is necessary that the so-and-so should *exist* (a term which will be explained shortly). It is false that the present King of France is the pres-ent King of France, or that the round square is the round square. When we substitute a description for a name, propositional functions which are "always true" may become false, if the description describes nothing. There is no mystery in this as soon as we realise (what was proved in the preceding paragraph) that when we substitute a description the result is not a value of the propositional function in question.

We are now in a position to define propositions in which a definite description occurs. The only thing that distinguishes "the so-and-so" from "a so-and-so" is the implication of uniqueness. We cannot speak of "*the* inhabitant of London," because inhabiting London is an attribute which is not unique. We cannot speak about "the present King of France," because there is none; but we can speak about "the present King of England." Thus propositions about "the so-and-so" always imply the corresponding propositions about "a so-and-so," with the addendum that there is not more than one so-and-so. Such a proposition as "Scott is the author of *Waverley*" could not be true if *Waverley* had never been written, or if several people had written it; and no more could any other proposition resulting from a propositional function *x* by the substitution of "the author of *Waverley*" for "*x*." We may say that "the author of *Waverley*" means "the value of *x* for which '*x* wrote *Waverley*' is true." Thus the proposition "the author of *Waverley* was Scotch," for example, involves:

(1) "*x* wrote *Waverley*" is not always false;

(2) "if *x* and *y* wrote *Waverley*, *x* and *y* are identical" is always true;

(3) "if *x* wrote *Waverley*, *x* was Scotch" is always true. These three propositions, translated into ordinary language, state:

(1) at least one person wrote *Waverley*;

(2) at most one person wrote *Waverley*;

(3) whoever wrote *Waverley* was Scotch.
All these three are implied by "the author of *Waverley* was Scotch." Conversely, the three together (but no two of them) imply that the author of *Waverley* was Scotch. Hence the three together may be taken as defining what is meant by the proposition "the author of *Waverley* was Scotch."

We may somewhat simplify these three propositions. The first and second together are equivalent to: "There is a term *c* such that '*x* wrote *Waverley*' is true when *x* is *c* and is false when *x* is not *c*." In other words, "There is a term *c* such that '*x* wrote *Waverley*' is always equivalent to '*x* is *c*.'" (Two propositions are "equivalent" when both are true or both are false.) We have here, to begin with, two functions of *x*, "*x* wrote *Waverley*" and "*x* is *c*," and we form a function of *c* by considering the equivalence of these two functions of *x* for all values of *x;* we then proceed to assert that the resulting function of *c* is "sometimes true," *i.e.* that it is true for at least one value of *c*. (It obviously cannot be true for more than one value of *c*.) These two conditions together are defined as giving the meaning of "the author of *Waverley* exists."

We may now define "the term satisfying the function ϕx exists." This is the general form of which the above is a particular case. "The author of *Waverley*" is "the term satisfying the function '*x* wrote *Waverley*.'" And "the so-and-so" will always involve reference to some propositional function, namely, that which defines the property that makes a thing a so-and-so. Our definition is as follows:—

"The term satisfying the function ϕx exists" means: "There is a term *c* such that ϕx is always equivalent to '*x* is *c*.'"

In order to define "the author of *Waverley* was Scotch," we have still to take account of the third of our three propositions, namely, "Whoever wrote *Waverley* was Scotch." This will be satisfied by merely adding that the *c* in question is to be Scotch. Thus "the author of *Waverley* was Scotch" is:

"There is a term *c* such that (1) '*x* wrote *Waverley*' is always equivalent to '*x* is *c*,' (2) *c* is Scotch."

And generally: "the term satisfying ϕx satisfies ψx" is defined as meaning:

"There is a term *c* such that (1) ϕx is always equivalent to '*x* is *c*,' (2) ψc is true."

This is the definition of propositions in which descriptions occur.

It is possible to have much knowledge concerning a term described, *i.e.* to know many propositions concerning "the so-and-so," without actually knowing what the so-and-so is, *i.e.* without knowing any proposition of the form "*x* is the so-and-so," where "*x*" is a name. In a detective story propositions about "the man who did the deed" are accumulated, in the hope that ultimately they will suffice to demonstrate that it was A who did the deed. We may even go so far as to say that, in all such knowledge as can be expressed in words—with the exception of "this" and "that" and a few other words of which the meaning varies on different occasions—no names, in the strict sense, occur, but what seem like names are really descriptions. We may inquire significantly whether Homer existed, which we could not do if "Homer" were a name. The proposition "the so-and-so exists" is significant, whether true or false; but if *a* is the so-and-so (where "*a*" is a name), the words "*a* exists" are meaningless. It is only of descriptions—definite or indefinite—that existence can be significantly asserted; for, if "*a*" is a name, it *must* name something: what does not name anything is not a name, and therefore, if intended to be a name, is a symbol devoid of meaning, whereas a description, like "the present King of France," does not become incapable of occurring significantly merely on the ground that it describes nothing, the reason being that it is a *complex* symbol, of which the meaning is derived from that of its constituent symbols. And so, when we ask whether Homer existed, we are using the word "Homer" as an abbreviated description: we may replace it by (say) "the author of the *Iliad* and the *Odyssey*." The same considerations apply to almost all uses of what look like proper names.

When descriptions occur in propositions, it is necessary to distinguish what may be called "primary" and "secondary" occurrences. The abstract distinction is as follows.

A description has a "primary" occurrence when the proposition in which it occurs results from substituting the description for "*x*" in some propositional function ϕx; a description has a "secondary" occurrence when the result of substituting the description for *x* in ϕx gives only *part* of the proposition concerned. An instance will make this clearer. Consider "the present King of France is bald." Here "the present King of France" has a primary occurrence, and the proposition is false. Every proposition in which a description which describes nothing has a primary occurrence is false. But now consider "the present King of France is not bald." This is ambiguous. If we are first to take "*x* is bald," then substitute "the present King of France" for "*x*," and then deny the result, the occurrence of "the present King of France" is secondary and our proposition is true; but if we are to take "*x* is not bald" and substitute "the present King of France" for "*x*," then "the present King of France" has a primary occurrence and the proposition is false. Confusion of primary and secondary occurrences is a ready source of fallacies where descriptions are concerned.

Descriptions occur in mathematics chiefly in the form of *descriptive functions, i.e.* "the term having the relation R to *y*," or "the R of *y*" as we may say, on the analogy of "the father of *y*" and similar phrases. To say "the father of *y* is rich," for example, is to say that the following propositional function of *c*: "*c* is rich, and '*x* begat *y*' is always equivalent to '*x* is *c*,'" is "sometimes true," *i.e.* is true for at least one value of *c*. It obviously cannot be true for more than one value.

The theory of descriptions, briefly outlined in the present chapter, is of the utmost importance both in logic and in theory of knowledge. But for purposes of mathematics, the more philosophical parts of the theory are not essential, and have therefore been omitted in the above account, which has confined itself to the barest mathematical requisites.

Paul Valéry

1871–1945

Paul Valéry, poet, essayist, critic, and man of letters, may also be the most consummate intellectual among poets since Coleridge and Goethe. His interest extended to virtually every subject, and his accomplishments generally matched his interests. His famous routine of rising early each day to meditate, recording his thoughts in notebooks, is reflected in one of his most celebrated (quasi) fictional characters, *Monsieur Teste* ("head"), and his longtime admiration for Leonardo da Vinci. Somewhat like Edmund Husserl, Valéry delighted in the intricacies of the lived experience of consciousness, a delight played out in his surprising and illuminating dialogues, almost all imaginary. Among the best is *Eupalinos, or, The Architect,* set in Hades as a conversation between Socrates and Phaedrus, who both ironically lament the loss and absence of physical sensation, not precisely what one might have expected of the Socrates who, in *Phaedo,* represented philosophy as "practicing death" inasmuch as it proceeds by separating the soul, the intellect, from the distractions of the body.

Phaedrus, however, calls attention to his friend, Eupalinos, who, as an architect, praised his own art in these terms: "the more I meditate on my art, the more I practice it; the more I think and act, the more I suffer and rejoice as an architect—and the more I feel my own being with an ever surer delight and clarity." The reason for this delight and clarity, moreover, is his sense of an "exact correspondence between my aims and my powers, that I seem to myself to have made of the existence that was given me a sort of human handiwork." He goes on, with a smile, "By dint of constructing, I truly believe that I have constructed myself." (*Collected Works* 4: 81) In this example lies an important dimension of Valéry's own conception of art, of *techné,* as a craft of construction that becomes in and through intense contemplation a form of self-construction. In the example of Leonardo, he finds this approach to art as constructive consciousness particularly exemplified, where the activity of thinking is not so much an affair of bodiless abstraction as a vivid sense of the materiality of thinking itself.

This peculiarity of Valéry's thought, moreover, is the characteristic fusion of the intellectually abstract with the concrete details of construction found in Valéry's best poems as well.

Valéry's *Complete Works* (in fourteen volumes, 1956–), edited by Jackson Matthews are available in English translation. A particularly interesting biographical study is by Valéry's daughter, Agathe Rouart Valéry, *Paul Valéry* (1966). See also Jean Hytier, *The Poetics of Paul Valéry* (1953, tr. 1966); Renée Green, *The Poetic Theory of Paul Valéry: Inspiration and Technique* (1962); W. N. Ince, *The Poetic Theory of Paul Valéry: Inspiration and Technique,* second edition (1970); William Kluback, *Paul Valéry: The Statesman of the Intellect* (1999) and *Paul Valéry: A Philosopher for Philosophers, the Sage* (2002).

Leonardo and the Philosophers

(Extracts)

One must admit that Esthetics is a great, even an irresistible, temptation. Almost all people who have a strong feeling for the arts do a little more than feel them; they cannot escape the necessity of closely examining their appreciation.

How can we endure to be mysteriously enchanted by certain aspects of the world or by certain works of man and not to explain to ourselves this accidental or calculated pleasure, which seems on the one hand independent of the intelligence,—of which it is, however, perhaps the hidden guiding principle—and on the other quite distinct from our ordinary tastes—the variety and depth of which it, nevertheless, sums up and deifies?

Philosophers could not fail to feel concerned about this strange type of emotion. Moreover they have a less naive and more methodical reason for giving it their attention, and for seeking out its causes, mechanism, significance and its core.

The vast undertaking of philosophy, when contemplated in the very heart of the philosopher, consists, after all, of an attempt to transmute all that we know and all that we would like to know, and that undertaking demands to be carried out, or at least presented, or at least to be made capable of presentation, in a definite order.

Philosophies are characterized by the system of their speculations, for in the philosophic mind there are not, and there cannot be, entirely independent and substantially isolated questions. On the contrary one finds in it, like an incessant bass accompaniment, the consciousness, the fundamental sound of a latent though quite proximate interdependence between all the thoughts it contains, or could ever contain. The realization of this profound liaison suggests and imposes the order and the order of questions leads of necessity to a supreme question, which is that of knowledge.

But once a philosophy has admitted or established, justified or discredited, knowledge—whether it has exalted it and developed it *ultra vires* by an effective combination of

logic and intuition, or whether it has measured it as if it were reduced to its component parts by the science of criticism—it is invariably forced to explain,—that is to express within its system, its personal system of comprehension—human activity in general, the intellectual understanding of which is, in short, only one of the modalities, although it represents the whole.

* * *

We are now at a critical point in the whole of philosophy.

Thoughts which are very exact and very pertinent, which, in reality, seek (whatever the content and the conclusions may be) the ideal of a uniform distribution of concepts around a certain attitude or singular and characteristic aspect of mind of the thinker, must nowadays try to recapture the diversity, the irregularity and the unexpectedness of bygone thoughts; and their order must set in order their apparent disorder.

They must re-establish the plurality and the autonomy of the mind as a result of their own unity and sovereignty. They must legitimize the existence of what they have convicted of error and destroyed as such, they must recognize the vitality of the absurd, and fecundity of the contradictory, and sometimes even feel themselves inspired as they are by the universality from which they believe themselves to spring, restricted to the particular state of mind or individual characteristics of a certain person. And this is the beginning of wisdom and, at the same time, the twilight of philosophy.

* * *

It is true that the existence of others is always disturbing to the magnificent egotism of a thinker. He cannot fail to be confronted by the great problem posed by the arbitrariness of others. The feelings, thoughts and actions of others almost always seem arbitrary to us. Every preference we give our own thoughts we justify by a necessity of which we believe ourselves the agent. But after all the other person does exist and the problem does confront us. It besets us in two forms, one of which consists in the difference in behavior and character, in the diversity of decisions and attitudes toward everything that has to do with the preservation of the body and its possessions; the other of which is manifested in the variety of tastes, expressions and creations of the sensibilities.

Leonardo and the Philosophers consists of extracts (made by Valéry himself) from Valéry's writings and notebooks on Leonardo da Vinci, translated by Anthony Bower. Reprinted from *Paul Valéry: Selected Writings* (New York: New Directions, 1950). This edition is based upon Valéry's *Morceaux choisis* (Paris: Gallimard, Éditions de la Nouvelle revue française, 1930).

* * *

The philosopher cannot decide not to absorb into his own intelligence all these realities which he wants to make similar to his own or reduce to potentialities within his scope. He wants to understand; he wants to understand them in every sense of the word. He then proceeds to meditate framing a science of the meaning of action, and a science of the meaning of the expressions and the creations of the emotions,—an *ethic* and an *esthetic*—as if the Palace of his Thoughts must seem to him imperfect without those two symmetrical wings in which his all-powerful and abstract Ego could hold passion, action, emotion and invention captive.

Every philosopher, when he has finished with God, with the Self, with Time, Space, Matter, with Categories and with Essences returns to man and his works.

* * *

Then as he had invented Truth, the Philosopher invented the Good and the Beautiful; and as he had invented the rules of agreement between an isolated thought and itself, he likewise undertook to prescribe rules for conformity of action and expression for the precepts and patterns which, through the contemplation of a unique and universal Principle, escaped the caprices and the doubts of the individual,—a Principle which must therefore, above all and independently of all personal experience, be defined and designated.

There are few more remarkable events in the history of the mind than this introduction of Ideals, in which one can see a completely European event. Their debasement in the mind coincides with that of the virtues typical of Europe.

However, in the same way that we are still quite attached to the conception of pure science, developed strictly according to tangible evidence which can be stretched indefinitely from identity to identity—so we are still half convinced of the existence of Ethics and Beauty independent of time, place, race, or people.

* * *

Nevertheless each day reveals a little more the ruin of this noble structure. We are watching this extraordinary phenomenon; the very development of the sciences is tending to diminish the idea of knowledge. I mean that that part of science which seemed unshakeable and which was common to it and to philosophy (that is to say to faith in the comprehensible and to belief in the real value of the attainments of

the mind) is little by little giving way to a new mode of understanding or evaluating knowledge. The efforts of the intellect can no longer be regarded as converging toward a spiritual limit, toward the Truth. One only has to examine oneself to recognize this contemporary conviction: that to *know* everything, which indicates no corresponding effective *power,* has only a conventional or arbitrary importance. To know everything is only worth while if it is the prescription or the receipt for real power. From now on all metaphysics and even any theory of knowledge, whatever they may be, will find themselves violently divided and removed from what is held to be, more or less consciously by everyone, the only real knowledge—payable in gold.

In the same way ethics and esthetics are themselves being distorted into problems of legislation, statistics, history and physiology—and into lost illusions.

* * *

Moreover on what grounds can one form or specify a plan for "creating an Esthetics"—A science of the Beautiful? But do the moderns still use this word? It seems to me that they only still use it lightly. Or perhaps . . . in thinking of the past. Beauty is a kind of corpse. Novelty, intensity, strangeness,—in a word all the values of surprise have supplanted it. Crude excitement is the ruling mistress of contemporary minds; and the actual purpose of any work is to tear us from the contemplative state, from the static happiness whose image was formerly part of the general conception of Beauty. People are more and more occupied with the most unstable and immediate characteristics of the psychic and sensitive life. The unconscious, the irrational, the temporary which are, and their names proclaim the fact, denials or negations of the intentional and sustained forms of mental activity, have been substituted for the patterns natural to the mind. One hardly ever sees any more a product of the desire for perfection. Let us note in passing that this superannuated desire must necessarily fade before the fixed idea and the insatiable thirst for originality. The ambition to reach perfection is confused with the idea of making a work independent of any particular time; but the desire to be new insists on making of it an event remarkable by its contrast to the present moment. The former admits of, and even demands, heredity, imitation or tradition, which are steps in its climb toward the absolute object it wishes to attain. The latter rejects them, and in so doing implies them still more strongly,—for its essence is to be different.

In our time a definition of 'Beauty' can only be considered as a historical or philological document. Taken in the former fullness of its meaning, this illustrious word is on its way to join many other kinds of verbal coinage, which are no longer in circulation, in the drawers of the numismatists of language.

* * *

What most obviously separates philosophical esthetics from the thoughts of the artist, is that it springs from a way of thinking which believes itself foreign to the arts and which feels itself to be of quite another species than that of a poet or a musician,—in which I shall say in a moment that it is deceived. Works of art are to it accidents, particular cases, the results of an active and industrious intelligence going blindly toward a principle of which Philosophy alone can possess the vision or the absolute and immediate understanding. This activity seems unnecessary to it, since its supreme object should be in the immediate realm of philosophic thought, and should be directly accessible only by attention applied to the knowledge of knowledge, or to a system of the perceptible world and the intelligible world combined. The philosopher does not recognize any particular necessity for it; he does not think much of the importance of the material means, of the ways and of the values of the execution, for he tends inevitably to distinguish them from the general conception. It is repugnant to him to think of an intimate, perpetual, equal interchange between what one wants and what one can do, between what he considers accidental and what he considers substantial, between 'form' and 'essence,' between consciousness and automatism, between the circumstances and the design, between 'matter' and the 'mind.' Now it is precisely this wonderful ability, the freedom acquired in these exchanges, the existence in the artist of a sort of common standard concealed beneath the extremely divergent elements of his temperament, it is the inevitable and indivisible collaboration, the coordination, at every moment and in every one of his acts, of the arbitrary and the necessary, of the expected and the unexpected, of his body, of his material, of his wishes, even of his absences—which finally allows him to endow nature (considered as a practically infinite source of subjects, models, means and pretexts) with some object which cannot be simplified and reduced to a simple and abstract thought in that it has its origin and its effect in a system which cannot be separated from independent conditions. One cannot summarize a poem as one summarizes . . . a universe. To summarize a thesis is to retain the essence of it. To summarize (or replace by a scheme) a work of art, is to lose its essence. One can see to what extent this fact (if one can understand its scope) makes an illusion of the analysis of the esthetic.

In fact one can only extract from an object or from a natural or artificial work certain esthetic characteristics, which could be found elsewhere, for use as a general formula for beautiful things. It is not that this method has not often been used; it is that one does not remember that this sort of research is only applied to an 'old discovery,' and moreover that the work under consideration cannot be reduced to any of its component properties without losing its intrinsic emotional value.

The philosopher cannot easily comprehend that the artist passes, almost with indifference, from form to content and from content to form; that form comes to the artist with the meaning that he wishes to give it, nor that the idea of form is the same thing to him as the idea which demands a form.

In a word, if esthetics could exist the arts would fade before it—that is to say before their essence.

What I am now saying should not be applied to technical studies which are only concerned with means and with particular solutions, and which have as their more or less direct object the production or the classification of works of art, but do not aim at reaching Beauty by a road that does not lie in their domain.

Perhaps one only really understands what one has created. Pascal tells us that he would not have invented painting. He could not see the reason for laboriously reproducing the most insignificant objects. However sometimes this great artist of language did apply himself to drawing, to painting the portrait of his thoughts in words. . . . It is true that he seems to have finished by rejecting all activities, save one, and by considering everything, with the exception of death, as something painted.

* * *

The philosopher took to the field to overcome the artist, to 'explain' what the artist feels and what he does; but quite the contrary took place and was discovered. Far from Philosophy enveloping and assimilating, in the name of the conception of Beauty, the whole domain of creative sensibility and making itself the mother and the mistress of esthetics, it so happens that it can no longer find its justification, the appeasement of its conscience or its real 'depth' except in its creative powers and in its abstract poetic freedom. Only an esthetic interpretation can save the venerable monuments of metaphysics from ruin by their more or less hidden postulates, or from the destructive effects of the analysis of language and of thought.

Perhaps it will seem very difficult at first to consider as artists certain philosophers whom up to now we have considered as seekers after truth, to transform into lies—into self-deceptions—the products of the deepest sincerity. . . . "What a state of affairs," one will say! Philosophers should set their minds at rest about this change, which is after all only a change of habit. I can only see in it a reform demanded by the course of events, of which I see a counterpart in the history of the ancient plastic arts. Once upon a time the likeness of a man or of an animal, even though it had been seen to come from the hands of the artist, was considered not only as a living thing, immobile and crude though it was, but also endowed with supernatural powers. Stones and pieces of wood which did not even resemble human beings were worshipped as gods. Images which were only very approximate likenesses were given food and were honored; and here is an extraordinary fact—the cruder they were the more they were worshipped—something that can also be observed in children playing with their dolls and lovers with their loved ones, and which is a profoundly significant fact. (Perhaps this is because we believe that the more we are obliged to give life to an object the more we receive from it in return). But as this communicated life became gradually weaker and weaker, and was little by little refused to such crude images, *the idol became beautiful.* Compelled to this by criticism, it lost its imaginary powers over events and persons in order to gain real power over the eyes. Sculpture became free and became itself.

Can I without shocking, without cruelly hurting philosophic feelings, compare its so idolized truths, its principles, its Ideas, its Entity, its Essence, its Categories, these Noumena, this Universe, this mass of conceptions which became successively necessary, to the idols of which I was speaking?—If one asks oneself how philosophy nowadays would compare to traditional philosophy the answer would be that it is as a fifth-century statue compared to the featureless gods of ancient times.

I sometimes think that as arrangements of ideas and abstract constructions without illusions—without recourse to the power of hypostasis—gradually become possible and acceptable, it will perhaps come about that this kind of untrammeled philosophy will prove itself more fruitful and more true than philosophy which was bound to primitive beliefs in explanations, more human and more seductive than that which demands a rigorous critical attitude. Perhaps it will allow us to begin again in a new spirit, with quite different aims, the great work undertaken by metaphysics in directing thought toward ends which criticism has greatly attenuated. For a long time mathematics has been independent of any aim foreign to the concept of itself found in the pure development of its technique, and in the value it has given to the value inherent in this development; and everyone knows to what extent this freedom in its practice, which seemed bound to lead it very far from reality into a world of make-believe, of difficulties and of useless elegances, has made it flexible and equipped it to aid the physicist.

Is an art of ideas, an art of the order of ideas, or of the plurality of the orders of ideas a vain conception? I allow myself to believe that all architecture is not concrete, that all music cannot be heard. There is a certain consciousness of ideas and of their analogies which seems to me to be able to act and to be developed in the same way as the consciousness of sound or of color; I should even be inclined, if I had to propose a definition of a philosopher, to base it on the predominance in his character of this type of sensibility.

I believe that one is born a philosopher, in the way that one is born a sculptor or a musician; and that this gift, if it takes the pursuit of any truth or reality as its justification and as its object, can nowadays be proud of itself and need no longer so much seek out as create. The philosopher should use freely the powers that he has acquired through discipline; and in an infinity of ways, and in an infinity of forms he should dispense the strength and the ability—which are his characteristics—to give life and movement to abstract things.

That is what will allow the Noumena to be saved by the simple understanding of their intrinsic harmonies.

Finally I say that there exists an excellent demonstration of what I have just proposed in the form of a question. Once it was only a possibility, but now it suffices to consider the fate of the great systems to find it already realized. In what way do we read the philosophers, and who ever consults them with the real hope of finding anything but a pleasure or an exercise for the mind? When we set out to read them, do we not have the feeling that we are submitting for a short time to the rules of an enjoyable game? What would become of these masterpieces of pointless discipline, if it were not for this convention which we accept for love of an exacting pleasure? If one refutes a Plato or a Spinoza would nothing remain of their astonishing works? Absolutely nothing—if there did not remain a work of art.

* * *

However in the field of philosophy, and on certain strategic points of the domain of the pursuit of intelligence, a few remarkable figures have appeared of whom one knows that their abstract thoughts, though extremely expert and capable of every variety of subtlety and depth, never wandered from their preoccupation with figurative creations, with applications and tangible proofs of their attentive abilities. They seem to have possessed an indefinable and intimate knowledge of the continual interchanges between the arbitrary and the necessary.

Leonardo da Vinci is the supreme example of these superior individuals.

Ludwig Wittgenstein

1889–1951

The precision and the finesse of Wittgenstein's philosophical writing, early and late, presents a particular difficulty in the context of an anthology such as this, and therefore warrants a somewhat unconventional introduction. For literary critics and others in the humanities, Wittgenstein's later writing, notably *Philosophical Investigations,* has long been preferred, for its apparent openness to adaptation, with such powerful ideas as the "language game," "family resemblances," and its treatment of such topics as pain and "private language," and more generally, the problems of representation and interpretation. It has been, accordingly, an almost irresistible temptation to sharply distinguish between the early Wittgenstein, of *Tractatus Logico-Philosophicus,* a work of unmistakable logical austerity, and late Wittgenstein, thereby introducing a serious distortion in the assessment of Wittgenstein's accomplishments.

This problem is twofold. First, it is a problem internal to Wittgenstein's own arguments, where the expansion of his position in the posthumously published *Philosophical Investigations* is not, in actuality, a reduction or lessening of philosophical rigor, but is, on the contrary, the direct consequence of it: the "picture theory" of meaning developed so meticulously in *Tractatus* is not simply in error, even though Wittgenstein later recognized "grave mistakes" in it, by following where his earlier thought led and not hesitating to question it. Thus, in the 1945 preface to *Philosophical Investigations,* Wittgenstein expresses the thought that he "should publish those old thoughts and the new ones together: that the latter could be seen in the right light only by contrast with and against the background of my old way of thinking" (vi). Unfortunately, this scheme was never realized, and without it, following the intellectual principle of *Tractatus* that propositions *show* their sense, it is not clear *a priori* what seeing Wittgenstein's later thoughts "in the right light" would be. The problem is more than a question of preserving what is *right* in the earlier work: it is also a question of tracking it, as a force in others' thoughts as well. For it is certain that *Tractatus* is among the relatively few genuinely great philosophical works, with profound consequences and effects. Wittgenstein concludes the Preface to *Philosophical Investigations* lamenting the fact that "the time is past" in which he could have improved the book, but expressing his primary hope in these terms: "I should not like my writing to spare other people the trouble of thinking" (vi).

This leads to the second problem of supposing there to be, in some way, two "Wittgensteins," early and late, as if one could simply choose one or the other. *Tractatus* is an intellectual watershed, even as it adopts an account of the *meaning* of language that fails, gravely, to capture its subtlety and power; but it is an unavoidable, even spectacular breakthrough on the question of *logical syntax,* just as it embodies a vision of the telos of philosophy *as an activity,* not a set of propositions, devoted to the elucidation of concepts. It is, in one respect, one of the peculiar ironies of history that the dramatic success of *Tractatus* in capturing the philosophical imagination, thereby eclipsed to a large degree Edmund Husserl's *Logical Investigations* (above, page 770), a work of different but equally impressive philosophical subtlety and scope. But in another, Wittgenstein's accomplishment was not merely in asserting, but in showing *why* philosophy could not be one among the sciences (as Husserl hoped), and in working out the idea and the schemata of the truth function of propositions in the complementary logic of tautology relative to contradiction, thereby opening a clearer path to the formalization of symbolic logic. In a simple but dazzling advance on both Frege and Russell, Wittgenstein irreversibly changed the course of philosophical discourse with a book that is a mere seventy-four pages long.

The resulting problem is this: if one proceeds as if "early" Wittgenstein were operating in the darkness of error, or merely presented one "interpretation" of the problem of signification and representation, such that business could go on as usual, what is lost is the fact that Wittgenstein's accomplishment pertained *not* to representations, but to the inescapable conditions of representability itself. The sharp implication of his work, in this context, is that to keep talking as if a transcendental discourse about "Being" made sense, or that Philosophy (capital *P*) could somehow once again appear as the Queen of the Sciences, was, at the worst, intellectually irresponsible, and at best, simply intellectually nonresponsive, as if one simply refused to listen to an inconvenient truth.

While one could argue that the issue is one of incommensurability between different views of what philosophy was or could be, taking such a position can only become (as it has, in fact, become) a way to decline to enter into conversation. Just as Frege had evidently severely shaken the confidence of Husserl in his devastating review of *Philosophie der Arithmetik*[1]—and as Russell later brought Frege's work on his system of logical representation in *Begriffsschrift und andere Aufsätze* to a standstill by pointing out a contradiction in the elaboration of set theory pertaining to sets of sets subsequently known simply as "Russell's Paradox"[2]—Wittgenstein opened up a genuinely new way to proceed, in which the "picture theory" of meaning is less important than the conception of logical syntax as a condition of representability (and thereby, of intelligibility itself) that it exemplifies. Wittgenstein's radical clarification of the status of the logical relations involved in contradiction and tautology, furthermore, cleared the way for a cleaner formal articulation of truth conditions as logical functions that could be represented in "truth tables."

From this point of view, the austerity of Wittgenstein's numbered propositions in *Tractatus,* including its use of mathematical and formal logical notation, has the immediate effect of increasing the degree of explicit expertise required to truly follow the argument, but the ultimate effect of making it essential that one at least try to do so. Otherwise one runs the risk of becoming an example of Wittgenstein's claim that statements which ignore the pivotal role of logical syntax render themselves meaningless.

In the selections here from *Tractatus* and *Philosophical Investigations,* the intent is to provide a sufficient framework in which not only to see the later work in a clearer light, but to preserve a substantive sense of the revolutionary quality of the earlier work, as it influenced such thinkers as Hans Reichenbach and Rudolph Carnap (below, page 978) of the Vienna Circle, and the subsequent development of analytic and linguistic philosophy, particularly in England and North America.

*   *   *

---

[1] Excerpted in Peter Geach and Max Black, eds., *Translations from the Philosophical Writings of Gottlob Frege* (Oxford: Blackwell, 1980).

[2] In brief, the result of positing a set of sets, *V,* consisting of all sets not members of themselves, such that asking whether *V* is a member of itself precipitates an antinomy.

During Wittgenstein's lifetime, *Tractatus Logico-Philosophicus* (1921) was his only published work, but works appearing after his death have included *Philosophical Investigations,* trans. G. E. M. Anscombe (New York: Macmillan Company, 1953); *On Certainty,* ed. G. E. M. Anscombe and G. H. von Wright, trans. Denis Paul and G. E. M. Anscombe (Oxford: Basil Blackwell, 1969); *Preliminary Studies for the "Philosophical Investigations", Generally Known as the Blue and Brown Books* (Oxford: Blackwell, 1969); *Lectures & Conversations on Aesthetics, Psychology, and Religious Belief,* ed. Cyril Barrett (Berkeley: University of California Press, 1972); and numerous other volumes of notes and correspondence. The critical literature on Wittgenstein is voluminous, but see especially Anthony Kenny, *Wittgenstein* (1973, reissued 1976) and *The Legacy of Wittgenstein* (1984, reprinted 1987); Peter Winch, ed., *Studies in the Philosophy of Wittgenstein* (1969); Gerd Brand, *The Essential Wittgenstein* (1979); Irving Block, ed., *Perspectives on the Philosophy of Wittgenstein* (1981, reprinted 1983); Derek Bolton, *An Approach to Wittgenstein's Philosophy* (1979); Max Black, *A Companion to Wittgenstein's "Tractatus"* (1964); Stuart Shanker, ed., *Ludwig Wittgenstein: Critical Assessments* (in four volumes, 1986); Gordon Baker, *Wittgenstein, Frege, and the Vienna Circle* (1988); Erich H. Reck, ed., *From Frege to Wittgenstein: Perspectives on Early Analytic Philosophy* (2002). Studies exploring Wittgenstein in other disciplinary contexts include: Henry Staten, *Wittgenstein and Derrida* (1984); Jorn K. Bramann, *Wittgenstein's Tractatus and the Modern Arts* (1985); Marjorie Perloff, *Wittgenstein's Ladder: Poetic Language and the Strangeness of the Ordinary* (1996); Frank Cioffi, *Wittgenstein on Freud and Frazer* (1998); Richard Allen and Malcolm Turvey, eds., *Wittgenstein, Theory and the Arts* (2001); Naomi Scheman and Peg O'Connor, eds., *Feminist Interpretations of Ludwig Wittgenstein* (2002); and Kenneth Dauber and Walter Jost, eds., *Ordinary Language Criticism: Literary Thinking after Cavell after Wittgenstein* (with an afterword by Stanley Cavell) (2003).

from

Tractatus Logico-Philosophicus

1   The world is all that is the case.

1.1   The world is the totality of facts, not of things.

1.11   The world is determined by the facts, and by their being *all* the facts.

1.12   For the totality of facts determines what is the case, and also whatever is not the case.

1.13   The facts in logical space are the world.

1.2   The world divides into facts.

1.21   Each item can be the case or not the case while everything else remains the same.

2   What is the case—a fact—is the existence of states of affairs.

2.01   A state of affairs (a state of things) is a combination of objects (things).

2.011   It is essential to things that they should be possible constituents of states of affairs.

Tractatus Logico-Philosophicus was first published in German in 1921. Reprinted, in part, from *Tractatus Logico-Philosophicus* with an Introduction by Bertrand Russell (London: K. Paul, Trench, Trubner & Co., Ltd., 1922). The reader is cautioned particularly to observe the marks of ellipsis in the selection here. We have endeavored to provide a sufficient indication of Wittgenstein's argument, up to the introduction of truth tables and his analysis of tautology and contradiction. Most of sections 5.xx and 6.xx are omitted, as are many illustrative and ampliative paragraphs in sections 2, 3, and 4.

2.012   In logic nothing is accidental: if a thing *can* occur in a state of affairs, the possibility of the state of affairs must be written into the thing itself.

2.0121   It would seem to be a sort of accident, if it turned out that a situation would fit a thing that could already exist entirely on its own.

If things can occur in states of affairs, this possibility must be in them from the beginning.

(Nothing in the province of logic can be merely possible. Logic deals with every possibility and all possibilities are its facts.)

Just as we are quite unable to imagine spatial objects outside space or temporal objects outside time, so too there is *no* object that we can imagine excluded from the possibility of combining with others.

If I can imagine objects combined in states of affairs, I cannot imagine them excluded from the *possibility of* such combinations.

2.0122   Things are independent in so far as they can occur in all *possible* situations, but this form of independence is a form of connexion with states of affairs, a form of dependence. (It is impossible for words to appear in two different roles: by themselves, and in propositions.)

* * *

2.013   Each thing is, as it were, in a space of possible states of affairs. This space I can imagine empty, but I cannot imagine the thing without the space.

* * *

2.014   Objects contain the possibility of all situations.

2.0141   The possibility of its occurring in states of affairs is the form of an object.

* * *

2.02   Objects are simple.

2.0201   Every statement about complexes can be resolved into a statement about their constituents and into the propositions that describe the complexes completely.

2.021   Objects make up the substance of the world. That is why they cannot be composite.

2.0211   If the world had no substance, then whether a proposition had sense would depend on whether another proposition was true.

2.0212   In that case we could not sketch any picture of the world (true or false).

2.022   It is obvious that an imagined world, however different it may be from the real one, must have *something—a* form—in common with it.

2.023   Objects are just what constitute this unalterable form.

* * *

2.024   Substance is what subsists independently of what is the case.

2.025   It is form and content.

* * *

2.04   The totality of existing states of affairs is the world.

2.05   The totality of existing states of affairs also determines which states of affairs do not exist.

2.06   The existence and non-existence of states of affairs is reality.

(We also call the existence of states of affairs a positive fact, and their non-existence a negative fact.)

2.061   States of affairs are independent of one another.

2.062   From the existence or non-existence of one state of affairs it is impossible to infer the existence or non-existence of another.

2.063   The sum-total of reality is the world.

2.1   We picture facts to ourselves.

2.11   A picture presents a situation in logical space, the existence and non-existence of states of affairs.

2.12   A picture is a model of reality.

2.13   In a picture objects have the elements of the picture corresponding to them.

2.131   In a picture the elements of the picture are the representatives of objects.

2.14   What constitutes a picture is that its elements are related to one another in a determinate way.

2.141   A picture is a fact.

* * *

2.16   If a fact is to be a picture, it must have something in common with what it depicts.

* * *

2.171   A picture can depict any reality whose form it has. A spatial picture can depict anything spatial, a coloured one anything coloured, etc.

2.172   A picture cannot, however, depict its pictorial form: it displays it.

* * *

2.18   What any picture, of whatever form, must have in common with reality, in order to be able to depict it—correctly or incorrectly—in any way at all, is logical form, i.e. the form of reality.

2.181   A picture whose pictorial form is logical form is called a logical picture.

2.182   Every picture is *at the same time* a logical one. (On the other hand, not every picture is, for example, a spatial one.)

2.19   Logical pictures can depict the world.

2.2   A picture has logico-pictorial form in common with what it depicts.

2.201   A picture depicts reality by representing a possibility of existence and non-existence of states of affairs.

* * *

2.21   A picture agrees with reality or fails to agree; it is correct or incorrect, true or false.

2.22   What a picture represents it represents independently of its truth or falsity, by means of its pictorial form.

2.221   What a picture represents is its sense.

2.222   The agreement or disagreement of its sense with reality constitutes its truth or falsity.

2.223   In order to tell whether a picture is true or false we must compare it with reality.

2.224   It is impossible to tell from the picture alone whether it is true or false.

2.225   There are no pictures that are true a priori.

3   A logical picture of facts is a thought.

3.001   'A state of affairs is thinkable': what this means is that we can picture it to ourselves.

3.01   The totality of true thoughts is a picture of the world.

3.02   A thought contains the possibility of the situation of which it is the thought. What is thinkable is possible too.

3.03   Thought can never be of anything illogical, since, if it were, we should have to think illogically.

3.031   It used to be said that God could create anything except what would be contrary to the laws of logic.—The truth is that we could not *say* what an 'illogical' world would look like.

* * *

3.04   If a thought were correct a priori, it would be a thought whose possibility ensured its truth.

3.05   A priori knowledge that a thought was true would be possible only if its truth were recognizable from the thought itself (without anything to compare it with).

3.1   In a proposition a thought finds an expression that can be perceived by the senses.

3.11   We use the perceptible sign of a proposition (spoken or written, etc.) as a projection of a possible situation.

The method of projection is to think of the sense of the proposition.

3.12   I call the sign with which we express a thought a propositional sign.—And a proposition is a propositional sign in its projective relation to the world.

3.13   A proposition includes all that the projection includes, but not what is projected.

Therefore, though what is projected is not itself included, its possibility is.

A proposition, therefore, does not actually contain its sense, but does contain the possibility of expressing it.

('The content of a proposition' means the content of a proposition that has sense.)

A proposition contains the form, but not the content, of its sense.

3.14   What constitutes a propositional sign is that in it its elements (the words) stand in a determinate relation to one another.

A propositional sign is a fact.

3.141   A proposition is not a blend of words.—(Just as a theme in music is not a blend of notes.) A proposition is articulate.

3.142   Only facts can express a sense, a set of names cannot.

*   *   *

3.2   In a proposition a thought can be expressed in such a way that elements of the propositional sign correspond to the objects of the thought.

3.201   I call such elements 'simple signs', and such a proposition 'completely analysed'.

3.202   The simple signs employed in propositions are called names.

3.203   A name means an object. The object is its meaning. ('A' is the same sign as 'A'.)

3.21   The configuration of objects in a situation corresponds to the configuration of simple signs in the propositional sign.

3.22   In a proposition a name is the representative of an object.

3.221   Objects can only be *named*. Signs are their representatives. I can only speak *about* them: I cannot *put them into words*. Propositions can only say *how* things are, not *what* they are.

3.23   The requirement that simple signs be possible is the requirement that sense be determinate.

*   *   *

3.25   A proposition has one and only one complete analysis.

3.251   What a proposition expresses it expresses in a determinate manner, which can be set out clearly: a proposition is articulate.

3.26   A name cannot be dissected any further by means of a definition: it is a primitive sign.

*   *   *

3.263   The meanings of primitive signs can be explained by means of elucidations. Elucidations are propositions that contain the primitive signs. So they can only be understood if the meanings of those signs are already known.

3.3   Only propositions have sense; only in the nexus of a proposition does a name have meaning.

3.31   I call any part of a proposition that characterizes its sense an expression (or a symbol).

(A proposition is itself an expression.)

Everything essential to their sense that propositions can have in common with one another is an expression.

An expression is the mark of a form and a content.

3.311   An expression presupposes the forms of all the propositions in which it can occur. It is the common characteristic mark of a class of propositions.

3.312   It is therefore presented by means of the general form of the propositions that it characterizes.

In fact, in this form the expression will be *constant* and everything else *variable*.

* * *

3.318   Like Frege and Russell I construe a proposition as a function of the expressions contained in it.

3.32   A sign is what can be perceived of a symbol.

3.321   So one and the same sign (written or spoken, etc.) can be common to two different symbols—in which case they will signify in different ways.

3.322   Our use of the same sign to signify two different objects can never indicate a common characteristic of the two, if we use it with two different *modes of signification.* For the sign, of course, is arbitrary. So we could choose two different signs instead, and then what would be left in common on the signifying side?

3.323   In everyday language it very frequently happens that the same word has different modes of signification—and so belongs to different symbols—or that two words that have different modes of signification are employed in propositions in what is superficially the same way.

Thus the word 'is' figures as the copula, as a sign for identity, and as an expression for existence; 'exist' figures as an intransitive verb like 'go', and 'identical' as an adjective; we speak of *something,* but also of *something's* happening.

(In the proposition, 'Green is green'—where the first word is the proper name of a person and the last an adjective—these words do not merely have different meanings: they are *different symbols.*)

3.324   In this way the most fundamental confusions are easily produced (the whole of philosophy is full of them).

3.325   In order to avoid such errors we must make use of a sign-language that excludes them by not using the same sign for different symbols and by not using in a superficially similar way signs that have different modes of signification: that is to say, a sign-language that is governed by *logical* grammar—by logical syntax.

(The conceptual notation of Frege and Russell is such a language, though, it is true, it fails to exclude all mistakes.)

3.326   In order to recognize a symbol by its sign we must observe how it is used with a sense.

3.327   A sign does not determine a logical form unless it is taken together with its logico-syntactical employment.

3.328   If a sign *is useless,* it is meaningless. That is the point of Occam's maxim.

(If everything behaves as if a sign had meaning, then it does have meaning.)

3.33   In logical syntax the meaning of a sign should never play a role. It must be possible to establish logical syntax without mentioning the *meaning* of a sign: *only* the description of expressions may be presupposed.

* * *

3.334   The rules of logical syntax must go without saying, once we know how each individual sign signifies.

* * *

3.342   Although there is something arbitrary in our notations, *this* much is not arbitrary—that *when* we have determined one thing arbitrarily, something else is necessarily the case. (This derives from the *essence* of notation.)

3.3421   A particular mode of signifying may be unimportant but it is always important that it is *a possible* mode of signifying. And that is generally so in philosophy: again and again the individual case turns out to be unimportant, but the possibility of each individual case discloses something about the essence of the world.

3.343   Definitions are rules for translating from one language into another. Any correct sign-language must be translatable into any other in accordance with such rules: it is *this* that they all have in common.

3.344   What signifies in a symbol is what is common to all the symbols that the rules of logical syntax allow us to substitute for it.

* * *

3.5   A propositional sign, applied and thought out, is a thought.

4   A thought is a proposition with a sense.

4.001   The totality of propositions is language.

4.002   Man possesses the ability to construct languages capable of expressing every sense, without having any idea how each word has meaning or what its meaning is—just as people speak without knowing how the individual sounds are produced.

Everyday language is a part of the human organism and is no less complicated than it.

It is not humanly possible to gather immediately from it what the logic of language is.

Language disguises thought. So much so, that from the outward form of the clothing it is impossible to infer the form of the thought beneath it, because the outward form of the clothing is not designed to reveal the form of the body, but for entirely different purposes.

The tacit conventions on which the understanding of everyday language depends are enormously complicated.

4.003   Most of the propositions and questions to be found in philosophical works are not false but nonsensical. Consequently we cannot give any answer to questions of this kind, but can only point out that they are nonsensical. Most of the propositions and questions of philosophers arise from our failure to understand the logic of our language.

(They belong to the same class as the question whether the good is more or less identical than the beautiful.)

And it is not surprising that the deepest problems are in fact *not* problems at all.

4.0031   All philosophy is a 'critique of language' (though not in Mauthner's sense). It was Russell who performed the service of showing that the apparent logical form of a proposition need not be its real one.

4.01   A proposition is a picture of reality.

A proposition is a model of reality as we imagine it.

4.011   At first sight a proposition—one set out on the printed page, for example—does not seem to be a picture of the reality with which it is concerned. But neither do written notes seem at first sight to be a picture of a piece of music, nor our phonetic notation (the alphabet) to be a picture of our speech.

And yet these sign-languages prove to be pictures, even in the ordinary sense, of what they represent.

4.012   It is obvious that a proposition of the form '*aRb*' strikes us as a picture. In this case the sign is obviously a likeness of what is signified.

4.013   And if we penetrate to the essence of this pictorial character, we see that it is *not* impaired *by apparent irregularities* (such as the use of # and ♭ in musical notation).

For even these irregularities depict what they are intended to express; only they do it in a different way.

4.014   A gramophone record, the musical idea, the written notes, and the sound-waves, all stand to one another in the same internal relation of depicting that holds between language and the world.

They are all constructed according to a common logical pattern.

* * *

4.0141   There is a general rule by means of which the musician can obtain the symphony from the score, and which makes it possible to derive the symphony from the groove on the gramophone record, and, using the first rule, to derive the score again. That is what constitutes the inner similarity between these things which seem to be constructed in such entirely different ways. And that rule is the law of projection which projects the symphony into the language of musical notation. It is the rule for translating this language into the language of gramophone records.

4.015   The possibility of all imagery, of all our pictorial modes of expression, is contained in the logic of depiction.

4.016   In order to understand the essential nature of a proposition, we should consider hieroglyphic script, which depicts the facts that it describes.

And alphabetic script developed out of it without losing what was essential to depiction.

4.02   We can see this from the fact that we understand the sense of a propositional sign without its having been explained to us.

4.021   A proposition is a picture of reality: for if I understand a proposition, I know the situation that it represents. And I understand the proposition without having had its sense explained to me.

4.022   A proposition *shows* its sense.

A proposition *shows* how things stand *if* it is true. And it *says that* they do so stand.

* * *

4.026   The meanings of simple signs (words) must be explained to us if we are to understand them.

With propositions, however, we make ourselves understood.

4.027 It belongs to the essence of a proposition that it should be able to communicate *a new* sense to us.

4.03 A proposition must use old expressions to communicate a new sense.

A proposition communicates a situation to us, and so it must be *essentially* connected with the situation.

And the connexion is precisely that it is its logical picture.

A proposition states something only in so far as it is a picture.

4.031 In a proposition a situation is, as it were, constructed by way of experiment.

Instead of, 'This proposition has such and such a sense', we can simply say, 'This proposition represents such and such a situation'.

4.0311 One name stands for one thing, another for another thing, and they are combined with one another. In this way the whole group—like a tableau vivant—presents a state of affairs.

4.0312 The possibility of propositions is based on the principle that objects have signs as their representatives.

My fundamental idea is that the 'logical constants' are not representatives; that there can be no representatives of the *logic* of facts.

4.032 It is only in so far as a proposition is logically articulated that it is a picture of a situation.

* * *

4.04 In a proposition there must be exactly as many distinguishable parts as in the situation that it represents.

The two must possess the same logical (mathematical) multiplicity. (Compare Hertz's *Mechanics* on dynamical models.)

4.041 This mathematical multiplicity, of course, cannot itself be the subject of depiction. One cannot get away from it when depicting.

* * *

4.05 Reality is compared with propositions.

4.06 A proposition can be true or false only in virtue of being a picture of reality.

* * *

4.062 Can we not make ourselves understood with false propositions just as we have done up till now with true ones?—So long as it is known that they are meant to be false.—No! For a proposition is true if we use it to say that things stand in a certain way, and they do; and If by '*p*' we mean '~*p*' and things stand as we mean that they do, then, construed in the w way, '*p*' is true and not false.

4.0621 But it is important that the signs '*p*' and '~*p*' *can* say the same thing. For it shows that nothing in reality corresponds to the sign '~'.

The occurrence of negation in a proposition is not enough to characterize its sense ($\sim\sim p = p$).

The propositions '*p*' and '~*p*' have opposite sense, but there corresponds to them one and the same reality.

* * *

4.1 Propositions represent the existence and non-existence of states of affairs.

4.11 The totality of true propositions is the whole of natural science (or the whole corpus of the natural sciences).

4.111 Philosophy is not one of the natural sciences.

(The word 'philosophy' must mean something whose place is above or below the natural sciences, not beside them.)

4.112 Philosophy aims at the logical clarification of thoughts. Philosophy is not a body of doctrine but an activity.

A philosophical work consists essentially of elucidations.

Philosophy does not result in 'philosophical propositions', but rather in the clarification of propositions.

Without philosophy thoughts are, as it were, cloudy and indistinct: its task is to make them clear and to give them sharp boundaries.

4.1121 Psychology is no more closely related to philosophy than any other natural science.

Theory of knowledge is the philosophy of psychology.

Does not my study of sign-language correspond to the

study of thought-processes, which philosophers used to consider so essential to the philosophy of logic? Only in most cases they got entangled in unessential psychological investigations, and with my method too there is an analogous risk.

4.1122   Darwin's theory has no more to do with philosophy than *any* other hypothesis in natural science.

4.113   Philosophy sets limits to the much disputed sphere of natural science.

4.114   It must set limits to what can be thought; and, in doing so, to what cannot be thought.
   It must set limits to what cannot be thought by working outwards through what can be thought.

4.115   It will signify what cannot be said, by presenting clearly what can be said.

4.116   Everything that can be thought at all can be thought clearly. Everything that can be put into words can be put clearly.

4.12   Propositions can represent the whole of reality, but they cannot represent what they must have in common with reality in order to be able to represent it—logical form.
   In order to be able to represent logical form, we should have to be able to station ourselves with propositions somewhere outside logic, that is to say outside the world.

4.121   Propositions cannot represent logical form: it is mirrored in them.
   What finds its reflection in language, language cannot represent.
   What expresses *itself* in language, *we* cannot express by means of language.
   Propositions *show* the logical form of reality. They display it.

*   *   *

4.1212   What *can* be shown, *cannot* be said.

4.1213   Now, too, we understand our feeling that once we have a sign-language in which everything is all right, we already have a correct logical point of view.

*   *   *

4.128   Logical forms are *without* number.
   Hence there are no pre-eminent numbers in logic, and hence there is no possibility of philosophical monism or dualism, etc.

4.2   The sense of a proposition is its agreement and disagreement with possibilities of existence and non-existence of states of affairs.

4.21   The simplest kind of proposition, an elementary proposition, asserts the existence of a state of affairs.

4.211   It is a sign of a proposition's being elementary that there can be no elementary proposition contradicting it.

4.22   An elementary proposition consists of names. It is a nexus, a concatenation, of names.

4.221   It is obvious that the analysis of propositions must bring us to elementary propositions which consist of names in immediate combination.
   This raises the question how such combination into propositions comes about.

4.2211   Even if the world is infinitely complex, so that every fact consists of infinitely many states of affairs and every state of affairs is composed of infinitely many objects, there would still have to be objects and states of affairs.

*   *   *

4.241   When I use two signs with one and the same meaning, I express this by putting the sign '=' between them. *So* '*a* = *b*' means that the sign '*b*' can be substituted for the sign '*a*'.
   (If I use an equation to introduce a new sign '*b*', laying down that it shall serve as a substitute for a sign '*a*' that is already known, then, like Russell, I write the equation—definition—in the form '*a* = *b* Def.' A definition is a rule dealing with signs.)

4.242   Expressions of the form '*a* = *b*' are, therefore, mere representational devices. They state nothing about the meaning of the signs '*a*' and '*b*'.

4.243   Can we understand two names without knowing whether they signify the same thing or two different things? Can we understand a proposition in which two names occur without knowing whether their meaning is the same or different?

Suppose I know the meaning of an English word and of a German word that means the same: then it is impossible for me to be unaware that they do mean the same; I must be capable of translating each into the other.

Expressions like '$a = a$', and those derived from them, are neither elementary propositions nor is there any other way in which they have sense. (This will become evident later.)

4.25 If an elementary proposition is true, the state of affairs exists; if an elementary proposition is false, the state of affairs does not exist.

4.26 If all true elementary propositions are given, the result is a complete description of the world. The world is completely described by giving all elementary propositions, and adding which of them are true and which false.

* * *

4.3 Truth-possibilities of elementary propositions mean possibilities of existence and non-existence of states of affairs.

4.31 We can represent truth-possibilities by schemata of the following kind ('T' means 'true', 'F' means 'false'; the rows of 'T's' and 'F's' under the row of elementary propositions symbolize their truth-possibilities in a way that can easily be understood):

p	q	r
T	T	T
F	T	T
T	F	T
T	T	F
F	F	T
F	T	F
T	F	F
F	F	F

,

p	q
T	T
F	T
T	F
F	F

,

p
T
F

4.4 A proposition is an expression of agreement and disagreement with truth-possibilities of elementary propositions.

4.41 Truth-possibilities of elementary propositions are the conditions of the truth and falsity of propositions.

* * *

4.43 We can express agreement with truth-possibilities by correlating the mark 'T' (true) with them in the schema. The absence of this mark means disagreement.

4.431 The expression of agreement and disagreement with the truth-possibilities of elementary propositions expresses the truth-conditions of a proposition.

A proposition is the expression of its truth-conditions.

(Thus Frege was quite right to use them as a starting point when he explained the signs of his conceptual notation. But the explanation of the concept of truth that Frege gives is mistaken: if 'the true' and 'the false' were really objects, and were the arguments in :p etc., then Frege's method of determining the sense of :p would leave it absolutely undetermined.)

4.44 The sign that results from correlating the mark 'T' with truth-possibilities is a propositional sign.

4.441 It is clear that a complex of the signs 'F' and 'T' has no object (or complex of objects) corresponding to it, just as there is none corresponding to the horizontal and vertical lines or to the brackets.—There are no 'logical objects'.

Of course the same applies to all signs that express what the schemata of 'T's' and 'F's' express.

4.442 For example, the following is a propositional sign:

'

p	q	
T	T	T
F	T	T
T	F	
F	F	$T.$

'

(Frege's judgment-stroke '|-' is logically quite meaningless: in the works of Frege (and Russell) it simply indicates that these authors hold the propositions marked with this sign to be true. Thus 'I-' is no more a component part of a proposition than is, for instance, the proposition's number. It is quite impossible for a proposition to state that it itself is true.)

If the order of the truth-possibilities in a schema is fixed once and for all by a combinatory rule, then the last column by itself will be an expression of the truth-conditions. If we now write this column as a row, the propositional sign will become

'(TT—T) (p,q)'

or more explicitly

'(TTFT) (p,q)'.

(The number of places in the left-hand pair of brackets is determined by the number of terms in the right-hand pair.)

4.45   For n elementary propositions there are L_n possible groups of truth-conditions.

The groups of truth-conditions that are obtainable from the truth-possibilities of a given number of elementary propositions can be arranged in a series.

4.46   Among the possible groups of truth-conditions there are two extreme cases.

In one of these cases the proposition is true for all the truth-possibilities of the elementary propositions. We say that the truth-conditions are *tautological.*

In the second case the proposition is false for all the truth-possibilities: the truth-conditions are *contradictory.*

In the first case we call the proposition a tautology; in the second, a contradiction.

4.461   Propositions show what they say: tautologies and contradictions show that they say nothing.

A tautology has no truth-conditions, since it is unconditionally true: and a contradiction is true on no condition.

Tautologies and contradictions lack sense.

(Like a point from which two arrows go out in opposite directions to one another.)

(For example, I know nothing about the weather when I know that it is either raining or not raining.)

4.4611   Tautologies and contradictions are not, however, nonsensical. They are part of the symbolism, much as '0' is part of the symbolism of arithmetic.

4.462   Tautologies and contradictions are not pictures of reality. They do not represent any possible situations. For the former admit *all* possible situations, and the latter *none.*

In a tautology the conditions of agreement with the world—the representational relations—cancel one another, so that it does not stand in any representational relation to reality.

4.463   The truth-conditions of a proposition determine the range that it leaves open to the facts.

(A proposition, a picture, or a model is, in the negative sense, like a solid body that restricts the freedom of movement of others, and, in the positive sense, like a space bounded by solid substance in which there is room for a body.)

A tautology leaves open to reality the whole—the infinite whole—of logical space: a contradiction fills the whole of logical space leaving no point of it for reality. Thus neither of them can determine reality in any way.

4.464   A tautology's truth is certain, a proposition's possible, a contradiction's impossible.

(Certain, possible, impossible: here we have the first indication of the scale that we need in the theory of probability.)

4.465   The logical product of a tautology and a proposition says the same thing as the proposition. This product, therefore, is identical with the proposition. For it is impossible to alter what is essential to a symbol without altering its sense.

4.466   What corresponds to a determinate logical combination of signs is a determinate logical combination of their meanings. It is only to the uncombined signs that *absolutely any* combination corresponds.

In other words, propositions that are true for every situation cannot be combinations of signs at all, since, if they were, only determinate combinations of objects could correspond to them.

(And what is not a logical combination has *no* combination of objects corresponding to it.)

Tautology and contradiction are the limiting cases—indeed the disintegration—of the combination of signs.

4.4661   Admittedly the signs are still combined with one another even in tautologies and contradictions—i.e. they stand in certain relations to one another: but these relations have no meaning, they are not essential to the *symbol.*

4.5   It now seems possible to give the most general propositional form: that is, to give a description of the propositions of *any* sign-language *whatsoever in* such a way that every possible sense can be expressed by a symbol satisfying the description, and every symbol satisfying the description can express a sense, provided that the meanings of the names are suitably chosen.

It is clear that *only* what is essential to the most general propositional form may be included in its description—for otherwise it would not be the most general form.

The existence of a general propositional form is proved by the fact that there cannot be a proposition whose form could not have been foreseen (i.e. constructed). The general form of a proposition is: This is how things stand.

4.51   Suppose that I am given *all* elementary propositions: then I can simply ask what propositions I can construct out of them. And there I have *all* propositions, and *that* fixes their limits.

4.52   Propositions comprise all that follows from the totality of all elementary propositions (and, of course, from its being the *totality* of them *all*). (Thus, in a certain sense, it could be said that *all* propositions were generalizations of elementary propositions.)

4.53   The general propositional form is a variable.

5   A proposition is a truth-function of elementary propositions.

(An elementary proposition is a truth-function of itself.)

5.01   Elementary propositions are the truth-arguments of propositions.

*   *   *

6.4   All propositions are of equal value.

6.41   The sense of the world must lie outside the world. In the world everything is as it is, and everything happens as it does happen: *in* it no value exists—and if it did exist, it would have no value.

If there is any value that does have value, it must lie outside the whole sphere of what happens and is the case. For all that happens and is the case is accidental.

What makes it non-accidental cannot lie *within* the world, since if it did it would itself be accidental.

It must lie outside the world.

6.42   So too it is impossible for there to be propositions of ethics.

Propositions can express nothing that is higher.

6.421   It is clear that ethics cannot be put into words. Ethics is transcendental. (Ethics and aesthetics are one and the same.)

6.422   When an ethical law of the form, 'Thou shalt . . .', is laid down, one's first thought is, 'And what if I do not do it?' It is clear, however, that ethics has nothing to do with punishment and reward in the usual sense of the terms. So our question about the *consequences* of an action must be unimportant.—At least those consequences should not be events. For there must be something right about the question we posed. There must indeed be some kind of ethical reward and ethical punishment, but they must reside in the action itself.

(And it is also clear that the reward must be something pleasant and the punishment something unpleasant.)

6.423   It is impossible to speak about the will in so far as it is the subject of ethical attributes.

And the will as a phenomenon is of interest only to psychology.

6.43   If the good or bad exercise of the will does alter the world, it can alter only the limits of the world, not the facts—not what can be expressed by means of language.

In short the effect must be that it becomes an altogether different world. It must, so to speak, wax and wane as a whole.

The world of the happy man is a different one from that of the unhappy man.

6.431   So too at death the world does not alter, but comes to an end.

6.4311   Death is not an event in life: we do not live to experience death.

If we take eternity to mean not infinite temporal duration but timelessness, then eternal life belongs to those who live in the present.

Our life has no end in just the way in which our visual field has no limits.

6.4312   Not only is there no guarantee of the temporal immortality of the human soul, that is to say of its eternal survival after death; but, in any case, this assumption completely fails to accomplish the purpose for which it has always been intended. Or is some riddle solved by my surviving for ever? Is not this eternal life itself as much of a riddle as our present life? The solution of the riddle of life in space and time lies *outside* space and time.

(It is certainly not the solution of any problems of natural science that is required.)

6.432   *How* things are in the world is a matter of complete indifference for what is higher. God does not reveal himself *in* the world.

6.4321   The facts all contribute only to setting the problem, not to its solution.

6.44   It is not *how* things are in the world that is mystical, but *that* it exists.

6.45   To view the world sub specie aeterni is to view it as a whole—a limited whole.

Feeling the world as a limited whole—it is this that is mystical.

6.5   When the answer cannot be put into words, neither can the question be put into words.

The riddle does not exist.

If a question can be framed at all, it is also *possible* to answer it.

6.51   Scepticism *is not* irrefutable, but obviously nonsensical, when it tries to raise doubts where no questions can be asked.

For doubt can exist only where a question exists, a question only where an answer exists, and an answer only where something *can be said.*

6.52   We feel that even when all *possible* scientific questions have been answered, the problems of life remain completely untouched. Of course there are then no questions left, and this itself is the answer.

6.521   The solution of the problem of life is seen in the vanishing of the problem.

(Is not this the reason why those who have found after a long period of doubt that the sense of life became clear to them have then been unable to say what constituted that sense?)

6.522   There are, indeed, things that cannot be put into words. They *make themselves manifest.* They are what is mystical.

6.53   The correct method in philosophy would really be the following: to say nothing except what can be said, i.e. propositions of natural science—i.e. something that has nothing to do with philosophy—and then, whenever someone else wanted to say something metaphysical, to demonstrate to him that he had failed to give a meaning to certain signs in his propositions. Although it would not be satisfying to the other person—he would not have the feeling that we were teaching him philosophy—this method would be the only strictly correct one.

6.54   My propositions serve as elucidations in the following way: anyone who understands me eventually recognizes them as nonsensical, when he has used them—as steps—to climb up beyond them. (He must, so to speak, throw away the ladder after he has climbed up it.)

He must transcend these propositions, and then he will see the world aright.

7   What we cannot speak about we must pass over in silence.

from

Philosophical Investigations

1.   "Cum ipsi (majores homines) appellabant rem aliquam, et cum secundum eam vocem corpus ad aliquid movebant, videbam, et tenebam hoc ab eis vocari rem illam, quod sonabant, cum eam vellent ostendere. Hoc autem eos velle ex motu corporis aperiebatur: tamquam verbis naturalibus omnium genrium, quae fiunt vultu et nutu oculorum, ceterorumque membrorum actu, et sonitu vocis indicante affectionem animi in petendis, habendis, rejiciendis, fugiendisve rebus. Ita verba in variis sententiis locis suis posita, et crebro audita, quarum rerum signa essent, paulatim colligebam, measque jam voluntates, edomito in eis signis ore, per haec enuntiabam." (Augustine, *Confessions*, I. 8.)[1]

These words, it seems to me, give us a particular picture of the essence of human language. It is this: the individual words in language name objects—sentences are combinations of such names.—In this picture of language we find the roots of the following idea: Every word has a meaning. This meaning is correlated with the word. It is the object for which the word stands.

Augustine does not speak of there being any difference between kinds of words. If you describe the learning of language in this way you are, I believe, thinking primarily of nouns like "table", "chair", "bread", and of people's names, and only secondarily of the names of certain actions and

---

Excerpts from *Philosophical Investigations* are reprinted by permission of Basil Blackwell and Mott, © 1958, and the literary executors of the estate of Ludwig Wittgenstein.

[1]"When they (my elders) named some object, and accordingly moved towards something, I saw this and I grasped that the thing was called by the sound they uttered when they meant to point it out. Their intention was shewn by their bodily movements, as it were the natural language of all peoples; the expression of the face, the play of the eyes, the movement of other parts of the body, and the tone of voice which expresses our state of mind in seeking, having, rejecting, or avoiding something. Thus, as I heard words repeatedly used in their proper places in various sentences, I gradually learnt to understand what objects they signified; and after I had trained my mouth to form these signs, I used them to express my own desires." [Tr.]

properties; and of the remaining kinds of word as something that will take care of itself.

Now think of the following use of language: I send someone shopping. I give him a slip marked "five red apples". He takes the slip to the shopkeeper, who opens the drawer marked "apples"; then he looks up the word "red" in a table and finds a colour sample opposite it; then he says the series of cardinal numbers—I assume that he knows them by heart—up to the word "five", and for each number he takes an apple of the same colour as the sample out of the drawer.—It is in this and similar ways that one operates with words.—"But how does he know where and how he is to look up the word 'red' and what he is to do with the word 'five'?"—Well, I assume that he *acts* as I have described. Explanations come to an end somewhere.—But what is the meaning of the word "five"?—No such thing was in question here, only how the word "five" is used.

2. That philosophical concept of meaning has its place in a primitive idea of the way language functions. But one can also say that it is the idea of a language more primitive than ours.

Let us imagine a language for which the description given by Augustine is right. The language is meant to serve for communication between a builder A and an assistant B. A is building with building-stones; there are blocks, pillars, slabs and beams. B has to pass the stones, and that in the order in which A needs them. For this purpose they use a language consisting of the words "block", "pillar", "slab", "beam". A calls them out;—B brings the stone which he has learnt to bring at such-and-such a call.—Conceive this as a complete primitive language.

3. Augustine, we might say, does describe a system of communication; only not everything that we call language is this system. And one has to say this in many cases where the question arises "Is this an appropriate description or not?" The answer is "Yes, it is appropriate, but only for this narrowly circumscribed region, not for the whole of what you were claiming to describe."

It is as if someone were to say: "A game consists in moving objects about on a surface according to certain rules . . ."—and we replied: You seem to be thinking of board games, but there are others. You can make your definition correct by expressly restricting it to those games.

4. Imagine a script in which the letters were used to stand for sounds, and also as signs of emphasis and punctuation. (A script can be conceived as a language for describing sound-patterns.) Now imagine someone interpreting that script as if there were simply a correspondence of letters to

sounds and as if the letters had not also completely different functions. Augustine's conception of language is like such an over-simple conception of the script.

5. If we look at the example in §1, we may perhaps get an inkling how much this general notion of the meaning of a word surrounds the working of language with a haze which makes clear vision impossible. It disperses the fog to study the phenomena of language in primitive kinds of application in which one can command a clear view of the aim and functioning of the words.

A child uses such primitive forms of language when it learns to talk. Here the teaching of language is not explanation, but training.

6. We could imagine that the language of §2 was the *whole* language of A and B; even the whole language of a tribe. The children are brought up to perform *these* actions, to use *these* words as they do so, and to react in *this* way to the words of others.

An important part of the training will consist in the teacher's pointing to the objects, directing the child's attention to them, and at the same time uttering a word; for instance, the word "slab" as he points to that shape. (I do not want to call this "ostensive definition", because the child cannot as yet *ask* what the name is. I will call it "ostensive teaching of words".—I say that it will form an important part of the training, because it is so with human beings; not because it could not be imagined otherwise.) This ostensive teaching of words can be said to establish an association between the word and the thing. But what does this mean? Well, it may mean various things; but one very likely thinks first of all that a picture of the object comes before the child's mind when it hears the word. But now, if this does happen—is it the purpose of the word?— Yes, it *may* be the purpose.—I can imagine such a use of words (of series of sounds). (Uttering a word is like striking a note on the keyboard of the imagination.) But in the language of §2 it is *not* the purpose of the words to evoke images. (It may, of course, be discovered that that helps to attain the actual purpose.)

But if the ostensive teaching has this effect,—am I to say that it effects an understanding of the word? Don't you understand the call "Slab!" if you act upon it in such-and-such a way?—Doubtless the ostensive teaching helped to bring this about; but only together with a particular training. With different training the same ostensive teaching of these words would have effected a quite different understanding.

"I set the brake up by connecting up rod and lever."— Yes, given the whole of the rest of the mechanism. Only in conjunction with that is it a brake-lever, and separated from its support it is not even a lever; it may be anything, or nothing.

7. In the practice of the use of language (2) one party calls out the words, the other acts on them. In instruction in the language the following process will occur: the learner *names* the objects; that is, he utters the word when the teacher points to the stone.—And there will be this still simpler exercise: the pupil repeats the words after the teacher—both of these being processes resembling language.

We can also think of the whole process of using words in (2) as one of those games by means of which children learn their native language. I will call these games "language-games" and will sometimes speak of a primitive language as a language-game.

And the processes of naming the stones and of repeating words after someone might also be called language-games. Think of much of the use of words in games like ring-a-ring-a-roses.

I shall also call the whole, consisting of language and the actions into which it is woven, the "language-game".

8. Let us now look at an expansion of language (2). Besides the four words "block", "pillar", etc., let it contain a series of words used as the shopkeeper in (1) used the numerals (it can be the series of letters of the alphabet); further let there be two words, which may as well be "there" and "this" (because this roughly indicates their purpose), that are used in connexion with a pointing gesture; and finally a number of colour samples. A gives an order like: "d—slab—there". At the same time he shews the assistant a colour sample, and when he says "there" he points to a place on the building site. From the stock of slabs B takes one for each letter of the alphabet up to "d", of the same colour as the sample, and brings them to the place indicated by A.—On other occasions A gives the order "this—there". At "this" he points to a building stone. And so on.

9. When a child learns this language, it has to learn the series of 'numerals' a, b, c, . . . by heart. And it has to learn their use.—Will this training include ostensive teaching of the words?—Well, people will, for example, point to slabs and count; "a, b, c slabs".—Something more like the ostensive teaching of the words "block", "pillar", etc. would be the ostensive teaching of numerals that serve not to count but to refer to groups of objects that can be taken in at a glance. Children do learn the use of the first five or six cardinal numerals in this way.

Are "there" and "this" also taught ostensively?—Imagine how one might perhaps teach their use. One will point to

places and things—but in this case the pointing occurs in the *use* of the words too and not merely in learning the use.—

10. Now what do the words of this language *signify?*—What is supposed to shew what they signify, if not the kind of use they have? And we have already described that. So we are asking for the expression "This word signifies *this*" to be made a part of the description. In other words the description ought to take the form: "The word . . . . signifies . . . .".

Of course, one can reduce the description of the use of the word "slab" to the statement that this word signifies this object. This will be done when, for example, it is merely a matter of removing the mistaken idea that the word "slab" refers to the shape of building-stone that we in fact call a "block"—but the kind of '*referring*' this is, that is to say the use of these words for the rest, is already known.

Equally one can say that the signs "a", "b", etc. signify numbers; when for example this removes the mistaken idea that "a", "b", "c", play the part actually played in language by "block", "slab", "pillar". And one can also say that "c" means this number and not that one; when for example this serves to explain that the letters are to be used in the order a, b, c, d, etc. and not in the order a, b, d, c.

But assimilating the descriptions of the uses of words in this way cannot make the uses themselves any more like one another. For, as we see, they are absolutely unlike.

11. Think of the tools in a tool-box: there is a hammer, pliers, a saw, a screw-driver, a rule, a gluepot, glue, nails and screws.—The functions of words are as diverse as the functions of these objects. (And in both cases there are similarities.)

Of course what confuses us is the uniform appearance of words when we hear them spoken or meet them in script and print. For their *application* is not presented to us so clearly. Especially when we are doing philosophy!

12. It is like looking into the cabin of a locomotive. We see handles all looking more or less alike. (Naturally, since they are all supposed to be handled.) But one is the handle of a crank which can be moved continuously (it regulates the opening of a valve); another is the handle of a switch, which has only two effective positions, it is either off or on; a third is the handle of a brake-lever, the harder one pulls on it, the harder it brakes; a fourth, the handle of a pump: it has an effect only so long as it is moved to and fro.

13. When we say: "Every word in language signifies something" we have so far said *nothing whatever;* unless we have explained exactly *what* distinction we wish to make. (It might be, of course, that we wanted to distinguish the words

of language (8) from words 'without meaning' such as occur in Lewis Carroll's poems, or words like "Lilliburlero" in
songs.)

14. Imagine someone's saying: "*All* tools serve to
modify something. Thus the hammer modifies the position
of the nail, the saw the shape of the board, and so on."—
And what is modified by the rule, the glue-pot, the nails?—
"Our knowledge of a thing's length, the temperature of the
glue, and the solidity of the box."—Would anything be
gained by this assimilation of expressions?—

15. The word "to signify" is perhaps used in the most
straight-forward way when the object signified is marked
with the sign. Suppose that the tools A uses in building bear
certain marks. When A shews his assistant such a mark, he
brings the tool that has that mark on it.

It is in this and more or less similar ways that a name
means and is given to a thing.—It will often prove useful in
philosophy to say to ourselves: naming something is like attaching a label to a thing.

16. What about the colour samples that A shews to B:
are they part of the *language?* Well, it is as you please. They
do not belong among the words; yet when I say to someone:
"Pronounce the word 'the'", you will count the second "the"
as part of the sentence. Yet it has a role just like that of a
colour-sample in language-game (8); that is, it is a sample
of what the other is meant to say.

It is most natural, and causes least confusion, to reckon
the samples among the instruments of the language.

((Remark on the reflexive pronoun "*this* sentence".))

17. It will be possible to say: In language (8) we have
different *kinds of word*. For the function of the word "slab"
and the word "block" are more alike than those of "slab"
and "d". But how we group words into kinds will depend on
the aim of the classification,—and on our own inclination.

Think of the different points of view from which one
can classify tools or chess-men.

18. Do not be troubled by the fact that languages (2)
and (8) consist only of orders. If you want to say that this
shews them to be incomplete, ask yourself whether our language is complete;—whether it was so before the symbolism
of chemistry and the notation of the infinitesimal calculus
were incorporated in it; for these are, so to speak, suburbs of
our language. (And how many houses or streets does it take
before a town begins to be a town?) Our language can be seen
as an ancient city: a maze of little streets and squares, of old
and new houses, and of houses with additions from various
periods; and this surrounded by a multitude of new boroughs

with straight regular streets and uniform houses.

19. It is easy to imagine a language consisting only of
orders and reports in battle.—Or a language consisting only
of questions and expressions for answering yes and no. And
innumerable others.—And to imagine a language means to
imagine a form of life.

But what about this: is the call "Slab!" in example (2)
a sentence or a word?—If a word, surely it has not the same
meaning as the like-sounding word of our ordinary language, for in §2 it is a call. But if a sentence, it is surely not
the elliptical sentence: "Slab!" of our language.—As far as
the first question goes you can call "Slab!" a word and also
a sentence; perhaps it could be appropriately called a 'degenerate sentence' (as one speaks of a degenerate hyper-
bola); in fact it *is* our 'elliptical' sentence.—But that is
surely only a shortened form of the sentence "Bring me a
slab", and there is no such sentence in example (2).—But
why should I not on the contrary have called the sentence
"Bring me a slab" a *lengthening* of the sentence "Slab!"?—
Because if you shout "Slab!" you really mean: "Bring me a
slab".—But how do you do this: how do you *mean that*
while you *say* "Slab!"? Do you say the unshortened sentence to yourself? And why should I translate the call
"Slab!" into a different expression in order to say what
someone means by it? And if they mean the same thing—
why should I not say: "When he says 'Slab!' he means
'Slab!'"? Again, if you can mean "Bring me the slab", why
should you not be able to mean "Slab!"?—But when I call
"Slab!", then what I want is, *that he should bring me a
slab!*—Certainly, but does 'wanting this' consist in thinking
in some form or other a different sentence from the other
you utter?—

20. But now it looks as if when someone says "Bring
me a slab" he could mean this expression as *one* long word
corresponding to the single word "Slab!"—Then can one
mean it sometimes as one word and sometimes as four? And
how does one usually mean it?—I think we shall be inclined
to say: we mean the sentence as *four* words when we use it
in contrast with other sentences such as "*Hand* me a slab",
"Bring *him* a slab", "Bring *two* slabs", etc.; that is, in contrast with sentences containing the separate words of our
command in other combinations.—But what does using one
sentence in contrast with others consist in? Do the others,
perhaps, hover before one's mind? *All* of them? And *while*
one is saying the one sentence, or before, or afterwards?—
No. Even if such an explanation rather tempts us, we need
only think for a moment of what actually happens in order
to see that we are going astray here. We say that we use
the command in contrast with other sentences because *our*

language contains the possibility of those other sentences. Someone who did not understand our language, a foreigner, who had fairly often heard someone giving the order: "Bring me a slab!", might believe that this whole series of sounds was one word corresponding perhaps to the word for "building-stone" in his language. If he himself had then given this order perhaps he would have pronounced it differently, and we should say: he pronounces it so oddly because he takes it for a *single* word.—But then, is there not also something different going on in him when he pronounces it,—something corresponding to the fact that he conceives the sentence as a *single* word?—Either the same thing may go on in him, or something different. For what goes on in you when you give such an order? Are you conscious of its consisting of four words *while* you are uttering it? Of course you have a *mastery* of this language—which contains those other sentences as well—but is this having a mastery something that *happens* while you are uttering the sentence?— And I have admitted that the foreigner will probably pronounce a sentence differently if he conceives it differently; but what we call his wrong concept *need* not lie in anything that accompanies the utterance of the command.

The sentence is 'elliptical', not because it leaves out something that we think when we utter it, but because it is shortened—in comparison with a particular paradigm of our grammar.—Of course one might object here: "You grant that the shortened and the unshortened sentence have the same sense.—What is this sense, then? Isn't there a verbal expression for this sense?"—But doesn't the fact that sentences have the same sense consist in their having the same *use?*—(In Russian one says "stone red" instead of "the stone is red"; do they feel the copula to be missing in the sense, or attach it in *thought?*)

21. Imagine a language-game in which A asks and B reports the number of slabs or blocks in a pile, or the colours and shapes of the building-stones that are stacked in such-and-such a place.—such a report might run: "Five slabs". Now what is the difference between the report or statement "Five slabs" and the order "Five slabs!"?—Well, it is the part which uttering these words plays in the language-game. No doubt the tone of voice and the look with which they are uttered, and much else besides, will also be different. But we could also imagine the tone's being the same—for an order and a report can be spoken in a *variety* of tones of voice and with various expressions of face—the difference being only in the application. (Of course, we might use the words "statement" and "command" to stand for grammatical forms of sentence and intonations; we do in fact call "Isn't the weather glorious to-day?" a question, although it is used as a state-

ment.) We could imagine a language in which *all* statements had the form and tone of rhetorical questions; or every command the form of the question "Would you like to . . . ?" Perhaps it will then be said: "What he says has the form of a question but is really a command",—that is, has the function of a command in the technique of using the language. (Similarly one says "You will do this" not as a prophecy but as a command. What makes it the one or the other?)

22. Frege's idea that every assertion contains an assumption, which is the thing that is asserted, really rests on the possibility found in our language of writing every statement in the form: "It is asserted that such-and-such is the case."—But "that such-and-such is the case" is *not* a sentence in our language—so far it is not a *move* in the language-game. And if I write, not "It is asserted that . . . .", but "It is asserted: such-and-such is the case", the words "It is asserted" simply become superfluous.

We might very well also write every statement in the form of a question followed by a "Yes"; for instance: "Is it raining? Yes!" Would this shew that every statement contained a question?

Of course we have the right to use an assertion sign in contrast with a question-mark, for example, or if we want to distinguish an assertion from a fiction or a supposition. It is only a mistake if one thinks that the assertion consists of two actions, entertaining and asserting (assigning the truth-value, or something of the kind), and that in performing these actions we follow the propositional sign roughly as we sing from the musical score. Reading the written sentence loud or soft is indeed comparable with singing from a musical score, but *'meaning'* (thinking) the sentence that is read is not.

Frege's assertion sign marks the *beginning of the sentence*. Thus its function is like that of the full-stop. It distinguishes the whole period from a clause *within* the period. If I hear someone say "it's raining" but do not know whether I have heard the beginning and end of the period, so far this sentence does not serve to tell me anything.

23. But how many kinds of sentence are there? Say assertion, question, and command?—There are *countless* kinds: countless different kinds of use of what we call "symbols", "words", "sentences". And this multiplicity is not something fixed, given once for all; but new types of language, new language-games, as we may say, come into existence, and others become obsolete and get forgotten. (We can get a *rough picture* of this from the changes in mathematics.)

Here the term "language-*game*" is meant to bring into prominence the fact that the *speaking* of language is part of an activity, or of a form of life.

Review the multiplicity of language-games in the following examples, and in others:

Giving orders, and obeying them—
Describing the appearance of an object, or giving its measurements—
Constructing an object from a description (a drawing)—
Reporting an event—
Speculating about an event—

Imagine a picture representing a boxer in a particular stance. Now, this picture can be used to tell someone how he should stand, should hold himself; or how he should not hold himself; or how a particular man did stand in such-and-such a place; and so on. One might (using the language of chemistry) call this picture a propositional-radical. This will be how Frege thought of the "assumption".

Forming and testing a hypothesis—
Presenting the results of an experiment in tables and diagrams—
Making up a story; and reading it—
Play-acting—
Singing catches—
Guessing riddles—
Making a joke; telling it—
Solving a problem in practical arithmetic—
Translating from one language into another—
Asking, thanking, cursing, greeting, praying.

—It is interesting to compare the multiplicity of the tools in language and of the ways they are used, the multiplicity of kinds of word and sentence, with what logicians have said about the structure of language. (Including the author of the *Tractatus Logico-Philosophicus.*)

24. If you do not keep the multiplicity of language-games in view you will perhaps be inclined to ask questions like: "What is a question?"—Is it the statement that I do not know such-and-such, or the statement that I wish the other person would tell me . . . . ? Or is it the description of my mental state of uncertainty?—And is the cry "Help!" such a description?

Think how many different kinds of thing are called "description": description of a body's position by means of its co-ordinates; description of a facial expression; description of a sensation of touch; of a mood.

Of course it is possible to substitute the form of statement or description for the usual form of question: "I want to know whether . . . ." or "I am in doubt whether . . . ."—but this does not bring the different language-games any closer together.

The significance of such possibilities of transformation, for example of turning all statements into sentences beginning "I think" or "I believe" (and thus, as it were, into descriptions of *my* inner life) will become clearer in another place. (Solipsism.)

25. It is sometimes said that animals do not talk because they lack the mental capacity. And this means: "they do not think, and that is why they do not talk." But—they simply do not talk. Or to put it better: they do not use language—if we except the most primitive forms of language.—Commanding, questioning, recounting, chatting, are as much a part of our natural history as walking, eating, drinking, playing.

26. One thinks that learning language consists in giving names to objects. Viz, to human beings, to shapes, to colours, to pains, to moods, to numbers, etc. To repeat—naming is something like attaching a label to a thing. One can say that this is preparatory to the use of a word. But *what* is it a preparation *for?*

27. "We name things and then we can talk about them: can refer to them in talk."—As if what we did next were given with the mere act of naming. As if there were only one thing called "talking about a thing". Whereas in fact we do the most various things with our sentences. Think of exclamations alone, with their completely different functions.

Water!
Away!
Ow!
Help!
Fine!
No!

Are you inclined still to call these words "names of objects"?

In languages (2) and (8) there was no such thing as asking something's name. This, with its correlate, ostensive definition, is, we might say, a language-game on its own. That is really to say: we are brought up, trained, to ask: "What is that called?"—upon which the name is given. And there is also a language-game of inventing a name for something, and hence of saying, "This is . . . ." and then using the new name. (Thus, for example, children give names to their dolls and then talk about them and to them. Think in this connexion how singular is the use of a person's name to *call* him!)

* * *

40. Let us first discuss *this* point of the argument: that a word has no meaning if nothing corresponds to it.—It is important to note that the word "meaning" is being used illicitly if it is used to signify the thing that 'corresponds' to the word. That is to confound the meaning of a name with the *bearer* of the name. When Mr. N. N. dies one says that the bearer of the name dies, not that the meaning dies. And it would be nonsensical to say that, for if the name ceased to have meaning it would make no sense to say "Mr. N. N. is dead."

41. In §15 we introduced proper names into language (8). Now suppose that the tool with the name "N" is broken. Not knowing this, A gives B the sign "N". Has this sign meaning now or not?—What is B to do when he is given it?—We have not settled anything about this. One might ask: what *will* he do? Well, perhaps he will stand there at a loss, or shew A the pieces. Now one *might* say: "N" has become meaningless; and this expression would mean that the sign "N" no longer had a use in our language-game (unless we gave it a new one). "N" might also become meaningless because, for whatever reason, the tool was given another name and the sign "N" no longer used in the language-game.—But we could also imagine a convention whereby B has to shake his head in reply if A gives him the sign belonging to a tool that is broken.—In this way the command "N" might be said to be given a place in the language-game even when the tool no longer exists, and the sign "N" to have meaning even when its bearer ceases to exist.

42. But has for instance a name which has *never* been used for a tool also got a meaning in that game?—Let us assume that "X" is such a sign and that A gives this sign to B—well, even such signs could be given a place in the language-game, and B might have, say, to answer them too with a shake of the head. (One could imagine this as a sort of joke between them.)

43. For a *large* class of cases—though not for all—in which we employ the word "meaning" it can be defined thus: the meaning of a word is its use in the language.

And the *meaning* of a name is sometimes explained by pointing to its *bearer.*

44. We said that the sentence "Excalibur has a sharp blade" made sense even when Excalibur was broken in pieces. Now this is so because in this language-game a name is also used in the absence of its bearer. But we can imagine a language-game with names (that is, with signs which we should certainly include among names) in which they are used only in the presence of the bearer; and so could *always* be replaced by a demonstrative pronoun and the gesture of pointing.

45. The demonstrative "this" can never be without a bearer. It might be said: "so long as there is a *this,* the word 'this' has a meaning too, whether *this* is simple or complex."—But that does not make the word into a name. On the contrary: for a name is not used with, but only explained by means of, the gesture of pointing.

46. What lies behind the idea that names really signify simples?—Socrates says in the *Theaetetus:* "If I make no mistake, I have heard some people say this: there is no definition of the primary elements—so to speak—out of which we and everything else are composed; for everything exists[2] in its own right can only be *named,* no other determination is possible, neither that it *is* nor that it *is not* . . . . . But what exists in its own right has to be . . . . . named without any other determination. In consequence it is impossible to give an account of any primary element; for it, nothing is possible but the bare name; its name is all it has. But just as what consists of these primary elements is itself complex, so the names of the elements become descriptive language by being compounded together. For the essence of speech is the composition of names."

Both Russell's 'individuals' and my 'objects' *(Tractatus Logico-Philosophicus)* were such primary elements.

47. But what are the simple constituent parts of which reality is composed?—What are the simple constituent parts of a chair?—The bits of wood of which it is made? Or the molecules, or the atoms?—"Simple" means: not composite. And here the point is: in what sense 'composite'? It makes no sense at all to speak absolutely of the 'simple parts of a chair'.

Again: Does my visual image of this tree, of this chair, consist of parts? And what are its simple component parts? Multi-colouredness is one kind of complexity; another is, for example, that of a broken outline composed of straight bits. And a curve can be said to be composed of an ascending and a descending segment.

If I tell someone without any further explanation: "What I see before me now is composite", he will have the right to ask: "What do you mean by 'composite'? For there are all sorts of things that that can mean!"—The question "Is what you see composite?" makes good sense if it is already established what kind of complexity—that is, which particular use of the word—is in question. If it had been laid down that the visual image of a tree was to be called "composite" if one saw not just a single trunk, but also

---

[2]I have translated the German translation which Wittgenstein used rather than the original. [Tr.]

branches, then the question "Is the visual image of this tree simple or composite?", and the question "What are its simple component parts?", would have a clear sense—a clear use. And of course the answer to the second question is not "The branches" (that would be an answer to the *grammatical* question: "What are here called 'simple component parts'?") but rather a description of the individual branches.

But isn't a chessboard, for instance, obviously, and absolutely, composite?—You are probably thinking of the composition out of thirty-two white and thirty-two black squares. But could we not also say, for instance, that it was composed of the colours black and white and the schema of squares? And if there are quite different ways of looking at it, do you still want to say that the chessboard is absolutely 'composite'?—Asking "Is this object composite?" *outside* a particular language-game is like what a boy once did, who had to say whether the verbs in certain sentences were in the active or passive voice, and who racked his brains over the question whether the verb "to sleep" meant something active or passive.

We use the word "composite" (and therefore the word "simple") in an enormous number of different and differently related ways. (Is the colour of a square on a chessboard simple, or does it consist of pure white and pure yellow? And is white simple, or does it consist of the colours of the rainbow?—Is this length of 2 cm. simple, or does it consist of two parts, each 1 cm. long? But why not of one bit 3 cm. long, and one bit 1 cm. long measured in the opposite direction?)

To the *philosophical* question: "Is the visual image of this tree composite, and what are its component parts?" the correct answer is: "That depends on what you understand by 'composite'." (And that is of course not an answer but a rejection of the question.)

48. Let us apply the method of §2 to the account in the *Theaetetus*. Let us consider a language-game for which this account is really valid. The language serves to describe combinations of coloured squares on a surface. The squares form a complex like a chessboard. There are red, green, white and black squares. The words of the language are (correspondingly) "R", "G", "W", "B", and a sentence is a series of these words. They describe an arrangement of squares in the order:

1	2	3
4	5	6
7	8	9

And so for instance the sentence "RRBGGGRWW" describes an arrangement of this sort:

red	red	black
green	green	green
red	white	white

Here the sentence is a complex of names, to which corresponds a complex of elements. The primary elements are the coloured squares. "But are these simple?"—I do not know what else you would have me call "the simples", what would be more natural in this language-game. But under other circumstances I should call a monochrome square "composite", consisting perhaps of two rectangles, or of the elements colour and shape. But the concept of complexity might also be so extended that a smaller area was said to be 'composed' of a greater area and another one subtracted from it. Compare the 'composition of forces', the 'division' of a line by a point outside it; these expressions shew that we are sometimes even inclined to conceive the smaller as the result of a composition of greater parts, and the greater as the result of a division of the smaller.

But I do not know whether to say that the figure described by our sentence consists of four or of nine elements! Well, does the sentence consist of four letters or of nine?—And which are *its* elements, the types of letter, or the letters? Does it matter which we say, so long as we avoid misunderstandings in any particular case?

49. But what does it mean to say that we cannot define (that is, describe) these elements, but only name them? This might mean, for instance, that when in a limiting case a complex consists of only *one* square, its description is simply the name of the coloured square.

Here we might say—though this easily leads to all kinds of philosophical superstition—that a sign "R" or "B", etc. may be sometimes a word and sometimes a proposition. But whether it 'is a word or a proposition' depends on the situation in which it is uttered or written. For instance, if A has to describe complexes of coloured squares to B and he uses the word "R" *alone,* we shall be able to say that the word is a description—a proposition. But if he is memorizing the words and their meanings, or if he is teaching someone else the use of the words and uttering them in the course of ostensive teaching, we shall not say that they are propositions. In this situation the word "R", for instance, is not a description; it *names* an element—but it would be queer to make that a reason for saying that an element can *only* be named! For naming and describing do not stand on the same level: naming is a preparation for description. Naming is so far not a move in the language-game—any more than putting a piece in its place on the board is a move in chess. We may say: *nothing* has so far been done, when a thing has been named. It has not even *got* a name except in the language-game. This was what Frege meant too, when he said that a word had meaning only as part of a sentence.

50. What does it mean to say that we can attribute neither being nor non-being to elements?—One might say: if everything that we call "being" and "non-being" consists in the existence and non-existence of connexions between elements, it makes no sense to speak of an element's being (non-being); just as when everything that we call "destruction" lies in the separation of elements, it makes no sense to speak of the destruction of an element.

One would, however, like to say: existence cannot be attributed to an element, for if it did not *exist,* one could not even name it and so one could say nothing at all of it.—But let us consider an analogous case. There is *one* thing of which one can say neither that it is one metre long, nor that it is not one metre long, and that is the standard metre in Paris.—But this is, of course, not to ascribe any extraordinary property to it, but only to mark its peculiar role in the language-game of measuring with a metre-rule.—Let us imagine samples of colour being preserved in Paris like the standard metre. We define: "sepia" means the colour of the standard sepia which is there kept hermetically sealed. Then it will make no sense to say of this sample either that it is of this colour or that it is not.

We can put it like this: This sample is an instrument of the language used in ascriptions of colour. In this language-game it is not something that is represented, but is a means of representation.—And just this goes for an element in language-game (48) when we name it by uttering the word "R": this gives this object a role in our language-game; it is now a *means* of representation. And to say "If it did not *exist,* it could have no name" is to say as much and as little as: if this thing did not exist, we could not use it in our language-game.—What looks as if it *had* to exist, is part of the language. It is a paradigm in our language-game; something with which comparison is made. And this may be an important observation; but it is none the less an observation concerning our language-game—our method of representation.

51. In describing language-game (48) I said that the words "R", "B", etc. corresponded to the colours of the squares. But what does this correspondence consist in; in what sense can one say that certain colours of squares corre-

spond to these signs? For the account in (48) merely set up a connexion between those signs and certain words of our language (the names of colours).—Well, it was presupposed that the use of the signs in the language-game would be taught in a different way, in particular by pointing to paradigms. Very well; but what does it mean to say that in the *technique of using the language* certain elements correspond to the signs?—Is it that the person who is describing the complexes of coloured squares always says "R" where there is a red square; "B" when there is a black one, and so on? But what if he goes wrong in the description and mistakenly says "R" where he sees a black square—what is the criterion by which this is a *mistake?*—Or does "R"'s standing for a red square consist in this, that when the people whose language it is use the sign "R" a red square always comes before their minds?

In order to see more clearly, here as in countless similar cases, we must focus on the details of what goes on; must look at them *from close to.*

52. If I am inclined to suppose that a mouse has come into being by spontaneous generation out of grey rags and dust, I shall do well to examine those rags very closely to see how a mouse may have hidden in them, how it may have got there and so on. But if I am convinced that a mouse cannot come into being from these things, then this investigation will perhaps be superfluous.

But first we must learn to understand what it is that opposes such an examination of details in philosophy.

53. Our language-game (48) has *various* possibilities; there is a variety of cases in which we should say that a sign in the game was the name of a square of such-and-such a colour. We should say so if, for instance, we knew that the people who used the language were taught the use of the signs in such-and-such a way. Or if it were set down in writing, say in the form of a table, that this element corresponded to this sign, and if the table were used in teaching the language and were appealed to in certain disputed cases.

We can also imagine such a table's being a tool in the use of the language. Describing a complex is then done like this: the person who describes the complex has a table with him and looks up each element of the complex in it and passes from this to the sign (and the one who is given the description may also use a table to translate it into a picture of coloured squares). This table might be said to take over here the role of memory and association in other cases. (We do not usually carry out the order "Bring me a red flower" by looking up the colour red in a table of colours and then bringing a flower of the colour that we find in the table; but when it is a question of choosing or mixing a particular shade of red, we do sometimes make use of a sample or table.)

If we call such a table the expression of a rule of the language-game, it can be said that what we call a rule of a language-game may have very different roles in the game.

54. Let us recall the kinds of case where we say that a game is played according to a definite rule.

The rule may be an aid in teaching the game. The learner is told it and given practice in applying it.—Or it is an instrument of the game itself.—Or a rule is employed neither in the teaching nor in the game itself; nor is it set down in a list of rules. One learns the game by watching how others play. But we say that it is played according to such-and-such rules because an observer can read these rules off from the practice of the game—like a natural law governing the play.—But how does the observer distinguish in this case between players' mistakes and correct play?—There are characteristic signs of it in the players' behaviour. Think of the behaviour characteristic of correcting a slip of the tongue. It would be possible to recognize that someone was doing so even without knowing his language.

55. "What the names in language signify must be indestructible; for it must be possible to describe the state of affairs in which everything destructible is destroyed. And this description will contain words; and what corresponds to these cannot then be destroyed, for otherwise the words would have no meaning." I must not saw off the branch on which I am sitting.

One might, of course, object at once that this description would have to except itself from the destruction.—But what corresponds to the separate words of the description and so cannot be destroyed if it is true, is what gives the words their meaning—is that without which they would have no meaning.—In a sense, however, this man is surely what corresponds to his name. But he is destructible, and his name does not lose its meaning when the bearer is destroyed.—An example of something corresponding to the name, and without which it would have no meaning, is a paradigm that is used in connexion with the name in the language-game.

56. But what if no such sample is part of the language, and we *bear in mind* the colour (for instance) that a word stands for?—"And if we bear it in mind then it comes before our mind's eye when we utter the word. So, if it is always supposed to be possible for us to remember it, it must be in itself indestructible."—But what do we regard as the criterion for remembering it right?—When we work with a sample instead of our memory there are circumstances in which we say that the sample has changed colour and we judge of this by memory. But can we not sometimes speak of a dark-ening (for example) of our memory-image? Aren't we as much at the mercy of memory as of a sample? (For someone might feel like saying: "If we had no memory we should be at the mercy of a sample".)—Or perhaps of some chemical reaction. Imagine that you were supposed to paint a particular colour "C", which was the colour that appeared when the chemical substances X and Y combined.—Suppose that the colour struck you as brighter on one day than on another; would you not sometimes say: "I must be wrong, the colour is certainly the same as yesterday"? This shews that we do not always resort to what memory tells us as the verdict of the highest court of appeal.

57. "Something red can be destroyed, but red cannot be destroyed, and that is why the meaning of the word 'red' is independent of the existence of a red thing."—Certainly it makes no sense to say that the colour red is torn up or pounded to bits. But don't we say "The red is vanishing"? And don't clutch at the idea of our always being able to bring red before our mind's eye even when there is nothing red any more. That is just as if you chose to say that there would still always be a chemical reaction producing a red flame.—For suppose you cannot remember the colour any more?—When we forget which colour this is the name of, it loses meaning for us; that is, we are no longer able to play a particular language-game with it. And the situation then is comparable with that in which we have lost a paradigm which was an instrument of our language.

* * *

65. Here we come up against the great question that lies behind all these considerations.—For someone might object against me: "You take the easy way out! You talk about all sorts of language-games, but have nowhere said what the essence of a language-game, and hence of language, is: what is common to all these activities, and what makes them into language or parts of language. So you let yourself off the very part of the investigation that once gave you yourself most headache, the part about the *general form of propositions* and of language."

And this is true.—Instead of producing something common to all that we call language, I am saying that these phenomena have no one thing in common which makes us use the same word for all,—but that they are *related* to one another in many different ways. And it is because of this relationship, or these relationships, that we call them all "language". I will try to explain this.

66. Consider for example the proceedings that we call "games". I mean board-games, card-games, ball-games, Olympic games, and so on. What is common to them all?—

Don't say: "There *must* be something common, or they would not be called 'games'"—but *look and see* whether there is anything common to all.—For if you look at them you will not see something that is common to *all,* but similarities, relationships, and a whole series of them at that. To repeat: don't think, but look!—Look for example at board-games, with their multifarious relationships. Now pass to card-games; here you find many correspondences with the first group, but many common features drop out, and others appear. When we pass next to ball-games, much that is common is retained, but much is lost.—Are they all 'amusing'? Compare chess with noughts and crosses. Or is there always winning and losing, or competition between players? Think of patience. In ball-games there is winning and losing; but when a child throws his ball at the wall and catches it again, this feature has disappeared. Look at the parts played by skill and luck; and at the difference between skill in chess and skill in tennis. Think now of games like ring-a-ring-a-roses; here is the element of amusement, but how many other characteristic features have disappeared! And we can go through the many, many other groups of games in the same way; can see how similarities crop up and disappear.

And the result of this examination is: we see a complicated network of similarities overlapping and criss-crossing: sometimes overall similarities, sometimes similarities of detail.

67. I can think of no better expression to characterize these similarities than "family resemblances"; for the various resemblances between members of a family: build, features, colour of eyes, gait, temperament, etc. etc. overlap and criss-cross in the same way.—And I shall say: 'games' form a family.

And for instance the kinds of number form a family in the same way. Why do we call something a "number"? Well, perhaps because it has a—direct—relationship with several things that have hitherto been called number; and this can be said to give it an indirect relationship to other things we call the same name. And we extend our concept of number as in spinning a thread we twist fibre on fibre. And the strength of the thread does not reside in the fact that some one fibre runs through its whole length, but in the overlapping of many fibres.

But if someone wished to say: "There is something common to all these constructions—namely the disjunction of all their common properties"—I should reply: Now you are only playing with words. One might as well say: "Something runs through the whole thread—namely the continuous overlapping of those fibres".

68. "All right: the concept of number is defined for you as the logical sum of these individual interrelated concepts: cardinal numbers, rational numbers, real numbers, etc.; and in the same way the concept of a game as the logical sum of a corresponding set of sub-concepts."—It need not be so. For I *can* give the concept 'number' rigid limits in this way, that is, use the word "number" for a rigidly limited concept, but I can also use it so that the extension of the concept is *not* closed by a frontier. And this is how we do use the word "game". For how is the concept of a game bounded? What still counts as a game and what no longer does? Can you give the boundary? No. You can *draw* one; for none has so far been drawn. (But that never troubled you before when you used the word "game".)

"But then the use of the word is unregulated, the 'game' we play with it is unregulated."—It is not everywhere circumscribed by rules; but no more are there any rules for how high one throws the ball in tennis, or how hard; yet tennis is a game for all that and has rules too.

69. How should we explain to someone what a game is? I imagine that we should describe *games* to him, and we might add: "This *and similar things* are called 'games'". And do we know any more about it ourselves? Is it only other people whom we cannot tell exactly what a game is?—But this is not ignorance. We do not know the boundaries because none have been drawn. To repeat, we can draw a boundary—for a special purpose. Does it take that to make the concept usable? Not at all! (Except for that special purpose.) No more than it took the definition: 1 pace = 75 cm. to make the measure of length 'one pace' usable. And if you want to say "But still, before that it wasn't an exact measure", then I reply: very well, it was an inexact one.—Though you still owe me a definition of exactness.

70. "But if the concept 'game' is uncircumscribed like that, you don't really know what you mean by a 'game'."—When I give the description: "The ground was quite covered with plants"—do you want to say I don't know what I am talking about until I can give a definition of a plant?

My meaning would be explained by, say, a drawing and the words "The ground looked roughly like this". Perhaps I even say "it looked *exactly* like this."—Then were just *this* grass and *these* leaves there, arranged just like this? No, that is not what it means. And I should not accept any picture as exact in *this* sense.

Someone says to me: "Shew the children a game." I teach them gaming with dice, and the other says "I didn't mean that sort of game." Must the exclusion of the game with dice have come before his mind when he gave me the order?

71. One might say that the concept 'game' is a concept with blurred edges.—"But is a blurred concept a concept at all?"—Is an indistinct photograph a picture of a person at all? Is it even always an advantage to replace an indistinct picture by a sharp one? Isn't the indistinct one often exactly what we need?

Frege compares a concept to an area and says that an area with vague boundaries cannot be called an area at all. This presumably means that we cannot do anything with it.—But is it senseless to say: "Stand roughly there"? Suppose that I were standing with someone in a city square and said that. As I say it I do not draw any kind of boundary, but perhaps point with my hand—as if I were indicating a particular *spot*. And this is just how one might explain to someone what a game is. One gives examples and intends them to be taken in a particular way.—I do not, however, mean by this that he is supposed to see in those examples that common thing which I—for some reason—was unable to express; but that he is now to *employ* those examples in a particular way. Here giving examples is not an *indirect* means of explaining—in default of a better. For any general definition can be misunderstood too. The point is that *this* is how we play the game. (I mean the language-game with the word "game".)

72. *Seeing what is common.* Suppose I shew someone various multicoloured pictures, and say: "The colour you see in all these is called 'yellow ochre'".—This is a definition, and the other will get to understand it by looking for and seeing what is common to the pictures. Then he can look *at,* can point *to,* the common thing.

Compare with this a case in which I shew him figures of different shapes all painted the same colour, and say: "What these have in common is called 'yellow ochre'".

And compare this case: I shew him samples of different shades of blue and say: "The colour that is common to all these is what I call 'blue'".

73. When someone defines the names of colours for me by pointing to samples and saying "This colour is called 'blue', this 'green'. . . . ." this case can be compared in many respects to putting a table in my hands, with the words written under the colour-samples.—Though this comparison may mislead in many ways.—One is now inclined to extend the comparison: to have understood the definition means to have in one's mind an idea of the thing defined, and that is a sample or picture. So if I am shewn various different leaves and told "This is called a 'leaf'", I get an idea of the shape of a leaf, a picture of it in my mind.—But what does the picture of a leaf look like when it does not shew us any particular shape, but 'what is common to all shapes of leaf'? Which

shade is the 'sample in my mind' of the colour green—the sample of what is common to all shades of green?

"But might there not be such 'general' samples? Say a schematic leaf, or a sample of *pure* green?"—Certainly there might. But for such a schema to be understood as a *schema,* and not as the shape of a particular leaf, and for a slip of pure green to be understood as a sample of all that is greenish and not as a sample of pure green—this in turn resides in the way the samples are used.

Ask yourself: what *shape* must the sample of the colour green be? Should it be rectangular? Or would it then be the sample of a green rectangle?—So should it be 'irregular' in shape? And what is to prevent us then from regarding it—that is, from using it—only as a sample of irregularity of shape?

74. Here also belongs the idea that if you see this leaf as a sample of 'leaf shape in general' you *see* it differently from someone who regards it as, say, a sample of this particular shape. Now this might well be so—though it is not so—for it would only be to say that, as a matter of experience, if you *see* the leaf in a particular way, you use it in such-and-such a way or according to such-and-such rules. Of course, there is such a thing as seeing in *this* way or *that;* and there are also cases where whoever sees a sample like *this* will in general use it in *this* way, and whoever sees it otherwise in another way. For example, if you see the schematic drawing of a cube as a plane figure consisting of a square and two rhombi you will, perhaps, carry out the order "Bring me something like this" differently from someone who sees the picture three-dimensionally.

75. What does it mean to know what a game is? What does it mean, to know it and not be able to say it? Is this knowledge somehow equivalent to an unformulated definition? So that if it were formulated I should be able to recognize it as the expression of my knowledge? Isn't my knowledge, my concept of a game, completely expressed in the explanations that I could give? That is, in my describing examples of various kinds of game; shewing how all sorts of other games can be constructed on the analogy of these; saying that I should scarcely include this or this among games; and so on.

76. If someone were to draw a sharp boundary I could not acknowledge it as the one that I too always wanted to draw, or had drawn in my mind. For I did not want to draw one at all. His concept can then be said to be not the same as mine, but akin to it. The kinship is that of two pictures, one of which consists of colour patches with vague contours, and the other of patches similarly shaped and distributed, but with clear contours. The kinship is just as undeniable as the difference.

77. And if we carry this comparison still further it is clear that the degree to which the sharp picture *can* resemble the blurred one depends on the latter's degree of vagueness. For imagine having to sketch a sharply defined picture 'corresponding' to a blurred one. In the latter there is a blurred red rectangle: for it you put down a sharply defined one. Of course—several such sharply defined rectangles can be drawn to correspond to the indefinite one.—But if the colours in the original merge without a hint of any outline won't it become a hopeless task to draw a sharp picture corresponding to the blurred one? Won't you then have to say: "Here I might just as well draw a circle or heart as a rectangle, for all the colours merge. Anything—and nothing—is right."—And this is the position you are in if you look for definitions corresponding to our concepts in aesthetics or ethics.

In such a difficulty always ask yourself: How did we *learn* the meaning of this word ("good" for instance)? From what sort of examples? in what language-games? Then it will be easier for you to see that the word must have a family of meanings.

* * *

489. Ask yourself: On what occasion, for what purpose, do we say this?

What kind of actions accompany these words? (Think of a greeting.) In what scenes will they be used; and what for?

490. How do I know that *this line of thought* has led me to this action?—Well, it is a particular picture: for example, of a calculation leading to a further experiment in an experimental investigation. It looks like *this*—and now I could describe an example.

491. Not: "without language we could not communicate with one another"—but for sure: without language we cannot influence other people in such-and-such ways; cannot build roads and machines, etc. And also: without the use of speech and writing people could not communicate.

492. To invent a language could mean to invent an instrument for a particular purpose on the basis of the laws of nature (or consistently with them); but it also has the other sense, analogous to that in which we speak of the invention of a game.

Here I am stating something about the grammar of the word "language" by connecting it with the grammar of the word "invent".

493. We say: "The cock calls the hens by crowing"—but doesn't a comparison with our language lie at the bottom of this?—Isn't the aspect quite altered if we imagine the crowing to set the hens in motion by some kind of physical causation?

But if it were shewn how the words "Come to me" act on the person addressed, so that finally, given certain conditions, the muscles of his legs are innervated, and so on—should we feel that that sentence lost the character of a *sentence?*

494. I want to say: It is *primarily* the apparatus of our ordinary language, of our word-language, that we call language; and then other things by analogy or comparability with this.

495. Clearly, I can establish by experience that a human being (or animal) reacts to one sign as I want him to, and to another not. That, e.g., a human being goes to the right at the sign "$->$" and goes to the left at the sign "$<-$"; but that he does not react to the sign "$\circ-|$" as to "$<-$".

I do not even need to fabricate a case, I only have to consider what is in fact the case; namely, that I can direct a man who has learned only German, only by using the German language. (For here I am looking at learning German as adjusting a mechanism to respond to a certain kind of influence; and it may be all one to us whether someone else has learned the language, or was perhaps from birth constituted to react to sentences in German like a normal person who has learned German.)

496. Grammar does not tell us how language must be constructed in order to fulfill its purpose, in order to have such-and-such an effect on human beings. It only describes and in no way explains the use of signs.

497. The rules of grammar may be called "arbitrary", if that is to mean that the *aim* of the grammar is nothing but that of the language.

If someone says "If our language had not this grammar, it could not express these facts"—it should be asked what *"could"* means here.

498. When I say that the orders "Bring me sugar" and "Bring me milk" make sense, but not the combination "Milk me sugar", that does not mean that the utterance of this combination of words has no effect. And if its effect is that the other person stares at me and gapes, I don't on that account call it the order to stare and gape, even if that was precisely the effect that I wanted to produce.

499. To say "This combination of words makes no sense" excludes it from the sphere of language and thereby bounds the domain of language. But when one draws a boundary it may be for various kinds of reason. If I surround

an area with a fence or a line or otherwise, the purpose may be to prevent someone from getting in or out; but it may also be part of a game and the players be supposed, say, to jump over the boundary; or it may shew where the property of one man ends and that of another begins; and so on. So if I draw a boundary line that is not yet to say what I am drawing it for.

500. When a sentence is called senseless, it is not as it were its sense that is senseless. But a combination of words is being excluded from the language, withdrawn from circulation.

* * *

xi. Two uses of the word "see".

The one: "What do you see there?"—"I see *this*" (and then a description, a drawing, a copy). The other: "I see a likeness between these two faces"—let the man I tell this to be seeing the faces as clearly as I do myself.

The importance of this is the difference of category between the two 'objects' of sight.

The one man might make an accurate drawing of the two faces, and the other notice in the drawing the likeness which the former did not see.

I contemplate a face, and then suddenly notice its likeness to another. I *see* that it has not changed; and yet I see it differently. I call this experience "noticing an aspect".

Its *causes* are of interest to psychologists.

We are interested in the concept and its place among the concepts of experience.

You could imagine the illustration

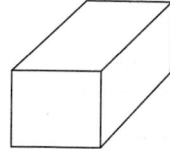

appearing in several places in a book, a text-book for instance. In the relevant text something different is in question every time: here a glass cube, there an inverted open box, there a wire frame of that shape, there three boards forming a solid angle. Each time the text supplies the interpretation of the illustration.

But we can also *see* the illustration now as one thing now as another.—So we interpret it, and *see* it as we *interpret* it.

Here perhaps we should like to reply: The description of what is got immediately, i.e. of the visual experience, by

means of an interpretation—is an indirect description. "I see the figure as a box" means: I have a particular visual experience which I have found that I always have when I interpret the figure as a box or when I look at a box. But if it meant this I ought to know it. I ought to be able to refer to the experience directly, and not only indirectly. (As I can speak of red without calling it the colour of blood.)

I shall call the following figure, derived from Jastrow,[3] the duck-rabbit. It can be seen as a rabbit's head or as a duck's.

And I must distinguish between the 'continuous seeing' of an aspect and the 'dawning' of an aspect.

The picture might have been shewn me, and I never have seen anything but a rabbit in it.

Here it is useful to introduce the idea of a picture-object. For instance

would be a 'picture-face'.

In some respects I stand towards it as I do towards a human face. I can study its expression, can react to it as to the expression of the human face. A child can talk to picture-men or picture-animals, can treat them as it treats dolls.

I may, then, have seen the duck-rabbit simply as a picture-rabbit from the first. That is to say, if asked "What's that?" or "What do you see here?" I should have replied: "A picture-rabbit". If I had further been asked what that was, I should have explained by pointing to all sorts of pictures of rabbits, should perhaps have pointed to real rabbits, talked abut their habits, or given an imitation of them.

I should not have answered the question "What do you see here?" by saying: "Now I am seeing it as a picture-rabbit". I should simply have described my perception: just

[3] *Fact and Fable in Psychology.* [Au.]

as if I had said "I see a red circle over there."—

Nevertheless someone else could have said of me: "He is seeing the figure as a picture-rabbit."

It would have made as little sense for me to say "Now I am seeing it as . . ." as to say at the sight of a knife and fork "Now I am seeing this as a knife and fork". This expression would not be understood.—And more than: "Now it's a fork" or "It can be a fork too".

One doesn't *'take'* what one knows as the cutlery at a meal *for* cutlery; any more than one ordinarily tries to move one's mouth as one eats, or aims at moving it.

If you say "Now it's a face for me", we can ask: "What change are you alluding to?"

I see two pictures, with the duck-rabbit surrounded by rabbits in one, by ducks in the other. I do not notice that they are the same. Does it *follow* from this that I *see* something different in the two cases?—It gives us a reason for using this expression here.

"I saw it quite differently, I should never have reocognized it!" Now, that is an exclamation. And there is also a justification for it.

I should never have thought of superimposing the heads like that, of making *this* comparison between them. For they suggest a different mode of comparison.

Nor has the head seen like *this* the slightest similarity to the head seen like *this*—although they are congruent.

I am shewn a picture-rabbit and asked what it is; I say "It's a rabbit". Not "Now it's a rabbit". I am reporting my perception.—I am shewn the duck-rabbit and asked what it is; I *may* say "It's a duck-rabbit". But I may also react to the question quite differently.—The answer that it is a duck-rabbit is again the report of a perception; the answer "Now it's a rabbit" is not. Had I replied "It's a rabbit", the ambiguity would have escaped me, and I should have been reporting my perception.

The change of aspect. "But surely you would say that the picture is altogether different now!"

But what is different: my impression? my point of view?—Can I say? I *describe* the alteration like a perception; quite as if the object had altered before my eyes.

"Now I am seeing *this*", I might say (pointing to another picture, for example). This has the form of a report of a new perception.

The expression of a change of aspect is the expression of a *new* perception and at the same time of the perception's being unchanged.

I suddenly see the solution of a puzzle-picture. Before, there were branches there; now there is a human shape. My visual impression has changed and now I recognize that it has not only shape and colour but also a quite particular 'organization'.—My visual impression has changed;—what was it like before and what is it like now?—If I represent it by means of an exact copy—and isn't that a good representation of it?—no change is shewn.

And above all do *not* say "After all my visual impression isn't the *drawing;* it is *this*—which I can't shew to anyone."—Of course it is not the drawing, but neither is it anything of the same category, which I carry within myself.

The concept of the 'inner picture' is misleading, for this concept uses the '*outer* picture' as a model; and yet the uses of the words for these concepts are no more like one another than the uses of 'numeral' and 'number'. (And if one chose to call numbers 'ideal numerals', one might produce a similar confusion.)

If you put the 'organization' of a visual impression on a level with colours and shapes, you are proceeding from the idea of the visual impression as an inner object. Of course this makes this object into a chimera; a queerly shifting construction. For the similarity to a picture is now impaired.

If I know that the schematic cube has various aspects and I want to find out what someone else sees, I can get him to make a model of what he sees, in addition to a copy, or to point to such a model; even though *he* has no idea of my purpose in demanding two accounts.

But when we have a changing aspect the case is altered. Now the only possible expression of our experience is what before perhaps seemed, or even was, a useless specification when once we had the copy.

And this by itself wrecks the comparison of 'organization' with colour and shape in visual impressions.

If I saw the duck-rabbit as a rabbit, then I saw: these shapes and colours (I give them in detail)—and I saw besides something like this: and here I point to a number of different pictures of rabbits.—This shews the difference between the concepts.

'Seeing as . . . .' is not part of perception. And for that reason it is like seeing and again not like.

I look at an animal and am asked: "What do you see?" I answer: "A rabbit".—I see a landscape; suddenly a rabbit runs past. I exclaim "A rabbit!"

Both things, both the report and the exclamation, are expressions of perception and of visual experience. But the exclamation is so in a different sense from the report: it is forced from us.—It is related to the experience as a cry is to pain.

But since it is the description of a perception, it can also be called the expression of thought.—If you are looking at the object, you need not think of it; but if you are having the visual experience expressed by the exclamation, you are also *thinking* of what you see.

Hence the flashing of an aspect on us seems half visual experience, half thought.

Someone suddenly sees an appearance which he does not recognize (it may be a familiar object, but in an unusual position or lighting); the lack of recognition perhaps lasts only a few seconds. Is it correct to say he has a different visual experience from someone who knew the object at once?

For might not someone be able to describe an unfamiliar shape that appeared before him just as *accurately* as I, to whom it is familiar? And isn't that the answer?—Of course it will not generally be so. And his description will run quite differently. (I say, for example, "The animal had long ears"—he: "There were two long appendages", and then he draws them.)

I meet someone whom I have not seen for years; I see him clearly, but fail to know him. Suddenly I know him, I see the old face in the altered one. I believe that I should do a different portrait of him now if I could paint.

Now, when I know my acquaintance in a crowd, perhaps after looking in his direction for quite a while,—is this a special sort of seeing? Is it a case of both seeing and thinking? or an amalgam of the two, as I should almost like to say?

The question is: *why* does one want to say this?

The very expression which is also a report of what is seen, is here a cry of recognition.

What is the criterion of the visual experience?—The criterion? What do you suppose?

The representation of 'what is seen'.

The concept of a representation of what is seen, like that of a copy, is very elastic, and so *together with it* is the concept of what is seen. The two are intimately connected. (Which is *not* to say that they are alike.)

How does one tell that human beings *see* three-dimensionally?—I ask someone about the lie of the land

(over there) of which he has a view. "Is it like *this?*" (I shew him with my hand)—"Yes."—"How do you know?"—"It's not misty, I see it quite clear."—He does not give reasons for the surmise. The only thing that is natural to us is to represent what we see three-dimensionally; special practice and training are needed for two-dimensional representation whether in drawing or in words. (The queerness of children's drawings.)

If someone sees a smile and does not know it for a smile, does not understand it as such, does he see it differently from someone who understands it?—He mimics it differently, for instance.

Hold the drawing of a face upside down and you can't recognize the expression of the face. Perhaps you can see that it is smiling, but not exactly what *kind* of smile it is. You cannot imitate the smile or describe it more exactly.

And yet the picture which you have turned round may be a most exact representation of a person's face.

The figure (a)

is the reverse of the figure (b)

As (c)

is the reverse of (d)

But—I should like to say—there is a different difference between my impressions of (c) and (d) and between those of (a) and (b). (d), for example, looks neater than (c). (Compare a remark of Lewis Carroll's.) (d) is easy, (c) hard to copy.

Imagine the duck-rabbit hidden in a tangle of lines. Now I suddenly notice it in the picture, and notice it simply as the head of a rabbit. At some later time I look at the same picture and notice the same figure, but see it as the duck, without necessarily realizing that it was the same figure both times.—If I later see the aspect change—can I say that the duck and rabbit aspects are now seen quite differently from when I recognized them separately in the tangle of lines? No.

But the change produces a surprise not produced by the recognition.

If you search in a figure (1) for another figure (2), and then find it, you see (1) in a new way. Not only can you give a new kind of description of it, but noticing the second figure was a new visual experience.

But you would not necessarily want to say "Figure (1) looks quite different now; it isn't even in the least like the figure I saw before, though they are congruent!"

There are here hugely many interrelated phenomena and possible concepts.

Then is the copy of the figure an *incomplete* description of my visual experience? No.—But the circumstances decide whether, and what, more detailed specifications are necessary.—It *may* be an incomplete description; if there is still something to ask.

Of course we can say: There are certain things which fall equally under the concept 'picture-rabbit' and under the concept 'picture-duck'. And a picture, a drawing, is such a thing.—But the *impression* is not simultaneously of a picture-duck and a picture-rabbit.

"What I really *see* must surely be what is produced in me by the influence of the object"—Then what is produced in me is a sort of copy, something that in its turn can be looked at, can be before one; almost something like a *materialization.*

And this materialization is something spatial and it must be possible to describe it in purely spatial terms. For instance (if it is a face) it can smile; the concept of friendliness, however, has no place in an account of it, but is *foreign* to such an account (even though it may subserve it).

If you ask me what I saw, perhaps I shall be able to make a sketch which shews you; but I shall mostly have no recollection of the way my glance shifted in looking at it.

The concept of 'seeing' makes a tangled impression. Well, it is tangled.—I look at the landscape, my gaze ranges over it, I see all sorts of distinct and indistinct movement; *this* impresses itself sharply on me, *that* is quite hazy. After all, how completely ragged what we see can appear! And

now look at all that can be meant by "description of what is seen".—But this just is what is called description of what is seen. There is not *one genuine* proper case of such description—the rest being just vague, something which awaits clarification, or which must just be swept aside as rubbish.

Here we are in enormous danger of wanting to make fine distinctions.—It is the same when one tries to define the concept of a material object in terms of 'what is really seen'.—What we have rather to do is to *accept* the everyday language-game, and to note *false* accounts of the matter *as* false. The primitive language-game which children are taught needs no justification; attempts at justification need to be rejected.

Take as an example the aspects of a triangle. This triangle

can be seen as a triangular hole, as a solid, as a geometrical drawing; as standing on its base, as hanging from its apex; as a mountain, as a wedge, as an arrow or pointer, as an overturned object which is meant to stand on the shorter side of the right angle, as a half parallelogram, and as various other things.

"You can think now of *this* now of *this* as you look at it, can regard it now as *this* now as *this,* and then you will see it now *this* way, now *this.*"—*What* way? There *is* no further qualification.

But how is it possible to *see* an object according to an *interpretation?*—The question represents it as a queer fact; as if something were being forced into a form it did not really fit. But no squeezing, no forcing took place here.

When it looks as if there were no room for such a form between other ones you have to look for it in another dimension. If there is no room here, there *is* room in another dimension.

*   *   *

Do I really see something different each time, or do I only interpret what I see in a different way? I am inclined to say the former. But why?—To interpret is to think, to do something; seeing is a state.

Now it is easy to recognize cases in which we are *interpreting.* When we interpret we form hypotheses, which may prove false.—"I am seeing this figure as a . . . ." can be verified as little as (or in the same sense as) "I am seeing bright red". So there is a similarity in the use of "seeing" in the two contexts. Only do not think you knew in advance what the "*state* of seeing" means here! Let the use *teach* you the meaning.

We find certain things about seeing puzzling, because we do not find the whole business of seeing puzzling enough.

If you look at a photograph of people, houses and trees, you do not feel the lack of the third dimension in it. We should not find it easy to describe a photograph as a collection of colour-patches on a flat surface; but what we see in a stereoscope looks three-dimensional in a different way again.

(It is anything but a matter of course that we see 'three-dimensionally' with two eyes. If the two visual images are amalgamated, we might expect a blurred one as a result.)

The concept of an aspect is akin to the concept of an image. In other words: the concept 'I am now seeing it as . . . .' is akin to 'I am now having *this* image'.

Doesn't it take imagination to hear something as a variation on a particular theme? And yet one is perceiving something in so hearing it.

"Imagine this changed like this, and you have this other thing." One can use imagining in the course of proving something.

Seeing an aspect and imagining are subject to the will. There is such an order as "Imagine *this*", and also: "Now see the figure like *this*"; but not: "Now see this leaf green".

The question now arises: Could there be human beings lacking in the capacity to see something *as something*—and what would that be like? What sort of consequences would it have?—Would this defect be comparable to colour-blindness or to not having absolute pitch?—We will call it "aspect-blindness"—and will next consider what might be meant by this. (A conceptual investigation.) The aspect-blind man is supposed not to see the aspects A change. But is he also supposed not to recognize that the double cross contains both a black and a white cross? So if told "Shew me figures containing a black cross among these examples" will he be unable to manage it? No, he should be able to do that; but he will not be supposed to say: "Now it's a black cross on a white ground!"

Is he supposed to be blind to the similarity between two faces?—And so also to their identity or approximate identity? I do not want to settle this. (He ought to be able to execute such orders as "Bring me something that looks like *this*.")

Ought he to be unable to see the schematic cube as a cube?—It would not follow from that that he could not recognize it as a representation (a working drawing for instance) of a cube. But for him it would not jump from one aspect to the other.—Question: Ought he to be able to *take* it as a cube in certain circumstances, as we do?—If not, this could not very well be called a sort of blindness.

The 'aspect-blind' will have an altogether different relationship to pictures from ours.

(Anomalies of *this* kind are easy for us to imagine.)

Aspect-blindness will be *akin* to the lack of a 'musical ear'.

The importance of this concept lies in the connexion between the concepts of 'seeing an aspect' and 'experiencing the meaning of a word'. For we want to ask "What would you be missing if you did not *experience* the meaning of a word?"

What would you be missing, for instance, if you did not understand the request to pronounce the word "till" and to mean it as a verb,—or if you did not feel that a word lost its meaning and became a mere sound if it was repeated ten times over?

In a law-court, for instance, the question might be raised how someone meant a word. And this can be inferred from certain facts.—It is a question of *intention*. But could how he experienced a word—the word "bank" for instance—have been significant in the same way?

Suppose I had agreed on a code with someone; "tower" means bank. I tell him "Now go to the tower"—he understands me and acts accordingly, but he feels the word "tower" to be strange in this use, it has not yet 'taken on' the meaning.

"When I read a poem or narrative with feeling, surely something goes on in me which does not go on when I merely skim the lines for information."—What processes am I alluding to?—The sentences have a different *ring*. I pay careful attention to my intonation. Sometimes a word has the wrong intonation, I emphasize it too much or too little. I notice this and shew it in my face. I might later talk about my reading in detail, for example about the mistakes in my tone of voice. Sometimes a picture, as it were an illustration, comes to me. And this seems to help me to read with the correct expression. And I could mention a good deal more of the same kind.—I can also give a word a tone of voice which brings out the meaning of the rest, almost as if this word were a picture of the whole thing. (And this may, of course, depend on sentence-formation.)

When I pronounce this word while reading with expression it is completely filled with its meaning.—"How can this be, if meaning is the use of the word?" Well, what I said was intended figuratively. Not that I chose the figure: it forced itself on me.—But the figurative employment of the word can't get into conflict with the original one.

Perhaps it could be explained why precisely *this* picture suggests itself to me. (Just think of the expression, and the meaning of the expression: "the word that hits it off".)

But if a sentence can strike me as like a painting in words, and the very individual word in the sentence as like a picture, then it is no such marvel that a word uttered in isolation and without purpose can seem to carry a particular meaning in itself.

Think here of a special kind of illusion which throws light on these matters.—I go for a walk in the environs of a city with a friend. As we talk it comes out that I am imagining the city to lie on our right. Not only have I *no* conscious reason for this assumption, but some quite simple consideration was enough to make me realize that the city lay rather to the left ahead of us. I can at first give no answer to the question *why* I imagine the city in *this* direction. I had *no reason* to think it. But though I see no reason still I seem to see certain psychological causes for it. In particular, certain associations and memories. For example, we walked along a canal, and once before in similar circumstances I had followed a canal and that time the city lay on our right.—I might try as it were psychoanalytically to discover the causes of my unfounded conviction.

"But what is this queer experience?"—Of course it is not queerer than any other; it simply differs in kind from those experiences which we regard as the most fundamental ones, our sense impressions for instance.

"I feel as if I knew the city lay over there."—"I feel as if the name 'Schubert' fitted Schubert's works and Schubert's face."

You can say the word "March" to yourself and mean it at one time as an imperative at another as the name of a month. And now say "March!"—and then "March *no further!*"—Does the *same* experience accompany the word both times—are you sure?

If a sensitive ear shews me, when I am playing this game, that I have now *this* now *that* experience of the word—doesn't it also shew me that I often do not have *any*

experience of it in the course of talking?—For the fact that I then also mean it, intend it, now like *this* now like *that,* and maybe also say so later is, of course, not in question.

But the question now remains why, in connexion with this *game* of experiencing a word, we also speak of 'the meaning' and of 'meaning it'.—This is a different kind of question.—It is the phenomenon which is characteristic of this language-game that in *this* situation we use this expression: we say we pronounced the word with *this* meaning and take this expression over from that other language-game.

Call it a dream. It does not change anything.

Given the two ideas 'fat' and 'lean', would you be rather inclined to say that Wednesday was fat and Tuesday lean, or *vice versa?* (I incline decisively towards the former.) Now have "fat" and "lean" some different meaning here from their usual one?—They have a different use.—So ought I really to have used different words? Certainly not that.—I want to use *these* words (with their familiar meanings) here.—Now, I say nothing about the causes of this phenomenon. They *might* be associations from my childhood. But that is a hypothesis. Whatever the explanation,—the inclination is there.

Asked "What do you really mean here by 'fat' and 'lean'?"—I could only explain the meanings in the usual way. I could *not* point to the examples of Tuesday and Wednesday.

Here one might speak of a 'primary' and 'secondary' sense of a word. It is only if the word has the primary sense for you that you use it in the secondary one.

Only if you have learnt to calculate—on paper or out loud—can you be made to grasp, by means of this concept, what calculating in the head is.

The secondary sense is not a 'metaphorical' sense. If I say "For me the vowel *e* is yellow" I do not mean: 'yellow' in a metaphorical sense,—for I could not express what I want to say in any other way than by means of the idea 'yellow'.

Someone tells me: "Wait for me by the bank". Question: Did you, *as you were saying the word,* mean this bank?—This question is of the same kind as "Did you intend to say such-and-such to him on your way to meet him?" It refers to a definite time (the time of walking, as the former question refers to the time of speaking)—but not to an *experience* during that time. Meaning is as little an experience as intending.

But what distinguishes them from experience?—They have no experience-content. For the contents (images for instance) which accompany and illustrate them are not the meaning or intending.

The intention *with which* one acts does not 'accompany' the action any more than the thought 'accompanies' speech. Thought and intention are neither 'articulated' nor 'non-articulated'; to be compared neither with a single note which sounds during the acting or speaking, nor with a tune.

'Talking' (whether out loud or silently) and 'thinking' are not concepts of the same kind; even though they are in closest connexion.

The *interest* of the experiences one has while speaking and of the intention is not the same. (The experiences might perhaps inform a psychologist about the *'unconscious'* intention.)

"At that word we both thought of him." Let us assume that each of us said the same words to himself—and how can it mean MORE than that?—But wouldn't even those words be only a *germ?* They must surely belong to a language and to a context, in order really to be the expression of the thought *of* that man.

If God had looked into our minds he would not have been able to see there whom we were speaking of.

"Why did you look at me at that word, were you thinking of . . . .?"—So there is a reaction at a certain moment and it is explained by saying "I thought of . . . . ." or "I suddenly remembered . . . ."

In saying this you refer to that moment in the time you were speaking. It makes a difference whether you refer to this or to that moment.

Mere explanation of a word does not refer to an occurrence at the moment of speaking.

The language-game "I mean (or meant) *this*" (subsequent explanation of a word) is quite different from this one: "I thought of . . . . as I said it." The latter is akin'to "It reminded me of . . . ."

"I have already remembered three times today that I must write to him." Of what importance is it what went on in me then?—On the other hand what is the importance, what the interest, of the statement itself?—It permits certain conclusions.

"At these words *he* occurred to me."—What is the primitive reaction with which the language-game begins— which can then be translated into these words? How do people get to use these words?

The primitive reaction may have been a glance or a gesture, but it may also have been a word.

"Why did you look at me and shake your head?"—"I wanted to give you to understand that you . . . . ." This is supposed to express not a symbolic convention but the purpose of my action.

Meaning it is not a process which accompanies a word. For no *process* could have the consequences of meaning.

(Similarly, I think, it could be said: a calculation is not an experiment, for no experiment could have the peculiar consequences of a multiplication.)

There are important accompanying phenomena of talking which are often missing when one talks without thinking, and this is characteristic of talking without thinking. But *they* are not the thinking.

"Now I know!" What went on here?—So did I *not* know, when I declared that now I knew?
You are looking at it wrong.
(What is the signal for?)
And could the 'knowing' be called an accompaniment of the exclamation?

The familiar physiognomy of a word, the feeling that it has taken up its meaning into itself, that it is an actual likeness of its meaning—there could be human beings to whom all this was alien. (They would not have an attachment to their words.)—And how are those feelings manifested among us?—By the way we choose and value words.

I. A. Richards

1893–1979

The influence of Richards on criticism in the twentieth century rivaled that of T. S. Eliot (above, page 806). He first developed his position in *Principles of Literary Criticism* (1924). *Science and Poetry* followed in 1926, and *Practical Criticism* in 1929. These books remained influential into the forties. A psychologist and semanticist, Richards displays an interest in the effect of poems on the reader and, like Matthew Arnold (above, page 586), in a possible cultural or therapeutic role for poetry. The poem's value lies, for Richards, in the balancing and organizing of what are usually conflicting impulses. He held that in an age when canons of moral and social authority are crumbling, the conquest of warring impulses is more difficult than in a reasonably stable one. Richards's psychologizing, though some of its language crept into criticism, turned out to be less influential than his address to certain other issues. In *Principles* he had decisive things to say about the condition of literary theory in his time (chaos), language as communication, and the availability of the poet's experience, including the question of authorial intention (see Wimsatt and Beardsley, below, page 1026). He also mounted an attack on what he called the "phantom aesthetic state," objecting to the tradition of aesthetics that emerged from Kant. In *Science and Poetry,* he offered the notion of pseudo-statements (see also Carnap, below, page 978), reflecting a positivistic streak that accompanied his materialistic psychologizing. Poetry is effective because it contains pseudo-statements, which may be entertained in a different way from unpoetic statements, the latter being referable to empirical evidence. It provides a way of satisfying a need to "cut our pseudo-statements free from belief, and yet retain them, in this released state, as the main instruments by which we order our attitudes as to one another and to the world." In *Practical Criticism,* where he analyzed responses by his students to poems he had given to them without indicating author or title, he raised the question of how belief or doctrine properly or improperly affected reader response, positing a difference between good and bad reading.

It is not surprising that with his theory of the balancing of conflicting impulses Richards should value most highly a poetry of irony, of "bringing in the opposite." In this preference he is aligned with T. S. Eliot and the New Critics.

Richards's works include *The Foundations of Aesthetics* (with C. K. Ogden, 1922); *Principles of Literary Criticism* (1924); *Science and Poetry* (1926), later reissued with commentary; *The Meaning of Meaning: A Study of the Influence of Language Upon Thought and of the Science of Symbolism,* with C. K. Ogden (rev. ed., 1927); *Practical Criticism* (1929); *Mencius on the Mind* (1932); *Coleridge on Imagination* (1934); *The Philosophy of Rhetoric* (1936); *Interpretation in Teaching* (1938); and *How to Read a Page* (1942). See J. C. Ransom, *The New Criticism* (1941); R. S. Crane, "I. A. Richards on the Art of Interpretation," in Crane, ed., *Critics and Criticism* (1952); Murray

Krieger, *The New Apologists for Poetry* (1956); M. H. Abrams, ed., *Literature and Belief* (1958); W. H. N. Hotopf, *Language, Thought, and Comprehension* (1965); J. P. Schiller, *I. A. Richards' Theory of Literature* (1970); John Needham, *The Completest Mode: I. A. Richards and the Continuity of English Literary Criticism* (1982); John Paul Russo, *I. A. Richards: His Life and Work* (1989).

from

Principles of Literary Criticism

Chapter II

The Phantom Æsthetic State

None of his follies will he repent, none will he wish to repeat; no happier lot can be assigned to man.
WILHELM MEISTER

A more serious defect in æsthetics is the avoidance of considerations as to value.[1] It is true that an ill-judged introduction of value considerations usually leads to disaster, as in Tolstoy's case.[2] But the fact that some of the experiences to which the arts give rise are valuable and take the form they do because of their value is not irrelevant. Whether this fact is of service in analysis will naturally depend upon the theory of value adopted. But to leave it out of account altogether is to run the risk of missing the clue to the whole matter. And the clue has in fact been missed.

All modern æsthetics rests upon an assumption which has been strangely little discussed, the assumption that there is a distinct *kind* of mental activity present in what are called æsthetic experiences. Ever since "the first rational word concerning beauty"[3] was spoken by Kant, the attempt to define the 'judgment of taste' as concerning pleasure which is disinterested, universal, unintellectual, and not to be confused with the pleasures of sense or of ordinary emotions, in short to make it a thing *sui generis*,[4] has continued. Thus

arises the phantom problem of the æsthetic mode or æsthetic state, a legacy from the days of abstract investigation into the Good, the Beautiful and the True.

The temptation to align this tripartite division with a similar division into Will, Feeling and Thought was irresistible. "All the faculties of the Soul, or capacities, are reducible to three, which do not admit of any further derivation from a common ground: the *faculty of knowledge,* the *feeling of pleasure or displeasure,* and the *faculty of desire*"[5] said Kant. Legislative for each of these faculties stood Understanding, Judgment and Reason respectively. "Between the faculties of knowledge and desire stands the feeling of pleasure, just as judgment is intermediate between understanding and reason." And he went on to discuss æsthetics as appertaining to the province of judgment, the middle one of these three, the first and last having already occupied him in his two other Critiques of Pure and Practical Reason respectively. The effect was virtually to annex æsthetics to Idealism, in which fabric it has ever since continued to serve important purposes.

This accident of formal correspondence has had an influence upon speculation which would be ridiculous if it had not been so disastrous. It is difficult even now to get out of ruts which have been seen to lead nowhere. With the identification of the provinces of Truth and Thought no quarrel arises, and the Will and the Good are, as we shall see, intimately connected, but the attempts to fit Beauty into a neat pigeon-hole with Feeling have led to calamitous distortions. It is now generally abandoned,[6] although echoes of it can be heard everywhere in critical writings. The peculiar use of 'emotion' by reviewers, and the prevalence of the phrase 'æsthetic emotion' is one of them. In view, then, of the objections to Feeling, something else, some special mode of mental activity, had to be found, to which Beauty could belong. Hence arose the æsthetic mode. Truth was the object of

---

The Principles of Literary Criticism was published in 1924 in New York by Harcourt, Brace.
[1] Richards relates aesthetics to the idea that there is such a thing as a special aesthetic affective response.
[2] Tolstoy (above, page 757).
[3] [Richards] Hegel's *dictum, History of Philosophy,* iii, 543 (Kant, above, page 420).
[4] Of its own making.

[5] [Richards] *Critique of Judgment,* trans. by Meredith, p. 15.
[6] [Richards] Dr. Bosanquet [English philosopher, 1848–1923] was one of the last adherents. See his *Three Lectures on Aesthetics.*

the inquiring activity, of the Intellectual or Theoretical part of the mind, and the Good that of the willing, desiring, practical part; what part could be found for the Beautiful? Some activity that was neither inquisitive nor practical, that did not question and did not seek to use. The result was the æsthetic, the contemplative, activity which is still defined, in most treatments,[7] by these negative conditions alone, as that mode of commerce with things which is neither intellectual inquiry into their nature, nor an attempt to make them satisfy our desire. The experiences which arise in contemplating objects of art were then discovered to be describable in some such terms, and system secured a temporary triumph.

It is true that many of these experiences do present peculiarities, both in the intellectual interest which is present and in the way in which the development of desires within them takes place, and these peculiarities—detachment, impersonality, serenity and so forth—are of great interest. They will have to be carefully examined in the sequel.

We shall find that two entirely different sets of characters are involved. They arise from quite different causes but are hard to distinguish introspectively. Taken as marking off a special province for inquiry they are most unsatisfactory. They would yield for our purposes, even if they were not so ambiguous, a diagonal or slant classification. Some of the experiences which most require to be considered would be left out and many which are without importance brought in. To choose the Æsthetic State as the starting-point for an inquiry into the values of the arts is in fact somewhat like choosing 'rectangular, and red in parts' as a definition of a picture. We should find ourselves ultimately discussing a different collection of things from those we intended to discuss.

But the problem remains—Is there any such thing as the æsthetic state, or any æsthetic character of experiences which is *sui generis?* Not many explicit arguments have ever been given for one. Vernon Lee, it is true, in *Beauty and Ugliness,* p. 10, argues that "a relation entirely *sui generis* between visible and audible forms and ourselves" can be deduced from the fact "that given proportions, shapes, patterns, compositions have a tendency to recur in art." How this can be done it is hard to divine. Arsenic tends to recur in murder cases, and tennis in the summer, but no characters or relations *sui generis* anywhere are thereby proved. Obviously you can only tell whether anything is like or unlike other things by examining it and them, and to notice that

one case of it is like another case of it, is not helpful. It may be suspected that where the argument is so confused, the original question was not very clear.

The question is whether a certain kind of experience is or is not *like* other kinds of experience. Plainly it is a question as to degree of likeness. Be it granted at once, to clear the air, that there are all sorts of experiences involved in the values of the arts, and that attributions of Beauty spring from all sorts of causes. Is there among these one kind of experience as different from experiences which don't so occur as, say, envy is from remembering, or as mathematical calculation is from eating cherries? And what degree of difference would make it specific? Put this way it is plainly not an easy question to answer. These differences, none of them measurable, are of varying degree, and all are hard to estimate. Yet the vast majority of post-Kantian writers, and many before him, have unhesitatingly replied, "Yes! the æsthetic experience is peculiar and specific." And their grounds, when not merely verbal, have usually been those of direct inspection.

It requires some audacity to run counter to such a tradition, and I do not do so without reflection. Yet, after all, the matter is one of classification, and when so many other divisions in psychology are being questioned and reorganized, this also may be re-examined.

The case for a distinct æsthetic species of experience can take two forms. It may be held that there is some unique kind of mental element which enters into æsthetic experiences and into no others. Thus Mr. Clive Bell[8] used to maintain the existence of an unique emotion 'æsthetic emotion' as the *differentia.* But psychology has no place for such an entity. What other will be suggested? Empathy, for example, as Vernon Lee herself insists, enters into innumerable other experiences as well as into æsthetic experiences. I do not think any will be proposed.

Alternatively, the æsthetic experience may contain no unique constituent, and be of the usual stuff but with a special form. This is what it is commonly supposed to be. Now the special form as it is usually described—in terms of disinterestedness, detachment, distance, impersonality, subjective universality, and so forth—this form, I shall try to show later, is sometimes no more than a consequence of the incidence of the experience, a condition or an effect of communication. But sometimes a structure which can be described in the same terms is an essential feature of the experience, the feature in fact upon which its value depends. In other

[7][Richards] E.g. Vernon Lee [Violet Paget, English aesthetician and writer, 1856–1935], *The Beautiful.*

[8]Clive Bell (1881–1964), English art critic.

words, at least two different sets of characters, due to different causes, are, in current usage, ambiguously covered by the term 'æsthetic.' It is very necessary to distinguish the sense in which merely putting something in a frame or writing it in verse gives it an 'æsthetic character,' from a sense in which value is implied. This confusion, together with other confusions,[9] has made the term nearly useless.

The æsthetic mode is generally supposed to be a peculiar way of regarding things which can be exercised, whether the resulting experiences are valuable, disvaluable or indifferent. It is intended to cover the experience of ugliness as well as that of beauty, and also intermediate experiences. What I wish to maintain is that there is no such mode, that the experience of ugliness has nothing in common with that of beauty, which both do not share with innumerable other experiences no one (except Croce;[10] but this qualification is often required) would dream of calling æsthetic. But a narrower sense of æsthetic is also found in which it *is* confined to experiences of beauty and does imply value. And with regard to this, while admitting that such experiences can be distinguished, I shall be at pains to show that they are closely similar to many other experiences, that they differ chiefly in the connections between their constituents, and that they are only a further development, a finer organisation of ordinary experiences, and not in the least a new and different kind of thing. When we look at a picture, or read a poem, or listen to music, we are not doing something quite unlike what we were doing on our way to the Gallery or when we dressed in the morning. The fashion in which the experience is caused in us is different, and as a rule the experience is more complex and, if we are successful, more unified. But our activity is not of a fundamentally different kind. To assume that it is, puts difficulties in the way of describing and explaining it, which are unnecessary and which no one has yet succeeded in overcoming.

The point here raised, and particularly the distinction between the two quite different sets of characters, on the ground of which an experience may be described as æsthetic or impersonal and disinterested, will become clearer at a later stage.[11]

A further objection to the assumption of a peculiar æsthetic attitude is that it makes smooth the way for the idea of a peculiar æsthetic value, a pure art value. Postulate a peculiar kind of experience, æsthetic experience, and it is an easy step to the postulation of a peculiar unique value, different in kind and cut off from the other values of ordinary experiences. "To appreciate a work of art we need bring with us nothing from life, no knowledge of its ideas and affairs, no familiarity with its emotions."[12] So runs a recent extreme statement of the Æsthetic Hypothesis, which has had much success. To quote another example less drastic but also carrying with it the implication that æsthetic experiences are *sui generis,* and their value not of the same kind as other values. "Its nature is to be not a part, nor yet a copy, of the real world (as we commonly understand that phrase), but a world in itself independent, complete, autonomous."[13]

This view of the arts as providing a private heaven for æsthetes is, as will appear later, a great impediment to the investigation of their value. The effects upon the general attitudes of those who accept it uncritically are also often regrettable; while the effects upon literature and the arts have been noticeable, in a narrowing and restriction of the interests active, in preciousness, artificiality and spurious aloofness. **Art** envisaged as a mystic, ineffable virtue is a close relative of the 'æsthetic mood', and may easily be pernicious in its effects, through the habits of mind which, as an idea, it fosters, and to which, as a mystery, it appeals.

* * *

. . . language has succeeded until recently in hiding from us almost all the things we talk about. Whether we are discussing music, poetry, painting, sculpture or architecture, we are forced to speak as though certain physical objects— vibrations of strings and of columns of air, marks printed on paper, canvasses and pigments, masses of marble, fabrics of freestone, are what we are talking about. And yet the remarks we make as critics do not apply to such objects but to states of mind, to experiences.

A certain strangeness about this view is often felt but diminishes with reflection. If anyone says that 'The May Queen'[14] is sentimental, it is not difficult to agree that he is referring to a state of mind. But if he declares that the masses in a Giotto[15] exactly balance one another, this is less

---

[9][Richards] E.g. any choice for which the chooser cannot give his reasons tends in the laboratory to be called an 'aesthetic choice.'

[10]Benedetto Croce (1866–1952), Italian philosopher, author of *Aesthetic.*

[11][Richards] Cf. Chapters X and XXXII, and Impersonality, *Index.*

[12][Richards] Clive Bell, *Art,* p. 25.

[13][Richards] A. C. Bradley [English literary scholar and critic, 1851–1935], *Oxford Lectures on Poetry,* p. 5.

[14]"The May Queen," a poem by Alfred Lord Tennyson.

[15]Giotto (c. 1267–1337), Italian painter.

apparent, and, if he goes on to discuss time in music, form in visual art, plot in drama, the fact that he is all the while talking about mental happenings becomes concealed. The verbal apparatus comes between us and the things with which we are really dealing. Words which are useful, indeed invaluable, as handy stop-gaps and makeshifts in conversation, but which need elaborate expansions before they can be used with precision, are treated as simply as people's proper names. So it becomes natural to seek for the things these words appear to stand for, and thus arise innumerable subtle investigations, doomed *ab initio* as regards their main intent to failure.

* * *

Most critical remarks state in an abbreviated form that an object causes certain experiences, and as a rule the form of the statement is such as to suggest that the object has been said to possess certain qualities. But often the critic goes further and affirms that the effect in his mind is due to special particular features of the object. In this case he is pointing out something about the object in addition to its effect upon him, and this fuller kind of criticism is what we desire. Before his insight can greatly benefit, however, a very clear demarcation between the object, with its features, and his experience, which is the effect of contemplating it, is necessary. The bulk of critical literature is unfortunately made up of examples of their confusion.

It will be convenient at this point to introduce two definitions. In a full critical statement which states not only that an experience is valuable in certain ways, but also that it is caused by certain features in a contemplated object, the part which describes the value of the experience we shall call the *critical* part. That which describes the object we shall call the *technical* part.[16] Thus to say that we feel differently towards wooden crosses and stone crosses is a technical remark. And to say that metre is more suited to the tender passion than is prose would be, as it stands, a technical remark, but here it is evident that a critical part might easily be also present. All remarks as to the ways and means by which experiences arise or are brought about are technical, but critical remarks are about the values of experiences and the reasons for regarding them as valuable, or not valuable. We shall endeavour in what follows to show that critical remarks are merely a branch of psychological remarks, and that no special ethical or metaphysical ideas need be introduced to explain value.

---

[16] R. P. Blackmur (below, page 976) may have picked up this term from Richards.

from

Science and Poetry

VI. Poetry and Beliefs

Control of the passes was, he saw, the Key
To this new district, but who would get it?
He, the trained spy, had walked into the trap
For a bogus guide, seduced with the old tricks.

W. H. AUDEN[1]

The business of the poet, as we have seen, is to give order and coherence, and so freedom, to a body of experience. To do so through words which act as its skeleton, as a structure by which the impulses which make up the experience are adjusted to one another and act together. The means by which words do this are many and varied. To work them out is a problem for linguistic psychology, that embarrassed young heir to philosophy. What little can be done shows already that most critical dogmas of the past are either false or nonsense. A little knowledge is not here a danger, but clears the air in a remarkable way.

Roughly and inadequately, even in the dim light of present knowledge, we can say that words work in the poem in two main fashions: as sensory stimuli and as (in the *widest* sense) symbols. We must refrain from considering the sensory side of the poem, remarking only that it is *not* in the least independent of the other side, and that it has for definite reasons prior importance in most poetry. We must confine ourselves to the other function of words in the poem, or rather, omitting much that is of secondary relevance, to one form of that function, let me call it *pseudo-statement*.[2]

It will be admitted—by those who distinguish between scientific statement, where truth is ultimately a matter of verification as this is understood in the laboratory, and emotive utterance, where "truth" is primarily acceptability *by* some attitude, and more remotely is the acceptability *of* this attitude itself—that it is *not* the poet's business to make scientific statements. Yet poetry has constantly the air of making statements, and important ones; which is one reason why some mathematicians can-

---

Poetry and Science was published in 1926 and reissued in New York by W. W. Norton & Co. in 1970 under the new title *Poetries and Sciences*.
[1] W. H. Auden (1907–1973), English, then American poet.
[2] For use of this term, see also Carnap (below, page 980).

not read it. They find the alleged statements to be *false*. It will be agreed that their approach to poetry and their expectations from it are mistaken. But what exactly is the other, the right, the poetic, approach and how does it differ from the mathematical?

The poetic approach evidently limits the framework of possible consequences into which the pseudo-statement is taken. For the scientific approach this framework is unlimited. Any and every consequence is relevant. If any of the consequences of a statement conflicts with acknowledged fact then so much the worse for the statement. Not so with the pseudo-statement when poetically approached. The problem is—just how does the limitation work? One tempting account is in terms of a supposed universe of discourse, a world of make-believe, of imagination, of recognized fictions common to the poet and his readers. A pseudo-statement which fits into this system of assumptions would be regarded as "poetically true"; one which does not, as "poetically false." This attempt to treat "poetic truth" on the model of general "coherence theories" is very natural for certain schools of logicians but is inadequate, on the wrong lines from the outset. To mention two objections, out of many; there is no means of discovering what the "universe of discourse" is on any occasion, and the kind of coherence which must hold within it, supposing it to be discoverable, is not an affair of logical relations. Attempt to define the system of propositions into which

O Rose, thou art sick![3]

must fit, and the logical relations which must hold between them if it is to be "poetically true"; the absurdity of the theory becomes evident.

We must look further. In the poetic approach the relevant consequences are not logical or to be arrived at by a partial relaxation of logic. Except occasionally and by accident logic does not enter at all. The relevant consequences are those which arise through our emotional organization. The acceptance which a pseudo-statement receives is entirely governed by its effects upon our feelings and attitudes. Logic only comes in, if at all, in subordination, as a servant to our emotional response. It is an unruly servant, however, as poets and readers are constantly discovering. A pseudo-statement is "true" if it suits and serves some attitude or links together attitudes which on other ground are desirable. This kind of "truth" is so opposed to scientific "truth" that it is a pity to use so similar a word, but at present it is difficult to avoid the malpractice.[4]

This brief analysis may be sufficient to indicate the fundamental disparity and opposition between pseudo-statements as they occur in poetry and statements as they occur in science. A pseudo-statement is a form of words which is justified entirely by its effect in releasing or organizing our impulses and attitudes (due regard being had for the better or worse organizations of these *inter se*); a statement, on the other hand, is justified by its truth, *i.e.,* its correspondence, in a highly technical sense, with the fact to which it points.

Statements true and false alike do, of course, constantly touch off attitudes and action. Our daily practical existence is largely guided by them. On the whole true statements are of more service to us than false ones. None the less we do not and, at present, cannot order our emotions and attitudes by true statements alone. Nor is there any probability that we ever shall contrive to do so. This is one of the great new dangers to which civilization is exposed. Countless pseudo-statements—about God, about the universe, about human nature, the relations of mind to mind, about the soul, its rank and destiny—pseudo-statements which are pivotal points in the organization of the mind, vital to its well-being, have suddenly become, for sincere, honest and informed minds, impossible to believe as for centuries they have been believed.[5] The accustomed incidences of the modes of believing are changed irrecoverably; and the knowledge which has displaced them is not of a kind upon which an equally fine organization of the mind can be based.

This is the contemporary situation. The remedy, since there is no prospect of our gaining adequate knowledge, and since indeed it is fairly clear that scientific knowledge cannot meet this need, is to cut our pseudo-statements free

---

[3]"The Sick Rose" by William Blake (1757–1827), English poet and artist.

[4][Richards] A pseudo-statement, as I use the term, is not necessarily false in any sense. It is merely a form of words whose scientific truth or falsity is irrelevant to the purpose in hand.

"Logic" in this paragraph is, of course, being used in a limited and conventional, or popular, sense.

[5][Richards] For the mind I am considering here the question "Do I believe *x?*" is no longer the same. Not only the "What" that is to be believed but the "How" of the believing has changed—through the segregation of science and its clarification of the techniques of proof. This is the danger; and the remedy suggested is a further differentiation of the "Hows." To these differences correspond differences in the senses of "is so" and "being" where, as is commonly the case, "is so" and "being" assert believings. As we admit this, the world that "is" divides into worlds incommensurable in respect to so called "degrees of reality." Yet, and this is all-important, these worlds have an order, with regard to one another, which is the order of the mind; and interference between them imperils sanity.

from that kind of belief which is appropriate to verified statements. So released they will be changed, of course, but they can still be the main instruments by which we order our attitudes to one another and to the world. This is not a desperate remedy, for, as poetry conclusively shows, even the most important among our attitudes can be aroused and maintained without any believing of a factual or verifiable order entering in at all. We need no such beliefs, and indeed we must have none, if we are to read *King Lear*. Pseudo-statements to which we attach no belief and statements proper, such as science provides, cannot conflict. It is only when we introduce inappropriate kinds of believing into poetry that danger arises. To do so is from this point of view a profanation of poetry.

Yet an important branch of criticism which has attracted the best talents from prehistoric times until today consists of the endeavour to persuade men that the functions of science and poetry are identical, or that the one is a "higher form" of the other, or that they conflict and we must choose between them.

The root of this persistent endeavour has still to be mentioned; it is the same as that from which the Magical View of the world arose. If we give to a pseudo-statement the kind of unqualified acceptance which belongs by right only to certified scientific statements—and those judgments of the routine of perception and action from which science derives—if we can contrive to do this, the impulses and attitudes with which we respond to it gain a notable stability and vigour. Briefly, if we can contrive to believe poetry, then the world *seems,* while we do so, to be transfigured. It used to be comparatively easy to do this, and the habit has become well established. With the extension of science and the neutralization of nature it has become difficult as well as dangerous. Yet it is still alluring; it has many analogies with drug-taking. Hence the endeavours of the critics referred to. Various subterfuges have been devised along the lines of regarding Poetic Truth as figurative, symbolic; or as more immediate, as a truth of intuition transcending common knowledge; or as a higher form of the same truth that science yields. Such attempts to use poetry as a denial or as a corrective of science are very common. One point can be made against them all: they are never worked out in detail. There is no equivalent of Mill's *Logic*[6] expounding any of them. The language in which they are framed is usually a blend of obsolete psychology and emotive exclamations.

The long-established and much-encouraged habit of giving to emotive utterances—whether pseudo-statements simple, or looser and larger wholes taken as saying something figuratively–the kind of assent which we give to unescapable facts, has for most people debilitated a wide range of their responses. A few scientists, caught young and brought up in the laboratory, are free from it; but then, as a rule, they pay no *serious* attention to poetry. For most men the recognition of the neutrality of nature brings about—through this habit—a divorce from poetry. They are so used to having their responses propped up by beliefs, however vague, that when these shadowy supports are removed they are no longer able to respond. Their attitudes to so many things have been forced in the past, over-encouraged. And when the world-picture ceases to assist there is a collapse. Over whole tracts of natural emotional response we are today like a bed of dahlias whose sticks have been removed. And this effect of the neutralization of nature is perhaps only in its beginnings. However, human nature has a prodigious resilience. Love poetry seems able to out-play psychoanalysis.

A sense of desolation, of uncertainty, of futility, of the groundlessness of aspirations, of the vanity of endeavour, and a thirst for a life-giving water which seems suddenly to have failed, are the signs in consciousness of this necessary reorganization of our lives.[7] Our attitudes and impulses are being compelled to become self-supporting; they are being driven back upon their biological justification, made once again sufficient to themselves. And the only impulses which seem strong enough to continue unflagging are commonly so crude that, to more finely developed individuals, they hardly seem worth having. Such people cannot live by warmth, food, fighting, drink and sex alone. Those who are least affected by the change are those who are emotionally least removed from the animals. As we shall see at the close of this essay, even a con-

---

[6]John Stuart Mill (1806–1873), English philosopher and economist.

---

[7][Richards] My debt to *The Waste Land* here will be evident. The original footnote seems to have puzzled Mr. Eliot and some other readers. Well it might! In saying, though, that he "had effected a complete severance between his poetry and all beliefs" I was referring not to the poet's own history, but to the technical detachment of the poetry. And the way in which he seemed to me to have "realized what might otherwise have remained a speculative possibility" was by finding a new order through the contemplation and exhibition of disorder.

"Yes! Very funny this terrible thing is. A man that is born falls into a dream like a man who falls into the sea. If he tries to climb out into the air as inexperienced people endeavour to do, he drowns—*nicht wahr?* . . . No! I tell you! The way is to the destructive element submit yourself, and with the exertions of your hands and feet in the water make the deep, deep sea keep you up. So if you ask me how to be? In the destructive element immerse . . . that was the way." *Lord Jim,* p. 216. Mr. Eliot's later verse has sometimes shown less "dread of the unknown depths." That, at least, seems in part to explain to me why *Ash Wednesday* is better poetry than even the best sections of *The Waste Land*.

siderable poet may attempt to find relief by a reversion to primitive mentality.

It is important to diagnose the disease correctly and to put the blame in the right quarter. Usually it is some alleged "materialism" of science which is denounced. This mistake is due partly to clumsy thinking, but chiefly to relics of the Magical View. For even if the Universe were "spiritual" all through (whatever that assertion might mean; all such assertions are probably nonsense), that would not make it any more accordant to human attitudes. It is not what the universe is made of but how it works, the law it follows, which makes verifiable knowledge of it incapable of spurring on our emotional responses, and further, the nature of knowledge itself makes it inadequate. The contact with things which we therein establish is too sketchy and indirect to help us. We are beginning to know too much about the bond which unites the mind to its object in knowledge[8] for that old dream of a perfect knowledge which would guarantee perfect life to retain its sanction. What was thought to be pure knowledge we see now to have been shot through with hope and desire, with fear and wonder; and these intrusive elements indeed gave it all its power to support our lives. In knowledge, in the "How?" of events, we can find hints by which to take advantage of circumstances in our favour and avoid mischances. But we cannot get from it a *raison d'être* or a justification of more than a relatively lowly kind of life.

The justification, or the reverse, of any attitude lies, not in the object, but in itself, in its serviceableness to the whole personality. Upon its place in the whole system of attitudes, which is the personality, all its worth depends. This is as true for the subtle, finely compounded attitudes of the civilized individual as for the simpler attitudes of the child.

In brief, the imaginative life is its own justification; and this fact must be faced, although sometimes—by a lover, for example—it may be very difficult to accept. When it is faced, it is apparent that all the attitudes to other human beings and to the world in all its aspects, which have been serviceable to humanity, remain as they were, as valuable as ever. Hesitation felt in admitting this is a measure of the strength of the evil habit I have been describing. But many of these attitudes, valuable as ever, are, now that they are being set free, more difficult to maintain, because we still hunger after a basis in belief.

Practical Criticism

from

Chapter I

The Four Kinds of Meaning

The all-important fact for the study of literature—or any other mode of communication—is that there are several kinds of meaning. Whether we know and intend it or not, we are all jugglers when we converse, keeping the billiard balls in the air while we balance the cue on our nose. Whether we are active, as in speech or writing, or passive,[1] as readers or listeners, the total meaning we are engaged with is, almost always, a blend, a combination of several contributory meanings of different types. Language—and preeminently language as it is used in poetry—has not one but several tasks to perform simultaneously, and we shall misconceive most of the difficulties of criticism unless we understand this point and take note of the differences between these functions. For our purposes here a division into four types of function, four kinds of meaning, will suffice.

It is plain that most human utterances and nearly all articulate speech can be profitably regarded from four points of view. Four aspects can be easily distinguished. Let us call them *sense, feeling, tone,* and *intention.*

I. Sense

We speak *to say something,* and when we listen we expect something to be said. We use words to direct our hearers' attention upon some state of affairs, to present to them some items for consideration and to excite in them some thoughts about these items.

II. Feeling[2]

But we also, as a rule, have some feelings *about these items,* about the state of affairs we are referring to. We have an attitude towards it, some special direction, bias, or accentuation of interest towards it, some personal flavor or coloring

---

[8][Richards] Verifiable scientific knowledge, of course. Shift the sense of "knowledge" to include hope and desire and fear as well as reference, and what I am saying would no longer be true. But then the relevant sense of "true" would have changed too. Its sanction would no longer be verifiability.

Practical Criticism was first published in 1929. The text is from *Practical Criticism* (New York: Harcourt, Brace, 1929).

[1][Richards] Relatively, or technically, "passive" only; a fact that our protocols [see footnote 4] will help us not to forget. The reception (or interpretation) of a meaning is an activity, which may go astray; in fact, there is always some degree of loss and distortion in transmission. For an account of "understanding," see Part IV.

[2][Richards] Under *feeling* I group for convenience the whole conative-affective aspect of life—emotions, emotional attitudes, the will, desire, pleasure-unpleasure, and the rest. *Feeling* is shorthand for any or all of this.

of feeling; and we use language to *express* these feelings, this nuance of interest. Equally, when we listen we pick it up, rightly or wrongly; it seems inextricably part of what we receive; and this whether the speaker be conscious himself of his feelings towards what he is talking about or not. I am, of course, here describing the normal situation; my reader will be able without difficulty to think of exceptional cases (mathematics for example) where no feeling enters.

III. Tone

Furthermore, the speaker has ordinarily *an attitude to his listener.* He chooses or arranges his words differently as his audience varies, in automatic or deliberate *recognition of his relation to them.* The tone of his utterance reflects his awareness of this relation, his sense of how he stands towards those he is addressing. Again the exceptional case of dissimulation, or instances in which the speaker unwittingly reveals an attitude he is not consciously desirous of expressing, will come to mind.

IV. Intention[3]

Finally, apart from what he says (sense), his attitude to what he is talking about (feeling), and his attitude to his listener (tone), there is the speaker's intention, his aim, *conscious or unconscious,* the effect he is endeavoring to promote. Ordinarily he speaks for a purpose, and his purpose modifies his speech. The understanding of it is part of the whole business of apprehending his meaning. Unless we know what he is trying to do, we can hardly estimate the measure of his success. Yet the number of readers who omit such considerations might make a fainthearted writer despair. Sometimes, of course, he will purpose no more than to state his thoughts (I), or to express his feelings about what he is thinking of, e.g. Hurrah! Damn! (II), or to express his attitude to his listener (III). With this last case we pass into the realm of endearments and abuse.

Frequently his intention operates through and satisfies itself in a combination of the other functions. Yet it has effects not reducible to their effects. It may govern the stress laid upon points in an argument for example, shape the arrangement, and even call attention to itself in such phrases as *for contrast's sake* or *lest it be supposed.* It controls the plot in the largest sense of the word, and is at work whenever the author is "hiding his hand." And it has especial importance in dramatic and semidramatic literature. Thus the influence of his intention upon the language he uses is additional to, and separable from, the other three influences, and its effects can profitably be considered apart.

We shall find in the protocols[4] instances, in plenty, of failure on the part of one or other of these functions. Sometimes all four fail together; a reader garbles the sense, distorts the feeling, mistakes the tone and disregards the intention; and often a partial collapse of one function entails aberrations in the others. The possibilities of human misunderstanding make up indeed a formidable subject for study, but something more can be done to elucidate it than has yet been attempted. Whatever else we may do by the light of nature it would be folly to maintain that we should read by it. But before turning back to scrutinize our protocols some further explanation of these functions will be in place.

If we survey our uses of language as a whole, it is clear that, at times, now one now another of the functions may become predominant. It will make the possible situations clearer if we briefly review certain typical forms of composition. A man writing a scientific treatise, for example, will put the sense of what he has to say first, he will subordinate his feelings about his subject or about other views upon it and be careful not to let them interfere to distort his argument or to suggest bias. His tone will be settled for him by academic convention; he will, if he is wise, indicate respect for his readers and a moderate anxiety to be understood accurately and to win acceptance for his remarks. It will be well if his intention, as it shows itself in the work, be on the whole confined to the clearest and most adequate statement of what he has to say (function 1, sense). But, if the circumstances warrant it, further relevant aims—an intention to reorientate opinion, to direct attention to new aspects, or to encourage or discourage certain methods of work or ways of approach—are obviously fitting. Irrelevant aims—the acceptance of the work as a thesis for a Ph.D., for example—come in a different category.

Consider now a writer engaged upon popularizing some of the results and hypotheses of science. The principles governing his language are not nearly so simple, for the furtherance of his intention will properly and inevitably interfere with the other functions.

In the first place, precise and adequate statement of the sense may have to be sacrificed, to some degree, in the interests of general intelligibility. Simplifications and distortions

---

[3][Richards] This function plainly is not on all fours with the others. See Part IV, section 16 and Appendix A, where a further discussion of these four functions is attempted.

[4]Reports by Richards's students in response to poems given them for discussion. The students were not given the names of the authors, and the titles of the poems were withheld.

may be necessary if the reader is to "follow." Secondly, a much more lively exhibition of feelings on the part of the author towards his subject matter is usually appropriate and desirable, in order to awaken and encourage the reader's interest. Thirdly, more variety of tone will be called for; jokes and humorous illustrations, for example, are admissible, and perhaps a certain amount of cajolery. With this increased liberty, tact, the subjective counterpart of tone, will be urgently required. A human relation between the expert and his lay audience must be created, and the task, as many specialists have discovered, is not easy. These other functions will interfere still more with strict accuracy of statement; and if the subject has a "tendency," if political, ethical or theological implications are at all prominent, the intention of the work will have further opportunities to intervene.

This leads us to the obvious instance of political speeches. What rank and precedence shall we assign to the four language functions if we analyze public utterances made in the midst of a General Election? Function 4, the furtherance of intentions (of all grades of worthiness) is unmistakably predominant. Its instruments are function 2, the expression of feelings about causes, policies, leaders and opponents, and function 3, the establishment of favorable relations with the audience ("the great heart of the people"). Recognizing this, ought we to be pained or surprised that function 1, the presentation of facts (or of objects of thought to be regarded as facts are regarded), is equally subordinated?[5] But further consideration of this situation would lead us into a topic that must be examined later, that of *sincerity,* a word with several important meanings. (See Chapter 7.)

In conversation, perhaps, we get the clearest examples of these shifts of function, the normal verbal apparatus of one function being taken over by another. Intention, we have seen, may completely subjugate the others; so, on occasion, may feeling or tone express themselves through sense, translating themselves into explicit statements about feelings and attitudes towards things and people—statements sometimes belied by their very form and manner. Diplomatic formulae are often good examples, together with much of the social language (Malinowski's "phatic communion"),[6] the *thank you so very muches,* and *pleased to meet yous,* that help us to live amicably with one another. (But see Appendix A, note 1.)

Under this head, too, may be put the psychological analyses, the introspective expatiations that have recently flourished so much in fiction as well as in sophisticated conversation. Does it indicate a confusion or a tenuousness in our feelings that we should now find ourselves so ready to make statements about them, to translate them into disquisitions, instead of expressing them in more direct and natural ways? Or is this phenomenon simply another result of the increased study of psychology? It would be rash to decide as yet. Certainly some psychologists lay themselves open to a charge of emptiness, of having so dealt with themselves that they have little left within them to talk about. "Putting it into words," if the words are those of a psychological textbook, is a process which may well be damaging to the feelings. I shall be lucky if my reader does not murmur *de te fabula*[7] at this point.

But feeling (and sometimes tone) may take charge of and operate through sense in another fashion, one more constantly relevant in poetry. (If indeed the shift just dealt with above might not be better described as sense interfering with and dominating feeling and tone.)

When this happens, the statements which appear in the poetry are there for the sake of their effects upon feelings, not for their own sake. Hence to challenge their truth or to question whether they deserve serious attention *as statements claiming truth,* is to mistake their function. The point is that many, if not most, of the statements in poetry are there *as a means* to the manipulation[8] and expression of feelings and attitudes, not as contributions to any body of doctrine of any type whatever. With narrative poetry there is little danger of any mistake arising, but with "philosophical" or meditative poetry there is great danger of a confusion which may have two sets of consequences.

On the one hand there are very many people who, if they read any poetry at all, try to take all its statements seriously—and find them silly. "My soul is a ship in full sail," for example, seems to them a very profitless kind of contribution to psychology. This may seem an absurd mistake but, alas! It is nonetheless common. On the other hand there are those who succeed too well, who swallow "Beauty is truth, truth beauty. . . . ,"[9] as the quintessence of an aesthetic philosophy, not as the expression of a certain blend of feelings, and proceed into a complete stalemate of muddle-mindedness as a result of

---

[5][Richards] The ticklish point is, of course, the implication that the speaker believes in the "facts"—not only as powerful arguments but *as facts. Belief* here has to do with function 2, and, as such examples suggest, is also a word with several senses, at least as many as attach to the somewhat analogous word *love.* Some separation and ventilation of them, beyond that attempted in Chapter 7 below, is very desirable, and I hope to explore this subject in a future work.

[6]Bronislaw Malinownski (1884–1942), Polish, later American anthropologist. [Richards] See *The Meaning of Meaning* [by Richards and C. K. Ogden], Supplement I, section iv.

[7]"The fable is told concerning yourself."

[8][Richards] I am not assuming that the poet is conscious of any distinction between his means and his ends.

[9]From "Ode on a Grecian Urn" by John Keats (1795–1821), English poet.

their linguistic naivety. It is easy to see what those in the first group miss; the losses of the second group, though the accountancy is more complicated, are equally lamentable.

A temptation to discuss here some further intricacies of this shift of function must be resisted. An overflow into Appendix A, which may serve as a kind of technical workshop for those who agree with me that the matter is important enough to be examined *with pains,* will be the best solution. I am anxious to illustrate these distinctions from the protocols before tedium too heavily assails us. It will be enough here to note that this subjugation of statement to emotive purposes has innumerable modes. A poet may distort his statements which have logically nothing to do with the subject under treatment; he may, by metaphor and otherwise, present objects for thought which are logically quite irrelevant; he may perpetrate logical nonsense, be as trivial or as silly, logically, as it is possible to be; all in the interests of the other functions of his language—to express feeling or adjust tone or further his other intentions. If his success in these other aims justify him, no reader (of the kind at least to take his meaning as it should be taken) can validly say anything against him.

But these indirect devices for expressing feeling through logical irrelevance and nonsense, through statements not to be taken strictly, literally or seriously, though preeminently apparent in poetry, are not peculiar to it. A great part of what passes for criticism comes under this head. It is much harder to obtain statements about poetry, than expressions of feelings towards it and towards the author. Very many apparent statements turn out on examination to be only these disguised forms, indirect expressions, of feeling, tone and intention. Dr. Bradley's remark that *poetry is a spirit,* and Dr. Mackail's that it is *a continuous substance or energy whose progress is immortal* are eminent examples that I have made use of elsewhere, so curious that I need no apology for referring to them again.[10] Remembering them, we may be more ready to apply to the protocols every instrument of interpretation we possess. May we avoid if possible in our own reading of the protocols those errors of misunderstanding which we are about to watch being committed towards the poems.

---

[10]For a criticism of A. C. Bradley (1851–1935), English scholar and critic, see Chapter 10 of Richards's *Principles of Literary Criticism.* J. W. Mackail's *Lectures on Poetry* is referred to in Chapter 3.

Boris Eichenbaum

1886–1959

With Roman Jakobson, who later founded the Prague school of structuralist linguistics, Eichenbaum was a main figure of the Russian Formalist movement, which flourished until its forced demise under political pressure in the 1920s. The attack that destroyed the movement began in 1924 with Leon Trotsky's *Literature and Revolution* and was carried on more vehemently by lesser figures. Members of the movement were charged with lack of interest in the social causes and effects of literature and advocating a form of art for art's sake.

Eichenbaum's essay is an attempt to summarize the movement's achievements and to defend it against Marxist attacks. There is an element of conciliation in the essay that somewhat distorts the picture. The movement was never as communal and orderly in its development and aims as Eichenbaum would have his readers believe. Also, there is considerably more emphasis on scientific, positivistic procedures in his essay than was evident in the work of the Formalist critics themselves. The standard history of the movement, Victor Erlich's *Russian Formalism: History-Doctrine* (rev. ed. 1964), offers a more detached summary.

Eichenbaum's reader cannot help being struck by the similarities of the movement to the American New Criticism. Almost all of the general principles he enunciates are shared by that movement: the attack on irresponsible mixing of various disciplines and their problems, the distinction between "practical language" and language with "independent value," the insistence that form is not simply an "envelope" for content, the assertion that explanation of the genesis of a phenomenon does not clarify our view of the phenomenon as a literary fact, the idea of a literary work as a "self-determined use of material," and the sense of the expansive meaning of a literary work.

The Formalists began, according to Eichenbaum, by rejecting old assumptions about beauty as an external ideal, worked through the idea of the literary object as a unified technical accomplishment, and came to the idea of a truly *literary* history. In this last phase, they spoke much as T. S. Eliot did in *Tradition and the Individual Talent* (above, page 807). In their view, a work of art is defined by its relation to other works. Literary history points out these relationships and thus is not using literature as a document but actually giving to aesthetic theory and to literary meaning a historical dimension.

When the Formalist movement died, many of its principles were carried, mainly by Jakobson, into structuralist linguistics. Combined with the ideas of Ferdinand de Saussure's *Course in General Linguistics* (1915), they contributed to structuralism in a variety of fields, including anthropology and, again, literary theory.

Essays by Eichenbaum can be found in *Michigan Slavic Materials* II (1963), in *Russian Formalist Criticism: Four Essays,* edited and translated by L. T. Lemon and M. J. Reis 1965), and in C. Pike, ed., *The Futurists, the Formalists, and the Marxist Cri-*

tique (1979). Eichenbaum's *O. Henry: The Theory of the "Formal Method" and the Theory of the Short Story* was translated in 1968, and his *Lermontov* in 1981. See A. N. Vognesenski, "Problems of Method in the Study of Literature in Russia," *Slavonic Review* VI (1927), 168–77; Manfred Kridl, "Russian Formalism," *The American Bookman* I (1944), 19–30; W. E. Harkins, "Slavonic Formalist Theories in Literary Scholarship," *Word* VII (1951), 177–85; Mark Slonim, *Modern Russian Literature* (1953); Victor Erlich, *Russian Formalism: History-Doctrine* (rev. ed. 1964); Harold K. Schefski, *Boris M. Eichenbaum: The Evaluation of His Critical Method* (unpub. diss., 1976).

The Theory of the "Formal Method"

The worst, in my opinion, are those who describe science as if it were settled.[1]

A. de Candolle

The so-called formal method grew out of a struggle for a science of literature that would be both independent and factual; it is not the outgrowth of a particular methodology. The notion of a method has been so exaggerated that it now suggests too much. In principle the question for the Formalist[2] is not how to study literature, but what the subject matter of literary study actually is. We neither discuss methodology nor quarrel about it. We speak and may speak only about theoretical principles suggested to us not by this or that ready-made methodology, but by the examination of specific material in its specific context. The Formalists' works in literary theory and literary history show this clearly enough, but during the past ten years so many new questions and old misunderstandings have accumulated that I feel it advisable to try to summarize some of our work—not as a dogmatic system but as a historical summation. I wish to show how the work of the Formalists began, how it evolved, and what it evolved into.

The evolutionary character of the development of the formal method is important to an understanding of its history; our opponents and many of our followers overlook it. We are surrounded by eclectics and latecomers who would turn the formal method into some kind of inflexible formalistic system in order to provide themselves with a working vocabulary, a program, and a name. A program is a very handy thing for critics, but not at all characteristic of our method. Our scientific approach has had no such prefabricated program or doctrine, and has none. In our studies we value a theory only as a working hypothesis to help us discover and interpret facts; that is, we determine the validity of the facts and use them as the material of our research. We are not concerned with definitions, for which the latecomers thirst; nor do we build general theories, which so delight eclectics. We posit specific principles and adhere to them insofar as the material justifies them. If the material demands their refinements or change, we change or refine them. In this sense we are quite free from our own theories—as science must be free to the extent that theory and conviction are distinct. There is no ready-made science; science lives not by settling on truth, but by overcoming error.

This essay is not intended to argue our position. The initial period of scientific struggle and journalistic polemics is past. Such attacks as that in *The Press and the Revolution*[3] (with which I was honored) can be answered only by new scientific works. My chief purpose here is to show how the formal method, by gradually evolving and broadening its field of research, spread beyond the usual "methodological" limits and became a special science of literature, a specific ordering of facts. Within the limits of this science, the most diverse methods may develop, if only because we focus on the empirical study of the material. Such study was, essentially, the aim of the Formalists from the very beginning,

---

Eichenbaum's "The Theory of the 'Formal Method'" was first published in Ukranian in 1926. The text is from *Russian Formalist Criticism: Four Essays,* edited and translated by Lee T. Lemon and Marion J. Reis (Lincoln: University of Nebraska Press, 1965).

[1] Le pire, à mon avis, est celui qui représente la science comme fait. Alphonse de Candolle (1806–1893).

[2] [Eichenbaum] By *Formalist* I mean in this essay only that group of theoreticians who made up the Society for the Study of Poetic Language (the OPOYAZ) and who began to publish their studies in 1916. [Lemon and Reis] Actually Eichenbaum also includes as Formalists members of the Moscow Linguistic Circle.

---

[3] An essay by Anatoly Lunacharsky (1875–1933), Soviet Commissar for Education, which attacked Formalism on the ground of its decadence.

and precisely that was the significance of our quarrel with the old traditions. The name *formal method,* bestowed upon the movement and now firmly attached to it, may be tentatively understood as a historical term; it should not be taken as an accurate description of our work. Neither *Formalism* as an aesthetic theory nor *methodology* as a finished scientific system characterizes us; we are characterized only by the attempt to create an independent science of literature which studies specifically literary material. We ask only for recognition of the theoretical facts of literary art as such.

Representatives of the formal method were frequently reproached by various groups for their lack of clarity or for the inadequacy of their principles—for indifference to general questions of aesthetics, sociology, psychology, and so on. These reproofs, despite their varying merit, are alike in that they correctly grasp that the chief characteristic of the Formalists is indeed their deliberate isolation both from "aesthetics from above" and from all ready-made or self-styled general theories. This isolation (particularly from aesthetics) is more or less typical of all contemporary studies of art. Dismissing a whole group of general problems (problems of beauty, the aims of art, etc.), the contemporary study of art concentrates on the concrete problems of aesthetics [*Kunstwissenschaft*]. Without reference to socio-aesthetic premises, it raises questions about the idea of artistic form and its evolution. It thereby raises a series of more specific theoretical and historical questions. Such familiar slogans as Wölfflin's "history of art without names" [*Kunstgeschichte ohne Nahmen*][4] characterized experiments in the empirical analysis of style and technique (like Voll's[5] "experiment in the comparative study of paintings"). In Germany especially the study of the theory and history of the visual arts, which had had there an extremely rich history of tradition and experiment, occupied a central position in art studies and began to influence the general theory of art and its separate disciplines—in particular, the study of literature. In Russia, apparently for local historical reasons, literary studies occupied a place analogous to that of the visual arts in Germany.

The formal method has attracted general attention and become controversial not, of course, because of its distinctive methodology, but rather because of its characteristic attitude towards the understanding and the study of technique. The Formalists advocated principles which violated solidly entrenched traditional notions, notions which had appeared to be axiomatic not only in the study of literature, but in the study of art generally. Because they adhered to their princi-

ples so strictly, they narrowed the distance between particular problems of literary theory and general problems of aesthetics. The ideas and principles of the Formalists, for all their concreteness, were pointedly directed towards a general theory of aesthetics. Our creation of a radically unconventional poetics, therefore, implied more than a simple reassessment of particular problems; it had an impact on the study of art generally. It had its impact because of a series of historical developments, the most important of which were the crisis in philosophical aesthetics and the startling innovations in art (in Russia most abrupt and most clearly defined in poetry). Aesthetics seemed barren and art deliberately denuded—in an entirely primitive condition. Hence, Formalism and Futurism seemed bound together by history.

But the general historical significance of the appearance of Formalism comprises a special theme; I must speak of something else here because I intend to show how the principles and problems of the formal method evolved and how the Formalists came to their present position.

Before the appearance of the Formalists, academic research, quite ignorant of theoretical problems, made use of antiquated aesthetic, psychological, and historical axioms and had so lost sight of its proper subject that its very existence as a science had become illusory. There was almost no struggle between the Formalists and the Academicians, not because the Formalists had broken in the door (there were no doors), but because we found an open passageway instead of a fortress. The theoretical heritage which Potebnya and Veselovsky[6] left to their disciples seemed to lie like dead capital—a treasure which they were afraid to touch, the brilliance of which they had allowed to fade. In fact, authority and influence had gradually passed from academic scholarship to the "scholarship" of the journals, to the work of the Symbolist critics and theoreticians. Actually, between 1907 and 1912 the books and essays of Vyacheslav Ivanov, Bryusov Merezhkovsky, Chukovsky,[7] and others, were much more influential than the scholarly studies and dissertations of the university professors. This journalistic scholarship, with all its subjectivity and tendentiousness, was supported by the theoretical principles and slogans of the new artistic movements and their propagandists. Such books as Bely's *Simvolizm* (1910)[8] naturally meant much more to the younger generation than the monographs on the history of literature which sprang up from no set of principles and

---

[4][Lemon and Reis] See Heinrich Wölfflin's *Kunstgeschichtliche Grundbegriffe* (Munich 1915). Wölfflin was one of the originators of the stylistic analysis of art.

[5]Karl Voll (1867–1917), German art historian.

[6]Alexander Potebnya (1836–1891), Alexander Veselovsky (1838–1906), Russian literary scholars.

[7]Vyaschlev Ivanov (1866–1949), Valery Bryusov (1873–1924), Dimitry Merzhkovski (1865–1941), Korney Chukovsky (1882–1969), Russian poets.

[8]Andrey Bely (1880–1934), Russian Symbolist poet.

which showed that the authors completely lacked both a scientific temperament and a scientific point of view.

The historical battle between the two generations [the Symbolists and the Formalists]—a battle which was fought over principles and was extraordinarily intense—was therefore resolved in the journals, and the battle line was drawn over Symbolist theory and Impressionistic criticism rather than over any work being done by the Academicians. We entered the fight against the Symbolists in order to wrest poetics from their hands—to free it from its ties with their subjective philosophical and aesthetic theories and to direct it toward the scientific investigation of facts. We were raised on their works, and we saw their errors with the greatest clarity. At this time, the struggle became even more urgent because the Futurists (Khlebnikov, Kruchenykh, and Mayakovsky),[9] who were on the rise, opposed the Symbolist poetics and supported the Formalists.

The original group of Formalists was united by the idea of liberating poetic diction from the fetters of the intellectualism and moralism which more and more obsessed the symbolists. The dissension among the Symbolist theoreticians (1910–11) and the appearance of the Acmeists[10] prepared the way for our decisive rebellion. We knew that all compromises would have to be avoided, that history demanded of us a really revolutionary attitude—a categorical thesis, merciless irony, and bold rejections of whatever could not be reconciled with our position. We had to oppose the subjective aesthetic principles espoused by the Symbolists with an objective consideration of the facts. Hence our Formalist movement was characterized by a new passion for scientific positivism—a rejection of philosophical assumptions of psychological and aesthetic interpretations, etc. Art, considered apart from philosophical aesthetics and ideological theories, dictated its own position on things. We had to turn to facts and, abandoning general systems and problems, to begin "in the middle," with the facts which art forced upon us. Art demanded that we approach it closely; science, that we deal with the specific.

The establishment of a specific and factual literary science was basic to the organization of the formal method. All of our efforts were directed toward disposing of the earlier position which, according to Alexander Veselovsky, made of literature an abandoned thing [a *res nullius*].[11] This is why

the position of the Formalists could not be reconciled with other approaches and was so unacceptable to the eclectics. In rejecting these other approaches, the Formalists actually rejected and still reject not the methods, but rather the irresponsible mixing of various disciplines and their problems. The basis of our position was and is that the object of literary science, as such, must be the study of those specifics which distinguish it from any other material. (The secondary, incidental features of such material, however, may reasonably and rightly be used in a subordinate way by other scientific disciplines.) Roman Jakobson formulated this view with perfect clarity:

> The object of the science of literature is not literature, but literariness—that is, that which makes a given work a work of literature. Until now literary historians have preferred to act like the policeman who, intending to arrest a certain person, would, at any opportunity, seize any and all persons who chanced into the apartment, as well as those who passed along the street. The literary historians used everything—anthropology, psychology, politics, philosophy. Instead of a science of literature, they created a conglomeration of homespun disciplines. They seemed to have forgotten that their essays strayed into related disciplines—the history of philosophy, the history of culture, of psychology, etc.—and that these could rightly use literary masterpieces, only as defective, secondary documents.[12]

To apply and strengthen this principle of specificity and to avoid speculative aesthetics, we had to compare literary facts with other kinds of facts, extracting from a limitless number of important orders of fact that order which would pertain to literature and would distinguish it from the others by its function. This was the method Leo Jakubinsky followed in his essays in the first *Opoyaz* collection, in which he worked out the contrast between poetic and practical language that served as the basic principle of the Formalists' work on key problems of poetics.[13] As a result, the Formalists did not look, as literary students usually had, to-

[9]Velemir Khlebnikov (1885–1922), Aleksey Kruchenykh (1886–1968), Vladimir Mayakovsky (1893–1930), Russian Futurist poets.

[10][Lemon and Reis] The Acmeists, like the Futurists, rebelled against the principles and practices of the Symbolists. But unlike the Futurists, they attempted a highly controlled, polished style of poetry. The best-known Acmeists were Anna Akhmatova [1888–1966] and Osip Mandelstam [1892–1942?]. The movement did not survive World War II.

[11]Literally a nonexistent thing.

[12][Eichenbaum] Roman Jakobson [1896–1982], *Noveshaya russkaya poeziya* [*Modern Russian Poetry*] (Prague, 1921), p. 11. [Lemon and Reis] Roman Jakobson, it should be stressed, is not arguing that literature is unrelated to history, psychology, and so forth. He is, rather, insisting that the study of literature, if it is to be a distinct discipline, must have its own particular subject.

[13]Leo Jakubinsky, early-twentieth-century Russian literary theorist of the OPOYAZ group.

wards history, culture, sociology, psychology, or aesthetics, etc., but toward linguistics, a science bordering on poetics and sharing material with it, but approaching it from a different perspective and with different problems. Linguistics, for its part, was also interested in the formal method in that what was discovered by comparing poetic and practical language could be studied as a purely linguistic problem, as part of the general phenomena of language. The relationship between linguistics and the formal method was somewhat analogous to that relation of mutual use and delimitation that exists, for example, between physics and chemistry. Against this background, the problems posed earlier by Potebnya and taken for granted by his followers were reviewed and reinterpreted.

Leo Jakubinsky's first essay, *On the Sounds of Poetic Language,* compared practical and poetic language and formulated the difference between them:

> The phenomena of language must be classified from the point of view of the speaker's particular purpose as he forms his own linguistic pattern. If the pattern is formed for the purely practical purpose of communication, then we are dealing with a system of *practical language* (the language of thought) in which the linguistic pattern (sounds, morphological features, etc.) have no independent value and are merely a *means* of communication. But other linguistic systems, systems in which the practical purpose is in the background (although perhaps not entirely hidden) are conceivable; they exist, and their linguistic patterns acquire *independent value.*

The establishment of this distinction was important both for the construction of a poetics and for understanding the Futurist's preference for nonsense language as revealing the furthest extension of the sheer independent value of words, the kind of value partially observed in the language of children, in the glossolalia of religious sects, and so on. The Futurist experiments in nonsense language were of prime significance as a demonstration against Symbolism which, in its theories, went no further than to use the idea of instrumentation to indicate the accompaniment of meaning by sound and so to de-emphasize the role of sound in poetic language. The problem of sound in verse was especially crucial because it was on this point that the Formalists and Futurists united to confront the theorists of Symbolism. Naturally, the Formalists gave battle at first on just that issue; the question of sound had to be disposed of first if we were to oppose the aesthetic and philosophical tendencies of the Symbolists with a system of pre-

cise observations and to reach the underlying scientific conclusions. This accounts for the content of the first volume of *Opoyaz,* a content devoted entirely to the problem of sound and nonsense language.

Victor Shklovsky, along with Jakubinsky, in *On Poetry and Nonsense Language,* cited a variety of examples which showed that "even words without meaning are necessary." He showed such meaninglessness to be both a widespread linguistic fact and a phenomenon characteristic of poetry. "The poet does not decide to use the meaningless word; usually 'nonsense' is disguised as some kind of frequently delusive, deceptive content. Poets are forced to acknowledge that they themselves do not understand the content of their own verses." Shklovsky's essay, moreover, transfers the question from the area of pure sound, from the acoustical level (which provided the basis for impressionistic interpretations of the relation between sound and the description of objects or the emotion represented) to the level of pronunciation and articulation. "In the enjoyment of a meaningless 'nonsense word,' the articulatory aspect of speech is undoubtedly important. Perhaps generally a great part of the delight of poetry consists in pronunciation, in the independent dance of the organs of speech." The question of meaningless language thus became a serious scientific concern, the solution of which would help to clarify many problems of poetic language in general. Shklovsky also formulated the general question:

> If we add to our demand of the word as such that it serve to clarify understanding, that it be generally meaningful, then of course "meaningless" language, as a relatively superficial language, falls by the wayside. But it does not fall alone; a consideration of the facts forces one to wonder whether words always have a meaning, not only in meaningless speech, but also in simple poetic speech—or whether this notion is only a fiction resulting from our inattention.

The natural conclusion of these observations and principles was that poetic language is not only a language of images, that sounds in verse are not at all merely elements of superficial euphony, and that they do not play a mere "accompaniment" to meaning, but rather that they have an independent significance. The purpose of this work was to force a revision of Potebnya's general theory, which had been built on the conviction that poetry is "thought in images." Potebnya's analysis of poetry, the analysis which the Symbolists had adopted, treated the sound of verse as expressive of something behind it. Sound was merely onomatopoetic, merely "aural description." The works of

Andrey Bely (who discovered the complete sound picture that champagne makes when poured from a bottle into a glass in two lines from Pushkin,[14] and who also discovered the "noisomeness of a hangover" in Blok's repetition of the consonantal cluster *rdt*) were quite typical.[15] Such attempts to explain alliteration, bordering on parody, required a rebuff and an attempt to produce concrete evidence showing that sounds in verse exist apart from any connection with imagery, that they have an independent oral function.

Leo Jakubinsky, in his essays, provided linguistic support for [our arguments in favor of] the independent value of sound in verse. Osip Brik's[16] essay on *Sound Repetitions* illustrated the same point with quotations from Pushkin and Lermontov[17] arranged to present a variety of models. Brik doubted the correctness of the common opinion that poetic language is a language of images:

> No matter how one looks at the interrelationship of image and sound, there is undoubtedly only one conclusion possible—the sounds, the harmonies, are not only euphonious accessories to meaning; they are also the result of an independent poetic purpose. The superficial devices of euphony do not completely account for the instrumentation of poetic speech. Such instrumentation represents on the whole an intricate product of the interaction of the general laws of harmony. Rhyme, alliteration, etc., are only obvious manifestations, particular cases, of the basic laws of euphony.

In opposing the work of Bely, Brik, in the same essay, made no comment at all on the meaning of this or that use of alliteration, but merely affirmed that repetition in verse is analogous to tautology in folklore—that is, that repetition itself plays something of an aesthetic role: "Obviously we have here diverse forms of one general principle, the principle of simple combination, by which either the sounds of the words or their meanings, or now one and now the other, serve as the material of the combination." Such an extension of one device to cover the various forms of poetic material is quite characteristic of the work of the Formalists during their initial period. After the presentation of Brik's essay the

question of sound in verse lost something of its urgency, and the Formalists turned to questions of poetics in general.

The Formalists began their work with the question of the sounds of verse—at that time the most controversial and most basic question. Behind this particular question of poetics stood more general theses which had to be formulated. The distinction between systems of poetic and practical language, which defined the work of the Formalists from the very beginning, was bound to result in the formulation of a whole group of basic questions. The idea of poetry as "thought by means of images" and the resulting formula, poetry = imagery, clearly did not coincide with our observations and contradicted our tentative general principles. Rhythm, sound, syntax—all of these seemed secondary from such a point of view; they seemed uncharacteristic of poetry and necessarily extraneous to it. The Symbolists accepted Potebnya's general theory because it justified the supremacy of the image-symbol; yet they could not rid themselves of the notorious theory of the "harmony of form and content" even though it clearly contradicted their bent for formal experimentation and discredited it by making it seem mere aestheticism. The Formalists, when they abandoned Potebnya's point of view, also freed themselves from the traditional correlation of form and content and from the traditional idea of form as an envelope, a vessel into which one pours a liquid (the content). The facts of art demonstrate that art's uniqueness consists not in the parts which enter into it but in their original *use*. Thus the notion of form was changed; the new notion of form required no companion idea, no correlative.

Even before the formation of the *Opoyaz* in 1914, at the time of the public performances of the Futurists, Shklovsky had published a monograph, *The Resurrection of the Word,* in which he took exception partly to the concepts set forth by Potebnya and partly to those of Veselovsky (the question of imagery was not then of major significance) to advance the principle of perceptible form as the specific sign of artistic awareness:

> We do not experience the commonplace, we do not see it; rather, we recognize it. We do not see the walls of our room; and it is very difficult for us to see errors in proofreading, especially if the material is written in a language we know well, because we cannot force ourselves to see, to read, and not to "recognize" the familiar word. If we have to define specifically "poetic" perception and artistic perception in general, then we suggest this definition: "Artistic" perception is that perception in which we experience form—perhaps not form alone, but certainly form.

---

[14] Alexander Sergeyevich Pushkin (1799–1837), Russian poet.
[15] Alexander Alexandrovich Blok (1880–1921), Russian Symbolist poet. [Eichenbaum] See the essay "A. Bely," *Skifi* [*Scythians*] (1917), and *Vetv* [*Branch*] (1917); see also my essay "O zvukakh v stikhe" ["On the Sound of Verse"], reprinted in *Skvoz literaturu* [*Through Literature*] (Leningrad, 1924).
[16] Osip Brik (1888–1945), Russian poet.
[17] Mikhail Yurevich Lermontov (1814–1841), Russian poet.

Perception here is clearly not to be understood as a simple psychological concept (the perception peculiar to this or that person), but, since art does not exist outside of perception, as an element in art itself. The notion of *form* here acquires new meaning; it is no longer an envelope, but a complete thing, something concrete, dynamic, self-contained, and without a correlative of any kind. Here we made a decisive break with the Symbolist principle that some sort of content is to shine through the form. And we broke with aestheticism—the preference for certain elements of form consciously isolated from "content."

But these general acknowledgments that there are differences between poetic and practical language and that the specific quality of art is shown in its particular use of the material were not adequate when we tried to deal with specific works. We had to find more specific formulations of the principle of perceptible form so that they could make possible the analysis of form itself—the analysis of form understood as content. We had to show that the perception of form results from special artistic techniques which force the reader to experience the form. Shklovsky's *Art as Technique,* presenting its own manifesto of the Formalist method, offered a perspective for the concrete analysis of form. Here was a really clear departure from Potebnya and Potebnyaism and, at the same time, from the theoretical principles of Symbolism. The essay began with objections to Potebnya's basic view of imagery and its relation to content. Shklovsky indicates, among other things, that images are almost always static:

> The more you understand an age, the more convinced you become that the images a given poet used and which you thought his own were taken almost unchanged from another poet. The works of poets are classified or grouped according to the new techniques they discover and share, and according to their arrangement and development of the resources of language; poets are much more concerned with arranging images than creating them. Images are given to poets; the ability to remember them is far more important than the ability to create them. Imagistic thought does not, in any case, include all aspects of art or even all aspects of verbal art. A change in imagery is not essential to the development of poetry.[18]

He further pointed out the difference between poetic and nonpoetic images. The poetic image is defined as one of the

devices of poetic language—as a device which, depending upon the problem, is as important as such other devices of poetic language as simple and negative parallelism, comparison, repetition, symmetry, hyperbole, etc., but no more important. Thus imagery becomes a part of a system of poetic devices and loses its theoretical dominance.

Shklovsky likewise repudiated the principle of artistic economy, a principle which had been strongly asserted in aesthetic theory, and opposed it with the device of defamiliarization and the notion of roughened form. That is, he saw art as increasing the difficulty and span of perception "because the process of perception is an aesthetic end in itself and must be prolonged"; he saw art as a means of destroying the automatism of perception; the purpose of the image is not to present the approximate meaning of its object to our understanding, but to create a special perception of the object—the creation of its vision, and not the recognition of its meaning. Hence the image is usually connected with the process of defamiliarization.

The break with Potebnya was formulated definitely in Shklovsky's essay *Potebnya.* He repeats once more that imagery—symbolization—does not constitute the specific difference between poetic and prosaic (practical) language:

> Poetic language is distinguished from practical language by the perception of its structure. The acoustical, articulatory, or semantic aspects of poetic language may be felt. Sometimes one feels the verbal structure, the arrangement of the words, rather than their texture. The poetic image is one of the ways, but only one of the ways, of creating a perceptible structure designed to be experienced within its very own fabric. . . . The creation of a scientific poetics must begin inductively with a hypothesis built on an accumulation of evidence. That hypothesis is that poetic and prosaic languages exist, that the laws which distinguish them exist, and finally, that these differences are to be analyzed.

These essays are to be read as the summation of the first phase of the Formalists' work. The main achievement of this period consisted in our establishment of a series of theoretical principles which provided working hypotheses for a further investigation of the data for the defeat of the current theories based on Potebnyaism. The chief strength of the Formalists, as these essays show, was neither the direction of their study of so-called forms nor the construction of a special method; their strength was founded securely on the fact that the specific features of the verbal arts had to be studied and that to do so it was first necessary to sort out the differing uses of

---

[18] Shklovsky (above, page 797).

poetic and practical language. Concerning form, the Formalists thought it important to change the meaning of this muddled term. It was important to destroy these traditional correlatives and so to enrich the idea of form with new significance. *The notion of technique, because has to do directly with the distinguishing features of poetic and practical speech, is much more significant in the long-range evolution of Formalism than is the notion of form.*

The preliminary stage of our theoretical work had passed. We had proposed general principles bearing directly upon factual material. We now had to move closer to the material and to make the problems themselves specific. At the center stood those questions of theoretical poetics that had previously been outlined only in general form. We had to move from questions about the sound of verse to a general theory of verse. The questions about the sound of verse, when originally posed, were meant only as illustrations of the difference between poetic and practical language. We had to move from questions about technique-in-general to the study of the specific devices of composition, to inquiry about plot, and so on. Our interest in opposing Veselovsky's general view and, specifically, in opposing his theory of plot, developed side by side with our interest in opposing Potebnya's.

At this time, the Formalists quite naturally used literary works only as material for supporting and testing their theoretical hypotheses; we had put aside questions of convention, literary evolution, etc. Now we felt it important to widen the scope of our study, to make a preliminary survey of the data, and to allow it to establish its own kind of laws. In this way we freed ourselves from the necessity of resorting to abstract premises and at the same time mastered the materials without losing ourselves in details.

Shklovsky, with his theory of plot and fiction, was especially important during this period. He demonstrated the presence of special devices of "plot construction" and their relation to general stylistic devices in such diverse materials as the *skaz,* Oriental tales, Cervantes' *Don Quixote,* Tolstoy's works, Sterne's *Tristram Shandy,* and so on.[19] I do not wish to go into details—those should be treated in specialized works and not in a general essay such as this on the Formalist method—but I do wish to cover those ideas in Shklovsky's treatment of plot which have a theoretical significance beyond any relationship they might have to particular problems of plots as such. Traces of those ideas can be found in the most advanced pieces of Formalist criticism.

The first of Shklovsky's works on plot, *The Relation of Devices of Plot Construction to General Devices of Style,* raised a whole series of such ideas. In the first place, the

proof that special devices of plot arrangement exist, a proof supported by the citation of great number of devices, changed the traditional notion of plot as a combination of a group of motifs and made plot a compositional rather than a thematic concept. Thus the very concept of plot was changed; *plot* was no longer synonymous with *story.*[20] Plot construction became the natural subject of Formalist study, since plot constitutes the specific peculiarity of narrative *art.* The idea of form had been enriched, and as it lost its former abstractness, it also lost its controversial meaning. Our idea of form had begun to coincide with our idea of literature as such, with the idea of the literary fact.

Furthermore, the analogies which we established between the devices of plot construction and the devices of style had theoretical significance, for the step-by-step structure usually found in the epic was found to be analogous to sound repetition, tautology, tautological parallelism, and so on. All illustrated a general principle of verbal art based on parceling out and impeding the action.

For instance, Roland's three blows on the stone in the *Song of Roland*[21] and the similar triple repetition common in tales may be compared, as a single type of phenomenon, with Gogol's use of synonyms and with such linguistic structures as *hoity-toity, a diller, a dollar,*[22] etc. "These variations of step-by-step construction usually do not all occur together, and attempts have been made to give each case a special explanation." Shklovsky shows how we attempt to demonstrate that the same device may reappear in diverse materials. Here we clashed with Veselovsky, who in such cases usually avoided theory and resorted to historical-genetic hypotheses. For instance, he explained epic repetition as a mechanism for the original performance (as embryonic song). But an explanation of the genetics of such a phenomenon, even if true, does not clarify the phenomenon as a fact of literature. Veselovsky and other members of the ethnographic school used to explain the peculiar motifs and plots of the *skaz* by relating literature and custom; Shklovsky did not object to making the relationship but challenged it only as an explanation of the peculiarities of the *skaz*—he challenged it as an explanation of a specifically literary fact. The study of literary genetics can clarify only the origin of a device, nothing more; poetics must explain its literary function. The genetic point of view fails to consider the device as a self-determined use of material; it

---

[19] *Skaz:* use of provincialisms, dialects, and grotesqueries.

[20] Aristotle (above, page 55), where plot is the artistic arrangement of the incidents rather than their chronological arrangement.

[21] French epic poem, eleventh or twelfth century.

[22] [Lemon and Reis] Eichenbaum gives two nonsense phrases here, *kudy-mudy* and *plyushkimlkushki.* The point is, of course, that repetition of sound alone may keep alive certain otherwise meaningless expressions.

does not consider how conventional materials are selected by an author, how conventional devices are transformed, or how they are made to play a structural role. The genetic point of view does not explain how a convention may disappear and its literary function remain. The literary function remains not as a simple [customary or social] experience but as a literary device retaining a significance over and beyond its connection with the convention. Characteristically, Veselovsky had contradicted himself by considering the adventures of the Greek romance as purely stylistic devices.

The Formalists naturally opposed Veselovsky's ethnographism because it ignored the special characteristic of the literary device and because it replaced the theoretical and evolutionary point of view with a genetic point of view.

Veselovsky saw syncretism as a phenomenon of primitive poetry, a result of custom, and he later was censured for this in B. Kazansky's *The Concept of Historical Poetics.* Kazansky repudiated the ethnographic point of view by affirming the presence of syncretic tendencies in the very nature of each art, a presence especially obvious in some periods. The Formalists naturally could not agree with Veselovsky when he touched upon general questions of literary evolution. If the clash with the Potebnyaists clarified basic principles of poetics, the clash with Veselovsky's general view and with that of his followers clarified the Formalist's views on literary evolution and, thereby, on the structure of literary history.

Shklovsky began to deal with the subject of literary evolution in the essay I cited previously, *The Relation of Devices of Plot Construction to General Devices of Style.* He had encountered Veselovsky's formula, a formula broadly based on the ethnographic principle that "the purpose of new form is to express new content," and he decided to advance a completely different point of view:

> The work of art arises from a background of other works and through association with them. The form of a work of art is defined by its relation to other works of art, to forms existing prior to it. . . . Not only parody, but also any kind of art is created parallel to and opposed to some kind of form. *The purpose of the new form is not to express new content, but to change an old form which has lost its aesthetic quality.*

Shklovsky supported this thesis with B[roder] Christiansen's[23] demonstration of "differentiated perceptions" or "perceptions of difference." He sees that the dynamism characteristic of art is based on this and is manifested in repeated violations of established rules. At the close of his essay, he quotes F[erdinand] Brunetière's[24] statements that "of all the influences active in the history of literature, the chief is the influence of *work on work*," and that "one should not, without good cause, increase the number of influences upon literature, under the assumption that literature is the expression of society, nor should one confuse the history of literature with the history of morals and manners. These are entirely different things."

Shklovsky's essay marked the changeover from our study of theoretical poetics to our study of the history of literature. Our original assumptions about form had been complicated by our observation of new features of evolutionary dynamics and their continuous variability. Our moving into the area of the history of literature was no simple expansion of our study; it resulted from the evolution of our concept of form. We found that we could not see the literary work in isolation, that we had to see its form against a background of other works rather than by itself. Thus the Formalists definitely went beyond "Formalism," if by *Formalism* one means (as some poorly informed critics usually did) some fabricated system which permitted us to be classified, some system which zealously adapted itself to logic-chopping, or some system which joyously welcomed any dogma. Such scholastic Formalism was neither historical nor essentially connected with the work of the *Opoyaz.* We were not responsible for it; on the contrary, we were irreconcilably its enemies on principle.

Later I shall return to the historical-literary work of the Formalists, but now I wish to conclude the survey of those theoretical principles and problems contained in the early work of the *Opoyaz.* The Shklovsky essay I referred to above contains still another idea which figured prominently in the subsequent study of the novel—the idea of motivation.[25] The discovery of various techniques of plot construction (step-by-step structure, parallelism, framing, the weaving of motifs, etc.) clarified the difference between the elements used in the construction of a work and the elements comprising its material (its story, the choice of motifs, the characters, the themes, etc.) Shklovsky stressed this difference at that time because the basic problem was to show the identity of individual structural devices in the most diverse materials imaginable. The old scholarship worked exclusively with the material, taking it as the content and treating the remainder as an external form either totally without interest or of interest only to

---

[23] Broder Christiansen, German aesthetician, author of *Philosophie der Kunst* (1909).

[24] Ferdinand Brunetière (1849–1906), French critic.

[25] Not necessarily the character's motivation, but the author's or the work's.

the dilettante. Hence the naive and pathetic aesthetics of our older literary critics and historians, who found "neglect of form" in Tyutchev's poetry and simply "bad form" in Nekrasov and Dostoevsky.[26] The literary reputations of these authors were saved because their intensity of thought and mood excused their formlessness. Naturally, during the years of struggle and polemics against such a position, the Formalists directed all their forces to showing the significance of such compositional devices as motivation and ignored all other considerations. In speaking of the formal method and its evolution, we must constantly remember that many of the principles advanced by the Formalists in the years of tense struggle were significant not only as scientific principles, but also as slogans, as paradoxes sharpened for propaganda and controversy. To ignore this fact and to treat the work of the *Opoyaz* (between 1916 and 1921) in the same way as one would treat the academic scholarship is to ignore history.

The concept of motivation permitted the Formalists to approach literary works (in particular, novels and short stories) more closely and to observe the details of their structure, which Shklovsky did in two later works, *Plot Development* and *Sterne's* Tristram Shandy *and the Theory of the Novel*. In these works, he studied the relationship between technique and motivation in Cervantes' *Don Quixote* and Sterne's *Tristram Shandy* as material for the study of the structure of the short story and the novel apart from literary history, and he studied *Don Quixote* as an instance of the transition from collections of tales (like the *Decameron*[27]) to the novel with a single hero whose travels justify or motivate its episodic structure. *Don Quixote* was chosen because the devices it contains and their motivation are not fully integrated into the entire context of the novel. Material is often simply inserted, not welded in; devices of plot construction and methods of using material to further the plot structure stand out sharply, whereas later structures tend "more and more to integrate the material tightly into the very body of the novel." While analyzing "how *Don Quixote* was made," Shklovsky also showed the instability of the hero and concluded that his type appeared "as the result of the business of constructing the novel." Thus the dominance of structure, of plot over material, was emphasized.

Neither a work fully motivated nor an art which deliberately does away with motivation and exposes the structure provides the most suitable material for the illumination of such theoretical problems. But the very existence of a work

such as *Don Quixote,* with a deliberately exposed structure, confirms the relevance of these problems, confirms the fact that the problems need to be stated as problems, and confirms the fact that they are *significant* literary problems. Moreover, we were able to explain works of literature entirely in the light of these theoretical problems and principles, as Shklovsky did with *Tristram Shandy*. Shklovsky not only used the book to illustrate our theoretical position, he gave it new significance and once more attracted attention to it. Studied against the background of an interest in the *structure* of the novel, Sterne became a contemporary; people spoke about him, people who previously had found in his novel only boring chatter or eccentricities, or who had prejudged it from the point of view of its notorious sentimentalism, a characteristic for which Sterne is as little to blame as Gogol[28] for realism.

Shklovsky pointed out Sterne's deliberate laying bare of his methods of constructing *Tristram Shandy* and asserted that Sterne had exaggerated the structure of the novel. He had shown his awareness of form by his manner of violating it and by his manner of assembling the novel's contents. In his conclusion to the essay, Shklovsky formulated the difference between plot and story.

> The idea of plot is too often confused with the description of events—with what I propose provisionally to call the *story*. The story is, in fact, only material for plot formulation. The plot of *Eugeny Onegin* is, therefore, not the romance of the hero with Tatyana, but the fashioning of the subject of this story as produced by the introduction of interrupting digressions. . . .
>
> The forms of art are explainable by the laws of art; they are not justified by their realism. Slowing the action of a novel is not accomplished by introducing rivals, for example, but by simply *transposing* parts. In so doing the artist makes us aware of the aesthetic laws which underlie both the transposition and the slowing down of the action.

My essay *How Gogol's* Greatcoat *Was Made* also considers the structure of the novel, comparing the problem of plot with the problem of the *skaz*—the problem of structure based upon the narrator's manner of telling what had happened. I tried to show that Gogol's text "was made up of living speech patterns and vocalized emotions," that words and sentences are selected and joined by Gogol as they are in the

[26]Feodor Ivanovich Tyutchev (1803–1873), Nikolai Alexeyevich Nekrasov (1821–1878), Russian poets; Feodor Mikhailovich Dostoyevsky (1821–1881), Russian novelist.
[27]Laurence Sterne (1713–1768), Miguel de Cervantes Saavedra (1547–1616); *The Decameron* by Giovanni Boccaccio (above, page 157).
[28]Nikolai Vaselyevich Gogol (1809–1852), Russian writer.

oral *skaz,* in which articulation, mimicry, sound gestures, and so on, play a special role. From this point of view I showed how the structure of *The Greatcoat* imparts a grotesque tone to the tale by replacing the usual humor of the *skaz* (with its anecdotes, puns, etc.) with sentimental-melodramatic declamation, I discussed, in this connection, the end of *The Greatcoat* as the apotheosis of the grotesque—not unlike the mute scene in *The Inspector General.*[29] The traditional line of argument about Gogol's romanticism and realism proved unnecessary and unilluminating.

Thus we began to make some progress with the problem of the study of prose. The line between the idea of plot as structure and the idea of the story as material was drawn; this explanation of the typical techniques of plot construction opened the door for work on the history and theory of the novel; and furthermore, the *skaz* was treated as the structural basis of the plotless short story. These works have influenced a whole series of recent studies by persons not directly connected with the *Opoyaz.*

As our theoretical work broadened and deepened it naturally became specialized—the more so because persons who were only beginning their work or who had been working independently joined the *Opoyaz* group. Some of them specialized in the problems of poetry, others in the problems of prose. The Formalists insisted upon keeping clear the demarcation between poetry and prose in order to counterbalance the Symbolists, who were then attempting to erase the boundary line both in theory and in practice by painstakingly attempting to discover meter in prose.[30]

The earlier sections of this essay show the intensity of our work on prose. We were pioneers in the area. Several Western works resembled ours (in particular, such observations on story material as Wilhelm Dibelius' *'Englische Romankunst,* 1910), but they had little relevance to our theoretical problems and principles. In our work on prose we felt almost free from tradition, but in dealing with verse the situation was different. The great number of works by Western and Russian literary theorists, the numerous practical and theoretical experiments of the Symbolists, and the special literature of the controversies over the concepts of rhythm and meter (produced between 1910 and 1917) complicated our study of poetry. The Futurists, in that same period, were creating new verse forms, and this complicated things still more. Given such conditions, it was difficult for us to pose the right problems. Many persons, instead of returning to basic questions, were concerned with special problems of

metrics or with trying to put the accumulation of systems and opinions in good order. Meanwhile, we had no general theory of poetry: no theoretical elucidations of verse rhythm, of the connection of rhythm and syntax, of the sounds of verse (the Formalists had indicated only a few linguistic premises), of poetic diction and semantics, and so on. In other words, the nature of verse as such remained essentially obscure. We had to draw away from particular problems of metrics and to approach verse from some more disciplined perspective. We had, first of all, to pose the problem of rhythm so that it did not rest on metrics and would include a more substantial part of poetic speech.

Here, as in the previous section, I shall dwell upon the problem of verse only insofar as its exploration led to a new theoretical view of verbal art or a new view of the nature of poetic speech. Our position was stated first in Osip Brik's *On Rhythmic-Syntactic Figures,* an unpublished lecture delivered before the *Opoyaz* group and, apparently, not even written out.[31] Brik demonstrated that verse contained stable syntactical figures indissolubly connected with rhythm. Thus rhythm was no longer thought of as an abstraction; it was made relevant to the very linguistic fabric of verse—the phrase. Metrics became a kind of background, significant, like the alphabet, for the reading and writing of verse. Brik's step was as important for the study of verse as the discovery of the relation of plot to structure was for the study of prose. The discovery that rhythmic patterns are related to the grammatical patterns of sentences destroyed the notion that rhythm is a superficial appendage, something floating on the surface of speech. Our theory of verse was founded on the analysis of rhythm as the structural basis of verse, a basis which of itself determined all of its parts—both acoustical and unacoustical. A superior theory of verse, which would make metrics but a kindergarten preparation, was in sight. The Symbolists and the group led by Bely, despite their attempts, could not travel our road because they still saw the central problem as metrics isolation.

But Brik's work merely hinted at the possibility of a new way; like his first essay, *Sound Repetitions,* it was limited to showing examples and arranging them into groups. From Brik's lecture one could move either into new problems or into the simple classification and cataloging, or systematizing, of the material. The lecture was not necessarily an expression of the formal method. V[ictor] Zhirmunsky[32] continued the work of classification in *The Composition of Lyric Verse.* Zhirmunsky, who did not share the theoretical principles of the *Opoyaz,* was interested in the formal

---

[29] By Gogol. [Lemon and Reis] The final scene, in which not a word is spoken for a minute and a half as the curtain slowly falls.
[30] [Lemon and Reis] See especially Andrey Bely's *Simvolizm* (Moscow, 1910).

[31] [Lemon and Reis] 1920. Brik's lecture was published in 1927 in *New Left.*
[32] Viktor Zhirmunsky (1889–1971), Russian literary theorist.

method as only one of the possible scientific approaches to the division of materials into various groups and headings. Given his understanding of the formal method, he could do nothing else; he accepted any superficial feature as a basis for the grouping of materials. Hence the unvarying cataloging and the pedantic tone of all of Zhirmunsky's theoretical work. Such works were not a major influence in the general evolution of the formal method; in themselves they merely emphasized the tendency (evidently historically inevitable) to give the formal method an academic quality. It is not surprising, therefore, that Zhirmunsky later completely withdrew from the *Opoyaz* over a difference of opinion about the principles he stated repeatedly in his last works (especially in his introduction to the translation of O[skar] Walzel's *The Problem of Form in Prose* [1923]).

My book, *Verse Melody*, which was prepared as a study of the phonetics of verse and so was related to a whole group of Western works (by Sievers, Saran, etc.), was relevant to Brik's work on rhythmic-syntactic figures. I maintained that stylistic differences were usually chiefly lexical:

With that we drop the idea of versification as such, and take up poetic language in general. . . . We have to find something related to the *poetic phrase* that does not also lead us away from the *poetry* itself, something bordering on both phonetics and semantics. This "something" is syntax.

I did not examine the rhythmic-syntactic phenomena in isolation, but as part of an examination of the structural significance of metrical and vocal intonation. I felt it especially important both to assert the idea of a *dominant,* upon which a given poetic style is organized, and to isolate the idea of melody as a system of intonations from the idea of the general musicality of verse. On this basis, I proposed to distinguish three fundamental styles of lyric poetry: declamatory (oratorical), melodic, and conversational. My entire book is devoted to the peculiarities of the melodic style—to peculiarities in the material of the lyrics of Zhukovsky, Tyutchev, Lermontov, and Fet.[33] Avoiding ready-made schematizations, I ended the book with the conviction that "in scientific work, I consider the ability to see facts far more important than the construction of a system. Theories are necessary to clarify facts; in reality, theories are made of facts. Theories perish and change, but the facts they help discover and support remain."

The tradition of specialized metrical studies still continued among the Symbolist theoreticians (Bely, Bryusov, Bobrov, Chukovsky,[34] and others), but it gradually turned into precise statistical enumeration and lost what had been its dominant characteristic. Here the metrical studies of Boris Tomashevsky,[35] concluded in his text *Russian Versification,* played the most significant role. Thus, as the study of metrics became secondary, a subsidiary discipline with a very limited range of problems, the general theory of verse entered its first stage.

Tomashevsky's *Pushkin's Iambic Pentameter* outlined the entire previous course of developments within the formal method, including its attempt to broaden and enrich the notion of poetic rhythm and to relate it to the structure of poetic language. The essay also attempted to go beyond the idea of meter in language. Hence the basic charge against Bely and his school: "The problem of rhythm is not conformity to imaginary meters; it is rather the distribution of expiratory energy within a single wave—the line itself." In *The Problems of Poetic Rhythm* Tomashevsky expressed this with perfect clarity of principle. Here the earlier conflict between meter and rhythm is resolved by applying the idea of rhythm in verse to all of the elements of speech that play a part in the structure of verse. The rhythms of phrasal intonation and euphony (alliterations, etc.) are placed side by side with the rhythm of word accent. Thus we came to see the line as *a special form of speech* which functions as a single unit in the creation of poetry. We no longer saw the line as something which could create a rhythmic variation by resisting or adjusting to the metrical form (a view which Zhirmunsky continued to defend in his new work, *Introduction to Metrics*). Tomashevsky wrote that:

Poetic speech is *organized* in terms of its sounds. Taken singly, any phonetic element is subject to rules and regulations, but sound is a *complex* phenomenon. Thus classical metrics singles out accent and normalizes it by its rules. . . . But it takes little effort to shake the authority of traditional forms, because the notion persisted that the nature of verse is not fully explained by a single distinguishing feature, that poetry exists in "secondary" features, that a recognizable rhythm exists alongside meter, that poetry can be created by imposing a pattern on only these secondary features, and *that speech without meter may sound like poetry.*

[33] Vasily Zhukovsky (1783–1952), Afanasii Afenesevich Fet (1820–1892), Russian poets.

[34] Valery Yakovlevich Bryusov (1873–1924), Russian poet; Sergei Bobrov (1889–1971), Russian poet and critic.
[35] Boris Tomashevsky (1890–1957), Russian Formalist theorist.

The important idea of a rhythmic impulse (which had figured earlier in Brik's work) with a general rhythmic function is maintained here:

> Rhythmic devices may participate in various degrees in the creation of an artistic-rhythmic effect; this or that device may dominate various works— this or that means may be the *dominant.* The use of a given rhythmic device determines the character of the particular rhythm of the work. On this basis poetry may be classified as accented-metrical poetry (e.g., the description of the Battle of Poltava[36]), intoned-melodic poetry (the verses of Zhukovsky), or harmonic poetry (common during the recent years of Russian Symbolism).

Poetic form, so understood, is not contrasted with anything outside itself—with a content which has been laboriously set inside this form—but is understood as the genuine content of poetic speech. Thus the very idea of form, as it had been understood in earlier works, emerged with a new and more adequate meaning.

In his essay *On Czech Versification* Roman Jakobson pointed out new problems in the general theory of poetic rhythm. He opposed the [earlier] theory that "verse adapts itself completely to the spirit of the language," that is, that "form does not resist the material [it shapes]" with the theory that "poetic form is the organized coercion of language." He applied this refinement of the more orthodox view—a refinement in keeping with the Formalist method—to the question of the difference between the phonetic qualities of practical language and those of poetic language. Although Jakubinsky had [for example] noted that the dissimilation of liquid consonants [*l* and *r*] is relatively infrequent in poetry, Jakobson showed that it existed in both poetical and practical language but that in practical language it is "accidental"; in poetic language it is, "so to speak, contrived; these are two distinct phenomena."[37]

In the same essay Jakobson also clarified the principal distinction between emotional and poetic language (a distinction he had previously considered in his first book, *Modern Russian Poetry*):

> Although poetry may use the methods of emotive language, it uses them only for *its own* purposes.

The similarities between the two kinds of language and the use of poetic language in the way that emotive language is used frequently lead to the assumption that the two are identical. The assumption is mistaken because it fails to consider the radical difference of *function* between the two kinds of language.

In this connection Jakobson refuted the attempts of [Maurice] Grammont[38] and other prosodists to explain the phonetic structure of poetry in terms either of onomatopoeia or of the emotional connection between sounds and images. "Phonetic structure," he wrote, "is not always a structure of audible images, nor is a structure of audible images always a method of emotional language." Jakobson's book was typical because it constantly went beyond the limits of its particular, special theme (the prosody of Czech verse) and shed light on general questions about the theory of poetic language and verse. Thus his book ends with a whole essay on Mayakovsky, an essay complemented by his earlier piece on Khlebnikov.

In my own work on Anna Akhmatova I also attempted to raise basic theoretical questions about the theory of verse—questions of the relation of rhythm to syntax and intonation, the relation of the sound of verse to its articulation, and, lastly, the relation of poetic diction to semantics. Referring to a book which Yury Tynyanov[39] was then preparing, I pointed out that "as words get into verse they are, as it were, taken out of ordinary speech. They are surrounded by a new aura of meaning and perceived not against the background of speech in general but against the background of poetic speech." I also indicated that the formation of collateral meanings, which disrupts ordinary verbal associations, is the chief peculiarity of the semantics of poetry.

Until then, the original connection between the formal method and linguistics had been growing considerably weaker. The difference that had developed between our problems was so great that we no longer needed the special support of the linguists, especially the support of those who were psychologically oriented. In fact, some of the work of the linguists was objectionable in principle. Tynyanov's *The Problem of Poetic Language,* which had appeared just then, emphasized the difference between the study of psychological linguistics and the study of poetic language and style. This book showed the intimate relation that exists between the meaning of words and the poetic structure itself; it added new meaning to the idea of poetic rhythm and initi-

[36] In Pushkin's *Poltava.*
[37] [Eichenbaum] Jakubinsky had already pointed out the excessive complexity of the idea of practical speech and the impossibility of analyzing it in terms of function (conversational, oratorical, scientific, and so on); see his essay "O dialogicheskoy rechi" ["On Dialogic Speech"], *Ruskaya rech* [*Russian Speech*] I (1923).

[38] Maurice Grammont (1866–1946), French linguist.
[39] Yuri Tynyanov (1894–1943), Russian literary theorist and novelist.

ated the Formalists' investigation not only of acoustics and syntax, but also of the shades of meaning peculiar to poetic speech. In the introduction Tynyanov says:

> The study of poetry has of late been quite reward-
> ing. Undoubtedly the prospect in the near future is
> for development in the whole field, although we
> all remember the systematic beginning of the
> study. But the study of poetry has been kept iso-
> lated from questions of poetic language *and* style;
> the study of the latter is kept isolated from the
> study of the former. The impression is given that
> neither the poetic language itself nor the poetic
> style itself has any connection with poetry, that
> the one does not depend upon the other. The idea
> of poetic language, which was advanced not so
> long ago and is now changing, undoubtedly in-
> vited a certain looseness by its breadth and by the
> vagueness of its content, a content based on psy-
> chological linguistics.

Among the general questions of poetics revived and illuminated by this book, that of the idea of the material is most
fundamental. The generally accepted view saw an opposition between form and content; when the distinction was
made purely verbal, it lost its meaning. In fact, as I have already mentioned, our view gave form the significance of a
thing complete in itself and strengthened it by considering
the work of art in relation to its purpose. Our concept of
form required no complement—except that other, artistically insignificant, kind of form. Tynyanov showed that the
materials of verbal art were neither all alike nor all equally
important, that "one feature may be prominent at the expense of the rest, so that the remainder is deformed and
sometimes degraded to the level of a neutral prop." Hence
the conclusion that "the idea of material does not lie beyond
the limits of form; the material itself is a formal element. To
confuse it with external structural features is a mistake." After this, Tynyanov could make the notion of form more complex by showing that form is dynamic: "The unity of the
work is not a closed, symmetrical whole, but an unfolding,
dynamic whole. Its elements are not static indications of
equality and complexity, but always dynamic indications of
correlation and integration. The form of literary works must
be thought of as dynamic."[40]

Rhythm is here presented as the fundamental specific
factor which permeates all the elements of poetry. The

objective sign of poetic rhythm is the establishment of a
rhythmic group whose *unity* and *richness* exist side by side
with each other. And again, Tynyanov affirms the principal
distinction between prose and poetry:

> Poetry, as opposed to prose, tends toward unity and
> richness ranged around an uncommon object. This
> very "uncommonness" prevents the main point of
> the poem from being smoothed over. Indeed, it as-
> serts the object with a new force. . . . Any element
> of prose brought into the poetic pattern is trans-
> formed into verse by that feature of it which asserts
> its function and which thus has two aspects: the
> emphasis of the structure—the versification—and
> the deformation of the uncommon object.

Tynyanov also raises the question of semantics: "In verse
are not the ordinary semantic meanings of the words so
distorted (a fact which makes complete paraphrase impossible) that the usual principles governing their arrangement no longer apply?" The entire second part of
Tynyanov's book answers this question by defining the
precise relation between rhythm and semantics. The facts
show clearly that oral presentations are unified in part by
rhythm. "This is shown in a more forceful and more compact integration of connectives than occurs in ordinary
speech; words are made correlative by their positions";
prose lacks this feature.

Thus the Formalists abandoned Potebnya's theory and
accepted the conclusions connected with it on a new basis,
and a new perspective opened on to the theory of verse.
Tynyanov's work permitted us to grasp even the remotest
implications of these new problems. It became clear even to
those only casually acquainted with the *Opoyaz* that the
essence of our work consisted not in some kind of static
"formal method," but in a study of the specific peculiarities
of verbal art—we were not advocates of a method, but students of an object. Again, Tynyanov stated this:

> The object of a study claiming to be a study of art
> ought to be so specific that it is distinguished from
> other areas of intellectual activity and uses them
> for its own materials and tools. Each work of art
> represents a complex interaction of many factors;
> consequently, the job of the student is the defini-
> tion of the specific character of this interaction.

Earlier I noted that the problem of the diffusion and
change of form—the problem of literary evolution—is
raised naturally along with theoretical problems. The prob-

---

[40]This statement is worth comparison to various statements by English Romantic writers, especially Coleridge (above, page 496).

lem of literary evolution arises in connection with a reconsideration of Veselovsky's view of *skaz* motifs and devices; the answer ("new form is not to express new content, but to replace old form") led to a new understanding of form. If form is understood as the very content, constantly changing according to its dependence upon previous images, then we naturally had to approach it without abstract, ready-made, unalterable, classical schemes; and we had to consider specifically its historical sense and significance. The approach developed its own kind of dual perspective: the perspective of theoretical study (like Shklovsky's *Development of Plot* and my *Verse Melody*), which centered on a given theoretical problem and its applicability to the most diverse materials, and the perspective of historical studies—studies of literary evolution as such. The combination of these two perspectives, both organic to the subsequent development of the formal school, raised a series of new and very complex problems, many of which are still unsolved and even undefined.

Actually, the original attempt of the Formalists to take a particular structural device and to establish its identity in diverse materials became an attempt to differentiate, to understand, the *function* of a device in each given case. This notion of functional significance was gradually pushed toward the foreground and the original idea of the device pushed into the background. This kind of sorting out of its own general ideas and principles has been characteristic of our work throughout the evolution of the formal method. We have no dogmatic position to bind us and shut us off from facts. We do not answer for our schematizations; they may require change, refinement, or correction when we try to apply them to previously unknown facts. Work on specific materials compelled us to speak of functions and thus to revise our idea of the device. The theory itself demanded that we turn to history.

Here again we were confronted with the traditional academic sciences and the preferences of critics. In our student days the academic history of literature was limited chiefly to biographical and psychological studies of various writers—only the "greats," of course. Critics no longer made attempts to construct a history of Russian literature as a whole, attempts which evidenced the intention of bringing the great historical materials into a system; nevertheless, the traditions established by earlier histories (like A. N. Pypin's *History of Russian Literature*) retained their scholarly authority, the more so because the following generation had decided not to pursue such broad themes. Meanwhile, the chief role was played by such general and somewhat vague notions as realism and romanticism (realism was said to be better than romanticism); evolution was understood as grad-

ual perfection, as progress (from Romanticism to realism); succession [of literary schools] as the peaceful transfer of the inheritance from father to son. But generally, there was no notion of literature as such; material taken from the history of social movements, from biography, etc. had replaced it entirely.

This primitive historicism, which led away from literature, naturally provoked the Symbolist theoreticians and critics into a denial of any kind of historicism. Their own discussions of literature, consequently, developed into impressionistic *"études"* and "silhouettes," and they indulged in a widespread "modernization" of old writers, transforming them into "eternal companions." The history of literature was silently (and sometimes aloud) declared unnecessary.

We had to demolish the academic tradition and to eliminate the bias of the journalists [the Symbolist theoreticians]. We had to advance against the first a new understanding of literary evolution and of literature itself—without the idea of progress and peaceful succession, without the ideas of realism and romanticism, without materials foreign to literature—as a specific order of phenomena, a specific order of material. We had to act against the second by pointing out concrete historical facts, fluctuating and changing forms, by pointing to the necessity of taking into account the specific functions of this or that device—in a word, we had to draw the line between the literary work as a definite historical fact and a free interpretation of it from the standpoint of contemporary literary needs, tastes, or interests. Thus the basic passion for our historical literary work had to be a passion for destruction and negation, and such was the original tone of our theoretical attacks; our work later assumed a calmer note when we went on to solutions of particular problems.

That is why the first of our historical-literary pronouncements came in the form of theses expressed almost against our will in connection with some specific material. A particular question would unexpectedly lead to the formulation of a general problem, a problem that inextricably mixed theoretical and historical considerations. In this sense Tynyanov's *Dostoevsky and Gogol* and Shklovsky's *Rozanov* were typical.

Tynyanov's basic problem was to show that Dostoevsky's *The Village of Stepanchikovo* is a parody, that behind its first level is hidden a second—it is a parody of Gogol's *Correspondence with Friends*. But his treatment of this particular question was overshadowed by a whole theory of parody [which he developed to solve the particular problem], a theory of parody as a stylistic device (stylized parody) and as one of the manifestations (having great historical-literary significance) of the dialectical development of literary groups. With this arose the problem of succession and tradition and, hence, the basic problems of literary evolution were posed [as part of the study of style]:

> When one speaks of literary tradition or succession . . . usually one implies a certain kind of direct line uniting the younger and older representatives of a known literary branch. Yet the matter is much more complicated. There is no continuing direct line; there is rather a departure, a pushing away from the known point—a struggle. . . . Any literary succession is first of all a struggle, a destruction of old values and a reconstruction of old elements.

Literary evolution was complicated by the notion of struggle, of periodic uprisings, and so lost its old suggestion or peaceful and gradual development. Against this background, the literary relationship between Dostoevsky and Gogol was shown to be that of a complicated struggle.

In his *Rozanov*, Shklovsky showed, almost in the absence of basic themes, a whole theory of literary evolution which even then reflected the current discussion of such problems in *Opoyaz*. Shklovsky showed that literature moves forward in a broken line.

> In each literary epoch there is not one literary school, but several. They exist simultaneously, with one of them representing the high point of the current orthodoxy. The others exist uncanonized, mutely; in Pushkin's time, for example, the courtly tradition of [Wilhelm] Kuchelbecker and [Alexander] Greboyedov existed simultaneously with the tradition of Russian vaudeville verse and with such other traditions as that of the pure adventure novel of Bulgarin.

The moment the old art is canonized, new forms are created on a lower level. A "young line" is created which

> grows up to replace the old, as the vaudevillist Belopyatkin is transformed into a Nekrasov (see Brik's discussion of the relationship); a direct descendant of the eighteenth century, Tolstoy, creates a new novel (see the work of Boris Eichenbaum); Blok makes the themes and times of the gypsy ballad acceptable, and Chekhov introduces the "alarm clock" into Russian literature. Dostoevsky introduced the devices of the dime novel

into the mainstream of literature. Each new literary school heralds a revolution, something like the appearance of a new class. But, of course, this is only an analogy. The vanquished line is not obliterated, it does not cease to exist. It is only knocked from the crest; it lies dormant and may again arise as a perennial pretender to the throne. Moreover, in reality the matter is complicated by the fact that the new hegemony is usually not a pure revival of previous forms but is made more complex by the presence of features of the younger schools and with features, now secondary, inherited from its predecessors on the throne.

Shklovsky is discussing the dynamism of genres, and he interprets Rosanov's books as embodiments of a new genre, as a new type of novel in which the parts are unconnected by motivation. "Thematically, Rozanov's books are characterized by the elevation of new themes; compositionally, by the revealed device." As part of this general theory, we introduced the notion of the dialectical self-creation of new forms, that is, hidden in the new form we saw both analogies with other kinds of cultural development and proof of the independence of the phenomena of literary evolution. In a simplified form, this theory quickly changed hands and, as always happens, became a simple and fixed scheme—very handy for critics. Actually, we have here only a general outline of evolution surrounded by a whole series of complicated conditions. From this general outline the Formalists moved on to a more consistent solution of historical-literary problems and facts, specifying and refining their original theoretical premises.

Given our understanding of literary evolution as the dialectical change of forms, we did not go back to the study of those materials which had held the central position in the old-fashioned historical-literary work. We studied literary evolution insofar as it bore a distinctive character and only to the extent that it stood alone, quite independent of other aspects of culture. In other words, we stuck exclusively to facts in order not to pass into an endless number of indefinite connections and correspondences which would do nothing at all to explain literary evolution. We did not take up questions of the biography and psychology of the artist because we assumed that these questions, in themselves serious and complex, must take their places in other sciences. We felt it important to find indications of historical regularity in evolution—that is why we ignored all that seemed, from this point of view, circumstantial, not concerned with [literary] history. We were interested in the very process of evolution, in the very *dynamics* of literary form, insofar as it was possible to observe them in the facts of the past. For us, the central problem of the history of literature is the problem of evolution without personality—the study of literature as a *self-formed social phenomenon*. As a result, we found extremely significant both the question of the formation and changes of genres and the question of how second rate and popular literature contributed to the formation of genres. Here we had only to distinguish that popular literature which prepared the way for the formation of new genres from that which arose out of their decay and which offered material for the study of historical inertia.

On the other hand, we were not interested in the past, in isolated historical facts, as such; we did not busy ourselves with the restoration of this or that epoch because we happened to like it. History gave us what the present could not—a stable body of material. But, precisely for this reason, we approached it with a stock of theoretical problems and principles suggested in part by the facts of contemporary literature. The Formalists, then, characteristically had a close interest in contemporary literature and also reconciled criticism and scholarship. The earlier literary historians had, to a great extent, kept themselves aloof from contemporary literature; the Symbolists had subordinated scholarship to criticism. We saw in the history of literature not so much a special theoretical *subject* as a special *approach,* a special cross section of literature. The character of our historical-literary work involved our being drawn not only to historical conclusions, but also to theoretical conclusions—to the posing of new theoretical problems and to the testing of old.

From 1922 to 1924 a whole series of Formalist studies of literary history was written, many of which, because of contemporary market conditions, remain unpublished and are known only as reports. . . .[41] There is, of course, not space enough here to speak of such works in detail. They usually took up secondary writers (those who form the background of literature) and carefully explained the traditions of their work, noting changes in genres, styles, and so on. As a result, many forgotten names and facts came to

light, current estimates were shown to be inaccurate, traditional ideas changed, and, chiefly, the very process of literary evolution became clearer. The working out of this material has only begun. A new series of problems is before us: further differentiation of theoretical and historical literary ideas, introduction of new material, posing new questions, and so on.

I shall conclude with a general summary. The evolution of the formal method, which I have tried to present, has the look of a sequential development of theoretical principles—apart from the individual roles each of us played. Actually, the work of the *Opoyaz* group was genuinely collective. It was this way, obviously, because from the very beginning we understood the historical nature of our task; we did not see it as the personal affair of this or that individual. This was our chief connection with the times. Science itself is still evolving, and we are evolving with it. I shall indicate briefly the evolution of the formal method during these ten years:

1. From the original outline of the conflict of poetic language with practical we proceeded to differentiate the idea of practical language by its various functions (Jakubinsky) and to delimit the methods of poetic and emotional languages (Jakobson). Along with this we became interested in studying oratorical speech because it was close to practical speech but distinguished from it by function, and we spoke about the necessity of a revival of the poetic of rhetoric.

2. From the general idea of form, in its new sense, we proceeded to the idea of technique, and from here, to the idea of function.

3. From the idea of poetic rhythm as opposed to meter we proceeded to the idea of rhythm as a constructive element in the total poem and thus to an understanding of verse as a special form of speech having special linguistic (syntactical, lexical, and semantic) features.

4. From the idea of plot as structure we proceeded to an understanding of material in terms of its motivation, and from here to an understanding of material as an element participating in the construction but subordinate to the character of the dominant formal idea.

5. From the ascertainment of a single device applicable to various materials we proceeded to differentiate techniques according to function and from here to the question of the evolution of form—that is, to the problem of historical-literary study.

A whole new series of problems faces us, as Tynyanov's latest essay, *Literary Fact,* shows. Here the question of the relation between life and literature is posed, a question which many persons answer on the basis of a simple-minded dilettantism. Examples of how life becomes

---

[41] [Lemon and Reis] The deleted material contains a listing of some Formalist works, including: Yury Tynyov's *Verse Forms of Nekrasov, The Question of Tyutchev, Tyutchev and Pushkin, Tyutchev and Heine, The Ode as a Declamatory Gesture;* Boris Tomashevsky's *Gavriliada, Pushkin, A Reader of French Poets, Pushkin, Pushkin and Boileau, Pushkin and La Fontaine;* Boris Eichenbaum's *Lermontov, Problems of the Poetics of Pushkin, Pushkin's Path to Prose, Nekrasov;* Victor Vinogradov's *Plot and Structure of Gogol's* The Nose, *Plot and Architectonics of Dostoevsky's Novel* Poor People, *Gogol and The Realistic School, Studies on the Style of Gogol;* and Victor Zhimursky, *Byron and Pushkin.*

literature are shown and, conversely, of how literature passes into life "During the period of its deterioration a given genre is shoved from the center toward the periphery, but in its place, from the trivia of literature, from literature's backyard, and from life itself, new phenomena flow into the center."

Although I deliberately called this essay *The Theory of the "Formal Method,"* I gave, obviously, a sketch of its evolution. We have no theory that can be laid out as a fixed, ready-made system. For us theory and history merge not only in words, but in fact. We are too well trained by history itself to think that it can be avoided. When we feel that we have a theory that explains everything, a ready-made theory explaining all past and future events and therefore needing neither evolution nor anything like it—then we must recognize that the formal method has come to an end, that the spirit of scientific investigation has departed from it. As yet that has not happened.

Virginia Woolf

1882–1941

One of the major novelists of the twentieth century, Virginia Woolf was also a perceptive critical essayist who wrote frequently for the *Times Literary Supplement, The Dial, Life and Letters,* and other journals and newspapers. She wrote essays frequently on English women writers and on modern fiction, the best known of the latter being "Modern Fiction" and "Mr. Bennett and Mrs. Brown." Today, as an essayist she is, however, best known for her feminist writings in *A Room of One's Own* and *Three Guineas,* where she discusses directly the situation of women writers throughout modern history. Woolf's feminism always displayed its own kind of independence. She was a feminist who disliked the word "feminist," and she has been attacked by some feminists in later generations. She was not an activist and had some considerable skepticism about Emmeline Pankhurst's single-minded emphasis on obtaining the vote. Woolf did not see it as a panacea. Her concerns were deeper, as any novelist's would be: men's anger at women, misunderstandings between the sexes, and above all the psychological conditions under which women—and men—were brought up. In this last respect she belongs to a tradition of writers on the subject going back to Mary Wollstonecraft (above, page 441) and John Stuart Mill. Virtually all her novels touch on this matter, and *A Room of One's Own* deals with it directly. Woolf addresses the question of why a sister of Shakespeare would not likely have been able to write anything, let alone a play. She would have had none of the material resources—breadth of human experience, money, time— to do so. She would have been discouraged by everyone.

Woolf's feminism went in its own direction. It did not go beyond her own upper middle class and it held for important differences between men and women when the feminist trend of her time was toward absolute equality with men and the erasure of differences. Woolf held for radical changes that would or should occur as women's freedom and their suppressed values began to affect conceptions of power, family, and social life, in the past shaped by men. Woolf sometimes imagined a society in which men and women would come together in purpose and desire. Thus the theme of androgyny recurs in her work. Some recent feminist critics have wished that Woolf had given greater vent in her writings to her anger, but as the kind of writer she believed herself to be, she would have rejected this notion as a betrayal of her art and also of the effectiveness of her polemic, which gains much of its rhetorical strength from its ironic, and sometimes sarcastic, tone. However, *Three Guineas* seems to release more bitterness, though the cunning remains. Late in her career, she came somewhat to regret its presence, but it never entirely left her. In 1941, with the world on the brink of war, the avowed pacifist took her own life.

Virginia Woolf's many works are published by Hogarth Press. The *Collected Essays,* edited by Leonard Woolf in four volumes, appeared in 1966–1967. In addition to *A Room of One's Own,* see also *The Common Reader* (1925), *The Second Common*

Reader (1932), and *Three Guineas* (1938). See Harvena Richier, *Virginia Woolf: The Inward Voyage* (1970); Nancy Topping Bazin, *Virginia Woolf and the Androgynous Vision* (1973); Carolyn Heilburn, *Towards Androgyny: Aspects of Male and Female in Literature* (1973); Elaine Showalter, *A Literature of Their Own* (1977); several essays by Jane Marcus including " 'No More Horses': Virginia Woolf on Art and Propaganda," *Women Studies* 4 (1977) and "Art and Anger," *Feminist Studies* 4 (1978); Phyllis Rose, *Woman of Letters: A Life of Virginia Woolf* (1978); Jane Marcus, ed., *New Feminist Essays on Virginia Woolf* (1981); Jane Marcus, *Virginia Woolf: A Feminist Slant* (1983); Lyndall Gordon, *Virginia Woolf: A Writer's Life* (1984); Alex Zwerdling, *Virginia Woolf and the Real World* (1986); Jane Goldman, *The Feminist Aesthetics of Virginia Woolf* (1998); Nigel Nicolson, *Virginia Woolf* (2000).

A Room of One's Own

Chapter 4

That one would find any woman in that state of mind in the sixteenth century was obviously impossible.[1] One has only to think of the Elizabethan tombstones with all those children kneeling with clasped hands; and their early deaths; and to see their houses with their dark, cramped rooms, to realise that no woman could have written poetry then. What one would expect to find would be that rather later perhaps some great lady would take advantage of her comparative freedom and comfort to publish something with her name to it and risk being thought a monster. Men, of course, are not snobs, I continued, carefully eschewing "the arrant feminism" of Miss Rebecca West;[2] but they appreciate with sympathy for the most part the efforts of a countess to write verse. One would expect to find a lady of title meeting with far greater encouragement than an unknown Miss Austen or a Miss Brontë[3] at that time would have met with. But one would also expect to find that her mind was disturbed by alien emotions like fear and hatred and that her poems showed traces of that disturbance. Here is Lady Winchilsea,[4] for example, I thought, taking down her poems. She was born in the year 1661; she was noble both by birth and by marriage; she was childless; she wrote poetry,

and one has only to open her poetry to find her bursting out in indignation against the position of women:

> *How are we fallen! fallen by mistaken rules,*
> *And Education's more than Nature's fools;*
> *Debarred from all improvements of the mind,*
> *And to be dull, expected and designed;*
> *And if some one would soar above the rest,*
> *With warmer fancy, and ambition pressed,*
> *So strong the opposing faction still appears,*
> *The hopes to thrive can ne'er outweigh the fears.*[5]

Clearly her mind has by no means "consumed all impediments and become incandescent." On the contrary, it is harrassed and distracted with hates and grievances. The human race is split up for her into two parties. Men are the "opposing faction"; men are hated and feared, because they have the power to bar her way to what she wants to do—which is to write.

> *Alas! a woman that attempts the pen,*
> *Such an intruder on the rights of men,*
> *Such a presumptuous creature is esteemed,*
> *The fault can by no virtue be redeemed.*
> *They tell us we mistake our sex and way;*
> *Good breeding, fashion, dancing, dressing, play,*
> *Are the accomplishments we should desire;*
> *To write, or read, or think, or to enquire,*
> *Would cloud our beauty, and exhaust our time,*
> *And interrupt the conquests of our prime,*
> *Whilst the dull manage of a servile house*
> *Is held by some our utmost art and use.*[6]

The lectures comprising *A Room of One's Own* were delivered at Girton College, Cambridge, in October 1928. Chapter 4 is reprinted from *A Room of One's Own* (New York: Harcourt Brace, 1929).

[1] In the previous chapter Woolf imagines what the fate of an extraordinarily gifted sister of William Shakespeare might have been. She then characterizes Shakespeare's mind as "incandescent" and "unimpeded."

[2] Pseudonym of Cecily Fairfield (1892–1983), English novelist and critic.

[3] Jane Austen (1775–1817) and the Brontë sisters (Charlotte, 1816–1855; Emily, 1818–1848; and Anne, 1820–1849), English novelists.

[4] Anne Finch, Countess of Winchelsea (1661–1720), English poet.

[5] "The Introduction," 51–58.

[6] Ll. 9–20.

Indeed she has to encourage herself to write by supposing that what she writes will never be published; to soothe herself with the sad chant:

> To some few friends, and to thy sorrows sing,
> For groves of laurel thou wert never meant;
> Be dark enough thy shades, and be thou there content.[7]

Yet it is clear that could she have freed her mind from hate and fear and not heaped it with bitterness and resentment, the fire was hot within her. Now and again words issue of pure poetry:

> Nor will in fading silks compose,
> Faintly the inimitable rose.[8]

—they are rightly praised by Mr. Murry, and Pope,[9] it is thought, remembered and appropriated those others:

> Now the jonquille o'ercomes the feeble brain;
> We faint beneath the aromatic pain.[10]

It was a thousand pities that the woman who could write like that, whose mind was turned to nature and reflection, should have been forced to anger and bitterness. But how could she have helped herself? I asked, imagining the sneers and the laughter, the adulation of the toadies, the scepticism of the professional poet. She must have shut herself up in a room in the country to write, and been torn asunder by bitterness and scruples perhaps, though her husband was of the kindest, and their married life perfection. She "must have," I say, because when one comes to seek out the facts about Lady Winchilsea, one finds, as usual, that almost nothing is known about her. She suffered terribly from melancholy, which we can explain at least to some extent when we find her telling us how in the grip of it she would imagine:

> My lines decried, and my employment thought,
> An useless folly or presumptuous fault:[11]

The employment, which was thus censured, was, as far as one can see, the harmless one of rambling about the fields and dreaming:

> My hand delights to trace unusual things,
> And deviates from the known and common way,
> Nor will in fading silks compose,
> Faintly the inimitable rose.[12]

Naturally, if that was her habit and that was her delight, she could only expect to be laughed at; and, accordingly, Pope or Gay is said to have satirised her "as a blue-stocking with an itch for scribbling." Also it is thought that she offended Gay[13] by laughing at him. She said that his *Trivia* showed that "he was more proper to walk before a chair than to ride in one." But this is all "dubious gossip" and, says Mr. Murry, "uninteresting." But there I do not agree with him, for I should have liked to have had more even of dubious gossip so that I might have found out or made up some image of this melancholy lady, who loved wandering in the fields and thinking about unusual things and scorned, so rashly, so unwisely, "the dull manage of a servile house." But she became diffuse, Mr. Murry says. Her gift is all grown about with weeds and bound with briars. It had no chance of showing itself for the fine distinguished gift it was. And so, putting her back on the shelf, I turned to the other great lady, the Duchess whom Lamb[14] loved, harebrained, fantastical Margaret of Newcastle,[15] her elder, but her contemporary. They were very different, but alike in this that both were noble and both childless, and both were married to the best of husbands. In both burnt the same passion for poetry and both are disfigured and deformed by the same causes. Open the Duchess and one finds the same outburst of rage, "Women live like Bats or Owls, labour like Beasts, and die like Worms. . . ."[16] Margaret too might have been a poet; in our day all that activity would have turned a wheel of some sort. As it was, what could bind, tame or civilise for human use that wild, generous, untutored intelligence? It poured itself out, higgledy-piggledy, in torrents of rhyme and prose, poetry and philosophy which stand congealed in quartos and folios that nobody ever reads. She should have had a microscope put in her hand. She should have been taught to look at the stars and reason scientifically. Her wits were turned with solitude and freedom. No one checked her. No one taught her. The professors fawned on her. At Court they jeered at her. Sir Egerton Brydges[17] complained of her coarseness—"as flowing from a female of high rank brought up in the Courts." She shut herself up at Welbeck alone.

---

[7]Ll. 62–64.
[8]"The Spleen," 85–86.
[9]John Middleton Murry (1889–1957), English critic; Alexander Pope (above, page 297).
[10]"The Spleen," 40–41.
[11]Ll. 79–80.

[12]Ll. 83–86.
[13]John Gay (1685–1732), English poet and dramatist.
[14]Charles Lamb (1775–1834), English essayist.
[15]Margaret Cavendish, Duchess of Newcastle (1624–1674), English writer.
[16]*Female Orations* I.
[17]Egerton Brydges (1762–1837), English genealogist and writer.

What a vision of loneliness and riot the thought of Margaret Cavendish brings to mind! as if some giant cucumber had spread itself over all the roses and carnations in the garden and choked them to death. What a waste that the woman who wrote "the best bred women are those whose minds are civilest" should have frittered her time away scribbling nonsense and plunging ever deeper into obscurity and folly till the people crowded round her coach when she issued out. Evidently the crazy Duchess became a bogey to frighten clever girls with. Here, I remembered, putting away the Duchess and opening Dorothy Osborne's letters, is Dorothy writing to Temple about the Duchess's new book. "Sure the poore woman is a little distracted, shee could never bee soe rediculous else as to venture at writeing book's and in verse too, if I should not sleep this fortnight I should not come to that."[18]

And so, since no woman of sense and modesty could write books, Dorothy, who was sensitive and melancholy, the very opposite of the Duchess in temper, wrote nothing. Letters did not count. A woman might write letters while she was sitting by her father's sick-bed. She could write them by the fire whilst the men talked without disturbing them. The strange thing is, I thought, turning over the pages of Dorothy's letters, what a gift that untaught and solitary girl had for the framing of a sentence, for the fashioning of a scene. Listen to her running on:

"After dinner wee sitt and talk till Mr. B. com's in question and then I am gon. The heat of the day is spent in reading or working and about six or seven a Clock, I walke out into a Common that lyes hard by the house where a great many young wenches keep Sheep and Cow's and sitt in the shades singing of Ballads; I goe to them and compare their voyces and Beauty's to some Ancient Shepherdesses that I have read of and finde a vaste difference there, but trust mee I think these are as innocent as those could bee. I talke to them, and finde they want nothing to make them the happiest People in the world, but the knoledge that they are soe. most commonly when we are in the middest of our discourse one looks aboute her and spyes her Cow's goeing into the Corne and then away they all run, as if they had wing's at theire heels. I that am not soe nimble stay behinde, and when I see them driveing home theire Cattle I think tis time for mee to retyre too. when I have supped I goe into the Garden and soe to the syde of a small River that runs by it where I sitt downe and wish you with mee. . . ."

One could have sworn that she had the makings of a writer in her. But "if I should not sleep this fortnight I should not come to that"—one can measure the opposition that was in the air to a woman writing when one finds that even a woman with a great turn for writing has brought herself to believe that to write a book was to be ridiculous, even to show oneself distracted. And so we come, I continued, replacing the single short volume of Dorothy Osborne's letters upon the shelf, to Mrs. Behn.[19]

And with Mrs. Behn we turn a very important corner on the road. We leave behind, shut up in their parks among their folios, those solitary great ladies who wrote without audience or criticism, for their own delight alone. We come to town and rub shoulders with ordinary people in the streets. Mrs. Behn was a middle-class woman with all the plebeian virtues of humour, vitality and courage; a woman forced by the death of her husband and some unfortunate adventures of her own to make her living by her wits. She had to work on equal terms with men. She made, by working very hard, enough to live on. The importance of that fact outweighs anything that she actually wrote, even the splendid "A Thousand Martyrs I have made," or "Love in Fantastic Triumph sat," for here begins the freedom of the mind, or rather the possibility that in the course of time the mind will be free to write what it likes. For now that Aphra Behn had done it, girls could go to their parents and say, You need not give me an allowance; I can make money by my pen. Of course the answer for many years to come was, Yes, by living the life of Aphra Behn! Death would be better! and the door was slammed faster than ever. That profoundly interesting subject, the value that men set upon women's chastity and its effect upon their education, here suggests itself for discussion, and might provide an interesting book if any student at Girton or Newnham cared to go into the matter. Lady Dudley, sitting in diamonds among the midges of a Scottish moor, might serve for frontispiece. Lord Dudley, *The Times* said when Lady Dudley died the other day, "a man of cultivated taste and many accomplishments, was benevolent and bountiful, but whimsically despotic. He insisted upon his wife's wearing full dress, even at the remotest shooting-lodge in the Highlands; he loaded her with gorgeous jewels," and so on, "he gave her everything—always excepting any measure of responsibility." Then Lord Dudley had a stroke and she nursed him and ruled his estates with supreme confidence for ever after. That whimsical despotism was in the nineteenth century too.

But to return. Aphra Behn proved that money could be made by writing at the sacrifice, perhaps, of certain agreeable

[18] Dorothy Osborne (1627–1695), writer of letters to her husband-to-be Sir William Temple (1628–1699), English statesman and commentator on Sidney. Osborne's letters appear in Woolf's *The Second Common Reader.*

[19] Aphra Behn (1640–1689), English writer.

qualities; and so by degrees writing became not merely a sign of folly and a distracted mind, but was of practical importance. A husband might die, or some disaster overtake the family. Hundreds of women began as the eighteenth century drew on to add to their pin money, or to come to the rescue of their families by making translations or writing the innumerable bad novels which have ceased to be recorded even in text-books, but are to be picked up in the fourpenny boxes in the Charing Cross Road. The extreme activity of mind which showed itself in the later eighteenth century among women—the talking, and the meeting, the writing of essays on Shakespeare, the translating of the classics—was founded on the solid fact that women could make money by writing. Money dignifies what is frivolous if unpaid for. It might still be well to sneer at "blue-stockings with an itch for scribbling," but it could not be denied that they could put money in their purses. Thus, towards the end of the eighteenth century a change came about which, if I were rewriting history, I should describe more fully and think of greater importance than the Crusades or the Wars of the Roses. The middle-class woman began to write. For if *Pride and Prejudice* matters, and *Middlemarch* and *Villette* and *Wuthering Heights* matter, then it matters far more than I can prove in an hour's discourse that women generally, and not merely the lonely aristocrat shut up in her country house among her folios and her flatterers, took to writing. Without those forerunners, Jane Austen and the Brontës and George Eliot[20] could no more have written than Shakespeare could have written without Marlowe, or Marlowe without Chaucer, or Chaucer[21] without those forgotten poets who paved the ways and tamed the natural savagery of the tongue. For masterpieces are not single and solitary births; they are the outcome of many years of thinking in common, of thinking by the body of the people, so that the experience of the mass is behind the single voice. Jane Austen should have laid a wreath upon the grave of Fanny Burney,[22] and George Eliot done homage to the robust shade of Eliza Carter[23]—the valiant old woman who tied a bell to her bedstead in order that she might wake early and learn Greek. All women together ought to let flowers fall upon the tomb of Aphra Behn which is, most scandalously but rather appropriately, in Westminster Abbey, for it was she who earned them the right to speak their minds. It is she—shady and amorous as she was—who makes it not quite fantastic for me to say to you tonight: Earn five hundred a year by your wits.

Here, then, one had reached the early nineteenth century. And here, for the first time, I found several shelves given up entirely to the works of women. But why, I could not help asking, as I ran my eyes over them, were they, with very few exceptions, all novels? The original impulse was to poetry. The "supreme head of song" was a poetess. Both in France and in England the women poets precede the women novelists. Moreover, I thought, looking at the four famous names, what had George Eliot in common with Emily Brontë? Did not Charlotte Brontë fail entirely to understand Jane Austen? Save for the possibly relevant fact that not one of them had a child, four more incongruous characters could not have met together in a room—so much so that it is tempting to invent a meeting and a dialogue between them. Yet by some strange force they were all compelled, when they wrote, to write novels. Had it something to do with being born of the middle class, I asked; and with the fact, which Miss Emily Davies a little later was so strikingly to demonstrate, that the middle-class family in the early nineteenth century was possessed only of a single sitting-room between them? If a woman wrote, she would have to write in the common sitting-room. And, as Miss Nightingale[24] was so vehemently to complain,—"women never have an half hour . . . that they can call their own"—she was always interrupted. Still it would be easier to write prose and fiction there than to write poetry or a play. Less concentration is required. Jane Austen wrote like that to the end of her days. "How she was able to effect all this," her nephew writes in his Memoir, "is surprising, for she had no separate study to repair to, and most of the work must have been done in the general sitting-room, subject to all kinds of casual interruptions. She was careful that her occupation should not be suspected by servants or visitors or any persons beyond her own family party."[25] Jane Austen hid her manuscripts or covered them with a piece of blotting-paper. Then, again, all the literary training that a woman had in the early nineteenth century was training in the observation of character, in the analysis of emotion. Her sensibility had been educated for centuries by the influences of the common sitting-room. People's feelings were impressed on her; personal relations were always before her eyes. Therefore, when the middle-class woman took to writing, she naturally wrote novels, even though, as seems evident enough, two of the four famous women here named were not by nature novelists. Emily Brontë should have written poetic plays; the overflow of George Eliot's capacious mind should have spread itself

---

[20] George Eliot (Mary Ann Evans, 1819–1893), English novelist.
[21] Shakespeare (1564–1616), Christopher Marlowe (1564–1593), Geoffrey Chaucer (c. 1340–1400).
[22] Fanny Burney (1752–1840), English novelist.
[23] Eliza (Elizabeth) Carter (1717–1806), English poet.

---

[24] Florence Nightingale (1820–1910), English nurse.
[25] [Woolf] *Memoir* of Jane Austen, by her nephew, James Edward Austen-Leigh.

when the creative impulse was spent upon history or biography. They wrote novels, however; one may even go further, I said, taking *Pride and Prejudice* from the shelf, and say that they wrote good novels. Without boasting or giving pain to the opposite sex, one may say that *Pride and Prejudice* is a good book. At any rate, one would not have been ashamed to have been caught in the act of writing *Pride and Prejudice*. Yet Jane Austen was glad that a hinge creaked, so that she might hide her manuscript before any one came in. To Jane Austen there was something discreditable in writing *Pride and Prejudice*. And, I wondered, would *Pride and Prejudice* have been a better novel if Jane Austen had not thought it necessary to hide her manuscript from visitors? I read a page or two to see; but I could not find any signs that her circumstances had harmed her work in the slightest. That, perhaps, was the chief miracle about it. Here was a woman about the year 1800 writing without hate, without bitterness, without fear, without protest, without preaching. That was how Shakespeare wrote, I thought, looking at *Antony and Cleopatra;* and when people compare Shakespeare and Jane Austen, they may mean that the minds of both had consumed all impediments; and for that reason we do not know Jane Austen and we do not know Shakespeare, and for that reason Jane Austen pervades every word that she wrote, and so does Shakespeare.[26] If Jane Austen suffered in any way from her circumstances it was in the narrowness of life that was imposed upon her. It was impossible for a woman to go about alone. She never travelled; she never drove through London in an omnibus or had luncheon in a shop by herself. But perhaps it was the nature of Jane Austen not to want what she had not. Her gift and her circumstances matched each other completely. But I doubt whether that was true of Charlotte Brontë, I said, opening *Jane Eyre* and laying it beside *Pride and Prejudice.*

I opened it at chapter twelve and my eye was caught by the phrase, "Anybody may blame me who likes." What were they blaming Charlotte Brontë for, I wondered? And I read how Jane Eyre used to go up on to the roof when Mrs. Fairfax was making jellies and looked over the fields at the distant view. And then she longed—and it was for this that they blamed her—that "then I longed for a power of vision which might overpass that limit; which might reach the busy world, towns, regions full of life I had heard of but never seen: that then I desired more of practical experience than I possessed; more of intercourse with my kind, of acquaintance with variety of character than was here within my

reach. I valued what was good in Mrs. Fairfax, and what was good in Adèle; but I believed in the existence of other and more vivid kinds of goodness, and what I believed in I wished to behold.

"Who blames me? Many, no doubt, and I shall be called discontented. I could not help it: the restlessness was in my nature; it agitated me to pain sometimes. . . .

"It is vain to say human beings ought to be satisfied with tranquillity: they must have action; and they will make it if they cannot find it. Millions are condemned to a stiller doom than mine, and millions are in silent revolt against their lot. Nobody knows how many rebellions ferment in the masses of life which people earth. Women are supposed to be very calm generally: but women feel just as men feel; they need exercise for their faculties and a field for their efforts as much as their brothers do; they suffer from too rigid a restraint, too absolute a stagnation, precisely as men would suffer; and it is narrow-minded in their more privileged fellow-creatures to say that they ought to confine themselves to making puddings and knitting stockings, to playing on the piano and embroidering bags. It is thoughtless to condemn them, or laugh at them, if they seek to do more or learn more than custom has pronounced necessary for their sex.

"When thus alone I not unfrequently heard Grace Poole's laugh. . . ."

That is an awkward break, I thought. It is upsetting to come upon Grace Poole all of a sudden. The continuity is disturbed. One might say, I continued, laying the book down beside *Pride and Prejudice,* that the woman who wrote those pages had more genius in her than Jane Austen; but if one reads them over and marks that jerk in them, that indignation, one sees that she will never get her genius expressed whole and entire. Her books will be deformed and twisted. She will write in a rage where she should write calmly. She will write foolishly where she should write wisely. She will write of herself where she should write of her characters. She is at war with her lot. How could she help but die young, cramped and thwarted?

One could not but play for a moment with the thought of what might have happened if Charlotte Brontë had possessed say three hundred a year—but the foolish woman sold the copyright of her novels outright for fifteen hundred pounds; had somehow possessed more knowledge of the busy world, and towns and regions full of life; more practical experience, and intercourse with her kind and acquaintance with a variety of character. In those words she puts her finger exactly not only upon her own defects as a novelist but upon those of her sex at that time. She knew, no one better, how enormously her genius would have profited if it had

---

[26]This may be compared to Keats (above, page 536) and to Coleridge on Shakespeare (above, page 494).

not spent itself in solitary visions over distant fields; if experience and intercourse and and travel had been granted her. But they were not granted; they were withheld; and we must accept the fact that all those good novels, *Villette, Emma, Wuthering Heights, Middlemarch,* were written by women without more experience of life than could enter the house of a respectable clergyman; written too in the common sitting-room of that respectable house and by women so poor that they could not afford to buy more than a few quires of paper at a time upon which to write *Wuthering Heights* or *Jane Eyre.* One of them, it is true, George Eliot, escaped after much tribulation, but only to a secluded villa in St. John's Wood. And there she settled down in the shadow of the world's disapproval. "I wish it to be understood," she wrote, "that I should never invite any one to come and see me who did not ask for the invitation"; for was she not living in sin with a married man and might not the sight of her damage the chastity of Mrs. Smith or whoever it might be that chanced to call? One must submit to the social convention, and be "cut off from what is called the world." At the same time, on the other side of Europe, there was a young man living freely with this gipsy or with that great lady; going to the wars; picking up unhindered and uncensored all that varied experience of human life which served him so splendidly later when he came to write his books. Had Tolstoi[27] lived at the Priory in seclusion with a married lady "cut off from what is called the world," however edifying the moral lesson, he could scarcely, I thought, have written *War and Peace.*

But one could perhaps go a little deeper into the question of novel-writing and the effect of sex upon the novelist. If one shuts one's eyes and thinks of the novel as a whole, it would seem to be a creation owning a certain looking-glass likeness to life, though of course with simplifications and distortions innumerable. At any rate, it is a structure leaving a shape on the mind's eye, built now in squares, now pagoda shaped, now throwing out wings and arcades, now solidly compact and domed like the Cathedral of Saint Sofia at Constantinople. This shape, I thought, thinking back over certain famous novels, starts in one the kind of emotion that is appropriate to it. But that emotion at once blends itself with others, for the "shape" is not made by the relation of stone to stone, but by the relation of human being to human being. Thus a novel starts in us all sorts of antagonistic and opposed emotions. Life conflicts with something that is not life. Hence the difficulty of coming to any agreement about novels, and the immense sway that our private prejudices have upon us. On the one hand, we feel You—John the

hero—must live, or I shall be in the depths of despair. On the other, we feel, Alas, John, you must die, because the shape of the book requires it. Life conflicts with something that is not life. Then since life it is in part, we judge it as life. James is the sort of man I most detest, one says. Or, This is a farrago of absurdity. I could never feel anything of the sort myself. The whole structure, it is obvious, thinking back on any famous novel, is one of infinite complexity, because it is thus made up of so many different judgments, of so many different kinds of emotion. The wonder is that any book so composed holds together for more than a year or two, or can possibly mean to the English reader what it means for the Russian or the Chinese. But they do hold together occasionally very remarkably. And what holds them together in these rare instances of survival (I was thinking of *War and Peace*) is something that one calls integrity, though it has nothing to do with paying one's bills or behaving honourably in an emergency. What one means by integrity, in the case of the novelist, is the conviction that he gives one that this is the truth. Yes, one feels, I should never have thought that this could be so; I have never known people behaving like that. But you have convinced me that so it is, so it happens. One holds every phrase, every scene to the light as one reads— for Nature seems, very oddly, to have provided us with an inner light by which to judge of the novelist's integrity or disintegrity. Or perhaps it is rather that Nature, in her most irrational mood, has traced in invisible ink on the walls of the mind a premonition which these great artists confirm; a sketch which only needs to be held to the fire of genius to become visible. When one so exposes it and sees it come to life one exclaims in rapture, But this is what I have always felt and known and desired! And one boils over with excitement, and, shutting the book even with a kind of reverence as if it were something very precious, a stand-by to return to as long as one lives, one puts it back on the shelf, I said, taking *War and Peace* and putting it back in its place. If, on the other hand, these poor sentences that one takes and tests rouse first a quick and eager response with their bright colouring and their dashing gestures but there they stop: something seems to check them in their development: or if they bring to light only a faint scribble in that corner and a blot over there, and nothing appears whole and entire, then one heaves a sigh of disappointment and says, Another failure. This novel has come to grief somewhere.

And for the most part, of course, novels do come to grief somewhere. The imagination falters under the enormous strain. The insight is confused; it can no longer distinguish between the true and the false; it has no longer the strength to go on with the vast labour that calls at every moment for the use of so many different faculties. But how

---

[27] Tolstoy (above, page 757).

would all this be affected by the sex of the novelist, I wondered, looking at *Jane Eyre* and the others. Would the fact of her sex in any way interfere with the integrity of a woman novelist—that integrity which I take to be the backbone of the writer? Now, in the passages I have quoted from *Jane Eyre*, it is clear that anger was tampering with the integrity of Charlotte Brontë the novelist. She left her story, to which her entire devotion was due, to attend to some personal grievance. She remembered that she had been starved of her proper due of experience—she had been made to stagnate in a parsonage mending stockings when she wanted to wander free over the world. Her imagination swerved from indignation and we feel it swerve. But there were many more influences than anger tugging at her imagination and deflecting it from its path. Ignorance, for instance. The portrait of Rochester is drawn in the dark. We feel the influence of fear in it; just as we constantly feel an acidity which is the result of oppression, a buried suffering smouldering beneath her passion, a rancour which contracts those books, splendid as they are, with a spasm of pain.

And since a novel has this correspondence to real life, its values are to some extent those of real life. But it is obvious that the values of women differ very often from the values which have been made by the other sex; naturally, this is so. Yet it is the masculine values that prevail. Speaking crudely, football and sport are "important"; the worship of fashion, the buying of clothes "trivial." And these values are inevitably transferred from life to fiction. This is an important book, the critic assumes, because it deals with war. This is an insignificant book because it deals with the feelings of women in a drawing-room. A scene in a battlefield is more important than a scene in a shop—everywhere and much more subtly the difference of value persists. The whole structure, therefore, of the early nineteenth-century novel was raised, if one was a woman, by a mind which was slightly pulled from the straight, and made to alter its clear vision in deference to external authority. One has only to skim those old forgotten novels and listen to the tone of voice in which they are written to divine that the writer was meeting criticism; she was saying this by way of aggression, or that by way of conciliation. She was admitting that she was "only a woman," or protesting that she was "as good as a man." She met that criticism as her temperament dictated, with docility and diffidence, or with anger and emphasis. It does not matter which it was; she was thinking of something other than the thing itself. Down comes her book upon our heads. There was a flaw in the centre of it. And I thought of all the women's novels that lie scattered, like small pock-marked apples in an orchard, about the secondhand book shops of London. It was the flaw in the centre that had rot-

ted them. She had altered her values in deference to the opinion of others.

But how impossible it must have been for them not to budge either to the right or to the left. What genius, what integrity it must have required in face of all that criticism, in the midst of that purely patriarchal society, to hold fast to the thing as they saw it without shrinking. Only Jane Austen did it and Emily Brontë. It is another feather, perhaps the finest, in their caps. They wrote as women write, not as men write. Of all the thousand women who wrote novels then, they alone entirely ignored the perpetual admonitions of the eternal pedagogue—write this, think that. They alone were deaf to that persistent voice, now grumbling, now patronising, now domineering, now grieved, now shocked, now angry, now avuncular, that voice which cannot let women alone, but must be at them, like some too conscientious governess, adjuring them, like Sir Egerton Brydges, to be refined; dragging even into the criticism of poetry criticism of sex;[28] admonishing them, if they would be good and win, as I suppose, some shiny prize, to keep within certain limits which the gentleman in question thinks suitable: ". . . female novelists should only aspire to excellence by courageously acknowledging the limitations of their sex."[29] That puts the matter in a nutshell, and when I tell you, rather to your surprise, that this sentence was written not in August 1828 but in August 1928, you will agree, I think, that however delightful it is to us now, it represents a vast body of opinion—I am not going to stir those old pools, I take only what chance has floated to my feet—that was far more vigorous and far more vocal a century ago. It would have needed a very stalwart young woman in 1828 to disregard all those snubs and chidings and promises of prizes. One must have been something of a firebrand to say to oneself, Oh, but they can't buy literature too. Literature is open to everybody. I refuse to allow you, Beadle though you are, to turn me off the grass.[30] Lock up your libraries if you like; but there is no gate, no lock, no bolt that you can set upon the freedom of my mind.

But whatever effect discouragement and criticism had upon their writing—and I believe that they had a very great

---

28 [Woolf] "[She] has a metaphysical purpose, and that is a dangerous obsession, especially with a woman, for women rarely possess men's healthy love of rhetoric. It is a strange lack in the sex which is in other things more primitive and materialistic."

29 [Woolf] "If, like the reporter, you believe that female novelists should only aspire to excellence by courageously acknowledging the limitations of their sex (Jane Austen [has] demonstrated how gracefully this gesture can be accomplished) . . . ," *Life and Letters*, August 1928.

30 *A Room of One's Own* begins with a brief account of Woolf's having been turned off the grass as an outsider when she visited "Oxbridge" and then having been forbidden the library because unaccompanied by a Fellow or not possessing a letter of introduction.

effect—that was unimportant compared with the other diffi-culty which faced them (I was still considering those early nineteenth-century novelists) when they came to set their thoughts on paper—that is that they had no tradition behind them, or one so short and partial that it was of little help. For we think back through our mothers if we are women. It is useless to go to the great men writers for help, however much one may go to them for pleasure. Lamb, Browne, Thackeray, Newman, Sterne, Dickens, De Quincey[31]—who-ever it may be—never helped a woman yet, though she may have learnt a few tricks of them and adapted them to her use. The weight, the pace, the stride of a man's mind are too un-like her own for her to lift anything substantial from him successfully. The ape is too distant to be sedulous. Perhaps the first thing she would find, setting pen to paper, was that there was no common sentence ready for her use. All the great novelists like Thackeray and Dickens and Balzac[32] have written a natural prose, swift but not slovenly, expres-sive but not precious, taking their own tint without ceasing to be common property. They have based it on the sentence that was current at the time. The sentence that was current at the beginning of the nineteenth century ran something like this perhaps. "The grandeur of their works was an argu-ment with them, not to stop short, but to proceed. They could have no higher excitement or satisfaction than in the exercise of their art and endless generations of truth and beauty. Success prompts to exertion; and habit facilitates success." That is a man's sentence; behind it one can see Johnson, Gibbon[33] and the rest. It was a sentence that was unsuited for a woman's use. Charlotte Brontë, with all her splendid gift for prose, stumbled and fell with that clumsy weapon in her hands. George Eliot committed atrocities with it that beggar description. Jane Austen looked at it and laughed at it and devised a perfectly natural, shapely sen-tence proper for her own use and never departed from it. Thus, with less genius for writing than Charlotte Brontë, she got infinitely more said. Indeed, since freedom and fullness of expression are of the essence of the art, such a lack of tra-dition, such a scarcity and inadequacy of tools, must have told enormously upon the writing of women. Moreover, a book is not made of sentences laid end to end, but of sen-tences built, if an image helps, into arcades or domes. And this shape too has been made by men out of their own needs for their own uses. There is no reason to think that the form of the epic or of the poetic play suits a woman any more than the sentence suits her. But all the older forms of litera-ture were hardened and set by the time she became a writer. The novel alone was young enough to be soft in her hands—another reason, perhaps, why she wrote novels. Yet who shall say that even now "the novel" (I give it inverted com-mas to mark my sense of the words' inadequacy), who shall say that even this most pliable of all forms is rightly shaped for her use? No doubt we shall find her knocking that into shape for herself when she has the free use of her limbs; and providing some new vehicle, not necessarily in verse, for the poetry in her. For it is the poetry that is still denied out-let. And I went on to ponder how a woman nowadays would write a poetic tragedy in five acts—would she use verse—would she not use prose rather?

But these are difficult questions which lie in the twi-light of the future. I must leave them, if only because they stimulate me to wander from my subject into trackless forests where I shall be lost and, very likely, devoured by wild beasts. I do not want, and I am sure that you do not want me, to broach that very dismal subject, the future of fiction, so that I will only pause here one moment to draw your attention to the great part which must be played in that future so far as women are concerned by physical condi-tions. The book has somehow to be adapted to the body, and at a venture one would say that women's books should·be shorter, more concentrated, than those of men, and framed so that they do not need long hours of steady and uninter-rupted work. For interruptions there will always be. Again, the nerves that feed the brain would seem to differ in men and women, and if you are going to make them work their best and hardest, you must find out what treatment suits them—whether these hours of lectures, for instance, which the monks devised, presumably, hundreds of years ago, suit them—what alternations of work and rest they need, inter-preting rest not as doing nothing but as doing something but something that is different; and what should that difference be? All this should be discussed and discovered; all this is part of the question of women and fiction. And yet, I contin-ued, approaching the bookcase again, where shall I find that elaborate study of the psychology of women by a woman? If through their incapacity to play football women are not going to be allowed to practise medicine—

Happily my thoughts were now given another turn.

[31] Sir Thomas Browne (1605–1682), English author and physician; William Makepeace Thackeray (1811–1863), English novelist; John Henry (Cardi-nal) Newman (1801–1890), English clergyman and writer; Laurence Sterne (1713–1768), English writer; Charles Dickens (1812–1870), English nov-elist; Thomas DeQuincey (1785–1859), English essayist.
[32] Honoré de Balzac (1799–1850), French novelist.
[33] Johnson (above, page 357); Edward Gibbon (1737–1794), English historian.

William Empson

1906–1984

Empson published his influential *Seven Types of Ambiguity* in 1930 and a revised edition in 1947 with a preface responding to critics and with footnotes in which he himself often criticized his text. Empson's work reflects the growing interest in language analysis of his time, part of which he inherited from one of his teachers, I. A. Richards (above, page 856). The book led a generation of critics in both England and America toward close verbal analysis, especially of lyric poetry. The methods developed were then extended by others to drama and prose fiction.

Ambiguity before Empson and usually after was described as syntactical, as in a verbal situation where there are two possible conflicting readings. Empson very much broadened use of the term to include: 1. Where a detail is effective in several ways at once; 2. Where two or more alternative meanings are fully resolved into one; 3. Where two apparently unconnected meanings are given simultaneously; 4. Where alternative meanings combine to make clear a complicated state of mind in the author; 5. Where there is a fortunate confusion; 6. Where what is said is contradictory or irrelevant and the reader is forced to invent interpretations; 7. Where a full contradiction marks a division in the author's mind. These types, which are taken almost verbatim from Empson's explanatory table of contents, are not claimed to exhaust the possibilities of ambiguity. Nor does Empson deny that they may overlap.

The selection below is from the chapter on the first type. That chapter ends with an "annex," a discussion of dramatic irony (not included here) as belonging to the type. However, irony might apply to more than one of the types.

Empson helped to generate the emphasis on irony among the New Critics, especially Cleanth Brooks (below, page 1043), and he is usually regarded as part of the movement that included them as well as Eliot and Richards. There are, however, significant differences. Empson, for example, includes reference to the author's intention in his seventh type and the reader's participation in the sixth, whereas the New Critics tended to objectify the poem apart from author and reader.

Empson is one of the wittiest and yet most plain-speaking of critics. His book is best read with the preface to the 1947 edition and its footnotes, to be followed by his later *Some Versions of Pastoral* and *The Structure of Complex Words*.

Empson's major works are *Seven Types of Ambiguity* (1930, rev. 1947), *Some Versions of Pastoral* (published in England as *The English Pastoral Poem*) (1935); and *The Structure of Complex Words* (1951), though he published much else including poetry. There are numerous collections of essays on Empson in recent years. See J. H. Willis, *William Empson* (1969); Christopher Norris, *William Empson and the Philosophy of Literary Criticism* (1978); James Haffenden, *Argufying: Essays on Literature and Culture/William Empson* (1987); Paul H. Fry, *William Empson: Prophet Against Sacrifice* (1991); C. Norris and N. Mapp, eds., *William Empson: The Critical Achievement* (1993); John Constable, ed., *Critical Essays on William Empson* (1993).

from
Seven Types of Ambiguity

Chapter I

An ambiguity, in ordinary speech, means something very pronounced, and as a rule witty or deceitful. I propose to use the word in an extended sense, and shall think relevant to my subject any verbal nuance, however slight, which gives room for alternative reactions to the same piece of language.[1] Sometimes, especially in this first chapter, the word may be stretched absurdly far, but it is descriptive because it suggests the analytical mode of approach, and with that I am concerned.

In a sufficiently extended sense any prose statement could be called ambiguous. In the first place it can be analysed. Thus, 'The brown cat sat on the red mat' may be split up into a series: 'This is a statement about a cat. The cat the statement is about is brown,' and so forth. Each such simple statement may be translated into a complicated statement which employs other terms; thus you are now faced with the task of explaining what a 'cat' is; and each such complexity may again be analysed into a simple series; thus each of the things that go to make up a 'cat' will stand in some spatial relation to the 'mat.' 'Explanation,' by choice of terms, may be carried in any direction the explainer wishes; thus to translate and analyse the notion of 'sat' might involve a course of anatomy; the notion of 'on' a theory of gravitation. Such a course, however, would be irrelevant not only to my object in this essay but to the context implied by the statement, the person to whom it seems to be addressed, and the purpose for which it seems to be addressed to him; nor would you be finding out anything very fundamental about the sentence by analysing it in this way; you would merely be making another sentence, stating the same fact, but designed for a different purpose, context, and person. Evidently, the literary critic is much concerned with implications of this last sort, and must regard them as a main part of the meaning. There is a difference (you may say that between thought

and feeling) between the fact stated and the circumstance of the statement, but very often you cannot know one without knowing the other, and an apprehension of the sentence involves both without distinguishing between them. Thus I should consider as on the same footing the two facts about this sentence, that it is about a cat and that it is suited to a child. And I should only isolate two of its 'meanings,' to form an ambiguity worth notice; it has contradictory associations, which might cause some conflict in the child who heard it, in that it might come out of a fairy story and might come out of *Reading without Tears*.

In analysing the statement made by a sentence (having, no doubt, fixed on the statement by an apprehension of the implications of the sentence), one would continually be dealing with a sort of ambiguity due to metaphors, made clear by Mr. Herbert Read in *English Prose Style*;[2] because metaphor, more or less far-fetched, more or less complicated, more or less taken for granted (so as to be unconscious), is the normal mode of development of a language. 'Words used as epithets are words used to *analyse* a direct statement,' whereas 'metaphor is the synthesis of several units of observation into one commanding image; it is the expression of a complex idea, not by analysis, nor by direct statement, but by a sudden perception of an objective relation.' One thing is said to be like another, and they have several different properties in virtue of which they are alike. Evidently this, as a verbal matter, yields more readily to analysis than the social ambiguities I have just considered; and I shall take it as normal to the simplest type of ambiguity, which I am considering in this chapter. The fundamental situation, whether it deserves to be called ambiguous or not, is that a word or a grammatical structure is effective in several ways at once. To take a famous example, there is no pun, double syntax, or dubiety of feeling, in

Bare ruined choirs, where late the sweet birds sang,[3]

but the comparison holds for many reasons; because ruined monastery choirs are places in which to sing, because they involve sitting in a row, because they are made of wood, are carved into knots and so forth, because they used to be surrounded by a sheltering building crystallised out of the likeness of a forest, and coloured with stained glass and painting like flowers and leaves, because they are now abandoned by all but the grey walls coloured like the skies of winter, because the cold and Narcissistic charm suggested by choirboys suits well with Shakespeare's feeling for the object of

---

Seven Types of Ambiguity was first published in England in 1930. It appeared revised in 1947. The selection is from the 1947 edition (New York: New Directions, 1947).

[1][Empson] In the first edition I made it 'adds some nuance to the direct statement of prose.' This, as was pointed out, begs a philosophical question and stretches the term 'ambiguity' so far that it becomes almost meaningless. The new phrase is not meant to be decisive but to avoid confusing the reader; naturally the question of what would be the best definition of 'ambiguity' (whether the example in hand should be called ambiguous) crops up all through the book.

[2] Herbert Read (1893–1968), English poet and critic.
[3] Sonnet by William Shakespeare (1564–1616).

the Sonnets, and for various sociological and historical reasons (the protestant destruction of monasteries; fear of puritanism), which it would be hard now to trace out in their proportions; these reasons, and many more relating the simile to its place in the Sonnet, must all combine to give the line its beauty, and there is a sort of ambiguity in not knowing which of them to hold most clearly in mind. Clearly this is involved in all such richness and heightening of effect, and the machinations of ambiguity are among the very roots of poetry.

Such a definition of the first type of ambiguity covers almost everything of literary importance, and this chapter ought to be my longest and most illuminating, but it is the most difficult. The important meanings of this sort, as may be seen from the example about the cat, are hard to isolate, or to be sure of when you have done so; and there is a sort of meaning, the sort that people are thinking of when they say 'this poet will mean more to you when you have had more experience of life,' which is hardly in reach of the analyst at all. They mean by this not so much that you will have more information (which could be given at once) as that the information will have been digested; that you will be more experienced in the apprehension of verbal subtleties or of the poet's social tone; that you will have become the sort of person that can feel at home in, or imagine, or extract experience from, what is described by the poetry; that you will have included it among the things you are prepared to apprehend. There is a distinction here of the implied meanings of a sentence into what is to be assimilated at the moment and what must already be part of your habits; in arriving at the second of these the educator (that mysterious figure) rather than the analyst would be helpful. In a sense it cannot be explained in language, because to a person who does not understand it any statement of it is as difficult as the original one, while to a person who does understand it a statement of it has no meaning because no purpose.

Meanings of this kind, indeed, are conveyed, but they are conveyed much more by poets than by analysts; that is what poets are for, and why they are important. For poetry has powerful means of imposing its own assumptions, and is very independent of the mental habits of the reader; one might trace its independence to the ease with which it can pass from the one to the other of these two sorts of meaning. A single word, dropped where it comes most easily, without being stressed, and as if to fill out the sentence, may signal to the reader what he is meant to be taking for granted; if it is already in his mind the word will seem natural enough and will not act as an unnecessary signal. Once it has gained its point, on further readings, it will take for granted that you always took it for granted; only very delicate people are as tactful in this matter as the printed page. Nearly all statements assume in this way that you know something but not everything about the matter in hand, and would tell you something different if you knew more; but printed commonly differ from spoken ones in being intended for a greater variety of people, and poetical from prosaic ones in imposing the system of habits they imply more firmly or more quickly.

As examples of the things that are taken for granted in this way, and assume a habit, rather than a piece of information, in the reader, one might give the fact that a particular section of the English language is being used; the fact that English is being used, which you can be conscious of if you can use French; the fact that a European language is used, which you can be conscious of if you can use Chinese. The first of these 'facts' is more definite than it sounds; a word in a speech which falls outside the expected vocabulary will cause an uneasy stir in all but the soundest sleepers; many sermons use this with painful frankness. Evidently such a section is defined by its properties rather than by enumeration, and so alters the character of the words it includes; for instance, one would bear it in mind when considering whether the use of a word demands that one should consider its derivation. Regional or dialect poets are likely to use words flatly from that point of view. No single example of so delicate and continuous a matter can be striking; I shall take one at random out of the Synge *Deirdre,* to make clear that a word need not be unpoetical merely because its meaning has been limited:

> DEIRDRE. . . . It should be a sweet thing to have what is best and richest, if it's for a short space only.
> NAISI. And we've a short space only to be triumphant and brave.[4]

The language here seems rich in implications; it certainly carries much feeling and conveys a delicate sense of style. But if one thinks of the Roman or medieval associations of *triumphant,* even of its normal use in English, one feels a sort of unexplained warning that these are irrelevant; the word here is a thin counter standing for a notion not fully translated out of Irish; it is used to eke out that alien and sliding speech-rhythm, which puts no weight upon its single words.[5]

The process of becoming accustomed to a new author is very much that of learning what to exclude in this way,

---

[4]From *Deirdre of the Sorrows* by J. M. Synge (1871–1909), Anglo-Irish dramatist.
[5][Empson] Not a clear example, and I am not sure that what I said is true; but a borderline example was needed here to show that fine shades can be concerned.

and this first of the three 'facts,' hard as it may be to explain in detail, is one with which appreciative critics are accustomed to deal very effectively. But the other two are more baffling; one can say little about the quality of a language, if only because the process of describing it in its own language is so top-heavy, and the words of another language will not describe it. The English prepositions, for example, from being used in so many ways and in combination with so many verbs, have acquired not so much a number of meanings as a body of meaning continuous in several dimensions; a tool-like quality, at once thin, easy to the hand, and weighty, which a mere statement of their variety does not convey. In a sense all words have a body of this sort; none can be reduced to a finite number of points, and if they could the points could not be conveyed by words.

Thus a word may have several distinct meanings; several meanings connected with one another; several meanings which need one another to complete their meaning; or several meanings which unite together so that the word means one relation or one process. This is a scale which might be followed continuously. 'Ambiguity' itself can mean an indecision as to what you mean, an intention to mean several things, a probability that one or other or both of two things has been meant, and the fact that a statement has several meanings.[6] It is useful to be able to separate these if you wish, but it is not obvious that in separating them at any particular point you will not be raising more problems than you solve. Thus I shall often use the ambiguity of 'ambiguity,' and pronouns like 'one,' to make statements covering both reader and author of a poem, when I want to avoid raising irrelevant problems as to communication. To be less ambiguous would be like analysing the sentence about the cat into a course of anatomy. In the same way the words of the poet will, as a rule, be more justly words, what they represent will be more effectively a unit in the mind, than the more numerous words with which I shall imitate their meaning so as to show how it is conveyed.

And behind this notion of the word itself, as a solid tool rather than as a collection of meanings, must be placed a notion of the way such a word is regarded as a member of the language; this seems still darker and less communicable in any terms but its own. For one may know what has been put into the pot, and recognise the objects in the stew, but the juice in which they are sustained must be regarded with a peculiar respect because they are all in there too, some-

how, and one does not know how they are combined or held in suspension. One must feel the respect due to a profound lack of understanding for the notion of a potential, and for the poet's sense of the nature of a language.

These examples of the 'meanings' of an English sentence should make clear that no explanation, certainly no explanation written in English, can be conceived to list them completely; and that there may be implications (such as I should call meanings) of which a statement would be no use. Neither of these are objections to my purpose, because I can assume that my readers already understand and enjoy the examples I shall consider, and I am concerned only to conduct a sufficient analysis of their enjoyment to make it seem more understandable.

It is possible that there are some writers who write very largely with this sense of a language as such, so that their effects would be almost out of reach of analysis. Racine[7] always seems to me to write with the whole weight of the French language, to remind one always of the latent assumptions of French, in a way that I am not competent to analyse in any case, but that very possibly could not be explained in intelligible terms. Dryden is a corresponding English figure in this matter;[8] Miss Gertrude Stein,[9] too, at this point, implores the passing tribute of a sigh. To understand their methods one might have to learn a great deal about the mode of action of language which is not yet known, and it might always be quicker to use habit than analysis, to learn the language than to follow the explanation.

I propose, then, to consider a series of definite and detachable ambiguities, in which several large and crude meanings can be separated out, and to arrange them in order of increasing distance from simple statement and logical exposition. There is much danger of triviality in this, because it requires a display of ingenuity such as can easily be used to escape from the consciousness of one's ignorance; because it ignores the fact that the selection of meanings is more important to the poet than their multitude, and harder to understand; and because it gives no means of telling how much has been done by meanings latent in the mode of action of the language, which may be far more elaborate and fundamental than those that can be written up. My methods can only be applied at intervals; I shall frequently pounce on the least interesting aspect of a poem, as being large enough for my forceps; and the atoms which build up the compounds I analyse will always be more complex than they.

---

[6][Empson] It would seem pedantic to alter the phrase 'has several meanings.' But it is treacherous. If the simplest statement has a subject and a predicate it may be said to include two meanings. There would be no point in calling it ambiguous unless it gave room for alternative reactions.

[7] Jean Baptiste Racine (1639–1699), French dramatist.
[8] Dryden (above, page 253).
[9] Gertrude Stein (1874–1946), American expatriate writer.

But in so far as anything can be said about this mysterious and important matter, to say it ought not to require apology.

I shall almost always take poems that I admire, and write with pleasure about their merits; you might say that, from the scientific point of view, this is a self-indulgence, and that as much is to be learnt from saying why bad poems are bad. This would be true if the field were of a known size; if you knew the ways in which a poem *might* be good, there would be a chance of seeing why it had failed. But, in fact, you must rely on each particular poem to show you the way in which it is trying to be good; if it fails you cannot know its object; and it would be trivial to explain why it had failed at something it was not trying to achieve. Of course, it may succeed in doing something that you understand and hate, and you may then explain your hatred; but all you can explain about the poem is its success. And even then, you can only have understood the poem by a stirring of the imagination, by something like an enjoyment of it from which you afterwards revolt in your own mind. It is more self-centred, therefore, and so less reliable, to write about the poems you have thought bad than about the poems you have thought good.

But, before I start to do this, I must consider two fundamental objections to my purpose, which many critics would raise; the objection that the meaning of poetry does not matter, because it is apprehended as Pure Sound, and the objection that what really matters about poetry is the Atmosphere. These two opinions are very similar, but are best answered in different ways.

The main argument for Pure Sound is the extreme oddity of the way poetry acts; the way lines seem beautiful without reason; the way you can decide (or at any rate people in practice do decide) whether a poem deserves further attention by a mere glance at the way it uses its words. This certainly is an important piece of evidence, and makes one feel that very strange things may be true about the mode of action of poetry, but it shows very little as to what these things may be. I shall myself try to bully my readers into a belief in the importance of ambiguity, for just this same reason.

There was a period of the cult of Pure Sound when infants were read passages from Homer, and then questioned as to their impressions, not unlike Darwin[10] playing the trombone to his French beans. And, indeed, conclusive evidence was collected in this way that a vague impression as to the subject of a poem may be derived from a study of its reciter; one can only question how far this is relevant to the question at issue. There is a crux here (to revive a rather stale contro-versy) which makes experiment difficult; on the one hand, it is no use telling a person who does not know Greek to read Homer for himself, because he does not know how to pronounce it (even if he knows how to pronounce the words, he will not pronounce them as a sentence); on the other hand, if you tell him how to pronounce the sentence, it is impossible to be sure you have not told him how to feel about it by the tone of your voice. Certainly it is no use denying that feelings can be conveyed, even between animals of different species, by grunts and screams; and there are those who say that language itself was at first a self-explanatory symbolism, based on these expressions of feeling, on onomatopoeia, and on that use of the tongue to point at matters of interest, or to imitate and so define a difficult action, which may be seen in a child learning to write. Certainly, too, one would expect language in poetry to retain its primitive uses more than elsewhere. But this sort of thing is no use to the admirers of Pure Sound in poetry, because a grunt is at once too crude and too subtle to be conveyed by the alphabet at all. Any word can be either screamed or grunted, so if you have merely a word written on paper you have to know not only its meaning but something about its context before it can tell you whether to grunt or to scream. Most admirers of Pure Sound, indeed, will admit that you have to be experienced in the words used by a poet before their sound can be appreciated, and evidently this admission makes all the difference.

They are the more willing to admit this because they are usually appreciative critics, persons of an extreme delicacy of sensibility who have to guard this delicacy in unusual ways. A first-rate wine-taster may only taste small amounts of wine, for fear of disturbing his palate, and I dare say it would really be unwise for an appreciative critic to use his intelligence too freely; but there is no reason why these specialised habits should be imposed on the ordinary drinker or reader. Specialists usually have a strong Trades Union sense, and critics have been perhaps too willing to insist that the operation of poetry is something magical, to which only their own method of incantation can be applied, or like the growth of a flower, which it would be folly to allow analysis to destroy by digging the roots up and crushing out the juices into the light of day. Critics, as 'barking dogs,' on this view, are of two sorts: those who merely relieve themselves against the flower of beauty, and those, less continent, who afterwards scratch it up. I myself, I must confess, aspire to the second of these classes; unexplained beauty arouses an irritation in me, a sense that this would be a good place to scratch; the reasons that make a line of verse likely to give pleasure, I believe, are like the reasons for anything else; one can reason about them; and while it may be true that the roots of beauty ought not to be violated, it

[10]Charles Darwin (1809–1882), English naturalist.

seems to me very arrogant of the appreciative critic to think that he could do this, if he chose, by a little scratching.

One reason, by the way, that the belief in Pure Sound is plausible seems interesting; it is that people often test it by experiments within their own family of languages. They know, say, a novel-reading amount of French, a public-school amount of Latin, half-forgotten, and a smattering of Italian; they try reading the *Oxford Book of Spanish Verse,* and are impressed by the discovery that they can get a great deal of pleasure out of individual lines without understanding the 'meaning' at all. Now such poetry is in a tradition to which they are accustomed; they know roughly what to look for in the poetry of a Latin language; they know what the syntax connecting one or two large words is likely to be; and they are almost sure to know the root meaning (though not the precise meaning) of the one or two large words. It seems to be true that with this equipment one has a very fair chance of seeing what I may call the 'lyrical point' of one or two lines. This may be an important piece of evidence about the mode of action of poetry, but as far as it concerns Pure Sound one must remember that such people will be pronouncing the lines entirely wrong. (And Vergil[11] remains the most melodious of poets through all the vagaries of official pronunciation.)

Such points would be admitted by most reasonable people, and it may seem an evasion on my part to attack Pure Sound as a defence of the opposite fallacy of Pure Meaning. But the situation about Pure Sound is like that about crude materialism; both beliefs lead a sort of underground existence, and at a low level of organisation have much vitality. Crude materialism is the first rough idea that people tumble into when they are interested in the sciences. In the same way, if you ask people in general about the interpretation of poetry, they are likely to say that it is no use talking because what they like is the sheer beauty of the sound.

The official, and correct, view, I take it, is that 'the sound must be an echo to the sense,' that we do not know what this condition may be, but that if we knew a great deal it could be analysed in detail. Thus

Tendebantque manus ripae ulterioris amore
(*Aeneid,* VI.)

(the stock line to try on the dog) is beautiful because *ulterioris,* the word of their banishment, is long, and so shows that they have been waiting a long time; and because the repeated vowel-sound (itself the moan of hopeless sorrow) in *oris amore* connects the two words as if of their own natures, and makes desire belong necessarily to the unattain-

able. This I think quite true, but it is no use deducing from it Tennyson's[12] simple and laborious cult of onomatopoeia. Once you abandon the idea that sounds are valuable in themselves you are thrown far towards the other extreme; you must say that the sounds are valuable because they suggest incidental connections of meaning. If this be true, one can do a great deal to make poetry intelligible by discussing the variety of resultant meanings, without committing oneself very deeply as to how they have been suggested by the sounds.

In claiming so much for analysis I shall seem to be aligning myself with the 'scientific' mode of literary criticism, with 'psychological' explanations of everything, and columns of a reader's sensitivity-coefficients. There is coming into existence a sort of party-system among critics; those critics will soon be considered mere shufflers who are not either only interested in Truth or only interested in Beauty; and Goodness, the third member of that indissoluble trinity, has somehow got attached only to Truth, so that aesthetes are expected to profess a playful indifference to the principles on which they in fact (one is to assume) order their own lives. It is odd, and I think harmful, that this *fin-de-siècle* squabble is still going on. Somewhere in the eighties of the last century the idea got about that Physics, and those sciences that might be conceived as derivatives of Physics, held a monopoly of Reason; aesthetes had therefore to eschew Reason. Now there are serious difficulties about applying the scientific view of truth to the arts; I shall attempt to restate them in my last chapter. But the belief that Reason can be applied to the arts is as old as criticism, and fundamental to it; there is no more materialism about it than there is about Aristotle. And if one is to be forced to take sides, as a matter of mere personal venom, I must confess I find the crudity and latent fallacy of a psychologist discussing verses that he does not enjoy less disagreeable than the blurred and tasteless refusal to make statements of an aesthete who conceives himself to be only interested in Taste.

Johnson's[13] remarks about the correspondence theory are not to be despised, particularly in the 92nd *Rambler:*

> There is nothing in the art of versifying so much exposed to the power of imagination as the accommodation of the sound to the sense. It is scarcely to be doubted that on many occasions we make the music that we imagine ourselves to hear, that we modulate the poem by our own disposition, and ascribe to the numbers the effects of the sense.

---

[11] Publius Virgilius Maro (17–19 B.C.), Roman poet.

[12] Alfred Lord Tennyson (1809–1992), English poet.
[13] Johnson (above, page 357).

But on the other hand:

> The measure of time in pronouncing may be varied so as very strongly to represent, not only the modes of external motion, but the quick or slow succession of ideas, and consequently the passions of the mind.

His examples certainly show very clearly that there is no *single* mode of correspondence; that very similar devices of sound may correspond effectively to very different meanings. And often enough in Milton, for instance, it is the opposite of onomatopoeia which is employed; thus in the lines about Vulcan—

> thrown by angry Jove
> Sheer o'er the crystal battlements; from morn
> To noon he fell, from noon to dewy eve,
> A summer's day; and with the setting sun
> Dropped from the zenith—[14]

Milton is extremely cool about the matter; one is made to sit with him pleasantly in the shade, all day long, needing no further satisfaction; it is delightfully soothing to feel that the devil is all the time falling faster and faster. But this is only to say that a sound effect must be interpreted. I think myself its most important mode of action is to connect two words by similarity of sound so that you are made to think of their possible connections.

Another of Johnson's remarks brings up some questions which deserve mention:

> Dionysius himself tells us, that the sound of Homer's verses sometimes exhibits the idea of corporal bulk: is not this a discovery nearly approaching to that of the blind man, who, after long enquiry into the nature of the scarlet colour, found that it represented nothing so much as the clangour of a trumpet?

The blind man seems to have anticipated Miss Sitwell,[15] who has actually used this comparison, I think very justly. She also writes

> The light is braying like an ass,

which of course depends for its effect on the whole scene described. In such cases, apprehension in terms of one of the senses is described in terms of, or compared with, one of the others; this has been called synaesthesia, and is clearly sometimes effective. It throws back the reader upon the undifferentiated affective states which are all that such sensations have in common; perhaps recalls him to an infantile state before they had been distinguished from one another; and may actually induce a sort of rudimentary disorder into his modes of sensation (so that the 'images' of the visualiser are transformed sounds) like those due to migraine or epilepsy or drugs like mescal. Mescal-eaters have just that impression common among readers of 'pure' poetry, that they are seeing very delightful but quite new colours, or knowing something which would be very important and interesting if they could make out just what it was. But how such a disturbance can be of serious importance to a reader of poetry it is not easy to see; or how one is to be sure when it is occurring. Often it is no more than a device for insisting on ambiguities of the first type; the main comparison is neither true nor false, and one is thrown back on a series of possible associations, as to the social setting in which these sensations would be expected, or the mood in which they would be sought out. Miss Sitwell seemed often to use the device rather as a flag of defiance, to insist that the main meaning is not what she valued, and the reader must put himself into a poetic or receptive frame of mind. ('These two things are alike in that, for quite different reasons, they harmonise with my mood.') But in a way this is only to push the notion of correspondence further back; how do these sensations come to seem proper to their social setting or their mood? Poe often seems excited about colours in a way that reminds one of people's reports from mescal, but then it is a Mexican drug and he had probably tried it; one cannot deduce anything very profound about poetry from that. And Swinburne[16] often uses devices that seem to demand synaesthesia;

> Thy voice is an odour that fades in a flame,

and suchlike; but that is only part of his diffused use of grammar, by which several precise conceits can be dissolved into a vagueness; it would probably be a misreading here to confuse the modes of sensation. Nor, so far as I can see, is his use of the device at all similar to that made of it by Miss Sitwell.

Of course, when a poet is describing paintings, as Spenser[17] does so often, the colours mentioned are supposed to act on one as they would do in a painting. Now, it is natu-

---

[14] John Milton (1608–1674), *Paradise Lost* I, 741–45.
[15] Edith Sitwell (1887–1964), English poet.
[16] Algernon Charles Swinburne (1837–1909), English poet and critic.
[17] Edmund Spenser (c. 1552–1599), English poet.

rally harder to analyse the visual arts than poetry, because their modes of satisfaction are further removed from the verbal system on which the discursive intelligence usually supports itself. In any case, I am not competent to do such a thing and shall not attempt it here; I mention this mysterious matter as a way in which poetry might be taking effect, but which I shall assume I can ignore. And it seems worth uttering the pious hope that such effects do not really depend on an obscure physiological perversion, which could be exploited separately, so as to 'deceive'; but that there is a field for analysis in the way the paintings admired by a particular school of poets are assumed as elements of sensibility, and referred to covertly, in their poetry.

So the *discovery of the blind man* may have its importance, but we must now turn to what *Dionysius himself said,* which may be very important indeed. I mentioned a moment ago the theory that language is fundamentally a system of gestures with the tongue; there is no doubt that, once the advocate of Pure Sound has admitted that sound has *some* connection with meaning, Sir Richard Paget's[18] method of interpretation gives him a great deal of rational support. Every one feels that, quite apart from words like 'pop,' which are like their meaning, there are words like 'wee,' which are fitted to their meaning; the Paget theory would explain this (taking only the vowel, for this brief example) by saying that while 'huge' moves the tongue back from the teeth so as to make as large a space as it can, 'wee' moves the tongue near to the teeth so as to leave as small a space as it can. In this way, not the sound itself, but our experience of the way it is produced, does, in fact, continually *exhibit the idea of corporal bulk,* which is just what Johnson thought impossible. All the sounds may be reduced to gestures in this way, more or less fancifully; they all, then, carry some suggestion of size, or shape, or movement, or pressure, up, down, forward, or backward, and, in themselves, that is all they can convey. This theory would have a peculiar charm for the materialists who wanted to explain everything in terms of Euclid and Newton; it offers a sort of guarantee that the explanation will be a picture on the blackboard. It is rather bad luck that it should be developed so late, when the faith even of physicists in pictures on the blackboard is not what it was, but that it explains *some* part of the effect of language it would be hard to deny.

Evidently there is here another field for the future analysis of poetry; when it becomes possible to list the root notions that the words must by their own nature be suggesting, it will be possible and profitable to discuss in some de-

tail how far their sound is an echo to their sense. But such a process will always be subject to curious limitations;

> . . . owing to the comparative paucity of different mouth-gestures, each mouth-gesture—which produces its own particular sound or root word—has to stand for a considerable number of hand- (or other bodily) gestures; to put it in another way, each root word is naturally liable to bear many different meanings. . . . One other point may be noted; the same mouth-gesture may be naturally construed in several different ways. Thus, the movement of tongue or lips may represent a pantomimic movement, symbolising a real movement, or a spatial relation of some kind, *e.g.* above, below, around, *or* it may represent a shape of some kind drawn in outline. Finally, any of these meanings may be used figuratively instead of concretely.
>
> (Sir RICHARD PAGET, *Human Speech.*)

Apart, then, from the ambiguities in the fully-developed language, such as I propose to consider, one would have also to consider the ambiguities (of the same sort, but entirely different in their details) which are always latent in the fundamental symbolism of the sound.

This suggests that the process of analysing the effect of a poem, not indeed completely, but sufficiently to be any use, must be one of altogether impossible complexity; that one must instead give up all hope of doing such a thing, and fall back on a doctrinaire irrationalism. It is true that no explanation can be adequate, but, on the other hand, any one valid reason that can be found is worth giving; the more one understands one's own reactions the less one is at their mercy.

Thus it seems to be fairly true, as a matter of introspection, that one judges the quality of a poem by something felt as 'sound' and something felt as 'rhythm,' but there are no necessary deductions from this fact, and it is liable to be misleading. One might use a spatial metaphor and a tautology to make it seem less important; 'the sound of words does not enter that part of the mind where it is effective, except in so far as the words take effect as words.' What this 'taking effect' may be like I shall try to discuss in my last chapter.

It has been deduced from the belief in Pure Sound that the resultant meaning of the words need not be known, that it is enough to know the meaning of the words in isolation and enough of their syntax to read them aloud rightly. In a degree this is often true, but it is better to regard this state of limited knowledge as a complicated state of indecision which involves much estimating of probabilities, and is less

---

[18]Richard Paget (b. 1869), English language scholar.

ignorance than an ordered suspension of judgment. Secondly, and more seriously, it has been deduced from this belief that you are liable to destroy the poem if its meaning is discovered, that it is important to preserve one's innocence about the meaning of verses, that one must use sensibility, and as little intelligence as possible. This, also, is often true, but I take a moral line here, and say it is true only of bad poetry. People suspect analysis, often rightly, as the refuge of the emotionally sterile, but that is only to say that analysis is often done badly. In so far as such a destruction occurs because you have used your intelligence it must be accepted, and you may reasonably expect to become interested in another poem, so that the loss is not permanent, because that is the normal process of learning to appreciate poetry.

As for the belief in Atmosphere, about which I shall now make some inadequate remarks, it may be viewed as a third deduction from the belief in Pure Sound. Critics often say or imply casually that some poetic effect conveys a direct 'physical' quality, something mysteriously intimate, something which it is strange a poet could convey, something like a sensation which is not attached to any one of the senses. This may only be a statement of how they themselves applied their conscious attention when reading the poem; thus a musical chord is a direct sensation, but not therefore unanalysable into its separate notes even at the moment of sensing. It can be either felt or thought; the two things are similar but different; and it requires practice to do both at once. Or the statement might, one cannot deny, mean that there has been some confusion of the senses. But it may mean something more important, involving a distinction between 'sensation' and 'feeling'; that what the poet has conveyed is no assembly of grammatical meanings, capable of analysis, but a 'mood,' an 'atmosphere,' a 'personality,' an attitude to life, an undifferentiated mode of being.

Probably it is in this way, as a sort of taste in the head, that one remembers one's own past experiences, including the experience of reading a particular poet. Probably, again, this mode of apprehension is connected with the condition of the whole body, and is as near as one can get to an immediate self-knowledge. You may say, then, that any grammatical analysis of poetry, since it must ignore atmosphere, is trivial; that atmosphere is conveyed in some unknown and fundamental way as a by-product of meaning; that analysis cannot hope to do anything but ignore it; and that criticism can only state that it is there.

This belief may in part explain the badness of much nineteenth-century poetry, and how it came to be written by critically sensitive people. They admired the poetry of previous generations, very rightly, for the taste it left in the head, and, failing to realise that the process of putting such a taste into a reader's head involves a great deal of work which does not feel like a taste in the head while it is being done, attempting, therefore, to conceive a taste in the head and put it straight on to their paper, they produced tastes in the head which were in fact blurred, complacent, and unpleasing. But to say that the consequences of a critical formula have been unfortunate is not to say that it is untrue or even unusable; it is very necessary for a critic to remember about the atmosphere, chiefly because he must concentrate on the whole of the poem he is talking about rather than on the particular things that he can find to say.

In wishing to apply verbal analysis to poetry the position of the critic is like that of the scientist wishing to apply determinism to the world. It may not be valid everywhere; though it be valid everywhere it may not explain everything; but in so far as he is to do any work he must assume it is valid where he is working, and will explain what he is trying to explain. I assume, therefore, that the 'atmosphere' is the consciousness of what is implied by the meaning, and I believe that this assumption is profitable in many more cases than one would suppose.

I shall try to recommend this opinion by giving what seems to me a striking example; a case, that is, where an affective state is conveyed particularly vividly by devices of particular irrelevance. Macbeth, in these famous lines, may easily seem to be doing something physiological and odd, something outside the normal use of words. It is when he is spurring on his jaded hatred to the murder of Banquo and Fleance.

> Come, seeling Night,
> Skarfe up the tender Eye of pitiful Day
> And with thy bloddie and invisible Hand
> Cancel and teare to pieces that great Bond
> That keepes me pale.
> *Light thickens, and the Crow*
> *Makes Wing to th' Rookie Wood.*
> Good things of Day begin to droope, and drowse,
> While Night's black Agents to their Prey's doe rowse,
> Thou marvell'st at my words, but hold thee still;
> Things bad begun, make strong themselves by ill:
> So prythee go with me.
>
> (III. ii. 50.)

The condition of his skin (By the pricking of my thumbs Something wicked this way comes), the sense of being withdrawn far within his own flesh (like an old lecher, a small fire at his heart, all the rest on's body cold), the sense that the affair is prosaic, it need not be mentioned, and yet an occasional squawking of the nerves (Hobbididance croaks in Tom's belly), in short the whole frame of body, as I read the lines, is lit up and imposed upon the reader, from which Macbeth lashes his exhausted energies into a new, into the accustomed, readiness for murder.

I have tried by these almost irrelevant quotations to show how much work the reader of Shakespeare is prepared to do for him, how one is helped by the rest of his work to put a great deal into any part of it, but this seems to explain very little. Various similar sound effects or associations may be noted; there is a suggestion of witches' broth, or curdling blood, about *thickens,* which the vowel sound of *light,* coming next to it, with the movement of stirring treacle, and the cluck of the k-sounds, intensify; a suggestion, too, of harsh, limpid echo, and, under careful feet of poachers, an abrupt crackling of sticks. The vowel sounds at the end make an increasing darkness as the *crow* goes forward. But, after all, one would be very surprised if two people got the same result from putting a sound-effect into words in this way.

It is safer to point out that *rooks* were, in any case, creatures of foreboding:

Augurs, and understood Relations, have
By Magot-Pyes, and Choughes, and Rookes, brought forth
The secret'st man of Blood;

(III. iv. 125.)

that Macbeth looked out of the window because Banquo was to be killed soon after dusk, so he wanted to know how the time was going; and that a dramatic situation is always heightened by breaking off the dialogue to look out of the window, especially if some kind of Pathetic Fallacy[19] is to be observed outside. But to notice this particular pathetic fallacy you must withdraw yourself from the apprehension of its effect, and be ready to notice irrelevant points which may act as a clue. I believe it is that the peaceful solitary *crow,* moving towards bed and the other crows, is made unnaturally like Macbeth and a murderer who is coming against them; this is suggested by the next lines, which do not say whether the *crow* is one of the *good things of day* or one of *night's black agents* (it is, at any rate, *black*), by the eerie way that *light* itself is *thickening,* as a man turns against men, a *crow* against *crows,* perhaps by the portentous way a *crow's* voice will carry at such a time, and by the sharpness of its wings against the even glow of a sky after sundown; but mainly, I think, by the use of the two words *rook* and *crow.*

Rooks live in a crowd and are mainly vegetarian; *crow* may be either another name for a *rook,* especially when seen alone, or it may mean the solitary Carrion crow. This subdued pun is made to imply here that Macbeth, looking out of the window, is trying to see himself as a murderer, and can only see himself as in the position of the *crow;* that his *day* of power, now, is closing; that he has to distinguish himself from the other *rooks* by a difference of name, *rook-crow,* like the kingly title, only; that he is anxious, at bottom, to be at one with the other *rooks,* not to murder them; that he can no longer, or that he may yet, be united with the rookery; and that he is murdering Banquo in a forlorn attempt to obtain peace of mind.[20]

Interest in 'atmospheres' is a critical attitude designed for, and particularly suited to, the poets of the nineteenth century; this may tell us something about them, and in part explain why they are so little ambiguous in the sense with which I am concerned. For a variety of reasons, they found themselves living in an intellectual framework with which it was very difficult to write poetry, in which poetry was rather improper, or was irrelevant to business, especially the business of becoming Fit to Survive, or was an indulgence of one's lower nature in beliefs the scientists knew were untrue. On the other hand, they had a large public which was as anxious to escape from this intellectual framework, on holiday, as they were themselves. Almost all of them, therefore, exploited a sort of tap-root into the world of their childhood, where they were able to conceive things poetically, and whatever they might be writing about they would suck up from this limited and perverted world an unvarying sap which was their poetical inspiration. Mr. Harold Nicolson[21] has written excellently about Swinburne's fixation on to the excitements of his early reading and experience, and about the unique position in the life of Tennyson occupied by the moaning of cold wind round a child frightened for its identity upon the fens. Wordsworth frankly had no inspiration other than his use, when a boy, of the mountains as a totem or father-substitute, and Byron only at the end of his life, in the first cantos of *Don Juan* in particular, escaped from the infantile incest-fixation upon his sister which was till then all that he had got to say. As for Keats's desire for death and his mother, it has become a byword among the learned. Shelley, perhaps, does not strike one as keeping so sharp a distinction between the world he considered real and

---

[19] A term coined by the English art critic John Ruskin (1819–1900) to mean a figure of speech that attributes human feelings to inanimate things.

[20] [Empson] It was stupid of me to present this example as a sort of test case, with a tidy solution drawn from the names of birds. Obviously the passage is still impressive if you have no opinions at all about the difference between crows and rooks. But it is at least a good example of a heavy Atmosphere, and I don't think my treatment of it was wrong as far as it went.

[21] Harold Nicolson (1886–1968), English writer.

the world from which he wrote poetry, but this did not in his case improve either of them; while Browning and Meredith,[22] who did write from the world they lived in, affect me as novel-writers of merit with no lyrical inspiration at all. Coleridge, it is true, relied on opium rather than the nursery. But of all these men an imposed excitement, a sense of uncaused warmth, achievement, gratification, a sense of hugging to oneself a private dream-world, is the main interest and material.[23]

In that age, too, began the doubt as to whether this man or that was 'grown-up,' which has ever since occupied so deeply the minds of those interested in their friends. Macaulay complains somewhere that in his day a man was sure to be accused of a child-mind if no doubt could be cast 'either on the ability of his intelligence or the innocence of his character'; now nobody seems to have said this in the eighteenth century. Before the Romantic Revival the possibilities of not growing up had never been exploited so far as to become a subject for popular anxiety.

Of course, these pat little theories are ridiculously simple; fantasy gratifications and a protective attitude towards one's inner life are in some degree essential for the production of poetry, and I have no wish to pretend the Romantics were not great poets. But I think this will be admitted, that they were making a use of language very different from that of their predecessors; imagine Shakespeare or Pope keeping a tap-root in this way. One might expect, then, that they would not need to use ambiguities of the kind I shall consider to give vivacity to their language, or even ambiguities with which the student of language, as such, is concerned; that the mode of approach to them should be psychological rather than grammatical, and that their distortions of meaning will belong to darker regions of the mind.

This introduction has grown too long and too portentous; it is time I settled down to the little I can do in this chapter, which is to list a few examples of ambiguity of the first type. Many of the preceding paragraphs are designed merely for defence; if it is said that the verbal analyst is a crude irrelevant fellow who should be thinking about the atmosphere, the reply is that though there may be an atmosphere to which analysis is irrelevant, it is not necessarily anything very respectable.

I have already considered the comparison of two things which does not say in virtue of what they are to be com-

pared. Of the same sort, though less common, is the ornamental use of false antithesis, which places words as if in opposition to one another without saying in virtue of what they are to be opposed. Cases in which several ways of opposing them are implied will be found in my later chapters as examples of more advanced ambiguity; but the device may be used to deny such an antithesis altogether. There is a rather trivial example of this in Peacock's[24] *War Song:*

> We there, in strife bewildring,
>   Spitt blood enough to swim in;
> We orphaned many children
>   And widowed many women.
> The eagles and the ravens
>   We glutted with our foemen;
> The heroes and the cravens,
>   The spearmen and the bowmen.

In the last two lines he is not concerned to be thinking, to decide something or convince somebody; he makes a cradle and rocks himself in it; it is the tone of a man imagining himself in a mood wholly alien to him, and looking round with an amused complacent absence of reflection. The lines also give finality in that the impulse is shown to be dying away; some reflection has been implied on the difference between *heroes* and *cravens,* on their equal deaths, and on the relations between *eagles* and *heroes, ravens* and *cravens,* but the irrelevant calm of the last line says 'these distinctions may be made at other times, but they are irrelevant to our slaughter and the reaction to it of Nature,' he proceeds to another merely technical way of separating the dead into classes, and by the failure of the antithesis shows he is merely thinking of them as a huge pile.

> How loved, how honoured once, avails thee not,
> To whom related, or by whom begot;
> A heap of dust is all remains of thee;
> 'Tis all thou art, and all the proud shall be.
>   (POPE, *Unfortunate Lady.*)[25]

The two parts of the second line make a claim to be alternatives which is not obviously justified, and this I think implies a good deal. If the antithesis is to be serious, *or* must mean 'one of her relations was grand but her father was humble,' or the other way about; thus one would take *how* to mean 'whether much or little' (it could mean 'though you were so

---

[22] Wordsworth (above, page 481), George Gordon Lord Byron (1788–1824), John Keats (above, page 534), Shelley (above, page 537), English poets of the Romantic age.

[23] [Empson] Byron I understand did not meet his half-sister at all until he was grown up. It seems no good trying to improve this paragraph, and I still think that the last sentence summing it up is sufficiently true.

[24] Thomas Love Peacock (1785–1866), English novelist and poet.

[25] Pope (above, page 297).

greatly'), and the last line to contrast her with the *proud,* so as to imply that she is humble (it could unite her with the *proud,* and deduce the death of all of them from the death of one). This obscurity is part of the 'Gothic' atmosphere that Pope wanted: 'her birth was high, but there was a mysterious stain on it'; or 'though you might not think it, her birth was high'; or 'her birth was high, but not higher than births to which I am accustomed.' Here, however, the false antithesis is finding another use, to convey the attitude of Pope to the subject. 'How simple, how irrelevant to the merits of the unfortunate lady, are such relationships; everybody has had both a relation and a father; how little I can admire the arrogance of great families on this point; how little, too, the snobbery of my reader, who is unlikely to belong to a great family; to how many people this subject would be extremely fruitful of antithesis; how little fruitful of antithesis it seems to an independent soul like mine.' What is important about such devices is that they leave it to the reader vaguely to invent something, and make him leave it at the back of his mind.

Not unlike the use of a comparison which does not say in virtue of what the two things are to be compared is the use of a comparative adjective which does not say what its noun is to be compared with; since all adjectives are in a sense comparative, this source of ambiguity is a sufficiently general one. In particular, it is the chief source of euphuistic conceits and the paradoxes cultivated in the 'nineties, which give a noun two contradictory adjectives and leave it to the reader to see how the adjectives are used.[26] Examples of this sort are too well known, and are generally thought too trivial, to be worth quoting. I shall give an example from one of Mr. Waley's[27] Chinese translations, to insist upon the profundity of feeling which such a device may enshrine.

Swiftly the years, beyond recall.
Solemn the stillness of this spring morning.

The human mind has two main scales on which to measure time. The large one takes the length of a human life as its unit, so that there is nothing to be done about life, it is of an animal dignity and simplicity, and must be regarded from a peaceable and fatalistic point of view. The small one takes as its unit the conscious moment, and it is from this that you consider the neighbouring space, an activity of the will, delicacies of social tone, and your personality. The scales are

so far apart as almost to give the effect of defining two dimensions; they do not come into contact because what is too large to be conceived by the one is still too small to be conceived by the other. Thus, taking the units as a century and the quarter of a second, their ratio is ten to the tenth and their mean is the standard working day; or taking the smaller one as five minutes, their mean is the whole of summer. The repose and self-command given by the use of the first are contrasted with the speed at which it shows the years to be passing from you, and therefore with the fear of death; the fever and multiplicity of life, as known by the use of the second, are contrasted with the calm of the external space of which it gives consciousness, with the absolute or extra-temporal value attached to the brief moments of self-knowledge with which it is concerned, and with a sense of security in that it makes death so far off.

Both these time-scales and their contrasts are included by these two lines in a single act of apprehension, because of the words *swift* and *still.* Being contradictory as they stand, they demand to be conceived in different ways; we are enabled, therefore, to meet the open skies with an answering stability of self-knowledge; to meet the brevity of human life with an ironical sense that it is morning and springtime, that there is a whole summer before winter, a whole day before night.

I call *swift* and *still* here ambiguous, though each is meant to be referred to one particular time-scale, because between them they put two time-scales into the reader's mind in a single act of apprehension. But these scales, being both present, are in some degree used for each adjective, so that the words are ambiguous in a more direct sense; the *years* of a man's life seem *swift* even on the small scale, like the mist from the mountains which 'gathers a moment, then scatters'; the *morning* seems *still* even on the large scale, so that this moment is apocalyptic and a type of heaven.

Lacking rhyme, metre, and any overt device such as comparison, these lines are what we should normally call poetry only by virtue of their compactness; two statements are made as if they were connected, and the reader is forced to consider their relations for himself. The reason why these facts should have been selected for a poem is left for him to invent; he will invent a variety of reasons and order them in his own mind. This, I think, is the essential fact about the poetical use of language.

Among metaphors effective from several points of view one may include, by no great extension, those metaphors which are partly recognised as such and partly received simply as words in their acquired sense. All languages are composed of dead metaphors as the soil of corpses, but English is perhaps uniquely full of metaphors of this sort, which are not dead but sleeping, and, while

---

[26] [Empson] Such a trick has usually one meaning which is the answer of the puzzle, but while you are puzzling the words have possible alternative meanings, and even to those who see the answers at once the alternatives are in a way present as being denied. They may appear as the views of commonplace people, who are thereby snubbed; but they can also make a real ambiguity when the denial is not felt to be complete.

[27] Arthur Waley (1889–1966), English translator.

making a direct statement, colour it with an implied comparison. The school rule against mixed metaphor, which in itself is so powerful a weapon, is largely necessary because of the presence of these sleepers, who must be treated with respect; they are harder to use than either plain word or metaphor because if you mix them you must show you are conscious of their meaning, and are not merely being insensitive to the possibilities of the language.

> Beauty is but a flower
> Which wrinkles will devour.
> Brightness falls from the air.
> Queens have died young and fair.
> Dust hath closed Helen's eye.
> I am sick, I must die.
>   Lord, have mercy upon us.
>   (NASH, *Summer's Last Will and Testament*.)[28]

I call it a subdued metaphor here that *devour* should mean 'remove' or 'replace,' with no more than an overtone of cruelty and the unnatural. This may seem very different from the less evident subdued metaphor in the derivation of a word like 'apprehension,' say, but a reader may ignore the consequences even of so evident a metaphor as *devour*. If you go into the metaphor it may make Time the *edax rerum,* and wrinkles only time's tooth-marks; more probably it compares long curving wrinkles on the face to rodent ulcers, caterpillars on petals, and the worms that are to gnaw it in the grave. Of these, the caterpillar (from *flower*) are what the comparison insists upon, but the Elizabethan imagination would let slip no chance of airing its miraculous corpse-worm.

On the other hand.

Brightness falls from the air

is an example of ambiguity by vagueness, such as was used to excess by the Pre-Raphaelites. Evidently there are a variety of things the line may be about. The sun and moon pass under the earth after their period of shining, and there are stars falling at odd times; Icarus and the prey of hawks, having soared upwards towards heaven, *fall* exhausted or dead; the glittering turning things the sixteenth century put on the top of a building may have *fallen* too often. In another sense, hawks, lightning, and meteorites *fall* flashing from heaven upon their prey. Taking *brightness* as abstract, not as meaning something bright, it is as a benefit that light *falls,* diffusely reflected, from the sky. In so far as the sky is brighter than the earth (especially at twilight), brightness is

natural to it; in so far as the earth may be bright when the clouds are dark, *brightness falls* from the sky to the earth when there is a threat of thunder. 'All is unsafe, even the heavens are not sure of their brightness,' or 'the qualities in man that deserve respect are not natural to him but brief gifts from God; they fall like manna, and melt as soon.' One may extract, too, from the oppression in the notion of thunder the idea that now, 'in time of pestilence,' the generosity of Nature is mysteriously interrupted; even at the scene of brilliant ecclesiastical festivity for which the poem was written there is a taint of darkness in the very *air.*

It is proper to mention a rather cynical theory that Nash wrote or meant 'hair'; still, though less imaginative, this is very adequate; oddly enough (it is electricity and the mysterious vitality of youth which have *fallen* from the *hair*) carries much the same suggestion as the other version; and gives the relief of a single direct meaning. Elizabethan pronunciation was very little troubled by snobbery, and it is conceivable that Nash meant both words to take effect in some way. Now that all this fuss has been made about aitches it is impossible to imagine what such a line would sound like.

For a final meaning of this line one must consider the line which follows it; there is another case of poetry by juxtaposition. In

Dust hath closed Helen's eye

one must think of Helen in part as an undecaying corpse or a statue; it is *dust* from outside which settles on her eyelids, and shows that it is long since they have been opened; only in the background, as a truth which could not otherwise be faced, is it suggested that the *dust* is generated from her own corruption. As a result of this ambiguity, the line imposes on *brightness* a further and more terrible comparison; on the one hand, it is the *bright* motes dancing in sunbeams, which *fall* and become dust which is dirty and infectious; on the other, the lightness, gaiety, and activity of humanity, which shall come to *dust* in the grave.

When a word is selected as a 'vivid detail,' as particular for general, a reader may suspect alternative reasons why it has been selected; indeed the author might find it hard to say. When there are several such words there may be alternative ways of viewing them in order of importance.

> Pan is our All, by him we breathe, we live,
> We move, we are; . . .
> But when he frowns, the sheep, alas,
> The shepherds wither, and the grass.
>   (BEN JONSON, *Pan's Anniversary*.)[29]

---

[28] Thomas Nashe (1567–1601), English dramatist.

[29] Ben Jonson (c. 1573–1637), English dramatist and poet.

Alas, the word explaining which of the items in this list we are to take most seriously, belongs to the *sheep* by proximity and the break in the line, to the *grass* by rhyming with it, and to the *shepherds,* humble though they may be, by the processes of human judgment; so that all three are given due attention, and the balance of the verse is maintained. The Biblical suggestions of *grass* as symbolic of the life of man ('in the mornings it is green and groweth up; in the evening it is cut down, dried up, and withered') add to the solemnity; or from another point of view make the passage absurdly blasphemous, because Pan here is James I. The grace, the pathos, the 'sheer song' of the couplet is given by an enforced subtlety of intonation, from the difficulty of saying it so as to bring out all the implications.

This last consideration is important, because it gives some hint as to why these devices belong to poetry rather than to prose, or indeed why poetry seems different from prose. A metrical scheme imposes a sort of intensity of interpretation upon the grammar, which makes it fruitful even when there is no 'song.'

> I want to know a butcher paints,
> A baker rhymes for his pursuit,
> Candlestick-maker, much acquaints
> His soul with song, or, haply mute,
> Blows out his brains upon the flute.   (BROWNING.)

'I want to know that the whole class of butchers paints,' or 'I want to know that some one butcher paints,' or 'I want to know personally a butcher who paints'; any of these may be taken as the meaning, and their resultant is something like, 'I want to know that a member of the class of butchers is moderately likely to be a man who paints, or at any rate that he can do so if he wishes.' The demands of metre allow the poet to say something which is not normal colloquial English, so that the reader thinks of the various colloquial forms which are near to it, and puts them together; weighting their probabilities in proportion to their nearness. It is for such reasons as this that poetry can be more compact, while seeming to be less precise, than prose.

It is for these reasons, too, among others, that an insensitivity in a poet to the contemporary style of speaking, into which he has been trained to concentrate his powers of apprehension, is so disastrous, can be noticed so quickly, and produces that curious thinness or blurring of texture one finds in William Morris.[30] And that is why the practice of putting single words into italics for emphasis (again the Victorians are guilty) is so vulgar; a well-constructed sentence

should be able to carry a stress on any of its words and should show in itself how these stresses are to be compounded. Both in prose and poetry, it is the impression that implications of this sort have been handled with more judgment than you yourself realise, that with this language as text innumerable further meanings, which you do not know, could be deduced, that forces you to feel respect for a style.

Also I have considered the 'implications' of sentences so far mainly as what they take for granted, as what must already be in mind if they are to be suitable. The stock example of this is, 'Have you stopped beating your wife?', which claims to know already that it has been your habit to do so. A complementary sort of implication may be defined: what must *not* be in mind if the sentence is to be suitable, what it leaves vague, or is not thinking about, or does not feel. The negative here assumes you might expect this particular thing to be in mind, because otherwise you would not have thought of it as an implication. You might think it lessened the importance of a negative implication that one is only conscious of it if its assumption is unjustified; but the mind is a destroyer; any assumption may chance to be questioned; and most people are conscious that they, therefore, can to some extent impose what they assume. In speaking of 'implications' one thinks as much of negative as of positive ones, indeed it would often be difficult to make the distinction. One would notice, to discover a negative implication, the degree to which stock phrases were used which did not fit the situation very closely, as if it did not need to be, or could not safely be, defined further, or the degree to which a form of words had been selected which only said so much and no more. For such reasons as these, private letters often seem most exquisitely adapted to their setting when written most casually; it is exactly the extent to which their language is careless, the proportion of carelessness they give to the different matters in hand, which is so precise. Similarly in conversation this more refined sort of implication is very highly developed. It is comparable to the use of facial muscles, intended for different or immensely cruder uses (such as the muscles round the eyes designed to prevent them from being gorged with blood when you scream), to convey fine shades of 'expression.' They are comparable, again, in that there are fewer verbal devices, as there are fewer ways of moving facial muscles, than there are sorts of feeling to convey by them; this gives an inherent opportunity for ambiguity which is regularly exploited. The cult of careless ease in literature, where one is less sure of the audience, is more treacherous, but its advantages and dangers are of the same kind.

It is because of the wealth of implication which must be carried by sentences in poetry, because they must start from scratch and put the reader in possession of the entire

---

[30] William Morris (1834–1896), English poet and designer.

attitude they assume, that the notion of 'sincerity' is important, and that it is so hard to imitate a style. A poem can be cross-questioned, and one must know, to feel sure that it will survive the process with undiminished reputation, that for a wide variety of possible assumptions in the reader the assumptions of the writer will seem reasonable enough to be adopted; and further that, for a hierarchy of degrees of care in the reader, the assumptions discovered in the writer will not show themselves to be self-conflicting in a way which to such a reader will seem absurd.

The reason, then, that ambiguity is more elaborate in poetry than in prose, other than the fact that the reader is trained to expect it, seems to be that the presence of metre and rhyme, admittedly irrelevant to the straightforward process of conveying a statement, makes it seem sensible to diverge from the colloquial order of statement, and so imply several colloquial orders from which the statement has diverged. But rhythm is a powerful weapon in itself, which needs to be considered separately; I have discussed negative implications here by way of a sidelong approach to it.

Rhythm allows one, by playing off the possible prose rhythms against the super-imposed verse rhythms, to combine a variety of statements in one order. Its direct effect seems a matter for physiology; in particular, a rhythmic beat taken faster than the pulse seems controllable, exhilarating, and not to demand intimate sympathy; a rhythmic beat almost synchronous with the pulse seems sincere and to demand intimate sympathy; while a rhythmic beat slower than the pulse, like a funeral bell, seems portentous and uncontrollable. But even if it is a simple rhythm which is apprehended, rather than something much more complex which involves the meaning, still it is the meaning which must show at what pace the verse is to be read. And, of course, it is not one rhythmical beat, like a bell tolling, which is apprehended; or if it is (since the ear insists on imposing rhythms, and cocaine can make one stroke into a series), then the word should be used in the plural; the foot, the grammatical clause, the line, the sentence, the stanza or paragraph, and the whole canto or subject-heading, are all rhythmical units; the total rhythmical line which results from them must be regarded as of an immense complexity entirely defined by the meaning; and even then it is the meaning which must imply how it is to be interpreted. So that rhythm is chiefly useful as a means of insisting upon, and then limiting, the possible implications; and though I may seem to be ignoring the rhythm through most of this book, I shall always be using it, so to speak, among the calculations on the margin, as a means of understanding the grammar.

However, one can oppose the use of rhythm to the use of ambiguity, because an interest in rhythm makes a poet long-winded, and ambiguity is a phenomenon of compression. Thus it is seldom that one finds relevant ambiguities in Spenser or Marlowe,[31] because their method is by a variety of means to sustain a poetic effect for so long that the poetic knot can be spread out at length, and one does not see that the separate uses of a word would be a pun if they were drawn together. When Marlowe brings off his triumphs of simplicity and the delight in rhythm it is often a matter of separating the implications of a sentence and using them at different times.

> MEANDER.   Your majesty shall shortly have your wish
>   And ride in triumph through Persepolis.
>   (*Exeunt all except* TAMBURLANE *and his followers.*)
> TAMBURLANE.   And ride in triumph through Persepolis.
>   Is it not brave to be a king, Techelles,
>   Usumcasane and Theridamas,
>   Is it not passing brave to be a king,
>   And ride in triumph through Persepolis?

Tamburlane can only use the same words again and again, because his mind is glutted with astonishment at them; Marlowe's idea of the heroic soul has extreme simplicity and unbounded appetite, so that after however great an expression of his desire for glory, after one subordinate clause has opened out of another, with unalterable energy, it can still roar at the close with the same directness as in its opening line. Thus the lack of variety in his rhythm is in itself a device of some rhythmical subtlety. It is for this sort of reason that the same line is repeated here in three tones, of obsequiousness, of astonishment, and of triumph, which Shakespeare could have included in a single line.

> Faustus, these books, thy wit, and our experience,
> Shall make all nations to canonise us.
> As Indian Moors obey their Spanish lords
> So shall the spirits of every element
> Be always serviceable to us three;
> Like lions shall they guard us when we please,
> Like Almain rutters, with their horsemen's staves,
> Or Lapland giants, trotting by our sides;
> Sometimes like women, or unwedded maids,
> Shadowing more beauty in their airy brows
> Than have the white breasts of the Queen of Love:
> From Venice shall they drag huge argosies,
> And from America the golden fleece
> That yearly stuffs old Philip's treasury;
> If learned Faustus will be resolute.

---

[31] Christopher Marlowe (1564–1593), English dramatist.

At first sight the last line is an afterthought expressing anxiety, but when immersed in the style one accepts it as a part of the sentence always intended, that might have been put in between the second line and the third. That a conditional clause should have been held back through all these successive lightnings of poetry, that after their achievement it should still be present with the same conviction and *resolution,* is itself a statement of heroic character. One's total impression of the character of Valdes is obtained by combining these two interpretations. Where so much can be said by the mere order of single mighty lines there is no need for much subtlety of implication within them.

I am considering here such ambiguities of rhythm as act without implying an ambiguity of grammar, or noticeable ambiguity in the use of words. This last example in result belongs to a later chapter, because it implies two different opinions of Valdes and leaves them to be reconciled; so does the following example, because it implies two different sentiments in the author. I put them here for the slightness of the machinery; it is a machinery continually used for ambiguities of the first type, and these examples may be prominent enough to show that it is powerful.

> Aye, look, high heaven and earth ail from their prime
> foundation.
>   All thoughts to rive the heart are there, and all are
> vain;
> Horror and scorn and hate and fear and indignation;
> Oh why did I awake, when shall I sleep again?
>   (A. E. HOUSMAN, *Last Poems.*)[32]

The main rhythm of the third line (the crest of the wave) takes *hate* as its chief stress, and the first three nouns as a group together. *Fear* gives the second emphasis, allowed by the extra foot, *fear and indignation* act as a unit balancing the first three, and by attraction the *fear* meant is seen to be of a dignified kind. But behind the energy and determination of this treatment of the line as a unit, there is a rocking, broken, agitated, and impotent grouping, which takes the first four nouns as two pairs, associates *fear* with *hate* so as to make it weak and snarling, and throws in *indignation* as an isolated and squeaking disapproval.

I have mentioned Spenser, whom no discussion of rhythm can ignore. To show the scale of his rhythm, it may be enough to list some of the ways in which he gave movement to the stanza of the *Faerie Queene;* it is by the delicacy of this movement that he shows his attitude towards his sentences, rather than by devices of implication in the sentences themselves. At the same time, once such an attitude has been fixed, it is more easily described in terms of the meaning of the words than in terms of the meaning of the rhythm; in the next example, from Sidney, I shall use this other mode of approach.

Spenser concentrates the reader's attention on to the movement of his stanza: by the use of archaic words and constructions, so that one is at a safe distance from the exercise of an immediate judgment, by the steady untroubled flow of similar lines, by making no rapid change of sense or feeling, by sustained alliteration, parallel adjectives, and full statement of the accessories of a thought, and by the dreamy repetition of the great stanza perpetually pausing at its close. *Ababbcbcc* is a unit which may be broken up into a variety of metrical forms, and the ways in which it is successively broken up are fitted into enormous patterns. The first quatrain usually gratifies the ear directly and without surprise, and the stanzas may then be classified by the grammatical connections of the crucial fifth line, which must give a soft bump to the dying fall of the first quatrain, keep it in the air, and prevent it from falling apart from the rest of the stanza.

It may complete the sense of the quatrain, for instance, with a couplet, and the stanza will then begin with a larger, more narrative unit, *ababb,* and wander garrulously down a perspective to the alexandrine. Or it may add to the quatrain as by an afterthought, as if with a childish earnestness it made sure of its point without regard to the metre, and one is relieved to find that the metre recovers itself after all. For more energetic or serious statements it will start a new quatrain at the fifth line, with a new sentence; there are then two smaller and tighter, repeatedly didactic, or logically opposed, or historically advancing, units, whose common rhyme serves to insist upon their contrast, which are summed up and reconciled in the final solemnity of the alexandrine. In times of excitement the fifth line will be connected both ways, so as to ignore the two quatrains, and, by flowing straight on down the stanza with an insistence on its unity, show the accumulated energy of some enormous climax; and again, by being connected with neither, it will make the stanza into an unstressed conversational device without overtones of rhythm, picking up stray threads of the story with almost the relief of prose. It would be interesting to take one of the vast famous passages of the work and show how these devices are fitted together into larger units of rhythm, but having said that every use of the stanza includes all these uses in the reader's apprehension of it I may have said enough to show the sort of methods Spenser had under his control; why it was not necessary for him to concentrate on the lightning flashes of ambiguity.

The size, the possible variety, and the fixity of this unit give something of the blankness that comes from fixing your

---

[32] A. E. Housman (1859–1936), English poet.

eyes on a bright spot; you have to yield yourself to it very completely to take in the variety of its movement, and, at the same time, there is no need to concentrate the elements of the situation into a judgment as if for action. As a result of this, when there are ambiguities of idea, it is whole civilisations rather than details of the moment which are their elements; he can pour into the even dreamwork of his fairyland Christian, classical, and chivalrous materials with an air, not of ignoring their differences, but of holding all their systems of values floating as if at a distance, so as not to interfere with one another, in the prolonged and diffused energies of his mind.

Nowhere in English literature can this use of diffuseness as an alternative to, or peculiar branch of, ambiguity be seen more clearly than in those lovely sestines of Sidney, which are so curiously foreign to the normal modes or later developments of the language. This time I must do some serious quotation.

STREPHON.   KLAIUS.

STREPHON   You Gote-heard Gods, that love the grassie
    mountaines,
    You nimphes that haunt the springs in pleasant vallies,
    You Satyrs joyd with free and quiet forrests,
    Vouchsafe your silent eares to playning musique,
    Which to my woes gives still an early morning:
    And draws the dolor on till wery evening.

KLAIUS.   O Mercurie, foregoer to the evening,
    O heavenlie huntresse of the savage mountaines,
    O lovelie starre, entitled of the morning,
    While that my voice doth fill the woeful vallies
    Vouchsafe your silent eares to playning musique,
    Which oft hath *Echo* tir'd in secrete forrests.

STREPHON.   I that was once free-burgess of the forrests
    Where shade from Sunne, and sports I sought at
      evening,
    I that was once esteemed for pleasant musique,
    Am banisht now amongst the monstrous mountaines
    Of huge despaire, and foul afflictions vallies,
    Am growne a skrich-owle to myself each morning.

KLAIUS.   I that was once delighted every morning,
    Hunting the wild inhabiters of forrests,
    I that was once the musique of these vallies,
    So darkened am, that all my day is evening,
    Hart-broken so, that mole-hills seem high mountaines,
    And fill the vales with cries in stead of musique.

STREPHON.   Long since alas, my deadly Swannish
    musique

Hath made itself a crier of the morning,
    And hath with wailing strength climbed highest
      mountaines:
    Long since my thoughts more desert be than forrests:
    Long since I see my joyes come to their evening,
    And state throwen down to over-troden vallies.

KLAIUS.   Long since the happie dwellers of these vallies,
    Have praide me leave my strange exclaiming musique,
    Which troubles their dayes worke, and joyes of
      evening:
    Long since I hate the night, more hate the morning:
    Long since my thoughts chase me like beasts in for
      rests,
    And make me wish myself laid under mountaines.

STREPHON.   Me seemes I see the high and stately
    mountaines,
    Transforme themselves to lowe dejected vallies:
    Me seemes I heare in these ill-changed forrests,
    The nightingales doo learne of Owles their musique:
    Me seemes I feele the comfort of the morning
    Turnde to the mortal serene of an evening.

KLAIUS.   Me seemes I see a filthie cloudie evening,
    As soone as Sunne begins to climbe the mountaines:
    Me seemes I feel a noisome scent, the morning
    When I do smell the flowers of these vallies:
    Me seemes I heare, when I doo heare sweet musique,
    The dreadful cries of murdered men in forrests.

STREPHON.   I wish to fire the trees of all these forrests;
    I give the Sunne a last farewell each evening;
    I curse the fiddling finders out of musique:
    With envy doo I hate the lofty mountaines;
    And with despite despise the humble vallies:
    I doo detest night evening, day, and morning.

KLAIUS.   Curse to myself my prayer is, the morning:
    My fire is more, than can be made with forrests;
    My state more base, than are the basest vallies:
    I wish no evenings more to see, each evening;
    Shamed I have myself in sight of mountaines,
    And stoppe mine eares, lest I go mad with musique.

STREPHON.   For she, whose parts maintained a perfect
    musique,
    Whose beauty shin'de more than the blushing morning,
    Who much did pass in state the stately mountaines,
    In straightness past the Cedars of the forrests,
    Hath cast me wretch into eternal evening,
    By taking her two Sunnes from these dark vallies.

KLAIUS.   For she, to whom compared, the Alps are vallies,
    She, whose lest word brings from the spheares their
        musique
    At whose approach the Sunne rose in the evening,
    Who, where she went, bare in her forehead morning,
    Is gone, is gone from these our spoiled forrests,
    Turning to deserts our best pastur'de mountaines.

STREPHON.   These mountaines witness shall, so shall
    these vallies,
KLAIUS.   These forrests eke, made wretched by our
    musique,
STREPHON.   Our morning hymn is this,
KLAIUS.   and song at evening.
                        (SIDNEY, *Arcadia*.)[33]

The poem beats, however rich its orchestration, with a
wailing and immovable monotony, for ever upon the same
doors in vain. *Mountaines, vallies, forrests; musique,
evening, morning;* it is at these words only that Klaius and
Strephon pause in their cries; these words circumscribe their
world; these are the bones of their situation; and in tracing
their lovelorn pastoral tedium through thirteen repetitions,
with something of the aimless multitudinousness of the sea
on a rock, we seem to extract all the meaning possible from
these notions; we are at last, therefore, in possession of all
that might have been implied by them (if we had understood
them) in a single sentence; of all, in fact, that is implied by
them, in the last sentence of the poem. I must glance, to
show this, at the twelve other occasions on which each word
is used.

Mountaines are haunts of Pan for lust and Diana for
chastity, to both of these the lovers appeal; they suggest being shut in, or banishment; impossibility and impotence, or
difficulty and achievement; greatness that may be envied or
may be felt as your own (so as to make you feel helpless, or
feel powerful); they give you the peace, or the despair, of
the grave; they are the distant things behind which the sun
rises and sets, the too near things which shut in your valley;
deserted wastes, and the ample pastures to which you drive
up the cattle for the summer.

Vallies hold nymphs to which you may appeal, and yet
are the normal places where you live; are your whole world,
and yet limited so that your voice can affect the whole of
them; are opposed to *mountaines,* either as places of shelter
and comfort, or as places of humility and affliction; are rich

with flowers and warmth, or are dark hollows between the
hills.

Forests, though valuable and accustomed, are desolate
and hold danger; there are both nightingales and owls in
them; their beasts, though savage, give the strong pleasures
of hunting; their burning is either useful or destructive;
though wild and sterile they give freedom for contemplation, and their trunks are symbols of pride.

Music may express joy or sorrow; is at once more and
less direct than talking, and so is connected with one's permanent feeling about the characters of pastoral that they are
at once very rustic and rather over-civilised; it may please
or distress the bystanders; and while belonging to despair
and to the deaths of swans, it may share the living beauty of
the lady, and be an inmate of the celestial spheres.

Morning brings hope, light and labour, *evening* rest,
play and despair; they are the variety of Nature, or the tedious repetition of a day; their patrons Venus, whom one
dare not name, and Mercury, who will bring no news of her.
Morning, too, has often attached to it a meaning which, by
an intelligent and illuminating misprint, is insisted upon in
the eleventh (and subsequent) editions:

> At whose approach the sun rose in the evening,
> Who where she went bore in her forehead *mourning,*
> Is gone, is gone, from these our spoiled forrests,
> Turning to deserts our best *pastor'd* mountaines.

The form takes its effect by concentrating on these
words and slowly building up our interest in them; all their
latent implications are brought out by the repetitions; and
each in turn is used to build up some simple conceit. So that
when the static conception of the complaint has been finally
brought into light (I do not mean by this to depreciate the
sustained magnificence of its crescendo, but to praise the
singleness of its idea), a whole succession of feelings about
the local scenery, the whole way in which it is taken for
granted, has been enlisted into sorrow and beats as a single
passion of the mind.

I have put this poem at the end of a discussion ostensibly about rhythm, and shall mention its rhythm only to remark that it is magnificent; my point is that one can best illustrate its rhythm by showing the cumulative way it uses its
words. It is seldom that the meaning of a poet's words is
built up so flatly and steadily in the course of using them.
And limited as this form may be, the capacity to accept a
limitation so unflinchingly, the capacity even to conceive so
large a form as a unit of sustained feeling, is one that has
been lost since that age.

---

[33] Sidney (above, page 185).

Mikhail M. Bakhtin

1895–1975

Bakhtin's work came to be known to English-speakers only in the sixties with publication of *Rabelais and His World* (1965, tr. 1968). The situation in the Soviet Union had made his own world at least uneasy. Until *Rabelais,* he had published but one work under his own name, *Problems of Dostoyevski's Poetics* (1929), though others of which he had written at least part appeared under the names of V. H. Volosinov and P. N. Medvedev. Bakhtin spent six years in exile in the thirties, and his work on Rabelais, submitted for the doctorate in 1940, was finally refused in 1949. When at last it appeared in translation, *Rabelais* had a considerable influence. It offered the provocative notion of "carnival" as a quality to be identified with the sources and development of the novel. Carnival is connected, for Bakhtin, with laughter, travesty, parody, comedy, improvisation, and the breaking down of hierarchy. Its roots lie in an "excess of humanness." Close to its beginnings are Menippean satire, named for the Greek writer Menippus, whose works are lost, and the Socratic dialogues.

In an essay written in the thirties, "Discourse in the Novel," Bakhtin contrasts the novel to the poem. The poem is "monological"; the novel is "polyphonic" and allows for "the point of view of others" to be revealed in their own voices. Bakhtin also calls the novel "dialogical." This characteristic can be traced back to the carnivalistic, with its "joyful relativity," vitality, and heterogenic creativity. In the essay reprinted in part here, Bakhtin contrasts the novel to the epic, principally on the ground that the epic is a closed form and the novel a dynamic open one. It produces a "surplus" in which voices can struggle with each other. In the epic, character does not change, and the text presents a past that is distanced, fully shaped, and thus "absolute." In the novel, character is always in the process of formation. The epic's emphasis is on memory, while the novel's is on experience and knowledge. The epic's voice, like the lyric poem's, is singular and internalized. The novel expresses what Bakhtin calls "heteroglossia," the merging of a variety of external and internal forces to make meaning. It is a democratic form, even bordering on the happily anarchic.

Clearly, Bakhtin identifies the novel with the modern. It is the hero of the "drama of literary development." All other literary genres have seemed to reach their ultimate forms, but the novel has not. Indeed, its dynamism indicates that it will continue to be open to change and that other genres are becoming "novelized."

Major works of Bakhtin translated into English are *Rabelais and His World* (1965, tr. 1969); *Problems of Dostoyevski's Poetics* (1929, rev. 1963, tr. 1973, 1984); [V. N. Volosinov] *Marxism and the Philosophy of Language* (1929, 1930, tr. 1973); [V. N. Volosinov] *Freudianism: A Marxist Critique* (1927, tr. 1976); [P. N. Medvedev] *The Formal Method in Literary Scholarship* (1928, tr. 1978); *The Dialogic Imagination* (essays written in the thirties, tr. 1981); and *Speech Genres and Other Essays* (1984). Among the many studies of Bakhtin in recent years, see Katerina Clark and Michael

Holquist, *Mikhail Bakhtin* (1984); Tzvetan Todorov, *Mikhail Bakhtin: The Dialogical Principle* (1985); Gary Saul Morson, ed., *Bakhtin: Essays and Dialogues on His Work* (1986); Gary Saul Morson and Caryl Emerson, *Mikhail Bakhtin: Creation of a Prosaics* (1990); David K. Danow, *The Thought of Bakhtin* (1991); Sue Vice, *Introducing Bakhtin* (1997); Caryl Emerson, ed., *Critical Essays on Bakhtin* (1999).

from

Epic and Novel: Toward a Methodology for the Study of the Novel

The study of the novel as a genre is distinguished by peculiar difficulties. This is due to the unique nature of the object itself: the novel is the sole genre that continues to develop, that is as yet uncompleted. The forces that define it as a genre are at work before our eyes: the birth and development of the novel as a genre takes place in the full light of the historical day. The generic skeleton of the novel is still far from having hardened, and we cannot foresee all its plastic possibilities.[1]

We know other genres, as genres, in their completed aspect, that is, as more or less fixed pre-existing forms into which one may then pour artistic experience. The primordial process of their formation lies outside historically documented observation. We encounter the epic as a genre that has not only long since completed its development, but one that is already antiquated. With certain reservations we can say the same for the other major genres, even for tragedy. The life they have in history, the life with which we are familiar, is the life they have lived as already completed genres, with a hardened and no longer flexible skeleton. Each of them has developed its own canon that operates in literature as an authentic historical force.

All these genres, or in any case their defining features, are considerably older than written language and the book, and to the present day they retain their ancient oral and auditory characteristics. Of all the major genres only the novel is younger than writing and the book: it alone is organically receptive to new forms of mute perception, that is, to reading. But of critical importance here is the fact that the novel has no canon of its own, as do other genres; only individual examples of the novel are historically active, not a generic canon as such. Studying other genres is analogous to studying dead languages; studying the novel, on the other hand, is like studying languages that are not only alive, but still young.

This explains the extraordinary difficulty inherent in formulating a theory of the novel. For such a theory has at its heart an object of study completely different from that which theory treats in other genres. The novel is not merely one genre among other genres. Among genres long since completed and in part already dead, the novel is the only developing genre. It is the only genre that was born and nourished in a new era of world history and therefore it is deeply akin to that era, whereas the other major genres entered that era as already fixed forms, as an inheritance, and only now are they adapting themselves—some better, some worse—to the new conditions of their existence. Compared with them, the novel appears to be a creature from an alien species. It gets on poorly with other genres. It fights for its own hegemony in literature; wherever it triumphs, the other older genres go into decline. Significantly, the best book on the history of the ancient novel—that by Erwin Rohde[2]—does not so much recount the history of the novel as it does illustrate the process of disintegration that affected all major genres in antiquity.

The mutual interaction of genres within a single unified literary period is a problem of great interest and importance. In certain eras—the Greek classical period, the Golden Age of Roman literature, the neoclassical period—all genres in "high" literature (that is, the literature of ruling social groups) harmoniously reinforce each other to a significant extent; the whole of literature, conceived as a totality of genres, becomes an organic unity of the highest order. But it is characteristic of the novel that it never enters into this whole,

---

"Epic and Novel: Toward a Methodology for the Study of the Novel" was written sometime in the 1930s. It is reprinted from *The Dialogic Imagination*, translated by Caryl Emerson and Michael Holquist. Copyright by the University of Texas Press, 1981. Reprinted with permission.

[1] See Aristotle (above, page 54), where Aristotle treats various genres as completed forms.

[2] [Emerson and Holquist] Erwin Rohde (1845–1898), *Der Griechesche Roman und seine Vorläufer* (1876, but many later editions, most recently that published by F. Olds [Hildesheim, 1960]), one of the greatest monuments of nineteenth-century classical scholarship in Germany. It has never been superseded. But see: Ben F. Perry, *The Ancient Romances* (Berkeley, 1967), and Arthur Heiserman, *The Novel Before the Novel* (Chicago, 1977).

it does not participate in any harmony of the genres. In these eras the novel has an unofficial existence, outside "high" literature. Only already completed genres, with fully formed and well-defined generic contours, can enter into such a literature as a hierarchically organized, organic whole. They can mutually delimit and mutually complement each other, while yet preserving their own generic natures. Each is a unit, and all units are interrelated by virtue of certain features of deep structure that they all have in common.

The great organic poetics of the past—those of Aristotle, Horace, Boileau[3]—are permeated with a deep sense of the wholeness of literature and of the harmonious interaction of all genres contained within this whole. It is as if they literally hear this harmony of the genres. In this is their strength—the inimitable, all-embracing fullness and exhaustiveness of such poetics. And they all, as a consequence, ignore the novel. Scholarly poetics of the nineteenth century lack this integrity: they are eclectic, descriptive; their aim is not a living and organic fullness but rather an abstract and encyclopedic comprehensiveness. They do not concern themselves with the actual possibility of specific genres coexisting within the living whole of literature in a given era; they are concerned rather with their coexistence in a maximally complete anthology. Of course these poetics can no longer ignore the novel—they simply add it (albeit in a place of honor) to already existing genres (and thus it enters the roster as merely one genre among many; in literature conceived as a living whole, on the other hand, it would have to be included in a completely different way).

We have already said that the novel gets on poorly with other genres. There can be no talk of a harmony deriving from mutual limitation and complementariness. The novel parodies other genres (precisely in their role as genres); it exposes the conventionality of their forms and their language; it squeezes out some genres and incorporates others into its own peculiar structure, reformulating and reaccentuating them. Historians of literature sometimes tend to see in this merely the struggle of literary tendencies and schools. Such struggles of course exist, but they are peripheral phenomena and historically insignificant. Behind them one must be sensitive to the deeper and more truly historical struggle of genres, the establishment and growth of a generic skeleton of literature.

Of particular interest are those eras when the novel becomes the dominant genre. All literature is then caught up in the process of "becoming," and in a special kind of "generic criticism." This occurred several times in the Hel-

lenic period, again during the late Middle Ages and the Renaissance, but with special force and clarity beginning in the second half of the eighteenth century. In an era when the novel reigns supreme, almost all the remaining genres are to a greater or lesser extent "novelized": drama (for example Ibsen, Hauptmann, the whole of Naturalist drama), epic poetry (for example, *Childe Harold* and especially Byron's *Don Juan*), even lyric poetry (as an extreme example, Heine's lyrical verse).[4] Those genres that stubbornly preserve their old canonic nature begin to appear stylized. In general any strict adherence to a genre begins to feel like a stylization, a stylization taken to the point of parody, despite the artistic intent of the author. In an environment where the novel is the dominant genre, the conventional languages of strictly canonical genres begin to sound in new ways, which are quite different from the ways they sounded in those eras when the novel was *not* included in "high" literature.

Parodic stylizations of canonized genres and styles occupy an essential place in the novel. In the era of the novel's creative ascendency—and even more so in the periods of preparation preceding this era—literature was flooded with parodies and travesties of all the high genres (parodies precisely of genres, and not of individual authors or schools)—parodies that are the precursors, "companions" to the novel, in their own way studies for it. But it is characteristic that the novel does not permit any of these various individual manifestations of itself to stabilize. Throughout its entire history there is a consistent parodying or travestying of dominant or fashionable novels that attempt to become models for the genre: parodies on the chivalric romance of adventure (*Dit d'aventures*, the first such parody, belongs to the thirteenth century), on the Baroque novel, the pastoral novel (Sorel's *Le Berger extravagant*),[5] the Sentimental novel (Fielding, and *The Second Grandison*,[6] of Musäus) and so forth. This ability of the novel to criticize itself is a remarkable feature of this ever-developing genre.

---

[3] Horace (above, page 78); Nicolas Boileau-Despréaux (1636–1711), French poet.

[4] Henrik Ibsen (1828–1906), Norwegian dramatist; Gerhart Hauptmann (1862–1946), German dramatist; George Gordon Lord Byron (1788–1824), English poet; Heinrich Heine (1977–1856), German poet.

[5] [Emerson and Holquist] Charles Sorel (1599–1674), an important figure in the reaction to the *preciosité* of such figures as Honoré d'Urfé (1567–1625), whose *L'Astrée* (1607–1627), a monstrous 5,500-page volume overflowing with highflown language, is parodied in *Le Berger extravagant* (1627). The latter book's major protagonist is a dyed-in-the-wool Parisian who reads too many pastoral novels; intoxicated by these, he attempts to live the rustic life as they describe it—with predictably comic results.

[6] [Emerson and Holquist] Johann Karl August Musaus (1735–1787), along with Tieck and Brentano, one of the great collectors of German folktales and author of several *Kunstmärchen* of his own (translated into English by Carlyle). Reference here is to his *Grandison der Zweite* (1760–1762), rewritten as *Der deutsche Grandison*, 1781–1782), a satire on Richardson [English novelist 1689–1761].

What are the salient features of this novelization of other genres suggested by us above? They become more free and flexible, their language renews itself by incorporating extraliterary heteroglossia and the "novelistic" layers of literary language, they become dialogized, permeated with laughter, irony, humor, elements of self-parody and finally—this is the most important thing—the novel inserts into these other genres an indeterminacy, a certain semantic openendedness, a living contact with unfinished, still-evolving contemporary reality (the openended present). As we will see below, all these phenomena are explained by the transposition of other genres into this new and peculiar zone for structuring artistic models (a zone of contact with the present in all its openendedness), a zone that was first appropriated by the novel.

It is of course impossible to explain the phenomenon of novelization purely by reference to the direct and unmediated influence of the novel itself. Even where such influence can be precisely established and demonstrated, it is intimately interwoven with those direct changes in reality itself that also determine the novel and that condition its dominance in a given era. The novel is the only developing genre and therefore it reflects more deeply, more essentially, more sensitively and rapidly, reality itself in the process of its unfolding. Only that which is itself developing can comprehend development as a process. The novel has become the leading hero in the drama of literary development in our time precisely because it best of all reflects the tendencies of a new world still in the making; it is, after all, the only genre born of this new world and in total affinity with it. In many respects the novel has anticipated, and continues to anticipate, the future development of literature as a whole. In the process of becoming the dominant genre, the novel sparks the renovation of all other genres, it infects them with its spirit of process and inconclusiveness. It draws them ineluctably into its orbit precisely because this orbit coincides with the basic direction of the development of literature as a whole. In this lies the exceptional importance of the novel, as an object of study for the theory as well as the history of literature.

Unfortunately, historians of literature usually reduce this struggle between the novel and other already completed genres, all these aspects of novelization, to the actual real-life struggle among "schools" and "trends." A novelized poem, for example, they call a "romantic poem" (which of course it is) and believe that in so doing they have exhausted the subject. They do not see beneath the superficial hustle and bustle of literary process the major and crucial fates of literature and language, whose great heroes turn out to be first and foremost genres, and whose "trends" and "schools" are but second- or third-rank protagonists.

The utter inadequacy of literary theory is exposed when it is forced to deal with the novel. In the case of other genres literary theory works confidently and precisely, since there is a finished and already formed object, definite and clear. These genres preserve their rigidity and canonic quality in all classical eras of their development; variations from era to era, from trend to trend or school to school are peripheral and do not affect their ossified generic skeleton. Right up to the present day, in fact, theory dealing with these already completed genres can add almost nothing to Aristotle's formulations. Aristotle's poetics, although occasionally so deeply embedded as to be almost invisible, remains the stable foundation for the theory of genres. Everything works as long as there is no mention of the novel. But the existence of novelized genres already leads theory into a blind alley. Faced with the problem of the novel, genre theory must submit to a radical re-structuring.

Thanks to the meticulous work of scholars, a huge amount of historical material has accumulated and many questions concerning the evolution of various types of novels have been clarified—but the problem of the novel genre as a whole has not yet found anything like a satisfactory principled resolution. The novel continues to be seen as one genre among many; attempts are made to distinguish it as an already completed genre from other already completed genres, to discover its internal canon—one that would function as a well-defined system of rigid generic factors. In the vast majority of cases, work on the novel is reduced to mere cataloging, a description of all variants on the novel—albeit as comprehensive as possible. But the results of these descriptions never succeed in giving us as much as a hint of comprehensive formula for the novel as a genre. In addition, the experts have not managed to isolate a single definite, stable characteristic of the novel—without adding a reservation, which immediately disqualifies it altogether as a generic characteristic.

Some examples of such "characteristics with reservations" would be: the novel is a multi-layered genre (although there also exist magnificent single-layered novels); the novel is a precisely plotted and dynamic genre (although there also exist novels that push to its literary limits the art of pure description); the novel is a complicated genre (although novels are mass produced as pure and frivolous entertainment like no other genre); the novel is a love story (although the greatest examples of the European novel are utterly devoid of the love element); the novel is a prose genre (although there exist excellent novels in verse). One could of course mention a large number of additional "generic characteristics" for the novel similar to those given above, which are immediately annulled by some reservation innocently appended to them.

Of considerably more interest and consequence are those normative definitions of the novel offered by novelists themselves, who produce a specific novel and then declare *it* the only correct, necessary and authentic form of the novel. Such, for instance, is Rousseau's foreword to his *La Nouvelle Héloise*,[7] Wieland's to his *Agathon*,[8] Wezel's to his *Tobias Knouts*,[9] in such a category belong the numerous declarations and statements of principle by the Romantics on *Wilhelm Meister, Lucinda*[10] and other texts. Such statements are not attempts to incorporate all the possible variants of the novel into a single eclectic definition, but are themselves part and parcel of the living evolution of the novel as a genre. Often they deeply and faithfully reflect the novel's struggle with other genres and with itself (with other dominant and fashionable variants of the novel) at a particular point in its development. They come closer to an understanding of the peculiar position of the novel in literature, a position that is not commensurate with that of other genres.

Especially significant in this connection is a series of statements that accompanied the emergence of a new novel-type in the eighteenth century. The series opens with Fielding's reflections on the novel and its hero in *Tom Jones*.[11] It continues in Wieland's foreword to *Agathon,* and the most essential link in the series is Blankenburg's *Versuch über den Roman*.[12] By the end of this series we have, in fact, that theory of the novel later formulated by Hegel. In all these statements, each reflecting the novel in one of its critical stages *(Tom Jones, Agathon, Wilhelm Meister),* the following prerequisites for the novel are characteristic: (1) the novel should not be "poetic," as the word "poetic" is used in other genres of imaginative literature; (2) the hero of a novel should not be "heroic" in either the epic or the tragic sense of the word: he should combine in himself negative as well as positive features, low as well as lofty, ridiculous as well as serious; (3) the hero should not be portrayed as an already completed and unchanging person but as one who is evolving and developing, a person who learns from life; (4) the novel should become for the contemporary world what the epic was for the ancient world (an idea that Blankenburg expressed very precisely, and that was later repeated by Hegel).[13]

All these positive prerequisites have their substantial and productive side—taken together, they constitute a criticism (from the novel's point of view) of other genres and of the relationship these genres bear to reality: their stilted heroizing, their narrow and unlifelike poeticalness, their monotony and abstractness, the pre-packaged and unchanging nature of their heroes. We have here, in fact, a rigorous critique of the literariness and poeticalness inherent in other genres and also in the predecessors of the contemporary novel (the heroic Baroque novel and the Sentimental novels of Richardson). These statements are reinforced significantly by the practice of these novelists themselves. Here the novel—its texts as well as the theory connected with it—emerges consciously and unambiguously as a genre that is both critical and self-critical, one fated to revise the fundamental concepts of literariness and poeticalness dominant at the time. On the one hand, the contrast of novel with epic (and the novel's opposition to the epic) is but one moment in the criticism of other literary genres (in particular, a criticism of epic heroization); but on the other hand, this contrast aims to elevate the significance of the novel, making of it the dominant genre in contemporary literature.

The positive prerequisites mentioned above constitute one of the high-points in the novel's coming to self-consciousness. They do not yet of course provide a theory of the novel. These statements are also not distinguished by any great philosophical depth. They do however illustrate the nature of the novel as a genre no less—if perhaps no more—than do other existing theories of the novel.

I will attempt below to approach the novel precisely as a genre-in-the-making, one in the vanguard of all modern literary development. I am not constructing here a functional definition of the novelistic canon in literary history, that is, a definition that would make of it a system of fixed generic characteristics. Rather, I am trying to grope my way toward the basic structural characteristics of this most fluid of genres, characteristics that might determine the direction

---

[7] Jean Jacques Rousseau (1712–1778).

[8] [Emerson and Holquist] Christoph Martin Wieland (1733–1813) is the author of *Geschichte des Agathon* (1767, first of many versions), an autobiographical novel in the guise of a Greek romance, considered by many to be the first in the long line of German *Bildungsromane.*

[9] [Emerson and Holquist] Reference here is to Johann Carl Wezel (1747–1819), *Lebensgeschichte Tobias Knouts, des Weisen, sonst der Stammler genannt* (733), a novel that has not received the readership that it deserves. A four-volume reprint was published by Metzler (Stuttgart, Afterword by Viktor Lange) in 1971. Also see Elizabeth Holzberg-Pfenniger, *Der disorientierte Erzähler: Studien zu J. C. Wezels Lebensgeschichte des Tobias Knouts* (Bern, 1976).

[10] By Johann Wolfgang von Goethe (1749–1832) and Friedrich Schlegel (above, page 473) respectively.

[11] Henry Fielding (1707–1754).

[12] [Emerson and Holquist] Friedrich von Blankenburg (1744–1796), *Versuch über den Roman* (1774), an enormous work (over 500 pages) that attempts to define the novel in terms of a rudimentary psychology, a concern for *Tugend* in the heroes. A facsimile edition was published by Metzler (Stuttgart) in 1965. Little is known about Blumenburg, who is also the author of an unfinished novel with the imposing title *Beytrage zur Geschichte deutschen Reichs und deutschen Sitten,* the first part of which appeared a year after the *Versuch* in 1775.

[13] Hegel (above, page 552).

of its peculiar capacity for change and of its influence and effect on the rest of literature.

I find three basic characteristics that fundamentally distinguish the novel in principle from other genres: (1) its stylistic three-dimensionality, which is linked with the multi-languaged consciousness realized in the novel; (2) the radical change it effects in the temporal coordinates of the literary image; (3) the new zone opened by the novel for structuring literary images, namely, the zone of maximal contact with the present (with contemporary reality) in all its openendedness.

These three characteristics of the novel are all organically interrelated and have all been powerfully affected by a very specific rupture in the history of European civilization: its emergence from a socially isolated and culturally deaf semipatriarchal society, and its entrance into international and interlingual contacts and relationships. A multitude of different languages, cultures and times became available to Europe, and this became a decisive factor in its life and thought.

In another work[14] I have already investigated the first stylistic peculiarity of the novel, the one resulting from the active polyglossia of the new world, the new culture and its new creative literary consciousness. I will summarize here only the basic points.

Polyglossia had always existed (it is more ancient than pure, canonic monoglossia), but it had not been a factor in literary creation; an artistically conscious choice between languages did not serve as the creative center of the literary and language process. Classical Greeks had a feeling both for "languages" and for the epochs of language, for the various Greek literary dialects (tragedy is a polyglot genre), but creative consciousness was realized in closed, pure languages (although in actual fact they were mixed). Polyglossia was appropriated and canonized among all the genres.

The new cultural and creative consciousness lives in an actively polyglot world. The world becomes polyglot, once and for all and irreversibly. The period of national languages, coexisting but closed and deaf to each other, comes to an end. Languages throw light on each other: one language can, after all, see itself only in the light of another language. The naive and stubborn coexistence of "languages" within a given national language also comes to an end—that is, there is no more peaceful coexistence between territorial dialects, social and professional dialects and jargons, literary language, generic languages within literary language, epochs in language and so forth.

All this set into motion a process of active, mutual cause-and-effect and interillumination. Words and language began to have a different feel to them; objectively they ceased to be what they had once been. Under these conditions of external and internal interillumination, each given language—even if its linguistic composition (phonetics, vocabulary, morphology, etc.) were to remain absolutely unchanged—is, as it were, reborn, becoming qualitatively a different thing for the consciousness that creates in it.

In this actively polyglot world, completely new relationships are established between language and its object (that is, the real world)—and this is fraught with enormous consequences for all the already completed genres that had been formed during eras of closed and deaf monoglossia. In contrast to other major genres, the novel emerged and matured precisely when intense activation of external and internal polyglossia was at the peak of its activity; this is its native element. The novel could therefore assume leadership in the process of developing and renewing literature in its linguistic and stylistic dimension.

In the above-mentioned work I tried to elucidate the profound stylistic originality of the novel, which is determined by its connection with polyglossia.

Let us move on to the two other characteristics, both concerned with the thematic aspect of structure in the novel as a genre. These characteristics can be best brought out and clarified through a comparison of the novel with the epic.

The epic as a genre in its own right may, for our purposes, be characterized by three constitutive features: (1) a national epic past—in Goethe's and Schiller's terminology the "absolute past"—serves as the subject for the epic;[15] (2) national tradition (not personal experience and the free thought that grows out of it) serves as the source for the epic; (3) an absolute epic distance separates the epic world from contemporary reality, that is, from the time in which the singer (the author and his audience) lives.

We will deal in more detail with each of these constitutive features of the epic.

The world of the epic is the national heroic past: it is a world of "beginnings" and "peak times" in the national history, a world of fathers and of founders of families, a world of "firsts" and "bests." The important point here is not that

---

[14] [Bakhtin] Cf. The article "From the Prehistory of Novelistic Discourse" [in *The Dialogic Imagination*].

[15] [Emerson and Holquist] Reference here is to "Über epische und dramatische Dichtung," co-signed by Schiller and Goethe, but probably written by the latter in 1797, although not published until 1827. The actual term used by Goethe for what Bakhtin is calling "absolute past" is *Volkommen vergangen,* which is opposed not to the novel, but to drama, which is defined as *Volkommen gegenwartig.* The essay can be found in Goethe's *Sämliche Werke* (Jubiläums-Ausgabe, Stuttgart and Berlin [1902–1907]), vol. 36, pp. 149–52.

the past constitutes the content of the epic. The formally constitutive feature of the epic as a genre is rather the transferral of a represented world into the past, and the degree to which this world participates in the past. The epic was never a poem about the present, about its own time (one that became a poem about the past only for those who came later). The epic, as the specific genre known to us today, has been from the beginning a poem about the past, and the authorial position immanent in the epic and constitutive for it (that is, the position of the one who utters the epic word) is the environment of a man speaking about a past that is to him inaccessible, the reverent point of view of a descendent. In its style, tone and manner of expression, epic discourse is infinitely far removed from discourse of a contemporary about a contemporary addressed to contemporaries ("Onegin, my good friend, was born on the banks of the Neva, where perhaps you were also born, or once shone, my reader. . . .")[16] Both the singer and the listener, immanent in the epic as a genre, are located in the same time and on the same evaluative (hierarchical) plane, but the represented world of the heroes stands on an utterly different and inaccessible time-and-value plane, separated by epic distance. The space between them is filled with national tradition. To portray an event on the same time-and-value plane as oneself and one's contemporaries (and an event that is therefore based on personal experience and thought) is to undertake a radical revolution, and to step out of the world of epic into the world of the novel.

It is possible, of course, to conceive even "my time" as heroic, epic time, when it is seen as historically significant; one can distance it, look at it as if from afar (not from one's own vantage point but from some point in the future), one can relate to the past in a familiar way (as if relating to "my" present). But in so doing we ignore the presentness of the present and the pastness of the past; we are removing ourselves from the zone of "my time," from the zone of familiar contact with me.

We speak of the epic as a genre that has come down to us already well defined and real. We come upon it when it is already completely finished, a congealed and half-moribund genre. Its completedness, its consistency and its absolute lack of artistic naiveté bespeak its old age as a genre and its lengthy past. We can only conjecture about this past, and we must admit that so far our conjectures have been rather poor. Those hypothetical primordial songs that preceded both the epic and the creation of a generic epic tradition, songs about contemporaries that directly echoed events that had just oc-

curred—such songs we do not know, although we must presume they existed. We can only guess at the nature of those original aëdonic songs, or of the cantilenas. And we have no reason to assume that they are any more closely related to the later and better-known epic songs than to our topical feuilletons or popular ditties. Those heroicized epic songs about contemporaries that *are* available to us and that we *do* know existed arose only after the epic was already an established form, and arose on the basis of an already ancient and powerful epic tradition. These songs transfer to contemporary events and contemporaries the ready-made epic form; that is, they transfer to these events the time-and-value contour of the past, thus attaching them to the world of fathers, of beginnings and peak time—canonizing these events, as it were, while they are still current. In a patriarchal social structure the ruling class does, in a certain sense, belong to the world of "fathers" and is thus separated from other classes by a distance that is almost epic. The epic incorporation of the contemporary hero into a world of ancestors and founders is a specific phenomenon that developed out of an epic tradition long since completed, and that therefore is as little able to explain the origin of the epic as is, say, the neoclassical ode.

Whatever its origins, the epic as it has come down to us is an absolutely completed and finished generic form, whose constitutive feature is the transferral of the world it describes to an absolute past of national beginnings and peak times. The absolute past is a specifically evaluating (hierarchical) category. In the epic world view, "beginning," "first," "founder," "ancestor," "that which occurred earlier" and so forth are not merely temporal categories but *valorized* temporal categories, and valorized to an extreme degree. This is as true for relationships among people as for relations among all the other items and phenomena of the epic world. In the past, everything is good: all the really good things (i.e., the "first" things) occur *only* in this past. The epic absolute past is the single source and beginning of everything good for all later times as well.

In ancient literature it is memory, and not knowledge, that serves as the source and power for the creative impulse. That is how it was, it is impossible to change it: the tradition of the past is sacred. There is as yet no consciousness of the possible relativity of any past.

The novel, by contrast, is determined by experience, knowledge and practice (the future). In the era of Hellenism a closer contact with the heroes of the Trojan epic cycle began to be felt; epic is already being transformed into novel. Epic material is transposed into novelistic material, into precisely that zone of contact that passes through the intermediate stages of familiarization and laughter. When the novel

[16] A. S. Pushkin (1799–1837), *Eugene Onegin*.

becomes the dominant genre, epistemology becomes the dominant discipline.

The epic past is called the "absolute past" for good reason: it is both monochronic and valorized (hierarchical); it lacks any relativity, that is, any gradual, purely temporal progressions that might connect it with the present. It is walled off absolutely from all subsequent times, and above all from those times in which the singer and his listeners are located. This boundary, consequently, is immanent in the form of the epic itself and is felt and heard in its every word.

To destroy this boundary is to destroy the form of the epic as a genre. But precisely because it is walled off from all subsequent times, the epic past is absolute and complete. It is as closed as a circle; inside it everything is finished, already over. There is no place in the epic world for any openendedness, indecision, indeterminacy. There are no loopholes in it through which we glimpse the future, it suffices unto itself, neither supposing any continuation nor requiring it. Temporal and valorized definitions are here fused into a single inseparable whole (as they are also fused in the semantic layers of ancient languages). Everything incorporated into this past was simultaneously incorporated into a condition of authentic essence and significance, but therefore also took on conclusiveness and finality, depriving itself, so to speak, of all rights and potential for a real continuation. Absolute conclusiveness and closedness is the outstanding feature of the temporally valorized epic past.

Let us move on to tradition. The epic past, walled off from all subsequent times by an impenetrable boundary, is preserved and revealed only in the form of national tradition. The epic relies entirely on this tradition. Important here is not the fact that tradition is the factual source for the epic—what matters rather is that a reliance on tradition is immanent in the very form of the epic, just as the absolute past is immanent in it. Epic discourse is a discourse handed down by tradition. By its very nature the epic world of the absolute past is inaccessible to personal experience and does not permit an individual, personal point of view or evaluation. One cannot glimpse it, grope for it, touch it; one cannot look at it from just any point of view; it is impossible to experience it, analyze it, take it apart, penetrate into its core. It is given solely as tradition, sacred and sacrosanct, evaluated in the same way by all and demanding a pious attitude toward itself. Let us repeat: the important thing is not the factual sources of the epic, not the content of its historical events, nor the declarations of its authors—the important thing is this formal constitutive characteristic of the epic as a genre (to be more precise, the formal-substantive characteristic): its reliance on impersonal and sacrosanct tradition, on a commonly held evaluation and point of view—which excludes any possibility of another approach—and which therefore displays a profound piety toward the subject described and toward the language used to describe it, the language of tradition.

The absolute past as the subject for epic and sacrosanct tradition as its sole source also determines the nature of epic distance—that is, the third constitutive characteristic of the epic as a genre. As we have already pointed out, the epic past is locked into itself and walled off from all subsequent times by an impenetrable boundary, isolated (and this is most important) from the eternal present of children and descendents in which the epic singer and his listeners are located, which figures in as an event in their lives and becomes the epic performance. On the other hand, tradition isolates the world of the epic from personal experience, from any new insights, from any personal initiative in understanding and interpreting, from new points of view and evaluations. The epic world is an utterly finished thing, not only as an authentic event of the distant past but also on its own terms and by its own standards; it is impossible to change, to re-think, to re-evaluate anything in it. It is completed, conclusive and immutable, as a fact, an idea and a value. This defines absolute epic distance. One can only accept the epic world with reverence; it is impossible to really touch it, for it is beyond the realm of human activity, the realm in which everything humans touch is altered and rethought. This distance exists not only in the epic material, that is, in the events and the heroes described, but also in the point of view and evaluation one assumes toward them; point of view and evaluation are fused with the subject into one inseparable whole. Epic language is not separable from its subject, for an absolute fusion of subject matter and spatial-temporal aspects with valorized (hierarchical) ones is characteristic of semantics in the epic. This absolute fusion and the consequent unfreedom of the subject was first overcome only with the arrival on the scene of an active polyglossia and interillumination of languages (and then the epic became a semiconventional, semimoribund genre).

Thanks to this epic distance, which excludes any possibility of activity and change, the epic world achieves a radical degree of completedness not only in its content but in its meaning and its values as well. The epic world is constructed in the zone of an absolute distanced image, beyond the sphere of possible contact with the developing, incomplete and therefore re-thinking and re-evaluating present.

The three characteristics of the epic posited by us above are, to a greater or lesser extent, also fundamental to the other high genres of classical antiquity and the Middle Ages. At the heart of all these already completed high genres lie the same evaluation of time, the same role for tradition, and a similar hierarchical distance. Contemporary reality as such does not figure in as an available object of representation in any of these high genres. Contemporary reality may enter into the high genres only in its hierarchically highest levels, already distanced in its relationship to reality itself. But the events, victors and heroes of "high" contemporary reality are, as it were, appropriated by the past as they enter into these high genres (for example, Pindar's odes or the works of Simonides);[17] they are woven by various intermediate links and connective tissue into the unified fabric of the heroic past and tradition. These events and heroes receive their value and grandeur precisely through this association with the past, the source of all authentic reality and value. They withdraw themselves, so to speak, from the present day with all its inconclusiveness, its indecision, its openness, its potential for re-thinking and re-evaluating. They are raised to the valorized plane of the past, and assume there a finished quality. We must not forget that "absolute past" is not to be confused with time in our exact and limited sense of the word; it is rather a temporally valorized hierarchical category.

It is impossible to achieve greatness in one's own time. Greatness always makes itself known only to descendents, for whom such a quality is always located in the past (it turns into a distanced image); it has become an object of memory and not a living object that one can see and touch. In the genre of the "memorial," the poet constructs his image in the future and distanced plane of his descendents (cf. the inscriptions of oriental despots, and of Augustus). In the world of memory, a phenomenon exists in its own peculiar context, with its own special rules, subject to conditions quite different from those we meet in the world we see with our own eyes, the world of practice and familiar contact. The epic past is a special form for perceiving people and events in art. In general the act of artistic perception and representation is almost completely obscured by this form. Artistic representation here is representation *sub specie aeternitatis*.[18] One may, and in fact one must, memorialize with artistic language only that which is worthy of being remembered, that which should be preserved in the memory of descendents; an image is created for descendents, and this image is projected on to their sublime and distant horizon. Contemporaneity for its own sake (that is to say, a contemporaneity that makes no claim on future memory) is molded in clay; contemporaneity for the future (for descendents) is molded in marble or bronze.

The interrelationship of times is important here. The valorized emphasis is not on the future and does not serve the future, no favors are being done it (such favors face an eternity outside time); what is served here is the future memory of a past, a broadening of the world of the absolute past, an enriching of it with new images (at the expense of contemporaneity)—a world that is always opposed in principle to any *merely transitory* past.

In the already completed high genres, tradition also retains its significance—although under conditions of open and personal creativity, its role becomes more conventionalized than in the epic.

In general, the world of high literature in the classical era was a world projected into the past, on to the distanced plane of memory, but not into a real, relative past tied to the present by uninterrupted temporal transitions; it was projected rather into a valorized past of beginnings and peak times. This past is distanced, finished and closed like a circle. This does not mean, of course, that there is no movement within it. On the contrary, the relative temporal categories within it are richly and subtly worked out (nuances of "earlier," "later," sequences of moments, speeds, durations, etc.); there is evidence of a high level of artistic technique in matters of time. But within this time, completed and locked into a circle, all points are equidistant from the real, dynamic time of the present; insofar as this time is whole, it is not localized in an actual historical sequence; it is not relative to the present or to the future; it contains within itself, as it were, the entire fullness of time. As a consequence all high genres of the classical era, that is, its entire high literature, are structured in the zone of the distanced image, a zone outside any possible contact with the present in all its openedness.

As we have said, contemporaneity as such (that is, one that preserves its own living contemporary profile) cannot become an object of representation for the high genres. Contemporaneity was reality of a "lower" order in comparison with the epic past. Least of all could it serve as the starting point for artistic ideation or evaluation. The focus for such an idea of evaluation could only be found in the absolute past. The present is something transitory, it is flow, it is an eternal continuation without beginning or end; it is denied an authentic conclusiveness and consequently lacks an essence as well. The future as well is perceived either as an essentially indifferent continuation of the present, or as an end, a final destruction, a catastrophe. The temporally valorized categories of absolute beginning and absolute end are extremely significant in our sense of time and in the ideologies of past times. The beginning is idealized, the end is darkened (catastrophe, "the twilight of the gods"). This sense of time and the hierarchy of times described by us here

---

[17] Pindar (c. 522–443 B.C.), Greek poet; Simonides (fifth c. B.C.), Greek poet.
[18] Under the aspect of eternity.

permeate all the high genres of antiquity and the Middle Ages. They permeated so deeply into the basic foundation of these genres that they continue to live in them in subsequent eras—up to the nineteenth century, and even further.

This idealization of the past in high genres has something of an official air. All eternal expressions of the dominant force and truth (the expression of everything conclusive) were formulated in the valorized-hierarchical category of the past, in a distanced and distant image (everything from gesture and clothing to literary style, for all are symbols of authority). The novel, however, is associated with the eternally living element of unofficial language and unofficial thought (holiday forms, familiar speech, profanation).

The dead are loved in a different way. They are removed from the sphere of contact, one can and indeed must speak of them in a different style. Language about the dead is stylistically quite distinct from language about the living.

In the high genres all authority and privilege, all lofty significance and grandeur, abandon the zone of familiar contact for the distanced plane (clothing, etiquette, the style of a hero's speech and the style of speech about him). It is in this orientation toward completeness that the classicism of all non-novel genres is expressed.

Contemporaneity, flowing and transitory, "low," present—this "life without beginning or end" was a subject of representation only in the low genres. Most importantly, it was the basic subject matter in that broadest and richest of realms, the common people's creative culture of laughter. In the aforementioned work I tried to indicate the enormous influence exercised by this realm—in the ancient world as well as the Middle Ages—on the birth and formation of novelistic language. It was equally significant for all other historical factors in the novelistic genre, during their emergence and early formation. Precisely here, in popular laughter, the authentic folkloric roots of the novel are to be sought. The present, contemporary life as such, "I myself" and "my contemporaries," "my time"—all these concepts were originally the objects of ambivalent laughter, at the same time cheerful and annihilating. It is precisely here that a fundamentally new attitude toward language and toward the word is generated. Alongside direct representation—laughing at living reality—there flourish parody and travesty of all high genres and of all lofty models embodied in national myth. The "absolute past" of gods, demigods and heroes is here, in parodies and even more so in travesties, "contemporized": it is brought low, represented on a plane equal with contemporary life, in an everyday environment, in the low language of contemporaneity.

In classical times this elemental popular laughter gave rise directly to a broad and varied field of ancient literature, one that the ancients themselves expressively labeled *spoudogeloion,* that is, the field of "serio-comical." The weakly plotted mimes of Sophron,[19] all the bucolic poems, the fable, early memoir literature (the *Epidēmiai* of Ion of Chios,[20] the *Homilae* of Critias),[21] pamphlets all belong to this field; here the ancients themselves included the "Socratic dialogues" (as a genre), here belong Roman satire (Lucilius,[13] Horace, Persius,[14] Juvenal),[22] the extensive literature of the "Symposia" and finally Menippean satire[23] (as a genre) and dialogues of the Lucianic type. All these genres, permeated with the "serio-comical," are authentic predecessors of the novel. In addition, several of these genres are thoroughly novelistic, containing in embryo and sometimes in developed form the basic elements characteristic of the most important later prototypes of the European novel. The authentic spirit of the novel as a developing genre is present in them to an incomparably greater degree than in the so-called Greek novels (the sole ancient genre bearing the name). The Greek novel [Greek romance] had a powerful influence on the European novel precisely in the Baroque era, that is, precisely at that time when novel theory was beginning to be reworked (Abbé Huet)[24] and when the very term "novel" was being tightened and made more precise. Out of all novelistic works of antiquity, the term "novel" was, therefore, attached to the Greek novel alone. Nevertheless, the

---

[19] [Emerson and Holquist] Sophron (fl. fifth century B.C.) was probably the first writer to give literary form to the mime. He was greatly admired by Plato. The mimes were written in rhythmic prose and took as their subject matter events of everyday life.

[20] [Emerson and Holquist] Ion of Chios (490–421 B.C.), a Greek poet who, when he won first for tragedy in the Great Dionysia, made a present of Chian wine to every Athenian. His memoirs have not come down to us, but Atheaeus (*q. v.*) gives long quotes, including the description of an evening Sophocles spent with him in his home on Chios. It has been said no other Greek before Socrates has been presented so vividly. The title of these *Epidēmiai* probably refers to the visits of distinguished Athenians who came to see Ion on Chios.

[21] [Emerson and Holquist] Critias (460–403 B.C.), one of the Thirty Tyrants, also active as a writer. He wrote mostly elegies and tragedies. Fragments of *Homilai* ("discussions") have come down to us. Galen is cited by the editors of the *Pauly Wissowa* (vol. II of the 1910 ed., p. 1910) as calling the two books of the original *Homilai* "aimless discussions" *(zwanglose Unterhaltungen).*

[22] [Emerson and Holquist] Lucilius Gaius (?–102 B.C.), member of one of the greatest Roman families, author of several important satires, chiefly remarkable for the personal, almost autobiographical tone he introduces into them. [Horace, above, page 78]. Persius, Flaccus Aulus (34–62 A.D.), satirist heavily influenced by Stoic philosophy. [Juvenal (c. 60–c. 140 A.D.), Roman satirical poet.]

[23] [Emerson and Holquist] Menippus was a Greek Cynic writer of the third century B.C. His works are lost.

[24] [Emerson and Holquist] Abbé Huet (1630–1731), Bishop of Avranches, learned scholar who write numerous works on a wide variety of subjects. His *Traité de l'origine des romans* (1670) was first published as an introduction to Mme. de Lafayette's *Zaide,* a novel written while its author was still influenced by ideas of the *précieux* society.

serio-comical genres mentioned above anticipate the more essential historical aspects in the development of the novel in modern times, even though they lack that sturdy skeleton of plot and composition that we have grown accustomed to demand from the novel as a genre. This applies in particular to the Socratic dialogues, which may be called—to rephrase Friedrich Schlegel—"the novels of their time," and also to Menippean satire (including the *Satyricon* of Petronius),[25] whose role in the history of the novel is immense and as yet inadequately appreciated by scholarship. These serio-comical genres were the first authentic and essential step in the evolution of the novel as the genre of becoming.

Precisely what is this novelistic spirit in these serio-comical genres, and on what basis do we claim them as the first step in the development of the novel? It is this: contemporary reality serves as their subject, and—even more important—it is the starting point for understanding, evaluating and formulating such genres. For the first time, the subject of serious literary representation (although, it is true, at the same time comical) is portrayed without any distance, on the level of contemporary reality, in a zone of direct and even crude contact. Even where the past or myth serves as the subject of representation in these genres there is no epic distance, and contemporary reality provides the point of view. Of special significance in this process of demolishing distance is the comical origin of these genres: they derive from folklore (popular laughter). It is precisely laughter that destroys the epic, and in general destroys any hierarchical (distancing and valorized) distance. As a distanced image a subject cannot be comical; to be made comical, it must be brought close. Everything that makes us laugh is close at hand, all comical creativity works in a zone of maximal proximity. Laughter has the remarkable power of making an object come up close, of drawing it into a zone of crude contact where one can finger it familiarly on all sides, turn it upside down, inside out, peer at it from above and below, break open its external shell, look into its center, doubt it, take it apart, dismember it, lay it bare and expose it, examine it freely and experiment with it. Laughter demolishes fear and piety before an object, before a world, making of it an object of familiar contact and thus clearing the ground for an absolutely free investigation of it. Laughter is a vital factor in laying down that prerequisite for fearlessness without which it would be impossible to approach the world realistically. As it draws an object to itself and makes it familiar, laughter delivers the object into the fearless hands of investigative experiment—both scientific and artistic—and into the hands of free experimental fantasy.

Familiarization of the world through laughter and popular speech is an extremely important and indispensable step in making possible free, scientifically knowable and artistically realistic creativity in European civilization.

The plane of comic (humorous) representation is a specific plane in its spatial as well as its temporal aspect. Here the role of memory is minimal; in the comic world there is nothing for memory and tradition to do. One ridicules in order to forget. This is the zone of maximally familiar and crude contact; laughter means abuse, and abuse could lead to blows. Basically this is uncrowning, that is, the removal of an object from the distanced plane, the destruction of epic distance, an assault on and destruction of the distanced plane in general. In this plane (the plane of laughter) one can disrespectfully walk around whole objects; therefore, the back and rear portion of an object (and also its innards, not normally accessible for viewing) assume a special importance. The object is broken apart, laid bare (its hierarchical ornamentation is removed): the naked object is ridiculous; its "empty" clothing, stripped and separated from its person, is also ridiculous. What takes place is a comical operation of dismemberment.

One can play games with the comical (that is, contemporize it); serving as the objects of the game we have the primordial artistic symbols of space and time—above, below, in front of, behind, earlier, later, first, last, past, present, brief (momentary), long and so forth. What reigns supreme here is the artistic logic of analysis, dismemberment, turning things into dead objects.

We possess a remarkable document that reflects the simultaneous birth of scientific thinking and of a new artistic prose model for the novel. These are the Socratic dialogues. For our purposes, everything in this remarkable genre, which was born just as classical antiquity was drawing to a close, is significant. Characteristically it arises as *pomnemoneumata*,[26] that is, as a genre of the memoir type, as transcripts based on personal memories of real conversations among contemporaries;[27] characteristic, also, is the fact that a speaking and conversing man is the central image of the genre. Characteristic, too, is the combination of the image of Socrates, the

---

[25] Petronius Gaius (first century A.D.), Roman satirist.

[26] [Emerson and Holquist] *Apomnemoneumata,* or *Hypomnemata* (literally, "recollections"). It is thought by some that a work of this title ascribed to Ion of Chios may be identical with the *Epidémiai.*

[27] [Bakhtin] "Memory" in memoirs and autobiographies is of a special sort: it is memory of one's own contemporaniety and of one's own self. It is a deheroizing memory; there is an element of the mechanical in it, of mere transcription (nonmonumental). What results is personal memory without preexisting chronological pattern, bounded only by the termini of a single personal life (there are no fathers or generations). This "memoir quality" was already inherent in Socratic dialogue.

central hero of the genre, wearing the popular mask of a be-wildered fool (almost a *Margit*)[28] with the image of a wise man of the most elevated sort (in the spirit of legends about seven wise men); this combination produces the ambivalent image of wise ignorance. Characteristic also is the ambivalent self-praise in the Socratic dialogue: I am wiser than everyone, because I know that I know nothing. In the image of Socrates one can detect a new type of prose heroization. Around this image, carnivalized legends spring up (for example, Socrates' relationship with Xanthippe);[29] the hero turns into a jester (compare the more recent carnivalization of legends sur-rounding Dante, Pushkin,[30] etc.).

Characteristic, even canonic, for the genre is the spo-ken dialogue framed by a dialogized story. Characteristic also is the proximity of its language to popular spoken lan-guage, as near as was possible for classical Greece; these dialogues in fact opened the path to Attic prose, and are con-nected with the essential renovation of the literary-prose language—and with a shift in languages in general. Charac-teristically this genre is at the same time a rather complex system of styles and dialects, which enter it as more-or-less parodied models of languages and styles (we have before us therefore a multi-styled genre, as is the authentic novel). Moreover the figure of Socrates himself is characteristic for the genre—he is an outstanding example of heroization in novelistic prose (so very different from epic heroization). It is, finally, profoundly characteristic—and for us this is of utmost importance—that we have laughter, Socratic irony, the entire system of Socratic degradations combined with a serious, lofty and for the first time truly free investigation of the world, of man and of human thought. Socratic laughter (reduced of irony) and Socratic degradations (an entire sys-tem of metaphors and comparisons borrowed from the lower spheres of life—from tradespeople, from everyday life, etc.) bring the world closer and familiarize it in order to investigate it fearlessly and freely. As our starting point we have contemporary reality, the living people who occupy it together with their opinions. From this vantage point, from this contemporary reality with its diversity of speech and voice, there comes about a new orientation in the world and in time (including the "absolute past" of tradition) through personal experience and investigation. It is canonical for the genre that even an accidental and insignificant pretext can ordinarily and deliberately serve as the external and most immediate starting point for a dialogue; the "todayness" of the day was emphasized in all its randomness (accidental encounters, etc.).

In other serio-comical genres we will come upon other aspects, nuances and consequences of this radical shift of the temporally valorized center of artistic orientation, and of the revolution in the hierarchy of times. A few words now about Menippean satire. Its folklore roots are identical with those of the Socratic dialogue, to which it is genetically re-lated (it is usually considered a product of the disintegration of the Socratic dialogue). The familiarizing role of laughter is here considerably more powerful, sharper and coarser. The liberty to crudely degrade, to turn inside out the lofty aspects of the world and world views, might sometimes seem shocking. But to this exclusive and comic familiarity must be added an intense spirit of inquiry and a utopian fan-tasy. Nothing is left of the distant epic image of the absolute past; the entire world and everything sacred in it is offered to us without any distancing at all, in a zone of crude con-tact, where we can grab at everything with our own hands. In this world, utterly familiarized, the subject moves with extreme and fantastic freedom; from heaven to earth, from earth to the nether world, from the present into the past, from the past into the future. In the comic afterlife visions of Menippean satire, the heroes of the absolute past, real-life figures from various eras of the historic past (for exam-ple, Alexander of Macedonia[31]) and living contemporaries jostle one another in a most familiar way, to talk, even to brawl; this confrontation of times from the point of view of the present is extremely characteristic. In Menippean satire the unfettered and fantastic plots and situations all serve one goal—to put to the test and to expose ideas and ideologues. These are experimental and provocative plots.

The appearance of the utopian element in this genre is symptomatic, although it is, to be sure, timid and shallow. The inconclusive present begins to feel closer to the future than to the past, and begins to seek some valorized support in the future, even if this future is as yet pictured merely as a return to the Golden Age of Saturn (in Roman times, Menippean satire was closely associated with the Saturnalia and with the freedom of Saturnalian laughter).

Menippean satire is dialogic, full of parodies and trav-esties, multi-styled, and does not fear elements of bilingual-

---

[28] [Emerson and Holquist] *Margit,* Greek "fool," subject of a work frequently cited by Bakhtin, the *Margites (q. v.).*

[29] Xanthippe, wife of Socrates.

[30] Dante Alighieri (1265–1321), Italian poet. [Emerson and Holquist] A good example of what Bakhtin has in mind here is provided by the leader of the *Oberuity,* Daniil Kharms (1905–1942), "Anecdotes about Pushkin." They are difficult to appreciate in translation, but are all similar to the following: "Pushkin loved to throw rocks. As soon as he saw a rock, he would throw it. Sometimes he became so excited that he stood, all red in the face, waving his arms, throwing rocks, simply something awful."—from *Russia's Lost Literature of the Absurd,* tr. and ed. by George Gibian (New York, 1974), 67.

[31] Alexander the Great (356 b.c.–323 b.c.), Macedonian king.

ism (in Varro,[32] and especially in Boethius' *The Consolation of Philosophy*). The *Satyricon* of Petronius is good proof that Menippean satire can expand into a huge picture, offering a realistic reflection of the socially varied and heteroglot world of contemporary life.

For almost all the above-mentioned genres, the "serio-comical" is characterized by a deliberate and explicit autobiographical and memoirist approach. The shift of the temporal center of artistic orientation, which placed on the same temporally valorized plane the author and his readers (on the one hand) and the world and heroes described by him (on the other), making them contemporaries, possible acquaintances, friends, familiarizing their relations (we again recall the novelistic opening of *Onegin*), permits the author, in all his various masks and faces, to move freely onto the field of his represented world, a field that in the epic had been absolutely inaccessible and closed.

The field available for representing the world changes from genre to genre and from era to era as literature develops. It is organized in different ways and limited in space and time by different means. But this field is always specific.

The novel comes into contact with the spontaneity of the inconclusive present; this is what keeps the genre from congealing. The novelist is drawn toward everything that is not yet completed. He may turn up on the field of representation in any authorial pose, he may depict real moments in his own life or make allusions to them, he may interfere in the conversations of his heroes, he may openly polemicize with his literary enemies and so forth. This is not merely a matter of the author's image appearing within his own field of representation—important here is the fact that the underlying, original formal author (the author of the authorial image) appears in a new relationship with the represented world. Both find themselves now subject to the same temporally valorized measurements, for the "depicting" authorial language now lies on the same plane as the "depicted" language of the hero, and may enter into dialogic relations and hybrid combinations with it (indeed, it cannot help but enter into such relations).

It is precisely this new situation, that of the original formally present author in a zone of contact with the world he is depicting, that makes possible at all the appearance of the authorial image on the field of representation. This new positioning of the author must be considered one of

the most important results of surmounting epic (hierarchical) distance. The enormous formal, compositional and stylistic implications this new positioning of the author has for the specific evolution of the novel as a genre require no further explanation.

* * *

We will summarize with some conclusions.

The present, in its all openendedness, taken as a starting point and center for artistic and ideological orientation, is an enormous revolution in the creative consciousness of man. In the European world this reorientation and destruction of the old hierarchy of temporalities received its crucial generic expression on the boundary between classic antiquity and Hellenism, and in the new world during the late Middle Ages and Renaissance. The fundamental constituents of the novel as a genre were formed in these eras, although some of the separate elements making up the novel were present much earlier, and the novel's roots must ultimately be sought in folklore. In these eras all other major genres had already long since come to completion, they were already old and almost ossified genres. They were all permeated from top to bottom with a more ancient hierarchization of temporalities. The novel, from the very beginning, developed as a genre that had at its core a new way of conceptualizing time. The absolute past, tradition, hierarchical distance played no role in the formation of the novel as a genre (such spatiotemporal categories did play a role, though insignificant, in certain periods of the novel's development, when it was slightly influenced by the epic—for example in the Baroque novel). The novel took shape precisely at the point when epic distance was disintegrating, when both the world and man were assuming a degree of comic familiarity, when the object of artistic representation was being degraded to the level of a contemporary reality that was inconclusive and fluid. From the very beginning the novel was structured not in the distanced image of the absolute past but in the zone of direct contact with inconclusive present-day reality. At its core lay personal experience and free creative imagination. Thus a new, sober artistic-prose novelistic image and a new critical scientific perception came into being simultaneously. From the very beginning, then, the novel was made of different clay than the other already completed genres; it is a different breed, and with it and in it is born the future of all literature. Once it came into being, it could never be merely one genre among others, and it could not erect rules for interrelating with others in peaceful and harmonious coexistence. In the presence of the novel, all other genres somehow have a different resonance. A lengthy battle for the novelization of the other genres be-

---

[32] [Emerson and Holquist] Marcus Terentius Varro (fl. first century B.C.), politician and scholar, a pupil of Stilo—the first Roman philologist—who had made himself known through research on the genuineness of Plautus' comedies. Varro wrote numerous works on the Latin language, but Bakhtin refers to him as author of the lost work *Statuarum Menippearum libri*, humorous essays in the Menippean style satirizing the luxury of his age.

gan, a battle to drag them into a zone of contact with reality. The course of this battle has been complex and tortuous.

The novelization of literature does not imply attaching to already completed genres a generic canon that is alien to them, not theirs. The novel, after all, has no canon of its own. It is, by its very nature, not canonic. It is plasticity itself. It is a genre that is ever questing, ever examining itself and subjecting its established forms to review. Such, indeed, is the only possibility open to a genre that structures itself in a zone of direct contact with developing reality. Therefore, the novelization of other genres does not imply their subjection to an alien generic canon; on the contrary, novelization implies their liberation from all that serves as a brake on their unique development, from all that would change them along with the novel into some sort of stylization of forms that have outlived themselves.

I have developed my various positions in this essay in a somewhat abstract way. There have been few illustrations, and even these were taken only from an ancient period in the novel's development. My choice was determined by the fact that the significance of that period has been greatly underestimated. When people talk about the ancient period of the novel they have traditionally had in mind the "Greek novel" alone. The ancient period of the novel is enormously significant for a proper understanding of the genre. But in ancient times the novel could not really develop all its potential; this potential came to light only in the modern world. We indicated that in several works of antiquity, the inconclusive present begins to sense a greater proximity to the future than to the past. The absence of a temporal perspective in ancient society assured that this process of reorientation toward a real future could not complete itself; after all, there was no real concept of a future. Such a reorientation occurred for the first time during the Renaissance. In that era, the present (that is, a reality that was contemporaneous) for the first time began to sense itself not only as an incomplete continuation of the past, but as something like a new and heroic beginning. To reinterpret reality on the level of the contemporary present now meant not only to degrade, but to raise reality into a new and heroic sphere. It was in the Renaissance that the present first began to feel with great clarity and awareness an incomparably closer proximity and kinship to the future than to the past.

The process of the novel's development has not yet come to an end. It is currently entering a new phase. For our era is characterized by an extraordinary complexity and a deepening in our perception of the world; there is an unusual growth in demands on human discernment, on mature objectivity and the critical faculty. These are features that will shape the further development of the novel as well.

Valentin N. Volosinov

1895–?

Valentin N. Volosinov's *Marxism and the Philosophy of Language* appeared in Leningrad in 1929 and 1930, in the context of a group of scholars and critics with an interest in semiotics, the most notable of whom is Mikhail Bakhtin (above, page 912), but an uncertain relation to emerging orthodoxy among Marxist scholars and thinkers. Volosinov's work, evidently closely related to Bakhtin's (including speculations that the work might have been merely published under Volosinov's name), was read and circulated by members of the Prague Linguistic Circle, though Volosinov himself was evidently the victim of political suppression, with no mention of his work (and no record of his own subsequent life) until the 1970s.

Volosinov's treatment of linguistic utterances fruitfully expanded beyond merely linguistic analysis, to take on the whole of the utterance, including its social, political, and psychological context. He challenges the view that language (in the sense of Saussure's [above, page 786] *langage*) should be considered as an abstract, objective form, seeing it instead as an *"always changeable and adaptable sign"* that is directly responsive to ideological, psychological, and other real-life practices. It is significant in this respect that Volosinov's book takes advantage of the fact that there is no clear position in the works of Marx and Engels (above, page 607) concerning the philosophy of language—just as its relative heterodoxy with respect to emerging Soviet standards was a factor in its suppression.

In addition to *Marxism and the Philosophy of Language,* Volosinov was the author of *Freudianism: A Marxist Critique* (1976; reprinted 1986, as *Freudianism: A Critical Sketch*), translated by I. R. Titunik, edited with the collaboration of Neal Bruss. See also Ladislav Matejka and Krystyna Pomorska, eds., *Readings in Russian Poetics: Formalist and Structuralist Views* (1971).

Verbal Interaction

Individualistic subjectivism and its theory of expression. Criticism of the theory of expression. The sociological structure of experience and expression. The problem of behavioral ideology. The utterance as the basic unit in the generative process of speech. Approaches to the solution of the problem of the actual mode of existence of language. The utterance as a whole entity and its forms.

The second trend of thought in the philosophy of language was associated, as we saw, with rationalism and neoclassicism. The first trend—individualistic subjectivism—is associated with *romanticism*. Romanticism, to a considerable degree, was a reaction against the alien word and the categories of thought promoted by the alien word. More particularly and more immediately, romanticism was a reaction against the last resurgences of the cultural power of the alien word—the epochs of the Renaissance and neoclassicism. The romanticists were the first philologists of native language, the first to attempt a radical restructuring of linguistic thought. Their restructuring was based on experience with native language as the medium through which consciousness and ideas are generated. True, the romanticists

---

Verbal Interaction was first published in 1929. It is reprinted from *Marxism and the Philosophy of Language,* translated by Ladislav Matejka and I. R. Titunik (New York: Seminar Press, 1973).

remained philologists in the strict sense of the word. It was, of course, beyond their power to restructure a mode of thinking about language that had taken shape and had been sustained over the course of centuries. Nevertheless, new categories were introduced into that thinking, and these new categories were precisely what gave the first trend its specific characteristics. Symptomatically, even recent representatives of individualistic subjectivism have been specialists in modern languages, chiefly the Romance languages (Vossler, Leo Spitzer, Lorch, *et al.*).[1]

However, individualistic subjectivism also took the monologic utterance as the ultimate reality and the point of departure for its thinking about language. To be sure, it did not approach the monologic utterance from the viewpoint of the passively understanding philologists but, rather, approached it from within, from the viewpoint of the person speaking and expressing himself.

What does the monologic utterance amount to, then, in the view of individualistic subjectivism? We have seen that it is a purely individual act, the expression of an individual consciousness, its ambitions, intentions, creative impulses, tastes, and so on. The category of expression for individualistic subjectivism is the highest and broadest category under which the speech act—the utterance—may be subsumed.

But what is expression?

Its simplest, rough definition is: something which, having in some way taken shape and definition in the psyche of an individual, is outwardly objectified for others with the help of external signs of some kind.

Thus there are two elements in expression: that inner something which is *expressible,* and its *outward objectification* for others (or possibly for oneself). Any theory of expression, however complex or subtle a form it may take, inevitably presupposes these two elements—the whole event of expression is played out between them. Consequently, any theory of expression inevitably presupposes that the expressible is something that can somehow take shape and exist apart from expression; that it exists first in one form and then switches to another form. This would have to be the case; otherwise, if the expressible were to exist from the very start in the form of expression, with quantitative transition between the two elements (in the sense of clarification, differentiation, and the like), the whole theory of expression would collapse. The theory of expression inevitably presupposes a certain dualism between the inner and outer elements and the explicit primacy of the former, since each act of objectification (expression) goes from inside out. Its sources are within. Not for nothing were idealistic and spiritualistic grounds the only grounds on which the theory of individualistic subjectivism and all theories of expression in general arose. Everything of real importance lies within; the outer element can take on real importance only by becoming a vessel for the inner, by becoming expression of spirit.

To be sure, by becoming external, by expressing itself outwardly, the inner element does undergo alteration. After all, it must gain control of outer material that possesses a validity of its own apart from the inner element. In this process of gaining control, of mastering outer material and making it over into a compliant medium of expression, the experiential, expressible element itself undergoes alteration and is forced to make a certain compromise. Therefore, idealistic grounds, the grounds on which all theories of expression have been established, also contain provision for the radical negation of expression as something that deforms the purity of the inner element.[2] In any case, all the creative and organizing forces of expression are within. Everything outer is merely passive material for manipulation by the inner element. Expression is formed basically within and then merely shifts to the outside. The understanding, interpretation, and explanation of an ideological phenomenon, it would follow from this argument, must also be directed inward; it must traverse a route the reverse of that for expression. Starting from outward objectification, the explanation must work down into its inner, organizing bases. That is how individualistic subjectivism understands expression.

The theory of expression underlying the first trend of thought in philosophy of language is fundamentally untenable.

The experiential, expressible element and its outward objectification are created, as we know, out of one and the same material. After all, there is no such thing as experience outside of embodiment in signs. Consequently, the very notion of a fundamental, qualitative difference between the inner and the outer element is invalid to begin with. Furthermore, the location of the organizing and formative center is not within (i.e., not in the material of inner signs) but outside. It is not experience that organizes expression, but the other way around—*expression organizes experience.* Expression is what first gives experience its form and specificity of direction.

---

[1] Karl Vossler (1872–1949), German literary critic; Leo Spitzer (1887–1960), German literary historian, critic, and philologist; Lorch—Volosinov evidently means J. Etienne Lorck (1860–?), German scholar of Italian and Romance languages. All footnotes are from the author and translators.

[2] [Volosinov] "Spoken thought is a lie" (Tjutčev); "Oh, if one could speak from the soul without words" (Fet). These statements are extremely typical of idealistic romanticism.

Indeed, from whichever aspect we consider it, expression-utterance is determined by the actual conditions of the given utterance—above all, by its *immediate social situation.*

Utterance, as we know, is constructed between two socially organized persons, and in the absence of a real addressee, an addressee is presupposed in the person, so to speak, of a normal representative of the social group to which the speaker belongs. The *word is oriented toward an addressee,* toward *who* that addressee might be: a fellow-member or not of the same social group, of higher or lower standing (the addressee's hierarchical status), someone connected with the speaker by close social ties (father, brother, husband, and so on) or not. There can be no such thing as an abstract addressee, a man unto himself, so to speak. With such a person, we would indeed have no language in common, literally and figuratively. Even though we sometimes have pretensions to experiencing and saying things *urbi et orbi,* actually, of course, we envision this "world at large" through the prism of the concrete social milieu surrounding us. In the majority of cases, we presuppose a certain typical and stabilized *social purview* toward which the ideological creativity of our own social group and time is oriented, i.e., we assume as our addressee a contemporary of our literature, our science, our moral and legal codes.

Each person's inner world and thought has its stabilized *social audience* that comprises the environment in which reasons, motives, values, and so on are fashioned. The more cultured a person, the more closely his inner audience will approximate the normal audience of ideological creativity; but, in any case, specific class and specific era are limits that the ideal of addressee cannot go beyond.

Orientation of the word toward the addressee has an extremely high significance. In point of fact, *word is a two-sided act.* It is determined equally by *whose* word it is and *for whom* it is meant. As word, it is precisely *the product of the reciprocal relationship between speaker and listener, addresser and addressee.* Each and every word expresses the "one" in relation to the "other." I give myself verbal shape from another's point of view, ultimately, from the point of view of the community to which I belong. A word is a bridge thrown between myself and another. If one end of the bridge depends on me, then the other depends on my addressee. A word is territory shared by both addresser and addressee, by the speaker and his interlocutor.

But what does being the speaker mean? Even if a word is not entirely his, constituting, as it were, the border zone between himself and his addressee—still, it does in part belong to him.

There is one instance of the situation wherein the speaker is the undoubted possessor of the word and to which, in this instance, he has full rights. This instance is the physiological act of implementing the word. But insofar as the act is taken in purely physiological terms, the category of possession does not apply.

If, instead of the physiological act of implementing sound, we take the implementation of word as sign, then the question of proprietorship becomes extremely complicated. Aside from the fact that word as sign is a borrowing on the speaker's part from the social stock of available signs, the very individual manipulation of this social sign in a concrete utterance is wholly determined by social relations. The stylistic individualization of an utterance that the Vosslerites speak about represents a reflection of social interrelationships that constitute the atmosphere in which an utterance is formed. *The immediate social situation and the broader social milieu wholly determine—and determine from within, so to speak—the structure of an utterance.*

Indeed, take whatever kind of utterance we will, even the kind of utterance that is not a referential message (communication in the narrow sense) but the verbal expression of some need—for instance, hunger—we may be certain that it is socially oriented in its entirety. Above all, it is determined immediately and directly by the participants of the speech event, both explicit and implicit participants, in connection with a specific situation. That situation shapes the utterance, dictating that it sound one way and not another—like a demand or request, insistence on one's rights or a plea for mercy, in a style flowery or plain, in a confident or hesitant manner, and so on.

The immediate social situation and its immediate social participants determine the "occasional" form and style of an utterance. The deeper layers of its structure are determined by more sustained and more basic social connections with which the speaker is in contact.

Even if we were to take an utterance still in process of generation "in the soul," it would not change the essence of the matter, since the structure of experience is just as social as is the structure of its outward objectification. The degree to which an experience is perceptible, distinct, and formulated is directly proportional to the degree to which it is socially oriented.

In fact, not even the simplest, dimmest apprehension of a feeling—say, the feeling of hunger not outwardly expressed—can dispense with some kind of ideological form. Any apprehension, after all, must have inner speech, inner intonation and the rudiments of inner style: one can apprehend one's hunger apologetically, irritably, angrily, indignantly, etc. We have indicated, of course, only the grosser, more egregious directions that inner intonation may take; actually, there is an extremely subtle and complex set of possibilities for intoning an experience. Outward expression in most cases only continues and makes more distinct the direction already taken by inner speech and the intonation already embedded in it.

Which way the intoning of the inner sensation of hunger will go depends upon the hungry person's general social standing as well as upon the immediate circumstances of the experience. These are, after all, the circumstances that determine in what evaluative context, within what social purview, the experience of hunger will be apprehended. The immediate social context will determine possible addressees, friends or foes, toward whom the consciousness and the experience of hunger will be oriented: whether it will involve dissatisfaction with cruel Nature, with oneself, with society, with a specific group within society, with a specific person, and so on. Of course, various degrees of perceptibility, distinctiveness, and differentiation in the social orientation of an experience are possible; but without some kind of evaluative social orientation there is no experience. Even the cry of a nursing infant is "oriented" toward its mother. There is the possibility that the experience of hunger may take on political coloring, in which case its structure will be determined along the lines of a potential political appeal or a reason for political agitation. It may be apprehended as a form of protest, and so on.

With regard to the potential (and sometimes even distinctly sensed) addressee, a distinction can be made between two poles, two extremes between which an experience can be apprehended and ideologically structured, tending now toward the one, now toward the other. Let us label these two extremes the *"I-experience"* and the *"we-experience."*

The "I-experience" actually tends toward extermination: the nearer it approaches its extreme limit, the more it loses its ideological structuredness and, hence, its apprehensible quality, reverting to the physiological reaction of the animal. In its course toward this extreme, the experience relinquishes all its potentialities, all outcroppings of social orientation, and, therefore, also loses its verbal delineation. Single experiences or whole groups of experiences can approach this extreme, relinquishing, in doing so, their ideological clarity and structuredness and testifying to the inability of the consciousness to strike social roots.[3]

The "we-experience" is not by any means a nebulous herd experience; it is differentiated. Moreover, ideological differentiation, the growth of consciousness, is in direct proportion to the firmness and reliability of the social orienta-tion. The stronger, the more organized, the more differentiated the collective in which an individual orients himself, the more vivid and complex his inner world will be.

The "we-experience" allows of different degrees and different types of ideological structuring.

Let us suppose a case where hunger is apprehended by one of a disparate set of hungry persons whose hunger is a matter of chance (the man down on his luck, the beggar, or the like). The experience of such a declassé loner will be colored in some specific way and will gravitate toward certain particular ideological forms with a range potentially quite broad: humility, shame, enviousness, and other evaluative tones will color his experience. The ideological forms along the lines of which the experience would develop would be either the individualistic protest of a vagabond or repentant, mystical resignation.

Let us now suppose a case in which the hungry person belongs to a collective where hunger is not haphazard and does bear a collective character—but the collective of these hungry people is not itself tightly bound together by material ties, each of its members experiencing hunger on his own. This is the situation most peasants are in. Hunger is experienced "at large," but under conditions of material disparateness, in the absence of a unifying economic coalition, each person suffers hunger in the small, enclosed world of his own individual economy. Such a collective lacks the unitary material frame necessary for united action. A resigned but unashamed and undemeaning apprehension of one's hunger will be the rule under such conditions—"everyone bears it, you must bear it, too." Here grounds are furnished for the development of the philosophical and religious systems of the nonresistor or fatalist type (early Christianity, Tolstoyanism).

A completely different experience of hunger applies to a member of an objectively and materially aligned and united collective (a regiment of solders; workers in their association within the walls of a factory; hired hands on a large-scale, capitalist farm; finally, a whole class once it has matured to the point of "class unto itself"). The experience of hunger this time will be marked predominantly by overtones of active and self-confident protest with no basis for humble and submissive intonation. These are the most favorable grounds for an experience to achieve ideological clarity and structuredness.[4]

---

[3][Volosinov] On the possibility of a set of human sexual experiences falling out of social context with concomitant loss of verbal cognizance, see our book, *Frejdizm* (Freudianism) (1927), pp. 135–136.

[4][Volosinov] Interesting material about expressions of hunger can be found in Leo Spitzer's books, *Italienische Kriegsgefangenenbriefe* and *Die Umschreibungen des Begriffes Hunger*. The basic concern in these studies is the adaptability of word and image to the conditions of an exceptional situation. The author does not, however, operate with a genuine sociological approach.

All these types of expression, each with its basic intonations, come rife with corresponding terms and corresponding forms of possible utterances. The social situation in all cases determines which term, which metaphor, and which form may develop in an utterance expressing hunger out of the particular intonational bearings of the experience.

A special kind of character marks the individualistic *self-experience*. It does not belong to the "I-experience" in the strict sense of the term as defined above. The individualistic experience is fully differentiated and structured. Individualism is a special ideological form of the "we-experience" of the bourgeois class (there is also an analogous type of individualistic self-experience for the feudal aristocratic class). The individualistic type of experience derives from a steadfast and confident social orientation. Individualistic confidence in oneself, one's sense of personal value, is drawn not from within, not from the depths of one's personality, but from the outside world. It is the ideological interpretation of one's social recognizance and tenability by rights, and of the objective security and tenability provided by the whole social order, of one's individual livelihood. The structure of the conscious, individual personality is just as social a structure as is the collective type of experience. It is a particular kind of interpretation, projected into the individual soul, of a complex and sustained socioeconomic situation. But there resides in this type of individualistic "we-experience," and also in the very order to which it corresponds, an inner contradiction that sooner or later will demolish its ideological structuredness.

An analogous structure is presented in solitary self-experience ("the ability and strength to stand alone in one's rectitude"), a type cultivated by Romain Rolland and, to some extent, by Tolstoj. The pride involved in this solitude also depends upon "we." It is a variant of the "we-experience" characteristic of the modern-day West European intelligentsia. Tolstoj's remarks about there being different kinds of thinking—"for oneself" and "for the public"—merely juxtapose two different conceptions of "public." Tolstoj's "for oneself" actually signifies only another social conception of addressee peculiar to himself. There is no such thing as thinking outside orientation toward possible expression and, hence, outside the social orientation of that expression and of the thinking involved.

Thus the personality of the speaker, taken from within, so to speak, turns out to be wholly a product of social interrelations. Not only its outward expression but also its inner experience are social territory. Consequently, the whole route between inner experience (the "expressible") and its outward objectification (the "utterance") lies entirely across social territory. When an experience reaches the stage of actualization in a full-fledged utterance, its social orientation acquires added complexity by focusing on the immediate social circumstances of discourse and, above all, upon actual addressees.

Our analysis casts a new light upon the problem of consciousness and ideology that we examined earlier.

Outside objectification, outside embodiment in some particular material (the material of gesture, inner word, outcry), *consciousness is a fiction.* It is an improper ideological construct created by way of abstraction from the concrete facts of social expression. But consciousness as organized, material expression (in the ideological material of word, a sign, drawing, colors, musical sound, etc.)—consciousness, so conceived, is an objective fact and a tremendous social force. To be sure, this kind of consciousness is not a supraexistential phenomenon and cannot determine the constitution of existence. It itself is part of existence and one of its forces, and for that reason it possesses efficacy and plays a role in the arena of existence. Consciousness, while still inside a conscious person's head as inner-word embryo of expression, is as yet too tiny a piece of existence, and the scope of its activity is also as yet too small. But once it passes through all the stages of social objectification and enters into the power system of science, art, ethics, or law, it becomes a real force, capable even of exerting in turn an influence on the economic bases of social life. To be sure, this force of consciousness is incarnated in specific social organizations, geared into steadfast ideological modes of expression (science, art, and so on), but even in the original, vague form of glimmering thought and experience, it had already constituted a social event on a small scale and was not an inner act on the part of the individual.

From the very start experience is set toward fully actualized outward expression and, from the very start, tends in that direction. The expression of an experience may be realized or it may be held back, inhibited. In the latter case, the experience is inhibited expression (we shall not go into the extremely complex problem of the causes and conditions of inhibition). Realized expression, in its turn, exerts a powerful, reverse influence on experience: it begins to tie inner life together, giving it more definite and lasting expression.

This reverse influence by structured and stabilized expression on experience (i.e., inner expression) has tremendous importance and must always be taken into account. The claim can be made that it is a matter *not so much of expression accomodating itself to our inner world but rather of our inner world accomodating itself to the potentialities of our expression, its possible routes and directions.*

To distinguish it from the established systems of ideology—the systems of art, ethics, law, etc.—we shall use the term *behavioral ideology* for the whole aggregate of life experiences and the outward expressions directly connected with it. Behavioral ideology is that atmosphere of unsystematized and unfixed inner and outer speech which endows our every instance of behavior and action and our every "conscious" state with meaning. Considering the sociological nature of the structure of expression and experience, we may say that behavioral ideology in our conception corresponds basically to what is termed "social psychology" in Marxist literature. In the present context, we should prefer to avoid the word "psychology," since we are concerned exclusively with the content of the psyche and the consciousness. That content is ideological through and through, determined not by individual, organismic (biological or physiological) factors, but by factors of a purely sociological character. The individual, organismic factor is completely irrelevant to an understanding of the basic creative and living lineaments of the content of consciousness.

The established ideological systems of social ethics, science, art, and religion are crystallizations of behavioral ideology, and these crystallizations, in turn, exert a powerful influence back upon behavioral ideology, normally setting its tone. At the same time, however, these already formalized ideological products constantly maintain the most vital organic contact with behavioral ideology and draw sustenance from it; otherwise, without that contact, they would be dead, just as any literary work or cognitive idea is dead without living, evaluative perception of it. Now, this ideological perception, for which alone any ideological piece of work can and does exist, is carried out in the language of behavioral ideology. Behavioral ideology draws the work into some particular social situation. The work combines with the whole content of the consciousness of those who perceive it and derives its apperceptive values only in the context of that consciousness. It is interpreted in the spirit of the particular content of consciousness (the consciousness of the perceiver) and is illuminated by it anew. This is what constitutes the vitality of an ideological production. In each period of its historical existence, a work must enter into close association with the changing behavioral ideology, become permeated with it, and draw new sustenance from it. Only to the degree that a work can enter into that kind of integral, organic association with the behavioral ideology of a given period is it viable for that period (and of course, for a given social group). Outside its connection with behavioral ideology it ceases to exist, since it ceases to be experienced as something ideologically meaningful.

We must distinguish several different strata in behavioral ideology. These strata are defined by the social scale on which experience and expression are measured, or by the social forces with respect to which they must directly orient themselves.

The purview in which an experience or expression comes into being may, as we know, vary in scope. The world of an experience may be narrow and dim; its social orientation may be haphazard and ephemeral and characteristic only for some adventitious and loose coalition of a small number of persons. Of course, even these erratic experiences are ideological and sociological, but their position lies on the borders of the normal and the pathological. Such an experience will remain an isolated fact in the psychological life of the person exposed to it. It will not take firm root and will not receive differentiated and full-fledged expression; indeed, if it lacks a socially grounded and stable audience, where could it possibly find bases for its differentiation and finalization? Even less likely would such an adventitious experience be set down, in writing or even more so in print. Experiences of that kind, experiences born of a momentary and accidental state of affairs, have, of course, no chance of further social impact of efficacy.

The lowest, most fluid, and quickly changing stratum of behavioral ideology consists of experiences of that kind. To this stratum, consequently, belong all those vague and undeveloped experiences, thoughts, and idle, accidental words that flash across our minds. They are all of them cases of miscarriages of social orientations, novels without heroes, performances without audiences. They lack any sort of logic or unity. The sociological regulatedness in these ideological scraps is extremely difficult to detect. In this lowest stratum of behavioral ideology only statistical regularity is detectable; given a huge quantity of products of this sort, the outlines of socioeconomic regulatedness could be revealed. Needless to say, it would be a practical impossibility to descry in any one such accidental experience or expression its socioeconomic premises.

The upper strata of behavioral ideology, the ones directly linked with ideological systems, are more vital, more serious and bear a creative character. Compared to an established ideology, they are a great deal more mobile and sensitive: they convey changes in the socioeconomic basis more quickly and more vividly. Here, precisely, is where those creative energies build up through whose agency partial or radical restructuring of ideological systems comes about. Newly emerging social forces find ideological expression and take shape first in these upper strata of behavioral ideology before they can succeed in dominating the arena of some organized, official ideology. Of course, in the process of this struggle, in the process of their gradual infiltration into ideological organizations (the press, literature, and science), these new currents in behavioral ideology, no matter how revolutionary they may be, undergo the influence of the established ideological systems and, to some extent, incorporate forms, ideological practices, and approaches already in stock.

What usually is called "creative individuality" is nothing but the expression of a particular person's basic, firmly grounded, and consistent line of social orientation. This concerns primarily the uppermost, fully structured strata of inner speech (behavioral ideology), each of whose terms and intonations have gone through the stage of expression and have, so to speak, passed the test of expression. Thus what is involved here are words, intonations, and inner-word gestures that have undergone the experience of outward expression on a more or less ample social scale and have acquired, as it were, a high social polish and lustre by the effect of reactions and responses, resistance or support, on the part of the social audience.

In the lower strata of behavioral ideology, the biological-biographical factor does, of course, play a crucial role, but its importance constantly diminishes as the utterance penetrates more deeply into an ideological system. Consequently, while bio-biographical explanations are of some value in the lower strata of experience and expression (utterance), their role in the upper strata is extremely modest. Here the objective sociological method takes full command.

So, then, the theory of expression underlying individualistic subjectivism must be rejected. *The organizing center of any utterance, of any experience, is not within but outside—in the social milieu surrounding the individual being.* Only the inarticulate cry of an animal is really organized from inside the physiological apparatus of an individual creature. Such a cry lacks any positive ideological factor vis-à-vis the physiological reaction. Yet, even the most primitive human utterance produced by the individual organism is, from the point of view of its content, import, and meaning, organized outside the organism, in the extraorganismic conditions of the social milieu. Utterance as such is wholly a product of social interaction, both of the immediate sort as determined by the circumstances of the discourse, and of the more general kind, as determined by the whole aggregate of conditions under which any given community of speakers operates.

The individual utterance *(parole)*, despite the contentions of abstract objectivism, is by no means an individual fact not susceptible to sociological analysis by virtue of its individuality. Indeed, if this were so, neither the sum total of these individual acts nor any abstract features common to all such individual acts (the "normatively identical forms") could possibly engender a social product.

Individualistic subjectivism is *correct* in that individual utterances *are* what constitute the actual, concrete reality of language, and in that they *do have* creative value in language.

But individualistic subjectivism is *wrong* in ignoring and failing to understand the social nature of the utterance and in attempting to derive the utterance from the speaker's inner world as an expression of that inner world. The structure of the utterance and of the very experience being expressed is a *social structure.* The stylistic shaping of an utterance is shaping of a social kind, and the very verbal stream of utterances, which is what the reality of language actually amounts to, is a social stream. Each drop of that stream is social and the entire dynamics of its generation are social.

Individualistic subjectivism is also completely *correct* in that linguistic form and its ideological impletion are *not* severable. Each and every word is ideological and each and every application of language involves ideological change. But individualistic subjectivism is *wrong* insofar as it also derives this ideological impletion of the word from the conditions of the individual psyche.

Individualistic subjectivism is *wrong* in taking the monologic utterance, just as abstract objectivism does, as its basic point of departure. Certain Vosslerites, it is true, have begun to consider the problem of dialogue and so to approach a more correct understanding of verbal interaction. Highly symptomatic in this regard is one of Leo Spitzer's books we have already cited—his *Italienische Umgangssprache,* a book that attempts to anlyze the forms of Italian conversational language in close connection with the conditions of discourse and above all with the issue of the addressee.[5] However, Leo Spitzer utilizes a *descriptive psychological* method. He does not draw from his analysis the fundamentally sociological conclusions it suggests. For the Vosslerites, therefore, the monologic utterance still remains the basic reality.

The problem of verbal interaction has been posed clearly and distinctly by Otto Dietrich.[6] He proceeds by way of subjecting to criticism the theory of utterance as expression. For him, the basic function of language is not expression but *communication* (in the strict sense), and this leads him to consider the role of the addressee. The minimal con-

---

[5][Volosinov] In this respect, the very organization of the book is symptomatic. The book divides into four main chapters. Their titles are as follows: I. *Eröffnungsformen des Gesprächs,* II. *Sprecher und Hörer;* A. *Höflchkelt (Rücksicht ouf den Partner).* B. *Sparsamkelt und Verschwendung im Ausdruck;* C. *In elnandeingreifen von Rede und Gegenrede.* III. *Sprecher und Situation.* IV. *Der Abschluss des Gesprächs.* Spitzer's predecessor in the study of conversational language under conditions of real-life discourse was Herman Wunderlich. See his book, *Unsere Umgangssprache* (1894).

[6][Volosinov] See *Die Probleme der Sprachpsychologie* (1914).

dition for a linguistic manifestation is, according to Dietrich, *twofold* (speaker and listener). However, Dietrich shares assumptions of a general psychological type with individualistic subjectivism. Dietrich's investigations likewise lack any determinate sociological basis.

Now we are in a position to answer the question we posed at the end of the first chapter of this section of our study. *The actual reality of language-speech is not the abstract system of linguistic forms, not the isolated monologic utterance, and not the psychophysiological act of its implementation, but the social event of verbal interaction implemented in an utterance or utterances.*

Thus, verbal interaction is the basic reality of language.

Dialogue, in the narrow sense of the word, is, of course, only one of the forms—a very important form, to be sure—of verbal interaction. But dialogue can also be understood in a broader sense, meaning not only direct, face-to-face, vocalized verbal communication between persons, but also verbal communication of any type whatsoever. A book, i.e., a *verbal performance in print,* is also an element of verbal communication. It is something discussable in actual, real-life dialogue, but aside from that, it is calculated for active perception, involving attentive reading and inner responsiveness, and for organized, *printed* reaction in the various forms devised by the particular sphere of verbal communication in question (book reviews, critical surveys, defining influence on subsequent works, and so on). Moreover, a verbal performance of this kind also inevitably orients itself with respect to previous performances in the same sphere, both those by the same author and those by other authors. It inevitably takes its point of departure from some particular state of affairs involving a scientific problem or a literary style. Thus the printed verbal performance engages, as it were, in ideological colloquy of large scale: it responds to something, objects to something, affirms something, anticipates possible responses and objections, seeks support, and so on.

Any utterance, no matter how weighty and complete in and of itself, *is only a moment in the continuous process of verbal communication.* But that continuous verbal communication is, in turn, itself only a moment in the continuous, all-inclusive, generative process of a given social collective. An important problem arises in this regard: the study of the connection between concrete verbal interaction and the extraverbal situation—both the immediate situation and, through it, the broader situation. The forms this connection takes are different, and different factors in a situation may, in association with this or that form, take on different meanings (for instance, these connections differ with the different factors of situation in literary or in scientific communi-

cation). *Verbal communication can never be understood and explained outside of this connection with a concrete situation.* Verbal intercourse is inextricably interwoven with communication of other types, all stemming from the common ground of production communication. It goes without saying that word cannot be divorced from this eternally generative, unified process of communication. In its concrete connection with a situation, verbal communication is always accompanied by social acts of a nonverbal character (the performance of labor, the symbolic acts of a ritual, a ceremony, etc.), and is often only an accessory to these acts, merely carrying out an auxiliary role. *Language acquires life and historically evolves precisely here, in concrete verbal communication, and not in the abstract linguistic system of language forms, nor in the individual psyche of speakers.*

From what has been established, it follows that the methodologically based order of study of language ought to be: (1) the forms and types of verbal interaction in connection with their concrete conditions; (2) forms of particular utterances, of particular speech performances, as elements of a closely linked interaction—i.e., the genres of speech performance in human behavior and ideological creativity as determined by verbal interaction; (3) a reexamination, on this new basis, of language forms in their usual linguistic presentation.

This is the order that the actual generative process of language follows: *social intercourse is generated* (stemming from the basis); *in it verbal communication and interaction are generated; and in the latter, forms of speech performances are generated; finally, this generative process is reflected in the change of language forms.*

One thing that emerges from all that has been said is the extreme importance of the problem of the forms of an utterance *as a whole.* We have already pointed out that contemporary linguistics lacks any approach to the utterance itself. Its analysis goes no further than the elements that constitute an utterance. Meanwhile, utterances are the real units that make up the stream of language-speech. What is necessary in order to study the forms of this real unit is precisely that it not be isolated from the historical stream of utterances. As a whole entity, the utterance is implemented only in the stream of verbal intercourse. The whole is, after all, defined by its boundaries, and these boundaries run along the line of contact between a given utterance and the extraverbal and verbal (i.e., made up of other utterances) milieu.

The first and last words, the beginning and end points of real-life utterance—that is what already constitutes the problem of the whole. The process of speech, broadly understood as the process of inner and outer verbal life, goes on continuously. It knows neither beginning nor end. The outwardly actualized utterance is an island rising from the boundless sea of inner speech; the dimensions and forms of this island are determined by the particular *situation* of the utterance and its *audience*. Situation and audience make inner speech undergo actualization into some kind of specific outer expression that is directly included into an unverbalized behavioral context and in that context is amplified by actions, behavior, or verbal responses of other participants of the utterance. The full-fledged question, exclamation, command, request—these are the most typical forms of wholes in behavioral utterances. All of them (especially the command and request) require an extraverbal complement and, indeed, an extraverbal commencement. The very type of structure these little behavioral *genres* will achieve is determined by the effect, upon a word, of its coming up against the extraverbal milieu and against another word (i.e., the words of other people). Thus, the form a command will take is determined by the obstacles it may encounter, the degree of submissiveness expected, and so on. The structure of the genre in these instances will be in accord with the accidental and unique features of behavioral situations. Only when social custom and circumstances have fixed and stabilized certain forms in behavioral interchange to some appreciable degree, can one speak of specific types of structure in genres of behavioral speech. So, for instance, an entirely special type of structure has been worked out for the genre of the light and casual causerie of the drawing room where everyone "feels at home" and where the basic differentiation within the gathering (the audience) is that between men and women. Here we find devised special forms of insinuation, half-sayings, allusions to little tales of an intentionally nonserious character, and so on. A different type of structure is worked out in the case of conversation between husband and wife, brother and sister, etc. In the case where a random assortment of people gathers—while waiting in a line or conducting some business—statements and exchanges of words will start and finish and be constructed in another, completely different way. Village sewing circles, urban carouses, workers' lunchtime chats, etc., will all have their own types. Each situation, fixed and sustained by social custom, commands a particular kind of organization of audience and, hence, a particular repertoire of little behavioral genres. The behavioral genre fits everywhere into the channel of social intercourse assigned to it and functions as an ideological reflection of its type, structure, goal, and social composition. The behavioral genre is a fact of the social milieu: of holiday, leisure time, and of social con-

tact in the parlor, the workshop, etc. It meshes with that milieu and is delimited and defined by it in all its internal aspects.

The production processes of labor and the processes of commerce know different forms for constructing utterances.

As for the forms of ideological intercourse in the strict sense of the term—forms for political speeches, political acts, laws, regulations, manifestos, and so forth; and forms for poetic utterances, scientific treatises, etc.—these have been the object of special investigation in rhetoric and poetics, but, as we have seen, these investigations have been completely divorced from the problem of language on the one hand, and from the problem of social intercourse on the other.[7] Productive analysis of the forms of the whole of utterances as the real units in the stream of speech is possible only on a basis that regards the individual utterance as a purely sociological phenomenon. Marxist philosophy of language should and must stand squarely on the utterance as the real phenomenon of language-speech and as a socio-ideological structure.

Now that we have outlined the sociological structure of the utterance, let us return to the two trends in philosophical linguistic thought and make a final summing up.

R. Šor, a Moscow linguist and an adherent of the second trend of thought in philosophy of language, ends a brief sketch of the contemporary state of linguistics with the following words:

> "Language is not an artifact *(ergon)* but a natural and congenital activity of mankind"—so claimed the romanticist linguistics of the 19th century. Theoretical linguistics of modern times claims otherwise: "Language is not individual activity *(energlea)* but a cultural-historical legacy of mankind *(ergon).*[8]

This conclusion is amazing in its bias and one-sidedness. On the factual side, it is completely untrue. Modern theoretical linguistics includes, after all, the Vossler school, one of Germany's most powerful movements in contemporary linguistic thought. It is impermissible to identify modern linguistics with only one of its trends.

---

[7][Volosinov] On the topic of disjuncture of a literary work of art with conditions of artistic communication and the resulting inertness of the work, see our study, "Slovo v zizni i slovo v poèzii" [Word in Life and Word in Poetry], *Zvezda*, 6 (1926).

[8][Volosinov] R. Šor, "Krizis sovremennoj linvistiki" [The Crisis in Contemporary Linguistics], *Jafetičeskij sbornik*, V (1927), p. 71.

From the theoretical point of view, both the thesis and the antithesis made up by Šor must equally be rejected, since they are equally inadequate to the real nature of language.

Let us conclude the argument with an attempt to formulate our own point of view in the following set of propositions:

1. *Language as a stable system of normatively identical forms is merely a scientific abstraction,* productive only in connection with certain particular practical and theoretical goals. This abstraction is not adequate to the concrete reality of language.

2. *Language is a continuous generative process implemented in the social-verbal interaction of speakers.*

3. *The laws of the generative process of language are not at all the laws of individual psychology, but neither can they be divorced from the activity of speakers.* The laws of language generation are *sociological* laws.

4. *Linguistic creativity does not coincide with artistic creativity nor with any other type of specialized ideological creativity. But, at the same time, linguistic creativity cannot be understood apart from the ideological meanings and values that fill it.* The generative process of language, as is true of any historical generative process, can be perceived as blind mechanical necessity, but it can also become "free necessity" once it has reached the position of a conscious and desired necessity.

5. *The structure of the utterance is a purely sociological structure.* The utterance, as such, obtains between speakers. The individual speech act (in the strict sense of the word "individual") is *contradictio in adjecto.*

Antonio Gramsci

1891–1937

In 1921, after almost a decade of association with various Socialist groups in Italy, Antonio Gramsci took steps to found the Italian Communist party, subsequently spending almost two years in the Soviet Union. A gifted writer and journalist, Gramsci had early on established a public presence through his columns and review in *Avanti!* and, after 1919, *The New Order.* After his return from Moscow (as an Italian delegate to the Communist International), he was elected to the Chamber of Deputies in 1924 but served only two years until the fascists outlawed the Communist Party and placed Gramsci in solitary confinement, with brutal irony, in the Regina Coeli prison until 1928, when he was sentenced to a term of more than twenty years, served in various prisons and hospitals in Turi, Formia, and Rome, until his death in 1937. His influence on Italian politics, however, was not stopped by his incarceration, as he communicated by letters and papers carefully couched to evade the censors. Following the end of World War II, selections from Gramsci's notebooks began to appear, culminating in the publication of *Selections from Prison Notebooks* in 1971.

The Notebooks offer sustained commentary and reflections on society and politics, including extremely provocative and influential discussions of the social role of the intellectual, and especially the complex concept of "hegemony," which does not mean, in Gramsci's writing, simply the asserted power of a dominant class or party, but more subtly, the conditions under which social institutions, from the church to schools and political parties, educe and sustain social coherence and assent to a practical program of action. In this respect, hegemony is at once a subject for critical caution, but a desirable, indeed an essential objective for any political program, since without securing the assent of the populace, one cannot effectively govern or lead. The complication in the concept, moreover, extends to two related ideas, the distinction between the "state" and "civil society" and between dominant ("hegemonic") groups and nonhegemonic or "subaltern" groups. For Gramsci, the social and political role of the intellectual is all the more important as at once a source of leadership and of mediation, particularly in times of social struggle or revolution, when the historical hegemony of a ruling group cannot be reconciled with the legitimate desires of a subaltern group.

Particularly after 1968, Gramsci's importance for critics and theorists concerned with postcolonial culture and politics, and the interests and rights of marginalized groups has been particularly prominent, in large measure because of the subtlety and scope of his reflections on what he termed a "philosophy of praxis," which attempts to integrate historical, speculative, and philosophical elements within the framework of radical politics.

The principal works of Gramsci available in English translation include: *The Modern Prince and Other Writings by Antonio Gramsci,* trans. Louis Marks (1957); *Selections from the Prison Notebooks of Antonio Gramsci,* ed. and trans. Quintin Hoare and

Geoffrey Nowell-Smith (1971); *Further Selections from the Prison Notebooks,* ed. and trans. Derek Boothman (1995); *Letters from Prison,* selected by Lynn Lawner, trans. (1973); *Selections from Cultural Writings,* ed. David Forgacs and Geoffrey Nowell-Smith, trans. William Boelhower (1985); and *An Antonio Gramsci Reader: Selected Writings, 1916–1935,* ed. David Forgacs (1988). Critical studies of Gramsci include: Walter L. Adamson, *Hegemony and Revolution: A Study of Antonio Gramsci's Political and Cultural Theory* (1980); Anne Showstack Sassoon, ed., *Approaches to Gramsci* (1982); John Hoffman, *The Gramscian Challenge: Coercion and Consent in Marxist Political Theory* (1984); Robert S. Dombroski, *Antonio Gramsci* (1989); James Martin, *Gramsci's Political Analysis: A Critical Introduction* (1998).

from
Prison Notebooks*

The Intellectuals

*[Hoare and Nowell-Smith] Terminology: Questions of censorship apart, Gramsci's terminology presents a number of difficulties to the translator. Wherever possible we have tried to render each term of Gramsci's with a single equivalent, as close as possible to the original. In one particular set of cases this has proved impossible, and that is with the group of words centred around the verb *dirigere* (*dirigente, direttivo, direzione,* etc.). Here we have in part followed the normal English usage dictated by the context (e.g. *direzione* = leadership; *class dirigente* = ruling class) but in certain cases we have translated *dirigente* and *direttivo* as "directive" in order to preserve what for Gramsci is a crucial conceptual distinction, between power based on "domination" and the exercise of "direction" or "hegemony." In this context it is also worth noting that the term "hegemony" in Gramsci itself has two faces. On the one hand it is contrasted with "domination" (and as such bound up with the opposition State/Civil Society) and on the other hand "hegemonic" is sometimes used as an opposite of "corporate" or "economic-corporate" to designate an historical phase in which a given group moves beyond a position of corporate existence and defence of its economic position and aspires to a position of leadership in the political and social arena. Nonhegemonic groups or classes are also called by Gramsci "subordinate," "subaltern" or sometimes "instrumental." Here again we have preserved Gramsci's original terminology despite the strangeness that some of these words have in English and despite the fact that it is difficult to discern any systematic difference in Gramsci's usage between, for instance, subaltern and subordinate. The Hegelian sense of the word "momento," meaning an aspect of a situation in its concrete (not necessarily temporal) manifestations, has generally been rendered as "moment" but sometimes as "aspect." Despite Marx's strictures (in *The German Ideology*) on the abuse of this word, it occurs frequently in Gramsci in both its senses, and confusion is made worse by the fact that Italian, unlike German, does not distinguish the two senses of the word according to gender. In particular cases where there seemed to us any difficulty with a word or concept we have referred the reader to a footnote, as also with any passage where the translation is at all uncertain. In general we have preferred to footnote too much rather than too little, on the assumption that readers familiar with, say, the history of the Third International might nevertheless find useful some explanation, however elementary, of the specialised vocabulary of Kantian philosophy, while philosophers who know their Hegel and Marx might be less at home in the history of the Italian Risorgimento.

The translation and notes for the writings on the Risorgimento and on politics are by Quintin Hoare; those for the essay on the Intellectuals are by Geoffrey Nowell-Smith.

The Formation of the Intellectuals

Are intellectuals an autonomous and independent social group, or does every social group have its own particular specialised category of intellectuals? The problem is a complex one, because of the variety of forms assumed to date by the real historical process of formation of the different categories of intellectuals.

The most important of these forms are two:

1. Every social group, coming into existence on the original terrain of an essential function in the world of economic production, creates together with itself, organically, one or more strata[1] of intellectuals which give it homogeneity and an awareness of its own function not only in the economic but also in the social and political fields. The capitalist entrepreneur creates alongside himself the industrial technician, the specialist in political economy, the organisers of a new culture, of a new legal system, etc. It should be

---

Selections from "The Intellectuals," "Notes on Italian History," and "State and Civil Society" were composed between 1929 and 1935, reprinted here from Antonio Gramsci, *Selections from Prison Notebooks,* edited and translated by Quintin Hoare and Geoffrey Nowell-Smith (London: Lawrence and Wishart, 1971).

[1] [Hoare and Nowell-Smith] The Italian word here is *"ceti"* which does not carry quite the same connotations as "strata," but which we have been forced to translate in that way for lack of alternatives. It should be noted that Gramsci tends, for reasons of censorship, to avoid using the word class in contexts where its Marxist overtones would be apparent, preferring (as for example in this sentence) the more neutral "social group." The word "group," however, is not always a euphemism for "class," and to avoid ambiguity Gramsci uses the phrase "fundamental social group" when he wishes to emphasise the fact that he is referring to one or other of the major social classes (bourgeoisie, proletariat) defined in strict Marxist terms by its position in the fundamental relations of production. Class groupings which do not have this fundamental role are often described as "castes" (aristocracy, etc.). The word "category," on the other hand, which also occurs on this page, Gramsci tends to use in the standard Italian sense of members of a trade or profession, though also more generally. Throughout this edition we have rendered Gramsci's usage as literally as possible.

noted that the entrepreneur himself represents a higher level of social elaboration, already characterised by a certain directive [*dirigente*][2] and technical (i.e. intellectual) capacity: he must have a certain technical capacity, not only in the limited sphere of his activity and initiative but in other spheres as well, at least in those which are closest to economic production. He must be an organiser of masses of men; he must be an organiser of the "confidence" of investors in his business, of the customers for his product, etc.

If not all entrepreneurs, at least an *élite* amongst them must have the capacity to be an organiser of society in general, including all its complex organism of services, right up to the state organism, because of the need to create the conditions most favourable to the expansion of their own class; or at the least they must possess the capacity to choose the deputies (specialised employees) to whom to entrust this activity of organising the general system of relationships external to the business itself. It can be observed that the "organic" intellectuals which every new class creates alongside itself and elaborates in the course of its development, are for the most part "specialisations" of partial aspects of the primitive activity of the new social type which the new class has brought into prominence.[3]

Even feudal lords were possessors of a particular technical capacity, military capacity, and it is precisely from the moment at which the aristocracy loses its monopoly of technico-military capacity that the crisis of feudalism begins. But the formation of intellectuals in the feudal world and in the preceding classical world is a question to be examined separately: this formation and elaboration follows ways and means which must be studied concretely. Thus it is to be noted that the mass of the peasantry, although it performs an essential function in the world of production, does not elaborate its own "organic" intellectuals, nor does it "assimilate" any stratum of "traditional" intellectuals, although it is from the peasantry that other social groups draw many

of their intellectuals and a high proportion of traditional intellectuals are of peasant origin.[5]

2. However, every "essential" social group which emerges into history out of the preceding economic structure, and as an expression of a development of this structure, has found (at least in all of history up to the present) categories of intellectuals already in existence and which seemed indeed to represent an historical continuity uninterrupted even by the most complicated and radical changes in political and social forms.

The most typical of these categories of intellectuals is that of the ecclesiastics, who for a long time (for a whole phase of history, which is partly characterised by this very monopoly) held a monopoly of a number of important services: religious ideology, that is the philosophy and science of the age, together with schools, education, morality, justice, charity, good works, etc. The category of ecclesiastics can be considered the category of intellectuals organically bound to the landed aristocracy. It had equal status juridically with the aristocracy, with which it shared the exercise of feudal ownership of land, and the use of state privileges connected with property.[6] But the monopoly held by the ecclesiastics in the superstructural field[7] was not exercised without a struggle or without limitations, and hence there took place the birth, in various forms (to be gone into and studied concretely), of other categories, favoured and enabled to expand by the growing strength of the central power of the monarch, right up to absolutism. Thus we find

---

[2][Hoare and Nowell-Smith] See note on Gramsci's Terminology.

[3][Gramsci] Mosca's *Elementi di Scienza Politica* (new expanded edition, 1923) are worth looking at in this connection. Mosca's so-called "political class"[4] is nothing other than the intellectual category of the dominant social group. Mosca's concept of "political class" can be connected with Pareto's concept of the *élite*, which is another attempt to interpret the historical phenomenon of the intellectuals and their function in the life of the state and of society. Mosca's book is an enormous hotch-potch, of a sociological and positivistic character, plus the tendentiousness of immediate politics which makes it less indigestible and livelier from a literary point of view.

[4][Hoare and Nowell-Smith] Usually translated in English as "ruling class," which is also the title of the English version of Mosca's *Elementi* (G. Mosca, *The Ruling Class*, New York 1939). Gaetano Mosca (1858–1941) was, together with Pareto and Michels, one of the major early Italian exponents of the theory of political *élites*. Although sympathetic to fascism, Mosca was basically a conservative, who saw the *élite* in rather more static terms than did some of his fellows.

[5][Hoare and Nowell-Smith] Notably in Southern Italy. See below, "The Different Position of Urban and Rural-type Intellectuals," pp. 14–23. Gramsci's general argument, here as elsewhere in the *Quoderni*, is that the person of peasant origin who becomes an "intellectual" (priest, lawyer, etc.) generally thereby ceases to be organically linked to his class of origin. One of the essential differences between, say, the Catholic Church and the revolutionary party of the working class lies in the fact that, ideally, the proletariat should be able to generate its own "organic" intellectuals within the class and who remain intellectuals *of* their class.

[6][Gramsci] For one category of these intellectuals, possibly the most important after the ecclesiastical for its prestige and the social function it performed in primitive societies, the category of *medical men* in the wide sense, that is all those who "struggle" or seem to struggle against death and disease, compare the *Storia della medicina* of Arturo Castiglioni. Note that there has been a connection between religion and medicine, and in certain areas there still is: hospitals in the hands of religious orders for certain organisational functions, apart from the fact that wherever the doctor appears, so does the priest (exorcism, various forms of assistance, etc.). Many great religious figures were and are conceived of as great "healers": the idea of miracles, up to the resurrection of the dead. Even in the case of kings the belief long survived that they could heal with the laying on of hands, etc.

[7][Gramsci] From this has come the general sense of "intellectual" or "specialist" of the word *"chierico"* (clerk, cleric) in many languages of romance origin or heavily influenced, through church Latin, by the romance languages, together with its correlative *"laico"* (lay, layman) in the sense of profane, non-specialist.

the formation of the *noblesse de robe,* with its own privileges, a stratum of administrators, etc., scholars and scientists, theorists, non-ecclesiastical philosophers, etc.

Since these various categories of traditional intellectuals experience through an *"esprit de corps"* their uninterrupted historical continuity and their special qualification, they thus put themselves forward as autonomous and independent of the dominant social group. This self-assessment is not without consequences in the ideological and political field, consequences of wide-ranging import. The whole of idealist philosophy can easily be connected with this position assumed by the social complex of intellectuals and can be defined as the expression of that social utopia by which the intellectuals think of themselves as "independent," autonomous, endowed with a character of their own, etc.

One should note however that if the Pope and the leading hierarchy of the Church consider themselves more linked to Christ and to the apostles than they are to senators Agnelli and Benni,[8] the same does not hold for Gentile and Croce, for example: Croce in particular feels himself closely linked to Aristotle and Plato, but he does not conceal, on the other hand, his links with senators Agnelli and Benni, and it is precisely here that one can discern the most significant character of Croce's philosophy.

What are the "maximum" limits of acceptance of the term "intellectual"? Can one find a unitary criterion to characterise equally all the diverse and disparate activities of intellectuals and to distinguish these at the same time and in an essential way from the activities of other social groupings? The most widespread error of method seems to me that of having looked for this criterion of distinction in the intrinsic nature of intellectual activities, rather than in the ensemble of the system of relations in which these activities (and therefore the intellectual groups who personify them) have their place within the general complex of social relations. Indeed the worker or proletarian, for example, is not specifically characterised by his manual or instrumental work, but by performing this work in specific conditions and in specific social relations (apart from the consideration that purely physical labour does not exist and that even Taylor's phrase of "trained gorilla"[9] is a metaphor to indicate a limit in a certain direction: in any physical work, even the most degraded and mechanical, there exists a minimum of technical qualification, that is, a minimum of creative intellectual activity.) And we have already observed that the entrepreneur, by virtue of his very function, must have to some degree a certain number of qualifications of an intellectual nature although his part in society is determined not by these, but by the general social relations which specifically characterise the position of the entrepreneur within industry.

All men are intellectuals, one could therefore say: but not all men have in society the function of intellectuals.[10]

When one distinguishes between intellectuals and non-intellectuals, one is referring in reality only to the immediate social function of the professional category of the intellectuals, that is, one has in mind the direction in which their specific professional activity is weighted, whether towards intellectual elaboration or towards muscular-nervous effort. This means that, although one can speak of intellectuals, one cannot speak of non-intellectuals, because non-intellectuals do not exist. But even the relationship between efforts of intellectual-cerebral elaboration and muscular-nervous effort is not always the same, so that there are varying degrees of specific intellectual activity. There is no human activity from which every form of intellectual participation can be excluded: *homo faber* cannot be separated from *homo sapiens.*[11] Each man, finally, outside his professional activity, carries on some form of intellectual activity, that is, he is a "philosopher," an artist, a man of taste, he participates in a particular conception of the world, has a conscious line of moral conduct, and therefore contributes to sustain a conception of the world or to modify it, that is, to bring into being new modes of thought.

The problem of creating a new stratum of intellectuals consists therefore in the critical elaboration of the intellectual activity that exists in everyone at a certain degree of development, modifying its relationship with the muscular-nervous effort towards a new equilibrium, and ensuring that the muscular-nervous effort itself, in so far as it is an element of a general practical activity, which is perpetually innovating the physical and social world, becomes the foundation of a new and integral conception of the world. The traditional and vulgarised type of the intellectual is given by the man of letters, the philosopher, the artist. Therefore journalists, who claim to be men of letters, philosophers, artists, also regard themselves as the "true" intellectuals. In the modern world, technical education, closely bound to industrial labour even at the most primitive and unqualified level, must form the basis of the new type of intellectual.

---

[8] [Hoare and Nowell-Smith] Heads of FIAT and Montecatini (Chemicals) respectively. For Agnelli, of whom Gramsci had direct experience during the *Ordine Nuovo* period, see note 11 on p. 286.

[9] [Hoare and Nowell-Smith] For Frederick Taylor and his notion of the manual worker as a "trained gorilla," see Gramsci's essay *Americanism and Fordism,* pp. 277–318 of this volume.

[10] [Gramsci] Thus, because it can happen that everyone at some time fries a couple of eggs or sews up a tear in a jacket, we do not necessarily say that everyone is a cook or a tailor.

[11] [Hoare and Nowell-Smith] I.e. Man the maker (or tool-bearer) and Man the thinker.

On this basis the weekly *Ordine Nuovo*[12] worked to develop certain forms of new intellectualism and to determine its new concepts, and this was not the least of the reasons for its success, since such a conception corresponded to latent aspirations and conformed to the development of the real forms of life. The mode of being of the new intellectual can no longer consist in eloquence, which is an exterior and momentary mover of feelings and passions, but in active participation in practical life, as constructor, organiser, "permanent persuader" and not just a simple orator (but superior at the same time to the abstract mathematical spirit); from technique-as-work one proceeds to technique-as-science and to the humanistic conception of history, without which one remains "specialised" and does not become "directive"[13] (specialised and political).

Thus there are historically formed specialised categories for the exercise of the intellectual function. They are formed in connection with all social groups, but especially in connection with the more important, and they undergo more extensive and complex elaboration in connection with the dominant social group. One of the most important characteristics of any group that is developing towards dominance is its struggle to assimilate and to conquer "ideologically" the traditional intellectuals, but this assimilation and conquest is made quicker and more efficacious the more the group in question succeeds in simultaneously elaborating its own organic intellectuals.

The enormous development of activity and organisation of education in the broad sense in the societies that emerged from the medieval world is an index of the importance assumed in the modern world by intellectual functions and categories. Parallel with the attempt to deepen and to broaden the "intellectuality" of each individual, there has also been an attempt to multiply and narrow the various specialisations. This can be seen from educational institutions at all levels, up to and including the organisms that exist to promote so-called "high culture" in all fields of science and technology.

School is the instrument through which intellectuals of various levels are elaborated. The complexity of the intellectual function in different states can be measured objectively by the number and gradation of specialised schools: the more extensive the "area" covered by education and the more numerous the "vertical" "levels" of schooling, the more complex is the cultural world, the civilisation, of a particular state. A point of comparison can be found in the sphere of industrial technology: the industrialisation of a country can be measured by how well equipped it is in the production of machines with which to produce machines, and in the manufacture of ever more accurate instruments for making both machines and further instruments for making machines, etc. The country which is best equipped in the construction of instruments for experimental scientific laboratories and in the construction of instruments with which to test the first instruments, can be regarded as the most complex in the technical-industrial field, with the highest level of civilisation, etc. The same applies to the preparation of intellectuals and to the schools dedicated to this preparation; schools and institutes of high culture can be assimilated to each other. In this field also, quantity cannot be separated from quality. To the most refined technical-cultural specialisation there cannot but correspond the maximum possible diffusion of primary education and the maximum care taken to expand the middle grades numerically as much as possible. Naturally this need to provide the widest base possible for the selection and elaboration of the top intellectual qualifications—i.e. to give a democratic structure to high culture and top-level technology—is not without its disadvantages: it creates the possibility of vast crises of unemployment for the middle intellectual strata, and in all modern societies this actually takes place.

It is worth noting that the elaboration of intellectual strata in concrete reality does not take place on the terrain of abstract democracy but in accordance with very concrete traditional historical processes. Strata have grown up which traditionally "produce" intellectuals and these strata coincide with those which have specialised in "saving," i.e. the petty and middle landed bourgeoisie and certain strata of the petty and middle urban bourgeoisie. The varying distribution of different types of school (classical and professional)[14] over the "economic" territory and the varying aspirations of different categories within these strata determine, or give form to, the production of various branches of intellectual specialisation. Thus in Italy the rural bourgeoisie produces in particular state functionaries and profes-

---

12 [Hoare and Nowell-Smith] The *Ordine Nuovo*, the magazine edited by Gramsci during his days as a militant in Turin, ran as a "weekly review of Socialist culture" in 1919 and 1920. See Introduction, pp. xxxv ff.

13 [Hoare and Nowell-Smith] *"Dirigente."* This extremely condensed and elliptical sentence contains a number of key Gramscian ideas: on the possibility of proletarian cultural hegemony through domination of the work process, on the distinction between organic intellectual of the working class and traditional intellectuals from outside, on the unity of theory and practice as a basic Marxist postulate, etc.

14 [Hoare and Nowell-Smith] The Italian school system above compulsory level is based on a division between academic ("classical" and "scientific") education and vocational training for professional purposes. Technical and, at the academic level, "scientific" colleges tend to be concentrated in the Northern industrial areas.

sional people, whereas the urban bourgeoisie produces technicians for industry. Consequently it is largely northern Italy which produces technicians and the South which produces functionaries and professional men.

The relationship between the intellectuals and the world of production is not as direct as it is with the fundamental social groups but is, in varying degrees, "mediated" by the whole fabric of society and by the complex of superstructures, of which the intellectuals are, precisely, the "functionaries." It should be possible both to measure the "organic quality" [*organicità*] of the various intellectual strata and their degree of connection with a fundamental social group, and to establish a gradation of their functions and of the superstructures from the bottom to the top (from the structural base upwards). What we can do, for the moment, is to fix two major superstructural "levels": the one that can be called "civil society," that is the ensemble of organisms commonly called "private," and that of "political society" or "the State." These two levels correspond on the one hand to the function of "hegemony" which the dominant group exercises throughout society and on the other hand to that of "direct domination" or command exercised through the State and "juridical" government. The functions in question are precisely organisational and connective. The intellectuals are the dominant group's "deputies" exercising the subaltern functions of social hegemony and political government. These comprise:

1. The "spontaneous" consent given by the great masses of the population to the general direction imposed on social life by the dominant fundamental group; this consent is "historically" caused by the prestige (and consequent confidence) which the dominant group enjoys because of its position and function in the world of production.

2. The apparatus of state coercive power which "legally" enforces discipline on those groups who do not "consent" either actively or passively. This apparatus is, however, constituted for the whole of society in anticipation of moments of crisis of command and direction when spontaneous consent has failed.

This way of posing the problem has as a result a considerable extension of the concept of intellectual, but it is the only way which enables one to reach a concrete approximation of reality. It also clashes with preconceptions of caste. The function of organising social hegemony and state domination certainly gives rise to a particular division of labour and therefore to a whole hierarchy of qualifications in some of which there is no apparent attribution of directive or organisational functions. For example, in the apparatus of social and state direction there exist a whole series of jobs of a manual and instrumental character (non-executive

work, agents rather than officials or functionaries).[15] It is obvious that such a distinction has to be made just as it is obvious that other distinctions have to be made as well. Indeed, intellectual activity must also be distinguished in terms of its intrinsic characteristics, according to levels which in moments of extreme opposition represent a real qualitative difference—at the highest level would be the creators of the various sciences, philosophy, art, etc., at the lowest the most humble "administrators" and divulgators of pre-existing, traditional, accumulated intellectual wealth.[16]

In the modern world the category of intellectuals, understood in this sense, has undergone an unprecedented expansion. The democratic-bureaucratic system has given rise to a great mass of functions which are not all justified by the social necessities of production, though they are justified by the political necessities of the dominant fundamental group. Hence Loria's[18] conception of the unproductive "worker" (but unproductive in relation to whom and to what mode of production?), a conception which could in part be justified if one takes account of the fact that these masses exploit their position to take for themselves a large cut out of the national income. Mass formation has standardized individuals both psychologically and in terms of individual qualification and has produced the same phenomena as with other standardised masses: competition which makes necessary organisations for the defence of professions, unemployment, over-production in the schools, emigration, etc.

The Different Position of Urban and Rural-Type Intellectuals

Intellectuals of the urban type have grown up along with industry and are linked to its fortunes. Their function can be compared to that of subaltern officers in the army. They have no autonomous initiative in elaborating plans for construc-

---

[15] [Hoare and Nowell-Smith] *"funzionari":* in Italian usage the word is applied to the middle and higher echelons of the bureaucracy. Conversely "administrators" (*"administratori"*) is used here (end of paragraph) to mean people who merely "administer" the decisions of others. The phrase "non-executive work" is a translation of "[*impiego*] *di ordine e non di concetto*" which refers to distinctions within clerical work.

[16] [Gramsci] Here again military organisation offers a model of complex gradations between subaltern officers, senior officers and general staff, not to mention the NCO's, whose importance is greater than is generally admitted. It is worth observing that all these parts feel a solidarity and indeed that it is the lower strata that display the most blatant *esprit de corps*, from which they derive a certain "conceit"[17] which is apt to lay them open to jokes and witticisms.

[17] [Hoare and Nowell-Smith] *"Boria."* This is a reference to an idea of Vico.

[18] [Hoare and Nowell-Smith] The notion of the "unproductive labourer" is not in fact an invention of Loria's but has its origins in Marx's definitions of productive and unproductive labour in *Capital*, which Loria, in his characteristic way, both vulgarised and claimed as his own discovery.

tion. Their job is to articulate the relationship between the entrepreneur and the instrumental mass and to carry out the immediate execution of the production plan decided by the industrial general staff, controlling the elementary stages of work. On the whole the average urban intellectuals are very standardised, while the top urban intellectuals are more and more identified with the industrial general staff itself.

Intellectuals of the rural type are for the most part "traditional," that is they are linked to the social mass of country people and the town (particularly small-town) petite bourgeoisie, not as yet elaborated and set in motion by the capitalist system. This type of intellectual brings into contact the peasant masses with the local and state administration (lawyers, notaries, etc.). Because of this activity they have an important politico-social function, since professional mediation is difficult to separate from political. Furthermore: in the countryside the intellectual (priest, lawyer, notary, teacher, doctor, etc.), has on the whole a higher or at least a different living standard from that of the average peasant and consequently represents a social model for the peasant to look to in his aspiration to escape from or improve his condition. The peasant always thinks that at least one of his sons could become an intellectual (especially a priest), thus becoming a gentleman and raising the social level of the family by facilitating its economic life through the connections which he is bound to acquire with the rest of the gentry. The peasant's attitude towards the intellectual is double and appears contradictory. He respects the social position of the intellectuals and in general that of state employees, but sometimes affects contempt for it, which means that his admiration is mingled with instinctive elements of envy and impassioned anger. One can understand nothing of the collective life of the peasantry and of the germs and ferments of development which exist within it, if one does not take into consideration and examine concretely and in depth this effective subordination to the intellectuals. Every organic development of the peasant masses, up to a certain point, is linked to and depends on movements among the intellectuals.

With the urban intellectuals it is another matter. Factory technicians do not exercise any political function over the instrumental masses, or at least this is a phase that has been superseded. Sometimes, rather, the contrary takes place, and the instrumental masses, at least in the person of their own organic intellectuals, exercise a political influence on the technicians.

The central point of the question remains the distinction between intellectuals as an organic category of every fundamental social group and intellectuals as a traditional category. From this distinction there flow a whole series of problems and possible questions for historical research.

The most interesting problem is that which, when studied from this point of view, relates to the modern political party, its real origins, its developments and the forms which it takes. What is the character of the political party in relation to the problem of the intellectuals? Some distinctions must be made:

1. The political party for some social groups is nothing other than their specific way of elaborating their own category of organic intellectuals directly in the political and philosophical field and not just in the field of productive technique. These intellectuals are formed in this way and cannot indeed be formed in any other way, given the general character and the conditions of formation, life and development of the social group.[19]

2. The political party, for all groups, is precisely the mechanism which carries out in civil society the same function as the State carries out, more synthetically and over a larger scale, in political society. In other words it is responsible for welding together the organic intellectuals of a given group—the dominant one—and the traditional intellectuals.[20] The party carries out this function in strict dependence on its basic function, which is that of elaborating its own component parts—those elements of a social group which has been born and developed as an "economic" group—and of turning them into qualified political intellectuals, leaders [*dirigenti*] and organisers of all the activities and functions inherent in the organic development of an integral society, both civil and political. Indeed it can be said that within its field the political party accomplishes its function more completely and organically than the State does within its admittedly far larger field. An intellectual who joins the political party of a particular social group is merged with the organic intellectuals of the group itself, and is linked tightly with the group. This takes place through participation in the life of the State only to a limited degree and often not at all. Indeed it happens that many intellectuals think that they *are* the State, a belief which, given the magnitude of the category, occasionally has important consequences and leads to unpleasant complications for the fundamental economic group which *really* is the State.

---

[19] [Gramsci] Within productive technique those strata are formed which can be said to correspond to NCO's in the army, that is to say, for the town, skilled and specialised workers and, for the country (in a more complex fashion) share-cropping and tenant farmers—since in general terms these types of farmer correspond more or less to the type of the artisan, who is the skilled worker of a mediaeval economy.

[20] [Hoare and Nowell-Smith] Although this passage is ostensibly concerned with the sociology of political parties in general, Gramsci is clearly particularly interested here in the theory of the revolutionary party and the role within it of the intellectuals. See Introduction to this Section.

That all members of a political party should be regarded as intellectuals is an affirmation that can easily lend itself to mockery and caricature. But if one thinks about it nothing could be more exact. There are of course distinctions of level to be made. A party might have a greater or lesser proportion of members in the higher grades or in the lower, but this is not the point. What matters is the function, which is directive and organisational, i.e. educative, i.e. intellectual. A tradesman does not join a political party in order to do business, nor an industrialist in order to produce more at lower cost, nor a peasant to learn new methods of cultivation, even if some aspects of these demands of the tradesman, the industrialist or the peasant can find satisfaction in the party.[21]

For these purposes, within limits, there exists the professional association, in which the economic-corporate activity of the tradesman, industrialist or peasant is most suitably promoted. In the political party the elements of an economic social group get beyond that moment of their historical development and become agents of more general activities of a national and international character. This function of a political party should emerge even more clearly from a concrete historical analysis of how both organic and traditional categories of intellectuals have developed in the context of different national histories and in that of the development of the various major social groups within each nation, particularly those groups whose economic activity has been largely instrumental.

The formation of traditional intellectuals is the most interesting problem historically. It is undoubtedly connected with slavery in the classical world and with the position of freed men of Greek or Oriental origin in the social organisation of the Roman Empire.

Note.   The change in the condition of the social position of the intellectuals in Rome between Republican and Imperial times (a change from an aristocratic-corporate to a democratic-bureaucratic régime) is due to Caesar, who granted citizenship to doctors and to masters of liberal arts so that they would be more willing to live in Rome and so that others should be persuaded to come there. (*"Omnesque medicinam Romae professos et liberalium artium doctores, quo libentius et ispi urbem incolerent et coeteri appeterent civitate donavit."* Suetonius, *Life of Caesar*, XLII.) Caesar therefore proposed: 1. to establish in Rome those

intellectuals who were already there, thus creating a permanent category of intellectuals, since without their permanent residence there no cultural organisation could be created; and 2. to attract to Rome the best intellectuals from all over the Roman Empire, thus promoting centralisation on a massive scale. In this way there came into being the category of "imperial" intellectuals in Rome which was to be continued by the Catholic clergy and to leave so many traces in the history of Italian intellectuals, such as their characteristic "cosmopolitanism," up to the eighteenth century.

This not only social but national and racial separation between large masses of intellectuals and the dominant class of the Roman Empire is repeated after the fall of the Empire in the division between Germanic warriors and intellectuals of romanised origin, successors of the category of freedmen. Interweaved with this phenomenon are the birth and development of Catholicism and of the ecclesiastical organisation which for many centuries absorbs the major part of intellectual activities and exercises a monopoly of cultural direction with penal sanctions against anyone who attempted to oppose or even evade the monopoly. In Italy we can observe the phenomenon, whose intensity varies from period to period, of the cosmopolitan function of the intellectuals of the peninsula. I shall now turn to the differences which are instantly apparent in the development of the intellectuals in a number of the more important countries, with the proviso that these observations require to be controlled and examined in more depth.

As far as Italy is concerned the central fact is precisely the international or cosmopolitan function of its intellectuals, which is both cause and effect of the state of disintegration in which the peninsula remained from the fall of the Roman Empire up to 1870.

France offers the example of an accomplished form of harmonious development of the energies of the nation and of the intellectual categories in particular. When in 1789 a new social grouping makes its political appearance on the historical stage, it is already completely equipped for all its social functions and can therefore struggle for total dominion of the nation. It does not have to make any essential compromises with the old classes but instead can subordinate them to its own ends. The first intellectual cells of the new type are born along with their first economic counterparts. Even ecclesiastical organisation is influenced (gallicanism, precocious struggles between Church and State). This massive intellectual construction explains the function of culture in France in the eighteenth and nineteenth centuries. It was a function of international and cosmopolitan

---

[21] [Gramsci] Common opinion tends to oppose this, maintaining that the tradesman, industrialist or peasant who engages in "politicking" loses rather than gains, and is the worst type of all—which is debatable.

outward radiation and of imperialistic and hegemonic expansion in an organic fashion, very different therefore from the Italian experience, which was founded on scattered personal migration and did not react on the national base to potentiate it but on the contrary contributed to rendering the constitution of a solid national base impossible.

In England the development is very different from France. The new social grouping that grew up on the basis of modern industrialism shows a remarkable economic-corporate development but advances only gropingly in the intellectual-political field. There is a very extensive category of organic intellectuals—those, that is, who come into existence on the same industrial terrain as the economic group—but in the higher sphere we find that the old land-owning class preserves its position of virtual monopoly. It loses its economic supremacy but maintains for a long time a politico-intellectual supremacy and is assimilated as "traditional intellectuals" and as directive [*dirigente*] group by the new group in power. The old land-owning aristocracy is joined to the industrialists by a kind of suture which is precisely that which in other countries unites the traditional intellectuals with the new dominant classes.

The English phenomenon appears also in Germany, but complicated by other historical and traditional elements. Germany, like Italy, was the seat of an universalistic and supranational institution and ideology, the Holy Roman Empire of the German Nation, and provided a certain number of personnel for the mediaeval cosmopolis, impoverishing its own internal energies and arousing struggles which distracted from problems of national organisation and perpetuated the territorial disintegration of the Middle Ages. Industrial development took place within a semi-feudal integument that persisted up to November 1918, and the *Junkers* preserved a politico-intellectual supremacy considerably greater even than that of the corresponding group in England. They were the traditional intellectuals of the German industrialists, but retained special privileges and a strong consciousness of being an independent social group, based on the fact that they held considerable economic power over the land, which was more "productive"[22] than in England. The Prussian *Junkers* resemble a priestly-military caste, with a virtual monopoly of directive-organisational functions in political society, but possessing at the same time an economic base of its own and so not exclusively dependent on the liberality of the dominant economic group. Furthermore, unlike the English land-owning aristocracy, the *Junkers* constituted the officer class

of a large standing army, which gave them solid organisational cadres favouring the preservation of an *esprit de corps* and of their political monopoly.[23]

In Russia various features: the political and economico-commercial organisation was created by the Norman (Varangians), and religious organisation by the Byzantine Greeks. In a later period the Germans and the French brought to Russia the European experience and gave a first consistent skeleton to the protoplasm of Russian history. National forces were inert, passive and receptive, but perhaps precisely for this reason they assimilated completely the foreign influences and the foreigners themselves, Russifying them. In the more recent historical period we find the opposite phenomenon. An *élite* consisting of some of the most active, energetic, enterprising and disciplined members of the society emigrates abroad and assimilates the culture and historical experiences of the most advanced countries of the West, without however losing the most essential characteristics of its own nationality, that is to say without breaking its sentimental and historical links with its own people. Having thus performed its intellectual apprenticeship it returns to its own country and compels the people to an enforced awakening, skipping historical stages in the process. The difference between this *élite* and that imported from Germany (by Peter the Great, for example) lies in its essentially national-popular character. It could not be assimilated by the inert passivity of the Russian people, because it was itself an energetic reaction of Russia to her own historical inertia.

On another terrain, and in very different conditions of time and place, the Russian phenomenon can be compared to the birth of the American nation (in the United States). The Anglo-Saxon immigrants are themselves an intellectual, but more especially a moral, *élite*. I am talking, naturally, of the first immigrants, the pioneers, protagonists of the political and religious struggles in England, defeated but not humiliated or laid low in their country of origin. They import into America, together with themselves, apart from moral energy and energy of the will, a certain level of civilisation, a certain stage of European historical evolution,

---

[22] [Hoare and Nowell-Smith] Gramsci is probably using the word "productive" here in the specifically Marxian sense of productive of surplus value or at any rate of surplus.

[23] [Gramsci] In Max Weber's book, *Parliament and Government in the New Order in Germany*[24] can be found a number of elements to show how the political monopoly of the nobility impeded the elaboration of an extensive and experienced bourgeois political personnel and how it is at the root of the continual parliamentary crises and of the fragmentation of the liberal and democratic parties. Hence the importance of the Catholic centre and of Social democracy, which succeeded during the period of the Empire[25] in building up to a considerable extent their own parliamentary and directive strata, etc.

[24] [Hoare and Nowell-Smith] Max Weber, *Parlament und Regierung im neugeordnetem Deutschland*. English translation in *From Max Weber: Essays in Sociology*, ed. H. H. Gerth and C. Wright Mills.

[25] [Hoare and Nowell-Smith] I.e. up to the formation of the Weimar Republic in 1919.

which, when transplanted by such men into the virgin soil of America, continues to develop the forces implicit in its nature but with an incomparably more rapid rhythm than in Old Europe, where there exists a whole series of checks (moral, intellectual, political, economic, incorporated in specific sections of the population, relics of past régimes which refuse to die out) which generate opposition to speedy progress and give to every initiative the equilibrium of mediocrity, diluting it in time and in space.

One can note, in the case of the United States, the absence to a considerable degree of traditional intellectuals, and consequently a different equilibrium among the intellectuals in general. There has been a massive development, on top of an industrial base, of the whole range of modern superstructures. The necessity of an equilibrium is determined, not by the need to fuse together the organic intellectuals with the traditional, but by the need to fuse together in a single national crucible with a unitary culture the different forms of culture imported by immigrants of differing national origins. The lack of a vast sedimentation of traditional intellectuals such as one finds in countries of ancient civilisation explains, at least in part, both the existence of only two major political parties, which could in fact easily be reduced to one only (contrast this with the case of France, and not only in the post-war period when the multiplication of parties became a general phenomenon), and at the opposite extreme the enormous proliferation of religious sects.[26]

One further phenomenon in the United States is worth studying, and that is the formation of a surprising number of negro intellectuals who absorb American culture and technology. It is worth bearing in mind the indirect influence that these negro intellectuals could exercise on the backward masses in Africa, and indeed direct influence if one or other of these hypotheses were ever to be verified: 1. that American expansionism should use American negroes as its agents in the conquest of the African market and the extension of American civilisation (something of the kind has already happened, but I don't know to what extent); 2. that the struggle for the unification of the American people should intensify in such a way as to provoke a negro exodus and the return to Africa of the most independent and energetic intellectual elements, the ones, in other words, who would be least inclined to submit to some possible future legislation that was even more humiliating than are the present widespread social customs. This development would give rise to two fundamental questions: 1. linguistic: whether English could become the educated language of Africa, bringing unity in the place of the existing swarm of dialects? 2. whether this intellectual stratum could have sufficient assimilating and organising capacity to give a "national" character to the present primitive sentiment of being a despised race, thus giving the African continent a mythic function as the common fatherland of all the negro peoples? It seems to me that, for the moment, American negroes have a national and racial spirit which is negative rather than positive, one which is a product of the struggle carried on by the whites in order to isolate and depress them. But was not this the case with the Jews up to and throughout the eighteenth century? Liberia, already Americanised and with English as its official language, could become the Zion of American negroes, with a tendency to set itself up as an African Piedmont.[27]

In considering the question of the intellectuals in Central and South America, one should, I think, bear in mind certain fundamental conditions. No vast category of traditional intellectuals exists in Central or South America either, but the question does not present itself in the same terms as with the United States. What in fact we find at the root of development of these countries are the patterns of Spanish and Portuguese civilisation of the sixteenth and seventeenth century, characterised by the effects of the Counter Reformation and by military parasitism. The change-resistant crystallisations which survive to this day in these countries are the clergy and a military caste, two categories of traditional intellectuals fossilised in a form inherited from the European mother country. The industrial base is very restricted, and has not developed complicated superstructures. The majority of intellectuals are of the rural type, and, since the latifundium is dominant, with a lot of property in the hands of the Church, these intellectuals are linked with the clergy and the big landowners. National composition is very unbalanced even among the white population and is further complicated by the great masses of Indians who in some countries form the majority of the inhabitants. It can be said that in these regions of the American continent there still exists a situation of the *Kulturkampf* and of the Dreyfus trial,[28]

---

[26] [Gramsci] More than two hundred of these have, I think, been counted. Again one should compare the case of France and the fierce struggles that went on to maintain the religious and moral unity of the French people.

[27] [Hoare and Nowell-Smith] The reference here is to the role of leadership among the Italian States assumed by Piedmont during the Risorgimento. For Gramsci's analysis of this phenomenon, see "The Function of Piedmont," pp. 104–106.

[28] [Hoare and Nowell-Smith] "*Kulturkampf*" was the name given to the struggle waged by Bismarck, in the 1870s, with Liberal support, against Catholic opposition to Prussian hegemony. The Dreyfus case in France, which lasted from Dreyfus' first condemnation in 1894 to his final acquittal in 1906, coincided with a major battle fully to laicise the French educational system and had the effect of polarising French society into a militaristic, pro-Catholic, anti-Semitic Right, and an anti-Catholic Liberal and Socialist Left. Both *Kulturkampf* and Dreyfus case can also be seen as aspects of the bourgeois-democratic struggle against the residues of reactionary social forces.

that is to say a situation in which the secular and bourgeois element has not yet reached the stage of being able to subordinate clerical and militaristic influence and interests to the secular politics of the modern State. It thus comes about that Free Masonry and forms of cultural organisation like the "positivist Church" are very influential in the opposition to Jesuitism. Most recent events (November 1930), from the *Kulturkampf* of Calles in Mexico[29] to the military-popular insurrections in Argentina, Brazil, Peru, Chile and Bolivia, demonstrate the accuracy of these observations.

Further types of formation of the categories of intellectuals and of their relationship with national forces can be found in India, China and Japan. In Japan we have a formation of the English and German type, that is an industrial civilisation that develops within a feudal-bureaucratic integument with unmistakable features of its own.

In China there is the phenomenon of the script, an expression of the complete separation between the intellectuals and the people. In both India and China the enormous gap separating intellectuals and people is manifested also in the religious field. The problem of different beliefs and of different ways of conceiving and practising the same religion among the various strata of society, but particularly as between clergy, intellectuals and people, needs to be studied in general, since it occurs everywhere to a certain degree; but it is in the countries of East Asia that it reaches its most extreme form. In Protestant countries the difference is relatively slight (the proliferation of sects is connected with the need for a perfect suture between intellectuals and people, with the result that all the crudity of the effective conceptions of the popular masses is reproduced in the higher organisational sphere). It is more noteworthy in Catholic countries, but its extent varies. It is less in the Catholic parts of Germany and in France; rather greater in Italy, particularly in the South and in the islands; and very great indeed in the Iberian peninsula and in the countries of Latin America. The phenomenon increases in scale in the Orthodox countries where it becomes necessary to speak of three degrees of the same religion: that of the higher clergy and the monks, that of the secular clergy and that of the people. It reaches a level of absurdity in East Asia, where the religion of the people often has nothing whatever to do with that of books, although the two are called by the same name.

Notes on Italian History

History of the Subaltern Classes: Methodological Criteria

The historical unity of the ruling classes is realised in the State, and their history is essentially the history of States and of groups of States. But it would be wrong to think that this unity is simply juridical and political (though such forms of unity do have their importance too, and not in a purely formal sense); the fundamental historical unity, concretely, results from the organic relations between State or political society and "civil society."[1]

The subaltern classes, by definition, are not unified and cannot unite until they are able to become a "State": their history, therefore, is intertwined with that of civil society, and thereby with the history of States and groups of States. Hence it is necessary to study: 1. the objective formation of the subaltern social groups, by the developments and transformations occurring in the sphere of economic production; their quantitative diffusion and their origins in pre-existing social groups, whose mentality, ideology and aims they conserve for a time; 2. their active or passive affiliation to the dominant political formations, their attempts to influence the programmes of these formations in order to press claims of their own, and the consequences of these attempts in determining processes of decomposition, renovation or neo-formation; 3. the birth of new parties of the dominant groups, intended to conserve the assent of the subaltern groups and to maintain control over them; 4. the formations which the subaltern groups themselves produce, in order to press claims of a limited and partial character; 5. those new formations which assert the autonomy of the subaltern groups, but within the old framework; 6. those formations which assert the integral autonomy, . . . etc.[2]

The list of these phases can be broken down still further, with intermediate phases and combinations of several phases. The historian must record, and discover the causes of, the line of development towards integral autonomy, starting from the most primitive phases; he must note every manifestation of the Sorelian "spirit of cleavage."[3] Therefore, the history of the parties of the subaltern groups is very complex too. It must include all the repercussions of party activity, throughout the area of the subaltern groups themselves taken

---

[29][Hoare and Nowell-Smith] Plutarco Elias Calles was President of Mexico from 1924–28. It was under his Presidency that the religious and educational provisions of the new constitution were carried through, against violent Catholic opposition.

[1][Hoare and Nowell-Smith] For Gramsci's use of the term "civil society", see introduction to *State and Civil Society*, pp. 206–9.

[2][Hoare and Nowell-Smith] The last three categories refer presumably to trade unions, reformist parties, and communist parties respectively.

[3][Hoare and Nowell-Smith] See note 4 on p. 126.

globally, and also upon the attitudes of the dominant group; it must include as well the repercussions of the far more effective actions (effective because backed by the State) of the dominant groups upon the subaltern groups and their parties. Among the subaltern groups, one will exercise or tend to exercise a certain hegemony through the mediation of a party; this must be established by studying the development of all the other parties too, in so far as they include elements of the hegemonic group or of the other subaltern groups which undergo such hegemony.

Numerous principles of historical research can be established by examining the innovatory forces which led the national Risorgimento in Italy: these forces took power and united in the modern Italian State, in struggle against specific other forces and helped by specific auxiliaries or allies. In order to become a State, they had to subordinate or eliminate the former and win the active or passive assent of the latter. A study of how these innovatory forces developed, from subaltern groups to hegemonic and dominant groups, must therefore seek out and identify the phases through which they acquired: 1. autonomy *vis-à-vis* the enemies they had to defeat, and 2. support from the groups which actively or passively assisted them; for this entire process was historically necessary before they could unite in the form of a State. It is precisely by these two yardsticks that the level of historical and political consciousness which the innovatory forces progressively attained in the various phases can be measured—and not simply by the yardstick of their separation from the formerly dominant forces. Usually the latter is the only criterion adopted, and the result is a unilateral history—or sometimes total incomprehension, as in the case of the history of Italy, since the era of the Communes. The Italian bourgeoisie was incapable of uniting the people around itself, and this was the cause of its defeats and the interruptions in its development.[4]

In the Risorgimento too, the same narrow egoism prevented a rapid and vigorous revolution like the French one. This is one of the most important problems, one of the most fertile causes of serious difficulties, in writing the history of the subaltern social groups and hence the (past) history *tout court* of the Italian States.

The history of subaltern social groups is necessarily fragmented and episodic. There undoubtedly does exist a tendency to (at least provisional stages of) unification in the historical activity of these groups, but this tendency is continually interrupted by the activity of the ruling groups; it therefore can only be demonstrated when an historical cycle is completed and this cycle culminates in a success. Subaltern groups are always subject to the activity of ruling groups, even when they rebel and rise up: only "permanent"

---

[4] [Hoare and Nowell-Smith] Clearly the fate of the mediaeval communes in Italy—i.e. the autonomous city-states—and the failure of their bourgeoisies to unite nationally is one of the fundamental problems for Italian historiography, and it recurs throughout the Prison Notebooks, though in particularly fragmentary form, e.g. "This book of Barbadoro's [on the finances of the Florentine Commune] is indispensable for seeing precisely how the communal bourgeoisie did not succeed in transcending the economic-corporate phase, i.e. in creating a State 'with the consent of the governed' and capable of developing. The development of the State proved possible only as a principality, not as a communal republic." (Ris., p. 9). "On the fact that the communal bourgeoisie did not succeed in transcending the corporative phase and hence cannot be said to have created a State, since it was rather the Church and the Empire which constituted States, i.e. on the fact that the Communes did not transcend feudalism, it is necessary before writing anything, to read Gioacchino Volpe's book *Il Medioevo*." (Ris., p. 10). "It is necessary to determine what significance the 'State' had in the Communal State: a limited 'corporative' significance, which meant that it was unable to develop beyond middle feudalism, i.e. that which succeeded the absolute feudalism—without a third estate, so to speak—which had existed before the year A.D. 1000, and which was itself succeeded by the absolute monarchy in the fifteenth century, up to the French Revolution. There was an organic transition from the Commune to a system that was no longer feudal in the Low Countries, and there alone. In Italy, the Communes were unable to go beyond the corporative phase, feudal anarchy triumphed in a form appropriate to the new situation and then came the period of foreign domination." (Ris., p. 18). In a note in which Gramsci sketches out a plan of historical research (*Il Risorgimento e la Storia Precedente,* Ris., p. 3), he devotes a section to "Middle Ages, or epoch of the Communes, in which the new urban social groups are formed in molecular fashion, without the process reaching the higher phase of maturation as in France, Spain, etc." Despite their fragmentary character, Gramsci's notes on "The Mediaeval Commune as the economic-corporative phase of the modern State" are clearly fundamental to his entire analysis of the specificity of Italian historical development. See also, e.g. "A further criterion of research must be borne in mind, in order to emphasise the dangers inherent in the method of historical analogy as an interpretative criterion. In the ancient and mediaeval State alike, centralisation, whether political-territorial or social (and the one is merely a function of the other), was minimal. The State was, in a certain sense, a mechanical bloc of social groups, often of different race: within the circle of political-military compression, which was only exercised harshly at certain moments, the subaltern groups had a life of their own, institutions of their own, etc., and sometimes these institutions had State functions which made of the State a federation of social groups with disparate functions not subordinated in any way—a situation which in periods of crisis highlighted with extreme clarity the phenomenon of 'dual power.' The only group excluded from any organised collective life of its own was that of the slaves (and such proletarians as were not slaves) in the classical world, and is that of the serfs and the peasants in the mediaeval world. However, even though, from many points of view, the slaves of the ancient world and the mediaeval proletariat were in the same conditions, their situation was not identical: the attempted revolt by the Ciompi [in Florence in 1378] certainly did not have the impact that a similar attempt by the slaves of antiquity would have produced (Spartacus demanding to be taken into the government in collaboration with the plebs, etc.). While in the Middle Ages an alliance between proletarians and people, and even more so the support of the proletarians for the dictatorship of a prince, was possible, nothing similar was possible for the slaves of the classical world. The modern State substitutes for the mechanical bloc of social groups their subordination to the active hegemony of the directive and dominant group, hence abolishes certain autonomies, which nevertheless are reborn in other forms, as parties, trade unions, cultural associations. The contemporary dictatorships legally abolish these new forms of autonomy as well, and strive to incorporate them within State activity: the legal centralisation of the entire national life in the hands of the dominant group becomes 'totalitarian.' " (Ris., pp. 195–6.)

victory breaks their subordination, and that not immediately. In reality, even when they appear triumphant, the subaltern groups are merely anxious to defend themselves (a truth which can be demonstrated by the history of the French Revolution at least up to 1830). Every trace of independent initiative on the part of subaltern groups should therefore be of incalculable value for the integral historian. Consequently, this kind of history can only be dealt with monographically, and each monograph requires an immense quantity of material which is often hard to collect. [1934–35]

State and Civil Society

Observations on Certain Aspects of the Structure of Political Parties in Periods of Organic Crisis

At a certain point in their historical lives, social classes become detached from their traditional parties. In other words, the traditional parties in that particular organisational form, with the particular men who constitute, represent, and lead them, are no longer recognised by their class (or fraction of a class) as its expression. When such crises occur, the immediate situation becomes delicate and dangerous, because the field is open for violent solutions, for the activities of unknown forces, represented by charismatic "men of destiny."

These situations of conflict between "represented and representatives" reverberate out from the terrain of the parties (the party organisations properly speaking, the parliamentary-electoral field, newspaper organisation) throughout the State organism, reinforcing the relative power of the bureaucracy (civil and military), of high finance, of the Church, and generally of all bodies relatively independent of the fluctuations of public opinion. How are they created in the first place? In every country the process is different, although the content is the same. And the content is the crisis of the ruling class's hegemony, which occurs either because the ruling class has failed in some major political undertaking for which it has requested, or forcibly extracted, the consent of the broad masses (war, for example), or because huge masses (especially of peasants and petit-bourgeois intellectuals) have passed suddenly from a state of political passivity to a certain activity, and put forward demands which taken together, albeit not organically formulated, add up to a revolution. A "crisis of authority"[1] is spoken of: this is precisely the crisis of hegemony, or general crisis of the State.

The crisis creates situations which are dangerous in the short run, since the various strata of the population are not all capable of orienting themselves equally swiftly, or of reorganizing with the same rhythm. The traditional ruling class, which has numerous trained cadres, changes men and programmes and, with greater speed than is achieved by the subordinate classes, reabsorbs the control that was slipping from its grasp. Perhaps it may make sacrifices, and expose itself to an uncertain future by demagogic promises; but it retains power, reinforces it for the time being, and uses it to crush its adversary and disperse his leading cadres, who cannot be very numerous or highly trained. The passage of the troops of many different parties under the banner of a single party, which better represents and resumes the needs of the entire class, is an organic and normal phenomenon, even if its rhythm is very swift—indeed almost like lightning in comparison with periods of calm. It represents the fusion of an entire social class under a single leadership, which alone is held to be capable of solving an overriding problem of its existence and of fending off a mortal danger. When the crisis does not find this organic solution, but that of the charismatic leader, it means that a static equilibrium exists (whose factors may be disparate, but in which the decisive one is the immaturity of the progressive forces); it means that no group, neither the conservatives nor the progressives, has the strength for victory, and that even the conservative group needs a master. [1932–1934: 1st version 1930–1932.] See *The Eighteenth Brumaire of Louis Bonaparte*. This order of phenomena is connected to one of the most important questions concerning the political party—i.e. the party's capacity to react against force of habit, against the tendency to become mummified and anachronistic. Parties come into existence, and constitute themselves as organisations, in order to influence the situation at moments which are historically vital for their class; but they are not always capable of adapting themselves to new tasks and to new epochs, nor of evolving *pari passu* with the overall relations of force (and hence the relative position of their class) in the country in question, or in the international field. In analysing the development of parties, it is necessary to distinguish: their social group; their mass membership; their bureaucracy and General Staff. The bureaucracy is the most dangerously hidebound and conservative force; if it ends up by constituting a compact body, which stands on its own and feels itself independent of the mass of members, the party ends up by becoming anachronist and at moments of acute crisis it is voided of its social content and left as though suspended in mid-air. One can see what has happened to a number of German parties as a result of the expansion of Hitlerism. French parties are a rich field for such

---

[1] [Hoare and Nowell-Smith] See " 'Wave of Materialism' and 'Crisis of Authority,'" on pp. 275–6, *Selections from Prison Notebooks*.

research: they are all mummified and anachronistic—historico-political documents of the various phases of past French history, whose outdated terminology they continue to repeat; their crisis could become even more catastrophic than that of the German parties. [1932–34: 1st version 1930–32.]

In examining such phenomena people usually neglect to give due importance to the bureaucratic element, both civil and military; furthermore they forget that not only actual military and bureaucratic elements, but also the social strata from which, in the particular national structure, the bureaucracy is traditionally recruited, must be included in such analyses. A political movement can be of a military character even if the army as such does not participate in it openly; a government can be of a military character even if the army as such does not take part in it. In certain situations it may happen that it suits better not to "reveal" the army, not to have it cross the bounds of what is constitutional, not to introduce politics into the ranks, as the saying goes—so that the homogeneity between officers and other ranks is maintained, on a terrain of apparent neutrality and superiority to the factions; yet it is nonetheless the army, that is to say the General Staff and the officer corps, which determines the new situation and dominates it. However, it is not true that armies are constitutionally barred from making politics; the army's duty is precisely to defend the Constitution—in other words the legal form of the State together with its related institutions. Hence so-called neutrality only means support for the reactionary side; but in such situations, the question has to be posed in such terms to prevent the unrest in the country being reproduced within the army, and the determining power of the General Staff thus evaporating through the disintegration of its military instrument. Obviously, none of these observations is absolute; at various moments of history and in various countries they have widely differing significance.

The first problem to be studied is the following: does there exist, in a given country, a widespread social stratum in whose economic life and political self-assertion (effective participation in power, even though indirectly, by "blackmail") the bureaucratic career, either civil or military, is a very important element? In modern Europe this stratum can be identified in the medium and small rural bourgeoisie, which is more or less numerous from one country to another—depending on the development of industrial strength on the one hand, and of agrarian reform on the other. Of course the bureaucratic career (civil and military) is not the monopoly of this social stratum; however, it is particularly well suited to the social function which this stratum carries out, and to the psychological tendencies which such a func-

tion produces or encourages. These two elements impart to the entire social stratum a certain homogeneity and energy in its aims—and hence a political value, and an often decisive function within the entire social organism. The members of this stratum are accustomed to direct command over nuclei of men, however tiny, and to commanding "politically," not "economically." In other words, their art of command implies no aptitude for ordering "things," for ordering "men and things" into an organic whole, as occurs in industrial production—since this stratum has no economic functions in the modern sense of the word. It has an income, because legally it is the owner of a part of the national soil, and its function consists in opposing "politically" the attempts of the peasant farmer to ameliorate his existence—since any improvement in the relative position of the peasant would be catastrophic for its social position. The chronic poverty and prolonged labour of the peasant, with the degradation these bring, are a primordial necessity for it. This is the explanation for the immense energy it shows in resisting and counterattacking whenever there is the least attempt at autonomous organisation of peasant labour, or any peasant cultural movement which leaves the bounds of official religion. This social stratum finds its limits, and the reasons for its ultimate weakness, in its territorial dispersal and in the "non-homogeneity" which is intimately connected to this dispersal. This explains some of its other characteristics too: its volubility, the multiplicity of ideological systems it follows, even the bizarre nature of the ideologies it sometimes follows. Its will is directed towards a specific end—but it is retarded, and usually requires a lengthy process before it can become politically and organisationally centralised. This process accelerates when the specific "will" of this stratum coincides with the will and the immediate interests of the ruling class; not only that, but its "military strength" then at once reveals itself, so that sometimes, when organised, it lays down the law to the ruling class, at least as far as the "form" of solution is concerned, if not the content. The same laws can be seen functioning here as have been observed in relations between town and countryside in the case of the subordinate classes.[2] Power in the towns automatically becomes power in the countryside. But the absence of economic margins and the normally heavier repression exercised from the top downwards in the countryside cause conflicts there immediately to assume an acute and "personal" form, so that counterattacks have to be more rapid and determined. The stratum under consideration understands and sees that the origin of its troubles is in the

---

[2] [Hoare and Nowell-Smith] See "The City-Countryside Relationship" on pp. 90–102, *Selections from Prison Notebooks*.

towns, in urban power; it therefore understands that it "must" dictate a solution to the urban ruling classes, so that the principal hot-bed will be extinguished—even if this does not immediately suit the urban ruling classes themselves, either because it is too costly, or because it is dangerous in the long term (these classes see longer cycles of development, in which it is possible to manoeuvre, instead of simply following "material" interests). It is in that sense, rather than in an absolute one, that the function of this stratum should be seen as directive;[3] all the same, it is no light matter.[4] It must be noted how this "military" character of the social group in question—traditionally a spontaneous reaction to certain specific conditions of its existence—is now consciously cultivated and organically formed in anticipation. To this conscious process belong the systematic efforts to create and reinforce various associations of reservists and ex-combatants from the various corps and branches of the services, especially of officers. These associations are linked to the respective General Staffs, and can be mobilised when required, without the need to mobilise the conscript army. The latter can thus preserve its character of a reserve force—forewarned, reinforced, and immunised from the political gangrene by these "private" forces which cannot fail to influence its morale, sustaining and stiffening it. It could be said that the result is a movement of the "cossack" type—with its formations ranged not along the frontiers of nationality, as was the case with the Tsarist cossacks, but along the "frontiers" of the social class.

In a whole series of countries, therefore, military influence in national life means not only the influence and weight of the military in the technical sense, but the influence and weight of the social stratum from which the latter (especially the junior officers) mostly derives its origin. This

series of observations is indispensable for any really profound analysis of the specific political form usually termed Caesarism or Bonapartism—to distinguish it from other forms in which the technical military element as such predominates, in conformations perhaps still more visible and exclusive.

Spain and Greece offer two typical examples, with both similar and dissimilar characteristics. In Spain it is necessary to take certain peculiarities into account: the size of the national territory, and the low density of the peasant population. Between the latifundist aristocrat and the peasant there does not exist a numerous rural bourgeoisie; hence, minor importance of the junior officer corps as a force in itself. (On the other hand, a certain oppositional importance was possessed by the officers of the technical corps—artillery and engineers; these, of urban bourgeois origin, opposed the generals and attempted to have a policy of their own.) Hence military governments in Spain are governments of "great" generals. Passivity of the peasant masses, as citizens and as soldiers. If political disintegration occurs in the army, it does so in a vertical rather than a horizontal sense, through rivalries between cliques at the top: the rank and file splits up behind the various competing leaders. Military government is a parenthesis between two constitutional governments. The military are the permanent reserves of order and conservation; they are a political force which comes into action "publicly" when "legality" is in danger. The course of events is similar in Greece, with the difference that Greek territory is scattered over a whole system of islands, and that a part of its more energetic and active population is always at sea, which makes military intrigue and conspiracy easier. The peasantry is passive in Greece as in Spain; but in the context of the total population—the most energetic and active Greeks being sailors, and almost always far from the centre of their political life—the general passivity must be analysed differently in each case, nor can the solution to the problem be the same in both countries. When the members of a deposed government were shot in Greece some years ago,[6] this was probably to be explained as an outburst of rage on the part of the energetic and active element referred to above, with the intention of imparting a bloody lesson. The most important observation to be made is that neither in Greece nor in Spain

---

[3] [Hoare and Nowell-Smith] See note 5 on p. 55. Gramsci's argument here is that the North Italian capitalists might have preferred to continue with Giolitti's strategy of alliance with the reformist working-class leaders after 1920, but that they were "led" by their landlord allies to switch to a policy of total repression of the organized working class. (It is true that "agrarian fascism" did precede urban repression.) "Absolute" hegemony within the ruling-class bloc, however, remained of course with the urban bourgeoisie.

[4] [Gramsci] A reflection of this stratum can be seen in the ideological activity of the conservative intellectuals of the Right. Gaetano Mosca's book *Teorica dei governi e governo parlamentare* (second edition 1925, first edition 1883) is typical in this respect;[5] even in 1883 Mosca was terrified at the possibility of a contact between the towns and the countryside. Mosca, because of his defensive position (of counterattack), understood the political technique of the subaltern classes better in 1883 than the representatives of those same classes, even in the towns, understood it themselves even several decades later.

[5] [Hoare and Nowell-Smith] Mosca (1858–1941) was together with Pareto and Michels an originator of the sociological theory of "*elites.*" His basic concept was that of the "political class", and his main object of attack was the Marxist theory of class struggle and concept of "ruling class." (See NM. p. 140, etc.)

---

[6] [Hoare and Nowell-Smith] In 1920, Greece was torn between two ruling class factions. On the one hand the supporters of the deposed King Constantine, who leaned towards Germany. On the other the "liberals" headed by Venizelos, supported by the British. After several alternations in power, an attempt was made to assassinate Venizelos—who was Prime Minister at the time—in August 1920, and its failure was followed by savage reprisals. Among those massacred was the royalist ex-minister Dragoumis.

has the experience of military government created a permanent, and formally organic, political and social ideology—as does on the other hand occur in those countries which are, so to speak, potentially Bonapartist. The general historical conditions of the two types are the same: an equilibrium of the conflicting urban classes, which obstructs the mechanism of "normal" democracy—i.e. parliamentarism. But the influence of the countryside in this equilibrium is diverse in the two cases. In countries like Spain, the total passivity of the countryside enables the generals of the land-owning aristocracy to utilise the army politically to restabilise the threatened equilibrium—in other words the supremacy of the ruling classes. In other countries the countryside is not passive, but the peasant movement is not coordinated politically with the urban movement: here the army has to remain neutral (up to a certain point, of course), since otherwise it might split horizontally; instead the bureacratic military class comes into action. This class, by military means, stifles the (more immediately dangerous) movement in the countryside. In this struggle, it finds a certain political and ideological unification; it finds allies in the urban middle classes (middle in the Italian sense)[7]—reinforced by students of rural origin now living in the towns; and it imposes its political methods on the upper classes, which are compelled to make numerous concessions to it, and to allow some legislation favourable to its interests. In short, continuing to maintain itself under arms amidst the general disarmament, and brandishing the danger of a civil war between its own troops and the regular, conscripted army if the ruling class shows too great an itch for resistance, it succeeds in permeating the State with its interests, up to a certain

point, and in replacing a part of the leading personnel. These observations must not be conceived of as rigid schemata, but merely as practical criteria of historical and political interpretation. In concrete analyses of real events, the historical forms are individualised and can almost be called "unique." Caesar represents a very different combination of real circumstances from that represented by Napoleon I, as does Primo de Rivera from that of Živkovič, etc.[8] [1933–34; 1st version 1930–32]

In analysing the third level or moment of the system of relations of force which exists in a given situation,[9] one may usefully have recourse to the concept which in military science is called the "strategic conjuncture"—or rather, more precisely, the level of strategic preparation of the theatre of struggle. One of the principal factors of this "strategic conjuncture" consists in the qualitative condition of the leading personnel, and of what may be called the "front-line" (and assault) forces. The level of strategic preparation can give the victory to forces which are "apparently" (i.e. quantatively) inferior to those of the enemy. It could be said that strategic preparation tends to reduce to zero the so-called "imponderable factors"—in other words, the immediate, unpremeditated reactions at a given moment of the traditionally inert and passive forces. Among the factors involved in the preparation of a favourable strategic conjuncture, there must precisely be included those already studied in our earlier observations on the existence and organisation of a military social stratum, side by side with the national army in the technical sense.[10]

Further points could be developed out of the following extract from the speech which General Gazzera, Minister of War, delivered in the Senate on 19 May 1932 (see *Corriere della Sera,* 20 May): "The disciplinary régime obtaining in our army thanks to Fascism, today sets a guiding

---

[7][Hoare and Nowell-Smith] On NM. pp. 148–49, Gramsci writes: "The meaning of the expression 'middle class' changes from country to country. . . . The term came from English social development. It seems that in England the bourgeoisie was never conceived of as an integral part of the people, but always as an entity separate from the latter: it thus came to pass, in English history, that instead of the bourgeoisie leading the people and winning the latter's support to abolish feudal privileges, the nobility (or a fraction of it) formed the national-popular bloc first against the Crown and later against the industrial bourgeoisie. English tradition of a popular "Toryism" (Disraeli, etc.). After the great liberal reforms, which brought the State into conformity with the interests and needs of the middle class, the two basic parties of English political life were differentiated on internal questions regarding the same class; the nobility increasingly acquired the specific character of a "bourgeois aristocracy" tied to certain functions of civil society and of political society (the State)—concerning tradition, the education of the ruling stratum, the preservation of a particular mentality which protects the system from sudden upheavals, etc., the consolidation of the imperial structure, etc. . . . In Italy, where the feudal aristocracy was destroyed by the mediaeval Communes (physically destroyed in the civil wars, except in Southern Italy and Sicily), since the traditional 'high' class is missing, the term 'middle' has gone down a rung. 'Negatively,' middle class means non-popular, i.e. those not workers or peasants; positively, it means the intellectual strata, the professional strata, the public employees."

[8][Hoare and Nowell-Smith] Primo de Rivera (1870–1930) was dictator of Spain 1923–30, with the support of the monarchy. Petar Živkovič (1879–1947) was Yugoslav prime minister 1929–32, and the instrument of King Alexander's dictatorial rule during those years.

[9][Hoare and Nowell-Smith] See "Analysis of Situations," *Selections,* pp. 175–185.

[10][Gramsci] In connection with the "military stratum," what T. Tittoni writes in *Ricordi personali di politica interna* (Nuova Antologia, 1–16 April 1929) is interesting. Tittoni recounts how he meditated on the fact that, in order to assemble the forces of order required to confront disturbances which had broken out in one place, it was necessary to plunder other regions. During the Red Week of June 1914, in order to repress the troubles in Ancona, Ravenna was plundered in this way; and subsequently the Prefect of Ravenna, deprived of his forces of order, was obliged to shut himself up in the Prefecture, abandoning the city to the rebels. "Several times I wondered what the government could have done if a movement of revolt had broken out simultaneously all over the peninsula." Tittoni proposed to the government that it should enrol ex-combatants under the command of retired officers as "public order volunteers." His project seemed to merit consideration, but it was not followed up.

norm valid for the entire nation. Other armies have had, and still retain, a formal and rigid discipline. We keep the principle constantly before us that the army is made for war, and that it is for war that it must prepare; peacetime discipline must be the same as wartime discipline, and it is in peacetime that the latter must find its spiritual foundations. Our discipline is based on a spirit of cohesion between leaders and followers which is a spontaneous product of the system adopted. This system resisted magnificently throughout a long and very hard war until the final victory; it is the merit of the Fascist régime to have extended to the entire Italian people so distinguished a disciplinary tradition. It is on individual discipline that the outcome of strategic conceptions and of tactical operations depends. War has taught us many things, among them that there is a deep gulf between peacetime preparation and wartime reality. It is certain that, whatever preparations may have been made, the initial operations of a campaign place the belligerents before new problems, which produce surprises on both sides. It should not for that reason be concluded that it is useless to have any *a priori* conceptions, and that no lessons can be derived from past wars. A theory of war can in fact be extracted from them, a theory which must be understood through intellectual discipline—understood as a means for promoting modes of reasoning which are not discordant, and uniformity of language such as will enable all to understand and make themselves understood. If, on occasions, theoretical unity has threatened to degenerate into schematism, there has at once been a prompt reaction, enforcing a rapid renovation of tactics—also made necessary by technical advances. Such a system of rules is therefore not static and traditional, as some people think. Tradition is considered only as a force, and the rules are constantly in the process of revision—not simply for the sake of change, but in order to fit them to reality." (An example of "preparation of the strategic conjuncture" is to be found in Churchill's *Memoirs,* where he speaks of the battle of Jutland.) [1933–34: 1st version 1932]

John Crowe Ransom

1888–1974

Most influential of the America New Critics, Ransom was a teacher at Vanderbilt University of some of the most prominent among them. He was also a distinguished poet and editor of the *Kenyon Review.* Ransom entitled his 1941 collection of essays *The New Criticism,* from which the name of the movement came. An earlier book, *The World's Body* (1938), expressed in its title his desire for a poetry emphasizing poetry's "sense of the real density and contingency of the world in which arguments and plans have to be pursued." This amounts to favoring particularity over generality, and it leads Ransom in *Poetry: A Note in Ontology,* reprinted below, to attack what he calls "Platonic" poetry, in which images are employed to express abstract ideas. But Ransom does not advocate the extreme particularity of "physical" poetry, like that of the Imagists, espoused by T. E. Hulme in his influential book *Speculations.* Ransom did not believe poetry is pure perception or pure emotion any more than he thought it is moral or scientific discourse clothed in tropes; in his view no discourse is ever pure, though it is clear that scientific and logical discourse tries to be. If poetry, however, should succeed in becoming pure it would fail. This view was taken up by his student Robert Penn Warren in an essay titled *Pure and Impure Poetry.* In a later essay, *Criticism as Pure Speculation,* Ransom was critical of those, like I. A. Richards (above, page 856), who tended to locate the poem in the feelings of the reader, for "the feelings are grossly inarticulate if we try to abstract them and take their testimony in their own language." The critic's discriminations, therefore, must be "among the objects." Ransom argues that poetry, like a democracy, must allow the "free exercise . . . of private and independent characters," while scientific discourse has a single totalitarian end. With this distinction, he recalls Kant's notion of internal purposiveness (above, page 427). His interest in language allies him to some extent with the Russian formalists.

For Ransom the poem has a central logic, situation, or "paraphrasable core," and a "context of lively local details." The poem differs from scientific discourse because the details of scientific discourse are always properly subordinate to the thesis. In the poem, detail may struggle with and change any apparent concept in the poem and make expression of the concept not the poem's ultimate purpose. Ransom's terms are designed to encourage discussion of a poem in its fullness without reducing it to its paraphrase. Despite all of his cautions, however, the phrases Ransom used sounded to his student Cleanth Brooks too much like the old ones, form and content. In Brooks's essay *The Heresy of Paraphrase* (below, page 1036), he was critical of Ransom and struggled with this problem.

Ransom's influence can be seen clearly in much criticism up through the 1960s— criticism sometimes called "objective" or "contextualist," as in that of Murray Krieger, who wrote the first account of the New Criticism. Both of these terms imply the critic's acknowledgment that all the parts of a poem that can be isolated for comment are affected by and affect all the other parts. There is a sense, then, in which criticism must be an examination of the poem's "being" rather than its "meaning," thus Ransom's use of the term "ontology."

Ransom's critical writings include *God Without Thunder* (1930), *The World's Body* (1938), *The New Criticism* (1941), and a selection *Poems and Essays* (1955). See Murray Krieger, *The New Apologists for Poetry* (1956); J. L. Stewart, *John Crowe Ransom* (1962) and *The Burden of Time* (1965); Robert Buffington, *The Equilibrist: A Study of John Crowe Ransom's Poetry* (1967); Thornton H. Parsons, *John Crowe Ransom* (1969); James E. Magner, *John Crowe Ransom* (1971); Thomas Daniel Young, *Gentleman in a Dustcoat* (1976); Kieran Quinlan, *John Crowe Ransom's Secular Faith* (1989); Mark Malvasi, *The Unrepentant South: The Agrarian Thought of John Crowe Ransom, Allen Tate, and Donald Davidson* (1997).

Poetry: A Note in Ontology

A poetry may be distinguished from a poetry by virtue of subject matter, and subject matter may be differentiated with respect to its ontology, or the reality of its being. An excellent variety of critical doctrine arises recently out of this differentiation, and thus perhaps criticism leans again upon ontological analysis as it was meant to do by Kant.[1] The recent critics remark in effect that some poetry deals with things, while some other poetry deals with ideas. The two poetries will differ from each other as radically as a thing differs from an idea.

The distinction in the hands of critics is a fruitful one. There is apt to go along with it a principle of valuation, which is the consequence of a temperament, and therefore basic. The critic likes things and intends that his poet shall offer them; or likes ideas and intends that he shall offer them; and approves him as he does the one or the other. Criticism cannot well go much deeper than this. The critic has carried to the last terms his analysis of the stuff of which poetry is made, and valued it frankly as his temperament or his need requires him to value it.

So philosophical a critic seems to be highly modern. He is; but this critic as a matter of fact is peculiarly on one side of the question. (The implication is unfavorable to the other side of the question.) He is in revolt against the tyranny of ideas, and against the poetry which celebrates ideas, and which may be identified—so far as his usual generalization may be trusted—with the hateful poetry of the Victorians. His bias is in favor of the things. On the other hand the critic

who likes Victorian verse, or the poetry of ideas, has probably not thought of anything of so grand a simplicity as electing between the things and the ideas, being apparently not quite capable of the ontological distinction. Therefore he does not know the real or constitutional ground of his liking, and may somewhat ingenuously claim that his predilection is for those poets who give him inspiration, or comfort, or truth, or honest meters, or something else equally "worthwhile." But Plato, who was not a modern, was just as clear as we are about the basic distinction between the ideas and the things, and yet stands far apart from the aforesaid conscious modern in passionately preferring the ideas over the things.[2] The weight of Plato's testimony would certainly fall on the side of the Victorians, though they may scarcely have thought of calling him as their witness. But this consideration need not conclude the hearing.

I. Physical Poetry

The poetry which deals with things was much in favor a few years ago with the resolute body of critics. And the critics affected the poets. If necessary, they became the poets, and triumphantly illustrated the new mode. The imagists[3] were important figures in the history of our poetry, and they were both theorists and creators. It was their intention to present things in their thinginess, or *Dinge* in their *Dinglichkeit;* and to such an extent had the public lost its sense of *Dinglichkeit* that their redirection was wholesome. What the public was inclined to seek in poetry was ideas, whether large ones or

---

Ransom's *Poetry: A Note in Ontology* was first published in 1934. The text is from *The World's Body* (Charles Scribner's Sons, 1938, ren. 1966).
[1]Kant (above, page 416).

[2]Plato (above, page 8).
[3]For a statement of Imagist principles see Ezra Pound, "A Retrospect," in *Literary Essays of Ezra Pound* (1954); also T. E. Hulme, *Speculations* (posth. 1924).

small ones, grand ones or pretty ones, certainly ideas to live by and die by, but what the imagists identified with the stuff of poetry was, simply, things.

Their application of their own principle was sufficiently heroic, though they scarcely consented to be as extreme in the practice as in the theory. They had artistic talent, every one of the original group, and it was impossible that they should make of poetry so simple an exercise as in doctrine they seemed to think it was. Yet Miss Lowell[4] wrote a poem on *Thompson's Lunch Room, Grand Central Station;* it is admirable if its intention is to show the whole reach of her courage. Its detail goes like this:

Jagged greenwhite bowls of pressed glass
Rearing snow-peaks of chipped sugar
Above the lighthouse-shaped castors
Of gray pepper and gray-white salt.

For most of us as for the public idealist, with his "values," this is inconsequential. Unhappily it seems that the things as things do not necessarily interest us, and that in fact we are not quite constructed with the capacity for a disinterested interest. But it must be noted even here that the things are on their good behavior, looking rather well, and arranged by lines into something approaching a military formation. More technically, there is cross-imagery in the snowpeaks of sugar, and in the lighthouse-shaped castors, and cross-imagery involves association, and will presently involve dissociation and thinking. The meter is but a vestige, but even so it means something, for meter is a powerful intellectual determinant marshaling the words and, inevitably, the things. The *Dinglichkeit* of this imagist specimen, or the realism, was therefore not pure. But it was nearer pure than the world was used to in poetry, and the exhibit was astonishing.

For the purpose of this note I shall give to such poetry, dwelling as exclusively as it dares upon physical things, the name *physical poetry*. It is to stand opposite to that poetry which dwells as firmly as it dares upon ideas.

But perhaps thing versus idea does not seem to name an opposition precisely. Then we might phrase it a little differently: image versus idea. The idealistic philosophies are not sure that things exist, but they mean the equivalent when they refer to images. (Or they may consent to perceptions; or to impressions, following Hume, and following Croce,[5] who remarks that they are preintellectual and independent of concepts. It is all the same, unless we are extremely tech-

nical.) It is sufficient if they concede that image is the raw material of idea. Though it may be an unwieldy and useless affair for the idealist as it stands, much needing to be licked into shape, nevertheless its relation to idea is that of a material cause, and it cannot be dispossessed of its priority.

It cannot be dispossessed of a primordial freshness, which idea can never claim. An idea is derivative and tamed. The image is in the natural or wild state, and it has to be discovered there, not put there, obeying its own law and none of ours. We think we can lay hold of image and take it captive, but the docile captive is not the real image but only the idea, which is the image with its character beaten out of it.

But we must be very careful: idealists are nothing if not dialectical. They object that an image in an original state of innocence is a delusion and cannot exist, that no image ever comes to us which does not imply the world of ideas, that there is "no percept without a concept." There is something in it. Every property discovered in the image is a universal property, and nothing discovered in the image is marvelous in kind though it may be pinned down historically or statistically as a single instance. But there is this to be understood too: the image which is not remarkable in any particular property is marvelous in its assemblage of many properties, a manifold of properties, like a mine or a field, something to be explored for the properties; yet science can manage the image, which is infinite in properties, only by equating it to the one property with which the science is concerned; for science at work is always *a science,* and committed to a special interest. It is not by refutation but by abstraction that science destroys the image.[6] It means to get its "value" out of the image, and we may be sure that it has no use for the image in its original state of freedom. People who are engrossed with their pet "values" become habitual killers. Their game is the images, or the things, and they acquire the ability to shoot them as far off as they can be seen, and do. It is thus that we lose the power of imagination, or whatever faculty it is by which we are able to contemplate things as they are in their rich and contingent materiality. But our dreams reproach us, for in dreams they come alive again. Likewise our memory; which makes light of our science by recalling the images in their panoply of circumstance and with their morning freshness upon them.

It is the dream, the recollection, which compels us to poetry, and to deliberate aesthetic experience. It can hardly be argued, I think, that the arts are constituted automatically out of original images, and arise in some early age of innocence. (Though Croce seems to support this view, and to

---

[4]Amy Lowell (1874–1925), American Imagist poet.
[5]Hume, (above, page 322); see Benedetto Croce, *Aesthetic* (1900).

[6]This statement can be compared to Cassirer's (below, page 1018).

make art a preadult stage of experience.) Art is based on second love, not first love. In it we make a return to something which we had willfully alienated. The child is occupied mostly with things, but it is because he is still unfurnished with systematic ideas, not because he is a ripe citizen by nature and comes along already trailing clouds of glory.[7] Images are clouds of glory for the man who has discovered that ideas are a sort of darkness. Imagism, that is, the recent historical movement, may resemble a naive poetry of mere things, but we can read the theoretical pronouncements of Imagists, and we can learn that Imagism is motivated by a distaste for the systematic abstractedness of thought. It presupposes acquaintance with science; that famous activity which is "constructive" with respect to the tools of our economic role in this world, and destructive with respect to nature. Imagists wish to escape from science by immersing themselves in images.

Not far off the simplicity of Imagism was, a little later, the subtler simplicity of Mr. George Moore's project shared with several others, in behalf of "pure poetry."[8] In Moore's house on Ebury Street they talked about poetry, with an after dinner warmth if not an early morning discretion, and their tastes agreed almost perfectly and reinforced one another. The fruit of these conversations was the volume *Pure Poetry*. It must have been the most exclusive anthology of English poetry that had yet appeared, since its room was closed to all the poems that dallied visibly with ideas, so that many poems that had been coveted by all other anthologists do not appear there. Nevertheless the book is delicious, and something more deserves to be said for it.

First, that "pure poetry" is a kind of physical poetry. Its visible content is a thing-content. Technically, I suppose, it is effective in this character if it can exhibit its material in such a way that an image or set of images and not an idea must occupy the foreground of the reader's attention. Thus: "Full fathom five thy father lies / Of his bones are coral made."[9] Here it is difficult for anybody (except the perfect idealist who is always theoretically possible and who would expect to take a return from anything whatever) to receive any experience except that of a very distinct image, or set of images. It has the configuration of image, which consists in being sharp of edges, and the modality of image, which consists in being given and nonnegotiable, and the density, which consists in being full, a plenum of qualities. What is to be done with it? It is pure exhibit; it is to be contemplated; perhaps it is to be enjoyed. The art of poetry depends more frequently on this faculty than on any other in its repertory; the faculty of presenting images so whole and clean that they resist the catalysis of thought.

And something else must be said, going in the opposite direction. "Pure poetry," all the same; is not as pure as it is claimed to be, though on the whole it is physical poetry. (All true poetry is a phase of physical poetry.) It is not as pure as imagism is, or at least it is not as pure as imagism would be if it lived up to its principles; and in fact it is significant that the volume does not contain any imagist poems, which argues a difference in taste somewhere. Imagism may take trifling things for its material, presumably it will take the first things the poet encounters, since "importance" and "interest" are not primary qualities which a thing possesses but secondary or tertiary ones which the idealist attributes to it by virtue of his own requirements. "Pure poetry" as Moore conceives it, and as the lyrics of Poe[10] and Shakespeare offer it, deals with the more dramatic materials, and here dramatic means human, or at least capable of being referred to the critical set of human interests. Employing this sort of material the poet cannot exactly intend to set the human economists in us actually into motion, but perhaps he does intend to comfort us with the fleeting sense that it is potentially our kind of material.

In the same way "pure poetry" is nicely metered, whereas imagism was free. Technique is written on it. And, by the way, the anthology contains no rugged anonymous Scottish ballad either, and probably for a like reason; because it would not be technically finished. Now both Moore and De La Mare[11] are accomplished conservative artists, and what they do or what they approve may be of limited range but it is sure to be technically admirable, and it is certain that they understand what technique in poetry is though they do not define it. Technique takes the thing-content and meters and orders it. Meter is not an original property of things. It is artificial, and conveys the sense of human control, even if it does not wish to impair the thinginess of the things. Metric is a science, and so far as we attend to it we are within the scientific atmosphere. Order is the logical arrangement of things. It involves the dramatic "form" which selects the things, and brings out their appropriate qualities, and carries them through a systematic course of predication until the total impression is a unit of logic and not merely a solid lump of thing-content. The "pure poems" which Moore admires are studied, though it would be fatal if they looked studious.

---

[7]Ransom quotes here words from William Wordsworth's *Ode: Intimations of Immortality from Early Childhood.*
[8]George Moore (1852–1933), Anglo-Irish novelist, editor of *An Anthology of Pure Poetry* (1924).
[9]Shakespeare, *The Tempest* I, ii, 397–98.
[10]Poe (above, page 580); Ransom is probably thinking of, among others, Poe's poem *The Bells.*
[11]Walter de la Mare (1873–1956), English poet.

A sustained effort of ideation effected these compositions. It is covered up, and communicates itself only on a subliminal plane of consciousness. But experienced readers are quite aware of it; they know at once what is the matter when they encounter a realism shamelessly passing for poetry, or a well-planned but blundering poetry.

As critics we should have every good will toward physical poetry: it is the basic constituent of any poetry. But the product is always something short of a pure or absolute existence, and it cannot quite be said that it consists of nothing but physical objects. The fact is that when we are more than usually satisfied with a physical poetry our analysis will probably disclose that it is more than usually impure.

II. Platonic Poetry

The poetry of ideas I shall denominate: *Platonic poetry.* This also has grades of purity. A discourse which employed only abstract ideas with no images would be a scientific document and not a poem at all, not even a Platonic poem. Platonic poetry dips heavily into the physical. If physical poetry tends to employ some ideation surreptitiously while still looking innocent of idea, Platonic poetry more than returns the compliment, for it tries as hard as it can to look like physical poetry, as if it proposed to conceal its medicine, which is the idea to be propagated, within the sugar candy of objectivity and *Dinglichkeit.* As an instance, it is almost inevitable that I quote a famous Victorian utterance:

> The year's at the spring
> And day's at the morn;
> Morning's at seven;
> The hill-side's dew-pearled;
>
> The lark's on the wing;
> The snail's on the thorn:
> God's in his heaven—
> All's right with the world![12]

which is a piece of transparent homiletics; for in it six pretty, coordinate images are marched, like six little lambs to the slaughter, to a colon and a powerful text. Now the exhibits of this poetry in the physical kind are always large, and may take more of the attention of the reader than is desired, but they are meant mostly to be illustrative of the ideas. It is on this ground that idealists like Hegel[13] detect something unworthy, like a pedagogical trick, in poetry af-

ter all, and consider that the race will abandon it when it has outgrown its childishness and is enlightened.

The ablest arraignment of Platonic poetry that I have seen, as an exercise which is really science but masquerades as poetry by affecting a concern for physical objects, is that of Mr. Allen Tate in a series of studies recently in *The New Republic.*[14] I will summarize. Platonic poetry is allegory, a discourse in things, but on the understanding that they are translatable at every point into ideas. (The usual ideas are those which constitute the popular causes, patriotic, religious, moral, or social.) Or Platonic poetry is the elaboration of ideas as such, but in proceeding introduces for ornament some physical properties after the style of physical poetry; which is rhetoric. It is positive when the poet believes in the efficacy of the ideas. It is negative when he despairs of their efficacy, because they have conspicuously failed to take care of him, and utters his personal wail: "I fall upon the thorns of life! I bleed!"[15] This is "Romantic irony,"[16] which comes at occasional periods to interrupt the march of scientific optimism. But it still falls under the category of Platonism; it generally proposes some other ideas to take the place of those which are in vogue.

But why Platonism? To define Platonism we must remember that it is not the property of the historical person who reports dialogues about it in an academy, any more than "pure poetry" is the property of the talkers who describe it from a house on Ebury Street. Platonism, in the sense I mean, is the name of an impulse that is native to us all, frequent, tending to take a too complete possession of our minds. Why should the spirit of mortal be proud? The chief explanation is that modern mortal is probably a Platonist. We are led to believe that nature is rational and that by the force of reasoning we shall possess it. I have read upon high authority: "Two great forces are persistent in Plato: the love of truth and zeal for human improvement." The forces are one force. We love to view the world under universal or scientific ideas to which we give the name truth; and this is because the ideas seem to make not for righteousness but for mastery. The Platonic view of the world is ultimately the predatory, for it reduces to the scientific, which we know. The Platonic idea becomes the logos which science worships, which is the occidental god, whose minions we are, and whose children, claiming a large share in his powers for patrimony.

---

[12]Robert Browning (1812–1889), *Pippa Passes,* 221–28.
[13]Hegel (above, page 552).

[14]Allen Tate (1899–1979), American poet, one of the New Critics and a student of Ransom. Ransom refers here to his "Three Types of Poetry," *On the Limits of Poetry* (1948).
[15]From Percy Bysshe Shelley's *Ode to the West Wind,* 54. Throughout Ransom's essay pieces of Romantic and Victorian poetry are looked on with a distaste typical of the New Critics.
[16]On Romantic irony see Schlegel (above, page 480).

Now the fine Platonic world of ideas fails to coincide with the original world of perception, which is the world populated by the stubborn and contingent objects, and to which as artists we fly in shame. The sensibility manifested by artists makes fools of scientists, if the latter are inclined to take their special and quite useful form of truth as the whole and comprehensive article. A dandified pagan worldling like Moore can always defeat Platonism; he does it every hour; he can exhibit the savor of his fish and wines, the fragrance of his coffee and cigars, and the solidity of the images in his favorite verse. These are objects which have to be experienced, and cannot be reported, for what is their simple essence that the Platonist can abstract? Moore may sound mystical but he is within the literal truth when he defends "pure poetry" on the ground that the things are constant, and it is the ideas which change— changing according to the latest mode under which the species indulges its grandiose expectation of subjugating nature. The things are constant in the sense that the ideas are never emancipated from the necessity of referring back to them as their original; and the sense that they are not altered nor diminished no matter which ideas may take off from them as a point of departure. The way to obtain the true *Dinglichkeit* of a formal dinner or a landscape or a beloved person is to approach the object as such, and in humility; then it unfolds a nature which we are unprepared for if we have put our trust in the simple idea which attempted to represent it.

The special antipathy of Moore is to the ideas as they put on their moral complexion, the ideas that relate everything to that insignificant center of action, the human "soul" in its most Platonic and Pharisaic aspect. Nothing can darken perception better than a repetitive moral earnestness, based on the reputed superiority and higher destiny of the human species. If morality is the code by which we expect the race to achieve the more perfect possession of nature, it is an incitement to a more heroic science, but not to aesthetic experience, nor religious; if it is the code of humility, by which we intend to know nature as nature is, that is another matter; but in an age of science morality is inevitably for the general public the former; and so transcendent a morality as the latter is now unheard of. And therefore:

> O love, *they* die in yon rich sky,
>   *They* faint on hill or field of river;
>   *Our* echoes roll from soul to soul,
>   And grow forever and forever.[17]

The italics are mine. These lines conclude an otherwise innocent poem, a candidate for the anthology, upon which Moore remarks: "The Victorian could never reconcile himself to finishing a poem without speaking about the soul, and the lines are particularly vindictive." Vindictive is just. By what right did the Laureate[18] exult in the death of the physical echoes and call upon his love to witness it, but out of the imperiousness of his savage Platonism? Plato himself would have admired this ending, and considered that it redeemed an otherwise vicious poem.

Why do persons who have ideas to promulgate risk the trial by poetry? If the poets are hired to do it, which is the polite conception of some Hegelians, why do their employers think it worth the money, which they hold in public trust for the cause? Does a science have to become a poetry too? A science is the less effective as a science when it muddies its clear waters with irrelevance, a sermon becomes less cogent when it begins to quote the poets. The moralist, the scientist, and the prophet of idealism think evidently that they must establish their conclusions in poetry, though they reach these conclusions upon quite other evidence. The poetry is likely to destroy the conclusions with a sort of death by drowning, if it is a free poetry.

When that happens the Platonists may be cured of Platonism. There are probably two cures, of which this is the better. One cure is by adversity, by the failure of the ideas to work, on account of treachery or violence, or the contingencies of weather, constitution, love, and economics; leaving the Platonist defeated and bewildered, possibly humbled, but on the other hand possibly turned cynical and worthless. Very much preferable is the cure which comes by education in the fine arts, erasing his Platonism more gently, leading him to feel that that is not a becoming habit of mind which dulls the perceptions.

The definition which some writers have given to art is: the reference of the idea to the image. The implication is that the act is not for the purpose of honest comparison so much as for the purpose of proving the idea by the image. But in the event the idea is not disproved so much as it is made to look ineffective and therefore foolish. The ideas will not cover the objects upon which they are imposed, they are too attenuated and threadlike; for ideas have extension and objects have intension, but extension is thin while intension is thick.[19]

There must be a great deal of genuine poetry which started in the poet's mind as a thesis to be developed, but in

---

[17]Alfred Lord Tennyson (1809–1892), *The Splendour Falls on Castle Walls*, 13–16.

[18]Tennyson was Poet Laureate of Britain from 1850 to 1892.

[19]On "extension" and "intension" see Allen Tate, "Tension in Poetry," *On the Limits of Poetry* (1948).

which the characters and the situations have developed faster than the thesis, and of their own accord. The thesis disappears; or it is recaptured here and there and at the end, and lodged sententiously with the reader, where every successive reading of the poem will dislodge it again. Like this must be some plays, even some play out of Shakespeare, whose thesis would probably be disentangled with difficulty out of the crowded pageant; or some narrative poem with a moral plot but much pure detail; perhaps some "occasional" piece of a Laureate or official person, whose purpose is compromised but whose personal integrity is saved by his wavering between the sentiment which is a public duty and the experience which he has in his own right; even some proclaimed allegory, like Spenser's,[20] unlikely as that may seem, which does not remain transparent and everywhere translatable into idea but makes excursions into the territory of objectivity. These are hybrid performances. They cannot possess beauty of design, though there may be a beauty in detailed passages. But it is common enough, and we should be grateful. The mind is a versatile agent, and unexpectedly stubborn in its determination not really to be hardened in Platonism. Even in an age of science like the nineteenth century the poetic talents are not so loyal to its apostolic zeal as they and it suppose, and do not deserve the unqualified scorn which it is fashionable to offer them, now that the tide has turned, for their performance is qualified.

But this may not be stern enough for concluding a note on Platonic poetry. I refer again to that whose Platonism is steady and malignant. This poetry is an imitation of physical poetry, and not really a poetry. Platonists practice their bogus poetry in order to show that an image will prove an idea, but the literature which succeeds in this delicate mission does not contain real images but illustrations.

III. Metaphysical Poetry

"Most men," Mr. Moore observes,

> read and write poetry between fifteen and thirty and afterwards very seldom, for in youth we are attracted by ideas, and modern poetry being concerned almost exclusively with ideas we live on duty, liberty, and fraternity as chameleons are said to live on light and air, till at last we turn from ideas to things, thinking that we have lost our taste for poetry, unless, perchance, we are classical scholars.

Much is conveyed in this characteristic sentence, even in proportion to its length. As for the indicated chronology, the cart is put after the horse, which is its proper sequence. And it is pleasant to be confirmed in the belief that many men do recant from their Platonism and turn back to things. But it cannot be exactly a *volte-face*,[21] for there are qualifications. If pure ideas were what these men turn from, they would have no poetry at all in the first period, and if pure things were what they turn to, they would be having not a classical poetry but a pure imagism, if such a thing is possible, in the second.

The mind does not come unscathed and virginal out of Platonism. Ontological interest would have to develop curiously, or wastefully and discontinuously, if men through their youth must cultivate the ideas so passionately that upon its expiration they are done with ideas forever and ready to become as little (and prelogical) children. Because of the foolishness of idealists are ideas to be taboo for the adult mind? And, as critics, what are we to do with those poems (like *The Canonization* and *Lycidas*)[22] which could not obtain admission by Moore into the anthology but which very likely are the poems we cherish beyond others?

The reputed "innocence" of the aesthetic moment, the knowledge without desire" which Schopenhauer[23] praises, must submit to a little scrutiny, like anything else that looks too good to be true. We come into this world as aliens come into a land which they must conquer if they are to live. For native endowment we have an exacting "biological" constitution which knows precisely what it needs and determines for us our inevitable desires. There can be no certainty that any other impulses are there, for why should they be? They scarcely belong in the biological picture. Perhaps we are simply an efficient animal species, running smoothly, working fast, finding the formula of life only too easy, and after a certain apprenticeship piling up power and wealth far beyond the capacity of our appetites to use. What will come next? Perhaps poetry, if the gigantic effort of science begins to seem disproportionate to the reward, according to a sense of diminishing returns. But before this pretty event can come to pass, it is possible that every act of attention which is allowed us is conditioned by a gross and selfish interest.

Where is innocence then? The aesthetic moment appears as a curious moment of suspension; between the Platonism in us, which is militant, always sciencing and devouring, and a starved inhibited aspiration towards

---

[20]Edmund Spenser (1552?–1599), English poet. Ransom is referring to Spenser's *Faerie Queene*.

[21]About-face.
[22]By John Donne (1572–1631) and John Milton (1608–1674) respectively. Concerning *Lycidas* see Ransom's essay *A Poem Nearly Anonymous*.
[23]Arthur Schopenhauer (1788–1860), German philosopher.

innocence which, if it could only be free, would like to respect and know the object as it might of its own accord reveal itself.

The poetic impulse is not free, yet it holds out stubbornly against science for the enjoyment of its images. It means to reconstitute the world of perceptions. Finally there is suggested some such formula as the following:

Science gratifies a rational or practical impulse and exhibits the minimum of perception. Art gratifies a perceptual impulse and exhibits the minimum of reason.

Now it would be strange if poets did not develop many technical devices for the sake of increasing the volume of the percipienda or sensibilia. I will name some of them.

First Device: meter. Meter is the most obvious device. A formal meter impresses us as a way of regulating very drastically the material, and we do not stop to remark (that is, as readers) that it has no particular aim except some nominal sort of regimentation. It symbolizes the predatory method, like a sawmill which intends to reduce all the trees to fixed unit timbers, and as business men we require some sign of our business. But to the Platonic censor in us it gives a false security, for so long as the poet appears to be working faithfully at his metrical engine he is left comparatively free to attend lovingly to the things that are being metered, and metering them need not really hurt them. Meter is the gentlest violence he can do them, if he is expected to do some violence.

Second Device: fiction. The device of the fiction is probably no less important and universal in poetry. Over every poem which looks like a poem is a sign which reads: This road does not go through to action; fictitious. Art always sets out to create an "aesthetic distance" between the object and the subject, and art takes pains to announce that it is not history. The situation treated is not quite an actual situation, for science is likely to have claimed that field, and exiled art; but a fictive or hypothetical one, so that science is less greedy and perception may take hold of it. Kant asserted that the aesthetic judgment is not concerned with the existence or nonexistence of the object, and may be interpreted as asserting that it is so far from depending on the object's existence that it really depends on the object's nonexistence.[24] Sometimes we have a certain melancholy experience. We enjoy a scene which we receive by report only, or dream, or meet with in art; but subsequently find ourselves in the presence of an actual one that seems the very same scene; only to discover that we have not now the power to enjoy it, or to receive it aesthetically, because the economic tension is upon us and will not indulge us in the proper mood. And it is generally easier to obtain our aesthetic experience from art than from nature, because nature is actual, and communication is forbidden. But in being called fictive or hypothetical the art object suffers no disparagement. It cannot be true in the sense of being actual, and therefore it may be despised by science. But it is true in the sense of being fair or representative, in permitting the "illusion of reality"; just as Schopenhauer discovered that music may symbolize all the modes of existence in the world; and in keeping with the customary demand of the readers of fiction proper, that it shall be "true to life." The defenders of art must require for it from its practitioners this sort of truth, and must assert of it before the world this dignity. If jealous science succeeds in keeping the field of history for its own exclusive use, it does not therefore annihilate the arts, for they reappear in a field which may be called real though one degree removed from actuality. There the arts perform their function with much less interference, and at the same time with about as much fidelity to the phenomenal world as history has.

Third Device: tropes. I have named two important devices; I am not prepared to offer the exhaustive list. I mention but one other kind, the device which comprises the figures of speech. A proper scientific discourse has no mention of employing figurative language for its definitive sort of utterance.[25] Figures of speech twist accidence away from the straight course, as if to intimate astonishing lapses of rationality beneath the smooth surface of discourse, inviting perceptual attention, and weakening the tyranny of science over the senses. But I skip the several easier and earlier figures, which are timid, and stop on the climactic figure, which is the metaphor; with special reference to its consequence, a poetry which once in our history it produced in a beautiful and abundant exhibit, called *metaphysical poetry*.

And what is metaphysical poetry? The term was added to the official vocabulary of criticism by Johnson, who probably took it from Pope, who probably took it from Dryden, who used it to describe the poetry of a certain school of poets, thus: "He [John Donne] affects the metaphysics, not only in his satires, but in his amorous verses, where nature only should reign. . . . In this Mr. Cowley has copied him to a fault." But the meaning of *metaphysical* which was common in Dryden's time, having come down from the Middle Ages through Shakespeare, was simply: supernatural; *miraculous*. The context of the Dryden passage indicates it.[26]

---

[24]This takes a certain liberty with Kant's views.

[25]Compare Locke (above, page 296).

[26]Pope (above, page 297); Dryden (above, page 253); Johnson (above, page 357); Abraham Cowley (1618–1687), English poet; Dryden's remark about Donne appears in his *Discourse on the Original and Progress of Satire* (1693); Johnson's criticism of the Metaphysical Poets is in his essay on Cowley in his *Lives of the English Poets* (1779–1781).

Dryden, then, noted a miraculism in poetry and repudiated it; except where it was employed for satire, where it was not seriously intended and had the effect of wit. Dryden himself employs miraculism wittily, but seems rather to avoid it if he will be really committed by it; he may employ it in his translations of Ovid,[27] where the responsibility is Ovid's and not Dryden's, and in an occasional classical piece where he is making polite use of myths well known to be pagan errors. In his "amorous" pieces he finds the reign of nature sufficient, and it is often the worse for his amorous pieces. He is not many removes from a naturalist. (A naturalist is a person who studies nature not because he loves it but because he wants to use it, approaches it from the standpoint of common sense, and sees it thin and not thick.) Dryden might have remarked that Donne himself had a change of heart and confined his miraculism at last to the privileged field of a more or less scriptural revelation. Perhaps Dryden found his way to accepting Milton because Milton's miraculism was mostly not a contemporary sort but classical and scriptural, pitched in a time when the age of miracles had not given way to the age of science. He knew too that Cowley had shamefully recanted from his petty miraculism, which formed the conceits, and turned to the scriptural or large order of miraculism to write his heroic (but empty) verses about David; and had written a Pindaric ode in extravagant praise of "Mr. Hobs,"[28] whose naturalistic account of nature seemed to render any other account fantastic if not contrary to the social welfare.

Incidentally, we know how much Mr. Hobbes affected Dryden too, and the whole of Restoration literature. What Bacon[29] with his disparagement of poetry had begun, in the cause of science and Protestantism, Hobbes completed. The name of Hobbes is critical in any history that would account for the chill which settled upon the poets at the very moment that English poetry was attaining magnificently to the fullness of its powers. The name stood for common sense and naturalism, and the monopoly of the scientific spirit over the mind. Hobbes was the adversary, the Satan, when the latter first intimidated the English poets. After Hobbes his name is legion.

"Metaphysics," or miraculism, informs a poetry which is the most original and exciting, and intellectually perhaps the most seasoned, that we know in our literature, and very probably it has few equivalents in other literatures. But it is evident that the metaphysical effects may be large scale or they may be small scale. (I believe that generically, or ontologically, no distinction is to be made between them.) If Donne and Cowley illustrate the small scale effects, Milton will illustrate the large scale ones, probably as a consequence of the fact that he wrote major poems. Milton, in the *Paradise Lost,* told a story which was heroic and miraculous in the first place. In telling it he dramatized it, and allowed the scenes and characters to develop of their own native energy. The virtue of a long poem on a "metaphysical" subject will consist in the dramatization or substantiation of all the parts, the poet not being required to devise fresh miracles on every page so much as to establish the perfect "naturalism" of the material upon which the grand miracle is imposed. The *Paradise Lost* possesses this virtue nearly everywhere:

> Thus *Adam* to himself lamented loud
> Through the still night, not now, as ere man fell,
> Wholesome and cool, and mild, but with black air
> Accompanied, with damps and dreadful gloom,
> Which to his evil conscience represented
> All things with double terror: On the ground
> Outstretched he lay, on the cold ground, and oft
> Cursed his creation, death as oft accused
> Of tardy execution, since denounced
> The day of his offense. Why comes not death,
> Said he, with one thrice acceptable stroke
> To end me?[30]

This is exactly the sort of detail for a large scale metaphysical work, but it would hardly serve the purpose with a slighter and more naturalistic subject; with "amorous" verses. For the critical mind metaphysical poetry refers perhaps almost entirely to the so-called conceits that constitute its staple. To define the conceit is to define small scale metaphysical poetry.

It is easily defined, upon a little citation. Donne exhibits two conceits, or two branches of one conceit in the familiar lines:

> Our hands were firmly cemented
> By a fast balm which thence did spring;
> Our eye-beams twisted, and did thread
> Our eyes upon one double string.[31]

[27]Publius Ovidius Naso (43 B.C.–18 A.D.), Roman poet.
[28]Thomas Hobbes (1588–1679), English philosopher.
[29]Bacon (above, page 234).

[30]X, 845–56.
[31]*The Ecstacy,* 5–8.

The poem which follows sticks to the topic; it represents the lovers in precisely that mode of union and no other. Cowley is more conventional yet still bold in the lines:

Oh take my heart, and by that means you'll prove
  Within, too stored enough of love:
Give me but yours, I'll by that change so thrive
  That love in all my parts shall live.
So powerful is this change, it render can,
My outside woman, and your inside man.[32]

A conceit originates in a metaphor; and in fact the conceit is but a metaphor if the metaphor is meant; that is, if it is developed so literally that it must be meant, or predicated so baldly that nothing else can be meant. Perhaps this will do for a definition.

Clearly the seventeenth century had the courage of its metaphors, and imposed them imperially on the nearest things, and just as clearly the nineteenth century lacked this courage, and was halfheartedly metaphorical, or content with similes. The difference between the literary qualities of the two periods is the difference between the metaphor and the simile. (It must be admitted that this like other generalizations will not hold without exceptions.) One period was pithy and original in its poetic utterance, the other was prolix and predictable. It would not quite commit itself to the metaphor even if it came upon one. Shelley is about as vigorous as usual when he says in *Adonais:* "Thou young dawn, / Turn all thy dew to splendor. . . ."[33] But splendor is not the correlative of dew, it has the flat tone of a Platonic idea, while physically it scarcely means more than dew with sunshine upon it. The seventeenth century would have said: "Turn thy dew, which is water, into fire, and accomplish the transmutation of the elements." Tennyson in his boldest lyric sings: "Come into the garden, Maud, / For the black bat, night, has flown,"[34] and leaves us unpersuaded of the bat. The predication would be complete without the bat, "The black night has flown," and a flying night is not very remarkable. Tennyson is only affecting a metaphor. But later in the same poem he writes:

The red rose cries, "She is near, she is near";
  And the white rose weeps, "She is late";
The larkspur listens, "I hear, I hear";
  And the lily whispers, "I wait."[35]

[32]*The Change,* 19–24.
[33]Ll. 362–63.
[34]*Maud* XXII, 850–51.
[35]*Maud* XXII, 912–15.

And this is a technical conceit. But it is too complicated for this author, having a plurality of images which do not sustain themselves individually. The flowers stand for the lover's thoughts, and have been prepared for carefully in an earlier stanza, but their distinctness is too arbitrary, and these are like a schoolgirl's made-up metaphors. The passage will not compare with one on a very similar situation in *Green Candles,* by Mr. Humbert Wolfe:[36]

"I know her little foot," gray carpet said:
"Who but I should know her light tread?"
"She shall come in," answered the open door,
"And not," said the room, "go out any more."

Wolfe's conceit works and Tennyson's does not, and though Wolfe's performance seems not very daring or important, and only pleasant, he employs the technique of the conceit correctly: he knows that the miracle must have a basis of verisimilitude.

Such is metaphysical poetry; the extension of a rhetorical device; as one of the most brilliant successes in our poetry, entitled to long and thorough examination; and even here demanding somewhat by way of a more ontological criticism. I conclude with it.

We may consult the dictionary, and discover that there is a miraculism or supernaturalism in a metaphorical assertion if we are ready to mean what we say, or believe what we hear. Or we may read Mr. Hobbes, the naturalist, who was very clear upon it: "II. The second cause of absurd assertions I ascribe to the giving of names of 'bodies' to 'accidents,' or of 'accidents' to 'bodies,' as they do that say 'faith is infused' or 'inspired,' when nothing can be 'poured' or 'breathed' into anything but body . . . and that 'phantasms' are 'spirits,' etc." Translated into our present terms, Hobbes is condemning the confusion of single qualities with whole things; or the substitution of concrete images for simple ideas.

Specifically, the miraculism arises when the poet discovers by analogy an identity between objects which is partial, though it should be considerable, and proceeds to an identification which is complete. It is to be contrasted with the simile, which says "as if" or "like," and is scrupulous to keep the identification partial. In Cowley's passage above, the lover is saying, not for the first time in his literature: "She and I have exchanged our hearts." What has actually been exchanged is affections, and affections are only in a limited sense the same as hearts. Hearts are unlike affections in be-

[36]Humbert Wolfe (1885–1940), English poet.

ing engines that pump blood and form body; and it is a miracle if the poet represents the lady's affection as rendering her inside into man. But he succeeds, with this mixture, in depositing with us the image of a very powerful affection.

From the strict point of view of literary criticism it must be insisted that the miraculism which produces the humblest conceit is the same miraculism which supplies to religions their substantive content. (This is said to assert the dignity not of the conceits but of the religions.) It is the poet and nobody else who gives to the God a nature, a form, faculties, and a history; to the God, most comprehensive of all terms, which, if there were no poetic impulse to actualize or "find" him, would remain the driest and deadest among Platonic ideas, with all intension sacrificed to infinite extension. The myths are conceits, born of metaphors. Religions are periodically produced by poets and destroyed by naturalists. Religion depends for its ontological validity upon a literary understanding, and that is why it is frequently misunderstood. The metaphysical poets, perhaps like their spiritual fathers the medieval schoolmen, were under no illusions about this. They recognized myth, as they recognized the conceits, as a device of expression; its sanctity as the consequence of its public or social importance.

But whether the topics be gods or amorous experiences, why do poets resort to miraculism? Hardly for the purpose of controverting natural fact or scientific theory. Religion pronounces about God only where science is silent and philosophy is negative; for a positive is wanted, that is, a God who has his being in the physical world as well as in the world of principles and abstractions. Likewise with the little secular enterprises of poetry too. Not now are the poets so brave, not for a very long time have they been so

brave, as to dispute the scientists on what they call their "truth"; though it is a pity that the statement cannot be turned round. Poets will concede that every act of science is legitimate, and has its efficacy. The metaphysical poets of the seventeenth century particularly admired the methodology of science, and in fact they copied it, and their phrasing is often technical, spare, and polysyllabic, though they are not repeating actual science but making those metaphorical substitutions that are so arresting.

The intention of metaphysical poetry is to complement science, and improve discourse. Naturalistic discourse is incomplete, for either of two reasons. It has the minimum of physical content and starves the sensibility, or it has the maximum, as if to avoid the appearance of evil, but is laborious and pointless. Platonic poetry is too idealistic, but physical poetry is too realistic, and realism is tedious and does not maintain interest. The poets therefore introduce the psychological device of the miracle. The predication which it permits is clean and quick but it is not a scientific predication. For scientific predication concludes an act of attention but miraculism initiates one. It leaves us looking, marveling, and reveling in the thick *dinglich* substance that has just received its strange representation.

Let me suggest as a last word, in deference to a common Puritan scruple, that the predication of metaphysical poetry is true enough. It is not true like history, but no poetry is true in that sense, and only a part of science. It is true in the pragmatic sense in which some of the generalizations of science are true: it accomplishes precisely the sort of representation that it means to. It suggests to us that the object is perceptually or physically remarkable, and we had better attend to it.

R. P. Blackmur

1904–1965

The self-consciousness with which critics began to examine what they do became pronounced after the work of T. S. Eliot (above, page 806) and I. A. Richards (above, page 856) in the 1920s. This was perhaps inevitable with the developments in the analysis of language. Solipsistic impressionism had come to a standstill, and a new objectification of the literary work seemed to be required if criticism were to have any pretensions to be a recognizable discipline. But the psychologism of Richards and various pronouncements of Eliot came under criticism by the New Critics.

Blackmur, an autodidact who had no academic degrees yet became a professor at Princeton University, was a practicing critic allied with the New Criticism. In the tradition of Kant's analysis of how we make aesthetic judgments, Blackmur and other critics of his time analyzed critical practices, inventing what was the criticism of criticism. Implicit in Blackmur's view is a sense of the literary work as distinct from poet, reader, and world. He assumes that as an object with a degree of autonomy the work should generate a mode of criticism that will approach but never violate "the thing in itself from its own point of view." Thus, for Blackmur, criticism is provisional and pragmatic. It is also ironic in that the critic should be at a certain psychical distance from the work.

In Blackmur's ironic phrase, criticism should be the "formal discourse of an amateur." By this he does not mean that the critic should be a dilettante, but that he should be the opposite of a professional insofar as he is not "professing" a doctrine. He must use all the knowledge that he can gain but at the same time "discount, absorb, or dominate the doctrine for the life that goes with it." For Blackmur, doctrine is the death of, not the completion or the source, of insight. The literary work is cut off from its own full worth as an initiator of new forms of understanding when it is reduced by a critic to illustration of doctrine. In these matters Blackmur is allied with John Crowe Ransom (above, page 953) and the New Criticism.

A large part of Blackmur's essay *A Critic's Job of Work* is devoted to discussing modes of literary analysis that have "ulterior" purposes and thus, in his view, are severely limited in the breadth of their possible insights: George Santayana reduces Lucretius's *On the Nature of Things* to the terms of moral philosophy; Van Wyck Brooks reduces Henry James's work to representations of the author's psychological problems; in *The Great Tradition* Granville Hicks judges all American literature on whether or not it represents the class struggle from a Marxist point of view. All of these critics are interested in what Blackmur calls the "separable content" of a literary work.

After discussing the critical methods of Richards, Kenneth Burke, and S. Foster Damon, Blackmur describes his own approach, the "technical approach," which seeks not to separate out any content of the work for special attention. He employs "technical" in a broad sense, and he seems to imply that intuition and expression are inseparable from the available technical modes of externalization. Blackmur would recognize, above all, that there are limits to what the critic can accomplish in analysis: "After all, it is only the facts about a poem, a play, a novel that can be reduced to tractable form, talked about, and examined. The rest can only be known, not talked about." He would agree with the attack of Cleanth Brooks (below, page 1036) on paraphrase, and he would take a cue from Henry James's remark that the novelist's aim is simply to make a perfect work. But Blackmur would shift the import of this remark to induce reflection on the critic's special responsibility to the work.

Among Blackmur's critical writings are *The Double Agent: Essays in Craft and Elucidation* (1935), *The Expense of Greatness* (1940), *Language as Gesture* (1952), *The Lion and the Honeycomb* (1955), *Form and Value in Modern Poetry* (1957), *Eleven Essays on the European Novel* (1964), and *The Outsider at the Heart of Things: Selected Essays* (1986). See Robert Boyers, *R. P. Blackmur, Poet-Critic* (1980); Russell Fraser, *A Mingled Yarn: The Life of R. P. Blackmur* (1981); Gerald J. Pannick, *Richard Palmer Blackmur* (1981); James T. Jones, *Wayward Skeptic* (1986).

A Critic's Job of Work

I

Criticism, I take it, is the formal discourse of an amateur. When there is enough love and enough knowledge represented in the discourse it is a self-sufficient but by no means an isolated art. It witnesses constantly in its own life its interdependence with the other arts. It lays out the terms and parallels of appreciation from the outside in order to convict itself of internal intimacy; it names and arranges what it knows and loves, and searches endlessly with every fresh impulse or impression for better names and more orderly arrangements. It is only in this sense that poetry (or some other art) is a criticism of life; poetry names and arranges, and thus arrests and transfixes its subject in a form which has a life which confronts it. Poetry is life at the remove of form and meaning; not life lived but life framed and identified. So the criticism of poetry is bound to be occupied at once with the terms and modes by which the remove was made and with the relation between—in the ambiguous stock phrase—content and form; which is to say with the establishment and appreciation of human or moral value. It will be the underlying effort of this essay to indicate approaches to criticism wherein these two problems—of form and value—will appear inextricable but not confused—like the stones in an arch or the timbers in a building.

These approaches—these we wish to eulogize—are not the only ones, nor the only good ones, nor are they complete. No approach opens on anything except from its own point of view and in terms of its own prepossessions. Let us set against each other for a time the facts of various approaches to see whether there is a residue, not of fact but of principle.

The approaches to—or the escapes from—the central work of criticism are as various as the heresies of the Christian church, and like them testify to occasional needs, fanatic emphasis, special interest, or intellectual pride, all flowing from and even the worst of them enlightening the same body of insight. Every critic like every theologian and every philosopher is a casuist in spite of himself. To escape or surmount the discontinuity of knowledge, each resorts to a particular heresy and makes it predominant and even omnivorous.[1]

For most minds, once doctrine is sighted and is held to be the completion of insight, the doctrinal mode of thinking seems the only one possible. When doctrine totters it seems it can fall only into the gulf of bewilderment; few minds risk the fall; most seize the remnants and swear the edifice remains, when doctrine becomes intolerable dogma.[2] All fall notwithstanding; for as knowledge itself is a fall from the paradise of undifferentiated sensation, so equally every

---

Blackmur's essay *A Critic's Job of Work* appeared first in book form in *The Double Agent: Essays in Craft and Elucidation* (1935). The text is from *Language as Gesture* (New York: Harcourt Brace Jovanovich, 1952).

[1] [Blackmur] The rashest heresy of our day and climate is exemplified by T. S. Eliot when he postulates an orthodoxy which exists whether anyone knows it or not.

[2] [Blackmur] Baudelaire's sonnet *Le Gouffre* dramatizes this sentiment at once as he saw it surmounted in Pascal and as it occurred insurmountably in himself.

formula of knowledge must fall the moment too much weight is laid upon it—the moment it becomes omnivorous and pretends to be omnipotent—the moment, in short, it is taken literally.[3] Literal knowledge is dead knowledge; and the worst bewilderment—which is always only comparative—is better than death. Yet no form, no formula, of knowledge ought to be surrendered merely because it runs the risk in bad or desperate hands of being used literally; and similarly, in our own thinking, whether it is carried to the point of formal discourse or not, we cannot only afford, we ought scrupulously to risk the use of any concept that seems propitious or helpful in getting over gaps. Only the use should be consciously provisional, speculative, and dramatic. The end virtue of humility comes only after a long train of humiliations; and the chief labor of humbling is the constant, resourceful restoration of ignorance.

The classic contemporary example of use and misuse is attached to the name of Freud.[4] Freud himself has constantly emphasized the provisional, dramatic character of his speculations: they are employed as imaginative illumination, to be relied on no more and no less than the sailor relies upon his buoys and beacons.[5] But the impetus of Freud was so great that a school of literalists arose with all the mad consequence of schism and heresy and fundamentalism which have no more honorable place in the scientific than the artistic imagination. Elsewhere, from one point of view, Caesarism in Rome and Berlin is only the literalist conception of the need for a positive state. So, too, the economic insights of Marxism, merely by being taken literally in their own field, are held to affect the subject and value of the arts, where actually they offer only a limited field of interest and enliven an irrelevant purpose. It is an amusing exercise—as it refreshes the terms of bewilderment and provides a common clue to the secrets of all the modes of thinking—to restore the insights of Freud and Fascism and Marxism to the terms of the church; when the sexual drama in Freud becomes the drama of original sin, and the politics of Hitler and Lenin becomes the politics of the City of God in the sense that theology provides both the sanctions of economics and the values of culture. Controversy is in terms absolutely held, when the problems argued are falsely conceived because necessarily abstracted from "real" experience. The vital or fatal nexus is in interest

and emotion and is established when the terms can be represented dramatically, almost, as it were for their own sakes alone and with only a pious or ritualistic regard for the doctrines in which they are clothed. The simple, and fatal, example is in the glory men attach to war; the vital, but precarious example, is in the intermittent conception of free institutions and the persistent reformulation of the myth of reason. Then the doctrines do not matter, since they are taken only for what they are worth (whatever rhetorical pretensions to the contrary) as guides and props, as aids to navigation. What does matter is the experience, the life represented and the value discovered, and both dramatized or enacted under the banner of doctrine. All banners are wrongheaded, but they make rallying points, free the impulse to cry out, and give meaning to the cry itself simply by making it seem appropriate.

It is on some analogue or parallel to these remarks alone that we understand and use the thought and art of those whose doctrines differ from our own. We either discount, absorb, or dominate the doctrine for the sake of the life that goes with it, for the sake of what is *formed* in the progressive act of thinking. When we do more—when we refine or elaborate the abstracted notion of form—we play a different game which has merit of its own like chess, but which applied to the world we live in produces false dilemmas like solipsism and infant damnation. There is, taking solipsism for example, a fundamental distinction. Because of the logical doctrine prepared to support it, technical philosophers employ years[6] to get around the impasse in which it leaves them; whereas men of poetic imagination merely use it for the dramatic insight it contains—as Eliot[7] uses it in the last section of the *Wasteland;* or as, say, everyone uses the residual mythology of the Greek religion—which its priests nevertheless used as literal sanctions for blood and power.

Fortunately, there exist archetypes of unindoctrinated thinking. Let us incline our minds like reflectors to catch the light of the early Plato and the whole Montaigne.[8] Is not the inexhaustible stimulus and fertility of the dialogues and the essays due as much as anything to the absence of positive doctrine? Is it not that the early Plato always holds conflicting ideas in shifting balance, presenting them in contest and evolution, with victory only the last shift? Is it not that Montaigne is always making room for another idea, and

---

[3] By this Blackmur seems to mean "the moment it is taken with absolute belief." The notion has little or nothing to do with the "literal" level of interpretation in Dante (above, page 154), or Frye (below, page 1139).

[4] Freud (above, page 746).

[5] [Blackmur] Santayana's essay *A Long Way Round to Nirvana* (in *Some Turns of Thought in Modern Philosophy*) illustrates the poetic-philosophic character of Freud's insight into death by setting up its analogues in Indian philosophy, and by his comparison only adds to the stimulus of Freud.

[6] [Blackmur] Santayana found it necessary to resort to his only sustained labor of dialectic, *Skepticism and Animal Faith,* which, though a beautiful monument of intellectual play, is ultimately valuable for its *incidental* moral wisdom.

[7] T. S. Eliot (above, page 806).

[8] Michel Eyqueem, seigneur de Montaigne (1533–1592), French essayist.

implying always a third for provisional, adjudicating irony? Are not the forms of both men themselves ironic, betraying in its most intimate recesses the duplicity of every thought, pointing it out, so to speak, in the act of self-incrimination, and showing it not paled on a pin but in the buff life? . . . Such an approach, such an attempt at vivid questing, borrowed and no doubt adulterated by our own needs, is the only rational approach to the multiplication of doctrine and arrogant technologies which fills out the body of critical thinking. Anything else is a succumbing, not an approach; and it is surely the commonest of ironies to observe a man altogether out of his depth do his cause fatal harm merely because, having once succumbed to an idea, he thinks it necessary to stick to it. Thought is a beacon, not a life raft, and to confuse the functions is tragic. The tragic character of thought—as any perspective will show—is that it takes a rigid mold too soon; chooses destiny like a Calvinist, in infancy, instead of waiting slowly for old age, and hence for the most part works against the world, good sense, and its own object: as anyone may see by taking a perspective of any given idea of democracy, of justice, or the nature of the creative act.

Imaginative skepticism and dramatic irony—the modes of Montaigne and Plato—keep the mind athletic and the spirit on the stretch. Hence the juvenescence of the *Tempest,* and hence, too, perhaps, the air almost of precocity in *Back to Methuselah.*[9] Hence, at any rate, the sustaining power of such varied works as *The Brothers Karamazov, Cousine Bette,* and *The Magic Mountain.*[10] Dante, whom the faithful might take to the contrary, is yet "the chief imagination of Christendom";[11] he took his doctrine once and for all from the church and from St. Thomas[12] and used it as a foil (in the painter's sense) to give recessiveness, background, and contrast. Virgil and Aristotle, Beatrice and Bertrans de Born, have in their way as much importance as St. Thomas and the church.[13] It was this security of reference that made Dante so much more a free spirit than were, say, Swift and Laurence Sterne.[14] Dante had a habit (not a theory) of imagination which enabled him to dramatize with equal ardor and effect what his doctrine blessed, what it assailed, and what,

at heart, it was indifferent to. Doctrine was the seed and structure of vision, and for his poems (at least to us) never more. The *Divine Comedy* no less than the dialogues and the essays[15] is a true *speculum mentis.*[16]

With lesser thinkers and lesser artists—and in the defective works of the greater—we have in reading, in criticizing, to supply the skepticism and the irony, or, as may be, the imagination and the drama, to the degree, which cannot be complete since then we should have had no prompts, that they are lacking. We have to rub the looking glass clear. With *Hamlet,* for example, we have to struggle and guess to bring the motive out of obscurity; a struggle which, aiming at the wrong end, the psychoanalysts have darkened with counsel.[17] With Shelley we have to flesh out the Platonic ideas, as with Blake we have to cut away, since it cannot be dramatized, all the excrescence of doctrine.[18] With Baudelaire we have sometimes to struggle with and sometimes to suppress the problem of belief, working out the irony implicit in either attitude.[19] Similarly, with a writer like Pascal, in order to get the most out of him, in order to compose an artistic judgment, we must consider such an idea as that of the necessity of the wager, not solemnly as Pascal took it, but as a dramatized possibility, a savage, but provisional irony;[20] and we need to show that the skepticisms of Montaigne and Pascal are not at all the same thing—that where one produced serenity the other produced excruciation.

Again, speaking of André Gide, we should remind ourselves not that he has been the apologist of homosexuality, not that he has become a communist, but that he is par excellence the French puritan chastened by the wisdom of the body, and that he has thus an acutely scrupulous ethical sensibility.[21] It is by acknowledging the sensibility that we feel the impact of the apologetics and the political conversion. Another necessity in the apprehension of Gide might be put as the recognition of similarity in difference of the precocious small boys in Dostoevski and Gide, e.g. Kolya in *Karamazov* and young George in *The Counterfeiters:*[22] they are small, cruel engines, all naked sensibility and no scruple, demonically possessed, and used to keep things going. And these in turn may remind us of another writer who had a predilection for presenting the *terrible* quality of the

[9]By William Shakespeare and George Bernard Shaw respectively.

[10]By Fyodor Dostoyevsky, Honoré de Balzac, and Thomas Mann respectively.

[11]Dante (above, page 153). Blackmur quotes W. B. Yeats's poem *Ego Dominus Tuus.*

[12]St. Thomas Aquinas (above, page 149).

[13]Publius Virgilius Maro (70–19 B.C.), Roman poet; Aristotle (above, page 48); Beatrice, a major figure in Dante's *Divine Comedy;* Bertrans de Born (twelfth–thirteenth centuries), French troubador.

[14]Jonathan Swift (1667–1745), Anglo-Irish writer; Laurence Sterne (1713–1768), English writer.

[15]The dialogues of Plato and the essays of Montaigne.

[16]Reflection of the mind.

[17]Blackmur refers here to interpretations of *Hamlet* emphasizing Freud's notion of the Oedipus complex (above, page 753).

[18]Shelley (above, page 537).

[19]Baudelaire (above, page 604).

[20]Blaise Pascal (1623–1662), French philosopher.

[21]André Gide (1869–1951), French novelist.

[22]*The Brothers Karamazov* by Dostoyevsky; *The Counterfeiters* by Gide.

young intelligence: of Henry James, of the children in *The Turn of the Screw,* of Maisie,[23] and all the rest, all beautifully efficient agents of dramatic judgment and action, in that they take all things seriously for themselves, with the least prejudice of preparation, candidly, with an intelligence life has not yet violated.

Such feats of agility and attention as these remarks illustrate seem facile and even commonplace, and from facile points of view there is no need to take them otherwise. Taken superficially they provide escape from the whole labor of specific understanding; or, worse, they provide an easy vault from casual interpretation to an omnivorous world view. We might take solemnly and as of universal application the two notions of demonic possession and inviolate intelligence in the children of Gide, Dostoevski, and James, and on that frail nexus build an unassailable theory of the sources of art, wisdom, and value; unassailable because affording only a stereotyped vision, like that of conservative capitalism, without reference in the real world. The maturity of Shakespeare and of Gertrude Stein[24] would then be found on the same childish level.

But we need not go so far in order to draw back. The modes of Montaigne and Plato contain their own safety. Any single insight is good only at and up to a certain point of development and not beyond, which is to say that it is a provisional and tentative and highly selective approach to its field. Furthermore, no observation, no collection of observations, ever tells the whole story; there is always room for more, and at the hypothetical limit of attention and interest there will always remain, quite untouched, the thing itself.[25] Thus, the complex character—I say nothing of the value—of the remarks above reveals itself. They flow from a dramatic combination of all the skills and conventions of the thinking mind. They are common-place only as criticism—as an end-product of function. Like walking, criticism is a pretty nearly universal art; both require a constant intricate shifting and catching of balance; neither can be questioned much in process; and few perform either really well. For either a new terrain is fatiguing and awkward, and in our day most men prefer paved walks or some form of rapid transit—some easy theory or outmastering dogma. A good critic keeps his criticism from becoming either instinctive or vicarious, and the labor of his understanding is always spe-

cific, like the art which he examines; and he knows that the sum of his best work comes only to the pedagogy of elucidation and appreciation. He observes facts and he delights in discriminations. The object remains and should remain, itself, only made more available and seen in a clearer light. The imagination of Dante is for us only equal to what we can know of it at a given time.

Which brings us to what, as T. S. Eliot would say,[26] I have been leading up to all the time, and what has indeed been said several times by the way. Any rational approach is valid to literature and may be properly called critical which fastens at any point upon the work itself. The utility of a given approach depends partly upon the strength of the mind making it and partly upon the recognition of the limits appropriate to it. Limits may be of scope, degree, or relevance, and may be either plainly laid out by the critic himself, or may be determined by his readers; and it is, by our argument, the latter case that commonly falls, since an active mind tends to overestimate the scope of its tools and to take as necessary those doctrinal considerations which habit has made seem instinctive. No critic is required to limit himself to a single approach, nor is he likely to be able to do so; facts cannot be exhibited without comment, and comment involves the generality of the mind. Furthermore, a consciously complex approach like that of Kenneth Burke[27] or T. S. Eliot, by setting up parallels of reference, affords a more flexible, more available, more stimulating standard of judgment—though of course at a greater risk of prejudice—than a single approach. What produces the evil of stultification and the malice of controversy is the confused approach, when the limits are not seen because they tend to cancel each other out, and the driving power becomes emotional.

The worse evil of fanatic falsification—of arrogant irrationality and barbarism in all its forms—arises when a body of criticism is governed by an *idée fixe,* a really exaggerated heresy, when a notion of genuine but small scope is taken literally as of universal application. This is the body of tendentious criticism where, since something is assumed proved before the evidence is in, distortion, vitiation, and absolute assertion become supreme virtues. I cannot help feeling that such writers as Maritain and Massis—no less

---

[23] Henry James (1843–1916), American novelist.

[24] Gertrude Stein (1874–1946), American writer.

[25] This view is common among the New Critics, who hold that no criticism (or paraphrase—see Brooks, below, page 1036) can adequately stand for a poem. The phrase recalls Kant's notion of the unknowability of the thing-in-itself (above, page 416).

[26] [Blackmur] . . . that when "morals cease to be a matter of tradition and *orthodoxy*—that is, of the habits of the community formulated, corrected, and elevated by the continuous thought and direction of the church—and when each man is to elaborate his own, then *personality* becomes a thing of alarming importance." *(After Strange Gods).* Thus Mr. Eliot becomes one of those viewers-with-alarm whose next step forward is the very hysteria of disorder they wish to escape. The hysteria of institutions is more dreadful than that of individuals.

[27] Kenneth Burke (below, page 1011).

than Nordau before them—are tendentious in this sense.[28] But even here, in this worst order of criticism, there is a taint of legitimacy. Once we reduce, in a man like Irving Babbitt,[29] the magnitude of application of such notions as the inner check and the higher will, which were for Babbitt paramount—that is, when we determine the limits within which he really worked—then the massive erudition and acute observation with which his work is packed become permanently available.

And there is no good to be got in objecting to and of allowing those orders of criticism which have an ulterior purpose. Ulterior is not in itself a pejorative, but only so when applied to an enemy. Since criticism is not autonomous—not a light but a process of elucidation—it cannot avoid discovering constantly within itself a purpose or purposes ulterior in the good sense. The danger is in not knowing what is ulterior and what is not, which is much the same as the cognate danger in the arts themselves. The arts serve purposes beyond themselves; the purposes of what they dramatize or represent at that remove from the flux which gives them order and meaning and value; and to deny those purposes is like asserting that the function of a handsaw is to hang above a bench and that to cut wood is to belittle it. But the purposes are varied and so bound in his subject that the artist cannot always design for them. The critic, if that is his bent, may concern himself with those purposes or with some one among them which obsess him; but he must be certain to distinguish between what is genuinely ulterior to the works he examines and what is merely irrelevant; and he must further not assume except within the realm of his special argument that other purposes either do not exist or are negligible or that the works may not be profitably discussed apart from ulterior purposes and as examples of dramatic possibility alone.

II

Three examples of contemporary criticism primarily concerned with the ulterior purposes of literature should, set side by side, exhibit both the defects and the unchastened virtues of that approach; though they must do so only tentatively and somewhat invidiously—with an exaggeration for effect. Each work is assumed to be a representative ornament of its kind, carrying within it the seeds of its own death and multiplication. Let us take then, with an eye sharpened by the dangers involved, Santayana's essay on Lucretius (in *Three Philosophical Poets*), Van Wyck Brooks' *Pilgrimage of Henry James,* and Granville Hicks' *The Great Tradition.*[30] Though that of the third is more obvious in our predicament, the urgency in the approach is equal in all three.

Santayana's essay represents a conversion or transvaluation of an actually poetic ordering of nature to the terms of a moral philosophy which, whatever its own responsibilities, is free of the special responsibility of poetry.[31] So ably and so persuasively is it composed, his picture seems complete and to contain so much of what was important in Lucretius that *De Rerum Natura* itself can be left behind. The philosophical nature of the insight, its moral scope and defect, the influence upon it of the Democritan[32] atom, once grasped intellectually as Santayana shows us how to grasp them, seem a good substitute for the poem and far more available. But, what Santayana remembers but does not here emphasize since it was beyond his immediate interest, there is no vicar[33] for poetry on earth. Poetry is idiom, a special and fresh saying, and cannot for its life be said otherwise; and there is, finally, as much difference between words used about a poem and the poem as there is between words used about a painting and the painting. The gap is absolute. Yet I do not mean to suggest that Santayana's essay—that any philosophical criticism—is beside the point. It is true that the essay may be taken as a venture in philosophy for its own sake, but it is also true that it reveals a body of facts about an ulterior purpose in Lucretius' poem—doubtless the very purpose Lucretius himself would have chosen to see enhanced. If we return to the poem it will be warmer as the facts come alive in verse. The reconversion comes naturally in this instance in that, through idioms differently construed but equally imaginative, philosophy and poetry both buttress and express moral value. The one enacts or represents in the flesh what the other reduces to principle or raises to the ideal. The only precaution the critic of poetry need take is negative: that neither poetry nor philosophy can ever fully satisfy the other's purposes,[34] though each may seem to do so if taken in an ulterior fashion. The relationship is mutual but not equivalent.

---

[28] Jacques Maritain (1882–1978), French philosopher; Henri Massis (1886–1970), French essayist; Max Nordau (1849–1943), German writer.

[29] Irving Babbitt (1865–1933), American critic.

[30] George Santayana (1863–1952), American philosopher; Van Wyck Brooks (1886–1963), American critic; Granville Hicks (1901–1982), American critic.

[31] These remarks can be compared to Santayana's own theoretical comments in his *The Sense of Beauty* (1896).

[32] Democritus (c. 480–c. 370 B.C.), Greek philosopher, known through Aristotle for his atomic theory of matter.

[33] In the sense of something acting for something else.

[34] This reflects the views of Ransom (above, page 957).

When we turn deliberately from Santayana on Lucretius to Van Wyck Brooks on Henry James, we turn from the consideration of the rational ulterior purpose of art to the consideration of the irrational underlying predicament of the artist himself, not only as it predicts his art and is reflected in it, but also, and in effect predominantly, as it represents the conditioning of nineteenth-century American culture. The consideration is sociological, the method of approach that of literary psychology, and the burden obsessive. The conversion is from literary to biographical values. Art is taken not as the objectification or mirroring of social experience but as a personal expression and escape-fantasy of the artist's personal life in dramatic extension. The point for emphasis is that the cultural situations of Henry James' America stultified the expression and made every escape ineffectual—even that of Europe. This theme—the private tragedy of the unsuccessful artist—was one of Henry James' own; but James saw it as typical or universal—as a characteristic tragedy of the human spirit—illustrated, as it happened for him, against the Anglo-American background. Brooks, taking the same theme, raises it to an obsession, an omnivorous concept, under which all other themes can be subsumed. Applied to American cultural history, such obsessive thinking is suggestive in the very exaggeration of its terms, and applied to the predicament of Henry James the man it dramatically emphasizes—uses for all and more than it is worth—an obvious conflict that tormented him. As history or as biography the book is a persuasive imaginative picture, although clearly not the only one to be seen. Used as a nexus between James the man and the novels themselves, the book has only possible relevance and cannot be held as material. *Hamlet,* by a similar argument, could be shown to be an unsuccessful expression of Shakespeare's personality. To remain useful in the field of literary criticism, Brooks' notions ought to be kept parallel to James' novels but never allowed to merge with them. The corrective, the proof of the gap, is perhaps in the great air of freedom and sway of mastery that pervades the prefaces James wrote to his collected edition.[35] For James art was enough because it molded and mirrored and valued all the life he knew. What Brooks' parallel strictures can do is to help us decide from another point of view whether to choose the values James dramatized. They cannot affect or elucidate but rather—if the gap is closed by will—obfuscate the values themselves.

In short, the order of criticism of which Brooks is a masterly exponent, and which we may call the psychosociological order, is primarily and in the end concerned less with the purpose, ulterior or not, of the arts than with some of the ulterior *uses* to which the arts can be appropriately put. Only what is said in the meantime, by the way—and does not depend upon the essence of argument but only accompanies it—can be applied to the arts themselves. There is nothing, it should be added, in Brooks' writings to show that he believes otherwise or would claim more; he is content with that scope and degree of value to which his method and the strength of his mind limit him; and his value is the greater and more urgent for that.

Such tacit humility, such implicit admission of contingency, are not immediate characteristics of Granville Hicks' *The Great Tradition,* though they may, so serious is his purpose, be merely virtues of which he deliberately, for the time being and in order to gain his point, deprives himself of the benefit. If that is so, however expedient his tactics may seem on the short view, they will defeat him on the long. But let us examine the book on the ground of our present concern alone. Like Brooks, Hicks presents an interpretation of American literature since the Civil War, dealing with the whole body rather than single figures. Like Brooks he has a touchstone in an obsessive idea, but where we may say that Brooks *uses* his idea—as we think for more than it is worth—we must say that Hicks is victimized by his idea to the point where the travail of judgment is suspended and becomes the mere reiteration of a formula. He judges literature as it expressed or failed to express the economic conflict of classes sharpened by the industrial revolution, and he judges individual writers as they used or did not use an ideology resembling the Marxist analysis as prime clue to the clear representation of social drama. Thus Howells comes off better than Henry James, and Frank Norris better than Mark Twain, and, in our own day, Dos Passos is struck on a thin eminence that must alarm him.[36]

Controversy is not here a profitable exercise, but it may be said for the sake of the record that although every period of history presents a class struggle, some far more acute than our own, the themes of great art have seldom lent themselves to propaganda for an economic insight, finding, as it happened, religious, moral, or psychological—that is to say, interpretative—insights more appropriate impulses. If *Piers Plowman* dealt with the class struggle, *The Canterbury Tales*[37] did not, and Hicks would be hard put, if he looked sharp, to make out a better case of social implication in Dostoevski than in Henry James.

---

[35] Blackmur edited a collection of James's prefaces, *The Art of the Novel* (1948).

[36] Frank Norris (1870–1902), Mark Twain (Samuel Clemens, 1835–1910), John Dos Passos (1896–1970), American novelists.

[37] Attributed to William Langland (c. 1332–c. 1400) and by Geoffrey Chaucer (c. 1340–1400), respectively.

What vitiates *The Great Tradition* is its tendentiousness. Nothing could be more exciting, nothing more vital, than a book by Hicks which discovered and examined the facts of a literature whose major theme hung on an honest, dramatic view of the class struggle—and there is indeed such a literature now emerging from the depression. And on the other hand it would be worthwhile to have Hicks sharpen his teeth on all the fraudulent or pseudo art which actually slanders the terms of the class and every other struggle.

The book with which he presents us performs a very different operation. There is an initial hortatory assumption that American literature ought to represent the class struggle from a Marxist view point, and that it ought thus to be the spur and guide to political action. Proceeding, the point is either proved or the literature dismissed and its authors slandered. Hicks is not disengaging for emphasis and contemporary need an ulterior purpose; he is not writing criticism at all; he is writing a fanatic's history and a casuist's polemic, with the probable result—which is what was meant by suggesting above that he had misconceived his tactics—that he will convert no one who retains the least love of literature or the least knowledge of the themes which engage the most of life. It should be emphasized that there is no more quarrel with Hicks' economic insight as such than there was with the insights of Santayana and Van Wyck Brooks. The quarrel is deeper. While it is true and good that the arts may be used to illustrate social propaganda—though it is not a great use—you can no more use an economic insight as your chief critical tool than you can make much out of the Mass by submitting the doctrine of transubstantiation to chemical analysis.

These three writers have one great formal fact in common, which they illustrate as differently as may be. They are concerned with the separable content of literature, with what may be said without consideration of its specific setting and apparition in a form; which is why, perhaps, all three leave literature so soon behind. The quantity of what can be said directly about the content alone of a given work of art is seldom great, but the least saying may be the innervation of an infinite intellectual structure, which, however valuable in itself, has for the most part only an asserted relation with the works from which it springs. The sense of continuous relationship, of sustained contact with the works nominally in hand is rare and when found uncommonly exhilarating; it is the fine object of criticism: as it seems to put us in direct possession of the principles whereby the works move without injuring or disintegrating the body of the works themselves. This sense of intimacy by inner contact cannot arise from methods of approach which hinge on seized separable content. We have constantly—if our interest is really in literature—to prod ourselves back, to remind ourselves that there was a poem, play, or a novel of some initial and we hope terminal concern, or we have to falsify facts and set up fictions[38] to the effect that no matter what we are saying we are really talking about art after all. The question must often be whether the prodding and reminding is worth the labor, whether we might not better assign the works that require it to a different category than that of criticism.

III

Similar strictures and identical precautions are necessary in thinking of other, quite different approaches to criticism, where if there are no ulterior purposes to allow for there are other no less limiting features—there are certainly such, for example, for me in thinking of my own. The ulterior motive, or the limiting feature, whichever it is, is a variable constant. One does not always know what it is, nor what nor how much work it does; but one always knows it is there—for strength or weakness. It may be only the strength of emphasis—which is necessarily distortion; or it may be the worse strength of a simplifying formula, which skeletonizes and transforms what we want to recognize in the flesh. It may be only the weakness of what is unfinished, undeveloped, or unseen—the weakness that follows on emphasis; or it may be the weakness that shows when pertinent things are deliberately dismissed or ignored, which is the corresponding weakness of the mind strong in formula. No mind can avoid distortion and formula altogether, nor would wish to; but most minds rush to the defense of qualities they think cannot be avoided, and that, in itself, is an ulterior motive, a limiting feature of the mind that rushes. I say nothing of one's personal prepossessions, of the damage of one's private experience, of the malice and false tolerance they inculcate into judgment. I know that my own essays suffer variously, but I cannot bring myself to specify the indulgences I would ask; mostly, I hope, that general indulgence which consists in the task of bringing my distortions and emphases and opinions into balance with other distortions, other emphases, and better opinions.

---

[38] [Blackmur] Such a fiction, if not consciously so contrived, is the fiction of an organic community of all literature as expounded by T. S. Eliot in his essay *Tradition and the Individual Talent* [see above, page 807]. The locus is famous and represents that each new work of art slightly alters the relationships among the whole order of existing works. The notion has truth, but it is a mathematical truth and has little relevance to the arts. Used as Eliot uses it, it is an experimental conceit and pushes the mind forward. Taken seriously it is bad constitutional law, in the sense that it would provoke numberless artificial and insoluble problems.

But rather than myself, let us examine briefly, because of their differences from each other and from the three critics already handled, the modes of approach to the act of criticism and habits of critical work of I. A. Richards, Kenneth Burke, and S. Foster Damon.[39] It is to characterize them and to judge the *character* of their work—its typical scope and value—that we want to examine them. With the objective validity of their varying theories we are not much here concerned. Objective standards of criticism, as we hope them to exist at all, must have an existence anterior and superior to the practice of particular critics. The personal element in a given critic—what he happens to know and happens to be able to understand—is strong or obstinate enough to reach into his aesthetic theories; and as most critics do not have the coherence of philosophers it seems doubtful if any outsider could ever reach the same conclusions as the critic did by adopting his aesthetics. Aesthetics sometimes seems only as implicit in the practice of criticism as the atomic physics is present in sunlight when you feel it.

But some critics deliberately expand the theoretic phase of every practical problem. There is a tendency to urge the scientific principle and the statistical method, and in doing so to bring in the whole assorted world of thought. That Mr. Richards, who is an admirable critic and whose love and knowledge of poetry are incontestable, is a victim of the expansiveness of his mind in these directions, is what characterizes, and reduces, the scope of his work as literary criticism. It is possible that he ought not to be called a literary critic at all. If we list the titles of his books we are in a quandary: *The Foundations of Aesthetics, The Meaning of Meaning* (these with C. K. Ogden),[40] *The Principles of Literary Criticism, Science and Poetry, Practical Criticism, Mencius on the Mind,* and *Coleridge on Imagination.* The apparatus is so vast, so labyrinthine, so inclusive—and the amount of actual literary criticism is so small that it seems almost a by-product instead of the central target. The slightest volume, physically, *Science and Poetry,* contains proportionally the most literary criticism, and contains, curiously, his one obvious failure in appreciation—since amply redressed—his misjudgment of the nature of Yeats'[41] poetry. His work is for the most part *about* a department of the mind which includes the pedagogy of sensibility and the practice of literary criticism. The matters he investigates are the problems of belief, of meaning, of communication, of the nature of controversy,

and of poetic language as the supreme mode of imagination. The discussion of these problems is made to focus for the most part on poetry because poetry provides the only great monuments of imagination available to verbal imagination. His bottom contention might I think be put as this: that words have a synergical power, in the realms of feeling, emotion, and value, to create a reality, or the sense of it, not contained in the words separately; and that the power and the reality as experienced in great poetry make the chief source of meaning and value for the life we live. This contention I share; except that I should wish to put on the same level, as sources of meaning and value, modes of imagination that have no medium in words—though words may call on them—and are not susceptible of verbal reformulation: the modes of great acting, architecture, music, and painting. Thus I can assent to Mr. Richards' positive statement of the task of criticism, because I can add to it positive tasks in analogous fields: "To recall that poetry is the supreme use of language, man's chief coordinating instrument, in the service of the most integral purposes of life; and to explore, with thoroughness, the intricacies of the modes of language as working modes of the mind." But I want this criticism, engaged in this task, constantly to be confronted with examples of poetry, and I want it so for the very practical purpose of assisting in pretty immediate appreciation of the use, meaning, and value of the language in that particular poetry. I want it to assist in doing for me what it actually assists Mr. Richards in doing, whatever that is, when he is reading poetry for its own sake.

Mr. Richards wants it to do that, too, but he wants it to do a great deal else first. Before it gets to actual poetry (from which it is said to spring) he wants literary criticism to become something else and much more: he wants it to become, indeed, the master department of the mind. As we become aware of the scope of poetry, we see, according to Mr. Richards, that

> the study of the modes of language becomes, as it attempts to be thorough, the most fundamental and extensive of all inquiries. It is no preliminary or preparation for other profounder studies. . . . The very formation of the objects which these studies propose to examine takes place through the processes (of which imagination and fancy are modes) by which the words they use acquire their meanings. Criticism is the science of these meanings. . . . Critics in the future must have a theoretical equipment which has not been felt to be necessary in the past . . . But the critical

[39] I. A. Richards (above, page 856); S. Foster Damon, American literary scholar, author of *William Blake: His Philosophy and Symbols* (1924).
[40] C. K. Ogden (1889–1957), British semanticist.
[41] William Butler Yeats (1865–1939), Anglo-Irish poet.

equipment will not be *primarily* philosophical. It will be rather a command *of the methods of general linguistic analysis.*[42]

I think we may take it that *Mencius on the Mind* is an example of the kind of excursion on which Mr. Richards would lead us. It is an excursion into multiple definition, and it is a good one if that is where you want to go and are in no hurry to come back: you learn the enormous variety and complexity of the operations possible in the process of verbally describing and defining brief passages of imaginative language and the equal variety and complexity of the result; you learn the practical impossibility of verbally ascertaining what an author means—and you hear nothing of the other ways of apprehending meaning at all. The instance is in the translation of Mencius,[43] because Mr. Richards happens to be interested in Mencius, and because it is easy to see the difficulties of translating Chinese; but the principles and method of application would work as well on passages from Milton or Rudyard Kipling.[44] The real point of Mr. Richards' book is the impossibility of understanding, short of a lifetime's analysis and compensation, the mechanism of meaning in even a small body of work. There is no question of the exemplary value and stimulus of Mr. Richards' work; but there is no question either that few would care to emulate him for any purpose of literary criticism. In the first place it would take too long, and in the second he does not answer the questions literary criticism would put. The literal adoption of Mr. Richards' approach to literary criticism would stultify the very power it was aimed to enhance—the power of imaginative apprehension, of imaginative coordination of varied and separate elements. Mr. Richards' work is something to be aware of, but deep awareness is the limit of use. It is notable that in his admirable incidental criticism of such poets as Eliot, Lawrence, Yeats, and Hopkins,[45] Mr. Richards does not himself find it necessary to be more than aware of his own doctrines of linguistic analysis. As philosophy from Descartes to Bradley[46] transformed itself into a study of the modes of knowing, Mr. Richards would transform literary criticism into the science of linguistics. Epistemology is a great subject, and so is linguistics; but they come neither in first nor final places; the one is only a fragment of wisdom

and the other only a fraction of the means of understanding. Literary criticism is not a science—though it may be the object of one; and to try to make it one is to turn it upside down. Right side up, Mr. Richards' contribution shrinks in weight and dominion but remains intact and preserves its importance. We may conclude that it was the newness of his view that led him to exaggerate it, and we ought to add the probability that had he not exaggerated it we should never have seen either that it was new or valuable at all.

From another point of view than that of literary criticism, and as a contribution to a psychological theory of knowledge, Mr. Richards' work is not heretical, but is integral and integrating, and especially when it incorporates poetry into its procedure; but from our point of view the heresy is profound—and is far more distorting than the heresies of Santayana, Brooks, and Hicks, which carry with them obviously the impetus for their correction. Because it is possible to apply scientific methods to the language of poetry, and because scientific methods engross their subject matter, Mr. Richards places the whole burden of criticism in the application of a scientific approach, and asserts it to be an implement for the judgment of poetry. Actually, it can handle only the language and its words and cannot touch—except by assertion—the imaginative product of the words which is poetry: which is the object revealed or elucidated by criticism. Criticism must be concerned, first and last—whatever comes between—with the poem as it is read and as what it represents as felt. As no amount of physics and physiology can explain the *feeling* of things seen as green or even certify their existence, so no amount of linguistic analysis can explain the *feeling* or existence of a poem. Yet the physics in the one case and the linguistics in the other may be useful both to the poet and the reader. It may be useful, for example, in extracting the facts of meaning from a poem, to show that, whether the poet was aware of it or not, the semantic history of a word was so and so; but only if the semantics can be resolved into the ambiguities and precisions created by the poem. Similarly with any branch of linguistics; and similarly with the applications of psychology—Mr. Richards' other emphasis. No statistical description can either explain or demean a poem unless the description is translated back to the imaginative apprehension or feeling which must have taken place without it. The light of science is parallel or in the background where feeling or meaning is concerned. The Oedipus complex does not explain *Oedipus Rex;*[47] not that Mr. Richards would think it did. Otherwise he could not believe that "poetry is the supreme use of

[42] [Blackmur] All quoted material is from the last four pages of *Coleridge on Imagination.*

[43] Mencius (372–c. 288 B.C.), Chinese philosopher.

[44] John Milton (1608–1674), Rudyard Kipling (1865–1936), English poets.

[45] D. H. Lawrence (1885–1930), English novelist; Gerard Manley Hopkins (1844–1889), English poet.

[46] René Descartes (1596–1650), French philosopher; F. H. Bradley (1846–1924), English philosopher.

[47] By Sophocles (c. 496–406 B.C.), Greek tragic dramatist.

language" and more, could not convey in his comments on T. S. Elliot's *Ash Wednesday* the actuality of his belief that poetry is the supreme use.

It is the interest and fascination of Mr. Richards' work in reference to different levels of sensibility, including the poetic, that has given him both a wide and a penetrating influence. No literary critic can escape his influence; an influence that stimulates the mind as much as anything by showing the sheer excitement as well as the profundity of the problems of language—many of which he has himself made genuine problems, at least for readers of poetry: an influence, obviously, worth deliberately incorporating by reducing it to one's own size and needs. In T. S. Eliot the influence is conspicuous if slight. Mr. Kenneth Burke is considerably indebted, partly directly to Mr. Richards, partly to the influences which acted upon Mr. Richards (as Bentham's[48] theory of fictions) and partly to the frame of mind which helped mold them both. But Mr. Burke is clearly a different person—and different from anyone writing today; and the virtues, the defects, and the élan of his criticism are his own.

Some years ago, when Mr. Burke was an animating influence on the staff of *The Dial*, Miss Marianne Moore[49] published a poem in that magazine called *Picking and Choosing* which contained the following lines:

> and Burke is a
> psychologist—of acute and raccoon-
>   like curiosity. *Summa diligentia;*
> to the humbug, whose name is
>   so very amusing—very young
>   and ve-
> ry rushed, Caesar crossed the Alps on the 'top of a
> *diligence.'* We are not daft about the meaning but this
>   familiarity
> with wrong meanings puzzles one.

In the index of Miss Moore's *Observations,* we find under Burke that the reference is to Edmund,[50] but it is really to Kenneth just the same. There is no acuter curiosity than Mr. Burke's engaged in associating the meanings, right and wrong, of the business of literature with the business of life and vice versa. No one has a greater awareness—not even Mr. Richards—of the important part wrong meanings play in establishing the consistency of right ones. The writer of

whom he reminds us, for the buoyancy and sheer remarkableness of his speculations, is Charles Santiago Sanders Peirce;[51] one is enlivened by them without any *necessary* reference to their truth; hence they have truth for their own purposes, that is, for their own uses. Into what these purposes or uses are it is our present business to inquire.

As Mr. Richards in fact uses literature as a springboard or source for a scientific method of a philosophy of value, Mr. Burke uses literature, not only as a springboard but also as a resort or home, for a philosophy or psychology of moral possibility. Literature is the hold-all and the persuasive form for the patterns of possibility. In literature we see unique possibilities enacted, actualized, and in the moral and psychological philosophies we see the types of possibility generalized, see their abstracted, convertible forms. In some literature, and in some aspects of most literature of either great magnitude or great possibility, we see, so to speak, the enactment or dramatic representation of the type or patterns. Thus Mr. Burke can make a thrilling intellectual pursuit of the subintelligent writing of Erskine Caldwell:[52] where he shows that Caldwell gains a great effect of humanity by putting in *none himself,* appealing to the reader's common stock: i.e., what is called for so desperately by the pattern of the story must needs be generously supplied. Exactly as thrilling is his demonstration of the great emotional role of the outsider as played in the supremely intelligent works of Thomas Mann and André Gide. His common illustrations of the pervasive spread of symbolic pattern are drawn from Shakespeare and from the type of the popular or pulp press. I think that on the whole his method could be applied with equal fruitfulness either to Shakespeare, Dashiell Hammett, or Marie Corelli;[53] as indeed he does apply it with equal force both to the field of anarchic private morals and to the outline of a secular conversion to communism—as in, respectively, *Toward a Better Life* and *Permanence and Change.*

The real harvest that we barn from Mr. Burke's writings is his presentation of the types of ways the mind works in the written word. He is more interested in the psychological means of the meaning, and how it might mean (and often really does) something else, than in the meaning itself. Like Mr. Richards, but for another purpose, he is engaged largely in the meaning of meaning, and is therefore much bound up with considerations of language, but on the plane of emotional and intellectual patterns rather than on the

---

[48]Jeremy Bentham (1748–1832). Ogden collected and edited Bentham's writings on fictions in *Bentham's Theory of Fictions* (1932).
[49]Marianne Moore (1887–1972), American poet.
[50]Edmund Burke (above, page 332).

[51]C. S. Peirce (above, page 652)
[52]Erskine Caldwell (1903–1987), American novelist.
[53]Dashiel Hammett (1894–1961), American novelist; Marie Corelli (Mary Mackay, 1885–1925), English novelist.

emotional plane; which is why his essays deal with literature (or other writings) as it dramatizes or unfolds character (a character is a pattern of emotions and notions) rather than with lyric or meditative poetry which is Mr. Richards' field. So we find language containing felt character as well as felt coordination. The representation of character, and of aspiration and symbol, must always be rhetorical; and therefore we find that for Mr. Burke the rightly rhetorical is the profoundly hortatory. Thus literature may be seen as an inexhaustible reservoir of moral or character philosophies in action.

It is the technique of such philosophies that Mr. Burke explores, as he pursues it through curiosities of development and conversion and duplicity; it is the technique of the notions that may be put into or taken out of literature, but it is only a part of the technique of literature itself. The final reference is to the psychological and moral possibilities of the mind, and these certainly do not exhaust the technique or the reality of literature. The reality in literature is an object of contemplation and of feeling, like the reality of a picture or a cathedral, not a route of speculation. If we remember this and make the appropriate reductions here as elsewhere, Mr. Burke's essays become as pertinent to literary criticism as they are to the general ethical play of the mind. Otherwise they become too much a methodology for its own sake on the one hand, and too much a philosophy at one remove on the other. A man writes as he can; but those who use his writings have the further responsibility of redefining their scope, an operation (of which Mr. Burke is a master) which alone uses them to the full.

It is in relation to these examples which I have so unjustly held up of the philosophical, the sociological or historical, the tendentious, the semasiological, and the psychological approaches to criticism that I wish to examine an example of what composes, after all, the great bulk of serious writings about literature: a work of literary scholarship. Upon scholarship all other forms of literary criticism depend, so long as they are criticism, in much the same way that architecture depends on engineering. The great editors of the last century—men such as Dyce and Skeat and Gifford and Furness[54]—performed work as valuable to the use of literature, and with far less complement of harm, as men like Hazlitt and Arnold and Pater.[55] Scholarship, being bent on the collection, arrangement, and scrutiny of facts, has the positive advantage over other forms of criticism that it is a

cooperative labor, and may be completed and corrected by subsequent scholars; and it has the negative advantage that it is not bound to investigate the mysteries of meaning or to connect literature with other departments of life—it has only to furnish the factual materials for such investigations and connections. It is not surprising to find that the great scholars are sometimes good critics, though usually in restricted fields; and it is a fact, on the other hand, that the great critics are themselves either good scholars or know how to take great advantage of scholarship. Perhaps we may put it that for the most part dead critics remain alive in us to the extent that they form part of our scholarship. It is Dr. Johnson's[56] statements of fact that we preserve of him as a critic; his opinions have long since become a part of that imaginative structure, his personality. A last fact about scholarship is this, that so far as its conclusions are sound they are subject to use and digestion not debate by those outside the fold. And of bad scholarship as of bad criticism we have only to find means to minimize what we cannot destroy.

It is difficult to find an example of scholarship pure and simple, of high character, which can be made to seem relevant to the discussion in hand. What I want is to bring into the discussion the omnipresence of scholarship as a background and its immediate and necessary availability to every other mode of approach. What I want is almost anonymous. Failing that, I choose S. Foster Damon's *William Blake* (as I might have taken J. L. Lowe's *Road to Xanadu*)[57] which, because of its special subject matter, brings its scholarship a little nearer the terms of discussion than a Shakespeare commentary would have done. The scholar's major problem with Blake happened to be one which many scholars could not handle, some refused to see, and some fumbled. A great part of Blake's meaning is not open to ordinarily well-instructed readers, but must be brought out by the detailed solution of something very like an enormous and enormously complicated acrostic puzzle. Not only earnest scrutiny of the poems as printed, but also a study of Blake's reading, a reconstruction of habits of thought, and an industrious piecing together into a consistent key of thousands of clues throughout the work, were necessary before many even of the simplest appearing poems could be explained. It is one thing to explain a mystical poet, like Crashaw,[58] who was attached to a recognized church, and difficult enough; but it is a far more difficult thing to explain a mystical poet like Blake, who was so much an eclectic in his sources that

---

[54] Alexander Dyce (1798–1869); Sheet (Blackmur must have meant W. W. Skeat, nineteenth-century editor); William Gifford (1756–1826); Horace Howard Furness (1833–1912), all editors of Shakespeare and other writers.

[55] William Hazlitt (1778–1830), English critic; Arnold (above, page 586); Pater (above, page 617).

[56] Johnson (above, page 357)

[57] John Livingston Lowes (1867–1945), American literary scholar.

[58] Richard Crashaw (1612?–1649), English poet.

his mystery as well as his apprehension of it was practically his own. All Mr. Damon had to go on besides the texts, and the small body of previous scholarship that was pertinent, were the general outlines of insight to which all mystics apparently adhere. The only explanation would be in the facts of what Blake meant to mean when he habitually said one thing in order to hide and enhance another; and in order to be convincing—poetry being what it is—the facts adduced had to be self-evident. It is not a question here whether the mystery enlightened was worth it. The result for emphasis is that Mr. Damon made Blake exactly what he seemed least to be, perhaps the most intellectually consistent of the greater poets in English. Since the chief weapons used are the extended facts of scholarship, the picture Mr. Damon produced cannot be destroyed even though later and other scholarship modifies, rearranges, or adds to it with different or other facts. The only suspicion that might attach is that the picture is too consistent and that the facts are made to tell too much, and direct, but instructed, apprehension not enough.

My point about Mr. Damon's work is typical and double. First, that the same sort of work, the adduction of ultimately self-evident facts, can be done and must be done in other kinds of poetry than Blake's. Blake is merely an extreme and obvious example of an unusually difficult poet who hid his facts on purpose. The work must be done to the appropriate degree of digging out the facts in all orders of poetry—and especially perhaps in contemporary poetry, where we tend to let the work go either because it seems too easy or because it seems supererogatory. Self-evident facts are paradoxically the hardest to come by; they are not evident till they are seen; yet the meaning of a poem—the part of it which is intellectually formulable—must invariably depend on this order of facts, the facts about the meanings of the elements aside from their final meaning in combination. The rest of the poem, what it is, what it shows, its final value as a created emotion, its meanings, if you like, *as* a poem, cannot in the more serious orders of poetry develop itself to the full without this factual or intellectual meaning to show the way. The other point is already made, and has been made before in this essay, but it may still be emphasized. Although the scholarly account is indispensable it does not tell the whole story. It is only the basis and perhaps ultimately the residue of all the other stories. But it must be seen to first.

My own approach, such as it is, and if it can be named, does not tell the whole story either; the reader is conscientiously left with the poem with the real work yet to do; and I wish to advance it—as indeed I have been advancing it *seriatim*—only in connection with the reduced and compensated approaches I have laid out; and I expect, too, that if

my approach is used at all it will require its own reduction as well as its compensations. Which is why this essay has taken its present form, preferring for once, in the realm of theory and apologetics, the implicit to the explicit statement. It is, I suppose, an approach to literary criticism—to the discourse of an amateur—primarily through the technique, in the widest sense of that word, of the examples handled; technique on the plane of words and even of linguistics in Mr. Richards' sense, but also technique on the plane of intellectual and emotional patterns in Mr. Burke's sense, and technique, too, in that there is a technique of securing and arranging and representing a fundamental view of life. The advantage of the technical approach is I think double. It readily admits other approaches and is anxious to be complemented by them. Furthermore, in a sense, it is able to incorporate the technical aspect, which always exists, of what is secured by other approaches—as I have argued elsewhere that so unpromising a matter as T. S. Eliot's religious convictions may be profitably considered as a dominant element in his technique of revealing the actual. The second advantage of the technical approach is a consequence of the first; it treats of nothing in literature except in its capacity of reduction to literary fact, which is where it resembles scholarship, only passing beyond it in that its facts are usually further into the heart of the literature than the facts of most scholarship. Aristotle, curiously, is here the type and master; as the *Poetics* is nothing but a collection and explanation of the facts of Greek poetry,[59] it is the factual aspect that is invariably produced. The rest of the labor is in the effort to find understandable terms to fit the composition of the facts. After all, it is only the facts about a poem, a play, a novel, that can be reduced to tractable form, talked about, and examined; the rest is the product of the facts, from the technical point of view, and not a product but the thing itself from its own point of view. The rest, whatever it is, can only be known, not talked about.

But facts are not simple or easy to come at; not all the facts will appear to one mind, and the same facts appear differently in the light of different minds. No attention is undivided, no single approach sufficient, no predilection guaranteed, when facts or what their arrangements create are in question. In short, for the arts, *mere* technical scrutiny of any order, is not enough without the direct apprehension—which may come first or last—to which all scrutinies that show facts contribute.

It may be that there are principles that cover both the direct apprehension and the labor of providing modes for the understanding of the expressive arts. If so, they are Socratic

---

[59] An odd judgment of Aristotle's work.

977 A Critic's Job of Work

and found within, and subject to the fundamental skepticism as in Montaigne. There must be seeds, let us say—seeds, germs, beginning forms upon which I can rely and to which I resort. When I use a word, an image, a notion, there must be in its small nodular apparent form, as in the peas I am testing on my desk, at least prophetically, the whole future growth, the whole harvested life; and not rhetorically nor in a formula, but stubbornly, pervasively, heart-hidden, materially, in both the anterior and the eventual prospect as well as in the small handled form of the nub. What is it, what are they, these seeds of understanding? And if I know, are they logical? Do they take the processional form of the words I use? Or do they take a form like that of the silver backing a glass, a dark that enholds all brightness? Is every metaphor—and the assertion of understanding is our great metaphor—mixed by the necessity of its intention? What is the mixture of a word, an image, a notion?

The mixture, if I may start a hare so late, the mixture, even in the fresh use of an old word, is made in the preconscious, and is by hypothesis unascertainable. But let us not use hypotheses, let us not desire to ascertain. By intuition we adventure in the preconscious; and there, where the adventure is, there is no need or suspicion of certainty or meaning; there is the living, expanding, *prescient* substance without the tags and handles of conscious form. Art is the looking glass of the preconscious, and when it is deepest seems to participate in it sensibly. Or better, for purposes of criticism, our sensibility resumes the division of the senses and faculties at the same time that it preens itself into conscious form. Criticism may have as an object the establishment and evaluation (comparison and analysis) of the modes of making the preconscious *consciously* available.

But this emphasis upon the preconscious need not be insisted on; once recognized it may be tacitly assumed, and the effort of the mind will be, as it were, restored to its own plane—only a little sensitive to the taproots below. On its own plane—that is the plane where almost everything is taken for granted in order to assume adequate implementation in handling what is taken for granted by others; where because you can list the items of your bewilderment and can move from one to another you assert that the achievement of motion is the experience of order; where, therefore, you must adopt always an attitude of provisional skepticism; where, imperatively, you must scrutinize until you have revealed, if it is there, the inscrutable divination, or, if it is not, the void of personal ambition; where, finally, you must stop short only when you have, with all the facts you can muster, indicated, surrounded, detached, somehow found the way demonstrably to get at, in pretty conscious terms which others may use, the substance of your chosen case.

Rudolph Carnap

1891–1970

Perhaps the only thing more surprising than the inclusion in this anthology of Rudolph Carnap, one of the principal exponents and theorists of Logical Positivism (and significantly, an auditor of the lectures of Gottlob Frege [above, page 734] at Jena) is his conspicuous absence in debates within literary studies where the very positions he adopted and advocated were the main concern. For the Anglo-American New Critics, for example, their acute, sometimes obsessional concern with questions of meaning in poetry as being other than "scientific" but equally valid would make little sense were it not for the remarkable ascendancy of logical positivism and closely related forms of analytical philosophy in British and North American universities. For the predominantly dialectical traditions of Continental philosophy, on the other hand, the assaults of such figures as Frege and Carnap on Husserl (above, page 770) and Heidegger (below, page 1051), attempting to turn the attention of professional philosophers to precise logical representation and away from seemingly unproductive metaphysical topics, appear to have been met with an equally puzzling silence. Though the reasons are complex in both cases, the questions that Carnap and the philosophers of the Vienna Circle (founded by Mortiz Schlick in 1926) posed for contemporary philosophers were acute, embarrassing (if not scandalous), and exceptionally difficult to answer without appearing to be merely evasive.

It is a telling coincidence, moreover, that one of Carnap's first publications in English, *Philosophy and Logical Syntax* (1935), appeared in the *Psyche Miniatures* series, under the general editorship of C. K. Ogden; and that its argument hinged on a term popularized almost a decade earlier by I. A. Richards (above, page 856) in his *Science and Poetry* (1926), the "pseudo-statement." In his little book, Carnap offered a general outline of logical empiricism, following in part Wittgenstein's *Tractatus Logico-Philosophicus* (above, page 825), foregrounding the insistence on precise logical and empirical verification of statements, and attacking traditional metaphysics as meaningless. Carnap's early position and his opposition to traditional metaphysics, from Plato (above, page 8) to Heidegger, is fully elaborated in the essay reprinted here, but without the rhetorical punch of the shorter and less careful *Philosophy and Logical Syntax*. There he says bluntly that "the propositions of metaphysics . . . are without sense" and (using another distinction of Richards's, between the representative or scientific and expressive or emotive functions of language) admits that they may be expressive, "but nevertheless they have no sense, no theoretical content" (26–27). Even granting Hegel's (above, page 552) well-known advice that philosophy should give up the effort to be merely edifying, Carnap's attack, like the case of The Emperor's New Clothes, seems to strip traditional philosophy of its pretensions without any worry at all about a sense of conventional intellectual propriety; Carnap simply presents his case:

> The meaning of our anti-metaphysical thesis may now be more clearly explained. This
> thesis asserts that metaphysical propositions—like lyrical verses—have only an expres-

sive function, but no representative function. Metaphysical propositions are neither true nor false, because they assert nothing, they contain neither knowledge nor error, they lie completely outside the field of knowledge, of theory, outside the discussion of truth or falsehood. They are, like laughing, lyrics, and music, expressive.

This is a statement with something to offend virtually all the parties involved, deflating conventional metaphysics (including efforts to reshape it) in its long-established presumption to be in principle the queen of the disciplines, superior especially to mere poets, while denying in toto any claim that poetry might make to knowledge or theoretical significance.

While it is easiest to respond to such a position polemically, it remains to say that the questions are fundamental and will not be vanquished by rhetorical bluster or disarmed by the skillful manipulation of terms. The double divide, between analytical philosophy and traditional metaphysics on the one hand, and between philosophy of any sort and poetry on the other, shows up with particular clarity as the fault lines in a great deal of twentieth-century intellectual history. The force of Carnap's attack, first of all, is arguably as important as any other single feature in shaping Anglo-American New Criticism, in its worried opposition between the literary and the scientific, as if it were somehow set in the nature of things, just as it has been a significant factor in isolating the main traditions of Continental philosophy from meaningful participation in crucial debates concerning modern science and technology.

Perhaps even more important is that the extreme position of Carnap and the early logical positivists has been subject to very dramatic internal challenges to a strict verificationist program, just as Carnap himself, in the later "Empiricism, Semantics, and Ontology," comes to terms with the problem of simply rejecting metaphysics, as it appears to undermine the justification of empirical science—which was a main point of the logical positivist movement all along. The advantage of following, even in outline, the unfolding of these problems within analytical philosophy is that radical questions are thereby neither evaded nor rejected polemically. In some respects, the alacrity with which Anglo-American literary theorists and critics embraced Continental philosophical models in the 1960s coincides with the virtual collapse of those models in the poststructuralist, postmodern emergence of the radical countercritique of deconstruction and cultural criticism. Throughout his entire career, Carnap, by both his own publications and his pivotal role in serial publications such as the journal *Erkentniss,* published between 1930 and 1940 with Hans Riechenbach, and his editorship with Otto Neurath and Charles Morris of *The Encyclopedia of Unified Science,* from 1938 to the 1960s, served as the leading figure of a crucial philosophical movement that has shaped professional philosophy dramatically, no matter the view one may take of the result. A renewed attention to the role of Logical Positivism in the context of literary criticism and the humanities may well serve to clarify current theoretical perplexities on both sides.

Among Carnap's most important works for a general audience are *Logische Syntax der Sprache* (1934; *The Logical Syntax of Language,* 1937) and *Meaning and Necessity* (1947; second enlarged ed., 1956). For a very clear summary of Carnap's career, with bibliography, see Norman M. Martin, "Carnap" in *The Encyclopedia of Philosophy,* ed. Paul Edwards, vol. 2 (1967). See also P. A. Schilpp, ed., *The Philosophy of Rudolph Carnap* (1963).

The Elimination of Metaphysics Through Logical Analysis of Language

1. Introduction

There have been many *opponents of metaphysics* from the Greek skeptics to the empiricists of the 19th century. Criticisms of very diverse kinds have been set forth. Many have declared that the doctrine of metaphysics is *false,* since it contradicts our empirical knowledge. Others have believed it to be *uncertain,* on the ground that its problems transcend the limits of human knowledge. Many antimetaphysicians have declared that occupation with metaphysical questions is *sterile.* Whether or not these questions can be answered, it is at any rate unnecessary to worry about them; let us devote ourselves entirely to the practical tasks which confront active men every day of their lives!

The development of *modern logic* has made it possible to give a new and sharper answer to the question of the validity and justification of metaphysics. The researches of applied logic or the theory of knowledge, which aim at clarifying the cognitive content of scientific statements and thereby the meanings of the terms that occur in the statements, by means of logical analysis, lead to a positive and to a negative result. The positive result is worked out in the domain of empirical science; the various concepts of the various branches of science are clarified; their formal-logical and epistemological connections are made explicit. In the domain of *metaphysics,* including all philosophy of value and normative theory, logical analysis yields the negative result *that the alleged statements in this domain are entirely meaningless.* Therewith a radical elimination of metaphysics is attained, which was not yet possible from the earlier antimetaphysical standpoints. It is true that related ideas may be found already in several earlier trains of thought, e.g. those of a nominalistic kind; but it is only now when the development of logic during recent decades provides us with a sufficiently sharp tool that the decisive step can be taken.

In saying that the so-called statements of metaphysics are *meaningless,* we intend this word in its strictest sense. In a loose sense of the word a statement or a question is at times called meaningless if it is entirely sterile to assert or ask it. We might say this for instance about the question "what is the average weight of those inhabitants of Vienna whose telephone number ends with '3'?" or about a statement which is quite obviously false like "in 1910 Vienna had 6 inhabitants" or about a statement which is not just empirically, but logically false, a contradictory statement such as "persons A and B are each a year older than the other." Such sentences are really meaningful, though they are pointless or false; for it is only meaningful sentences that are even divisible into (theoretically) fruitful and sterile, true and false. In the strict sense, however, a sequence of words is *meaningless* if it does not, within a specified language, constitute a statement. It may happen that such a sequence of words looks like a statement at first glance; in that case we call it a *pseudo-statement.* Our thesis, now, is that logical analysis reveals the alleged statements of metaphysics to be pseudo-statements.

A language consists of a vocabulary and a syntax, i.e. a set of words which have meanings and rules of sentence formation. These rules indicate how sentences may be formed out of the various sorts of words. Accordingly, there are two kinds of pseudo-statements: either they contain a word which is erroneously believed to have meaning, or the constituent words are meaningful, yet are put together in a counter-syntactical way, so that they do not yield a meaningful statement. We shall show in terms of examples that pseudo-statements of both kinds occur in metaphysics. Later we shall have to inquire into the reasons that support our contention that metaphysics in its entirety consists of such pseudo-statements.

2. The Significance of a Word

A word which (within a definite language) has a meaning, is usually also said to designate a concept; if it only seems to have a meaning while it really does not, we speak of a "pseudo-concept." How is the origin of a pseudo-concept to be explained? Has not every word been introduced into the language for no other purpose than to express something or other, so that it had a definite meaning from the very beginning of its use? How, then, can a traditional language contain meaningless words? To be sure, originally every word (excepting rare cases which we shall illustrate later) had a meaning. In the course of historical development a word frequently changes its meaning. And it also happens at times that a word loses its old sense without acquiring a new one. It is thus that a pseudo-concept arises.

"The Elimination of Metaphysics Through Logical Analysis of Language" originally appeared as "Überwindung der Metaphysik durch Logisce Analyse der Sprache" in *Erkenntnis* II (1932). The translation here, by Arthur Pap, is reprinted from A. J. Ayer, ed., *Logical Positivism* (Glencoe, Illinois: The Free Press, 1959), 60–81.

What, now, is *the meaning of a word?* What stipulations concerning a word must be made in order for it to be significant? (It does not matter for our investigation whether these stipulations are explicitly laid down, as in the case of some words and symbols of modern science, or whether they have been tacitly agreed upon, as is the case for most words of traditional language.) First, the *syntax* of the word must be fixed, i.e. the mode of its occurrence in the simplest sentence form in which it is capable of occurring; we call this sentence form its *elementary sentence.* The elementary sentence form for the word "stone" e.g. is "x is a stone"; in sentences of this form some designation from the category of things occupies the place of "x," e.g. "this diamond," "this apple." Secondly, for an elementary sentence S containing the word an answer must be given to the following question, which can be formulated in various ways:

(1.) What sentences is S *deducible* from, and what sentences are deducible from S?

(2.) Under what conditions is S supposed to be true, and under what conditions false?

(3.) How is S to be *verified?*

(4.) What is the *meaning* of S?

(1) is the correct formulation; formulation (2) accords with the phraseology of logic, (3) with the phraseology of the theory of knowledge, (4) with that of philosophy (phenomenology). Wittgenstein has asserted that (2) expresses what philosophers mean by (4): the meaning of a sentence consists in its truth-condition. ((1) is the "metalogical" formulation; it is planned to give elsewhere a detailed exposition of metalogic as the theory of syntax and meaning, i.e. relations of deducibility.)

In the case of many words, specifically in the case of the overwhelming majority of scientific words, it is possible to specify their meaning by reduction to other words ("constitution," definition). E.g. " 'arthropodes' are animals with segmented bodies and jointed legs." Thereby the above-mentioned question for the elementary sentence form of the word "arthropode," that is for the sentence form "the thing x is an arthropode," is answered: it has been stipulated that a sentence of this form is deducible from premises of the form "x is an animal," "x has a segmented body," "x has jointed legs," and that conversely each of these sentences is deducible from the former sentence. By means of these stipulations about deducibility (in other words: about the truth-condition, about the method of verification, about the meaning) of the elementary sentence about "arthropode" the meaning of the word "arthropode" is fixed. In this way every word of the language is reduced to other words and finally to the words which occur in the so-called "observation sentences" or "protocol sentences." It is through this reduction that the word acquires its meaning.

For our purposes we may ignore entirely the question concerning the content and form of the primary sentences (protocol sentences) which has not yet been definitely settled. In the theory of knowledge it is customary to say that the primary sentences refer to "the given"; but there is no unanimity on the question what it is that is given. At times the position is taken that sentences about the given speak of the simplest qualities of sense and feeling (e.g. "warm," "blue," "joy" and so forth); others incline to the view that basic sentences refer to total experiences and similarities between them; a still different view has it that even the basic sentences speak of things. Regardless of this diversity of opinion it is certain that a sequence of words has a meaning only if its relations of deducibility to the protocol sentences are fixed, whatever the characteristics of the protocol sentences may be; and similarly, that a word is significant only if the sentences in which it may occur are reducible to protocol sentences.

Since the meaning of a word is determined by its criterion of application (in other words: by the relations of deducibility entered into by its elementary sentence-form, by its truth-conditions, by the method of its verification), the stipulation of the criterion takes away one's freedom to decide what one wishes to "mean" by the word. If the word is to receive an exact meaning, nothing less than the criterion of application must be given; but one cannot, on the other hand, give more than the criterion of application, for the latter is a sufficient determination of meaning. The meaning is implicitly contained in the criterion; all that remains to be done is to make the meaning explicit.

Let us suppose, by way of illustration, that someone invented the new word "teavy" and maintained that there are things which are teavy and things which are not teavy. In order to learn the meaning of this word, we ask him about its criterion of application: how is one to ascertain in a concrete case whether a given thing is teavy or not? Let us suppose to begin with that we get no answer from him: there are no empirical signs of teavyness, he says. In that case we would deny the legitimacy of using this word. If the person who uses the word says that all the same there are things which are teavy and there are things which are not teavy, only it remains for the weak, finite intellect of man an eternal secret which things are teavy and which are not, we shall regard this as empty verbiage. But perhaps he will assure us that he means, after all, something by the word "teavy." But from this we only learn the psychological fact that he associates some kind of images and feelings with the word. The word does not acquire a meaning through such associations. If no criterion of application for the word is stipulated, then nothing is asserted by the sentences in which it occurs, they are but pseudo-statements.

Secondly, take the case when we are given a criterion of application for a new word, say "toovy"; in particular, let the sentence "this thing is toovy" be true if and only if the thing is quadrangular (It is irrelevant in this context whether the criterion is explicitly stated or whether we derive it by observing the affirmative and the negative uses of the word). Then we will say: the word "toovy" is synonymous with the word "quadrangular." And we will not allow its users to tell us that nevertheless they "intended" something else by it than "quadrangular"; that though every quadrangular thing is also toovy and conversely, this is only because quadrangularity is the visible manifestation of toovyness, but that the latter itself is a hidden, not itself observable property. We would reply that after the criterion of application has been fixed, the synonymy of "toovy" and "quadrangular" is likewise fixed, and that we are no further at liberty to "intend" this or that by the word.

Let us briefly summarize the result of our analysis. Let "a" be any word and "S(a)" the elementary sentence in which it occurs. Then the sufficient and necessary condition for "a" being meaningful may be given by each of the following formulations, which ultimately say the same thing:

1. The *empirical criteria* for a are known.
2. It has been stipulated from what protocol sentences "S(a)" is *deducible*.
3. The *truth-conditions* for "S(a)" are fixed.
4. The method of *verification* of "S(a)" is known.[1]

3. Metaphysical Words Without Meaning

Many words of metaphysics, now, can be shown not to fulfill the above requirement, and therefore to be devoid of meaning.

Let us take as an example the metaphysical term "principle" (in the sense of principle of being, not principle of knowledge or axiom). Various metaphysicians offer an answer to the question which is the (highest) "principle of the world" (or of "things," of "existence," of "being"), e.g. water, number, form, motion, life, the spirit, the idea, the unconscious, activity, the good, and so forth. In order to discover the meaning of the word "principle" in this metaphysical question we must ask the metaphysician un-

der what conditions a statement of the form "x is the principle of y" would be true and under what conditions it would be false. In other words: we ask for the criteria of application or for the definition of the word "principle." The metaphysician replies approximately as follows: "x is the principle of y" is to mean "y arises out of x," "the being of y rests on the being of x," "y exists by virtue of x" and so forth. But these words are ambiguous and vague. Frequently they have a clear meaning; e.g., we say of a thing or process y that it "arises out of" x when we observe that things or processes of kind x are frequently or invariably followed by things or processes of kind y (causal connection in the sense of a lawful succession). But the metaphysician tells us that he does not mean this empirically observable relationship. For in that case his metaphysical theses would be merely empirical propositions of the same kind as those of physics. The expression "arising from" is not to mean here a relation of temporal and causal sequence, which is what the word ordinarily means. Yet, no criterion is specified for any other meaning. Consequently, the alleged "metaphysical" meaning, which the word is supposed to have here in contrast to the mentioned empirical meaning, does not exist. If we reflect on the original meaning of the word "principium" (and of the corresponding Greek word "ἀρχή"), we notice the same development. The word is explicitly deprived of its original meaning "beginning"; it is not supposed to mean the temporally prior any more, but the prior in some other, specifically metaphysical, respect. The criteria for this "metaphysical respect," however, are lacking. In both cases, then, the word has been deprived of its earlier meaning without being given a new meaning; there remains the word as an empty shell. From an earlier period of significant use, it is still associatively connected with various mental images; these in turn get associated with new mental images and feelings in the new context of usage. But the word does not thereby become meaningful; and it remains meaningless as long as no method of verification can be described.

Another example is the word "God." Here we must, apart from the variations of its usage within each domain, distinguish the linguistic usage in three different contexts or historical epochs, which however overlap temporally. In its *mythological* use the word has a clear meaning. It, or parallel words in other languages, is sometimes used to denote physical beings which are enthroned on Mount Olympus, in Heaven or in Hades, and which are endowed with power, wisdom, goodness and happiness to a greater or lesser extent. Sometimes the word also refers to spiritual beings which, indeed, do not have manlike bodies, yet manifest themselves nevertheless somehow in the things or processes of the visible world and are therefore empirically verifiable.

---

[1] [Carnap] For the logical and epistemological conception which underlies our exposition, but can only briefly be intimated here, cf. Wittgenstein, *Tractatus Logico-Philosophicus*, 1922, and Carnap, *Der logische Aufbau der Welt*, 1928.

In its *metaphysical* use, on the other hand, the word "God" refers to something beyond experience. The word is deliberately divested of its reference to a physical being or to a spiritual being that is immanent in the physical. And as it is not given a new meaning, it becomes meaningless. To be sure, it often looks as though the word "God" had a meaning even in metaphysics. But the definitions which are set up prove on closer inspection to be pseudo-definitions. They lead either to logically illegitimate combinations of words (of which we shall treat later) or to other metaphysical words (e.g. "primordial basis," "the absolute," "the unconditioned," "the autonomous," "the self-dependent" and so forth), but in no case to the truth-conditions of its elementary sentences. In the case of this word not even the first requirement of logic is met, that is the requirement to specify its syntax, i.e. the form of its occurrence in elementary sentences. An elementary sentence would here have to be of the form "x is a God"; yet, the metaphysician either rejects this form entirely without substituting another, or if he accepts it he neglects to indicate the syntactical category of the variable x. (Categories are, for example, material things, properties of things, relations between things, numbers etc.)

The *theological* usage of the word "God" falls between its mythological and its metaphysical usage. There is no distinctive meaning here, but an oscillation from one of the mentioned two uses to the other. Several theologians have a clearly empirical (in our terminology, "mythological") concept of God. In this case there are no pseudo-statements; but the disadvantage for the theologian lies in the circumstance that according to this interpretation the statements of theology are empirical and hence are subject to the judgment of empirical science. The linguistic usage of other theologians is clearly metaphysical. Others again do not speak in any definite way, whether this is because they follow now this, now that linguistic usage, or because they express themselves in terms whose usage is not clearly classifiable since it tends towards both sides.

Just like the examined examples "principle" and "God," most of the other *specifically metaphysical terms are devoid of meaning*, e.g. "the Idea," "the Absolute," "the Unconditioned," "the Infinite," "the being of being," "nonbeing," "thing in itself," "absolute spirit," "objective spirit," "essence," "being-in-itself," "being-in-and-for-itself," "emanation," "manifestation," "articulation," "the Ego," "the non-Ego," etc. These expressions are in the same boat with "teavy," our previously fabricated example. The metaphysician tells us that empirical truth-conditions cannot be specified; if he adds that nevertheless he "means" something, we know that this is merely an allusion to associated images and feelings which, however, do not bestow a meaning on

the word. The alleged statements of metaphysics which contain such words have no sense, assert nothing, are mere pseudo-statements. Into the explanation of their historical origin we shall inquire later.

4. The Significance of a Sentence

So far we have considered only those pseudo-statements which contain a meaningless word. But there is a second kind of pseudo-statement. They consist of meaningful words, but the words are put together in such a way that nevertheless no meaning results. The syntax of a language specifies which combinations of words are admissible and which inadmissible. The grammatical syntax of natural languages, however, does not fulfill the task of elimination of senseless combinations of words in all cases. Let us take as examples the following sequences of words:

1. "Caesar is and"
2. "Caesar is a prime number"

The word sequence (1) is formed countersyntactically; the rules of syntax require that the third position be occupied, not by a conjunction, but by a predicate, hence by a noun (with article) or by an adjective. The word sequence "Caesar is a general," e.g., is formed in accordance with the rules of syntax. It is a meaningful word sequence, a genuine sentence. But, now, word sequence (2) is likewise syntactically correct, for it has the same grammatical form as the sentence just mentioned. Nevertheless (2) is meaningless. "Prime number" is a predicate of numbers; it can be neither affirmed nor denied of a person. Since (2) looks like a statement yet is not a statement, does not assert anything, expresses neither a true nor a false proposition, we call this word sequence a "pseudo-statement." The fact that the rules of grammatical syntax are not violated easily seduces one at first glance into the erroneous opinion that one still has to do with a statement, albeit a false one. But "a is a prime number" is false if and only if a is divisible by a natural number different from a and from 1; evidently it is illicit to put here "Caesar" for "a." This example has been so chosen that the nonsense is easily detectable. Many so-called statements of metaphysics are not so easily recognized to be pseudo-statements. The fact that natural languages allow the formation of meaningless sequences of words without violating the rules of grammar, indicates that grammatical syntax is, from a logical point of view, inadequate. If grammatical syntax corresponded exactly to logical syntax, pseudo-statements could not arise. If grammatical syntax differentiated not only the word-categories of nouns, adjectives, verbs, conjunctions etc., but within each of these categories made the further distinctions that are logically indispensable, then no pseudo-statements could be formed. If, e.g., nouns were grammatically subdivided into several kinds of words, according as they designated properties of physical objects, of numbers etc., then the words "general" and "prime number" would belong to grammatically different word-categories, and (2) would be just as linguistically incorrect as (1). In a correctly constructed language, therefore, all nonsensical sequences of words would be of the kind of example (1). Considerations of grammar would already eliminate them as it were automatically; i.e. in order to avoid nonsense, it would be unnecessary to pay attention to the meanings of the individual words over and above their syntactical type (their "syntactical category," e.g. things, property of things, relation between things, number, property of numbers, relation between numbers, and so forth). It follows that if our thesis that the statements of metaphysics are pseudo-statements is justifiable, then metaphysics could not even be expressed in a logically constructed language. This is the great philosophical importance of the task, which at present occupies the logicians, of building a logical syntax.

5. Metaphysical Pseudo-statements

Let us now take a look at some examples of metaphysical pseudo-statements of a kind where the violation of logical syntax is especially obvious, though they accord with historical-grammatical syntax. We select a few sentences from that metaphysical school which at present exerts the strongest influence in Germany.[2]

"What is to be investigated is being only and—*nothing else; being alone and further—nothing; solely being, and beyond being—nothing. What about this Nothing? . . . Does the Nothing exist only because the Not, i.e. the Negation, exists? Or is it the other way around? Does Negation and the Not exist only because the Nothing exists? . . .* We assert: *the Nothing is prior to the Not and the Negation. . . .* Where do we seek the Nothing? How do we find the Nothing. . . . We know the Nothing. . . . *Anxiety reveals the Nothing. . . .* That for which and because of which we were anxious, was 'really'—nothing. Indeed: the Nothing itself—as such—was present. . . . *What about this Nothing?—The Nothing itself nothings.*"

In order to show that the possibility of forming pseudo-statements is based on a logical defect of language, we set up the schema below. The sentences under I are grammatically as well as logically impeccable, hence meaningful. The sentences under II (excepting B3) are in grammatical respects perfectly analogous to those under I. Sentence form IIA (as question and answer) does not, indeed, satisfy the requirements to be imposed on a logically correct language. But it is nevertheless meaningful, because it is translatable into correct language. This is shown by sentence IIIA, which has the same meaning as IIA. Sentence form IIA then proves to be undesirable because we can be led from it, by means of grammatically faultless operations, to the meaningless sentence forms IIB, which are taken from the above quotation. These forms cannot even be constructed in the correct language of Column III. Nonetheless, their nonsensicality is not obvious at first glance, because one is easily deceived by the analogy with the meaningful sentences IB. The fault of our language identified here lies, therefore, in the circumstance that, in contrast to a logically correct language, it admits of the same grammatical form for meaningful and meaningless word sequences. To each sentence in words we have added a corresponding formula in the notation of symbolic logic; these formulae facilitate recognition of the undesirable analogy between IA and IIA and therewith of the origin of the meaningless constructions IIB.

I. Meaningful Sentences of Ordinary Language	II. Transition from Sense to Nonsense in Ordinary Language	III. Logically Correct Language
A. What is outside? Ou(?) Rain is outside Ou(r)	A. What is outside Ou(?) Nothing is outside Ou(no)	A. There is nothing (does not exist anything) which is outside. $\sim(\exists x).Ou(x)$
B. What about this rain? (i.e. what does the rain do? or: what else can be said about this rain? ?(r)	B. "What about this Nothing?" ? (no)	B. None of these forms can even be constructed.
1. We know the rain K(r)	1. "We seek the Nothing" "We find the	

[2][Carnap] The following quotations (original italics) are taken from M. Heidegger, *Was Ist Metaphysik?* 1929. We could just as well have selected passages from any other of the numerous metaphysicians of the present or of the past; yet the selected passages seem to us to illustrate our thesis especially well.

Nothing"
We know the
Nothing"
K(no)

2. The rain rains
R(r)

2. "The Nothing
nothings"
No(no)
3. "The Nothing
exists only
because . . ."
Ex(no)

On closer inspection of the pseudo-statements under IIB, we also find some differences. The construction of sentence (1) is simply based on the mistake of employing the word "nothing" as a noun, because it is customary in ordinary language to use it in this form in order to construct a negative existential statement (see IIA). In a correct language, on the other hand, it is not a particular *name,* but a certain *logical form* of the sentence that serves this purpose (see IIIA). Sentence IIB2 adds something new, viz. the fabrication of the meaningless word "to nothing." This sentence, therefore, is senseless for a twofold reason. We pointed out before that the meaningless words of metaphysics usually owe their origin to the fact that a meaningful word is deprived of its meaning through its metaphorical use in metaphysics. But here we confront one of those rare cases where a new word is introduced which never had a meaning to begin with. Likewise sentence IIB3 must be rejected for two reasons. In respect of the error of using the word "nothing" as a noun, it is like the previous sentences. But in addition it involves a contradiction. For even if it were admissible to introduce "nothing" as a name or description of an entity, still the existence of this entity would be denied in its very definition, whereas sentence (3) goes on to affirm its existence. This sentence, therefore, would be contradictory, hence absurd, even if it were not already meaningless.

In view of the gross logical errors which we find in sentences IIB, we might be led to conjecture that perhaps the word "nothing" has in Heidegger's treatise a meaning entirely different from the customary one. And this presumption is further strengthened as we go on to read there that anxiety reveals the Nothing, that the Nothing itself is present as such in anxiety. For here the word "nothing" seems to refer to a certain emotional constitution, possibly of a religious sort, or something or other that underlies such emotions. If such were the case, then the mentioned logical errors in sentences IIB would not be committed. But the first

sentence of the quotation at the beginning of this section proves that this interpretation is not possible. The combination of "only" and "nothing else" shows unmistakably that the word "nothing" here has the usual meaning of a logical particle that serves for the formulation of a negative existential statement. This introduction of the word "nothing" is then immediately followed by the leading question of the treatise: "What about this Nothing?".

But our doubts as to a possible misinterpretation get completely dissolved as we note that the author of the treatise is clearly aware of the conflict between his questions and statements, and logic. "*Question and answer* in regard to the Nothing are equally *absurd* in themselves. . . . The fundamental rule of thinking commonly appealed to, the law of prohibited contradiction, general *'logic,'* destroys this question." All the worse for logic! We must abolish its sovereignty: "If thus the power of the *understanding* in the field of questions concerning Nothing and Being is broken, then the fate of the sovereignty of 'logic' within philosophy is thereby decided as well. The very idea of 'logic' dissolves in the whirl of a more basic questioning." But will sober science condone the whirl of counter-logical questioning? To this question too there is a ready answer: "The alleged sobriety and superiority of science becomes ridiculous if it does not take the Nothing seriously." Thus we find here a good confirmation of our thesis; a metaphysician himself here states that his questions and answers are irreconcilable with logic and the scientific way of thinking.

The difference between our thesis and that of the *earlier antimetaphysicians* should now be clear. We do not regard metaphysics as "mere speculation" or "fairy tales." The statements of a fairy tale do not conflict with logic, but only with experience; they are perfectly meaningful, although false. Metaphysics is not *"superstition";* it is possible to believe true and false propositions, but not to believe meaningless sequences of words. Metaphysical statements are not even acceptable as *"working hypotheses";* for an hypothesis must be capable of entering into relations of deducibility with (true or false) empirical statements, which is just what pseudo-statements cannot do.

With reference to the so-called *limitation of human knowledge* an attempt is sometimes made to save metaphysics by raising the following objection: metaphysical statements are not, indeed, verifiable by man nor by any other finite being; nevertheless they might be construed as conjectures about the answers which a being with higher or even perfect powers of knowledge would make to our questions, and as such conjectures they would, after all, be meaningful. To counter this objection, let us consider the following. If the meaning of a word cannot be specified, or if the sequence of words does not accord with the rules of syntax, then one has not even asked a question. (Just think of the pesudo-questions: "Is this table teavy?", "is the number 7 holy?", "which numbers are darker, the even or the odd ones?"). Where there is no question, not even an omniscient being can give an answer. Now the objector may say: just as one who can see may communicate new knowledge to the blind, so a higher being might perhaps communicate to us metaphysical knowledge, e.g. whether the visible world is the manifestation of a spirit. Here we must reflect on the meaning of "new knowledge." It is, indeed, conceivable that we might encounter animals who tell us about a new sense. If these beings were to prove to us Fermat's theorem or were to invent a new physical instrument or were to establish a hitherto unknown law of nature, then our knowledge would be increased with their help. For this sort of thing we can test, just the way even a blind man can understand and test the whole of physics (and therewith any statement made by those who can see). But if those hypothetical beings tell us something which we cannot verify, then we cannot understand it either; in that case no information has been communicated to us, but mere verbal sounds devoid of meaning though possibly associated with images. It follows that our knowledge can only be quantitatively enlarged by other beings, no matter whether they know more or less or everything, but no knowledge of an essentially different kind can be added. What we do not know for certain, we may come to know with greater certainty through the assistance of other beings; but what is unintelligible, meaningless for us, cannot become meaningful through someone else's assistance, however vast his knowledge might be. Therefore no god and no devil can give us metaphysical knowledge.

6. Meaninglessness of all Metaphysics

The examples of metaphysical statements which we have analyzed were all taken from just one treatise. But our results apply with equal validity, in part even in verbally identical ways, to other metaphysical systems. That treatise is completely in the right in citing approvingly a statement by Hegel ("pure Being and pure Nothing, therefore, are one and the same"). The metaphysics of Hegel has exactly the same logical character as this modern system of metaphysics. And the same holds for the rest of the metaphysical systems, though the kind of phraseology and therewith the kind of logical errors that occur in them deviate more or less from the kind that occurs in the examples we discussed.

It should not be necessary here to adduce further examples of specific metaphysical sentences in diverse systems and submit them to analysis. We confine ourselves to an indication of the most frequent kinds of errors.

Perhaps the majority of the logical mistakes that are committed when pseudo-statements are made, are based on the logical faults infecting the use of the word "to be" in our language (and of the corresponding words in other languages, at least in most European languages). The first fault is the ambiguity of the word "to be." It is sometimes used as copula prefixed to a predicate ("I am hungry"), sometimes to designate existence ("I am"). This mistake is aggravated by the fact that metaphysicians often are not clear about this ambiguity. The second fault lies in the form of the verb in its second meaning, the meaning of *existence*. The verbal form feigns a predicate where there is none. To be sure, it has been known for a long time that existence is not a property (cf. Kant's refutation of the ontological proof of the existence of God). But it was not until the advent of modern logic that full consistency on this point was reached: the syntactical form in which modern logic introduces the sign for existence is such that it cannot, like a predicate, be applied to signs for objects, but only to predicates (cf. e.g. sentence IIIA in the above table). Most metaphysicians since antiquity have allowed themselves to be seduced into pseudo-statements by the verbal, and therewith the predicative form of the word "to be," e.g. "I am," "God is."

We meet an illustration of this error in Descartes' "cogito, ergo sum." Let us disregard here the material objections that have been raised against the premise—viz. whether the sentence "I think" adequately expresses the intended state of affairs or contains perhaps an hypostasis—and consider the two sentences only from the formal-logical point of view. We notice at once two essential logical mistakes. The first lies in the conclusion "I am." The verb "to be" is undoubtedly meant in the sense of existence here; for a copula cannot be used without predicate; indeed, Descartes' "I am" has always been interpreted in this sense. But in that case this sentence violates the above-mentioned logical rule that existence can be predicated only in conjunction with a predicate, not in conjunction with a name (subject, proper name). An existential statement does not have the form "*a* exists" (as in "I am," i.e. "I exist"), but "there exists something of such and such a kind." The second error lies in the transition from "I think" to "I exist." If from the statement "P(a)" ("*a* has the property P") an existential statement is to be deduced, then the latter can assert existence only with respect to the predicate P, not with respect to the subject *a* of the premise. What follows from "I am a European" is not "I exist," but "a European exists." What follows from "I think" is not "I am" but "there exists something that thinks."

The circumstance that our languages express existence by a verb ("to be" or "to exist") is not in itself a logical fault; it is only inappropriate, dangerous. The verbal form easily misleads us into the misconception that existence is a predicate. One then arrives at such logically incorrect and hence senseless modes of expression as were just examined. Likewise such forms as "Being" or "Not-Being," which from time immemorial have played a great role in metaphysics, have the same origin. In a logically correct language such forms cannot even be constructed. It appears that in the Latin and the German languages the forms "ens" or "das Seiende" were, perhaps under the seductive influence of the Greek example, introduced specifically for use by metaphysicians; in this way the language deteriorated logically whereas the addition was believed to represent an improvement.

Another very frequent violation of logical syntax is the so-called *"type confusion"* of concepts. While the previously mentioned mistake consists in the predicative use of a symbol with non-predicative meaning, in this case a predicate is, indeed, used as predicate yet as predicate of a different type. We have here a violation of the rules of the so-called theory of types. An artificial example is the sentence we discussed earlier: "Caesar is a prime number." Names of persons and names of numbers belong to different logical types, and so do accordingly predicates of persons (e.g. "general") and predicates of numbers ("prime number"). The error of type confusion is, unlike the previously discussed usage of the verb "to be," not the prerogative of metaphysics but already occurs very often in conversational language also. But here it rarely leads to nonsense. The typical ambiguity of words is here of such a kind that it can be easily removed.

Example: 1. "This table is larger than that." 2. "The height of this table is larger than the height of that table." Here the word "larger" is used in (1) for a relation between objects, in (2) for a relation between numbers, hence for two distinct syntactical categories. The mistake is here unimportant; it could, e.g., be eliminated by writing "larger1" and "larger2"; "larger1" is then defined in terms of "larger2" by declaring statement form (1) to be synonymous with (2) (and others of a similar kind).

Since the confusion of types causes no harm in conversational language, it is usually ignored entirely. This is, indeed, expedient for the ordinary use of language, but has had unfortunate consequences in metaphysics. Here the conditioning by everyday language has led to confusions of types which, unlike those in everyday language, are no longer translatable into logically correct form. Pseudo-statements of this kind are encountered in especially large quantity, e.g.,

in the writings of Hegel and Heidegger. The latter has adopted many peculiarities of the Hegelian idiom along with their logical faults (e.g. predicates which should be applied to objects of a certain sort are instead applied to predicates of these objects or to "being" or to "existence" or to a relation between these objects).

Having found that many metaphysical statements are meaningless, we confront the question whether there is not perhaps a core of meaningful statements in metaphysics which would remain after elimination of all the meaningless ones.

Indeed, the results we have obtained so far might give rise to the view that there are many dangers of falling into nonsense in metaphysics, and that one must accordingly endeavor to avoid these traps with great care if one wants to do metaphysics. But actually the situation is that meaningful metaphysical statements are impossible. This follows from the task which metaphysics sets itself: to discover and formulate a kind of knowledge which is not accessible to empirical science.

We have seen earlier that the meaning of a statement lies in the method of its verification. A statement asserts only so much as is verifiable with respect to it. Therefore a sentence can be used only to assert an empirical proposition, if indeed it is used to assert anything at all. If something were to lie, in principle, beyond possible experience, it could be neither said nor thought nor asked.

(Meaningful) statements are divided into the following kinds. First there are statements which are true solely by virtue of their form ("tautologies" according to Wittgenstein; they correspond approximately to Kant's "analytic judgments"). They say nothing about reality. The formulae of logic and mathematics are of this kind. They are not themselves factual statements, but serve for the transformation of such statements. Secondly there are the negations of such statements (*"contradictions"*). They are self-contradictory, hence false by virtue of their form. With respect to all other statements the decision about truth or falsehood lies in the protocol sentences. They are therefore (true or false) *empirical statements* and belong to the domain of empirical science. Any statement one desires to construct which does not fall within these categories becomes automatically meaningless. Since metaphysics does not want to assert analytic propositions, nor to fall within the domain of empirical science, it is compelled to employ words for which no criteria of application are specified and which are therefore devoid of sense, or else to combine meaningful words in such a way that neither an analytic (or contradictory) statement nor an empirical statement is produced. In either case pseudo-statements are the inevitable product.

Logical analysis, then, pronounces the verdict of meaninglessness on any alleged knowledge that pretends to reach above or behind experience. This verdict hits, in the first place, any speculative metaphysics, any alleged knowledge by *pure thinking* or by *pure intuition* that pretends to be able to do without experience. But the verdict equally applies to the kind of metaphysics which, starting from experience, wants to acquire knowledge about that which *transcends experience* by means of special *inferences* (e.g. the neo-vitalist thesis of the directive presence of an "entelechy" in organic processes, which supposedly cannot be understood in terms of physics; the question concerning the "essence of causality," transcending the ascertainment of certain regularities of succession; the talk about the "thing in itself"). Further, the same judgment must be passed on all *philosophy of norms,* or *philosophy of value,* on any ethics or esthetics as a normative discipline. For the objective validity of a value or norm is (even on the view of the philosophers of value) not empirically verifiable nor deducible from empirical statements; hence it cannot be asserted (in a meaningful statement) at all. In other words: Either empirical criteria are indicated for the use of "good" and "beautiful" and the rest of the predicates that are employed in the normative sciences, or they are not. In the first case, a statement containing such a predicate turns into a factual judgment, but not a value judgment; in the second case, it becomes a pseudo-statement. It is altogether impossible to make a statement that expresses a value judgment.

Finally, the verdict of meaninglessness also hits those metaphysical movements which are usually called, improperly, epistemological movements, that is *realism* (insofar as it claims to say more than the empirical fact that the sequence of events exhibits a certain regularity, which makes the application of the inductive method possible) and its opponents: subjective *idealism,* solipsism, phenomenalism, and *positivism* (in the earlier sense).

But what, then, is left over for *philosophy,* if all statements whatever that assert something are of an empirical nature and belong to factual science? What remains is not statements, nor a theory, nor a system, but only a *method:* the method of logical analysis. The foregoing discussion has illustrated the negative application of this method: in that context it serves to eliminate meaningless words, meaningless pseudo-statements. In its positive use it serves to clarify meaningful concepts and propositions, to lay logical foundations for factual science and for mathematics. The negative application of the method is necessary and important in the present historical situation. But even in its present practice, the positive application is more fertile. We cannot here discuss it in greater detail. It is the indicated task of logical

analysis, inquiry into logical foundations, that is meant by *"scientific philosophy"* in contrast to metaphysics.

The question regarding the logical character of the statements which we obtain as the result of a logical analysis, e.g. the statements occurring in this and other logical papers, can here be answered only tentatively: such statements are partly analytic, partly empirical. For these statements about statements and parts of statements belong in part to pure *metalogic* (e.g. "a sequence consisting of the existence-symbol and a noun, is not a sentence"), in part to descriptive metalogic (e.g. "the word sequence at such and such a place in such and such a book is meaningless"). Metalogic will be discussed elsewhere. It will also be shown there that the metalogic which speaks about the sentences of a given language can be formulated in that very language itself.

7. Metaphysics as Expression of an Attitude Toward Life

Our claim that the statements of metaphysics are entirely meaningless, that they do not assert anything, will leave even those who agree intellectually with our results with a painful feeling of strangeness: how could it be explained that so many men in all ages and nations, among them eminent minds, spent so much energy, nay veritable fervor, on metaphysics if the latter consisted of nothing but mere words, nonsensically juxtaposed? And how could one account for the fact that metaphysical books have exerted such a strong influence on readers up to the present day, if they contained not even errors, but nothing at all? These doubts are justified since metaphysics does indeed have a content; only it is not theoretical content. The (pseudo)-statements of metaphysics do not serve for the *description of states of affairs,* neither existing ones (in that case they would be true statements) nor non-existing ones (in that case they would be at least false statements). They serve for the *expression of the general attitude of a person towards life* ("Lebenseinstellung, Lebensgefühl").

Perhaps we may assume that metaphysics originated from *mythology.* The child is angry at the "wicked table" which hurt him. Primitive man endeavors to conciliate the threatening demon of earthquakes, or he worships the deity of the fertile rains in gratitude. Here we confront personifications of natural phenomena, which are the quasi-poetic expression of man's emotional relationship to his environment. The heritage of mythology is bequeathed on the one hand to poetry, which produces and intensifies the effects of mythology on life in a deliberate way; on the other hand, it is handed down to theology, which develops mythology into a system.

Which, now, is the historical role of metaphysics? Perhaps we may regard it as a substitute for theology on the level of systematic, conceptual thinking. The (supposedly) transcendent sources of knowledge of theology are here replaced by natural, yet supposedly trans-empirical sources of knowledge. On closer inspection the same content as that of mythology is here still recognizable behind the repeatedly varied dressing: we find that metaphysics also arises from the need to give expression to a man's attitude in life, his emotional and volitional reaction to the environment, to society, to the tasks to which he devotes himself, to the misfortunes that befall him. This attitude manifests itself, unconsciously as a rule, in everything a man does or says. It also impresses itself on his facial features, perhaps even on the character of his gait. Many people, now, feel a desire to create over and above these manifestations a special expression of their attitude, through which it might become visible in a more succinct and penetrating way. If they have artistic talent they are able to express themselves by producing a work of art. Many writers have already clarified the way in which the basic attitude is manifested through the style and manner of a work of art (e.g. Dilthey and his students). [In this connection the term "world view" ("Weltanschauung") is often used; we prefer to avoid it because of its ambiguity, which blurs the difference between attitude and theory, a difference which is of decisive importance for our analysis.] What is here essential for our considerations is only the fact that art is an adequate, metaphysics an inadequate means for the expression of the basic attitude. Of course, there need be no intrinsic objection to one's using any means of expression one likes. But in the case of metaphysics we find this situation: through the form of its works it pretends to be something that it is not. The form in question is that of a system of statements which are apparently related as premises and conclusions, that is, the form of a theory. In this way the fiction of theoretical content is generated, whereas, as we have seen, there is no such content. It is not only the reader, but the metaphysician himself who suffers from the illusion that the metaphysical statements say something, describe states of affairs. The metaphysician believes that he travels in territory in which truth and falsehood are at stake. In reality, however, he has not asserted anything, but only expressed something, like an artist. That the metaphysician is thus deluding himself cannot be inferred from the fact that he selects language as the medium of expression and declarative sentences as the form of expression; for lyrical poets do the same without succumbing to self-delusion. But the metaphysician supports his statements by arguments, he claims assent to their content, he polemicizes against metaphysicians, of divergent persuasion by attempting to refute their assertions in his treatise. Lyrical poets, on the other hand, do not try to refute in their poem the statements in a poem by some other lyrical poet; for they know they are in the domain of art and not in the domain of theory.

Perhaps music is the purest means of expression of the basic attitude because it is entirely free from any reference to objects. The harmonious feeling or attitude, which the metaphysician tries to express in a monistic system, is more clearly expressed in the music of Mozart. And when a metaphysician gives verbal expression to his dualistic-heroic attitude towards life in a dualistic system, is it not perhaps because he lacks the ability of a Beethoven to express this attitude in an adequate medium? Metaphysicians are musicians without musical ability. Instead they have a strong inclination to work within the medium of the theoretical, to connect concepts and thoughts. Now, instead of activating, on the one hand, this inclination in the domain of science, and satisfying, on the other hand, the need for expression in art, the metaphysician confuses the two and produces a structure which achieves nothing for knowledge and something inadequate for the expression of attitude.

Our conjecture that metaphysics is a substitute, albeit an inadequate one, for art, seems to be further confirmed by the fact that the metaphysician who perhaps had artistic talent to the highest degree, viz. Nietzsche, almost entirely avoided the error of that confusion. A large part of his work has predominantly empirical content. We find there, for instance, historical analyses of specific artistic phenomena, or an historical-psychological analysis of morals. In the work, however, in which he expresses most strongly that which others express through metaphysics or ethics, in *Thus Spake Zarathustra*, he does not choose the misleading theoretical form, but openly the form of art, of poetry.

Jacques Lacan

1901–1981

Lacan, the French psychoanalyst, was an unconventional interpreter of Freud and eccentric in his psychoanalytical practices. In 1953, he delivered at the meeting of the International Psychoanalytical Association a speech now known as the *Discours de Rome,* which led to his break with that group. The *Discours* appears in English translation as "The Function and Field of Speech and Language in Pyschoanalysis" in *Écrits,* a collection of his essays. Lacan's principal departure from mainline psychoanalytical theory was his embrace of Saussure's structuralist theory of the signifier (above, page 787), Lévi-Strauss's structuralist anthropology, and to some extent phenomenology. In an important essay, "The Agency of the Letter in the Unconscious or Reason Since Freud," Lacan remarks, ". . . what the psychoanalytical experience discovers in the unconscious is the whole structure of language." As in Saussure, the signifier is privileged over the signified, and thus language and the unconscious become to a degree freed from reference to externality.

Lacan tells a story, in the selection below, of the child's entrance into the domain of the signifier. He posits three stages: the mirror stage, the imaginary, and the symbolic. These stages overlap in the child's development. Indeed, Lacan treats them at times as synchronous. The mirror stage is that in which the child discovers its image. This begins the child's alienation, for the image is the Other; the child thus enters into the imaginary. The symbolic marks entry into language and constant deferral of the self along the Saussurean chain of signification. As a result the self can never be complete and known; it is enmeshed in language. Lacan rejects the notion of a simple Cartesian subject and opposes "any philosophy directly issuing from the *Cogito.*" There is generated in the mirror stage "a primordial Discord" in human beings.

Lacan's translated writings include *Écrits: A Selection* (1977); *The Four Fundamental Concepts of Psycholanalysis* (the eleventh seminar, 1964, tr. 1978); *Feminine Sexuality* (1982); *The Language of the Self (Discours de Rome)* (1968); "Seminar on the Purloined Letter," *Yale French Studies* 48 (1972). Other seminars have been published in France and translated. See Stuart Schneiderman, *The Death of an Intellectual Hero* (1983); Catherine Clément, *The Lives and Legends of Jacques Lacan* (1983); Bice Benvenute and Roger Kennedy, *The Works of Jacques Lacan: An Introduction* (1986); Ellen Ragland-Sullivan and Mark Brasher, *Lacan and the Subject of Language* (1991); Jean-Luc Nancy and Philippe Lacoue-Labarthe, *The Title of the Letter* (1992); Mark Brasher et al., ed., *Lacanian Theory of Discourse* (1994); Ben Stoltzfus, *Lacan and Literature* (1996); Tim Dean, *Beyond Sexuality* (2000); Jean-Michel Rabaté, *Jacques Lacan and the Subject of Literature* (2001).

The Mirror Stage as Formative of the Function of the I as Revealed in Psychoanalytic Experience

The conception of the mirror stage that I introduced at our last congress, thirteen years ago, has since become more or less established in the practice of the French group. However, I think it worthwhile to bring it again to your attention, especially today, for the light it sheds on the formation of the *I* as we experience it in psychoanalysis. It is an experience that leads us to oppose any philosophy directly issuing from the *Cogito*.[1]

Some of you may recall that this conception originated in a feature of human behaviour illuminated by a fact of comparative psychology. The child, at an age when he is for a time, however short, outdone by the chimpanzee in instrumental intelligence, can nevertheless already recognize as such his own image in a mirror. This recognition is indicated in the illuminative mimicry of the *Aha-Erlebnis*, which Köhler[2] sees as the expression of situational apperception, an essential stage of the act of intelligence.

This act, far from exhausting itself, as in the case of the monkey, once the image has been mastered and found empty, immediately rebounds in the case of the child in a series of gestures in which he experiences in play the relation between the movements assumed in the image and the reflected environment, and between this virtual complex and the reality it reduplicates—the child's own body, and the persons and things, around him.

This event can take place, as we have known since Baldwin,[3] from the age of six months, and its repetition has often made me reflect upon the startling spectacle of the infant in front of the mirror. Unable as yet to walk, or even to stand up, and held tightly as he is by some support, human or artificial (what, in France, we call a *'trotte-bébé'*), he nevertheless overcomes, in a flutter of jubilant activity, the obstructions of his support and, fixing his attitude in a slightly leaning-forward position, in order to hold it in his gaze, brings back an instantaneous aspect of the image.

For me, this activity retains the meaning I have given it up to the age of eighteen months. This meaning discloses a libidinal dynamism, which has hitherto remained problematic, as well as an ontological structure of the human world that accords with my reflections on paranoiac knowledge.

We have only to understand the mirror stage *as an identification,* in the full sense that analysis gives to the term: namely, the transformation that takes place in the subject when he assumes an image—whose predestination to this phase-effect is sufficiently indicated by the use, in analytic theory, of the ancient term *imago.*

This jubilant assumption of his specular image by the child at the *infans* stage, still sunk in his motor incapacity and nursling dependence, would seem to exhibit in an exemplary situation the symbolic matrix in which the *I* is precipitated in a primordial form, before it is objectified in the dialectic of identification with the other, and before language restores to it, in the universal, its function as subject.

This form would have to be called the Ideal-I,[4] if we wished to incorporate it into our usual register, in the sense that it will also be the source of secondary identifications, under which term I would place the functions of libidinal normalization. But the important point is that this form situates the agency of the ego, before its social determination, in a fictional direction, which will always remain irreducible for the individual alone, or rather, which will only rejoin the coming-into-being (*le devenir*) of the subject asymptotically, whatever the success of the dialectical syntheses by which he must resolve as *I* his discordance with his own reality.

The fact is that the total form of the body by which the subject anticipates in a mirage the maturation of his power is given to him only as *Gestalt,*[5] that is to say, in an exteriority in which this form is certainly more constituent than constituted, but in which it appears to him above all in a constrasting size (*un relief de stature*) that fixes it and in a symmetry that inverts it, in contrast with the turbulent movements that the subject feels are animating him. Thus, this *Gestalt*—whose pregnancy should be regarded as bound up with the species, though its motor style remains

---

[1] The phrase *Cogito ergo sum* (I think, therefore I am) was uttered by René Descartes (1596–1650), French philosopher and mathematician. Lacan refers to the Cartesian establishment of a divorce between subject and world.

[2] Wolfgang Köhler (1887–1967), American psychologist.

[3] James Baldwin (1861–1934), American psychologist.

[4] [Lacan] Throughout this article I leave in its peculiarity the translation I have adopted for Freud's *Ideal-Ich* [i.e. *'je-idéal'*], without further comment, other than to say that I have not maintained it since.

[5] *Gestalt:* In psychology the idea that a response is a whole rather than a congeries of responses.

scarcely recognizable—by these two aspects of its appearance, symbolizes the mental permanence of the *I*, at the same time as it prefigures its alienating destination; it is still pregnant with the correspondences that unite the *I* with the statue in which man projects himself, with the phantoms that dominate him, or with the automaton in which, in an ambiguous relation, the world of his own making tends to find completion.

Indeed, for the *imagos*—whose veiled faces it is our privilege to see in outline in our daily experience and in the penumbra of symbolic efficacity[6]—the mirror-image would seem to be the threshold of the visible world, if we go by the mirror disposition that the *imago of one's own body* presents in hallucinations or dreams, whether it concerns its individual features, or even its infirmities, or its object-projections; or if we observe the role of the mirror apparatus in the appearances of the *double,* in which physical realities, however heterogeneous, are manifested.

That a *Gestalt* should be capable of formative effects in the organism is attested by a piece of biological experimentation that is itself so alien to the idea of psychical causality that it cannot bring itself to formulate its results in these terms. It nevertheless recognizes that it is a necessary condition for the maturation of the gonad of the female pigeon that it should see another member of its species, of either sex; so sufficient in itself is this condition that the desired effect may be obtained merely by placing the individual within reach of the field of reflection of a mirror. Similarly, in the case of the migratory locust, the transition within a generation from the solitary to the gregarious form can be obtained by exposing the individual, at a certain stage, to the exclusively visual action of a similar image, provided it is animated by movements of a style sufficiently close to that characteristic of the species. Such facts are inscribed in an order of homeomorphic identification that would itself fall within the larger question of the meaning of beauty as both formative and erogenic.

But the facts of mimicry are no less instructive when conceived as cases of heteromorphic identification, in as much as they raise the problem of the signification of space for the living organism—psychological concepts hardly seem less appropriate for shedding light on these matters than ridiculous attempts to reduce them to the supposedly supreme law of adaptation. We have only to recall how Roger Caillois[7] (who was then very young, and still fresh from his breach with the sociological school in which he was trained) illuminated the subject by using the term '*legendary psychasthenia*' to classify morphological mimicry as an obsession with space in its derealizing effect.

I have myself shown in the social dialectic that structures human knowledge as paranoiac[8] why human knowledge has greater autonomy than animal knowledge in relation to the field of force of desire, but also why human knowledge is determined in that 'little reality' *(ce peu de ré-alité),* which the Surrealists, in their restless way, saw as its limitation. These reflections lead me to recognize in the spatial captation manifested in the mirror-stage, even before the social dialectic, the effect in man of an organic insufficiency in his natural reality—in so far as any meaning can be given to the word 'nature.'

I am led, therefore, to regard the function of the mirror-stage as a particular case of the function of the *imago,* which is to establish a relation between the organism and its reality—or, as they say, between the *Innenwelt* and the *Umwelt.*

In man, however, this relation to nature is altered by a certain dehiscence at the heart of the organism, a primordial Discord betrayed by the signs of uneasiness and motor unco-ordination of the neonatal months. The objective notion of the anatomical incompleteness of the pyramidal system and likewise the presence of certain humoral residues of the maternal organism confirm the view I have formulated as the fact of a real *specific prematurity of birth* in man.

It is worth noting, incidentally, that this is a fact recognized as such by embryologists, by the term *foetalization,* which determines the prevalence of the so-called superior apparatus of the neurax, and especially of the cortex, which psycho-surgical operations lead us to regard as the intraorganic mirror.

This development is experienced as a temporal dialectic that decisively projects the formation of the individual into history. The *mirror stage* is a drama whose internal thrust is precipitated from insufficiency to anticipation—and which manufactures for the subject, caught up in the lure of spatial identification, the succession of phantasies that extends from a fragmented body-image to a form of its totality that I shall call orthopaedic—and, lastly, to the assumption of the armour of an alienating identity, which will mark with is rigid structure the subject's entire mental development. Thus, to break out of the circle of the *Innenwelt* into the *Umwelt* generates the inexhaustible quadrature of the ego's verifications.

6 Cf. Claude Lévi-Strauss, *Structural Anthropology,* Chapter X. See also Lévi-Strauss (below, page 1119).
7 Roger Callois (1917–1978), French critic and poet.
8 [Lacan] Cf. 'Aggressivity in Psychoanalysis,' p. 8, and *Écrits,* p. 180.

This fragmented body—which term I have also introduced into our system of theoretical references—usually manifests itself in dreams when the movement of the analysis encounters a certain level of aggressive disintegration in the individual. It then appears in the form of disjointed limbs, or of those organs represented in exoscopy, growing wings and taking up arms for intestinal persecutions—the very same that the visionary Hieronymus Bosch[9] has fixed, for all time, in painting, in their ascent from the fifteenth century to the imaginary zenith of modern man. But this form is even tangibly revealed at the organic level, in the lines of 'fragilization' that define the anatomy of phantasy, as exhibited in the schizoid and spasmodic symptoms of hysteria.

Correlatively, the formation of the *I* is symbolized in dreams by a fortress, or a stadium—its inner arena and enclosure, surrounded by marshes and rubbish-tips, dividing it into two opposed fields of contest where the subject flounders in quest of the lofty, remote inner castle whose form (sometimes juxtaposed in the same scenario) symbolizes the id in a quite startling way. Similarly, on the mental plane, we find realized the structures of fortified works, the metaphor of which arises spontaneously, as if issuing from the symptoms themselves, to designate the mechanisms of obsessional neurosis—inversion, isolation, reduplication, cancellation and displacement.

But if we were to build on these subjective givens alone—however little we free them from the condition of experience that makes us see them as partaking of the nature of a linguistic technique—our theoretical attempts would remain exposed to the charge of projecting themselves into the unthinkable of an absolute subject. This is why I have sought in the present hypothesis, grounded in a conjunction of objective data, the guiding grid for a *method of symbolic reduction*.

It establishes in the *defences of the ego* a genetic order, in accordance with the wish formulated by Miss Anna Freud,[10] in the first part of her great work, and situates (as against a frequently expressed prejudice) hysterical repression and its returns at a more archaic stage than obsessional inversion and its isolating processes, and the latter in turn as preliminary to paranoic alienation, which dates from the deflection of the specular *I* into the social *I*.

This moment in which the mirror-stage comes to an end inaugurates, by the identification with the *imago* of the counterpart and the drama of primordial jealousy (so well brought out by the school of Charlotte Bühler[11] in the phenomenon of infantile *transitivism*), the dialectic that will henceforth link the *I* to socially elaborated situations.

It is this moment that decisively tips the whole of human knowledge into mediatization through the desire of the other, constitutes its objects in an abstract equivalence by the co-operation of others, and turns the I into that apparatus for which every instinctual thrust constitutes a danger, even though it should correspond to a natural maturation—the very normalization of this maturation being henceforth dependent, in man, on a cultural mediation as exemplified, in the case of the sexual object, by the Oedipus complex.

In the light of this conception, the term primary narcissism, by which analytic doctrine designates the libidinal investment characteristic of that moment, reveals in those who invented it the most profound awareness of semantic latencies. But it also throws light on the dynamic opposition between this libido and the sexual libido, which the first analysts tried to define when they invoked destructive and, indeed, death instincts, in order to explain the evident connection between the narcissistic libido and the alienating function of the *I*, the aggressivity it releases in any relation to the other, even in a relation involving the most Samaritan of aid.

In fact, they were encountering that existential negativity whose reality is so vigorously proclaimed by the contemporary philosophy of being and nothingness.

But unfortunately that philosophy grasps negativity only within the limits of a self-sufficiency of consciousness, which, as one of its premises, links to the *méconnaissances* that constitute the ego, the illusion of autonomy to which it entrusts itself. This flight of fancy, for all that it draws, to an unusual extent, on borrowings from psychoanalytic experience, culminates in the pretension of providing an existential psychoanalysis.

At the culmination of the historical effort of a society to refuse to recognize that it has any function other than the utilitarian one, and in the anxiety of the individual confronting the 'concentrational'[12] form of the social bond that seems to arise to crown this effort, existentialism must be judged by the explanations it gives of the subjective impasses that have indeed resulted from it; a freedom that is never more authentic than when it is within the walls of a prison; a demand for commitment, expressing the impotence of a pure consciousness to master any situation; a voyeuristic-sadistic idealization of the sexual relation; a per-

---

[9]Hieronymus Bosch (c. 1462–1516), Flemish painter.
[10]Anna Freud (1895–1982), British child psychologist, daughter of Sigmund Freud.
[11]Charlotte Bühler (1893–1974), German psychologist.

[12][Sheridan] 'Concentrationnairre,' an adjective coined after World War II (this article was written in 1949) to describe the life of the concentration-camp. In the hands of certain writers it became, by extension, applicable to many aspects of 'modern' life.

sonality that realizes itself only in suicide; a consciousness of the other that can be satisfied only by Hegelian murder.

These propositions are opposed by all our experience, in so far as it teaches us not to regard the ego as centered on the *perception-consciousness system,* or as organized by the 'reality principle'—a principle that is the expression of a scientific prejudice most hostile to the dialectic of knowledge. Our experience shows that we should start instead from the *function of méconnaissance* that characterizes the ego in all is structures, so markedly articulated by Miss Anna Freud. For, if the *Verneinung*[13] represents the patent form of that function, its effects will, for the most part, remain latent, so long as they are not illuminated by some light reflected on to the level of fatality, which is where the id manifests itself.

We can thus understand the inertia characteristic of the formations of the *I,* and find there the most extensive definition of neurosis—just as the captation of the subject by the situation gives us the most general formula for madness, not only the madness that lies behind the walls of asylums, but also the madness that deafens the world with its sound and fury.

The sufferings of neurosis and psychosis are for us a schooling in the passions of the soul, just as the beam of the psychoanalytic scales, when we calculate the tilt of its threat to entire communities, provides us with an indication of the deadening of the passions in society.

At this junction of nature and culture, so persistently examined by modern anthropology, psychoanalysis alone recognizes this knot of imaginary servitude that love must always undo again, or sever.

For such a task, we place no trust in altruistic feeling, we who lay bare the aggressivity that underlies the activity of the philanthropist, the idealist, the pedagogue, and even the reformer.

In the recourse of subject to subject that we preserve, psychoanalysis may accompany the patient to the ecstatic limit of the *'Thou art that,'* in which is revealed to him the cipher of his mortal destiny, but it is not in our mere power as practitioners to bring him to that point where the real journey begins.

---

[13]*Verneinung:* negation.

Walter Benjamin

1892–1940

Walter Benjamin, who in 1940 took his own life in order to escape capture by the Nazis, was never an institutional critic, nor was his criticism limited to literature. Without institutional affiliation, he completed only one book, the now highly praised *Ursprung des deutschen Trauerspiels (The Origin of German Tragic Drama)*. The manuscript was rejected for a doctorate at Frankfurt in 1925 but published as a whole in 1928. Benjamin had connections with the later Frankfurt school of social critics, though this relationship was always ambivalent, as was his relation to Marxism. Theodor Adorno (below, page 1101) criticized Benjamin's views as static rather than dialectical and accused him of a retreat into metaphor.

The fact is that Benjamin was a *critic,* and as one he ranged far for subject matter and remained open to many insights from many intellectual quarters. His acquaintance among intellectuals included Bertolt Brecht and Gershom Scholem. He knew both Marxism and Kabbalah. Though he identifies himself in the selection below with historical materialism, he seems generally wary of any theory that might harden into oppressive form. Historians should not try to blot out the past that intervenes between them and the past events they study. Rather than redemption of the future, Benjamin desires redemption of the dead. Historical materialism "supplies a unique experience with the past," that is, it sees the past in its own perspective. This view, though connected, is somewhat different from that taken up by later critics, who see interpretation as always a negotiation between present and past. Benjamin's view embraces the notion of class struggle, and his aim is to free history of the story imposed by those in power. The critic, for Benjamin, is never removed from the social moment, never above the scene of conflict, and to think one is is a dangerous delusion. Thus, he is wary of any single all-encompassing theory.

Benjamin's range can be seen by comparing the selection below and his Marxist essay "The Author as Producer" with the earlier "On Language as Such and On the Language of Man." The last reveals his knowledge of a tradition of thinking about language that grew out of Kant and romanticism. One even finds some affinities with Heidegger (below, page 1051). He does not flinch from considering language in the light of what the Bible tells us about it, even if he is deeply suspicious of any view claiming transcendence.

A translation of *The Origin of German Tragic Drama* was published in 1977. *Illuminations* and *Reflections* came out in 1969 and 1978 respectively. See especially Hannah Arendt's introductory essay in *Illuminations* and Geoffrey H. Hartman, *Criticism in the Wilderness* (1980), 63–85. Of the large amount of more recent work, see Michael W. Jennings, *Dialectical Images* (1987); John McCole, *Walter Benjamin and the Antinomies of Tradition* (1993); Richard Wolin, *Walter Benjamin, an Aesthetics of Redemption* (1994); David S. Ferris, *Walter Benjamin: Theoretical Questions* (1996); Michael

P. Steinberg, *Walter Benjamin and the Demands of History* (1996); Laura Marcus and Lynda Nead, eds., *The Actuality of Walter Benjamin* (1998); Lutz Koepnick, *Walter Benjamin and the Aesthetics of Power* (1999); Carol Jacobs, *In the Language of Walter Benjamin* (1999).

Theses on the Philosophy of History

I

The story is told of an automation constructed in such a way that it could play a winning game of chess, answering each move of an opponent with a countermove. A puppet in Turkish attire and with a hookah in its month sat before a chessboard placed on a large table. A system of mirrors created the illusion that this table was transparent from all sides. Actually, a little hunchback who was an expert chess player sat inside and guided the puppet's hand by means of strings. One can imagine a philosophical counterpart to this device. The puppet called "historical materialism" is to win all the time. It can easily be a match for anyone if it enlists the services of theology, which today, as we know, is wizened and has to keep out of sight.

II

"One of the most remarkable characteristics of human nature," writes Lotze,[1] "is, alongside so much selfishness in specific instances, the freedom from envy which the present displays toward the future." Reflection shows us that our image of happiness is thoroughly colored by the time to which the course of our own existence has assigned us. The kind of happiness that could arouse envy in us exists only in the air we have breathed, among people we could have talked to, women who could have given themselves to us. In other words, our image of happiness is indissolubly bound up with the image of redemption. The same applies to our view of the past, which is the concern of history. The past carries with it a temporal index by which it is referred to redemption. There is a secret agreement between past generations and the present one. Our coming was expected on earth. Like every generation that preceded us, we have been endowed with a *weak* Messianic power, a power to which the past has a claim. That claim cannot be settled cheaply. Historical materialists are aware of that.

III

A chronicler who recites events without distinguishing between major and minor ones acts in accordance with the following truth: nothing that has ever happened should be regarded as lost for history. To be sure, only a redeemed mankind receives the fullness of its past—which is to say, only for a redeemed mankind has its past become citable in all its moments. Each moment it has lived becomes a *citation a l'ordre du jour*[2]—and that day is Judgment Day.

IV

Seek for food and clothing first, then the Kingdom of God shall be added unto you.

—HEGEL, 1807[3]

The class struggle, which is always present to a historian influenced by Marx,[4] is a fight for the crude and material things without which no refined and spiritual things could exist. Nevertheless, it is not in the form of the spoils which fall to the victor that the latter make their presence felt in the class struggle. They manifest themselves in this struggle as courage, humor, cunning, and fortitude. They have retroactive force and will constantly call in question every victory, past and present, of the rulers. As flowers turn toward the sun, by dint of a secret heliotropism the past strives to turn toward that sun which is rising in the sky of history. A historical materialist must be aware of this most inconspicuous of all transformations.

"Theses on the Philosophy of History" is reprinted from *Illuminations* by Walter Benjamin, Harry Zohn, tr. (New York: Schocken Books, 1969).
[1] Rudolph Hermann Lotze (1817–1881), German philosopher and psychologist, who attempted to reconcile the principles of romanticism with mechanistic science.

---

[2] "Summons to the order of the day."
[3] Hegel (above, page 552).
[4] Marx (above, page 607).

V

The true picture of the past flits by. The past can be seized only as an image which flashes up at the instant when it can be recognized and is never seen again. "The truth will not run away from us": in the historical outlook of historicism these words of Gottfried Keller[5] mark the exact point where historical materialism cuts through historicism. For every image of the past that is not recognized by the present as one of its own concerns threatens to disappear irretrievably. (The good tidings which the historian of the past brings with throbbing heart may be lost in a void the very moment he opens his mouth.)

VI

To articulate the past historically does not mean to recognize it "the way it really was" (Ranke).[6] It means to seize hold of a memory as it flashes up at a moment of danger. Historical materialism wishes to retain that image of the past which unexpectedly appears to man singled out by history at a moment of danger. The danger affects both the content of the tradition and its receivers. The same threat hangs over both: that of becoming a tool of the ruling classes. In every era the attempt must be made anew to wrest tradition away from a conformism that is about to overpower it. The Messiah comes not only as the redeemer, he comes as the subduer of Antichrist. Only that historian will have the gift of fanning the spark of hope in the past who is firmly convinced that *even the dead* will not be safe from the enemy if he wins. And this enemy has not ceased to be victorious.

VII

Consider the darkness and the great
     cold
In this vale which resounds with
     mystery.

BRECHT, *THE THREEPENNY OPERA*[7]

To historians who wish to relive an era, Fustel de Coulanges[8] recommends that they blot out everything they know about the later course of history. There is no better way of characterizing the method with which historical materialism has broken. It is a process of empathy whose origin is the indolence of the heart, *acedia,* which despairs of grasping and holding the genuine historical image as it flares up briefly. Among medieval theologians it was regarded as the root cause of sadness. Flaubert, who was familiar with it, wrote: *"Peu de gens devineront combien il a fallu être triste pour ressusciter Carthage."*[9] The nature of this sadness stands out more clearly if one asks with whom the adherents of historicism actually empathize. The answer is inevitable: with the victor. And all rulers are the heirs of those who conquered before them. Hence, empathy with the victor invariably benefits the rulers. Historical materialists know what that means. Whoever has emerged victorious participates to this day in the triumphal procession in which the present rulers step over those who are lying prostrate. According to traditional practice, the spoils are carried along in the procession. They are called cultural treasures, and a historical materialist views them with cautious detachment. For without exception the cultural treasures he surveys have an origin which he cannot contemplate without horror. They owe their existence not only to the efforts of the great minds and talents who have created them, but also to the anonymous toil of their contemporaries. There is no document of civilization which is not at the same time a document of barbarism. And just as such a document is not free of barbarism, barbarism taints also the manner in which it was transmitted from one owner to another. A historical materialist therefore dissociates himself from it as far as possible. He regards it as his task to brush history against the grain.

VIII

The tradition of the oppressed teaches us that the "state of emergency" in which we live is not the exception but the rule. We must attain to a conception of history that is in keeping with this insight. Then we shall clearly realize that it is our task to bring about a real state of emergency, and this will improve our position in the struggle against Fascism. One reason why Fascism has a chance is that in the name of progress its opponents treat it as a historical norm. The current amazement that the things we are experiencing are "still" possible in the twentieth century is *not* philosophical. This amazement is not the beginning of knowledge—

---

[5]Gottfried Keller (1819–1890), Swiss novelist, short-story writer, and poet.
[6]Leopold von Ranke (1795–1886), German historian.
[7]Bertolt Brecht (1898–1956), German dramatist.
[8]Numa Denis Fustel de Coulanges (1830–1889), French historian who argued against the presumed German origins of feudalism and the manorial system in favor of primarily Roman influences.

---

[9][Zohn] "Few will be able to guess how sad one had to be in order to resuscitate Carthage."

unless it is the knowledge that the view of history which gives rise to it is untenable.

IX

Mein Flügel ist zum Schwung bereit,
ich kehrte gern zurück,
denn blieb ich auch lebendige Zeit,
ich hätte wenig Glück.
　　　—Gerhard Scholem, "Gruss vom Angelus"[10]

A Klee[11] painting named "Angelus Novus" shows an angel looking as though he is about to move away from something he is fixedly contemplating. His eyes are staring, his mouth is open, his wings are spread. This is how one pictures the angel of history. His face is turned toward the past. Where we perceive a chain of events, he sees one single catastrophe which keeps piling wreckage upon wreckage and hurls it in front of his feet. The angel would like to stay, awaken the dead, and make whole what has been smashed. But a storm is blowing from Paradise; it has got caught in his wings with such violence that the angel can no longer close them. This storm irresistibly propels him into the future to which his back is turned, while the pile of debris before him grows skyward. This storm is what we call progress.

X

The themes which monastic discipline assigned to friars for meditation were designed to turn them away from the world and its affairs. The thoughts which we are developing here originate from similar considerations. At a moment when the politicians in whom the opponents of Fascism had placed their hopes are prostrate and confirm their defeat by betraying their own cause, these observations are intended to disentangle the political worldlings from the snares in which the traitors have entrapped them. Our consideration proceeds from the insight that the politicians' stubborn faith in progress, their confidence in their "mass basis," and, finally, their servile integration in an uncontrollable apparatus have been three aspects of the same thing. It seeks to convey an idea of the high price our accustomed thinking will have to pay for a conception of history that avoids any complicity with the thinking to which these politicians continue to adhere.

XI

The conformism which has been part and parcel of Social Democracy from the beginning attaches not only to its political tactics but to its economic views as well. It is one reason for its later breakdown. Nothing has corrupted the German working class so much as the notion that it was moving with the current. It regarded technological developments as the fall of the stream with which it thought it was moving. From there it was but a step to the illusion that the factory work which was supposed to tend toward technological progress constituted a political achievement. The old Protestant ethics of work was resurrected among German workers in secularized form. The Gotha Program[12] already bears traces of this confusion, defining labor as "the source of all wealth and all culture." Smelling a rat, Marx countered that ". . . the man who possesses no other property than his labor power" must of necessity become "the slave of other men who have made themselves the owners. . . ." However, the confusion spread, and soon thereafter Josef Dietzgen[13] proclaimed: "The savior of modern times is called work. The . . . improvement . . . of labor constitutes the wealth which is now able to accomplish what no redeemer has ever been able to do." This vulgar-Marxist conception of the nature of labor bypasses the question of how its products might benefit the workers while still not being at their disposal. It recognizes only the progress in the mastery of nature, not the retrogression of society; it already displays the technocratic features later encountered in Fascism. Among these is a conception of nature which differs ominously from the one in the Socialist utopias before the 1848 revolution. The new conception of labor amounts to the exploitation of nature, which with naïve complacency is contrasted with the exploitation of the proletariat. Compared with this positivistic conception, Fourier's[14] fantasies, which have so often been ridiculed, prove to be surprisingly sound. According to Fourier, as a result of efficient cooperative labor, four moons would illuminate the earthly night, the ice would recede from the poles, sea water would no longer taste salty, and beasts of prey would do man's bidding. All this illustrates a kind of labor which, far from exploiting nature, is capable of delivering her of the creations which lie dormant in her womb as potentials. Nature, which, as Dietzgen puts it, "exists gratis," is a complement to the corrupted conception of labor.

---

[10]Gershom Gerhard Scholem (1897–1982), Jewish scholar and professor. "My wing is ready for flight, / I would like to turn back. / If I stayed timeless time, / I would have little luck."
[11]Paul Klee (1879–1940), Swiss painter.

[12]The Gotha Congress of 1875 united two socialist parties, one led by Marx, who later attacked the Program.
[13]Josef Dietzgen (1828–1888), German philosopher.
[14]Charles Fourier (1772–1837), French socialist thinker.

XII

We need history, but not the way a spoiled loafer in the garden of knowledge needs it.
—NIETZSCHE, *OF THE USE AND ABUSE OF HISTORY*[15]

Not man or men but the struggling, oppressed class itself is the depository of historical knowledge. In Marx it appears as the last enslaved class, as the avenger that completes the task of liberation in the name of generations of the downtrodden. This conviction, which had a brief resurgence in the Spartacist group,[16] has always been objectionable to Social Democrats. Within three decades they managed virtually to erase the name of Blanqui,[17] though it had been the rallying sound that had reverberated through the preceding century. Social Democracy thought fit to assign to the working class the role of the redeemer of future generations, in this way cutting the sinews of its greatest strength. This training made the working class forget both its hatred and its spirit of sacrifice, for both are nourished by the image of enslaved ancestors rather than that of liberated grandchildren.

XIII

Every day our cause becomes clearer and people get smarter.
—WILHELM DIETZGEN, *DIE RELIGION DER SOZIALDEMOKRATIE*

Social Democratic theory, and even more its practice, have been formed by a conception of progress which did not adhere to reality but made dogmatic claims. Progress as pictured in the minds of Social Democrats was, first of all, the progress of mankind itself (and not just advances in men's ability and knowledge). Secondly, it was something boundless, in keeping with the infinite perfectibility of mankind. Thirdly, progress was regarded as irresistible, something that automatically pursued a straight or spiral course. Each of these predicates is controversial and open to criticism. However, when the chips are down, criticism must penetrate beyond these predicates and focus on something that they have in common. The concept of the historical progress of mankind cannot be sundered from the concept of its progression through a homogeneous, empty time. A critique of the concept of such a progression must be the basis of any criticism of the concept of progress itself.

XIV

Origin is the goal.
—KARL KRAUS,[18] *WORTE IN VERSEN*, Vol. I

History is the subject of a structure whose site is not homogeneous, empty time, but time filled by the presence of the now [*Jetztzeit*].[19] Thus, to Robespierre[20] ancient Rome was a past charged with the time of the now which he blasted out of the continuum of history. The French Revolution viewed itself as Rome reincarnate. It evoked ancient Rome the way fashion evokes costumes of the past. Fashion has a flair for the topical, no matter where it stirs in the thickets of long ago; it is a tiger's leap into the past. This jump, however, takes place in an arena where the ruling class gives the commands. The same leap in the open air of history is the dialectical one, which is how Marx understood the revolution.

XV

The awareness that they are about to make the continuum of history explode is characteristic of the revolutionary classes at the moment of their action. The great revolution introduced a new calendar. The initial day of a calendar serves as a historical time-lapse camera. And, basically, it is the same day that keeps recurring in the guise of holidays, which are days of remembrance. Thus the calendars do not measure time as clocks do; they are monuments of a historical consciousness of which not the slightest trace has been apparent in Europe in the past hundred years. In the July revolution an incident occurred which showed this consciousness still alive. On the first evening of fighting it turned out that the clocks in towers were being fired on simultaneously and independently from several places in Paris. An eye-witness, who may have owed his insight to the rhyme, wrote as follows:

> Qui le croirait! on dit, qu'irrités contre l'heure
> De nouveaux Josués au píed de chaque tour,
> Tiraient sur les cadrans pour arrêter le jour.[21]

---

[15] Nietzsche (above, page 686).
[16] A Leftist group founded at the beginning of World War I, later absorbed by the Communist Party.
[17] Auguste Blanqui (1805–1881), French socialist.
[18] Karl Kraus (1874–1936), Austrian writer.
[19] [Zohn] Benjamin says "jetztzeit" and indicates by the quotation marks that he does not simply mean an equivalent to *Gegenwart,* that is, present. He clearly is thinking of the mythical *nunc stans.*
[20] Maximillien Robespierre (1759–1794), French revolutionary.
[21] [Zohn] "Who would have believed it! We are told that new Joshuas / at the foot of every tower, as though irritated with / time itself, fired at the dials in order to stop the day."

XVI

A historical materialist cannot do without the notion of a present which is not a transition, but in which time stands still and has come to a stop. For this notion defines the present in which he himself is writing history. Historicism gives the "eternal" image of the past; historical materialism supplies a unique experience with the past. The historical materialist leaves it to others to be drained by the whore called "Once upon a time" in historicism's bordello. He remains in control of his powers, man enough to blast open the continuum of history.

XVII

Historicism rightly culminates in universal history. Materialistic historiography differs from it as to method more clearly than from any other kind. Universal history has no theoretical armature. Its method is additive; it musters a mass of data to fill the homogeneous, empty time. Materialistic historiography, on the other hand, is based on a constructive principle. Thinking involves not only the flow of thoughts, but their arrest as well. Where thinking suddenly stops in a configuration pregnant with tensions, it gives that configuration a shock, by which it crystallizes into a monad. A historical materialist approaches a historical subject only where he encounters it as a monad. In this structure he recognizes the sign of a Messianic cessation of happening, or, put differently, a revolutionary chance in the fight for the oppressed past. He takes cognizance of it in order to blast a specific era out of the homogeneous course of history—blasting a specific life out of the era or a specific work out of the lifework. As a result of this method the lifework is preserved in this work and at the same time canceled;[22] in the lifework, the era; and in the era, the entire course of history. The nourishing fruit of the historically understood contains time as a precious but tasteless seed.

---

[22]The Hegelian term *aufheben* in its threefold meaning: to preserve, to elevate, to cancel.

XVIII

"In relation to the history of organic life on earth," writes a modern biologist, "the paltry fifty millennia of *homo sapiens* constitute something like two seconds at the close of a twenty-four-hour day. On this scale, the history of civilized mankind would fill one-fifth of the last second of the last hour." The present, which, as a model of messianic time, comprises the entire history of mankind in an enormous abridgment, coincides exactly with the stature which the history of mankind has in the universe.

A

Historicism contents itself with establishing a causal connection between various moments in history. But no fact that is a cause is for that very reason historical. It became historical post-humously, as it were, through events that may be separated from it by thousands of years. A historian who takes this as his point of departure stops telling the sequence of events like the beads of a rosary. Instead, he grasps the constellation which his own era has formed with a definite earlier one. Thus he establishes a conception of the present as the "time of the now" which is shot through with chips of Messianic time.

B

The soothsayers who found out from time what it had in store certainly did not experience time as either homogeneous or empty. Anyone who keeps this in mind will perhaps get an idea of how past times were experienced in remembrance—namely, in just the same way. We know that the Jews were prohibited from investigating the future. The Torah and the prayers instruct them in remembrance, however. This stripped the future of its magic, to which all those succumb who turn to the soothsayers for enlightenment. This does not imply, however, that for the Jews the future turned into homogeneous, empty time. For every second of time was the strait gate through which the Messiah might enter.

William Carlos Williams

1883–1963

For virtually all of his professional career, poet William Carlos Williams practiced medicine in his hometown of Rutherford, New Jersey, while also maintaining very active alliances with artists, musicians, and small magazine publishers in New York City and elsewhere. In addition to publishing more than thirty-five volumes of poetry, short stories, plays, and novels, Williams published numerous critical essays addressed particularly to the theory of the imagination. Throughout his career, Williams was devoted to the idea of the universality of the local, attending with scrupulous detail to the sources and roots of life that are unique to a place. His collection of historical sketches, *In the American Grain* (1925), offers a profoundly imaginative reinterpretation, sometimes a reinhabitation of historical documents, experimentally displaced, in an effort to follow the contours of American experience as a series of encounters between the old and the new. Early in his career, he carried out numerous literary experiments, such as *Kora in Hell* (1920), composed of brief entries, written sometimes on prescription pads, collected over the course of a year, and then revised, with added commentaries; or *Spring and All* (1924), composed of interspersed poetry and prose, developing as he goes a far-reaching theory of imagination as a force of renewal, always attending precisely to what is closest at hand. His most ambitious work, *Paterson* (1946–1963), originally in four books with an added fifth and notes for a sixth, is a metamorphic local epic, following the course of the Passaic River, through Paterson to the Atlantic coast, modeled roughly on James Joyce's *Finnegans Wake,* as the dream of mythic figures who walk up and down through their local domains. The essay selected for inclusion here, "Against the Weather: A Study of the Artist," originally published in 1939 in *Twice-A-Year,* was an invited essay on the brink of war. Williams was a lifelong admirer of Walt Whitman, and this essay follows generally in the line of Whitman's speculations in *Democratic Vistas* (above, page 674), though Williams frames his essay with the figure of the artist attending to and confronting his "weather," always local, and always calling for an immediate response. On the first page of the essay, Williams offers a sentence written "with all the art I can muster" that is demonstrably easy to misread, asserting, not as many readers expect, that a work of art creates a new world, but rather, that "A work of art is important only as evidence, in its structure, of a new world which it has been created to affirm." Williams's position is that the world has no choice but always to be new, at each moment, and that the artist's work is affirmation of that world. His conclusion calls attention to the importance of close attention to the art, the *techne* of construction to ensure that "the best thought is built newly, in a comprehensive form of the day, into the structure of the work." Williams was posthumously awarded the Pulitzer Prize in poetry in 1963 for his *Pictures from Breughel and Other Poems* (1962).

New Directions, Williams's career-long publisher, has reissued over the last decade most of his books in new, frequently augmented editions. Especially important are *The

Collected Poems, Volumes I & II (1986); *Paterson* (1992); *Imaginations* (1971), containing *Kora in Hell, Spring and All, The Great American Novel, The Descent of Winter,* and *A Novelette and Other Prose; In the American Grain* (1956); and *Pictures from Breughel and Other Poems* (1967). Also important is his *Selected Essays* (1954). Critical and biographical studies include: Reed Whittemore, *William Carlos Williams, Poet from New Jersey* (1975); Bram Dijkstra, *Cubism, Steiglitz, and the Early Poetry of William Carlos Williams* (1978); David Frail et al., *The Early Politics and Poetics of William Carlos Williams* (1987); Thomas Whitaker, *William Carlos Williams,* rev. ed. (1989); T. Hugh Crawford, *Modernism, Medicine, and William Carlos Williams* (1993); Brian Bremen, *William Carlos Williams and the Diagnostics of Culture* (1993); Helen Deese et al., *Critical Essays on William Carlos Williams* (1994); John Beck, *Writing the Radical Center: William Carlos Williams, John Dewey, and American Cultural Politics* (2001).

Against the Weather

A Study of the Artist

What should the artist be today? What must he be? What can he do? To what purpose? What does he effect? How does he function? What enters into it? The economic, the sociological: how is he affected? How does his being a man or a woman, one of a certain race, an American enter into it?

If there were more air smelling of the crispness, the chill, the faint flowerless odor of ice and sunlight that reigns here, March 9, 1938, in the neighborhood of New York City today—I could do, and under like circumstances could always have done, any imaginable thing that might unreasonably be or has been expected of a man. But all days are not like today nor is my mind of a consequence always so moved. Quite the contrary.

I've been writing a sentence, with all the art I can muster. Here it is: A work of art is important only as evidence, in its structure, of a new world which it has been created to affirm.

Let me explain.

A life that is here and now is timeless. That is the universal I am seeking: to embody that in a work of art, a new world that is always "real."

All things otherwise grow old and rot. By long experience the only thing that remains unchanged and unchangeable is the work of art. It is because of the element of time-lessness in it, its sensuality. The only world that exists is the world of the senses. The world of the artist.

That is the artist's work. He might well be working at it during a bombardment, for the bombardment will stop. After a while they will run out of bombs. Then they will need something to fall back on: today. Only the artist can invent it. Without today everything would be lost and they would have to start bombing again as they always do, to hide the lack. If the artist can finish before the attack is over it will be lucky. He is the most important artisan they have.

The work an artist has to do is the most important creation of civilization. It is also its creator.

It is a world of men.

It is not an "essence," a philosophic or physiochemical derivative I am seeking but a sensual "reality." Though it *might* be war, it had better be a work of art.

The artist is to be understood not as occupying some outlying section of the field of action but the whole field, at a different level howbeit from that possessed by grosser modes. The artist is to be conceived as a universal man of action—restricted by circumstances to a field in which only he can remain alive, whole and effective. He is the most effective of all men, by test of time, in proving himself able to resist circumstances and bring the load through. Dig up his carvings in the center of the Sahara Desert, where there was once a lake and forests, his effectiveness remains intact.

He differs from the philosopher in point of action. He is the whole man, not the breaker up but the compactor. He does not translate the sensuality of his materials into symbols but deals with them directly. By this he belongs to his world and time, sensually, realistically. His work might and finally must be expanded—holds the power of expansion at any time—into new conceptions of government. It is not the passive "to be" but the active "I am."

"Against the Weather: A Study of the Artist" was first published in *Twice-A-Year* (1939) and is reprinted from William Carlos Williams, *Selected Essays* (New York: New Directions, 1954).

Being an artist I can produce, if I am able, universals of general applicability. If I succeed in keeping myself objective enough, sensual enough, I can produce the factors, the concretions of materials by which others shall understand and so be led to use—that they may the better see, touch, taste, enjoy—their own world *differing as it may* from mine. By mine, they, different, can be discovered to be the same as I, and, thrown into contrast, will see the implications of a general enjoyment through me.

That—all my life I have striven to emphasize it—is what is meant by the universality of the local. From me where I stand to them where they stand in their here and now—where I cannot be—I do in spite of that arrive! through their work which complements my own, each sensually local.

This is the generosity also of art. It closes up the ranks of understanding. It shows the world at one with itself. And it solves, it is the solvent—or it can be—of old antagonisms. It is theoretical, as opposed to philosophy, most theoretical when it is most down on the ground, most sensual, most real. Picking out a flower or a bird in detail that becomes an abstract term of enlightenment.

This paper is full of electricity, I can hardly pick it up or lay it down.

Another characteristic of all art is its compactness. It is not, at its best, the mirror—which is far too ready a symbol. It is the life—but transmuted to another tighter form.

The compactness implies restriction but does not mean loss of parts; it means compact, restricted to essentials. Neither does it mean the extraction of a philosophic essence. The essence remains in the parts proper to life, in all their sensual reality.

The grossly active agent of the moment, possessing the government, less whole than the artist, usually a party—that is to say partial or a part—tries to break the artist from his complete position to make him serve an incomplete function. And the *way* they attack him in order to make him serve their purpose is to accuse him of being inactive or reserved to the aesthetic. To which he can have only one answer which is to be active, to practice his unnicked art. For this they will kill him proving his point—and if they have not been successful in destroying all he has done, which is unlikely, he will end by destroying them.

The extreme example of the principle of sabotage as practiced by parties upon the arts was the destruction of the library at Alexandria. So valuable was the work of the artist there that to this day we unglue the backs of old books and even pick apart the lids of sarcophagi in order to find perhaps one line of Sappho.

What does the artist do? And what has the world of varying events to do with what he does? He attacks, con-

stantly toward a full possession of life by himself as a man. Those who possess the world will have it their way but in the conceit of the artist, generous enough, the actual and necessary government occupies only an incomplete segment of that which is just, in the full sense, and possible.

The artist is, by that, called very often a revolutionist and is threatened, as it may be Shakespeare was threatened by the Protestant power, which he had to please being himself a Papist. At the same time *he wrote plays.* And if, in *The Tempest,* he approached the ideology of his bringing up, during his full intervening years *he still wrote plays.* That is the artist, the man of action, as laid against the man of ideas.

Imagine a world without the effects of art. Take it ten years before Shakespeare wrote a play or Dante placed on paper his *Divina Commedia.* Such a world might well be and was in either case governed by laws, but what should be the general applicability of them if it had not been for works of art existing earlier? Without conceptions of art the world might well be and has usually been a shambles of groups lawful enough but bent upon nothing else than mutual destruction. This comes of their partiality. They lack that which must draw them together—without destruction of their particular characteristics; the thing that will draw them together because in their disparateness it discovers an identity. Nowhere will this be found save in the sensual, the real, world of the arts.

Every masterwork liberates while it draws the world closer in mutual understanding and tolerance. This is its aroma of the whole. For these are the pure characteristics, in tremendous concentration, of the work itself, made, demonstrated, as imitated in the laboratory, in which we believe so much today, by the trivial artist. It is the cement of the sensual world. Or even less destructible, it is more the cementless joining itself of the parts, as in the examples of Inca masonry.

As the world is unimaginable without the effects of art—that is to say without art there would be no Chartres, no Parthenon, no *Oedipus Rex,* no pyramids, *Matthew's Passion, Divina Commedia, Quixote* or *Lear*—which make it one, so a man walks the streets but he is none without the agency of the artist. He may be a "soul" or a "citizen," a "member of the party," an example of certain philosophic concepts in operation or one of the genus *Homo sapiens* but a MAN—lacking art—never! Only that preserves him in his full sensuality, the man himself.

And today, after the same fashion, he is everything imaginable. There are a hundred names and might just as well be five hundred or a thousand—and the reasons one way or the other are often logical (Why not?), cogent, inevitable and overwhelming. But it has an effect, this positivity. It blinds! It deafens, confuses and destroys. Catholic or Protestant can never be more than half a man in the eyes of the artist—each in himself "perfect." A man, to be, emerges through them into a region common to both. He knows them by what they *do*—in relation to each other—to make up the whole.

2

These are some conditions an artist must face and react to: There are two great Spanish epics that illustrate this life of man preserved in the arts. They will serve as examples. Both the *Poema del Cid*[1] and the *Book of Love*[2] are distinguished and live by what is called the "ethical detachment" of the poet exhibited there. He, the poet, saw a specific action, he experienced and he recorded, as a man of sense, directly after the deed without preconception.

The poet saw a sword flash! It lit the field. He did not see a CASTILIAN sword flash or a MOORISH sword flash. He saw a SWORD flash. The effect of that flashing did not immediately concern either Spain or Arabia, it concerned a man. The sword rose or it fell and the work was done or missed. The poet recorded it with a power that took it out of the partial, a power which derived from his passion as an artist to know, in full. This is good.

With the author of the *Libro de Buen Amor,* the fat archpriest of Hita the same. His work was not war but love, love of God and love of women—almost indistinguishable to the poet though he made ample gestures both ways. But the *poem* was the thing—this was his good—as he confesses very clearly. He came, this amorous archpriest, of a time when Moslem, Christian and Jew mingled, as it has been said, in one great fraternity of mirth and pleasure, whatever ends each otherwise was also seeking. They mingled without prejudice, a resemblance to the conditions of art. They mingled and *El Libro de Buen Amor* took it up and lives.

A more complex example than the *Book of Love,* Dante's *Divina Commedia* throws into even greater relief this compelling force which takes possession of a man and causes him to act in a certain manner producing works of art—its conditions and significances. In the *Book of Love,* untouched by morals, the artist's impulse carries the day un-

opposed. But the *Divina Commedia* presents three facts, the moral, that of formal religion and that other whose character, in itself, I wish to define. The comment of the artist illuminates the other two—a good place to witness it at work. Dante upon Dante.

Full stop.

Nothing is under consideration but the artist's concern in these things, enlightenment upon the artist's significance. And the reason for going into such seemingly remote matters (as the poetry of Dante) in the search for present-day solutions is the question of origins. As writers we shall find in writing our most telling answers and as writers it is we who should uncover them. That is our business. If, as writers, we are stuck somewhere, along with others, we must go back to the place, if we can, where a blockage may have occurred. We must go back in established writing, as far as necessary, searching out the elements that occur there. We must go to the bottom.

If we suspect that, in past writing, archaic forms give the significance a false cast we are under an obligation to go back to that place where the falsity clings and whence it works. We must unravel it to the last shred; nothing is more important, nothing must stand in the way and no time that is taken to it could be better spent. We have to dig. For by repeating an early misconception it gains acceptance and may be found running through many, or even all, later work. It has to be rooted out at the site of its first occurrence.

We know that what we are seeking, as writing, lies in the form or in the substance or both, of what is before us. It lies there undeciphered but active, malevolent it may be, and from it steam up the forces which are obstructing the light. Furthermore it is quite likely to be defended under the title of "beauty."

It is distinctly important that in the face of "beauty" we go in and expose the lesion. Nothing could be more timely. If we do not take the time for it but think to press on to more advanced matters we leave a basis for destruction in our rear. While we are using the old forms we unwittingly do ourselves a damage if they carry over within them that which undermines our own enlightened effectiveness.

The first and obvious contrast between the *Book of Love* and the *Commedia* is the scrupulous order maintained throughout the latter both in content and structure as against the carefree disorder of the Spanish work. One is closely clipt within ascertained bounds while the other runs away, going along from point to point, like a child picking flowers under a hedge.

This is very bad, this looseness, according to one of the major tenets of art, conscious restriction to prescribed form, and very good according to another—unconfined accep-

---

[1] *Poema del Cid,* also known as *Cantar de Mio Cid,* a twelfth-century Castilian epic poem, celebrating the life and exploits of Rodrigo Díaz de Vivar (1043–1099), a nobleman and military leader who became a Spanish national hero.

[2] *Book of Love* or *Libro de Buen Amor,* completed about 1330, by Juan Ruiz (1283–c. 1350), a poet and clergyman, who served as archpriest in the village of Hita.

tance of experience. Close order makes for penetration. Looseness is likely to prove weakness, having little impact upon the mind. But it is wise, always, to beware of that sort of order which cuts away too much.

The *Divina Commedia* has since the twelfth century exerted a lasting influence on Western poetry. What sort of influence? Good or bad? Which of the characters it presents has been the most influential? What of it relates to the art and how much masks under the colors of art and to other effect?

This begins to give an inkling of what, to the artist, is meant, as Rembrandt might conceivably have used the term, by "the great tradition"—an inkling of what is good and what is evil relating to his world by which he lives and acts beyond the aesthetic in his person as an artist.

Good and evil are the conjoint theme of the *Divina Commedia,* full of prejudice as between the blessed and the damned and structurally full of the mystical forms of religious ritual—in which it closely resembles Gothic architecture. But it is also a great work of art in that the same lack of ethical prejudice prevails as in the *Book of Love.* The blessed and the damned are treated by Dante, the *artist,* with scrupulous impartiality. The drawing is the same, the intense application toward veracity, the same meticulous care for "the good" whether in heaven or hell, the same address toward the truth—throughout its gamut.

I am comparing two poetical works of diverse character to discover wherein the practices of the artist are significant. These works are not arbitrarily chosen but represent two casts of thought stemming from them which stand confronting each other also today.

But my purpose in contrasting these works is the opposite of an attempt to weigh one against the other. Rather I want to draw out the same metal from both to see what its influence there is and has been.

Both the *Commedia* and the *Libro de Buen Amor* have love as their theme, earthly and heavenly. But earthly love, in its own right (Paolo and Francesca) is condemned in the *Commedia* and celebrated to the full in the *Book*—free to the winds.

Dante restricts, the archpriest expands. Dante fastened upon his passion a whole hierarchy of formal beliefs. The fat priest slighted the formality of his beliefs in favor of the sensual thing itself to its full length and breadth.

In the structure of their works will stand revealed that they, as artists, conceived of their material. In the structure the artist speaks as an artist purely. There he cannot lie. The artist as a man of action perpetuates his deed and records himself as a reality in the structure of his work—for which the content is merely useful.

The artist addresses himself to life as a whole. By reason of this he is constantly questioned and attacked. He is attacked by the closed lobbies of thought, those who have special solutions. Those who wish to halt the mutations of truth under a single aegis fixing it to a complexion of their private manufacture in search of a way through to order as against the modern lostness and distress.

But the general reason for our distress seems to be that we are stopped in our tracks by the dead masquerading as life. We are stopped by the archaic lingering in our laboring forms of procedure—which interested parties, parts, having or getting the power will defend with explosives—seeking to prevent the new life from generating in the decay of the old.

Those who see it one way call it the defense of tradition. Others see tradition belied in that tradition once was new—now only a wall.

In Dante and the fat archpriest of Hita, two artists look at good and evil; as artist they agree, unbiased. Dante condemned not only usurers and murderers to hell but lovers also unless formally blest. Yet as an artist he seems to pity Paolo and Francesca by the grace with which he has portrayed them.

To the other there are no barriers, only a glowing at the center which extends in all directions equally, resembling in that the grace of Paradise. To Dante the passion was restricted by the narrow corset of the times, the *Commedia* by its constriction to a set of special symbols standing to lose much of its availability as time passes and knowledge increases. Their harsh, restrictive and archaic nature approaches the malevolent today—in face of the great tradition.

There is likely to prove as time passes more good in the *Book of Love* than could ever be contained in Dante's *Paradiso.* That is why the *Paradiso* is so much weaker than the *Inferno.* The artist is belied there. There Dante set himself to limit virtue by a set of narrow symbols.

Just what is wrong with the *Paradiso* becomes clearer when the whole place of the sensual artist in sacred works is better understood. Pan is the artist's patron. How have morality and the Church compromised to bring him in and be saved? It is an unnatural alliance. The structure of the work must reveal it. The structure shows this struggle between the artist and his material, to wrestle his content out of the narrow into the greater meaning.

Dante was the agent of art facing a time and place and enforcement which were his "weather." Taking this weather as his starting point, as an artist, he had to deal with it to affirm that which to him was greater than it. By his structure he shows this struggle.

All I say is that the artist's is the great master pattern which all others approach and that in this Dante and the archpriest are the same. The moral good and bad approach the good and bad of the arts. Formal patterns of all sorts represent arrests of the truth in some particular phase of its mutations, and immediately thereafter, unless they change, become mutilations.

The great pattern is difficult to approach: This is the principal objective of a work of art—to maintain this against the weather of the other conditions—so that though they warp and bend it the effect will be still the supersedure of that above these effects.

And so when a life approaches the conditions of art we have clement weather, when it recedes from them the weather is vile and tormented.

The absolute is art with its sharp distinction of good and bad, the great tradition; nothing is wholly good which has no place for every part.

Dante was a craftsman of supreme skill, his emphasis upon a triple unity is an emphasis upon structure. All his elements are in threes. In the solid structure of the Spaniard, far less skillfully made, it is important to note the flat-footed quadruple rhyme scheme as opposed to the unfinished three of the Italian dogmatist. The emphasis is upon structure, the sensual structure of the verse.

Without such sensuality the dogmatism of the *Commedia* would have killed all attempts at a work of art—as it limits it and, except for the skill of the artist (had the faintest prejudice intervened), would have submerged it. It is only as the artist has clung fast to his greatness in sensual portrayal, without influence from the content of his work, that he is able to give the content whatever secondary value it possesses. The real significance of the *Commedia* today is that it is a work of art—its meaning shifting steadily with time more and more away from the smallness, the narrowness of special pressures of its dogmatic significance. Just as the whole Renaissance has a flavor of fading dogmatism about it, perversion—which the artist leaning upon Hellenic originals—rescued sacrilegiously while painting Christian models.

This must show somewhere in the structure. There is an undercurrent, a hidden—mystical!—quality about the whole Renaissance. This is the missing part that is not named. In the *Commedia,* Dante, like the painters, fused the two, the Hellenic and the mystic, but in doing so had to seem to sacrifice the wholeness which made pagan art universal, the charge of Pan whom the Church hates.

To realize these two in Dante, as typifying what the artist has to do, to sense the point of fusion and how it tortures the handling (as in El Greco), is to realize the in-evitable direction art took following the Renaissance. The archpriest, freed by geography from the dominance of Christian dogma, was closer to the artist of today than the abler Florentine.

Today is the day in question. Does the work of Dante instruct or maim today? He must be split and the artist rescued from the dogmatist first. When this is done he gives life, when we fail to do so he inspires death. The sunnier scatterings of the amorous archpriest at least manure the entire poetic field.

Look at the structure if you will truly grasp the significance of a poem. The dogmatist in Dante chose a triple multiple for his poem, the craftsman skilfully followed orders—but the artist?

Note that beginning with the first line of the *terza rima* at any given onset, every four lines following contain a dissonance. In the *Book of Love* four rhymes are continuous, one piled upon the next four in the manner of masonry. Throughout the *Commedia* this fourth unrhymed factor, unobserved, is the entrance of Pan to the Trinity which restores it to the candid embrace of love underlying the peculiar, faulty love of the great poem which makes remote, by virtue, that which possessed, illuminates the Spanish epic.

This fault, this celebration of denial, that enters into the archaic structure of the Renaissance as against the broader Hellenic which it copies, the necessities of art correct.

It is not until today that we see the full bearing of this, the elemental significance of the work of the supreme artist shouldering through the impediments of his time. For if the poem set out to punish the wicked and reward the virtuous, it had better have been on the basis of fulfilled love than unfulfilled.

All these things, all things relating to the world of art are to be unraveled, not to be swallowed whole with amazed eyes.

Both materials and structure have a meaning that is to be discovered, one in relation to the other, not in an esoteric, special sense but in a general sense hidden by the other, a full sense which the partial, selective sense seeks to hide and is put there to hide.

The natural corrective is the salutary mutation in the expression of all truths, the continual change without which no symbol remains permanent. It must change, it must reappear in another form, to remain permanent. It is the image of the Phoenix. To stop the flames that destroy the old nest prevents the rebirth of the bird itself. All things rot and stink, nothing stinks more than an old nest, if not recreated.

This is the essence of what art is expected to do and cannot live without doing. These are some conditions which an artist must face and react to.

3

How does this apply here, today?

Take America. When America became the escape for the restless and confined of Europe the significance, as a historic moment, was not guessed. It has never been clarified. The commonly accepted symbol for it, naturally enough, was "freedom," in which the sense of an escape from a tyrannical restriction was emphasized. This was inevitable and in the first flush of release seemed thoroughly justified, but it left a great deal to be desired.

Liberty is the better word. It was liberty they needed, not so much liberty for freedom's sake but liberty to partake of, to be included in and to conserve. Liberty, in this sense, has the significance of inclusion rather than a breaking away. It is the correct sense for the understanding of America, a sense which the word has had difficulty to convey and which few properly interpret.

But to have liberty one must be first a man, cultured by circumstances to maintain oneself under adverse weather conditions as still part of the whole. Discipline is implied.

But freedom remained the commonly accepted and much copied cliché, implying lack of discipline, dispersion.

As a matter of fact, men and women isolated in Europe found each other here and banded together to resist official restrictions of the people to join on points of common agreement. The impulse was toward joint action. It was a drawing together.

The real character of the people became their joint and skilful resistance to the weather. Some broke away, but their leaders usually hanged those. They had banded together to resist it in Europe and, in a transmuted form, the same applied here. The real character of the people is not toward dispersion except as a temporary phase for the gathering of power, but to unite. To form a union. To work toward a common purpose—to resist the weather.

For what? On the principle that only in this way can that which is common, commonly possessed—be preserved among differences. Commonwealth Avenue was the center of Boston. The common persists among New England towns.

Man has only one enemy: the weather. It came to America, this philosophy, largely from the northern countries where the weather is bad. Being able to resist individually *taught them* to work toward a stronger union so that they could better resist as a whole. It comes from boats and the sea, from the north, through England to us. It is interesting that the Icelanders who lived in perishable ships should have been among the first to be governed by common councils. It came also from Norway.

There were certain effects.

Braddock[3] in Pennsylvania was advancing down a narrow, wooded road with his men in close formation. They were among the finest troops in the world. Suddenly being picked off panic-stricken from behind trees, they stampeded to the rear until Washington—whose advice had been earlier put to scorn—sick as he was, grabbed a horse, rode up and got his Americans out among the trees to fight the enemy at its own game. He gave each man his liberty, under orders, to look out for himself in open formation. The result was to save the day—to whatever extent it could be saved.

Later when Von Steuben,[4] trained in the army of Frederick the Great, came to drill the American troops at Valley Forge he was not blind to the advantages of certain native tactics. It was he who wrote the first American Manual at Arms, the *Army Blue Book.* When he did so he adopted from America the open formation, therefore unheard of, now the common usage of all armies of the world and likely to become more and more important as warfare progresses and trees get wings.

The weather changes and man adapts his methods that he may survive, one by one, in order to be there for agreements later. In this sense only is the artist an individualist. The whole material has shrunk back before attack into him. It is with him as with the Chinese today: the front has to be broken up and guerilla tactics adopted. Let them hunt us out individually and kill us one by one because we carry the destiny of united action within us, action on the plane of a whole man. Not to be alone for individual reasons but only in that it is sheer suicide to advance in phalanx and be destroyed. Disperse and survive.

The artist is the servant of need.

The need is to resist the cracking weather on all fronts. There is more destruction in a pleasant day than in a stormy one because the storm carries a greater emphasis of its intent. We live under attack by various parties against the whole. And all in the name of order! But never an order discovered in its living character of today, always an order imposed in the senseless image of yesterday—for a purpose of denial.

Parties exist to impose such governments. The result is inevitably to cut off and discard that part of the whole which does not come within the order they affect.

---

[3] Edward Braddock (1695–1755), British commander during the French and Indian Wars. Williams refers to Braddock's disastrous battle against the French at Fort Duquesne (the site of present-day Pittsburgh) in 1755. George Washington served under Braddock in that campaign.
[4] Frederick Wilhelm von Steuben (1730–1794), German officer and gentleman who was largely responsible for turning the American revolutionary brigades into a disciplined army.

By this it is to be observed that even the ordinary political mind finds important what the composition of a work of art may be. It must be measured to the same measure that the political situation calls for or suffer—by which its dangerous interest is made clear.

Then let those who would force the artist to conform to their party—in the broadest sense—but especially let such poets realize, such pretty orderists as seek to impose a fixed order from without, that the acts of today, the brutalities and bigotries of the various segmentary regimes are a direct moral consequence upon their own faithless acts of a generation previous. Of course their affectation is a faith! Faith! Since they are the betrayers of the great tradition nothing but to affect a faith (in *something*) will excuse them.

England has lopped off that Spain where loyalty to the dangerous present is assertive—a Spain that does not fit that "order" which conveniences her, just as Russia periodically lops off those men who do not convenience the party.

Chamberlain had to make a choice, black or white, to defend the best of English tradition fighting for its life in Spain or to defend the British Empire under Tory rule. He chose the latter. This is a choice no artist could make without sacrificing his status as an artist.

There is a sharp cleavage between the true and the false in art; that illustrates it.

The responsibility of the artist in face of the world is toward inclusion when others sell out to a party. Nations may be said to have to take what is and to be convenient liars for a purpose, because they have to do something and only by so doing can they exist. But the artist, for that very reason and all the more so because of it, can never be a liar. He has to perpetuate his trust on an unlying scale. If he fails, the character of his failure lies precisely there, his crime, for which I condemn him to the eighth circle of hell, dry rot. Of all moral hells that of the faithless artist is the worst since his responsibility is the greatest: as England murders Spanish babies, dextrously, behind the back of opinion, and censors the terrors of Disney's *Snow White* from its children.

This is the sort of thing an artist is incapable of performing.

The poet must see before and behind—if he will know what he sees in front of him or comprehend its significance—for the art forms of today open the way to the intelligence of tomorrow.

The understanding of Walt Whitman is after the same nature. Verse is measure, there is no free verse. *But* the measure must be one of more trust, greater liberty, than has been permitted in the past. It must be an open formation. Whitman was never able fully to realize the significance of his structural innovations. As a result he fell back to the overstuffed catalogues of his later poems and a sort of looseness that was not freedom but lack of measure. Selection, structural selection was lacking.

And so about a generation ago, when under the influence of Whitman the prevalent verse forms had gone to the free-verse pole, the countering cry of Order! Order! reawakened. That was the time of the new Anglo-Catholicism.

The result was predictable. Slash down the best life of the day to bring it into the lines of control.

It comes to this: Murder can't be murder—it has to be some special sort of murder—with a quasi-secret, cabalistic significance—not understood by everyone. It has to be murder *in the cathedral*—whose momentum is lost, at the full, except to the instructed few. And instructed poetry is all secondary in the exact sense that Dante's *Commedia* is secondary where it is archaic and fettered against a broad application of the great tradition. Nothing can be simply beautiful, it must be so beautiful that no one can understand it *except* by the assistance of the cult. It must be a "mystery."

Man is mysterious in his own right and does not submit to more than his common sensual relationships to "explain" him. Anything else approaches the trivial.

He is a man to be judged, to live or die, like other men by what he does. No symbolism is acceptable. No symbolism can be permitted to obscure the real purpose, to lift the world of the senses to the level of the imagination and so give it new currency. If the time can possess itself of such a man, such an actor, to make it aware of its own values to which through lack of imagination it remains blind, amorphous, it can gain such a momentum toward life that its dominance will be invincible.

The imagination is the transmuter. It is the changer. Without imagination life cannot go on, for we are left staring at the empty casings where truth lived yesterday while the creature itself has escaped behind us. It is the power of mutation which the mind possesses to rediscover the truth.

So that the artist is dealing with actualities not with dreams. But do not be deceived, there is no intention to depict the artist, the poet, as a popular leader in the Rousseauian sense. Rather he builds a structure of government using for this the materials of his verse. His objective is an order. It is through this structure that the artist's permanence and effectiveness are proven.

Judged equitably by the great tradition, of which the processes of art are the active front—obviously it is the artist's business to call attention to the imbecilities, the imperfections, the partialities as well as the excellence of his time.

Obviously—all defects are officially neglected by those in power; never studied or even mentioned—for clear reasons!

The trick is delay; to involve the mind in discussions likely to last a lifetime and so withdraw the active agent from performance. The answer is, an eye to judge.—When the deer is running between the birches one doesn't get out a sextant but a gun—a flash of insight with proof by performance—and let discussion follow. If the result is a work of art the effect is permanent.

Meanwhile twenty or thirty generations have died stupefied by it. The genius of the colored would have started singing it off before any one of them was twelve.

Obviously the trick of postponement needs to knock one leg from under the table so that it will wobble—to keep everyone scurrying about for a prop instead of sitting down at the table and eating. Finally they put a living caryatid in the form of a Mexican-Spanish-Russian-Chinese peasant under the loose corner to take the brunt of it on his shoulders while SOMEBODY gorges.

Why are we dull other than that the best minds are inoperative, blocked by the half minds.

Obviously—"It's *his* money and a man can do what he pleases with his own money." "He doesn't really *own* the money, my dear. After all, you must know *that*. It's really in all our pockets . . ." and "$500,000 may seem impressive to you but we are in the habit of dealing with a weekly balance of $35,000,000, or more, so that to me $500,000 might be something easily overlooked."

Obviously—a man of quite ordinary intelligence sees at once what is at stake. Somebody ought to offer a prize.

Obviously—the economic imbecilities of the age are reflected in everything save the artist's judgments:

The political, the social. Fascism is helpless without compromise with capital-credit just as Russia is the same. Both come out of the same pot. The revolution that will be a revolution is still to be made. It will have a complexion of the great tradition, cannot have any other, which capital-credit traduces in the name of "masterpieces," to them no more than conspicuous waste.

"What heavenly blue on those Gutenberg Bibles! We haven't anything like that nowadays."

Obviously—the Church sold out in 325 A.D. at the council of Nicaea. The writing shows it—the secrecy and all the rest of it when compared with the directness and clarity of the first century. Leo shows his good heart—or showed his good heart in the encyclical *Rerum Organum* addressed to Spain forty years ago, in which he warned of what was to happen, and has since happened! if the peasants were to be continually robbed as they were being robbed at that time

under the Church's dominion. Splendid! But it does not for a moment wipe out the systematic economic policy upon which the institution of which A. Vetti is the official head was founded.[5]

Invest in the N.Y. market and count on inside information to get your funds out before the crash without comment on the character of the market. These things are obviously marked with their origin.

Obviously every little cleric who happens to bleat and consider himself an artist because of his association with the Church has no title whatever to consider himself so for that reason. Rather the Church is likely to be a insuperable barrier today if the major function of the artist—to lift to the imagination and give new currency to the sensual world at our feet—is envisaged.

Obviously the artist cannot ignore the economic dominance in his time. He is all but suppressed by it—which should mean something—but never converted. On the contrary he attacks and his attack is basic, the only basic one.

It was not I or even my day that brought the Church into the discussion touching poetry but by their adoption of its authority, those seeking order from it, do not by that remove the question of its revelance there.

Modern painting and the State have divorced themselves from clerical alliances to good effect—good being the inclusive sweep of the great tradition. If poetry is to be tied into it anew it should show in the structural breadth of its receptors—not a narrowing lilt and a content of "mysteries."

All formal religions, in spite of their varieties, embrace one final and damning evil; founded on the immanence of a religious experience, they tend rather to be monopolies using religion to bring a man under an economic yoke of one sort or another for the perpetuation of a priesthood—largely predatory in character.

The simple teaching, "Give all thy goods to feed the poor" was in spite of great examples, such as that of St. Francis, turned into—the draining of every cent from the Russian serfs, the Mexican peon and the Spanish peasantry to their everlasting misery and impoverishment—murders, wars. No wonder they hate the Church.

When Chamberlain in England—while the poor man, poor in ways not to be more than half-guessed, starves—plays for the dominance of the banking class before the obvious dread that were Italy and Germany and Franco, *not*-triumphant England must, of necessity, reform her internal economy. To which the Church supported by the Bishop

---

[5] A. Vetti, not traced, but Williams appears to be speaking of the New York Stock Exchange.

Mannings of America in pay of those who have to build his heap of stone—sends out a large mouthed, Aye!

A curious anomaly is the suppression of the Jew for practical reasons—on borrowed ethical grounds—today in Germany as throughout past history. But a Jew as a Jew does not exist. He is a man, an oriental somewhat characterized by certain manners and physiologic peculiarities perhaps, but no different from any others in that. But a Jew as party to a tribal-religious cult is something else again. Judaism in *that* sense, he must not forget, is precisely the equivalent of *that* aspect of Fascism today.

Communism is the obverse of that facet. And in spite of the poetic and theoretical solidity of Marxist teaching the effects, so far, do not warrant unthinking obedience to it.

How will the artist show the side he has taken? as a man? By subjecting himself, like Lorca, to attack—to be dragged gutless through Granada and burned with his books on the public square? Or to be an exile like Thomas Mann?

All I say is that, unless all this is already in his writing—in the materials and structure of it—he might better have been a cowhand. The effect of the aristocratic revolution that the artist knows is necessary and intended—must be in his work, in the structure of his work. Everything else is secondary, but for the artist *that,* which has made all the greatest art one and permanent, that continual reassertion of structure, is first.

The mutability of the truth, Ibsen said it. Jefferson said it. We should have a revolution of some sort in America every ten years. The truth has to be redressed, re-examined, reaffirmed in a new mode. There has to be new poetry. But the thing is that the change, the greater material, the altered structure of the inevitable revolution must be *in* the poem, in it. Made of it. It must shine in the structural body of it.

There is a bookish quality too patent in Communism today, taken from a book that appears not to have been properly related to its object—man. Raw. And I'll back, as I regret, the faces of some of my young compatriots, with scars on their backs and faces, from policeman's fists and clubs, showing the part they have taken in strikes. They've seen the froth at the mouths of the men who club women in the belly with night sticks and seen how they bare their upper teeth as they attack. But—when I look at their poems, I wonder. The structure is weak.

The poet is a special sort of fool. He only has the one talent in most cases which can't be spent to effect but once.

Think of a work of art—a poem—as a structure. A form is a structure consciously adopted for an effect. How then can a man seriously speak of order when the most that he is doing is to impose a structural character taken over from the habits of the past upon his content? This is sheer bastardy. Where in that is the work, the creation which gives the artist his status as a man? And what is a man saying of moment as an artist when he neglects his major opportunity, to build his living, complex day into the body of his poem?

Unless he discovers and builds anew he is betraying his contemporaries in all other fields of intellectual realization and achievement and must bring their contempt upon himself and his fellow artists.

Who cares anything about propaganda, about alliances with the broad front of a life that seeks to assert itself in any age when lived to the hilt—unless the best thought is built newly, in a comprehensive form of the day, into the structure of the work? And if such a basis is accepted then, indeed, propaganda can be thoroughly welcomed. Built into the structure of a work, propaganda is always acceptable for by that it has been transmuted into the materials of art. It has no life unless to live or die judged by an artist's standards.

But if, imposing an exposed, a depleted, restrictive and unrealized form, the propagandist thinks he can make what he has to say convincing by merely filling in that wooden structure with some ideas he wants to put over—he turns up not only as no artist but a weak fool.

Whitman, a key man to whom I keep returning, was tremendously important in the history of modern poetry. But who has seen through his structure to a clear reason for his values and his limitations? No one that I have encountered. They begin to speak of his derivations, of his personal habits, of his putative children. For God's sake! He broke through the deadness of copied forms which keep shouting above everything that wants to get said today drowning out one man with the accumulated weight of a thousand voices in the past—re-establishing the tyrannies of the past, the very tyrannies that we are seeking to diminish. The structure of the old is active, it says no! to everything in propaganda and poetry that wants to say yes. Whitman broke through that. That was basic and good.

Kenneth Burke

1897–1993

Kenneth Burke was one of the most interesting, far-reaching, eclectic, and inquisitive critics of his age. He was a theory-builder whose theory was always in development. He has been compared to Coleridge for the breadth of his undertakings. Indeed there is some similarity in spite of the fact that Coleridge was an idealist and Burke was influenced by Marxist materialism, especially in his early book *Attitudes Toward History*. However, no particular philosophy or theory ever captured him. He was like Coleridge also in his tendency toward digressions and long footnotes, often more interesting than the part of the text to which they referred. Coleridge's plans for books often remained but plans. Burke's books were usually arguments put together from separate essays.

In addition to Marxism, Burke appropriated insights from anthropological studies of myth and ritual, psychology, psychoanalysis, and sociology; but he evaded attachment to any school. He was a friend of many of the New Critics, but his relation to that movement was only peripheral. As sociological criticism, Burke's work is more concerned with aesthetic questions than one would expect. As analytic criticism, it is more concerned with art as a social act than is that of the New Critics.

In "Literature as Equipment for Living," reprinted below, each work of art is "the addition of a word to an informal dictionary." Works of art are strategic namings of situations that enable one to gain control over things that assignment of a name brings. Sociological criticism should "codify the various strategies which artists have developed with relation to the naming of situations." Burke proposes a method of classification based on "social strategies," believing that the advantage of this would be to cut across previously established disciplines.

Burke's criticism is lively, even joyous, as if every connection he makes is a source of celebration. At the same time, he seems suspicious of any attempt to specialize critical practice or encompass it in a grand theory.

Among Burke's works are *Counter-Statement* (1931), *Permanence and Change* (1935), *Attitudes Toward History* (1937), *The Philosophy of Literary Form* (1941), *A Grammar of Motives* (1945), *A Rhetoric of Motives* (1950), *The Rhetoric of Religion* (1961), *Perspectives by Incongruity* (1964), *Terms for Order* (1964), and *Language as Symbolic Action* (1966). See George Knox, *Critical Moments* (1957); W. H. Rueckert, *Kenneth Burke and the Drama of Human Relations* (1963); W. H. Rueckert, ed., *Critical Responses to Kenneth Burke* (1969); M. E. Brown, *Kenneth Burke* (1969); Armin Paul Frank, *Kenneth Burke* (1969); Frank Lentricchia, *Criticism and Social Change* (1983); Grieg E. Henderson, *Kenneth Burke: Literature and Language as Symbolic Action* (1988); Stephen Bygrave, *Kenneth Burke: Rhetoric and Ideology* (1993); Ross Wolin, *The Rhetorical Imagination of Kenneth Burke* (2001).

Literature as Equipment for Living

Here I shall put down, as briefly as possible, a statement in behalf of what might be catalogued, with a fair degree of accuracy, as a *sociological* criticism of literature. Sociological criticism in itself is certainly not new. I shall here try to suggest what partially new elements or emphasis I think should be added to this old approach. And to make the "way in" as easy as possible, I shall begin with a discussion of proverbs.

I

Examine random specimens in *The Oxford Dictionary of English Proverbs.* You will note, I think, that there is no "pure" literature here. Everything is "medicine." Proverbs are designed for consolation or vengeance, for admonition or exhortation, for foretelling.

Or they name typical, recurrent situations. That is, people find a certain social relationship recurring so frequently that they must "have a word for it." The Eskimos have special names for many different kinds of snow (fifteen, if I remember rightly) because variations in the quality of snow greatly affect their living. Hence, they must "size up" snow much more accurately than we do. And the same is true of social phenomena. Social structures give rise to "type" situations, subtle subdivisions of the relationships involved in competitive and cooperative acts. Many proverbs seek to chart, in more or less homey and picturesque ways, these "type" situations. I submit that such naming is done, not for the sheer glory of the thing, but because of its bearing upon human welfare. A different name for snow implies a different kind of hunt. Some names for snow imply that one should not hunt at all. And similarly, the names for typical, recurrent social situations are not developed out of "disinterested curiosity," but because the names imply a command (what to expect, what to look out for).

To illustrate with a few representative examples:

Proverbs designed for consolation: "The sun does not shine on both sides of the hedge at once." "Think of ease, but work on." "Little troubles the eye, but far less the soul." "The worst luck now, the better another time." "The wind in one's face makes one wise." "He that hath lands hath quarrels." "He knows how to carry the dead cock home." "He is

not poor that hath little, but he that desireth much."

For vengeance: "At length the fox is brought to the furrier." "Shod in the cradle, barefoot in the stubble." "Sue a beggar and get a louse." "The higher the ape goes, the more he shows his tail." "The moon does not heed the barking of dogs." "He measures another's corn by his own bushel." "He shuns the man who knows him well." "Fools tie knots and wise men loose them."

Proverbs that have to do with foretelling: (The most obvious are those to do with the weather.) "Sow peas and beans in the wane of the moon, Who soweth them sooner, he soweth too soon." "When the wind's in the north, the skillful fisher goes not forth." "When the sloe tree is as white as a sheet, sow your barley whether it be dry or wet." "When the sun sets bright and clear, An easterly wind you need not fear. When the sun sets in a bank, A westerly wind we shall not want."

In short: "Keep your weather eye open": be realistic about sizing up today's weather, because your accuracy has bearing upon tomorrow's weather. And forecast not only the meteorological weather, but also the social weather: "When the moon's in the full, then wit's in the wane." "Straws show which way the wind blows." "When the fish is caught, the net is laid aside." "Remove an old tree, and it will wither to death." "The wolf may lose his teeth, but never his nature." "He that bites on every weed must needs light on poison." "Whether the pitcher strikes the stone, or the stone the pitcher, it is bad for the pitcher." "Eagles catch no flies." "The more laws, the more offenders."

In this foretelling category we might also include the recipes for wise living, sometimes moral, sometimes technical: "First thrive, and then wive." "Think with the wise but talk with the vulgar." "When the fox preacheth, then beware your geese." "Venture a small fish to catch a great one." "Respect a man, he will do the more."

In the class of "typical, recurrent situations" we might put such proverbs and proverbial expressions as: "Sweet appears sour when we pay." "The treason is loved but the traitor is hated." "The wine in the bottle does not quench thirst." "The sun is never the worse for shining on a dunghill." "The lion kicked by an ass." "The lion's share." "To catch one napping." "To smell a rat." "To cool one's heels."

By all means, I do not wish to suggest that this is the only way in which the proverbs could be classified. For instance, I have listed in the "foretelling" group the proverb, "When the fox preacheth, then beware your geese." But it could obviously be "taken over" for vindictive purposes. Or consider a proverb like, "Virtue flies from the heart of a mercenary man." A poor man might obviously use it either to console himself for being poor (the implication being, "Because I am poor in money I am rich in virtue") or to

"Literature as Equipment for Living" is reprinted from *The Philosophy of Literary Form* (Baton Rouge: Louisiana State University Press, 1941).

strike at another (the implication being, "When he got money, what else could you expect of him but deterioration?"). In fact, we could even say that such symbolic vengeance would itself be an aspect of solace. And a proverb like "The sun is never the worse for shining on a dunghill" (which I have listed under "typical recurrent situations") might as well be put in the vindictive category.

The point of issue is not to find categories that "place" the proverbs once and for all. What I want is categories that suggest their active nature. Here there is no "realism for its own sake." There is realism for promise, admonition, solace, vengeance, foretelling, instruction, charting, all for the direct bearing that such acts have upon matters of welfare.

II

Step two: Why not extend such analysis of proverbs to encompass the whole field of literature? Could the most complex and sophisticated works of art legitimately be considered somewhat as "proverbs writ large"? Such leads, if held admissible, should help us to discover important facts about literary organization (thus satisfying the requirements of technical criticism). And the kind of observation from this perspective should apply beyond literature to life in general (thus helping to take literature out of its separate bin and give it a place in a general "sociological" picture).

The point of view might be phrased in this way: Proverbs are *strategies* for dealing with *situations*. Insofar as situations are typical and recurrent in a given social structure, people develop names for them and strategies for handling them. Another name for strategies might be *attitudes*.

People have often commented on the fact that there are contrary *proverbs*. But I believe that the above approach to proverbs suggests a necessary modification of that comment. The apparent contradictions depend upon differences in *attitude*, involving a correspondingly different choice of *strategy*. Consider, for instance, the *apparently* opposite pair: "Repentance comes too late" and "Never too late to mend." The first is admonitory. It says in effect: "You'd better look out, or you'll get yourself too far into this business." The second is consolatory, saying in effect: "Buck up, old man, you can still pull out of this."

Some critics have quarreled with me about my selection of the word *strategy* as the name for this process. I have asked them to suggest an alternative term, so far without profit. The only one I can think of is *method*. But if *strategy* errs in suggesting to some people an overly *conscious* procedure, *method* errs in suggesting an overly *"methodical"* one. Anyhow, let's look at the documents:

Concise Oxford Dictionary: "Strategy: Movement of an army or armies in a campaign, art of so moving or disposing troops or ships as to impose upon the enemy the place and time and conditions for fighting preferred by oneself" (from a Greek word that refers to the leading of an army).

New English Dictionary: "Strategy: The art of projecting and directing the larger military movements and operations of a campaign."

André Cheron, *Traité complet d'Échecs: "On entend par stratégie les manoeuvres qui ont pour but la sortie et le bon arrangement des pièces."*[1]

Looking at these definitions, I gain courage. For surely, the most highly alembicated and sophisticated work of art, arising in complex civilizations, could be considered as designed to organize and command the army of one's thoughts and images, and to so organize them that one "imposes upon the enemy the time and place and conditions for fighting preferred by oneself." One seeks to "direct the larger movements and operations" in one's campaign of living. One "maneuvers," and the maneuvering is an "art."

Are not the final results one's "strategy"? One tries, as far as possible, to develop a strategy whereby one "can't lose." One tries to change the rules of the game until they fit his own necessities. Does the artist encounter disaster? He will "make capital" of it. If one is a victim of competition, for instance, if one is elbowed out, if one is willy-nilly more jockeyed against than jockeying, one can by the solace and vengeance of art convert this very "liability" into an "asset." One tries to fight on his own terms, developing a strategy for imposing the proper "time, place, and conditions."

But one must also, to develop a full strategy, be *realistic*. One must *size things up* properly. One cannot accurately know how things *will be,* what is promising and what is menacing, unless he accurately knows how things *are.* So the wise strategist will not be content with strategies of merely a self-gratifying sort. He will "keep his weather eye open." He will not too eagerly "read into" a scene an attitude that is irrelevant to it. He won't sit on the side of an active volcano and "see" it as a dormant plain.

Often, alas, he will. The great allurement in our present popular "inspirational literature," for instance, may be largely of this sort. It is strategy for easy consolation. It "fills a need," since there is always a need for easy consolation—and in an era of confusion like our own the need is especially keen. So people are only too willing to "meet a man halfway" who will *play down* the realistic naming of

---

[1] [Burke] *Complete Treatise on Chess.* "One understands by strategy the maneuvers which are designed for the attack and the grand arrangement of pieces."

our situation and *play up* such strategies as make solace cheap. However, I should propose a reservation here. We usually take it for granted that people who consume our current output of books on "How to Buy Friends and Bamboozle Oneself and Other People" are reading as *students* who will attempt applying the recipes given. Nothing of the sort. *The reading of a book on the attaining of success is in itself the symbolic attaining of that success.* It is *while they read* that these readers are "succeeding." I'll wager that, in by far the great majority of cases, such readers make no serious attempt to apply the book's recipes. The lure of the book resides in the fact that the reader, while reading it, is then living in the aura of success. What he wants is *easy* success; and he gets it in symbolic form by the mere reading itself. To attempt applying such stuff in real life would be very difficult, full of many disillusioning difficulties.

Sometimes a different strategy may arise. The author may remain realistic, avoiding too easy a form of solace—yet he may get as far off the track in his own way. Forgetting that realism is an aspect for foretelling, he may take it as an end in itself. He is tempted to do this by two factors: (1) an *ill-digested* philosophy of science, leading him mistakenly to assume that "relentless" naturalistic "truthfulness" is a proper end in itself, and (2) a merely *competitive* desire to outstrip other writers by being "more realistic" than they. Works thus made "efficient" by tests of competition internal to the book trade are a kind of academicism not so named (the writer usually thinks of it as the *opposite* of academicism). Realism thus stepped up competitively might be distinguished from the proper sort by the name of "naturalism." As a way of "sizing things up," the naturalistic tradition tends to become as inaccurate as the "inspirational" strategy, though at the opposite extreme.

Anyhow, the main point is this: A work like *Madame Bovary* (or its homely America translation, *Babbitt*),[2] is the strategic naming of a situation. It singles out a pattern of experience that is sufficiently representative of our social structure, that recurs sufficiently often *mutandis mutatis,* for people to "need a word for it" and to adopt an attitude towards it. Each work of art is the addition of a word to an informal dictionary (or, in the case of purely derivative artists, the addition of a subsidiary meaning to a word already given by some originating artist). As for *Madame Bovary,* the French critic Jules de Gaultier[3] proposed to add it to our *for-*

mal dictionary by coining the word "Bovarysme" and writing a whole book to say what he meant by it.

Mencken's book on *The American Language,*[4] I hate to say, is splendid. I console myself with the reminder that Mencken didn't write it. Many millions of people wrote it, and Mencken was merely the amanuensis who took it down from their dictation. He found a true "vehicle" (that is, a book that could be greater than the author who wrote it). He gets the royalties, but the job was done by a collectivity. As you read that book, you see a people who were up against a new set of typical recurrent situations, situations typical of their business, their politics, their criminal organizations, their sports. Either there were no words for these in standard English, or people didn't know them, or they didn't "sound right." So a new vocabulary arose, to "give us a word for it." I see no reason for believing that Americans are unusually fertile in word coinage. American slang was not developed out of some exceptional gift. It was developed out of the fact that new typical situations had arisen and people needed names for them. They had to "size things up." They had to console and strike, to promise and admonish. They had to describe for purposes of forecasting. And "slang" was the result. It is, by this analysis, simply *proverbs not so named,* a kind of "folk criticism."

III

With what, then, would "sociological criticism" along these lines be concerned? It would seek to codify the various strategies which artists have developed with relation to the naming of situations. In a sense, much of it would even be "timeless," for many of the "typical, recurrent situations" are not peculiar to our own civilization at all. The situations and strategies framed in Aesop's *Fables,* for instance, apply to human relations now just as fully as they applied in ancient Greece. They are, like philosophy, sufficiently "generalized" to extend far beyond the particular combination of events named by them in any one instance. They name an "essence." Or, as Korzybski[5] might say, they are on a "high level of abstraction." One doesn't usually think of them as "abstract," since they are usually so concrete in their stylistic expression. But they invariably aim to discern the "general behind the particular" (which would suggest that they are good Goethe).[6]

---

[2] By Gustave Flaubert (1821–1880), French novelist; by Sinclair Lewis (1885–1951), American novelist.
[3] Jules de Gaultier (1858–1942).

[4] H. L. Mencken (1880–1957), American editor and writer.
[5] Alfred Korzybski (1879–1950), American scientist and philosopher.
[6] Johann Wolfgang von Goethe (1749–1832), German poet.

The attempt to treat literature from the standpoint of situations and strategies suggests a variant of Spengler's notion of the "contemporaneous." By "contemporaneity" he meant corresponding stages of different cultures. For instance, if modern New York is much like decadent Rome, then we are "contemporaneous" with decadent Rome, or with some corresponding decadent city among the Mayas, etc. It is in this sense that situations are "timeless," "nonhistorical," "contemporaneous." A given human relationship may be at one time named in terms of foxes and lions, if there are foxes and lions about; or it may now be named in terms of salesmanship, advertising, the tactics of politicians, etc. But beneath the change in particulars, we may often discern the naming of the one situation.

So sociological criticism, as here understood, would seek to assemble and codify this lore. It might occasionally lead us to outrage good taste, as we sometimes found exemplified in some great sermon or tragedy or abstruse work of philosophy the same strategy as we found exemplified in a dirty joke. At this point, we'd put the sermon and the dirty joke together, thus "grouping by situation" and showing the range of possible particularizations. In his exceptionally discerning essay, *A Critic's Job of Work,* R. P. Blackmur says, "I think on the whole his (Burke's) method could be applied with equal fruitfulness to Shakespeare, Dashiell Hammett, or Marie Corelli."[7] When I got through wincing, I had to admit that Blackmur was right. This article is an attempt to say for the method what can be said. As a matter of fact, I'll go a step further and maintain: you can't properly put Marie Corelli and Shakespeare apart until you have first put them together. First genus, then differentia. The strategy in common is the genus. The *range* or *scale* or *spectrum* of particularizations is the differentia.

Anyhow, that's what I'm driving at. And that's why reviewers sometime find in my work "intuitive" leaps that are dubious as "science." They are not "leaps" at all. They are classifications, groupings, made on the basis of some strategic element common to the items grouped. They are neither more nor less "intuitive" than *any* grouping or classification of social events. Apples can be grouped with bananas as fruits, and they can be grouped with tennis balls as round. I am simply proposing, in the social sphere, a method of classification with reference to *strategies.*

The method has these things to be said in its favor: it gives definite insight into the organization of literary works; and it automatically breaks down the barriers erected about literature as a specialized pursuit. People can classify novels by reference to three kinds, eight kinds, seventeen kinds. It doesn't matter. Students patiently copy down the professor's classification and pass examinations on it, because the range of possible academic classifications is endless. Sociological classification, as herein suggested, would derive its relevance from the fact that it should apply both to works of art and to social situations outside of art.

It would, I admit, violate current pieties, break down current categories, and thereby "outrage good taste." But "good taste" has become *inert.* The classifications I am proposing would be *active.* I think that what we need is active categories.

These categories will lie on the bias across the categories of modern specialization. The new alignment will outrage in particular those persons who take the division of faculties in our universities to be an exact replica of the way in which God himself divided up the universe. We have had the philosophy of the being; and we have had the philosophy of the becoming. In contemporary specialization, we have been getting the philosophy of the bin. Each of these mental localities has had its own peculiar way of life, its own values, even its own special idiom for seeing, thinking, and "proving." Among other things, a sociological approach should attempt to provide a reintegrative point of view, a broader empire of investigation encompassing the lot.

What would such sociological categories be like? They would consider works of art, I think, as strategies for selecting enemies and allies, for socializing losses, for warding off evil eye, for purification, propitiation, and desanctification, consolation and vengeance, admonition and exhortation, implicit commands or instructions of one sort or another. Art forms like "tragedy" or "comedy" or "satire" would be treated as *equipments for living,* that size up situations in various ways and in keeping with correspondingly various attitudes. The typical ingredients of such forms would be sought. Their relation to typical situations would be stressed. Their comparative values would be considered, with the intention of formulating a "strategy of strategies," the "overall" strategy obtained by inspection of the lot.

[7]R. P. Blackmur (above, page 974); Dashiell Hammett (1894–1961), American mystery writer; Marie Corelli (1855–1924), British novelist.

Ernst Cassirer

1874–1945

Cassirer was a member of the so-called Marburg School of neo-Kantian philosophers in Germany, but had to leave the country to escape persecution by the Nazis. He came eventually to the United States, where he taught at Columbia University. He was a philosopher of science as well as one of culture and wrote one of the first books on Einstein's theory of relativity. Cassirer's *An Essay on Man,* written in America in English, is a development from his monumental three-volume *Philosophy of Symbolic Forms* (1923–1929). That earlier work was divided into studies of language, mythical thought, and the phenomenology of knowledge (the last covering the development of science). This and the *Essay* completed a movement, which included Von Humboldt (above, page 523), in the Kantian tradition from pure epistemology to the notion that our knowledge is always mediated by systems of symbols. These systems are the "symbolic forms" by which we constitute our reality. Language and mythical thinking, which for Cassirer is similar to Giambattista Vico's "poetic logic" (above, page 313), are the two basic forms, the interrelated sources of which are lost in prehistory. *An Essay on Man* includes chapters on history, religion, art, and science as symbolic forms. Cassirer's is an "anthropological" philosophy, and early in the *Essay* he remarks,

> Man cannot escape from his own achievement. He cannot but adopt the conditions of his own life. No longer in a merely physical universe, man lives in a symbolic universe. . . . He has so enveloped himself in linguistic forms, in archaic images, in mythical symbols or religious rites that he cannot see or know anything except by interposition of this artificial medium. His situation is the same in the theoretical as in the practical sphere.

In the chapter on art, Cassirer offers a discussion of the major theories of art beginning with an analysis of the history of imitation and the shift of emphasis from imitative to expressive theories early reflected in the writings of Rousseau and Goethe. He proceeds to a critique of various metaphysical and psychological theories, arguing that art is itself a "universe of discourse" or symbolic form with its own nature. He is critical of any division between expression and externalization, as in Benedetto Croce's *Aesthetic* (1900). Expression is properly the product of the artist's struggle with formal and material problems and is not prior to externalization in form (see Blake, above, page 447). He argues that art always tends toward the particular and sensuous and seeks to overcome the gap between subject and object, whereas language and science move toward abstraction and divide object from subject. This conclusion leads him to be critical of subjectivist theories or notions that art expresses the infinite. Though he eschews analogies between art and science offered by Zola (above, page 698) and the naturalists, he respects their practice of looking closely at actual experience. He holds that art is not an imitation but a discovery. Indeed, it is more than that; it constitutes and organizes our experience according to its own formal principles. It exists in a tension of Heraclitan opposition with the other symbolic forms.

However, for literary critics, Cassirer's view presents a problem. Except in a very few places he seems to ignore the fact that there is an art of language, and he tends to identify language with science and abstraction as if language followed the model proposed by logical positivism. (In the chapter excerpted below he distinguishes in one place between the "symbols of art and the linguistic terms of ordinary speech or writing," but he does not expand on this.) Yet both Vico and Humboldt clearly influenced Cassirer. Thus one must look back to Vico and then to certain critics who come after Cassirer (for example, Philip Wheelwright in *The Burning Fountain* [1954] and Frye [below, page 1136]) to find out how the identification of language with Cassirer's "mythical thought" came into literary criticism.

Cassirer has certain affinities with the American New Criticism in his contrast of poetry to science, his emphasis on particularity, his remarks about the structure of a poem, and his treatment of the question of belief, much discussed in early-twentieth-century criticism. For him, an important difference between art and the symbolization of mythical thinking is that the latter contains a strong element of naïve belief, while the artist's forms cause the work to differ from an extractable abstract content subject to empirical analysis. The New Critics, however, were probably not aware of Cassirer's work until late in their careers, and his thought in the end has more affinities with that of Frye, who argues that literature requires a criticism not derived from other disciplines but instead one appropriate to literature's unique nature.

Cassirer's neo-Kantian views separate him from the phenomenological tradition and from Heidegger, with whom he had a notorious debate; and he does not hold that language inevitably lies or fails to attain truth, as in some postmodernists. Rather, he sees symbolic forms as containers of what truth we can constitute as real according to the specific categories of each. As in Kant, things in themselves are unknowable.

Some of Cassirer's many works are *The Philosophy of Symbolic Forms* (1923–1929, tr. 1953–1957), *Language and Myth* (1925, tr. 1946), *Individual and Cosmos in the Philosophy of the Renaissance* (1927, tr. 1963), *The Platonic Renaissance in England and the School of Cambridge* (1932, tr. 1953), *The Philosophy of the Enlightenment* (1932, tr. 1951), *An Essay on Man* (1944), *Rousseau, Kant, Goethe* (1945), *The Myth of the State* (1946), *Symbol, Myth, and Culture: Essays of Ernst Cassirer, 1935–1945* (1979). See P. A. Schilpp, ed., *The Philosophy of Ernst Cassirer* (1949); Carl H. Hamburg, *Symbol and Myth: Studies in the Philosophy of Ernst Cassirer* (1956); Seymour Itzkoff, *Ernst Cassirer: Philosopher of Culture* (1977); John Michael Krois, *Cassirer, Symbolic Forms, and History* (1987); Ivan Strenski, *Four Theories of Myth in Twentieth-Century History: Cassirer, Eliade, Lévi-Strauss and Malinowski* (1987); Sylvia Ferretti, *Cassirer, Panofsky, and Warburg: Symbol, Art, and History* (tr. 1989); S. G. Lofts, *Ernst Cassirer: A "Repetition" of Modernity* (2000); Thora Ilin Bayer, *Cassirer's Metaphysics of Symbolic Forms* (2001).

from

An Essay on Man

Like all the other symbolic forms art is not the mere reproduction of a ready-made, given reality. It is one of the ways leading to an objective view of things and of human life. It is not an imitation but a discovery of reality. We do not, however, discover nature through art in the same sense in which the scientist uses the term *nature*. Language and science are the two main processes by which we ascertain and determine our concepts of the external world.[1] We must classify our sense perceptions and bring them under general notions and general rules in order to give them an objective meaning. Such classification is the result of a persistent effort toward simplification. The work of art in like manner implies such an act of condensation and concentration. When Aristotle wanted to describe the real difference between poetry and history he insisted upon this process. What a drama gives us, he asserts, is a single action ($\mu\acute{\iota}\alpha$ $\pi\rho\hat{\alpha}\xi\iota\varsigma$) which is a complete whole in itself, with all the organic unity of a living creature; whereas the historian has to deal not with one action but with one period and all that happened therein to one or more persons, however disconnected the several events may have been.[2]

In this respect beauty as well as truth may be described in terms of the same classical formula: they are "a unity in the manifold." But in the two cases there is a difference of stress. Language and science are abbreviations of reality; art is an intensification of reality. Language and science depend upon one and the same process of abstraction; art may be described as a continuous process of concretion.[3] In our scientific description of a given object we begin with a great number of observations which at first sight are only a loose conglomerate of detached facts. But the farther we proceed the more these individual phenomena tend to assume a definite shape and become a systematic whole. What science is searching for is some central features of a given object from which all its particular qualities may be derived. If a chemist knows the atomic number of a certain element he possesses a clue to a full insight into its structure and constitution. From this number he may deduce all the characteristic properties of the element. But art does not admit of this sort of

conceptual simplification and deductive generalization. It does not inquire into the qualities or causes of things; it gives us the intuition of the form of things. But this too is by no means a mere repetition of something we had before. It is a true and genuine discovery. The artist is just as much a discoverer of the forms of nature as the scientist is a discoverer of facts or natural laws. The great artists of all times have been cognizant of this special task and special gift of art. Leonardo da Vinci spoke of the purpose of painting and sculpture in the words *"saper vedere."*[4] According to him the painter and sculptor are the great teachers in the realm of the visible world. For the awareness of pure forms of things is by no means an instinctive gift, a gift of nature. We may have met with an object of our ordinary sense experience a thousand times without ever having "seen" its form. We are still at a loss if asked to describe not its physical qualities or effects but its pure visual shape and structure. It is art that fills this gap. Here we live in the realm of pure forms rather than in that of the analysis and scrutiny of sense objects or the study of their effects.

From a merely theoretical point of view we may subscribe to the words of Kant that mathematics is the "pride of human reason." But for this triumph of scientific reason we have to pay a very high price. Science means abstraction, and abstraction is always an impoverishment of reality. The forms of things as they are described in scientific concepts tend more and more to become mere formulae. These formulae are of a surprising simplicity. A single formula, like the Newtonian law of gravitation, seems to comprise and explain the whole structure of our material universe. It would seem as though reality were not only accessible to our scientific abstractions but exhaustible by them. But as soon as we approach the field of art this proves to be an illusion. For the aspects of things are innumerable, and they vary from one moment to another. Any attempt to comprehend them within a simple formula would be in vain. Heraclitus'[5] saying that the sun is new every day is true for the sun of the artist if not for the sun of the scientist. When the scientist describes an object he characterizes it by a set of numbers, by its physical and chemical constants. Art has not only a different aim but a different object. If we say of two artists that they paint "the same" landscape we describe our aesthetic experience very inadequately. From the point of view of art such a pretended sameness is quite illusory. We cannot speak of one and the same thing as the subject matter of both painters. For the artist does not portray or copy a

---

An Essay on Man. The selection is from "Art," Chapter 9 of *An Essay on Man* (New Haven: Yale University Press, 1944).
[1] In addition to the chapters mentioned in the headnote, Cassirer's book has several introductory chapters on symbolism.
[2] *Poetics* (above, page 57).
[3] See Blake (above, page 449).

---

[4] Leonardo da Vinci (1452–1519), Italian painter; "to know how to see."
[5] Heraclitus (fifth century B.C.), Greek philosopher.

certain empirical object—a landscape with its hills and mountains, its brooks and rivers. What he gives us is the individual and momentary physiognomy of the landscape. He wishes to express the atmosphere of things, the play of light and shadow. A landscape is not "the same" in early twilight, in midday heat, or on a rainy or sunny day. Our aesthetic perception exhibits a much greater variety and belongs to a much more complex order than our ordinary sense perception. In sense perception we are content with apprehending the common and constant features of the objects of our surroundings. Aesthetic experience is incomparably richer. It is pregnant with infinite possibilities which remain unrealized in ordinary sense experience. In the work of the artist these possibilities become actualities; they are brought into the open and take on a definite shape. The revelation of this inexhaustibility of the aspects of things is one of the great privileges and one of the deepest charms of art.

The painter Ludwig Richter[6] relates in his memoirs how once when he was in Tivoli as a young man he and three friends set out to paint the same landscape. They were all firmly resolved not to deviate from nature; they wished to reproduce what they had seen as accurately as possible. Nevertheless the result was four totally different pictures, as different from one another as the personalities of the artist. From this experience the narrator concluded that there is no such thing as objective vision, and that form and color are always apprehended according to individual temperament.[7] Not even the most determined champions of a strict and uncompromising naturalism could overlook or deny this factor. Émile Zola defines the work of art as *"un coin de la nature vu à travers un tempérament."*[8] What is referred to here as temperament is not merely singularity or idiosyncrasy. When absorbed in the intuition of a great work of art we do not feel a separation between the subjective and the objective worlds. We do not live in our plain commonplace reality of physical things, nor do we live wholly within an individual sphere. Beyond these two spheres we detect a new realm, the realm of plastic, musical, poetical forms; and these forms have a real universality. Kant distinguishes sharply between what he calls *"aesthetic* universality" and the "objective validity" which belongs to our local and scientific judgments.[9] In our aesthetic judgments, he

contends, we are not concerned with the object as such but with the pure contemplation of the object. Aesthetic universality means that the predicate of beauty is not restricted to a special individual but extends over the whole field of judging subjects. If the work of art were nothing but the freak and frenzy of an individual artist it would not possess this universal communicability. The imagination of the artist does not arbitrarily invent the forms of things. It shows us these forms in their true shape, making them visible and recognizable. The artist chooses a certain aspect of reality, but this process of selection is at the same time a process of objectification. Once we have entered into his perspective we are forced to look on the world with his eyes. It would seem as if we had never before seen the world in this peculiar light. Yet we are convinced that this light is not merely a momentary flash. By virtue of the work of art it has become durable and permanent. Once reality has been disclosed to us in this particular way, we continue to see it in this shape.

A sharp distinction between the objective and the subjective, the representative and the expressive arts is thus difficult to maintain. The Parthenon frieze or a Mass by Bach, Michelangelo's Sistine Chapel or a poem of Leopardi, a sonata of Beethoven or a novel of Dostoevski are neither merely representative nor merely expressive.[10] They are symbolic in a new and deeper sense. The works of the great lyrical poets—of Goethe or Hölderlin, of Wordsworth or Shelley—do not give us *disjecti membra poetae,* scattered and incoherent fragments of the poet's life.[11] They are not simply a momentary outburst of passionate feeling; they reveal a deep unity and continuity. The great tragic and comic writers on the other hand—Euripides and Shakespeare, Cervantes and Molière[12]—do not entertain us with detached scenes from the spectacle of life. Taken in themselves these scenes are but fugitive shadows. But suddenly we begin to see behind these shadows and to envisage a new reality. Through his characters and actions the comic and the tragic poet reveals his view of human life as a whole, of its greatness and weakness, its sublimity and its absurdity. "Art," wrote Goethe,

> does not undertake to emulate nature in its breadth and depth. It sticks to the surface of nat-

---

[6]Gustav Karl Ludwig Richter (1823–1884), German painter.

[7][Cassirer] I take this account from Heinrich Wölfflin's *Principles of Art History.*

[8]Zola (above, page 698). "A corner of nature seen through a temperament."

[9][Cassirer] In Kant's terminology the former is called *Gemeingültigkeit* whereas the latter is called *Allgemeingültigkeit*—a distinction that is difficult to render in corresponding English terms. For a systematic interpretation of the two terms see H. W. Cassirer, *A Commentary on Kant's "Critique of Judgment"* (London, 1938), pp. 190ff.

[10]Johann Sebastian Bach (1685–1750), German composer; Michelangelo Buonarroti (1475–1564), Italian artist; Giacomo Leopardi (1798–1837), Italian poet; Ludwig Beethoven (1770–1827), German composer; Fyodor Dostoyevsky (1821–1881), Russian novelist.

[11]Friedrich Hölderlin (1770–1843), German poet; Wordsworth (above, page 481); Shelley (above, page 537).

[12]Euripides (c. 480–406 B.C.), Greek dramatist; Shakespeare (1564–1616); Miguel de Cervantes Saavedra (1547–1616), Spanish novelist; Molière (Jean Baptiste Poquelin, 1622–1673), French dramatist.

ural phenomena; but it has its own depth, its own power; it crystallizes the highest moments of these superficial phenomena by recognizing in them the character of lawfulness, the perfection of harmonious proportion, the summit of beauty, the dignity of significance, the height of passion.[13]

This fixation of the "highest moments of phenomena" is neither an imitation of physical things nor a mere overflow of powerful feelings.[14] It is an interpretation of reality—not by concepts but by intuitions; not through the medium of thought but through that of sensuous forms.

From Plato to Tolstoy art has been accused of exciting our emotions and thus of disturbing the order and harmony of our moral life. Poetical imagination, according to Plato, waters our experience of lust and anger, of desire and pain, and makes them grow when they ought to starve with drought.[15] Tolstoy sees in art a source of infection. "Not only is infection," he says, "a sign of art, but the degree of infectiousness is also the sole measure of excellence in art."[16] But the flaw in this theory is obvious. Tolstoy suppresses a fundamental moment of art, the moment of form. The aesthetic experience—the experience of contemplation—is a different state of mind from the coolness of our theoretical and the sobriety of our moral judgment. It is filled with the liveliest energies of passion, but passion itself is here transformed both in its nature and in its meaning. Wordsworth defines poetry as "emotion recollected in tranquility."[17] But the tranquility we feel in great poetry is not that of recollection. The emotions aroused by the poet do not belong to a remote past. They are "here"—alive and immediate. We are aware of their full strength, but this strength tends in a new direction. It is rather seen than immediately felt. Our passions are no longer dark and impenetrable powers; they become, as it were, transparent. Shakespeare never gives us an aesthetic theory. He does not speculate about the nature of art. Yet in the only passage in which he speaks of the character and function of dramatic art the whole stress is laid upon this point. "The purpose of playing," as Hamlet explains, "both at the first and now, was and is, to hold as 'twere, the mirror up to nature; to show virtue her own feature, scorn her own image, and the very age and body of the time his form and pressure."[18] But the image of a passion is not the passion itself. The poet who represents a passion does not infect us with this passion. At a Shakespeare play we are not infected with the ambition of Macbeth, with the cruelty of Richard III, or with the jealousy of Othello. We are not at the mercy of these emotions; we look through them; we seem to penetrate into their very nature and essence. In this respect Shakespeare's theory of dramatic art, if he had such a theory, is in complete agreement with the conception of the fine arts of the great painters and sculptors of the Renaissance. He would have subscribed to the words of Leonardo da Vinci that *saper vedere* is the highest gift of the artist. The great painters show us the forms of outward things; the great dramatists show us the forms of our inner life. Dramatic art discloses a new breadth and depth of life. It conveys an awareness of human things and human destinies, of human greatness and misery, in comparison to which our ordinary existence appears poor and trivial. All of us feel, vaguely and dimly, the infinite potentialities of life, which silently await the moment when they are to be called forth from dormancy into the clear and intense light of consciousness. It is not the degree of infection but the degree of intensification and illumination which is the measure of the excellence of art.

If we accept this view of art we can come to a better understanding of a problem first encountered in the Aristotelian theory of catharsis. We need not enter here into all the difficulties of the Aristotelian term or into the innumerable efforts of the commentators to clear up these difficulties.[19] What seems to be clear and what is now generally admitted is that the cathartic process described by Aristotle does not mean a purification or a change in the character and quality of the passions themselves but a change in the human soul. By tragic poetry the soul acquires a new attitude toward its emotions. The soul experiences the emotions of pity and fear, but instead of being disturbed and disquieted by them it is brought to a state of rest and peace. At first sight this would seem to be a contradiction. For what Aristotle looks upon as the effect of tragedy is a synthesis of two moments which in real life, in our practical existence, exclude each other. The highest intensification of our emotional life is thought of as at the same time giving us a sense of repose. We live through all our passions feeling their full range and highest tension. But what we leave behind when passing the threshold of art is the hard pressure, the compulsion of our emotions. The tragic poet is not the slave but the master of his emotions; and he is able to transfer this mastery to the spectators. In his work we are not swayed and

---

[13] [Cassirer] Goethe, notes to a translation of Diderot's "Essai sur le peinture," *Werke* XLV, 260.

[14] Wordsworth's phrase (above, page 490).

[15] Plato, *Republic* (above, page 16).

[16] Tolstoy (above, page 757).

[17] Wordsworth's phrase (above, page 490).

[18] III, ii, 22–27.

[19] [Cassirer] For details see Jakob Bernays, *Zwei Abhandlungen über die Arostotelische Theorie des Dramas* (Berlin, 1880), and Ingram Bywater, *Aristotle on the Art of Poetry* (Oxford, 1909), pp. 152ff.

carried away by our emotions. Aesthetic freedom is not the absence of passions, not Stoic apathy, but just the contrary. It means that our emotional life acquires its greatest strength, and that in this very strength it changes its form. For here we no longer live in the immediate reality of things but in a world of pure sensuous forms. In this world all our feelings undergo a sort of transubstantiation with respect to their essence and their character. The passions themselves are relieved of their material burden. We feel their form and their life but not their encumbrance. The calmness of the work of art is, paradoxically, a dynamic, not a static calmness. Art gives us the motions of the human soul in all their depth and variety. But the form, the measure and rhythm, of these motions is not comparable to any single state of emotion. What we feel in art is not a simple or single emotional quality. It is the dynamic process of life itself—the continuous oscillation between opposite poles, between joy and grief, hope and fear, exultation and despair. To give aesthetic form to our passions is to transform them into a free and active state. In the work of the artist the power of passion itself has been made a formative power.

It may be objected that all this applies to the artist but not to ourselves, the spectators and auditors. But such an objection would imply a misunderstanding of the artistic process. Like the process of speech the artistic process is a dialogical and dialectic one. Not even the spectator is left to a merely passive role. We cannot understand a work of art without, to a certain degree, repeating and reconstructing the creative process by which it has come into being. By the nature of this creative process the passions themselves are turned into actions. If in real life we had to endure all those emotions through which we live in Sophocles' *Oedipus* or in Shakespeare's *King Lear* we should scarcely survive the shock and strain. But art turns all these pains and outrages, these cruelties and atrocities, into a means of self-liberation, thus giving us an inner freedom which cannot be attained in any other way.

The attempt to characterize a work of art by some particular emotional feature must, therefore, inevitably fail to do it justice. If what art tries to express is no special state but the very dynamic process of our inner life, then any such qualification could hardly be more than perfunctory and superficial. Art must always give us motion rather than mere emotion. Even the distinction between tragic and comic art is much more a conventional than a necessary one. It relates to the content and motives but not to the form and essence of art. Plato had long since denied the existence of these artificial and traditional boundaries. At the end of the *Symposium* he describes Socrates as engaged in a conversation with Agathon, the tragic poet, and Aristophanes, the comic poet.

Socrates compels the two poets to admit that the true tragedian is the true artist in comedy, and vice versa.[20] A commentary on this passage is given in the *Philebus.*[21] In comedy as well in tragedy, Plato maintains in this dialogue, we always experience a mixed feeling of pleasure and pain. In this the poet follows the rules of nature itself since he portrays "the whole comedy and tragedy of life." In every great poem—in Shakespeare's plays, in Dante's *Commedia,* in Goethe's *Faust*—we must indeed pass through the whole gamut of human emotions. If we were unable to grasp the most delicate nuances of the different shades of feeling, unable to follow the continuous variations in rhythm and tone, if unmoved by sudden dynamic changes, we could not understand and feel the poem. We may speak of the individual temperament of the artist, but the work of art, as such, has no special temperament. We cannot subsume it under any traditional psychological class concept. To speak of Mozart's[22] music as cheerful or serene, of Beethoven's as grave, somber, or sublime would betray an unpenetrating taste. Here too the distinction between tragedy and comedy becomes irrelevant. The question whether Mozart's *Don Giovanni* is a tragedy or an *opera buffa*[23] is scarcely worth answering. Beethoven's composition based on Schiller's[24] *Hymn to Joy* expresses the highest degree of exultation. But when listening to it we do not for a moment forget the tragic accents of the Ninth Symphony. All these contrasts must be present and they must be felt in their full strength. In our aesthetic experience they coalesce into one indivisible whole. What we hear is the whole scale of human emotions from the lowest to the highest note; it is the motion and vibration of our whole being. The greatest comedians themselves can by no means give us an easy beauty. Their work is often filled with great bitterness. Aristophanes is one of the sharpest and sternest critics of human nature; Moliére is nowhere greater than in his *Misanthrope* or *Tartuffe.* Nevertheless the bitterness of the great comic writers is not the acerbity of the satirist or the severity of the moralist. It does not lead to a moral verdict upon human life. Comic art possesses in the highest degree that faculty shared by all art, sympathetic vision. By virtue of this faculty it can accept human life with all its defects and foibles, its follies and vices. Great comic art has always been a sort of *encomium moriae,* a praise of folly. In comic perspective all things begin to take on a new face. We are perhaps never

---

[20] Agathon (c. 450–c. 400 B.C.), Aristophanes (c. 448–after 388 B.C.), Greek dramatists. [Cassirer] Plato, *Symposium,* 223 (Jowett translation).
[21] [Cassirer] *Philebus,* 48ff. (Jowett translation).
[22] Wolfgang Amadeus Mozart (1756–1791), Austrian composer.
[23] "Comic opera."
[24] Schiller (above, page 460).

nearer to our human world than in the works of a great comic writer—in Cervantes' *Don Quixote,* Sterne's *Tristram Shandy,* or in Dickens' *Pickwick Papers.*[25] We become observant of the minutest details; we see this world in all its narrowness, its pettiness, and silliness. We live in this restricted world, but we are no longer imprisoned by it. Such is the peculiar character of the comic catharsis. Things and events begin to lose their material weight; scorn is dissolved into laughter and laughter is liberation.

That beauty is not an immediate property of things that it necessarily involves a relation to the human mind, is a point which seems to be admitted by almost all aesthetic theories. In his essay *Of the Standard of Taste* Hume declares: "Beauty is no quality in things themselves: it exists merely in the mind which contemplates them."[26] But this statement is ambiguous. If we understand *mind* in Hume's own sense, and think of self as nothing but a bundle of impressions, it would be very difficult to find in such a bundle that predicate which we call beauty. Beauty cannot be defined by its mere *percipi,* as "being perceived"; it must be defined in terms of an activity of the mind, of the function of perceiving and by a characteristic direction of this function. It does not consist of passive percepts; it is a mode, a process of perceptualization. But this process is not merely subjective in character; on the contrary, it is one of the conditions of our intuition of an objective world. The artistic eye is not a passive eye that receives and registers the impression of things. It is a constructive eye, and it is only by constructive acts that we can discover the beauty of natural things. The sense of beauty is the susceptibility to the dynamic life of forms, and this life cannot be apprehended except by a corresponding dynamic process in ourselves.

To be sure, in the various aesthetic theories this polarity, which as we have seen is an inherent condition of beauty, has led to diametrically opposed interpretations. According to Albrecht Dürer the real gift of the artist is to "elicit" beauty from nature.[27] *"Denn wahrhaftig steckt die Kunst in der Natur, wer sie heraus kann reissen, der hat sie."*[28] On the other hand we find spiritualistic theories which deny any connection between the beauty of art and the so-called beauty of nature. The beauty of nature is understood as merely a metaphor. Croce thinks it sheer rhetoric to speak of a beautiful river or tree.[29] Nature to him

is stupid when compared with art; she is mute save when man makes her speak. The contradiction between these conceptions may perhaps be resolved by distinguishing sharply between organic beauty and aesthetic beauty. There are many natural beauties with no specific aesthetic character. The organic beauty of a landscape is not the same as that aesthetic beauty which we feel in the works of the great landscape painters. Even we, the spectators, are fully aware of this difference. I may walk through a landscape and feel its charms. I may enjoy the mildness of the air, the freshness of the meadows, the variety and cheerfulness of the coloring, and the fragrant odor of the flowers. But I may then experience a sudden change in my frame of mind. Thereupon I see the landscape with an artist's eye—I begin to form a picture of it. I have now entered a new realm—the realm not of living things but of "living forms." No longer in the immediate reality of things, I live now in the rhythm of spatial forms, in the harmony and contrast of colors, in the balance of light and shadow. In such absorption in the dynamic aspect of form consists the aesthetic experience.

II

All the controversies between the various aesthetic schools may in a sense be reduced to one point. What all these schools have to admit is that art is an independent "universe of discourse."[30] Even the most radical defenders of a strict realism who wished to limit art to a mimetic function alone have had to make allowance for the specific power of the artistic imagination. But the various schools differed widely in their evaluation of this power. The classical and neoclassical theories did not encourage the free play of imagination. From their point of view the imagination of the artist is a great but rather questionable gift. Boileau himself did not deny that, psychologically speaking, the gift of imagination is indispensable for every true poet.[31] But if the poet indulges in the mere play of this natural impulse and instinctive power, he will never achieve perfection. The poet's imagination must be guided and controlled by reason and subjected to its rules. Even when deviating from the natural the poet must respect the laws of reason, and these laws restrict him to the field of the probable. French classicism defined this field in purely objective terms. The dramatic unities of space and time became physical facts measurable by a linear standard or by a clock.[32]

---

[25]Laurence Sterne (1713–1768), Charles Dickens (1812–1870), English novelists.

[26]Hume (above, page 324).

[27]Albrecht Dürer (1471–1528), German artist.

[28][Cassirer] "For art standeth firmly fixed in nature—and who can rend her from thence, he only possesseth her." See William N. Conway, *Literary Remains of Albrecht Dürer* (1889), p. 182.

[29]Croce, *Aesthetic,* Chapter 13.

[30]Or symbolic form.

[31]Nicolas Boileau-Despréaux (1636–1710), *Art of Poetry.*

[32]See Castelvetro (above, page 176), Corneille (above, page 244).

An entirely different conception of the character and function of poetic imagination was introduced by the Romantic theory of art. This theory is not the work of the so-called "romantic school" in Germany. It had been developed much earlier and had begun to play a decisive role in both French and English literature during the eighteenth century. One of the best and most concise expressions of this theory is to be found in Edward Young's *Conjectures on Original Composition* (1759). "The pen of an original writer," says Young, "like Armida's wand out of a barren waste calls a blooming spring."[33] From this time on the classical views of the probable were supplanted more and more by their opposite. The marvelous and miraculous are now believed to be the only subjects that admit of true poetical portraiture. In eighteenth-century aesthetics we can trace step by step the rise of this new ideal. The Swiss critics Bodmer and Breitinger appeal to Milton in justification of the "wonderful in poetry."[34] The wonderful gradually outweighs and eclipses the probable as a literary subject. The new theory seemed to be embodied in the works of the greatest poets. Shakespeare himself had illustrated it in his description of the poet's imagination.

> The lunatic, the lover, and the poet
> Are of imagination all compact.
> One sees more devils than vast hell can hold,
> That is the madman; the lover, all as frantic,
> Sees Helen's beauty in a brow of Egypt.
> The poet's eye, in a fine frenzy rolling,
> Doth glance from heaven to earth, from earth to heaven;
> And, as imagination bodies forth
> The forms of things unknown, the poet's pen
> Turns them to shapes, and gives to airy nothing
> A local habitation and a name.[35]

Yet the Romantic conception of poetry found no solid support in Shakespeare. If we stood in need of proof that the world of the artist is not a merely "fantastic" universe, we could find no better, no more classical, witness than Shakespeare. The light in which he sees nature and human life is no mere "fancy light in fancy caught." But there is still another form of imagination with which poetry seems to be indissolubly connected. When Vico made his first systematic attempt to create a "logic of the imagination" he turned back

to the world of myth.[36] He speaks of three different ages: the age of gods, the age of heroes, and the age of man. It is in the two former ages, he declared, that we have to look for the true origin of poetry. Mankind could not begin with abstract thought or with a rational language. It had to pass through the era of the symbolic language of myth and poetry. The first nations did not think in concepts but in poetic images; they spoke in fables and wrote in hieroglyphs. The poet and the maker of myth seem, indeed, to live in the same world. They are endowed with the same fundamental power, the power of personification. They cannot contemplate any object without giving to it an inner life and a personal shape. The modern poet often looks back at the mystical, the "divine" or "heroic" ages, as at a lost paradise. In his poem *The Gods of Greece* Schiller expressed this feeling. He wished to recall the times of the Greek poets, for whom myth was not an empty allegory but a living power. The poet yearns for this golden age of poetry in which all things were still full of gods, in which every hill was the dwelling place of an oread, every tree the home of a dryad.

But this complaint of the modern poet appears to be unfounded. For it is one of the greatest privileges of art that it can never lose this "divine age." Here the source of imaginative creation never dries up, for it is indestructible and inexhaustible. In every age and in every great artist the operation of the imagination reappears in new forms and in new force. In the lyrical poets, first and foremost, we feel this continuous rebirth and regeneration. They cannot touch a thing without imbuing it with their own inner life. Wordsworth has described this gift as the inherent power of his poetry:

> To every natural form, rock, fruits or flower,
> Even the loose stones that cover the highway,
> I gave a moral life: I saw them feel,
> Or linked them to some feeling: the great mass
> Lay imbedded in a quickening soul, and all
> That I beheld respired with inward meaning.[37]

But with these powers of invention and of universal animation we are only in the anteroom of art. The artist must not only feel the "inward meaning" of things and their moral life, he must externalize his feelings. The highest and most characteristic power of artistic imagination appears in this latter act. Externalization[38] means visible or tangible embodiment not simply in a particular material medium—

---

[33] Young (above, page 349).
[34] [Cassirer] Bodmer and Breitinger, *Discurs der Maler* (1721–1723). John Milton (1608–1674), English poet.
[35] *A Midsummer Night's Dream* V, I, 7–17.

[36] See Vico (above, page 313).
[37] *The Prelude*, 111, 127–132.
[38] Croce, *Aesthetic*, Chapter 15.

in clay, bronze, or marble—but in sensuous forms, in rhythms, in color pattern, in lines and design, in plastic shapes. It is the structure, the balance and order, of these forms which affect us in the work of art. Every art has is own characteristic idiom, which is unmistakable and unexchangeable. The idioms of the various arts may be interconnected, as, for instance, when a lyric is set to music or a poem is illustrated; but they are not translatable into each other. Each idiom has a special task to fulfill in the "architectonic" of art. "The problems of form arising from this architectonic structure," states Adolf Hildebrand,

> though they are not given us immediately and self-evidently by nature, are yet the true problems of art. Material acquired through a direct study of nature is, by the architectonic process, transformed into an artistic unity. When we speak of the imitative aspect of art, we are referring to material which has not yet been developed in this manner. Through architectonic development, then, sculpture and painting emerge from the sphere of mere naturalism into the realm of true art.[39]

Even in poetry we find this architectonic development. Without it poetical imitation or invention would lose its force. The horrors of Dante's "Inferno" would remain unalleviated horrors, the raptures of his "Paradiso" would be visionary dreams were they not molded into a new shape by the magic of Dante's diction and verse.

In his theory of tragedy Aristotle stressed the invention of the tragic plot. Of all the necessary ingredients of tragedy—spectacle, characters, fable, diction, melody, and thought—he thought the combination of the incidents of the story (ἡ τῶν πραγμάτων σύστασις) the most important. For tragedy is essentially an imitation not of persons but of action and life. In a play the persons do not act in order to portray the characters; the characters are represented for the sake of the action. A tragedy is impossible without action, but there may be tragedy without character.[40] French classicism adopted and emphasized this Aristotelian theory. Corneille in the prefaces to his plays everywhere insists upon this point. He speaks with pride of his tragedy *Heraclius* because here the plot was so complicated that it needed a special intellectual effort to understand and unravel it. It is clear, however, that this sort of intellectual activity and intellectual pleasure is no necessary element of the artistic process. To enjoy the plots of Shakespeare—to follow with the keenest interest "the combination of the incidents of the story" in *Othello, Macbeth,* or *Lear*—does not necessarily mean that one understands and feels the tragic art of Shakespeare. Without Shakespeare's language, without the power of his dramatic diction, all this would remain unimpressive. The context of a poem cannot be separated from its form—from the verse, the melody, the rhythm. These formal elements are not merely external or technical means to reproduce a given intuition; they are part and parcel of the artistic intuition itself.

In Romantic thought the theory of poetic imagination had reached its climax. Imagination is no longer that special human activity which builds up the human world of art. It now has universal metaphysical value. Poetic imagination is the only clue to reality. Fichte's[41] idealism is based upon his conception of "productive imagination." Schelling declared in his *System of Transcendental Idealism* that art is the consummation of philosophy.[42] In nature, in morality, in history we are still living in the propylaeum of philosophical wisdom; in art we enter into the sanctuary itself. Romantic writers in both verse and prose expressed themselves in the same vein. The distinction between poetry and philosophy was felt to be shallow and superficial. According to Friedrich Schlegel the highest task of a modern poet is to strive after a new form of poetry which he describes as "transcendental poetry." No other poetic genre can give us the essence of the poetic spirit, the "poetry of poetry."[43] To poeticize philosophy and to philosophize poetry—such was the highest aim of all the Romantic thinkers. The true poem is not the work of the individual artist; it is the universe itself, the one work of art which is forever perfecting itself. Hence all the deepest mysteries of all the arts and sciences appertain to poetry.[44] "Poetry," said Novalis, "is what is absolutely and genuinely real. That is the kernel of my philosophy. The more poetic, the more true."[45]

By this conception poetry and art seemed to be elevated to a rank and dignity they had never before possessed.

---

[39] [Cassirer] Adolph Hildebrand, *Das Problem der Form in der bildenden Kunst.* English translation by Max Meyer and R. M. Ogden, *The Problem of Form in Painting and Sculpture* (New York, G. E. Stechert Co., 1907), p. 12.

[40] *Poetics* (above, page 56). Aristotle does not say that there may be tragedy without character.

[41] Johann Gottlieb Fichte (1762–1814), German philosopher.

[42] Friedrich Wilhelm Joseph Schelling (1775–1864), German philosopher.

[43] [Cassirer] Cf. Schlegel, *Athenaumsfragmente,* 238, in *Prosaische Jugendschriften,* ed. J. Minor (second ed. Vienna, 1906), II, 242 [above, page 473].

[44] [Cassirer] Schlegel [above, page 473], *Gespräch über die Poesie* (1800), *op. cit.,* II, 364.

[45] [Cassirer] Novalis, ed. J. Minor, III, II. Cf. O. Walzel, *German Romanticism,* English translation by Alma E. Lussky (New York, 1932), p. 28.

They became a *novum organum* for discovering the wealth and depth of the universe. Nevertheless this exuberant and ecstatic praise of poetic imagination had its strict limitations. In order to achieve their metaphysical aim the Romanticists had to make a serious sacrifice. The infinite had been declared to be the true, indeed the only, subject of art. The beautiful was conceived as a symbolic representation of the infinite. He can only be an artist, according to Friedrich Schlegel, who has a religion of his own, an original conception of the infinite.[46] But in this event what becomes of our finite world, the world of sense experience? Clearly this world as such has no claim to beauty. Over against the true universe, the universe of the poet and artist, we find our common and prosaic world deficient in all poetic beauty. A dualism of this kind is an essential feature in all Romantic theories of art. When Goethe began to publish *Wilhelm Meister's Lehrjahre* the first Romantic critics hailed the work with extravagant expressions of enthusiasm. Novalis saw in Goethe "the incarnation of the poetic spirit on earth." But as the work continued, as the Romantic figure of Mignon and the harpist were overshadowed by more realistic characters and more prosaic events, Novalis grew deeply disappointed. He not only revoked his first judgment; he went so far as to call Goethe a traitor to the cause of poetry. *Wilhelm Meister* came to be looked upon as a satire, a "*Candide*[47] against poetry." When poetry loses sight of the wonderful, it loses its significance and justification. Poetry cannot thrive in our trivial and commonplace world. The miraculous, the marvelous, and the mysterious are the only subjects that admit of a truly poetic treatment.

This conception of poetry is, however, rather a qualification and limitation than a genuine account of the creative process of art. Curiously enough the great realists of the nineteenth century had in this respect a keener insight into the art process than their Romantic adversaries. They maintained a radical and uncompromising naturalism. But it was precisely this naturalism which led them to a more profound conception of artistic form. Denying the "pure forms" of the idealistic schools they concentrated upon the material aspect of things. By virtue of this sheer concentration they were able to overcome the conventional dualism between the poetic and the prosaic spheres. The nature of a work of art, according to the realists, does not depend on the greatness or smallness of its subject matter. No subject whatever is impermeable to the formative energy of art. One of the greatest triumphs of art is to make us see commonplace things in their real shape and in

their true light. Balzac plunged into the most trifling features of the "human comedy,"[48] Flaubert made profound analyses of the meanest characters.[49] In some of Émile Zola's novels we discover minute descriptions of the structure of a locomotive, of a department store, or of a coal mine.[50] No technical detail, however insignificant, was omitted from these accounts. Nevertheless, running through the works of all these realists great imaginative power is observable, which is by no means inferior to that of the Romantic writers. The fact that this power could not be openly acknowledged was a serious drawback to the naturalistic theories of art. In their attempts to refute the Romantic conceptions of a transcendental poetry they reverted to the old definition of art as an imitation of nature.[51] In so doing they missed the principal point, since they failed to recognize the symbolic character of art. If such a characterization of art were admitted, there seemed to be no escape from the metaphysical theories of Romanticism. Art is, indeed, symbolism, but the symbolism of art must be understood in an immanent, not in a transcendent sense. Beauty is "the infinite finitely presented" according to Schelling.[52] The real subject of art is not, however, the metaphysical infinite of Schelling, nor is it the absolute of Hegel.[53] It is to be sought in certain fundamental structural elements of our sense experience itself—in lines, design, in architectural, musical forms. These elements are, so to speak, omnipresent. Free of all mystery, they are patent and unconcealed; they are visible, audible, tangible. In this sense Goethe did not hesitate to say that art does not pretend to show the metaphysical depth of things, it merely sticks to the surface of natural phenomena. But this surface is not immediately given. We do not know it before we discover it in the works of the great artists. This discovery, however, is not confined to a special field. To the extent that human language can express everything, the lowest and the highest things, art can embrace and pervade the whole sphere of human experience. Nothing in the physical or moral world, no natural thing and no human action, is by its nature and essence excluded from the realm of art, because nothing resists its formative and creative process. "*Quicquid essentia dignum est,*" says Bacon in his *Novum Organum,* "*id etiam scientia dignum est.*"[54] This dictum holds for art as well as for science.

---

[46] [Cassirer] *Ideen,* 18, in *Prosaische Jugendschriften,* II, 290.

[47] *Candide,* a novel by Voltaire.

[48] Honoré de Balzac (1799–1850), French novelist. The collection of his novels and stories was called "the human comedy."

[49] Gustave Flaubert (1821–1880), French novelist.

[50] An observation made about Zola by Mallarmé (above, page 729).

[51] See Zola (above, page 698).

[52] Friedrich Wilhelm Joseph Schelling (1775–1854), German philosopher.

[53] See Hegel (above, page 552).

[54] [Cassirer] Bacon, *Novum Organum,* Liber I, Aphor. CXX. "Whatever is essential is fitting." "Science is also fitting."

W. K. Wimsatt

1907–1975

◇ ◇ ◇

Monroe C. Beardsley

1915–1985

The history of literary theory is replete with accusations of heresy and fallacy. Edgar Allan Poe found heresy in didacticism, Cleanth Brooks in paraphrase. In twentieth-century criticism the two best-known accusations of fallacy were made by Wimsatt and Beardsley in "The Intentional Fallacy," reprinted below, and a later essay called "The Affective Fallacy." These essays were written out of the assumption that a literary work had an ontological status of its own—that it was an object with a certain identity. In this the authors were following the lead of John Crowe Ransom (above, page 953). They reflected objectivist principles current in the New Criticism, concisely discussed by Abrams (below, page 1099).

By "intentional fallacy" Wimsatt and Beardsley mean a confusion between a poem and its origins. Their argument is that true authorial intention is not only unavailable to a critic but also undesirable. For them, what is internal to the poem is public and available; what is external, that is, biographical information and the like, is private. The poem belongs to the public and not to the poet. Wimsatt and Beardsley thus represent the New Criticism's rejection of much romantic criticism, which often saw the poem as an expression of the author's self, the interior made exterior, and thrust the ultimate interest back on the author, using the poem as evidence for biographical or psychological conclusions. Before the romantic period, biographical criticism was rare and of little importance; afterward biography came to be a dominant form of literary scholarship. For Wimsatt and Beardsley, what the author did accomplish is before us as the poem, although they did allow that biography had its own interest. But it did not really belong to criticism. Later attacks on the notion of the author, far more radical than that of Wimsatt and Beardsley, were mounted by Barthes (below, page 1256) and Foucault (below, page 1260).

In the companion essay, the phrase "affective fallacy" means a confusion between the poem and its results in the reader. It is a "special case of epistemological skepticism." It ends in "impressionism and relativism." This fallacy was committed, in the view of Wimsatt and Beardsley, by I. A. Richards (above, page 856), though he exerted an influence on the New Criticism. In more recent times there has been a revival of reader-oriented criticism in the work of Jauss (below, page 1237) and Fish (below, page 1395) in quite different ways. Ultimately all theories of catharsis, therapy, didacticism, and delight take in the role of the reader to some extent.

Works by Wimsatt include *The Prose Style of Dr. Johnson* (1941); *Philosophical Words* (1948); *The Verbal Icon* (1954); *Literary Criticism: A Short History* (with Cleanth Brooks, 1957); *Hateful Contraries* (1965); *The Portraits of Alexander Pope* (1965); and *Day of the Leopards* (1976). Beardsley's work includes *Aesthetics: Problems in the Philosophy of Criticism* (1958); *Aesthetics from Classical Greece to the Present* (1966); *Aesthetic Inquiry* (1967); *The Possibility of Criticism* (1970); *The Aesthetic Point of View* (1982). See John Fisher, ed., *Essays on Aesthetics: Perspectives on the Work of Monroe C. Beardsley* (1983).

The Intentional Fallacy

I

The claim of the author's "intention" upon the critic's judgment has been challenged in a number of recent discussions, notably in the debate entitled *The Personal Heresy,* between Professors Lewis and Tillyard.[1] But it seems doubtful if this claim and most of its Romantic corollaries are as yet subject to any widespread questioning. The present writers, in a short article entitled *Intention* for a dictionary[2] of literary criticism, raised the issue but were unable to pursue its implications at any length. We argued that the design or intention of the author is neither available nor desirable as a standard for judging the success of a work of literary art, and it seems to us that this is a principle which goes deep into some differences in the history of critical attitudes. It is a principle which accepted or rejected points to the polar opposites of classical "imitation" and Romantic expression. It entails many specific truths about inspiration, authenticity, biography, literary history and scholarship, and about some trends of contemporary poetry, especially its allusiveness. There is hardly a problem of literary criticism in which the critic's approach will not be qualified by his view of "intention."

Intention, as we shall use the term, corresponds to *what he intended* in a formula which more or less explicitly has had wide acceptance. "In order to judge the poet's performance, we must know *what he intended.*" Intention is design or plan in the author's mind. Intention has obvious affinities for the author's attitude toward his work, the way he felt, what made him write.

We begin our discussion with a series of propositions summarized and abstracted to a degree where they seem to as axiomatic.

1. A poem does not come into existence by accident. The words of a poem, as Professor Stoll[3] has remarked, come out of a head, not out of a hat. Yet to insist on the designing intellect as a *cause* of a poem is not to grant the design or intention as a *standard* by which the critic is to judge the worth of the poet's performance.

2. One must ask how a critic expects to get an answer to the question about intention. How is he to find out what the poet tried to do? If the poet succeeded in doing it, then the poem itself shows what he was trying to do. And if the poet did not succeed, then the poem is not adequate evidence, and the critic must go outside the poem—for evidence of an intention that did not become effective in the poem. "Only one caveat must be borne in mind," says an eminent intentionalist[4] in a moment when his theory repudiates itself; "the poet's aim must be judged at the moment of the creative act, that is to say, by the art of the poem itself."

3. Judging a poem is like judging a pudding or a machine. One demands that it work. It is only because an artifact works that we infer the intention of an artificer. "A poem should not mean but be."[5] A poem can *be* only through its *meaning*—since its medium is words—yet it *is,* simply *is,* in the sense that we have no excuse for inquiring what part is intended or meant. Poetry is a feat of style by which a complex of meaning is handled all at once. Poetry succeeds because all or most of what is said or implied is relevant; what is irrelevant has been excluded, like lumps from pudding and "bugs" from machinery. In this respect poetry differs from practical messages, which are successful if and only if we correctly infer the intention. They are more abstract than poetry.

"The Intentional Fallacy" was first published in 1966. The text is from *The Verbal Icon* by W. K. Wimsatt (Lexington: University of Kentucky Press, 1954).

[1] 1939, by C. S. Lewis (1898–1963) and E. M. W. Tillyard (1889–1962).
[2] [Wimsatt and Beardsley] *Dictionary of World Literature,* Joseph T. Shipley, ed. (New York, 1942), pp. 326–29.

[3] E. E. Stoll (1874–1959), American scholar and critic.
[4] [Wimsatt and Beardsley] J. E. Spingarn, *The New Criticism,* in *Criticism in America* (New York, 1924), 24–25. [Spingarn is referring to the criticism of an earlier generation than that of the New Critics.]
[5] "Ars Poetica" by Archibald MacLeish (1892–1982), American poet.

4. The meaning of a poem may certainly be a personal one, in the sense that a poem expresses a personality or state of soul rather than a physical object like an apple. But even a short lyric poem is dramatic, the response of a speaker (no matter how abstractly conceived) to a situation (no matter how universalized). We ought to impute the thoughts and attitudes of the poem immediately to the dramatic *speaker*, and if to the author at all, only by an act of biographical inference.

5. There is a sense in which an author, by revision, may better achieve his original intention. But it is a very abstract sense. He intended to write a better work, or a better work of a certain kind, and now has done it. But it follows that his former concrete intention was not his intention. "He's the man we were in search of, that's true," says Hardy's rustic constable, "and yet he's not the man we were in search of. For the man we were in search of was not the man we wanted."

"Is not a critic," asks Professor Stoll, "a judge, who does not explore his own consciousness, but determines the author's meaning of intention, as if the poem were a will, a contract, or the constitution? The poem is not the critic's own." He has accurately diagnosed two forms of irresponsibility, one of which he prefers. Our view is yet different. The poem is not the critic's own and not the author's (it is detached from the author at birth and goes about the world beyond his power to intend about it or control it). The poem belongs to the public. It is embodied in language, the peculiar possession of the public, and it is about the human being, an object of public knowledge. What is said about the poem is subject to the same scrutiny as any statement in linguistics or in the general science of psychology.

A critic of our dictionary article, Ananda K. Coomaraswamy, has argued[6] that there are two kinds of inquiry about a work of art: (1) whether the artist achieved his intentions; (2) whether the work of art "ought ever to have been undertaken at all" and so "whether it is worth preserving." Number 2, Coomaraswamy maintains, is not "criticism of any work of art qua work of art," but is rather moral criticism; number 1 is artistic criticism. But we maintain that 2 need not be moral criticism: that there is another way of deciding whether works of art are worth preserving and whether, in a sense, they "ought" to have been undertaken, and this is the way of objective criticism of works of art as such, the way which enables us to distinguish between a skillful murder and a skillful poem. A skillful murder is an example which Coomaraswamy uses,

and in his system the difference between the murder and the poem is simply a "moral" one, not an "artistic" one, since each if carried out according to plan is "artistically" successful. We maintain that 2 is an inquiry of more worth than 1, and since 2 and not 1 is capable of distinguishing poetry from murder, the name "artistic criticism" is properly given to 2.

II

It is not so much a historical statement as a definition to say that the intentional fallacy is a Romantic one. When a rhetorician of the first century AD writes: "Sublimity is the echo of a great soul,"[7] or when he tells us that "Homer enters into the sublime actions of his heroes" and "shares the full inspiration of the combat," we shall not be surprised to find this rhetorician considered as a distant harbinger of Romanticism and greeted in the warmest terms by Saintsbury. One may wish to argue whether Longinus should be called Romantic, but there can hardly be a doubt that in one important way he is.

Goethe's three questions for "constructive criticism" are "What did the author set out to do? Was his plan reasonable and sensible, and how far did he succeed in carrying it out?" If one leaves out the middle question, one has in effect the system of Croce[8]—the culmination and crowning philosophic expression of Romanticism. The beautiful is the successful intuition-expression, and the ugly is the unsuccessful; the intuition or private part of art is *the* aesthetic fact, and the medium or public part is not the subject of aesthetic at all. The Madonna of Cimabue[9] is still in the Church of Santa Maria Novella; but does she speak to the visitor of today as to the Florentines of the thirteenth century? "*Historical interpretation* labors . . . to reintegrate in us the psychological conditions which have changed in the course of history. It . . . enables us to see a work of art (a physical object) as its *author saw it* in the moment of production."[10] The first italics are Croce's, the second ours. The upshot of Croce's system is an ambiguous emphasis on history. With such passages as a point of departure a critic may write a nice analysis of the meaning or "spirit" of a play by

[6][Wimsatt and Beardsley] Ananda Coomaraswamy, *Intention*, in *American Bookman*, I (1944), 41–48.

[7]Longinus (above, page 98).
[8]Benedetto Croce (1866–1952), Italian philosopher.
[9]Giovanni Cimabue (c. 1240–c.1302), Florentine painter.
[10][Wimsatt and Beardsley] It is true that Croce himself in his *Ariosto, Shakespeare, and Corneille* (London, 1920), Chapter 7, "The Practical Personality and the Poetical Personality," and in his *Defense of Poetry* (Oxford, 1933), 24, and elsewhere, early and late, has delivered telling attacks on emotive geneticism, but the main drive of the *Aesthetic* is surely toward a kind of cognitive intentionalism.

Shakespeare or Corneille[11]—a process that involves close historical study but remains aesthetic criticism—or he may, with equal plausibility, produce an essay in sociology, biography, or other kinds of nonaesthetic history.

III

> I went to the poets; tragic, dithyrambic, and all sorts. . . . I took them some of the most elaborate passages in their own writings, and asked what was the meaning of them. . . . Will you believe me? . . . there is hardly a person present who would not have talked better about their poetry than they did themselves. Then I knew that not by wisdom do poets write poetry, but by a sort of genius and inspiration.[12]

That reiterated mistrust of the poets which we hear from Socrates may have been part of a rigorously ascetic view in which we hardly wish to participate, yet Plato's Socrates saw a truth about the poetic mind which the world no longer commonly sees—so much criticism, and that the most inspirational and most affectionately remembered, has proceeded from the poets themselves.

Certainly the poets have had something to say that the critic and professor could not say; their message has been more exciting: that poetry should come as naturally as leaves to a tree, that poetry is the lava of the imagination, or that it is emotion recollected in tranquility. But it is necessary that we realize the character and authority of such testimony. There is only a fine shade of difference between such expressions and a kind of earnest advice that authors often give. Thus Edward Young, Carlyle, Walter Pater: "I know two golden rules from ethics, which are no less golden in composition, than in life. I. Know thyself; 2dly, Reverence thyself."[13] This is the grand secret for finding readers and retaining them: let him who would move and convince others, be first moved and convinced himself. Horace's rule, *Si vis me flere,* is applicable in a wider sense than the literal one. To every poet, to every writer, we might say: Be true, if you would be believed. "Truth! There can be no merit, no craft at all, without that. And further, all beauty is in the long run only *fineness* of truth, or what we call expression, the finer accommodation of speech to that vision within."

And Housman's little handbook to the poetic mind[14] yields this illustration:

> Having drunk a pint of beer at luncheon—beer is a sedative to the brain, and my afternoons are the least intellectual portion of my life—I would go out for a walk of two or three hours. As I went along, thinking of nothing in particular, only looking at things around me and following the progress of the seasons, there would flow into my mind, with sudden and unaccountable emotion, sometimes a line or two of verse, sometimes a whole stanza at once.

This is the logical terminus of the series already quoted. Here is a confession of how poems were written which would do as a definition of poetry just as well as "emotion recollected in tranquility"[15]—and which the young poet might equally well take to heart as a practical rule. Drink a pint of beer, relax, go walking, think on nothing in particular, look at things, surrender yourself to yourself, search for the truth in your own soul, listen to the sound of your own inside voice, discover and express the *vraie vérité.*

It is probably true that all this is excellent advice for poets. The young imagination fired by Wordsworth and Carlyle[16] is probably closer to the verge of producing a poem than the mind of the student who has been sobered by Aristotle or Richards.[17] The art of inspiring poets, or at least of inciting something like poetry in young persons, has probably gone further in our day than ever before. Books of creative writing such as those issued from the Lincoln School are interesting evidence of what a child can do.[18] All this, however, would appear to belong to an art separate from criticism—to a psychological discipline, a system of self-development, a yoga, which the young poet perhaps does well to notice, but which is something different from the public art of evaluating poems.

---

[11] Corneille (above, page 244).
[12] Plato, *Apology.*
[13] Young (above, page 347).

[14] A. E. Housman (1859–1936), English poet, *The Name and Nature of Poetry* (1933).
[15] Wordsworth (above, page 490).
[16] Thomas Carlyle (1795–1881), Scottish writer.
[17] Aristotle (above, page 48); Richards (above, page 856).
[18] [Wimsatt and Beardsley] See Hughes Mearns, *Creative Youth* (Garden City, 1925), especially 10, 27–29. The technique of inspiring has apparently been outdone more recently by the study of inspiration in successful poets and other artists. See, for instance, Rosamond E. M. Harding, *An Anatomy of Inspiration* (Cambridge, 1940); Julius Portnoy, *A Psychology of Art Creation* (Philadelphia, 1942); Rudolf Arnheim and others, *Poets at Work* (New York, 1947); Phyllis Bartlett, *Poems in Process* (New York, 1951); Brewster Ghiselin, ed., *The Creative Process: A Symposium* (Berkeley and Los Angeles, 1952).

Coleridge and Arnold[19] were better critics than most poets have been, and if the critical tendency dried up the poetry in Arnold and perhaps in Coleridge, it is not inconsistent with our argument, which is that judgment of poems is different from the art of producing them. Coleridge has given us the classic "anodyne" story, and tells what he can about the genesis of a poem which he calls a "psychological curiosity," but his definitions of poetry and of the poetic quality "imagination" are to be found elsewhere and in quite other terms.

It would be convenient if the passwords of the intentional school, *sincerity, fidelity, spontaneity, authenticity, genuineness, originality,* could be equated with terms such as *integrity, relevance, unity, function, maturity, subtlety, adequacy,* and other more precise terms of evaluation—in short, if *expression* always meant aesthetic achievement. But this is not so.

"Aesthetic" art, says Professor Curt Ducasse, an ingenious theorist of expression, is the conscious objectification of feelings, in which an intrinsic part is the critical moment. The artist corrects the objectification when it is not adequate. But this may mean that the earlier attempt was not successful in objectifying the self, or "it may also mean that it was a successful objectification of a self which, when it confronted us clearly, we disowned and repudiated in favor of another."[20] What is the standard by which we disown or accept the self? Professor Ducasse does not say. Whatever it may be, however, this standard is an element in the definition of art which will not reduce to terms of objectification. The evaluation of the work of art remains public; the work is measured against something outside the author.

IV

There is criticism of poetry and there is author psychology, which when applied to the present or future takes the form of inspirational promotion; but author psychology can be historical too, and then we have literary biography, a legitimate and attractive study in itself, one approach, as Professor Tillyard would argue, to personality, the poem being only a parallel approach. Certainly it need not be with a derogatory purpose that one points out personal studies, as distinct from poetic studies, in the realm of literary scholarship. Yet there is danger of confusing personal and poetic studies; and there is the fault of writing the personal as if it were poetic.

There is a difference between internal and external evidence for the meaning of a poem. And the paradox is only verbal and superficial that what is (1) internal is also public: it is discovered through the semantics and syntax of a poem, through our habitual knowledge of the language, through grammars, dictionaries, and all the literature which is the source of dictionaries, in general through all that makes a language and culture; while what is (2) external is private or idiosyncratic; not a part of the work as a linguistic fact: it consists of revelations (in journals, for example, or letters or reported conversations) about how or why the poet wrote the poem—to what lady, while sitting on what lawn, or at the death of what friend or brother. There is (3) an intermediate kind of evidence about the character of the author or about private or semiprivate meanings attached to words or topics by an author or by a coterie of which he is a member. The meaning of words is the history of words, and the biography of an author, his use of a word, and the associations which the word had for *him,* are part of the word's history and meaning.[21] But the three types of evidence, especially 2 and 3, shade into one another so subtly that it is not always easy to draw a line between examples, and hence arises the difficulty for criticism. The use of biographical evidence need not involve intentionalism, because while it may be evidence of what the author intended, it may also be evidence of the meaning of his words and the dramatic character of his utterance. On the other hand, it may not be all this. And a critic who is concerned with evidence of type 1 and moderately with that of type 3 will in the long run produce a different sort of comment from that of the critic who is concerned with 2 and with 3 where it shades into 2.

The whole glittering parade of Professor Lowes' *Road to Xanadu,*[22] for instance, runs along the border between types 2 and 3 or boldly traverses the Romantic region of 2. "Kubla Khan," says Professor Lowes, "is the fabric of a vision, but every image that rose up in its weaving had passed that way before. And it would seem that there is nothing haphazard or fortuitous in their return." This is not quite clear—not even when Professor Lowes explains that there were clusters of associations, like hooked atoms, which were drawn into complex relation with other clusters in the deep well of Coleridge's memory, and which then coalesced and issued forth as poems. If there was nothing "haphazard or fortuitous" in the way the images returned to the surface, that may mean (1) that Coleridge could not produce what he

---

[19]Coleridge (above, page 493); Arnold (above, page 586).
[20][Wimsatt and Beardsley] Curt Ducasse [1881–1969], *The Philosophy of Art* (New York, 1929), 116.

[21][Wimsatt and Beardsley] And the history of words *after* a poem is written may contribute meanings which if relevant to the original pattern should not be ruled out by a scruple about intention.
[22]John Livingston Lowes (1867–1945), American literary scholar.

did not have, that he was limited in his creation by what he had read or otherwise experienced, or (2) that having received certain clusters of associations, he was bound to return them in just the way he did, and that the value of the poem may be described in terms of the experiences on which he had to draw. The latter pair of propositions (a sort of Hartleyan associationism[23] which Coleridge himself repudiated in the *Biographia*) may not be assented to. There were certainly other combinations, other poems, worse or better, that might have been written by men who had read Bartram and Purchas and Bruce and Milton.[24] And this will be true no matter how many times we are able to add to the brilliant complex of Coleridge's reading. In certain flourishes (such as the sentence we have quoted) and in chapter headings like "The Shaping Spirit," "The Magical Synthesis," "Imagination Creatrix," it may be that Professor Lowes pretends to say more about the actual poems than he does. There is a certain deceptive variation in these fancy chapter titles; one expects to pass on to a new stage in the argument, and one finds—more and more sources, more and more about "the streamy nature of association."[25]

"Wohin der Weg?" quotes Professor Lowes, for the motto of his book. *"Kein Weg! Ins Unbetretene."*[26] Precisely because the way is *unbetreten,* we should say, it leads away from the poem. Bartram's *Travels* contains a good deal of the history of certain words and of certain Romantic Floridian conceptions that appear in *Kubla Khan*. And a good deal of that history has passed and was then passing into the very stuff of our language. Perhaps a person who has read Bartram appreciates the poem more than one who has not. Or, by looking up the vocabulary of *Kubla Khan* in the *Oxford English Dictionary,* or by reading some of the other books there quoted, a person may know the poem better. But it would seem to pertain little to the poem to know that Coleridge had read Bartram. There is a gross body of life, of sensory and mental experience, which lies behind and in some sense causes every poem, but can never be and need not be known in the verbal and hence intellectual composition which is the poem. For all the objects of our manifold experience, for every unity, there is an action of the mind which cuts off roots, melts away context—or indeed we should never have objects or ideas or anything to talk about.

It is probable that there is nothing in Professor Lowes' vast book which could detract from anyone's appreciation of either *The Ancient Mariner* or *Kubla Khan*. We next present a case where preoccupation with evidence of type 3 has gone so far as to distort a critic's view of a poem (yet a case not so obvious as those that abound in our critical journals).

In a well-known poem by John Donne appears this quatrain:

> Moving of th' earth brings harms and fears,
>   Men reckon what it did and meant,
> But trepidation of the spheres,
>   Though greater far, is innocent.[27]

A recent critic in an elaborate treatment of Donne's learning has written of this quatrain as follows:

> He touches the emotional pulse of the situation by a skillful allusion to the new and the old astronomy.... Of the new astronomy, the "moving of the earth" is the most radical principle, of the old, the "trepidation of the spheres" is the motion of the greatest complexity.... The poet must exhort his love to quietness and calm upon his departure; and for this purpose the figure based upon the latter motion (trepidation), long absorbed into the tradiional astronomy, fittingly suggests the tension of the moment without arousing the "harms and fears" implicit in the figure of the moving earth.[28]

The argument is plausible and rests on a well-substantiated thesis that Donne was deeply interested in the new astronomy and its repercussions in the theological realm. In various works Donne shows his familiarity with Kepler's *De Stella Nova,* with Galileo's *Siderius Nuncius,* with William Gilbert's *De Magnete,* and with Clavius' commentary on the *De Sphaera* of Sacrobosco.[29] He refers to the new science in his sermon at Paul's Cross and in a letter to Sir Henry Goodyer. In *The First Anniversary* he says the "new philosophy calls all in doubt." In the *Elegy on Prince Henry* he says that the "least moving of the center" makes "the world to shake."

---

[23] David Hartley (1705–1757), English physician and psychologist.

[24] William Bartram, *Travels* (1791); Samuel Purchas (1577–1626), *Purchas His Pilgrimes* (1625); James Bruce (1730–1794), *Travels to Discover the Source of the Nile* (1790). John Milton (1608–1674), English poet.

[25] [Wimsatt and Beardsley] Chapters 8, "The Pattern," and 16, "The Known and Familiar Landscape," will be found of most help to the student of the poem.

[26] "Where does the path lead?" "There is no path! Into the untraveled."

[27] John Donne (1573–1631), English poet, "A Valediction: Forbidding Mourning."

[28] [Wimsatt and Beardsley] Charles M. Coffin, *John Donne and the New Philosophy* (New York, 1927), 97–98.

[29] Johannes Kepler (1571–1630), German astronomer; Galileo Galilei (1564–1642), Italian astronomer; Christopher Clavius (1537–1612), German astronomer; Johannes de Sacrobosco (1200–1250), English astronomer.

It is difficult to answer argument like this, and impossible to answer it with evidence of like nature. There is no reason why Donne might not have written a stanza in which the two kinds of celestial motion stood for two sorts of emotion at parting. And if we become full of astronomical ideas and see Donne only against the background of the new science, we may believe that he did. But the text itself remains to be dealt with, the analyzable vehicle of a complicated metaphor. And one may observe: (1) that the movement of the earth according to the Copernican theory is a celestial motion, smooth and regular, and while it might cause religious or philosophic fears, it could not be associated with the crudity and earthiness of the kind of commotion which the speaker in the poem wishes to discourage; (2) that there is another moving of the earth, an earthquake, which has just these qualities and is to be associated with the tear-floods and sigh-tempests of the second stanza of the poem; (3) that "trepidation" is an appropriate opposite of earthquake, because each is a shaking or vibratory motion; and "trepidation of the spheres" is "greater far" than an earthquake, but not much greater (if two such motions can be compared as to greatness) than the annual motion of the earth; (4) that reckoning what it "did and meant" shows that the event has passed, like an earthquake, not like the incessant celestial movement of the earth. Perhaps a knowledge of Donne's interest in the new science may add another shade of meaning, an overtone to the stanza in question, though to say even this runs against the words. To make the geocentric and heliocentric antithesis the core of the metaphor is to disregard the English language, to prefer private evidence to public, external to internal.

V

If the distinction between kinds of evidence has implications for the historical critic, it has them no less for the contemporary poet and his critic. Or, since every rule for a poet is but another side of a judgment by a critic, and since the past is the realm of the scholar and critic, and the future and present that of the poet and the critical leaders of taste, we may say that the problems arising in literary scholarship from the intentional fallacy are matched by others which arise in the world of progressive experiment.

The question of "allusiveness," for example, as acutely posed by the poetry of Eliot, is certainly one where a false judgment is likely to involve the intentional fallacy. The frequency and depth of literary allusion in the poetry of Eliot and others has driven so many in pursuit of full meanings to the *Golden Bough*[30] and the Elizabethan drama that it has become a kind of commonplace to suppose that we do not know what a poet means unless we have traced him in his reading—a supposition redolent with intentional implications. The stand taken by F. O. Matthiessen is a sound one and partially forestalls the difficulty.

> If one reads these lines with an attentive ear and is sensitive to their sudden shifts in movement, the contrast between the actual Thames and the idealized vision of it during an age before it flowed through a megalopolis is sharply conveyed by that movement itself, whether or not one recognizes the refrain to be from Spenser.[31]

Eliot's allusions work when we know them—and to a great extent even when we do not know them, through their suggestive power.

But sometimes we find allusions supported by notes, and it is a nice question whether the notes function more as guides to send us where we may be educated, or more as indications in themselves about the character of the allusions. "Nearly everything of importance . . . that is apposite to an appreciation of *The Waste Land*," writes Matthiessen of Miss Weston's[32] book, "has been incorporated into the structure of the poem itself, or into Eliot's notes." And with such an admission it may begin to appear that it would not much matter if Eliot invented his sources (as Sir Walter Scott invented chapter epigraphs from "old plays" and "anonymous" authors, or as Coleridge wrote marginal glosses for *The Ancient Mariner*). Allusions to Dante, Webster, Marvell, or Baudelaire[33] doubtless gain something because these writers existed, but it is doubtful whether the same can be said for an allusion to an obscure Elizabethan: "The sound of horns and motors, which shall bring / Sweeney to Mrs. Porter in the spring." "Cf. Day, *Parliament of Bees:*"[34] says Eliot.

> When of a sudden, listening, you shall hear,
> A noise of horns and hunting, which shall bring
> Actaeon to Diana in the spring,
> Where all shall see her naked skin.

---

[30] (1890) by James G. Frazer (1854–1941), British anthropologist.

[31] F. O. Matthiessen (1902–1950), American literary critic, *The Achievement of T. S. Eliot.*

[32] Jessie L. Weston (1850–1928), *From Ritual to Romance* (1920).

[33] Dante Aligieri (above, page 153); John Webster (c. 1580–c. 1625), English dramatist; Andrew Marvell (1621–1678), English poet; Baudelaire (above, page 604).

[34] John Day (fl. 1606), English dramatist.

The irony is completed by the quotation itself; had Eliot, as is quite conceivable, composed these lines to furnish his own background, there would be no loss of validity. The conviction may grow as one reads Eliot's next note: "I do not know the origin of the ballad from which these lines are taken: it was reported to me from Sydney, Australia." The important word in this note—on Mrs. Porter and her daughter who washed their feet in soda water—is *ballad*. And if one should feel from the lines themselves their "ballad" quality, there would be little need for the note. Ultimately, the inquiry must focus on the integrity of such notes as parts of the poem, for where they constitute special information about the meaning of phrases in the poem, they ought to be subject to the same scrutiny as any of the other words in which it is written. Matthiessen believes the notes were the price Eliot "had to pay in order to avoid what he would have considered muffling the energy of his poem by extended connecting links in the text itself." But it may be questioned whether the notes and the need for them are not equally muffling. F. W. Bateson[35] has plausibly argued that Tennyson's *The Sailor Boy* would be better if half the stanzas were omitted, and the best versions of ballads like *Sir Patrick Spens* owe their power to the very audacity with which the minstrel has taken for granted the story upon which he comments. What then if a poet finds he cannot take so much for granted in a more recondite context and rather than write informatively, supplies notes? It can be said in favor of this plan that at least the notes do not pretend to be dramatic, as they would if written in verse. On the other hand, the notes may look like unassimilated material lying loose beside the poem, necessary for the meaning of the verbal symbol, but not integrated, so that the symbol stands incomplete.

We mean to suggest by the above analysis that whereas notes tend to seem to justify themselves as external indexes to the author's *intention,* yet they ought to be judged like any other parts of a composition (verbal arrangement special to a particular context), and when so judged their reality as parts of the poem, or their imaginative integration with the rest of the poem, may come into question. Matthiessen, for instance, sees that Eliot's titles for poems and his epigraphs are informative apparatus, like the notes. But while he is worried by some of the notes and thinks that Eliot "appears to be mocking himself for writing the note at the same time that he wants to convey something by it," Matthiessen believes that the "device" of epigraphs "is not at all open to the objection of not being sufficiently struc-

tural." "The *intention,*" he says, "is to enable the poet to secure a condensed expression in the poem itself." "In each case the epigraph is *designed* to form an integral part of the effect of the poem." And Eliot himself, in his notes, has justified his poetic practice in terms of intention.

> The Hanged Man, a member of the traditional pack, fits my purpose in two ways: because he is associated in my mind with the Hanged God of Frazer, and because I associate him with the hooded figure in the passage of the disciples to Emmaus in Part V. . . . The man with Three Staves (an authentic member of the Tarot pack) I associate, quite arbitrarily, with the Fisher King himself.

And perhaps he is to be taken more seriously here, when off guard in a note, than when in his Norton lectures he comments on the difficulty of saying what a poem means and adds playfully that he thinks of prefixing to a second edition of *Ash Wednesday* some lines from *Don Juan:*

> I don't pretend that I quite understand
> My own meaning when I would be *very* fine;
> But the fact is that I have nothing planned
> Unless it were to be a moment merry.

If Eliot and other contemporary poets have any characteristic fault, it may be in *planning* too much.

Allusiveness in poetry is one of several critical issues by which we have illustrated the more abstract issue of intentionalism, but it may be for today the most important illustration. As a poetic practice allusiveness would appear to be in some recent poems an extreme corollary of the Romantic intentionalist assumption, and as a critical issue it challenges and brings to light in a special way the basic premise of intentionalism. The following instance from the poetry of Eliot may serve to epitomize the practical implications of what we have been saying. In Eliot's *Love Song of J. Alfred Prufrock,* toward the end, occurs the line: "I have heard the mermaids singing, each to each," and this bears a certain resemblance to a line in a song by John Donne, "Teach me to hear mermaids singing," so that for the reader acquainted to a certain degree with Donne's poetry, the critical question arises: Is Eliot's line an allusion to Donne's? Is Prufrock thinking about Donne? Is Eliot thinking about Donne? We suggest that there are two radically different ways of looking for an answer to this question. There is (1) the way of poetic analysis and exegesis, which inquires whether it makes any sense if Eliot-Prufrock *is* thinking about Donne. In an earlier part of the poem, when

---

[35] F. W. Bateson (1901–1978), English literary critic.

Prufrock asks, "Would it have been worthwhile, . . . To have squeezed the universe into a ball," his words take half their sadness and irony from certain energetic and passionate lines of Marvel *To His Coy Mistress*. But the exegetical inquirer may wonder whether mermaids considered as "strange sights" (to hear them is in Donne's poem analogous to getting with child a mandrake root) have much to do with Prufrock's mermaids, which seem to be symbols of romance and dynamism, and which incidentally have literary authentication, if they need it, in a line of a sonnet by Gérard de Nerval.[36] This method of inquiry may lead to the conclusion that the given resemblance between Eliot and Donne is without significance and is better not thought of, or the method may have

---

[36] Gérard de Nerval (1808–1855), French poet.

the disadvantage of providing no certain conclusion. Nevertheless, we submit that this is the true and objective way of criticism, as contrasted to what the very uncertainty of exegesis might tempt a second kind of critic to undertake: (2) the way of biographical or genetic inquiry, in which, taking advantage of the fact that Eliot is still alive, and in the spirit of a man who would settle a bet, the critic writes to Eliot and asks what he meant, or if he had Donne in mind. We shall not here weigh the probabilities—whether Eliot would answer that he meant nothing at all, had nothing at all in mind—a sufficiently good answer to such a question—or in an unguarded moment might furnish a clear and, within its limit, irrefutable answer. Our point is that such an answer to such an inquiry would have nothing to do with the poem *Prufrock;* it would not be a critical inquiry. Critical inquiries, unlike bets, are not settled in this way. Critical inquiries are not settled by consulting the oracle.

Cleanth Brooks

1906–1994

Brooks's essays, particularly those collected in *The Well Wrought Urn*, were at one time, and may still be, the most widely read works of the American New Criticism. Like Wimsatt and Beardsley's "intentional fallacy" and "affective fallacy," the phrase "heresy of paraphrase," the title of one of the essays below, became associated with the movement. Brooks is heavily indebted to the work of his teacher John Crowe Ransom (above, page 953), and his essays may be profitably compared to Ransom's. Following Coleridge, he is fond of metaphors of organicism to describe a poem. He insists that statements occurring in poems cannot be treated out of the context of the whole poem, for the total structure controls the poem's meaning. In *Irony as a Principle of Structure*, Brooks defines irony, the central term of his criticism, very broadly as the poem's implicit acknowledgment at all times of the pressure of the whole on any part of it. The meaning, or perhaps better "being" (if we were to follow Ransom), of the poem lies in its formal structure, not in a paraphrase abstracted from it. Brooks therefore criticizes Ransom's assertion that the poem has a "paraphrasable core." His organicism leads him to insist that the paraphrasable core is not an element of the poem but instead an inevitably inadequate creation of the poem's interpreter. One of Brooks's complaints against Romantic and Victorian poetry is that much of it seems to insist on its most portentous statements being taken out of context, as if the rest of the poem were merely a surrounding embellishment. Perhaps the most useful analogy that Brooks draws is his identification of the poem with drama, emphasizing (1) the difference between the poem's fictive speaker and the author and thus (2) the contextualization of anything said in the poem. Brooks, himself, was a professor of drama at Yale University.

Brooks's views were reflected in two influential textbooks by Brooks and Robert Penn Warren, *Understanding Poetry* and *Understanding Fiction*. He also produced *Understanding Drama* with Robert B. Heilman. Because of these books he is usually identified as the critic most responsible for the movement of the New Criticism into the college classroom in the 1940s.

In addition to his collaborations with Warren and Heilman, Brooks wrote with W. K. Wimsatt *Literary Criticism: A Short History* (1957). His other works include *Modern Poetry and the Tradition* (1939), *The Well Wrought Urn* (1947), *The Hidden God* (1963), *William Faulkner: The Yoknapatawpha Country* (1963), *A Shaping Joy* (1972), *William Faulkner: Toward Yoknapatawpha and Beyond* (1978), *William Faulkner: First Encounters* (1983), *The Language of the American South* (1985), *On the Prejudices, Predilections, and Firm Beliefs of William Faulkner* (1987). See Lewis P. Simpson, ed., *The Possibilities of Order: Cleanth Brooks and His Work* (1976); Mark Royden Winchell, *Cleanth Brooks and the Rise of Modern Criticism* (1996).

The Heresy of Paraphrase

The ten poems that have been discussed[1] were not selected because they happened to express a common theme or to display some particular style or to share a special set of symbols. It has proved, as a matter of fact, somewhat surprising to see how many items they do have in common: the light symbolism as used in *L'Allegro—Il Penseroso* and in the *Intimations* ode, for example; or, death as a sexual metaphor in *The Canonization* and in *The Rape of the Lock;* or the similarity of problem and theme in the *Intimations* ode and *Among School Children.*

On reflection, however, it would probably warrant more surprise if these ten poems did not have much in common. For they are all poems which most of us will feel are close to the central stream of the tradition. Indeed, if there is any doubt on this point, it will have to do with only the first and last members of the series [Donne's *The Canonization,* and Yeats's *Among School Children*]—poems whose relation to the tradition I shall, for reasons to be given a little later, be glad to waive. The others, it will be granted, are surely in the mainstream of the tradition.

As a matter of fact, a number of the poems discussed in this book were not chosen by me but were chosen for me. But having written on these, I found that by adding a few poems I could construct a chronological series which (though it makes no pretension to being exhaustive of periods or types) would not leave seriously unrepresented any important period since Shakespeare. In filling the gaps I tried to select poems which had been held in favor in their own day and which most critics still admire. There were, for example, to be no "metaphysical" poems beyond the first exhibit and no "modern" ones other than the last. But the intervening poems were to be read as one has learned to read Donne and the moderns. One was to attempt to see, in terms of this approach, what the masterpieces had in common rather than to see how the poems of different historical periods differed—and in particular to see whether they had any-

thing in common with the "metaphysicals" and with the moderns.

The reader will by this time have made up his mind as to whether the readings are adequate. (I use the word advisedly, for the readings do not pretend to be exhaustive, and certainly it is highly unlikely that they are not in error in one detail or another.) If the reader feels that they are seriously inadequate, then the case has been judged; for the generalizations that follow will be thoroughly vitiated by the inept handling of the particular cases on which they depend.

If, however, the reader does feel them to be adequate, it ought to be readily apparent that the common goodness which the poems share will have to be stated, not in terms of *content* or *subject matter* in the usual sense in which we use these terms, but rather in terms of structure. The "content" of the poems is various, and if we attempt to find one *quality* of content which is shared by all the poems—a "poetic" subject matter or diction or imagery—we shall find that we have merely confused the issues. For what is it to be poetic? Is the schoolroom of Yeats's poem poetic or unpoetic? Is Shakespeare's "new-borne babe / Striding the blast" poetic whereas the idiot of his "Life is a tale tolde by an idiot" is unpoetic? If Herrick's "budding boy or girl" is poetic, then why is not that monstrosity of the newspaper's society page, the "society bud," poetic too?

To say this is not, of course, to say that all materials have precisely the same potentialities (as if the various pigments on the palette had the same potentialities, any one of them suiting the given picture as well as another). But what has been said, on the other hand, requires to be said: for, if we are to proceed at all, we must draw a sharp distinction between the attractiveness or beauty of any particular item taken as such and the "beauty" of the poem considered as a whole. The latter is the effect of a total pattern, and of a kind of pattern which can incorporate within itself items intrinsically beautiful or ugly, attractive or repulsive. Unless one asserts the primacy of the pattern, a poem becomes merely a bouquet of intrinsically beautiful items.

But though it is in terms of structure that we must describe poetry, the term *structure* is certainly not altogether satisfactory as a term. One means by it something far more internal than the metrical pattern, say, or than the sequence of images. The structure meant is certainly not *form* in the conventional sense in which we think of form as a kind of envelope which "contains" the "content." The structure obviously is everywhere conditioned by the nature of the material which goes into the poem. The nature of the material sets the problem to be solved, and the solution is the ordering of the material.

The Heresy of Paraphrase is the last chapter of *The Well Wrought Urn.* It is reprinted from *The Well Wrought Urn* (New York: Harcourt Brace, 1947).

[1] John Donne (1572–1631), *The Canonization;* William Shakespeare (1564–1616), *Macbeth;* John Milton (1608–1674), *L'Allegro* and *Il Penseroso;* Robert Herrick (1591–1674), *Corinna's Going a-Maying;* Alexander Pope (1688–1744), *The Rape of the Lock;* Thomas Gray (1716–1771), *Elegy Written in a Country Churchyard;* William Wordsworth (1770–1850), *Ode: Intimations of Immortality from Recollections of Early Childhood;* John Keats (1795–1821), *Ode on a Grecian Urn;* Alfred Lord Tennyson (1809–1892), *Tears, Idle Tears;* William Butler Yeats (1865–1939), *Among School Children.* Brooks deliberately picked poems from different periods of English literature to show that his approach was not limited to the Metaphysical Poets of the seventeenth century and the twentieth-century poets.

Pope's *Rape of the Lock* will illustrate: the structure is not the heroic couplet as such, or the canto arrangement; for, important as is Pope's use of the couplet as one means by which he secures the total effect, the heroic couplet can be used—has been used many times—as an instrument in securing very different effects. The structure of the poem, furthermore, is not that of the mock-epic convention, though here, since the term *mock-epic* has implications of attitude, we approach a little nearer to the kind of structure of which we speak.

The structure meant is a structure of meanings, evaluations, and interpretations; and the principle of unity which informs it seems to be one of balancing and harmonizing connotations, attitudes, and meanings.[2] But even here one needs to make important qualifications: the principle is not one which involves the arrangement of the various elements into homogeneous groupings, pairing like with like. It unites the like with the unlike. It does not unite them, however, by the simple process of allowing one connotation to cancel out another nor does it reduce the contradictory attitudes to harmony by a process of subtraction. The unity is not a unity of the sort to be achieved by the reduction and simplification appropriate to an algebraic formula. It is a positive unity, not a negative; it represents not a residue but an achieved harmony.

The attempt to deal with a structure such as this may account for the frequent occurrence in the preceding chapters of such terms as *ambiguity, paradox, complex of attitudes,* and—most frequent of all, and perhaps most annoying to the reader—*irony.* I hasten to add that I hold no brief for these terms as such. Perhaps they are inadequate. Perhaps they are misleading. It is to be hoped in that case that we can eventually improve upon them. But adequate terms—whatever those terms may turn out to be—will certainly have to be terms which do justice to the special kind of structure which seems to emerge as the common structure of poems so diverse on other counts as are *The Rape of the Lock* and *Tears, Idle Tears.*

The conventional terms are much worse than inadequate: they are positively misleading in their implication that the poem constitutes a "statement" of some sort, the statement being true or false, and expressed more or less clearly or eloquently or beautifully; for it is from this formula that most of the common heresies about poetry derive. The formula begins by introducing a dualism which thenceforward is rarely overcome, and which at best can be overcome only by the most elaborate and clumsy qualifications. Where it is not overcome, it leaves the critic lodged upon one or the other

of the horns of a dilemma: the critic is forced to judge the poem by its political or scientific or philosophical truth; or, he is forced to judge the poem by its form as conceived externally and detached from human experience. Mr. Alfred Kazin,[3] for example, to take an instance from a recent and popular book, accuses the "new formalists"—his choice of that epithet is revealing—of accepting the latter horn of the dilemma because he notices that they have refused the former. In other words, since they refuse to rank poems by their messages, he assumes that they are compelled to rank them by their formal embellishments.

The omnipresence of this dilemma, a false dilemma, I believe, will also account for the fact that so much has been made in the preceding chapters of the resistance which any good poem sets up against all attempts to paraphrase it. The point is surely not that we cannot describe adequately enough for many purposes what the poem in general is "about" and what the general effect of the poem is: *The Rape of the Lock* is *about* the foibles of an eighteenth-century belle. The effect of *Corinna's Going a-Maying* is one of gaiety tempered by the poignance of the fleetingness of youth. We can very properly use paraphrases as pointers and as shorthand references provided that we know what we are doing. But it is highly important that we know what we are doing and that we see plainly that paraphrase is not the real core of meaning which constitutes the essence of the poem.

For the imagery and the rhythm are not merely the instruments by which this fancied core-of-meaning-which-can-be-expressed-in-a-paraphrase is directly rendered. Even in the simplest poem their mediation is not positive and direct. Indeed, whatever statement we may seize upon as incorporating the "meaning" of the poem, immediately the imagery and the rhythm seem to set up tensions with it, warping and twisting it, qualifying and revising it. This is true of Wordsworth's *Ode* no less than of Donne's *Canonization.* To illustrate: if we say that the *Ode* celebrates the spontaneous "naturalness" of the child, there is the poem itself to indicate that nature has a more sinister aspect—that the process by which the poetic lamb becomes the dirty old sheep or the child racing over the meadows becomes the balding philosopher is a process that is thoroughly "natural." Or, if we say that the thesis of the *Ode* is that the child brings into the natural world a supernatural glory which acquaintance with the world eventually and inevitably quenches in the light of common day, there is the last stanza and the drastic qualifications which it asserts: it is significant that the thoughts that lie too deep for tears are mentioned in this sunset stanza of the *Ode* and that they are thoughts, not of the child, but of the man.

---

[2] The remark is similar to that of Coleridge (above, page 508).

[3] Alfred Kazin (1915–2001), American critic.

We have precisely the same problem if we make our example *The Rape of the Lock.* Does the poet assert that Belinda is a goddess? Or does he say that she is brainless chit? Whichever alternative we take, there are elaborate qualifications to be made. Moreover, if the simple propositions offered seem in their forthright simplicity to make too easy the victory of the poem over any possible statement of its meaning, then let the reader try to formulate a proposition that will say what the poem "says." As his proposition approaches adequacy, he will find, not only that it has increased greatly in length, but that it has begun to fill itself up with reservations and qualifications—and most significant of all—the formulator will find that he has himself begun to fall back upon metaphors of his own in his attempt to indicate what the poem "says." In sum, his proposition, as it approaches adequacy, ceases to be a proposition.

Consider one more case, *Corinna's Going a-Maying.* Is the doctrine preached to Corinna throughout the first four stanzas true? Or is it damnably false? Or is it a "harmless folly"? Here perhaps we shall be tempted to take the last option as the saving mean—what the poem really *says*—and my account of the poem at the end of the third chapter is perhaps susceptible of this interpretation—or misinterpretation. If so, it is high time to clear the matter up. For we mistake matters grossly if we take the poem to be playing with opposed extremes, only to point the golden mean in a doctrine which, at the end, will correct the falsehood of extremes. The reconcilement of opposites[4] which the poet characteristically makes is not that of a prudent splitting of the difference between antithetical overemphases.

It is not so in Wordsworth's poem nor in Keats's nor in Pope's. It is not so even in this poem of Herrick's. For though the poem reflects, if we read it carefully, the primacy of the Christian mores, the pressure exerted throughout the poem is upon the pagan appeal; and the poem ends, significantly, with a reiteration of the appeal to Corinna to go a-Maying, an appeal which, if qualified by the Christian view, still, in a sense, has been deepened and made more urgent by that very qualification. The imagery of loss and decay, it must be remembered, comes in this last stanza after the admission that the May-Day rites are not a real religion but a "harmless folly."

If we are to get all these qualifications into our formulation of what the poem says—and they are relevant—then, our formulation of the "statement" made by Herrick's poem will turn out to be quite as difficult as that of Pope's mock-epic. The truth of the matter is that all such formulations lead away from the center of the poem—not toward it; that the prose-sense" of the poem is not a rack on which the stuff of the poem is hung; that it does not represent the "inner" structure or the "essential" structure or the "real" structure of the poem. We may use—and in many connections must use—such formulations as more or less convenient ways of referring to parts of the poem. But such formulations are scaffoldings which we may properly for certain purposes throw about the building. We must not mistake them for the internal and essential structure of the building itself.

Indeed, one may sum up by saying that most of the distempers of criticism come about from yielding to the temptation to take certain remarks which we make *about* the poem—statements about what it says or about what truth it gives or about what formulations it illustrates—for the essential core of the poem itself. As W. M. Urban[5] puts it in his *Language and Reality:*

> The general principle of the inseparability of intuition and expression holds with special force for the aesthetic intuition. Here it means that form and content, or content and medium, are inseparable. The artist does not first intuit his object and then find the appropriate medium. It is rather in and through his medium that he intuits the object.

So much for the process of composition. As for the critical process: "To pass from the intuitible to the nonintuitible is to negate the function and meaning of the symbol." For it "is precisely because the more universal and ideal relations cannot be adequately expressed directly that they are indirectly expressed by means of the more intuitible." The most obvious examples of such error (and for that reason those which are really least dangerous) are those theories which frankly treat the poem as propaganda. The most subtle (and the most stubbornly rooted in the ambiguities of language) are those which, beginning with the "paraphrasable" elements of the poem, refer the other elements of the poem finally to some role subordinate to the paraphrasable elements. (The relation between all the elements must surely be an organic one—there can be no question about that. There is, however, a very serious question as to whether the paraphrasable elements have primacy.)

Mr. Winters'[6] position will furnish perhaps the most respectable example of the paraphrastic heresy. He assigns

---

[4]Coleridge (above, page 508).

[5]W. M. Urban (1873–1952), American philosopher.
[6]Yvor Winters (1900–1968), American critic.

primacy to the "rational meaning" of the poem. "The relationship, in the poem, between rational statement and feeling," he remarks in his latest book, "is thus seen to be that of motive to emotion." He goes on to illustrate his point by a brief and excellent analysis of the following lines from Browning: "So wore night; the East was gray, / White the broadfaced hemlock flowers. . . ."[7]

"The verb *wore*," he continues,

> means literally that the night passed, but it carries with it connotations of exhaustion and attrition which belong to the condition of the protagonist; and grayness is a color which we associate with such a condition. If we change the phrase to read: "Thus night passed," we shall have the same rational meaning, and a meter quite as respectable, but no trace of the power of the line: the connotation of *wore* will be lost, and the connotation of *gray* will remain in a state of ineffective potentiality.

But the word *wore* does not mean *literally* "that the night passed," it means literally "that the night *wore*"—whatever *wore* may mean, and as Winters' own admirable analysis indicates, *wore* "means," whether *rationally* or *irrationally,* a great deal. Furthermore, "So wore night" and "Thus night passed" can be said to have "the same rational meaning" only if we equate *rational meaning* with the meaning of a loose paraphrase. And can a loose paraphrase be said to be the "motive to emotion"? Can it be said to "generate" the feelings in question? (Or, would Mr. Winters not have us equate *rational statement* and *rational meaning?*)

Much more is at stake here than any quibble. In view of the store which Winters sets by rationality and of his penchant for poems which make their evaluations overtly, and in view of his frequent blindness to those poems which do not—in view of these considerations, it is important to see what "So wore night" and "Thus night passed" have in common as their "rational meaning" is not the "rational meaning" of each but the lowest common denominator of both. To refer the structure of the poem to what is finally a paraphrase of the poem is to refer it to something outside the poem.

To repeat, most of our difficulties in criticism are rooted in the heresy of paraphrase. If we allow ourselves to be misled by it, we distort the relation of the poem to its "truth," we raise the problem of belief in a vicious and crip-

pling form, we split the poem between its "form" and its "content"—we bring the statement to be conveyed into an unreal competition with science or philosophy or theology. In short, we put our questions about the poem in a form calculated to produce the battles of the last twenty-five years over the "use of poetry."[8]

If we allow ourselves to be misled by the heresy of paraphrase, we run the risk of doing even more violence to the internal order of the poem itself. By taking the paraphrase as our point of stance, we misconceive the function of metaphor and meter. We demand logical coherences where they are sometimes irrelevant, and we fail frequently to see imaginative coherences on levels where they are highly relevant.

But what would be a positive theory? We tend to embrace the doctrine of a logical structure the more readily because, to many of us, the failure to do so seems to leave the meaning of the poem hopelessly up in the air. The alternative position will appear to us to lack even the relative stability of an Ivory Tower: it is rather commitment to a free balloon. For, to deny the possibility of pinning down what the poem "says" to some "statement" will seem to assert that the poem really says nothing. And to point out what has been suggested in earlier chapters and brought to a head in this one, namely, that one can never measure a poem against the scientific or philosophical yardstick for the reason that the poem, when laid along the yardstick, is never the "full poem" but an abstraction from the poem—such an argument will seem to such readers a piece of barren logic-chopping—a transparent dodge.

Considerations of strategy then, if nothing more, dictate some positive account of what a poem is and does. And some positive account can be given, though I cannot promise to do more than suggest what a poem is, nor will my terms turn out to be anything more than metaphors.[9]

The essential structure of a poem (as distinguished from the rational or logical structure of the "statement" which we abstract from it) resembles that of architecture or

---

[7] Robert Browning (1812–1889), English poet, *A Serenade in a Villa*, 21–22.

[8] [Brooks] I do not, of course, intend to minimize the fact that some of these battles have been highly profitable, or to imply that the foregoing paragraphs could have been written except for the illuminations shed by the discussions of the last twenty-five years.

[9] [Brooks] For those who cannot be content with metaphors (or with the particular metaphors which I can give) I recommend Rene Wellek's excellent "The Mode of Existence of a Work of Art," *The Southern Review* (Spring 1942). I shall not try to reproduce here as a handy, thumbnail definition his account of a poem as "a stratified system of norms," for the definition would be relatively meaningless without the further definitions which he assigns to the individual terms which he uses. I have made no special use of his terms in this chapter, but I believe that the generalizations about poetry outlined here can be thoroughly accommodated to the position which his essay sets forth.

painting: it is a pattern of resolved stresses. Or, to move closer still to poetry by considering the temporal arts, the structure of a poem resembles that of a ballet or musical composition. It is a pattern of resolutions and balances and harmonizations developed through a temporal scheme.[10]

Or, to move still closer to poetry, the structure of a poem resembles that of a play. This last example, of course, risks introducing once more the distracting element, since drama, like poetry, makes use of words. Yet, on the whole, most of us are less inclined to force the concept of "statement" on drama than on a lyric poem: for the very nature of drama is that of something "acted out"—something which arrives at its conclusion through conflict—something which builds conflict into its very being. The dynamic nature of drama, in short, allows us to regard it as *an action* rather than as a formula for action or as a statement about action. For this reason, therefore, perhaps the most helpful analogy by which to suggest the structure of poetry is that of the drama, and for many readers at least, the least confusing way in which to approach a poem is to think of it as a drama.

The general point, of course, is not that either poetry or drama makes no use of ideas, or that either is "merely emotional"—whatever *that* is—or that there is not the closest and most important relationship between the intellectual materials which they absorb into their structure and other elements in the structure. The relationship between the intellectual and the nonintellectual elements in a poem is actually far more intimate than the conventional accounts would represent it to be: the relationship is not that of an idea "wrapped in emotion" or a "prose-sense decorated by sensuous imagery."

The dimension in which the poem moves is not one which excludes ideas, but one which does include atti-

tudes. The dimension includes ideas, to be sure; we can always abstract an "idea" from a poem—even from the simplest poem—even from a lyric so simple and unintellectual as

> Western wind, when wilt thou blow
>   That the small rain down can rain?
> Christ, that my love were in my arms
>   And I in my bed again.[11]

But the idea which we abstract—assuming that we can all agree on what that idea is—will always be *abstracted*: it will always be the projection of a plane along a line or the projection of a cone upon a plane.

If this analogy proves to be more confusing than illuminating let us return to the analogy with drama. We have argued that any proposition asserted in a poem is not to be taken in abstraction but is justified, in terms of the poem, if it is justified at all, not by virtue of its scientific or historical or philosophical truth, but is justified in terms of a principle analogous to that of dramatic propriety. Thus, the proposition that "Beauty is truth, truth beauty"[12] is given its precise meaning and significance by its relation to the total context of the poem.

This principle is easy enough to see when the proposition is asserted overtly in the poem—that is, when it constitutes a specific detail of the poem. But the reader may well ask: is it not possible to frame a proposition, a statement, which will adequately represent the total meaning of the poem; that is, is it not possible to elaborate a summarizing proposition which will "say," briefly and in the form of a proposition, what the poem "says" as a poem, a proposition which will say it fully and will say it exactly, no more and no less? Could not the poet, if he had chosen, have framed such a proposition? Cannot we as readers and critics frame such a proposition?

The answer must be that the poet himself obviously did not—else he would not have had to write his poem. We as readers can attempt to frame such a proposition in our effort to understand the poem; it may well help toward an understanding. Certainly, the efforts to arrive at such propositions can do no harm *if we do not mistake them for the inner core of the poem*—if we do not mistake them for "what the poem *really* says." For, if we take one of them to represent the essential poem, we have to disregard the qualifications exerted by the total context as of no account, or else we have

---

[10] [Brooks] In recent numbers of *Accent,* two critics for whose work I have high regard have emphasized the dynamic character of poetry. Kenneth Burke argues that if we are to consider a poem as a poem, we must consider it as a "mode of action." R. P. Blackmur asks us to think of it as gesture, "the outward and dramatic play of inward and imagined meaning." I do not mean to commit either of these critics to my own interpretation of dramatic or symbolic action; and I have on my own part, several rather important reservations with respect to Mr. Burke's position. But there are certainly large areas of agreement among our positions. The reader might also compare the account of poetic structure given in this chapter with the following passage from Susanne Langer's *Philosophy in a New Key:*

> . . . though the *material* is verbal its import is not the literal assertion made in the words, but *the way the assertion is made,* and this involves the sound, the tempo, the aura of associations of the words, the long or short sequences of ideas, the wealth or poverty of transient imagery that contains them, the sudden arrest of fantasy, the suspense of literal meaning by a sustained ambiguity resolved in a long-awaited key word, and the unifying, all-embracing artifice of rhythm.

[11] Anonymous medieval ballad.
[12] Keats, *Ode on a Grecian Urn.*

assumed that we can reproduce the effect of the total context in a condensed prose statement.[13]

But to deny that the coherence of a poem is reflected in a logical paraphrase of its "real meaning" is not, of course, to deny coherence to poetry; it is rather to assert that its coherence is to be sought elsewhere. The characteristic unity of a poem (even of those poems which may accidentally possess a logical unity as well as this poetic unity) lies in the unification of attitudes into a hierarchy subordinated to a total and governing attitude. In the unified poem, the poet has "come to terms" with his experience. The poem does not merely eventuate in a logical conclusion. The conclusion of the poem is the working out of the various tensions—set up by whatever means—by propositions, metaphors, symbols. The unity is achieved by a dramatic process, not a logical; it represents an equilibrium of forces, not a formula. It is "proved" as a dramatic conclusion is proved: by its ability to resolve the conflicts which have been accepted as the *données* of the drama.

Thus, it is easy to see why the relation of each item to the whole context is crucial, and why the effective and essential structure of the poem has to do with the complex of attitudes achieved. A scientific proposition can stand alone. If it is true, it is true. But the expression of an attitude, apart from the occasion which generates it and the situation which it encompasses, is meaningless. For example, the last two lines of the *Intimations* ode, "To me the meanest flower that blows can give / Thoughts that do often lie too deep for tears," when taken in isolation—I do not mean quoted in isolation by one who is even vaguely acquainted with the context—makes a statement which is sentimental if taken in reference to the speaker, and one which is patent nonsense if taken with a general reference. The man in the street (of whom the average college freshman is a good enough replica) knows that the meanest flower that grows does not give *him* thoughts that lie too deep for tears; if he thinks about the matter at all, he is inclined to feel that the person who can make such an assertion is a very fuzzy sentimentalist.

We have already seen the ease with which the statement "Beauty is truth, truth beauty" becomes detached from its context, even in the hands of able critics; and we have seen the misconceptions that ensue when this detachment occurs. To take one more instance: the last stanza of Herrick's *Corinna*, taken in isolation, would probably not impress the average reader as sentimental nonsense. Yet it would suffer quite as much by isolation from its context as would the lines from Keats's *Ode*. For, as mere statement, it would become something flat and obvious—of course our lives are short! And the conclusion from the fact would turn into an obvious truism for the convinced pagan, and, for the convinced Christian, equally obvious, though damnable, nonsense.

Perhaps this is why the poet, to people interested in hard-and-fast generalizations, must always seem to be continually engaged in blurring out distinctions only after provoking and unnecessary delays. But this last position is merely another variant of the paraphrastic heresy: to assume it is to misconceive the end of poetry—to take its meanderings as negative, or to excuse them (with the comfortable assurance that the curved line is the line of beauty) because we can conceive the purpose of a poem to be only the production, in the end, of a proposition—of a statement.

But the meanderings of a good poem (they are meanderings only from the standpoint of the prose paraphrase of the poem) are not negative, and they do not have to be excused; and most of all, we need to see what their positive function is; for unless we can assign them a positive function, we shall find it difficult to explain why one divergence from "the prose line of the argument" is not as good as another. The truth is that the apparent irrelevancies which metrical pattern and metaphor introduce do become relevant when we realize that they function in a good poem to modify, qualify, and develop the total attitude which we are to take in coming to terms with the total situation.

If the last sentence seems to take a dangerous turn toward some special "use of poetry"—some therapeutic value for the sake of which poetry is to be cultivated—I can only say that I have in mind no special ills which poetry is to cure. Uses for poetry are always to be found, and doubtless will continue to be found. But my discussion of the structure of poetry is not being conditioned at this point by some new and special role which I expect poetry to assume in the future or some new function to which I would assign it. The structure described—a structure of "gestures" or attitudes—seems to me to describe the essential structure of both the

---

[13] [Brooks] We may, it is true, be able to adumbrate what the poem says if we allow ourselves enough words, and if we make enough reservations and qualifications, thus attempting to come nearer the meaning of the poem by successive approximations and refinements, gradually encompassing the meaning and pointing to the area in which it lies rather than realizing it. The earlier chapters of this book, if they are successful, are obviously illustrations of this process. But such adumbrations will lack, not only the tension—the dramatic force—of the poem; they will be at best crude approximations of the poem. Moreover—and this is the crucial point—they will be compelled to resort to the methods of the poem—analogy, metaphor, symbol, etc.—in order to secure even this near approximation.

Urban's comment on this problem is interesting: he says that if we expand the symbol,

> We lose the "sense" or value of the symbol *as symbol*. The solution . . . seems to me to lie in an adequate theory of interpretation of the symbol. It does not consist in substituting *literal* for symbol sentences, in other words substituting "blunt" truth for symbolic truth, but rather in deepening and enriching the meaning of the symbol.

Odyssey and *The Waste Land.* It seems to be the kind of structure which the ten poems considered in this book possess in common.

If the structure of poetry is a structure of the order described, that fact may explain (if not justify) the frequency with which I have had to have recourse, in the foregoing chapters, to terms like *irony* and *paradox.* By using the term *irony,* one risks, of course, making the poem seem arch and self-conscious, since irony, for most readers of poetry, is associated with satire, *vers de société,* and other "intellectual" poetries. Yet, the necessity for some such term ought to be apparent; and *irony* is the most general term that we have for the kind of qualification which the various elements in a context receive from the context. This kind of qualification, as we have seen, is of tremendous importance in any poem. Moreover, *irony* is our most general term for indicating that recognition of incongruities—which, again, pervades all poetry to a degree far beyond what our conventional criticism has been heretofore willing to allow.

Irony in this general sense, then, is to be found in Tennyson's *Tears, Idle Tears* as well as in Donne's *Canonization.* We have, of course, been taught to expect to find irony in Pope's *Rape of the Lock,* but there is a profound irony in Keats's *Ode on a Grecian Urn;* and there is irony of a very powerful sort in Wordsworth's *Intimations* ode. For the thrusts and pressures exerted by the various symbols in this poem are not avoided by the poet: they are taken into account and played, one against the other. Indeed, the symbols—from a scientific point of view—are used perversely: it is the child who is the best philosopher; it is from a kind of darkness—from something that is "shadowy"—that the light proceeds; growth into manhood is viewed, not as an extrication from, but as an incarceration within, a prison.

There should be no mystery as to why this must be so. The terms of science are abstract symbols which do not change under the pressure of the context. They are pure (or aspire to be pure) denotations; they are defined in advance. They are not to be warped into new meanings. But where is the dictionary which contains the terms of a poem? It is a truism that the poet is continually forced to remake language. As Eliot has put it, his task is to "dislocate language into meaning." And, from the standpoint of a scientific vocabulary, this is precisely what he performs: for, rationally considered, the ideal language would contain one term for each meaning, and the relation between term and meaning would be constant. But the word, as the poet uses it, has to be conceived of, not as a discrete particle of meaning, but as potential of meaning, a nexus or cluster of meanings.

What is true of the poet's language in detail is true of the larger wholes of poetry. And therefore, if we persist in approaching the poem as primarily a rational statement, we ought not to be surprised if the statement seems to be presented to us always in the ironic mode. When we consider the statement immersed in the poem, it presents itself to us, like the stick immersed in the pool of water, warped and bent. Indeed, whatever the statement, it will always show itself as deflected away from a positive, straightforward formulation.

It may seem perverse, however, to maintain, in the face of our revived interest in Donne, that the essential structure of poetry is not logical. For Donne has been appealed to of late as the great master of metaphor who imposes a clean logic on his images beside which the ordering of the images in Shakespeare's sonnets is fumbling and loose. It is perfectly true that Donne makes a great show of logic; but two matters need to be observed. In the first place, the elaborated and "logical" figure is not Donne's only figure or even his staple one. "Telescoped" figures like "Made one another's hermitage" are to be found much more frequently than the celebrated comparison of the souls of the lovers to the legs of a pair of compasses. In the second place, where Donne uses "logic," he regularly uses it to justify illogical positions. He employs it to overthrow a conventional position or to "prove" an essentially illogical one.

Logic, as Donne uses it, is nearly always an ironic logic to state the claims of an idea or attitude which we have agreed, with our everyday logic, is false. This is not to say, certainly, that Donne is not justified in using his logic so, or that the best of his poems are not "proved" in the only senses in which poems can be proved.

But the proof is not a logical proof. *The Canonization* will scarcely prove to the hard-boiled naturalist that the lovers, by giving up the world, actually attain a better world. Nor will the argument advanced in the poem convince the dogmatic Christian that Donne's lovers are really saints.

In using logic, Donne as a poet is fighting the devil with fire. To adopt Robert Penn Warren's metaphor (which, though I lift it somewhat scandalously out of another context, will apply to this one):

> The poet, somewhat less spectacularly [than the saint], proves his vision by submitting it to the fires of irony—to the drama of the structure—in the hope that the fires will refine it. In other words, the poet wishes to indicate that his vision has been earned, that it can survive reference to the complexities and contradictions of experience.[14]

---

[14] In his essay *Pure and Impure Poetry.*

The same principle that inspires the presence of irony in so many of our great poems also accounts for the fact that so many of them seem to be built around paradoxes. Here again the conventional associations of the term may prejudice the reader just as the mention of Donne may prejudice him. For Donne, as one type of reader knows all too well, was of that group of poets who wished to impress their audience with their cleverness. All of us are familiar with the censure passed upon Donne and his followers by Dr. Johnson,[15] and a great many of us still retain it as our own, softening only the rigor of it and the thoroughness of its application, but not giving it up as a principle.

Yet there are better reasons than that of rhetorical vainglory that have induced poet after poet to choose ambiguity and paradox rather than plain, discursive simplicity. It is not enough for the poet to analyze his experience as the scientist does, breaking it up into parts, distinguishing part from part, classifying the various parts. His task is finally to unify experience. He must return to us the unity of the experience itself as man knows it in his own experience. The poem, if it be a true poem is a simulacrum of reality—in this sense, at least, it is an "imitation"—by *being* an experience rather than any mere statement about experience or any mere abstraction from experience.

Tennyson cannot be content with *saying* that in memory the poet seems both dead *and* alive; he must dramatize its life-in-death for us, and his dramatization involves, necessarily, ironic shock and wonder. The dramatization demands that the antithetical aspects of memory be coalesced into one entity which—if we take it on the level of statement—is a paradox, the assertion of the union of opposites. Keats's Urn must express a life which is above life and its vicissitudes, but it must also bear witness to the fact that its life is not life at all but is a kind of death. To put it in other terms, the Urn must, in its role as historian, assert that myth is truer than history. Donne's lovers must reject the world in order to possess the world.

Or, to take one further instance: Wordsworth's light must serve as the common symbol for aspects of man's vision which seem mutually incompatible—intuition and analytic reason. Wordsworth's poem, as a matter of fact, typifies beautifully the poet's characteristic problem itself. For even this poem, which testifies so heavily to the way in which the world is split up and parceled out under the growing light of reason, cannot rest in this fact as its own mode of perception, and still be a poem. Even after the worst has been said about man's multiple vision, the poet must somehow prove that the child is father to the man, that the dawn light is still somehow the same light as the evening light.

If the poet, then, must perforce dramatize the oneness of the experience, even though paying tribute to its diversity, then his use of paradox and ambiguity is seen as necessary. He is not simply trying to spice up, with a superficially exciting or mystifying rhetoric, the old stale stockpot (though doubtless this will be what the inferior poet does generally and what the real poet does in his lapses). He is rather giving us an insight which preserves the unity of experience and which, at its higher and more serious levels, triumphs over the apparently contradictory and conflicting elements of experience by unifying them into a new pattern.

Wordsworth's *Intimations* ode, then, is not only a poem, but, among other things, a parable about poetry. Keats's *Ode on a Grecian Urn* is quite obviously such a parable. And, indeed, most of the poems which we have discussed in this study may be taken as such parables.

In one sense, Pope's treatment of Belinda raises all the characteristic problems of poetry. For Pope, in dealing with his "goddess," must face the claims of naturalism and of common sense which would deny divinity to her. Unless he faces them, he is merely a sentimentalist. He must do an even harder thing: he must transcend the conventional and polite attributions of divinity which would be made to her as an acknowledged belle. Otherwise, he is merely trivial and obvious. He must "prove" her divinity against the commonsense denial (the brutal denial) and against the conventional assertion (the polite denial). The poetry must be wrested from the context: Belinda's lock, which is what the rude young man wants and which Belinda rather prudishly defends and which the naturalist asserts is only animal and which displays in its curled care the style of a particular era of history, must be given a place of permanence among the stars.

Irony as a Principle of Structure

One can sum up modern poetic technique by calling it the rediscovery of metaphor and the full commitment to metaphor. The poet can legitimately step out into the universal only by first going through the narrow door of the particular.[1] The poet does not select an abstract theme and then embellish it

---

[15] In his life of Alexander Cowley.

"Irony as a Principle of Structure" was written in 1949 and is reprinted from M. D. Zabel, ed., *Literary Opinion in America.*
[1] See Blake (above, page 452), in contrast to Johnson (above, page 361) and Reynolds (above, page 394).

with concrete details. On the contrary, he must establish the details, must abide by the details, and through his realization of the details attain to whatever general meaning he can attain. The meaning must issue from the particulars; it must not seem to be arbitrarily forced upon the particulars. Thus, our conventional habits of language have to be reversed when we come to deal with poetry. For here it is the tail that wags the dog. Better still, here it is the tail of the kite—the tail that makes the kite fly—the tail that renders the kite more than a frame of paper blown crazily down the wind.

The tail of the kite, it is true, seems to negate the kite's function: it weights down something made to rise; and in the same way, the concrete particulars with which the poet loads himself seem to deny the universal to which he aspires. The poet wants to "say" something. Why, then, doesn't he say it directly and forthrightly? Why is he willing to say it only through his metaphors? Through his metaphors, he risks saying it partially and obscurely, and risks not saying it at all. But the risk must be taken, for direct statement leads to abstraction and threatens to take us out of poetry altogether.

The commitment to metaphor thus implies, with respect to general theme, a principle of indirection. With respect to particular images and statements, it implies a principle of organic relationship. That is, the poem is not a collection of beautiful or "poetic" images. If there really existed objects which were somehow intrinsically "poetic," still the mere assemblage of these would not give us a poem. For in that case, one might arrange bouquets of these poetic images and thus create poems by formula. But the elements of a poem are related to each other, not as blossoms juxtaposed in a bouquet, but as the blossoms are related to the other parts of growing plant. The beauty of the poem is the flowering of the whole plant, and needs the stalk, the leaf, and the hidden roots.

If this figure seems somewhat highflown, let us borrow an analogy from another art: the poem is like a little drama. The total effect proceeds from all the elements in the drama, and in a good poem, as in a good drama, there is no wasted motion and there are no superfluous parts.

In coming to see that the parts of a poem are related to each other organically, and related to the total theme indirectly, we have come to see the importance of context. The memorable verses in poetry—even those which seem somehow intrinsically "poetic"—show on inspection that they derive their poetic quality from their relation to a particular context. We may, it is true, be tempted to say that Shakespeare's "Ripeness is all"[2] is poetic because it is a sublime thought, or because it possesses simple eloquence; but that is to forget the

context in which the passage appears. The proof that this is so becomes obvious when we contemplate such unpoetic lines as "vitality is all," "serenity is all," "maturity is all,"—statements whose philosophical import in the abstract is about as defensible as that of "ripeness is all." Indeed, the commonplace word *never* repeated five times becomes one of the most poignant lines in *Lear,* but it becomes so because of the supporting context.[3] Even the "meaning" of any particular item is modified by the context. For what is said is said in a particular situation and by a particular dramatic character.

The last instances adduced can be most properly regarded as instances of "loading" from the context. The context endows the particular word or image or statement with significance. Images so charged become symbols; statements so charged become dramatic utterances. But there is another way in which to look at the impact of the context upon the part. The part is modified by the pressure of the context.

Now the *obvious* warping of a statement by the context we characterize as "ironical." To take the simplest instance, we say "this is a fine state of affairs," and in certain contexts the statement means quite the opposite of what it purports to say literally. This is sarcasm, the most obvious kind of irony. Here a complete reversal of meaning is effected: effected by the context, and pointed, probably, by the tone of voice. But the modification can be most important even though it falls far short of sarcastic reversal, and it need not be underlined by the tone of voice at all. The tone of irony can be effected by the skillful disposition of the context. Gray's *Elegy* will furnish an obvious example.

> Can storied urn or animated bust
> Back to its mansion call the fleeting breath?
> Can Honor's voice provoke the silent dust,
> Or Flatt'ry soothe the dull cold ear of death?[4]

In its context, the question is obviously rhetorical. The answer has been implied in the characterization of the breath as fleeting and of the ear of death as dull and cold. The form is that of a question, but the manner in which the question has been asked shows that it is no true question at all.

These are obvious instances of irony, and even on this level, much more poetry is ironical than the reader may be disposed to think. Many of Hardy's poems and nearly all of Housman's, for example, reveal irony quite as definite and overt as this.[5] Lest these examples, however, seem to specialize irony in the direction of the sardonic, the reader

[2] Shakespeare, *King Lear* V, ii, 9.

[3] *King Lear* V, iii, 307.
[4] *Elegy Written in a Country Churchyard.*
[5] Thomas Hardy (1840–1928), A. E. Housman (1859–1936).

ought to be reminded that irony, even in its obvious and conventionally recognized forms, comprises a wide variety of modes: tragic irony, self-irony, playful, arch, mocking, or gentle irony, etc. The body of poetry which may be said to contain irony in the ordinary senses of the term stretches from *Lear,* on the one hand, to *Cupid and Campaspe Played,*[6] on the other.

What indeed would be a statement wholly devoid of an ironic potential—a statement that did not show any qualification of the context? One is forced to offer statements like "Two plus two equals four," or "The square on the hypotenuse of a right triangle is equal to the sum of the squares on the two sides." The meaning of these statements is unqualified by any context; if they are true, they are equally true in any possible context.[7] These statements are properly abstract, and their terms are pure denotations. (If "two" or "four" actually happened to have connotations for the fancifully minded, the connotations would be quite irrelevant: they do not participate in the meaningful structure of the statement.)

But connotations are important in poetry and do enter significantly into the structure of meaning which is the poem. Moreover, I should claim also—as a corollary of the foregoing proposition—that poems never contain abstract statements. That is, any "statement" made in the poem bears the pressure of the context and has its meaning modified by the context. In other words, the statements made—including those which appear to be philosophical generalizations—are to be read as if they were speeches in a drama. Their relevance, their propriety, their rhetorical force, even their meaning, cannot be divorced from the context in which they are imbedded.

The principle I state may seem a very obvious one, but I think that it is nonetheless very important. It may throw some light upon the importance of the term *irony* in modern criticism. As one who has certainly tended to overuse the term *irony* and perhaps, on occasion, has abused the term, I am closely concerned here. But I want to make quite clear what that concern is: it is not to justify the term *irony* as

such, but rather to indicate why modern critics are so often tempted to use it. We have doubtless stretched the term too much, but it has been almost the only term available by which to point to a general and important aspect of poetry.

Consider this example: The speaker in Matthew Arnold's *Dover Beach* states that the world, "which seems to lie before us like a land of dreams . . . hath really neither joy nor love nor light. . . ." For some readers the statement will seem an obvious truism. (The hero of a typical Hemingway[8] short story or novel, for example, will say this, though of course in a rather different idiom.) For other readers, however, the statement will seem false, or at least highly questionable. In any case, if we try to "prove" the proposition, we shall raise some very perplexing metaphysical questions, and in doing so, we shall certainly also move away from the problems of the poem and, finally, from a justification of the poem. For the lines are to be justified in the poem in terms of the context: the speaker is standing beside his loved one, looking out of the window on the calm sea, listening to the long withdrawing roar of the ebbing tide, and aware of the beautiful delusion of moonlight which "blanches" the whole scene. The "truth" of the statement, and of the poem itself, in which it is imbedded, will be validated, not by a majority report of the association of sociologists, or a committee of physical scientists, or of a congress of metaphysicians who are willing to stamp the statement as proved. How is the statement to be validated? We shall probably not be able to do better than to apply T. S. Eliot's[9] test: does the statement seem to be that which the mind of the reader can accept as coherent, mature, and founded on the facts of experience? But when we raise such a question, we are driven to consider the poem as drama. We raise such further questions as these: Does the speaker seem carried away with his own emotions? Does he seem to oversimplify the situation? Or does he, on the other hand, seem to have won to a kind of detachment and objectivity? In other words, we are forced to raise the question as to whether the statement grows properly out of a context; whether it acknowledges the pressures of the context; whether it is "ironical"—or merely callow, glib, and sentimental.

I have suggested elsewhere that the poem which meets Eliot's test comes to the same thing as I. A. Richards' "poetry of synthesis"[10]—that is, a poetry which does not leave out what is apparently hostile to its dominant tone, and which, because it is able to fuse the irrelevant and discordant, has come to terms with itself and is invulnerable to

---

[6]John Lyly (1554?–1606), "Cupid and my Campaspe played," from his play *Alexander and Campaspe.*

[7][Brooks] This is not to say, of course, that such statements are not related to a particular "universe of discourse." They are indeed, as are all statements of whatever kind. But I distinguish here between "context" and "universe of discourse." "Two plus two equals four" is not dependent on a special dramatic context in the way in which a "statement" made in a poem is. Compare "two plus two equals four" and the same "statement" as contained in Housman's poem:

—To think that two and two are four
 And neither five nor three
The Heart of man has long been sore
 And long 'tis like to be.

[8]Ernest Hemingway (1889–1961), American novelist.
[9]In connection with this see Eliot's essay on Dante (1929).
[10]Richards (above, page 856).

irony. Irony, then, in this further sense, is not only an acknowledgment of the pressures of a context. Invulnerability to irony is the stability of a context in which the internal pressures balance and mutually support each other. The stability is like that of the arch: the very forces which are calculated to drag the stones to the ground actually provide the principle of support—a principle in which thrust and counterthrust become the means of stability.

In many poems the pressures of the context emerge in obvious ironies. Marvell's *To His Coy Mistress* or Raleigh's *Nymph's Reply*[11] or even Gray's *Elegy* reveal themselves as ironical, even to readers who use irony strictly in the conventional sense.

But can other poems be subsumed under this general principle, and do they show a comparable basic structure? The test case would seem to be presented by the lyric, and particularly the simple lyric. Consider, for example, one of Shakespeare's songs:

> Who is Silvia: what is she
>> That all our swains commend her?
> Holy, fair, and wise is she;
>> The heavens such grace did lend her,
> That she might admired be.
>
> Is she kind as she is fair?
>> For beauty lives with kindness.
> Love doth to her eyes repair,
>> To help him of his blindness,
> And, being help'd, inhabits there.
>
> Then to Silvia let us sing,
>> That Silvia is excelling;
> She excels each mortal thing
>> Upon the dull earth dwelling:
> To her let us garlands bring.[12]

On one level the song attempts to answer the question, who is Silvia? and the answer given makes her something of an angel and something of a goddess. She excels each mortal thing "Upon the dull earth dwelling." Silvia herself, of course, dwells upon that dull earth, though it is presumably her own brightness which makes it dull by comparison. (The dull earth, for example, yields bright garlands which the swains are bringing to her.) Why does she excel each mortal thing? Because of her virtues

("Holy, fair, and wise is she"), and these are a celestial gift. She is heaven's darling ("The heavens such grace did lend her").

Grace, I suppose, refers to grace of movement, and some readers will insist that we leave it at that. But since Silvia's other virtues include holiness and wisdom, and since her grace has been lent from above, I do not think that we can quite shut out the theoretical overtones. Shakespeare's audience would have found it even more difficult to do so. At any rate, it is interesting to see what happens if we are aware of these overtones. We get a delightful richness, and we also get something very close to irony.

The motive for the bestowal of grace—that she might admired be—is oddly untheological. But what follows is odder still, for the love that "doth to her eyes repair" is not, as we might expect, Christian "charity" but the little pagan god Cupid ("Love doth to her eyes repair, / To help him of his blindness.") But if Cupid lives in her eyes, then the second line of the stanza takes on another layer of meaning. "For beauty lives with kindness" becomes not merely a kind of charming platitude—actually often denied in human experience. (The Petrarchan[13] lover, for example, as Shakespeare well knew, frequently found a beautiful and *cruel* mistress.) The second line, in this context, means also that the love god lives with the kind Silvia, and indeed has taken these eyes that sparkle with kindness for his own.

Is the mixture of pagan myth and Christian theology, then, an unthinking confusion into which the poet has blundered, or is it something wittily combined? It is certainly not a confusion, and if blundered into unconsciously, it is a happy mistake. But I do not mean to press the issue of the poet's self-consciousness (and with it, the implication of a kind of playful irony). Suffice it to say that the song is charming and delightful, and that the mingling of elements is proper to a poem which is a deft and light-fingered attempt to suggest the quality of divinity with which lovers perennially endow maidens who are finally mortal. The touch is light, there is a lyric grace, but the tone is complex, nonetheless.

I shall be prepared, however, to have this last example thrown out of court since Shakespeare, for all his universality, was a contemporary of the metaphysical poets, and may have incorporated more of their ironic complexity than is necessary or normal. One can draw more innocent and therefore more convincing examples from Wordsworth's[14] Lucy poems.

---

[11] Sir Walter Raleigh (1554?–1618), English courtier and man of letters.
[12] From *Love's Labours Lost* IV, ii, 40.
[13] Francesco Petrarch (1304–1374), Italian poet.
[14] Wordsworth (above, page 481).

She dwelt among the untrodden ways
Beside the springs of Dove,
A maid whom there were none to praise
And very few to love;

A violet by a mossy stone
Half hidden from the eye!
Fair as a star, when only one
Is shining in the sky.

She lived unknown, and few could know
When Lucy ceased to be;
But she is in her grave, and, oh,
The difference to me.

Which is Lucy really like—the violet or the star? The context in general seems to support the violet comparison. The violet, beautiful but almost unnoticed, already half hidden from the eye, is now, as the poem ends, completely hidden in its grave, with none but the poet to grieve for its loss. The star comparison may seem only vaguely relevant—a conventional and here a somewhat anomalous compliment. Actually, it is not difficult to justify the star comparison: to her lover's eyes, she is the solitary star. She has no rivals, nor would the idea of rivalry, in her unselfconscious simplicity, occur to her.

The violet and the star thus balance each other and between themselves define the situation: Lucy was, from the viewpoint of the great world, unnoticed, shy, modest, and half hidden from the eye, but from the standpoint of her lover, she is the single star, completely dominating that world, not arrogantly like the sun, but sweetly and modestly, like the star. The implicit contrast is that so often developed ironically by John Donne in his poems where the lovers, who amount to nothing in the eyes of the world, become, in their own eyes, each the other's world—as in *The Good-Morrow,* where their love makes "one little room an everywhere," or as in *The Canonization,* where the lovers drive into the mirrors of each other's eyes the "towns, countries, courts"—which make up the great world; and thus find that world in themselves. It is easy to imagine how Donne would have exploited the contrast between the violet and the star, accentuating it, developing the irony, showing how the violet was really like its antithesis, the star, etc.

Now one does not want to enter an Act of Uniformity against the poets. Wordsworth is entitled to his method of simple juxtaposition with no underscoring of the ironical contrast. But it is worth noting that the contrast with its ironic potential is there in his poem. It is there in nearly all of Wordsworth's successful lyrics. It is certainly to be found in "A slumber did my spirit seal."

A slumber did my spirit seal;
I had no human fears:
She seemed a thing that could not feel
The touch of earthly years.

No motion has she now, no force;
She neither hears nor sees,
Rolled round in earth's diurnal course,
With rocks, and stones, and trees.[15]

The lover's insensitivity to the claims of mortality is interpreted as a lethargy of spirit—a strange slumber. Thus the "human fears" that he lacked are apparently the fears normal to human beings. But the phrase has a certain pliability. It could mean fears *for* the loved one as a mortal human being; and the lines that follow tend to warp the phrase in this direction: it does not occur to the lover that he needs to fear for one who cannot be touched by "earthly years." We need not argue that Wordsworth is consciously using a witty device, a purposed ambiguity; nor need we conclude that he is confused. It is enough to see that Wordsworth has developed, quite "normally," let us say, a context calculated to pull "human fears" in opposed directions, and that the slightest pressure of attention on the part of the reader precipitates an ironical effect.

As we move into the second stanza, the potential irony almost becomes overt. If the slumber has sealed the lover's spirit, a slumber, immersed in which he thought it impossible that his loved one could perish, so too a slumber has now definitely sealed *her* spirit: "No motion has she now, no force; / She neither hears nor sees." It is evident that it is her unnatural slumber that has waked him out of his. It is curious to speculate on what Donne or Marvell[16] would have made of this.

Wordsworth, however, still does not choose to exploit the contrast as such. Instead, he attempts to suggest something of the lover's agonized shock at the loved one's present lack of motion—of his response to her utter and horrible inertness. And how shall he suggest this? He chooses to suggest it, not by saying that she lies as quiet as marble or as a lump of clay; on the contrary, he attempts to suggest it by imagining her in violent motion—violent, but imposed motion, the same motion indeed which the very stones share, whirled about as they are in earth's diurnal course. Why does the image convey so powerfully the sense of something inert and helpless? Part of the effect, of course, resides in the fact that a dead lifelessness is suggested more sharply by

---

[15] Another of the Lucy poems.
[16] Andrew Marvell (1621–1678), English poet.

an object's being whirled about by something else than by an image of the object in repose. But there are other matters which are at work here: the sense of the girl's falling back into the clutter of things, companioned by things chained like a tree to one particular spot, or by things completely inanimate, like rocks and stones. Here, of course, the concluding figure leans upon the suggestion made in the first stanza, that the girl once seemed something not subject to earthly limitations at all. But surely, the image of the whirl itself is important in its suggestion of something meaningless—motion that mechanically repeats itself. And there is one further element: the girl, who to her lover seemed a thing that could not feel the touch of earthly years, is caught up helplessly into the empty whirl of the earth which measure and makes time. She is touched by and held by earthly time in its most powerful and horrible image. The last figure thus seems to me to summarize the poem—to offer to almost every facet of meaning suggested in the earlier lines a concurring and resolving image which meets and accepts and reduces each item to its place in the total unity.

Wordsworth, as we have observed above, does not choose to point up specifically the ironical contrast between the speaker's former slumber and the loved one's present slumber. But there is one ironical contrast which he does stress: this is the contrast between the two senses in which the girl becomes insulated against the "touch of earthly years." In the first stanza, she "could not feel / The touch of earthly years" because she seemed divine and immortal. But in the second stanza, now in her grave, she still does not "feel the touch of earthly years," for, like the rocks and stones, she feels nothing at all. It is true that Wordsworth does not repeat the verb "feels"; instead he writes "She neither *hears* nor *sees*." But the contrast, though not commented upon directly by any device of verbal wit, is there nonetheless, and is bound to make itself felt in any sensitive reading of the poem. The statement of the first stanza has been literally realized in the second, but its meaning has been ironically reversed.

Ought we, then, to apply the term *ironical* to Wordsworth's poem? Not necessarily. I am trying to account for my temptation to call such a poem ironical—not to justify my yielding to the temptation—least of all to insist that others so transgress. Moreover, Wordsworth's poem seems to me admirable, and I entertain no notion that it might have been more admirable still had John Donne written it rather than William Wordsworth. I shall be content if I can make a much more modest point: namely, that since both Wordsworth and Donne are poets, their work has at basis a similar structure, and that the dynamic structure—the pattern of thrust and counterthrust—which we associate with Donne has its coun-

terpart in Wordsworth. In the work of both men, the relation between part and part is organic, which means that each part modifies and is modified by the whole.

Yet to intimate that there are potential ironies in Wordsworth's lyric may seem to distort it. After all, is it not simple and spontaneous? With these terms we encounter two of the critical catchwords of the nineteenth century, even as *ironical* is in danger of becoming a catchword of our own period. Are the terms *simple* and *ironical* mutually exclusive? What after all do we mean by *simple* or by *spontaneous?*[17] We may mean that the poem came to the poet easily and even spontaneously: very complex poems may—indeed have—come just this way. Or the poem may seem in its effect on the reader a simple and spontaneous utterance: some poems of great complexity possess this quality. What is likely to cause trouble here is the intrusion of a special theory of composition. It is fairly represented as an intrusion since a theory as to how a poem is written is being allowed to dictate to us how the poem is to be read. There is no harm in thinking of Wordsworth's poem as simple and spontaneous unless these terms deny complexities that actually exist in the poem, and unless they justify us in reading the poem with only half our minds. A slumber ought not to seal the *reader's* spirit as he reads this poem, or any other poem.

I have argued that irony, taken as the acknowledgment of the pressures of context, is to be found in poetry of every period and even in simple lyrical poetry. But in the poetry of our own time, this pressure reveals itself strikingly. A great deal of modern poetry does use irony as its special and perhaps its characteristic strategy. For this there are reasons, and compelling reasons. To cite only a few of these reasons: there is the breakdown of a common symbolism; there is the general skepticism as to universals; not least important, there is the depletion and corruption of the very language itself, by advertising and by the mass-produced arts of radio, the moving picture, and pulp fiction. The modern poet has the task of rehabilitating a tired and drained language so that it can convey meanings once more with force and with exactitude. This task of qualifying and modifying language is perennial; but it is imposed on the modern poet as a special burden. Those critics who attribute the use of ironic techniques to the poet's own bloodless sophistication and tired skepticism would be better advised to refer these vices to his potential readers, a public corrupted by Hollywood and the Book of the Month Club. For the modern poet is not addressing simple primitives but a public sophisticated by

---

[17] Wordsworth (above, page 490).

commercial art.

At any rate, to the honor of the modern poet be it said that he has frequently succeeded in using his ironic techniques to win through to clarity and passion. Randall Jarrell's *Eighth Air Force* represents a success of this sort.[18]

> If, in an odd angle of the hutment,
> A puppy laps the water from a can
> Of flowers, and the drunk sergeant shaving
> Whistles *O Paradiso!*—shall I say that man
> Is not as men have said: a wolf to man?
>
> The other murderers troop in yawning;
> Three of them play pitch, one sleeps, and one
> Lies counting missions, lies there sweating
> Till even his heart beats: One; One; One.
> *O murderers!* . . . Still, this is how it's done:
>
> This is a war. . . . But since these play, before they die,
> Like puppies with their puppy; since, a man,
> I did as these have done, but did not die—
> I will content the people as I can
> And give up these to them: Behold the man!
>
> I have suffered, in a dream, because of him,
> Many things; for this last savior, man,
> I have lied as I lie now. But what is lying?
> Men wash their hands, in blood, as best they can:
> I find no fault in this just man.

There are no superfluous parts, no dead or empty details. The airmen in their hutment are casual enough and honest enough to be convincing. The raw building is domesticated: there are the flowers in water from which the mascot, a puppy, laps. There is the drunken sergeant, whistling an opera aria as he shaves. These "murderers," as the poet is casually to call the airmen in the next stanza, display a touching regard for the human values. How, then, can one say that man is a wolf to man, since these men "play before they die, like puppies with their puppy." But the casual presence of the puppy in the hutment allows us to take the stanza both ways, for the dog is a kind of tamed and domesticated wolf, and his presence may prove on the contrary that the hutment is the wolf den. After all, the timber wolf plays with its puppies.

The second stanza takes the theme to a perfectly explicit conclusion. If three of the men play pitch, and one is asleep, at least one man is awake and counts himself and his

companions murderers. But his unvoiced cry "O murderers" is met, countered, and dismissed with the next two lines: ". . . Still this is how it's done: / This is a war. . . ."

The note of casuistry and cynical apology prepares for a brilliant and rich resolving image, the image of Pontius Pilate, which is announced specifically in the third stanza: "I will content the people as I can / And give up these to them: behold the man!" Yet if Pilate, as he is first presented, is a jesting Pilate, who asks, what is truth? it is a bitter and grieving Pilate who concludes the poem. It is the integrity of man himself that is at stake. Is man a cruel animal, a wolf, or is he the last savior, the Christ of our secular religion of humanity?

The Pontius Pilate metaphor, as the poet uses it, becomes a device for tremendous concentration. For the speaker (presumably the young airman who cried "O murderers") is himself the confessed murderer under judgment, and also the Pilate who judges, and, at least as a representative of man, the savior whom the mob would condemn. He is even Pilate's better nature, his wife, for the lines "I have suffered, in a dream, because of him, / Many things" is merely a rearrangement of Matthew 27:19, the speech of Pilate's wife to her husband. But this last item is more than a reminiscence of the scriptural scene. It reinforces the speaker's present dilemma. The modern has had high hopes for man; are the hopes merely a dream? Is man incorrigible, merely a cruel beast? The speaker's present torture springs from that hope and from his reluctance to dismiss it as an empty dream. This Pilate is even harder pressed than was the Roman magistrate. For he must convince himself of this last savior's innocence. But he had lied for him before. He will lie for him now. "Men wash their hands in blood, as best they can: / I find no fault in this just man."

What is the meaning of "Men wash their hands in blood, as best they can"? It can mean "Since my own hands are bloody, I have no right to condemn the rest." It can mean "I know that man can love justice, even though his hands are bloody, for there is blood on mine." It can mean "Men are essentially decent: they try to keep their hands clean even if they have only blood in which to wash them."

None of these meanings cancels out the others. All are relevant, and each meaning contributes to the total meaning. Indeed, there is not a facet of significance which does not receive illumination from the figure.

Some of Jarrell's weaker poems seem weak to me because they lean too heavily upon this concept of the goodness of man. In some of them, his approach to the theme is too direct. But in this poem, the affirmation of man's essential justness by a Pilate who contents the people as he washes his hands in blood seems to me to supply every qualification that

---

[18] Randall Jarrell (1914–1965), American poet.

is required. The sense of self-guilt, the yearning to believe in man's justness, the knowledge of the difficulty of so believing—all work to render accurately and dramatically the total situation.

It is easy at this point to misapprehend the function of irony. We can say that Jarrell's irony pares his theme down to acceptable dimensions. The theme of man's goodness has here been so qualified that the poet himself does not really believe in it. But this is not what I am trying to say. We do not ask a poet to bring his poem into line with our personal beliefs—still less to flatter our personal beliefs. What we do ask is that the poem dramatize the situation so accurately, so honestly, with such fidelity to the total situation that it is no longer a question of our beliefs, but of our participation in the poetic experience. At his best, Jarrell manages to bring us by an act of imagination, to the most penetrating insight. Participating in that insight, we doubtless become better citizens. (One of the "uses" of poetry, I should agree, is to make us better citizens.) But poetry is not the eloquent rendition of the citizen's creed. It is not even the accurate rendition of his creed. Poetry must carry us beyond the abstract creed into the very matrix out of which, and from which, our creeds are abstracted. That is what *The Eighth Air Force* does. That is what, I am convinced, all good poetry does.

For the theme in a genuine poem does not confront us as abstraction—that is, as one man's generalization from the relevant particulars. Finding its proper symbol, defined and refined by the participating metaphors, the theme becomes a part of the reality in which we live—an insight, rooted in and growing out of concrete experience, many-sided, three-dimensional. Even the resistance to generalization has its part in this process—even the drag of the particulars away from the universal—even the tension of opposing themes—play their parts. The kite properly loaded, tension maintained along the kite string, rises steadily *against* the thrust of the wind.

Martin Heidegger

1889–1976

There is perhaps no figure who exemplifies the problematic character of twentieth-century philosophy and criticism as fully and as agonizingly as Martin Heidegger. As the student and eventually professorial successor of Edmund Husserl (above, page 770), Heidegger was (and was aware of being) in a position of historical privilege, as far as a particular conception of the enterprise of Western thinking was concerned. In Husserl's expansive and open style, the drama of thinking had found its rigor not in logistical technique, but in the open pursuit of transcendence, though for Husserl, the point of origin lay not in the immemoriality of time, but quite specifically in the idea of *logical investigations* in the most intimate contact with the dynamic of consciousness itself. For Heidegger, on the other hand, the lure of the immeasurable problems of Being and Time, joined in his first great book, comprise something very different from a phenomenological *epoché* or bracketing, but a veritable plunge into a metaphysical crisis of the times, appearing all the more so, not as an event attributable to such historical inconveniences as wars and economic catastrophes, but as a revelation about the shuddering faithlessness of contemporary philosophy, before its own great question of Being.

Whatever position one may at length settle upon with respect to the outcome, it is impossible to deny that Heidegger was faithful to this question with a tenacity and thoroughness that ensures his ranking among the great philosophers. Yet therein also lies the enormous difficulty that Heidegger presents, not merely in the all but incomprehensible embarrassment of his involvement with National Socialism in the 1930s, and his apparent reluctance to admit any fundamental error, despite having acknowledged *mistakes,* even at the time. While the episodes are amply discussed elsewhere, the persistent problem is not circumstantial, does not lie in any possible indictment or conviction of wrongdoing, but in the most intimate way with Heidegger's root conception of thinking and its relation to Being. The selection reprinted in part here, the *Letter on Humanism,* originally addressed to Jean Beaufret and first published in 1947, was written at least partly in answer to Jean Paul Sartre's *Existentialism Is a Humanism* of 1946, but it provides an eloquent and important statement of virtually all the themes of Heidegger's long philosophical career. Coming as it did after the end of the war, after the horrific disclosures of the Holocaust, the *Letter on Humanism* is all the more remarkable for the tenacity with which Heidegger reiterates his conception of *Dasein,* of Language as the House of Being, and of Thinking in its own element as the revelation of essence and not a *technical* pursuit of calculation or ordinary discourse. Though the trait is evident elsewhere also, Heidegger in the *Letter* repeatedly cites his own work, especially *Being and Time,* as if it were an independent agent: "*Being and Time* says . . ." and so on, with the effect of attributing to it a degree of monumental inevitability very much in keeping with his own undiminished sense of *his* project of thinking the essence of Being as not a choice but an arguably tragic destiny, as if in the very voice of Being itself.

From an earlier work, *An Introduction to Metaphysics* (1935), a less modulated or distanced approach to this issue articulates both the philosophical commitment and the felt urgency of the historical moment, as Heidegger frames his question, "How does it stand with being?"[1] allowing ironically that the question is "a very useless one." He goes on:

> And yet a *question, the* question: is "being" a mere word and its meaning a vapor or is it the spiritual destiny of the Western world?
>
> This Europe, in its ruinous blindness forever on the point of cutting its own throat, lies today in a great pincers, squeezed between Russia on one side and America on the other. From a metaphysical point of view, Russia and America are the same; the same dreary technological frenzy, the same unrestricted organization of the average man.

It is worth recalling that at approximately the same time, Rudolph Carnap published his carefully destructive critique of metaphysics (reprinted here, above, page 980), with Heidegger very much the target, insisting that the "question of being" was not so much "useless" as simply *meaningless*. It is not difficult to appreciate just how dark to Heidegger must have seemed "the darkening of the world, the flight of the gods, the destruction of the earth, the transformation of men into a mass, the hatred and suspicion of everything free and creative" (*Introduction,* 38), but at the same time, this is almost the language of rapture, of the fervently hoped-for apotheosis, or at least a *glimpse* of the lighting of Being that refused to come.

In the more sober and patient laying out of the argument in the *Letter on Humanism,* there remains the same irreversible opposition to the merely technical, to a sense of logic as mechanical or of thinking, out of its element, as the quotidian stuff of education and training: "By and by," Heidegger writes, "philosophy becomes a technique for explaining from highest causes. One no longer thinks; one occupies himself with 'philosophy.' " In this position, so unwaveringly held, Heidegger puts himself not so much in opposition to other schools, other philosophers (for example, Carnap), but to modernity itself, at war with the Century, the Epoch, tragically nostalgic for a greatness that "begins great, maintains itself only through the free recurrence of greatness within it, and if it is great ends also in greatness" (*Introduction,* 15). In the same way, Heidegger declines any easy agreement or conciliation with other versions of "existentialism," certainly not Sartre's, with its too-easy depiction of action as something that individuals *do.* In this respect, the Heidegger of the *Letter on Humanism* presents a heroic enactment of opposition not merely to one's enemies but to one's ostensible friends, certainly here to the tame philosophy of Sartre, but beyond that to any acknowledgment that the *techné* of formal argument, the less sweeping give and take of professional discourse within a civil community, is one of the ways that Being has of protecting us from our own *hubris*. While Carnap might represent the out-of-date metaphysician as like a musician without any musical talent, the expressiveness in Heidegger lies in the irreducible complexity of his defense of philosophy as the love of wisdom and thinking as an illimitable activity with the disclosure of being as its ultimate destination. Like the very

---

[1] *An Introduction to Metaphysics,* tr. Ralph Mannheim (1959), 37.

century he seems to oppose, Heidegger's relentlessness does not, in itself, come to any easy resolution or catharsis but remains, in root and branch, a kind of insistent, organic witness to the profound uneasiness of being and time, in our time.

Translations from Heidegger's voluminous writings continue to appear, drawn from the collected *Works, 1975–2000,* still in progress. Especially recommended is *Basic Writings from Being and Time (1927) to The Task of Thinking (1964),* ed. David Farrell Krell (1977). His major works in translation include: *Being and Time* (1927, tr. 1962); *An Introduction to Metaphysics* (1935, tr. 1959); *Kant and the Problem of Metaphysics* (1951, tr. 1990); *Existence and Being,* including "Hölderlin and the Essence of Poetry," (1956); *Nietzsche* (1961, tr. 1979); *What Is Called Thinking?* (1968); *Early Greek Thinking* (1975); *The Question Concerning Technology and Other Essays* (1977); and *Parmenides* (1982, tr. 1992). Studies of Heidegger include: Arne Naess, *Four Modern Philosophers: Carnap, Heidegger, Wittgenstein, Sartre* (1968); Michael Murray, ed., *Heidegger and Modern Philosophy* (1978); Steven L. Bindeman, *Heidegger and Wittgenstein, The Politics of Silence* (1981); Richard Polt, *Heidegger: An Introduction* (1999); Daniela Vallega-Neu, *Heidegger's Contributions to Philosophy: An Introduction* (2003); Miguel de Beistegui, *Thinking with Heidegger: Displacements* (2003). For an introduction to the vexed question of Heidegger's involvement with the Third Reich, see Richard Wolin, *The Heidegger Controversy: A Critical Reader* (1993).

from

Letter on Humanism[1]

We are still far from pondering the essence of action decisively enough. We view action only as causing an effect. The actuality of the effect is valued according to its utility. But the essence of action is accomplishment. To accomplish means to unfold something into the fullness of its essence, to lead it forth into this fullness—*producere.* Therefore only

what already is can really be accomplished. But what "is" above all is Being. Thinking accomplishes the relation of Being to the essence of man. It does not make or cause the relation. Thinking brings this relation to Being solely as something handed over to it from Being. Such offering consists in the fact that in thinking Being comes to language. Language is the house of Being. In its home man dwells. Those who think and those who create with words are the guardians of this home. Their guardianship accomplishes the manifestation of Being insofar as they bring the manifestation to language and maintain it in language through their speech. Thinking does not become action only because some effect issues from it or because it is applied. Thinking acts insofar as it thinks. Such action is presumably the simplest and at the same time the highest, because it concerns the relation of Being to man. But all working or effecting lies in Being and is directed toward beings. Thinking, in contrast, lets itself be claimed by Being so that it can say the truth of Being. Thinking accomplishes this letting.

* * *

... Thinking is not merely *l'engagement dans l'action* for and by beings, in the sense of the actuality of the present situation. Thinking is *l'engagement* by and for the truth of Being.

"Letter on Humanism" was first published in German in 1947. The edition reprinted in part here was translated by Frank A. Capuzzi and J. Glenn Gray. Reprinted from Martin Heidegger, *Basic Writings from Being and Time (1927) to The Task of Thinking (1964),* ed. David Farrell Krell (New York: Harper & Row, 1977).

[1] [Krell] This new translation of *Brief über den Humanismus* by Frank A. Capuzzi in collaboration with J. Glenn Gray appears here in its entirety. I have edited it with reference to the helpful French bilingual edition, Martin Heidegger, *Lettre sur l'humanisme,* translated by Roger Munier, revised edition (Paris: Aubier Montaigne, 1964). A previous English translation by Edgar Lohner is included in *Philosophy in the Twentieth Century,* edited by William Barrett and Henry D. Aiken (New York: Random House, 1962), III, 271–302. The German text was first published in 1947 by A. Francke Verlag, Bern; the present translation is based on the text in Martin Heidegger, *Wegmarken* (Frankfurt am Main: Vittorio Klostermann Verlag, 1967), pp. 145–194.

The history of Being is never past but stands ever before; it sustains and defines every *condition et situation humaine*. In order to learn how to experience the aforementioned essence of thinking purely, and that means at the same time to carry it through, we must free ourselves from the technical interpretation of thinking. The beginnings of that interpretation reach back to Plato and Aristotle.[2] They take thinking itself to be a *technē*, a process of reflection in service to doing and making. But here reflection is already seen from the perspective of *praxis* and *poiēsis*. For this reason thinking, when taken for itself, is not "practical." The characterization of thinking as *theōria* and the determination of knowing as "theoretical" behavior occur already within the "technical" interpretation of thinking. Such characterization is a reactive attempt to rescue thinking and preserve its autonomy over against acting and doing. Since then "philosophy" has been in the constant predicament of having to justify its existence before the "sciences." It believes it can do that most effectively by elevating itself to the rank of a science. But such an effort is the abandonment of the essence of thinking. Philosophy is hounded by the fear that it loses prestige and validity if it is not a science. Not to be a science is taken as a failing which is equivalent to being unscientific. Being, as the element of thinking, is abandoned by the technical interpretation of thinking. "Logic," beginning with the Sophists and Plato, sanctions this explanation. Thinking is judged by a standard that does not measure up to it. Such judgment may be compared to the procedure of trying to evaluate the nature and powers of a fish by seeing how long it can live on dry land. For a long time now, all too long, thinking has been stranded on dry land. Can then the effort to return thinking to its element be called "irrationalism"?

Surely the questions raised in your letter would have been better answered in direct conversation. In written form thinking easily loses its flexibility. But in writing it is difficult above all to retain the multidimensionality of the realm peculiar to thinking. The rigor of thinking, in contrast to that of the sciences, does not consist merely in an artificial, that is, technical-theoretical exactness of concepts. It lies in the fact that speaking remains purely in the element of Being and lets the simplicity of its manifold dimensions rule. On the other hand, written composition exerts a wholesome pressure toward deliberate linguistic formulation. Today I would like to grapple with only one of your questions. Perhaps its discussion will also shed some light on the others.

You ask: *Comment redonner un sens au mot 'Humanisme'?* [How can we restore meaning to the word "human-

ism"?] This question proceeds from your intention to retain the word "humanism." I wonder whether that is necessary. Or is the damage caused by all such terms still not sufficiently obvious? True, "-isms" have for a long time now been suspect. But the market of public opinion continually demands new ones. We are always prepared to supply the demand. Even such names as "logic," "ethics," and "physics" begin to flourish only when original thinking comes to an end. During the time of their greatness the Greeks thought without such headings. They did not even call thinking "philosophy." Thinking comes to an end when it slips out of its element. The element is what enables thinking to be a thinking.

* * *

When thinking comes to an end by slipping out of its element it replaces this loss by procuring a validity for itself as *technē*, as an instrument of education and therefore as a classroom matter and later a cultural concern. By and by philosophy becomes a technique for explaining from highest causes. One no longer thinks; one occupies himself with "philosophy." In competition with one another, such occupations publicly offer themselves as "-isms" and try to offer more than the others. The dominance of such terms is not accidental. It rests above all in the modern age upon the peculiar dictatorship of the public realm. However, so-called "private existence" is not really essential, that is to say free, human being. It simply insists on negating the public realm. It remains an offshoot that depends upon the public and nourishes itself by a mere withdrawal from it. Hence it testifies, against its own will, to its subservience to the public realm. But because it stems from the dominance of subjectivity the public realm itself is the metaphysically conditioned establishment and authorization of the openness of individual beings in their unconditional objectification. Language thereby falls into the service of expediting communication along routes where objectification—the uniform accessibility of everything to everyone—branches out and disregards all limits. In this way language comes under the dictatorship of the public realm which decides in advance what is intelligible and what must be rejected as unintelligible.

* * *

. . . The widely and rapidly spreading devastation of language not only undermines aesthetic and moral responsibility in every use of language; it arises from a threat to the essence of humanity. A merely cultivated use of language is still no proof that we have as yet escaped the danger to our essence.

---

[2] Plato (above, page 8); Aristotle (above, page 48).

These days, in fact, such usage might sooner testify that we have not yet seen and cannot see the danger because we have never yet placed ourselves in view of it. Much bemoaned of late, and much too lately, the downfall of language is, however, not the grounds for, but already a consequence of, the state of affairs in which language under the dominance of the modern metaphysics of subjectivity almost irremediably falls out of its element. Language still denies us its essence: that it is the house of the truth of Being. Instead, language surrenders itself to our mere willing and trafficking as an instrument of domination over beings. Beings themselves appear as actualities in the interaction of cause and effect. We encounter beings as actualities in a calculative business-like way, but also scientifically and by way of philosophy, with explanations and proofs. Even the assurance that something is inexplicable belongs to these explanations and proofs. With such statements we believe that we confront the mystery. As if it were already decided that the truth of Being lets itself at all be established in causes and explanatory grounds or, what comes to the same, in their incomprehensibility.

But if man is to find his way once again into the nearness of Being he must first learn to exist in the nameless. In the same way he must recognize the seductions of the public realm as well as the impotence of the private. Before he speaks man must first let himself be claimed again by Being, taking the risk that under this claim he will seldom have much to say. Only thus will the preciousness of its essence be once more bestowed upon the word, and upon man a home for dwelling in the truth of Being.

But in the claim upon man, in the attempt to make man ready for this claim, is there not implied a concern about man? Where else does "care" tend but in the direction of bringing man back to his essence?[3] What else does that in turn betoken but that man *(homo)* become human *(humanus)?* Thus *humanitas* really does remain the concern of such thinking. For this is humanism: meditating and caring, that man be human and not inhumane, "inhuman," that is, outside his essence. But in what does the humanity of man consist? It lies in his essence.

---

[3] [Krell] In the final chapter of division one of *Being and Time* Heidegger defines "care" as the Being of Dasein. It is a name for the structural whole of existence in all its modes and for the broadest and most basic possibilities of discovery and disclosure of self and world. Most poignantly experienced in the phenomenon of anxiety—which is not fear of anything at hand but awareness of my being-in-the-world as such—"care" describes the sundry ways I get involved in the issue of my birth, life, and death, whether by my projects, inclinations, insights, or illusions. "Care" is the all-inclusive name for my concern for other people, preoccupations with things, and awareness of my proper Being. It expresses the movement of my life out of a past, into a future, through the present. In section 65 the ontological meaning of the Being of care proves to be *temporality.*

* * *

Humanitas, explicitly so called, was first considered and striven for in the age of the Roman Republic. *Homo humanus* was opposed to *homo barbarus. Homo humanus* here means the Romans, who exalted and honored Roman *virtus* through the "embodiment" of the *paideia* [education] taken over from the Greeks. These were the Greeks of the Hellenistic age, whose culture was acquired in the schools of philosophy. It was concerned with *eruditio et institutio in bonas artes* [scholarship and training in good conduct]. *Paideia* thus understood was translated as *humanitas.* The genuine *romanitas* of *homo romanus* consisted in such *humanitas.* We encounter the first humanism in Rome: it therefore remains in essence a specifically Roman phenomenon which emerges from the encounter of Roman civilization with the culture of late Greek civilization. The so-called Renaissance of the fourteenth and fifteenth centuries in Italy is a *renascentia romanitatis.* Because *romanitas* is what matters, it is concerned with *humanitas* and therefore with Greek *paideia.* But Greek civilization is always seen in its later form and this itself is seen from a Roman point of view. The *homo romanus* of the Renaissance also stands in opposition to *homo barbarus.* But now the in-humane is the supposed barbarism of gothic Scholasticism in the Middle Ages. Therefore a *studium humanitatis,* which in a certain way reaches back to the ancients and thus also becomes a revival of Greek civilization, always adheres to historically understood humanism. For Germans this is apparent in the humanism of the eighteenth century supported by Winckelmann, Goethe, and Schiller.[4] On the other hand, Hölderlin does not belong to "humanism" precisely because he thought the destiny of man's essence in a more original way than "humanism" could.

But if one understands humanism in general as a concern that man become free for his humanity and find his worth in it, then humanism differs according to one's conception of the "freedom" and "nature" of man. So too are there various paths toward the realization of such conceptions. The humanism of Marx[5] does not need to return to antiquity any more than the humanism which Sartre[6] conceives existentialism to be. In this broad sense Christianity too is a humanism, in that according to its teaching everything depends on man's salvation *(salus aeterna);* the

---

[4] Johann Joachim Winckelmann (1717–1768), German archaeologist and art historian; Wolfgang von Goethe (1749–1832), German poet and dramatist; Schiller (above, page 460).
[5] Marx (above, page 607).
[6] Sartre (below, page 1175).

history of man appears in the context of the history of re-demption. However different these forms of humanism may be in purpose and in principle, in the mode and means of their respective realizations, and in the form of their teach-ing, they nonetheless all agree in this, that the *humanitas* of *homo humanus* is determined with regard to an already es-tablished interpretation of nature, history, world, and the ground of the world, that is, of beings as a whole.

Every humanism is either grounded in a metaphysics or is itself made to be the ground of one. Every determina-tion of the essence of man that already presupposes an inter-pretation of being without asking about the truth of Being, whether knowingly or not, is metaphysical. The result is that what is peculiar to all metaphysics, specifically with respect to the way the essence of man is determined, is that it is "hu-manistic." Accordingly, every humanism remains metaphys-ical. In defining the humanity of man humanism not only does not ask about the relation of Being to the essence of man; because of its metaphysical origin humanism even im-pedes the question by neither recognizing nor understand-ing it. On the contrary, the necessity and proper form of the question concerning the truth of Being, forgotten in and through metaphysics, can come to light only if the question "What is metaphysics?" is posed in the midst of meta-physics' domination. Indeed every inquiry into Being, even the one into the truth of Being, must at first introduce its in-quiry as a "metaphysical" one.

The first humanism, Roman humanism, and every kind that has emerged from that time to the present, has presup-posed the most universal "essence" of man to be obvious. Man is considered to be an *animal rationale*. This definition is not simply the Latin translation of the Greek *zōon logon echon* but rather a metaphysical interpretation of it. This es-sential definition of man is not false. But it is conditioned by metaphysics. The essential provenance of metaphysics, and not just its limits, became questionable in *Being and Time*. What is questionable is above all commended to thinking as what is to be thought, but not at all left to the gnawing doubts of an empty skepticism.

Metaphysics does indeed represent beings in their Be-ing, and so it thinks the Being of beings. But it does not think the difference of both.[7] Metaphysics does not ask about the truth of Being itself. Nor does it therefore ask in what way the essence of man belongs to the truth of Being. Metaphysics has not only failed up to now to ask this ques-tion, the question is inaccessible to metaphysics as such. Being is still waiting for the time when it will become thought-provoking to man. With regard to the definition of man's essence, however one may determine the *ratio* of the *animal* and the reason of the living being, whether as a "fac-ulty of principles," or a "faculty of categories," or in some other way, the essence of reason is always and in each case grounded in this: for every apprehending of beings in their Being, Being itself is already illumined and comes to pass in its truth. So too with *animal, zōon,* an interpretation of "life" is already posited which necessarily lies in an inter-pretation of beings as *zōē* and *physis,* within which what is living appears. Above and beyond everything else, however, it finally remains to ask whether the essence of man primor-dially and most decisively lies in the dimension of *animali-tas* at all. Are we really on the right track toward the essence of man as long as we set him off as one living creature among others in contrast to plants, beasts, and God? We can proceed in that way; we can in such fashion locate man within being as one being among others. We will thereby al-ways be able to state something correct about man. But we must be clear on this point, that when we do this we aban-don man to the essential realm of *animalitas* even if we do not equate him with beasts but attribute a specific difference to him. In principle we are still thinking of *homo animalis*—even when *anima* [soul] is posited as *animus sive mens* [spirit or mind], and this in turn is later posited as subject, person, or spirit [*Geist*]. Such positing is the manner of metaphysics. But then the essence of man is too little heeded and not thought in its origin, the essential prove-nance that is always the essential future for historical mankind. Metaphysics thinks of man on the basis of *animal-itas* and does not think in the direction of his *humanitas*.

Metaphysics closes itself to the simple essential fact that man essentially occurs only in his essence, where he is claimed by Being. Only from that claim "has" he found that wherein his essence dwells. Only from this dwelling "has" he "language" as the home that preserves the ecstatic for his essence.[8] Such standing in the lighting of Being I call the ek-sistence of man. This way of Being is proper only to man. Ek-sistence so understood is not only the ground of the

[7][Heidegger] Cf. Martin Heidegger, *Vom Wesen des Grundes* (1929), p. 8; *Kant and the Problem of Metaphysics,* trans. J. Churchill (Bloomington, Ind.: Indiana University Press, 1962), p. 243; and *Being and Time,* section 44, p. 230.

[8][Krell] In *Being and Time* "ecstatic" (from the Greek *ekstasis*) means the way Dasein "stands out" in the various moments of the temporality of care, being "thrown" out of a past and "projecting" itself toward a future by way of the present. The word is closely related to another Heidegger introduces now to capture the unique sense of man's Being—*ek-sistence.* This too means the way man "stands out" into the truth of Being and so is excep-tional among beings that are on hand only as things of nature or human pro-duction. Cf. Heidegger's definition of "existence" in *Being and Time,* and his use of ek-sistence in Reading III.

possibility of reason, *ratio,* but is also that in which the essence of man preserves the source that determines him.

* * *

What man is—or, as it is called in the traditional language of metaphysics, the "essence" of man—lies in his ek-sistence. But ek-sistence thought in this way is not identical with the traditional concept of *existentia,* which means actuality in contrast to the meaning of *essentia* as possibility. In *Being and Time* this sentence is italicized: "The 'essence' of Dasein lies in its existence." However, here the opposition between *existentia* and *essentia* is not under consideration, because neither of these metaphysical determinations of Being, let alone their relationship, is yet in question. Still less does the sentence contain a universal statement about *Dasein,* since the word came into fashion in the eighteenth century as a name for "object," intending to express the metaphysical concept of the actuality of the actual. On the contrary, the sentence says: man occurs essentially in such a way that he is the "there" [*das "Da"*], that is, the lighting of Being. The "Being" of the *Da,* and only it, has the fundamental character of ek-sistence, that is, of an ecstatic inherence in the truth of Being. The ecstatic essence of man consists in ek-sistence, which is different from the metaphysically conceived *existentia.* Medieval philosophy conceives the latter as *actualitas.* Kant represents *existentia* as actuality in the sense of the objectivity of experience. Hegel defines *existentia* as the self-knowing Idea of absolute subjectivity. Nietzsche grasps *existentia* as the eternal recurrence of the same. Here it remains an open question whether through *existentia*—in these explanations of it as actuality, which at first seem quite different—the Being of a stone or even life as the Being of plants and animals is adequately thought. In any case living creatures are as they are without standing outside their Being as such and within the truth of Being, preserving in such standing the essential nature of their Being. Of all the beings that are, presumably the most difficult to think about are living creatures, because on the one hand they are in a certain way most closely related to us, and on the other are at the same time separated from our ek-sistent essence by an abyss. However, it might also seem as though the essence of divinity is closer to us than what is foreign in other living creatures, closer, namely, in an essential distance which however distant is nonetheless more familiar to our ek-sistent essence than is our appalling and scarcely conceivable bodily kinship with the beast. Such reflections cast a strange light upon the current and therefore always still premature designation of man as *animal rationale.* Because plants and animals are lodged in their respective environments but are never placed freely in the lighting of Being which alone is "world," they lack language. But in being denied language they are not thereby suspended worldlessly in their environment. Still, in this word "environment" converges all that is puzzling about living creatures. In its essence language is not the utterance of an organism; nor is it the expression of a living thing. Nor can it ever be thought in an essentially correct way in terms of its symbolic character, perhaps not even in terms of the character of signification. Language is the lighting-concealing advent of Being itself.

Ek-sistence, thought in terms of *ecstasis,* does not coincide with *existentia* in either form or content. In terms of content ek-sistence means standing out into the truth of Being. *Existentia (existence)* means in contrast *actualitas,* actuality as opposed to mere possibility as Idea. Ek-sistence identifies the determination of what man is in the destiny of truth. *Existentia* is the name for the realization of something that is as it appears in its Idea. The sentence "Man ek-sists" is not an answer to the question of whether man actually is or not; rather, it responds to the question concerning man's "essence." We are accustomed to posing this question with equal impropriety whether we ask what man is or who he is. For in the *Who?* or the *What?* we are already on the lookout for something like a person or an object. But the personal no less than the objective misses and misconstrues the essential unfolding of ek-sistence in the history of Being. That is why the sentence cited from *Being and Time* is careful to enclose the word "essence" in quotation marks. This indicates that "essence" is now being defined from neither *esse essentiae* nor *esse existentiae* but rather from the ek-static character of Dasein. As ek-sisting, man sustains Da-sein in that he takes the *Da,* the lighting of Being, into "care." But Da-sein itself occurs essentially as "thrown." It unfolds essentially in the throw of Being as the fateful sending.

But it would be the ultimate error if one wished to explain the sentence about man's ek-sistent essence as if it were the secularized transference to human beings of a thought that Christian theology expresses about God (*Deus est suum esse* [God is His Being]); for ek-sistence is not the realization of an essence, nor does ek-sistence itself even effect and posit what is essential. If we understand what *Being and Time* calls "projection" as a representational positing, we take it to be an achievement of subjectivity and do not think it in the only way the "understanding of Being" in the context of the "existential analysis" of "being-in-the-world" can be thought—namely as the ecstatic relation to the lighting of Being. The adequate execution and completion of this other thinking that abandons subjectivity is surely made more difficult by the fact that in the publication of *Being and Time* the third division of the first part, "Time and Being," was held back (cf. *Being and Time*, p. 88). Here everything is reversed. The section in question was held back because thinking failed in the adequate saying of this turning [*Kehre*] and did not succeed with the help of the language of metaphysics. The lecture "On the Essence of Truth," thought out and delivered in 1930 but not printed until 1943, provides a certain insight into the thinking of the turning from "Being and Time" to "Time and Being." This turning is not a change of standpoint from *Being and Time,* but in it the thinking that was sought first arrives at the location of that dimension out of which *Being and Time* is experienced, that is to say, experienced from the fundamental experience of the oblivion of Being.

By way of contrast, Sartre expresses the basic tenet of existentialism in this way: Existence precedes essence.[9] In this statement he is taking *existentia* and *essentia* according to their metaphysical meaning, which from Plato's time on has said that *essentia* precedes *existentia*. Sartre reverses this statement. But the reversal of a metaphysical statement remains a metaphysical statement. With it he stays with metaphysics in oblivion of the truth of Being. For even if philosophy wishes to determine the relation of *essentia* and *existentia* in the sense it had in medieval controversies, in Leibniz's sense, or in some other way, it still remains to ask first of all from what destiny of Being this differentiation in Being as *esse essentiae* and *esse existentiae* comes to appear to thinking. We have yet to consider why the question about the destiny of Being was never asked and why it could never be thought. Or is the fact that this is how it is with the differentiation of *essentia* and *existentia* not at all a sign of forgetfulness of Being? We must presume that this destiny does not rest upon a mere failure of human thinking, let alone upon a lesser capacity of early Western thinking. Concealed in its essential provenance, the differentiation of *essentia* (essentiality) and *existentia* (actuality) completely dominates the destiny of Western history and of all history determined by Europe.

Sartre's key proposition about the priority of *existentia* over *essentia* does, however, justify using the name "existentialism" as an appropriate title for a philosophy of this sort. But the basic tenet of "existentialism" has nothing at all in common with the statement from *Being and Time*— apart from the fact that in *Being and Time* no statement about the relation of *essentia* and *existentia* can yet be expressed since there it is still a question of preparing something precursory. As is obvious from what we have just said, that happens clumsily enough. What still today remains to be said could perhaps become an impetus for guiding the essence of man to the point where it thoughtfully attends to that dimension of the truth of Being which thoroughly governs it. But even this could take place only to the honor of Being and for the benefit of Dasein which man eksistingly sustains; not, however, for the sake of man so that civilization and culture through man's doings might be vindicated.

But in order that we today may attain to the dimension of the truth of Being in order to ponder it, we should first of all make clear how Being concerns man and how it claims him. Such an essential experience happens to us when it dawns on us that man is in that he eksists. Were we now to say this in the language of the tradition, it would run: the eksistence of man is his substance. That is why in *Being and Time* the sentence often recurs, "The 'substance' of man is existence." But "substance," thought in terms of the history of Being, is already a blanket translation of *ousia,* a word that designates the presence of what is present and at the same time, with puzzling ambiguity, usually means what is present itself. If we think the metaphysical term "substance" in the sense already suggested in accordance with the "phenomenological destruction" carried out in *Being and Time,* then the statement "The 'substance' of man is ek-sistence" says nothing else but that the way that man in his proper essence becomes present to Being is ecstatic inherence in the truth of Being. Through this determination of the essence of man the humanistic interpretations of man as *animal rationale,* as "person," as spiritual-ensouled-bodily being, are not declared false and thrust aside. Rather, the sole implication is that the highest determinations of the essence of man in humanism still do not realize the proper dignity of man. To that extent the thinking in *Being and Time* is against humanism. But this opposition does not mean that such thinking aligns itself against the humane and advocates the inhuman, that it promotes the inhumane and deprecates the dignity of man. Humanism is opposed because it does not set the *humanitas* of man high enough. Of course the essential worth of man does not consist in his being the substance of beings, as the "Subject" among them, so that as the tyrant of Being he may deign to release the beingness of beings into an all too loudly bruited "objectivity."

Man is rather "thrown" from Being itself into the truth of Being, so that ek-sisting in this fashion he might guard the truth of Being, in order that beings might appear in the light of Being as the beings they are. Man does not decide whether and how beings appear, whether and how God and the gods or history and nature come forward into the lighting of Being, come to presence and depart. The advent of

---

[9][Krell] Cf. Jean-Paul Sartre, *L'Existentialisme est un humanisme* (Paris: Nagel, 1946), pp. 17, 21, and elsewhere.

beings lies in the destiny of Being. But for man it is ever a question of finding what is fitting in his essence which corresponds to such destiny; for in accord with this destiny man as ek-sisting has to guard the truth of Being. Man is the shepherd of Being. It is in this direction alone that *Being and Time* is thinking when ecstatic existence is experienced as "care" (cf. section 44 C).

Yet Being—what is Being? It is It itself. The thinking that is to come must learn to experience that and to say it. "Being"—that is not God and not a cosmic ground. Being is farther than all beings and is yet nearer to man than every being, be it a rock, a beast, a work of art, a machine, be it an angel or God. Being is the nearest. Yet the near remains farthest from man. Man at first clings always and only to beings. But when thinking represents beings as beings it no doubt relates itself to Being. In truth, however, it always thinks only of beings as such; precisely not, and never, Being as such. The "question of Being" always remains a question about beings. It is still not at all what its elusive name indicates: the question in the direction of Being. Philosophy, even when it becomes "critical" through Descartes and Kant,[10] always follows the course of metaphysical representation. It thinks from beings back to beings with a glance in passing toward Being. For every departure from beings and every return to them stands already in the light of Being.

But metaphysics recognizes the lighting of Being either solely as the view of what is present in "outward appearance" *(idea)* or critically as what is seen as a result of categorial representation on the part of subjectivity. This means that the truth of Being as the lighting itself remains concealed for metaphysics. However, this concealment is not a defect of metaphysics but a treasure withheld from it yet held before it, the treasure of its own proper wealth. But the lighting itself is Being. Within the destiny of Being in metaphysics the lighting first affords a view by which what is present comes into touch with man, who is present to it, so that man himself can in apprehending *(noein)* first touch upon Being *(thigein,* Aristotle, *Met.* IX, 10). This view first gathers the aspect to itself. It yields to such aspects when apprehending has become a setting-forth-before-itself in the *perceptio* of the *res cogitans* taken as the *subiectum* of *certitudo.*

But how—provided we really ought to ask such a question at all—how does Being relate to ek-sistence? Being itself is the relation to the extent that It, as the location of the truth of Being amid beings, gathers to itself and embraces

ek-sistence in its existential, that is, ecstatic, essence. Because man as the one who ek-sists comes to stand in this relation that Being destines for itself, in that he ecstatically sustains it, that is, in care takes it upon himself, he at first fails to recognize the nearest and attaches himself to the next nearest. He even thinks that this is the nearest. But nearer than the nearest and at the same time for ordinary thinking farther than the farthest is nearness itself: the truth of Being.

Forgetting the truth of Being in favor of the pressing throng of beings unthought in their essence is what ensnarement [*Verfallen*] means in *Being and Time.*[11] This word does not signify the Fall of Man understood in a "moral-philosophical" and at the same time secularized way; rather, it designates an essential relationship of man to Being within Being's relation to the essence of man. Accordingly, the terms "authenticity" and "inauthenticity," which are used in a provisional fashion, do not imply a moral-existential or an "anthropological" distinction but rather a relation which, because it has been hitherto concealed from philosophy, has yet to be thought for the first time, an "ecstatic" relation of the essence of man to the truth of Being. But this relation is as it is not by reason of ek-sistence; on the contrary, the essence of ek-sistence derives existentially-ecstatically from the essence of the truth of Being.

The one thing thinking would like to attain and for the first time tries to articulate in *Being and Time* is something simple. As such, Being remains mysterious, the simple nearness of an unobtrusive governance. The nearness occurs essentially as language itself. But language is not mere speech, insofar as we represent the latter at best as the unity of phoneme (or written character), melody, rhythm, and meaning (or sense). We think of the phoneme and written character as a verbal body for language, of melody and rhythm as its soul, and whatever has to do with meaning as its mind. We usually think of language as corresponding to the essence of man represented as *animal rationale,* that is, as the unity of body-soul-mind. But just as ek-sistence—and through it the relation of the truth of Being to man—

---

[10]René Descartes (1596–1650), French philosopher and mathematician; Kant (above, page 416).

[11] [Krell] In *Being and Time* (cf. esp. sections 25–27, 38, and 68 C) *Verfallen,* literally a "falling" or "lapsing," serves as a third constitutive moment of being-in-the-world. Dasein is potentiality for Being, directed toward a future in which it can realize its possibilities: this is its "existentiality." But existence is always "thrown" out of a past that determines its trajectory: this is its "facticity." Meanwhile, Dasein usually busies itself in quotidien affairs, losing itself in the present, forgetting what is most its own: this is its *Verfallensein.* (The last-named is not simply a matter of "everyday" dealings, however, since the tendency to let theoretical problems slip into the readymade solutions of a tradition affects interpretation itself.) To forget what is most its own is what Heidegger means by *Uneigentlichkeit,* usually rendered as "inauthenticity."

remains veiled in the humanitas of *homo animalis,* so does the metaphysical-animal explanation of language cover up the essence of language in the history of Being. According to this essence language is the house of Being which comes to pass from Being and is pervaded by Being. And so it is proper to think the essence of language from its correspondence to Being and indeed as this correspondence, that is, as the home of man's essence.

But man is not only a living creature who possesses language along with other capacities. Rather, language is the house of Being in which man ek-sists by dwelling, in that he belongs to the truth of Being, guarding it.

So the point is that in the determination of the humanity of man as ek-sistence what is essential is not man but Being—as the dimension of the *ecstasis* of ek-sistence. However, the dimension is not something spatial in the familiar sense. Rather, everything spatial and all space-time occur essentially in the dimensionality which Being itself is.

Thinking attends to these simple relationships. It tries to find the right word for them within the long traditional language and grammar of metaphysics. But does such thinking—granted that there is something in a name—still allow itself to be described as humanism? Certainly not so far as humanism thinks metaphysically. Certainly not if humanism is existentialism and is represented by what Sartre expresses: *précisément nous sommes sur un plan où il y a seulement des hommes* [We are precisely in a situation where there are only human beings].[12] Thought from *Being and Time,* this should say instead: *précisément nous sommes sur un plan où il y a principalement l'Être* [We are precisely in a situation where principally there is Being]. But where does *le plan* come from and what is it? *L'Être et le plan* are the same. In *Being and Time* (p. 212) we purposely and cautiously say, *il y a l'Être:* "there is / it gives" [*"es gibt"*] Being. *Il y a* translates "it gives" imprecisely. For the "it" that here "gives" is Being itself. The "gives" names the essence of Being that is giving, granting its truth. The self-giving into the open, along with the open region itself, is Being itself.

At the same time "it gives" is used preliminarily to avoid the locution "Being is"; for "is" is commonly said of some thing which is. We call such a thing a being. But Being "is" precisely not "a being." If "is" is spoken without a closer interpretation of Being, then Being is all too easily represented as a "being" after the fashion of the familiar sort of beings which act as causes and are actualized as effects. And yet Parmenides,[13] in the early age of thinking, says, *esti gar einai,* "for there is Being." The primal mystery for all thinking is concealed in this phrase. Perhaps "is" can be said only of Being in an appropriate way, so that no individual being ever properly "is." But because thinking should be directed only toward saying Being in its truth instead of explaining it as a particular being in terms of beings, whether and how Being is must remain an open question for the careful attention of thinking.

The *esti gar einai* of Parmenides is still unthought today. That allows us to gauge how things stand with the progress of philosophy. When philosophy attends to its essence it does not make forward strides at all. It remains where it is in order constantly to think the Same. Progression, that is, progression forward from this place, is a mistake that follows thinking as the shadow which thinking itself casts. Because Being is still unthought, *Being and Time* too says of it, "there is / it gives." Yet one cannot speculate about this *il y a* precipitously and without a foothold. This "there is / it gives" rules as the destiny of Being. Its history comes to language in the words of essential thinkers. Therefore the thinking that thinks into the truth of Being is, as thinking, historical. There is not a "systematic" thinking and next to it an illustrative history of past opinions. Nor is there, as Hegel[14] thought, only a systematics which can fashion the law of its thinking into the law of history and simultaneously subsume history into the system. Thought in a more primordial way, there is the history of Being to which thinking belongs as recollection of this history that unfolds of itself. Such recollective thought differs essentially from the subsequent presentation of history in the sense of an evanescent past. History does not take place primarily as a happening. And its happening is not evanescence. The happening of history occurs essentially as the destiny of the truth of Being and from it.[15] Being comes to destiny in that It, Being, gives itself. But thought in terms of such destiny this says: it gives itself and refuses itself simultaneously. Nonetheless, Hegel's definition of history as the development of "Spirit" is not untrue. Neither is it partly correct and

---

[12] [Krell] Heidegger cites Sartre's *L'Existentialisme est un humanisme,* p. 36. The context of Sartre's remark is as follows. He is arguing (pp. 33 ff.) "that God does not exist, and that it is necessary to draw the consequences to the end." To those who assert that the death of God leaves traditional values and norms untouched—and humanism is one such value—Sartre rejoins "that it is very distressing that God does not exist because with him vanishes every possibility of finding values in some intelligible heaven; we can no longer locate an *a priori* Good since there is no infinite and perfect consciousness to think it; it is nowhere written that the Good exists, that we must be honest, that we mustn't lie, precisely because we are in a situation where there are only human beings."

[13] Parmenides (fifth century B.C.), Greek philosopher.

[14] Hegel (above, page 552).

[15] [Heidegger] See the lecture on Hölderlin's hymn, "Wie wenn am Feiertage . . ." in Martin Heidegger, *Erläuterungen zu Hölderlins Dichtung,* fourth, expanded ed. (Frankfurt am Main: V. Klostermann, 1971), p. 76.

partly false. It is as true as metaphysics, which through Hegel first brings to language its essence—thought in terms of the absolute—in the system. Absolute metaphysics, with its Marxian and Nietzschean[16] inversions, belongs to the history of the truth of Being. Whatever stems from it cannot be countered or even cast aside by refutations. It can only be taken up in such a way that its truth is more primordially sheltered in Being itself and removed from the domain of mere human opinion. All refutation in the field of essential thinking is foolish. Strife among thinkers is the "lovers' quarrel" concerning the matter itself. It assists them mutually toward a simple belonging to the Same, from which they find what is fitting for them in the destiny of Being.

Assuming that in the future man will be able to think the truth of Being, he will think from ek-sistence. Man stands ek-sistingly in the destiny of Being. The ek-sistence of man is historical as such, but not only or primarily because so much happens to man and to things human in the course of time. Because it must think the ek-sistence of Dasein, the thinking of *Being and Time* is essentially concerned that the historicity of Dasein be experienced.

But does not *Being and Time* say, where the "there is / it gives" comes to language, "Only so long as Dasein is, is there [*gibt es*] Being"? To be sure. It means that only so long as the lighting of Being comes to pass does Being convey itself to man. But the fact that the *Da*, the lighting as the truth of Being itself, comes to pass is the dispensation of Being itself. This is the destiny of the lighting. But the sentence does not mean that the Dasein of man in the traditional sense of *existentia,* and thought in modern philosophy as the actuality of the *ego cogito,* is that being through which Being is first fashioned. The sentence does not say that Being is the product of man. The "Introduction" to *Being and Time* says simply and clearly, even in italics, "Being is the *transcendens* pure and simple." Just as the openness of spatial nearness seen from the perspective of a particular thing exceeds all things near and far, so is Being essentially broader than all beings, because it is the lighting itself. For all that, Being is thought on the basis of beings, a consequence of the approach—at first unavoidable—within a metaphysics that is still dominant. Only from such a perspective does Being show itself in and as a transcending.

The introductory definition, "Being is the *transcendens* pure and simple," articulates in one simple sentence the way the essence of Being hitherto has illumined man. This retrospective definition of the essence of Being from the lighting of beings as such remains indispensable for the prospective approach of thinking toward the question concerning the truth of Being. In this way thinking attests to its essential unfolding as destiny. It is far from the arrogant presumption that wishes to begin anew and declares all past philosophy false. But whether the definition of Being as the *transcendens* pure and simple really does express the simple essence of the truth of Being—this and this alone is the primary question for a thinking that attempts to think the truth of Being. That is why we also say that how Being *is* is to be understood chiefly from its "meaning" [*"Sinn"*], that is, from the truth of Being. Being is illumined for man in the ecstatic projection [*Entwurf*]. But this projection does not create Being.

Moreover, the projection is essentially a thrown projection. What throws in projection is not man but Being itself, which sends man into the ek-sistence of Da-sein that is his essence. This destiny comes to pass as the lighting of Being, as which it is. The lighting grants nearness to Being. In this nearness, in the lighting of the *Da,* man dwells as the ek-sisting one without yet being able properly to experience and take over this dwelling. In the lecture on Hölderlin's elegy "Homecoming" (1943) this nearness "of" Being, which the *Da* of Dasein is, is thought on the basis of *Being and Time;* it is perceived as spoken from the minstrel's poem; from the experience of the oblivion of Being it is called the "homeland." The word is thought here in an essential sense, not patriotically or nationalistically but in terms of the history of Being. The essence of the homeland, however, is also mentioned with the intention of thinking the homelessness of contemporary man from the essence of Being's history. Nietzsche was the last to experience this homelessness. From within metaphysics he was unable to find any other way out than a reversal of metaphysics. But that is the height of futility. On the other hand, when Hölderlin[17] composes "Homecoming" he is concerned that his "countrymen" find their essence. He does not at all seek that essence in an egoism of his nation. He sees it rather in the context of a belongingness to the destiny of the West. But even the West is not thought regionally as the Occident in contrast to the Orient, nor merely as Europe, but rather world-historically out of nearness to the source. We have still scarcely begun to think of the mysterious relations to the East which found expression in Hölderlin's poetry.[18] "German" is not spoken to the world so that the world might be reformed through the German essence; rather, it is spoken to

---

[16] Nietzsche (above, page 686).

[17] Johann Christian Friedrich Hölderlin (1770–1843), German poet.

[18] [Heidegger] Cf. "The Ister" and "The Journey" [*Die Wanderung*], third stanza and ff. [In the translations by Michael Hamburger (Ann Arbor: University of Michigan Press, 1966), pp. 492 ff. and 392 ff.]

the Germans so that from a fateful belongingness to the nations they might become world-historical along with them.[19] The homeland of this historical dwelling is nearness to Being.

In such nearness, if at all, a decision may be made as to whether and how God and the gods withhold their presence and the night remains, whether and how the day of the holy dawns, whether and how in the upsurgence of the holy an epiphany of God and the gods can begin anew. But the holy, which alone is the essential sphere of divinity, which in turn alone affords a dimension for the gods and for God, comes to radiate only when Being itself beforehand and after extensive preparation has been illuminated and is experienced in its truth. Only thus does the overcoming of homelessness begin from Being, a homelessness in which not only man but the essence of man stumbles aimlessly about.

* * *

In the face of the essential homelessness of man, man's approaching destiny reveals itself to thought on the history of Being in this, that man find his way into the truth of Being and set out on this find. Every nationalism is metaphysically an anthropologism, and as such subjectivism. Nationalism is not overcome through mere internationalism; it is rather expanded and elevated thereby into a system. Nationalism is as little brought and raised to *humanitas* by internationalism as individualism is by an ahistorical collectivism. The latter is the subjectivity of man in totality. It completes subjectivity's unconditioned self-assertion, which refuses to yield. Nor can it be even adequately experienced by a thinking that mediates in a one-sided fashion. Expelled from the truth of Being, man everywhere circles round himself as the *animal rationale.*

But the essence of man consists in his being more than merely human, if this is represented as "being a rational creature." "More" must not be understood here additively as if the traditional definition of man were indeed to remain basic, only elaborated by means of an existentiell postscript. The "more" means: more originally and therefore more essentially in terms of his essence. But here something enigmatic manifests itself: man is in thrownness. This means that man, as the ek-sisting counter-throw [*Gegenwurf*] of Being, is more than *animal rationale* precisely to the extent that he is less bound up with man conceived from subjectivity. Man is not the lord of beings. Man is the shepherd of Being. Man loses noth-

ing in this "less"; rather, he gains in that he attains the truth of Being. He gains the essential poverty of the shepherd, whose dignity consists in being called by Being itself into the preservation of Being's truth. The call comes as the throw from which the thrownness of Da-sein derives. In his essential unfolding within the history of Being, man is the being whose Being as ek-sistence consists in his dwelling in the nearness of Being. Man is the neighbor of Being.

But—as you no doubt have been wanting to rejoin for quite a while now—does not such thinking think precisely the *humanitas* of *homo humanus?* Does it not think *humanitas* in a decisive sense, as no metaphysics has thought it or can think it? Is this not "humanism" in the extreme sense? Certainly. It is a humanism that thinks the humanity of man from nearness to Being. But at the same time it is a humanism in which not man but man's historical essence is at stake in its provenance from the truth of Being. But then doesn't the ek-sistence of man also stand or fall in this game of stakes? So it does.

In *Being and Time* it is said that every question of philosophy "recoils upon existence." But existence here is not the actuality of the *ego cogito.* Neither is it the actuality of subjects who act with and for each other and so become who they are. "Ek-sistence," in fundamental contrast to every *existentia* and *"existence,"* is ecstatic dwelling in the nearness of Being. It is the guardianship, that is, the care for Being. Because there is something simple to be thought in this thinking it seems quite difficult to the representational thought that has been transmitted as philosophy. But the difficulty is not a matter of indulging in a special sort of profundity and of building complicated concepts; rather, it is concealed in the step back that lets thinking enter into a questioning that experiences—and lets the habitual opining of philosophy fall away.

It is everywhere supposed that the attempt in *Being and Time* ended in a blind alley. Let us not comment any further upon that opinion. The thinking that hazards a few steps in *Being and Time* has even today not advanced beyond that publication. But perhaps in the meantime it has in one respect come farther into its own matter. However, as long as philosophy merely busies itself with continually obstructing the possibility of admittance into the matter for thinking, i.e., into the truth of Being, it stands safely beyond any danger of shattering against the hardness of that matter. Thus to "philosophize" about being shattered is separated by a chasm from a thinking that is shattered. If such thinking were to go fortunately for a man no misfortune would befall him. He would receive the only gift that can come to thinking from Being.

---

[19][Heidegger] Cf. Hölderlin's poem "Remembrance" [*Andenken*] in the *Tübingen Memorial* (1943), p. 322. [Hamburger, pp. 488 ff.]

But it is also the case that the matter of thinking is not achieved in the fact that talk about the "truth of Being" and the "history of Being" is set in motion. Everything depends upon this alone, that the truth of Being come to language and that thinking attain to this language. Perhaps, then, language requires much less precipitous expression than proper silence. But who of us today would want to imagine that his attempts to think are at home on the path of silence? At best, thinking could perhaps point toward the truth of Being, and indeed toward it as what is to be thought. It would thus be more easily weaned from mere supposing and opining and directed to the now rare handicraft of writing. Things that really matter, although they are not defined for all eternity, even when they come very late still come at the right time.

Whether the realm of the truth of Being is a blind alley or whether it is the free space in which freedom conserves its essence is something each one may judge after he himself has tried to go the designated way, or even better, after he has gone a better way, that is, a way befitting the question. On the penultimate page of *Being and Time* stand the sentences: "The *conflict* with respect to the interpretation of Being (that is, therefore, not the interpretation of beings or of the Being of man) cannot be settled, *because it has not yet been kindled.* And in the end it is not a question of 'picking a quarrel,' since the kindling of the conflict does demand some preparation. To this end alone the foregoing investigation is under way." Today after two decades these sentences still hold. Let us also in the days ahead remain as wanderers on the way into the neighborhood of Being. The question you pose helps to clarify the way.

You ask, *Comment redonner un sens au mot 'Humanisme'?* "How can some sense be restored to the word 'humanism'?" Your question not only presupposes a desire to retain the word "humanism" but also contains an admission that this word has lost its meaning.

It has lost it through the insight that the essence of humanism is metaphysical, which now means that metaphysics not only does not pose the question concerning the truth of Being but also obstructs the question, insofar as metaphysics persists in the oblivion of Being. But the same thinking that has led us to this insight into the questionable essence of humanism has likewise compelled us to think the essence of man more primordially. With regard to this more essential *humanitas* of *homo humanus* there arises the possibility of restoring to the word "humanism" a historical sense that is older than its oldest meaning chronologically reckoned. The restoration is not to be understood as though the word "humanism" were wholly without meaning and a mere *flatus vocis* [empty sound]. The *"humanum"* in the word points to *humanitas,* the essence of man; the "-ism" indicates that the essence of man is meant to be taken essentially. This is the sense that the word "humanism" has as such. To restore a sense to it can only mean to redefine the meaning of the word. That requires that we first experience the essence of man more primordially; but it also demands that we show to what extent this essence in its own way becomes fateful. The essence of man lies in ek-sistence. That is what is essentially—that is, from Being itself—at issue here, insofar as Being appropriates man as ek-sisting for guardianship over the truth of Being into this truth itself. "Humanism" now means, in case we decide to retain the word, that the essence of man is essential for the truth of Being, specifically in such a way that the word does not pertain to man simply as such. So we are thinking a curious kind of "humanism." The word results in a name that is a *lucus a non lucendo* [literally, a grove where no light penetrates].

Should we still keep the name "humanism" for a "humanism" that contradicts all previous humanism—although it in no way advocates the inhuman? And keep it just so that by sharing in the use of the name we might perhaps swim in the predominant currents, stifled in metaphysical subjectivism and submerged in oblivion of Being? Or should thinking, by means of open resistance to "humanism," risk a shock that could for the first time cause perplexity concerning the *humanitas* of *homo humanus* and its basis? In this way it could awaken a reflection—if the world-historical moment did not itself already compel such a reflection—that thinks not only about man but also about the "nature" of man, not only about his nature but even more primordially about the dimension in which the essence of man, determined by Being itself, is at home. Should we not rather suffer a little while longer those inevitable misinterpretations to which the path of thinking in the element of Being and Time has hitherto been exposed and let them slowly dissipate? These misinterpretations are natural reinterpretations of what was read, or simply mirrorings of what one believes he knows already before he reads. They all betray the same structure and the same foundation.

Because we are speaking against "humanism" people fear a defense of the inhuman and a glorification of barbaric brutality. For what is more "logical" than that for somebody who negates humanism nothing remains but the affirmation of inhumanity?

Because we are speaking against "logic" people believe we are demanding that the rigor of thinking be renounced and in its place the arbitrariness of drives and feelings be installed and thus that "irrationalism" be proclaimed as true. For what is more "logical" than that whoever speaks against the logical is defending the alogical?

Because we are speaking against "values" people are horrified at a philosophy that ostensibly dares to despise humanity's best qualities. For what is more "logical" than that a thinking that denies values must necessarily pronounce everything valueless?

Because we say that the Being of man consists in "being-in-the-world" people find that man is downgraded to a merely terrestrial being, whereupon philosophy sinks into positivism. For what is more "logical" than that whoever asserts the worldliness of human being holds only this life as valid, denies the beyond, and renounces all "Transcendence"?

Because we refer to the word of Nietzsche on the "death of God" people regard such a gesture as atheism. For what is more "logical" than that whoever has experienced the death of God is godless?

Because in all the respects mentioned we everywhere speak against all that humanity deems high and holy our philosophy teaches an irresponsible and destructive "nihilism." For what is more "logical" than that whoever roundly denies what is truly in being puts himself on the side of nonbeing and thus professes the pure nothing as the meaning of reality?

What is going on here? People hear talk about "humanism," "logic," "values," "world," and "God." They hear something about opposition to these. They recognize and accept these things as positive. But with hearsay—in a way that is not strictly deliberate—they immediately assume that what speaks against something is automatically its negation and that this is "negative" in the sense of destructive. And somewhere in *Being and Time* there is explicit talk of "the phenomenological destruction." With the assistance of logic and *ratio*—so often invoked—people come to believe that whatever is not positive is negative and thus that it seeks to degrade reason—and therefore deserves to be branded as depravity. We are so filled with "logic" that anything that disturbs the habitual somnolence of prevailing opinion is automatically registered as a despicable contradiction. We pitch everything that does not stay close to the familiar and beloved positive into the previously excavated pit of pure negation which negates everything, ends in nothing, and so consummates nihilism. Following this logical course we let everything expire in a nihilism we invented for ourselves with the aid of logic.

But does the "against" which a thinking advances against ordinary opinion necessarily point toward pure negation and the negative? This happens—and then, to be sure, happens inevitably and conclusively, that is, without a clear prospect of anything else—only when one posits in advance what is meant by the "positive" and on this basis

makes an absolute and absolutely negative decision about the range of possible opposition to it. Concealed in such a procedure is the refusal to subject to reflection this presupposed "positive" in which one believes himself saved, together with its position and opposition. By continually appealing to the logical one conjures up the illusion that he is entering straightforwardly into thinking when in fact he has disavowed it.

It ought to be somewhat clearer now that opposition to "humanism" in no way implies a defense of the inhuman but rather opens other vistas.

"Logic" understands thinking to be the representation of beings in their Being, which representation proposes to itself in the generality of the concept. But how is it with meditation on Being itself, that is, with the thinking that thinks the truth of Being? This thinking alone reaches the primordial essence of *logos* which was already obfuscated and lost in Plato and in Aristotle, the founder of "logic." To think against "logic" does not mean to break a lance for the illogical but simply to trace in thought the *logos* and its essence which appeared in the dawn of thinking, that is, to exert ourselves for the first time in preparing for such reflection. Of what value are even far-reaching systems of logic to us if, without really knowing what they are doing, they recoil before the task of simply inquiring into the essence of *logos?* If we wished to bandy about objections, which is of course fruitless, we could say with more right: irrationalism, as a denial of *ratio,* rules unnoticed and uncontested in the defense of "logic," which believes it can eschew meditation on *logos* and on the essence of *ratio* which has its ground in *logos.*

To think against "values" is not to maintain that everything interpreted as "a value"—"culture," "art," "science," "human dignity," "world," and "God"—is valueless. Rather, it is important finally to realize that precisely through the characterization of something as "a value" what is so valued is robbed of its worth. That is to say, by the assessment of something as a value what is valued is admitted only as an object for man's estimation. But what a thing is in its Being is not exhausted by its being an object, particularly when objectivity takes the form of value. Every valuing, even where it values positively, is a subjectivizing. It does not let beings: be. Rather, valueing lets beings: be valid—solely as the objects of its doing. The bizarre effort to prove the objectivity of values does not know what it is doing. When one proclaims "God" the altogether "highest value," this is a degradation of God's essence. Here as elsewhere thinking in values is the greatest blasphemy imaginable against Being. To think against values therefore does not mean to beat the drum for the valuelessness and nullity of beings. It means rather to bring the lighting of the truth of Being before thinking, as against subjectivizing beings into mere objects.

The reference to "being-in-the-world" as the basic trait of the *humanitas* of *homo humanus* does not assert that man is merely a "worldly" creature understood in a Christian sense, thus a creature turned away from God and so cut loose from "Transcendence." What is really meant by this word could be more clearly called "the transcendent." The transcendent is supersensible being. This is considered the highest being in the sense of the first cause of all beings. God is thought as this first cause. However, in the name "being-in-the-world," "world" does not in any way imply earthly as opposed to heavenly being, nor the "worldly" as opposed to the "spiritual." For us "world" does not at all signify beings or any realm of beings but the openness of Being. Man is, and is man, insofar as he is the ek-sisting one. He stands out into the openness of Being. Being itself, which as the throw has projected the essence of man into "care," is as this openness. Thrown in such fashion, man stands "in" the openness of Being. "World" is the lighting of Being into which man stands out on the basis of his thrown essence. "Being-in-the-world" designates the essence of ek-sistence with regard to the lighted dimension out of which the "ek-" of ek-sistence essentially unfolds. Thought in terms of ek-sistence, "world" is in a certain sense precisely "the beyond" within existence and for it. Man is never first and foremost man on the hither side of the world, as a "subject," whether this is taken as "I" or "We." Nor is he ever simply a mere subject which always simultaneously is related to objects, so that his essence lies in the subject-object relation. Rather, before all this, man in his essence is ek-sistent into the openness of Being, into the open region that lights the "between" within which a "relation" of subject to object can "be."

The statement that the essence of man consists in being-in-the-world likewise contains no decision about whether man in a theologico-metaphysical sense is merely a this-worldly or an otherworldly creature.

With the existential determination of the essence of man, therefore, nothing is decided about the "existence of God" or his "non-being," no more than about the possibility or impossibility of gods. Thus it is not only rash but also an error in procedure to maintain that the interpretation of the essence of man from the relation of his essence to the truth of Being is atheism. And what is more, this arbitrary classification betrays a lack of careful reading. No one bothers to notice that in the article *Vom Wesen des Grundes* the following appears: "Through the ontological interpretation of Dasein as being-in-the-world no decision, whether positive or negative, is made concerning a possible being toward God. It is, however, the case that through an illumination of tran-

scendence we first achieve an *adequate concept of Dasein,* with respect to which it can now be asked how the relationship of Dasein to God is ontologically ordered."[20] If we think about this remark too quickly, as is usually the case, we will declare that such a philosophy does not decide either for or against the existence of God. It remains stalled in indifference. Thus it is unconcerned with the religious question. Such indifferentism ultimately falls prey to nihilism.

But does the foregoing observation teach indifferentism? Why then are particular words in the note italicized— and not just random ones? For no other reason than to indicate that the thinking that thinks from the question concerning the truth of Being questions more primordially than metaphysics can. Only from the truth of Being can the essence of the holy be thought. Only from the essence of the holy is the essence of divinity to be thought. Only in the light of the essence of divinity can it be thought or said what the word "God" is to signify. Or should we not first be able to hear and understand all these words carefully if we are to be permitted as men, that is, as eksistent creatures, to experience a relation of God to man? How can man at the present stage of world history ask at all seriously and rigorously whether the god nears or withdraws, when he has above all neglected to think into the dimension in which alone that question can be asked? But this is the dimension of the holy, which indeed remains closed as a dimension if the open region of Being is not lighted and in its lighting is near man. Perhaps what is distinctive about this world-epoch consists in the closure of the dimension of the hale [*des Heilen*]. Perhaps that is the sole malignancy [*Unheil*].

But with this reference the thinking that points toward the truth of Being as what is to be thought has in no way decided in favor of theism. It can be theistic as little as atheistic. Not, however, because of an indifferent attitude, but out of respect for the boundaries that have been set for thinking as such, indeed set by what gives itself to thinking as what is to be thought, by the truth of Being. Insofar as thinking limits itself to its task it directs man at the present moment of the world's destiny into the primordial dimension of his historical abode. When thinking of this kind speaks the truth of Being it has entrusted itself to what is more essential than all values and all types of beings. Thinking does not overcome metaphysics by climbing still higher, surmounting it, transcending it somehow or other; thinking overcomes metaphysics by climbing back down into the nearness of the nearest. The descent, particularly where man has strayed into subjectivity, is more arduous and more dangerous than the as-

---

[20] [Heidegger] Martin Heidegger, *Vom Wesen des Grundes,* p. 28 n. 1.

cent. The descent leads to the poverty of the ek-sistence of *homo humanus.* In ek-sistence the region of *homo animalis,* of metaphysics, is abandoned. The dominance of that region is the mediate and deeply rooted basis for the blindness and arbitrariness of what is called "biologism," but also of what is known under the heading "pragmatism." To think the truth of Being at the same time means to think the humanity of *homo humanus.* What counts is *humanitas* in the service of the truth of Being, but without humanism in the metaphysical sense.

But if *humanitas* must be viewed as so essential to the thinking of Being, must not "ontology" therefore be supplemented by "ethics"? Is not that effort entirely essential which you express in the sentence *"Ce que je cherche à faire, depuis longtemps déjà, c'est préciser le rapport de l'ontologie avec une éthique possible"* ["What I have been trying to do for a long time now is to determine precisely the relation of ontology to a possible ethics"]?

Soon after *Being and Time* appeared a young friend asked me, "When are you going to write an ethics?" Where the essence of man is thought so essentially, i.e., solely from the question concerning the truth of Being, but still without elevating man to the center of beings, a longing necessarily awakens for a peremptory directive and for rules that say how man, experienced from eksistence toward Being, ought to live in a fitting manner. The desire for an ethics presses ever more ardently for fulfillment as the obvious no less than the hidden perplexity of man soars to immeasurable heights. The greatest care must be fostered upon the ethical bond at a time when technological man, delivered over to mass society, can be kept reliably on call only by gathering and ordering all his plans and activities in a way that corresponds to technology.

Who can disregard our predicament? Should we not safeguard and secure the existing bonds even if they hold human beings together ever so tenuously and merely for the present? Certainly. But does this need ever release thought from the task of thinking what still remains principally to be thought and, as Being prior to all beings, is their guarantor and their truth? Even further, can thinking refuse to think Being after the latter has lain hidden so long in oblivion but at the same time has made itself known in the present moment of world history by the uprooting of all beings?

Before we attempt to determine more precisely the relationship between "ontology" and "ethics" we must ask what "ontology" and "ethics" themselves are. It becomes necessary to ponder whether what can be designated by both terms still remains near and proper to what is assigned to thinking, which as such has to think above all the truth of Being.

Of course if both "ontology" and "ethics," along with all thinking in terms of disciplines, become untenable, and if our thinking therewith becomes more disciplined, how then do matters stand with the question about the relation between these two philosophical disciplines?

Along with "logic" and "physics," "ethics" appeared for the first time in the school of Plato. These disciplines arose at a time when thinking was becoming "philosophy," philosophy, *epistēmē* (science), and science itself a matter for schools and academic pursuits. In the course of a philosophy so understood, science waxed and thinking waned. Thinkers prior to this period knew neither a "logic" nor an "ethics" nor "physics." Yet their thinking was neither illogical nor immoral. But they did think *physis* in a depth and breadth that no subsequent "physics" was ever again able to attain. The tragedies of Sophocles—provided such a comparison is at all permissible—preserve the *ēthos* in their sagas more primordially than Aristotle's lectures on "ethics." A saying of Heraclitus which consists of only three words says something so simply that from it the essence of the *ēthos* immediately comes to light.

The saying of Heraclitus[21] (Frag. 119) goes: *ēthos anthrōpōi daimōn.* This is usually translated, "A man's character is his daimon." This translation thinks in a modern way, not a Greek one. *Ethos* means abode, dwelling place. The word names the open region in which man dwells. The open region of his abode allows what pertains to man's essence, and what in thus arriving resides in nearness to him, to appear. The abode of man contains and preserves the advent of what belongs to man in his essence. According to Heraclitus' phrase this is *daimōn,* the god. The fragment says: Man dwells, insofar as he is man, in the nearness of god. A story that Aristotle reports (*De parte animalium,* I, 5, 645a 17) agrees with this fragment of Heraclitus.

> The story is told of something Heraclitus said to some strangers who wanted to come visit him. Having arrived, they saw him warming himself at a stove. Surprised, they stood there in consternation—above all because he encouraged them, the astounded ones, and called for them to come in with the words, "For here too the gods are present."

The story certainly speaks for itself, but we may stress a few aspects.

---

[21]Heraclitus (c. 540–c. 480 B.C.), Greek philosopher.

The group of foreign visitors, in their importunate curiosity about the thinker, are disappointed and perplexed by their first glimpse of his abode. They believe they should meet the thinker in circumstances which, contrary to the ordinary round of human life, everywhere bear traces of the exceptional and rare and so of the exciting. The group hopes that in their visit to the thinker they will find things that will provide material for entertaining conversation—at least for a while. The foreigners who wish to visit the thinker expect to catch sight of him perchance at that very moment when, sunk in profound meditation, he is thinking. The visitors want this "experience" not in order to be overwhelmed by thinking but simply so they can say they saw and heard someone everybody says is a thinker.

Instead of this the sightseers find Heraclitus by a stove. That is surely a common and insignificant place. True enough, bread is baked here. But Heraclitus is not even busy baking at the stove. He stands there merely to warm himself. In this altogether everyday place he betrays the whole poverty of his life. The vision of a shivering thinker offers little of interest. At this disappointing spectacle even the curious lose their desire to come any closer. What are they supposed to do here? Such an everyday and unexciting occurrence—somebody who is chilled warming himself at a stove—anyone can find any time at home. So why look up a thinker? The visitors are on the verge of going away again. Heraclitus reads the frustrated curiosity in their faces. He knows that for the crowd the failure of an expected sensation to materialize is enough to make those who have just arrived leave. He therefore encourages them. He invites them explicitly to come in with the words *Einai gar kai entautha theous,* "Here too the gods are present."

This phrase places the abode *(ēthos)* of the thinker and his deed in another light. Whether the visitors understood this phrase at once—or at all—and then saw everything differently in this other light the story doesn't say. But the story was told and has come down to us today because what it reports derives from and characterizes the atmosphere surrounding this thinker. *Kai entautha,* "even here," at the stove, in that ordinary place where every thing and every condition, each deed and thought is intimate and commonplace, that is, familiar [*geheuer*], "even there" in the sphere of the familiar, *einai theous,* it is the case that "the gods are present."

Heraclitus himself says, *ēthos anthrōpōi daimōn,* "The (familiar) abode is for man the open region for the presencing of god (the unfamiliar one)."

If the name "ethics," in keeping with the basic meaning of the word *ēthos,* should now say that "ethics" ponders the abode of man, then that thinking which thinks the truth of Be-

ing as the primordial element of man, as one who eksists, is in itself the original ethics. However, this thinking is not ethics in the first instance, because it is ontology. For ontology always thinks solely the being *(on)* in its Being. But as long as the truth of Being is not thought all ontology remains without its foundation. Therefore the thinking which in *Being and Time* tries to advance thought in a preliminary way into the truth of Being characterizes itself as "fundamental ontology." [Cf. *Being and Time,* sections 3 and 4, above.] It strives to reach back into the essential ground from which thought concerning the truth of Being emerges. By initiating another inquiry this thinking is already removed from the "ontology" of metaphysics (even that of Kant).

"Ontology" itself, however, whether transcendental or precritical, is subject to criticism, not because it thinks the Being of beings and thereby reduces Being to a concept, but because it does not think the truth of Being and so fails to recognize that there is a thinking more rigorous than the conceptual. In the poverty of its first breakthrough, the thinking that tries to advance thought into the truth of Being brings only a small part of that wholly other dimension to language. This language is still faulty insofar as it does not yet succeed in retaining the essential help of phenomenological seeing and in dispensing with the inappropriate concern with "science" and "research." But in order to make the attempt at thinking recognizable and at the same time understandable for existing philosophy, it could at first be expressed only within the horizon of that existing philosophy and its use of current terms.

In the meantime I have learned to see that these very terms were bound to lead immediately and inevitably into error. For the terms and the conceptual language corresponding to them were not rethought by readers from the matter particularly to be thought; rather, the matter was conceived according to the established terminology in its customary meaning. The thinking that inquires into the truth of Being and so defines man's essential abode from Being and toward Being is neither ethics nor ontology. Thus the question about the relation of each to the other no longer has any basis in this sphere. Nonetheless, your question, thought in a more original way, retains a meaning and an essential importance.

For it must be asked: If the thinking that ponders the truth of Being defines the essence of *humanitas* as eksistence from the latter's belongingness to Being, then does thinking remain only a theoretical representation of Being and of man, or can we obtain from such knowledge directives that can be readily applied to our active lives?

The answer is that such thinking is neither theoretical nor practical. It comes to pass before this distinction. Such thinking is, insofar as it is, recollection of Being and nothing else. Belonging to Being, because thrown by Being into the preservation of its truth and claimed for such preservation, it thinks Being. Such thinking has no result. It has no effect. It satisfies its essence in that it is. But it is by saying its matter. Historically, only one Saying [*Sage*] belongs to the matter of thinking, the one that is in each case appropriate to its matter. Its material relevance is essentially higher than the validity of the sciences, because it is freer. For it lets Being—be.

Thinking builds upon the house of Being, the house in which the jointure of Being fatefully enjoins the essence of man to dwell in the truth of Being. This dwelling is the essence of "being-in-the-world." The reference in *Being and Time* to "being-in" as "dwelling" is no etymological game.[22] The same reference in the 1936 essay on Hölderlin's verse, "Full of merit, yet poetically, man dwells on this earth," is no adornment of a thinking that rescues itself from science by means of poetry. The talk about the house of Being is no transfer of the image "house" to Being. But one day we will, by thinking the essence of Being in a way appropriate to its matter, more readily be able to think what "house" and "to dwell" are.

And yet thinking never creates the house of Being. Thinking conducts historical eksistence, that is, the *humanitas* of *homo humanus,* into the realm of the upsurgence of the healing [*des Heilens*].

With healing, evil appears all the more in the lighting of Being. The essence of evil does not consist in the mere baseness of human action but rather in the malice of rage. Both of these, however, healing and the raging, can essentially occur only in Being, insofar as Being itself is what is contested. In it is concealed the essential provenance of nihilation. What nihilates illuminates itself as the negative. This can be addressed in the "no." The "not" in no way arises from the no-saying of negation. Every "no" that does not mistake itself as willful assertion of the positing power of subjectivity, but rather remains a letting-be of ek-sistence, answers to the claim of the nihilation illumined. Every "no" is simply the affirmation of the "not." Every affirmation consists in acknowledgment. Acknowledgment lets that toward which it goes come toward it. It is believed that nihilation is nowhere to be found in beings themselves. This is correct as long as one seeks nihilation as some kind of being, as an existing quality in beings. But in so seeking,

one is not seeking nihilation. Neither is Being any existing quality which allows itself to be fixed among beings. And yet Being is more in being than any being. Because nihilation occurs essentially in Being itself we can never discern it as a being among beings. Reference to this impossibility never in any way proves that the origin of the not is no-saying. This proof appears to carry only if one posits beings as what is objective for subjectivity. From this alternative it follows that every "not," because it never appears as something objective, must inevitably be the product of a subjective act. But whether no-saying first posits the "not" as something merely thought, or whether nihilation first requires the "no" as what is to be said in the letting-be of beings—this can never be decided at all by a subjective reflection of a thinking already posited as subjectivity. In such a reflection we have not yet reached the dimension where the question can be appropriately formulated. It remains to ask, granting that thinking belongs to ek-sistence, whether every "yes" and "no" are not themselves already dependent upon Being. As these dependents, they can never first posit the very thing to which they themselves belong.

Nihilation unfolds essentially in Being itself, and not at all in the existence of man—so far as this is thought as the subjectivity of the *ego cogito.* Dasein in no way nihilates as a human subject who carries out nihilation in the sense of denial; rather, Da-sein nihilates inasmuch as it belongs to the essence of Being as that essence in which man ek-sists. Being nihilates—as Being. Therefore the "not" appears in the absolute Idealism of Hegel and Schelling[23] as the negativity of negation in the essence of Being. But there Being is thought in the sense of absolute actuality as unconditioned will that wills itself and does so as the will of knowledge and of love. In this willing Being as will to power is still concealed. But just why the negativity of absolute subjectivity is "dialectical," and why nihilation comes to the fore through this dialectic but at the same time is veiled in its essence, cannot be discussed here.

The nihilating in Being is the essence of what I call the nothing. Hence because it thinks Being, thinking thinks the nothing.

To healing Being first grants ascent into grace; to raging its compulsion to malignancy.

Only so far as man, ek-sisting into the truth of Being, belongs to Being can there come from Being itself the assignment of those directions that must become law and rule for man. In Greek to assign is *nemein. Nomos* is not only law but more originally the assignment contained in the

---

[22] [Krell] Citing an analysis of the word "in" by Jacob Grimm, Heidegger relates "being-in" to *innan, wohnen,* inhabit, reside, or dwell. To be *in* the world means to dwell and be at home there, i.e., to be familiar with meaningful structures that articulate people and things.

[23] Friedrich Wilhelm Joseph von Schelling (1775–1864), German philosopher.

dispensation of Being. Only the assignment is capable of dispatching man into Being. Only such dispatching is capable of supporting and obligating. Otherwise all law remains merely something fabricated by human reason. More essential than instituting rules is that man find the way to his abode in the truth of Being. This abode first yields the experience of something we can hold on to. The truth of Being offers a hold for all conduct. "Hold" in our language means protective heed. Being is the protective heed that holds man in his ek-sistent essence to the truth of such protective heed—in such a way that it houses ek-sistence in language. Thus language is at once the house of Being and the home of human beings. Only because language is the home of the essence of man can historical mankind and human beings not be at home in their language, so that for them language becomes a mere container for their sundry preoccupations.

But now in what relation does the thinking of Being stand to theoretical and practical behavior? It exceeds all contemplation because it cares for the light in which a seeing, as *theoria,* can first live and move. Thinking attends to the lighting of Being in that it puts its saying of Being into language as the home of eksistence. Thus thinking is a deed. But a deed that also surpasses all *praxis.* Thinking towers above action and production, not through the grandeur of its achievement and not as a consequence of its effect, but through the humbleness of its inconsequential accomplishment.

For thinking in its saying merely brings the unspoken word of Being to language.

The usage "bring to language" employed here is now to be taken quite literally. Being comes, lighting itself, to language. It is perpetually under way to language. Such arriving in its turn brings ek-sisting thought to language in a saying. Thus language itself is raised into the lighting of Being. Language is only in this mysterious and yet for us always pervasive way. To the extent that language which has thus been brought fully into its essence is historical, Being is entrusted to recollection. Ek-sistence thoughtfully dwells in the house of Being. In all this it is as if nothing at all happens through thoughtful saying.

But just now an example of the inconspicuous deed of thinking manifested itself. For to the extent that we expressly think the usage "bring to language," which was granted to language, think only that and nothing further, to the extent that we retain this thought in the heedfulness of saying as what in the future continually has to be thought, we have brought something of the essential unfolding of Being itself to language.

What is strange in the thinking of Being is its simplicity. Precisely this keeps us from it. For we look for thinking—which has its world-historical prestige under the name "philosophy"—in the form of the unusual, which is accessible only to initiates. At the same time we conceive of thinking on the model of scientific knowledge and its research projects. We measure deeds by the impressive and successful achievements of *praxis.* But the deed of thinking is neither theoretical nor practical, nor is it the conjunction of these two forms of behavior.

Through its simple essence the thinking of Being makes itself unrecognizable to us. But if we become acquainted with the unusual character of the simple, then another plight immediately befalls us. The suspicion arises that such thinking of Being falls prey to arbitrariness; for it cannot cling to beings. Whence does thinking take its measure? What law governs its deed?

Here the third question of your letter must be entertained: *Comment sauver l'élément d'aventure que comporte toute recherche sans faire de la philosophie une simple aventurière?* [How can we preserve the element of adventure that all research contains without simply turning philosophy into an adventuress?] I shall mention poetry now only in passing. It is confronted by the same question, and in the same manner, as thinking. But Aristotle's words in the *Poetics,* although they have scarcely been pondered, are still valid—that poetic composition is truer than exploration of beings.

But thinking is an *aventure* not only as a search and an inquiry into the unthought. Thinking, in its essence as thinking of Being, is claimed by Being. Thinking is related to Being as what arrives (*l'avenant*).[24] Thinking as such is bound to the advent of Being, to Being as advent. Being has already been dispatched to thinking. Being *is* as the destiny of thinking. But destiny is in itself historical. Its history has already come to language in the saying of thinkers.

To bring to language ever and again this advent of Being which remains, and in its remaining waits for man, is the sole matter of thinking. For this reason essential thinkers always say the Same. But that does not mean the identical. Of course they say it only to him who undertakes to think back on them. Whenever thinking, in historical recollection, attends to the destiny of Being, it has already bound itself to what is fitting for it, in accord with its destiny. To flee into the identical is not dangerous. To risk discord in order to say the Same is the danger. Ambiguity threatens, and mere quarreling.

---

[24] [Krell] *L'avenant* (cf. the English *advenient*) is most often used as an adverbial phrase, *à l'avenant,* to be in accord, conformity, or relation to something. It is related to *l'aventure,* the arrival of some unforeseen challenge, and *l'avenir,* the future, literally, what is to come. Thinking is in relation to Being insofar as Being advenes or arrives. Being as arrival or presence is the "adventure" toward which Heidegger's thought is on the way.

The fittingness of the saying of Being, as of the destiny of truth, is the first law of thinking—not the rules of logic which can become rules only on the basis of the law of Being. To attend to the fittingness of thoughtful saying does not only imply, however, that we contemplate at every turn *what* is to be said of Being and *how* it is to be said. It is equally essential to ponder *whether* what is to be thought is to be said—to what extent, at what moment of the history of Being, in what sort of dialogue with this history, and on the basis of what claim, it ought to be said. The threefold thing mentioned in an earlier letter is determined in its cohesion by the law of the fittingness of thought on the history of Being: rigor of meditation, carefulness in saying, frugality with words.

It is time to break the habit of overestimating philosophy and of thereby asking too much of it. What is needed in the present world crisis is less philosophy, but more attentiveness in thinking; less literature, but more cultivation of the letter.

The thinking that is to come is no longer philosophy, because it thinks more originally than metaphysics—a name identical to philosophy. However, the thinking that is to come can no longer, as Hegel demanded, set aside the name "love of wisdom" and become wisdom itself in the form of absolute knowledge. Thinking is on the descent to the poverty of its provisional essence. Thinking gathers language into simple saying. In this way language is the language of Being, as clouds are the clouds of the sky. With its saying, thinking lays inconspicuous furrows in language. They are still more inconspicuous than the furrows that the farmer, slow of step, draws through the field.

R. S. Crane

1886–1967

R(onald) S(almon) Crane served from 1924 until his death as professor of English at the University of Chicago, where he was a leading figure in the development of a distinctive "neo-Aristotelian" approach to literary criticism. Together with his colleague Richard McKeon, Crane led the development of an approach to poetic form that relied on a recovery and reinterpretation of Aristotle's *Poetics*. It is of some interest to note that in the influential anthology of literary criticism edited by R. W. Stallman, *Critiques and Essays in Criticism, 1920–1948* (1949), work by members of the Chicago school is included as part of what was just coming to be known popularly as the "New Criticism," though in what served as a kind of demonstrative manifesto of Chicago criticism, edited by Crane, *Critics and Criticism: Ancient and Modern* (1952), Crane and his colleagues left no doubt about their opposition to such critics as Cleanth Brooks or William Empson.

The central tenet of Crane's neo-Aristotelian orientation, shared in part by Elder Olson, was that it was a fundamental error to reduce the study of poetic form to a single element—language, or, as he polemically stated it, "diction," in the essay reprinted here—when Aristotle with more reason and wisdom had insisted that a poem include six elements: plot, character, thought, diction, music, and spectacle. In Elder Olson's insistent formulation, poems are "not words *which;* poetry is *verbal.*" The polemical sharpness of Crane's attack on Cleanth Brooks, in this light, takes the New Criticism to task for making a fetish of the paradoxical or dramatically ironic quality of all poetic language, enacting a "monism" that would make it impossible, according to Crane, to make essential generic distinctions among different kinds of poetry. Thus, in finding that Brooks's dramatic irony is nothing more than a property of all connected discourse, he makes the pivotal point of his case the assertion that for New Critics like Brooks, Einstein's formula $E=mc^2$ would be indistinguishable from a modernist poem.

While Crane took this result to demonstrate the absurdity of attempting to theorize about poetry solely on the basis of its language (or "diction"), he was ironically close to a now familiar, post-structuralist perspective that taking Einstein's formula as a "modernist poem" reflects precisely the truth that "all connected discourse" *does* have the property Brooks found in poetry. Crane, however, went in the opposite direction, to recommend a radical version of critical pluralism, sketched out in his later *The Languages of Criticism and the Structure of Poetry* (1953)—significantly, a title partially borrowed later by Richard Macksey and Eugenio Donato for their eventful conference on "The Languages of Criticism and the Sciences of Man" in 1966—on the principle that the kind of answers one may get in criticism is precisely relative to the questions one asks. Borrowing a set of distinctions from Rudolph Carnap (above, page 978), Crane proposed that critics should think of their theories as "frameworks" within which questions of certain kinds could be asked and answered, treating the existence and character of the framework as a "practical" question—and to this end, offered a sober and thorough explanation of the advantage of treating poetic form, in an Aristotelian mode, as a "concrete whole."

Carnap's point, however, was that in any field, the adoption of a "framework" was contingent on two severe conditions: first, that the abstract entities in question, be they *numbers* or *poems,* be categorially identifiable by a general term; and second, that there be agreement about what *kinds* or *types* there may be (as even, odd, prime, transcendental *numbers;* or lyric, dramatic, narrative, or epic *poems*). These two agreements are the ground for actually making theoretically cogent statements about the subject. Crane's idea of critical pluralism, by contrast, does not require that either condition be observed, so Carnap's "practical question" can be posed only polemically: I *choose* to speak in this way about poems because it allows me to formulate just the kinds of questions that interest me—and ignore all others. What is left out of account is the question of the intellectual or social or other *function* of poetry, such that critical claims about it could be evaluated on theoretical grounds. In retrospect, it is of particular interest that the relatively rapid demise of both the neo-Aristotelian formalism advocated by Crane and the more language-oriented practice of the New Critics Crane opposed appears to hinge on the same ambiguity concerning the relation between critical theory and practice.

In addition to *Critics and Criticism* (1952) and *The Languages of Criticism and the Structure of Poetry* (1953), Crane is the author of *The Idea of the Humanities* (1967), and *Critical and Historical Principles of Literary History* (1971).

The Critical Monism of Cleanth Brooks[1]

Certain skeptical doubts which I have long felt concerning "the new criticism" have been considerably sharpened by Mr. Cleanth Brooks's latest volume, *The Well Wrought Urn,*[2] as well as by his recent essay on "Irony and 'Ironic' Poetry."[3] I am not happy about this, since on a number of points I am in sympathy with the purposes which differentiate Mr. Brooks and the writers commonly associated with him from most of the other critical schools of the day. I applaud them for having rejected the temptation to assimilate poetry, by large analogies, to metaphysics or rhetoric or history or the spirit of the age, and for having insisted on considering it, in Eliot's phrase, as poetry and not another thing. I welcome their efforts to shift the emphasis in practical criticism from generalities about authors to particularized studies of texts; and I have only praise for their de-

sire to rescue poetics from the dictatorship of factual science and relativism and to reorient it toward normative judgments. These seem to me valuable contributions, and, were it not for other and, as I think, more essential aspects of the philosophy common to the group, I should be inclined to let my gratitude for them outweigh my misgivings.

It is not so much the particular theses advanced by Brooks in "Irony and 'Ironic' Poetry" that disturb me as the tacit assumptions about critical theory and method which have made the questions debated in this essay seem of such crucial importance to him. On the immediate issues of his polemic against those who object to his enlargement of the term "irony" I think he is right. There is no reason why a critic who has chosen to make a common word like "irony" or "paradox" the central term of his system should not enjoy the privilege "of wrenching the word from its usual context—of at once specializing and broadening it"; all critics from the beginning have done this, and their readers can legitimately complain only when the wrenching is unsystematic or when the motive to it, as is sometimes the case in contemporary criticism, is merely ignorance of the existence in earlier literature of an equally good and, to the educated public, better-known word for the same idea. If Brooks is guilty of these faults, his detractors have not pointed it out. And he cannot be fairly accused, either, of

---

"The Critical Monism of Cleanth Brooks" is reprinted from *Critics and Criticism: Ancient and Modern* (Chicago: University of Chicago Press, 1952). All footnotes are the author's.
[1] Reprinted, with minor alterations, from *Modern Philology*, May, 1948.
[2] New York: Reynal & Hitchcock, [1947].
[3] *College English,* IX (1948), 231–37.

having so narrowed the meaning of "irony" as to deny the benefit of the concept to any poem, however apparently "simple," which he can convince himself is poetry. At all events, if there was ever substance to this charge, it is probable that few readers of his chapter on "Tears, Idle Tears" in *The Well Wrought Urn,* in which Tennyson's handling of ironic contrast and paradox is exhibited in detail, will care to press it in the future.

I do not question, either, that "irony," in Brooks's sense of the term, is a constant trait of all good poems, and I should have no quarrel with him had he been content to say so and to offer his analyses of texts as illustrations of one point, among others, in poetic theory. What troubles me is that, for Brooks, there are no other points. Irony, or paradox, is poetry, *tout simplement,* its form no less than its matter; or rather, in the critical system which he has constructed, there is no principle save that denoted by the words "irony" or "paradox" from which significant propositions concerning poems can be derived. It is the One in which the Many in his theory—and there are but few of these—are included as parts, the single source of all his predicates, the unique cause from which he generates all effects.

In this, it is true, he is not alone among the "new critics." The terms may differ, but the same tendency toward a monistic reduction of critical concepts is manifest in Allen Tate's doctrine of "tension," in John Crowe Ransom's principle of "texture," in Robert Penn Warren's obsession with symbols, above all in I. A. Richards' Pavlovian mythology concerning the "behavior" of words. The doubts which Brooks inspires thus become doubts about the general state of critical learning. I shall treat him, therefore, rather as a sign than as an individual, and I take him in place of any of the others, partly because he has expounded his position in full most recently, and partly because the position itself, as I shall indicate, is set forth in language which at once affords an easy clue to what has happened to critical theory in our age and at the same time is prophetic, however unconsciously, of new directions it may yet take.

I

It will be well to begin at the climactic point where Brooks's analysis of poetry leaves off. "One of the critical discoveries of our time—perhaps it is not a discovery but merely a recovery—" he says in his essay, "is that the parts of a poem have an organic relation to each other." It is "this general concept of organic structure which has been revolutionary in our recent criticism; our best 'practical criticism' has been based upon it; and upon it rests, in my opinion, the

best hope that we have for reviving the study of poetry and of the humanities generally."[4]

What the concept of organic structure means for him is made clear in *The Well Wrought Urn,* the subtitle of which is *Studies in the Structure of Poetry.* We must draw "a sharp distinction," he writes, "between the attractiveness or beauty of any particular item taken as such and the 'beauty' of the poem considered as a whole. . . . Unless one asserts the primacy of the pattern, a poem becomes merely a bouquet of intrinsically beautiful items." We must describe poetry, therefore, "in terms of structure"; but the nature of the "structure" which distinguishes poetry requires careful definition. "The structure meant is certainly not 'form' in the conventional sense in which we think of form as a kind of envelope which 'contains' the 'content.' " Nor is it a logical structure or a "rational meaning" which can be apprehended adequately by paraphrasing it in prose. Poetry, it must always be remembered, is the opposite of science.

> The structure meant is a structure of meanings, evaluations, and interpretations; and the principle of unity which informs it seems to be one of balancing and harmonizing connotations, attitudes, and meanings. But even here one needs to make important qualifications: the principle is not one which involves the arrangement of the various elements into homogeneous groupings, pairing like with like. It unites the like with the unlike. It does not unite them, however, by the simple process of allowing one connotation to cancel out another nor does it reduce the contradictory attitudes to harmony by a process of subtraction. . . . It is a positive unity, not a negative.

It is the presence in poetry of a structure such as this, he remarks, that accounts for his choice of key terms, and explains the recurrence in his pages of such words as "ambiguity," "paradox," "complex of attitudes," and, most frequently of all, "irony." These words may perhaps give way to other better ones in the future, but any substitutes for them will "have to be terms which do justice to the special kind of structure which seems to emerge as the common structure of poems so diverse on other counts as are *The Rape of the Lock* and 'Tears, Idle Tears.' "[5]

"The structure meant is a structure of meanings, evaluations, and interpretations; and the principle of unity which

---

[4] Ibid., pp. 231–32, 237.
[5] *The Well Wrought Urn,* pp. 178–79.

informs it seems to be one of balancing and harmonizing connotations, attitudes, and meanings." Whatever may be said of the first part of this formula, the second part will surely recall to every reader the famous passage in chapter xiv of the *Biographia literaria* in which Coleridge describes the operation of "that synthetic and magical power," constitutive of poetic genius, "to which we have exclusively appropriated the name of imagination":

> This power, first put in action by the will and understanding, and retained under their irremissive, though gentle and unnoticed, controul . . . reveals itself in the balance or reconciliation of opposite or discordant qualities: of sameness, with difference; of the general, with the concrete; the idea, with the image; the individual, with the representative; the sense of novelty and freshness, with old and familiar objects; a more than usual state of emotion, with more than usual order; judgement ever awake and steady self-possession, with enthusiasm and feeling profound or vehement; and while it blends and harmonizes the natural and the artificial, still subordinates art to nature; the manner to the matter; and our admiration of the poet to our sympathy with the poetry.[6]

Brooks prefers to talk about the structure of poetry rather than about the imagination, but the parallelism of his doctrine with that of Coleridge is none the less evident, and, what is more to the point, it has been acknowledged by Brooks himself, recently in *The Well Wrought Urn*[7] and earlier in *Modern Poetry and the Tradition*. There he was interested in defining metaphysical poetry in such a way as to reveal its community with all poetry, or at least all good poetry; and among the pronouncements of other critics which he finds most to his purpose he singles out particularly the passage I have quoted from Coleridge and, as a "development" from it, I. A. Richards' definition of the "poetry of synthesis," that is to say, the poetry in which impulses are brought ironically—the term is Richards'—into conflict with their opposites and the apparent discords finally resolved.[8] Brooks can hardly object, therefore, if I state my dissatisfaction with his critical method, first of all at least, in terms of its departures from the method of Coleridge.

II

The theory of poetry set forth in the *Biographia literaria* forms a coherent whole, but it is too good a theory, for all its limitations, to permit of reduction to a single principle or cause. For this reason various modern commentators, including I. A. Richards and Allen Tate, have naturally discovered that Coleridge, great as he was, had only a confused glimpse of the simple truth about his subject. The confusion, however, appears less glaring on a close reading of the text of the *Biographia* than in the pages of these recent interpreters; and much of the trouble disappears when it is observed that Coleridge had not one source for the distinctions he employs but several sources, which are nevertheless correlated in a scheme that allows him to discriminate aspects of poems as determined now by their medium or manner, now by their substance, now by their origin in the mental powers of the poet, now by their immediate or remote ends. The unity of his system derives, indeed, from the primacy of one of these causes relatively to the others: "I labored at a solid foundation," he says, "on which permanently to ground my opinions, in the component faculties of the human mind itself, and their comparative dignity and importance."[9] But the faculties of the mind, though ideally they form a hierarchy, can yet be distinguished as to their particular objects and operations, with the result that, whereas poetry can be analogized, on the philosophical level, to the other arts and to science and philosophy itself, a special consideration of it in criticism is still possible in terms of the variable factors which enter into its production.

Thus it is that Coleridge, as one can see from chapters i and xvi of the *Biographia,* as well as from many other passages, can make intelligible use of the old distinction, so abhorrent to modern critics, between the diction or language of poems and their "matter and substance." He knew from his own experience in writing verse, as well as from literary history, that the fitting of the right manner to the right objects, or vice versa, is a problem which poets actually face, and that in criticism, therefore, terms and distinctions are needed, on both sides of the disjunction, in order to formulate the degree of success achieved in its solution. The distinction is saved from becoming a merely sterile dichotomy by virtue of a further distinction, to which Coleridge himself attached great importance, but which has not been too well understood by some of the "new critics"[10]—the

---

[6]*Biographia literaria*, ed. J. Shawcross (Oxford, 1907), II, 12.
[7]Pp. 17, 230.
[8]*Modern Poetry and the Tradition* (Chapel Hill, 1919), pp. 40–43.

[9]*Biographia literaria*, I, 14.
[10]Cf., e.g., I. A. Richards, *Coleridge on Imagination* (New York, 1935), pp. 112–19; and Allen Tate, *Reason in Madness: Critical Essays* (New York, 1941), pp. 45–51.

distinction, which he insists is not a division, between "poetry" and "poem." I have quoted his definition of "poetry": it is a much wider term than "poem," since, on the one hand, what is essential to poetry may be found in writings, like those of Plato, Jeremy Taylor, and Thomas Burnet, which lack not only meter but also "the contra-distinguishing objects of a poem," and since, on the other hand, no poem of any length either can be or ought to be "all poetry." The reason is that "poetry" comes into being, no matter what the medium, whenever the images, thoughts, and emotions of the mind are brought into unity by the synthetic power of the secondary imagination. The definition of poetry, therefore, is the same as the definition of what "the poetic genius" does with whatever materials it operates upon: whenever "opposite or discordant qualities" of any sort are balanced or reconciled, poetry results, though we may call it, judging by other criteria, poetry (in the narrower sense) or philosophy or pictorial art. Poetry is thus architectonic thought, but a "poem," or "poetry" in its limited meaning, is a composition in words of a special kind; it contains the same elements—afforded by the mind interacting with the things of its experience—as a prose composition, but differs by virtue of "a different combination of them, in consequence of a different object being proposed." It is at this point, with the introduction of ends, that Coleridge's criticism becomes specifically poetic, and the result is a definition of poem in separation, first, from works of science and history and then from such works in prose as novels and romances: "A poem is that species of composition, which is opposed to works of science, by proposing for its *immediate* object pleasure, not truth; and from all other species (having *this* object in common with it) it is discriminated by proposing to itself such delight from the *whole,* as is compatible with a distinct gratification from each component *part.*"[11] Or again: "It [namely, poetry in the narrower sense] is an art . . . of representing, in words, external nature and human thoughts and affections, both relatively to human affections, by the production of as much immediate pleasure in parts, as is compatible with the largest sum of pleasure in the whole."[12]

The comprehensiveness of Coleridge's scheme is apparent. "Imagination" is the key term in the sense that it designates the common source in the mind from which poetry as the balancing and reconciliation of opposites necessarily derives, along with philosophy and other things; and as are the differences in the operation of the imagination, so are the major distinctions—evident, for example, in the contrast

between Shakespeare and Milton—which separate kinds of poetic genius. But poetry is also the art of making poems, and the consideration of these must take account, not merely of the imagination as the source of all excellence in thought, but of particular differences in ends pursued, objects represented, and kinds and qualities of language and verse selected for the purpose. Multiple and converging lines of differentiation are hence made possible, with the aid of which the critic—as Coleridge himself showed—can explore a wide variety of problems and arrive at solutions in which the obvious complexity of poetic composition is not obscured by the reduction of all effects to a single cause.

The scheme has a characteristically Platonic structure, but of the better sort, inasmuch as it formulates its idea of excellence in terms applicable to all synthetic activities of the mind and at the same time preserves the identity of poetry, as poetry and not another thing, by discriminating differences in ends, subject matters, and linguistic forms. It is a scheme with two levels, signified respectively by the words "poetry" and "poem," and the principle which relates the two is the principle, common to most of the Platonisms, of reflection or imitation. A poem in itself is a composite of diction with such-and-such qualities and of thought or matter determined by this or that faculty of the mind acting on the objects of human experience, the composite so organized as to produce as much immediate pleasure by its parts as is compatible with a maximum of pleasure from the whole. But a poem is likewise the work of a poet, and as such it reflects, in so far as it is successful, the secondary imagination "co-existing with the conscious will," just as this reflects the primary imagination operative in all human perception, and just as this in turn reflects "in the finite mind . . . the eternal act of creation in the infinite I AM."[13]

It is illuminating to see what has happened to this multidimensional and hence relatively sophisticated theory, to which he is admittedly indebted, in the criticism of Brooks. He has retained two of Coleridge's points: the proposition that the "imagination" reveals itself in the balance or reconciliation of opposite and discordant qualities; and the proposition that the contrary of poetry is science. But the new scheme in which these doctrines are embraced in a much simpler scheme than Coleridge's, and one capable of generating far fewer distinctions and criteria for the analysis and judgment of poems. The most obvious contrast is that, whereas Coleridge was concerned alike with indicating differences, both as between poems and other forms of composition and as between different sorts of poems (witness the

[11] *Biographia literaria.* II, 8–10.
[12] *Coleridge's Shakespearean Criticism,* ed. T. M. Raysor (London, 1910), II, 66–67.
[13] *Biographia literaria,* I, 202.

beginning of chap. xiv), and with establishing the unifying basis of all these distinctions in the powers and creative operations of the mind, Brooks is concerned solely with constituting poetry—that is, poems considered collectively—as homogeneous by attributing to poetry a "special kind of structure," to be found in all poems—in the *Odyssey* no less than in *The Waste Land*, as he says[14]—but distinctive of poems as opposed to works of science. His problem is one of literal differentiation, and he has no need, consequently, for the elaborate "Platonic" dialectic underlying the *Biographia*. But the result of his decision to look for differences only as between poetry and other things and not within poetry itself is a notable impoverishment of poetic theory.

The nature of this impoverishment will perhaps become clear if we observe the manner in which his two major propositions have been separated from the argumentative context in which their originals were placed in chapter xiv of the *Biographia*. In that context the antithesis of poetry and science formed a part, as we have seen, of Coleridge's definition of "a poem," and the concept of the balancing and reconciliation of opposites formed a part of his definition of "poetry" in terms of the "poet." And the two definitions were philosophically distinct, the term "poetry" being a much more inclusive term than "poem." Brooks has abolished this difference, and has done so by fusing the two concepts, with a consequent loss of analytical values on both sides. His discourse is uniformly of "poems" in Coleridge's sense, that is to say, compositions in words of a special kind, and these he opposes, as Coleridge did, to works of science and other similar modes of writing. He also follows Coleridge in assigning poems a peculiar kind of structure, or relationship of parts to whole. But—and this is the crucial shift—he derives his formula for this structure from what had been Coleridge's formula for "poetry" considered as the creative activity of the poet, and in doing so he decisively narrows the scope of the formula by dissociating it from the universal operations of the mind—the same, for Coleridge, wherever the highest excellence is achieved, whether in poetry, philosophy, eloquence, or science—and attaching it as a distinctive predicate to one species of linguistic objects. "Poems" thus become either all "poetry" or not-poems, and it would be an error to look for "poetry" elsewhere than in "poems."

One consequence of this is the disappearance from his treatment of poems in contrast with scientific works of Coleridge's differentiation of ends—truth for works of science, pleasure (entailing the special relationship, already noted, of parts and whole in the composition) for poems. So far as I have noticed, Brooks never treats poems in relation to the kinds or degrees of delight they afford; if the word "pleasure" occurs, it is surely only as a nonfunctional appendage to his system. It is otherwise with "truth"; being intent upon distinguishing poetry from science in terms of their different linguistic "structures," he is obliged to assume some common reference, and this turns out to be the term "truth" employed in a highly analogical sense, as one thing for the "rational" and "abstract" statements of science, and another thing for the "paradoxes" of poetry. Strictly speaking, however, poetry has no final cause, in his system, that is anyway analytically distinct from what poems read as ironic contexts "say"—even his remark that the "task" of the poet is to "unify experience"[15] signifies only that the parts of a poem necessarily have an organic—that is, an "ironic"—relation to each other.

Another consequence is the disappearance of the distinction between the "manner" and the "matter," or the "form" and the "substance," of poems. The warrant of this in the *Biographia* derives from the position that "poems," as distinct from "poetry," are compositions in words possessing the same "elements" as other kinds of composition and differing only, as we have seen, in "a different combination of them, in consequence of a different object being proposed." Poems may thus be characterized and differentiated specifically in terms of the varying mental faculties operative in them and the varying kinds of phenomena, human or natural, they represent, and questions may be raised concerning the appropriateness to these of the diction and meter: the reader of Coleridge's practical criticism will recall many passages in which precisely this is done. For Brooks, on the other hand, any such procedure is necessarily suspect; it is a sign that the critic who employs it is ignorant of the principle which essentially separates poetry from science. The distinction between language and thought is still reflected, to be sure, in his vocabulary, so that he can designate the "elements" of a poem sometimes as "attitudes," "evaluations," or "interpretations" and sometimes as "connotations" or "meanings." But the different words are merely names for different aspects of one thing—the "structure" which distinguishes poems. To treat them otherwise would be to revert to what he calls "the old form-content dualism" or to fall victim to "the heresy of paraphrase," with its

---

[14] *The Well Wrought Urn*, p. 191.

[15] Ibid., p. 194.

implication of a "logical structure" detachable from the poem. Most of our difficulties in criticism, he remarks,

> are rooted in the heresy of paraphrase. If we allow ourselves to be misled by it, we distort the relation of the poem to its "truth," we raise the problem of belief in a vicious and crippling form, we split the poem between its "form" and its "content"—we bring the statement to be conveyed into an unreal competition with science or philosophy or theology.

The most subtle examples of this error "are those which, beginning with the 'paraphrasable' elements of the poem, refer the other elements of the poem finally to some role subordinate to the paraphrasable elements."[16] But the parts of a poem are related "organically," and hence there can be nothing to which any of them can be said to be subordinate except the poetical "structure" itself which balances and harmonizes them.

The definition of this "structure," as we have observed, derives from Coleridge's definition, not of "poem," but of "poetry." But it, too, undergoes a profound change in its transfer from one system to the other. In Coleridge the concept of "poetry" is not a differentia of poems (since it may appear in works of philosophy and science) but a criterion of their value, the ideal of perfection to which they, or passages in them, are to be referred. They approach perfection whenever the poetic genius, or the imagination, put in action by the will and understanding and retained under their control, succeeds in reconciling or reducing to unity any of the various "opposite or discordant qualities" involved in the substance or the diction of a poem, and they depart from perfection in proportion as such unification is not achieved. It is in these terms, for example, that Coleridge distinguishes between the beauties and the defects of Wordsworth in chapter xxii of the *Biographia*. When Wordsworth is at his best, the unity is complete—there is a perfect appropriateness of the language to the meaning, there is a union of deep and subtle thought with sensibility, there is, above all, imagination. On the other hand, the unification does not always take place, and signs of the failure may be seen, throughout Wordsworth's poetry, in the occasional inconstancy of the style, in the unnecessary matter-of-factness of certain passages, or in thoughts and images too great for the subject.

In making what remains of Coleridge's definition of "poetry" the differentia of "poems" as contrasted with

works of science, Brooks has cut himself off from any such critical use of the concept as this. It is not strange, therefore, that he feels no need, as Coleridge did, for an analysis of the "component faculties of the mind and their comparative dignity and importance," or that, in speaking of poetic "structure," he introduces no distinctions that depend on a conception of the poetic process such as Coleridge expressed when he spoke of the "imagination" as being set in motion and kept under the control of the "will and understanding." Any such reference of poems or poetic values to the mental powers of the poet and their operations would be fatal to Brooks's central position, since it would derive the peculiar "structure" of poems from a cause in no way distinct from that which generates works of science, philosophy, theology, and rhetoric.

Some enabling cause of poetic "structure" must, however, be found; and what more natural—since this is the one remaining possibility—than to locate it in the poet's language as an instrument determined to poetry rather than to science or propaganda? That this is indeed Brooks's position is indicated by several passages in *The Well Wrought Urn*. Thus, after commenting on the quality of the "irony" in one stanza of Gray's *Elegy*, he remarks that "I am not here interested in enumerating the possible variations; I am interested rather in our seeing that *the paradoxes spring from the very nature of the poet's language:* it is a language in which the connotations play as great a part as the denotations." And again:[17]

> I have said that even the apparently simple and straightforward poet *is forced into paradoxes by the nature of his instrument.* Seeing this, we should not be surprised to find poets who consciously employ it to gain a compression and precision otherwise unobtainable. . . . The method is an extension of the normal language of poetry, not a perversion of it.[18]

The causal efficacy thus runs, not from the poet to the poem, but from "the language of poetry" to the ironical or paradoxical "structure of poetry," which the poet's choice of this kind of language, instead of that of science, makes inevitable. But "the language of poetry is the language of paradox";[19] in other words, the two terms signify the same thing, or at most different degrees of the same thing; and

---

[16] Ibid., pp. 184, 183.

[17] Ibid., p. 8; italics mine.
[18] Ibid., p. 10; italics mine.
[19] Ibid., p. 3.

thus all the multiple principles which Coleridge found it necessary to invoke—in proper subordination—for the adequate criticism of poetry are collapsed into one—the single principle, essentially linguistic in its formulation, which is designated as "irony" or "paradox." Brooks, in short, is a complete monist, and, given his choice of language rather than subject matter or the poet or the ends of poetry as the unique basis of all his explanations, a materialistic monist at that.

III

The last point can be put in another way by saying that whereas for Coleridge at least three sciences are necessary for criticism—grammar, logic, and psychology—Brooks finds it possible to get along with only one, namely, grammar; and with only one part of that, namely, its doctrine of qualification. His whole effort can be described not unfairly as an attempt to erect a theory of poetry by extending and analogizing from the simple proposition of grammar that the meaning of one word or group of words is modified by its juxtaposition in discourse with another word or group of words. The paradoxes and ironic oppositions and resolutions of discrepant "attitudes" which, in his system, distinguish poetry sharply from science and other nonpoetical modes of writing are merely the more striking forms which such qualification takes when it is considered, merely qua qualification of meaning by context, apart from, and in contrast with, what he takes to be the self-contained and "abstract" meaning, not dependent on any special context, of predications of fact or universal truth, such as "Two plus two equals four" or "The square on the hypotenuse of a right triangle is equal to the sum of the squares on the other two sides."[20] To talk about the "prose-sense" of poems is to reduce them, or some part of them, to the status of assertions of this kind; and it is for the sake of eradicating this error—the source of "the heresy of paraphrase"—that he insists on finding the essence of poetry in its exclusive reliance on properties of speech which in earlier analyses of language were treated between the consideration of individual words and the consideration of linguistic wholes determined differently by the different ends of logic, dialectic, poetic, and rhetoric; as, for example, in Aristotle's discussions of ambiguity and equivocation; the modes of opposition or contrariety; the different senses of sameness and difference; the kinds of metaphor, including that which involves an-

tithesis; amplification and depreciation in thought and words; the ways of making discourse lively and dramatic; the technique of the unexpected; and so on. Brooks has retained very little of the complexity and precision of this old "grammatical" teaching, and he presents what remains of it as peculiarly relevant to poetry rather than as applicable generally to discourse, and, indeed, as constitutive by itself of the whole of poetic theory. For all his simplification and distortion of the ancient analyses, however, it is clear that the apparatus of terms and distinctions he brings to the study of poetry is a composite of elements that can be traced historically to the pre-propositional sections of logic and dialectic, the theory of diction, merely qua diction, of poetic, and the stylistic part of rhetoric.

His key concepts, "paradox" and "irony," reflect unmistakably their grammatical origin. They are terms that designate the mutual "qualification"—and especially one mode of it—that inevitably occurs when the meanings of individual words or sentences or passages are not fixed by prior definition but are determined immediately, in the discourse itself, by the "contexts" in which they stand. "Irony," he says, "is the most general term that we have for the kind of qualification which the various elements in a context receive from the context. This kind of qualification . . . is of tremendous importance in any poem. Moreover, irony is our most general term for indicating that recognition of incongruities—which, again, pervades all poetry to a degree far beyond what our conventional criticism has been heretofore willing to allow."[21] And "paradox" would seem to differ from "irony" only as it signifies "irony" especially in its narrower sense—not the general phenomenon of contextual qualification (the importance of which, Brooks tells us, we, or at least the "new critics," have at last come to see)[22] but the special kind of qualification, so long neglected, which involves the resolution of opposites: in short, the antithetical metaphor of Aristotle, Johnson's "heterogeneous ideas yoked by violence together," and Coleridge's "imagination."

So much for the manner in which Brooks constitutes the distinctive "language of poetry." His main interest, however, is in its distinctive "structure," and this would seem, on first thought, to be something requiring formulation in different, and even nongrammatical, terms. He tells us indeed, in his recent essay, that the statements made in a poem—including those which look like philosophical generalizations—"are to be read as if they were speeches

---

[20] *College English.* IX. 233.

[21] *The Well Wrought Urn*, pp. 191–92.
[22] *College English*, IX, 232.

in a drama,"[23] and in *The Well Wrought Urn* he remarks that "the structure of a poem resembles that of a play."[24] This sounds promising—and the analogy does, in fact, as we shall see, imply one idea which, if Brooks had worked it out, might have led to a more adequate theory than the one he gives us; but the promise is dimmed when we recollect that a "drama" is after all, when considered apart from the specific emotional quality of its plot, merely a grammatical entity, that is, a sequence of speeches with conflicting contexts.

Again, he has much to say about "unity," as when he remarks that the poet "must peforce dramatize the oneness of the experience, even though paying tribute to its diversity," and that the poet gives us "an insight which preserves the unity of experience," his final task being, indeed, "to unify experience." "He must return to us the unity of the experience itself as man knows it in his own experience."[25] But this, too, is disappointing, for it merely attributes to the poet the same necessity for "balancing and harmonizing connotations, attitudes, and meanings" which elsewhere in Brooks—and more typically—is said to follow from the nature of the linguistic instrument the poet uses, as contrasted with the fixed statement-making language of science. It is not, therefore, any special principle of unity derived from the nature of the "experience" or object represented in a given kind of poem that determines poetical structure; rather it is the presence in poems of poetical structure—i.e., ironical opposition and resolution—that determines, and is the sign of, the unification of experience. And, as Brooks makes abundantly clear, the "structure of poetry" is a structure common to all poems.

Only one alternative remains: to get the "structure" of poems out of their linguistic elements or parts. And this is what Brooks tells us explicitly that he is doing. "The structure obviously is everywhere conditioned by the nature of the material which goes into the poem. The nature of the material sets the problem to be solved, and the solution is the ordering of the material."[26] And again, and most plainly: "What is true of the poet's language in detail is true of the larger wholes of poetry."[27] But what is true of the poet's language in detail, in Brooks's account of it, is that it is a language—"of paradox," as he says—which inevitably organizes itself, when two words are put together, into "organic" relations according to some pattern of ambiguity, metaphor,

or ironic contrast. And nothing less, or more, than this can be said about the total organization of parts—that is to say, of lines and passages—in the poem as a whole. Brooks devotes a short paragraph in *The Well Wrought Urn* to a familiar line of Gray's *Elegy:*

> Grandeur is not to smile at the "short and simple annals of the poor." Properly speaking, of course, the poor do not have "annals." Kingdoms have annals, and so do kings, but the peasantry does not. The choice of the term is ironical, and yet the "short and simple" records of the poor are their "annals"—the important records for them.[28]

Here is poetry, the whole of poetry, so far as its essence as "paradoxical" language is concerned, for here is ironic contrast and its resolution; and the only difference between this one line and the whole *Elegy* is merely a matter of the degree of complexity exhibited by the ironic interrelationships. We may speak, indeed, of partial "contexts" and of total "contexts," the latter being built up, as Brooks suggests in one place,[29] out of the former; but the two are completely homogeneous in their elements and structure, and the relation between them is best described as that of microcosm to macrocosm.

The limiting consequences of this radical reduction of poetics to grammar become apparent as soon as we consider what problems of criticism Brooks's system will not permit us to solve. Thus we cannot, by any legitimate extension of his principles, develop an apparatus for discriminating essentially and not solely in terms of accidents of subject matter or historical style—between poems so obviously different in the special kinds of pleasure they give us as are the *Odyssey* and *The Waste Land,* "Who Is Sylvia?" and "The Canonization," "Westminster Bridge" and Gray's *Elegy, The Rape of the Lock* and "Tears, Idle Tears." What is revealed, if we stay with Brooks, is merely the ironical "structure" which all these, and other, poems have in common as contrasted with nonpoetical works or bad poems. But this is to shut our eyes to a whole range of questions, turning on specific differences in poetic ends and the means suitable for their realization, which are real problems for poets writing poems and hence, one would suppose, important problems for critics. For, literally speaking at any rate, a poet does not write poetry but individual poems. And these are inevitably, as finished wholes, instances of one or another poetic kind,

---

[23] Ibid., p. 233.
[24] P. 186.
[25] *The Well Wrought Urn*, pp. 194–95.
[26] Ibid., p. 178.
[27] Ibid., p. 192.

[28] Ibid., p. 102.
[29] Ibid., p. 226.

differentiated not by any necessities of the linguistic instrument of poetry but primarily by the nature of the poet's conception, as finally embodied in his poem, of a particular form to be achieved through the representation, in speech used dramatically or otherwise, of some distinctive state of feeling, or moral choice, or action, complete in itself and productive of a certain emotion or complex of emotions in the reader. It is thus only relatively to the form of the poem, as the representation of a particularized human activity of a given emotional quality, that the poet can know whether his poem is too long or too short, whether the things to be said or left unsaid are properly chosen, whether the parts are rightly ordered and connected, or whether the words, metaphors, and "paradoxes" are appropriate or nor to the thought, emotion, character, situation, or general effect. In other words, the principles of the poet's artistic reasoning (however instinctive this may be) are always, and necessarily, ends or effects of some determinate sort to be accomplished in his poem, whether ultimately in the poem as a whole or mediately in some part of it; and the principles will differ, and along with them his decisions as to what must or can be done in constituting his action and its mode of representation, rendering his characters and their thoughts, and fashioning his diction, according as he is writing a simple lyric of feeling or a moral lyric of character, a tragedy or a mock-epic. A sign of the adequacy to its subject of any theory of poetry which aims, as Brooks's theory does, to treat poetry as poetry and not another thing, is surely the extent to which it is able to cope, in specific terms, with problems of this nature. The construction of an adequate theory is not an impossible task, but it requires a basic analysis that will take account, as Brooks never does, of more than one among the several variable "parts" which are combined in different ways in each of the many distinguishable species of poetic works.

It would be false to say that Brooks's preoccupation with language to the exclusion of the other more controlling causes of poetry deprives his criticism of any basis for judgments of value. He insists repeatedly, in fact, that they must be made. "The Humanities are in their present plight," he says, "largely because their teachers have more and more ceased to raise normative questions, have refrained from evaluation";[30] and he remarks that his studies of particular poems in *The Well Wrought Urn* are based on the assumption that "there are general criteria against which the poems may be measured."[31] The criteria as fi-

nally stated, however, turn out either to be excessively general or to have little direct applicability to individual poems. He refers to T. S. Eliot's test, which he puts in the form of the question, "Does the statement seem to be that which the mind of the reader can accept as coherent, mature, and founded on the facts of experience?"[32] We must indeed ask this question about poems, but the test is equally relevant to other kinds of works, as when one says of an argument that the conclusion seems true enough, but the conception of the subject is simple-minded. Elsewhere the standard is formulated in terms of deficiency and excess. On the one hand, poems lacking in irony are vulnerable to it, and hence "sentimental" and hence bad; on the other hand, as he suggests may be true of "Who Is Sylvia?" the "complexity" may be greater "than is necessary or normal."[33] Between these extremes, a hierarchy of poems, he thinks, may be established by the test of "complexity of attitude," with poems of simple affection at the bottom and probably tragedy at the top.[34] In so far as this reiterates the old doctrine that the excellence of art consists in a mean, there is no difficulty. But relatively to what is the too much or the too little to be determined in any particular case? Relatively to the maximizing, without diminishing returns, of the peculiar emotional effect proper to the object represented in a given poem? Or relatively to some standard of complexity fixed apart from the poet's problems in writing an individual poem of a certain form, and hence, in some sense, absolute? Brooks does not clearly say; but his notion of a hierarchy of poems based on the quantity and "sharpness" of the ironical oppositions they subsume suggests that he means by "normative" judgments the measurement of poems by a predetermined norm assumed to have general validity for all poems no matter what their kind or intended effect. He cannot, in fact, hold anything else but this, lacking any premises that would warrant judgments of individual poems founded on a mean relative to their peculiar ends and forms. And he lacks such premises because he has no concept of poems as concrete wholes the unity of which requires that the parts should be of a certain quality and magnitude and present in a certain order if the desired poetic effect is to be fully achieved.

But this is equivalent to saying that he has no distinctions for dealing with individual poems otherwise than as instances, to be grammatically construed, of a universal poetic "structure." His many *explications de textes* are

---

[30] Ibid., p. 212.
[31] Ibid., pp. 198–99.

[32] *College English*, IX, 234.
[33] Ibid., p. 235.
[34] *The Well Wrought Urn*, pp. 229–30.

accordingly better described, in his own term, as "readings" than as critical studies proper. Their method is the repeated application of his central paradigm of poetry to particular poems for the sake of uncovering, in the significances which can be attributed to their statements when taken in context, hitherto unnoticed occurrences of ironical "complexity," first on the level of single words and lines, and then on the level of the interrelationships between larger passages, until the end of the poem is reached.

A typical example of the method is the chapter on Gray's *Elegy* in *The Well Wrought Urn,* from which I have already quoted a passage illustrative of the manner in which the technique works in detail. The essay considers successively, first the effect of the many "echoes" of Milton and others in making the *Elegy* an ironical rather than a "simple" poem; then the ironic contrast implied in the opening description of the churchyard; then the ironic function of the personifications, together with their "supporting ironical devices" in phrases like "homely joys," "the short and simple annals of the poor," "animated bust," the stanza beginning "Full many a gem," and the lines on Hampden, Milton, and Cromwell; then the passage on the tombstones in the churchyard, which, according to Brooks, brings together opposites so far held apart; and, finally, the poet's lines about himself and his imagined epitaph, which are said to center in the speaker's "choice" between the two alternatives of burial contrasted earlier in the poem.

Brooks is concerned, in this chapter, to put us on guard against what he fears is the common temptation "to think of the prose-sense as the poetic content, a content which in this poem is transmitted, essentially unqualified, to the reader by means of the poetic form, which, in this case, merely supplies a discreet decoration to the content." This should certainly be discouraged; but Brooks appears to have fallen victim to an equally unfortunate temptation, which his critical principles, in fact, make irresistible, namely, to disregard the "poetic content" altogether. For surely there is a kind of "content," distinctive of poems like Gray's, which cannot be reduced, by paraphrase, to any proposition or idea, and which is not so much "transmitted" as represented: it is that which primarily constitutes the *Elegy* a complete and ordered serious lyric, productive of a special emotional pleasure, rather than simply a statement of thought. It is to be discovered by inquiring about the moral character of the speaker (as distinct from his "attitudes") and the particular problem which confronts him; about the relation between what Gray has chosen to present, namely, the calm and aphoristic but solemn deliberation in the churchyard, and the emotions which the speaker's situation and outlook had previously generated;

about the sequence of his thoughts and feelings as thus made probable or necessary; and so on.[35] Brooks raises none of these poetic questions. The *Elegy* as he exhibits it is indeed ironical discourse, in which the "prose-sense" (that is, what is contained in bad paraphrases of the poem) is "qualified" at each step. But it is still merely discourse, with an arrangement dictated solely by the contrast the speaker is supposed to be making between two possibilities of burial and his (at least in Brooks's account) unmotivated choice between them. It has an outline, to be sure, but an outline of the kind that any sermon might have, or any serious familiar essay. The "reading" gives us, in short, not a poem but simply a piece of moderately subtle dialectic: an inferior specimen of the genre represented—to choose an example consonant with the title of Brooks's volume—by Sir Thomas Browne's *Urn Burial.* What excitement and dramatic life the poem has, no less than its peculiar ethical quality, accordingly disappear, and we have instead an inconsequential and unmoving "theme"

---

[35] More explicitly, I take the poetic form of the *Elegy* to be that of an imitative lyric of moral choice (see below, p. 564), representing a situation in which a virtuous, sensitive, and ambitious young man of humble birth confronts the prospect of his death while still to "Fortune and to Fame unknown," and eventually, after much disturbance of mind, reconciles himself to his probable "fate" by reflecting that none of the rewards of successful ambition can "sooth the dull cold ear of Death," which comes as inevitably to the great as to the obscure; that a life passed "far from the madding crowd's ignoble strife," though circumscribing the exercise of virtue and talent, may yet be a means of preserving innocence; and that he can at any rate look forward to—what all men desire as a minimum—living on in the memory of at least one friend, while his merits and frailties alike repose "in trembling hope" on the bosom of his Father and his God. What is embodied in the words of the poem is the final stage of this "action"—the resolution of the speaker's internal conflict (hinted at in II. 101–8); with respect to this, his evening meditation in the churchyard on the "unhonour'd Dead" serves the double function of a dramatizing and externalizing device and, more importantly, of an analogy in his reconciling argument. He stands apart from both the great of the world and the humble rustics whose tombs are before him; but he resembles more closely, in his fortune, the latter than the former. Hence it is natural for him to infer that the advantages and consolations he finds in their lot can likewise be advantages and consolations for himself.

This is not, of course, the poem, or even a "paraphrase" of it; nor is it an attempt to state what Gray must have had explicitly in mind when he gave his *imprimatur* to the *Elegy* in its final form. It is rather an effort to formulate, hypothetically, the over-all principle of construction which appears to me to account most adequately for the detailed character and interrelations of the parts which the finished poem combines and for the effect which it is calculated to produce on a normally sensitive reader. Discussion of its value as a hypothesis in practical criticism would therefore turn on the extent to which, relative to alternative hypotheses, it, on the one hand, makes both grammatical and poetic sense out of the total succession of words and sentences in the *Elegy* and, on the other hand, receives further confirmation from repeated and independent considerations of these. The hypothesis itself is a correlation of three elements: the moral character of the speaker, the situation which compels his effort at resolution, and the steps of the meditation through which his choice is expressed; of these, only the last appears, abstracted from the others, in Brooks's "reading." Cf. below, pp. 632 ff.

(largely read into the poem) on modes of burial. Why is it, if it is, a great poem? Or is it that "irony," in Brooks's view, is really a final good and not merely, as he indicates at times, a means or device?

The neglect of poetic content or form—the words here mean the same—is responsible, furthermore, for difficulties in the "reading" itself. This is inevitably so since, without a clear principle of control, in an adequate hypothesis about the poetic whole, the purely grammatical scrutiny of a poem for instances of "ambiguity," "paradox," "complex of attitudes," or "irony" is bound to lead to *contresens*. Not all of Brooks's remarks about the *Elegy* fall into this class, and the chapter contains, indeed, a number of shrewd and sensitive observations which any student will be glad to have. But I am disturbed, among other things, by his misconstruction of the thought in lines 45–76—a misconstruction which a prior inquiry into the unifying action of the poem would have prevented—and especially by his much too respectful view of William Empson's commentary on stanza 14—a masterpiece of critical irresponsibility surely unmatched in modern times, except elsewhere in Empson.

IV

I have hitherto gone along with Brooks in his contention that the qualities he calls "paradox" or "irony" are somehow peculiar to poetry, and have been content to urge the inadequacy of his theory in terms of what his exclusive concern with "the language of poetry" forces him to leave out. I now want to examine the proofs on which this major proposition of his theory—as a theory of poetry—ultimately rests.

The first step in the argument is simple enough. It consists in a division of all discourse into two kinds: that in which the statements are "abstract," in the sense that their meaning is "unqualified by any context," and that in which the statements are not "abstract" but bear "the pressure of the context" and have their meanings "modified by the context"; an extreme form of the latter is discourse which achieves "the stability of a context in which the internal pressures balance and mutually support each other."[36] The term "irony" applies, as we have seen, to the second type of discourse: in its "obvious" meaning to the general phenomenon of contextual qualification, in a "further sense" to the degree of qualification which is manifest when opposing or discordant meanings are fused.

The initial problem is to demonstrate that this division corresponds to the distinction between "science" and "poetry." That scientific discourse is made up of "denotations," that is, terms with fixed meanings, and hence of "abstract" statements, is assumed rather than proved; that poetry, on the other hand, is discourse which never contains "abstract" statements is argued instantially by presenting "readings" of various poems so chosen as to embrace representatives of the whole English tradition from Shakespeare to Yeats and of the extremes, within this tradition, of admittedly witty poems and of poems apparently "simple" and "spontaneous." All these are analyzed exclusively with a view to the manner in which single words, phrases, lines, and passages have their meanings determined "ironically" (in both senses of the term) by contexts; whence the conclusion follows that "the special kind of structure" thus revealed—a structure from which "abstract statements" are necessarily excluded by the very technique of reading—is "the common structure" of poems of all kinds, since it occurs not only in those where we would expect it from obvious signs but also in those where its presence has often been denied. And it follows, as a corollary of this, that to read poems as expressions of "rational" meanings rather than as patterns of "ironical" qualification is to do violence to their true nature and to bring them "into an unreal competition with science or philosophy or theology" or, as other passages indicate, moral rhetoric and propaganda.

If we ask, then, what the "readings" prove, the answer must be that they prove what they were designed to prove, namely, the possession by poems of a kind of structure which, on Brooks's assumptions, poems must have inasmuch as there are only two kinds of structure possible and the other is preempted by science, of which poetry is, also by assumption, the necessary opposite. He has got himself into this difficult logical position, I would suggest, precisely because, although his analysis is set up in terms derived from Coleridge, he has insisted, unlike Coleridge, on identifying "the structure of poetry" literally with poems in the usual sense of that word, while retaining, but reducing to linguistic differences, the opposition, in Coleridge, of "poems" and "science." As a result, he is committed to saying, or at least implying, not merely that "irony" or "paradox" is universally present in poems—which, granted his definitions of the two words, is doubtless true—but that the "structure" these terms signify is the differentia of poems, the sufficient cause which distinguishes them essentially from all other kinds of works in which language is employed. If he does not mean this, then it is hard to understand why he gives instances of "irony" only from poems or why he supposes that recognition of "the concept of poetry as an organism" with its corollaries of "the ultimate importance of context and the fact of contextual qualification," is

---

[36] *College English*, IX, 234.

"the best hope that we have for reviving the study of poetry and of the humanities generally." But if he does mean that "irony" is a quality peculiar to poems, then—especially in view of the claims he makes for the novelty of the theory—we might reasonably expect him to offer some evidence that this is indeed the case. The evidence would consist in a series of "readings" of complete works other than poems leading to the conclusion that, when they are analyzed in the same way his poems are analyzed, the same phenomena of contextual qualification and "irony" do not appear. No such evidence, however, is forthcoming, with the result that what would seem to be the crucial proposition of his theory is advanced as a mere assertion, without argumentative support.

How, if he had raised the question, he could have resolved it in favor of his hypothesis, I confess I do not see. It is surely not a self-evident truth that it is only, or peculiarly, in poems that the "relevance," "propriety," "rhetorical force," and "meaning" of statements "cannot be divorced from the context in which they are imbedded," or only, or peculiarly, in poems that systematic ambiguities occur, or that "incongruities" are recognized, or extremes of opposition reconciled, or the claims of discordant and apparently irrelevant "attitudes" adjusted to one another. Merely to state the point should be sufficient, it would seem, to convince anyone that these are "structures" common not only to all poems but to all species of connected discourse—and necessarily, since all words as they present themselves to a writer are ambiguous (there being many more things or ideas than verbal symbols for them) and therefore have to have their significances fixed by the particular contexts, of whatever sort, in which they are used. There are many devices for doing this, but there are none, as far as I can recall, that have not been used indifferently in poems, essays, histories, orations, philosophic treatises, or scientific expositions. Nor is any meaningful distinction to be made in this connection, as Brooks supposes,[37] between "context" and "universe of discourse": the one is the grammarian's term, the other the logician's; but if we wish to talk about discourse apart from the various specific ends it serves (as Brooks talks about poetry), we must inevitably speak of contexts and of statements in relation to them, that being all that discourse, qua discourse, consists of.

Why, then, all the to-do about "irony" in poetry? Why not look for "irony" everywhere? For, if we look, it will assuredly be found. It even pervades this essay I am writing, from the "echo" in the opening phrase on through: there is no essential difference, in terms of anything Brooks's analy-

sis can show, between, for example, my "qualification" of Brooks by Coleridge and Gray's "qualification" of the graves in the churchyard by the tombs in the church. The full and proper meaning of "Beauty is truth, truth beauty," is no doubt dependent, as Brooks makes clear in some detail, upon the total context of the character and "attitude" of the speaker in Keats's ode; but it would take almost as many words to exhibit adequately the "pressure" of the context upon Gibbon's statement in his fifteenth chapter that he intended to write "a candid but rational inquiry into the progress and establishment of Christianity." And it would require many more words—Coleridge needed thirteen chapters—to trace the contribution of the context to the very rich meanings which the words "poem" and "poetry" have when they are opposed in the *Biographia literaria*.

But we may go farther than this. Brooks finds his extreme of "irony" in I. A. Richards' "poetry of synthesis"—"a poetry which does not leave out what is apparently hostile to its dominant tone, and which, because it is able to fuse the irrelevant and discordant, has come to terms with itself and is invulnerable to irony"—invulnerability to irony being "the stability of a context in which the internal pressures balance and mutually support each other."[38] This is excellent, but it is a perfect formula for what is achieved, more completely than in any poem I have ever read, by the dialectic of the *Phaedrus* or *Republic* or by Hume's *Dialogues concerning Natural Religion*. No more than for any poem can the "insights" communicated by these marvelous discourses be summed up in a "paraphrase," however elaborate: they are supreme instances of "irony" in every sense which Brooks attaches to the word; and, although it is true that his method of "reading" would exhibit only a few of their more material and hence less essential traits, it would certainly leave out no more than the same method does when applied to poems.

There is, finally, science—or rather, since the comparison must be made in terms of uses of language, scientific works. Brooks would have it that the words of science, unlike those of poetry, do not change under the pressure of the context. "They are pure (or aspire to be pure) denotations; they are defined in advance. They are not to be warped into new meanings. But where is the dictionary which contains the terms of a poem? It is a truism that the poet is continually forced to remake language."[39] In these statements we have the keystone of his whole position: remove it, and his account of the structure "characteristic" of poetry crumbles.

---

[37] Ibid., p. 233 n.

[38] Ibid., p. 234.

[39] *The Well Wrought Urn*, p. 192.

And at first sight this would seem hard to do. For it is undoubtedly the case that scientists, in the physical sciences at any rate, aspire to definitions of terms which will remain constant in all the treatises or papers in which the terms are used, and it is just as clearly the case that poets, in writing new poems, do nothing of the sort. But this difference follows as a consequence from the quite different ends which poets and scientists pursue and is not in any sense an antecedent cause of the differences between poetry and science. And in particular it is not a sign that the principle of "contextual qualification," which evidently operates in poetry, does not also function in scientific discourse, when this is considered, as Brooks considers poetry, purely in terms of interrelationships of significations. The terms of science, says Brooks, "are defined in advance." In advance of what? Surely not of the particular framework of meanings in which they are used: the definitions of Euclid are not separate from, but an integral part of, the "context" in which all his subsequent theorems are set up, and by the "pressure" of which the terms employed in the theorems are qualified in this way rather than in that. And what, for that matter, is a definition but a qualification of a common word, ambiguous otherwise, by a context? Moreover, as the context, in the sense of the total system of meanings, shifts, so do the meaning, propriety, relevance, and so on of any term or statement. Thus the vocabulary with which Aristotle discourses scientifically about poetry in the *Poetics* is in large part identical with the vocabulary of Plato in Books ii, iii, and x of the *Republic;* the meanings of the corresponding terms and statements in Aristotle, however, are entirely different, and the difference is produced (it is recorded in part, but only in part, in explicit definitions) by a radical change in "context," which can be described in the same grammatical fashion as Brooks describes differences or changes of "context" in poetry. And the shifts go on within the *Poetics* itself, as anyone can see, for example, who will trace what happens to the word *ethos* in chapter 6. Nor is modern science an exception. Where is the dictionary which contains the terms of Newton? He, too, like any innovating poet, inherited a vocabulary; but the *Principia* is an original system of verbal and ideational "contexts"—it is more than that, of course, but so, in a different way, is any good poem—under the pressure of which all the old words and "attitudes" take on new senses, with the consequence that the traditional language is completely "remade." In contemporary physics, also, as I am informed, contextual qualification occurs whenever a statement is moved from the macroscopic level of classical to the microscopic level of relativity mechanics. It is true that the rules for such shifts, in modern science, can be explicitly stated and are well known; but even this

has its analogue in poetry in the persistence of conventions and formularized techniques for getting "paradoxical" effects.

The syntheses of science, too, can be described, omitting questions of their truth, in much the same terms as Brooks uses to distinguish the "poetry of synthesis." One example will suffice—the formula in which Einstein brought together in a single unified equation the hitherto "discordant" qualities of mass and energy:

$$E = mc^2.$$

I offer this, judging it solely by Brooks's criterion for poetic "structure," as the greatest "ironical" poem written so far in the twentieth century.

The moral of all this is surely not that there is any fundamental similarity between poetry and science, or poetry and dialectic, which can be made to lead to fruitful and precise practical criticism, but simply that Brooks's attempt to differentiate "the structure of poetry" by deriving it from basic distinctions in language is self-defeating. He has assumed, in his initial divisions, with no warrant from the facts, what he has to prove, and he has thus begged the entire question.

V

His fundamental error, I suggest, is that he has begun to theorize about poetry at the wrong end—starting not with concrete poetic wholes of various kinds, the parts of which, with their possible interrelationships, can be inferred as consequences from inductively established principles, but rather with one only of the several internal causes of poems, and the cause which they have most completely in common with all other literary productions, namely, their linguistic matter: here he begins, and here also he ends. The choice is regrettable, since it prevents him from dealing adequately with poetic works in terms of the sufficient or distinguishing causes of their production and nature; but it would be unfair to blame him unduly for making it, inasmuch as it has been a characteristic methodological choice, as I have said before, in the school of "new critics" to which he belongs. Nor are the reasons hard to assign. Chief among them is what I can only call the morbid obsession of these writers with the problem of justifying and preserving poetry in an age of science. This has resulted in an extraordinary florescence of modern apologies for poesy, the majority of which, in spite of much diversity in the rhetorical topics, have turned on the antithesis expressed in the title of one of the most famous of them, science and poetry. The question of the differences between poetry and science is as old as the Greeks, but whereas, with earlier critics, it was only one among many problems—and, for most, a problem preliminary to criticism proper—it has become, for our contemporaries, *the* crucial issue upon the successful resolution of which the fate of poetry, and even of the humanities in general, is thought to depend. How, with science everywhere dominant and the method of science universally accepted as the one road to truth, can poetry still be made to seem a valuable and respectable form of mental activity, rather than merely a survival of prescientific modes of thought destined to disappear in the future? Obviously—so goes the common answer—only by returning to first principles and seeking to define afresh the nature and peculiar sphere of poetry in terms which will at once mark it off sharply from the factual and "rational" sphere of science and exhibit it as a natural, and hence permanent, effect of causes distinct from, but no less basic in, man's life than those which operate in the scientific sphere.

It is not strange, therefore, that critics thus preoccupied with the single problem of establishing a division of labor between science and poetry should largely give up, as irrelevant to their purpose, the discrimination of particular poetic kinds and effects. What has to be saved, or reconciled with science, is poetry itself *en bloc;* and, that being the case, the inquiry resolves itself into a search for some one fundamental difference between the two which can be shown to depend, not upon the arbitrary determinations of poets or critics, but upon divergent tendencies in the underlying natural conditions from which both science and poetry spring. Such a common basis was frequently found in earlier times in the faculties of the soul (as in Bacon and Macaulay); in the twentieth century, however, this will no longer do; the golden key which is counted on to unlock all doors is now not the mind but language. It is here, accordingly, and not either in the final character of poetic works as opposed to scientific, or in the differentiation of ends or subject matters or techniques, that most of the "new critics" have sought their first principles, in the simple faith, that, because language is the instrument of both scientists and poets, the high claims of poetry can be asserted most effectively by deriving all its essential characteristics from a consideration of those potentialities of language which are left over, once the specialized use of words in science has been defined. So everything turns, for I. A. Richards, on the opposition of "referential" and "emotive" speech; for John Crowe Ransom, on the antithesis of logical "structure" and poetic "texture"; and for Brooks, as we have seen, on the contrast between the "abstract" language of science and the "paradoxical" language of poetry. The words of poetry have thus become all-important, to the neglect or obscuration of all the factors in poetic production which determine, for the poet, what the words ought to be; and poetry, ironically enough, is defended against materialistic science by arguments which attempt, materialistically, to deduce poetic form from an examination of the medium alone.

I am convinced that this has led only to a blind alley and that a "newer" criticism is needed which will not worry so much about saving poetry—this, after all, has been with us a very long time and, besides, contains within itself powerful springs of natural human interest, surely not yet exhausted—but will devote itself to a scholarly and philosophically comprehensive study of poetry calculated to refine our instinctive response to poems by giving us an adequately sensitive critical apparatus for discriminating among them. I have tried to show how Brooks, having made a false start, is prevented, by the pressure of the limited context he has selected, from developing such an apparatus. Not everything he says or implies in his writings, however, is strictly functional in terms of his characteristic method; and among the pale ineffectual ghosts from earlier and better systems which hover, in the shapes of undefined and inoperative words, on the confines of his argument and make possible critical insights frequently much better than his theory, there are several which, if brought back to life, might do serviceable work. Among these peripheral terms we find "beauty," "unity," "propriety," "drama," "character," and, especially, "imitation." "The poem," he writes, "if it be a true poem is a simulacrum of reality—in this sense, at least, it is an 'imitation'—by *being* an experience rather than any mere statement about experience or any mere abstraction from experience."[40] If he had started here rather than with "the language of paradox," he might have got somewhere (and incidentally been able to give a better account of "irony" itself), for here is clearly a first principle by which poetry may be distinguished essentially, and not merely accidentally, from science, philosophy, history, and rhetoric, and precise consequences drawn concerning the construction and peculiar beauty of poems of different kinds. But the statement is isolated in his system: it does not follow from his theory of language, nor is it made a starting point for any significant deductions. So, too, with the other terms: they remain "irrelevant and discordant" elements, meaningful enough in other critical analyses, but never, in Brooks, subsumed under any general poetic principles. Yet the presence of such words in his exposition may be taken as a sign of his

---

[40]Ibid., p. 194.

own half-conscious awareness that grammar is not enough; and at all events we may regard them as encouraging portents, suggestive of a direction which criticism might take if only it freed itself from the despotism of linguistics and the unique cause and aimed at a multidimensional theory of poetry that would be, like Brooks's, literal rather than Platonic in method, but much more adequate than his to the discrimination of peculiarly poetic values and to the development of normative judgments relative to *all* the complex problems— of object, manner, and effect as well as of medium—that enter into the various poetic arts.

To reconstruct criticism in this way would obviously be to reverse the whole tendency of critical reasoning as practiced by the "new critics." It would be to substitute the matter-of-fact and concrete for the abstract; the a posteriori for the a priori; the argument from immediately sensible and particular poetic effects to their proximate poetic causes for the argument from remote and nonpoetic causes to only general and common poetic effects. It would be, in a word, to study poems as complete wholes possessed of distinctive powers rather than merely the materials and devices of poetry in a context of extrapoetic considerations. And that would be new indeed.

M. H. Abrams

b. 1912

M. H. Abrams's *The Mirror and the Lamp* and his later *Natural Supernaturalism* were two of the most influential books on romanticism published in the twentieth century. The first was a study of romantic criticism, which Abrams characterized as treating poetry as "expressive," that is, emphasizing the relation of the poem to its author with attention to the author's feelings and attitudes as projected into the poem. The first chapter of *The Mirror and the Lamp* provides a clear and concise description of what Abrams calls the four fundamental "orientations" of literary theory from the time of Plato to that of the New Critics: the mimetic, pragmatic, expressive, and objective. These orientations overlap each other and are rarely, if ever, seen in pure form in any critic or poet defending his practice. They provide, nevertheless, a valuable brief overview of the whole history of literary criticism and a means of analyzing the grounds of critical practice.

Abrams is also the author of a number of important essays, including "The Correspondent Breeze: A Romantic Metaphor" and "How to Do Things with Texts," the latter a criticism of deconstruction.

Abrams's principal works are *The Mirror and the Lamp: Romantic Theory and the Critical Tradition* (1953), *Natural Supernaturalism: Tradition and Revolution in Romantic Literature* (1971), and *The Correspondent Breeze* (1984), a collection of essays on romanticism. See Wayne Booth, "M. H. Abrams: Historian and Critic, Critic as Pluralist," *Critical Inquiry* 2 (Spring 1976).

from

Orientation of Critical Theories

i. Some Co-ordinates of Art Criticism

Four elements in the total situation of a work of art are discriminated and made salient, by one or another synonym, in almost all theories which aim to be comprehensive. First, there is the *work,* the artistic product itself. And since this is a human product, an artifact, the second common element is the artificer, the *artist.* Third, the work is taken to have a subject which, directly or deviously, is derived from existing things—to be about, or signify, or reflect something which either is, or bears some relation to, an objective state of affairs. This third element, whether held to consist of people and actions, ideas and feelings, material things and events, or super-sensible essences, has frequently been denoted by that word-of-all-work, 'nature'; but let us use the more neutral and comprehensive term, *universe,* instead. For the final element we have the *audience:* the listeners, spectators, or readers to whom the work is addressed, or to whose attention, at any rate, it becomes available.

On this framework of artist, work, universe, and audience I wish to spread out various theories for comparison. To emphasize the artificiality of the device, and at the same time make it easier to visualize the analyses, let us arrange the four co-ordinates in a convenient pattern. A triangle will

"Orientation of Critical Theories" is reprinted in part from *The Mirror and the Lamp: Romantic Theory and the Critical Tradition* (New York: Oxford University Press, 1953).

do, with the work of art, the thing to be explained, in the center.

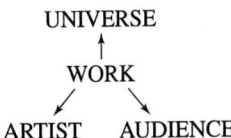

UNIVERSE

WORK

ARTIST   AUDIENCE

Although any reasonably adequate theory takes some account of all four elements, almost all theories, as we shall see, exhibit a discernible orientation toward one only. That is, a critic tends to derive from one of these terms his principal categories for defining, classifying, and analyzing a work of art, as well as the major criteria by which he judges its value. Application of this analytic scheme, therefore, will sort attempts to explain the nature and worth of a work of art into four broad classes. Three will explain the work of art principally by relating it to another thing: the universe, the audience, or the artist. The fourth will explain the work by considering it in isolation, as an autonomous whole, whose significance and value are determined without any reference beyond itself.

To find the major orientation of a critical theory, however, is only the beginning of an adequate analysis. For one thing, these four co-ordinates are not constants, but variables; they differ in significance according to the theory in which they occur. Take what I have called the *universe* as an example. In any one theory, the aspects of nature which an artist is said to imitate, or is exhorted to imitate, may be either particulars or types, and they may be only the beautiful or the moral aspects of the world, or else any aspect without discrimination. It may be maintained that the artist's world is that of imaginative intuition, or of common sense, or of natural science; and this world may be held to include, or not to include, gods, witches, chimeras, and Platonic Ideas. Consequently, theories which agree in assigning to the represented universe the primary control over a legitimate work of art may vary from recommending the most uncompromising realism to the most remote idealism. Each of our other terms, as we shall see, also varies, both in meaning and functioning, according to the critical theory in which it occurs, the method of reasoning which the theorist characteristically uses, and the explicit or implicit 'world-view' of which these theories are an integral part.

It would be possible, of course, to devise more complex methods of analysis which, even in a preliminary clas-

sification, would make more subtle distinctions.[1] By multiplying differentiae, however, we sharpen our capacity to discriminate at the expense both of easy manageability and the ability to make broad initial generalizations. For our historical purpose, the scheme I have proposed has this important virtue, that it will enable us to bring out the one essential attribute which most early nineteenth-century theories had in common: the persistent recourse to the poet to explain the nature and criteria of poetry. Historians have recently been instructed to speak only of 'romanticisms,' in the plural, but from our point of vantage there turns out to be one distinctively romantic criticism, although this remains a unity amid variety.

ii. Mimetic Theories

The mimetic orientation—the explanation of art as essentially an imitation of aspects of the universe—was probably the most primitive aesthetic theory, but mimesis is no simple concept by the time it makes its first recorded appearance in the dialogues of Plato. The arts of painting, poetry, music, dancing, and sculpture, Socrates says, are all imitations.[2] 'Imitation' is a relational term, signifying two items and some correspondence between them. But although in many later mimetic theories everything is comprehended in two categories, the imitable and the imitation, the philosopher in the Platonic dialogues characteristically operates with three categories. The first category is that of the eternal and unchanging Ideas; the second, reflecting this, is the world of sense, natural or artificial; and the third category, in turn reflecting the second, comprises such things as shadows, images in water and mirrors, and the fine arts.

Around this three-stage regress—complicated still further by various supplementary distinctions, as well as by his exploitation of the polysemism of his key terms—Plato weaves his dazzling dialectic.[3] But from the shifting arguments emerges a recurrent pattern, exemplified in the famous passage in the tenth book of the *Republic*. In discussing the nature of art, Socrates makes the point that there are three beds: the Idea which 'is the essence of the bed' and

[1] [Abrams] For a subtle and elaborate analysis of diverse critical theories, see Richard McKeon, "Philosophic Bases of Art and Criticism," *Critics and Criticism, Ancient and Modern,* ed. R. S. Crane (Chicago: University of Chicago Press, 1952).

[2] [Abrams] *Republic* (tr. Jowett) X. 596–97 [above, page 29]; *Laws* ii. 667–68, vii. 814–16.

[3] [Abrams] See Richard McKeon, "Literary Criticism and the Concept of Imitation in Antiquity," *Critics and Criticism,* ed. Crane, pp. 147–49. The article exhibits those multiple shifts in Plato's use of the term "imitation" which have trapped many later commentators as successfully as they once did the rash spirits who engaged Socrates in controversy.

is made by God, the bed made by the carpenter, and the bed found in a painting. How shall we describe the painter of this third bed?

> I think, he said, that we may fairly designate him as the imitator of that which the others make.
>
> Good, I said; then you call him who is third in the descent from nature an imitator?
>
> Certainly, he said.
>
> And the tragic poet is an imitator, and therefore, like all other imitators, he is thrice removed from the king and from the truth?
>
> That appears to be so.[4]

From the initial position that art imitates the world of appearance and not of Essence, it follows that works of art have a lowly status in the order of existing things. Furthermore, since the realm of Ideas is the ultimate locus not only of reality but of value, the determination that art is at second remove from the truth automatically establishes its equal remoteness from the beautiful and good. Despite the elaborate dialectic—or more accurately, by means of it—Plato's remains a philosophy of a single standard; for all things, including art, are ultimately judged by the one criterion of their relation to the same Ideas. On these grounds, the poet is inescapably the competitor of the artisan, the lawmaker, and the moralist; indeed, any one of these can be regarded as himself the truer poet, successfully achieving that imitation of the Ideas which the traditional poet attempts under conditions dooming him to failure. Thus the lawmaker is able to reply to the poets seeking admission to his city, 'Best of strangers—

> we also according to our ability are tragic poets, and our tragedy is the best and noblest; for our whole state is an imitation of the best and noblest life, which we affirm to be indeed the very truth of tragedy. You are poets and we are poets . . . rivals and antagonists in the noblest of dramas. . .[5]

And the poor opinion of ordinary poetry to which we are committed on the basis of its mimetic character, is merely confirmed when Plato points out that its effects on its auditors are bad because it represents appearance rather than truth, and nourishes their feelings rather than their reason; or by demonstrating that the poet in composing (as Socrates jockeys poor obtuse Ion into admitting) cannot depend on

his art and knowledge, but must wait upon the divine afflatus and the loss of his right mind.[6]

The Socratic dialogues, then, contain no aesthetics proper, for neither the structure of Plato's cosmos nor the pattern of his dialectic permits us to consider poetry as poetry—as a special kind of product having its own criteria and reason for being. In the dialogues there is only one direction possible, and one issue, that is, the perfecting of the social state and the state of man; so that the question of art can never be separated from questions of truth, justice, and virtue. 'For great is the issue at stake,' Socrates says in concluding his discussion of poetry in the *Republic*, 'greater than appears, whether a man is to be good or bad.'[7]

Aristotle in the *Poetics* also defines poetry as imitation. 'Epic poetry and Tragedy, as also Comedy, Dithyrambic poetry, and most flute-playing and lyre-playing, are all, viewed as a whole, modes of imitation'; and 'the objects the imitator represents are actions. . .'[8] But the difference between the way the term 'imitation' functions in Aristotle and in Plato distinguishes radically their consideration of art. In the *Poetics,* as in the Platonic dialogues, the term implies that a work of art is constructed according to prior models in the nature of things, but since Aristotle has shorn away the other world of criterion-Ideas, there is no longer anything invidious in that fact. Imitation is also made a term specific to the arts, distinguishing these from everything else in the universe, and thereby freeing them from rivalry with other human activities. Furthermore, in his analysis of the fine arts, Aristotle at once introduces supplementary distinctions according to the objects imitated, the medium of imitation, and the manner—dramatic, narrative, or mixed, for example—in which the imitation is accomplished. By successive exploitation of these distinctions in object, means, and manner, he is able first to distinguish poetry from other kinds of art, and then to differentiate the various poetic genres, such as epic and drama, tragedy and comedy. When he focuses on the genre of tragedy, the same analytic instrument is applied to the discrimination of the parts constituting the individual whole: plot, character, thought, and so on. Aristotle's criticism, therefore, is not only criticism of art as art, independent of statesmanship, being, and morality, but also of poetry as poetry, and of each kind of poem by the criteria appropriate to its particular nature. As a result of this procedure, Aristotle bequeathed an arsenal of instruments for

---

[4][Abrams] *Republic* x, 597 [above, page 31].
[5][Abrams] *Laws* vii. 817.

[6][Abrams] *Republic* x. 603–5 [above, page 29]; *Ion* 535–36 [above, page 13]; *Apology* 22.
[7][Abrams] *Republic* x. 608 [above, page 36].
[8][Abrams] *Poetics* (tr. Ingram Bywater) I. 1447a, 1448a. [above, page 52]. On imitation in Aristotle's criticism see McKeon, "The Concept of Imitation," op. cit., pp. 160–68.

technical analysis of poetic forms and their elements which have proved indispensable to critics ever since, however diverse the uses to which these instruments have been put.

A salient quality of the *Poetics* is the way it considers a work of art in various of its external relations, affording each its due function as one of the 'causes' of the work. This procedure results in a scope and flexibility that makes the treatise resist a ready classification into any one kind of orientation. Tragedy cannot be fully defined, for example, nor can the total determinants of its construction be understood, without taking into account its proper effect on the audience: the achievement of the specifically 'tragic pleasure,' which is 'that of pity and fear.'[9] It is apparent, however, that the mimetic concept—the reference of a work to the subject matter which it imitates—is primary in Aristotle's critical system, even if it is *primus inter pares*.[10] Their character as an imitation of human actions is what defines the arts in general, and the kind of action imitated serves as one important differentia of an artistic species. The historical genesis of art is traced to the natural human instinct for imitating, and to the natural tendency to find pleasure in seeing imitations. Even the unity essential to any work of art is mimetically grounded, since 'one imitation is always of one thing,' and in poetry 'the story, as an imitation of action, must represent one action, a complete whole. . .'[11] And the 'form' of a work, the presiding principle determining the choice and order and internal adjustments of all the parts, is derived from the form of the object that is imitated. It is the fable or plot 'that is the end and purpose of tragedy,' its 'life and soul, so to speak,' and this because

> tragedy is essentially an imitation not of persons but of action and life. . . We maintain that Tragedy is primarily an imitation of action, and that it is mainly for the sake of the action that it imitates the personal agents.[12]

If we refer again to our analytic diagram, one other general aspect of the *Poetics* presses on our attention, particularly when we have the distinctive orientation of romantic criticism in mind. While Aristotle makes a distribution (though an unequal one) among the objects imitated, the necessary emotional effects on an audience, and the internal demands of the product itself, as determinants of this or that aspect of a poem, he does not assign a determinative function to the poet himself. The poet is the indispensable efficient cause, the agent

who, by his skill, extracts the form from natural things and imposes it upon an artificial medium; but his personal faculties, feelings, or desires are not called on to explain the subject matter or form of a poem. In the *Poetics*, the poet is invoked only to explain the historical divergence of comic from serious forms, and to be advised of certain aids toward the construction of plot and the choice of diction.[13] In Plato, the poet is considered from the point of view of politics, not of art. When the poets make a personal appearance all the major ones are dismissed, with extravagant courtesy, from the ideal Republic; upon later application, a somewhat greater number are admitted to the second-best state of the *Laws*, but with a radically diminished repertory.[14]

'Imitation' continued to be a prominent item in the critical vocabulary for a long time after Aristotle—all the way through the eighteenth century, in fact. The systematic importance given to the term differed greatly from critic to critic; those objects in the universe that art imitates, or should imitate, were variously conceived as either actual or in some sense ideal; and from the first, there was a tendency to replace Aristotle's 'action' as the principal object of imitation with such elements as human character, or thought, or even inanimate things. But particularly after the recovery of the *Poetics* and the great burst of aesthetic theory in sixteenth-century Italy, whenever a critic was moved to get down to fundamentals and frame a comprehensive definition of art, the predicate usually included the word 'imitation,' or else one of those parallel terms which, whatever differences they might imply, all faced in the same direction: 'reflection,' 'representation,' 'counterfeiting,' 'feigning,' 'copy,' or 'image.'

Through most of the eighteenth century, the tenet that art is an imitation seemed almost too obvious to need iteration or proof. As Richard Hurd said in his 'Discourse on Poetical Imitation,' published in 1751, 'All *Poetry*, to speak with Aristotle and the Greek critics (if for so plain a point authorities be thought wanting) *is*, properly, *imitation*. It is, indeed, the noblest and most extensive of the mimetic arts; having all creation for its object, and ranging the entire circuit of universal being.'[15] Even the reputedly radical proponents of 'original genius' in the second half of the century commonly found that a work of genius was no less an imitation for being an original. '*Imitations*,' Young wrote in his *Conjectures on Original Composition*, 'are of two kinds: one of nature, one of authors. The first we call *Originals*. . .' The original genius in fact turns out to be a kind of scientific investigator: 'The wide field of nature lies open before it, where it may range

[9] [Abrams] *Poetics* 6, 1449b, 14. 1453b [above, page 55].
[10] First among equals.
[11] [Abrams] *Poetics* 8. 1451a [above, page 57].
[12] [Abrams] Ibid. 6. 1450a–1450b [above, page 55].

[13] [Abrams] Ibid. 4. 1448b, 17. 1455a–1455b [above, page 27].
[14] [Abrams] *Republic*, iii. 398, x. 606–8 [above, page 27]; *Laws* vii. 817.
[15] [Abrams] *The Works of Richard Hurd* (London, 1811), II, 111–12.

unconfined, make what discoveries it can . . . as far as visible nature extends. . .'[16] Later the Reverend J. Moir, an extremist in his demand for originality in poetry, conceived genius to lie in the ability to discover 'a thousand new variations, distinctions, and resemblances' in the 'familiar phenomena of nature,' and declared that original genius always gives 'the identical impression it receives.'[17] In this identification of the poet's task as novelty of discovery and particularity of description we have moved a long way from Aristotle's conception of mimesis, except in this respect, that criticism still looks to one or another aspect of the given world for the essential source and subject matter of poetry.

Instead of heaping up quotations, it will be better to cite a few eighteenth-century discussions of imitation that are of special interest. My first example is the French critic, Charles Batteux, whose *Les Beaux Arts réduits à un même principe* (1747) found some favor in England and had immense influence in Germany, as well as in his native country. The rules of art, Batteux thought, which are now so numerous, must surely be reducible to a single principle. 'Let us,' he cries, 'imitate the true physicists, who assemble experiments and then on these found a system which reduces them to a principle.'

That Batteux proposes for his procedure 'to begin with a clear and distinct idea'—a principle 'simple enough to be grasped instantly, and extensive enough to absorb all the little detailed rules'—is sufficient clue that he will follow in method not Newton, the physicist, but rather Euclid and Descartes.[18] In pursuance of his clear and distinct idea, he burrowed industriously through the standard French critics until, he says ingenuously, 'it occurred to me to open Aristotle, whose *Poetics* I had heard praised.' Then came the revelation; all details fell neatly into place. The source of illumination?—none other than 'the principle of imitation which the Greek philosopher established for the fine arts?[19] This imitation, however, is not

of crude everyday reality, but of 'la belle nature'; that is, 'le vrai-semblable,' formed by assembling traits taken from individual things to compose a model possessing 'all the perfections it is able to receive.'[20] From this principle Batteux goes on, lengthily and with great show of rigor, to extract one by one the rules of taste—both the general rules for poetry and painting and the detailed rules for the special genres. For

> the majority of known rules refer back to imitation, and form a sort of chain, by which the mind seizes at the same instant consequences and principle, as a whole perfectly joined, in which all the parts are mutually sustained.[21]

Next to this classic instance of a priori and deductive aesthetics I shall set a German document, Lessing's *Laokoön,* published in 1776.[22] Lessing undertook to undo the confusion in theory and practice between poetry and the graphic and plastic arts which, he believed, resulted from an uninquisitive acceptance of Simonides' maxim that 'painting is dumb poetry and poetry a speaking painting.'[23] His own procedure, he promises, will be continually to test abstract theory against 'the individual instance.' Repeatedly he derides German critics for their reliance on deduction. 'We Germans have no lack of systematic books. We are the most expert of any nation in the world at deducing, from a few given verbal explanations, and in the most beautiful order, anything whatever that we wish.' 'How many things would prove incontestable in theory, had not genius succeeded in proving the contrary in fact!'[24] Lessing's intention, then, is to establish aesthetic principles by an inductive logic which is deliberately opposed to the procedure of Batteux. Nevertheless, like Batteux, Lessing concludes that poetry, no less than painting, is imitation. The diversity between these arts follows from their difference in medium, which imposes necessary differences in the objects each is competent to imitate. But although poetry consists of a sequence of articulate sounds in time rather than of forms and colors fixed in space, and although, instead of being limited, like painting, to a static but pregnant moment, its special power is the reproduction of progressive action, Lessing reiterates for it the standard

---

[16] [Abrams] Edward Young, *Conjectures on Original Composition* [above, page 349], ed. Edith Morley (Manchester, 1918), pp. 6, 18. See also William Duff, *Essay on Original Genius* (London, 1767), p. 192n. John Ogilvie reconciles creative genius and original invention with "the great principle of *poetic imitation*" (*Philosophical and Critical Observations on the Nature, Characters, and Various Species of Composition*, London, 1774, I, 105–7). Joseph Warton, familiar proponent of a "boundless imagination," enthusiasm, and "the romantic, the wonderful, and the wild," still agrees with Richard Hurd that poetry is "an art, whose essence is imitation," and whose objects are "material or animate, extraneous or internal." (*Essay on the Writings and Genius of Pope*, London, 1756, I, 89–90). Cf. Robert Wood, *Essay on the Original Genius and Writings of Homer* (1769), London, 1824, pp. 6–7, 178.

[17] [Abrams] "Originality," *Gleanings* (London, 1785), I, 107, 109.

[18] Isaac Newton (1642–1727), English mathematician and physicist; Euclid (fl. 300 B.C.), Greek mathematician; René Descartes (1596–1650), French mathematician and philosopher.

[19] [Abrams] Charles Batteux, *Les Beaux Arts réduits á un même principe* (Paris, 1747), pp. I–viii.

[20] [Abrams] Ibid. pp. 9–27.

[21] [Abrams] Ibid. p. xiii. For the important place of imitation in earlier French neoclassic theories, see René Bray, *La Formation de la doctrine classique en France* (Lausanne, 1931), pp. 144ff.

[22] Lessing (above, page 379).

[23] Simonides (fl. fifth century B.C.), Greek poet.

[24] [Abrams] Lessing, *Laocoön*, ed. W. G. Howard (New York, 1910), pp. 235–42.

formula: 'Nachahmung' is still for the poet the attribute 'which constitutes the essence of his art.'[25]

As the century drew on, various English critics began to scrutinize the concept of imitation very closely, and they ended by finding (Aristotle to the contrary) that differences in medium between the arts were such as to disqualify all but a limited number from being classed as mimetic, in any strict sense. The trend may be indicated by a few examples. In 1744 James Harris still maintained, in 'A Discourse on Music, Painting, and Poetry,' that imitation was common to all three arts. 'They agree, by being all mimetic or imitative. They differ, as they imitate by different media. . . "[26] In 1762 Kames declared that 'of all the fine arts, painting only and sculpture are in their nature imitative'; music, like architecture, 'is productive of originals, and copies not from nature'; while language copies from nature only in those instances in which it 'is imitative of sound or motion.'[27] And by 1789, in two closely reasoned dissertations prefixed to his translation of the *Poetics,* Thomas Twining confirmed this distinction between arts whose media are 'iconic' (in the later terminology of the Chicago semiotician, Charles Morris[28]), in that they resemble what they denote, and those which are significant only by convention. Only works in which the resemblance between copy and object is both 'immediate' and 'obvious,' Twining says, can be described as imitative in a strict sense. Dramatic poetry, therefore, in which we mimic speech by speech, is the only kind of poetry which is properly imitation; music must be struck from the list of imitative arts; and he concludes by saying that painting, sculpture, and the arts of design in general are 'the only arts that are *obviously* and *essentially* imitative.'[29]

The concept that art is imitation, then, played an important part in neo-classic aesthetics; but closer inspection shows that it did not, in most theories, play the dominant part. Art, it was commonly said, is an imitation—but an imitation which is only instrumental toward producing effects upon an audience. In fact, the near-unanimity with which post-Renaissance critics lauded and echoed Aristotle's *Poetics* is deceptive. The focus of interest had shifted, and, on our diagram, this later criticism is primarily oriented, not from work to universe, but from work to audience. The na-

ture and consequences of this change of direction is clearly indicated by the first classic of English criticism, written sometime in the early 1580's, Sir Philip Sidney's *The Apologie for Poetry.*

iii. Pragmatic Theories

Poesy therefore [said Sidney] is an arte of imitation, for so Aristotle termeth it in the word Mimesis, *that is to say, a representing, counterfetting, or figuring foorth—to speake metaphorically, a speaking picture: with this end, to teach and delight.*[30]

In spite of the appeal to Aristotle, this is not an Aristotelian formulation. To Sidney, poetry, by definition, has a purpose—to achieve certain effects in an audience. It imitates only as a means to the proximate end of pleasing, and pleases, it turns out, only as a means to the ultimate end of teaching; for 'right poets' are those who 'imitate both to delight and teach, and delight to move men to take that goodnes in hande, which without delight they would flye as from a stranger. . .'[31] As a result, throughout this essay the needs of the audience become the fertile grounds for critical distinctions and standards. In order 'to teach and delight,' poets imitate not 'what is, hath been, or shall be,' but only 'what may be, and should be,' so that the very objects of imitation become such as to guarantee the moral purpose. The poet is distinguished from, and elevated above, the moral philosopher and the historian by his capacity to move his auditors more forcefully to virtue, since he couples 'the general notion' of the philosopher with 'the particular example' of the historian; while by disguising his doctrine in a tale, he entices even 'harde harted evil men,' unaware, into the love of goodness, 'as if they tooke a medicine of Cherries.' The genres of poetry are discussed and ranked from the point of view of the moral and social effect each is suited to achieve: the epic poem thus demonstrates itself to be the king of poetry because it 'most inflameth the mind with desire to be worthy,' and even the lowly love lyric is conceived as an instrument for persuading a mistress of the genuineness of her lover's passion.[32] A history of criticism could be written solely on the basis of successive interpretations of salient passages from Aristotle's *Poetics.* In this instance, with no sense of strain, Sidney follows his Italian guides (who in turn had read Aristotle through the spectacles of Horace, Cicero, and the Church fathers) in

[25] [Abrams] Ibid, pp. 99–102, 64.

[26] [Abrams] *Three Treatises* in *The Works of James Harris* (London, 1803), I. 58. Cf. Adam Smith, "Of the Nature of That Imitation Which Takes Place in What Are Called the Imitative Arts," *Essays Philosophical and Literary* (London, n.d.), pp. 405ff.

[27] [Abrams] Henry Home, Lord Kames [above, page 369], *Elements of Criticism* (Boston, 1796), II, I (chap. xviii).

[28] Charles Morris (1903–1979).

[29] [Abrams] Thomas Twining, ed., *Aristotle's Treatise on Poetry* (London, 1789), pp. 4, 21–22, 60–61.

[30] [Abrams] Sir Philip Sidney [above, page 189], "An Apology for Poetry," *Elizabethan Critical Essays,* ed. G. Gregory Smith (London, 1904), I, 158.

[31] [Abrams] Ibid. I, 159 [above, page 189].

[32] [Abrams] Ibid. I, 159, 161–64, 171–80, 201 [above, page 197].

bending one after another of the key statements of the *Poetics* to fit his own theoretical frame.[33]

For convenience we may name criticism that, like Sidney's, is ordered toward the audience, a 'pragmatic theory,' since it looks at the work of art chiefly as a means to an end, an instrument for getting something done, and tends to judge its value according to its success in achieving that aim. There is, of course, the greatest variance in emphasis and detail, but the central tendency of the pragmatic critic is to conceive a poem as something made in order to effect requisite responses in its readers; to consider the author from the point of view of the powers and training he must have in order to achieve this end; to ground the classification and anatomy of poems in large part on the special effects each kind and component is most competent to achieve; and to derive the norms of the poetic art and canons of critical appraisal from the needs and legitimate demands of the audience to whom the poetry is addressed.

The perspective, much of the basic vocabulary, and many of the characteristic topics of pragmatic criticism originated in the classical theory of rhetoric. For rhetoric had been universally regarded as an instrument for achieving persuasion in an audience, and most theorists agreed with Cicero that in order to persuade, the orator must conciliate, inform, and move the minds of his auditors.[34] The great classical exemplar of the application of the rhetorical point of view to poetry was, of course, the *Ars Poetica* of Horace. As Richard McKeon points out, 'Horace's criticism is directed in the main to instruct the poet how to keep his audience in their seats until the end, how to induce cheers and applause, how to please a Roman audience, and by the same token, how to please all audiences and win immortality.'[35]

In what became for later critics the focal passage of the *Ars Poetica*, Horace advised that 'the poet's aim is either to profit or to please, or to blend in one the delightful and the useful.' The context shows that Horace held pleasure to be the chief purpose of poetry, for he recommends the profitable merely as a means to give pleasure to the elders, who, in contrast to the young aristocrats, 'rail at what contains no serviceable lesson.'[36] But *prodesse*

and *delectare,* to teach and to please, together with another term introduced from rhetoric, *movere,* to move, served for centuries to collect under three heads the sum of aesthetic effects on the reader. The balance between these terms altered in the course of time. To the overwhelming majority of Renaissance critics, as to Sir Philip Sidney, the moral effect was the terminal aim, to which delight and emotion were auxiliary. From the time of the critical essays of Dryden through the eighteenth century, pleasure tended to become the ultimate end, although poetry without profit was often held to be trivial, and the optimistic moralist believed with James Beattie that if poetry instructs, it only pleases the more effectually.[37]

Looking upon a poem as a 'making,' a contrivance for affecting an audience, the typical pragmatic critic is engrossed with formulating the methods—the 'skill, or Crafte of making' as Ben Jonson called it—for achieving the effects desired. These methods, traditionally comprehended under the term *poesis,* or 'art' (in phrases such as 'the art of poetry'), are formulated as precepts and rules whose warrant consists either in their being derived from the qualities of works whose success and long survival have proved their adaptation to human nature, or else in their being grounded directly on the psychological laws governing the responses of men in general. The rules, therefore, are inherent in the qualities of each excellent work of art, and when excerpted and codified these rules serve equally to guide the artist in making and the critics in judging any future product. 'Dryden,' said Dr. Johnson, 'may be properly considered as the father of English criticism, as the writer who first taught us to determine upon principles the merit of composition.'[38] Dryden's method of establishing those principles was to point out that poetry, like painting, has an end, which is to please; that imitation of nature is the general means for attaining this end; and that rules serve to specify the means for accomplishing this end in detail:

> Having thus shewn that imitation pleases, and why it pleases in both these arts, it follows, that some rules of imitation are necessary to obtain the end; for without rules there can be no art, any more than there can be a house without a door to conduct you into it.[39]

---

[33][Abrams] See, e.g., his use of Aristotle's statement that poetry is more philosophical than history (I, 167–68) [above, page 57] and that painful things can be made pleasant by imitations (p. 171) [above, page 58]; and his wrenching of Aristotle's central term, *praxis*—the actions which are imitated by poetry—to signify the moral action which a poem moves the spectator to practice.

[34][Abrams] Cicero [above, page 74], *De oratore* II. xxviii.

[35][Abrams] "The Concept of Imitation," op. cit., p. 173.

[36][Abrams] Horace, *Ars Poetica,* tr. E. H. Blakeney, in *Literary Criticism: Plato to Dryden,* ed. Allan H. Gilbert (New York, 1940), p. 139 [above, page 83].

[37][Abrams] *Essays on Poetry and Music* (third ed.; London, 1779), p. 10.

[38][Abrams] "Dryden," *Lives of the English Poets,* ed. Birkbeck Hill (Oxford, 1905), I, 410.

[39][Abrams] "Parallel of Poetry and Painting" (1695), *Essays,* ed. W. P. Ker (Oxford, 1926), II. See Hoyt Trowbridge, "The Place of Rules in Dryden's Criticism," *Modern Philology,* XLIV (1946), 84ff.

Emphasis on the rules and maxims of an art is native to all criticism that grounds itself in the demands of an audience, and it survives today in the magazines and manuals devoted to teaching fledgling authors 'how to write stories that sell.' But rulebooks based on the lowest common denominator of the modern buying public are only gross caricatures of the complex and subtly rationalized neo-classic ideals of literary craftsmanship. Through the early part of the eighteenth century, the poet could rely confidently on the trained taste and expert connoisseurship of a limited circle of readers, whether these were Horace's Roman contemporaries under Emperor Augustus, or Vida's at the papal court of Leo X,[40] or Sidney's fellow-courtiers under Elizabeth, or the London audience of Dryden and Pope; while, in theory, the voices even of the best contemporary judges were subordinated to the voice of the ages. Some neo-classic critics were also certain that the rules of art, though empirically derived, were ultimately validated by conforming to that objective structure of norms whose existence guaranteed the rational order and harmony of the universe. In a strict sense, as John Dennis made explicit what was often implied, Nature 'is nothing but that Rule and Order, and Harmony, which we find in the visible Creation'; so 'Poetry, which is an imitation of Nature,' must demonstrate the same properties. The renowned masters among the ancients wrote not

> to please a tumultuous transitory Assembly, or a Handful of Men, who were call'd their Countrymen; They wrote to their Fellow-Citizens of the Universe, to all Countries, and to all Ages. . . They were clearly convinc'd, that nothing could transmit their Immortal Works to Posterity, but something like that harmonious Order which maintains the Universe. . .[41]

Although they disagreed concerning specific rules, and although many English critics repudiated such formal French requisites as the unity of time and place, and the purity of comedy and tragedy, all but a few eccentrics among eighteenth-century critics believed in the validity of some set of universal rules. At about mid-century, it became popular to demonstrate and expound all the major rules for poetry, or even for art in general, in a single inclusive critical

system. The pattern of the pragmatic reasoning usually employed may conveniently be studied in such a compendious treatment as James Beattie's *Essay on Poetry and Music as they affect the Mind* (1762), or more succinctly still, in Richard Hurd's 'Dissertation of the Idea of Universal Poetry' (1766). Universal poetry, no matter what the genre, Hurd says, is an art whose end is the maximum possible pleasure. 'When we speak of poetry, as an *art,* we mean *such a way or method of treating a subject, as is found most pleasing and delightful to us.'* And this idea 'if kept steadily in view, will unfold to us all the mysteries of the poetic art. There needs but to evolve the philosopher's idea, and to apply it, as occasion serves.' From this major premise Hurd evolves three properties, essential to all poetry if it is to effect the greatest possible delight: figurative language, 'fiction' (that is to say, a departure from what is actual, or empirically possible), and versification. The mode and degree in which these three universal qualities are to be combined in any one species of poetry, however, will depend on its peculiar end, because each poetic kind must exploit that special pleasure which it is generically adapted to achieve. 'For the art of every *kind* of poetry is only this general art so modified as the *nature* of each, that is, its more immediate and subordinate end, may respectively require.'

> For the name of poem will belong to every composition, whose primary end is to *please,* provided it be so constructed as to afford *all* the pleasure, which its kind or *sort* will permit.[42]

On the basis of isolated passages from his *Letters on Chivalry and Romance,* Hurd is commonly treated as a 'pre-romantic' critic. But in the summation of his poetic creed in the 'Idea of Universal Poetry,' the rigidly deductive logic which Hurd employs to 'unfold' the rules of poetry from a primitive definition, permitting 'the reason of the thing' to override the evidence of the actual practice of poets, brings him as close as anyone in England to the geometric method of Charles Batteux, though without that critic's Cartesian apparatus. The difference is that Batteux evolves his rules from the definition of poetry as the imitation of *la belle nature,* and Hurd, from its definition as the art of treating a subject so as to afford the reader a maximum pleasure; and this involves his assuming that he possesses an empirical knowledge of the psychology of the reader. For if the end of poetry is to gratify the mind of the reader, Hurd says, knowledge of the laws of

---

[40] Augustus (63 B.C.–14 A.D.), first Roman Emperor; Marco Giraloma Vida (c. 1490–1556) Italian Latin poet; Leo X (1475–1521), pope.

[41] [Abrams] *The Advancement and Reform of Modern Poetry* (1701), in *Critical Works of John Dennis,* ed. E. N. Hooker (Baltimore, 1939), I, 202–3. For Dennis' derivation of specific rules from the end of art, which is "to delight and reform the mind," see *The Grounds of Criticism in Poetry* (1704), ibid., pp. 336ff.

[42] [Abrams] "Dissertation on the Idea of Universal Poetry," *Works,* II, 3–4, 25–26, 7. For a parallel argument see Alexander Gerard, *An Essay on Taste* (London 1759), p. 40.

mind is necessary to establish its rules, which are 'but so many MEANS, which experience finds most conducive to that end.'[43] Since Batteux and Hurd, however, are both intent on rationalizing what is mainly a common body of poetic lore, it need not surprise us that, though they set out from different points of the compass, their paths often coincide.[44]

But to appreciate the power and illumination of which a refined and flexible pragmatic criticism is capable, we must turn from these abstract systematizers of current methods and maxims to such a practical critic as Samuel Johnson. Johnson's literary criticism assumes approximately the frame of critical reference I have described, but Johnson, who distrusts rigid and abstract theorizing, applies the method with a constant appeal to specific literary examples, deference to the opinions of other readers, but ultimately, reliance on his own expert responses to the text. As a result Johnson's comments on poets and poems have persistently afforded a jumping-off point for later critics whose frame of reference and particular judgments differ radically from his own. For an instance of Johnson's procedure which is especially interesting because it shows how the notion of the imitation of nature is co-ordinated with the judgment of poetry in terms of its end and effects, consider that monument of neo-classic criticism, Johnson's *Preface to Shakespeare.*

Johnson undertakes in his *Preface* to establish Shakespeare's rank among poets, and to do so, he is led to rate Shakespeare's native abilities against the general level of taste and achievement in the Elizabethan age, and to measure these abilities in turn 'by their proportion to the general and collective ability of man.'[45] Since the powers and excellence of an author, however, can only be inferred from the nature and excellence of the works he achieves, Johnson addresses himself to a general examination of Shakespeare's dramas. In this systematic appraisal of the works themselves, we find that mimesis retains for Johnson a measure of authority as criterion. Repeatedly Johnson maintains that 'this therefore is the praise of *Shakespeare,* that his drama is

the mirrour of life,' and of inanimate nature as well: 'He was an exact surveyor of the inanimate world. . . *Shakespeare,* whether life or nature be his subject, shews plainly, that he has seen with his own eyes. . .'[46] But, Johnson also claims, 'The end of writing is to instruct; the end of poetry is to instruct by pleasing.'[47] It is to this function of poetry, and to the demonstrated effect of a poem upon its audience, that Johnson awards priority as aesthetic criterion. If a poem fails to please, whatever its character otherwise, it is, as a work of art, nothing; though Johnson insists, with a strenuous moralism that must already have seemed old-fashioned to contemporary readers, it must please without violating the standards of truth and virtue. Accordingly, Johnson discriminates those elements in Shakespeare's plays which were introduced to appeal to the local and passing tastes of the rather barbarous audience of his own time ('He knew,' said Johnson, 'how he should most please'),[48] from those elements which are proportioned to the tastes of the common readers of all time. And since in works 'appealing wholly to observation and experience, no other test can be applied than length of duration and continuance of esteem,' Shakespeare's long survival as a poet 'read without any other reason than the desire for pleasure' is the best evidence for his artistic excellence. The reason for this survival Johnson explains on the subsidiary principle that 'nothing can please many, and please long, but just representations of general nature.' Shakespeare exhibits the eternal 'species' of human character, moved by 'those general passions and principles by which all minds are agitated.'[49] Thus Shakespeare's excellence in holding up the mirror to general nature turns out, in the long run, to be justified by the superior criterion of the appeal this achievement holds for the enduring tastes of the general literary public.

A number of Johnson's individual observations and judgments exhibit a play of the argument between the two principles of the nature of the world the poet must reflect, and the nature and legitimate requirements of the poet's audience. For the most part the two principles co-operate toward a single conclusion. For example, both the empirical nature of the universe and of the universal reader demonstrate the fallacy of those who censure Shakespeare for mixing his comic and tragic scenes. Shakespeare's plays, Johnson says, exhibit 'the real state of sublunary nature, which partakes of good and evil, joy and sorrow, mingled with endless variety.' In addition, 'the mingled drama may

---

[43] [Abrams] "Idea of Universal Poetry," *Works,* II, 3–4. On the rationale underlying the body of Hurd's criticism, see the article by Hoyt Trowbridge, "Bishop Hurd, A Reinterpretation," *PMLA,* LVIII (1943), 450ff.

[44] [Abrams] Batteux "deduces" from the idea that poetry is the imitation, not of unadorned reality, but of *la belle nature,* that its end can only be "to please, to move, to touch, in a word, pleasure" (*Les Beaux Art,* pp. 81, 151). Conversely, Hurd infers from the fact that the end of poetry is pleasure that the poet's duty is to "illustrate and adorn" reality, and to delineate it "in the most taking forms" ("Idea of Universal Poetry," *Works,* II, 8). For purposes of a specialized investigation into the evidence of plagiarism among poets, Hurd himself, in another essay, shifts his ground, and like Batteux, sets out from a definition of poetry as an imitation, specifically, of "the fairest forms of things" ("Discourse on Poetic Imitation," *Works,* II, 111).

[45] [Abrams] *Johnson on Shakespeare,* ed. Walter Raleigh (Oxford, 1908), pp. 10, 30–31.

[46] [Abrams] Ibid. pp. 14, 39. Cf. pp. 11, 31, 33, 37, etc.

[47] [Abrams] Ibid, p. 16.

[48] [Abrams] Ibid. pp. 31–33, 41.

[49] [Abrams] Ibid, pp. 9–12.

convey all the instruction of tragedy or comedy' by approaching nearer 'to the appearance of life'; while the objection that the change of scene 'wants at last the power to move' is a specious reasoning 'received as true even by those who in daily experience feel it to be false.'[50] But when the actual state of sublunary affairs conflicts with the poet's obligation to his audience, the latter is the court of final appeal. It is Shakespeare's defect, says Johnson,

> that he seems to write without any moral purpose
> . . . He makes no just distribution of good or evil,
> nor is always careful to shew in the virtuous a disapprobation of the wicked. . . It is always a
> writer's duty to make the world better, and justice
> is a virtue independant on time or place.[51]

The pragmatic orientation, ordering the aim of the artist and the character of the work to the nature, the needs, and the springs of pleasure in the audience, characterized by far the greatest part of criticism from the time of Horace through the eighteenth century. Measured either by its duration or the number of its adherents, therefore, the pragmatic view, broadly conceived, has been the principal aesthetic attitude of the Western world. But inherent in this system were the elements of its dissolution. Ancient rhetoric had bequeathed to criticism not only its stress on affecting the audience but also (since its main concern was with educating the orator) its detailed attention to the powers and activities of the speaker himself—his 'nature,' or innate powers and genius, as distinguished from his culture and art, and also the process of invention, disposition, and expression involved in his discourse.[52] In the course of time, and particularly after the psychological contributions of Hobbes and Locke[53] in the seventeenth century, increasing attention was

given to the mental constitution of the poet, the quality and degree of his 'genius,' and the play of his faculties in the act of composition. Through most of the eighteenth century, the poet's invention and imagination were made thoroughly dependent for their materials—their ideas and 'images'—on the external universe and the literary models the poet had to imitate; while the persistent stress laid on his need for judgment and art—the mental surrogates, in effect, of the requirements of a cultivated audience—held the poet strictly responsible to the audience for whose pleasure he exerted his creative ability. Gradually, however, the stress was shifted more and more to the poet's natural genius, creative imagination, and emotional spontaneity, at the expense of the opposing attributes of judgment, learning, and artful restraints. As a result the audience gradually receded into the background, giving place to the poet himself, and his own mental powers and emotional needs, as the predominant cause and even the end and test of art. By this time other developments, which we shall have occasion to talk about later, were also helping to shift the focus of critical interest from audience to artist and thus to introduce a new orientation into the theory of art.

iv. Expressive Theories

'Poetry,' Wordsworth announced in his Preface to the *Lyrical Ballads* of 1800, 'is the spontaneous overflow of powerful feelings.'[54] He thought well enough of this formulation to use it twice in the same essay, and on this, as the ground-idea, he founded his theory of the proper subjects, language, effects, and value of poetry. Almost all the major critics of the English romantic generation phrased definitions or key statements showing a parallel alignment from work to poet. Poetry is the overflow, utterance, or projection of the thought and feelings of the poet; or else (in the chief variant formulation) poetry is defined in terms of the imaginative process which modifies and synthesizes the images, thoughts, and feelings of the poet. This way of thinking, in which the artist himself becomes the major element generating both the artistic product and the criteria by which it is to be judged, I shall call the expressive theory of art.

Setting the date at which this point of view became predominant in critical theory, like marking the point at which orange becomes yellow in the color spectrum, must be a somewhat arbitrary procedure. As we shall see, an approach to the expressive orientation, though isolated in history and partial in scope, is to be found as early as Longinus' discus-

---

[50] [Abrams] Ibid. pp. 15–17. See Johnson's defense of Shakespeare for violating the decorum of character-types, by the appeal to "nature" as against "accident"; and for breaking the unities of time and place, by the appeal both to the actual experience of dramatic auditors, and to the principle that "the greatest graces of a play, are to copy nature and instruct life" (ibid. pp. 14–15, 25–30). Cf *Rambler* No. 156.

[51] [Abrams] Ibid. pp. 20–21. The logic appears even more clearly in Johnson's early paper on "works of fiction," in *Rambler* No. 4, 1750 (*The Works of Samuel Johnson*, ed. Arthur Murphy, London 1924, IV, 23): "It is justly considered as the greatest excellency of art, to imitate nature; but it is necessary to distinguish those parts of nature which are most proper for imitation," etc. For a detailed analysis of Johnson's critical methods, see W. R. Keats, "The Theoretical Foundations of Johnson's Criticism," *Critics and Criticism*, ed. R. S. Crane, pp. 389–407.

[52] [Abrams] See the masterly précis of the complex movements within English neoclassic criticism by R. S. Crane, "English Neoclassical Criticism, *"Critics and Criticism*, pp. 372–88.

[53] Thomas Hobbes (1588–1679), English philosopher; John Locke (above, page 281).

[54] Wordsworth (above, page 490).

sion of the sublime style[55] as having its main sources in the thought and emotions of the speaker; and it recurs in a variant form in Bacon's brief analysis of poetry as pertaining to the imagination and 'accommodating the shows of things to the desires of the mind.'[56] Even Wordsworth's theory, it will appear, is much more embedded in a traditional matrix of interests and emphases, and is, therefore, less radical than are the theories of his followers of the 1830's. The year 1800 is a good round number, however, and Wordsworth's Preface a convenient document, by which to signalize the displacement of the mimetic and pragmatic by the expressive view of art in English criticism.

In general terms, the central tendency of the expressive theory may be summarized in this way: A work of art is essentially the internal made external, resulting from a creative process operating under the impulse of feeling, and embodying the combined product of the poet's perceptions, thoughts, and feelings. The primary source and subject matter of a poem, therefore, are the attributes and actions of the poet's own mind; or if aspects of the external world, then these only as they are converted from fact to poetry by the feelings and operations of the poet's mind. ('Thus the Poetry . . .' Wordsworth wrote, 'proceeds whence it ought to do, from the soul of Man, communicating its creative energies to the images of the external world.')[57] The paramount cause of poetry is not, as in Aristotle, a formal cause, determined primarily by the human actions and qualities imitated; nor, as in neo-classic criticism, a final cause, the effect intended upon the audience; but instead an efficient cause—the impulse within the poet of feelings and desires seeking expression, or the compulsion of the 'creative' imagination which, like God the creator, has its internal source of motion. The propensity is to grade the arts by the extent to which their media are amenable to the undistorted expression of the feelings or mental powers of the artist, and to classify the species of an art, and evaluate their instances, by the qualities or states of mind of which they are a sign. Of the elements constituting a poem, the element of diction, especially figures of speech, becomes primary; and the burning question is, whether these are the natural utterance of emotion and imagination or the deliberate aping of poetic conventions. The first test any poem must pass is no longer, 'Is it true to nature?' or 'Is it appropriate to the requirements either of the best judges or the generality of mankind?' but a criterion looking in a different direction; namely, 'Is it sin-

cere? Is it genuine? Does it match the intention, the feeling, and the actual state of mind of the poet while composing?' The work ceases then to be regarded as primarily a reflection of nature, actual or improved; the mirror held up to nature becomes transparent and yields the reader insights into the mind and heart of the poet himself. The exploitation of literature as an index to personality first manifests itself in the early nineteenth century; it is the inevitable consequence of the expressive point of view.

The sources, details, and historical results of this reorientation of criticism, in its various forms, will be a principal concern of the rest of this book. Now, while we have some of the earlier facts fresh in mind, let me indicate what happened to salient elements of traditional criticism in the essays 'What Is Poetry?' and 'The Two Kinds of Poetry,' written by John Stuart Mill in 1833. Mill relied in large part on Wordsworth's Preface to the *Lyrical Ballads,* but in the intervening thirty years the expressive theory had emerged from the network of qualifications in which Wordsworth had carefully placed it, and had worked out its own destiny unhindered. Mill's logic in answering the question, 'What Is Poetry?' is not *more geometrico,* like that of Batteux, nor stiffly formal, like Richard Hurd's; nonetheless, his theory turns out to be just as tightly dependent upon a central principle as theirs. For whatever Mill's empirical pretensions, his initial assumption about the essential nature of poetry remains continuously though silently effective in selecting, interpreting, and ordering the facts to be explained.

The primitive proposition of Mill's theory is: Poetry is 'the expression or uttering forth of feeling.'[58] Exploration of the data of aesthetics from this starting point leads, among other things, to the following drastic alterations in the great commonplaces of the critical tradition:

(1) *The poetic kinds.* Mill reinterprets and inverts the neo-classic ranking of the poetic kinds. As the purest expression of feeling, lyric poetry is 'more eminently and peculiarly poetry than any other. . .' Other forms are all alloyed by non-poetic elements, whether descriptive, didactic, or narrative, which serve merely as convenient occasions for the poetic utterances of feeling either by the poet or by one of his invented characters. To Aristotle, tragedy had been the highest form of poetry, and the plot, representing the action being imitated, had been its 'soul'; while most neo-classic critics had agreed that, whether judged by greatness of subject matter or of effect, epic and tragedy are the king and queen of poetic forms. It serves as an index to the revolution

---

[55] Longinus, (above, page 94).

[56] Bacon (above, page 234).

[57] [Abrams] *Letters of William and Dorothy Wordsworth: The Middle Years,* ed. E. de Selincourt (Oxford, 1937), II, 705; 18 Jan. 1816.

[58] [Abrams] *Early Essays by John Stuart Mill,* ed. J. W. M. Gibbs (London, 1897), p. 208.

in critical norms to notice that to Mill, plot becomes a kind of necessary evil. An epic poem 'in so far as it is epic (i.e. narrative) . . . is not poetry at all,' but only a suitable frame for the greatest diversity of genuinely poetic passages; while the interest in plot and story 'merely as a story' characterizes rude stages of society, children, and the 'shallowest and emptiest' of civilized adults.[59] Similarly with the other arts; in music, painting, sculpture, and architecture Mill distinguishes between that which is 'simple imitation or description' and that which 'expresses human feeling' and is, therefore, poetry.[60]

(2) *Spontaneity as criterion.* Mill accepts the venerable assumption that a man's emotional susceptibility is innate, but his knowledge and skill—his art—are acquired. On this basis, he distinguishes poets into two classes: poets who are born and poets who are made, or those who are poets 'by nature,' and those who are poets 'by culture.' Natural poetry is identifiable because it 'is Feeling itself, employing Thought only as the medium of its utterance'; on the other hand, the poetry of 'a cultivated but not naturally poetic mind,' is written with 'a distinct aim,' and in it the thought remains the conspicuous object, however surrounded by 'a halo of feeling.' Natural poetry, it turns out, is 'poetry in a far higher sense, than any other; since . . . that which constitutes poetry, human feeling, enters far more largely into this than into the poetry of culture.' Among the moderns, Shelley represents the poet born and Wordsworth the poet made; and with unconscious irony Mill turns Wordsworth's own criterion, 'the spontaneous overflow of feeling,' against its sponsor. Wordsworth's poetry 'has little even of the appearance of spontaneousness: the well is never so full that it overflows.'[61]

(3) *The external world.* In so far as a literary product simply imitates objects, it is not poetry at all. As a result, reference of poetry to the external universe disappears from Mill's theory, except to the extent that sensible objects may serve as a stimulus or 'occasion for the generation of poetry,' and then, 'the poetry is not in the object itself,' but 'in the state of mind' in which it is contemplated. When a poet describes a lion he 'is describing the lion professedly, but the state of excitement of the spectator really,' and the poetry must be true not to the object, but to 'the human emotion.'[62] Thus severed from the external world, the objects signified by a poem tend to be regarded as no more than a

projected equivalent—an extended and articulated symbol—for the poet's inner state of mind. Poetry, said Mill, in a phrasing which anticipates T. E. Hulme and lays the theoretical groundwork for the practice of symbolists from Baudelaire through T. S. Eliot, embodies 'itself in symbols, which are the nearest possible representations of the feeling in the exact shape in which it exists in the poet's mind.'[63] Tennyson, Mill wrote in a review of that poet's early poems, excels in 'scene-painting, in the higher sense of the term'; and this is

> not the mere power of producing that rather vapid species of composition usually termed descriptive poetry . . . but the power of *creating* scenery, in keeping with some state of human feeling; so fitted to it as to be the embodied symbol of it, and to summon up the state of feeling itself, with a force not to be surpassed by anything but reality.[64]

And as an indication of the degree to which the innovations of the romantics persist as the commonplaces of modern critics—even of those who purport to found their theory on anti-romantic principles—notice how striking is the parallel between the passage above and a famous comment by T. S. Eliot:

> The only way of expressing emotion in the form of art is by finding an 'objective correlative'; in other words, a set of objects, a situation, a chain of events which shall be the formula of that *particular* emotion; such that when the external facts, which must terminate in sensory experience, are given, the emotion is immediately evoked.[65]

(4) *The audience.* No less drastic is the fate of the audience. According to Mill, 'Poetry is feeling, confessing itself to itself in moments of solitude. . .' The poet's audience is reduced to a single member, consisting of the poet himself. 'All poetry,' as Mill puts it, 'is of the nature of soliloquy.' The purpose of producing effects upon other men, which for centuries had been the defining character of the art of poetry, now serves precisely the opposite function: it

[59] [Abrams] Ibid. pp. 228, 205–6, 213, 203–4.
[60] [Abrams] Ibid. pp. 211–17.
[61] [Abrams] Ibid. pp. 222–231.
[62] [Abrams] Ibid. pp. 206–7.

[63] [Abrams] Ibid. pp. 208–9. Cf. Hulme [English 1888–1917], "If it is sincere in the accurate sense . . . the whole of the analogy is necessary to get out the exact curve of the feeling or thing you want to express . . ." ("Romanticism and Classicism," *Speculations,* London, 1936, p. 138).
[64] [Abrams] Review, written in 1835, of Tennyson's *Poems Chiefly Lyrical* (1830) and *Poems* (1833), in *Early Essays,* p. 242.
[65] [Abrams] "Hamlet," *Selected Essays 1917–32* (London, 1932), p. 145.

disqualifies a poem by proving it to be rhetoric instead. When the poet's

> act of utterance is not itself the end, but a means to an end—viz. by the feelings he himself expresses, to work upon the feelings, or upon the belief, or the will, of another,—when the expression of his emotions . . . is tinged also by that purpose, by that desire of making an impression upon another mind, then it ceases to be poetry, and becomes eloquence.[66]

There is, in fact, something singularly fatal to the audience in the romantic point of view. Or, in terms of historical causes, it might be conjectured that the disappearance of a homogeneous and discriminating reading public fostered a criticism which on principle diminished the importance of the audience as a determinant of poetry and poetic value. Wordsworth still insisted that 'Poets do not write for Poets alone, but for Men,' and that each of his poems 'has a worthy purpose'; even though it turns out that the pleasure and profit of the audience is an automatic consequence of the poet's *spontaneous* overflow of feeling, provided that the appropriate associations between thoughts and feelings have been established by the poet in advance.[67] Keats, however, affirmed roundly that 'I never wrote one single line of Poetry with the least Shadow of public thought.'[68] 'A poet is a nightingale,' according to Shelley, 'who sits in darkness and sings to cheer its own solitude with sweet sounds; his auditors are as men entranced by the melody of an unseen musician. . .'[69] For Carlyle, the poet utterly replaces the audience as the generator of aesthetic norms.

> On the whole, Genius has privileges of its own; it selects an orbit for itself; and be this never so eccentric, if it is indeed a celestial orbit, we mere star-gazers must at last compose ourselves; must cease to cavil at it, and begin to observe it, and calculate its laws.[70]

---

[66] [Abrams] *Early Essays*, pp. 208–9. Cf. John Keble, *Lectures on Poetry* (1832–1841), tr. E. K. Francis (Oxford, 1912), I, 48–49: "Cicero is always the orator" because "he always has in mind the theatre, the benches, the audience"; whereas Plato is "more poetical than Homer himself" because "he writes to please himself, not to win over others."

[67] [Abrams] Preface to the *Lyrical Ballads, Wordsworth's Literary Criticism,* ed. N. C. Smith (London, 1905), pp. 30, 15–16 [above, page 488].

[68] *Letters*, ed. Maurice Buxton Forman (third ed.; New York, 1948), p. 131 (to Reynolds, 9 April 1818).

[69] [Abrams] "Defence of Poetry," *Shelley's Literary and Philosophical Criticism*, ed. John Shawcross (London, 1909), p. 129 [above, page 541].

[70] Thomas Carlyle (1795–1881), Scottish writer. [Abrams] "Jean Paul Friedrich Richter" (1827), *Works*, ed. H. D. Traill (London, 1905), xxvi, 20.

The evolution is complete, from the mimetic poet, assigned the minimal role of holding a mirror up to nature, through the pragmatic poet who, whatever his natural gifts, is ultimately measured by his capacity to satisfy the public taste, to Carlyle's Poet as Hero, the chosen one who, because he is 'a Force of Nature,' writes as he must, and through the degree of homage he evokes, serves as the measure of his *reader's* piety and taste.[71]

v. Objective Theories

All types of theory described so far, in their practical applications, get down to dealing with the work of art itself, in its parts and their mutual relations, whether the premises on which these elements are discriminated and evaluated relate them primarily to the spectator, the artist, or the world without. But there is also a fourth procedure, the 'objective orientation,' which on principle regards the work of art in isolation from all these external points of reference, analyzes it as a self-sufficient entity constituted by its parts in their internal relations, and sets out to judge it solely by criteria intrinsic to its own mode of being.

This point of view has been comparatively rare in literary criticism. The one early attempt at the analysis of an art form which is both objective and comprehensive occurs in the central portion of Aristotle's *Poetics.* I have chosen to discuss Aristotle's theory of art under the heading of mimetic theories, because it sets out from, and makes frequent reference back to the concept of imitation. Such is the flexibility of Aristotle's procedure, however, that after he has isolated the species 'tragedy,' and established its relation to the universe as an imitation of a certain kind of action, and to the audience through its observed effect of purging pity and fear, his method becomes centripetal, and assimilates these external elements into attributes of the work proper. In this second consideration of tragedy as an object in itself, the actions and agents that are imitated re-enter the discussion as the plot, character, and thought which, together with diction, melody, and spectacle, make up the six elements of a tragedy; and even pity and fear are reconsidered as that pleasurable quality proper to tragedy, to be distinguished from the pleasures characteristic of comedy and

---

[71] [Abrams] See *Heroes, Hero-Worship, and the Heroic in History* in *Works*, V, esp. pp. 80–85, 108–12. Cf. Jones Very's indignant denial of the inference that because the general ear takes delight in Shakespeare, "his motive was to please . . . We degrade those whom the world has pronounced poets, when we assume any other cause of their song than the divine and original action of the soul in humble obedience to the Holy Spirit upon whom they call." ("Shakespeare" [1838], *Poems and Essays*, Boston and New York, 1886, pp. 45–46).

other forms.[72] The tragic work itself can now be analyzed formally as a self-determining whole made up of parts, all organized around the controlling part, the tragic plot—itself a unity in which the component incidents are integrated by the internal relations of 'necessity or probability.'

As an all-inclusive approach to poetry, the objective orientation was just beginning to emerge in the late eighteenth and early nineteenth century. We shall see later on that some critics were undertaking to explore the concept of the poem as a heterocosm, a world of its own, independent, of the world into which we are born, whose end is not to instruct or please but simply to exist. Certain critics, particularly in Germany, were expanding upon Kant's formula that a work of art exhibits *Zweckmässigkeit ohne Zweck* (purposiveness without purpose),[73] together with his concept that the contemplation of beauty is disinterested and without regard to utility, while neglecting Kant's characteristic reference of an aesthetic product to the mental faculties of its creator and receptor. The aim to consider a poem, as Poe expressed it, as a 'poem *per se* . . . written solely for the poem's sake,'[74] in isolation from external causes and ulterior ends, came to constitute one element of the diverse doctrines usually huddled together by historians under the heading 'Art for Art's Sake.' And with differing emphases and adequacy, and in a great variety of theoretical contexts, the objective approach to poetry has become one of the most prominent elements in the innovative criticism of the last two or three decades. T. S. Eliot's dictum of 1928, that 'when we are considering poetry we must consider it primarily as poetry and not another thing' is widely approved, however far Eliot's own criticism sometimes departs from this ideal; and it is often joined with MacLeish's verse aphorism, 'A poem should not mean But be.'[75] The subtle and incisive criticism of criticism by the Chicago Neo-Aristotelians and their advocacy of an instrument adapted to dealing with poetry as such have been largely effective toward a similar end.[76] In his 'ontological criticism,' John Crowe Ransom has been calling for recognition of 'the autonomy of the work itself as existing for its own sake';[77] campaigns have been organized against 'the personal heresy,' 'the intentional fallacy,' and 'the affective fallacy';[78] the widely influential handbook, *The Theory of Literature*, written by René Wellek and Austin Warren, proposes that criticism deal with a poem *qua* poem, independently of 'extrinsic' factors; and similar views are being expressed, with increasing frequency, not only in our literary but in our scholarly journals. In America, at least, some form of the objective point of view has already gone far to displace its rivals as the reigning mode of literary criticism.

According to our scheme of analysis, then, there have been four major orientations, each one of which has seemed to various acute minds adequate for a satisfactory criticism of art in general. And by and large the historic progression, from the beginning through the early nineteenth century, has been from the mimetic theory of Plato and (in a qualified fashion) Aristotle, through the pragmatic theory, lasting from the conflation of rhetoric with poetic in the Hellenistic and Roman era almost through the eighteenth century, to the expressive theory of English (and somewhat earlier, German) romantic criticism.

---

[72] [Abrams] "Not every kind of pleasure should be required of a tragedy, but only its own proper pleasure. The tragic pleasure is that of pity and fear . . ." (*Poetics* 14. 1453b) [above, page 59].

[73] Above, page 428.

[74] [Abrams] "The Poetic Principle," *Representative Selections*, eds. Margaret Alterton and Hardin Craig (New York, 1935), pp. 382–83 [above, page 583].

[75] Archibald MacLeish (1892–1982), "Ars Poetica."

[76] A group at the University of Chicago. See R. S. Crane, ed., *Critics and Criticism* (1952).

[77] [Abrams] See John Crowe Ransom [above, page 953], *The World's Body* (New York, 1938), esp. pp. 327ff., and "Criticism as Pure Speculation," *The Intent of the Critic*, ed. Donald Stauffer (Princeton, 1941).

[78] See Wimsatt and Beardsley (above, pp. 1026).

Theodor W. Adorno

1903–1969

From his early collaboration with Max Horkheimer (1895–1973), published under the title *Dialectic of Enlightenment* (1947), the work of Theodor W. Adorno has been marked by a tense and difficult style, showing its own dialectical boldness in the intimate engagement with the intellectual life of culture. Trained as a musician, with some promise as both a performer and composer, Adorno took a degree in philosophy at Johann Wolfgang Goethe University in Frankfurt in 1924, and in 1932 accepted a teaching position at the University of Frankfurt as an affiliate in the Institute for Social Research, founded by Carl Grünberg in 1923. In only two years, however, Adorno emigrated to England to escape the Nazi persecution of Jews, and subsequently moved with colleagues to the United States, where the Institute was temporarily housed at Columbia University (Adorno himself worked at Princeton until 1941), and later at the University of California. With Horkheimer and others, Adorno returned to Frankfurt in 1949 to resume the work of the Institute, better known in the United States as the "Frankfurt School."

In *Dialectic of Enlightenment,* Adorno and Horkheimer offer a brilliant paradigmatic study of internal conflicts and tensions inherent in the very idea of reason informing the Western project of enlightenment that show a disturbing potential of self-undoing and destruction. The model of cultural criticism Adorno later incisively practiced exhibits an even more intense kind of intellectual inhabitation, as the critic, abandoned, superbly intelligent, philosophically homeless, moves *inside* cultural problems, issues, and practices, to trace them relentlessly, and surprisingly, to their consequences. The dialectical distancing that results, manifest clearly, for example, in the disarming opening paragraphs of "Cultural Criticism and Society" reprinted here, has some resemblances of effect to deconstruction, though it is typically more earnest, less playful, and not infrequently ambiguous.

For Adorno, the status of the work of art and the category of the aesthetic generally had particular importance as exemplifying the idea of self-identity that stands apart from the omnivorous compulsions in everyday life to embrace the inauthentic. This does contribute to a frequent sense of austerity and ambivalence, possibly connected to Adorno's reluctance to engage protest movements of the late 1960s (unlike his colleague, Herbert Marcuse) and his notorious dislike of jazz. What is central, however, is a characteristic intensity of intellectual engagement, a kind of fierce commitment to seriousness, that is especially clear in his most ambitious philosophical work, *Negative Dialectics* (1966). In that work, a full-scale working out of the innovative and highly figural dialectic of his collaboration with Horkheimer, Adorno launches a searing indictment of traditional philosophy, particularly in its inclination to develop totalizing (and totalitarian) systems. Throughout, Adorno moves toward (and never forgets or lets his reader forget) the horror of the Holocaust exemplified by Auschwitz, not as an accidental or anomalous event, but a deep symptom that implicates philosophical thinking itself. In particular, Adorno sets out, in his words, to "use the strength of the subject to break through the fallacy of constitutive subjectivity" and to substitute "for the unity principle" the idea of "what would be outside the sway of such unity." While dialectic, since Parmenides and Plato, has always relied on negativity as an instrument of philosophical disclosure, Adorno radicalizes the principle to explore the possibility of a dialectics of freedom outside the oppressive idea of Hegel's "universal standpoint," and more particularly, opposes the potentially self-blinding absorption of Heidegger's insistence upon recuperating the primordiality of the question of Being. Indeed, the whole of *Negative Dialectics* can be read as a deeply subversive critique of Heidegger's *Being and Time,* not on the now familiar ground of Heidegger's apparently unrepentant relation to National Socialism, but more tellingly as a reading of what he characterizes as an "ontological need" through which we make ourselves susceptible to totalitarian disasters.

Adorno's major works available in translation include: *Dialectic of Enlightenment* (with Max Horkheimer, 1947, tr. 1967); *Philosophy of Modern Music* (1949, tr. 1973); *The Authoritarian Personality* (with others, 1950); *Negative Dialectics* (1966, tr. 1973); and *Aesthetic Theory* (1970, tr. 1983). Several collections of essays and papers have been published, including: *Prisms* (1955, tr. 1981); *Minima Moralia: Reflections from Damaged Life* (tr. 1974); *The Culture Industry: Selected Essays on Mass Culture,* ed. J. M. Bernstein (1991); *The Adorno Reader,* ed. Brian O'Conner (2000); and *Can One Live after Auschwitz? A Philosophical Reader,* ed. Rolf Tiedemann (2003). In addition to major studies of Alban Berg, Beethoven, Wagner, and Mahler, there is an important collection, selected by Richard Leppart, *Essays on Music* (2002). Critical studies include: Susan Buck-Morss, *The Origin of Negative Dialectics* (1977); Gillian Rose, *The Melancholy Science* (1978); Martin Jay, *Adorno* (1984); Peter Ewe Hohendahl, *Prismatic Thought: Theodor W. Adorno* (1995); Simon Jarvis, *Adorno: A Critical Introduction* (1998); Christoph Menke-Eggers, *The Sovereignty of Art: Aesthetic Negativity in Adorno and Derrida* (1998); Hauke Brunkhorst, *Adorno and Critical Theory* (1999); J. M. Bernstein, *Adorno: Disenchantment and Ethics* (2001); Robert W. Witkin, *Adorno on Popular Culture* (2003).

Cultural Criticism and Society

To anyone in the habit of thinking with his ears, the words 'cultural criticism' *(Kulturkritik)* must have an offensive ring, not merely because, like 'automobile,' they are pieced together from Latin and Greek. The words recall a flagrant contradiction. The cultural critic is not happy with civilization, to which alone he owes his discontent. He speaks as if he represented either unadulterated nature or a higher his-

torical stage. Yet he is necessarily of the same essence as that to which he fancies himself superior. The insufficiency of the subject—criticized by Hegel in his apology for the *status quo*—which in its contingency and narrowness passes judgment on the might of the existent, becomes intolerable when the subject itself is mediated down to its innermost make-up by the notion to which it opposes itself as independent and sovereign. But what makes the content of cultural criticism inappropriate is not so much lack of respect for that which is criticized as the dazzled and arrogant recognition which criticism surreptitiously confers on culture. The cultural critic can hardly avoid the imputation that he has the culture which culture lacks. His vanity aids that of culture; even in the accusing gesture, the critic clings to the notion of culture, isolated, unquestioned, dogmatic. He shifts

Cultural Criticism and Society first appeared in 1955. It is reprinted here translated by Samuel and Sherry Weber, from *Prisms* (Cambridge, Mass.: MIT Press, 1981).

the attack. Where there is despair and measureless misery, he sees only spiritual phenomena, the state of man's consciousness, the decline of norms. By insisting on this, criticism is tempted to forget the unutterable, instead of striving, however impotently, so that man may be spared.

The position of the cultural critic, by virtue of its difference from the prevailing disorder, enables him to go beyond it theoretically, although often enough he merely falls behind. But he incorporates this difference into the very culture industry which he seeks to leave behind and which itself needs the difference in order to fancy itself culture. Characteristic of culture's pretension to distinction, through which it exempts itself from evaluation against the material conditions of life, is that it is insatiable. The exaggerated claims of culture, which in turn inhere in the movement of the mind, remove it ever further from those conditions as the worth of sublimation becomes increasingly suspect when confronted both by a material fulfillment near enough to touch and by the threatening annihilation of uncounted human beings. The cultural critic makes such distinction his privilege and forfeits his legitimation by collaborating with culture as its salaried and honoured nuisance. This, however, affects the substance of criticism. Even the implacable rigour with which criticism speaks the truth of an untrue consciousness remains imprisoned within the orbit of that against which it struggles, fixated on its surface manifestations. To flaunt one's superiority is, at the same time, to feel in on the job. Were one to study the profession of critic in bourgeois society as it progressed towards the rank of cultural critic, one would doubtless stumble on an element of usurpation in its origins, an element of which a writer like Balzac was still aware. Professional critics were first of all 'reporters': they oriented people in the market of intellectual products. In so doing, they occasionally gained insights into the matter at hand, yet remained continually traffic agents, in agreement with the sphere as such if not with its individual products. Of this they bear the mark even after they have discarded the role of agent. That they should have been entrusted with the roles of expert and then of judge was economically inevitable although accidental with respect to their objective qualifications. Their agility, which gained them privileged positions in the general competition— privileged, since the fate of those judged depends largely on their vote—invests their judgments with the semblance of competence. While they adroitly slipped into gaps and won influence with the expansion of the press, they attained that very authority which their profession already presupposed. Their arrogance derives from the fact that, in the forms of competitive society in which all being is merely there *for* something else, the critic himself is also measured only in

terms of his marketable success—that is, in terms of his *being for* something else. Knowledge and understanding were not primary, but at most by-products, and the more they are lacking, the more they are replaced by Oneupmanship and conformity. When the critics in their playground—art—no longer understand what they judge and enthusiastically permit themselves to be degraded to propagandists or censors, it is the old dishonesty of trade fulfilling itself in their fate. The prerogatives of information and position permit them to express their opinion as if it were objectivity. But it is solely the objectivity of the ruling mind. They help to weave the veil.

The notion of the free expression of opinion, indeed, that of intellectual freedom itself in bourgeois society, upon which cultural criticism is founded, has its own dialectic. For while the mind extricated itself from a theological-feudal tutelage, it has fallen increasingly under the anonymous sway of the *status quo*. This regimentation, the result of the progressive societalization of all human relations, did not simply confront the mind from without; it immigrated into its immanent consistency. It imposes itself as relentlessly on the autonomous mind as heteronomous orders were formerly imposed on the mind which was bound. Not only does the mind mould itself for the sake of its marketability, and thus reproduce the socially prevalent categories. Rather, it grows to resemble ever more closely the *status quo* even where it subjectively refrains from making a commodity of itself. The network of the whole is drawn ever tighter, modelled after the act of exchange. It leaves the individual consciousness less and less room for evasion, preforms it more and more thoroughly, cuts it off *a priori* as it were from the possibility of differencing itself as all difference degenerates to a nuance in the monotony of supply. At the same time, the semblance of freedom makes reflection upon one's own unfreedom incomparably more difficult than formerly when such reflection stood in contradiction to manifest unfreedom, thus strengthening dependence. Such moments, in conjunction with the social selection of the 'spiritual and intellectual leaders,' result in the regression of spirit and intellect. In accordance with the predominant social tendency, the integrity of the mind becomes a fiction. Of its freedom it develops only the negative moment, the heritage of the planless-monadological condition, irresponsibility. Otherwise, however, it clings ever more closely as a mere ornament to the material base which it claims to transcend. The strictures of Karl Kraus[1] against freedom of the press are certainly not to be taken literally. To invoke

---

[1] Karl Krauss (1874–1936), Austrian writer.

seriously the censors against hack-writers would be to drive out the devil with Beelzebub. Nevertheless, the brutalization and deceit which flourish under the aegis of freedom of the press are not accidental to the historical march of the mind. Rather, they represent the stigma of that slavery within which the liberation of the mind—a false emancipation—has taken place. This is nowhere more striking than where the mind tears at its bonds: in criticism. When the German fascists defamed the word and replaced it with the inane notion of 'art appreciation,' they were led to do so only by the rugged interests of the authoritarian state which still feared the passion of a Marquis Posa[2] in the impertinence of the journalist. But the self-satisfied cultural barbarism which clamoured for the abolition of criticism, the incursion of the wild horde into the preserve of the mind, unawares repaid kind in kind. The bestial fury of the Brownshirt against 'carping critics' arises not merely from his envy of a culture which excludes him and against which he blindly rebels; nor is it merely his resentment of the person who can speak out the negative moment which he himself must repress. Decisive is that the critic's sovereign gesture suggests to his readers an autonomy which he does not have, and arrogates for itself a position of leadership which is incompatible with his own principle of intellectual freedom. This is innervated by his enemies. Their sadism was idiosyncratically attracted by the weakness, cleverly disguised as strength, of those who, in their dictatorial bearing, would have willingly excelled the less clever tyrants who were to succeed them. Except that the fascists succumbed to the same naivete as the critics, the faith in culture as such, which reduced it to pomp and approved spiritual giants. They regarded themselves as physicians of culture and removed the thorn of criticism from it. They thus not only degraded culture to the Official, but in addition, failed to recognize the extent to which culture and criticism, for better or for worse, are intertwined. Culture is only true when implicitly critical, and the mind which forgets this revenges itself in the critics it breeds. Criticism is an indispensable element of culture which is itself contradictory: in all its untruth still as true as culture is untrue. Criticism is not unjust when it dissects—this can be its greatest virtue—but rather when it parries by not parrying.

The complicity of cultural criticism with culture lies not in the mere mentality of the critic. Far more, it is dictated by his relation to that with which he deals. By making culture his object, he objectifies it once more. Its very meaning, however, is the suspension of objectification. Once cul-

ture itself has been debased to 'cultural goods,' with its hideous philosophical rationalization, 'cultural values,' it has already defamed its *raison d'être*. The distillation of such 'values'—the echo of commercial language is by no means accidental—places culture at the will of the market. Even the enthusiasm for foreign cultures includes the excitement over the rarity in which money may be invested. If cultural criticism, even at its best with Valéry, sides with conservativism, it is because of its unconscious adherence to a notion of culture which, during the era of late capitalism, aims at a form of property which is stable and independent of stock-market fluctuations. This idea of culture asserts its distance from the system in order, as it were, to offer universal security in the middle of a universal dynamic. The model of the cultural critic is no less the appraising collector than the art critic. In general, cultural criticism recalls the gesture of bargaining, of the expert questioning the authenticity of a painting or classifying it among the Master's lesser works. One devaluates in order to get more. The cultural critic evaluates and hence is inevitably involved in a sphere stained with 'cultural values,' even when he rants against the mortgaging of culture. His contemplative stance towards culture necessarily entails scrutinizing, surveying, balancing, selecting: this piece suits him, that he rejects. Yet his very sovereignty, the claim to a more profound knowledge of the object, the separation of the idea from its object through the independence of the critical judgment threatens to succumb to the thinglike form of the object when cultural criticism appeals to a collection of ideas on display, as it were, and fetishizes isolated categories such as mind, life and the individual.

But the greatest fetish of cultural criticism is the notion of culture as such. For no authentic work of art and no true philosophy, according to their very meaning, has ever exhausted itself in itself alone, in its being-in-itself. They have always stood in relation to the actual life-process of society from which they distinguished themselves. Their very rejection of the guilt of a life which blindly and callously reproduces itself, their insistence on independence and autonomy, on separation from the prevailing realm of purposes, implies, at least as an unconscious element, the promise of a condition in which freedom were realized. This remains an equivocal promise of culture as long as its existence depends on a bewitched reality and, ultimately, on control over the work of others. That European culture in all its breadth—that which reached the consumer and which today is prescribed for whole populations by managers and psychotechnicians—degenerated to mere ideology resulted from a change in its function with regard to material *praxis:* its renunciation of interference. Far from being culture's

---

[2] Marquis Posa, character in Schiller's *Don Karlos.*

'sin,' the change was forced upon culture by history. For it is only in the process of withdrawing into itself, only indirectly that is, that bourgeois culture conceives of a purity from the corrupting traces of a totalitarian disorder which embraces all areas of existence. Only in so far as it withdraws from a *praxis* which has degenerated into its opposite, from the ever-changing production of what is always the same, from the service of the customer who himself serves the manipulator—only in so far as it withdraws from Man, can culture be faithful to man. But such concentration on substance which is absolutely one's own, the greatest example of which is to be found in the poetry and theoretical writings of Paul Valéry, contributes at the same time to the impoverishment of that substance. Once the mind is no longer directed at reality, its meaning is changed despite the strictest preservation of meaning. Through its resignation before the facts of life and, even more, through its isolation as one 'field' among others, the mind aids the existing order and takes its place within it. The emasculation of culture has angered philosophers since the time of Rousseau and the 'ink-splattering age' of Schiller's *Robbers,* to Nietzsche and finally, to the preachers of commitment for its own sake. This is the result of culture's becoming self-consciously cultural, which in turn places culture in vigorous and consistent opposition to the growing barbarism of economic hegemony. What appears to be the decline of culture is its coming to pure self-consciousness. Only when neutralized and reified, does Culture allow itself to be idolized. Fetishism gravitates towards mythology. In general, cultural critics become intoxicated with idols drawn from antiquity to the dubious, long-evaporated warmth of the liberalist era, which recalled the origins of culture in its decline. Cultural criticism rejects the progressive integration of all aspects of consciousness within the apparatus of material production. But because it fails to see through the apparatus, it turns towards the past, lured by the promise of immediacy. This is necessitated by its own momentum and not merely by the influence of an order which sees itself obliged to drown out its progress in dehumanization with cries against dehumanization and progress. The isolation of the mind from material production heightens its esteem but also makes it a scapegoat in the general consciousness for that which is perpetrated in practice. Enlightenment as such—not as an instrument of actual domination—is held responsible. Hence, the irrationalism of cultural criticism. Once it has wrenched the mind out of its dialectic with the material conditions of life, it seizes it unequivocally and straightforwardly as the principle of fatality, thus undercutting the mind's own resistance. The cultural critic is barred from the insight that the reification of life results not from too much enlightenment but from too little, and that the mutilation of man which is the result of the present particularistic rationality is the stigma of the total irrationality. The abolition of this irrationality, which would coincide with the abolition of the divorce between mental and physical work, appears as chaos to the blindness of cultural criticism: whoever glorifies order and form as such, must see in the petrified divorce an archetype of the Eternal. That the fatal fragmentation of society might some day end is, for the cultural critic, a fatal destiny. He would rather that everything end than for mankind to put an end to reification. This fear harmonizes with the interests of those interested in the perpetuation of material denial. Whenever cultural criticism complains of 'materialism,' it furthers the belief that the sin lies in man's desire for consumer goods, and not in the organization of the whole which withholds these goods from man: for the cultural critic, the sin is satiety, not hunger. Were mankind to possess the wealth of goods, it would shake off the chains of that civilized barbarism which cultural critics ascribe to the advanced state of the human spirit rather than to the retarded state of society. The 'eternal values' of which cultural criticism is so fond reflect the perennial catastrophe. The cultural critic thrives on the mythical obduracy of culture.

Because the existence of cultural criticism, no matter what its content, depends on the economic system, it is involved in the fate of the system. The more completely the life-process, including leisure, is dominated by modern social orders—those in the East, above all—the more all spiritual phenomena bear the mark of the order. Either, they may contribute directly to the perpetuation of the system as entertainment or edification, and are enjoyed as exponents of the system precisely because of their socially preformed character. Familiar, stamped and Approved by Good Housekeeping as it were, they insinuate themselves into a regressive consciousness, present themselves as 'natural,' and permit identification with powers whose preponderance leaves no alternative but that of false love. Or, by being different, they become rarities and once again marketable. Throughout the liberalist era, culture fell within the sphere of circulation. Hence, the gradual withering away of this sphere strikes culture to the quick. With the elimination of trade and its irrational loopholes by the calculated distributive apparatus of industry, the commercialization of culture culminates in absurdity. Completely subdued, administered, thoroughly 'cultivated' in a sense, it dies out. Spengler's denunciation: that mind and money go together, proves correct.[3] But because of his sympathy with direct rule, he

---

[3] Oswald Spengler (1880–1936), German historian.

advocated a structure of existence divested of all economic as well as spiritual mediations. He maliciously threw the mind together with an economic type which was in fact obsolete. What Spengler failed to understand was that no matter to what extent the mind is a product of that type, it implies at the same time the objective possibility of overcoming it. Just as culture sprang up in the marketplace, in the traffic of trade, in communication and negotiation, as something distinct from the immediate struggle for individual self-preservation, just as it was closely tied to trade in the era of mature capitalism, just as its representatives were counted among the class of 'third persons' who supported themselves in life as middlemen, so culture, considered 'socially necessary' according to classical rules, in the sense of reproducing itself economically, is in the end reduced to that as which it began, to mere communication. Its alienation from human affairs terminates in its absolute docility before a humanity which has been enchanted and transformed into clientele by the suppliers. In the name of the consumer, the manipulators suppress everything in culture which enables it to go beyond the total immanence in the existing society and allow only that to remain which serves society's unequivocal purpose. Hence, 'consumer culture' can boast of being not a luxury but rather the simple extension of production. Political slogans, designed for mass manipulation, unanimously stigmatize, as 'luxury,' 'snobbism,' and 'highbrow,' everything cultural which displeases the commissars. Only when the established order has become the measure of all things does its mere reproduction in the realm of consciousness become truth. Cultural criticism points to this and rails against 'superficiality' and 'loss of substance.' But by limiting its attention to the entanglement of culture in commerce, such criticism itself becomes superficial. It follows the pattern of reactionary social critics who pit 'productive' against 'predatory' capital. In fact, all culture shares the guilt of society. It ekes out its existence only by virtue of injustice already perpetrated in the sphere of production, much as does commerce (cf. *Dialektik der Aufklärung*).[4] Consequently, cultural criticism shifts the guilt: such criticism is ideology as long as it remains mere criticism of ideology. Totalitarian regimes of both kinds, seeking to protect the *status quo* from even the last traces of insubordination which they ascribe to culture even at its most servile, can conclusively convict culture and its introspection of servility. They suppress the mind, in itself already grown intolerable, and so feel themselves to be purifiers and revolutionaries. The ideological function of cultural criticism

bridles its very truth which lies in its opposition to ideology. The struggle against deceit works to the advantage of naked terror. 'When I hear the word "culture," I reach for my gun,' said the spokesman of Hitler's Imperial Chamber of Culture.

Cultural criticism is, however, only able to reproach culture so penetratingly for prostituting itself, for violating in its decline the pure autonomy of the mind, because culture originates in the radical separation of mental and physical work. It is from this separation, the original sin as it were, that culture draws its strength. When culture simply denies the separation and feigns harmonious union, it falls back behind its own notion. Only the mind which, in the delusion of being absolute, removes itself entirely from the merely existent, truly defines the existent in its negativity. As long as even the least part of the mind remains engaged in the reproduction of life, it is its sworn bondsman. The anti-philistinism of Athens was both the most arrogant contempt of the man who need not soil his hands for the man from whose work he lives, and the preservation of an image of existence beyond the constraint which underlies all work. In projecting its own uneasy conscience on to its victims as their 'baseness,' such an attitude also accuses that which they endure: the subjugation of men to the prevailing form in which their lives are reproduced. All 'pure culture' has always been a source of discomfort to the spokesmen of power. Plato and Aristotle knew why they would not permit the notion to arise. Instead, in questions concerning the evaluation of art, they advocated a pragmatism which contrasts curiously with the *pathos* of the two great metaphysicians. Modern bourgeois cultural criticism has, of course, been too prudent to follow them openly in this respect. But such criticism secretly finds a source of comfort in the divorce between 'high' and 'popular' culture, art and entertainment, knowledge and non-committal *Weltanschauung*.[5] Its anti-philistinism exceeds that of the Athenian upper class to the extent that the proletariat is more dangerous than the slaves. The modern notion of a pure, autonomous culture indicates that the antagonism has become irreconcilable. This is the result both of an uncompromising opposition to being-for-something else, and of an ideology which in its hybris enthrones itself as being-in-itself.

Cultural criticism shares the blindness of its object. It is incapable of allowing the recognition of its frailty to arise, a frailty set in the division of mental and physical work. No society which contradicts its very notion—that of mankind—can have full consciousness of itself. A display of subjective

---

[4]*Dialectic of Enlightenment* (1947) by Adorno and Max Horkheimer.

[5]World-view, philosophy of life.

ideology is not required to obstruct this consciousness, although in times of historical upheaval it tends to contribute to the objective blindness. Rather, the fact that every form of repression, depending on the level of technology, has been necessary for the survival of society, and that society as it is, despite all absurdity, does indeed reproduce its life under the existing conditions, objectively produces the semblance of society's legitimation. As the epitome of the self-consciousness of an antagonistic society, culture can no more divest itself of this semblance than can cultural criticism, which measures culture against culture's own ideal. The semblance has become total in a phase in which irrationality and objective falsity hide behind rationality and objective necessity. Nevertheless, by virtue of their real force, the antagonisms reassert themselves in the realm of consciousness. Just because culture affirms the validity of the principle of harmony within an antagonistic society, albeit in order to glorify that society, it cannot avoid confronting society with its own notion of harmony and thereby stumbling on discord. The ideology which affirms life is forced into opposition to life by the immanent drive of the ideal. The mind which sees that reality does not resemble it in every respect but is instead subject to an unconscious and fatal dynamic, is impelled even against its will beyond apologetics. The fact that theory becomes real force when it moves men is founded in the objectivity of the mind itself which, through the fulfilment of its ideological function must lose faith in ideology. Prompted by the incompatibility of ideology and existence, the mind, in displaying its blindness also displays its effort to free itself of ideology. Disenchanted, the mind perceives naked existence in its nakedness and delivers it up to criticism. The mind either damns the material base, in accordance with the ever-questionable criterion of its 'pure principle,' or it becomes aware of its own questionable position, by virtue of its incompatibility with the base. As a result of the social dynamic, culture becomes cultural criticism, which preserves the notion of culture while demolishing its present manifestations as mere commodities and means of brutalization. Such critical consciousness remains subservient to culture in so far as its concern with culture distracts from the true horrors. From this arises the ambivalent attitude of social theory towards cultural criticism. The procedure of cultural criticism is itself the object of permanent criticism, both in its general presuppositions—its immanence in the existing society—and in its concrete judgments. For the subservience of cultural criticism is revealed in its specific content, and only in this may it be grasped conclusively. At the same time, a dialectical theory which does not wish to succumb to 'Economism,' the sentiment which holds that the transformation of the world is exhausted in the increase of production, must absorb cultural

criticism, the truth of which consists in bringing untruth to consciousness of itself. A dialectical theory which is uninterested in culture as a mere epiphenomenon, aids pseudo-culture to run rampant and collaborates in the reproduction of the evil. Cultural traditionalism and the terror of the new Russian despots are in basic agreement. Both affirm culture as a whole, sight-unseen, while at the same time proscribing all forms of consciousness which are not made-to-order. They are thus no less ideological than is criticism when it calls a disembodied culture before its tribunal, or holds the alleged negativity of culture responsible for real catastrophes. To accept culture as a whole is to deprive it of the ferment which is its very truth—negation. The joyous appropriation of culture harmonizes with a climate of military music and paintings of battle-scenes. What distinguishes dialectical from cultural criticism is that it heightens cultural criticism until the notion of culture is itself negated, fulfilled and surmounted in one.

Immanent criticism of culture, it may be argued, overlooks what is decisive: the role of ideology in social conflicts. To suppose, if only methodologically, anything like an independent logic of culture is to collaborate in the hypostasis of culture, the ideological *proton pseudos*. The substance of culture, according to this argument, resides not in culture alone but in its relation to something external, to the material life-process. Culture, as Marx observed of juridical and political systems, cannot be fully 'understood either in terms of itself . . . or in terms of the so-called universal development of the mind.' To ignore this, the argument concludes, is to make ideology the basic matter and thus to establish it firmly. And in fact, having taken a dialectical turn, cultural criticism must not hypostasize the criteria of culture. Criticism retains its mobility in regard to culture by recognizing the latter's position within the whole. Without such freedom, without consciousness transcending the immanence of culture, immanent criticism itself would be inconceivable: the spontaneous movement of the object can be followed only by someone who is not entirely engulfed by it. But the traditional demand of the ideology-critique is itself subject to a historical dynamic. The critique was conceived against idealism, the philosophical form which reflects the fetishization of culture. Today, however, the definition of consciousness in terms of being has become a means of dispensing with all consciousness which does not conform to existence. The objectivity of truth, without which the dialectic is inconceivable, is tacitly replaced by vulgar positivism and pragmatism—ultimately, that is, by bourgeois subjectivism. During the bourgeois era, the prevailing theory was the ideology and the opposing *praxis* was in direct contradiction. Today, theory hardly exists any longer and the ideology drones, as it were, from the gears of an irresistible *praxis*. No notion dares to be conceived any more which does not cheerfully include, in all camps, explicit instructions as to who its beneficiaries are—exactly what the polemics once sought to expose. But the unideological thought is that which does not permit itself to be reduced to 'operational terms' and instead strives solely to help the things themselves to that articulation from which they are otherwise cut off by the prevailing language. Since the moment arrived when every advanced economic and political council agreed that what was important was to change the world and that to interpret it was *allotria,* it has become difficult simply to invoke the *Theses* against Feuerbach.[6] Dialectics also includes the relation between action and contemplation. In an epoch in which bourgeois social science has, in Scheler's words, 'plundered' the Marxian notion of ideology and diluted it to universal relativism, the danger involved in overlooking the function of ideologies has become less than that of judging intellectual phenomena in a subsumptive, uninformed and administrative manner and assimilating them into the prevailing constellations of power which the intellect ought to expose. As with many other elements of dialectical materialism, the notion of ideology has changed from an instrument of knowledge into its straitjacket. In the name of the dependence of superstructure on base, all use of ideology is controlled instead of criticized. No one is concerned with the objective substance of an ideology as long as it is expedient.

Yet the very function of ideologies becomes increasingly abstract. The suspicion held by earlier cultural critics is confirmed: in a world which denies the mass of human beings the authentic experience of intellectual phenomena by making genuine education a privilege and by shackling consciousness, the specific ideological content of these phenomena is less important than the fact that there should be anything at all to fill the vacuum of the expropriated consciousness and to distract from the open secret. Within the context of its social effect, the particular ideological doctrine which a film imparts to its audience is presumably far less important than the interest of the homeward bound moviegoer in the names and marital affairs of the stars. Vulgar notions such as 'amusement' and 'diversion' are more appropriate than pretentious explanations which designate one writer as a representative of the lower-middle class, another of the upper-middle. Culture has become ideological not only as the quintessence of subjectively devised manifestations of the objective mind, but even more as the sphere of private life. The illusory importance and autonomy of private

life conceals the fact that private life drags on only as an appendage of the social process. Life transforms itself into the ideology of reification—a death mask. Hence, the task of criticism must be not so much to search for the particular interest-groups to which cultural phenomena are to be assigned, but rather to decipher the general social tendencies which are expressed in these phenomena and through which the most powerful interests realize themselves. Cultural criticism must become social physiognomy. The more the whole divests itself of all spontaneous elements, is socially mediated and filtered, is 'consciousness,' the more it becomes 'culture.' In addition to being the means of subsistence, the material process of production finally unveils itself as that which it always was, from its origins in the exchange-relationship as the false consciousness which the two contracting parties have of each other: ideology. Inversely, however, consciousness becomes at the same time increasingly a mere transitional moment in the functioning of the whole. Today, ideology means society as appearance. Although mediated by the totality behind which stands the rule of partiality, ideology is not simply reducible to a partial interest. It is, as it were, equally near the centre in all its pieces.

The alternatives—either calling culture as a whole into question from outside under the general notion of ideology, or confronting it with the norms which it itself has crystallized—cannot be accepted by critical theory. To insist on the choice between immanence and transcendence is to revert to the traditional logic criticized in Hegel's polemic against Kant. As Hegel argued, every method which sets limits and restricts itself to the limits of its object thereby goes beyond them. The position transcending culture is in a certain sense presupposed by dialectics as the consciousness which does succumb in advance to the fetishization of the intellectual sphere. Dialectics means intransigence towards all reification. The transcendent method, which aims at totality, seems more radical than the immanent method, which presupposes the questionable whole. The transcendent critic assumes an as it were Archimedean position above culture and the blindness of society, from which consciousness can bring the totality, no matter how massive, into flux. The attack on the whole draws strength from the fact that the semblance of unity and wholeness in the world grows with the advance of reification; that is, with division. But the summary dismissal of ideology which in the Soviet sphere has already become a pretext for cynical terror, taking the form of a ban on 'objectivism,' pays that wholeness too high an honour. Such an attitude buys up culture *en bloc* from society, regardless of the use to which it is put. If ideology is defined as socially necessary appearance, then the ideology today is society itself in so far as its integral power and inevitability, its

[6]Ludwig Feuerbach (1804–1872), German philosopher. Adorno alludes to Marx's *Theses on Feuerbach* (1845).

overwhelming existence-in-itself, surrogates the meaning which that existence has exterminated. The choice of a standpoint outside the sway of existing society is as fictitious as only the construction of abstract utopias can be. Hence, the transcendent criticism of culture, much like bourgeois cultural criticism, sees itself obliged to fall back upon the idea of 'naturalness,' which itself forms a central element of bourgeois ideology. The transcendent attack on culture regularly speaks the language of false escape, that of the 'nature boy.' It despises the mind and its works, contending that they are, after all, only man-made and serve only to cover up 'natural' life. Because of this alleged worthlessness, the phenomena allow themselves to be manipulated and degraded for purposes of domination. This explains the inadequacy of most socialist contributions to cultural criticism: they lack the experience of that with which they deal. In wishing to wipe away the whole as if with a sponge, they develop an affinity to barbarism. Their sympathies are inevitably with the more primitive, more undifferentiated, no matter how much it may contradict the level of intellectual productive forces. The blanket rejection of culture becomes a pretext for promoting what is crudest, 'healthiest,' even repressive; above all, the perennial conflict between individual and society, both drawn in like manner, which is obstinately resolved in favour of society according to the criteria of the administrators who have appropriated it. From there it is only a step to the official reinstatement of culture. Against this struggles the immanent procedure as the more essentially dialectical. It takes seriously the principle that it is not ideology in itself which is untrue but rather its pretension to correspond to reality. Immanent criticism of intellectual and artistic phenomena seeks to grasp, through the analysis of their form and meaning, the contradiction between their objective idea and that pretension. It names what the consistency or inconsistency of the work itself expresses of the structure of the existent. Such criticism does not stop at a general recognition of the servitude of the objective mind, but seeks rather to transform this knowledge into a heightened perception of the thing itself. Insight into the negativity of culture is binding only when it reveals the truth or untruth of a perception, the consequence or lameness of a thought, the coherence or incoherence of a structure, the substantiality or emptiness of a figure of speech. Where it finds inadequacies it does not ascribe them hastily to the individual and his psychology, which are merely the façade of the failure, but instead seeks to derive them from the irreconcilability of the object's moments. It pursues the logic of its aporias, the insolubility of the task itself. In such antinomies criticism perceives those of society. A successful work, according to immanent criticism, is not one which

resolves objective contradictions in a spurious harmony, but one which expresses the idea of harmony negatively by embodying the contradictions, pure and uncompromised, in its innermost structure. Confronted with this kind of work, the verdict 'mere ideology' loses its meaning. At the same time, however, immanent criticism holds in evidence the fact that the mind has always been under a spell. On its own it is unable to resolve the contradictions under which it labours. Even the most radical reflection of the mind on its own failure is limited by the fact that it remains only reflection, without altering the existence to which its failure bears witness. Hence immanent criticism cannot take comfort in its own idea. It can neither be vain enough to believe that it can liberate the mind directly by immersing itself in it, nor naïve enough to believe that unflinching immersion in the object will inevitably lead to truth by virtue of the logic of things if only the subjective knowledge of the false whole is kept from intruding from the outside, as it were, in the determination of the object. The less the dialectical method can today presuppose the Hegelian identity of subject and object, the more it is obliged to be mindful of the duality of the moments. It must relate the knowledge of society as a totality and of the mind's involvement in it to the claim inherent in the specific content of the object that it be apprehended as such. Dialectics cannot, therefore, permit any insistence on logical neatness to encroach on its right to go from one *genus* to another, to shed light on an object in itself hermetic by casting a glance at society, to present society with the bill which the object does not redeem. Finally, the very opposition between knowledge which penetrates from without and that which bores from within becomes suspect to the dialectical method, which sees in it a symptom of precisely that reification which the dialectic is obliged to accuse. The abstract categorizing and, as it were, administrative thinking of the former corresponds in the latter to the fetishism of an object blind to its genesis, which has become the prerogative of the expert. But if stubbornly immanent contemplation threatens to revert to idealism, to the illusion of the self-sufficient mind in command of both itself and of reality, transcendent contemplation threatens to forget the effort of conceptualization required and content itself instead with the prescribed label, the petrified invective, most often 'petty bourgeois,' the ukase dispatched from above. Topological thinking, which knows the place of every phenomenon and the essence of none, is secretly related to the paranoic system of delusions which is cut off from experience of the object. With the aid of mechanically functioning categories, the world is divided into black and white and thus made ready for the very domination against which concepts were once conceived. No theory, not even that which is true, is safe from perversion into delusion once it has renounced a spontaneous relation to the object. Dialectics must guard against this no less than against enthrallment in the cultural object. It can subscribe neither to the cult of the mind nor to hatred of it. The dialectical critic of culture must both participate in culture and not participate. Only then does he do justice to his object and to himself.

The traditional transcendent critique of ideology is obsolete. In principle, the method succumbs to the very reification which is its critical theme. By transferring the notion of causality directly from the realm of physical nature to society, it falls back behind its own object. Nevertheless, the transcendent method can still appeal to the fact that it employs reified notions only in so far as society itself is reified. Through the crudity and severity of the notion of causality, it claims to hold up a mirror to society's own crudity and severity, to its debasement of the mind. But the sinister, integrated society of today no longer tolerates even those relatively independent, distinct moments to which the theory of the causal dependence of superstructure on base once referred. In the open-air prison which the world is becoming, it is no longer so important to know what depends on what, such is the extent to which everything is one. All phenomena rigidify, become insignias of the absolute rule of that which is. There are no more ideologies in the authentic sense of false consciousness, only advertisements for the world through its duplication and the provocative lie which does not seek belief but commands silence. Hence, the question of the causal dependence of culture, a question which seems to embody the voice of that on which culture is thought only to depend, takes on a backwoods ring. Of course, even the immanent method is eventually overtaken by this. It is dragged into the abyss by its object. The materialistic transparency of culture has not made it more honest, only more vulgar. By relinquishing its own particularity, culture has also relinquished the salt of truth, which once consisted in its opposition to other particularities. To call it to account before a responsibility which it denies is only to confirm cultural pomposity. Neutralized and ready-made, traditional culture has become worthless today. Through an irrevocable process its heritage, hypocritically reclaimed by the Russians, has become expendable to the highest degree, superfluous, trash. And the hucksters of mass culture can point to it with a grin, for they treat it as such. The more total society becomes, the greater the reification of the mind and the more paradoxical its effort to escape reification on its own. Even the most extreme consciousness of doom threatens to degenerate into idle chatter. Cultural criticism finds itself faced with the final stage of the dialectic of culture and barbarism. To write poetry after Auschwitz is barbaric. And this corrodes even the knowledge of why it has become impossible to write poetry today. Absolute reification, which presupposed intellectual progress as one of its elements, is now preparing to absorb the mind entirely. Critical intelligence cannot be equal to this challenge as long as it confines itself to self-satisfied contemplation.

from

Negative Dialects

The Ontological Need

Question and Answer

The ontologies in Germany, Heidegger's in particular, remain effective to this day. Traces of the political past are no deterrent. Tacitly, ontology is understood as readiness to sanction a heteronomous order that need not be consciously justified, and that such interpretations are denied in higher places—as misconceptions, declines to the ontical sphere, deficient radicalism in formulating the question—serves but to enhance the dignity of their appeal. Ontology seems the more numinous the less it can be laid down in definite contents that would give the meddlesome intellect something to latch on to. Intangibility comes to be unassailability. He who refuses to follow suit is suspect, a fellow without a spiritual fatherland, without a home in Being—not so much different from the "baseness" for which the idealists Fichte and Schelling used to excoriate resisters to their metaphysics. In all its embattled trends, which mutually exclude each other as false versions, ontology is apologetical. Yet its effect would be unintelligible if it did not meet an emphatic need, a sign of something missed, a longing that Kant's verdict on a knowledge of the Absolute should not be the end of the matter.

The need was crudely but openly manifest in the early days of the neo-ontological movements, when theological sympathizers would talk of the resurrection of metaphysics. There was a touch of it in Husserl's will to replace the *intentio obliqua* with the *intentio recta;* what had delimited the cognitive possibilities in the critique of reason was nothing but the recollection of the cognitive powers themselves, a recollection which the phenomenological platform initially

"The Ontological Need," and "Meditations on Metaphysics" were first published in *Negative Dialectik* (1966), excerpted and reprinted here from *Negative Dialectics,* tr. E. B. Ashton (New York: The Seabury Press, 1979).

meant to dispense with. Plainly stirring in the "draft" of the ontological constitution of topical fields and regions, and finally of the "world as the entirety of all there is," was the will to grasp the whole without any limits being placed on its cognition. Husserl's εἴδη—later turned into *"existentialia"* by the Heidegger of *Being and Time*—were to anticipate encompassingly what those regions were, up to the highest. The implication behind them was that rational drafts might pre-design the structure of all the abundance of Being. It was a second reprise of the old philosophies of the Absolute, their first reprise having been post-Kantian idealism.

Yet the critical trend remained at work at the same time, though not so much as counter to dogmatic concepts. It continued as an effort in which the absolutes, now deprived of their systematic unity and delimited from each other, would no longer be posited or construed but received, accepted, and described in a posture following the lines of the positivistic scientific ideal. Once again, as for Schelling, absolute knowledge became intellectual visuality. One hoped to delete the transmissions instead of reflecting them. The nonconformist motive that philosophy need not resign itself within the bounds of an organized, usable science recoiled into conformism. The categorial structure that had been uncritically accepted as such, as the skeleton of extant conditions, was confirmed as absolute, and the unreflective immediacy of the method lent itself to any kind of license. The critique of criticism became pre-critical. Hence the mental posture of a permanent "back to." The Absolute became what it would least like to be, and what critical truth does call it: a matter of natural history that would quickly and crudely provide the norm of adjustment.

In comparison, the idealistic academic philosophy denied what will be expected of philosophy by anyone who goes in for it unprepared. That was the reverse of its Kant-enforced scientific self-responsibility. The awareness that a philosophy carried on as a specialty no longer has anything to do with people—with the people it trains to stop asking, as futile, the only questions for whose sake they turn to it—this awareness was already stirring in German idealism; it was voiced without professional discretion by Schopenhauer and Kierkegaard, and Nietzsche challenged any kind of accord with academicism. But what the present ontologies have done under this aspect is not simply to adopt the anti-academic philosophical tradition by asking, as Paul Tillich phrased it once, about that which concerns one absolutely. They have taken the nonacademic pathos and established it academically. They combined a pleasant shudder at the world's imminent end with a soothing sense of operating on solid ground, perhaps even on philologically fortified ground. Audacity, ever the prerogative of youth, knew itself covered by general agreement and by the most powerful educational institution. The movement as a whole became the opposite of what its germs seemed to promise: the treatment of relevant things relapsed into an abstractness unsurpassed by any neo-Kantian methodology.

This development is inseparable from the problematics of the ontological need itself. It can no more be quenched by that sort of philosophy than it could once be quenched by the transcendental system. This is why ontology has become shrouded in vapors. In line with an older German tradition, it puts the question above the answer; where it keeps owing what it promised, it has consolingly raised failure as such to existential rank. The weight of questions in philosophy differs indeed from the weight they have in special sciences, where the solution of questions removes them, while in philosophical history their rhythm would be more that of duration and oblivion. But this does not mean that—as some keep parroting Kierkegaard—the truth lies in the questioner's existence, in his mere futile search for an answer. Rather, in philosophy the authentic question will somehow almost always include its answer. Unlike science, philosophy knows no fixed sequence of question and answer. Its question must be shaped by its experience, so as to catch up with the experience. Its answers are not given, not made, not generated: they are the recoil of the unfolded, transparent question.

This is precisely what idealism would drown out in its constant endeavor to produce, to "deduce," its own form and, if possible, its every content. But thought does not preserve itself as an origin, and it ought not to hide the fact that it does not generate—that it merely returns what it already has as experience. The expressive moment in thought keeps it from proceeding *more mathematico* and serving up problems followed by pseudo-solutions. In philosophy, words like "problem" and "solution" have a mendacious ring because they postulate the thought's independence from thinking precisely where thinking and the thought transmit each other. Only the truth can really be philosophically understood. Our fulfilling concurrence in the judgment in which we understand something is the same as a decision about True or False. If we do not personally judge the stringency or nonstringency of a theorem, we do not understand it. The theorem's claim of such stringency is its own content of meaning, the very thing that is to be understood.

This distinguishes the relation of understanding and judgment from the usual order of time. The fact that we can no more understand without judging than we can judge without understanding invalidates the schema that the solution is the judgment and the problem is only the question, based on understanding. What is transmitted here is the fiber of the so-called philosophical demonstration, a mode of proof that contrasts with the mathematical model. And yet that model does not simply disappear, for the stringency of a philosophical thought requires its mode of proceeding to be measured by the forms of inference. Philosophical proof is the effort to give statements a binding quality by making them commensurable with the means of discursive thinking. But it does not purely follow from that thinking: the critical reflection of such cogitative productivity is itself a philosophical content.

In Hegel's case, despite the extreme enhancement of his claim to derive the nonidentical from identity, the thought structure of the great *Logic* implies the solutions in the way the problems are put, instead of presenting results after striking a balance. While Hegel's critique of analytical judgments is exacerbated to the thesis of their "falseness," everything is to him an analytical judgment, a turning to and fro of the thought without citation of anything extraneous to it. It is a moment of dialectics that the new is the old, and otherness is familiarity. The connection of that moment with the identity thesis is evident, but it is not circumscribed by the thesis. Paradoxically, the more a philosophical thought yields to its experience, the closer its approach to an analytical judgment. To grow fully aware of a desideratum of cognition is mostly to achieve the cognition itself; this is the counterpart of the idealistic principle of perpetual production. That it is by no means the Absolute is asserted in philosophy by doing without the traditional machinery of proof, by accentuating a knowledge that is known already.

Affirmative Character

The ontological need can no more guarantee its object than the agony of the starving assures them of food. But no doubts of such guarantees plague a philosophical movement once destined for better things; it was for this reason as much as for any other that it became untruthfully affirmative. "Dimming the world never takes us to the light of Being."[1] In the categories to which fundamental ontology owes its echo—and which it therefore either denies or sublimates until they will no longer serve for any unwelcome confrontation—we can read how much they are the imprints of something missing that is not to be produced, how much they are its complementary ideology. Yet the cult of Being, or at least the attraction of the word as of something superior, lives by the fact that in reality, as once upon a time in epistemology, concepts denoting function have more and more replaced the concepts denoting substance. Society has become the total functional context which liberalism used to think it was: to be is to be relative to other persons and things, and to be irrelevant in oneself. This frightening fact, this dawning awareness that it may be losing its substantiality, prepares the subject to listen to avowals that its unarticulated being—equated with that substantiality—cannot be lost, that it will survive the functional context.

What the conjurers of ontological philosophizing strive, as it were, to awaken is undermined by real processes, however: by the production and reproduction of social life. The effort to justify "man" and "being" and "time" theoretically, as primal phenomena, cannot stay the fate of the resurrected ideas. Concepts whose substrate is historically at an end have always been duly criticized as dogmatic hypostases, even in the specifically philosophical realm—as Kant, for example, criticized the transcendence of the empirical soul, the aura of the word *Dasein,* in his chapter on paralogisms, and the immediate recourse to Being in his chapter on the amphiboly of reflexive concepts.[2] But the exponents of the new ontology do not make that Kantian critique their own. They do not carry it forward by reflection. Instead, they act as if that critique belonged to a rationalistic consciousness of whose flaws genuine thought had to be cleansed as in a ritual bath.

Despite this, trying to hitch their wagon to critical philosophy as well, they directly impute to this philosophy an ontological content. Heidegger's reading of the antisubjectivist and "transcending" element in Kant was not quite unwarranted: in the Preface to the *Critique of Pure Reason* Kant does programmatically stress his objective way to pose questions, and leaves no doubt of it as he performs the deduction of pure intellectual concepts. The Copernican turn registered in conventional philosophical history does not exhaust him; the objective interest retains primacy over the subjective interest in the mere occurrence of cognition, in a dismembering of consciousness in empiricist style. By no means, however, can we equate this objective interest with a hidden ontology. Arguing against such an equation is not only Kant's critique of rationalist ontology—which might allow for the conception of another, if need be—but the train of thought of the critique of reason

[1][Adorno] Martin Heidegger, *Aus der Erfahrung des Denkens,* Pfullingen 1954, p. 7.

[2]See Immanuel Kant, *Critique of Pure Reason,* tr. Norman Kemp Smith, 363–83; 276–96. Paralogisms are syllogisms that are fallacious in form, their content notwithstanding. Amphiboly is a condition of uncertain ambiguity attributable to the mode or manner of the construction of a sentence or phrase, not necessarily an ambiguity attributable to words. Adorno's target here is Heidegger's notion of *Dasein.*

itself. Following this train of thought, we find that objectivity, the objectivity of knowledge as well as that of the totality of all things known, is subjectively transmitted. It allows us to assume an "in itself" beyond the subject-object polarity, but it intentionally leaves this assumption so indefinite that no sort of interpretation whatsoever would be able to extract an ontology from it. If Kant meant to rescue that *kosmos noetikos* which the turn to the subject was attacking, and if, therefore, there is an ontological element in his work, it is still an element, and not the central one. His philosophy is an attempt to accomplish the rescue by means of that which menaces what he would save.

Incapacitation of the Subject

A fact supporting the objectivistic resuscitation of ontology would indeed be the least compatible with its idea: the fact that to a great extent the subject came to be an ideology, a screen for society's objective functional context and a palliative for the subjects' suffering under society. In this sense—and not just today—the not-I has moved drastically ahead of the I. In Heidegger's philosophy the fact is detoured but registered; in his hands that historical primacy becomes an ontological precedence of "Being" pure and simple over all ontical and real things. He prudently refrained from reversing the Copernican turn, the turn to the idea, in plain view of all. He zealously set off his version of ontology from objectivism, and his anti-idealistic stand from realism, whether critical or naïve.[3] Unquestionably, the ontological need could not be planed down to an anti-idealism along the battle lines of academic debate. And yet, of all the impulses given by that need the most enduring may have been the disavowal of idealism.

The anthropocentric sense of life has been shaken. The subject in its philosophical self-reflection has, so to speak, made the centuries-old critique of geocentrism its own. This motive is more than a matter of weltanschauung, however easy it was to exploit as a weltanschauung. Extravagant syntheses between developments in philosophy and in the natural science are odious, of course; they ignore the increasingly independent language of physical-mathematical formulas, a language that has long ceased to be retrievable into visuality or any other categories directly commensurable to the consciousness of man. And yet, the results of recent cosmology have radiated far and wide. All notions to make the universe resemble the subject, if not indeed to derive it as positing the subject, have been relegated to a naïveté comparable to that of Boeotians or paranoiacs who regard their hamlet as the center of the world. The ground of philosophical idealism, the control of nature, has lost the certainty of its omnipotence precisely because of its immense expansion during the first half of the twentieth century; also because human consciousness has limped behind, leaving the order of human affairs irrational, and finally because it took the magnitude of the attainments to let us measure their infinitesimality in comparison with the unattainable. There is a universal feeling, a universal fear, that our progress in controlling nature may increasingly help to weave the very calamity it is supposed to protect us from, that it may be weaving that second nature into which society has rankly grown.

Ontology and the philosophy of Being are modes of reaction in which—along with other and cruder modes—consciousness hopes to escape from that entanglement. But they contain a fatal dialectics. The truth that expels man from the center of creation and reminds him of his impotence—this same truth will, as a subjective mode of conduct, confirm the sense of impotence, cause men to identify with it, and thus reinforce the spell of the second nature. Faith in Being, a dim weltanschauung derived from critical premonitions, really degenerates into a bondage to Being, as Heidegger incautiously defined it once. Feeling face to face with the cosmos, the believer clings without much ado to any kind of particular, if only it is forceful enough in convicting the subject of its weakness. The subjects' readiness to cringe before the calamity that springs from the subjective context itself is the punishment for their futile wish to fly the prison of their subjectivity. The philosophical leap, the primal gesture of Kierkegaard, is the very license from which the subject dreams it may escape by its submission to Being.

The spell is diminished only where the subject, in Hegel's language, is "involved"; it is perpetuated in whatever would be the subject's downright otherness, just as the *deus absconditus* always carried some of the irrational features of mythical deities. The corny exoticism of such decorative world views as the astonishingly consumable Zen Buddhist one casts light upon today's restorative philosophies. Like Zen, they simulate a thinking posture which the history stored in the subjects makes impossible to assume. Restricting the mind to thoughts open and attainable at the historical stage of its experience is an element of freedom; nonconceptual vagary represents the opposite of freedom. Doctrines which heedlessly run off from the subject to the universe, along with the philosophy of Being, are more easily brought into accord with the world's hardened condi-

---

[3][Adorno] Cf. Heidegger, *Vom Wesen des Grundes,* Frankfurt am Main 1949, p. 14; *The Essence of Reasons,* tr. Terence Malick (Evanston, Ill.: Northwestern University Press, 1969).

tion and with the chances of success in it than is the tiniest bit of self-reflection by a subject pondering upon itself and its real captivity.

Meditations on Metaphysics

1

After Auschwitz

We cannot say any more that the immutable is truth, and that the mobile, transitory is appearance. The mutual indifference of temporality and eternal ideas is no longer tenable even with the bold Hegelian explanation that temporal existence, by virtue of the destruction inherent in its concept, serves the eternal represented by the eternity of destruction. One of the mystical impulses secularized in dialectics was the doctrine that the intramundane and historic is relevant to what traditional metaphysics distinguished as transcendence—or at least, less gnostically and radically put, that it is relevant to the position taken by human consciousness on the questions which the canon of philosophy assigned to metaphysics. After Auschwitz, our feelings resist any claim of the positivity of existence as sanctimonious, as wronging the victims; they balk at squeezing any kind of sense, however bleached, out of the victims' fate. And these feelings do have an objective side after events that make a mockery of the construction of immanence as endowed with a meaning radiated by an affirmatively posited transcendence.

Such a construction would affirm absolute negativity and would assist its ideological survival—as in reality that negativity survives anyway, in the principle of society as it exists until its self-destruction. The earthquake of Lisbon sufficed to cure Voltaire of the theodicy of Leibniz,[1] and the visible disaster of the first nature was insignificant in comparison with the second, social one, which defies human imagination as it distills a real hell from human evil. Our metaphysical faculty is paralyzed because actual events have shattered the basis on which speculative metaphysical thought could be reconciled with experience. Once again, the dialectical motif of quantity recoiling into quality scores an unspeakable triumph. The administrative murder of mil-

lions made of death a thing one had never yet to fear in just this fashion. There is no chance any more for death to come into the individuals' empirical life as somehow conformable with the course of that life. The last, the poorest possession left to the individual is expropriated. That in the concentration camps it was no longer an individual who died, but a specimen—this is a fact bound to affect the dying of those who escaped the administrative measure.

Genocide is the absolute integration. It is on its way wherever men are leveled off—"polished off," as the German military called it—until one exterminates them literally, as deviations from the concept of their total nullity. Auschwitz confirmed the philosopheme of pure identity as death. The most far out dictum from Beckett's *End Game*,[2] that there really is not so much to be feared any more, reacts to a practice whose first sample was given in the concentration camps, and in whose concept—venerable once upon a time—the destruction of nonidentity is ideologically lurking. Absolute negativity is in plain sight and has ceased to surprise anyone. Fear used to be tied to the *principium individuationis* of self-preservation, and that principle, by its own consistency, abolishes itself. What the sadists in the camps foretold their victims, "Tomorrow you'll be wiggling skyward as smoke from this chimney," bespeaks the indifference of each individual life that is the direction of history. Even in his formal freedom, the individual is as fungible and replaceable as he will be under the liquidators' boots.

But since, in a world whose law is universal individual profit, the individual has nothing but this self that has become indifferent, the performance of the old, familiar tendency is at the same time the most dreadful of things. There is no getting out of this, no more than out of the electrified barbed wire around the camps. Perennial suffering has as much right to expression as a tortured man has to scream; hence it may have been wrong to say that after Auschwitz you could no longer write poems. But it is not wrong to raise the less cultural question whether after Auschwitz you can go on living—especially whether one who escaped by accident, one who by rights should have been killed, may go on living. His mere survival calls for the coldness, the basic principle of bourgeois subjectivity, without which there could have been no Auschwitz; this is the drastic guilt of him who was spared. By way of atonement he will be plagued by dreams such as that he is no longer living at all, that he was sent to the ovens in 1944

---

[1] See Voltaire, *Candide* (1759), a satirical novel opposing the philosophical optimism of Gottfried Wilhelm Leibniz (1646–1714), German philosopher and scientist. The particular tag phrase that Voltaire's naïve young hero, Candide, repeats from his master, Dr. Pangloss, is that this is "the best of all possible worlds." It is the catastrophe of the Lisbon earthquake that finally awakens Candide to the absurdity of such a view.

[2] *Fin de partie* (1957, tr. *Endgame*): A one-act play by Irish playwright Samuel Beckett (1906–1989), depicting the deterioration of the relation between a master, Hamm, and his servant, Clov, in an abstract setting that strongly suggests the inside of a skull.

and his whole existence since has been imaginary, an emanation of the insane wish of a man killed twenty years earlier.

Thinking men and artists have not infrequently described a sense of being not quite there, of not playing along, a feeling as if they were not themselves at all, but a kind of spectator. Others often find this repulsive; it was the basis of Kierkegaard's polemic against what he called the esthetic sphere. A critique of philosophical personalism indicates, however, that this attitude toward immediacy, this disavowal of every existential posture, has a moment of objective truth that goes beyond the appearance of the self-preserving motive. "What does it really matter?" is a line we like to associate with bourgeois callousness, but it is the line most likely to make the individual aware, without dread, of the insignificance of his existence. The inhuman part of it, the ability to keep one's distance as a spectator and to rise above things, is in the final analysis the human part, the very part resisted by its ideologists.

It is not altogether implausible that the immortal part is the one that acts in this fashion. The scene of Shaw on his way to the theater, showing a beggar his identification with the hurried remark, "Press," hides a sense of that beneath the cynicism. It would help to explain the fact that startled Schopenhauer: that affections in the face of death, not only other people's but our own, are frequently so feeble. People, of course, are spellbound without exception, and none of them are capable of love, which is why everyone feels loved too little. But the spectator's posture simultaneously expresses doubt that this could be all—when the individual, so relevant to himself in his delusion, still has nothing but that poor and emotionally animal-like ephemerality.

Spellbound, the living have a choice between involuntary ataraxy—an esthetic life due to weakness—and the bestiality of the involved. Both are wrong ways of living. But some of both would be required for the right *désinvolture* and sympathy. Once overcome, the culpable self-preservation urge has been confirmed, confirmed precisely, perhaps, by the threat that has come to be ceaselessly present. The only trouble with self-preservation is that we cannot help suspecting the life to which it attaches us of turning into something that makes us shudder: into a specter, a piece of the world of ghosts, which our waking consciousness perceives to be nonexistent. The guilt of a life which purely as a fact will strangle other life, according to statistics that eke out an overwhelming number of killed with a minimal number of rescued, as if this were provided in the theory of probabilities—this guilt is irreconcilable with living. And the guilt does not cease to reproduce itself, because not for an instant can it be made fully, presently conscious.

This, nothing else, is what compels us to philosophize. And in philosophy we experience a shock: the deeper, the more vigorous its penetration, the greater our suspicion that philosophy removes us from things as they are—that an unveiling of the essence might enable the most superficial and trivial views to prevail over the views that aim at the essence. This throws a glaring light on truth itself. In speculation we feel a certain duty to grant the position of a corrective to common sense, the opponent of speculation. Life feeds the horror of a premonition: what must come to be known may resemble the down-to-earth more than it resembles the sublime; it might be that this premonition will be confirmed even beyond the pedestrian realm, although the happiness of thought, the promise of its truth, lies in sublimity alone.

If the pedestrian had the last word, if it were the truth, truth would be degraded. The trivial consciousness, as it is theoretically expressed in positivism and unreflected nominalism, may be closer than the sublime consciousness to an *adaequatio rei aique cogitationis;*[3] its sneering mockery of truth may be truer than a superior consciousness, unless the formation of a truth concept other than that of *adaequatio* should succeed. The innervation that metaphysics might win only by discarding itself applies to such other truth, and it is not the last among the motivations for the passage to materialism. We can trace the leaning to it from the Hegelian Marx to Benjamin's rescue of induction; Kafka's work may be the apotheosis of the trend. If negative dialectics calls for the self-reflection of thinking, the tangible implication is that if thinking is to be true—if it is to be true today, in any case—it must also be a thinking against itself. If thought is not measured by the extremity that eludes the concept, it is from the outset in the nature of the musical accompaniment with which the SS liked to drown out the screams of its victims.

2

Metaphysics and Culture

A new categorical imperative has been imposed by Hitler upon unfree mankind: to arrange their thoughts and actions so that Auschwitz will not repeat itself, so that nothing similar will happen. When we want to find reasons for it, this imperative is as refractory as the given one of Kant was once upon a time. Dealing discursively with it would be an outrage, for the new imperative gives us a bodily sensation of the moral addendum—bodily, because it is now the

---

[3] Adequation of things together with thoughts.

practical abhorrence of the unbearable physical agony to which individuals are exposed even with individuality about to vanish as a form of mental reflection. It is in the unvarnished materialistic motive only that morality survives.

The course of history forces materialism upon metaphysics, traditionally the direct antithesis of materialism. What the mind once boasted of defining or construing as its like moves in the direction of what is unlike the mind, in the direction of that which eludes the rule of the mind and yet manifests that rule as absolute evil. The somatic, unmeaningful stratum of life is the stage of suffering, of the suffering which in the camps, without any consolation, burned every soothing feature out of the mind, and out of culture, the mind's objectification. The point of no return has been reached in the process which irresistibly forced metaphysics to join what it was once conceived against. Not since the youthful Hegel has philosophy—unless selling out for authorized cerebration—been able to repress how very much it slipped into material questions of existence.

Children sense some of this in the fascination that issues from the flayer's zone, from carcasses, from the repulsively sweet odor of putrefaction, and from the opprobrious terms used for that zone. The unconscious power of that realm may be as great as that of infantile sexuality; the two intermingle in the anal fixation, but they are scarcely the same. An unconscious knowledge whispers to the child what is repressed by civilized education; this is what matters, says the whispering voice. And the wretched physical existence strikes a spark in the supreme interest that is scarcely less repressed; it kindles a "What is that?" and "Where is it going?" The man who managed to recall what used to strike him in the words "dung hill" and "pig sty" might be closer to absolute knowledge than Hegel's chapter in which readers are promised such knowledge only to have it withheld with a superior mien. The integration of physical death into culture should be rescinded in theory—not, however, for the sake of an ontologically pure being named Death, but for the sake of that which the stench of cadavers expresses and we are fooled about by their transfiguration into "remains."

A child, fond of an innkeeper named Adam, watched him club the rats pouring out of holes in the courtyard; it was in his image that the child made its own image of the first man. That this has been forgotten, that we no longer know what we used to feel before the dogcatcher's van, is both the triumph of culture and its failure. Culture, which keeps emulating the old Adam, cannot bear to be reminded of that zone, and precisely this is not to be reconciled with the conception that culture has of itself. It abhors stench because it stinks—because, as Brecht put it in a magnificent line, its mansion is built of dogshit. Years after that line was written, Auschwitz demonstrated irrefutably that culture has failed.

That this could happen in the midst of the traditions of philosophy, of art, and of the enlightening sciences says more than that these traditions and their spirit lacked the power to take hold of men and work a change in them. There is untruth in those fields themselves, in the autarky that is emphatically claimed for them. All post-Auschwitz culture, including its urgent critique, is garbage. In restoring itself after the things that happened without resistance in its own countryside, culture has turned entirely into the ideology it had been potentially—had been ever since it presumed, in opposition to material existence, to inspire that existence with the light denied it by the separation of the mind from manual labor. Whoever pleads for the maintenance of this radically culpable and shabby culture becomes its accomplice, while the man who says no to culture is directly furthering the barbarism which our culture showed itself to be.

Not even silence gets us out of the circle. In silence we simply use the state of objective truth to rationalize our subjective incapacity, once more degrading truth into a lie. When countries of the East, for all their drivel to the contrary, abolished culture or transformed it into rubbish as a mere means of control, the culture that moans about it is getting what it deserves, and what on its part, in the name of people's democratic right to their own likeness, it is zealously heading for. The only difference is that when the apparatchiks over there acclaim their administrative barbarism as culture and guard its mischief as an inalienable heritage, they convict its reality, the infrastructure, of being as barbarian as the superstructure they are dismantling by taking it under their management. In the West, at least, one is allowed to say so.

The theology of the crisis registered the fact it was abstractly and therefore idly rebelling against: that metaphysics has merged with culture. The aureole of culture, the principle that the mind is absolute, was the same which tirelessly violated what it was pretending to express. After Auschwitz there is no word tinged from on high, not even a theological one, that has any right unless it underwent a transformation. The judgment passed on the ideas long before, by Nietzsche, was carried out on the victims, reiterating the challenge of the traditional words and the test whether God would permit this without intervening in his wrath.

A man whose admirable strength enabled him to survive Auschwitz and other camps said in an outburst against Beckett that if Beckett had been in Auschwitz he would be writing differently, more positively, with the front-line creed of the escapee. The escapee is right in a fashion other than he thinks. Beckett, and whoever else remained in control of himself, would have been broken in Auschwitz and probably forced to confess that front-line creed which the escapee clothed in the words "Trying to give men courage"—as if this were up to any structure of the mind; as if the intent to address men, to adjust to them, did not rob them of what is their due even if they believe the contrary. That is what we have come to in metaphysics.

* * *

12

Self-Reflection of Dialectics

The question is whether metaphysics as a knowledge of the absolute is at all possible without the construction of an absolute knowledge—without that idealism which supplied the title for the last chapter of Hegel's *Phenomenology*. Is a man who deals with the absolute not necessarily claiming to be the thinking organ with the capacity to do so, and thus the absolute himself? And on the other hand, if dialectics turned into a metaphysics that is not simply like dialectics, would it not violate its own strict concept of negativity?

Dialectics, the epitome of negative knowledge, will have nothing beside it; even a negative dialectics drags along the commandment of exclusiveness from the positive one, from the system. Such reasoning would require a non-dialectical consciousness to be negated as finite and fallible. In all its historical forms, dialectics prohibited stepping out of it. Willy-nilly, it played the part of a conceptual mediator between the unconditional spirit and the finite one; this is what intermittently kept making theology its enemy. Although dialectics allows us to think the absolute, the absolute as transmitted by dialectics remains in bondage to conditioned thinking. If Hegel's absolute was a secularization of the deity, it was still the deity's secularization; even as the totality of mind and spirit, that absolute remained chained to its finite human model.

But if our thought, fully aware of what it is doing, gropes beyond itself—if in otherness it recognizes something which is downright incommensurable with it, but which it thinks anyway—then the only shelter it will find lies in the dogmatic tradition. In such thoughts our thinking is estranged from its content, unreconciled, and newly condemned to two kinds of truth, and that in turn would be incompatible with the idea of truth. Metaphysics depends upon whether we can get out of this aporia otherwise than

by stealth. To this end, dialectics is obliged to make a final move: being at once the impression and the critique of the universal delusive context, it must now turn even against itself. The critique of every self-absolutizing particular is a critique of the shadow which absoluteness casts upon the critique; it is a critique of the fact that critique itself, contrary to its own tendency, must remain within the medium of the concept. It destroys the claim of identity by testing and honoring it; therefore, it can reach no farther than that claim. The claim is a magic circle that stamps critique with the appearance of absolute knowledge. It is up to the self-reflection of critique to extinguish that claim, to extinguish it in the very negation of negation that will not become a positing.

Dialectics is the self-consciousness of the objective context of delusion; it does not mean to have escaped from that context. Its objective goal is to break out of the context from within. The strength required from the break grows in dialectics from the context of immanence; what would apply to it once more is Hegel's dictum that in dialectics an opponent's strength is absorbed and turned against him, not just in the dialectical particular, but eventually in the whole. By means of logic, dialectics grasps the coercive character of logic, hoping that it may yield—for that coercion itself is the mythical delusion, the compulsory identity. But the absolute, as it hovers before metaphysics, would be the nonidentical that refuses to emerge until the compulsion of identity has dissolved. Without a thesis of identity, dialectics is not the whole; but neither will it be a cardinal sin to depart from it in a dialectical step.

It lies in the definition of negative dialectics that it will not come to rest in itself, as if it were total. This is its form of hope. Kant registered some of this in his doctrine of the transcendent thing-in-itself, beyond the mechanisms of identification. His successors, however stringently they criticized the doctrine, were reinforcing the spell, regressing like the post-revolutionary bourgeoisie as a whole: they hypostatized coercion itself as the absolute. Kant on his part, in defining the thing-in-itself as the intelligible being, had indeed conceived transcendence as nonidentical, but in equating it with the absolute subject he had bowed to the identity principle after all. The cognitive process that is supposed to bring us asymptotically close to the transcendent thing is pushing that thing ahead of it, so to speak, and removing it from our consciousness.

The identifications of the absolute transpose it upon man, the source of the identity principle. As they will admit now and then, and as enlightenment can strikingly point out to them every time, they are anthropomorphisms. This is why, at the approach of the mind, the absolute flees from the mind: its approach is a mirage. Probably, however, the successful elimination of any anthropomorphism, the elimination with which the delusive content seems removed, coincides in the end with that context, with absolute identity. Denying the mystery by identification, by ripping more and more scraps out of it, does not resolve it. Rather, as though in play, the mystery belies our control of nature by reminding us of the impotence of our power.

Enlightenment leaves practically nothing of the metaphysical content of truth—*presque rien,* to use a modern musical term. That which recedes keeps getting smaller and smaller, as Goethe describes it in the parable of New Melusine's box, designating an extremity. It grows more and more insignificant; this is why, in the critique of cognition as well as in the philosophy of history, metaphysics immigrates into micrology. Micrology is the place where metaphysics finds a haven from totality. No absolute can be expressed otherwise than in topics and categories of immanence, although neither in its conditionality nor as its totality is immanence to be deified.

According to its own concept, metaphysics cannot be a deductive context of judgments about things in being, and neither can it be conceived after the model of an absolute otherness terribly defying thought. It would be possible only as a legible constellation of things in being. From those it would get the material without which it would not be; it would not transfigure the existence of its elements, however, but would bring them into a configuration in which the elements unite to form a script. To that end, metaphysics must know how to wish. That the wish is a poor father to the thought has been one of the general theses of European enlightenment ever since Xenophanes,[4] and the thesis applies undiminished to the attempts to restore ontology. But thinking, itself a mode of conduct, contains the need—the vital need, at the outset—in itself. The need is what we think from, even where we disdain wishful thinking. The motor of the need is the effort that involves thought as action. The object of critique is not the need in thinking, but the relationship between the two.

Yet the need in thinking is what makes us think. It asks to be negated by thinking; it must disappear in thought if it is to be really satisfied; and in this negation it survives. Represented in the inmost cell of thought is that which is unlike thought. The smallest intramundane traits would be of relevance to the absolute, for the micrological view cracks the shells of what, measured by the subsuming cover concept, is helplessly isolated and explodes its identity, the delusion that it is but a specimen. There is solidarity between such thinking and metaphysics at the time of its fall.

---

[4]Xenophanes (c. 570–c.480 B.C.), Greek philosopher who opposed the anthropomorphic representations of the gods.

Claude Lévi-Strauss

1908–2001

Lévi-Strauss was unquestionably the best-known and most influential of structural anthropologists. Acknowledging the importance to him of N. S. Troubetskoy and Ferdinand de Saussure (above, page 786), he argued that traditional anthropology, like traditional diachronic or historical linguistics, looked at terms, but not the relations among them. Structuralism looks at the relations. In Lévi-Strauss's view, structuralist linguistics affected the social scientists in as revolutionary a way as did nuclear physics the physical scientists. In structuralism the relations among entities ("difference" in Saussure) take precedence over the entities themselves. Only by attention to relations can general laws of structure be grasped. Further, Lévi-Strauss emphasized the synchronic over the diachronic (or historical).

Perhaps Lévi-Strauss's best-known example of a structuralist approach to the interpretation of myths is his treatment of the myth of Oedipus. Rather than seeking an origin, recognized as impossible in any case, he argues that any myth is a congeries of all of its known versions (even, perhaps, his own interpretation). For him, there is not only no original, there is no pattern that leads to a certain significance, as say in Freudian psychology. In his view myths are not allegorical. Rather a myth is a set of relations that attempts to resolve in the structure an apparently unresolvable cultural problem. The Oedipus myth, for example, attempts a resolution between the notion of the autochthonous origin of human beings (birth from the earth) and a denial of that origin in favor of birth from two parents. This resolution is abstractable from the relations of the mythic units when they are freed from a purely diachronic reading.

Lévi-Strauss applied his method to a poem in a well-known essay, coauthored with Roman Jakobson (below, page 1132), "Charles Baudelaire's 'Les Chats'" (1962), which led to similar efforts by others. He saw structural analysis as a method stretching over different disciplines, in contrast to Clifford Geertz (below, page 1328), who later thought of it as part of a more general phenomenon in which the social sciences became interrelated in various ways with the humanities. Lévi-Strauss's structuralist view was analyzed and "deconstructed" by Jacques Derrida (below, page 1208) in an influential work.

The main works of Lévi-Strauss translated into English are *The Elementary Structures of Kinship* (1949, tr. 1969); *Race and History* (1952, tr. 1958); *Tristes Tropiques* (1955, tr. 1961); *Structural Anthropology* (1958, tr. 1963); *Mythologiques* (in three volumes, 1964–1968, tr. 1969ff.); *The Savage Mind* (1962, tr. 1966); *The Raw and the Cooked* (tr. 1969); *Anthropology and Myth: Lectures: 1951–1982* (tr. 1986); and *Myth and Meaning* (tr. 1995). See E. N. Hayes and T. Hayes, eds., *Claude Lévi-Strauss: The Anthropologist as Hero* (1970); James A. Boon, *From Symbolism to Structuralism: Lévi-Strauss in a Literary Tradition* (1972); Edmund Leach, *Claude Lévi-Strauss* (1976); Simon Clarke, *The Foundations of Structuralism: A Critique of Lévi-Strauss and the Structuralist Movement* (1981); David Pace, *Lévi-Strauss: The Bearer of Ashes* (1982); Robert A. Champagne, *Claude Lévi-Strauss* (1987).

The Structural Study of Myth

"It would seem that mythological worlds have been built up only to be shattered again, and that new worlds were built from the fragments."

FRANZ BOAS[1]

Despite some recent attempts to renew them, it seems that during the past twenty years anthropology has increasingly turned from studies in the field of religion. At the same time, and precisely because the interest of professional anthropologists has withdrawn from primitive religion, all kinds of amateurs who claim to belong to other disciplines have seized this opportunity to move in, thereby turning into their private playground what we had left as a wasteland. The prospects for the scientific study of religion have thus been undermined in two ways.

The explanation for this situation lies to some extent in the fact that the anthropological study of religion was started by men like Tylor, Frazer, and Durkheim,[2] who were psychologically oriented although not in a position to keep up with the progress of psychological research and theory. Their interpretations, therefore, soon became vitiated by the outmoded psychological approach which they used as their basis. Although they were undoubtedly right in giving their attention to intellectual processes, the way they handled these remained so crude that it discredited them altogether. This is much to be regretted, since, as Hocart so profoundly noted in his introduction to a posthumous book recently published,[3] psychological interpretations were withdrawn from the intellectual field only to be introduced again in the field of affectivity, thus adding to "the inherent defects of the psychological school . . . the mistake of deriving clear-cut ideas . . . from vague emotions." Instead of trying to enlarge the framework of our logic to include processes which, whatever their apparent differences, belong to the same kind of intellectual operation, a naïve attempt was made to reduce them to inarticulate emotional drives, which resulted only in hampering our studies.

Of all the chapters of religious anthropology probably none has tarried to the same extent as studies in the field of mythology. From a theoretical point of view the situation remains very much the same as it was fifty years ago, namely, chaotic. Myths are still widely interpreted in conflicting ways: as collective dreams, as the outcome of a kind of esthetic play, or as the basis of ritual. Mythological figures are considered as personified abstractions, divinized heroes, or fallen gods. Whatever the hypothesis, the choice amounts to reducing mythology either to idle play or to a crude kind of philosophic speculation.

In order to understand what a myth really is, must we choose between platitude and sophism? Some claim that human societies merely express, through their mythology, fundamental feelings common to the whole of mankind, such as love, hate, or revenge or that they try to provide some kind of explanations for phenomena which they cannot otherwise understand—astronomical, meteorological, and the like. But why should these societies do it in such elaborate and devious ways, when all of them are also acquainted with empirical explanations? On the other hand, psychoanalysts and many anthropologists have shifted the problems away from the natural or cosmological toward the sociological and psychological fields. But then the interpretation becomes too easy: If a given mythology confers prominence on a certain figure, let us say an evil grandmother, it will be claimed that in such a society grandmothers are actually evil and that mythology reflects the social structure and the social relations; but should the actual data be conflicting, it would be as readily claimed that the purpose of mythology is to provide an outlet for repressed feelings. Whatever the situation, a clever dialectic will always find a way to pretend that a meaning has been found.

Mythology confronts the student with a situation which at first sight appears contradictory. On the one hand it would seem that in the course of a myth anything is likely to happen. There is no logic, no continuity. Any characteristic can be attributed to any subject; every conceivable relation can be found. With myth, everything becomes possible. But on the other hand, this apparent arbitrariness is belied by the astounding similarity between myths collected in widely different regions. Therefore the problem: If the content of a myth is contingent, how are we going to explain the fact that myths throughout the world are so similar?

It is precisely this awareness of a basic antinomy pertaining to the nature of myth that may lead us toward its solution. For the contradiction which we face is very similar to that which in earlier times brought considerable worry to the first philosophers concerned with linguistic problems; linguistics could only begin to evolve as a science after this

---

"The Structural Study of Myth" was first published in *Journal of American Folklore* 78 (1955). It is reprinted from *Structural Anthropology* by Claude Lévi-Strauss, published by Basic Books in 1963.
[1][Lévi-Strauss] In Boas' Introduction to James Teit, "Traditions of the Thompson River Indians of British Columbia," *Memoirs of the American Folklore Society* VI (1898), p. 18.
[2]Edward Burnett Tylor (1832–1917), English anthropologist; James G. Frazer (1854–1941), Scottish anthropologist, author of *The Golden Bough;* Emil Durkheim (1858–1917), French sociologist.
[3][Lévi-Strauss] A. M. Hocart, *Social Origins* (London, 1954), p. 7.

contradiction had been overcome. Ancient philosophers reasoned about language the way we do about mythology. On the one hand, they did notice that in a given language certain sequences of sounds were associated with definite meanings, and they earnestly aimed at discovering a reason for the linkage between those *sounds* and that *meaning*. Their attempt, however, was thwarted from the very beginning by the fact that the same sounds were equally present in other languages although the meaning they conveyed was entirely different. The contradiction was surmounted only by the discovery that it is the combination of sounds, not the sounds themselves, which provides the significant data.[4]

It is easy to see, moreover, that some of the more recent interpretations of mythological thought originated from the same kind of misconception under which those early linguists were laboring. Let us consider, for instance, Jung's[5] idea that a given mythological pattern—the so-called archetype—possesses a certain meaning. This is comparable to the long-supported error that a sound may possess a certain affinity with a meaning; for instance, the "liquid" semi-vowels with water, the open vowels with things that are big, large, loud, or heavy, etc., a theory which still has its supporters.[6] Whatever emendations the original formulation may now call for, everybody will agree that the Saussurean principle of the *arbitrary character of linguistic signs* was a prerequisite for the accession of linguistics to the scientific level.[7]

To invite the mythologist to compare his precarious situation with that of the linguist in the pre-scientific stage is not enough. As a matter of fact we may thus be led only from one difficulty to another. There is a very good reason why myth cannot simply be treated as language if its specific problems are to be solved; myth *is* language: to be known, myth has to be told; it is a part of human speech. In order to preserve its specificity we must be able to show that it is both the same thing as language, and also something different from it. Here, too, the past experience of linguists may help us. For language itself can be analyzed into things which are at the same time similar and yet different. This is precisely what is expressed in Saussure's distinction between *langue* and *parole,* one being the structural side of language, the other the statistical aspect of it, *langue* belonging to a reversible time, *parole*

being non-reversible. If those two levels already exist in language, then a third one can conceivably be isolated.

We have distinguished *langue* and *parole* by the different time referents which they use. Keeping this in mind, we may notice that myth uses a third referent which combines the properties of the first two. On the one hand, a myth always refers to events alleged to have taken place long ago. But what gives the myth an operational value is that the specific pattern described is timeless; it explains the present and the past as well as the future. This can be made clear through a comparison between myth and what appears to have largely replaced it in modern societies, namely, politics. When the historian refers to the French Revolution, it is always as a sequence of past happenings, a non-reversible series of events the remote consequences of which may still be felt at present. But to the French politician, as well as to his followers, the French Revolution is both a sequence belonging to the past—as to the historian—and a timeless pattern which can be detected in the contemporary French social structure and which provides a clue for its interpretation, a lead from which to infer future developments. Michelet, for instance, was a politically minded historian. He describes the French Revolution thus: "That day . . . everything was possible. . . . Future became present . . . that is, no more time, a glimpse of eternity."[8] It is that double structure, altogether historical and ahistorical, which explains how myth, while pertaining to the realm of *parole* and calling for an explanation as such, as well as to that of *langue* in which it is expressed, can also be an absolute entity on a third level which, though it remains linguistic by nature, is nevertheless distinct from the other two.

A remark can be introduced at this point which will help to show the originality of myth in relation to other linguistic phenomena. Myth is the part of language where the formula *traduttore, traditore*[9] reaches its lowest truth value. From that point of view it should be placed in the gamut of linguistic expressions at the end opposite to that of poetry, in spite of all the claims which have been made to prove the contrary. Poetry is a kind of speech which cannot be translated except at the cost of serious distortions; whereas the mythical value of the myth is preserved even through the worst translation. Whatever our ignorance of the language and the culture of the people where it originated, a myth is still felt as a myth by any reader anywhere in the world. Its substance does not lie in its style, its original music, or its syntax, but in the *story* which it tells. Myth is language,

---

[4] See in this connection Saussure (above, page 788).

[5] Carl Gustav Jung (1875–1961), Swiss psychologist.

[6] [Lévi-Strauss] See, for instance Sir. R. A. Paget, "The Origin of Language," *Journal of World History* I, No. 2 (UNESCO, 1953).

[7] [Lévi-Strauss] See Émile Benveniste "Nature du signe linguistique," *Acta Linguistica* I, No. 1 (1939); and Chapter V *Structuralist Anthropology.* [Also Saussure (above, page 791). Unfortunately, Lévi-Strauss's discussion in the following paragraph confuses Saussure's distinction of *langue / parole* with synchronic / diachronic linguistic study.]

[8] [Lévi-Strauss] Jules Michelet, *Histoire de la revolution francaise* IV, 1. I took this quotation from M. Merleau-Ponty, *Les Aventures de la dialectique* (Paris, 1955), p. 273.

[9] *Traduttore, traditore:* To translate is to betray.

functioning on an especially high level where meaning succeeds practically at "taking off" from the linguistic ground on which it keeps on rolling.

To sum up the discussion at this point, we have so far made the following claims: (1) If there is a meaning to be found in mythology, it cannot reside in the isolated elements which enter into the composition of a myth, but only in the way those elements are combined. (2) Although myth belongs to the same category as language, being, as a matter of fact, only part of it, language in myth exhibits specific properties. (3) Those properties are only to be found *above* the ordinary linguistic level, that is, they exhibit more complex features than those which are to be found in any other kind of linguistic expression.

If the above three points are granted, at least as a working hypothesis, two consequences will follow: (1) Myth, like the rest of language, is made up of constituent units. (2) These constituent units pre-suppose the constituent units present in language when analyzed on other levels—namely, phonemes, morphemes, and sememes—but they, nevertheless, differ from the latter in the same way as the latter differ among themselves; they belong to a higher and more complex order. For this reason, we shall call them *gross constituent units.*

How shall we proceed in order to identify and isolate these gross constituent units or mythemes? We know that they cannot be found among phonemes, morphemes, or sememes, but only on a higher level; otherwise myth would become confused with any other kind of speech. Therefore, we should look for them on the sentence level. The only method we can suggest at this stage is to proceed tentatively, by trial and error, using as a check the principles which serve as a basis for any kind of structural analysis: economy of explanation; unity of solution; and ability to reconstruct the whole from a fragment, as well as later stages from previous ones.

The technique which has been applied so far by this writer consists in analyzing each myth individually, breaking down its story into the shortest possible sentences, and writing each sentence on an index card bearing a number corresponding to the unfolding of the story.

Practically each card will thus show that a certain function is, at a given time, linked to a given subject. Or, to put it otherwise, each gross constituent unit will consist of a *relation.*

However, the above definition remains highly unsatisfactory for two different reasons. First, it is well known to structural linguists that constituent units on all levels are made up of relations, and the true difference between our *gross* units and the others remains unexplained; second, we still find ourselves in the realm of a non-reversible

time, since the numbers of the cards correspond to the unfolding of the narrative. Thus the specific character of mythological time, which as we have seen is both reversible and non-reversible, synchronic and diachronic, remains unaccounted for. From this springs a new hypothesis, which constitutes the very core of our argument: The true constituent units of a myth are not the isolated relations but *bundles of such relations,* and it is only as bundles that these relations can be put to use and combined so as to produce a meaning. Relations pertaining to the same bundle may appear diachronically at remote intervals, but when we have succeeded in grouping them together we have reorganized our myth according to a time referent of a new nature, corresponding to the pre-requisite of the initial hypothesis, namely a two-dimensional time referent which is simultaneously diachronic and synchronic, and which accordingly integrates the characteristics of *langue* on the one hand, and those of *parole* on the other. To put it in even more linguistic terms, it is as though a phoneme were always made up of all its variants.

Two comparisons may help to explain what we have in mind.

Let us first suppose that archaeologists of the future coming from another planet would one day, when all human life had disappeared from the earth, excavate one of our libraries. Even if they were at first ignorant of our writing, they might succeed in deciphering it—an undertaking which would require, at some early stage, the discovery that the alphabet, as we are in the habit of printing it, should be read from left to right and from top to bottom. However, they would soon discover that a whole category of books did not fit the usual pattern—these would be the orchestra scores on the shelves of the music division. But after trying, without success, to decipher staffs one after the other, from the upper down to the lower, they would probably notice that the same patterns of notes recurred at intervals, either in full or in part, or that some patterns were strongly reminiscent of earlier ones. Hence the hypothesis: What if patterns showing affinity, instead of being considered in succession, were to be treated as one complex pattern and read as a whole? By getting at what we call *harmony,* they would then see that an orchestra score, to be meaningful, must be read diachronically along one axis—that is, page after page, and from left to right—and synchronically along the other axis, all the notes written vertically making up one gross constituent unit, that is, one bundle of relations.

The other comparison is somewhat different. Let us take an observer ignorant of our playing cards, sitting for a long time with a fortune-teller. He would know something of the visitors: sex, age, physical appearance, social situation, etc., in the same way as we know something of the different cultures whose myths we try to study. He would also listen to the séances and record them so as to be able to go over them and make comparisons—as we do when we listen to myth-telling and record it. Mathematicians to whom I have put the problem agree that if the man is bright and if the material available to him is sufficient, he may be able to reconstruct the nature of the deck of cards being used, that is, fifty-two or thirty-two cards according to the case, made up of four homologous sets consisting of the same units (the individual cards) with only one varying feature, the suit.

Now for a concrete example of the method we propose. We shall use the Oedipus myth, which is well known to everyone. I am well aware that the Oedipus myth has only reached us under late forms and through literary transmutations concerned more with esthetic and moral preoccupations than with religious or ritual ones, whatever these may have been. But we shall not interpret the Oedipus myth in literal terms, much less offer an explanation acceptable to the specialist. We simply wish to illustrate—and without reaching any conclusions with respect to it—a certain technique, whose use is probably not legitimate in this particular instance, owing to the problematic elements indicated above. The "demonstration" should therefore be conceived, not in terms of what the scientist means by this term, but at best in terms of what is meant by the street peddler, whose aim is not to achieve a concrete result, but to explain, as succinctly as possible, the functioning of the mechanical toy which he is trying to sell to the onlookers.

The myth will be treated as an orchestra score would be if it were unwittingly considered as a unilinear series; our task is to re-establish the correct arrangement. Say, for instance, we were confronted with a sequence of the type: 1, 2, 4, 7, 8, 2, 3, 4, 6, 8, 1, 4, 5, 7, 8, 1, 2, 5, 7, 3, 4, 5, 6, 8 . . . , the assignment being to put all the 1's together, all the 2's, the 3's, etc.; the result is a chart:

```
1   2       4           7   8
    2   3   4       6       8
1           4   5       7   8
1   2           5       7
        3   4   5   6       8
```

We shall attempt to perform the same kind of operation on the Oedipus myth, trying out several arrangements of the mythemes until we find one which is in harmony with the principles enumerated above. Let us suppose, for the sake of argument, that the best arrangement is the following

(although it might certainly be improved with the help of a specialist in Greek mythology):

Cadmos seeks his sister Europa, ravished by Zeus			
		Cadmos kills the dragon	
	The Spartoi kill one another		
			Labdacos (Laios' father) = *lame (?)*
	Oedipus kills his father, Laios		Laios (Oedipus's father) = *left-sided (?)*
		Oedipus kills the Sphinx	
			Oedipus = *swollen-foot (?)*
Oedipus marries his mother, Jocasta			
	Eteocles kills his brother, Polynices		
Antigone buries her brother, Polynices, despite prohibition			

We thus find ourselves confronted with four vertical columns, each of which includes several relations belonging to the same bundle. Were we to *tell* the myth, we would disregard the columns and read the rows from left to right and from top to bottom. But if we want to *understand* the myth, then we will have to disregard one half of the diachronic dimension (top to bottom) and read from left to right, column after column, each one being considered as a unit.

All the relations belonging to the same column exhibit one common feature which it is our task to discover. For instance, all the events grouped in the first column on the left have something to do with blood relations which are overemphasized, that is, are more intimate than they should be. Let us say, then, that the first column has as its common feature the *overrating of blood relations*. It is obvious that the second column expresses the same thing, but inverted: *underrating of blood relations*. The third column refers to monsters being slain. As to the fourth, a few words of clarification are needed. The remarkable connotation of the surnames in Oedipus' father-line has often been noticed. However, linguists usually disregard it, since to them the only way to define the meaning of a term is to investigate all the contexts in which it appears, and personal names, precisely because they are used as such, are not accompanied by any context. With the method we propose to follow the objection disappears, since the myth itself provides its own context. The significance is no longer to be sought in the eventual meaning of each name, but in the fact that all the names have a common feature: All the hypothetical meanings (which may well remain hypothetical) refer to *difficulties in walking straight and standing upright*.

What then is the relationship between the two columns on the right? Column three refers to monsters. The dragon is a chthonian being which has to be killed in order that mankind be born from the Earth; the Sphinx is a monster unwilling to permit men to live. The last unit reproduces the first one, which has to do with the *autochtonous origin* of mankind. Since the monsters are overcome by men, we may thus say that the common feature of the third column is *denial of the autochthonous origin of man*.[10]

This immediately helps us to understand the meaning of the fourth column. In mythology it is a universal characteristic of men born from the Earth that at the moment they emerge from the depth they either cannot walk or they walk clumsily. This is the case of the chthonian beings in the mythology of the Pueblo: Muyingwu, who leads the emergence, and the chthonian Shumaikoli are lame ("bleeding-foot," "sore-foot"). The same happens to the Koskimo of the Kwakiutl after they have been swallowed by the chthonian monster, Tsiakish: when they returned to the surface of the earth "they limped forward or tripped sideways." Thus the common feature of the fourth column is *the persistence of the autochthonous origin of man*. It follows that column four is to column three as column one is to column two. The inability to connect two kinds of relationships is overcome (or rather replaced) by the assertion that contradictory relationships are identical inasmuch as they are both self-contradictory in a similar way. Although this is still a provisional formulation of the structure of mythical thought, it is sufficient at this stage.

Turning back to the Oedipus myth, we may now see what it means. The myth has to do with the inability, for a culture which holds the belief that mankind is autochthonous (see, for instance, Pausanias,[11] VIII, xxix, 4: plants provide a *model* for humans), to find a satisfactory transition between this theory and the knowledge that human beings are actually born from the union of man and woman. Although the problem obviously cannot be solved, the Oedipus myth provides a kind of logical tool which relates the original problem—born from one or born from two?—to

---

[10] [Lévi-Strauss] We are not trying to become involved with specialists in an argument; this would be presumptuous and even meaningless on our part. Since the Oedipus myth is taken here merely as an example treated in arbitrary fashion, the chthonian nature ascribed to the Sphinx might seem surprising; We shall refer to the testimony of Marie Delcourt: "In the archaic legends [she is] certainly born of the earth itself" (*Oedipe ou la légende du conquérant* [Liége: 1944], p. 108). No matter how remote from Delcourt's our method may be (and our conclusions would be, no doubt, if we were competent to deal with the problem in depth), it seems to us that she has convincingly established the nature of the Sphinx in the archaic tradition, namely that of a female monster who attacks and rapes young men; in other

words, the personification of a female being with an inversion of the sign. This explains why, in the handsome iconography compiled by Delcourt at the end of her work, men and women are always found in an inverted "sky/earth" relationship.

As we shall point out below, we selected the Oedipus myth as our first example because of the striking analogies that seem to exist between certain aspects of archaic Greek thought and that of the Pueblo Indians, from whom we have borrowed the examples that follow. In this respect it should be noted that the figure of the Sphinx, as reconstructed by Delcourt, coincides with two figures of North American mythology (who probably merge into one). We are referring, on the one hand, to "the old hag," a repulsive witch whose physical appearance presents a "problem" to the young hero. If he "solves" this problem—that is, if he responds to the advances of the abject creature—he will find in his bed, upon awakening, a beautiful young woman who will confer power upon him (this is also a Celtic theme). The Sphinx, on the other hand, recalls even more "the child-protruding woman" of the Hopi Indians, that is, a phallic mother par excellence. This young woman was abandoned by her group in the course of a difficult migration, just as she was about to give birth. Henceforth she wanders in the desert as the "Mother of Animals," which she withholds from hunters. He who meets her in bloody clothes "is so frightened that he has an erection," of which she takes advantage to rape him, after which she rewards him with unfailing success in hunting. See H. R. Voth, "The Oraibi Summer Snake Ceremony," *Field Columbian Museum*, Publication No. 83, Anthropological Series, Vol. III, No. 4 (Chicago: 1903), pp. 352–3 and p. 353, *n* 1.

[11] Pausanius (second century A.D.), Greek geographer.

the derivative problem: born from different or born from same? By a correlation of this type, the overrating of blood relations is to the underrating of blood relations as the attempt to escape autochthony is to the impossibility to succeed in it. Although experience contradicts theory, social life validates cosmology by its similarity of structure. Hence cosmology is true.

Two remarks should be made at this stage.

In order to interpret the myth, we left aside a point which has worried the specialists until now, namely, that in the earlier (Homeric) versions of the Oedipus myth, some basic elements are lacking, such as Jocasta killing herself and Oedipus piercing his own eyes. These events do not alter the substance of the myth although they can easily be integrated, the first one as a new case of autodestruction (column three) and the second as another case of crippledness (column four). At the same time there is something significant in these additions, since the shift from foot to head is to be correlated with the shift from autochthonous origin to self-destruction.

Our method thus eliminates a problem which has, so far, been one of the main obstacles to the progress of mythological studies, namely, the quest for the *true* version, or the *earlier* one. On the contrary, we define the myth as consisting of all its versions; or to put it otherwise, a myth remains the same as long as it is felt as such. A striking example is offered by the fact that our interpretation may take into account the Freudian use of the Oedipus myth and is certainly applicable to it. Although the Freudian problem has ceased to be that of autochthony *versus* bisexual reproduction, it is still the problem of understanding how *one* can be born from *two:* How is it that we do not have only one procreator, but a mother plus a father? Therefore, not only Sophocles,[12] but Freud himself, should be included among the recorded versions of the Oedipus myth on a par with earlier or seemingly more "authentic" versions.

An important consequence follows. If a myth is made up of all its variants, structural analysis should take all of them into account. After analyzing all the known variants of the Theban version, we should thus treat the others in the same way: first, the tales about Labdacos' collateral line including Agave, Pentheus, and Jocasta herself; the Theban variant about Lycos with Amphion and Zetos as the city founders; more remote variants concerning Dionysus (Oedipus' matrilateral cousin); and Athenian legends where Cecrops takes the place of Cadmos, etc. For each of them a similar chart should be drawn and then compared

and reorganized according to the findings: Cecrops killing the serpent with the parallel episode of Cadmos; abandonment of Dionysus with abandonment of Oedipus; "Swollen Foot" with Dionysus' *loxias,* that is, walking obliquely; Europa's quest with Antiope's; the founding of Thebes by the Spartoi or by the brothers Amphion and Zetos; Zeus kidnapping Europa and Antiope and the same with Semele; the Theban Oedipus and the Argian Perseus, etc. We shall then have several two-dimensional charts, each dealing with a variant, to be organized in a three-dimensional order, as shown in the figure, so that three different readings become possible: left to right, top to bottom, front to back (or vice versa). All of these charts cannot be expected to be identical; but experience shows that any difference to be observed may be correlated with other differences, so that a logical treatment of the whole will allow simplifications, the final outcome being the structural law of the myth.

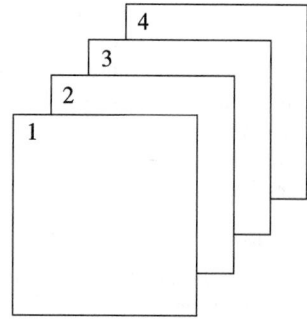

At this point the objection may be raised that the task is impossible to perform, since we can only work with known versions. Is it not possible that a new version might alter the picture? This is true enough if only one or two versions are available, but the objection becomes theoretical as soon as a reasonably large number have been recorded. Let us make this point clear by a comparison. If the furniture of a room and its arrangement were known to us only through its reflection in two mirrors placed on opposite walls, we should theoretically dispose of an almost infinite number of mirror images which would provide us with a complete knowledge. However, should the two mirrors be obliquely set, the number of mirror images would become very small; nevertheless, four or five such images would very likely give us, if not complete information, at least a sufficient coverage so that we would feel sure that no large piece of furniture is missing in our description.

---

[12]Sophocles (496?–406 B.C.), Greek dramatist, author of the Oedipus trilogy.

On the other hand, it cannot be too strongly emphasized that all available variants should be taken into account. If Freudian comments on the Oedipus complex are a part of the Oedipus myth, then questions such as whether Cushing's version of the Zuni origin myth should be retained or discarded become irrelevant. There is no single "true" version of which all the others are but copies or distortions. Every version belongs to the myth.

The reason for the discouraging results in works on general mythology can finally be understood. They stem from two causes. First, comparative mythologists have selected preferred versions instead of using them all. Second, we have seen that the structural analysis of *one* variant of *one* myth belonging to *one* tribe (in some cases, even *one* village) already requires two dimensions. When we use several variants of the same myth for the same tribe or village, the frame of reference becomes three-dimensional, and as soon as we try to enlarge the comparison, the number of dimensions required increases until it appears quite impossible to handle them intuitively. The confusions and platitudes which are the outcome of comparative mythology can be explained by the fact that multi-dimensional frames of reference are often ignored or are naïvely replaced by two- or three-dimensional ones. Indeed, progress in comparative mythology depends largely on the cooperation of mathematicians who would undertake to express in symbols multi-dimensional relations which cannot be handled otherwise.

To check this theory,[13] an attempt was made from 1952 to 1954 toward an exhaustive analysis of all the known versions of the Zuni origin and emergence myth: Cushing, 1883 and 1896; Stevenson, 1904; Parsons, 1923; Bunzel, 1932; Benedict, 1934.[14] Furthermore, a preliminary attempt was made at a comparison of the results with similar myths in other Pueblo tribes, Western and Eastern. Finally, a test was undertaken with Plains mythology. In all cases, it was found that the theory was sound; light was thrown, not only on North American mythology, but also on a previously unnoticed kind of logical operation, or one known so far only in a wholly different context. The bulk of material which needs to be handled practically at the outset of the work makes it impossible to enter into details, and we shall have to limit ourselves here to a few illustrations.

A simplified chart of the Zuni emergence myth would read:

CHANGE			DEATH
mechanical value of plants (used as ladders to emerge from lower world)	emergence led by Beloved Twins	sibling incest (origin of water)	gods kill children of men (by drowning)
food value of wild plants	migration led by the two Newekwe (ceremonial clowns)		magical contest with People of the Dew (collecting wild food *versus* cultivation)
		brother and sister sacrificed (to gain victory)	
food value of cultivated plants			
		brother and sister adopted (in exchange for corn)	
periodical character of agricultural work			
			war against the Kyanakwe (gardeners *versus* hunters)

---

[13][Lévi-Strauss] See *Annuaire de l'École pratique des Hautes Études,* section des Sciences religieuses, 1952–1953, pp. 19–21, and 1953–1954, pp. 27–9. Thanks are due here to an unrequested but deeply appreciated grant from the Ford Foundation.

[14]F. H. Cushing, *Zuni Fetiches,* Bureau of American Ethnology, Second Annual Report (1880–1881), Washington, D.C.: 1883; *Outlines of Zuni Creation Myths,* Bureau of American Ethnology, Thirteenth Annual Report, Washington, D.C.: 1896. M. C. Stevenson, *The Zuni Indians,* Bureau of American Ethnology, 23rd Annual Report, Washington, D.C.: 1905. E. C. Parsons, "The Origin Myth of Zuni," *Journal of American Folklore* XXXVI, 1923. R. L. Bunzel, *Introduction to Zuni Ceremonialism,* Bureau of American Ethnology, 47th Annual Report, Washington, D.C.: 1930. R. Benedict, *Zuni Mythology,* in two volumes, Columbia University Contributions to Anthropology, no. 21, New York, 1934.

food value
of game
(hunting)

       war led by
       the two
       War-Gods

inevitability
of warfare
                salvation of the
                tribe (center of
                the World found)

         brother
         and sister
         sacrificed
         (to avoid
         the Flood)

DEATH   PERMANENCE

As the chart indicates, the problem is the discovery of a life-death mediation. For the Pueblo, this is especially difficult; they understand the origin of human life in terms of the model of plant life (emergence from the earth). They share that belief with the ancient Greeks, and it is not without reason that we chose the Oedipus myth as our first example. But in the American Indian case, the highest form of plant life is to be found in agriculture which is periodical in nature, that is, which consists in an alternation between life and death. If this is disregarded, the contradiction appears elsewhere: Agriculture provides food, therefore life; but hunting provides food and is similar to warfare which means death. Hence there are three different ways of handling the problem. In the Cushing version, the difficulty revolves around an opposition between activities yielding an immediate result (collecting wild food) and activities yielding a delayed result—death has to become integrated so that agriculture can exist. Parsons' version shifts from hunting to agriculture, while Stevenson's version operates the other way around. It can be shown that all the differences between these versions can be rigorously correlated with these basic structures.

Thus the three versions describe the great war waged by the ancestors of the Zuni against a mythical population, the Kyanakwe, by introducing into the narrative significant variations which consist (1) in the friendship or hostility of the gods; (2) in the granting of final victory to one camp or the other; (3) in the attribution of the symbolic function to the Kyanakwe, described sometimes as hunters (whose bows are strung with animal sinews) and sometimes as gardeners (whose bows are strung with plant fibers).

CUSHING	PARSONS	STEVENSON
Gods, Kyanakwe } allied, use fiber string on their bows (gardeners)	Kyanakwe, alone, use fiber string	Gods, Men } allied, use fiber string
VICTORIOUS OVER	**VICTORIOUS OVER**	**VICTORIOUS OVER**
Men, alone, use sinew (until they shift to fiber)	Gods, Men } allied, use sinew string	Kyanakwe, alone, use sinew string

Since fiber string (agriculture) is always superior to sinew string (hunting), and since (to a lesser extent) the gods' alliance is preferable to their antagonism, it follows that in Cushing's version, men are seen as doubly underprivileged (hostile gods, sinew string); in the Stevenson version, doubly privileged (friendly gods, fiber string); while Parsons' version confronts us with an intermediary situation (friendly gods, but sinew strings, since men begin by being hunters). Hence:

OPPOSITIONS	CUSHING	PARSONS	STEVENSON
gods/men	−	+	+
fiber/sinew	−	−	+

Bunzel's version is of the same type as Cushing's from a structural point of view. However, it differs from both Cushing's and Stevenson's, inasmuch as the latter two explain the emergence as the result of man's need to evade his pitiful condition, while Bunzel's version makes it the consequence of a call from the higher powers—hence the inverted sequences of the means resorted to for the emergence: In both Cushing and Stevenson, they go from plants to animals; in Bunzel, from mammals to insects, and from insects to plants.

Among the Western Pueblo the logical approach always remains the same; the starting point and the point of arrival are simplest, whereas the intermediate stage is characterized by ambiguity:

LIFE (= INCREASE)

(Mechanical) value of the plant kingdom, taking growth alone into account	ORIGINS
Food value of the plant kingdom, limited to wild plants	FOOD-GATHERING
Food value of the plant kingdom, including wild and cultivated plants	AGRICULTURE
Food value of the animal kingdom, limited to animals *(but there is a contradiction here, owing to the negation of life = destruction, hence:)*	
Destruction of the animal kingdom, extended to human beings	HUNTING
	WARFARE

DEATH (= DECREASE)

The fact that contradiction appears in the middle of the dialectical process results in a double set of dioscuric pairs, the purpose of which is to mediate between conflicting terms:

1. 2 divine messengers	2 ceremonial clowns		2 war-gods
2. homogeneous pair: dioscuri (2 brothers)	siblings (brother and sister)	couple (husband and wife)	heterogeneous pair: (grandmother and grandchild)

We have here combinational variants of the same function in different contexts (hence the war attribute of the clowns, which has given rise to so many queries).

The problem, often regarded as insoluble, vanishes when it is shown that the clowns—gluttons who may with impunity make excessive use of agricultural products—have the same function in relation to food production as the war-gods. (This function appears, in the dialectical process, as *overstepping the boundaries* of hunting, that is, hunting for men instead of for animals for human consumption.)

Some central and Eastern Pueblos proceed the other way around. They begin by stating the identity of hunting and cultivation (first corn obtained by Game-Father sowing deer-dewclaws), and they try to derive both life and death from that central notion. Then, instead of extreme terms being simple and intermediary ones duplicated as among the Western groups, the extreme terms become duplicated (i.e., the two sisters of Eastern Pueblo) while a simple mediating term comes to the foreground (for instance, the Poshaiyanne of the Zia), but endowed with equivocal attributes. Hence the attributes of this "messiah" can be deduced from the place it occupies in the time sequence: good when at the beginning (Zuni, Cushing), equivocal in the middle (Central Pueblo), bad at the end (Zia), except in Bunzel's version, where the sequence is reversed as has been shown.

By systematically using this kind of structural analysis it becomes possible to organize all the known variants of a myth into a set forming a kind of permutation group, the two variants placed at the far ends being in a symmetrical, though inverted, relationship to each other.

Our method not only has the advantage of bringing some kind of order to what was previously chaos; it also enables us to perceive some basic logical processes which are at the root of mythical thought.[15] Three main processes should be distinguished.

The trickster of American mythology has remained so far a problematic figure. Why is it that throughout North America his role is assigned practically everywhere to either coyote or raven? If we keep in mind that mythical thought always progresses from the awareness of oppositions toward their resolution, the reason for these choices becomes clearer. We need only assume that two opposite terms with no intermediary always tend to be replaced by two equivalent terms which admit of a third one as a mediator; then

---

[15][Lévi-Strauss] For another application of this method, see our study "Four Winnebego Myths: A Structural Sketch," in Stanley Diamond, ed., *Culture in History: Essays in Honor of Paul Radin* (New York: 1960), pp. 351–62.

one of the polar terms and the mediator become replaced by a new triad, and so on. Thus we have a mediating structure of the following type:

INITIAL PAIR	FIRST TRIAD	SECOND TRIAD
Life		
	Agriculture	
		Herbivorous animals
		Carrion-eating animals
		(raven: coyote)
	Hunting	
	Warfare	Beasts of prey
Death		

The unformulated argument is as follows: carrion-eating animals are like beasts of prey (they eat animal food), but they are also like food-plant producers (they do not kill what they eat). Or to put it otherwise, Pueblo style (for Pueblo agriculture is more "meaningful" than hunting): ravens are to gardens as beasts of prey are to herbivorous animals. But it is also clear that herbivorous animals may be called first to act as mediators on the assumption that they are like collectors and gatherers (plant-food eaters), while they can be used as animal food though they are not themselves hunters. Thus we may have mediators of the first order, of the second order, and so on, where each term generates the next by a double process of opposition and correlation.

This kind of process can be followed in the mythology of the Plains, where we may order the data according to the set:

Unsuccessful mediator between Earth and Sky (Star-Husband's wife)

Heterogeneous pair of mediators (grandmother and grandchild)

Semi-homogeneous pair of mediators (Lodge-Boy and Thrown-away)

While among the Pueblo (Zuni) we have the corresponding set:

Successful mediator between Earth and Sky (Poshaiyanki)

Semi-homogeneous pair of mediators (Uyuyewi and Matsailema)

Homogeneous pair of mediators (the two Ahaiyuta)

On the other hand, correlations may appear on a horizontal axis (this is true even on the linguistic level; see the manifold connotation of the root *pose* in Tewa according to Parsons: coyote, mist, scalp, etc.). Coyote (a carrion-eater) is intermediary between herbivorous and carnivorous just as mist between Sky and Earth; as scalp between war and agriculture (scalp is a war crop); as corn smut between wild and cultivated plants; as garments between "nature" and "culture"; as refuse between village and outside; and as ashes (or soot) between roof (sky vault) and hearth (in the ground). This chain of mediators, if one may call them so, not only throws light on entire parts of North American mythology—why the Dew-God may be at the same time the Game-Master and the giver of raiments and be personified as an "Ash-Boy"; or why scalps are mist-producing; or why the Game-Mother is associated with corn smut; etc.—but it also probably corresponds to a universal way of organizing daily experience. See, for instance, the French for plant smut (*nielle,* from Latin *nebula*); the luck-bringing power attributed in Europe to refuse (old shoe) and ashes (kissing chimney sweeps); and compare the American Ash-Boy cycle with the Indo-European Cinderella: Both are phallic figures (mediators between male and female); masters of the dew and the game; owners of fine raiments; and social mediators (low class marrying into high class); but they are impossible to interpret through recent diffusion, as has been contended, since Ash-Boy and Cinderella are symmetrical but inverted in every detail (while the borrowed Cinderella tale in America—Zuni Turkey-Girl—is parallel to the prototype). Hence the chart:

	EUROPE	AMERICA
Sex	female	male
Family Status	double family (remarried father)	no family (orphan)
Appearance	pretty girl	ugly boy
Sentimental status	nobody likes her	unrequited love for girl

| Transformation | luxuriously clothed with supernatural help | stripped of ugliness with supernatural help |

Thus, like Ash-Boy and Cinderella, the trickster is a mediator. Since his mediating function occupies a position halfway between two polar terms, he must retain something of that duality—namely an ambiguous and equivocal character. But the trickster figure is not the only conceivable form of mediation; some myths seem to be entirely devoted to the task of exhausting all the possible solutions to the problem of bridging the gap between *two* and *one.* For instance, a comparison between all the variants of the Zuni emergence myth provides us with a series of mediating devices, each of which generates the next one by a process of opposition and correlation:

messiah > dioscuri > trickster > bisexual being > sibling pair > married couple > grandmother-grandchild > four-term group > triad

In Cushing's version, this dialectic is associated with a change from a spatial dimension (mediation between Sky and Earth) to a temporal dimension (mediation between summer and winter, that is, between birth and death). But while the shift is being made from space to time, the final solution (triad) re-introduces space, since a triad consists of a dioscuric pair *plus* a messiah, present simultaneously; and while the point of departure was ostensibly formulated in terms of a space referent (Sky and Earth), this was nevertheless implicitly conceived in terms of a time referent (first the messiah calls, *then* the dioscuri descend). Therefore the logic of myth confronts us with a double, reciprocal exchange of functions to which we shall return shortly.

Not only can we account for the ambiguous character of the trickster, but we can also understand another property of mythical figures the world over, namely, that the same god is endowed with contradictory attributes—for instance, he may be *good* and *bad* at the same time. If we compare the variants of the Hopi myth of the origin of Shalako, we may order them in terms of the following structure:

(Masauwu: x) ≅ (Muyingwu: Masauwu) ≅ (Shalako: Muyingwu) ≅ (y: Masauwu)

where x and y represent arbitrary values corresponding to

the fact that in the two "extreme" variants the god Masauwu, while appearing alone rather than associated with another god, as in variant two, or being absent, as in variant three, still retains intrinsically a relative value. In variant one, Masauwu (alone) is depicted as helpful to mankind (though not as helpful as he could be), and in version four, harmful to mankind (though not as harmful as he could be). His role is thus defined—at least implicitly—in contrast with another role which is possible but not specified and which is represented here by the values x and y. In version two, on the other hand, Muyingwu is relatively more helpful than Masauwu, and in version three, Shalako more helpful than Muyingwu. We find an identical series when ordering the Keresan variants:

(Poshaiyanki: x) ≅ (Lea: Poshaiyanki) ≅ (Poshaiyanki: Tiamoni) ≅ (y: Poshaiyanki)

This logical framework is particularly interesting, since anthropologists are already acquainted with it on two other levels—first, in regard to the problem of the pecking order among hens, and second, to what this writer has called *generalized exchange* in the field of kinship. By recognizing it also on the level of mythical thought, we may find ourselves in a better position to appraise its basic importance in anthropological studies and to give it a more inclusive theoretical interpretation.

Finally, when we have succeeded in organizing a whole series of variants into a kind of permutation group, we are in a position to formulate the law of that group. Although it is not possible at the present stage to come closer than an approximate formulation which will certainly need to be refined in the future, it seems that every myth (considered as the aggregate of all its variants) corresponds to a formula of the following type:

$$F_x(a): F_y(b) \cong F_x(b): F_{a-1}(y)$$

Here, with two terms, *a* and *b,* being given as well as two functions, *x* and *y,* of these terms, it is assumed that a relation of equivalence exists between two situations defined respectively by an inversion of *terms* and *relations,* under two conditions: (1) that one term be replaced by its opposite (in the above formula, *a* and *a* − *1*); (2) that an inversion be made between the *function value* and the *term value* of two elements (above, *y* and *a*).

This formula becomes highly significant when we recall that Freud considered that *two traumas* (and not one, as is so commonly said) are necessary in order to generate the individual myth in which a neurosis consists. By trying to apply the formula to the analysis of these traumas (and assuming that they correspond to conditions 1 and 2 respectively) we should not only be able to provide a more precise and rigorous formulation of the genetic law of the myth, but we would find ourselves in the much desired position of developing side by side the anthropological and the psychological aspects of the theory; we might also take it to the laboratory and subject it to experimental verification.

At this point it seems unfortunate that with the limited means at the disposal of French anthropological research no further advance can be made. It should be emphasized that the task of analyzing mythological literature, which is extremely bulky, and of breaking it down into its constituent units, requires team work and technical help. A variant of average length requires several hundred cards to be properly analyzed. To discover a suitable pattern of rows and columns for those cards, special devices are needed, consisting of vertical boards about six feet long and four and a half feet high, where cards can be pigeon-holed and moved at will. In order to build up three-dimensional models enabling one to compare the variants, several such boards are necessary, and this in turn requires a spacious workshop, a commodity particularly unavailable in Western Europe nowadays. Furthermore, as soon as the frame of reference becomes multi-dimensional (which occurs at an early stage, as has been shown above) the board system has to be replaced by perforated cards, which in turn require IBM equipment, etc.

THREE final remarks may serve as conclusion.

First, the question has often been raised why myths, and more generally oral literature, are so much addicted to duplication, triplication, or quadruplication of the same sequence. If our hypotheses are accepted, the answer is obvious: The function of repetition is to render the structure of the myth apparent. For we have seen that the synchronic-diachronic structure of the myth permits us to organize it into diachronic sequences (the rows in our tables) which should be read synchronically (the columns). Thus, a myth exhibits a "slated" structure, which comes to the surface, so to speak, through the process of repetition.

However, the slates are not absolutely identical. And since the purpose of myth is to provide a logical model capable of overcoming a contradiction (an impossible achievement if, as it happens, the contradiction is real), a theoretically infinite number of slates will be generated, each one slightly different from the others. Thus, myth grows spiralwise until the intellectual impulse which has produced it is exhausted. Its *growth* is a continuous process, whereas its *structure* remains discontinuous. If this is the case, we should assume that it closely corresponds, in the realm of the spoken word, to a crystal in the realm of physical matter. This analogy may help us to better understand the relationship of myth to both *langue* on the one hand and *parole* on the other. Myth is an intermediary entity between a statistical aggregate of molecules and the molecular structure itself.

Prevalent attempts to explain alleged differences between the so-called primitive mind and scientific thought have resorted to qualitative differences between the working processes of the mind in both cases, while assuming that the entities which they were studying remained very much the same. If our interpretation is correct, we are led toward a completely different view—namely, that the kind of logic in mythical thought is as rigorous as that of modern science, and that the difference lies, not in the quality of the intellectual process, but in the nature of the things to which it is applied.[16] This is well in agreement with the situation known to prevail in the field of technology: What makes a steel ax superior to a stone ax is not that the first one is better made than the second. They are equally well made, but steel is quite different from stone. In the same way we may be able to show that the same logical processes operate in myth as in science, and that man has always been thinking equally well; the improvement lies, not in an alleged progress of man's mind, but in the discovery of new areas to which it may apply its unchanged and unchanging powers.

---

[16]See Lévi-Strauss, *The Savage Mind* (1962, tr. 1966).

Roman Jakobson

1896–1982

Roman Jakobson's essay "The Metaphoric and Metonymic Poles" illustrates the complexity of relationships that may exist between the areas of psychological linguistics and literary criticism. Jakobson was a major scholar in both fields. He helped to found the Russian Formalist movement and later the Prague school of linguistics, both of which treated literature as fundamentally definable as language. Jakobson begins the essay, which is reprinted below, with a discussion of the relationship between metaphor and metonymy and the two polar types of aphasia, a brain disorder affecting speech. He then observes that the distinction between Romanticism and Realism lies in the relative dominance of metaphor in Romanticism and of metonymy in Realism. He suggests that though there has been much discussion of metaphor, there has been little study of metonymy. For a consideration of the language of Realism and of prose, a theory of metonymy is a necessity. In investigations such as Jakobson's, criticism, linguistics, and psychology contribute to each other.

Jakobson's emphasis on metonymy was taken up, with a somewhat different emphasis, by Paul de Man (below, page 1309) in a later influential essay, "The Rhetoric of Temporality," where metaphor is identified with symbolism and metonymy with allegory, with the latter preferred because, as de Man saw it, metonymy faces up to the reality of the arbitrary nature of the linguistic sign.

For a list of Jakobson's Formalist publications in Russian see Victor Erlich, *Russian Formalism: Theory, Practice* (1965), 288–89. For a bibliography of his many publications see Stephen Rudy, ed., *Roman Jakobson: A Complete Bibliography of His Writings* (1990). See Elmar Holenstein, *Roman Jakobson's Approach to Language* (tr. 1976); Linda R. Waugh, *Roman Jakobson's Science of Language* (1976); Rodney B. Sangster, *Roman Jakobson and Beyond* (1982); Richard Bradford, *Roman Jakobson: Life, Language, and Art* (1994).

The Metaphoric and Metonymic Poles

The varieties of aphasia are numerous and diverse, but all of them oscillate between the two polar types just described. Every form of aphasic disturbance consists in some impairment, more or less severe, either of the faculty for selection and substitution or for combination and contexture. The former affliction involves a deterioration of metalinguistic operations, while the latter damages the capacity for maintaining the hierarchy of linguistic units. The relation of similarity is suppressed in the former, the relation of contiguity in the latter type of aphasia. Metaphor is alien to the similarity disorder, and metonymy to the contiguity disorder.

The development of a discourse may take place along two different semantic lines: one topic may lead to another either through their similarity or through their contiguity. The metaphoric way would be the most appropriate term for the first case and the metonymic way for the second, since they find their most condensed expression in metaphor and

Jakobson's "The Metaphoric and Metonymic Poles" is Chapter 5 of *Fundamentals of Language,* coauthored with Morris Halle (1956). The essay is Jakobson's.

metonymy respectively. In aphasia one or the other of these two processes is restricted or totally blocked—an effect which makes the study of aphasia particularly illuminating for the linguist. In normal verbal behavior both processes are continually operative, but careful observation will reveal that under the influence of a cultural pattern, personality, and verbal style, preference is given to one of the two processes over the other.

In a well-known psychological test, children are confronted with some noun and told to utter the first verbal response that comes into their heads. In this experiment two opposite linguistic predilections are invariably exhibited; the response is intended either as a substitute for, or as a complement to the stimulus. In the latter case the stimulus and the response together form a proper syntactic construction, most usually a sentence. These two types of reaction have been labeled substitutive and predicative.

To the stimulus *hut* one response was *burnt out;* another, *is a poor little house*. Both reactions are predicative; but the first creates a purely narrative context, while in the second there is a double connection with the subject *hut:* on the one hand, a positional (namely, syntactic) contiguity, and on the other a semantic similarity.

The same stimulus produced the following substitutive reactions: the tautology *hut;* the synonyms *cabin* and *hovel,* the antonym *palace,* and the metaphors *den* and *burrow*. The capacity of two words to replace one another is an instance of positional similarity, and, in addition, all these responses are linked to the stimulus by semantic similarity (or contrast). Metonymical responses to the same stimulus, such as *thatch, litter,* or *poverty,* combine and contrast the positional similarity with semantic contiguity.

In manipulating these two kinds of connection (similarity and contiguity) in both their aspects (positional and semantic)—selecting, combining, and ranking them—an individual exhibits his personal style, his verbal predilections and preferences.

In verbal art the interaction of these two elements is especially pronounced. Rich material for the study of this relationship is to be found in verse patterns which require a compulsory parallelism between adjacent lines, for example in Biblical poetry or in the West Finnic and, to some extent, the Russian oral traditions. This provides an objective criterion of what in the given speech community acts as a correspondence. Since on any verbal level—morphemic, lexical, syntactic, and phraseological—either of these two relations (similarity and contiguity) can appear—and each in either of two aspects—an impressive range of possible configurations is created. Either of the two gravitational poles may prevail. In Russian lyrical songs, for example, metaphoric

constructions predominate, while in the heroic epics the metonymic way is preponderant.

In poetry there are various motives which determine the choice between these alternants. The primacy of the metaphoric process in the literary schools of Romanticism and symbolism has been repeatedly acknowledged, but it is still insufficiently realized that it is the predominance of metonymy which underlies and actually predetermines the so-called realistic trend, which belongs to an intermediary stage between the decline of Romanticism and the rise of symbolism and is opposed to both. Following the path of contiguous relationships, the realistic author metonymically digresses from the plot to the atmosphere and from the characters to the setting in space and time. He is fond of synecdochic details. In the scene of Anna Karenina's suicide Tolstoy's artistic attention is focused on the heroine's handbag; and in *War and Peace* the synecdoches "hair on the upper lip" or "bare shoulders" are used by the same writer to stand for the female characters to whom these features belong.[1]

The alternative predominance of one or the other of these two processes is by no means confined to verbal art. The same oscillation occurs in sign systems other than language.[2] A salient example from the history of painting is the manifestly metonymical orientation of cubism, where the object is transformed into a set of synecdoches; the surrealist painters responded with a patently metaphorical attitude. Ever since the productions of D. W. Griffith,[3] the art of the cinema, with its highly developed capacity for changing the angle, perspective and focus of "shots," has broken with the tradition of the theater and ranged an unprecedented variety of synecdochic "close-ups" and metonymic "set-ups" in general. In such pictures as those of Charlie Chaplin, these devices in turn were superseded by a novel, metaphoric "montage" with its "lap dissolves"—the filmic similes.[4]

The bipolar structure of language (or other semiotic systems), and, in aphasia, the fixation on one of these poles to the exclusion of the other require systematic comparative study. The retention of either of these alternatives in the two types of aphasia must be confronted with the predominance of the same pole in certain styles, personal habits, current

---

[1] Tolstoy (above, page 757).

[2] [Jakobson] I ventured a few sketchy remarks on the metonymical turn in verbal art ("Pro realizm u mystectvi," *Vaplite,* Kharkov, 1927, No. 2; "Randbemerkungen zur Prosa des Dichters Pasternak," *Slavische Rundschau,* VII, 1935), in painting ("Futurizm," *Iskusstvo,* Moscow, August 2, 1919) and in motion pictures ("Úpadek filmu," *Listy pro umení a kritiku,* I, Prague, 1933), but the crucial problem of the two polar processes awaits a detailed investigation.

[3] D. W. Griffith (1875–1948), American producer and director.

[4] Charlie Chaplin (1889–1977), British actor and producer. [Jakobson] Cf. B. Balazs, *Theory of the Film* (London, 1952).

fashions, etc. A careful analysis and comparison of these phenomena with the whole syndrome of the corresponding type of aphasia is an imperative task for joint research by experts in psychopathology, psychology, linguistics, poetics, and semiotic, the general science of signs. The dichotomy here discussed appears to be of primal significance and consequence for all verbal behavior and for human behavior in general.[5]

To indicate the possibilities of the projected comparative research, we choose an example from a Russian folk tale which employs parallelism as a comic device: "Thomas is a bachelor; Jeremiah is unmarried" (*"Fomá xólost; Erjóma neženát"*). Here the predicates in the two parallel clauses are associated by similarity: they are in fact synonymous. The subjects of both clauses are masculine proper names and hence morphologically similar, while on the other hand they denote two contiguous heroes of the same tale, created to perform identical actions and thus to justify the use of synonymous pairs of predicates. A somewhat modified version of the same construction occurs in a familiar wedding song in which each of the wedding guests is addressed in turn by his first name and patronymic: "Gleb is a bachelor; Ivanovič is unmarried." While both predicates here are again synonyms, the relationship between the two subjects is changed: both are proper names denoting the same man and are normally used contiguously as a mode of polite address.

In the quotation from the folk tale the two parallel clauses refer to two separate facts, the marital status of Thomas and the similar status of Jeremiah. In the verse from the wedding song, however, the two clauses are synonymous: they redundantly reiterate the celibacy of the same hero, splitting him into two verbal hypostases.

The Russian novelist Gleb Ivanovič Uspenskij (1840–1902) in the last years of his life suffered from a mental illness involving a speech disorder. His first name and patronymic, *Gleb Ivanovič,* traditionally combined in polite intercourse, for him split into two distinct names designating two separate beings: Gleb was endowed with all his virtues, while Ivanovič, the name relating the son to the father, became the incarnation of all Uspenskij's vices. The linguistic aspect of this split personality is the patient's inability to use two symbols for the same thing, and it is thus a similarity disorder. Since the similarity disorder is bound

up with the metonymical bent, an examination of the literary manner Uspenskij had employed as a young writer takes on particular interest. And the study of Anatolij Kamegulov, who analyzed Uspenskij's style, bears out our theoretical expectations. He shows that Uspenskij had a particular penchant for metonymy, and especially for synecdoche, and that he carried it so far that "the reader is crushed by the multiplicity of detail unloaded on him in a limited verbal space, and is physically unable to grasp the whole, so that the portrait is often lost."[6]

To be sure, the metonymical style in Uspenskij is obviously prompted by the prevailing literary canon of his time, late nineteenth-century "realism"; but the personal stamp of Gleb Ivanovič made his pen particularly suitable for this artistic trend in its extreme manifestations and finally left its mark upon the verbal aspect of his mental illness.

A competition between both devices, metonymic and metaphoric, is manifest in any symbolic process, either intrapersonal or social. Thus in an inquiry into the structure of dreams, the decisive question is whether the symbols and the temporal sequences used are based on contiguity (Freud's metonymic "displacement" and synecdochic "condensation") or on similarity (Freud's "identification and symbolism").[7] The principles underlying magic rites have been resolved by Frazer into two types: charms based on the law of similarity and those founded on association by contiguity. The first of these two great branches of sympathetic magic has been called homeopathic or imitative, and the second, contagious magic.[8] This bipartition is indeed illuminating. Nonetheless, for the most part, the question of the two poles is still neglected, despite its wide scope and importance for the study of any symbolic behavior, especially verbal, and of its impairments. What is the main reason for this neglect?

Similarity in meaning connects the symbols of a metalanguage with the symbols of the language referred to. Similarity connects a metaphorical term with the term for which it is substituted. Consequently, when constructing a metalanguage to interpret tropes, the researcher possesses more

---

[5][Jakobson] For the psychological and sociological aspects of this dichotomy see Bateson's views on "progressional" and "selective integration" and Parsons on the "conjunction-disjunction dichotomy" in children's development: J. Ruesch and G. Bateson, *Communication, The Social Matrix of Psychiatry* (New York, 1951), pp. 183 ff.; T. Parsons and R. F. Bates, *Family Socialization and Interaction Process* (Glencoe, 1955), pp. 119 ff.

[6][Jakobson] A. Kamegulov, *Stil' Gleba Unspenskogo* (Leningrad, 1930), p. 65, 145. One of such disintegrated portraits cited by the monograph:
From underneath an ancient straw cap with a black spot on its shield, there peeked two braids resembling the tusks of a wild boar; a chin grown fat and pendulous definitely spread over greasy collar of the calico dickey and in thick layer lay on the coarse collar of the canvas coat, firmly buttoned on the neck. From below this coat to the eyes of the observer there protruded massive hands with a ring, which had eaten into the fat finger, a cane with a copper top, a significant bulge of the stomach and the presence of very broad pants, almost of muslin quality, in the broad ends of which hid the toes of his boots.

[7][Jakobson] S. Freud, *Die Traumdeutung,* ninth ed. (Vienna, 1950).

[8][Jakobson] J. G. Frazer, *The Golden Bough: A Study of Magic and Religion,* Part I, third ed. (Vienna, 1950), Chapter 3.

homogeneous means to handle metaphor, whereas metonymy, based on a different principle, easily defies interpretation. Therefore nothing comparable to the rich literature on metaphor[9] can be cited for the theory of metonymy. For the same reason, it is generally realized that Romanticism is closely linked with metaphor, whereas the equally intimate ties of realism with metonymy usually remain unnoticed. Not only the tool of the observer but also the object of observation is responsible for the preponderance of metaphor over metonymy in scholarship. Since poetry is focused upon sign, and pragmatical prose primarily upon referent, tropes and figures were studied mainly as poetical devices. The principle of similarity underlies poetry; the metrical parallelism of lines or the phonic equivalence of rhyming words prompts the question of semantic similarity and contrast; there exist, for instance, grammatical and antigrammatical but never agrammatical rhymes. Prose, on the contrary, is forwarded essentially by contiguity. Thus, for poetry, metaphor, and for prose, metonymy is the line of least resistance and, consequently, the study of poetical tropes is directed chiefly toward metaphor. The actual bipolarity has been artificially replaced in these studies by an amputated, unipolar scheme which, strikingly enough, coincides with one of the two aphasic patterns, namely with the contiguity disorder.[10]

---

[9][Jakobson] C. F. P. Stutterheim, *Het begrip metaphoor* (Amsterdam, 1941).

[10][Jakobson] Thanks are due to Hugh McLean for his valuable assistance and to Justinia Besharov for her original observations on tropes and figures.

Northrop Frye

1912–1991

The Canadian critic Northrop Frye's *Ethical Criticism: Theory of Symbols* is the second of four interrelated essays that, with an introduction and conclusion, comprise his influential *Anatomy of Criticism.* He begins the book with an argument for a criticism the axioms and postulates of which grow out of the art it deals with. Thus Frye rejects various psychological and sociological approaches as imposing alien frameworks on literature when singly applied. Claiming that literature is an object, not a subject, of study and that we must learn about it through a conceptual framework, he proceeds to offer essays on various aspects of criticism as a subject. The first essay, *Historical Criticism: Theory of Modes,* establishes much of his terminology, including the five literary modes, which he also calls phases—myth, romance, the high mimetic, the low mimetic, and the ironic. These phases, historic and modal in the first essay, help to identify the range of literary symbolism in the second. Beginning with a distinction between "outward" and "inward" phases of symbolism, Frye distinguishes between verbal structures with a tendency toward the didactic or descriptive in their efforts to grasp an assumed external reality and those where the poet depends not on descriptive accuracy but on conformity to his own "hypothetical postulates." In making this distinction, however, Frye insists that in *all* literary verbal structures the final direction of meaning is inward, no matter how outward the technique may appear to be. (Indeed, at the end of his book Frye suggests that all systems of symbols, literary or not, are centripetal.) Literature, for Frye, is in this sense a "disembodied use of words." Thus Zola's novels and Mallarmé's poems belong to the same "system," though at opposite poles, as Mallarmé seems to have recognized (above, page 729).

There are three other phases of symbolism: the formal phase, where the symbol is seen as an "image"; the mythical phase, where it is seen as an "archetype"; and the anagogic phase, a term drawn from Aquinas (above, page 151) and Dante (above, page 154), where it is seen as a "monad." In his discussion of the formal phase, Frye imagines allegory as existing on a scale ranging from naïve allegory and extreme outwardness, where it is a simple device in discursive statement, to the extreme inwardness of private association. Unlike the Romantics, who tended to oppose symbolism to allegory, to the denigration of the latter, Frye considers allegory an aspect of symbolism. In the mythical phase, the idea of the symbol as something that is repeated throughout the body of literature is emphasized. In this phase, poems are regarded as imitations of other poems more than of nature. In the anagogic phase, the idea of literature as a total imaginative form dominates. In this phase, literature is seen no longer as looking outward to comment on life but as constituting life and reality in a system of verbal relationships.

The anagogic phase, and much else in Frye, is reminiscent of William Blake's (above, page 447) views (Frye's first book was a groundbreaking study of Blake). It also has affinities with Ernst Cassirer's (above, page 1016) notion of "symbolic forms." Indeed, Frye's system could be said to have resulted from a meditation on the symbolism of Blake's longer poems. At the same time it appropriates insights from a number of other writers, including Vico (above, page 313), Frazer, Freud (above, page 746), and Jung; but Frye's notion of the archetype is not Jungian, and he is not a Freudian.

Frye has been looked on as having provided an alternative in the late 1950s to the so-called contextualism of the American New Criticism, but it is more fruitful to consider his work an attempt to synthesize and ground in a general theory of literature the interests of that movement with the anthropological study of myth and ritual. It is instructive to see how Frye would seem to have assimilated (always with his own ends in mind) the insights of critics as diverse as Matthew Arnold (above, page 586), T. S. Eliot (above, page 806), Ronald S. Crane (above, page 1071), and Philip Wheelwright. Yet he remains apart from all of them. It is sometimes overlooked that Frye's book deliberately belongs to one of the genres it includes in its system, the anatomy. Thus what Frye says about the anatomy is relevant to understanding Frye's book.

Frye's many works include *Fearful Symmetry: A Study of William Blake* (1947), *Anatomy of Criticism* (1957), *The Well-Tempered Critic* (1963), *The Educated Imagination* (1963), *T. S. Eliot* (1963), *Fables of Identity* (1963), *A Natural Perspective* (1965), *The Return of Eden* (1965), *Five Essays on Milton's Epics* (1966), *Fools of Time* (1967), *The Modern Century* (1967), *The Bush Garden* (1971), *The Critical Path* (1971), *The Secular Scripture* (1976), *Spiritus Mundi* (1976), *Northrop Frye on Culture and Literature* (1978), *Creation and Recreation* (1980), *The Myth of Deliverance* (1981), *The Great Code* (1982), *Divisions on a Ground* (1982), *Northrop Frye on Shakespeare* (1986), *Northrop Frye on Education* (1988), *Words With Power (1990), The Eternal Act of Creation: Essays 1979–1990* (1993). See Murray Krieger, ed., *Northrop Frye in Modern Criticism* (1966); Ronald Bates, *Northrop Frye* (1971); Robert Denham, *Northrop Frye and Critical Method* (1978); David Cook, *Northrop Frye: A Vision of the New World* (1985); Ian Balfour, *Northrop Frye* (1988); John Ayre, *Northrop Frye: A Biography* (1989); A. C. Hamilton, *Northrop Frye: Anatomy of His Criticism* (1990); Alvin A. Lee and Robert D. Denham, eds., *The Legacy of Northrop Frye* (1994); Jonathan Locke Hart, *Northrop Frye: The Theoretical Imagination* (1994); Caterina Nella Cotrupi, *Northrop Frye and the Poetics of Process* (2000).

from

Anatomy of Criticism

Second Essay

Ethical Criticism: Theory of Symbols

Introduction

Of the problems arising from the lack of a technical vocabulary[1] of poetics, two demand special attention. The fact, already mentioned, that there is no word for a work of literary art is one that I find particularly baffling. One may invoke the authority of Aristotle[2] for using *poem* in this sense, but usage declares that a poem is a composition in meter, and to speak of *Tom Jones*[3] as a poem would be an abuse of ordinary language. One may discuss the question whether great works of prose deserve to be called poetry in some more extended sense, but the answer can only be a matter of taste in definitions. The attempt to introduce a value judgment into a definition of poetry (e.g., "What, after all, do we mean by a poem—that is, something worthy of the name of poem?") only adds to the confusion. So of course does the antique snobbery about the superiority of meter which has given *prosy* the meaning of tedious and *prosaic* the meaning of pedestrian. As often as I can, I use *poem* and its relatives by synecdoche, because they are short words; but where synecdoche would be confusing, the reader will have to put up with such cacophonous jargon as *hypothetical verbal structure* and the like.

The other matter concerns the use of the word *symbol* which in this essay means any unit of any literary structure that can be isolated for critical attention. A word, a phrase, or an image used with some kind of special reference (which is what a symbol is usually taken to mean) are all symbols when they are distinguishable elements in critical analysis. Even the letters a writer spells his words with form

part of his symbolism in this sense: they would be isolated only in special cases, such as alliteration or dialect spellings, but we are still aware that they symbolize sounds. Criticism as a whole, in terms of this definition, would begin with, and largely consist of, the systematizing of literary symbolism. It follows that other words must be used to classify the different types of symbolism.

For there must be different types: the criticism of literature can hardly be a simple or one-level activity. The more familiar one is with a great work of literature, the more one's understanding of it grows. Further, one has the feeling of growing in the understanding of the work itself, not in the number of things one can attach to it. The conclusion that a work of literary art contains a variety or sequence of meanings seems inescapable. It has seldom, however, been squarely faced in criticism since the Middle Ages, when a precise scheme of literal, allegorical, moral, and anagogic meanings was taken over from theology and applied to literature.[4] Today there is more of a tendency to consider the problem of literary meaning as subsidiary to the problems of symbolic logic and semantics. In what follows I try to work as independently of the latter subjects as I can, on the ground that the obvious place to start looking for a theory of literary meaning is in literature.

The principle of manifold or "polysemous" meaning, as Dante calls it,[5] is not a theory any more, still less an exploded superstition, but an established fact. The thing that has established it is the simultaneous development of several different schools of modern criticism, each making a distinctive choice of symbols in its analysis. The modern student of critical theory is faced with a body of rhetoricians who speak of texture and frontal assaults, with students of history who deal with traditions and sources, with critics using material from psychology and anthropology, with Aristotelians, Coleridgians, Thomists, Freudians, Jungians, Marxists, with students of myths, rituals, archetypes, metaphors, ambiguities, and significant forms. The student must either admit the principle of polysemous meaning, or choose one of these groups and then try to prove that all the others are less legitimate. The former is the way of scholarship, and leads to the advancement of learning; the latter is the way of pedantry, and gives us a wide choice of goals, the most conspicuous today being fantastical learning, or myth criticism, contentious learning, or historical criticism, and delicate learning, or "new" criticism.

Once we have admitted the principle of polysemous meaning, we can either stop with a purely relative and plu-

---

Ethical Criticism: Theory of Symbols first appeared in 1957. It is reprinted from *Anatomy of Criticism* (Princeton, N.J.: Princeton University Press, 1957).

[1] [Frye] The revival of the technical language of rhetoric would not only provide us with useful terms, but in many cases would revive the conceptions themselves which have been forgotten along with their names. It may be true that, as Samuel Butler said: ". . . all a rhetorician's rules teach nothing but to name his tools" but if a critic cannot name his tools, the world is not likely to concede much authority to his craft. We should not entrust our cars to a mechanic who lived entirely in a world of gadgets and doohickeys.

[2] Aristotle (above, page 48).

[3] By Henry Fielding (1707–1754), English novelist.

[4] Aquinas (above, page 151) and Dante (above, page 154).

[5] Above, page 154.

ralistic position, or we can go on to consider the possibility that there is a finite number of valid critical methods, and that they can all be contained in a single theory. It does not follow that all meanings can be arranged, as the medieval four-level scheme implies, in a hierarchical sequence, in which the first steps are comparatively elementary and apprehension gets more subtle and rarefied as one goes on. The term *level* is used here only for convenience, and should not be taken as indicating any belief on my part in a series of degrees of critical initiation. Again, there is a general reservation to be made about the conception of polysemous meaning: the meaning of a literary work forms a part of a larger whole. In the previous essay we saw that meaning or *dianoia* was one of three elements, the other two being *mythos* or narrative and *ethos* or characterization. It is better to think, therefore, not simply of a sequence of meanings, but of a sequence of contexts or relationships in which the whole work of literary art can be placed, each context having its characteristic *mythos* and *ethos* as well as its *dianoia* or meaning. I call these contexts or relationships *phases*.

Literal and Descriptive Phases: Symbols as Motif and as Sign

Whenever we read anything, we find our attention moving in two directions at once. One direction is outward or centrifugal, in which we keep going outside our reading, from the individual words to the things they mean, or, in practice, to our memory of the conventional association between them. The other direction is inward or centripetal, in which we try to develop from the words a sense of the larger verbal pattern they make. In both cases we deal with symbols, but when we attach an external meaning to a word we have, in addition to the verbal symbol, the thing represented or symbolized by it. Actually we have a series of such representations: the verbal symbol *cat* is a group of black marks on a page representing a sequence of noises representing an image or memory representing a sense experience representing an animal that says meow. Symbols so understood may here be called *signs,* verbal units which, conventionally and arbitrarily, stand for and point to things outside the place where they occur. When we are trying to grasp the context of words, however, the word *cat* is an element in a larger body of meaning. It is not primarily a symbol "of" anything, for in this aspect it does not represent, but connects.[6] We can hardly even say that it

represents a part of the author's intention in putting it there, for the author's intention ceases to exist as a separate factor as soon as he has finished revising.[7] Verbal elements understood inwardly or centripetally, as parts of a verbal structure, are, as symbols, simply and literally verbal elements, or units of a verbal structure. (The word *literally* should be kept in mind.) We may, borrowing a term from music, call such elements *motifs.*

These two modes of understanding take place simultaneously in all reading. It is impossible to read the word *cat* in a context without some representational flash of the animal so named; it is impossible to see the bare sign *cat* without wondering what context it belongs to. But verbal structures may be classified according to whether the *final* direction of meaning is outward or inward. In descriptive or assertive writing the final direction is outward. Here the verbal structure is intended to represent things external to it, and it is valued in terms of the accuracy with which it does represent them. Correspondence between phenomenon and verbal sign is truth; lack of it is falsehood; failure to connect is tautology, a purely verbal structure that cannot come out of itself.

In all literary verbal structures the final direction of meaning is inward. In literature the standards of outward meaning are secondary, for literary works do not pretend to describe or assert, and hence are not true, not false, and yet not tautological either, or at least not in the sense in which such a statement as "the good is better than the bad" is tautological. Literary meaning may best be described, perhaps, as hypothetical, and a hypothetical or assumed relation to the external world is part of what is usually meant by the word *imaginative.* This word is to be distinguished from *imaginary,* which usually refers to an assertive verbal structure that fails to make good its assertions. In literature, questions of fact or truth are subordinated to the primary literary aim of producing a structure of words for its own sake, and the sign-values of symbols are subordinated to their importance as a structure of interconnected motifs. Wherever we have an autonomous verbal structure of this kind, we have literature. Wherever this autonomous structure is lacking, we have language, words used instrumentally to help human consciousness do or understand something else. Literature is a specialized form of language, as language is of communication.

The reason for producing the literary structure is apparently that the inward meaning, the self-contained verbal pattern, is the field of the responses connected with pleasure, beauty, and interest. The contemplation of a detached

---

[6] Compare Saussure (above, page 787). Frye's use of the word "structure" is different from the structuralist use of it, where it applies initially to language as a structure, though Roland Barthes and Claude Lévi-Strauss are among those who extend its usage with the linguistic model in mind.

[7] See Wimsatt and Beardsley (above, page 1026).

pattern, whether of words or not, is clearly a major source of the sense of the beautiful, and of the pleasure that accompanies it. The fact that interest is most easily aroused by such a pattern is familiar to every handler of words, from the poet to the after-dinner speaker who digresses from an assertive harangue to present the self-contained structure of verbal interrelationships known as a joke. It often happens that an originally descriptive piece of writing, such as the histories of Fuller and Gibbon,[8] survives by virtue of its "style," or interesting verbal pattern, after its value as a representation of facts has faded.

The old precept that poetry is designed to delight and instruct[9] sounds like an awkward hendiadys, as we do not usually feel that a poem does two different things to us, but we can understand it when we relate it to these two aspects of symbolism. In literature, what entertains is prior to what instructs, or, as we may say, the reality-principle is subordinate to the pleasure-principle. In assertive verbal structures the priority is reversed. Neither factor can, of course, ever be eliminated from any kind of writing.

One of the most familiar and important features of literature is the absence of a controlling aim of descriptive accuracy. We should, perhaps, like to feel that the writer of a historical drama knew what the historical facts of his theme were, and that he would not alter them without good reason. But that such good reasons may exist in literature is not denied by anyone. They seem to exist only there: the historian selects his facts, but to suggest that he had manipulated them to produce a more symmetrical structure would be grounds for libel. Some other types of verbal structures, such as theology and metaphysics, are declared by some to be centripetal in final meaning, and hence to be tautological ("purely verbal").[10] I have no opinion on this, except that in literary criticism theology and metaphysics must be treated as assertive, because they are outside literature, and everything that influences literature from without creates a centrifugal movement in it, whether it is directed toward the nature of absolute being or advice on the raising of hops. It is clear, too, that the proportion between the sense of being pleasantly entertained and the sense of being instructed, or awakened to reality, will vary in different forms of literature. The sense of reality is, for instance, far higher in tragedy than in comedy, as in comedy the logic of events normally gives way to the audience's desire for a happy ending.

The apparently unique privilege of ignoring facts has given the poet his traditional reputation as a licensed liar, and explains why so many words denoting literary structure, *fable, fiction, myth,* and the like, have a secondary sense of untruth, like the Norwegian word *digter* which is said to mean liar as well as poet. But, as Sir Philip Sidney remarked, "the poet never affirmeth,"[11] and therefore does not lie any more than he tells the truth. The poet, like the pure mathematician, depends, not on descriptive truth, but on conformity to his hypothetical postulates. The appearance of a ghost in *Hamlet* presents the hypothesis "let there be a ghost in *Hamlet.*" It has nothing to do with whether ghosts exist or not, or whether Shakespeare or his audience thought they did. A reader who quarrels with postulates, who dislikes *Hamlet* because he does not believe that there are ghosts or that people speak in pentameters, clearly has no business in literature. He cannot distinguish fiction from fact, and belongs in the same category as the people who send checks to radio stations for the relief of suffering heroines in soap operas. We may note here, as the point will be important later, that the accepted postulate, the contract agreed on by the reader before he can start reading, is the same thing as a convention.

The person who cannot be brought to understand literary convention is often said to be "literal-minded." But as *literal* surely ought to have some connection with letters, it seems curious to use the phrase *literal-minded* for imaginative illiterates.[12] The reason for the anomaly is interesting, and important to our argument. Traditionally, the phrase *literal meaning* refers to descriptive meaning that is free from ambiguity. We usually say that the word cat "means literally" a cat when it is an adequate sign for a cat, when it stands in a simple representative relation to the animal that says meow. This sense of the term literal comes down from medieval times, and may be due to the theological origin of critical categories. In theology, the literal meaning of Scripture is usually the historical meaning, its accuracy as a record of facts or truths. Dante says, commenting on the verse in the Psalms, "When Israel went out of Egypt," "considering the letter only, the exodus of the Israelites to Palestine in the time of Moses is what is signified to us *(significatur nobis).*"[13] The word *signified* shows that the literal meaning here is the simplest kind of descriptive or representational meaning, as it would still be to a biblical "literalist."

---

[8] Thomas Fuller (1608–1661), English clergyman and author; Edward Gibbon (1737–1794), English historian.

[9] Horace (above, page 83).

[10] A view held, for example, by Carnap (above, page 978).

[11] Sidney (above, page 198).

[12] Frye's literal level is different from Aquinas's and Dante's, which are "historical" levels, pointing outward to people and events (fictional or otherwise in Dante), whereas for Frye the literal level is "centripetal," with words pointing to other words.

[13] Dante, *Letter to Can Grande* (above, page 154).

But this conception of literal meaning as simple descriptive meaning will not do at all for literary criticism. An historical event cannot be literally anything but an historical event; a prose narrative describing it cannot be literally anything but a prose narrative. The literal meaning of Dante's own *Commedia* is not historical, not at any rate a *simple* description of what "really happened" to Dante. And if a poem cannot be literally anything but a poem, then the literal basis of meaning in poetry can only be its letters, its inner structure of interlocking motifs. We are always wrong, in the context of criticism, when we say "this poem means literally"—and then give a prose paraphrase of it. All paraphrases abstract a secondary or outward meaning.[14] Understanding a poem literally means understanding the whole of it, as a poem, and as it stands. Such understanding begins in a complete surrender of the mind and senses to the impact of the work as a whole, and proceeds through the effort to unite the symbols toward a simultaneous perception of the unity of the structure. (This is a *logical* sequence of critical elements, the *integritas, consonantia,* and *claritas* of Stephen's argument in Joyce's *Portrait.*[15] I have no idea what the psychological sequence is, or whether there is a sequence—I suppose there would not be in a *Gestalt* theory.[16]) Literal understanding occupies the same place in criticism that observation, the direct exposure of the mind to nature, has in the scientific method. "Every poem must necessarily be a perfect unity," says Blake:[17] this, as the wording implies, is not a statement of fact about all existing poems, but a statement of the hypothesis which every reader adopts in first trying to comprehend even the most chaotic poem ever written.

Some principle of recurrence seems to be fundamental to all works of art, and this recurrence is usually spoken of as rhythm when it moves along in time, and as pattern when it is spread out in space. Thus we speak of the rhythm of music and the pattern of painting. But a slight increase of sophistication will soon start us talking about the pattern of music and the rhythm of painting. The inference is that all arts possess both a temporal and a spatial aspect, whichever takes the lead when they are presented. The score of a symphony may be studied all at once, as a spread-out pattern: a painting may be studied as the track of an intricate dance of the eye. Works of literature also move in time like music and spread out in images like painting. The word *narrative* or *mythos* conveys the sense of movement caught by the ear, and the word *meaning* or *dianoia* conveys, or at least preserves, the sense of simultaneity caught by the eye. We *listen to* the poem as it moves from beginning to end, but as soon as the whole of it is in our minds at once we "see" what it means. More exactly, this response is not simply to *the* whole *of* it, but to *a* whole *in* it: we have a vision of meaning or *dianoia* whenever any simultaneous apprehension is possible.

Now as a poem is literally a poem, it belongs, in its literal context, to the class of things called poems, which in their turn form part of the larger class known as works of art. The poem from this point of view presents a flow of sounds approximating music on one side, and an integrated pattern of imagery approximating the pictorial on the other. Literally, then, a poem's narrative is its rhythm or movement of words. If a dramatist writes a speech in prose, and then rewrites it in blank verse, he has made a strategic rhythmical change, and therefore a change in the literal narrative. Even if he alters *came a day* to *a day came* he has still made a tiny alteration of sequence, and so, literally, of his rhythm and narrative. Similarly, a poem's meaning is literally its pattern or integrity as a verbal structure. Its words cannot be separated and attached to sign-values: all possible sign-values of a word are absorbed into a complexity of verbal relationships.

The word's meaning is therefore, from the centripetal or inward-meaning point of view, variable or ambiguous, to use a term now familiar in criticism, a term which, significantly enough, is pejorative when applied to assertive writing. The word *wit* is said to be employed in Pope's *Essay on Criticism* in nine different senses.[18] In assertive writing, such a semantic theme with variations could produce nothing but hopeless muddle. In poetry, it indicates the ranges of meanings and contexts that a word may have. The poet does not equate a word with a meaning; he establishes the functions or powers of words. But when we look at the symbols of a poem as verbal *signs,* the poem appears in a different context altogether, and so do its narrative and meaning. Descriptively, a poem is not primarily a work of art, but primarily a *verbal* structure or set of representative words, to be classed with other verbal structures like books on gardening. In this context narrative means the relation of the order of words to events resembling the events in "life" outside; meaning means the relation of its pattern to a body of assertive propositions, and the conception of symbolism involved is the one which literature has in common, not with the arts, but with other structures in words.

---

[14] See Brooks (above, page 1036).

[15] James Joyce (1882–1941), Irish novelist, *A Portrait of the Artist as a Young Man.*

[16] A school of psychology emphasizing the perception of wholes, which take precedence over parts.

[17] Blake (above, page 447), *On Homer's Poetry.*

[18] Pope (above, page 298).

A considerable amount of abstraction enters at this stage. When we think of a poem's narrative as a description of events, we no longer think of the narrative as literally embracing every word and letter. We think rather of a sequence of gross events, of the obvious and externally striking elements in the word order. Similarly, we think of meaning as the kind of discursive meaning that a prose paraphrase of the poem might reproduce. Hence a parallel abstraction comes into the conception of symbolism. On the literal level, where the symbols are motifs, any unit whatever, down to the letters, may be relevant to our understanding. But only large and striking symbols are likely to be treated critically as signs: nouns and verbs, and phrases built up out of important words. Prepositions and conjunctions are almost pure connectives. A dictionary, which is primarily a table of conventional sign-values, can tell us nothing about such words unless we already understand them.

So literature in its descriptive context is a body of hypothetical verbal structures. The latter stand between the verbal structures that describe or arrange actual events, or histories, and those that describe or arrange actual ideas or represent physical objects, like the verbal structures of philosophy and science. The relation of the spatial to the conceptual world is one that we obviously cannot examine here; but from the point of view of literary criticism, descriptive writing and didactic writing, the representation of natural objects and of ideas, are simply two different branches of centrifugal meaning. We may use the word *plot* or *story* for the sequence of gross events, and the connection of story with history is indicated in its etymology. But it is more difficult to use *thought,* or even *thought-content,* for the representational aspect of pattern, or gross meaning, because *thought* also describes what we are here trying to distinguish it from. Such are the problems of a vocabulary of poetics.

The literal and the descriptive phases of symbolism are, of course, present in every work of literature. But we find (as we shall also find with the other phases) that each phase has a particularly close relationship to a certain kind of literature, and to a certain type of critical procedure as well. Literature deeply influenced by the descriptive aspect of symbolism is likely to tend toward the realistic in its narrative and toward the didactic or descriptive in its meaning. Its prevailing rhythm will be the prose of direct speech, and its main effort will be to give as clear and honest an impression of external reality as is possible with a hypothetical structure. In the documentary naturalism generally associated with such names as Zola and Dreiser,[19] literature goes about as far as representation of life, to be judged by its accuracy of description rather than by its integrity as a structure of words, as it could go and still remain literature. Beyond this point, the hypothetical or fictional element in literature would begin to dissolve. The limits of literary expression of this type are, of course, very wide, and nearly all the great empire of realistic poetry, drama, and prose fiction lies well within them. But we notice that the great age of documentary naturalism, the nineteenth century, was also the age of Romantic poetry, which, by concentrating on the process of imaginative creation, indicated a feeling of tension between the hypothetical and the assertive elements in literature.

This tension finally snaps off in the movement generally called *symbolisme,* a term which we expand here to take in the whole tradition which develops with a broad consistency through Mallarmé and Rimbaud to Valéry in France, Rilke in Germany, and Pound and Eliot[20] in England. In the theory of *symbolisme* we have the complement to extreme naturalism, an emphasis on the literal aspect of meaning, and a treatment of literature as centripetal verbal pattern, in which elements of direct or verifiable statement are subordinated to the integrity of that pattern. The conception of "pure" poetry,[21] or evocative verbal structure injured by assertive meaning, was a minor by-product of the same movement. The great strength of *symbolisme* was that it succeeded in isolating the hypothetical germ of literature, however limited it may have been in its earlier stages by its tendency to equate this isolation with the entire creative process. All its characteristics are solidly based on its conception of poetry as concerned with the centripetal aspect of meaning. Thus the achieving of an acceptable theory of literal meaning in criticism rests on a relatively recent development in literature.

Symbolisme, as expressed for instance in Mallarmé, maintains that the representational answer to the question, what does this mean? should not be pressed in reading poetry, for the poetic symbol means primarily itself in relation to the poem.[22] The unity of a poem, then, is best apprehended as a unity of mood, a mood being a phase of emotion, and emotion being the ordinary word for the state of mind directed toward the experiencing of pleasure or the contemplating of beauty. And as moods are not long sustained, literature, for *symbolisme,* is essentially discontinu-

---

[19] Zola (above, page 698); Theodore Dreiser (1871–1945), American novelist.

[20] Mallarmé (above, page 726); Arthur Rimbaud (1854–1891); Valéry (above, page 818); Rainer Maria Rilke (1875–1926); Ezra Pound (1885–1972); T. S. Eliot (above, page 806).

[21] Often associated with the anthology edited by George Moore (1852–1933), Irish novelist.

[22] Mallarmé (above, page 728).

ous, longer poems being held together only by the use of the grammatical structures more appropriate to descriptive writing. Poetic images do not state or point to anything, but, by pointing to each other, they suggest or evoke the mood which informs the poem. That is, they express or articulate the mood. The emotion is not chaotic or inarticulate: it merely would have remained so if it had not turned into a poem, and when it does so, it *is* the poem, not something else still behind it. Nevertheless the words suggest and evoke are appropriate, because in *symbolisme* the word does not echo the thing but other words, and hence the immediate impact *symbolisme* makes on the reader is that of incantation, a harmony of sounds and the sense of a growing richness of meaning unlimited by denotation.

Some philosophers who assume that all meaning is descriptive meaning tell us that, as a poem does not describe things rationally, it must be a description of an emotion. According to this the literal core of poetry would be a *cri de coeur,*[23] to use the elegant expression, the direct statement of a nervous organism confronted with something that seems to demand an emotional response, like a dog howling at the moon. *L'Allegro* and *Il Penseroso* would be respectively, according to this theory, elaborations of "I feel happy" and "I feel pensive."[24] We have found, however, that the real core of poetry is a subtle and elusive verbal pattern that avoids, and does not lead to, such bald statements. We notice too that in the history of literature the riddle, the oracle, the spell, and the kenning are more primitive than a presentation of subjective feelings. The critics who tell us that the basis of poetic expression is irony,[25] or a pattern of words that turns away from obvious (i.e., descriptive) meaning, are much closer to the facts of literary experience, at least on the literal level. The literary structure is ironic because "what it says" is always different in kind or degree from "what it means." In discursive writing what is said tends to approximate, ideally to become identified with, what is meant.

The criticism as well as the creation of literature reflects the distinction between literal and descriptive aspects of symbolism. The type of criticism associated with research and learned journals treats the poem as a verbal document, to be related as fully as possible to the history and the ideas that it reflects. The poem is most valuable to this kind of criticism when it is most explicit and descriptive, and when its core of imaginative hypothesis can be most easily separated. (Note that I am speaking of a kind of criticism, not of a kind of critic.) What is now called "new criticism,"[26] on the other hand, is largely criticism based on the conception of a poem as literally a poem. It studies the symbolism of a poem as an ambiguous structure of interlocking motifs; it sees the poetic pattern of meaning as a self-contained "texture," and it thinks of the external relations of a poem as being with the other arts, to be approached only with the Horatian warning of *favete linguis,*[27] and not with the historical or the didactic. The word *texture,* with its overtones of a complicated surface, is a most expressive one for this approach. These two aspects of criticism are often thought of as antithetical, as were, in the previous century, the corresponding groups of writers. They are of course complementary, not antithetical, but still the difference in emphasis between them is important to grasp before we go on to try to resolve the antithesis in a third phase of symbolism.

Formal Phase: Symbol as Image

We have now established a new sense of the term *literal meaning* for literary criticism, and have also assigned to literature, as one of its subordinate aspects of meaning, the ordinary descriptive meaning that works of literature share with all other structures of words. But it seems unsatisfactory to stop with this quizzical antithesis between delight and instruction, ironic withdrawal from reality and explicit connection with it. Surely, it will be said, we have overlooked the essential unity, in works of literature, expressed by the commonest of all critical terms, the word *form.* For the usual associations of *form*[28] seem to combine these apparently contradictory aspects. On the one hand, form implies what we have called the literal meaning, or unity of structure; on the other, it implies such complementary terms as content and matter, expressive of what it shares with external nature. The poem is not natural in form, but it relates itself naturally to nature, and so, to quote Sidney again, "doth grow in effect a second nature."[29]

Here we reach a more unified conception of narrative and meaning. Aristotle speaks of *mimesis praxeos,* an imitation of an action,[30] and it appears that he identifies this

---

[23] "Cry of the heart."

[24] Poems by John Milton (1608–1674), English poet.

[25] See, for example, Brooks (above, page 1043).

[26] [Frye] The account of literal meaning given here depends on I. A. Richards, Richard Blackmur, William Empson (ambiguity), Cleanth Brooks (literal irony), and John Crowe Ransom (texture) in particular [all represented above].

[27] "Don't speak badly." Horace (above, page 84).

[28] [Frye] For the theory of the formal phase, I have been considerably indebted to R. S. Crane [represented above], *The Languages of Criticism and the Structure of Poetry* (1953), as well as to *Critics and Criticism* (1952), edited by him.

[29] Sidney (above, page 188).

[30] Aristotle, *Poetics* VII, 2 (above, page 55).

mimesis praxeos with *mythos*. Aristotle's greatly abbreviated account here needs some reconstruction. Human action *(praxis)* is primarily imitated by histories, or verbal structures that describe specific and particular actions. A *mythos* is a secondary imitation of an action, which means, not that it is at two removes from reality, but that it describes typical actions, being more philosophical than history. Human thought *(theoria)* is primarily imitated by discursive writing, which makes specific and particular predications. A *dianoia* is a secondary imitation of thought, a *mimesis logou*, concerned with typical thought, with the images, metaphors, diagrams, and verbal ambiguities out of which specific ideas develop. Poetry is thus more historical than philosophy, more involved in images and examples. For it is clear that all verbal structures with meaning are verbal imitations of that elusive psychological and physiological process known as thought, a process stumbling through emotional entanglements, sudden irrational convictions, involuntary gleams of insight, rationalized prejudices, and blocks of panic and inertia, finally to reach a completely incommunicable intuition. Anyone who imagines that philosophy is not a verbal imitation of this process, but the process itself, has clearly not done much thinking.

The form of a poem, that to which every detail relates, is the same whether it is examined as stationary or as moving through the work from beginning to end, just as a musical composition has the same form when we study the score as it has when we listen to the performance. The *mythos* is the *dianoia* in movement; the *dianoia* is the *mythos* in stasis. One reason why we tend to think of literary symbolism solely in terms of meaning is that we have ordinarily no word for the *moving* body of imagery in a work of literature. The word *form* has normally two complementary terms, *matter* and *content,* and it perhaps makes some distinction whether we think of form as a shaping principle or as a containing one. As shaping principle, it may be thought of as narrative, organizing temporally what Milton called, in an age of more exact terminology, the "matter" of his song.[31] As containing principle it may be thought of as meaning, holding the poem together in a simultaneous structure.

The literary standards generally called "classical" or "neoclassical," which prevailed in Western Europe from the sixteenth to the eighteenth centuries, have the closest affinity with this formal phase. Order and clarity are particularly emphasized: order because of the sense of the importance of grasping a central form,[32] and clarity because of the feeling

that this form must not dissolve or withdraw into ambiguity, but must preserve a continuous relationship to the nature which is its own content. It is the attitude characteristic of "humanism" in the historical sense, an attitude marked on the one hand by a devotion to rhetoric and verbal craftsmanship, and on the other by a strong attachment to historical and ethical affairs.

Writers typical of the formal phase—Ben Jonson[33] for instance—are sure that they are in contact with reality and that they follow nature, yet the effect they produce is quite different from the descriptive realism of the nineteenth century, the difference being largely in the conception of imitation involved. In formal imitation, or Aristotelian mimesis, the work of art does not reflect external events and ideas, but exists between the example and the precept. Events and ideas are now aspects of its content, not external fields of observation. Historical fictions are not designed to give insight into a period of history, but are exemplary; they illustrate action, and are ideal in the sense of manifesting the universal form of human action. (The vagaries of language make *exemplary* the adjective for both example and precept.) Shakespeare and Jonson were keenly interested in history, yet their plays seem timeless: Jane Austen[34] did not write historical fiction, yet, because she represents a later and more externalized method of following nature, the picture she gives of Regency society has a specific historical value.

A poem, according to Hamlet, who, though speaking of action, is following a conventional Renaissance line of poetics, holds the mirror up to nature.[35] We should be careful to notice what this implies: the poem is not itself a mirror. It does not merely reproduce a shadow of nature; it causes nature to be reflected in its containing form. When the formal critic comes to deal with symbols, therefore, the units he isolates are those which show an analogy of proportion between the poem and the nature which it imitates. The symbol in this aspect may best be called the image. We are accustomed to associate the term *nature* primarily with the external physical world, and hence we tend to think of an image as primarily a replica of a natural object. But of course both words are far more inclusive: nature takes in the conceptual or intelligible order as well as the spatial one, and what is usually called an idea may be a poetic image also.

One could hardly find a more elementary critical principle than the fact that the events of a literary fiction are not real

---

[31] In the preface to his *Paradise Lost.*
[32] The phrase "central form" is employed by Reynolds (above, page 395) and complained about, with reservations, by Blake (above, page 451).
[33] Ben Jonson (1572–1637), English dramatist.
[34] Jane Austen (1775–1817), English novelist.
[35] *Hamlet* III, ii, 19.

but hypothetical events. For some reason it has never been consistently understood that the ideas of literature are not real propositions, but verbal formulas which imitate real propositions. The *Essay on Man* does not expound a system of metaphysical optimism founded on the chain of being: it uses such a system as a model on which to construct a series of hypothetical statements which are more or less useless as propositions, but inexhaustibly rich and suggestive when read in their proper context as epigrams. As epigrams, as solid, resonant, centripetal verbal structures, they may apply pointedly to millions of human situations which have nothing to do with metaphysical optimism. Wordsworth's pantheism, Dante's Thomism, Lucretius' Epicureanism, all have to be read in the same way, as do Gibbon or Macaulay or Hume when they are read for style instead of subject matter.[36]

Formal criticism begins with an examination of the imagery of a poem, with a view to bringing out its distinctive pattern. The recurring or most frequently repeated images form the tonality, so to speak, and the modulating, episodic and isolated images relate themselves to this in a hierarchic structure which is the critical analogy to the proportions of the poem itself. Every poem has its peculiar spectroscopic band of imagery, caused by the requirements of its genre, the predilections of its author, and countless other factors. In *Macbeth,* for instance, the images of blood and of sleeplessness have a thematic importance, as is very natural for a tragedy of murder and remorse. Hence in the line "Making the green one red,"[37] the colors are of different thematic intensities. Green is used incidentally and for contrast; red, being closer to the *key* of the play as a whole, is more like the repetition of a tonic chord in music. The opposite would be true of the contrast between red and green in Marvell's *The Garden.*[38]

The form of the poem is the same whether it is studied as narrative or as meaning, hence the structure of imagery in *Macbeth* may be studied as a pattern derived from the text, or as a rhythm of repetition falling on an audience's ear. There is a vague notion that the latter method produces a simpler result, and may therefore be used as a common-sense corrective to the niggling subtleties of textual study. The analogy of music again may be helpful. The average audience at a symphony knows very little about sonata form, and misses practically all the subtleties detected by an analysis of the score; yet those subtleties are really there, and as the audience can hear everything that is being played,

it gets them all as part of a linear experience; the awareness is less conscious, but not less real. The same is true of the response to the imagery of a highly concentrated poetic drama.

The analysis of recurrent imagery is, of course, one of the chief techniques of rhetorical or "new" criticism as well: the difference is that formal criticism, after attaching the imagery to the central form of the poem, renders an aspect of the form into the propositions of discursive writing. Formal criticism, in other words, is commentary, and commentary is the process of translating into explicit or discursive language what is implicit in the poem. Good commentary naturally does not read ideas into the poem; it reads and translates what is there, and the evidence that it is there is offered by the study of the structure of imagery with which it begins. The sense of tact, of the desirability of not pushing a point of interpretation "too far," is derived from the fact that the proportioning of emphasis in criticism should normally bear a rough analogy to the proportioning of emphasis in the poem.

The failure to make, in practice, the most elementary of all distinctions in literature, the distinction between fiction and fact, hypothesis and assertion, imaginative and discursive writing, produces what in criticism has been called the "intentional fallacy,"[39] the notion that the poet has a primary intention of conveying meaning to a reader, and that the first duty of a critic is to recapture that intention. The word *intention* is analogical; it implies a relation between two things, usually a conception and an act. Some related terms show this duality even more clearly: to *aim at* something means that a target and a missile are being brought into alignment. Hence such terms properly belong only to discursive writing, where the correspondence of a verbal pattern with what it describes is of primary importance. But a poet's primary concern is to produce a work of art, and hence his intention can only be expressed by some kind of tautology.

In other words, a poet's intention is centripetally directed. It is directed towards putting words together, not towards aligning words with meanings. If we had the privilege of Gulliver in Glubbdubdrib[40] to call up the ghost of, say, Shakespeare, to ask him what he meant by such and such a passage, we could only get, with maddening iteration, the same answer: "I meant it to form part of the play." One may pursue the centripetal intention as far as genre, as a poet intends to produce, not simply a poem, but a certain kind of poem. In reading, for instance, *Zuleika Dobson*[41] as a description of life in Oxford, we should be well advised to al-

---

[36] Wordsworth (above, page 481); Titus Lucretius Carus (c. 99–c. 55 B.C.), Roman poet; Thomas Babington Macauley (1800–1859), English historian.
[37] *Macbeth* II, ii, 63.
[38] Andrew Marvell (1621–1678), English poet.

[39] See Wimsatt and Beardsley (above, page 1027).
[40] A place in Jonathan Swift's (1667–1745), *Gulliver's Travels.*
[41] (1911), by Max Beerbohm (1872–1956).

low for ironic intention. One has to assume, as an essential heuristic axiom, that the work as produced constitutes the definitive record of the writer's intention. For many of the flaws which an inexperienced critic thinks he detects, the answer "But it's supposed to be that way" is sufficient. All other statements of intention, however fully documented, are suspect. The poet may change his mind or mood; he may have intended one thing and done another, and then rationalized what he did. (A cartoon in a *New Yorker* of some years back hit off this last problem beautifully: it depicted a sculptor gazing at a statue he had just made and remarking to a friend: "Yes, the head is too large. When I put it in exhibition I shall call it 'The Woman with the Large Head.' ") If intention is still thought to be apparent in the poem itself, the poem is being regarded as incomplete, like a freshman's essay where the reader has continually to speculate about what the author may have had in his mind. If the author has been dead for centuries, such speculation cannot get us very far, however irresistibly it may suggest itself.

What the poet meant to say, then, is, literally, the poem itself; what he meant to say in any given passage is, in its literal meaning, part of the poem. But literal meaning, we have seen, is variable and ambiguous. The reader may be dissatisfied with the ghost of Shakespeare's answer: he may feel that Shakespeare, unlike, say, Mallarmé, is a poet he can trust, and that he also meant his passage to be intelligible in itself (i.e., have descriptive or rephrasable meaning). Doubtless he did, but the relationship of the passage to the rest of the play creates myriads of new meanings for it. Just as a vivid sketch of a cat by a good draftsman may contain in a few crisp lines the entire feline experience of everyone who looks at it, so the powerfully constructed pattern of words that we know as *Hamlet* may contain an amount of meaning which the vast and constantly growing library of criticism on the play cannot begin to exhaust. Commentary, which translates the implicit into the explicit, can only isolate the aspect of meaning, large or small, which is appropriate or interesting for certain readers to grasp at a certain time. Such translation is an activity with which the poet has very little to do. The relation in bulk between commentary and a sacred book, such as the Bible or the Vedic hymns, is even more striking, and indicates that when a poetic structure attains a certain degree of concentration or social recognition, the amount of commentary it will carry is infinite. This fact is in itself no more incredible than the fact that a scientist can state a law illustrated by more phenomena than he could ever observe or count, and there is no occasion for wondering, like the yokels in Goldsmith,[42] how

one small poet's head can carry the amount of wit, wisdom, instruction, and significance that Shakespeare and Dante have given the world.

Still there is a genuine mystery in art, and a real place for wonder. In *Sartor Resartus* Carlyle distinguishes extrinsic symbols,[43] like the cross or the national flag, which are without value in themselves but are signs or indicators of something existential, from intrinsic symbols, which include works of art. On this basis we may distinguish two kinds of mystery. (A third kind, the mystery which is a puzzle, a problem to be solved and annihilated, belongs to discursive thought, and has little to do with the arts, except in matters of technique.) The mystery of the unknown or unknowable essence is an extrinsic mystery, which involves art only when art is also made illustrative of something else, as religious art is to the person concerned primarily with worship. But the intrinsic mystery is that which remains a mystery in itself no matter how fully known it is, and hence is not a mystery separated from what is known. The mystery in the greatness of *King Lear* or *Macbeth* comes not from concealment but from revelation, not from something unknown or unknowable in the work, but from something unlimited in it.

It could be said, of course, that poetry is the product not only of a deliberate and voluntary act of consciousness, like discursive writing, but of processes which are subconscious or preconscious or half-conscious or unconscious as well, whatever psychological metaphor one prefers. It takes a great deal of will power to write poetry, but part of that will power must be employed in trying to relax the will, so making a large part of one's writing involuntary. This is no doubt true, and it is also true that poetic technique, like all technique, is a habitual, and therefore an increasingly unconscious, skill. But I feel that literary data are in the long run only explicable within criticism, and I am reluctant to explain literary facts by psychological clichés. Still, it seems now almost impossible to avoid the term *creative*, with all the biological analogies it suggests, when speaking of the arts. And creation, whether of God, man, or nature, seems to be an activity whose only intention is to abolish intention, to eliminate final dependence on or relation to something else, to destroy the shadow that falls between itself and its conception.

One wishes that literary criticism had a Samuel Butler[44] to formulate some of the paradoxes involved in this parallel between the work of art and the organism. We can

---

[42] Oliver Goldsmith (1730?–1774), Anglo-Irish writer.

[43] Thomas Carlyle (1795–1881), English writer.
[44] Samuel Butler (1612–1680), English poet and satirist.

describe objectively what happens when a tulip blooms in spring and a chrysanthemum in autumn, but we cannot describe it from the inside of the plant, except by metaphors derived from human consciousness and ascribed to some agent like God or nature or environment or *élan vital,* or to the plant itself. It is projected metaphor to say that a flower "knows" when it is time for it to bloom, and of course to say that "nature knows" is merely to import a faded mother-goddess cult into biology. I can well understand that in their own field biologists would find such teleological metaphors both unnecessary and confusing, a fallacy of misplaced concreteness. The same would be true of criticism to the extent that criticism has to deal with imponderables other than consciousness or logically directed will. If one critic says that another has discovered a mass of subtleties in a poet of which that poet was probably quite unconscious, the phrase points up the biological analogy. A snowflake is probably quite unconscious of forming a crystal, but what it does may be worth study even if we are willing to leave its inner mental processes alone.

It is not often realized that all commentary is allegorical interpretation, an attaching of ideas to the structure of poetic imagery. The instant that any critic permits himself to make a genuine comment about a poem (e.g., "In *Hamlet* Shakespeare appears to be portraying the tragedy of irresolution") he has begun to allegorize. Commentary thus looks at literature as, in its formal phase, a potential allegory of events and ideas. The relation of such commentary to poetry itself is the source of the contrast which was developed by several critics of the Romantic period between *symbolism* and *allegory*,[45] symbolism here being used in the sense of thematically significant imagery. The contrast is between a "concrete" approach to symbols which begins with images of actual things and works outward to ideas and propositions, and an "abstract" approach which begins with the idea and then tries to find a concrete image to represent it.[46] This distinction is valid enough in itself, but it has deposited a large terminal moraine of confusion in modern criticism, largely because the term *allegory* is very loosely employed for a great variety of literary phenomena.

We have actual allegory when a poet explicitly indicates the relationship of his images to examples and precepts, and so tries to indicate how a commentary on him should proceed. A writer is being allegorical whenever it is clear that he is saying "by this I *also (allos)* mean that." If this seems to be done continuously, we may say, cautiously,

that what he is writing "is" an allegory. In *The Faerie Queene*,[47] for instance, the narrative systematically refers to historical examples and the meaning to moral precepts, besides doing their own work in the poem. Allegory, then, is a contrapuntal technique, like canonical imitation in music. Dante, Spenser, Tasso, and Bunyan use it throughout: their works are the masses and oratorios of literature. Ariosto, Goethe, Ibsen, Hawthorne[48] write in a *freistimmige* style in which allegory may be picked up and dropped again at pleasure. But even continuous allegory is still a structure of images, not of disguised ideas, and commentary has to proceed with it exactly as it does with all other literature, trying to see what precepts and examples are suggested by the imagery as a whole.

The commenting critic is often prejudiced against allegory without knowing the real reason, which is that continuous allegory prescribes the direction of his commentary, and so restricts its freedom. Hence he often urges us to read Spenser and Bunyan, for example, for the story alone and let the allegory go, meaning by that that he regards his own type of commentary as more interesting. Or else he will frame a definition of allegory that will exclude the poems he likes. Such a critic is often apt to treat all allegory as though it were naive allegory, or the translation of ideas into images.

Naive allegory is a disguised form of discursive writing, and belongs chiefly to educational literature on an elementary level: schoolroom moralities, devotional exempla, local pageants, and the like. Its basis is the habitual or customary ideas fostered by education and ritual, and its normal form is that of transient spectacle. Under the excitement of a particular occasion familiar ideas suddenly become sense experiences, and vanish with the occasion. The defeat of Sedition and Discord by Sound Government and Encouragement of Trade would be the right sort of theme for a pageant designed only to entertain a visiting monarch for half an hour. The apparatus of "mass media" and "audiovisual aids" plays a similar allegorical role in contemporary education. Because of this basis in spectacle, naive allegory has its center of gravity in the pictorial arts and is most successful as art when recognized to be a form of occasional wit, as it is in the political cartoon. The more solemn and permanent naive allegories of official murals and statuary show a marked tendency to date.

---

[45] See Blake (above, page 458) and Coleridge (above, page 519).
[46] See Vico (above, page 313).

[47] By Edmund Spenser (1552?–1599).
[48] Tasso (above, page 226); John Bunyan (1628–1688), *Pilgrim's Progress* (1666); Ludovico Ariosto (1474–1533), Italian poet, *Orlando Furioso* (1532); Johann Wolfgang Goethe (1749–1832), German writer; Henrik Ibsen (1828–1906), Norwegian dramatist; Nathaniel Hawthorne (1804–1864), American novelist.

At one extreme of commentary, then, there is the naive allegory so anxious to make its own allegorical points that it has no real literary or hypothetical center. When I say that naive allegory *dates,* I mean that any allegory which resists a primary analysis of imagery—that is, an allegory which is simply discursive writing with an illustrative image or two stuck into it—will have to be treated less as literature than as a document in the history of ideas. When the author of II Esdras, for instance, introduces an allegorical vision of an eagle, and then says, "Behold, on the right side there arose one feather, which reigned over all the earth," it is clear that he is not sufficiently interested in his eagle as a poetic image to remain within the normal boundaries of literary expression. The basis of poetic expression is the metaphor, and the basis of naive allegory is the mixed metaphor.

Within the boundaries of literature we find a kind of sliding scale, ranging from the most explicitly allegorical, consistent with being literature at all, at one extreme, to the most elusive, antiexplicit and antiallegorical at the other. First we meet the continuous allegories, like *The Pilgrim's Progress* and *The Faerie Queene,* and then the free-style allegories just mentioned. Next come the poetic structures with a large and insistent doctrinal interest, in which the internal fictions are exempla, like the epics of Milton. Then we have, in the exact center, works in which the structure of imagery, however suggestive, has an implicit relation only to events and ideas, and which includes the bulk of Shakespeare. Below this, poetic imagery begins to recede from example and precept and become increasingly ironic and paradoxical. Here the modern critic begins to feel more at home, the reason being that this type is more consistent with the modern literal view of art, the sense of the poem as withdrawn from explicit statement.

Several types of this ironic and antiallegorical imagery are familiar. One is the typical symbol of the metaphysical school of the Baroque period, the "conceit" or deliberately strained union of normally disparate things. The paradoxical techniques of metaphysical poetry are based on a sense of the breakdown of the internal relation of art and nature into an external one. Another is the substitute image of *symbolisme,* part of a technique for suggesting or evoking things and avoiding the explicit naming of them. Still another is the kind of image described by Mr. Eliot as an objective correlative,[49] the image that sets up an inward focus of emotion in poetry and at the same time substitutes itself for an idea. Still another, closely related to if not identical with the objective correlative, is the heraldic symbol, the central emblematic image which comes most readily to mind when we think of the word *symbol* in modern literature. We think, for example, of Hawthorne's scarlet letter, Melville's white whale, James's golden bowl, or Virginia Woolf's lighthouse.[50] Such an image differs from the image of the formal allegory in that there is no continuous relationship between art and nature. In contrast to the allegorical symbols of Spenser, for instance, the heraldic emblematic image is in a paradoxical and ironic relation to both narrative and meaning. As a unit of meaning, it arrests the narrative; as a unit of narrative, it perplexes the meaning. It combines the qualities of Carlyle's intrinsic symbol with significance in itself, and the extrinsic symbol which points quizzically to something else. It is a technique of symbolism which is based on a strong sense of a lurking antagonism between the literal and the descriptive aspects of symbols, the same antagonism that made Mallarmé and Zola so extreme a contrast in nineteenth-century literature.

Below this we run into still more indirect techniques, such as private association, symbolism intended not to be fully understood, the deliberate spoofing of Dadaism,[51] and kindred signs of another approaching boundary of literary expression. We should try to keep this whole range of possible commentary clearly in mind, so as to correct the perspective both of the medieval and Renaissance critics who assumed that all major poetry should be treated as far as possible as continuous allegory, and of the modern ones who maintain that poetry is essentially antiallegorical and paradoxical.

What we have now is a conception of literature as a body of hypothetical creations which is not necessarily involved in the worlds of truth and fact, not necessarily withdrawn from them, but which may enter into any kind of relationship to them, ranging from the most to the least explicit. We are strongly reminded of the relationship of mathematics to the natural sciences. Mathematics, like literature, proceeds hypothetically and by internal consistency, not descriptively and by outward fidelity to nature. When it is applied to external facts, it is not its truth but its applicability that is being verified. As I seem to have fastened on the cat for my semantic emblem in this essay, I note that this point comes out sharply in the discussion between Yeats and Sturge Moore over the problem of Ruskin's cat, the animal that was picked up and flung out of a window by Ruskin al-

---

[49] See Eliot (above, page 806).

[50] Herman Melville (1819–1891), American novelist, *Moby Dick* (1851); Henry James (1843–1916), American novelist, *The Golden Bowl* (1904); Virginia Woolf (1882–1941), English novelist, *To the Lighthouse* (1927).
[51] Dadaism, nihilistic artistic movement, 1916 ff.

though it was not there.[52] Anyone measuring his mind against an external reality has to fall back on an axiom of faith. The distinction between an empirical fact and an illusion is not a rational distinction, and cannot be logically proved. It is "proved" only by the practical and emotional necessity of assuming the distinction. For the poet, qua poet, this necessity does not exist, and there is no poetic reason why he should either assert or deny the existence of any cat, real or Ruskinian.

The conception of art as having a relation to reality which is neither direct nor negative, but potential, finally resolves the dichotomy between delight and instruction, the style and the message. "Delight" is not readily distinguishable from pleasure, and hence opens the way to that aesthetic hedonism we glanced at in the introduction, the failure to distinguish personal and impersonal aspects of valuation. The traditional theory of catharsis implies that the emotional response to art is not the raising of an actual emotion, but the raising and casting out of actual emotion on a wave of something else.[53] We may call this something else, perhaps, exhilaration or exuberance: the vision of something liberated from experience, the response kindled in the reader by the transmutation of experience into mimesis, of life into art, of routine into play. At the center of liberal education something surely ought to get liberated. The metaphor of creation suggests the parallel image of birth, the emergence of a newborn organism into independent life. The ecstasy of creation and its response produce, on one level of creative effort, the hen's cackle; on another, the quality that the Italian critics called *sprezzatura* and that Hoby's translation of Castiglione[54] calls "recklessness," the sense of buoyancy or release that accompanies perfect discipline, when we can no longer know the dancer from the dance.

It is impossible to understand the effect of what Milton called "gorgeous tragedy" as producing a real emotion of gloom or sorrow. Aeschylus's[55] *The Persians* and Shakespeare's *Macbeth* are certainly tragedies, but they are associated respectively with the victory of Salamis and the accession of James I,[56] both occasions of national rejoicing. Some critics carry the theory of real emotion over into Shakespeare himself, and talk about a "tragic period," in

which he is supposed to have felt dismal from 1600 to 1608. Most people, if they had just finished writing a play as good as *King Lear,* would be in a mood of exhilaration, and while we have no right to ascribe this mood of Shakespeare, it is surely the right way to describe our response to the play. On the other hand, it comes as something of a shock to realize that the blinding of Gloucester is primarily entertainment, the more so as the pleasure we get from it obviously has nothing to do with sadism. If any literary work is emotionally "depressing," there is something wrong with either the writing or the reader's response. Art seems to produce a kind of buoyancy which, though often called pleasure, as it is for instance by Wordsworth, is something more inclusive than pleasure. "Exuberance is beauty," said Blake.[57] That seems to me a practically definitive solution, not only of the minor question of what beauty is, but of the far more important problem of what the conceptions of catharsis and ecstasis really mean.

Such exuberance is, of course, as much intellectual as it is emotional: Blake himself was willing to define poetry as "allegory addressed to the intellectual powers."[58] We live in a world of threefold external compulsion: of compulsion on action, or law; of compulsion on thinking, or fact; of compulsion on feeling, which is the characteristic of all pleasure whether it is produced by the *Paradiso* or by an ice cream soda. But in the world of imagination a fourth power, which contains morality, beauty, and truth but is never subordinated to them, rises free of all their compulsions. The work of imagination presents us with a vision, not of the personal greatness of the poet, but of something impersonal and far greater: the vision of a decisive act of spiritual freedom, the vision of the recreation of man.

Mythical Phase: Symbol as Archetype

In the formal phase the poem belongs neither to the class "art," nor to the class "verbal": it represents its own class. There are thus two aspects to its form. In the first place, it is unique, a *techne* or artifact, with its own peculiar structure of imagery, to be examined by itself without immediate reference to the other things like it. The critic here begins with poems, not with a prior conception or definition of poetry. In the second place, the poem is one of a class of similar forms. Aristotle knows that *Oedipus Tyrannus*[59] is in one sense not like any other tragedy, but he also knows that it

---

[52][Frye] See *W. B. Yeats and T. Sturge Moore: Their Correspondence, 1901–1937* (1953).

[53] See Aristotle (above, page 55).

[54] Baldassare Castiglione (1478–1529), Italian writer, *Book of the Courtier* (1528).

[55] Aeschylus (525–456 B.C.), Greek dramatist.

[56] The Battle of Salamis, where the Greeks defeated the Persians in a sea battle (480 B.C.); James I reigned as king of Scotland from 1406 to 1437.

[57] Blake (above, page 454).

[58] Blake (above, page 448).

[59] By Sophocles (c. 496–406 B.C.), Greek dramatist.

belongs to the class called tragedy. We, who have experienced Shakespeare and Racine,[60] can add the corollary that tragedy is something bigger than a phase of Greek drama. We may also find tragedy in literary works which are not dramas. To understand what tragedy is, therefore, takes us beyond the merely historical into the question of what an aspect of literature as a whole is. With this idea of the external relations of a poem with other poems, two considerations in criticism for the first time become important: convention and genre.[61]

The study of genres is based on analogies in form. It is characteristic of documentary and historical criticism that it cannot deal with such analogies. It can trace influence with great plausibility, whether it exists or not, but confronted with a tragedy of Shakespeare and a tragedy of Sophocles, to be compared solely because they are both tragedies, the historical critic has to confine himself to general reflections about the seriousness of life. Similarly, nothing is more striking in rhetorical criticism than the absence of any consideration of genre: the rhetorical critic analyzes what is in front of him without much regard to whether it is a play, a lyric, or a novel. He may in fact even assert that there are no genres in literature. That is because he is concerned with his structure simply as a work of art, not as an artifact with a possible function. But there are many analogies in literature apart altogether from sources and influences (many of which, of course, are not analogous at all) and noticing such analogies forms a large part of our actual experience of literature, whatever its role so far in criticism.

The central principle of the formal phase, that a poem is an imitation of nature, is, though a perfectly sound one, still a principle which isolates the individual poem. And it is clear that any poem may be examined, not only as an imitation of nature, but as an imitation of other poems. Virgil discovered, according to Pope,[62] that following nature was ultimately the same thing as following Homer. Once we think of a poem in relation to other poems, as a unit of poetry, we can see that the study of genres has to be founded on the study of convention. The criticism which can deal with such matters will have to be based on that aspect of symbolism which relates poems to one another, and it will choose, as its main field of operations, the symbols that link poems together. Its ultimate object is to consider, not simply *a* poem as an imitation of nature, but the order of nature as a whole as imitated by a corresponding order of words.

All art is equally conventionalized, but we do not ordinarily notice this fact unless we are unaccustomed to the convention. In our day the conventional element in literature is elaborately disguised by a law of copyright pretending that every work of art is an invention distinctive enough to be patented. Hence the conventionalizing forces of modern literature—the way, for instance, that an editor's policy and the expectation of his readers combine to conventionalize what appears in a magazine—often go unrecognized. Demonstrating the debt of A to B is merely scholarship if A is dead, but a proof of moral delinquency if A is alive. This state of things makes it difficult to appraise a literature which includes Chaucer, much of whose poetry is translated or paraphrased from others; Shakespeare, whose plays sometimes follow their sources almost verbatim; and Milton, who asked for nothing better than to steal as much as possible out of the Bible. It is not only the inexperienced reader who looks for a *residual* originality in such works. Most of us tend to think of a poet's real achievement as distinct from, or even contrasted with, the achievement present in what he stole, and we are thus apt to concentrate on peripheral rather than on central critical facts. For instance, the central greatness of *Paradise Regained,* as a poem, is not the greatness of the rhetorical decorations that Milton added to his source, but the greatness of the theme itself, which Milton *passes on* to the reader from his source. This conception of the great poet's being entrusted with the great theme was elementary enough to Milton, but violates most of the low mimetic prejudices about creation that most of us are educated in.

The underestimating of convention appears to be a result of, may even be a part of, the tendency, marked from Romantic times on, to think of the individual as ideally prior to his society. The view opposed to this, that the new baby is conditioned by a hereditary and environmental kinship to a society which already exists, has, whatever doctrines may be inferred from it, the initial advantage of being closer to the facts it deals with. The literary consequence of the second view is that the new poem, like the new baby, is born into an already existing order of words, and is typical of the structure of poetry to which it is attached. The new baby *is* his own society appearing once again as a unit of individuality, and the new poem has a similar relation to its poetic society.

It is hardly possible to accept a critical view which confuses the original with the aboriginal, and imagines that a "creative" poet sits down with a pencil and some blank pa-

---

[60] Jean Racine (1639–1699), French dramatist.

[61] [Frye] The conception of the autonomy of form in art is essential to the argument of Andre Malraux, *The Voices of Silence,* translated by Stuart Gilbert (1953). In modern English criticism the archetypal approach is highly developed in both theory and practice. In theory the books of Maud Bodkin, Kenneth Burke, Gaston Bachelard, Francis Fergusson, and Philip Wheelwright are of obvious and exceptional usefulness. See the excellent bibliographies in René Wellek and Austin Warren, *Theory of Literature* (1942), Chapter 15.

[62] Pope, *Essay on Criticism* (above, page 299). See also Frye's essay "Nature and Homer" in his *Fables of Identity.*

per and eventually produces a new poem in a special act of creation *ex nihilo*. Human beings do not create in that way. Just as a new scientific discovery manifests something that was already latent in the order of nature, and at the same time is logically related to the total structure of the existing science, so the new poem manifests something that was already latent in the order of words. Literature may have life, reality, experience, nature, imaginative truth, social conditions, or what you will for its *content;* but literature itself is not made out of these things. Poetry can only be made out of other poems; novels out of other novels. Literature shapes itself, and is not shaped externally: the *forms* of literature can no more exist outside literature than the forms of sonata and fugue and rondo can exist outside music.

All this was much clearer before the assimilation of literature to private enterprise concealed so many of the facts of criticism. When Milton sat down to write a poem about Edward King,[63] he did not ask himself: "What can I find to say about King?" but "How does poetry require that such a subject should be treated?" The notion that convention shows a lack of feeling, and that a poet attains "sincerity" (which usually means articulate emotion) by disregarding it, is opposed to all the facts of literary experience and history. The origin of this notion is, again, the view that poetry is a description of emotion, and that its "literal" meaning is an assertion about the emotions held by the individual poet. But any serious study of literature soon shows that the real difference between the original and the imitative poet is simply that the former is more profoundly imitative. Originality returns to the origins of literature, as radicalism returns to its roots. The remark of Mr. Eliot that a good poet is more likely to steal than to imitate[64] affords a more balanced view of convention, as it indicates that the poem is specifically involved with other poems, not vaguely with such abstractions as tradition or style. The copyright law, and the mores attached to it, make it difficult for a modern novelist to steal anything except his title from the rest of literature: hence it is often only in such titles as *For Whom the Bell Tolls, The Grapes of Wrath,* or *The Sound and the Fury,*[65] that we can clearly see how much impersonal dignity and richness of association an author can gain by the communism of convention.

As with other products of divine activity, the father of a poem is much more difficult to identify than the mother. That the mother is always nature, the realm of the objective considered as a field of communication, no serious criticism can ever deny. But as long as the father of a poem is assumed to be the poet himself, we have once again failed to distinguish literature from discursive verbal structures. The discursive writer writes as an act of conscious will, and that conscious will, along with the symbolic system he employs for it, is set over against the body of things he is describing. But the poet, who writes creatively rather than deliberately, is not the father of his poem; he is at best a midwife, or, more accurately still, the womb of Mother Nature herself: her privates he, so to speak. The fact that revision is possible, that a poet can make changes in a poem not because he likes them better but because they are better, shows clearly that the poet has to give birth to the poem as it passes through his mind. He is responsible for delivering it in as uninjured a state as possible, and if the poem is alive, it is equally anxious to be rid of him, and screams to be cut loose from all the navel-strings and feeding-tubes of his ego.

The true father or shaping spirit of the poem is the form of the poem itself, and this form is a manifestation of the universal spirit of poetry, the "only begetter" of Shakespeare's sonnets who was not Shakespeare himself, much less that depressing ghost Mr. W. H.,[66] but Shakespeare's subject, the master-mistress of his passion. When a poet speaks of the *internal* spirit which shapes the poem, he is apt to drop the traditional appeal to female Muses and think of himself as in a feminine, or at least receptive, relation to some god or lord, whether Apollo, Dionysus, Eros, Christ, or (as in Milton) the Holy Spirit. *Est deus in nobis,* Ovid says: in modern times we may compare Nietzsche's remarks about his inspiration in *Ecce Homo.*[67]

The problem of convention is the problem of how art can be communicable, for literature is clearly as much a technique of communication as assertive verbal structures are. Poetry, taken as a whole, is no longer simply an aggregate of artifacts imitating nature, but one of the activities of human artifice taken as a whole. If we may use the word "civilization" for this, we may say that our fourth phase looks at poetry as one of the techniques of civilization. It is concerned, therefore, with the social aspect of poetry, with poetry as the focus of a community. The symbol in this phase is the communicable unit, to which I give the name archetype: that is, a typical or recurring image. I mean by an *archetype* a symbol which connects one poem with another and thereby helps to unify and integrate our literary experience. And as the archetype is the communicable symbol,

---

[63] Edward King, for whom Milton wrote the elegy *Lycidas*.
[64] [Frye] In his essay on Philip Massinger.
[65] By Ernest Hemingway (1889–1961), John Steinbeck (1902–1968), and William Faulkner (1897–1962), respectively, American novelists.

[66] The unknown person to whom Shakespeare's sonnets are dedicated.
[67] Nietzsche (above, page 686).

archetypal criticism is primarily concerned with literature as a social fact and as a mode of communication. By the study of conventions and genres, it attempts to fit poems into the body of poetry as a whole.

The repetition of certain common images of physical nature like the sea or the forest in a large number of poems cannot in itself be called even *coincidence,* which is the name we give to a piece of design when we cannot find a use for it. But it does indicate a certain unity in the nature that poetry imitates, and in the communicating activity of which poetry forms part. Because of the larger communicative context of education, it is possible for a story about the sea to be archetypal, to make a profound imaginative impact, on a reader who has never been out of Saskatchewan. And when pastoral images are deliberately employed in *Lycidas,* for instance, merely because they are conventional, we can see that the convention of the pastoral makes us assimilate these images to other parts of literary experience.

We think first of the pastoral's descent from Theocritus,[68] where the pastoral elegy first appears as a literary adaptation of the ritual of the Adonis lament,[69] and through Theocritus to Virgil and the whole pastoral tradition to *The Shepheardes Calender*[70] and beyond to *Lycidas* itself. Then we think of the intricate pastoral symbolism of the Bible and the Christian church, of Abel and the twenty-third psalm and Christ the Good Shepherd, of the ecclesiastical overtones of *pastor* and *flock,* and of the link between the Classical and Christian traditions in Virgil's Messianic eclogue.[71] Then we think of the extensions of pastoral symbolism into Sidney's *Arcadia, The Faerie Queene,* Shakespeare's forest comedies, and the like; then of the post-Miltonic development of pastoral elegy in Shelley, Arnold, Whitman, and Dylan Thomas;[72] perhaps too of pastoral conventions in painting and music. In short, we can get a whole liberal education simply by picking up one conventional poem and following its archetypes as they stretch out into the rest of literature. An avowedly conventional poem like *Lycidas* urgently demands the kind of criticism that will absorb it into the study of literature as a whole, and this activity is expected to begin at once, with the first cultivated reader. Here we have a situation in literature more like that of mathematics or science, where the work of genius is assimilated to the whole subject so

quickly that one hardly notices the difference between creative and critical activity.

If we do not accept the archetypal or conventional element in the imagery that links one poem with another, it is impossible to get any systematic mental training out of the reading of literature alone. But if we add to our desire to know literature a desire to know how we know it, we shall find that expanding images into conventional archetypes of literature is a process that takes place unconsciously in all our reading. A symbol like the sea or the heath cannot remain within Conrad or Hardy:[73] it is bound to expand over many works into an archetypal symbol of literature as a whole. Moby Dick cannot remain in Melville's novel: he is absorbed into our imaginative experience of leviathans and dragons of the deep from the Old Testament onward. And what is true for the reader is a fortiori true of the poet, who learns very quickly that there is no singing school for his soul except the study of the monuments of its own magnificence.[74]

In each phase of symbolism there is a point at which the critic is compelled to break away from the range of the poet's own knowledge. Thus the historical or documentary critic has sooner or later to call Dante a "medieval" poet, a notion unknown and unintelligible to Dante. In archetypal criticism, the poet's conscious knowledge is considered only so far as the poet may allude to or imitate other poets ("sources") or make a deliberate use of a convention. Beyond that, the poet's control over his poem stops with the poem. Only the archetypal critic can be concerned with its relationship to the rest of literature. But here again we have to distinguish between explicitly conventionalized literature, such as *Lycidas,* where the poet himself starts us off by referring to Theocritus, Virgil, Renaissance pastoralists, and the Bible, and literature which conceals or ignores its conventional links. The conception of copyright and the revolutionary nature of the low mimetic view of creation also extends to a general unwillingness on the part of authors of the copyright age to have their imagery studied conventionally, and in dealing with this period, most archetypes have to be established by critical inspection alone.

To give a random example, one very common convention of the nineteenth-century novel is the use of two heroines, one dark and one light. The dark one is as a rule passionate, haughty, plain, foreign or Jewish, and in some way associated with the undesirable or with some kind of forbidden fruit like incest. When the two are involved with the same hero, the plot usually has to get rid of the dark one or

---

[68] Theocritus (fl. c. 270 B.C.), Greek poet.
[69] [Frye] This phrase should be understood in the light of the general principle that *ritual* refers to content rather than source.
[70] By Edmund Spenser.
[71] The fourth eclogue, interpreted by some to prophesy Christ's birth.
[72] Shelley (above, page 537); Arnold (above, page 586); Whitman (above, page 673); Dylan Thomas (1914–1953), Welsh poet.

[73] Joseph Conrad (1857–1924), Thomas Hardy (1840–1928), English novelists.
[74] A phrase from W. B. Yeats's *Sailing to Byzantium.*

make her into a sister if the story is to end happily. Examples include *Ivanhoe, The Last of the Mohicans, The Woman in White, Ligeia, Pierre* (a tragedy because the hero chooses the dark girl, who is also his sister), *The Marble Faun,* and countless incidental treatments. A male version forms the symbolic basis of *Wuthering Heights.*[75] This device is as much a convention as Milton's calling Edward King by a name out of Virgil's *Eclogues,* but it shows a confused, or, as we say "unconscious" approach to conventions. Again, when we meet the images of a man, a woman, and a serpent in the ninth book of *Paradise Lost,* there is no doubt of their conventional links with similar figures in the Book of Genesis. In Hudson's *Green Mansions*[76] the hero and heroine first meet over a serpent in a quasi-Paradisal setting: here the conventional nature of the imagery is a matter on which the author gives us no help. When a critic meets St. George the Red-cross Knight in Spenser, bearing a red cross on a white ground, he has some idea what to do with this figure. When he meets a female in Henry James's *The Other House* called Rose Armiger with a white dress and a red parasol, he is in the current slang, clueless.[77] It is clear that a deficiency in contemporary education often complained of, the disappearance of a common cultural ground which makes a modern poet's allusions to the Bible or to Classical mythology fall with less weight than they should, has much to do with the decline in the explicit use of archetypes.

Whitman, as is well known, was a spokesman of an antiarchetypal view of literature, and urged the Muse to forget the matter of Troy and develop new themes. This is a low mimetic prejudice, and is consequently appropriate enough for Whitman, who is both right and wrong. He is wrong because the matter of Troy will always be, in the foreseeable future, an integral part of the Western cultural heritage, and hence references to Agamemnon in Yeats's *Leda* or Eliot's *Sweeney Among the Nightingales* have as much cumulative power as ever for the properly instructed reader. But he is of course perfectly right in feeling that the *content* of poetry is normally an immediate and contemporary environment. He was right, being the kind of poet he was, in making the content of his own *When Lilacs Last in the Dooryard Bloomed* an elegy on Lincoln and not a conventional Adonis lament. Yet his elegy is, in its *form,* as conventional as *Lycidas,* complete with purple flowers

thrown on coffins, a great star drooping in the west, imagery of "ever-returning spring" and all the rest of it. Poetry organizes the content of the world as it passes before the poet, but the forms in which that content is organized come out of the structure of poetry itself.

Archetypes are associative clusters, and differ from signs in being complex variables. Within the complex is often a large number of specific learned associations which are communicable because a large number of people in a given culture happen to be familiar with them. When we speak of "symbolism" in ordinary life we usually think of such learned cultural archetypes as the cross or the crown, or of conventional associations, as of white with purity or green with jealousy. As an archetype, green may symbolize hope or vegetable nature or a go sign in traffic or Irish patriotism as easily as jealousy, but the word *green* as a verbal sign always refers to a certain color. Some archetypes are so deeply rooted in conventional association that they can hardly avoid suggesting that association, as the geometrical figure of the cross inevitably suggests the death of Christ. A *completely* conventionalized art would be an art in which the archetypes, or communicable units, were essentially a set of esoteric signs. This can happen in the arts—for instance in some of the sacred dances of India—but it has not happened in Western literature yet, and the resistance of modern writers to having their archetypes "spotted," so to speak, is due to a natural anxiety to keep them as versatile as possible, not pinned down exclusively to one interpretation. A poet may be showing an esoteric tendency if he specifically points out one association, as Yeats does in his footnotes to some of his early poems. There are no *necessary* associations: there are some exceedingly obvious ones, such as the association of darkness with terror or mystery, but there are no intrinsic or inherent correspondences which must invariably be present. As we shall see later, there is a context in which the phrase *universal symbol* makes sense, but it is not this context. The stream of literature, however, like any other stream, seeks the easiest channels first: the poet who uses the expected associations will communicate more rapidly.

At one extreme of literature we have the pure convention, which a poet uses merely because it has often been used before in the same way. This is most frequent in naive poetry, in the fixed epithets and phrase tags of medieval romance and ballad, in the invariable plots and character types of naive drama, and, to a lesser degree, in the *topoi*[78] or

---

[75] By Sir Walter Scott, James Fenimore Cooper, Wilkie Collins, Edgar Allan Poe, Herman Melville, Nathaniel Hawthorne, and Emily Brontë respectively.

[76] W. H. Hudson (1841–1922), English author.

[77] [Frye] My only point is that there may not be any point, but as Rose Armiger is a sister to dragons rather than knights errant, there is a faint possibility of parody-symbolism, discussed below.

---

[78] [Frye] For these see E. R. Curtius, *European Literature and the Latin Middle Ages,* translated by Willard Trask (1953), 79 ff. An example of the point made in the text is the relation of Milton's first prolusion, "Whether Day is more excellent than Night," to *L'Allegro* and Il Penseroso.

rhetorical commonplaces which, like other ideas in literature, are so dull when stated as propositions, and so rich and variegated when they are used as structural principles in literature. At the other extreme we have the pure variable, where there is a deliberate attempt at novelty or unfamiliarity, and consequently a disguising or complicating of archetypes. Such techniques come very close to a distrust of communication itself as a function of literature. However, extremes meet, as Coleridge said, and anticonventional poetry soon becomes a convention in its turn, to be explored by hardy scholars accustomed to the dreariness of literary badlands. Between these extreme points conventions vary from the most explicit to the most indirect, along a scale parallel to the scale of allegory and paradox already dealt with. The two scales may be often confused or identified, but translating imagery into examples and precepts is a quite distinct process from following images into other poems.

Near the extreme of pure convention is translation, paraphrase, and the kind of use which Chaucer makes of Boccaccio[79] in *Troilus* and *The Knight's Tale*. Next we come to deliberate and explicit convention, such as we have noted in *Lycidas*. Next comes paradoxical or ironic convention, including parody—often a sign that certain vogues in handling conventions are getting worn out. Then comes the attempt to reach originality through turning one's back on explicit convention, an attempt which results in implicit convention of the kind we detected in Whitman. Then comes a tendency to identify originality with "experimental" writing, based in our day on an analogy with scientific discovery, and which is frequently spoken of as "breaking with convention." And, of course, at every stage of literature, including this last one, there is a great deal of superficial and inorganic convention, producing the kind of writing that most students of literature prefer to keep in the middle distance: run-of-the-mill Elizabethan sonnets and love lyrics, Plautine[80] comedy-formulas, eighteenth-century pastorals, nineteenth-century happy-ending novels, works of followers and disciples and schools and trends generally.

It is clear from all this that archetypes are most easily studied in highly conventionalized literature: that is, for the most part, naive, primitive, and popular literature. In suggesting the possibility of archetypal criticism, then, I am suggesting the possibility of extending the kind of comparative and morphological study now made of folk tales and ballads into the rest of literature. This should be more easily conceivable now that it is no longer fashionable to mark off

popular and primitive literature from ordinary literature as sharply as we used to do. Also, we shall find that superficial literature, of the kind just spoken of, is of great value to archetypal criticism simply because it is conventional. If throughout this book I refer to popular fiction as frequently as to the greatest novels and epics, it is for the same reason that a musician attempting to explain the rudimentary facts about counterpoint would be more likely, at least at first, to illustrate from *Three Blind Mice* than from a complex Bach[81] fugue.

Every phase of symbolism has its particular approach to narrative and to meaning. In the literal phase, narrative is a flow of significant sounds, and meaning an ambiguous and complex verbal pattern. In the descriptive phase, narrative is an imitation of real events, and meaning an imitation of actual objects or propositions. In the formal phase, poetry exists between the example and the precept. In the exemplary event there is an element of *recurrence;* in the precept, or statement about what ought to be, there is a strong element of *desire,* or what is called "wish-thinking." These elements of recurrence and desire come into the foreground in archetypal criticism, which studies poems as units of poetry as a whole and symbols as units of communication.

From such a point of view, the narrative aspect of literature is a recurrent act of symbolic communication: in other words a ritual. Narrative is studied by the archetypal critic as ritual or imitation of human action as a whole, and not simply as a *mimesis praxeos* or imitation of *an* action. Similarly, in archetypal criticism the significant content is the conflict of desire and reality which has for its basis the work of the dream.[82] Ritual and dream, therefore, are the narrative and significant content respectively of literature in its archetypal aspect. The archetypal analysis of the plot of a novel or play would deal with it in terms of the generic, recurring, or conventional actions which show analogies to rituals: the weddings, funerals, intellectual and social initiations, executions or mock executions, the chasing away of the scapegoat, villain, and so on. The archetypal analysis of the meaning or significance of such a work would deal with it in terms of the generic, recurring, or conventional shape indicated by its mood and resolution, whether tragic, comic, ironic, or what not, in which the relationship of desire and experience is expressed.

Recurrence and desire interpenetrate, and are equally important in both ritual and dream. In its archetypal phase,

---

[79] Boccaccio (above, page 157).

[80] Named after Titus Maccius Plautus (c. 254–184 B.C.), Roman comic poet.

[81] Johann Sebastian Bach (1685–1750), German composer.

[82] [Frye] Throughout this book *dream* is used in an extended sense to mean, not simply the fantasies of the sleeping mind, but the whole interpenetrating activity of desire and repugnance in shaping thought.

the poem imitates nature, not (as in the formal phase) nature as a structure or system, but nature as a cyclical process. The principle of recurrence in the rhythm of art seems to be derived from the repetitions in nature that make time intelligible to us. Rituals cluster around the cyclical movements of the sun, the moon, the seasons, and human life. Every crucial periodicity of experience: dawn, sunset, the phases of the moon, seed-time and harvest, the equinoxes and the solstices, birth, initiation, marriage, and death, get rituals attached to them. The pull of ritual is toward pure cyclical narrative, which, if there could be such a thing, would be automatic and unconscious repetition. In the middle of all this recurrence, however, is the central recurrent cycle of sleeping and waking life, the daily frustration of the ego, the nightly awakening of a titanic self.

The archetypal critic studies the poem as part of poetry and poetry as part of the total human imitation of nature that we call civilization. Civilization is not merely an imitation of nature, but the process of making a total human form out of nature, and it is impelled by the force that we have just called desire. The desire for food and shelter is not content with roots and caves: it produces the human forms of nature that we call farming and architecture. Desire is thus not a simple response to need, for an animal may need food without planting a garden to get it, nor is it a simple response to want, or desire *for* something in particular. It is neither limited to nor satisfied by objects, but is the energy that leads human society to develop its own form. Desire in this sense is the social aspect of what we met on the literal level as emotion, an impulse toward expression which would have remained amorphous if the poem had not liberated it by providing the form of its expression. The form of desire, similarly, is liberated and made apparent by civilization. The efficient cause of civilization is work, and poetry in its social aspect has the function of expressing, as a verbal hypothesis, a vision of the goal of work and the forms of desire.

There is however a moral dialectic in desire. The conception of a garden develops the conception *weed,* and building a sheepfold makes the wolf a greater enemy. Poetry in its social or archetypal aspect, therefore, not only tries to illustrate the fulfillment of desire, but to define the obstacles to it. Ritual is not only a recurrent act, but an act expressive of a dialectic of desire and repugnance: desire for fertility or victory, repugnance to drought or to enemies. We have rituals of social integration, and we have rituals of expulsion, execution, and punishment. In dream there is a parallel dialectic, as there is both the wish-fulfillment dream and the anxiety or nightmare dream of repugnance. Archetypal criticism, therefore, rests on two organizing rhythms or patterns, one cyclical, the other dialectic.

The union of ritual and dream in a form of verbal communication is myth. This is a sense of the term *myth* slightly different from that used in the previous essay.[83] But, first, the sense is equally familiar, and the ambiguity not mine but the dictionary's; and, second, there is a real connection between the two senses which will become more apparent as we go on. The myth accounts for, and makes communicable, the ritual and the dream. Ritual, by itself, cannot account for itself: it is prelogical, preverbal, and in a sense prehuman. Its attachment to the calendar seems to link human life to the biological dependence on the natural cycle which plants, and to some extent animals, still have. Everything in nature that we think of as having some analogy with works of art, like the flower or the bird's song, grows out of a synchronization between an organism and the rhythms of its natural environment, especially that of the solar year. With animals some expressions of synchronization, like the mating dances of birds, could almost be called rituals. Myth is more distinctively human, as the most intelligent partridge cannot tell even the most absurd story explaining why it drums in the mating season. Similarly, the dream, by itself, is a system of cryptic allusions to the dreamer's own life, not fully understood by him, or so far as we know of any real use to him. But in all dreams there is a mythical element which has a power of independent communication, as is obvious, not only in the stock example of Oedipus, but in any collection of folk tales. Myth, therefore, not only gives meaning to ritual and narrative to dream: it is the identification of ritual and dream, in which the former is seen to be the latter in movement. This would not be possible unless there were a common factor to ritual and dream which made one the social expression of the other; the investigation of this common factor we must leave for later treatment. All that we need to say here is that ritual is the archetypal aspect of *mythos* and dream the archetypal aspect of *dianoia.*

The same distinction in emphasis that we noted in the first essay between fictional and thematic literature recurs here. Some literary forms, such as drama, remind us with particular vividness of analogies to rituals, for the drama in literature, like the ritual in religion, is primarily a social or ensemble performance. Others, such as romance, suggest analogies to dreams. Ritual analogies are most easily seen, not in the drama of the educated audience and the settled theater, but in naive or spectacular drama: in the folk play, the puppet show, the pantomime, the farce, the pageant, and their descendants in masque, comic opera, commercial movie, and revue. Dream analogies are best studied in naive

---

[83] Where the term refers to stories about superhuman beings.

romance, which includes the folk tales and fairy tales that are so closely related to dreams of wonderful wishes coming true, and to nightmares of ogres and witches. Naive drama and naive romance, of course, also interpenetrate. What naive drama dramatizes is usually some kind of romance, and the close relation of romance to ritual can be seen in the number of medieval romances that are linked to some part of the calendar, the winter solstice, a May morning, or a saint's eve; or else to some class ritual like the tournament. The fact that the archetype is primarily a *communicable* symbol largely accounts for the ease with which ballads and folk tales and mimes travel through the world, like so many of their heroes, over all barriers of language and culture. We come back here to the fact that literature most deeply influenced by the archetypal phase of symbolism impresses us as primitive and popular.

By these words I mean possessing the ability to communicate in time and space respectively. Otherwise they mean much the same thing. Popular art is normally decried as vulgar by the cultivated people of its time; then it loses favor with its original audience as a new generation grows up; then it begins to merge into the softer lighting of "quaint," and cultivated people become interested in it, and finally it begins to take on the archaic dignity of the primitive. This sense of the archaic recurs whenever we find great art using popular forms, as Shakespeare does in his last period, or as the Bible does when it ends in a fairy tale about a damsel in distress, a hero killing dragons, a wicked witch, and a wonderful city glittering with jewels. Archaism is a regular feature of all social uses of archetypes. Soviet Russia is very proud of its production of tractors, but it will be some time before the tractor replaces the sickle on the Soviet flag.

It is at this point that we must notice and avoid the fallacy of a theory of mythological contract. That is, there may be such a thing as a social contract in political theory, if we keep the discussion to observable facts about the present structure of society. But when these facts are attached to a fable about something that happened in a past too remote for any evidence to disturb the fabler's assertions, and we are told that once upon a time men surrendered or delegated or were tricked into surrendering their power, political theory has merely become one of Plato's indoctrinating lies.[84] And because the only evidence for this remote event is its analogy to the present facts, the present facts are being compared with their own shadows. A precisely similar fabling process has taken place in the literary criticism concerned

with myth, which has hardly yet emerged from its historical contract stage.

As the archetypal critic is concerned with ritual and dream, it is likely that he would find much of interest in the work done by contemporary anthropology in ritual, and by contemporary psychology in dreams. Specifically, the work done on the ritual basis of naive drama in Frazer's *Golden Bough,* and the work done on the dream basis of naive romance by Jung and the Jungians, are of most direct value to him. But the three subjects of anthropology, psychology, and literary criticism are not yet clearly separated, and the danger of determinism has to be carefully watched. To the literary critic, ritual is the *content* of dramatic action, not the source or origin of it. The *Golden Bough* is, from the point of view of literary criticism, an essay on the ritual content of naive drama: that is, it reconstructs an archetypal ritual from which the structural and generic principles of drama may be logically, not chronologically, derived. It does not matter two pins to the literary critic whether such a ritual had any historical existence or not. It is very probable that Frazer's hypothetical ritual would have many and striking analogies to actual rituals, and collecting such analogies is part of his argument. But an analogy is not necessarily a source, an influence, a cause, or an embryonic form, much less an identity. The *literary* relation of ritual to drama, like that of any other aspect of human action to drama, is a relation of content to form only, not one of source to derivation.

The critic, therefore, is concerned only with the ritual or dream patterns which are actually in what he is studying, however they got there. The work of the Classical scholars who have followed Frazer's lead has produced a general theory of the spectacular or ritual content of Greek drama. *The Golden Bough* purports to be a work of anthropology, but it has had more influence on literary criticism than in its own alleged field, and it may yet prove to be really a work of literary criticism. If the ritual pattern is in the plays—and it is fact, not opinion, that one of the main themes of *Iphigeneia in Tauris,*[85] for example, is human sacrifice—the critic need not take sides in the quite separate historical controversy over the ritual *origin* of Greek drama. Hence ritual, as the content of action, and more particularly of dramatic action, is something continuously latent in the order of words, and is quite independent of direct influence. Even in the nineteenth century, we find that the instant drama becomes primitive and popular, as it does in *The Mikado,*[86] to repeat an example given before, back comes all Frazer's ap-

---

[84] See Plato, *Republic* (above, page 22).

[85] By Euripides (c. 480–406 B.C.), Greek tragic dramatist.
[86] (1885), comic operetta by William S. Gilbert (1836–1911) and Arthur Sullivan (1842–1900).

paratus, the king's son, the mock sacrifice, the analogy with the festival of the Sacaea, and many other things that Gilbert knew and cared nothing about. It comes back because it is still the best way of holding an audience's attention, and the experienced dramatist knows it.

The prestige of documentary criticism, which deals entirely with sources and historical transmission, has misled some archetypal critics into feeling that all such ritual elements ought to be traced directly, like the lineage of royalty, as far back as a willing suspension of disbelief will allow. The vast chronological gaps resulting are usually bridged by some theory of race memory, or by some conspiratorial conception of history involving secrets jealously guarded for centuries by esoteric cults or traditions. It is curious that when archetypal critics hang on to a historical framework they almost invariably produce some hypothesis of continuous degeneration from a golden age lost in antiquity. Thus the prelude to Thomas Mann's[87] Joseph series traces back several of our central myths to Atlantis, Atlantis being clearly more useful as an archetypal idea than as a historical one. When archetypal criticism revived in the nineteenth century with a vogue for sun myths, an attempt was made to ridicule it by proving with equal plausibility that Napoleon was a sun myth. The ridicule is effective only against the historical distortion of the method. Archetypally, we turn Napoleon into a sun myth whenever we speak of the rise of his career, the zenith of his fame, or the eclipse of his fortunes.

Social and cultural history, which is anthropology in an extended sense, will always be a part of the context of criticism, and the more clearly the anthropological and the critical treatments of ritual are distinguished, the more beneficial their influence on each other will be. The same is true of the relation of psychology to criticism. The first and most striking unit of poetry larger than the individual poem is the total work of the man who wrote the poem. Biography will always be a part of criticism, and the biographer will naturally be interested in his subject's poetry as a personal document, recording his private dreams, associations, ambitions, and expressed or repressed desires. Studies of such matters form an essential part of criticism. I am not of course speaking of the silly ones, which simply project the author's own erotica, in a rationalized clinical disguise, on his victim, but only of the serious studies which are technically competent both in psychology and in criticism, which are aware how much guesswork is involved and how tentative all the conclusions must be.

Such an approach is easiest, and most rewarding, with what we have called thematic writers of the low mimetic—that is, chiefly, the Romantic poets, where the poet's own psychological processes are often part of the theme. With other writers, say a dramatist who is aware from the first word he writes that "They who live to please must please to live," there is danger of making an unreal abstraction of the poet from his literary community. Suppose a critic finds that a certain pattern is repeated time and again in the plays of Shakespeare. If Shakespeare is unique or anomalous, or even exceptional, in using this pattern, the reason for his use of it may be at least partly psychological. If there were any evidence that he had persisted in using it when it failed to please an audience, the probability of a personal psychological element would be very high. But if we can find the same pattern in half a dozen of his contemporaries, we clearly have to allow for convention. And if we find it in a dozen dramatists of different ages and cultures, we have to allow for genre, for the structural requirements of drama itself. Now as a matter of fact we do find in Shakespeare's comedies that the same devices are used over and over, and it is the business of the literary critic to compare these devices with those of other dramatists, in a morphological study of comic form. Otherwise we shall deprive ourselves of the perfectly legitimate appreciation of the *scholarly* qualities of Shakespeare, of seeing in the repeated devices of his comedies a kind of *Art of Fugue* of comedy.

A psychologist examining a poem will tend to see in it what he sees in the dream, a mixture of latent and manifest content. For the literary critic the manifest content of the poem is its form, hence its latent content becomes simply its actual content, its *dianoia*[88] or theme. And this *dianoia* on the archetypal level is a dream, a presentation of the conflict of desire and actuality. We seem to be going around in a circle, but not quite. For the critic, a problem appears which does not exist for a purely psychological analysis, the problem of communicable latent content, of intelligible dream, Plato's conception of art as a dream for awakened minds. For the psychologist all dream symbols are private ones, interpreted by the personal life of the dreamer. For the critic there is no such thing as private symbolism, or, if there is, it is his job to make sure that it does not remain so.

This problem is already present in Freud's treatment of *Oedipus Tyrannus* as a play which owes much of its power to the fact that it dramatizes the Oedipus complex. The dramatic and psychological elements can be linked without any reference to the personal life of Sophocles, of which we

---

[87] Thomas Mann (1875–1955), German novelist.

[88] [Frye] The expression here is careless, as *dianoia* refers to form.

know nothing whatever. This emphasis on impersonal content has been developed by Jung and his school, where the communicability of archetypes is accounted for by a theory of a collective unconscious—an unnecessary hypothesis in literary criticism, so far as I can judge.

What we have found to be true of the writer's intention is also true of the audience's attention. Both are centripetally directed, and implications exist in the response to art as they do in the creation of it, implications of which the audience is not explicitly aware. Discrete conscious awareness can take in only a very few details of the complex of response. This state of things enabled Tennyson,[89] for instance, to be praised for the chastity of his language and read for his powerful erotic sensuousness. It also makes it possible for a contemporary critic to draw on the fullest resources of modern knowledge in explicating a work of art without any real fear of anachronism.

For instance, *Le Malade Imaginaire* is a play about a man who, in seventeenth-century terms, including no doubt Molière's[90] own terms, was not really sick but just thought he was. A modern critic might object that life is not so simple: that it is perfectly possible for a *malade imaginaire* to be a *malade véritable,* and that what is wrong with Argan is clearly an unwillingness to see his children grow up, an infantile regression which his wife—his second wife, incidentally—shows that she understands completely by coddling him and murmuring such phrases as *"pauvre petit fils."* Such a critic would find the clue to Argan's whole behavior in his unguarded remark after the scene with the little girl Louison (the erotic nature of which the critic would also notice): *"Il n'y a plus d'enfants."*[91] Now whether this reading is right or wrong, it does not swerve from Molière's text, yet it tells us nothing about Molière himself. The play is generically a comedy; it must therefore end happily; Argan must therefore be brought to see some reason; his wife, whose dramatic function it is to keep him within his obsession, must therefore be "exposed" as inimical to him. The plot is a ritual moving toward a scapegoat rejection followed by a marriage, and the theme is a dream-pattern of irrational desire in conflict with reality.

Another essay in this book will be concerned with the details and practice of archetypal criticism: here we are concerned only with its place in the context of criticism as a whole. In its archetypal aspect, art is a part of civilization, and civilization we defined as the process of making a human form out of nature. The shape of this human form is revealed by civilization itself as it develops: its major components are the city, the garden, the farm, the sheepfold, and the like, as well as human society itself. An archetypal symbol is usually a natural object with a human meaning, and it forms part of the critical view of art as a civilized product, a vision of the goals of human work.

Such a vision is bound to idealize some aspect of civilization and ridicule or ignore others; in other words the social context of art is also the moral context. All artists have to come to terms with their communities: many artists, and many great ones, are content to be the spokesmen of them. But in terms of his moral significance, the poet reflects, and follows at a distance, what his community really achieves through its work. Hence the moral view of the artist is invariably that he ought to assist the work of his society by framing workable hypotheses, imitating human action and thought in such a way as to suggest realizable modes of both. If he does not do this, his hypotheses should at least be clearly labeled as playful or fantastic. Marxism takes more or less this view of art, and thereby repeats the argument reached at the end of the *Republic.* We are told there, if we follow the argument simply as it stands, that according to justice, or social work properly done, the painter's bed is an external imitation of the craftsman's bed. The artist, therefore, is confined either to reflecting or to escaping from the world that the true worker is realizing.

We have adopted the principle in this essay that the events and ideas of poetry are hypothetical imitations of history and discursive writing respectively, which in their turn are verbal imitations of action and thought. This principle brings us close to the view of poetry as a secondary imitation of reality. We are interpreting mimesis, however, not as a Platonic "recollection" but as an emancipation of externality into image, nature into art. From this point of view the work of art must be its own object:[92] it cannot be ultimately descriptive of something, and can never be ultimately related to any other system of phenomena, standards, values, or final causes. All such external relations form part of the "intentional fallacy." Poetry is a vehicle for morality, truth, and beauty, but the poet does not aim at these things, but only at inner verbal strength. The poet qua poet intends only to write a poem, and as a rule it is not the artist, but the ego in the artist, who turns away from his proper work to go and chase these other seductive marshlights.

[89] Alfred Lord Tennyson (1809–1892), English poet.
[90] Molière (Jean Baptiste Poquelin, 1622–1673), French dramatist.
[91] "There are no more children."
[92] [Frye] I have taken this phrase from an oral lecture by M. Jacques Maritain.

It is an elementary axiom in criticism that morally the lion lies down with the lamb. Bunyan and Rochester, Sade and Jane Austen, *The Miller's Tale* and *The Second Nun's Tale*,[93] are all equally elements of a liberal education, and the only moral criterion to be applied to them is that of decorum. Similarly, the moral attitude taken by the poet in his work derives largely from the structure of that work. Thus the fact that *Le Malade Imaginaire* is a comedy is the only reason for making Argan's wife a hypocrite—she must be got rid of to make the play end happily.

The pursuit of beauty is much more dangerous nonsense than the pursuit of truth or goodness, because it affords a stronger temptation to the ego. Beauty, like truth and goodness, is a quality that may in one sense be predicated of all great art, but the deliberate attempt to beautify can, in itself, only weaken the creative energy. Beauty in art is like happiness in morals: it may accompany the act, but it cannot be the goal of the act, just as one cannot "pursue happiness, but only something else that may give happiness. Aiming at beauty produces, at best, the attractive: the quality of beauty represented by the word *loveliness,* a quality which depends on a carefully restricted choice of both subject and technique. A religious painter, for instance, can produce this quality only as long as churches keep commissioning Madonnas: if a church asks for a Crucifixion he must paint cruelty and horror instead.

When we speak of the human body as "beautiful," we usually mean the body of someone in good physical condition between eighteen and about thirty, and if Degas, for example, shows us pictures of thick-bottomed matrons squatting in hip baths, we interpret the shock to our propriety as an aesthetic judgment. Whenever the word *beauty* means loveliness or attractiveness, as it is bound to do whenever it is made the intention of art, it becomes reactionary: it tries to restrict either what the artist may choose for a subject or the method in which he may choose to treat it, and it marshals all the forces of prudery to keep him from expanding his vision beyond an arid and insipid pseudoclassicism. Ruskin spoiled many of his finest critical insights with this fallacy; Tennyson often hampered the vigor of his poetry by it, and in some of the lesser beauticians of the same period we can see clearly what the neurotic compulsion to beautify everything leads to. It leads to an exaggerated cult of style, a technique of making everything in a work of art, even drama, sound all alike, and like the author, and like the author at his most impressive. Here again the vanity of the ego has replaced the honest pride of the craftsman.

The formal or third phase of narrative and meaning, although it includes the external relations of literature to events and ideas, nevertheless brings us back ultimately to the aesthetic view of the work of art as an object of contemplation, a *techne* designed for ornament and pleasure rather than use. This view encourages us to separate aesthetic objects from other kinds of artifacts and to postulate an aesthetic experience different in kind from other experiences. Corresponding to the bibliographical view of literature as the aggregate or pile of all the books and plays and poems that have been written, we find the aesthetic view of criticism as a discrete series of special (sometimes vaguely sacramental) apprehensions. There is no reason for not granting this view of literary experience its own validity; one objects to it only when it excludes other approaches.

The archetypal view of literature shows us literature as a total form and literary experience as a part of the continuum of life, in which one of the poet's functions is to visualize the goals of human work. As soon as we add this approach to the other three, literature becomes an ethical instrument, and we pass beyond Kierkegaard's[94] "either/or" dilemma between aesthetic idolatry and ethical freedom, without any temptation to dispose of the arts in the process. Hence the importance, after accepting the validity of this view of literature, of rejecting the external goals of morality, beauty, and truth. The fact that they are external makes them ultimately idolatrous, and so demonic. But if no social, moral, or aesthetic standard is in the long run externally determinative of the value of art, it follows that the archetypal phase, in which art is part of civilization, cannot be the ultimate one. We need still another phase where we can pass from civilization, where poetry is still useful and functional, to culture, where it is disinterested and liberal, and stands on its own feet.

Anagogic Phase: Symbol as Monad

In tracing the different phases of literary symbolism, we have been going up a sequence parallel to that of medieval criticism. We have, it is true, established a different meaning for the word *literal*. It is our second or descriptive level that corresponds to the historical or literal one of the medieval scheme, or at any rate of Dante's version of it. Our third level, the level of commentary and interpretation, is the second or allegorical level of the Middle Ages. Our fourth

---

[93] John Wilmot, Earl of Rochester (1647–1680), English poet; the Marquis de Sade (1740–1814), French writer; two tales from Geoffrey Chaucer's *Canterbury Tales.*

[94] Søren Kierkegaard (1813–1855), Danish philosopher.

level, the study of myths, and of poetry as a technique of so-cial communication, is the third medieval level of moral and tropological meaning, concerned at once with the social and the figurative aspect of meaning. The medieval distinction between the allegorical as what one believes *(quid credas)* and the moral as what one does *(quid agas)* is also reflected in our conception of the formal phase as aesthetic or specu-lative and the archetypal phase as social and part of the con-tinuum of work. We have now to see if we can establish a modern parallel to the medieval conception of anagogy or universal meaning.

Again, the reader may have noticed a parallelism grad-ually shaping up between the five modes of our first essay and the phases of symbolism in this one. Literal meaning, as we expounded it, has much to do with the techniques of the-matic irony introduced by *symbolisme,* and with the view of many of the "new" critics that poetry is primarily (i.e., liter-ally) an ironic structure. Descriptive symbolism, shown at its most uncompromising in the documentary naturalism of the nineteenth century, seems to bear a close connection with the low mimetic, and formal symbolism, most easily studied in Renaissance and Neoclassical writers, with the high mimetic. Archetypal criticism seems to find its center of gravity in the mode of romance, when the interchange of ballads, folk tales, and popular stories was at its easiest. If the parallel holds, then, the last phase of symbolism will still be concerned, as the previous one was, with the mythopoeic aspect of literature, but with myth in its nar-rower and more technical sense of fictions and themes relat-ing to divine or quasi-divine beings and powers.

We have associated archetypes and myths particularly with primitive and popular literature. In fact we could al-most define popular literature, admittedly in a rather circu-lar way, as literature which affords an unobstructed view of archetypes. We can find this quality on every level of litera-ture: in fairy tales and folk tales, in Shakespeare (in most of the comedies), in the Bible (which would still be a popular book if it were not a sacred one), in Bunyan, in Richardson, in Dickens, in Poe,[95] and of course in a vast amount of ephemeral rubbish as well. We began this book by remark-ing that we cannot correlate popularity and value. But there is still the danger of reduction, or assuming that literature is *essentially* primitive and popular. This view had a great vogue in the nineteenth century, and is by no means dead yet, but if we were to adopt it we should cut off a third and most important source of supply for archetypal criticism.

We notice that many learned and recondite writers whose work requires patient study are explicitly mythopoeic writers. Instances include Dante and Spenser, and in the twentieth century embrace nearly all the "difficult" writers in both poetry and prose. Such work, when fictional, is of-ten founded on a basis of naive drama *(Faust, Peer Gynt)* or naive romance (Hawthorne, Melville: one may compare the sophisticated allegories of Charles Williams and C. S. Lewis[96] in our day, which are largely based on the formulas of the Boy's Own Paper).[97] Learned mythopoeia, as we have it in the last period of Henry James and in James Joyce, for example, may become bewilderingly complex; but the com-plexities are designed to reveal and not to disguise the myth. We cannot assume that a primitive and popular myth has been swathed like a mummy in elaborate verbiage, which is the assumption that the fallacy of reduction would lead to. The inference seems to be that the learned and the subtle, like the primitive and the popular, tend toward a center of imaginative experience.

Knowing that *The Two Gentlemen of Verona* is an early Shakespeare comedy and *The Winter's Tale* a late one, the student would expect the later play to be more subtle and complex; he might not expect it to be more archaic and primitive, more suggestive of ancient myths and rituals. The later play is also more popular, though not popular of course in the sense of giving a lower-middle-class audience what it thinks it wants. As a result of expressing the inner forms of drama with increasing force and intensity, Shakespeare ar-rived in his last period at the bedrock of drama, the roman-tic spectacle out of which all the more specialized forms of drama, such as tragedy and social comedy, have come, and to which they recurrently return. In the greatest moments of Dante and Shakespeare, in, say *The Tempest* or the climax of the *Purgatorio,* we have a feeling of converging signifi-cance, the feeling that here we are close to seeing what our whole literary experience has been about, the feeling that we have moved into the still center of the order of words. Criticism as knowledge, the criticism which is compelled to keep on talking about the subject, recognizes the fact that there *is* a center of the order of words.

Unless there is such a center, there is nothing to pre-vent the analogies supplied by convention and genre from being an endless series of free associations, perhaps sugges-tive, perhaps even tantalizing, but never creating a real structure. The study of archetypes is the study of literary symbols as parts of a whole. If there are such things as ar-

---

[95] John Bunyan (1628–1688), English moralist writer; Samuel Richardson (1689–1761), Charles Dickens (1812–1870), English novelists; Edgar Al-lan Poe (above, page 580).

[96] Charles Williams (1886–1945), C. S. Lewis (1898–1963), both English writers.
[97] *The Boy's Own Paper* (1879–1967), children's magazine.

chetypes at all, then, we have to take yet another step, and conceive the possibility of a self-contained literary universe. Either archetypal criticism is a will-o-the-wisp, an endless labyrinth without an outlet, or we have to assume that literature is a total form, and not simply the name given to the aggregate of existing literary works. We spoke before of the mythical view of literature as leading to the conception of an order of nature as a whole being imitated by a corresponding order of words.

If archetypes are communicable symbols, and there is a center of archetypes, we should expect to find, at that center, a group of universal symbols. I do not mean by this phrase that there is any archetypal code book which has been memorized by all human societies without exception. I mean that some symbols are images of things common to all men, and therefore have a communicable power which is potentially unlimited. Such symbols include those of food and drink, of the quest or journey, of light and darkness, and of sexual fulfillment, which would usually take the form of marriage. It is inadvisable to assume that an Adonis or Oedipus myth is universal, or that certain associations, such as the serpent with the phallus, are universal, because when we discover a group of people who know nothing of such matters we must assume that they did know and have forgotten, or do know and won't tell, or are not members of the human race. On the other hand, they may be confidently excluded from the human race if they cannot understand the conception of food, and so any symbolism founded on food is universal in the sense of having an indefinitely extensive scope. That is, there are no limits to its intelligibility.

In the archetypal phase the work of literary art is a myth, and unites the ritual and the dream. By doing so it limits the dream: it makes it plausible and acceptable to a social working consciousness. Thus as a moral fact in civilization, literature embodies a good deal of the spirit which in the dream itself is called the censor. But the censor stands in the way of the impetus of the dream. When we look at the dream as a whole, we notice three things about it. First, its limits are not the real, but the conceivable. Second, the limit of the conceivable is the world of fulfilled desire emancipated from all anxieties and frustrations. Third, the universe of the dream is entirely within the mind of the dreamer.

In the anagogic phase, literature imitates the total dream of man, and so imitates the thought of a human mind which is at the circumference and not at the center of its reality. We see here the completion of the imaginative revolution begun when we passed from the descriptive to the formal phase of symbolism. There, the imitation of nature shifted from a reflection of external nature to a formal organization of which nature was the content. But in the formal phase the poem is still contained by nature, and in the archetypal phase the whole of poetry is still contained within the limits of the natural, or plausible. When we pass into anagogy, nature becomes, not the container, but the thing contained, and the archetypal universal symbols, the city, the garden, the quest, the marriage, are no longer the desirable forms that man constructs inside nature, but are themselves the forms of nature. Nature is now inside the mind of an infinite man who builds his cities out of the Milky Way. This is not reality, but it is the conceivable or imaginative limit of desire, which is infinite, eternal, and hence apocalyptic. By an apocalypse I mean primarily the imaginative conception of the whole of nature as the content of an infinite and eternal living body which, if not human, is closer to being human than to being inanimate. "The desire of man being infinite," said Blake, "the possession is infinite and himself infinite."[98] If Blake is thought a prejudiced witness on this point, we may cite Hooker:[99] "That there is somewhat higher than either of these two (sensual and intellectual perfection), no other proof doth need than the very process of man's desire, which being natural should be frustrate, if there were not some farther thing wherein it might rest at the length contented, which in the former it cannot do."

If we turn to ritual, we see there an imitation of nature which has a strong element of what we call magic in it. Magic seems to begin as something of a voluntary effort to recapture a lost rapport with the natural cycle. This sense of a deliberate recapturing of something no longer possessed is a distinctive mark of human ritual. Ritual constructs a calendar and endeavors to imitate the precise and sensitive accuracy of the movements of the heavenly bodies and the response of vegetation to them. A farmer must harvest his crop at a certain time of the year, but because he must do this anyway, harvesting itself is not precisely a ritual. It is the expression of a will to synchronize human and natural energies at that time which produces the harvest songs, harvest sacrifices, and harvest folk customs that we associate with ritual. But the impetus of the magical element in ritual is clearly toward a universe in which a stupid and indifferent nature is no longer the container of human society, but is contained by that society, and must rain or shine at the pleasure of man. We notice too the tendency of ritual to become not only cyclical but encyclopedic, as already noted. In its anagogic phase, then, poetry imitates human action as total ritual, and so imitates the action of an omnipotent human society that contains all the powers of nature within itself.

---

[98] From Blake's *The Marriage of Heaven and Hell.*
[99] Richard Hooker (1554?–1600), English clergyman.

Anagogically, then, poetry unites total ritual, or unlimited social action, with total dream, or unlimited individual thought. Its universe is infinite and boundless hypothesis: it cannot be contained within any actual civilization or set of moral values, for the same reason that no structure of imagery can be restricted to one allegorical interpretation. Here the *dianoia* of art is no longer a *mimesis logou,* but the Logos, the shaping word which is both reason and, as Goethe's Faust speculated, *praxis* or creative act. The *ethos* of art is no longer a group of characters within a natural setting, but a universal man who is also a divine being, or a divine being conceived in anthropomorphic terms.

The form of literature most deeply influenced by the anagogic phase is the scripture or apocalyptic revelation. The god, whether traditional deity, glorified hero, or apotheosized poet, is the central image that poetry uses in trying to convey the sense of unlimited power in a humanized form. Many of these scriptures are documents of religion as well, and hence are a mixture of the imaginative and the existential. When they lose their existential content they become purely imaginative, as Classical mythology did after the rise of Christianity. They belong in general, of course, to the mythical or theogonic mode. We see the relation to anagogy also in the vast encyclopedic structure of poetry that seems to be a whole world in itself, that stands in its culture as an inexhaustible storehouse of imaginative suggestion, and seems, like theories of gravitation or relativity in the physical universe, to be applicable to, or have analogous connections with every part of the literary universe. Such works are definitive myths, or complete organizations of archetypes. They include what in the previous essay we called analogies of revelation: the epics of Dante and Milton and their counterparts in the other modes.

But the anagogic perspective is not to be confined only to works that seem to take in everything, for the principle of anagogy is not simply that everything is the subject of poetry, but that anything may be the subject of a poem. The sense of the infinitely varied unity of poetry may come, not only explicitly from an apocalyptic epic, but implicitly from any poem. We said that we could get a whole liberal education by picking up one conventional poem, *Lycidas* for example, and following its archetypes through literature. Thus the center of the literary universe is whatever poem we happen to be reading. One step further, and the poem appears as a microcosm of all literature, an individual manifestation of the total order of words. Anagogically, then, the symbol is a monad, all symbols being united in a single infinite and eternal verbal symbol which is, as *dianoia,* the logos, and, as *mythos,* total creative act. It is this conception which Joyce expresses, in terms of

subject matter, as "epiphany," and Hopkins, in terms of form, as "inscape."[100]

If we look at *Lycidas* anagogically, for example, we see that the subject of the elegy has been identified with a god who personifies both the sun that falls into the western ocean at night and the vegetable life that dies in the autumn. In the latter aspect Lycidas is the Adonis or Tammuz[101] whose "annual wound," as Milton calls it elsewhere, was the subject of a ritual lament in Mediterranean religion, and has been incorporated in the pastoral elegy since Theocritus, as the title of Shelley's *Adonais* shows more clearly. As a poet, Lycidas's archetype is Orpheus,[102] who also died young, in much the same role as Adonis, and was flung into the water. As priest, his archetype is Peter, who would have drowned on the "Galilean lake" without the help of Christ. Each aspect of *Lycidas* poses the question of premature death as it relates to the life of man, of poetry, and of the church. But all of these aspects are contained within the figure of Christ, the young dying god who is eternally alive, the Word that contains all poetry, the head and body of the church, the Good Shepherd whose pastoral world sees no winter, the Sun of Righteousness that never sets, whose power can raise Lycidas, like Peter, out of the waves, as it redeems souls from the lower world, which Orpheus failed to do. Christ does not enter the poem as a character, but he pervades every line of it so completely that the poem, so to speak, enters him.

Anagogic criticism is usually found in direct connection with religion, and is to be discovered chiefly in the more uninhibited utterances of poets themselves. It comes out in those passages of Eliot's quartets where the words of the poet are placed within the context of the incarnate Word. An even clearer statement is in a letter of Rilke,[103] where he speaks of the function of the poet as revealing a perspective of reality like that of an angel, containing all time and space, who is blind and looking into himself. Rilke's angel is a modification of the more usual god or Christ, and his statement is all the more valuable because it is explicitly not Christian, and illustrates the independence of the anagogic perspective, of the poet's attempt to speak from the circumference instead of from the center of reality, from the acceptance of any specific religion. Similar views are expressed or implied in Valéry's conception of a total intelligence

---

[100] Gerard Manley Hopkins (1844–1889), English poet.
[101] Adonis, in Greek mythology a beautiful youth loved by Aphrodite and Persephone and killed by a wild boar; Tammuz, in Babylonian religion a beautiful youth loved by Ishtar, who killed him and restored him to life.
[102] Orpheus, mythological Greek poet.
[103] [Frye] Letter to Ellen Delp, October 27, 1915.

which appears more fancifully in his figure of M. Teste; in Yeats's cryptic utterances about the artifice of eternity, and, in *The Tower* and elsewhere, about man as the creator of all creation as well as of both life and death; in Joyce's non-theological use of the theological term *epiphany;* in Dylan Thomas's exultant hymns to a universal human body.[104] We may note in passing that the more sharply we distinguish the poetic and the critical functions, the easier it is for us to take seriously what great writers have said about their work.

The anagogic view of criticism thus leads to the conception of literature as existing in its own universe, no longer a commentary on life or reality, but containing life and reality in a system of verbal relationships. From this point of view the critic can no longer think of literature as a tiny palace of art looking out upon an inconceivably gigantic "life." "Life" for him has become the seed-plot of literature, a vast mass of potential literary forms, only a few of which will grow up into the greater world of the literary universe. Similar universes exist for all the arts. "We make to ourselves pictures of facts," says Wittgenstein,[105] but by *pictures* he means representative illustrations, which are not pictures. Pictures as pictures are themselves facts, and exist only in a pictorial universe. *"Tout au monde,"* says Mallarmé, *"existe pour aboutir à un livre."*[106]

So far we have been dealing with symbols as isolated units, but clearly the unit of relationship between two symbols, corresponding to the phrase in music, is of equal importance. The testimony of critics from Aristotle on seems fairly unanimous that this unit of relationship is the metaphor. And the metaphor, in its radical form, is a statement of identity of the "A is B" type, or rather, putting it into its proper hypothetical form, of the "let *x* be *y*" type (letters altered for euphony). Thus the metaphor turns its back on ordinary descriptive meaning, and presents a structure which literally is ironic and paradoxical. In ordinary descriptive meaning, if A is B then B is A, and all we have really said is that A is itself. In the metaphor two things are identified while each retains its own form. Thus if we say "the hero was a lion" we identify the hero *with* the lion, while at the same time both the hero and the lion are identified *as* themselves. A work of literary art owes its unity to this process of identification *with,* and its variety, clarity, and intensity to identification *as.*

[104] [Frye] To these should be added the great meditation on time in the second part of *Le Temps retrouve* [by Marcel Proust]. One wonders if there is anything more than doubtful puns connecting the anagogic perspective in literature with Kant's conception of "transcendental aesthetic" as the a priori consciousness of space and time.
[105] Ludwig Wittgenstein (above, page 826).
[106] Mallarmé (above, page 729).

On the literal level of meaning, metaphor appears in its literal shape, which is simple juxtaposition. Ezra Pound, in explaining this aspect of metaphor, uses the illustrative figure of the Chinese ideogram, which expresses a complex image by throwing a group of elements together without predication. In Pound's famous blackboard example of such a metaphor, the two-line poem *In a Station of the Metro,* the images of the faces in the crowd and the petals on the black bough are juxtaposed with no predicate of any kind connecting them. Predication belongs to assertion and descriptive meaning, not to the literal structure of poetry.

On the descriptive level we have the double perspective of the verbal structure and the phenomena to which it is related. Here meaning is "literal" in the common sense which we explained would not do for criticism, an unambiguous alignment of words and facts. Descriptively, then, all metaphors are similes. When we are writing ordinary discursive prose and use a metaphor, we are not asserting that A is B; we are "really" saying that A is in some respects comparable with B; and similarly when we are extracting the descriptive or paraphrasable meaning of a poem. "The hero was a lion," then, on the descriptive level, is a simile with the word "like" omitted for greater vividness, and to show more clearly that the analogy is only a hypothetical one. In Whitman's poem *Out of the Cradle Endlessly Rocking,* we find shadows "twining and twisting as if they were alive," and the moon swollen, "as if with tears." As there is no *poetic* reason why shadows should not be alive or the moon tearful, we may perhaps see in the cautious *as if* the working of a low mimetic discursive prose conscience.

On the formal level, where symbols are images or natural phenomena conceived as matter or content, the metaphor is an analogy of natural proportion. Literally, metaphor is juxtaposition; we say simply "A; B." Descriptively we say "A is (like)B." But formally we say "A is as B." An analogy of proportion thus requires four terms, of which two have a common factor. Thus "the hero was a lion" means, as a form of expression which has nature for its internal content, that the hero is to human courage as the lion is to animal courage, courage being the factor common to the third and fourth terms.

Archetypally, where the symbol is an associative cluster, the metaphor unites two individual images, each of which is a specific representative of a class or genus. The rose in Dante's *Paradiso* and the rose in Yeats's early lyrics are identified *with* different things, but both stand for all roses—all poetic roses, of course, not all botanical ones. Archetypal metaphor thus involves the use of what has been called the concrete universal, the individual identified with its class, Wordsworth's "tree of many one." Of course there are no *real* universals in poetry, only poetic ones. All four of these aspects of metaphors are recognized in Aristotle's discussion of metaphor in the *Poetics,* though sometimes very briefly and elliptically.

In the anagogic aspect of meaning, the radical form of metaphor, "A is B," comes into its own. Here we are dealing with poetry in its totality, in which the formula "A is B" may be hypothetically applied to anything, for there is no metaphor, not even "black is white," which a reader has any right to quarrel with in advance. The literary universe, therefore, is a universe in which everything is potentially identical with everything else. This does not mean that any two things in it are separate and very similar, like peas in a pod, or in the slangy and erroneous sense of the word in which we speak of identical twins. If twins were really identical they would be the same person. On the other hand, a grown man feels identical with himself at the age of seven, although the two manifestations of this identity, the man and the boy, have very little in common as regards similarity or likeness. In form, matter, personality, time, and space, man and boy are quite unlike. This is the only type of image I can think of that illustrates the process of identifying two independent forms. All poetry, then, proceeds as though all poetic images were contained within a single universal body. Identity is the opposite of similarity or likeness, and total identity is not uniformity, still less monotony, but a unity of various things.

Finally, identification belongs not only to the structure poetry, but to the structure of criticism as well, at least of commentary. Interpretation proceeds by metaphor as well as creation, and even more explicitly. When St. Paul interprets the story of Abraham's wives in Genesis, for instance, he says that Hagar "is" Mount Sinai in Arabia. Poetry, said Coleridge, is the identity of knowledge.[107]

The universe of poetry, however, is a literary universe, and not a separate existential universe. Apocalypse means revelation, and when art becomes apocalyptic, it reveals. But it reveals only on its own terms, and in its own forms: it does not describe or represent a separate content of revelation. When poet and critic pass from the archetypal to the anagogic phase, they enter a phase of which only religion, or something as infinite in its range as religion, can possibly form an external goal. The poetic imagination, unless it disciplines itself in the particular way in which the imaginations of Hardy and Housman were disciplined, is apt to get claustrophobia when it is allowed to talk only about human

nature and subhuman nature; and poets are happier as servants of religion than of politics, because the transcendental and apocalyptic perspective of religion comes as a tremendous emancipation of the imaginative mind. If men were compelled to make the melancholy choice between atheism and superstition, the scientist, as Bacon pointed out long ago, would be compelled to choose atheism, but the poet would be compelled to choose superstition, for even superstition, by its very confusion of values, gives his imagination more scope than a dogmatic denial of imaginative infinity does. But the loftiest religion, no less than the grossest superstition, comes to the poet, qua poet, only as the spirits came to Yeats, to give him metaphors for poetry.

The study of literature takes us toward seeing poetry as the limitation of infinite social action and infinite human thought, the mind of a man who is all men, the universal creative word which is all words. About this man and word we can, speaking as critics, say only one thing ontologically: we have no reason to suppose either that they exist or that they do not exist. We can call them divine if by divine we mean the unlimited or projected human. But the critic, qua critic, has nothing to say for or against the affirmations that a religion makes out of these conceptions. If Christianity wishes to identify the infinite Word and Man of the literary universe with the Word of God, the person of Christ, the historical Jesus, the Bible or Church dogma, these identifications may be accepted by any poet or critic without injury to his work—the acceptance may even clarify and intensify his work, depending on his temperament and situation. But they can never be accepted by poetry as a whole, or by criticism as such. The literary critic, like the historian, is compelled to treat every religion in the same way that religions treat each other, as though it were a human hypothesis, whatever else he may in other contexts believe it to be. The discussion of the universal Word at the opening of the Chhandogya Upanishad (where it is symbolized by the sacred word "Aum") is exactly as relevant and as irrelevant to literary criticism as the discussion at the opening of the fourth gospel. Coleridge was right in thinking that the "logos" was the goal of his work as a critic, but not right in thinking that his poetic logos would so inevitably be absorbed into Christ as to make literary criticism a kind of natural theology.

The total logos of criticism by itself can never become an object of faith or an ontological personality. The conception of a total Word is the postulate that there is such a thing as an order of words, and that the criticism which studies it makes, or could make, complete sense. Aristotle's *Physics* leads to the conception of an unmoved first mover at the circumference of the physical universe. This, in itself, means

---

[107] [Frye] *Coleridge's Miscellaneous Criticism,* edited by T. M. Raysor (1936), 343.

essentially that physics *has* a universe. The systematic study of motion would be impossible unless all phenomena of motion could be related to unifying principles, and those in their turn to a total unifying principle of movement which is not itself merely another phenomenon of motion. If theology identifies Aristotle's unmoved mover with a creating God, that is the business of theology; physics as physics will be unaffected by it. Christian critics may see their total Word as an analogy of Christ, as medieval critics did, but as literature itself may be accompanied in culture by any religion, criticism must detach itself accordingly. In short, the study of literature belongs to the "humanities," and the humanities, as their name indicates, can take only the human view of the superhuman.

The close resemblance between the conceptions of anagogic criticism and those of religion has led many to assume that they can only be related by making one supreme and the other subordinate. Those who choose religion, like Coleridge, will, like him, try to make criticism a natural theology; those who choose culture, like Arnold, will try to reduce religion to objectified cultural myth. But for the purity of each the autonomy of each must be guaranteed. Culture interposes, between the ordinary and the religious life, a total vision of possibilities, and insists on its totality—for whatever is excluded from culture by religion or state will get its revenge somehow. Thus culture's essential service to a religion is to destroy intellectual idolatry, the recurrent tendency in religion to replace the object of its worship with its present understanding and forms of approach to that object. Just as no argument in favor of a religious or political doctrine is of any value unless it is an intellectually honest argument, and so guarantees the autonomy of logic, so no religious or political myth is either valuable or valid unless it assumes the autonomy of culture, which may be provisionally defined as the total body of imaginative hypothesis in a society and its tradition. To defend the autonomy of culture in this sense seems to me the social task of the "intellectual" in the modern world: if so, to defend its subordination to a total synthesis of any kind, religious or political, would be the authentic form of the *trahison des clercs.*[108]

Besides, it is of the essence of imaginative culture that it transcends the limits both of the naturally possible and of the morally acceptable. The argument that there is no room for poets in any human society which is an end in itself remains unanswerable even when the society is the people of God. For religion is also a social institution, and so far as it is one, it imposes limitations on the arts just as a Marxist or Platonic state would do. Christian theology is no less of a revolutionary dialectic, or indissoluble union of theory and social practice. Religions, in spite of their enlarged perspective, cannot as social institutions *contain* an art of unlimited hypothesis. The arts in their turn cannot help releasing the powerful acids of satire, realism, ribaldry, and fantasy in their attempt to dissolve all the existential concretions that get in their way. The artist often enough has to find that, as God says in *Faust,* he "muss als Teufel schaffen," which I suppose means rather more than he has to work like the devil. Between religion's "this is" and poetry's "but suppose *this* is," there must always be some kind of tension, until the possible and the actual meet at infinity. Nobody wants a poet in the perfect human state, and, as even the poets tell us, nobody but God himself can tolerate a poltergeist in the City of God.

---

[108] "Treachery of clerks."

Noam Chomsky

b. 1928

Noam Chomsky has arguably done more to shape the intellectual climate of the study of language than any single figure since Ferdinand de Saussure (above, page 786) or Leonard Bloomfield. Since his devastating review of B. F. Skinner's *Verbal Behavior* (1959), excerpted here, Chomsky has argued against many commonplace conceptions of the nature of language, primarily through his development of a sequence of theoretical insights concerning the structure and syntax of natural language. His work on the early theory of generative transformational grammar, calling attention to the sometimes startling fact that a native speaker, in discerning which utterances are grammatical, has a linguistic "competence" that evidently takes form in rules of operation that the speaker may not be able to formulate. Like Freud's hypothesis of the unconscious, Chomsky's idea of a tacit linguistic competence underlying observable linguistic performance, together with his hypothesis concerning the "deep structure" of sentences, revolutionized the field of linguistic theory as a discipline that required precise, logical analysis to describe the observable but frequently obscure regularities in grammatical utterances.

While the details of Chomsky's specific theories have changed in many particulars, what has remained consistent is his view that language competence is universal and species-specific: that our ability to learn and manipulate natural language, whatever particular language we may learn, is innate or genetically determined, and not simply the result of imitation and behavioral conditioning. In such books as *Language and Mind* and *Cartesian Linguistics,* Chomsky has argued vigorously for a kind of "mentalism" in opposition to behaviorism that is essential to the human ability to learn language, just as he has advanced the search for linguistic universals that are manifest in different sets of rules in all natural languages. His distinction between the base component or "deep structure" of an utterance, as a set of logical (and semantic) relations, operated upon to generate or produce the utterance that appears as a "surface structure" gained force through his frequently brilliant examples that show simply why it is that the observable structure of a sentence may not be a sufficient guide to its grammatical character—as in perhaps his most famous example of two sentences with the same structural shape, with profoundly different meaning: *"John is eager to please";* and *"John is easy to please."* For historical reasons, however, we have focused primarily on Chomsky's review of Skinner because it exemplifies dramatically his departure from behaviorist and merely empiricist conceptions of language.

While it must be said that the "revolution" in linguistics attributed to Chomsky has been neither easy nor universally acknowledged, it remains the case that contemporary linguistics is especially indebted to in his groundbreaking book, *Aspects of the Theory of Syntax* (1965). Particularly in the area of semantics, the standard of descriptive adequacy at which Chomsky early aimed, left open a broad (and deep) question pertaining to whether or not the meaning of utterances could be interpreted as *derived* from the "base component" (implying that an interpretive semantics might locate the meaning in the "deep structure" and not the "surface structure"), or whether meaning was affected by broader principles such as grammatical case (in the early work of Charles Fillmore) and by the variability of meaning introduced by transformations themselves. Such questions, it should be clear, could hardly be formulated without Chomsky's contributions to linguistic theory. On broader philosophical questions concerning the nature of language, Chomsky has also been at the center of numerous many-sided controversies, concerning the sense in which language (and language ability) depends upon properties of mind, with such philosophers as Daniel C. Dennett and John Searle.

Chomsky has also been, since the mid-1960s, an equally incisive and pervasive critic and theorist in the political domain, developing a sweeping theory of political power and a vigorous position of advocacy, in favor of radical democracy and against the influence of large institutional forces, in business and government alike. From the publication of *American Power and the New Mandarins* (1969) to *Power and Terror—Post 9-11 Talks and Interviews* (2003), Chomsky has published more than 50 books, monographs, and collections of essays and interviews on political subjects.

The historical importance of *Aspects of the Theory of Syntax* (1965) lies in the fact that it effected a major consolidation of linguistic theory, but Chomsky's work has moved a considerable distance beyond it. Other major works include: *Cartesian Linguistics: A Chapter in the History of Rationalist Thought* (1966); *Language and Mind* (1968); *The Logical Structure of Linguistic Theory* (1975); *Essays on Form and Interpretation* (1977); *Rules and Representations* (1980); *Knowledge of Language: Its Nature, Origins, and Use* (1986); *Language and Thought* (1993); *On Langauge,* with Mitsu Ronat (1998). Studies of Chomsky include: John Lyons, *Chomsky* (1970); Alexander George, ed., *Reflections on Chomsky* (1989); Vivian Cook and Mark Newson, *Chomsky's Universal Grammar: An Introduction* (1996); Alison Edgley, *The Social and Political Thought of Noam Chomsky* (2000); Morton Winston, *On Chomsky* (2002).

from

A Review of B. F. Skinner's
Verbal Behavior

I

A great many linguists and philosophers concerned with language have expressed the hope that their studies might ultimately be embedded in a framework provided by behaviorist psychology, and that refractory areas of investigation, particularly those in which meaning is involved, will in this way be opened up to fruitful exploration. Since this volume

"A Review of B. F. Skinner's *Verbal Behavior*" originally appeared in 1959, and is reprinted in part from *Language* 35, No. 1 (1959), 26–58.

is the first large-scale attempt to incorporate the major aspects of linguistic behavior within a behaviorist framework, it merits and will undoubtedly receive careful attention. Skinner is noted for his contributions to the study of animal behavior. The book under review is the product of study of linguistic behavior extending over more than twenty years. Earlier versions of it have been fairly widely circulated, and there are quite a few references in the psychological literature to its major ideas.

The problem to which this book is addressed is that of giving a "functional analysis" of verbal behavior. By functional analysis, Skinner means identification of the variables that control this behavior and specification of how they interact to determine a particular verbal response. Furthermore, the controlling variables are to be described completely in terms of such notions as *stimulus, reinforcement, deprivation,* which have been given a reasonably clear meaning in animal experimentation. In other words, the goal of the book is to provide a way to predict and control verbal behavior by observing and manipulating the physical environment of the speaker.

Skinner feels that recent advances in the laboratory study of animal behavior permit us to approach this problem with a certain optimism, since "the basic processes and relations which give verbal behavior its special characteristics are now fairly well understood . . . the results [of this experimental work] have been surprisingly free of species restrictions. Recent work has shown that the methods can be extended to human behavior without serious modification" (3).[1]

It is important to see clearly just what it is in Skinner's program and claims that makes them appear so bold and remarkable. It is not primarily the fact that he has set functional analysis as his problem, or that he limits himself to study of *observables,* i.e., input-output relations. What is so surprising is the particular limitations he has imposed on the way in which the observables of behavior are to be studied, and, above all, the particularly simple nature of the *function* which, he claims, describes the causation of behavior. One would naturally expect that prediction of the behavior of a complex organism (or machine) would require, in addition to information about external stimulation, knowledge of the internal structure of the organism, the ways in which it processes input information and organizes its own behavior. These characteristics of the organism are in general a complicated product of inborn structure, the genetically determined course of maturation, and past experience. Insofar as independent neurophysiological evidence is not available, it is obvious that inferences concerning the structure of the organism are based on observation of behavior and outside

events. Nevertheless, one's estimate of the relative importance of external factors and internal structure in the determination of behavior will have an important effect on the direction of research on linguistic (or any other) behavior, and on the kinds of analogies from animal behavior studies that will be considered relevant or suggestive.

Putting it differently, anyone who sets himself the problem of analyzing the causation of behavior will (in the absence of independent neurophysiological evidence) concern himself with the only data available, namely the record of inputs to the organism and the organism's present response, and will try to describe the function specifying the response in terms of the history of inputs. This is nothing more than the definition of his problem. There are no possible grounds for argument here, if one accepts the problem as legitimate, though Skinner has often advanced and defended this definition of a problem as if it were a thesis which other investigators reject. The differences that arise between those who affirm and those who deny the importance of the specific "contribution of the organism" to learning and performance concern the particular character and complexity of this function, and the kinds of observations and research necessary for arriving at a precise specification of it. If the contribution of the organism is complex, the only hope of predicting behavior even in a gross way will be through a very indirect program of research that begins by studying the detailed character of the behavior itself and the particular capacities of the organism involved.

Skinner's thesis is that external factors consisting of present stimulation and the history of reinforcement (in particular, the frequency, arrangement, and withholding of reinforcing stimuli) are of overwhelming importance, and that the general principles revealed in laboratory studies of these phenomena provide the basis for understanding the complexities of verbal behavior. He confidently and repeatedly voices his claim to have demonstrated that the contribution of the speaker is quite trivial and elementary, and that precise prediction of verbal behavior involves only specification of the few external factors that he has isolated experimentally with lower organisms.

Careful study of this book (and of the research on which it draws) reveals, however, that these astonishing claims are far from justified. It indicates, furthermore, that the insights that have been achieved in the laboratories of the reinforcement theorist, though quite genuine, can be applied to complex human behavior only in the most gross and superficial way, and that speculative attempts to discuss linguistic behavior in these terms alone omit from consideration factors of fundamental importance that are, no doubt, amenable to scientific study, although their specific character cannot at

---

[1] [Chomsky] Skinner's confidence in recent achievements in the study of animal behavior and their applicability to complex human behavior does not appear to be widely shared. In many recent publications of confirmed behaviorists there is a prevailing note of skepticism with regard to the scope of these achievements. For representative comments, see the contributions to *Modern Learning Theory* (by W. K. Estes et al.; New York: Appleton-Century-Crofts, Inc., 1954); B. R. Bugelski, *Psychology of Learning* (New York: Holt, Rinehart & Winston, Inc., 1956); S. Koch, in *Nebraska Symposium on Motivation,* 58 (Lincoln, 1956); W. S. Verplanck, "Learned and Innate Behavior," *Psych. Rev.,* 52, (1955), 139. Perhaps the strongest view is that of H. Harlow, who has asserted ("Mice, Monkeys, Men, and Motives," *Psych. Rev.,* 60, [1953] 23–32) that "a strong case can be made for the proposition that the importance of the psychological problems studied during the last 15 years has decreased as a negatively accelerated function approaching an asymptote of complete indifference." N. Tinbergen, a leading representative of a different approach to animal behavior studies (comparative ethology), concludes a discussion of *functional analysis* with the comment that "we may now draw the conclusion that the causation of behavior is immensely more complex than was assumed in the generalizations of the past. A number of internal and external factors act upon complex central nervous structures. Second, it will be obvious that the facts at our disposal are very fragmentary indeed"—*The Study of Instinct* (Toronto: Oxford Univ. Press, 1951), p. 74.

present be precisely formulated. Since Skinner's work is the most extensive attempt to accommodate human behavior involving higher mental faculties within a strict behaviorist schema of the type that has attracted many linguists and philosophers, as well as psychologists, a detailed documentation is of independent interest. The magnitude of the failure of this attempt to account for verbal behavior serves as a kind of measure of the importance of the factors omitted from consideration, and an indication of how little is really known about this remarkably complex phenomenon.

The force of Skinner's argument lies in the enormous wealth and range of examples for which he proposes a functional analysis. The only way to evaluate the success of his program and the correctness of his basic assumptions about verbal behavior is to review these examples in detail and to determine the precise character of the concepts in terms of which the functional analysis is presented. Section 2 of this review describes the experimental context with respect to which these concepts are originally defined. Sections 3 and 4 deal with the basic concepts—*stimulus, response,* and *reinforcement*—Sections 6 to 10 with the new descriptive machinery developed specifically for the description of verbal behavior. In Section 5 we consider the status of the fundamental claim, drawn from the laboratory, which serves as the basis for the analogic guesses about human behavior that have been proposed by many psychologists. The final section (Section 11) will consider some ways in which further linguistic work may play a part in clarifying some of these problems.

II

Although this book makes no direct reference to experimental work, it can be understood only in terms of the general framework that Skinner has developed for the description of behavior. Skinner divides the responses of the animal into two main categories. *Respondents* are purely reflex responses elicited by particular stimuli. *Operants* are emitted responses, for which no obvious stimulus can be discovered. Skinner has been concerned primarily with operant behavior. The experimental arrangement that he introduced consists basically of a box with a bar attached to one wall in such a way that when the bar is pressed, a food pellet is dropped into a tray (and the bar press is recorded). A rat placed in the box will soon press the bar, releasing a pellet into the tray. This state of affairs, resulting from the bar press, increases the *strength* of the bar-pressing operant. The food pellet is called a *reinforcer;* the event, a *reinforcing event*. The strength of an operant is defined by Skinner in terms of the rate of response during ex-

tinction (i.e., after the last reinforcement and before return to the pre-conditioning rate).

* * *

The notions *stimulus, response, reinforcement* are relatively well defined with respect to the bar-pressing experiments and others similarly restricted. Before we can extend them to real-life behavior, however, certain difficulties must be faced. We must decide, first of all, whether any physical event to which the organism is capable of reacting is to be called a stimulus on a given occasion, or only one to which the organism in fact reacts; and correspondingly, we must decide whether any part of behavior is to be called a response, or only one connected with stimuli in lawful ways. Questions of this sort pose something of a dilemma for the experimental psychologist. If he accepts the broad definitions, characterizing any physical event impinging on the organism as a stimulus and any part of the organism's behavior as a response, he must conclude that behavior has not been demonstrated to be lawful. In the present state of our knowledge, we must attribute an overwhelming influence on actual behavior to ill-defined factors of attention, set, volition, and caprice. If we accept the narrower definitions, then behavior is lawful by definition (if it consists of responses); but this fact is of limited significance, since most of what the animal does will simply not be considered behavior. Hence, the psychologist either must admit that behavior is not lawful (or that he cannot at present show that it is—not at all a damaging admission for a developing science), or must restrict his attention to those highly limited areas in which it is lawful (e.g., with adequate controls, bar-pressing in rats; lawfulness of the observed behavior provides, for Skinner, an implicit definition of a good experiment).

Skinner does not consistently adopt either course. He utilizes the experimental results as evidence for the scientific character of his system of behavior, and analogic guesses (formulated in terms of a metaphoric extension of the technical vocabulary of the laboratory) as evidence for its scope. This creates the illusion of a rigorous scientific theory with a very broad scope, although in fact the terms used in the description of real-life and of laboratory behavior may be mere homonyms, with at most a vague similarity of meaning. To substantiate this evaluation, a critical account of his book must show that with a literal reading (where the terms of the descriptive system have something like the technical meanings given in Skinner's definitions) the book covers almost no aspect of linguistic behavior, and that with a metaphoric reading, it is no more scientific than the traditional approaches to this subject matter, and rarely as clear and careful.[2]

III

Consider first Skinner's use of the notions *stimulus* and *response*. In *Behavior of Organisms* (9) he commits himself to the narrow definitions for these terms. A part of the environment and a part of behavior are called *stimulus* (eliciting, discriminated, or reinforcing) and *response,* respectively, only if they are lawfully related; that is, if the *dynamic laws* relating them show smooth and reproducible curves. Evidently, stimuli and responses, so defined, have not been shown to figure very widely in ordinary human behavior.[3] We can, in the face of presently available evidence, continue to maintain the lawfulness of the relation between stimulus and response only by depriving them of their objective character. A typical example of *stimulus control* for Skinner would be the response to a piece of music with the utterance *Mozart* or to a painting with the response *Dutch*. These responses are asserted to be "under the control of extremely subtle properties" of the physical object or event (108). Suppose instead of saying *Dutch* we had said *Clashes with the wallpaper, I thought you liked abstract work, Never saw it before, Tilted, Hanging too low, Beautiful, Hideous, Remember our camping trip last summer?,* or whatever else might come into our minds when looking at a picture (in Skinnerian translation, whatever other responses exist in sufficient strength). Skinner could only say that each of these responses is under the control of some other stimulus property of the physical object. If we look at a red chair and say *red*, the response is under the control of the stimulus *redness;* if we say *chair*, it is under the control of the collection of properties (for Skinner,

the object) *chairness* (110), and similarly for any other response. This device is as simple as it is empty. Since properties are free for the asking (we have as many of them as we have nonsynonymous descriptive expressions in our language, whatever this means exactly), we can account for a wide class of responses in terms of Skinnerian functional analysis by identifying the *controlling stimuli*. But the word *stimulus* has lost all objectivity in this usage. Stimuli are no longer part of the outside physical world; they are driven back into the organism. We identify the stimulus when we hear the response. It is clear from such examples, which abound, that the talk of *stimulus control* simply disguises a complete retreat to mentalistic psychology. We cannot predict verbal behavior in terms of the stimuli in the speaker's environment, since we do not know what the current stimuli are until he responds. Furthermore, since we cannot control the property of a physical object to which an individual will respond, except in highly artificial cases, Skinner's claim that his system, as opposed to the traditional one, permits the practical control of verbal behavior[4] is quite false.

* * *

V

* * *

As far as acquisition of language is concerned, it seems clear that reinforcement, casual observation, and natural in-

---

[2] [Chomsky] An analogous argument, in connection with a different aspect of Skinner's thinking, is given by M. Scriven in "A Study of Radical Behaviorism," *Univ. of Minn. Studies in Philosophy of Science,* I. Cf. Verplanck's contribution to *Modern Learning Theory, op. cit.* pp. 283–88, for more general discussion of the difficulties in formulating an adequate definition of *stimulus* and *response.* He concludes, quite correctly, that in Skinner's sense of the word, stimuli are not objectively identifiable independently of the resulting behavior, nor are they manipulable. Verplanck presents a clear discussion of many other aspects of Skinner's system, commenting on the untestability of many of the so-called "laws of behavior" and the limited scope of many of the others, and the arbitrary and obscure character of Skinner's notion of *lawful relation;* and, at the same time, noting the importance of the experimental data that Skinner has accumulated.

[3] [Chomsky] In *Behavior of Organisms,* Skinner apparently was willing to accept this consequence. He insists (41–42) that the terms of casual description in the popular vocabulary are not validly descriptive until the defining properties of stimulus and response are specified, the correlation is demonstrated experimentally, and the dynamic changes in it are shown to be lawful. Thus, in describing a child as hiding from a dog, "it will not be enough to dignify the popular vocabulary by appealing to essential properties of *dogness* or *hidingness* and to suppose them intuitively known." But this is exactly what Skinner does in the book under review, as we will see directly.

[4] [Chomsky] 253f. and elsewhere, repeatedly. As an example of how well we can control behavior using the notions developed in this book, Skinner shows here how he would go about evoking the response *pencil*. The most effective way, he suggests, is to say to the subject, "Please say *pencil*" (our chances would, presumably, be even further improved by use of "aversive stimulation," e.g., holding a gun to his head). We can also "make sure that no pencil or writing instrument is available, then hand our subject a pad of paper appropriate to pencil sketching, and offer him a handsome reward for a recognizable picture of a cat." It would also be useful to have voices saying *pencil* or *pen and . . .* in the background; signs reading *pencil* or *pen and . . .;* or to place a "large and unusual pencil in an unusual place clearly in sight." "Under such circumstances, it is highly probable that our subject will say *pencil*." "The available techniques are all illustrated in this sample." These contributions of behavior theory to the practical control of human behavior are amply illustrated elsewhere in the book, as when Skinner shows (113–14) how we can evoke the response *red* (the device suggested is to hold a red object before the subject and say, "Tell me what color this is").

In fairness, it must be mentioned that there are certain nontrivial applications of *operant conditioning* to the control of human behavior. A wide variety of experiments have shown that the number of plural nouns (for example) produced by a subject will increase if the experimenter says "right" or "good" when one is produced (similarly, positive attitudes on a certain issue, stories with particular content, etc.; cf. L. Krasner, "Studies of the Conditioning of Verbal Behavior," *Psych. Bull.,* 55 [1958], for a survey of several dozen experiments of this kind, mostly with positive results). It is of some interest that the subject is usually unaware of the process. Just what insight this gives into normal verbal behavior is not obvious. Nevertheless, it is an example of positive and not totally expected results using the Skinnerian paradigm.

quisitiveness (coupled with a strong tendency to imitate) are important factors, as is the remarkable capacity of the child to generalize, hypothesize, and "process information" in a variety of very special and apparently highly complex ways which we cannot yet describe or begin to understand, and which may be largely innate, or may develop through some sort of learning or through maturation of the nervous system. The manner in which such factors operate and interact in language acquisition is completely unknown. It is clear that what is necessary in such a case is research, not dogmatic and perfectly arbitrary claims, based on analogies to that small part of the experimental literature in which one happens to be interested.

The pointlessness of these claims becomes clear when we consider the well-known difficulties in determining to what extent inborn structure, maturation, and learning are responsible for the particular form of a skilled or complex performance.[5] To take just one example,[6] the gaping response of a nestling thrush is at first released by jarring of the nest, and, at a later stage, by a moving object of specific size, shape, and position relative to the nestling. At this later stage the response is directed toward the part of the stimulus object corresponding to the parent's head, and characterized by a complex configuration of stimuli that can be precisely described. Knowing just this, it would be possible to construct a speculative, learning-theoretic account of how this sequence of behavior patterns might have developed through a process of differential reinforcement, and it would no doubt be possible to train rats to do something similar. However, there appears to be good evidence that these responses to fairly complex "sign stimuli" are genetically determined and mature without learning. Clearly, the possibility cannot be discounted. Consider now the comparable case of a child imitating new words. At an early stage we may find rather gross correspondences. At a later stage, we find that repetition is of course far from exact (i.e., it is not mimicry, a fact which itself is interesting), but that it repro-

duces the highly complex configuration of sound features that constitute the phonological structure of the language in question. Again, we can propose a speculative account of how this result might have been obtained through elaborate arrangement of reinforcing contingencies. Here too, however, it is possible that ability to select out of the complex auditory input those features that are phonologically relevant may develop largely independently of reinforcement, through genetically determined maturation. To the extent that this is true, an account of the development and causation of behavior that fails to consider the structure of the organism will provide no understanding of the real processes involved.

It is often argued that experience, rather than innate capacity to handle information in certain specific ways, must be the factor of overwhelming dominance in determining the specific character of language acquisition, since a child speaks the language of the group in which he lives. But this is a superficial argument. As long as we are speculating, we may consider the possibility that the brain has evolved to the point where, given an input of observed Chinese sentences, it produces (by an *induction* of apparently fantastic complexity and suddenness) the *rules* of Chinese grammar, and given an input of observed English sentences, it produces (by, perhaps, exactly the same process of induction) the rules of English grammar; or that given an observed application of a term to certain instances, it automatically predicts the extension to a class of complexly related instances. If clearly recognized as such, this speculation is neither unreasonable nor fantastic; nor, for that matter, is it beyond the bounds of possible study. There is of course no known neural structure capable of performing this task in the specific ways that observation of the resulting behavior might lead us to postulate; but for that matter, the structures capable of accounting for even the simplest kinds of learning have similarly defied detection.[7] Summarizing this brief discussion, it seems that there is neither empirical evidence nor any known argument to support any specific claim about the relative importance of "feedback" from the environment and the "independent contribution of the organism" in the process of language acquisition.

---

[5][Chomsky] Tinbergen, *op.cit.,* Chap. VI, reviews some aspects of this problem, discussing the primary role of maturation in the development of many complex motor patterns (e.g., flying, swimming) in lower organisms, and the effect of an "innate disposition to learn" in certain specific ways and at certain specific times. Cf. also P. Schiller, "Innate Motor Action as a Basis for Learning," in C. H. Schiller, ed., *Instinctive Behavior* (New York: International Universities Press, 1957), pp. 265–88, for a discussion of the role of maturing motor patterns in apparently insightful behavior in the chimpanzee.

Lenneberg ("The Capacity for Language Acquisition," in J. A. Fodor, ed., *The Structure of Language* [Prentice-Hall, Inc., 1964]) presents a very interesting discussion of the part that biological structure may play in the acquisition of language, and the dangers in neglecting this possibility.

[6][Chomsky] From among many cited by Tinbergen, *op. cit.,* p. 85.

[7][Chomsky] Cf. K. S. Lashley, "In Search of the Engram," *Symposium of the Society for Experimental Biology,* 4 (1950), 454–82. R. Sperry, "On the Neural Basis of the Conditioned Response," *British Journal of Animal Behavior,* 3 (1955), 41–44, argues that to account for the experimental results of Lashley and others, and for other facts that he cites, it is necessary to assume that high-level cerebral activity of the type of insight, expectancy, and so on is involved even in simple conditioning. He states that "we still lack today a satisfactory picture of the underlying neural mechanism" of the conditioned response.

* * *

XI

The preceding discussion covers all the major notions that Skinner introduces in his descriptive system. My purpose in discussing the concepts one by one was to show that in each case, if we take his terms in their literal meaning, the description covers almost no aspect of verbal behavior, and if we take them metaphorically, the description offers no improvement over various traditional formulations. The terms borrowed from experimental psychology simply lose their objective meaning with this extension, and take over the full vagueness of ordinary language. Since Skinner limits himself to such a small set of terms for paraphrase, many important distinctions are obscured. I think that this analysis supports the view expressed in Section I, that elimination of the independent contribution of the speaker and learner (a result which Skinner considers of great importance, cf. 311–12) can be achieved only at the cost of eliminating all significance from the descriptive system, which then operates at a level so gross and crude that no answers are suggested to the most elementary questions.[8] The questions to which Skinner has addressed his speculations are hopelessly premature. It is futile to inquire into the causation of verbal behavior until much more is known about the specific character of this behavior; and there is little point in speculating about the process of acquisition without much better understanding of what is acquired.

Anyone who seriously approaches the study of linguistic behavior, whether linguist, psychologist, or philosopher, must quickly become aware of the enormous difficulty of stating a problem which will define the area of his investigations, and which will not be either completely trivial or hopelessly beyond the range of present-day understanding and technique. In selecting functional analysis as his problem, Skinner has set himself a task of the latter type. In an extremely interesting and insightful paper,[9] K. S. Lashley has implicitly delimited a class of problems which can be approached in a fruitful way by the linguist and psychologist, and which are clearly preliminary to those with which Skinner is concerned. Lashley recognizes, as anyone must who seriously considers the data, that the composition and production of an utterance is not simply a matter of stringing together a sequence of responses under the control of outside stimulation and intraverbal association, and that the syntactic organization of an utterance is not something directly represented in any simple way in the physical structure of the utterance itself. A variety of observations lead him to conclude that syntactic structure is "a generalized pattern imposed on the specific acts as they occur" (512), and that "a consideration of the structure of the sentence and other motor sequences will show . . . that there are, behind the overtly expressed sequences, a multiplicity of integrative processes which can only be inferred from the final results of their activity" (509). He also comments on the great difficulty of determining the "selective mechanisms" used in the actual construction of a particular utterance (522).

Although present-day linguistics cannot provide a precise account of these integrative processes, imposed patterns, and selective mechanisms, it can at least set itself the problem of characterizing these completely. It is reasonable to regard the grammar of a language L ideally as a mechanism that provides an enumeration of the sentences of L in something like the way in which a deductive theory gives an enumeration of a set of theorems. (*Grammar,* in this sense of the word, includes phonology.) Furthermore, the theory of language can be regarded as a study of the formal properties of such grammars, and, with a precise enough formulation, this general theory can provide a uniform method for determining, from the process of generation of

---

[8][Chomsky] E.g., what are in fact the actual units of verbal behavior? Under what conditions will a physical event capture the attention (be a stimulus) or be a reinforcer? How do we decide what stimuli are in "control" in a specific case? When are stimuli "similar"? And so on. (It is not interesting to be told, e.g., that we say *Stop* to an automobile or billiard ball because they are sufficiently similar to reinforcing people [46].) The use of unanalyzed notions like *similar* and *generalization* is particularly disturbing, since it indicates an apparent lack of interest in every significant aspect of the learning or the use of language in new situations. No one has ever doubted that in some sense, language is learned by generalization, or that novel utterances and situations are in some way similar to familiar ones. The only matter of serious interest is the specific "similarity." Skinner has, apparently, no interest in this. Keller and Schoenfeld, *op. cit.,* proceed to incorporate these notions (which they identify) into their Skinnerian "modern objective psychology" by defining two stimuli to be similar when "we make the same sort of response to them" (124; but when are responses of the "same sort"?). They do not seem to notice that this definition converts their "principle of generalization" (116), under any reasonable interpretation of this, into a tautology. It is obvious that such a definition will not be of much help in the study of language learning or construction of new responses in appropriate situations.

[9][Chomsky] "The Problem of Serial Order in Behavior," in L. A. Jeffress, ed., *Hixon Symposium on Cerebral Mechanisms in Behavior* (New York: John Wiley & Sons Inc., 1951). Reprinted in F. A. Beach, D. O. Hebb, C. T. Morgan, H. W. Nissen, eds., *The Neuropsychology of Lashley* (New York: McGraw-Hill Book Company, 1960). Page references are to the latter.

a given sentence, a structural description which can give a good deal of insight into how this sentence is used and understood. In short, it should be possible to derive from a properly formulated grammar a statement of the integrative processes and generalized patterns imposed on the specific acts that constitute an utterance. The rules of a grammar of the appropriate form can be subdivided into the two types, optional and obligatory; only the latter must be applied in generating an utterance. The optional rules of the grammar can be viewed, then, as the selective mechanisms involved in the production of a particular utterance. The problem of specifying these integrative processes and selective mechanisms is nontrivial and not beyond the range of possible investigation. The results of such a study might, as Lashley suggests, be of independent interest for psychology and neurology (and conversely). Although such a study, even if successful, would by no means answer the major problems involved in the investigation of meaning and the causation of behavior, it surely will not be unrelated to these. It is at least possible, furthermore, that such a notion as *semantic generalization,* to which such heavy appeal is made in all approaches to language in use, conceals complexities and specific structure of inference not far different from those that can be studied and exhibited in the case of syntax, and that consequently the general character of the results of syntactic investigations may be a corrective to oversimplified approaches to the theory of meaning.

The behavior of the speaker, listener, and learner of language constitutes, of course, the actual data for any study of language. The construction of a grammar which enumerates sentences in such a way that a meaningful structural description can be determined for each sentence does not in itself provide an account of this actual behavior. It merely characterizes abstractly the ability of one who has mastered the language to distinguish sentences from non-sentences, to understand new sentences (in part), to note certain ambiguities, etc. These are very remarkable abilities. We constantly read and hear new sequences of words, recognize them as sentences, and understand them. It is easy to show that the new events that we accept and understand as sentences are not related to those with which we are familiar by any simple notion of formal (or semantic or statistical) similarity or identity of grammatical frame. Talk of generalization in this case is entirely pointless and empty. It appears that we recognize a new item as a sentence not because it matches some familiar item in any simple way, but because it is generated by the grammar that each individual has somehow and in some form internalized. And we understand a new sentence, in part, because

we are somehow capable of determining the process by which this sentence is derived in this grammar.

Suppose that we manage to construct grammars having the properties outlined above. We can then attempt to describe and study the achievement of the speaker, listener, and learner. The speaker and the listener, we must assume, have already acquired the capacities characterized abstractly by the grammar. The speaker's task is to select a particular compatible set of optional rules. If we know, from grammatical study, what choices are available to him and what conditions of compatibility the choices must meet, we can proceed meaningfully to investigate the factors that lead him to make one or another choice. The listener (or reader) must determine, from an exhibited utterance, what optional rules were chosen in the construction of the utterance. It must be admitted that the ability of a human being to do this far surpasses our present understanding. The child who learns a language has in some sense constructed the grammar for himself on the basis of his observation of sentences and nonsentences (i.e., corrections by the verbal community). Study of the actual observed ability of a speaker to distinguish sentences from nonsentences, detect ambiguities, etc., apparently forces us to the conclusion that this grammar is of an extremely complex and abstract character, and that the young child has succeeded in carrying out what from the formal point of view, at least, seems to be a remarkable type of theory construction. Furthermore, this task is accomplished in an astonishingly short time, to a large extent independently of intelligence, and in a comparable way by all children. Any theory of learning must cope with these facts.

It is not easy to accept the view that a child is capable of constructing an extremely complex mechanism for generating a set of sentences, some of which he has heard, or that an adult can instantaneously determine whether (and if so, how) a particular item is generated by this mechanism, which has many of the properties of an abstract deductive theory. Yet this appears to be a fair description of the performance of the speaker, listener, and learner. If this is correct, we can predict that a direct attempt to account for the actual behavior of speaker, listener, and learner, not based on a prior understanding of the structure of grammars, will achieve very limited success. The grammar must be regarded as a component in the behavior of the speaker and listener which can only be inferred, as Lashley has put it, from the resulting physical acts. The fact that all normal children acquire essentially comparable grammars of great complexity with remarkable rapidity suggests that human beings are somehow specially designed to do this, with data-handling or "hypothesis-formulating" ability of unknown character and complexity.[10] The study of linguistic structure may ultimately lead to some significant insights into this matter. At the moment the question cannot be seriously posed, but in principle it may be possible to study the problem of determining what the built-in structure of an information-processing (hypothesis-forming) system must be to enable it to arrive at the grammar of a language from the available data in the available time. At any rate, just as the attempt to eliminate the contribution of the speaker leads to a "mentalistic" descriptive system that succeeds only in blurring important traditional distinctions, a refusal to study the contribution of the child to language learning permits only a superficial account of language acquisition, with a vast and unanalyzed contribution attributed to a step called *generalization* which in fact includes just about everything of interest in this process. If the study of language is limited in these ways, it seems inevitable that major aspects of verbal behavior will remain a mystery.

---

[10] [Chomsky] There is nothing essentially mysterious about this. Complex innate behavior patterns and innate "tendencies to learn in specific ways" have been carefully studied in lower organisms. Many psychologists have been inclined to believe that such biological structure will not have an important effect on acquisition of complex behavior in higher organisms, but I have not been able to find any serious justification for this attitude. Some recent studies have stressed the necessity for carefully analyzing the strategies available to the organism, regarded as a complex "information-processing system" (cf. J. S. Bruner, J. J. Goodnow, and G. A. Austin, *A Study of Thinking* [New York, 1956]; A. Newell, J. C. Shaw, and H. A. Simon, "Elements of a Theory of Human Problem Solving," *Psych. Rev.*, 65, [1958], 151–66), if anything significant is to be said about the character of human learning. These may be largely innate, or developed by early learning processes about which very little is yet known. (But see Harlow, "The Formation of Learning Sets," *Psych. Rev.*, 56, (1949), 51–65, and many later papers, where striking shifts in the character of learning are shown as a result of early training; also D. O. Hebb, *Organization of Behavior*, 109 ff.). They are undoubtedly quite complex. Cf. Lenneberg, *op. cit.*, and R. B. Lees, review of N. Chomsky's *Syntactic Structures* in *Language*, 33 (1957), 406f, for discussion of the topics mentioned in this section. [The foregoing discussion provides the foundation for Chomsky's conception of linguistic competence, elaborated in later work.]

Jean Paul Sartre

1905–1980

In 1964, Jean Paul Sartre was designated to receive the Nobel Prize in Literature, an honor he declined, but his lifelong production of extraordinary work as a philosopher, a novelist, a playwright, and a political theorist had already earned for him an exceptional position as both a master and a mediator between multiple discourses, not just in France but internationally. While teaching in Le Havre, he published his first novel, *La Nausée* (1938; *Nausea,* 1949). Following his early phenomenological studies of imagination and emotion in the 1930s, his *Being and Nothingness,* published in 1943, following his release from internment as a prisoner of war, was quickly recognized as one of the essential works of philosophical existentialism. For Sartre, unlike Heidegger (above, page 1051), for example, existentialism was treated both as a philosophical imperative, in response to a sense of metaphysical crisis (crudely encapsulated in the formula that existence precedes essence implying that the meaning or truth of being was not transcendentally sanctioned but must be made by radical, individual action)—and as the natural inheritor of humanism, attending to the concrete problems and dilemmas of humankind.

Sartre's version of existentialism, in this sense, places human freedom in the foreground, just as it points to social and political action, in which writers have inherent responsibilities. Following the war, Sartre turned to writing plays, then novels, projecting a large four-volume work *(Les Chemins de la Liberté* or *The Paths of Liberty),* of which three volumes were published: *L'Âge de raison* (1945; *The Age of Reason,* 1947), *Le Sursis* (1945; *The Reprieve,* 1947), and *La Mort dans l'âme* (1949; *Troubled Sleep,* 1950), followed by a series of plays for which he is possibly best known by international audiences, including *Les Mouches* (1943; *The Flies,* 1946); *Huis-clos* (1944; *No Exit,* 1946); *Les mains sales* (1948; *Dirty Hands,* 1949); and *Les Séquestrés d'Altona* (1959; *The Condemned of Altona,* 1960). He is also the author of scores of critical, political, and philosophical essays (many collected in the multiple volumes of *Situations*) and literary biography and criticism focusing on Baudelaire, Jean Genet, and Flaubert.

The work of Sartre's that is, however, the most pointed and, for subsequent theory, the most influential, is his political and philosophical works, starting with a popular booklet, *L'Existentialism est un humanisme* (1946; *Existentialism and Humanism,* 1948), and his ambitious *Critique de la raison dialectique* (1960; the introduction separately published as *Search for a Method,* 1963, and *Critique of Dialectical Reason,* in two volumes, 1990). This work attempts a full exposition and a critique of relations between existentialism and Marxism, setting forth a view of philosophy as always and necessarily reflective of and grounded in social reality and its material contestations, while confronting the growing evidence that Marxism, on the Soviet model, was untenable, just as the larger social objectives Marx had enunciated remained vital. In this context, Sartre's preeminent role in French intellectual life from before World War II, to the decades following it, should be seen against the background of extraordinary intellectual energy, directed to the reinterpretation of philosophical, political, psychological, and anthropological traditions, with competing revivals of interest in a critique of the philosophy of Hegel especially in lectures from the 1930s by Alexandre Kojeve, *Introduction to the Reading of Hegel* (1947; tr. 1969); and Jean Hyppolite's *Introduction to Hegel's Philosophy of History* (1948; tr. 1996). Thus, what might have been Sartre's most triumphant work appeared, instead, in the midst of a multifaceted and inherently problematizing intellectual revolution that brought such younger thinkers as Maurice Merleau-Ponty, Claude Lévi-Strauss, and Jean Piaget, to the fore, followed in their turn by a still more relentless critical style with such figures as Jacques Lacan, Jacques Derrida, and Michel Foucault.

Sartre's primary philosophical works include *Being and Nothingness: An Essay on Phenomenological Ontology,* tr. Hazel Barnes (1956); *Critique of Dialectical Reason,* in two volumes, tr. Quintin Hoare (1990); *The Transcendence of the Ego: An Existentialist Theory of Consciousness* (1957). Many collections of Sartre's literary, critical, and autobiographical essays are available, but see especially, *"What Is Literature" and Other Essays* (1988); *Situations,* tr. Benita Eisler (1965); *The Psychology of Imagination* (1948); and *The Words* (1966). Selected biographical and critical studies include: Alfred Stern, *Sartre, His Philosophy and Psychoanalyses* (1953); E. W. Knight, *Literature Considered as Philosophy* (1957); William Barrett, *Irrational Man* (1958); Philip Thody, *Jean-Paul Sartre: A Literary and Political Study* (1960), and *Jean-Paul Sartre* (1992); R. D. Laing and D. G. Cooper, *Reason & Violence: A Decade of Sartre's Philosophy, 1950–1960* (1964, reissued 1983); Benjamin Suhl, *The Philosopher as Literary Critic* (1970); Dominic LaCapra, *A Preface to Sartre* (1978); Christine Howells, *Sartre's Theory of Literature* (1979); Douglas Collins, *Sartre as Biographer* (1980); Kenneth and Margaret Thompson, *Sartre: Life and Works* (1984); Frederic Jameson, *Sartre: The Origins of a Style* (1984); Thomas C. Anderson, *Sartre's Two Ethics: From Authenticity to Integral Humanity* (1993); Andrew Dobson, *Jean Paul Sartre and the Politics of Reason: A Theory of History* (1993); Gregory McCulloch, *Using Sartre: An Analytical Introduction to Early Sartrean Themes* (1994); Thomas R. Flynn, *Sartre, Foucault, and Historical Reason* (1997); Ann Fulton, *Apostles of Sartre: Existentialism in America, 1945–1963* (1999); Tilottima Rajan, *Deconstruction and the Remainders of Phenomenology: Sartre, Derrida, Foucault, Baudrillard* (2002); Nik Farrell Fox, *The New Sartre: Explorations in Post-Modernism* (2003).

I. Marxism and Existentialism

Philsosphy appears to some people as a homogeneous milieu: there thoughts are born and die, there systems are built, and there, in turn, they collapse. Others take *Philosophy* for a spe-

cific attitude which we can freely adopt at will. Still others see it as a determined segment of culture. In our view *Philosophy* does not exist. In whatever form we consider it, this shadow of science, this Gray Eminence of humanity, is only a hypostatised abstraction. Actually, there are *philosophies.* Or rather—for you would never at the same time find more than one living philosophy—under certain well-defined circumstances a philosophy is developed for the purpose of giving expression to the general movement of the society. So long as a philosophy is alive, it serves as a cultural milieu for its contemporaries. This disconcerting object presents itself *at the same time* under profoundly distinct aspects, the unification of which it is continually effecting.

"Marxism and Existentialism" is reprinted from *Search for a Method,* translated by Hazel Barnes (New York: A. A. Knopf, 1963; Vintage Books, 1968). *Search for a Method* is the first part of *Critique of Dialectical Reason* (1960).

A philosophy is first of all a particular way in which the arising class becomes conscious of itself.[1] This consciousness may be clear or confused, indirect or direct. At the time of the *noblesse de robe*[2] and of mercantile capitalism, a bourgeoisie of lawyers, merchants, and bankers gained a certain self-awareness through Cartesianism; a century and a half later, in the primitive stage of industrialisation, a bourgeoisie of manufacturers, engineers, and scientists dimly discovered itself in the image of universal man which Kantianism offered to it.

But if it is to be truly philosophical, this mirror must be presented as the totalisation of contemporary Knowledge. The philosopher effects the unification of everything that is known, following certain guiding schemata which express the attitudes and techniques of the rising class regarding its own period and the world. Later, when the details of this Knowledge have been, one by one, challenged and destroyed by the advance of learning, the overall concept will still remain as an undifferentiated content. These achievements of knowing, after having been first bound together by principles, will in turn—crushed and almost undecipherable—bind together the principles. Reduced to its simplest expression, the philosophical object will remain in "the objective mind" in the form of a regulative Idea, pointing to an infinite task. Thus, in France one speaks of "the Kantian Idea" or in Germany of "Fichte's *Weltanschauung*." This is because a philosophy, when it is at the height of its power, is never presented as something inert, as the passive, already terminated unity of Knowledge. Born from the movement of society, it is itself a movement and acts upon the future. This concrete totalisation is at the same time the abstract project of pursuing the unification up to its final limits. In this sense philosophy is characterised as a method of investigation and explication. The confidence which it has in itself and in its future development merely reproduces the certitudes of the class which supports it. Every philosophy is practical, even the one which at first appears to be the most contemplative. Its method is a social and political weapon. The analytical, critical rationalism of the great Cartesians has survived them; born from conflict, it looked back to clarify the conflict. At the time when the bourgeoisie sought to

undermine the institutions of the Ancien Regime, it attacked the outworn significations which tried to justify them.[3] Later it gave service to liberalism, and it provided a doctrine for procedures that attempted to realize the "atomisation" of the Proletariat.

Thus a philosophy remains efficacious so long as the *praxis*[4] which has engendered it, which supports it, and which is clarified by it, is still alive. But it is transformed, it loses its uniqueness, it is stripped of its original, dated content to the extent that it gradually impregnates the masses so as to become in and through them a collective instrument of emancipation. In this way Cartesianism, in the eighteenth century, appears under two indissoluble and complementary aspects. On the one hand, as the Idea of reason, as an analytical method, it inspires Holbach, Helvetius, Diderot, even Rousseau;[5] it is Cartesianism which we find at the source of antireligious pamphlets as well as of mechanistic materialism. On the other hand, it passes into anonymity and conditions the attitudes of the Third Estate.[6] In each case universal, analytical Reason vanishes and reappears in the form of "spontaneity." This means that the immediate response of the oppressed to oppression will be critical. The abstract revolt precedes the French Revolution and armed insurrection by some years. But the directed violence of weapons will overthrow privileges which have already been dissolved in Reason. Things go so far that the philosophical mind crosses the boundaries of the bourgeoisie and infiltrates the ranks of the populace. This is the moment at which the French bourgeoisie claims that it is a universal class; the infiltrations of its philosophy will permit it to mask the struggles which are beginning to split the Third Estate and will allow it to find a language and common gestures for all revolutionary classes.

---

[1] [Sartre] If I do not mention here the *person* who is objectified and revealed in his work, it is because the philosophy of a period extends far beyond the philosopher who first gave it shape—no matter how great he may be. But conversely we shall see that the study of particular doctrines is inseparable from a real investigation of philosophies. Cartesianism illuminates the period and *situates* Descartes within the totalitarian development of analytical reason; in these terms, Descartes, taken as a person and as a philosopher, clarifies the historical (hence the particular) meaning of the new rationality up to the middle of the eighteenth century.

[2] [Barnes] *Noblesse de robe* was originally the designation given in France to those members of the bourgeoisie who were awarded titles of nobility in recognition of outstanding achievement or services to the State. Later it was used more loosely to refer to any "new" nobility.

[3] [Sartre] In the case of Cartesianism, the action of "philosophy" remains negative; it clears the ground, it destroys, and it enables men, across the infinite complexities and particularisms of the feudal system, to catch a glimpse of the abstract universality of bourgeois property. But under different circumstances, when the social struggle itself assumes other forms, the theory's contribution can be positive.

[4] [Barnes] The Greek work *praxis* means "deed" or "action." As Sartre uses it, *praxis* refers to any purposeful human activity. It is closely allied to the existential project which Sartre made so important a part of his philosophy in *Being and Nothingness*.

[5] Paul Henri Dietrich, baron d'Holbach (1723–1789), French encyclopedist and philosopher, noted for his espousal of materialism and atheism; Claude-Adrien Helvétius (1715–1771), French philosopher and radical educational theorist, host of the Philosophes; Denis Diderot (1713–1784), French philosopher, chief editor of the *Encyclopédie;* Jean-Jacques Rousseau (1712–1778), French philosopher, writer, political theorist whose works had a significant impact on the leaders of the French Revolution.

[6] One of the *"Estates-generale,"* consisting of three "estates" or classes with a voice in governance: the First Estate is royalty; the Second Estate is the clergy; the Third Estate is the general populace. The institution has a history extending back to Philip IV in 1302; in 1789, on the eve of the French Revolution, the "Third Estate" refused to vote as a block but claimed the right to vote as individuals, and declared themselves to be the National Assembly.

If philosophy is to be simultaneously a totalisation of knowledge, a method, a regulative Idea, an offensive weapon, and a community of language, if this "vision of the world" is also an instrument which ferments rotten societies, if this particular conception of a man or of a group of men becomes the culture and sometimes the nature of a whole class—then it is very clear that the periods of philosophical creation are rare. Between the seventeenth century and the twentieth, I see three such periods, which I would designate by the names of the men who dominated them: there is the "moment" of Descartes and Locke, that of Kant and Hegel, finally that of Marx. These three philosophies become, each in its turn, the humus of every particular thought and the horizon of all culture; there is no going beyond them so long as man has not gone beyond the historical moment which they express. I have often remarked on the fact that an "anti-Marxist" argument is only the apparent rejuvenation of a pre-Marxist idea. A so-called "going beyond" Marxism will be at worst only a return to pre-Marxism; at best, only the rediscovery of a thought already contained in the philosophy which one believes he has gone beyond. As for "revisionism," this is either a truism or an absurdity. There is no need to readapt a living philosophy to the course of the world; it adapts itself by means of thousands of new efforts, thousands of particular pursuits, for the philosophy is one with the movement of society. Despite their good intentions, those very people who believe themselves to be the most faithful spokesmen for their predecessors transform the thoughts which they want simply to repeat; methods are modified because they are applied to new objects. If this movement on the part of the philosophy no longer exists, one of two things is true: either the philosophy is dead or it is going through a "crisis." In the first case there is no question of revising, but of razing a rotten building; in the second case the "philosophical crisis" is the particular expression of a social crisis, and its immobility is conditioned by the contradictions which split the society. A so-called "revision," performed by "experts," would be, therefore, only an idealist mystification without real significance. It is the very movement of History, the struggle of men on all planes and on all levels of human activity, which will set free captive thought and permit it to attain its full development.

Those intellectuals who come after the great flowering and who undertake to set the systems in order to use the new methods to conquer territory not yet fully explored, those who provide practical applications for the theory and employ it as a tool to destroy and to construct—they should not be called philosophers. They cultivate the domain, they take an inventory, they erect certain structures there, they may even bring about certain internal changes; but they still get their nourishment from the living thought of the great dead. They are borne along by the crowd on the march, and it is the crowd which constitutes their cultural milieu and their future, which determines the field of their investigations, and even of their "creation." These *relative* men I propose to call "ideologists."[7] And since I am to speak of existentialism, let it be understood that I take it to be an "ideology." It is a parasitical system living on the margin of Knowledge, which at first it opposed but into which today it seeks to be integrated. If we are to understand its present ambitions and its function we must go back to the time of Kierkegaard.

The most ample philosophical totalisation is Hegelianism. Here Knowledge is raised to its most eminent dignity. It is not limited to viewing Being from the outside; it incorporates Being and dissolves it in itself. Mind objectifies itself, alienates itself, and recovers itself—without ceasing; it realises itself through its own history. Man externalises himself, he loses himself in things; but every alienation is surmounted by the absolute Knowledge of the philosopher. Thus those cleavages, those contradictions which cause our unhappiness are moments which are posited in order that they may be surpassed. We are not only *knowers;* in the triumph of intellectual self-consciousness, we appear as the *known.* Knowledge pierces us through and through; it situates us before dissolving us. We are integrated alive in the supreme totalisation. Thus the pure, lived aspect of a tragic experience, a suffering unto death, is absorbed by the system as a relatively abstract determination which must be mediated, as a passage toward the Absolute, the only genuine concrete.[8]

---

[7] [Barnes] Sartre's word is *ideologues.* I translate it "ideologists" after the analogy of words such as *philologue* (English "philologist").

[8] [Sartre] It is entirely possible, of course, to draw Hegel over to the side of existenialism, and Hyppolite endeavored to do so, not without success, in his *Studies in Marx and Hegel.* Was it not Hegel who first pointed out that "the appearance as such is a reality"? And is not his panlogicism complemented by a pantragicism? Can we not with good reason say that for Hegel "existences are enmeshed in the history which they make and which, as a concrete universality, is what judges and transcends them"? One can do this easily, but that is not the question. What Kierkegaard opposes in Hegel is the fact that for Hegel the tragedy of a particular life is always surpassed. The lived fades away into knowledge. Hegel talks to us about the slave and his fear of death. But the fear which was *felt* becomes the simple object of knowing, and the moment of a transformation which is itself surpassed. In Kierkegaard's view it is of no importance that Hegel speaks of "freedom to die" or that he correctly describes certain aspects of faith. What Kierkegaard complains of in Hegelianism is that it neglects the *unsurpassable opaqueness* of the lived experience. The disagreement is not only and not primarily at the level of concepts but rather has to do with the critique of knowledge and the delimitation of its scope. For example, it is perfectly correct to point out that Hegel is profoundly aware of the unity of life and consciousness an of the opposition between them. But it is also true that these are already recognized as incomplete *from the point of view of* the totality. Or, to use for the moment the terms of modern semeiology—for Hegel, the *Signifying* (at any moment of history) is the movement of Mind (which will be constituted as the signifying-signified and the signified-signifying; that is, as absolute-subject); the *Signified* is the living man and his objectification. For Kierkegaard, man is the Signifying; he himself produces the significations, and no signification points to him from outside (Abraham does not know whether he *is* Abraham); man is never the *signified* (not even by God).

Compared with Hegel, Kierkegaard[9] scarcely seems to count. He is certainly not a philosopher; moreover, he himself refused this title. In fact, he is a Christian who is not willing to let himself be enclosed in the system and who, against Hegel's "intellectualism," asserts unrelentingly the irreducibility and the specificity of what is lived. There is no doubt, as Jean Wahl has remarked, that a Hegelian would have assimilated this romantic and obstinate consciousness to the "unhappy consciousness," a moment which had already been surpassed and known in its essential characteristics. But it is precisely this objective knowledge which Kierkegaard challenges. For him the surpassing of the unhappy consciousness remains purely verbal. The *existing* man cannot be assimilated by a system of ideas. Whatever one may say or think about suffering, it escapes knowledge to the extent that it is suffered in itself, for itself, and to the degree that knowledge remains powerless to transform it. "The philosopher constructs a palace of ideas and lives in a hovel." Of course, it is religion which Kierkegaard wants to defend. Hegel was not willing for Christianity to be "surpassed," but for this very reason he made it the highest moment of human existence. Kierkegaard, on the contrary, insists on the transcendence of the Divine; between man and God he puts an infinite distance. The existence of the Omnipotent cannot be the object of an objective knowledge; it becomes the aim of a subjective faith. And this faith, in turn, with its strength and its spontaneous affirmation, will never be reduced to a moment which can be surpassed and classified, to a knowing. Thus Kierkegaard is led to champion the cause of pure, unique subjectivity against the objective universality of essence, the narrow, passionate intransigence of the immediate life against the tranquil mediation of all reality, faith, which stubbornly asserts itself, against scientific evidence—*despite* the scandal. He looks everywhere for weapons to aid him in escaping from the terrible "mediation"; he discovers within himself oppositions, indecisions, equivocations which cannot be surpassed: paradoxes, ambiguities, discontinuities, dilemmas, etc. In all these inward conflicts, Hegel would doubtless see only contradictions in formation or in process of development—but this is exactly what Kierkegaard reproaches him for: even before becoming aware of them, the philosopher of Jena[10] would have decided to consider them truncated ideas. In fact, the *subjective* life, just insofar as it is lived, can never be made the object of a knowledge. On principle it escapes knowing, and the relation of the believer to transcendence can only be conceived of in the form of a *going beyond*. This inwardness, which in its narrowness and its infinite depth claims to affirm itself against all philosophy, this subjectivity rediscovered beyond language as the personal adventure of each man in the face of others and of God—this is what Kierkegaard called *existence*.

We see that Kierkegaard is inseparable from Hegel, and that this vehement negation of every system can arise only within a cultural field entirely dominated by Hegelianism. The Dane feels himself hemmed in by concepts, by History, he fights for his life; it is the reaction of Christian romanticism against the rationalist humanisation of faith. It would be too easy to reject this work as simply subjectivism; what we ought rather to point out, in placing it back within the framework of its period, is that Kierkegaard has as much right on his side as Hegel has on his. Hegel is right: unlike the Danish ideologist, who obstinately fixed his stand on poor, frozen paradoxes ultimately referring to an empty subjectivity, the philosopher of Jena aims through his concepts at the veritable concrete; for him, mediation is always presented as an enrichment. Kierkegaard is right: grief, need, passion, the pain of men, are brute realities which can be neither surpassed nor changed by knowledge. To be sure, Kierkegaard's religious subjectivism can with good reason be taken as the very peak of idealism; but in relation to Hegel, he marks a progress toward realism, since he insists above all on the *primacy* of the specifically real over thought, that the real cannot be reduced to thought. There are today some psychologists and psychiatrists[11] who consider certain evolutions of our inward life to be the result of a work which it performs upon itself. In this sense Kierkegaardian *existence* is the *work* of our inner life—resistances overcome and perpetually reborn, efforts perpetually renewed, despairs surmounted, provisional failures and precarious victories—and this work is directly opposed to intellectual knowing. Kierkegaard was perhaps the first to point out, against Hegel and thanks to him, the incommensurability of the real and knowledge. This incommensurability maybe the origin of a conservative irrationalism; it is even one of the ways in which we may understand this ideologist's writings. But it can be seen also as the death of absolute idealism; ideas do not change men. Knowing the cause of a passion is not enough to overcome it; one must live it, one must oppose other passions to it, one must combat it tenaciously, in short one must "work oneself over."

It is striking that Marxism addresses the same reproach to Hegel though from quite another point of view. For Marx, indeed, Hegel has confused objectification, the simple externalisation of man in the universe, with the alienation which

---

[9]Søren Kierkegaard (1813–1855), Danish philosopher and religious writer, a critic of rationalism and generally regarded as one of the first Existentialist philosophers.

[10]That is, Hegel.

[11][Sartre] Cf. Lagache, *Le Travail du deul (The Work of Mourning).*

turns his externalisation back against man. Taken by itself— Marx emphasises this again and again—objectification would be an opening out; it would allow man, who produces and re-produces his life without ceasing and who transforms himself by changing nature, to "contemplate himself in a world which he has created." No dialectical sleight of hand can make alienation come out of it; this is why what is involved here is not a mere play of concepts but real History. "In the social production of their existence, men enter into relations which are determined, necessary, independent of their will; these relations of production correspond to a given stage of develop-ment of their material productive forces. The totality of these relations of production constitutes the real foundation upon which a legal and political superstructure arises and to which definite forms of social consciousness correspond."[12]

Now, in the present phase of our history, productive forces have entered into conflict with relations of produc-tion. Creative work is alienated; man does not recognise himself in his own product, and his exhausting labor ap-pears to him as a hostile force. Since alienation comes about as the result of this conflict, it is a historical reality and com-pletely irreducible to an idea. If men are to free themselves from it, and if their work is to become the pure objectifica-tion of themselves, it is not enough that "consciousness think itself"; there must be *material* work and revolutionary *praxis*. When Marx writes: "Just as we do not judge an indi-vidual by his own idea of himself, so we cannot judge a . . . pe-riod of revolutionary upheaval by its own self-consciousness," he is indicating the priority of action (work and social praxis) over *knowledge* as well as their heterogeneity. He too asserts that the human fact is irreducible to knowing, that it must be *lived* and *produced;* but he is not going to confuse it with the empty subjectivity of a puritanical and mystified petite bourgeoisie. He makes of it the immediate theme of the philosophical totalisation, and it is the concrete man whom he puts at the center of his research, that man who is defined simultaneously by his needs, by the material conditions of his existence, and by the nature of his work— that is, by his struggle against things and against men.

Thus Marx, rather than Kierkegaard or Hegel, is right, since he asserts with Kierkegaard the specificity of human *existence* and, along with Hegel, takes the concrete man in his objective reality. Under these circumstances, it would seem natural if existentialism, this idealist protest against idealism, had lost all usefulness and had not survived the decline of Hegelianism.

In fact, existentialism suffered an eclipse. In the gen-eral struggle which bourgeois thought leads against Marxist dialectic, it gets its support from the post-Kantians, from Kant himself, and from Descartes; it never thinks of ad-dressing itself to Kierkegaard. The Dane will reappear at the beginning of the twentieth century when people will take it into their heads to fight against Marxism by opposing to it pluralisms, ambiguities, paradoxes; that is, his revival dates back to the moment when for the first time bourgeois thought was reduced to being on the defensive. Between the two World Wars the appearance of a German existentialism certainly corresponds—at least in the work of Jaspers[13]—to a surreptitious wish to resuscitate the transcendent. Already—as Jean Wahl[14] has pointed out—one could won-der if Kierkegaard did not lure his readers into the depths of subjectivity for the sole purpose of making them discover there the unhappiness of man without God. This trap would be quite in keeping with the "great solitary" who denied communication between human beings and who saw no way to influence his fellow man except by "indirect action."

Jaspers himself put his cards on the table. He has done nothing except to comment upon his master; his originality consists especially in putting certain themes into relief and in hiding others. The transcendent, for example, appears at first to be absent from his thought, which in fact is haunted by it. We are taught to catch a presentiment of the transcendent in our failures; it is their profound meaning. This idea is already found in Kierkegaard, but it is less emphasised since this Christian thinks and lives within the compass of a revealed re-ligion. Jaspers, mute on Revelation, leads us back—through discontinuity, pluralism, and impotence—to the pure, formal subjectivity which is discovered and which discovers tran-scendence through its defeats. Success, indeed, as an *objecti-fication,* would enable the person to inscribe himself in things and finally would compel him to surpass himself. The medi-tation on failure is perfectly suited to a bourgeoisie which is partially de-Christianised but which regrets its past faith be-cause it has lost confidence in its rationalist, positivist ideol-ogy. Kierkegaard already considered that every victory is sus-pect because it turns man away from himself. Kafka took up this Christian theme again in his *Journal.* And one can find a certain truth in the idea, since in a world of alienation the

---

[12] [Barnes] Sartre has not given the source for this important quotation. It comes from Marx's *"Preface* to Contribution to a Critique of Political Economy." I am indebted for the discovery to Erich Fromm, who quotes the passage in *Marx's Concept of Man* (New York: Frederick Ungar, 1961), p. 17.

[13] [Sartre] The case of Heidegger is too complex for me to discuss here. [Eds.] Karl Jaspers (1883–1969), major German Existentialist philosopher and psychologist whose later work addressed issues in religion.

[14] Jean Wahl (1888–1974), French philosopher, author of *A Short History of Existentialism* (1949), and *Les philosophies de l'existence* (1954), among other works.

individual conqueror does not recognise himself in his victory and becomes its slave. But what is important to Jaspers is to derive from all this a subjective pessimism, which ultimately emerges as a theological optimism that dares not speak its name. The transcendent, indeed, remains veiled; it is attested only by its absence. One will never go beyond pessimism; one will have a presentiment of reconciliation while remaining at the level of an insurmountable contradiction and a total cleavage. This condemnation of dialectic is aimed no longer at Hegel, but at Marx. It is no longer the refusal of *Knowledge,* but the refusal of *praxis.* Kierkegaard was unwilling to play the role of a concept in the Hegelian system; Jaspers refuses to cooperate *as an individual* with the history which Marxists are making. Kierkegaard realised some progress over Hegel by affirming the *reality* of the lived; Jaspers regresses in the historical movement, for he flees from the real movement of *praxis* and takes refuge in an abstract subjectivity, whose sole aim is to achieve a certain inward *quality.*[15] This ideology of withdrawal expressed quite well only yesterday the attitude of a certain Germany fixed on its two defeats and that of a certain European bourgeoisie which wants to justify its privileges by an aristocracy of the soul, to find refuge from its objectivity in an exquisite subjectivity, and to let itself be fascinated by an ineffable present so as not to see its future. Philosophically this soft, devious thought is only a survival; it holds no great interest. But it is one more existentialism which has developed at the margin of Marxism and not against it. It is Marx with whom we claim kinship, and Marx of whom I wish to speak now.

By its *actual* presence, a philosophy transforms the structures of Knowledge, stimulates ideas; even when it defines the practical perspectives of an exploited class, it polarises the culture of the ruling classes and changes it. Marx wrote that the ideas of the dominant class are the dominant ideas. He is *absolutely* right. In 1925, when I was twenty years old, there was no chair of Marxism at the University, and Communist students were very careful not to appeal to Marxism or even to mention it in their examinations; had they done so, they would have failed. The horror of dialectic was such that Hegel himself was unknown to us. Of course, they allowed us to read Marx; they even advised us to read him; one had to know him "in order to refute him." But without the Hegelian tradition, without Marxist teachers, without any planned program of study, without the instruments of thought, our generation, like the preceding ones and like that which followed, was wholly ignorant of historical materialism.[16] On the other hand, they taught us Aristotelian and mathematical logic in great detail. It was at about this time that I read *Capital* and *German Ideology.* I found everything perfectly clear, and I really understood absolutely nothing. To understand is to change, to go beyond oneself. This reading did not change me. By contrast, what did begin to change me was the *reality* of Marxism, the heavy presence on my horizon of the masses of workers, an enormous, sombre body which *lived* Marxism, which *practiced* it, and which at a distance exercised an irresistible attraction on petit bourgeois intellectuals. When we read this philosophy in books, it enjoyed no privilege in our eyes. A priest, who has just written a voluminous and very interesting work on Marx, calmly states in the opening pages: "It is possible to study [his] thought just as securely as one studies that of any other philosopher or any other sociologist."[17] That was exactly what we believed. So long as this thought appeared to us through written words, we remained "objective." We said to ourselves: "Here are the conceptions of a German intellectual who lived in London in the middle of the last century." But when it was presented as a real determination of the Proletariat and as the profound meaning of its acts—for itself and in itself—then Marxism attracted us irresistibly without our knowing it, and it put all our acquired culture out of shape. I repeat, it was not the idea which unsettled us; nor was it the condition of the worker, which we knew abstractly but which we had not experienced. No, it was the two joined together. It was—as we would have said then in our idealist jargon even as we were breaking with idealism—the Proletariat as the incarnation and vehicle of an idea. And I believe that we must here complete Marx's statement: When the rising class becomes conscious of itself, this self-consciousness acts at a distance upon intellectuals and makes the ideas in their heads disintegrate. We rejected the official idealism in the name of "the tragic sense of life."[18] This Proletariat, far off, invisible, inaccessible, but conscious and acting, furnished the proof—obscurely for most of us—that not all conflicts had been resolved. We had been brought up in bourgeois humanism, and this optimistic humanism was shattered when we vaguely perceived around our town the immense crowd of "sub-men conscious of their subhumanity." But we sensed this shattering in a way that was still idealist and individualist.

---

[15] [Sartre] Jaspers gives the name "existence" to this quality which is at once immanent (since it extends throughout our lived subjectivity) and transcendent (since it remains beyond our reach).

[16] [Sartre] This explains why intellectual Marxists of my age (whether Communists or not) are such poor dialecticians; they have returned, without knowing it, to mechanistic materialism.

[17] [Sartre] [Jean-Yves] Calvez: *La Pensée de Karl Marx* (Le Seuil) [1970].

[18] [Sartre] This phrase was made popular by the Spanish philosopher Miguel de Unamuno [1864–1936]. Of course, this tragic sense had nothing in common with the true conflicts of our period.

At about that time, the writers whom we loved explained to us that existence is a *scandal*. What interested us, however, was real men with their labours and their troubles. We cried out for a philosophy which would account for everything, and we did not perceive that it existed already and that it was precisely this philosophy which provoked in us this demand. At that time one book enjoyed a great success among us—Jean Wahl's *Toward the Concrete*. Yet we were disappointed by this "toward." The total concrete was what we wanted to leave behind us; the absolute concrete was what we wanted to achieve. Still the work pleased us, for it embarrassed idealism by discovering in the universe paradoxes, ambiguities, conflicts, still unresolved. We learned to turn pluralism (that concept of the Right) against the optimistic, monistic idealism of our professors—in the name of a Leftist thought which was still ignorant of itself. Enthusiastically we adopted all those doctrines which divided men into watertight groups. "Petit bourgeois" democrats, we rejected racism, but we liked to think that "primitive mentality," the universe of the child and the madman, remained entirely impenetrable to us. Under the influence of war and the Russian Revolution, we offered violence—only theoretically, of course—in opposition to the sweet dreams of our professors. It was a wretched violence (insults, brawls, suicides, murders, irreparable catastrophes) which risked leading us to fascism; but in our eyes it had the advantage of highlighting the contradictions of reality. Thus Marxism as "a philosophy which had become the world" wrenched us away from the defunct culture of a bourgeoisie which was barely subsisting on its past. We plunged blindly down the dangerous path of a pluralist realism concerned with man and things in their "concrete" existence. Yet we remained within the compass of "dominating ideas." Although we wanted to know man in his real life, we did not as yet have the idea of considering him first a worker who produces the conditions of his life. For a long time we confused the *total* and the *individual*. Pluralism, which had served us so well against M. Brunschvicg's idealism, prevented us from understanding the dialectical totalisation. It pleased us to decry essences and artificially isolated types rather than to reconstitute the synthetic movement of a truth that had "become." Political events led us to employ the schema of the "class struggle" as a sort of grid, more convenient than veridical; but it took the whole bloody history of this half century to make us grasp the reality of the class struggle and to situate us in a split society. It was the war which shattered the worn structures of our thought—War, Occupation, Resistance, the years which followed. We wanted to fight at the side of the working class; we finally understood that the concrete is history and dialectical action. We had repudiated pluralist realism only to have found it again among the fascists, and we discovered the world.

Why then has "existentialism" preserved its autonomy? Why has it not simply dissolved in Marxism?

Lukács[19] believed that he had answered this question in a small book called *Existentialism and Marxism*. According to him, bourgeois intellectuals have been forced "to abandon the method of idealism while safeguarding its results and its foundations; hence the historical necessity of a 'third path' (between materialism and idealism) in actuality and in the bourgeois consciousness during the imperialistic period." I shall show later the havoc which this wish to conceptualise a priori has wrought at the center of Marxism. Here let us simply observe that Lukács fails absolutely to account for the principal fact: we were convinced at one and the same time that historical materialism furnished the only valid interpretation of history and that existentialism remained the only concrete approach to reality. I do not pretend to deny the contradictions in this attitude. I simply assert that Lukács does not even suspect it. Many intellectuals, many students, have lived and still live with the tension of this double demand. How does this come about? It is due to a circumstance which Lukács knew perfectly well but which he could not at that time even mention: Marxism, after drawing us to it as the moon draws the tides, after transforming all our ideas, after liquidating the categories of our bourgeois thought, abruptly left us stranded. It did not satisfy our need to understand. In the particular situation in which we were placed, it no longer had anything new to teach us, because it had come to a stop.

Marxism stopped. Precisely because this philosophy wants to change the world, because its aim is "philosophy-becoming-the-world," because it is and wants to be *practical*, there arose within it a veritable schism which rejected theory on one side and *praxis* on the other. From the moment the U.S.S.R., encircled and alone, undertook its gigantic effort at industrialisation, Marxism found itself unable to bear the shock of these new struggles, the practical necessities and the mistakes which are always inseparable from them. At this period of withdrawal (for the U.S.S.R.) and of ebb tide (for the revolutionary proletariats), the ideology itself was subordinated to a double need: security (that is, unity) and the construction of socialism *inside* the U.S.S.R. Concrete thought must be born from *praxis* and must turn back upon it in order to clarify it, not by chance and without rules, but—as in all sciences and all techniques—in conformity with principles. Now the Party leaders, bent on pushing the integration of the group to the limit, feared that the free process of truth, with all the discussions and all the conflicts which it involves, would break the unity of combat; they reserved for themselves the right to define the line and to interpret the event. In

---

[19] Georg Lukács (1885–1971), Hungarian Marxist theorist and critic; above, Léon Brunschvicg (1869–1944), French philosopher and educator.

addition, out of fear that the experience might not provide its own clarities, that it might put into question certain of their guiding ideas and might contribute to "weakening the ideological struggle," they put the doctrine out of reach. The separation of theory and practice resulted in transforming the latter into an empiricism without principles; the former into a pure, fixed knowledge. On the other hand, the economic planning imposed by a bureaucracy unwilling to recognise its mistakes became thereby a violence done to reality. And since the future production of a nation was determined in offices, often outside its own territory, this violence had as its counterpart an absolute idealism. Men and things had to yield to ideas—a priori; experience, when it did not verify the predictions, could only be wrong. Budapest's subway was real in Rakosi's[20] head. If Budapest's subsoil did not allow him to construct the subway, this was because the subsoil was counter-revolutionary. Marxism, as a philosophical interpretation of man and of history, necessarily had to reflect the preconceptions of the planned economy.

This fixed image of idealism and of violence did idealistic violence to facts. For years the Marxist intellectual believed that he served his party by violating experience, by overlooking embarrassing details, by grossly simplifying the data, and above all, by conceptualising the event *before* having studied it. And I do not mean to speak only of Communists, but of all the others—fellow travellers, Trotskyites, and Trotsky sympathisers—for they have been *created* by their sympathy for the Communist Party or by their opposition to it. On November 4, 1956, at the time of the second Soviet intervention in Hungary, each group already had its mind made up before it possessed any information on the situation. It had decided in advance whether it was witnessing an act of aggression on the part of the Russian bureaucracy against the democracy of Workers' Committees, with a revolt of the masses against the bureaucratic system, or with a counter-revolutionary attempt which Soviet moderation had known how to check. Later there was news, a great deal of news; but I have not heard it said that even one Marxist changed his opinion.

Among the interpretations which I have just mentioned, there is one which shows the method in all its nakedness, that which reduces the facts in Hungary to a "Soviet act of aggression against the democracy of Workers' Committees."[21] It is obvious that the Workers' Committees are a democratic institution; one can even maintain that they bear within them the future of the socialist society. But this does not alter the fact

that they did not exist in Hungary at the time of the first Soviet intervention; and their appearance during the Insurrection was much too brief and too troubled for us to be able to speak of an organised democracy. No matter. There were Workers' Committees, Soviet intervention took place. Starting from there, Marxist idealism proceeds to two simultaneous operations: conceptualisation and passage to the limit. They push the empirical notion to the perfection of the type, the germ to its total development. At the same time they reject the equivocal givens of experience; these could only lead one astray. We will find ourselves then in the presence of a typical contradiction between two Platonic ideas: on the one side, the wavering policy of the U.S.S.R. gave way to the rigorous and predictable action of that entity, "the Soviet Bureaucracy"; on the other side, the Workers' Committees disappeared before that other entity, "the direct Democracy." I shall call these two objects "general particularities"; they are made to pass for particular, historical realities when we ought not to see in them anything more than the purely formal unity of abstract, universal relations. The process of making them into fetishes will be complete when each one is endowed with real powers: the Democracy of Workers' Committees holds within itself the absolute negation of the Bureaucracy, which reacts by crushing its adversary.

Now there can be no doubt that the fruitfulness of living Marxism stemmed in part from its way of approaching experience. Marx was convinced that facts are never isolated appearances, that if they come into being together, it is always within the higher unity of a whole, that they are bound to each other by internal relations, and that the presence of one profoundly modifies the nature of the other. Consequently, Marx approached the study of the revolution of February 1848 or Louis Napoleon Bonaparte's *coup d'état*[22] with a synthetic intent; he saw in these events totalities produced and at the same time split apart by their internal contradiction. Of course, the physicist's hypothesis, before it has been confirmed by experimentation, is also an interpretation of experience; it rejects empiricism simply because it is mute. But the constitutive schema of this hypothesis is universalising, not totalising. It determines a relation, a function, and not a concrete totality. The Marxist approaches the historical process with universalising and totalising schemata. Naturally the totalisation was not made by chance. The theory had determined the choice of perspective and the order of the conditioning factors; it studied each particular process within the framework of a general system in evolution. But in no case, in Marx's own work, does this putting in perspective claim to

---

[20]Mátyás Rákosi (1892–1971), Communist party chief, secretary, and sometime prime minister of Hungary from 1945 to 1956, when he fled to the U.S.S.R. at the outbreak of the Budapest uprising.

[21][Sartre] Maintained by former Trotskyites.

---

[22]Louis Napoleon Bonaparte (1808–1873), son of Louis Bonaparte, nephew of Napoleon Bonaparte. In 1851, he led a coup, disbanded the Legislative Assembly, and was named Emperor Napoleon III.

prevent or to render useless the appreciation of the process as a *unique* totality. When, for example, he studies the brief and tragic history of the Republic of 1848,[23] he does not limit himself—as would be done today—to stating that the republican petite bourgeoisie betrayed its ally, the Proletariat. On the contrary, he tries to account for this tragedy in its detail and in the aggregate. If he subordinates anecdotal facts to the totality (of a movement, of an attitude), he also seeks to discover the totality by means of the facts. In other words, he gives to each event, in addition to its particular signification, the role of being revealing. Since the ruling principle of the inquiry is the search for the synthetic ensemble, each fact, once established, is questioned and interpreted as part of a whole. It is on the basis of the *fact,* through the study of its lacks and its "oversignifications," that one determines, by virtue of a hypothesis, the totality at the heart of which the fact will recover its truth. Thus living Marxism is heuristic; its principles and its prior knowledge appear as regulative in relation to its concrete research. In the work of Marx we never find entities. Totalities (e.g., "the petite bourgeoisie" of the *18th Brumaire*) are living; they furnish their own definitions within the framework of the research.[24] Otherwise we could not understand the importance which Marxists attach (even today) to "the analysis" of a situation. It goes without saying that this analysis is not enough and that it is but the first moment in an effort at synthetic reconstruction. But it is appar-

ent also that the analysis is indispensable to the later reconstruction of the total structures.

Marxist voluntarism, which likes to speak of analysis, has reduced this operation to a simple ceremony. There is no longer any question of studying facts within the general perspective of Marxism so as to enrich our understanding and to clarify action. Analysis consists solely in getting rid of detail, in forcing the signification of certain events, in denaturing facts or even in inventing a nature for them in order to discover it later underneath them, as their substance, as unchangeable, fetishised "synthetic notions." The open concepts of Marxism have closed in. They are no longer *keys,* interpretive schemata; they are posited for themselves as an already totalised knowledge. To use Kantian terms Marxism makes out of these particularised, fetishised types, constitutive concepts of experience. The real content of these typical concepts is always *past Knowledge;* but today's Marxist makes of it an eternal knowledge. His sole concern, at the moment of analysis, will be to "place" these entities. The more he is convinced that they represent truth a priori, the less fussy he will be about proof. The Kerstein Amendment, the appeals of Radio Free Europe, rumours—these are sufficient for the French Communists to "place" the entity "world imperialism" at the origin of the events in Hungary. The totalising investigation has given way to a Scholasticism of the totality. The heuristic principle—"to search for the whole in its parts"—has become the terrorist practice of "liquidating the particularity."[25] It is not by chance that Lukács—Lukács who so often violates history—has found in 1956 the best definition of this frozen Marxism. Twenty years of practice give him all the authority necessary to call this pseudo-philosophy a *voluntarist idealism.*

Today social and historical experience falls outside of Knowledge. Bourgeois concepts just manage to revive and quickly break down; those which survive lack any foundation. The real attainments of American Sociology cannot hide its theoretic uncertainty. Psychoanalysis, after a spectacular beginning, has stood still. It knows a great many details, but it lacks any firm foundation. Marxism possesses theoretical bases, it embraces all human activity; but it no longer *knows* anything. Its concepts are *dictates;* its goal is no longer to increase what it knows but to be itself constituted a priori as an absolute Knowledge. In view of this twofold ignorance, existentialism has been able to return and to maintain itself because it reaffirmed the reality of men as Kierkegaard asserted his own reality against Hegel. However, the Dane rejected the Hegelian conception of man

---

[23] The Republic of 1848, the Second Republic, came to power following a worker-led revolt, one of several throughout Europe in 1848, but the only one to succeed—but only briefly, until the 1851 coup of Louis Napoleon Bonaparte.

[24] [Sartre] The concept of "the petite bourgeoisie" exists in Marxist philosophy, of course, well before the study of Louis Napoleon's *coup d'état.* But this is because the petite bourgeoisie itself had already existed as a class for a long time. What is important is the fact that it evolves with history and that in 1848 it presents unique characteristics which the concept cannot derive from itself. We will see that Marx goes back to the general traits which defined it as a class and at the same time—in those terms and in the light of experience—he determines the specific traits which determined it as a unique reality in 1848. To take another example, see how he tries in 1853, in a series of articles *(The British Rule in India),* to portray the peculiar quality of Hindustand. Maximilien Rubel in his excellent book quotes this curious passage (so shocking to our contemporary Marxists). "This strange combination of Italy and Ireland, of a world of pleasure and a world of suffering, is anticipated in the old religious traditions of Hindustan, in that religion of sensual exuberance and savage asceticism . . ." (Rubel: *Karl Marx,* p. 302. The quotation from Marx appeared June 25, 1853, under the title *On India.)* Certainly we can find behind these words the true concepts and method: the social structure and the geographical aspect—that is what recalls Italy; English colonization—that is what recalls Ireland; etc. No matter. He gives a *reality* to these words—pleasure, suffering, sensual exuberance, and savage asceticism. Better yet, he shows the actual situation of Hindustan "anticipated" *(before the English)* by its old religious traditions. Whether Hindustan is actually this or something else matters little to us; what counts here is the synthetic view which *gives life* to the objects of the analysis.

[25] [Sartre] At one time this intellectual terror corresponded to "the physical liquidation" of particular peoples.

and of the real. Existentialism and Marxism, on the contrary, aim at the same object; but Marxism has reabsorbed man into the idea, and existentialism seeks him everywhere *where he is,* at his work, in his home, in the street. We certainly do not claim—as Kierkegaard did—that this real man is unknowable. We say only that he is not known. If for the time being he escapes Knowledge, it is because the only concepts at our disposal for understanding him are borrowed either from the idealism of the Right or from the idealism of the Left. We are careful not to confuse these two idealisms: the former merits its name by the *content* of its concepts, and the latter by the *use* which today it makes of its concepts. It is true also that among the masses Marxist *practice* does not reflect, or only slightly reflects, the sclerosis of its theory. But it is precisely the conflict between revolutionary action and the Scholastic justification of this action which prevents Communist man—in socialist countries as in bourgeois countries—from achieving any clear self-consciousness. One of the most striking characteristics of our time is the fact that history is made without self-awareness. No doubt someone will say this has always been the case; and this was true up until the second half of the last century—that is, until Marx. But what has made the force and richness of Marxism is the fact that it has been the most radical attempt to clarify the historical process in its totality. For the last twenty years, on the contrary, its shadow has obscured history; this is because it has ceased to live *with history* and because it attempts, through a bureaucratic conservatism, to reduce change to identity.[26]

Yet we must be clear about all this. This sclerosis does not correspond to a normal aging. It is produced by a worldwide combination of circumstances of a particular type. Far from being exhausted Marxism is still very young, almost in its infancy; it has scarcely begun to develop. It remains, therefore, the philosophy of our time. We cannot go beyond it because we have not gone beyond the circumstances which engendered it. Our thoughts, whatever they may be, can be formed only upon this humus; they must be contained within the framework which it furnishes for them or be lost in the void or retrogress. Existentialism, like Marxism, addresses itself to experience in order to discover there concrete syntheses; it can conceive of these syntheses only within a moving, dialectical totalisation which is nothing else but history or—from the strictly cultural point of view which we have adopted here—"philosophy-becoming-the-world." For us, truth is something which becomes, it *has* and *will have* become. It is a totalisation which is forever being totalised. Particular facts do not signify anything; they are neither true nor false so long as they are not related, through the mediation of various partial totalities, to the totalisation in process.

Let us go further. We agree with Garaudy[27] when he writes (*Humunite,* May 17, 1955): "Marxism forms today the system of coordinates which alone permits it to situate and to define a thought in any domain whatsoever—from political economy to physics, from history to ethics." And we should agree all the more readily if he had extended his statement (but this was not his subject) to the actions of individuals and masses, to specific works, to modes of life, to labor, to feelings, to the particular evolution of an institution or a character. To go further, we are also in full agreement with Engels when he wrote in that letter which furnished Plekhanov the occasion for a famous attack against Bernstein: "There does not exist, as one would like to imagine now and then, simply for convenience, any effect produced automatically by the economic situation. On the contrary, it is men themselves who make their history, but within a given environment which conditions them and on the basis of real, prior conditions among which economic conditions—no matter how much influenced they may be by other political and ideological conditions—are nevertheless, in the final analysis, the determining conditions, constituting from one end to the other the guiding thread which alone puts us in a position to understand." It is already evident that we do not conceive of economic conditions as the simple, static structure of an unchangeable society; it is the contradictions within them which form the driving force of history. It is amusing that Lukács, in the work which I have already quoted, believed he was distinguishing himself from us by recalling that Marxist definition of materialism: "the

---

[26] [Sartre] I have already expressed my opinion on the Hungarian tragedy, and I shall not discuss the matter again. From the point of view of what concerns us here, it matters little a priori that the Communist commentators believed that they had to justify the Soviet intervention. What is really heart-breaking is the fact that their "analyses" doubt that an insurrection at Budapest a dozen years after the war, less than five years after the death of Stalin, must present very particular characteristics. What do our "schematizers" do? They lay stress on the faults of the Party but without defining them. These indeterminate faults assume an abstract and eternal character which wrenches them from the historical context so as to make of them a universal entity; it is "human error." The writers indicate the presence of reactionary elements, but without showing their Hungarian *reality*. Suddenly these reactionaries pass over into eternal Reaction; they are brothers of the counter-revolutionaries of 1793, and their only distinctive trait is the will to injure. Finally, those commentators present world imperialism as an inexhaustible, formless force, whose essence does not vary regardless of its point of application. They construct an interpretation which serves as a skeleton key to everything from popular discontent, and the exploitation-of-this-situation-by-world-imperialism. This interpretation can be applied as well or as badly to all insurrections, including the disturbances in Vendée or at Lyon in 1793, by merely putting "aristocracy" in place of "imperialism." In short, nothing new has happened. That is what had to be demonstrated.

[27] Roger Garaudy (b. 1913), French philosopher, and writer; see his *Perspectives de l'homme: Existentialisme, Pensée Catholique, Marxisme* (1961).

primacy of existence over consciousness"—whereas existentialism, as its name sufficiently indicates, makes of this primacy the object of its fundamental affirmation.[28]

To be still more explicit, we support unreservedly that formulation in *Capital* by which Marx means to define his "materialism": "The mode of production of material life generally dominates the development of social, political,

and intellectual life." We cannot conceive of this conditioning in any form except that of a dialectical movement (contradictions, surpassing, totalisations). M. Rubel[29] criticises me for not making any allusion to this "Marxist materialism" in the article I wrote in 1946, "Materialism and Revolution."[30] But he himself supplies the reason for this omission. "It is true that this author is directing his comments at Engels rather than at Marx." Yes, and even more at contemporary French Marxists. But Marx's statement seems to me to point to a factual evidence which we cannot go beyond so long as the transformations of social relations and technical progress have not freed man from the yoke of scarcity. We are all acquainted with the passage in which Marx alludes to that far-off time: "This reign of freedom does not begin in fact until the time when the work imposed by necessity and external finality shall cease; it is found, therefore, beyond the sphere of material production proper" (*Capital,* III, p. 873). As soon as there will exist *for everyone* a margin of *real* freedom beyond the production of life, Marxism will have lived out its span; a philosophy of freedom will take its place. But we have no means, no intellectual instrument, no concrete experience which allow us to conceive of this freedom or of this philosophy.

---

[28] [Sartre] The *methodological* principle which holds that certitude begins with reflection in no way contradicts the *anthropological* principle which defines the concrete person by his materiality. For us, reflection is not reduced to the simple immanence of idealist subjectivism, it is a point of departure only if it throws us back immediately among things and men, in the world. The only theory of knowledge which can be valid today is one which is founded on that truth of microphysics: the experimenter is a part of the experimental system. This is the only position which allows us to get rid of all idealist illusion, the only one which shows the real man in the midst of the real world. But this realism necessarily implies a reflective point of departure; that is, the *revelation* of a situation is effected in and through the *praxis* which changes it. We do not hold that this first act of becoming conscious of the situation is the originating source of an action; we see in it a necessary moment of the action itself—the action, *in the course of its accomplishment,* provides its own clarification. That does not prevent this clarification from appearing in and by means of the attainment of awareness on the part of the agents; and this in turn necessarily implies that one must develop a theory of consciousness. Yet the theory of knowledge continues to be the weak point of Marxism. When Marx writes: "The materialist conception of the world signifies simply the conception of nature as it is without any foreign addition," he makes himself into an *objective observation* and claims to contemplate nature as it is absolutely. Having stripped away all subjectivity and having assimilated himself into pure objective truth he walks in a world of objects inhabited by object-men. By contrast, when Lenin speaks of our consciousness, he writes: "Consciousness is only the reflection of being, at best an approximately accurate reflection"; and by a single stroke he removes from himself the right to write what he is writing. In both cases it is a matter of suppressing subjectivity: with Marx, we are placed beyond it; with Lenin, on this side of it.

These two positions contradict each other. How can the "approximately accurate reflection" become the source of *materialistic rationalism?* The game is played on two levels: there is in Marxism a constituting consciousness which asserts *a priori* the rationality of the world (and which, consequently, falls into idealism); this constituting consciousness determines the constituted consciousness of particular men as a simple reflection (which ends up in a sceptical idealism). Both of these conceptions amount to breaking man's real relation with history, since in the first, knowing is pure theory, a non-situated observing, and in the second, it is a simple passivity. In the latter there is no longer any experimenting, there is only a sceptical empiricism; man vanishes and Hume's challenge is not taken up. In the former the experimenter transcends the experimental system. And let no one try to tie one to the other by a "dialectical theory of the reflection" the two concepts are essentially *anti-dialectical.* When knowing is made apodictic, and when it is constituted against all possible questioning without ever defining its scope or its rights, then it is cut off from the world and becomes a formal system. When it is reduced to a pure psycho-physiological determination, it loses its primary quality, which is its relation to the object, in order to become itself a pure object of knowing. No mediation can link Marxism as a declaration of principles and apodictic truths to psycho-physiological reflection (or dialectic). These two conceptions of knowing (dogmatism and the knowing-dyad) are both of them *pre-Marxist.* In the movement of Marxist "analyses" and especially in the process of totalisation, just as in Marx's remarks on the *practical* aspect of truth and on the general relations of theory and *praxis* it would be easy to discover the rudiments of a *realistic* epistemology which has never been developed. But what we can and

ought to construct on the basis of these scattered observations is a theory which *situates* knowing *in the world* (as the theory of the reflection attempts awkwardly to do) and which determines it in its negativity (that negativity which Stalinist dogmatism pushes to the absolute and which it transforms into a negation). Only then will it be understood that knowing is not a knowing of ideas but a practical knowing of *things;* then it will be possible to suppress the *reflection* as a useless and misleading intermediary. Then we will be able to account for the thought which is lost and alienated in the course of action so that it may be rediscovered by and in the action itself. But what are we to call this situated negativity, as a moment of praxis and as a pure relation to things themselves, if not exactly "consciousness"?

There are two ways to fall into idealism: The one consists of dissolving the real in subjectivity; the other in denying all real subjectivity in the interests of objectivity. The truth is that subjectivity is neither everything nor nothing; it represents a moment in the objective process (that in which externality is internalised), and this moment is perpetually eliminated only to be perpetually reborn. Now, each of these ephemeral moments—which rise up in the course of human history and which are never either the first or the last—is lived as a *point of departure* by the subject of history. "Class-consciousness" is not the simple lived contradiction which objectively characterises the class considered, it is that contradiction already surpassed by praxis and thereby preserved and denied all at once. But it is precisely this revealing negativity, this distance within immediate proximity, which simultaneously constitutes what existentialism calls "consciousness *of* the object" and "non-thetic self-consciousness."

[29] Maximilien Rubel (1905–1996), French biographer and historian of Marx and Marxism; see, for example, *Rubel on Marx: Five Essays,* edited by Joseph O'Malley and Keith Algozin (1971).

[30] [Barnes] "Matérialisme et revolution," *Les Temps modernes,* Vol. I, Nos. 9 and 10 (June–July 1946). The article has been translated into English by Annette Michelson and is included in Jean-Paul Sartre's *Literary and Philosophical Essays* (New York: Criterion Books, 1955).

Frantz Fanon

1925–1961

Born in Martinique and educated there and in France as a psychiatrist, Frantz Fanon experienced firsthand the injustices of which he was later to write so eloquently. In 1953, after having served in the French army in World War II, Fanon was appointed head of the psychiatry department at Blida-Joinville Hospital in Algeria. Within a year, he had joined the Algerian liberation movement, working as the editor of its principal newspaper, *El Moudjahid.* In 1960, he served as ambassador to Ghana for the Provisional Government in Algeria. As a physician and psychiatrist, Fanon led the way in proposing that certain mental illnesses and neuroses were socially induced, but as a writer, he was a fierce and moving advocate for social justice and the liberation of subjected peoples, by violence if need be. He argued consistently, however, for the acknowledgment and advancement of the essential role of the native intellectual, with commitments to the specific historical conditions of his or her society, as an essential component of meaningful political change.

Following his untimely death, Fanon's influence through his writing has grown steadily. He has been a major inspiration in the emergence of postcolonial studies and the Negritude movement in Africa, the West Indies, and elsewhere, and his careful yet passionate work has been a significant force in the developing world.

Fanon's three most important books are *Black Skin, White Masks* (1952); *The Wretched of the Earth* (1961); and *For the African Revolution* (1964). He was also the author of *Studies in a Dying Colonialism* (1965, a translation of *L'an V de la Révolution Algérienne*). Critical studies include: Anthony Alessandri, ed., *Frantz Fanon: Critical Perspectives* (1999); David Macey, *Frantz Fanon: A Biography* (2001); and Nigel C. Gibson, *Fanon: The Postcolonial Imagination* (2003).

On National Culture

To take part in the African revolution it is not enough to write a revolutionary song; you must fashion the revolution with the people. And if you fashion it with the people, the songs will come by themselves, and of themselves.

In order to achieve real action, you must yourself be a living part of Africa and of her thought; you must be an element of that popular energy which is entirely called forth for the freeing, the progress, and the happiness of Africa.

There is no place outside that fight for the artist or for the intellectual who is not himself concerned with and completely at one with the people in the great battle of Africa and of suffering humanity—SÉKOU TOURÉ.[1]

Each generation must out of relative obscurity discover its mission, fulfill it, or betray it. In underdeveloped countries the preceding generations have both resisted the work or erosion carried by colonialism and also helped on the maturing of the struggles of today. We must rid ourselves of the habit, now that we are in the thick of the fight, of minimizing the action of our fathers or of feigning incomprehension when

---

"On National Culture" was first presented as an address at the Second Congress of Black Artists and Writers, Rome, 1959. It is reprinted here from Frantz Fanon, *The Wretched of the Earth,* translated by Constance Farrington (New York: Grove Press, Inc., 1963).

[1] Sékou Touré, "The political leader as the representative of a culture," Address to the second Congress of Black Writers and Artists, Rome, 1959.

considering their silence and passivity. They fought as well as they could, with the arms that they possessed then; and if the echoes of their struggle have not resounded in the international arena, we must realize that the reason for this silence lies less in their lack of heroism than in the fundamentally different international situation of our time. It needed more than one native to say "We've had enough"; more than one peasant rising crushed, more than one demonstration put down before we could today hold our own, certain in our victory. As for we who have decided to break the back of colonialism, our historic mission is to sanction all revolts, all desperate actions, all those abortive attempts drowned in rivers of blood.

In this chapter we shall analyze the problem, which is felt to be fundamental, of the legitimacy of the claims of a nation. It must be recognized that the political party which mobilizes the people hardly touches on this problem of legitimacy. The political parties start from living reality and it is in the name of this reality, in the name of the stark facts which weigh down the present and the future of men and women, that they fix their line of action. The political party may well speak in moving terms of the nation, but what it is concerned with is that the people who are listening understand the need to take part in the fight if, quite simply, they wish to continue to exist.

Today we know that in the first phase of the national struggle colonialism tries to disarm national demands by putting forward economic doctrines. As soon as the first demands are set out, colonialism pretends to consider them, recognizing with ostentatious humility that the territory is suffering from serious underdevelopment which necessitates a great economic and social effort. And, in fact, it so happens that certain spectacular measures (centers of work for the unemployed which are opened here and there, for example) delay the crystallization of national consciousness for a few years. But, sooner or later, colonialism sees that it is not within its powers to put into practice a project of economic and social reforms which will satisfy the aspirations of the colonized people. Even where food supplies are concerned, colonialism gives proof of its inherent incapability. The colonialist state quickly discovers that if it wishes to disarm the nationalist parties on strictly economic questions then it will have to do in the colonies exactly what it has refused to do in its own country. It is not mere chance that almost everywhere today there flourishes the doctrine of Cartierism.[2]

The disillusioned bitterness we find in Cartier when up against the obstinate determination of France to link to herself peoples which she must feed while so many French people live in want shows up the impossible situation in which colonialism finds itself when the colonial system is called upon to transform itself into an unselfish program of aid and assistance. It is why, once again, there is no use in wasting time repeating that hunger with dignity is preferable to bread eaten in slavery. On the contrary, we must become convinced that colonialism is incapable of procuring for the colonized peoples the material conditions which might make them forget their concern for dignity. Once colonialism has realized where its tactics of social reform are leading, we see it falling back on its old reflexes, reinforcing police effectives, bringing up troops, and setting a reign of terror which is better adapted to its interests and its psychology.

Inside the political parties, and most often in offshoots from these parties, cultured individuals of the colonized race make their appearance. For these individuals, the demand for a national culture and the affirmation of the existence of such a culture represent a special battlefield. While the politicians situate their action in actual present-day events, men of culture take their stand in the field of history. Confronted with the native intellectual who decides to make an aggressive response to the colonialist theory of precolonial barbarism, colonialism will react only slightly, and still less because the ideas developed by the young colonized intelligentsia are widely professed by specialists in the mother country. It is in fact a commonplace to state that for several decades large numbers of research workers have, in the main, rehabilitated the African, Mexican, and Peruvian civilizations. The passion with which native intellectuals defend the existence of their national culture may be a source of amazement; but those who condemn this exaggerated passion are strangely apt to forget that their own psyche and their own selves are conveniently sheltered behind a French or German culture which has given full proof of its existence and which is uncontested.

I am ready to concede that on the plane of factual being the past existence of an Aztec civilization does not change anything very much in the diet of the Mexican peasant of today. I admit that all the proofs of a wonderful Songhai civilization will not change the fact that today the Songhais are underfed and illiterate, thrown between sky and water with empty heads and empty eyes. But it has been remarked several times that this passionate search for a national culture which existed before the colonial era finds its legitimate reason in the anxiety shared by native intellectuals to shrink away from that Western culture in which they

---

[2] A doctrine and attitude named for Raymond Cartier, author and editor in the 1950s and 1960s of *Paris Match,* who notoriously said "France first; Zambezi second." Cartierism is thus an unabashed expression of colonial superiority and preeminence.

all risk being swamped. Because they realize they are in danger of losing their lives and thus becoming lost to their people, these men, hotheaded and with anger in their hearts, relentlessly determine to renew contact once more with the oldest and most pre-colonial springs of life of their people.

Let us go further. Perhaps this passionate research and this anger are kept up or at least directed by the secret hope of discovering beyond the misery of today, beyond self-contempt, resignation, and abjuration, some very beautiful and splendid era whose existence rehabilitates us both in regard to ourselves and in regard to others. I have said that I have decided to go further. Perhaps unconsciously, the native intellectuals, since they could not stand wonderstruck before the history of today's barbarity, decided to back further and to delve deeper down; and, let us make no mistake, it was with the greatest delight that they discovered that there was nothing to be ashamed of in the past, but rather dignity, glory, and solemnity. The claim to a national culture in the past does not only rehabilitate that nation and serve as a justification for the hope of a future national culture. In the sphere of psycho-affective equilibrium it is responsible for an important change in the native. Perhaps we have not sufficiently demonstrated that colonialism is not simply content to impose its rule upon the present and the future of a dominated country. Colonialism is not satisfied merely with holding a people in its grip and emptying the native's brain of all form and content. By a kind of perverted logic, it turns to the past of the oppressed people, and distorts, disfigures, and destroys it. This work of devaluing pre-colonial history takes on a dialectical significance today.

When we consider the efforts made to carry out the cultural estrangement so characteristic of the colonial epoch, we realize that nothing has been left to chance and that the total result looked for by colonial domination was indeed to convince the natives that colonialism came to lighten their darkness. The effect consciously sought by colonialism was to drive into the natives' heads the idea that if the settlers were to leave, they would at once fall back into barbarism, degradation, and bestiality.

On the unconscious plane, colonialism therefore did not seek to be considered by the native as a gentle, loving mother who protects her child from a hostile environment, but rather as a mother who unceasingly restrains her fundamentally perverse offspring from managing to commit suicide and from giving free rein to its evil instincts. The colonial mother protects her child from itself, from its ego, and from its physiology, its biology, its own unhappiness which is its very essence.

In such a situation the claims of the native intellectual are not a luxury but a necessity in any coherent program.

The native intellectual who takes up arms to defend his nation's legitimacy and who wants to bring proofs to bear out that legitimacy, who is willing to strip himself naked to study the history of his body, is obliged to dissect the heart of his people.

Such an examination is not specifically national. The native intellectual who decides to give battle to colonial lies fights on the field of the whole continent. The past is given back its value. Culture, extracted from the past to be displayed in all its splendor, is not necessarily that of his own country. Colonialism, which has not bothered to put too fine a point on its efforts, has never ceased to maintain that the Negro is a savage; and for the colonist, the Negro was neither an Angolan nor a Nigerian, for he simply spoke of "the Negro." For colonialism, this vast continent was the haunt of savages, a country riddled with superstitions and fanaticism, destined for contempt, weighed down by the curse of God, a country of cannibals—in short, the Negro's country. Colonialism's condemnation is continental in its scope. The contention by colonialism that the darkest night of humanity lay over pre-colonial history concerns the whole of the African continent. The efforts of the native to rehabilitate himself and to escape from the claws of colonialism are logically inscribed from the same point of view as that of colonialism. The native intellectual who has gone far beyond the domains of Western culture and who has got it into his head to proclaim the existence of another culture never does so in the name of Angola or of Dahomey. The culture which is affirmed is African culture. The Negro, never so much a Negro as since he has been dominated by the whites, when he decides to prove that he has a culture and to behave like a cultured person, comes to realize that history points out a well-defined path to him: he must demonstrate that a Negro culture exists.

And it is only too true that those who are most responsible for this racialization of thought, or at least for the first movement toward that thought, are and remain those Europeans who have never ceased to set up white culture to fill the gap left by the absence of other cultures. Colonialism did not dream of wasting its time in denying the existence of one national culture after another. Therefore the reply of the colonized peoples will be straight away continental in its breadth. In Africa, the native literature of the last twenty years is not a national literature but a Negro literature. The concept of negritude, for example, was the emotional if not the logical antithesis of that insult which the white man flung at humanity. This rush of negritude against the white man's contempt showed itself in certain spheres to be the one idea capable of lifting interdictions and anathemas. Because the New Guinean or Kenyan intellectuals found themselves above all up against a general ostracism and delivered to the combined contempt of their overlords, their reaction was to sing praises in admiration of each other. The unconditional affirmation of African culture has succeeded the unconditional affirmation of European culture. On the whole, the poets of negritude oppose the idea of an old Europe to a young Africa, tiresome reasoning to lyricism, oppressive logic to high-stepping nature, and on one side stiffness, ceremony, etiquette, and scepticism, while on the other frankness, liveliness, liberty, and—why not?—luxuriance: but also irresponsibility.

The poets of negritude will not stop at the limits of the continent. From America, black voices will take up the hymn with fuller unison. The "black world" will see the light and Busia from Ghana, Birago Diop from Senegal, Hampaté Ba from the Soudan, and Saint-Clair Drake from Chicago will not hesitate to assert the existence of common ties and a motive power that is identical.

The example of the Arab world might equally well be quoted here. We know that the majority of Arab territories have been under colonial domination. Colonialism has made the same effort in these regions to plant deep in the minds of the native population the idea that before the advent of colonialism their history was one which was dominated by barbarism. The struggle for national liberty has been accompanied by a cultural phenomenon known by the name of the awakening of Islam. The passion with which contemporary Arab writers remind their people of the great pages of their history is a reply to the lies told by the occupying power. The great names of Arabic literature and the great past of Arab civilization have been brandished about with the same ardor as those of the African civilizations. The Arab leaders have tried to return to the famous Dar El Islam which shone so brightly from the twelfth to the fourteenth century.

Today, in the political sphere, the Arab League is giving palpable form to this will to take up again the heritage of the past and to bring it to culmination. Today, Arab doctors and Arab poets speak to each other across the frontiers, and strive to create a new Arab culture and a new Arab civilization. It is in the name of Arabism that these men join together, and that they try to think together. Everywhere, however, in the Arab world, national feeling has preserved even under colonial domination a liveliness that we fail to find in Africa. At the same time that spontaneous communion of each with all, present in the African movement, is not to be found in the Arab League. On the contrary, paradoxically, everyone tries to sing the praises of the achievements of his nation. The cultural process is freed from the indifferentiation which characterized it in the African world, but the

Arabs do not always manage to stand aside in order to achieve their aims. The living culture is not national but Arab. The problem is not as yet to secure a national culture, not as yet to lay hold of a movement differentiated by nations, but to assume an African or Arabic culture when confronted by the all-embracing condemnation pronounced by the dominating power. In the African world, as in the Arab, we see that the claims of the man of culture in a colonized country are all-embracing, continental, and in the case of the Arabs, worldwide.

This historical necessity in which the men of African culture find themselves to racialize their claims and to speak more of African culture than of national culture will tend to lead them up a blind alley. Let us take for example the case of the African Cultural Society. This society had been created by African intellectuals who wished to get to know each other and to compare their experiences and the results of their respective research work. The aim of this society was therefore to affirm the existence of an African culture, to evaluate this culture on the plane of distinct nations, and to reveal the internal motive forces of each of their national cultures. But at the same time this society fulfilled another need: the need to exist side by side with the European Cultural Society, which threatened to transform itself into a Universal Cultural Society. There was therefore at the bottom of this decision the anxiety to be present at the universal trysting place fully armed, with a culture springing from the very heart of the African continent. Now, this Society will very quickly show its inability to shoulder these different tasks, and will limit itself to exhibitionist demonstrations, while the habitual behavior of the members of this Society will be confined to showing Europeans that such a thing as African culture exists, and opposing their ideas to those of ostentatious and narcissistic Europeans. We have shown that such an attitude is normal and draws its legitimacy from the lies propagated by men of Western culture, but the degradation of the aims of this Society will become more marked with the elaboration of the concept of negritude. The African Society will become the cultural society of the black world and will come to include the Negro dispersion, that is to say the tens of thousands of black people spread over the American continents.

The Negroes who live in the United States and in Central or Latin America in fact experience the need to attach themselves to a cultural matrix. Their problem is not fundamentally different from that of the Africans. The whites of America did not mete out to them any different treatment from that of the whites who ruled over the Africans. We have seen that the whites were used to putting all Negroes in the same bag. During the first congress of the African

Cultural Society which was held in Paris in 1956, the American Negroes of their own accord considered their problems from the same standpoint as those of their African brothers. Cultured Africans, speaking of African civilizations, decreed that there should be a reasonable status within the state for those who had formerly been slaves. But little by little the American Negroes realized that the essential problems confronting them were not the same as those that confronted the African Negroes. The Negroes of Chicago only resemble the Nigerians or the Tanganyikans in so far as they were all defined in relation to the whites. But once the first comparisons had been made and subjective feelings were assuaged, the American Negroes realized that the objective problems were fundamentally heterogeneous. The test cases of civil liberty whereby both whites and blacks in America try to drive back racial discrimination have very little in common in their principles and objectives with the heroic fight of the Angolan people against the detestable Portuguese colonialism. Thus, during the second congress of the African Cultural Society the American Negroes decided to create an American society for people of black cultures.

Negritude therefore finds its first limitation in the phenomena which take account of the formation of the historical character of men. Negro and African-Negro culture broke up into different entities because the men who wished to incarnate these cultures realized that every culture is first and foremost national, and that the problems which kept Richard Wright[3] or Langston Hughes[4] on the alert were fundamentally different from those which might confront Leopold Senghor[5] or Jomo Kenyatta.[6] In the same way certain Arab states, though they had chanted the marvelous hymn of Arab renaissance, had nevertheless to realize that their geographical position and the economic ties of their region were stronger even than the past that they wished to revive. Thus we find today the Arab states organically linked once more with societies which are Mediterranean in their culture. The fact is that these states are submitted to modern pressure and to new channels of trade while the network of trade relations which was dominant during the great period of Arab history has disappeared. But above all there is the fact that the political regimes of certain Arab states are so different, and so far away from each other in their conception, that even a cultural meeting between these states is meaningless.

Thus we see that the cultural problem as it sometimes exists in colonized countries runs the risk of giving rise to serious ambiguities. The lack of culture of the Negroes, as proclaimed by colonialism, and the inherent barbarity of the Arabs ought logically to lead to the exaltation of cultural manifestations which are not simply national but continental, and extremely racial. In Africa, the movement of men of culture is a movement toward the Negro-African culture or the Arab-Moslem culture. It is not specifically toward a national culture. Culture is becoming more and more cut off from the events of today. It finds its refuge beside a hearth that glows with passionate emotion, and from there makes its way by realistic paths which are the only means by which it may be made fruitful, homogeneous, and consistent.

If the action of the native intellectual is limited historically, there remains nevertheless the fact that it contributes greatly to upholding and justifying the action of politicians. It is true that the attitude of the native intellectual sometimes takes on the aspect of a cult or of a religion. But if we really wish to analyze this attitude correctly we will come to see that it is symptomatic of the intellectual's realization of the danger that he is running in cutting his last moorings and of breaking adrift from his people. This stated belief in a national culture is in fact an ardent, despairing turning toward anything that will afford him secure anchorage. In order to ensure his salvation and to escape from the supremacy of the white man's culture the native feels the need to turn backward toward his unknown roots and to lose himself at whatever cost in his own barbarous people. Because he feels he is becoming estranged, that is to say because he feels that he is the living haunt of contradictions which run the risk of becoming insurmountable, the native tears himself away from the swamp that may suck him down and accepts everything, decides to take all for granted and confirms everything even though he may lose body and soul. The native finds that he is expected to answer for everything, and to all comers. He not only turns himself into the defender of his people's past; he is willing to be counted as one of them, and henceforward he is even capable of laughing at his past cowardice.

This tearing away, painful and difficult though it may be, is however necessary. If it is not accomplished there will be serious psycho-affective injuries and the result will be individuals without an anchor, without a horizon, colorless, stateless, rootless—a race of angels. It will be also quite normal to hear certain natives declare, "I speak as a Senegalese and as a Frenchman . . ." "I speak as an Algerian and as a Frenchman . . ." The intellectual who is Arab and

---

[3]Richard Wright (1908–1960), Black American novelist and short-story writer, author of *Native Son* (1940).
[4]Langston Hughes (1902–1967), Black American poet, active in the Harlem Renaissance.
[5]Leopold Senghor (1906–2001), African poet and teacher, first president of Senegal, and a major figure in the development of the Negritude movement.
[6]Jomo Kenyatta (1894–1978), African statesman and the first president of independent Kenya from 1964 to 1978.

French, or Nigerian and English, when he comes up against the need to take on two nationalities, chooses, if he wants to remain true to himself, the negation of one of these determinations. But most often, since they cannot or will not make a choice, such intellectuals gather together all the historical determining factors which have conditioned them and take up a fundamentally "universal standpoint."

This is because the native intellectual has thrown himself greedily upon Western culture. Like adopted children who only stop investigating the new family framework at the moment when a minimum nucleus of security crystallizes in their psyche, the native intellectual will try to make European culture his own. He will not be content to get to know Rabelais and Diderot, Shakespeare and Edgar Allan Poe;[7] he will bind them to his intelligence as closely as possible:

> La dame n'était pas seule
> Elle avait un mari
> Un mari très comme il faut
> Qui citait Racine et Corneille
> Et Voltaire et Rousseau
> Et le Père Hugo et le jeune Musset
> Et Gide et Valéry
> Et tant d'autres encore.[8]

But at the moment when the nationalist parties are mobilizing the people in the name of national independence, the native intellectual sometimes spurns these acquisitions which he suddenly feels make him a stranger in his own land. It is always easier to proclaim rejection than actually to reject. The intellectual who through the medium of culture has filtered into Western civilization, who has managed to become part of the body of European culture—in other words who has exchanged his own culture for another—will come to realize that the cultural matrix, which now he wishes to assume since he is anxious to appear original, can hardly supply any figureheads which will bear comparison with those, so many in number and so great in prestige, of the occupying power's civilization. History, of course, though nevertheless written by the Westerners and to serve their purposes, will be able to evaluate from time to time certain periods of the African past. But, standing face to face with his country at the present time, and observing clearly and objectively the events of today

throughout the continent which he wants to make his own, the intellectual is terrified by the void, the degradation, and the savagery he sees there. Now he feels that he must get away from the white culture. He must seek his culture elsewhere, anywhere at all; and if he fails to find the substance of culture of the same grandeur and scope as displayed by the ruling power, the native intellectual will very often fall back upon emotional attitudes and will develop a psychology which is dominated by exceptional sensitivity and susceptibility. This withdrawal, which is due in the first instance to a begging of the question in his internal behavior mechanism and his own character, brings out, above all, a reflex and contradiction which is muscular.

This is sufficient explanation of the style of those native intellectuals who decide to give expression to this phase of consciousness which is in the process of being liberated. It is a harsh style, full of images, for the image is the drawbridge which allows unconscious energies to be scattered on the surrounding meadows. It is a vigorous style, alive with rhythms, struck through and through with bursting life; it is full of color, too, bronzed, sunbaked, and violent. This style, which in its time astonished the peoples of the West, has nothing racial about it, in spite of frequent statements to the contrary; it expresses above all a hand-to-hand struggle and it reveals the need that man has to liberate himself from a part of his being which already contained the seeds of decay. Whether the fight is painful, quick, or inevitable, muscular action must substitute itself for concepts.

If in the world of poetry this movement reaches unaccustomed heights, the fact remains that in the real world the intellectual often follows up a blind alley. When at the height of his intercourse with his people, whatever they were or whatever they are, the intellectual decides to come down into the common paths of real life, he only brings back from his adventuring formulas which are sterile in the extreme. He sets a high value on the customs, traditions, and the appearances of his people; but his inevitable, painful experience only seems to be a banal search for exoticism. The sari becomes sacred, and shoes that come from Paris or Italy are left off in favor of pampooties, while suddenly the language of the ruling power is felt to burn your lips. Finding your fellow countrymen sometimes means in this phase to will to be a nigger, not a nigger like all other niggers but a real nigger, a Negro cur, just the sort of nigger that the white man wants you to be. Going back to your own people means to become a dirty wog, to go native as much as you can, to become unrecognizable, and to cut off those wings that before you had allowed to grow.

The native intellectual decides to make an inventory of the bad habits drawn from the colonial world, and hastens to

---

[7] François Rabelis (c. 1494–1553), French author; Diderot (above, page 383), Poe (above, page 580).

[8] Poem by René Depestre (b. 1926), Haitian poet; active in the Negritude movement. Translation: The lady was not alone / She had a husband / A very respectable husband / Who knew how to quote Racine and Corneille / And Voltaire and Rousseau / And the elder Hugo and the young Musset / and Gide and Valéry / And as many more again. From "Face à la Nuit."

remind everyone of the good old customs of the people, that people which he has decided contains all truth and goodness. The scandalized attitude with which the settlers who live in the colonial territory greet this new departure only serves to strengthen the native's decision. When the colonialists, who had tasted the sweets of their victory over these assimilated people, realize that these men whom they considered as saved souls are beginning to fall back into the ways of niggers, the whole system totters. Every native won over, every native who had taken the pledge not only marks a failure for the colonial structure when he decides to lose himself and to go back to his own side, but also stands as a symbol for the uselessness and the shallowness of all the work that has been accomplished. Each native who goes back over the line is a radical condemnation of the methods and of the regime; and the native intellectual finds in the scandal he gives rise to a justification and an encouragement to persevere in the path he has chosen.

If we wanted to trace in the works of native writers the different phases which characterize this evolution we would find spread out before us a panorama on three levels. In the first phase, the native intellectual gives proof that he has assimilated the culture of the occupying power. His writings correspond point by point with those of his opposite numbers in the mother country. His inspiration is European and we can easily link up these works with definite trends in the literature of the mother country. This is the period of unqualified assimilation. We find in this literature coming from the colonies the Parnassians, the Symbolists, and the Surrealists.

In the second phase we find the native is disturbed; he decides to remember what he is. This period of creative work approximately corresponds to that immersion which we have just described. But since the native is not a part of his people, since he only has exterior relations with his people, he is content to recall their life only. Past happenings of the byegone days of his childhood will be brought up out of the depths of his memory; old legends will be reinterpreted in the light of a borrowed estheticism and of a conception of the world which was discovered under other skies.

Sometimes this literature of just-before-the-battle is dominated by humor and by allegory; but often too it is symptomatic of a period of distress and difficulty, where death is experienced, and disgust too. We spew ourselves up; but already underneath laughter can be heard.

Finally in the third phase, which is called the fighting phase, the native, after having tried to lose himself in the people and with the people, will on the contrary shake the people. Instead of according the people's lethargy an honored place in his esteem, he turns himself into an awakener of the people; hence comes a fighting literature, a revolu-

tionary literature, and a national literature. During this phase a great many men and women who up till then would never have thought of producing a literary work, now that they find themselves in exceptional circumstances—in prison, with the Maquis, or on the eve of their execution—feel the need to speak to their nation, to compose the sentence which expresses the heart of the people, and to become the mouthpiece of a new reality in action.

The native intellectual nevertheless sooner or later will realize that you do not show proof of your nation from its culture but that you substantiate its existence in the fight which the people wage against the forces of occupation. No colonial system draws its justification from the fact that the territories it dominates are culturally nonexistent. You will never make colonialism blush for shame by spreading out little-known cultural treasures under its eyes. At the very moment when the native intellectual is anxiously trying to create a cultural work he fails to realize that he is utilizing techniques and language which are borrowed from the stranger in his country. He contents himself with stamping these instruments with a hallmark which he wishes to be national, but which is strangely reminiscent of exoticism. The native intellectual who comes back to his people by way of cultural achievements behaves in fact like a foreigner. Sometimes he has no hesitation in using a dialect in order to show his will to be as near as possible to the people; but the ideas that he expresses and the preoccupations he is taken up with have no common yardstick to measure the real situation which the men and the women of his country know. The culture that the intellectual leans toward is often no more than a stock of particularisms. He wishes to attach himself to the people; but instead he only catches hold of their outer garments. And these outer garments are merely the reflection of a hidden life, teeming and perpetually in motion. That extremely obvious objectivity which seems to characterize a people is in fact only the inert, already forsaken result of frequent, and not always very coherent, adaptations of a much more fundamental substance which itself is continually being renewed. The man of culture, instead of setting out to find this substance, will let himself be hypnotized by these mummified fragments which because they are static are in fact symbols of negation and outworn contrivances. Culture has never the translucidity of custom; it abhors all simplification. In its essence it is opposed to custom, for custom is always the deterioration of culture. The desire to attach oneself to tradition or bring abandoned traditions to life again does not only mean going against the current of history but also opposing one's own people. When a people undertakes an armed struggle or even a political struggle against a relentless colonialism, the significance of tradition changes. All that has made up the technique of passive resistance in the past may, during this phase, be radically condemned. In an underdeveloped country during the period of struggle traditions are fundamentally unstable and are shot through by centrifugal tendencies. This is why the intellectual often runs the risk of being out of date. The peoples who have carried on the struggle are more and more impervious to demagogy; and those who wish to follow them reveal themselves as nothing more than common opportunists, in other words, latecomers.

In the sphere of plastic arts, for example, the native artist who wishes at whatever cost to create a national work of art shuts himself up in a stereotyped reproduction of details. These artists who have nevertheless thoroughly studied modern techniques and who have taken part in the main trends of contemporary painting and architecture, turn their backs on foreign culture, deny it, and set out to look for a true national culture, setting great store on what they consider to be the constant principles of national art. But these people forget that the forms of thought and what it feeds on, together with modern techniques of information, language, and dress have dialectically reorganized the people's intelligences and that the constant principles which acted as safeguards during the colonial period are now undergoing extremely radical changes.

The artist who has decided to illustrate the truths of the nation turns paradoxically toward the past and away from actual events. What he ultimately intends to embrace are in fact the castoffs of thought, its shells and corpses, a knowledge which has been stabilized once and for all. But the native intellectual who wishes to create an authentic work of art must realize that the truths of a nation are in the first place its realities. He must go on until he has found the seething pot out of which the learning of the future will emerge.

Before independence, the native painter was insensible to the national scene. He set a high value on non-figurative art, or more often specialized in still lifes. After independence his anxiety to rejoin his people will confine him to the most detailed representation of reality. This is representative art which has no internal rhythms, an art which is serene and immobile, evocative not of life but of death. Enlightened circles are in ecstasies when confronted with this "inner truth" which is so well expressed; but we have the right to ask if this truth is in fact a reality, and if it is not already outworn and denied, called in question by the epoch through which the people are treading out their path toward history.

In the realm of poetry we may establish the same facts. After the period of assimilation characterized by rhyming poetry, the poetic tom-tom's rhythms break through. This is a poetry of revolt; but it is also descriptive and analytical poetry. The poet ought however to understand that nothing can replace the reasoned, irrevocable taking up of arms on the people's side. Let us quote Depestre once more:

> The lady was not alone;
> She had a husband,
> A husband who knew everything,
> But to tell the truth knew nothing,
> For you can't have culture without making concessions.
> You concede your flesh and blood to it,
> You concede your own self to others;
> By conceding you gain
> Classicism and Romanticism,
> And all that our souls are steeped in.[9]

The native poet who is preoccupied with creating a national work of art and who is determined to describe his people fails in his aim, for he is not yet ready to make that fundamental concession that Depestre speaks of. The French poet René Char shows his understanding of the difficulty when he reminds us that "the poem emerges out of a subjective imposition and an objective choice. A poem is the assembling and moving together of determining original values, in contemporary relation with someone that these circumstances bring to the front."[10]

Yes, the first duty of the native poet is to see clearly the people he has chosen as the subject of his work of art. He cannot go forward resolutely unless he first realizes the extent of his estrangement from them. We have taken everything from the other side; and the other side gives us nothing unless by a thousand detours we swing finally round in their direction, unless by ten thousand wiles and a hundred thousand tricks they manage to draw us toward them, to seduce us, and to imprison us. Taking means in nearly every case being taken: thus it is not enough to try to free oneself by repeating proclamations and denials. It is not enough to try to get back to the people in that past out of which they have already emerged; rather we must join them in that fluctuating movement which they are just giving a shape to, and which, as soon as it has started, will be the signal for everything to be called in question. Let there be no mistake about it; it is to this zone of occult instability where the people dwell that we must come; and it is there that our souls are crystallized and that our perceptions and our lives are transfused with light.

Keita Fodeba,[11] today Minister of Internal Affairs in the Republic of Guinea, when he was the director of the

---

[9] René Depestre, "Face à la Nuit."
[10] René Char (1907–1988), French poet. Quotation from *Partage Formel*.
[11] Keita Fodeba (also Modibo) (1915–1977), African poet, first president of Mali, 1960–1968.

"African Ballet" did not play any tricks with the reality which the people of Guinea offered him. He reinterpreted all the rhythmic images of his country from a revolutionary standpoint. But he did more. In this poetic works, which are not well known, we find a constant desire to define accurately the historic moments of the struggle and to mark off the field in which were to be unfolded the actions and ideas around which the popular will would crystallize. Here is a poem by Keita Fodeba which is a true invitation to thought, to de-mystification, and to battle:

African Dawn

(Guitar music)

Dawn was breaking. The little village, which had danced half the night to the sound of its tom-toms, was waking slowly. Ragged shepherds playing their flutes were leading their flocks down into the valley. The girls of the village with their canaries followed one by one along the winding path that leads to the fountain. In the marabout's courtyard a group of children were softly chanting in chorus some verses from the Koran.

(Guitar music)

Dawn was breaking—dawn, the fight between night and day. But the night was exhausted and could fight no more, and slowly died. A few rays of the sun, the forerunners of this victory of the day, still hovered on the horizon, pale and timid, while the last stars gently glided under the mass of clouds, crimson like the blooming flamboyant flowers.

(Guitar music)

Dawn was breaking. And down at the end of the vast plain with its purple contours, the silhouette of a bent man tilling the ground could be seen, the silhouette of Naman the laborer. Each time he lifted his hoe the frightened birds rose, and flew swiftly away to find the quiet banks of the Djoliba, the great Niger river. The man's gray cotton trousers, soaked by the dew, flapped against the grass on either side. Sweating, unresting, always bent over he worked with his hoe; for the seed had to be sown before the next rains came.

(Cora music)

Dawn was breaking, still breaking. The sparrows circled amongst the leaves announcing the day. On the damp track leading to the plain a child, carrying his little quiver of arrows round him like a bandolier, was running breathless toward Naman. He called out: "Brother Naman, the headman of the village wants you to come to the council tree."

(Cora music)

The laborer, surprised by such a message so early in the morning, laid down his hoe and walked toward the village which now was shining in the beams of the rising sun. Already the old men of the village were sitting under the tree, looking more solemn than ever. Beside them a man in uniform, a district guard, sat impassively, quietly smoking his pipe.

(Cora music)

Naman took his place on the sheepskin. The headman's spokesman stood up to announce to the assembly the will of the old men: "The white men have sent a district guard to ask for a man from the village who will go to the war in their country. The chief men, after taking counsel together, have decided to send the young man who is the best representative of our race, so that he may go and give proof to the white men of that courage which has always been a feature of our *Manding*."

(Guitar music)

Naman was thus officially marked out, for every evening the village girls praised his great stature and muscular appearance in musical couplets. Gentle Kadia, his young wife, overwhelmed by the news, suddenly ceased grinding corn, put the mortar away under the barn, and without saying a word shut herself into her hut to weep over her misfortune with stifled sobs. For death had taken her first husband; and she could not believe that now the white people had taken Naman from her, Naman who was the center of all her new-sprung hopes.

(Guitar music)

The next day, in spite of her tears and lamentations, the full-toned drumming of the war tom-toms accompanied Naman to the village's little harbor where he boarded a trawler which was going to the district capital. That night, instead of dancing in the marketplace as they usually did, the village girls came to keep watch in Naman's outer room, and there told their tales until morning around a wood fire.

(Guitar music)

Several months went by without any news of Naman reaching the village. Kadia was so worried that she went to the cunning fetish-worker from the neighboring village. The village elders themselves held a short secret council on the matter, but nothing came of it.

(Cora music)

At last one day a letter from Naman came to the village, to Kadia's address. She was worried as to what was happening to her husband, and so that same night she came, after hours of tiring walking, to the capital of the district, where a translator read the letter to her.

Naman was in North Africa; he was well, and he asked for news of the harvest, of the feastings, the river, the dances, the council tree . . . in fact, for news of all the village.

(Balafo music)

That night the old women of the village honored Kadia by allowing her to come to the courtyard of the oldest woman and listen to the talk that went on nightly among them. The headman of the village, happy to have heard news of Naman, gave a great banquet to all the beggars of the neighborhood.

(Balafo music)

Again several months went by and everyone was once more anxious, for nothing more was heard of Naman. Kadia was thinking of going again to consult the fetish-worker when she received a second letter. Naman, after passing through Corsica and Italy, was now in Germany and was proud of having been decorated.

(Balafo music)

But the next time there was only a postcard to say that Naman had been made prisoner by the Germans. This news weighed heavily on the village. The old men held council and decided that henceforward Naman would be allowed to dance the Douga, that sacred dance of the vultures that no one who has not performed some outstanding feat is allowed to dance, that dance of the Mali emperors of which every step is a stage in the history of the Mali race. Kadia found consolation in the fact that her husband had been raised to the dignity of a hero of his country.

(Guitar music)

Time went by. A year followed another, and Naman was still in Germany. He did not write any more.

(Guitar music)

One fine day, the village headman received word from Dakar that Naman would soon be home. The mutter of the tom-toms was at once heard. There was dancing and singing till dawn. The village girls composed new songs for his homecoming, for the old men who were the devotees of the Douga spoke no more about that famous dance of the *Manding.*

(Tom-toms)

But a month later, Corporal Moussa, a great friend of Naman's, wrote a tragic letter to Kadia: "Dawn was breaking. We were at Tiaroye-sur-Mer. In the course of a widespread dispute between us and our white officers from Dakar, a bullet struck Naman. He lies in the land of Senegal."

(Guitar music)

Yes; dawn was breaking. The first rays of the sun hardly touched the surface of the sea as they gilded its little foam-flecked waves. Stirred by the breeze, the palm trees gently bent their trunks down toward the ocean, as if saddened by the morning's battle. The crows came in noisy flocks to warn the neighborhood by their cawing of the tragedy that was staining the dawn at Tiaroye with blood. And in the flaming blue sky, just above Naman's body, a huge vulture was hovering heavily. It seemed to say to him "Naman! You have not danced that dance that is named after me. Others will dance it."

(Cora music)

If I have chosen to quote this long poem, it is on account of its unquestioned pedagogical value. Here, things are clear; it is a precise, forward-looking exposition. The understanding of the poem is not merely an intellectual advance, but a political advance. To understand this poem is to understand the part one has played, to recognize one's advance, and to furbish up one's weapons. There is not a single colonized person who will not receive the message that this poem holds. Naman, the hero of the battlefields of Europe, Naman who eternally ensures the power and perenniality of the mother country, Naman is machine-gunned by the police force at the very moment that he comes back to the country of his birth: and this is Sétif in 1945, this is Fort-le-France, this is Saigon, Dakar, and Lagos. All those niggers, all those wogs who fought to defend the liberty of France or for British civilization recognize themselves in this poem by Keita Fodeba.

But Keita Fodeba sees further. In colonized countries, colonialism, after having made use of the natives on the battlefields, uses them as trained soldiers to put down the movements of independence. The ex-service associations are in the colonies one of the most anti-nationalist elements which exist. The poet Keita Fodeba was training the Minister of Internal Affairs of the Republic of Guinea to frustrate the plots organized by French colonialism. The French secret service intend to use, among other means, the ex-servicemen to break up the young independent Guinean state.

The colonized man who writes for his people ought to use the past with the intention of opening the future, as an invitation to action and a basis for hope. But to ensure that hope and to give it form, he must take part in action and throw himself body and soul into the national struggle. You may speak about everything under the sun; but when you decide to speak of that unique thing in man's life that is represented by the fact of opening up new horizons, by bringing light to your own country, and by raising yourself and your people to their feet, then you must collaborate on the physical plane.

The responsibility of the native man of culture is not a responsibility vis-à-vis his national culture, but a global responsibility with regard to the totality of the nation, whose culture merely, after all, represents one aspect of that nation. The cultured native should not concern himself with choosing the level on which he wishes to fight or the sector where he decides to give battle for his nation. To fight for national culture means in the first place to fight for the liberation of the nation, that material keystone which makes the building of a culture possible. There is no other fight for culture which can develop apart from the popular struggle. To take an example: all those men and women who are fighting with their bare hands against French colonialism in Algeria are not by any means strangers to the national culture of Algeria. The national Algerian culture is taking on form and content as the battles are being fought out, in prisons, under the guillotine, and in every French outpost which is captured or destroyed.

We must not therefore be content with delving into the past of a people in order to find coherent elements which will counteract colonialism's attempts to falsify and harm. We must work and fight with the same rhythm as the people to construct the future and to prepare the ground where vigorous shoots are already springing up. A national culture is not a folklore, nor an abstract populism that believes it can discover the people's true nature. It is not made up of the inert dregs of gratuitous actions, that is to say actions which are less and less attached to the ever-present reality of the people. A national culture is the whole body of efforts made by a people in the sphere of thought to describe, justify, and praise the action through which that people has created itself and keeps itself in existence. A national culture in underdeveloped countries should therefore take its place at the very heart of the struggle for freedom which these countries are carrying on. Men of African cultures who are still fighting in the name of African-Negro culture and who have called many congresses in the name of the unity of that culture should today realize that all their efforts amount to is to make comparisons between coins and sarcophagi.

There is no common destiny to be shared between the national cultures of Senegal and Guinea; but there *is* a common destiny between the Senegalese and Guinean nations which are both dominated by the same French colonialism. If it is wished that the national culture of Senegal should come to resemble the national culture of Guinea, it is not enough for the rulers of the two peoples to decide to consider their problems—whether the problem of liberation is concerned, or the trade-union question, or economic difficulties—from similar viewpoints. And even here there does not seem to be complete identity, for the rhythm of the people and that of their rulers are not the same. There can be no two cultures which are completely identical. To believe that it is possible to create a black culture is to forget that niggers are disappearing, just as those people who brought them into being are seeing the breakup of their economic and cultural supremacy.[12] There will never be such a thing as black culture because there is not a single politician who feels he has a vocation to bring black republics into being. The problem is to get to know the place that these men mean to give their people, the kind of social relations that they decide to set up, and the conception that they have of the future of humanity. It is this that counts; everything else is mystification, signifying nothing.

In 1959, the cultured Africans who met at Rome never stopped talking about unity. But one of the people who was loudest in the praise of this cultural unity, Jacques Rabemananjara, is today a minister in the Madagascan government, and as such has decided, with his government, to oppose the Algerian people in the General Assembly of the United Nations. Rabemananjara, if he had been true to himself, ought to have resigned from the government and denounced those men who claim to incarnate the will of the Madagascan people. The ninety thousand dead of Madagascar have not given Rabemananjara authority to oppose the aspirations of the Algerian people in the General Assembly of the United Nations.

It is around the peoples' struggles that African-Negro culture takes on substance, and not around songs, poems, or folklore. Senghor, who is also a member of the Society of African Culture and who has worked with us on the question of African culture, is not afraid for his part either to give the order to his delegation to support French proposals on Algeria. Adherence to African-Negro culture and to the cultural unity of Africa is arrived at in the first place by

---

[12] [Fanon] At the last school prize giving in Dakar, the president of the Senegalese Republic, Leopold Senghor, decided to include the study of the idea of negritude in the curriculum. If this decision was due to a desire to study historical causes, no one can criticize it. But if on the other hand it was taken in order to create black self-consciousness, it is simply a turning of his back upon history which has already taken cognizance of the disappearance of the majority of Negroes.

upholding unconditionally the peoples' struggle for freedom. No one can truly wish for the spread of African culture if he does not give practical support to the creation of the conditions necessary to the existence of that culture; in other words, to the liberation of the whole continent.

I say again that no speech-making and no proclamation concerning culture will turn us from our fundamental tasks: the liberation of the national territory; a continual struggle against colonialism in its new forms; and an obstinate refusal to enter the charmed circle of mutual admiration at the summit.

Reciprocal Bases of National Culture and the Fight for Freedom

Colonial domination, because it is total and tends to oversimplify, very soon manages to disrupt in spectacular fashion the cultural life of a conquered people. This cultural obliteration is made possible by the negation of national reality, by new legal relations introduced by the occupying power, by the banishment of the natives and their customs to outlying districts by colonial society, by expropriation, and by the systematic enslaving of men and women.

Three years ago at our first congress I showed that, in the colonial situation, dynamism is replaced fairly quickly by a substantification of the attitudes of the colonizing power. The area of culture is then marked off by fences and signposts. These are in fact so many defense mechanisms of the most elementary type, comparable for more than one good reason to the simple instinct for preservation. The interest of this period for us is that the oppressor does not manage to convince himself of the objective non-existence of the oppressed nation and its culture. Every effort is made to bring the colonized person to admit the inferiority of his culture which has been transformed into instinctive patterns of behavior, to recognize the unreality of his "nation," and, in the last extreme, the confused and imperfect character of his own biological structure.

Vis-à-vis this state of affairs, the native's reactions are not unanimous. While the mass of the people maintain intact traditions which are completely different from those of the colonial situation, and the artisanal style solidifies into a formalism which is more and more stereotyped, the intellectual throws himself in frenzied fashion into the frantic acquisition of the culture of the occupying power and takes every opportunity of unfavorably criticizing his own national culture, or else takes refuge in setting out and substantiating the claims of that culture in a way that is passionate but rapidly becomes unproductive.

The common nature of these two reactions lies in the fact that they both lead to impossible contradictions. Whether a turncoat or a substantialist, the native is ineffectual precisely because the analysis of the colonial situation is not carried out on strict lines. The colonial situation calls a halt to national culture in almost every field. Within the framework of colonial domination there is not and there will never be such phenomena as new cultural departures or changes in the national culture. Here and there valiant attempts are sometimes made to reanimate the cultural dynamic and to give fresh impulses to its themes, its forms, and its tonalities. The immediate, palpable, and obvious interest of such leaps ahead is nil. But if we follow up the consequences to the very end we see that preparations are being thus made to brush the cobwebs off national consciousness, to question oppression, and to open up the struggle for freedom.

A national culture under colonial domination is a contested culture whose destruction is sought in systematic fashion. It very quickly becomes a culture condemned to secrecy. This idea of a clandestine culture is immediately seen in the reactions of the occupying power which interprets attachment to traditions as faithfulness to the spirit of the nation and as a refusal to submit. This persistence in following forms of cultures which are already condemned to extinction is already a demonstration of nationality; but it is a demonstration which is a throwback to the laws of inertia. There is no taking of the offensive and no redefining of relationships. There is simply a concentration on a hard core of culture which is becoming more and more shrivelled up, inert, and empty.

By the time a century or two of exploitation has passed there comes about a veritable emaciation of the stock of national culture. It becomes a set of automatic habits, some traditions of dress, and a few broken-down institutions. Little movement can be discerned in such remnants of culture; there is no real creativity and no overflowing life. The poverty of the people, national oppression, and the inhibition of culture are one and the same thing. After a century of colonial domination we find a culture which is rigid in the extreme, or rather what we find are the dregs of culture, its mineral strata. The withering away of the reality of the nation and the death pangs of the national culture are linked to each other in mutual dependence. This is why it is of capital importance to follow the evolution of these relations during the struggle for national freedom. The negation of the native's culture, the contempt for any manifestation of culture whether active or emotional, and the placing outside the pale of all specialized branches of organization contribute to breed aggressive patterns of conduct in the native. But these patterns of conduct are of the reflexive type; they are poorly differentiated, anarchic, and ineffective. Colonial exploitation, poverty, and endemic famine drive the native more and more to open, organized revolt. The necessity for an open and decisive breach is formed progressively and imperceptibly, and comes to be felt by the great majority of the people. Those tensions which hitherto were non-existent come into being. International events, the collapse of whole sections of colonial empires and the contradictions inherent in the colonial system strengthen and uphold the native's combativity while promoting and giving support to national consciousness.

These new-found tensions which are present at all stages in the real nature of colonialism have their repercussions on the cultural plane. In literature, for example, there is relative overproduction. From being a reply on a minor scale to the dominating power, the literature produced by natives becomes differentiated and makes itself into a will to particularism. The intelligentsia, which during the period of repression was essentially a consuming public, now themselves become producers. This literature at first chooses to confine itself to the tragic and poetic style; but later on novels, short stories, and essays are attempted. It is as if a kind of internal organization or law of expression existed which wills that poetic expression become less frequent in proportion as the objectives and the methods of the struggle for liberation become more precise. Themes are completely altered; in fact, we find less and less of bitter, hopeless recrimination and less also of that violent, resounding, florid writing which on the whole serves to reassure the occupying power. The colonialists have in former times encouraged these modes of expression and made their existence possible. Stinging denunciations, the exposing of distressing conditions and passions which find their outlet in expression are in fact assimilated by the occupying power in a cathartic process. To aid such processes is in a certain sense to avoid their dramatization and to clear the atmosphere.

But such a situation can only be transitory. In fact, the progress of national consciousness among the people modifies and gives precision to the literary utterances of the native intellectual. The continued cohesion of the people constitutes for the intellectual an invitation to go further than his cry of protest. The lament first makes the indictment; and then it makes an appeal. In the period that follows, the words of command are heard. The crystallization of the national consciousness will both disrupt literary styles and themes, and also create a completely new public. While at the beginning the native intellectual used to produce his work to be read exclusively by the oppressor, whether with the intention of charming him or of denouncing him through ethnic or subjectivist means, now the native writer progressively takes on the habit of addressing his own people.

It is only from that moment that we can speak of a national literature. Here there is, at the level of literary creation, the taking up and clarification of themes which are typically nationalist. This may be properly called a literature of combat, in the sense that it calls on the whole people to fight for their existence as a nation. It is a literature of combat, because it molds the national consciousness, giving it form and contours and flinging open before it new and boundless horizons; it is a literature of combat because it assumes responsibility, and because it is the will to liberty expressed in terms of time and space.

On another level, the oral tradition—stories, epics, and songs of the people—which formerly were filed away as set pieces are now beginning to change. The storytellers who used to relate inert episodes now bring them alive and introduce into them modifications which are increasingly fundamental. There is a tendency to bring conflicts up to date and to modernize the kinds of struggle which the stories evoke, together with the names of heroes and the types of weapons. The method of allusion is more and more widely used. The formula "This all happened long ago" is substituted with that of "What we are going to speak of happened somewhere else, but it might well have happened here today, and it might happen tomorrow." The example of Algeria is significant in this context. From 1952–53 on, the storytellers, who were before that time stereotyped and tedious to listen to, completely overturned their traditional methods of storytelling and the contents of their tales. Their public, which was formerly scattered, became compact. The epic, with its typified categories, reappeared; it became an authentic form of entertainment which took on once more a cultural value. Colonialism made no mistake when from 1955 on it proceeded to arrest these storytellers systematically.

The contact of the people with the new movement gives rise to a new rhythm of life and to forgotten muscular tensions, and develops the imagination. Every time the storyteller relates a fresh episode to his public, he presides over a real invocation. The existence of a new type of man is revealed to the public. The present is no longer turned in upon itself but spread out for all to see. The storyteller once more gives free rein to his imagination; he makes innovations and he creates a work of art. It even happens that the characters, which are barely ready for such a transformation—highway robbers or more or less antisocial vagabonds—are taken up and remodeled. The emergence of the imagination and of the creative urge in the songs and epic stories of a colonized country is worth following. The storyteller replies to the expectant people by successive approximations, and makes his way, apparently alone but in fact helped on by his public, toward the seeking out of new patterns, that is to say national patterns. Comedy and farce disappear, or lose their attraction. As for dramatization, it is no longer placed on the plane of the troubled intellectual and his tormented conscience. By losing its characteristics of despair and revolt, the drama becomes part of the common lot of the people and forms part of an action in preparation or already in progress.

Where handicrafts are concerned, the forms of expression which formerly were the dregs of art, surviving as if in a daze, now begin to reach out. Woodwork, for example, which formerly turned out certain faces and attitudes by the million, begins to be differentiated. The inexpressive or overwrought mask comes to life and the arms tend to be raised from the body as if to sketch an action. Compositions containing two, three, or five figures appear. The traditional schools are led on to creative efforts by the rising avalanche of amateurs or of critics. This new vigor in this sector of cultural life very often passes unseen; and yet its contribution to the national effort is of capital importance. By carving figures and faces which are full of life, and by taking as his theme a group fixed on the same pedestal, the artist invites participation in an organized movement.

If we study the repercussions of the awakening of national consciousness in the domains of ceramics and pottery-making, the same observations may be drawn. Formalism is abandoned in the craftsman's work. Jugs, jars, and trays are modified, at first imperceptibly, then almost savagely. The colors, of which formerly there were but few and which obeyed the traditional rules of harmony, increase in number and are influenced by the repercussion of the rising revolution. Certain ochres and blues, which seemed forbidden to all eternity in a given cultural area, now assert themselves without giving rise to scandal. In the same way the stylization of the human face, which according to sociologists is typical of very clearly defined regions, becomes suddenly completely relative. The specialist coming from the home country and the ethnologist are quick to note these changes. On the whole such changes are condemned in the name of a rigid code of artistic style and of a cultural life which grows up at the heart of the colonial system. The colonialist specialists do not recognize these new forms and rush to the help of the traditions of the indigenous society. It is the colonialists who become the defenders of the native style. We remember perfectly, and the example took on a certain measure of importance since the real nature of colonialism was not involved, the reactions of the white jazz specialists when after the Second World War new styles such as the be-bop took definite shape. The fact is that in their eyes jazz should only be the despairing, broken-down nostalgia of an old Negro who is trapped between five glasses of whiskey, the curse of his race, and the racial hatred of the white men. As soon as the Negro comes to an understanding of himself, and understands the rest of the world differently, when he gives birth to hope and forces back the racist universe, it is clear that his trumpet sounds more clearly and his voice less hoarsely. The new fashions in jazz are not simply born of economic competition. We must without any doubt see in them one of the consequences of the defeat, slow but sure, of the southern world of the United States. And it is not utopian to suppose that in fifty years' time the type of jazz howl hiccuped by a poor misfortunate Negro will be upheld only by the whites who believe in it as an expression of negritude, and who are faithful to this arrested image of a type of relationship.

We might in the same way seek and find in dancing, singing, and traditional rites and ceremonies the same upward-springing trend, and make out the same changes and the same impatience in this field. Well before the political or fighting phase of the national movement, an attentive spectator can thus feel and see the manifestation of new vigor and feel the approaching conflict. He will note unusual forms of expression and themes which are fresh and imbued with a power which is no longer that of invocation but rather of the assembling of the people, a summoning together for a precise purpose. Everything works together to awaken the native's sensibility and to make unreal and inacceptable the contemplative attitude, or the acceptance of defeat. The native rebuilds his perceptions because he renews the purpose and dynamism of the craftsmen, of dancing and music, and of literature and the oral tradition. His world comes to lose its accursed character. The conditions necessary for the inevitable conflict are brought together.

We have noted the appearance of the movement in cultural forms and we have seen that this movement and these new forms are linked to the state of maturity of the national consciousness. Now, this movement tends more and more to express itself objectively, in institutions. From thence comes the need for a national existence, whatever the cost.

A frequent mistake, and one which is moreover hardly justifiable, is to try to find cultural expressions for and to give new values to native culture within the framework of colonial domination. This is why we arrive at a proposition which at first sight seems paradoxical: the fact that in a colonized country the most elementary, most savage, and the most undifferentiated nationalism is the most fervent and efficient means of defending national culture. For culture is first the expression of a nation, the expression of its preferences, of its taboos and of its patterns. It is at every stage of the whole of society that other taboos, values, and patterns are formed. A national culture is the sum total of all these appraisals; it is the result of internal and external tensions exerted over society as a whole and also at every level of that society. In the colonial situation, culture, which is doubly deprived of the support of the nation and of the state, falls away and dies. The condition for its existence is therefore national liberation and the renaissance of the state.

The nation is not only the condition of culture, its fruitfulness, its continuous renewal, and its deepening. It is also a necessity. It is the fight for national existence which sets culture moving and opens to it the doors of creation. Later on it is the nation which will ensure the conditions and framework necessary to culture. The nation gathers together the various indispensable elements necessary for the creation of a culture, those elements which alone can give it credibility, validity, life, and creative power. In the same way it is its national character that will make such a culture open to other cultures and which will enable it to influence and permeate other cultures. A non-existent culture can hardly be expected to have bearing on reality, or to influence reality. The first necessity is the re-establishment of the nation in order to give life to national culture in the strictly biological sense of the phrase.

Thus we have followed the breakup of the old strata of culture, a shattering which becomes increasingly fundamental; and we have noticed, on the eve of the decisive conflict for national freedom, the renewing of forms of expression and the rebirth of the imagination. There remains one essential question: what are the relations between the struggle—whether political or military—and culture? Is there a suspension of culture during the conflict? Is the national struggle an expression of a culture? Finally, ought one to say that the battle for freedom however fertile *a posteriori* with regard to culture is in itself a negation of culture? In short, is the struggle for liberation a cultural phenomenon or not?

We believe that the conscious and organized undertaking by a colonized people to re-establish the sovereignty of that nation constitutes the most complete and obvious cultural manifestation that exists. It is not alone the success of the struggle which afterward gives validity and vigor to culture; culture is not put into cold storage during the conflict. The struggle itself in its development and in its internal progression sends culture along different paths and traces out entirely new ones for it. The struggle for freedom does not give back to the national culture its former value and shapes; this struggle which aims at a fundamentally different set of relations between men cannot leave intact either the form or the content of the people's culture. After the conflict there is not only the disappearance of colonialism but also the disappearance of the colonized man.

This new humanity cannot do otherwise than define a new humanism both for itself and for others. It is prefigured in the objectives and methods of the conflict. A struggle which mobilizes all classes of the people and which expresses their aims and their impatience, which is not afraid to count almost exclusively on the people's support, will of necessity triumph. The value of this type of conflict is that it supplies the maximum of conditions necessary for the development and aims of culture. After national freedom has been obtained in these conditions, there is no such painful cultural indecision which is found in certain countries which are newly independent, because the nation by its manner of coming into being and in the terms of its existence exerts a fundamental influence over culture. A nation which is born of the people's concerted action and which embodies the real aspirations of the people while changing the state cannot exist save in the expression of exceptionally rich forms of culture.

The natives who are anxious for the culture of their country and who wish to give to it a universal dimension ought not therefore to place their confidence in the single principle of inevitable, undifferentiated independence written into the consciousness of the people in order to achieve their task. The liberation of the nation is one thing; the methods and popular content of the fight are another. It seems to us that the future of national culture and its riches are equally also part and parcel of the values which have ordained the struggle for freedom.

And now it is time to denounce certain pharisees. National claims, it is here and there stated, are a phase that humanity has left behind. It is the day of great concerted actions, and retarded nationalists ought in consequence to set their mistakes aright. We however consider that the mistake, which may have very serious consequences, lies in wishing to skip the national period. If culture is the expression of national consciousness, I will not hesitate to affirm that in the case with which we are dealing it is the national consciousness which is the most elaborate form of culture.

The consciousness of self is not the closing of a door to communication. Philosophic thought teaches us, on the contrary, that it is its guarantee. National consciousness, which is not nationalism, is the only thing that will give us an international dimension. This problem of national consciousness and of national culture takes on in Africa a special dimension. The birth of national consciousness in Africa has a strictly contemporaneous connection with the African consciousness. The responsibility of the African as regards national culture is also a responsibility with regard to African Negro culture. This joint responsibility is not the fact of a metaphysical principle but the awareness of a simple rule which wills that every independent nation in an Africa where colonialism is still entrenched is an encircled nation, a nation which is fragile and in permanent danger.

If man is known by his acts, then we will say that the most urgent thing today for the intellectual is to build up his nation. If this building up is true, that is to say if it interprets the manifest will of the people and reveals the eager African peoples, then the building of a nation is of necessity accompanied by the discovery and encouragement of universaliz-ing values. Far from keeping aloof from other nations, therefore, it is national liberation which leads the nation to play its part on the stage of history. It is at the heart of national consciousness that international consciousness lives and grows. And this two-fold emerging is ultimately only the source of all culture.

Statement made at the Second Congress
of Black Artists and Writers, Rome, 1959

Jacques Derrida

b. 1930

For more than thirty years, Jacques Derrida has been at the forefront of developments in criticism and theory, as both a significant innovator and as a target for objections or a subject of controversy. As the principal theorist of "deconstruction," Derrida employed the term in connection with a very specific and important philosophical project of examining the status of the linguistic sign in the discourse of traditional (Continental) philosophy. His attention to the work of Ferdinand de Saussure (above, page 786) provided an eminently convenient vehicle for the exploration of these issues, just as it may have contributed to a centering of attention on the work of Saussure (particularly among nonlinguists) despite its obvious deficiencies and incompleteness as a theory of language. It is a measure, albeit ambiguous, of the scope of Derrida's influence, that the term deconstruction has now largely broken free of this philosophical context to revert, at least in English, to the simpler meaning applying to virtually any process involved in taking something apart. Derrida's importance, however, lies in his extraordinarily shrewd and insightful pursuit of philosophical issues in the context of the postwar intellectual environment of phenomenology, existentialism, and structuralism. As numerous selections in this anthology make clear, particularly in work by Husserl (above, page 770), Sartre (above, page 1175), Heidegger (above, page 1051), Lévi-Strauss (above, page 1119), and Althusser (below, page 1297), this was an environment haunted by the sense of a continuing *and* impending intellectual crisis, articulated first and perhaps most clearly by Husserl in his frequently translated and reprinted *Die Krisis der europäischen Wissenschaften und die transzendentale Phänomenologie: Eine Einleitung in die phänomenologische Philosophie* (1936, *The Crisis of European Sciences and Transcendental Phenomenology,* 1970), his last work, based on lectures given after his expulsion from the German university system during Hitler's rise to power. It is worth noting here the disappearance of Husserl's subtitle, *A Prelude to Phenomenological Philosophy,* in the English translation as a perhaps coincidental indicator of the fact that the "crisis" to which he alluded, concerning the apparent breakdown of the historically valorized sense of purpose in philosophy, has seemed more like the prelude to the reiteration of crisis as a virtually permanent condition of philosophical criticism, a point detailed by Paul de Man in *Blindness and Insight* (1971). For Derrida, that sense of "crisis" seems a much closer sense of impending disclosure of something uncannily already known, situated not outside but within the very processes of our thinking, writing, and speaking, in the endless making and unmaking of sense discernible at whatever level of detail one chooses to examine.

In this connection, Derrida is also frequently associated with the development of "postmodern" and "poststructuralist" positions, largely because of his incisive and very influential essay, "Structure, Sign and Play in the Discourse of the Human Sciences." This widely reprinted essay was first delivered at the 1966 conference, significantly titled (with a nod to R. S. Crane's work—above, page 1071) "The Languages of Criticism and the Sciences of Man," at John Hopkins University, meant to introduce recent work by European structuralist theorists to an American audience. Derrida's paper, however, carried out with great precision and acuity what remains a paradigmatic instance of deconstruction in practice, disclosing the contradictions and inconsistencies in the very idea of "structure," with special attention to the work of Claude Lévi-Strauss. The proceedings for the conference were subsequently renamed *The Structuralist Controversy* (1972) to capture at least a part of what ensued. While it is surely the case that the sense of crisis and controversy was already an unavoidable figure in commentary on the times, from student uprisings in Paris and around the world in the late 1960s, the rise of the civil rights movement in the United States, opposition to the war in Vietnam, in conjunction with the spread of wars of national liberation throughout the third world, the political foregrounding of feminism on an international scale, and so on, Derrida's centrality to subsequent discussions was by no means merely coincidental.

What is perhaps easiest to overlook, given the notoriety of Derrida's work, is precisely its philosophical precision, even its modesty—which is in no way inconsistent with its philosophical ambitions. *Of Grammatology* (1967, tr. 1972) makes particularly clear that the work of deconstruction must *inhabit* the very structures it analyzes, staying close enough to them to know their most intimate characteristics. With some distant similarities to the practices of "close reading" developed among the New Critics—see for example, William Empson (above, page 894) and Cleanth Brooks (above, page 1035)—Derrida is much more acutely aware of the subtle problems of philosophical language in which the assumptions that enable thinking are the very elements that escape detection. As one in a long series of thinkers to whom the notion of the "linguistic turn" can apply, Derrida is distinctive in that he does not assume that the turn to language will yield a decisive clarification, a reduction of ambiguity, or issue in some form of technical innovation in specialized vocabulary—despite his own contribution to the debate of his term of differing / deferring, differ-*a*-nce, to indicate the very point at which such a nailing-down of meaning might be the strongest temptation. On the contrary, he sees instead the fundamental perplexity of language as a reflection of metaphysical commitments that so saturate all traditions of Western thinking as to be virtually invisible. In particular, Derrida has focused on the problematic of writing without privileging the primacy of voice or direct intuition, thereby revealing both the pervasiveness of constructedness, in the sense that our thoughts never stand in a simple relation to some transcendental object of which they are the representation but are always being constituted, and the limitlessness of signification without a reachable origin or end. In his earlier work, emphasized in our selections here, deconstruction is a radical opening up of the problems of representation in an encounter with a tradition of thinking built on a metaphysical model that presupposes the accessibility of pure *immediate* intuition, just as Derrida shows with fateful accuracy and frequently dazzling agility, is everywhere and always in the midst of mediation. Derrida has not, however, taken it as his task to build some alternative "system," but to occupy that liminal space in the discourse of philosophy where problems are neither solved, nor, as the early Wittgenstein would have had it, "dissolved," but persist in a kind of perpetual kaleidoscopic surprise. In this respect, Derrida's career has not followed a kind of paradigmatic trajectory to abstract architectonic mastery, but instead has branched out incessantly to literary texts and tropes, to aspects of culture ranging from postcards to television, to reflections on politics and ethics, and so on.

The still startling effect of Derrida's analytical practice, early and later, of opening up fundamental assumptions that if not already in a state of contradiction are on the brink of it has contributed not a little to the controversies that have surrounded his work all along. In the early 1990s, for example, Derrida was nominated for an honorary doctorate at Cambridge University, leading to a remarkable collapse of well-established British intellectual manners, in the fierce opposition to the nomination, leading to a vote in 1992 (which carried, 336 to 204) to confer the degree, the first such vote in decades.

When read in the historical context of such other philosophers and theorists for whom language has been a crucial issue, such as Husserl (above, page 770), Russell (above, page 811), Wittgenstein (above, page 823), and Carnap (above, page 978), Derrida may appear far less alarming but still one of the great radical thinkers on this topic, for his fundamental insight that the dream of intellectual intuition, of perfect adequation between word and thought or word and object, is vexed by a fundamental dilemma in the search for intellectual origins or ends that is in almost every way inconsistent with the very process of signification, and hence, of thinking itself. In this respect, he appears as a logical, but hardly expected, successor to both Husserl and Heidegger, who may appear, in this light, as the very last of the would-be system builders who have dominated philosophical thinking since Plato and Aristotle. The selections included here, beginning with a chapter from Derrida's meticulous critique of Husserl in *Speech and Phenomena and Other Essays on Husserl's Theory of Signs* (1967; tr. 1973), his essay "Structure, Sign and Play in the Discourse of the Human Sciences," and a section from *Of Grammatology* (1967, tr. 1976), offer a substantive introduction to principal issues in Derrida's thinking, but they can only suggest the extraordinary range of topics and subjects upon which he has written, or, for that matter, the rhetorical subtlety, exuberance, and playfulness of his writing—or of his practical commitments to the concrete politics of education and the support of colleagues, sometimes barely noticed in the glare of his extraordinary international visibility.

Derrida has been so enormously prolific that we can here mention only a few his most important books translated into English. Readers are urged to consult William R. Schultz and Lewis L. B. Fried, *Jacques Derrida: An Annotated Primary and Secondary Bibliography* (1992), and Derek Attridge's "A Selected Bibliography of Jacques Derrida's Writing, with Particular Reference to the Question of Literature" in his *Acts of Literature* (1992). Major works of Derrida include: *Writing and Difference* (1967, tr. 1978); *Of Grammatology* (1967, tr. 1976); *Speech and Phenomena* (1967, tr. 1974); *Dissemination* (1972, tr. 1981); *Margins of Philosophy* (1972); *Glas* (1974); *The Post Card: From Socrates to Freud and Beyond* (1980); *Limited, Inc.* (1988); *The Other Heading: Reflections on Today's Europe* (1991, tr. 1992); *Acts of Literature,* ed. Derek Attridge (1992); *Specters of Marx: The State of Debt, the Work of Mourning, and the New International* (1993, tr. 1994); *Politics of Friendship* (1994, tr. 1997); *Adieu to Emmanuel Lévinas* (1997, tr. 1999); and *Negotiations: Interventions and Interviews, 1971–2001,* ed. Elizabeth Rottenberg (2002). Critical works on Derrida include: Christopher Norris, *Deconstruction: Theory and Practice;* Paul de Man, "The Rhetoric of Blindness," in *Blindness and Insight* (1971); Geoffrey H. Hartman, *Saving the Text: Literature/Derrida/Philosophy* (1981); Henry Staten, *Wittgenstein and Derrida* (1984); Gregory J. Ulmer, *Applied Grammatology* (1985); Rodolph Gauché, *The Tain of the Mirror: Derrida* and the Philosophy of Reflection (1986); Simon Critchley, The Ethics of Deconstruction: Derrida and Levinas (1992); Christopher Johnson, System and Writing in the Philosophy of Jacques Derrida (1993); William R. McKenna and J. Claude Evans, eds., Derrida and Phenomenology (1995); Geoffrey Bennington, Interrupting Derrida (2000); Herman Rapaport, Later Derrida: Reading the Recent Work (2003).

Structure, Sign and Play in the Discourse of the Human Sciences

We need to interpret interpretations
more than to interpret things.
MONTAIGNE

Perhaps something has occurred in the history of the concept of structure that could be called an "event," if this loaded word did not entail a meaning which it is precisely the function of structural—or structuralist—thought to reduce or to suspect. Let us speak of an "event," nevertheless, and let us use quotation marks to serve as a precaution. What would this event be then? Its exterior form would be that of a *rupture* and a redoubling.

It would be easy enough to show that the concept of structure and even the word "structure" itself are as old as the *epistēmē*[1]—that is to say, as old as Western science and Western philosophy—and that their roots thrust deep into the soil of ordinary language, into whose deepest recesses the *epistēmē* plunges in order to gather them up and to make them part of itself in a metaphorical displacement. Nevertheless, up to the event which I wish to mark out and define, structure—or rather the structurality of structure—although it has always been at work, has always been neutralized or reduced, and this by a process of giving it a center or of referring it to a point of presence, a fixed origin. The function of this center was not only to orient, balance, and organize the structure—one cannot in fact conceive of an unorganized structure—but above all to make sure that the organizing principle of the structure would limit what we might call the *play* of the structure. By orienting and organizing the coherence of the system, the center of a structure permits the play of its elements inside the total form. And even today the notion of a structure lacking any center represents the unthinkable itself.

Nevertheless, the center also closes off the play which it opens up and makes possible. As center, it is the point at which the substitution of contents, elements, or terms is no longer possible. At the center, the permutation or the transformation of elements (which may of course be structures enclosed within a structure) is forbidden. At least this permutation has always remained *interdicted* (and I am using this word deliberately). Thus it has always been thought that the center, which is by definition unique, constituted that very thing within a structure which while governing the structure, escapes structurality. This is why classical thought concerning structure could say that the center is, paradoxically, *within* the structure and *outside it*. The center is at the center of the totality, and yet, since the center does not belong to the totality (is not part of the totality), the totality *has its center elsewhere*. The center is not the center. The concept of centered structure—although it represents coherence itself, the condition of the *epistēmē* as philosophy or science—is contradictorily coherent. And as always, coherence in contradiction expresses the force of a desire.[2] The concept of centered structure is in fact the concept of a play based on a fundamental ground, a play constituted on the

---

"Structure, Sign and Play in the Discourse of the Human Sciences" was first given as a lecture at the Johns Hopkins University in 1966, at a conference titled "The Languages of Criticism and the Sciences of Man." The essay was subsequently published in the proceedings titled *The Structuralist Controversy: The Languages of Criticism and the Sciences of Man* (1970). A revised edition was published in *Writing and Difference* (1967, tr. Alan Bass, 1978). The essay here is reprinted from *Writing and Difference,* tr. Alan Bass (Chicago: University of Chicago Press, 1978).
[1] *epistēmē*: Greek, wisdom, scientific or philosophical knowledge.

[2] [Bass] The reference, in a restricted sense, is to the Freudian theory of neurotic symptoms and of dream interpretation in which a given symbol is understood contradictorily as both the desire to fulfill an impulse and the desire to suppress the impulse. In a general sense the reference is to Derrida's thesis that logic and coherence themselves can only be understood contradictorily, since they presuppose the suppression of *différance,* "writing" in the sense of the general economy. Cf. "La pharmacie de Platon," in *La dissemination,* pp. 125–26, where Derrida uses the Freudian model of dream interpretation in order to clarify the contradictions embedded in philosophical coherence.

basis of a fundamental immobility and a reassuring certitude, which itself is beyond the reach of play. And on the basis of this certitude anxiety can be mastered, for anxiety is invariably the result of a certain mode of being implicated in the game, of being caught by the game, of being as it were at stake in the game from the outset. And again on the basis of what we call the center (and which, because it can be either inside or outside, can also indifferently be called the origin or end, *archē* or *telos*), repetitions, substitutions, transformations, and permutations are always *taken* from a history of meaning [*sens*]—that is, in a word, a history—whose origin may always be reawakened or whose end may always be anticipated in the form of presence. This is why one perhaps could say that the movement of any archaeology, like that of any eschatology, is an accomplice of this reduction of the structurality of structure and always attempts to conceive of structure on the basis of a full presence which is beyond play.

If this is so, the entire history of the concept of structure, before the rupture of which we are speaking, must be thought of as a series of substitutions of center for center, as a linked chain of determinations of the center. Successively, and in a regulated fashion, the center receives different forms or names. The history of metaphysics, like the history of the West, is the history of these metaphors and metonymies. Its matrix—if you will pardon me for demonstrating so little and for being so elliptical in order to come more quickly to my principal theme—is the determination of Being as *presence* in all senses of this word. It could be shown that all the names related to fundamentals, to principles, or to the center have always designated an invariable presence—*eidos, archē, telos, energeia, ousia* (essence, existence, substance, subject) *alētheia,* transcendentality, consciousness, God, man, and so forth.

The event I called a rupture, the disruption I alluded to at the beginning of this paper, presumably would have come about when the structurality of structure had to begin to be thought, that is to say, repeated, and this is why I said that this disruption was repetition in every sense of the word. Henceforth, it became necessary to think both the law which somehow governed the desire for a center in the constitution of structure, and the process of signification which orders the displacements and substitutions for this law of central presence—but a central presence which has never been itself, has always already been exiled from itself into its own substitute. The substitute does not substitute itself for anything which has somehow existed before it. Henceforth, it was necessary to begin thinking that there was no center, that the center could not be thought in the form of a present-being, that the center had no natural site, that it was not a

fixed locus but a function, a sort of nonlocus in which an infinite number of sign-substitutions came into play. This was the moment when language invaded the universal problematic, the moment when, in the absence of a center or origin, everything became discourse—provided we can agree on this word—that is to say, a system in which the central signified, the original or transcendental signified, is never absolutely present outside a system of differences. The absence of the transcendental signified extends the domain and the play of signification infinitely.

Where and how does this decentering, this thinking the structurality of structure, occur? It would be somewhat naïve to refer to an event, a doctrine, or an author in order to designate this occurrence. It is no doubt part of the totality of an era, our own, but still it has always already begun to proclaim itself and begun to *work*. Nevertheless, if we wished to choose several "names," as indications only, and to recall those authors in whose discourse this occurrence has kept most closely to its most radical formulation, we doubtless would have to cite the Nietzschean critique of metaphysics, the critique of the concepts of Being and truth, for which were substituted the concepts of play, interpretation, and sign (sign without present truth); the Freudian critique of self-presence, that is, the critique of consciousness, of the subject, of self-identity and of self-proximity or self-possession; and, more radically, the Heideggerean destruction of metaphysics, of onto-theology, of the determination of Being as presence. But all these destructive discourses and all their analogues are trapped in a kind of circle. This circle is unique. It describes the form of the relation between the history of metaphysics and the destruction of the history of metaphysics. There is no sense in doing without the concepts of metaphysics in order to shake metaphysics. We have no language—no syntax and no lexicon—which is foreign to this history; we can pronounce not a single destructive proposition which has not already had to slip into the form, the logic, and the implicit postulations of precisely what it seeks to contest. To take one example from many: the metaphysics of presence is shaken with the help of the concept of *sign*. But, as I suggested a moment ago, as soon as one seeks to demonstrate in this way that there is no transcendental or privileged signified and that the domain or play of signification henceforth has no limit, one must reject even the concept and word "sign" itself—which is precisely what cannot be done. For the signification "sign" has always been understood and determined, in its meaning, as sign-of, a signifier referring to a signified, a signifier different from its signified. If one erases the radical difference between signifier and signified, it is the word "signifier" itself which must be abandoned as a metaphysical concept. When Lévi-Strauss says in the preface to *The Raw and the Cooked* that he has "sought to transcend the opposition between the sensible and the intelligible by operating from the outset at the level of signs,"[3] the necessity, force, and legitimacy of his act cannot make us forget the concept of the sign cannot in itself surpass this opposition between the sensible and the intelligible. The concept of the sign, in each of its aspects, has been determined by this opposition throughout the totality of its history. It has lived only on this opposition and its system. But we cannot do without the concept of the sign, for we cannot give up this metaphysical complicity without also giving up the critique we are directing against this complicity, or without the risk of erasing difference in the self-identity of a signified reducing its signifier into itself or, amounting to the same thing, simply expelling its signifier outside itself. For there are two heterogeneous ways of erasing the difference between the signifier and the signified: one, the classic way, consists in reducing or deriving the signifier, that is to say, ultimately in *submitting* the sign to thought; the other, the one we are using here against the first one, consists in putting into question the system in which the preceding reduction functioned: first and foremost, the opposition between the sensible and the intelligible. For the *paradox* is that the metaphysical reduction of the sign needed the opposition it was reducing. The opposition is systematic with the reduction. And what we are saying here about the sign can be extended to all the concepts and all the sentences of metaphysics, in particular to the discourse on "structure." But there are several ways of being caught in this circle. They are all more or less naïve, more or less empirical, more or less systematic, more or less close to the formulation—that is, to the formalization—of this circle. It is these differences which explain the multiplicity of destructive discourses and the disagreement between those who elaborate them. Nietzsche, Freud, and Heidegger, for example, worked within the inherited concepts of metaphysics. Since these concepts are not elements or atoms, and since they are taken from a syntax and a system, every particular borrowing brings along with it the whole of metaphysics. This is what allows these destroyers to destroy each other reciprocally—for example, Heidegger regarding Nietzsche, with as much lucidity and rigor as bad faith and misconstruction, as the last metaphysician, the last "Platonist." One could do the same for Heidegger himself, for Freud, or for a number of others. And today no exercise is more widespread.

What is the relevance of this formal schema when we turn to what are called the "human sciences"? One of them perhaps occupies a privileged place—ethnology. In fact one can assume that ethnology could have been born as a science only at the moment when a decentering had come about: at the moment when European culture—and, in consequence, the history of metaphysics and of its concepts—had been *dislocated,* driven from its locus, and forced to stop considering itself as the culture of reference. This moment is not first and foremost a moment of philosophical or scientific discourse. It is also a moment which is political, economic, technical, and so forth. One can say with total security that there is nothing fortuitous about the fact that the critique of ethnocentrism—the very condition for ethnology—should be systematically and historically contemporaneous with the destruction of the history of metaphysics. Both belong to one and the same era. Now, ethnology—like any science—comes about within the element of discourse. And it is primarily a European science employing traditional concepts, however much it may struggle against them. Consequently, whether he wants to or not—and this does not depend on a decision on his part—the ethnologist accepts into his discourse the premises of ethnocentrism at the very moment when he denounces them. This necessity is irreducible; it is not a historical contingency. We ought to consider all its implications very carefully. But if no one can escape this necessity, and if no one is therefore responsible for giving in to it, however little he may do so, this does not mean that all the ways of giving in to it are of equal pertinence. The quality and fecundity of a discourse are perhaps measured by the critical rigor with which this relation to the history of metaphysics and to inherited concepts is thought. Here it is a question both of a critical relation to the language of the social sciences and a critical responsibility of the discourse itself. It is a question of explicitly and systematically posing the problem of the status of a discourse which borrows from a heritage the resources necessary for the deconstruction of that heritage itself. A problem of *economy* and *strategy.*

If we consider, as an example, the texts of Claude Lévi-Strauss, it is not only because of the privilege accorded to ethnology among the social sciences, nor even because the thought of Lévi-Strauss weighs heavily on the contemporary theoretical situation. It is above all because a certain choice has been declared in the work of Lévi-Strauss and because a certain doctrine has been elaborated there, and precisely, in a *more or less explicit manner,* as concerns both this critique of language and this critical language in the social sciences.

In order to follow this movement in the text of Lévi-Strauss, let us choose as one guiding thread among others the

---

[3][Derrida] *The Raw and the Cooked,* trans. John and Doreen Wightman (New York: Harper and Row, 1969), p. 14. [Bass] (Translation somewhat modified.)

opposition between nature and culture. Despite all its rejuvenations and disguises, this opposition is congenital to philosophy. It is even older than Plato. It is at least as old as the Sophists. Since the statement of the opposition *physics/nomos, physis/technē,*[4] it has been relayed to us by means of a whole historical chain which opposes "nature" to law, to education, to art, to technics—but also to liberty, to the arbitrary, to history, to society, to the mind, and so on. Now, from the outset of his researches, and from his first book *(The Elementary Structures of Kinship)* on, Lévi-Strauss simultaneously has experienced the necessity of utilizing this opposition and the impossibility of accepting it. In the *Elementary Structures,* he begins from this axiom or definition: that which is *universal* and spontaneous, and not dependent on any particular culture or on any determinate norm, belongs to nature. Inversely, that which depends upon a system of *norms* regulating society and therefore is capable of *varying* from one social structure to another, belongs to culture. These two definitions are of the traditional type. But in the very first pages of the *Elementary Structures* Lévi-Strauss, who has begun by giving credence to these concepts, encounters what he calls a *scandal,* that is to say, something which no longer tolerates the nature/culture opposition he has accepted, something which *simultaneously* seems to require the predicates of nature and of culture. This scandal is the *incest prohibition.* The incest prohibition is universal; in this sense one could call it natural. But it is also a prohibition, a system of norms and interdicts; in this sense one could call it cultural:

> Let us suppose then that everything universal in man relates to the natural order, and is characterized by spontaneity, and that everything subject to a norm is cultural and is both relative and particular. We are then confronted with a fact, or rather, a group of facts, which, in the light of previous definitions, are not far removed from a scandal: we refer to that complex group of beliefs, customs, conditions and institutions described succinctly as the prohibition of incest, which presents, without the slightest ambiguity, and inseparably combines, the two characteristics in which we recognize the conflicting features of two mutually exclusive orders. It constitutes a rule, but a rule which, alone among all the social rules, possesses at the same time a universal character.[5]

Obviously there is no scandal except within a system of concepts which accredits the difference between nature and culture. By commencing his work with the *factum* of the incest prohibition, Lévi-Strauss thus places himself at the point at which this difference, which has always been assumed to be self-evident, finds itself erased or questioned. For from the moment when the incest prohibition can no longer be conceived within the nature/culture opposition, it can no longer be said to be a scandalous fact, a nucleus of opacity within a network of transparent significations. The incest prohibition is no longer a scandal one meets with or comes up against in the domain of traditional concepts; it is something which escapes these concepts and certainly precedes them—probably as the condition of their possibility. It could perhaps be said that the whole of philosophical conceptualization, which is systematic with the nature/culture opposition, is designed to leave in the domain of the unthinkable the very thing that makes this conceptualization possible: the origin of the prohibition of incest.

This example, too cursorily examined, is only one among many others, but nevertheless it already shows that language bears within itself the necessity of its own critique. Now this critique may be undertaken along two paths, in two "manners." Once the limit of the nature/culture opposition makes itself felt, one might want to question systematically and rigorously the history of these concepts. This is a first action. Such a systematic and historic questioning would be neither a philological nor a philosophical action in the classic sense of these words. To concern oneself with the founding concepts of the entire history of philosophy, to deconstitute them, is not to undertake the work of the philologist or of the classic historian of philosophy. Despite appearances, it is probably the most daring way of making the beginnings of a step outside of philosophy. The step "outside philosophy" is much more difficult to conceive than is generally imagined by those who think they made it long ago with cavalier ease, and who in general are swallowed up in metaphysics in the entire body of discourse which they claim to have disengaged from it.

The other choice (which I believe corresponds more closely to Lévi-Strauss's manner), in order to avoid the possibly sterilizing effects of the first one, consists in conserving all these old concepts within the domain of empirical discovery while here and there denouncing their limits, treating them as tools which can still be used. No longer is any truth value attributed to them; there is a readiness to abandon them, if necessary, should other instruments appear more useful. In the meantime, their relative efficacy is exploited, and they are employed to destroy the old machinery to which they belong and of which they themselves are

---

[4] *physis, nomos, technē:* Greek, physical reality, custom, art.
[5] [Derrida/Bass] *The Elementary Structures of Kinship,* trans. James Bell, John von Sturmer, and Rodney Needham (Boston, Beacon Press, 1969), p. 8.

pieces. This is how the language of the social sciences criticizes *itself*. Lévi-Strauss thinks that in this way he can separate *method* from *truth,* the instruments of the method and the objective significations envisaged by it. One could almost say that this is the primary affirmation of Lévi-Strauss; in any event, the first words of the *Elementary Structures* are: "Above all, it is beginning to emerge that this distinction between nature and society ('nature' and 'culture' seem preferable to us today), while of no acceptable historical significance, does contain a logic, fully justifying its use by modern sociology as a methodological tool."[6]

Lévi-Strauss will always remain faithful to this double intention: to preserve as an instrument something whose truth value he criticizes.

On the one hand, he will continue, in effect, to contest the value of the nature/culture opposition. More than thirteen years after the *Elementary Structures, The Savage Mind* faithfully echoes the text I have just quoted: "The opposition between nature and culture to which I attached much importance at one time . . . now seems to be of primarily methodological importance." And this methodological value is not affected by its "ontological" nonvalue (as might be said, if this notion were not suspect here): "However, it would not be enough to reabsorb particular humanities into a general one. This first enterprise opens the way for others which . . . are incumbent on the exact natural sciences: the reintegration of culture in nature and finally of life within the whole of its physico-chemical conditions."[7]

On the other hand, still in *The Savage Mind,* he presents as what he calls *bricolage* what might be called the discourse of this method. The *bricoleur,* says Lévi-Strauss, is someone who uses "the means at hand," that is, the instruments he finds at his disposition around him, those which are already there, which had not been especially conceived with an eye to the operation for which they are to be used and to which one tries by trial and error to adapt them, not hesitating to change them whenever it appears necessary, or to try several of them at once, even if their form and their origin are heterogenous—and so forth. There is therefore a critique of language in the form of *bricolage,* and it has even been said that *bricolage* is critical language itself. I am thinking in particular of the article of G. Genette, "Structuralisme et critique littéraire," published in homage to Lévi-Strauss in a special issue of *L'Arc* (no. 26, 1965), where it is stated that the analysis of *bricolage* could "be applied almost word for word" to criticism, and especially to "literary criticism."

If one calls *bricolage* the necessity of borrowing one's concepts from the text of a heritage which is more or less coherent or ruined, it must be said that every discourse is *bricoleur.* The engineer, whom Lévi-Strauss opposes to the *bricoleur,* should be the one to construct the totality of his language, syntax, and lexicon. In this sense the engineer is a myth. A subject who supposedly would be the absolute origin of his own discourse and supposedly would construct it "out of nothing," "out of whole cloth," would be the creator of the verb, the verb itself. The notion of the engineer who supposedly breaks with all forms of *bricolage* is therefore a theological idea; and since Lévi-Strauss tells us elsewhere that *bricolage* is mythopoetic, the odds are that the engineer is a myth produced by the *bricoleur.* As soon as we cease to believe in such an engineer and in a discourse which breaks with the received historical discourse, and as soon as we admit that every finite discourse is bound by a certain *bricolage* and that the engineer and the scientist are also species of *bricoleurs,* then the very idea of *bricolage* is menaced and the difference in which it took on its meaning breaks down.

This brings us to the second thread which might guide us in what is being contrived here.

Lévi-Strauss describes *bricolage* not only as an intellectual activity but also as a mythopoetical activity. One reads in *The Savage Mind,* "Like *bricolage* on the technical plane, mythical reflection can reach brilliant unforeseen results on the intellectual plane. Conversely, attention has often been drawn to the mythopoetical nature of *bricolage.*"[8]

But Lévi-Strauss's remarkable endeavor does not simply consist in proposing, notably in his most recent investigations, a structural science of myths and of mythological activity. His endeavor also appears—I would say almost from the outset—to have the status which he accords to his own discourse on myths, to what he calls his "mythologicals." It is here that his discourse on the myth reflects on itself and criticizes itself. And this moment, this critical period, is evidently of concern to all the languages which share the field of the human sciences. What does Lévi-Strauss say of his "mythologicals"? It is here that we rediscover the mythopoetical virtue of *bricolage.* In effect, what appears most fascinating in this critical search for a new status of discourse is the stated abandonment of all reference to a *center,* to a *subject,* to a privileged *reference,* to an origin, or to an absolute *archia.* The theme of this decentering could be followed throughout the "Overture" to his last

---

[6] [Derrida/Bass] Ibid., p. 3.
[7] [Derrida] *The Savage Mind* (London: George Weidenfeld and Nicolson; Chicago: The University of Chicago Press, 1966), p. 247.

[8] [Derrida] Ibid., p. 17.

book, *The Raw and the Cooked.* I shall simply remark on a few key points.

1. From the very start, Lévi-Strauss recognizes that the Bororo myth which he employs in the book as the "reference myth" does not merit this name and this treatment. The name is specious and the use of the myth improper. This myth deserves no more than any other its referential privilege: "In fact, the Bororo myth, which I shall refer to from now on as the key myth, is, as I shall try to show, simply a transformation, to a greater or lesser extent, of other myths originating either in the same society or in neighboring or remote societies. I could, therefore, have legitimately taken as my starting point any one representative myth of the group. From this point of view, the key myth is interesting not because it is typical, but rather because of its irregular position within the group."[9]

2. There is no unity or absolute source of the myth. The focus and the source of the myth are always shadows and virtualities which are elusive, unactualizable, and nonexistent in the first place. Everything begins with structure, configuration, or relationship. The discourse on the acentric structure that myth itself is, cannot itself have an absolute subject or an absolute center. It must avoid the violence that consists in centering a language which describes an acentric structure if it is not to shortchange the form and movement of myth. Therefore it is necessary to forgo scientific or philosophical discourse, to renounce the *epistēmē* which absolutely requires, which is the absolute requirement that we go back to the source, to the center, to the founding basis, to the principle, and so on. In opposition to *epistemic* discourse, structural discourse on myths—*mythological* discourse—must itself be *mythomorphic.* It must have the form of that of which it speaks. This is what Lévi-Strauss says in *The Raw and the Cooked,* from which I would now like to quote a long and remarkable passage:

> The study of myths raises a methodological problem, in that it cannot be carried out according to the Cartesian principle of breaking down the difficulty into as many parts as may be necessary for finding the solution. There is no real end to methodological analysis, no hidden unity to be grasped once the breaking-down process has been completed. Themes can be split up *ad infinitum.* Just when you think you have disentangled and separated them, you realize that they are knitting together again in response to the operation of un-

expected affinities. Consequently the unity of the myth is never more than tendential and projective and cannot reflect a state or a particular moment of the myth. It is a phenomenon of the imagination, resulting from the attempt at interpretation; and its function is to endow the myth with synthetic form and to prevent its disintegration into a confusion of opposites. The science of myths might therefore be termed "anaclastic," if we take this old term in the broader etymological sense which includes the study of both reflected rays and broken rays. But unlike philosophical reflection, which aims to go back to its own source, the reflections we are dealing with here concern rays whose only source is hypothetical. . . . And in seeking to imitate the spontaneous movement of mythological thought, this essay, which is also both too brief and too long, has had to conform to the requirements of that thought and to respect its rhythm. It follows that this book on myths is itself a kind of myth.[10]

This statement is repeated a little farther on: "As the myths themselves are based on secondary codes (the primary codes being those that provide the substance of language), the present work is put forward as a tentative draft of a tertiary code, which is intended to ensure the reciprocal translatability of several myths. This is why it would not be wrong to consider this book itself as a myth: it is, as it were, the myth of mythology."[11] The absence of a center is here the absence of a subject and the absence of an author. "Thus the myth and the musical work are like conductors of an orchestra, whose audience becomes the silent performers. If it is now asked where the real center of work is to be found, the answer is that this is impossible to determine. Music and mythology bring man face to face with potential objects of which only the shadows are actualized. . . . Myths are anonymous."[12] The musical model chosen by Lévi-Strauss for the composition of his book is apparently justified by this absence of any real and fixed center of the mythical or mythological discourse.

Thus it is at this point that ethnographic *bricolage* deliberately assumes its mythopoetic function. But by the same token, this function makes the philosophical or epistemological requirement of a center appear as mythological, that is to say, as a historical illusion.

[9][Derrida] *The Raw and the Cooked,* p. 2.

[10][Derrida] Ibid., pp. 5–6.
[11][Derrida] Ibid., p. 12.
[12][Derrida] Ibid., pp. 17–18.

Nevertheless, even if one yields to the necessity of what Lévi-Strauss has done, one cannot ignore its risks. If the mythological is mythomorphic, are all discourses on myths equivalent? Shall we have to abandon any epistemological requirement which permits us to distinguish between several qualities of discourse on the myth? A classic, but inevitable question. It cannot be answered—and I believe that Lévi-Strauss does not answer it—for as long as the problem of the relations between the philosopheme or the theorem, on the one hand, and the mytheme or the mythopoem, on the other, has not been posed explicitly, which is no small problem. For lack of explicitly posing this problem, we condemn ourselves to transforming the alleged transgression of philosophy into an unnoticed fault within the philosophical realm. Empiricism would be the genus of which these faults would always be the species. Transphilosophical concepts would be transformed into philosophical naïvetés. Many examples could be given to demonstrate this risk: the concepts of sign, history, truth, and so forth. What I want to emphasize is simply that the passage beyond philosophy does not consist in turning the page of philosophy (which usually amounts to philosophizing badly), but in continuing to read philosophers *in a certain way.* The risk I am speaking of is always assumed by Lévi-Strauss, and it is the very price of this endeavor. I have said that empiricism is the matrix of all faults menacing a discourse which continues, as with Lévi-Strauss in particular, to consider itself scientific. If we wanted to pose the problem of empiricism and *bricolage* in depth, we would probably end up very quickly with a number of absolutely contradictory propositions concerning the status of discourse in structural ethnology. On the one hand, structuralism justifiably claims to be the critique of empiricism. But at the same time there is not a single book or study by Lévi-Strauss which is not proposed as an empirical essay which can always be completed or invalidated by new information. The structural schemata are always proposed as hypotheses resulting from a finite quantity of information and which are subjected to the proof of experience. Numerous texts could be used to demonstrate this double postulation. Let us turn once again to the "Overture" of *The Raw and the Cooked,* where it seems clear that if this postulation is double, it is because it is a question here of a language on language:

> If critics reproach me with not having carried out an exhaustive inventory of South American myths before analyzing them, they are making a grave mistake about the nature and function of these documents. The total body of myth belonging to a given community is comparable to its speech. Unless the population dies out physically or morally, this totality is never complete. You might as well criticize a linguist for compiling the grammar of a language without having complete records of the words pronounced since the language came into being, and without knowing what will be said in it during the future part of its existence. Experience proves that a linguist can work out the grammar of a given language from a remarkably small number of sentences. . . . And even a partial grammar or an outline grammar is a precious acquisition when we are dealing with unknown languages. Syntax does not become evident only after a (theoretically limitless) series of events has been recorded and examined, because it is itself the body of rules governing their production. What I have tried to give is an outline of the syntax of South American mythology. Should fresh data come to hand, they will be used to check or modify the formulation of certain grammatical laws, so that some are abandoned and replaced by new ones. But in no instance would I feel constrained to accept the arbitrary demand for a total mythological pattern, since, as has been shown, such a requirement has no meaning.[13]

Totalization, therefore, is sometimes defined as *useless,* and sometimes as *impossible.* This is no doubt due to the fact that there are two ways of conceiving the limit of totalization. And I assert once more that these two determinations coexist implicitly in Lévi-Strauss's discourse. Totalization can be judged impossible in the classical style: one then refers to the empirical endeavor of either a subject or a finite richness which it can never master. There is too much, more than one can say. But nontotalization can also be determined in another way: no longer from the standpoint of a concept of finitude as relegation to the empirical, but from the standpoint of the concept of *play.* If totalization no longer has any meaning, it is not because the infiniteness of a field cannot be covered by a finite glance or a finite discourse, but because the nature of the field—that is, language and a finite language—excludes totalization. This field is in effect that of *play,* that is to say, a field of infinite substitutions only because it is finite, that is to say, because instead of being an inexhaustible field, as in the classical hypothesis, instead of being too large, there is something missing from it: a center which arrests and grounds the play of substitutions. One could say—rigorously using that word whose scandalous signifi-

13 [Derrida] Ibid., pp. 7–8.

cation is always obliterated in French—that this movement of play, permitted by the lack or absence of a center or origin, is the movement of *supplementarity*. One cannot determine the center and exhaust totalization because the sign which replaces the center, which supplements it, taking the center's place in its absence—this sign is added, occurs as a surplus, as a *supplement*.[14] The movement of signification adds something, which results in the fact that there is always more, but this addition is a floating one because it comes to perform a vicarious function, to supplement a lack on the part of the signified. Although Lévi-Strauss in his use of the word "supplementary" never emphasizes, as I do here, the two directions of meaning which are so strangely compounded within it, it is not by chance that he uses this word twice in his "Introduction to the Work of Marcel Mauss," at one point where he is speaking of the "overabundance of signifier, in relation to the signifieds to which this overabundance can refer":

> In his endeavor to understand the world, man therefore always has at his disposal a surplus of signification (which he shares out amongst things according to the laws of symbolic thought—which is the task of ethnologists and linguists to study). This distribution of a *supplementary* allowance [*ration supplémentaire*]—if it is permissible to put it that way—is absolutely necessary in order that on the whole the available signifier and the signified it aims at may remain in the relationship of complementarity which is the very condition of the use of symbolic thought."[15]

(It could no doubt be demonstrated that this *ration supplémentaire* of signification is the origin of the *ratio* itself.) The word reappears a little further on, after Lévi-Strauss has mentioned "this floating signifier, which is the servitude of all finite thought":

> In other words—and taking as our guide Mauss's precept that all social phenomena can be assimi-

lated to language—we see in *mana, Wakau, oranda* and other notions of the same type, the conscious expression of a semantic function, whose role it is to permit symbolic thought to operate in spite of the contradiction which is proper to it. In this way are explained the apparently insoluble antinomies attached to this notion. . . . At one and the same time force and action, quality and state, noun and verb; abstract and concrete, omnipresent and localized—*mana* is in effect all these things. But is it not precisely because it is none of these things that *mana* is a simple form, or more exactly, a symbol in the pure state, and therefore capable of becoming charged with any sort of symbolic content whatever? In the system of symbols constituted by all cosmologies, *mana* would simply be a zero symbolic value, that is to say, a sign marking the necessity of a symbolic content *supplementary* [my italics] to that with which the signified is already loaded, but which can take on any value required, provided only that this value still remains part of the available reserve and is not, as phonologists put it, a "group-term."

Lévi-Strauss adds the note:
"Linguists have already been led to formulate hypotheses of this type. For example: 'A zero phoneme is opposed to all the other phonemes in French in that it entails no differential characters and no constant phonetic value. On the contrary, the proper function of the zero phoneme is to be opposed to phoneme absence.' (R. Jakobson and J. Lutz, "Notes on the French Phonemic Pattern," *Word* 5, no. 2 [August 1949]: 155). Similarly, if we schematize the conception I am proposing here, it could almost be said that the function of notions like *mana* is to be opposed to the absence of signification, without entailing by itself any particular signification."[16]

The *overabundance* of the signifier, its *supplementary* character, is thus the result of a finitude, that is to say, the result of a lack which must be *supplemented*.

It can now be understood why the concept of play is important in Lévi-Strauss. His references to all sorts of games, notably to roulette, are very frequent, especially in his *Conversations*,[17] in *Race and History*,[18] and in *The*

---

[14] [Bass] This double sense of supplement—to supply something which is missing, or to supply something additional—is at the center of Derrida's deconstruction of traditional linguistics in *De la grammatologie*. In a chapter entitled, "The Violence of the Letter: From Lévi-Strauss to Rousseau" (pp. 149 ff.), Derrida expands the analysis of Lévi-Strauss begun in this essay in order to further clarify the ways in which the contradictions of traditional logic "program" the most modern conceptual apparatuses of linguistics and the social sciences.

[15] [Derrida] "Introduction à l'oeuvre de Marcel Mauss," in Marcel Mauss, *Sociologie et anthropologie* (Paris: P.U.F., 1950), p. xlix.

[16] [Derrida] Ibid., pp. xlix–1.

[17] [Derrida] George Charbonnier, *Entretiens avec Claude Lévi-Strauss* (Paris: Plon, 1961).

[18] [Derrida] *Race and History* (Paris: UNESCO Publications, 1958).

Savage Mind. Further, the reference to play is always caught up in tension.

Tension with history, first of all. This is a classical problem, objections to which are now well worn. I shall simply indicate what seems to me the formality of the problem: by reducing history, Lévi-Strauss has treated as it deserves a concept which has always been in complicity with a teleological and eschatological metaphysics, in other words, paradoxically, in complicity with that philosophy of presence to which it was believed history could be opposed. The thematic of historicity, although it seems to be a somewhat late arrival in philosophy, has always been required by the determination of Being as presence. With or without etymology, and despite the classic antagonism which opposes these significations throughout all of classical thought, it could be shown that the concept of *epistēmē* has always called forth that of *historia,* if history is always the unity of becoming, as the tradition of truth or the development of science or knowledge oriented toward the appropriation of truth in presence and self-presence, toward knowledge in consciousness-of-self. History has always been conceived as the movement of a resumption of history, as a detour between two presences. But if it is legitimate to suspect this concept of history, there is a risk, if it is reduced without an explicit statement of the problem I am indicating here, of falling back into an ahistoricism of a classical type, that is to say, into a determined moment of the history of metaphysics. Such is the algebraic formality of the problem as I see it. More concretely, in the work of Lévi-Strauss it must be recognized that the respect for structurality, for the internal originality of the structure, compels a neutralization of time and history. For example, the appearance of a new structure, of an original system, always comes about—and this is the very condition of its structural specificity—by a rupture with its past, its origin, and its cause. Therefore one can describe what is peculiar to the structural organization only by not taking into account, in the very moment of this description, its past conditions; by omitting to posit the problem of the transition from one structure to another, by putting history between brackets. In this "structuralist" moment, the concepts of chance and discontinuity are indispensable. And Lévi-Strauss does in fact often appeal to them, for example, as concerns that structure of structures, language, of which he says in the "Introduction to the Work of Marcel Mauss" that it "could only have been born in one fell swoop":

Whatever may have been the moment and the circumstances of its appearance on the scale of ani-

mal life, language could only have been born in one fell swoop. Things could not have set about acquiring signification progressively. Following a transformation the study of which is not the concern of the social sciences, but rather of biology and psychology, a transition came about from a stage where nothing had a meaning to another where everything possessed it.[19]

This standpoint does not prevent Lévi-Strauss from recognizing the slowness, the process of maturing, the continuous toil of factual transformations, history (for example, *Race and History*). But, in accordance with a gesture which was also Rousseau's and Husserl's, he must "set aside all the facts" at the moment when he wishes to recapture the specificity of a structure. Like Rousseau, he must always conceive of the origin of a new structure on the model of catastrophe—an overturning of nature in nature, a natural interruption of the natural sequence, a setting aside *of* nature.

Besides the tension between play and history, there is also the tension between play and presence. Play is the disruption of presence. The presence of an element is always a signifying and substitutive reference inscribed in a system of differences and the movement of a chain. Play is always play of absence and presence, but if it is to be thought radically, play must be conceived of before the alternative of presence and absence. Being must be conceived as presence or absence on the basis of the possibility of play and not the other way around. If Lévi-Strauss, better than any other, has brought to light the play of repetition and the repetition of play, one no less perceives in his work a sort of ethic of presence, an ethic of nostalgia for origins, an ethic of archaic and natural innocence, of a purity of presence and self-presence in speech—an ethic, nostalgia, and even remorse, which he often presents as the motivation of the ethnological project when he moves toward the archaic societies which are exemplary societies in his eyes. These texts are well known.[20]

Turned towards the lost or impossible presence of the absent origin, this structuralist thematic of broken immediacy is therefore the saddened, *negative,* nostalgic, guilty, Rousseauistic side of the thinking of play whose other side would be the Nietzschean *affirmation,* that is the joyous af-

[19][Derrida] "Introduction à l'oeuvre de Marcel Mauss," p. xlvi.
[20][Bass] The reference is to *Tristes tropique,* trans. John Russell (London: Hutchinson and Co., 1961).

firmation of the play of the world and of the innocence of becoming, the affirmation of a world of signs without fault, without truth, and without origin which is offered to an active interpretation. *This affirmation then determines the noncenter otherwise than as loss of the center.* And it plays without security. For there is a *sure* play: that which is limited to the *substitution* of *given* and *existing, present,* pieces. In absolute chance, affirmation also surrenders itself to *genetic* indetermination, to the *seminal* adventure of the trace.

There are thus two interpretations of interpretation, of structure, of sign, of play. The one seeks to decipher, dreams of deciphering a truth or an origin which escapes play and the order of the sign, and which lives the necessity of interpretation as an exile. The other, which is no longer turned toward the origin, affirms play and tries to pass beyond man and humanism, the name of man being the name of that being who, throughout the history of metaphysics or of ontotheology—in other words, throughout his entire history—has dreamed of full presence, the reassuring foundation, the origin and the end of play. The second interpretation of interpretation, to which Nietzsche pointed the way, does not seek in ethnography, as Lévi-Strauss does, the "inspiration of a new humanism" (again citing the "Introduction to the Work of Marcel Mauss").

There are more than enough indications today to suggest we might perceive that these two interpretations of interpretation—which are absolutely irreconcilable even if we live them simultaneously and reconcile them in an obscure economy—together share the field which we call, in such a problematic fashion, the social sciences.

For my part, although these two interpretations must acknowledge and accentuate their difference and define their irreducibility, I do not believe that today there is any question of *choosing*—in the first place because here we are in a region (let us say, provisionally, a region of historicity) where the category of choice seems particularly trivial; and in the second, because we must first try to conceive of the common ground, and the *différance* of this irreducible difference. Here there is a kind of question, let us still call it historical, whose *conception, formation, gestation,* and *labor* we are only catching a glimpse of today. I employ these words, I admit, with a glance toward the operations of childbearing—but also with a glance toward those who, in a society from which I do not exclude myself, turn their eyes away when faced by the as yet unnamable which is proclaiming itself and which can do so, as is necessary whenever a birth is in the offing, only under the species of the nonspecies, in the formless, mute, infant, and terrifying form of monstrosity.

Meaning and Representation

Let us recall the object and crux of this demonstration: the pure function of expression and meaning is not to communicate, inform, or manifest, that is, to indicate. "Solitary mental life" would prove that such an expression without indication is possible. In solitary discourse the subject learns nothing about himself, manifests nothing to himself. To support this demonstration, whose consequences for phenomenology will be limitless, Husserl invokes two kinds of argument.

1. In inward speech, I communicate nothing to myself, I indicate nothing to myself. I can at most imagine myself doing so; I can only represent myself as manifesting something to myself. This, however, is only *representation* and *imagination.*

2. In inward speech I communicate nothing to myself *because there is no need of it;* I can only pretend to do so. Such an operation, the self-communication of the self, could not take place because it would make no sense, and it would make no sense because there would be *no finality* to it. The existence of mental acts does not have to be indicated (let us recall that in general only an existence can be indicated) because it is immediately present to the subject in the present moment.

Let us first read the paragraph that ties these two arguments together:

> One of course *speaks,* in a certain sense, even in soliloquy, and it is certainly possible to think of oneself as speaking, and even as speaking to oneself, as, e.g., when someone says to himself: "You have gone wrong, you can't go on like that." But in the genuine sense of communication, there is no speech in such cases, nor does one tell oneself anything: one merely conceives of *(man stellt sich vor)* oneself as speaking and communicating. In a monologue words can perform no function of indicating the existence *(Dasein)* of mental acts, since such indication would there be quite purposeless *(ganz zwecklos wäre).* For the acts in question are themselves

"Meaning and Representation" is chapter four from *La Voix et le Phénomène* (1967). It is reprinted here from *Voice and Phenomenon and Other Essays on Husserl's Theory of Signs,* tr. David B. Allison (Evanston, Ill.: Northwestern University Press, 1973). All notes are by Derrida.

experienced by us at that very moment *(im selben Augenblick)* (First Investigation, § 8; ET, pp. 279–80).

These affirmations raise some very diverse questions, all concerned with the status of *representation* in language. Representation can be understood in the general sense of *Vorstellung,* but also in the sense of re-presentation, as repetition or reproduction of presentation, as the *Vergegenwärtigung* which modifies a *Präsentation* or *Gegenwärtigung.* And it can be understood as what takes the place of, what occupies the place of, another *Vorstellung (Repräsentation, Repräsentant, Stellvertreter).*[1]

Let us consider the first argument. In monologue, nothing is communicated; one represents oneself *(man stellt sich vor)* as a speaking and communicating subject. Husserl thus seems here to apply the fundamental distinction between reality and representation to language. Between effective communication (indication) and "represented" communication there would be a difference in essence, a simple exteriority. Moreover, in order to reach inward language (in the sense of communication) as pure representation *(Vorstellung),* a certain fiction, that is, a particular type of representation, would have to be employed: the imaginary representation, which Husserl will later define as neutralizing representation *(Vergegenwärtigung).*

Can this system of distinctions be applied to language? From the start we would have to suppose that representation (in every sense of the term) is neither essential to nor constitutive of communication, the "effective" practice of language, but is only an accident eventually occurring in the practice of discourse. But there is every reason to believe that representation and reality are not merely added together here and there in language, for the simple reason that it is impossible in principle to rigorously distinguish them. And it doesn't help to say that this happens *in* language; language in general—and language alone—*is* this.

Husserl himself gives us the motives for the opposing position. When in fact I *effectively* use words, and whether or not I do it for communicative ends (let us consider signs in general, prior to this distinction), I must from the outset operate (within) a structure of repetition whose basic element can only be representative. A sign is never an event, if by event we mean an irreplaceable and irreversible empirical particular. A sign which would take place but "once" would not be a sign; a purely idiomatic sign would not be a sign. A signifier (in general) must be formally recognizable in spite of, and through, the diversity of empirical characteristics which may modify it. It must remain the *same,* and be able to be repeated as such, despite and across the deformations which the empirical event necessarily makes it undergo. A phoneme or grapheme is necessarily always to some extent different each time that it is presented in an operation or a perception. But, it can function as a sign, and in general as language, only if a formal identity enables it to be issued again and to be recognized. This identity is necessarily ideal. It thus necessarily implies representation: as *Vorstellung,* the locus of ideality in general, as *Vergegenwärtigung,* the possibility of reproductive repetition in general, and as *Repräsentation,* insofar as each signifying event is a substitute (for the signified as well as for the ideal form of the signifier). Since this representative structure is signification itself, I cannot enter into an "effective" discourse without being from the start involved in unlimited representation.

One might object that it is precisely this exclusively representative character of expression that Husserl wants to bring out by his hypothesis of solitary discourse, which would retain the essence of speech while dropping its communicative and indicative shell. Moreover, one might object that we have precisely formulated our question with Husserlian concepts. We have indeed. But according to Husserl's description, it is only expression and not signification in general that belongs to the order of representation as *Vorstellung.* However, we have just suggested that the latter—and its other representative modifications—is implied by any sign whatsoever. On the other hand, and more importantly, as soon as we admit that speech belongs essentially to the order of representation, the distinction between "effective" speech and the representation of speech becomes suspect, whether the speech is purely "expressive" or engaged in "communication." By reason of the primordially repetitive structure of signs in general, there is every likelihood that "effective" language is just as imaginary as imaginary speech and that imaginary speech is just as effective as effective speech. In both expression and indicative communication the difference between reality and representation, between the veridical and the imaginary, and between simple presence and repetition has already begun to wear away. Does not the maintaining of this difference—in the history of metaphysics and for Husserl as well—answer to the obstinate desire to save presence and to reduce or derive the sign, and with it all powers of repetition? Which comes to living *in* the ef-

---

[1] Cf. on this subject the note by the French translators of the *Logical Investigations* (French ed., Vol. II, pt. I, p. 276) and that by the French translators of *The Phenomenology of Internal Time-Consciousness* (French ed., p. 26).

fect—the assured, consolidated, constituted effect of repetition and representation, of the difference which removes presence. To assert, as we have been doing, that within the sign *the difference does not take place* between reality and representation, etc., amounts to saying that the gesture that confirms this difference is the very obliteration of the sign. But there are two ways of eliminating the primordiality of the sign; we must be attentive to the instability of all these moves, for they pass quickly and surreptitiously into one another. Signs can be eliminated in the classical manner in a philosophy of intuition and presence. Such a philosophy eliminates signs by making them derivative; it annuls reproduction and representation by making signs a modification of a simple presence. But because it is just such a philosophy—which is, in fact, *the* philosophy and history of the West—which has so constituted and established the very concept of signs, the sign is from its origin and to the core of its sense marked by this will to derivation or effacement. Thus, to restore the original and nonderivative character of signs, in opposition to classical metaphysics, is, by an apparent paradox, at the same time to eliminate a concept of signs whose whole history and meaning belong to the adventure of the metaphysics of presence. This also holds for the concepts of representation, repetition, difference, etc., as well as for the system they form. For the present and for some time to come, the movement of that schema will only be capable of working over the language of metaphysics from within, from a certain sphere of problems inside that language. No doubt this work has always already begun. We shall have to grasp what happens inside language when the closure of metaphysics is announced.

With the difference between real presence and presence in representation as *Vorstellung,* a whole system of differences involved in language is implied in the same deconstruction: the differences between the represented and the representative in general, the signified and signifier, simple presence and its reproduction, presentation as *Vorstellung* and re-presentation as *Vergegenwärtigung,* for what is represented in the re-presentation is a presentation *(Präsentation)* as *Vorstellung.* We thus come—against Husserl's express intention—to make the *Vorstellung* itself, and as such, depend on the possibility of re-presentation *(Vergegenwärtigung).* The presence-of-the-present is derived from repetition and not the reverse. While this is against Husserl's express intention, it does take into account what is implied by his description of the movement of temporalization and of the relation with the other, as will perhaps become clear later on.

The concept of *ideality* naturally has to be at the center of such a question. According to Husserl, the structure

of speech can only be described in terms of ideality. There is the ideality of the sensible form of the signifier (for example, the word), which must remain *the same* and can do so only as an ideality. There is, moreover, the ideality of the signified (of the *Bedeutung*) or intended sense, which is not to be confused with the act of intending or with the object, for the latter two need not necessarily be ideal. Finally, in certain cases there is the ideality of the object itself, which then assures the ideal transparency and perfect univocity of language; this is what happens in the exact sciences.[2] But this ideality, which is but another name for the permanence of the same and the possibility of its repetition, *does not exist* in the world, and it does not come from another world; it depends entirely on the possibility of acts of repetition. It is constituted by this possibility. Its "being" is proportionate to the power of repetition; absolute ideality is the correlate of a possibility of indefinite repetition. It could therefore be said that being is determined by Husserl as ideality, that is, as repetition. For Husserl, historical progress always has as its essential form the constitution of idealities whose repetition, and thus tradition, would be assured *ad infinitum,* where repetition and tradition are the transmission and reactivation of origins. And this determination of being as ideality is properly a *valuation,* an ethico-theoretical act that revives the decision that founded philosophy in its Platonic form. Husserl occasionally admits this; what he always opposed was a conventional Platonism. When he affirms the nonexistence or nonreality of ideality, it is always to acknowledge that ideality *is* a way of being that is irreducible to sensible existence or empirical reality and their fictional counterparts.[3] In determining the *ontōs on* as *eidos,* Plato himself was affirming the same thing.

Now (and here again the commentary must take its bearing from the interpretation) this determination of being as ideality is paradoxically one with the determination of being as presence. This occurs not only because pure ideality is always that of an ideal "ob-ject" which stands in

---

[2]Cf. on this subject *The Origin of Geometry* and the Introduction to the French translation, pp. 60–69.

[3]The assertion implied by the whole of phenomenology is that the Being *(Sein)* of the *Ideal* is nonreality, nonexistence. This predetermination is the first word of phenomenology. Although it does not exist, ideality is anything but a nonbeing. "Each attempt to transform the being of what is ideal *(das Sein des Idealen)* into the possible being of what is real, must obviously suffer shipwreck on the fact that possibilities themselves are ideal objects. Possibilities can as little be found in the real world, as can numbers in general, or triangles in general" (*Logical Investigations,* Second Investigation, Chap. I, § 4; ET, p. 345). "It is naturally not our intention to put the *being of what is ideal* on a level with the *being-thought-of which characterizes the fictitious or the absurd Widersinnigen)*" (*ibid.,* § 8; ET, p. 352).

front of, which is pre-sent before the act of repetition (*Vorstellung* being the general form of presence as proximity to a viewing), but also because only a temporality determined on the basis of the living present as its source (the now as "source-point") can ensure the purity of ideality, that is, openness for the infinite repeatability of the same. For, in fact, what is signified by phenomenology's "principle of principles"? What does the value of primordial presence to intuition as source of sense and evidence, as the *a priori* of *a prioris,* signify? First of all it signifies the certainty, itself ideal and absolute, that the universal form of all experience *(Erlebnis),* and therefore of all life, has always been and will always be the *present.* The present alone is and ever will be. Being is presence or the modification of presence. The relation with the presence of the present as the ultimate form of being and of ideality is the move by which I transgress empirical existence, factuality, contingency, worldliness, etc.—first of all, *my own* empirical existence, factuality, contingency, worldliness, etc. To think of presence as the universal form of transcendental life is to open myself to the knowledge that in my absence, beyond my empirical existence, before my birth and after my death, *the present is.* I can empty all empirical content, imagine an absolute overthrow of the *content* of every possible experience, a radical transformation of the world. I have a strange and unique certitude that this universal form of presence, since it concerns no determined being, will not be affected by it. The relationship with *my death* (my disappearance in general) thus lurks in this determination of being as presence, ideality, the absolute possibility of repetition. The possibility of the sign is this relationship with death. The determination and elimination of the sign in metaphysics is the dissimulation of this relationship with death, which yet produced signification.

If the possibility of my disappearance in general must somehow be experienced in order for a relationship with presence in general to be instituted, we can no longer say that the experience of the possibility of my absolute disappearance (my death) affects me, occurs to an *I am,* and modifies a subject. The *I am,* being experienced only as an *I am present,* itself presupposes the relationship with presence in general, with being as presence. The appearing of the *I* to itself in the *I am* is thus originally a relation with its own possible disappearance. Therefore, *I am* originally means *I am mortal. I am immortal* is an impossible proposition.[4] We can even go further: as a linguistic statement "I am he who am"

is the admission of a mortal. The move which leads from the *I am* to the determination of my being as *res cogitans* (thus, as an immortality) is a move by which the origin of presence and ideality is concealed in the very presence and ideality it makes possible.

The effacement (or derivation) of signs is thereby confused with the reduction of the imagination. Husserl's position with respect to tradition is here ambiguous. No doubt he profoundly renewed the question of imagination, and the role he reserves for fiction in the phenomenological method clearly shows that for him imagination is not just one faculty among others. Yet without neglecting the novelty and rigor of the phenomenological description of images, we should certainly be cognizant of their origin. Husserl continually emphasizes that, unlike a memory, an image is not "propositional"; it is a "neutralizing" re-presentation. While this gives it a privilege in "phenomenological" practice, both an image and a memory are classified under the general concept "re-presentation" *(Vergegenwärtigung),* that is, the reproduction of a presence, even if the product is a purely fictitious object. It follows that imagination is not a simple "modification of neutrality," even if it is neutralizing ("We must protect ourselves here against a very closely besetting confusion, namely, that between *neutrality-modification* and *imagination*" [*Ideas I,* Section III, § III; ET, p. 309, modified]). Its neutralizing operation modifies a positional re-presentation *(Vergegenwärtigung),* which is memory. "More closely stated, *imagination* in general is the *neutrality-modification applied to 'positional' presentification (Vergegenwärtigung),* and therefore of remembering in the widest conceivable sense of the term" *(ibid.).* Consequently, even if it is a good auxiliary instrument of phenomenological neutralization, the image is not a pure neutralization. It retains a primary reference to a primordial presentation, that is, to a perception and positing of existence, to a belief in general.

This is why pure ideality, reached through neutralization, is not fictitious. This theme appears very early,[5] and it will continually serve to feed the polemic against Hume.

---

[4]Employing distinctions from "pure logical grammar" and the *Formal and Transcendental Logic,* this impossibility must be expressed as follows: this proposition certainly makes sense, it constitutes intelligible speech, it is not *sinnlos;* but within this intelligibility and for the reason indicated, it is "absurd" (with the absurdity of contradiction—*Widersinnigkeit*) and *a fortiori* "false." But as the classical idea of truth, which guides these distinctions, has itself issued from such a concealment of the relationship with death, this "falsity" is the very truth of truth. Hence, it is in other completely different "categories" (if such thoughts can still be labeled thus) that these movements have to be interpreted.

[5]Cf., particularly, *Logical Investigations,* Second Investigation, Chap. II.

But it is no accident that Hume's thought fascinated Husserl more and more. The power of pure repetition that opens up ideality and the power which liberates the imaginative reproduction of empirical perception cannot be foreign to each other; nor can their products.

In this respect, the First Investigation also remains most disconcerting in more than one way:

1. Expressive phenomena in their expressive purity are, from the start, taken to be imaginative representations (*Phantasievorstellungen*).

2. In the inner sphere thus disengaged by this fiction, the communicative discourse that a subject may occasionally address to himself ("You have gone wrong") is called "fictitious." This leads one to think that a purely expressive and noncommunicative discourse can *effectively* take place in "solitary mental life."

3. By the same token, it is supposed that in communication, where the same words, the same expressive cores are at work, where, consequently, pure idealities are indispensable, a rigorous distinction can be drawn between the fictitious and the effective and between the ideal and the real. It is consequently supposed that effectiveness comes like an empirical and exterior cloak to expression, like a body to a soul. And these are indeed the notions Husserl uses, even when he stresses the unity of the body and soul in intentional *animation*. This unity does not impair the essential distinction, for it always remains a unity of composition.

4. Inside the pure interior "representation," in "solitary mental life," certain kinds of speech could effectively take place, as *effectively* representative (this would be the case with expressive language and, we can already specify, language with a purely objective, theoretico-logical character), while certain others would remain purely *fictitious* (those fictions located in fiction would be the acts of indicative communication between the self and the self, between the self taken as other and the self taken as self, etc.).

However, if it is admitted that, as we have tried to show, every sign whatever is of an originally repetitive structure, the general distinction between the fictitious and effective usages of the sign is threatened. *The sign is originally wrought by fiction.* From this point on, whether with respect to indicative communication or expression, there is no sure criterion by which to distinguish an outward language from an inward language or, in the hypothesis of an inward language, an effective language from a fictitious language. Such a distinction, however, is indispensable to Husserl for proving that indication is exterior to expression, with all that this entails. In declaring this distinction illegiti-

mate, we anticipate a whole chain of formidable consequences for phenomenology.

What we have just said concerning the sign holds, by the same token, for the act of the speaking subject. "But," as Husserl says, "in the genuine sense of communication, there is no speech in such cases, nor does one tell oneself anything: one merely conceives of oneself *(man stellt sich vor)* as speaking and communicating" (*LI*, § 8; ET, p. 280). This leads to the second argument proposed.

Between effective communication and the representation of the self as speaking subject, Husserl must suppose a difference such that the representation of the self can only be added on to the act of communication contingently and from the outside. But the primordial structure of repetition that we just evoked for signs must govern all acts of signification. The subject cannot speak without giving himself a representation of his speaking, and this is no accident. We can no more imagine effective speech without there being self-representation than we can imagine a representation of speech without there being effective speech. This representation may no doubt be modified, complicated, and be reflected in the primary modes that are studied by the linguist, the semiologist, the psychologist, the theoretician of literature or of art, or even the philosopher. They may be quite primary, but they all suppose the primordial unity of speech and the representation of speech. Speech represents itself; it *is* its representation. Even better, speech is *the* representation of itself.[6]

More generally, Husserl seems to allow that the subject as he is in his effective experience and the subject as he represents himself to be can be simply external to each other. The subject may think that he is talking to himself and communicating something; in truth he is doing nothing of the kind. Where consciousness is thus entirely overcome by the belief or illusion of speaking to itself, an entirely false consciousness, one might be tempted to conclude that the truth of experience would belong to the order of the nonconscious. Quite the contrary: consciousness is the self-presence of the living, the *Erleben,* of experience. Experience thus understood is simple and is in

_____

[6]But if the *re-* of this re-presentation does not signify the simple—repetitive or reflexive—reduplication that *befalls* a simple presence (which is what the word *representation* has always *meant*), then what we are approaching or advancing here concerning the relation between presence and representation must be approached in other terms. What we are describing as primordial representation can be provisionally designated with this term only within the closure whose limits we are here seeking to transgress by setting down and demonstrating various contradictory or untenable propositions within it, attempting thereby to institute a kind of insecurity and to open it up to the outside. This can only be done from a certain inside.

its essence free of illusion, since it relates only to itself in an absolute proximity. The illusion of speaking to oneself would float on the surface of experience as an empty, peripheral, and secondary consciousness. Language and its representation is added on to a consciousness that is simple and simply present to itself, or in any event to an experience which could reflect its own presence in silence.

As Husserl will say in *Ideas I,* § III,

> every experience generally (every really living one, so to speak) is an experience according to the mode of "being present." It belongs to its very essence that it should be able to reflect upon that same essence in which it is necessarily characterized as *being* certain and present (ET, p. 310, modified).

Signs would be foreign to this self-presence, which is the ground of presence in general. It is because signs are foreign to the self-presence of the living present that they may be called foreign to presence in general in (what is currently styled) intuition or perception.

If the representation of indicative speech in the monologue is false, it is because it is useless; this is the ultimate basis of the argumentation in this section (§ 8) of the First Investigation. If the subject indicates nothing to himself, it is because he cannot do so, and he cannot do so because there is no need of it. Since lived experience is immediately self-present in the mode of certitude and absolute necessity, the manifestation of the self to the self through the delegation or representation of an indicative sign is impossible because it is superfluous. It would be, in every sense of the term, *without reason*—thus without cause. Without cause because without purpose: *zwecklos,* Husserl says.

This *Zwecklosigkeit* of inward communication is the nonalterity, the nondifference in the identity of presence as self-presence. Of course this concept of *presence* not only involves the enigma of a being appearing in absolute proximity to oneself; it also designates the temporal essence of this proximity—which does not serve to dispel the enigma. The self-presence of experience must be produced in the present taken as a now. And this is just what Husserl says: if "mental acts" are not announced to themselves through the intermediary of a *"Kundgabe,"* if they do not have to be informed about themselves through the intermediary of indications, it is because they are "lived by us in the same instant" *(im selben Augenblick).* The present of self-presence would be as indivisible as the *blink of an eye.*

from
Of Grammatology

Linguistics and Grammatology

The Outside and the Inside[1]

On the one hand, true to the Western tradition that controls not only in theory but in practice *(in the principle of its practice)* the relationships between speech and writing, Saussure does not recognize in the latter more than a *narrow* and *derivative* function. Narrow because it is nothing but one modality among others, a modality of the events which can befall a language whose essence, as the facts seem to show, can remain forever uncontaminated by writing. "Language does have an . . . oral tradition that is independent of writing" *(Cours de linguistique générale,* p. 46). Derivative because *representative:* signifier of the first signifier, representation of the self-present voice, of the immediate, natural, and direct signification of the meaning (of the signified, of the concept, of the ideal object or what have you). Saussure takes up the traditional definition of writing which, already in Plato and Aristotle, was restricted to the model of phonetic script and the language of

---

Of Grammatication (De la grammatologie) was first published in 1967 and translated by Gayatri C. Spivak in 1976. The selection below is from part I, chapter 2, reprinted in part from *Of Grammatology* (Baltimore: The Johns Hopkins University Press, 1977).

[1]The introductory portion of this chapter sketches Derrida's notion of grammatology as "a science of writing," on the principle that "The concept of writing should define the field of a science" (p. 27). Derrida distinguishes between linguistics and grammatology by asserting that the "scientific" status for linguistics is grounded on phonology, leading to a conception of the primary task to be demonstrating the "unity" of sound and meaning. Under this view, which we specifically note is *not* a proposition that would have been viewed so complacently after Chomsky's *Syntactic Structures* (1957) and would very likely have been rejected outright after his *Aspects of the Theory of Syntax,* it is Derrida's view that the problem of writing would remain "outside" the field of linguistics, as "the sign of a sign" while the essential task has been taken to be demonstrating the "unity" of sound and meaning, which therefore appears to place writing "outside" the field of linguistics proper, as "the sign of a sign." It is, we think, of more than slight importance to note that this disparity of conception is *not* fundamental, no doubt implicated in some controversies in the reception of Derrida's work, despite the fact that Derrida's point *could* be recast relative to the distinction between "deep" and "surface" structure, or in the difficulty of determining the precise nature of the semantic relation between the base component and explicit expressions.

[Spivak]The title of the next section is "The Outside I̶s̶ the Inside." In French, "is" *(est)* and "and" *(et)* "sound the same." For Derrida's discussion of the complicity between supplementation (and) and the copula (is), see, particularly, "Le supplément de copule: la philosophie devant la linguistique," in *Margins of Philosophy.*

words. Let us recall the Aristotelian definition: "Spoken words are the symbols of mental experience and written words are the symbols of spoken words." Saussure: "Language and writing are two distinct systems of signs; the second *exists for the sole purpose of representing* the first" (p. 45; italics added) [p. 23].[2] This representative determination, beside communicating without a doubt essentially with the idea of the sign, does not translate a choice or an evaluation, does not betray a psychological or metaphysical presupposition peculiar to Saussure; it describes or rather reflects the structure of a certain type of writing: phonetic writing, which we use and within whose element the *epistémè* in general (science and philosophy), and linguistics in particular, could be founded. One should, moreover, say *model* rather than *structure;* it is not a question of a system constructed and functioning perfectly, but of an ideal explicitly directing a functioning which *in fact* is never completely phonetic. In fact, but also for reasons of essence to which I shall frequently return.

To be sure this factum of phonetic writing is massive; it commands our entire culture and our entire science, and it is certainly not just one fact among others. Nevertheless it does not respond to any necessity of an absolute and universal essence. Using this as a point of departure, Saussure defines the project and object of general linguistics: "The linguistic object is not defined by the combination of the written word and the spoken word: *the spoken form alone constitutes the object*" (p. 45; italics added) [pp. 23–24].

The form of the question to which he responded thus entailed the response. It was a matter of knowing what sort of *word* is the object of linguistics and what the relationships are between the atomic unities that are the written and the spoken word. Now the word *(vox)* is already a unity of sense and sound, of concept and voice, or, to speak a more rigorously Saussurian language, of the signified and the signifier. This last terminology was moreover first proposed in the domain of spoken language alone, of linguistics in the narrow sense and not in the domain of semiology ("I propose to retain the word *sign* [*signe*] to designate the whole and to replace *concept* and *sound-image* respectively by *signified* [*signifié*] and *signifier* [*signifiant*]" p. 99 [p. 67]). The *word* is thus already a constituted unity, an effect of "the somewhat mysterious fact . . . that 'thought-sound' implies divisions" (p. 156) [p. 112]. Even if the word is in its turn articulated, even if it implies other divisions, as long as one poses the question of the re-

lationships between speech and writing in the light of the indivisible units of the "thought-sound," there will always be the ready response. Writing will be "phonetic," it will be the outside, the exterior representation of language and of this "thought-sound." It must necessarily operate from already constituted units of signification, in the formation of which it has played no part.

Perhaps the objection will be made that writing up to the present has not only not contradicted, but indeed confirmed the linguistics of the word. Hitherto I seem to have maintained that only the fascination of the unit called *word* has prevented giving to writing the attention that it merited. By that I seemed to suppose that, by ceasing to accord an absolute privilege to the word, modern linguistics would become that much more attentive to writing and would finally cease to regard it with suspicion. André Martinet comes to the opposite conclusion. In his study "The Word,"[3] he describes the necessity that contemporary linguistics obeys when it is led, if not to dispense everywhere with the concept of the word, at least to make its usage more flexible, to associate it with the concepts of smaller or greater units (monemes or syntagms). In accrediting and consolidating the division of language into words in certain areas of linguistics, writing would thus have encouraged classical linguistics in its prejudices. Writing would have constructed or at least condensed the "screen of the word."

What a contemporary linguist can say of the word well illustrates the general revision of traditional concepts that the functionalist and structuralist research of the last thirty-five years had to undertake in order to give a scientific basis to the observation and description of languages. Certain applications of linguistics, like the researches relating to mechanical translation, by the emphasis

---

[2][Spivak] Hereafter, page numbers in parentheses refer to the original work and those in brackets to the English translation.

[3][Derrida / Spivak] *Diogène* 51, 1965, [p. 54]. [Parallel English, French, and Spanish editions of this journal are published simultaneously. My references are to the English *Diogenes.*] André Martinet alludes to the "courage" which would formerly have been "needed" to "foresee that the term 'word' itself might have to be put aside if . . . researches showed that this term could not be given a universally applicable definition" (p. 39) [p. 39]. "Semiology, as revealed by recent studies, has no need of the word" (p. 40) [p. 39]. . . . "Grammarians and linguists have long known that the analysis of utterances can be pursued beyond the word without going into phonetics, that is, ending with segments of speech, such as syllables or phonemes, which have nothing to do with meaning" (p. 41) [p. 40]. "We are touching here on what renders the notion of the word so suspect to all true linguists. They cannot accept traditional writing without verifying first whether it reproduces faithfully the true structure of the language which it is supposed to record" (p. 48) [p. 48]. In conclusion Martinet proposes the replacement "in linguistic practice" of the notion of word by that of "syntagm," any "group of several minimal signs" that will be called "monemes."

they place on the written form of language, could make us believe in the fundamental importance of the divisions of the written text and make us forget that one must always start with the oral utterance in order to understand the real nature of human language. Also it is more than ever indispensable to insist on the necessity of pushing the examination beyond the immediate appearances and the structures most familiar to the researcher. It is behind the screen of the word that the truly fundamental characteristics of human language often appear.

One cannot but subscribe to this caution. Yet it must always be recognized that it throws suspicion only on a certain type of writing: phonetic writing conforming to the empirically determined and practiced divisions of ordinary oral language. The processes of mechanical translation to which it alludes conform similarly to that spontaneous practice. Beyond that model and that concept of writing, this entire demonstration must, it seems, be reconsidered. For it remains trapped in the Saussurian limitation that we are attempting to explore.

In effect Saussure limits the number of systems of writing to two, both defined as systems of representation of the oral language, either representing *words* in a synthetic and global manner, or representing *phonetically* the elements of sounds constituting words:

> There are only two systems of writing: 1) In an ideographic system each word is represented by a single sign that is unrelated to the component sounds of the word itself. Each written sign stands for a whole word and, indirectly, for the idea expressed by the word. The classic example of an ideographic system of writing is Chinese. 2) The system commonly known as "phonetic" tries to reproduce the succession of sounds that make up a word. Phonetic systems are sometimes syllabic, sometimes alphabetic, i.e., based on the irreducible elements of speech. Moreover, ideographic systems freely become mixtures when certain ideograms lose their original value and become symbols of isolated sounds. (p. 47) [pp. 25–26].

This limitation is at bottom justified, in Saussure's eyes, by the notion of the arbitrariness of the sign. Writing being defined as "a system of signs," there is no "symbolic" writing (in the Saussurian sense), no figurative writing;

there is no *writing* as long as graphism keeps a relationship of natural figuration and of some resemblance to what is then not *signified* but represented, drawn, etc. The concept of pictographic or natural writing would therefore be contradictory for Saussure. If one considers the now recognized fragility of the notions of pictogram, ideogram, etc., and the uncertainty of the frontiers between so-called pictographic, ideographic, and phonetic scripts, one realizes not only the un-wiseness of the Saussurian limitation but the need for general linguistics to abandon an entire family of concepts inherited from metaphysics—often through the intermediary of a psychology—and clustering around the concept of arbitrariness. All this refers, beyond the nature/culture opposition, to a supervening opposition between *physis* and *nomos, physis* and *techné,* whose ultimate function is perhaps to *derive* historicity; and, paradoxically, not to recognize the rights of history, production, institutions etc., except in the form of the arbitrary and in the substance of naturalism. But let us keep that question provisionally open: perhaps this gesture, which in truth presides over metaphysics, is also inscribed in the concept of history and even in the concept of time.

In addition, Saussure introduces another massive limitation: "I shall limit discussion to the phonetic system and especially to the one used today, the system that stems from the Greek alphabet" (p. 48) [p. 26].

These two limitations are all the more reassuring because they are just what we need at a specific point to fulfill the most legitimate of exigencies; in fact, the condition for the scientificity of linguistics is that the field of linguistics have hard and fast frontiers, that it be a system regulated by an *internal* necessity, and that in a certain way its structure be closed. The representativist concept of writing facilitates things. If writing is nothing but the "figuration" (p. 44) [p. 23] of the language, one has the right to exclude it from the interiority of the system (for it must be believed that there is an *inside* of the language), as the image may be excluded without damage from the system of reality. Proposing as his theme "the representation of language by writing" Saussure thus begins by positing that writing is "unrelated to [the] . . . inner system" of language (p. 44) [p. 23]. External/internal, image/reality, representation/presence, such is the old grid to which is given the task of outlining the domain of a science. And of what science? Of a science that can no longer answer to the classical concept of the *epistémè* because the originality of its field—an originality that it inaugurates—is that the opening of the "image" within it appears as the condition of "reality"; a relationship that can no longer be thought within the simple difference and the uncompromising exteriority of "image" and "reality," of "outside" and "inside," of "appearance" and "essence," with the entire system of oppositions which necessarily follows from it. Plato, who said basically the same thing about the relationship between writing, speech, and being (or idea), had at least a more subtle, more critical, and less complacent theory of image, painting, and imitation than the one that presides over the birth of Saussurian linguistics.

It is not by chance that the exclusive consideration of phonetic writing permits a response to the exigencies of the "internal system." The basic functional principle of phonetic writing is precisely to respect and protect the integrity of the "internal system" of the language, even if in fact it does not succeed in doing so. *The Saussurian limitation does not respond, by a mere happy convenience, to the scientific exigency of the "internal system." That exigency is itself constituted, as the epistemological exigency in general, by the very possibility of phonetic writing and by the exteriority of the "notation" to internal logic.*

But let us not simplify: on that point Saussure too is not quite complacent. Why else would he give so much attention to that external phenomenon, that exiled figuration, that outside, that double? Why does he judge it impossible "to simply disregard" [literally "make abstraction of"] what is nevertheless designated as the abstract itself with respect to the inside of language? "Writing, though unrelated to its inner system, is used continually to represent language. We cannot simply disregard it. We must be acquainted with its usefulness, shortcomings, and dangers" (p. 44) [p. 23].

Writing would thus have the exteriority that one attributes to utensils; to what is even an imperfect tool and a dangerous, almost maleficent, technique. One understands better why, instead of treating this exterior figuration in an appendix or marginally, Saussure devotes so laborious a chapter to it almost at the beginning of the *Course*. It is less a question of outlining than of protecting, and even of restoring the internal system of the language in the purity of its concept against the gravest, most perfidious, most permanent contamination which has not ceased to menace, even to corrupt that system, in the course of what Saussure strongly wishes, in spite of all opposition, to consider as an external history, as a series of accidents affecting the language and befalling it *from without,* at the moment of "notation" (p. 45) [p. 24], as if writing began and ended with notation. Already in the *Phaedrus,* Plato says that the evil of writing comes from without (275a). The contamination by writing, the fact or the threat of it, are denounced in the accents of the moralist or preacher by the linguist from Geneva. The tone counts; it is as if, at the moment when the modern science of the logos would come into its

autonomy and its scientificity, it became necessary again to attack a heresy. This tone began to make itself heard when, at the moment of already tying the *epistémè* and the *logos* within the same possibility, the *Phaedrus* denounced writing as the intrusion of an artful technique, a forced entry of a totally original sort, an archetypal violence: eruption of the *outside* within the *inside,* breaching into the interiority of the soul, the living self-presence of the soul within the true logos, the help that speech lends to itself. Thus incensed, Saussure's vehement argumentation aims at more than a theoretical error, more than a moral fault: at a sort of stain and primarily at a sin. Sin has been defined often—among others by Malebranche[4] and by Kant—as the inversion of the natural relationship between the soul and the body through passion. Saussure here points at the inversion of the natural relationship between speech and writing. It is not a simple analogy: writing, the letter, the sensible inscription, has always been considered by Western tradition as the body and matter external to the spirit, to breath, to speech, and to the logos. And the problem of soul and body is no doubt derived from the problem of writing from which it seems—conversely—to borrow its metaphors.

Writing, sensible matter and artificial exteriority: a "clothing." It has sometimes been contested that speech clothed thought. Husserl, Saussure, Lavelle have all questioned it. But has it ever been doubted that writing was the clothing of speech? For Saussure it is even a garment of perversion and debauchery, a dress of corruption and disguise, a festival mask that must be exorcised, that is to say warded off, by the good word: "Writing veils the appearance of language; it is not a guise for language but a disguise" (p. 51) [p. 30]. Strange "image." One already suspects that if writing is "image" and exterior "figuration," this "representation" is not innocent. The outside bears with the inside a relationship that is, as usual, anything but simple exteriority. The meaning of the outside was always present within the inside, imprisoned outside the outside, and vice versa.

Thus a science of language must recover the *natural*— that is, the simple and original—relationships between speech and writing, that is, between an inside and an outside. It must restore its absolute youth, and the purity of its origin, short of a history and a fall which would have perverted the relationships between outside and inside. Therefore there would be a *natural order* of relationships between linguistic and graphic signs, and it is the theoretician of the

---

[4] Nicolas Malebranche (1638–1715), French philosopher.

arbitrariness of the sign who reminds us of it. According to the historico-metaphysical presuppositions evoked above, there would be first a *natural* bond of sense to the senses and it is this that passes from sense to sound: "the natural bond," Saussure says, "the only true bond, the bond of sound" (p. 46) [p. 25]. This natural bond of the signified (concept or sense) to the phonic signifier would condition the natural relationship subordinating writing (visible image) to speech. It is this natural relationship that would have been inverted by the original sin of writing: "The graphic form [*image*] manages to force itself upon them at the expense of sound . . . and the natural sequence is reversed" (p. 47) [p. 25]. Malebranche explained original sin as inattention, the temptation of ease and idleness, by that *nothing* that was Adam's "distraction," alone culpable before the innocence of the divine word: the latter exerted no force, no efficacy, since *nothing* had taken place. Here too, one gave in to *ease,* which is curiously, but as usual, on the side of technical artifice and not within the bent of the natural movement thus thwarted or deviated:

> First, the graphic form [*image*] of words strikes us as being something permanent and stable, better suited than sound to constitute the unity of language throughout time. Though it creates a purely *fictitious* unity, the *superficial* bond of writing is much *easier* to grasp than the natural bond, the only true bond, the bond of sound (p. 46; italics added) [p. 25].

That "the graphic form of words strikes us as being something permanent and stable, better suited than sound to constitute the unity of language throughout time," is that not a natural phenomenon too? In fact a bad nature, "superficial" and "fictitious" and "easy," effaces a good nature by imposture; that which ties sense to sound, the "thought-sound." Saussure is faithful to the tradition that has always associated writing with the fatal violence of the political institution. It is clearly a matter, as with Rousseau for example, of a break with nature, of a usurpation that was coupled with the theoretical blindness to the natural essence of language, at any rate to the natural bond between the "instituted signs" of the voice and "the first language of man," the "cry of nature" (*Second Discourse*).[5] Saussure: "But the spoken word is so intimately bound to its written image that the latter manages

to usurp the main role" (p. 45; italics added) [p. 24]. Rousseau: "Writing is nothing but the representation of speech; it is *bizarre* that one gives more care to the determining of the *image* than to the *object.*" Saussure: "Whoever says that a certain letter must be pronounced a certain way is mistaking the written *image* of a sound for the sound itself. . . . [One] attribute[s] the oddity [*bizarrerie*] to an exceptional pronunciation" (p. 52) [p. 30].[6] What is intolerable and fascinating is indeed the intimacy intertwining image and thing, *graph, i.e.,* and phonè, to the point where by a mirroring, inverting, and perverting effect, speech seems in its turn the speculum of writing, which "manages to usurp the main role." Representation mingles with what it represents, to the point where one speaks as one writes, one thinks as if the represented were nothing more than the shadow or reflection of the representer. A dangerous promiscuity and a nefarious complicity between the reflection and the reflected which lets itself be seduced narcissistically. In this play of representation, the point of origin becomes ungraspable. There are things like reflecting pools, and images, an infinite reference from one to the other, but no longer a source, a spring. There is no longer a simple origin. For what is reflected is split *in itself* and not only as an addition to itself of its image. The reflection, the image, the double, splits what it doubles. The origin of the speculation becomes a difference. What can look at itself is not one; and the law of the addition of the origin to its representation, of the thing to its image, is that one plus one makes at least three. The historical usurpation and theoretical oddity that install the image within the rights of reality are determined as the *forgetting* of a simple origin. By Rousseau but also for Saussure. The displacement is hardly anagrammatic: "The result is that people forget that they learn to speak before they learn to write and the natural sequence is reversed" (p. 47) [p. 25]. The violence of forgetting. Writing, a mnemotechnic means, supplanting good memory, spontaneous memory, signifies forgetfulness. It is exactly what Plato

---

[5] [Spivak]"Discours sur l'origine et les fondements de l'inégalité." Derrida's references are to the Pléiade edition, vol. 3, mine, placed within brackets, to "A Discourse on the Origin of Inequality," *The Social Contract and Discourses,* tr. G. D. H. Cole (London, 1913).

[6] [Derrida] Let us extend our quotation to bring out the tone and the affect of these theoretical propositions. Saussure *puts the blame on* writing: "Another result is that the less writing represents what it is supposed to represent, the stronger the tendency to use it as a basis becomes. Grammarians never fail to draw attention to the written form. Psychologically, the tendency is easily explained, but its consequences are annoying. Free use of the words 'pronounce' and 'pronunciation' sanctions the abuse and reverses the real, legitimate relationship between writing and language. Whoever says that a certain letter must be pronounced a certain way is mistaking the written image of a sound for the sound itself. For French *oi* to be pronounced *wa,* this spelling would have to exist independently; actually *wa* is written *oi.*" Instead of meditating upon this strange proposition, the *possibility* of such a text ("actually *wa* is written *oi*"), Saussure argues: "To attribute the oddity to an exceptional pronunciation of *o* and *i* is also misleading, for this implies that language depends on its written form and that certain liberties may be taken in writing, as if the graphic symbols were the norm" (p. 52) [p. 30].

said in the *Phaedrus,* comparing writing to speech as *hypomnesis* to *mnémè,* the auxilliary aide-mémoire to the living memory. Forgetfulness because it is a mediation and the departure of the logos from itself. Without writing, the latter would remain in itself. Writing is the dissimulation of the natural, primary, and immediate presence of sense to the soul within the logos. Its violence befalls the soul as unconsciousness. Deconstructing this tradition will therefore not consist of reversing it, of making writing innocent. Rather of showing why the violence of writing does not *befall* an innocent language. There is an originary violence of writing because language is first, in a sense I shall gradually reveal, writing. "Usurpation" has always already begun. The sense of the right side appears in a mythological effect of return.

"The sciences and the arts" have elected to live within this violence, their "progress" has consecrated forgetfulness and "corrupted manners [*moeurs*]." Saussure again anagrammatizes Rousseau: "The literary language adds to the undeserved importance of writing. . . . Thus writing assumes undeserved importance [*une importance à laquelle elle n'a pas droit*]" (p. 47) [p. 25]. When linguists become embroiled in a theoretical mistake in this subject, when they are taken in, they are *culpable,* their fault is above all *moral;* they have yielded to imagination, to sensibility, to passion, they have fallen into the "trap" (p. 46) [p. 25] of writing, have let themselves be fascinated by the "influence [*prestige*] of the written form" (ibid.), of that custom, that second nature. "The language does have a definite and stable oral tradition that is independent of writing, but the influence [*prestige*] of the written form prevents our seeing this." We are thus not blind to the visible, but blinded by the visible, dazzled by writing. "The first linguists confused language and writing, just as the humanists had done before them. Even Bopp.[7] . . . His immediate successors fell into the same trap." Rousseau had already addressed the same reproach to the Grammarians: "For the Grammarians, the art of speech seems to be very little more than the art of writing."[8] As usual, the "trap" is artifice dissimulated in nature. This explains why *The Course in General Linguistics* treats this strange external system that is writing. As necessary preamble to restoring the natural to itself, one must first disassemble the trap. We read a little further on:

To substitute immediately what is natural for what is artificial would be necessary; but this is impossible without first studying the sounds of what is language; detached from their graphic signs, sounds represent only vague notions, and the prop provided by writing, though deceptive, is still preferable. The first linguists, who knew nothing about the physiology of articulated sounds, were constantly falling into a trap; to let go of the letter was for them to lose their foothold; to me, it means a first step in the direction of truth (p. 55, Opening of the chapter on Phonology) [p. 32].

For Saussure, to give in to the "prestige of the written form" is, as I have just said, to give in to *passion*. It is passion—and I weigh my word—that Saussure analyzes and criticizes here, as a moralist and a psychologist of a very old tradition. As one knows, passion is tyrannical and enslaving: "Philological criticism is still deficient on one point: it follows the written language slavishly and neglects the living language" (p. 14) [pp. 1–2]. "The tyranny of writing," Saussure says elsewhere (p. 53) [p. 31]. That tyranny is at bottom the mastery of the body over the soul, and passion is a passivity and sickness of the soul, the moral perversion is *pathological*. The reciprocal effect of writing on speech is "wrong [*vicieuse*]," Saussure says, "such mistakes are really pathological" (p. 53) [p. 31]. The inversion of the natural relationships would thus have engendered the perverse cult of the letter-image: sin of idolatry, "superstition of the letter" Saussure says in the *Anagrams*[9] where he has difficulty in proving the existence of a "phoneme anterior to all writing." The perversion of artifice engenders monsters. Writing, like all artificial languages one would wish to fix and remove from the living history of the natural language, participates in the monstrosity. It is a deviation from nature. The characteristic of the Leibnizian type and Esperanto would be here in the same position. Saussure's irritation with such possibilities drives him to pedestrian comparisons: "A man proposing a fixed language that posterity would have to accept for what it is would be like a hen hatching a duck's egg" (p. 111) [p. 76]. And Saussure wishes to save not only the *natural life* of language, but the natural habits of writing. Spontaneous life must be protected. Thus, the introduction of scientific exigencies and the taste for exactitude into ordinary phonetic writing must be avoided. In this case, rationality would bring

---

[7] Franz Bopp (1791–1867), German philologist of Indo-European languages.

[8] [Derrida] Manuscript included in the *Pléiade* edition under the title *Prononciation* (11, p. 1248). Its composition is placed circa 1761 (cf. editors' note in the *Pléiade*). The sentence that I have just cited is the last one of the fragment as published in the *Pléiade*. It does not appear in the comparable edition of the same group of notes by [M. G.] Streckeisen-Moultou, under the title of "Fragment d'un Essai sur les langues" and "Notes détachées <xx> sur le mème sujet," in *Oeuvres et correspondances inédites de J. J. Rousseau* ([Paris], 1861), p. 295.

[9] [Derrida / Spivak] Text presented by Jean Starobinski in "Les anagrammes de Ferdinand de Saussure: textes inédits," *Mercure de France* (February 1964), [vol. 350; now published as *Les mots sous les mots: les anagrammes de Ferdinand de Saussure,* ed. Starobinski (Paris, 1971)].

death, desolation, and monstrousness. That is why common orthography must be kept away from the notations of the linguist and *the multiplying of diacritical signs must be avoided:*

> Are there grounds for substituting a phonologic alphabet for a system [*l'orthographe*] already in use? Here I can only broach this interesting subject. I think that phonological writing should be for the use of linguists only. First, how would it be possible to make the English, Germans, French, etc. adopt a uniform system! Next, an alphabet applicable to all languages would probably be weighed down by diacritical marks; and—to say nothing of the distressing appearance of a page of phonological writing—attempts to gain precision would obviously confuse the reader by obscuring what the writing was designed to express. The advantages would not be sufficient to compensate for the inconveniences. Phonological exactitude is not very desirable outside science (p. 57) [p. 34].

I hope my intention is clear. I think Saussure's reasons are good. I do not question, *on the level on which he says it,* the truth of *what Saussure says* in such a tone. And as long as an explicit problematics, a *critique* of the relationships between speech and writing, is not elaborated, what he denounces as the blind prejudice of classical linguists or of common experience indeed remains a blind prejudice, on the basis of a general presupposition which is no doubt common to the accused and the prosecutor.

I would rather announce the limits and the presuppositions of what seems here to be self-evident and what seems to me to retain the character and validity of evidence. The limits have already begun to appear: Why does a project of *general* linguistics, concerning the *internal system in general of language in general,* outline the limits of its field by excluding, as *exteriority in general, a particular* system of writing, however important it might be, even were it to be *in fact* universal?[10] A particular system which has precisely for its *principle* or at least for its *declared* project to be exterior to the spoken language. Declaration of principle, pious wish and

historical violence of a speech dreaming its full self-presence, living itself as its own resumption; self-proclaimed language, auto-production of a speech declared alive, capable, Socrates said, of helping itself, a logos which believes itself to be its own father, being lifted thus above written discourse, *infans* (speechless) and infirm at not being able to respond when one questions it and which, since its "parent['s help] is [always] needed" (toū patrōs áeī deītai boīthoū—*Phaedrus* 275d) must therefore be born out of a primary gap and a primary *expatriation,* condemning it to wandering and blindness, to mourning. Self-proclaimed language but actually speech, deluded into believing itself completely alive, and violent, for it is not "capable of protect[ing] or defend[ing] [itself]" (dunatōs mēn amūnai éauto) except through expelling the other, and especially *its own* other, throwing it *outside* and *below,* under the name of writing. But however important it might be, and were it in fact universal or called upon to become so, that particular model which is phonetic writing *does not exist;* no practice is ever totally faithful to its principle. Even before speaking, as I shall do further on, of a radical and a priori necessary infidelity, one can already remark its massive phenomenon in mathematical script or in punctuation, in *spacing* in general, which it is difficult to consider as simple accessories of writing. That a speech supposedly alive can lend itself to spacing in its own writing is what relates it originarily to its own death.

Finally, the "usurpation" of which Saussure speaks, the violence by which writing would substitute itself for its own origin, for that which ought not only to have engendered it but to have been engendered from itself—such a reversal of power cannot be an accidental aberration. Usurpation necessarily refers us to a profound possibility of essence. This is without a doubt inscribed within speech itself and he should have questioned it, perhaps even started from it.

Saussure confronts the system of the spoken language with the system of phonetic (and even alphabetic) writing as though with the telos of writing. This teleology leads to the interpretation of all eruptions of the nonphonetic within writing as transitory crisis and accident of passage, and it is right to consider this teleology to be a Western ethnocentrism, a premathematical primitivism, and a preformalist intuitionism. Even if this teleology responds to some absolute necessity, it should be problematized as such. The scandal of "usurpation" invites us expressly and intrinsically to do that. How was the trap and the usurpation possible? Saussure never replies to this question beyond a psychology of the passions or of the imagination; a psychology reduced to its most conventional diagrams. This best explains why all linguistics, a determined sector inside semiology, is placed under the authority and superiority of psychology: "To determine the exact place of

---

[10] [Derrida] Rousseau is seemingly more cautious in the fragment on *Pronunciation:* "Thought is analyzed by speech, speech by writing; speech represents thought by conventional signs, and writing represents speech in the same way; thus the art of writing is nothing but a mediated representation of thought, *at least in the vocalic languages, the only ones that we use*" (p. 1249; italics added). Only seemingly, for even if, unlike Saussure, Rousseau here forbids himself to speak *in general* of the entire system, the notions of mediacy and of "vocalic languages" leave the enigma intact. I shall be obliged to return to this.

semiology is the task of the psychologist" (p. 33) [p. 16]. The affirmation of the essential and "natural" bond between the *phonè* and the sense, the privilege accorded to an order of signifier (which then becomes the major signified of all other signifiers) depend expressly, and in contradiction to the other levels of the Saussurian discourse, upon a psychology of consciousness and of intuitive consciousness. What Saussure does not question here is the essential possibility of nonintuition. Like Husserl, Saussure determines this nonintuition teleologically as *crisis*. The *empty* symbolism of the written notation—in mathematical technique for example—is also for Husserlian intuitionism that which exiles us far from the *clear* evidence of the sense, that is to say from the full presence of the signified in its truth, and thus opens the possibility of crisis. This is indeed a crisis of the logos. Nevertheless, for Husserl, this possibility remains linked with the very moment of truth and the production of ideal objectivity: it has in fact an essential need for writing.[11] By one entire aspect of his text, Husserl makes us think that the negativity of the crisis is not a mere accident. But it is then the concept of crisis that should be suspect, by virtue of what ties it to a dialectical and teleological determination of negativity.

On the other hand, to account for "usurpation" and the origin of "passion," the classical and very superficial argument of the solid permanence of the written thing, not to be simply false, calls forth descriptions which are precisely no longer within the province of psychology. Psychology will never be able to accommodate within its space that which constitutes the absence of the signatory, to say nothing of the absence of the referent. Writing is the name of these two absences. Besides, is it not contradictory to what is elsewhere affirmed about language having "a definite and [far more] stable oral tradition that is independent of writing" (p. 46) [p. 24], to explain the usurpation by means of writing's power of *duration,* by means of the *durability* of the substance of writing? If these two "stabilities" were of the same nature, and if the stability of the spoken language were superior and independent, the origin of writing, its "prestige" and its supposed harmfulness, would remain an inexplicable mystery. It seems then as if Saussure wishes *at the same time* to demonstrate the corruption of speech by writing, to denounce the harm that the latter does to the former, *and* to underline the inalterable and natural independence of language. "Languages are independent of writing" (p. 45) [p. 24]. Such is the truth of nature. And yet nature is affected—from without—by an overturning which modifies it in its interior, denatures it and obliges it to be separated from itself. Nature denaturing itself, being sepa-

rated *from itself,* naturally gathering its outside into its inside, is *catastrophe,* a natural event that overthrows nature, or *monstrosity,* a natural deviation within nature. The function assumed in Rousseau's discourse by the catastrophe (as we shall see), is here delegated to monstrousness. Let us cite the entire conclusion of Chapter VI of the *Course* ("Graphic Representation of Language"), which must be compared to Rousseau's text on *Pronunciation:*

> But the tyranny of writing goes even further. By imposing itself upon the masses, spelling influences and modifies language. This happens only in highly literary languages where written texts play an important role. Then visual images lead to wrong [*vicieuses*] pronunciations; such mistakes are really pathological. Spelling practices cause mistakes in the pronunciation of many French words. For instance, there were two spellings for the surname Lefèvre (from latin *faber*), one popular and simple, the other learned and etymological: *Lefèvre* and *Lefèbvre.* Because *v* and *u* were not kept apart in the old system of writing, *Lefèbvre* was read as *Lefébure,* with a *b* that has never really existed and a *u* that was the result of ambiguity. Now, the latter form is actually pronounced (pp. 53–54) [p. 31].

Where is the evil? one will perhaps ask. And what has been invested in the "living word," that makes such "aggressions" of writing intolerable? What investment begins by determining the constant action of writing as a deformation and an aggression? What prohibition has thus been transgressed? Where is the sacrilege? Why should the mother tongue be protected from the operation of writing? Why determine that operation as a violence, and why should the transformation be only a deformation? Why should the mother tongue not have a history, or, what comes to the same thing, produce its own history in a perfectly natural, autistic, and domestic way, without ever being affected by any outside? Why wish to punish writing for a monstrous crime, to the point of wanting to reserve for it, even within scientific treatments, a "special compartment" that holds it at a distance? For it is indeed within a sort of intralinguistic leper colony that Saussure wants to contain and concentrate the problem of deformations through writing. And, in order to be convinced that he would take in very bad part the innocent questions that I have just asked—for after all *Lefébure is not a bad name* and we can love this play—let us read the following. The passage below explains to us that the "play" is not "natural," and its accents are pessimistic: "Mispronunciations due to spelling will

[11] [Derrida] Cf. *L'origine de la géométrie,* 1962.

probably appear more frequently and as time goes on, the number of useless letters pronounced by speakers will probably increase." As in Rousseau in the same context, the Capital is accused: "Some Parisians already pronounce the *t* in *sept femmes* 'seven women.' " Strange example. The historical gap—for it is indeed history that one must stop in order to protect language from writing—will only widen:

> Darmsteter foresees the day when even the last two letters of *vingt* "twenty" will be pronounced—truly an orthographic *monstrosity*. Such phonic *deformations* belong to language but *do not stem from its natural functioning*. They are due to an *external* influence. Linguistics should put them into a *special compartment* for observation: they are *teratological* cases (p. 54; italics added) [pp. 31–32].

It is clear that the concepts of stability, permanence, and duration, which here assist thinking the relationships between speech and writing, are too lax and open to every uncritical investiture. They would require more attentive and minute analyses. The same is applicable to an explanation according to which "most people pay more attention to visual impressions simply because these are sharper and more lasting than aural impressions" (p. 46) [p. 25]. This explanation of "usurpation" is not only empirical in its form, it is problematic in its content, it refers to a metaphysics and to an old physiology of sensory faculties constantly disproved by science, as by the experience of language and by the body proper as language. It imprudently makes of visibility the tangible, simple, and essential element of writing. Above all, in considering the audible as the *natural* milieu within which language must *naturally* fragment and articulate its instituted signs, thus exercising its arbitrariness, this explanation excludes all possibility of some natural relationship between speech and writing at the very moment that it affirms it. Instead of deliberately dismissing the notions of nature and institution that it constantly uses, which ought to be done first, it thus confuses the two. It finally and most importantly contradicts the principal affirmation according to which "the thing that constitutes language [*l'essentiel de la langue*] is . . . unrelated to the phonic character of the linguistic sign" (p. 21) [p. 7]. This affirmation will soon occupy us; within it the other side of the Saussurian proposition denouncing the "illusions of script" comes to the fore.

What do these limits and presuppositions signify? First that a linguistics is not *general* as long as it defines its outside and inside in terms of *determined* linguistic models; as long as it does not rigorously distinguish essence from fact in their respective degrees of generality. The system of writing in general is not exterior to the system of language in general, unless it is granted that the division between exterior and interior passes through the interior of the interior or the exterior of the exterior, to the point where the immanence of language is essentially exposed to the intervention of forces that are apparently alien to its system. For the same reason, writing in general is not "image" or "figuration" of language in general, except if the nature, the logic, and the functioning of the image within the system from which one wishes to exclude it be reconsidered. Writing is not a sign of a sign, except if one says it of all signs, which would be more profoundly true. If every sign refers to a sign, and if "sign of a sign" signifies writing, certain conclusions—which I shall consider at the appropriate moment—will become inevitable. What Saussure saw without seeing, knew without being *able* to take into account, following in that the entire metaphysical tradition, is that a certain model of writing was necessarily but provisionally imposed (but for the inaccuracy in principle, insufficiency of fact, and the permanent usurpation) as instrument and technique of representation of a system of language. And that this movement, unique in style, was so profound that it permitted the thinking, *within language,* of concepts like those of the sign, technique, representation, language. The system of language associated with phonetic-alphabetic writing is that within which logocentric metaphysics, determining the sense of being as presence, has been produced. This logocentrism, this *epoch* of the full speech, has always placed in parenthesis, *suspended,* and suppressed for essential reasons, all free reflection on the origin and status of writing, all science of writing which was not *technology* and the *history of a technique,* itself leaning upon a mythology and a metaphor of a natural writing.[12] It is this logocentrism which, limiting the internal system of language in general by a bad abstraction, prevents Saussure and the majority of his successors[13] from determining fully and explicitly that which is called "the integral and concrete object of linguistics" (p. 23) [p. 7].

---

[12] [Spivak] A play on "époque" (epoch) and "epoche," the Husserlian term for "bracketting" or "putting out of play" that constitutes phenomenological reduction.

[13] [Derrida / Spivak] "The signifier aspect of the system of language can consist only of rules according to which the phonic aspect of the act of speech is ordered," [N.S.] Troubetzkoy, *Principes de phonologie,* tr. fr. [J. Cantineau (Paris, 1949); *Principles of Phonology,* tr. Christiane A. M. Baltaxe (Berkeley and Los Angeles, 1969)], p. 2. It is in the "Phonologie et phonétique" of Jakobson and Halle (the first part of *Fundamentals of Language,* collected and translated in *Essais de linguistique générale* [tr. Nicolas Ruwet (Paris, 1963)], p. 103) that the phonologistic strand of the Saussurian project seems to be most systematically and most rigorously defended, notably against Hjelmslev's "algebraic" point of view.

But conversely, as I announced above, it is when he is not expressly dealing with writing, when he feels he has closed the parentheses on that subject, that Saussure opens the field of a general grammatology. Which would not only no longer be excluded from general linguistics, but would dominate it and contain it within itself. Then one realizes that what was chased off limits, the wandering outcast of linguistics, has indeed never ceased to haunt language as its primary and most intimate possibility. Then something which was never spoken and which is nothing other than writing itself as the origin of language writes itself within Saussure's discourse. Then we glimpse the germ of a profound but indirect explanation of the usurpation and the traps condemned in Chapter VI. This explanation will overthrow even the form of the question to which it was a premature reply.

The Outside ~~Is~~ the Inside

The thesis of the *arbitrariness* of the sign (so grossly misnamed, and not only for the reasons Saussure himself recognizes)[14] must forbid a radical distinction between the linguistic and the graphic sign. No doubt this thesis concerns only the necessity of relationships between specific signifiers and signifieds *within* an allegedly natural relationship between the voice and sense in general, between the order of phonic signifiers and the content of the signifieds ("the only natural bond, the only true bond, the bond of sound"). Only these relationships between specific signifiers and signifieds would be regulated by arbitrariness. Within the "natural" relationship between phonic signifiers and their signifieds *in general,* the relationship between each determined signifier and its determined signified would be "arbitrary."

Now from the moment that one considers the totality of determined signs, spoken, and a fortiori written, as unmotivated institutions, one must exclude any relationship of natural subordination, any natural hierarchy among signifiers or orders of signifiers. If "writing" signifies inscription and especially the durable institution of a sign (and that is the only irreducible kernel of the concept of writing), writing in general covers the entire field of linguistic signs. In that field a certain sort of instituted signifiers may then appear, "graphic" in the narrow and derivative sense of the word, ordered by a

certain relationship with other instituted—hence "written," even if they are "phonic"—signifiers. The very idea of institution—hence of the arbitrariness of the sign—is unthinkable before the possibility of writing and outside of its horizon. Quite simply, that is, outside of the horizon itself, outside the world as space of inscription, as the opening to the emission and to the spatial *distribution* of signs, to the *regulated play* of their differences, even if they are "phonic."

Let us now persist in using this opposition of nature and institution, of *physis* and *nomos* (which also means, of course, a distribution and division regulated in fact by *law*) which a meditation on writing should disturb although it functions everywhere as self-evident, particularly in the discourse of linguistics. We must then conclude that only the signs called *natural,* those that Hegel and Saussure call "symbols," escape semiology as grammatology. But they fall a fortiori outside the field of linguistics as the region of general semiology. The thesis of the arbitrariness of the sign thus indirectly but irrevocably contests Saussure's declared proposition when he chases writing to the outer darkness of language. This thesis successfully accounts for a conventional relationship between the phoneme and the grapheme (in phonetic writing, between the phoneme, signifier-signified, and the grapheme, pure signifier), but by the same token it forbids that the latter be an "image" of the former. Now it was indispensable to the exclusion of writing as "external system," that it come to impose an "image," a "representation," or a "figuration," an exterior reflection of the reality of language.

It matters little, here at least, that there is in fact an ideographic filiation of the alphabet. This important question is much debated by historians of writing. What matters here is that in the synchronic structure and systematic principle of alphabetic writing—and phonetic writing in general—no relationship of "natural" representation, none of resemblance or participation, no "symbolic" relationship in the Hegelian-Saussurian sense, no "iconographic" relationship in the Peircian sense, be implied.

One must therefore challenge, in the very name of the arbitrariness of the sign, the Saussurian definition of writing as "image"—hence as natural symbol—of language. Not to mention the fact that the phoneme is the *unimaginable* itself, and no visibility can *resemble* it, it suffices to take into account what Saussure says about the difference between the symbol and the sign (p. 101) [pp. 68–69] in order to be completely baffled as to how he can at the same time say of writing that it is an "image" or "figuration" of language and define language and writing elsewhere as "two distinct systems of signs" (p. 45) [p. 23]. For the property of the sign is not to be an image. By a process exposed by Freud in *The Interpretation of Dreams,* Saussure thus accumulates contradictory

---

[14] [Derrida] Page 101. Beyond the scruples formulated by Saussure himself, an entire system of intralinguistic criticism can be opposed to the thesis of the "arbitrariness of the sign." Cf. Jakobson, "A la recherche de l'essence du langage," ["Quest for the Essence of Language"] *Diogène,* 51, and Martinet, *La linguistique synchronique* [Paris 1965], p. 34. But these criticisms do not interfere—and, besides, do not pretend to interfere—with Saussure's profound intention directed at the discontinuity and immotivation proper to the structure if not the origin of the sign.

arguments to bring about asatisfactory decision: the exclusion of writing. In fact, even within so-called phonetic writing, the "graphic" signifier refers to the phoneme through a web of many dimensions which binds it, like all signifiers, to other written and oral signifiers, within a "total" system open, let us say, to all possible investments of sense. We must begin with the possibility of that total system.

Saussure was thus never able to think that writing was truly an "image," a "figuration," a "representation" of the spoken language, a symbol. If one considers that he nonetheless needed these inadequate notions to decide upon the exteriority of writing, one must conclude that an entire stratum of his discourse, the intention of Chapter VI ("Graphic Representation of Language"), was not at all scientific. When I say this, my quarry is not primarily Ferdinand de Saussure's intention or motivation, but rather the entire uncritical tradition which he inherits. To what zone of discourse does this strange functioning of argumentation belong, this coherence of desire producing itself in a near-oneiric way—although it clarifies the dream rather than allow itself to be clarified by it—through a contradictory logic? How is this functioning articulated with the entirety of theoretical discourse, throughout the history of science? Better yet, how does it work from within the concept of science itself? It is only when this question is elaborated— if it is some day—when the concepts required by this functioning are defined outside of all psychology (as of all sciences of man), outside metaphysics (which can now be "Marxist" or "structuralist"); when one is able to respect all its levels of generality and articulation—it is only then that one will be able to state rigorously the problem of the articulated appurtenance of a text (theoretical or otherwise) to an entire set: I obviously treat the Saussurian text at the moment only as a telling example within a given situation, without professing to use the concepts required by the functioning of which I have just spoken. My justification would be as follows: this and some other indices (in a general way the treatment of the concept of writing) already give us the assured means of broaching the deconstruction of *the greatest totality*—the concept of the *epistémè* and logocentric metaphysics—within which are produced, without ever posing the radical question of writing, all the Western methods of analysis, explication, reading, or interpretation.

Now we must think that writing is at the same time more exterior to speech, not being its "image" or its "symbol," and more interior to speech, which is already in itself a writing. Even before it is linked to incision, engraving, drawing, or the letter, to a signifier referring in general to a signifier signified by it, the concept of the *graphie* [unit of a possible graphic system] implies the framework of the *instituted trace,* as the possibility common to all systems of sig-

nification. My efforts will now be directed toward slowly detaching these two concepts from the classical discourse from which I necessarily borrow them. The effort will be laborious and we know a priori that its effectiveness will never be pure and absolute.

The instituted trace is "unmotivated" but not capricious. Like the word "arbitrary" according to Saussure, it "should not imply that the choice of the signifier is left entirely to the speaker" (p. 101) [pp. 68–69]. Simply, it has no "natural attachment" to the signified within reality. For us, the rupture of that "natural attachment" puts in question the idea of naturalness rather than that of attachment. That is why the word "institution" should not be too quickly interpreted within the classical system of oppositions.

The instituted trace cannot be thought without thinking the retention of difference within a structure of reference where difference appears *as such* and thus permits a certain liberty of variations among the full terms. The absence of *another* here-and-now, of another transcendental present, of *another* origin of the world appearing as such, presenting itself as irreducible absence within the presence of the trace, is not a metaphysical formula substituted for a scientific concept of writing. This formula, beside the fact that it is the questioning of metaphysics itself, describes the structure implied by the "arbitrariness of the sign," from the moment that one thinks of its possibility *short of* the derived opposition between nature and convention, symbol and sign, etc. These oppositions have meaning only after the possibility of the trace. The "unmotivatedness" of the sign requires a synthesis in which the completely other is announced as such—without any simplicity, any identity, any resemblance or continuity— within what is not it. *Is announced as such:* there we have all *history,* from what metaphysics has defined as "non-living" up to "consciousness," passing through all levels of animal organization. The trace, where the relationship with the other is marked, articulates its possibility in the entire field of the entity [*étant*], which metaphysics has defined as the being-present starting from the occulted movement of the trace. The trace must be thought before the entity. But the movement of the trace is necessarily occulted, it produces itself as self-occultation. When the other announces itself as such, it presents itself in the dissimulation of itself. This formulation is not theological, as one might believe somewhat hastily. The "theological" is a determined moment in the total movement of the trace. The field of the entity, before being determined as the field of presence, is structured according to the diverse possibilities—genetic and structural—of the trace. The presentation of the other as such, that is to say the dissimulation of its "as such," has always already begun and no structure of the entity escapes it.

That is why the movement of "unmotivatedness" passes from one structure to the other when the "sign" crosses the stage of the "symbol." It is in a certain sense and according to a certain determined structure of the "as such" that one is authorized to say that there is yet no immotivation in what Saussure calls "symbol" and which, according to him, does not—at least provisionally—interest semiology. The general structure of the unmotivated trace connects within the same possibility, and they cannot be separated except by abstraction, the structure of the relationship with the other, the movement of temporalization, and language as writing. Without referring back to a "nature," the immotivation of the trace has always *become*. In fact, there is no unmotivated trace: the trace is indefinitely its own becoming-unmotivated. In Saussurian language, what Saussure does not say would have to be said: there is neither symbol nor sign but a becoming-sign of the symbol.

Thus, as it goes without saying, the trace whereof I speak is not more *natural* (it is not the mark, the natural sign, or the index in the Husserlian sense) than *cultural,* not more physical than psychic, biological than spiritual. It is that starting from which a becoming-unmotivated of the sign, and with it all the ulterior oppositions between *physis* and its other, is possible.

In his project of semiotics, Peirce seems to have been more attentive than Saussure to the irreducibility of this becoming-unmotivated. In his terminology, one must speak of a becoming-unmotivated of the *symbol,* the notion of the symbol playing here a role analogous to that of the sign which Saussure opposes precisely to the symbol:

> Symbols grow. They come into being by development out of other signs, particularly from icons, or from mixed signs partaking of the nature of icons and symbols. We think only in signs. These mental signs are of mixed nature; the symbol parts of them are called concepts. If a man makes a new symbol, it is by thoughts involving concepts. So it is only out of symbols that a new symbol can grow. Omne symbolum de symbolo.[15]

Peirce complies with two apparently incompatible exigencies. The mistake here would be to sacrifice one for the other. It must be recognized that the symbolic (in Peirce's sense: of "the arbitrariness of the sign") is rooted in the nonsymbolic, in an anterior and related order of signification:

"Symbols grow. They come into being by development out of other signs, particularly from icons, or from mixed signs." But these roots must not compromise the structural originality of the field of symbols, the autonomy of a domain, a production, and a play: "So it is only out of symbols that a new symbol can grow. Omne symbolum de symbolo."

But in both cases, the genetic root-system refers from sign to sign. No ground of nonsignification—understood as insignificance or an intuition of a present truth—stretches out to give it foundation under the play and the coming into being of signs. Semiotics no longer depends on logic. Logic, according to Peirce, is only a semiotic: "Logic, in its general sense, is, as I believe I have shown, only another name for semiotics *(semeiotike),* the quasi-necessary, or formal, doctrine of signs." And logic in the classical sense, logic "properly speaking," nonformal logic commanded by the value of truth, occupies in that semiotics only a determined and not a fundamental level. As in Husserl (but the analogy, although it is most thought-provoking, would stop there and one must apply it carefully), the lowest level, the foundation of the possibility of logic (or semiotics) corresponds to the project of the *Grammatica speculativa* of Thomas d'Erfurt,[16] falsely attributed to Duns Scotus.[17] Like Husserl, Peirce expressly refers to it. It is a matter of elaborating, in both cases, a formal doctrine of conditions which a discourse must satisfy in order to have a sense, in order to "mean," even if it is false or contradictory. The general morphology of that meaning[18] *(Bedeutung, vouloir-dire)* is independent of all logic of truth.

> The science of semiotic has three branches. The first is called by Duns Scotus *grammatica speculativa.* We may term it *pure grammar.* It has for its task to ascertain what must be true of the representamen used by every scientific intelligence in order that they may embody any *meaning.* The second is logic proper. It is the science of what is quasi-necessarily true of the representamina of any scientific intelligence in order that they may hold good of any *object,* that is, may be true. Or say, logic proper is the formal science of the conditions of the truth of representations. The third, in imitation of Kant's fashion of preserving old associations of words in finding nomenclature for new conceptions, I call *pure rhetoric.* Its task is to ascertain the laws by which in every scien-

---

[15] [Derrida] *Elements of Logic,* Bk. II [*Collected Papers,* ed. Charles Hartshorne and Paul Weiss (Cambridge, Mass., 1931–1958), vol. 2], p. 169, paragraph 302. [Eds.] See Peirce (above, page 652).

[16] [Eds.] Thomas d'Erfurt, thirteenth-century Scholastic philosopher.
[17] [Eds.] John Duns Scotus (c. 1266–1308), Scholastic philosopher and theologian.
[18] [Derrida] I justify the translation of *bedeuten* by *vouloir-dire* [meaning, literally "wish-to-say"] in *La voix et le phénomène.*

tific intelligence one sign gives birth to another, and especially one thought brings forth another.[19]

Peirce goes very far in the direction that I have called the de-construction of the transcendental signified, which, at one time or another, would place a reassuring end to the reference from sign to sign. I have identified logocentrism and the metaphysics of presence as the exigent, powerful, systematic, and irrepressible desire for such a signified. Now Peirce considers the indefiniteness of reference as the criterion that allows us to recognize that we are indeed dealing with a system of signs. *What broaches the movement of signification is what makes its interruption impossible. The thing itself is a sign.* An unacceptable proposition for Husserl, whose phenomenology remains therefore—in its "principle of principles"—the most radical and most critical restoration of the metaphysics of presence. The difference between Husserl's and Peirce's phenomenologies is fundamental since it concerns the concept of the sign and of the manifestation of presence, the relationships between the re-presentation and the originary presentation of the thing itself (truth). On this point Peirce is undoubtedly closer to the inventor of the word *phenomenology:* Lambert proposed in fact to "reduce *the theory of things* to the *theory of signs.*" According to the "phaneroscopy" or "phenomenology" of Peirce, *manifestation* itself does not reveal a presence, it makes a sign. One may read in the *Principle of Phenomenology* that "the idea of *manifestation* is the idea of a sign."[20] There is thus no phenomenality reducing the sign or the representer so that the thing signified may be allowed to glow finally in the luminosity of its presence. The so-called "thing itself" is always already a *representamen* shielded from the simplicity of intuitive evidence. The *representamen* functions only by giving rise to an *interpretant* that itself becomes a sign and so on to infinity. The self-identity of the signified conceals itself unceasingly and is always on the move. The property of the *representamen* is to be itself and another, to be produced as a structure of reference, to be separated from itself. The property of the *representamen* is not to be *proper* [*propre*], that is to say absolutely *proximate* to itself (*prope, proprius*). The *represented* is always already a *representamen.* Definition of the sign:

Anything which determines something else (its interpretant) to refer to an object to which itself refers (its object) in the same way, this interpretant becoming in turn a sign, and so on ad infinitum. . . . If the series of successive interpretants comes to an end, the sign is thereby rendered imperfect, at least.[21]

From the moment that there is meaning there are nothing but signs. We *think only in signs.* Which amounts to ruining the notion of the sign at the very moment when, as in Nietzsche, its exigency is recognized in the absoluteness of its right. One could call *play* the absence of the transcendental signified as limitlessness of play, that is to say as the destruction of ontotheology and the metaphysics of presence. It is not surprising that the shock, shaping and undermining metaphysics since its origin, lets itself *be named as such* in the period when, refusing to bind linguistics to semantics (which all European linguists, from Saussure to Hjemslev, still do), expelling the problem of *meaning* outside of their researches, certain American linguists constantly refer to the model of a game. Here one must think of writing as a game within language. (The *Phaedrus* (277e) condemned writing precisely as play— *paidia*—and opposed such childishness to the adult gravity [*spoudè*] of speech.) This *play,* thought as absence of the transcendental signified, is not a play *in the world,* as it has always been defined, for the purposes of *containing* it, by the philosophical tradition and as the theoreticians of play also consider it (or those who, following and going beyond Bloomfield, refer semantics to psychology or some other local discipline). To think play radically the ontological and transcendental problematics must first be seriously *exhausted*; the question of the meaning of being, the being of the entity and of the transcendental origin of the world—of the world-ness of the world—must be patiently and rigorously worked through, the critical movement of the Husserlian and Heideggerian questions must be effectively followed to the very end, and their effectiveness and legibility must be conserved. Even if it were crossed out, without it the concepts of play and writing to which I shall have recourse will remain caught within regional limits and an empiricist, positivist, or metaphysical discourse. The counter-move that the holders of such a discourse would oppose to the precritical tradition and to metaphysical speculation would be nothing but the worldly representation of their own operation. It is therefore *the game of*

---

[19] [Derrida] *The Philosophy of Peirce: Selected Writings* [ed. Justus Buchler (New York and London, 1940)], ch. 7, p. 99.

[20] [Derrida] Page 93. Let us recall that Lambert opposes phenomenology to aletheiology. [Eds.] Johann Heinrich Lambert (1728–1777), German mathematician and philosopher.

[21] [Derrida] *Elements of Logic,* Bk. I, 2, p. 302. [Eds.] See Peirce (above, page 652).

the world that must be first thought; before attempting to understand all the forms of play in the world.[22]

From the very opening of the game, then, we are within the becoming-unmotivated of the symbol. With regard to this becoming, the opposition of diachronic and synchronic is also derived. It would not be able to command a grammatology pertinently. The immotivation of the trace ought now to be understood as an operation and not as a state, as an active movement, a demotivation, and not as a given structure. Science of "the arbitrariness of the sign," science of the immotivation of the trace, science of writing before speech and in speech, grammatology would thus cover a vast field within which linguistics would, by abstraction, delineate its own area, with the limits that Saussure prescribes to its internal system and which must be carefully reexamined in each speech/writing system in the world and history.

By a substitution which would be anything but verbal, one may replace semiology by grammatology in the program of the Course in General Linguistics:

> I shall call it [grammatology]. . . . Since the science does not yet exist, no one can say what it would be; but it has a right to existence, a place staked out in advance. Linguistics is only a part of [that] general science . . . ; the laws discovered by [grammatology] will be applicable to linguistics (p. 33) [p. 16].

The advantage of this substitution will not only be to give to the theory of writing the scope needed to counter logocentric repression and the subordination to linguistics. It will liberate the semiological project itself from what, in spite of its greater theoretical extension, remained *governed* by linguistics, organized as if linguistics were at once its center and its telos. *Even though semiology was in fact more general and more comprehensive than linguistics, it continued to be regulated as if it were one of the areas of linguistics. The linguistic sign remained exemplary for semiology,* it dominated it as the master-sign and as the generative model: the pattern [*patron*].

One could therefore say that signs that are wholly arbitrary realize better than the others the ideal of the semiological process; that is why language, the most complex and universal of all systems of expression, is also the most characteristic; in this sense linguistics can become *the master-pattern for all branches* of *semiology* although language is only one particular semiological system (p. 101; italics added) [p. 68].

Consequently, reconsidering the order of dependence prescribed by Saussure, apparently inverting the relationship of the part to the whole, Barthes in fact carries out the profoundest intention of the *Course:*

> From now on we must admit the possibility of reversing Saussure's proposition some day: linguistics is not a part, even if privileged, of the general science of signs, it is semiology that is a part of linguistics.[23]

This coherent reversal, submitting semiology to a "translinguistics," leads to its full explication as linguistics historically dominated by logocentric metaphysics, for which in fact there is not and there should not be "any meaning except as named" (ibid.). Dominated by the so-called "civilization of writing" that we inhabit, a civilization of so-called phonetic writing, that is to say of the logos where the sense of being is, in its telos, determined as parousia. The Barthesian reversal is fecund and indispensable for the description of the *fact and the vocation of signification* within the closure of this epoch and this civilization that is in the process of disappearing in its very globalization.

Let us now try to go beyond these formal and architectonic considerations. Let us ask in a more intrinsic and concrete way, how language is not merely a sort of writing, "comparable to a system of writing" (p. 33) [p. 16]—Saussure writes curiously—but a species *of* writing. Or rather, since writing no longer relates to language as an extension or frontier, let us ask how language is a possibility founded on the general possibility of writing. Demonstrating this, one would give at the same time an account of that alleged "usurpation" which could not be an unhappy accident. It supposes on the contrary a common root and thus excludes the resemblance of the "image," derivation, or representative reflexion. And thus one would bring back to its true meaning, to its primary possibility, the apparently innocent and didactic analogy which makes Saussure say:

> Language is [comparable to] a system of signs that express ideas, and is therefore *comparable to*

---

22 [Derrida / Spivak] These Heideggerian themes obviously refer back to Nietzsche (cf. *La chose* [1950], Spivak fr. in *Essais et conférences* [tr. André Préau (Paris, 1958)], p. 214 ["Das Ding," *Vorträge und Aufsätze* (Pfüllingen, 1954)], *Le principe de raison* (1955–1956), tr. fr. [André Préau, Paris, 1962], pp. 240 f. [*Der Satz vom Grund* (Pfüllingen, 1957)]. Such themes are presented also in Eugen Fink (*Le jeu comme symbole du monde* [*Spiel als Weltsymbol,* Stuttgart, 1960]), and, in France, in Kostas Axelos, *Vers la pensée planétaire* ([Paris], 1964), and *Einführung in ein künftiges Denken: über Marx und Heidegger* (Tübingen, 1966).

23 [Derrida] *Communications,* 4 (1964), p. 2.

1234 ◇ Jacques Derrida

writing, the alphabet of deaf-mutes, symbolic rites, polite formulas, military signals, etc. But it is the most important of all these systems (p. 33; italics added) [p. 16].

Further, it is not by chance that, a hundred and thirty pages later, at the moment of explaining *phonic difference* as the condition of linguistic *value* ("from a material viewpoint"),[24] he must again borrow all his pedagogic resources from the example of writing:

Since an identical state of affairs is observable in writing, another system of signs, we shall use writing to draw some comparisons that will clarify the whole issue (p. 165) [p. 119].

Four demonstrative items, borrowing pattern and content from writing, follow.[25]

Once more, then, we definitely have to oppose Saussure to himself. Before being or not being "noted," "represented," "figured," in a *"graphie,"* the linguistic sign implies an originary writing. Henceforth, it is not to the thesis of the arbitrariness of the sign that I shall appeal directly, but to what Saussure associates with it as an indispensable correlative and which would seem to me rather to lay the foundations for it: the thesis of *difference* as the source of linguistic value.[26]

What are, from the grammatological point of view, the consequences of this theme that is now so well-known (and upon which Plato already reflected in the *Sophist*)?

By definition, difference is never in itself a sensible plenitude. Therefore, its necessity contradicts the allegation of a naturally phonic essence of language. It contests by the same token the professed natural dependence of the graphic signifier. That is a consequence Saussure himself draws against the premises defining the internal system of language. He must now exclude the very thing which had permitted him to exclude writing: sound and its "natural bond" [*lien naturel*] with meaning. For example: "The thing that constitutes language is, as I shall show later, unrelated to the phonic character of the linguistic sign" (p. 21) [p. 7]. And in a paragraph on difference:

It is impossible for sound alone, a material element, to belong to language. It is only a secondary thing, substance to be put to use. All our conventional values have the characteristic of not being confused with the tangible element which supports them.... The linguistic signifier ... is not [in essence] phonic but incorporeal—constituted not by its material substance but the differences that separate its sound-image from all others (p. 164) [pp. 118–19]. The idea or phonic substance that a sign contains is of less importance than the other signs that surround it (p. 166) [p. 120].

Without this reduction of phonic matter, the distinction between language and speech, decisive for Saussure, would have no rigor. It would be the same for the oppositions that happened to descend from it: between code and message, pattern and usage, etc. Conclusion: "Phonology—this bears repeating—is only an auxiliary discipline [of the science of language] and belongs exclusively to speaking" (p. 56) [p. 33]. Speech thus draws from this stock of writing, noted or not, that language is, and it is here that one must meditate upon the complicity between the two "stabilities." The reduction of the *phonè* reveals this complicity. What Saussure says, for example, about the sign in general and what he "confirms" through the example of writing, applies also to language: "Signs are governed by a principle of general semiology: continuity in time is coupled to change in time; this is confirmed by orthographic systems, the speech of deaf-mutes, etc." (p. 111) [p. 16].

The reduction of phonic substance thus does not only permit the distinction between phonetics on the one hand (and a fortiori acoustics or the physiology of the phonating organs) and phonology on the other. It also makes of phonology itself an "auxiliary discipline." Here the direction indicated by Saussure takes us beyond the phonologism of those who profess to follow him on this point: in

---

[24] [Derrida] "The conceptual side of value is made up solely of relations and differences with respect to the other terms of language, and the same can be said of its material side. The important thing in the word is not the sound alone but the phonic differences that make it possible to distinguish this word from all others, for differences carry signification.... A segment of language can never in the final analysis be based on anything except its noncoincidence with the rest" (p. 163) [pp. 117–18].

[25] [Derrida] "Since an identical state of affairs is observable in writing, another system of signs, we shall use writing to draw some comparisons that will clarify the whole issue. In fact: (1) The signs used in writing are arbitrary; there is no connection, for example, between the letter *t* and the sound that it designates. (2) The value of letters is purely negative and differential. The same person can write for instance, in different ways: *t* & t. The only requirement is that the sign for *t* not be confused in his script with the signs used for *l, d,* etc. (3) Values in writing function only through reciprocal opposition within a fixed system that consists of a set number of letters. This third characteristic, though not identical to the second, is closely related to it, for both depend on the first. Since the graphic sign is arbitrary, its form matters little or rather matters only within the limitations imposed by the system. (4) The means by which the sign is produced is completely unimportant, for it does not affect the system (this also follows from characteristic 1). Whether I make the letters in white or black, raised or engraved, with pen or chisel—all this is of no importance with respect to their signification" (pp. 165–66) [pp. 119–20].

[26] [Derrida] *"Arbitrary and differential* are two correlative qualities" (p. 163) [p. 118].

fact, Jakobson believes indifference to the phonic substance of expression to be impossible and illegitimate. He thus criticizes the glossematics of Hjelmslev which requires and practices the neutralizing of sonorous substance. And in the text cited above, Jakobson and Halle maintain that the "theoretical requirement" of a research of invariables placing sonorous substance in parenthesis (as an empirical and contingent content) is:

1. *impracticable* since, as "Eli Fischer-Jorgensen exposes [it]," "the sonorous substance [is taken into account] at every step of the analysis."[27] But is that a "troubling discrepancy," as Jakobson and Halle would have it? Can one not account for it as a fact serving as an example, as do the phenomenologists who always need, keeping it always within sight, an exemplary empirical content in the reading of an essence which is independent of it by right?

2. *inadmissible in principle* since one cannot consider "that in language form is opposed to substance as a constant to a variable." It is in the course of this second demonstration that the literally Saussurian formulas reappear within the question of the relationships between speech and writing; the order of writing is the order of exteriority, of the "occasional," of the "accessory," of the "auxiliary," of the *"parasitic"* (pp. 116–17; italics added) [pp. 16–17]. The argument of Jakobson and Halle appeals to the factual genesis and invokes the secondariness of writing in the colloquial sense: "Only after having mastered speech does one graduate to reading and writing." Even if this commonsensical proposition were rigorously proved—something that I do not believe (since each of its concepts harbors an immense problem)—one would still have to receive assurance of its pertinence to the argument. Even if "after" were here a facile representation, if one knew perfectly well what one thought and stated while assuring that one learns to write *after* having learned to speak, would that suffice to conclude that what thus comes "after" is parasitic? And what is a parasite? And what if writing were precisely that which makes us reconsider our logic of the parasite?

In another moment of the critique, Jakobson and Halle recall the imperfection of graphic representation; that imperfection is due to "the cardinally dissimilar patterning of letters and phonemes":

Letters never, or only partially, reproduce the different distinctive features on which the phonemic pattern is based and unfailingly disregard the

structural relationship of these features (p. 116) [p. 17].

I have suggested it above: does not the radical dissimilarity of the two elements—graphic and phonic—exclude derivation? Does not the inadequacy of graphic representation concern only common alphabetic writing, to which glossematic formalism does not essentially refer? Finally, if one accepts all the phonologist arguments thus presented, it must still be recognized that they oppose a "scientific" concept of the spoken word to a vulgar concept of writing. What I would wish to show is that one cannot exclude writing from the general experience of "the structural relationship of these features." Which amounts, of course, to reforming the concept of writing.

In short, if the Jakobsonian analysis is faithful to Saussure in this matter, is it not especially so to the Saussure of Chapter VI? Up to what point would Saussure have maintained the inseparability of matter and form, which remains the most important argument of Jakobson and Halle (p. 117), [p. 17]? The question may be repeated in the case of the position of André Martinet who, in this debate, follows Chapter VI of the *Course* to the letter.[28] And only Chapter VI, from which Martinet expressly dissociates the doctrine of what, in the *Course,* effaces the privilege of phonic substance. After

---

27 [Spivak] Jakobson and Halle, *Fundamentals of Language* (1956), p. 16.

28 [Derrida] This literal fidelity is expressed: 1. In the critical exposition of Hjelmslev's attempt ("Au sujet des fondements de la théorie linguistique de L. Hjelmslev," *Bulletin de la Société Linguistique de Paris,* vol. 42, p. 40): "Hjelmslev is perfectly consistent with himself when he declares that a written text has for the linguist exactly the same value as a spoken text, since the choice of the substance is not important. He refuses even to admit that the spoken substance is primitive and the written substance derived. It seems as if it would suffice to make him notice that, but for certain pathological exceptions, all human beings speak, but few know how to write, or that children know how to speak long before they learn how to write. *I shall therefore not press the point*" (italics added). 2. In the *Eléments de linguistique générale* [(Paris, 1961); *Elements of General Linguistics,* tr. Elisabeth Palmer (London, 1964)], where all the chapters on the vocal character of language pick up the words and arguments of Chapter VI of the *Course:* "[One learns to speak before learning to read:] reading comes as a reflection of spoken usage: *the reverse is never true*" (italics added. This proposition seems to me to be thoroughly debatable, even on the level of that common experience which has the force of law within this argument). Martinet concludes: "The study of writing is a discipline distinct from linguistics proper, although practically speaking it is one of its dependencies. Thus the linguist in principle operates without regard for written forms" (p. 11) [p. 17]. We see how the concepts of *dependency* and *abstraction* function: writing and its science are alien but not independent; which does not stop them from being, conversely, immanent but not essential. Just enough "outside" not to affect the integrity of the language *itself,* in its pure original self-identity, in its property; just enough "inside" not to have the right to any practical or epistemological independence. And vice versa. 3. In "The Word" (already cited): ". . . it is from speech that one should always start in order to understand the real nature of human language" (p. 53) [p. 54]. 4. And finally and above all in "La double articulation du langage," *La linguistique synchronique,* pp. 8 f. and 18 f.

having explained why "a dead language with a perfect ideography," that is to say a communication effective through the system of a generalized script, "could not have any real autonomy," and why *nevertheless*, "such a system would be something so particular that one can well understand why linguists *want to exclude* it from the domain of their science" (*La linguistique syncronique*, p. 18; italics added), Martinet criticizes those who, following a certain trend in Saussure, question the essentially phonic character of the linguistic sign: "Much will be attempted to prove that Saussure is right when he announces that 'the thing that constitutes language [*l'essentiel de la langue*] is . . . unrelated to the phonic character of the linguistic sign,' and, going beyond the teaching of the master, to declare that the linguistic sign does not necessarily have that phonic character" (p. 19).

On that precise point, it is not a question of "going beyond" the master's teaching but of following and extending it. Not to do it is to cling to what in Chapter VI greatly limits its formal and structural research and contradicts the least contestable findings of Saussurian doctrine. To avoid "going beyond," one risks returning to a point that falls short.

I believe that generalized writing is not just the idea of a system to be invented, an hypothetical characteristic or a future possibility. I think on the contrary that oral language already belongs to this writing. But that presupposes a modification of the concept of writing that we for the moment merely anticipate. Even supposing that one is not given that modified concept, supposing that one is considering a system of pure writing as an hypothesis for the future or a working hypothesis, faced with that hypothesis, should a linguist refuse himself the means of thinking it and of integrating its formulation within his theoretical discourse? Does the fact that most linguists do so create a theoretical right? Martinet seems to be of that opinion. After having elaborated a purely "dactylological" hypothesis of language, he writes, in effect:

> It must be recognized that the parallelism between this "dactylology" and phonology is complete as much in synchronic as in diachronic material, and that the terminology associated with the latter may be used for the former, except of course when the terms refer to the phonic substance. Clearly, if we do not *desire* to exclude from the domain of linguistics the systems of the type we have just imagined, it is most important to modify traditional terminology relative to the articulation of signifiers so as to eliminate all reference to phonic substance; as does Louis Hjelm-

slev when he uses "ceneme" and "cenematics" instead of "phoneme" and "phonematics." *Yet it is understandable that the majority of linguists hesitate to modify completely the traditional terminological edifice for the only theoretical advantages of being able to include in the field of their science some purely hypothetical systems. To make them agree to envisage such a revolution,* they must be persuaded that, in attested linguistic systems, they have no advantage in considering the phonic substance of units of expression as to be of direct interest (pp. 20–21; italics added).

Once again, we do not doubt the value of these phonological arguments, the presuppositions behind which I have attempted to expose above. Once one assumes these presuppositions, it would be absurd to reintroduce confusedly a derivative writing, in the area of oral language and within the system of this derivation. Not only would ethnocentrism not be avoided, but all the frontiers within the sphere of its legitimacy would then be confused. It is not a question of rehabilitating writing in the narrow sense, nor of reversing the order of dependence when it is evident. Phonologism does not brook any objections as long as one conserves the colloquial concepts of speech and writing which form the solid fabric of its argumentation. Colloquial and quotidian conceptions, inhabited besides—uncontradictorily enough—by an old history, limited by frontiers that are hardly visible yet all the more rigorous by that very fact.

I would wish rather to suggest that the alleged derivativeness of writing, however real and massive, was possible only on one condition: that the "original," "natural," etc. language had never existed, never been intact and untouched by writing, that it had itself always been a writing. An arche-writing whose necessity and new concept I wish to indicate and outline here; and which I continue to call writing only because it essentially communicates with the vulgar concept of writing. The latter could not have imposed itself historically except by the dissimulation of the arche-writing, by the desire for a speech displacing its other and its double and working to reduce its difference. If I persist in calling that difference writing, it is because, within the work of historical repression, writing was, by its situation, destined to signify the most formidable difference. It threatened the desire for the living speech from the closest proximity, it *breached* living speech from within and from the very beginning. And as we shall begin to see, difference cannot be thought without the *trace*.

Hans Robert Jauss

b. 1921

Jauss's essay below is one of the most, if not the most, important writings on what has come to be known as reception theory. Its first form was a lecture given in 1967 titled "What is and for what purpose does one study literary history?" The title was meant to recall Friedrich Schillers's 1798 oration "What is and for what purpose does one study universal history?" Both address the question of interpretation and deal with the confrontation of the present with the past.

Jauss sees literary interpretation in his time caught in a conflict between Marxist historicism and an ahistorical aesthetic formalism. For him, the solution is to introduce the role of the reader, neglected in theories that emphasize author and/or work. However, this new emphasis raises numerous problems. How is the reader to be characterized? Is it in some sense the public? Is it the reader or readers contemporary with the author? Or is it today's reader? Or is it some idealized reader, some critically constituted fiction?

Jauss's answer is first to see reception itself as a historical process without a teleology. The literary work's meaning is unfolded through time and is actualized in historical moments in which the "horizon" of the text (that is, its own temporal context) meets the horizon of the reading public. The notion of horizon is derived from the work of Hans-Georg Gadamer and his influential book *Wahrheit und Methode (Truth and Method),* in which all interpretation is a conversation of horizons. But Jauss does not accept Gadamer's idea of the so-called classics as a standard by which all horizons must be judged.

Jauss's reception theory breaks decisively with any objectivist position, including that of traditional literary history, in that it refuses to accept a position of observation that is not itself historically horizonal and this finally fleeting, though part of the history of the text's reception. It is worthwhile to compare with Jauss's the work of I. A. Richards (above, page 856), whose position was objectivistic, and Stanley Fish (below, page 1395), who developed a theory of interpretive communities. Worthwhile also is the essay of Stephen J. Greenblatt (below, page 1476), representing another view of literary history.

The reprinting here does not include the first four sections, which critique previous theories of literary history and formalism.

Some of Jauss's most important essays are gathered together in *Toward an Aesthetic of Reception* (1982) and *Aesthetic Experience and Literary Hermeneutics* (1982), where Jauss revises the theory developed here. See Paul de Man's introduction to the former volume. See also Jauss's *Question and Answer: Forms of Dialogic Understanding* (1989) and Robert C. Holub, *Reception Theory: A Critical Introduction* (1984).

from

Literary History as a Challenge to Literary Theory

V

In the question thus posed, I see the challenge to literary studies of taking up once again the problem of literary history, which was left unresolved in the dispute between Marxist and Formalist methods.[1] My attempt to bridge the gap between literature and history, between historical and aesthetic approaches, begins at the point at which both schools stop. Their methods conceive the *literary fact* within the closed circle of an aesthetics of production and of representation. In doing so, they deprive literature of a dimension that inalienably belongs to its aesthetic character as well as to its social function: the dimension of its reception and influence. Reader, listener, and spectator—in short, the factor of the audience—play an extremely limited role in both literary theories. Orthodox Marxist aesthetics treats the reader—if at all—no differently from the author: it inquires about his social position or seeks to recognize him in the structure of a represented society. The Formalist school needs the reader only as a perceiving subject who follows the directions in the text in order to distinguish the [literary] form or discover the [literary] procedure. It assumes that the reader has the theoretical understanding of the philologist who can reflect on the artistic devices, already knowing them; conversely, the Marxist school candidly equates the spontaneous experience of the reader with the scholarly interest of historical materialism, which would discover relationships between superstructure and basis in the literary work. However, as Walther Bulst has stated, "no text was ever written to be read and interpreted philologically by philologists,"[2] nor, may I add, historically by historians. Both methods lack the reader in his genuine role, a role as unalterable for aesthetic as for historical knowledge: as the addressee for whom the literary work is primarily destined.

For even the critic who judges a new work, the writer who conceives of his work in light of positive or negative norms of an earlier work, and the literary historian who classifies a work in its tradition and explains it historically are first simply readers before their reflexive relationship to literature can become productive again. In the triangle of author, work, and public the last is no passive part, no chain of mere reactions, but rather itself an energy formative of history. The historical life of a literary work is unthinkable without the active participation of its addressees. For it is only through the process of its mediation that the work enters into the changing horizon-of-experience of a continuity in which the perpetual inversion occurs from simple reception to critical understanding, from passive to active reception, from recognized aesthetic norms to a new production that surpasses them. The historicity of literature as well as its communicative character presupposes a dialogical and at once processlike relationship between work, audience, and new work that can be conceived in the relations between message and receiver as well as between question and answer, problem and solution. The closed circle of production and of representation within which the methodology of literary studies has mainly moved in the past must therefore be opened to an aesthetics of reception and influence if the problem of comprehending the historical sequence of literary works as the coherence of literary history is to find a new solution.

The perspective of the aesthetics of reception mediates between passive reception and active understanding, experience formative of norms, and new production. If the history of literature is viewed in this way within the horizon of a dialogue between work and audience that forms a continuity, the opposition between its aesthetic and its historical aspects is also continually mediated. Thus the thread from the past appearance to the present experience of literature, which historicism had cut, is tied back together.

The relationship of literature and reader has aesthetic as well as historical implications. The aesthetic implication lies in the fact that the first reception of a work by the reader includes a test of its aesthetic value in comparison with works already read.[3] The obvious historical implication of this is that the understanding of the first reader will be sustained and enriched in a chain of receptions from generation to generation; in this way the historical significance of a work will be decided and its aesthetic value made evident. In this process of the history of reception, which the literary

---

"Literary History as a Challenge to Literary Theory" was first published in Germany in 1967. It is reprinted here from *Toward an Aesthetic of Reception*, tr. Timothy Bahti (Minneapolis: University of Minnesota Press, 1982).

[1]In connection with this opposition see Raymond Williams (below, page 1356).

[2][Jauss] "Bedenken eines Philologen," *Stadium generale* 7 (1954), 321–23. The new approach to literary tradition that R. Guiette has sought in a series of pioneering essays (partly in *Questions de littérature* [Ghent, 1960]), using his own method of combining aesthetic criticism with historical knowledge, corresponds almost literally to his [unpublished] axiom, "The greatest error of philologists is to believe that literature has been made for philologists." See also his "Eloge de la lecture," *Revue générale belge* (January, 1966), pp. 3–14.

[3][Jauss] This thesis is one of the main points of the *Introduction à une esthétique de la littérature* by G. Picon (Paris, 1953); see esp. pp. 90ff.

historian can only escape at the price of leaving unquestioned the presuppositions that guide his understanding and judgment, the reappropriation of past works occurs simultaneously with the perpetual mediation of past and present art and of traditional evaluation and current literary attempts. The merit of a literary history based on an aesthetics of reception will depend upon the extent to which it can take an active part in the ongoing totalization of the past through aesthetic experience. This demands on the one hand—in opposition to the objectivism of positivist literary history—a conscious attempt at the formation of a canon, which, on the other hand—in opposition to the classicism of the study of traditions—presupposes a critical revision if not destruction of the received literary canon. The criterion for the formation of such a canon and the ever necessary retelling of literary history is clearly set out by the aesthetics of reception. The step from the history of the reception of the individual work to the history of literature has to lead to seeing and representing the historical sequence of works as they determine and clarify the coherence of literature, to the extent that it is meaningful for us, as the prehistory of its present experience.[4]

From this premise, the question as to how literary history can today be methodologically grounded and written anew will be addressed in the following seven theses.

VI

Thesis I. A renewal of literary history demands the removal of the prejudices of historical objectivism and the grounding of the traditional aesthetics of production and representation in an aesthetics of reception and influence. The historicity of literature rests not on an organization of "literary facts" that is established *post festum,* but rather on the preceding experience of the literary work by its readers.

R. G. Collingwood's postulate, posed in his critique of the prevailing ideology of objectivity in history—"History is nothing but the re-enactment of past thought in the historian's mind"[5]—is even more valid for literary history. For the positivistic view of history as the "objective" description of a series of events in an isolated past neglects the artistic

character as well as the specific historicity of literature. A literary work is not an object that stands by itself and that offers the same view to each reader in each period.[6] It is not a monument that monologically reveals its timeless essence. It is much more like an orchestration that strikes ever new resonances among its readers and that frees the text from the material of the words and brings it to a contemporary existence: "words that must, at the same time that they speak to him, create an interlocutor capable of understanding them."[7] This dialogical character of the literary work also establishes why philological understanding can exist only in a perpetual confrontation with the text, and cannot be allowed to be reduced to a knowledge of facts.[8] Philological understanding always remains related to interpretation that must set as its goal, along with learning about the object, the reflection on and description of the completion of this knowledge as a moment of new understanding.

History of literature is a process of aesthetic reception and production that takes place in the realization of literary texts on the part of the receptive reader, the reflective critic, and the author in his continuing productivity. The endlessly growing sum of literary "facts" that winds up in the conventional literary histories is merely left over from this process; it is only the collected and classified past and therefore not history at all, but pseudo-history. Anyone who considers a series of such literary facts as a piece of the history of literature confuses the eventful character of a work of art with that of historical matter-of-factness. The *Perceval* of Chrétien de Troyes,[9] as a literary event, is not "historical" in the same sense as, for example, the Third Crusade, which was

---

[4] [Jauss] Correspondingly, Walter Benjamin (above, page 995) (1931) formulated: "For it is not a question of representing the written works in relation to their time but of bringing to representation the time that knows them—that is our time—in the time when they originated. Thus literature becomes an organon of history and the task of literary history is to make it this—and not to make written works the material of history" (*Angelus Novus* [Frankfurt a.M., 1966], p. 456).

[5] [Jauss] *The Idea of History* (New York and Oxford, 1956), p. 228.

[6] [Jauss] Here I am following A. Nisin in his criticism of the latent Platonism of philological methods, that is, of their belief in the timeless substance of a literary work and in a timeless point of view of the reader: "for the work of art, if it cannot incarnate the essence of art, is also not an object which we can regard according to the Cartesian rule 'without putting anything of ourselves into it but what can apply indiscriminately to all objects.' " *La Littérature et le lecteur* (Paris, 1959), p. 57 (see also my review in *Archiv für das Studium der neueren Sprachen* 197 [1960], 223–35).

[7] [Jauss] Picon, *Introduction,* p. 34. This view of the dialogical mode of being of a literary work of art is found in Malraux (*Les voix du silence*) as well as in Picon, Nison, and Guitte—a tradition of literary aesthetics which is still alive in France and to which I am especially indebted; it finally goes back to a famous sentence in Valéry's poetics, "It is the execution of the poem which is the poem." [For a view of the dialogical see Bakhtin (above, page 912)].

[8] [Jauss] Peter Szondi, "Über philologische Erkenntnis," *Hölderlin-Studien* (Frankfurt a.M., 1967), rightly sees in this the decisive difference between literary and historical studies, p. 11: "No commentary, no stylistic examination of a poem should aim to give a description of the poem that could be taken by itself. Even the least critical reader will want to confront it with the poem and will not understand it until he has traced the claim back to the acts of knowledge whence they originated." Guitte says something very similar in "Eloge de la lecture" (see note 2).

[9] Chrétien de Troyes (1140?–1191), French poet.

occurring at about the same time.[10] It is not a "fact" that could be explained as caused by a series of situational preconditions and motives, by the intent of a historical action as it can be reconstructed, and by the necessary and secondary consequences of this deed. The historical context in which a literary work appears is not a factical, independent series of events that exists apart from an observer. *Perceval* becomes a literary event only for its reader, who reads this last work of Chrétien with a memory of his earlier works and who recognizes its individuality in comparison with these and other works that he already knows, so that he gains a new criterion for evaluating future works. In contrast to a political event, a literary event has no unavoidable consequences subsisting on their own that no succeeding generation can ever escape. A literary event can continue to have an effect only if those who come after it still or once again respond to it—if there are readers who again appropriate the past work or authors who want to imitate, outdo, or refute it. The coherence of literature as an event is primarily mediated in the horizon of expectations of the literary experience of contemporary and later readers, critics, and authors. Whether it is possible to comprehend and represent the history of literature in its unique historicity depends on whether this horizon of expectations can be objectified.

VII

Thesis 2. The analysis of the literary experience of the reader avoids the threatening pitfalls of psychology if it describes the reception and the influence of a work within the objectifiable system of expectations that arises for each work in the historical moment of its appearance, from a preunderstanding of the genre, from the form and themes of already familiar works, and from the opposition between poetic and practical language.

My thesis opposes a widespread skepticism that doubts whether an analysis of aesthetic influence can approach the meaning of a work of art at all or can produce, at best, more than a simple sociology of taste. René Wellek in particular directs such doubts against the literary theory of I. A. Richards.[11] Wellek argues that neither the individual state of consciousness, since it is momentary and only personal, nor a collective state of consciousness, as Jan Mukarovsky as-

sumes the effect a work of art to be, can be determined by empirical means.[12] Roman Jakobson wanted to replace the "collective state of consciousness" by a "collective ideology" in the form of a system of norms that exists for each literary work as *langue* and that is actualized as *parole* by the receiver—although incompletely and never as a whole.[13] This theory, it is true, limits the subjectivity of the influence, but it still leaves open the question of which data can be used to comprehend the influence of a particular work on a certain public and to incorporate it into a system of norms. In the meantime there are empirical means that had never been thought of before—literary data that allow one to ascertain a specific disposition of the audience for each work (a disposition that precedes the psychological reaction as well as the subjective understanding of the individual reader). As in the case of every actual experience, the first literary experience of a previously unknown work also demands a "foreknowledge which is an element of the experience itself, and on the basis of which anything new that we come across is available to experience at all, i.e., as it were readable in a context of experience."[14]

A literary work, even when it appears to be new, does not present itself as something absolutely new in an informational vacuum, but predisposes its audience to a very specific kind of reception by announcements, overt and covert signals, familiar characteristics, or implicit allusions. It awakens memories of that which was already read, brings the reader to a specific emotional attitude, and with its beginning arouses expectations for the "middle and end," which can then be maintained intact or altered, reoriented, or even fulfilled ironically in the course of the reading according to specific rules of the genre or type of text. The psychic process in the reception of a text is, in the primary horizon of aesthetic experience, by no means only an arbitrary series of merely subjective impressions, but rather the carrying out of specific instructions in a process of directed perception, which can be comprehended according to its constitutive motivations and triggering signals, and which also can be described by a textual linguistics. If, along with W. D. Stempel, one defines the initial horizon of expectations of a text as paradigmatic isotopy, which is transposed

---

[10] [Jauss] Note also J. Storost, "Das Problem der Literaturgeschichte," *Dante-Jahrbuch* 38 (1960), pp. 1–17, who simply equates the historical event with the literary event ("A work of art is first of all an artistic act hence historical like the Battle of Isos").

[11] I. A. Richards (above, page 856).

[12] [Jauss] René Wellek, "The Theory of Literary History," *Études dediées au quatrieme Congres de linguistes—Travaux du Cercle Linguistique de Prague* (1936), p. 179.

[13] [Jauss] In *Slovo a slovemost*, I, p. 192, cited by Wellek (1936), pp. 179ff.

[14] [Jauss] G. Buck, *Lernen und Erfabrung* (Stuttgart, 1967), p. 56, who refers here to Husserl [above, page 770] (*Erfabrung und Urteil*, esp. Sn. 8) but who more broadly goes beyond Husserl in a determination of the negativity in the process of experience that is of significance for the horizontal structure of aesthetic experience.

into an immanent syntagmatic horizon of expectations to the extent that the utterance grows, then the process of reception becomes describable in the expansion of a semiotic system that accomplishes itself between the development and the correction of a system.[15] A corresponding process of the continuous establishing and altering of horizons also determines the relationship of the individual text to the succession of texts that forms the genre. The new text evokes for the reader (listener) the horizon of expectations and rules familiar from earlier texts, which are then varied, corrected, altered, or even just reproduced. Variation and correction determine the scope, whereas alteration and reproduction determine the borders of a genre-structure.[16] The interpretative reception of a text always presupposes the context of experience of aesthetic perception: the question of the subjectivity of the interpretation and of the taste of different readers or levels of readers can be asked meaningfully only when one has first clarified which transsubjective horizon of understanding conditions the influence of the text.

The ideal cases of the objective capability of such literary-historical frames of reference are works that evoke the reader's horizon of expectations, formed by a convention of genre, style, or form, only in order to destroy it step by step—which by no means serves a critical purpose only, but can itself once again produce poetic effects. Thus Cervantes allows the horizon of expectations of the favorite old tales of knighthood to arise out of the reading of *Don Quixote,* which the adventure of his last knight then seriously parodies.[17] Thus Diderot, at the beginning of *Jacques le Fataliste,* evokes the horizon of expectations of the popular novelistic schema of the "journey" (with the fictive questions of the reader to the narrator) along with the (Aristotelian) convention of the romanesque fable and the providence unique to it, so that he can then provocatively oppose to the promised journey- and love-novel a completely unromanesque "vérité de l'histoire": the bizarre reality and moral casuistry of the enclosed stories in which the truth of life continually denies the mendacious character of poetic fiction.[18] Thus Nerval in the *Chimères*

cites, combines, and mixes a quintessence of well-known romantic and occult motifs to produce the horizon of expectations of a mythical metamorphosis of the world only in order to signify his renunciation of romantic poetry. The identifications and relationships of the mythic state that are familiar or disclosable to the reader dissolve into an unknown to the same degree as the attempted private myth of the lyrical "I" fails, the law of sufficient information is broken, and the obscurity that has become expressive itself gains a poetic function.[19]

There is also the possibility of objectifying the horizon of expectations in works that are historically less sharply delineated. For the specific disposition toward a particular work that the author anticipates from the audience can also be arrived at, even if explicit signals are lacking, through three generally presupposed factors: first, through familiar norms or the immanent poetics of the genre; second, through the implicit relationships to familiar works of the literary-historical surroundings; and third, through the opposition between fiction and reality, between the poetic and the practical function of language, which is always available to the reflective reader during the reading as a possibility of comparison. The third factor includes the possibility that the reader of a new work can perceive it within the narrower horizon of literary expectations, as well as within the wider horizon of experience of life. I shall return to this horizontal structure, and its ability to be objectified by means of the hermeneutics of question and answer, in the discussion of the relationship between literature and lived praxis (see XII).

VIII

Thesis 3. Reconstructed in this way, the horizon of expectations of a work allows one to determine its artistic character by the kind and the degree of its influence on a presupposed audience. If one characterizes as aesthetic distance the disparity between the given horizon of expectations and the appearance of a new work, whose reception can result in a "change of horizons" through negation of familiar experiences or through raising newly articulated experiences to the level of consciousness, then this aesthetic distance can be objectified historically along the spectrum of the audience's reactions and criticism's judgment (spontaneous success, rejection or shock, scattered approval, gradual or belated understanding).

---

[15] [Jauss] Wolf Dieter Stempel, "Pour une description de genres littéraires," in *Actes du XIIe Congres international de linguistique Romane* (Bucharest, 1968), also in *Beiträge zur Textlinguistik,* ed. W. D. Stempel (Munich, 1970).

[16] [Jauss] Here I can refer to my study, "Theory of Genres and Medieval Literature," Chapter 3, *Toward an Aesthetic of Reception.*

[17] Miguel de Cervantes (1547–1616), Spanish novelist and dramatist. [Jauss] According to the interpretation of H. J. Neuschafer, *Der Sinn der Parodie im Don Quijote,* Studia Romanica 5 (Heidelberg, 1963).

[18] Denis Diderot (above, page 383). [Jauss] According to the interpretation of Rainer Warning, *Illusion und Wirklichkeit in Tristram Shandy und Jacques le Fataliste,* Theorie und Geschichte der Literatur und der schönen Künste 4 (Munich, 1965), esp. pp. 80ff.

[19] [Jauss] According to the interpretation of Karl Heinz Stierle, *Dunkelheit und Form in Gérard de Nervals "Chimeres,"* Theorie und Geschichte der Literatur und der schönen Künste 5 (Munich, 1967), esp. pp. 55 and 91.

The way in which a literary work, at the historical moment of its appearance, satisfies, surpasses, disappoints, or refutes the expectations of its first audience obviously provides a criterion for the determination of its aesthetic value. The distance between the horizon of expectations and the work, between the familiarity of previous aesthetic experience and the "horizontal change"[20] demanded by the reception of the new work, determines the artistic character of a literary work, according to an aesthetics of reception: to the degree that this distance decreases, and no turn toward the horizon of yet-unknown experience is demanded of the receiving consciousness, the closer the work comes to the sphere of "culinary" or entertainment art [*Unterhaltungskunst*]. This latter work can be characterized by an aesthetics of reception as not demanding any horizonal change, but rather as precisely fulfilling the expectations prescribed by a ruling standard of taste, in that it satisfies the desire for the reproduction of the familiarly beautiful; confirms familiar sentiments; sanctions wishful notions; makes unusual experiences enjoyable as "sensations"; or even raises moral problems, but only to "solve" them in an edifying manner as predecided questions.[21] If, conversely, the artistic character of a work is to be measured by the aesthetic distance with which it opposes the expectations of its first audience, then it follows that this distance, at first experienced as a pleasing or alienating new perspective, can disappear for later readers, to the extent that the original negativity of the work has become self-evident and has itself entered into the horizon of future aesthetic experience, as a henceforth familiar expectation. The classical character of the so-called masterworks especially belongs to this second horizontal change;[22] their beautiful form that has become self-evident, and their seemingly unquestionable "eternal meaning" bring them,

according to an aesthetics of reception, dangerously close to the irresistibly convincing and enjoyable "culinary" art, so that it requires a special effort to read them "against the grain" of the accustomed experience to catch sight of their artistic character once again (see section X).

The relationship between literature and audience includes more than the facts that every work has its own specific, historically and sociologically determinable audience, that every writer is dependent on the milieu, views, and ideology of his audience, and that literary success presupposes a book "which expresses what the group expects, a book which presents the group with its own image."[23] This objectivist determination of literary success according to the congruence of the work's intention with the expectations of a social group always leads literary sociology into a dilemma whenever later or ongoing influence is to be explained. Thus R. Escarpit wants to presuppose a "collective basis in space or time" for the "illusion of the lasting quality" of a writer, which in the case of Molière[24] leads to an astonishing prognosis: "Molière is still young for the Frenchman of the twentieth century because his world still lives, and a sphere of culture, views, and language still binds us to him. . . . But the sphere becomes ever smaller, and Molière will age and die when the things which our culture still has in common with the France of Molière die" (p. 117). As if Molière had only mirrored the "mores of his time" and had only remained successful through this supposed intention! Where the congruence between work and social group does not exist, or no longer exists, as for example with the reception of a work in a foreign language, Escarpit is able to help himself by inserting a "myth" in between: "myths that are invented by a later world for which the reality that they substitute for has become alien" (p. 111). As if all reception beyond the first, socially determined audience for a work were only a "distorted echo," only a result of "subjective myths," and did not itself have its objective a priori once again in the received work as the limit and possibility of later understanding! The sociology of literature does not view its object dialectically enough when it determines the circle of author, work, and audience so one-sidedly.[25] The

---

[20] [Jauss] On this Husserlian concept see Buck, *Lernen und Erfahrung,* pp. 64ff.

[21] [Jauss] Here I am incorporating results of the discussion of "kitsch," as a borderline phenomenon of the aesthetic, which took place during the third colloquium of the research group "Poetic und Hermeneutic" (now in the volume *Die nicht mehr schönen Künste—Grenzphänomene des Ästhetischen,* ed. H. R. Jauss [Munich, 1968]). For the "culinary" approach, which presupposes mere entertainment art, the same thing holds as for kitsch, namely, that here the "demands of the consumer are *a priori* satisfied" (P. Beylin), that "the fulfilled expectation becomes the norm of the product" (Wolfgang Iser), or that "its work, without having or solving a problem, presents the appearance of a solution to a problem" (M. Imdahl), pp. 651–67.

[22] [Jauss] As also the epigonal; on this see Boris Tomaschevsky, in *Théorie de la littérature. Textes des formalistes russes,* ed. T. Todorov (Paris, 1965), p. 306, n. 53: "The appearance of a genius always equals a literary revolution which dethrones the dominant canon and gives power to processes subordinated until then. . . . The epigones repeat a worn-out combination of processes, and as original and revolutionary as it was, this combination becomes stereotypical and traditional. Thus then epigones kill, sometimes for a long time, the aptitude of their contemporaries to sense the aesthetic force of the examples they imitate: they discredit their masters."

[23] [Jauss] R. Escarpit, *Das Buch und der Leser: Entwurf einer Literatursoziologie* (Cologne and Opladen, 1961); first expanded German edition of *Sociologie de la littérature* [Paris, 1958], p. 116

[24] Jean Baptiste Poquelin (1622–1673), French dramatist.

[25] [Jauss] K. H. Bender, *König und Vasall: Untersuchungen zur Chanson de Geste des XII. Jahrhunderts,* Studia Romanica 13 (Heidelberg, 1967), shows what step is necessary to get beyond this one-sided determination. In this history of the early French epic, the apparent congruence of feudal society and epic ideality is represented as a process that is maintained through a continually changing discrepancy between "reality" and "ideology," that is, between the historical constellations of feudal conflicts and the poetic responses of the epics.

determination is reversible: there are works that at the moment of their appearance are not yet directed at any specific audience, but that break through the familiar horizon of literary expectations so completely that an audience can only gradually develop for them.[26] When, then, the new horizon of expectations has achieved more general currency, the power of the altered aesthetic norm can be demonstrated in that the audience experiences formerly successful works as outmoded, and withdraws its appreciation. Only in view of such horizontal change does the analysis of literary influence achieve the dimension of a literary history of readers,[27] and do the statistical curves of the bestsellers provide historical knowledge.

A literary sensation from the year 1857 may serve as an example. Alongside Flaubert's *Madame Bovary,*[28] which has since become world-famous, appeared his friend Feydeau's *Fanny,*[29] today forgotten. Although Flaubert's novel brought with it a trial for offending public morals, *Madame Bovary* was at first overshadowed by Feydeau's novel: *Fanny* went through thirteen editions in one year, achieving a success the likes of which Paris had not experienced since Chateaubriand's *Atala.*[30] Thematically considered, both novels met the expectations of a new audience that—in Baudelaire's analysis—had foresworn all romanticism, and despised great as well as naive passions equally:[31] they treated a trivial subject, infidelity in a bourgeois and provincial milieu. Both authors understood how to give to the conventional, ossified triangular relationship a sensational twist that went beyond the expected details of the erotic scenes. They put the worn-out theme of jealousy in a new light by reversing the expected relationship between the three classic roles: Feydeau has the youthful lover of the *femme de trente ans* become jealous of his lover's husband despite his having already fulfilled his desires, and perishing over this agonizing situation; Flaubert gives the adulteries of the doctor's wife in the provinces—interpreted by Baudelaire as a sublime form of *dandysme*—the surprise ending that precisely the laughable figure of the cuckolded Charles Bovary takes on dignified traits at the end. In the official criticism of the time, one finds voices that reject *Fanny* as well as *Madame Bovary* as a product of the new school of *réalisme,* which they reproach for denying everything ideal and attacking the ideas on which the social order of the Second Empire was founded.[32] The audience's horizon of expectations in 1857, here only vaguely sketched in, which did not expect anything great from the novel after Balzac's death,[33] explains the different success of the two novels only when the question of the effect of their narrative form is posed. Flaubert's formal innovation, his principle of "impersonal narration" *(impassibilité)*—attacked by Barbey d'Aurevilly with the comparison that if a story-telling machine could be cast of English steel it would function no differently than Monsieur Flaubert[34]—must have shocked the same audience that was offered the provocative contents of *Fanny* in the inviting tone of a confessional novel. It could also find incorporated in Feydeau's descriptions the modish ideals and surpressed desires of a stylish level of society,[35] and could delight without restraint in the lascivious central scene which Fanny (without suspecting that her lover is watching from the balcony) seduces her husband—for the moral indignation was already diminished for them through the reaction of the unhappy witness. As *Madame Bovary,* however, became a worldwide success, when at first it was understood and appreciated as a turning-point in the history of the novel by only a small circle of connoisseurs, the

---

[26] [Jauss] The incomparably more promising literary sociology of Eric Auerbach brought these aspects to light in the variety of epoch-making breaks in the relationship between author and reader; for this see the evaluation of Fritz Schalk in his edition of Auerbach's *Gesammelte Aufsätze zur romanischen Philologie* (Bern and Munich, 1967), pp. 11ff.

[27] [Jauss] See Harald Wewinrich, "Für eine Literaturgeschichte des Lesers," *Merkur* 21 (November, 1967), an attempt arising from the same intent as mine, which, analogously, is the way that linguistics of the speaker, customary earlier, has been replaced by the linguists of the listener, argues for a methodological consideration of the perspective of the reader in literary history and thereby most happily supports my aims. Weinrich shows above all how the empirical methods of literary sociology can be supplemented by the linguistic and literary interpretation of the role of the reader implicit in the work.

[28] Gustave Flaubert (1821–1880), French novelist.

[29] Ernest Aimé Feydeau (1862–1921), French novelist.

[30] Francois René de Chateaubriand (1768–1648), French writer.

[31] [Jauss] In *"Madame Bovary* par Gustave Flaubert, Baudelaire, *Oeuvres completes,* Pléade ed. (Paris, 1951), p. 998: "The last years of Louis-Philippe witnessed the last explosions of a spirit still excitable by the play of the imagination; but the new novelist found himself faced with a completely worn-out society—worse than worn-out—stupified and gluttonous, with a horror only of fiction, and love only for possession."

[32] [Jauss] Cf. ibid., p. 999, as well as the accusation, speech for the defense, and verdict of the *Bovary* trial in Flaubert, *Oeuvres,* Pléade ed. (Paris, 1951), I, pp. 649–717, esp. p. 717; also about *Fanny,* E. Montégut, "Le roman intime de la littérature réaliste," *Revue des deux mondes* 18 (1858), pp. 196–213, esp. pp. 201 and 209ff.

[33] [Jauss] As Baudelaire declares, *Oeuvres completes,* p. 996: "for since the disappearance of Balzac . . . all curiosity relative to the novel has been pacified and put to rest."

[34] [Jauss] For these and other contemporary verdicts see H. R. Jauss, "Die beiden Fassungen von Flauberts *Education sentimentale,"* *Heidelberger Jahrbücher* 2 (1958), pp. 96–116, esp. p. 97.

[35] [Jauss] On this, see the excellent analysis by the contemporary critic E. Montégut (see note 32 above), who explains in detail why the dream-world and the figures in Feydeau's novel are typical for the audience in the neighborhoods "between the Bourse and the boulevard Montmartre" (p. 209) that needs an "alcool poétique," enjoys "seeing their vulgar adventures of yesterday, and their vulgar projects of tomorrow poeticized" (p. 210), and subscribes to an "idolatry of the material," by which Montégut understands the ingredients of the "dream factory" of 1858—"a sort of sanctimonious admiration, almost devout, for furniture, wallpaper, dress, escapes like a perfume of patchouli from each of its pages" (p. 201).

audience of novel-readers that was formed by it came to sanction the new canon of expectations; this canon made Feydeau's weaknesses—his flowery style, his modish effects, his lyrical-confessional cliches—unbearable, and allowed *Fanny* to fade into yesterday's bestseller.

IX

Thesis 4. The reconstruction of the horizon of expectations, in the face of which a work was created and received in the past, enables one on the other hand to pose questions that the text gave an answer to, and thereby to discover how the contemporary reader could have viewed and understood the work. This approach corrects the mostly unrecognized norms of a classicist or modernizing understanding of art, and avoids the circular recourse to a general "spirit of the age." It brings to view the hermeneutic difference between the former and the current understanding of a work; it raises to consciousness the history of its reception, which mediates both positions; and it thereby calls into question as a platonizing dogma of philological metaphysics the apparently self-evident claims that in the literary text, literature [Dichtung] is eternally present, and that its objective meaning, determined once and for all, is at all times immediately accessible to the interpreter.

The method of historical reception[36] is indispensable for the understanding of literature from the distant past. When the author of a work is unknown, his intent undeclared, and his relationship to sources and models only indirectly accessible, the philological question of how the text is "properly" —that is, "from its intention and time"—to be understood can best be answered if one foregrounds it against those works that the author explicitly or implicitly presupposed his contemporary audience to know. The creator of the oldest branches of the *Roman de Renart,* for example, assumes—as his prologue testifies—that his listeners know romances like the story of Troy and *Tristan,* heroic epics

(chansons de geste), and verse fables *(fabliaux),* and that they are therefore curious about the "unprecedented war between the two barons, Renart and Ysengrin," which is to overshadow everything already known. The works and genres that are evoked are then all ironically touched on in the course of the narrative. From this horizonal change one can probably also explain the public success, reaching far beyond France, of this rapidly famous work that for the first time took a position opposed to all the long-reigning heroic and courtly poetry.[37]

Philological research long misunderstood the originally satiric intention of the medieval *Reineke Fuchs* and, along with it, the ironic-didactic meaning of the analogy between animal and human natures, because ever since Jacob Grimm[38] it had remained trapped within the romantic notion of pure nature poetry and naive animal tales. Thus, to give yet a second example of modernizing norms, one could also rightly reproach French research into the epic since Bédier for living—unconsciously—by the criteria of Boileau's poetics,[39] and judging a nonclassical literature by the norms of simplicity, harmony of part and whole, probability, and still others.[40] The philological-critical method is obviously not protected by its historical objectivism from the interpreter who, supposedly bracketing himself, nonetheless raises his own aesthetic preconceptions to an unacknowledged norm and unreflectively modernizes the meaning of the past text. Whoever believes that the "timelessly true" meaning of a literary work must immediately, and simply through one's mere absorption in the text, disclose itself to the interpreter as if he had a standpoint outside of history and beyond all "errors" of his predecessors and of the historical reception—whoever believes this "conceals the involvement of the historical consciousness itself in the history of influence." He denies "those presuppositions—certainly not arbitrary but rather fundamental—that govern his own understanding," and can only feign an objectivity "that in truth depends upon the legitimacy of the questions asked."[41]

In *Truth and Method* Hans-Georg Gadamer, whose critique of historical objectivism I am assuming here, described the principle of the history of influence, which seeks to present the reality of history in understanding itself,[42] as

---

[36] [Jauss] Examples of this method, which not only follow the success, fame, and the influence of a writer through history but also examine the historical conditions and changes in understanding him, are rare. The following should be mentioned: G. F. Ford, *Dickens and His Readers* (Princeton, 1955); A. Nisin, *Les Oeuvres at les siecles* (Paris, 1960), which discusses "Virgil, Dante, et nous," Ronsard, Corneille, Racine; E. Lämmert, "Zur Wirkungsgeschichte Eichendorffs in Deutschland," *Festschrift für Richard Alewyn,* ed. H. Singer and B. von Wiese (Cologne and Graz, 1967). The methodological problem of the step from the influence to the reception of a work was indicated most sharply by F. Vodicka already in 1941 in his study "Die Problematik der Rezeption von Nerudas Werk" (now in *Struktur vývoje* Prague, 1969) with the question of the changes in the work that are realized in its successive aesthetic preceptions.

[37] [Jauss] See H. R. Jauss, *Untersuchungen zur mittelalterlichen Tierdichtung* (Tübingen, 1959), esp. chap. IV A and D.
[38] Jakob Grimm (1785–1863), German philologist, collector, and writer of fairy tales.
[39] Joseph Bédier (1864–1938), French medieval scholar; Nicolas Boileau-Despréaux (1636–1711), French poet and critic.
[40] [Jauss] A. Vinaver, "A la recherche d'une poétique médiévale," *Cahiers de Civilisation médiévale* 2 (1959), 1–16.
[41] [Jauss] Gadamer, *Wahrheit und Methode,* pp. 284, 285; Eng., p. 268.
[42] [Jauss] Ibid., p. 283; Eng., p. 267.

an application of the logic of question and answer to the historical tradition. In a continuation of Collingwood's thesis that "one can understand a text only when one has understood the question to which it is an answer,"[43] Gadamer demonstrates that the reconstructed question can no longer stand within its original horizon because this historical horizon is always already enveloped within the horizon of the present: "Understanding is always the process of the fusion of these horizons that we suppose to exist by themselves."[44] The historical question cannot exist for itself; it must merge with the question "that the tradition is for us."[45] One thereby solves the question with which René Wellek described the aporia of literary judgment: should the philologist evaluate a literary work according to the perspective of the past, the standpoint of the present, or the "verdict of the ages"?[46] The actual standards of a past could be so narrow that their use would only make poorer a work that in the history of its influence had unfolded a rich semantic potential. The aesthetic judgment of the present would favor a canon of works that correspond to modern taste, but would unjustly evaluate all other works only because their function in their time is no longer evident. And the history of influence itself, as instructive as it might be, is as "authority open to the same objections as the authority of the author's contemporaries."[47] Wellek's conclusion—that there is no possibility of avoiding our own judgment; one must only make this judgment as objective as possible in that one does what every scholar does, namely, "isolate the object"[48]—is no solution to the aporia, but rather a relapse into objectivism. The "verdict of the ages" on a literary work is more than merely "the accumulated judgment of other readers, critics, viewers, and even professors";[49] it is the successive unfolding of the potential for meaning that is embedded in a work and actualized in the stages of its historical reception as it discloses itself to understanding judgment, so long as this faculty achieves in a controlled fashion the "fusion of horizons" in the encounter with the tradition.

The agreement between my attempt to establish a possible literary history on the basis of an aesthetics of reception and H.-G. Gadamer's principle of the history of influence nonetheless reaches its limit where Gadamer would like to elevate the concept of the classical to the status of

prototype for all historical mediation of past with present. His definition, that "what we call 'classical' does not first require the overcoming of historical distance—for in its own constant mediation it achieves this overcoming,"[50] falls out of the relationship of question and answer that is constitutive of all historical tradition. If classical is "what says something to the present as if it were actually said to it,"[51] then for the classical text one would not first seek the question to which it gives an answer. Doesn't the classical, which "signifies itself and interprets itself,"[52] merely describe the result of what I called the "second horizontal change": the unquestioned, self-evident character of the so-called "masterwork," which conceals its original negativity within the retrospective horizon of an exemplary tradition, and which necessitates our regaining the "right horizon of questioning" once again in the face of the confirmed classicism? Even with the classical work, the receiving consciousness is not relieved of the task of recognizing the "tensional relationship between the text and the present."[53] The concept of the classical that interprets itself, taken over from Hegel, must lead to a reversal of the historical relationship of question and answer,[54] and contradicts the principle of the history of influence that understanding is "not merely a reproductive, but always a productive attitude as well."[55]

This contradiction is evidently conditioned by Gadamer's holding fast to a concept of classical art that is not capable of serving as a general foundation for an aesthetics of reception beyond the period of its origination, namely, that of humanism. It is the concept of *mimesis,* understood as "recognition," as Gadamer demonstrates in his ontological explanation of the experience of art: "What one actually experiences in a work of art and what one is directed toward is rather how true it is, that is, to what extent one knows and recognizes something and oneself."[56] This concept of art can be validated for the humanist period of art, but not for its preceding medieval period and not at all for its succeeding period of our modernity, in which the aesthetics of mimesis has lost its obligatory character, along with the substantialist metaphysics ("knowledge of essence") that founded it. The epistemological significance of art does not, however, come to an end with this period-change,

[43][Jauss] Ibid., p. 352; Eng., p. 333.
[44][Jauss] Ibid., p. 289; Eng. p. 273.
[45][Jauss] Ibid., p. 356; Eng. p. 337.
[46][Jauss] Wellek, 1936, p. 184; ibid., "The Concept of Evolution in Literary History," *Concepts of Criticism* (New Haven, 1963), pp. 17–20.
[47][Jauss] Ibid. p. 17.
[48][Jauss] Ibid.
[49][Jauss] Ibid.

[50][Jauss] *Wahrheit und Methode,* p. 274; Eng., p. 257.
[51][Jauss] Ibid.
[52][Jauss] Ibid.
[53][Jauss] Ibid., p. 290; Eng., p. 273.
[54][Jauss] This reversal becomes obvious in the chapter "Die Logik von Frage und Antwort" (ibid., pp. 351–60; Eng., pp. 333–41); see my "History of Art and Pragmatic History," Chapter 2 of *Toward an Aesthetic of Reception.*
[55][Jauss] Ibid., p. 280; Eng. p. 264.
[56][Jauss] Ibid., p. 109; Eng. p. 102.

whence it becomes evident that art was in no way bound to the classical function of recognition.[57] The work of art can also mediate knowledge that does not fit into the Platonic schema if it anticipates paths of future experience, imagines as-yet-untested models of perception and behavior, or contains an answer to newly posed questions.[58] It is precisely concerning this virtual significance and productive function in the process of experience that the history of the influence of literature is abbreviated when one gathers the mediation of past art and the present under the concept of the *classical*. If, according to Gadamer, the classical *itself* is supposed to achieve the overcoming of historical distance through its constant mediation, it must, as a perspective of the hypostatized tradition, displace the insight that classical art at the time of its production did not yet appear "classical": rather, it could open up new ways of seeing things and preform new experiences that only in historical distance—in the recognition of what is now familiar—give rise to the appearance that a timeless truth expresses itself in the work of art.

The influence of even the great literary works of the past can be compared neither with a self-mediating event nor with an emanation: the tradition of art also presupposes a dialogical relationship of the present to the past, according to which the past work can answer and "say something" to us only when the present observer has posed the question that draws it back out of its seclusion. When, in *Truth and Method,* understanding is conceived—analogous to Heidegger's[59] "event of being" [*Seinsgeschehen*]—as "the placing of oneself within a process of tradition in which past and present are constantly mediated,"[60] the "productive moment which lies in understanding"[61] must be shortchanged. This productive function of progressive understanding, which necessarily also includes criticizing the tradition and forgetting it, shall in the following sections establish the basis for the project of a literary history according to an aesthetics of reception. This project must consider the historicity of literature in a threefold manner: diachronically in the interrelationships of the reception of literary works (see X), synchronically in the frame of reference of literature of the same moment, as well as in the sequence of such frames (see XI), and finally in the relationship of the immanent literary development to the general process of history (see XII).

X

Thesis 5. The theory of the aesthetics of reception not only allows one to conceive the meaning and form of a literary work in the historical unfolding of its understanding. It also demands that one insert the individual work into its "literary series" to recognize its historical position and significance in the context of the experience of literature. In the step from a history of the reception of works to an eventful history of literature, the latter manifests itself as a process in which the passive reception is on the part of authors. Put another way, the next work can solve formal and moral problems left behind by the last work, and present new problems in turn.

How can the individual work, which positivistic literary history determined in a chronological series and thereby reduced to the status of a "fact," be brought back into its historical-sequential relationship and thereby once again be understood as an "event"? The theory of the Formalist school, as already mentioned, would solve this problem with its principle of "literary evolution," according to which the new work arises against the background of preceding or competing works, reaches the "high point" of a literary period as a successful form, is quickly reproduced and thereby increasingly automatized, until finally, when the next form has broken through, the former vegetates on as a used-up genre in the quotidian sphere of literature. If one were to analyze and describe a literary period according to this program—which to date has hardly been put into use[62]—one could expect a representation that would in various respects be superior to that of the conventional literary history. Instead of the works standing in closed series, themselves standing one after another and unconnected, at best framed by a sketch of general history—for example, the series of the works of an author, a particular school, or one kind of style, as well as the series of various genres—the Formalist method would relate the series to one another and *discover the evolutionary alternating relationship of functions and*

---

[57] [Jauss] See ibid., p. 110; Eng. p. 103.

[58] [Jauss] This also follows from Formalist aesthetics and especially from Viktor Shklovsky's theory of "deautomatization"; cf. Victor Erlich's summary, *Russian Formalism,* p. 76: "As the 'twisted, deliberately impeded form' interposes artificial obstacles between the perceiving subject and the object perceived, the chain of habitual association and of automatic responses is broken; thus, we become able to *see* things instead of merely *recognizing* them."

[59] Heidegger (above, page 1051).

[60] [Jauss] *Wahrheit und Methode,* p. 275; Eng. p. 258.

[61] [Jauss] Ibid., p. 280; Eng, p. 264.

[62] [Jauss] In the 1927 article, "Über literarische Evolution," by Jurij Tynjanov (in *Die literarischen Künstmittel und die Evolution in der Literatur,* pp. 37–60), this program is most pregnantly presented. It was only partially fulfilled—as Jurij Striedter informed me—in the treatment of problems of structural change in the history of literary genres, as for example in the volume *Russkaja poza,* Voprosy poetiki 8 (Leningrad, 19260, or J. Tynjanov, "Die Ode als rhetorische Gattung" (1922), now in *Texte der russischen Formalisten,* II, ed. J. Striedter (Munich, 1970).

forms.[63] The works that thereby stand out from, correspond to, or replace one another would appear as moments of a process that no longer needs to be construed as tending toward some end point, since as the *dialectical self-production of new forms* it requires no teleology. Seen in this way, the autonomous dynamics of literary evolution would furthermore eliminate the dilemma of the criteria of selection: the criterion here is the work as a new form in the literary series, and not the self-reproduction of worn-out forms, artistic devices, and genres, which pass into the background until at a new moment in the evolution they are made "perceptible" once again. Finally, in the Formalist project of a literary history that understands itself as "evolution" and—contrary to the usual sense of this term—excludes any directional course, the historical character of a work becomes synonymous with literature's historical character: the "evolutionary" significance and characteristics of a literary phenomenon presuppose innovation as the decisive feature, just as a work of art is perceived against the background of other works of art.[64]

The Formalist theory of "literary evolution" is certainly one of the most significant attempts at a renovation of literary history. The recognition that historical changes also occur within a system in the field of literature, the attempted functionalization of literary development, and, not least of all, the theory of automatization—these are achievements that are to be held onto, even if the one-sided canonization of change requires a correction. Criticism has already displayed the weaknesses of the Formalist theory of evolution: mere opposition or aesthetic variation does not suffice to explain the growth of literature; the question of the direction of change of literary forms remains unanswerable; innovation for itself does not alone make up artistic character; and the connection between literary evolution and social change does not vanish from the face of the earth through its mere negation.[65] My thesis XII responds to the last question; the problematic of the remaining questions demands that the descriptive literary theory of the Formalists be opened up, through an aesthetics of reception, to the dimension of historical experience that must also include the historical standpoint of the present observer, that is, the literary historian.

The description of literary evolution as a ceaseless struggle between the new and the old, or as the alternation of the canonization and automatization of forms reduces the historical character of literature to the one-dimensional actuality of its changes and limits historical understanding to their perception. The alterations in the literary series nonetheless only become a historical sequence when the opposition of the old and new form also allows one to recognize their specific mediation. This mediation, which includes the step from the old to the new form in the interaction of work and recipient (audience, critic, new producer) as well as that of past event and successive reception, can be methodologically grasped in the formal and substantial problem "that each work of art, as the horizon of the 'solutions' which are possible after it, poses and leaves behind."[66] The mere description of the altered structure and the new artistic devices of a work does not necessarily lead to this problem, nor, therefore, back to its function in the historical series. To determine this, that is, to recognize the problem left behind to which the new work in the historical series is the answer, the interpreter must bring his own experience into play, since the past horizon of old and new forms, problems and solutions, is only recognizable in its further mediation, within the present horizon of the received work. Literary history as "literary evolution" presupposes the historical process of aesthetic reception and production up to the observer's present as the condition for the mediation of all formal oppositions or "differential qualities" [*"Differenzqualitäten"*].[67]

Founding "literary evolution" on an aesthetics of reception thus not only returns its lost direction insofar as the standpoint of the literary historian becomes the vanishing point—but not the goal!—of the process. It also opens to view the temporal depths of literary experience, in that it allows one to recognize the variable distance between the actual and the virtual significance of a literary work. This means that the artistic character of a work, whose semantic potential Formalism reduces to innovation as the single criterion of value, must in no way always be immediately perceptible within the horizon of its first appearance, let alone that it could then also already be exhausted in the pure opposition between the old and the new form. The distance between the actual first perception of a work and its virtual

---

[63] [Jauss] J. Tynjanov, "Über literarische Evolution," p. 59.

[64] [Jauss] "A work of art will appear as a positive value when it regroups the structure of the preceding period, it will appear as a negative value if it takes over the structure without changing it." (Jan Mukarovský, cited by R. Wellek, 1963, pp. 48, 49).

[65] [Jauss] See V. Erlich, *Russian Formalism,* pp. 254–57, R. Wellek, 1963, pp. 48ff., and J. Striedter, *Texte der Russischen Formalisten,* I, Introduction, Sn X.

[66] [Jauss] Hans Blumenberg, in *Poetik und Hermeneutik* 3 (see note 21), p. 692.

[67] [Jauss] According to V. Erlich, *Russian Formalism,* p. 252, this concept meant three things to the Formalists: "on the level of the representation of reality, *Differenzqualität* stood for the 'divergence' from the actual, i. e., for creative deformation. On the level of language it meant a departure from current linguistic usage. Finally, on the place of literary dynamics, a . . . modification of the prevailing artistic norm."

significance, or, put another way, the resistance that the new work poses to the expectations of its first audience, can be so great that it requires a long process of reception to gather in that which was unexpected and unusable within the first horizon. It can thereby happen that a virtual significance of the work remains long unrecognized until the "literary evolution," through the actualization of a newer form, reaches the horizon that now for the first time allows one to find access to the understanding of the misunderstood older form. Thus the obscure lyrics of Mallarmé[68] and his school prepared the ground for the return to baroque poetry, long since unappreciated and therefore forgotten, and in particular for the philological reinterpretation and "rebirth" of Góngora.[69] One can line up the examples of how a new literary form can reopen access to forgotten literature. These include the so-called "renaissances"—so-called, because the word's meaning gives rise to the appearance of an automatic return, and often prevents one from recognizing that literary tradition can not transmit itself alone. That is, a literary past can return only when a new reception draws it back into the present, whether an altered aesthetic attitude willfully reaches back to reappropriate the past, or an unexpected light falls back on forgotten literature from the new moment of literary evolution, allowing something to be found that one previously could not have sought in it.[70]

The new is thus not only an *aesthetic* category. It is not absorbed into the factors of innovation, surprise, surpassing, rearrangement, or alienation, to which the Formalist theory assigned exclusive importance. The new also becomes a *historical* category when the diachronic analysis of literature is pushed further to ask which historical moments are really the ones that first make new that which is new in a literary phenomenon; to what degree this new element is already perceptible in the historical instant of its emergence; which distance, path, or detour of understanding were required for its realization in content; and whether the moment of its full actualization was so influential that it could alter the perspective on the old, and thereby the canonization of the literary past.[71] How the relationship of poetic theory to aes-

thetically productive praxis is represented in this light has already been discussed in another context.[72] The possibilities of the interaction between production and reception in the historical change of aesthetic attitudes are admittedly far from exhausted by these remarks. Here they should above all illustrate the dimension into which a diachronic view of literature leads when it would no longer be satisfied to consider a chronological series of literary facts as already the historical appearance of literature.

XI

Thesis 6. The achievements made in linguistics through the distinction and methodological interrelation of diachronic and synchronic analysis are the occasion for overcoming the diachronic perspective—previously the only one practiced—in literary history as well. If the perspective of the history of reception always bumps up against the functional connections between the understanding of new works and the significance of older ones when changes in aesthetic attitudes are considered, it must also be possible to take a synchronic cross-section of a moment in the development, to arrange the heterogeneous multiplicity of contemporaneous works in equivalent, opposing, and heirarchical structures, and thereby to discover an overarching system of relationships in the literature of a historical moment. From this the principle of representation of a new literary history could be developed, if further cross-sections diachronically before and after were so arranged as to articulate historically the change in literary structures in its epoch-making moments.

Siegfried Kracauer has most decisively questioned the primacy of the diachronic perspective in historiography. His study "Time and History"[73] disputes the claim of "General History" to render comprehensible events from all spheres of life within a homogeneous medium of chronological time as a unified process, consistent in each historical moment. This understanding of history, still standing under the influence of Hegel's concept of the "objective spirit," presupposes that everything that happens contemporaneously is equally informed by the significance of this moment, and it thereby conceals the actual noncontemporaneity of the con-

---

[68] Mallarmé (above, page 726).

[69] Góngora: a style named for Gongora y Argote (d. 1627), Spanish poet.

[70] [Jauss] For the first possibility the (antiromantic) reevaluation of Boileau and of the classical *contrainte* poetics by Gide and Valéry can be introduced; for the second, the belated discovery of Hölderlin's hymns or Novalis's concept of future poetry (on the latter see H. R. Jauss n *Romanische Forschungen* 77 [1965], pp. 174–83).

[71] [Jauss] Thus, since the reception of the "minor romantic" Nerval, whose *Chimeres* only attracted attention under the influence of Mallarmé, the canonized "major romantics" Lamartine, Vigny, Musset and a large part of the "rhetorical" lyrics of Victor Hugo have been increasingly forced into the background.

[72] [Jauss] *Poetik und Hermeneutik 2 (Immanente Ästhetik—Ästhetische Reflexion)*, ed. W. Iser (Munich, 1966), esp. 395–418.

[73] [Jauss] In *Zeugnisse—Theodor W. Adorno zum 60. Geburtstag* (Frankfurt a.M., 1963), pp. 50–64, and also in "General History and the Aesthetic Approach," *Poetik und Hermeneutik 3*. See *History: The Last Things Before the Last* (New York, 1969), esp. chap. 6: "Ahaseurus, or the Riddle of Time," pp. 139–63.

temporaneous.[74] For the multiplicity of events of one historical moment, which the universal historian believes can be understood as exponents of a unified content, are de facto moments of entirely different time-curves, conditioned by the laws of their "special history,"[75] as becomes immediately evident in the discrepancies of the various "histories" of the arts, law, economics, politics, and so forth: "The shaped times of the diverse areas overshadow the uniform flow of time. Any historical period must therefore be imagined as a mixture of events which emerge at different moments of their own time."[76]

It is not in question here whether this state of affairs presupposes a primary inconsistency to history, so that the consistency of general history always only arises retrospectively from the unifying viewpoint and representation of the historian; or whether the radical doubt concerning "historical reason," which Kracauer extends from the pluralism of chronological and morphological courses of time to the fundamental antinomy of the general and the particular in history, in fact proves that universal history is philosophically illegitimate today. For the sphere of literature in any case, one can say that Kracauer's insights into the "coexistence of the contemporaneous and non-contemporaneous,"[77] far from leading historical knowledge into an aporia, rather make apparent the necessity and possibility of discovering the historical dimension of literary phenomena in synchronic cross-sections. For it follows from these insights that the chronological fiction of the moment that informs all contemporaneous phenomena corresponds as little to the historicity of literature as does the morphological fiction of a homogeneous literary series, in which all phenomena in their sequential order only follow immanent laws. The purely diachronic perspective, however conclusively it might explain changes in, for example, the histories of genres according to the immanent logic of innovation and automatization, problem and solution, nonetheless only arrives at the properly historical dimension when it breaks through the morphological canon, to confront the work that is important in historical influence with the historically worn-out, conventional works of the genre, and at the same time does not ignore its relationship to the literary milieu in which it had to make its way alongside works of other genres.

The historicity of literature comes to light at the intersections of diachrony and synchrony. Thus it must also be possible to make the literary horizon of a specific historical moment comprehensible as that synchronic system in relation to which literature that appears contemporaneously could be received diachronically in relations of noncontemporaneity, and the work could be received as current or not, as modish, outdated, or perennial, as premature or belated.[78] For if, from the point of view of an aesthetics of production, literature that appears contemporaneously breaks down into a heterogeneous multiplicity of the noncontemporaneous, that is, of works informed by the various moments of the "shaped time" of their genre (as the seemingly present heavenly constellations move apart astronomically into points of the most different temporal distance), this multiplicity of literary phenomena nonetheless, when seen from the point of view of an aesthetics of reception, coalesces again for the audience that perceives them and relates them to one another as works of *its* present, in the unity of a common horizon of literary expectations, memories, and anticipations that establishes their significance.

Since each synchronic system must contain its past and its future as inseparable structural elements,[79] the synchronic cross-section of the literary production of a historical point in time necessarily implies further cross-sections that are diachronically before and after. Analogous to the history of language, constant and variable factors are thereby brought to light that can be localized as functions of a system. For literature as well is a kind of grammar or syntax, with relatively fixed relations of its own: the arrangement of the traditional and the uncanonized genres; modes

---

[74] [Jauss] "First, in identifying history as a process in chronological time, we tacitly assume that our knowledge of the moment at which an event emerges from the flow of time will help us to account for its appearance. The date of the event is a value-laden fact. Accordingly, all events in the history of a people, a nation, or a civilization that take place at a given moment are supposed to occur then and there for reasons bound up, somehow, with that moment. (Kracauer, *History*, p. 141).

[75] [Jauss] This concept goes back to H. Foccillon, *The Life of Forms in Art*, (New York, 1948), and G. Kubler, *The Shape of Time: Remarks on the History of Things* (New Haven, 1962).

[76] [Jauss] Kracauer, *History*, p. 53.

[77] [Jauss] *Poetik und Hermeneutik* 3, p. 569. The formula of "the contemporaneity of the different," with which F. Sengle, "Aufgaben de heutigen Literaturgeschichtsschreibung," 1964, pp. 247ff, refers to the same phenomenon, fails to grasp one dimension of the problem, which becomes evident in his belief that this difficulty of literary history can be solved by simply combining comparative methods and modern interpretation ("that is, carrying out comparative interpretation on a broader basis," p. 249).

[78] [Jauss] In 1960 Roman Jakobson also made this claim in a lecture that now constitutes chap. 11, "Linguistique et poétique," of his book, *Essais de linguistique générale* (Paris, 1963). Cf. p. 212: "Synchronic description envisages not only the literary production of a given period, but also that part of the literary tradition which has remained alive or been resuscitated in the period in question. . . . Historical poetics, exactly like the history of language, if it wants to be truly comprehensive, ought to be conceived as a superstructure built upon a series of successive synchronic descriptions."

[79] [Jauss] Jurij Tynjanov and Roman Jakobson, "Probleme der Literatur—und Sprachforschung" (1928), now in *Kursbuch* 5 (Frankfurt a.M., 1966), p. 75: "The history of the system itself represents another system. Pure synchrony now proves to be illusory; each synchronic system has its past and its future as inseparable structural elements of this system."

of expression, kinds of style, and rhetorical figures; contrasted with this arrangement is the much more variable realm of a semantics: the literary subjects, archetypes, symbols, and metaphors. One can therefore seek to erect for literary history an analogy to that which Hans Blumenberg has postulated for the history of philosophy, elucidating it through examples of the change in periods and, in particular, the successional relationship of Christian theology and philosophy, and grounding it in his historical logic of question and answer: a "formal system of the explanation of the world . . . , within which structure the reshufflings can be localized which make up the process-like character of history up to the radicality of period-changes."[80] Once the substantialist notion of a self-reproducing literary tradition has been overcome through a functional explanation of the processlike relationships of production and reception, it must also be possible to recognize behind the *transformation* of literary forms and contents those *reshufflings* in a literary system of world-understanding that make the horizontal change in the process of aesthetic experience comprehensible.

From these premises one could develop the principle of representation of a literary history that would neither have to follow the all too familiar high road of the traditional great books, not have to lose itself in the lowlands of the sum-total of all texts that can no longer be historically articulated. The problem of selecting that which is important for a new history of literature can be solved with the help of the synchronic perspective in a manner that has not yet been attempted: a horizontal change in the historical process of "literary evolution" need not be pursued only throughout the web of all the diachronic facts and filiations, but can also be established in the altered remains of the synchronic literary system and read out of further cross-sectional analyses. In principle, a representation of literature in the historical succession of such systems would be possible through a series of arbitrary points of intersection between diachrony and synchrony. The historical dimension of literature, its eventful continuity that is lost in traditionalism as in positivism, can meanwhile be recovered only if the literary historian finds points of intersection and brings works to light that articulate the processlike character of "literary evolution" in its moments formative of history as well as its caesurae between periods. But neither statistics nor the subjective willfulness of the literary historian decides on this historical articulation, but rather the history of influence: that "which

results from the event" and which from the perspective of the present constitutes the coherence of literature as the prehistory of its present manifestation.

XII

Thesis 7. The task of literary history is thus only completed when literary production is not only represented synchronically and diachronically in the succession of its systems, but also seen as "special history" in its own unique relationship to "general history." This relationship does not end with the fact that a typified, idealized, satiric, or utopian image of social existence can be found in the literature of all times. The social function of literature manifests itself in its genuine possibility only where the literary experience of the reader enters into the horizon of expectations of his lived praxis, preforms his understanding of the world, and thereby also has an effect on his social behavior.

The functional connection between literature and society is for the most part demonstrated in traditional literary sociology within the narrow boundaries of a method that has only superficially replaced the classical principle of *imitatio naturae* with the determination that literature is the representation of a pregiven reality, which therefore must elevate a concept of style conditioned by a particular period—the "realism" of the nineteenth century—to the status of the literary category par excellence. But even the literary "structuralism" now fashionable,[81] which appeals, often with dubious justification, to the archetypal criticism of Northrop Frye[82] or to the structural anthropology of Claude Lévi-Strauss,[83] still remains quite dependent on this basically classicist aesthetics of representation with its schematizations of "reflection" [*Wiederspiegelung*] and "typification." By interpreting the findings of linguistic and literary structuralism as archaic anthropological constants disguised in literary myths—which it not infrequently manages only with the help of an obvious allegorization of the text[84]—it reduces on the one hand historical existence to the structures of an original social nature, on the other hand literature to this nature's mythic or symbolic expression. But with this

---

[80] [Jauss] First in "Epochenschwelle und Rezeption," *Philosophische Rundschau* 6 (1958), pp. 101ff., most recently in *Die Legitimität der Neuzeit* (Frankfurt a.M., 1966); see esp. pp. 41ff.

[81] [Bahti] N.B. This was composed in 1967.

[82] Frye (above, page 1136).

[83] Lévi-Strauss (above, page 1119).

[84] [Jauss] Lévi-Strauss himself testifies to this involuntarily but extremely impressively in his attempt to "interpret" with the help of his structural method a linguistic description of Baudelaire's poem, "Les Chats," provided by Roman Jakobson. See *L'Homme* 2 (1962), pp. 5–21; Eng. in *Structuralism*, ed. Jacques Ehrmann (Garden City, N.Y., 1971), a reprint of *Yale French Studies* nos. 36–37 (1966).

viewpoint, it is precisely the eminently social, i.e., socially *formative* function of literature that is missed. Literary structuralism—as little as the Marxist and Formalist literary studies that came before it—does not inquire as to how literature "itself turns around to help inform . . . the idea of society which it presupposes" and has helped to inform the processlike character of history. With these words, Gerhard Hess formulated in his lecture on "The Image of Society in French Literature" (1954) the unsolved problem of a union of literary history and sociology, and then explained to what extent French literature, in the course of its modern development, could claim for itself to have first discovered certain law-governed characteristics of social existence.[85] To answer the question of the socially formative function of literature according to an aesthetics of reception exceeds the competence of the traditional aesthetics of representation. The attempt to close the gap between literary-historical and sociological research through the methods of an aesthetics of reception is made easier because the concept of the *horizon of expectations* that I introduced into literary-historical interpretation[86] also has played a role in the axiomatics of the social sciences since Karl Mannheim.[87] It likewise stands in the center of a methodological essay on "Natural Laws and Theoretical Systems" by Karl R. Popper, who would anchor the scientific formation of theory in the prescientific experience of lived praxis. Popper here develops the problem of observation from out of the presupposition of a "horizon of expectations," thereby offering a basis of comparison for my attempt to determine the specific achievement of literature in the general process of the formation of experience, and to delimit it vis-à-vis other forms of social behavior.[88]

According to Popper, progress in science has in common with prescientific experience the fact that each hypothesis, like each observation, always presupposes expectations, "namely those that constitute the horizon of expectations which first makes those observations significant and thereby grants them the status of observations."[89] For progress in science as for that in the experience of life, the most important moment is the "disappointment of

expectations": "It resembles the experience of a blind person, who runs into an obstacle and thereby experiences its existence. Through the falsification of our assumptions we actually make contact with 'reality.' The refutation of our errors is the positive experience that we gain from reality."[90] This model certainly does not sufficiently explain the process of the scientific formation of theory,[91] and yet it can well illustrate the "productive meaning of negative experience" in lived praxis,[92] as well as shed a clearer light upon the specific function of literature in social existence. For the reader is privileged above the (hypothetical) nonreader because the reader—to stay with Popper's image—does not first have to bump into a new obstacle to gain a new experience of reality. The experience of reading can liberate one from adaptations, prejudices, and predicaments of a lived praxis in that it compels one to a new perception of things. The horizon of expectations of literature distinguishes itself before the horizon of expectations of historical lived praxis in that it not only preserves actual experiences, but also anticipates unrealized possibility, broadens the limited space of social behavior for new desires, claims, and goals, and thereby opens paths of future experience.

The pre-orientation of our experience through the creative capability of literature rests not only on its artistic character, which by virtue of a new form helps one to break through the automatism of everyday perception. The new form of art is not only "perceived against the background of other art works and through association with them." In this famous sentence, which belongs to the core of the Formalist

---

[85] [Jauss] Now in *Gesellschaft—Literatur—Wissenschafty: Gesammelte Schriften 1938–1966*, eds. H. R. Jauss and C. Müller-Daehn (Munich, 1967), pp. 1–13, esp. pp. 2 and 4.

[86] [Jauss] First in *Untersuchungen zur mittelalterlichen Tierdichtung*, see pp. 153, 180, 225, 271; further in *Archiv für das Stadium der neuren Sprachen* 197 (1961), pp. 223–25.

[87] [Jauss] Karl Mannheim, *Mensch und Gesellschaft in Zeitalter des Umbaus* (Darmstadt, 1958), pp. 212ff.

[88] [Jauss] in *Theorie und Realität*, ed. H. Albert (Tübingen, 1964), pp. 87–102.

[89] [Jauss] Ibid., p. 91.

[90] [Jauss] Ibid., p. 102.

[91] [Jauss] Popper's example of the blind man does not distinguish between the two possibilities of a merely reactive behavior and an experimenting mode of action under specific hypotheses. If the second possibility characterizes reflected scientific behavior in distinction to the unreflected behavior in lived praxis, the researcher would be "creative" on his part, and thus to be placed above the "blind man" and more appropriately compared with the writer as a creator of new expectations.

[92] [Jauss] G. Buck, *Lernen und Erfahrung*, pp. 70ff.: "[Negative experience] has its instructive effect not only by causing us to revise the context of our subsequent experience so that the new fits into the corrected unity of an objective meaning. . . . Not only is the object of the experience differently represented, but the experiencing consciousness itself reverses itself. The work of negative experience is one of becoming conscious of oneself. What one becomes conscious of are the motifs which have been guiding experience and which have remained unquestioned in this guiding function. Negative experience thus has primarily the character of self-experience, which frees one for a qualitatively new kind of experience." From these premises Buck developed the concept of a hermeneutics, which, as a "relationship of lived praxis that is guided by the highest interest of lived praxis—the agent's self-information," legitimizes the specific experience of the so-called humanities [*Geisteswissenschaften*] in contrast to the empiricism of the natural sciences. See his "Bildung durch Wissenschaft," in *Wissenschaft, Bildung, und pädagogische Wirklichkeit* (Heidenhein, 1969), p. 24.

credo, Viktor Shklovsky[93] remains correct only insofar as he turns against the prejudice of classicist aesthetics that defines the beautiful as *harmony of form and content* and accordingly reduces the new form of the secondary function of giving shape to a pregiven content. The new form, however, does not appear just "in order to relieve the old form that already is no longer artistic." It also can make possible a new perception of things by preforming the content of a new experience first brought to light in the form of literature. The relationship between literature and reader can actualize itself in the sensorial realm as an incitement to aesthetic perception as well as in the ethical realm as a summons to moral reflection.[94] The new literary work is received and judged against the background of other works of art as well as against the background of the everyday experience of life. Its social function in the ethical realm is to be grasped according to an aesthetics of reception in the same modalities of question and answer, problem and solution, under which it enters into the horizon of its historical influence.

How a new aesthetic form can have moral consequences at the same time, or, put another way, how it can have the greatest conceivable impact on a moral question, is demonstrated in an impressive manner by the case of *Madame Bovary,* as reflected in the trial that was instituted against the author Flaubert after the prepublication of the work in the *Révue de Paris* in 1857. The new literary form that compelled Flaubert's audience to an unfamiliar perception of the "well-thumbed fable" was the principle of impersonal (or uninvolved) narration, in conjunction with the artistic device of the so-called *style indirect libre,* handled by Flaubert like a virtuoso and in a perspectively consequential manner. What is meant by this can be made clear with a quotation from the book, a description that the prosecuting attorney Pinard accused in his indictment as being immoral in the highest degree. In the novel it follows upon Emma's first "false step" and relates how she catches sight of herself in the mirror after her adultery:

> Seeing herself in the mirror she wondered at her face. Never had her eyes been so large, so black, or so deep. Something subtle spread about her being transfigured her.

She repeated: "I have a lover! a lover!", delighting at the idea as at that of a second puberty that had come to her. So at last she was going to possess those joys of love, that fever of happiness of which she had despaired. She was entering upon something marvelous where all would be passion, ecstasy, delirium.

The prosecuting attorney took the last sentences for an objective depiction that included the judgment of the narrator and was upset over the "glorification of adultery" which he held to be even much more dangerous and immoral than the false step itself.[95] Yet Flaubert's accuser thereby succumbed to an error, as the defense immediately demonstrated. For the incriminating sentences are not any objective statement of the narrator's to which the reader can attribute belief, but rather a subjective opinion of the character, who is thereby to be characterized in her feelings that are formed according to novels. The artistic device consists in bringing forth a mostly inward discourse of the represented character without the signals of direct discourse ("So I am at last going to possess") or indirect discourse ("She said to herself that she was therefore at last going to possess"), with the effect that the reader himself has to decide whether he should take the sentence for a true declaration or understand it as an opinion characteristic of this character. Indeed, Emma Bovary is "judged, simply through a plain description of her existence, out of her own feelings."[96] This result of a modern stylistic analysis agrees exactly with the counterargument of the defense attorney Sénard, who emphasized that the disillusion began for Emma already from the second day onward: "The dénouement for morality is found in each line of the book"[97] (only that Sénard himself could not yet name the artistic device that was not yet recorded at this time!). The consternating effect of the formal innovations of Flaubert's narrative style became evident in the trial: the impersonal form of narration not only compelled his readers to perceive things differently—"photographically exact," according to the judgment of the time—but at the same time thrust them into an alienating uncertainty of judgment. Since the new artistic

---

[93] Shklovsky (above, page 796).

[94] [Jauss] Juruj Strieter has pointed out that in the diaries and examples from the prose of Leo Tolstoy to which Shklovsky referred in his first explanation of the procedure of "alienation," the purely aesthetic aspect was still bound up with an epistemological and ethical aspect. "Shklovsky was interested—in contrast to Tolstoy—above all in the artistic 'procedure' and not in the question of its ethical presuppositions and effects." (*Poetic und Hermeneutik* 2, pp. 288ff.).

[95] [Jauss] Flaubert, *Oeuvres,* I. p. 657: "thus, as early as this first mistake, as early as this first fall, she glorified adultery, its poetry, its voluptuousness. Voilá, gentlemen, what for me is more dangerous, much more immoral than the fall itself!"

[96] [Jauss] Erich Auerbach, *Mimesis: Dargestellte Wirklichkeit in der abendländischen Literatur* (Bern, 1946), p. 430. Eng., *Mimesis: The Representation of Reality in Western Literature,* tr. Willard R. Trask (Princeton, 1953), p. 485.

[97] [Jauss] Flaubert, *Oeuvres,* I. p. 6734.

device broke through an old novelistic convention—the moral judgment of the represented characters that is always unequivocal and confirmed in the description—the novel was able to radicalize or to raise new questions of lived praxis, which during the proceedings caused the original occasion for the accusation—alleged lasciviousness—to recede wholly into the background. The question with which the defense went on its counterattack turned the reproach, that the novel provides nothing other than the "story of a provincial woman's adulteries," against the society: whether, then, the subtitle to *Madame Bovary* must not more properly read, "story of the education too often provided in the provinces."[98] But the question with which the prosecuting attorney's *réquisitoire*[99] reaches its peak is nonetheless not yet thereby answered: "Who can condemn that woman in the book? No one. Such is the conclusion. In the book there is not a character who can condemn her. If you find a wise character there, if you find a single principle there by virtue of which the adultery might be stigmatized, I am in error."[100]

If in the novel none of the represented characters could break the staff across Emma Bovary, and if no moral principle can be found valid in whose name she would be condemnable, then is not the ruling "public opinion" and its basis in "religious feeling" at once called into question along with the "principle of marital fidelity"? Before what court could the case of *Madame Bovary* be brought if the formerly valid social norms—public opinion, religious sentiment, public morals, good manners—are no longer sufficient to reach a verdict in this case?[101] These open and implicit questions by no means indicate an aesthetic lack of understanding and moral philistinism on the part of the prosecuting attorney. Rather, it is much more that in them the unsuspected influence of a new art form comes to be expressed, which through a new *manière de voir les choses* was able to jolt the reader of *Madame Bovary* out of the self-evident character of his moral judgment, and turned a predecided question of public morals back into an open problem. In the face of the vexation that Flaubert, thanks to the artistry of his impersonal style, did not offer any handhold with which to ban his novel on grounds of the author's immorality, the court to that extent acted consistently when it acquitted Flaubert as writer, but condemned the literary school that he was supposed to represent, but that in truth was the as yet unrecognized artistic device:

Whereas it is not permitted, under the pretext of portraying character and local color, to reproduce in their errors the facts, utterances and gestures of the characters whom the author's mission it is to portray; that a like system, applied to works of the spirit as well as to productions of the fine arts, leads to a realism which would be the negation of the beautiful and the good, and which, giving birth to works equally offensive to the eye and to the spirit, would commit continual offences against public morals and good manners.[102]

Thus a literary work with an unfamiliar aesthetic form can break through the expectations of its readers and at the same time confront them with a question, the solution to which remains lacking for them in the religiously or officially sanctioned morals. Instead of further examples, let one only recall here that it was not first Bertolt Brecht, but rather already the Enlightenment that proclaimed the competitive relationship between literature and canonized morals, as Friedrich Schiller not least of all bears witness to when he expressly claims for the bourgeois drama: "The laws of the stage begin where the sphere of worldly laws end."[103] But the literary work can also—and in the history of literature this possibility characterizes the latest period of our modernity—reverse the relationship of question and answer and in the medium of art confront the reader with a new, "opaque" reality that no longer allows itself to be understood from a pregiven horizon of expectations. Thus, for example, the latest genre of novels, the much-discussed *nouveau roman,* presents itself as a form of modern art that according to Edgar Wind's formulation, represents the paradoxical case "that the solution is given, but the problem is given up, so that the solution might be understood as a problem."[104] Here the reader is excluded from the situation of the immediate audience and put in the position of an uninitiated third party who in the face of a reality still without significance must himself find the questions that will decode for him the perception of the world and the interpersonal problem toward which the answer of the literature is directed.

It follows from all of this that the specific achievement of literature in social existence is to be sought exactly where

---

[98] [Jauss] Ibid., p. 670.
[99] Charge.
[100] [Jauss] Ibid., p. 666.
[101] [Jauss] Cf. ibid., pp. 666–67.

---

[102] [Jauss] Ibid., p. 717.
[103] [Jauss] "Die Schaubühne als eine moralische Anstalt betractet," in *Schiller's Sämtliche Werke,* Säkularaugabe, XI, p. 99. See also R. Koselleck, *Kritik und Krise* (Freiburg and Munich, 1959), pp. 82ff.
[104] [Jauss] "Zur Systematik der künstlerischen Probleme," *Jahrbuch für Ästhetik* (1925), p. 440; for the application of this principle to works of art of the present, see M. Imdahl, *Poetik und Hermeneutik* 3, pp. 493–505, 663–64.

literature is not absorbed into the function of a *representational* art. If one looks at the moments in history when literary works toppled the taboos of the ruling morals or offered the reader new solutions for the moral casuistry of his lived praxis, which thereafter could be sanctioned by the consensus of all readers in the society, then a still-little-studied area of research opens itself up to the literary historian. The gap between literature and history, between aesthetic and historical knowledge, can be bridged if literary history does not simply describe the process of general history in the reflection of its works one more time, but rather when it discovers in the course of "literary evolution" that properly *socially formative* function that belongs to literature as it competes with other arts and social forces in the emancipation of mankind from its natural, religious, and social bonds.

If it is worthwhile for the literary scholar to jump over his ahistorical shadow for the sake of this task, then it might well also provide an answer to the question: toward what end and with what right can one today still—or again—study literary history?

Roland Barthes

1915–1980

Structuralism is prominently associated in linguistics with Ferdinand de Saussure (above, page 786) and in anthropology with Claude Lévi-Strauss (above, page 1119). Among literary and cultural critics perhaps the most prominent name is Roland Barthes, who did much to popularize structuralist approaches, not only to literature but also to other things, from fashion to wrestling, regarded as "texts." To trace Barthes's career is to read the history of French criticism from structuralism and semiology into the post-structuralist era, the beginning of which is often identified with Jacques Derrida's (above, page 1203) critiques of Saussure and Lévi-Strauss in the sixties. In an early essay titled "The Structuralist Activity," Barthes set forth his version of structuralist principles, particularly the emphasis on function rather than substance. Objects as such, reduced to functions, are terms in sets of relations, thus emphasizing, after Saussure, difference or the relational "space" between objects rather than the objects themselves. In Barthes, emphasis is on the creative or "reconstructive" activity endlessly productive of meaning, meaning itself receding down the differential chain of signifiers.

In "The Death of the Author," reprinted below, Barthes proceeds to a poststructuralist view of the author, who is dissolved as an ego controlling the book or as the center of attention by means of which one interprets a text. Barthes sees a text's language controlling any sense of what an author is rather than the other way around. For this linguistically constituted and contained author, Barthes invents the depersonalizing term "scriptor." His privileging of the text over the author may be compared to Michel Foucault's treatment of the author (below, page 1260), written at about the same time. Both offer the notion that the author is a modern invention, just as Raymond Williams (below, page 1356) offers the notion that literature is a historical term.

Barthes's rejection of the author is part of a general attack on a previous biographically oriented French criticism. It is of interest to compare it with the American New Criticism's critique of authorial intention as a ground for interpretation (Wimsatt and Beardsley, above, page 1026), almost thirty years before.

Among Barthes's translated works are *Writing Degree Zero* (1953, tr. 1967); *Mythologies* (1957, tr. 1972); *On Racine* (1963, tr. 1964); *Elements of Semiology* (1964, tr. 1967); *Critical Essays* (1964, tr. 1972); *Criticism and Truth* (1966, tr. 1987); *Empire of Signs* (1970, tr. 1982); *S/Z* (1970, tr. 1974); *Sade, Fourier, Loyola* (1971, tr. 1976); *New Critical Essays* (1971, tr. 1976); *The Pleasure of the Text* (1973, tr. 1975); *Roland Barthes by Roland Barthes* (1975, tr. 1977); *A Lover's Discourse* (1977, tr. 1978); *Image-Music-Text* (tr. 1977); *Sollers Writer* (1979, tr. 1987); *The Grain of the Voice* (1981, tr. 1985); *The Responsibilities of Form* (1982, tr. 1985); and *The Rustle of Language* (1984, tr. 1986). See George B. Wasserman, *Roland Barthes* (1981); Annette Lavers, *Roland Barthes: Structuralism and After* (1982); Jonathan Culler, *Roland Barthes* (1983); Mary Bittner Wiseman, *The Ecstasies of Roland Barthes* (1989); Andrew Brown, *Roland Barthes: Figures of Writing* (1992); D. A. Miller, *Bringing Out Roland Barthes* (1992).

The Death of the Author

In his tale *Sarrasine*. Balzac,[1] speaking of a castrato disguised as a woman, writes this sentence: "She was Woman, with her sudden fears, her inexplicable whims, her instinctive fears, her meaningless bravado, her defiance, and her delicious delicacy of feeling." Who speaks in this way? Is it the hero of the tale, who would prefer not to recognize the castrato hidden beneath the "woman"? Is it Balzac the man, whose personal experience has provided him with a philosophy of Woman? Is it Balzac the author, professing certain "literary" ideas about femininity? Is it universal wisdom? Romantic psychology? We can never know, for the good reason that writing is the destruction of every voice, every origin. Writing is that neuter, that composite, that obliquity into which our subject flees, the black-and-white where all identity is lost, beginning with the very identity of the body that writes.

No doubt it has always been so: once a fact is *recounted*—for intransitive purposes, and no longer to act directly upon reality, i.e., exclusive of any function except that exercise of the symbol itself—this gap appears, the voice loses its origin, the author enters into his own death, writing begins. However, the affect of this phenomenon has been variable; in ethnographic societies, narrative is never assumed by a person but by a mediator, shaman, or reciter, whose "performance" (i.e., his mastery of the narrative code) can be admired, but never his "genius." The *author* is a modern character, no doubt produced by our society as it emerged from the Middle Ages, influenced by English empiricism, French rationalism, and the personal faith of the Reformation, thereby discovering the prestige of the individual, or, as we say more nobly, of the "human person." Hence, it is logical that in literary matters it should be positivism, crown and conclusion of capitalist ideology, which has granted the greatest importance to the author's "person." The *author* still reigns in manuals of literary history, in biographies of writers, magazine interviews, and in the very consciousness of literateurs eager to unite, by means of private journals, their person and their work; the image of literature to be found in contemporary culture is tyrannically centered on the author, his person, his history, his tastes, his passions; criticism still largely consists in saying that Baudelaire's oeuvre is the failure of the man Baudelaire, Van Gogh's is his madness, Tchaikovsky's his

vice: *explanation* of the work is still sought in the person of its producer, as if, through the more or less transparent allegory of fiction, it was always, ultimately, the voice of one and the same person, the *author,* which was transmitting his "confidences."[2]

Though the Author's empire is still very powerful (the new criticism has quite often merely consolidated it), we know that certain writers have already tried to subvert it. In France, Mallarmé,[3] no doubt the first, saw and foresaw in all its scope the necessity to substitute language itself for the subject hitherto supposed to be its owner; for Mallarmé, as for us, it is language which speaks, not the author; to write is to reach, through a preliminary impersonality—which we can at no moment identify with the realistic novelist's castrating "objectivity"—that point where not "I" but only language functions, "performs": Mallarmé's whole poetics consists in suppressing the author in favor of writing (and thereby restoring, as we shall see, the reader's place). Valéry,[4] entangled in a psychology of the ego, greatly edulcorated Mallarmean theory, but led by a preference for classicism to conform to the lessons of Rhetoric, he continued to cast the Author into doubt and derision, emphasized the linguistic and "accidental" nature of his activity, and throughout his prose works championed the essentially verbal condition of literature, as opposed to which any resort to the writer's interiority seemed to him pure superstition. Proust himself, despite the apparently psychological character of what is called his *analyses,* visibly undertook to blur by an extreme subtilization the relation of the writer and his characters: by making the narrator not the one who has seen or felt, or even the one who writes, but the one who *is going to write* (the young man of the novel—but, as a matter of fact, how old is he and *who* is he?—wants to write but cannot, and the novel ends when writing finally becomes possible). Proust has given modern writing its epic: by a radical reversal, instead of putting his life into his novel, as is so often said, he made his life itself a work of which his own book was the model, so that it is quite clear to us that it is not Charlus who imitates Montesquiou, but Montesquiou, in his anecdotal, historical reality, who is only a secondary, derived fragment of Charlus.[5] Finally Surrealism, to keep to this prehistory of modernity, could doubtless not attribute a sovereign place to language, since language is system, and what this movement sought was, romantically, a direct sub-

"The Death of the Author" first appeared in French in 1968. It is reprinted from *Image-Music-Text,* tr. Stephen Heath (New York: Hill and Wang, 1977).
[1] Honoré de Balzac (1799–1850), French novelist.

[2] Baudelaire (above, page 604); Vincent van Gogh (1853–1890), Dutch painter; Petr Ilich Tchaikovsky (1840–1983), Russian composer.
[3] Mallarmé (above, page 726).
[4] Valéry (above, page 818).
[5] Marcel Proust (1871–1922), French novelist; Baron de Charlus in *The Guermantes Way* is modeled on Count Robert de Montesquiou (1855–1951), French poet and aesthete.

version of the codes—an illusory subversion, moreover, for a code cannot be destroyed, only "flouted"; yet, by constantly striving to disappoint expected meanings (this was the famous surrealist "shock"), by urging the hand to write as fast as possible what the head was unaware of (this was automatic writing), by accepting the principle and the experiment of collective writing, Surrealism helped desacralize the image of the Author. Last, outside literature itself (in fact, such distinctions are becoming quite dated), linguistics furnishes the destruction of the Author with a precious analytic instrument, showing that the speech-act in its entirety is an "empty" process, which functions perfectly without its being necessary to "fill" it with the person of the interlocutors; linguistically, the author is nothing but the one who writes, just as *I* is nothing but the one who says *I:* language knows a "subject," not a "person," and this subject, empty outside of the very speech-act which defines it, suffices to "hold" language, i.e., to exhaust it.

The removal of the Author (with Brecht,[6] we might speak here of a veritable *distancing,* the Author diminishing like a figure at the far end of the literary stage) is not only a historical fact or an act of writing: it utterly transforms the modern text (or—which is the same thing—the text is henceforth produced and read so that the author absents himself from it at every level). Time, first of all, is no longer the same. The Author, when we believe in him, is always conceived as the past of his own book: book and author are voluntarily placed on one and the same line, distributed as a *before* and an *after:* the Author is supposed to *feed* the book, i.e., he lives before it, thinks, suffers, lives for it; he has the same relation of antecedence with his work that a father sustains with his child. Quite the contrary, the modern *scriptor* is born *at the same time* as his text; he is not furnished with a being which precedes or exceeds his writing, he is not the subject of which his book would be the predicate; there is no time other than that of the speech-act, and every text is written eternally *here* and *now.* This is because (or it follows that) *writing* can no longer designate an operation of recording, of observation, of representation, of "painting" (as the Classics used to say), but instead what the linguists, following Oxfordian philosophy,[7] call a performative, a rare verbal form (exclusively found in the first person and in the present), in which the speech-act has no other content (no other statement) than the act by which it is uttered: something like the *I declare* of kings or the *I sing* of the earliest poets; the modern *scriptor,* having buried the Author, can therefore no

longer believe, according to the pathos of his predecessors, that his hand is slower than his passion and that in consequence, making a law of necessity, he must emphasize this delay and endlessly "elaborate" his form; for him, on the contrary, his hand, detached from any voice, borne by a pure gesture of inscription (and not of expression), traces a field without origin—or at least with no origin but language itself, i.e., the very thing which ceaselessly calls any origin into question.

We know now that a text consists not of a line of words, releasing a single "theological" meaning (the "message" of the Author-God), but of a multi-dimensional space in which are married and contested several writings, none of which is original; the text is a fabric of quotations, resulting from a thousand sources of culture. Like Bouvard and Pécuchet,[8] those eternal copyists, at once sublime and comical, whose profound absurdity *precisely* designates the truth of writing, the writer can only imitate an ever anterior, never original gesture; his sole power is to mingle writings, to counter some by others, so as never to rely on just one; if he seeks to *express himself,* at least he knows that the interior "thing" he claims to "translate" is itself no more than a ready-made lexicon, whose words can be explained only through other words, and this ad infinitum; an adventure which exemplarily befell young Thomas De Quincey,[9] so versed in his Greek that in order to translate certain absolutely modern ideas and images into this dead language, Baudelaire[10] tells us, "he had a dictionary made for himself, one much more complex and extensive than the kind produced by the vulgar patience of purely literary themes" *(Les Paradis artificiels);* succeeding the Author, the *scriptor* no longer contains passions, moods, sentiments, impressions, but that immense dictionary from which he draws a writing which will be incessant: life merely imitates the book, and this book itself is but a tissue of signs, endless imitation, infinitely postponed.

Once the Author is distanced, the claim to "decipher" a text becomes entirely futile. To assign an Author to a text is to impose a brake on it, to furnish it with a final signified, to close writing. This conception is quite suited to criticism, which then undertakes the important task of discovering the Author (or his hypostases: society, history, the psyche, freedom) beneath the work: once the Author is found, the text is "explained," the critic has won; hence, it is hardly surprising that historically the Author's empire has been the

---

[6] Bertolt Brecht (1898–1956), German dramatist.
[7] Cf. J. L. Austin, *How to Do Things with Words* (1962).

[8] Characters in the novel of the same name by Gustave Flaubert (1821–1880), French novelist.
[9] Thomas De Quincey (1785–1859), English writer.
[10] Baudelaire (above, page 604).

Critic's as well, and also that (even new) criticism is today unsettled at the same time in the Author. In multiple writing, in effect, everything is to be *disentangled,* but nothing *deciphered,* structure can be followed, "threaded" (as we say of a run in a stocking) in all its reprises, all its stages, but there is no end to it, no bottom; the space of writing is to be traversed, not pierced; writing constantly posits meaning, but always in order to evaporate it: writing seeks a systematic exemption of meaning. Thereby, literature (it would be better, from now on, to say *writing*), by refusing to assign to the text (and to the world-as-text) a "secret," i.e., an ultimate meaning, liberates an activity we may call countertheological, properly revolutionary, for to refuse to halt meaning is finally to refuse God and his hypostases, reason, science, the law.

To return to Balzac's sentence. No one (i.e., no "person") says it: its source, its voice is not the true site of writing, it is reading. Another very specific example will help us here: recent investigations (J. P. Vernant[11]) have shed some light on the constitutively ambiguous nature of Greek tragedy, whose text is "woven" of words with double meanings, words which each character understands unilaterally (this perpetual misunderstanding is precisely what we call the "tragic"); there is, however, someone who understands each word in its duplicity, and further understands, one may say, the very deafness of the characters speaking in his presence; this "someone" is precisely the reader (or here the listener). Here we discern the total being of writing: a text consists of multiple writings, proceeding from several cultures and entering into dialogue, into parody, into contestation; but there is a site where this multiplicity is collected, and this site is not the author, as has hitherto been claimed, but the reader: the reader is the very space in which are inscribed, without any of them being lost, all the citations out of which a writing is made; the unity of a text is not in its origin but in its destination, but this destination can no longer be personal: the reader is a man without history, without biography, without psychology; he is only that *someone* who holds collected into one and the same field all of the traces from which writing is constituted. That is why it is absurd to hear the new writing condemned in the name of a humanism which hypocritically claims to champion the reader's rights. Classical criticism has never been concerned with the reader; for that criticism, there is no other man in literature than the one who writes. We are no longer so willing to be the dupes of such antiphrases, by which a society proudly recriminates in favor of precisely what it discards, ignores, muffles, or destroys; we know that in order to restore writing to its future, we must reverse the myth: the birth of the reader must be requited by the death of the Author.

---

[11] Jean Pierre Vernant (b. 1914), twentieth-century French critic.

Michel Foucault

1926–1984

Michel Foucault's earlier "archeological" studies dealt with institutional "practices that systematically form the objects of which they speak." In *Madness and Civilization* (1961), for example, he studied the asylum as a system and madness as it is discursively constituted. His early work revealed a connection to structuralism that he was quickly prepared to disavow, for he was not at all content with structuralism's ahistorical or synchronic emphasis. Neither was he content with the linguistic model, which dematerialized everything into relations of signifier and signified; but he seems to have displaced the emphasis on relations (or differences; see Saussure, above, page 786) to one on what he called power relations. He wished to probe beneath abstract systems to study where discursive practices are interwoven with social practices in the circulation of power. Structuralism he came to regard as a discursive practice related to power.

Foucault abandoned the notion of archeology and called his later investigations "genealogical," adopting the term from Friedrich Nietzsche's *Genealogy of Morals,* again rejecting the static, synchronic, and descriptive. Genealogy implies development and change, and Foucault's interests had always been nothing if not historical and concerned with events. In his later work, his principal interest became the ways in which power is diffused in systems of authority and how "effects of truth are produced within discourses which in themselves are neither true nor false." Truth, then, is the product of power relations and of the system in which power is distributed and flows. It changes as systems change. Power itself has no origin, but is a diffusion within the social system. Because part of the same historical process, the old epistemological subject (together with the object) is no longer of importance except as a historical development, it cannot be presumed as truth in any genealogical account. The term "subject," for Foucault, refers to someone "subject to someone else by control or dependence, and tied to his own identity by a conscience or self-knowledge."

The essay "What Is an Author?" was published a year after Roland Barthes's "The Death of the Author" (above, page 1256), but though it agrees about the author's disappearance, it treats the matter differently, raising numerous questions about authority. It is Foucault's aim to reduce the author to a "function of discourse," with the reservation that even the "author-function," as he calls it, is neither universal in discourse nor constant in nature when it exists. He imagines, once the traditional author is dispensed with, a whole new series of questions to be asked, if one looks not to the author but to the social fabric and the functions of discourse.

Foucault's work has been particularly influential in culture studies generally and in the New Historicism, where the circulation of power in specific historical moments has been a topic of study.

Books by Foucault available in English include *Madness and Civilization* (1961, tr. 1965); *The Birth of the Clinic* (1963, rev. 1972, tr. 1975); *The Order of Things* (1966, tr.

1970); *The Archeology of Knowledge* (1969, tr. 1972); *Discipline and Punish* (1975, tr. 1977); *The History of Sexuality* (1976, tr. 1978); *Language, Counter-Memory, Practice: Selected Essays and Interviews* (1977); and *Power/Knowledge* (1980). See Alan Sheridan, *Michel Foucault: The Will to Truth* (1980); Charles C. Lemert and Garth Gillan, *Michel Foucault: Social Theory and Transgression* (1982); Herbert L. Dreyfuss and Paul Robinow, *Michel Foucault: Beyond Structuralism and Hermeneutics* (1983); R. John Rajchman, *Michel Foucault, The Freedom of Philosophy* (1987); Michael Clark, *Michel Foucault: A Bibliography* (1983); Mark Poster, *Foucault, Marxism, and History* (1984); Gilles Deleuze, *Foucault* (1986, tr. 1988); David Carroll, *Paraesthetics, Foucault, Lyotard, Derrida* (1987); David R. Shumway, *Michel Foucault* (1989); Simon During, *Foucault and Literature: Towards a Genealogy of Writing* (1992); Rudi Visker, *Michel Foucault: Genealogy as Critique* (1995); Philip Barker, *Michel Foucault: An Introduction* (1998); Alison Leigh Brown, *On Foucault* (2000); Barry Smart, *Michel Foucault* (2002); Gary Shapiro, *Archeologies of Vision: Foucault and Nietzsche on Seeing and Saying* (2003).

What Is an Author?

In proposing this slightly odd question, I am conscious of the need for an explanation. To this day, the "author" remains an open question both with respect to its general function within discourse and in my own writings; that is, this question permits me to return to certain aspects of my own work which now appear ill-advised and misleading. In this regard, I wish to propose a necessary criticism and reevaluation.

For instance, my objective in *The Order of Things*[1] had been to analyse verbal clusters as discursive layers which fall outside the familiar categories of a book, a work, or an author. But while I considered "natural history," the "analysis of wealth," and "political economy" in general terms, I neglected a similar analysis of the author and his works; it is perhaps due to this omission that I employed the names of authors throughout this book in a naive and often crude fashion. I spoke of Buffon, Cuvier, Ricardo, and others as well, but failed to realize that I had allowed their names to function ambiguously.[2] This has proved an embarrassment to me in that my oversight has served to raise two pertinent objections.

It was argued that I had not properly described Buffon or his work and that my handling of Marx was pitifully inadequate in terms of the totality of his thought.[3] Although these objections were obviously justified, they ignored the task I had set myself: I had no intention of describing Buffon or Marx or of reproducing their statements or implicit meanings, but, simply stated, I wanted to locate the rules that formed a certain number of concepts and theoretical relationships in their works. In addition, it was argued that I had created monstrous families by bringing together names as disparate as Buffon and Linnaeus or in placing Cuvier next to Darwin in defiance of the most readily observable family resemblances and natural ties.[4] This objection also seems inappropriate since I had never tried to establish a genealogical table of exceptional individuals, nor was I concerned in forming an intellectual daguerreotype of the scholar or naturalist of the seventeenth and eighteenth century. In fact, I had no intention of forming any family, whether holy or perverse. On the contrary, I wanted to determine—a much more modest task—the functional conditions of specific discursive practices.

Then why did I use the names of authors in *The Order of Things?* Why not avoid their use altogether, or, short of that, why not define the manner in which they were used? These questions appear fully justified and I have tried to gauge their implications and consequences in a

---

"What Is an Author?" first appeared in the *Bulletin de la Société francaise de Philosophie* in 1969. It is reprinted from Foucault's *Language, Counter-Memory, Practice,* translated by Donald F. Bouchard and Sherry Simon, ed. Donald F. Bouchard (Ithaca: Cornell University Press, 1977).
[1] The book that first brought Foucault to prominence; original title, *Les mots et choses* (1966).
[2] Georges Buffon (1707–1788), French naturalist; Georges Cuvier (1769–1832), French naturalist; David Ricardo (1772–1823), English economist.

[3] Marx (above, page 607).
[4] Linnaeus (Karl von Linne, 1707–1778), Swedish botanist.

book that will appear shortly.[5] These questions have determined my effort to situate comprehensive discursive units, such as "natural history" or "political economy," and to establish the methods and instruments for delimiting, analyzing, and describing these unities. Nevertheless, as a privileged moment of individualization in the history of ideas, knowledge, and literature, or in the history of philosophy and science, the question of the author demands a more direct response. Even now, when we study the history of a concept, a literary genre, or a branch of philosophy, these concerns assume a relatively weak and secondary position in relation to the solid and fundamental role of an author and his works.

For the purposes of this paper, I will set aside a socio-historical analysis of the author as an individual and the numerous questions that deserve attention in this context: how the author was individualized in a culture such as ours; the status we have given the author, for instance, when we began our research into authenticity and attribution; the systems of valorization in which he was included; or the moment when the stories of heroes gave way to an author's biography; the conditions that fostered the formulation of the fundamental critical category of "the man and his work." For the time being, I wish to restrict myself to the singular relationship that holds between an author and a text, the manner in which a text apparently points to this figure who is outside and precedes it.

Beckett supplies a direction: "What matter who's speaking, someone said, what matter who's speaking."[6] In an indifference such as this we must recognize one of the fundamental ethical principles of contemporary writing. It is not simply "ethical" because it characterizes our way of speaking and writing, but because it stands as an immanent rule, endlessly adopted and yet never fully applied. As a principle, it dominates writing as an ongoing practice and slights our customary attention to the finished product. For the sake of illustration, we need only consider two of its major themes. First, the writing of our day has freed itself from the necessity of "expression"; it only refers to itself, yet it is not restricted to the confines of interiority. On the contrary, we recognize it in its exterior deployment. This reversal transforms writing into an interplay of signs, regulated less by the content it signifies than by the very nature of the signifier. Moreover, it implies an action that is always testing

the limits of its regularity, transgressing and reversing an order that it accepts and manipulates. Writing unfolds like a game that inevitably moves beyond its own rules and finally leaves them behind. Thus, the essential basis of this writing is not the exalted emotions related to the act of composition or the insertion of a subject into language. Rather, it is primarily concerned with creating an opening where the writing subject endlessly disappears.

The second theme is even more familiar: it is the kinship between writing and death. This relationship inverts the age-old conception of Greek narrative or epic, which was designed to guarantee the immortality of a hero. The hero accepted an early death because his life, consecrated and magnified by death, passed into immortality; and the narrative redeemed his acceptance of death. In a different sense, Arabic stories, and *The Arabian Nights* in particular, had as their motivation, their theme and pretext, this strategy for defeating death. Storytellers continued their narratives late into the night to forestall death and to delay the inevitable moment when everyone must fall silent. Scheherazade's story is a desperate inversion of murder; it is the effort, throughout all those nights, to exclude death from the circle of existence. This conception of a spoken or written narrative as a protection against death has been transformed by our culture. Writing is now linked to sacrifice and to the sacrifice of life itself; it is a voluntary obliteration of the self that does not require representation in books because it takes place in the everyday existence of the writer. Where a work had the duty of creating immortality, it now attains the right to kill, to become the murderer of its author. Flaubert, Proust, and Kafka[7] are obvious examples of this reversal. In addition, we find the link between writing and death manifested in the total effacement of the individual characteristics of the writer; the quibbling and confrontations that a writer generates between himself and his text cancel out the signs of his particular individuality. If we wish to know the writer in our day, it will be through the singularity of his absence and in his link to death, which has transformed him into a victim of his own writing. While all of this is familiar in philosophy, as in literary criticism, I am not certain that the consequences derived from the disappearance or death of the author have been fully explored or that the importance of this event has been appreciated. To be specific, it seems to me that the themes destined to replace the privileged position accorded the author have merely served to arrest the

[5][Bouchard and Simon] *The Archeology of Knowledge* tr. A. M. Sheridan Smith (London: Tavistock, 1972), was published in France in 1969; for discussion of the author, see esp. 92–96, 122.

[6][Bouchard and Simon] Samuel Beckett, *Texts for Nothing,* tr. Beckett (London: Calder and Boyars, 1974), p. 16.

[7]Gustave Flaubert (1821–1880), Marcel Proust (1871–1922), French novelists; Franz Kafka (1883–1924), Austrian novelist.

possibility of genuine change. Of these, I will examine two that seem particularly important.

To begin with, the thesis concerning a work. It has been understood that the task of criticism is not to reestablish the ties between an author and his work or to reconstitute an author's thought and experience through his works and, further, that criticism should concern itself with the structures of a work, its architectonic forms, which are studied for their intrinsic and internal relationships. Yet, what of a context that questions the concept of a work? What, in short, is the strange unit designated by the term, work? What is necessary to its composition, if a work is not something written by a person called an "author"? Difficulties arise on all sides if we raise the question in this way. If an individual is not an author, what are we to make of those things he has written or said, left among his papers or communicated to others? Is this not properly a work? What, for instance, were Sade's papers before he was consecrated as an author? Little more, perhaps, than rolls of paper on which he endlessly unravelled his fantasies while in prison.

Assuming that we are dealing with an author, is everything he wrote and said, everything he left behind, to be included in his work? This problem is both theoretical and practical. If we wish to publish the complete works of Nietzsche,[8] for example, where do we draw the line? Certainly, everything must be published, but can we agree on what "everything" means? We will, of course, include everything that Nietzsche himself published, along with the drafts of his work, his plans for aphorisms, his marginal notations and corrections. But what if, in a notebook filled with aphorisms, we find a reference, a reminder of an appointment, an address, or a laundry bill, should this be included in his works? Why not? These practical considerations are endless once we consider how a work can be extracted from the millions of traces left by an individual after his death. Plainly, we lack a theory to encompass the questions generated by a work and the empirical activity of those who naively undertake the publication of the complete works of an author often suffers from the absence of this framework. Yet more questions arise. Can we say that *The Arabian Nights,* and *Stromates* of Clement of Alexandria, or the *Lives* of Diogenes Laertes constitute works?[9] Such questions only begin to suggest the range of our difficulties, and, if some have found it convenient to bypass the individuality of the writer or his status as an author to concentrate on a work, they have

failed to appreciate the equally problematic nature of the word "work" and the unity it designates.

Another thesis has detained us from taking full measure of the author's disappearance. It avoids confronting the specific event that makes it possible and, in subtle ways, continues to preserve the existence of the author. This is the notion of *écriture.*[10] Strictly speaking, it should allow us not only to circumvent references to an author, but to situate his recent absence. The conception of *écriture,* as currently employed, is concerned with neither the act of writing nor the indications, as symptoms or signs within a text, of an author's meaning; rather, it stands for a remarkably profound attempt to elaborate the conditions of any text, both the conditions of its spatial dispersion and its temporal deployment.

It appears, however, that this concept, as currently employed, has merely transposed the empirical characteristics of an author to a transcendental anonymity. The extremely visible signs of the author's empirical activity are effaced to allow the play, in parallel or opposition, of religious and critical modes of characterization. In granting a primordial status to writing, do we not, in effect, simply reinscribe in transcendental terms the theological affirmation of its sacred origin or a critical belief in its creative nature? To say that writing, in terms of the particular history it made possible, is subjected to forgetfulness and repression, is this not to reintroduce in transcendental terms the religious principle of hidden meanings (which require interpretation) and the critical assumption of implicit significations, silent purposes, and obscure contents (which give rise to commentary)? Finally, is not the conception of writing as absence a transposition into transcendental terms of the religious belief in a fixed and continuous tradition or the aesthetic principle that proclaims the survival of the work as a kind of enigmatic supplement of the author beyond his own death?[11]

This conception of *écriture* sustains the privileges of the author through the safeguard of the a priori; the play of representations that formed a particular image of the author is extended within a gray neutrality. The disappearance of the author—since Mallarmé,[12] an event of our time—is held in check by the transcendental. Is it not necessary to draw a

---

[8] Nietzsche (above, page 686).

[9] *The Thousand and One Nights,* Arabic series of stories; Clement (d. c. 215), Greek theologian; Diogenes Laertius (third century), Greek biographer.

[10] [Bouchard and Simon] We have kept the French *écriture,* with its double reference to the act of writing and to the primordial (and metaphysical) nature of writing as an entity in itself, since it is the term that best identifies the program of Jacques Derrida. Like the theme of self-referential writing, it too builds on a theory of the sign and denotes writing as the interplay of presence and absence in that "signs represent the present in its absence."

[11] [Bouchard and Simon] On "supplement" see Jacques Derrida, *Speech and Phenomena,* pp. 88–104. [Derrida, above, page 1203].

[12] Mallarmé (above, page 726).

line between those who believe that we can continue to situate our present discontinuities within the historical and transcendental tradition of the nineteenth century and those who are making a great effort to liberate themselves, once and for all, from this conceptual framework?

It is obviously insufficient to repeat empty slogans: the author has disappeared; God and man died a common death.[13] Rather, we should reexamine the empty space left by the author's disappearance; we should attentively observe, along its gaps and fault lines, its new demarcations, and the reapportionment of this void; we should await the fluid functions released by this disappearance. In this context we can briefly consider the problems that arise in the use of an author's name. What is the name of an author? How does it function? Far from offering a solution, I will attempt to indicate some of the difficulties related to these questions.

The name of an author poses all the problems related to the category of the proper name. (Here, I am referring to the work of John Searle,[14] among others.) Obviously not a pure and simple reference, the proper name (and the author's name as well) has other than indicative functions. It is more than a gesture, a finger pointed at someone; it is, to a certain extent, the equivalent of a description. When we say "Aristotle," we are using a word that means one or a series of definite descriptions of the type: "the author of the *Analytics*," or "the founder of ontology," and so forth.[15] Furthermore, a proper name has other functions than that of signification: when we discover that Rimbaud[16] has not written *La Chasse spirituelle,* we cannot maintain that the meaning of the proper name or this author's name has been altered. The proper name and the name of an author oscillate between the poles of description and designation, and, granting that they are linked to what they name, they are not totally determined either by their descriptive or designative functions.[17] Yet—and it is here that the specific difficulties attending an author's name appear—the link between a proper name and the individual being named and the link between an author's name and that which it names are not isomorphous and do not function in the same way; and these differences require clarification.

To learn, for example, that Pierre Dupont does not have blue eyes, does not live in Paris, and is not a doctor does not invalidate the fact that the name, Pierre Dupont, continues

to refer to the same person; there has been no modification of the designation that links the name to the person. With the name of an author, however, the problems are far more complex. The disclosure that Shakespeare was not born in the house that tourists now visit would not modify the functioning of the author's name, but, if it were proved that he had not written the sonnets that we attribute to him, this would constitute a significant change and affect the manner in which the author's name functions. Moreover, if we establish that Shakespeare wrote Bacon's[18] *Organon* and that the same author was responsible for both the works of Shakespeare and those of Bacon, we would have introduced a third type of alteration which completely modifies the functioning of the author's name. Consequently, the name of an author is not precisely a proper name among others.

Many other factors sustain this paradoxical singularity of the name of an author. It is altogether different to maintain that Pierre Dupont does not exist and that Homer or Hermes Trismegistus[19] have never existed. While the first negation merely implies that there is no one by the name of Pierre Dupont, the second indicates that several individuals have been referred to by one name or that the real author possessed none of the traits traditionally associated with Homer or Hermes. Neither is it the same thing to say that Jacques Durand, not Pierre Dupont, is the real name of X and that Stendhal's name was Henri Beyle.[20] We could also examine the function and meaning of such statements as "Bourbaki is this or that person," and "Victor Eremita, Climacus, Anticlimacus, Frater Taciturnus, Constantin Constantius, all of these are Kierkegaard."[21]

These differences indicate that an author's name is not simply an element of speech (as a subject, a complement, or an element that could be replaced by a pronoun or other parts of speech). Its presence is functional in that it serves as a means of classification. A name can group together a number of texts and thus differentiate them from others. A name also establishes different forms of relationships among texts. Neither Hermes nor Hippocrates[22] existed in the sense that we can say Balzac[23] existed, but the fact that a number of texts were attached to a single name implies that relationships of homogeneity, filiation, reciprocal explanation, authentification, or of common utilization were estab-

[13][Foucault] Nietzsche, *The Gay Science,* III, 108.

[14][Bouchard and Simon] John Searle, *Speech Acts: An Essay in the Philosophy of Language* (Cambridge: Cambridge University Press, 1969), pp. 162–74.

[15][Bouchard and Simon] *Speech Acts,* p. 169. [See also Russell (above, page 811).]

[16]Arthur Rimbaud (1854–1891), French poet.

[17][Bouchard and Simon] *Speech Acts,* p. 172.

[18]Bacon (above, page 234). Foucault here plays upon the frequently repeated conjecture that Bacon is the author of works attributed to Shakespeare.

[19]Hermes Trismegistus, fictitious author of the occult so-called *Corpus Hermeticum* of the early Christian era.

[20]Henri Beyle (Stendhal, 1783–1842), French novelist.

[21]Søren Kierkegaard (1813–1855), Danish philosopher and theologian. "Bourbaki" is the authorial designation for a celebrated series of mathematical treatises, written by many mathematicians whose biographical identities are meticulously concealed.

[22]Said to be a Greek physician of the fifth century B.C.

[23]Honoré de Balzac (1799–1850), French novelist.

lished among them. Finally, the author's name characterizes a particular manner of existence of discourse. Discourse that possesses an author's name is not to be immediately consumed and forgotten; neither is it accorded the momentary attention given to ordinary, fleeting words. Rather, its status and its manner of reception are regulated by the culture in which it circulates.

We can conclude that, unlike a proper name, which moves from the interior of a discourse to the real person outside who produced it, the name of the author remains at the contours of texts—separating one from the other, defining their form, and characterizing their mode of existence. It points to the existence of certain groups of discourse and refers to the status of this discourse within a society and culture. The author's name is not a function of a man's civil status, nor is it fictional; it is situated in the breach, among the discontinuities, which gives rise to new groups of discourse and their singular mode of existence. Consequently, we can say that in our culture, the name of an author is a variable that accompanies only certain texts to the exclusion of others: a private letter may have a signatory, but it does not have an author; a contract can have an underwriter, but not an author; and, similarly, an anonymous poster attached to a wall may have a writer, but he cannot be an author. In this sense, the function of an author is to characterize the existence, circulation, and operation of certain discourses within a society.

In dealing with the "author" as a function of discourse, we must consider the characteristics of a discourse that support this use and determine its difference from other discourses. If we limit our remarks to only those books or texts with authors, we can isolate four different features.

First, they are objects of appropriation; the form of property they have become is of a particular type whose legal codification was accomplished some years ago. It is important to notice, as well, that its status as property is historically secondary to the penal code controlling its appropriation. Speeches and books were assigned real authors, other than mythical or important religious figures, only when the author became subject to punishment and to the extent that his discourse was considered transgressive. In our culture—undoubtedly in others as well—discourse was not originally a thing, a product, or a possession, but an action situated in a bipolar field of sacred and profane, lawful and unlawful, religious and blasphemous. It was a gesture charged with risks long before it became a possession caught in a circuit of property values. But it was at the moment when a system of ownership and strict copyright rules were established (toward the end of the eighteenth and be-

ginning of the nineteenth century) that the transgressive properties always intrinsic to the act of writing became the forceful imperative of literature. It is as if the author, at the moment he was accepted into the social order of property which governs our culture, was compensating for his new status by reviving the older bipolar field of discourse in a systematic practice of transgression and by restoring the danger of writing which, on another side, had been conferred the benefits of property.

Secondly, the "author-function" is not universal or constant in all discourse. Even within our civilization, the same types of texts have not always required authors; there was a time when those texts which we now call "literary" (stories, folk tales, epics, and tragedies) were accepted, circulated, and valorized without any question about the identity of their author. Their anonymity was ignored because their real or supposed age was a sufficient guarantee of their authenticity. Texts, however, that we now call "scientific" (dealing with cosmology and the heavens, medicine or illness, the natural sciences or geography) were only considered truthful during the Middle Ages if the name of the author was indicated. Statements on the order of "Hippocrates said . . ." or "Pliny[24] tells us that . . ." were not merely formulas for an argument based on authority; they marked a proven discourse. In the seventeenth and eighteenth centuries, a totally new conception was developed when scientific texts were accepted on their own merits and positioned within an anonymous and coherent conceptual system of established truths and methods of verification. Authentification no longer required reference to the individual who had produced them; the role of the author disappeared as an index of truthfulness and, where it remained as an inventor's name, it was merely to denote a specific theorem or proposition, a strange effect, a property, a body, a group of elements, or pathological syndrome.

At the same time, however, "literary" discourse was acceptable only if it carried an author's name; every text of poetry or fiction was obliged to state its author and the date, place, and circumstance of its writing. The meaning and value attributed to the text depended on this information. If by accident or design a text was presented anonymously, every effort was made to locate its author. Literary anonymity was of interest only as a puzzle to be solved as, in our day, literary works are totally dominated by the sovereignty of the author. (Undoubtedly, these remarks are far too categorical. Criticism has been concerned for some time now with aspects of a text not fully dependent on the notion of an individual creator;

---

[24]Gaius Plinius Secundus (23–79).

studies of genre or the analysis of recurring textual motifs and their variations from a norm other than the author. Furthermore, where in mathematics the author has become little more than a handy reference for a particular theorem or group of propositions, the reference to an author in biology and medicine, or to the date of his research has a substantially different bearing. This latter reference, more than simply indicating the source of information, attests to the "reliability" of the evidence, since it entails an appreciation of the techniques and experimental materials available at a given time and in a particular laboratory.)

The third point concerning this "author-function" is that it is not formed spontaneously through the simple attribution of a discourse to an individual. It results from a complex operation whose purpose is to construct the rational entity we call an author. Undoubtedly, this construction is assigned a "realistic" dimension as we speak of an individual's "profundity" or "creative" power, his intentions or the original inspiration manifested in writing. Nevertheless, these aspects of an individual, which we designate as an author (or which comprise an individual as an author), are projections, in terms always more or less psychological, of our way of handling texts: in the comparisons we make, the traits we extract as pertinent, the continuities we assign, or the exclusions we practice. In addition, all these operations vary according to the period and the form of discourse concerned. A "philosopher" and a "poet" are not constructed in the same manner; and the author of an eighteenth-century novel was formed differently from the modern novelist. There are, nevertheless, transhistorical constants in the rules that govern the construction of an author.

In literary criticism, for example, the traditional methods for defining an author—or, rather, for determining the configuration of the author from existing texts—derive in large part from those used in the Christian tradition to authenticate (or to reject) the particular texts in its possession. Modern criticism, in its desire to "recover" the author from a work, employs devices strongly reminiscent of Christian exegesis when it wished to prove the value of a text by ascertaining the holiness of its author. In *De Viris Illustribus*, Saint Jerome[25] maintains that homonymy is not proof of the common authorship of several works, since many individuals could have the same name or someone could have perversely appropriated another's name. The name, as an individual mark, is not sufficient as it relates to a textual tradition. How, then, can several texts be attributed to an individual author? What norms, related to the function of the author, will disclose the involvement of several authors? According to Saint Jerome, there are four criteria: the texts that must be eliminated from the list of works attributed to a single author are those inferior to the others (thus, the author is defined as a standard level of quality); those whose ideas conflict with the doctrine expressed in the others (here the author is defined as a certain field of conceptual or theoretical coherence); those written in a different style and containing words and phrases not ordinarily found in the other works (the author is seen as a stylistic uniformity); and those referring to events or historical figures subsequent to the death of the author (the author is thus a definite historical figure in which a series of events converge). Although modern criticism does not appear to have these same suspicions concerning authentication, its strategies for defining the author present striking similarities. The author explains the presence of certain events within a text, as well as their transformations, distortions, and their various modifications (and this through an author's biography or by reference to his particular point of view, in the analysis of his social preferences and his position within a class or by delineating his fundamental objectives). The author also constitutes a principle of unity in writing where any unevenness of production is ascribed to changes caused by evolution, maturation, or outside influence. In addition, the author serves to neutralize the contradictions that are found in a series of texts. Governing this function is the belief that there must be—at a particular level of an author's thought, of his conscious or unconscious desire—a point where contradictions are resolved, where the incompatible elements can be shown to relate to one another or to cohere around a fundamental and originating contradiction. Finally, the author is a particular source of expression who, in more or less finished forms, is manifested equally well, and with similar validity, in a text, in letters, fragments, drafts, and so forth. Thus, even while Saint Jerome's four principles of authenticity might seem largely inadequate to modern critics, they, nevertheless, define the critical modalities now used to display the function of the author.

However, it would be false to consider the function of the author as a pure and simple reconstruction after the fact of a text given as passive material, since a text always bears a number of signs that refer to the author. Well known to grammarians, these textual signs are personal pronouns, adverbs of time and place, and the conjugation of verbs. But it is important to note that these elements have a different bearing on texts with an author and on those without one. In the latter, these "shifters" refer to a real speaker and to an actual deictic situation, with certain exceptions such as the case of indirect speech in the first person. When discourse is linked to an

---

[25] Saint Jerome (340?–420), church scholar.

author, however, the role of "shifters" is more complex and variable. It is well known that in a novel narrated in the first person, neither the first person pronoun, the present indicative tense, nor, for that matter, its signs of localization refer directly to the writer, either to the time when he wrote, or to the specific act of writing; rather, they stand for a "second self" whose similarity to the author is never fixed and undergoes considerable alteration within the course of a single book. It would be as false to seek the author in relation to the actual writer as to the fictional narrator; the "author-function" arises out of their scission—in the division and distance of the two. One might object that this phenomenon only applies to novels or poetry, to a context of "quasi-discourse," but, in fact, all discourse that supports this "author-function" is characterized by this plurality of egos. In a mathematical treatise, the ego who indicates the circumstances of composition in the preface is not identical, either in terms of his position or his function, to the "I" who concludes a demonstration within the body of the text. The former implies a unique individual who, at a given time and place, succeeded in completing a project, whereas the latter indicates an instance and plan of demonstration that anyone could perform provided the same set of axioms, preliminary operations, and an identical set of symbols were used. It is also possible to locate a third ego: one who speaks of the goals of his investigation, the obstacles encountered, its results, and the problems yet to be solved and this "I" would function in a field of existing or future mathematical discourses. We are not dealing with a system of dependencies where a first and essential use of the "I" is reduplicated, as a kind of fiction, by the other two. On the contrary, the "author-function" in such discourses operates so as to effect the simultaneous dispersion of the three egos.

Further elaboration would, of course, disclose other characteristics of the "author-function," but I have limited myself to the four that seemed the most obvious and important. They can be summarized in the following manner: the "author-function" is tied to the legal and institutional systems that circumscribe, determine, and articulate the realm of discourses; it does not operate in a uniform manner in all discourses, at all times, and in any given culture; it is not defined by the spontaneous attribution of a text to its creator, but through a series of precise and complex procedures; it does not refer, purely and simply, to an actual individual insofar as it simultaneously gives rise to a variety of egos and to a series of subjective positions that individuals of any class may come to occupy.

I am aware that until now I have kept my subject within unjustifiable limits; I should also have spoken of the "author-function" in painting, music, technical fields, and so forth.

Admitting that my analysis is restricted to the domain of discourse, it seems that I have given the term "author" an excessively narrow meaning. I have discussed the author only in the limited sense of a person to whom the production of a text, a book, or a work can be legitimately attributed. However, it is obvious that even within the realm of discourse a person can be the author of much more than a book—of a theory, for instance, of a tradition or a discipline within which new books and authors can proliferate. For convenience, we could say that such authors occupy a "transdiscursive" position.

Homer, Aristotle, and the Church Fathers played this role, as did the first mathematicians and the originators of the Hippocratic tradition. This type of author is surely as old as our civilization. But I believe that the nineteenth century in Europe produced a singular type of author who should not be confused with "great" literary authors, or the authors of canonical religious texts, and the founders of sciences. Somewhat arbitrarily, we might call them "initiators of discursive practices."

The distinctive contribution of these authors is that they produced not only their own work, but the possibility and the rules of formation of other texts. In this sense, their role differs entirely from that of a novelist, for example, who is basically never more than the author of his own text. Freud is not simply the author of *The Interpretation of Dreams* or of *Wit and its Relation to the Unconscious* and Marx is not simply the author of the *Communist Manifesto* or *Capital:* they both established the endless possibility of discourse. Obviously, an easy objection can be made. The author of a novel may be responsible for more than his own text; if he acquires some "importance" in the literary world, his influence can have significant ramifications. To take a very simple example, one could say that Ann Radcliffe did not simply write *The Mysteries of Udolpho* and a few other novels, but also made possible the appearance of Gothic Romances at the beginning of the nineteenth century.[26] To this extent, her function as an author exceeds the limits of her work. However, this objection can be answered by the fact that the possibilities disclosed by the initiators of discursive practices (using the examples of Marx and Freud, whom I believe to be the first and the most important) are significantly different from those suggested by novelists. The novels of Ann Radcliffe put into circulation a certain number of resemblances and analogies patterned on her work—various characteristic signs, figures, relationships, and structures that could be integrated into other books. In short, to say that Ann Radcliffe created the Gothic Romance means that

---

[26] Ann Radcliffe (1764–1823), English novelist.

there are certain elements common to her works and to the nineteenth-century Gothic romance: the heroine ruined by her own innocence, the secret fortress that functions as a counter-city, the outlaw-hero who swears revenge on the world that has cursed him, etc. On the other hand, Marx and Freud, as "initiators of discursive practices," not only made possible a certain number of analogies that could be adopted by future texts, but, as importantly, they also made possible a certain number of differences. They cleared a space for the introduction of elements other than their own, which, nevertheless, remain within the field of discourse they initiated. In saying that Freud founded psychoanalysis, we do not simply mean that the concept of libido or the techniques of dream analysis reappear in the writings of Karl Abraham or Melanie Klein,[27] but that he made possible a certain number of differences with respect to his books, concepts, and hypotheses, which all arise out of psychoanalytic discourse.

Is this not the case, however, with the founder of any new science or of any author who successfully transforms an existing science? After all, Galileo[28] is indirectly responsible for the texts of those who mechanically applied the laws he formulated, in addition to having paved the way for the production of statements far different from his own. If Cuvier is the founder of biology and Saussure of linguistics, it is not because they were imitated or that an organic concept or a theory of the sign was uncritically integrated into new texts, but because Cuvier, to a certain extent, made possible a theory of evolution diametrically opposed to his own system and because Saussure[29] made possible a generative grammar radically different from his own structural analysis. Superficially, then, the initiation of discursive practices appears similar to the founding of any scientific endeavor, but I believe there is a fundamental difference.

In a scientific program, the founding act is on an equal footing with its future transformations: it is merely one among the many modifications that it makes possible. This interdependence can take several forms. In the future development of a science, the founding act may appear as little more than a single instance of a more general phenomenon that has been discovered. It might be questioned, in retrospect, for being too intuitive or empirical and submitted to the rigors of new theoretical operations in order to situate it in a formal domain. Finally, it might be thought a hasty generalization whose validity should be restricted. In other words,

the founding act of a science can always be rechanneled through the machinery of transformations it has instituted.

On the other hand, the initiation of a discursive practice is heterogeneous to its ulterior transformations. To extend psychoanalytic practice, as initiated by Freud, is not to presume a formal generality that was not claimed at the outset; it is to explore a number of possible applications. To limit it is to isolate in the original texts a small set of propositions or statements that are recognized as having an inaugurative value and that mark other Freudian concepts or theories as derivative. Finally, there are no "false" statements in the work of these initiators; those statements considered inessential or "prehistoric," in that they are associated with another discourse, are simply neglected in favor of the more pertinent aspects of the work. The initiation of a discursive practice, unlike the founding of a science, overshadows and is necessarily detached from its later developments and transformations. As a consequence, we define the theoretical validity of a statement with respect to the work of the initiator, whereas in the case of Galileo or Newton, it is based on the structural and intrinsic norms established in cosmology or physics. Stated schematically, the work of these initiators is not situated in relation to a science or in the space it defines; rather, it is science or discursive practice that relate to their works as the primary points of reference.

In keeping with this distinction, we can understand why it is inevitable that practitioners of such discourses must "return to the origin." Here, as well, it is necessary to distinguish a "return" from scientific "rediscoveries" or "reactivations." "Rediscoveries" are the effects of analogy or isomorphism with current forms of knowledge that allow the perception of forgotten or obscured figures. For instance, Chomsky in his book on Cartesian grammar[30] "rediscovered" a form of knowledge that had been in use from Cordemoy to Humboldt.[31] It could only be understood from the perspective of generative grammar because this later manifestation held the key to its construction: in effect, a retrospective codification of an historical position. "Reactivation" refers to something quite different: the insertion of discourse into totally new domains of generalization, practice, and transformations. The history of mathematics abounds in examples of this phenomenon as the work of Michel Serres on mathematical anamnesis shows.[32]

[27] Karl Abraham (1877–1925), German psychoanalyst; Melanie Klein (1882–1960), English psychoanalyst.

[28] Galileo Galilei (1564–1642), Italian astronomer.

[29] Saussure (above, page 786); Foucault is alluding here to Noam Chomsky (b. 1928), American linguist and "initiator" of transformational-generative grammar.

[30] Chomsky (above, page 1166). [Bouchard and Simon] *Cartesian Linguistics* (New York: Harper & Row, 1966).

[31] Géraud de Cordemoy (1620–1684), French historian and philsosopher; Humboldt (above, page 523).

[32] [Bouchard and Simon] *La Communication: Hermes I* (Paris: Editions de Minuit, 1968), pp. 78–112.

The phrase, "return to," designates a movement with its proper specificity, which characterizes the initiation of discursive practices. If we return, it is because of a basic and constructive omission, an omission that is not the result of accident or incomprehension. In effect, the act of initiation is such, in its essence, that it is inevitably subjected to its own distortions; that which displays this act and derives from it is, at the same time, the root of its divergences and travesties. This nonaccidental omission must be regulated by precise operations that can be situated, analysed, and reduced in a return to the act of initiation. The barrier imposed by omission was not added from the outside; it arises from the discursive practice in question, which gives it its law. Both the cause of the barrier and the means for its removal, this omission—also responsible for the obstacles that prevent returning to the act of initiation—can only be resolved by a return. In addition, it is always a return to a text in itself, specifically, to a primary and unadorned text with particular attention to those things registered in the interstices of the text, its gaps and absences. We return to those empty spaces that have been masked by omission or concealed in a false and misleading plenitude. In these rediscoveries of an essential lack, we find the oscillation of two characteristic responses: "This point was made—you can't help seeing it if you know how to read"; or, inversely, "No, that point is not made in any of the printed words in the text, but it is expressed through the words, in their relationships and in the distance that separates them." It follows naturally that this return, which is a part of the discursive mechanism, constantly introduces modifications and that the return to a text is not a historical supplement that would come to fix itself upon the primary discursivity and redouble it in the form of an ornament which, after all, is not essential. Rather, it is an effective and necessary means of transforming discursive practice. A study of Galileo's works could alter our knowledge of the history, but not the science, of mechanics; whereas, a reexamination of the books of Freud or Marx can transform our understanding of psychoanalysis or Marxism.

A last feature of these returns is that they tend to reinforce the enigmatic link between an author and his works. A text has an inaugurative value precisely because it is the work of a particular author, and our returns are conditioned by this knowledge. The rediscovery of an unknown text by Newton or Cantor[33] will not modify classical cosmology or group theory; at most, it will change our appreciation of their historical genesis. Bringing to light, however, *An Out-*

line of Psychoanalysis, to the extent that we recognize it as a book by Freud, can transform not only our historical knowledge, but the field of psychoanalytic theory—if only through a shift of accent or of the center of gravity. These returns, an important component of discursive practices, form a relationship between "fundamental" and mediate authors, which is not identical to that which links an ordinary text to its immediate author.

These remarks concerning the initiation of discursive practices have been extremely schematic, especially with regard to the opposition I have tried to trace between this initiation and the founding of sciences. The distinction between the two is not readily discernible, moreover, there is no proof that the two procedures are mutually exclusive. My only purpose in setting up this opposition, however, was to show that the "author-function," sufficiently complex at the level of a book or a series of texts that bear a definite signature, has other determining factors when analysed in terms of larger entities—groups of works or entire disciplines.

Unfortunately, there is a decided absence of positive propositions in this essay, as it applies to analytic procedures or directions for future research, but I ought at least to give the reasons why I attach such importance to a continuation of this work. Developing a similar analysis could provide the basis for a typology of discourse. A typology of this sort cannot be adequately understood in relation to the grammatical features, formal structures, and objects of discourse, because there undoubtedly exist specific discursive properties or relationships that are irreducible to the rules of grammar and logic and to the laws that govern objects. These properties require investigation if we hope to distinguish the larger categories of discourse. The different forms of relationships (or nonrelationships) that an author can assume are evidently one of these discursive properties.

This form of investigation might also permit the introduction of an historical analysis of discourse. Perhaps the time has come to study not only the expressive value and formal transformations of discourse, but its mode of existence: the modifications and variations, within any culture, of modes of circulation, valorization, attribution, and appropriation. Partially at the expense of themes and concepts that an author places in his work, the "author-function" could also reveal the manner in which discourse is articulated on the basis of social relationships.

Is it not possible to reexamine, as a legitimate extension of this kind of analysis, the privileges of the subject? Clearly, in undertaking an internal and architectonic analysis of a work (whether it be a literary text, a philosophical

---

[33]Isaac Newton (1642–1727), English mathematician; Georg Cantor (1845–1918), German mathematician.

system, or a scientific work) and in delimiting psychological and biographical references, suspicions arise concerning the absolute nature and creative role of the subject. But the subject should not be entirely abandoned. It should be reconsidered, not to restore the theme of an originating subject, but to seize its functions, its intervention in discourse, and its system of dependencies. We should suspend the typical questions: how does a free subject penetrate the density of things and endow them with meaning; how does it accomplish its design by animating the rules of discourse from within? Rather, we should ask: under what conditions and through what forms can an entity like the subject appear in the order of discourse; what position does it occupy; what functions does it exhibit; and what rules does it follow in each type of discourse? In short, the subject (and its substitutes) must be stripped of its creative role and analysed as a complex and variable function of discourse.

The author—or what I have called the "author-function"—is undoubtedly only one of the possible specifications of the subject and, considering past historical transformations, it appears that the form, the complexity, and even the existence of this function are far from immutable. We can easily imagine a culture where discourse would circulate without any need for an author. Discourses, whatever their status, form, or value, and regardless of our manner of handling them, would unfold in a pervasive anonymity. No longer the tiresome repetitions:

"Who is the real author?"

"Have we proof of his authenticity and originality?"

"What has he revealed of his most profound self in his language?"

New questions will be heard:

"What are the modes of existence of this discourse?"

"Where does it come from; how is it circulated; who controls it?"

"What placements are determined for possible subjects?"

"Who can fulfill these diverse functions of the subject?"

Behind all these questions we would hear little more than the murmur of indifference:

"What matter who's speaking?"

Truth and Power

Could you briefly outline the route which led you from your work on madness in the Classical age to the study of criminality and delinquency?

When I was studying during the early 1950s, one of the great problems that arose was that of the political status of science and the ideological functions which it could serve. It wasn't exactly the Lysenko[1] business which dominated everything, but I believe that around the sordid affair—which had long remained buried and carefully hidden—a whole number of interesting questions were provoked. These can all be summed up in two words: power and knowledge. I believe I wrote *Madness and Civilisation* to some extent within the horizon of these questions. For me, it was a matter of saying this: if, concerning a science like theoretical physics or organic chemistry, one poses the problem of its relations with the political and economic structures of society, isn't one posing an excessively complicated question? Doesn't this set the threshold of possible explanations impossibly high? But on the other hand, if one takes a form of knowledge *(savior)* like psychiatry, won't the question be much easier to resolve, since the epistemological profile of psychiatry is a low one and psychiatric practice is linked with a whole range of institutions, economic requirements and political issues of social regulation? Couldn't the interweaving of effects of power and knowledge be grasped with greater certainty in the case of a science as 'dubious' as psychiatry? It was this same question which I wanted to pose concerning medicine in *The Birth of the Clinic*: medicine certainly has a much more solid scientific armature than psychiatry, but it too is profoundly enmeshed in social structures. What rather threw me at the time was the fact that the question I was posing totally failed to interest those to whom I addressed it. They regarded it as a problem which was politically unimportant and epistemologically vulgar.

I think there were three reasons for this. The first is that for Marxist intellectuals in France (and there they were playing the role prescribed for them by the PCF[2]) the

---

"Truth and Power," an interview with Alessandro Fontana and Pasquele Pasquino, originally appeared as "Intervista a Michel Foucault" in *Microfiseca del Potere* (Turin, 1977). It is translated by the interviewers. A shortened version appeared as "Vérité et Pouvoir" in *L'Arc* 70 (1977). It is reprinted here from *Power/Knowledge: Selected Interviews and Other Writings: 1972–1977*, ed. Colin Gordon (New York: Pantheon Books, 1977).
[1] T. D. Lysenko (1896–1976), Head of Soviet Institute of Genetics, rejected Mendel's theory of genetics.
[2] The French Communist Party.

problem consisted in gaining for themselves the recognition of the university institutions and establishment. Consequently they found it necessary to pose the same theoretical questions as the academic establishment, to deal with the same problems and topics: 'We may be Marxists, but for all that we are not strangers to your preoccupations, rather we are the only ones able to provide new solutions for your old concerns.' Marxism sought to win acceptance as a renewal of the liberal university tradition—just as, more broadly, during the same period the Communists presented themselves as the only people capable of taking over and reinvigorating the nationalist tradition. Hence, in the field we are concerned with here, it followed that they wanted to take up the 'noblest,' most academic problems in the history of the sciences: mathematics and physics, in short the themes valorised by Duhem, Husserl and Koyré.[3] Medicine and psychiatry didn't seem to them to be very noble or serious matters, nor to stand on the same level as the great forms of classical rationalism.

The second reason is that post-Stalinist Stalinism, by excluding from Marxist discourse everything that wasn't a frightened repetition of the already said, would not permit the broaching of uncharted domains. There were no ready-made concepts, no approved terms of vocabulary available for questions like the power-effects of psychiatry or the political function of medicine, whereas on the contrary innumerable exchanges between Marxists and academics, from Marx via Engels and Lenin down to the present, had nourished a whole tradition of discourse on 'science,' in the nineteenth-century sense of that term.[4] The price Marxists paid for their fidelity to the old positivism was a radical deafness to a whole series of questions posed by science.

Finally, there is perhaps a third reason, but I can't be absolutely sure that it played a part. I wonder nevertheless whether among intellectuals in or close to the PCF there wasn't a refusal to pose the problem of internment, of the political use of psychiatry and, in a more general sense, of the disciplinary grid of society. No doubt little was then known in 1955–60 of the real extent of the Gulag, but I believe that many sensed it, in any case many had a feeling that it was better not to talk about those things: it was a danger zone, marked by warning signs. Of course, it's difficult in retrospect to judge people's degree of awareness. But in any case, you well know how easily the Party leadership—which knew everything of course—could circulate

instructions preventing people from speaking about this or that, or precluding this or that line of research. At any rate, if the question of Pavlovian psychiatry[5] did get discussed among a few doctors close to the PCF, psychiatric politics and psychiatry as politics were hardly considered to be respectable topics.

What I myself tried to do in this domain was met with a great silence among the French Intellectual Left. And it was only around 1968, and in spite of the Marxist tradition and the PCF, that all these questions came to assume their political significance, with a sharpness that I had never envisaged, showing how timid and hesitant those early books of mine had still been. Without the political opening created during those years, I would surely never have had the courage to take up these problems again and pursue my research in the direction of penal theory, prisons and disciplines.

> So there is a certain 'discontinuity' in your theoretical trajectory. Incidentally, what do you think today about this concept of discontinuity, on the basis of which you have been all too rapidly and readily labelled as a 'structuralist' historian?

This business about discontinuity has always rather bewildered me. In the new edition of the *Petit Larousse* it says: 'Foucault: a philosopher who founds his theory of history on discontinuity.' That leaves me flabbergasted. No doubt I didn't make myself sufficiently clear in *The Order of Things,* though I said a good deal there about this question. It seemed to me that in certain empirical forms of knowledge like biology, political economy, psychiatry, medicine etc., the rhythm of transformation doesn't follow the smooth, continuist schemas of development which are normally accepted. The great biological image of a progressive maturation of science still underpins a good many historical analyses; it does not seem to me to be pertinent to history. In a science like medicine, for example, up to the end of the eighteenth century one has a certain type of discourse whose gradual transformation, within a period of twenty-five or thirty years, broke not only with the 'true' propositions which it had hitherto been possible to formulate but also, more profoundly, with the ways of speaking and seeing, the whole ensemble of practices which served as supports for medical knowledge. These are not simply new discoveries, there is a whole new 'régime' in discourse and forms of knowledge. And all this happens in the space of a

---

[3]Pierre Duhem (1861–1916), French scientist and cosmologist; Husserl (above, page 770); Alexandre Koyré (1892–1964), French philosopher and historian of science.
[4]Marx and Engels (above, page 607); V. I. Lenin (1870–1924), Russian revolutionary, premier of Soviet Union (1918–1924).

[5]Ivan Petrovich Pavlov (1849–1936), Russian physiologist and early behaviorist. Cf. Chomsky (above, page 1166).

few years. This is something which is undeniable, once one has looked at the texts with sufficient attention. My problem was not at all to say, '*Voilà,* long live discontinuity, we are in the discontinuous and a good thing too,' but to pose the question, 'How is it that at certain moments and in certain orders of knowledge, there are these sudden take-offs, these hastenings of evolution, these transformations which fail to correspond to the calm, continuist image that is normally accredited?' But the important thing here is not that such changes can be rapid and extensive, or rather it is that this extent and rapidity are only the sign of something else: a modification in the rules of formation of statements which are accepted as scientifically true. Thus it is not a change of content (refutation of old errors, recovery of old truths), nor is it a change of theoretical form (renewal of a paradigm, modification of systematic ensembles). It is a question of what *governs* statements, and the way in which they *govern* each other so as to constitute a set of propositions which are scientifically acceptable, and hence capable of being verified or falsified by scientific procedures.[6] In short, there is a problem of the régime, the politics of the scientific statement. At this level it's not so much a matter of knowing what external power imposes itself on science, as of what effects of power circulate among scientific statements, what constitutes, as it were, their internal régime of power, and how and why at certain moments that régime undergoes a global modification.

It was these different régimes that I tried to identify and describe in *The Order of Things,* all the while making it clear that I wasn't trying for the moment to explain them, and that it would be necessary to try and do this in a subsequent work. But what was lacking here was this problem of the 'discursive régime,' of the effects of power peculiar to the play of statements. I confused this too much with systematicity, theoretical form, or something like a paradigm. This same central problem of power, which at that time I had not yet properly isolated, emerges in two very different aspects at the point of junction of *Madness and Civilisation* and *The Order of Things.*

> We need, then, to locate the notion of discontinuity in its proper context. And perhaps there is another concept which is both more difficult and more central to your thought, the concept of an event. For in relation to the event a whole generation was long trapped in an *impasse,* in that following the works of ethnologists, some of them great ethnologists, a dichotomy was established

between structures (the *thinkable*) and the event considered as the site of the irrational, the unthinkable, that which doesn't and cannot enter into the mechanism and play of analysis, at least in the form which this took in structuralism. In a recent discussion published in the journal '*L'Homme,*' three eminent anthropologists posed this question once again about the concept of event, and said: the event is what always escapes our rational grasp, the domain of 'absolute contingency'; we are thinkers who analyse structures, history is no concern of ours, what could we be expected to have to say about it, and so forth. This opposition then between event and structure is the site and the product of a certain anthropology. I would say this has had devastating effects among historians who have finally reached the point of trying to dismiss the event and the '*évènementiel*' as an inferior order of history dealing with trivial facts, chance occurrences and so on. Whereas it is a fact that there are nodal problems in history which are neither a matter of trivial circumstances nor of those beautiful structures that are so orderly, intelligible and transparent to analysis. For instance, the 'great internment' which you described in *Madness and Civilisation* perhaps represents one of these nodes which elude the dichotomy of structure and event. Could you elaborate from our present standpoint on this renewal and reformulation of the concept of event?

One can agree that structuralism formed the most systematic effort to evacuate the concept of the event, not only from ethnology but from a whole series of other sciences and in the extreme case from history. In that sense, I don't see who could be more of an anti-structuralist than myself. But the important thing is to avoid trying to do for the event what was previously done with the concept of structure. It's not a matter of locating everything on one level, that of the event, but of realising that there are actually a whole order of levels of different types of events differing in amplitude, chronological breadth, and capacity to produce effects.

The problem is at once to distinguish among events, to differentiate the networks and levels to which they belong, and to reconstitute the lines along which they are connected and engender one another. From this follows a refusal of analyses couched in terms of the symbolic field or the domain of signifying structures, and a resource to analyses in terms of the genealogy of relations of force, strategic developments, and tactics. Here I believe one's point of reference

---

[6]See, in this context, Kuhn (below, page 1280).

should not be to the great model of language *(langue)* and signs, but to that of war and battle. The history which bears and determines us has the form of a war rather than that of a language: relations of power, not relations of meaning. History has no 'meaning,' though this is not to say that it is absurd or incoherent. On the contrary, it is intelligible and should be susceptible of analysis down to the smallest detail—but this in accordance with the intelligibility of struggles, of strategies and tactics. Neither the dialectic, as logic of contradictions, nor semiotics, as the structure of communication, can account for the intrinsic intelligibility of conflicts. 'Dialectic' is a way of evading the always open and hazardous reality of conflict by reducing it to a Hegelian[7] skeleton, and 'semiology' is a way of avoiding its violent, bloody and lethal character by reducing it to the calm Platonic form of language and dialogue.

> In the context of this problem of discursivity, I think one can be confident in saying that you were the first person to pose the question of power regarding discourse, and that at a time when analyses in terms of the concept or object of the 'text,' along with the accompanying methodology of semiology, structuralism, etc., were the prevailing fashion. Posing for discourse the question of power means basically to ask whom does discourse serve? It isn't so much a matter of analysing discourse into its unsaid, its implicit meaning, because (as you have often repeated) discourses are transparent, they need no interpretation, no one to assign them a meaning. If one reads 'texts' in a certain way, one perceives that they speak clearly to us and require no further supplementary sense or interpretation. This question of power that you have addressed to discourse naturally has particular effects and implications in relation to methodology and contemporary historical researches. Could you briefly situate within your work this question you have posed—if indeed it's true that you have posed it?

I don't think I was the first to pose the question. On the contrary, I'm struck by the difficulty I had in formulating it. When I think back now, I ask myself what else it was that I was talking about, in *Madness and Civilisation* or *The Birth of the Clinic,* but power? Yet I'm perfectly aware that I scarcely ever used the word and never had such a field of analyses at my disposal. I can say that this was an incapacity linked undoubtedly with the political situation we found ourselves in. It is hard to see where, either on the Right or the Left, this problem of power could then have been posed. On the Right, it was posed only in terms of constitution, sovereignty, etc., that is, in juridical terms; on the Marxist side, it was posed only in terms of the State apparatus.[8] The way power was exercised—concretely and in detail—with its specificity, its techniques and tactics, was something that no one attempted to ascertain; they contented themselves with denouncing it in a polemical and global fashion as it existed among the 'others,' in the adversary camp. Where Soviet socialist power was in question, its opponents called it totalitarianism; power in Western capitalism was denounced by the Marxists as class domination; but the mechanics of power in themselves were never analysed. This task could only begin after 1968, that is to say on the basis of daily struggles at grass roots level, among those whose fight was located in the fine meshes of the web of power. This was where the concrete nature of power became visible, along with the prospect that these analyses of power would prove fruitful in accounting for all that had hitherto remained outside the field of political analysis. To put it very simply, psychiatric internment, the mental normalisation of individuals, and penal institutions have no doubt a fairly limited importance if one is only looking for their economic significance. On the other hand, they are undoubtedly essential to the general functioning of the wheels of power. So long as the posing of the question of power was kept subordinate to the economic instance and the system of interests which this served, there was a tendency to regard these problems as of small importance.

> So a certain kind of Marxism and a certain kind of phenomenology constituted an objective obstacle to the formulation of this problematic?

Yes, if you like, to the extent that it's true that, in our student days, people of my generation were brought up on these two forms of analysis, one in terms of the constituent subject, the other in terms of the economic in the last instance, ideology and the play of superstructures and infrastructures.

> Still within this methodological context, how would you situate the genealogical approach? As a questioning of the conditions of possibility, modalities and constitution of the 'objects' and domains you have successively analysed, what makes it necessary?

---

[7]Hegel (above, page 552).

[8]See Althusser (below, page 1297).

I wanted to see how these problems of constitution could be resolved within a historical framework, instead of referring them back to a constituent object (madness, criminality or whatever). But this historical contextualisation needed to be something more than the simple relativisation of the phenomenological subject. I don't believe the problem can be solved by historicising the subject as posited by the phenomenologists, fabricating a subject that evolves through the course of history. One has to dispense with the constituent subject, to get rid of the subject itself, that's to say, to arrive at an analysis which can account for the constitution of the subject within a historical framework. And this is what I would call genealogy, that is, a form of history which can account for the constitution of knowledges, discourses, domains of objects etc., without having to make reference to a subject which is either transcendental in relation to the field of events or runs in its empty sameness throughout the course of history.

Marxist phenomenology and a certain kind of Marxism have clearly acted as a screen and an obstacle; there are two further concepts which continue today to act as a screen and an obstacle, ideology on the one hand and repression on the other.

All history comes to be thought of within these categories which serve to assign a meaning to such diverse phenomena as normalisation, sexuality and power. And regardless of whether these two concepts are explicitly utilised, in the end one always comes back, on the one hand to ideology—where it is easy to make the reference back to Marx—and on the other to repression, which is a concept often and readily employed by Freud throughout the course of his career. Hence I would like to put forward the following suggestion. Behind these concepts and among those who (properly or improperly) employ them, there is a kind of nostalgia; behind the concept of ideology, the nostalgia for a quasi-transparent form of knowledge, free from all error and illusion, and behind the concept of repression, the longing for a form of power innocent of all coercion, discipline and normalisation. On the one hand, a power without a bludgeon, and on the other hand knowledge without deception. You have called these two concepts, ideology and repression, negative, 'psychological,' insufficiently analytical. This is particularly the case in *Discipline and Punish* where, even if there isn't an extended discussion of these concepts, there is nevertheless a kind of analysis that allows one to go beyond the traditional forms of explanation and in-

telligibility which, in the last (and not only the last) instance rest on the concepts of ideology and repression. Could you perhaps use this occasion to specify more explicitly your thoughts on these matters? With *Discipline and Punish,* a kind of positive history seems to be emerging which is free of all the negativity and psychologism implicit in those two universal skeleton-keys.

The notion of ideology appears to me to be difficult to make use of, for three reasons. The first is that, like it or not, it always stands in virtual opposition to something else which is supposed to count as truth. Now I believe that the problem does not consist in drawing the line between that in a discourse which falls under the category of scientificity or truth, and that which comes under some other category, but in seeing historically how effects of truth are produced within discourses which in themselves are neither true nor false. The second drawback is that the concept of ideology refers, I think necessarily, to something of the order of a subject. Thirdly, ideology stands in a secondary position relative to something which functions as its infrastructure, as its material, economic determinant, etc. For these three reasons, I think that this is a notion that cannot be used without circumspection.

The notion of repression is a more insidious one, or at all events I myself have had much more trouble in freeing myself of it, in so far as it does indeed appear to correspond so well with a whole range of phenomena which belong among the effects of power. When I wrote *Madness and Civilisation,* I made at least an implicit use of this notion of repression. I think indeed that I was positing the existence of a sort of living, voluble and anxious madness which the mechanisms of power and psychiatry were supposed to have come to repress and reduce to silence. But it seems to me now that the notion of repression is quite inadequate for capturing what is precisely the productive aspect of power. In defining the effects of power as repression, one adopts a purely juridical conception of such power, one identifies power with a law which says no, power is taken above all as carrying the force of a prohibition. Now I believe that this is a wholly negative, narrow, skeletal conception of power, one which has been curiously widespread. If power were never anything but repressive, if it never did anything but to say no, do you really think one would be brought to obey it? What makes power hold good, what makes it accepted, is simply the fact that it doesn't only weigh on us as a force that says no, but that it traverse and produces things, it induces pleasure, forms knowledge, produces discourse. It needs to be considered as a productive network which runs through the whole social body, much more than as a negative instance whose function is repression. In *Discipline and Punish* what I wanted to show was how, from the seventeenth and eighteenth centuries onwards, there was a veritable technological take-off in the productivity of power. Not only did the monarches of the Classical period develop great state apparatuses (the army, the police and fiscal administration), but above all there was established at this period what one might call a new 'economy' of power, that is to say procedures which allowed the effects of power to circulate in a manner at once continuous, uninterrupted, adapted and 'individualised' throughout the entire social body. These new techniques are both much more efficient and much less wasteful (less costly economically, less risky in their results, less open to loopholes and resistances) than the techniques previously employed which were based on a mixture of more or less forced tolerances (from recognised privileges to endemic criminality) and costly ostentation (spectacular and discontinuous interventions of power, the most violent form of which was the 'exemplary,' because exceptional, punishment).

> Repression is a concept used above all in relation to sexuality. It was held that bourgeois society represses sexuality, stifles sexual desire, and so forth. And when one considers for example the campaign launched against masturbation in the eighteenth century, or the medical discourse on homosexuality in the second half of the nineteenth century, or discourse on sexuality in general, one does seem to be faced with a discourse of repression. In reality however this discourse serves to make possible a whole series of interventions, tactical and positive interventions of surveillance, circulation, control and so forth, which seem to have been intimately linked with techniques that give the appearance of repression, or are at least liable to be interpreted as such. I believe the crusade against masturbation is a typical example of this.

Certainly. It is customary to say that bourgeois society repressed infantile sexuality to the point where it refused even to speak of it or acknowledge its existence. It was necessary to wait until Freud for the discovery at last to be made that children have a sexuality. Now if you read all the books on pedagogy and child medicine—all the manuals for parents that were published in the eighteenth century—you find that children's sex is spoken of constantly and in every possible context. One might argue that the purpose of these discourses was precisely to prevent children from having a sex-

uality. But their *effect* was to din it into parents' heads that their children's sex constituted a fundamental problem in terms of their parental educational responsibilities, and to din it into children's heads that their relationship with their own body and their own sex was to be a fundamental problem as far as *they* were concerned; and this had the consequence of sexuality exciting the bodies of children while at the same time fixing the parental gaze and vigilance on the peril of infantile sexuality. The result was a sexualising of the infantile body, a sexualising of the bodily relationship between parent and child, a sexualising of the familial domain. 'Sexuality' is far more of a positive product of power than power was ever repression of sexuality. I believe that it is precisely these positive mechanisms that need to be investigated, and here one must free oneself of the juridical schematism of all previous characterisations of the nature of power. Hence a historical problem arises, namely that of discovering why the West has insisted for so long on seeing the power it exercises as juridical and negative rather than as technical and positive.

> Perhaps this is because it has always been thought that power is mediated through the forms prescribed in the great juridical and philosophical theories, and that there is a fundamental, immutable gulf between those who exercise power and those who undergo it.

I wonder if this isn't bound up with the institution of monarchy. This developed during the Middle Ages against the backdrop of the previously endemic struggles between feudal power agencies. The monarchy presented itself as a referee, a power capable of putting an end to war, violence and pillage and saying no to these struggles and private feuds. It made itself acceptable by allocating itself a juridical and negative function, albeit one whose limits it naturally began at once to overstep. Sovereign, law and prohibition formed a system of representation of power which was extended during the subsequent era by the theories of right: political theory has never ceased to be obsessed with the person of the sovereign. Such theories still continue today to busy themselves with the problem of sovereignty. What we need, however, is a political philosophy that isn't erected around the problem of sovereignty, nor therefore around the problems of law and prohibition. We need to cut off the King's head: in political theory that has still to be done.

> The King's head still hasn't been cut off, yet already people are trying to replace it by discipline, that vast system instituted in the seventeenth cen-

tury comprising the functions of surveillance, normalisation and control and, a little later, those of punishment, correction, education and so on. One wonders where this system comes from, why it emerges and what its use is. And today there is rather a tendency to attribute a subject to it, a great, molar, totalitarian subject, namely the modern State, constituted in the sixteenth and seventeenth centuries and bringing with it (according to the classical theories) the professional army, the police and the administrative bureaucracy.

To pose the problem in terms of the State means to continue posing it in terms of sovereign and sovereignty, that is to say in terms of law. If one describes all these phenomena of power as dependent on the State apparatus, this means grasping them as essentially repressive: the Army as a power of death, police and justice as punitive instances, etc. I don't want to say that the State isn't important; what I want to say is that relations of power, and hence the analysis that must be made of them, necessarily extend beyond the limits of the State. In two senses: first of all because the State, for all the omnipotence of its apparatuses, is far from being able to occupy the whole field of actual power relations, and further because the State can only operate on the basis of other, already existing power relations. The State is superstructural in relation to a whole series of power networks that invest the body, sexuality, the family, kinship, knowledge, technology and so forth. True, these networks stand in a conditioning-conditioned relationship to a kind of 'meta-power' which is structured essentially round a certain number of great prohibition functions; but this meta-power with its prohibitions can only take hold and secure its footing where it is rooted in a whole series of multiple and indefinite power relations that supply the necessary basis for the great negative forms of power. That is just what I was trying to make apparent in my book.

> Doesn't this open up the possibility of overcoming the dualism of political struggles that eternally feed on the opposition between the State on the one hand and Revolution on the other? Doesn't it indicate a wider field of conflicts than that of those where the adversary is the State?

I would say that the State consists in the codification of a whole number of power relations which render its functioning possible, and that Revolution is a different type of codification of the same relations. This implies that there are many different kinds of revolution, roughly speaking as

many kinds as there are possible subversive recodifications of power relations, and further that one can perfectly well conceive of revolutions which leave essentially untouched the power of relations which form the basis for the functioning of the State.

> You have said about power as an object of research that one has to invert Clausewitz's[9] formula so as to arrive at the idea that politics is the continuation of war by other means. Does the military model seem to you on the basis of your most recent researches to be the best one for describing power; is war here simply a metaphorical model, or is it the literal, regular, everyday mode of operation of power?

This is the problem I now find myself confronting. As soon as one endeavours to detach power with its techniques and procedures from the form of law within which it has been theoretically confined up until now, one is driven to ask this basic question: isn't power simply a form of warlike domination? Shouldn't one therefore conceive all problems of power in terms of relations of war? Isn't power a sort of generalised war which assumes at particular moments the forms of peace and the State? Peace would then be a form of war, and the State a means of waging it.

A whole range of problems emerge here. Who wages war against whom? Is it between two classes, or more? Is it a war of all against all? What is the role of the army and military institutions in this civil society where permanent war is waged? What is the relevance of concepts of tactics and strategy for analysing structures and political processes? What is the essence and mode of transformation of power relations? All these questions need to be explored. In any case it's astonishing to see how easily and self-evidently people talk of war-like relations of power or of class struggle without ever making it clear whether some form of war is meant, and if so what form.

> We have already talked about this disciplinary power whose effects, rules and mode of constitution you describe in *Discipline and Punish*. One might ask here, why surveillance? What is the use of surveillance? Now there is a phenomenon that emerges during the eighteenth century, namely the discovery of population as an object of scientific investigation; people begin to inquire into birth-rates, death-rates and changes in population

---

[9]Karl von Klausewitz (1780–1831), Prussian general and military writer.

and to say for the first time that it is impossible to govern a State without knowing its population. Moheau[10] for example, who was one of the first to organise this kind of research on an administrative basis, seems to see its goal as lying in the problems of political control of a population. Does this disciplinary power then act alone and of itself, or doesn't it rather draw support from something more general, namely this fixed conception of a population that reproduces itself in the proper way, composed of people who marry in the proper way and behave in the proper way, according to precisely determined norms? One would then have on the one hand a sort of global, molar body, the body of the population, together with a whole series of discourses concerning it, and then on the other hand and down below, the small bodies, the docile, individual bodies, the micro-bodies of discipline. Even if you are only perhaps at the beginning of your researches here, could you say how you see the nature of the relationships (if any) which are engendered between these different bodies: the molar body of the population and the micro-bodies of individuals?

Your question is exactly on target.[11] I find it difficult to reply because I am working on this problem right now. I believe one must keep in view the fact that along with all the fundamental technical inventions and discoveries of the seventeenth and eighteenth centuries, a new technology of the exercise of power also emerged which was probably even more important than the constitutional reforms and new forms of government established at the end of the eighteenth century. In the camp of the Left, one often hears people saying that power is that which abstracts, which negates the body, represses, suppresses, and so forth. I would say instead that what I find most striking about these new technologies of power introduced since the seventeenth and eighteenth centuries is their concrete and precise character, their grasp of a multiple and differentiated reality. In feudal societies power functioned essentially through signs and levies. Signs of loyalty to the feudal lords, rituals, ceremonies and so forth, and levies in the form of taxes, pillage, hunting, war etc. In the seventeenth and eighteenth centuries a form of power comes into being that begins to exercise itself through social production and social service. It be-

comes a matter of obtaining productive service from individuals in their concrete lives. And in consequence, a real and effective 'incorporation' of power was necessary, in the sense that power had to be able to gain access to the bodies of individuals, to their acts, attitudes and modes of everyday behaviour. Hence the significance of methods like school discipline, which succeeded in making children's bodies the object of highly complex systems of manipulation and conditioning. But at the same time, these new techniques of power needed to grapple with the phenomena of population, in short to undertake the administration, control and direction of the accumulation of men (the economic system that promotes the accumulation of capital and the system of power that ordains the accumulation of men are, from the seventeenth century on, correlated and inseparable phenomena): hence there arise the problems of demography, public health, hygiene, housing conditions, longevity and fertility. And I believe that the political significance of the problem of sex is due to the fact that sex is located at the point of intersection of the discipline of the body and the control of the population.

> Finally, a question you have been asked before: the work you do, these preoccupations of yours, the results you arrive at, what use can one finally make of all this in everyday political struggles? You have spoken previously of local struggles as the specific site of confrontation with power, outside and beyond all such global, general instances as parties or classes. What does this imply about the role of intellectuals? If one isn't an 'organic' intellectual acting as the spokesman for a global organisation, if one doesn't purport to function as the bringer, the master of truth, what position is the intellectual to assume?

For a long period, the 'left' intellectual spoke and was acknowledged the right of speaking in the capacity of master of truth and justice. He was heard, or purported to make himself heard, as the spokesman of the universal. To be an intellectual meant something like being the consciousness/conscience of us all. I think we have here an idea transposed from Marxism, from a faded Marxism indeed. Just as the proletariat, by the necessity of its historical situation, is the bearer of the universal (but its immediate, unreflected bearer, barely conscious of itself as such), so the intellectual, through his moral, theoretical and political choice, aspires to be the bearer of this universality in its conscious, elaborated form. The intellectual is thus taken as the clear, individual figure of a universality whose obscure, collective form is embodied in the proletariat.

---

[10]Moheau (fl. 1778), French writer on statistics.
[11][Fontana and Pasquino] Foucault's response to this final question was given in writing.

Some years have now passed since the intellectual was called upon to play this role. A new mode of the 'connection between theory and practice' has been established. Intellectuals have got used to working, not in the modality of the 'universal,' the 'exemplary,' the 'just-and-true-for-all,' but within specific sectors, at the precise points where their own conditions of life or work situate them (housing, the hospital, the asylum, the laboratory, the university, family and sexual relations). This has undoubtedly given them a much more immediate and concrete awareness of struggles. And they have met here with problems which are specific, 'non-universal,' and often different from those of the proletariat or the masses. And yet I believe intellectuals have actually been drawn closer to the proletariat and the masses, for two reasons. Firstly, because it has been a question of real, material, everyday struggles, and secondly because they have often been confronted, albeit in a different form, by the same adversary as the proletariat, namely the multinational corporations, the judicial and police apparatuses, the property speculators, etc. This is what I would call the 'specific' intellectual as opposed to the 'universal' intellectual.

This new configuration has a further political significance. It makes it possible, if not to integrate, at least to rearticulate categories which were previously kept separate. The intellectual *par excellence* used to be the writer: as a universal consciousness, a free subject, he was counterposed to those intellectuals who were merely *competent instances* in the service of the State or Capital—technicians, magistrates, teachers. Since the time when each individual's specific activity began to serve as the basis for politicisation, the threshold of *writing,* as the sacralising mark of the intellectual, has disappeared. And it has become possible to develop lateral connections across different forms of knowledge and from one focus of politicisation to another. Magistrates and psychiatrists, doctors and social workers, laboratory technicians and sociologists have become able to participate, both within their own fields and through mutual exchange and support, in a global process of politicisation of intellectuals. This process explains how, even as the writer tends to disappear as a figurehead, the university and the academic emerge, if not as principal elements, at least as 'exchangers,' privileged points of intersection. If the universities and education have become politically ultrasensitive areas, this is no doubt the reason why. And what is called the crisis of the universities should not be interpreted as a loss of power, but on the contrary as a multiplication and re-inforcement of their power-effects as centres in a polymorphous ensemble of intellectuals who virtually all pass through and relate themselves to the academic system. The whole relentless theorisation of writing which we saw in the 1960s was doubtless only a swansong. Through it, the writer was fighting for the preservation of his political privilege; but the fact that it was precisely a matter of theory, that he needed scientific credentials, founded in linguistics, semiology, psychoanalysis, that this theory took its references from the direction of Saussure, or Chomsky, etc., and that it gave rise to such mediocre literary products, all this proves that the activity of the writer was no longer at the focus of things.

It seems to me that this figure of the 'specific' intellectual has emerged since the Second World War. Perhaps it was the atomic scientist (in a word, or rather a name: Oppenheimer) who acted as the point of transition between the universal and the specific intellectual. It's because he had a direct and localised relation to scientific knowledge and institutions that the atomic scientist could make his intervention; but, since the nuclear threat affected the whole human race and the fate of the world, his discourse could at the same time be the discourse of the universal. Under the rubric of this protest, which concerned the entire world, the atomic expert brought into play his specific position in the order of knowledge. And for the first time, I think, the intellectual was hounded by political powers, no longer on account of a general discourse which he conducted, but because of the knowledge at his disposal: it was at this level that he constituted a political threat. I am only speaking here of Western intellectuals. What happened in the Soviet Union is analogous with this on a number of points, but different on many others. There is certainly a whole study that needs to be made of scientific dissidence in the West and the socialist countries since 1945.

It is possible to suppose that the 'universal' intellectual, as he functioned in the nineteenth and early twentieth centuries was in fact derived from a quite specific historical figure: the man of justice, the man of law, who counterposes to power, despotism and the abuses and arrogance of wealth the universality of justice and the equity of an ideal law. The great political struggles of the eighteenth century were fought over law, right, the constitution, the just in reason and law, that which can and must apply universally. What we call today 'the intellectual' (I mean the intellectual in the political, not the sociological sense of the word, in other words the person who utilises his knowledge, his competence and his relation to truth in the field of political struggles) was, I think, an offspring of the jurist, or at any rate of the man who invoked the universality of a just law, if necessary against the legal professions themselves (Voltaire,[12] in France, is the prototype of such intellectuals). The

---

[12]Francois Marie Arouet (1694–1778), French writer.

'universal' intellectual derives from the jurist or notable, and finds his fullest manifestation in the writer, the bearer of values and significations in which all can recognise themselves. The 'specific' intellectual derives from quite another figure, not the jurist or notable, but the savant or expert. I said just now that it's with the atomic scientists that this latter figure comes to the forefront. In fact, it was preparing in the wings for some time before, and was even present on at least a corner of the stage from about the end of the nineteenth century. No doubt it's with Darwin or rather with the post-Darwinian evolutionists that this figure begins to appear clearly. The stormy relationship between evolutionism and the socialists, as well as the highly ambiguous effects of evolutionism (on sociology, criminology, psychiatry and eugenics, for example) mark the important moment when the savant begins to intervene in contemporary political struggles in the name of a 'local' scientific truth—however important the latter may be. Historically, Darwin represents this point of inflection in the history of the Western intellectual. (Zola[13] is very significant from this point of view: he is the type of the 'universal' intellectual, bearer of law and militant of equity, but he ballasts his discourse with a whole invocation of nosology and evolutionism, which he believes to be scientific, grasps very poorly in any case, and whose political effects on his own discourse are very equivocal.) If one were to study this closely, one would have to follow how the physicists, at the turn of the century, re-entered the field of political debate. The debates between the theorists of socialism and the theorists of relativity are of capital importance in this history.

At all events, biology and physics were to a privileged degree the zones of formation of this new personage, the specific intellectual. The extension of technico-scientific structures in the economic and strategic domain was what gave him his real importance. The figure in which the functions and prestige of this new intellectual are concentrated is no longer that of the 'writer of genius,' but that of the 'absolute savant,' no longer he who bears the values of all, opposes the unjust sovereign or his ministers and makes his cry resound even beyond the grave. It is rather he who, along with a handful of others, has at his disposal, whether in the service of the State or against it, powers which can either benefit or irrevocably destroy life. He is no longer the rhapsodist of the eternal, but the strategist of life and death. Meanwhile we are at present experiencing the disappearance of the figure of the 'great writer.'

Now let's come back to more precise details. We accept, alongside the development of technico-scientific structures in contemporary society, the importance gained by the specific intellectual in recent decades, as well as the acceleration of this process since around 1960. Now the specific intellectual encounters certain obstacles and faces certain dangers. The danger of remaining at the level of conjunctural struggles, pressing demands restricted to particular sectors. The risk of letting himself be manipulated by the political parties or trade union apparatuses which control these local struggles. Above all, the risk of being unable to develop these struggles for lack of a global strategy or outside support; the risk too of not being followed, or not by very limited groups. In France we can see at the moment an example of this. The struggle around the prisons, the penal system and the police-judicial system, because it has developed 'in solitary,' among social workers and ex-prisoners, has tended increasingly to separate itself from the forces which would have enabled it to grow. It has allowed itself to be penetrated by a whole naive, archaic ideology which makes the criminal at once into the innocent victim and the pure rebel—society's scapegoat—and the young wolf of future revolutions. This return to anarchist themes of the late nineteenth century was possible only because of a failure of integration of current strategies. And the result has been a deep split between this campaign with its monotonous, lyrical little chant, heard only among a few small groups, and the masses who have good reason not to accept it as valid political currency, but who also—thanks to the studiously cultivated fear of criminals—tolerate the maintenance, or rather the reinforcement, of the judicial and police apparatuses.

It seems to me that we are now at a point where the function of the specific intellectual needs to be reconsidered. Reconsidered but not abandoned, despite the nostalgia of some for the great 'universal' intellectuals and the desire for a new philosophy, a new world-view. Suffice it to consider the important results which have been achieved in psychiatry: they prove that these local, specific struggles haven't been a mistake and haven't led to a dead end. One may even say that the role of the specific intellectual must become more and more important in proportion to the political responsibilities which he is obliged willy-nilly to accept, as a nuclear scientist, computer expert, pharmacologist, etc. It would be a dangerous error to discount him politically in his specific relation to a local form of power, either on the grounds that this is a specialist matter which doesn't concern the masses (which is doubly wrong: they are already aware of it, and in any case implicated in it), or that the specific intellectual serves the interests of State or Capital (which is true, but at the same time shows the strategic position he occupies), or, again, on the grounds that he

---

[13]Charles Darwin (1809–1882), English naturalist; Émile Zola (above, page 698).

propagates a scientific ideology (which isn't always true, and is anyway certainly a secondary matter compared with the fundamental point: the effects proper to true discourses).

The important thing here, I believe, is that truth isn't outside power, or lacking in power: contrary to a myth whose history and functions would repay further study, truth isn't the reward of free spirits, the child of protracted solitude, nor the privilege of those who have succeeded in liberating themselves. Truth is a thing of this world: it is produced only by virtue of multiple forms of constraint. And it induces regular effects of power. Each society has its régime of truth, its 'general politics' of truth: that is, the types of discourse which it accepts and makes function as true; the mechanisms and instances which enable one to distinguish true and false statements, the means by which each is sanctioned; the techniques and procedures accorded value in the acquisition of truth; the status of those who are charged with saying what counts as true.

In societies like ours, the 'political economy' of truth is characterised by five important traits. 'Truth' is centered on the form of scientific discourse and the institutions which produce it; it is subject to constant economic and political incitement (the demand for truth, as much for economic production as for political power); it is the object, under diverse forms, of immense diffusion and consumption (circulating through apparatuses of education and information whose extent is relatively broad in the social body, not withstanding certain strict limitations); it is produced and transmitted under the control, dominant if not exclusive, of a few great political and economic apparatuses (university, army, writing, media); lastly, it is the issue of a whole political debate and social confrontation ('ideological' struggles).

It seems to me that what must now be taken into account in the intellectual is not the 'bearer of universal values.' Rather, it's the person occupying a specific position—but whose specificity is linked, in a society like ours, to the general functioning of an apparatus of truth. In other words, the intellectual has a three-fold specificity: that of his class position (whether as petty-bourgeois in the service of capitalism or 'organic' intellectual of the proletariat); that of his conditions of life and work, linked to his condition as an intellectual (his field of research, his place in a laboratory, the political and economic demands to which he submits or against which he rebels, in the university, the hospital, etc.); lastly, the specificity of the politics of truth in our societies. And it's with this last factor that his position can take on a general significance and that his local, specific struggle can have effects and implications which are not simply professional or sectoral. The intellectual can operate and struggle at the general level of that régime of truth which is so essential to the structure and functioning of our society. There is a battle 'for truth,' or at least 'around truth'—it being understood once again that by truth I do not mean 'the ensemble of truths which are to be discovered and accepted,' but rather 'the ensemble of rules according to which the true and the false are separated and specific effects of power attached to the true,' it being understood also that it's not a matter of a battle 'on behalf' of the truth, but of a battle about the status of truth and the economic and political role it plays. It is necessary to think of the political problems of intellectuals not in terms of 'science' and 'ideology,' but in terms of 'truth' and 'power.' And thus the question of the professionalisation of intellectuals and the division between intellectual and manual labour can be envisaged in a new way.

All this must seem very confused and uncertain. Uncertain indeed, and what I am saying here is above all to be taken as a hypothesis. In order for it to be a little less confused, however, I would like to put forward a few 'propositions'—not firm assertions, but simply suggestions to be further tested and evaluated.

'Truth' is to be understood as a system of ordered procedures for the production, regulation, distribution, circulation and operation of statements.

'Truth' is linked in a circular relation with systems of power which produce and sustain it, and to effects of power which it induces and which extend it. A 'régime' of truth.

This régime is not merely ideological or superstructural; it was a condition of the formation and development of capitalism. And it's this same régime which, subject to certain modifications, operates in the socialist countries (I leave open here the question of China, about which I know little).

The essential political problem for the intellectual is not to criticise the ideological contents supposedly linked to science, or to ensure that his own scientific practice is accompanied by a correct ideology, but that of ascertaining the possibility of constituting a new politics of truth. The problem is not changing people's consciousness—or what's in their heads—but the political, economic, institutional régime of the production of truth.

It's not a matter of emancipating truth from every system of power (which would be a chimera, for truth is already power) but of detaching the power of truth from the forms of hegemony, social, economic and cultural, within which it operates at the present time.

The political question, to sum up, is not error, illusion, alienated consciousness or ideology; it is truth itself. Hence the importance of Nietzsche.

Thomas S. Kuhn

1922–1996

Though contemporary readers may not notice the connection, Thomas Kuhn's *The Structure of Scientific Revolutions* (1962) was published as the last volume in the great project of Logical Positivism, *The Encyclopedia of Unified Science,* under the general editorship of Rudolph Carnap (above, page 978) and Otto Neurath. That project had sought to provide a comprehensive survey of modern scientific theory, on the assumption that the use of a strict logical formalism applied to scrupulously verified empirical observations was essential for the grounding of science. In that context, Kuhn's argument well deserves to be considered something of a revolution itself, since his own historical studies of science revealed a rather different picture, foregrounding the importance of the scientific groups that develop in the pursuit of exemplary scientific achievements. In a stroke that is at once brilliant and problematic, Kuhn employs the grammatical metaphor of the "paradigm," the model in a language, for example, indicating a general type of verb conjugation, to characterize the collective commitments that inform the pursuit of science. In the selection here, Kuhn notes that reviewers found this term troublesome, with one counting more than twenty distinct uses of "paradigm," though he also points out that it is probably not as great a problem as this might suggest.

The reason is that Kuhn's focus in *The Structure of Scientific Revolutions* is upon the characteristic historical patterns by which relatively desultory investigations of a subject attain their distinctive "scientific" character as organized, methodical, and expansive inquiries—including, perhaps most significantly, the high degree of verifiability that the *Encyclopedia of Unified Science* valorized above all else. What Kuhn's work showed, however, was by no means a slow and gradual ascent to verified truth, but rather a complex relativity between the elements of scientific practice, ranging from crucial experiments, and elegant and precise theories, to the sociological organization of science as a professional pursuit. By using a single term, "paradigm," Kuhn gains the advantage of calling attention to the complex interaction among such elements, all of which go into modeling what is understood to be good scientific practice in a given field.

The dramatic success of Kuhn's terms is evident in the dubious implicit compliment of being frequently quoted without citation (or, one might sometimes suspect, without reading his book), to the point that the idea of a "paradigm shift" has become a commonplace in contemporary language. It is, however, of some interest that this phrase was merely mentioned by Kuhn, whose concern is with the dynamics of scientific revolutions, where an older paradigm collapses and a new, usually incommensurable one emerges. The general pattern Kuhn traces typically begins with an exemplary scientific accomplishment, sufficiently interesting to attract a group of adherents—whose own work follows some generative possibility within the original exemplary work. What follows Kuhn calls "normal science," consisting predominantly of "puzzle-solving" activity that continues to an indefinite point of institutional consolidation for the scientific community. The idea of the "scientific revolutions" in Kuhn's title stems from the emergence of a crisis over some anomaly in contemporary research that resists solution (or cannot be reduced to a solvable puzzle) by using established models and procedures. A scientific "revolution" is not then certain, by any means: a new model, a new "paradigm" may or may not emerge, such that the field of examination may decline or even cease to be viable as science. In this sense, what one expects is that paradigms break and are replaced, not that they "shift."

In later work, notably the essays included in his *The Essential Tension,* Kuhn explores other implications of paradigms and the scientific practices they support. In one essay in particular, "Objectivity, Value Judgment, and Theory Choice," Kuhn considers five general properties that appear to be implicit in the choice of theories, including *accuracy, consistency, broad scope, simplicity,* and *fruitfulness,* for further research. As Kuhn points out, each of these does involve a value judgment, which is not only consistent with scientific *objectivity,* but almost the condition of it. As a sample set of axiological criteria, these five concepts all favor the continuation of science as organized inquiry, foregrounding the work of the group, not just the individual contributor.

The dramatic success of Kuhn's book as a model for thinking about other disciplines, from sociology to literary study, is but a part of a broader effort to understand science in philosophical and historical terms. Along with the very different work of Karl Popper, Imre Lakatos, Gerald Holton, Paul Feyerabend, and Bruno Latour, Kuhn's work has been at the forefront of the critical examination of science and remains a dominant force in the history and philosophy of science.

Kuhn's principal works are: *The Copernican Revolution: Planetary Astronomy in the Development of Western Thought* (1957); *The Structure of Scientific Revolutions* (1962, 1970); *The Essential Tension: Selected Studies in Scientific Tradition and Change* (1977); *The Road since Structure: Philosophical Essays, 1970–1993,* ed. by James Conant and John Haugeland (2000). Of special importance is a collection of essays edited by Imre Lakatos and Alan Musgrave, *Criticism and the Growth of Knowledge* (1970), based on a conference convened to consider in large measure Kuhn's contributions to contemporary history and philosophy of science, with a very important concluding essay by Kuhn, "Reflections on My Critics." For a particularly strident example of objections to Kuhn, see Israel Scheffler, *Science and Subjectivity* (1982). For a clear introduction to logical and philosophical issues pertaining to Kuhn, see Harold I. Brown, *Perception, Theory, and Commitment: The New Philosophy of Science* (1977). More recent studies of Kuhn include: Paul Hoyingen-Huene, *Reconstructing Scientific Revolutions: Thomas S. Kuhn's Philosophy of Science* (1993); Paul Horwich, ed., *World Changes: Thomas Kuhn and the Nature of Science* (1993); Steve Fuller, *Thomas Kuhn: A Philosophical History for Our Time* (2000); Thomas Nickels, ed., *Thomas Kuhn* (2003).

from

Postscript—1969

It has now been almost seven years since this book was first published. In the interim both the response of critics and my own further work have increased my understanding of a number of the issues it raises. On fundamentals my viewpoint is very nearly unchanged, but I now recognize aspects of its initial formulation that create gratuitous difficulties and misunderstandings. Since some of those misunderstandings have been my own, their elimination enables me to gain ground that should ultimately provide the basis for a new version of the book. Meanwhile, I welcome the chance to sketch needed revisions, to comment on some reiterated criticisms, and to suggest directions in which my own thought is presently developing.[1]

Several of the key difficulties of my original text cluster about the concept of a paradigm, and my discussion begins with them.[2] In the subsection that follows at once, I suggest the desirability of disentangling that concept from the notion of a scientific community, indicate how this may be done, and discuss some significant consequences of the resulting analytic separation. Next I consider what occurs when paradigms are sought by examining the behavior of the members of a *previously determined* scientific community. That procedure quickly discloses that in much of the book the term 'paradigm' is used in two different senses. On the one hand, it stands for the entire constellation of beliefs, values, techniques, and so on shared by the members of a given community. On the other, it denotes one sort of element in that constellation, the concrete puzzle-solutions which, employed as models or examples, can replace explicit rules as a basis for the solution of the remaining puzzles of normal science. The first sense of the term, call it

the sociological, is the subject of Subsection 2, below; Subsection 3 is devoted to paradigms as exemplary past achievements.

Philosophically, at least, this second sense of 'paradigm' is the deeper of the two, and the claims I have made in its name are the main sources for the controversies and misunderstandings that the book has evoked, particularly for the charge that I make of science a subjective and irrational enterprise. These issues are considered in Subsections 4 and 5. The first argues that terms like 'subjective' and 'intuitive' cannot appropriately be applied to the components of knowledge that I have described as tacitly embedded in shared examples. Though such knowledge is not, without essential change, subject to paraphrase in terms of rules and criteria, it is nevertheless systematic, time tested, and in some sense corrigible. Subsection 5 applies that argument to the problem of choice between two incompatible theories, urging in brief conclusion that men who hold incommensurable viewpoints be thought of as members of different language communities and that their communication problems be analyzed as problems of translation. Three residual issues are discussed in the concluding Subsections, 6 and 7. The first considers the charge that the view of science developed in this book is through-and-through relativistic. The second begins by inquiring whether my argument really suffers, as has been said, from a confusion between the descriptive and the normative modes; it concludes with brief remarks on a topic deserving a separate essay: the extent to which the book's main theses may legitimately be applied to fields other than science.

1. Paradigms and Community Structure

The term 'paradigm' enters the preceding pages early, and its manner of entry is intrinsically circular. A paradigm is what the members of a scientific community share, *and,* conversely, a scientific community consists of men who share a paradigm. Not all circularities are vicious (I shall defend an argument of similar structure late in this postscript), but this one is a source of real difficulties. Scientific communities can and should be isolated without prior recourse to paradigms; the latter can then be discovered by scrutinizing the behavior of a given community's members. If this book were being rewritten, it would therefore open with a discussion of the community structure of science, a topic that has recently become a significant subject of sociological research and that historians of science are also beginning to take seriously. Preliminary results, many of them still unpublished, suggest that the empirical techniques required for its exploration are non-trivial, but some are in hand and

---

Postscript—1969 was first published in the second edition, enlarged, of Thomas S. Kuhn's *The Structure of Scientific Revolutions* (Chicago: University of Chicago Press, 1970). It is reprinted from that edition.

[1] [Kuhn] Other indications will be found in two recent essays of mine: "Reflection on My Critics," in Imre Lakatos and Alan Musgrave (eds.), *Criticism and the Growth of Knowledge* (Cambridge, 1970); and "Second Thoughts on Paradigms," in Frederick Suppe (ed.), *The Structure of Scientific Theories* (Urbana, Ill., 1970 or 1971), both currently in press. I shall cite the first of these essays below as "Reflections" and the volume in which it appears as *Growth of Knowledge;* the second essay will be referred to as "Second Thoughts."

[2] [Kuhn] For particularly cogent criticism of my initial presentation of paradigms see: Margaret Masterman, "The Nature of a Paradigm," in *Growth of Knowledge;* and Dudley Shapere, "The Structure of Scientific Revolutions," *Philosophical Review,* LXXIII (1964), 383–94.

others are sure to be developed.[3] Most practicing scientists respond at once to questions about their community affiliations, taking for granted that responsibility for the various current specialties is distributed among groups of at least roughly determinate membership. I shall therefore here assume that more systematic means for their identification will be found. Instead of presenting preliminary research results, let me briefly articulate the intuitive notion of community that underlies much in the earlier chapters of this book. It is a notion now widely shared by scientists, sociologists, and a number of historians of science.

A scientific community consists, on this view, of the practitioners of a scientific specialty. To an extent unparalleled in most other fields, they have undergone similar educations and professional initiations; in the process they have absorbed the same technical literature and drawn many of the same lessons from it. Usually the boundaries of that standard literature mark the limits of a scientific subject matter, and each community ordinarily has a subject matter of its own. There are schools in the sciences, communities, that is, which approach the same subject from incompatible viewpoints. But they are far rarer there than in other fields; they are always in competition; and their competition is usually quickly ended. As a result, the members of a scientific community see themselves and are seen by others as the men uniquely responsible for the pursuit of a set of shared goals, including the training of their successors. Within such groups communication is relatively full and professional judgment relatively unanimous. Because the attention of different scientific communities is, on the other hand, focused on different matters, professional communication across group lines is sometimes arduous, often results in misunderstanding, and may, if pursued, evoke significant and previously unsuspected disagreement.

Communities in this sense exist, of course, at numerous levels. The most global is the community of all natural scientists. At an only slightly lower level the main scientific professional groups are communities: physicists, chemists, astronomers, zoologists, and the like. For these major groupings, community membership is readily established except at the fringes. Subject of highest degree, membership in professional societies, and journals read are ordinarily more than sufficient. Similar techniques will also isolate major subgroups: organic chemists, and perhaps protein chemists among them, solid-state and high-energy physicists, radio astronomers, and so on. It is only at the next lower level that empirical problems emerge. How, to take a contemporary example, would one have isolated the phage group prior to its public acclaim? For this purpose one must have recourse to attendance at special conferences, to the distribution of draft manuscripts or galley proofs prior to publication, and above all to formal and informal communication networks including those discovered in correspondence and in the linkages among citations.[4] I take it that the job can and will be done, at least for the contemporary scene and the more recent parts of the historical. Typically it may yield communities of perhaps one hundred members, occasionally significantly fewer. Usually individual scientists, particularly the ablest, will belong to several such groups either simultaneously or in succession.

Communities of this sort are the units that this book has presented as the producers and validators of scientific knowledge. Paradigms are something shared by the members of such groups. Without reference to the nature of these shared elements, many aspects of science described in the preceding pages can scarcely be understood. But other aspects can, though they are not independently presented in my original text. It is therefore worth noting, before turning to paradigms directly, a series of issues that require reference to community structure alone.

Probably the most striking of these is what I have previously called the transition from the pre- to the post-paradigm period in the development of a scientific field. That transition is the one sketched above in Section II. Before it occurs, a number of schools compete for the domination of a given field. Afterward, in the wake of some notable scientific achievement, the number of schools is greatly reduced, ordinarily to one, and a more efficient mode of scientific practice begins. The latter is generally esoteric and oriented to puzzle-solving, as the work of a group can be only when its members take the foundations of their field for granted.

The nature of that transition to maturity deserves fuller discussion than it has received in this book, particularly from those concerned with the development of the contemporary social sciences. To that end it may help to point out

---

[3] [Kuhn] W. O. Hagstrom, *The Scientific Community* (New York, 1965), chaps. iv and v; D. J. Price and D. de B. Beaver, "Collaboration in an Invisible College," *American Psychologist,* XXI (1966), 1011–18; Diana Crane, "Social Structure in a Group of Scientists: A Test of the 'Invisible College' Hypothesis," *American Sociological Review,* XXXIV (1969), 335–52; N. C. Mullins, *Social Networks among Biological Scientists,* (Ph.D. diss., Harvard University, 1966), and "The Micro-Structure of an Invisible College: The Phage Group" (paper delivered at an annual meeting of the American Sociological Association, Boston, 1968).

[4] [Kuhn] Eugene Garfield, *The Use of Citation Data in Writing the History of Science* (Philadelphia: Institute of Scientific Information, 1964); M. M. Kessler, "Comparison of the Results of Bibliographic Coupling and Analytic Subject Indexing," *American Documentation,* XVI (1965), 223–33; D. J. Price, "Networks of Scientific Papers," *Science,* CIL (1965), 510–15.

that the transition need not (I now think should not) be associated with the first acquisition of a paradigm. The members of all scientific communities, including the schools of the "pre-paradigm" period, share the sorts of elements which I have collectively labelled 'a paradigm.' What changes with the transition to maturity is not the presence of a paradigm but rather its nature. Only after the change is normal puzzle-solving research possible. Many of the attributes of a developed science which I have above associated with the acquisition of a paradigm I would therefore now discuss as consequences of the acquisition of the sort of paradigm that identifies challenging puzzles, supplies clues to their solution, and guarantees that the truly clever practitioner will succeed. Only those who have taken courage from observing that their own field (or school) has paradigms are likely to feel that something important is sacrificed by the change.

A second issue, more important at least to historians, concerns this book's implicit one-to-one identification of scientific communities with scientific subject matters. I have, that is, repeatedly acted as though, say, 'physical optics,' 'electricity,' and 'heat' must name scientific communities because they do name subject matters for research. The only alternative my text has seemed to allow is that all these subjects have belonged to the physics community. Identifications of that sort will not, however, usually withstand examination, as my colleagues in history have repeatedly pointed out. There was, for example, no physics community before the mid-nineteenth century, and it was then formed by the merger of parts of two previously separate communities, mathematics and natural philosophy (*physique expérimentale*). What is today the subject matter for a single broad community has been variously distributed among diverse communities in the past. Other narrower subjects, for example heat and the theory of matter, have existed for long periods without becoming the special province of any single scientific community. Both normal science and revolutions are, however, community-based activities. To discover and analyze them, one must first unravel the changing community structure of the sciences over time. A paradigm governs, in the first instance, not a subject matter but rather a group of practitioners. Any study of paradigm-directed or of paradigm-shattering research must begin by locating the responsible group or groups.

When the analysis of scientific development is approached in that way, several difficulties which have been foci for critical attention are likely to vanish. A number of commentators have, for example, used the theory of matter to suggest that I drastically overstate the unanimity of scientists in their allegiance to a paradigm. Until comparatively recently, they point out, those theories have been topics for continuing disagreement and debate. I agree with the description but think it no counter-example. Theories of matter were not, at least until about 1920, the special province or the subject matter for any scientific community. Instead, they were tools for a large number of specialists' groups. Members of different communities sometimes chose different tools and criticized the choice made by others. Even more important, a theory of matter is not the sort of topic on which the members of even a single community must necessarily agree. The need for agreement depends on what it is the community does. Chemistry in the first half of the nineteenth century provides a case in point. Though several of the community's fundamental tools—constant proportion, multiple proportion, and combining weights—had become common property as a result of Dalton's atomic theory, it was quite possible for chemists, after the event, to base their work on these tools and to disagree, sometimes vehemently, about the existence of atoms.

Some other difficulties and misunderstandings will, I believe, be dissolved in the same way. Partly because of the examples I have chosen and partly because of my vagueness about the nature and size of the relevant communities, a few readers of this book have concluded that my concern is primarily or exclusively with major revolutions such as those associated with Copernicus, Newton, Darwin, or Einstein. A clearer delineation of community structure should, however, help to enforce the rather different impression I have tried to create. A revolution is for me a special sort of change involving a certain sort of reconstruction of group commitments. But it need not be a large change, nor need it seem revolutionary to those outside a single community, consisting perhaps of fewer than twenty-five people. It is just because this type of change, little recognized or discussed in the literature of the philosophy of science, occurs so regularly on this smaller scale that revolutionary, as against cumulative, change so badly needs to be understood.

One last alteration, closely related to the preceding, may help to facilitate that understanding. A number of critics have doubted whether crisis, the common awareness that something has gone wrong, precedes revolutions so invariably as I have implied in my original text. Nothing important to my argument depends, however, on crises' being an absolute prerequisite to revolutions; they need only be the usual prelude, supplying, that is, a self-correcting mechanism which ensures that the rigidity of normal science will not forever go unchallenged. Revolutions may also be induced in other ways, though I think they seldom are. In addition, I would now point out what the absence of an adequate discussion of community structure has obscured above: crises need not be generated by the work of the community that experiences them and that sometimes undergoes revolution as a result. New instruments like the electron microscope or new laws like Maxwell's may develop in one specialty and their assimilation create crisis in another.

2. Paradigms as the Constellation of Group Commitments

Turn now to paradigms and ask what they can possibly be. My original text leaves no more obscure or important question. One sympathetic reader, who shares my conviction that 'paradigm' names the central philosophical elements of the book, prepared a partial analytic index and concluded that the term is used in at least twenty-two different ways.[5] Most of those differences are, I now think, due to stylistic inconsistencies (e.g., Newton's Laws are sometimes a paradigm, sometimes parts of a paradigm, and sometimes paradigmatic), and they can be eliminated with relative ease. But, with that editorial work done, two very different usages of the term would remain, and they require separation. The more global use is the subject of this subsection; the other will be considered in the next.

Having isolated a particular community of specialists by techniques like those just discussed, one may usefully ask: What do its members share that accounts for the relative fulness of their professional communication and the relative unanimity of their professional judgments? To that question my original text licenses the answer, a paradigm or set of paradigms. But for this use, unlike the one to be discussed below, the term is inappropriate. Scientists themselves would say they share a theory or set of theories, and I shall be glad if the term can ultimately be recaptured for this use. As currently used in philosophy of science, however, 'theory' connotes a structure far more limited in nature and scope than the one required here. Until the term can be freed from its current implications, it will avoid confusion to adopt another. For present purposes I suggest 'disciplinary matrix': 'disciplinary' because it refers to the common possession of the practitioners of a particular discipline; 'matrix' because it is composed of ordered elements of various sorts, each requiring further specification. All or most of the objects of group commitment that my original text makes paradigms, parts of paradigms, or paradigmatic are constituents of the disciplinary matrix, and as such they form a whole and function together. They are, however, no longer to be discussed as though they were all of a piece. I shall not here attempt an exhaustive list, but noting the main sorts of

components of a disciplinary matrix will both clarify the nature of my present approach and simultaneously prepare for my next main point.

One important sort of component I shall label 'symbolic generalizations,' having in mind those expressions, deployed without question or dissent by group members, which can readily be cast in a logical form like $(x)(y)(z) \phi (x, y, z)$. They are the formal or the readily formalizable components of the disciplinary matrix. Sometimes they are found already in symbolic form: $f = ma$ or $I = V / R$. Others are ordinarily expressed in words: "elements combine in constant proportion by weight, or "action equals reaction." If it were not for the general acceptance of expressions like these, there would be no points at which group members could attach the powerful techniques of logical and mathematical manipulation in their puzzle-solving enterprise. Though the example of taxonomy suggests that normal science can proceed with few such expressions, the power of a science seems quite generally to increase with the number of symbolic generalizations its practitioners have at their disposal.

These generalizations look like laws of nature, but their function for group members is not often that alone. Sometimes it is: for example the Joule-Lenz Law, $H = RI^2$. When that law was discovered, community members already knew what H, R, and I stood for, and these generalizations simply told them something about the behavior of heat, current, and resistance that they had not known before. But more often, as discussion earlier in the book indicates, symbolic generalizations simultaneously serve a second function, one that is ordinarily sharply separated in analyses by philosophers of science. Like $f = ma$ or $I = V / R$, they function in part as laws but also in part as definitions of some of the symbols they deploy. Furthermore, the balance between their inseparable legislative and definitional force shifts over time. In another context these points would repay detailed analysis, for the nature of the commitment to a law is very different from that of commitment to a definition. Laws are often corrigible piecemeal, but definitions, being tautologies, are not. For example, part of what the acceptance of Ohm's Law demanded was a redefinition of both 'current' and 'resistance'; if those terms had continued to mean what they had meant before, Ohm's Law could not have been right; that is why it was so strenuously opposed as, say, the Joule-Lenz Law was not.[6] Probably that situation is typical. I currently suspect

---

[5][Kuhn] Masterman, *op. cit.*

[6][Kuhn] For significant parts of this episode see: T. M. Brown, "The Electric Current in Early Nineteenth-Century French Physics," *Historical Studies in the Physical Sciences*, I (1969), 61–103, and Morton Schagrin, "Resistance to Ohm's Law," *American Journal of Physics*, XXI (1963), 536–47.

that all revolutions involve, among other things, the abandonment of generalizations the force of which had previously been in some part that of tautologies. Did Einstein show that simultaneity was relative or did he alter the notion of simultaneity itself? Were those who heard paradox in the phrase 'relativity of simultaneity' simply wrong?

Consider next a second type of component of the disciplinary matrix, one about which a good deal has been said in my original text under such rubrics as 'metaphysical paradigms' or 'the metaphysical parts of paradigms.' I have in mind shared commitments to such beliefs as: heat is the kinetic energy of the constituent parts of bodies; all perceptible phenomena are due to the interaction of qualitatively neutral atoms in the void, or, alternatively, to matter and force, or to fields. Rewriting the book now I would describe such commitments as beliefs in particular models, and I would expand the category models to include also the relatively heuristic variety: the electric circuit may be regarded as a steady-state hydrodynamic system; the molecules of a gas behave like tiny elastic billiard balls in random motion. Though the strength of group commitment varies, with nontrivial consequences, along the spectrum from heuristic to ontological models, all models have similar functions. Among other things they supply the group with preferred or permissible analogies and metaphors. By doing so they help to determine what will be accepted as an explanation and as a puzzle-solution; conversely, they assist in the determination of the roster of unsolved puzzles and in the evaluation of the importance of each. Note, however, that the members of scientific communities may not have to share even heuristic models, though they usually do so. I have already pointed out that membership in the community of chemists during the first half of the nineteenth century did not demand a belief in atoms.

A third sort of element in the disciplinary matrix I shall here describe as values. Usually they are more widely shared among different communities than either symbolic generalizations or models, and they do much to provide a sense of community to natural scientists as a whole. Though they function at all times, their particular importance emerges when the members of a particular community must identify crisis or, later, choose between incompatible ways of practicing their discipline. Probably the most deeply held values concern predictions: they should be accurate; quantitative predictions are preferable to qualitative ones; whatever the margin of permissible error, it should be consistently satisfied in a given field; and so on. There are also, however, values to be used in judging whole theories: they must, first and foremost, permit puzzle-formulation and solution; where possible they should be simple, self-consistent, and plausible, compatible, that is, with other theories currently deployed. (I now think it a weakness of my original text that so little attention is given to such values as internal and external consistency in considering sources of crisis and factors in theory choice.) Other sorts of values exist as well—for example, science should (or need not) be socially useful—but the preceding should indicate what I have in mind.

One aspect of shared values does, however, require particular mention. To a greater extent than other sorts of components of the disciplinary matrix, values may be shared by men who differ in their application. Judgments of accuracy are relatively, though not entirely, stable from one time to another and from one member to another in a particular group. But judgments of simplicity, consistency, plausibility, and so on often vary greatly from individual to individual. What was for Einstein an insupportable inconsistency in the old quantum theory, one that rendered the pursuit of normal science impossible, was for Bohr and others a difficulty that could be expected to work itself out by normal means. Even more important, in those situations where values must be applied, different values, taken alone, would often dictate different choices. One theory may be more accurate but less consistent or plausible than another; again the old quantum theory provides an example. In short, though values are widely shared by scientists and though commitment to them is both deep and constitutive of science, the application of values is sometimes considerably affected by the features of individual personality and biography that differentiate the members of the group.

To many readers of the preceding chapters, this characteristic of the operation of shared values has seemed a major weakness of my position. Because I insist that what scientists share is not sufficient to command uniform assent about such matters as the choice between competing theories or the distinction between an ordinary anomaly and a crisis-provoking one, I am occasionally accused of glorifying subjectivity and even irrationality.[7] But that reaction ignores two characteristics displayed by value judgments in any field. First, shared values can be important determinants of group behavior even though the members of the group do not all apply them in the same way. (If that were not the case, there would be no *special* philosophic problems about value theory or aesthetics.) Men did not all paint alike dur-

---

[7][Kuhn] See particularly: Dudley Shapere, "Meaning and Scientific Change," in *Mind and Cosmos: Essays in Contemporary Science and Philosophy,* The University of Pittsburgh Series in the Philosophy of Science, III (Pittsburgh, 1966), 41–85; Israel Scheffler, *Science and Subjectivity* (New York, 1967); and the essays of Sir Karl Popper and Imre Lakatos in *Growth of Knowledge.*

ing the periods when representation was a primary value, but the developmental pattern of the plastic arts changed drastically when that value was abandoned. Imagine what would happen in the sciences if consistency ceased to be a primary value. Second, individual variability in the application of shared values may serve functions essential to science. The points at which values must be applied are invariably also those at which risks must be taken. Most anomalies are resolved by normal means; most proposals for new theories do prove to be wrong. If all members of a community responded to each anomaly as a source of crisis or embraced each new theory advanced by a colleague, science would cease. If, on the other hand, no one reacted to anomalies or to brand-new theories in high-risk ways, there would be few or no revolutions. In matters like these the resort to shared values rather than to shared rules governing individual choice may be the community's way of distributing risk and assuring the long-term success of its enterprise.

Turn now to a fourth sort of element in the disciplinary matrix, not the only other kind but the last I shall discuss here. For it the term 'paradigm' would be entirely appropriate, both philologically and autobiographically; this is the component of a group's shared commitments which first led me to the choice of that word. Because the term has assumed a life of its own, however, I shall here substitute 'exemplars.' By it I mean, initially, the concrete problem-solutions that students encounter from the start of their scientific education, whether in laboratories, on examinations, or at the ends of chapters in science texts. To these shared examples should, however, be added at least some of the technical problem-solutions found in the periodical literature that scientists encounter during their post-educational research careers and that also show them by example how their job is to be done. More than other sorts of components of the disciplinary matrix, differences between sets of exemplars provide the community fine-structure of science. All physicists, for example, begin by learning the same exemplars: problems such as the inclined plane, the conical pendulum, and Keplerian orbits; instruments such as the vernier, the calorimeter, and the Wheatstone bridge. As their training develops, however, the symbolic generalizations they share are increasingly illustrated by different exemplars. Though both solid-state and field-theoretic physicists share the Schrödinger equation, only its more elementary applications are common to both groups.

3. Paradigms as Shared Examples

The paradigm as shared example is the central element of what I now take to be the most novel and least understood

aspect of this book. Exemplars will therefore require more attention than the other sorts of components of the disciplinary matrix. Philosophers of science have not ordinarily discussed the problems encountered by a student in laboratories or in science texts, for these are thought to supply only practice in the application of what the student already knows. He cannot, it is said, solve problems at all unless he has first learned the theory and some rules for applying it. Scientific knowledge is embedded in theory and rules; problems are supplied to gain facility in their application. I have tried to argue, however, that this localization of the cognitive content of science is wrong. After the student has done many problems, he may gain only added facility by solving more. But at the start and for some time after, doing problems is learning consequential things about nature. In the absence of such exemplars, the laws and theories he has previously learned would have little empirical content.

To indicate what I have in mind I revert briefly to symbolic generalizations. One widely shared example is Newton's Second Law of Motion, generally written as $f = ma$. The sociologist, say, or the linguist who discovers that the corresponding expression is unproblematically uttered and received by the members of a given community will not, without much additional investigation, have learned a great deal about what either the expression or the terms in it mean, about how the scientists of the community attach the expression to nature. Indeed, the fact that they accept it without question and use it as a point at which to introduce logical and mathematical manipulation does not of itself imply that they agree at all about such matters as meaning and application. Of course they do agree to a considerable extent, or the fact would rapidly emerge from their subsequent conversation. But one may well ask at what point and by what means they have come to do so. How have they learned, faced with a given experimental situation, to pick out the relevant forces, masses, and accelerations?

In practice, though this aspect of the situation is seldom or never noted, what students have to learn is even more complex than that. It is not quite the case that logical and mathematical manipulation are applied directly to $f = ma$. That expression proves on examination to be a law-sketch or a law-schema. As the student or the practicing scientist moves from one problem situation to the next, the symbolic generalization to which such manipulations apply changes. For the case of free fall, $f = ma$ becomes $mg = m\dfrac{d^2s}{dt^2}$; for the simple pendulum it is transformed to $mg \sin\theta = -ml\dfrac{d^2\theta}{dt^2}$; for a pair of interacting harmonic oscillators it becomes two equations, the first of which may be written $m_1 \dfrac{d^2 s_1}{dt^2} + k_1 s_1 = k_2(s_2 - s_1 + d)$; and for more complex situations, such as the gyroscope, it takes still other forms, the family resemblance of which to $f = ma$ is still harder to discover. Yet, while learning to identify forces, masses, and accelerations in a variety of physical situations not previously encountered, the student has also learned to design the appropriate version of $f = ma$ through which to interrelate them, often a version for which he has encountered no literal equivalent before. How has he learned to do this?

A phenomenon familiar to both students of science and historians of science provides a clue. The former regularly report that they have read through a chapter of their text, understood it perfectly, but nonetheless had difficulty solving a number of the problems at the chapter's end. Ordinarily, also, those difficulties dissolve in the same way. The student discovers, with or without the assistance of his instructor, a way to see his problem as *like* a problem he has already encountered. Having seen the resemblance, grasped the analogy between two or more distinct problems, he can interrelate symbols and attach them to nature in the ways that have proved effective before. The law-sketch, say $f = ma$, has functioned as a tool, informing the student what similarities to look for, signaling the gestalt in which the situation is to be seen. The resultant ability to see a variety of situations as like each other, as subjects for $f = ma$ or some other symbolic generalization, is, I think, the main thing a student acquires by doing exemplary problems, whether with a pencil and paper or in a well-designed laboratory. After he has completed a certain number, which may vary widely from one individual to the next, he views the situations that confront him as a scientist in the same gestalt as other members of his specialists' group. For him they are no longer the same situations he had encountered when his training began. He has meanwhile assimilated a time-tested and group-licensed way of seeing.

The role of acquired similarity relations also shows clearly in the history of science. Scientists solve puzzles by modeling them on previous puzzle-solutions, often with only minimal recourse to symbolic generalizations. Galileo found that a ball rolling down an incline acquires just enough velocity to return it to the same vertical height on a second incline of any slope, and he learned to see that experimental situation as like the pendulum with a point-mass for a bob. Huyghens then solved the problem of the center of oscillation of a physical pendulum by imagining that the extended body of the latter was composed of Galilean point-pendula, the bonds between which could be instantaneously released at any point in the swing. After the bonds were released, the individual point-pendula would swing freely, but their collective center of gravity when each attained its highest point would, like that of Galileo's pendulum, rise only to the height from which the center of gravity of the extended pendulum had begun to fall. Finally, Daniel Bernoulli discovered how to make the flow of water from an orifice resemble Huyghens' pendulum. Determine the descent of the center of gravity of the water in tank and jet during an infinitesimal interval of time. Next imagine that each particle of water afterward moves separately upward to the maximum height attainable with the velocity acquired during that interval. The ascent of the center of gravity of the individual particles must then equal the descent of the center of gravity of the water in tank and jet. From that view of the problem the long-sought speed of efflux followed at once.[8]

That example should begin to make clear what I mean by learning from problems to see situations as like each other, as subjects for the application of the same scientific law or law-sketch. Simultaneously it should show why I refer to the consequential knowledge of nature acquired while learning the similarity relationship and thereafter embodied in a way of viewing physical situations rather than in rules or laws. The three problems in the example, all of them exemplars for eighteenth-century mechanicians, deploy only one law of nature. Known as the Principle of *vis viva*, it was usually stated as: "Actual descent equals potential ascent." Bernoulli's application of the law should suggest how consequential it was. Yet the verbal statement of the law, taken by itself, is virtually impotent. Present it to a contemporary student of physics, who knows the words and can do all these problems but now employs different means. Then imagine what the words, though all well known, can have said to a man who did not know even the problems. For him the generalization could begin to function only when he learned to recognize "actual descents" and "potential ascents" as ingredients of nature, and that is to learn something, prior to the law, about the situations that nature does and does not present. That sort of learning is not acquired by exclusively verbal means. Rather it comes as one is given

---

[8] [Kuhn] For the example, see: René Dugas, *A History of Mechanics,* trans. J. R. Maddox (Neuchatel, 1955), pp. 135–36, 186–93, and Daniel Bernoulli, *Hydrodynamica, sive de viribus et motibus fluidorum, commentarii opus academicum* (Strasbourg, 1738), Sec. iii. For the extent to which mechanics progressed during the first half of the eighteenth century by modelling one problem-solution on another, see Clifford Truesdell, "Reactions of Late Baroque Mechanics to Success, Conjecture, Error, and Failure in Newton's *Principia*," *Texas Quarterly,* X (1967), 238–58.

words together with concrete examples of how they function in use; nature and words are learned together. To borrow once more Michael Polanyi's useful phrase, what results from this process is "tacit knowledge" which is learned by doing science rather than by acquiring rules for doing it.

4. Tacit Knowledge and Intuition

That reference to tacit knowledge and the concurrent rejection of rules isolates another problem that has bothered many of my critics and seemed to provide a basis for charges of subjectivity and irrationality. Some readers have felt that I was trying to make science rest on unanalyzable individual intuitions rather than on logic and law. But that interpretation goes astray in two essential respects. First, if I am talking at all about intuitions, they are not individual. Rather they are the tested and shared possessions of the members of a successful group, and the novice acquires them through training as a part of his preparation for group-membership. Second, they are not in principle unanalyzable. On the contrary, I am currently experimenting with a computer program designed to investigate their properties at an elementary level.

About that program I shall have nothing to say here,[9] but even mention of it should make my most essential point. When I speak of knowledge embedded in shared exemplars, I am not referring to a mode of knowing that is less systematic or less analyzable than knowledge embedded in rules, laws, or criteria of identification. Instead I have in mind a manner of knowing which is misconstrued if reconstructed in terms of rules that are first abstracted from exemplars and thereafter function in their stead. Or, to put the same point differently, when I speak of acquiring from exemplars the ability to recognize a given situation as like some and unlike others that one has seen before, I am not suggesting a process that is not potentially fully explicable in terms of neuro-cerebral mechanism. Instead I am claiming that the explication will not, by its nature, answer the question, "Similar with respect to what?" That question is a request for a rule, in this case for the criteria by which particular situations are grouped into similarity sets, and I am arguing that the temptation to seek criteria (or at least a full set) should be resisted in this case. It is not, however, system but a particular sort of system that I am opposing.

To give that point substance, I must briefly digress. What follows seems obvious to me now, but the constant re-

course in my original text to phrases like "the world changes" suggests that it has not always been so. If two people stand at the same place and gaze in the same direction, we must, under pain of solipsism, conclude that they receive closely similar stimuli. (If both could put their eyes at the same place, the stimuli would be identical.) But people do not see stimuli; our knowledge of them is highly theoretical and abstract. Instead they have sensations, and we are under no compulsion to suppose that the sensations of our two viewers are the same. (Sceptics might remember that color blindness was nowhere noticed until John Dalton's description of it in 1794.) On the contrary, much neural processing takes place between the receipt of a stimulus and the awareness of a sensation. Among the few things that we know about it with assurance are: that very different stimuli can produce the same sensations; that the same stimulus can produce very different sensations; and, finally, that the route from stimulus to sensation is in part conditioned by education. Individuals raised in different societies behave on some occasions as though they saw different things. If we were not tempted to identify stimuli one-to-one with sensations, we might recognize that they actually do so.

Notice now that two groups, the members of which have systematically different sensations on receipt of the same stimuli, do *in some sense* live in different worlds. We posit the existence of stimuli to explain our perceptions of the world, and we posit their immutability to avoid both individual and social solipsism. About neither posit have I the slightest reservation. But our world is populated in the first instance not by stimuli but by the objects of our sensations, and these need not be the same, individual to individual or group to group. To the extent, of course, that individuals belong to the same group and thus share education, language, experience, and culture, we have good reason to suppose that their sensations are the same. How else are we to understand the fulness of their communication and the communality of their behavioral responses to their environment? They must see things, process stimuli, in much the same ways. But where the differentiation and specialization of groups begins, we have no similar evidence for the immutability of sensation. Mere parochialism, I suspect, makes us suppose that the route from stimuli to sensation is the same for the members of all groups.

Returning now to exemplars and rules, what I have been trying to suggest, in however preliminary a fashion, is this. One of the fundamental techniques by which the members of a group, whether an entire culture or a specialists' sub-community within it, learn to see the same things when confronted with the same stimuli is by being shown examples of situations that their predecessors in the group have

---

[9][Kuhn] Some information on this subject can be found in "Second Thoughts."

already learned to see as like each other and as different from other sorts of situations. These similar situations may be successive sensory presentations of the same individual—say of mother, who is ultimately recognized on sight as what she is and as different from father or sister. They may be presentations of the members of natural families, say of swans on the one hand and of geese on the other. Or they may, for the members of more specialized groups, be examples of the Newtonian situation, of situations, that is, that are alike in being subject to a version of the symbolic form $f = ma$ and that are different from those situations to which, for example, the law-sketches of optics apply.

Grant for the moment that something of this sort does occur. Ought we say that what has been acquired from exemplars is rules and the ability to apply them? That description is tempting because our seeing a situation as like ones we have encountered before must be the result of neural processing, fully governed by physical and chemical laws. In this sense, once we have learned to do it, recognition of similarity must be as fully systematic as the beating of our hearts. But that very parallel suggests that recognition may also be involuntary, a process over which we have no control. If it is, then we may not properly conceive it as something we manage by applying rules and criteria. To speak of it in those terms implies that we have access to alternatives, that we might, for example, have disobeyed a rule, or misapplied a criterion, or experimented with some other way of seeing.[10] Those, I take it, are just the sorts of things we cannot do.

Or, more precisely, those are things we cannot do until after we have had a sensation, perceived something. Then we do often seek criteria and put them to use. Then we may engage in interpretation, a deliberative process by which we choose among alternatives as we do not in perception itself. Perhaps, for example, something is odd about what we have seen (remember the anomalous playing cards). Turning a corner we see mother entering a downtown store at a time we had thought she was home. Contemplating what we have seen we suddenly exclaim, "That wasn't mother, for she has red hair!" Entering the store we see the woman again and cannot understand how she could have been taken for mother. Or, perhaps we see the tail feathers of a waterfowl feeding from the bottom of a shallow pool. Is it a swan or a goose? We contemplate what we have seen, mentally comparing the tail feathers with those of swans and geese we have seen before. Or, perhaps, being proto-scientists, we simply want to know some general characteristic (the whiteness of swans, for example) of the members of a natural family we can already recognize with ease. Again, we contemplate what we have previously perceived, searching for what the members of the given family have in common.

These are all deliberative processes, and in them we do seek and deploy criteria and rules. We try, that is, to interpret sensations already at hand, to analyze what is for us the given. However we do that, the processes involved must ultimately be neural, and they are therefore governed by the same *physico-chemical* laws that govern perception on the one hand and the beating of our hearts on the other. But the fact that the system obeys the same laws in all three cases provides no reason to suppose that our neural apparatus is programmed to operate the same way in interpretation as in perception or in either as in the beating of our hearts. What I have been opposing in this book is therefore the attempt, traditional since Descartes but not before, to analyze perception as an interpretive process, as an unconscious version of what we do after we have perceived.

What makes the integrity of perception worth emphasizing is, of course, that so much past experience is embodied in the neural apparatus that transforms stimuli to sensations. An appropriately programmed perceptual mechanism has survival value. To say that the members of different groups may have different perceptions when confronted with the same stimuli is not to imply that they may have just any perceptions at all. In many environments a group that could not tell wolves from dogs could not endure. Nor would a group of nuclear physicists today survive as scientists if unable to recognize the tracks of alpha particles and electrons. It is just because so very few ways of seeing will do that the ones that have withstood the tests of group use are worth transmitting from generation to generation. Equally, it is because they have been selected for their success over historic time that we must speak of the experience and knowledge of nature embedded in the stimulus-to-sensation route.

Perhaps 'knowledge' is the wrong word, but there are reasons for employing it. What is built into the neural process that transforms stimuli to sensations has the following characteristics: it has been transmitted through education; it has, by trial, been found more effective than its historical competitors in a group's current environment; and, finally, it is subject to change both through further education and through the discovery of misfits with the environment. Those are characteristics of knowledge, and they explain why I use the term. But it is strange usage, for one other

---

[10] [Kuhn] This point might never have needed making if all laws were like Newton's and all rules like the Ten Commandments. In that case the phrase 'breaking a law' would be nonsense, and a rejection of rules would not seem to imply a process not governed by law. Unfortunately, traffic laws and similar products of legislation can be broken, which makes the confusion easy.

characteristic is missing. We have no direct access to what it is we know, no rules or generalizations with which to express this knowledge. Rules which could supply that access would refer to stimuli not sensations, and stimuli we can know only through elaborate theory. In its absence, the knowledge embedded in the stimulus-to-sensation route remains tacit.

Though it is obviously preliminary and need not be correct in all details, what has just been said about sensation is meant literally. At the very least it is a hypothesis about vision which should be subject to experimental investigation though probably not to direct check. But talk like this of seeing and sensation here also serves metaphorical functions as it does in the body of the book. We do not *see* electrons, but rather their tracks or else bubbles of vapor in a cloud chamber. We do not *see* electric currents at all, but rather the needle of an ammeter or galvanometer. Yet in the preceding pages, particularly in Section X, I have repeatedly acted as though we did perceive theoretical entities like currents, electrons, and fields, as though we learned to do so from examination of exemplars, and as though in these cases too it would be wrong to replace talk of seeing with talk of criteria and interpretation. The metaphor that transfers 'seeing' to contexts like these is scarcely a sufficient basis for such claims. In the long run it will need to be eliminated in favor of a more literal mode of discourse.

The computer program referred to above begins to suggest ways in which that may be done, but neither available space nor the extent of my present understanding permits my eliminating the metaphor here.[11] Instead I shall try briefly to bulwark it. Seeing water droplets or a needle against a numerical scale is a primitive perceptual experience for the man unacquainted with cloud chambers and ammeters. It thus requires contemplation, analysis, and interpretation (or else the intervention of external authority) before conclusions can be reached about electrons or currents. But the position of the man who has learned about these instruments and had much exemplary experience with them is very different, and there are corresponding differences in the way he processes the stimuli that reach him from them. Regarding the vapor in his breath on a cold winter afternoon, his sensation may be the same as that of a layman, but viewing a cloud chamber he sees (here literally) not droplets but the tracks of electrons, alpha particles, and so on. Those tracks are, if you will, criteria that he interprets as indices of the presence of the corresponding particles, but that route is both shorter and different from the one taken by the man who interprets droplets.

Or consider the scientist inspecting an ammeter to determine the number against which the needle has settled. His sensation probably is the same as the layman's, particularly if the latter has read other sorts of meters before. But he has seen the meter (again often literally) in the context of the entire circuit, and he knows something about its internal structure. For him the needle's position is a criterion, but only of *the value* of the current. To interpret it he need determine only on which scale the meter is to be read. For the layman, on the other hand, the needle's position is not a criterion of anything except itself. To interpret it, he must examine the whole layout of wires, internal and external, experiment with batteries and magnets, and so on. In the metaphorical no less than in the literal use of 'seeing,' interpretation begins where perception ends. The two processes are not the same, and what perception leaves for interpretation to complete depends drastically on the nature and amount of prior experience and training.

5. Exemplars, Incommensurability, and Revolutions

What has just been said provides a basis for clarifying one more aspect of the book: my remarks on incommensurability and its consequences for scientists debating the choice between successive theories.[12] In Sections X and XII I have argued that the parties to such debates inevitably see differently certain of the experimental or observational situations to which both have recourse. Since the vocabularies in which they discuss such situations consist, however, predominantly of the same terms, they must be attaching some of those terms to nature differently, and their communication is inevitably only partial. As a result, the superiority of one theory to another is something that cannot be proved in

---

[11][Kuhn] For readers of "Second Thoughts" the following cryptic remarks may be leading. The possibility of immediate recognition of the members of natural families depends upon the existence, after neural processing, of empty perceptual space between the families to be discriminated. If, for example, there were a perceived continuum of waterfowl ranging from geese to swans, we should be compelled to introduce a specific criterion for distinguishing them. A similar point can be made for unobservable entities. If a physical theory admits the existence of nothing else like an electric current, then a small number of criteria, which may vary considerably from case to case, will suffice to identify currents even though there is no set of rules that specifies the necessary and sufficient conditions for the identification. That point suggests a plausible corollary which may be more important. Given a set of necessary and sufficient conditions for identifying a theoretical entity, that entity can be eliminated from the ontology of a theory by substitution. In the absence of such rules, however, these entities are not eliminable; the theory then demands their existence.

[12][Kuhn] The points that follow are dealt with in more detail in Secs. v and vi of "Reflections."

the debate. Instead, I have insisted, each party must try, by persuasion, to convert the other. Only philosophers have seriously misconstrued the intent of these parts of my argument. A number of them, however, have reported that I believe the following:[13] the proponents of incommensurable theories cannot communicate with each other at all; as a result, in a debate over theory-choice there can be no recourse to *good* reasons; instead theory must be chosen for reasons that are ultimately personal and subjective; some sort of mystical apperception is responsible for the decision actually reached. More than any other parts of the book, the passages on which these misconstructions rest have been responsible for charges of irrationality.

Consider first my remarks on proof. The point I have been trying to make is a simple one, long familiar in philosophy of science. Debates over theory-choice cannot be cast in a form that fully resembles logical or mathematical proof. In the latter, premises and rules of inference are stipulated from the start. If there is disagreement about conclusions, the parties to the ensuing debate can retrace their steps one by one, checking each against prior stipulation. At the end of that process one or the other must concede that he has made a mistake, violated a previously accepted rule. After that concession he has no recourse, and his opponent's proof is then compelling. Only if the two discover instead that they differ about the meaning or application of stipulated rules, that their prior agreement provides no sufficient basis for proof, does the debate continue in the form it inevitably takes during scientific revolutions. That debate is about premises, and its recourse is to persuasion as a prelude to the possibility of proof.

Nothing about that relatively familiar thesis implies either that there are no good reasons for being persuaded or that those reasons are not ultimately decisive for the group. Nor does it even imply that the reasons for choice are different from those usually listed by philosophers of science: accuracy, simplicity, fruitfulness, and the like. What it should suggest, however, is that such reasons function as values and that they can thus be differently applied, individually and collectively, by men who concur in honoring them. If two men disagree, for example, about the relative fruitfulness of their theories, or if they agree about that but disagree about the relative importance of fruitfulness and, say, scope in reaching a choice, neither can be convicted of a mistake. Nor is either being unscientific. There is no neutral algorithm for theory-choice, no systematic decision procedure which, properly applied, must lead each individual in the group to the same decision. In this sense it is the community of specialists rather than its individual members that makes the effective decision. To understand why science develops as it does, one need not unravel the details of biography and personality that lead each individual to a particular choice, though that topic has vast fascination. What one must understand, however, is the manner in which a particular set of shared values interacts with the particular experiences shared by a community of specialists to ensure that most members of the group will ultimately find one set of arguments rather than another decisive.

That process is persuasion, but it presents a deeper problem. Two men who perceive the same situation differently but nevertheless employ the same vocabulary in its discussion must be using words differently. They speak, that is, from what I have called incommensurable viewpoints. How can they even hope to talk together much less to be persuasive? Even a preliminary answer to that question demands further specification of the nature of the difficulty. I suppose that, at least in part, it takes the following form.

The practice of normal science depends on the ability, acquired from exemplars, to group objects and situations into similarity sets which are primitive in the sense that the grouping is done without an answer to the question, "Similar with respect to what?" One central aspect of any revolution is, then, that some of the similarity relations change. Objects that were grouped in the same set before are grouped in different ones afterward and vice versa. Think of the sun, moon, Mars, and earth before and after Copernicus; of free fall, pendular, and planetary motion before and after Galileo; or of salts, alloys, and a sulphur-iron filing mix before and after Dalton. Since most objects within even the altered sets continue to be grouped together, the names of the sets are usually preserved. Nevertheless, the transfer of a subset is ordinarily part of a critical change in the network of interrelations among them. Transferring the metals from the set of compounds to the set of elements played an essential role in the emergence of a new theory of combustion, of acidity, and of physical and chemical combination. In short order those changes had spread through all of chemistry. Not surprisingly, therefore, when such redistributions occur, two men whose discourse had previously proceeded with apparently full understanding may suddenly find themselves responding to the same stimulus with incompatible descriptions and generalizations. Those difficulties will not be felt in all areas of even their scientific discourse, but they will arise and will then cluster most densely about the phenomena upon which the choice of theory most centrally depends.

Such problems, though they first become evident in communication, are not merely linguistic, and they cannot

---

[13] [Kuhn] See the works cited in note 7, above, and also the essay by Stephen Touimin in *Growth of Knowledge*.

be resolved simply by stipulating the definitions of troublesome terms. Because the words about which difficulties cluster have been learned in part from direct application to exemplars, the participants in a communication breakdown cannot say, "I use the word 'element' (or 'mixture,' or 'planet,' or 'unconstrained motion') in ways determined by the following criteria." They cannot, that is, resort to a neutral language which both use in the same way and which is adequate to the statement of both their theories or even of both those theories' empirical consequences. Part of the difference is prior to the application of the languages in which it is nevertheless reflected.

The men who experience such communication breakdowns must, however, have some recourse. The stimuli that impinge upon them are the same. So is their general neural apparatus, however differently programmed. Furthermore, except in a small, if all-important, area of experience even their neural programming must be very nearly the same, for they share a history, except the immediate past. As a result, both their everyday and most of their scientific world and language are shared. Given that much in common, they should be able to find out a great deal about how they differ. The techniques required are not, however, either straightforward, or comfortable, or parts of the scientist's normal arsenal. Scientists rarely recognize them for quite what they are, and they seldom use them for longer than is required to induce conversion or convince themselves that it will not be obtained.

Briefly put, what the participants in a communication breakdown can do is recognize each other as members of different language communities and then become translators.[14] Taking the differences between their own intra- and inter-group discourse as itself a subject for study, they can first attempt to discover the terms and locutions that, used unproblematically within each community, are nevertheless foci of trouble for inter-group discussions. (Locutions that present no such difficulties may be homophonically translated.) Having isolated such areas of difficulty in scientific communication, they can next resort to their shared everyday vocabularies in an effort further to elucidate their troubles. Each may, that is, try to discover what the other would see and say when presented with a stimulus to which his own verbal response would be different. If they can sufficiently refrain from explaining anomalous behavior as the consequence of mere error or madness, they may in time become very good predictors of each other's behavior. Each will have learned to translate the other's theory and its consequences into his own language and simultaneously to describe in his language the world to which that theory applies. That is what the historian of science regularly does (or should) when dealing with out-of-date scientific theories.

Since translation, if pursued, allows the participants in a communication breakdown to experience vicariously something of the merits and defects of each other's points of view, it is a potent tool both for persuasion and for conversion. But even persuasion need not succeed, and, if it does, it need not be accompanied or followed by conversion. The two experiences are not the same, an important distinction that I have only recently fully recognized.

To persuade someone is, I take it, to convince him that one's own view is superior and ought therefore supplant his own. That much is occasionally achieved without recourse to anything like translation. In its absence many of the explanations and problem-statements endorsed by the members of one scientific group will be opaque to the other. But each language community can usually produce from the start a few concrete research results that, though describable in sentences understood in the same way by both groups, cannot yet be accounted for by the other community in its own terms. If the new viewpoint endures for a time and continues to be fruitful, the research results verbalizable in this way are likely to grow in number. For some men such results alone will be decisive. They can say: I don't know how the proponents of the new view succeed, but I must learn; whatever they are doing, it is clearly right. That reaction comes particularly easily to men just entering the profession, for they have not yet acquired the special vocabularies and commitments of either group.

Arguments statable in the vocabulary that both groups use in the same way are not, however, usually decisive, at least not until a very late stage in the evolution of the opposing views. Among those already admitted to the profession, few will be persuaded without some recourse to the more extended comparisons permitted by translation. Though the price is often sentences of great length and complexity (think of the Proust-Berthollet controversy conducted without recourse to the term 'element'), many additional research results can be *translated* from one community's language into the other's. As translation proceeds, furthermore, some members of each community may also begin vicariously to understand how a statement previously opaque could seem an explanation to members of the opposing group. The availability of techniques like these does not, of

---

[14] [Kuhn] The already classic source for most of the relevant aspects of translation is W. V. O. Quine, *Word and Object* (Cambridge, Mass., and New York, 1960), chaps. i and ii. But Quine seems to assume that two men receiving the same stimulus must have the same sensation and therefore has little to say about the extent to which a translator must be able to *describe* the world to which the language being translated applies. For the latter point see, E. A. Nida, "Linguistics and Ethnology in Translation Problems," in Del Hymes (ed.), *Language and Culture in Society* (New York, 1964), pp. 90–97.

course, guarantee persuasion. For most people translation is a threatening process, and it is entirely foreign to normal science. Counter-arguments are, in any case, always available, and no rules prescribe how the balance must be struck. Nevertheless, as argument piles on argument and as challenge after challenge is successfully met, only blind stubbornness can at the end account for continued resistance.

That being the case, a second aspect of translation, long familiar to both historians and linguists, becomes crucially important. To translate a theory or worldview into one's own language is not to make it one's own. For that one must go native, discover that one is thinking and working in, not simply translating out of, a language that was previously foreign. That transition is not, however, one that an individual may make or refrain from making by deliberation and choice, however good his reasons for wishing to do so. Instead, at some point in the process of learning to translate, he finds that the transition has occurred, that he has slipped into the new language without a decision having been made. Or else, like many of those who first encountered, say, relativity or quantum mechanics in their middle years, he finds himself fully persuaded of the new view but nevertheless unable to internalize it and be at home in the world it helps to shape. Intellectually such a man has made his choice, but the conversion required if it is to be effective eludes him. He may use the new theory nonetheless, but he will do so as a foreigner in a foreign environment, an alternative available to him only because there are natives already there. His work is parasitic on theirs, for he lacks the constellation of mental sets which future members of the community will acquire through education.

The conversion experience that I have likened to a gestalt switch remains, therefore, at the heart of the revolutionary process. Good reasons for choice provide motives for conversion and a climate in which it is more likely to occur. Translation may, in addition, provide points of entry for the neural reprogramming that, however inscrutable at this time, must underlie conversion. But neither good reasons nor translation constitute conversion, and it is that process we must explicate in order to understand an essential sort of scientific change.

6. Revolutions and Relativism

One consequence of the position just outlined has particularly bothered a number of my critics.[15] They find my

viewpoint relativistic, particularly as it is developed in the last section of this book. My remarks about translation highlight the reasons for the charge. The proponents of different theories are like the members of different language-culture communities. Recognizing the parallelism suggests that in some sense both groups may be right. Applied to culture and its development that position is relativistic.

But applied to science it may not be, and it is in any case far from *mere* relativism in a respect that its critics have failed to see. Taken as a group or in groups, practitioners of the developed sciences are, I have argued, fundamentally puzzle-solvers. Though the values that they deploy at times of theory-choice derive from other aspects of their work as well, the demonstrated ability to set up and to solve puzzles presented by nature is, in case of value conflict, the dominant criterion for most members of a scientific group. Like any other value, puzzle-solving ability proves equivocal in application. Two men who share it may nevertheless differ in the judgments they draw from its use. But the behavior of a community which makes it preeminent will be very different from that of one which does not. In the sciences, I believe, the high value accorded to puzzle-solving ability has the following consequences.

Imagine an evolutionary tree representing the development of the modern scientific specialties from their common origins in, say, primitive natural philosophy and the crafts. A line drawn up that tree, never doubling back, from the trunk to the tip of some branch would trace a succession of theories related by descent. Considering any two such theories, chosen from points not too near their origin, it should be easy to design a list of criteria that would enable an uncommitted observer to distinguish the earlier from the more recent theory time after time. Among the most useful would be: accuracy of prediction, particularly of quantitative prediction; the balance between esoteric and everyday subject matter; and the number of different problems solved. Less useful for this purpose, though also important determinants of scientific life, would be such values as simplicity, scope, and compatibility with other specialties. Those lists are not yet the ones required, but I have no doubt that they can be completed. If they can, then scientific development is, like biological, a unidirectional and irreversible process. Later scientific theories are better than earlier ones for solving puzzles in the often quite different environments to which they are applied. That is not a relativist's position, and it displays the sense in which I am a convinced believer in scientific progress.

Compared with the notion of progress most prevalent among both philosophers of science and laymen, however, this position lacks an essential element. A scientific theory

---

[15][Kuhn] Shapere, "Structure of Scientific Revolutions," and Popper in *Growth of Knowledge.*

is usually felt to be better than its predecessors not only in the sense that it is a better instrument for discovering and solving puzzles but also because it is somehow a better representation of what nature is really like. One often hears that successive theories grow ever closer to, or approximate more and more closely to, the truth. Apparently generalizations like that refer not to the puzzle-solutions and the concrete predictions derived from a theory but rather to its ontology, to the match, that is, between the entities with which the theory populates nature and what is "really there."

Perhaps there is some other way of salvaging the notion of 'truth' for application to whole theories, but this one will not do. There is, I think, no theory-independent way to reconstruct phrases like 'really there'; the notion of a match between the ontology of a theory and its "real" counterpart in nature now seems to me illusive in principle. Besides, as a historian, I am impressed with the implausability of the view. I do not doubt, for example, that Newton's mechanics improves on Aristotle's and that Einstein's improves on Newton's as instruments for puzzle-solving. But I can see in their succession no coherent direction of ontological development. On the contrary, in some important respects, though by no means in all, Einstein's general theory of relativity is closer to Aristotle's than either of them is to Newton's. Though the temptation to describe that position as relativistic is understandable, the description seems to me wrong. Conversely, if the position be relativism, I cannot see that the relativist loses anything needed to account for the nature and development of the sciences.

7. The Nature of Science

I conclude with a brief discussion of two recurrent reactions to my original text, the first critical, the second favorable, and neither, I think, quite right. Though the two relate neither to what has been said so far nor to each other, both have been sufficiently prevalent to demand at least some response.

A few readers of my original text have noticed that I repeatedly pass back and forth between the descriptive and the normative modes, a transition particularly marked in occasional passages that open with, "But that is not what scientists do," and close by claiming that scientists ought not do so. Some critics claim that I am confusing description with prescription, violating the time-honored philosophical theorem: 'Is' cannot imply 'ought.'[16]

That theorem has, in practice, become a tag, and it is no longer everywhere honored. A number of contemporary philosophers have discovered important contexts in which the normative and the descriptive are inextricably mixed.[17] 'Is' and 'ought' are by no means always so separate as they have seemed. But no recourse to the subtleties of contemporary linguistic philosophy is needed to unravel what has seemed confused about this aspect of my position. The preceding pages present a viewpoint or theory about the nature of science, and, like other philosophies of science, the theory has consequences for the way in which scientists should behave if their enterprise is to succeed. Though it need not be right, any more than any other theory, it provides a legitimate basis for reiterated 'oughts' and 'shoulds.' Conversely, one set of reasons for taking the theory seriously is that scientists, whose methods have been developed and selected for their success, do in fact behave as the theory says they should. My descriptive generalizations are evidence for the theory precisely because they can also be derived from it, whereas on other views of the nature of science they constitute anomalous behavior.

The circularity of that argument is not, I think, vicious. The consequences of the viewpoint being discussed are not exhausted by the observations upon which it rested at the start. Even before this book was first published, I had found parts of the theory it presents a useful tool for the exploration of scientific behavior and development. Comparison of this postscript with the pages of the original may suggest that it has continued to play that role. No merely circular point of view can provide such guidance.

To one last reaction to this book, my answer must be of a different sort. A number of those who have taken pleasure from it have done so less because it illuminates science than because they read its main theses as applicable to many other fields as well. I see what they mean and would not like to discourage their attempts to extend the position, but their reaction has nevertheless puzzled me. To the extent that the book portrays scientific development as a succession of tradition-bound periods punctuated by non-cumulative breaks, its theses are undoubtedly of wide applicability. But they should be, for they are borrowed from other fields. Historians of literature, of music, of the arts, of political development, and of many other human activities have long described their subjects in the same way. Periodization in terms of revolutionary breaks in style, taste, and institutional structure have been among their standard tools. If I

---

[16] [Kuhn] For one of many examples, see P. K. Feyerabend's essay in *Growth of Knowledge*.

[17] [Kuhn] Stanley Cavell, *Must We Mean What We Say?* (New York, 1969), chap. i.

have been original with respect to concepts like these, it has mainly been by applying them to the sciences, fields which had been widely thought to develop in a different way. Conceivably the notion of a paradigm as a concrete achievement, an exemplar, is a second contribution. I suspect, for example, that some of the notorious difficulties surrounding the notion of style in the arts may vanish if paintings can be seen to be modeled on one another rather than produced in conformity to some abstracted canons of style.[18]

This book, however, was intended also to make another sort of point, one that has been less clearly visible to many of its readers. Though scientific development may resemble that in other fields more closely than has often been supposed, it is also strikingly different. To say, for example, that the sciences, at least after a certain point in their development, progress in a way that other fields do not, cannot have been all wrong, whatever progress itself may be. One of the objects of the book was to examine such differences and begin accounting for them.

Consider, for example, the reiterated emphasis, above, on the absence or, as I should now say, on the relative scarcity of competing schools in the developed sciences. Or

remember my remarks about the extent to which the members of a given scientific community provide the only audience and the only judges of that community's work. Or think again about the special nature of scientific education, about puzzle-solving as a goal, and about the value system which the scientific group deploys in periods of crisis and decision. The book isolates other features of the same sort, none necessarily unique to science but in conjunction setting the activity apart.

About all these features of science there is a great deal more to be learned. Having opened this postcript by emphasizing the need to study the community structure of science, I shall close by underscoring the need for similar and, above all, for comparative study of the corresponding communities in other fields. How does one elect and how is one elected to membership in a particular community, scientific or not? What is the process and what are the stages of socialization to the group? What does the group collectively see as its goals; what deviations, individual or collective, will it tolerate; and how does it control the impermissible aberration? A fuller understanding of science will depend on answers to other sorts of questions as well, but there is no area in which more work is so badly needed. Scientific knowledge, like language, is intrinsically the common property of a group or else nothing at all. To understand it we shall need to know the special characteristics of the groups that create and use it.

---

[18] [Kuhn] For this point as well as a more extended discussion of what is special about the sciences, see T. S. Kuhn, "Comment [on the Relations of Science and Art]," *Comparative Studies in Philosophy and History,* XI (1969), 403–12.

Louis Althusser

1918–1990

To say of Louis Althusser that he was a prominent French Marxist philosopher would be to miss the extraordinary impact of his way of *reading* Marx. For Althusser, reading Marx (above, page 607) was itself a dialectical enterprise, expanding, shifting the focus of, and clarifying the problematic of Marx's writings in the light of concrete, material historical events. The selection reprinted here on "Ideological State Apparatuses," from *Lenin and Philosophy, and Other Essays* has become, over the last twenty-five years, one of the indispensable works of contemporary theory, in no small measure because its approach to the question of ideology refuses to be confined by conventional Marxist doctrine. For Althusser, ideology was not a passive relation between the economic base and superstructure, but a pervasive set of dynamic conditions suffusing the institutional apparatus of the state and shaping not just the idea of the person *as subject,* but more important for theorists to follow, clarifying in structural terms the idea of a *subject position,* wherein political and psychological forces converge to define possibilities of action and forces of constraint and repression.

Together with earlier work by Antonio Gramsci (above, page 936), Althusser's reflections on Ideological State Apparatuses have shaped not only the work of Althusser's most famous student, Michel Foucault (above, page 1259), but an entire generation of critics and theorists, with interests in feminism, postcolonialism, and the sociological study of culture. It is of particular interest that for Althusser (like Gramsci before him), the most telling examples of the operation of ideology are religious, including his vivid term for how the subject is "called" or "hailed," *interpellation,* transferred to the political domain. In Althusser's account, ideology as such has no history since it is carried in the material, institutional forms of social life and is always submerged back into them. The analytical problem is to preserve a critical focus on the moment of "calling," as the *interpellated* subject is both created as a subject by being called, and subsumed by the very acknowledgment that, as he puts it, *"It is I"* who is being called. In this sense, one is always dealing with ideolog*ies,* not a monolithic doctrine, that may show up in any arena of social life, in the family, the school, the church, political parties, government, and so on. Althusser's accomplishment is to have provided an example of ideological analysis that is, in Thomas Kuhn's sense of the term, "paradigmatic," by pointing the way to other applications of the same kind of analysis. In this respect, by reading Marx expansively, Althusser recontextualizes Marxist thinking by freeing it from the dogmas of doctrine or limitations of subject matter, by linking the position of the subject to the institutional apparatus that at once sustains and vexes identity. A particularly salient characteristic of his analytical method lies in the fact that it does not insist on a barrier between the political and the psychoanalytic, pointing the way to treatments (such as Fredric Jameson's in *The Political Unconscious: Narrative as a Socially Symbolic Act,* [1981]) that bring both fruitfully together for the purposes of criticism.

Most of Althusser's major writing is available in translation. See especially: *For Marx* (1965; trans. Ben Brewster, 1969); *Lenin and Philosophy and other essays,* tr. Ben Brewster (1971); *Reading 'Capital' / Louis Althusser, Étienne Balibar;* tr. Ben Brewster (1979); *Essays on Ideology* (1984, c. 1976); and *Althusser: A Critical Reader,* ed. Gregory Elliott (1994). A good indication of the scope and importance of Althusser's influence can be seen in *Postmodern Materialism and the Future of Marxist Theory: Essays in the Althusserian Tradition,* edited by Antonio Callari and David F. Ruccio (1996). Critical studies include: Alex Callinicos, *Althusser's Marxism* (1979); Stephen B. Smith, *Reading Althusser: An Essay on Structural Marxism* (1984); Gregory Elliott, *Althusser: The Detour of Theory* (1992); Robert P. Resch, *Althusser and the Renewal of Marxist Social Theory* (1992); and Andrew Levine, *A Future for Marxism?: Althusser, The Analytical Turn and The Revival of Socialist Theory* (2003).

from

Ideology and Ideological State Apparatuses

On Ideology

When I put forward the concept of an Ideological State Apparatus, when I said that the ISAs 'function by ideology,' I invoked a reality which needs a little discussion: ideology.

It is well known that the expression 'ideology' was invented by Cabanis,[1] Destutt de Tracy[2] and their friends, who assigned to it as an object the (genetic) theory of ideas. When Marx took up the term fifty years later, he gave it a quite different meaning, even in his Early Works. Here, ideology is the system of the ideas and representations which dominate the mind of a man or a social group. The ideologico-political struggle conducted by Marx as early as his articles in the *Rheinische Zeitung* inevitably and quickly brought him face to face with this reality and forced him to take his earliest intuitions further.

However, here we come upon a rather astonishing paradox. Everything seems to lead Marx to formulate a theory of ideology. In fact, *The German Ideology* does offer us, after the *1844 Manuscripts,* an explicit theory of ideology, but . . . it is not Marxist (we shall see why in a moment). As for *Capital,* although it does contain many hints towards a theory of ideologies (most visibly, the ideology of the vulgar economists), it does not contain the theory itself, which depends for the most part on a theory of ideology in general.

I should like to venture a first and very schematic outline of such a theory. The theses I am about to put forward are certainly not off the cuff, but they cannot be sustained and tested, i.e. confirmed or rejected, except by much thorough study and analysis.

Ideology Has No History

One word first of all to expound the reason in principle which seems to me to found, or at least to justify, the project of a theory of ideology *in general,* and not a theory of particular ideologies, which, whatever their form (religious, ethical, legal, political), always express *class positions.*

It is quite obvious that it is necessary to proceed towards a theory of ideolog*ies* in the two respects I have just suggested.[3] It will then be clear that a theory of ideolog*ies* depends in the last resort on the history of social formations, and thus of the modes of production combined in social formations, and of the class struggles which develop in them. In this sense it is clear that there can be no question of a theory of ideolog*ies in general,* since ideolog*ies* (defined in the double respect suggested above: regional and class) have a his-

---

Ideology and Ideological State Apparatuses (Notes Towards an Investigation), reprinted in part here, first appeared in French in *La Pensée* in 1970. It is reprinted from *Lenin and Philosophy and other essays,* tr. Ben Brewster (New York: New Left Books, 1971). Reprinted by permission of Monthly Review Foundation.
[1] Pierre-Jean-Georges Cabanis (1757–1808), French philosopher, author of *On the Relations Between the Physical and Moral Aspects of Man* (1802; tr. 1981).
[2] Destutt de Tracy (1854–1836), French philosopher, founder of the School of Ideology, pursuing a Locke-influenced "science of ideas."

---

[3] Althusser earlier has distinguished between state power and state apparatus, representing the direct manifestation of power, and ideological state apparatuses, which are subtler forms of power and repression, including religious denominations and churches, schools, the ideology of the law, political parties, trade unions, the arts, and so on.

tory, whose determination in the last instance is clearly situated outside ideologies alone, although it involves them.

On the contrary, if I am able to put forward the project of a theory of ideology *in general,* and if this theory really is one of the elements on which theories of ideolo*gies* depend, that entails an apparently paradoxical proposition which I shall express in the following terms: *ideology has no history.*

As we know, this formulation appears in so many words in a passage from *The German Ideology.* Marx utters it with respect to metaphysics, which, he says, has no more history than ethics (meaning also the other forms of ideology).

In *The German Ideology,* this formulation appears in a plainly positivist context. Ideology is conceived as a pure illusion, a pure dream, i.e. as nothingness. All its reality is external to it. Ideology is thus thought as an imaginary construction whose status is exactly like the theoretical status of the dream among writers before Freud. For these writers, the dream was the purely imaginary, i.e. null, result of 'day's residues,' presented in an arbitrary arrangement and order, sometimes even 'inverted,' in other words, in 'disorder.' For them, the dream was the imaginary, it was empty, null and arbitrarily 'stuck together' *(bricolé),* once the eyes had closed, from the residues of the only full and positive reality, the reality of the day. This is exactly the status of philosophy and ideology (since in the book philosophy is ideology *par excellence*) in *The German Ideology.*

Ideology, then, is for Marx an imaginary assemblage *(bricolage),* a pure dream, empty and vain, constituted by the 'day's residues' from the only full and positive reality, that of the concrete history of concrete material individuals materially producing their existence. It is on this basis that ideology has no history in *The German Ideology,* since its history is outside it, where the only existing history is, the history of concrete individuals, etc. In *The German Ideology,* the thesis that ideology has no history is therefore a purely negative thesis, since it means both:

1. ideology is nothing insofar as it is a pure dream (manufactured by who knows what power: if not by the alienation of the division of labour, but that, too, is a *negative* determination);

2. ideology has no history, which emphatically does not mean that there is no history in it (on the contrary, for it is merely the pale, empty and inverted reflection of real history) but that it has no history *of its own.*

Now, while the thesis I wish to defend formally speaking adopts the terms of *The German Ideology* ('ideology has no history'), it is radically different from the positivist and historicist thesis of *The German Ideology.*

For on the one hand, I think it is possible to hold that ideolo*gies have a history of their own* (although it is deter-

mined in the last instance by the class struggle); and on the other, I think it is possible to hold that ideology *in general has no history,* not in a negative sense (its history is external to it), but in an absolutely positive sense.

This sense is a positive one if it is true that the peculiarity of ideology is that it is endowed with a structure and a functioning such as to make it a non-historical reality, i.e. an *omni-historical* reality, in the sense in which that structure and functioning are immutable, present in the same form throughout what we can call history, in the sense in which the *Communist Manifesto* defines history as the history of class struggles, i.e. the history of class societies.

To give a theoretical reference-point here, I might say that, to return to our example of the dream, in its Freudian conception this time, our proposition: ideology has no history, can and must (and in a way which has absolutely nothing arbitrary about it, but, quite the reverse, is theoretically necessary, for there is an organic link between the two propositions) be related directly to Freud's proposition that the *unconscious is eternal,* i.e. that it has no history.

If eternal means, not transcendent to all (temporal) history, but omnipresent, trans-historical and therefore immutable in form throughout the extent of history, I shall adopt Freud's expression word for word, and write *ideology is eternal,* exactly like the unconscious. And I add that I find this comparison theoretically justified by the fact that the eternity of the unconscious is not unrelated to the eternity of ideology in general.

That is why I believe I am justified, hypothetically at least, in proposing a theory of ideology *in general,* in the sense that Freud presented a theory of the unconscious *in general.*

To simplify the phrase, it is convenient, taking into account what has been said about ideologies, to use the plain term ideology to designate ideology in general, which I have just said has no history, or, what comes to the same thing, is eternal, i.e. omnipresent in its immutable form throughout history (the history of social formations containing social classes). For the moment I shall restrict myself to 'class societies' and their history.

Ideology Is a 'Representation' of the Imaginary Relationship of Individuals to Their Real Conditions of Existence

In order to approach my central thesis on the structure and functioning of ideology, I shall first present two theses, one negative, the other positive. The first concerns the object which is 'represented' in the imaginary form of ideology, the second concerns the materiality of ideology.

We commonly call religious ideology, ethical ideology, legal ideology, political ideology, etc., so many 'world outlooks.' Of course, assuming that we do not live one of these ideologies as the truth (e.g. 'believe' in God, Duty, Justice, etc. . . .), we admit that the ideology we are discussing from a critical point of view, examining it as the ethnologist examines the myths of a 'primitive society,' that these 'world outlooks' are largely imaginary, i.e. do not 'correspond to reality.'

However, while admitting that they do not correspond to reality, i.e. that they constitute an illusion, we admit that they do make allusion to reality, and that they need only be 'interpreted' to discover the reality of the world behind their imaginary representation of that world (ideology=*illusion / allusion*).

There are different types of interpretation, the most famous of which are the *mechanistic* type, current in the eighteenth century (God is the imaginary representation of the real King), and the *'hermeneutic'* interpretation, inaugurated by the earliest Church Fathers, and revived by Feuerbach[4] and the theologico-philosophical school which descends from him, e.g. the theologian Barth (to Feuerbach, for example, God is the essence of real Man). The essential point is that on condition that we interpret the imaginary transposition (and inversion) of ideology we arrive at the conclusion that in ideology 'men represent their real conditions of existence to themselves in an imaginary form.'

Unfortunately, this interpretation leaves one small problem unsettled: why do men 'need' this imaginary transposition of their real conditions of existence in order to 'represent to themselves' their real conditions of existence?

The first answer (that of the eighteenth century) proposes a simple solution: Priests or Despots are responsible. They 'forged' the Beautiful Lies so that, in the belief that they were obeying God, men would in fact obey the Priests and Despots, who are usually in alliance in their imposture, the Priests acting in the interests of the Despots or *vice versa,* according to the political positions of the 'theoreticians' concerned. There is therefore a cause for the imaginary transposition of the real conditions of existence: that cause is the existence of a small number of cynical men who base their domination and exploitation of the 'people' on a

falsified representation of the world which they have imagined in order to enslave other minds by dominating their imaginations.

The second answer (that of Feuerbach, taken over word for word by Marx in his Early Works) is more 'profound,' i.e. just as false. It, too, seeks and finds a cause for the imaginary transposition and distortion of men's real conditions of existence, in short, for the alienation in the imaginary of the representation of men's conditions of existence. This cause is no longer Priests or Despots, nor their active imagination and the passive imagination of their victims. This cause is the material alienation which reigns in the conditions of existence of men themselves. This is how, in *The Jewish Question* and elsewhere, Marx defends the Feuerbachian idea that men make themselves an alienated (=imaginary) representation of their conditions of existence because these conditions of existence are themselves alienating (in the *1844 Manuscripts:* because these conditions are dominated by the essence of alienated society—*'alienated labour'*).

All these interpretations thus take literally the thesis which they presuppose, and on which they depend, i.e. that what is reflected in the imaginary representation of the world found in an ideology is the conditions of existence of men, i.e. their real world.

Now I can return to a thesis which I have already advanced: it is not their real conditions of existence, their real world, that 'men' 'represent to themselves' in ideology, but above all it is their relation to those conditions of existence which is represented to them there. It is this relation which is at the centre of every ideological, i.e. imaginary, representation of the real world. It is this relation that contains the 'cause' which has to explain the imaginary distortion of the ideological representation of the real world. Or rather, to leave aside the language of causality it is necessary to advance the thesis that it is the *imaginary nature of this relation* which underlies all the imaginary distortion that we can observe (if we do not live in its truth) in all ideology.

To speak in a Marxist language, if it is true that the representation of the real conditions of existence of the individuals occupying the posts of agents of production, exploitation, repression, ideologization and scientific practice, does in the last analysis arise from the relations of production, and from relations deriving from the relations of production, we can say the following: all ideology represents in its necessarily imaginary distortion not the existing relations of production (and the other relations that derive from them), but above all the (imaginary) relationship of individuals to the relations of production and the relations that derive from

---

[4]Ludwig Andreas Feuerbach (1804–1872), post-Hegelian German philosopher, later a materialist and an influence on Marx.

them. What is represented in ideology is therefore not the system of the real relations which govern the existence of individuals, but the imaginary relation of those individuals to the real relations in which they live.

If this is the case, the question of the 'cause' of the imaginary distortion of the real relations in ideology disappears and must be replaced by a different question: why is the representation given to individuals of their (individual) relation to the social relations which govern their conditions of existence and their collective and individual life necessarily an imaginary relation? And what is the nature of this imaginariness? Posed in this way, the question explodes the solution by a 'clique'[5] by a group of individuals (Priests or Despots) who are the authors of the great ideological mystification, just as it explodes the solution by the alienated character of the real world. We shall see why later in my exposition. For the moment I shall go no further.

THESIS II: *Ideology Has a Material Existence*

I have already touched on this thesis by saying that the 'ideas' or 'representations,' etc., which seem to make up ideology do not have an ideal *(idéale* or *idéelle)* or spiritual existence, but a material existence. I even suggested that the ideal *(idéale / idéelle)* and spiritual existence of 'ideas' arises exclusively in an ideology of the 'idea' and of ideology, and let me add, in an ideology of what seems to have 'founded' this conception since the emergence of the sciences, i.e. what the practicians of the sciences represent to themselves in their spontaneous ideology as 'ideas,' true or false. Of course, presented in affirmative form, this thesis is unproven. I simply ask that the reader be favourably disposed towards it, say, in the name of materialism. A long series of arguments would be necessary to prove it.

This hypothetical thesis of the not spiritual but material existence of 'ideas' or other 'representations' is indeed necessary if we are to advance in our analysis of the nature of ideology. Or rather, it is merely useful to us in order the better to reveal what every at all serious analysis of any ideology will immediately and empirically show to every observer, however critical.

While discussing the ideological State apparatuses and their practices, I said that each of them was the realization of an ideology (the unity of these different regional ideologies—religious, ethical, legal, political, aesthetic, etc.—

being assured by their subjection to the ruling ideology). I now return to this thesis: an ideology always exists in an apparatus, and its practice, or practices. This existence is material.

Of course, the material existence of the ideology in an apparatus and its practices does not have the same modality as the material existence of a paving-stone or a rifle. But, at the risk of being taken for a Neo-Aristotelian (NB Marx had a very high regard for Aristotle), I shall say that 'matter is discussed in many senses,' or rather that it exists in different modalities, all rooted in the last instance in 'physical' matter.

Having said this, let me move straight on and see what happens to the 'individuals' who live in ideology, i.e. in a determinate (religious, ethical, etc.) representation of the world whose imaginary distortion depends on their imaginary relation to their conditions of existence, in other words, in the last instance, to the relations of production and to class relations (ideology=an imaginary relation to real relations). I shall say that this imaginary relation is itself endowed with a material existence.

Now I observe the following.

An individual believes in God, or Duty, or Justice, etc. This belief derives (for everyone, i.e. for all those who live in an ideological representation of ideology, which reduces ideology to ideas endowed by definition with a spiritual existence) from the ideas of the individual concerned, i.e. from him as a subject with a consciousness which contains the ideas of his belief. In this way, i.e. by means of the absolutely ideological 'conceptual' device *(dispositif)* thus set up (a subject endowed with a consciousness in which he freely forms or freely recognizes ideas in which he believes), the (material) attitude of the subject concerned naturally follows.

The individual in question behaves in such and such a way, adopts such and such a practical attitude, and, what is more, participates in certain regular practices which are those of the ideological apparatus on which 'depend' the ideas which he has in all consciousness freely chosen as a subject. If he believes in God, he goes to Church to attend Mass, kneels, prays, confesses, does penance (once it was material in the ordinary sense of the term) and naturally repents and so on. If he believes in Duty, he will have the corresponding attitudes, inscribed in ritual practices 'according to the correct principles.' If he believes in Justice, he will submit unconditionally to the rules of the Law, and may even protest when they are violated, sign petitions, take part in a demonstration, etc.

Throughout this schema we observe that the ideological representation of ideology is itself forced to recognize that every 'subject' endowed with a 'consciousness' and believing in the 'ideas' that his 'consciousness' inspires in him and

---

[5][Althusser] I use this very modern term deliberately. For even in Communist circles, unfortunately, it is a commonplace to 'explain' some political deviation (left or right opportunism) by the action of a 'clique.'

freely accepts, must '*act* according to his ideas,' must therefore inscribe his own ideas as a free subject in the actions of his material practice. If he does not do so, 'that is wicked.'

Indeed, if he does not do what he ought to do as a function of what he believes, it is because he does something else, which, still as a function of the same idealist scheme, implies that he has other ideas in his head as well as those he proclaims, and that he acts according to these other ideas, as a man who is either 'inconsistent' ('no one is willingly evil') or cynical, or perverse.

In every case, the ideology of ideology thus recognizes, despite its imaginary distortion, that the 'ideas' of a human subject exist in his actions, or ought to exist in his actions, and if that is not the case, it lends him other ideas corresponding to the actions (however perverse) that he does perform. This ideology talks of actions: I shall talk of actions inserted into *practices. And* I shall point out that these practices are governed by the *rituals* in which these practices are inscribed, within the *material existence of an ideological apparatus,* be it only a small part of that apparatus: a small mass in a small church, a funeral, a minor match at a sports' club, a school day, a political party meeting, etc.

Besides, we are indebted to Pascal's[6] defensive 'dialectic' for the wonderful formula which will enable us to invert the order of the notional schema of ideology. Pascal says more or less: 'Kneel down, move your lips in prayer, and you will believe.' He thus scandalously inverts the order of things, bringing, like Christ, not peace but strife, and in addition something hardly Christian (for woe to him who brings scandal into the world!)—scandal itself. A fortunate scandal which makes him stick with Jansenist defiance to a language that directly names the reality.

I will be allowed to leave Pascal to the arguments of his ideological struggle with the religious ideological State apparatus of his day. And I shall be expected to use a more directly Marxist vocabulary, if that is possible, for we are advancing in still poorly explored domains.

I shall therefore say that, where only a single subject (such and such an individual) is concerned, the existence of the ideas of his belief is material in that *his ideas are his material actions inserted into material practices governed by material rituals which are themselves defined by the material ideological apparatus from which derive the ideas of that subject.* Naturally, the four inscriptions of the adjective 'material' in my proposition must be affected by different modalities: the materialities of a displacement for going to mass, of kneeling down, of the gesture of the sign of the cross, or of the *mea culpa,* of a sentence, of a prayer, of an act of contrition, of a penitence, of a gaze, of a hand-shake, of an external verbal discourse or an 'internal' verbal discourse (consciousness), are not one and the same materiality. I shall leave on one side the problem of a theory of the differences between the modalities of materiality.

It remains that in this inverted presentation of things, we are not dealing with an 'inversion' at all, since it is clear that certain notions have purely and simply disappeared from our presentation, whereas others on the contrary survive, and new terms appear.

Disappeared: the term *ideas.*
Survive: the terms *subject, consciousness, belief, actions.*
Appear: the terms *practices, rituals, ideological apparatus.*

It is therefore not an inversion or overturning (except in the sense in which one might say a government or a glass is overturned), but a reshuffle (of a non-ministerial type), a rather strange reshuffle, since we obtain the following result.

Ideas have disappeared as such (insofar as they are endowed with an ideal or spiritual existence), to the precise extent that it has emerged that their existence is inscribed in the actions of practices governed by rituals defined in the last instance by an ideological apparatus. It therefore appears that the subject acts insofar as he is acted by the following system (set out in the order of its real determination): ideology existing in a material ideological apparatus, prescribing material practices governed by a material ritual, which practices exist in the material actions of a subject acting in all consciousness according to his belief.

But this very presentation reveals that we have retained the following notions: subject, consciousness, belief, actions. From this series I shall immediately extract the decisive central term on which everything else depends: the notion of the *subject.*

And I shall immediately set down these two conjoint theses:

1. there is no practice except by and in an ideology;
2. there is no ideology except by the subject and for subjects.

I can now come to my central thesis.

Ideology Interpellates Individuals as Subjects

This thesis is simply a matter of making my last proposition explicit: there is no ideology except by the subject and

---

[6]Blaise Pascal (1623–1662), French philosopher, author of *Pensées.*

for subjects. Meaning, there is no ideology except for concrete subjects, and this destination for ideology is only made possible by the subject: meaning, *by the category of the subject* and its functioning.

By this I mean that, even if it only appears under this name (the subject) with the rise of bourgeois ideology, above all with the rise of legal ideology,[7] the category of the subject (which may function under other names: e.g., as the soul in Plato, as God, etc.) is the constitutive category of all ideology, whatever its determination (regional or class) and whatever its historical date—since ideology has no history.

I say: the category of the subject is constitutive of all ideology, but at the same time and immediately I add that *the category of the subject is only constitutive of all ideology insofar as all ideology has the function (which defines it) of 'constituting' concrete individuals as subjects.* In the interaction of this double constitution exists the functioning of all ideology, ideology being nothing but its functioning in the material forms of existence of that functioning.

In order to grasp what follows, it is essential to realize that both he who is writing these lines and the reader who reads them are themselves subjects, and therefore ideological subjects (a tautological proposition), i.e. that the author and the reader of these lines both live 'spontaneously' or 'naturally' in ideology in the sense in which I have said that 'man is an ideological animal by nature.'

That the author, insofar as he writes the lines of a discourse which claims to be scientific, is completely absent as a 'subject' from 'his' scientific discourse (for all scientific discourse is by definition a subject-less discourse, there is no 'Subject of science' except in an ideology of science) is a different question which I shall leave on one side for the moment.

As St. Paul admirably put it, it is in the 'Logos,' meaning in ideology, that we 'live, move and have our being.' It follows that, for you and for me, the category of the subject is a primary 'obviousness' (obviousnesses are always primary): it is clear that you and I are subjects (free, ethical, etc. . . .). Like all obviousnesses, including those that make a word 'name a thing' or 'have a meaning' (therefore including the obviousness of the 'transparency' of language), the 'obviousness' that you and I are subjects—and that that does not cause any problems—is an ideological effect, the elementary ideological effect.[8] It is indeed a peculiarity of ide-

ology that it imposes (without appearing to do so, since these are 'obviousnesses') obviousnesses as obviousnesses, which we cannot *fail to recognize* and before which we have the inevitable and natural reaction of crying out (aloud or in the 'still, small voice of conscience'): 'That's obvious! That's right! That's true!'

At work in this reaction is the ideological *recognition* function which is one of the two functions of ideology as such (its inverse being the function of *misrecognition—méconnaissance*).

To take a highly 'concrete' example, we all have friends who, when they knock on our door and we ask, through the door, the question 'Who's there?' answer (since 'it's obvious') 'It's me.' And we recognize that 'it is him,' or 'her.' We open the door, and 'it's true, it really was she who was there.' To take another example, when we recognize somebody of our (previous) acquaintance ((*re*)-*connaissance*) in the street, we show him that we have recognized him (and have recognized that he has recognized us) by saying to him 'Hello, my friend,' and shaking his hand (a material ritual practice of ideological recognition in everyday life in France, at least; elsewhere, there are other rituals).

In this preliminary remark and these concrete illustrations, I only wish to point out that you and I are *always already* subjects, and as such constantly practice the rituals of ideological recognition, which guarantee for us that we are indeed concrete, individual, distinguishable and (naturally) irreplaceable subjects. The writing I am currently executing and the reading you are currently[9] performing are also in this respect rituals of ideological recognition, including the 'obviousness' with which the 'truth' or 'error' of my reflections may impose itself on you.

But to recognize that we are subjects and that we function in the practical rituals of the most elementary everyday life (the hand-shake, the fact of calling you by your name, the fact of knowing, even if I do not know what it is, that you 'have' a name of your own, which means that you are recognized as a unique subject, etc.)—this recognition only gives us the 'consciousness' of our incessant (eternal) practice of ideological recognition—its consciousness, i.e. its *recognition*—but in no sense does it give us the (scientific) *knowledge* of the mechanism of this recognition. Now it is this knowledge that we have to reach, if you will, while speaking in ideology, and from within ideology we have to outline a discourse which tries to break with ideology, in

---

[7][Althusser] Which borrowed the legal category of 'subject in law' to make an ideological notion: man is by nature a subject.

[8][Althusser] Linguists and those who appeal to linguistics for various purposes often run up against difficulties which arise because they ignore the action of the ideological effects in all discourses—including even scientific discourses.

[9][Althusser] NB: this double 'currently' is one more proof of the fact that ideology is 'eternal,' since these two 'currentlys' are separated by an indefinite interval; I am writing these lines on 6 April 1969, you may read them at any subsequent time.

order to dare to be the beginning of a scientific (i.e. subject-less) discourse on ideology.

Thus in order to represent why the category of the 'subject' is constitutive of ideology, which only exists by constituting concrete subjects as subjects, I shall employ a special mode of exposition: 'concrete' enough to be recognized, but abstract enough to be thinkable and thought, giving rise to knowledge.

As a first formulation I shall say: *all ideology hails or interpellates concrete individuals as concrete subjects,* by the functioning of the category of the subject.

This is a proposition which entails that we distinguish for the moment between concrete individuals on the one hand and concrete subjects on the other, although at this level concrete subjects only exist insofar as they are supported by a concrete individual.

I shall then suggest that ideology 'acts' or 'functions' in such a way that it 'recruits' subjects among the individuals (it recruits them all), or 'transforms' the individuals into subjects (it transforms them all) by that very precise operation which I have called *interpellation* or hailing, and which can be imagined along the lines of the most commonplace everyday police (or other) hailing: 'Hey, you there!'[10]

Assuming that the theoretical scene I have imagined takes place in the street, the hailed individual will turn round. By this mere one-hundred-and-eighty-degree physical conversion, he becomes a *subject.* Why? Because he has recognized that the hail was 'really' addressed to him, and that 'it was *really him* who was hailed' (and not someone else). Experience shows that the practical telecommunication of hailings is such that they hardly ever miss their man: verbal call or whistle, the one hailed always recognizes that it is really him who is being hailed. And yet it is a strange phenomenon, and one which cannot be explained solely by 'guilt feelings,' despite the large numbers who 'have something on their consciences.'

Naturally for the convenience and clarity of my little theoretical theatre I have had to present things in the form of a sequence, with a before and an after, and thus in the form of a temporal succession. There are individuals walking along. Somewhere (usually behind them) the hail rings out: 'Hey, you there!' One individual (nine times out of ten it is the right one) turns round, believing/suspecting/knowing that it is for him, i.e. recognizing that 'it really is he' who is meant by the hailing. But in reality these things happen without any succession. The existence of ideology and the hailing or interpellation of individuals as subjects are one and the same thing.

I might add: what thus seems to take place outside ideology (to be precise, in the street), in reality takes place in ideology. What really takes place in ideology seems therefore to take place outside it. That is why those who are in ideology believe themselves by definition outside ideology: one of the effects of ideology is the practical *denegation* of ideological character of ideology by ideology: ideology never says, 'I am ideological.' It is necessary to be outside ideology, i.e. in scientific knowledge, to be able to say: I am in ideology (a quite exceptional case) or (the general case): I was in ideology. As is well known, the accusation of being in ideology only applies to others, never to oneself (unless one is really a Spinozist or a Marxist, which, in this matter, is to be exactly the same thing). Which amounts to saying that ideology *has no outside* (for itself), but at the same time *that it is nothing but outside* (for science and reality).

Spinoza[11] explained this completely two centuries before Marx, who practised it but without explaining it in detail. But let us leave this point, although it is heavy with consequences, consequences which are not just theoretical, but also directly political, since, for example, the whole theory of criticism and self-criticism, the golden rule of the Marxist-Leninist practice of the class struggle, depends on it.

Thus ideology hails or interpellates individuals as subjects. As ideology is eternal, I must now suppress the temporal form in which I have presented the functioning of ideology, and say: ideology has always-already interpellated individuals as subjects, which amounts to making it clear that individuals are always-already interpellated by ideology as subjects, which necessarily leads us to one last proposition: *individuals are always-already subjects.* Hence individuals are 'abstract' with respect to the subjects which they always-already are. This proposition might seem paradoxical.

That an individual is always-already a subject, even before he is born, is nevertheless the plain reality, accessible to everyone and not a paradox at all. Freud shows that individuals are always 'abstract' with respect to the subjects they always-already are, simply by noting the ideological ritual that surrounds the expectation of a 'birth,' that 'happy event.' Everyone knows how much and in what way an unborn child is expected. Which amounts to saying, very prosaically, if we agree to drop the 'sentiments,' i.e. the forms of family ideology (paternal/maternal/conjugal/fraternal) in

---

[10][Althusser] Hailing as an everyday practice subject to a precise ritual takes quite 'special' form in the policeman's practice of 'hailing' which concerns the hailing of 'suspects.'

[11]Baruch (or Benedict) Spinoza (1632–1677), Jewish-Dutch philosopher, follower of Descartes and originator of Pantheism.

which the unborn child is expected: it is certain in advance that it will bear its Father's Name, and will therefore have an identity and be irreplaceable. Before its birth, the child is therefore always-already a subject, appointed as a subject in and by the specific familial ideological configuration in which it is 'expected' once it has been conceived. I hardly need add that this familial ideological configuration is, in its uniqueness, highly structured, and that it is in this implacable and more or less 'pathological' (presupposing that any meaning can be assigned to that term) structure that the former subject-to-be will have to 'find' 'its' place, i.e. 'become' the sexual subject (boy or girl) which it already is in advance. It is clear that this ideological constraint and preappointment, and all the rituals of rearing and then education in the family, have some relationship with what Freud studied in the forms of the pre-genital and genital 'stages' of sexuality, i.e. in the 'grip' of what Freud registered by its effects as being the unconscious. But let us leave this point, too, on one side.

Let me go one step further. What I shall now turn my attention to is the way the 'actors' in this *mise en scene* of interpellation, and their respective roles, are reflected in the very structure of all ideology.

An Example: The Christian Religious Ideology

As the formal structure of all ideology is always the same, I shall restrict my analysis to a single example, one accessible to everyone, that of religious ideology, with the proviso that the same demonstration can be produced for ethical, legal, political, aesthetic ideology, etc.

Let us therefore consider the Christian religious ideology. I shall use a rhetorical figure and 'make it speak,' i.e. collect into a fictional discourse what it 'says' not only in its two Testaments, its Theologians, Sermons, but also in its practices, its rituals, its ceremonies and its sacraments. The Christian religious ideology says something like this:

It says: I address myself to you, a human individual called Peter (every individual is called by his name, in the passive sense, it is never he who provides his own name), in order to tell you that God exists and that you are answerable to Him. It adds: God addresses himself to you through my voice (Scripture having collected the Word of God, Tradition having transmitted it, Papal Infallibility fixing it for ever on 'nice' points). It says: this is who you are: you are Peter! This is your origin, you were created by God for all eternity, although you were born in the 1920th year of Our Lord! This is your place in the world! This is what you must do! By these means, if you observe the 'law of love' you

will be saved, you, Peter, and will become part of the Glorious Body of Christ! Etc. . . .

Now this is quite a familiar and banal discourse, but at the same time quite a surprising one.

Surprising because if we consider that religious ideology is indeed addressed to individuals,[12] in order to 'transform them into subjects,' by interpellating the individual, Peter, in order to make him a subject, free to obey or disobey the appeal, i.e. God's commandments; if it calls these individuals by their names, thus recognizing that they are always-already interpellated as subjects with a personal identity (to the extent that Pascal's Christ says: 'It is for you that I have shed this drop of my blood!'); if it interpellates them in such a way that the subject responds: *'Yes, it really is me!'* if it obtains from them the *recognition* that they really do occupy the place it designates for them as theirs in the world, a fixed residence: 'It really is me, I am here, a worker, a boss or a soldier!' in this vale of tears; if it obtains from them the recognition of a destination (eternal life or damnation) according to the respect or contempt they show to 'God's Commandments,' Law become Love; if everything does happen in this way (in the practices of the well-known rituals of baptism, confirmation, communion, confession and extreme unction, etc. . . .), we should note that all this 'procedure' to set up Christian religious subjects is dominated by a strange phenomenon: the fact that there can only be such a multitude of possible religious subjects on the absolute condition that there is a Unique, Absolute, *Other Subject,* i.e. God.

It is convenient to designate this new and remarkable Subject by writing Subject with a capital S to distinguish it from ordinary subjects, with a small s.

It then emerges that the interpellation of individuals as subjects presupposes the 'existence' of a Unique and central Other Subject, in whose Name the religious ideology interpellates all individuals as subjects. All this is clearly[13] written in what is rightly called the Scriptures. 'And it came to pass at that time that God the Lord (Yahweh) spoke to Moses in the cloud. And the Lord cried to Moses, "Moses!" And Moses replied "It is (really) I! I am Moses thy servant, speak and I shall listen!" And the Lord spoke to Moses and said to him, *"I am that I am."*'

God thus defines himself as the Subject *par excellence,* he who is through himself and for himself ('I am that I am'),

---

[12] [Althusser] Although we know that the individual is always already a subject, we go on using this term, convenient because of the contrasting effect it produces.

[13] [Althusser] I am quoting in a combined way, not to the letter but 'in spirit and truth.'

and he who interpellates his subject, the individual subjected to him by his very interpellation, i.e. the individual named Moses. And Moses, interpellated-called by his Name, having recognized that it 'really' was he who was called by God, recognizes that he is a subject, a subject *of* God, a subject subjected to God, *a subject through the Subject and subjected to the Subject*. The proof: he obeys him, and makes his people obey God's Commandments.

God is the Subject, and Moses and the innumerable subjects of God's people, the Subject's interlocutors-interpellates: his *mirrors,* his *reflections.* Were not men made *in the image* of God? As all theological reflection proves, whereas He 'could' perfectly well have done without men, God needs them, the Subject needs the subjects, just as men need God, the subjects need the Subject. Better: God needs men, the great Subject needs subjects, even in the terrible inversion of his image in them (when the subjects wallow in debauchery, i.e. sin).

Better: God duplicates himself and sends his Son to the Earth, as a mere subject 'forsaken' by him (the long complaint of the Garden of Olives which ends in the Crucifixion), subject but Subject, man but God, to do what prepares the way for the final Redemption, the Resurrection of Christ. God thus needs to 'make himself' a man, the Subject needs to become a subject, as if to show empirically, visibly to the eye, tangibly to the hands (see St. Thomas)[14] of the subjects, that, if they are subjects, subjected to the Subject, that is solely in order that finally, on Judgement Day, they will re-enter the Lord's Bosom, like Christ, i.e. re-enter the Subject.[15]

Let us decipher into theoretical language this wonderful necessity for the duplication of *the Subject into subjects* and of *the Subject itself into a subject-Subject.*

We observe that the structure of all ideology, interpellating individuals as subjects in the name of a Unique and Absolute Subject is *speculary,* i.e. a mirror-structure, and *doubly* speculary: this mirror duplication is constitutive of ideology and ensures its functioning. Which means that all ideology is *centred,* that the Absolute Subject occupies the unique place of the Centre, and interpellates around it the infinity of individuals into subjects in a double mirror-connexion such that it *subjects* the subjects to the Subject, while giving them in the Subject in which each subject can contemplate its own image (present and future) the *guarantee* that this really concerns them and Him, and that since everything takes place in the Family (the Holy Family: the Family is in essence Holy), 'God will *recognize* his own in it,' i.e. those who have recognized God, and have recognized themselves in Him, will be saved.

Let me summarize what we have discovered about ideology in general.

The duplicate mirror-structure of ideology ensures simultaneously:

1. the interpellation of 'individuals' as subjects;

2. their subjection to the Subject;

3. the mutual recognition of subjects and Subject, the subjects' recognition of each other, and finally the subject's recognition of himself;[16]

4. the absolute guarantee that everything really is so, and that on condition that the subjects recognize what they are and behave accordingly, everything will be all right; Amen—'*So be it.*'

Result: caught in this quadruple system of interpellation as subjects, of subjection to the Subject, of universal recognition and of absolute guarantee, the subjects 'work,' they 'work by themselves' in the vast majority of cases, with the exception of the 'bad subjects' who on occasion provoke the intervention of one of the detachments of the (repressive) State apparatus. But the vast majority of (good) subjects work all right 'all by themselves,' i.e. by ideology (whose concrete forms are realized in the Ideological State Apparatuses). They are inserted into practices governed by the rituals of the ISAs. They 'recognize' the existing state of affairs *(das Bestehende),* that 'it really is true that it is so and not otherwise,' and that they must be obedient to God, to their conscience, to the priest, to de Gaulle, to the boss, to the engineer, that thou shalt 'love thy neighbour as thyself,' etc. Their concrete, material behaviour is simply the inscription in life of the admirable words of the prayer: '*Amen—So be it.*'

Yes, the subjects 'work by themselves.' The whole mystery of this effect lies in the first two moments of the quadruple system I have just discussed, or, if you prefer, in the ambiguity of the term *subject.* In the ordinary use of the term, subject in fact means: (1) a free subjectivity, a centre of initiatives, author of and responsible for its actions; (2) a subjected being, who submits to a higher authority, and is therefore stripped of all freedom except that of freely accepting his submission. This last note gives us the meaning

---

[14] Aquinas (above, page 149), philosopher and churchman.

[15] [Althusser] The dogma of the Trinity is precisely the theory of the duplication of the Subject (the Father) into a subject (the Son) and of their mirror connexion (the Holy Spirit).

[16] [Althusser] Hegel is (unknowingly) an admirable 'theoretician' of ideology insofar as he is a 'theoretician' of Universal Recognition who unfortunately ends up in the ideology of Absolute Knowledge. Feuerbach is an astonishing 'theoretician' of the mirror connexion, who unfortunately ends up in the ideology of the Human Essence. To find the material with which to construct a theory of the guarantee, we must turn to Spinoza.

of this ambiguity, which is merely a reflection of the effect which produces it: the individual *is interpellated as a (free) subject in order that he shall submit freely to the commandments of the Subject, i.e .in order that he shall (freely) accept his subjection,* i.e. in order that he shall make the gestures and actions of his subjection 'all by himself.' *There are no subjects except by and for their subjection.* That is why they 'work all by themselves.'

'*So be it!* . . .' This phrase which registers the effect to be obtained proves that it is not 'naturally' so ('naturally': outside the prayer, i.e. outside the ideological intervention). This phrase proves that it *has* to be so if things are to be what they must be, and let us let the words slip: if the reproduction of the relations of production is to be assured, even in the processes of production and circulation, every day, in the 'consciousness,' i.e. in the attitudes of the individual-subjects occupying the posts which the socio-technical division of labour assigns to them in production, exploitation, repression, ideologization, scientific practice, etc. Indeed, what is really in question in this mechanism of the mirror recognition of the Subject and of the individuals interpellated as subjects, and of the guarantee given by the Subject to the subjects if they freely accept their subjection to the Subject's 'commandments'? The reality in question in this mechanism, the reality which is necessarily *ignored (méconnue)* in the very forms of recognition (ideology=misrecognition/ignorance) is indeed, in the last resort, the reproduction of the relations of production and of the relations deriving from them.

January–April 1969

P.S. If these few schematic theses allow me to illuminate certain aspects of the functioning of the Superstructure and its mode of intervention in the Infrastructure, they are obviously *abstract* and necessarily leave several important problems unanswered, which should be mentioned:

1. The problem of the *total process* of the realization of the reproduction of the relations of production.

As an element of this process, the ISAs *contribute* to this reproduction. But the point of view of their contribution alone is still an abstract one.

It is only within the processes of production and circulation that this reproduction is *realized.* It is realized by the mechanisms of those processes, in which the training of the workers is 'completed,' their posts assigned them, etc. It is in the internal mechanisms of these processes that the effect of the different ideologies is felt (above all the effect of legal-ethical ideology).

But this point of view is still an abstract one. For in a class society the relations of production are relations of ex-

ploitation, and therefore relations between antagonistic classes. The reproduction of the relations of production, the ultimate aim of the ruling class, cannot therefore be a merely technical operation training and distributing individuals for the different posts in the 'technical division' of labour except in the ideology of the ruling class: every 'technical' division, every 'technical' organization of labour is the form and mask of a *social* (=class) division and organization of labour. The reproduction of the relations of production can therefore only be a class undertaking. It is realized through a class struggle which counterposes the ruling class and the exploited class.

The *total process* of the realization of the reproduction of the relations of production is therefore still abstract, insofar as it has not adopted the point of view of this class struggle. To adopt the point of view of reproduction is therefore, in the last instance, to adopt the point of view of the class struggle.

2. The problem of the class nature of the ideologies existing in a social formation.

The 'mechanism' of ideology *in general* is one thing. We have seen that it can be reduced to a few principles expressed in a few words (as 'poor' as those which, according to Marx, define production *in general,* or in Freud, define *the* unconscious *in general*). If there is any truth in it, this mechanism must be *abstract* with respect to every real ideological formation.

I have suggested that the ideologies were *realized* in institutions, in their rituals and their practices, in the ISAs. We have seen that on this basis they contribute to that form of class struggle, vital for the ruling class, the reproduction of the relations of production. But the point of view itself, however real, is still an abstract one.

In fact, the State and its Apparatuses only have meaning from the point of view of the class struggle, as an apparatus of class struggle ensuring class oppression and guaranteeing the conditions of exploitation and its reproduction. But there is no class struggle without antagonistic classes. Whoever says class struggle of the ruling class says resistance, revolt and class struggle of the ruled class.

That is why the ISAs are not the realization of ideology *in general,* nor even of the conflict-free realization of the ideology of the ruling class. The ideology of the ruling class does not become the ruling ideology by the grace of God, nor even by virtue of the seizure of State power alone. It is by the installation of the ISAs in which this ideology is realized and realizes itself that it becomes the ruling ideology. But this installation is not achieved all by itself; on the contrary, it is the stake in a very bitter and continuous class struggle: first against the former ruling classes and their positions in the old and new ISAs, then against the exploited class.

But this point of view of the class struggle in the ISAs is still an abstract one. In fact, the class struggle in the ISAs is indeed an aspect of the class struggle, sometimes an important and symptomatic one: e.g. the anti-religious struggle in the eighteenth century, or the 'crisis' of the educational ISA in every capitalist country today. But the class struggles in the ISAs is only one aspect of a class struggle which goes beyond the ISAs. The ideology that a class in power makes the ruling ideology in its ISAs is indeed 'realized' in those ISAs, but it goes beyond them, for it comes from elsewhere. Similarly, the ideology that a ruled class manages to defend in and against such ISAs goes beyond them, for it comes from elsewhere.

It is only from the point of view of the classes, i.e. of the class struggle, that it is possible to explain the ideologies existing in a social formation. Not only is it from this starting-point that it is possible to explain the realization of the ruling ideology in the ISAs and of the forms of class struggle for which the ISAs are the seat and the stake. But it is also and above all from this starting-point that it is possible to understand the provenance of the ideologies which are realized in the ISAs and confront one another there. For if it is true that the ISAs represent the *form* in which the ideology of the ruling class must *necessarily* be realized, and the form in which the ideology of the ruled class must *necessarily* be measured and confronted, ideologies are not 'born' in the ISAs but from the social classes at grips in the class struggle: from their conditions of existence, their practices, their experience of the struggle, etc.

April 1970

Paul de Man

1919–1983

In the early 1960s, Paul de Man achieved a considerable and well-deserved reputation as a brilliant reader of texts, but perhaps more important was his early role in shaping the reception of deconstruction in the United States. His collection of essays, *Blindness and Insight: Essays in the Rhetoric of Contemporary Criticism,* articulated the frequently confusing relation between critics' theoretical commitments and their actual critical insights, owing much to phenomenological criticism and existentialism, generally following Jean Paul Sartre (above, page 1175). From his earliest essays, but particularly in "The Intentional Structure of the Romantic Image," the central philosophical preoccupation in de Man's work was the problem of mystification, treated in the essay just mentioned, for example, in the commitment of Hölderlin to a conception of the poetic image that treated it as constitutive and generative, like organic nature. The contradiction, however, seems obvious: a word or image is not and apparently cannot be self-originating as a flower is. Yet the power of Hölderlin's poetry depends upon this apparent impossibility. The pursuit of this and related problems led de Man to his most widely recognized insight, that critics may be essentially blind to the very belief that enables their best insights.

After the publication of *Blindness and Insight,* however, de Man became increasingly identified with deconstruction, despite the fact that his primary interest in the rhetoric of criticism and the problem of mystification / demystification did not have the same basis as the work of Jacques Derrida, the primary theoretical source for deconstruction as a specifically philosophical undertaking. It may be, however, that de Man's exceptional lucidity and rhetorical ingenuity as a reader provided a point of access to deconstruction as a critical practice for literary scholars and critics more immediately influential than Derrida's more philosophical work would have been alone.

The subsequent trajectory of de Man's career, moreover, shows a heightening of interest in the subject of rhetoric, set quite explicitly in contrast to poetics, as the inevitable center for criticism once it confronts what de Man took to be the inescapable truth about the inherent rhetoricity of language as such. In this connection, de Man's work is very deeply tied to the study of Romanticism, in no small measure as the study of a pervasive mystification, which de Man took to be the work of a more enlightened rhetorical criticism to expose. In "The Rhetoric of Temporality" (1969), for example, de Man locates the problematic of Romanticism in the seemingly irreconcilable tropes of symbol and allegory, where the former posits an identification with, and the latter, an unbridgeable distance from its own origins. De Man sees this as leading inevitably to a contradiction between irreconcilable positions that assert the priority of the mind and self over nature, or nature over the self, a contradiction in which he sees a "genuine impasse." The form of rhetorical criticism that emerges from confronting this impasse, while it resembles the language of deconstruction following Derrida, differs in the role it gives to irony as a particular predicament of the self, constantly asserting its integrity before its experience of the world and of language, which undermines it.

In the selections reprinted here, the first from *Blindness and Insight,* and the second, "The Resistance of Theory," an essay written for but rejected by the Modern Language Association, together frame this problem in explicitly linguistic and rhetorical terms. The fate of rhetorical criticism, as de Man outlines it, is the tragic recognition that an aesthetic orientation to language cannot survive the insight that the linguistic sign is arbitrary and never adequate to its intentional objects.

Paul de Man's major books include: *Blindness and Insight: Essays in the Rhetoric of Contemporary Criticism* (1971, second ed. revised, 1983); *Allegories of Reading: Figural Language in Rousseau, Nietzsche, Rilke, and Proust* (1979); *The Rhetoric of Romanticism* (1984); and *The Resistance to Theory* (1986). Several collections have appeared since his death, including the highly controversial *Wartime Journalism, 1939–1943,* ed. Werner Hamacher, Neil Hertz, and Thomas Keenan (1988); *Critical Writings, 1953–1978,* ed. Lindsay Waters (1989); *Romanticism and Contemporary Criticism: The Gauss Seminar and Other Papers,* ed. E. S. Burt, Kevin Newmark, and Andrzej Warminski (1993); and *Aesthetic Ideology,* ed. Andrzej Warminski (1996). Studies of de Man include: Jonathan Arac, Wlad Godzich, and Wallace Martin, eds., *The Yale Critics: Deconstruction in America* (1983); Christopher Norris, *Paul de Man: Deconstruction and the Critique of Ideology* (1988); David Lehman, *Signs of the Times: Deconstruction and the Fall of Paul de Man* (1991); John Guillory, on de Man and teaching, in *Cultural Capital: The Problem of Literary Canon Formation* (1993); Rodolphe Gauché, *The Wild Card of Reading: Paul de Man* (1998).

Criticism and Crisis

When the French poet Stéphane Mallarmé[1] visited Oxford in 1894 to deliver a lecture entitled *La Musique et les lettres* and dealing with the state of French poetry at the time, he exclaimed, with mock sensationalism:

"I am indeed bringing you news. The most surprising news ever. Nothing like it ever happened before. They have tampered with the rules of verse . . . *On a touché au vers"* (Pléiade ed., 643).

In 1970, one might well feel tempted to echo Mallarmé's words, this time with regard not to poetry, but to literary criticism. *On a touché à la critique.* . . . Well-established rules and conventions that governed the discipline of criticism and made it a cornerstone of the intellectual establishment have been so badly tampered with that the entire edifice threatens to collapse. One is tempted to speak of recent developments in Continental criticism in terms of *crisis.* To confine oneself for the moment to purely outward symptoms, the crisis-aspect of the situation is apparent, for instance, in the incredible swiftness with which often conflicting tendencies succeed each other, condemning to immediate obsolescence what might have appeared as the extreme point of avant-gardisme briefly before. Rarely has the dangerous word "new" been used so freely; a few years ago, for very different reasons, there used to be in Paris a *Nouvelle Nouvelle Revue Française,* but today almost every new book that appears inaugurates a new kind of *nouvelle nouvelle critique.* It is hard to keep up with the names and the trends that succeed each other with bewildering rapidity. Not much more than ten years ago, names such as those of Bachelard, Sartre, Blanchot, or Poulet seemed to be those of daring pioneers, and younger men such as Jean-Pierre Richard or Jean Starobinski[2] proudly considered themselves as continuators

---

Criticism and Crisis was originally presented as a lecture at the University of Texas, Austin, and first appeared in *Arion* (Spring 1967). It is reprinted from *Blindness and Insight: Essays in the Rhetoric of Contemporary Criticism* (New York: Oxford University Press, 1971).

[1] Mallarmé (above, page 726).

[2] Gaston Bachelard (1884–1962), French existentialist and phenomenological critic; Jean Paul Sartre (above, page 1175); Maurice Blanchot (1907–2003), French writer and critic; Georges Poulet (1902–1991), French proponent of *le nouvelle critique;* Jean-Pierre Richard (b. 1922), French critic and literary scholar; Jean Starobinski (b. 1920), French critic and scholar of eighteenth-century and Romantic literature.

of the novel approaches that originated with their immediate predecessors. At that time, the main auxiliary discipline for literary criticism was undoubtedly philosophy. At the Sorbonne, which then as now saw its role primarily as one of conservation and even reaction, the theses considered too bold and experimental to be handled by the chairs of literature would quite naturally find their home among the philosophers. These philosophers were themselves engaged in working out a difficult synthesis between the vitalism of Bergson and the phenomenological method of Husserl;[3] this tendency proved quite congenial to the combined use of the categories of sensation, consciousness and temporality that is prevalent among the literary critics of this group. Today, very little remains, at least on the surface, of this cooperation between phenomenology and literary criticism. Philosophy, in the classical form of which phenomenology was, in France, the most recent manifestation, is out of fashion and has been replaced by the social sciences.

But it is by no means clear which one of the social sciences has taken its place, and the hapless and impatient new new critic is hard put deciding in which discipline he should invest his reading time. For a while, after Lucien Goldman's[4] theses on the sociology of Jansenism[5] in the seventeenth century, it seemed as if sociology was in the lead, and the name of Lukács[6] was being mentioned in Parisian intellectual circles with the same awe that used to surround the figures of Kierkegaard and Hegel[7] a few years earlier. But then Lévi-Strauss'[8] *Tristes tropiques* appeared, and anthropology definitely edged out sociology as the main concern of the literary critic. Hardly had he mastered the difficult terminology of tribal intersubjectivity when linguistics appeared over the horizon with an even more formidable technical jargon. And with the somewhat subterranean influence of Jacques Lacan,[9] psychoanalysis has made a comeback, giving rise to a neo-Freudian rebirth that seems to be quite germane to the concerns of several critics.

This sudden expansion of literary studies outside their own province and into the realm of the social sciences was perhaps long overdue. What is nowadays labeled "structuralism" in France is, on a superficial level, nothing but an attempt to formulate a general methodology of the sciences of man. Literary studies and literary criticism naturally play a certain part in this inquiry. There is nothing particularly new or crisis-like about this. Such attempts to situate literary studies in relation to the social sciences are a commonplace of nineteenth-century thought, from Hegel to Taine and Dilthey.[10] What seems crisis-like is, among outer signs, the sense of urgency, the impatient competitiveness with which the various disciplines vie for leadership.

What interest can this Gallic turbulence have for literary studies in America? The irony of Mallarmé's situation at his Oxford lecture was that his English listeners had little awareness of the emergency by which he claimed to be so disturbed. English prosody had not waited for some rather disreputable foreigners to start tampering with verse; free and blank verse were nothing very new in the country of Shakespeare and Milton, and English literary people thought of the alexandrine as the base supporting the column of the Spenserian stanza rather than as a way of life. They probably had difficulty understanding the rhetoric of crisis that Mallarmé was using, with an ironic slant that would not have been lost in Paris, but that certainly baffled his foreign audience. Similarly, speaking of a crisis in criticism in the United States today, one is likely to appear equally out of tone. Because American criticism is more eclectic, less plagued than its European counterpart by ideology, it is very open to impulses from abroad but less likely to experience them with the same crisis-like intensity. We have some difficulty taking seriously the polemical violence with which methodological issues are being debated in Paris. We can invoke the authority of the best historians to point out that what was considered a crisis in the past often turns out to be a mere ripple, that changes first experienced as upheavals tend to become absorbed in the continuity of much slower movements as soon as the temporal perspective broadens.

This kind of pragmatic common sense is admirable, up to the point where it lures the mind into self-satisfied complacency and puts it irrevocably to sleep. It can always be shown, on all levels of experience, that what other people experience as a crisis is perhaps not even a change; such observations depend to a very large extent on the standpoint of the observer. Historical "changes" are not like changes in nature, and the vocabulary of change and movement as it applies to historical process is a mere metaphor, not devoid of meaning, but without an objective correlative that can unambiguously

---

[3] Henri Bergson (1859–1941), French philosopher; Husserl (above, page 770).

[4] Lucien Goldmann (b. 1913), French sociological critic.

[5] Reformist doctrine of moral determinism, late seventeenth century.

[6] Georg Lukács (1885–1971), critical theorist.

[7] Søren Kierkegaard (1813–1855), Danish philosopher; Hegel (above, page 552).

[8] Lévi-Strauss (above, page 1119).

[9] Lacan (above, p. 990).

[10] Taine (above, page 639); Wilhelm Dilthey (1833–1911), German philosopher and theorist of the "human sciences" or humanities.

be pointed to in empirical reality, as when we speak of a change in the weather or a change in a biological organism. No set of arguments, no enumeration of symptoms will ever prove that the present effervescence surrounding literary criticism is in fact a crisis that, for better or worse, is reshaping the critical consciousness of a generation. It remains relevant, however, that these people are experiencing it as a crisis and that they are constantly using the language of crisis in referring to what is taking place. We must take this into account when reflecting on the predicament of others as a preliminary before returning to ourselves.

Again, Mallarmé's text of his Oxford lecture, very closely linked to another prose text of his that was written a little later on the same subject and is entitled *Crise de vers,* can give us a useful hint. Apparently, in these texts, Mallarmé is speaking about the experiments in prosody undertaken by a group of younger poets who call themselves (often without his direct encouragement) his disciples, and whom he designates by name: Henri de Régnier, Moréas, Vielé-Griffin, Gustave Kahn, Charles Morice, Emile Verhaeren, Dujardin, Albert Mockel,[11] and so on. And he pretends to believe that their partial rejection of traditional verse, in favor of free verse forms that he calls "polymorphic," represents a major crisis, the kind of apocalyptic tempest that often reappears as a central symbol in much of his own later poetry. It is obvious, for any historian of French literature, that Mallarmé exaggerates the importance of what is happening around him, to the point of appearing completely misled, not only in the eyes of his more phlegmatic British audience, but in the eyes of future historians as well. The poets he mentions are hardly remembered today, and certainly not praised for the explosive renovation with which Mallarmé seems to credit them. Moreover, one can rightly point out that Mallarmé not only overstates their importance, but that he seems to be blind to the forces within his own time that were indeed to have a lasting effect: he makes only a passing reference to Laforgue,[12] who is somewhat incongruously linked with Henri de Régnier, but fails to mention Rimbaud.[13] In short, Mallarmé seems to be entirely mystified into over-evaluating his own private circle of friends, and his use of the term "crisis" seems to be inspired by propaganda rather than by insight.

It does not take too attentive a reading of the text, however, to show that Mallarmé is in fact well aware of the relative triviality of what his disciples are taking so seriously. He is using them as a screen, a pretext to talk about something that concerns him much more; namely, his own experiments with poetic language. That is what he is referring to when he describes the contemporary condition of poetry as follows: "Orage, lustral, et dans des bouleversements, tout à l'acquit de la génération, récente, l'acte d'écrire se scruta jusqu'en l'origine. Très avant, au moins, quant au point, je le formule;—à savoir s'il y a lieu d'écrire." Freely translated and considerably flattened by filling in the elliptic syntax this becomes: "A tempest cleared the air: the new generation deserves credit for bringing this about. The act of writing scrutinized itself to the point of reflecting on its own origin, or, at any rate, far enough to reach the point where it could ask whether it is necessary for this act to take place." It matters little whether the "recent" generation to which Mallarmé refers indicates his younger disciples or his own contemporaries such as Verlaine, Villiers or even potentially Rimbaud.[14] We know with certainty that something crisis-like was taking place at that moment, making practices and assumptions problematic that had been taken for granted.

We have, to a large extent, lost interest in the actual event that Mallarmé was describing as a crisis, but we have not at all lost interest in a text that pretends to designate a crisis when it is, in fact, itself the crisis to which it refers. For here, as in all of Mallarmé's later prose and poetic works, the act of writing reflects indeed upon its own origin and opens up a cycle of questions that none of his real successors have been allowed to forget. We can speak of crisis when a "separation" takes place, by self-reflection, between what, in literature, is in conformity with the original intent and what has irrevocably fallen away from this source. Our question in relation to contemporary criticism then becomes: Is criticism indeed engaged in scrutinizing itself to the point of reflecting on its own origin? Is it asking whether it is necessary for the act of criticism to take place?

The matter is still further complicated by the fact that such scrutiny defines, in effect, the act of criticism itself. Even in its most naïve form, that of evaluation, the critical act is concerned with conformity to origin or specificity: when we say of art that it is good or bad, we are in fact judg-

---

[11] Henri de Régnier (1864–1936), distinguished French poet, member of the *Académie Française;* Jean Moréas (1856–1910), Greek-born French symbolist poet; Francis Vieleé-Griffin (1864–1937), American-born French symbolist poet; Gustave Kahn (1859–1936), French poet and critic, claimed to be the inventor of free verse; Charles Morice (1861–1919), French writer and art critic; Émile Verhaeren (1855–1916), Francophone Belgian poet, sometimes compared to Walt Whitman; Édouard Dujardin (1861–1949), French poet, advocate of free verse; Albert Mockel (1866–1945), French symbolist poet.

[12] Jules Laforgue (1860–1887), French symbolist poet, superb poetic craftsman.

[13] Arthur Rimbaud (1854–1891), French symbolist poet, broad influence on European writers.

[14] Paul Verlaine (1844–1896), influential French poet, associated with Parnassian movement, and the symbolists; Villiers de L'Isle-Adam (1838–1889), French poet and dramatist.

ing a certain degree of conformity to an original intent called artistic. We imply that bad art is barely art at all; good art, on the contrary, comes close to our preconceived and implicit notion of what art ought to be. For that reason, the notion of crisis and that of criticism are very closely linked, so much so that one could state that all true criticism occurs in the mode of crisis. To speak of a crisis of criticism is then, to some degree, redundant. In periods that are not periods of crisis, or in individuals bent on avoiding crisis at all cost, there can be all kinds of approaches to literature: historical, philological, psychological, etc., but there can be no criticism. For such periods or individuals will never put the act of writing into question by relating it to its specific intent. The Continental criticism of today is doing just that, and it therefore deserves to be called genuine literary criticism. It will become clear, I hope, that this is not to be considered as an evaluative but as a purely descriptive statement. Whether authentic criticism is a liability or an asset to literary studies as a whole remains an open question. One thing, however, is certain; namely, that literary studies cannot possibly refuse to take cognizance of its existence. It would be as if historians refused to acknowledge the existence of wars because they threaten to interfere with the serenity that is indispensable to an orderly pursuit of their discipline.

The trend in Continental criticism, whether it derives its language from sociology, psychoanalysis, ethnology, linguistics, or even from certain forms of philosophy, can be quickly summarized: it represents a methodologically motivated attack on the notion that a literary or poetic consciousness is in any way a privileged consciousness, whose use of language can pretend to escape, to some degree, from the duplicity, the confusion, the untruth that we take for granted in the everyday use of language. We know that our entire social language is an intricate system of rhetorical devices designed to escape from the direct expression of desires that are, in the fullest sense of the term, unnameable—not because they are ethically shameful (for this would make the problem a very simple one), but because unmediated expression is a philosophical impossibility. And we know that the individual who chose to ignore this fundamental convention would be slated either for crucifixion, if he were aware, or, if he were naïve, destined to the total ridicule accorded such heroes as Candide[15] and all other fools in fiction or in life. The contemporary contribution to this age-old problem comes by way of a rephrasing of the problem that develops when a consciousness gets involved in interpreting another

consciousness, the basic pattern from which there can be no escape in the social sciences (if there is to be such a thing). Lévi-Strauss, for instance, starts out from the need to protect anthropologists engaged in the study of a so-called "primitive" society from the error made by earlier positivistic anthropologists when they projected upon this society assumptions that remained nonconsciously determined by the inhibitions and shortcomings of their own social situation. Prior to making any valid statement about a distant society, the observing subject must be as clear as possible about his attitude towards his own. He will soon discover, however, that the only way in which he can accomplish this self-demystification is by a (comparative) study of his own social self as it engages in the observation of others, and by becoming aware of the pattern of distortions that this situation necessarily implies. The observation and interpretation of others is always also a means of leading to the observation of the self; true anthropological knowledge (in the ethnological as well as in the philosophical, Kantian sense of the term) can only become worthy of being called knowledge when this alternating process of mutual interpretation between the two subjects has run its course. Numerous complications arise, because the observing subject is no more constant than the observed, and each time the observer actually succeeds in interpreting his subject he changes it, and changes it all the more as his interpretation comes closer to the truth. But every change of the observed subject requires a subsequent change in the observer, and the oscillating process seems to be endless. Worse, as the oscillation gains in intensity and in truth, it becomes less and less clear who is in fact doing the observing and who is being observed. Both parties tend to fuse into a single subject as the original distance between them disappears. The gravity of this development will at once be clear if I allow myself to shift, for a brief moment, from the anthropological to the psychoanalytical or political model. In the case of a genuine analysis of the psyche, it means that it would no longer be clear who is analyzing and who is being analyzed; consequently the highly embarrassing question arises, who should be paying whom. And on a political level, the equally distressing question as to who should be exploiting whom, is bound to arise.

The need to safeguard reason from what might become a dangerous *vertige,* a dizziness of the mind caught in an infinite regression, prompts a return to a more rational methodology. The fallacy of a finite and single interpretation derives from the postulate of a privileged observer; this leads, in turn, to the endless oscillation of an intersubjective demystification. As an escape from this predicament, one can propose a radical relativism that operates from the most empirically specific to the most loftily general level of

---

[15] *Candide,* novel by François-Marie Arouat Voltaire (1694–1778), French writer.

human behavior. There are no longer any standpoints that can a priori be considered privileged, no structure that functions validly as a model for other structures, no postulate of ontological hierarchy that can serve as an organizing principle from which particular structures derive in the manner in which a deity can be said to engender man and the world. All structures are, in a sense, equally fallacious and are therefore called myths. But no myth ever has sufficient coherence not to flow back into neighboring myths or even has an identity strong enough to stand out by itself without an arbitrary act of interpretation that defines it. The relative unity of traditional myths always depends on the existence of a privileged point of view to which the method itself denies any status of authenticity. "Contrary to philosophical reflection, which claims to return to the source," writes Claude Lévi-Strauss in *Le Cru et le cuit,* "the reflective activities involved in the structural study of myths deal with light rays that issue from a virtual focal point. . . ." The method aims at preventing this virtual focus from being made into a *real* source of light. The analogy with optics is perhaps misleading, for in literature everything hinges on the existential status of the focal point; and the problem is more complex when it involves the disappearance of the self as a constitutive subject.

These remarks have made the transition from anthropology to the field of language and, finally, of literature. In the act of anthropological intersubjective interpretation, a fundamental discrepancy always prevents the observer from coinciding fully with the consciousness he is observing. The same discrepancy exists in everyday language, in the impossibility of making the actual expression coincide with what has to be expressed, of making the actual sign coincide with what it signifies. It is the distinctive privilege of language to be able to hide meaning behind a misleading sign, as when we hide rage or hatred behind a smile. But it is the distinctive curse of all language, as soon as any kind of interpersonal relation is involved, that it is forced to act this way. The simplest of wishes cannot express itself without hiding behind a screen of language that constitutes a world of intricate intersubjective relationships, all of them potentially inauthentic. In the everyday language of communication, there is no a priori privileged position of sign over meaning or of meaning over sign; the act of interpretation will always again have to establish this relation for the particular case at hand. The interpretation of everyday language is a Sisyphean task, a task without end and without progress, for the other is always free to make what he wants differ from what he says he wants. The methodology of structural anthropology and that of post-Saussurian linguistics thus share the common problem of a built-in discrepancy within the intersubjective relationship. As Lévi-Strauss, in order to protect the rationality of his science, had to come to the conclusion of a myth without an author, so the linguists have to conceive of a meta-language without speaker in order to remain rational.

Literature, presumably, is a form of language, and one can argue that all other art forms, including music, are in fact proto-literary languages. This, indeed, was Mallarmé's thesis in his Oxford lecture, as it is Lévi-Strauss' when he states that the language of music, as a language without speaker, comes closest to being the kind of meta-language of which the linguists are dreaming. If the radical position suggested by Lévi-Strauss is to stand, if the question of structure can only be asked from a point of view that is not that of a privileged subject, then it becomes imperative to show that literature constitutes no exception, that its language is in no sense privileged in terms of unity and truth over everyday forms of language. The task of structuralist literary critics then becomes quite clear: in order to eliminate the constitutive subject, they have to show that the discrepancy between sign and meaning (*signifiant* and *signifié*) prevails in literature in the same manner as in everyday language.

Some contemporary critics have more or less consciously been doing this. Practical criticism, in France and in the United States, functions more and more as a demystification of the belief that literature is a privileged language. The dominant strategy consists of showing that certain claims to authenticity attributed to literature are in fact expressions of a desire that, like all desires, falls prey to the duplicities of expression. The so-called "idealism" of literature is then shown to be an idolatry, a fascination with a false image that mimics the presumed attributes of authenticity when it is in fact just the hollow mask with which a frustrated, defeated consciousness tries to cover up its own negativity.

Perhaps the most specific example of this strategy is the use made by structuralist critics of the historical term "romantic"; the example also has the virtue of revealing the historical scheme within which they are operating, and which is not always openly stated. The fallacy of the belief that, in the language of poetry, sign and meaning can coincide, or at least be related to each other in the free and harmonious balance that we call beauty, is said to be a specifically romantic delusion. The unity of appearance (sign) and idea (meaning)—to use the terminology that one finds indeed among the theoreticians of romanticism when they speak of *Schein* and *Idee*—is said to be a romantic myth embodied in the recurrent topos of the "Beautiful Soul." The *schöne Seele,* a predominant theme of pietistic origin in eighteenth- and nineteenth-century literature, functions indeed as the *figura* of a privileged kind of language. Its outward appearance receives its beauty from an inner glow (or *feu sacré*) to which it is so finely attuned that, far from hiding it from sight, it gives it just the right balance of opacity and transparency, thus allowing the holy fire to shine without burning. The romantic imagination embodies this figure at times in the shape of a person, feminine, masculine or hermaphrodite, and seems to suggest that it exists as an actual, empirical subject: one thinks, for instance, of Rousseau's *Julie*, of Hölderlin's *Diotima*, or of the beautiful soul that appears in Hegel's *Phenomenology of the Spirit* and in Goethe's *Wilhelm Meister*.[16]

At this point, it is an irresistible temptation for the demystifying critic, from Voltaire down to the present, to demonstrate that this person, this actual subject, becomes ludicrous when it is transplanted in the fallen world of our facticity. The beautiful soul can be shown to spring from fantasies by means of which the writer sublimates his own shortcomings; it suffices to remove the entity for a moment from the fictional world in which it exists to make it appear even more ridiculous than Candide. Some authors, writing in the wake of the romantic myth, have been well aware of this. One can see how certain developments in nineteenth-century realism, the ironic treatment of the Rousseauistic figure by Stendhal, of the quixotic figure by Flaubert, or of the "poetic" figure by Proust, can be interpreted as a gradual demystification of romantic idealism.[17] This leads to a historical scheme in which romanticism represents, so to speak, the point of maximum delusion in our recent past, whereas the nineteenth and twentieth centuries represent a gradual emerging from this aberration, culminating in the breakthrough of the last decades that inaugurates a new form of insight and lucidity, a cure from the agony of the romantic disease. Refining on what may appear too crude in such a historical scheme, some modern critics transpose this movement within the consciousness of a single writer and show how the development of a novelist can best be understood as a successive process of mystifications and partial demystifications. The process does not necessarily move in one single direction, from delusion to insight; there can be an intricate play of relapses and momentary recoveries. All the same, the fundamental movement of the literary mind espouses the pattern of a demystifying consciousness; literature finally comes into its own, and becomes authentic,

when it discovers that the exalted status it claimed for its language was a myth. The function of the critic then naturally becomes coextensive with the intent at demystification that is more or less consciously present in the mind of the author.

This scheme is powerful and cogent, powerful enough, in fact, to go to the root of the matter and consequently to cause a crisis. To reject it convincingly would require elaborate argument. My remarks are meant to indicate some reasons, however, for considering the conception of literature (or literary criticism) as demystification the most dangerous myth of all, while granting that it forces us, in Mallarmé's terms, to scrutinize the act of writing "jusqu'en l'origine."

For reasons of economy, my starting point will have to be oblique, for in the language of polemics the crooked path often travels faster than the straight one. We must ask ourselves if there is not a recurrent epistemological structure that characterizes all statements made in the mood and the rhetoric of crisis. Let me take an example from philosophy. On May 7 and May 10 of 1935, Edmund Husserl, the founder of phenomenology, delivered in Vienna two lectures entitled "Philosophy and the Crisis of European Humanity"; the title was later changed to "The Crisis of European Humanity and Philosophy," to stress the priority of the concept of crisis as Husserl's main concern. The lectures are the first version of what was to become Husserl's most important later work, the treatise entitled *The Crisis of the European Sciences and Transcendental Phenomenology,* now the sixth volume of the complete works edited by Walter Biemel. In these various titles, two words remain constant: the word "crisis" and the word "European"; it is in the interaction of these two concepts that the epistemological structure of the crisis-statement is fully revealed.

Reading this text with the hindsight that stems from more than thirty years of turbulent history, it strikes one as both prophetic and tragic. Much of what is being stated seems relevant today. It is not by a mere freak of language that the key word "demythification" *(Entmythisierung),* that was destined to have such an important career, appears in the text (VI. 340.4), although the context in which the term is used, designating what takes place when the superior theoretical man observes the inferior natural man, is highly revealing. There is a very modern note in Husserl's description of philosophy as a process by means of which naïve assumptions are made accessible to consciousness by an act of critical self-understanding. Husserl conceived of philosophy primarily as a self-interpretation by means of which we eliminate what he calls *Selbstverhülltheit,* the tendency of the self to hide from the light it can cast on itself. The universality of philosophical knowledge stems from a persistently reflective attitude that

---

[16] Jean-Jacques Rousseau (1712–1778), French writer; Friedrich Hölderlin (1770–1843), German poet; Johann Wilhelm von Goethe (1749–1832), German poet and dramatist.

[17] Stendhal (Marie-Henri Beyle, 1783–1842); Gustave Flaubert (1821–1880); Marcel Proust (1871–1922), all French novelists.

can take philosophy itself for its theme. He describes philosophy as a prolegomenon to a new kind of praxis, a "universal critique of all life and all the goals of life, of all the man-created cultural systems and achievements" and, consequently, "a criticism of man himself (*Kritik der Menschheit selbst*) and of the values by which he is consciously or pre-consciously being governed."

Alerted by this convincing appeal to self-critical vigilance, Husserl's listeners and his present-day readers may well be tempted to turn this philosophical criticism on Husserl's own text, especially on the numerous sections in which philosophy is said to be the historical privilege of European man. Husserl speaks repeatedly of non-European cultures as primitive, prescientific and pre-philosophical, myth-dominated and congenitally incapable of the disinterested distance without which there can be no philosophical meditation. This, although by his own definition philosophy, as unrestricted reflection upon the self, necessarily tends toward a universality that finds its concrete, geographical correlative in the formation of supratribal, supranational communities such as, for instance, Europe. Why this geographical expansion should have chosen to stop, once and forever, at the Atlantic Ocean and at the Caucasus, Husserl does not say. No one could be more open to Lévi-Strauss' criticism of the mystified anthropologist than Husserl when he warns us, with the noblest of intentions, that we should not assume a potential for philosophical attitudes in non-European cultures. The privileged viewpoint of the post-Hellenic, European consciousness is never for a moment put into question; the crucial, determining examination on which depends Husserl's right to call himself, by his own terms, a philosopher, is in fact never undertaken. As a European, it seems that Husserl escapes from the necessary self-criticism that is prior to all philosophical truth about the self. He is committing precisely the mistake that Rousseau did not commit when he carefully avoided giving his concept of natural man, the basis of his anthropology, any empirical status whatever. Husserl's claim to European supremacy hardly stands in need of criticism today. Since we are speaking of a man of superior good will, it suffices to point to the pathos of such a claim at a moment when Europe was about to destroy itself as center in the name of its unwarranted claim to be the center.

The point, however, transcends the personal situation. Speaking in what was in fact a state of urgent personal and political crisis about a more general form of crisis, Husserl's text reveals with striking clarity the structure of all crisis-determined statements. It establishes an important truth: the fact that philosophical knowledge can only come into being when it is turned back upon itself. But it immediately proceeds, in the very same text, to do the opposite. The rhetoric of crisis states its own truth in the mode of error. It is itself radically blind to the light it emits. It could be shown that the same is true of Mallarmé's *Crise de vers,* which served as our original starting point—although it would be a great deal more complex to demonstrate the self-mystification of as ironical a man as Mallarmé than of as admirably honest a man as Husserl.

Our question, rather, is the following: How does this pattern of self-mystification that accompanies the experience of crisis apply to literary criticism? Husserl was demonstrating the urgent philosophical necessity of putting the privileged European standpoint into question, but remained himself entirely blind to this necessity, behaving in the most unphilosophical way possible at the very moment when he rightly understood the primacy of philosophical over empirical knowledge. He was, in fact, stating the privileged status of philosophy as an authentic language, but withdrawing at once from the demands of this authenticity as it applied to himself. Similarly, demystifying critics are in fact asserting the privileged status of literature as an authentic language, but withdrawing from the implications by cutting themselves off from the source from which they receive their insight.

For the statement about language, that sign and meaning can never coincide, is what is precisely taken for granted in the kind of language we call literary. Literature, unlike everyday language, begins on the far side of this knowledge; it is the only form of language free from the fallacy of unmediated expression. All of us know this, although we know it in the misleading way of a wishful assertion of the opposite. Yet the truth emerges in the foreknowledge we possess of the true nature of literature when we refer to it as *fiction.* All literatures, including the literature of Greece, have always designated themselves as existing in the mode of fiction; in the *Iliad,* when we first encounter Helen, it is as the emblem of the narrator weaving the actual war into the tapestry of a fictional object. Her beauty prefigures the beauty of all future narratives as entities that point to their own fictional nature. The self-reflecting mirror-effect by means of which a work of fiction asserts, by its very existence, its separation from empirical reality, its divergence, as a sign, from a meaning that depends for its existence on the constitutive activity of this sign, characterizes the work of literature in its essence. It is always against the explicit assertion of the writer that readers degrade the fiction by confusing it with a reality from which it has forever taken leave. "Le pays des chimères est en ce monde le seul digne d'être habité," Rousseau has Julie write, "et tel est le néant des choses humaines qu'hors l'Etre existant par lui-même, il n'y a rien de beau que ce qui n'est pas" (*La Nouvelle Heloïse*, Pléiade ed. II, 693). One entirely misunderstands this assertion of the priority of fiction over reality, of imagination over perception, if one considers it as the compensatory expression of a shortcoming, of a deficient sense of reality. It is attributed to a fictional character who knows all there is to know of human happiness and who is about to face death with Socratic equanimity. It transcends the notion of a nostalgia or a desire, since it discovers desire as a fundamental pattern of being that discards any possibility of satisfaction. Elsewhere, Rousseau speaks in similar terms of the nothingness of fiction *(le néant de mes chimères):* "If all my dreams had turned into reality, I would still remain unsatisfied: I would have kept on dreaming, imagining, desiring. In myself, I found an unexplainable void that nothing could have filled; a longing of the heart towards another kind of fulfillment of which I could not conceive but of which I nevertheless felt the attraction" (Letter to Malesherbes, Pléiade ed. I, 1140).

These texts can be called romantic, and I have purposely chosen them within the period and the author that many consider the most deluded of all. But one hesitates to use terms such as nostalgia or desire to designate this kind of consciousness, for all nostalgia or desire is desire of something or for someone; here, the consciousness does not result from the absence of something, but consists of the presence of a nothingness. Poetic language names this void with ever-renewed understanding and, like Rousseau's longing, it never tires of naming it again. This persistent naming is what we call literature. In the same manner that the poetic lyric originates in moments of tranquility, in the absence of actual emotions, and then proceeds to invent fictional emotions to create the illusion of recollection, the work of fiction invents fictional subjects to create the illusion of the reality of others. But the fiction is not myth, for it knows and names itself as fiction. It is not a demystification, it is demystified from the start. When modern critics think they are demystifying literature, they are in fact being demystified by it; but since this necessarily occurs in the form of a crisis, they are blind to what takes place within themselves. At the moment that they claim to do away with literature, literature is everywhere; what they call anthropology, linguistics, psychoanalysis is nothing but literature reappearing, like the Hydra's head, in the very spot where it had supposedly been suppressed. The human mind will go through amazing feats of distortion to avoid facing "the nothingness of human matters." In order not to see that the failure lies in the nature of things, one chooses to locate it in the individual, "romantic" subject, and thus retreats behind a historical scheme which, apocalyptic as it may sound, is basically reassuring and bland.

Lévi-Strauss had to give up the notion of subject to safeguard reason. The subject, he said, in fact, is a "foyer virtuel," a mere hypothesis posited by the scientists to give consistency to the behavior of entities. The metaphor in his statement that "the reflective activities [of the structuralists] deal with light that issues from a virtual focal point . . ." stems from the elementary laws of optical refraction. The image is all the more striking since it plays on the confusion between the imaginary loci of the physicist and the *fictional* entities that occur in literary language. The virtual focus is a quasi-objective structure posited to give rational integrity to a process that exists independently of the self. The subject merely fills in, with the dotted line of geometrical construction, what natural reason had not bothered to make explicit; it has a passive and unproblematic role. The "virtual focus" is, strictly speaking, a nothing, but its nothingness concerns us very little, since a mere act of reason suffices to give it a mode of being that leaves the rational order unchallenged. The same is not true of the imaginary source of fiction. Here the human self has experienced the void within itself and the invented fiction, far from filling the void, asserts itself as pure nothingness, *our* nothingness stated and restated by a subject that is the agent of its own instability. Lévi-Strauss' suppression of the subject is perfectly legitimate as an attempt to protect the scientific status of ethnology; by the same token, however, it leads directly into the larger question of the ontological status of the self. From this point on, a philosophical anthropology would be inconceivable without the consideration of literature as a primary source of knowledge.

The Resistance to Theory

This essay was not originally intended to address the question of teaching directly, although it was supposed to have a didactic and an educational function—which it failed to achieve. It was written at the request of the Committee on Research Activities of the Modern Language Association as a contribution to a collective volume entitled *Introduction to Scholarship in Modern Languages and Literatures.* I was asked to write the section on literary theory. Such essays are expected to follow a clearly determined program: they are supposed to provide the reader with a select but comprehensive list of the main trends and publications in the field, to

The Resistance to Theory was first published in *Yale French Studies* 63 (1982). It is reprinted here from *The Resistance to Theory* (Minneapolis: University of Minnesota Press, 1986).

synthesize and classify the main problematic areas and to lay out a critical and programmatic projection of the solutions which can be expected in the foreseeable future. All this with a keen awareness that, ten years later, someone will be asked to repeat the same exercise.

I found it difficult to live up, in minimal good faith, to the requirements of this program and could only try to explain, as concisely as possible, why the main theoretical interest of literary theory consists in the impossibility of its definition. The Committee rightly judged that this was an inauspicious way to achieve the pedagogical objectives of the volume and commissioned another article. I thought their decision altogether justified, as well as interesting in its implications for the teaching of literature.

I tell this for two reasons. First, to explain the traces in the article of the original assignment which account for the awkwardness of trying to be more retrospective and more general than one can legitimately hope to be. But, second, because the predicament also reveals a question of general interest: that of the relationship between the scholarship (the key word in the title of the MLA volume), the theory, and the teaching of literature.

Overfacile opinion notwithstanding, teaching is not primarily an intersubjective relationship between people but a cognitive process in which self and other are only tangentially and contiguously involved. The only teaching worthy of the name is scholarly, not personal; analogies between teaching and various aspects of show business or guidance counseling are more often than not excuses for having abdicated the task. Scholarship has, in principle, to be eminently teachable. In the case of literature, such scholarship involves at least two complementary areas: historical and philological facts as the preparatory condition for understanding, and methods of reading or interpretation. The latter is admittedly an open discipline, which can, however, hope to evolve by rational means, despite internal crises, controversies and polemics. As a controlled reflection on the formation of method, theory rightly proves to be entirely compatible with teaching, and one can think of numerous important theoreticians who are or were also prominent scholars. A question arises only if a tension develops between methods of understanding and the knowledge which those methods allow one to reach. If there is indeed something about literature, as such, which allows for a discrepancy between truth and method, between *Wahrheit* and *Methode*,[1] then scholarship and theory are no longer necessarily compatible; as a first casualty of this com-

plication, the notion of "literature as such" as well as the clear distinction between history and interpretation can no longer be taken for granted. For a method that cannot be made to suit the "truth" of its object can only teach delusion. Various developments, not only in the contemporary scene but in the long and complicated history of literary and linguistic instruction, reveal symptoms that suggest that such a difficulty is an inherent focus of the discourse about literature. These uncertainties are manifest in the hostility directed at theory in the name of ethical and aesthetic values, as well as in the recuperative attempts of theoreticians to reassert their own subservience to these values. The most effective of these attacks will denounce theory as an obstacle to scholarship and, consequently, to teaching. It is worth examining whether, and why, this is the case. For if this is indeed so, then it is better to fail in teaching what should not be taught than to succeed in teaching what is not true.

A general statement about literary theory should not, in theory, start from pragmatic considerations. It should address such questions as the definition of literature (what is literature?) and discuss the distinction between literary and non-literary uses of language, as well as between literary and non-verbal forms of art. It should then proceed to the descriptive taxonomy of the various aspects and species of the literary genus and to the normative rules that are bound to follow from such a classification. Or, if one rejects, a scholastic for a phenomenological model, one should attempt a phenomenology of the literary activity as writing, reading or both, or of the literary work as the product, the correlate of such an activity. Whatever the approach taken (and several other theoretically justifiable starting-points can be imagined) it is certain that considerable difficulties will arise at once, difficulties that cut so deep that even the most elementary task of scholarship, the delimitation of the corpus and the *état présent* of the question, is bound to end in confusion, not necessarily because the bibliography is so large but because it is impossible to fix its borderlines. Such predictable difficulties have not prevented many writers on literature from proceeding along theoretical rather than pragmatic lines, often with considerable success. It can be shown however that, in all cases, this success depends on the power of a system (philosophical, religious or ideological) that may well remain implicit but that determines an *a priori* conception of what is "literary" by starting out from the premises of the system rather than from the literary thing itself—if such a "thing" indeed exists. This last qualification is of course a real question which in fact accounts for the predictability of the difficulties just alluded to: if the condition of existence of an entity is itself particularly critical, then the theory of this entity is bound

---

[1] De Man alludes here to Hans-Georg Gadamer (1900–2002), German philosopher and theorist of hermeneutics, whose principal work was *Warheit und Methode* (1960; tr. *Truth and Method,* 1989).

to fall back into the pragmatic. The difficult and inconclusive history of literary theory indicates that this is indeed the case for literature in an even more manifest manner than for other verbalized occurrences such as jokes, for example, or even dreams. The attempt to treat literature theoretically may as well resign itself to the fact that it has to start out from empirical considerations.

Pragmatically speaking, then, we know that there has been, over the last fifteen to twenty years, a strong interest in something called literary theory and that, in the United States, this interest has at times coincided with the importation and reception of foreign, mostly but not always continental, influences. We also know that this wave of interest now seems to be receding as some satiation or disappointment sets in after the initial enthusiasm. Such an ebb and flow is natural enough, but it remains interesting, in this case, because it makes the depth of the resistance to literary theory so manifest. It is a recurrent strategy of any anxiety to defuse what it considers threatening by magnification or minimization, by attributing to it claims to power of which it is bound to fall short. If a cat is called a tiger it can easily be dismissed as a paper tiger; the question remains however why one was so scared of the cat in the first place. The same tactic works in reverse: calling the cat a mouse and then deriding it for its pretense to be mighty. Rather than being drawn into this polemical whirlpool, it might be better to try to call the cat a cat and to document, however briefly, the contemporary version of the resistance to theory in this country.

The predominant trends in North American literary criticism, before the nineteen sixties, were certainly not averse to theory, if by theory one understands the rooting of literary exegesis and of critical evaluation in a system of some conceptual generality. Even the most intuitive, empirical and theoretically low-key writers on literature made use of a minimal set of concepts (tone, organic form, allusion, tradition, historical situation, etc.) of at least some general import. In several other cases, the interest in theory was publicly asserted and practiced. A broadly shared methodology, more or less overtly proclaimed, links together such influential text books of the era as *Understanding Poetry* (Brooks and Warren), *Theory of Literature* (Wellek and Warren) and *The Fields of Light* (Reuben Brower) or such theoretically oriented works as *The Mirror and the Lamp, Language as Gesture* and *The Verbal Icon.*[2]

Yet, with the possible exception of Kenneth Burke and, in some respects, Northrop Frye, none of these authors would have considered themselves theoreticians in the post-1960 sense of the term, nor did their work provoke as strong reactions, positive or negative, as that of later theoreticians.[3] There were polemics, no doubt, and differences in approach that cover a wide spectrum of divergencies, yet the fundamental curriculum of literary studies as well as the talent and training expected for them were not being seriously challenged. New Critical approaches experienced no difficulty fitting into the academic establishments without their practitioners having to betray their literary sensibilities in any way; several of its representatives pursued successful parallel careers as poets or novelists next to their academic functions. Nor did they experience difficulties with regard to a national tradition which, though certainly less tyrannical than its European counterparts, is nevertheless far from powerless. The perfect embodiment of the New Criticism remains, in many respects, the personality and the ideology of T. S. Eliot,[4] a combination of original talent, traditional learning, verbal wit and moral earnestness, an Anglo-American blend of intellectual gentility not so repressed as not to afford tantalizing glimpses of darker psychic and political depths, but without breaking the surface of an ambivalent decorum that has its own complacencies and seductions. The normative principles of such a literary ambiance are cultural and ideological rather than theoretical, oriented towards the integrity of a social and historical self rather than towards the impersonal consistency that theory requires. Culture allows for, indeed advocates, a degree of cosmopolitanism, and the literary spirit of the American Academy of the fifties was anything but provincial. It had no difficulty appreciating and assimilating outstanding products of a kindred spirit that originated in Europe: Curtius, Auerbach, Croce, Spitzer, Alonso, Valéry[5] and also, with the exception of some of his works, J. P. Sartre. The inclusion of Sartre in this list is important, for it indicates that the dominant cultural code we are trying to evoke cannot simply be assimilated to a political polarity of the left and the right, of the academic and non-academic, of Greenwich Village and Gambier, Ohio. Politically oriented and predominantly non-academic journals, of which the *Partisan Review* of the fifties remains the best example, did not (after due allowance is made for all proper reservations and distinctions) stand in any genuine opposition to the New Critical approaches. The broad,

---

[2] The methodology in question is the American "New Criticism." In addition to Cleanth Brooks (above, page 1035) and Robert Penn Warren (1905–1989), de Man mentions his own mentor at Harvard, Reuben Brower (b. 1908), and works (in order) by M. H. Abrams (above, page 1087), R. P. Blackmur (above, page 964), and W. K. Wimsatt (above, page 1026).

[3] Burke (above, page 1011); Frye (above, page 1136).
[4] Eliot (above, page 806).
[5] Ernst Robert Curtius (1886–1956), German literary historian and philologist; Eric Auerbach (1892–1957), German literary critic, author of *Mimesis* (1953); Benedetto Croce (1866–1952), Italian philosopher and aesthetician; Valéry (above, page 818).

though negative, consensus that brings these extremely diverse trends and individuals together is their shared resistance to theory. This diagnosis is borne out by the arguments and complicities that have since come to light in a more articulate opposition to the common opponent.

The interest of these considerations would be at most anecdotal (the historical impact of twentieth-century literary discussion being so slight) if it were not for the theoretical implications of the resistance to theory. The local manifestations of this resistance are themselves systematic enough to warrant one's interest.

What is it that is being threatened by the approaches to literature that developed during the sixties and that now, under a variety of designations, make up the ill-defined and somewhat chaotic field of literary theory? These approaches cannot be simply equated with any particular method or country. Structuralism was not the only trend to dominate the stage, not even in France, and structuralism as well as semiology are inseparable from prior tendencies in the Slavic domain. In Germany, the main impulses have come from other directions, from the Frankfurt school and more orthodox Marxists, from post-Husserlian phenomenology and post-Heideggerian hermeneutics, with only minor inroads made by structural analysis. All these trends have had their share of influence in the United States, in more or less productive combinations with nationally rooted concerns. Only a nationally or personally competitive view of history would wish to hierarchize such hard-to-label movements. The possibility of doing literary theory, which is by no means to be taken for granted, has itself become a consciously reflected-upon question and those who have progressed furthest in this question are the most controversial but also the best sources of information. This certainly includes several of the names loosely connected with structuralism, broadly enough defined to include Saussure, Jakobson and Barthes as well as Greimas and Althusser, that is to say, so broadly defined as to be no longer of use as a meaningful historical term.[6]

Literary theory can be said to come into being when the approach to literary texts is no longer based on non-linguistic, that is to say historical and aesthetic, considerations or, to put it somewhat less crudely, when the object of discussion is no longer the meaning or the value but the modalities of production and of reception of meaning and of value prior to their establishment—the implication being that this establishment

is problematic enough to require an autonomous discipline of critical investigation to consider its possibility and its status. Literary history, even when considered at the furthest remove from the platitudes of positivistic historicism, is still the history of an understanding of which the possibility is taken for granted. The question of the relationship between aesthetics and meaning is more complex, since aesthetics apparently has to do with the *effect* of meaning rather than with its content *per se*. But aesthetics is in fact, ever since its development just before and with Kant,[7] a phenomenalism of a process of meaning and understanding, and it may be naive in that it postulates (as its name indicates) a phenomenology of art and of literature which may well be what is at issue. Aesthetics is part of a universal system of philosophy rather than a specific theory. In the nineteenth-century philosophical tradition, Nietzsche's[8] challenge of the system erected by Kant, Hegel and their successors is a version of the general question of philosophy. Nietzsche's critique of metaphysics includes, or starts out from, the aesthetic, and the same could be argued for Heidegger. The invocation of prestigious philosophical names does not intimate that the present-day development of literary theory is a by-product of larger philosophical speculations. In some rare cases, a direct link may exist between philosophy and literary theory. More frequently, however, contemporary literary theory is a relatively autonomous version of questions that also surface, in a different context, in philosophy, though not necessarily in a clearer and more rigorous form. Philosophy, in England as well as on the Continent, is less freed from traditional patterns than it sometimes pretends to believe and the prominent, though never dominant, place of aesthetics among the main components of the system is a constitutive part of this system. It is therefore not surprising that contemporary literary theory came into being from outside philosophy and sometimes in conscious rebellion against the weight of its tradition. Literary theory may now well have become a legitimate concern of philosophy but it cannot be assimilated to it, either factually or theoretically. It contains a necessarily pragmatic moment that certainly weakens it as theory but that adds a subversive element of unpredictability and makes it something of a wild card in the serious game of the theoretical disciplines.

The advent of theory, the break that is now so often being deplored and that sets it aside from literary history and from literary criticism, occurs with the introduction of linguistic terminology in the metalanguage about literature. By linguistic terminology is meant a terminology that desig-

---

[6] Saussure (above, page 786); Jakobson (above, page 1132); Barthes (above, page 1255); A. J. Greimas (1917–2002), French critic and theorist of narrative; Althusser (above, page 1297).

[7] Kant (above, page 416).
[8] Nietzsche (above, page 686).

nates reference prior to designating the referent and takes into account, in the consideration of the world, the referential function of language or, to be somewhat more specific, that considers reference as a function of language and not necessarily as an intuition. Intuition implies perception, consciousness, experience, and leads at once into the world of logic and of understanding with all its correlatives, among which aesthetics occupies a prominent place. The assumption that there can be a science of language which is not necessarily a logic leads to the development of a terminology which is not necessarily aesthetic. Contemporary literary theory comes into its own in such events as the application of Saussurian linguistics to literary texts.

The affinity between structural linguistics and literary texts is not as obvious as, with the hindsight of history, it now may seem. Peirce, Saussure, Sapir and Bloomfield[9] were not originally concerned with literature at all but with the scientific foundations of linguistics. But the interest of philologists such as Roman Jakobson or literary critics such as Roland Barthes in semiology reveals the natural attraction of literature to a theory of linguistic signs. By considering language as a system of signs and of signification rather than as an established pattern of meanings, one displaces or even suspends the traditional barriers between literary and presumably non-literary uses of language and liberates the corpus from the secular weight of textual canonization. The results of the encounter between semiology and literature went considerably further than those of many other theoretical models—philological, psychological or classically epistemological—which writers on literature in quest of such models had tried out before. The responsiveness of literary texts to semiotic analysis is visible in that, whereas other approaches were unable to reach beyond observations that could be paraphrased or translated in terms of common knowledge, these analyses revealed patterns that could only be described in terms of their own, specifically linguistic, aspects. The linguistics of semiology and of literature apparently have something in common that only their shared perspective can detect and that pertains distinctively to them. The definition of this something, often referred to as literariness, has become the object of literary theory.

Literariness, however, is often misunderstood in a way that has provoked much of the confusion which dominates today's polemics. It is frequently assumed, for instance, that literariness is another word for, or another mode of, aesthetic response. The use, in conjunction with literariness, of such

terms as style and stylistics, form or even "poetry" (as in "the poetry of grammar"), all of which carry strong aesthetic connotations, helps to foster this confusion, even among those who first put the term in circulation. Roland Barthes, for example, in an essay properly and revealingly dedicated to Roman Jakobson, speaks eloquently of the writer's quest for a perfect coincidence of the phonic properties of a word with its signifying function. "We would also wish to insist on the Cratylism[10] of the name (and of the sign) in Proust. . . . Proust sees the relationship between signifier and signified as motivated, the one copying the other and representing in its material form the signified essence of the thing (and not the thing itself). . . . This realism (in the scholastic sense of the word), which conceives of names as the 'copy' of the ideas, has taken, in Proust, a radical form. But one may well ask whether it is not more or less consciously present in all writing and whether it is possible to be a writer without some sort of belief in the natural relationship between names and essences. The poetic function, in the widest sense of the word, would thus be defined by a Cratylian awareness of the sign, and the writer would be the conveyor of this secular myth which wants language to imitate the idea and which, contrary to the teachings of linguistic science, thinks of signs as motivated signs."[11] To the extent that Cratylism assumes a convergence of the phenomenal aspects of language, as sound, with its signifying function as referent, it is an aesthetically oriented conception; one could, in fact, without distortion, consider aesthetic theory, including its most systematic formulation in Hegel, as the complete unfolding of the model of which the Cratylian conception of language is a version. Hegel's somewhat cryptic reference to Plato, in the *Aesthetics,* may well be interpreted in this sense. Barthes and Jakobson often seem to invite a purely aesthetic reading, yet there is a part of their statement that moves in the opposite direction. For the convergence of sound and meaning celebrated by Barthes in Proust and, as Gérard Genette has decisively shown,[12] later dismantled by Proust himself as a seductive temptation to mystified minds, is also considered here to be a mere *effect* which language can perfectly well achieve, but which bears no substantial relationship, by analogy or by ontologically grounded imitation, to anything beyond that particular effect. It is a rhetorical rather than an aesthetic function of language, an identifiable trope (paronomasis) that operates on the level of the signifier and contains no

---

[9]Peirce (above, page 652); Edward Sapir (1884–1939) and Leonard Bloomfield (1887–1949), American linguists.

[10]Pertaining to Cratylus; see Plato (above, page 41).

[11][de Man] Roland Barthes, "Proust et les noms," in *To Honor Roman Jakobson* (The Hague: Mouton, 1976), part 1, pp. 157–58.

[12][de Man] [Gérard Genette (b. 1930)], "Proust et le language indirect," in *Figures II* (Paris: Seuill, 1969).

responsible pronouncement on the nature of the world—despite its powerful potential to create the opposite illusion. The phenomenality of the signifier, as sound, is unquestionably involved in the correspondence between the name and the thing named, but the link, the relationship between word and thing, is not phenomenal but conventional.

This gives the language considerable freedom from referential restraint, but it makes it epistemologically highly suspect and volatile, since its use can no longer be said to be determined by considerations of truth and falsehood, good and evil, beauty and ugliness, or pleasure and pain. Whenever this autonomous potential of language can be revealed by analysis, we are dealing with literariness and, in fact, with literature as the place where this negative knowledge about the reliability of linguistic utterance is made available. The ensuing foregrounding of material, phenomenal aspects of the signifier creates a strong illusion of aesthetic seduction at the very moment when the actual aesthetic function has been, at the very least, suspended. It is inevitable that semiology or similarly oriented methods be considered formalistic, in the sense of being aesthetically rather than semantically valorized, but the inevitability of such an interpretation does not make it less aberrant. Literature involves the voiding, rather than the affirmation, of aesthetic categories. One of the consequences of this is that, whereas we have traditionally been accustomed to reading literature by analogy with the plastic arts and with music, we now have to recognize the necessity of a non-perceptual, linguistic moment in painting and music, and learn to *read* pictures rather than to *imagine* meaning.

If literariness is not an aesthetic quality, it is also not primarily mimetic. Mimesis becomes one trope among others, language choosing to imitate a non-verbal entity just as paronomasis "imitates" a sound without any claim to identity (or reflection on difference) between the verbal and non-verbal elements. The most misleading representation of literariness, and also the most recurrent objection to contemporary literary theory, considers it as pure verbalism, as a denial of the reality principle in the name of absolute fictions, and for reasons that are said to be ethically and politically shameful. The attack reflects the anxiety of the aggressors rather than the guilt of the accused. By allowing for the necessity of a non-phenomenal linguistics, one frees the discourse on literature from naive oppositions between fiction and reality, which are themselves an offspring of an uncritically mimetic conception of art. In a genuine semiology as well as in other linguistically oriented theories, the referential function of language is not being denied—far from it; what is in question is its authority as a model for natural or phenomenal cognition. Literature is fiction not because it

somehow refuses to acknowledge "reality," but because it is not *a priori* certain that language functions according to principles which are those, or which are *like* those, of the phenomenal world. It is therefore not *a priori* certain that literature is a reliable source of information about anything but its own language.

It would be unfortunate, for example, to confuse the materiality of the signifier with the materiality of what it signifies. This may seem obvious enough on the level of light and sound, but it is less so with regard to the more general phenomenality of space, time or especially of the self; no one in his right mind will try to grow grapes by the luminosity of the word "day," but it is very difficult not to conceive the pattern of one's past and future existence as in accordance with temporal and spatial schemes that belong to fictional narratives and not to the world. This does not mean that fictional narratives are not part of the world and of reality; their impact upon the world may well be all too strong for comfort. What we call ideology is precisely the confusion of linguistic with natural reality, of reference with phenomenalism. It follows that, more than any other mode of inquiry, including economics, the linguistics of literariness is a powerful and indispensable tool in the unmasking of ideological aberrations, as well as a determining factor in accounting for their occurrence. Those who reproach literary theory for being oblivious to social and historical (that is to say ideological) reality are merely stating their fear at having their own ideological mystifications exposed by the tool they are trying to discredit. They are, in short, very poor readers of Marx's *German Ideology*.[13]

In these all too summary evocations of arguments that have been much more extensively and convincingly made by others, we begin to perceive some of the answers to the initial question: what is it about literary theory that is so threatening that it provokes such strong resistances and attacks? It upsets rooted ideologies by revealing the mechanics of their workings; it goes against a powerful philosophical tradition of which aesthetics is a prominent part; it upsets the established canon of literary works and blurs the borderlines between literary and non-literary discourse. By implication, it may also reveal the links between ideologies and philosophy. All this is ample enough reason for suspicion, but not a satisfying answer to the question. For it makes the tension between contemporary literary theory and the tradition of literary studies appear as a mere historical conflict between two modes of thought that happen to hold the stage at the same time. If the conflict is merely histori-

---

[13] Marx (above, page 607).

cal, in the literal sense, it is of limited theoretical interest, a passing squall in the intellectual weather of the world. As a matter of fact, the arguments in favor of the legitimacy of literary theory are so compelling that it seems useless to concern oneself with the conflict at all. Certainly, none of the objections to theory, presented again and again, always misinformed or based on crude misunderstandings of such terms as mimesis, fiction, reality, ideology, reference and, for that matter, relevance, can be said to be of genuine rhetorical interest.

It may well be, however, that the development of literary theory is itself overdetermined by complications inherent in its very project and unsettling with regard to its status as a scientific discipline. Resistance may be a built-in constituent of its discourse, in a manner that would be inconceivable in the natural sciences and unmentionable in the social sciences. It may well be, in other words, that the polemical opposition, the systematic non-understanding and misrepresentation, the unsubstantial but eternally recurrent objections, are the displaced symptoms of a resistance inherent in the theoretical enterprise itself. To claim that this would be sufficient reason not to envisage doing literary theory would be like rejecting anatomy because it has failed to cure mortality. The real debate of literary theory is not with its polemical opponents but rather with its own methodological assumptions and possibilities. Rather than asking why literary theory is threatening, we should perhaps ask why it has such difficulty going about its business and why it lapses so readily either into the language of self-justification and self-defense or else into the overcompensation of a programmatically euphoric utopianism. Such insecurity about its own project calls for self-analysis, if one is to understand the frustrations that attend upon its practitioners, even when they seem to dwell in serene methodological self-assurance. And if these difficulties are indeed an integral part of the problem, then they will have to be, to some extent, a-historical in the temporal sense of the term. The way in which they are encountered on the present local literary scene as a resistance to the introduction of linguistic terminology in aesthetic and historical discourse about literature is only one particular version of a question that cannot be reduced to a specific historical situation and called modern, post-modern, post-classical or romantic (not even in Hegel's sense of the term), although its compulsive way of forcing itself upon us in the guise of a system of historical periodization is certainly part of its problematic nature. Such difficulties can be read in the text of literary theory at all times, at whatever historical moment one wishes to select. One of the main achievements of the present theoretical trends is to have restored some awareness of this fact. Clas-

sical, medieval and Renaissance literary theory is now often being read in a way that knows enough about what it is doing not to wish to call itself "modern."

We return, then, to the original question in an attempt to broaden the discussion enough to inscribe the polemics inside the question rather than having them determine it. The resistance to theory is a resistance to the use of language about language. It is therefore a resistance to language itself or to the possibility that language contains factors or functions that cannot be reduced to intuition. But we seem to assume all too readily that, when we refer to something called "language," we know what it is we are talking about, although there is probably no word to be found in the language that is as overdetermined, self-evasive, disfigured and disfiguring as "language." Even if we choose to consider it at a safe remove from any theoretical model, in the pragmatic history of "language," not as a concept, but as a didactic assignment that no human being can bypass, we soon find ourselves confronted by theoretical enigmas. The most familiar and general of all linguistic models, the classical *trivium,* which considers the sciences of language as consisting of grammar, rhetoric, and logic (or dialectics), is in fact a set of unresolved tensions powerful enough to have generated an infinitely prolonged discourse of endless frustration of which contemporary literary theory, even at its most self-assured, is one more chapter. The difficulties extend to the internal articulations between the constituent parts as well as the articulation of the field of language with the knowledge of the world in general, the link between the *trivium* and the *quadrivium,* which covers the non-verbal sciences of number (arithmetic), of space (geometry), of motion (astronomy), and of time (music). In the history of philosophy, this link is traditionally, as well as substantially, accomplished by way of logic, the area where the rigor of the linguistic discourse about itself matches up with the rigor of the mathematical discourse about the world. Seventeenth-century epistemology, for instance, at the moment when the relationship between philosophy and mathematics is particularly close, holds up the language of what it calls geometry *(mos geometricus),* and which in fact includes the homogeneous concatenation between space, time and number, as the sole model of coherence and economy. Reasoning *more geometrico* is said to be "almost the only mode of reasoning that is infallible, because it is the only one to adhere to the true method, whereas all other ones are by natural necessity in a degree of confusion of which only geometrical minds can be aware."[14] This is a clear instance of the interconnection

---

[14] [de Man] Blaise Pascal, "De l'esprit géométrique et de l'art de persuader," in *Oeuvers completes,* L. Lafuma, ed. (Paris: Seuil, 1963), pp. 349 ff.

between a science of the phenomenal world and a science of language conceived as definitional logic, the pre-condition for a correct axiomatic-deductive, synthetic reasoning. The possibility of thus circulating freely between logic and mathematics has its own complex and problematic history as well as its contemporary equivalences with a different logic and a different mathematics. What matters for our present argument is that this articulation of the sciences of language with the mathematical sciences represents a particularly compelling version of a continuity between a theory of language, as logic, and the knowledge of the phenomenal world to which mathematics gives access. In such a system, the place of aesthetics is preordained and by no means alien, provided the priority of logic, in the model of the *trivium,* is not being questioned. For even if one assumes, for the sake of argument and against a great deal of historical evidence, that the link between logic and the natural sciences is secure, this leaves open the question, within the confines of the *trivium* itself, of the relationship between grammar, rhetoric and logic. And this is the point at which literariness, the use of language that foregrounds the rhetorical over the grammatical and the logical function, intervenes as a decisive but unsettling element which, in a variety of modes and aspects, disrupts the inner balance of the model and, consequently, its outward extension to the nonverbal world as well.

Logic and grammar seem to have a natural enough affinity for each other and, in the tradition of Cartesian linguistics, the grammarians of Port-Royal experienced little difficulty at being logicians as well. The same claim persists today in very different methods and terminologies that nevertheless maintain the same orientation toward the universality that logic shares with science. Replying to those who oppose the singularity of specific texts to the scientific generality of the semiotic project, A. J. Greimas disputes the right to use the dignity of "grammar" to describe a reading that would not be committed to universality. Those who have doubts about the semiotic method, he writes, "postulate the necessity of constructing a grammar for each particular text. But the essence *(le propre)* of a grammar is its ability to account for a large number of texts, and the metaphorical use of the term . . . fails to hide the fact that one has, in fact, given up on the semiotic project."[15] There is no doubt that what is here prudently called "a large number" implies the hope at least of a future model that would in fact be applicable to the generation of all texts. Again, it is not our present purpose to discuss the validity of this methodological optimism, but merely to offer it as an instance of

the persistent symbiosis between grammar and logic. It is clear that, for Greimas as for the entire tradition to which he belongs, the grammatical and the logical functions of language are co-extensive. Grammar is an isotope of logic.

It follows that, as long as it remains grounded in grammar, any theory of language, including a literary one, does not threaten what we hold to be the underlying principle of all cognitive and aesthetic linguistic systems. Grammar stands in the service of logic which, in turn, allows for the passage to the knowledge of the world. The study of grammar, the first of the *artes liberales,* is the necessary precondition for scientific and humanistic knowledge. As long as it leaves this principle intact, there is nothing threatening about literary theory. The continuity between theory and phenomenalism is asserted and preserved by the system itself. Difficulties occur only when it is no longer possible to ignore the epistemological thrust of the rhetorical dimension of discourse, that is, when it is no longer possible to keep it in its place as a mere adjunct, a mere ornament within the semantic function.

The uncertain relationship between grammar and rhetoric (as opposed to that between grammar and logic) is apparent, in the history of the *trivium,* in the uncertain status of figures of speech or tropes, a component of language that straddles the disputed borderlines between the two areas. Tropes used to be part of the study of grammar but were also considered to be the semantic agent of the specific function (or effect) that rhetoric performs as persuasion as well as meaning. Tropes, unlike grammar, pertain primordially to language. They are text-producing functions that are not necessarily patterned on a non-verbal entity, whereas grammar is by definition capable of extra-linguistic generalization. The latent tension between rhetoric and grammar precipitates out in the problem of reading, the process that necessarily partakes of both. It turns out that the resistance to theory is in fact a resistance to reading, a resistance that is perhaps at its most effective, in contemporary studies, in the methodologies that call themselves theories of reading but nevertheless avoid the function they claim as their object.

What is meant when we assert that the study of literary texts is necessarily dependent on an act of reading, or when we claim that this act is being systematically avoided? Certainly more than the tautology that one has to have read at least some parts, however small, of a text (or read some part, however small, of a text about this text) in order to be able to make a statement about it. Common as it may be, criticism by hearsay is only rarely held up as exemplary. To stress the by no means self-evident necessity of reading implies at least two things. First of all, it implies that literature

[15] [de Man] A. J. Greimas, *Du Sens* (Paris: Seuil, 1970), p. 13.

is not a transparent message in which it can be taken for granted that the distinction between the message and the means of communication is clearly established. Second, and more problematically, it implies that the grammatical decoding of a text leaves a residue of indetermination that has to be, but cannot be, resolved by grammatical means, however extensively conceived. The extension of grammar to include para-figural dimensions is in fact the most remarkable and debatable strategy of contemporary semiology, especially in the study of syntagmatic and narrative structures. The codification of contextual elements well beyond the syntactical limits of the sentence leads to the systematic study of metaphrastic dimensions and has considerably refined and expanded the knowledge of textual codes. It is equally clear, however, that this extension is always strategically directed towards the replacement of rhetorical figures by grammatical codes. This tendency to replace a rhetorical by a grammatical terminology (to speak of hypotaxis, for instance, to designate anamorphic or metonymic tropes) is part of an explicit program, a program that is entirely admirable in its intent since it tends towards the mastering and the clarification of meaning. The replacement of a hermeneutic by a semiotic model, of interpretation by decoding, would represent, in view of the baffling historical instability of textual meanings (including, of course, those of canonical texts), a considerable progress. Much of the hesitation associated with "reading" could thus be dispelled.

The argument can be made, however, that no grammatical decoding, however refined, could claim to reach the determining figural dimensions of a text. There are elements in all texts that are by no means ungrammatical, but whose semantic function is not grammatically definable, neither in themselves nor in context. Do we have to interpret the genitive in the title of Keats' unfinished epic *The Fall of Hyperion* as meaning "Hyperion's Fall," the case story of the defeat of an older by a newer power, the very recognizable story from which Keats indeed started out but from which he increasingly strayed away, or as "Hyperion Falling," the much less specific but more disquieting evocation of an actual process of falling, regardless of its beginning, its end or the identity of the entity to whom it befalls to be falling? This story is indeed told in the later fragment entitled *The Fall of Hyperion,* but it is told about a character who resembles Apollo rather than Hyperion, the same Apollo who, in the first version (called *Hyperion*), should definitely be triumphantly standing rather than falling if Keats had not been compelled to interrupt, for no apparent reason, the story of Apollo's triumph. Does the title tell us that Hyperion is fallen and that Apollo stands, or does it tell us that Hyperion and Apollo (and Keats, whom it is hard to distinguish, at times, from Apollo) are interchangeable in that all of them are necessarily and constantly falling? Both readings are grammatically correct, but it is impossible to decide from the context (the ensuing narrative) which version is the right one. The narrative context suits neither and both at the same time, and one is tempted to suggest that the fact that Keats was unable to complete either version manifests the impossibility, for him as for us, of reading his own title. One could then read the word "Hyperion" in the title *The Fall of Hyperion* figurally, or, if one wishes, intertextually, as referring not to the historical or mythological character but as referring to the title of Keats' own earlier text *(Hyperion).* But are we then telling the story of the failure of the first text as the success of the second, the Fall of *Hyperion* as the Triumph of *The Fall of Hyperion*? Manifestly, yes, but not quite, since the second text also fails to be concluded. Or are we telling the story of why all texts, as texts, can always be said to be falling? Manifestly yes, but not quite, either, since the story of the fall of the first version, as told in the second, applies to the first version only and could not legitimately be read as meaning also the fall of *The Fall of Hyperion.* The undecidability involves the figural or literal status of the proper name Hyperion as well as of the verb falling, and is thus a matter of figuration and not of grammar. In "Hyperion's Fall," the word "fall" is plainly figural, the representation of a figural fall, and we, as readers, read this fall standing up. But in "Hyperion Falling," this is not so clearly the case, for if Hyperion can be Apollo and Apollo can be Keats, then he can also be us and his figural (or symbolic) fall becomes his and our literal falling as well. The difference between the two readings is itself structured as a trope. And it matters a great deal how we read the title, as an exercise not only in semantics, but in what the text actually does to us. Faced with the ineluctable necessity to come to a decision, no grammatical or logical analysis can help us out. Just as Keats had to break off his narrative, the reader has to break off his understanding at the very moment when he is most directly engaged and summoned by the text. One could hardly expect to find solace in this "fearful symmetry" between the author's and reader's plight since, at this point, the symmetry is no longer a formal but an actual trap, and the question no longer "merely" theoretical.

This undoing of theory, this disturbance of the stable cognitive field that extends from grammar to logic to a general science of man and of the phenomenal world, can in its turn be made into a theoretical project of rhetorical analysis that will reveal the inadequacy of grammatical models of non-reading. Rhetoric, by its actively negative relationship to grammar and to logic, certainly undoes the claims of the *trivium* (and by extension, of language) to be an epistemologically stable construct. The resistance to theory is a resistance to the rhetorical or tropological dimension of language, a dimension which is perhaps more explicitly in the foreground in literature (broadly conceived) than in other verbal manifestations or—to be somewhat less vague—which can be revealed in any verbal event when it is read textually. Since grammar as well as figuration is an integral part of reading, it follows that reading will be a negative process in which the grammatical cognition is undone, at all times, by its rhetorical displacement. The model of the *trivium* contains within itself the pseudo-dialectic of its own undoing and its history tells the story of this dialectic.

This conclusion allows for a somewhat more systematic description of the contemporary theoretical scene. This scene is dominated by an increased stress on reading as a theoretical problem or, as it is sometimes erroneously phrased, by an increased stress on the reception rather than on the production of texts. It is in this area that the most fruitful exchanges have come about between writers and journals of various countries and that the most interesting dialogue has developed between literary theory and other disciplines, in the arts as well as in linguistics, philosophy and the social sciences. A straightforward *report* on the present state of literary theory in the United States would have to stress the emphasis on reading, a direction which is already present, moreover, in the New Critical tradition of the forties and the fifties. The methods are now more technical, but the contemporary interest in a poetics of literature is clearly linked, traditionally enough, to the problems of reading. And since the models that are being used certainly are no longer *simply* intentional and centered on an identifiable self, nor *simply* hermeneutic in the postulation of a single originary, pre-figural and absolute text, it would appear that this concentration on reading would lead to the rediscovery of the theoretical difficulties associated with rhetoric. This is indeed the case, to some extent; but not quite. Perhaps the most instructive aspect of contemporary theory is the refinement of the techniques by which the threat inherent in rhetorical analysis is being avoided at the very moment when the efficacy of these techniques has progressed so far that the rhetorical obstacles to understanding can no longer be mistranslated in thematic and phenomenal commonplaces. The resistance to theory which, as we saw, is a resistance to reading, appears in its most rigorous and theoretically elaborated form among the theoreticians of reading who dominate the contemporary theoretical scene.

It would be a relatively easy, though lengthy, process to show that this is so for theoreticians of reading who, like Greimas or, on a more refined level, Riffaterre or, in a very

different mode, H. R. Jauss or Wolfgang Iser[16]—all of whom have a definite, though sometimes occult, influence on literary theory in this country—are committed to the use of grammatical models or, in the case of *Rezeptionsästhetik,* to traditional hermeneutic models that do not allow for the problematization of the phenomenalism of reading and therefore remain uncritically confined within a theory of literature rooted in aesthetics. Such an argument would be easy to make because, once a reader has become aware of the rhetorical dimensions of a text, he will not be amiss in finding textual instances that are irreducible to grammar or to historically determined meaning, provided only he is willing to acknowledge what he is bound to notice. The problem quickly becomes the more baffling one of having to account for the shared reluctance to acknowledge the obvious. But the argument would be lengthy because it has to involve a textual analysis that cannot avoid being somewhat elaborate; one can succinctly suggest the grammatical indetermination of a title such as *The Fall of Hyperion,* but to confront such an undecidable enigma with the critical reception and reading of Keats' text requires some space.

The demonstration is less easy (though perhaps less ponderous) in the case of the theoreticians of reading whose avoidance of rhetoric takes another turn. We have witnessed, in recent years, a strong interest in certain elements in language whose function is not only not dependent on any form of phenomenalism but on any form of cognition as well, and which thus excludes, or postpones, the consideration of tropes, ideologies, etc., from a reading that would be primarily performative. In some cases, a link is reintroduced between performance, grammar, logic, and stable referential meaning, and the resulting theories (as in the case of Ohmann) are not in essence distinct from those of avowed grammarians or semioticians. But the most astute practitioners of a speech act theory of reading avoid this relapse and rightly insist on the necessity to keep the actual performance of speech acts, which is conventional rather than cognitive, separate from its causes and effects—to keep, in their terminology, the illocutionary force separate from its perlocutionary function. Rhetoric, understood as persuasion, is forcefully banished (like Coriolanus) from the performative moment and exiled in the affective area of perlocution. Stanley Fish, in a masterful essay, convincingly makes this point.[17] What awakens one's suspicion about this

---

[16] Michael Riffaterre (b. 1924), American theorist; Jauss (above, page 1237); German theorist; Iser (b. 1926), German theorist.

[17] [de Man] Stanley Fish, "How to Do Things with Austin and Searle: Speech Act Theory and Literary Criticism," in *MLN* 91 (1976), pp. 983–1025. See especially p. 1008.

conclusion is that it relegates persuasion, which is indeed inseparable from rhetoric, to a purely affective and intentional realm and makes no allowance for modes of persuasion which are no less rhetorical and no less at work in literary texts, but which are of the order of persuasion by *proof* rather than persuasion by seduction. Thus to empty rhetoric of its epistemological impact is possible only because its tropological, figural functions are being bypassed. It is as if, to return for a moment to the model of the *trivium,* rhetoric could be isolated from the generality that grammar and logic have in common and considered as a mere correlative of an illocutionary power. The equation of rhetoric with psychology rather than with epistemology opens up dreary prospects of pragmatic banality, all the drearier if compared to the brilliance of the performative analysis. Speech act theories of reading in fact repeat, in a much more effective way, the grammatization of the *trivium* at the expense of rhetoric. For the characterization of the performative as sheer convention reduces it in effect to a grammatical code among others. The relationship between trope and performance is actually closer but more disruptive than what is here being proposed. Nor is this relationship properly captured by reference to a supposedly "creative" aspect of performance, a notion with which Fish rightly takes issue. The performative power of language can be called positional, which differs considerably from conventional as well as from "creatively" (or, in the technical sense, intentionally) constitutive. Speech act oriented theories of reading read only to the extent that they prepare the way for the rhetorical reading they avoid.

But the same is still true even if a "truly" rhetorical reading that would stay clear of any undue phenomenalization or of any undue grammatical or performative codification of the text could be conceived—something which is not necessarily impossible and for which the aims and methods of literary theory should certainly strive. Such a reading would indeed appear as the methodical undoing of the grammatical construct and, in its systematic disarticulation of the *trivium,* will be theoretically sound as well as effective. Technically correct rhetorical readings may be boring, monotonous, predictable and unpleasant, but they are irrefutable. They are also totalizing (and potentially totalitarian) for since the structures and functions they expose do not lead to the knowledge of an entity (such as language) but are an unreliable process of knowledge production that prevents all entities, including linguistic entities, from coming into discourse as such, they are indeed universals, consistently defective models of language's impossibility to be a model language. They are, always in theory, the most elastic theoretical and dialectical model to end all models and they can rightly claim to contain within their own defective selves all the other defective models of reading-avoidance, referential, semiological, grammatical, performative, logical, or whatever. They are theory and not theory at the same time, the universal theory of the impossibility of theory. To the extent however that they are theory, that is to say teachable, generalizable and highly responsive to systematization, rhetorical readings, like the other kinds, still avoid and resist the reading they advocate. Nothing can overcome the resistance to theory since theory *is* itself this resistance. The loftier the aims and the better the methods of literary theory, the less possible it becomes. Yet literary theory is not in danger of going under; it cannot help but flourish, and the more it is resisted, the more it flourishes, since the language it speaks is the language of self-resistance. What remains impossible to decide is whether this flourishing is a triumph or a fall.

Clifford Geertz

b. 1926

In 1980, the anthropologist Clifford Geertz published an article titled "Blurred Genres: The Refiguration of Social Thought," which outlined a significant change in intellectual life and specifically in the social sciences. He observed a change in the latter from a "laws and instances ideal of explanation" to one of "cases and interpretations," and he noted that the social sciences were employing analogies drawn from the humanities. This he saw as part of a general change: "Something is happening to the way we think about the way we think." In the bulk of his article he discussed three analogies that had begun to dominate: game (including play), drama (including ritual and symbolization), and text (reflecting the turn to emphasis on language). The latter two especially had been derived in large part from literary criticism. Much of what Geertz wrote in this article is more or less taken for granted today.

In an earlier and longer essay, appearing here, Geertz makes a distinction, borrowed from the philosopher Gilbert Ryle, between "thin" and "thick" descriptions. The latter are those that give attention to the particularity of an event rather than submission of it to a theory. Events are unique and have unique contexts that require interpretation, not submission to "abstract regularities." Geertz writes of "delicacies of distinctions." "Refinement of debate" rather than "perfection of consensus" is the proper direction of anthropological thought. An interpretation should take us into the heart of the thing interpreted.

Geertz would seem to hold that anthropology should be like practical literary criticism, and in the essay below he treats as a sort of drama the example he gives of human interaction across cultural divides.

It is profitable to compare Geertz's approach to that of Claude Lévi-Strauss (above, page 1119), who champions a quite different method derived from structuralist linguistics and is critical of those "amateurs" who would move into anthropology from other disciplines.

Geertz's major writings include *Islam Observed: Religious Development in Morocco and Indonesia* (1968); *The Interpretation of Cultures* (1973); *Kinship in Bali* (with Hildred Geertz, 1975); *Person, Time, and Conduct in Bali* (1977); *Meaning and Order in Moroccan Society* (1979); *Local Knowledge: Selected Essays in Interpretive Anthropology* (1983); *Works and Lives: The Anthropologist as Author* (1988); *After the Fact: Two Countries, Four Decades, One Anthropologist* (1995); *Available Light: Anthropological Reflections on Philosophical Topics* (2000). See Kenneth A. Rice, *Geertz and Culture* (1980); James Clifford, *The Predicament of Culture* (1988); Fred Inglis, *Clifford Geertz: Culture, Custom, and Ethics* (2000). For a critique of Geertz's view of interpretation see Victor Crapanzano, *Hermes' Dilemma and Hamlet's Desire: On the Epistemology of Interpretation* (1992).

Thick Description: Toward an Interpretive Theory of Culture

I

In her book, *Philosophy in a New Key,* Susanne Langer[1] remarks that certain ideas burst upon the intellectual landscape with a tremendous force. They resolve so many fundamental problems at once that they seem also to promise that they will resolve all fundamental problems, clarify all obscure issues. Everyone snaps them up as the open sesame of some new positive science, the conceptual center-point around which a comprehensive system of analysis can be built. The sudden vogue of such a *grande idée,* crowding out almost everything else for a while, is due, she says, "to the fact that all sensitive and active minds turn at once to exploiting it. We try it in every connection, for every purpose, experiment with possible stretches of its strict meaning, with generalizations and derivatives."

After we have become familiar with the new idea, however, after it has become part of our general stock of theoretical concepts, our expectations are brought more into balance with its actual uses, and its excessive popularity is ended. A few zealots persist in the old key-to-the-universe view of it; but less driven thinkers settle down after a while to the problems the idea has really generated. They try to apply it and extend it where it applies and where it is capable of extension; and they desist where it does not apply or cannot be extended. It becomes, if it was, in truth, a seminal idea in the first place, a permanent and enduring part of our intellectual armory. But it no longer has the grandiose, all-promising scope, the infinite versatility of apparent application, it once had. The second law of thermodynamics, or the principle of natural selection, or the notion of unconscious motivation, or the organization of the means of production does not explain everything, not even everything human, but it still explains something; and our attention shifts to isolating just what that something is, to disentangling ourselves from a lot of pseudoscience to which, in the first flush of its celebrity, it has also given rise.

Whether or not this is, in fact, the way all centrally important scientific concepts develop, I don't know. But certainly this pattern fits the concept of culture, around which the whole discipline of anthropology arose, and whose domination that discipline has been increasingly concerned to limit, specify, focus, and contain. It is to this cutting of the culture concept down to size, therefore actually insuring its continued importance rather than undermining it, that the essays below are all, in their several ways and from their several directions, dedicated.[2] They all argue, sometimes explicitly, more often merely through the particular analysis they develop, for a narrowed, specialized, and, so I imagine, theoretically more powerful concept of culture to replace E. B. Tylor's famous "most complex whole,"[3] which, its originative power not denied, seems to me to have reached the point where it obscures a good deal more than it reveals.

The conceptual morass into which the Tylorean kind of *pot-au-feu* theorizing about culture can lead, is evident in what is still one of the better general introductions to anthropology, Clyde Kluckhohn's *Mirror for Man.*[4] In some twenty-seven pages of his chapter on the concept, Kluckhohn managed to define culture in turn as: (1) "the total way of life of a people"; (2) "the social legacy the individual acquires from his group"; (3) "a way of thinking, feeling, and believing"; (4) "an abstraction from behavior"; (5) a theory on the part of the anthropologist about the way in which a group of people in fact behave; (6) a "storehouse of pooled learning"; (7) "a set of standardized orientations to recurrent problems"; (8) "learned behavior"; (9) a mechanism for the normative regulation of behavior; (10) "a set of techniques for adjusting both to the external environment and to other men"; (11) "a precipitate of history"; and turning, perhaps in desperation, to similes, as a map, as a sieve, and as a matrix. In the face of this sort of theoretical diffusion, even a somewhat constricted and not entirely standard concept of culture, which is at least internally coherent and, more important, which has a definable argument to make is (as, to be fair, Kluckhohn himself keenly realized) an improvement. Eclecticism is self-defeating not because there is only one direction in which it is useful to move, but because there are so many: it is necessary to choose.

The concept of culture I espouse, and whose utility the essays below attempt to demonstrate, is essentially a semiotic one. Believing, with Max Weber,[5] that man is an animal

"Thick Description: Toward an Interpretive Theory of Culture" is reprinted from *The Interpretation of Cultures: Selected Essays* (New York: Basic Books, 1973).
[1] Susanne K. Langer (1895–1985), American philosopher.

[2] *The Interpretation of Cultures: Selected Essays* (1973).
[3] E. B. Tylor (1832–1917), English anthropologist.
[4] Clyde Kluckhohn (1905–1960), American anthropologist.
[5] Max Weber (1864–1920), German sociologist.

suspended in webs of significance he himself has spun. I take culture to be those webs, and the analysis of it to be therefore not an experimental science in search of law but an interpretive one in search of meaning. It is explication I am after, construing social expressions on their surface enigmatical. But this pronouncement, a doctrine in a clause, demands itself some explication.

II

Operationalism as a methodological dogma never made much sense so far as the social sciences are concerned, and except for a few rather too well-swept corners—Skinnerian[6] behaviorism, intelligence testing, and so on—it is largely dead now. But it had, for all that, an important point to make, which, however we may feel about trying to define charisma or alienation in terms of operations, retains a certain force: if you want to understand what a science is, you should look in the first instance not at its theories or its findings, and certainly not at what its apologists say about it; you should look at what the practitioners of it do.

In anthropology, or anyway social anthropology, what the practioners do is ethnography. And it is in understanding what ethnography is, or more exactly *what doing ethnography is,* that a start can be made toward grasping what anthropological analysis amounts to as a form of knowledge. This, it must immediately be said, is not a matter of methods. From one point of view, that of the textbook, doing ethnography is establishing rapport, selecting informants, transcribing texts, taking genealogies, mapping fields, keeping a diary, and so on. But it is not these things, techniques and received procedures, that define the enterprise. What defines it is the kind of intellectual effort it is: an elaborate venture in, to borrow a notion from Gilbert Ryle, "thick description."[7]

Ryle's discussion of "thick description" appears in two recent essays of his (now reprinted in the second volume of his *Collected Papers*) addressed to the general question of what, as he puts it, *"Le Penseur"* is doing: "Thinking and Reflecting" and "The Thinking of Thoughts." Consider, he says, two boys rapidly contracting the eyelids of their right eyes. In one, this is an involuntary twitch; in the other, a conspiratorial signal to a friend. The two movements are, as movements, identical; from an I-am-a-camera, "phenomenalistic" observation of them alone, one could not tell which was twitch and which was wink, or indeed whether both or either was twitch or wink. Yet the difference, however unphotographable, between a twitch and a wink is vast; as anyone unfortunate enough to have had the first taken for the second knows. The winker is communicating, and indeed communicating in a quite precise and special way: (1) deliberately, (2) to someone in particular, (3) to impart a particular message, (4) according to a socially established code, and (5) without cognizance of the rest of the company. As Ryle points out, the winker has done two things, contracted his eyelids and winked, while the twitcher has done only one, contracted his eyelids. Contracting your eyelids on purpose when there exists a public code in which so doing counts as a conspiratorial signal *is* winking. That's all there is to it: a speck of behavior, a fleck of culture, and— *voilà!*—a gesture.

That, however, is just the beginning. Suppose, he continues, there is a third boy, who, "to give malicious amusement to his cronies," parodies the first boy's wink, as amateurish, clumsy, obvious, and so on. He, of course, does this in the same way the second boy winked and the first twitched: by contracting his right eyelids. Only this boy is neither winking nor twitching, he is parodying someone else's, as he takes it, laughable, attempt at winking. Here, too, a socially established code exists (he will "wink" laboriously, overobviously, perhaps adding a grimace—the usual artifices of the clown); and so also does a message. Only now it is not conspiracy but ridicule that is in the air. If the others think he is actually winking, his whole project misfires as completely, though with somewhat different results, as if they think he is twitching. One can go further: uncertain of his mimicking abilities, the would-be satirist may practice at home before the mirror, in which case he is not twitching, winking, or parodying, but rehearsing; though so far as what a camera, a radical behaviorist, or a believer in protocol sentences would record he is just rapidly contracting his right eyelids like all the others. Complexities are possible, if not practically without end, at least logically so. The original winker might, for example, actually have been fake-winking, say, to mislead outsiders into imagining there was a conspiracy afoot when there in fact was not, in which case our descriptions of what the parodist is parodying and the rehearser rehearsing of course shift accordingly. But the point is that between what Ryle calls the "thin description" of what the rehearser (parodist, winker, twitcher . . .) is doing ("rapidly contracting his right eyelids") and the "thick description" of what he is doing ("practicing a burlesque of a friend faking a wink to deceive an innocent into thinking a conspiracy is in motion") lies the object of ethnography: a stratified hierarchy of meaningful structures in terms of which twitches, winks, fake-winks, parodies, rehearsals of parodies are produced, perceived,

---

[6]B. F. Skinner (1904–1990), American behaviorist psychologist.
[7]Gilbert Ryle (1900–1976), English philosopher.

and interpreted, and without which they would not (not even the zero-form twitches, which, *as a cultural category,* are as much nonwinks as winks are nontwitches) in fact exist, no matter what anyone did or didn't do with his eyelids.

Like so many of the little stories Oxford philosophers like to make up for themselves, all this winking, fake-winking, burlesque-fake-winking, rehearsed-burlesque-fake-winking, may seem a bit artificial. In way of adding a more empirical note, let me give, deliberately unpreceded by any prior explanatory comment at all, a not untypical excerpt from my own field journal to demonstrate that, however evened off for didactic purposes, Ryle's example presents an image only too exact of the sort of piled-up structures of inference and implication through which an ethnographer is continually trying to pick his way:

The French [the informant said] had only just arrived. They set up twenty or so small forts between here, the town, and the Marmusha area up in the middle of the mountains, placing them on promontories so they could survey the countryside. But for all this they couldn't guarantee safety, especially at night, so although the *mezrag,* trade-pact, system was supposed to be legally abolished it in fact continued as before.

One night, when Cohen (who speaks fluent Berber), was up there, at Marmusha, two other Jews who were traders to a neighboring tribe came by to purchase some goods from him. Some Berbers, from yet another neighboring tribe, tried to break into Cohen's place, but he fired his rifle in the air. (Traditionally, Jews were not allowed to carry weapons; but at this period things were so unsettled many did so anyway.) This attracted the attention of the French and the marauders fled.

The next night, however, they came back, one of them disguised as a woman who knocked on the door with some sort of a story. Cohen was suspicious and didn't want to let "her" in, but the other Jews said, "oh, it's all right, it's only a woman." So they opened the door and the whole lot came pouring in. They killed the two visiting Jews, but Cohen managed to barricade himself in an adjoining room. He heard the robbers planning to burn him alive in the shop after they removed his goods, and so he opened the door and, laying about him wildly with a club, managed to escape through a window.

He went up to the fort, then, to have his wounds dressed, and complained to the local commandant, one Captain Dumari, saying he wanted his *'ar*—i.e., four or five times the value of the merchandise stolen from him. The robbers were from a tribe which had not yet submitted to French authority and were in open rebellion against it, and he wanted authorization to go with his *mezrag*-holder, the Marmusha tribal *sheikh,* to collect the indemnity that, under traditional rules, he had coming to him. Captain Dumari couldn't officially give him permission to do this, because of the French prohibition of the *mezrag* relationship, but he gave him verbal authorization, saying, "If you get killed, it's your problem."

So the *sheikh,* the Jew, and a small company of armed Marmushans went off ten or fifteen kilometers up into the rebellious area, where there were of course no French, and, sneaking up, captured the thief-tribe's shepherd and stole its herds. The other tribe soon came riding out on horses after them, armed with rifles and ready to attack. But when they saw who the "sheep thieves" were, they thought better of it and said, "all right, we'll talk." They couldn't really deny what had happened—that some of their men had robbed Cohen and killed the two visitors—and they weren't prepared to start the serious feud with the Marmusha a scuffle with the invading party would bring on. So the two groups talked, and talked, and talked, there on the plain amid the thousands of sheep, and decided finally on five-hundred-sheep damages. The two armed Berber groups then lined up on their horses at opposite ends of the plain, with the sheep herded between them, and Cohen, in his black gown, pillbox hat, and flapping slippers, went out alone among the sheep, picking out, one by one and at his own good speed, the best ones for his payment.

So Cohen got his sheep and drove them back to Marmusha. The French, up in their fort, heard them coming from some distance ("Ba, ba, ba" said Cohen, happily, recalling the image) and said, "What the hell is that?" And Cohen said, "That is my *'ar.*" The French couldn't believe he had actually done what he said he had done, and accused him of being a spy for the rebellious Berbers, put him in prison, and took his sheep. In the town, his family, not having heard from him in so long a time, thought he was dead. But after a while the French released him and he came back home, but without his sheep. He then went to the Colonel in

1332 ◇ CLIFFORD GEERTZ

the town, the Frenchman in charge of the whole region, to complain. But the Colonel said, "I can't do anything about the matter. It's not my problem."

Quoted raw, a note in a bottle, this passage conveys, as any similar one similarly presented would do, a fair sense of how much goes into ethnographic description of even the most elemental sort—how extraordinarily "thick" it is. In finished anthropological writings, including those collected here, this fact—that what we call our data are really our own constructions of other people's constructions of what they and their compatriots are up to—is obscured because most of what we need to comprehend a particular event, ritual, custom, idea, or whatever is insinuated as background information before the thing itself is directly examined. (Even to reveal that this little drama took place in the highlands of central Morocco in 1912—and was recounted there in 1968—is to determine much of our understanding of it.) There is nothing particularly wrong with this, and it is in any case inevitable. But it does lead to a view of anthropological research as rather more of an observational and rather less of an interpretive activity than it really is. Right down at the factual base, the hard rock, insofar as there is any, of the whole enterprise, we are already explicating: and worse, explicating explications. Winks upon winks upon winks.

Analysis, then, is sorting out the structures of signification—what Ryle called established codes, a somewhat misleading expression, for it makes the enterprise sound too much like that of the cipher clerk when it is much more like that of the literary critic—and determining their social ground and import. Here, in our text, such sorting would begin with distinguishing the three unlike frames of interpretation ingredient in the situation, Jewish, Berber, and French, and would then move on to show how (and why) at that time, in that place, their copresence produced a situation in which systematic misunderstanding reduced traditional form to social farce. What tripped Cohen up, and with him the whole, ancient pattern of social and economic relationships within which he functioned, was a confusion of tongues.

I shall come back to this too-compacted aphorism later, as well as to the details of the text itself. The point for now is only that ethnography is thick description. What the ethnographer is in fact faced with—except when (as, of course, he must do) he is pursuing the more automatized routines of data collection—is a multiplicity of complex conceptual structures, many of them superimposed upon or knotted into one another, which are at once strange, irregular, and inexplicit, and which he must contrive somehow first to grasp and then to render. And this is true at the most down-to-earth, jungle field work levels of his activity: inter-

viewing informants, observing rituals, eliciting kin terms, tracing property lines, censusing households . . . writing his journal. Doing ethnography is like trying to read (in the sense of "construct a reading of") a manuscript—foreign, faded, full of ellipses, incoherencies, suspicious emendations, and tendentious commentaries, but written not in conventionalized graphs of sound but in transient examples of shaped behavior.

III

Culture, this acted document, thus is public, like a burlesqued wink or a mock sheep raid. Though ideational, it does not exist in someone's head; though unphysical, it is not an occult entity. The interminable, because unterminable, debate within anthropology as to whether culture is "subjective" or "objective," together with the mutual exchange of intellectual insults ("idealist!"—"materialist!"; "mentalist!"—"behaviorist!"; "impressionist!"—"positivist!") which accompanies it, is wholly misconceived. Once human behavior is seen as (most of the time; there *are* true twitches) symbolic action[8]—action which, like phonation in speech, pigment in painting, line in writing, or sonance in music, signifies—the question as to whether culture is patterned conduct or a frame of mind, or even the two somehow mixed together, loses sense. The thing to ask about a burlesqued wink or a mock sheep raid is not what their ontological status is. It is the same as that of rocks on the one hand and dreams on the other—they are things of this world. The thing to ask is what their import is: what it is, ridicule or challenge, irony or anger, snobbery or pride, that, in their occurrence and through their agency, is getting said.

This may seem like an obvious truth, but there are a number of ways to obscure it. One is to imagine that culture is a self-contained "super-organic" reality with forces and purposes of its own; that is, to reify it. Another is to claim that it consists in the brute pattern of behavioral events we observe in fact to occur in some identifiable community or other; that is, to reduce it. But though both these confusions still exist, and doubtless will be always with us, the main source of theoretical muddlement in contemporary anthropology is a view which developed in reaction to them and is right now very widely held—namely, that, to quote Ward Goodenough,[9] perhaps its leading proponent, "culture [is located] in the minds and hearts of men."

---

[8] A phrase established by Kenneth Burke (above, page 1011).
[9] Ward Goodenough, contemporary American anthropologist.

Variously called ethnoscience, componential analysis, or cognitive anthropology (a terminological wavering which reflects a deeper uncertainty), this school of thought holds that culture is composed of psychological structures by means of which individuals or groups of individuals guide their behavior. "A society's culture," to quote Goodenough again, this time in a passage which has become the *locus classicus* of the whole movement, "consists of whatever it is one has to know or believe in order to operate in a manner acceptable to its members." And from this view of what culture is follows a view, equally assured, of what describing it is—the writing out of systematic rules, an ethnographic algorithm, which, if followed, would make it possible so to operate, to pass (physical appearance aside) for a native. In such a way, extreme subjectivism is married to extreme formalism, with the expected result: an explosion of debate as to whether particular analyses (which come in the form of taxonomies, paradigms, tables, trees, and other ingenuities) reflect what the natives "really" think or are merely clever simulations, logically equivalent but substantively different, of what they think.

As, on first glance, this approach may look close enough to the one being developed here to be mistaken for it, it is useful to be explicit as to what divides them. If, leaving our winks and sheep behind for the moment, we take, say, a Beethoven[10] quartet as an, admittedly rather special but, for these purposes, nicely illustrative, sample of culture, no one would, I think, identify it with its score, with the skills and knowledge needed to play it, with the understanding of it possessed by its performers or auditors, nor, to take care, *en passant,* of the reductionists and reifiers, with a particular performance of it or with some mysterious entity transcending material existence. The "no one" is perhaps too strong here, for there are always incorrigibles. But that a Beethoven quartet is a temporally developed tonal structure, a coherent sequence of modeled sound—in a word, music— and not anybody's knowledge of or belief about anything, including how to play it, is a proposition to which most people are, upon reflection, likely to assent.

To play the violin it is necessary to possess certain habits, skills, knowledge, and talents, to be in the mood to play, and (as the old joke goes) to have a violin. But violin playing is neither the habits, skills, knowledge, and so on, nor the mood, nor (the notion believers in "material culture" apparently embrace) the violin. To make a trade pact in Morocco, you have to do certain things in certain ways (among others, cut, while chanting Quranic Arabic, the throat of a lamb before the assembled, undeformed, adult male members of your tribe) and to be possessed of certain psychological characteristics (among others, a desire for distant things). But a trade pact is neither the throat cutting nor the desire, though it is real enough, as seven kinsmen of our Marmusha sheikh discovered when, on an earlier occasion, they were executed by him following the theft of one mangy, essentially valueless sheepskin from Cohen.

Culture is public because meaning is. You can't wink (or burlesque one) without knowing what counts as winking or how, physically, to contract your eyelids, and you can't conduct a sheep raid (or mimic one) without knowing what it is to steal a sheep and how practically to go about it. But to draw from such truths the conclusion that knowing how to wink is winking and knowing how to steal a sheep is sheep raiding is to betray as deep a confusion as, taking thin descriptions for thick, to identify winking with eyelid contractions or sheep raiding with chasing woolly animals out of pastures. The cognitivist fallacy—that culture consists (to quote another spokesman for the movement, Stephen Tyler)[11] of "mental phenomena which can [he means "should"] be analyzed by formal methods similar to those of mathematics and logic"—is as destructive of an effective use of the concept as are the behaviorist and idealist fallacies to which it is a misdrawn correction. Perhaps, as its errors are more sophisticated and its distortions subtler, it is even more so.

The generalized attack on privacy theories of meaning is, since early Husserl and late Wittgenstein,[12] so much a part of modern thought that it need not be developed once more here. What is necessary is to see to it that the news of it reaches anthropology; and in particular that it is made clear that to say that culture consists of socially established structures of meaning in terms of which people do such things as signal conspiracies and join them or perceive insults and answer them, is no more to say that it is a psychological phenomenon, a characteristic of someone's mind, personality, cognitive structure, or whatever, than to say that Tantrism, genetics, the progressive form of the verb, the classification of wines, the Common Law, or the notion of "a conditional curse" (as Westermarck[13] defined the concept of *'ar* in terms of which Cohen pressed his claim to damages) is. What, in a place like Morocco, most prevents those of us who grew up winking other winks or attending other sheep from grasping what people are up to is not ignorance as to how cognition works (though, especially as, one

---

[10]Ludwig von Beethoven (1770–1827), German composer.

[11]Stephen Tyler (b. 1932), American anthropologist.
[12]Husserl (above, page 770); Wittgenstein (above, page 823).
[13]Edward Westermarck (1862–1939), Finnish sociologist.

assumes, it works the same among them as it does among us, it would greatly help to have less of that too) as a lack of familiarity with the imaginative universe within which their acts are signs. As Wittgenstein has been invoked, he may as well be quoted:

> We . . . say of some people that they are transparent to us. It is, however, important as regards this observation that one human being can be a complete enigma to another. We learn this when we come into a strange country with entirely strange traditions; and, what is more, even given a mastery of the country's language. We do not *understand* the people. (And not because of not knowing what they are saying to themselves.) We cannot find our feet with them.

IV

Finding our feet, an unnerving business which never more than distantly succeeds, is what ethnographic research consists of as a personal experience; trying to formulate the basis on which one imagines, always excessively, one has found them is what anthropological writing consists of as a scientific endeavor. We are not, or at least I am not, seeking either to become natives (a compromised word in any case) or to mimic them. Only romantics or spies would seem to find point in that. We are seeking, in the widened sense of the term in which it encompasses very much more than talk, to converse with them, a matter a great deal more difficult, and not only with strangers, than is commonly recognized. "If speaking *for* someone else seems to be a mysterious process," Stanley Cavell[14] has remarked, "that may be because speaking *to* someone does not seem mysterious enough."

Looked at in this way, the aim of anthropology is the enlargement of the universe of human discourse. That is not, of course, its only aim—instruction, amusement, practical counsel, moral advance, and the discovery of natural order in human behavior are others; nor is anthropology the only discipline which pursues it. But it is an aim to which a semiotic concept of culture is peculiarly well adapted. As interworked systems of construable signs (what, ignoring provincial usages, I would call symbols), culture is not a power, something to which social events, behaviors, institutions, or processes can be causally attributed; it is a context, something within which they can be intelligibly—that is, thickly—described.

The famous anthropological absorption with the (to us) exotic—Berber horsemen, Jewish peddlers, French Legionnaires—is, thus, essentially a device for displacing the dulling sense of familiarity with which the mysteriousness of our own ability to relate perceptively to one another is concealed from us. Looking at the ordinary in places where it takes unaccustomed forms brings out not, as has so often been claimed, the arbitrariness of human behavior (there is nothing especially arbitrary about taking sheep theft for insolence in Morocco), but the degree to which its meaning varies according to the pattern of life by which it is informed. Understanding a people's culture exposes their normalness without reducing their particularity. (The more I manage to follow what the Moroccans are up to, the more logical, and the more singular, they seem.) It renders them accessible: setting them in the frame of their own banalities, it dissolves their opacity.

It is this maneuver, usually too casually referred to as "seeing things from the actor's point of view," too bookishly as "the *verstehen*[15] approach," or too technically as "emic analysis," that so often leads to the notion that anthropology is a variety of either long-distance mind reading or cannibalisle fantasizing, and which, for someone anxious to navigate past the wrecks of a dozen sunken philosophies, must therefore be executed with a great deal of care. Nothing is more necessary to comprehending what anthropological interpretation is, and the degree to which it *is* interpretation, than an exact understanding of what it means—and what it does not mean—to say that our formulations of other peoples' symbol systems must be actor-oriented.[16]

What it means is that descriptions of Berber, Jewish, or French culture must be cast in terms of the constructions we imagine Berbers, Jews, or Frenchmen to place upon what they live through, the formulae they use to define what happens to them. What it does not mean is that such descriptions are themselves Berber, Jewish, or French—that is, part of the reality they are ostensibly describing; they are anthropological—that is, part of a developing system of scientific analysis. They must be cast in terms of the interpretations to which persons of a particular denomination subject their experience, because that is what they profess to be descriptions of; they are anthropological because it is, in fact, anthropologists who profess them. Normally, it is not necessary to point out quite so laboriously that the object of study is one thing and the

---

[14] Stanley Cavell (b. 1926), American philosopher.

[15] *Verstehen*: to understand.

[16] [Geertz] Not only other people's: anthropology *can* be trained on the culture of which it is itself a part, and it increasingly is; a fact of profound importance, but which, as it raises a few tricky and rather special second order problems, I shall put to the side for the moment.

study of it another. It is clear enough that the physical world is not physics and *A Skeleton Key to Finnegan's Wake* not *Finnegan's Wake*.[17] But, as, in the study of culture, analysis penetrates into the very body of the object—that is, *we begin with our own interpretations of what our informants are up to, or think they are up to, and then systematize those*—the line between (Moroccan) culture as a natural fact and (Moroccan) culture as a theoretical entity tends to get blurred. All the more so, as the latter is presented in the form of an actor's-eye description of (Moroccan) conceptions of everything from violence, honor, divinity, and justice, to tribe, property, patronage, and chiefship.

In short, anthropological writings are themselves interpretations, and second and third order ones to boot. (By definition, only a "native" makes first order ones: it's *his* culture.)[18] They are, thus, fictions; fictions, in the sense that they are "something made," "something fashioned"—the original meaning of *fictiō*—not that they are false, unfactual, or merely "as if" thought experiments. To construct actor-oriented descriptions of the involvements of a Berber chieftain, a Jewish merchant, and a French soldier with one another in 1912 Morocco is clearly an imaginative act, not all that different from constructing similar descriptions of, say, the involvements with one another of a provincial French doctor, his silly, adulterous wife, and her feckless lover in nineteenth century France.[19] In the latter case, the actors are represented as not having existed and the events as not having happened, while in the former they are represented as actual, or as having been so. This is a difference of no mean importance; indeed, precisely the one Madame Bovary had difficulty grasping. But the importance does not lie in the fact that her story was created while Cohen's was only noted. The conditions of their creation, and the point of it (to say nothing of the manner and the quality) differ. But the one is as much a *fictiō*—"a making"—as the other.

Anthropologists have not always been as aware as they might be of this fact: that although culture exists in the trading post, the hill fort, or the sheep run, anthropology exists in the book, the article, the lecture, the museum display, or,

sometimes nowadays, the film. To become aware of it is to realize that the line between mode of representation and substantive content is as undrawable in cultural analysis as it is in painting; and that fact in turn seems to threaten the objective status of anthropological knowledge by suggesting that its source is not social reality but scholarly artifice.

It does threaten it, but the threat is hollow. The claim to attention of an ethnographic account does not rest on its author's ability to capture primitive facts in faraway places and carry them home like a mask or a carving, but on the degree to which he is able to clarify what goes on in such places, to reduce the puzzlement—what manner of men are these?—to which unfamiliar acts emerging out of unknown backgrounds naturally give rise. This raises some serious problems of verification, all right—or, if "verification" is too strong a word for so soft a science (I, myself, would prefer "appraisal"), of how you can tell a better account from a worse one. But that is precisely the virtue of it. If ethnography is thick description and ethnographers those who are doing the describing, then the determining question for any given example of it, whether a field journal squib or a Malinowski-sized monograph,[20] is whether it sorts winks from twitches and real winks from mimicked ones. It is not against a body of uninterpreted data, radically thinned descriptions, that we must measure the cogency of our explications, but against the power of the scientific imagination to bring us into touch with the lives of strangers. It is not worth it, as Thoreau[21] said, to go round the world to count the cats in Zanzibar.

V

Now, this proposition, that it is not in our interest to bleach human behavior of the very properties that interest us before we begin to examine it, has sometimes been escalated into a larger claim: namely, that as it is only those properties that interest us, we need not attend, save cursorily, to behavior at all. Culture is most effectively treated, the argument goes, purely as a symbolic system (the catch phrase is, "in its own terms"), by isolating its elements, specifying the internal relationships among those elements, and then characterizing the whole system in some general way—according to the core symbols around which it is organized, the underlying structures of which it is a surface expression, or the ideological principles upon which it is based. Though a distinct improvement over "learned behavior" and "mental

---

[17] 1944, by James Campbell and Henry Morton Robinson, the first book on James Joyce's *Finnegans Wake* (1939).

[18] [Geertz] The order problem is, again, complex. Anthropological works based on other anthropological works (Lévi-Strauss, for example) may, of course, be fourth order or higher, and informants frequently, even habitually, make second order interpretations—what have come to be known as "native models." In literate cultures, where "native" interpretation can proceed to higher levels—in connection with the Magreb, one has only to think of Ibn Khaldun; within the United States, Margaret Mead—these matters become intricate indeed.

[19] Geertz refers here to *Madame Bovary* by Gustave Flaubert (1821–1880), French novelist.

[20] Bronislaw Malinowski (1884–1942), American anthropologist.

[21] Henry David Thoreau (1817–1892), American writer.

phenomena" notions of what culture is, and the source of some of the most powerful theoretical ideas in contemporary anthropology, this hermetical approach to things seems to me to run the danger (and increasingly to have been overtaken by it) of locking cultural analysis away from its proper object, the informal logic of actual life. There is little profit in extricating a concept from the defects of psychologism only to plunge it immediately into those of schematicism.

Behavior must be attended to, and with some exactness, because it is through the flow of behavior—or, more precisely, social action—that cultural forms find articulation. They find it as well, of course, in various sorts of artifacts, and various states of consciousness; but these draw their meaning from the role they play (Wittgenstein would say their "use") in an ongoing pattern of life, not from any intrinsic relationships they bear to one another. It is what Cohen, the sheikh, and "Captain Dumari" were doing when they tripped over one another's purposes—pursuing trade, defending honor, establishing dominance—that created our pastoral drama, and that is what the drama is, therefore, "about." Whatever, or wherever, symbol systems "in their own terms" may be, we gain empirical access to them by inspecting events, not by arranging abstracted entities into unified patterns.

A further implication of this is that coherence cannot be the major test of validity for a cultural description. Cultural systems must have a minimal degree of coherence, else we would not call them systems; and, by observation, they normally have a great deal more. But there is nothing so coherent as a paranoid's delusion or a swindler's story. The force of our interpretations cannot rest, as they are now so often made to do, on the tightness with which they hold together, or the assurance with which they are argued. Nothing has done more, I think, to discredit cultural analysis than the construction of impeccable depictions of formal order in whose actual existence nobody can quite believe.

If anthropological interpretation is constructing a reading of what happens, then to divorce it from what happens—from what, in this time or that place, specific people say, what they do, what is done to them, from the whole vast business of the world—is to divorce it from its applications and render it vacant. A good interpretation of anything—a poem, a person, a history, a ritual, an institution, a society—takes us into the heart of that of which it is the interpretation. When it does not do that, but leads us instead somewhere else—into an admiration of its own elegance, of its author's cleverness, or of the beauties of Euclidean order—it may have its intrinsic charms; but it is something else than what the task at hand—figuring out what all that rigamarole with the sheep is about—calls for.

The rigamarole with the sheep—the sham theft of them, the reparative transfer of them, the political confiscation of them—is (or was) essentially a social discourse, even if, as I suggested earlier, one conducted in multiple tongues and as much in action as in words.

Claiming his 'ar,' Cohen invoked the trade pact; recognizing the claim, the sheikh challenged the offenders' tribe; accepting responsibility, the offenders' tribe paid the indemnity; anxious to make clear to sheikhs and peddlers alike who was now in charge here, the French showed the imperial hand. As in any discourse, code does not determine conduct, and what was actually said need not have been. Cohen might not have, given its illegitimacy in Protectorate eyes, chosen to press his claim. The sheikh might, for similar reasons, have rejected it. The offenders' tribe, still resisting French authority, might have decided to regard the raid as "real" and fight rather than negotiate. The French, were they more *habile* and less *dur* (as, under Mareschal Lyautey's[22] seigniorial tutelage, they later in fact became), might have permitted Cohen to keep his sheep, winking—as we say—at the continuance of the trade pattern and its limitation to their authority. And there are other possibilities: the Marmushans might have regarded the French action as too great an insult to bear and gone into dissidence themselves; the French might have attempted not just to clamp down on Cohen but to bring the sheikh himself more closely to heel; and Cohen might have concluded that between renegade Berbers and Beau Geste soldiers, driving trade in the Atlas highlands was no longer worth the candle and retired to the better-governed confines of the town. This, indeed, is more or less what happened, somewhat further along, as the Protectorate moved toward genuine sovereignty. But the point here is not to describe what did or did not take place in Morocco. (From this simple incident one can widen out into enormous complexities of social experience.) It is to demonstrate what a piece of anthropological interpretation consists in: tracing the curve of a social discourse; fixing it into an inspectable form.

The ethnographer "inscribes" social discourse; *he writes it down*. In so doing, he turns it from a passing event, which exists only in its own moment of occurrence, into an account, which exists in its inscriptions and can be reconsulted. The sheikh is long dead, killed in the process of being, as the French called it, "pacified"; "Captain Dumari," his pacifier, lives, retired to his souvenirs, in the south of France; and Cohen went last year, part refugee, part pilgrim,

---

[22]Louis-Hubert-Gonsalve Lyautey (1854–1934), French statesman and soldier.

part dying patriarch, "home" to Israel. But what they, in my extended sense, "said" to one another on an Atlas plateau sixty years ago is—very far from perfectly—preserved for study. "What," Paul Ricoeur,[23] from whom this whole idea of the inscription of action is borrowed and somewhat twisted, asks, "what does writing fix?"

> Not the event of speaking, but the "said" of speaking, where we understand by the "said" of speaking that intentional exteriorization constitutive of the aim of discourse thanks to which the *sagen*—the saying—wants to become *Aus-sage*—the enunciation, the enunciated. In short, what we write is the *noema* ["thought," "content," "gist"] of the speaking. It is the meaning of the speech event, not the event as event.

This is not itself so very "said"—if Oxford philosophers run to little stories, phenomenological ones run to large sentences; but it brings us anyway to a more precise answer to our generative question, "What does the ethnographer do?"—he writes.[24] This, too, may seem a less than startling discovery, and to someone familiar with the current "literature," an implausible one. But as the standard answer to our question has been, "He observes, he records, he analyzes"—a kind of *veni, vidi, vici* conception of the matter— it may have more deep-going consequences than are at first apparent, not the least of which is that distinguishing these three phases of knowledge-seeking may not, as a matter of fact, normally be possible; and, indeed, as autonomous "operations" they may not in fact exist.

The situation is even more delicate, because, as already noted, what we inscribe (or try to) is not raw social discourse, to which, because, save very marginally or very specially, we are not actors, we do not have direct access, but only that small part of it which our informants can lead us into understanding.[25] This is not as fatal as it sounds, for, in fact, not all

Cretans are liars, and it is not necessary to know everything in order to understand something. But it does make the view of anthropological analysis as the conceptual manipulation of discovered facts, a logical reconstruction of a mere reality, seem rather lame. To set forth symmetrical crystals of significance, purified of the material complexity in which they were located, and then attribute their existence to autogenous principles of order, universal properties of the human mind, or vast, a priori *weltanschauungen,* is to pretend a science that does not exist and imagine a reality that cannot be found. Cultural analysis is (or should be) guessing at meanings, assessing the guesses, and drawing explanatory conclusions from the better guesses, not discovering the Continent of Meaning and mapping out its bodiless landscape.

VI

So, there are three characteristics of ethnographic description: it is interpretive; what it is interpretive of is the flow of social discourse; and the interpreting involved consists in trying to rescue the "said" of such discourse from its perishing occasions and fix it in perusable terms. The *kula* is gone or altered; but, for better or worse, *The Argonauts of the Western Pacific* remains. But there is, in addition, a fourth characteristic of such description, at least as I practice it: it is microscopic.

This is not to say that there are no large-scale anthropological interpretations of whole societies, civilizations, world events, and so on. Indeed, it is such extension of our analyses to wider contexts that, along with their theoretical implications, recommends them to general attention and justifies our constructing them. No one really cares anymore, not even Cohen (well . . . maybe, Cohen), about those sheep as such. History may have its unobtrusive turning points, "great noises in a little room"; but this little go-round was surely not one of them.

It is merely to say that the anthropologist characteristically approaches such broader interpretations and more abstract analyses from the direction of exceedingly extended acquaintances with extremely small matters. He confronts the same grand realities that others—historians, economists, political scientists, sociologists—confront in more fateful settings: Power, Change, Faith, Oppression, Work, Passion, Authority, Beauty, Violence, Love, Prestige; but he confronts them in contexts obscure enough—places like Marmusha and lives like Cohen's—to take the capital letters off them. These all-too-human constancies, "those big words that make us all afraid," take a homely form in such homely contexts. But that is exactly the advantage. There are enough profundities in the world already.

---

[23] Paul Ricoeur (b. 1913), French philosopher.

[24] [Geertz] Or, again, more exactly, "inscribes." Most ethnography is in fact to be found in books and articles, rather than in films, records, museum displays, or whatever; but even in them there are, of course, photographs, drawings, diagrams, tables, and so on. Self-consciousness about modes of representation (not to speak of experiments with them) has been very lacking in anthropology.

[25] [Geertz] So far as it has reinforced the anthropologist's impulse to engage himself with his informants as persons rather than as objects, the notion of "participant observation" has been a valuable one. But, to the degree it has led the anthropologist to block from his view the very special, culturally bracketed nature of his own role and to imagine himself something more than an interested (in both senses of that word) sojourner, it has been our most powerful source of bad faith.

Yet, the problem of how to get from a collection of ethnographic miniatures on the order of our sheep story—an assortment of remarks and anecdotes—to wall-sized culturescapes of the nation, the epoch, the continent, or the civilization is not so easily passed over with vague allusions to the virtues of concreteness and the down-to-earth mind. For a science born in Indian tribes, Pacific islands, and African lineages and subsequently seized with grander ambitions, this has come to be a major methodological problem, and for the most part a badly handled one. The models that anthropologists have themselves worked out to justify their moving from local truths to general visions have been, in fact, as responsible for undermining the effort as anything their critics—sociologists obsessed with sample sizes, psychologists with measures, or economists with aggregates—have been able to devise against them.

Of these, the two main ones have been: the Jonesville-is-the-USA "microcosmic" model; and the Easter-Island-is-a-testing-case "natural experiment" model. Either heaven in a grain of sand, or the farther shores of possibility.

The Jonesville-is-America writ small (or America-is-Jonesville writ large) fallacy is so obviously one that the only thing that needs explanation is how people have managed to believe it and expected others to believe it. The notion that one can find the essence of national societies, civilizations, great religions, or whatever summed up and simplified in so-called "typical" small towns and villages is palpable nonsense. What one finds in small towns and villages is (alas) small-town or village life. If localized, microscopic studies were really dependent for their greater relevance upon such a premise—that they captured the great world in the little—they wouldn't have any relevance.

But, of course, they are not. The locus of study is not the object of study. Anthropologists don't study villages (tribes, towns, neighborhoods . . .); they study in villages. You can study different things in different places, and some things—for example, what colonial domination does to established frames of moral expectation—you can best study in confined localities. But that doesn't make the place what it is you are studying. In the remoter provinces of Morocco and Indonesia I have wrestled with the same questions other social scientists have wrestled with in more central locations—for example, how comes it that men's most importunate claims to humanity are cast in the accents of group pride?—and with about the same conclusiveness. One can add a dimension—one much needed in the present climate of size-up-and-solve social science; but that is all. There is a certain value, if you are going to run on about the exploitation of the masses in having seen a Javanese sharecropper turning earth in a tropical downpour or a Moroccan tailor embroidering kaftans by the light of a twenty-watt bulb. But the notion that this gives you the thing entire (and elevates you to some moral vantage ground from which you can look down upon the ethically less privileged) is an idea which only someone too long in the bush could possibly entertain.

The "natural laboratory" notion has been equally pernicious, not only because the analogy is false—what kind of a laboratory is it where *none* of the parameters are manipulable?—but because it leads to a notion that the data derived from ethnographic studies are purer, or more fundamental, or more solid, or less conditioned (the most favored word is "elementary") than those derived from other sorts of social inquiry. The great natural variation of cultural forms is, of course, not only anthropology's great (and wasting) resource, but the ground of its deepest theoretical dilemma: how is such variation to be squared with the biological unity of the human species? But it is not, even metaphorically, experimental variation, because the context in which it occurs varies along with it, and it is not possible (though there are those who try) to isolate the y's from x's to write a proper function.

The famous studies purporting to show that the Oedipus complex was backwards in the Trobriands, sex roles were upside down in Tchambuli, and the Pueblo Indians lacked aggression (it is characteristic that they were all negative—"but not in the South"), are, whatever their empirical validity may or may not be, not "scientifically tested and approved" hypotheses. They are interpretations, or misinterpretations, like any others, arrived at in the same way as any others, and as inherently inconclusive as any others, and the attempt to invest them with the authority of physical experimentation is but methodological sleight of hand. Ethnographic findings are not privileged, just particular: another country heard from. To regard them as anything more (*or anything less*) than that distorts both them and their implications, which are far profounder than mere primitivity, for social theory.

Another country heard from: the reason that protracted descriptions of distant sheep raids (and a really good ethnographer would have gone into what kind of sheep they were) have general relevance is that they present the sociological mind with bodied stuff on which to feed. The important thing about the anthropologist's findings is their complex specificness, their circumstantiality. It is with the kind of material produced by long-term, mainly (though not exclusively) qualitative, highly participative, and almost obsessively fine-comb field study in confined contexts that the mega-concepts with which contemporary social science is afflicted—legitimacy, modernization, integration, conflict, charisma, structure, . . . meaning—can be given the sort of sensible actuality that makes it possible to think not only re-alistically and concretely *about* them, but, what is more im-portant, creatively and imaginatively *with* them.

The methodological problem which the microscopic nature of ethnography presents is both real and critical. But it is not to be resolved by regarding a remote locality as the world in a teacup or as the sociological equivalent of a cloud chamber. It is to be resolved—or, anyway, decently kept at bay—by realizing that social actions are comments on more than themselves; that where an interpretation comes from does not determine where it can be impelled to go. Small facts speak to large issues, winks to epistemology, or sheep raids to revolution, because they are made to.

VII

Which brings us, finally, to theory. The besetting sin of in-terpretive approaches to anything—literature, dreams, symptoms, culture—is that they tend to resist, or to be per-mitted to resist, conceptual articulation and thus to escape systematic modes of assessment. You either grasp an inter-pretation or you do not, see the point of it or you do not, accept it or you do not. Imprisoned in the immediacy of its own detail, it is presented as self-validating, or, worse, as validated by the supposedly developed sensitivities of the person who presents it; any attempt to cast what it says in terms other than its own is regarded as a travesty—as, the anthropologist's severest term of moral abuse, ethnocentric.

For a field of study which, however timidly (though I, myself, am not timid about the matter at all), asserts itself to be a science, this just will not do. There is no reason why the conceptual structure of a cultural interpretation should be any less formulable, and thus less susceptible to explicit canons of appraisal, than that of, say, a biological observa-tion or a physical experiment—no reason except that the terms in which such formulations can be cast are, if not wholly nonexistent, very nearly so. We are reduced to insin-uating theories because we lack the power to state them.

At the same time, it must be admitted that there are a number of characteristics of cultural interpretation which make the theoretical development of it more than usually difficult. The first is the need for theory to stay rather closer to the ground than tends to be the case in sciences more able to give themselves over to imaginative abstraction. Only short flights of ratiocination tend to be effective in anthro-pology; longer ones tend to drift off into logical dreams, academic bemusements with formal symmetry. The whole point of a semiotic approach to culture is, as I have said, to aid us in gaining access to the conceptual world in which

our subjects live so that we can, in some extended sense of the term, converse with them. The tension between the pull of this need to penetrate an unfamiliar universe of symbolic action and the requirements of technical advance in the the-ory of culture, between the need to grasp and the need to an-alyze, is, as a result, both necessarily great and essentially irremovable. Indeed, the further theoretical development goes, the deeper the tension gets. This is the first condition for cultural theory: it is not its own master. As it is unsever-able from the immediacies thick description presents, its freedom to shape itself in terms of its internal logic is rather limited. What generality it contrives to achieve grows out of the delicacy of its distinctions, not the sweep of its abstractions.

And from this follows a peculiarity in the way, as a sim-ple matter of empirical fact, our knowledge of culture . . . cul-tures . . . a culture . . . grows: in spurts. Rather than following a rising curve of cumulative findings, cultural analysis breaks up into a disconnected yet coherent sequence of bolder and bolder sorties. Studies do build on other studies, not in the sense that they take up where the others leave off, but in the sense that, better informed and better conceptualized, they plunge more deeply into the same things. Every serious cul-tural analysis starts from a sheer beginning and ends where it manages to get before exhausting its intellectual impulse. Previously discovered facts are mobilized, previously devel-oped concepts used, previously formulated hypotheses tried out; but the movement is not from already proven theorems to newly proven ones, it is from an awkward fumbling for the most elementary understanding to a supported claim that one has achieved that and surpassed it. A study is an advance if it is more incisive—whatever that may mean—than those that preceded it; but it less stands on their shoulders than, chal-lenged and challenging, runs by their side.

It is for this reason, among others, that the essay, whether of thirty pages or three hundred, has seemed the natural genre in which to present cultural interpretations and the theories sustaining them, and why, if one looks for sys-tematic treatises in the field, one is so soon disappointed, the more so if one finds any. Even inventory articles are rare here, and anyway of hardly more than bibliographical inter-est. The major theoretical contributions not only lie in spe-cific studies—that is true in almost any field—but they are very difficult to abstract from such studies and integrate into anything one might call "culture theory" as such. Theoreti-cal formulations hover so low over the interpretations they govern that they don't make much sense or hold much inter-est apart from them. This is so, not because they are not gen-eral (if they are not general, they are not theoretical), but be-cause, stated independently of their applications, they seem either commonplace or vacant. One can, and this in fact is how the field progresses conceptually, take a line of theoretical attack developed in connection with one exercise in ethnographic interpretation and employ it in another, pushing it forward to greater precision and broader relevance; but one cannot write a "General Theory of Cultural Interpretation." Or, rather, one can, but there appears to be little profit in it, because the essential task of theory building here is not to codify abstract regularities but to make thick description possible, not to generalize across cases but to generalize within them.

To generalize within cases is usually called, at least in medicine and depth psychology, clinical inference. Rather than beginning with a set of observations and attempting to subsume them under a governing law, such inference begins with a set of (presumptive) signifiers and attempts to place them within an intelligible frame. Measures are matched to theoretical predictions, but symptoms (even when they are measured) are scanned for theoretical peculiarities—that is, they are diagnosed. In the study of culture the signifiers are not symptoms or clusters of symptoms, but symbolic acts or clusters of symbolic acts, and the aim is not therapy but the analysis of social discourse. But the way in which theory is used—to ferret out the unapparent import of things—is the same.

Thus we are led to the second condition of cultural theory: it is not, at least in the strict meaning of the term, predictive. The diagnostician doesn't predict measles; he decides that someone has them, or at the very most *anticipates* that someone is rather likely shortly to get them. But this limitation, which is real enough, has commonly been both misunderstood and exaggerated, because it has been taken to mean that cultural interpretation is merely post facto: that, like the peasant in the old story, we first shoot the holes in the fence and then paint the bull's-eyes around them. It is hardly to be denied that there is a good deal of that sort of thing around, some of it in prominent places. It is to be denied, however, that it is the inevitable outcome of a clinical approach to the use of theory.

It is true that in the clinical style of theoretical formulation, conceptualization is directed toward the task of generating interpretations of matters already in hand, not toward projecting outcomes of experimental manipulations or deducing future states of a determined system. But that does not mean that theory has only to fit (or, more carefully, to generate cogent interpretations of) realities past; it has also to survive—intellectually survive—realities to come. Although we formulate our interpretation of an outburst of winking or an instance of sheep-raising after its occurrence, sometimes long after, the theoretical framework in terms of

which such an interpretation is made must be capable of continuing to yield defensible interpretations as new social phenomena swim into view. Although one starts any effort at thick description, beyond the obvious and superficial, from a state of general bewilderment as to what the devil is going on—trying to find one's feet—one does not start (or ought not) intellectually empty-handed. Theoretical ideas are not created wholly anew in each study; as I have said, they are adopted from other, related studies, and, refined in the process, applied to new interpretive problems. If they cease being useful with respect to such problems, they tend to stop being used and are more or less abandoned. If they continue being useful, throwing up new understandings, they are further elaborated and go on being used.[26]

Such a view of how theory functions in an interpretive science suggests that the distinction, relative in any case, that appears in the experimental or observational sciences between "description" and "explanation" appears here as one, even more relative, between "inscription" ("thick description") and "specification" ("diagnosis")—between setting down the meaning particular social actions have for the actors whose actions they are, and stating, as explicitly as we can manage, what the knowledge thus attained demonstrates about the society in which it is found and, beyond that, about social life as such. Our double task is to uncover the conceptual structures that inform our subjects' acts, the "said" of social discourse, and to construct a system of analysis in whose terms what is generic to those structures, what belongs to them because they are what they are, will stand out against the other determinants of human behavior. In ethnography, the office of theory is to provide a vocabulary in which what symbolic action has to say about itself—that is, about the role of culture in human life—can be expressed.

Aside from a couple of orienting pieces concerned with more foundational matters, it is in such a manner that theory operates in the essays collected here. A repertoire of very general, made-in-the-academy concepts and systems of

---

[26][Geertz] Admittedly this has been something of an idealization. Because theories are seldom if ever decisively disproved in clinical use but merely grow increasingly awkward, unproductive, strained, or vacuous, they often persist long after all but a handful of people (though *they* are often most passionate) have lost much interest in them. Indeed, so far as anthropology is concerned, it is almost more of a problem to get exhausted ideas out of the literature than it is to get productive ones in, and so a great deal more of theoretical discussion than one would prefer is critical rather than constructive, and whole careers have been devoted to hastening the demise of moribund notions. As the field advances one would hope that this sort of intellectual weed control would become a less prominent part of our activities. But, for the moment, it remains true that old theories tend less to die than to go into second editions.

concepts—"integration," "rationalization," "symbol," "ideology," "ethos," "revolution," "identity," "metaphor," "structure," "ritual," "world view," "actor," "function," "sacred," and, of course, "culture" itself—is woven into the body of thick-description ethnography in the hope of rendering mere occurrences scientifically eloquent. The aim is to draw large conclusions from small, but very densely textured facts; to support broad assertions about the role of culture in the construction of collective life by engaging them exactly with complex specifics.

Thus it is not only interpretation that goes all the way down to the most immediate observational level: the theory upon which such interpretation conceptually depends does so also. My interest in Cohen's story, like Ryle's in winks, grew out of some very general notions indeed. The "confusion of tongues" model—the view that social conflict is not something that happens when, out of weakness, indefiniteness, obsolescence, or neglect, cultural forms cease to operate, but rather something which happens when, like burlesqued winks, such forms are pressed by unusual situations or unusual intentions to operate in unusual ways—is not an idea I got from Cohen's story. It is one, instructed by colleagues, students, and predecessors, I brought to it.

Our innocent-looking "note in a bottle" is more than a portrayal of the frames of meaning of Jewish peddlers, Berber warriors, and French proconsuls, or even of their mutual interference. It is an argument that to rework the pattern of social relationships is to rearrange the coordinates of the experienced world. Society's forms are culture's substance.

VIII

There is an Indian story—at least I heard it as an Indian story—about an Englishman who, having been told that the world rested on a platform which rested on the back of an elephant which rested in turn on the back of a turtle, asked (perhaps he was an ethnographer; it is the way they behave), what did the turtle rest on? Another turtle. And that turtle? "Ah, Sahib, after that it is turtles all the way down."

Such, indeed, is the condition of things. I do not know how long it would be profitable to meditate on the encounter of Cohen, the sheikh, and "Dumari" (the period has perhaps already been exceeded); but I do know that however long I did so I would not get anywhere near to the bottom of it. Nor have I ever gotten anywhere near to the bottom of anything I have ever written about, either in the essays below or elsewhere. Cultural analysis is intrinsically incomplete. And, worse than that, the more deeply it goes the less complete it is: It is a strange science whose most telling assertions are its most tremulously based, in which to get somewhere with the matter at hand is to intensify the suspicion, both your own and that of others, that you are not quite getting it right. But that, along with plaguing subtle people with obtuse questions, is what being an ethnographer is like.

There are a number of ways to escape this—turning culture into folklore and collecting it, turning it into traits and counting it, turning it into institutions and classifying it, turning it into structures and toying with it. But they *are* escapes. The fact is that to commit oneself to a semiotic concept of culture and an interpretive approach to the study of it is to commit oneself to a view of ethnographic assertion as, to borrow W. B. Gallie's by now famous phrase, "essentially contestable."[27] Anthropology, or at least interpretive anthropology, is a science whose progress is marked less by a perfection of consensus than by a refinement of debate. What gets better is the precision with which we vex each other.

This is very difficult to see when one's attention is being monopolized by a single party to the argument. Monologues are of little value here, because there are no conclusions to be reported; there is merely a discussion to be sustained. Insofar as the essays here collected have any importance, it is less in what they say than what they are witness to: an enormous increase in interest, not only in anthropology, but in social studies generally, in the role of symbolic forms in human life. Meaning, that elusive and ill-defined pseudoentity we were once more than content to leave philosophers and literary critics to fumble with, has now come back into the heart of our discipline. Even Marxists are quoting Cassirer, even positivists, Kenneth Burke.[28]

My own position in the midst of all this has been to try to resist subjectivism on the one hand and cabbalism on the other, to try to keep the analysis of symbolic forms as closely tied as I could to concrete social events and occasions, the public world of common life, and to organize it in such a way that the connections between theoretical formulations and descriptive interpretations were unobscured by appeals to dark sciences. I have never been impressed by the argument that, as complete objectivity is impossible in these matters (as, of course, it is), one might as well let one's sentiments run loose. As Robert Solow[29] has remarked, that is like saying that as a perfectly aseptic environment is impossible, one might as well conduct surgery in a sewer. Nor, on the other hand, have I been impressed with claims that structural linguistics, computer engineering, or some other

---

[27] W. B. Gallie (b. 1912), American philosopher.
[28] Cassirer (above, page 1016); Burke (above, page 1011).
[29] Robert Solow (b. 1924), American economist.

advanced form of thought is going to enable us to understand men without knowing them. Nothing will discredit a semiotic approach to culture more quickly than allowing it to drift into a combination of intuitionism and alchemy, no matter how elegantly the intuitions are expressed or how modern the alchemy is made to look.

The danger that cultural analysis, in search of all-too-deep-lying turtles, will lose touch with the hard surfaces of life—with the political, economic, stratificatory realities within which men are everywhere contained—and with the biological and physical necessities on which those surfaces rest, is an ever-present one. The only defense against it, and against, thus, turning cultural analysis into a kind of sociological aestheticism, is to train such analysis on such realities and such necessities in the first place. It is thus that I have written about nationalism, about violence, about identity, about human nature, about legitimacy, about revolution, about ethnicity, about urbanization, about status, about death, about time, and most of all about particular attempts by particular peoples to place these things in some sort of comprehensible, meaningful frame.

To look at the symbolic dimensions of social action—art, religion, ideology, science, law, morality, common sense—is not to turn away from the existential dilemmas of life for some empyrean realm of deemotionalized forms; it is to plunge into the midst of them. The essential vocation of interpretive anthropology is not to answer our deepest questions, but to make available to us answers that others, guarding other sheep in other valleys, have given, and thus to include them in the consultable record of what man has said.

Mary Louise Pratt

b. 1948

Mary Louise Pratt's *Toward a Speech Act Theory of Literary Discourse* is a significant effort to apply to literary texts the theory of speech acts developed in "ordinary language" philosophy, which grew out of the British tradition of John R. Searle, P. F. Strawson, and H. P. Grice. Pratt is careful to distinguish "ordinary language" in this sense from ordinary or everyday language as referred to in structuralist poetics (for example, Shklovsky, above, page 796). She writes, "The former is conceived in opposition to formal logic, the latter in opposition to 'poetic language.'" It is her thesis that it is not possible to find actual linguistic characteristics special to poetic language that are not also present in language as generally used. She argues that speech act theory, applied to literary texts, allows one to discuss context, intention, attitudes, expectations, and conventions of utterance: "Literature itself is a speech context." Pratt gives attention, for example, to genre as a context, but she is mainly concerned with emphasizing the importance of the disposition of speaker and audience (speaking directed inside and speaking directed outside the text) over the "morphological and syntactical structure of the language," the latter being the approach, for example, of Roman Jakobson (above, page 1132).

Pratt observes that the application of speech act theory blurs the difference between so-called fictivity and nonfiction. Fictively organized utterances take place both inside and outside what we call literature. This kind of discussion of fiction and linguistic characteristics has helped to lead to a general blurring of the difference between literature and other kinds of discourse. For example, Hayden White in his *Metahistory* (1973) and other writings argued on totally different grounds that the historians he studied employed tropes that were fundamental to the nature of their historical views, resulting in a sort of fiction. Indeed, theories since Jeremy Bentham and, later, Hans Vaihinger emphasized the fictive nature of virtually all discourse. Pratt's argument comes from the opposite direction in that her aim is not to fictionalize all discourse but to erase a false opposition.

Pratt's work includes *Toward a Speech Act Theory of Literary Discourse* (1977); *Linguistics for Students* (with Elizabeth Traugott, 1980); *Imperial Eyes: Travel Writing and Transculturation* (1992). Fundamental works of speech act theory include J. L. Austin, *How to Do Things with Words* (1962), and John R. Searle, *Speech Acts* (1969).

from

Toward a Speech Act Theory of Literary Discourse

from
Chapter One

The *"Poetic Language" Fallacy*

It is of the utmost importance to overcome naive antinomies of sacred and secular. They prevail not only in historiography but also in personal and even national psychoses. Anthropology has helped to overcome them by showing that the sacred is not a class of special things but rather a special class of things.

GEOFFREY HARTMAN,
"Structuralism: The Anglo-
American Adventure"

In his 1926 article, "The Theory of the Formal Method," Boris Èjxenbaum explains the role played in Russian Formalist literary theory by the opposition between poetic and nonpoetic language:

> Their [the Formalists'] basic point was, and still is, that the object of literary science, as literary science, ought to be the investigation of the specific properties of literary material, of the properties that distinguish such material from material of any other kind. . . . To establish this principle of specificity without resorting to speculative aesthetics required the juxtaposing of the literary order of facts with another such order. For this purpose one order had to be selected from among existent orders which, while contiguous with the literary order, would contrast with it in terms of function. It was just such a methodological procedure that produced the opposition between "poetic" language and "practical" language. . . . Thus, instead of an orientation toward a history of culture or of social life, toward psychology, or aesthetics and so on, as had been customary for literary scholars, the Formalists came up with their own characteristic orientation toward linguistics.[1]

According to Èjxenbaum, then, the opposition between poetic and practical language was supposed to provide "literary scientists" with a method of empirical verification, a kind of external evaluative criterion against which their observations about literature could be tested. By establishing a systematic relation between literary and nonliterary data on which to base their work, poeticians would be able to claim for their observation the same empirical validity granted to the statements of general linguistics. Notice, however, that Èjxenbaum makes a number of assumptions about the nature of that relation that are not obvious. Among other things, he assumes that (1) language functions in literature differently than it does elsewhere, (2) the relation between the literary and nonliterary functions of language is one of opposition, and (3) this opposition is fully manifested in the observable properties of literary and nonliterary data; thus, literature has properties that other utterances do not possess and is defined by those properties. Literature, in other words, is linguistically autonomous. And literature and nonliterature can be taken as self-consistent, homogenous bodies of data, at least in their relation to each other.

In his 1919 article, "Potebnja," Viktor Šklovskij[2] makes the same set of assumptions and in addition claims that "massive evidence" exists to support them:

> If a scientific poetics is to be brought about, it must start with the factual assertion, founded on massive evidence, that there are such things as "poetic" and "prosaic" languages, each with their different laws.

("Prosaic" in Šklovskij's terminology is synonymous with "everyday.")[3] There is no question in Šklovskij's mind that the poetic/nonpoetic distinction, the different laws, and the massive evidence exist. Throughout the seventy-five-year history of modern poetics their existence has hardly ever been questioned. They have existed as presuppositions without, to my knowledge, ever having been tested as hypotheses. The verification procedure which Èjxenbaum claims motivated the comparison of literature with nonliterature in the first place was never actually applied.

I mean simply this: throughout the exhaustive literature this century has produced on metrics, rhythm, syllabification, metaphor, rhyme, and parallelism of every kind, the role these devices do play in real utterances outside litera-

---

"The 'Poetic Language' Fallacy" is Chapter One and "The Linguistics of Use" Chapter Three of *Toward a Speech Act Theory of Literary Discourse* (Bloomington: Indiana University Press, 1977). Both are reprinted in part here.
[1] Eichenbaum (above, page 867).

[2] Shklovsky (above, page 796).
[3] [Pratt] Tzvetan Todorov, ed. and tr., *Théorie de la littérature: Textes des formalistes russes* (Paris, Seuil, 1965), p. 81.

ture was never seriously examined or recognized. Likewise, throughout the brilliant body of Formalist scholarship on prose fiction, nary a scholar seriously poses the question of whether or to what extent devices like palpableness of form, estrangement, foregrounding, and laying bare of devices do exist outside literature. Not a single reference can be found to the myriad types of narrative utterances which make up a formidable part of everyone's day-to-day verbal behavior. Examples from literature are virtually never accompanied by data from extraliterary discourse. Instead, devices observed in literature were assumed to be "literary," to constitute "literariness" (the term is Jakobson's[4]) because nonliterature was assumed a priori not to possess the properties of literature. Hence even terminologically, the right-hand term of the poetic/nonpoetic dichotomy scarcely mattered at all. "Nonpoetic" could be specified variously as "practical," "utilitarian," "spoken," "prosaic," "scientific," "everyday," "communicative," "referential," or any combination of these without in the least disturbing the notion of what "poetic" was. That the poeticians themselves have never been able to agree on a term for designating nonliterature should have led them to doubt the existence of any such monolith. That they have so far felt no need to resolve the question of how nonliterature should be baptized is, as I shall show shortly, an important symptom of the vacuous role this concept plays in their theory.

Had the Formalists and their descendants used their verification procedure, had they actually asked whether their so-called literary properties really did "distinguish literary material from material of any other kind," they would have found Šklovskij's "massive evidence" seriously lacking. One simple negative proof of this is the fact that texts cannot always be identified as literature on sight. In addition, even the most cursory glance at the day-to-day behavior of a speech community can tell us that neither the formal nor the functional distinctiveness that the Formalists attributed to literature has any factual basis. Before I develop and illustrate this claim, however, I should like to show in a little more detail what the real motivation for the poetic/nonpoetic duality was and what happens to the Formalist argument when that duality begins to break down.

We could begin by posing two questions. First, since the Formalists were only interested in the structural properties of literary utterances, why bring nonliterary discourse into the picture at all? Secondly, since their claims about nonliterary discourse are almost never supported by real data in their writings and since linguistic theory at the time

of the Formalists had specifically excluded the question of language use from its scope of inquiry, where did the Formalist assumptions about the nonliterary uses of language come from, and on what basis was the category of "practical" language defined in the first place?

Èjxenbaum, in the passage quoted earlier, provides us with his answer to the first question: "practical language" was introduced to "establish a principle of specificity without resorting to speculative aesthetics." Èjxenbaum here appears to be proposing the comparison of two types of data, but his statement (quoted in full on p. 3) makes sense only if one assumes the existence of a pre-established "order of facts" called "practical language" whose identity has been defined without the devious intervention of "speculative aesthetics."

And so we face question two: where did this "order of facts" come from? Èjxenbaum and his colleagues evidently believed it came from linguistics. Linguistics provided the facts about nonliterary language; the job of poetics was to juxtapose those facts and the facts about literary language. In other words, coupling "poetic" and "ordinary" language was a way of coupling poetics and linguistics and thus of laying claim to a respectable empirical basis for observations which had previously only been "speculative." Notice, however, that this "methodological procedure" entails a rather drastic redefinition of what linguistics is. For, as I have already suggested, the linguistics of the Saussurian[5] structural tradition does not claim to describe real utterances of any kind but rather the abstract set of rules which underlies real utterances. While a structuralist grammar can make statements about the grammatical relations which obtain among elements in a given real utterance, it emphatically does not claim to make statements about that utterance's function or use and remains effectively blind to those aspects of an utterance's organization which may have been determined by its intended function in its speech situation. By means of the *langue/parole* distinction, Saussurian linguistics intentionally "brackets" all structures other than basic, rule-governed grammatical and phonological ones. Prague School[6] structural linguistics, though it made a point of calling itself "functional," was, like Saussure, almost uniquely concerned with the function of elements within the linguistic system rather than with the functions the language serves within the speech community. In the pre-World War II days of the Prague School, the poeticians

---
[4] Jakobson (above, page 1132).

---
[5] Saussure (above, page 786).
[6] The Prague School included Roman Jakobson.

themselves were virtually the only members interested in this latter question,[7] with the result that in the all-important Prague School Theses of 1929, the poetic/nonpoetic opposition is built right into the pronouncement on the social function of language:

> In its social role, language [*le langage*] must be specified [*distinguer*] according to its relation to extralinguistic reality. It has either a communicative function, that is, it is directed toward the signified, or a poetic function, that is, it is directed toward the sign itself.[8]

Given the limited scope of structural linguistics, then, the Formalist and structuralist belief that statements arising from general linguistics were available as evidence in support of a theory of linguistic aesthetics rested on a number of questionable assumptions. Schematically, we could say that the Formalists established their "principle of specificity" by:

1. defining literature as a linguistic category
2. postulating an opposing linguistic category containing all and only nonliterature
3. redefining grammar in such a way that its domain is all and only nonliterature
4. ascribing to nonliterature all and only those properties described by structuralist grammar.

Obviously, I am not suggesting that these four points represent the stages of a conscious attempt to mislead the public. Rather, they represent a set of assumptions, in some cases only attitudes, which gave rise to the poetic/nonpoetic opposition in the first place and which underlie its various manifestations today. It is worth examining more closely how this relation between poetics and linguistics came to be. Consider the following statement by Jakobson and Bogatyrev concerning the relation of a work of folk literature to its tradition:

> A folklore work is extraindividual and exists only potentially; . . . it is a skeleton of actual traditions which the implementers embellish with the tracery of individual creation, in much the same way as the producers of a verbal message (*la parole* in the Saussurian sense) act with respect to the verbal code (*la langue*).[9]

Here, the Saussurian *langue/parole* distinction is used as an analogy. The folklore work is to its tradition as the individual utterance is to its grammar. In an earlier article, Tynjanov and Jakobson apply the analogy to all literature. Referring to *langue* and *parole,* they write:

> The principles involved in relating these two categories (i.e., the existing norm and individual utterances) as applied to literature must now be elaborated. In this latter case, the individual utterance cannot be considered without reference to the existing complex of norms.[10]

René Wellek elaborates the same argument in his 1936 article, "The Theory of Literary History." Discussing the problem of a work's relation to the individual, he says:

> Roman Jakobson has supplied the necessary corrective meeting the objections here voiced. He prefers to speak of "collective ideology," a system of norms which is implied in every work of art though not every individual may be able to materialize these norms. The parallel between language (*langue*) and speech (*parole*) in the sense defined by de Saussure is instructive. A system of actual norms (*langue*) is materialized only in the individual pronouncements (*parole*), but only the existence of this system of norms makes the individual pronouncements possible and comprehensible. So every work of art materializes (becomes effective) only in the minds of individuals, but no individual ever realizes it as a whole, just as he will never "materialize" the whole of his language.[11]

---

[7] [Pratt] One important exception here is Vilém Mathesius, whose interest in language as a social phenomenon crystallized even before the Russian Formalists were in existence (see, for example, his 1911 paper in Vachek, 1964). However, Mathesius himself showed little interest in the poetic language question, and I have found almost no reference to his work among the poeticians. In addition Professor E. J. Brown has called to my attention a still untranslated essay by L. P. Jakubinsky titled "On dialogic discourse" (Russkaya rech', 1923), in which Jakubinsky criticizes the inadequacies of the poetic/practical language opposition and tries to produce a more detailed inventory of the uses of language.

[8] [Pratt] Here and throughout, references to the Prague Circle's Theses refer to the French original in the *Travaux de Cercle linguistique de Prague,* vol. I (1929). Since the Theses are not available in English, translations are my own and are as literal as possible.

[9] [Pratt] Roman Jakobson and Petr Bogatyrev, "On the Boundary Between Studies of Folklore and Literature" (1929). Translated by Herbert Eagle. In Ladislav Matejka and Krystyna Pomorska, eds., *Readings in Russian Poetics: Formalist and Structuralist Views,* Cambridge, Mass.: MIT Press, 1971, p. 91.

[10] [Pratt] Juri Tynjanov and Roman Jakobson, "Problems in the Study of Literature and Language" (1928), in Matejka and Pomorska, *Readings.*

[11] [Pratt] René Wellek, "The Theory of Literary History," *Travaux du Cercle linguistique de Prague* 4 (1936), p. 180.

Wellek, you will notice, posits not one analogy here but two. The *langue/parole* distinction is used to represent both the relation of a given work to the literary canon of its time and the relation of an individual reading of a work to the work itself.

The fact that, analogies aside, there is a real *langue* shared by literary and nonliterary utterances alike is quite overlooked and seems almost irrelevant to the line of argument these quotations indicate. But the analogy is flawed in a more serious way, for it implies that this metaphorical *langue/parole* relationship is unique to literature, that only literary utterances are subject to norms other than the rules of grammar. But this is clearly false. In addition to the rules of grammar (or *langue*), any utterance is subject to rules governing the use of language in the context in question. All utterances take place against the background of a whole range of contemporary norms governing what styles, what subject matter, what degrees of formality, politeness, and so on are appropriate in different contexts. The *langue/parole* analogy used in these quotations obscures the fact that such norms exist for extraliterary discourse and are of the same type as those making up the so-called *langue* of literature. Indeed, the two overlap to a significant extent.

In a 1935 lecture, Jakobson developed the analogy even further by attributing to this hypothetical poetic *langue* its own peculiar set of minimal units: "Each concrete poetic canon, every set of temporal poetic norms, however, comprises indispensable distinctive elements without which the work cannot be identified as poetic."[12] Here the analogy becomes more concrete. The literary norms that are compared to *langue* in the first three quotations are here depicted as configurations of discrete minimal units ("distinctive elements"), in the same way that morphemes are configurations of phonemes. The *langue* of poetry, it seems, has its own universal categories and units of analysis, just like the *langue* . . . the language of what? "Of practical language," is Èjxenbaum's answer; "of everyday language," is Šklovskij's answer; "of communicative language," is the Prague Circle's answer. It is exactly at this point that the analogy becomes a distortion, for it is taken here as a fact. Postulating a separate grammar of poetry which is related analogically to the grammar of language very easily obscures the real relation that holds between poetic utterances and the grammar of the language in which they are written, namely that of *parole* to *langue,* the relation that all utterances in a given language hold with respect to the grammar. It was a simple step indeed for the poeticians to lose sight of

this fact and to establish their relation to linguistics on the basis of their analogy instead. It is the analogy that leads to the belief that there *is* a poetic language with its own laws, which poeticians discover and specify, and a nonpoetic language with its laws, which linguists discover and specify (cf. Šklovskij, quoted above). According to the analogy, grammatically is to linguistics what poeticality is to poetics, and the difference between the linguist's grammar and the poetician's grammar is the difference between literature and nonliterature.

Notice that at this point the methodological parallel ceases to be an analogy at all. The definition of poetic language offered by the Prague Circle in its Theses of 1929 bears no traces of its metaphorical underpinnings:

> It is necessary to develop principles for the synchronic description of poetic language [*langue*] without making the common mistake of identifying the language [*langue*] of poetry with that of communication. Poetic discourse [*langage*] has, from a synchronic point of view, the form of speech [*parole*], that is, the form of an individual creative act, which is realized on the one hand against the background of existing poetic tradition (poetic language [*langue*]), and on the other hand against the background of contemporary communicative language. . . . All levels of the linguistic system, which have only a subordinate role [*rôle de service*] in communicative discourse, take on in poetic discourse some degree of autonomous value.[13]

The poetic *langue* here is regarded not as a metaphor but as an autonomous phenomenon of the same order as, but also contrasting with, the *langue* of nonpoetry, here labeled "communicative language." The following statement made by Tomaševskij in 1928 illustrates what happens when the results of the linguist's and the poetician's procedures are compared as facts of the same order:

> The chief trait of poetry is that it no longer presents an expression merely as a means or the action of an automatic mechanism, but as an element which has gained an original aesthetic value and has become an end in itself of the discourse.[14]

---

[12] [Pratt] "The Dominant" (1935), in Matejka and Pomorska, *Readings.*

[13] [Pratt] Prague Linguistic Circle, *Theses,* p. 19.

[14] [Pratt] Boris Tomaševskij, "La nouvelle école d'histoire littéraire en Russie," *Revue des Études Slaves* 8 (1928), p. 230.

The implication, obviously, is that nonpoetry does present an expression "merely as a means or the action of an automatic mechanism." But of course it is structural linguistics that presents language in this way (Saussure's chapter on syntax is titled *Mécanisme de la langue*). What Tomaševskij takes to be characteristics of nonpoetic utterances are actually characteristics of a structuralist grammar.

Similarly, Osip Brik describes the interaction of rhythm and syntax in the following terms:

> Syntax is the system of word combination in ordinary speech. Inasmuch as verse language is still subject to the basic laws of prose syntax, the laws of word combination are laws of rhythm. And these rhythmic laws complicate the syntactic nature of verse. . . . Verse is regulated not simply by the laws of syntax, but by the laws of rhythmic syntax, that is, a syntax in which the usual syntactic laws are complicated by rhythmic requirements. . . . The very fact that a certain number of words coexist with the two sets of laws constitutes the peculiarity of poetry.[15]

Assuming that syntax, as it is specified in a grammar, constitutes a description of how words are combined in spoken discourse is for Brik a way of assuming that rhythmic organization is alien to nonliterary discourse and can thus be taken as a distinctive feature of the poetic language. Hence, according to Brik, one can "translate" an utterance from poetic to nonpoetic language by wiping out its rhythmic organization: "By rearranging words we can deprive any line of poetry of its poetic shape and turn it into a phrase from the sphere of ordinary speech" (p. 124).

But of course the syntacticians who formulated the "laws of word combination" had never *posed the question* of rhythmic organization and in fact located such questions squarely outside their concerns, along with everything else that concerned the use of language. Brik's comparison is thus illegitimate.

Nearly forty years later, Samuel Levin makes the same mistake in his influential monograph, *Linguistic Structures in Poetry*. "In poetry," writes Levin, "structures are not merely dummies to be filled in by just any form as long as it is grammatical and communication is effected."[16] Once

again, note the implication: outside poetry, constructions *are* "merely dummies to be filled in by just any form. . . ." Within the context of the linguistics which invented it, the dummy construction (whereby a sentence is conceived as a series of slots, each to be filled in by a given part of speech) is no more a characteristic of nonliterary discourse than it is of literary. It is a descriptive device used in specifying grammatical relations. Besides being an inadequate representation of the way syntax works, as Chomsky[17] has shown, the dummy construction was never intended to represent the aesthetic structure of any real utterance and was obviously not conceived with aesthetics in mind at all. In fact, it was above all a device linguists could use in field research to elicit responses from informants (by asking them to "fill in the blank" in the sentence). It was designated, in short, by and for linguists whose concern was to derive the phonological, syntactic, and morphological systems of (often unwritten) languages up to the level of word order within the sentence, linguists who were very far indeed from *posing the question* of aesthetic organization either within literature or outside it.

Levin, Tomaševskij, and Brik all make the same far-reaching mistake. They derive their view of what extraliterary utterances are like from structural linguistics' idea of what a grammar is like. In the process of defining poetics by analogy to linguistics, they in effect redefine linguistics in the way I outlined earlier; the domain of grammar is taken to be all and only extraliterary discourse; extraliterary discourse is assumed to possess all and only the properties attributed to it by the grammar.

In point of fact, let me repeat, the structural linguist's grammar is not a description of any set of utterances at all, and it is even more emphatically not a description of how language is used in a given utterance and context. A structuralist grammar—an inventory of phonemes, morphemes, and rules for combining them—bears no substantive resemblance at all to the inventory of devices, conventions, and norms which makes up the *langue* the poeticians were postulating for literature. Nor are there grounds for equating the two. The so-called grammar of communicative language can exist apart from the so-called grammar of poetry, but the reverse is not so; the latter exists only by contrast to the former. The often voiced claim that "poetic language must be studied in and of itself" is thus meaningless. The "poetic morphology, phonology and syntax" which the Prague Circle outlined in their Theses[18] can only consist of the search

---

[15][Pratt] Osip M. Brik, "Contributions to the Study of Verse Language" (1927). Translated by C. H. Severens in Matjka and Pomorska, *Readings*, pp. 121–22.
[16][Pratt] Samuel Levin, *Linguistic Structures in Poetry*. The Hague: Mouton, 1962, p. 34.

[17]Chomsky (above, page 1166).
[18][Pratt] *Theses*, pp. 18ff.

for points of contrast. Attempts to define the terms positively seem unintelligible: "Poetic phonology deals with the degree to which the phonological repertoire is utilized in comparison with [*par rapport au*] communicative discourse [*langage*]."

In short, it is clearly illegitimate to infer that a linguistic theory asking the question "Is this utterance grammatical?" should have answered, in the realm of nonliterary discourse, the question "Is this utterance poetic?" And although this inference does not always emerge as blatantly as in the examples I have cited, it lies at the center of the structural poetic conception of "ordinary language." The faulty analogy I have been discussing underlies the overwhelming tendency to view style as an exclusively or predominantly literary phenomenon and to equate style outside literature with mere grammaticality and conventional appropriateness. "Ordinary language" looks utilitarian, prosaic, mechanical, practical, and automatized to poeticians not because it is, but because structural linguistics is utilitarian, prosaic, and mechanical in the sense that it only undertakes to describe those aspects of language that can be accounted for in terms of dummy constructions, grammaticality, *rôles de service* and the "action of a mechanism." Small wonder that poetic language should seem to "impose on the discourse some structure in addition to that which derives from ordinary language"[19] or that rhythmic structure should appear to be a second set of syntactic laws. These are not structures in addition to those nonliterary utterances possess. They are structures in addition to those which structural grammar describes.

* * *

from

Chapter Three

The Linguistics of Use

For speech act theoreticians, "speaking a language is engaging in a (highly complex) rule-governed form of behavior" (Searle).[20] To make an utterance is to perform an act. A person who performs a speech act does at least two and possibly three things. First, he performs a *locutionary act,* the act of producing a recognizable grammatical utterance in the given language. Second, he performs an *illocutionary act* of a certain type. "Promising," "warning," "greeting," "reminding," "informing," or "commanding" are all kinds of illocutionary acts.

There have been numerous attempts to classify illocutionary acts according to the kind of communication they represent, that is, the way in which the speaker is using the language. Searle,[21] for example, proposes that illocutionary acts be classified into five basic categories:

1. *representatives:* illocutionary acts that undertake to represent a state of affairs, whether past, present, future, or hypothetical, e.g. stating, claiming, hypothesizing, describing, predicting, telling, insisting, suggesting, or swearing that something is the case

2. *directives:* illocutionary acts designed to get the addressee to do something, e.g. requesting, commanding, pleading, inviting, daring

3. *commissives:* illocutionary acts that commit the speaker to doing something, e.g. promising, threatening, vowing

4. *expressives:* illocutionary acts that express only the speaker's psychological state, e.g. congratulating, thanking, deploring, condoling, welcoming

5. *declarations:* illocutionary acts that bring about the state of affairs they refer to, e.g. blessing, firing, baptizing, bidding, passing sentence.

Finally, a speaker who performs an illocutionary act may also be performing a *perlocutionary act;* that is, by saying what he says, he may be achieving certain intended effects in his hearer in addition to those achieved by the illocutionary act. By warning a person one may frighten him, by arguing one may convince, and so on.

To perform a speech act correctly, however, it is not enough merely to utter a grammatical sentence. Speech acts, like all behavior, are correctly or felicitously performed only if certain conditions obtain. The illocutionary act of promising, for example, is only felicitously carried out if the speaker is able to fulfill the promise, sincerely intends to do so, and believes that what he is promising to do is something the hearer would like him to do. (This latter condition is what distinguishes promising from threatening.) Promising, in other words, depends on more than just saying the sentence "I promise to do X," and speakers of the language know it. These conditions on which the felicity of a speech

---

[19] [Pratt] Levin, p. 18.

[20] [Pratt] John R. Searle, *Speech Acts: An Essay in the Philosophy of Language,* Cambridge; Cambridge University Press, 1969, p. 12.

[21] [Pratt] John R. Searle, "A Classification of Illocutionary Acts," *Language in Society* 5 (1976), pp. 1–23.

act depends are called *appropriateness conditions* or *felicity conditions*. They represent rules which users of the language assume to be in force in their verbal dealings with each other; they form part of the knowledge which speakers of a language share and on which they rely in order to use the language correctly and effectively, both in producing and understanding utterances. An account of the appropriateness conditions for the illocutionary act of asking a question, for example, would include the following statements:

1. speaker does not know the answer
2. speaker believes it is possible hearer knows the answer
3. it is not obvious that hearer will provide the answer at the time without being asked
4. speaker wants to know the answer

A speaker who utters a question implies that these conditions have been met, and the addressee assumes the speaker has implied this. If the conditions have not been met, the speaker's question is inappropriate or infelicitous. Searle proposes that appropriateness conditions be classified as either preparatory, essential, or sincerity conditions.[22] Conditions (1) to (3) above would be preparatory conditions, condition (4) is the sincerity condition. The essential condition is the definition of a question as an undertaking to elicit information from the addressee. Similarly, the illocutionary act of making a statement carries the following appropriateness conditions:

1. speaker believes p (where p is the proposition being asserted)
2. speaker has evidence for the truth of p (or reasons for believing p)
3. it is not obvious to both speaker and addressee that the addressee knows p (or does not need to be reminded of p)
4. speaker has some reason for wanting addressee to know p (or to remember p)

Each of the five main categories of illocutionary acts mentioned above encompasses a wide range of illocutionary acts, which can be differentiated from each other in terms of their appropriateness conditions. Thus, pleading, commanding, and requesting are all directives, but they differ according to the relationship that must exist between speaker and addressee. The illocutionary act of commanding, for example, has an appropriateness condition requiring that the speaker be in a position of authority; for pleading, the addressee must be in authority; for requesting, either speaker and addressee must be peers, or the addressee must have some measure of authority.

Suggesting, insisting, and hypothesizing (that something is the case) are all illocutionary acts belonging to the class of representatives, but they differ in that in each case the speaker is expressing a different degree of belief or commitment toward the truth of what he is representing. These distinctions would likewise be stated as appropriateness conditions. Concluding, replying, and disagreeing are all representatives, but they differ in that they each express a different relationship between what is being said and prior discourse. Many declarations have appropriateness conditions requiring that the speaker be endowed with institutional authority to perform the act in question, as with marrying, excommunicating, or sentencing someone to prison.

As speakers of the language, we rely at every moment on our knowledge of appropriateness conditions, both when we produce utterances and when we decode utterances of others. It is our knowledge of appropriateness conditions that lets us know, for example, that the sentence "You must have another piece of cake," uttered by our hostess at a tea party, is an invitation and not a command;[23] that the sentence "Could you take out the garbage?" in spite of its interrogative form is not a question about our physical capacities; or that in most contexts, there would be something odd about the sentence "Thank you for the hideous sweater."

From a linguist's point of view, appropriateness conditions are a crucial component of the grammar of a language, even though they represent aspects of an utterance which are not part of the explicit verbal structure. The appropriateness conditions for questions, for example, will form part of a linguist's description of what a question is along with his description of the explicit syntactic and phonological configurations given to questions. In this regard, speech act theory supplies an important corrective to the overwhelming concentration on syntax and phonology which has accompanied Chomskyan linguistics. If, as Chomsky claimed, the goal of linguistics is to describe what a speaker knows about his language that enables him to produce and understand new utterances (his competence), such a description must specify not only our knowledge of grammatical rules but also our "ability to handle possible linguistic structures appropriately in specific contexts, that is, what Hymes has called our 'communicative competence.' "[24] This contextual knowledge is exactly what appropriateness conditions

---

[22][Pratt] Searle, *Speech Acts.*

[23][Pratt] Robin Lakoff, "Language in Context," *Language* 48 (1972), pp. 907–27.

[24][Pratt] Elizabeth Traugott, "Generative Semantics and the Concept of Literary Discourse," *Journal of Literary Semantics* 2 (1973), p. 6.

express. The post-Chomskyan linguistic movement known as generative semantics, developed since about 1968 by G. Lakoff, R. Lakoff, C. Fillmore, and many others, has undertaken to devise formal linguistic models based on this expanded notion of competence and has relied a great deal on the approach taken by speech act theory.[25]

As is probably already clear, many appropriateness conditions are shared by large numbers and classes of illocutionary acts. All directives, for example, have a preparatory condition to the effect that the addressee must be able to carry out what is being asked of him. Some appropriateness conditions apply even more generally. No illocutionary act can be felicitous if the addressee does not speak the language in question, is out of earshot, or is otherwise incapable of understanding the utterance. Appropriateness conditions would specify that utterances performed in such contexts are infelicitous. It is both impractical and counterintuitive to view appropriateness conditions such as these as separate rules attaching to specific illocutionary acts; rather, they are to be construed as rules for language use of a more general kind.

Similarly, there are many cases in which it is impractical and counterintuitive to view appropriateness conditions as applying only at the level of the sentence. Searle claims that "the characteristic grammatical form of an illocutionary act is the complete sentence (it can be a one-word sentence)," and indeed, speech acts have been discussed mostly in terms of single-sentence utterances.[26] Nevertheless, it is clear that the appropriateness conditions for explaining, thanking, or persuading, for example, must at some level of analysis be seen as applying to explanations, thankings, or persuadings that are many sentences long. This is an issue to which few speech act philosophers (and few linguists) have addressed themselves, and to which I will be returning in the next chapter. For the moment, we need only say that in cases of multisentence utterances that have a single point or purpose, there will be appropriateness conditions that, by virtue of that overall purpose, apply across the entire utterance. An individual sentence within such an utterance will be subject to these larger appropriateness conditions as well as to the sentence-level ones that apply to it alone. In other words while we must be able to treat any single sentence as a single speech act, subject to a given set of appropriateness conditions, we must also be able to view appropriateness conditions as applying at the level of discourse. At this level,

for example, the contrast I mentioned earlier between telling a story and testifying in court is the result of contrasting appropriateness conditions. The court requires that the witness *not* evaluate the events he recounts; the appropriateness conditions on natural narrative require that he do so. In addition, the appropriateness conditions for natural narrative require that the speaker tell a complete narrative (with complicating action and resolution) and that he orient it adequately with respect to his audience. Thus, example (3) in chapter two, if analyzed as a natural narrative, would fail to fulfill the conditions requiring adequate orientation and evaluation. But if analyzed as an answer to a request (the interviewer's request to "tell me as much about it as you can"), the appropriateness conditions requiring orientation and evaluation would not apply, and (3) would be viewed as perfectly felicitous.

In sum, speech act theory provides a way of talking about utterances not only in terms of their surface grammatical properties but also in terms of the context in which they are made, the intentions, attitudes, and expectations of the participants, the relationships existing between participants, and generally, the unspoken rules and conventions that are understood to be in play when an utterance is made and received.

There are enormous advantages to talking about literature in this way, too, for literary works, like all our communicative activities, are context-dependent. Literature itself is a speech context. And as with any utterance, the way people produce and understand literary works depends enormously on unspoken, culturally-shared knowledge of the rules, conventions, and expectations that are in play when language is used in that context. Just as a definition of explaining, thanking, or persuading must include the unspoken contextual information on which the participants are relying, so must a definition of literature.

One of the most obvious kinds of contextual information we bring to bear in confronting a literary work is our knowledge of its genre. As Traugott[27] notes, genres and subgenres can to a great extent be defined as systems of appropriateness conditions. Thus elegies, for example, presuppose that someone has died and that the dead person was known to the speaker of the poem. Unless otherwise indicated, we assume the "you" of an elegy refers to the dead person and that the death in question was a human one, hence the (obviously intentional) inappropriateness of an elegy to the death of a mad dog. Fairy tales and fables allow for supernatural events and objects but have rather strict

---

[25] [Pratt] For the literary scholar, Elizabeth Traugott's article (above, fn. 24) is the best introduction to generative semantics and its implications for literary studies.

[26] [Pratt] Searle, *Speech Acts,* p. 25.

[27] [Pratt] Traugott, "Generative Semantics."

rules about what kinds of supernatural events may occur and how they may come about. It is very likely that these conventions, too, can be formulated as appropriateness conditions.

More generally, appropriateness conditions provide a way of building into the description of an utterance the contextual norms which Riffaterre, Halliday, and the others were seeking, so that style in any kind of discourse can be represented as the context-dependent phenomenon it is.[28] Each aspect of an utterance's context can be formulated as a subset of appropriateness conditions interacting with all the others. With respect to a given literary work, we may be called upon to study "the complex interplay of appropriateness conditions of the language of the author's time, of the genre of literary discourse, of the world the author sets up, and of the interplay between these and our expectations at this point in time when we are attempting to establish a theory of the author's work" (Traugott).[29] By the same token, many kinds of literary deviance can be described as violations of specific appropriateness conditions.

Notice that by treating literary works as speech acts of a certain type that occur in a speech situation of a certain type and that presuppose certain knowledge shared by the participants, a speech act approach to literature overcomes the main fault I found with structural poetics, namely the necessity of associating "literariness" directly with formal textual properties. Speech act theory lets us say meaningfully and legitimately what I think any theory of literary discourse is obliged to say, that, as Richard Ohmann puts it, "Our readiness to discover and dwell on the implicit meanings in literary works—and to judge them important—is a consequence of our knowing them to *be* literary works, rather than that which tells us they are such."[30] Ohmann offers this statement to refute Beardsley's definition of literature as "discourse with important implicit meaning."[31] With a context-dependent linguistics, the essence of literariness or poeticality can be said to reside not in the message but in a particular disposition of speaker and audience with regard to the message, one that is characteristic of the literary speech situation. This view has considerably more explanatory power than the view

that asks us to regard "poetic resources" as "concealed in the morphological and syntactic structure of the language."[32] Clearly, it is the reader who focuses on the message in a literary speech situation, not the message that focuses on itself. Likewise it is the speaker, not the text, who invites and attempts to control or manipulate this focusing according to his own, not the text's, intention. Finally, once we are able to make explicit the speech situation itself, we are in a position to account for something Šklovskij noted but could not explain, the fact that "a work may be (1) intended as prosaic [i.e., 'ordinary'] and accepted as poetic, or (2) intended as poetic and accepted as prosaic."[33] As hearers and readers, we are free to lend our aesthetic attention to any text at all. In principle, there is no utterance on whose message (or "implicit meaning" or "style" or "poetic structure") we may not choose to focus.

Finally, and perhaps most important of all, a speech act approach to literature enables and indeed requires us to describe and define literature *in the same terms* used to describe and define all other kinds of discourse. It thus does away with the distortive and misleading concepts of "poetic" and "ordinary" language. Speech act theory views a person's ability to deal with literary works as part of his general "ability to handle possible linguistic structures in specific contexts." Similarities between literary and nonliterary utterance types (such as the similarities between natural and literary narrative discussed earlier) can be linked quite naturally to similarities in the linguistic context and the communicative purposes of the participants. Their differences can be specified in the same terms. In such a description, then, the relations holding between the many kinds of literary discourse and the many kinds of nonliterary discourse are no different in kind from the relations holding between any two speech act types. In short, a speech act approach to literature offers the important possibility of integrating literary discourse into the same basic model of language as all our other communicative activities. The remainder of this study can be taken as an attempt to explore this possibility and to lay some groundwork for a context-dependent theory of literature.

The first attempt to apply speech act theory to the literary speech situation was made by Richard Ohmann in his 1971 article, "Speech Acts and the Definition of Literature,"[34] an article that is of prime importance to anyone interested in the linguistics of literature. Ultimately, the argument

---

[28] [Pratt] Michael Riffaterre, "Criteria for Style Analysis," *Word* 15 (1959), pp. 156–75; Michael A. K. Halliday, "Linguistic Function and Literary Style: An Inquiry into the Language of William Golding's *The Inheritors*," in Seymour Chatman, ed., *Literary Style: A Symposium*, London: Oxford University Press, 1971, pp. 330–68.

[29] [Pratt] Traugott, "Generative Semantics," p. 20.

[30] [Pratt] Richard Ohmann, "Speech Acts and the Definition of Literature," *Philosophy and Rhetoric* 4 (1971), p. 6.

[31] Beardsley (above, page 1027).

[32] [Pratt] "Closing Statement: Linguistics and Poetics." In Thomas A. Sebeok, ed., *Style in Language* (Cambridge, Mass.: MIT Press, 1960) p. 375.

[33] [Pratt] Shklovsky [above, page 798], "Art as Technique."

[34] [Pratt] Ohmann, "Speech Acts," pp. 1–19.

Ohmann presents falls down, but its failure is a most instructive one and merits our close attention.[35]

The "literature" Ohmann aims to define in his paper corresponds to the traditional category "imaginative literature" (novels, stories, poems, plays) in what he calls its "non-honorific" sense, which includes all such works regardless of quality. Ohmann's definition of this category of utterances rests on his observation that the appropriateness conditions outlined by Austin for illocutionary acts do not seem to apply to statements made in works of literature.[36] Of a declarative sentence in a lyric poem, for example, we cannot meaningfully ask whether the person making the assertion was qualified to do so, whether he believed what he said and made the statement under appropriate circumstances, whether objects are referred to correctly and really exist, whether all relevant information has been included, and so on. Ohmann concludes that these appropriateness conditions fail to apply to literary utterances because the latter do not have any illocutionary force. They are "quasi-speech-acts":

> The writer *pretends* to report discourse, and the reader accepts the pretense. Specifically, the reader constructs (imagines) a speaker and a set of circumstances to accompany the quasi-speech-act, and makes it felicitous (or infelicitous—for there are unrealiable narrators, etc.). . . . A *literary work is a discourse whose sentences lack the illocutionary forces that would normally attach to them. Its illocutionary force is mimetic.* By "mimetic" I mean purportedly imitative. Specifically, a literary work *purportedly imitates* (or reports) a series of speech acts, which in fact have no other existence. By so doing, it leads the reader to imagine a speaker, a situation, a set of ancillary events, and so on.[37]

As Ohmann suggests, his definition is mainly an elaboration of the very old observation that the poet nothing affirmeth; however, in Ohmann's view, that observation acquires a great deal of explanatory power when it is restated in speech act terms. For Ohmann, it is the suspension of normal illocutionary force that allows speech acts to be "exhibited" in literary works and that underlies our tendency, when reading literature, to "focus on the message," to attend to implicit or secondary meaning, or to respond emotively to the text:

> Since the quasi-speech-acts of literature are not carrying on the world's business—describing, urging, contracting, etc.—the reader may well attend to them in a non-pragmatic way, and thus allow them to realize their emotive potential. In other words, the suspension of normal illocutionary forces tends to shift a reader's attention to the locutionary acts themselves and to their perlocutionary effects. (p. 17)

The speech act analysis, Ohmann claims, adds "concreteness and precision" to the traditional critical claims that literature is play, presentational symbolism, or rhetoric, that it is essentially dramatic, mimetic, or world-creating, and that it is autonomous.

Many literary critics will find Ohmann's observations about literature entirely acceptable. It is true that authors of fictional literary works are not bound by the appropriateness conditions for the speech acts they invent. It is true that literary works are speech acts which are on exhibit. Literary works indeed do not "carry on the world's business" in the same way many other kinds of speech acts do, and this fact does encourage us to respond aesthetically and emotively to literary texts. However, if we are to use these characteristics to define literature, they must be shown to be unique to literature. And they are not.

The basic criterion on which Ohmann's definition depends is fictivity, and his definition could only stand if it were true that all and only the fictive utterances in a language were literature. Mukařovský, you will recall, posited this same criterion when he was looking for a distinguishing literary feature of prose fiction. Ohmann acknowledges that such a definition of literature would have to include "jokes, ironic rejoinders, parables and fables within political speeches, some advertisements, and many other such," but he is not much troubled by these intruders since they "actually *are* very close to being literature." Poeticians have always been comfortable admitting jokes and fables into literature, but our daily discourse is full of other kinds of fictive speech acts that I am sure would cause even Ohmann to hesitate. For example, in addition to hyperbole, teasing, "kidding around," imitations, and other verbal play, hypotheses of any kind are as immune to Austin's appropriateness conditions as any poem. The "scenarios" in the Oval

---

[35] [Pratt] Ohmann has changed his position somewhat in his more recent but equally important publication, "Speech, Literature and the Space Between" (*New Literary History*, 1974), to which I also refer here. I have chosen to focus on the 1971 paper, however, because it represents a position which many critics would be tempted to adopt vis-à-vis the status of literature in a theory of speech acts.

[36] [Pratt] J. L. Austin, *How to Do Things with Words*. New York: Oxford University Press, 1962.

[37] [Pratt] Ohmann, "Speech Acts," p. 14.

Office, the hypothetical situations used in mathematical problems and philosophical arguments, assumptions made "for the sake of the discussion," speculation about "what he'll do next" or "what might have happened if only. . . ." are all fictional, as indeed are imaginings, plannings, dreams, wishings, and fantasizings of almost any kind. It is "suspended illocutionary force" in Ohmann's sense that distinguishes teasing from insulting, irony from deceit, devil's advocating from real advocating, and hypotheses from claims. A conventional reductio ad absurdum argument is, by Ohmann's own criteria, every bit as "mimetic" a speech act as a novel. If fictivity were indeed the distinguishing characteristic of literature, we would have to describe such speech acts as these *in terms of* their similarity to works of literature. But why should we? This would be nothing short of absurd, like describing apples in terms of oranges without reference to the category "fruit." Does it not make more sense to say that our ability to conceive and manipulate hypothetical worlds or states of affairs, possible or impossible, real or unreal, and to mediate between those worlds and our own is part of our normal cognitive and linguistic competence? And the capacity to use that imaginative faculty in aesthetically and rhetorically effective ways is also a part of our normal linguistic competence. The technique of juxtaposing possible states of affairs to the given situation by means of the "comparators" was, you will recall, an important evaluation device used by Labov's narrators.[38]

Labov's data show that the kind of narrative rhetoric that we tend to think of as exclusively literary does not in fact derive from an utterance's being literature, and the same is clearly true for fictivity or, as Ohmann puts it, the suspension of normal illocutionary force. Labov's data make it necessary to account for narrative rhetoric in terms that are not exclusively literary; the fact that fictive or mimetically organized utterances can occur in almost any realm of extraliterary discourse requires that we do the same for fictivity or mimesis. In other words, the relation between a work's fictivity and its literariness is indirect. The same is true of all the characteristics of literature that Ohmann (and most proponents of fictivity theories of literature) claims to derive from the suspension of illocutionary force.

Let me offer an example. On several occasions, Ohmann uses Truman Capote's *In Cold Blood* (1965) as an example of a discourse in which normal illocutionary forces are *not* suspended, meaning the book is not to be defined as

literature.[39] In the case of *In Cold Blood*, Ohmann claims, "It makes sense to ask all of the questions implied by Austin's rules." Of any assertion in Capote's book then, I can meaningfully ask questions like the following: Do these people and places really exist? Does Capote know what he is talking about? Is he telling the truth? Is all the relevant information included? Now, it is meaningful to ask these questions in the sense that I could appropriately address them to Mr. Capote, whereas I could perhaps not appropriately have asked Emily Brontë (or Ellis Bell) for Heathcliff's middle name. Notice, however, that when I read *In Cold Blood*, I do not have the answers to these questions, nor do I have access to them, nor do I need them to execute my side of the speech act felicitously. I have only Capote's claim that all the pertinent conditions have been met, and I accept his claim automatically, in the same way I accept the "pretense" of the fiction writer the way Ohmann describes it. For this reason, Capote's claim that his utterance does indeed have "normal illocutionary force" does not affect my participation in the speech act in the way Ohmann's analysis predicts. It does not prevent me from focusing on the message, noticing secondary meanings, and generally attending to the utterance in the "non-pragmatic" way Ohmann describes for literature. In fact, my position with respect to Capote's report is necessarily almost exactly the same as that of Ohmann's fiction reader (except for the *quasi,* of course): "The reader constructs (imagines) a speaker and a set of circumstances to accompany the quasi-speech-act and make it felicitous." Obviously, this reconstructive imagining is as much a part of my role when I read *In Cold Blood* as when I read *Emma*. Pragmatically speaking, I have no more knowledge of the situations reported and the reporting circumstances in the former case than I do in the latter, and Capote knows it. Unless I am otherwise acquainted with Capote or his characters, the events and the speaker of *In Cold Blood,* like those of *Emma,* do not exist for me outside the text. The only difference for me between the two speech situations is my knowledge in the first case that Capote intends me to believe his story really happened, and the only effect this has on my reading experience is perhaps an intensification of certain perlocutionary effects— the same perlocutionary effects Conrad tries to capture by having Marlow tell us *Lord Jim*.

Should we classify *In Cold Blood* as literature, then? This would hardly solve the problem, for the claims I have been making with regard to *In Cold Blood* apply identically

---

[38] William Labov, American sociolinguist, discussed by Pratt earlier in the book, especially in connection with his *The Social Stratification of English in New York City* (1966) and *Language in the Inner City* (1972).

[39] [Pratt] *In Cold Blood* is, in Capote's own words, "a true account of a multiple murder and its consequences."

to natural narratives, too. Narrative (2) quoted earlier was nonfiction to you only because I said that Labov said that his informant said it was true. It was part of our job in reading that narrative to reconstruct mentally both the circumstances surrounding the fight and the circumstances under which the informant told his story to the interviewer, at least insofar as such reconstruction was necessary to make the narrative speech act felicitous. And we did so automatically. Nor is such reconstruction or filling in peculiar to our dealings with written texts. "Making felicitous" is equally part of our role in decoding natural narratives in natural oral situations. Thus, natural narratives do not become infelicitous when they concern people and places the audience has never heard of. Without the slightest hint of infelicity, I can recount an anecdote I heard from someone else whose name I can't remember to an audience I don't know about events I didn't witness that happened somewhere I've never been. And all the time I am talking, those in my audience who do not know me will be busy not just filling in my narrative, but making assessments about me, my background, my social class, my personality, and my reliability, just as we do with the first person narrator of a novel.

Raymond Williams

1922–1988

Perhaps the leading social critic of his time in England, Raymond Williams had Welsh working-class roots. His *The Country and the City* (1973) examined the nostalgia for an idyllic rural earlier age that never existed for most people, yet has been endlessly eulogized in literature, "the recurrent myth of a happier and more natural past." Left out of this picture, as Williams pointed out, is the real life of the rural working poor. What has frequently been identified with natural social order was never natural, usually not of as great an age as claimed, and always exploitative of those at the bottom who supported the hierarchy of ownership and privilege. The growth that followed Feudalism was but the substitution of one form of domination for another. Williams's intellectual orientation was Marxist, but he was different from most European Marxist critics in that his background was rural and theirs was metropolitan.

Williams's *Marxism and Literature* (1977), while certainly in Marx's debt and committed to a social theory of culture, goes beyond most Marxist theorizing, deemphasizing its militant aspects while yet maintaining emphasis on historical movement. Thus, for example, the notions of literature and aesthetics are both "culturally specific," that is, creations of certain historical and cultural moments. For Williams, it is the role of social theory to analyze the development of such terms, what they have included and excluded, and why, with emphasis on the concepts of production and consumption. As for literary theory, at any time it tends to confuse or diminish what Williams calls "the real multiplicity of writing," that is, the great variety of it in favor of a certain definition of what is literature or what is aesthetic.

Williams does not reject such terms, but in historicizing them he limits the possible life and value of meanings given to them. At the same time, he sees certain theories as dangerous when they dominate a field: literature viewed reductively as ideology or literature viewed reductively as aesthetic. Nevertheless, these views performed certain historical tasks, responding to worn-out theories and practices. Certain views of language also have their births and declines. For example, a reductive formalism, as in Russian formalism (Eichenbaum, above, page 867) or structuralist linguistics (Saussure, above, page 786), led to the reduction of language to abstract system, then decipherment, then deconstruction, all ideological responses to prior ideological historical movements.

Perhaps the best example of a critical movement emerging in part from Marxist historical analysis is the New Historicism (Greenblatt, below, page 1476), which emphasizes the historical specificity of a literary text.

Among Williams's writings are *Culture and Society, 1780–1950* (1958); *Border Country* (1960); *The Long Revolution* (1961); *Reading and Criticism* (1966); *Drama in Performance* (1968); *Drama from Ibsen to Brecht* (1969); *The English Novel from Dickens to Lawrence* (1970); *The Country and the City* (1973); *Keywords* (1976); *Marxism and Literature* (1977); *Politics and Letters: Interviews with the New Left Review* (1979);

Problems in Materialism and Culture (1980); *Culture* (1981); *The Sociology of Culture* (1982); *Writing in Society* (1983); and *The Fight for Manod* (1988). See Jan Gorek, *The Alien Mind of Raymond Williams* (1988); Alan O'Connor, *Raymond Williams: Writing, Culture, Politics* (1989); Terry Eagleton, ed., *Raymond Williams: Critical Perspectives* (1989); Fred Inglis, *Raymond Williams* (1995); John Higgins, *Raymond Williams, Marxism, and Cultural Materialism* (1999); Stephen Woodham, *History in the Making: Raymond Williams, Edward Thompson, and Radical Intellectuals* (2001).

from
Marxism and Literature, Part III

1. The Multiplicity of Writing

Literary theory cannot be separated from cultural theory, though it may be distinguished within it. This is the central challenge of any social theory of culture. Yet while this challenge has to be sustained at every point, in general and in detail, it is necessary to be precise about the modes of distinction which then follow. Some of these become modes of effective separation, with important theoretical and practical consequences. But there is equal danger in an opposite kind of error, in which the generalizing and connecting impulse is so strong that we lose sight of real specificities and distinctions of practice, which are then neglected or reduced to simulations of more general forms.

The theoretical problem is that two very powerful modes of distinction are deeply implanted in modern culture. These are the supposedly distinctive categories of 'literature' and of 'the aesthetic.' Each, of course, is historically specific: a formulation of bourgeois culture at a definite period of its development, from the mid-eighteenth to the mid-nineteenth century. But we cannot say this merely dismissively. In each mode of distinction, and in many of the consequent particular definitions, there are elements which cannot be surrendered, either to historical reaction or to a confused projective generalization. Rather, we have to try to analyse the very complicated pressures and limits which, in their weakest forms, these definitions falsely stabilized, yet which, in their strongest forms, they sought to emphasize as new cultural practice.

We have already examined the historical development of the concept of 'literature': from its connections with literacy to an emphasis on polite learning and on printed

books, and then, in its most interesting phase, to an emphasis on 'creative' or 'imaginative' writing as a special and indispensable kind of cultural practice. It is important that elements of this new definition of literature were dragged back to older concepts, as in the attempted isolation of 'the literary tradition' as a form of the tradition of 'polite learning.' But it is more important that the most active elements of the new definition were both specialized and contained, in quite new ways.

The specialization was the interpretation of 'creative' or 'imaginative' writing through the weak and ambiguous concept of 'fiction,' or through the grander but even more questionable concepts of 'imagination' and 'myth.' The containment partly followed from this specialization, but was decisively reinforced by the concept of 'criticism': in part the operative procedure of a selecting and containing 'tradition'; in part also the key shift from creativity and imagination as active productive processes to categorical abstractions demonstrated and ratified by conspicuous humanistic consumption: criticism as 'cultivation,' 'discrimination,' or 'taste.'

Neither the specialization nor the containment has ever been completed. Indeed, in the continuing reality of the practice of writing this is strictly impossible. But each has done significant harm, and in their domination of literary theory have become major obstacles to the understanding of both theory and practice. It is still difficult, for example, to prevent any attempt at literary theory from being turned, almost a priori, into critical theory, as if the only major questions about literary production were variations on the question "how do we judge?" At the same time, in looking at actual writing, the crippling categorizations and dichotomies of 'fact' and 'fiction,' or of 'discursive' and 'imaginative' or 'referential' and 'emotive,' stand regularly not only between works and readers (whence they feed back, miserably, into the complications of 'critical theory') but between writers and works, at a still active and shaping stage.

The multiplicity of writing is its second most evident characteristic, the first being its distinctive practice of the objectified material composition of language. But of course

---

Raymond Williams's *Marxism and Literature* was published in 1977 by Oxford University Press.

this multiplicity is a matter of interpretation as well as of fact. Indeed multiplicity can be realized in weak ways as often as strong. Where the specializing and containing categories operate at an early stage, multiplicity is little more than a recognition of varying 'forms of literature'—poetry, drama, novel—or of forms within these forms—'lyric,' 'epic,' 'narrative,' and so on. The point is not that these recognitions of variation are unimportant; on the contrary they are necessary, though not always in these received and often residual forms. The really severe limitation is the line drawn between all these variations and other 'non-literary' forms of writing. Prebourgeois categorization was normally in terms of the writing itself, as in the relatively evident distinction between verse and other forms of composition, usually drawn in characteristically feudal or aristocratic terms of 'elevation' or 'dignity.' It is significant that while that distinction held, verse normally included what would now be called 'historical' or 'philosophical' or 'descriptive' or 'didactic' or even 'instructional' writing, as well as what would now be called 'imaginative' or 'dramatic' or 'fictional' or 'personal' writing and experience.

The bourgeois drawing and redrawing of all these lines was a complex process. On the one hand it was the result, or more strictly the means, of a decisive secularization, rationalization, and eventually popularization of a wide area of experience. Different values can be attached to each of these processes at different stages, but in history, philosophy, and social and scientific description it is clear that new kinds of distinction about forms and methods of writing were radically connected with new kinds of distinction about intention. 'Elevation' and 'dignity' gave place, inevitably, in certain selected fields, to 'practicality,' 'effectiveness,' or 'accuracy.' Intentions other than these were either willingly conceded or contemptuously dismissed. 'Literature' as a body of 'polite learning' was still used to unite these varying intentions, but under pressure, especially in the late eighteenth and early nineteenth centuries, this broke down. 'Literature' became either the conceded or the contemptuous alternative—the sphere of imagination or fancy, or of emotional substance and effect—or, at the insistence of its practitioners, the relatively removed but again 'higher' dimension—the 'creative' as distinguished from the rational or the practical. In this complex interaction it is of course significant that the separated literature itself changed, in many of its immediate forms. In the 'realist' novel, especially in its distinction from 'romance,' in the new drama (socially extended, secular and contemporary), and in the new special forms of biography and autobiography, many of the same secular, rational, or popular impulses changed particular forms of writing from the inside, or created new literary forms.

Two major consequences followed from this. There was a falsification—false distancing—of the 'fictional' or the 'imaginary' (and connected with these the 'subjective'). And there was a related suppression of the fact of writing—active signifying composition—in what was distinguished as the 'practical,' the 'factual,' or the 'discursive.' These consequences are profoundly related. To move, by definition, from the 'creative' to the 'fictional,' or from the 'imaginative' to the 'imaginary,' is to deform the real practices of writing under the pressure of the interpretation of certain specific forms. The extreme negative definition of 'fiction' (or of 'myth')—an account of 'what did not (really) happen'—depends, evidently, on a pseudo-positive isolation of the contrasting definition, 'fact.' The real range in the major forms—epic, romance, drama, narrative—in which this question of 'fact' and 'fiction' arises is the more complex series: what really happened; what might (could) have happened; what really happens; what might happen; what essentially (typically) happened/happens. Similarly the extreme negative definition of 'imaginary persons'—'who did not/do not exist'—modulates in practice into the series: who existed in this way; who might (could) have existed; who might (could) exist; who essentially (typically) exist. The range of actual writing makes use, implicitly or explicitly, of all these propositions, but not only in the forms that are historically specialized as 'literature.' The characteristically 'difficult' forms (difficult because of the deformed definition) of history, memoir, and biography use a significant part of each series, and given the use of real characters and events in much major epic, romance, drama, and narrative, the substantial overlap—indeed in many areas the substantial community—is undeniable.

The range of actual writing similarly surpasses any reduction of 'creative imagination' to the 'subjective,' with its dependent propositions: 'literature' as 'internal' or 'inner' truth; other forms of writing as 'external' truth. These depend, ultimately, on the characteristic bourgeois separation of 'individual' and 'society' and on the older idealist separation of 'mind' and 'world.' The range of writing, in most forms, crosses these artificial categories again and again, and the extremes can even be stated in an opposite way: autobiography ('what I experienced,' 'what happened to me') is 'subjective' but (ideally) 'factual' writing; realist fiction or naturalist drama ('people as they are,' 'the world as it is') is 'objective' (the narrator or even the fact of narrative occluded in the form) but (ideally) 'creative' writing.

The full range of writing extends even further. Argument, for example, can be distinguished from narrative or characterizing forms, but in practice certain forms of narrative (exemplary instances) or forms of characterization (this kind of person, this kind of behaviour) are radically embedded in many forms of argument. Moreover, the very fact of address—a crucial element in argument—is a stance (at times sustained, at times varying) strictly comparable to elements that are elsewhere isolated as narrative or dramatic. This is true even of the apparently extreme case, in which the stance is 'impersonal' (the scientific paper), where it is the practical mode of writing that establishes this (conventional) absence of personality, in the interest of the necessary creation of the 'impersonal observer.' Thus over a practical range from stance to selection, and in the employment of the vast variety of explicit or implicit propositions which define and control composition, this real multiplicity of writing is continually evident, and much of what has been known as literary theory is a way either of confusing or of diminishing it. The first task of any social theory is then to analyse the forms which have determined certain (interpreted) inclusions and certain (categorical) exclusions. Subject always to the effect of residual categorization, the development of these forms is in the end a social history. The dichotomies fact/fiction and objective/subjective are then the theoretical and historical keys to the basic bourgeois theory of literature, which has controlled and specialized the actual multiplicity of writing.

Yet there is another necessary key. The multiplicity of productive practice was in one way acknowledged, and then effectively occluded, by a transfer of interest from intention to effect. The replacement of the disciplines of grammar and rhetoric (which speak to the multiplicities of intention and performance) by the discipline of criticism (which speaks of effect, and only through effect to intention and performance) is a central intellectual movement of the bourgeois period. Each kind of discipline moved, in the period of change, to a particular pole: grammar and rhetoric to writing; criticism to reading. Any social theory, by contrast, requires the activation of both poles: not merely their interaction-movement from one fixed point, stance, or intention to and from another; but their profound interlocking in actual composition. Something of this kind is now being attempted in what is known (but residually) as communication theory and aesthetics.

And it is on the delineation of 'aesthetics' that we have first to fix our attention. From the description of a theory of perception aesthetics became, in the eighteenth and especially the nineteenth century, a new specializing form of description of the response to 'art' (itself newly generalized from skill to 'imaginative' skill). What emerged in bourgeois economics as the 'consumer'—the abstract figure corresponding to the abstraction of (market and commodity) 'production'—emerged in cultural theory as 'aesthetics' and 'the aesthetic response.' All problems of the multiplicities of intention and performance could then be undercut, or bypassed, by the transfer of energy to this other pole. Art, including literature, was to be defined by its capacity to evoke this special response: initially the perception of beauty; then the pure contemplation of an object, for its own sake and without other ('external') considerations; then also the perception and contemplation of the 'making' of an object: its language, its skill of construction, its 'aesthetic properties.' Such response (power to evoke response) could be as present in a work of history or philosophy as in a play or poem or novel (and all were then 'literature'). Equally, it could be absent in this play or this poem or this novel (and these were then 'not literature' or 'not really literature' or 'bad literature'). The specializing concept of 'literature,' in its modern forms, is thus a central example of the controlling and categorizing specialization of 'the aesthetic.'

2. Aesthetic and Other Situations

Yet it is clear, historically, that the definition of 'aesthetic' response is an affirmation, directly comparable with the definition and affirmation of 'creative imagination,' of certain human meanings and values which a dominant social system reduced and even tried to exclude. Its history is in large part a protest against the forcing of all experience into instrumentality ('utility'), and of all things into commodities. This must be remembered even as we add, necessarily, that the form of this protest, within definite social and historical conditions, led almost inevitably to new kinds of privileged instrumentality and specialized commodity. The humane response was nevertheless there. It has remained important, and still necessary, in controversies within twentieth-century Marxism, where, for example, the (residual bourgeois) reduction of art to social engineering ('ideology') or superstructural reflection (simple 'realism') has been opposed by a tendency, centred on Lukács,[1] to distinguish and defend 'the specificity of the aesthetic.' ('Specificity' is used to translate Lukács's key term kulonosseg-Hungarianor besonderheit-German; the translation, as Fekete (1972)[2] has shown, isdifficult, and 'speciality' and 'particularity,' which have both been used, are misleading; Fekete's own translation is 'peculiarity.')

Lukács sought to define art in ways which would distinguish it, categorically, from both the 'practical' and the 'magical.' 'Practical,' here, is seen as limited by its

---

[1] Georg Lukács (1885–1971), Hungarian philosopher.
[2] Williams refers to an Oxford Ph.D. dissertation *A Theoretical Critique of Some Aspects of North American Critical Theory* (1972) by John Fekete.

containment within specific historical forms: for example, the reduced practice of capitalist society, which is ordinarily reified as 'reality' and to which art is then a necessary alternative. (This repeats, as often in Lukács, the radical idealism of the beginnings of this movement). But, equally, the aesthetic must be distinguished from the 'magical' or 'religious.' These offer their images as objectively real, transcendent, and demanding belief. Art offers its images as images, closed and real in themselves (following a familiar isolation of the 'aesthetic'), but at the same time represents a human generality: a real mediation between (isolated) subjectivity and (abstract) universality; a specific process of the 'identical subject/object.'

This definition is the strongest contemporary form of the affirmation of genuine 'aesthetic' practice as against a reduced 'practicality' or a displaced 'myth-making.' But it raises fundamental problems. It is, intrinsically, a categorical proposition, defensible at that level but immediately subject to major difficulties when it is taken into the multiple world of social and cultural process. Indeed its difficulties are similar to those which confronted formalism after its critical attempt to isolate the art-object as a thing in itself, to be examined only in its own terms and through its own 'means' or 'devices': an attempt founded on the hypothesis of a specifically distinguishable 'poetic language.' It is never the categorical distinction between aesthetic intentions, means, and effects and other intentions, means, and effects which presents difficulties. The problem is to sustain such a distinction through the inevitable extension to an indissoluble social material process: not only indissoluble in the social conditions of the making and reception of art, within a general social process from which these can not be excised; but also indissoluble in the actual making and reception, which are connecting material processes within a social system of the use and transformation of material (including language) by material means. The formalists, seeking 'specificity,' in their detailed studies, not in a category but in what they claimed to show as a specific 'poetic language,' reached this crucial impasse earlier and more openly. One way out (or back) was the conversion of all social and cultural practice to 'aesthetic' forms in this sense: a solution, or displacement, since widely evident in the 'closed forms' of structuralist linguistics and in structuralist-semiotic literary and cultural studies. Another and more interesting way out was to move definition of the aesthetic to a 'function', and therefore a 'practice,' as distinct from its location in special objects or special means.

The best representative of this more interesting apparent solution is Mukarovsky;[3] for example in his *Aesthetic*

---

[3] Jan Mukarovský (1891–1975), a member of the Prague school of structural linguistics.

Function, Norm and Value as Social Facts. Mukarovsky, facing the multiplicity of practice, had little difficulty in showing that

> there are no objects or actions which, by virtue of their essence or organization would, regardless of time, place or the person evaluating them, possess an aesthetic function, and others which, again by their very nature, would be necessarily immune to the aesthetic function. (p. 1)

He took examples not only from the recognized arts, in which the aesthetic function which appears to be their primary definition may be displaced and overridden, or destroyed and lost, but also from the 'borderline' cases of the decorative arts, craft production, the continuum of processes in building and architecture, landscape, social manners, the preparation and presentation of food and drink, and the varied functions of dress. He conceded that there are

> within art and outside of it—objects which, by virtue of their organization are meant to have an aesthetic effect. This is actually the essential property of art. But an active capacity for the aesthetic function is not a real property of an object, even if the object has been deliberately composed with the aesthetic function in mind. Rather, the aesthetic function manifests itself only under certain conditions, i.e. in a certain social context. (p. 3)

What then is the aesthetic function? Mukarovsky's elaborately differentiated argument ends in the radical diversification of what had been singular terms, which yet he retains. Art is not a special kind of object but one in which the aesthetic function, usually mixed with other functions, is dominant. Art, with other things (landscape and dress, most evidently), gives aesthetic pleasure, but this cannot be transliterated as a sense of beauty or a sense of perceived form, since while these are central in the aesthetic function they are historically and socially variable, and in all real instances concrete. At the same time the aesthetic function is "not an epiphenomenon of other functions" but a "codeterminant of human reaction to reality."

Mukarovsky's important work is best seen as the penultimate stage of the critical dissolution of the specializing and controlling categories of bourgeois aesthetic theory. Almost all the original advantages of this theory have been quite properly, indeed necessarily, abandoned. 'Art' as a categorically separate dimension, or body of objects; 'the aesthetic' as an isolable extra-social phenomenon: each has been broken up by a return to the variability, the relativity, and the multiplicity of actual cultural practice. We can then see more clearly the ideological function of the specializing abstractions of 'art' and 'the aesthetic.' What they represent, in an abstract way, is a particular stage of the division of labour. 'Art' is a kind of production which has to be seen as separate from the dominant bourgeois productive norm: the making of commodities. It has then, in fantasy, to be separated from 'production' altogether; described by the new term 'creation'; distinguished from its own material processes; distinguished, finally, from other products of its own kind or closely related kinds—'art' from 'non-art'; 'literature' from 'para-literature' or 'popular literature'; 'culture' from 'mass culture.' The narrowing abstraction is then so powerful that, in its name, we find ways of neglecting (or of dismissing as peripheral) that relentless transformation of art works into commodities, within the dominant forms of capitalist society. Art and thinking about art have to separate themselves, by ever more absolute abstraction, from the social processes within which they are still contained. Aesthetic theory is the main instrument of this evasion. In its concentration on receptive states, on psychological responses of an abstractly differentiated kind, it represents the division of labour in consumption corresponding to the abstraction of art as the division of labour in production.

Mukarovsky, from within this tradition, in effect destroyed it. He restored real connections even while retaining the terms of the deliberate disconnection. Aesthetic function, aesthetic norms, aesthetic values: each in turn was scrupulously followed through to historical social practice, yet each, as a category, was almost desperately retained. The reason is evident. While the dominant elements of human practice, within a specific and dominant form of society, exclude or undervalue known and pressing elements of human intention and response, a specialized and privileged area— 'art' and 'the aesthetic'—has, it can seem, to be defined and defended, even after the point at which it is realized that interrelationship and interpenetration are radically inevitable: the point at which the 'area' is redefined as a 'function.'

The next step in the argument has now to be taken. What Mukarovsky abstracted as a function has to be seen, rather, as a series of situations, in which specific intentions and responses combine, within discoverable formations, to produce a true range of specific facts and effects. It is obvious that one primary feature of such situations is the availability of works which are specifically designed to occasion them, and of specific institutions which are intended to be such actual occasions; (an occasion, however, is only potentially a function). Yet such situations are still, as history shows us, highly variable and commonly mixed, and the works and institutions vary accordingly. It is in this sense that we have to replace the specializing category of 'the aesthetic,' and its dependent and circulating categories of 'the arts,' by the radically different vocabulary of 'the dominant,' the 'associated,' and the 'subordinate' which, in the last phase of rigorous specialization, the formalists and the social formalists necessarily developed. What the formalists saw as a hierarchy within specific forms, and the social formalists as a hierarchy of specific practices, has to be extended to the area in which these hierarchies are both determined and contested: the full social material process itself.

Apart from the complications of received theory, this is not really difficult. Anyone who is in contact with the real multiplicity of writing, and with the no less real multiplicity of those forms of writing that have been specialized as literature, is already aware of the range of intentions and responses which are continually and variably manifest and latent. The honest muddle that so often arises is a consequence of pressure from both ends of a range of received and incompatible theories. If we are asked to believe that all literature is 'ideology,' in the crude sense that its dominant intention (and then our only response) is the communication or imposition of 'social' or 'political' meanings and values, we can only, in the end, turn away. If we are asked to believe that all literature is 'aesthetic,' in the crude sense that its dominant intention (and then our only response) is the beauty of language or form, we may stay a little longer but will still in the end turn away. Some people will lurch from one position to the other. More, in practice, will retreat to an indifferent acknowledgement of complexity, or assert the autonomy of their own (usually consensual) response.

But it is really much simpler to face the facts of the range of intentions and effects, and to face it as a range. All writing carries references, meanings, and values. To suppress or displace them is in the end impossible. But to say 'all writing carries' is only a way of saying that language and form are constitutive processes of reference, meaning, and value, and that these are not necessarily identical with, or exhausted by, the kinds of reference, meaning, and value that correspond or can be grouped with generalized references, meanings and values that are also evident, in other senses and in summary, elsewhere.

This recognition is lost if it is specialized to 'beauty,' though to suppress or displace the real experience to which that abstraction points is also in the end impossible. The true effects of many kinds of writing are indeed quite physical: specific alterations of physical rhythms, physical organization: experiences of quickening and slowing, of expansion and of intensification. It was to these experiences, more varied and more intricate than any general naming can indicate, that the categorization of 'the aesthetic' appeared to speak, and that the reduction to 'ideology' tried and failed to deny or make incidental. Yet the categorization was complicit with a deliberately dividing society, and could then not admit what is also evident: the dulling, the lulling, the chiming, the overbearing, which are also, in real terms, 'aesthetic' experiences: aesthetic effects but also aesthetic intentions. What we can practically though variably recognize in specific works has to be linked with the complex formations, situations, and occasions in which such intentions and such responses are made possible, are modified, and are encouraged or deflected.

Thus we have to reject 'the aesthetic' both as a separate abstract dimension and as a separate abstract function. We have to reject 'Aesthetics' to the large extent that it is posited on these abstractions. At the same time we have to recognize and indeed emphasize the specific variable intentions and the specific variable responses that have been grouped as aesthetic in distinction from other isolated intentions and responses, and in particular from information and suasion, in their simplest senses. Indeed, we cannot rule out, theoretically, the possibility of discovering certain invariant combinations of elements within this grouping, even while we recognize that such invariant combinations as have hitherto been described depend on evident processes of supra-historical appropriation and selection. Moreover, the grouping is not a way of assigning value, even relative value. Any concentration on language or form, in sustained or temporary priority over other elements and other ways of realizing meaning and value; is specific: at times an intense and irreplaceable experience in which these fundamental elements of human process are directly stimulated, reinforced, or extended; at times, at a different extreme, an evasion of other immediate connections, an evacuation of immediate situation, or a privileged indifference to the human process as a whole. ("Does a man die at your feet, your business is not to help him, but to note the colour of his lips.")[4]

Value cannot reside in the concentration or in the priority or in the elements which provoke these. The argument of values is in the variable encounters of intention and response in specific situations. The key to any analysis, and from analysis back to theory, is then the recognition of precise situations in which what have been isolated, and displaced, as 'the aesthetic intention' and 'the aesthetic response' have occurred. Such 'situations' are not only

'moments.' In the varied historical development of human culture they are almost continuously both organized and disorganized, with precise but highly variable formations initiating, sustaining, enclosing, or destroying them. The history of such formations is the specific and highly varied history of art. Yet to enter any part of this history, in an active way, we have to learn to understand the specific elements—conventions and notations—which are the material keys to intention and response, and, more generally, the specific elements which socially and historically determine and signify aesthetic and other situations.

3. From Medium to Social Practice

Any description of 'situations' is manifestly social, but as a description of cultural practice it is still evidently incomplete. What is ordinarily added (or what in an earlier and persistent kind of theory was taken as definitive) is a specification of cultural practice in terms of its 'medium.' Literature, it is said, is a particular kind of work in the medium of language. Anything else, though important, is peripheral to this: a situation in which the real work is begun, or in which it is received. The work itself is in 'the medium.'

Some emphasis of this kind is indeed necessary, but we have to look very carefully at its definition as work in a 'medium.' We saw earlier the inherent dualism in the idea of 'mediation,' but in most of its uses it continues to denote an activity: an active relationship or, more interestingly, a specific transformation of material. What is interesting about 'medium' is that it began as a definition of an activity by an apparently autonomous object or force. This was particularly clear when the word acquired the first element of its modern sense in the early seventeenth century. Thus 'to the Sight three things are required, the Object, the Organ and the Medium.' Here a description of the practical activity of seeing, which is a whole and complex process of relationship between the developed organs of sight and the accessible properties of things seen, is characteristically interrupted by the invention of a third term which is given its own properties, in abstraction from the practical relationship. This general notion of intervening and in effect causal substances, on which various practical operations were believed to depend, had a long course in scientific thought, down to 'phlogiston' and 'caloric.' But in the case of a hypothetical substance, in some natural operation, it was accessible to and could be corrected by continued observation.

It was a different matter when the same hypothesis was applied to human activities, and especially to language. Ba-

---

[4][Williams] John Ruskin in the manuscript printed as an appendix to *Modern Painters* (Library Edition, London, 1903–1912, ii), 388–89.

con[5] wrote of thoughts 'expressed by the Medium of Wordes,' and this is an example of the familiar position, already examined, in which thoughts exist before language and are then expressed through its 'medium.' A constitutive human activity is thus abstracted and objectified. Words are seen as objects, things, which men take up and arrange into particular forms to express or communicate information which, before this work in the 'medium,' they already possess. This notion, in many different forms, has persisted even into some modern communications theory. It reaches its extreme in the assumption of the independent properties of the 'medium,' which, in one kind of theory, is seen as determining not only the 'content' of what is communicated but also the social relationships within which the communication takes place. In this influential kind of technological determinism (for example, in McLuhan[6]) the 'medium' is (metaphysically) the master.

Two other developments in the idea of a 'medium' must also be noted. From the eighteenth century it was often used to describe what we would now ordinarily call a means of communication. It was particularly used of newspapers: "through the medium . . . of your publication"; "your journal one of the best possible mediums." In the twentieth century, the description of a newspaper as a 'medium' for advertising became common, and the extended description of the press and broadcasting as 'the media' was affected by this. 'A medium' or 'the media' is then, on the one hand, a term for a social organ or institution of general communication—a relatively neutral use—and, on the other hand, a term for a secondary or derived use (as in advertising) of an organ or institution with another apparently primary purpose. Yet in either case the 'medium' is a form of social organization, something essentially different from the idea of an intermediate communicative substance.

However, the notion of an intermediate substance was also extensively and simultaneously developed, especially in the visual arts: 'the medium of oils' or 'the medium of water-colour': in fact as a development from a relatively neutral scientific sense of the carrier of some active substance. The 'medium' in painting had been any liquid with which pigments could be mixed; it was then extended to the active mixture and so to the specific practice. There was then an important extended use in all the arts. 'Medium' became the specific material with which a particular kind of artist worked. To understand this 'medium' was obviously a condition of professional skill and prac-

tice. Thus far there was not, and is not, any real difficulty. But a familiar process of reification occurred, reinforced by the influence of formalism. The properties of 'the medium' were abstracted as if they defined the practice, rather than being its means. This interpretation then suppressed the full sense of practice, which has always to be defined as work on a material for a specific purpose within certain necessary social conditions. Yet this real practice is easily displaced (often by only a small extension from the necessary emphasis on knowing how to handle the material) to an activity defined, not by the material, which would be altogether too crude, but by that particular projection and reification of work on the material which is called 'the medium.'

Yet this is still a projection and reification of a practical operation. Even in this diminished form, concentration on 'the medium,' as at least the location of a process of work, is very much preferable to those conceptions of 'art' which had become almost wholly divorced from its original general sense of skilled work (as 'poetry' had also been moved from a sense which contained a central emphasis on 'making' and 'the maker'). In fact the two processes—the idealization of art and the reification of the medium—were connected, through a specific and strange historical development. Art was idealized to distinguish it from 'mechanical' work. One motive, undoubtedly, was a simple class emphasis, to separate 'higher' things—the objects of interest to free men, the 'liberal arts'—from the 'ordinary' business ('mechanical' as manual work, and then as work with machines) of the 'everyday world.' A later phase of the idealization, however, was a form of oblique (and sometimes direct) protest against what work had become, within capitalist production. An early manifesto of English Romanticism, Young's *Conjectures on Original Composition* (1759), defined original art as rising

> spontaneously from the vital root of genius; it grows, it is not made. Imitations are often a sort of manufacture, wrought up by those mechanics, art and labour, out of pre-existent materials not their own.[7]

From a similar position Blake attacked "the Monopolizing Trader who Manufactures Art by the Hands of Ignorant journeymen till . . . he is Counted the Greatest Genius who can sell a Good-for-Nothing Commodity for a Great Price."[8]

---

[5] Bacon (above, page 234).
[6] Marshall McLuhan (1911–1980), Canadian author of works on communication theory.

[7] Young (above, page 348).
[8] Blake (above, page 447).

All the traditional terms were now in fact confused, under the pressure of changes in the general mode of production, and the steady extension of these changes to the production of 'art,' when both art and knowledge, as Adam Smith[9] realistically observed, were

> purchased, in the same manner as shoes or stockings, from those whose business it is to make up and prepare for the market that particular species of goods.

Both the dominant bourgeois definition of work as the production of commodities, and the steady practical inclusion of works of art as commodities among others, led to this special form of a general protest.

A practical alienation was being radically experienced, at two interconnecting levels. There was the loss of connection between a worker's own purposes, and thus his 'original' identity, and the actual work he was hired to perform. There was also the loss of the 'work' itself, which when it was made, within this mode of production, necessarily became a commodity. The protest in the name of 'art' was then at one level the protest of craftsmen—most of them literally hand-craftsmen—against a mode of production which steadily excluded them or profoundly altered their status. But at another level it was a claim for a significant meaning of work—that of using human energy on material for an autonomous purpose—which was being radically displaced and denied, in most kinds of production, but which could be more readily and more confidently asserted, in the case of art, by association with the 'life of the spirit' or 'our general humanity.'

The argument was eventually consciously articulated and generally applied by William Morris.[10] But the orthodox development of the original perception was an idealization, in which 'art' was exempted from, made exceptional to, what 'work' had been made to mean. At the same time, however, no artist could dispense with his working skills. Still, as before, the making of art was experienced, tangibly, as a craft, a skill, a long working process. The special senses of 'medium' were then exceptionally reinforced: medium as intermediate agency, between an 'artistic impulse' and a complete 'work'; or medium as the objectified properties of the working process itself. To have seen the working process differently, not with the specializing senses of 'medium,' but as a particular case of conscious practice, and thus 'practical consciousness,' would have endangered the precious reservation of art from the conditions, not only of practical everyday work—that relation which had once, in a different social order, been accepted—but of the capitalist system of material production for a market.

Yet painters and sculptors remained manual workers. Musicians remained involved with the material performance and material notation of instruments which were the products of conscious and prolonged manual skills. Dramatists remained involved with the material properties of stages and the physical properties of actors and voices. Writers, in ways which we must examine and distinguish, handled material notations on paper. Necessarily, inside any art, there is this physical and material consciousness. It is only when the working process and its results are seen or interpreted in the degraded forms of material commodity production that the significant protest—the denial of materiality by these necessary workers with material—is made and projected into abstracted 'higher' or 'spiritual' forms. The protest is understandable, but these 'higher' forms of production, embodying many of the most intense and most significant forms of human experience, are more clearly understood when they are recognized as specific objectifications, in relatively durable material organizations, of what are otherwise the least durable though often the most powerful and affective human moments. The inescapable materiality of works of art is then the irreplaceable materialization of kinds of experience, including experience of the production of objects, which, from our deepest sociality, go beyond not only the production of commodities but also our ordinary experience of objects.

At the same time, beyond this, material cultural production has a specific social history. Much of the evident crisis of 'literature,' in the second half of the twentieth century, is the result of altered processes and relationships in basic material production. I do not mean only the radical material changes in printing and publishing, though these have had direct effects. I mean also the development of new material forms of dramatization and narrative in the specific technologies of motion pictures, sound broadcasting, and television, involving not only new intrinsic material processes, which in the more complex technologies bring with them quite new problems of material notation and realization, but also new working relationships on which the complex technologies depend. In one phase of material literary production, most typically from the seventeenth to the midtwentieth century, the author was a solitary handworker, alone with his 'medium.' Subsequent material processes—printing and distribution—could then be seen as simple accessories. But in other phases, earlier and later, the work was from the beginning undertaken in

---

[9] Adam Smith (1723–1790), Scottish economist.
[10] William Morris (1834–1896), English poet and artist.

relation with others (for example in the Elizabethan theatre or in a motion-picture or broadcasting unit) and the immediate material process was more than notation as a stage of transcription or publication. It was, and is, co-operative material production involving many processes of a material and physical kind. The reservation of 'literature' to the specific technology of pen and paper, linked to the printed book, is then an important historical phase, but not, in relation to the many practices which it offers to represent, any kind of absolute definition.

Yet these are not, except in a kind of shorthand, problems of 'the medium' or of 'new media.' Every specific art has dissolved into it, at every level of its operations, not only specific social relationships, which in a given phase define it (even at its most apparently solitary), but also specific material means of production, on the mastery of which its production depends. It is because they are dissolved that they are not 'media.' The form of social relationship and the form of material production are specifically linked. Not always, however, in some simple identity. The contradiction between an increasingly collaborative production and the learned skills and values of individual production is now especially acute in several kinds of writing (the dramatic most evidently, but also much narrative and argument), and not only as a publishing or distributing problem, as which it is often most identifiable, but right back in the processes of writing itself.

Significantly, since the late nineteenth century, crises of technique—which can be isolated as problems of the 'medium' or of the 'form'—have been directly linked with a sense of crisis in the relationship of art to society, or in the very purposes of art which had previously been agreed or even taken for granted. A new technique has often been seen, realistically, as a new relationship, or as depending on a new relationship. Thus what had been isolated as a medium, in many ways rightly as a way of emphasizing the material production which any art must be, came to be seen, inevitably, as social practice; or, in the crisis of modern cultural production, as a crisis of social practice. This is the crucial common factor, in otherwise diverse tendencies, which links the radical aesthetics of modernism and the revolutionary theory and practice of Marxism.

4. Signs and Notations

Language, then, is not a medium; it is a constitutive element of material social practice. But if this is so, it is clearly also a special case. For it is at once a material practice and a process in which many complex activities, of a less manifestly material kind—from information to interaction, from

representation to imagination, and from abstract thought to immediate emotion—are specifically realized. Language is in fact a special kind of material practice: that of human sociality. And then, to the extent that material practice is limited to the production of objects, or that social practice is taken to exclude or to contrast with individual practice, language can become unrecognizable in its real forms. Within this failure of recognition, alternative partial accounts of language are made the basis of, among other matters, alternative kinds of literary theory. The two major alternative kinds, in our own culture, are on the one hand 'expressivism,' in its simple forms of 'psychological realism' or the writing of 'personal experience,' or its disguised forms of naturalism and simple realism—expressing the truth of an observed situation or fact—and on the other hand, 'formalism,' in its variants of instances of a form, assemblies of literary devices, or 'texts' of a 'system of signs.'[11] Each of these general theories grasps real elements of the practice of writing, but commonly in ways which deny other real elements and even make them inconceivable.

Thus formalism focuses our attention on what is evidently present and might well be overlooked in writing: the specific and definitive uses of literary forms of many kinds, from the most general to the most local, which have always to be seen as more than simple 'vehicles' or 'scaffolding' for the expression of an independent experience. At the same time it deflects our attention, and in doing so becomes incredible beyond certain limited circles, from the more than formal meanings and values, and in this sense the defining experiences, of almost all actual works. The impatient 'commonsense' reaction, that literature does, quite evidently, describe events, depict situations, express the experiences of real men and women, is in this context understandable and persuasive. Yet the reaction is still not a possible literary theory, that is to say, a consciousness of real literary practice. We have to learn to look in the space between the deflection and the reaction if we are to grasp the significance of the practice as a whole. What we then find is that we have been dealing with complementary errors.

The central error of expressivist theory—an error common to descriptions of naturalism or simple realism and to descriptions of psychological realism or literature as personal experience (descriptions which are in fact often opposed to each other and which contend for significance and priority)—is the failure to acknowledge the fact that meaning is always produced; it is never simply expressed.

There are indeed crucial variations in the methods of its production, from a relatively complete reliance on al-

---

[11] See Saussure (above, page 786).

ready established meanings and interrelations of meanings to a relatively complete reworking of available meanings and the discovery of new combinations of meanings. In fact neither of these methods is as complete, as self-contained, as it may at first sight appear. The 'orthodox' work is still always a specific production. 'Experimental' work depends, even predominantly, on a shared consciousness of already available meanings. For these are the defining characteristics and then the real determinations of the process of language as such. No expression, that is to say—no account, description, depiction, portrait—is 'natural' or 'straightforward.' These are at most socially relative terms. Language is not a pure medium through which the reality of a life or the reality of an event or an experience or the reality of a society can 'flow.' It is a socially shared and reciprocal activity, already embedded in active relationships, within which every move is an activation of what is already shared and reciprocal or may become so.

Thus to address an account to another is, explicitly or potentially, as in any act of expression, to evoke or propose a relationship. It is also, through this, to evoke or propose an active relationship to the experience being expressed, whether this condition of relationship is seen as the truth of a real event or the significance of an imagined event, the reality of a social situation or the significance of a response to it, the reality of a private experience or the significance of its imaginative projection, or the reality of some part of the physical world or the significance of some element of perception or response to it.

Every expression proposes this complex relationship, on which, but to variable degrees of consciousness and conscious attention, it depends. It is then important that the complex relationship implicit in any expression should not be reduced to categorical or general (for example, abstracted political and economic) factors, as some of the simpler Marxist theories propose. But it remains essential to grasp the full social significance that is always active and inherent in any apparently 'natural' or 'straightforward' account. Crucial assumptions and propositions, not simply in ideology or in conscious stance, but in the ebb and flow of feeling from and to others, in assumed situations and relationships, and in the relationships implied or proposed within the immediate uses of language, are always present and are always directly significant. In many instances, and especially in class-divided societies, it is necessary to make them explicit, by analysis, and to show, in detail, that this is not a case of going 'beyond' the literary work, but of going more thoroughly into its full (and not arbitrarily protected) expressive significance.

It was a version of this procedure which one tendency in formalism proposed. Other variants of formalism underlined the general forms within which particular expressions occurred, or drew attention to the devices, seen as active elements of form or formation, through which presentation of the expression was affected. A more radical formalism, reacting against notions of language and expression as 'natural,' reduced the whole process to what it saw as its basic constituents; to 'signs,' and then to a 'system of signs,' concepts which it had borrowed from one kind of linguistics (see I, 2 above).

The sense of a production of meanings was then notably strengthened. Any unit of expression can be shown, by analysis, to depend on the formal signs which are words and not persons or things, and on their formal arrangement. 'Natural' expression of 'reality' or 'experience' can be convincingly shown to be a myth, occluding this real and demonstrable activity. Yet what then usually happened was the production (itself not scrutinized) of a new myth, based on the following assumptions: that all 'signs' are arbitrary; that the 'system of signs' is determined by its formal internal relations;[12] that 'expression' is not only not 'natural' but is a form of 'codification'; and that the appropriate response to 'codification' is 'decipherment,' 'deconstruction.'[13] Each of these assumptions is in fact ideological, to be sure in response to another and more pervasive ideology.

For the 'sign' is 'arbitrary' only from a position of conscious or unconscious alienation. Its apparent arbitrariness is a form of social distance, itself a form of relationship. The social history of philology and of comparative linguistics, based so largely in residual or in colonizing formations, prepared the way for this alienation, and, ironically, naturalized it. Every expression, every utterance, is within its procedures an 'alien' fact. The formal quality of words as 'signs,' which was correctly perceived, was rendered as 'arbitrary' by a privileged withdrawal from the lived and living relationships which, within any native language (the languages of real societies, to which all men belong), make all formal meanings significant and substantial, in a world of reciprocal reference which moves, as it must, beyond the signs. To reduce words to 'arbitrary' signs, and to reduce language to a 'system' of signs, is then either a realized alienation (the position of the alien observer of another people's language or of the conscious linguist deliberately abstracting lived and living forms for scientific analysis) or an unrealized alienation, in which a specific group, for understandable reasons, overlooks its privileged relationship to the real and active language and society all around it and in fact within

---

[12] Saussure again.

[13] See Derrida (above, page 1203).

it, and projects onto the activities of others its own forms of alienation. There is a respectable variant of this latter position, in which the society or form of society within which the privileged group operates is seen as 'alienated,' in Marxist or post-Marxist terms, and the 'arbitrary' signs and the 'codes' they compose are seen as forms of bourgeois society. But even this is unacceptable because the theoretical assumptions within which the diagnosis is made—the arbitrariness of all 'signs,' for example—are fundamentally incompatible with recognition of any specific kinds of alienation. Indeed, what really follows is the universality of alienation, the position of a closely associated bourgeois idealist formation, drawing its assumptions from a universalist (mainly Freudian) psychology.

Again, if a 'system of signs' has only internal formal rules, there can be no specific social formations, in historical or sociological terms, to institute, vary, or alter this kind of (social) practice. Nor, finally, can there be full social practice of any kind. The description of active practice in language as 'codification,' while appearing to point to the relationships and references which the description of 'natural' expression occludes, then in its own way occludes them, by withdrawing attention from a continuous and varied material social practice, and rendering all this practice into formal terms. 'Code' has a further irony, in that it implies, somewhere, the existence of the same message 'in clear.' But this, even as a formal account of language, is radically wrong, and the simple notion of 'decoding' the messages of others is then a privileged fantasy. The (alienated) reference to the 'science' of such deconstruction is a displacement from the social situation, in which specific formations, and specific individuals, in highly differential but discoverable ways, are all (including the decoders) using, offering, testing, amending, and altering this central and substantial element of their own material and social relationships. To occlude these relationships, by reducing their expressed forms to a linguistic system, is a kind of error closely related, in effect, to that made by the theorist of 'pure' expression, for whom, also, there was no materially and socially differential world of lived and living practice; a human world of which language, in and through its own forms, is itself always a form.

To understand the materiality of language we have of course to distinguish between spoken words and written notations. This distinction, which the concept of 'sign' fundamentally obscures, has to be related to a development in means of production. Spoken words are a process of human activity using only immediate, constitutive, physical resources. Written words, with their continuing but not necessarily direct relation to speech, are a form of material pro-

duction, adapting non-human resources to a human end.

There are now intermediate cases, in the mechanical and electronic recording, reproduction, and composition of speech, yet these are not, of course, notations, though difficult problems of notation are at times involved in their preparation. But the central characteristic of writing is the production of material notations, though the purposes and therefore the means of production are variable. Thus the written play is a notation of intended speech, and sometimes also of intended movement and scene (I have analysed these variations in *Drama in Performance*). Some written forms are a record of speech, or a text for speech, (speeches, lectures, sermons). But the characteristic 'literary' form is written notation for reading. It is characteristic of such notations, in printing obviously but also in copying, that they are reproducible. They are unlike normal forms of produced material objects, even such related forms as paintings. For their essential material existence is in the reproducible notations, which are then radically dependent on the cultural system within which the notations are current, as well as, in a secondary way, on the social and economic system within which they are distributed. It is thus in the whole and complex process of notation that we find the reality of this specific material and social process. Once again the linguistic elements are not signs; they are the notations of actual productive relationships.

The most basic kind of notation is of course the alphabetic. In highly literate cultures this means of production is in effect almost naturalized, but the more we learn about the processes of reading the more we realize the active and interactive relationship which this apparently settled kind of notation involves. Thus the notation is not, even at this level, simple transfer; it depends upon the active grasping, often by repeated trial and error, of shapes and relationships which the notation promotes but does not guarantee. Reading, then, is as active as writing, and the notation, as means of production, depends on both these activities and upon their effective relationship. What is true but general at this basic level remains true but highly specific in more specifying forms of notation within this general process.

Consider, for example, the complex notations of source: the indications, at times quite direct, at times highly indirect, of the identity of the writer, in all its possible senses. Such notations are often closely involved with indications of situation, the combinations of situation and identity often constituting crucial notations of part of the relationship into which the writing is intended to enter. The process of reading, in anything more than its most literal sense, is radically dependent on these indications: not only as an answer to the necessary question, 'who "speaks"?', but as answers to the necessary range of related questions: 'from what situation?'; 'with what authority?'; 'with what intention?'

Such questions are often answered by technical analysis: the identification of 'devices.' But the technical observations—whether arrived at analytically or, as much more commonly, through the understanding of conventional indications within a shared culture—are always methods of establishing, in what is really a simultaneous movement, the nature of the specific productive process and of the inherent relationship which it proposes. The indications may be very general; to show whether we are reading novel, biography, autobiography, memoir, or historical account. But many of the most significant notations are particular: indications of speech, reported speech and dialogue; indications of explicit and implicit thought processes; indications of displaced or suspended monologue, dialogue, or thought; indications of direct or of 'characterized' observation. All extended reading and all developed writing depend on an understanding of the range of these indications, and the indications depend on both received and possible relationships, locally materialized by processes of complex notation. And this is to see the matter only at the level of the specification of persons, events, and experiences. Some of the most important notations are indications of writing for reading in more immediate ways, within the productive process itself. Notations of order, arrangement, and the mutual relationship of parts; notations of pause, of break, of transition; notations of emphasis: all these can be said to control, but are better described as ways of realizing, the process of the specific productive relationship that is at once, in its character as notation, a way of writing and a way of reading.

It was the specific contribution of formalist studies, as of a much older tradition of rhetoric, to identify and to demonstrate the operation of such notations. At the same time, by reducing them to elements of a formal system, they occluded the extending relationships of which these elements are always and inevitably the productive means. Expressivist studies, on the other hand, reduced notations, where they noticed them at all, to mechanical elements—means to other ends—or to elements of decoration or the simple formalities of address. To the extent that this can sustain attention to the full human experiences and relationships which are in fact always in process in and through the notations, it can seem the lesser error. But the errors of each tendency are complementary, and can be corrected only by a fully social theory of literature. For the notations are relationships, expressed, offered, tested, and amended in a whole social process, in which device, expression, and the substance of expression are in the end inseparable. To look at this conclusion in another way, we must look at the nature of literary conventions.

Edward W. Said

1935–2003

Born in Palestine, educated there and in Egypt, as well as in the United States, Edward Said did not augur in his earliest works, including *Joseph Conrad and the Fiction of Autobiography* (1966) and *Beginnings: Intention and Method* (1975), the kind of emphatic, sometimes dazzling innovations and penetrating insights of the series of books starting in 1978 with *Orientalism,* without doubt his best-known work. The impact of this book was immediate and profound, as Said captured the deeply interpenetrating aspects of the politics of colonialism and the academic study of non-European culture. More than any single work, *Orientalism* articulated a framework for the integration of philosophical, anthropological, literary, and political aspects of the study of culture in a postcolonial era. Whereas earlier work, such as Frantz Fanon's *The Wretched of the Earth* (above, page 1187) or Antonio Gramsci's *Prison Notebooks* (above, page 936), addressed urgent practical matters pertaining to wars of national liberation, or the analysis of the domination of subaltern peoples, Said's integrative model effected an alignment of interests both within the academic professions and on the ground. Needless to say, his work also provoked criticism and opposition, since the same alignment that made it exemplary, work of the sort that younger scholars and critics could emulate, called attention to the sometimes deep and intricate complicity between the academic study of other peoples (in this case by "Orientalists") and attitudes of political condescension or the countenancing of exploitation by professional intellectuals.

In many ways like the counter-career of Noam Chomsky as a political analyst and commentator, Said's work after *Orientalism,* particularly concerning the world of Islam and the situation of Palestine, was increasingly involved both directly and indirectly with practical political matters. In this too, Said's active participation, especially in Palestinian issues, was both exemplary and intensely controversial. But with a remarkable mixture of cosmopolitan urbanity and passionate political commitment, Said exerted a broad and deep influence on the contemporary culture. Throughout this palpably political work, however, Said continued to pursue literary, artistic, and aesthetic concerns, as evinced in his *Musical Elaborations* (1991), and a more than methodological interest in the idea of counterpoint as an approach to the integration of academic and practical matters so richly manifest in his career.

Edward Said's works include: *Joseph Conrad and the Fiction of Autobiography* (1966); *Beginnings: Intention and Method* (1975); *Orientalism* (1978); *The Question of Palestine* (1979); *Covering Islam: How the Media and the Experts Determine How We See the Rest of the World* (1981); *The World, the Text, and the Critic* (1983); coeditor with Christopher Hitchens, *Blaming the Victims: Spurious Scholarship and the Palestinian Question* (1988); *Musical Elaborations* (1991); *Culture and Imperialism* (1993); *The Politics of Dispossession* (1994); and *Peace and Its Discontents: Essays on Palestine in the Middle East Peace Process* (1995). Critical responses include: Keith Ansell-Pearson,

Bonita Parry, and Judith Squires, eds., *Cultural Readings of Imperialism: Edward Said and the Gravity of History* (1997); Paul Bové, ed., *Edward Said and the Work of the Critic: Speaking Truth to Power* (2000); and Robert J. C. Young, *Postcolonialism: An Historical Introduction* (2001).

from

Orientalism

Introduction

I

On a visit to Beirut during the terrible civil war of 1975–1976 a French journalist wrote regretfully of the gutted downtown area that "it had once seemed to belong to . . . the Orient of Chateaubriand and Nerval."[1] He was right about the place, of course, especially so far as a European was concerned. The Orient was almost a European invention, and had been since antiquity a place of romance, exotic beings, haunting memories and landscapes, remarkable experiences. Now it was disappearing; in a sense it had happened, its time was over. Perhaps it seemed irrelevant that Orientals themselves had something at stake in the process, that even in the time of Chateaubriand and Nerval Orientals had lived there, and that now it was they who were suffering; the main thing for the European visitor was a European representation of the Orient and its contemporary fate, both of which had a privileged communal significance for the journalist and his French readers.

Americans will not feel quite the same about the Orient, which for them is much more likely to be associated very differently with the Far East (China and Japan, mainly). Unlike the Americans, the French and the British—less so the Germans, Russians, Spanish, Portuguese, Italians, and Swiss—have had a long tradition of what I shall be calling *Orientalism,* a way of coming to terms with the Orient that is based on the Orient's special place in European Western experience. The Orient is not only adjacent to Europe; it is also the place of Europe's greatest and richest and oldest colonies, the source of its civilizations and languages, its cultural contestant, and one

of its deepest and most recurring images of the Other. In addition, the Orient has helped to define Europe (or the West) as its contrasting image, idea, personality, experience. Yet none of this Orient is merely imaginative. The Orient is an integral part of European *material* civilization and culture. Orientalism expresses and represents that part culturally and even ideologically as a mode of discourse with supporting institutions, vocabulary, scholarship, imagery, doctrines, even colonial bureaucracies and colonial styles. In contrast, the American understanding of the Orient will seem considerably less dense, although our recent Japanese, Korean, and Indochinese adventures ought now to be creating a more sober, more realistic "Oriental" awareness. Moreover, the vastly expanded American political and economic role in the Near East (the Middle East) makes great claims on our understanding of that Orient.

It will be clear to the reader (and will become clearer still throughout the many pages that follow) that by Orientalism I mean several things, all of them, in my opinion, interdependent. The most readily accepted designation for Orientalism is an academic one, and indeed the label still serves in a number of academic institutions. Anyone who teaches, writes about, or researches the Orient—and this applies whether the person is an anthropologist, sociologist, historian, or philologist—either in its specific or its general aspects, is an Orientalist, and what he or she does is Orientalism. Compared with *Oriental studies* or *area studies,* it is true that the term *Orientalism* is less preferred by specialists today, both because it is too vague and general and because it connotes the high-handed executive attitude of nineteenth-century and early-twentieth-century European colonialism. Nevertheless books are written and congresses held with "the Orient" as their main focus, with the Orientalist in his new or old guise as their main authority. The point is that even if it does not survive as it once did, Orientalism lives on academically through its doctrines and theses about the Orient and the Oriental.

Related to this academic tradition, whose fortunes, transmigrations, specializations, and transmissions are in part the subject of this study, is a more general meaning for Orientalism. Orientalism is a style of thought based upon an ontological and epistemological distinction made between "the Orient" and (most of the time) "the Occident." Thus a very large mass of writers, among whom are poets, novelists,

---

This is the opening chapter, complete, reprinted from *Orientalism* (New York: Random House, 1978).

[1] [Said] Thierry Desjardins, *Le Martyre du Liban* (Paris: Plon, 1976), p. 14. [François-Auguste-Rene de Chateaubriand (1768–1848), French author; Gérard de Nerval (1808–1855), French poet.]

philosophers, political theorists, economists, and imperial administrators, have accepted the basic distinction between East and West as the starting point for elaborate theories, epics, novels, social descriptions, and political accounts concerning the Orient, its people, customs, "mind," destiny, and so on. *This* Orientalism can accommodate Aeschylus, say, and Victor Hugo, Dante and Karl Marx. A little later in this introduction I shall deal with the methodological problems one encounters in so broadly construed a "field" as this.

The interchange between the academic and the more or less imaginative meanings of Orientalism is a constant one, and since the late eighteenth century there has been a considerable, quite disciplined—perhaps even regulated—traffic between the two. Here I come to the third meaning of Orientalism, which is something more historically and materially defined than either of the other two. Taking the late eighteenth century as a very roughly defined starting point Orientalism can be discussed and analyzed as the corporate institution for dealing with the Orient—dealing with it by making statements about it, authorizing views of it, describing it, by teaching it, settling it, ruling over it: in short, Orientalism as a Western style for dominating, restructuring, and having authority over the Orient. I have found it useful here to employ Michel Foucault's notion of a discourse, as described by him in *The Archaeology of Knowledge* and in *Discipline and Punish,* to identify Orientalism.[2] My contention is that without examining Orientalism as a discourse one cannot possibly understand the enormously systematic discipline by which European culture was able to manage— and even produce—the Orient politically, sociologically, militarily, ideologically, scientifically, and imaginatively during the post-Enlightenment period. Moreover, so authoritative a position did Orientalism have that I believe no one writing, thinking, or acting on the Orient could do so without taking account of the limitations on thought and action imposed by Orientalism. In brief, because of Orientalism the Orient was not (and is not) a free subject of thought or action. This is not to say that Orientalism unilaterally determines what can be said about the Orient, but that it is the whole network of interests inevitably brought to bear on (and therefore always involved in) any occasion when that peculiar entity "the Orient" is in question. How this happens is what this book tries to demonstrate. It also tries to show that European culture gained in strength and identity by setting itself off against the Orient as a sort of surrogate and even underground self.

Historically and culturally there is a quantitative as well as a qualitative difference between the Franco-British involvement in the Orient and—until the period of American ascendancy after World War II—the involvement of every other European and Atlantic power. To speak of Orientalism therefore is to speak mainly, although not exclusively, of a British and French cultural enterprise, a project whose dimensions take in such disparate realms as the imagination itself, the whole of India and the Levant, the Biblical texts and the Biblical lands, the spice trade, colonial armies and a long tradition of colonial administrators, a formidable scholarly corpus, innumerable Oriental "experts" and "hands," an Oriental professorate, a complex array of "Oriental" ideas (Oriental despotism, Oriental splendor, cruelty, sensuality), many Eastern sects, philosophies, and wisdoms domesticated for local European use—the list can be extended more or less indefinitely. My point is that Orientalism derives from a particular closeness experienced between Britain and France and the Orient, which until the early nineteenth century had really meant only India and the Bible lands. From the beginning of the nineteenth century until the end of World War II France and Britain dominated the Orient and Orientalism; since World War II America has dominated the Orient, and approaches it as France and Britain once did. Out of that closeness, whose dynamic is enormously productive even if it always demonstrates the comparatively greater strength of the Occident (British, French, or American), comes the large body of texts I call Orientalist.

It should be said at once that even with the generous number of books and authors that I examine, there is a much larger number that I simply have had to leave out. My argument, however, depends neither upon an exhaustive catalogue of texts dealing with the Orient nor upon a clearly delimited set of texts, authors, and ideas that together make up the Orientalist canon. I have depended instead upon a different methodological alternative—whose backbone in a sense is the set of historical generalizations I have so far been making in this Introduction—and it is these I want now to discuss in more analytical detail.

II

I have begun with the assumption that the Orient is not an inert fact of nature. It is not merely *there,* just as the Occident itself is not just *there* either. We must take seriously Vico's[3] great observation that men make their own history, that what they can know is what they have made, and extend

---

[2]Foucault (above, page 1260). *The Archaeology of Knowledge* (tr. 1972); *Discipline and Punish* (tr. 1977).

[3]Vico (above, page 313).

it to geography: as both geographical and cultural entities—
to say nothing of historical entities—such locales, regions,
geographical sectors as "Orient" and "Occident" are man-
made. Therefore as much as the West itself, the Orient is an
idea that has a history and a tradition of thought, imagery,
and vocabulary that have given it reality and presence in and
for the West. The two geographical entities thus support and
to an extent reflect each other.

Having said that, one must go on to state a number of
reasonable qualifications. In the first place, it would be
wrong to conclude that the Orient was *essentially* an idea, or
a creation with no corresponding reality. When Disraeli said
in his novel *Tancred* that the East was a career, he meant
that to be interested in the East was something bright young
Westerners would find to be an all-consuming passion; he
should not be interpreted as saying that the East was *only* a
career for Westerners. There were—and are—cultures and
nations whose location is in the East, and their lives, histories, and customs have a brute reality obviously greater than
anything that could be said about them in the West. About
that fact this study of Orientalism has very little to contribute, except to acknowledge it tacitly. But the phenomenon of Orientalism as I study it here deals principally, not
with a correspondence between Orientalism and Orient, but
with the internal consistency of Orientalism and its ideas
about the Orient (the East as career) despite or beyond any
correspondence, or lack thereof, with a "real" Orient. My
point is that Disraeli's statement about the East refers
mainly to that created consistency, that regular constellation
of ideas as the pre-eminent thing about the Orient, and not
to its mere being, as Wallace Stevens's phrase has it.

A second qualification is that ideas, cultures, and histories cannot seriously be understood or studied without
their force, or more precisely their configurations of power,
also being studied. To believe that the Orient was created—
or, as I call it, "Orientalized"—and to believe that such
things happen simply as a necessity of the imagination, is to
be disingenuous. The relationship between Occident and
Orient is a relationship of power, of domination, of varying
degrees of a complex hegemony, and is quite accurately indicated in the title of K. M. Panikkar's classic *Asia and
Western Dominance.*[4] The Orient was Orientalized not only
because it was discovered to be "Oriental" in all those ways
considered commonplace by an average nineteenth-century
European, but also because it *could be*—that is, submitted
to being—*made* Oriental. There is very little consent to be
found, for example, in the fact that Flaubert's encounter

with an Egyptian courtesan[5] produced a widely influential
model of the Oriental woman; she never spoke of herself,
she never represented her emotions, presence, or history. *He*
spoke for and represented her. He was foreign, comparatively wealthy, male, and these were historical facts of domination that allowed him not only to possess Kuchuk Hanem
physically but to speak for her and tell his readers in what
way she was "typically Oriental." My argument is that
Flaubert's situation of strength in relation to Kuchuk Hanem
was not an isolated instance. It fairly stands for the pattern
of relative strength between East and West, and the discourse about the Orient that it enabled.

This brings us to a third qualification. One ought never
to assume that the structure of Orientalism is nothing more
than a structure of lies or of myths which, were the truth
about them to be told, would simply blow away. I myself
believe that Orientalism is more particularly valuable as a
sign of European-Atlantic power over the Orient than it is as
a veridic discourse about the Orient (which is what, in its
academic or scholarly form, it claims to be). Nevertheless,
what we must respect and try to grasp is the sheer knitted-
together strength of Orientalist discourse, its very close ties
to the enabling socio-economic and political institutions,
and its redoubtable durability. After all, any system of ideas
that can remain unchanged as teachable wisdom (in academies, books, congresses, universities, foreign-service institutes) from the period of Ernest Renan[6] in the late 1840s until the present in the United States must be something more
formidable than a mere collection of lies. Orientalism,
therefore, is not an airy European fantasy about the Orient,
but a created body of theory and practice in which, for many
generations, there has been a considerable material investment. Continued investment made Orientalism, as a system
of knowledge about the Orient, an accepted grid for filtering
through the Orient into Western consciousness, just as that
same investment multiplied—indeed, made truly productive—the statements proliferating out from Orientalism into
the general culture.

Gramsci has made the useful analytic distinction between civil and political society in which the former is made
up of voluntary (or at least rational and noncoercive) affiliations like schools, families, and unions, the latter of state institutions (the army, the police, the central bureaucracy)

---

[4][Said] K. M. Panikkar, *Asia and Western Dominance* (London: George Allen & Unwin, 1959).

[5]The source for this incident is Gustave Flaubert (1821–1880), *Flaubert in Egypt: A Sensibility on Tour; A Narrative Drawn from Gustave Flaubert's Travel Notes & Letters,* translated from the French and edited by Francis Steegmuller (1972).

[6]Ernest Renan (1823–1892), French writer, best known for his popular *Life of Jesus* (tr. 1927).

whose role in the polity is direct domination. Culture, of course, is to be found operating within civil society, where the influence of ideas, of institutions, and of other persons works not through domination but by what Gramsci calls consent. In any society not totalitarian, then, certain cultural forms predominate over others, just as certain ideas are more influential than others; the form of this cultural leadership is what Gramsci has identified as *hegemony,* an indispensable concept for any understanding of cultural life in the industrial West.[7] It is hegemony, or rather the result of cultural hegemony at work, that gives Orientalism the durability and the strength I have been speaking about so far. Orientalism is never far from what Denys Hay has called the idea of Europe,[8] a collective notion identifying "us" Europeans as against all "those" non-Europeans, and indeed it can be argued that the major component in European culture is precisely what made that culture hegemonic both in and outside Europe: the idea of European identity as a superior one in comparison with all the non-European peoples and cultures. There is in addition the hegemony of European ideas about the Orient, themselves reiterating European superiority over Oriental backwardness, usually overriding the possibility that a more independent, or more skeptical, thinker might have had different views on the matter.

In a quite constant way, Orientalism depends for its strategy on this flexible *positional* superiority, which puts the Westerner in a whole series of possible relationships with the Orient without ever losing him the relative upper hand. And why should it have been otherwise, especially during the period of extraordinary European ascendancy from the late Renaissance to the present? The scientist, the scholar, the missionary, the trader, or the soldier was in, or thought about, the Orient because he *could be there,* or could think about it, with very little resistance on the Orient's part. Under the general heading of knowledge of the Orient, and within the umbrella of Western hegemony over the Orient during the period from the end of the eighteenth century, there emerged a complex Orient suitable for study in the academy, for display in the museum, for reconstruction in the colonial office, for theoretical illustration in anthropological, biological, linguistic, racial, and historical theses about mankind and the universe, for instances of economic and sociological theories of development, revolution, cultural personality, national or religious character. Additionally, the imaginative examination of things Oriental was based more or less exclusively upon a sovereign Western

consciousness out of whose unchallenged centrality an Oriental world emerged, first according to general ideas about who or what was an Oriental, then according to a detailed logic governed not simply by empirical reality but by a battery of desires, repressions, investments, and projections. If we can point to great Orientalist works of genuine scholarship like Silvestre de Sacy's *Chrestomathie arabe* or Edward William Lane's *Account of the Manners and Customs of the Modern Egyptians,*[9] we need also to note that Renan's and Gobineau's[10] racial ideas came out of the same impulse, as did a great many Victorian pornographic novels (see the analysis by Steven Marcus of "The Lustful Turk").[11]

And yet, one must repeatedly ask oneself whether what matters in Orientalism is the general group of ideas overriding the mass of material—about which who could deny that they were shot through with doctrines of European superiority, various kinds of racism, imperialism, and the like, dogmatic views of "the Oriental" as a kind of ideal and unchanging abstraction?—or the much more varied work produced by almost uncountable individual writers, whom one would take up as individual instances of authors dealing with the Orient. In a sense the two alternatives, general and particular, are really two perspectives on the same material: in both instances one would have to deal with pioneers in the field like William Jones,[12] with great artists like Nerval or Flaubert. And why would it not be possible to employ both perspectives together, or one after the other? Isn't there an obvious danger of distortion (of precisely the kind that academic Orientalism has always been prone to) if either too general or too specific a level of description is maintained systematically?

My two fears are distortion and inaccuracy, or rather the kind of inaccuracy produced by too dogmatic a generality and too positivistic a localized focus. In trying to deal with these problems I have tried to deal with three main aspects of my own contemporary reality that seem to me to point the way out of the methodological or perspectival difficulties I have been discussing, difficulties that might force one, in the first instance, into writing a coarse polemic on so

---

[7] Gramsci (above, page 936).

[8] Denys Hay, *Europe: The Emergence of an Idea,* second ed. (Edinburgh: Edinburgh University Press, 1968).

[9] Baron Silvestre de Sacy (1758–1838), French scholar of Arabic and Semitic languages, author of *"Chrestomathie arabe"* (in three volumes, 1806); *"Grammaire arabe"* (in two volumes, 1810); Edward William Lane (1801–1876), *Account of the Manners and Customs of the Modern Egyptians* (1833, tr. 1936).

[10] Arthur, Comte de Gobineau (1816–1882), French novelist and essayist; focused frequently on Asiatic subjects.

[11] [Said] Steven Marcus, *The Other Victorians: A Study of Sexuality and Pornography in Mid-Nineteenth-Century England* (1966; reprint ed., New York: Bantam Books, 1967), pp. 200–19.

[12] Sir William Jones (1746–1794), English writer, traveler, and linguist; author of *Persian Grammar* (1771), among other works.

unacceptably general a level of description as not to be worth the effort, or in the second instance, into writing so detailed and atomistic a series of analyses as to lose all track of the general lines of force informing the field, giving it its special cogency. How then to recognize individuality and to reconcile it with its intelligent, and by no means passive or merely dictatorial, general and hegemonic context?

III

I mentioned three aspects of my contemporary reality: I must explain and briefly discuss them now, so that it can be seen how I was led to a particular course of research and writing.

1. *The distinction between pure and political knowledge.* It is very easy to argue that knowledge about Shakespeare or Wordsworth is not political whereas knowledge about contemporary China or the Soviet Union is. My own formal and professional designation is that of "humanist," a title which indicates the humanities as my field and therefore the unlikely eventuality that there might be anything political about what I do in that field. Of course, all these labels and terms are quite unnuanced as I use them here, but the general truth of what I am pointing to is, I think, widely held. One reason for saying that a humanist who writes about Wordsworth, or an editor whose specialty is Keats, is not involved in anything political is that what he does seems to have no direct political effect upon reality in the everyday sense. A scholar whose field is Soviet economics works in a highly charged area where there is much government interest, and what he might produce in the way of studies or proposals will be taken up by policymakers, government officials, institutional economists, intelligence experts. The distinction between "humanists" and persons whose work has policy implications, or political significance, can be broadened further by saying that the former's ideological color is a matter of incidental importance to politics (although possibly of great moment to his colleagues in the field, who may object to his Stalinism or fascism or too easy liberalism), whereas the ideology of the latter is woven directly into his material—indeed, economics, politics, and sociology in the modern academy are ideological sciences—and therefore taken for granted as being "political."

Nevertheless the determining impingement on most knowledge produced in the contemporary West (and here I speak mainly about the United States) is that it be nonpolitical, that is, scholarly, academic, impartial, above partisan or small-minded doctrinal belief. One can have no quarrel with such an ambition in theory, perhaps, but in practice the reality is much more problematic. No one has ever devised a method for detaching the scholar from the circumstances of life, from the fact of his involvement (conscious or unconscious) with a class, a set of beliefs, a social position, or from the mere activity of being a member of a society. These continue to bear on what he does professionally, even though naturally enough his research and its fruits do attempt to reach a level of relative freedom from the inhibitions and the restrictions of brute, everyday reality. For there is such a thing as knowledge that is less, rather than more, partial than the individual (with his entangling and distracting life circumstances) who produces it. Yet this knowledge is not therefore automatically nonpolitical.

Whether discussions of literature or of classical philology are fraught with—or have unmediated—political significance is a very large question that I have tried to treat in some detail elsewhere.[13] What I am interested in doing now is suggesting how the general liberal consensus that "true" knowledge is fundamentally nonpolitical (and conversely, that overtly political knowledge is not "true" knowledge) obscures the highly if obscurely organized political circumstances obtaining when knowledge is produced. No one is helped in understanding this today when the adjective "political" is used as a label to discredit any work for daring to violate the protocol of pretended suprapolitical objectivity. We may say, first, that civil society recognizes a gradation of political importance in the various fields of knowledge. To some extent the political importance given a field comes from the possibility of its direct translation into economic terms; but to a greater extent political importance comes from the closeness of a field to ascertainable sources of power in political society. Thus an economic study of long-term Soviet energy potential and its effect on military capability is likely to be commissioned by the Defense Department, and thereafter to acquire a kind of political status impossible for a study of Tolstoi's[14] early fiction financed in part by a foundation. Yet both works belong in what civil society acknowledges to be a similar field, Russian studies, even though one work may be done by a very conservative economist, the other by a radical literary historian. My point here is that "Russia" as a general subject matter has political priority over nicer distinctions such as "economics" and "literary history," because political society in Gramsci's sense reaches into such realms of civil society as the academy and saturates them with significance of direct concern to it.

---

[13] [Said] See my "Criticism Between Culture and System." [An essay published in *The World, the Text, and the Critic,* Cambridge, Mass.: Harvard University Press, 1983.]
[14] Tolstoy (above, page 757).

I do not want to press all this any further on general theoretical grounds: it seems to me that the value and credibility of my case can be demonstrated by being much more specific, in the way, for example, Noam Chomsky has studied the instrumental connection between the Vietnam War and the notion of objective scholarship as it was applied to cover state-sponsored military research.[15] Now because Britain, France, and recently the United States are imperial powers, their political societies impart to their civil societies a sense of urgency, a direct political infusion as it were, where and whenever matters pertaining to their imperial interests abroad are concerned. I doubt that it is controversial, for example, to say that an Englishman in India or Egypt in the later nineteenth century took an interest in those countries that was never far from their status in his mind as British colonies. To say this may seem quite different from saying that all academic knowledge about India and Egypt is somehow tinged and impressed with, violated by, the gross political fact—and yet *that is what I am saying* in this study of Orientalism. For if it is true that no production of knowledge in the human sciences can ever ignore or disclaim its author's involvement as a human subject in his own circumstances, then it must also be true that for a European or American studying the Orient there can be no disclaiming the main circumstances of *his* actuality: that he comes up against the Orient as a European or American first, as an individual second. And to be a European or an American in such a situation is by no means an inert fact. It meant and means being aware, however dimly, that one belongs to a power with definite interests in the Orient, and more important, that one belongs to a part of the earth with a definite history of involvement in the Orient almost since the time of Homer.

Put in this way, these political actualities are still too undefined and general to be really interesting. Anyone would agree to them without necessarily agreeing also that they mattered very much, for instance, to Flaubert as he wrote *Salammbô*, or to H. A. R. Gibb as he wrote *Modern Trends in Islam*.[16] The trouble is that there is too great a distance between the big dominating fact, as I have described it, and the details of everyday life that govern the minute discipline of a novel or a scholarly text as each is being written. Yet if we eliminate from the start any notion that "big"

facts like imperial domination can be applied mechanically and deterministically to such complex matters as culture and ideas, then we will begin to approach an interesting kind of study. My idea is that European and then American interest in the Orient was political according to some of the obvious historical accounts of it that I have given here, but that it was the culture that created that interest, that acted dynamically along with brute political, economic, and military rationales to make the Orient the varied and complicated place that it obviously was in the field I call Orientalism.

Therefore, Orientalism is not a mere political subject matter or field that is reflected passively by culture, scholarship, or institutions; nor is it a large and diffuse collection of texts about the Orient; nor is it representative and expressive of some nefarious "Western" imperialist plot to hold down the "Oriental" world. It is rather a *distribution* of geopolitical awareness into aesthetic, scholarly, economic, sociological, historical, and philological texts; it is an *elaboration* not only of a basic geographical distinction (the world is made up of two unequal halves, Orient and Occident) but also of a whole series of "interests" which, by such means as scholarly discovery, philological reconstruction, psychological analysis, landscape and sociological description, it not only creates but also maintains; it *is*, rather than expresses, a certain *will* or *intention* to understand, in some cases to control, manipulate, even to incorporate, what is a manifestly different (or alternative and novel) world; it is, above all, a discourse that is by no means in direct, corresponding relationship with political power in the raw, but rather is produced and exists in an uneven exchange with various kinds of power, shaped to a degree by the exchange with power political (as with a colonial or imperial establishment), power intellectual (as with reigning sciences like comparative linguistics or anatomy, or any of the modern policy sciences), power cultural (as with orthodoxies and canons of taste, texts, values), power moral (as with ideas about what "we" do and what "they" cannot do or understand as "we" do). Indeed, my real argument is that Orientalism is—and does not simply represent—a considerable dimension of modern political-intellectual culture, and as such has less to do with the Orient than it does with "our" world.

Because Orientalism is a cultural and a political fact, then, it does not exist in some archival vacuum; quite the contrary, I think it can be shown that what is thought, said, or even done about the Orient follows (perhaps occurs within) certain distinct and intellectually knowable lines. Here too a considerable degree of nuance and elaboration can be seen working as between the broad superstructural pressures and the details of composition, the facts of textuality.

---

[15] [Said] Principally in his *American Power and the New Mandarins: Historical and Political Essays* (New York: Pantheon Books, 1969) and *For Reasons of State* (New York: Pantheon Books, 1973). [Chomsky (above, page 1166).]

[16] Gustave Flaubert (1821–1880), French novelist; H[amilton] A. R. Gibb (1895–1971), British Arabic and Islamic scholar. *Modern Trends in Islam* was published in 1947.

Most humanistic scholars are, I think, perfectly happy with the notion that texts exist in contexts, that there is such a thing as intertextuality, that the pressures of conventions, predecessors, and rhetorical styles limit what Walter Benjamin once called the "overtaxing of the productive person in the name of . . . the principle of 'creativity,'" in which the poet is believed on his own, and out of his pure mind, to have brought forth his work.[17] Yet there is a reluctance to allow that political, institutional, and ideological constraints act in the same manner on the individual author. A humanist will believe it to be an interesting fact to any interpreter of Balzac that he was influenced in the *Comédie humaine* by the conflict between Geoffroy Saint-Hilaire and Cuvier,[18] but the same sort of pressure on Balzac of deeply reactionary monarchism is felt in some vague way to demean his literary "genius" and therefore to be less worth serious study. Similarly—as Harry Bracken has been tirelessly showing—philosophers will conduct their discussions of Locke, Hume, and empiricism without ever taking into account that there is an explicit connection in these classic writers between their "philosophic" doctrines and racial theory, justifications of slavery, or arguments for colonial exploitation.[19] These are common enough ways by which contemporary scholarship keeps itself pure.

Perhaps it is true that most attempts to rub culture's nose in the mud of politics have been crudely iconoclastic; perhaps also the social interpretation of literature in my own field has simply not kept up with the enormous technical advances in detailed textual analysis. But there is no getting away from the fact that literary studies in general, and American Marxist theorists in particular, have avoided the effort of seriously bridging the gap between the superstructural and the base levels in textual, historical scholarship; on another occasion I have gone so far as to say that the literary-cultural establishment as a whole has declared the serious study of imperialism and culture off limits.[20] For Orientalism brings one up directly against that question—that is, to realizing that political imperialism governs an entire field of study, imagination, and scholarly institutions—in such a way as to make its avoidance an intellectual and historical impossibility. Yet there will always remain the perennial escape mechanism of saying that a literary scholar and a philosopher, for example, are trained in literature and philosophy respectively, not in politics or ideological analysis. In other words, the specialist argument can work quite effectively to block the larger and, in my opinion, the more intellectually serious perspective.

Here it seems to me there is a simple two-part answer to be given, at least so far as the study of imperialism and culture (or Orientalism) is concerned. In the first place, nearly every nineteenth-century writer (and the same is true enough of writers in earlier periods) was extraordinarily well aware of the fact of empire: this is a subject not very well studied, but it will not take a modern Victorian specialist long to admit that liberal cultural heroes like John Stuart Mill, Arnold, Carlyle, Newman, Macaulay, Ruskin, George Eliot, and even Dickens had definite views on race and imperialism, which are quite easily to be found at work in their writing. So even a specialist must deal with the knowledge that Mill, for example, made it clear in *On Liberty* and *Representative Government* that his views there could not be applied to India (he was an India Office functionary for a good deal of his life, after all) because the Indians were civilizationally, if not racially, inferior. The same kind of paradox is to be found in Marx, as I try to show in this book. In the second place, to believe that politics in the form of imperialism bears upon the production of literature, scholarship, social theory, and history writing is by no means equivalent to saying that culture is therefore a demeaned or denigrated thing. Quite the contrary: my whole point is to say that we can better understand the persistence and the durability of saturating hegemonic systems like culture when we realize that their internal constraints upon writers and thinkers were *productive,* not unilaterally inhibiting. It is this idea that Gramsci, certainly, and Foucault and Raymond Williams in their very different ways have been trying to illustrate. Even one or two pages by Williams on "the uses of the Empire" in *The Long Revolution* tell us more about nineteenth-century cultural richness than many volumes of hermetic textual analyses.[21]

Therefore I study Orientalism as a dynamic exchange between individual authors and the large political concerns shaped by the three great empires—British, French, American—in whose intellectual and imaginative territory the

---

[17] Walter Benjamin (above, page 995), *Charles Baudelaire: A Lyric Poet in the Era of High Capitalism,* tr. Harry Zohn (London: New Left Books, 1973), p. 71.

[18] Honoré de Balzac (1799–1850), French novelist, author of the *Comédie humaine;* Étienne Geoffroy Saint-Hilaire (1772–1844), French naturalist, noted for studies of animal development, in some ways anticipating theories of organic evolution; Georges Cuvier (1769–1832), French zoologist and anatomist, whose views of anatomy diverged sharply from Saint-Hilaire's over the question of whether or not animal kinds were immutable.

[19] [Said] Harry Bracken, "Essence, Accident and Race," *Hermathena* 116 (Winter 1973): 81–96. [Locke (above, page 281); Hume (above, page 322).]

[20] [Said] In an interview published in *Diacritics* 6, no. 3 (Fall 1976): 38.

[21] [Said] Raymond Williams [above, page 1356], *The Long Revolution* (London: Chatto & Windus, 1961), pp. 66–67.

writing was produced. What interests me most as a scholar is not the gross political verity but the detail, as indeed what interests us in someone like Lane or Flaubert or Renan is not the (to him) indisputable truth that Occidentals are superior to Orientals, but the profoundly worked over and modulated evidence of his detailed work within the very wide space opened up by that truth. One need only remember that Lane's *Manners and Customs of the Modern Egyptians* is a classic of historical and anthropological observation because of its style, its enormously intelligent and brilliant details, not because of its simple reflection of racial superiority, to understand what I am saying here.

The kind of political questions raised by Orientalism, then, are as follows: What other sorts of intellectual, aesthetic, scholarly, and cultural energies went into the making of an imperialist tradition like the Orientalist one? How did philology, lexicography, history, biology, political and economic theory, novel-writing, and lyric poetry come to the service of Orientalism's broadly imperial view of the world? What changes, modulations, refinements, even revolutions take place within Orientalism? What is the meaning of originality, of continuity, of individuality, in this context? How does Orientalism transmit or reproduce itself from one epoch to another? In fine, how can we treat the cultural, historical phenomenon of Orientalism as a kind of *willed human work*—not of mere unconditioned ratiocination—in all its historical complexity, detail, and worth without at the same time losing sight of the alliance between cultural work, political tendencies, the state, and the specific realities of domination? Governed by such concerns a humanistic study can responsibly address itself to politics *and* culture. But this is not to say that such a study establishes a hard-and-fast rule about the relationship between knowledge and politics. My argument is that each humanistic investigation must formulate the nature of that connection in the specific context of the study, the subject matter, and its historical circumstances.

2. *The methodological question.* In a previous book I gave a good deal of thought and analysis to the methodological importance for work in the human sciences of finding and formulating a first step, a point of departure, a beginning principle.[22] A major lesson I learned and tried to present was that there is no such thing as a merely given, or simply available, starting point: beginnings have to be made for each project in such a way as to *enable* what follows from them. Nowhere in my experience has the difficulty of

this lesson been more consciously lived (with what success—or failure—I cannot really say) than in this study of Orientalism. The idea of beginning, indeed the act of beginning, necessarily involves an act of delimitation by which something is cut out of a great mass of material, separated from the mass, and made to stand for, as well as be, a starting point, a beginning; for the student of texts one such notion of inaugural delimitation is Louis Althusser's idea of the *problematic,* a specific determinate unity of a text, or group of texts, which is something given rise to by analysis.[23] Yet in the case of Orientalism (as opposed to the case of Marx's texts, which is what Althusser studies) there is not simply the problem of finding a point of departure, or problematic, but also the question of designating which texts, authors, and periods are the ones best suited for study.

It has seemed to me foolish to attempt an encyclopedic narrative history of Orientalism, first of all because if my guiding principle was to be "the European idea of the Orient" there would be virtually no limit to the material I would have had to deal with; second, because the narrative model itself did not suit my descriptive and political interests; third, because in such books as Raymond Schwab's *La Renaissance orientale,* Johann Fück's *Die Arabischen Studien in Europa bis in den Anfang des 20. Jahrhunderts,* and more recently, Dorothee Metlitzki's *The Matter of Araby in Medieval England*[24] there already exist encyclopedic works on certain aspects of the European-Oriental encounter such as make the critic's job, in the general political and intellectual context I sketched above, a different one.

There still remained the problem of cutting down a very fat archive to manageable dimensions, and more important, outlining something in the nature of an intellectual order within that group of texts without at the same time following a mindlessly chronological order. My starting point therefore has been the British, French, and American experience of the Orient taken as a unit, what made that experience possible by way of historical and intellectual background, what the quality and character of the experience has been. For reasons I shall discuss presently I limited that already limited (but still inordinately large) set of questions to the Anglo-French-American experience of the Arabs and Islam, which for almost a thousand years together stood for the Orient. Immediately upon doing that, a large part of the

[22] [Said] In my *Beginnings: Intention and Method* (New York: Basic Books, 1975).

[23] [Said] Louis Althusser [above, page 1297], *For Marx,* tr. Ben Brewster (New York: Pantheon Books, 1969), pp. 65–67.

[24] [Said] Raymond Schwab, *La Renaissance orientale* (Paris: Payot, 1950); Johann W. Fück, *Die Arabischen Studien in Europa bis in den Anfang des 20. Jahrhunderts* (Leipzig: Otto Harrassowitz, 1955); Dorothee Metlitzki, *The Matter of Araby in Medieval England* (New Haven, Conn.: Yale University Press, 1977).

Orient seemed to have been eliminated—India, Japan, China, and other sections of the Far East—not because these regions were not important (they obviously have been) but because one could discuss Europe's experience of the Near Orient, or of Islam, apart from its experience of the Far Orient. Yet at certain moments of that general European history of interest in the East, particular parts of the Orient like Egypt, Syria, and Arabia cannot be discussed without also studying Europe's involvement in the more distant parts, of which Persia and India are the most important; a notable case in point is the connection between Egypt and India so far as eighteenth- and nineteenth-century Britain was concerned. Similarly the French role in deciphering the Zend-Avesta, the pre-eminence of Paris as a center of Sanskrit studies during the first decade of the nineteenth century, the fact that Napoleon's interest in the Orient was contingent upon his sense of the British role in India: all these Far Eastern interests directly influenced French interest in the Near East, Islam, and the Arabs.

Britain and France dominated the Eastern Mediterranean from about the end of the seventeenth century on. Yet my discussion of that domination and systematic interest does not do justice to *(a)* the important contributions to Orientalism of Germany, Italy, Russia, Spain, and Portugal and *(b)* the fact that one of the important impulses toward the study of the Orient in the eighteenth century was the revolution in Biblical studies stimulated by such variously interesting pioneers as Bishop Lowth, Eichhorn, Herder, and Michaelis.[25] In the first place, I had to focus rigorously upon the British-French and later the American material because it seemed inescapably true not only that Britain and France were the pioneer nations in the Orient and in Oriental studies, but that these vanguard positions were held by virtue of the two greatest colonial networks in pre-twentieth-century history; the American Oriental position since World War II has fit—I think, quite self-consciously—in the places excavated by the two earlier European powers. Then too, I believe that the sheer quality, consistency, and mass of British, French, and American writing on the Orient lifts it above the doubtless crucial work done in Germany, Italy, Russia, and elsewhere. But I think it is also true that the major steps in Oriental scholarship were first taken in either Britain and France, then elaborated upon by Germans. Silvestre de Sacy,[26] for example, was not only the first modern and insti-

tutional European Orientalist, who worked on Islam, Arabic literature, the Druze religion, and Sassanid Persia; he was also the teacher of Champollion and of Franz Bopp, the founder of German comparative linguistics. A similar claim of priority and subsequent pre-eminence can be made for William Jones and Edward William Lane.

In the second place—and here the failings of my study of Orientalism are amply made up for—there has been some important recent work on the background in Biblical scholarship to the rise of what I have called modern Orientalism. The best and the most illuminatingly relevant is E. S. Shaffer's impressive *"Kubla Khan" and The Fall of Jerusalem*,[27] an indispensable study of the origins of Romanticism, and of the intellectual activity underpinning a great deal of what goes on in Coleridge, Browning, and George Eliot. To some degree Shaffer's work refines upon the outlines provided in Schwab, by articulating the material of relevance to be found in the German Biblical scholars and using that material to read, in an intelligent and always interesting way, the work of three major British writers. Yet what is missing in the book is some sense of the political as well as ideological edge given the Oriental material by the British and French writers I am principally concerned with; in addition, unlike Shaffer I attempt to elucidate subsequent developments in academic as well as literary Orientalism that bear on the connection between British and French Orientalism on the one hand and the rise of an explicitly colonial-minded imperialism on the other. Then too, I wish to show how all these earlier matters are reproduced more or less in American Orientalism after the Second World War.

Nevertheless there is a possibly misleading aspect to my study, where, aside from an occasional reference, I do not exhaustively discuss the German developments after the inaugural period dominated by Sacy. Any work that seeks to provide an understanding of academic Orientalism and pays little attention to scholars like Steinthal, Müller, Becker, Goldziher, Brockelmann, Nöldeke[28]—to mention only a handful—needs to be reproached, and I freely reproach myself. I particularly regret not taking more account of the great scientific prestige that accrued to German scholarship by the middle of the nineteenth century, whose neglect was made into a denunciation of insular British scholars by

---

[25] Robert Lowth (1710–1787), English churchman, author of *The Sacred Poetry of the Hebrews;* Johann Gottfried Eichhorn (1752–1827), German biblical scholar; Johann Gottfried Herder (1744–1803), German philosopher and theologian; Johann David Michaelis (1717–1791), German orientalist.
[26] A.I. Sylvestri de Sacy (1758–1838), French scholar.

[27] [Said] E. S. Shaffer, *"Kubla Khan" and The Fall of Jerusalem: The Mythological School in Biblical Criticism and Secular Literature, 1770–1880* (Cambridge: Cambridge University Press, 1975).
[28] Hegmann Steinthal (1823–1899), German philologist; Friedrick Max Müller (1823–1900), German orientalist; Wilhelm Adolph Becker (1796–1846), German classical archeologist; Ignás Goldziher (1850–1921), Hungarian scholar; Carl Brackelmann (1868–1956), German philologist; Theodor Nöldeke (1836–1930), German orientalist.

George Eliot. I have in mind Eliot's unforgettable portrait of Mr. Casaubon in *Middlemarch*. One reason Casaubon cannot finish his Key to All Mythologies is, according to his young cousin Will Ladislaw, that he is unacquainted with German scholarship. For not only has Casaubon chosen a subject "as changing as chemistry: new discoveries are constantly making new points of view": he is undertaking a job similar to a refutation of Paracelsus because "he is not an Orientalist, you know."[29]

Eliot was not wrong in implying that by about 1830, which is when *Middlemarch* is set, German scholarship had fully attained its European pre-eminence. Yet at no time in German scholarship during the first two-thirds of the nineteenth century could a close partnership have developed between Orientalists and a protracted, sustained *national* interest in the Orient. There was nothing in Germany to correspond to the Anglo-French presence in India, the Levant, North Africa. Moreover, the German Orient was almost exclusively a scholarly, or at least a classical, Orient: it was made the subject of lyrics, fantasies, and even novels, but it was never actual, the way Egypt and Syria were actual for Chateaubriand, Lane, Lamartine, Burton, Disraeli, or Nerval.[30] There is some significance in the fact that the two most renowned German works on the Orient, Goethe's *Westöstlicher Diwan* and Friedrich Schlegel's *Über die Sprache und Weisheit der Indier*, were based respectively on a Rhine journey and on hours spent in Paris libraries. What German Oriental scholarship did was to refine and elaborate techniques whose application was to texts, myths, ideas, and languages almost literally gathered from the Orient by imperial Britain and France.

Yet what German Orientalism had in common with Anglo-French and later American Orientalism was a kind of intellectual *authority* over the Orient within Western culture. This authority must in large part be the subject of any description of Orientalism, and it is so in this study. Even the name *Orientalism* suggests a serious, perhaps ponderous style of expertise; when I apply it to modern American social scientists (since they do not call themselves Orientalists, my use of the word is anomalous), it is to draw attention to the way Middle East experts can still draw on the vestiges of Orientalism's intellectual position in nineteenth-century Europe.

There is nothing mysterious or natural about authority. It is formed, irradiated, disseminated; it is instrumental, it is persuasive; it has status, it establishes canons of taste and value; it is virtually indistinguishable from certain ideas it dignifies as true, and from traditions, perceptions, and judgments it forms, transmits, reproduces. Above all, authority can, indeed must, be analyzed. All these attributes of authority apply to Orientalism, and much of what I do in this study is to describe both the historical authority in and the personal authorities of Orientalism.

My principal methodological devices for studying authority here are what can be called *strategic location*, which is a way of describing the author's position in a text with regard to the Oriental material he writes about, and *strategic formation*, which is a way of analyzing the relationship between texts and the way in which groups of texts, types of texts, even textual genres, acquire mass, density, and referential power among themselves and thereafter in the culture at large. I use the notion of strategy simply to identify the problem every writer on the Orient has faced: how to get hold of it, how to approach it, how not to be defeated or overwhelmed by its sublimity, its scope, its awful dimensions. Everyone who writes about the Orient must locate himself vis-à-vis the Orient; translated into his text, this location includes the kind of narrative voice he adopts, the type of structure he builds, the kinds of images, themes, motifs that circulate in his text—all of which add up to deliberate ways of addressing the reader, containing the Orient, and finally, representing it or speaking in its behalf. None of this takes place in the abstract, however. Every writer on the Orient (and this is true even of Homer) assumes some Oriental precedent, some previous knowledge of the Orient, to which he refers and on which he relies. Additionally, each work on the Orient *affiliates* itself with other works, with audiences, with institutions, with the Orient itself. The ensemble of relationships between works, audiences, and some particular aspects of the Orient therefore constitutes an analyzable formation—for example, that of philological studies, of anthologies of extracts from Oriental literature, of travel books, of Oriental fantasies—whose presence in time, in discourse, in institutions (schools, libraries, foreign services) gives it strength and authority.

It is clear, I hope, that my concern with authority does not entail analysis of what lies hidden in the Orientalist text, but analysis rather of the text's surface, its exteriority to what it describes. I do not think that this idea can be overemphasized. Orientalism is premised upon exteriority, that is, on the fact that the Orientalist, poet or scholar, makes the Orient speak, describes the Orient, renders its mysteries plain for and to the West. He is never concerned with the Orient except as

---

[29] [Said] George Eliot, *Middlemarch: A Study of Provincial Life* (1872; reprint ed., Boston: Houghton Mifflin Co., 1956), p. 164. [Paracelsus (Theophrastus von Hohenheim, 1493–1541), Swiss alchemist and physician.]

[30] Edward William Lane (1801–1876), English orientalist; Alphonse de Lamartine (1790–1869), French poet; Richard Francis Burton (1821–1890), English orientalist; Benjamin Disraeli (1804–1881), British statesman and novelist.

the first cause of what he says. What he says and writes, by virtue of the fact that it is said or written, is meant to indicate that the Orientalist is outside the Orient, both as an existential and as a moral fact. The principal product of this exteriority is of course representation: as early as Aeschylus's play *The Persians* the Orient is transformed from a very far distant and often threatening Otherness into figures that are relatively familiar (in Aeschylus's case, grieving Asiatic women). The dramatic immediacy of representation in *The Persians* obscures the fact that the audience is watching a highly artificial enactment of what a non-Oriental has made into a symbol for the whole Orient. My analysis of the Orientalist text therefore places emphasis on the evidence, which is by no means invisible, for such representations *as representations,* not as "natural" depictions of the Orient. This evidence is found just as prominently in the so-called truthful text (histories, philological analyses, political treatises) as in the avowedly artistic (i.e., openly imaginative) text. The things to look at are style, figures of speech, setting, narrative devices, historical and social circumstances, *not* the correctness of the representation nor its fidelity to some great original. The exteriority of the representation is always governed by some version of the truism that if the Orient could represent itself, it would; since it cannot, the representation does the job, for the West, and *faute de mieux,* for the poor Orient. "Sie können sich nicht vertreten, sie müssen vertreten werden,"[31] as Marx wrote in *The Eighteenth Brumaire of Louis Bonaparte.*

Another reason for insisting upon exteriority is that I believe it needs to be made clear about cultural discourse and exchange within a culture that what is commonly circulated by it is not "truth" but representations. It hardly needs to be demonstrated again that language itself is a highly organized and encoded system, which employs many devices to express, indicate, exchange messages and information, represent, and so forth. In any instance of at least written language, there is no such thing as a delivered presence, but a *re-presence,* or a representation. The value, efficacy, strength, apparent veracity of a written statement about the Orient therefore relies very little, and cannot instrumentally depend, on the Orient as such. On the contrary, the written statement is a presence to the reader by virtue of its having excluded, displaced, made supererogatory any such *real thing* as "the Orient." Thus all of Orientalism stands forth and away from the Orient: that Orientalism makes sense at all depends more on the West than on the Orient, and this sense is directly indebted to various Western techniques of representation that make the Orient visible, clear, "there" in

discourse about it. And these representations rely upon institutions, traditions, conventions, agreed-upon codes of understanding for their effects, not upon a distant and amorphous Orient.

The difference between representations of the Orient before the last third of the eighteenth century and those after it (that is, those belonging to what I call modern Orientalism) is that the range of representation expanded enormously in the later period. It is true that after William Jones and Anquetil-Duperron,[32] and after Napoleon's Egyptian expedition, Europe came to know the Orient more scientifically, to live in it with greater authority and discipline than ever before. But what mattered to Europe was the expanded scope and the much greater refinement given its techniques for receiving the Orient. When around the turn of the eighteenth century the Orient definitively revealed the age of its languages—thus outdating Hebrew's divine pedigree—it was a group of Europeans who made the discovery, passed it on to other scholars, and preserved the discovery in the new science of Indo-European philology. A new powerful science for viewing the linguistic Orient was born, and with it, as Foucault has shown in *The Order of Things,* a whole web of related scientific interests. Similarly William Beckford, Byron, Goethe, and Hugo[33] restructured the Orient by their art and made its colors, lights, and people visible through their images, rhythms, and motifs. At most, the "real" Orient provoked a writer to his vision; it very rarely guided it.

Orientalism responded more to the culture that produced it than to its putative object, which was also produced by the West. Thus the history of Orientalism has both an internal consistency and a highly articulated set of relationships to the dominant culture surrounding it. My analyses consequently try to show the field's shape and internal organization, its pioneers, patriarchal authorities, canonical texts, doxological ideas, exemplary figures, its followers, elaborators, and new authorities; I try also to explain how Orientalism borrowed and was frequently informed by "strong" ideas, doctrines, and trends ruling the culture. Thus there was (and is) a linguistic Orient, a Freudian Orient, a Spenglerian Orient, a Darwinian Orient, a racist Orient—and so on. Yet never has there been such a thing as a pure, or unconditional, Orient; similarly, never has there been a nonmaterial form of Orientalism, much less something so innocent as an "idea" of the Orient. In this underlying conviction

---

[31] "They cannot represent themselves, they must be represented."

[32] A.H. Anquetil-Duperron (1731–1803), French orientalist.

[33] Foucault (above, page 1260); William Beckford (1760–1844), English novelist; George Gordon Lord Byron (1788–1824), English poet; Johann Wolfgang von Goethe (1749–1832), German poet and dramatist; Victor-Marie Hugo (1802–1885), French poet and novelist.

and in its ensuing methodological consequences do I differ from scholars who study the history of ideas. For the emphases and the executive form, above all the material effectiveness, of statements made by Orientalist discourse are possible in ways that any hermetic history of ideas tends completely to scant. Without those emphases and that material effectiveness Orientalism would be just another idea, whereas it is and was much more than that. Therefore I set out to examine not only scholarly works but also works of literature, political tracts, journalistic texts, travel books, religious and philological studies. In other words, my hybrid perspective is broadly historical and "anthropological," given that I believe all texts to be worldly and circumstantial in (of course) ways that vary from genre to genre, and from historical period to historical period.

Yet unlike Michel Foucault, to whose work I am greatly indebted, I do believe in the determining imprint of individual writers upon the otherwise anonymous collective body of texts constituting a discursive formation like Orientalism. The unity of the large ensemble of texts I analyze is due in part to the fact that they frequently refer to each other: Orientalism is after all a system for citing works and authors. Edward William Lane's *Manners and Customs of the Modern Egyptians* was read and cited by such diverse figures as Nerval, Flaubert, and Richard Burton. He was an authority whose use was an imperative for anyone writing or thinking about the Orient, not just about Egypt: when Nerval borrows passages verbatim from *Modern Egyptians* it is to use Lane's authority to assist him in describing village scenes in Syria, not Egypt. Lane's authority and the opportunities provided for citing him discriminately as well as indiscriminately were there because Orientalism could give his text the kind of distributive currency that he acquired. There is no way, however, of understanding Lane's currency without also understanding the peculiar features of *his* text; this is equally true of Renan, Sacy, Lamartine, Schlegel,[34] and a group of other influential writers. Foucault believes that in general the individual text or author counts for very little; empirically, in the case of Orientalism (and perhaps nowhere else) I find this not to be so. Accordingly my analyses employ close textual readings whose goal is to reveal the dialectic between individual text or writer and the complex collective formation to which his work is a contribution.

Yet even though it includes an ample selection of writers, this book is still far from a complete history or general account of Orientalism. Of this failing I am very conscious. The fabric of as thick a discourse as Orientalism has survived and functioned in Western society because of its richness: all I have done is to describe parts of that fabric at certain moments, and merely to suggest the existence of a larger whole, detailed, interesting, dotted with fascinating figures, texts, and events. I have consoled myself with believing that this book is one installment of several, and hope there are scholars and critics who might want to write others. There is still a general essay to be written on imperialism and culture; other studies would go more deeply into the connection between Orientalism and pedagogy, or into Italian, Dutch, German, and Swiss Orientalism, or into the dynamic between scholarship and imaginative writing, or into the relationship between administrative ideas and intellectual discipline. Perhaps the most important task of all would be to undertake studies in contemporary alternatives to Orientalism, to ask how one can study other cultures and peoples from a libertarian, or a nonrepressive and nonmanipulative, perspective. But then one would have to rethink the whole complex problem of knowledge and power. These are all tasks left embarrassingly incomplete in this study.

The last, perhaps self-flattering, observation on method that I want to make here is that I have written this study with several audiences in mind. For students of literature and criticism, Orientalism offers a marvelous instance of the interrelations between society, history, and textuality; moreover, the cultural role played by the Orient in the West connects Orientalism with ideology, politics, and the logic of power, matters of relevance, I think, to the literary community. For contemporary students of the Orient, from university scholars to policymakers, I have written with two ends in mind: one, to present their intellectual genealogy to them in a way that has not been done; two, to criticize—with the hope of stirring discussion—the often unquestioned assumptions on which their work for the most part depends. For the general reader, this study deals with matters that always compel attention, all of them connected not only with Western conceptions and treatments of the Other but also with the singularly important role played by Western culture in what Vico called the world of nations. Lastly, for readers in the so-called Third World, this study proposes itself as a step towards an understanding not so much of Western politics and of the non-Western world in those politics as of the *strength* of Western cultural discourse, a strength too often mistaken as merely decorative or "superstructural." My hope is to illustrate the formidable structure of cultural domination and, specifically for formerly colonized peoples, the dangers and temptations of employing this structure upon themselves or upon others.

---

[34]Joseph Ernest Renan (1823–1892), French philologist and historian; Schlegel (above, page 473).

The three long chapters and twelve shorter units into which this book is divided are intended to facilitate exposition as much as possible. Chapter One, "The Scope of Orientalism," draws a large circle around all the dimensions of the subject, both in terms of historical time and experiences and in terms of philosophical and political themes. Chapter Two, "Orientalist Structures and Restructures," attempts to trace the development of modern Orientalism by a broadly chronological description, and also by the description of a set of devices common to the work of important poets, artists, and scholars. Chapter Three, "Orientalism Now," begins where its predecessor left off, at around 1870. This is the period of great colonial expansion into the Orient, and it culminates in World War II. The very last section of Chapter Three characterizes the shift from British and French to American hegemony; I attempt there finally to sketch the present intellectual and social realities of Orientalism in the United States.

3. *The personal dimension.* In the *Prison Notebooks* Gramsci says: "The starting-point of critical elaboration is the consciousness of what one really is, and is 'knowing thyself' as a product of the historical process to date, which has deposited in you an infinity of traces, without leaving an inventory." The only available English translation inexplicably leaves Gramsci's comment at that, whereas in fact Gramsci's Italian text concludes by adding, "therefore it is imperative at the outset to compile such an inventory."[35]

Much of the personal investment in this study derives from my awareness of being an "Oriental" as a child growing up in two British colonies. All of my education, in those colonies (Palestine and Egypt) and in the United States, has been Western, and yet that deep early awareness has persisted. In many ways my study of Orientalism has been an attempt to inventory the traces upon me, the Oriental subject, of the culture whose domination has been so powerful a factor in the life of all Orientals. This is why for me the Islamic Orient has had to be the center of attention. Whether what I have achieved is the inventory prescribed by Gramsci is not for me to judge, although I have felt it important to be conscious of trying to produce one. Along the way, as severely and as rationally as I have been able, I have tried to maintain a critical consciousness, as well as employing those instruments of historical, humanistic, and cultural research of which my education has made me the fortunate

beneficiary. In none of that, however, have I ever lost hold of the cultural reality of, the personal involvement in having been constituted as, "an Oriental."

The historical circumstances making such a study possible are fairly complex, and I can only list them schematically here. Anyone resident in the West since the 1950s, particularly in the United States, will have lived through an era of extraordinary turbulence in the relations of East and West. No one will have failed to note how "East" has always signified danger and threat during this period, even as it has meant the traditional Orient as well as Russia. In the universities a growing establishment of area-studies programs and institutes has made the scholarly study of the Orient a branch of national policy. Public affairs in this country include a healthy interest in the Orient, as much for its strategic and economic importance as for its traditional exoticism. If the world has become immediately accessible to a Western citizen living in the electronic age, the Orient too has drawn nearer to him, and is now less a myth perhaps than a place crisscrossed by Western, especially American, interests.

One aspect of the electronic, postmodern world is that there has been a reinforcement of the stereotypes by which the Orient is viewed. Television, the films, and all the media's resources have forced information into more and more standardized molds. So far as the Orient is concerned, standardization and cultural stereotyping have intensified the hold of the nineteenth-century academic and imaginative demonology of "the mysterious Orient." This is nowhere more true than in the ways by which the Near East is grasped. Three things have contributed to making even the simplest perception of the Arabs and Islam into a highly politicized, almost raucous matter: one, the history of popular anti-Arab and anti-Islamic prejudice in the West, which is immediately reflected in the history of Orientalism; two, the struggle between the Arabs and Israeli Zionism, and its effects upon American Jews as well as upon both the liberal culture and the population at large; three, the almost total absence of any cultural position making it possible either to identify with or dispassionately to discuss the Arabs or Islam. Furthermore, it hardly needs saying that because the Middle East is now so identified with Great Power politics, oil economics, and the simple-minded dichotomy of freedom-loving, democratic Israel and evil, totalitarian, and terroristic Arabs, the chances of anything like a clear view of what one talks about in talking about the Near East are depressingly small.

My own experiences of these matters are in part what made me write this book. The life of an Arab Palestinian in the West, particularly in America, is disheartening. There

---

[35] [Said] Antonio Gramsci [above, page 936], *The Prison Notebooks: Selections,* tr. and ed. Quintin Hoare and Geoffrey Nowell-Smith (New York: International Publishers, 1971), p. 324. The full passage, unavailable in the Hoare and Nowell-Smith translation, is to be found in Gramsci, *Quaderni del Carcere,* ed. Valentino Gerratana (Turin: Einaudi Editore, 1975), 2: 1363.

exists here an almost unanimous consensus that politically he does not exist, and when it is allowed that he does, it is either as a nuisance or as an Oriental. The web of racism, cultural stereotypes, political imperialism, dehumanizing ideology holding in the Arab or the Muslim is very strong indeed, and it is this web which every Palestinian has come to feel as his uniquely punishing destiny. It has made matters worse for him to remark that no person academically involved with the Near East—no Orientalist, that is—has ever in the United States culturally and politically identified himself wholeheartedly with the Arabs; certainly there have been identifications on some level, but they have never taken an "acceptable" form as has liberal American identification with Zionism, and all too frequently they have been radically flawed by their association either with discredited political and economic interests (oil-company and State Department Arabists, for example) or with religion.

The nexus of knowledge and power creating "the Oriental" and in a sense obliterating him as a human being is therefore not for me an exclusively academic matter. Yet it is an *intellectual* matter of some very obvious importance. I have been able to put to use my humanistic and political concerns for the analysis and description of a very worldly matter, the rise, development, and consolidation of Orientalism. Too often literature and culture are presumed to be politically, even historically innocent; it has regularly seemed otherwise to me, and certainly my study of Orientalism has convinced me (and I hope will convince my literary colleagues) that society and literary culture can only be understood and studied together. In addition, and by an almost inescapable logic, I have found myself writing the history of a strange, secret sharer of Western anti-Semitism. That anti-Semitism and, as I have discussed it in its Islamic branch, Orientalism resemble each other very closely is a historical, cultural, and political truth that needs only to be mentioned to an Arab Palestinian for its irony to be perfectly understood. But what I should like also to have contributed here is a better understanding of the way cultural domination has operated. If this stimulates a new kind of dealing with the Orient, indeed if it eliminates the "Orient" and "Occident" altogether, then we shall have advanced a little in the process of what Raymond Williams has called the "unlearning" of "the inherent dominative mode."[36]

---

[36][Said] Raymond Williams [above, page 1356], *Culture and Society, 1780–1950* (London: Chatto & Windus, 1958), p. 376.

Annette Kolodny

b. 1941

Written in 1979, Annette Kolodny's essay below remains in its first part a valuable account of modern twentieth-century feminist criticism and theory. It then goes on to offer a program for future feminist work. Kolodny first discusses the accomplishments of feminist criticism: the recovery of lost or neglected works by women, a new sense of literary history, the recognition and expression of a feminine consciousness, a new scrutiny of writing by men, the analysis of language particularly with respect to patriarchal social structure, the analysis of women's language. She notes the speed of accomplishment of feminist criticism in addressing these issues while noting the paucity of feminist critics in English departments of universities and colleges (a situation that has changed markedly since she wrote).

In the later part of her essay, after discussing the male domination of the so-called literary canon, she first proposes reexamination of literary history with a recognition of its always fictive nature, invoking the notion of inevitably changing horizons (see Jauss, above, page 1240, on horizons). Second, she seeks recognition that in our readings we engage not texts but paradigms and learned interpretive strategies (see Fish, below, page 1395). Finally, she would have us reexamine our aesthetic assumptions. All three of these ideas were fairly common in mid-twentieth-century literary theory, the first arising in the work of Hans-Georg Gadamer, but not with a feminist perspective, the second in Fish, and the third in many critics beginning roughly with I. A. Richards (above, page 856). The important difference in each case is that Kolodny saw these moves as ones necessary to establish feminist power in a field in which feminist readings and paradigms had been suppressed and aesthetic assumptions had been those of men.

The last few pages of Kolodny's essay are not included here. In them, she argues for critical pluralism on the ground that no "single system of analysis" can possibly do justice to literary experience and that all approaches are perspectival. Here her aim was to allow for perspectives to contain a variety of feminist approaches, whether in conflict or logically independent. She insisted also that literary criticism be related to the larger political and social feminist movement. Kolodny's views here met occasional resistance from feminists suspicious of a pluralistic attitude. This may have been in part because she synthesized in her three proposals diverse approaches first offered by men.

Among Kolodny's works are *The Lay of the Land: Metaphor as Experience and History in American Life and Letters* (1975); *The Land Before Her: Fantasy and Experience of the American Frontier, 1630–1860* (1984), and a book on higher education, *Failing the Future* (1998). See also her "A Map for Rereading: Gender and the Interpretation of Literary Texts," *New Literary History* 11 (1980).

from

Dancing Through the Minefield: Some Observations on the Theory, Practice, and Politics of a Feminist Literary Criticism

Had anyone had the prescience, in 1969, to pose the question of defining a "feminist" literary criticism, she might have been told, in the wake of Mary Ellmann's *Thinking About Women,*[1] that it involved exposing the sexual stereotyping of women in both our literature and our literary criticism and, as well, demonstrating the inadequacy of established critical schools and methods to deal fairly or sensitively with works written by women. In broad outline, such a prediction would have stood well the rest of time, and, in fact, Ellmann's book continues to be widely read and to point us in useful directions. What could not have been anticipated in 1969, however, was the catalyzing force of an ideology that, for many of us, helped to bridge the gap between the world as we found it and the world as we wanted it to be. For those of us who studied literature, a previously unspoken sense of exclusion from authorship, and a painfully personal distress at discovering whores, bitches, muses, and heroines dead in childbirth where we had once hoped to discover ourselves, could—for the first time—begin to be understood as more than "a set of disconnected, unrealized private emotions."[2] With a renewed courage to make public our otherwise private discontents, what had once been "felt individually as personal insecurity" came at last to be "viewed collectively as structural inconsistency"[3] within the very disciplines we studied. Following unflinchingly the full implications of Ellmann's percipient observations, and emboldened by the liberating energy of feminist ideology—in all its various forms and guises—feminist criticism very quickly moved

beyond merely "expos[ing] sexism in one work of literature after another,"[4] and promised instead that we might at last "begin to record new choices in a new literary history."[5] So powerful was that impulse that we experienced it, along with Adrienne Rich, as much more than "a chapter in cultural history"; it became, rather, "an act of survival."[6] What was at stake was not so much literature or criticism as such, but the historical, social, and ethical consequences of women's participation in, or exclusion from, either enterprise.

The pace of inquiry in the 1970s was fast and furious—especially after Kate Millett's 1970 analysis of the sexual politics of literature[7] added a note of urgency to what had earlier been Ellmann's sardonic anger—while the diversity of that inquiry easily outstripped all efforts to define feminist literary criticism as either a coherent system or a unified set of methodologies. Under its wide umbrella, everything was thrown into question: our established canons, our aesthetic criteria, our interpretative strategies, our reading habits, and most of all, ourselves as critics and as teachers. To delineate its full scope would require nothing less than a book—a book that would be outdated even as it was being composed. For the sake of brevity, therefore, let me attempt only a summary outline.

Perhaps the most obvious success of this new scholarship has been the return to circulation of previously lost or otherwise ignored works by women writers. Following fast upon the initial success of the Feminist Press in reissuing gems such as Rebecca Harding Davis's 1861 novella, *Life in the Iron Mills,* and Charlotte Perkins Gilman's 1892 short story "The Yellow Wallpaper," published in 1972 and 1973 respectively,[8] commercial trade and reprint houses vied with one another in the reprinting of anthologies of lost texts and, in some cases, in the reprinting of whole series. For those of

---

"Dancing Through the Minefield: Some Observations on the Theory, Practice, and Politics of a Feminist Literary Criticism" was published in *Feminist Studies* (1980). It is reprinted here in part with some later changes made by the author.

[1] [Kolodny] Mary Ellmann, *Thinking About Women* (New York: Harcourt, Brace & World, 1968).

[2] [Kolodny] See Clifford Geertz, "Ideology as a Cultural System," *The Interpretation of Cultures: Selected Essays* (New York: Basic Books, 1973), p. 232.

[3] [Kolodny] Ibid., p. 204.

[4] [Kolodny] Lillian S. Robinson, "Cultural Criticism and the *Horror Vacui,*" *College English* 33 (October 1972); reprinted as "The Critical Task" in her *Sex, Class, and Culture* (Bloomington: Indiana University Press, 1978), p. 51.

[5] [Kolodny] Elaine Showalter, *A Literature of Their Own: British Women Novelists from Brontë to Lessing* (Princeton: Princeton University Press, 1977), p. 36.

[6] [Kolodny] Adrienne Rich, "When We Dead Awaken: Writing as Re-Vision," *College English* 34 (October 1972); reprinted in *Adrienne Rich's Poetry,* ed. Barbara Charlesworth Gelpi and Albert Gelpi (New York: W. W. Norton, 1975), p. 90.

[7] [Kolodny] Kate Millett, *Sexual Politics* (Garden City: Doubleday, 1970).

[8] [Kolodny] Rebecca Harding Davis, *Life in the Iron Mills,* originally published in the *Atlantic Monthly,* April 1861; reprinted with "A Biographical Interpretation" by Tillie Olsen (Old Westbury: Feminest Press, 1972). Charlotte Perkins Gilman, "The Yellow Wallpaper," originally published in the *New England Magazine,* May 1892; reprinted with an Afterword by Elaine R. Hedges (Old Westbury: Feminist Press, 1973).

us in American literature especially, the phenomenon promised a radical reshaping of our concepts of literary history and, at the very least, a new chapter in understanding the development of women's literary traditions. So commercially successful were these reprintings, and so attuned were the reprint houses to the political attitudes of the audiences for which they were offered, that many of us found ourselves wooed to compose critical introductions, which would find in the pages of nineteenth-century domestic and sentimental fictions some signs of either muted rebellions or overt radicalism, in anticipation of the current wave of "New Feminism." In rereading with our students these previously lost works, we inevitably raised perplexing questions as to the reasons for their disappearance from the canons of "major works," and we worried over the aesthetic and critical criteria by which they had been accorded diminished status.

This increased availability of works by women writers led, of course, to an increased interest in what elements, if any, might constitute some sort of unity or connection among them. The possibility that women had developed either a unique or at least a related tradition of their own especially intrigued those of us who specialized in one national literature or another, or in historical periods. Nina Baym's *Woman's Fiction: A Guide to Novels by and about Women in America, 1820–1870* [9] demonstrated the Americanist's penchant for examining what were once the "best-sellers" of their day, the ranks of the popular fiction writers, among which women took a dominant place throughout the nineteenth century, while the feminist studies of British literature emphasized instead the wealth of women writers who have been regarded as worthy of canonization. Not so much building upon one another's work as clarifying, successively, the parameters of the questions to be posed, Sydney Janet Kaplan, Ellen Moers, Patricia Meyer Spacks, and Elaine Showalter, among many others, concentrated their energies on delineating an internally consistent "body of work" by women that might stand as a female counter-tradition. For Kaplan, in 1975, this entailed examining women writers' various attempts to portray feminine consciousness and self-consciousness, not as a psychological category, but as a stylistic or rhetorical device. [10] That same year, arguing essen-

tially that literature publicizes the private, Spacks placed her consideration of a "female imagination" within social and historical frames, to conclude that "for readily discernible historical reasons women have characteristically concerned themselves with matters more or less peripheral to male concerns," and she attributed to this fact an inevitable difference in the literary emphases and subject matters of female and male writers. [11] The next year, Moers's *Literary Women: The Great Writers* focused on the pathways of literary influence that linked the English novel in the hands of women. [12] And finally, in 1977, Showalter took up the matter of a "female literary tradition in the English novel from the generation of the Brontës to the present day" by arguing that because women in general constitute a kind of "subculture within the framework of a larger society," the work of women writers, in particular, would thereby demonstrate a unity of "values, conventions, experiences, and behaviors impinging on each individual" as she found her sources of "self-expression relative to a dominant [and, by implication, male] society." [13]

At the same time that women writers were being reconsidered and reread, male writers were similarly subjected to a new feminist scrutiny. The continuing result—to put years of difficult analysis into a single sentence—has been nothing less than an acute attentiveness to the ways in which certain power relations, usually those in which males wield various forms of influence over females, are inscribed in the texts (both literary and critical) that we have inherited, not merely as subject matter, but as the unquestioned, often unacknowledged *given* of the culture. Even more important than the new interpretations of individual texts are the probings into the consequences (for women) of the conventions that inform those texts. For example, in surveying selected nineteenth- and early-twentieth-century British novels which employ what she calls "the two-suitors convention," Jean E. Kennard sought to understand why and how the structural demands of the convention, even in the hands of women writers, inevitably work to imply "the inferiority and necessary subordination of women." Her 1978 study, *Victims of Convention*, points out that the symbolic nature of the marriage which conventionally concludes such novels "indicates the adjustment of the protagonist to society's values, a condition which is equated with her maturity."

---

[9] [Kolodny] Nina Baym, *Women's Fiction: A Guide to Novels by and About Women in America, 1820–1870* (Ithaca: Cornell University Press, 1978).

[10] [Kolodny] In her *Feminine Consciousness in the Modern British Novel* (Urbana: University of Illinois Press, 1975), p. 3, Sydney Janet Kaplan explains that she is using the term "feminine consciousness" "not simply as some general attitude of women toward their own femininity, and not as something synonymous with a particular sensibility among female writers. I am concerned with it as a literary device: a method of characterization of females in fiction."

[11] [Kolodny] Patricia Meyer Spacks, *The Female Imagination* (New York: Avon Books, 1975), p. 6.

[12] [Kolodny] Ellen Moers, *Literary Women: The Great Writers* (Garden City: Doubleday, 1976).

[13] [Kolodny] Showalter, *A Literature of Their Own*, p. 11.

Kennard's concern, however, is with the fact that the structural demands of the form too often sacrifice precisely those "virtues of independence and individuality," or, in other words, the very "qualities we have been invited to admire in" the heroines.[14] Kennard appropriately cautions us against drawing from her work any simplistically reductive thesis about the mimetic relations between art and life. Yet her approach nonetheless suggests that what is important about a fiction is not whether it ends in a death or a marriage, but what the symbolic demands of that particular conventional ending imply about the values and beliefs of the world that engendered it.

Her work thus participates in a growing emphasis in feminist literary study on the fact of literature as a social institution, embedded not only within its own literary traditions but also within the particular physical and mental artifacts of the society from which it comes. Adumbrating Millett's 1970 decision to anchor her "literary reflections" to a preceding analysis of the historical, social, and economic contexts of sexual politics,[15] more recent work—most notably Lillian Robinson's—begins with the premise that the process of artistic creation "consists not of ghostly happenings in the head but of a matching of the states and processes of symbolic models against the states and processes of the wider world."[16] The power relations inscribed in the form of conventions within our literary inheritance, these critics argue, reify the encodings of those same power relations in the culture at large. And the critical examination of rhetorical codes becomes, in their hands, the pursuit of ideological codes, because both embody either value systems or the dialectic of competition between value systems. More often than not, these critics insist upon examining not only the mirroring of life in art but also the normative impact of art on life. Addressing herself to the popular art available to working women, for example, Robinson is interested in understanding not only "the forms it uses" but, more important, "the myths it creates, the influence it exerts." "The way art helps people to order, interpret, mythologize, or dispose of their own experience," she declares, may be "complex and often ambiguous, but it is not impossible to define."[17]

Whether its focus be upon the material or the imaginative contexts of literary invention; single texts or entire canons; the relations between authors, genres, or historical circumstances; lost authors or well-known names, the variety and diversity of all feminist literary criticism finally coheres in its stance of almost defensive rereading. What Adrienne Rich had earlier called "revision," that is, "the act of looking back, of seeing with fresh eyes, of entering an old text from a new critical direction,"[18] took on a more actively self-protective coloration in 1978, when Judith Fetterley called upon the woman reader to learn to "resist" the sexist designs a text might make upon her—asking her to identify against herself, so to speak, by manipulating her sympathies on behalf of male heroes but against female shrew or bitch characters.[19] Underpinning a great deal of this critical rereading has been the not-unexpected alliance between feminist literary study and feminist studies in linguistics and language acquisition. Tillie Olsen's commonsense observation of the danger of "perpetuating—by continued usage—entrenched, centuries-old oppressive power realities, early-on incorporated into language,"[20] has been given substantive analysis in the writings of feminists who study "language as a symbolic system closely tied to a patriarchal social structure." Taken together, their work demonstrates "the importance of language in establishing, reflecting, and maintaining an asymmetrical relationship between women and men."[21]

To consider what this implies for the fate of women who essay the craft of language is to ascertain, perhaps for the first time, the real dilemma of the poet who finds her most cherished private experience "hedged by taboos, mined with false-namings."[22] It also explains the dilemma of the male reader who, in opening the pages of a woman's book, finds himself entering a strange and unfamiliar world of symbolic significance. For if, as Nelly Furman insists, neither language use nor language acquisition is "gender-neutral," but is, instead, "imbued with our sex-inflected cultural values;"[23] and if, additionally, reading is a process of

[14] [Kolodny] Jean E. Kennard, *Victims of Convention* (Hamden: Archon Books, 1978), pp. 164, 18, 14.

[15] [Kolodny] See Millett, *Sexual Politics,* pt. 3, "The Literary Reflection," pp. 235–361.

[16] [Kolodny] The phrase is Geertz's; see "Ideology as a Cultural System," p. 214.

[17] [Kolodny] Lillian S. Robinson, "Criticism—and Self-Criticism," *College English* 36 (January 1974), and "Criticism: Who Needs It?" in *The Uses of Criticism,* ed. A. P. Foulkes (Bern and Frankfurt: Lang, 1976); both reprinted in *Sex, Class, and Culture,* pp. 67, 80.

[18] [Kolodny] Rich, "When We Dead Awaken," p. 90.

[19] [Kolodny] Judith Fetterly, *The Resisting Reader: A Feminist Approach to American Fiction* (Bloomington: Indiana University Press, 1978).

[20] [Kolodny] Tillie Olsen, *Silences* (New York: Delacorte Press, 1978), pp. 239–40.

[21] [Kolodny] See Cheris Kramer, Barrie Thorne, and Nancy Henley, "Perspectives on Language and Communication," Review Essay, *Signs* 3 (Summer 1978), p. 646.

[22] [Kolodny] See Adrienne Rich's discussion of the difficulty in finding authentic language for her experience as a mother in *Of Woman Born: Motherhood as Experience and Institution* (New York: W. W. Norton, 1976), p. 15.

[23] [Kolodny] Nelly Furman, "The Study of Women and Language: Comment on Vol. 3, no. 3," *Signs* 4 (Fall 1978), p. 184.

"sorting out the structures of signification"[24] in any text, then male readers who find themselves outside of and unfamiliar with the symbolic systems that constitute female experience in women's writings will necessarily dismiss those systems as undecipherable, meaningless, or trivial. And male professors will find no reason to include such works in the canons of "major authors." At the same time, women writers, coming into a tradition of literary language and conventional forms already appropriated, for centuries, to the purposes of male expression, will be forced virtually to "wrestle" with that language in an effort "to remake it as a language adequate to our conceptual processes."[25] To all of this, feminists concerned with the politics of language and style have been acutely attentive. "Language conceals an invincible adversary," observes French critic Hélène Cixous, "because it's the language of men and their grammar."[26] But equally insistent, as in the work of Sandra Gilbert and Susan Gubar, has been the understanding of the need for *all* readers, male and female alike, to learn to penetrate the otherwise unfamiliar universes of symbolic action that comprise women's writings, past and present.[27]

To have attempted so many difficult questions and to have accomplished so much—even acknowledging the inevitable false starts, overlapping, and repetition—in so short a time, should certainly have secured feminist literary criticism an honored berth on that ongoing intellectual journey which we loosely term in academia "critical analysis." Instead of being welcomed onto the train, however, we have been forced to negotiate a minefield. The very energy and diversity of our enterprise have rendered us vulnerable to attack on the grounds that we lack both definition and coherence; while our particular attentiveness to the ways in which literature encodes and disseminates cultural value systems calls down upon us imprecations echoing those heaped upon the Marxist critics of an earlier generation. If we are scholars dedicated to rediscovering a lost body of writings by women, then our finds are questioned on aesthetic grounds. And if we are critics determined to practice revisionist readings, it is claimed that our focus is too narrow and our results are only distortions or, worse still, polemical misreadings.

The very vehemence of the outcry, coupled with our total dismissal in some quarters,[28] suggests not our deficiencies, however, but the potential magnitude of our challenge. For what we are asking be scrutinized are nothing less than shared cultural assumptions so deeply rooted and so long ingrained that, for the most part, our critical colleagues have ceased to recognize them as such. In other words, what is really being bewailed in the claims that we distort texts or threaten the disappearance of the great Western literary tradition itself[29] is not so much the disappearance of either text or tradition but, instead, the eclipse of that particular *form* of the text and that particular *shape* of the canon which previously reified male readers' sense of power and significance in the world. Analogously, by asking whether, as readers, we ought to be "really satisfied by the marriage of Dorothea Brooke to Will Ladislaw? of Shirley Keeldar to Louis Moore?" or whether, as Kennard suggests, we must reckon with the ways in which "the qualities we have been invited to admire in these heroines [have] been sacrificed to structural neatness,"[30] is to raise difficult and profoundly perplexing questions about the ethical implications of our otherwise unquestioned aesthetic pleasures. It is, after all, an imposition of high order to ask the viewer to attend to Ophelia's sufferings in a scene where, before, he had always so comfortably kept his eye fixed firmly on Hamlet. To understand all this, then, as the real nature of the challenge we have offered and, in consequence, as the motivation for the often overt hostility we have aroused, should help us learn

---

[24] [Kolodny] Again my phrasing comes from Geertz, "Thick Description: Toward an Interpretive Theory of Culture" [above, page 1329], *Interpretation of Cultures*, p. 9.

[25] [Kolodny] Julia Penelope Stanley and Susan W. Robbins, "Toward a Feminist Aesthetic," *Chrysalis*, no. 6 (1977), p. 63.

[26] [Kolodny] Hélène Cixous, "The Laugh of the Medusa," tr. Keith Cohen and Paula Cohen, *Signs* 1 (Summer 1976), p. 887.

[27] [Kolodny] In *The Madwoman in the Attic: The Woman Writer and the Nineteenth-Century Literary Imagination* (New Haven: Yale University Press, 1979) Sandra M. Gilbert and Susan Gubar suggest that women's writings are in some sense "palimpsestic" in that their "surface designs conceal or obscure deeper, less accessible (and less socially acceptable) levels of meaning" (p. 73). It is, in their view, an art designed "both to express and to camouflage" (p. 81).

---

[28] [Kolodny] Consider, for example, Robert Boyer's reductive and inaccurate generalization that "what distinguishes ordinary books and articles about women from feminist writing is the feminist insistence on asking the same question of every work and demanding ideologically satisfactory answers to those questions as a means of evaluating it," in "A Case Against Feminist Criticism," *Partisan Review* 43 (1976): 602. It is partly as a result of such misconceptions that we have the paucity of feminist critics who are granted a place in English departments that otherwise pride themselves on the variety of their critical orientations.

[29] [Kolodny] Ambivalent though he is about the literary continuity that begins with Homer, Harold Bloom nonetheless somewhat ominously prophesies "that the first true break . . . will be brought about in generations to come, if the burgeoning religion of Liberated Woman spreads from its clusters of enthusiasts to dominate the West," in *A Map of Misreading* (New York: Oxford University Press, 1975), p. 33. On p. 36, he acknowledges that while something "as violent [as] a quarrel would ensue if I expressed my judgment" on Robert Lowell and Norman Mailer, "it would lead to something more intense than quarrels if I expressed my judgment upon . . . the literature of Women's Liberation."

[30] [Kolodny] Kennard, *Victims of Convention*, p. 14.

to negotiate the minefield, if not with grace, then with at least a clearer comprehension of its underlying patterns.

The ways in which objections to our work are usually posed, of course, serve to obscure their deeper motivations. But this may, in part, be due to our own reticence at taking full responsibility for the truly radicalizing premises that lie at the theoretical core of all we have so far accomplished. It may be time, therefore, to redirect discussion, forcing our adversaries to deal with the substantive issues and pushing ourselves into a clearer articulation of what, in fact, we are about. Up until now, I fear, we have dealt only piecemeal with the difficulties inherent in challenging the authority of established canons and then justifying the excellence of women's traditions, sometimes in accord with standards to which they have no intrinsic relation.

At the very point at which we must perforce enter the discourse—that is, claiming excellence or importance for our "finds"—all discussion has already, we discover, long ago been closed. "If Kate Chopin[31] were *really* worth reading," an Oxford-trained colleague once assured me, "she'd have lasted—like Shakespeare"; and he then proceeded to vote against the English department's crediting a women's studies seminar I was offering in American women writers. The canon, for him, conferred excellence; Chopin's exclusion demonstrated only her lesser worth. As far as he was concerned, I could no more justify giving English-department credit for the study of Chopin than I could dare publicly to question Shakespeare's genius. Through hindsight, I have now come to view that discussion as not only having posed fruitless oppositions but also having entirely evaded the much more profound problem lurking just beneath the surface of our disagreement. That is, that the fact of canonization puts any work beyond questions of establishing its merit and, instead, invites students to offer only increasingly more ingenious readings and interpretations, the purpose of which is to validate the greatness already imputed by canonization.

Had I only understood it for what it was then, into this circular and self-serving set of assumptions I might have interjected some statement of my right to question why *any* text is revered and my need to know what it tells us about "how we live, how we have been living, how we have been led to imagine ourselves, [and] how our language has trapped as well as liberated us."[32] The very fact of our critical training within the strictures imposed by an established canon of major works and authors, however, repeatedly deflects us from such questions. Instead, we find ourselves endlessly responding to the riposte that the overwhelmingly male presence among canonical authors was only an accident of history and never intentionally sexist, coupled with claims to the "obvious" aesthetic merit of those canonized texts. It is, as I say, a fruitless exchange, serving more to obscure than to expose the territory being protected and dragging us, again and again, through the minefield.

It is my contention that current hostilities might be transformed into a true dialogue with our critics if we at last made explicit what appear, to this observer, to constitute the three crucial propositions to which our special interests inevitably give rise. They are, moreover, propositions which, if handled with care and intelligence, could breathe new life into now moribund areas of our profession: (1) literary history (and with that, the historicity of literature) is a fiction; (2) insofar as we are taught how to read, what we engage are not texts but paradigms; and finally, (3) since the grounds upon which we assign aesthetic value to texts are never infallible, unchangeable, or universal, we must reexamine not only our aesthetics but, as well, the inherent biases and assumptions informing the critical methods which (in part) shape our aesthetic responses. For the sake of brevity, I will not attempt to offer the full arguments for each but, rather, only sufficient elaboration to demonstrate what I see as their intrinsic relation to the potential scope of and present challenge implied by feminist literary study.

1. *Literary history (and with that, the historicity of literature) is a fiction.* To begin with, an established canon functions as a model by which to chart the continuities and discontinuities, as well as the influences upon and the interconnections between works, genres, and authors. That model we tend to forget, however, is of our own making. It will take a very different shape, and explain its inclusions and exclusions in very different ways, if the reigning critical ideology believes that new literary forms result from some kind of ongoing internal dialectic within preexisting styles and traditions or if, by contrast, the ideology declares that literary change is dependent upon societal development and therefore determined by upheavals in the social and economic organization of the culture at large.[33] Indeed, whenever in the previous century of English and American literary scholarship one alternative replaced the other, we saw dramatic alterations in canonical "wisdom."

This suggests, then, that our sense of a "literary history," and, by extension, our confidence in a "historical"

---

[31] Kate Chopin (1851–1904), American author.
[32] [Kolodny] Rich, "When We Dead Awaken," p. 90.

[33] [Kolodny] The first is a proposition currently expressed by some structuralists and formalist critics; the best statement of the second probably appears in Georg Lukács, *Writer and Critic* (New York: Grosset & Dunlap, 1970), p. 119.

canon, is rooted not so much in any definitive understanding of the past as it is in our need to call up and utilize the past on behalf of a better understanding of the present. Thus, to paraphrase David Couzens Hoy, it becomes necessary "to point out that the understanding of art and literature is such an essential aspect of the present's self-understanding that this self-understanding conditions what even gets taken" as constituting that artistic and literary past. To quote Hoy fully, "this continual reinterpretation of the past goes hand in hand with the continual reinterpretation by the present of itself."[34] In our own time, uncertain as to which, if any, model truly accounts for our canonical choices or accurately explains literary history, and pressured further by the feminists' call for some justification of the criteria by which women's writings were largely excluded from both that canon and history, we suffer what Harold Bloom has called "a remarkable dimming" of "our mutual sense of canonical standards."[35]

Into this apparent impasse, feminist literary theorists implicitly introduce the observation that our choices and evaluations of current literature have the effect either of solidifying or of reshaping our sense of the past. The authority of any established canon, after all, is reified by our perception that current work seems to grow almost inevitably out of it (even in opposition or rebellion), and is called into question when what we read appears to have little or no relation to what we recognize as coming before. So, were the larger critical community to begin to attend seriously to the recent outpouring of fine literature by women, this would surely be accompanied by a concomitant researching of the past, by literary historians, in order to account for the present phenomenon. In that process, literary history would itself be altered: works by seventeenth-, eighteenth-, or nineteenth-century women to which we had not previously attended might be given new importance as "precursors" or as prior influences upon present-day authors; while selected male writers might also be granted new prominence as figures whom women today, or even yesterday, needed to reject. I am arguing, in other words, that the choices we make in the present inevitably alter our sense of the past that led to them.

Related to this is the feminist challenge to that patently mendacious critical fallacy that we read the "classics" in order to reconstruct the past "the way it really was," and that we read Shakespeare and Milton in order to apprehend the meanings that they intended. Short of time machines or miraculous resurrections, there is simply no way to know, precisely or surely, what "really was," what Homer intended when he sang, or Milton when he dictated. Critics more acute than I have already pointed up the impossibility of grounding a reading in the imputation of authorial intention because the further removed the author is from us, so too must be her or his systems of knowledge and belief, points of view, and structures of vision (artistic and otherwise).[36] (I omit here the difficulty of finally either proving or disproving the imputation of intentionality because, inescapably, the only appropriate authority is unavailable: deceased.) What we have really come to mean when we speak of competence in reading historical texts, therefore, is the ability to recognize literary conventions which have survived through time—so as to remain operational in the mind of the reader—and, where these are lacking, the ability to translate (or perhaps transform?) the text's ciphers into more current and recognizable shapes. But we never really reconstruct the past in its own terms. What we gain when we read the "classics," then, is neither Homer's Greece nor George Eliot's[37] England *as they knew it* but, rather, an approximation of an already fictively imputed past made available, through our interpretative strategies, for present concerns. Only by understanding this can we put to rest that recurrent delusion that the "continuing relevance" of the classics serves as "testimony to perennial features of human experience."[38] The only "perennial feature" to which our ability to read and reread texts written in previous centuries testifies to our inventiveness—in the sense that all of literary history is a fiction which we daily re-create as we reread it. What distinguishes feminists in this regard is their desire to alter and extend what we take as historically relevant from out of that vast storehouse of our literary inheritance and, further, feminists' recognition of the storehouse for what it really is: a resource for remodeling our literary history, past, present, and future.

---

[36] John Dewey offered precisely this argument in 1934 when he insisted that a work of art "is recreated every time it is esthetically experienced. . . . It is absurd to ask what an artist 'really' meant by his product: he himself would find different meanings in it at different days and hours and in different stages of his own development." Further, he explained, "It is simply an impossibility that anyone today should experience the Parthenon as the devout Athenian contemporary citizen experienced it, any more than the religious statuary of the twelfth century can mean, esthetically, just what it meant to the worshipers of the old period." *Art as Experience* (New York: Capricorn Books, 1958), pp. 108–9.

[37] George Eliot (Mary Ann Evans, 1819–1880), English novelist.

[38] [Kolodny] Charles Altieri, "The Hermeneutics of Literary Indeterminacy: A Dissent from the New Orthodoxy," *New Literary History* 10 (Fall 1978), p. 90.

---

[34] [Kolodny] David Couzens Hoy, "Hermeneutic Circularity, Indeterminacy, and Incommensurability," *New Literary History* 10 (Fall 1978), pp. 166–67.

[35] [Kolodny] Bloom, *Map of Misreading*, p. 36.

2. *Insofar as we are taught how to read, what we engage are not texts but paradigms.* To pursue the logical consequences of the first proposition leads, however uncomfortably, to the conclusion that we appropriate meaning from a text according to what we need (or desire), or in other words, according to the critical assumptions or predispositions (conscious or not) that we bring to it. And we appropriate different meanings, or report different gleanings, at different times—even from the same text—according to our changed assumptions, circumstances, and requirements. This, in essence, constitutes the heart of the second proposition. For insofar as literature is itself a social institution, so, too, reading is a highly socialized—or learned—activity. What makes it so exciting, of course, is that it can be constantly relearned and refined, so as to provide either an individual or an entire reading community, over time, with infinite variations of the same text. It *can* provide that, but, I must add, too often it does not. Frequently our reading habits become fixed, so that each successive reading experience functions, in effect, normatively, with one particular kind of novel stylizing our expectations of those to follow, the stylistic devices of any favorite author (or group of authors) alerting us to the presence or absence of those devices in the works of others, and so on. "Once one has read his first poem," Murray Krieger has observed, "he turns to his second and to the others that will follow thereafter with an increasing series of preconceptions about the sort of activity in which he is indulging. In matters of literary experience, as in other experiences," Krieger concludes, "one is a virgin but once."[39]

For most readers, this is a fairly unconscious process, and not unnaturally, what we are taught to read well and with pleasure when we are young predisposes us to certain specific kinds of adult reading tastes. For the professional literary critic, the process may be no different, but it is at least more conscious. Graduate schools, at their best, are training grounds for competing interpretative paradigms or reading techniques: affective stylistics, structuralism, and semiotic analysis, to name only a few of the more recent entries. The delight we learn to take in the mastery of these interpretative strategies is then often mistakenly construed as our delight in reading specific texts, especially in the case of works that would otherwise be unavailable or even offensive to us. In my own graduate career, for example, with superb teachers to guide me, I learned to take great pleasure in *Paradise Lost,* even though, as both a Jew and a feminist, I can

subscribe neither to its theology nor to its hierarchy of sexual valuation. If, within its own terms (as I have been taught to understand them), the text manipulates my sensibilities and moves me to pleasure—as I will affirm it does—then, at least in part, that must be because, in spite of my real-world alienation from many of its basic tenets, I have been able to enter that text through interpretative strategies which allow me to displace less comfortable observations with others to which I have been taught pleasurably to attend. Though some of my teachers may have called this process "learning to read the text properly," I have now come to see it as learning to effectively manipulate the critical strategies which they taught me so well. Knowing, for example, the poem's debt to epic conventions, I am able to discover in it echoes and reworkings of both lines and situations from Virgil and Homer; placing it within the ongoing Christian debate between Good and Evil, I comprehend both the philosophic and the stylistic significance of Satan's ornate rhetoric as compared with God's majestic simplicity in Book III. But in each case, an interpretative model, already assumed, had guided my discovery of the evidence for it.[40]

When we consider the implications of these observations for the processes of canon formation and for the assignment of aesthetic value, we find ourselves locked in a chicken-and-egg dilemma, unable easily to distinguish as primary the importance of *what* we read as opposed to *how* we have learned to read it. For, simply put, we read well, and with pleasure, what we already know how to read; and what we know how to read is to a large extent dependent upon what we have already read (works from which we developed our expectations and learned our interpretative strategies). What we then choose to read—and, by extension, teach and thereby "canonize"—usually follows upon our previous reading. Radical breaks are tiring, demanding, uncomfortable, and sometimes wholly beyond our comprehension.

Though the argument is not usually couched in precisely these terms, a considerable segment of the most recent feminist rereadings of women writers allows the conclusion that, where those authors have dropped out of sight, it may be due not to any lack of merit in the work but, instead, to an incapacity of predominantly male readers to properly interpret and appreciate women's texts—due, in large part, to a lack of prior acquaintance. The fictions that women compose about the worlds they inhabit may owe a debt to prior, influential works by other women or, simply

---

[39] [Kolodny] Murray Krieger, *Theory of Criticism: A Tradition and Its System* (Baltimore: Johns Hopkins University Press, 1976), p. 6.

[40] [Kolodny] See Stanley Fish, "Normal Circumstances, Literal Language, Direct Speech Acts, the Ordinary, the Everyday, the Obvious, What Goes without Saying, and Other Special Cases," *Critical Inquiry* 4 (Summer 1978), pp. 627–28.

enough, to the daily experience of the writer herself or, more usually, to some combination of the two. The reader coming upon such fiction with knowledge of neither its informing literary traditions nor its real-world contexts will find himself hard pressed, though he may recognize the words on the page, to competently decipher its intended meanings. And this is what makes the studies by Spacks, Moers, Showalter, Gilbert and Gubar, and others so crucial. For, by attempting to delineate the connections and interrelations that make for a female literary tradition, they provide us invaluable aids for recognizing and understanding the unique literary traditions and sex-related contexts out of which women write.

The (usually male) reader who, both by experience and by reading, has never made acquaintance with those contexts—historically, the lying-in room, the parlor, the nursery, the kitchen, the laundry, and so on—will necessarily lack the capacity to fully interpret the dialogue or action embedded therein; for, as every good novelist knows, the meaning of any character's action or statement is inescapably a function of the specific situation in which it is embedded.[41] Virginia Woolf therefore quite properly anticipated the male reader's disposition to write off what he could not understand, abandoning women's writings as offering "not merely a difference of view, but a view that is weak, or trivial, or sentimental because it differs from his own." In her 1929 essay "Women and Fiction," Woolf grappled most obviously with the ways in which male writers and male subject matter had already preempted the language of literature. Yet she was also tacitly commenting on the problem of (male) audience and conventional reading expectations when she speculated that the woman writer might well "find that she is perpetually wishing to alter the established values [in literature]—to make serious what appears insignificant to a man, and trivial what is to him important."[42] "The 'competence' necessary for understanding [a] literary message . . . depends upon a great number of codices," after all; as Cesare Segre has pointed out, to be competent, a reader must either share or at least be familiar with, "in addition to the code language . . . the codes of custom, of society, and of conceptions of the world"[43] (what Woolf meant by "values"). Males ignorant of women's "values" or conceptions of the world will, necessarily, be poor readers of works that in any sense recapitulate their codes.

The problem is further exacerbated when the language of the literary text is largely dependent upon figuration. For it can be argued, as Ted Cohen has shown, that while "in general, and with some obvious qualifications . . . all literal use of language is accessible to all whose language it is . . . figurative use can be inaccessible to all but those who share information about one another's knowledge, beliefs, intentions, and attitudes."[44] There was nothing fortuitous, for example, in Charlotte Perkins Gilman's decision to situate the progressive mental breakdown and increasing incapacity of the protagonist of "The Yellow Wallpaper" in an upstairs room that had once served as a nursery (with barred windows, no less). But a reader unacquainted with the ways in which women have traditionally inhabited a household might not take the initial description of the setting as semantically relevant, and the progressive infantilization of the adult protagonist would thereby lose some of its symbolic implications. Analogously, the contemporary poet who declares, along with Adrienne Rich, the need for "a whole new poetry beginning here" is acknowledging that the materials available for symbolization and figuration from women's contexts will necessarily differ from those that men have traditionally utilized.

> *Vision begins to happen in such a life*
> *as if a woman quietly walked away*
> *from the argument and jargon in a room*
> *and sitting down in the kitchen, began*
> *turning in her lap*
> *bits of yarn, calico and velvet scraps,*
>
>   *   *   *
>
> *pulling the tenets of a life together*
> *with no mere will to mastery,*
> *only care for the many-lived, unending*
> *forms in which she finds herself.*[45]

What, then, is the fate of the woman writer whose competent reading community is composed only of members of her own sex? And what, then, the response of the male critic who, on first looking into Virginia Woolf or Doris Lessing,[46] finds all of the interpretative strategies at his command inadequate to a full and pleasurable deciphering of their

---

[41][Kolodny] Ibid., p. 643.

[42][Kolodny] Virginia Woolf, "Women and Fiction," *Granite and Rainbow: Essays* (London: Hogarth Press, 1958), p. 81.

[43][Kolodny] Cesare Segre, "Narrative Structures and Literary History," *Critical Inquiry* 3 (Winter 1976), pp. 272–73.

[44][Kolodny] Ted Cohen, 'Metaphor and the Cultivation of Intimacy," *Critical Inquiry* 5 (Fall 1978), p. 9.

[45][Kolodny] From Adrienne Rich's "Transcendental Etude," *The Dream of a Common Language: Poems 1974–1977* (New York: W. W. Norton, 1978) pp. 76–77.

[46]Woolf (above, page 885); Doris Lessing (b. 1919), English novelist.

pages? Historically, the result has been the diminished status of women's products and their consequent absence from major canons. Nowadays, however, by pointing out that the act of "interpreting language is no more sexually neutral than language use or the language system itself," feminist students of language like Nelly Furman help us better understand the crucial linkage between our gender and our interpretative, or reading, strategies. Insisting upon "the contribution of the ... reader [in] the active attribution of significance to formal signifiers,"[47] Furman and others promise to shake us all—female and male alike—out of our canonized and conventional aesthetic assumptions.

3. *Since the grounds upon which we assign aesthetic value to texts are never infallible, unchangeable, or universal, we must reexamine not only our aesthetics but, as well, the inherent biases and assumptions informing the critical methods which (in part) shape our aesthetic responses.* I am, on the one hand, arguing that men will be better readers, or appreciators, of women's books when they have read more of them (as women have always been taught to become astute readers of men's texts). On the other hand, it will be noted, the emphasis of my remarks shifts the act of critical judgment from assigning aesthetic valuations to texts and directs it, instead, to ascertaining the adequacy of any interpretative paradigm to a full reading of both female and male writing. My third proposition—and, I admit, perhaps the most controversial—thus calls into question that recurrent tendency in criticism to establish norms for the evaluation of literary works when we might better serve the cause of literature by developing standards for evaluating the adequacy of our critical methods.[48] This does not mean that I wish to discard aesthetic valuation. The choice, as I see it, is not between retaining or discarding aesthetic values; rather, the choice is between having some awareness of what constitutes (at least in part) the bases of our aesthetic responses and going without such an awareness. For it is my view that insofar as aesthetic responsiveness continues to be an integral aspect of our human response system—in part spontaneous, in part learned and educated—we will inevitably develop theories to help explain, formalize, or even initiate those responses.

In challenging the adequacy of received critical opinion or the imputed excellence of established canons, feminist literary critics are essentially seeking to discover how aesthetic value is assigned in the first place, where it resides (in the text or in the reader), and, most important, what validity may really be claimed by our aesthetic "judgments." What ends do those judgments serve, the feminist asks; and what conceptions of the world or ideological stances do they (even if unwittingly) help to perpetuate? In so doing, she points out, among other things, that any response labeled "aesthetic" may as easily designate some immediate experienced moment or event as it may designate a species of nostalgia, a yearning for the components of a simpler past when the world seemed known or at least understandable. Thus the value accorded an opera or a Shakespeare play may well reside in the viewer's immediate viewing pleasure, or it may reside in the play's nostalgic evocation of a once comprehensible and ordered world. At the same time, the feminist confronts, for example, the reader who simply cannot entertain the possibility that women's worlds are symbolically rich, the reader who, like the male characters in Susan Glaspell's 1917 short story "A Jury of Her Peers," has already assumed the innate "insignificance of kitchen things."[49] Such a reader, she knows, will prove himself unable to assign significance to fictions that attend to "kitchen things" and will, instead, judge such fictions as trivial and as aesthetically wanting. For her to take useful issue with such a reader, she must make clear that what appears to be a dispute about aesthetic merit is, in reality, a dispute about the *contexts of judgment;* and what is at issue, then, is the adequacy of the prior assumptions and reading habits brought to bear on the text. To put it bluntly: we have had enough pronouncements of aesthetic valuation for a time; it is now our task to evaluate the imputed norms and normative reading patterns that, in part, led to those pronouncements.

By and large, I think I have made my point. Only to clarify it do I add this coda: when feminists turn their attention to the works of male authors which have traditionally been accorded high aesthetic value and, where warranted, follow Olsen's advice that we assert our "right to say: this is surface, this falsifies reality, this degrades,"[50] such statements do not necessarily mean that we will end up with a diminished canon. To question the source of the aesthetic pleasures we have gained from reading Spenser, Shakespeare, Milton, and so on does not imply that we must deny those pleasures. It means only that aesthetic response is once more invested

---

[47] [Kolodny] Furman, "Study of Women and Language," p. 184.

[48] [Kolodny] "A recurrent tendency in criticism is the establishment of false norms for evaluation of literary works," notes Robert Scholes in *Structuralism in Literature: An Introduction* (New Haven: Yale University Press, 1974), p. 131.

[49] [Kolodny] For a full discussion of the Glaspell short story that takes this problem into account, please see my "A Map for Rereading: Gender and Interpretation of Literary Texts," *New Literary History* 11 (Spring 1980), pp. 451–67.

[50] [Kolodny] Olsen, *Silences*, p. 45.

with epistemological, ethical, and moral concerns. It means, in other words, that readings of *Paradise Lost* which analyze its complex hierarchal structures but fail to note the implications of gender within that hierarchy; or which insist upon the inherent (or even inspired) perfection of Milton's figurative language but fail to note the consequences, for Eve, of her specifically gender-marked weakness, which, like the flowers she attends, requires "propping up"; or which concentrate on the poem's thematic reworking of classical notions of martial and epic prowess into Christian (moral) heroism but fail to note that Eve is stylistically edited out of that process—all such readings, however useful, will no longer be deemed wholly adequate. The pleasures we had earlier learned to take in the poem will not be diminished thereby, but they will be come part of an altered reading attentiveness.

These three propositions I believe to be at the theoretical core of most current feminist literary criticism, whether acknowledged as such or not. If I am correct in this, then that criticism represents more than a profoundly skeptical stance toward all other preexisting and contemporaneous schools and methods, and more than an impassioned demand that the variety and variability of women's literary expression be taken into full account, rather than written off as a caprice and exception, the irregularity in an otherwise regular design. It represents that locus in literary study where, in unceasing effort, female self-consciousness turns in upon itself, attempting to grasp the deepest conditions of its own unique and multiplicitous realities, in the hope, eventually, of altering the very forms through which the culture perceives, expresses, and knows itself. For, if what the larger women's movement looks for in the future is a transformation of the structures of primarily male power which now order our society, then the feminist literary critic demands that we understand the ways in which those structures have been—and continue to be—reified by our literature and by our literary criticism. Thus, along with other "radical" critics and critical schools, though our focus remains the power of the word to both structure and mirror human experience, our overriding commitment is to a radical alteration—an improvement, we hope—in the nature of that experience.

Stanley Fish

b. 1938

Fish's work in the 1960s and 1970s was a major part of developments in reader-oriented criticism. His career charts in many ways the different aspects of the movement. In his early work the aim was, for the most part, to oppose and overcome the objectivist influence of the New Criticism and its attack on the so-called "affective fallacy" (Wimsatt and Beardsley, above, page 1027). For Fish, meaning was a product of the reader's movement through the text so that the whole process of reading became the meaning's locus. Fish remained committed to the stability of the text, however, accepting the notion that the text controlled readers' responses. This led to the problem of subjective relativism unless one could develop some idea of readerly competence (as in Chomsky [above, page 1166] for example). But this move tended to return Fish to the literary object (as it seems to have done in Richards [above, page 856]).

Soon Fish submerged the text entirely in the reader, for he came to regard it as the product of interpretation rather than the object of it. Along with this came the notion of "interpretive communities," which he held controlled what is to be regarded as literature at any given time. Readers always read out of interpretive conventions, being unable to do otherwise. This was Fish's effort to escape from the charge of radical subjectivity, indeed to lay it aside for good.

The next question was how such communities are formed and by whom. This led Fish to issues of power and authority. For him, criticism established "by political and persuasive means" the conventions and interpretive assumptions on which it was grounded. This was for Fish never a critical approach to be advocated; it was inevitable and was a condition that has always existed.

Fish disassociated himself from a common characterization of poststructuralist deconstruction that claimed it led to absolute indeterminacy of meaning. His answer was that "determinacy and decidability are always available, not, however, because of the constraints imposed by language or the world—that is, by entities independent of context—but because of the constraints built into the context or contexts in which we find ourselves operating."

Books by Fish include *John Skelton's Poetry* (1965); *Surprised by Sin* (1971); *Self-Consuming Artifacts* (1972); *The Living Temple* (1978); *Is There a Text in This Class?* (1980); *Doing What Comes Naturally: Change, Rhetoric, and the Nature of Theory in Literary and Legal Studies* (1989); *There Is No Such Thing as Free Speech, and It's a Good Thing* (1994); *Professional Correctness: Literary Study and Political Change* (1995); *The Trouble with Principle* (1999); and *How Milton Works* (2001). See Phillip J. Donnelly, *Rhetorical Faith: The Literary Hermeneutics of Stanley Fish* (2000); Gary A. Olson, *Justifying Belief: Stanley Fish and the Work of Rhetoric* (2002).

Is There a Text in This Class?

On the first day of the new semester a colleague at Johns Hopkins University was approached by a student who, as it turned out, had just taken a course from me. She put to him what I think you would agree is a perfectly straightforward question: "Is there a text in this class?" Responding with a confidence so perfect that he was unaware of it (although in telling the story, he refers to this moment as "walking into the trap"), my colleague said, "Yes; it's the *Norton Anthology of Literature,*" whereupon the trap (set not by the student but by the infinite capacity of language for being appropriated) was sprung: "No, no," she said, "I mean in this class do we believe in poems and things, or is it just us?" Now it is possible (and for many tempting) to read this anecdote as an illustration of the dangers that follow upon listening to people like me who preach the instability of the text and the unavailability of determinate meanings; but in what follows I will try to read it as an illustration of how baseless the fear of these dangers finally is.

Of the charges levied against what Meyer Abrams has recently called the New Readers (Derrida, Bloom, Fish) the most persistent is that these apostles of indeterminacy and undecidability ignore, even as they rely upon, the "norms and possibilities" embedded in language, the "linguistic meanings" words undeniably have, and thereby invite us to abandon "our ordinary realm of experience in speaking, hearing, reading and understanding" for a world in which "no text can mean anything in particular" and where "we can never say just what anyone means by anything he writes."[1] The charge is that literal or normative meanings are overriden by the actions of willful interpreters. Suppose we examine this indictment in the context of the present example. What, exactly, is the normative or literal or linguistic meaning of "Is there a text in this class?"

Within the framework of contemporary critical debate (as it is reflected in the pages, say, of *Critical Inquiry*) there would seem to be only two ways of answering this question: either there *is* a literal meaning of the utterance and we should be able to say what it is, or there are as many meanings as there are readers and no one of them is literal. But the answer suggested by my little story is that the utterance has *two* literal meanings: within the circumstances assumed by my colleague (I don't mean that he took the step of assuming them, but that he was already stepping within them) the utterance is obviously a question about whether or not there is a required textbook in this particular course; but within the circumstances to which he was alerted by his student's corrective response, the utterance is just as obviously a question about the instructor's position (within the range of positions available in contemporary literary theory) on the status of the text. Notice that we do not have here a case of indeterminacy or undecidability but of a determinacy and decidability that do not always have the same shape and that can, and in this instance do, change. My colleague was not hesitating between two (or more) possible meanings of the utterance; rather, he immediately apprehended what seemed to be an inescapable meaning, given his prestructured understanding of the situation, and then he immediately apprehended another inescapable meaning when that understanding was altered. Neither meaning was imposed (a favorite word in the anti-new-reader polemics) on a more normal one by a private, idiosyncratic interpretive act; both interpretations were a function of precisely the public and constituting norms (of language and understanding) invoked by Abrams. It is just that these norms are not embedded in the language (where they may be read out by anyone with sufficiently clear, that is, unbiased, eyes) but inhere in an institutional structure within which one hears utterances as already organized with reference to certain assumed purposes and goals. Because both my colleague and his student are situated in that institution, their interpretive activities are not free, but what constrains them are the understood practices and assumptions of the institution and not the rules and fixed meanings of a language system.

Another way to put this would be to say that neither reading of the question—which we might for convenience's sake label as "Is there a text in this class?"$_1$ and "Is there a text in this class?"$_2$—would be immediately available to any native speaker of the language. "Is there a text in this class?"$_1$ is interpretable or readable only by someone who already knows what is included under the general rubric "first day of class" (what concerns animate students, what bureaucratic matters must be attended to before instruction begins) and who therefore hears the utterance under the aegis of that knowledge, which is not applied after the fact but is responsible for the shape the fact immediately has. To someone whose consciousness is not already informed by that knowledge, "Is there a text in this class?"$_1$ would be just as unavailable as "Is there a text in this class?"$_2$ would be to someone who was not already aware of the disputed issues in contemporary literary theory. I am not saying that for some readers or hearers the question would be wholly unin-

---

"Is There a Text in This Class?" is reprinted from *Is There a Text in This Class?*, published by Harvard University Press, 1980.
[1][Fish] M. H. Abrams [above, page 1087], "The Deconstructive Angel," *Critical Inquiry* 3, no. 3 (Spring 1977), 431, 434.

telligible (indeed, in the course of this essay I will be arguing that unintelligibility, in the strict or pure sense, is an impossibility), but that there are readers and hearers for whom the intelligibility of the question would have neither of the shapes it had, in a temporal succession, for my colleague. It is possible, for example, to imagine someone who would hear or intend the question as an inquiry about the location of an object, that is, "I think I left my text in this class; have you seen it?" We would then have an "Is there a text in this class?"$_3$ and the possibility, feared by the defenders of the normative and determinate, of an endless succession of numbers, that is, of a world in which every utterance has an infinite plurality of meanings. But that is not what the example, however it might be extended, suggests at all. In any of the situations I have imagined (and in any that I might be able to imagine) the meaning of the utterance would be severely constrained, not after it was heard but in the ways in which it *could,* in the first place, be heard. An infinite plurality of meanings would be a fear only if sentences existed in a state in which they were not already embedded in, and had come into view as a function of, some situation or other. That state, if it could be located, would be the normative one, and it would be disturbing indeed if the norm were free-floating and indeterminate. But there is no such state; sentences emerge only in situations, and within those situations, the normative meaning of an utterance will always be obvious or at least accessible, although within another situation that same utterance, no longer the same, will have another normative meaning that will be no less obvious and accessible. (My colleague's experience is precisely an illustration.) This does not mean that there is no way to discriminate between the meanings an utterance will have in different situations, but that the discrimination will already have been made by virtue of our being in a situation (we are never not in one) and that in another situation the discrimination will also have already been made, but differently. In other words, while at any one point it is always possible to order and rank "Is there a text in this class?"$_1$ and "Is there a text in this class?"$_2$ (because they will always have already been ranked), it will never be possible to give them an immutable once-and-for-all ranking, a ranking that is independent of their appearance or nonappearance in situations (because it is only in situations that they do or do not appear).

Nevertheless, there is a distinction to be made between the two that allows us to say that, in a limited sense, one is more normal than the other: for while each is perfectly normal in the context in which their literalness is immediately obvious (the successive contexts occupied by my colleague), as things stand now, one of those contexts is surely more available, and therefore more likely to be the perspec-

tive within which the utterance is heard, than the other. Indeed, we seem to have here an instance of what I would call "institutional nesting": if "Is there a text in this class?"$_1$ is hearable only by those who know what is included under the rubric "first day of class," and if "Is there a text in this class?"$_2$ is hearable only by those whose categories of understanding include the concerns of contemporary literary theory, then it is obvious that in a random population presented with the utterance, more people would "hear" "Is there a text in this class?"$_1$ than "Is there a text in this class?"$_2$; and, moreover, that while "Is there a text in this class?"$_1$ could be immediately hearable by someone for whom "Is there a text in this class?"$_2$ would have to be laboriously explained, it is difficult to imagine someone capable of hearing "Is there a text in this class?"$_2$ who was not already capable of hearing "Is there a text in this class."$_1$ (One is hearable by anyone in the profession and by most students and by many workers in the book trade, and the other only by those in the profession who would not think it peculiar to find, as I did recently, a critic referring to a phrase "made popular by Lacan.")[2] To admit as much is not to weaken my argument by reinstating the category of the normal, because the category as it appears in that argument is not transcendental but institutional; and while no institution is so universally in force and so perdurable that the meanings it enables will be normal for ever, some institutions or forms of life are so widely lived in that for a great many people the meanings they enable seem "naturally" available and it takes a special effort to see that they are the products of circumstances.

The point is an important one, because it accounts for the success with which an Abrams or an E. D. Hirsch can appeal to a shared understanding of ordinary language and argue from that understanding to the availability of a core of determinate meanings. When Hirsch offers "The air is crisp" as an example of a "verbal meaning" that is accessible to all speakers of the language, and distinguishes what is shareable and determinate about it from the associations that may, in certain circumstances, accompany it (for example, "I should have eaten less at supper." "Crisp air reminds me of my childhood in Vermont"),[3] he is counting on his readers to agree so completely with his sense of what that shared and normative verbal meaning is that he does not bother even to specify it; and although I have not taken a survey, I would venture to guess that his optimism, with respect to this particular example, is well founded. That is,

---

[2] Lacan (above, page 990).

[3] [Fish] E. D. Hirsch, *Validity in Interpretation* (New Haven: Yale University Press, 1967), pp. 218–19.

most, if not all, of his readers immediately understand the utterance as a rough meteorological description predicting a certain quality of the local atmosphere. But the "happiness" of the example, far from making Hirsch's point (which is always, as he has recently reaffirmed, to maintain "the stable determinacy of meaning")[4] makes mine. The obviousness of the utterance's meaning is not a function of the values its words have in a linguistic system that is independent of context; rather, it is because the words are heard as already embedded in a context that they have a meaning that Hirsch can then cite as obvious. One can see this by embedding the words in another context and observing how quickly another "obvious" meaning emerges. Suppose, for example, we came upon "The air is crisp" (which you are even now hearing as Hirsch assumes you hear it) in the middle of a discussion of music ("When the piece is played correctly the air is crisp"); it would immediately be heard as a comment on the performance by an instrument or instruments of a musical air. Moreover, it would *only* be heard that way, and to hear it in Hirsch's way would require an effort on the order of a strain. It could be objected that in Hirsch's text "The air is crisp"$_1$ has no contextual setting at all; it is merely presented, and therefore any agreement as to its meaning must be because of the utterance's acontextual properties. But there *is* a contextual setting and the sign of its presence is precisely the absence of any reference to it. That is, it is impossible even to think of a sentence independently of a context, and when we are asked to consider a sentence for which no context has been specified, we will automatically hear it in the context in which it has been most often encountered. Thus Hirsch invokes a context by not invoking it; by not surrounding the utterance with circumstances, he directs us to imagine it in the circumstances in which it is most likely to have been produced; and to so imagine it is already to have given it a shape that seems at the moment to be the only one possible.

What conclusions can be drawn from these two examples? First of all, neither my colleague nor the reader of Hirsch's sentence is constrained by the meanings words have in a normative linguistic system; and yet neither is free to confer on an utterance any meaning he likes. Indeed, "confer" is exactly the wrong word because it implies a two stage procedure in which a reader or hearer first scrutinizes an utterance and *then* gives it a meaning. The argument of the preceding pages can be reduced to the assertion that there is no such first stage, that one hears an utterance within, and not as preliminary to determining, a knowledge

of its purposes and concerns, and that to so hear it is already to have assigned it a shape and given it a meaning. In other words, the problem of how meaning is determined is only a problem if there is a point at which its determination has not yet been made, and I am saying that there is no such point.

I am *not* saying that one is never in the position of having to self-consciously figure out what an utterance means. Indeed, my colleague is in just such a position when he is informed by his student that he has not heard her question as she intended it ("No, No, I mean in this class do we believe in poems and things, or is it just us?") and therefore must now figure it out. But the "it" in this (or any other) case is not a collection of words waiting to be assigned a meaning but an utterance whose already assigned meaning has been found to be inappropriate. While my colleague has to begin all over again, he does not have to begin from square one; and indeed he never was at square one, since from the very first his hearing of the student's question was informed by his assumption of what its concerns could possibly be. (That is why he is not "free" even if he is unconstrained by determinate meanings.) It is that assumption rather than his performance within it that is challenged by the student's correction. She tells him that he has mistaken her meaning, but this is not to say that he has made a mistake in combining her words and syntax into a meaningful unit; it is rather that the meaningful unit he immediately discerns is a function of a mistaken identification (made before she speaks) of her intention. He was prepared as she stood before him to hear the kind of thing students ordinarily say on the first day of class, and therefore that is precisely what he heard. He has not misread the text (his is not an error in calculation) but mis*pre*read the text, and if he is to correct himself he must make another (pre)determination of the structure of interests from which her question issues. This, of course, is exactly what he does and the question of how he does it is a crucial one, which can best be answered by first considering the ways in which he *didn't* do it.

He didn't do it by attending to the literal meaning of her response. That is, this is not a case in which someone who has been misunderstood clarifies her meaning by making more explicit, by varying or adding to her words in such a way as to render their sense inescapable. Within the circumstances of utterance as he has assumed them her words are perfectly clear, and what she is doing is asking him to imagine other circumstances in which the same words will be equally, but differently, clear. Nor is it that the words she does add ("No, No, I mean . . .") direct him to those circumstances by picking them out from an inventory of all possible ones. For this to be the case there would have to be an inherent relationship between the words she speaks and a

[4] [Fish] E. D. Hirsch, *The Aims of Interpretation* (Chicago: University of Chicago Press, 1976), p. 1.

particular set of circumstances (this would be a higher level literalism) such that any competent speaker of the language hearing those words would immediately be referred to that set. But I have told the story to several competent speakers of the language who simply didn't get it, and one friend—a professor of philosophy—reported to me that in the interval between his hearing the story and my explaining it to him (and just how I was able to do that is another crucial question) he found himself asking "What kind of joke is this and have I missed it?" For a time at least he remained able only to hear "Is there a text in this class" as my colleague first heard it; the student's additional words, far from leading him to another hearing, only made him aware of his distance from it. In contrast, there are those who not only get the story but get it before I tell it; that is, they know in advance what is coming as soon as I say that a colleague of mine was recently asked, "Is there a text in this class?" Who are these people and what is it that makes their comprehension of the story so immediate and easy? Well, one could say, without being the least bit facetious, that they are the people who come to hear me speak because they are the people who already know my position on certain matters (or know that I will *have* a position). That is, they hear, "Is there a text in this class?" even as it appears at the beginning of the anecdote (or for that matter as a title of an essay) in the light of their knowledge of what I am likely to do with it. They hear it coming from *me,* in circumstances which have committed me to declaring myself on a range of issues that are sharply delimited.

My colleague was finally able to hear it in just that way, as coming from me, not because I was there in his classroom, nor because the words of the student's question pointed to me in a way that would have been obvious to any hearer, but because he was able to think of me in an office three doors down from his telling students that there are no determinate meanings and that the stability of the text is an illusion. Indeed, as he reports it, the moment of recognition and comprehension consisted of his saying to himself, "Ah, there's one of Fish's victims!" He did not say this because her words identified her as such but because his ability to see her as such informed his perception of her words. The answer to the question "How did he get from her words to the circumstances within which she intended him to hear them?" is that he must already be thinking within those circumstances in order to be able to hear her words as referring to them. The question, then, must be rejected, because it assumes that the construing of sense leads to the identification of the context of utterance rather than the other way around. This does not mean that the context comes first and that once it has been identified the construing of sense can begin.

This would be only to reverse the order of precedence, whereas precedence is beside the point because the two actions it would order (the identification of context and the making of sense) occur simultaneously. One does not say "Here I am in a situation; now I can begin to determine what these words mean." To be in a situation is to see the words, these or any other, as already meaningful. For my colleague to realize that he may be confronting one of my victims is *at the same time* to hear what she says as a question about his theoretical beliefs.

But to dispose of one "how" question is only to raise another: if her words do not lead him to the context of her utterance, how does he get there? Why did he think of me telling students that there were no determinate meanings and not think of someone or something else? First of all, he might well have. That is, he might well have guessed that she was coming from another direction (inquiring, let us say, as to whether the focus of this class was to be the poems and essays or our responses to them, a question in the same line of country as hers but quite distinct from it) or he might have simply been stymied, like my philosopher friend, confined, in the absence of an explanation, to his first determination of her concerns and unable to make any sense of her words other than the sense he originally made. How, then, did he do it? In part, he did it because he *could* do it; he was able to get to this context because it was already part of his repertoire for organizing the world and its events. The category "one of Fish's victims" was one he already had and didn't have to work for. Of course, *it* did not always have *him,* in that his world was not always being organized by it, and it certainly did not have him at the beginning of the conversation; but it was available to him, and he to it, and all he had to do was to recall it or be recalled to it for the meanings it subtended to emerge. (Had it not been available to him, the career of his comprehension would have been different and we will come to a consideration of that difference shortly.)

This, however, only pushes our inquiry back further. How or why was he recalled to it? The answer to this question must be probabilistic and it begins with the recognition that when something changes, not everything changes. Although my colleague's understanding of his circumstances is transformed in the course of this conversation, the circumstances are still understood to be academic ones, and within that continuing (if modified) understanding, the directions his thought might take are already severely limited. He still presumes, as he did at first, that the student's question has something to do with university business in general, and with English literature in particular, and it is the organizing rubrics associated with these areas of experience that are likely to occur to him. One of those rubrics is "what-goes-on-in-other-classes" and one of those other classes is mine. And so, by a route that is neither entirely unmarked nor wholly determined, he comes to me and to the notion "one of Fish's victims" and to a new construing of what his student has been saying.

Of course that route would have been much more circuitous if the category "one of Fish's victims" was not already available to him as a device for producing intelligibility. Had that device not been part of his repertoire, had he been incapable of being recalled to it because he never knew it in the first place, how would he have proceeded? The answer is that he could not have proceeded at all, which does not mean that one is trapped forever in the categories of understanding at one's disposal (or the categories at whose disposal one is), but that the introduction of new categories or the expansion of old ones to include new (and therefore newly seen) data must always come from the outside or from what is perceived, for a time, to be the outside. In the event that he was unable to identify the structure of her concerns because it had never been his (or he its), it would have been her obligation to explain it to him. And here we run up against another instance of the problem we have been considering all along. She could not explain it to him by varying or adding to her words, by being more explicit, because her words will only be intelligible if he already has the knowledge they are supposed to convey, the knowledge of the assumptions and interests from which they issue. It is clear, then, that she would have to make a new start, although she would not have to start from scratch (indeed, starting from scratch is never a possibility); but she would have to back up to some point at which there was a shared agreement as to what was reasonable to say so that a new and wider basis for agreement could be fashioned. In this particular case, for example, she might begin with the fact that her interlocutor already knows what a text is; that is, he has a way of thinking about it that is responsible for his hearing of her first question as one about bureaucratic classroom procedures. (You will remember that "he" in these sentences is no longer my colleague but someone who does not have his special knowledge.) It is that way of thinking that she must labor to extend or challenge, first, perhaps, by pointing out that there are those who think about the text in other ways, and then by trying to find a category of his own understanding which might serve as an analogue to the understanding he does not yet share. He might, for example, be familiar with those psychologists who argue for the constitutive power of perception, or with Gombrich's theory of the beholder's share, or with that philosophical tradition in which the stability of objects has always been a matter of dispute. The

example must remain hypothetical and skeletal, because it can only be fleshed out after a determination of the particular beliefs and assumptions that would make the explanation necessary in the first place; for whatever they were, they would dictate the strategy by which she would work to supplant or change them. It is when such a strategy has been successful that the import of her words will become clear, not because she has reformulated or refined them but because they will now be read or heard within the same system of intelligibility from which they issue.

In short, this hypothetical interlocutor will in time be brought to the same point of comprehension my colleague enjoys when he is able to say to himself, "Ah, there's one of Fish's victims," although presumably he will say something very different to himself if he says anything at all. The difference, however, should not obscure the basic similarities between the two experiences, one reported, the other imagined. In both cases the words that are uttered are immediately heard within a set of assumptions about the direction from which they could possibly be coming, and in both cases what is required is that the hearing occur within another set of assumptions in relation to which the same words ("Is there a text in this class?") will no longer be the same. It is just that while my colleague is able to meet that requirement by calling to mind a context of utterance that is already a part of his repertoire, the repertoire of his hypothetical stand-in must be expanded to include that context so that should he some day be in an analogous situation, he would be able to call it to mind.

The distinction, then, is between already having an ability and having to acquire it, but it is not finally an essential distinction, because the routes by which that ability could be exercised on the one hand, and learned on the other, are so similar. They are similar first of all because they are similarly *not* determined by words. Just as the student's words will not direct my colleague to a context he already has, so will they fail to direct someone not furnished with that context to its discovery. And yet in neither case does the absence of such a mechanical determination mean that the route one travels is randomly found. The change from one structure of understanding to another is not a rupture but a modification of the interests and concerns that are already in place; and because they are already in place, they constrain the direction of their own modification. That is, in both cases the hearer is already in a situation informed by tacitly known purposes and goals, and in both cases he ends up in another situation whose purposes and goals stand in some elaborated relation (of contrast, opposition, expansion, extension) to those they supplant. (The one relation in which they could not stand is no relation at all.) It is just that in one case the network of elaboration (from the text as an obviously physical object to the question of whether or not the text is a physical object) has already been articulated (although not all of its articulations are in focus at one time; selection is always occurring), while in the other the articulation of the network is the business of the teacher (here the student) who begins, necessarily, with what is already given.

The final similarity between the two cases is that in neither is success assured. It was no more inevitable that my colleague tumble to the context of his student's utterance than it would be inevitable that she could introduce that context to someone previously unaware of it; and, indeed, had my colleague remained puzzled (had he simply not thought of me), it would have been necessary for the student to bring him along in a way that was finally indistinguishable from the way she would bring someone to a new knowledge, that is, by beginning with the shape of his present understanding.

I have lingered so long over the unpacking of this anecdote that its relationship to the problem of authority in the classroom and in literary criticism may seem obscure. Let me recall you to it by recalling the contention of Abrams and others that authority depends upon the existence of a determinate core of meaning because in the absence of such a core there is no normative or public way of construing what anyone says or writes, with the result that interpretation becomes a matter of individual and private construings none of which is subject to challenge or correction. In literary criticism this means that no interpretation can be said to be better or worse than any other, and in the classroom this means that we have no answer to the student who says my interpretation is as valid as yours. It is only if there is a shared basis of agreement at once guiding interpretation and providing a mechanism for deciding between interpretations that a total debilitating relativism can be avoided.

But the point of my analysis has been to show that while "Is there a text in this class?" does not have a determinate meaning, a meaning that survives the sea change of situations, in any situation we might imagine the meaning of the utterance is either perfectly clear or capable, in the course of time, of being clarified. What is it that makes this possible, if it is not the "possibilities and norms" already encoded in language? How does communication ever occur if not by reference to a public and stable norm? The answer, implicit in everything I have already said, is that communication occurs within situations and that to be in a situation is already to be in possession of (or to be possessed by) a structure of assumptions, of practices understood to be relevant in relation to purposes and goals that are already in place; and it is within the assumption of these purposes and

goals that any utterance is *immediately* heard. I stress immediately because it seems to me that the problem of communication, as someone like Abrams poses it, is a problem only because he assumes a distance between one's receiving of an utterance and the determination of its meaning—a kind of dead space when one has only the words and then faces the task of construing them. If there were such a space, a moment before interpretation began, then it would be necessary to have recourse to some mechanical and algorithmic procedure by means of which meanings could be calculated and in relation to which one could recognize mistakes. What I have been arguing is that meanings come already calculated, not because of norms embedded in the language but because language is always perceived, from the very first, within a structure of norms. That structure, however, is not abstract and independent but social; and therefore it is not a single structure with a privileged relationship to the process of communication as it occurs in any situation but a structure that changes when one situation, with its assumed background of practices, purposes, and goals, has given way to another. In other words, the shared basis of agreement sought by Abrams and others is never not already found, although it is not always the same one.

Many will find in this last sentence, and in the argument to which it is a conclusion, nothing more than a sophisticated version of the relativism they fear. It will do no good, they say, to speak of norms and standards that are context specific, because this is merely to authorize an infinite plurality of norms and standards, and we are still left without any way of adjudicating between them and between the competing systems of value of which they are functions. In short, to have many standards is to have no standards at all.

On one level this counterargument is unassailable, but on another level it is finally beside the point. It is unassailable as a general and theoretical conclusion: the positing of context- or institution-specific norms surely rules out the possibility of a norm whose validity would be recognized by everyone, no matter what his situation. But it is beside the point for any particular individual, for since everyone is situated somewhere, there is no one for whom the absence of an asituational norm would be of any practical consequence, in the sense that his performance or his confidence in his ability to perform would be impaired. So that while it is generally true that to have many standards is to have none at all, it is not true for anyone in particular (for there is no one in a position to speak "generally"), and therefore it is a truth of which one can say "it doesn't matter."

In other words, while relativism is a position one can entertain, it is not a position one can occupy. No one can *be* a relativist, because no one can achieve the distance from his own beliefs and assumptions which would result in their being no more authoritative *for him* than the beliefs and assumptions held by others, or, for that matter, the beliefs and assumptions he himself used to hold. The fear that in a world of indifferently authorized norms and values the individual is without a basis for action is groundless because no one is indifferent to the norms and values that enable his consciousness. It is in the name of personally held (in fact they are doing the holding) norms and values that the individual acts and argues, and he does so with the full confidence that attends belief. When his beliefs change, the norms and values to which he once gave unthinking assent will have been demoted to the status of opinions and become the objects of an analytical and critical attention; but that attention will itself be enabled by a new set of norms and values that are, for the time being, as unexamined and undoubted as those they displace. The point is that there is never a moment when one believes nothing, when consciousness is innocent of any and all categories of thought, and whatever categories of thought are operative at a given moment will serve as an undoubted ground.

Here, I suspect, a defender of determinate meaning would cry "solipsist" and argue that a confidence that had its source in the individual's categories of thought would have no public value. That is, unconnected to any shared and stable system of meanings, it would not enable one to transact the verbal business of everyday life; a shared intelligibility would be impossible in a world where everyone was trapped in the circle of his own assumptions and opinions. The reply to this is that an individual's assumptions and opinions are not "his own" in any sense that would give body to the fear of solipsism. That is, *he* is not their origin (in fact it might be more accurate to say that they are his); rather, it is their prior availability which delimits in advance the paths that his consciousness can possibly take. When my colleague is in the act of construing his student's question ("Is there a text in this class?"), none of the interpretive strategies at his disposal are uniquely his, in the sense that he thought them up; they follow from his preunderstanding of the interests and goals that could possibly animate the speech of someone functioning within the institution of academic America, interests and goals that are the particular property of no one in particular but which link everyone for whom their assumption is so habitual as to be unthinking. They certainly

link my colleague and his student, who are able to communicate and even to reason about one another's intentions, not, however, because their interpretive efforts are constrained by the shape of an independent language but because their shared understanding of what could possibly be at stake in a classroom situation results in language appearing to them in the same shape (or successions of shapes). That shared understanding is the basis of the confidence with which they speak and reason, but its categories are their own only in the sense that as actors within an institution they automatically fall heir to the institution's way of making sense, its systems of intelligibility. That is why it is so hard for someone whose very being is defined by his position within an institution (and if not this one, then some other) to explain to someone outside it a practice or a meaning that seems to him to require no explanation, because he regards it as natural. Such a person, when pressed, is likely to say, "but that's just the way it's done" or "but isn't it obvious" and so testify that the practice or meaning in question is community property, as, in a sense, he is too.

We see then that (1) communication does occur, despite the absence of an independent and context-free system of meanings, that (2) those who participate in this communication do so confidently rather than provisionally (they are not relativists), and that (3) while their confidence has its source in a set of beliefs, those beliefs are not individual-specific or idiosyncratic but communal and conventional (they are not solipsists).

Of course, solipsism and relativism are what Abrams and Hirsch fear and what lead them to argue for the necessity of determinate meaning. But if, rather than acting on their own, interpreters act as extensions of an institutional community, solipsism and relativism are removed as fears because they are not possible modes of being. That is to say, the condition required for someone to be a solipsist or relativist, the condition of being independent of institutional assumptions and free to originate one's own purposes and goals, could never be realized, and therefore there is no point in trying to guard against it. Abrams, Hirsch, and company spend a great deal of time in a search for the ways to limit and constrain interpretation, but if the example of my colleague and his student can be generalized (and obviously I think it can be), what they are searching for is never not already found. In short, my message to them is finally not challenging, but consoling—not to worry.

Pierre Bourdieu

1930–2002

French sociologist and theorist Pierre Bourdieu taught in Moulins, Algeria, and the University of Paris before accepting a position in 1964 at L'École des Hautes Études en Sciences Sociales, where he founded the very influential Center for the Sociology of Education and Culture. From 1982 until his death, he taught at the Collège de France. From his earliest sociological study, *Sociologie de l'Algérie* (1958; *The Algerians,* 1962), Bourdieu resisted the systematizing tendencies of other social scientific (and particularly anthropological) thinkers, to attend to the socially acquired dispositions *(habitus)* and the subtle, practical modes of institution formation that shape daily life, well exemplified in his *Le Sens pratique* (1980; *The Logic of Practice,* 1990).

Bourdieu's studies of art, particularly *La Distinction* (1979; *Distinction,* 1984), *Les Règles de l'Art* (1992; *The Rules of Art,* 1996), and *The Field of Cultural Production: Essays on Art and Literature* (1993), are characterized by his insistence on examining the social function of artistic practices, from his tracing of aesthetic judgment as a fact of social distinction (in a hierarchical sense), to the role of art in shaping the idea of intellectual autonomy. More broadly, Bourdieu's studies of the logic of social practice and his models of cultural institutions, from museums and schools to professional organizations, foreground the generative idea of "cultural capital," explored in detail in his work with Jean-Claude Passeron, *Héritiers, les étudiants et la culture* (1966; *The Inheritors: French Students and Their Relation to Culture,* 1979). Bourdieu's approach to sociology, being reflective as well as empirical, places his work in a sometimes uneasy relation both to more quantitatively determined views of the field and to disciplines in the humanities and arts. The extraordinary range of his studies, however, and his ability to fuse the immediate and practical with the philosophical, has made his work particularly attractive as a model, most evidently in the United States in the work of John Guillory (below, page 1500). In all of his studies, he is particularly attuned to the nuances of social and political power as it shapes and conditions identity—and like Louis Althusser (above, page 1297), he finds the evidence of such shaping virtually everywhere in the social fabric.

A substantial portion of Bourdieu's work is available in translation. See especially: *Academic Discourse: Linguistic Misunderstanding and Professorial Power,* by Pierre Bourdieu, Jean-Claude Passeron, and Monique de Saint Martin, with contributions by Christian Baudelot and Guy Vincent, tr. Richard Teese (1965, tr. 1994); *Distinction: A Social Critique of the Judgement of Taste,* tr. Richard Nice (1979, tr. 1984); *The Logic of Practice,* tr. Richard Nice (1990); *Language and Symbolic Power,* edited and introduced by John B. Thompson, tr. Gino Raymond and Matthew Adamson (1991); *The Field of Cultural Production: Essays on Art and Literature,* ed. Randal Johnson (1993); *Homo Academicus,* tr. Peter Collier (1984, tr. 1988); *In Other Words: Essays Towards a Reflexive Sociology,* tr. Matthew Adamson (1990); *The Political Ontology of Martin*

Heidegger, tr. Peter Collier (1991); *The Rules of Art: Genesis and Structure of the Literary Field,* tr. Susan Emanuel (1996); *Masculine Domination,* tr. Richard Nice (2001). Useful critical studies include: Derek Robbins, *The Work of Pierre Bourdieu: Recognizing Society* (1991) and *Bourdieu and Culture* (2000); David Swartz, *Culture & Power: The Sociology of Pierre Bourdieu* (1997); Michael Grenfell and David James, with Philip Hodkinson, Diane Reay, and Derek Robbins, *Bourdieu and Education: Acts of Practical Theory* (1998); Jeremy F. Lane, *Pierre Bourdieu: A Critical Introduction* (2000).

from

Language and Symbolic Power

The Production and Reproduction of Legitimate Language

'As you say, my good knight! There ought to be laws to protect the body of acquired knowledge.

Take one of our good pupils, for example: modest and diligent, from his earliest grammar classes he's kept a little notebook full of phrases.

After hanging on the lips of his teachers for twenty years, he's managed to build up an intellectual stock in trade; doesn't it belong to him as if it were a house, or money?'

P. Claudel, Le Soulier de Satin

'Language forms a kind of wealth, which all can make use of at once without causing any diminution of the store, and which thus admits a complete community of enjoyment; for all, freely participating in the general treasure, unconsciously aid in its preservation.'[1] In describing symbolic appropriation as a sort of mystical participation, universally and uniformly accessible and therefore excluding any form of dispossession, Auguste Comte offers an exemplary expression of the illusion of linguistic communism which haunts all linguistic theory. Thus, Saussure[2] resolves the question of the social and economic conditions of the appropriation of language without ever needing to raise it. He

does this by resorting, like Comte, to the metaphor of treasure, which he applies indiscriminately to the 'community' and the individual: he speaks of 'inner treasure,' of a 'treasure deposited by the practice of speech in subjects belonging to the same community,' of 'the sum of individual treasures of language,' and of the 'sum of imprints deposited in each brain.'

Chomsky has the merit of explicitly crediting the speaking subject in his universality with the perfect competence which the Saussurian tradition granted him tacitly: 'Linguistic theory is concerned primarily with an *ideal speaker-listener, in a completely homogeneous speech-community, who knows its language perfectly* and is unaffected by such *grammatically irrelevant* conditions as memory limitations, distractions, shifts of attention or interest, and errors (random or characteristic) in applying his knowledge of the language in actual performance. This seems to me to have been the position of the founders of modern general linguistics, and no cogent reason for modifying it has been offered.'[3] In short, from this standpoint, Chomskyan 'competence' is simply another name for Saussure's *langue.*[4] Corresponding to language as a 'universal treasure,' as the collective property of the whole group, there is linguistic competence as the 'deposit' of this 'treasure' in each individual or as the participation of each member of the 'linguistic community' in this public good. The shift in vocabulary conceals the *fictio juris* through which Chomsky, converting the immanent laws of legitimate discourse into universal norms of correct linguistic practice, sidesteps the question of the economic and social conditions of the acquisition of the legitimate

---

"The Production and Reproduction of Legitimate Language" is Chapter One of *Language and Symbolic Power* (Cambridge, Mass.: Harvard University Press, 1991).

[1] [Bourdieu] A. Comte [1798–1857], *System of Positive Polity,* 4 vols (London: Longmans Green and Co., 1875–77), vol. 2, p. 213.

[2] Saussure (above, page 786).

[3] [Bourdieu] N. Chomsky [above, page 1166], *Aspects of the Theory of Syntax* (Cambridge, Mass.: MIT Press, 1965), p. 3 (my italics). See also N. Chomsky and M. Halle, *The Sound Pattern of English* (New York: Harper and Row, 1968), p. 3.

[4] [Bourdieu] Chomsky himself makes this identification explicitly, at least in so far as competence is 'knowledge of grammar' (Chomsky and Halle, *The Sound Pattern of English*) or 'generative grammar internalized by someone' (N. Chomsky, *Current Issues in Linguistic Theory* (London and The Hague: Mouton, 1964), p. 10).

competence and of the constitution of the market in which this definition of the legitimate and the illegitimate is established and imposed.[5]

Official Language and Political Unity

As a demonstration of how linguists merely incorporate into their theory a pre-constructed object, ignoring its *social laws of construction* and masking its social genesis, there is no better example than the passage in his *Course in General Linguistics* in which Saussure discusses the relation between language and space.[6] Seeking to prove that it is not space which defines language but language which defines its space, Saussure observes that neither dialects nor languages have natural limits, a phonetic innovation (substitution of 's' for Latin 'c,' for example) determining its own area of diffusion by the intrinsic force of its autonomous logic, through the set of speaking subjects who are willing to make themselves its bearers. This philosophy of history, which makes the internal dynamics of a language the sole principle of the limits of its diffusion, conceals the properly political process of unification whereby a determinate set of 'speaking subjects' is led in practice to accept the official language.

Saussure's *langue,* a code both legislative and communicative which exists and subsists independently of its users ('speaking subjects') and its uses *(parole),* has in fact all the properties commonly attributed to official language. As opposed to dialect, it has benefited from the institutional conditions necessary for its generalized codification and imposition. Thus known and recognized (more or less completely) throughout the whole jurisdiction of a certain political authority, it helps in turn to reinforce the authority which is the source of its dominance. It does this by ensuring among all members of the 'linguistic community,' traditionally defined,

since Bloomfield, as a 'group of people who use the same system of linguistic signs,'[7] the minimum of communication which is the precondition for economic production and even for symbolic domination.

To speak of *the* language, without further specification, as linguists do, is tacitly to accept the *official* definition of the *official* language of a political unit. This language is the one which, within the territorial limits of that unit, imposes itself on the whole population as the only legitimate language, especially in situations that are characterized in French as more *officielle* (a very exact translation of the word 'formal' used by English-speaking linguists).[8] Produced by authors who have the authority to write, fixed and codified by grammarians and teachers who are also charged with the task of inculcating its mastery, the language is a *code,* in the sense of a cipher enabling equivalences to be established between sounds and meanings, but also in the sense of a system of norms regulating linguistic practices.

The official language is bound up with the state, both in its genesis and in its social uses. It is in the process of state formation that the conditions are created for the constitution of a unified linguistic market, dominated by the official language. Obligatory on official occasions and in official places (schools, public administrations, political institutions, etc.), this state language becomes the theoretical norm against which all linguistic practices are objectively measured. Ignorance is no excuse; this linguistic law has its body of jurists—the grammarians—and its agents of regulation and imposition—the teachers—who are empowered *universally* to subject the linguistic performance of speaking subjects to examination and to the legal sanction of academic qualification.

In order for one mode of expression among others (a particular language in the case of bilingualism, a particular use of language in the case of a society divided into classes) to impose itself as the only legitimate one, the linguistic market has to be unified and the different dialects (of class, region or ethnic group) have to be measured practically against the legitimate language or usage. Integration into a

---

[5] [Bourdieu] The fact that Habermas [below, page 1429] crowns his pure theory of 'communicative competence'—an essentialist analysis of the situation of communication—with a declaration of intentions regarding the degree of repression and the degree of development of the productive forces does not mean that he escapes from the ideological effect of absolutizing the relative which is inscribed in the silences of the Chomskyan theory of competence (J. Habermas, 'Toward a theory of communicative competence,' in H. P. Dreitzel (ed.), *Recent Sociology,* no. 2 (New York: Macmillan, 1970), pp. 114–48). Even if it is purely methodological and provisional, and intended only to 'make possible' the study of 'the distortions of pure intersubjectivity,' *idealization* (which is clearly seen in the use of notions such as 'mastery of the dialogue-constitutive universals' or 'speech situation determined by pure subjectivity') has the practical effect of removing from relations of communication the power relations which are implemented within them in a transfigured form. This is confirmed by the uncritical borrowing of concepts such as 'illocutionary force,' which tends to locate the power of words in words themselves rather than in the institutional conditions of their use.

[6] [Bourdieu] F. de Saussure, *Course in General Linguistics,* tr. W. Baskin (Glasgow: Collins, 1974), pp. 199–203.

[7] [Bourdieu] L. Bloomfield, *Language* (London: George Allen, 1958), p. 29. Just as Saussure's theory of language forgets that a language does not impose itself by its own force but derives its geographical limits from a political act of institution, an arbitrary act misrecognized as such (and misrecognized by the science of language), so Bloomfield's theory of the 'linguistic community' ignores the political and institutional conditions of 'intercomprehension.'

[8] [Bourdieu] The adjective 'formal,' which can be used to describe a language that is guarded, polished and tense, as opposed to one that is familiar and relaxed, or a person that is starchy, stiff and formalist, can also mean the same as the French adjective *officiel* (as in 'a formal dinner'), that is, conducted in full accordance with the rules, in due and proper order, by formal agreement.

single 'linguistic community,' which is a product of the political domination that is endlessly reproduced by institutions capable of imposing universal recognition of the dominant language, is the condition for the establishment of relations of linguistic domination.

The 'Standard' Language: A 'Normalized' Product

Like the different crafts and trades which, before the advent of large-scale industry, constituted, in Marx's[9] phrase, so many separate 'enclosures,' local variants of the *langue d'oïl* differed from one parish to another until the eighteenth century. This is still true today of the regional dialects and, as the dialecticians' maps show, the phonological, morphological and lexicological features are distributed in patterns which are never entirely superimposable and which only ever correspond to religious or administrative boundaries through rare coincidence.[10] In fact, in the absence of *objectification* in writing and especially of the quasi-legal *codification* which is inseparable from the constitution of an official language, 'languages' exist only in the practical state, i.e. in the form of so many linguistic habitus which are at least partially orchestrated, and of the oral productions of these habitus.[11] So long as a language is only expected to ensure a minimum of mutual understanding in the (very rare) encounters between people from neighbouring villages or different regions, there is no question of making one usage the norm for another (despite the fact that the differences perceived may well serve as pretexts for declaring one superior to the other).

> Until the French Revolution, the process of linguistic unification went hand in hand with the process of constructing the monarchical state. The 'dialects,' which often possessed some of the properties attributed to 'languages' (since most of

them were used in written form to record contracts, the minutes of local assemblies, etc.), and literary languages (such as the poetic language of the *pays d'oc*), like artificial languages distinct from each of the dialects used over the whole territory in which they were current, gave way progressively, from the fourteenth century on, at least in the central provinces of the *pays d'oïl,* to the common language which was developed in Paris in cultivated circles and which, having been promoted to the status of official language, was used in the form given to it by scholarly, i.e. written, uses. Correlatively, the popular and purely oral uses of all the regional dialects which had thus been supplanted degenerated into *patois,* as a result of the compartmentalization (linked to the abandonment of the written form) and internal disintegration (through lexical and syntactic borrowing) produced by the social devaluation which they suffered. Having been abandoned to the peasants, they were negatively and pejoratively defined in opposition to distinguished or literate usages. One indication of this, among many others, is the shift in the meaning assigned to the word *patois,* which ceased to mean 'incomprehensible speech' and began to refer to 'corrupted and coarse speech, such as that of the common people' (Furetière's Dictionary, 1690).

The linguistic situation was very different in the *langue d'oc* regions. Not until the sixteenth century, with the progressive constitution of an administrative organization linked to royal power (involving the appearance of a multitude of subordinate administrative agents, lieutenants, provosts, magistrates, etc.), did the Parisian dialect begin to take over from the various *langue d'oc* dialects in legal documents. The imposition of French as the official language did not result in the total abolition of the written use of dialects, whether in administrative, political or even literary texts (dialect literature continued to exist during the *ancien régime*), and their oral uses remained predominant. A situation of bilingualism tended to arise. Whereas the lower classes, particularly the peasantry, were limited to the local dialect, the aristocracy, the commercial and business bourgeoisie and particularly the literate petite bourgeoisie (precisely those who responded to Abbé Grégoire's survey and who had, to varying degrees, attended the Jesuit colleges, which were

---

[9] Marx (above, page 607).

[10] [Bourdieu] Only by transposing the representation of the national language is one led to think that regional dialects exist, themselves divided into subdialects—an idea flatly contradicted by the study of dialectics (see F. Brunot, *Histoire de la langue française des origines à nos jours* (Paris: Colin, 1968), pp. 77–78). And it is no accident that nationalism almost always succumbs to this illusion since, once it triumphs, it inevitably reproduces the process of unification whose effects it denounced.

[11] [Bourdieu] This is seen in the difficulties raised by the translation of decrees during the Revolutionary period in France. Because the practical language was devoid of political vocabulary and divided into dialects, it was necessary to forge an intermediate language. (The advocates of the *langues d'oc* do the same thing nowadays, fixing and standardizing orthography and thereby producing a language not readily accessible to ordinary speakers.)

institutions of linguistic unification) had access much more frequently to the use of the official language, written or spoken, while at the same time possessing the dialect (which was still used in most private and even public situations), a situation in which they were destined to fulfil the function of intermediaries.

The members of these local bourgeoisies of priests, doctors or teachers, who owed their position to their mastery of the instruments of expression, had everything to gain from the Revolutionary policy of linguistic unification. Promotion of the official language to the status of national language gave them that *de facto* monopoly of politics, and more generally of communication with the central government and its representatives, that has defined local notables under all the French republics.

The imposition of the legitimate language in opposition to the dialects and *patois* was an integral part of the political strategies aimed at perpetuating the gains of the Revolution through the production and the reproduction of the 'new man.' Condillac's theory, which saw language as a *method,* made it possible to identify revolutionary language with revolutionary thought. To reform language, to purge it of the usages linked to the old society and impose it in its purified form, was to impose a thought that would itself be purged and purified. It would be naïve to attribute the policy of linguistic unification solely to the technical needs of communication between the different parts of the territory, particularly between Paris and the provinces, or to see it as the direct product of a state centralism determined to crush 'local characteristics.' The conflict between the French of the revolutionary intelligentsia and the dialects or *patois* was a struggle for symbolic power in which what was at stake was the *formation* and *re-formation* of mental structures. In short, it was not only a question of communicating but of gaining recognition for a new language of authority, with its new political vocabulary, its terms of address and reference, its metaphors, its euphemisms and the representation of the social world which it conveys, and which, because it is linked to the new interests of new groups, is inexpressible in the local idioms shaped by usages linked to the specific interests of peasant groups.

Thus, only when the making of the 'nation,' an entirely abstract group based on law, creates new usages and functions does it become indispensable to forge a *standard* language, impersonal and anonymous like the official uses it has to serve, and by the same token to undertake the work of normalizing the products of the linguistic habitus. The dictionary is the exemplary result of this labour of codification and normalization. It assembles, by scholarly recording, the totality of the *linguistic resources* accumulated in the course of time and, in particular, all the possible uses of the same word (or all the possible expressions of the same sense), juxtaposing uses that are socially at odds, and even mutually exclusive (to the point of marking those which exceed the bounds of acceptability with a sign of exclusion such as *Obs., Coll.* or *Sl.*). It thereby gives a fairly exact image of language as Saussure understands it, 'the sum of individual treasuries of language,' which is predisposed to fulfil the functions of a 'universal' code. The *normalized* language is capable of functioning outside the constraints and without the assistance of the situation, and is suitable for transmitting and decoding by any sender and receiver, who may know nothing of one another. Hence it concurs with the demands of bureaucratic predictability and calculability, which presuppose universal functionaries and clients, having no other qualities than those assigned to them by the administrative definition of their condition.

In the process which leads to the construction, legitimation and imposition of an official language, the educational system plays a decisive role: 'fashioning the similarities from which that community of consciousness which is the cement of the nation stems.' And Georges Davy goes on to state the function of the schoolmaster, a *maître à parler* (teacher of speaking) who is thereby also a *maître à penser* (teacher of thinking): 'He [the primary school teacher], by virtue of his function, works daily on the faculty of expression of every idea and every emotion: on language. In teaching the same clear, fixed language to children who know it only very vaguely or who even speak various dialects or *patois,* he is already inclining them quite naturally to see and feel things in the same way; and he works to build the common consciousness of the nation.'[12] The Whorfian—or, if you like, Humboldtian—theory of language which underlies this view of education as an instrument of 'intellectual and moral integration,' in Durkheim's sense, has an affinity with the Durkheimian theory of consensus, an affinity which is also indicated by the shift of the word 'code' from law to

---

[12] [Bourdieu] G. Davy, *Éléments de sociologie* (Paris: Vrin, 1950), p. 233.

linguistics.[13] The code, in the sense of cipher, that governs written language, which is identified with correct language, as opposed to the implicitly inferior conversational language, acquires the force of law in and through the educational system.[14]

The educational system, whose scale of operations grew in extent and intensity throughout the nineteenth century,[15] no doubt directly helped to devalue popular modes of expression, dismissing them as 'slang' and 'gibberish' (as can be seen from teachers' marginal comments on essays) and to impose recognition of the legitimate language. But it was doubtless the dialectical relation between the school system and the labour market—or, more precisely, between the unification of the educational (and linguistic) market, linked to the introduction of educational qualifications valid nation-wide, independent (at least officially) of the social or regional characteristics of their bearers, and the unification of the labour market (including the development of the state administration and the civil service)—which played the most decisive role in devaluing dialects and establishing the new hierarchy of linguistic practices.[16] To induce the holders of dominated linguistic competences to collaborate in the destruction of their instruments of expression, by endeavouring for example to speak 'French' to their children or requiring them to speak 'French' at home, with the more or less explicit intention of increasing their value on the educational market, it was necessary for the school system to be perceived as the principal (indeed, the only) means of access to administrative positions which were all the more attractive in areas where industrialization was least developed. This conjunction of circumstances was found in the regions of 'dialect' (except the east of France) rather than in the *patois* regions of northern France.

Unification of the Market and Symbolic Domination

In fact, while one must not forget the contribution which the political will to unification (also evident in other areas, such as law) makes to the *construction* of the language which linguists accept as a natural datum, one should not regard it as the sole factor responsible for the generalization of the use of the dominant language. This generalization is a dimension of the unification of the market in symbolic goods which accompanies the unification of the economy and also of cultural production and circulation. This is seen clearly in the case of the market in matrimonial exchanges, in which 'products' which would previously have circulated in the protected enclosure of local markets, with their own laws of price formation, are suddenly devalued by the generalization of the dominant criteria of evaluation and the discrediting of 'peasant values,' which leads to the collapse of the value of the peasants, who are often condemned to celibacy. Visible in all areas of practice (sport, song, clothing, housing, etc.), the process of unification of both the production and the circulation of economic and cultural goods entails the progressive obsolescence of the earlier mode of production of the habitus and its products. And it is clear why, as sociolinguists have often observed, women are more disposed to adopt the legitimate language (or the legitimate pronunciation): since they are inclined towards docility with regard to the dominant usages both by the sexual division of labour, which makes them specialize in the sphere of consumption, and by the logic of marriage, which is their main if not their only avenue of social advancement and through which they circulate upwards, women are predisposed to accept, from school onwards, the new demands of the market in symbolic goods.

Thus the effects of domination which accompany the unification of the market are always exerted through a whole set of specific institutions and mechanisms, of which the specifically linguistic policy of the state and even the overt interventions of pressure groups form only the most superficial aspect. The fact that these mechanisms presuppose the political or economic unification which they help in turn to reinforce in no way implies that the progress of the official language is to be attributed to the direct effectiveness of legal or

---

[13] Benjamin Lee Whorf (1897–1941), American linguist; Humboldt (above, page 523); Émile Durkheim (1858–1917), French sociologist. [Bourdieu] Humboldt's linguistic theory, which was generated from the celebration of the linguistic 'authenticity' of the Basque people and the exaltation of the language–nation couplet, has an intelligible relationship with the conception of the unifying mission of the university which Humboldt deployed in the creation of the University of Berlin.

[14] [Bourdieu] Grammar is endowed with real legal effectiveness via the educational system, which places its power of certification at its disposal. If grammar and spelling are sometimes the object of ministerial decrees (such as that of 1900 on the agreement of the past participle conjugated with *avoir*), this is because, through examinations and the qualifications which they make it possible to obtain, they govern access to jobs and social positions.

[15] [Bourdieu] Thus, in France, the numbers of schools and of pupils enrolled and, correlatively, the volume and spatial dispersion of the teaching profession increased steadily after 1816—well before the official introduction of compulsory schooling.

[16] [Bourdieu] This would probably explain the apparently paradoxical relationship between the linguistic remoteness of the different regions in the nineteenth century and their contribution to the ranks of the civil service in the twentieth century. The regions which, according to the survey carried out by Victor Duruy in 1864, had the highest proportion of adults who could not speak French, and of 7- to 13-year-olds unable to read or speak it, were providing a particularly high proportion of civil servants in the first half of the twentieth century, a phenomenon which is itself known to be linked to a high rate of secondary schooling.

quasi-legal constraints. (These can at best impose the acquisition, but not the generalized use and therefore the autonomous reproduction, of the legitimate language.) All symbolic domination presupposes, on the part of those who submit to it, a form of complicity which is neither passive submission to external constraint nor a free adherence to values. The recognition of the legitimacy of the official language has nothing in common with an explicitly professed, deliberate and revocable belief, or with an intentional act of accepting a 'norm.' It is inscribed, in a practical state, in dispositions which are impalpably inculcated, through a long and slow process of acquisition, by the sanctions of the linguistic market, and which are therefore adjusted, without any cynical calculation or consciously experienced constraint, to the chances of material and symbolic profit which the laws of price formation characteristic of a given market objectively offer to the holders of a given linguistic capital.[17]

The distinctiveness of symbolic domination lies precisely in the fact that it assumes, of those who submit to it, an attitude which challenges the usual dichotomy of freedom and constraint. The 'choices' of the habitus (for example, using the 'received' uvular 'r' instead of the rolled 'r' in the presence of legitimate speakers) are accomplished without consciousness or constraint, by virtue of the dispositions which, although they are unquestionably the product of social determinisms, are also constituted outside the spheres of consciousness and constraint. The propensity to reduce the search for causes to a search for responsibilities makes it impossible to see that *intimidation,* a symbolic violence which is not aware of what it is (to the extent that it implies no *act of intimidation*) can only be exerted on a person predisposed (in his habitus) to feel it, whereas others will ignore it. It is already partly true to say that the cause of the timidity lies in the relation between the situation or the intimidating person (who may deny any intimidating intention) and the person intimidated, or rather, between the social conditions of production of each of them. And little by little, one has to take account thereby of the whole social structure.

There is every reason to think that the factors which are most influential in the formation of the habitus are transmitted without passing through language and consciousness, but through suggestions inscribed in the most apparently insignificant aspects of the things, situations and practices of everyday life. Thus the modalities of practices, the ways of looking, sitting, standing, keeping silent, or even of speaking ('reproachful looks' or 'tones,' 'disapproving glances' and so

on) are full of injunctions that are powerful and hard to resist precisely because they are silent and insidious, insistent and insinuating. (It is this *secret code* which is explicitly denounced in the crises characteristic of the domestic unit, such as marital or teenage crises: the apparent disproportion between the violence of the revolt and the causes which provoke it stems from the fact that the most anodyne actions or words are now seen for what they are—as injunctions, intimidations, warnings, threats—and denounced as such, all the more violently because they continue to act below the level of consciousness and beneath the very revolt which they provoke.) The power of suggestion which is exerted through things and persons and which, instead of telling the child what he must do, tells him what he is, and thus leads him to become durably what he has to be, is the condition for the effectiveness of all kinds of symbolic power that will subsequently be able to operate on a habitus predisposed to respond to them. The relation between two people may be such that one of them has only to appear in order to impose on the other, without even having to want to, let alone formulate any command, a definition of the situation and of himself (as intimidated, for example), which is all the more absolute and undisputed for not having to be stated.

The recognition extorted by this invisible, silent violence is expressed in explicit statements, such as those which enable Labov to establish that one finds the same *evaluation* of the phoneme 'r' among speakers who come from different classes and who therefore differ in their actual *production* of 'r.' But it is never more manifest than in all the corrections, whether *ad hoc* or permanent, to which dominated speakers, as they strive desperately for correctness, consciously or unconsciously subject the stigmatized aspects of their pronunciation, their diction (involving various forms of euphemism) and their syntax, or in the disarray which leaves them 'speechless,' 'tongue-tied,' 'at-a loss for words,' as if they were suddenly dispossessed of their own language.[18]

Distinctive Deviations and Social Value

Thus, if one fails to perceive both the special value objectively accorded to the legitimate use of language and the social foundations of this privilege, one inevitably falls into one or other of two opposing errors. Either one unconsciously absolutizes that which is objectively relative and in that sense arbitrary, namely the dominant usage, failing to look beyond

---

[17] [Bourdieu] This means that 'linguistic customs' cannot be changed by decree as the advocates of an interventionist policy of 'defence of the language' often seem to imagine.

[18] [Bourdieu] The 'disintegrated' language which surveys record when dealing with speakers from the dominated classes is thus a product of the survey relationship.

the properties of language itself, such as the complexity of its syntactic structure, in order to identify the basis of the value that is accorded to it, particularly in the educational market; or one escapes this form of fetishism only to fall into the naïvety *par excellence* of the scholarly relativism which forgets that the naïve gaze is not relativist, and ignores the fact of legitimacy, through an arbitrary relativization of the dominant usage, which is socially recognized as legitimate, and not only by those who are dominant.

> To reproduce in scholarly discourse the fetishizing of the legitimate language which actually takes place in society, one only has to follow the example of Basil Bernstein, who describes the properties of the 'elaborated code' without relating this social product to the social conditions of its production and reproduction, or even, as one might expect from the sociology of education, to its academic conditions. The 'elaborated code' is thus constituted as the absolute norm of all linguistic practices which then can only be conceived in terms of the logic of *deprivation*. Conversely, ignorance of what popular and educated usage owe to their objective relations and to the structure of the relation of domination between classes, which they reproduce in their own logic, leads to the *canonization* as such of the 'language' of the dominated classes. Labov leans in this direction when his concern to rehabilitate 'popular speech' against the theorists of deprivation leads him to contrast the verbosity and pompous verbiage of middle-class adolescents with the precision and conciseness of black children from the ghettos. This overlooks the fact that, as he himself has shown (with the example of recent immigrants who judge deviant accents, including their own, with particular severity), the linguistic 'norm' is imposed on all members of the same 'linguistic community,' most especially in the educational market and in all formal situations in which verbosity is often *de rigueur.*

Political unification and the accompanying imposition of an official language establish relations between *the different uses of the same language* which differ fundamentally from the theoretical relations (such as that between *mouton* and 'sheep' which Saussure cites as the basis for the arbitrariness of the sign) between different languages, spoken by politically and economically independent groups. All linguistic practices are measured against the legitimate practices, i.e. the practices of those who are dominant. The probable

value objectively assigned to the linguistic productions of different speakers and therefore the relation which each of them can have to the language, and hence to his own production, is defined within the system of practically competing variants which is actually established whenever the extra-linguistic conditions for the constitution of a linguistic market are fulfilled.

Thus, for example, the linguistic differences between people from different regions cease to be incommensurable particularisms. Measured *de facto* against the single standard of the 'common' language, they are found wanting and cast into the outer darkness of *regionalisms,* the 'corrupt expressions and mispronunciations' which schoolmasters decry.[19] Reduced to the status of quaint or vulgar jargons, in either case unsuitable for formal occasions, popular uses of the official language undergo a systematic devaluation. A system of *sociologically pertinent* linguistic oppositions tends to be constituted, which has nothing in common with the system of *linguistically pertinent* linguistic oppositions. In other words, the differences which emerge from the confrontation of speech varieties are not reducible to those the linguist constructs in terms of his own criterion of pertinence. However great the proportion of the functioning of a language that is not subject to variation, there exists, in the area of pronunciation, diction and even grammar, a whole set of differences significantly associated with social differences which, though negligible in the eyes of the linguist, are pertinent from the sociologist's standpoint because they belong to a system of linguistic oppositions which is the *retranslation* of a system of social differences. A structural sociology of language, inspired by Saussure but constructed in opposition to the abstraction he imposes, must take as its object *the relationship between the structured systems of sociologically pertinent linguistic differences and the equally structured systems of social differences.*

The social uses of language owe their specifically social value to the fact that they tend to be organized in systems of differences (between prosodic and articulatory or lexical and syntactic variants) which reproduce, in the symbolic order of differential deviations, the system of social

---

[19] [Bourdieu] Conversely, when a previously dominated language achieves the status of an official language, it undergoes a *revaluation* which profoundly changes its users' relationship with it. So-called linguistic conflicts are therefore not so unrealistic and irrational (which does not mean that they are directly inspired by self-interest) as is supposed by those who only consider the (narrowly defined) economic stakes. The reversal of the symbolic relations of power and of the hierarchy of the values placed on the competing languages has entirely real economic and political effects, such as the appropriation of positions and economic advantages reserved for holders of the legitimate competence, or the symbolic profits associated with possession of a prestigious, or at least unstigmatized, social identity.

differences. To speak is to appropriate one or other of the expressive styles already constituted in and through usage and objectively marked by their position in a hierarchy of styles which expresses the hierarchy of corresponding social groups. These styles, systems of differences which are both classified and classifying, ranked and ranking, mark those who appropriate them. And a spontaneous stylistics, armed with a practical sense of the equivalences between the two orders of differences, apprehends social classes through classes of stylistic indices.

In emphasizing the linguistically pertinent constants at the expense of the sociologically significant variations in order to construct that artefact which is the 'common' language, the linguist proceeds as if the *capacity to speak,* which is virtually universal, could be identified with *the socially conditioned way of realizing this natural capacity,* which presents as many variants as there are social conditions of acquisition. The competence adequate to produce sentences that are likely to be understood may be quite inadequate to produce sentences that are likely to be *listened to,* likely to be recognized as *acceptable* in all the situations in which there is occasion to speak. Here again, social acceptability is not reducible to mere grammaticality. Speakers lacking the legitimate competence are *de facto* excluded from the social domains in which this competence is required, or are condemned to silence. What is rare, then, is not the capacity to speak, which, being part of our biological heritage, is universal and therefore essentially non-distinctive,[20] but rather the competence necessary in order to speak the legitimate language which, depending on social inheritance, re-translates social distinctions into the specifically symbolic logic of differential deviations, or, in short, distinction.[21]

The constitution of a linguistic market creates the conditions for an objective competition in and through which the legitimate competence can function as linguistic capital, producing a *profit of distinction* on the occasion of each social exchange. Because it derives in part from the scarcity of the products (and of the corresponding competences), this profit does not correspond solely to the cost of training.

The cost of training is not a simple, socially neutral notion. To an extent which varies depending on national traditions in education, the historical period and the academic discipline in question, it includes expenditure which may far exceed the minimum 'technically' required in order to ensure the transmission of the strictly defined competence (if indeed it is possible to give a purely technical definition of the training necessary and sufficient to fulfil a function and of the function itself, bearing in mind that 'role distance'—distance from the function—enters increasingly into the definition of the function as one moves up the hierarchy of functions). In some cases, for example, the duration of study (which provides a good measure of the economic cost of training) tends to be valued for its own sake, independently of the result it produces (encouraging, among the 'elite schools,' a kind of competition in the sheer length of courses). In other cases—not that the two options are mutually exclusive—the social quality of the competence acquired, which is reflected in the symbolic modality of practices, i.e. in the *manner* of performing technical acts and implementing the competence, appears as inseparable from the *slowness* of the acquisition, short or 'crash' courses always being suspected of leaving on their products the marks of 'cramming' or the stigmata of 'catching up.' This conspicuous consumption of training (i.e. of time), an apparent technical wastage which fulfils social functions of legitimation, enters into the value socially attributed to a socially guaranteed competence (which means, nowadays, one 'certified' by the educational system).

Since the profit of distinction results from the fact that the supply of products (or speakers) corresponding to a given level of linguistic (or, more generally, cultural) qualification is lower than it would be if all speakers had benefited from the conditions of acquisition of the legitimate competence to the same extent as the holders of the rarest competence,[22] it is logically distributed as a function of the chances of access to these conditions, that is, as a function of the position occupied in the social structure.

---

[20] [Bourdieu] Only the *optional* can give rise to effects of *distinction.* As Pierre Encrevé has shown, in the case of obligatory liaisons—those which are always observed by all speakers, including the lower classes—there is no room for manoeuvre. When the structural constraints of the language are suspended, as with optional liaisons, the leeway reappears, with the associated effects of distinction.

[21] [Bourdieu] There is clearly no reason to take sides in the debate between the nativists (over or not), for whom the acquisition of the capacity to speak presupposes the existence of an innate disposition, and the empiricists, who emphasize the learning process. So long as not everything is inscribed in nature and the acquisition process is something more than a simple maturation, there exist linguistic differences capable of functioning as signs of social distinction.

[22] [Bourdieu] The hypothesis of equal chances of access to the conditions of acquisition of the legitimate linguistic competence is a simple *mental experiment* designed to bring to light one of the *structural effects* of inequality.

Despite certain appearances, we could not be further from the Saussurian model of *homo linguisticus* who, like the economic subject in the Walrasian tradition, is formally free to do as he likes in his verbal productions (free, for example, to say 'tat' for 'hat,' as children do) but can be understood, can exchange and communicate only on condition that he conforms to the rules of the common code. This market, which knows only pure, perfect competition among agents who are as interchangeable as the products they exchange and the 'situations' in which they exchange, and who are all identically subject to the principle of the maximization of informative efficiency (analogous to the principle of the maximization of utilities), is, as will shortly become clearer, as remote from the real linguistic market as the 'pure' market of the economists is from the real economic market, with its monopolies and oligopolies.

Added to the specific effect of distinctive rarity is the fact that, by virtue of the relationship between the system of linguistic differences and the system of economic and social differences, one is dealing not with a relativistic universe of differences capable of relativizing one another, but with a hierarchical universe of deviations with respect to a form of speech that is (virtually) universally recognized as legitimate, i.e. as the standard measure of the value of linguistic products. The dominant competence functions as linguistic capital, securing a profit of distinction in its relation to other competences only in so far as certain conditions (the unification of the market and the unequal distribution of the chances of access to the means of production of the legitimate competence, and to the legitimate places of expression) are continuously fulfilled, so that the groups which possess that competence are able to impose it as the only legitimate one in the formal markets (the fashionable, educational, political and administrative markets) and in most of the linguistic interactions in which they are involved.[23]

It is for this reason that those who seek to defend a threatened linguistic capital, such as knowledge of the clas-

sical languages in present-day France, are obliged to wage a total struggle. One cannot save the *value* of a competence unless one saves the market, in other words, the whole set of political and social conditions of production of the producers/consumers. The defenders of Latin or, in other contexts, of French or Arabic, often talk as if the language they favour could have some value outside the market, by intrinsic virtues such as its 'logical' qualities; but, in practice, they are defending the market. The position which the educational system gives to the different languages (or the different cultural contents) is such an important issue only because this institution has the monopoly in the large-scale production of producers/consumers, and therefore in the reproduction of the market without which the social value of the linguistic competence, its capacity to function as linguistic capital, would cease to exist.

The Literary Field and the Struggle for Linguistic Authority

Thus, through the medium of the structure of the linguistic field, conceived as a system of specifically linguistic relations of power based on the unequal distribution of linguistic capital (or, to put it another way, of the chances of assimilating the objectified linguistic resources), the structure of the space of expressive styles reproduces in its own terms the structure of the differences which objectively separate conditions of existence. In order fully to understand the structure of this field and, in particular, the existence, within the field of linguistic production, of a sub-field of restricted production which derives its fundamental properties from the fact that the producers within it produce first and foremost for other producers, it is necessary to distinguish between the capital necessary for the simple production of more or less legitimate ordinary speech, on the one hand, and the capital of instruments of expression (presupposing appropriation of the resources deposited in objectified form in libraries—books, and in particular in the 'classics,' grammars and dictionaries) which is needed to produce a written discourse worthy of being published, that is to say, made official, on the other. This production of instruments of production, such as rhetorical devices, genres, legitimate styles and manners and, more generally, all the formulations destined to be 'authoritative' and to be cited as examples of 'good usage,' confers on those who engage in it a power over language and thereby over the ordinary users of language, as well as over their capital.

The legitimate language no more contains within itself the power to ensure its own perpetuation in time than it has

---

[23] [Bourdieu] Situations in which linguistic productions are explicitly subjected to evaluation, such as examinations or job interviews, recall the evaluation which takes place in every linguistic exchange. Numerous surveys have shown that linguistic characteristics have a very strong influence on academic success, employment opportunities, career success, the attitude of doctors (who pay more attention to bourgeois patients and their discourse, e.g. giving them less pessimistic diagnoses), and more generally on the recipients' inclination to co-operate with the sender, to assist him or give credence to the information he provides.

the power to define its extension in space. Only the process of continuous creation, which occurs through the unceasing struggles between the different authorities who compete within the field of specialized production for the monopolistic power to impose the legitimate mode of expression, can ensure the permanence of the legitimate language and of its value, that is, of the recognition accorded to it. It is one of the generic properties of fields that the struggle for specific stakes masks the objective collusion concerning the principles underlying the game. More precisely, the struggle tends constantly to produce and reproduce the game and its stakes by reproducing, primarily in those who are directly involved, but not in them alone, the practical commitment to the value of the game and its stakes which defines the recognition of legitimacy. What would become of the literary world if one began to argue, not about the value of this or that author's style, but about the value of arguments about style? The game is over when people start wondering if the cake is worth the candle. The struggles among writers over the legitimate art of writing contribute, through their very existence, to producing both the legitimate language, defined by its distance from the 'common' language, and belief in its legitimacy.

It is not a question of the symbolic power which writers, grammarians or teachers may exert over the language in their personal capacity, and which is no doubt much more limited than the power they can exert over culture (for example, by imposing a new definition of legitimate literature which may transform the 'market situation'). Rather, it is a question of the contribution they make, independently of any intentional pursuit of distinction, to the production, consecration and imposition of a distinct and distinctive language. In the collective labour which is pursued through the struggles for what Horace called *arbitrium et just et norma loquendi*, writers—more or less authorized authors—have to reckon with the grammarians, who hold the monopoly of the consecration and canonization of legitimate writers and writing. They play their part in constructing the legitimate language by selecting, from among the products on offer, those which seem to them worthy of being consecrated and incorporated into the legitimate competence through educational inculcation, subjecting them, for this purpose, to a process of normalization and codification intended to render them consciously assimilable and therefore easily reproducible. The grammarians, who, for their part, may find allies among

establishment writers and in the academies, and who take upon themselves the power to set up and impose norms, tend to consecrate and codify a particular use of language by rationalizing it and 'giving reason' to it. In so doing they help to determine the value which the linguistic products of the different users of the language will receive in the different markets—particularly those most directly subject to their control, such as the educational market—by delimiting the universe of acceptable pronunciations, words or expressions, and fixing a language censored and purged of all popular usages, particularly the most recent ones.

The variations corresponding to the different configurations of the relation of power between the authorities, who constantly clash in the field of literary production by appealing to very different principles of legitimation, cannot disguise the structural invariants which, in the most diverse historical situations, impel the protagonists to resort to the same strategies and the same arguments in order to assert and legitimate their right to legislate on language and in order to denounce the claims of their rivals. Thus, against the 'fine style' of high society and the writers' claim to possess an instinctive art of good usage, the grammarians always invoke 'reasoned usage,' the 'feel for the language' which comes from knowledge of the principles of 'reason' and 'taste' which constitute grammar. Conversely, the writers, whose pretensions were most confidently expressed during the Romantic period, invoke genius against the rule, flouting the injunctions of those whom Hugo disdainfully called 'grammatists.'[24]

The objective dispossession of the dominated classes may never be intended as such by any of the actors engaged in literary struggles (and there have, of course, always been

---

[24] [Bourdieu] Rather than rehearse innumerable quotations from writers or grammarians which would only take on their full meaning if accompanied by a thorough historical analysis of the state of the field in which they were produced in each case, I shall refer readers who would like to get a concrete idea of this permanent struggle to B. Quemada, *Les dictionnaires du français moderne, 1539–1863* (Paris: Didier, 1968), pp. 193, 204, 207, 210, 216, 226, 228, 229, 230 n. 1, 231, 233, 237, 239, 241, 242, and Brunot, *Histoire de la langue française,* 11–13 and *passim*. A similar division of roles and strategies between writers and grammarians emerges from Haugen's account of the struggle for control over the linguistic planning of Norwegian: see E. Haugen, *Language Conflict and Language Planning; The Case of Norwegian* (Cambridge, Mass.: Harvard University Press, 1966), esp. pp. 296ff.

writers who, like Hugo, claimed to 'revolutionize dictionaries' or who sought to mimic popular speech). The fact remains that this dispossession is inseparable from the existence of a body of professionals, objectively invested with the monopoly of the legitimate use of the legitimate language, who produce for their own use a special language predisposed to fulfil, *as a by-product,* a social function of distinction in the relations between classes and in the struggles they wage on the terrain of language. It is not unconnected, moreover, with the existence of the educational system which, charged with the task of sanctioning heretical products in the name of grammar and inculcating the specific norms which block the effects of the laws of evolution, contributes significantly to constituting the dominated uses of language as such by consecrating the dominant use as the only legitimate one, by the mere fact of inculcating it. But one would obviously be missing the essential point if one related the activity of artists or teachers directly to the effect to which it objectively contributes, namely, the devaluation of the common language which results from the very existence of a literary language. Those who operate in the literary field contribute to symbolic domination only because the effects that their position in the field and its associated interests lead them to pursue always conceal from themselves and from others the external effects which are a by-product of this very misrecognition.

The properties which characterize linguistic excellence may be summed up in two words: distinction and correctness. The work performed in the literary field produces the appearances of an original language by resorting to a set of derivations whose common principle is that of a deviation from the most frequent, i.e. 'common,' 'ordinary,' 'vulgar,' usages. Value always arises from deviation, *deliberate or not,* with respect to the most widespread usage, 'commonplaces,' 'ordinary sentiments,' 'trivial' phrases, 'vulgar' expressions, 'facile' style.[25] In the uses of language as in lifestyles, all definition is relational. Language that is 'recherché,' 'well chosen,' 'elevated,' 'lofty,' 'dignified' or 'distinguished' contains a negative reference (the very words used to name it show this) to 'common' 'everyday,' 'ordinary,' 'spoken,' 'colloquial,' 'familiar' language and, beyond this, to 'popular,' 'crude,' 'coarse,' 'vulgar,' 'sloppy,' 'loose,' 'trivial,' 'uncouth' language (not to mention the un-

speakable, 'gibberish,' 'pidgin' or 'slang'). The oppositions from which this series is generated, and which, being derived from the legitimate language, is organized from the standpoint of the dominant users, can be reduced to two: the opposition between 'distinguished' and 'vulgar' (or 'rare' and 'common') and the opposition between 'tense' (or 'sustained') and 'relaxed' (or 'loose'), which no doubt represents the specifically linguistic version of the first, very general, opposition. It is as if the principle behind the ranking of class languages were nothing other than the degree of *control* they manifested and the intensity of the *correctness* they presupposed.

It follows that the legitimate language is a semi-artificial language which has to be sustained by a permanent effort of correction, a task which falls both to institutions specially designed for this purpose and to individual speakers. Through its grammarians, who fix and codify legitimate usage, and its teachers who impose and inculcate it through innumerable acts of correction, the educational system tends, in this area as elsewhere, to produce the need for its own services and its own products, i.e. the labour and instruments of correction.[26] The legitimate language owes its (relative) constancy in time (as in space) to the fact that it is continuously protected by a prolonged labour of inculcation against the inclination towards the economy of effort and tension which leads, for example, to analogical simplification (e.g. of irregular verbs in French—*vous faisez* and *vous disez* for *vous faites* and *vous dites*). Moreover, the correct, i.e. corrected, expression owes the essential part of its social properties to the fact that it can be produced only by speakers possessing practical mastery of scholarly rules, explicitly constituted by a process of codification and expressly inculcated through pedagogic work. Indeed, the paradox of all institutionalized pedagogy is that it aims to implant, as schemes that function in a practical state, rules which grammarians have laboured to extract from the practice of the professionals of written expression (from the past), by a process of retrospective formulation and codification. 'Correct usage' is the product of a competence which is an *incorporated grammar,* the word grammar being used explicitly (and not tacitly, as it is by the linguists) in its true sense of a system

---

[25] [Bourdieu] One might contrast a 'style-in-itself,' the objective product of an unconscious or even forced 'choice' (like the objectively aesthetic 'choice' of a piece of furniture or a garment, which is imposed by economic necessity), with a 'style-for-itself,' the product of a choice which, even when experienced as free and 'pure,' is equally determined, but by the specific constraints of the economy of symbolic goods, such as explicit or implicit reference to the forced choices of those who have no choice, luxury itself having no sense except in relation to necessity.

[26] [Bourdieu] Of the errors induced by the use of concepts like 'apparatus' or 'ideology' (whose naïve teleology is taken a degree further in the notion of 'ideological state apparatuses'), one of the most significant is neglect of the *economy* of the institutions of production of cultural goods. One only has to think, for example, of the *cultural industry,* oriented towards producing services and instruments of linguistic correction (e.g. manuals, grammars, dictionaries, guides to correspondence and public speaking, children's books, etc.), and of the thousands of agents in the public and private sectors whose most vital material and symbolic interests are invested in the competitive struggles which lead them to contribute, incidentally and often unwittingly, to the defence and exemplification of the legitimate language.

of scholarly rules, derived *ex post facto* from expressed discourse and set up as imperative norms for discourse yet to be expressed. It follows that one cannot fully account for the properties and social effects of the legitimate language unless one takes account, not only of the social conditions of the production of literary language and its grammar, but also of the social conditions in which this scholarly code is imposed and inculcated as the principle of the production and evaluation of speech.[27]

The Dynamics of the Linguistic Field

The laws of the transmission of linguistic capital are a particular case of the laws of the legitimate transmission of cultural capital between the generations, and it may therefore be posited that the linguistic competence measured by academic criteria depends, like the other dimensions of cultural capital, on the level of education (measured in terms of qualifications obtained) and on the social trajectory. Since mastery of the legitimate language may be acquired through familiarization, that is, by more or less prolonged exposure to the legitimate language, or through the deliberate inculcation of explicit rules, the major classes of modes of expression correspond to classes of modes of acquisition, that is, to different forms of the combination between the two principal factors of production of the legitimate competence, namely, the family and the educational system.

In this sense, like the sociology of culture, the sociology of language is logically inseparable from a sociology of education. As a linguistic market strictly subject to the verdicts of the guardians of legitimate culture, the educational market is strictly dominated by the linguistic products of the dominant class and tends to sanction the pre-existing differences in capital. The combined effect of low cultural capital and the associated low propensity to increase it through educational investment condemns the least favoured classes to the negative sanctions of the scholastic market,

i.e. exclusion or early self-exclusion induced by lack of success. The initial disparities therefore tend to be reproduced since the length of inculcation tends to vary with its efficiency: those least inclined and least able to accept and adopt the language of the school are also those exposed for the shortest time to this language and to educational monitoring, correction and sanction.

Given that the educational system possesses the delegated authority necessary to engage in a universal process of durable inculcation in matters of language, and given that it tends to vary the duration and intensity of this inculcation in proportion to inherited cultural capital, it follows that the social mechanisms of cultural transmission tend to reproduce the structural disparity between the very unequal *knowledge* of the legitimate language and the much more uniform *recognition* of this language. This disparity is one of the determinant factors in the dynamics of the linguistic field and therefore in changes in the language. For the linguistic struggles which are the ultimate source of these changes presuppose that speakers have virtually the same recognition of authorized usage, but very unequal knowledge of this usage. Thus, if the linguistic strategies of the petite bourgeoisie, and in particular its tendency to hypercorrection—a very typical expression of 'cultural goodwill' which is manifested in all areas of practice—have sometimes been seen as the main factor in linguistic change, this is because the disparity between knowledge and recognition, between aspirations and the means of satisfying them—a disparity that generates tension and pretension—is greatest in the intermediate regions of the social space. This pretension, a recognition of distinction which is revealed in the very effort to deny it by appropriating it, introduces a permanent pressure into the field of competition which inevitably induces new strategies of distinction on the part of the holders of distinctive marks that are socially recognized as distinguished.

The petit-bourgeois hypercorrection which seeks its models and instruments of correction from the most consecrated arbiters of legitimate usage—Academicians, grammarians, teachers—is defined in the subjective and objective relationship to popular 'vulgarity' and bourgeois 'distinction.' Consequently, the contribution which this striving for assimilation (to the bourgeois classes) and, at the same time, dissimilation (with respect to the lower classes) makes to linguistic change is simply more visible than the dissimilation strategies which, in turn, it provokes from the holders of a rarer competence. Conscious or unconscious avoidance of the most visible marks of the linguistic tension and exertion of petit-bourgeois speakers (for example, in French, spoken use of the past

---

[27] [Bourdieu] The social conditions of production and reproduction of the legitimate language are responsible for another of its properties: the autonomy with regard to practical functions, or, more precisely, the neutralized and neutralizing relation to the 'situation,' the object of discourse or the interlocutor, which is implicitly required on all the occasions when solemnity calls for a controlled and tense use of language. The spoken use of 'written language' is only acquired in conditions in which it is objectively inscribed in the situation, in the form of freedoms, facilities and, above all, *leisure,* in the sense of the neutralization of practical urgencies; and it presupposes the disposition which is acquired in and through exercises in which language is manipulated without any other necessity than that arbitrarily imposed for pedagogic purposes.

historic, associated with old-fashioned schoolmasters) can lead the bourgeois and the intellectuals towards the controlled hypocorrection which combines confident relaxation and lofty ignorance of pedantic rules with the exhibition of ease on the most dangerous ground.[28] Showing tension where the ordinary speaker succumbs to relaxation, facility where he betrays effort, and the ease in tension which differs utterly from petit-bourgeois or popular tension and ease: these are all strategies of distinction (for the most part unconscious) giving rise to endless refinements, with constant reversals of value which tend to discourage the search for non-relational properties of linguistic styles.

> Thus, in order to account for the new style of speaking adopted by intellectuals, which can be observed in America as well as in France—a somewhat hesitant, even faltering, interrogative manner (*'non?,'* 'right?,' 'OK?' etc.)—one would have to take into account the whole *structure of usages* in relation to which it is differentially defined. On the one hand, there is the old academic manner (with—in French—its long periods, imperfect subjunctives, etc.), associated with a devalued image of the professorial role; on the other, the new petit-bourgeois usages resulting from wider diffusion of scholarly usage and ranging from 'liberated' usage, a blend of tension and relaxation which tends to characterize the new petite bourgeoisie, to the hypercorrection of an over-refined speech, immediately devalued by an all-too-visible ambition, which is the mark of the upwardly mobile petite bourgeoisie.

The fact that these distinctive practices can be understood only in relation to the universe of possible practices does not mean that they have to be traced back to a conscious concern to distinguish oneself from them. There is every reason to believe that they are rooted in a practical sense of the rarity of distinctive marks (linguistic or otherwise) and of its evolution over time. Words which become popularized lose their *discriminatory power* and thereby tend to be perceived as intrinsically banal, common, *facile*—or (since diffusion

is linked to time) as *worn out*. It is no doubt the weariness deriving from repeated exposure which, combined with the sense of rarity, gives rise to the unconscious drift towards more 'distinguished' stylistic features or towards rarer usages of common features.

Thus distinctive deviations are the driving force of the unceasing movement which, though intended to annul them, tends in fact to reproduce them (a paradox which is in no way surprising once one realizes that constancy may presuppose change). Not only do the strategies of assimilation and dissimilation which underlie the changes in the different uses of language not affect the structure of the distribution of different uses of language, and consequently the system of the systems of distinctive deviations (expressive styles) in which those uses are manifested, but they tend to reproduce it (albeit in a superficially different form). Since the very motor of change is nothing less than the whole linguistic field or, more precisely, the whole set of actions and reactions which are continuously generated in the universe of competitive relations constituting the field, the centre of this perpetual movement is everywhere and nowhere. Those who remain trapped in a philosophy of cultural diffusion based on a hydraulic imagery of 'two-step flow' or 'trickle-down,' and who persist in locating the principle of change in a determinate site in the linguistic field, will always be greatly disappointed. What is described as a phenomenon of diffusion is nothing other than the process resulting from the *competitive struggle* which leads each agent, through countless strategies of assimilation and dissimilation (*vis-à-vis* those who are ahead of and behind him in the social space and in time) constantly to change his substantial properties (here, pronunciation, diction, syntactic devices, etc.), while maintaining, precisely by running in the race, the disparity which underlies the race. This structural constancy of the social values of the uses of the legitimate language becomes intelligible when one knows that the logic and the aims of the strategies seeking to modify it are governed by the structure itself, through the position occupied in the structure by the agent who performs them. The 'interactionist' approach, which fails to go beyond the actions and reactions apprehended in their directly visible immediacy, is unable to discover that the different agents' linguistic strategies are strictly dependent on their positions in the structure of the distribution of linguistic capital, which can in turn be shown to depend, via the structure of chances of access to the educational system, on the structure of class relations. Hence, interactionism can know nothing of the deep mechanisms which, through surface changes, tend to reproduce the structure of distinctive deviations and to maintain the profits accruing to those who possess a rare and therefore distinctive competence.

---

[28] [Bourdieu] It is therefore no accident that, as Troubetzkoy notes, 'casual articulation' is one of the most universally observed ways of marking distinction: see N. S. Troubetzkoy, *Principes de Phonologie* (Paris: Klincksieck, 1957), p. 22. In reality, as Pierre Encrevé has pointed out to me, the strategic relaxation of tension only exceptionally extends to the phonetic level; spuriously denied distinction continues to be marked in pronunciation. And writers such as Raymond Queneau have, of course, been able to derive literary effects from systematic use of similar discrepancies in level between the different aspects of discourse.

Jean François Lyotard

1924–1998

Prior to the Paris riots in 1968, Jean François Lyotard was best known for his frequently reprinted *Phenomenology,* with at least nine editions and numerous translations published between 1954 and 1982, and frequent essays, interviews, and books on politics (particularly Algeria), psychoanalysis, and the arts. In subsequent years, Lyotard became even more celebrated as arguably the premier thinker and writer on the subject of the postmodern, a term he helped to define and shape with his *The Post-Modern Condition: A Report on Knowledge,* first published in 1979, translated into English in 1984. The fundamental proposition Lyotard elaborates in that influential book is that our fundamental conceptions of knowledge, the large organizing stories or "metanarratives" by which we make the pursuit of research and thinking intelligible, had reached a condition of impasse or collapse. The "postmodern" world, accordingly, faced the daunting (but exhilarating) task of reconceiving fundamental relations of politics, education, art, and social life without a quasi-automatic reliance upon traditional models.

While many of these themes were anticipated by earlier work, especially *Libidinal Economy* (1974; tr. 1993), Lyotard followed them with considerable intellectual courage and thoughtfulness in *The Différend: Phrases in Dispute* (1983; tr. 1988), which takes on the seemingly intractable problem of trying to resolve difference when there is no applicable rule of judgment that applies to both sides. The problem itself dictates an inventive and, we may say, "postmodern" mode of exposition, to explore the difficulty even when there is no certainty that it can be resolved. In a similar way, his *Au Juste* (1979, tr. as *Just Gaming,* 1984) in the form of conversations with Jean-Loup Thébaud, carries out a sustained reflection on the philosophical discourse of justice in a contemporary light.

The essay reprinted here, "Answering the Question: What Is Postmodernism?" ranges over these issues, together with provocative remarks on the aesthetic, particularly the sublime, which also figure prominently in Lyotard's collection of essays translated as *The Inhuman: Reflections on Time* (1991).

A superb on-line year-by-year bibliography of works by and about Lyotard, compiled by Eddie Yeghiayan, is available through the University of California at Irvine Critical Theory Institute. Lyotard's principal books in translation include: *Libidinal Economy* (1974, tr. 1993); *The Post-Modern Condition: A Report on Knowledge* (1979, tr. 1984); *Just Gaming* (1979, tr. 1984); *The Différend: Phrases in Dispute* (1983, tr. 1988); and *The Inhuman: Reflections on Time* (1991).

Answering the Question: What Is Postmodernism?

A Demand

This is a period of slackening—I refer to the color of the times. From every direction we are being urged to put an end to experimentation, in the arts and elsewhere. I have read an art historian who extols realism and is militant for the advent of a new subjectivity. I have read an art critic who packages and sells "Transavantgardism" in the marketplace of painting.[1] I have read that under the name of postmodernism, architects are getting rid of the Bauhaus project, throwing out the baby of experimentation with the bathwater of functionalism. I have read that a new philosopher is discovering what he drolly calls Judaeo-Christianism, and intends by it to put an end to the impiety which we are supposed to have spread. I have read in a French weekly that some are displeased with *Mille Plateaux* [by Deleuze and Guattari, below, page 1442] because they expect, especially when reading a work of philosophy, to be gratified with a little sense. I have read from the pen of a reputable historian that writers and thinkers of the 1960 and 1970 avant-gardes spread a reign of terror in the use of language, and that the conditions for a fruitful exchange must be restored by imposing on the intellectuals a common way of speaking, that of the historians. I have been reading a young philosopher of language who complains that Continental thinking, under the challenge of speaking machines, has surrendered to the machines the concern for reality, that it has substituted for the referential paradigm that of "adlinguisticity" (one speaks about speech, writes about writing, intertextuality), and who thinks that the time has now come to restore a solid anchorage of language in the referent. I have read a talented theatrologist for whom postmodernism, with its games and fantasies, carries very little weight in front of political authority, especially when a worried public opinion encourages authority to a politics of totalitarian surveillance in the face of nuclear warfare threats.

I have read a thinker of repute who defends modernity against those he calls the neoconservatives. Under the ban-

ner of postmodernism, the latter would like, he believes, to get rid of the uncompleted project of modernism, that of the Enlightenment. Even the last advocates of *Aufklärung*, such as Popper or Adorno, were only able, according to him, to defend the project in a few particular spheres of life—that of politics for the author of *The Open Society,* and that of art for the author of *Asthetische Theorie.*[2] Jürgen Habermas[3] (everyone had recognized him) thinks that if modernity has failed, it is in allowing the totality of life to be splintered into independent specialties which are left to the narrow competence of experts, while the concrete individual experiences "desublimated meaning" and "destructured form," not as a liberation but in the mode of that immense *ennui* which Baudelaire[4] described over a century ago.

Following a prescription of Albrecht Wellmer,[5] Habermas considers that the remedy for this splintering of culture and its separation from life can only come from "changing the status of aesthetic experience when it is no longer primarily expressed in judgments of taste," but when it is "used to explore a living historical situation," that is, when "it is put in relation with problems of existence." For this experience then "becomes a part of a language game which is no longer that of aesthetic criticism"; it takes part "in cognitive processes and normative expectations"; "it alters the manner in which those different moments *refer* to one another." What Habermas requires from the arts and the experiences they provide is, in short, to bridge the gap between cognitive, ethical, and political discourses, thus opening the way to a unity of experience.

My question is to determine what sort of unity Habermas has in mind. Is the aim of the project of modernity the constitution of sociocultural unity within which all the elements of daily life and of thought would take their places as in an organic whole? Or does the passage that has to be charted between heterogeneous language games—those of cognition, of ethics, of politics—belong to a different order from that? And if so, would it be capable of effecting a real synthesis between them?

The first hypothesis, of a Hegelian inspiration, does not challenge the notion of a dialectically totalizing *experience;* the second is closer to the spirit of Kant's *Critique of*

"Answering the Question: What Is Postmodernism?" was first published as "Réponse à la question: qu'est-ce que le postmoderne?" in *Critique* (April 1982), 38(419), 357–67. The translation by Régis Durand is reprinted from Ihab Hassan and Sally Hassan, eds., *Innovation/Renovation: New Perspectives on the Humanities,* pp. 329–41 (Madison: University of Wisconsin Press, 1983).

[1] See Achille Bonito Oliva (b. 1939), Italian "creative critic."

[2] That is, Karl Popper (1902–1994), Austrian-born British philosopher of science, author of *The Open Society and Its Enemies* (1945), including a stinging critique of Plato as anticipating fascism and other forms of totalitarian government; and Theodor W. Adorno (above, page 1101).

[3] Jürgen Habermas (below, page 1429).

[4] Baudelaire (above, page 604).

[5] Albrecht Wellmer, German philosopher and social critic, professor at the Free University of Berlin.

Judgment;[6] but must be submitted, like the *Critique,* to that severe reexamination which postmodernity imposes on the thought of the Enlightenment, on the idea of a unitary end of history and of a subject. It is this critique which not only Wittgenstein and Adorno[7] have initiated, but also a few other thinkers (French or other) who do not have the honor to be read by Professor Habermas—which at least saves them from getting a poor grade for their neoconservatism.

Realism

The demands I began by citing are not all equivalent. They can even be contradictory. Some are made in the name of postmodernism, others in order to combat it. It is not necessarily the same thing to formulate a demand for some referent (and objective reality), for some sense (and credible transcendence), for an addressee (and audience), or an addressor (and subjective expressiveness) or for some communicational consensus (and a general code of exchanges, such as the genre of historical discourse). But in the diverse invitations to suspend artistic experimentation, there is an identical call for order, a desire for unity, for identity, for security, or popularity (in the sense of *Öffentlichkeit,* of "finding a public"). Artists and writers must be brought back into the bosom of the community, or at least, if the latter is considered to be ill, they must be assigned the task of healing it.

There is an irrefutable sign of this common disposition: it is that for all those writers nothing is more urgent than to liquidate the heritage of the avant-gardes. Such is the case, in particular, of the so-called transavantgardism. The answers given by Achille Bonito Oliva to the questions asked by Bernard Lamarche-Vadel and Michel Enric leave no room for doubt about this. By putting the avant-gardes through a mixing process, the artist and critic feel more confident that they can suppress them than by launching a frontal attack. For they can pass off the most cynical eclecticism as a way of going beyond the fragmentary character of the preceding experiments; whereas if they openly turned their backs on them, they would run the risk of appearing ridiculously neoacademic. The *Salons* and the *Académies,* at the time when the bourgeoisie was establishing itself in history, were able to function as purgation and to grant awards for good plastic and literary conduct under the cover of realism. But capitalism inherently possesses the power to derealize familiar objects, social roles, and institutions to such a degree that the so-called realistic representations can

no longer evoke reality except as nostalgia or mockery, as an occasion for suffering rather than for satisfaction. Classicism seems to be ruled out in a world in which reality is so destabilized that it offers no occasion for experience but one for ratings and experimentation.

This theme is familiar to all readers of Walter Benjamin.[8] But it is necessary to assess its exact reach. Photography did not appear as a challenge to painting from the outside, any more than industrial cinema did to narrative literature. The former was only putting the final touch to the program of ordering the visible elaborated by the quattrocento; while the latter was the last step in rounding off diachronies as organic wholes, which had been the ideal of the great novels of education since the eighteenth century. That the mechanical and the industrial should appear as substitutes for hand or craft was not in itself a disaster—except if one believes that art is in its essence the expression of an individuality of genius assisted by an elite craftsmanship.

The challenge lay essentially in that photographic and cinematographic processes can accomplish better, faster, and with a circulation a hundred thousand times larger than narrative or pictorial realism, the task which academicism had assigned to realism: to preserve various consciousnesses from doubt. Industrial photography and cinema will be superior to painting and the novel whenever the objective is to stabilize the referent, to arrange it according to a point of view which endows it with a recognizable meaning, to reproduce the syntax and vocabulary which enable the addressee to decipher images and sequences quickly, and so to arrive easily at the consciousness of his own identity as well as the approval which he thereby receives from others—since such structures of images and sequences constitute a communication code among all of them. This is the way the effects of reality, or if one prefers, the fantasies of realism, multiply.

If they too do not wish to become supporters (of minor importance at that) of what exists, the painter and novelist must refuse to lend themselves to such therapeutic uses. They must question the rules of the art of painting or of narrative as they have learned and received them from their predecessors. Soon those rules must appear to them as a means to deceive, to seduce, and to reassure, which makes it impossible for them to be "true." Under the common name of painting and literature, an unprecedented split is taking place. Those who refuse to reexamine the rules of art pursue successful careers in mass conformism by communicating, by means of the "correct rules," the endemic desire for real-

---

[6] Kant (above, page 416).
[7] Wittgenstein (above, page 823); Adorno (above, page 1101).

[8] Walter Benjamin (above, page 995).

ity with objects and situations capable of gratifying it. Pornography is the use of photography and film to such an end. It is becoming a general model for the visual or narrative arts which have not met the challenge of the mass media.

As for the artists and writers who question the rules of plastic and narrative arts and possibly share their suspicions by circulating their work, they are destined to have little credibility in the eyes of those concerned with "reality" and "identity"; they have no guarantee of an audience. Thus it is possible to ascribe the dialectics of the avant-gardes to the challenge posed by the realisms of industry and mass communication to painting and the narrative arts. Duchamp's "ready made" does nothing but actively and parodistically signify this constant process of dispossession of the craft of painting or even of being an artist. As Thierry de Duve[9] penetratingly observes, the modern aesthetic question is not "What is beautiful?" but "What can be said to be art (and literature)?"

Realism, whose only definition is that it intends to avoid the question of reality implicated in that of art, always stands somewhere between academicism and kitsch. When power assumes the name of a party, realism and its neoclassical complement triumph over the experimental avant-garde by slandering and banning it—that is, provided the "correct" images, the "correct" narratives, the "correct" forms which the party requests, selects, and propagates can find a public to desire them as the appropriate remedy for the anxiety and depression that public experiences. The demand for reality—that is, for unity, simplicity, communicability, etc.—did not have the same intensity nor the same continuity in German society between the two world wars and in Russian society after the Revolution: this provides a basis for a distinction between Nazi and Stalinist realism.

What is clear, however, is that when it is launched by the political apparatus, the attack on artistic experimentation is specifically reactionary: aesthetic judgment would only be required to decide whether such or such work is in conformity with the established rules of the beautiful. Instead of the work of art having to investigate what makes it an art object and whether it will be able to find an audience, political academicism possesses and imposes a priori criteria of the beautiful, which designate some works and a public at a stroke and forever. The use of categories in aesthetic judgment would thus be of the same nature as in cognitive judgment. To speak like Kant, both would be determining

judgments: the expression is "well formed" first in the understanding, then the only cases retained in experience are those which can be subsumed under this expression.

When power is that of capital and not that of a party, the "transavantgardist" or "postmodern" (in Jencks's sense) solution proves to be better adapted than the antimodern solution. Eclecticism is the degree zero of contemporary general culture: one listens to reggae, watches a western, eats McDonald's food for lunch and local cuisine for dinner, wears Paris perfume in Tokyo and "retro" clothes in Hong Kong; knowledge is a matter for TV games. It is easy to find a public for eclectic works. By becoming kitsch, art panders to the confusion which reigns in the "taste" of the patrons. Artists, gallery owners, critics, and public wallow together in the "anything goes," and the epoch is one of slackening. But this realism of the "anything goes" is in fact that of money; in the absence of aesthetic criteria, it remains possible and useful to assess the value of works of art according to the profits they yield. Such realism accommodates all tendencies, just as capital accommodates all "needs," providing that the tendencies and needs have purchasing power. As for taste, there is no need to be delicate when one speculates or entertains oneself.

Artistic and literary research is doubly threatened, once by the "cultural policy" and once by the art and book market. What is advised, sometimes through one channel, sometimes through the other, is to offer works which, first, are relative to subjects which exist in the eyes of the public they address, and second, works so made ("well made") that the public will recognize what they are about, will understand what is signified, will be able to give or refuse its approval knowingly, and if possible, even to derive from such work a certain amount of comfort.

The interpretation which has just been given of the contact between the industrial and mechanical arts, and literature and the fine arts is correct in its outline, but it remains narrowly sociologizing and historicizing—in other words, one-sided. Stepping over Benjamin's and Adorno's reticences, it must be recalled that science and industry are no more free of the suspicion which concerns reality than are art and writing. To believe otherwise would be to entertain an excessively humanistic notion of the mephistophelian functionalism of sciences and technologies. There is no denying the dominant existence today of techno-science, that is, the massive subordination of cognitive statements to the finality of the best possible performance, which is the technological criterion. But the mechanical and the industrial, especially when they enter fields traditionally reserved for artists, are carrying with them much more than power effects. The objects and the thoughts which originate in

---

[9]Thierry de Duve, French art critic and historian, author of several studies of Marcel Duchamp (1887–1968), French modernist painter and sculptor.

scientific knowledge and the capitalist economy convey with them one of the rules which supports their possibility: the rule that there is no reality unless testified by a consensus between partners over a certain knowledge and certain commitments.

This rule is of no little consequence. It is the imprint left on the politics of the scientist and the trustee of capital by a kind of flight of reality out of the metaphysical, religious, and political certainties that the mind believed it held. This withdrawal is absolutely necessary to the emergence of science and capitalism. No industry is possible without a suspicion of the Aristotelian theory of motion, no industry without a refutation of corporatism, of mercantilism, and of physiocracy. Modernity, in whatever age it appears, cannot exist without a shattering of belief and without discovery of the "lack of reality" of reality, together with the invention of other realities.

What does this "lack of reality" signify if one tries to free it from a narrowly historicized interpretation? The phrase is of course akin to what Nietzsche calls nihilism. But I see a much earlier modulation of Nietzschean perspectivism in the Kantian theme of the sublime. I think in particular that it is in the aesthetic of the sublime that modern art (including literature) finds its impetus and the logic of avant-gardes finds its axioms.

The sublime sentiment, which is also the sentiment of the sublime, is, according to Kant, a strong and equivocal emotion: it carries with it both pleasure and pain. Better still, in it pleasure derives from pain. Within the tradition of the subject, which comes from Augustine and Descartes and which Kant does not radically challenge, this contradiction, which some would call neurosis or masochism, develops as a conflict between the faculties of a subject, the faculty to conceive of something and the faculty to "present" something. Knowledge exists if, first, the statement is intelligible, and second, if "cases" can be derived from the experience which "corresponds" to it. Beauty exists if a certain "case" (the work of art), given first by the sensibility without any conceptual determination, the sentiment of pleasure independent of any interest the work may elicit, appeals to the principle of a universal consensus (which may never be attained).

Taste, therefore, testifies that between the capacity to conceive and the capacity to present an object corresponding to the concept, an undetermined agreement, without rules, giving rise to a judgment which Kant calls reflective, may be experienced as pleasure. The sublime is a different sentiment. It takes place, on the contrary, when the imagination fails to present an object which might, if only in principle, come to match a concept. We have the Idea of the world (the totality of what is), but we do not have the capacity to

show an example of it. We have the Idea of the simple (that which cannot be broken down, decomposed), but we cannot illustrate it with a sensible object which would be a "case" of it. We can conceive the infinitely great, the infinitely powerful, but every presentation of an object destined to "make visible" this absolute greatness or power appears to us painfully inadequate. Those are Ideas of which no presentation is possible. Therefore, they impart no knowledge about reality (experience); they also prevent the free union of the faculties which gives rise to the sentiment of the beautiful; and they prevent the formation and the stabilization of taste. They can be said to be unpresentable.

I shall call modern the art which devotes its "little technical expertise" *(son "petit technique"),* as Diderot[10] used to say, to present the fact that the unpresentable exists. To make visible that there is something which can be conceived and which can neither be seen nor made visible: this is what is at stake in modern painting. But how to make visible that there is something which cannot be seen? Kant himself shows the way when he names "formlessness, the absence of form," as a possible index to the unpresentable. He also says of the empty "abstraction" which the imagination experiences when in search for a presentation of the infinite (another unpresentable): this abstraction itself is like a presentation of the infinite, its "negative presentation." He cites the commandment, "Thou shalt not make graven images" *(Exodus),* as the most sublime passage in the Bible in that it forbids all presentation of the Absolute. Little needs to be added to those observations to outline an aesthetic of sublime paintings. As painting, it will of course "present" something though negatively; it will therefore avoid figuration or representation. It will be "white" like one of Malevitch's[11] squares; it will enable us to see only by making it impossible to see; it will please only by causing pain. One recognizes in those instructions the axioms of avant-gardes in painting, inasmuch as they devote themselves to making an allusion to the unpresentable by means of visible presentations. The systems in the name of which, or with which, this task has been able to support or to justify itself deserve the greatest attention; but they can originate only in the vocation of the sublime in order to legitimize it, that is, to conceal it. They remain inexplicable without the incommensurability of reality to concept which is implied in the Kantian philosophy of the sublime.

It is not my intention to analyze here in detail the manner in which the various avant-gardes have, so to speak,

---

[10] Diderot (above, page 383).

[11] Kazimar Malevitch (1878–1935), Russian painter.

humbled and disqualified reality by examining the pictorial techniques which are so many devices to make us believe in it. Local tone, drawing, the mixing of colors, linear perspective, the nature of the support and that of the instrument, the treatment, the display, the museum: the avant-gardes are perpetually flushing out artifices of presentation which make it possible to subordinate thought to the gaze and to turn it away from the unpresentable. If Habermas, like Marcuse, understands this task of derealization as an aspect of the (repressive) "desublimation" which characterizes the avant-garde, it is because he confuses the Kantian sublime with Freudian sublimation, and because aesthetics has remained for him that of the beautiful.

The Postmodern

What, then, is the postmodern? What place does it or does it not occupy in the vertiginous work of the questions hurled at the rules of image and narration? It is undoubtedly a part of the modern. All that has been received, if only yesterday (*modo, modo,* Petronius[12] used to say), must be suspected. What space does Cézanne challenge?[13] The Impressionists.' What object do Picasso and Braque attack?[14] Cézanne's. What presupposition does Duchamp[15] break with in 1912? That which says one must make a painting, be it cubist. And Buren[16] questions that other presupposition which he believes had survived untouched by the work of Duchamp: the place of presentation of the work. In an amazing acceleration, the generations precipitate themselves. A work can become modern only if it is first postmodern. Postmodernism thus understood is not modernism at its end but in the nascent state, and this state is constant.

Yet I would like not to remain with this slightly mechanistic meaning of the word. If it is true that modernity takes place in the withdrawal of the real and according to the sublime relation between the presentable and the conceivable, it is possible, within this relation, to distinguish two modes (to use the musician's language). The emphasis can be placed on the powerlessness of the faculty of presentation, on the nostalgia for presence felt by the human subject, on the obscure and futile will which inhabits him in spite of everything. The emphasis can be placed, rather, on the power of the faculty to conceive, on its "inhuman-

ity" so to speak (it was the quality Apollinaire[17] demanded of modern artists), since it is not the business of our understanding whether or not human sensibility or imagination can match what it conceives. The emphasis can also be placed on the increase of being and the jubilation which result from the invention of new rules of the game, be it pictorial, artistic, or any other. What I have in mind will become clear if we dispose very schematically a few names on the chessboard of the history of avant-gardes: on the side of melancholia, the German Expressionists, and on the side of *novatio,* Braque and Picasso, on the former Malevitch and on the latter Lissitsky, on the one Chirico[18] and on the other Duchamp. The nuance which distinguishes these two modes may be infinitesimal; they often coexist in the same piece, are almost indistinguishable; and yet they testify to a difference (*un différend*) on which the fate of thought depends and will depend for a long time, between regret and assay.

The work of Proust and that of Joyce both allude to something which does not allow itself to be made present.[19] Allusion, to which Paolo Fabbri recently called my attention, is perhaps a form of expression indispensable to the works which belong to an aesthetic of the sublime. In Proust, what is being eluded as the price to pay for this allusion is the identity of consciousness, a victim to the excess of time (*au trop de temps*). But in Joyce, it is the identity of writing which is the victim of an excess of the book (*au trop de livre*) or of literature.

Proust calls forth the unpresentable by means of a language unaltered in its syntax and vocabulary and of a writing which in many of its operators still belongs to the genre of novelistic narration. The literary institution, as Proust inherits it from Balzac and Flaubert, is admittedly subverted in that the hero is no longer a character but the inner consciousness of time, and in that the diegetic diachrony, already damaged by Flaubert,[20] is here put in question because of the narrative voice. Nevertheless, the unity of the book, the odyssey of that consciousness, even if it is deferred from chapter to chapter, is not seriously challenged: the identity of the writing with itself throughout the labyrinth of the interminable narration is enough to connote such unity, which has been compared to that of *The Phenomenology of Mind.*[21]

---

[12] Titus Petronius Niger (d.66 A.D.), Roman artist.

[13] Paul Cézanne (1839–1906), French painter.

[14] Pablo Picasso (1888–1973), Spanish painter and sculptor; George Braque (1882–1963), French painter.

[15] Marcel Duchamp (1887–1968), French painter.

[16] Daniel Buren (b. 1938), French artist.

[17] Guillaume Appollinaire (1880–1918), French poet.

[18] El Lissitsky (1890–1941), Russian painter and designer; Giorgio Chirico (1888–1978), Italian painter.

[19] Marcel Proust (1871–1922), French novelist; James Joyce (1882–1941), Irish novelist.

[20] Gustave Flaubert (1821–1880), French novelist.

[21] By Hegel (above, page 552).

Joyce allows the unpresentable to become perceptible in his writing itself, in the signifier. The whole range of available narrative and even stylistic operators is put into play without concern for the unity of the whole, and new operators are tried. The grammar and vocabulary of literary language are no longer accepted as given; rather, they appear as academic forms, as rituals originating in piety (as Nietzsche[22] said) which prevent the unpresentable from being put forward.

Here, then, lies the difference: modern aesthetics is an aesthetic of the sublime, though a nostalgic one. It allows the unpresentable to be put forward only as the missing contents; but the form, because of its recognizable consistency, continues to offer to the reader or viewer matter for solace and pleasure. Yet these sentiments do not constitute the real sublime sentiment, which is in an intrinsic combination of pleasure and pain: the pleasure that reason should exceed all presentation, the pain that imagination or sensibility should not be equal to the concept.

The postmodern would be that which, in the modern, puts forward the unpresentable in presentation itself; that which denies itself the solace of good forms, the consensus of a taste which would make it possible to share collectively the nostalgia for the unattainable; that which searches for new presentations, not in order to enjoy them but in order to impart a stronger sense of the unpresentable. A postmodern artist or writer is in the position of a philosopher: the text he writes, the work he produces are not in principle governed by preestablished rules, and they cannot be judged according to a determining judgment, by applying familiar categories to the text or to the work. Those rules and categories are what the work of art itself is looking for. The artist and the writer, then, are working without rules in order to formulate the rules of what *will have been done.* Hence the fact that work and text have the characters of an *event;* hence also, they always come too late for their author, or, what amounts to the same thing, their being put into work, their realization *(mise en oeuvre)* always begin too soon. *Post modern* would have to be understood according to the paradox of the future *(post)* anterior *(modo).*

It seems to me that the essay (Montaigne) is postmodern, while the fragment *(The Athaeneum)* is modern.[23]

Finally, it must be clear that it is our business not to supply reality but to invent allusions to the conceivable which cannot be presented. And it is not to be expected that this task will effect the last reconciliation between language games (which, under the name of faculties, Kant[24] knew to be separated by a chasm), and that only the transcendental illusion (that of Hegel) can hope to totalize them into a real unity. But Kant also knew that the price to pay for such an illusion is terror. The nineteenth and twentieth centuries have given us as much terror as we can take. We have paid a high enough price for the nostalgia of the whole and the one, for the reconciliation of the concept and the sensible, of the transparent and the communicable experience. Under the general demand for slackening and for appeasement, we can hear the mutterings of the desire for a return of terror, for the realization of the fantasy to seize reality. The answer is: Let us wage a war on totality; let us be witnesses to the unpresentable; let us activate the differences and save the honor of the name.

---

[22] Nietzsche (above, page 686).

[23] Michel Eyquem de Montaigne (1533–1592), French essayist; *Athaeneum* edited by A. W. and Friedrich Schlegel (above, page 473) from 1798 to 1800.
[24] Kant (above, page 416).

Benedict Anderson

b. 1936

Even though the initial focus of Benedict Anderson's *Imagined Communities: Reflections on the Origin and Spread of Nationalism* (1983) was political history, the subject quickly found a place in multiple discourse communities and disciplines, from communications to postcolonial studies. Anderson's attention to the peculiar nature of self-identification by Nation serves usefully to put in perspective a wide range of cultural and political processes, seen all the more clearly through the lens of his work on the history, culture, and politics of Indonesia and South Asia.

In the brief selection reprinted here, the focus is upon the indispensable role of print media—and by implication, literacy—in the development and consolidation of national identities. The pivotal part played by national languages and all the cultural institutions dependent upon them, including national literatures and political organizations is sufficiently obvious as to be commonly ignored. Anderson's work is a clear corrective.

Besides *Imagined Communities: Reflections on the Origin and Spread of Nationalism* (1983, 1991), Benedict Anderson's other work includes: *Java in a Time of Revolution: Occupation and Resistance, 1944–1946* (1972); as editor, *Interpreting Indonesian Politics: Thirteen Contributions to the Debate* (1982); and *Language and Power: Exploring Political Cultures in Indonesia* (1990).

The Origins of National Consciousness

If the development of print-as-commodity is the key to the generation of wholly new ideas of simultaneity, still, we are simply at the point where communities of the type 'horizontal-secular, transverse-time' become possible. Why, within that type, did the nation become so popular? The factors involved are obviously complex and various. But a strong case can be made for the primacy of capitalism.

As already noted, at least 20,000,000 books had already been printed by 1500,[1] signalling the onset of Benjamin's 'age of mechanical reproduction.' If manuscript knowledge was scarce and arcane lore, print knowledge lived by reproducibility and dissemination.[2] If, as Febvre and Martin believe, possibly as many as 200,000,000 volumes had been manufactured by 1600, it is no wonder that Francis Bacon[3] believed that print had changed 'the appearance and state of the world.'[4]

One of the earlier forms of capitalist enterprise, book-publishing felt all of capitalism's restless search for markets. The early printers established branches all over Europe: 'in this way a veritable "international" of publishing houses, which ignored national [sic] frontiers, was created.'[5] And since the years 1500–1550 were a period of exceptional

---

"The Origins of National Consciousness" is Chapter 3 in Benedict Anderson, *Imagined Communities: Reflections on the Origin and Spread of Nationalism* (New York: Verso, 1983, 1991). Reprinted from the 1991 revised edition.
[1] [Anderson] The population of that Europe where print was then known was about 100,000,000. Febvre and Martin, *The Coming of the Book*, pp. 248–49.

[2] [Anderson] Emblematic is Marco Polo's *Travels,* which remained largely unknown till its first printing in 1559. Polo, *Travels,* p. xiii.
[3] Bacon (above, page 234).
[4] [Anderson] Quoted in Eisenstein, 'Some Conjectures,' p. 56.
[5] [Anderson] Febvre and Martin, *The Coming of the Book*, p. 122. (The original text, however, speaks simply of 'par-dessus les frontières.' *L'Apparition*, p. 184.)

European prosperity, publishing shared in the general boom. 'More than at any other time' it was 'a great industry under the control of wealthy capitalists.'[6] Naturally, 'book-sellers were primarily concerned to make a profit and to sell their products, and consequently they sought out first and foremost those works which were of interest to the largest possible number of their contemporaries.'[7]

The initial market was literate Europe, a wide but thin stratum of Latin-readers. Saturation of this market took about a hundred and fifty years. The determinative fact about Latin—aside from its sacrality—was that it was a language of bilinguals. Relatively few were born to speak it and even fewer, one imagines, dreamed in it. In the sixteenth century the proportion of bilinguals within the total population of Europe was quite small; very likely no larger than the proportion in the world's population today, and—proletarian internationalism notwithstanding—in the centuries to come. Then and now the bulk of mankind is monoglot. The logic of capitalism thus meant that once the elite Latin market was saturated, the potentially huge markets represented by the monoglot masses would beckon. To be sure, the Counter-Reformation encouraged a temporary resurgence of Latin-publishing, but by the mid-seventeenth century the movement was in decay, and fervently Catholic libraries replete. Meantime, a Europe-wide shortage of money made printers think more and more of peddling cheap editions in the vernaculars.[8]

The revolutionary vernacularizing thrust of capitalism was given further impetus by three extraneous factors, two of which contributed directly to the rise of national consciousness. The first, and ultimately the least important, was a change in the character of Latin itself. Thanks to the labours of the Humanists in reviving the broad literature of pre-Christian antiquity and spreading it through the print-market, a new appreciation of the sophisticated stylistic achievements of the ancients was apparent among the trans-European intelligentsia. The Latin they now aspired to write became more and more Ciceronian, and, by the same token, increasingly removed from ecclesiastical and everyday life. In this way it acquired an esoteric quality quite different from that of Church Latin in mediaeval times. For the older Latin was not arcane because of its subject matter or style, but simply because it was written at all, i.e. because of its status as *text*. Now it became arcane because of what was written, because of the language-in-itself.

Second was the impact of the Reformation, which, at the same time, owed much of its success to print-capitalism. Before the age of print, Rome easily won every war against heresy in Western Europe because it always had better internal lines of communication than its challengers. But when in 1517 Martin Luther nailed his theses to the chapel-door in Wittenberg, they were printed up in German translation, and 'within 15 days [had been] seen in every part of the country.'[9] In the two decades 1520–1540 three times as many books were published in German as in the period 1500–1520, an astonishing transformation to which Luther was absolutely central. His works represented no less than one third of *all* German-language books sold between 1518 and 1525. Between 1522 and 1546, a total of 430 editions (whole or partial) of his Biblical translations appeared. 'We have here for the first time a truly mass readership and a popular literature within everybody's reach.'[10] In effect, Luther became the first best-selling author *so known*. Or, to put it another way, the first writer who could 'sell' his *new* books on the basis of his name.[11]

Where Luther led, others quickly followed, opening the colossal religious propaganda war that raged across Europe for the next century. In this titanic 'battle for men's minds,' Protestantism was always fundamentally on the offensive, precisely because it knew how to make use of the expanding vernacular print-market being created by capitalism, while the Counter-Reformation defended the citadel of Latin. The emblem for this is the Vatican's *Index Librorum Prohibitorum*—to which there was no Protestant counterpart—a novel catalogue made necessary by the sheer volume of printed subversion. Nothing gives a better sense of this siege mentality than François I's panicked 1535 ban on the printing of *any* books in his realm—on pain of death by hanging! The reason for both the ban and its unenforceability was that by then his realm's eastern borders were ringed with Protestant states and cities producing a massive stream of smugglable print. To take Calvin's[12] Geneva alone: between 1533 and 1540 only 42 editions were published there, but the numbers swelled to

---

[6][Anderson] Ibid., p. 187. The original text speaks of 'puissants' (powerful) rather than 'wealthy' capitalists. *L'Apparition*, p. 281.

[7][Anderson] 'Hence the introduction of printing was in this respect a stage on the road to our present society of mass consumption and standardisation.' Ibid., pp. 259–60. (The original text has 'une civilisation de masse et de standardisation,' which may be better rendered 'standardised, mass civilization.' *L'Apparition*, p. 394).

[8][Anderson] Ibid., p. 195.

[9][Anderson] Ibid., pp. 289–90.

[10][Anderson] Ibid., pp. 291–95.

[11][Anderson] From this point it was only a step to the situation in seventeenth-century France where Corneille, Molière, and La Fontaine could sell their manuscript tragedies and comedies directly to publishers, who bought them as excellent investments in view of their authors' market reputations. Ibid., p. 161.

[12]John Calvin (1509–1564), French theologian.

527 between 1550 and 1564, by which latter date no less than 40 separate printing-presses were working overtime.[13]

The coalition between Protestantism and print-capitalism, exploiting cheap popular editions, quickly created large new reading publics—not least among merchants and women, who typically knew little or no Latin—and simultaneously mobilized them for politico-religious purposes. Inevitably, it was not merely the Church that was shaken to its core. The same earthquake produced Europe's first important non-dynastic, non-city states in the Dutch Republic and the Commonwealth of the Puritans. (François I's panic was as much political as religious.)

Third was the slow, geographically uneven, spread of particular vernaculars as instruments of administrative centralization by certain well-positioned would-be absolutist monarchs. Here it is useful to remember that the universality of Latin in mediaeval Western Europe never corresponded to a universal political system. The contrast with Imperial China, where the reach of the mandarinal bureaucracy and of painted characters largely coincided, is instructive. In effect, the political fragmentation of Western Europe after the collapse of the Western Empire meant that no sovereign could monopolize Latin and make it his-and-only-his language-of-state, and thus Latin's religious authority never had a true political analogue.

The birth of administrative vernaculars predated both print and the religious upheaval of the sixteenth century, and must therefore be regarded (at least initially) as an independent factor in the erosion of the sacred imagined community. At the same time, nothing suggests that any deepseated ideological, let alone proto-national, impulses underlay this vernacularization where it occurred. The case of 'England'—on the northwestern periphery of Latin Europe—is here especially enlightening. Prior to the Norman Conquest, the language of the court, literary and administrative, was Anglo-Saxon. For the next century and a half virtually all royal documents were composed in Latin. Between about 1200 and 1350 this state-Latin was superseded by Norman French. In the meantime, a slow fusion between this language of a foreign ruling class and the Anglo-Saxon of the subject population produced Early English. The fusion made it possible for the new language to take its turn, after 1362, as the language of the courts—and for the opening of Parliament. Wycliffe's vernacular *manuscript* Bible followed in 1382.[14] It is essential to bear in mind that this sequence was a series of 'state,' not 'national,' languages;

and that the state concerned covered at various times not only today's England and Wales, but also portions of Ireland, Scotland *and France.* Obviously, huge elements of the subject populations knew little or nothing of Latin, Norman French, or Early English.[15] Not till almost a century *after* Early English's political enthronement was London's power swept out of 'France.'

On the Seine, a similar movement took place, if at a slower pace. As Bloch wrily puts it, 'French, that is to say a language which, since it was regarded as merely a corrupt form of Latin, took several centuries to raise itself to literary dignity,'[16] only became the official language of the courts of justice in 1539, when François I issued the Edict of Villers-Cotterets.[17] In other dynastic realms Latin survived much longer—under the Habsburgs well into the nineteenth century. In still others, 'foreign' vernaculars took over: in the eighteenth century the languages of the Romanov court were French and German.[18]

In every instance, the 'choice' of language appears as a gradual, unselfconscious, pragmatic, not to say haphazard development. As such, it was utterly different from the self-conscious language policies pursued by nineteenth-century dynasts confronted with the rise of hostile popular linguistic-nationalisms. (See below, Chapter 6). One clear sign of the difference is that the old administrative languages were *just that:* languages used by and for officialdoms for their own inner convenience. There was no idea of systematically imposing the language on the dynasts' various subject populations.[19] Nonetheless, the elevation of these vernaculars to the status of languages-of-power, where, in one sense, they were competitors with Latin (French in Paris, [Early] English in London), made its own contribution to the decline of the imagined community of Christendom.

At bottom, it is likely that the esotericization of Latin, the Reformation, and the haphazard development of administrative vernaculars are significant, in the present context, primarily in a negative sense—in their contributions to the dethronement of Latin. It is quite possible to conceive of the emergence of the new imagined national communities without any one, perhaps all, of them being present. What, in a positive sense, made the new communities imaginable was

---

[13] [Anderson] Ibid., pp. 310–15.

[14] [Anderson] Seton-Watson, *Nations and States,* pp. 28–29; Bloch, *Feudal Society,* I, p. 75.

[15] [Anderson] We should not assume that administrative vernacular unification was immediately or fully achieved. It is unlikely that the Guyenne ruled from London was ever primarily administered in Early English.

[16] [Anderson] Bloch, *Feudal Society,* I, p. 98.

[17] [Anderson] Seton-Watson, *Nations and States,* p. 48.

[18] [Anderson] Ibid., p. 83.

[19] [Anderson] An agreeable confirmation of this point is provided by François I, who, as we have seen, banned all printing of books in 1535 and made French the language of his courts four years later!

a half-fortuitous, but explosive, interaction between a system of production and productive relations (capitalism), a technology of communications (print), and the fatality of human linguistic diversity.[20]

The element of fatality is essential. For whatever superhuman feats capitalism was capable of, it found in death and languages two tenacious adversaries.[21] Particular languages can die or be wiped out, but there was and is no possibility of humankind's general linguistic unification. Yet this mutual incomprehensibility was historically of only slight importance until capitalism and print created monoglot mass reading publics.

While it is essential to keep in mind an idea of fatality, in the sense of a *general* condition of irremediable linguistic diversity, it would be a mistake to equate this fatality with that common element in nationalist ideologies which stresses the primordial fatality of *particular* languages and their association with *particular* territorial units. The essential thing is the *interplay* between fatality, technology, and capitalism. In pre-print Europe, and, of course, elsewhere in the world, the diversity of spoken languages, those languages that for their speakers were (and are) the warp and woof of their lives, was immense; so immense, indeed, that had print-capitalism sought to exploit each potential oral vernacular market, it would have remained a capitalism of petty proportions. But these varied idiolects were capable of being assembled, within definite limits, into print-languages far fewer in number. The very arbitrariness of any system of signs for sounds facilitated the assembling process.[22] (At the same time, the more ideographic the signs, the vaster the potential assembling zone. One can detect a sort of descending hierarchy here from algebra through Chinese and English, to the regular syllabaries of French or Indonesian.) Nothing served to 'assemble' related vernaculars more than capitalism, which, within the limits imposed by grammars and syn-

taxes, created mechanically reproduced print-languages capable of dissemination through the market.[23]

These print-languages laid the bases for national consciousnesses in three distinct ways. First and foremost, they created unified fields of exchange and communication below Latin and above the spoken vernaculars. Speakers of the huge variety of Frenches, Englishes, or Spanishes, who might find it difficult or even impossible to understand one another in conversation, became capable of comprehending one another via print and paper. In the process, they gradually became aware of the hundreds of thousands, even millions, of people in their particular language-field, and at the same time that *only those* hundreds of thousands, or millions, so belonged. These fellow-readers, to whom they were connected through print, formed, in their secular, particular, visible invisibility, the embryo of the nationally imagined community.

Second, print-capitalism gave a new fixity to language, which in the long run helped to build that image of antiquity so central to the subjective idea of the nation. As Febvre and Martin remind us, the printed book kept a permanent form, capable of virtually infinite reproduction, temporally and spatially. It was no longer subject to the individualizing and 'unconsciously modernizing' habits of monastic scribes. Thus, while twelfth-century French differed markedly from that written by Villon in the fifteenth, the rate of change slowed decisively in the sixteenth. 'By the 17th century languages in Europe had generally assumed their modern forms.'[24] To put it another way, for three centuries now these stabilized print-languages have been gathering a darkening varnish; the words of our seventeenth-century forebears are accessible to us in a way that to Villon his twelfth-century ancestors were not.

Third, print-capitalism created languages-of-power of a kind different from the older administrative vernaculars. Certain dialects inevitably were 'closer' to each print-language and dominated their final forms. Their disadvantaged cousins, still assimilable to the emerging print-language, lost caste, above all because they were unsuccessful (or only relatively successful) in insisting on their own print-form. 'Northwestern German' became Platt Deutsch, a largely spoken, thus sub-standard, German, because it was assimilable to print-German in a way that Bohemian spoken-

---

[20] [Anderson] It was not the first 'accident' of its kind. Febvre and Martin note that while a visible bourgeoisie already existed in Europe by the late thirteenth century, paper did not come into general use until the end of the fourteenth. Only paper's smooth plane surface made the mass reproduction of texts and pictures possible—and this did not occur for still another seventy-five years. But paper was not a European invention. It floated in from another history—China's—through the Islamic world. *The Coming of the Book,* pp. 22, 30, and 45.

[21] [Anderson] We still have no giant multinationals in the world of publishing.

[22] [Anderson] For a useful discussion of this point, see S. H. Steinberg, *Five Hundred Years of Printing,* chapter 5. That the sign *ough* is pronounced differently in the words although, bough, lough, rough, cough, and hiccough, shows both the idiolectic variety out of which the now-standard spelling of English emerged, and the ideographic quality of the final product.

[23] [Anderson] I say 'nothing served . . . more than capitalism' advisedly. Both Steinberg and Eisenstein come close to theomorphizing 'print' *qua* print as the genius of modern history. Febvre and Martin never forget that behind print stand printers and publishing firms. It is worth remembering in this context that although printing was invented first in China, possibly 500 years before its appearance in Europe, it had no major, let alone revolutionary impact—precisely because of the absence of capitalism there.

[24] [Anderson] *The Coming of the Book,* p. 319. Cf. *L'Apparition,* p. 477; 'Au XVIIe siècle, les langues nationales apparaissent un peu partout cristallisées.'

Czech was not. High German, the King's English, and, later, Central Thai, were correspondingly elevated to a new politico-cultural eminence. (Hence the struggles in late-twentieth-century Europe by certain 'sub-'nationalities to change their subordinate status by breaking firmly into print—and radio.)

It remains only to emphasize that in their origins, the fixing of print-languages and the differentiation of status between them were largely unselfconscious processes resulting from the explosive interaction between capitalism, technology and human linguistic diversity. But as with so much else in the history of nationalism, once 'there,' they could become formal models to be imitated, and, where expedient, consciously exploited in a Machiavellian spirit. Today, the Thai government actively discourages attempts by foreign missionaries to provide its hill-tribe minorities with their own transcription-systems and to develop publications in their own languages: the same government is largely indifferent to what these minorities *speak*. The fate of the Turkic-speaking peoples in the zones incorporated into today's Turkey, Iran, Iraq, and the USSR is especially exemplary. A family of spoken languages, once everywhere assemblable, thus comprehensible, within an Arabic orthography, has lost that unity as a result of conscious manipulations. To heighten Turkish–Turkey's national consciousness at the expense of any wider Islamic identification, Atatürk imposed compulsory romanization.[25] The Soviet authorities followed suit, first with an anti-Islamic, anti-Persian compulsory romanization, then, in Stalin's 1930s, with a Russifying compulsory Cyrillicization.[26]

---

[25] [Anderson] Hans Kohn, *The Age of Nationalism*, p. 108. It is probably only fair to add that Kemal also hoped thereby to align Turkish nationalism with the modern, romanized civilization of Western Europe.

[26] [Anderson] Seton-Watson, *Nations and States*, p. 317.

We can summarize the conclusions to be drawn from the argument thus far by saying that the convergence of capitalism and print technology on the fatal diversity of human language created the possibility of a new form of imagined community, which in its basic morphology set the stage for the modern nation. The potential stretch of these communities was inherently limited, and, at the same time, bore none but the most fortuitous relationship to existing political boundaries (which were, on the whole, the highwater marks of dynastic expansionisms).

Yet it is obvious that while today almost all modern self-conceived nations—and also nation-states—have 'national print-languages,' many of them have these languages in common, and in others only a tiny fraction of the population 'uses' the national language in conversation or on paper. The nation-states of Spanish America or those of the 'Anglo-Saxon family' are conspicuous examples of the first outcome; many ex-colonial states, particularly in Africa, of the second. In other words, the concrete formation of contemporary nation-states is by no means isomorphic with the determinate reach of particular print-languages. To account for the discontinuity-in-connectedness between print-languages, national consciousness, and nation-states, it is necessary to turn to the large cluster of new political entities that sprang up in the Western hemisphere between 1776 and 1838, all of which self-consciously defined themselves as nations, and, with the interesting exception of Brazil, as (non-dynastic) republics. For not only were they historically the first such states to emerge on the world stage, and therefore inevitably provided the first real models of what such states should 'look like,' but their numbers and contemporary births offer fruitful ground for comparative enquiry.

Jürgen Habermas

b. 1929

When Jürgen Habermas's *Knowledge and Human Interests* appeared in translation in 1971, one reviewer wrote, "It is not altogether easy to assess the work of a scholar whose professional competence extends from the logic of science to the sociology of knowledge. . . . The baffling thing about Habermas is that, at an age when most of his colleagues had painfully established control over one corner of the field, he has made himself master of the whole. . . ." It is true that Habermas is an intellectual historian, an analytic critic of theorists, and a philosopher in his own right. One of his aims, as he has said, has been to "reconstruct the history of modern positivism" so as to understand better the intellectual life of modernity and what has emerged from it, the postmodern critique of reason and of the so-called autonomous subject.

Habermas criticizes especially two aspects of that critique: the attack on the distinction between philosophy and literature on behalf of a single textual context for all linguistic expression and the claim that reason is but an expression and tool of the Nietzschean will to power, however it may be disguised. In the selection below from *The Philosophical Discourse of Modernity,* Habermas begins with a discussion of philosophers who have sought to criticize subject-centered reason by trying to escape the use of reason to do so (avoiding a version of Russell's paradox). But the critique made by Heidegger is, for Habermas, vague and evasive, and in others reason generally returns in the form of relativism. Habermas agrees with those he criticizes that subject-centered reason is long dead, and he offers a new version as communicative action and problem-solving without recourse to transcendent truth. Thus reason is embodied in communication and dialogue toward specific ends.

Against a deconstructive overcoming of logic and ordinary discourse by rhetoric, as in Derrida and de Man, Habermas argues that there is a discourse in which the poetic is dominant and another in which it is subordinate and put to solving problems that may involve processes of verification. In this he returns rhetoric to its classical meaning, as, for example, in Aristotle, where it is a tool of persuasion, and so on. In poetically dominant language practical action is secondary to "world-disclosure," a phrase reminiscent of Heidegger.

With respect to a Nietzschean theory of power, from which Foucault's views in part emerged, Habermas argues that morality and law do not just represent the domination of power but can also be emancipatory from specific powers. What is needed is not the wholesale rejection of reason, but rather a reason based on intersubjective communication and dialogue, all absolutes rejected in favor of necessary but provisional idealizations. The old notion of an ideal transcendental subjective consciousness is dismissed but not at the expense of humanly made acceptable standards.

This selection from Habermas is valuable in part because of its clear, brief descriptions of certain postmodern positions.

Among Habermas's many books are *Theory and Practice* (tr. 1973); *Communication and the Evolution of Society* (tr. 1979); *Philosophical-Political Profiles* (tr. 1983); *Theory of Communicative Action* (tr. 1987); *Knowledge and Human Interests* (tr. 1987); *The Philosophical Discourse of Modernity* (tr. 1987); *On the Logic of the Social Sciences* (1988); *Postmetaphysical Thinking* (1992); *Justification and Application: Remarks on Discourse Ethics* (tr. 1993); *Between Facts and Norms* (tr. 1996); *The Habermas Reader* (1996); *On the Pragmatics of Communication* (tr. 1998); *On the Pragmatics of Social Interaction* (tr. 2001); *Religion and Rationality: Essays on Reason, God, and Modernity* (tr. 2002); *The Future of Human Nature* (tr. 2003); *Philosophy in a Time of Terror: Dialogues with Jürgen Habermas and Jacques Derrida* (2003). See Richard J. Bernstein, ed., *Habermas and Modernity* (1985); Tom Rockmore, *Habermas on Historical Materialism* (1989); William Rehg, *Insight and Solidarity: A Study in the Discourse Ethics of Jürgen Habermas* (1994); Michael Kelly, ed., *Critique and Power: Recasting the Foucault-Habermas Debate* (1994); J. M. Bernstein, *Recovering Ethical Life: Jürgen Habermas and the Future of Critical Theory* (1995); Jósef Niznik and John T. Sanders, eds., *Debating the State of Philosophy: Habermas, Rorty, and Kolakowsky* (1996).

Excursus on Leveling the Genre Distinction Between Philosophy and Literature

I

Adorno's "negative dialectics" and Derrida's "deconstruction" can be seen as different answers to the same problem.[1] The totalizing self-critique of reason gets caught in a performative contradiction since subject-centered reason can be convicted of being authoritarian in nature only by having recourse to its own tools. The tools of thought, which miss the "dimension of nonidentity" and are imbued with the "metaphysics of presence," are nevertheless the only available means for uncovering their own insufficiency. Heidegger[2] flees from this paradox to the luminous heights of an esoteric, special discourse, which absolves itself of the restrictions of discursive speech generally and is immunized by vagueness against any specific objections. He makes use of metaphysical concepts for purposes of a critique of metaphysics, as a ladder he casts away once he has mounted the rungs. Once on the heights, however, the late Heidegger does not, as did the

early Wittgenstein,[3] withdraw into the mystic's silent intuition; instead, with the gestures of the seer and an abundance of words, he lays claim to the authority of the initiate.

Adorno operates differently. He does not slip out of the paradoxes of the self-referential critique of reason; he makes the performative contradiction within which this line of thought has moved since Nietzsche,[4] and which he acknowledges to be unavoidable, into the organizational form of indirect communication. Identity thinking turned against itself becomes pressed into continual self-denial and allows the wounds it inflicts on itself and its objects to be seen. This exercise quite rightly bears the name negative dialectics because Adorno practices determinate negation unremittingly, even though it has lost any foothold in the categorial network of Hegelian Logic[5]—as a fetishism of demystification, so to speak. This fastening upon a critical procedure that can no longer be sure of its foundations is explained by the fact that Adorno (in contrast to Heidegger) bears no elitist contempt for discursive thought. Like exiles, we wander about lost in the discursive zone; and yet it is only the insistent force of a groundless reflection turned against itself that preserves our connection with the utopia of a long since lost, uncoerced and intuitive knowledge belonging to the primal past.[6] Discursive thought cannot identify itself as the decadent form

---

"Excursus on Leveling the Genre Distinction Between Literature" follows Chapter VII of *The Philosophical Discourse of Modernity,* translated by Frederick Lawrence (Cambridge, Mass.: The MIT Press, 1987).
[1] Adorno (above, page 1110); Derrida (above, page 1203).
[2] Heidegger (above, page 1051).

[3] Wittgenstein (above, page 825).
[4] Nietzsche (above, page 686).
[5] Hegel (above, page 552).
[6] [Habermas] H. Schnädelbach, "Dialektik als Vernunftkritik," in L. von Friedenburg and J. Habermas, eds., *Adorno-Konferenz 1983* (Frankfurt, 1983), pp. 66ff.

of this knowledge by means of its own resources; for this purpose, the aesthetic experience gained in contact with avant-garde art is needed. The promise for which the surviving philosophic tradition is no longer a match has withdrawn into the mirror-writing of the esoteric work of art and requires a negativistic deciphering. From this labor of deciphering, philosophy sucks the residue of that paradoxical trust in reason with which negative dialectics executes (in the double sense of this word) its performative contradiction.

Derrida cannot share Adorno's aesthetically certified, residual faith in a de-ranged reason that has been expelled from the domains of philosophy and become, literally, utopian [having no place]. He is just as little convinced that Heidegger actually escaped the conceptual constraints of the philosophy of the subject by using metaphysical concepts in order to "cancel them out." Derrida does, to be sure, want to advance the already forged path of the critique of metaphysics; he, too, would just as soon break out of the paradox as broodingly encircle it. But like Adorno, he guards against the gestures of profundity that Heidegger unhesitatingly imitates from his opposite number, the philosophy of origins. And so there are also parallels between Derrida and Adorno.

This affinity in regard to their thought gestures calls for a more precise analysis. Adorno and Derrida are sensitized in the same way against definitive, totalizing, all-incorporating models, especially against the organic dimension in works of art. Thus, both stress the primacy of the allegorical over the symbolic, of metonymy over metaphor, of the Romantic over the Classical. Both use the fragment as an expository form; they place any system under suspicion. Both are abundantly insightful in decoding the normal case from the point of view of its limit cases; they meet in a negative extremism, finding the essential in the marginal and incidental, the right on the side of the subversive and the outcast, and the truth in the peripheral and the inauthentic. A distrust of everything direct and substantial goes along with an intransigent tracing of mediations, of hidden presuppositions and dependencies. The critique of origins, of anything original, of first principles, goes together with a certain fanaticism about showing what is merely produced, imitated, and secondary in everything. What pervades Adorno's work as a materialist motif—his unmasking of idealist positings, his reversal of false constitutive connections, his thesis about the primacy of the object—even for this there is a parallel in Derrida's logic of the supplement. The rebellious labor of deconstruction aims indeed at dismantling smuggled-in basic conceptual hierarchies, at overthrowing foundational relationships and conceptual relations of domination, such as those between speech and writing, the intelligible and the

sensible, nature and culture, inner and outer, mind and matter, male and female. Logic and rhetoric constitute one of these conceptual pairs. Derrida is particularly interested in standing the primacy of logic over rhetoric, canonized since Aristotle, on its head.

It is not as though Derrida concerned himself with these controversial questions in terms of viewpoints familiar from the history of philosophy. If he had done so, he would have had to relativize the status of his own project in relation to the tradition that was shaped from Dante to Vico, and kept alive through Hamann, Humboldt, and Droysen, down to Dilthey and Gadamer.[7] For the protest against the Platonic-Aristotelian primacy of the logical over the rhetorical that is raised anew by Derrida was articulated in this tradition. Derrida wants to expand the sovereignty of rhetoric over the realm of the logical in order to solve the problem confronting the totalizing critique of reason. As I have indicated, he is satisfied neither with Adorno's negative dialectics nor with Heidegger's critique of metaphysics—the one remaining tied to the rational bliss of the dialectic, the other to the elevation of origins proper to metaphysics, all protestations to the contrary notwithstanding, Heidegger only escapes the paradoxes of a self-referential critique of reason by claiming a special status for *Andenken,*[8] that is, its release from discursive obligations. He remains completely silent about the privileged access to truth. Derrida strives to arrive at the same esoteric access to truth, but he does not want to admit it as a privilege—no matter for what or for whom. He does not place himself in lordly fashion above the objection of pragmatic inconsistency, but renders it *objectless*.

There can only be talk about "contradiction" in the light of consistency requirements, which lose their authority or are at least subordinated to other demands—of an aesthetic nature, for example—if logic loses its conventional primacy over rhetoric. Then the deconstructionist can deal with the works of philosophy as works of literature and adapt the critique of metaphysics to the standards of a literary criticism that does not misunderstand itself in a scientistic way. As soon as we take the *literary* character of Nietzsche's writings seriously, the suitableness of his critique of reason has to be assessed in accord with the standards of rhetorical success and not those of logical consistency. Such

---

[7]Dante (above, page 153); Vico (above, page 313); Johann Georg Hamann (1730–1788), German philosopher; Humboldt (above, page 523); Johann Gustav Droysen (1808–1884), German historian; Wilhelm Dilthey (1833–1911), German philosopher; Hans-Georg Gadamer (1900–2003), German philosopher.
[8]Memory.

a critique (which is more adequate to its object) is not immediately directed toward the network of discursive relationships of which arguments are built, but toward the figures that shape style and are decisive for the literary and rhetorical power of a text. A literary criticism that in a certain sense merely *continues* the literary process of its objects cannot end up in science. Similarly, the deconstruction of great philosophical texts, carried out as literary criticism in this broader sense, is not subject to the criteria of problem-solving, purely cognitive undertakings.

Hence, Derrida *undercuts* the very problem that Adorno acknowledged as unavoidable and turned into the starting point of his reflectively self-transcending identity-thinking. For Derrida, this problem has no object since the deconstructive enterprise cannot be pinned down to the discursive obligations of philosophy and science. He calls his procedure deconstruction because it is supposed to *clear away* the ontological *scaffolding* erected by philosophy in the course of its subject-centered history of reason. However, in his business of deconstruction, Derrida does not proceed analytically, in the sense of identifying hidden presuppositions or implications. This is just the way in which each successive generation has critically reviewed the works of the preceding ones. Instead, Derrida proceeds by a critique of style, in that he finds something like indirect communications, by which the text itself denies its manifest content, in the rhetorical surplus of meaning inherent in the literary strata of texts that present themselves as nonliterary. In this way, he compels texts by Husserl, Saussure, or Rousseau to confess their guilt, against the explicit interpretations of their authors. Thanks to their rhetorical content, texts combed against the grain contradict what they state, such as the explicitly asserted primacy of signification over the sign, of the voice in relation to writing, of the intuitively given and immediately present over the representative and the postponed-postponing. In a philosophical text, the blind spot cannot be identified on the level of manifest content any more than it can in a literary text. "Blindness and insight"[9] are rhetorically interwoven with one another. Thus, the constraints constitutive for knowledge of a philosophical text only become accessible when the text is handled as what it would not like to be—as a literary text.

If, however, the philosophical (or scholarly) text were thereby only *extraneously turned* into an apparently literary one, deconstruction would still be an arbitrary act. Derrida can only attain Heidegger's goal of bursting metaphysical thought-forms from the inside by means of his essentially rhetorical procedure if the philosophical text is *in truth* a literary one—if one can *demonstrate* that the genre distinction between philosophy and literature dissolves upon closer examination. This demonstration is supposed to be carried out by way of deconstruction itself; in every single case we see anew the impossibility of so specializing the language of philosophy and science for cognitive purposes that they are cleansed of everything metaphorical and merely rhetorical, and kept free of literary admixtures. The frailty of the genre distinction between philosophy and literature is evidenced in the practice of deconstruction; in the end, *all* genre distinctions are submerged in one comprehensive, all-embracing context of texts—Derrida talks in a hypostatizing manner about a "universal text." What remains is self-inscribing writing as the medium in which each text is woven together with everything else. Even before it makes its appearance, every text and every particular genre has already lost its autonomy to an all-devouring context and an uncontrollable happening of spontaneous text production. This is the ground of the primacy of rhetoric, which is concerned with the qualities of texts in general, over logic, as a system of rules to which only certain types of discourse are subjected in an exclusive manner—those bound to argumentation.

II

This—at first glance inconspicuous—transformation of the "destruction" into the "deconstruction" of the philosophical tradition transposes the radical critique of reason into the domain of rhetoric and thereby shows it a way out of the aporia of self-referentiality: Anyone who still wanted to attribute paradoxes to the critique of metaphysics after this transformation would have misunderstood it in a scientistic manner. This argument holds good only if the following propositions are true:

1. Literary criticism is not primarily a scientific (or scholarly: *wissenschaftliches*) enterprise but observes the same rhetorical criteria as its literary objects.

2. Far from there being a genre distinction between philosophy and literature, philosophical texts can be rendered accessible in their essential contents by literary criticism.

3. The primacy of rhetoric over logic means the overall responsibility of rhetoric for the general qualities of an all-embracing context of texts, within which all genre distinctions are ultimately dissolved; philosophy and science no more constitute their own proper universes than art and literature constitute a realm of fiction that could assert its autonomy vis-à-vis the universal text.

---

[9]Phrase made well-known by Paul de Man's book by that name (above, page 1309).

Proposition 3 explicates propositions 2 and 1 by despecializing the meaning of "literary criticism." Literary criticism does serve as a model that clarifies itself through a long tradition; but it is considered precisely as a model case of something more universal, namely, a criticism suited to the rhetorical qualities of everyday discourse as well as of discourse outside the everyday. The procedure of deconstruction deploys this generalized criticism to bring to light the suppressed surpluses of rhetorical meaning in philosophical and scientific texts—against their manifest sense. Derrida's claim that "deconstruction" is an instrument for bringing Nietzsche's radical critique of reason out of the dead end of its paradoxical self-referentiality therefore stands—or falls—along with thesis number 3.

Just this thesis has been the centerpoint of the lively reception Derrida's work has enjoyed in the literature faculties of prominent American universities.[10] In the United States, literary criticism has for a long time been institutionalized as an academic discipline, that is, within the scholarly-scientific enterprise. From the very start, the self-tormenting question about the scholarly-scientific character of literary criticism was institutionalized along with it. This endemic self-doubt forms the background for the reception of Derrida, along with the dissolution of the decades-long domination of the New Criticism, which was convinced of the autonomy of the literary work of art and drew nourishment from the scientific pathos of structuralism. The idea of "deconstruction" could catch on in this constellation because it opened up to literary criticism a task of undoubted significance, under exactly the opposite premises: Derrida disputes the autonomy of the linguistic work of art and the independent meaning of the aesthetic illusion no less energetically than he does the possibility of criticism's ever being able to attain scientific status. At the same time, literary criticism serves him as the model for a procedure that takes on an almost world-historical mission with its overcoming of the thinking of the metaphysics of presence and of the age of logocentrism.

The leveling of the genre distinction between literary criticism and literature frees the critical enterprise from the unfortunate compulsion to submit to pseudo-scientific standards; it simultaneously lifts it above science to the level of creative activity. Criticism does not need to consider itself as something secondary; it gains literary status. In the texts

of Hillis Miller, Geoffrey Hartman, and Paul de Man we can find the new self-awareness: "that critics are no more parasites than the texts they interpret, since both inhabit a host-text of pre-existing language which itself parasitically feeds on their host-like willingness to receive it."[11] Deconstructionists break with the traditional Arnoldian conception of criticism's function as a mere servant: "Criticism is now crossing over into literature, rejecting its subservient, Arnoldian stance and taking on the freedom of interpretive style with a matchless gusto."[12] Thus, in perhaps his most brilliant book, Paul de Man deals with critical texts by Lukács, Barthes, Blanchot, and Jakobson with a method and finesse that are usually reserved only for literary texts: "Since they are not scientific, critical texts have to be read with the same awareness of ambivalence that is brought to the study of non-critical literary texts."[13]

Just as important as the equation of literary criticism with creative literary production is the increase in significance enjoyed by literary criticism as sharing in the business of the critique of metaphysics. This upgrading to the critique of metaphysics requires a counterbalancing supplement to Derrida's interpretation of the leveling of the genre distinction between philosophy and literature. Jonathan Culler recalls the strategic meaning of Derrida's treatment of philosophical texts through literary criticism in order to suggest that, in turn, literary criticism treat literary texts also as philosophical texts. Simultaneously maintaining and relativizing the distinction between the two genres "is essential to the demonstration that the most truly philosophical reading of a philosophical text . . . is one that treats the work as literature, as a fictive, rhetorical construct whose elements and order are determined by various textual exigencies." Then he continues: "Conversely, the most powerful and opposite readings of literary works may be those that treat them as philosophical gestures by teasing out the implications of their dealings with the philosophical oppositions that support them."[14] Proposition 2 is thus varied in the following sense:

2′. Far from there being a genre distinction between philosophy and literature, literary texts can be rendered accessible in their essential contents by a critique of metaphysics.

---

[10][Habermas] This is especially true of the Yale critics, Paul de Man, Geoffrey Hartman, J. Hillis Miller, and Harold Bloom. See J. Arac, W. Godzich, and W. Martin, eds., *The Yale Critics: Deconstruction in America* (Minneapolis, 1983). In addition to Yale, important centers of deconstructionism are located at Johns Hopkins and Cornell universities.

[11]The notion of the parasite is developed by J. Hillis Miller in "The Critic as Host," in which to describe deconstructive reading he cites a use of the term by Wayne Booth. The essay appears in *Deconstruction and Criticism,* ed. Harold Bloom, 1979.
[12][Habermas] Christopher Norris, *Deconstruction: Theory and Practice* (New York and London, 1982), pp. 93, 98.
[13][Habermas] Paul de Man, *Blindness and Insight,* 2d. ed. (Minneapolis, 1983), p. 110.
[14][Habermas] Jonathan Culler, *On Deconstruction* (London, 1983), p. 150.

Of course, the two propositions, 2 and 2′, point in the direction of the primacy of rhetoric over logic, which is asserted in proposition 3. Consequently, American literary critics are concerned to develop a concept of *general* literature, equal in overall scope to rhetoric, which would correspond to Derrida's "universal text." The notion of literature as confined to the realm of the fictive is deconstructed at the same time as the conventional notion of philosophy that denies the metaphorical basis of philosophical thought: "The notion of literature or literary discourse is involved in several of the hierarchical oppositions on which deconstruction has focussed: serious/non-serious, literal/metaphorical, truth/fiction. . . . Deconstruction's demonstration that these hierarchies are undone by the working of the texts that propose them alters the standing of literary language." There now follows, in the form of a conditional statement, the thesis on which everything depends—both the self-understanding of a literary criticism upgraded to the critique of metaphysics and the deconstructionist dissolution of the performative contradiction of a self-referential critique of reason: "If serious language is a special case of non-serious, if truths are fictions whose fictionality has been forgotten, then literature is not a deviant, parasitical instance of language. On the contrary, other discourses can be seen as cases of a generalized literature, or archi-literature."[15] Since Derrida does not belong to those philosophers who like to argue, it is expedient to take a closer look at his disciples in literary criticism within the Anglo-Saxon climate of argument in order to see whether this thesis really can be held.

Jonathan Culler reconstructs in a very clear way the somewhat impenetrable discussion between Derrida and Searle in order to show by the example of Austin's[16] speech-act theory that any attempt to demarcate the ordinary domain of normal speech from an "unusual" use of language, "deviating" from the standard cases, is doomed to failure. Culler's thesis is expanded and indirectly confirmed in a study of speech-act theory by Mary Louise Pratt,[17] who wants to prove, by the example of the structuralist theory of poetics, that even the attempt to delimit the extraordinary domain of fictive discourse from everyday discourse fails (see section III below). But first let us take a look at the debate between Derrida and Searle.[18]

From this complex discussion, Culler selects as the central issue the question of whether Austin does in fact, as it seems he does, make a totally unprejudiced, provisory, and purely methodical move. Austin wants to analyze the rules intuitively mastered by competent speakers, in accordance with which typical speech acts can be successfully executed. He undertakes this analysis with respect to sentences from *normal* everyday practice that are uttered *seriously* and used as *simply* and *literally* as possible. Thus, the unit of analysis, the standard speech act, is the result of certain abstractions. The theoretician of speech acts directs his attention to a sample of normal linguistic utterances from which all complex, derivative, parasitic, and deviant cases have been filtered out. A concept of "usual" or normal linguistic practice underpins this isolation, a concept of "ordinary language" whose harmlessness and consistency Derrida puts in doubt. Austin's intention is clear: He wants to analyze the universal properties of "promises," for example, with respect to cases in which the utterance of corresponding sentences actually *functions* as a promise. Now there are contexts in which the same sentences lose the illocutionary force of a promise. Spoken by an actor on the stage, as part of a poem, or even in a monologue, a promise, according to Austin, becomes "null and void in a unique manner." The same holds true for a promise that comes up in a quotation, or one merely mentioned. In these contexts, there is no *serious* or *binding* use, and sometimes not even a *literal* use, of the respective performative sentence, but a derivative or parasitic use instead. As Searle constantly repeats, these fictive or simulated or indirect modes of use are "parasitic" in the sense that logically they presuppose the possibility of a serious, literal, and binding use of sentences grammatically appropriate for making promises. Culler extracts what are in essence three objections from Derrida's texts; they point toward the impossibility of such an operation and are meant to show that the common distinctions between serious and simulated, literal and metaphorical, everyday and fictional, usual and parasitic modes of speech break down.

(a) In his initial argument, Derrida posits a not very clear link between quotability and repeatability on the one hand, and fictionality on the other. The quotation of a promise is only apparently something secondary in comparison to the directly made promise, for the indirect rendition of a performative utterance in a quote is a form of repetition, and as quotability presupposes the possibility of repetition in accord with a rule, that is, conventionality, it belongs to the nature of any conventionally generated utterance (including performative ones) that it can be quoted—and fictively imitated, in a broader sense: "If it were not possible

[15] [Habermas] Ibid., p. 181.
[16] John Searle (b. 1932), J. L. Austin (1911–1960), American and English philosophers respectively.
[17] Pratt (above, page 1344).
[18] [Habermas] In his essay "Signature Event Context," in *Margins of Philosophy* (Chicago, 1982), pp. 307–30, Derrida devotes the last section to a discussion of Austin's theory. Searle refers to this in "Reiterating the Differences: A Reply to Derrida," *Glyph* 1 (1977); 198ff. Derrida's response appeared in *Glyph* 2 (1977): 202ff. Under the title "Limited, Inc."

for a character in a play to make a promise, there could be no promise in real life, for what makes it possible to promise, as Austin tells us, is the existence of a conventional procedure, of formulas one can repeat. For me to be able to make a promise in real life, there must be iterable procedures or formulas such as are used on stage. Serious behavior is a case of role-playing."[19]

In this argument, Derrida obviously already presupposes what he wants to prove: that any convention which permits the repetition of exemplary actions possesses from the outset not only a symbolic, but also a fictional character. But it must first be shown that the conventions of a game are ultimately indistinguishable from norms of action. Austin introduces the quotation of a promise as an example of a derivative or parasitic form because the illocutionary force is removed from the quoted promise by the form of indirect rendition; it is thereby taken out of the context in which it "functions," that is, in which it coordinates the actions of the different participants in interaction and has consequences relevant to action. Only the actually performed speech act is *effective as action;* the promise mentioned or reported in a quote depends grammatically upon this. A setting that deprives it of its illocutionary force constitutes the bridge between quotation and fictional representation. Even action on the stage rests on a basis of everyday action (on the part of the actors, director, stage-workers, and theater people); and in the context of this framework, promises can function *in another mode* than they do "on stage," that is, with obligations and consequences relevant for action. Derrida makes no attempt to "deconstruct" this distinctive functional mode of ordinary speech within communicative action. In the illocutionary binding force of linguistic utterances Austin discovered a mechanism for coordinating action that places normal speech, as part of everyday practice, under constraints different from those of fictional discourse, simulation, and interior monologue. The constraints under which illocutionary acts develop a force for coordinating action and have consequences relevant to action define the domain of "normal" language. They can be analyzed as the kinds of idealizing suppositions we have to make in communicative action.

(b) The second argument brought forward by Culler, with Derrida, against Austin and Searle relates to just such idealizations. Any generalizing analysis of speech acts has to be able to specify general contextual conditions for the illocutionary success of standardized speech acts. Searle has been especially occupied with this task.[20] Linguistic expressions, however, change their meanings depending on shifting contexts; moreover, contexts are so constituted as to be open to ever wider-reaching specification. It is one of the peculiarities of our language that we can separate utterances from their original contexts and transplant them into different ones—Derrida speaks of "grafting." In this manner, we can think of a speech act, such as a "marriage vow," in ever new and more improbable contexts; the specification of universal contextual conditions does not run into any natural limits: "Suppose that the requirements for a marriage ceremony were met but that one of the parties were under hypnosis, or that the ceremony were impecabble in all respects but had been called a 'rehearsal,' or finally, that while the speaker was a minister licensed to perform weddings and the couple had obtained a license, that three of them were on this occasion acting in a play that, coincidentally, included a wedding ceremony."[21] These variations of context that change meaning cannot in principle be arrested or controlled, because contexts cannot be exhausted, that is, they cannot be theoretically mastered once and for all. Culler shows clearly that Austin cannot escape this difficulty by taking refuge in the intentions of speakers and listeners. It is not the thoughts of bride, bridegroom, or priest that decide the validity of the ceremony, but their actions and the circumstances under which they are carried out: "What counts is the plausibility of the description: whether or not the features of the context adduced create a frame that alters the illocutionary force of the utterances."[22]

Searle reacted to this difficulty by introducing a qualification to the effect that the literal meaning of a sentence does not completely fix the validity conditions of the speech act in which it is employed; it depends, rather, on tacit supplementation by a system of background assumptions regarding the normality of general world conditions. These parareflective background certainties have a holistic nature; they cannot be exhausted by a countably finite set of specifications. Meanings of sentences, however well analyzed, are thus valid only relative to a shared background knowledge that is constitutive of the lifeworld of a linguistic community. But Searle makes clear that the addition of this relational moment does not bring with it the relativism of meaning that Derrida is after. As long as language games are functioning and the preunderstanding constitutive of the lifeworld has not broken down, participants rightly count on world conditions being what is understood in their linguistic community as "normal." And in cases where individual background convictions do become problematic, they

---

[19] [Habermas] Culler, *On Deconstruction,* p. 119.

[20] [Habermas] John Searle, *Speech Acts* (Cambridge, 1969), and *Expression and Meaning* (Cambridge, 1979).

[21] [Habermas] Culler, *On Deconstruction,* pp. 121ff.

[22] [Habermas] Ibid., p. 123.

assume that they could reach a rationally motivated agreement. Both are strong, that is to say idealizing, suppositions; but these idealizations are not arbitrary, logocentric acts brought to bear by theoreticians on unmanageable contexts in order to give the illusion of mastery; rather, they are presuppositions that the participants themselves have to make if communicative action is to be at all possible.

(c) The role of idealizing suppositions can also be clarified in connection with some other consequences of this same state of affairs. Because contexts are changeable and can be expanded in any desired direction, the same text can be open to different readings; it is the text itself that makes possible its uncontrollable effective history. Still, Derrida's purposely paradoxical statement that any interpretation is inevitably a false interpretation, and any understanding a misunderstanding, does not follow from this venerable hermeneutic insight. Culler justifies the statement "Every reading is a misreading" as follows: "If a text can be understood, it can in principle be understood repeatedly, by different readers in different circumstances. These acts of reading or understanding are not, of course, identical. They involve modifications and differences, but differences which are deemed not to matter. We can thus say that understanding is a special case of misunderstanding, a particular deviation or determination of misunderstanding. It is a misunderstanding whose misses do not matter."[23] Yet Culler leaves one thing out of consideration. The productivity of the process of understanding remains unproblematic only so long as all participants stick to the reference point of possibly achieving a mutual understanding in which the *same* utterances are assigned the same meaning. As Gadamer has shown, the hermeneutic effort that would bridge over temporal and cultural distances remains oriented toward the idea of a possible consensus being brought about in the present.

Under the pressure for decisions proper to the communicative practice of everyday life, participants are dependent upon agreements that coordinate their actions. The more removed interpretations are from the "seriousness of this type of situation," the more they can prescind from the idealizing supposition of an achievable consensus. But they can never be wholly absolved of the idea that wrong interpretations must in principle be criticizable in terms of consensus to be aimed for ideally. The interpreter does not impose this idea on his object; rather, with the performative attitude of a participant observer, he takes it over from the direct participants, *who can act communicatively only under the presupposition of intersubjectively identical ascriptions of meaning.* I do not

mean to marshal a Wittgensteinian positivism of language games against Derrida's thesis. It is not habitual linguistic practice that determines just what meaning is attributed to a text or an utterance.[24] Rather, language games only work because they presuppose idealizations that transcend any particular language game; as a necessary condition of possibly reaching understanding, these idealizations give rise to the perspective of an agreement that is open to criticism on the basis of validity claims. A language operating under these kinds of constraints is subject to an ongoing test. Everyday communicative practice, in which agents have to reach an understanding about something in the world, stands under the need to prove its worth, and it is the idealizing suppositions that make such testing possible in the first place. It is in relation to this need for standing the test within ordinary practice that one may distinguish, with Austin and Searle, between "usual" and "parasitic" uses of language.

III

Up to this point, I have criticized Derrida's third and fundamental assumption only to the extent that (against Culler's reconstruction of Derrida's arguments) I have defended the possibility of demarcating normal speech from *derivative* forms. I have not yet shown how fictional discourse can be separated from the normal (everyday) use of language. This aspect is the most important for Derrida. If "literature" and "writing" constitute the model for a universal context of texts, which cannot be surpassed and within which all genre distinctions are ultimately dissolved, they cannot be separated from other discourses as an autonomous realm of fiction. For the literary critics who follow Derrida in the United States, the thesis of the autonomy of the linguistic work of art is, as I mentioned, also unacceptable, because they want to set themselves off from the formalism of the New Criticism and from structuralist aesthetics.

The Prague Structuralists originally tried to distinguish poetic from ordinary language in view of their relations to extralinguistic reality. Insofar as language occurs in *communicative functions,* it has to produce relations between linguistic expression and speaker, hearer, and the state of affairs represented. Bühler articulated this in his semiotic scheme as the sign-functions of expression, appeal, and representation.[25] However, when language fulfills a poetic function, it does so in virtue of a reflexive relation of the lin-

---

[23] [Habermas] Ibid., p. 176.

[24] [Habermas] Compare ibid., pp. 130ff.
[25] [Habermas] Karl Bühler, *Semiotic Foundations of Language Theory* (New York, 1982).

guistic expression to itself. Consequently, reference to an object, informational content, and truth-value—conditions of validity in general—are extrinsic to poetic speech; an utterance can be poetic to the extent that it is directed to the linguistic medium itself, to its own linguistic form. Roman Jakobson integrated this characterization into an expanded scheme of functions; in addition to the basic functions— expressing the speaker's intentions, establishing interpersonal relations, and representing states of affairs—which go back to Bühler, and two more functions related to making contact and to the code, he ascribes to linguistic utterances a poetic function, which directs our attention to "the message as such."[26] We are less concerned here with a closer characterization of the poetic function (in accord with which the principle of equivalence is projected from the axis of selection to the axis of combination) than with an interesting consequence that is important for our problem of delimiting normal from other instances of speech: "Any attempt to reduce the sphere of the poetic function would be a deceptive oversimplification. The poetic function is not the only function of verbal artistry, merely a *predominant* and *structurally determinative* one, whereas in all other linguistic activities it plays a subordinate and supplementary role. Inasmuch as it *directs our attention to the sign's perceptibility,* this function deepens the fundamental dichotomy between signs and objects. For this reason, linguistics should not, when it studies the poetic function, restrict itself solely to the field of poetry."[27] Poetic speech, therefore, is to be distinguished only in virtue of the primacy and structure-forming force of a certain function that is always fulfilled together with other linguistic functions.

Richard Ohmann makes use of Austin's approach to specify poetic language in this sense. For him, the phenomenon in need of clarification is the fictionality of the linguistic work of art, that is, the generation of aesthetic illusion by which a second, specifically de-realized arena is opened up on the basis of a continued everyday practice. What distinguishes poetic language is its "world-generating" capacity: "A literary work creates a world . . . by providing the reader with *impaired* and incomplete speech acts which he completes by supplying the appropriate circumstances."[28] The unique *impairment* of speech acts that generates fictions arises when they are robbed of their illocutionary force, or

maintain their illocutionary meanings only as in the refraction of indirect repetition or quotation: "A literary work is a discourse whose sentences lack the illocutionary forces that would normally attach to them. Its illocutionary force is mimetic. . . . Specifically, a literary work purportedly imitates a series of speech acts, which in fact have no other existence. By doing so, it leads the reader to imagine a speaker, a situation, a set of ancillary events, and so on."[29] The bracketing of illocutionary force virtualizes the relations to the world in which the speech acts are involved due to their illocutionary force, and releases the participants in interaction from reaching agreement about something in the world on the basis of idealizing understandings in such a way that they coordinate their plans of action and thus enter into obligations relevant to the outcomes of action: "Since the quasi-speech acts of literature are not *carrying on the world's business*—describing, urging, contracting, etc.—the reader may well attend to them in a non-pragmatic way."[30] Neutralizing their binding force releases the disempowered illocutionary acts from the pressure to decide proper to everyday communicative practice, removes them from the sphere of usual discourse, and thereby empowers them for the playful creation of new worlds—or, rather, for the pure demonstration of the world-disclosing force of innovative linguistic expressions. This specialization in the world-disclosive function of speech explains the unique self-reflexivity of poetic language to which Jakobson refers and which leads Geoffrey Hartman to pose the rhetorical question: "Is not literary language the name we give to a diction whose frame of reference is such that the words stand out as words (even as sounds) rather than being, at once, assimilable meanings?"[31]

Mary L. Pratt makes use of Ohmann's studies[32] to refute, by means of speech-act theory, the thesis of the independence of the literary work of art in Derrida's sense. She does not consider fictionality, the bracketing of illocutionary force, and the disengagement of poetic language from everyday communicative practice to be adequate selective criteria, because fictional speech elements such as jokes, irony, wish-fantasies, stories, and parables pervade our everyday discourse and by no means constitute an autonomous universe apart from "the world's business." Conversely, nonfiction works, memoirs, travel reports, historical romances, even *romans à clef* or thrillers that, like Truman

---

[26] [Habermas] Roman Jakobson [above, page 1132], "Linguistics and Poetics," in Thomas A. Sebeok, editor, *Style in Language* (Cambridge, Mass.: 1960), pp. 350–58.
[27] [Habermas] Ibid.
[28] [Habermas] R. Ohmann, "Speech-Acts and the Definition of Literature," *Philosophy and Rhetoric* 4 (1971), p. 17.

[29] [Habermas] Ibid., p. 14.
[30] [Habermas] Ibid, p. 17.
[31] [Habermas] Geoffrey Hartman, *Saving the Text* (Baltimore, 1981), p. xxi.
[32] [Habermas] See also "Speech, Literature, and the Space Between," *New Literary History* 5 (1974), p. 34ff. [See Pratt (above, page 1352).]

Capote's *In Cold Blood*,[33] adapt a factually documented case, by no means create an unambiguously fictional world, even though we often relegate these productions, for the most part at least, to "literature." Pratt uses the results of studies in sociolinguistics by W. Labov[34] to prove that natural narratives, that is, the "stories" told spontaneously or upon request in everyday life, follow the same rhetorical laws of construction as and exhibit structural characteristics similar to literary narratives: "Labov's data make it necessary to account for narrative rhetoric in terms that are not exclusively literary; the fact that fictive or mimetically organized utterances can occur in almost any realm of extraliterary discourse requires that we do the same for fictivity or mimesis. In other words, the relation between a work's fictivity and its literariness is indirect."[35]

Nonetheless, the fact that normal language is permeated with fictional, narrative, metaphorical, and, in general, with rhetorical elements does not yet speak against the attempt to explain the autonomy of the linguistic work of art by the bracketing of illocutionary forces, for, according to Jakobson, the mark of fictionality is suited for demarcating literature from everyday discourses only to the degree that the world-disclosing function of language predominates over the other linguistic functions and determines the structure of the linguistic artifact. In a certain respect, it is the refraction and partial elimination of illocutionary validity claims that distinguishes the story from the statement of the eyewitness, teasing from insulting, being ironic from misleading, the hypothesis from the assertion, wish-fantasy from perception, a training maneuver from an act of warfare, and a scenario from a report of an actual catastrophe. But in none of these cases do the illocutionary acts lose their binding force for coordinating action. Even in the cases adduced for the sake of comparison, the communicative functions of the speech acts remain intact insofar as the fictive elements cannot be separated from contexts of life practice. The world-disclosive function of language does not gain independence over against the expressive, regulative, and informative functions. By contrast, in Truman Capote's literary elaboration of a notorious and carefully researched incident, precisely this may be the case. That is to say, what grounds the *primacy* and the structuring force of the poetic function is not the deviation of a fictional representation

from the documentary report of an incident, but the exemplary elaboration that takes the case out of its context and makes it the occasion for an innovative, world-disclosive, and eye-opening representation in which the rhetorical means of representation depart from communicative routines and take on a life of their own.

It is interesting to see how Pratt is compelled to work out this poetic function against her will. Her sociolinguistic counterproposal begins with the analysis of a speech situation that poetic discourse shares with other discourses—the kind of arrangement in which a narrator or lecturer turns to a public and calls its attention to a text. The text undergoes certain procedures of preparation and selection before it is ready for delivery. Before a text can lay claim to the patience and discretion of the audience, it has also to satisfy certain criteria of relevance: it *has to be worth telling*. The tellability is to be assessed in terms of the manifestation of some significant exemplary experience. In its content, a tellable text reaches beyond the local context of the immediate speech situation and is open to further elaboration: "As might be expected, these two features—contextual detachability and susceptibility to elaboration—are equally important characteristics of literature." Of course, literary texts share these characteristics with "display texts" in general. The latter are characterized by their special communicative functions: "They are designed to serve a purpose I have described as that of verbally representing states of affairs and experiences which are held to be *unusual* or *problematic* in such a way that the addressee will respond affectively in the intended way, adopt the intended evaluation and interpretation, take pleasure in doing so, and *generally find the whole undertaking worth it*."[36] One sees how the pragmatic linguistic analyst creeps up on literary texts from outside, as it were. The latter have still to satisfy a final condition; in the case of literary texts, tellability must gain a preponderance over other functional characteristics: "In the end, tellability can take precedence over assertability itself."[37] Only in this case do the functional demands and structural constraints of everyday communicative practice (which Pratt defines by means of Grice's[38] conversation postulates) lose their force. The concern to give one's contribution an informative shape, to say what is relevant, to be straightforward and to avoid obscure, ambiguous, and prolix utterances are idealizing presuppositions of the communicative action *of normal speech,* but not of poetic discourse: "Our tolerance, indeed propensity, for elaboration when dealing with the tellable

[33] Truman Capote (1924–1984), American novelist; *In Cold Blood* was published in 1965.

[34] [Habermas] William Labov, *Language in the Inner City* (Philadelphia, 1972).

[35] [Habermas] Mary Louise Pratt, *A Speech-Act Theory of Literary Discourse* (Bloomington, 1977), p. 92; I am grateful to Jonathan Culler for his reference to this interesting book.

[36] [Habermas] Ibid., p. 148.

[37] [Habermas] Ibid., p. 147.

[38] Paul Grice (1913–1988), British philosopher.

suggests that, in Gricean terms, the standards of quantity, quality and manner for display texts differ from those Grice suggests for declarative speech in his maxims."

In the end, the analysis leads to a confirmation of the thesis it would like to refute. To the degree that the poetic, world-disclosing function of language gains primacy and structuring force, language escapes the structural constraints and communicative functions of everyday life. The space of fiction that is opened up when linguistic forms of expression become reflexive results from suspending illocutionary binding forces and those idealizations that make possible a use of language oriented toward mutual understanding— and hence make possible a coordination of plans of action that operates via the intersubjective recognition of criticizable validity claims. One can read Derrida's debate with Austin also as a denial of this independently structured domain of everyday communicative practice; it corresponds to the denial of an autonomous realm of fiction.

IV

Because Derrida denies both, he can analyze any given discourse in accord with the model of poetic language, and do so as if language generally were determined by the poetic use of language specialized in world-disclosure. From this viewpoint, language as such converges with literature or indeed with "writing." This *aestheticizing of language, which is purchased with the twofold denial of the proper senses of normal and poetic discourse,* also explains Derrida's insensitivity toward the tension-filled polarity between the poetic-world-disclosive function of language and its prosaic, innerworldly functions, which a modified version of Bühler's functional scheme takes into consideration.[39]

Linguistically mediated processes such as the acquisition of knowledge, the transmission of culture, the formation of personal identity, and socialization and social integration involve mastering problems posed by the world; the independence of learning processes that Derrida cannot acknowledge is due to the independent logics of these problems and the linguistic medium tailored to deal with them. For Derrida, linguistically mediated processes within the world are embedded in a *world-constituting* context that prejudices everything; they are fatalistically delivered up to the unmanageable happening of text production, overwhelmed by the poetic-creative transformation of a background designed by archewriting, and condemned to be provincial. An aesthetic contextualism blinds

him to the fact that everyday communicative practice makes learning processes possible (thanks to built-in idealizations) in relation to which the world-disclosive force of interpreting language has in turn to prove its worth. These learning processes unfold an independent logic that transcends all local constraints, because experiences and judgments are formed only in the light of criticizable validity claims. Derrida neglects the potential for negation inherent in the validity basis of action oriented toward reaching understanding; he permits the capacity to solve problems to disappear behind the world-creating capacity of language; the former capacity is possessed by language as the medium through which those acting communicatively get involved in relations to the world whenever they agree with one another about something in the objective world, in their common social world, or in the subjective worlds to which each has privileged access.

Richard Rorty[40] proposes a similar leveling; unlike Derrida, however, he does not remain idealistically fixated upon the history of metaphysics as a transcendent happening that determines everything intramundane. According to Rorty, science and morality, economics and politics, are delivered up to a process of language-creating protuberances *in just the same way* as art and philosophy. Like Kuhnian[41] history of science, the flux of interpretations beats rhythmically between revolutions and normalizations of language. He observes this back-and-forth between two situations in all fields of cultural life: "One is the sort of situation encountered when people pretty much agree on what is wanted, and are talking about how best to get it. In such a situation there is no need to say anything terribly unfamiliar, for argument is typically about the truth of assertions rather than about the utility of vocabularies. The contrasting situation is one in which everything is up for grabs at once—in which the motives and terms of discussions are a central subject of argument. . . . In such periods people begin to toss around old words in new senses, to throw in the occasional neologism, and thus to hammer out a new idiom which initially attracts attention to itself and only later gets put to work."[42] One notices how the Nietzschean pathos of a *Lebensphilosophie* that has made the linguistic turn beclouds the sober insights of pragmatism; in the picture painted by Rorty, the renovative process of linguistic world-disclosure no longer has a *counterpoise* in the testing processes of intramundane practice. The "Yes" and "No" of

---

[39] [Habermas] See Jürgen Habermas, *Theory of Communicative Action,* volume 1 (Boston, 1984), pp. 273ff.

[40] Rorty (below, page 1457).

[41] Kuhn (above, page 1280).

[42] [Habermas] Richard Rorty, "Deconstruction and Circumvention" (manuscript, 1983); and *Consequences of Pragmatism* (Minneapolis, 1982), especially the introduction and chapters 6, 7, and 9.

communicatively acting agents is so prejudiced and rhetorically overdetermined by their linguistic contexts that the anomalies that start to arise during the phases of exhaustion are taken to represent only symptoms of waning vitality, or aging processes analogous to processes of nature—and are not seen as the result of *deficient* solutions to problems and *invalid* answers.

Intramundane linguistic practice draws its power of negation from validity claims that go beyond the horizons of any currently given context. But the contextualist concept of language, laden as it is with *Lebensphilosophie*, is impervious to the very real force of the counterfactual, which makes itself felt in the idealizing presuppositions of communicative action. Hence Derrida and Rorty are also mistaken about the unique status of discourses differentiated from ordinary communication and tailored to a single validity dimension (truth or normative rightness), or to a single complex of problems (questions of truth or justice). In modern societies, the spheres of science, morality, and law have crystallized around these forms of argumentation. The corresponding cultural systems of action administer *problem-solving capacities* in a way similar to that in which the enterprises of art and literature administer *capacities for world-disclosure*. Because Derrida overgeneralizes this one linguistic function—namely, the poetic—he can no longer see the complex relationship of the ordinary practice of normal speech to the two extraordinary spheres, differentiated, as it were, in opposite directions. The polar tension between world-disclosure and problem-solving is held together within the functional matrix of ordinary language; but art and literature on the one side, and science, morality, and law on the other, are specialized for experiences and modes of knowledge that can be shaped and worked out within the compass of *one* linguistic function and *one* dimension of validity at a time. Derrida holistically levels these complicated relationships in order to equate philosophy with literature and criticism. He fails to recognize the special status that both philosophy and literary criticism, each in its own way, assume as mediators between expert cultures and the everyday world.

Literary criticism, institutionalized in Europe since the eighteenth century, has contributed to the differentiation of art. It has responded to the increasing autonomy of linguistic works of art by means of a discourse specialized for questions of taste. In it, the claims with which literary texts appear are submitted to examination—claims to "artistic truth," aesthetic harmony, exemplary validity, innovative force, and authenticity. In this respect, aesthetic criticism is similar to argumentative forms specialized for propositional truth and the rightness of norms, that is, to theoretical and practical discourse. It is, however, not merely an esoteric component of expert culture but, beyond this, has the job of mediating between expert culture and everyday world.

This *bridging function* of art criticism is more obvious in the cases of music and the plastic arts than in that of literary works, which are already formulated in the medium of language, even if it is a poetic, self-referential language. From this second, exoteric standpoint, criticism performs a translating activity of a unique kind. It brings the experiential content of the work of art into normal language; the innovative potential of art and literature for the lifeworlds and life histories that reproduce themselves through everyday communicative practice can only be unleashed in this maieutic way. This is then deposited in the changed configuration of the evaluative vocabulary, in a renovation of value orientations and need interpretations, which alters the color of modes of life by way of altering modes of perception.

Philosophy also occupies a position with two fronts similar to that of literary criticism—or at least this is true of modern philosophy, which no longer promises to redeem the claims of religion in the name of theory. On the one hand, it directs its interest to the foundations of science, morality, and law and attaches theoretical claims to its statements. Characterized by universalist problematics and strong theoretical strategies, it maintains an intimate relationship with the sciences. And yet philosophy is not simply an esoteric component of an expert culture. It maintains just as intimate a relationship with the totality of the lifeworld and with sound common sense, even if in a subversive way it relentlessly shakes up the certainties of everyday practice. Philosophical thinking represents the lifeworld's interest in the whole complex of functions and structures connected and combined in communicative action, and it does so in the face of knowledge systems differentiated out in accord with particular dimensions of validity. Of course, it maintains this relationship to totality with a reflectiveness lacking in the intuitively present background proper to the lifeworld.

If one takes into consideration the two-front position of criticism and philosophy that I have only sketched here—toward the everyday world on the one side, and on the other toward the specialized cultures of art and literature, science and morality—it becomes clear what the leveling of the genre distinction between philosophy and literature, and the assimilation of philosophy to literature and of literature to philosophy, as affirmed in propositions 2 and 2′, mean. This leveling and this assimilation confusedly jumble the constellations in which the rhetorical elements of language assume *entirely different* roles. The rhetorical element occurs in its *pure form* only in the self-referentiality of the poetic expression, that is, in the language of fiction specialized for world-disclosure. Even the normal language of everyday life is ineradicably rhetorical; but within the matrix of different linguistic functions, the rhetorical elements recede here. The world-disclosive linguistic framework is almost at a standstill in the routines of everyday practice. The same holds true of the specialized languages of science and technology, law and morality, economics, political science, etc. They, too, live off of the illuminating power of metaphorical tropes; but the rhetorical elements, which are by no means expunged, are tamed, as it were, and enlisted for special purposes of problem-solving.

The rhetorical dimension plays a different and far more important role in the language of literary criticism and philosophy. They are both faced with tasks that are paradoxical in similar ways. They are supposed to feed the contents of expert cultures, in which knowledge is accumulated under one aspect of validity at a time, into an everyday practice in which all linguistic functions and aspects of validity are intermeshed to form one syndrome. And yet literary criticism and philosophy are supposed to accomplish this task of mediation with means of expression taken from languages specialized in questions of taste or of truth. They can only resolve this paradox by rhetorically expanding and enriching their special languages to the extent that is required to link up indirect communications with the manifest contents of statements, and to do so in a deliberate way. That explains the strong rhetorical strain characteristic of studies by literary critics and philosophers alike. Significant critics and great philosophers are also noted writers. Literary criticism and philosophy have a family resemblance to literature—and to this extent to one another as well—in their rhetorical achievements. But their family relationship stops right there, for in each of these enterprises the tools of rhetoric are subordinated to the discipline of a *distinct* form of argumentation.

If, following Derrida's recommendation, philosophical thinking were to be relieved of the duty of solving problems and shifted over to the function of literary criticism, it would be robbed not merely of its seriousness, but of its productivity. Conversely, the literary-critical power of judgment loses its potency when, as is happening among Derrida's disciples in literature departments, it gets displaced from appropriating aesthetic experiential contents into the critique of metaphysics. The false assimilation of one enterprise to the other robs both of their substance. And so we return to the issue with which we started. Whoever transposes the radical critique of reason into the domain of rhetoric in order to blunt the paradox of self-referentiality,

also dulls the sword of the critique of reason itself. The false pretense of eliminating the genre distinction between philosophy and literature cannot lead us out of this aporia.[43]

---

[43] [Habermas] Our reflections have brought us to a point from which we can see why Heidegger, Adorno, and Derrida get into this aporia at all. They all still defend themselves as if they were living in the shadow of the "last" philosopher, as did the first generation of Hegelian disciples. They are still battling against the "strong" concepts of theory, truth, and system that have actually belonged to the past for over a century and a half. They still think they have to arouse philosophy from what Derrida calls "the dream of its heart." They believe that they have to tear philosophy away from the madness of expounding a theory that has the last word. Such a comprehensive, closed, and definitive system of propositions would have to be formulated in a language that is self-explanatory, that neither needs nor permits commentary, and thus that brings to a standstill the effective history in which interpretations are heaped upon interpretations without end. In this connection, Rorty speaks about the demand for a language "which can receive no gloss, requires no interpretation, cannot be distanced, cannot be sneered at by later generations. It is the hope for a vocabulary which is intrinsically and self-evidently final, not only the most comprehensive and fruitful vocabulary we have come up with so far." (Rorty, *Consequences of Pragmatism*, pp. 93ff.).

If reason were bound, under penalty of demise, to hold on to these goals of metaphysics classically pursued from Parmenides to Hegel, if reason as such (even after Hegel) stood before the alternative of either maintaining the strong concepts of theory, truth, and system that were common in the great tradition or of throwing in the sponge, then an *adequate* critique of reason would really have to grasp the roots at such a depth that it could scarcely avoid the paradoxes of self-referentiality. Nietzsche viewed the matter in this way. And, unfortunately, Heidegger, Adorno, and Derrida all still seem to confuse the universalist *problematics still maintained* in philosophy with the long since *abandoned status claims* that philosophy once alleged its answers to have. Today, however, it is clear that the scope of universalist questions—for instance, questions of the necessary conditions for the rationality of utterances, or of the universal pragmatic presuppositions of communicative action and argumentation—does indeed have to be reflected in the grammatical form of universal propositions—but not in any unconditional validity or "ultimate foundations" claimed for themselves or their theoretical framework. The fallibilist consciousness of the sciences caught up with philosophy, too, a long time ago.

With this kind of fallibilism, we, philosophers and nonphilosophers alike, do not by any means eschew truth claims. Such claims cannot be raised in the performative attitude of the first person other than as transcending space and time—precisely as claims. But we are also aware that there is no zero-context for truth claims. They are raised here and now and are open to criticism. Hence we reckon upon the trivial *possibility* that they will be revised tomorrow or some place else. Just as it always has, philosophy understands itself as the defender of rationality in the sense of the claim of reason endogenous to our form of life. In its work, however, it prefers a combination of strong presuppositions with weak status claims; so little is this totalitarian, that there is no call for a totalizing critique of reason against it. On this point see my "Die Philosophie als Platzhalter und Interpret," in *Moralbewusstsein und kommunikatives Handeln* (Frankfurt, 1983), pp. 7ff. (English translation forthcoming).

Gilles Deleuze

1925–1995

◇ ◇ ◇

Félix Guattari

1930–1992

Gilles Deleuze, a philosopher and theorist, collaborated over a period of more than twenty years with Félix Guattari, a radical psychoanalyst, in an exuberant and variegated critical and philosophical project, taking much of its original inspiration from political events in 1968. Their first major book together, *Anti-Oedipus: Capitalism and Schizophrenia* (1972), took aim at a general and widely disseminated conception of philosophy and psychoanalysis that contributed to a kind of "state" philosophy, a mode of propriety as control, seen as inimical to the existence of free thought and action, which they describe as "nomadic thought." Deleuze's earlier work in philosophy had concentrated on issues of perception and sense (informing his later work on film theory), generally within the orbit of academic philosophy, but actuated by a persistent resistance to the formalist constraints of the discipline. Guattari, on his part, was a student of Jacques Lacan (above, page 990) and an early colleague and associate of Jean Oury, founder of an experimental clinic at La Borde, notable for its practice of including psychiatric patients as active participants in their own treatment and in the affairs of the clinic.

The selection included here, from *A Thousand Plateaus* (1980), itself a continuation of *Anti-Oedipus* and bearing the same subtitle, *Capitalism and Schizophrenia,* serves as the introduction to a book that at times resembles a happening, a rock concert, a series of eruptive digressions and connections, with the general aim of disrupting a conventional sense of order in the interest of freeing thought and enabling connections in readers' minds, all the while claiming the book to have "neither object nor subject." Yet for all its deliberate, even extravagant deployment of metaphor and essentially catachrestic rhetorical figures, the philosophical strategy of this work emerges clearly and insistently in the vigorous insight that thought *always* lags behind nature, revealing the cognitive impulse to tidiness in ferocious tension with a creative, eruptive, and libidinal energy that is also of the nature of thinking. Treating writing in whatever genre as a process of assemblage, Deleuze and Guattari, in their joint detestation of dialectic as an argumentative machine, nevertheless ensure what is more properly conceived as a dialogic, an unpredictable dialogue, that de-centers thinking as a condition for its renewal.

Collaborative works (translated into English) by Deleuze and Guattari include *Anti-Oedipus: Capitalism and Schizophrenia* (1977); *Kafka: Toward a Minor Literature*

(1986); *Nomadology: The War Machine* (1986); *A Thousand Plateaus: Capitalism and Schizophrenia* (1987); *What Is Philosophy?* (1994). Works by Deleuze alone include: *Nietzsche and Philosophy* (1962; tr. 1983); *The Critical Philosophy of Kant* (1963, tr. 1984); *Difference and Repetition* (1968, tr. 1994); *The Logic of Sense* (1969, tr. 1990); and *Cinema 1: The Movement-Image* (1983, tr. 1986). Guattari is the author of *Molecular Revolution: Psychiatry and Politics* (1984). Critical studies include Ronald Bogue's *Deleuze and Guattari* (1989); Brian Massumi's *A User's Guide to Capitalism and Schizophrenia: Deviations from Deleuze and Guattari* (1992); Charles J. Stivale's *The Twofold Thought of Deleuze and Guattari: Intersections and Animations* (1998); and *A Shock to Thought: Expression after Deleuze and Guattari* (2002), edited by Brian Massumi.

1. Introduction: Rhizome

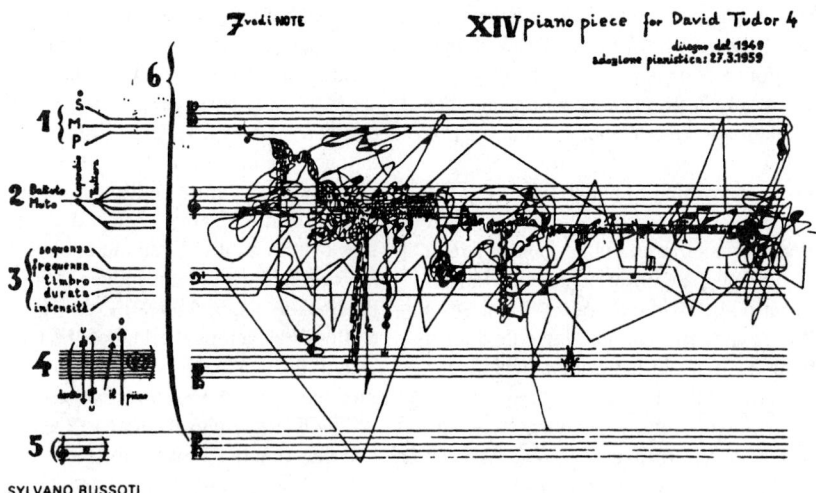

SYLVANO BUSSOTI

The two of us wrote *Anti-Oedipus* together. Since each of us was several, there was already quite a crowd. Here we have made use of everything that came within range, what was closest as well as farthest away. We have assigned clever pseudonyms to prevent recognition. Why have we kept our own names? Out of habit, purely out of habit. To make ourselves unrecognizable in turn. To render imperceptible, not ourselves, but what makes us act, feel, and think. Also because it's nice to talk like everybody else, to say the sun rises, when everybody knows it's only a manner of speaking. To reach, not the point where one no longer says I, but the point where it is no longer of any importance whether one says I. We are no longer ourselves. Each will know his own. We have been aided, inspired, multiplied.

A book has neither object nor subject; it is made of variously formed matters, and very different dates and speeds. To attribute the book to a subject is to overlook this working of matters, and the exteriority of their relations. It is to fabricate a beneficent God to explain geological movements. In a book, as in all things, there are lines of articulation or segmentarity, strata and territories; but also lines of flight, movements of deterritorialization and destratification. Comparative rates of flow on these lines produce phenomena of relative slowness and viscosity, or, on the contrary, of acceleration and rupture. All this, lines and measurable speeds, constitutes an *assemblage.* A book is an assemblage of this kind, and as such is unattributable. It is a multiplicity—but we don't know yet what the multiple entails when it is no longer attributed, that is, after it has been elevated to the status of a substantive. One side of a machinic assemblage faces the strata, which doubtless make it a kind of organism, or signifying totality, or determination attributable to a subject; it also has a side facing a *body without organs,* which is continually dismantling the organism, causing asignifying particles or pure intensities to pass or circulate, and attributing to itself subjects that it leaves with nothing more than a name as the trace of an intensity. What is the body without organs of a book? There are several, depending on the nature of the lines considered, their particular grade or density, and the possibility of their converging on a "plane of consistency" assuring their selection. Here, as elsewhere, the units of measure are what is essential: *quantify writing.* There is no difference between what a book talks about and how it is made. Therefore a book also has no object. As an assemblage, a book has only itself, in connection with other assemblages and in relation to other bodies without organs. We will never ask what a book means, as signified or signifier; we will not look for anything to understand in it. We will ask what it functions with, in connection with what other things it does or does not transmit intensities, in which other multiplicities its own are inserted and metamorphosed, and with what bodies without organs it makes its own converge. A book exists only through the outside and on the outside. A book itself is a little machine; what is the relation (also measurable) of this literary machine to a war machine, love machine, revolutionary machine, etc.—and an *abstract machine* that sweeps them along? We have been criticized for overquoting literary authors. But when one writes, the only question is which other machine the literary machine can be plugged into, must be plugged into in order to work. Kleist and a mad war machine, Kafka and a most extraordinary bureaucratic machine[1] . . . (What if one became animal or plant *through* literature, which certainly does not mean literally? Is it not first through the voice that one becomes animal?) Literature is an assemblage. It has nothing to do with ideology. There is no ideology and never has been.

All we talk about are multiplicities, lines, strata and segmentarities, lines of flight and intensities, machinic assemblages and their various types, bodies without organs and their construction and selection, the plane of consis-

tency, and in each case the units of measure. *Stratometers, deleometers, BwO units of density, BwO units of convergence:* Not only do these constitute a quantification of writing, but they define writing as always the measure of something else. Writing has nothing to do with signifying. It has to do with surveying, mapping, even realms that are yet to come.

A first type of book is the root-book. The tree is already the image of the world, or the root the image of the world-tree. This is the classical book, as noble, signifying, and subjective organic interiority (the strata of the book). The book imitates the world, as art imitates nature: by procedures specific to it that accomplish what nature cannot or can no longer do. The law of the book is the law of reflection, the One that becomes two. How could the law of the book reside in nature, when it is what presides over the very division between world and book, nature and art? One becomes two: whenever we encounter this formula, even stated strategically by Mao[2] or understood in the most "dialectical" way possible, what we have before us is the most classical and well reflected, oldest, and weariest kind of thought. Nature doesn't work that way: in nature, roots are taproots with a more multiple, lateral, and circular system of ramification, rather than a dichotomous one. Thought lags behind nature. Even the book as a natural reality is a taproot, with its pivotal spine and surrounding leaves. But the book as a spiritual reality, the Tree or Root as an image, endlessly develops the law of the One that becomes two, then of the two that become four . . . Binary logic is the spiritual reality of the root-tree. Even a discipline as "advanced" as linguistics retains the root-tree as its fundamental image, and thus remains wedded to classical reflection (for example, Chomsky[3] and his grammatical trees, which begin at a point S and proceed by dichotomy). This is as much as to say that this system of thought has never reached an understanding of multiplicity: in order to arrive at two following a spiritual method it must assume a strong principal unity. On the side of the object, it is no doubt possible, following the natural method, to go directly from One to three, four, or five, but only if there is a strong principal unity available, that of the pivotal taproot supporting the secondary roots. That doesn't get us very far. The binary logic of dichotomy has simply been replaced by biunivocal relationships between successive circles. The pivotal taproot provides no better understanding of multiplicity than the dichotomous root. One operates in the object, the other in the subject.

---

[1] Heinrich Wilhelm von Kleist (1777–1811), German dramatist; Franz Kafka (1883–1924), Czech novelist.

[2] Mao Zedong (1893–1976), Chinese People's Republic leader.
[3] Chomsky (above, page 1166).

Binary logic and biunivocal relationships still dominate psychoanalysis (the tree of delusion in the Freudian interpretation of Schreber's case), linguistics, structuralism, and even information science.

The radicle-system, or fascicular root, is the second figure of the book, to which our modernity pays willing allegiance. This time, the principal root has aborted, or its tip has been destroyed; an immediate, indefinite multiplicity of secondary roots grafts onto it and undergoes a flourishing development. This time, natural reality is what aborts the principal root, but the root's unity subsists, as past or yet to come, as possible. We must ask if reflexive, spiritual reality does not compensate for this state of things by demanding an even more comprehensive secret unity, or a more extensive totality. Take William Burroughs's[4] cut-up method: the folding of one text onto another, which constitutes multiple and even adventitious roots (like a cutting), implies a supplementary dimension to that of the texts under consideration. In this supplementary dimension of folding, unity continues its spiritual labor. That is why the most resolutely fragmented work can also be presented as the Total Work or Magnum Opus. Most modern methods for making series proliferate or a multiplicity grow are perfectly valid in one direction, for example, a linear direction, whereas a unity of totalization asserts itself even more firmly in another, circular or cyclic, dimension. Whenever a multiplicity is taken up in a structure, its growth is offset by a reduction in its laws of combination. The abortionists of unity are indeed angel makers, *doctores angelici,* because they affirm a properly angelic and superior unity. Joyce's[5] words, accurately described as having "multiple roots," shatter the linear unity of the word, even of language, only to posit a cyclic unity of the sentence, text, or knowledge. Nietzsche's[6] aphorisms shatter the linear unity of knowledge, only to invoke the cyclic unity of the eternal return, present as the nonknown in thought. This is as much as to say that the fascicular system does not really break with dualism, with the complementarity between a subject and an object, a natural reality and a spiritual reality: unity is consistently thwarted and obstructed in the object, while a new type of unity triumphs in the subject. The world has lost its pivot; the subject can no longer even dichotomize, but accedes to a higher unity, of ambivalence or overdetermination, in an always supplementary dimension to that of its object. The world has become chaos, but the book remains the image of the world: radicle-

chaosmos rather than root-cosmos. A strange mystification: a book all the more total for being fragmented. At any rate, what a vapid idea, the book as the image of the world. In truth, it is not enough to say, "Long live the multiple," difficult as it is to raise that cry. No typographical, lexical, or even syntactical cleverness is enough to make it heard. The multiple *must be made,* not by always adding a higher dimension, but rather in the simplest of ways, by dint of sobriety, with the number of dimensions one already has available—always $n - 1$ (the only way the one belongs to the multiple: always subtracted). Subtract the unique from the multiplicity to be constituted; write at $n - 1$ dimensions. A system of this kind could be called a rhizome. A rhizome as subterranean stem is absolutely different from roots and radicles. Bulbs and tubers are rhizomes. Plants with roots or radicles may be rhizomorphic in other respects altogether: the question is whether plant life in its specificity is not entirely rhizomatic. Even some animals are, in their pack form. Rats are rhizomes. Burrows are too, in all of their functions of shelter, supply, movement, evasion, and breakout. The rhizome itself assumes very diverse forms, from ramified surface extension in all directions to concretion into bulbs and tubers. When rats swarm over each other. The rhizome includes the best and the worst: potato and couchgrass, or the weed. Animal and plant, couchgrass is crabgrass. We get the distinct feeling that we will convince no one unless we enumerate certain approximate characteristics of the rhizome.

1 and 2. Principles of connection and heterogeneity: any point of a rhizome can be connected to anything other, and must be. This is very different from the tree or root, which plots a point, fixes an order. The linguistic tree on the Chomsky model still begins at a point S and proceeds by dichotomy. On the contrary, not every trait in a rhizome is necessarily linked to a linguistic feature: semiotic chains of every nature are connected to very diverse modes of coding (biological, political, economic, etc.) that bring into play not only different regimes of signs but also states of things of differing status. *Collective assemblages of enunciation* function directly within *machinic assemblages;* it is not impossible to make a radical break between regimes of signs and their objects. Even when linguistics claims to confine itself to what is explicit and to make no presuppositions about language, it is still in the sphere of a discourse implying particular modes of assemblage and types of social power. Chomsky's grammaticality, the categorical S symbol that dominates every sentence, is more fundamentally a marker of power than a syntactic marker: you will construct grammatically correct sentences, you will divide each statement into a noun phrase and a verb phrase (first dichotomy . . .).

---

[4] William Burroughs (1914–1997), American novelist.
[5] James Joyce (1882–1941), Irish novelist; the reference is to *Finnegans Wake* (1939).
[6] Nietzsche (above, page 686); see *Thus Spoke Zarathustra* (1883 to 1885) and *The Gay Science* (1882).

Our criticism of these linguistic models is not that they are too abstract but, on the contrary, that they are not abstract enough, that they do not reach the *abstract machine* that connects a language to the semantic and pragmatic contents of statements, to collective assemblages of enunciation, to a whole micropolitics of the social field. A rhizome ceaselessly establishes connections between semiotic chains, organizations of power, and circumstances relative to the arts, sciences, and social struggles. A semiotic chain is like a tuber agglomerating very diverse acts, not only linguistic, but also perceptive, mimetic, gestural, and cognitive: there is no language in itself, nor are there any linguistic universals, only a throng of dialects, patois, slangs, and specialized languages. There is no ideal speaker-listener, any more than there is a homogeneous linguistic community. Language is, in Weinreich's words, "an essentially heterogeneous reality."[7] There is no mother tongue, only a power takeover by a dominant language within a political multiplicity. Language stabilizes around a parish, a bishopric, a capital. It forms a bulb. It evolves by subterranean stems and flows, along river valleys or train tracks; it spreads like a patch of oil.[8] It is always possible to break a language down into internal structural elements, an undertaking not fundamentally different from a search for roots. There is always something genealogical about a tree. It is not a method for the people. A method of the rhizome type, on the contrary, can analyze language only by decentering it onto other dimensions and other registers. A language is never closed upon itself, except as a function of impotence.

3. Principle of multiplicity: it is only when the multiple is effectively treated as a substantive, "multiplicity," that it ceases to have any relation to the One as subject or object, natural or spiritual reality, image and world. Multiplicities are rhizomatic, and expose arborescent pseudomultiplicities for what they are. There is no unity to serve as a pivot in the object, or to divide in the subject. There is not even the unity to abort in the object or "return" in the subject. A multiplicity has neither subject nor object, only determinations, magnitudes, and dimensions that cannot increase in number without the multiplicity changing in nature (the laws of combination therefore increase in number as the multiplicity grows). Puppet strings, as a rhizome or multiplicity, are tied not to the supposed will of an artist or puppeteer but to a multiplicity of nerve fibers, which form another puppet in other dimensions connected to the first: "Call the strings or rods that move the puppet the weave. It might be objected that *its multiplicity* resides in the person of the actor, who projects it into the text. Granted; but the actor's nerve fibers in turn form a weave. And they fall through the gray matter, the grid, into the undifferentiated. . . . The interplay approximates the pure activity of weavers attributed in myth to the Fates or Norns."[9] An assemblage is precisely this increase in the dimensions of a multiplicity that necessarily changes in nature as it expands its connections. There are no points or positions in a rhizome, such as those found in a structure, tree, or root. There are only lines. When Glenn Gould[10] speeds up the performance of a piece, he is not just displaying virtuosity, he is transforming the musical points into lines, he is making the whole piece proliferate. The number is no longer a universal concept measuring elements according to their emplacement in a given dimension, but has itself become a multiplicity that varies according to the dimensions considered (the primacy of the domain over a complex of numbers attached to that domain). We do not have units (*unités*) of measure, only multiplicities or varieties of measurement. The notion of unity (*unité*) appears only when there is a power takeover in the multiplicity by the signifier or a corresponding subjectification proceeding: This is the case for a pivot-unity forming the basis for a set of biunivocal relationships between objective elements or points, or for the One that divides following the law of a binary logic of differentiation in the subject. Unity always operates in an empty dimension supplementary to that of the system considered (overcoding). The point is that a rhizome or multiplicity never allows itself to be overcoded, never has available a supplementary dimension over and above its number of lines, that is, over and above the multiplicity of numbers attached to those lines. All multiplicities are flat, in the sense that they fill or occupy all of their dimensions: we will therefore speak of a *plane of consistency* of multiplicities, even though the dimensions of this "plane" increase with the number of connections that are made on it. Multiplicities are defined by the outside: by the abstract line, the line of flight or deterritorialization according to which they change in nature and connect with other multiplicities. The plane of consistency (grid) is the outside of all multiplicities. The line of flight marks: the reality of a finite number of dimensions that the multiplicity effectively fills; the

[7][Deleuze and Guattari] [Tr.] U. Weinreich, W. Labov, and M. Herzog, "Empirical Foundations for a Theory of Language," in W. Lehmann and Y. Malkeiel, eds., *Directions for Historical Linguistics* (1968), p. 125; cited by Françoise Robert, "Aspects sociaux du changement dans une grammaire générative," *Languages,* no. 32 (December 1973), p. 90.

[8][Deleuze and Guattari] Bertil Malmberg, *New Trends in Linguistics,* tr. Edward Carners (Stockholm: Lund, 1964), pp. 65–67 (the example of the Castilian dialect).

[9][Deleuze and Guattari] Ernst Jünger, *Approaches: drogues et ivresse* (Paris: Table Ronde, 1974), p. 304, sec. 218.

[10]Glenn Gould (1932–1982), Canadian pianist.

impossibility of a supplementary dimension, unless the multiplicity is transformed by the line of flight; the possibility and necessity of flattening all of the multiplicities on a single plane of consistency or exteriority, regardless of their number of dimensions. The ideal for a book would be to lay everything out on a plane of exteriority of this kind, on a single page, the same sheet: lived events, historical determinations, concepts, individuals, groups, social formations. Kleist invented a writing of this type, a broken chain of affects and variable speeds, with accelerations and transformations, always in a relation with the outside. Open rings. His texts, therefore, are opposed in every way to the classical or romantic book constituted by the interiority of a substance or subject. The war machine-book against the State apparatus-book. *Flat multiplicities of n dimensions* are asignifying and asubjective. They are designated by indefinite articles, or rather by partitives (*some* couchgrass, *some* of a rhizome . . .).

4. Principle of asignifying rupture: against the oversignifying breaks separating structures or cutting across a single structure. A rhizome may be broken, shattered at a given spot, but it will start up again on one of its old lines, or on new lines. You can never get rid of ants because they form an animal rhizome that can rebound time and again after most of it has been destroyed. Every rhizome contains lines of segmentarity according to which it is stratified, territorialized, organized, signified, attributed, etc., as well as lines of deterritorialization down which it constantly flees. There is a rupture in the rhizome whenever segmentary lines explode into a line of flight, but the line of flight is part of the rhizome. These lines always tie back to one another. That is why one can never posit a dualism or a dichotomy, even in the rudimentary form of the good and the bad. You may make a rupture, draw a line of flight, yet there is still a danger that you will reencounter organizations that restratify everything, formations that restore power to a signifier, attributions that reconstitute a subject—anything you like, from Oedipal resurgences to fascist concretions. Groups and individuals contain microfascisms just waiting to crystallize. Yes, couchgrass is also a rhizome. Good and bad are only the products of an active and temporary selection, which must be renewed.

How could movements of deterritorialization and processes of reterritorialization not be relative, always connected, caught up in one another? The orchid deterritorializes by forming an image, a tracing of a wasp; but the wasp reterritorializes on that image. The wasp is nevertheless deterritorialized, becoming a piece in the orchid's reproductive apparatus. But it reterritorializes the orchid by transporting its pollen. Wasp and orchid, as heterogeneous elements, form

a rhizome. It could be said that the orchid imitates the wasp, reproducing its image in a signifying fashion (mimesis, mimicry, lure, etc.). But this is true only on the level of the strata—a parallelism between two strata such that a plant organization on one imitates an animal organization on the other. At the same time, something else entirely is going on: not imitation at all but a capture of code, surplus value of code, an increase in valence, a veritable becoming, a becoming-wasp of the orchid and a becoming-orchid of the wasp. Each of these becomings brings about the deterritorialization of one term and the reterritorialization of the other; the two becomings interlink and form relays in a circulation of intensities pushing the deterritorialization ever further. There is neither imitation nor resemblance, only an exploding of two heterogeneous series on the line of flight composed by a common rhizome that can no longer be attributed to or subjugated by anything signifying. Rémy Chauvin expresses it well: "the *aparallel evolution* of two beings that have absolutely nothing to do with each other."[11] More generally, evolutionary schemas may be forced to abandon the old model of the tree and descent. Under certain conditions, a virus can connect to germ cells and transmit itself as the cellular gene of a complex species; moreover, it can take flight, move into the cells of an entirely different species, but not without bringing with it "genetic information" from the first host (for example, Benveniste and Todaro's current research on a type C virus, with its double connection to baboon DNA and the DNA of certain kinds of domestic cats). Evolutionary schemas would no longer follow models of arborescent descent going from the least to the most differentiated, but instead a rhizome operating immediately in the heterogeneous and jumping from one already differentiated line to another.[12] Once again, there is *aparallel evolution,* of the baboon and the cat; it is obvious that they are not models or copies of each other (a becoming-baboon in the cat does not

---

[11] [Deleuze and Guattari] Rémy Chauvin in *Entretiens sur la sexualité,* ed. Max Aron, Robert Courrier, and Etienne Wolff (Paris: Plon, 1969), p. 205.

[12] [Deleuze and Guattari] On the work of R. E. Benveniste and G. J. Todaro, see Yves Christen, "Le role des virus dans l'évolution," *La Recherche,* no. 54 (March 1975): "After integration-extraction in a cell, viruses may, due to an error in excision, carry off fragments of their host's DNA and transmit them to new cells: this in fact is the basis for what we call 'genetic engineering.' As a result, the genetic information of one organism may be transferred to another by means of viruses. We could even imagine an extreme case where this transfer of information would go from a more highly evolved species to one that is less evolved or was the progenitor of the more evolved species. This mechanism, then, would run in the opposite direction to evolution in the classical sense. If it turns out that this kind of transferral of information has played a major role, we would in certain cases have to *substitute reticular schemas (with communications between branches after they have become differentiated) for the bush or tree schemas currently used to represent evolution*" (p. 271).

mean that the cat "plays" baboon). We form a rhizome with our viruses, or rather our viruses cause us to form a rhizome with other animals. As François Jacob says, transfers of genetic material by viruses or through other procedures, fusions of cells originating in different species, have results analogous to those of "the abominable couplings dear to antiquity and the Middle Ages."[13] Transversal communications between different lines scramble the genealogical trees. Always look for the molecular, or even submolecular, particle with which we are allied. We evolve and die more from our polymorphous and rhizomatic flus than from hereditary diseases, or diseases that have their own line of descent. The rhizome is an antigenealogy.

The same applies to the book and the world: contrary to a deeply rooted belief, the book is not an image of the world. It forms a rhizome with the world, there is an aparallel evolution of the book and the world; the book assures the deterritorialization of the world, but the world effects a reterritorialization of the book, which in turn deterritorializes itself in the world (if it is capable, if it can). Mimicry is a very bad concept, since it relies on binary logic to describe phenomena of an entirely different nature. The crocodile does not reproduce a tree trunk, any more than the chameleon reproduces the colors of its surroundings. The Pink Panther imitates nothing, it reproduces nothing, it paints the world its color, pink on pink; this is its becoming-world, carried out in such a way that it becomes imperceptible itself, asignifying, makes its rupture, its own line of flight, follows its "aparallel evolution" through to the end. The wisdom of the plants: even when they have roots, there is always an outside where they form a rhizome with something else—with the wind, an animal, human beings (and there is also an aspect under which animals themselves form rhizomes, as do people, etc.). "Drunkenness as a triumphant irruption of the plant in us." Always follow the rhizome by rupture; lengthen, prolong, and relay the line of flight; make it vary, until you have produced the most abstract and tortuous of lines of n dimensions and broken directions. Conjugate deterritorialized flows. Follow the plants: you start by delimiting a first line consisting of circles of convergence around successive singularities; then you see whether inside that line new circles of convergence establish themselves, with new points located outside the limits and in other directions. Write, form a rhizome, increase your territory by deterritorialization, extend the line of flight to the point where it becomes an abstract machine covering the entire plane of consistency. "Go first to your old plant and watch carefully the watercourse made by the rain. By now the rain must have carried the seeds far away. Watch the crevices made by the runoff, and from them determine the direction of the flow. Then find the plant that is growing at the farthest point from your plant. All the devil's weed plants that are growing in between are yours. Later . . . you can extend the size of your territory by following the watercourse from each point along the way."[14] Music has always sent out lines of flight, like so many "transformational multiplicities," even overturning the very codes that structure or arborify it; that is why musical form, right down to its ruptures and proliferations, is comparable to a weed, a rhizome.[15]

5 and 6. Principle of cartography and decalcomania: a rhizome is not amenable to any structural or generative model. It is a stranger to any idea of genetic axis or deep structure. A genetic axis is like an objective pivotal unity upon which successive stages are organized; a deep structure is more like a base sequence that can be broken down into immediate constituents, while the unity of the product passes into another, transformational and subjective, dimension. This does not constitute a departure from the representative model of the tree, or root—pivotal taproot or fascicles (for example, Chomsky's "tree" is associated with a base sequence and represents the process of its own generation in terms of binary logic). A variation on the oldest form of thought. It is our view that genetic axis and profound structure are above all infinitely reproducible principles of *tracing*. All of tree logic is a logic of tracing and reproduction. In linguistics as in psychoanalysis, its object is an unconscious that is itself representative, crystallized into codified complexes, laid out along a genetic axis and distributed within a syntagmatic structure. Its goal is to describe a de facto state, to maintain balance in intersubjective relations, or to explore an unconscious that is already there from the start, lurking in the dark recesses of memory and language. It consists of tracing, on the basis of an overcoding structure or supporting axis, something that comes ready-made. The tree articulates and hierarchizes tracings; tracings are like the leaves of a tree.

The rhizome is altogether different, a *map and not a tracing*. Make a map, not a tracing. The orchid does not re-

---

[13] [Deleuze and Guattari] François Jacob, *The Logic of Life,* tr. Betty E. Spillmann (New York: Pantheon, 1973), pp. 291–92, 311 (quote).

[14] [Deleuze and Guattari] Carlos Castaneda, *The Teachings of Don Juan* (Berkeley: University of California Press, 1971), p. 88.

[15] [Deleuze and Guattari] Pierre Boulez, *Conversations with Celestin Deliège* (London: Eulenberg Books, 1976): "a seed which you plant in compost, and suddenly it begins to proliferate like a weed" (p. 15); and on musical proliferation: "a music that floats, and in which the writing itself makes it impossible for the performer to keep in with a pulsed time" (p. 69 [translation modified]).

produce the tracing of the wasp; it forms a map with the wasp, in a rhizome. What distinguishes the map from the tracing is that it is entirely oriented toward an experimentation in contact with the real. The map does not reproduce an unconscious closed in upon itself; it constructs the unconscious. It fosters connections between fields, the removal of blockages on bodies without organs, the maximum opening of bodies without organs onto a plane of consistency. It is itself a part of the rhizome. The map is open and connectable in all of its dimensions; it is detachable, reversible, susceptible to constant modification. It can be torn, reversed, adapted to any kind of mounting, reworked by an individual, group, or social formation. It can be drawn on a wall, conceived of as a work of art, constructed as a political action or as a meditation. Perhaps one of the most important characteristics of the rhizome is that it always has multiple entryways; in this sense, the burrow is an animal rhizome, and sometimes maintains a clear distinction between the line of flight as passageway and storage or living strata (cf. the muskrat). A map has multiple entryways, as opposed to the tracing, which always comes back "to the same." The map has to do with performance, whereas the tracing always involves an alleged "competence." Unlike psychoanalysis, psychoanalytic competence (which confines every desire and statement to a genetic axis or overcoding structure, and makes infinite, monotonous tracings of the stages on that axis or the constituents of that structure), schizoanalysis rejects any idea of pretraced destiny, whatever name is given to it—divine, anagogic, historical, economic, structural, hereditary, or syntagmatic. (It is obvious that Melanie Klein[16] has no understanding of the cartography of one of her child patients, Little Richard, and is content to make ready-made tracings—Oedipus, the good daddy and the bad daddy, the bad mommy and the good mommy—while the child makes a desperate attempt to carry out a performance that the psychoanalyst totally misconstrues.)[17] Drives and part-objects are neither stages on a genetic axis nor positions in a deep structure; they are political options for problems, they are entryways and exits, impasses the child lives out politically, in other words, with all the force of his or her desire.

Have we not, however, reverted to a simple dualism by contrasting maps to tracings, as good and bad sides? Is it not

of the essence of the map to be traceable? Is it not of the essence of the rhizome to intersect roots and sometimes merge with them? Does not a map contain phenomena of redundancy that are already like tracings of its own? Does not a multiplicity have strata upon which unifications and totalizations, massifications, mimetic mechanisms, signifying power takeovers, and subjective attributions take root? Do not even lines of flight, due to their eventual divergence, reproduce the very formations their function it was to dismantle or outflank? But the opposite is also true. It is a question of method: *the tracing should always be put back on the map.* This operation and the previous one are not at all symmetrical. For it is inaccurate to say that a tracing reproduces the map. It is instead like a photograph or X ray that begins by selecting or isolating, by artificial means such as colorations or other restrictive procedures, what it intends to reproduce. The imitator always creates the model, and attracts it. The tracing has already translated the map into an image; it has already transformed the rhizome into roots and radicles. It has organized, stabilized, neutralized the multiplicities according to the axes of significance and subjectification belonging to it. It has generated, structuralized the rhizome, and when it thinks it is reproducing something else it is in fact only reproducing itself. That is why the tracing is so dangerous. It injects redundancies and propagates them. What the tracing reproduces of the map or rhizome are only the impasses, blockages, incipient taproots, or points of structuration. Take a look at psychoanalysis and linguistics: all the former has ever made are tracings or photos of the unconscious, and the latter of language, with all the betrayals that implies (it's not surprising that psychoanalysis tied its fate to that of linguistics). Look at what happened to Little Hans already, an example of child psychoanalysis at its purest: they kept on BREAKING HIS RHIZOME and BLOTCHING HIS MAP, setting it straight for him, blocking his every way out, until he began to desire his own shame and guilt, until they had rooted shame and guilt in him, PHOBIA (they barred him from the rhizome of the building, then from the rhizome of the street, they rooted him in his parents' bed, they radicled him to his own body, they fixated him on Professor Freud). Freud explicitly takes Little Hans's cartography into account, but always and only in order to project it back onto the family photo. And look what Melanie Klein did to Little Richard's geopolitical maps: she developed photos from them, made tracings of them. Strike the pose or follow the axis, genetic stage or structural destiny—one way or the other, your rhizome will be broken. You will be allowed to live and speak, but only after every outlet has been obstructed. Once a rhizome has been obstructed, arborified, it's all over, no desire stirs; for

---

[16]Melanie Klein (1882–1916), British psychoanalyst.

[17][Deleuze and Guattari] See Melanie Klein, *Narrative of a Child Analysis* (London: Hogarth Press, 1961): the role of war maps in Richard's activities. [TR: Deleuze and Guattari, with Claire Parnet and André Scala, analyze Klein's Richard and Freud's Little Hans in "The Interpretation of Utterances," in *Language, Sexuality and Subversion,* tr. Paul Foss and Meaghan Morris (Sydney: Feral Publications, 1978), pp. 141–57.]

it is always by rhizome that desire moves and produces. Whenever desire climbs a tree, internal repercussions trip it up and it falls to its death; the rhizome, on the other hand, acts on desire by external, productive outgrowths.

That is why it is so important to try the other, reverse but nonsymmetrical, operation. Plug the tracings back into the map, connect the roots or trees back up with a rhizome. In the case of Little Hans, studying the unconscious would be to show how he tries to build a rhizome, with the family house but also with the line of flight of the building, the street, etc.; how these lines are blocked, how the child is made to take root in the family, be photographed under the father, be traced onto the mother's bed; then how Professor Freud's intervention assures a power takeover by the signifier, a subjectification of affects; how the only escape route left to the child is a becoming-animal perceived as shameful and guilty (the becoming-horse of Little Hans, a truly political option). But these impasses must always be resituated on the map, thereby opening them up to possible lines of flight. The same applies to the group map: show at what point in the rhizome there form phenomena of massification, bureaucracy, leadership, fascization, etc., which lines nevertheless survive, if only underground, continuing to make rhizome in the shadows. Deligny's method: map the gestures and movements of an autistic child, combine several maps for the same child, for several different children.[18] If it is true that it is of the essence of the map or rhizome to have multiple entryways, then it is plausible that one could even enter them through tracings or the root-tree, assuming the necessary precautions are taken (once again, one must avoid any Manichaean dualism). For example, one will often be forced to take dead ends, to work with signifying powers and subjective affections, to find a foothold in formations that are Oedipal or paranoid or even worse, rigidified territorialities that open the way for other transformational operations. It is even possible for psychoanalysis to serve as a foothold, in spite of itself. In other cases, on the contrary, one will bolster oneself directly on a line of flight enabling one to blow apart strata, cut roots, and make new connections. Thus, there are very diverse map-tracing, rhizome-root assemblages, with variable coefficients of deterritorialization. There exist tree or root structures in rhizomes; conversely, a tree branch or root division may begin to burgeon into a rhizome. The coordinates are determined not by theoretical analyses implying universals but by a pragmatics composing multiplicities or aggregates of intensities. A new

rhizome may form in the heart of a tree, the hollow of a root, the crook of a branch. Or else it is a microscopic element of the root-tree, a radicle, that gets rhizome production going. Accounting and bureaucracy proceed by tracings: they can begin to burgeon nonetheless, throwing out rhizome stems, as in a Kafka novel. An intensive trait starts working for itself, a hallucinatory perception, synesthesia, perverse mutation, or play of images shakes loose, challenging the hegemony of the signifier. In the case of the child, gestural, mimetic, ludic, and other semiotic systems regain their freedom and extricate themselves from the "tracing," that is, from the dominant competence of the teacher's language—a microscopic event upsets the local balance of power. Similarly, generative trees constructed according to Chomsky's syntagmatic model can open up in all directions, and in turn form a rhizome.[19] To be rhizomorphous is to produce stems and filaments that seem to be roots, or better yet connect with them by penetrating the trunk, but put them to strange new uses. We're tired of trees. We should stop believing in trees, roots, and radicles. They've made us suffer too much. All of arborescent culture is founded on them, from biology to linguistics. Nothing is beautiful or loving or political aside from underground stems and aerial roots, adventitious growths and rhizomes. Amsterdam, a city entirely without roots, a rhizome-city with its stem-canals, where utility connects with the greatest folly in relation to a commercial war machine.

Thought is not arborescent, and the brain is not a rooted or ramified matter. What are wrongly called "dendrites" do not assure the connection of neurons in a continuous fabric. The discontinuity between cells, the role of the axons, the functioning of the synapses, the existence of synaptic microfissures, the leap each message makes across these fissures, make the brain a multiplicity immersed in its plane of consistency or neuroglia, a whole uncertain, probabilistic system ("the uncertain nervous system"). Many people have a tree growing in their heads, but the brain itself is much more a grass than a tree. "The axon and the dendrite twist around each other like bindweed around brambles, with synapses at each of the thorns."[20] The same goes for memory. Neurologists and psychophysiologists distinguish between long-term memory and short-term memory (on the order of a minute). The difference between them is not sim-

---

[18] [Deleuze and Guattari] Fernand Deligny, *Cahiers de l'immuable,* vol. 1, *Voix et voir, Recherches,* no. 8 (April 1975).

[19] [Deleuze and Guattari] See Dieter Wunderlich, "Pragmatique, situation d'énonciation et Deixis," in *Languages,* no. 26 (June 1972), pp. 50ff.: MacCawley, Sadock, and Wunderlich's attempts to integrate "pragmatic properties" into Chomskian trees.

[20] [Deleuze and Guattari] Steven Rose, *The Conscious Brain* (New York: Knopf, 1975), p. 76; on memory, see pp. 185–219.

ply quantitative: short-term memory is of the rhizome or diagram type, and long-term memory is arborescent and centralized (imprint, engram, tracing, or photograph). Short-term memory is in no way subject to a law of contiguity or immediacy to its object; it can act at a distance, come or return a long time after, but always under conditions of discontinuity, rupture, and multiplicity. Furthermore, the difference between the two kinds of memory is not that of two temporal modes of apprehending the same thing; they do not grasp the same thing, memory, or idea. The splendor of the short-term Idea: one writes using short-term memory, and thus short-term ideas, even if one reads or rereads using long-term memory of long-term concepts. Short-term memory includes forgetting as a process; it merges not with the instant but instead with the nervous, temporal, and collective rhizome. Long-term memory (family, race, society, or civilization) traces and translates, but what it translates continues to act in it, from a distance, off beat, in an "untimely" way, not instantaneously.

The tree and root inspire a sad image of thought that is forever imitating the multiple on the basis of a centered or segmented higher unity. If we consider the set, branches-roots, the trunk plays the role of *opposed segment* for one of the subsets running from bottom to top: this kind of segment is a "link dipole," in contrast to the "unit dipoles" formed by spokes radiating from a single center.[21] Even if the links themselves proliferate, as in the radicle system, one can never get beyond the One-Two, and fake multiplicities. Regenerations, reproductions, returns, hydras, and medusas do not get us any further. Arborescent systems are hierarchical systems with centers of significance and subjectification, central automata like organized memories. In the corresponding models, an element only receives information from a higher unit, and only receives a subjective affection along preestablished paths. This is evident in current problems in information science and computer science, which still cling to the oldest modes of thought in that they grant all power to a memory or central organ. Pierre Rosenstiehl and Jean Petitot, in a fine article denouncing "the imagery of command trees" (centered systems or hierarchical structures), note that "accepting the primacy of hierarchical structures amounts to giving arborescent structures privileged status. . . . The arborescent form admits of topological explanation. . . . In a hierarchical system, an individual has only one active neighbor, his or her hierarchical superior. . . . The channels of transmission are preestablished: the arborescent system preexists the individual, who is integrated into it at an allotted place" (significance and subjectification). The authors point out that even when one thinks one has reached a multiplicity, it may be a false one—of what we call the radicle type—because its ostensibly nonhierarchical presentation or statement in fact only admits of a totally hierarchical solution. An example is the famous *friendship theorem:* "If any two given individuals in a society have precisely one mutual friend, then there exists an individual who is the friend of all the others." (Rosenstiehl and Petitot ask who that mutual friend is. Who is "the universal friend in this society of couples: the master, the confessor, the doctor? These ideas are curiously far removed from the initial axioms." Who is this friend of humankind? Is it the *philo*sopher as he appears in classical thought, even if he is an aborted unity that makes itself felt only through its absence or subjectivity, saying all the while, I know nothing, I am nothing?) Thus the authors speak of dictatorship theorems. Such is indeed the principle of roots-trees, or their outcome: the radicle solution, the structure of Power.[22]

To these centered systems, the authors contrast acentered systems, finite networks of automata in which communication runs from any neighbor to any other, the stems or channels do not preexist, and all individuals are interchangeable, defined only by their *state* at a given moment—such that the local operations are coordinated and the final, global result synchronized without a central agency. Transduction of intensive states replaces topology, and "the graph regulating the circulation of information is in a way the opposite of the hierarchical graph. . . . There is no reason for the graph to be a tree" (we have been calling this kind of

---

[21] [Deleuze and Guattari] See Julien Pacotte, *Le réseau arborescent, schème primordial de la pensée* (Paris: Hermann, 1936). This book analyzes and develops various schemas of the arborescent form, which is presented not as a mere formalism but as the "real foundation of formal thought." It follows classical thought through to the end. It presents all of the forms of the "One-Two," the theory of the dipole. The set, trunk-roots-branches, yields the following schema:

opposed ⊢ segment

More recently, Michel Serres has analyzed varieties and sequences of trees in the most diverse scientific domains: how a tree is formed on the basis of a "network." *La traduction* (Paris: Minuit, 1974), pp. 27ff.; *Feux et signaux de brume* (Paris: Grasset, 1975), pp. 35ff.

[22] [Deleuze and Guattari] Pierre Rosenstiehl and Jean Petitot, "Automate asocial et systèmes acentrés," *Communications*, no. 22 (1974), pp. 45–62. On the friendship theorem, see Herbert S. Wilf, *The Friendship Theorem in Combinatorial Mathematics* (Welsh Academic Press); and on a similar kind of theorem, called the theorem of group indecision, see Kenneth J. Arrow, *Social Choice and Individual Values* (New York: Wiley, 1963).

graph a map). The problem of the war machine, or the firing squad: is a general necessary for *n* individuals to manage to fire in unison? The solution without a General is to be found in an acentered multiplicity possessing a finite number of states with signals to indicate corresponding speeds, from a war rhizome or guerrilla logic point of view, without any tracing, without any copying of a central order. The authors even demonstrate that this kind of machinic multiplicity, assemblage, or society rejects any centralizing or unifying automaton as an "asocial intrusion."[23] Under these conditions, *n* is in fact always *n* − 1. Rosenstiehl and Petitot emphasize that the opposition, centered-acentered, is valid less as a designation for things than as a mode of calculation applied to things. Trees may correspond to the rhizome, or they may burgeon into a rhizome. It is true that the same thing is generally susceptible to both modes of calculation or both types of regulation, but not without undergoing a change in state. Take psychoanalysis as an example again: it subjects the unconscious to arborescent structures, hierarchical graphs, recapitulatory memories, central organs, the phallus, the phallus-tree—not only in its theory but also in its practice of calculation and treatment. Psychoanalysis cannot change its method in this regard: it bases its own dictatorial power upon a dictatorial conception of the unconscious. Psychoanalysis's margin of maneuverability is therefore very limited. In both psychoanalysis and its object, there is always a general, always a leader (General Freud). Schizoanalysis, on the other hand, treats the unconscious as an acentered system, in other words, as a machinic network of finite automata (a rhizome), and thus arrives at an entirely different state of the unconscious. These same remarks apply to linguistics; Rosenstiehl and Petitot are right to bring up the possibility of an "acentered organization of a society of words." For both statements and desires, the issue is never to reduce the unconscious or to interpret it or to make it signify according to a tree model. The issue is to *produce the unconscious,* and with it new statements, different desires: the rhizome is precisely this production of the unconscious.

It is odd how the tree has dominated Western reality and all of Western thought, from botany to biology and anatomy, but also gnosiology, theology, ontology, all of philosophy . . . : the root-foundation, *Grund, racine, fondement.* The West has a special relation to the forest, and deforestation; the fields carved from the forest are populated with seed plants produced by cultivation based on species lineages of the arborescent type; animal raising, carried out on fallow fields, selects lineages forming an entire animal arborescence. The East presents a different figure: a relation to the steppe and the garden (or in some cases, the desert and the oasis), rather than forest and field; cultivation of tubers by fragmentation of the individual; a casting aside or bracketing of animal raising, which is confined to closed spaces or pushed out onto the steppes of the nomads. The West: agriculture based on a chosen lineage containing a large number of variable individuals. The East: horticulture based on a small number of individuals derived from a wide range of "clones." Does not the East, Oceania in particular, offer something like a rhizomatic model opposed in every respect to the Western model of the tree? André Haudricourt even sees this as the basis for the opposition between the moralities or philosophies of transcendence dear to the West and the immanent ones of the East: the God who sows and reaps, as opposed to the God who replants and unearths (replanting of offshoots versus sowing of seeds).[24] Transcendence: a specifically European disease. Neither is music the same, the music of the earth is different, as is sexuality: seed plants, even those with two sexes in the same plant, subjugate sexuality to the reproductive model; the rhizome, on the other hand, is a liberation of sexuality not only from reproduction but also from genitality. Here in the West, the tree has implanted itself in our bodies, rigidifying and stratifying even the sexes. We have lost the rhizome, or the grass. Henry Miller: "China is the weed in the human cabbage patch. . . . The weed is the Nemesis of human endeavor. . . . Of all the imaginary existences we attribute to plant, beast and star the weed leads the most satisfactory life of all. True, the weed produces no lilies, no battleships, no Sermons on the Mount. . . . Eventually the weed gets the upper hand. Eventually things fall back into a state of China. This condi-

---

[23] [Deleuze and Guattari] Rosenstiehl and Petitot, "Automate asocial." The principal characteristic of the acentered system is that local initiatives are coordinated independently of a central power, with the calculations made throughout the network (multiplicity). "That is why the only place files on people can be kept is right in each person's home, since they alone are capable of filling in the description and keeping it up to date: society itself is the only possible data bank on people. A naturally acentered society rejects the centralizing automaton as an asocial intrusion" (p. 62). On the "Firing Squad Theorem," see pp. 51–57. It even happens that generals, dreaming of appropriating the formal techniques of guerrilla warfare, appeal to *multiplicities* "of synchronous modules . . . based on numerous but independent lightweight cells" having in theory only a minimum of central power and "hierarchical relaying"; see Guy Brossollet, *Essai sur la non-bataille* (Paris: Belin, 1975).

[24] [Deleuze and Guattari] On Western agriculture of grain plants and Eastern horticulture of tubers, the opposition between sowing of seeds and replanting of offshoots, and the contrast to animal raising, see André Haudricourt, "Domestication des animaux, culture des plantes et traitement d'autrui," *L'Homme,* vol. 2, no. 1 (January–April 1962), pp. 40–50, and "Nature et culture dans la civilisation de l'igname: l'origine des clones et des clans," *L'Homme,* vol. 4, no. 1 (January–April 1964), pp. 93–104. Maize and rice are no exception: they are cereals "adopted at a late date by tuber cultivators" and were treated in a similar fashion; it is probable that rice "first appeared as a weed in taro ditches."

tion is usually referred to by historians as the Dark Age. Grass is the only way out. . . . The weed exists only to fill the waste spaces left by cultivated areas. *It grows between,* among other things. The lily is beautiful, the cabbage is provender, the poppy is maddening—but the weed is rank growth . . .: it points a moral."[25] Which China is Miller talking about? The old China, the new, an imaginary one, or yet another located on a shifting map?

America is a special case. Of course it is not immune from domination by trees or the search for roots. This is evident even in the literature, in the quest for a national identity and even for a European ancestry or genealogy (Kerouac[26] going off in search of his ancestors). Nevertheless, everything important that has happened or is happening takes the route of the American rhizome: the beatniks, the underground, bands and gangs, successive lateral offshoots in immediate connection with an outside. American books are different from European books, even when the American sets off in pursuit of trees. The conception of the book is different. *Leaves of Grass.*[27] And directions in America are different: the search for arborescence and the return to the Old World occur in the East. But there is the rhizomatic West, with its Indians without ancestry, its ever-receding limit, its shifting and displaced frontiers. There is a whole American "map" in the West, where even the trees form rhizomes. America reversed the directions: it put its Orient in the West, as if it were precisely in America that the earth came full circle; its West is the edge of the East.[28] (India is not the intermediary between the Occident and the Orient, as Haudricourt[29] believed: America is the pivot point and mechanism of reversal.) The American singer Patti Smith sings the bible of the American dentist: Don't go for the root, follow the canal . . .

Are there not also two kinds of bureaucracy, or even three (or still more)? Western bureaucracy: its agrarian, cadastral origins; roots and fields; trees and their role as frontiers; the great census of William the Conqueror; feudalism; the policies of the kings of France; making property the basis of the State; negotiating land through warfare, litigation, and marriages. The kings of France chose the lily because it is a plant with deep roots that clings to slopes. Is bureaucracy the same in the Orient? Of course it is all too easy to depict an Orient of rhizomes and immanence; yet it is true that in the Orient the State does not act following a schema of arborescence corresponding to preestablished, arborified, and rooted classes; its bureaucracy is one of channels, for example, the much-discussed case of hydraulic power with "weak property," in which the State engenders channeled and channelizing classes (cf. the aspects of Wittfogel's work that have not been refuted).[30] The despot acts as a river, not as a fountainhead, which is still a point, a tree-point or root; he flows with the current rather than sitting under a tree; Buddha's tree itself becomes a rhizome; Mao's river and Louis's tree. Has not America acted as an intermediary here as well? For it proceeds both by internal exterminations and liquidations (not only the Indians but also the farmers, etc.), and by successive waves of immigration from the outside. The flow of capital produces an immense channel, a quantification of power with immediate "quanta," where each person profits from the passage of the money flow in his or her own way (hence the reality-myth of the poor man who strikes it rich and then falls into poverty again): in America everything comes together, tree and channel, root and rhizome. There is no universal capitalism, there is no capitalism in itself; capitalism is at the crossroads of all kinds of formations, it is neocapitalism by nature. It invents its eastern face and western face, and reshapes them both—all for the worst.

At the same time, we are on the wrong track with all these geographical distributions. An impasse. So much the better. If it is a question of showing that rhizomes also have their own, even more rigid, despotism and hierarchy, then fine and good: for there is no dualism, no ontological dualism between here and there, no axiological dualism between good and bad, no blend or American synthesis. There are knots of arborescence in rhizomes, and rhizomatic offshoots in roots. Moreover, there are despotic formations of immanence and channelization specific to rhizomes, just as there are anarchic deformations in the transcendent system of trees, aerial roots, and subterranean stems. The important point is that the root-

---

[25] [Deleuze and Guattari] Henry Miller, in Henry Miller and Michael Fraenkel, *Hamlet* (New York: Carrefour, 1939), pp. 105–106.

[26] Jack Kerouac (1922–1969), American novelist.

[27] By Walt Whitman (above, page 673).

[28] [Deleuze and Guattari] See Leslie Fiedler, *The Return of the Vanishing American* (New York: Stein and Day, 1968). This book contains a fine analysis of geography and its role in American mythology and literature, and of the reversal of directions. In the East, there was the search for a specifically American code and for a recoding with Europe (Henry James, Eliot, Pound, etc.); in the South, there was the overcoding of the slave system, with its ruin and the ruin of the plantations during the Civil War (Faulkner, Caldwell); from the North came capitalist decoding (Dos Passos, Dreiser); the West, however, played the role of a line of flight combining travel, hallucination, madness, the Indians, perceptive and mental experimentation, the shifting of frontiers, the rhizome (Ken Kesey and his "fog machine," the beat generation, etc.). Every great American author creates a cartography, even in his or her style; in contrast to what is done in Europe, each makes a map that is directly connected to the real social movements crossing America. An example is the indexing of geographical directions throughout the work of Fitzgerald.

[29] Andre Haudricourt, twentieth-century French linguist.

[30] [Deleuze and Guattari] [Tr.] Karl Wittfogel, *Oriental Despotism* (New Haven, Conn.: Yale University Press, 1957).

tree and canal-rhizome are not two opposed models: the first operates as a transcendent model and tracing, even if it engenders its own escapes; the second operates as an immanent process that overturns the model and outlines a map, even if it constitutes its own hierarchies, even if it gives rise to a despotic channel. It is not a question of this or that place on earth, or of a given moment in history, still less of this or that category of thought. It is a question of a model that is perpetually in construction or collapsing, and of a process that is perpetually prolonging itself, breaking off and starting up again. No, this is not a new or different dualism. The problem of writing: in order to designate something exactly, anexact expressions are utterly unavoidable. Not at all because it is a necessary step, or because one can only advance by approximations: anexactitude is in no way an approximation; on the contrary, it is the exact passage of that which is under way. We invoke one dualism only in order to challenge another. We employ a dualism of models only in order to arrive at a process that challenges all models. Each time, mental correctives are necessary to undo the dualisms we had no wish to construct but through which we pass. Arrive at the magic formula we all seek—PLURALISM = MONISM—via all the dualisms that are the enemy, an entirely necessary enemy, the furniture we are forever rearranging.

Let us summarize the principal characteristics of a rhizome: unlike trees or their roots, the rhizome connects any point to any other point, and its traits are not necessarily linked to traits of the same nature; it brings into play very different regimes of signs, and even nonsign states. The rhizome is reducible neither to the One nor the multiple. It is not the One that becomes Two or even directly three, four, five, etc. It is not a multiple derived from the One, or to which One is added ($n + 1$). It is composed not of units but of dimensions, or rather directions in motion. It has neither beginning nor end, but always a middle *(milieu)* from which it grows and which it overspills. It constitutes linear multiplicities with n dimensions having neither subject nor object, which can be laid out on a plane of consistency, and from which the One is always subtracted ($n - 1$). When a multiplicity of this kind changes dimension, it necessarily changes in nature as well, undergoes a metamorphosis. Unlike a structure, which is defined by a set of points and positions, with binary relations between the points and biunivocal relationships between the positions, the rhizome is made only of lines: lines of segmentarity and stratification as its dimensions, and the line of flight or deterritorialization as the maximum dimension after which the multiplicity undergoes metamorphosis, changes in nature. These lines, or lineaments, should not be confused with lineages of the arborescent type, which are merely localizable linkages between points and positions. Unlike the tree, the rhizome is not the object of reproduction: neither external reproduction as image-tree nor internal reproduction as tree-structure. The rhizome is an antigenealogy. It is a short-term memory, or antimemory. The rhizome operates by variation, expansion, conquest, capture, offshoots. Unlike the graphic arts, drawing, or photography, unlike tracings, the rhizome pertains to a map that must be produced, constructed, a map that is always detachable, connectable, reversible, modifiable, and has multiple entryways and exits and its own lines of flight. It is tracings that must be put on the map, not the opposite. In contrast to centered (even polycentric) systems with hierarchical modes of communication and preestablished paths, the rhizome is an acentered, nonhierarchical, nonsignifying system without a General and without an organizing memory or central automaton, defined solely by a circulation of states. What is at question in the rhizome is a relation to sexuality—but also to the animal, the vegetal, the world, politics, the book, things natural and artificial—that is totally different from the arborescent relation: all manner of "becomings."

A plateau is always in the middle, not at the beginning or the end. A rhizome is made of plateaus. Gregory Bateson uses the word "plateau" to designate something very special: a continuous, self-vibrating region of intensities whose development avoids any orientation toward a culmination point or external end. Bateson cites Balinese culture as an example: mother-child sexual games, and even quarrels among men, undergo this bizarre intensive stabilization. "Some sort of continuing plateau of intensity is substituted for [sexual] climax," war, or a culmination point. It is a regrettable characteristic of the Western mind to relate expressions and actions to exterior or transcendent ends, instead of evaluating them on a plane of consistency on the basis of their intrinsic value.[31] For example, a book composed of chapters has culmination and termination points. What takes place in a book composed instead of plateaus that communicate with one another across microfissures, as in a brain? We call a "plateau" any multiplicity connected to other multiplicities by superficial underground stems in such a way as to form or extend a rhizome. We are writing this book as a rhizome. It is composed of plateaus. We have given it a circular form, but only for laughs. Each morning we would wake up, and each of us

---

[31] [Deleuze and Guattari] Gregory Bateson, *Steps to an Ecology of Mind* (New York: Ballantine Books, 1972), p. 113. It will be noted that the word "plateau" is used in classical studies of bulbs, tubers, and rhizomes; see the entry for "Bulb" in M. H. Baillon, *Dictionnaire de botanique* (Paris: Hachette, 1876–1892).

would ask himself what plateau he was going to tackle, writing five lines here, ten there. We had hallucinatory experiences, we watched lines leave one plateau and proceed to another like columns of tiny ants. We made circles of convergence. Each plateau can be read starting anywhere and can be related to any other plateau. To attain the multiple, one must have a method that effectively constructs it; no typographical cleverness, no lexical agility, no blending or creation of words, no syntactical boldness, can substitute for it. In fact, these are more often than not merely mimetic procedures used to disseminate or disperse a unity that is retained in a different dimension for an image-book. Technonarcissism. Typographical, lexical, or syntactic creations are necessary only when they no longer belong to the form of expression of a hidden unity, becoming themselves dimensions of the multiplicity under consideration; we only know of rare successes in this.[32] We ourselves were unable to do it. We just used words that in turn function for us as plateaus. RHIZOMATICS = SCHIZOANALYSIS = STRATOANALYSIS = PRAGMATICS = MICROPOLITICS. These words are concepts, but concepts are lines, which is to say, number systems attached to a particular dimension of the multiplicities (strata, molecular chains, lines of flight or rupture, circles of convergence, etc.). Nowhere do we claim for our concepts the title of a science. We are no more familiar with scientificity than we are with ideology; all we know are assemblages. And the only assemblages are machinic assemblages of desire and collective assemblages of enunciation. No significance, no subjectification: writing to the *n*th power (all individuated enunciation remains trapped within the dominant significations, all signifying desire is associated with dominated subjects). An assemblage, in its multiplicity, necessarily acts on semiotic flows, material flows, and social flows simultaneously (independently of any recapitulation that may be made of it in a scientific or theoretical corpus). There is no longer a tripartite division between a field of reality (the world) and a field of representation (the book) and a field of subjectivity (the author). Rather, an assemblage establishes connections between certain multiplicities drawn from each of these orders, so that a book has no sequel nor the world as its object nor one or several authors as its subject. In short, we think that one cannot write sufficiently in the name of an outside. The outside has no image, no signification, no subjectivity. The book as assemblage with the outside, against the book as image of the world. A rhizome-book, not a dichotomous, pivotal, or fasci-

cular book. Never send down roots, or plant them, however difficult it may be to avoid reverting to the old procedures. "Those things which occur to me, occur to me not from the root up but rather only from somewhere about their middle. Let someone then attempt to seize them, let someone attempt to seize a blade of grass and hold fast to it when it begins to grow only from the middle."[33] Why is this so difficult? The question is directly one of perceptual semiotics. It's not easy to see things in the middle, rather than looking down on them from above or up at them from below, or from left to right or right to left: try it, you'll see that everything changes. It's not easy to see the grass in things and in words (similarly, Nietzsche said that an aphorism had to be "ruminated"; never is a plateau separable from the cows that populate it, which are also the clouds in the sky).

History is always written from the sedentary point of view and in the name of a unitary State apparatus, at least a possible one, even when the topic is nomads. What is lacking is a Nomadology, the opposite of a history. There are rare successes in this also, for example, on the subject of the Children's Crusades: Marcel Schwob's book multiplies narratives like so many plateaus with variable numbers of dimensions. Then there is Andrzejewski's book, *Les portes du paradis* (The gates of paradise), composed of a single uninterrupted sentence; a flow of children; a flow of walking with pauses, straggling, and forward rushes; the semiotic flow of the confessions of all the children who go up to the old monk at the head of the procession to make their declarations; a flow of desire and sexuality, each child having left out of love and more or less directly led by the dark posthumous pederastic desire of the count of Vendôme; all this with circles of convergence. What is important is not whether the flows are "One or multiple"—we're past that point: there is a collective assemblage of enunciation, a machinic assemblage of desire, one inside the other and both plugged into an immense outside that is a multiplicity in any case. A more recent example is Armand Farrachi's book on the Fourth Crusade, *La dislocation,* in which the sentences space themselves out and disperse, or else jostle together and coexist, and in which the letters, the typography begin to dance as the crusade grows more delirious.[34] These are

---

[32] [Deleuze and Guattari] For example, Joëlle de La Casinière, *Absolument nécessaire. The Emergency Book* (Paris: Minuit, 1973), a truly nomadic book. In the same vein, see the research in progress at the Montfaucon Research Center.

[33] [Deleuze and Guattari] *The Diaries of Franz Kafka,* ed. Max Brod, tr. Joseph Kresh (New York: Schocken, 1948), p. 12.

[34] [Deleuze and Guattari] Marcel Schwob, *The Children's Crusade,* tr. Henry Copley (Boston: Small, Maynard, 1898); Jersy Andrzejewski, *Les portes du paradis* (Paris: Gallimard, 1959); Armand Farrachi, *La dislocation* (Paris: Stock, 1974). It was in the context of Schwob's book that Paul Alphandéry remarked that literature, in certain cases, could revitalize history and impose upon it "genuine research directions"; *La chrétienté et l'idée de croisade* (Paris: Albin Michel, 1959), vol. 2, p. 116.

models of nomadic and rhizomatic writing. Writing weds a war machine and lines of flight, abandoning the strata, segmentarities, sedentary, the State apparatus. But why is a model still necessary? Aren't these books still "images" of the Crusades? Don't they still retain a unity, in Schwob's case a pivotal unity, in Farrachi's an aborted unity, and in the most beautiful example, *Les portes du paradis,* the unity of the funereal count? Is there a need for a more profound nomadism than that of the Crusades, a nomadism of true nomads, or of those who no longer even move or imitate anything? The nomadism of those who only assemble *(agencent).* How can the book find an adequate outside with which to assemble in heterogeneity, rather than a world to reproduce? The cultural book is necessarily a tracing: already a tracing of itself, a tracing of the previous book by the same author, a tracing of other books however different they may be, an endless tracing of established concepts and words, a tracing of the world present, past, and future. Even the anticultural book may still be burdened by too heavy a cultural load: but it will use it actively, for forgetting instead of remembering, for underdevelopment instead of progress toward development, in nomadism rather than sedentarity, to make a map instead of a tracing. RHIZOMATICS = POP ANALYSIS, even if the people have other things to do besides read it, even if the blocks of academic culture or pseudoscientificity in it are still too painful or ponderous. For science would go completely mad if left to its own devices. Look at mathematics: it's not a science, it's a monster slang, it's nomadic. Even in the realm of theory, especially in the realm of theory, any precarious and pragmatic framework is better than tracing concepts, with their breaks and progress changing nothing. Imperceptible rupture, not signifying break. The nomads invented a war machine in opposition to the State apparatus. History has never comprehended nomadism, the book has never comprehended the outside. The State as the model for the book and for thought has a long history: logos, the philosopher-king, the transcendence of the Idea, the interiority of the concept, the republic of minds, the court of reason, the functionaries of thought, man as legislator and subject. The State's pretension to be a world order, and to root man. The war machine's relation to an outside is not another "model"; it is an assemblage that makes thought itself nomadic, and the book a working part in every mobile machine, a stem for a rhizome (Kleist and Kafka against Goethe).[35]

Write to the *n*th power, the *n* − 1 power, write with slogans: Make rhizomes, not roots, never plant! Don't sow, grow offshoots! Don't be one or multiple, be multiplicities! Run lines, never plot a point! Speed turns the point into a line![36] Be quick, even when standing still! Line of chance, line of hips, line of flight. Don't bring out the General in you! Don't have just ideas, just have an idea (Godard). Have short-term ideas. Make maps, not photos or drawings. Be the Pink Panther and your loves will be like the wasp and the orchid, the cat and the baboon. As they say about old man river:

> He don't plant 'tatos
> Don't plant cotton
> Them that plants them is soon forgotten
> But old man river he just keeps rollin' along

A rhizome has no beginning or end; it is always in the middle, between things, interbeing, *intermezzo.* The tree is filiation, but the rhizome is alliance, uniquely alliance. The tree imposes the verb "to be," but the fabric of the rhizome is the conjunction, "and . . . and . . . and . . ." This conjunction carries enough force to shake and uproot the verb "to be." Where are you going? Where are you coming from? What are you heading for? These are totally useless questions. Making a clean slate, starting or beginning again from ground zero, seeking a beginning or a foundation—all imply a false conception of voyage and movement (a conception that is methodical, pedagogical, initiatory, symbolic. . .). But Kleist, Lenz, and Büchner have another way of traveling and moving: proceeding from the middle, through the middle, coming and going rather than starting and finishing.[37] American literature, and already English literature, manifest this rhizomatic direction to an even greater extent; they know how to move between things, establish a logic of the AND, overthrow ontology, do away with foundations, nullify endings and beginnings. They know how to practice pragmatics. The middle is by no means an average; on the contrary, it is where things pick up speed. *Between* things does not designate a localizable relation going from one thing to the other and back again, but a perpendicular direction, a transversal movement that sweeps one *and* the other away, a stream without beginning or end that undermines its banks and picks up speed in the middle.

---

[35] Johann Wolfgang von Goethe (1749–1832), German poet and dramatist.

[36] [Deleuze and Guattari] See Paul Virilio, "Véhiculaire," in *Nomades et vagabonds,* ed. Jacques Bergue (Paris: Union Générale d'Editions, 1975), p. 43, on the appearance of linearity and the disruption of perception by speed.

[37] [Deleuze and Guattari] See Jean-Cristophe Bailly's description of movement in German Romanticism, in his introduction to *La légende dispersée. Anthologie du romantisme allemand* (Paris: Union Générale d'Editions, 1976), pp. 18ff. [Jacob Michael Reinhold Lienz (1751–1792), German poet; Georg Büchner (1813–1837), German dramatist.]

Richard Rorty

b. 1931

Richard Rorty's work represents one type of philosophy identified as pragmatism, a term coined by C. S. Peirce (above, page 668) and adopted (without Peirce's concurrence) by William James and John Dewey. Rorty's brand explicitly identifies pragmatism as culturally allied with art and politics. Indeed, he divides philosophers roughly into two groups: 1. those who regard philosophy as a handmaiden to science and technology, and 2. those who argue that philosophy does not describe an "outer" world. This second group emerged out of epistemological idealism, which (as in Hegel [above, page 552]) still thought that "spirit" could be represented, even if the outer world could not. This evolved toward pragmatism, which in Rorty's version is deeply involved with the "linguistic turn," a phrase first used by Gustav Bergmann which supplied the title for a collection of philosophical essays that Rorty edited in 1967.

Rather than being descriptive of the world, language, for Rorty, is a workable tool. What he regards as needed is a philosophy that acknowledges that the world is "out there" but that "truth" is made by human beings, especially in language. It follows that descriptions of the world may be true or false depending on their workability, but the world as such is neither true nor false, these categories belonging only to language. This is not to say that there is no truth, but that questions like that of the nature of truth are unprofitable to pursue. The world does not speak Aristotelian, Newtonian, Einsteinian, Freudian, Marxian, or anything. It does not speak at all. People speak.

Rorty regards language not as a medium conveying prior meanings but a making, which is always in process. It is fundamentally metaphorical, and what we think of as literality is dead metaphor no longer recognized as such. New metaphor is disruptive of dead metaphorical or habitual thought that has come to seem literal and correspondent to some external or internal "reality." Literal is but what is familiar; metaphor is the unfamiliar that may drive a new theory. As a result, for Rorty, philosophy of interest is not part of a debate over "pros and cons of a thesis" but rather a "contest between an entrenched vocabulary that has become a nuisance and a half-formed vocabulary which vaguely promises great things."

One sees in Rorty, as he himself points out, the influence of Wittgenstein's notion of language games and workability, and more generally the whole "linguistic turn," stretching back at least to Von Humboldt in its idealistic phase and coming up through structuralism and deconstruction. This form of pragmatism may be seen in rather simplified form applied to literary texts in Fish (above, page 1395), and it is strictly opposed to the positivism represented by Russell (above, page 811) and Carnap (above, page 978) and on the other hand to various forms of idealism emerging from Hegel.

Works by Rorty include *The Linguistic Turn* (ed., 1967), *Philosophy and the Mirror of Nature* (1979); *Consequences of Pragmatism* (1982); *Contingency, Irony, and Solidarity* (1989); *Essays on Heidegger and Others* (1991); *Philosophical Papers* (1991, 1998);

Philosophy and Social Hope (1999). See David L. Hall, *Richard Rorty: Prophet and Poet of the New Pragmatism* (1994); Norman Geras, *Solidarity in the Conversation of Humankind: The Ungroundable Liberalism of Richard Rorty* (1995); H. O. Mounse, *The Two Pragmatisms: Peirce to Rorty* (1997); Richard Rumana, *On Rorty* (2000) and *Richard Rorty: An Annotated Bibliography of Secondary Literature* (2002); Robert B. Brandon, ed., *Rorty and His Critics* (2000); Alan Malachowski, *Richard Rorty* (2002).

The Contingency of Language

About two hundred years ago, the idea that truth was made rather than found began to take hold of the imagination of Europe. The French Revolution had shown that the whole vocabulary of social relations, and the whole spectrum of social institutions, could be replaced almost overnight. This precedent made utopian politics the rule rather than the exception among intellectuals. Utopian politics sets aside questions about both the will of God and the nature of man and dreams of creating a hitherto unknown form of society.

At about the same time, the Romantic poets were showing what happens when art is thought of no longer as imitation but, rather, as the artist's self-creation. The poets claimed for art the place in culture traditionally held by religion and philosophy, the place which the Enlightenment had claimed for science. The precedent the Romantics set lent initial plausibility to their claim. The actual role of novels, poems, plays, paintings, statues, and buildings in the social movements of the last century and a half has given it still greater plausibility.

By now these two tendencies have joined forces and have achieved cultural hegemony. For most contemporary intellectuals, questions of ends as opposed to means—questions about how to give a sense to one's own life or that of one's community—are questions for art or politics, or both, rather than for religion, philosophy, or science. This development has led to a split within philosophy. Some philosophers have remained faithful to the Enlightenment and have continued to identify themselves with the cause of science. They see the old struggle between science and religion, reason and unreason, as still going on, having now taken the form of a struggle between reason and all those forces within culture which think of truth as made rather than found. These philosophers take science as the paradigmatic human activity, and they insist that natural science discovers truth rather than makes it. They regard "making truth" as a merely metaphorical, and thoroughly misleading, phrase. They think of politics and art as spheres in which the notion of "truth" is out of place. Other philosophers, realizing that the world as it is described by the physical sciences teaches no moral lesson, offers no spiritual comfort, have concluded that science is no more than the handmaiden of technology. These philosophers have ranged themselves alongside the political utopian and the innovative artist.

Whereas the first kind of philosopher contrasts "hard scientific fact" with the "subjective" or with "metaphor," the second kind sees science as one more human activity, rather as the place at which human beings encounter a "hard," nonhuman reality. On this view, great scientists invent descriptions of the world which are useful for purposes of predicting and controlling what happens, just as poets and political thinkers invent other descriptions of it for other purposes. But there is no sense in which *any* of these descriptions is an accurate representation of the way the world is in itself. These philosophers regard the very idea of such a representation as pointless.

Had the first sort of philosopher, the sort whose hero is the natural scientist, always been the only sort, we should probably never have had an autonomous discipline called "philosophy"—a discipline as distinct from the sciences as it is from theology or from the arts. As such a discipline, philosophy is no more than two hundred years old. It owes its existence to attempts by the German idealists to put the sciences in their place and to give a clear sense to the vague idea that human beings make truth rather than find it. Kant[1] wanted to consign science to the realm of second-rate truth—truth about a phenomenal world. Hegel[2] wanted to think of natural science as a description of spirit not yet fully conscious of its own spiritual nature, and thereby to elevate the sort of truth offered by the poet and the political revolutionary to first-rate status.

German idealism, however, was a short-lived and unsatisfactory compromise. For Kant and Hegel went only

---

"The Contingency of Language" is Chapter One of *Contingency, Irony, and Solidarity,* published by Cambridge University Press in 1989.

[1] Kant (above, page 416).
[2] Hegel (above, page 552).

halfway in their repudiation of the idea that truth is "out there." They were willing to view the world of empirical science as a made world—to see matter as constructed by mind, or as consisting in mind insufficiently conscious of its own mental character. But they persisted in seeing mind, spirit, the depths of the human self, as having an intrinsic nature—one which could be known by a kind of nonempirical super science called philosophy. This meant that only half of truth—the bottom, scientific half—was made. Higher truth, the truth about mind, the province of philosophy, was still a matter of discovery rather than creation.

What was needed, and what the idealists were unable to envisage, was a repudiation of the very idea of anything—mind or matter, self or world—having an intrinsic nature to be expressed or represented. For the idealists confused the idea that nothing has such a nature with the idea that space and time are unreal, that human beings cause the spatiotemporal world to exist.

We need to make a distinction between the claim that the world is out there and the claim that truth is out there. To say that the world is out there, that it is not our creation, is to say, with common sense, that most things in space and time are the effects of causes which do not include human mental states. To say that truth is not out there is simply to say that where there are no sentences there is no truth, that sentences are elements of human languages, and that human languages are human creations.

Truth cannot be out there—cannot exist independently of the human mind—because sentences cannot so exist, or be out there. The world is out there, but descriptions of the world are not. Only descriptions of the world can be true or false. The world on its own—unaided by the describing activities of human beings—cannot.

The suggestion that truth, as well as the world, is out there is a legacy of an age in which the world was seen as the creation of a being who had a language of his own. If we cease to attempt to make sense of the idea of such a nonhuman language, we shall not be tempted to confuse the platitude that the world may cause us to be justified in believing a sentence true with the claim that the world splits itself up, on its own initiative, into sentence-shaped chunks called "facts." But if one clings to the notion of self-subsistent facts, it is easy to start capitalizing the word "truth" and treating it as something identical either with God or with the world as God's project. Then one will say, for example, that Truth is great, and will prevail.

This conflation is facilitated by confining attention to single sentences as opposed to vocabularies. For we often let the world decide the competition between alternative sentences (e.g., between "Red wins" and "Black wins" or between "The butler did it" and "The doctor did it"). In such cases, it is easy to run together the fact that the world contains the causes of our being justified in holding a belief with the claim that some nonlinguistic state of the world is itself an example of truth, or that some such state "makes a belief true" by "corresponding" to it. But it is not so easy when we turn from individual sentences to vocabularies as wholes. When we consider examples of alternative language games—the vocabulary of ancient Athenian politics versus Jefferson's, the moral vocabulary of Saint Paul versus Freud's, the jargon of Newton versus that of Aristotle, the idiom of Blake versus that of Dryden—it is difficult to think of the world as making one of these better than another, of the world as deciding between them.[3] When the notion of "description of the world" is moved from the level of criterion-governed sentences within language games to language games as wholes, games which we do not choose between by reference to criteria, the idea that the world decides which descriptions are true can no longer be given a clear sense. It becomes hard to think that that vocabulary is somehow already out there in the world, waiting for us to discover it. Attention (of the sort fostered by intellectual historians like Thomas Kuhn and Quentin Skinner)[4] to the vocabularies in which sentences are formulated, rather than to individual sentences, makes us realize, for example, that the fact that Newton's vocabulary lets us predict the world more easily than Aristotle's does not mean that the world speaks Newtonian.

The world does not speak. Only we do. The world can, once we have programmed ourselves with a language, cause us to hold beliefs. But it cannot propose a language for us to speak. Only other human beings can do that. The realization that the world does not tell us what language games to play should not, however, lead us to say that a decision about which to play is arbitrary, nor to say that it is the expression of something deep within us. The moral is not that objective criteria for choice of vocabulary are to be replaced with subjective criteria, reason with will or feeling. It is rather that the notions of criteria and choice (including that of "arbitrary" choice) are no longer in point when it comes to changes from one language game to another. Europe did not *decide* to accept the idiom of Romantic poetry, or of socialist politics, or of Galilean mechanics. That sort of shift was

---

[3] Thomas Jefferson (1743–1826), U.S. president; Freud (above, page 746); Isaac Newton (1642–1727), English mathematician and philosopher; Aristotle (above, page 48); Blake (above, page 447); Dryden (above, page 253).
[4] Thomas S. Kuhn (1922–1996; above, page 1280), historian of science, author of *The Structure of Scientific Revolutions* (1962) and other works; Quentin Skinner (b. 1940), British historian.

no more an act of will than it was a result of argument. Rather, Europe gradually lost the habit of using certain words and gradually acquired the habit of using others.

As Kuhn argues in *The Copernican Revolution,*[5] we did not decide on the basis of some telescopic observations, or on the basis of anything else, that the earth was not the center of the universe, that macroscopic behavior could be explained on the basis of microstructural motion, and that prediction and control should be the principal aim of scientific theorizing. Rather, after a hundred years of inconclusive muddle, the Europeans found themselves speaking in a way which took these interlocked theses for granted. Cultural change of this magnitude does not result from applying criteria (or from "arbitrary decision") any more than individuals become theists or atheists, or shift from one spouse or circle of friends to another, as a result either of applying criteria or of *actes gratuits.* We should not look within ourselves for criteria of decision in such matters any more than we should look to the world.

The temptation to look for criteria is a species of the more general temptation to think of the world, or the human self, as possessing an intrinsic nature, an essence. That is, it is the result of the temptation to privilege some one among the many languages in which we habitually describe the world or ourselves. As long as we think that there is some relation called "fitting the world" or "expressing the real nature of the self" which can be possessed or lacked by vocabularies-as-wholes, we shall continue the traditional philosophical search for a criterion to tell us which vocabularies have this desirable feature. But if we could ever become reconciled to the idea that most of reality is indifferent to our descriptions of it, and that the human self is created by the use of a vocabulary rather than being adequately or inadequately expressed in a vocabulary, then we should at last have assimilated what was true in the Romantic idea that truth is made rather than found. What is true about this claim is just that *languages* are made rather than found, and that truth is a property of linguistic entities, of sentences.[6]

I can sum up by redescribing what, in my view, the revolutionaries and poets of two centuries ago were getting at. What was glimpsed at the end of the eighteenth century was that anything could be made to look good or bad, important or unimportant, useful or useless, by being redescribed. What Hegel describes as the process of spirit gradually becoming self-conscious of its intrinsic nature is better described as the process of European linguistic practices changing at a faster and faster rate. The phenomenon Hegel describes is that of more people offering more radical redescriptions of more things than ever before, of young people going through half a dozen spiritual gestalt-switches before reaching adulthood. What the Romantics expressed as the claim that imagination, rather than reason, is the central human faculty was the realization that a talent for speaking differently, rather than for arguing well, is the chief instrument of cultural change. What political utopians since the French Revolution have sensed is not that an enduring, substratal human nature has been suppressed or repressed by "unnatural" or "irrational" social institutions but rather that changing languages and other social practices may produce human beings of a sort that had never before existed. The German idealists, the French revolutionaries, and the Romantic poets had in common a dim sense that human beings whose language changed so that they no longer spoke of themselves as responsible to nonhuman powers would thereby become a new kind of human beings.

The difficulty faced by a philosopher who, like myself, is sympathetic to this suggestion—one who thinks of himself as auxiliary to the poet rather than to the physicist—is to avoid hinting that this suggestion gets something right, that my sort of philosophy corresponds to the way things really are. For this talk of correspondence brings back just the idea my sort of philosopher wants to get rid of, the idea that the world or the self has an intrinsic nature. From our point of view, explaining the success of science, or the desirability of political liberalism, by talk of "fitting the world" or "expressing human nature" is like explaining why opium makes you sleepy by talking about its dormitive power. To say that Freud's vocabulary gets at the truth about human nature, or Newton's at the truth about the heavens, is not an explanation of anything. It is just an empty compliment—one traditionally paid to writers whose novel jargon we have found useful. To say that there is no such thing as intrinsic nature is not to say that the intrinsic nature of reality has turned out, surprisingly enough, to be extrinsic. It is to say that the term "intrinsic nature" is one which it would pay us not to use, an expression which has caused more trouble than it has been worth. To say that we should drop the idea of truth as out there waiting to be discovered is not to say

---

[5]Published 1957.

[6][Rorty] I have no criterion for distinct languages or vocabularies to offer, but I am not sure that we need one. Philosophers have used phrases like "in the language L" for a long time without worrying too much about how one can tell where one natural language ends and another begins, nor about when "the scientific vocabulary of the sixteenth century" ends and "the vocabulary of the New Science" begins. Roughly, a break of this sort occurs when we start using "translation" rather than "explanation" in talking about geographical or chronological differences. This will happen whenever we find it handy to start mentioning words rather than using them—to highlight the difference between two sets of human practices by putting quotation marks around elements of those practices.

that we have discovered that, out there, there is no truth.[7] It is to say that our purposes would be served best by ceasing to see truth as a deep matter, as a topic of philosophical interest, or "true" as a term which repays "analysis." "The nature of truth" is an unprofitable topic, resembling in this respect "the nature of man" and "the nature of God," and differing from "the nature of the positron," and "the nature of Oedipal fixation." But this claim about relative profitability, in turn, is just the recommendation that we in fact *say* little about these topics, and see how we get on.

On the view of philosophy which I am offering, philosophers should not be asked for arguments against, for example, the correspondence theory of truth or the idea of the "intrinsic nature of reality." The trouble with arguments against the use of a familiar and time-honored vocabulary is that they are expected to be phrased in that very vocabulary. They are expected to show that central elements in that vocabulary are "inconsistent in their own terms" or that they "deconstruct themselves." But that can *never* be shown. Any argument to the effect that our familiar use of a familiar term is incoherent, or empty, or confused, or vague, or "merely metaphorical" is bound to be inconclusive and question-begging. For such use is, after all, the paridigm of coherent, meaningful, literal, speech. Such arguments are always parasitic upon, and abbreviations for, claims that a better vocabulary is available. Interesting philosophy is rarely an examination of the pros and cons of a thesis. Usually it is, implicitly or explicitly, a contest between an entrenched vocabulary which has become a nuisance and a half-formed new vocabulary which vaguely promises great things.

The latter "method" of philosophy is the same as the "method" of utopian politics or revolutionary science (as opposed to parliamentary politics, or normal science). The method is to redescribe lots and lots of things in new ways, until you have created a pattern of linguistic behavior which will tempt the rising generation to adopt it, thereby causing them to look for appropriate new forms of nonlinguistic behavior, for example, the adoption of new scientific equipment or new social institutions. This sort of philosophy does not work piece by piece, analyzing concept after concept, or testing thesis after thesis. Rather, it works holistically and pragmatically. It says things like "try thinking of it this way"—or more specifically, "try to ignore the apparently

futile traditional questions by substituting the following new and possibly interesting questions." It does not pretend to have a better candidate for doing the same old things which we did when we spoke in the old way. Rather, it suggests that we might want to stop doing those things and do something else. But it does not argue for this suggestion on the basis of antecedent criteria common to the old and the new language games. For just insofar as the new language really is new, there will be no such criteria.

Conforming to my own precepts, I am not going to offer arguments against the vocabulary I want to replace. Instead, I am going to try to make the vocabulary I favor look attractive by showing how it may be used to describe a variety of topics. More specifically, in this chapter I shall be describing the work of Donald Davidson[8] in philosophy of language as a manifestation of a willingness to drop the idea of "intrinsic nature," a willingness to face up to the *contingency* of the language we use. In subsequent chapters, I shall try to show how a recognition of that contingency leads to a recognition of the contingency of conscience, and how both recognitions lead to a picture of intellectual and moral progress as a history of increasingly useful metaphors rather than of increasing understanding of how things really are.

I begin, in this first chapter, with the philosophy of language because I want to spell out the consequences of my claims that only sentences can be true, and that human beings make truths by making languages in which to phrase sentences. I shall concentrate on the work of Davidson because he is the philosopher who has done most to explore these consequences.[9] Davidson's treatment of truth ties in with his treatment of language learning and of metaphor to form the first systematic treatment of language which breaks *completely* with the notion of language as something which can be adequate or inadequate to the world or to the self. For Davidson breaks with the notion that language is a *medium*— a medium either of representation or of expression.

I can explain what I mean by a medium by noting that the traditional picture of the human situation has been one in which human beings are not simply networks of beliefs and desires but rather beings which *have* those beliefs and

---

[7] [Rorty] Nietzsche has caused a lot of confusion by inferring from "truth is not a matter of correspondence to reality" to "what we call 'truths' are just useful lies." The same confusion is occasionally found in Derrida, in the inference from "there is no such reality as the metaphysicians have hoped to find" to "what we call 'real' is not really real." Such confusions make Nietzsche and Derrida liable to the charges of self-referential inconsistency—to claiming to know what they themselves claim cannot be known.

[8] Donald Davidson (1917–2003), American philosopher, author, among other things, of *Essays on Actions and Events* (1980) and *Inquiries into Truth and Interpretation* (1984).

[9] [Rorty] I should remark that Davidson cannot be held responsible for the interpretation I am putting on his views, nor for the further views I extrapolate from his. For an extended statement of that interpretation, see my "Pragmatism, Davidson, and Truth," in Ernest Lepore, ed., *Truth and Interpretation: Perspectives on the Philosophy of Donald Davidson* (Oxford: Blackwell, 1984). For Davidson's reaction to this interpretation see his "After-thoughts" to "A Coherence Theory of Truth and Knowledge" in Alan Malachowski, *Reading Rorty* (Oxford: Blackwell).

desires. The traditional view is that there is a core self which can look at, decide among, use, and express itself by means of, such beliefs and desires. Further, these beliefs and desires are criticizable not simply by reference to their ability to cohere with one another, but by reference to something exterior to the network within which they are strands. Beliefs are, on this account, criticizable because they fail to correspond to reality. Desires are criticizable because they fail to correspond to the essential nature of the human self—because they are "irrational" or "unnatural." So we have a picture of the essential core of the self on one side of this network of beliefs and desires, and reality on the other side. In this picture, the network is the product of an interaction between the two, alternately expressing the one and representing the other. This is the traditional subject-object picture which idealism tried and failed to replace, and which Nietzsche, Heidegger, Derrida, James, Dewey, Goodman, Sellars, Putnam, Davidson[10] and others have tried to replace without entangling themselves in the idealists' paradoxes.

One phase of this effort of replacement consisted in an attempt to substitute "language" for "mind" or "consciousness" as the medium out of which beliefs and desires are constructed, the third, mediating, element between self and world. This turn toward language[11] was thought of as a progressive, naturalizing move. It seemed so because it seemed easier to give a causal account of the evolutionary emergence of language-using organisms than of the metaphysical emergence of consciousness out of nonconsciousness. But in itself this substitution is ineffective. For if we stick to the picture of language as a medium, something standing between the self and the nonhuman reality with which the self seeks to be in touch, we have made no progress. We are still using a subject-object[12] picture, and we are still stuck with issues about skepticism, idealism, and realism. For we are still able to ask questions about language of the same sort we asked about consciousness.

These are such questions as: "Does the medium between the self and reality get them together or keep them apart?" "Should we see the medium primarily as a medium of expression—of articulating what lies deep within the self? Or should we see it as primarily a medium of representation—showing the self what lies outside it?" Idealist theories of knowledge and Romantic notions of the imagination

can, alas, easily be transposed from the jargon of "consciousness" into that of "language." Realistic and moralistic reactions to such theories can be transposed equally easily. So the seesaw battles between romanticism and moralism, and between idealism and realism, will continue as long as one thinks there is a hope of making sense of the question of whether a given language is "adequate" to a task—either the task of properly expressing the nature of the human species, or the task of properly representing the structure of nonhuman reality.

We need to get off this seesaw. Davidson helps us do so. For he does not view language as a medium for either expression or representation. So he is able to set aside the idea that both the self and reality have intrinsic natures, natures which are out there waiting to be known. Davidson's view of language is neither reductionist nor expansionist. It does not, as analytical philosophers sometimes have, purport to give reductive definitions of semantical notions like "truth" or "intentionality" or "reference." Nor does it resemble Heidegger's attempt to make language into a kind of divinity, something of which human beings are mere emanations. As Derrida has warned us, such an apotheosis of language is merely a transposed version of the idealists' apotheosis of consciousness.

In avoiding both reductionism and expansionism, Davidson resembles Wittgenstein.[13] Both philosophers treat alternative vocabularies as more like alternative tools than like bits of a jigsaw puzzle. To treat them as pieces of a puzzle is to assume that all vocabularies are dispensable, or reducible to other vocabularies, or capable of being united with all other vocabularies in one grand unified super vocabulary. If we avoid this assumption, we shall not be inclined to ask questions like "What is the place of consciousness in a world of molecules?" "Are colors more mind-dependent than weights?" "What is the place of value in a world of fact?" "What is the place of intentionality in a world of causation?" "What is the relation between the solid table of common sense and the unsolid table of microphysics?" or "What is the relation of language to thought?" We should not try to answer such questions, for doing so leads either to the evident failures of reductionism or to the short-lived successes of expansionism. We should restrict ourselves to questions like "Does our use of these words get in the way of our use of those other words?" This is a question about whether our use of tools is inefficient, not a question about whether our beliefs are contradictory.

---

[10]Nietzsche (above, page 686); Heidegger (above, page 1051); Derrida (above, page 1203); William James (1842–1910), American philosopher and psychologist; John Dewey (1859–1952), Nelson Goodman (1906–1998), Wilfrid Sellars (1912–1989), and Hilary Putnam (b. 1926), American philosophers.

[11]See Rorty, ed., *The Linguistic Turn* (1967).

[12]See Locke (above, page 281).

[13]Wittgenstein (above, page 823).

"Merely philosophical" questions, like Eddington's[14] question about the two tables, are attempts to stir up a factitious theoretical quarrel between vocabularies which have proved capable of peaceful coexistence. The questions I have recited above are all cases in which philosophers have given their subject a bad name by seeing difficulties nobody else sees. But this is not to say that vocabularies never do get in the way of each other. On the contrary, revolutionary achievements in the arts, in the sciences, and in moral and political thought typically occur when somebody realizes that two or more of our vocabularies are interfering with each other, and proceeds to invent a new vocabulary to replace both. For example, the traditional Aristotelian vocabulary got in the way of the mathematized vocabulary that was being developed in the sixteenth century by students of mechanics. Again, young German theology students of the late eighteenth century—like Hegel and Hölderlin[15]—found that the vocabulary in which they worshiped Jesus was getting in the way of the vocabulary in which they worshiped the Greeks. Yet again, the use of Rossetti-like tropes got in the way of the early Yeats's use of Blakean tropes.[16]

The gradual trial-and-error creation of a new, third, vocabulary—the sort of vocabulary developed by people like Galileo,[17] Hegel, or the later Yeats—is not a discovery about how old vocabularies fit together. That is why it cannot be reached by an inferential process—by starting with premises formulated in the old vocabularies. Such creations are not the result of successfully fitting together pieces of a puzzle. They are not discoveries of a reality behind the appearances, of an undistorted view of the whole picture with which to replace myopic views of its parts. The proper analogy is with the invention of new tools to take the place of old tools. To come up with such a vocabulary is more like discarding the lever and the chock because one has envisaged the pully, or like discarding gesso and tempera because one has now figured out how to size canvas properly.

This Wittgensteinian analogy between vocabularies and tools has one obvious drawback. The craftsman typically knows what job he needs to do before picking or inventing tools with which to do it. By contrast, someone like Galileo, Yeats, or Hegel (a "poet" in my wide sense of the term—the sense of "one who makes things new") is typically unable to make clear exactly what it is that he wants to do before developing the language in which he succeeds in doing it. His new vocabulary makes possible, for the first time, a formulation of its own purpose. It is a tool for doing something which could not have been envisaged prior to the development of a particular set of descriptions, those which it itself helps to provide. But I shall, for the moment, ignore this disanalogy. I want simply to remark that the contrast between the jigsaw-puzzle and the "tool" models of alternative vocabularies reflects the contrast between—in Nietzsche's slightly misleading terms—the will to truth and the will to self-overcoming. Both are expressions of the contrast between the attempt to represent or express something that was already there and the attempt to make something that never had been dreamed of before.

Davidson spells out the implications of Wittgenstein's treatment of vocabularies as tools by raising explicit doubts about the assumptions underlying traditional pre-Wittgensteinian accounts of language. These accounts have taken for granted that questions like "Is the language we are presently using the 'right' language—is it adequate to its task as a medium of expression or representation?" "Is our language a transparent or an opaque medium?" make sense. Such questions assume there are relations such as "fitting the world" or "being faithful to the true nature of the self" in which language might stand to nonlanguage. This assumption goes along with the assumption that "our language"—the language we speak now, the vocabulary at the disposal of educated inhabitants of the twentieth century—is somehow a unity, a third thing which stands in some determinate relation with two other unities—the self and reality. Both assumptions are natural enough, once we accept the idea that there are nonlinguistic things called "meanings" which it is the task of language to express, as well as the idea that there are nonlinguistic things called "facts" which it is the task of language to represent. Both ideas enshrine the notion of language as medium.

Davidson's polemics against the traditional philosophical uses of the terms "fact" and "meaning," and against what he calls "the scheme-content model" of thought and inquiry, are parts of a larger polemic against the idea that there is a fixed task for language to perform, and an entity called "language" or "the language" or "our language" which may or may not be performing this task efficiently. Davidson's doubt that there is any such entity parallels Gilbert Ryle's and Daniel Dennett's doubts about whether there is anything called "the mind" or "consciousness."[18] Both sets of doubts

---

[14] Arthur Stanley Eddington (1882–1944), English physicist. The allusion is to *The Nature of the Physical World* (1928); the "two tables" are the commonplace object and the table described according to scientific conceptions of matter.

[15] Johann Christian Friedrich Hölderlin (1770–1843), German poet.

[16] Dante Gabriel Rossetti (1828–1882), English poet and painter; William Butler Yeats (1865–1939), Irish poet; Blake (above, page 447).

[17] Galileo Galilei (1564–1642), Italian astronomer.

[18] Gilbert Ryle (1900–1976), English philosopher; Daniel Dennett, contemporary American philosopher. [Rorty] For an elaboration of these doubts, see my "Contemporary Philosophy of Mind," *Synthesis* 53 (1982).

are doubts about the utility of the notion of a medium between the self and reality—the sort of medium which realists see as transparent and skeptics as opaque.

In a recent paper, nicely entitled "A Nice Derangement of Epitaphs,"[19] Davidson tries to undermine the notion of languages as entities by developing the notion of what he calls "a passing theory" about the noises and inscriptions presently being produced by a fellow human. Think of such a theory as part of a larger "passing theory" about this person's total behavior—a set of guesses about what she will do under what conditions. Such a theory is "passing" because it must constantly be corrected to allow for mumbles, stumbles, malapropisms, metaphors, tics, seizures, psychotic symptoms, egregious stupidity, strokes of genius, and the like. To make things easier, imagine that I am forming such a theory about the current behavior of a native of an exotic culture into which I have unexpectedly parachuted. This strange person, who presumably finds me equally strange, will simultaneously be busy forming a theory about my behavior. If we ever succeed in communicating easily and happily, it will be because her guesses about what I am going to do next, including what noises I am going to make next, and my own expectations about what I shall do or say under certain circumstances, come more or less to coincide, and because the converse is also true. She and I are coping with each other as we might cope with mangoes or boa constrictors—we are trying not to be taken by surprise. To say that we come to speak the same language is to say, as Davidson puts it, that "we tend to converge on passing theories." Davidson's point is that all "two people need, if they are to understand one another through speech, is the ability to converge on passing theories from utterance to utterance."

Davidson's account of linguistic communication dispenses with the picture of language as a third thing intervening between self and reality, and of different languages as barriers between persons or cultures. To say that one's previous language was inappropriate for dealing with some segment of the world (for example, the starry heavens above, or the raging passions within) is just to say that one is now, having learned a new language, able to handle that segment more easily. To say that two communities have trouble getting along because the words they use are so hard to translate into each other is just to say that the linguistic behavior of inhabitants of one community may, like the rest of their behavior, be hard for inhabitants of the other community to predict. As Davidson puts it,

We should realize that we have abandoned not only the ordinary notion of a language, but we have erased the boundary between knowing a language and knowing our way around the world generally. For there are no rules for arriving at passing theories that work. . . . There is no more chance of regularizing, or teaching, this process than there is of regularizing or teaching the process of creating new theories to cope with new data—for that is what this process involves. . . .

There is no such thing as a language, not if a language is anything like what philosophers, at least, have supposed. There is therefore no such thing to be learned or mastered. We must give up the idea of a clearly defined shared structure which language users master and then apply to cases . . . We should give up the attempt to illuminate how we communicate by appeal to conventions.[20]

This line of thought about language is analogous to the Ryle-Dennett view that when we use a mentalistic terminology we are simply using an efficient vocabulary—the vocabulary characteristic of what Dennett calls the "intentional stance"—to predict what an organism is likely to do or say under various sets of circumstances. Davidson is a nonreductive behaviorist about language in the same way that Ryle was a nonreductive behaviorist about mind. Neither has any desire to give equivalents in Behaviorese for talk about beliefs or about reference. But both are saying: Think of the term "mind" or "language" not as the name of a medium between self and reality but simply as a flag which signals the desirability of using a certain vocabulary when trying to cope with certain kinds of organisms. To say that a given organism—or, for that matter, a given machine—has a mind is just to say that, for some purposes, it will pay to think of it as having beliefs and desires. To say that it is a language user is just to say that pairing off the marks and noises it makes with those we make will prove a useful tactic in predicting and controlling its future behavior.

This Wittgensteinian attitude, developed by Ryle and Dennett for minds and by Davidson for languages, naturalizes mind and language by making all questions about the relation of either to the rest of universe *causal* questions, as opposed to questions about adequacy of representation or expression. It makes perfectly good sense to ask how we got from the relative mindlessness of the monkey to the full-

---

[19] [Rorty] This essay can be found in Lepore, ed., *Truth and Interpretation* [1986].

[20] [Rorty] "A Nice Derangement of Epitaphs," in Lepore, ed., *Truth and Interpretation*, p. 446. Italics added.

fledged mindedness of the human, or from speaking Neanderthal to speaking postmodern, if these are construed as straightforward causal questions. In the former case the answer takes us off into neurology and thence into evolutionary biology. But in the latter case it takes us into intellectual history viewed as the history of metaphor. For my purposes in this book, it is the latter which is important. So I shall spend the rest of this chapter sketching an account of intellectual and moral progress which squares with Davidson's account of language.

To see the history of language, and thus of the arts, the sciences, and the moral sense, as the history of metaphor is to drop the picture of the human mind, or human languages, becoming better and better suited to the purposes for which God or Nature designed them, for example, able to express more and more meanings or to represent more and more facts. The idea that language has a purpose goes once the idea of language as medium goes. A culture which renounced both ideas would be the triumph of those tendencies in modern thought which began two hundred years ago, the tendencies common to German idealism, Romantic poetry, and utopian politics.

A nonteleological view of intellectual history, including the history of science, does for the theory of culture what the Mendelian, mechanistic, account of natural selection did for evolutionary theory. Mendel[21] let us see mind as something which just happened rather than as something which was the point of the whole process. Davidson lets us think of the history of language, and thus of culture, as Darwin taught us to think of the history of a coral reef. Old metaphors are constantly dying off into literalness, and then serving as a platform and foil for new metaphors. This analogy lets us think of "our language"—that is, of the science and culture of twentieth-century Europe—as something that took shape as a result of a great number of sheer contingencies. Our language and our culture are as much a contingency, as much a result of thousands of small mutations finding niches (and millions of others finding no niches), as are the orchids and the anthropoids.

To accept this analogy, we must follow Mary Hesse in thinking of scientific revolutions as "metaphoric redescriptions" of nature rather than insights into the intrinsic nature of nature.[22] Further, we must resist the temptation to think that the redescriptions of reality offered by contemporary physical or biological science are somehow closer to "the things themselves," less "mind-dependent," than the redescriptions of history offered by contemporary culture criticism. We need to see the constellations of causal forces which produced talk of DNA or of the Big Bang as of a piece with the causal forces which produced talk of "secularization" or of "late capitalism."[23] These various constellations are the random factors which have made some things subjects of conversation for us and others not, have made some projects and not others possible and important.

I can develop the contrast between the idea that the history of culture has a *telos*—such as the discovery of truth, or the emancipation of humanity—and the Nietzschean and Davidsonian picture which I am sketching by noting that the latter picture is compatible with a bleakly mechanical description of the relation between human beings and the rest of the universe. For genuine novelty can, after all, occur in a world of blind, contingent, mechanical forces. Think of novelty as the sort of thing which happens when, for example, a cosmic ray scrambles the atoms in a DNA molecule, thus sending things off in the direction of the orchids or the anthropoids. The orchids, when their time came, were no less novel or marvelous for the sheer contingency of this necessary condition of their existence. Analogously, for all we know, or should care, Aristotle's metaphorical use of *ousia,* Saint Paul's metaphorical use of *agapē,* and Newton's metaphorical use of *gravitas,* were the results of cosmic rays scrambling the fine structure of some crucial neurons in their respective brains. Or, more plausibly, they were the result of some odd episodes in infancy—some obsessional kinks left in these brains by idiosyncratic traumata. It hardly matters how the trick was done. The results were marvelous. There had never been such things before.

This account of intellectual history chimes with Nietzsche's definition of "truth" as "a mobile army of metaphors." It also chimes with the description I offered earlier of people like Galileo and Hegel and Yeats, people in whose minds new vocabularies developed, thereby equipping them with tools for doing things which could not even have been envisaged before these tools were available. But in order to accept this picture, we need to see the distinction between the literal and the metaphorical in the way Davidson sees it: not as a distinction between two sorts of meaning, nor as a distinction

---

[21] Gregor Johann Mendel (1822–1884), Austrian founder of genetics.
[22] [Rorty] See "The Explanatory Function of Metaphor," in Hesse, *Revolutions and Reconstructions in the Philosophy of Science* (Bloomington: Indiana University Press, 1980).

[23] [Rorty] This coalescence is resisted in Bernard Williams's discussion of Davidson's and my views in chap. 6 of his *Ethics and the Limits of Philosophy* (Cambridge, Mass.: Harvard University Press, 1985). For a partial reply to Williams, see my "Is Natural Science a Natural Kind?" in Ernan McMullin, ed., *Construction and Constraint: The Shaping of Scientific Rationality* (Notre Dame, Ind.: University of Notre Dame Press, 1988).

between two sorts of interpretation, but as a distinction between familiar and unfamiliar uses of noises and marks. The literal uses of noises and marks are the uses we can handle by our old theories about what people will say under various conditions. Their metaphorical use is the sort which makes us get busy developing a new theory.

Davidson puts this point by saying that one should not think of metaphorical expressions as having meanings distinct from their literal ones. To have a meaning is to have a place in a language game. Metaphors, by definition, do not. Davidson denies, in his words, "the thesis that associated with a metaphor is a cognitive content that its author wishes to convey and that the interpreter must grasp if he is to get the message."[24] In his view, tossing a metaphor into a conversation is like suddenly breaking off the conversation long enough to make a face, or pulling a photograph out of your pocket and displaying it, or pointing at a feature of the surroundings, or slapping your interlocutor's face, or kissing him. Tossing a metaphor into a text is like using italics, or illustrations, or odd punctuation or formats.

All these are ways of producing effects on your interlocutor or your reader, but not ways of conveying a message. To none of these is it appropriate to respond with "What exactly are you trying to say?" If one had wanted to say something—if one had wanted to utter a sentence with a meaning—one would presumably have done so. But instead one thought that one's aim could be better carried out by other means. That one uses familiar words in unfamiliar ways—rather than slaps, kisses, pictures, gestures, or grimaces—does not show that what one said must have a meaning. An attempt to state that meaning would be an attempt to find some familiar (that is, literal) use of words—some sentence which already had a place in the language game—and, to claim that one might just as well have *that*. But the unparaphrasability[25] of metaphor is just the unsuitability of any such familiar sentence for one's purpose.

Uttering a sentence without a fixed place in a language game is, as the positivists rightly have said, to utter something which is neither true nor false—something which is not, in Ian Hacking's terms, a "truth-value candidate."[26] This is because it is a sentence which one cannot confirm or disconfirm, argue for or against. One can only savor it or spit it out. But this is not to say that it may not, in time, *become* a truth-value candidate. If it *is* savored rather than spat

out, the sentence may be repeated, caught up, bandied about. Then it will gradually require a habitual use, a familiar place in the language game. It will thereby have ceased to be a metaphor—or, if you like, it will have become what most sentences of our language are, a dead metaphor. It will be just one more, literally true or literally false, sentence of the language. That is to say, our theories about the linguistic behavior of our fellows will suffice to let us cope with its utterance in the same unthinking way in which we cope with most of their other utterances.

The Davidsonian claim that metaphors do not have meanings may seem like a typical philosopher's quibble, but it is not.[27] It is part of an attempt to get us to stop thinking of language as a medium. This, in turn, is part of a larger attempt to get rid of the traditional philosophical picture of what it is to be human. The importance of Davidson's point can perhaps best be seen by contrasting his treatment of metaphor with those of the Platonist and the positivist on the one hand and the Romantic on the other. The Platonist and the positivist share a reductionist view of metaphor: They think metaphors are either paraphrasable or useless for the one serious purpose which language has, namely, representing reality. By contrast, the Romantic has an expansionist view: He thinks metaphor is strange, mystic, wonderful. Romantics attribute metaphor to a mysterious faculty called the "imagination," a faculty they suppose to be at the very center of the self, the deep heart's core. Whereas the metaphorical looks irrelevant to Platonists and positivists, the literal looks irrelevant to Romantics. For the former think that the point of language is to represent a hidden reality which lies outside us, and the latter thinks its purpose is to express a hidden reality which lies within us.

Positivist history of culture thus sees language as gradually shaping itself around the contours of the physical world. Romantic history of culture sees language as gradually bringing Spirit to self-consciousness. Nietzschean history of culture, and Davidsonian philosophy of language, see language as we now see evolution, as new forms of life constantly killing off old forms—not to accomplish a higher purpose, but blindly. Whereas the positivist sees Galileo as making a discovery—finally coming up with the words which were needed to fit the world properly, words Aristotle missed—the Davidsonian sees him as having hit upon a tool which happened to work better for certain purposes than any previous tool. Once we found out what could be done with

---

[24] [Rorty] Davidson, "What Metaphors Mean," in his *Inquiries into Truth and Interpretation* (Oxford University Press, 1984), p. 262.

[25] Cf. Brooks (above, page 1036) on the heresy of paraphrase, referring to whole poems.

[26] Ian Hacking (b. 1936), Canadian philosopher.

[27] [Rorty] For a further defense of Davidson against the charge of quibbling, and various other charges, see my "Unfamiliar Noises: Hesse and Davidson on Metaphor," *Proceedings of the Aristotelian Society,* supplementary vol. 61 (1987): 283–96.

a Galilean vocabulary, nobody was much interested in doing the things which used to be done (and which Thomists thought should still be done) with an Aristotelian vocabulary.

Similarly, whereas the Romantic sees Yeats as having gotten at something which nobody had previously gotten at, expressed something which had long been yearning for expression, the Davidsonian sees him as having hit upon some tools which enabled him to write poems which were not just variations on the poems of his precursors. Once we had Yeats's later poems in hand, we were less interested in reading Rossetti's. What goes for revolutionary, strong scientists and poets goes also for strong philosophers—people like Hegel and Davidson, the sort of philosophers who are interested in dissolving inherited problems rather than in solving them. In this view, substituting dialectic for demonstration as the method of philosophy, or getting rid of the correspondence theory of truth, is not a discovery about the nature of a preexistent entity called "philosophy" or "truth." It is changing the way we talk, and thereby changing what we want to do and what we think we are.

But in a Nietzschean view, one which drops the reality-appearance distinction, to change how we talk is to change what, for our own purposes, we are. To say, with Nietzsche, that God is dead, is to say that we serve no higher purposes. The Nietzschean substitution of self-creation for discovery substitutes a picture of the hungry generations treading each other down for a picture of humanity approaching closer and closer to the light. A culture in which Nietzschean metaphors were literalized would be one which took for granted that philosophical problems are as temporary as poetic problems, that there are no problems which bind the generations together into a single natural kind called "humanity." A sense of human history as the history of successive metaphors would let us see the poet, in the generic sense of the maker of new words, the shaper of new languages, as the vanguard of the species.

I shall try to develop this last point in Chapters 2 and 3 in terms of Harold Bloom's notion of the "strong poet." But I shall end this first chapter by going back to the claim, which has been central to what I have been saying, that the world does not provide us with any criterion of choice between alternative metaphors, that we can only compare languages or metaphors with one another, not with something beyond language called "fact."

The only way to argue for this claim is to do what philosophers like Goodman, Putnam, and Davidson have done: exhibit the sterility of attempts to give a sense to phrases like "the way the world is" or "fitting the facts." Such efforts can be supplemented by the work of philosophers of science such as Kuhn and Hesse. These philosophers explain why there is no way to explain the fact that a Galilean vocabulary enables us to make better predictions than an Aristotelian vocabulary by the claim that the book of nature is written in the language of mathematics.

These sorts of arguments by philosophers of language and of science should be seen against the background of the work of intellectual historians: historians who, like Hans Blumenberg, have tried to trace the similarities and dissimilarities between the Age of Faith and the Age of Reason.[28] These historians have made the point I mentioned earlier: The very idea that the world or the self has an intrinsic nature—one which the physicist or the poet may have glimpsed—is a remnant of the idea that the world is a divine creation, the work of someone who had something in mind, who Himself spoke some language in which He described His own project. Only if we have some such picture in mind, some picture of the universe as either itself a person or as created by a person, can we make sense of the idea that the world has an "intrinsic nature." For the cash value of that phrase is just that some vocabularies are better representations of the world than others, as opposed to being better tools for dealing with the world for one or another purpose.

To drop the idea of languages as representations, and to be thoroughly Wittgensteinian in our approach to language, would be to de-divinize the world. Only if we do that can we fully accept the argument I offered earlier—the argument that since truth is a property of sentences, since sentences are dependent for their existence upon vocabularies, and since vocabularies are made by human beings, so are truths. For as long as we think that "the world" names something we ought to respect as well as cope with, something personlike in that it has a preferred description of itself, we shall insist that any philosophical account of truth save the "intuition" that truth is "out there." This intuition amounts to the vague sense that it would be *hybris* on our part to abandon the traditional language of "respect for fact" and "objectivity"—that it would be risky, and blasphemous, not to see the scientist (or the philosopher, or the poet, or *somebody*) as having a priestly function, as putting us in touch with a realm which transcends the human.

On the view I am suggesting, the claim that an "adequate" philosophical doctrine must make room for our intuitions is a reactionary slogan, one which begs the question

---

[28] [Rorty] See Hans Blumenberg, *The Legitimacy of the Modern Age,* tr. Robert Wallace (Cambridge, Mass.: MIT Press, 1982).

at hand.[29] For it is essential to my view that we have no prelinguistic consciousness to which language needs to be adequate, no deep sense of how things are which it is the duty of philosophers to spell out in language. What is described as such a consciousness is simply a disposition to use the language of our ancestors, to worship the corpses of their metaphors. Unless we suffer from what Derrida calls "Heideggerian nostalgia," we shall not think of our "intuitions" as more than platitudes, more than the habitual use of a certain repertoire of terms, more than old tools which as yet have no replacements.

I can crudely sum up the story which historians like Blumenberg tell by saying that once upon a time we felt a need to worship something which lay beyond the visible world. Beginning in the seventeenth century we tried to substitute a love of truth for a love of God, treating the world described by science as a quasi divinity. Beginning at the end of the eighteenth century we tried to substitute a love of ourselves for a love of scientific truth, a worship of our own deep spiritual or poetic nature, treated as one more quasi divinity.

The line of thought common to Blumenberg, Nietzsche, Freud, and Davidson suggests that we try to get to the point where we no longer worship *anything,* where we treat *nothing* as a quasi divinity, where we treat *everything*—our language, our conscience, our community—as a product of time and chance. To reach this point would be, in Freud's words, to "treat chance as worthy of determining our fate." In the next chapter I claim that Freud, Nietzsche, and Bloom[30] do for our conscience what Wittgenstein and Davidson do for our language, namely, exhibit its sheer contingency.

---

[29] [Rorty] For an application of this dictum to a particular case, see my discussion of the appeals to intuition found in Thomas Nagel's view of "subjectivity" and in John Searle's doctrine of "intrinsic intentionality," in "Contemporary Philosophy of Mind." For further criticisms of both, criticism which harmonizes with my own, see Daniel Dennett, "Setting Off on the Right Foot" and "Evolution, Error, and Intentionality," in Dennett, *The Intentional Stance* (Cambridge, Mass.: MIT Press, 1987).

---

[30] Harold Bloom (b. 1930), American literary critic.

Eve Kosofsky Sedgwick

b. 1950

As Eve Kososky Sedgwick says of her very influential *Epistemology of the Closet* (1990), perhaps the entire book "constitutes an extended introduction." Yet as she also notes, it is an introduction to an intricate theme with an extended, though generally submerged, history of the role of sexuality in human identity. More specifically, Sedgwick argues that the contemporary shape of that theme in homoerotic love and the idea of homosexuality cuts across a multitude of other themes, of power, of justice, of knowledge and ignorance, that are crucial for defining our own time. Drawing upon the work of Michel Foucault (above, page 1259) in his three-volume *History of Sexuality* (1976–1984), Sedgwick explores the dynamics of knowledge and the politics of sexual and gender identity through the organizing metaphor of the closet, and "coming out" of the closet as a unique moment of disclosure, not merely of one's sexual orientation, but as the revelation of social, psychic, and political structures within which identities are negotiated. A crucial dimension of her work is to make explicit the political, legal, and constitutional issues concerning individual rights, the protection of privacy, and protection against violence, by both others and the state, that emerge with particularly virulence around the topic of homosexuality. In this respect, the issue is not merely a matter of discourse, but a route by which broader social and cultural issues are registered concretely. Using the strategies of deconstruction, however, Sedgwick is chiefly concerned with exploring the manifold "puzzles" of sexual identity wherein the categories of gender and sex comprise a matrix, sometimes a maze, that seems, as she puts it, to create "a field of intractable, highly structured discursive incoherence" at the crucial node "at which *any* gender is discriminated." In a universalizing and inclusive mode, Sedgwick's vision of the question of sexual and gender identity through the lens of contemporary gay and lesbian studies and queer theory shows the subject to be one that not only cannot stay in the closet but intersects the entire field wherein individual identity is created.

Sedgwick's works include: *The Coherence of Gothic Conventions* (1980); *Between Men: English Literature and Male Homosocial Desire* (1985); *Epistemology of the Closet* (1990); *Tendencies* (1993); and *Touching Feeling: Affect, Pedagogy, Performativity* (2003). For critical discussions of Sedgwick's work, see especially Stephen M. Barber and David L. Clark, eds., *Regarding Sedgwick: Essays on Queer Culture and Critical Theory* (2002).

from

Epistemology of the Closet

Introduction: Axiomatic

Epistemology of the Closet proposes that many of the major nodes of thought and knowledge in twentieth-century Western culture as a whole are structured—indeed, fractured—by a chronic, now endemic crisis of homo/heterosexual definition, indicatively male, dating from the end of the nineteenth century. The book will argue that an understanding of virtually any aspect of modern Western culture must be, not merely incomplete, but damaged in its central substance to the degree that it does not incorporate a critical analysis of modern homo/heterosexual definition; and it will assume that the appropriate place for that critical analysis to begin is from the relatively decentered perspective of modern gay and antihomophobic theory.

The passage of time, the bestowal of thought and necessary political struggle since the turn of the century have only spread and deepened the long crisis of modern sexual definition, dramatizing, often violently, the internal incoherence and mutual contradiction of each of the forms of discursive and institutional "common sense" on this subject inherited from the architects of our present culture. The contradictions I will be discussing are not in the first place those between prohomosexual and antihomosexual people or ideologies, although the book's strongest motivation is indeed the gay-affirmative one. Rather, the contradictions that seem most active are the ones internal to all the important twentieth-century understandings of homo/heterosexual definition, both heterosexist and antihomophobic. Their outlines and something of their history are sketched in Chapter 1. Briefly, they are two. The first is the contradiction between seeing homo/heterosexual definition on the one hand as an issue of active importance primarily for a small, distinct, relatively fixed homosexual minority (what I refer to as a minoritizing view), and seeing it on the other hand as an issue of continuing, determinative importance in the lives of people across the spectrum of sexualities (what I refer to as a universalizing view). The second is the contradiction between seeing same-sex object choice on the one hand as a matter of liminality or transitivity between genders, and seeing it on the other hand as reflecting an impulse of separatism—though by no means necessarily political separatism—within each gender. The

purpose of this book is not to adjudicate between the two poles of either of these contradictions, for, if its argument is right, no epistemological grounding now exists from which to do so. Instead, I am trying to make the strongest possible introductory case for a hypothesis about the centrality of this nominally marginal, conceptually intractable set of definitional issues to the important knowledges and understandings of twentieth-century Western culture as a whole.

The word "homosexual" entered Euro-American discourse during the last third of the nineteenth century—its popularization preceding, as it happens, even that of the word "heterosexual."[1] It seems clear that the sexual behaviors, and even for some people the conscious identities, denoted by the new term "homosexual" and its contemporary variants already had a long, rich history. So, indeed, did a wide range of other sexual behaviors and behavioral clusters. What *was* new from the turn of the century was the world-mapping by which every given person, just as he or she was necessarily assignable to a male or a female gender, was now considered necessarily assignable as well to a homo- or a hetero-sexuality, a binarized identity that was full of implications, however confusing, for even the ostensibly least sexual aspects of personal existence. It was this new development that left no space in the culture exempt from the potent incoherences of homo/heterosexual definition.

New, institutionalized taxonomic discourses—medical, legal, literary, psychological—centering on homo/heterosexual definition proliferated and crystallized with exceptional rapidity in the decades around the turn of the century, decades in which so many of the other critical nodes of the culture were being, if less suddenly and newly, nonetheless also definitively reshaped. Both the power relations between the genders and the relations of nationalism and imperialism, for instance, were in highly visible crisis. For this reason, and because the structuring of same-sex bonds can't, in any historical situation marked by inequality and contest *between* genders, fail to be a site of intensive regulation that intersects virtually every issue of power and gender,[2] lines can never be drawn to circumscribe within some proper domain of sexuality (whatever that might be) the consequences of a shift in sexual discourse. Furthermore, in accord with Foucault's demonstration, whose results I will take to be axiomatic, that modern Western culture has placed what it calls sexuality in a

---

"Introduction: Axiomatic" is part of the introduction to Eve Kosofsky Sedgwick's *Epistemology of the Closet* (Berkeley: University of California Press, 1990). Except as indicated, all footnotes are the author's.

[1] [Sedgwick] On this, see Jonathan Katz, *Gay/Lesbian Almanac: A New Documentary* (New York: Harper & Row, 1983), pp. 147–50; for more discussion, David M. Halperin, *One Hundred Years of Homosexuality* (New York: Routledge, 1989), p. 155*n*.1 and pp. 158–59*n*.17.

[2] [Sedgwick] This is an argument of my *Between Men: English Literature and Male Homosocial Desire* (New York: Columbia University Press, 1985).

more and more distinctively privileged relation to our most prized constructs of individual identity, truth, and knowledge, it becomes truer and truer that the language of sexuality not only intersects with but transforms the other languages and relations by which we know.

Accordingly, one characteristic of the readings in this book is to attend to performative aspects of texts, and to what are often blandly called their "reader relations," as sites of definitional creation, violence, and rupture in relation to particular readers, particular institutional circumstances. An assumption underlying the book is that the relations of the closet—the relations of the known and the unknown, the explicit and the inexplicit around homo/heterosexual definition—have the potential for being peculiarly revealing, in fact, about speech acts more generally. It has felt throughout this work as though the density of their social meaning lends any speech act concerning these issues—and the outlines of that "concern," it turns out, are broad indeed—the exaggerated propulsiveness of wearing flippers in a swimming pool: the force of various rhetorical effects has seemed uniquely difficult to calibrate.

But, in the vicinity of the closet, even what *counts* as a speech act is problematized on a perfectly routine basis. As Foucault says: "there is no binary division to be made between what one says and what one does not say; we must try to determine the different ways of not saying such things. . . . There is not one but many silences, and they are an integral part of the strategies that underlie and permeate discourses."[3] "Closetedness" itself is a performance initiated as such by the speech act of a silence—not a particular silence, but a silence that accrues particularity by fits and starts, in relation to the discourse that surrounds and differentially constitutes it. The speech acts that coming out, in turn, can comprise are as strangely specific. And they may have nothing to do with the acquisition of new information. I think of a man and a woman I know, best friends, who for years canvassed freely the emotional complications of each other's erotic lives—the man's eroticism happening to focus exclusively on men. But it was only after one particular conversational moment, fully a decade into this relationship, that it seemed to either of these friends that permission had been given to the woman to refer to the man, in their conversation together, as *a gay man*. Discussing it much later, both agreed they had felt at the time that this one moment had constituted a clear-cut act of coming out, even in the context of years and years beforehand of exchange predicated on the man's *being* gay. What was said to make this difference?

Not a version of "I am gay," which could only have been bathetic between them. What constituted coming out for this man, in this situation, was to use about himself the phrase "coming out"—to mention, as if casually, having come out to someone else. (Similarly, a T-shirt that ACT UP sells in New York bearing the text, "I am out, therefore I am," is meant to do for the wearer, not the constative work of reporting that s/he *is* out, but the performative work of coming out in the first place.) And as Chapter 1 will discuss, the fact that silence is rendered as pointed and performative as speech, in relations around the closet, depends on and highlights more broadly the fact that ignorance is as potent and as multiple a thing there as is knowledge.

Knowledge, after all, is not itself power, although it is the magnetic field of power. Ignorance and opacity collude or compete with knowledge in mobilizing the flows of energy, desire, goods, meanings, persons. If M. Mitterrand knows English but Mr. Reagan lacks—as he did lack—French, it is the urbane M. Mitterrand who must negotiate in an acquired tongue, the ignorant Mr. Reagan who may dilate in his native one. Or in the interactive speech model by which, as Sally McConnell-Ginet puts it, "the standard . . . meaning can be thought of as what is recognizable solely on the basis of interlocutors' mutual knowledge of established practices of interpretation," it is the interlocutor who has or pretends to have the *less* broadly knowledgeable understanding of interpretive practice who will define the terms of the exchange. So, for instance, because "men, with superior extralinguistic resources and privileged discourse positions, are often less likely to treat perspectives different from their own as mutually available for communication," their attitudes are "thus more likely to leave a lasting imprint on the common semantic stock than women's."[4]

Such ignorance effects can be harnessed, licensed, and regulated on a mass scale for striking enforcements—perhaps especially around sexuality, in modern Western culture the most meaning-intensive of human activities. The epistemological asymmetry of the laws that govern rape, for instance, privileges at the same time men and ignorance, inasmuch as it matters not at all what the raped woman perceives or wants just so long as the man raping her can claim not to have noticed (ignorance in which male sexuality receives careful education).[5] And the rape machinery that is organized by this

---

[3][Sedgwick] Michel Foucault [above, p. 1259], *The History of Sexuality.* Volume I: *An Introduction,* tr. Robert Hurley (New York: Pantheon, 1978), p. 27.

[4][Sedgwick] Sally McConnell-Ginet, "The Sexual (Re)Production of Meaning: A Discourse-Based Theory," manuscript, pp. 387–88, quoted in Cheris Kramarae and Paula A. Treichler, *A Feminist Dictionary* (Boston: Pandora Press, 1985), p. 264; emphasis added. [Sedgwick refers in the example to then U.S. President Ronald Reagan and French Prime Minister François Mitterand.]

[5][Sedgwick] Catherine A. MacKinnon makes this point more fully in "Feminism, Marxism, Method, and the State: An Agenda for Theory," *Signs* 7, no. 3 (Spring 1982): 515–44.

epistemological privilege of unknowing in turn keeps disproportionately under discipline, of course, women's larger ambitions to take more control over the terms of our own circulation.[6] Or, again, in an ingenious and patiently instructive
orchestration of ignorance, the U.S. Justice Department ruled
in June, 1986, that an employer may freely fire persons with
AIDS exactly so long as the employer can claim to be ignorant of the medical fact, *quoted in the ruling,* that there is no
known health danger in the workplace from the disease.[7]
Again, it is clear in political context that the effect aimed at—
in this case, it is hard to help feeling, aimed at with some
care—is the ostentatious declaration, for the private sector, of
an organized open season on gay men.[8]

Although the simple, stubborn fact or pretense of ignorance (one meaning, the Capital one, of the word
"stonewall") can sometimes be enough to enforce discursive
power, a far more complex drama of ignorance and knowledge is the more usual carrier of political struggle. Such a
drama was enacted when, only a few days after the Justice

Department's private-sector decision, the U.S. Supreme
Court correspondingly opened the public-sector bashing
season by legitimating state antisodomy laws in *Bowers v.
Hardwick.*[9] In a virulent ruling whose language made from
beginning to end an insolent display of legal illogic—of
what Justice Blackmun in dissent called "the most willful
blindness"[10]—a single, apparently incidental word used in
Justice White's majority opinion became for many gay or
antihomophobic readers a focus around which the inflammatory force of the decision seemed to pullulate with peculiar density.[11] In White's opinion,

> to claim that a right to engage in sodomy is
> "deeply rooted in this nation's history and tradi-
> tion" or "implicit in the concept of ordered lib-
> erty" is, at best, facetious.[12]

What lends the word "facetious" in this sentence such an unusual power to offend, even in the context of a larger legal offense whose damage will be much more indelible, has to be
the economical way it functions here as switchpoint for the
cyclonic epistemological undertows that encompass power in
general and issues of homosexual desire in particular.

One considers: (1) *prima facie,* nobody could, of
course, actually for an instant mistake the intent of the gay
advocates as facetious. (2) *Secunda facie,* it is thus the court
itself that is pleased to be facetious. Trading on the assertion's very (3) transparent stupidity (not just the contemptuous demonstration that powerful people don't have to be
acute or right, but even more, the contemptuous demonstration—this is palpable throughout the majority opinions, but

---

[6][Sedgwick] Susan Brownmiller made the most forceful and influential presentation of this case in *Against Our Will: Men, Women, and Rape* (New
York: Simon & Schuster, 1975).

[7][Sedgwick] Robert Pear, "Rights Laws Offer Only Limited Help on AIDS,
U.S. Rules," *New York Times,* June 23, 1986. That the ruling was calculated
to offer, provoke, and legitimize harm and insult is clear from the language
quoted in Pear's article: "A person," the ruling says, for instance, "cannot
be regarded as handicapped [and hence subject to federal protection] simply
because others shun his company. Otherwise, a host of personal traits, from
ill temper to poor personal hygiene, would constitute handicaps."

[8][Sedgwick] Not that gay men were intended to be the only victims of this
ruling. In even the most conscientious discourse concerning AIDS in the
United States so far there has been the problem, to which this essay does not
pretend to offer any solution, of doing justice at once to the relative (and
increasing) heterogeneity of those who actually have AIDS and to the
specificity with which AIDS discourse at every level has until very recently
focused on male homosexuality. In its worldwide epidemiology, of course,
AIDS has no distinctive association with gay men, nor is it likely to for long
here either. The acknowledgment/management of this fact was the
preoccupation of a strikingly sudden media-wide discursive shift in the
winter and early spring of 1987. If the obsessionally homophobic focus of
AIDS phobia up to that moment scapegoated gay men by (among other
things) subjecting their sexual practice and lifestyles to a glaring and
effectually punitive visibility, however, it worked in an opposite way to
expunge the claims by expunging the visibility of most of the disease's other
victims. So far, here, these victims have been among groups already the
most vulnerable—intravenous drug users, sex workers, wives and
girlfriends of closeted men—on whom invisibility, or a public subsumption
under the incongruous heading of gay men, can have no protective effect.
(It has been notable, for instance, that media coverage of prostitutes with
AIDS has shown no interest in the health of the women themselves, but only
in their potential for infecting men. Again, the campaign to provide drug
users with free needles had not until early 1987 received even the exiguous
state support given to safer-sex education for gay men.) The damages of
homophobia on the one hand, of classism/racism/sexism on the other; of
intensive regulatory visibility on the one hand, of discursive erasure on the
other: these pairings are not only incommensurable (and why measure them
against each other rather than against the more liberating possibilities they
foreclose?) but very hard to interleave with each other conceptually. The
effect has been perhaps most dizzying when the incommensurable damages

are condensed upon a single person, e.g., a nonwhite gay man. The focus
of this book is on the specific damages of homophobia; but to the extent
that it is impelled by (a desire to resist) the public pressures of AIDS phobia, I must at least make clear how much that is important even to its own
ambitions is nonetheless excluded from its potential for responsiveness.

[9][Sedgwick] Graphic encapsulation of this event on the front page of the
Times: at the bottom of the three-column lead story on the ruling, a photo
ostensibly about the influx of various navies into a welcoming New York
for "the Liberty celebration" shows two worried but extremely good-
looking sailors in alluring whites, "asking directions of a police officer"
(*New York Times,* July 1, 1986). [The U.S. Supreme Court, in Lawrence
and Garner v. Texas, case No. 02-0102 (2003), ruled such state antisodomy
laws unconstitutional.]

[10][Sedgwick] "The Supreme Court Opinion. Michael J. Bowers, Attorney
General of Georgia, Petition v. Michael Hardwick and John and Mary Doe,
Respondents," text in *New York Native,* no. 169 (July 14, 1986): 15.

[11][Sedgwick] The word is quoted, for instance, in isolation, in the sixth
sentence of the *Times*'s lead article announcing the decision (July 1, 1986).
The *Times* editorial decrying the decision (July 2, 1986) remarks on the
crudity of this word before outlining the substantive offensiveness of the
ruling. The *New York Native* and the gay leaders it quoted also gave the
word a lot of play in the immediate aftermath of the ruling (e.g., no. 169
[July 14, 1986]: 8, 11).

[12][Sedgwick] *New York Native,* no. 169 (July 14, 1986): 13.

only in this word does it bubble up with active pleasure—of how obtuseness itself arms the powerful against their enemies), the court's joke here (in the wake of the mock-ignorant mock-jocose threat implicit in "at best") is (4) the clownish claim to be able at will to "read"—i.e., project into—the minds of the gay advocates. This being not only (5) a parody of, but (6) more intimately a kind of aggressive jamming technique against, (7) the truth/paranoid fantasy that it is gay people who can read, or project their own desires into, the minds of "straight" people.

Inarguably, there is a satisfaction in dwelling on the degree to which the power of our enemies over us is implicated, not in their command of knowledge, but precisely in their ignorance. The effect is a real one, but it carries dangers with it as well. The chief of these dangers is the scornful, fearful, or patheticizing reification of "ignorance"; it goes with the unexamined Enlightenment assumptions by which the labeling of a particular force as "ignorance" seems to place it unappealably in a demonized space on a never quite explicit ethical schema. (It is also dangerously close in structure to the more palpably sentimental privileging of ignorance as an originary, passive innocence.) The angles of view from which it can look as though a political fight is a fight against ignorance are invigorating and maybe revelatory ones but dangerous places for dwelling. The writings of, among others, Foucault, Derrida, Thomas Kuhn, and Thomas Szasz[13] have given contemporary readers a lot of practice in questioning both the ethical/political disengagement and, beyond that, the ethical/political simplicity of the category of "knowledge," so that a writer who appeals too directly to the redemptive potential of simply upping the cognitive wattage on any question of power seems, now, naive. The corollary problems still adhere to the category of "ignorance," as well, but so do some additional ones: there are psychological operations of shame, denial, projection around "ignorance" that make it an especially galvanizing category for the individual reader, even as they give it a rhetorical potency that it would be hard for writers to forswear and foolhardy for them to embrace.

Rather than sacrifice the notion of "ignorance," then, I would be more interested at this point in trying, as we are getting used to trying with "knowledge," to pluralize and specify it. That is, I would like to be able to make use in sexual-political thinking of the deconstructive understanding that particular insights generate, are lined with, and at the same time are themselves structured by particular opacities. If ig-

norance is not—as it evidently is not—a single Manichaean, aboriginal maw of darkness from which the heroics of human cognition can occasionally wrestle facts, insights, freedoms, progress, perhaps there exists instead a plethora of *ignorances,* and we may begin to ask questions about the labor, erotics, and economics of their human production and distribution. Insofar as ignorance is ignorance *of* a knowledge—a knowledge that may itself, it goes without saying, be seen as either true or false under some other regime of truth—these ignorances, far from being pieces of the originary dark, are produced by and correspond to particular knowledges and circulate as part of particular regimes of truth. We should not assume that their doubletting with knowledges means, however, that they obey identical laws identically or follow the same circulatory paths at the same pace.[14]

Historically, the framing of *Epistemology of the Closet* begins with a puzzle. It is a rather amazing fact that, of the very many dimensions along which the genital activity of one person can be differentiated from that of another (dimensions that include preference for certain acts, certain zones or sensations, certain physical types, a certain frequency, certain symbolic investments, certain relations of age or power, a certain species, a certain number of participants, etc. etc. etc.), precisely one, the gender of object choice, emerged from the turn of the century, and has remained, as *the* dimension denoted by the now ubiquitous category of "sexual orientation." This is not a development that would have been foreseen from the viewpoint of the fin de siècle itself, where a rich stew of male algolagnia, child-love, and autoeroticism, to mention no more of its components, seemed to have as indicative a relation as did homosexuality to the whole, obsessively entertained problematic of sexual "perversion" or, more broadly, "decadence." Foucault, for instance, mentions the hysterical woman and the masturbating child, along with "entomologized" sexological categories such as zoophiles, zooerasts, auto-monosexuals, and gynecomasts, as typifying the new sexual taxonomies, the *"specification of individuals"* that facilitated the modern freighting of sexual definition with epistemological and power relations.[15] True as his notation is, it suggests without beginning to answer the further question: why the category of "the masturbator," to choose only one example, should by now have entirely lost its diacritical potential for specifying a particular kind of person, an identity, at the same time as it

---

[13] Derrida (above, page 1203); Kuhn (above, p. 1280); Thomas Szasz (b. 1920), American psychiatrist and psychotherapist, best known for his *The Myth of Mental Illness: Foundations of a Theory of Personal Conduct* (1961).

[14] [Sedgwick] For an essay that makes these points more fully, see my "Privilege of Unknowing," *Genders,* no. 1 (Spring 1988): 102–24, a reading of Diderot's *La Religieuse,* from which the preceding six paragraphs are taken.

[15] [Sedgwick] Foucault, *History of Sexuality,* pp. 105, 43.

continues to be true—becomes increasingly true—that, for a crucial strain of Western discourse, in Foucault's words "the homosexual was now a species."[16] So, as a result, is the heterosexual, and between *these* species the human species has come more and more to be divided. *Epistemology of the Closet* does not have an explanation to offer for this sudden, radical condensation of sexual categories; instead of speculating on its causes, the book explores its unpredictably varied and acute implications and consequences.

At the same time that this process of sexual specification or species-formation was going on, the book will argue, less stable and identity-bound understandings of sexual choice also persisted and developed, often among the same people or interwoven in the same systems of thought. Again, the book will not suggest (nor do I believe there currently exists) any standpoint of thought from which the rival claims of these minoritizing and universalizing understandings of sexual definition could be decisively arbitrated as to their "truth." Instead, the performative effects of the self-contradictory discursive field of force created by their overlap will be my subject. And, of course, it makes every difference that these impactions of homo/heterosexual definition took place in a setting, not of spacious emotional or analytic impartiality, but rather of urgent homophobic pressure to devalue one of the two nominally symmetrical forms of choice.

As several of the formulations above would suggest, one main strand of argument in this book is deconstructive, in a fairly specific sense. The analytic move it makes is to demonstrate that categories presented in a culture as symmetrical binary oppositions—heterosexual/homosexual, in this case—actually subsist in a more unsettled and dynamic tacit relation according to which, first, term B is not symmetrical with but subordinated to term A; but, second, the ontologically valorized term A actually depends for its meaning on the simultaneous subsumption and exclusion of term B; hence, third, the question of priority between the supposed central and the supposed marginal category of each dyad is irresolvably unstable, an instability caused by the fact that term B is constituted as at once internal and external to term A. Harold Beaver, for instance, in an influential 1981 essay sketched the outlines of such a deconstructive strategy:

The aim must be to reverse the rhetorical opposition of what is "transparent" or "natural" and what is "derivative" or "contrived" by demonstrating that the qualities predicated of "homosexuality" (as a dependent term) are in fact a condition

of "heterosexuality"; that "heterosexuality," far from possessing a privileged status, must itself be treated as a dependent term.[17]

To understand these conceptual relations as irresolvably unstable is not, however, to understand them as inefficacious or innocuous. It is at least premature when Roland Barthes prophesies that "once the paradigm is blurred, utopia begins: meaning and sex become the objects of free play, at the heart of which the (polysemant) forms and the (sensual) practices, liberated from the binary prison, will achieve a state of infinite expansion."[18] To the contrary, a deconstructive understanding of these binarisms makes it possible to identify them as sites that are *peculiarly* densely charged with lasting potentials for powerful manipulation—through precisely the mechanisms of self-contradictory definition or, more succinctly, the double bind. Nor is a deconstructive analysis of such definitional knots, however necessary, at all sufficient to disable them. Quite the opposite: I would suggest that an understanding of their irresolvable instability has been continually available, and has continually lent discursive authority, to antigay as well as to gay cultural forces of this century. Beaver makes an optimistic prediction that "by disqualifying the autonomy of what was deemed spontaneously immanent, the whole sexual system is fundamentally decentred and exposed."[19] But there is reason to believe that the oppressive sexual system of the past hundred years was if anything born and bred (if I may rely on the pith of a fable whose value doesn't, I must hope, stand or fall with its history of racist uses) in the briar patch of the most notorious and repeated decenterings and exposures.

These deconstructive contestations can occur, moreover, only in the context of an entire cultural network of normative definitions, definitions themselves equally unstable but responding to different sets of contiguities and often at a different rate. The master terms of a particular historical moment will be those that are so situated as to entangle most inextricably and at the same time most differentially the filaments of other important definitional nexuses. In arguing that homo/heterosexual definition has been a presiding master term of the past century, one that has the same, primary importance for all modern Western identity and social organization (and not merely for homosexual identity and culture) as do the more traditionally visible cruxes of gender, class, and race, I'll argue that the now chronic modern crisis of

---

[16] [Sedgwick] Foucault, *History of Sexuality,* p. 43.

[17] [Sedgwick] Harold Beaver, "Homosexual Signs," *Critical Inquiry* 8 (Autumn 1981): 115.
[18] [Sedgwick] *Roland Barthes by Roland Barthes,* tr. Richard Howard (New York: Hill and Wang, 1977), p. 133.
[19] [Sedgwick] Beaver, "Homosexual Signs," pp. 115–16.

homo/heterosexual definition has affected our culture through its ineffaceable marking particularly of the categories secrecy/disclosure, knowledge/ignorance, private/public, masculine/feminine, majority/minority, innocence/initiation, natural/artificial, new/old, discipline/terrorism, canonic/non-canonic, wholeness/decadence, urbane/provincial, domestic/foreign, health/illness, same/different, active/passive, in/out, cognition/paranoia, art/ kitsch, utopia/apocalypse, sincerity/sentimentality, and voluntarity/addiction.[20] And rather than embrace an idealist faith in the necessarily, immanently self-corrosive efficacy of the contradictions inherent to these definitional binarisms, I will suggest instead that contests for discursive power can be specified as competitions for the material or rhetorical leverage required to set the terms of, and to profit in some way from, the operations of such an incoherence of definition.

Perhaps I should say something about the project of hypothesizing that certain binarisms that structure meaning in a culture may be "ineffaceably marked" by association with this one particular problematic—ineffaceably even when invisibly. Hypothesizing is easier than proving, but indeed I cannot imagine the protocol by which such hypotheses might be *tested;* they must be deepened and broadened—not the work of one book—and used, rather than proved or disproved by a few examples. The collecting of instances of each binarism that would appear to "common sense" to be unmarked by issues of homo/heterosexual definition, though an inexhaustibly stimulating heuristic, is not, I believe, a good test of such a hypothesis. After all, the particular kinds of skill that might be required to produce the most telling interpretations have hardly been a valued part of the "common sense" of this epistemologically cloven culture. If a painstaking process of accumulative reading and historical de- and recontextualization does not render these homologies resonant and productive, that is the only test they can directly fail, the only one they need to pass.

The structure of the present book has been markedly affected by this intuition—by a sense that the cultural interrogations it aims to make imperative will be trivialized or evacuated, at this early stage, to the degree that their procedures seem to partake of the a priori. I've wanted the book to be inviting (as well as imperative) but resolutely nonalgo-rithmic. A point of the book is *not to know* how far its insights and projects are generalizable, not to be able to say in advance where the semantic specificity of these issues gives over to (or: itself structures?) the syntax of a "broader" or more abstractable critical project. In particular, the book aims to resist in every way it can the deadening pretended knowingness by which the chisel of modern homo/heterosexual definitional crisis tends, in public discourse, to be hammered most fatally home.

Perhaps to counter that, it seems now that the book not only has but constitutes an extended introduction. It is organized, not as a chronological narrative, but as a series of essays linked closely by their shared project and recurrent topics. The Introduction, situating this project in the larger context of gay/lesbian and antihomophobic theory, and Chapter 1, outlining its basic terms, are the only parts that do not comprise extended readings. Chapter 2 (on *Billy Budd*) and Chapter 3 (on Wilde and Nietzsche),[21] which were originally conceived as a single unit, offer a different kind of introduction: an assay, through the specificity of these texts and authors, of most of the bravely showy list of binarized cultural nexuses about which the book makes, at other places, more generalized assertions. Chapter 4 discusses at length, through a reading of James's[22] "The Beast in the Jungle," the elsewhere recurrent topos of male homosexual panic. And Chapter 5, on Proust,[23] focuses more sharply on the book's preoccupation with the speech-act relations around the closet.

In consonance with my emphasis on the performative relations of double and conflicted definition, the theorized prescription for a *practical* politics implicit in these readings is for a multi-pronged movement whose idealist and materialist impulses, whose minority-model and universalist-model strategies, and for that matter whose gender-separatist and gender-integrative analyses would likewise proceed in parallel without any high premium placed on ideological rationalization between them. In effect this is how the gay movements of this century have actually been structured, if not how they have often been perceived or evaluated. The breadth and fullness of the political gestalt of gay-affirmative struggle give a powerful resonance to the voice of each of its constituencies. The cost in ideological rigor, though high indeed, is very simply inevitable: this is not a conceptual landscape in which ideological rigor across levels, across constituencies is at all possible, be it ever so desirable. . . .

---

[20] [Sedgwick] My casting of all these definitional nodes in the form of binarisms, I should make explicit, has to do not with a mystical faith in the number two but, rather, with the felt need to schematize in some consistent way the treatment of social vectors so exceedingly various. The kind of falsification necessarily performed on each by this reduction cannot, unfortunately, itself be consistent. But the scope of the kind of hypotheses I want to pose does seem to require a drastic reductiveness, at least in its initial formulations.

[21] *Billy Budd* by Herman Melville (1819–1891), American novelist; Wilde (above, page 711); Nietzsche (above, page 686).

[22] Henry James (1843–1916), American novelist.

[23] Marcel Proust (1871–1922), French novelist.

Stephen J. Greenblatt

b. 1943

Greenblatt is generally regarded as the founder and namer of the movement known as the New Historicism, which came to prominence with the generation of American literary scholars who had been college students during the late 1960s and early 1970s. He responded negatively to a literary training dominated by the methods of the New Criticism when it had become institutionalized and systematized by the followers of its founders, and he rejected critical and historical writings that claimed to withhold judgment. Thus he contrasted the New Historicism with historicism as usually defined. For him the old historicism's failure was not to connect present with past, for the past reveals the genealogy of present judgments. Greenblatt describes three characteristics of historicism that his work specifically opposes, attacking particularly a historical understanding too narrow by virtue of choice of the objects it studies and the tendency to isolate them.

Greenblatt concludes the essay reprinted below with a discussion of the two words that compose its title: resonance and wonder. Resonance, which is really the fundamental interest of New Historicism, is the power of objects to "reach beyond [their] formal boundaries to a larger world, to evoke in the viewer the complex, dynamic cultural forces from which it has emerged." Wonder is the "power of the object . . . to stop the viewer in his tracks, to convey an arresting sense of uniqueness." This is all that is left of the New Criticism's formalism and what Greenblatt calls the "mystique of the object"; but Greenblatt would extend wonder "beyond the formal boundaries of works of art."

"Wonder" is not a new term in criticism. It was employed in Renaissance criticism and by some nineteenth-century writers, but it was usually associated with the phantastic. For Greenblatt, it is obviously not only that, nor is it "beauty" in its usually aestheticist definitions. It is more like the sublime in Longinus (above, page 94). Wonder Greenblatt sees as an attitude responding to all sorts of objects. But wonder is not really his interest as a professional scholar. Where he mentions it here he is responding to critics of his work who fault him for ignoring what are usually called the formal aspects of a work. A comparison of Greenblatt's use of the term "object" to that of Ransom (above, page 953) is instructive. One may also profit from noting the similarity of Benjamin's (above, page 995) identification of his own work with historical materialism and his insisting on the relation of present to past, though Greenblatt's relation to Marxism is less evident in his later work. The New Historicism has a significant relationship to what has been called cultural materialism in England.

It should be added that Greenblatt's theory, if that is what it should be called, also arose, not so much out of a concern with critical approach as it did out of his interest in Renaissance culture.

Among Greenblatt's works are *Renaissance Self-Fashioning* (1980); *Shakespearean Negotiations* (1988); *Learning to Curse* (1990); *Marvelous Possessions: The*

Wonder of the New World (1991); *Practicing New Historicism* (with Catherine Gallagher, 2000); and *Hamlet in Purgatory* (2001). See Jürgen Pieters, ed., *Critical Self-Fashioning: Stephen Greenblatt and the New Historicism* (1999).

Resonance and Wonder

In a small glass case in the library of Christ Church, Oxford, there is a round, broad-brimmed cardinal's hat; a note card identifies it as having belonged to Cardinal Wolsey.[1] It is altogether appropriate that this hat should have wound up at Christ Church, for the college owed its existence to Wolsey, who had decided at the height of his power to found in his own honor a magnificent new Oxford college. But the hat was not a direct bequest; historical forces, as we sometimes say—in this case, taking the ominous form of Henry VIII—intervened, and Christ Church, like Hampton Court Palace, was cut off from its original benefactor. Instead, as the note informs us, after it had passed through the hands of various owners—including Bishop Burnet, Burnet's son, Burnet's son's housekeeper, the Dowager Countess of Albemarle's butler, the countless herself, and Horace Walpole—the hat was acquired for Christ Church in the nineteenth century, purchased, we are told, for the sum of sixty-three pounds, from the daughter of the actor Charles Kean. Kean is said to have worn the hat when he played Wolsey in Shakespeare's *Henry VIII*. If this miniature history of an artifact is too slight to be of much consequence, it nonetheless evokes a vision of cultural production that I find compelling. The peregrinations of Wolsey's hat suggest that cultural artifacts do not stay still, that they exist in time, and that they are bound up with personal and institutional conflict, negotiations, and appropriations.

The term culture has, in the case of the hat, a convenient material referent—a bit of red cloth stitched together—but that referent is only a tiny element in a complex symbolic construction that originally marked the transformation of Wolsey from a butcher's son to a prince of the church. Wolsey's gentleman usher, George Cavendish, has left a remarkably circumstantial contemporary account of that construction, an account that enables us even to glimpse the hat in its place among all the other ceremonial regalia:

And after Mass he would return in his privy chamber again and, being advertized of the furniture of his chamber without with noblemen and gentlemen . . . , would issue out into them apparelled all in red in the habit of a Cardinal; which was either of fine scarlet or else of crimson satin, taffeta, damask, or caffa [a rich silk cloth], the best that he could get for money; and upon his head a round pillion with a neck of black velvet, set to the same in the inner side. . . . There was also borne before him first the Great Seal of England, and then his Cardinal's hat by a nobleman or some worthy gentleman right solemnly, bareheaded. And as soon as he was entered into his chamber of presence where was attending his coming to await upon him to Westminster Hall, as well noblemen and other worthy gentlemen as noblemen and gentlemen of his own family; thus passing forth with two great crosses of silver borne before him, with also two great pillars of silver, and his sergeant at arms with a great mace of silver gilt. Then his gentlemen ushers cried and said, 'On my lords and masters, make way for my lord's grace!'[2]

The extraordinary theatricality of this manifestation of clerical power did not escape the notice of the Protestant reformers who called the Catholic church "the Pope's playhouse." When the Reformation in England dismantled the histrionic apparatus of Catholicism, they sold some of its gorgeous properties to the professional players—not only a mark of thrift but a polemical gesture, signifying that the sanctified vestments were in reality mere trumpery whose proper place was a disreputable world of illusion-mongering. In exchange for this polemical service, the theatrical joint-stock companies received more than an attractive, cut-rate wardrobe; they acquired the tarnished but still potent

---

"Resonance and Wonder" is reprinted from *Learning to Curse: Essays in Early Modern Culture*, published in 1990 by Routledge.

[1] Thomas Cardinal Wolsey (1475?–1530), English statesman and churchman.

[2] [Greenblatt] George Cavendish, *The Life and Death of Cardinal Wolsey* in *Two Early Tudor Lives*, ed. Richard S. Sylvester and Davis P. Harding (New Haven and London: Yale University Press, 1962), pp. 24–25. We get another glimpse of the symbolism of hats later in the text, when Wolsey is beginning his precipitous fall from power: "And talking with Master Norris upon his knees in the mire, he would have pulled off his under cap of velvet, but he could not undo the knot under his chin. Wherefore with violence he rent the laces and pulled it from his head and so kneeled bareheaded" (p. 106). I am grateful to Anne Barton for correcting my description of the hat in Christ Church and for transcribing the note card that details its provenance.

charisma that clung to the old vestments, charisma that in paradoxical fashion the players at once emptied out and heightened. By the time Wolsey's hat reached the library at Christ Church, its charisma must have been largely exhausted, but the college could confer upon it the prestige of an historical curiosity, as a trophy of the distant founder. And in its glass case it still radiates a tiny quantum of cultural energy.

Tiny indeed—I may already have seemed to make much more of this trivial relic than it deserves. But I am fascinated by transmigrations of the kind I have just sketched here—from theatricalized rituals to the stage to the university library or museum—because they seem to reveal something critically important about the *textual* relics with which my profession is obsessed. They enable us to glimpse the social process through which objects, gestures, rituals, and phrases are fashioned and moved from one zone of display to another. The display cases with which I am most involved—books—characteristically conceal this process, so that we have a misleading impression of fixity and little sense of the historical transactions through which the great texts we study have been fashioned. Let me give a literary example, an appropriately tiny textual equivalent of Wolsey's hat. At the close of Shakespeare's *Midsummer Night's Dream,* the Fairy King Oberon declares that he and his attendants are going to bless the beds of the three couples who have just been married. This ritual of blessing will ensure the happiness of the newlyweds and ward off moles, harelips and other prodigious marks that would disfigure their offspring. "With this field-dew consecrate," the Fairy King concludes,

> Every fairy take his gait,
> And each several chamber bless,
> Through this palace, with sweet peace,
> And the owner of it blest
> Ever shall in safety rest.
>
> (5.1.415–20)

Oberon himself, we are told, will conduct the blessing upon the "best bride-bed," that of the ruler Theseus and his Amazon queen Hippolyta.

The ceremony—manifestly the sanctification of ownership and caste, as well as marriage—is a witty allusion to the traditional Catholic blessing of the bride-bed with holy water, a ceremony vehemently attacked as pagan superstition and banned by English Protestants. But the conventional critical term "allusion" seems inadequate, for the term usually implies a bloodless, bodiless thing, while even the tiny, incidental detail of the field dew bears a more active charge. Here, as with Wolsey's hat, I want to ask what is at stake in the shift from one zone of social practice to another, from the old religion to public theater, from priests to fairies, from holy water to field dew, or rather to theatrical fairies and theatrical field dew on the London stage. When the Catholic ritual is made into theatrical representation, the transposition at once naturalizes, denaturalizes, mocks, and celebrates. It naturalizes the ritual by transforming the specially sanctified water into ordinary dew; it denaturalizes the ritual by removing it from human agents and attributing it to the fairies; it mocks Catholic practice by associating it with notorious superstition and then by enacting it on the stage where it is revealed as a histrionic illusion; and it celebrates such practice by reinvesting it with the charismatic magic of the theater.

Several years ago, intending to signal a turn away from the formal, decontextualized analysis that dominates new criticism, I used the term "new historicism" to describe an interest in the kinds of issues I have been raising—in the embeddedness of cultural objects in the contingencies of history—and the term has achieved a certain currency. But like most labels, this one is misleading. The new historicism, like the Holy Roman Empire, constantly belies its own name. *The American Heritage Dictionary* gives three meanings for the term "historicism":

1. The belief that processes are at work in history that man can do little to alter.
2. The theory that the historian must avoid all value judgments in his study of past periods or former cultures.
3. Veneration of the past or of tradition.

Most of the writing labelled new historicist, and certainly my own work, has set itself resolutely against each of these positions.

1. *The belief that processes are at work in history that man can do little to alter.* This formulation rests upon a simultaneous abstraction and evacuation of human agency. The men and women who find themselves making concrete choices in given circumstances at particular times are transformed into something called "man." And this colorless, nameless collective being cannot significantly intervene in the "processes . . . at work in history," processes that are thus mysteriously alienated from all of those who enact them.

New historicism, by contrast, eschews the use of the term "man"; interest lies not in the abstract universal but in particular, contingent cases, the selves fashioned and acting according to the generative rules and conflicts of a given culture. And these selves, conditioned by the expectations of their class, gender, religion, race and national identity, are constantly effecting changes in the course of history. Indeed if there is any inevitability in the new historicism's vision of history it is this insistence on agency, for even inaction or extreme marginality is understood to possess meaning and therefore to imply intention. Every form of behavior, in this view, is a strategy: taking up arms or taking flight is a significant social action, but so is staying put, minding one's business, turning one's face to the wall. Agency is virtually inescapable.

Inescapable but not simple: new historicism, as I understand it, does not posit historical processes as unalterable and inexorable, but it does tend to discover limits or constraints upon individual intervention. Actions that appear to be single are disclosed as multiple; the apparently isolated power of the individual genius turns out to be bound up with collective, social energy; a gesture of dissent may be an element in a larger legitimation process, while an attempt to stabilize the order of things may turn out to subvert it. And political valences may change, sometimes abruptly: there are no guarantees, no absolute, formal assurances that what seems progressive in one set of contingent circumstances will not come to seem reactionary in another.

The new historicism's insistence on the pervasiveness of agency has apparently led some of its critics to find in it a Nietzschean[3] celebration of the ruthless will to power, while its ironic and skeptical reappraisal of the cult of heroic individualism has led others to find in it a pessimistic doctrine of human helplessness. Hence, for example, from a Marxist perspective one critic characterizes the new historicism as a "liberal disillusionment" that finds that "any apparent site of resistance ultimately serves the interests of power" (33), while from a liberal humanist perspective, another critic proclaims that "anyone who, like me, is reluctant to accept the will to power as the defining human essence will probably have trouble with the critical procedures of the new historicists and with their interpretive conclusions."[4] But the very idea of a "defining human essence" is precisely what new historicists find vacuous and untenable, as I do the counter-claim that love rather than power makes the world go round. The Marxist critique is more plausible, but it rests

upon an assertion that new historicism argues that "*any* apparent site of resistance" is ultimately coopted. Some are, some aren't.

I argued in an essay published some years ago that the sites of resistance in Shakespeare's second tetralogy are coopted in the plays' ironic, complex, but finally celebratory affirmation of charismatic kingship. That is, the formal structure and rhetorical strategy of the plays make it difficult for audiences to withhold their consent from the triumph of Prince Hal. Shakespeare shows that the triumph rests upon a claustrophobic narrowing of pleasure, a hypocritical manipulation of appearances, and a systematic betrayal of friendship, and yet these manifestations of bad faith only contrive to heighten the spectators' knowing pleasure and the ratification of applause. The subversive perceptions do not disappear, but insofar as they remain within the structure of the play, they are contained and indeed serve to heighten a power they would appear to question.

I did not propose that all manifestation of resistance in all literature (or even in all plays by Shakespeare) were coopted—one can readily think of plays where the forces of ideological containment break down. And yet characterizations of this essay in particular, and new historicism in general, repeatedly refer to a supposed argument that any resistance is impossible.[5] A particularizing argument about the subject position projected by a set of plays is at once simplified and turned into a universal principle from which contingency and hence history itself is erased.

Moreover, even my argument about Shakespeare's second tetralogy is misunderstood if it is thought to foreclose the possibility of dissent or change or the radical alteration of the processes of history. The point is that certain aesthetic and political structures work to contain the subversion perceptions they generate, not that those perceptions simply wither away. On the contrary, they may be pried loose from the order with which they were bound up and may serve to fashion a new and radically different set of structures. How else could change ever come about? No one is forced—except perhaps in school—to take aesthetic or political wholes as sacrosanct. The order of things is never simply a given: it takes labor to produce, sustain,

---

[3] Nietzsche (above, page 686).

[4] [Greenblatt] Walter Cohen, "Political Criticism of Shakespeare" in *Shakespeare Reproduced: The Text in History and Ideology,* ed. Jean E. Howard and Marion F. O'Connor (New York and London: Methuen, 1987), p. 33; Edward Pechter, "The New Historicism and Its Discontents," in *PMLA* 102 (1987), p. 301.

[5] [Greenblatt] "The new historicists and cultural materialists," one typical summary puts it, "represent, and by representing, reproduce in their *new* history of ideas, a world which is hierarchical, authoritarian, hegemonic, unsubvertable. . . . In this world picture, Stephen Greenblatt has poignantly asserted, there can be no subversion—and certainly not for *us!*" Poignantly or otherwise, I asserted no such thing; I argued that the spectator of the history plays was continually tantalized by a resistance simultaneously powerful and deferred.

reproduce, and transmit the way things are, and this labor may be withheld or transformed. Structures may be broken in pieces, the pieces altered, inverted, rearranged. Everything can be different than it is; everything could have been different than it was. But it will not do to imagine that this alteration is easy, automatic, without cost or obligation. My objection was to the notion that the rich ironies in the history plays were themselves inherently liberating, that to savor the tetralogy's skeptical cunning was to participate in an act of political resistance. In general I find dubious the assertion that certain rhetorical features in much-loved literary works constitute authentic acts of political liberation; the fact that this assertion is now heard from the left, where in my college days it was more often heard from the right, does not make it in most instances any less fatuous and presumptuous. I wished to show, at least in the case of Shakespeare's histories and in several analogous discourses, how a set of representational and political practices in the late sixteenth century could produce and even batten upon what appeared to be their own subversion.

To show this is not to give up on the possibility of altering historical processes—if this is historicism I want no part of it—but rather to eschew an aestheticized and idealized politics of the imagination.

2. *The theory that the historian must avoid all value judgments in his study of past periods or former cultures.* Once again, if this is an essential tenet of historicism, then the new historicism belies its name. My own critical practice and that of many others associated with new historicism was decisively shaped by the American 1960s and early 70s, and especially by the opposition to the Viet Nam War. Writing that was not engaged, that withheld judgments, that failed to connect the present with the past seemed worthless. Such connection could be made either by analogy or causality; that is, a particular set of historical circumstances could be represented in such a way as to bring out homologies with aspects of the present or, alternatively, those circumstances could be analyzed as the generative forces that led to the modern condition. In either mode, value judgments were implicated, because a neutral or indifferent relation to the present seemed impossible. Or rather it seemed overwhelmingly clear that neutrality was itself a political position, a decision to support the official policies in both the state and the academy.

To study the culture of sixteenth-century England did not present itself as an escape from the turmoil of the present; it seemed rather an intervention, a mode of relation. The fascination for me of the Renaissance was that it seemed to be powerfully linked to the present both analogically and causally. This doubled link at once called forth and qualified my value judgments: called them forth because my response to the past was inextricably bound up with my response to the present; qualified them because the analysis of the past revealed the complex, unsettling historical genealogy of the very judgments I was making. To study Renaissance culture then was simultaneously to feel more rooted and more estranged in my own values.[6]

Other critics associated with the new historicism have written directly and forcefully about their own subject position and have made more explicit than I the nature of this engagement.[7] If I have not done so to the same extent, it is not because I believe that my values are somehow suspended in my study of the past but because I believe they are pervasive: in the textual and visual traces I choose to analyze, in the stories I choose to tell, in the cultural conjunctions I attempt to make, in my syntax, adjectives, pronouns. "The new historicism," someone has written in a lively critique, "needs at every point to be more overtly self-conscious of its methods and its theoretical assumptions, since what one discovers about the historical place and function of literary texts is in large measure a function of the angle from which one looks and the assumptions that enable the investigation."[8] I am certainly not opposed to methodological self-consciousness, but I am less inclined to see overtness—an explicit articulation of one's values and methods—as inherently necessary or virtuous. Nor, though I believe that my values are everywhere engaged in my work, do I think that there need be a perfect integration of those values and the objects I am studying. On the contrary, some of the most interesting and powerful ideas in cultural criticism occur precisely at moments of disjunction, disintegration, unevenness. A criticism that never encounters obstacles, that celebrates predictable heroines and rounds up the usual suspects, that finds con-

---

[6][Greenblatt] See my *Renaissance Self-Fashioning: From More to Shakespeare* (Chicago: University of Chicago Press, 1980), pp. 174–75. "We are situated at the close of the cultural movement initiated in the Renaissance; the places in which our social and psychological world seems to be cracking apart are those structural joints visible when it was first constructed."

[7][Greenblatt] Louis Adrian Montrose, "Renaissance Literary Studies and the Subject of History," in *English Literary Renaissance* 16 (1986), pp. 5–12. Don Wayne, "Power, Politics, and the Shakespearean Text: Recent Criticism in England and the United States," in *Shakespeare Reproduced: The Text in History and Ideology,* ed. Howard and O'Connor, pp. 47–67; Catherine Gallagher, "Marxism and the New Historicism," in *The New Historicism,* ed. Harold Veeser (New York and London, Routledge, 1989).

[8][Greenblatt] Jean E. Howard, "The New Historicism in Renaissance Studies," in *Renaissance Historicism: Selections from "English Literary Renaissance,"* ed. Arthur F. Kinney and Dan S. Collins (Amherst: University of Massachusetts Press, 1987), pp. 32–33.

firmation of its values everywhere it turns, is quite simply boring.[9]

3. *Veneration of the past or of tradition.* The third definition of historicism obviously sits in a strange relation to the second, but they are not simply alternatives. The apparent eschewing of value judgments was often accompanied by a still more apparent admiration, however cloaked as objective description, of the past. One of the more irritating qualities of my own literary training had been its relentlessly celebratory character: literary criticism was and largely remains a kind of secular theodicy. Every decision made by a great artist could be shown to be a brilliant one; works that had seemed flawed and uneven to an earlier generation of critics bent on displaying discriminations in taste were now revealed to be organic masterpieces. A standard critical assignment in my student years was to show how a text that seemed to break in parts was really a complex whole: thousands of pages were dutifully churned out to prove that the bizarre subplot of *The Changeling* was cunningly integrated into the tragic mainplot or that every tedious bit of clowning in *Doctor Faustus* was richly significant. Behind these exercises was the assumption that great works of art were triumphs of resolution, that they were, in Bakhtin's[10] term, monological—the mature expression of a single artistic intention. When this formalism was combined, as it often was, with both ego psychology and historicism, it posited aesthetic integration as the reflection of the artist's psychic integration and posited that psychic integration as the triumphant expression of a healthy, integrated community. Accounts of Shakespeare's relation to Elizabethan culture were particularly prone to this air of veneration, since the Romantic cult of poetic genius could be conjoined with the still older political cult that had been created around the figure of the Virgin Queen.

Here again new historicist critics have swerved in a different direction. They have been more interested in unre-

solved conflict and contradiction than in integration; they are as concerned with the margins as with the center; and they have turned from a celebration of achieved aesthetic order to an exploration of the ideological and material bases for the production of this order. Traditional formalism and historicism, twin legacies of early nineteenth-century Germany, shared a vision of high culture as a harmonizing domain of reconciliation based upon an aesthetic labor that transcends specific economic or political determinants. What is missing is psychic, social, and material resistance, a stubborn, unassimilable otherness, a sense of distance and difference. New historicism has attempted to restore this distance; hence its characteristic concerns have seemed to some critics off-center or strange. "New historicists," writes a Marxist observer, "are likely to seize upon something out of the way, obscure, even bizarre: dreams, popular or aristocratic festivals, denunciations of witchcraft, sexual treatises, diaries and autobiographies, descriptions of clothing, reports on disease, birth and death records, accounts of insanity."[11] What is fascinating to me is that concerns like these should have come to seem bizarre, especially to a critic who is committed to the historical understanding of culture. That they have done so indicates how narrow the boundaries of historical understanding had become, how much these boundaries needed to be broken.

For none of the cultural practices on this list (and one could extend it considerably) is or should be "out of the way" in a study of Renaissance literature or art; on the contrary, each is directly in the way of coming to terms with the period's methods of regulating the body, its conscious and unconscious psychic strategies, its ways of defining and dealing with marginals and deviants, its mechanisms for the display of power and the expression of discontent, its treatment of women. If such concerns have been rendered "obscure," it is because of a disabling idea of causality that confines the legitimate field of historical agency within absurdly restrictive boundaries. The world is parceled out between a predictable group of stereotypical causes and a large, dimly lit mass of raw materials that the artist chooses to fashion.

The new historicist critics are interested in such cultural expressions as witchcraft accusations, medical manuals, or clothing not as raw materials but as "cooked"[12]—complex symbolic and material articulations of the imaginative and ideological structures of the society that produced them. Consequently, there is a tendency in at least some new

---

[9][Greenblatt] If there is then no suspension of value judgments in the new historicism, there is at the same time a complication of those judgments, what I have called a sense of estrangement. This estrangement is bound up with the abandonment of a belief in historical inevitability, for, with this abandonment, the values of the present could no longer seem the necessary outcome of an irreversible teleological progression, whether of enlightenment or decline. An older historicism that proclaimed self-consciously that it had avoided all value judgments in its account of the past—that it had given us historical reality *wie es eigentlich gewesen*—did not thereby avoid all value judgments; it simply provided a misleading account of what it had actually done. In this sense the new historicism, for all its acknowledgment of engagement and partiality, may be slightly less likely than the older historicism to impose its values belligerently on the past, for those values seem historically contingent.

[10]Bakhtin (above, page 912).

[11][Greenblatt] Cohen, in *Shakespeare Reproduced,* pp. 33–34.

[12]Cf. Claude Lévi-Strauss (above, page 1119); the reference is to *The Raw and the Cooked.*

historicist writings (certainly in my own) for the focus to be partially displaced from the work of art that is their formal occasion onto the related practices that had been adduced ostensibly in order to illuminate that work. It is difficult to keep those practices in the background if the very concept of historical background has been called into question.

I have tried to deal with the problem of focus by developing a notion of cultural negotiation and exchange, that is, by examining the points at which one cultural practice intersects with another, borrowing its forms and intensities or attempting to ward off unwelcome appropriations or moving texts and artifacts from one place to another. But it would be misleading to imagine that there is a complete homogenization of interest; my own concern remains centrally with imaginative literature, and not only because other cultural structures resonate powerfully within it. If I do not approach works of art in a spirit of veneration, I do approach them in a spirit that is best described as wonder. Wonder has not been alien to literary criticism, but it has been associated (if only implicitly) with formalism rather than historicism. I wish to extend this wonder beyond the formal boundaries of works of art, just as I wish to intensify resonance within those boundaries.

It will be easier to grasp the concepts of resonance and wonder if we think of the way in which our culture presents to itself not the textual traces of its past but the surviving visual traces, for the latter are put on display in galleries and museums specially designed for the purpose. By resonance I mean the power of the object displayed to reach out beyond its formal boundaries to a larger world, to evoke in the viewer the complex, dynamic cultural forces from which it has emerged and for which as metaphor or more simply as metonymy it may be taken by a viewer to stand. By wonder I mean the power of the object displayed to stop the viewer in his tracks, to convey an arresting sense of uniqueness, to evoke an exalted attention.

The new historicism obviously has distinct affinities with resonance; that is, its concern with literary texts has been to recover as far as possible the historical circumstances of their original production and consumption and to analyze the relationship between these circumstances and our own. New historicist critics have tried to understand the intersecting circumstances not as a stable, prefabricated background against which the literary texts can be placed, but as a dense network of evolving and often contradictory social forces. The idea is not to find outside the work of art some rock onto which literary interpretation can be securely chained but rather to situate the work in relation to other representational practices operative in the culture at a given moment in both its history and our own. In Louis Montrose's convenient formulation, the goal has been to grasp simultaneously the historicity of texts and the textuality of history.

Insofar as this approach, developed for literary interpretation, is at all applicable to visual traces, it would call for an attempt to reduce the isolation of individual "masterpieces," to illuminate the conditions of their making, to disclose the history of their appropriation and the circumstances in which they come to be displayed, to restore the tangibility, the openness, the permeability of boundaries that enabled the objects to come into being in the first place. An actual restoration of tangibility is obviously in most cases impossible, and the frames that enclose pictures are only the ultimate formal confirmation of the closing of the borders that marks the finishing of a work of art. But we need not take that finishing so entirely for granted; museums can and on occasion do make it easier imaginatively to recreate the work in its moment of openness.

That openness is linked to a quality of artifacts that museums obviously dread, their precariousness. But though it is perfectly reasonable for museums to protect their objects—I would not wish it any other way—precariousness is a rich source of resonance. Thomas Greene, who has written a sensitive book on what he calls the "vulnerable text," suggests that the symbolic wounding to which literature is prone may confer upon it power and fecundity. "The vulnerability of poetry," Greene argues, "stems from four basic conditions of language: its historicity, its dialogic function, its referential function, and its dependence on figuration."[13] Three of these conditions are different for the visual arts, in ways that would seem to reduce vulnerability: painting and sculpture may be detached more readily than language from both referentiality and figuration, and the pressures of contextual dialogue are diminished by the absence of an inherent *logos,* a constitutive word. But the fourth condition— historicity—is in the case of material artifacts vastly increased, indeed virtually literalized. Museums function, partly by design and partly in spite of themselves, as monuments to the fragility of cultures, to the fall of sustaining institutions and noble houses, the collapse of rituals, the evacuation of myths, the destructive effects of warfare, neglect, and corrosive doubt.

I am fascinated by the signs of alteration, tampering, even destructiveness which many museums try simply to efface: first and most obviously, the act of displacement

---

[13] [Greenblatt] Thomas Greene, *The Vulnerable Text: Essays on Renaissance Literature* (New York: Columbia University Press, 1986), p. 100.

that is essential for the collection of virtually all older artifacts and most modern ones—pulled out of chapels, peeled off church walls, removed from decaying houses, seized as spoils of war, stolen, "purchased" more or less fairly by the economically ascendent from the economically naive, the poor, the hard-pressed heirs of fallen dynasties and impoverished religious orders. Then too there are the marks on the artifacts themselves: the attempt to scratch out or deface the image of the devil in numerous late-medieval and Renaissance paintings, the concealing of the genitals in sculptured and painted figures, the iconoclastic smashing of human or divine representations, the evidence of cutting or reshaping to fit a new frame or purpose, the cracks or scorch marks or broken-off noses that indifferently record the grand disasters of history and the random accidents of trivial incompetence. Even these accidents— the marks of a literal fragility—can have their resonance: the climax of an absurdly hagiographical Proust exhibition several years ago was a display case holding a small, patched, modest vase with a notice, "This vase broken by Marcel Proust."

As this comical example suggests, wounded artifacts may be compelling not only as witnesses to the violence of history but as signs of use, marks of the human touch, and hence links with the openness to touch that was the condition of their creation. The most familiar way to recreate the openness of aesthetic artifacts without simply renewing their vulnerability is through a skillful deployment of explanatory texts in the catalogue, on the walls of the exhibit, or on cassettes. The texts so deployed introduce and in effect stand in for the context that has been effaced in the process of moving the object into the museum. But insofar as that context is partially, often primarily, visual as well as verbal, textual contextualism has its limits. Hence the mute eloquence of the display of the palette, brushes, and other implements that an artist of a given period would have employed or of objects that are represented in the exhibited paintings or of materials and images that in some way parallel or intersect with the formal works of art.

Among the most resonant moments are those in which the supposedly contextual objects take on a life of their own, make a claim that rivals that of the object that is formally privileged. A table, a chair, a map, often seemingly placed only to provide a decorative setting for a grand work, become oddly expressive, significant not as "background" but as compelling representational practices in themselves. These practices may in turn impinge upon the grand work, so that we begin to glimpse a kind of circulation: the cultural practice and social energy implicit in map-making drawn into the aesthetic orbit of a painting which has itself enabled us to register some of the representational significance of the map. Or again the threadbare fabric on the old chair or the gouges in the wood of a cabinet juxtapose the privileged painting or sculpture with marks not only of time but of use, the imprint of the human body on the artifact, and call attention to the deliberate removal of certain exalted aesthetic objects from the threat of that imprint.

For the effect of resonance does not necessarily depend upon a collapse of the distinction between art and non-art; it can be achieved by awakening in the viewer a sense of the cultural and historically contingent construction of art objects, the negotiations, exchanges, swerves, exclusions by which certain representational practices come to be set apart from other representational practices that they partially resemble. A resonant exhibition often pulls the viewer away from the celebration of isolated objects and toward a series of implied, only half-visible relationships and questions. How have the objects come to be displayed? What is at stake in categorizing them as of "museum-quality"? How were they originally used? What cultural and material conditions made possible their production? What were the feelings of those who originally held these objects, cherished them, collected them, possessed them? What is the meaning of my relationship to these same objects now that they are displayed here, in this museum, on this day?

It is time to give a more sustained example. Perhaps the most purely resonant museum I have ever seen is the State Jewish Museum in Prague. This is housed not in a single building but in a cluster of old synagogues scattered through the city's former Jewish Town. The oldest of these—known as the Old-New Synagogue—is a twin-nave medieval structure dating to the last third of the 13th century; the others are mostly Renaissance and Baroque. In these synagogues are displayed Judaica from 153 Jewish communities throughout Bohemia and Moravia. In one there is a permanent exhibition of synagogue silverworks, in another there are synagogue textiles, in a third there are Torah scrolls, ritual objects, manuscripts and prints illustrative of Jewish beliefs, traditions, and customs. One of the synagogues shows the work of the physician and artist Karel Fleischmann, principally drawings done in the Terezin concentration camp during his months of imprisonment prior to his deportation to Auschwitz. Next door in the Ceremonial Hall of the Prague Burial Society there is a wrenching exhibition of children's drawings from Terezin. Finally, one synagogue, closed at the time of my visit to Prague, has simply a wall of names—thousands of them—to commemorate the Jewish victims of Nazi persecution in Czechoslovakia.

"The Museum's rich collections of synagogue art and the historic synagogue buildings of Prague's Jewish town," says the catalogue of the State Jewish Museum, "form a memorial complex that has not been preserved to the same extent anywhere else in Europe." "A memorial complex"— this museum is not so much about artifacts as about memory, and the form the memory takes is a secularized kaddish, a commemorative prayer for the dead. The atmosphere has a peculiar effect on the act of viewing. It is mildly interesting to note the differences between the mordant Grosz-like lithographs of Karel Fleischmann in the pre-war years and the tormented style, at once detached and anguished, of the drawings in the camps, but aesthetic discriminations feel weird, out-of-place. And it seems wholly absurd, even indecent, to worry about the relative artistic merits of the drawings that survive by children who did not survive.

The discordance between viewing and remembering is greatly reduced with the older, less emotionally charged artifacts, but even here the ritual objects in their glass cases convey an odd and desolate impression. The oddity, I suppose, should be no greater than in seeing a Mayan god or, for that matter, a pyx or a ciborium, but we have become so familiarized to the display of such objects, so accustomed to considering them works of art, that even pious Catholics, as far as I know, do not necessarily feel disconcerted by their transformation from ritual function to aesthetic exhibition. And until very recently the voices of the tribal peoples who might have objected to the display of their religious artifacts have not been heard and certainly not attended to.

The Jewish objects are neither sufficiently distant to be absorbed into the detached ethos of anthropological display nor sufficiently familiar to be framed and encased alongside the altarpieces and reliquaries that fill Western museums. And moving as they are as mnemonic devices, most of the ritual objects in the State Jewish Museum are not, by contrast with Christian liturgical art, particularly remarkable either for their antiquity or their extraordinary beauty. They are the products of a people with a resistance to joining figural representation to religious observance, a strong anti-iconic bias. The objects have, as it were, little will to be observed; many of them are artifacts—ark curtains, Torah crowns, breastplates, pointers, and the like—whose purpose was to be drawn back or removed in order to make possible the act that mattered: not vision but reading.

But the inhibition of viewing in the Jewish Museum is paradoxically bound up with its resonance. This resonance depends not upon visual stimulation but upon a felt intensity of names, and behind the names, as the very term resonance suggests, of voices: the voices of those who chanted, studied, muttered their prayers, wept, and then were forever silenced. And mingled with these voices are others—of those Jews in 1389 who were murdered in the Old-New Syna-

gogue where they were seeking refuge; of the great sixteenth-century Kabbalist, Jehuda ben Bezalel, known as Rabbi Loew, who is fabled to have created the Golem; of the twentieth century's ironic Kabbalist, Franz Kafka.

It is Kafka who would be most likely to grasp imaginatively the State Jewish Museum's ultimate source of resonance: the fact that most of the objects are located in the museum—were displaced, preserved, and transformed categorically into works of art—because the Nazis stored the articles they confiscated in the Prague synagogues that they chose to preserve for this very purpose. In 1941 the Nazi Hochschule in Frankfurt had established an Institute for the Exploration of the Jewish Question which in turn had initiated a massive effort to confiscate Jewish libraries, archives, religious artifacts, and personal property. By the middle of 1942 Heydrich as Hitler's chief officer within the so-called Protectorate of Bohemia and Moravia, had chosen Prague as the site of the Central Bureau for Dealing with the Jewish Question, and an SS officer, Untersturmführer Karl Rahm, had assumed control of the small existing Jewish museum, founded in 1912, which was renamed the Central Jewish Museum. The new charter of the museum announced that "the numerous, hitherto scattered Jewish possessions of both historical and artistic value, on the territory of the entire Protectorate, must be collected and stored."[14]

During the following months, tens of thousands of confiscated items arrived, the dates of the shipments closely coordinated with the "donors' " deportation to the concentration camps. The experts formally employed by the original Jewish museum were compelled to catalogue the items, and the Nazis compounded this immense task by also ordering the wretched, malnourished curators to prepare a collections guide and organize private exhibitions for SS staff. Between September 1942 and October 1943 four major exhibitions were mounted. Since these required far more space than the existing Jewish Museum's modest location, the great old Prague synagogues—made vacant by the Nazi prohibition of Jewish public worship—were partially refurbished for the occasion. Hence in March 1943, for example, in the seventeenth-century Klaus Synagogue, there was an exhibition of Jewish festival and life-cycle observances; "when Sturmbannführer Günther first toured the collection on April 6, he demanded various changes, including the translation of all Hebrew texts and the addition of an exhibit on

---

[14][Greenblatt] Quoted in Linda A. Altshuler and Anna R. Cohn, "The Precious Legacy," in David Altshuler, ed., *The Precious Legacy: Judaic Treasures from the Czechoslovac State Collections* (New York: Summit Books, 1983), p. 24. My sketch of the genesis of the State Jewish Museum is largely paraphrased from this chapter.

kosher butchering" (*Precious Legacy,* p. 36). Plans were drawn up for other exhibitions, but the curators—who had given themselves to the task with a strange blend of selflessness, irony, helplessness, and heroism—were themselves at this point sent to concentration camps and murdered.

After the war, the few survivors of the Czech Jewish community apparently felt they could not sustain the ritual use of the synagogues or maintain the large collections. In 1949 the Jewish Community Council offered as a gift to the Czechoslovak government both the synagogues and their contents. These became the resonant, impure "memorial complex" they are—a cultural machine that generates an uncontrollable oscillation between homage and desecration, longing and hopelessness, the voices of the dead and silence. For resonance, like nostalgia, is impure, a hybrid forged in the barely acknowledged gaps, the cesurae, between words like State, Jewish, and Museum.

I want to avoid the implication that resonance must be necessarily linked to destruction and absence; it can be found as well in unexpected survival. The key is the intimation of a larger community of voices and skills, an imagined ethnographic thickness. Here another example will serve: in the Yucatan there is an extensive, largely unexcavated late-Classic Maya site called Coba, whose principal surviving feature is a high pyramid known as Nahoch Mul. After a day of tramping around the site, I was relaxing in the pool of the nearby Club Med Archaeological Villa in the company of a genial structural engineer from Little Rock. To make conversation, I asked my pool-mate what he as a structural engineer thought of Nahoch Mul. "From an engineer's point of view," he replied, "a pyramid is not very interesting—it's just an enormous gravity structure." "But," he added, "did you notice that Coca Cola stand on the way in? That's the most impressive example of contemporary Maya architecture I've ever seen." I thought it quite possible that my leg was being pulled, but I went back the next day to check—I had, of course, completely blocked out the Coke stand on my first visit. Sure enough, some enterprising Mayan had built a remarkably elegant shelter with a soaring pyramidal roof constructed out of ingeniously intertwining sticks and branches. Places like Coba are thick with what Spenser called the Ruins of Time—with a nostalgia for a lost civilization, in a state of collapse long before Cortés or Montejo cut their paths through the jungle.[15]

But, despite frequent colonial attempts to drive them or imagine them out of existence, the Maya have not in fact vanished, and a single entrepreneur's architectural improvisation suddenly had more resonance for me than the mounds of the 'lost' city.

My immediate thought was that the whole Coca Cola stand could be shipped to New York and put on display in the Museum of Modern Art. And that impulse moves us away from resonance and toward wonder. For the MOMA is one of the great contemporary places not for the hearing of intertwining voices, not for historical memory, not for ethnographic thickness, but for intense, indeed enchanting looking. Looking may be called enchanted when the act of attention draws a circle around itself from which everything but the object is excluded, when intensity of regard blocks out all circumambient images, stills all murmuring voices. To be sure, the viewer may have purchased a catalogue, read an inscription on the wall, switched on a cassette, but in the moment of wonder all of this apparatus seems mere static.

The so-called boutique lighting that has become popular in recent years—a pool of light that has the surreal effect of seeming to emerge from within the object rather than to focus upon it from without—is an attempt to provoke or to heighten the experience of wonder, as if modern museum designers feared that wonder was increasingly difficult to arouse or perhaps that it risked displacement entirely onto the windows of designer dress shops and antique stores. The association of that lighting—along with transparent plastic rods and other devices to create the magical illusion of luminous, weightless suspension—with commerce would seem to suggest that wonder is bound up with acquisition and possession, yet the whole experience of most art museums is about *not* touching, *not* carrying home, *not* owning the marvelous objects. Modern museums in effect at once evoke the dream of possession and evacuate it.[16] (Alternatively, we could say that they displace that dream onto the museum gift shop, where the boutique lighting once again serves to heighten acquisition, now of reproductions that stand for the unattainable works of art.)

That evacuation or displacement is an historical rather than structural aspect of the museum's regulation of wonder: that is, collections of objects calculated to arouse wonder arose precisely in the spirit of personal acquisition and were only subsequently detached from it. In the Middle

---

[15]Edmund Spenser (1552?–1599), English poet; Hernando Cortés (1485–1547), Spanish conqueror of Mexico; Francesco de Montejo (c.1479–1548), Spanish conquistador.

[16][Greenblatt] In effect that dream of possessing wonder is at once aroused and evacuated in commerce as well, since the minute the object—shoe or dress or soup tureen—is removed from its magical pool of light, it loses its wonder and returns to the status of an ordinary purchase.

Ages and Renaissance we characteristically hear about wonders in the context of those who possessed them (or who gave them away). Hence, for example, in his *Life of Saint Louis,* Joinville writes that "during the king's stay at Saida someone brought him a stone that split into flakes":

> It was the most marvelous stone in the world, for when you lifted one of the flakes you found the form of a sea-fish between the two pieces of stone. This fish was entirely of stone, but there was nothing lacking in its shape, eyes, bones, or colour to make it seem otherwise than if it had been alive. The king gave me one of these stones. I found a tench inside; it was brown in colour, and in every detail exactly as you would expect a tench to be.[17]

The wonder-cabinets of the Renaissance were at least as much about possession as display. The wonder derived not only from what could be seen but from the sense that the shelves and cases were filled with unseen wonders, all the prestigious property of the collector. In this sense, the cult of wonder originated in close conjunction with a certain type of resonance, a resonance bound up with the evocation not of an absent culture but of the great man's superfluity of rare and precious things. Those things were not necessarily admired for their beauty; the marvelous was bound up with the excessive, the surprising, the literally outlandish, the prodigious. They were not necessarily the manifestations of the artistic skill of human makers: technical virtuosity could indeed arouse admiration, but so could nautilus shells, ostrich eggs, uncannily large (or small) bones, stuffed crocodiles, fossils. And, most importantly, they were not necessarily objects set out for careful viewing.

The experience of wonder was not initially regarded as essentially or even primarily *visual; reports* of marvels had a force equal to the seeing of them. Seeing was important and desirable, of course, but precisely in order to make reports possible, reports which then circulated as virtual equivalents of the marvels themselves. The great medieval collections of marvels are almost entirely textual: Friar Jordanus's *Marvels of the East,* Marco Polo's *Book of Marvels,* Mandeville's *Travels.* Some of the manuscripts, to be sure, were illuminated, but these illuminations were almost always ancillary to the textual record of wonders, just as emblem books were originally textual and only subsequently illustrated. Even in the sixteenth century, when the power of direct visual experience was increasingly valued, the marvelous was principally theorized as a textual phenomenon, as it had been in antiquity. "No one can be called a poet," writes the influential Italian critic Minturno in the 1550s, "who does not excel in the power of arousing wonder."[18] For Aristotle wonder was associated with pleasure as the end of poetry, and in the *Poetics* he examined the strategies by which tragedians and epic poets employ the marvelous to arouse wonder.[19] For the Platonists too wonder was conceived as an essential element in literary art: in the sixteenth century, the Neo-Platonist Francesco Patrizi defined the poet as principal "maker of the marvelous," and the marvelous is found, as he put it, when men "are astounded, ravished in ecstasy." Patrizi goes so far as to posit marvelling as a special faculty of the mind, a faculty which in effect mediates between the capacity to think and the capacity to feel.[20]

Modern art museums reflect a profound transformation of the experience: the collector—a Getty or a Mellon—may still be celebrated, and market value is even more intensely registered, but the heart of the mystery lies with the uniqueness, authenticity, and visual power of the masterpiece, ideally displayed in such a way as to heighten its charisma, to compel and reward the intensity of the viewer's gaze, to manifest artistic genius. Museums display works of art in such a way as to imply that no one, not even the nominal owner or donor, can penetrate the zone of light and actually possess the wonderful object. The object exists not principally to be owned but to be viewed. Even the *fantasy* of possession is no longer central to the museum-gaze, or rather it has been inverted, so that the object in its essence seems not to be a possession but rather to be itself the possessor of what is most valuable and enduring.[21] What the work possesses is the power to arouse wonder, and that power, in the dominant aesthetic ideology of the West, has been infused into it by the creative genius of the artist.

---

18 [Greenblatt] Quoted in J. V. Cunningham, *Woe and Wonder: The Emotional Effect of Shakespearean Tragedy* (Denver: Alan Swallow, 1960; orig. ed. 1951), p. 82.

19 Aristotle (above, page 66).

20 [Greenblatt] Hathaway's [Baxter Hathaway, *The Age of Criticism*] account of Patrizi is taken largely from Bernard Weinberg, *A History of Literary Criticism in the Italian Renaissance,* 2 vols. (Chicago: University of Chicago Press, 1961). [Unlikely, as Hathaway's book was published in 1962.]

21 [Greenblatt] It is a mistake to associate the gaze of the museum-goer with the appropriative male gaze about which so much has been written recently. But then I think that the discourse of the appropriative male gaze is itself in need of considerable qualification.

---

17 [Greenblatt] Joinville, *Life of Saint Louis,* in *Chronicles of the Crusades,* tr. M. R. B. Shaw (Harmondsworth: Penguin, 1963), p. 315.

It is beyond the scope of this essay to account for the transformation of the experience of wonder from the spectacle of proprietorship to the mystique of the object[22]—an exceedingly complex, overdetermined history centering on institutional and economic shifts—but I think it is important to say that at least in part this transformation was shaped by the collective project of Western artists and reflects their vision. Already in the early sixteenth century, when the marvelous was still principally associated with the prodigious, Dürer begins, in a famous journal entry describing Mexican objects sent to Charles V by Cortés, to reconceive it:

> I saw the things which have been brought to the King from the new golden land: a sun all of gold a whole fathom broad, and a moon all of silver of the same size, also two rooms full of the armour of the people there, and all manner of wondrous weapons of theirs, harness and darts, wonderful shields, strange clothing, bedspreads, and all kinds of wonderful objects of various uses, much more beautiful to behold than prodigies. These things were all so precious that they have been valued at one hundred thousand gold florins. All the days of my life I have seen nothing that has gladdened my heart so much as these things, for I saw amongst them wonderful works of art, and I marvelled at the subtle *ingenia* of men in foreign lands. Indeed, I cannot express all that I thought there.[23]

Dürer's description is full of the conventional marks of his period's sense of wonder: he finds it important that the artifacts have been brought as a kind of tribute to the king, that large quantities of precious metals have been used, that their market value has been reckoned; he notes the strangeness of them, even as he uncritically assimilates that strangeness to his own culture's repertory of objects (which include harness and bedspreads). But he also notes, in perceptions highly unusual for his own time, that these objects are "much more beautiful to behold than prodigies." Dürer relocates the source of wonder from the outlandish to the aesthetic, and he understands the effect of beauty as a testimony to creative genius: "I saw amongst them wonderful

works of art, and I marvelled at the subtle *ingenia* of men in foreign lands."

It would be misleading to strip away the relations of power and wealth that are encoded in the artist's response, but it would be still more misleading, I think, to interpret that response as an unmediated expression of those relations. For Dürer gives voice to an aesthetic understanding—a form of wondering and admiring and knowing—that is at least partly independent of the structures of politics and the marketplace.

This understanding—by no means autonomous and yet not reducible to the institutional and economic forces by which it is shaped—is centered on a certain kind of looking, a looking whose origins lie in the cult of the marvelous and hence in the art work's capacity to generate in the spectator surprise, delight, admiration, and intimations of genius. The knowledge that derives from this kind of looking may not be very useful in the attempt to understand another culture, but it is vitally important in the attempt to understand our own. For it is one of the distinctive achievements of our culture to have fashioned this type of gaze, and one of the most intense pleasures that it has to offer. This pleasure does not have an inherent and necessary politics, either radical or imperialist, but Dürer's remarks suggest that it originates at least in respect and admiration for the *ingenia* of others. This respect is a response worth cherishing and enhancing. Hence, for all of my academic affiliations and interests, I am skeptical about the recent attempt to turn our museums from temples of wonder into temples of resonance.

Perhaps the most startling instance of this attempt is the transfer of the paintings in the Jeu de Paume and the Louvre to the new Musée d'Orsay. The Musée d'Orsay is at once a spectacular manifestation of French cultural *dépense*[24] and a highly self-conscious, exceptionally stylish generator of resonance, including the literal resonance of voices in an enormous vaulted railway station. By moving the Impressionist and Post-Impressionist masterpieces into proximity with the work of far less well-known painters—Jean Béraud, Guillaume Dubuffe, Paul Sérusier,[25] and so forth—and into proximity as well with the period's sculpture and decorative arts, the museum remakes a remarkable group of highly individuated geniuses into engaged participants in a vital, conflict-ridden, immensely productive period in French cultural history. The reimagining is guided by many well-designed informative

---

[22] This is a term that Greenblatt associates with the New Criticism, possibly because of Ransom's (above, page 961) secular appropriation of the word "miraculous" to describe the poetic.

[23] [Greenblatt] Quoted in Hugh Honour, *The New Golden Land: European Images of America from the Discoveries to the Present Time* (New York: Pantheon Books, 1975), p. 28.

---

[24] *Dépense:* expenditure.

[25] Jean Béraud (1849–1935), Guillaume Dubuffe (1837–1895), Paul Sérusier (1863?–1927), all French painters.

boards—cue cards, in effect—along, of course, with the extraordinary building itself.

All of this is intelligently conceived and dazzlingly executed—on a cold winter day in Paris, the museum-goer may look down from one of the high balconies by the old railway clocks and savor the swirling pattern formed by the black and gray raincoats of the spectators below, as they pass through the openings in the massive black stone partitions of Gay Aulenti's interior.[26] The pattern seems spontaneously to animate the period's style—if not Manet, then at least Caillebotte;[27] it is as if a painted scene had recovered the power to move and to echo.

But what has been sacrificed on the altar of cultural resonance is visual wonder centered on the aesthetic masterpiece. Attention is dispersed among a wide range of lesser objects that collectively articulate the impressive creative achievement of French culture in the late nineteenth century, but the experience of the old Jeu de Paume—intense looking at Manet, Monet, Cézanne and so forth[28]—has been radically reduced. The paintings are there, but they are mediated by the resonant contextualism of the building itself and its myriad objects and its descriptive and analytical plaques. Moreover, many of the greatest paintings have been demoted, as it were, to small spaces where it is difficult to view them adequately—as if the design of the museum were trying to assure the triumph of resonance over wonder.

But is a triumph of one over the other necessary? I have, for the purposes of this exposition, obviously exaggerated the extent to which these are alternative models for museums (or for the reading of texts): in fact, almost every exhibition worth the viewing has strong elements of both. I think that the impact of most exhibitions is likely to be greater if the initial appeal is wonder, a wonder that then leads to the desire for resonance, for it is easier to pass from wonder to resonance than from resonance to wonder. Why this should be so is suggested by a remarkable passage in his *Commentary on the Metaphysics of Aristotle* by Aquinas's teacher, Albert the Great:

> wonder is defined as a constriction and suspension of the heart caused by amazement at the sensible appearance of something so portentous, great, and unusual, that the heart suffers a systole. Hence wonder is something like fear in its effect on the heart. This effect of wonder, then, this constriction and systole of the heart, spring from an unfulfilled but felt desire to know the cause of that which appears portentous and unusual; so it was in the beginning when men, up to that time unskilled, began to philosophize. . . . Now the man who is puzzled and wonders apparently does not know. Hence wonder is the movement of the man who does not know on his way to finding out, to get at the bottom of that at which he wonders and to determine its cause. . . . Such is the origin of philosophy.[29]

Such too, from the perspective of the new historicism, is the origin of a meaningful desire for cultural resonance. But while philosophy would seek to supplant wonder with secure knowledge, it is the function of the new historicism continually to renew the marvelous at the heart of the resonant.

---

[26]Gae Aulenti (b. 1927), Italian architect.
[27]Édouard Manet (1832–1883), Gustave Caillebotte (1848–1894), French painters.
[28]Claude Monet (1840–1926), Paul Cézanne (1839–1906), French painters.

[29][Greenblatt] Quoted in Cunningham, pp. 77–78.

Judith Butler

b. 1956

In a very powerful pair of books, *Gender Trouble: Feminism and the Subversion of Identity* (1990) and *Bodies that Matter: On the Discursive Limits of "Sex"* (1993), Judith Butler outlined an array of issues at the intersection of contemporary feminism and the politics and philosophy of gender that continue to generate lively critical debate. Writing as a philosopher and a critic, Butler brought to the foreground the problematics of the concept of gender as always including a performative dimension, not only complicating categorical conceptions of identity and sex, but the idea of identity itself. While Butler has long identified herself as primarily a feminist theorist, the "trouble" with gender is that it is too prone to fixed assignment into such categories as "masculine" or "feminine," without taking into account that gender is constituted by the repetition of social acts. In this light, the danger of a politics grounded on fixed notions of identity, particularly gender identity, can entail a significant loss of freedom. In *Bodies that Matter,* Butler extends (and to some degree alters) her position as a guard against the supposition that if gender is socially constructed and based on the performative, then the physicality, the materiality of bodies may be neglected. Here too, however, Butler's concern is to avoid categorial habits precisely because they play out across the entire social field as a loss of motility, a reduction of choice.

There is, of course, no small irony in the fact that just as Butler argues strenuously to keep notions of identity from being captured by practically obligatory forms, whether masculine or feminine, hetero- or homosexual, her work is identified in just such terms for constituencies to whom the questions are vital—as they evidently are to her own work as well. Thus her prominent role in queer theory, even as she problematizes the idea, is a reflection of the scope of the issue of gender and sexual identity. In the essay reprinted here, she keeps these questions in play with philosophical dexterity and a ready command of political and psychoanalytic conceptual registers.

Butler's works include: *Subjects of Desire: Hegelian Reflections in Twentieth-Century France* (1986); *Gender Trouble: Feminism and the Subversion of Identity* (1990); *Bodies that Matter: On the Discursive Limits of "Sex"* (1993); *Excitable Speech: A Politics of the Performative* (1996); and *The Psychic Life of Power: Theories in Subjection* (1997). See also her wide-ranging work in collaboration with Slavoj Žižek and Ernseto Laclau, *Contingency, Hegemony, Universality: Contemporary Dialogues on the Left* (2000). For further critical interactions, see *Feminist Contentions: A Philosophical Exchange* (1995), with Seyla Benhabib, Nancy Fraser, Drucilla Cornell, and Linda Nicholson.

Imitation and Gender Insubordination[1]

So what is this divided being introduced into language through gender? It is an impossible being, it is a being that does not exist, an ontological joke.

MONIQUE WITTIG[2]

Beyond physical repetition and the psychical or metaphysical repetition, is there an ontological *repetition? . . . This ultimate repetition, this ultimate theatre, gathers everything in a certain way; and in another way, it destroys everything; and in yet another way, it selects from everything.*

GILLES DELEUZE[3]

To Theorize as a Lesbian?

At first I considered writing a different sort of essay, one with a philosophical tone: the "being" of being homosexual. The prospect of *being* anything, even for pay, has always produced in me a certain anxiety, for "to be" gay, "to be" lesbian seems to be more than a simple injunction to become who or what I already am. And in no way does it settle the anxiety for me to say that this is "part" of what I am. To write or speak *as a lesbian* appears a paradoxical appearance of this "I," one which feels neither true nor false. For it is a production, usually in response to a request, to come out or write in the name of an identity which, once produced, sometimes functions as a politically efficacious phantasm. I'm not at ease with "lesbian theories, gay theories," for as I've argued elsewhere,[4] identity categories tend to be instruments of regulatory regimes, whether as the normalizing categories of oppressive structures or as the rallying points for a liberatory contestation of that very oppression. This is not to say that I will not appear at political occasions under the sign of lesbian, but that I would like to have it permanently unclear what precisely that sign signifies. So it is unclear how it is that I can contribute to this book and appear under its title, for it announces a set of terms that I propose to contest. One risk I take is to be recolonized by the sign under which I write, and so it is this risk that I seek to thematize. To propose that the invocation of identity is always a risk does not imply that resistance to it is always or only symptomatic of a self-inflicted homophobia. Indeed, a Foucaultian perspective might argue that the affirmation of "homosexuality" is itself an extension of a homophobic discourse. And yet "discourse," he writes on the same page, "can be both an instrument and an effect of power, but also a hindrance, a stumbling-block, a point of resistance and a starting point for an opposing strategy."[5]

So I am skeptical about how the "I" is determined as it operates under the title of the lesbian sign, and I am no more comfortable with its homophobic determination than with those normative definitions offered by other members of the "gay or lesbian community." I'm permanently troubled by identity categories, consider them to be invariable stumbling-blocks, and understand them, even promote them, as sites of necessary trouble. In fact, if the category were to offer no trouble, it would cease to be interesting to me: it is precisely the *pleasure* produced by the instability of those categories which sustains the various erotic practices that make me a candidate for the category to begin with. To install myself within the terms of an identity category would be to turn against the sexuality that the category purports to describe; and this might be true for any identity category which seeks to control the very eroticism that it claims to describe and authorize, much less "liberate."

And what's worse, I do not understand the notion of "theory," and am hardly interested in being cast as its defender, much less in being signified as part of an elite gay/lesbian theory crowd that seeks to establish the legitimacy and domestication of gay/lesbian studies within the academy. Is there a pregiven distinction between theory, politics, culture, media? How do those divisions operate to quell a certain intertextual writing that might well generate wholly different epistemic maps? But I am writing here now: is it too late? Can this writing, can any writing, refuse the terms by which it is appropriated even as, to some extent, that very colonizing discourse enables or produces this stumbling-block, this resistance? How do I relate the paradoxical situation of this dependency and refusal?

If the political task is to show that theory is never merely *theoria,* in the sense of disengaged contemplation, and to insist that it is fully political (*phronesis* or even *praxis*), then why not simply call this operation *politics,* or some necessary permutation of it?

"Imitation and Gender Insubordination" was published in 1991 drawing upon an earlier presentation at Yale University in 1989. It is reprinted here from *Inside / Out: Lesbian Theories, Gay Theories,* ed. Diana Fuss (New York: Routledge, 1991).

[1] [Butler] Parts of this essay were given as a presentation at the Conference on Homosexuality at Yale University in October 1989.

[2] [Butler] "The Mark of Gender," *Feminist Issues* 5 no. 2 (1985), 6.

[3] [Butler] *Différence et répétition* (Paris: PUF, 1968), 374; my translation. [Deleuze (above, page 1442)].

[4] [Butler] *Gender Trouble: Feminism and the Subversion of Identity* (New York and London: Routledge, 1990).

[5] [Butler] Michel Foucault, *The History of Sexuality, Vol. I,* tr. John Hurley (New York: Random House, 1980), 101. [Foucault (above, page 1259)].

I have begun with confessions of trepidation and a series of disclaimers, but perhaps it will become clear that *disclaiming,* which is no simple activity, will be what I have to offer as a form of affirmative resistance to a certain regulatory operation of homophobia. The discourse of "coming out" has clearly served its purposes, but what are its risks? And here I am not speaking of unemployment or public attack or violence, which are quite clearly and widely on the increase against those who are perceived as "out" whether or not of their own design. Is the "subject" who is "out" free of its subjection and finally in the clear? Or could it be that the subjection that subjectivates the gay or lesbian subject in some ways continues to oppress, or oppresses most insidiously, once "outness" is claimed? What or who is it that is "out," made manifest and fully disclosed, when and if I reveal myself as lesbian? What is it that is now known, anything? What remains permanently concealed by the very linguistic act that offers up the promise of a transparent revelation of sexuality? Can sexuality even remain sexuality once it submits to a criterion of transparency and disclosure, or does it perhaps cease to be sexuality precisely when the semblance of full explicitness is achieved?[6] Is sexuality of any kind even possible without that opacity designated by the unconscious, which means simply that the conscious "I" who would reveal its sexuality is perhaps the last to know the meaning of what it says?

To claim that this is what I *am* is to suggest a provisional totalization of this "I." But if the I can so determine itself, then that which it excludes in order to make that determination remains constitutive of the determination itself. In other words, such a statement presupposes that the "I" exceeds its determination, and even produces that very excess in and by the act which seeks to exhaust the semantic field of that "I." In the act which would disclose the true and full content of that "I," a certain radical *concealment* is thereby produced. For it is always finally unclear what is meant by invoking the lesbian-signifier, since its signification is always to some degree out of one's control, but also because its *specificity* can only be demarcated by exclusions that return to disrupt its claim to coherence. What, if anything, can lesbians be said to share? And who will decide this question, and in the name of whom? If I claim to be a lesbian, I "come out" only to produce a new and different "closet." The "you" to whom I come out now has access to a different region of opacity. Indeed, the locus of opacity has simply shifted: before, you did not know whether I

"am," but now you do not know what that means, which is to say that the copula is empty, that it cannot be substituted for with a set of descriptions.[7] And perhaps that is a situation to be valued. Conventionally, one comes out *of* the closet (and yet, how often is it the case that we are "outted" when we are young and without resources?); so we are out of the closet, but into what? what new unbounded spatiality? the room, the den, the attic, the basement, the house, the bar, the university, some new enclosure whose door, like Kafka's[8] door, produces the expectation of a fresh air and a light of illumination that never arrives? Curiously, it is the figure of the closet that produces this expectation, and which guarantees its dissatisfaction. For being "out" always depends to some extent on being "in"; it gains its meaning only within that polarity. Hence, being "out" must produce the closet again and again in order to maintain itself as "out." In this sense, *outness* can only produce a new opacity; and *the closet* produces the promise of a disclosure that can, by definition, never come. Is this infinite postponement of the disclosure of "gayness," produced by the very act of "coming out," to be lamented? Or is this very deferral of the signified *to be valued,* a site for the production of values, precisely because the term now takes on a life that cannot be, can never be, permanently controlled?

It is possible to argue that whereas no transparent or full revelation is afforded by "lesbian" and "gay," there remains a political imperative to use these necessary errors or category mistakes, as it were (what Gayatri Spivak might call "catachrestic" operations: to use a proper name improperly[9]), to rally and represent an oppressed political constituency. Clearly, I am not legislating against the use of the term. My question is simply: which use will be legislated, and what play will there be between legislation and use such that the instrumental uses of "identity" do not become regulatory imperatives? If it is already true that "lesbians" and "gay men" have been traditionally designated as impossible identities, errors of classification, unnatural disasters within juridico-medical discourses, or, what perhaps amounts to the same, the very paradigm of what calls to be classified, regulated, and controlled, then perhaps these sites of disruption, error, confusion, and trouble can be the very rallying points for a certain resistance to classification and to identity as such.

---

[6] [Butler] Here I would doubtless differ from the very fine analysis of Hitchcock's *Rope* offered by D. A. Miller in this volume [i.e., *Inside / Out*].

[7] [Butler] For an example of "coming out" that is strictly unconfessional and which, finally, offers no content for the category of lesbian, see Barbara Johnson's deftly constructed "Sula Passing: No Passing" presentation at UCLA, May 1990.

[8] Franz Kafka (1883–1924), Czech novelist; see the parable "Before the Law" in *The Trial* (1925).

[9] [Butler] Gayatri Ghakravorty Spivak, "Displacement and the Discourse of Woman." In *Displacement: Derrida and After,* ed. Mark Krupnick (Bloomington: Indiana University Press, 1983). [Spivak (below, page 1509)].

The question is not one of *avowing* or *disavowing* the category of lesbian or gay, but, rather, why it is that the category becomes the site of this "ethical" choice? What does it mean to *avow* a category that can only maintain its specificity and coherence by performing a prior set of *disavowals?* Does this make "coming out" into the avowal of disavowal, that is, a return to the closet under the guise of an escape? And it is not something like heterosexuality or bisexuality that is disavowed by the category, but a set of identificatory and practical crossings between these categories that renders the discreteness of each equally suspect. Is it not possible to maintain and pursue heterosexual identifications and aims within homosexual practice, and homosexual identifications and aims within heterosexual practices? If a sexuality is to be disclosed, what will be taken as the true determinant of its meaning: the phantasy structure, the act, the orifice, the gender, the anatomy? And if the practice engages a complex interplay of all of those, which one of these erotic dimensions will come to stand for the sexuality that requires them all? Is it the *specificity* of a lesbian experience or lesbian desire or lesbian sexuality that lesbian theory needs to elucidate? Those efforts have only and always produced a set of contests and refusals which should by now make it clear that there is no necessarily common element among lesbians, except perhaps that we all know something about how homophobia works against women—although, even then, the language and the analysis we use will differ.

To argue that there might be a *specificity* to lesbian sexuality has seemed a necessary counterpoint to the claim that lesbian sexuality is just heterosexuality once removed, or that it is derived, or that it does not exist. But perhaps the claim of specificity, on the one hand, and the claim of derivativeness or non-existence, on the other, are not as contradictory as they seem. Is it not possible that lesbian sexuality is a process that reinscribes the power domains that it resists, that it is constituted in part from the very heterosexual matrix that it seeks to displace, and that its specificity is to be established, not *outside* or *beyond* that reinscription or reiteration, but in the very modality and effects of that reinscription. In other words, the negative constructions of lesbianism as a fake or a bad copy can be occupied and reworked to call into question the claims of heterosexual priority. In a sense I hope to make clear in what follows, lesbian sexuality can be understood to redeploy its 'derivativeness' in the service of displacing hegemonic heterosexual norms. Understood in this way, the political problem is not to establish the specificity of lesbian sexuality over and against its derivativeness, but to turn the homophobic construction of the bad copy against the framework that privileges heterosexuality as origin, and so 'derive' the former

from the latter. This description requires a reconsideration of imitation, drag, and other forms of sexual crossing that affirm the internal complexity of a lesbian sexuality constituted in part within the very matrix of power that it is compelled both to reiterate and to oppose.

On the Being of Gayness as Necessary Drag

The professionalization of gayness requires a certain performance and production of a "self" which is the *constituted effect* of a discourse that nevertheless claims to "represent" that self as a prior truth. When I spoke at the conference on homosexuality in 1989,[10] I found myself telling my friends beforehand that I was off to Yale to be a lesbian, which of course didn't mean that I wasn't one before, but that somehow then, as I spoke in that context, I *was* one in some more thorough and totalizing way, at least for the time being. So I *am* one, and my qualifications are even fairly unambiguous. Since I was sixteen, being a lesbian is what I've been. So what's the anxiety, the discomfort? Well, it has something to do with that redoubling, the way I can say, I'm going to Yale to be a lesbian; a lesbian is what I've been being for so long. How is it that I can

---

[10] [Butler] Let me take this occasion to apologize to the social worker at that conference who asked a question about how to deal with those clients with AIDS who turned to Bernie Segal and others for the purposes of psychic healing. At the time, I understood this questioner to be suggesting that such clients were full of self-hatred because they were trying to find the causes of AIDS in their own selves. The questioner and I appear to agree that any effort to locate the responsibility for AIDS in those who suffer from it is politically and ethically wrong. I thought the questioner, however, was prepared to tell his clients that they were self-hating, and I reacted strongly (too strongly) to the paternalistic prospect that this person was going to pass judgment on someone who was clearly not only suffering, but already passing judgment on him or herself. To call another person self-hating is itself an act of power that calls for some kind of scrutiny, and I think in response to someone who is already dealing with AIDS, that is perhaps the last thing one needs to hear. I also happened to have a friend who sought out advice from Bernie Segal, not with the belief that there is an exclusive or even primary psychic cause or solution for AIDS, but that there might be a psychic contribution to be made to surviving with AIDS. Unfortunately, I reacted quickly to this questioner, and with some anger. And I regret now that I didn't have my wits about me to discuss the distinctions with him that I have just laid out.

Curiously, this incident was invoked at a CLAGS (Center for Lesbian and Gay Studies) meeting at CUNY sometime in December of 1989 and, according to those who told me about it, my angry denunciation of the social worker was taken to be symptomatic of the political insensitivity of a "theorist" in dealing with someone who is actively engaged in AIDS work. That attribution implies that I do not do AIDS work, that I am not politically engaged, and that the social worker in question does not read theory. Needless to say, I was reacting angrily on behalf of an absent friend with AIDS who sought out Bernie Segal and company. So as I offer this apology to the social worker, I wait expectantly that the CLAGS member who misunderstood me will offer me one in turn. [Cf. Bernie S. Siegel, *Love, Medicine & Miracles* (1986).]

both "be" one, and yet endeavor to be one at the same time? When and where does my being a lesbian come into play, when and where does this playing a lesbian constitute something like what I am? To say that I "play" at being one is not to say that I am not one "really"; rather, how and where I play at being one is the way in which that "being" gets established, instituted, circulated, and confirmed. This is not a performance from which I can take radical distance, for this is deep-seated play, psychically entrenched play, *and this "I" does not play its lesbianism as a role.* Rather, it is through the repeated play of this sexuality that the "I" is insistently reconstituted as a lesbian "I"; paradoxically, it is precisely the *repetition* of that play that establishes as well the *instability* of the very category that it constitutes. For if the "I" is a site of repetition, that is, if the "I" only achieves the semblance of identity through a certain repetition of itself, then the I is always displaced by the very repetition that sustains it. In other words, does or can the "I" ever repeat itself, cite itself, faithfully, or is there always a displacement from its former moment that establishes the permanently non-self-identical status of that "I" or its "being lesbian"? What "performs" does not exhaust the "I"; it does not lay out in visible terms the comprehensive content of that "I," for if the performance is "repeated," there is always the question of what differentiates from each other the moments of identity that are repeated. And if the "I" is the effect of a certain repetition, one which produces the semblance of a continuity or coherence, then there is no "I" that precedes the gender that it is said to perform; the repetition, and the failure to repeat, produce a string of performances that constitute and contest the coherence of that "I."

But *politically,* we might argue, isn't it quite crucial to insist on lesbian and gay identities precisely because they are being threatened with erasure and obliteration from homophobic quarters? Isn't the above theory *complicitous* with those political forces that would obliterate the possibility of gay and lesbian identity? Isn't it "no accident" that such theoretical contestations of identity emerge within a political climate that is performing a set of similar obliterations of homosexual identities through legal and political means?

The question I want to raise in return is this: ought such threats of obliteration dictate the terms of the political resistance to them, and if they do, do such homophobic efforts to that extent win the battle from the start? There is no question that gays and lesbians are threatened by the violence of public erasure, but the decision to counter that violence must be careful not to reinstall another in its place. Which version of lesbian or gay ought to be rendered visible, and which in-

ternal exclusions will that rendering visible institute? Can the visibility of identity *suffice* as a political strategy, or can it only be the starting point for a strategic intervention which calls for a transformation of policy? Is it not a sign of despair over public politics when identity becomes its own policy, bringing with it those who would 'police' it from various sides? And this is not a call to return to silence or invisibility, but, rather, to make use of a category that can be called into question, made to account for what it excludes. That any consolidation of identity requires some set of differentiations and exclusions seems clear. But which ones ought to be valorized? That the identity-sign I use now has its purposes seems right, but there is no way to predict or control the political uses to which that sign will be put in the future. And perhaps this is a kind of openness, regardless of its risks, that ought to be safeguarded for political reasons. If the rendering visible of lesbian/gay identity now presupposes a set of exclusions, then perhaps part of what is necessarily excluded is *the future uses of the sign.* There is a political necessity to use some sign now, and we do, but how to use it in such a way that its futural significations are not *foreclosed?* How to use the sign and avow its temporal contingency at once?

In avowing the sign's strategic provisionality (rather than its strategic essentialism), that identity can become a site of contest and revision, indeed, take on a future set of significations that those of us who use it now may not be able to foresee. It is in the safeguarding of the future of the political signifiers—preserving the signifier as a site of rearticulation—that Laclau and Mouffe discern its democratic promise.

Within contemporary U.S. politics, there are a vast number of ways in which lesbianism in particular is understood as precisely that which cannot or dare not *be.* In a sense, Jesse Helms's attack on the NEA for sanctioning representations of "homoeroticism" focuses various homophobic fantasies of what gay men are and do on the work of Robert Mapplethorpe.[11] In a sense, for Helms, gay men exist as objects of prohibition; they are, in his twisted fantasy, sadomasochistic exploiters of children, the paradigmatic exemplars of "obscenity"; in a sense, the lesbian is not even produced within this discourse as a prohibited object. Here it becomes important to recognize that oppression works not merely through acts of overt prohibition, but covertly, through the constitution of viable subjects and through the corollary constitution of a domain of unviable (un)-

---

[11] [Butler] See my "The Force of Fantasy: Feminism, Mapplethorpe, and Discursive Excess," *differences* 2, no. 2 (Summer 1990). Since the writing of this essay, lesbian artists and representations have also come under attack.

subjects—*abjects,* we might call them—who are neither named nor prohibited within the economy of the law. Here oppression works through the production of a domain of unthinkability and unnameability. Lesbianism is not explicitly prohibited in part because it has not even made its way into the thinkable, the imaginable, that grid of cultural intelligibility that regulates the real and the nameable. How, then, to "be" a lesbian in a political context in which the lesbian does not exist? That is, in a political discourse that wages its violence against lesbianism in part by excluding lesbianism from discourse itself? To be prohibited explicitly is to occupy a discursive site from which something like a reverse-discourse can be articulated; to be implicitly proscribed is not even to qualify as an object of prohibition.[12] And though homosexualities of all kinds in this present climate are being erased, reduced, and (then) reconstituted as sites of radical homophobic fantasy, it is important to retrace the different routes by which the unthinkability of homosexuality is being constituted time and again.

It is one thing to be erased from discourse, and yet another to be present within discourse as an abiding falsehood. Hence, there is a political imperative to render lesbianism visible, but how is that to be done outside or through existing regulatory regimes? Can the exclusion from ontology itself become a rallying point for resistance?

Here is something like a confession which is meant merely to thematize the impossibility of confession: As a young person, I suffered for a long time, and I suspect many people have, from being told, explicitly or implicitly, that what I "am" is a copy, an imitation, a derivative example, a shadow of the real. Compulsory heterosexuality sets itself up as the original, the true, the authentic; the norm that determines the real implies that "being" lesbian is always a kind of miming, a vain effort to participate in the phantasmatic plenitude of naturalized heterosexuality which will always and only fail.[13] And yet, I remember quite distinctly when I first read in Esther Newton's *Mother Camp:*

Female Impersonators in America[14] that drag is not an imitation or a copy of some prior and true gender; according to Newton, drag enacts the very structure of impersonation by which *any gender* is assumed. Drag is not the putting on of a gender that belongs properly to some other group, i.e. an act of *expropriation* or *appropriation* that assumes that gender is the rightful property of sex, that "masculine" belongs to "male" and "feminine" belongs to "female." There is no "proper" gender, a gender proper to one sex rather than another, which is in some sense that sex's cultural property. Where that notion of the "proper" operates, it is always and only *improperly* installed as the effect of a compulsory system. Drag constitutes the mundane way in which genders are appropriated, theatricalized, worn, and done; it implies that all gendering is a kind of impersonation and approximation. If this is true, it seems, there is no original or primary gender that drag imitates, but *gender is a kind of imitation for which there is no original;* in fact, it is a kind of imitation that produces the very notion of the original as an *effect* and consequence of the imitation itself. In other words, the naturalistic effects of heterosexualized genders are produced through imitative strategies; what they imitate is a phantasmatic ideal of heterosexual identity, one that is produced by the imitation as its effect. In this sense, the "reality" of heterosexual identities is performatively constituted through an imitation that sets itself up as the origin and the ground of all imitations. In other words, heterosexuality is always in the process of imitating and approximating its own phantasmatic idealization of itself—*and failing.* Precisely because it is bound to fail, and yet endeavors to succeed, the project of heterosexual identity is propelled into an endless

---

[12] [Butler] It is this particular ruse of erasure which Foucault for the most part fails to take account of in his analysis of power. He almost always presumes that power takes place through discourse as its instrument, and that oppression is linked with subjection and subjectivication that is, that it is installed as the formative principle of the identity of subjects.

[13] [Butler] Although miming suggests that there is a prior model which is being copied, it can have the effect of exposing that prior model as purely phantasmatic. In Jacques Derrida's "The Double Session" in *Dissemination,* tr. Barbara Johnson (Chicago: University of Chicago Press, 1981), he considers the textual effect of the mime in Mallarmé's "Mimique." There Derrida argues that the mime does not imitate or copy some prior phenomenon, idea, or figure, but constitutes—some might say *performatively*—the phantasm of the original in and through the mime:

He represents nothing, imitates nothing, does not have to conform to any prior referent with the aim of achieving adequation or verisimilitude. One can here foresee an objection: since the mime imitates nothing, reproduces nothing, opens up in its origin the very thing he is tracing out, presenting, or producing, he must be the very movement of truth. Not, of course, truth in the form of adequation between the representation and the present of the thing itself, or between the imitator and the imitated, but truth as the present unveiling of the present. . . . But this is not the case. . . . We are faced then with mimicry imitating nothing: faced, so to speak, with a double that couples no simple, a double that nothing anticipates, nothing at least that is not itself already double. There is no simple reference. . . . This speculum reflects no reality: it produces mere "reality-effects". . . . In this speculum with no reality, in this mirror of a mirror, a difference or dyad does exist, since there are mimes and phantoms. But it is a difference without reference, or rather reference without a referent, without any first or last unit, a ghost that is the phantom of no flesh . . . (206)

[14] [Butler] Esther Newton, *Mother Camp: Female Impersonators in America* (Chicago: University of Chicago Press, 1972).

repetition of itself. Indeed, in its efforts to naturalize itself as the original, heterosexuality must be understood as a compulsive and compulsory repetition that can only produce the *effect* of its own originality; in other words, compulsory heterosexual identities, those ontologically consolidated phantasms of "man" and "woman," are theatrically produced effects that posture as grounds, origins, the normative measure of the real.[15]

Reconsider then the homophobic charge that queens and butches and femmes are imitations of the heterosexual real. Here "imitation" carries the meaning of "derivative" or "secondary," a copy of an origin which is itself the ground of all copies, but which is itself a copy of nothing. Logically, this notion of an "origin" is suspect, for how can something operate as an origin if there are no secondary consequences which retrospectively confirm the originality of that origin? The origin requires its derivations in order to affirm itself as an origin, for origins only make sense to the extent that they are differentiated from that which they produce as derivatives. Hence, if it were not for the notion of the homosexual *as* copy, there would be no construct of heterosexuality *as* origin. Heterosexuality here presupposes homosexuality. And if the homosexual *as* copy *precedes* the heterosexual as *origin,* then it seems only fair to concede that the copy comes before the origin, and that homosexuality is thus the origin, and heterosexuality the copy.

But simple inversions are not really possible. For it is only *as* a copy that homosexuality can be argued to *precede* heterosexuality as the origin. In other words, the entire framework of copy and origin proves radically unstable as each position inverts into the other and confounds the possibility of any stable way to locate the temporal or logical priority of either term.

But let us then consider this problematic inversion from a psychic/political perspective. If the structure of gender imitation is such that the imitat*ed* is to some degree produced—or, rather, *re*produced—by imitation (see again Derrida's[16] inversion and displacement of mimesis in "The Double Session"), then to claim that gay and lesbian identities are implicated in heterosexual norms or in hegemonic culture generally is not to *derive* gayness from straightness. On the contrary, *imitation* does not copy that which is prior, but produces and *inverts* the very terms of priority and derivativeness. Hence, if gay identities are implicated in heterosexuality, that is not the same as claiming that they are determined or derived from heterosexuality, and it is not the same as claiming that that heterosexuality is the only cultural network in which they are implicated. These are, quite literally, *inverted* imitations, ones which invert the order of imitated and imitation, and which, in the process, expose the fundamental dependency of "the origin" on that which it claims to produce as its secondary effect.

What follows if we concede from the start that gay identities as derivative inversions are in part defined in terms of the very heterosexual identities from which they are differentiated? If heterosexuality is an impossible imitation of itself, an imitation that performatively constitutes itself as the original, then the imitative parody of "heterosexuality"—when and where it exists in gay cultures—is always and only an imitation of an imitation, a copy of a copy, for which there is no original. Put in yet a different way, the parodic or imitative effect of gay identities works neither to copy nor to emulate heterosexuality, but rather, to expose heterosexuality as an incessant and *panicked* imitation of its own naturalized idealization. That heterosexuality is always in the act of elaborating itself is evidence that it is perpetually at risk, that is, that it "knows" its own possibility of becoming undone: hence, its compulsion to repeat which is at once a foreclosure of that which threatens its coherence. That it can never eradicate that risk attests to its profound dependency upon the homosexuality that it seeks fully to eradicate and never can or that it seeks to make second, but which is always already there as a prior possibility.[17] Although this failure of naturalized heterosexuality might constitute a source of pathos for heterosexuality itself—what its theorists often refer to as its constitutive malaise—it can become an occasion for a subversive and proliferating parody of gender norms in which the very claim to originality and to the real is shown to be the effect of a certain kind of naturalized gender mime.

It is important to recognize the ways in which heterosexual norms reappear within gay identities, to affirm that

---

[15] [Butler] In a sense, one might offer a redescription of the above in Lacanian terms. The sexual "positions" of heterosexually differentiated "man" and "woman" are part of the *Symbolic,* that is, an ideal embodiment of the Law of sexual difference which constitutes the object of imaginary pursuits, but which is always thwarted by the "real." These symbolic positions for Lacan are by definition impossible to occupy even as they are impossible to resist as the structuring telos of desire. I accept the former point, and reject the latter one. The imputation of universal necessity to such positions simply encodes compulsory heterosexuality at the level of the Symbolic, and the "failure" to achieve it is implicitly lamented as a source of heterosexual pathos.

[16] Derrida (above, page 1203).

[17] [Butler] Of course, it is Eve Kosofsky Sedgwick's *Epistemology of the Closet* (Berkeley: University of California Press, 1990) which traces the subleties of this kind of panic in Western heterosexual epistemes. [See above, page 1470.]

gay and lesbian identities are not only structured in part by dominant heterosexual frames, but that they are *not* for that reason *determined* by them. They are running commentaries on those naturalized positions as well, parodic replays and resignifications of precisely those heterosexual structures that would consign gay life to discursive domains of unreality and unthinkability. But to be constituted or structured in part by the very heterosexual norms by which gay people are oppressed is not, I repeat, to be claimed or determined by those structures. And it is not necessary to think of such heterosexual constructs as the pernicious intrusion of "the straight mind," one that must be rooted out in its entirety. In a way, the presence of heterosexual constructs and positionalities in whatever form in gay and lesbian identities presupposes that there is a gay and lesbian repetition of straightness, a recapitulation of straightness—which is itself a repetition and recapitulation of its own ideality—within its own terms, a site in which all sorts of resignifying and parodic repetitions become possible. The parodic replication and resignification of heterosexual constructs within nonheterosexual frames brings into relief the utterly constructed status of the so-called original, but it shows that heterosexuality only constitutes itself as the original through a convincing act of repetition. The more that "act" is expropriated, the more the heterosexual claim to originality is exposed as illusory.

Although I have concentrated in the above on the reality-effects of gender practices, performances, repetitions, and mimes, I do not mean to suggest that drag is a "role" that can be taken on or taken off at will. There is no volitional subject behind the mime who decides, as it were, which gender it will be today. On the contrary, the very possibility of becoming a viable subject requires that a certain gender mime be already underway. The "being" of the subject is no more self-identical than the "being" of any gender; in fact, coherent gender, achieved through an apparent repetition of the same, produces as its *effect* the illusion of a prior and volitional subject. In this sense, gender is not a performance that a prior subject elects to do, but gender is *performative* in the sense that it constitutes as an effect the very subject it appears to express. It is a *compulsory* performance in the sense that acting out of line with heterosexual norms brings with it ostracism, punishment, and violence, not to mention the transgressive pleasures produced by those very prohibitions.

To claim that there is no performer prior to the performed, that the performance is performative, that the performance constitutes the appearance of a "subject" as its effect is difficult to accept. This difficulty is the result of a predisposition to think of sexuality and gender as "expressing" in some indirect or direct way a psychic reality that precedes it. The denial of the *priority* of the subject, however, is not the denial of the subject; in fact, the refusal to conflate the subject with the psyche marks the psychic as that which exceeds the domain of the conscious subject. This psychic excess is precisely what is being systematically denied by the notion of a volitional "subject" who elects at will which gender and/or sexuality to be at any given time and place. It is this excess which erupts within the intervals of those repeated gestures and acts that construct the apparent uniformity of heterosexual positionalities, indeed which compels the repetition itself, and which guarantees its perpetual failure. In this sense, it is this excess which, within the heterosexual economy, implicitly includes homosexuality, that perpetual threat of a disruption which is quelled through a reenforced repetition of the same. And yet, if repetition is the way in which power works to construct the illusion of a seamless heterosexual identity, if heterosexuality is compelled to *repeat itself* in order to establish the illusion of its own uniformity and identity, then this is an identity permanently at risk, for what if it fails to repeat, or if the very exercise of repetition is redeployed for a very different performative purpose? If there is, as it were, always a compulsion to repeat, repetition never fully accomplishes identity. That there is a need for a repetition at all is a sign that identity is not self-identical. It requires to be instituted again and again, which is to say that it runs the risk of becoming *de*-instituted at every interval.

So what is this psychic excess, and what will constitute a subversive or *de*-instituting repetition? First, it is necessary to consider that sexuality always exceeds any given performance, presentation, or narrative which is why it is not possible to derive or read off a sexuality from any given gender presentation. And sexuality may be said to exceed any definitive narrativization. Sexuality is never fully "expressed" in a performance or practice; there will be passive and butchy femmes, femmy and aggressive butches, and both of those, and more, will turn out to describe more or less anatomically stable "males" and "females." There are no direct expressive or causal lines between sex, gender, gender presentation, sexual practice, fantasy and sexuality. None of those terms captures or determines the rest. Part of what constitutes sexuality is precisely that which does not appear and that which, to some degree, can never appear. This is perhaps the most fundamental reason why sexuality is to some degree always closeted, especially to the one who would express it through acts of self-disclosure. That which is excluded for a given gender presentation to "succeed" may be precisely what is played out sexually, that is, an "inverted" relation, as it were, between gender and gender presentation, and gender presentation and sexuality. On the other hand, both gender presentation and sexual practices may corollate such that it appears that the former "expresses" the latter, and yet both are jointly constituted by the very sexual possibilities that they exclude.

This logic of inversion gets played out interestingly in versions of lesbian butch and femme gender stylization. For a butch can present herself as capable, forceful, and all-providing, and a stone butch may well seek to constitute her lover as the exclusive site of erotic attention and pleasure. And yet, this "providing" butch who seems *at first* to replicate a certain husband-like role, can find herself caught in a logic of inversion whereby that "providingness" turns to a self-sacrifice, which implicates her in the most ancient trap of feminine self-abnegation. She may well find herself in a situation of radical need, which is precisely what she sought to locate, find, and fulfill in her femme lover. In effect, the butch inverts into the femme or remains caught up in the specter of that inversion, or takes pleasure in it. On the other hand, the femme who, as Amber Hollibaugh has argued, "orchestrates" sexual exchange,[18] may well eroticize a certain dependency only to learn that the very power to orchestrate that dependency exposes her own incontrovertible power, at which point she inverts into a butch or becomes caught up in the specter of that inversion, or perhaps delights in it.

Psychic Mimesis

What stylizes or forms an erotic style and/or a gender presentation—and that which makes such categories inherently unstable—is a set of *psychic identifications* that are not simple to describe. Some psychoanalytic theories tend to construe identification and desire as two mutually exclusive relations to love objects that have been lost through prohibition and/or separation. Any intense emotional attachment thus divides into either wanting to have someone or wanting to be that someone, but never both at once. It is important to consider that identification and desire can coexist, and that their formulation in terms of mutually exclusive oppositions serves a heterosexual matrix. But I would like to focus attention on yet a different construal of that scenario, namely, that "wanting to be" and "wanting

to have" can operate to differentiate mutually exclusive positionalities internal to lesbian erotic exchange. Consider that identifications are always made in response to loss of some kind, and that they involve a certain *mimetic practice* that seeks to incorporate the lost love within the very "identity" of the one who remains. This was Freud's thesis in "Mourning and Melancholia" in 1917 and continues to inform contemporary psychoanalytic discussions of identification.[19]

For psychoanalytic theorists Mikkel Borch-Jacobsen and Ruth Leys, however, identification and, in particular, identificatory mimetism, *precedes* "identity" and constitutes identity as that which is fundamentally "other to itself." The notion of this Other *in* the self, as it were, implies that the self/Other distinction is *not* primarily external (a powerful critique of ego psychology follows from this); the self is from the start radically implicated in the "Other." This theory of primary mimetism differs from Freud's account of melancholic incorporation. In Freud's view, which I continue to find useful, incorporation—a kind of psychic miming—is a response to, and refusal of, *loss*. Gender as the site of such psychic mimes is thus constituted by the variously gendered Others who have been loved and lost, where the loss is suspended through a melancholic and imaginary incorporation (and preservation) of those Others into the psyche. Over and against this account of psychic mimesis by way of incorporation and melancholy, the theory of primary mimetism argues an even stronger position in favor of the non-self-identity of the psychic subject. Mimetism is not motivated by a drama of loss and wishful recovery, but appears to precede and constitute desire (and motivation) itself; in this sense, mimetism would be prior to the possibility of loss and the disappointments of love.

Whether loss or mimetism is primary (perhaps an undecidable problem), the psychic subject is nevertheless constituted internally by differentially gendered Others and is, therefore, never, as a gender, self-identical.

In my view, the self only becomes a self on the condition that it has suffered a separation (grammar fails us here, for the "it" only becomes differentiated through that separation), a loss which is suspended and provisionally resolved through a melancholic incorporation of some "Other." That "Other" installed in the self thus establishes the permanent incapacity of that "self" to achieve self-identity; it is as it were always already disrupted by that

---

18[Butler] Amber Hollibaugh and Cherríe Moraga, "What We're Rollin Around in Bed With: Sexual Silences in Feminism," in *Powers of Desire: The Politics of Sexuality,* ed. Ann Snitow, Christine Stansell, and Sharon Thompson (New York: Monthly Review Press, 1983), 394–405.

19[Butler] Mikkel Borch-Jacobsen, *The Freudian Subject* (Stanford: Stanford University Press, 1988); for citations of Ruth Leys's work, see the following two footnotes.

Other; the disruption of the Other at the heart of the self is the very condition of that self's possibility.[20]

Such a consideration of psychic identification would vitiate the possibility of any stable set of typologies that explain or describe something like gay or lesbian identities. And any effort to supply one—as evidenced in Kaja Silverman's recent inquiries into male homosexuality—suffer from simplification, and conform, with alarming ease, to the regulatory requirements of diagnostic epistemic regimes. If incorporation in Freud's sense in 1914 is an effort to *preserve* a lost and loved object and to refuse or postpone the recognition of loss and, hence, of grief, then to become *like* one's mother or father or sibling or other early "lovers" may be an act of love and/or a hateful effort to replace or displace. How would we "typologize" the ambivalence at the heart of mimetic incorporations such as these?[21]

How does this consideration of psychic identification return us to the question, what constitutes a subversive repetition? How are troublesome identifications apparent in cultural practices? Well, consider the way in which heterosexuality naturalizes itself through setting up certain illusions of continuity between sex, gender, and desire. When Aretha Franklin sings, "you make me feel like a natural woman," she seems at first to suggest that some natural potential of her biological sex is actualized by her participation in the cultural position of "woman" as object of heterosexual recognition. Something in her "sex" is thus expressed by her "gender" which is then fully known and consecrated within the heterosexual scene. There is no breakage, no discontinuity between "sex" as biological facticity and essence, or between gender and sexuality. Although Aretha appears to be all too glad to have her naturalness confirmed, she also seems fully and paradoxically mindful that that confirmation is never guaranteed, that the effect of naturalness is only achieved as a consequence of that moment of heterosexual recognition. After all, Aretha sings, you make me feel *like* a natural woman, suggesting that this is a kind of metaphorical substitution, an act of imposture, a kind of sublime and momentary participation in an ontological illusion produced by the mundane operation of heterosexual drag.

But what if Aretha were singing to me? Or what if she were singing to a drag queen whose performance somehow confirmed her own?

How do we take account of these kinds of identifications? It's not that there is some kind of *sex* that exists in hazy biological form that is somehow *expressed* in the gait, the posture, the gesture; and that some sexuality then expresses both that apparent gender or that more or less magical sex. If gender is drag, and if it is an imitation that regularly produces the ideal it attempts to approximate, then gender is a performance that *produces* the illusion of an inner sex or essence or psychic gender core; it *produces* on the skin, through the gesture, the move, the gait (that array of corporeal theatrics understood as gender presentation), the illusion of an inner depth. In effect, one way that genders gets naturalized is through being constructed as an inner psychic or physical *necessity*. And yet, it is always a surface sign, a signification on and with the public body that produces this illusion of an inner depth, necessity or essence that is somehow magically, causally expressed.

To dispute the psyche as *inner depth,* however, is not to refuse the psyche altogether. On the contrary, the psyche calls to be rethought precisely as a compulsive repetition, as that which conditions and disables the repetitive performance of identity. If every performance repeats itself to institute the effect of identity, then every repetition requires an interval between the acts, as it were, in which risk and excess threaten to disrupt the identity being constituted. The unconscious is this excess that enables and contests every performance, and which never fully appears within the performance itself. The psyche is not "in" the body, but in the very signifying process through which that body comes to appear; it is the lapse in repetition as well as its compulsion, precisely what the performance seeks to deny, and that which compels it from the start.

To locate the psyche within this signifying chain as the instability of all iterability is not the same as claiming that it is inner core that is awaiting its full and liberatory expression. On the contrary, the psyche is the permanent failure of expression, a failure that has its values, for it impels repetition and so reinstates the possibility of disruption. What then does it mean to pursue disruptive repetition within compulsory heterosexuality?

---

[20] [Butler] For a very fine analysis of primary mimetism with direct implications for gender formation, see Ruth Leys, "The Real Miss Beauchamp: The History and Sexual Politics of the Multiple Personality Concept," in *Feminists Theorize the Political,* eds. Judith Butler and Joan W. Scott (New York and London: Routledge, forthcoming 1991). For Leys, a primary mimetism or suggestibility requires that the "self" from the start is constituted by its incorporations; the effort to differentiate oneself from that by which one is constituted is, of course, impossible, but it does entail a certain "incorporative violence," to use her term. The violence of identification is in this way in the service of an effort at differentiation, to take the place of the Other who is, as it were, installed at the foundation of the self. That this replacement, which seeks to be a displacement, fails, and must repeat itself endlessly, becomes the trajectory of one's psychic career.

[21] [Butler] Here again, I think it is the work of Ruth Leys which will clarify some of the complex questions of gender constitution that emerge from a close psychoanalytic consideration of imitation and identification. Her forthcoming book manuscript will doubtless galvanize this field: *The Subject of Imitation.*

Although compulsory heterosexuality often presumes that there is first a sex that is expressed through a gender and then through a sexuality, it may now be necessary fully to invert and displace that operation of thought. If a regime of sexuality mandates a compulsory performance of sex, then it may be only through that performance that the binary system of gender and the binary system of sex come to have intelligibility at all. It may be that the very categories of sex, of sexual identity, of gender are produced or maintained in the *effects* of this compulsory performance, effects which are disingenuously renamed as causes, origins, disingenuously lined up within a causal or expressive sequence that the heterosexual norm produces to legitimate itself as the origin of all sex. How then to expose the causal lines as retrospectively and performatively produced fabrications, and to engage gender itself as an inevitable fabrication, to fabricate gender in terms which reveal every claim to the origin, the inner, the true, and the real as nothing other than the effects of *drag,* whose subversive possibilities ought to be played and replayed to make the "sex" of gender into a site of insistent political play? Perhaps this will be a matter of working sexuality *against* identity, even against gender, and of letting that which cannot fully appear in any performance persist in its disruptive promise.

John Guillory

b. 1952

John Guillory's *Cultural Capital,* making excellent use of the historical studies of cultural institutions by Pierre Bourdieu (above, page 1403) is a highly significant and much discussed commentary not just on the long-running controversy in literature departments concerning the expansion of the literary canon in North America and elsewhere, but upon the presently troubled and tenuous status of literary institutions in culture. Guillory's analysis shows that the selection of preferred or "canonical" texts reflects the historicity of curricular and cultural decisions that are rarely fully evident, while a seeming assault on the existing literary canon exposes the vulnerability of literary education generally. In a widely disseminated essay, "Preprofessionalism: What Graduate Students Want" (in *Profession 1996*), Guillory explores this problem in very cogent reflections on the role of literary education in the current socioeconomic climate, where apparently decreasing chances for full academic employment distort the trajectory of professional careers, while encouraging an increasing politicization of a professional discourse in danger of losing contact with any audience other than other professionals—or preprofessionals.

The central problem, however, appears to be, as the selection below argues, that literary study, in endeavoring to expand the canon, is now confronting a serious perplexity about the appropriate object of literary study generally. In this selection, which begins with a long discussion of the theories and pedagogy of the late Paul de Man, calls urgent attention to the need to reconsider "the task of literary criticism," with attention to conceptualizing a "new disciplinary domain."

John Guillory is the author of *Poetic Authority: Spenser, Milton, and Literary History* (1983), and *Cultural Capital: The Problem of Literary Canon Formation* (1993), from which the selection reprinted here is drawn. He was also a coeditor, with Judith Butler and Kendall Thomas, of *What's Left of Theory: New Work on the Politics of Literary Theory* (2000).

from

Literature after Theory

... I have already alluded in Chapter 1 to the significance of the relative autonomy of pedagogic practice in the context of appropriating Bourdieu and Passeron's contention that "by ignoring all demands other than that of its own reproduction, the school most effectively contributes to the reproduction of the social order."[1] The question before us now is somewhat more complex. Bourdieu and Passeron insist in *Reproduction* on the theoretical distinctiveness of the "autonomy" specific to the educational system, and they are thus resistant to any reduction of pedagogic action to a species of the bureaucratic. They object in particular to the argument of Michel Crozier in *The Bureaucratic Phenomenon* (1964) that "we should find, in the French educational

---

Selections from "Literature after Theory" are reprinted from *Cultural Capital: The Problem of Literary Canon Formation* (Chicago: University of Chicago Press, 1993).

[1] Pierre Bourdieu (above, page 1403) and Jean-Claude Passeron, *Reproduction in Education, Society and Culture* (London: Sage, 1990).

system, the main characteristic patterns of the bureaucratic system of organization," a thesis they regard as construing the formal features of the educational institution merely as reflections of the dominant mode of social organization:

> Thus, for example, Crozier is only able to grasp characteristic features of the school institution, such as the ritualization of pedagogic action or the distance between master and pupil, insofar as he recognizes in them manifestations of the logic of bureaucracy, i.e. fails to recognize what is specifically scholastic about them, in that it expresses tendencies or requirements proper to all institutionalized educational systems, even when scarcely or not at all bureaucratized: the tendency toward "routinization" of pedagogic work, which is expressed in, among other things, the production of intellectual and material instruments devised by and for the School, manuals, corpuses, topics, etc., appears, alongside the first signs of institutionalization, in traditional schools like the rhetoric and philosophy schools of Antiquity or the Koran schools, which exhibit none of the features of bureaucratic organization. (190)

The argument of *Reproduction* is explicitly here, as it is implicitly throughout, a description of the transhistorical structure of the educational institution, and in the terms of this project, the concept of autonomy emerges as the single most significant concept defining the transhistorical identity of the school as an institution. The routinization effect exhibited in the school's formal procedures is thus only accidentally congruent with the historical form of bureaucracy, which is a mode of social relation specifically *modern:*

> when Crozier sees in the institutional guarantees of university "independence" no more than a form of the guarantees statutorily written into the bureaucratic definition of official posts, he lumps together two facts as irreducible to one another as the systems of relations to which they belong, on the one hand the autonomy which teachers have claimed and obtained as civil servants subject to the common legislation of a Government department, and on the other hand, the pedagogic autonomy inherited from the medieval corporation. (190–91)

The distinction drawn by Bourdieu and Passeron between bureaucratic and pedagogic autonomy is indeed the crucial

one, but that does not mean that in practice, in the pedagogic imaginary, the two forms of autonomy are not actually *confused.* It is not a question of "lumping together" the two autonomies, when they are "irreducible to one another," much less of reducing the pedagogic to the bureaucratic, but of acknowledging the overdetermination of the concept of "autonomy" in the contemporary school by the complex interaction of the two relative autonomies, the pedagogic and the bureaucratic. In the situation of the bureaucratized educational institution, pedagogic autonomy must defend itself against the heteronomous pressure of the *educational institution itself,* insofar as it bureaucratically administers pedagogy, and not only against the pressures that seek to constrain or determine pedagogy from outside the school. The defense of pedagogic autonomy has taken the form of an aggressive defense of "professionalism," whose social function we can now identify as an attempt to compensate for the bureaucratic constraints upon pedagogic autonomy. In these circumstances, the career of the college professor is increasingly structured as a mimesis of the bureaucratic career (even sometimes, as a movement "up" from teaching to administration). It would not otherwise be possible to explain the subordination of even the most rarefied intellectual inquiry to norms of "productivity" which usually determine the trajectory of the bureaucratic career.[2]

The larger question of the relation between the professional and the bureaucratic has been addressed recently in an excellent study by Magali Scarfatti Larson, *The Rise of Professionalism.*[3] Larson points out that while the profession has always been represented as "the antithesis of bureaucracy," all professions are now "bureaucratized to a greater or lesser extent" (xvii), and further, "in a bureaucratized world, professions can no longer be interpreted as inherently antibureaucratic" (199). While a greater measure of "work autonomy" can still be said to define the professional mode of work organization, a condition which characterizes such institutions as "the medical clinic, the graduate school, the large legal or accounting firm, large architectural offices, and research institutes," the existence of common standards of "technical competence" governing all the "professional bureaucracies" suggests that bureaucracy and profession can be regarded as "two subtypes of a larger category—that of rational administration" (191). This proposition may seem at first

---

[2] [Guillory] David Harvey makes this point in his essay "Flexibility: Threat or Opportunity?" *Socialist Review* 12 (1991): "University-based intellectuals, for example, now find themselves faced with far shorter turnover times in the realm of ideas and far stronger pressures to increase output than was the case in the 1960s" (77).

[3] [Guillory] Magali Scarfatti Larson, *The Rise of Professionalism: A Sociological Analysis* (Berkeley: University of California Press, 1977).

glance only to reassert a Weberian thesis, but its implications are profound. Larson argues finally that "the alleged conflict between bureaucracy and profession as modes of work organization is not so much a conflict between two structures as it is a contrast between the structure of bureaucratic organizations and an ideology promoted by some of their members" (219). In the case of the university teacher, the claim to professional autonomy can thus be asserted *against the school itself,* despite the fact that accomplishments in the professional field are compensated by the usual rewards only a bureaucratically organized institution can offer. In reality, then, the "personal talent and charisma" of the professor, though they are established in the seminar or in the professional field, are never entirely distinguishable from the status hierarchy of the institution:

> The more incorporated into heteronomous organizations a profession is, the more its members' prestige is determined by the organization: thus, the pattern of academic mobility—by "horizontal upward displacement" from campus to more prestigious campus—appears *prima facie* to replicate the pattern of the careers of executives in the private or public sector, or across both.
>
> However, the individualization of organizational prestige is different in consulting or academic professions from what it is in technobureaucratic careers. The fact that achievements in the former are personalized seems to allow for an ideological blending of personal and organizational *prestige.* (205)

Such "ideological blending" is paradoxical in that bureaucratic organizations like the modern university tend to encourage the very professionalist ideology that denies the subordination of professional activity to merely bureaucratic ends. Professionalism is thus lodged within bureaucracy as the affirmation of the principle antithetical to bureaucracy itself, the principle Weber[4] called "charisma" and which Larson recognizes as a form of "individualism":

> Typically, professions maintain indeterminate and untestable cognitive areas in order to assert, collectively, the uniqueness of *individual* capacities. Collectively they solicit trust in *individual* professionals and *individual* freedom from external controls. . . .

> This individualism is, I believe, one of the powerful factors that make professions continue to appear, in the eyes of the public and of most social scientists, as the "anti-bureaucracy." (206)

At the least Larson's argument implies that discussions of the academic "profession" which do not acknowledge its incorporation into a heteronomous bureaucracy simply disseminate an *ideology* of professionalism and not an analysis of its real institutional conditions. It is just such an ideology which has subtended the claims for the subversiveness of literary theory, and rhetorical reading in particular, by naming the "institution" as the object of subversive teaching by charismatic master theorists. Such charisma is always a "blending of personal and organizational prestige." Yet within the ideology of professionalism, the charisma of the master theorist appears to constitute a realm of *absolute* autonomy, and therefore, as we have noted, an "other scene" of politics.

Nothing confirms this point more certainly than the mutation of the master theorists in the 1980s into "superstars," into the free agents of pure charisma. It is not difficult to see that the deployment of this category was driven by the interests of competitive university administrations, for whom the content of theory, subversive or otherwise, was largely irrelevant. What mattered was that the charisma of the master theorists could be converted into bureaucratic prestige. The social horizon circumscribing and conditioning the emergence of the academic superstar is thus nothing less than the total socioeconomic order, within which the pervasive mass-cultural form of the celebrity system is directly (but at the same time invisibly) correlated to the disappearance of "work autonomy" at every level and in every sphere of the work force. For the professoriate, it is only in the superstar as a form of *celebrity* that autonomy or free agency truly resides, an autonomy ratified by "horizontal upward mobility." Such mobility signifies an imaginary transcendence of institutional heteronomy by means of *professionalism itself,* by the deliberate cultivation of charismatic authority.[5] But the figure in whom so large an imaginary investment is deposited, so far from representing a real autonomy, is the site of the maximum determination of the university teacher's "professional activity" by external so-

---

[4] Max Weber (1864–1920), German sociologist.

[5] [Guillory] A similar point has been argued by Alvin Gouldner in *The Future of Intellectuals and the Rise of the New Class:* "Unlike the older bureaucrats, the new intelligentsia have extensive cultural capital which increases their mobility. . . . They need not, moreover, seek status solely within their own organization and from its staff or clients. Rather, they also seek status in professional associations; they wish the good regard of the knowledgeable" (51).

cial forces, namely (as everyone also knows) the forces of
the market. The invisible hand which gives the charismatic
celebrity "mobility" is thus the same hand which makes a
given commodity irresistible in a given time and place, especially when that commodity signifies (as so many commodities do) autonomy itself.

"the task of literary criticism"

The foregoing argument confirms, if it needs confirming,
that the institutional position of the master theorist, as the
person in whom institutional and personal prestige is
"blended," and in whom the concept of "autonomy" is maximally overdetermined, was always a condition for the emergence of theory. In the case of de Man,[6] his institutional affiliation was never merely incidental, it was essential to the
propagation of rhetorical reading as a school, and therefore
also to the construction of his personal "charisma." The same
circumstances explain why the waning of deconstruction
was a consequence not of its successful refutation, but of its
successful dissemination, the transference onto the methodology. Theory itself is burdened with the task of "subverting"
the very institutional conditions that permit it to construct itself as the vehicle of an anti-institutional, charismatic authority. This paradox is only intelligible from the point of view
of a sociological analysis: as the pedagogic transference
moves out of the seminar into the larger institutional field, it
produces the phenomenon of *factions,* the internecine bureaucratic conflict that is misrecognized as "institutional resistance" to deconstruction. Hence deconstructive theory is
vulnerable, as the object of transference transferred, to the
same bureaucratic and market forces the theorist experiences
in his or her career. This point has been underscored in the
wake of the scandal of de Man's wartime collaboration, since
the scandal itself has absurdly but inevitably discredited deconstructive theory, as though the theory and the theorist
were the same.

More consequential than the decline of deconstruction,
however, is the current "crisis" of theory itself,[7] with which
the name "deconstruction" is inseparably entangled. So far
from recognizing here only the supposedly "journalistic"

misapprehensions about a monolithic theory,[8] we must insist again that de Man himself always endorsed deconstruction's claim to be the most exemplary of theories ("always
in theory, the most elastic theoretical and dialectical model
to end all models"), in other words, that theory in which the
name of theory is at stake. The resistance to theory was
never anything other than the resistance to deconstruction.
Are not the consequences of this gamble still with us? Why
else should the fortunes of theory itself rise or fall *after deconstruction?* I do not imagine that any challenge to the authority of a monolithic "theory" (on behalf of, for example,
a neorelativism or neopragmatism) would have the slightest
chance of succeeding if theory itself were not capable of being experienced *as* monolithic, even by its advocates. There
is no answer, then, to the question "What is theory?" because the concept of theory inhabits (like the concept of
rigor), the pedagogic imaginary, where it does indeed mean
one thing, however different that thing may be to different
factions within the profession. If deconstruction no longer
establishes the terms by which certain texts, of whatever
provenance, can be integrated into the corpus of literary theory, that is preeminently because it no longer offers to the
pedagogic imaginary a resolution to the problem of professional autonomy, a resolution which begins to fail in rhetorical reading as soon as the problem itself becomes visible in
de Man's later essays as an uneasy reflection on pedagogy,
on the dilemma of discipleship. To the demonstration of this
point we now turn.

The nature of this problem has been well described by
Bourdieu: "Intellectual labour carried out collectively,
within technically and socially differentiated production
units, can no longer surround itself with the charismatic
aura attaching to traditional independent production."[9] The
increasingly technobureaucratic organization of the
professional field of literary criticism was a condition for
the emergence of theory, which we can understand in

---

[6] Paul de Man (above, page 1317). The text under discussion here is *The Resistance to Theory* (1986), cited as RT.

[7] [Guillory] In addition to *The Future of Literary Theory* and *The Textual
Sublime,* from which I have already cited, see also Joseph Natoli, ed.,
Literary Theory's Future(s) (Urbana: University of Illinois Press, 1989),
and Thomas M. Kavanagh, ed., *The Limits of Theory* (Stanford: Stanford
University Press, 1989). See also Steven Knapp and Walter Benn
Michaels's "Against Theory," *Critical Inquiry* 8 (1982), 723–42, and the
subsequent controversy over this argument.

[8] [Guillory] I emphasize once again that "theory" and "deconstruction" were
virtually synonymous in both the "journalistic" accounts of deconstruction
and the various specifically academic media of dissemination. Journalism
can hardly be held responsible for this confusion, since the journalists only
confirmed the considerable homogenization of theory in the graduate
schools, the solidification of an epistemic rhetoricism which colored the
practice of many different and on the surface conflicting theories. The vil-
lainizing of journalism in the wake of the de Man scandal is only a belated
consequence of this homogenization effect, the inverse mirror image of deconstruction's self-image as the premier theory of its day. The level of
anathema heaped upon the journalistic accounts of the de Man scandal is
convincing testimony to how crucial the celebrity system always was to the
dissemination of theory, how thoroughly theory's dissemination conformed
to the cultural paradigms of the mass media.

[9] [Guillory] Pierre Bourdieu, "The Market of Symbolic Goods," *Poetics* 14
(1985), 33.

retrospect as the reassertion of charismatic authority in the face of that technobureaucratic domination. In the graduate schools of the last quarter-century, a *contradiction* appeared to open up between an enlarged sphere of intellectual auton-omy—a kind of extra-institutional space occupied by the master theorists—and the bureaucratization of professional life. The deconstructive resolution to this contradiction was to model the work of theory on bureaucratic work, and thus to reproduce *as theory* the mutual nonrecognition of the bu-reaucratic and the charismatic. It was of the essence of this theory that its dissemination could be attributed to a "cogni-tive process" and not to the effects of the transference, the "madness of authority," for only by means of such a formal-ization of its method could theoretical discourse be dissemi-nated beyond the immediate institutional sphere of charis-matic authority, the graduate seminar. Theory's constitutive "impersonality" was achieved not simply by the deconstruc-tion of illusions of autonomous agency but by the transfor-mation of the work of reading into an *unconscious mimesis* of the form of bureaucratic labor: "Technically correct rhetorical readings may be boring, monotonous, predictable, and unpleasant, but they are irrefutable" (RT, 19). There is no lack of overdetermination in this sentence; it character-izes rhetorical reading as "technical" in a quasi-scientific sense of "rigorous," but also as a specific kind of *work,* the work of the office. For the disciples, the transference is transferred not only onto the methodology of rhetorical reading, but onto the sheer "technicality" of that method, its iterability, which can then take on the properties of rou-tinized labor in the bureaucratic sphere.[10] In this way the transference finds what appears to be the same object to cathect in both the intellectual and the bureaucratic fields, the routinization-effect it knows as "rigor." Only in this way can boredom, monotony, predictability, and unpleasantness be revalued as *positive* qualities of rhetorical reading, as the objects of a psychic investment. And the question of "bor-ing to whom" is of course not the issue at all, since the ref-erent of these terms is not some real, experiential boredom but the "technical" iterability of rhetorical reading. Just as transference transferred in the pedagogic sphere imparts to "rigor" the eros, the sexiness, of the master teacher, so in the bureaucratic sphere it signifies a *charisma of routinization,* the cathexis of routine.

To return to the lexicon of deconstructive terms, we can easily give a de Manian equivalent for the "charisma of rou-tinization": it is the *pathos of rigor.* The puzzle of Hertz's[11] "lurid figures" is solved by reading the terms "pathos" and "rigor" as equally overdetermined, provided we recognize that the concept of the "lurid" or the "pathetic" governs not only its spectacular instances—beheading, castration, and the like—but most of all the "pathos" of the method, its boredom, its predictability, its unpleasantness, the "tedium of its tech-niques"[12] (RT, 106). At this point we may go on to contextu-alize the entire de Manian thematic by turning it inside out, as it were, by correlating the terms which are internal to its dis-course with the terms defining the conditions of its institu-tional practice:

rhetoric vs. grammar
metaphor vs. metonymy
necessity vs. chance
pathos vs. rigor
↓
literary texts vs. philosophical texts
↓
charisma vs. routine
profession vs. bureaucracy
autonomy vs. heteronomy

By means of this diagram we can see that the development of a dual syllabus of literary and philosophical texts served as a kind of hinge between the rhetorical/thematic terminol-ogy, internal to the discourse of rhetorical reading, and its institutional conditions, the conditions of intellectual labor for literary critics in general. Our analysis has already re-vealed that the terms on the left-hand side of the diagram are entirely governed by the terms on the right: just as agency is deconstructed by the "effet machinal" of lan-guage, just as metaphor is "metonymized," just as meta-physical necessity is displaced by the mechanical causality of chance, so pathos is determined to be nothing other than the effect of rigor, the inexorable rigor of the deconstructive method. It is crucial nevertheless that what does not and cannot appear within deconstructive discourse is the *mean-ing* of these terms in their institutional context, what the lower half of the diagram reveals: the subversion of charisma, of the claims to professional autonomy, by the heteronomous organization of the school. Such heteronomy

---

[10][Guillory] The only critic I have encountered who has remarked on the "cathexis" of boredom in the practice of rhetorical reading is D. A. Miller, who detects and exposes such a cathexis in J. Hillis Miller's citation of pre-cisely this passage from de Man's work. See "The Profession of English: An Exchange," J. Hillis Miller and D. A. Miller, *ADE Bulletin* 88 (1987), 42–58.

[11]Neil Hertz, "Lurid Figures," *Reading de Man Reading,* Li Waters and W. Godzich; eds. (Minneapolis: University of Minnesota Press, 1989).
[12]Paul de Man, *The Resistance to Theory* (Minneapolis: University of Minnesota Press, 1986), page 106.

rather appears within rhetorical reading only as a symptomatic doctrine: the *linguistic determinism* which somehow determines, without the intervention of any authoritative agent, of any "intersubjective relation," the protocols of rhetorical reading as a disciplinary practice: "But there is absolutely no reason why analyses of the kind here suggested for Proust would not be applicable, with proper modifications of technique, to Milton or to Dante or to Hölderlin. This will in fact be the task of literary criticism in the coming years."[13] The supreme confidence with which this prophecy is offered as a fact is staked on nothing other than a "blending" of personal and institutional authority in the figure of de Man; but that hindsight observation scarcely begins to confront the statement's rhetorical mode. By the latter term, I do not mean that these artfully dry sentences perform the same deconstruction to which all of canonical literature is to be submitted. The rhetorical mode of the passage is rather more homely and familiar: it resonates with the style of the *memo,* the humblest text of bureaucracy. It reports on the future *productivity* of rhetorical reading. But to whom is the memo addressed? It is as though de Man were merely reporting, as though he were merely passing on instructions from somewhere higher or deeper within the institution itself, and not setting an agenda for his disciples, for the school (and faction) of rhetorical reading. The denial of the master theorist's charismatic authority, his reabsorption into the company of nameless critical laborers, is enacted in the erasure of any agency, any higher authority, directing "the task of criticism." No one can claim credit for the setting of this agenda, not even de Man.

If the mask of impersonality conceals the "madness of authority," that is no more than what is to be expected of bureaucratic domination. The denial of the charismatic network (and its factions) belongs to the official ideology of the bureaucratic organization, to its language of "impersonal" relations and merely "technical" standards of competence; and it is under cover of this ideology that charismatic authority can be cultivated to an extreme degree, can be given the maximum field of play. At the same time, the transferential dynamic can only be unofficially acknowledged, reduced to the language of gossip, which dominates everyday working life and is like talk about the weather, at once tedious and compelling. At this point we can offer a summary reading of the de Manian oeuvre as a *symptomatic* discourse, a discourse that registers at the heart of its terminology the historical moment of the fusion of the university teacher's autonomous

"professional activity" with the technobureaucratic organization of intellectual labor. Within the larger discourse of "theory," rhetorical reading has the important symptomatic function of figuring a rapprochement with the institutional conditions of criticism, by acknowledging the loss of intellectual autonomy as a theory of linguistic determinism—at the same time that autonomy is continually reinvested in the figure of the master theorist. But this is an autonomy which exists only on the imaginary *outside* of the institution, as an "anti-institutional" charisma.[14]

We are now prepared to take an even longer view of the moment of theory, and the symptomatic role of rhetorical reading in that moment. For what we have attempted to understand is a historically specific routinization effect—the "rigor" of rhetorical reading—that was always articulated on the preexisting routinization effects of literary education, the most important of which is the literary curriculum itself. On the syllabus as routinization effect, Bourdieu and Passeron have commented: "Because sacerdotal practice can never so entirely escape stereotyping as can pedagogic practice (the manipulation of secularized goods), priestly charisma can never rest so entirely as teacherly charisma on the technique of ritual deritualization, the juggling with the syllabus that is implicitly *on* the syllabus" (66–67). Rhetorical reading has vigorously endorsed the "scheduled improvisation" of theory, its "juggling" with the syllabus, and at the same time tacitly returned in its practice to the syllabus of literature. The latter motive is expressed without apology in de Man's injunction to "apply" the techniques of rhetorical reading to "the whole of literature" (AR, 16). As I have already argued, the theory of rhetorical reading can provide no rationale for limiting the syllabus to works of literature, and no rationale is available in de Man for the deconstructive reading of nonliterary texts, except by extending the quality of "literariness" to those texts. While departmental inertia may ultimately limit the extent of curricular "improvisation," the larger context of a general and well publicized curricular crisis of the "humanities" suggests that the ambivalence of theory with respect to the literary

---

[13] Paul de Man, *Allegories of Reading* (New Haven: Yale University Press), page 17. Cited as AR.

[14] [Guillory] It seems evident in retrospect that deconstruction's solution to the problem of autonomy has been displaced in recent years by a more openly professionalist discourse that vehemently reasserts professional autonomy by celebrating precisely the "blending of personal and organizational prestige." Such an ideology of professionalism once again represses the bureaucratic determination of professional activity, though it is no less troubled by the omnipresence of such heteronomy; it wishes rather to play the game well, "pragmatically." Most importantly it no longer needs to project its solution to the problem of work autonomy onto a theory of *reading.* Indeed, the versions of pragmatism and relativism now circulating in the wake of theory can display a relaxed disdain for theory's "rigor," as that term signifies a kind of prior restraint upon professional activity. In that sense pragmatism is the theory of which professionalism is the practice.

syllabus is itself related to long-term developments in the educational institution. For the "canon of theory" introduces into the institutional context of literary pedagogy (the graduate seminar) a syllabus whose symptomatic function is to signify precisely methodological "rigor," rather than the taste or discrimination which for so long determined the ideological protocols of literary criticism. In no other circumstance would it have been possible for deconstruction to circulate as the other *name* of theory, the name given by de Man himself in the Preface to *Allegories of Reading.* At a certain moment, then, the syllabus of literary texts, constituting the traditional "routinization" of literary education, could be perceived as inadequate to support a practice that possessed "rigor"; and that inadequacy could only be compensated by another syllabus, one which in effect signified rigor.

Those authors or texts designated as "theoretical" are now increasingly capable of being introduced to students in traditional routinized forms, even by means of anthologies. It is difficult to imagine how graduate education could proceed at the present moment without recourse to a relatively standardized set of theoretical texts, which are employed not only in the context of "application" to works of literature, but also in the seminar on theory. These arrangements are hardly to be deplored in themselves. The routinization of theory does not necessarily represent, as Gerald Graff worries, only the rise of another specialization within literature: "It is largely the institutionalization of literary theory as a special field that lends truth to the complaint that literary theory has become a private enclave in which theorists only talk to one another."[15] Graff points out that theory is no more specialized than any other specialization in a period or an author, and he recommends that it become more like work on a set of problems that concern all critics. But I would suggest that theory has already become just that, with the qualification that the problem which is negotiated (unconsciously) in the language of theory, its language of "rigor," *is* the problem of "specialization," or the effects of the technobureaucratic organization of intellectual labor on the discipline of criticism. The interesting historical question remains what institutional conditions produced the secondary routinization effect by which theory was constituted as a syllabus both supplementary to the literary syllabus and in a necessarily pendant relation to that syllabus.

We can emphasize, to begin with, that it is only in the graduate seminar that theory can emerge as such, as a distinctive "canon" of writers and texts. The institutional conditions for the emergence of literary theory are therefore related to the institutional distinction between the graduate and undergraduate levels of the educational system. The signal feature of that distinction will already have been apparent: the relatively greater autonomy of the graduate teacher, which is in turn the condition for the transferential cathexes necessary for the propagation of theory. The relative nondetermination of the graduate syllabus by any higher administrative power is the sine qua non of theory, and for that reason theory itself is the vehicle of a claim to autonomy; it is the discursive field in which that autonomy can be negotiated, even when it is negotiated ideologically, as the perennial theoretical problem of the relation between language and the agency of the subject. The development of theory was always premised on the inviolability of the graduate seminar, the site of an autonomy not possible at the undergraduate level, where the syllabus of literature was subject to much greater oversight. At the same time it seems unlikely that theory would have been permitted to achieve so extensively a routinized a form in the graduate schools if an exclusively literary curriculum were still the norm at the graduate level. The indifference of university administrators to the graduate curriculum reflects less their respect for the traditional autonomy of the graduate teacher as it does an accurate estimation of the diminished significance of the literary curriculum in the context of the university's perceived social function, the perceived demand for the knowledges it disseminates.

The ultimate social horizon of the latter development is the hegemony of that technobureaucratic organization of intellectual life which has rendered the literary curriculum socially marginal by transforming the university into the institution designed to produce a new class of technical/managerial specialists possessed of purely technical/managerial knowledge. It is in this context that we shall have to understand the ambivalent position of literary theory with respect to literature, since theory is both indissolubly bound to that curriculum and yet opposed to reproducing it as the vehicle of universal "humanist values" constituting a knowledge of a nonspecialist nature. The project of literary theory in its premier deconstructive form was therefore to discard one ideological rationale for the literary curriculum, and then immediately to install another in its place. Rhetorical reading identified this rationale with the practice of *rhetoric,* but the invocation of that premodern discipline should not disguise the function of rhetoric as an ideological discourse when it is deployed as the means of transforming the method of reading into a rigorously iterable *technical* procedure. The refunctioning of rhetoric's *techne* as a kind of technology directly incorporated into the protocols of rhetorical reading a mimesis of

---

[15] [Guillory] Gerald Graff, *Professing Literature: An Institutional History* (Chicago: University of Chicago Press, 1987), 1987.

the technobureaucratic itself. Deconstructive literary theory testified to the obsolescence of the "humanist" rationale of literary study not only, then, by attacking that rationale directly, but by reproducing in the form of its practice the form of that hegemonic rationality which had *already* rendered the traditional ideological rationale of the literary curriculum obsolete. The failure of deconstructive theory to produce a new rationale for the literary curriculum accounts for the tenacity of the concept of the "literary" in its discourse, the fact that its syllabus was in practice confined to a specific set of literary and philosophical texts selected for their capacity to foreground (or thematize) rhetorical reading's ideological motifs and methodological procedures.

The absence of a rationale for the literary curriculum has up to this point meant nothing but the absence of an *ideological* rationale. This is necessarily so because the syllabus of literary works always demanded an essentialist concept of literature to ground it. Theory replaced the "humanistic" thematic of literature with an equally universalizing, if antihumanistic, thematic of *language;* the important point is that theory belongs to the long-term historical project of providing a rationale for the literary curriculum that would effectively establish a syllabus of study. Can essentializing concepts of literature be discarded without resorting to the kind of ideological debunking of literary works sometimes characterizing the critique of the canon? Perhaps it is time to reconsider the implications of Raymond Williams's "cultural materialist" critique of literature, a critique which is opposed both to the traditionalist ideological defense of literature and to the rhetoricism of theory: "It is in a way surprising that the specialized concept of 'literature,' developed in precise forms of correspondence with a particular social class, a particular technology of print, should be so often invoked in retrospective, nostalgic, or reactionary moods, as a form of opposition to what is correctly seen as a new phase of civilization."[16] Yet the progressive critical movements of the 1980s took as the object of their critique not the historical category of literature but "the canon." We are in a position now to recognize that the career of theory had everything to do with the status of literature in "a new phase of civilization."

A preliminary attempt at reconsidering the category of literature might begin with the observation that while the original ideological rationale of literature justified the social project of producing a standard vernacular by presenting literature as the repository of the most universal truths of the human condition, this project was always belied by the actual structure of the educational system. The contradiction between the politico-administrative requirement of linguistic homogeneity and the socioeconomic necessity of distributing unequally every form of cultural capital (including Standard English) burdened the educational system throughout its modern history with the impossible task of at once democratizing the distribution of knowledges and maintaining class distinctions. This contradiction marks in familiar ways the complex interrelations between public and private schools, and between the various levels of the educational system. At the present moment, the nation-state still requires a relatively homogeneous language to administer its citizenry, but it no longer requires that a distinctive practice of that language identify a culturally homogeneous bourgeoisie. That class has long since been replaced by a culturally heterogeneous New Class, which has in turn been fully integrated into mass culture, a media culture mediating the desires of every class and group. In this "new phase of civilization," the historical function of the literary curriculum—to produce at the lower levels of the educational system a practice of Standard English, and at the higher levels a more refined bourgeois language, a "literary" English—is no longer crucially important to the social order. We might even speculate that it is the *absence* of such a crucial social function which the professors of literature experience as powerlessness in the face of a political entity—the state—which they misrecognize as the source of disempowerment. For the same reason the absence of a central social function for the literary curriculum has become the occasion of an anxious thematizing of the political in literary critical discourse, as well as the occasion of an undervaluation of the field in which teachers do possess agency, namely, the school itself. What appears to be a politically significant fact from the point of view of a "cultural materialism" may be something rather different than the question of which social groups are represented in the canon: for example, the fact that the function of producing in a segment of the populace a minimal degree of linguistic uniformity (in ideological terms, "competence") has been given over to the field of composition, which has developed a nonfictional prose syllabus specific to its function, a syllabus which seems to have no necessary relation to the study of literature. As we have seen in Chapter 1, the new institutional significance of composition marks the appearance of a new social function for the university, the task of providing the future technobureaucratic elite with precisely and only the linguistic competence necessary for the performance of its specialized functions.

The study of literature has taken its place in the undergraduate curriculum, then, as one apparent specialization among many others, but a specialization without a rationale specific to its syllabus. It is still a specialization with a *universalist* rationale, and this was true even of rhetorical

---

[16] [Guillory] Williams, *Marxism and Literature,* 54. [See above, page 1357.]

reading, which expressed this contradiction as the discrepancy between its mimetically technobureaucatic methodology and its universalist theory of language, a theory which rediscovered in works of literature an expression of the universal human condition. If deconstructive theory did not provide an enduring new rationale for literary study, that was in part because it was incapable of seeing the relation between its practice of *supplementing* the literary syllabus at the level of the graduate school, and composition's practice of *displacing* it at the entry level of university study. Rhetorical reading was entirely symptomatic of theory in general in its incapacity to rationalize its syllabus, except by falling back upon the textual preferences of de Man himself, or by generalizing the concept of literariness to a particular set of philosophical texts. The weakness of this rationalization was only too apparent when it had to confront the demand from other factions of the profession to "open the canon." But the diminished significance of the literary syllabus in the university is in reality a systemic institutional effect, and not the result of a deconstructive (or any other) attack upon the universality of the values supposed to be expressed in the literary canon. Here, then, is a new "political" question: What is the systemic relation between the syllabus of composition and the syllabus of theory? Both of these practices have invoked in highly charged ideological contexts the precedent of rhetoric, and both have refunctioned rhetoric in practices which are overdetermined by the technobureaucratic conditions themselves responsible for the social marginality of the literary curriculum.[17] What de Man considered to be the cultural irrelevance of the university describes a real condition, perhaps, not of the university but of the literary curriculum, a condition which has given rise, among other things, to the canon of theory.

The difficulty of imagining what might succeed the curricular forms of literature and theory is well indicated in the following comment of John Frow, from his *Marxism and Literary History*:

> The whole weight of recent literary theory has been on the *constitutive* status of language, on the impossibility of linguistic transparency, on the agonistic rhetorical strategies of discourse, and on the shaping of language by the forces of power and desire. The effect of this emphasis should be in the first place to redefine the traditional objects of literary knowledge, and in particular the forms of valorization of writing which have prevailed in most forms of literary study.[18]

Frow recommends a "general poetics" or "general rhetoric" which would not be addressed exclusively to the traditional canon of literary texts but would take as its object noncanonical genres and forms, including popular romances, journalism, film, television, scientific discourses, and even "everyday language." But the recourse to "poetics" and "rhetoric" confirms once again how nearly impossible it is to imagine what lies beyond the rhetoricism of literary theory, and hence beyond the problematic of literariness. It is not yet clear whether a "cultural studies" curriculum has been conceived which does not replicate the theoretical and hermeneutic paradigms of literary interpretation. There is also evidence to suggest that cultural studies' new "opening" of the syllabus to popular or mass cultural works has been accompanied by a closure of the syllabus to the same High Cultural philosophical texts which were so important to the dissemination of theory. Such a cultural studies syllabus would certainly not be inclusive of cultural products generally.[19] If literary criticism is ever to conceptualize a new disciplinary domain, it will have to undertake first a much more thorough reflection on the historical category of literature; otherwise I suggest that new critical movements will continue to register their agendas symptomatically, by ritually overthrowing a continually resurgent literariness and literary canon. At the same time it is unquestionably the case that the several recent crises of the literary canon—its "opening" to philosophical works, to works by minorities, and now to popular and mass cultural works—amounts to a terminal crisis, more than sufficient evidence of the urgent need to reconceptualize the object of literary study. One may predict, without resorting to prophecy, that such reconceptualization will become "the task of literary criticism in the coming years."

---

[17] [Guillory] On the relation between technical knowledges and the practice of composition, see the interesting remarks of Stanley Aronowitz and Henry A. Giroux, *Education Under Siege: The Conservative, Liberal, and Radical Debate over Schooling* (Hadley, Mass.: Bergin and Garvey, 1985), 52ff.

[18] [Guillory] John Frow, *Marxism and Literary History* (Oxford: Basil Blackwell, 1986), 234.

[19] [Guillory] Raymond Williams has always argued forcefully for maintaining a sense of the historical interrelation between High and Low Cultural works. See his comment in "The Future of Cultural Studies," in *The Politics of Modernism: Against the New Conformists* (London: Verso, 1989): "It is necessary and wholly intellectually defensible to analyse serials and soap operas. Yet I do wonder about the courses where at least the teachers—and I would say also the students—have not themselves encountered the problems of the whole development of naturalist and realist drama, of social-problem drama, or of certain kinds of serial form in the nineteenth century, which are elements in the constitution of these precise contemporary forms, so that the tension between that social history of forms and these forms in a contemporary situation, with their partly new and partly old content, partly new and partly old techniques, can be explored with weight on both sides" (159).

Gayatri Chakravorty Spivak

b. 1942

It is very difficult to characterize the work of Gayatri Chakravorty Spivak for many reasons, not the least of which is its rich variety of subject and orientation. Equally important, however, is the intellectual tension everywhere evident in her prose, sometimes like the sprung rhythms of Gerard Manley Hopkins, but always at once bristlingly abstract and rooted in the concrete details of practice. From her undergraduate education at Presidency College, Calcutta, to advanced study at Cambridge University and a Ph.D. from Cornell, Spivak has taken the intellectual professions, emphatically including her own, very seriously as being always subject to incursions and interventions by which intellectual issues reveal their practical, political, and moral dimension. As the translator of Jacques Derrida's *Of Grammatology* (1967, tr. 1976) and author of a lengthy introduction to that volume, Spivak's own practice of deconstruction has been distinctive. It is, in multiple ways, interventionist, activist, always enlivened by a concrete sense of the situations in which deconstruction discloses not a merely abstract complicity, but particular, frequently personal injury or suppression. Her characteristic skepticism about *isms,* particularly those to which she is profoundly committed, notably feminism and Marxism, reflects her vivid sense that one's own practice as a cultural and literary analyst offers may venues for evasion. For this reason, she has for many years carried out a daunting schedule of "field work," actual *working* trips to the places where women in other cultures work and teach as part of her pursuit of "the global history of the present."

The essay selected here reflects these complications vividly. For what is most striking and consistent in Spivak's work is that she is always and everywhere a teacher, alert to subtleties in concrete teaching situations—which are all situations whatsoever—of the intricate passageways between commitments that the practice of deconstruction, at its best, discloses in language. In one of her most important (and difficult) essays, "Can the Subaltern Speak?" Spivak provides one of the best and most articulate defenses of deconstruction by rejecting the easy judgment (as advanced, for example, by Terry Eagleton, but widely shared) that, in Spivak's words, "Foucault deals with real history, real politics, real social problems; Derrida is inaccessible, esoteric, and textualistic." The error lies in supposing that such matters are easily accessible to intuition, that what is "real" is obvious or that what requires action is self-evident. But it is precisely that "textualistic" particular that gives Spivak's "interventionist" deconstruction its sharp and surprising edge: the situations of "real" politics must be read with even more care, more cunning, so as not to follow apparent passageways to change that in fact go nowhere. "Teaching for the Times" in this respect affords a rich figure for justifying critical procedures that, on a first reading, may seem "inaccessible, esoteric," but which, with that primary form of intervention, good teaching, yield their complex meaning exactly as texts do. As a teacher, Spivak has the remarkable virtue of not forgetting the power of learning to read, the importance of teaching it to others in times of change.

Spivak's principal works include: *In Other Worlds: Essays in Cultural Politics* (1987); *The Post-Colonial Critic* (1990); *Thinking Academic Freedom in Gendered Post-Coloniality* (1992); *Outside in the Teaching Machine* (1993); and most recently, *A Critique of Postcolonial Reason: Toward a History of the Vanishing Present* (1999) and *Death of a Discipline* (2003). Her essays and addresses are widely anthologized, for use in many fields—feminist criticism, subaltern and postcolonial studies, literary theory, and cultural studies.

Teaching for the Times

This essay was originally written for the annual convention of the Midwestern Modern Language Association in the United States. I have not removed the signs that show that I am speaking to fellow teachers; in other words, it is a practical piece. I have also kept its local flavor. I think these signs and marks can be of some interest to readers from various parts of the world, if only because their presence might then produce some effort to work out how, in readers' own contexts, the teaching of literature can be transnational.[1]

The word "transnational" now bears the weight of the untrammeled financialization of the globe in the recent post-Soviet years. I will not offer a detailed discussion of this abundantly discussed phenomenon here, except to remark that, in this dispensation, the integrity of particular states has become much more fluid, especially in the South, and especially since capitalism is being reterritorialized as "democracy." It seems obvious that the always precarious hyphen between nation and state is now rather more so; and that this hyphen is being inhabited by multifarious mobilizers of identity politics. It is within this broad context that the words were first uttered; the exhortation was for new immigrant American college and university teachers of English to locate themselves in it: and

that effortful location was called transnational literacy.[2] It would, I think, be less useful to read "transnational" only by the rules of an older lexicon, where it stands for a globality in conflict with the nation-state, although that lexicon is by no means obsolete.

It should also be kept in mind that we are speaking here of college and university teaching of English, not of subaltern projects of literacy or pedagogy of the oppressed. In an effort to understand how diversified yet related transnational teaching must be, I have attempted to travel the course, starting from rural or specifically aboriginal literacy under different national circumstances, all the way to international conferences—again under various national determinations, with situations of national(ized) education systems somewhere in the middle. If it has taught me anything, it is that nothing applies everywhere. I speak of the invention of unity for the new immigrant teacher in the body of the piece. That is a strategic unity. I do not believe we can have any more globalized a vision within the boundaries of the varieties of academic practice.

When I wrote the piece, we in the United States were still caught between "liberal multiculturalism," on the one hand, and white cultural supremacy—the anti-"politically correct" (pc)—on the other.[3] If the reader wishes to tease out a presupposition from the following pages, here is one: at a

---

"Teaching for the Times" has appeared in many different versions. We reprint here the third revision, from *Dangerous Liasons: Gender, Nation, & Postcolonial Perspectives,* ed. Anne McClintock, Aamir Mufti, and Ella Shohat (Minneapolis: The University of Minnesota Press, 1997). All footnotes are by the author.

[Spivak] This essay was first published in *MMLA Quarterly* 25, no. 1 (1992): 3–22; reprinted with extensive revisions in Jan Nederveen Pieterse, ed., *The Decolonization of Imagination* (London: Zed Books, 1995), 177–202. This version has been further revised. I thank Thomas W. Keenan for reading the first and Vincent Cheng for reading the final versions.

[1] Now that this essay is being reprinted stateside, I want to keep the contextual sedimentation intact. It is because the "U.S. as such" (it means something in capital logic) is also "local," not merely its multicultural neighborhoods or its municipal issues.

[2] As always, by "new immigrants" I mean the continuing influx of immigrants since, by "[t]he Immigration and Nationality Act of October 1, 1965," Lyndon Johnson "swept away both the national-origin system and the Asia-Pacific Triangle"; these are precisely the groups escaping decolonization, one way or another. "That the Act would, for example, create a massive brain drain from developing countries and increase Asian immigration 500 per cent was entirely unexpected" (Maldwyn Allen Jones, *American Immigration,* 2d ed. [Chicago: University of Chicago Press, 1992], 266, 267). For purposes of definition, I have repeated this footnote in other writing. It goes without saying that, in the post-Soviet phase, the patterns of this "new" immigration have a fast-changing dynamic. The increasing legislative and electoral rage against immigrants should strengthen the argument in my essay. A superficial understanding of this rage has, however, exacerbated the unexamined culturalist competition that is my target.

[3] Darryl J. Gless and Barbara Herrnstein Smith, eds., *The Politics of Liberal Education* (Durham, N.C.: Duke University Press, 1992), gives a sense of the debate. A great many documents can now be cited, but I am revising on press deadline.

certain limit, the two sides of the debate feed each other. The

colonial*ism,* it can only be a transnational literacy; for post-coloniali*ty* is a failure of decolonization. Is decolonization possible? In the broadest possible sense, once and for all, no; but this is what it shares with everything else.[7] Yet, given the situation of the self-representation of multicultural teaching of literature in the United States, it seems more canny to stop (or start) with prospects for decolonization, presumably a condition before *post*coloniality (or ism) can be declared. As far as I can tell, and for all practical purposes, a general condition of postcoloniality is a future anterior, something that will have happened, if one concerned oneself with the persistent crafty details of the calculus of decolonization, in the sphere in which one is contractually engaged, not excluding tacit affective contracts, of course.

Since its inception, the United States has been a nation of immigrants. The winners among the first set of European immigrants claimed, often with violence, that the land belonged to them, because the industrial revolution was in their pocket. And the story of its origin has been re-presented as an escape from old feudalism, in a general de Tocquevillian way. It is well known that in the founders' Constitution, African slaves and the Original Nations were inscribed as property in order to get around the problem of the representation of slaves as wealth: "The key slogan in the struggle against the British had been 'no taxation without representation. . . .' The acceptance that slaves as wealth should entitle Southern voters to extra representation built an acknowledgement of slavery into the heart of the Constitution."[8]

Here we have extreme cases of marginalization where the term itself gives way: dehumanization, transportation, genocide. I will not begin in that scene of violence at the origin, but rather with the phenomenon that has gradually kicked us—marginal voices—from opposition to the perceived dominant in the U.S. cultural space: new immigration in the new world order.

These important books can obviously not be discussed in an endnote. Here suffice it to say that the three texts have something like a relationship with the civilizing mission of imperialism seriously credited. Ackerman's position is so muscle-bound with learning as to be least examined, and it is not surprising that, at the 1994 Pacific American Philosophical Association convention, he advanced his position as a justification both for foreign aid and for the emancipation of the women of developing nations. His book is specifically addressed to the needs of the new world order; "The Meaning of 1989" (113–23) is one of his chapters. Charles Taylor reduces the value of his thoughtful study by deducing the subject of multiculturalism (difficult for me to imagine as a unicity) from the "European" historical narrative of the emergence of secularism. And John Rawls, by far the most astute of the three, recognizes the limits of liberalism as politics in order to save it as philosophy. "The hearts of innumerable men and women respond . . . with idealistic fervour to [t]his clarion, because it [goes] . . without saying that it would be good for . . anywhere . . to be made [American]. At this point it might be useful to wonder which of the ideals that make our hearts beat faster will seem wrong-headed to people a hundred years from now" (Doris Lessing, *African Laughter: Four Visits to Zimbabwe* [New York: HarperCollins, 1992], 3; she is writing about Cecil Rhodes and "Southern Rhodesia"). I have not yet read Duncan Kennedy, *Sexy Dressing Etc.: Essays on the Power and Politics of Cultural Identity* (Cambridge, Mass.: Harvard University Press, 1993).

[7] I insist upon this point, trivially but crucially true. It is so often neglected that I take the liberty of self-citation: "The fact that socialism can never fully (adequately) succeed is what it has in common with everything. It is *after* that fact that one starts to make the choices, especially after the implosion of the Bolshevik experiment" ("Marginality in the Teaching Machine," in Spivak, *Outside in the Teaching Machine,* New York, Routledge, 1993, 68). What follows in the text about the foundation of the United States is a condensed version of the final chapter of *Outside.* Mindful of Kathy E. Ferguson's critique of my apparent claim to authority in *The Man Question: Visions of Subjectivity in Feminist Theory* (Berkeley: University of California Press, 1993), 201, I controlled my habit of self-referencing for a while. Weighing this against many complaints of overburdened, cryptic, and incomprehensible writing, I have thought it best to revert to a modified version of my original practice.

[8] Robin Blackburn, *The Overthrow of Colonial Slavery: 1776–1848* (London: Verso, 1988), 123, 124.

Let us rewrite "cultural identity" as "national-origin validation." Let us not use "cultural identity" as a permission to difference and an instrument for disavowing that Eurocentric economic migration (and eventually even political exile) persists in the hope of justice under capitalism. That unacknowledged and scandalous secret is the basis of our unity. Let us reinvent this basis as a springboard for a teaching that counterpoints these times. This is what unites the "illegal alien" and the aspiring academic. I am arguing that this is all the more important because "we"—that vague, menaced, and growing body of the teachers of culture and literature who question the canon—are not *oppositional* any more. We are being actively opposed because what used to be the dominant literary-cultural voice—the male-dominated, white, Eurocentric voice—obviously feels its shaping and molding authority slipping away. We seem to be perceived as the emerging dominant. What is the role and task of the emerging dominant teacher? Since one of the major functions of professional organizations in the United States is to facilitate employment, let us also consider the problems of educating the educators of the emerging dominant field: in other words, let us consider both the undergraduate and the graduate curriculum.

Access to the Universal/National-Origin Validation on the Undergraduate Curriculum

In a powerful paper entitled "The Campaign against Political Correctness: What's Really at Stake?" Joan Wallach Scott lays bare the shoddy techniques of what was the opposition at the beginning of the 1980s:

> Serious intellectuals have only to read the self-assured, hopelessly ill-informed, and simply wrong descriptions of deconstruction, psychoanalysis, feminism, or any other serious theory by the likes of D'Souza, Richard Bernstein, David Lehman, Roger Kimball, Hilton Kramer, George Will—and even Camille Paglia—to understand the scam. . . . [T]heir anger at the very scholars they long to emulate . . . seems to have worked in some quarters. That is partly because the publicists have assumed another persona beside that of the intellectual: they pretend to represent the common man—whom, as elitists, they also loathe.[9]

This brilliant and shrewd paper focuses on the contemporary American scene. And as such its writer shows that the opposition is desperately claiming a "universality" that, in my view, has already slipped out of their grasp. She quotes S. P. Mohanty who "calls for an alternative to pluralism that would make difference and conflict the center of a history 'we' all share." She quotes Christopher Fynsk as offering "the French word *partage,* [meaning] . . . both to divide and to share," as an informing metaphor of community. I will keep these suggestions in mind in this first section, most specifically confined to the undergraduate curriculum in the United States.

Emergence into an at best precarious dominant does not for a moment mean that our battle for national-origin validation in the United States is over. First, we as new immigrants must rethink the battle lines. Since the "national origins" of new immigrants, as fantasized by themselves, have not, so far, contributed to the unacknowledged and remoter historical culture of the United States, what we are demanding is that the United States recognize *our* rainbow as part of its history of the present. Since most of our countries were not *territorially* colonized by the United States, this is a transaction that relates to our status as new Americans, not primarily to the countries of our origin. (In this respect our struggle is similar to as well as different from that of the new European immigrants.) Second, we must realize that, in the post-Soviet, post-Fordist world, we as a specific part of the collective of marginals are currently fighting from a different position. We face the need to consolidate ourselves in new ways, which I have tried to indicate in my opening words. Being reactive to the dominant is no longer the only issue. I agree with Scott's and Mohanty's and Fynsk's general point: conflict, relationality, dividing, and sharing. In the American context these are good marching orders. But difference and conflict are hard imperatives. Difference becomes competition, for we live and participate—even as dissidents—within institutions anchored in a transnational capitalist economy. Our "limited physical supply of what is at stake makes it easy to overlook the fact that the functioning of the economic game itself presupposes adherence to the game and *belief in the value of its stakes.*"[10]

The stakes in question are not just institutional but generally social. Eurocentric economic migration as a critical mass is based on hope for justice under capitalism. The task of the teacher is as crucial as it is chancy, for there is no guarantee that to know it is to be able to act on it (especially since our self-representation as marginal in the United States might involve a disavowed dominant status with re-

---

[9] Joan Wallach Scott, "The Campaign against Political Correctness: What's Really at Stake?" *Change* 23, no. 6 (November/December 1991): 32–33. The passages from Mohanty and Fynsk are from pp. 39 and 43, respectively.

[10] Pierre Bourdieu [above, page 1403], "The Philosophical Institution," in Alan Montefiore, ed., *Philosophy in France Today* (Cambridge: Cambridge University Press, 1983), 2; emphasis added.

spect to our countries of national origin). To continue with the quotation above:

> [H]ow is it possible to produce that minimal invest-ment which is the condition of economic produc-tion without resorting to competition and without reproducing individuation? As long as the logic of social games is not explicitly recognized (and even if it is . . .), even the apparently freest and most cre-ative of actions is never more than an encounter be-tween reified and embodied history, . . . a necessity which the agent *constitutes* as such and for which [s]he provides the scene of action without actually being its subject.

"Reified history" is in this case our monumentalized national-cultural history of origin combined with ideas of a miracu-lated resistant hybridity; "embodied history" our disavowed articulation within the history of the present of our chosen new nation-state.[11] This "encounter" does not translate to the scene of violence at the origin—slavery and genocide, black and red—that I laid aside at the opening of my essay.

In the U.S. classroom I spend some time on Pierre Bourdieu's caution: "and even if it is [recognized] . . ." I draw it out into the difference between knowing and learn-ing. Without falling into too strict an adherence to the iron distinction between the constative and the performative, I still have to hang on to a working difference between know-ing about something and learning to do something. The re-lationship between knowing and learning is crucial as we move from the space of opposition to the menaced space of the emerging dominant.

An anthology piece in an international collection will not allow the meditative tempo of the classroom. Let me therefore ignore Bourdieu's parenthesis and emphasize the point Bourdieu makes, keeping myself, for the moment, confined to our role within the academic institution. I will return to the more general social point of new-immigration-in-capitalism later.

As long as we are interested, and we *must* be interested, in hiring and firing, in grants, in allocations, in budgets, in funding new job descriptions, in *publishing* radical texts, in fighting for tenure and recommending for jobs, we are *in* cap-italism, and we cannot avoid competition and individuation. Under these circumstances, essentializing difference, how-ever sophisticated we might be at it, may lead to unproductive conflict among ourselves. If we are not merely the opposition any more, we must not lose the possibility of our swing into power by crumbling into interest groups in the name of dif-ference. We must find some basis for unity. It is a travesty of philosophy, a turning of philosophy into a direct blueprint for policy making, to suggest that the search for a situational unity goes against the lesson of deconstruction. If we perceive our emergence into the dominant as a situation, we see the importance of inventing a unity that depends upon that situa-tion. I am not a situational relativist. No situation is saturated. But imperatives arise out of situations, and, however unthink-ingly, we act by imagining imperatives. We must therefore scrupulously imagine a situation in order to act. Pure differ-ence cannot appear. Difference cannot provide an adequate theory of practice. "Left to itself, the incalculable and giving idea of justice [here as justice to difference] is always very close to the bad, even to the worst, for it can always be reap-propriated by the most perverse calculation."[12]

In the interest of space I am collapsing a few philo-sophical moves needed to make this argument acceptable. I can only ask you to take it on trust that those moves can be made.[13] What is important for me, in order, later, to pass into the second part of my remarks, is simply the convic-tion: we, the new immigrant teachers of so-called opposi-tional discourses in the United States, must today find a practical basis for unity at this crucial moment.

Consider this good passage from Jonathan Culler, also quoted by Joan Scott:

> A particular virtue of literature, of history, of an-thropology is instruction in otherness: vivid, com-pelling evidence of differences in cultures, mores,

---

[11] In this connection, the phrase "colonial subject" may be misleadingly laden with pathos. In my estimation, the constitution of the so-called colonial subject can also be described as the violent and necessary constitution of an abstract subject of a limited-access civil society—the core of the colo-nial infrastructure. Eurocentric economic migration and its struggle for full access to civil rights accompanied by a validated if phantasmatic national-cultural origin can then be seen as a document continuous with that consti-tution. For a Foucauldian elaboration of this theme, see Spivak, "Narratives of Multiculturalism," in Thomas W. Keenan, ed., *Cultural Diversities* (forthcoming); for an elaboration of this in terms of the old multicultural imperial formations in Eurasia, see "Response to Anahid Kasabian and David Kasanjian," *Armenian Review*.

[12] Jacques Derrida, "Force of Law: the 'Mystical Foundation of Authority,' " \in *Deconstruction and the Possibility of Justice,* vol. 11, nos. 5–6 of *Car-dozo Law Review* (July–August 1990): 971.

[13] Some of these philosophical moves are to be found, with reference to a general social context, in the discussion of the aporia between the experience of the impossible and the possibility of the political in Jacques Derrida, *The Other Heading: Reflections on Today's Europe,* tr. Pascale-Anne Brault and Michael B. Naas (Bloomington: Indiana University Press, 1992), 44–46; and, with reference to the academic institutional context, in Derrida, "Mochlos; or, The Conflict of the Faculties," in Richard Rand, ed., *Logomachia: The Conflict of the Faculties* (Lincoln: University of Nebraska Press, 1992), 3–34.

assumptions, values. At their best, these subjects make otherness palpable and make it comprehensible without reducing it to an inferior version of the same, as a universalizing humanism threatens to do.[14]

I repeat, good words, words with which we should certainly claim alliance. Yet, today in particular, we must also ask: Who speaks here? Who is the implied reader of this literature, the researcher of this history, the investigator of this anthropology? For whose benefit is this knowledge being produced, so that he or she can have *our* otherness made palpable and comprehensible, without reducing it into an inferior version of *their* same, through the choice of studying literature, history, and anthropology "at their best"? Shall we, today, be satisfied with the promise of liberal multiculturalism that these disciplines will remain "at their best," with a now-contrite universal humanism in the place of the same, and us being studied as examples of otherness? Or should we remind ourselves of Herbert Marcuse's wise words in the 1960s? I will speak of our difference from the 1960s in a while, but Marcuse's words are still resonant over against the promises of liberal multiculturalism: "Equality of tolerance becomes abstract, spurious. . . . The opposition is insulated in small and frequently insulated groups who, even when tolerated within the narrow limits set by the hierarchical structure of society, are powerless while they keep within these limits."[15]

This does not mean that we should be opposed to small victories: it is certainly important that some Third World literature job descriptions—"global" rather than "insular" English—now appear on the job lists issued by our national professional organization, the Modern Language Association of America. Yet it is possible that we will remain powerless collaborators in repressive tolerance if, in higher education in the humanities, we do not rethink our agency. Predictably, my agenda in the end will be the persistent and shifting pursuit of the global history of the present.

Other voices are asking questions similar to mine. I would cite here Aihwa Ong's piece "Colonialism and Modernity: Feminist Re-presentations of Women in Non-Western Society," which ends with these important words: "We begin a dialogue when we recognize other forms of gender- and culture-based subjectivities, and accept that others often choose to conduct their lives separate from our

particular vision of the future."[16] To claim agency in the emerging dominant is to *recognize* agency in others, not simply to comprehend otherness.

A distorted version of this recognition is produced in liberal multiculturalism. Yet we have to claim some alliance with it, for on the other side, as the article by Joan Scott that I have already cited will make abundantly clear, are the white-supremacist critics of "political correctness," a major phenomenon on the U.S. scene. It is no secret that liberal multiculturalism is determined by the demands of contemporary transnational capitalisms. It is an important public relations move in the apparent winning of consent from developing countries in the dominant project of the financialization of the globe. (I am arguing that, having shifted our lives from those nations to this, we become part of the problem if we continue to disavow its responsibility.) Procter and Gamble, a large U.S. multinational corporation, sends students specializing in business administration abroad to learn language and culture. Already in 1990, the National Governors' Association report queried: "How are we to sell our product in a global economy when we are yet to learn the language of the customers?"[17] If we are to question this distorting rationale for multiculturalism while utilizing its material support, we have to recognize also that the virulent backlash from the current *racist* dominant in this country is out of step with contemporary geopolitics. *We* are caught in a larger struggle where one side devises newer ways to exploit transnationality through a distorting culturalism and the other knows rather little what transnational script drives, writes, and operates it. It is within this ignorant clash that we have to find and locate our agency and attempt, again and again, to unhinge the clashing machinery.

What actually happens in a typical liberal-multicultural classroom "at its best"? On a given day we are reading a text from one national origin. The group in the classroom from that particular national origin in the general polity can identify with the richness of the texture of the "culture" in question, often through a haze of nostalgia. (I am not even bringing up the question of the definition of culture.) People from other national origins in the classroom (other, that is, than Anglo) relate sympathetically but superficially, in an aura of same difference. The Anglo relates benevolently to everything, "knowing about other cultures" in a relativist glow.

---

[14] Scott, "Campaign," 43.

[15] Herbert Marcuse, "Repressive Tolerance," in Robert Paul Wolff and Barrington Moore Jr., eds., *A Critique of Pure Tolerance* (Boston: Beacon Press, 1965), 116.

[16] Aihwa Ong, "Colonialism and Modernity: Feminist Re-presentations of Women in Non-Western Societies," *Inscriptions* 3, no. 4 (1988): 90. Although I have some problems with the details of Ong's argument, I am fully in accord with her general point.

[17] Much the most successful effort is from the great UN Women's Conferences (Nairobi 1985, Cairo 1994, Beijing 1995). I have discussed this in "Love, Cruelty, and Cultural Talks in the Hot Peace," *Parallax* (forthcoming) and "Who Claims Sexuality?" *New Literary History*.

What is the basis of the sympathy and the feeling of same difference among the various national origins in such a best-case scenario? Here the general social case writes our script. To pick up on my earlier argument, the basis for that feeling is that we have all come with the hope of finding justice or welfare within a capitalist society. (The place of women within this desire merits a separate discussion.)[18] We have come to avoid wars, to avoid political oppression, to escape from poverty, to find opportunity for ourselves and, more important, for our children: with the hope of finding justice within a capitalist society. Strictly speaking, we have left the problems of postcoloniality, located in the former colony (now a "developing nation" trying to survive the ravages of colonialism), *only* to discover that the white-supremacist culture wants to claim the entire agency of capitalism—recoded as the rule of law within a democratic heritage—*only* for itself; to find that the *only* entry is through a forgetfulness or a museumization of national origin in the interest of class mobility. In the liberal-multicultural classroom we go for the second alternative, thinking of it as resistance to forgetfulness, but necessarily in the long-term interest of our often disavowed common faith in democratic capitalism: "a necessity [as Bourdieu reminded us] which the agent *constitutes* as such and for which [s]he provides the scene of action without actually being its subject." This necessity is what unites us, and unless we acknowledge it ("and even if we do . . .") we cannot hope to undertake the responsibility of the emerging dominant.

Let me digress for a moment on a lesson such an acknowledgment can draw from history. If by teaching ourselves and our students to acknowledge our part and hope in capitalism we can bring that hope to a persistent and principled crisis, we can set ourselves on the way to intervening in an unfinished chapter of history that was mired in Eurocentric national disputes.

"The Law is the element of calculation, and it is just that there be Law, but justice is incalculable, it requires us to calculate with the incalculable."[19] Now that the Bolshevik experiment has imploded, we cannot afford to forget that the incalculable dreams of the vestiges of Second International Communism (rather than the overt history of its demise in national competition), placed within the calculus of the welfare state, are daily eroded by the forces of what is politely called "liberalization" in the Third World and the new Second World (the old Eastern bloc)—and by privatization in the First.

(In the first version of this essay, delivered in the United States and addressed to teachers of the humanities, I used the term "Second International" in rather a loose way. In a European and social-scientific context, the steps leading to this loose use should be spelled out.)

In *Imperialism,* Lenin writes: "The boom at the end of the nineteenth century and the crisis of 1900–03. Cartels become one of the foundations of the whole of economic life. Capitalism has been transformed into imperialism."[20] The description sounds old-fashioned in its terms precisely because the transformation has moved into spectacular determinations. The post-Soviet world order is an example of the timeliness of Lenin's harsh proposition. His scathing critique of Karl Kautsky and the Second International in the same text, in contrast, has lost some of its point precisely because of the astuteness of his judgment that imperialism does not resemble its nineteenth-century lineaments today. Today the United States left turns toward "radical democracy" rather than socialism because the project is a transformation of capitalist imperialism everywhere, not a claim to the culture of postcoloniality in the multicultural United States of Europe and America.[21] When liberalism claims its revolution in the name of capitalism in the social sciences [see my discussion of Bruce Ackerman in note 6], it is time for us, humanist academics marked by recent other-national origin but integrated into developed civil societies, to take note; for we teach a large sector of the growing electorate the uncertain grounds of choice: the singular and unverifiable witnessing of literature.

I will quote Immanuel Wallerstein because the narrative here is conveniently put together, not because I necessarily subscribe to his position on world-systems or movements of ethnic identity. I should also mention that the invocation of specifically the *Second* International was to distinguish myself from those academic leftists in the United States who were concentrating on a Trotskyist critique of the Soviet system, precisely because such a concentration did not seem productive of a specific plan of action for the new immigrant academic. Given the absence of a serious state-level left in the United States, I must confess I did not see the need, in a hortatory piece, to distinguish

---

[18] I have attempted such a separate discussion in "Diasporas Old and New: Women in the Transnational World," *Textual Practices.* Suffice it here to say that even within economic migration, women often remain exilic. The definition is, as usual, gender-sensitive.

[19] Derrida, "Force of Law," 947.

[20] V. I. Lenin, *Imperialism: The Highest Stage of Capitalism: A Popular Outline* (New York: International Publishers, 1939), 22.

[21] Stanley Aronowitz, "The Situation of the Left in the United States," *Socialist Review* 93, no. 3 (January–March 1994): 5–79. See also the collection of responses in the subsequent issue.

carefully between the Second International as such and the specific party positions and histories of social democracy and democratic socialism. It should be also be remembered that the closest thing to a serious left party in the United States had been the Democratic Socialists of America under the leadership of Michael Harrington. With regard to new immigrants the point is that, whereas the original Second International Socialist movement had come to an end in European nationalisms, and the Third International Communist movement now shows itself to have had, in many respects, the lineaments and problems of a species of colonialism in the name of internationalism, this particular U.S. group, with what I am calling its "negotiable" national sentiments straddling the periphery and the center, can, especially through its contingent of radical humanist teachers, teach not only for a nostalgic culturalism but also for a progressivist socialism. Here is the passage from Wallerstein:

> [D]uring the period between the First and Second World Wars [there] exist[ed] . . . two rival and fiercely competitive Internationals, the Second and the Third, also known as the conflict between Social Democrats and Communists. . . . It is less that the social-democratic parties came to be seen as one of the alternating groups which could legitimately govern than that the main program of the Social Democrats, the welfare state, came to be accepted by even the conservative parties [of northwestern Europe], even if begrudgingly.[22]

I now return to the original essay.)

The calculations with the incalculable dream of communism are concealed in many passages of the later Marx, the most memorable being the long paragraph at the end of the chapter entitled "The Illusion Created by Competition" in *Capital,* vol. 3, where, in a series of five massive "ifs" (the rhetorical bulwark of the element of calculation), Marx comes to the conclusion: "*[T]hen* nothing of these [capitalist] forms remains, but simply those foundations of the forms that are common to all social modes of production."[23] If, if, if, if, if. The line between "democratic" capitalism and democratic socialism is here being undone, with a certain set of impossible conditions. Persistent critique is being replaced by blueprint. The new immigrant ideologue today

acts out the impossibility of that blueprint. It is in the face of that impossibility that she must persistently investigate the possibility of the push from democratic capitalism into a globally responsible democratic socialism, the only struggle that fits the post-Soviet scene.[24] It is no secret that, in the developing countries, it is the forces of feminist activism and the non-Eurocentric ecology movement that are attempting to regenerate the critical element into that dream of displacement from capitalism to socialism. Ethnicity, striking at the very heart of identity, is the incalculable and mystical principle that is open for the "most perverse calculation" in that larger field. The role and agency of the U.S.-based marginal movement and its claims to ethnicity are therefore up for reinvention. That is indeed my theme. But by sounding this motif too soon, I am short-circuiting into my second movement, where I will speak of educating the educators. Let us return to the undergraduate classroom.

In spite of our commonsense estimation of the best-case scenario, national-origin validation in the general multicultural classroom remains crucially important, *for* the various national origins, if only to undermine the symbolic importance, all out of proportion to its content and duration, of the test in American history and civilization administered by the Immigration and Naturalization Services (INS) for new citizens, which establishes that, from now on, the history of the racial dominant in the United States is the migrant's own.

I have already suggested that the place of women within the desire for justice under capitalism may be different. Amy Tan's controversial *Joy Luck Club* animates this difference in every possible way.[25] The competitive difference among marginal groups, the difference between economic migration (to the United States) and political exile (in China), the necessity and impossibility of the representation of the "culture of origin," culture as negotiable systems of representation between mothers and daughters, the role of the university and corporatism in "moving West to reach the East" (*JLC* 205), the extreme ungroundedness of identity in the obsessive pursuit of perspectives, all thematized in this first novel, can be used for political pedagogy in the invention of unity.

---

[22]Immanuel Wallerstein et al., *Antisystemic Movements* (New York: Verso, 1989), 32, 34–35.

[23]Karl Marx, *Capital,* tr. David Fernbach (New York: Vintage, 1981), 3:1015–16.

[24]For the argument that socialism and capitalism are each other's *différance,* see Spivak, "Supplementing Marxism," in Steven Cullenberg and Bernd Magnus, eds., *Whither Marxism?* (New York: Routledge, 1995).

[25]Amy Tan, *The Joy Luck Club* (New York: Ivy Books, 1989). Hereafter cited in the text as *JLC,* followed by the page number(s). For specific criticism of this text and other "ethnic minority" texts from specific ethnic groups, see my description of the liberal multiculturalist classroom above. By contrast, I am speaking of the text's witnessing to the U.S. commonality of the migrant, "the same difference."

Let me indicate the inaugural staging of the economic argument, rehearsed many times in the novel:

> After everybody votes unanimously for the Canada gold stock, I go into the kitchen to ask Auntie An-mei why the Joy Luck Club started investing in stocks. . . . "We got smart. Now we can all win and lose equally. We can have stock market luck. And we can play mah jong for fun, just for a few dollars, winner take all. Losers take home left-overs! So everyone can have some joy. Smart-hanh?" (*JLC* 18)

Contrast this egalitarian "joy luck" by way of investment to the original Joy Luck Club, four women attempting to contain political exile by force of spirit. This is the frame-narrator remembering the reminiscence of her recently dead mother. The women are refugees from the Japanese, in Kweilin:

> I knew which women I wanted to ask. They were all young like me, with wishful faces. . . . Each week we could forget past wrongs done to us. We weren't allowed to think a bad thought. We feasted, we laughed, we played games, lost and won, we told the best stories. And each week, we could hope to be lucky. That hope was our only joy. . . . I won tens of thousands of *yuan*. But I wasn't rich. No. By then paper money had become worthless. Even toilet paper was worth more. And that made us laugh harder, to think a thousand-*yuan* note wasn't even good enough to rub on our bottoms. (*JLC* 10, 12)

In this perspectivized field of identity, only the Polaroid produces the final ID. Here is the last scene of the novel, where the Chinese-American frame-narrator meets her long-lost Chinese half-sisters. No attempt is made to provide interior representations of their memories:

> I look at their faces again and I see no trace of my mother in them. Yet they still look familiar. . . . The flash of the Polaroid goes off and my father hands me the snapshot. . . . The gray-green surface changes to the bright colors of our three images, sharpening and deepening all at once. And although we don't speak, I know we all see it. Together we look like our mother. Her same eyes, her same mouth, open in surprise to see, at last, her long-cherished wish. (*JLC* 331, 332)

It is at her peril that the reader forgets the authoritative cherished wish that is given in the opening epigraphic tale:

> The old woman remembered a swan she had bought many years ago in Shanghai for a foolish sum. This bird, boasted the market vendor, was once a duck that stretched its neck in hopes of becoming a goose. . . . When she arrived in the new country, the immigration officials pulled her swan away from her, leaving the woman . . . with only one swanfeather for a memory. . . . For a long time now the woman had wanted to give her daughter the single swan feather and tell her, "This feather may look worthless, but it comes from afar and carries with it all my good intentions." And she waited, year after year, for the day she could tell her daughter this in perfect American English. (*JLC* 3–4)

Tan's risk-taking book offers us a timely concept-metaphor: the dead mother's voice achieves perfect American English in the regularizing graph of the Polaroid. It is left to us to decode the scandal with sympathy and responsibility.

The Earlier Scene

Since Reconstruction and the first major change in the Constitution after the Civil War, the various waves of immigrants have mingled with one of the supportive, original agents of the production of American origins: the African-American (not the Original Nations). But even here, the emphasis on assimilation given in the melting-pot theory followed the pattern of Anglocentrism first and a graduated *Euro*centrism next, with the lines of dominance radiating out of that presumptive center. Indeed, this is why the older immigrant elements in the multicultural classroom may or may not strengthen the undermining of the INS test, if the issue is the invention of unity rather than difference. This is the pedagogic imperative, the persuasive force-field of the classroom, to change the "may not" to "may," among the descendants of the older white immigrants, in the interest of a different unity. We are not disuniting America. If we are not aware of this as participating agents, the tremendous force of American ethnicity can be used in the service of consolidating the new world order out of the ashes of the Soviet Union, simply by recoding capitalism as democracy.

I have so far put aside the uprooting of the African and the redefining of the Original Nations in the interest of the new (and old) immigrants. Also to be placed here is the itinerary of the Chicano/Latino, unevenly straddling the history of two empires, the Spanish and the U.S., one on the cusp of the transition to capitalism, the other active today.

For me, an outsider who came to the United States in 1961, the voice that still echoes from the civil rights/black power movement is from the Ocean Hill–Brownsville School District Struggle of 1968.[26] I had received my Ph.D. the previous year. My own school days in India, a newly independent country attempting to decolonize its curriculum, were not far behind. Perhaps this is why words from that less famous struggle have been retained by the force of my memory. I am not even sure who it was that said them. It may have been the Reverend Galamaison: "This is a struggle against educational colonization." The other day I caught a voice on television, of an African-American woman who had been a student in that school district, now a mature woman who spoke of her experience and remarked: "We became Third World. We became international."

Let me propose what may at first sight seem odd: in the struggle against *internal* colonization, it is the African-American who is *post*colonial in the United States. To imply that postcoloniality is a step beyond colonialism is the new immigrant's reactive and unexamined disavowal of the move (however justified) away from the postcolonial scene to embrace the American dream—the civilizing mission of the new colonizing power. In its own context, postcoloniality is the achievement of an independence that removes the legal subject-status of a people as the result of struggle, armed or otherwise. In terms of internal colonization, the Emancipation, Reconstruction, and civil rights were just such an achievement. Furthermore, postcoloniality is no guarantee of prosperity for all but rather a signal for the consolidation of recolonization. In that respect as well, the condition of the African-American fits the general picture of postcoloniality much more accurately than the unearned claims of the Eurocentric well-placed migrant. Paradoxically, the rising racist backlash is an acknowledgment of this. In the so-called postcolonial countries, postcoloniality is not a signal for an end to struggle

but rather a shifting of the struggle to the persistent register of decolonization. Here, too, the situation of the African-American struggle offers a parallel. The second wave of backlash rage is on the rise. With an awareness of that register Joan Scott asks her astute question and makes her judgments in terms of class:

> [T]he special treatment that came with high social status never seems to have been seen as a compromise of university standards. (One has to wonder why it was that, for example, the test scores of blacks are stolen from the admissions office at Georgetown Law School and published by disgruntled conservatives, while those of alumni children of influential politicians were not. One can only conclude that the call for a return to a meritocracy that never was is a thinly veiled manifestation of racism.)[27]

I am claiming postcoloniality for the African-American, then, not because I want to interfere with her self-representation but because I want to correct the self-representation of the new immigrant academic as postcolonial, indeed as the source of postcolonial theory.

In terms of internal colonization in the United States, the original three groups have not emerged equally into postcoloniality. If I read the signs right (and I may not), the Latino/Chicano segment has, on one side, been moving for some time toward a recognition, in literary-cultural studies, of "our America" in the entire (North-Central-South) American continental context, not contained within *internal* U.S. colonization, as the African-American must be. The *différance* of unity and difference between African and African-American Pan-Africanism is the authoritative text here.[28] The Latino/Chicano move toward "our America" may be read as a move toward globality. This is particularly interesting today because, given U.S. economic policy toward Latin America, "illegal immigration," especially in the case of Mexico, *is* transnationality. *On that level*—the level of the subaltern *as* "illegal immigrant" un-

[26] The fact that this struggle did not mean the same thing for the Jewish and the black sectors of the district brings forth both the element of competition and the pedagogically negotiable epistemic space of the old immigrants that I have touched on above. These examples make clear that abstract talk of the politics of difference and different histories does not go too far unless we consider only the "white" as dominant. For details of the event, see Maurice R. Berube and Marilyn Gittell, eds., *Confrontation at Ocean Hill–Brownsville: The New York School Strikes of 1968* (New York: Praeger, 1969). For a testament on the continuing struggle in the field of black-Jewish unity, consider Thurgood Marshall's choice of Jack Greenberg in 1949 (Jack Greenberg, *Crusaders in the Courts: How a Dedicated Band of Lawyers Fought for the Civil Rights Revolution* [New York: Basic Books, 1994]).

[27] Scott, "Campaign," 36.
[28] For an account of the party debate on the internal colonization of the African-American, see Philip S. Foner and James S. Allen, eds., *American Communism and Black Americans: A Documentary History, 1919–1929* (Philadelphia: Temple University Press, 1986), vii–xvi, 163–201; and Philip S. Foner and Herbert Shapero, eds., *American Communism and Black Americans: A Documentary History, 1930–1934* (Philadelphia: Temple University Press, 1991), xi–xxix, 1–50, 93–107. I thank Brent Edwards for making these volumes known to me. The debate plays out the difference between Lenin's notion of (capitalist) territorial imperialism and Stalin's notion of (precapitalist) multinational empires in another setting.

der limited surveillance by the border patrol—the local *is* the global.[29] By contrast, specifically the Chicano engagement in the restoration of the major voices within internal colonization belongs within diasporic discourse studies.[30]

The thought of sublating internal colonization (another description of postcoloniality) is articulated differently in the context of the Original Nations.

At a recent conference on the literature of ethnicity, John Mohawk anguished that Native American writing was not yet stylistically competitive with the kind of sexy postmodernism that some of our best-known colleagues celebrate in the name of postcoloniality.[31] The embattled phrase "stylistically competitive" was not his. But I will use that phrase again before I end.

Since the Native American voice has been most rigorously marginalized even within marginality, I want to spend some time on the work of a Native American scholar, Jack D. Forbes, who is claiming a new unity with African-Americans. Unity in this sphere cannot be based on an initial, often disavowed, *choice* for justice under capitalism, as in the case of the new immigrants; but rather it must be based in the investigation of the institution of the so-called origins of the white-supremacist United States: a sublation of internal colonization.[32] Before making the claim to this divided unity, Forbes lays bare the mechanics of constructing another unity, in another political interest. He gets behind dictionaries to capture the elusive lexical space in-between meaning shifts, by sheer empirical obstinacy. He teases out usage to show the emergence of juridico-legal practice and rational classification. This is an invaluable quarry, on the level of aggregative apparatuses (power) and of propositions (knowledge), for a future Foucauldian who will dare to try to take these further below, into the utterables *(énoncés)* that form the archival ground-level (not ground) of knowledge and the nonsymbolizable force-field that shapes the shifting ground-levels of power.[33] I cannot readily imagine such a person, for the *pouvoir-savoir* (ability to make sense) in question involves

> 300 to 400 years of intermixture of a very complex sort, [and] varying amounts of African and American ancestry derived at different intervals and from extremely diverse sources—as from American nations as different as Narragansett or Pequot and the Carib or Arawak, or from African nations as diverse as the Mandinka, Yoruba, and Malagasy. *(BA* 270–71)

For the perceptive reader, then, Forbes's book at once opens the horizons of Foucault's work, shows the immense, indeed perhaps insuperable complexity of the task once we let go of "pure" European outlines, and encourages a new generation of scholars to acquire the daunting skills for robust cultural history. This work is rather different from the primitivist patronage of orality. It is in the context of this complexity that a new "unity" is claimed:

> In an article published in the *Journal of Negro History* [James Hugo] Johnston remarked: "Where the Negro was brought into contact with the American Indian the blood of the two races intermingled, the Indian has not disappeared from the land, but is now part of the Negro population of the United States." The latter statement might offend many Indians today, who still survive, of course, in great numbers as Native Americans, but nonetheless the significance of Johnston's thesis as regards the extent of Native American–African intermixture remains before us. *(BA* 191)

This point of view is to be contrasted with the persuasive and representative usual view of the substitution of one collective identity by another: that the Indian population dwindled, was exported, and was replaced by Africans and imported slaves

---

[29] On limited surveillance by the border patrol, see Michael Kearney, "Borders and Boundaries of State and Self at the End of Empire," *Journal of Historical Sociology* 4, no. 1 (March 1991): 52–74. Illegal immigration is so volatile a public issue in California that descriptive generalizations may become obsolete rather quickly.

[30] Diaspora and transnationality are investigated, respectively, in José Saldívar, *The Dialectics of Our America: Genealogy, Cultural Critique, and Literary History* (Durham, N.C.: Duke University Press, 1991), and *Border Matters* (Berkeley: University of California Press, forthcoming). For an appropriately gendered perspective, see Jean Franco, *Border Patrol* (Cambridge. Mass.: Harvard University Press, forthcoming).

[31] With texts such as Leslie Silko, *Almanac of the Dead* (New York: Simon and Schuster, 1991), and the work of younger writers like Drew Taylor, such anguish seems slightly anachronistic as I revise, although it is still appropriate in the larger context.

[32] Jack D. Forbes, *Black Africans and Native Americans: Color, Race and Caste in the Evolution of Red Black Peoples* (New York: Blackwell, 1988). Hereafter cited in the text as *BA,* followed by the page number(s).

[33] It would, for example, be interesting to play this narrative in counterpoint with Hortense Spillers, "The Tragic Mulatta," in Elizabeth A. Meese and Alice Parker, eds., *The Difference Within: Feminism and Critical Theory* (Amsterdam: John Benjamin, 1989), or with the more extensive work in Deborah E. McDowell and Arnold Rampersad, eds., *Slavery and the Literary Imagination: Selected Papers from the English Institute, 1987* (Baltimore: Johns Hopkins University Press, 1989). Since this is a slightly idiosyncratic reading of Foucault, I am obliged to cite my own "More on Power/Knowledge," in Spivak, *Outside,* 25–95.

from the West Indies.[34] It is in the pores of such identity-based arguments that Forbes discovers the survival of the Native American, in the male and female line. By focusing on the vast heterogeneity and textuality of the description of mixed groups, Forbes shows that the emergence of the "other," as the other of the white, may be, at best, an unwitting legitimation by reversal of the very dominant positions it is supposed to contest. My argument thus is a corollary of Forbes's. Forbes points out what we caricature by defining ourselves as the "other (of the white dominant in metropolitan space)": "It would appear that both Americans and Africans began to appear in exotic pageants and entertainments staged in London during the seventeenth century. It is not always possible to clearly ascertain the ethnicity of the performers, since Africans were sometimes dressed up as Americans, or perhaps vice versa" (*BA* 56).

In the discontinuous narrative of the development of racism, how are we to compute the relationship between that usage and the 1854 California State Supreme Court statement that "expresses a strong tendency in the history of the United States, a tendency to identify two broad classes of people: white and non-white, citizen and non-citizen (or semi-citizen)" (*BA* 65)? Are we, once again, to become complicit with this tendency by identifying ourselves, single ethnic group by group, or as migrant collectivity, only as the "other" of the white dominant? Shall we, "like so many Europeans, [remain] utterly transfixed by the black-white nexus either as 'opposites' or as real people" (*BA* 172)? Given that, in the literally postcolonial areas like Algeria or India, white racism is no longer the chief problem, Forbes's historical reasoning is yet another way of bringing together the intuitions of global resistance.[35]

Yet even in this work, where isolationist concerns broaden out into the global decolonization of scholarship, one must note the absence of a feminist impulse. The Native American woman, being legally free, was often the enslaved man's access to "freedom" in the United States. And slavery itself is "matrilineal." These two facts provide the motor for a great deal of Forbes's narrative of interaction. Yet *Black Africans and Native Americans,* so resourceful and imaginative in probing the pores of the hide of history, never questions the gender secrets hidden in them. It is correctly mentioned that Native American practices included the thought of "individual freedom and utopian socialism" (*BA* 266). But it is not noticed that there is feminism in those practices as well. What is it to define as "free"—*after* enslavement, genocide, colonization, theft of land, and tax-imposition—women who had, before these acts (masquerading today as social cohesion), been culturally inscribed as "freer"? What is it to become, then, a passageway to freedom after the fact? What is the "meaning" of matrilineage-in-slavery, mentioned in parentheses—"(generally slavery was inherited in the female line)" (*BA* 240)—where lineage itself is devastated?[36]

The Global Field/Transnational Literacy on the Graduate Curriculum

With the name of "woman" I pass from "access to the universal" into "the global field" of uneven decolonization and make an appeal to decolonize feminism as it studies feminism in decolonization. With plenty of help from feminist historians and social scientists, I teach myself to teach a course entitled "Feminism in Decolonization." From personal experience, then, I know how much education an educator (in this case myself) needs in this venture. "Feminism in Decolonization" is a political re-writing of the title "Women in Development." I am encouraged to see that a critique of the metropolitan feminist focus on women in development is one of the main premises of the piece by Aihwa Ong that I have already cited. This gives me an opportunity to recite once again that, in this effort, we have to *learn* interdisciplinary teaching by supplementing our work with that of the social scientists, and supplementing theirs with ours.

It is through the literature of ethnicity that we customarily approach the question of globality within literary-cultural studies when they are defined along humanist disciplinary lines. The Greek-English Lexicon tells us that the word *ethnos* meant "a number of people accustomed to live together"—one's *own* kind of people, in other words—and therefore, after Homer, "nation." Side-by-side with the

---

[34] This argument is generally present in extant scholarship. For a random and superior example, I offer Russell R. Menard, "The Africanization of the Lowcountry Labor Force, 1670–1730," in Winthrop D. Jordan and Sheila L. Skemp, eds., *Race and Family in the Colonial South* (Jackson: University Press of Mississippi, 1987), 81–108.

[35] Contrary to some established opinion, Forbes makes a convincing case that the crucial descriptive *mulat(t)o* is a displacement of the Arabic *muwallad-maula* (*BA* 141–42). The importance of Islam in discussions of imperial formations is illustrated here from below as elsewhere from above. For the general reader, the sourcebooks are Samir Amin, *Unequal Development: An Essay on the Social Formations of Peripheral Capitalism,* tr. Brian Pearce (Boston: Monthly Review Press, 1976), and the last chapter of Perry Anderson, *Lineages of the Absolutist State* (London: New Left Books, 1974). To this must now be added Jan Nederveen Pieterse, *Empire and Emancipation: Power and Liberation on a World Scale* (New York: Praeger, 1989).

[36] The portions on Forbes are excerpted from Gayatri Spivak, "Race before Racism and the Disappearance of the American," *Plantation Society* 3, no. 2 (summer 93): 73–91.

Greek word *ethnos* was the word *ethnikos*—other people, often taken to mean "heathen, pagan, foreign." It is not hard to see how the New Testament would use these already available words to mean "all but Jews and Christians." Like many ideas belonging to Christianity, these words were pressed into pejorative service in English, to mean "other (lesser) peoples," in the Age of Conquest. In the nineteenth century, as conquest consolidated itself into imperialism, the word becomes "scientific," especially in the forms "ethnography" and "ethnology." We are aware of the debates between the British ethnologist-ethnographers, on the one hand, and anthropologists, on the other, as to whether their study should be based on language or on physical characteristics. In any event, the discipline concerned itself, of course, with ideas of race, culture, and religion. The connections between *national* origin and "ethnicity" are, at best, dubious and, at worst, a site of violent contestation. In the cultural politics of the United States, they are now firmly in place without question.

I think the literature of ethnicity writes itself between *ethnos*—a writer writing for her *own* people (whatever that means) without deliberated self-identification as such—and *ethnikos,* the pejoratively defined other reversing the charge, (de)anthropologizing herself by separating herself into a staged identity. The literature of ethnicity in this second sense thus carries, paradoxically, the writer's signature as divided against itself, for the staging of the displacing of the dominant must somehow be indexed there. A woman's relationship to a patriarchal or patriarchalized ethnicity makes her access to this signature even more complex.

The standard world-system estimation of ethnicity, not unrelated to the failures of systemic communism, is something like the following: "Seen in long historical time and broad world space, [nations and ethnic groups] fade into one another, becoming only 'groups.' Seen in short historical time and narrow world space, they become clearly defined and so form distinctive structures." [37] Although I am in general sympathy with the resistance to "the intellectual pressure to reify groups," I cannot work with this world-system view of ethnicities in globality. The long view and the broad space are so perspectivized that to learn to acquire them in order to produce correct descriptions may be useful only if supplemented unceasingly, not just by way of the popular U.S. T-shirt slogan, "Think globally act locally," although it is not bad for a start.

Sublimation (and what Lacan calls the symbolic circuit) stands over against what Freud represents as cultural-ethical pathogenic repressions that may be represented as movements against the individual or social-psychic system. On the literary-critical side, Fredric Jameson represents such representations. And therefore he has been reading Third World literature for some time now as *allegories* of transnational capitalism. It is because I agree with Jameson in a general way that I would like to insist here upon a different definition of allegory, one that sees it as not just a symbolic order of semiosis. Otherwise, caught between accusations of political correctness and liberal multiculturalism, we are denied the right to say, "Heresy by itself is no token of truth." [38]

I take as my motto the opening words of *Abarodh-bāshini* (Lady-Prisoner), a critique of veiled female life published by Rokeya Sakhawat Hossain, an Indian Muslim woman, between 1915 and 1917. She shows that not only the signature of the writer of ethnicity, but also the signature of the patriarchally imprisoned woman, is self-separated: "We have become habituated after living for so long in prison; therefore, against the prison we, especially I myself, have nothing to say. If the fishwife is asked, 'Is the stink of rotten fish good or bad?' what will she respond? Here I will make a gift of a few of our personal experiences to our reader-sisters, and I hope they will be pleased." [39]

Hossain allows me to produce a more responsible sense of allegory: the fishwife-as-feminist who, like Hossain, admits to being unable to distance herself from her own imprisonment, "admits," in other words, "to the impossibility of reading [her] own text, . . ." and can only produce, as she herself says, fragmentary instances "against the inherent logic which animate[s] the development of the narrative [of imprisonment], and disarticulates it in a way that seems perverse." [40] On that model, since *we* are imprisoned in and habituated to capitalism, we might try to look at the *allegory* of capitalism not in terms of capitalism as the source of authoritative reference but in terms of the constant small failures in and interruptions to its logic, which help to recode it and produce our unity. "Allegory" here "speaks out with the referential efficacy of a praxis."

Learning this *praxis* that may produce interruptions to capitalism from within requires us to make future educators in the humanities transnationally literate, so that they can distinguish between the varieties of decolonization on the agenda, rather than collapse them as "postcoloniality." I am

[37] Wallerstein, *Antisystemic Movements,* 21; the following phrase is on 20.

[38] Marcuse, "Repressive Tolerance," 91.

[39] Begum Rokeya Sakhawat Hossain, *Abarodh-bāshini,* in *Rokeya-achanābali* (Dhaka: Bangla Akademi, 1984), 473; translation mine.

[40] Paul de Man, *Allegories of Reading: Figural Language in Rousseau, Nietzsche, Rilke, and Proust* (New Haven: Yale University Press, 1979), 205; the following phrase is from 208-9.

speaking of transnational *literacy*. We must remember that to achieve literacy in a language is not to become an expert in it. I am therefore not making an impossible demand upon the graduate curriculum. Literacy produces the skill to differentiate between letters, so that an articulated script can be read, reread, written, rewritten. Literacy is poison as well as medicine. It allows us to sense that the other is not just a "voice"—others also produce articulated texts, even as they, like us, are written in and by a text not of our own making. It is through transnational literacy that we can invent grounds for an interruptive praxis from within our disavowed hope in justice under capitalism.

If we were transnationally literate, we might read sectors that are stylistically noncompetitive with the spectacular experimental fiction of certain sections of hybridity or postcoloniality with a disarticulating rather than a comparative point of view. Native American fiction would then allegorically intervene in reminding us of the economic peripheralization of the originary, communist, precapitalist ethnicities of the Fourth World. We can link it to the fact that, even as we admire the sophistication of Indian writing in English, we have not yet seen a non-Christian *tribal* Indo-Anglican fiction writer in English.[41] And we will also discover that all stylistically noncompetitive literature cannot be relegated to the same transnational allegory in the crude sense.

Take, for example, the case of Bangladesh. You will hardly ever find an entry from Bangladesh in a course on postcolonial or Third World literature. Its literature is stylistically noncompetitive on the international market. The UN has written it off as the lowest on its list of developing countries, its women at the lowest rung of development. Our students will not know that, as a result of decolonization from the British in 1947 and liberation from West Pakistan in 1971, Bangladesh had to go through a double decolonization; that as a result of the appropriation of its language by the primarily Hindu Bengali nationalists in the nineteenth century, and the adherence of upper-class Bangladeshis to Arabic and Urdu, the Bangladeshis have to win back their language inch by inch. Some of this may be gleaned from Naila Kabeer's essay on Bangladesh in Deniz Kandiyoti's *Women, Islam, and the State*.[42] But apart from a rather mysterious paragraph on "progressive

non-government organizations" that would be incomprehensible to most graduate students of modern languages, there is no mention of the fact that, because of the timing and manner of Bangladesh's liberation, the country fell into the clutches of the transnational global economy in a way significantly different from the situation of both the Asia-Pacific *and* the older postcolonial countries.[43] The transnationally illiterate student might not know that the worst victim of the play of the multinational pharmaceuticals in the name of population control is the woman's body; that in the name of development, international monetary organizations are substituting the impersonal and incomprehensible state for the older, more recognizable enemies-cum-protectors (the patriarchal family), a process broadly comparable, in women's history, to the transition from feudalism to capitalism.[44] In this situation, the most dynamic minds are engaged in alternative development work, not literary production. And class-fixed literary production as such in Bangladesh is concerned not with the place of the nation in transnationality but rather with a nation-fixed view that does not produce the energy of translation.[45]

About twelve years ago, in an essay that was refused entry into the Norton Critical Edition of *Jane Eyre* because it was allegedly too oppositional, I wrote these words:

> A full literary reinscription cannot easily flourish in the imperialist fracture or discontinuity, covered over by an alien legal system masquerading as Law as such, an alien ideology established as only Truth, and a set of human sciences busy establishing the "native" as self-consolidating Other. . . . To reopen the fracture without succumbing to a nostalgia for lost origins, the literary critic must turn to the archives of imperial governance.[46]

Over the last decade, I have painfully learned that literary reinscription cannot easily flourish, not only in the inaugura-

---

[41] Here I refer the reader to a more extended discussion of the cultural politics of Indian writing in English in Gayatri Spivak, "How to Teach a 'Culturally Different' Book," in Peter Hulme, ed., *Colonial Discourse/Postcolonial Theory* (Manchester: University of Manchester Press, 1994).

[42] Naila Kabeer, "The Quest for National Identity: Women, Islam and the State in Bangladesh," in Deniz Kandiyoti, ed., *Women, Islam, and the State* (Philadelphia: Temple University Press, 1991), 115–43; the quoted phrase is on 138.

[43] For a convenient description of the qualitative change in global exploitation to manage the recession of 1973, see David Harvey, *The Condition of Postmodernity: An Enquiry into the Origins of Cultural Change* (Cambridge: Blackwell, 1989), 141–72.

[44] Woman's position within the patriarchal family as a feudal mode of production has been argued forcefully by Harriet Fraad et al., in *Bringing It All Back Home: Class, Gender and Power in the Household Today* (London: Pluto Press, 1994).

[45] A striking exception is the poetry of Farhad Mazhar. A selection will be available in my translation, forthcoming from *Third Text*.

[46] Gayatri Spivak, "Three Women's Texts and a Critique of Imperialism," in Henry Louis Gates Jr., ed., *Race, Writing, and Difference* (Chicago: University of Chicago Press, 1986), 272.

tion of imperialism but also in the discontinuity of recolonization. The literary critic and educator must acquire and transmit transnational literacy in a system that must be allegorized by its failures. There is a mad scramble on among highly placed intellectuals to establish their "colonial origins" these days. Such efforts belong with the impatience of world-systems literary theory, with portmanteau theories of post-coloniality, with the isolationism of both multiculturalism and antiracism; they cannot keep the fracture or wound open. This is the infinite responsibility of the emergent dominant engaged in graduate education in the humanities. Otherwise we side with the sanctimonious pronouncement of a Lynn Cheney: of course I support multicultural education; I want each child to know that he can succeed.[47] Woodrow Wilson had, I believe, suggested at some point that he wanted each American to be a captain of industry! Faith in capitalism gone mad in the name of individualism and competition.

Over against this superindividualist faith, let me quote the *Declaration of Comilla* (1989), drawn up in Bangladesh, by the Feminist International Network of Resistance to Reproductive and Genetic Engineering, under the auspices of UBINIG, a Bangladesh development-alternative collective, proposing once again an interruptive literate practice within development:

> We live in a limited world. In the effort to realise [the] illusion [of unlimited progress leading to unlimited growth] within a limited world, it is necessary that some people [be] exploited so that others can grow; Woman is exploited so that Man can grow; South is exploited so that North can grow; Animals are exploited so that people can grow! The Good Life of some is always at the expense of others. Health of some is based on the disease of others. Fertility of some is based on the infertility of others. . . . What is good for the ruling class should be good for everybody![48]

I can just hear world-system theorists murmuring, "moralism." But then, the unexamined moralism of liberal multiculturalism allows us to forget these women's admonition. Like the fishwife, we cannot tell if the stink of rotten fish is good or bad when we disavow our own part or hope in U.S. capitalism.

I heard a colleague say recently, only half in jest, that the newest criticism no longer considered the "literary" part

of literature to be that important. On the contrary. We expand the definition of literature to include social inscription. Farida Akhter intervening angrily against "the agenda of developing countries enforcing population policies on others" at the third plenary of the World Women's Congress for a Healthy Planet on November 11, 1991, has something like a relationship with the absence of classy postcolonial women's literary texts from Bangladesh on the U.S. curriculum. If those of us who write dissertations and teach future teachers still peddle something called "culture" on the model of national-origin validation (crucial to the general *undergraduate* curriculum), we have failed to grasp the moment of the emerging dominant, to rend time with the urgency of justice. Indeed, in the era of global capital rampant, it is the new immigrant intellectual's negotiable nationality that might act as a lever to undo the nation-based conflict that killed the Second International.

Conclusion

I close with two passages I often quote these days, from Assia Djebar's novel *Fantasia.*[49] Algeria, like India, is an older postcolonial state. The old modes of decolonization at the time of national liberation are crumbling in both. Transnational literacy allows us to recognize that we hear a different *kind* of voice from these countries, especially from singular women, from Mahasweta Devi, from Assia Djebar.

In the case of Djebar, that crumbling can be staged as a profound critique of Fanon's false hopes for unveiling in *A Dying Colonialism.* Here are Fanon's famous words: "There is the much discussed status of the Algerian woman . . . today . . . receiving the only valid challenge: the experience of revolution. Algerian woman's ardent love of the home is not a limit imposed by the universe. . . . Algerian society reveals itself not to be the woman-less society that had been so convincingly described."[50]

And here is Djebar, in *Fantasia.* Staging herself as an Algerian Muslim woman denied access to classical Arabic, she gives a fragmented version of the graphing of her bio in French, of which I quote the following fragments:

> The overlay of my oral culture wearing dangerously thin . . . Writing of the most anodyne of

[47] Discussion with National Press Club, broadcast on CSPAN, September 28, 1991.

[48] *Declaration of Comilla* (Dhaka: UBINIG, 1991), xiii.

[49] Assia Djebar, *Fantasia: An Algerian Cavalcade,* tr. Dorothy S. Blair (New York: Quartet Books, 1985); translation modified in all cited passages; hereafter cited in the text as *F,* followed by page number(s). This concluding passage is a modified version of the opening of "Acting Bits/Identity Talk," *Critical Inquiry* 28, no. 4 (summer 1992): 770–803.

[50] Frantz Fanon, *A Dying Colonialism,* tr. Haakan Chevalier (New York: Grove Weidenfeld, 1965), 65–66, 67.

childhood memories leads back to a body bereft of voice. To attempt an autobiography in French words alone is to show more than its skin under the slow scalpel of a live autopsy. Its flesh peels off and with it, seemingly, the speaking of childhood which can no longer be written is torn to shreds. Wounds are reopened, veins weep, the blood of the self flows and that of others, a blood which has never dried. (*F* 156, 178)

Identity is here exposed as a wound, exposed by the historically hegemonic imperial languages, for those who have learned the double-binding "practice of [their] writing" (*F* 181). This double-bind, felt by feminists *in* decolonizing countries rather than in Eurocentric economic migration, is not ours. The wound of our split identity is not this specific wound, for this wound is not necessarily, indeed rarely, opened by a hope in Anglo-U.S.-EEC–based capitalism.

One of the major motifs of *Fantasia* is a meditation upon the possibility that to achieve autobiography in the double-bind of the practice of the conqueror's writing is not for the well-placed marginal to "tell her own story," but to learn, to learn to be taken seriously by the gendered subaltern, the woman in radical disenfranchisement, who has not had the chance to master that practice. And therefore, hidden in the many-sectioned third part of the book, there is the single episode where the central character speaks in the ethical singularity of the *tu-toi* to Zohra, an eighty-year-old rural *muj hida* (female freedom fighter) who has been devastated both by her participation in the nationalist struggle and by the neglect of woman's claims in decolonized Algeria. The achievement of the autobiographer-in-fiction is to be fully fledged as a storyteller to this intimate interlocutor. Telling one's own story is not the continuist imperative of identity upon the privileged feminist in decolonization.

Rokeya Sakhawat Hossain, an upper-class Indian woman, had not kept a journal, but spoke as the fishwife. Djebar's French-educated heroine attempts to animate the story of two nineteenth-century Algerian prostitutes, Fatma and Meriem, allegorically interrupting Eugène Fromentin's *Un été au Sahara,* a masterpiece of Orientalism. She succeeds, for Zohra's curiosity flares up: " 'And Fatma? And Meriem?' Lla Zhora interrupted, catching herself following the story as if it were a legend recounted by a bard. 'Where did you hear this story?' she went on, impatiently." The "I" (now at last articulated because related and responsible to "you") replies simply: " 'I read it!' I retorted. 'An eyewitness told it to a friend who wrote it down' " (*F* 166).

This unemphatic short section ends simply: "I, your cousin, translate this account into the mother tongue, and re-

port it to you. So I try my self out, as ephemeral teller, close to you little mother, in front of your vegetable patch" (*F* 167). The central character shares her mother-tongue as instrument of translation with the other woman.

In the rift of this divided field of identity, the tale shared in the mother-tongue forever interrupts (in every act of reading) and is forever absent, for it is in the mother tongue. The authority of the "now" inaugurates this absent autobiography in every "here" of the book: the fleeting framed moment undoes the "blank [*blanc*] in the memory" of the narrator's *personal* childhood, which only yields the image of an old crone whose muttered Qur'anic curses could not be understood (*F* 10).

The final movement of *Fantasia* is in three short bits, what remains of an autobiography when it has been unraveled strand by strand. First a tribute to Pauline Rolland, the French revolutionary of 1848, exiled in Algeria, as the true ancestress of the *mujāhidāt.*[51] Revolutionary discourse for women cannot rely upon indigenous cultural production. If the tale told to Zohra is a divided moment of access to autobiography as the telling of an absent story, here autobiography is the possibility of writing or giving writing to the other identifiable only as a mutilated metonym of violence, as part object. The interrupted continuous source is, once again, Eugène Fromentin. There is one unexplained Arabic word in the following passage, a word that means, in fact, pen:

> Eugène Fromentin offers me an unexpected hand—the hand of an unknown woman he was never able to draw. He describes in sinister detail: as he is leaving the oasis which six months after the massacre is still filled with its stench, Fromentin picks up out of the dust the severed hand of an anonymous Algerian woman. He throws it down again in his path. Later, I seize on this living hand, hand of mutilation and of memory, and I attempt to bring it the *qalam.* (*F* 226)

Everything in this essay has been a meditation upon the possibility that, at this divided moment, we not only should work mightily to take up the pen in our own hands but should also attempt to pick up the *qalam* offered us in uneven decolonization and, with the help of our Polaroid, attempt to figure forth the world's broken and shifting alphabet.

---

[51] It would be interesting to work out the itinerary of Rolland's exile from the energetic analysis of 1848 by Marx, "The Eighteenth Brumaire of Louis Bonaparte," in *Surveys from Exile,* tr. Ben Fowkes (New York: Vintage Books, 1974), 143–249.

Ernesto Laclau

b. 1935

The work of political philosopher Ernesto Laclau, educated in Argentina and England, has for two decades concentrated on an interconnected set of problems concerning hegemony, socialism, and democracy. His best-known work, coauthored with Chantal Mouffe, *Hegemony and Socialist Strategy: Towards a Radical Democratic Politics* (1985), employs the work of Antonio Gramsci (above, page 936) as an instrument to open a radical reexamination of current political options. Laclau's distinctive dialectical style, tough and rigorous, typically eschews the discussion of current themes and topics as already settled, in axiological terms, to work through the logic of political desires and strategies. He frequently has recourse, in this connection, to the example of Peronist Argentina, where he finds very rich and sobering analogues to the circumstances of postmodern politics in the North Atlantic nations (and elsewhere). In particular, Laclau has argued forcefully (as in the selection reprinted here) that political conceptualizations depend fundamentally on a universal/particular dialectic—but with the difference that in the political domain, the universal turns out to be empty, even as it is inescapable. In the context of contemporary critiques of the Enlightenment since the early work of Horkheimer and Adorno (above, page 1101), and subsequent objections to "essentialism" as potential instruments of political oppression, Laclau points out the deep paradoxes that emerge when a culture commits itself to a respect for difference, only to find that all differences tend to become equivalent, with no real possibility for achieving or expressing an imagined cultural or ethnic identity. This is especially true in cases such as Argentinian Perónism, where Perón as idea returns from exile "not as an empty signifier but as the president of the country" who had to carry out specific policies—which led directly to the military dictatorship of 1976. In a similar way, Laclau shows how the apparently comforting logic of difference in contemporary models of multiculturalism or assertions of the universal right of nations to self-determination enact the same logic that can lead to genocide on the one hand, and apartheid on the other. Such paradoxes, moreover, exhibit hegemonic situations between particular claims and some universal principle, in which the activity of opposition alone is insufficient protection. This requires not only a rethinking of the relation between particular and universal, but a reconsideration of "hegemony" along Gramscian lines, so as not to lose sight of the practical reality of political policy. As Laclau puts it in the conclusion of the essay reprinted here, the particular (whether a group or an individual) "can only fully realize itself if it constantly keeps open, and constantly redefines, its relation to the universal."

Laclau's major works include: *Politics and Ideology in Marxist Theory: Capitalism, Fascism, Populism* (1979); *Hegemony and Socialist Strategy: Towards a Radical Democratic Politics,* with Chantal Mouffe (1985); *New Reflections on the Revolution of Our Time* (1990); *The Making of Political Identities,* as editor (1994); and *Emancipation(s)* (1996). See especially *Contingency, Hegemony, Universality: Contemporary Dialogues on the Left,* with Judith Butler and Slavoj Žižek (2000).

Subject of Politics, Politics of the Subject

The question of the relationship (complementarity? tension? mutual exclusion?) between universalism and particularism occupies a central place on the current political and theoretical agenda. Universal values are seen either as dead or—at the very least—as threatened. What is more important, the positive character of those values is no longer taken for granted. On the one hand, under the banner of multiculturalism, the classical values of the Enlightenment are under fire, and considered as little more than the cultural preserve of Western imperialism. On the other hand, the whole debate concerning the end of modernity, the assault on foundationalism in its various expressions, has tended to establish an essential link between the obsolete notion of a ground of history and society, and the *actual contents* which, from the Enlightenment onwards, have played that role of ground. It is important, however, to realize that these two debates have not advanced along symmetrical lines, that argumentative strategies have tended to move from one to the other in unexpected ways, and that many apparently paradoxical combinations have been shown to be possible. Thus, the so-called postmodern approaches can be seen as weakening the imperialist foundationalism of Western Enlightenment and opening the way to a more democratic cultural pluralism; but they can also be perceived as underpinning a notion of 'weak' identity which is incompatible with the strong cultural attachments required by a 'politics of authenticity.' And universal values can be seen as a strong assertion of the 'ethnia of the West' (as in the later Husserl[1]), but also as a way of fostering—at least tendentially—an attitude of respect and tolerance *vis-à-vis* cultural diversity.

It would certainly be a mistake to think that concepts such as 'universal' and 'particular' have exactly the same meaning in both debates; but it would also be mistaken to assume that the continuous interaction of both debates has had no effect on the central categories of each. This interaction has given way to ambiguities and displacements of meaning which are—I think—the source of a certain political productivity. It is to these displacements and interactions that I want to refer in this essay. My question, put in its simplest terms, is

the following: what happens with the categories of 'universal' and 'particular' once they become tools in the language games that shape contemporary politics? What is performed through them? What displacements of meaning are at the root of their current political productivity?

Multiculturalism

Let us take both debates successively and see the points in which each cuts across the central categories of the other. Multiculturalism first. The question can be formulated in these terms: is a pure culture of difference possible, a pure particularism which does away entirely with any kind of universal principle? There are various reasons to doubt that this is possible. In the first place, to assert a purely separate and differential identity is to assert that this identity is constituted *through* cultural pluralism and difference. There is no way that a particular group living in a wider community can live a monadic existence—on the contrary, part of the definition of its own identity is the construction of a complex and elaborated system of relations with other groups. And these relations will have to be regulated by norms and principles which transcend the particularism of *any* group. To assert, for instance, the right of all ethnic groups to cultural autonomy is to make an argumentative claim which can only be justified on universal grounds. The assertion of one's own particularity requires the appeal of something transcending it. The more particular a group is, the less it will be able to control the global communitarian terrain within which it operates, and the more universally grounded will have to be the justification of its claims.

But there is another reason why a politics of pure difference would be self-defeating. To assert one's own *differential* identity involves, as we have just argued, the inclusion in that identity of the other, as that from whom one delimits oneself. But it is easy to see that a fully achieved differential identity would involve the sanctioning of the existing *status quo* in the relation between groups. For an identity which is purely differential *vis-à-vis* other groups has to assert the identity of the other at the same time as its own and, as a result, cannot have identity claims in relation to those other groups. Let us suppose that a group *has* such claims—for instance, the demand for equal opportunities in employment and education, or even the right to have confessional schools. In so far as these are claims presented as rights that I share as a member of the community with all other groups, they presuppose that I am not simply different from the others but, in some fundamental respects, equal to them. If it is asserted that all particular groups have the right to respect of their own particularity, this means that they are

"Subject of Politics, Politics of the Subject" was first delivered as a lecture in 1995 at the University of Hawaii, subsequently published in *Differences* 7.1, Spring 1995. It is reprinted here from chapter 4 (complete) in Ernesto Laclau, *Emancipation(s)* (London: Verso, 1996).
[1] Husserl (above, page 770).

equal to each other in some ways. Only in a situation in which all groups were different from each other, and in which none of them wanted to be anything other than what they are, would the pure logic of difference exclusively govern the relations between groups. In all other scenarios the logic of difference will be interrupted by a logic of equivalence and equality. It is not for nothing that a pure logic of difference—the notion of separate developments—lies at the root of apartheid.

This is the reason why the struggle of *any* group that attempts to assert its own identity against a hostile environment is always confronted by two opposite but symmetrical dangers for which there is no logical solution, no square circle—only precarious and contingent attempts of mediation. If the group tries to assert its identity *as it is at that moment,* as its location within the community at large is defined by the system of exclusions dictated by the dominant groups, it condemns itself to a perpetually marginalized and ghettoized existence. Its cultural values can be easily retrieved as 'folklore' by the establishment. If, on the other hand, it struggles to change its location within the community and to break with its situation of marginalization, it has to engage in a plurality of political initiatives which take it beyond the limits defining its present identity—for instance, struggles within the existing institutions. As these institutions are, however, ideologically and culturally moulded by the dominant groups, the danger is that the differential identity of the struggling group will be lost. Whether the new groups will manage to transform the institutions, or whether the logic of the institutions will manage to dilute—via co-option—the identity of those groups is something which, of course, cannot be decided beforehand and depends on a hegemonic struggle. But what is certain is that there is no major historical change in which the identity of *all* intervening forces is not transformed. There is no possibility of victory in terms of an *already acquired* cultural authenticity. The increasing awareness of this fact explains the centrality of the concept of 'hybridization' in contemporary debates.

If we look for an example of the early emergence of this alternative in European history, we can refer to the opposition between social-democrats and revolutionary syndicalists in the decades preceding the First World War. The classical Marxist solution to the problem of the disadjustment between the particularism of the working class and the universality of the task of socialist transformation had been the assumption of an increasing simplification of the social structure under capitalism: as a result, the working class as a homogeneous subject would embrace the vast majority of the population and could take up the task of universal trans-

formation. With this type of prognostic discredited at the turn of the century, two possible solutions remained open: either to accept a dispersion of democratic struggles only loosely unified by a semi-corporative working class, or to foster a politics of pure identity by a working class unified through revolutionary violence. The first road led to what has been depicted as social-democratic integration: the working class was co-opted by a State in whose management it participated but whose mechanisms it could not master. The second road led to working-class segregationism through violence and the rejection of all participation in democratic institutions. It is important to realize that the myth of the general strike in Sorel[2] was not a device to keep a purely working-class identity as a condition for a revolutionary victory. As the revolutionary strike was a regulative idea rather than an actual possible event, it was not a real strategy for the seizure of power: its function was exhausted in being a mechanism endlessly recreating the workers' separate identity. In the option between a politics of identity and the transformation of the relations of force between groups, Sorelianism can be seen as an extreme form of unilateralization of the first alternative.

If, however, we renounce a unilateral solution, then the tension between these two contradictory extremes cannot be eradicated: it is there to stay, and a strategic calculation can only consist of the pragmatic negotiations between them. Hybridization[3] is not a marginal phenomenon but the very terrain in which contemporary political identities are constructed. Let us just consider a formula such as 'strategic essentialism'[4] which has been much used lately. For a variety of reasons, I am not entirely satisfied with it, but it has the advantage of bringing to the fore the antinomic alternatives to which we have been referring and the need for a politically negotiated equilibrium between them. 'Essentialism' alludes to a strong identity politics, without which there can be no bases for political calculation and action. But that essentialism is only strategic—that is it points, at the very moment of its constitution, to its own contingency and its own limits.

This contingency is central to understanding what is perhaps the most prominent feature of contemporary poli-

---

[2] Georges Sorel (1847–1922), French socialist/syndicalist, an admirer of Lenin, who propounded a theory of "social myths" including the idea of a "general strike" as inspirations for progressive politics, coupled with a belief in the necessity of violent revolutionary action.

[3] See, for example, Homi K. Bhabha, *The Location of Culture* (1994).

[4] Cf., Gayatri Spivak, *The Spivak Reader* (1996); also *In Other Worlds: Essays in Cultural Politics* (1987). "Strategic essentialism" is the use of positivist essentialism for a specific political purpose. See also Rob Cover, "Strategic Subjects: The Sexual Binary, Transgression and the Ethics of Strategic Essentialism" in *Colloquy,* Issue six.

tics: the full recognition of the limited and fragmented character of its historical agents. Modernity started with the aspiration to a limitless historical actor, who would be able to ensure the fullness of a perfectly instituted social order. Whatever the road leading to that fullness—an 'invisible hand' which would hold together a multiplicity of disperse individual wills, or a universal class who would ensure a transparent and rational system of social relations—it always implied that the agents of that historical transformation would be able to overcome all particularism and all limitation and bring about a society reconciled with itself. That is what, for modernity, true universality meant. The starting point of contemporary social and political struggles is, on the contrary, the strong assertion of their particularity, the conviction that none of them is capable, on its own, of bringing about the fullness of the community. But precisely because of that, as we have seen, this particularity cannot be constructed through a pure 'politics of difference' but has to appeal, as the very condition of its own assertion, to universal principles. The question that at this point arises is to what extent this universality is the same as the universality of modernity, to what extent the very idea of a fullness of society experiences, in this changed political and intellectual climate, a radical mutation that—while maintaining the double reference to the universal and the particular—entirely transforms the logic of their articulation. Before answering this question, however, we have to move to our second debate, that related to the critique of foundationalism.

Contexts and the Critique of Foundationalism

Let us start our discussion with a very common proposition: that there is no truth or value independent of the context, that the validity of any statement is only contextually determined. In one sense, of course, this proposition is uncontroversial and a necessary corollary of the critique of foundationalism. To pass from it to assert the incommensurability of contexts and to draw from there an argument in defense of cultural pluralism seems to be only a logical move, and I am certainly not prepared to argue otherwise. There is, however, one difficulty that this whole reasoning does not contemplate, and it is the following: how to determine the limits of a context. Let us accept that all identity is a differential identity. In that case two consequences follow: (1) that, as in a Saussurean[5] *system*, each identity is what it is only through its differences from all the others; (2) that

the context has to be a closed one—if all identities depend on the differential *system*, unless the latter defines its own limits, no identity would be finally constituted. But nothing is more difficult—from a logical point of view—than defining those limits. If we had a foundational perspective we could appeal to an ultimate ground which would be the source of all differences; but if we are dealing with a true pluralism of differences, if the differences are *constitutive*, we cannot go, in the search for the systematic limits that define a context, beyond the differences themselves. Now, the only way of defining a context is, as we have said, through its limits, and the only way of defining those limits is to point out what is beyond them. But what is beyond the limits can only be other differences, and in that case—given the constitutive character of all differences—it is impossible to establish whether these new differences are internal or external to the context. The very possibility of a limit and, *ergo,* a context, is thus jeopardized.

As I have argued elsewhere, the only way out of this difficulty is to postulate a beyond which is not one more difference but something which poses a threat to (that is negates) all the differences within that context—or, better, that the context constitutes itself as such through the act of exclusion of something alien, of a radical otherness. Now, this possibility has three consequences which are capital for our argument:

1. The first is that antagonism and exclusion are constitutive of all identity. Without limits through which a (non-dialectical) negativity is constructed, we would have an indefinite dispersion of differences whose absence of systematic limits would make any differential identity impossible. But this very function of constituting differential identities through antagonistic limits is what, at the same time, destabilizes and subverts those differences. For if the limit poses an equal threat to all the differences, it makes them all equivalent to each other, interchangeable with each other as far as the limit is concerned. This already announces the possibility of a relative universalization through equivalential logics, which is not incompatible with a differential particularism, but is required by the very logic of the latter.

2. The system is what is required for the differential identities to be constituted, but the only thing—exclusion—which can constitute the system and thus make possible those identities, is also what subverts them. (In deconstructive terms: the conditions of possibility of the system are also its conditions of impossibility.) Contexts have to be internally subverted in order to become possible. The system (as in Jacques Lacan's[6] object *petit a*) is that which the very

---

[5] Saussure (above, page 786).

[6] Lacan (above, page 990).

logic of the context requires but which is, however, impossible. It is present, if you want, through its absence. But this means two things. First, that all differential identity will be constitutively split; it will be the crossing point between the logic of difference and the logic of equivalence. This introduces into it a radical undecidability. Second, that although the fullness and universality of society is unachievable, its need does not disappear: it will always show itself through the presence of its absence. Again, what we see announcing itself here is an intimate connection between the universal and the particular which does not consist, however, in the subsumption of the latter in the former.

3. Finally, if that impossible object—the system—cannot be represented but needs, however, to show itself within the field of representation, the means of that representation will be constitutively inadequate. Only the particulars are such means. As a result the systematicity of the system, the moment of its impossible totalization, will be symbolized by particulars which contingently assume such a representative function. This means, first, that the particularity of the particular is subverted by this function of representing the universal, but second, that a certain particular, by making its own particularity the signifying body of a universal representation, comes to occupy—within the system of differences as a whole—a hegemonic role. This anticipates our main conclusion: in a society (and this is finally the case of *any* society) in which its fullness—the moment of its universality—is unachievable, the relation between the universal and the particular is a hegemonic relation.

Let us see in more detail the logic of that relation. I will take as an example the 'universalization' of the popular symbols of Perónism[7] in the Argentina of the 1960s and 1970s. After the coup of 1955 which overthrew the Perónist regime, Argentina entered a period of institutional instability which lasted for over twenty years. Perónism and other popular organizations were proscribed, and the succession of military governments and fraudulent civilian regimes which occupied the government were clearly incapable of meeting the popular demands of the masses through the existing institutional channels. So, there was a succession of less and less representative regimes and an accumulation of unfulfilled democratic demands. These demands were certainly particular ones and came from very different groups. The fact that all of them were rejected by the dominant regimes established an increasing relation of equivalence between them. This equiva-

lence, it is important to realize, did not express any essential a priori unity. On the contrary, its only ground was the rejection of all those demands by successive regimes. In terms of our previous terminology, their unification within a context or system of differences was the pure result of all of them being antagonized by the dominant sectors.

Now, as we have seen, this contextual unification of a system of differences can only take place at the price of weakening the purely differential identities, through the operation of a logic of equivalence which introduces a dimension of relative universality. In our example, people felt that through the differential particularity of their demands—housing, union rights, level of wages, protection of national industry, etcetera—something equally present in all of them was expressed, which was opposition to the regime. It is important to realize that this dimension of universality was not at odds with the particularism of the demands—or even of the groups entering into the equivalential relation—but grew out of it. A certain more universal perspective, which developed out of the inscription of particular demands in a wider popular language of resistance, was the result of the expansion of the equivalential logic. A pure particularism of the demands of the groups, which had entirely avoided the equivalential logic, would have been possible only if the regime had succeeded in dealing separately with the particular demands and had absorbed them in a 'transformistic' way. But in any process of hegemonic decline, this transformistic absorption becomes impossible and the equivalential logics interrupt the pure particularism of the individual democratic demands.

As we can see, this dimension of universality reached through equivalence is very different from the universality which results from an underlying essence or an unconditioned a priori principle. It is not a regulative idea either—empirically unreachable but with an unequivocal teleological content—because it cannot exist apart from the system of equivalences from which it proceeds. But this has important consequences for both the content and the function of that universality. We have seen before that the moment of totalization or universalization of the community—the moment of its fullness—is an impossible object which can only acquire a discursive presence through a particular content which divests itself of its particularity in order to represent that fullness. To return to our Argentinian example, this was precisely the role that, in the 1960s and 1970s, was played by the popular symbols of Perónism. As I said earlier, the country had entered into a rapid process of de-institutionalization, so the equivalential logics could operate freely. The Perónist movement itself lacked a real organization and was rather a series of symbols and a loose language unifying a variety of political initiatives. Finally, Perón himself was in exile in

---

[7]The political movement in Argentina led by Juan Domingo Perón (1895–1974), military officer who served as president from 1946 to 1955 and, after exile in Spain, in 1973–1974.

Madrid, intervening only in a distant way in his movement's actions, being very careful not to take any definitive stand in the factional struggles within Perónism. In those circumstances, he was in ideal conditions to become the 'empty signifier' incarnating the moment of universality in the chain of equivalences which unified the popular camp. And the ulterior destiny of Perónism in the 1970s clearly illustrates the essential ambiguity inherent in any hegemonic process: on the one hand, the fact that the symbols of a particular group at some point assume a function of universal representation certainly gives a hegemonic power to that group; but, on the other hand, the fact that this function of universal representation has been acquired at the price of weakening the differential particularism of the original identity, leads necessarily to the conclusion that this hegemony is going to be precarious and threatened. The wild logic of emptying the signifiers of universality through the expansion of the equivalential chains means that no fixing and particular limitation on the sliding of the signified under the signifier is going to be permanently assured. This is what happened to Perónism after the electoral victory of 1973 and Perón's return to Argentina. Perón was no longer an empty signifier but the president of the country, who had to carry out concrete politics. Yet the chains of equivalences constructed by the different factions of his movements had gone beyond any possibility of control—even by Perón himself. The result was the bloody process which led to the military dictatorship in 1976.

The Dialectics of Universality

The previous developments lead us to the following conclusion: the dimension of universality—resulting from the incompletion of all differential identities—cannot be eliminated so long as a community is not entirely homogeneous (if it *were* homogeneous, what would disappear is not only universality but also the very distinction universality/particularity). This dimension is, however, just an empty place unifying a set of equivalential demands. We have to determine the nature of this place both in terms of its contents and of its function. As far as the content is concerned, it does not have one of its own but just that which is given to it by a transient articulation of equivalential demands. There is a paradox implicit in the formulation of universal principles, which is that all of them have to present themselves as valid without exception, while, even in its own terms, this universality can easily be questioned and can never be actually maintained. Let us take a universal principle such as the right of nations to self-determination. As a universal right, it claims to be valid in any

circumstance. Let us suppose now that within a nation genocidal practices are taking place: in that case has the international community the duty to intervene, or is the principle of self-determination an unconditionally valid one? The paradox is that while the principle has to be formulated as universally valid, there will always be exceptions to that universal validity. But perhaps the paradox proceeds from believing that this universality has a content of its own, whose logical implications can be analytically deduced, without realizing that its own function—within a particular language game—is to make discursively possible a chain of equivalential effects, but without pretending that this universality can operate beyond the context of its emergence. There are innumerable contexts in which the principle of national self-determination is a perfectly valid way of totalizing and universalizing a historical experience.

But in that case, if we always know beforehand that no universalization will live up to its task, if it will always fail to deliver the goods, why does the equivalential aggregation have to express itself through the universal? The answer is to be found in what we said before about the formal structure on which the aggregation depends. The 'something identical' shared by all the terms of the equivalential chain—that which makes the equivalence possible—cannot be something positive (that is one more difference which could be defined in its particularity), but proceeds from the unifying effects that the external threat poses to an otherwise perfectly heterogeneous set of differences (particularities). The 'something identical' can only be the pure, abstract, absent fullness of the community, which lacks, as we have seen, any direct form of representation and expresses itself through the equivalence of the differential terms. But, in that case, it is essential that the chain of equivalences remains open: otherwise its closure could only be the result of one more difference specifiable in its particularity and we would not be confronted with the fullness of the community as an absence. The open character of the chain means that what is expressed through it has to be universal and not particular. Now, this universality needs—for its expression—to be incarnated in something essentially incommensurable with it: a particularity (as in our example of the right to self-determination). This is the source of the tension and ambiguities surrounding all these so-called 'universal' principles: all of them *have* to be formulated as limitless principles, expressing a universality transcending them: but they all, for essential reasons, sooner or later become entangled in their own contextual particularism and are incapable of fulfilling their universal function.

As far as the function (as different from the content) of the 'universal' is concerned, we have said enough to make clear what it consists of: it is exhausted in introducing chains of equivalence in an otherwise purely differential world. This is the moment of hegemonic aggregation and articulation and can operate in two ways. The first is to inscribe particular identities and demands as links in a wider chain of equivalences, thereby giving each of them a 'relative' universalization. If, for instance, feminist demands enter into chains of equivalence with those of black groups, ethnic minorities, civil rights activists, etcetera, they acquire a more global perspective than is the case where they remain restricted to their own particularism. The second is to give a particular demand a function of universal representation—that is to give it the value of a horizon giving coherence to the chain of equivalences and, at the same time, keeping it indefinitely open. To give just a few examples: the socialization of the means of production was not considered as a narrow demand concerning the economy but as the 'name' for a wide variety of equivalential effects radiating over the whole society. The introduction of a market economy played a similar role in Eastern Europe after 1989. The return of Perón, in our Argentinian example, was also conceived in the early 1970s as the prelude to a much wider historical transformation. Which particular demand, or set of demands, are going to play this function of universal representation is something which cannot be determined by a priori reasons (if we could do so, this would mean that there is something in the particularity of the demand which predetermined it to fulfil that role, and that would be in contradiction to our whole argument).

We can now return to the two debates which were the starting point of our reflection. As we can see, there are several points in which they interact and in which parallelism can be detected. We have said enough about multiculturalism for our argument concerning the limits of particularism to be clear. A *pure* particularistic stand is self-defeating because it has to provide a ground for the constitution of the differences *as* differences, and such a ground can only be a new version of an essentialist universalism. (If we have a *system* of differences A/B/C, etcetera, we have to account for this systemic dimension and that leads us straight into the discourse of ground. If we have a plurality of *separate* elements A, B, C, etcetera, which do not constitute a system, we still have to account for this separation—to be separated is also a form of relation between objects—and we are again entangled, as Leibnitz[8] knew well, in the positing of a ground. The pre-established harmony of the monads is as essential a ground as the Spinozean[9] totality.) So, the only

way out of this dilemma is to maintain the dimension of universality but to propose a different form for its articulation with the particular. This is what we have tried to provide in the preceding pages through the notion of the universal as an empty but ineradicable place.

It is important, however, to realize that this type of articulation would be theoretically unthinkable if we did not introduce into the picture some of the central tenets of the contemporary critique of foundationalism (it would be unthinkable, for instance, in a Habermasian[10] perspective). If meaning is fixed beforehand either, in a strong sense, by a radical ground (a position that fewer and fewer people would sustain today) or, in a weaker version, through the regulative principle of an undistorted communication, the very possibility of the ground as an empty place which is politically and contingently filled by a variety of social forces disappears. Differences would not be constitutive because something previous to their play *already* fixes the limit of their possible variation and establishes an external tribunal to *judge* them. Only the critique of a universality which is determined in all its essential dimensions by the metaphysics of presence opens the way for a *theoretical* apprehension of the notion of 'articulation' that we are trying to elaborate—as different from a purely impressionistic apprehension, in terms of a discourse structured through concepts which are perfectly incompatible with it. (We always have to remember Pascal's critique of those who think that they are already converted because they have just started thinking of getting converted.)

But if the debate concerning multiculturalism can draw clear advantages from the contemporary critique of foundationalism (broadly speaking, the whole range of intellectual developments embraced by labels such as 'postmodernism' and 'poststructuralism'), these advantages also work in the opposite direction. For the requirements of a politics based on a universality compatible with an increasing expansion of cultural differences are clearly incompatible with some versions of postmodernism—particularly those which conclude from the critique of foundationalism that there is an implosion of all meaning and the entry into a world of 'simulation' (Baudrillard[11]). I don't think that this is a conclusion which follows at all. As we have argued, the impossibility of a universal ground does not eliminate its need: it just transforms the ground into an empty place which can be partially filled in a variety of ways (the strategies of this filling is what politics is about). Let us go back for a moment to the question of

---

[8] Gottfried Wilhelm Leibnitz (1646–1716), German philosopher and mathematician.
[9] Benedict (Baruch) Spinoza (1632–1677), Dutch philosopher.

[10] Habermas (above, page 1429).
[11] Jean Baudrillard (b. 1929), French social philosopher.

contextualization. If we could have a 'saturated' context we would indeed be confronted with a plurality of incommensurable spaces without any possible tribunal deciding between them. But, as we have seen, any such saturated context is impossible. Yet, the conclusion which follows from this verification is not that there is a formless dispersion of meaning without even any possible kind of relative articulation but, rather, that whatever plays such an articulating role is not predetermined to it by the form of the dispersion as such. This means first that all articulation is contingent and, second, that the articulating moment as such is always going to be an empty place—the various attempts at filling it being transient and submitted to contestation. As a result, at any historical moment, whatever dispersion of differences exists in society is going to be submitted to contradictory processes of contextualization and de-contextualization. For instance, those discourses attempting to close a context around certain principles or values will be confronted and limited by discourses of *rights,* which try to limit the closure of any context. This is what makes so unconvincing the attempts by contemporary neo-Aristotelians such as McIntyre at accepting only the contextualizing dimension and closing society around a substantive vision of the common good. Contemporary social and political struggles open, I think, strategies of filling the empty place of the common good. The ontological implications of the thought accompanying these 'filling' strategies clarifies, in turn, the horizon of possibilities opened by the antifoundationalist critique. It is to these strategic logics that I want to devote the rest of this essay.

Ruling and Universality: Four Moments

We can start with some conclusions which could easily be derived from our previous analysis concerning the status of the universal. The first is that if the place of the universal is an empty one and there is no a priori reason for it not to be filled by *any* content, if the forces which fill that place are constitutively split between the concrete politics that they advocate and the ability of those politics to fill the empty place, the political language of any society whose degree of institutionalization has, to some extent, been shaken or undermined, will also be split. Let us just take a term such as 'order' (social order). What are the conditions of its universalization? Simply, that the experience of a radical disorder makes *any* order preferable to the continuity of disorder. The experience of a lack, of an absence of fullness in social relations, transforms 'order' into the signifier of an absent fullness. This explains the split we were referring to: any concrete politics, if it is capable of bringing about social order, will be judged not only

according to its merits in the abstract, independently of any circumstance, but mainly in terms of that ability to bring about 'order'—a name for the absent fullness of society. ('Change,' 'revolution,' 'unity of the people,' etcetera are other signifiers which have historically played the same role.) Since, for essential reasons as we have pointed out, the fullness of society is unreachable, this split in the identity of political agents is an absolutely constitutive 'ontological difference'—in a sense not entirely unrelated to Heidegger's use of this expression. The universal is certainly empty, and can only be filled in different contexts by concrete particulars. But, at the same time, it is absolutely essential for any kind of *political* interaction, for if the latter took place without universal reference, there would be no political interaction at all: we would only have either a complementarity of differences which would be totally non-antagonistic, or a totally antagonistic one, one where differences entirely lack any commensurability, and whose only possible resolution is the mutual destruction of the adversaries.

Now, it is our contention that politico-philosophical reflection since the ancient world has been largely conscious of this constitutive split, and has tried to provide various ways of dealing with it. These ways follow one or the other of the logical possibilities pointed out in the previous analysis. To suggest how this took place, we will briefly refer to four moments in the politico-philosophical tradition of the West in which images of the ruler have emerged which combine universality and particularity in different ways. We will refer successively to Plato's philosopher-king, to Hobbes's[12] sovereign, to Hegel's hereditary monarch, and to Gramsci's[13] hegemonic class.

In Plato the situation is unambiguous. There is no possible tension or antagonism between the universal and the particular. Far from being an empty place, the universal is the location of all possible meaning, and it absorbs the particular within itself. Now, for him however, there is only *one* articulation of the particularities which actualize the essential form of the community. The universal is not 'filled' from outside, but is the fullness of its own origin and expresses itself in all aspects of social organization. There can be no 'ontological difference' here between the fullness of the community and its actual political and social arrangements. Only *one* kind of social arrangement, which extends itself to the most minute aspects of social life, is compatible with what the community in its last instance is. Other forms of social organization can,

---

[12] Thomas Hobbes (1588–1679), English political theorist and philosopher, author of *Leviathan, or the Matter, Form, and Power of a Commonwealth, Ecclesiastical and Civil* (1651).
[13] Gramsci (above, page 936).

of course, factually exist, but they do not have the status of alternative forms among which one has to choose according to the circumstances. They are just degenerate forms, pure corruption of being, derived from obfuscation of the mind. In so far as there is true knowledge, only one particular form of social organization realizes the universal. And if ruling is a matter of knowledge and not of prudence, only the bearer of that knowledge, the philosopher, has the right to rule. *Ergo:* a philosopher-king.

With Hobbes we are apparently at the antipodes of Plato. Far from being the sovereign, the one who has the knowledge of what the community is before any political decision, his decisions are the only source of social order. Hobbes is well aware of what we have called the 'ontological difference.' Inasmuch as the anarchy of the state of nature threatens society with radical disorder, the unification of the will of the community in the will of the ruler (or rather, the will of the ruler as the only unified will that the community can have) will count in so far as it imposes order, whatever the contents of the latter could be. Any order will be better than radical disorder. There is something close to a complete indifference here to the *content* of the social order imposed by the ruler, and an exclusive concentration on the *function* of the latter: ensuring order as such. 'Order' certainly becomes an empty place, but there is in Hobbes no hegemonic theory about the transient forms of its filling: the sovereign, the 'mortall God,' fills the empty place once and forever.

So, Plato and Hobbes are apparently at the antipodes of the theoretical spectrum. For Plato, the universal is the *only* full place; for Hobbes, it is an absolutely empty place which has to be filled by the will of the sovereign. But if we look more closely at the matter, we will see that this difference between them is overshadowed by what they actually share, which is not to allow the particular any dynamics of its own *vis-à-vis* the full/empty place of the universal. In the first case, the particular has to actualize in its own body a universality transcending it; in the second case equally, although by artificial means, a particular has detached itself from the realm of particularities and has become the unchallengeable law of the community.

For Hegel, the problem is posed in different terms. Since, for him, the particularism of each stage of social organization is *aufgehoben* at a higher level, the problem of the incommensurability between particular content and universal function cannot actually arise. But the problem of the empty place emerges in relation to the moment in which the community has to *signify* itself as a totality—that is the moment of its *individuality*. This signification is obtained, as we know, through the constitutional monarch, whose physical body represents a rational totality absolutely dissimilar to that body. (This representation, in Hegel, of something which has no content of its own through something else which is its exact reverse, has very often been stressed by Slavoj Žižek,[14] who has contributed several other examples such as the assertion, in the *Phenomenology of Spirit,* that 'the Spirit is a bone.') But this relation, by which a physical content can represent, in its pure alienation of any spiritual content, this last content, entirely depends on the community having reached, through successive sublations of its partial contents, the highest form of rationality achievable in its own sphere. For such a fully rational community no *content* can be added and it only remains, as a requirement for its completion, *the signification of the achievement of that functional rationality:* Because of that, the rational monarch cannot be an elected monarch: he has to be a hereditary one. If he were elected, *reasons* would have to be given for that election, and this process of argumentation would mean that the rationality of society would not have been achieved independently of the monarch, and that the latter would have to play a greater role than a pure function of ceremonial representation.

Finally Gramsci. The hegemonic class can only become such by linking a particular content to a universality transcending it. If we say—as Gramsci did—that the task of the Italian working class is to fulfil the tasks of national unification that the Italian people had posed themselves since the time of Machiavelli and, in some way, to complete the historical project of the *Risorgimento,* we have a double order of reference.[15] On the one hand, a concrete political programme—that of the workers—as different from those of other political forces; but, on the other hand, that programme—that is that set of demands and political proposals—is presented as a historical vehicle for a task transcending it: the unity of the Italian nation. Now, if this 'unity of the Italian nation' was a concrete content, specifiable in a particular context, it could not be something which extended over a period of centuries and that different historical forces could bring about. However, if this *can* happen, it is because 'unity of the Italian nation' is just the name or the symbol of a lack. Precisely because it is a *constitutive* lack, there is no content which is a priori destined to fill it, and it is open to the most diverse articulations. But this means that the 'good' articulation, the one that would finally suture the link between universal task and concrete historical forces will never be found, and that all partial victory

---

[14]Slavoj Žižek (b. 1949), Slovenian philosopher.

[15]Niccolò Machiavelli (1469–1627), Italian political theorist, author of *The Prince* (1513), a treatise on statecraft notorious for its apparently amoral view of power and rule. The idea of *Risorgimento* (literally, "rising again") is associated with the movement for the unification of Italy, resulting in the establishment of the Kingdom of Italy in 1861.

will always take place against the background of an ultimate and unsurpassable impossibility.

Viewed from this perspective the Gramscían project can be seen as a double displacement, *vis-à-vis* both Hegel and Hobbes. In one sense it is more Hobbesian than Hegelian, because, as society and State are less self-structured than in Hegel, they require a dimension of political constitution in which the representation of the unity of the community is not separated from its construction. There is a remainder of particularity which cannot be eliminated from the representation of that unity (unity = individuality in the Hegelian sense). The presence of this remainder is what is specific to the hegemonic relation. The hegemonic class is somewhere in between the Hegelian monarch and the Leviathan. But it can equally be said that Gramsci is more Hegelian than Hobbesian, in the sense that the political moment in his analysis presupposes an image of social crises which is far less radical than in Hobbes. Gramsci's 'organic crises' fall far short, in terms of their degrees of social structuring, from the Hobbesian state of nature. In some senses, the succession of hegemonic regimes can be seen as a series of 'partial covenants'—partial because, as society is more structured than in Hobbes, people have more conditions under which to enter into the political covenant: but partial also because, as the result of that, they also have more reasons to substitute the sovereign.

These last points allow us to go back to our earlier discussion concerning contemporary particularistic struggles and to inscribe it within the politico-philosophical tradition. In the same way that we have presented Gramsci's problematic through the displacements that he introduces *vis-à-vis* the two approaches that we have symbolized in Hobbes and Hegel, we could present the political alternatives open to multicultural struggles through similar displacements *vis-à-vis* Gramsci's approach. The first and most obvious displacement is to conceive a society which is more particularistic and fragmented and less amenable than Gramsci's to enter into unified hegemonic articulations. The second is that the loci from which the articulation takes place—for Gramsci they were locations such as the Party, or the State (in an expanded sense)—are also going to be more plural and less likely to generate a chain of totalizing effects. What we have called the remainder of particularism inherent in any hegemonic centrality grows thicker but also more plural. Now, this has mixed effects from the viewpoint of a democratic politics. Let us imagine a Jacobinic scenario. The public sphere is one, the place of power is one but is empty, and a plurality of political forces can occupy the latter. In one sense we can say that this is an ideal situation for democracy, because the place of power is empty and we can conceive the democratic process as a partial articulation of

the empty universality of the community and the particularism of the transient political forces incarnating it. This is true, but precisely because the universal place is empty, it can be occupied by any force, not necessarily democratic. As is well known, this is one of the roots of contemporary totalitarianism (Lefort).

If, on the contrary, the place of power is not unique, the remainder, as we said, will be weightier, and the possibility of constructing a common public sphere through a series of equivalential effects cutting across communities will clearly be less. This has ambiguous results. On the one hand, communities are certainly more protected in the sense that a Jacobinic totalitarianism is less likely. But, on the other hand, for reasons that have been pointed out earlier, this also favours the maintenance of the *status quo*. We can perfectly well imagine a modified Hobbesian scenario in which the law respects communities—no longer individuals—in their private sphere, while the main decisions concerning the future of the community as a whole are the preserve of a neo-Leviathan—for instance a quasi-omnipotent technocracy. To realize that this is not at all an unrealistic scenario, we only have to think of Samuel Huntington[16] and, more generally, of contemporary corporatist approaches.

The other alternative is more complex but it is the only one, I think, compatible with a true democratic politics. It wholly accepts the plural and fragmented nature of contemporary societies but, instead of remaining in this particularistic moment, it tries to inscribe this plurality in equivalential logics which make possible the construction of new public spheres. Difference and particularisms are the necessary starting point, but out of it, it is possible to open the way to a relative universalization of values which can be the basis for a popular hegemony. This universalization and its open character certainly condemns all identity to an unavoidable hybridization, but hybridization does not necessarily mean decline through the loss of identity: it can also mean empowering existing identities through the opening of new possibilities. Only a conservative identity, closed on itself, could experience hybridization as a loss. But this democratico-hegemonic possibility has to recognize the constitutive contextualized/decontextualized terrain of its constitution and take full advantage of the political possibilities that this undecidability opens.

All this finally amounts to saying is that the particular can only fully realize itself if it constantly keeps open, and constantly redefines, its relation to the universal.

---

[16] Samuel Huntington, American political scientist and author of *The Clash of Civilizations and the Remaking of the World Order* (1988); see also his widely circulated essay, "The Clash of Civilizations?" in *Public Affairs* (Summer 1993).

INDEX

A

Abject, 1494

Acting, paradox of, 384 ff.

Actor, has no character, 391

Aesthetic(s), and restoration of humanity, 469; categorizing and control, 1359; concerned with effects of meaning, 1320; disinterest, 420; distance, 960; empirical and pure, 426; excellence, 470; experience, 858; function in bourgeois theory, 1360; judgment, 420, 1019; rejection of, 1362; state, phantom, 857; value and reception, 1242

Affirmation, of new world, 1002

African culture, racialized, not national, 1190

African-American, as postcolonial in the U.S., 1518

Agency, pervasiveness of, 1479; recognize in others, 1514

Allegory, 319, 1149; addressed to intellectual powers, 448; and religions, 539; and interpretation, 151, 154, 1147; and Platonic poetry, 957; and symbol, 519; and symbol in Adorno and Derrida, 1431; fable and vision, 458–59; in ancient poetry, 237–38; in painting, 403

Ambiguity, 741; and indecision, 897; and obscurity, 291; and paradox, 1037; in scripture, 145; types of, 895 ff.

Anagnorisis, see Discovery, 58, 60

Anagogy, 151, 154, 1159; as universal meaning, 1160; imitates total dream of man, 1161; and religion, 1165

Ancients, as artistic people of God, 476; wisdom of, 316

Ancients and Moderns, 256, 263, 299, 330, 350, 354, 395, 455, 461, 475, 476, 546; imposing new on old, 294

Anthropology, aims to enlarge universe of human discourse, 1334; writings are interpretations, 1335

Aphasia, similarity and contiguity disorder, 1132, 1135

Apocalypse, and revelation, 1162–64

Apologetic tradition, 621

Appollonian-Dionysiac, 687 ff.

Archetypes, 139; and ritual, 1154; as associative clusters, 1153; as communicable symbols, 1161; integrates literary experience, 1151; Jungian, 1121

Architecture, 414, 559–60; and beauty, 129

Art, and abstraction, 554; and creation of civilization, 1002; and idea, 554; and understanding, 51; as key to wisdom and religion, 553, 761; as subject of scientific inquiry, 553; expresses only itself, 722; for art's sake, 620; generosity of, 1003; independent universe of discourse, 1022; infection theory of, 759, 1020; not divine gift, 399; path of creator to work, 578; rules of, founded on experience, 325; symbolic, classical, romantic, 553 ff.; unites people, 767; work, importance in structure, 1002

Artifice, modes of, 216

Artificer, inner, 210

Artist, differs from philosopher, 1002; man of action, 1003

Association, and indication, 775; of ideas, 442

Associative relations, 795

Atomism, logical, 811

Auschwitz, and new categorical imperative, 1115; metaphysical faculty paralyzed by, 1114; writing poetry barbaric, after, 1110; wrong to say no more poetry, 1114

Authority, in classroom and in criticism, 1401

Auto-erotic, oral and anal, 753

Avant-gardes, and the postmodern, 1421–22

B

Beautiful, and agreeable, 497; and sublime, 418; pleasant and good, 421–22

Beauty, a kind of corpse, 820; a social quality, 340; and love, 130; and moral freedom, 472; and necessity, 573; and pleasure, 425; and purification, 131; as the Good, 131; as whole, 128; consummation of humanity, 467; derives from Soul, 128; ideal of, 429; is truth, 1040–41; not a quality of things, 324, 1022; reduces many to one, 497, 500; self unfolding idea, 561

Behaviorism, critique of, 1167 ff.

Being, concept arises in propositions, 657; as presence, relation to death, 1217–18; as *transcendens,* 1061; inapplicable to a subject, 656; man "thrown" from, 1058; three modes of, 663; truth of and theism / atheism, 1065; truth of, forgetting, 1059

Blindness, and insight, states truth in mode of error, 1316

Bondage, as truth of independent consciousness, 564

Books, all existence to be in a, 729; for inspiration, 567; theory of, 567

Bricolage, 1210

Bureaucracy, kinds of, 1453

C

Canon, and women writers, 1388–89; formation and aesthetic valuation, 1391; in Scripture, 146; literary, *see* Curriculum, 628; of theory, and in graduate seminar, 1506–08

Capital, 611

Capitalism, adversaries: death and language, 1427; industrial, 612; print, 1426; print, and languages of power, 1427; reterritorialized as "democracy," 1510; world market, 609

Care *(Sorge)*, 1055

Catachresis, 262, 1491

Categories, 416; firstness: quality, feeling, ground, 657; secondness: correlate, object, 657–58; thirdness: mediation, interpretant, 658–59

Catharsis, 55, 1020; as purgation, 183; as purification, 127

Cause, 208; and principle, 209; Aristotelian, 49; efficient, 209, 220; final (*see* Teleology), 210

Center, as virtual focal point, a nothing, 1317; Europe as, crisis of, 1316

Character, good and bad, 53; in tragedy, 59

Civil faculty, 219–22, 408; and wit, 475

Civil society, 936, 1372; and hegemony, 941; and state, 941

Civilization, and barbarism, documents of, 997; makes total human form, 1155, 1158; wound of, 462

Class, dominated, dispossession of, 1413; hegemonic, 1533; oppressed, repository of historical knowledge, 999; political, 938 n3–4; struggle, 609 ff., 996; political struggle, 612; revolutionary and continuum of history, 999

Closet (gay), 1470 ff.; and performativity, 1471, 1475; and speech act of silence, 1471; deferred promise of disclosure, 1491

Colonialism, and Cartierism, superiority, 1188; and national struggle, 1188; native culture accused of barbarism, 1190

Coming out, 1491

Common sense, and common understanding, 432; and standard of taste, 373

Common understanding, 622, 629

Commonplaces, and dialectic, 630; as profound questions, 606

Communism, Spectre of, 608

Community, imagined, and print culture, 1424 ff.

Complication, in drama, 79, 247

Composition, original, 348 ff.; rules not *a priori,* 324

Concept, and blurred edges, 847; and judgment of taste, 428; and unity of consciousness, 655

Conceptualism, and nominalism, 663–64

Consciousness, and social being, 607; position of, 563; romantic, as presence of a nothingness, 1317

Continental philosophy, isolation of, 979

Contraries, 456

Convention, and genre, 1150

Crisis, of humanities and ambivalence of theory, 1505; of literary studies, 1508; of theory, 1503; rhetoric of, 1316; scientific revolutions, 1284

Critic, qualities needed by, 329

Criticism, and author psychology, 1030; and demystification, 1315; and disinterestedness, 592; and free play of mind, 592; and heresies, 956; and *idée fixe,* 968; and intellectual sphere, 593; and politics, religion, 598; and psychological theory of knowledge, 973; and social / cultural history, 1157; and tendentiousness, 971; and ulterior purposes, 969 ff.; and valuable experiences, 860; as bricolage, 1210; as creative and primary, not parasite, 1433; as rational science, 371; bridging function of, 1440; clarified by long tradition, or a universal rhetoric, 1433; continental, attack on privileged consciousness, 1313; critical and technical parts, 860; differs from "approaches" to literature, 1313; feminist, 1385 ff.; formal discourse of amateur, 956; function of, 475, 587 ff., 598; historical, 474; lower rank than creativity, 588; other sciences needed for, 1078; practical, 863; reader response, 1395; sociological, 1014–15; support for morality, 372; to *see* object as it really is, 587, 589, 618; true, calls act of writing into question, 1313

Cultural capital, 1403 ff.

Cultural criticism, 1102 ff.; and economic system, 1105; and ideology, 1106; complicity with culture, 1104; inadequacy of socialist contributions to, 1109

Cultural legitimation, 628–29

Cultural studies, a continuation of literary history, 628; and criticism, 625; curriculum closed to texts that enabled it, 1508

Culture, and barbarism, 1110; and configurations of power, 1372; as the enemy, 680; has failed, 1116; high *vs.* popular, 1106; national 1187 ff.; semiotic conception of, 1329

Curriculum (*see also* Canon), expansion of, 628; literary, absence of *ideological* rationale, 1507; literary, diminished social significance of, 1506; literary, social marginality of, 1508

D

Dasein, Being "there," 1057

Deconstruction, 5, 624; and "close reading," 1204; and negative dialectics, 1430; Peirce anticipates, 1232; reflection of earlier episodes, 631

Defamiliarizing, 800 ff.

Definition, and genus, 285; danger of, 334

Delight and teach, 83, 87, 169, 174, 178, 229, 364, 1092, 1140

Democracy, and literature, 675 ff.

Demystification, radical, as cause of crisis, 1315

Denotation, and connotation, 785

Dénouement, 61

Descriptions, ambiguous, 814; definite and indefinite, 812; incomplete, 852; thick, 1329 ff.

Desire, coherence in contradiction, 1206

Dialectic, intransigent toward reification, 1108; negative, 1430; of universality, 1530 ff.; social, 992

Dialectic of Enlightenment, 1101

Dialectical tradition, untheoretical nature of, 630

Dialectics, and negative knowledge, 117

Dialogic, 923

Diction, 61, 62, 64; and thought, 62; poetic, 484–85, 488–89

Différance, and monstrosity, 1215

Dionysian / Dionysiac, 130; music and will, 690

Disbelief, willing suspension of, 505

Discourse, and unlimited representation, 1216; solitary, 1216

Discovery, *see* Anagnorisis, 58–60

Disinterestedness, 586, 592, 627

Distinction, profit of, 1411

Division, and generalization, 37; of poetry, 52

Dominant class, *see* Ruling class; and race, 943

Domination, symbolic, 1408 ff.

Drama, 54, 245 ff., 256, 363, 384; comedy and tragedy, 25; English and French, 263–71; number of scenes, 248; Shakespeare, neither tragedy nor comedy, 364

Dream, and intoxication, 687

Dream work, 748

Drives, sensuous and formal, 462–63

E

Economy, and the state, 942

Education, 16, 29; aesthetic, 460 ff; and poetry, 35; by criticism, 371; literary and philosophical, 633

Egotism, necessary to human dignity, 712

Eidos (*see* Idea, Form), 219, 631; and ontology, 1217

Einstein, formulae and "ironical" poem, 1084

Elevated language (*see* Sublime), sources, 98

Elite, moral and intellectual, 940–43

Emotion, recollected in tranquility, 490

Emotive language, 879

Epic, and heroic, 227; and tragedy, 65; completed form, 918; transformation into novel, 918

Episteme, 1206, 1222; and history, 1214

Erotic, and defamiliarization, 803

Essence, real and nominal, 287

Ethics, and ethos, 1067; cannot be put into words, 835; development, 752

Ethnography, as form of knowledge, 1330; interpretive of flow of social discourse, 1337

Evening star / morning star, 735

Evolution, a-parallel, 1447; and experimental novel, 703; literary, 882

Existence, a *scandal,* 1182; and essence, 1057–58; as work of inner life, 1179; definition of, 814

Existentialism, and Kierkegaard, 1179; Sartre and Heidegger differ, 1058

Expenditure, and economy in poetic language, 799

Experiment, 241–42, 515; central, protophaenomenon (*see* Paradigm(s)), 519

Experimental method, and feeling, 706; and literary history, 639

Expression, adequate is rare, 571; and meaning: ideal unities, 779; critique of, 926–27; determined by social situation, 928; errors of expressivist theory, 1365; organizes experience, 927

Expressions, and meaningful signs, 775; in solitary life, 777

Externalization, and inward meaning, 1023

F

Fable, divine, 317

Fascism, 951–52, 998

Faculties, senses, imagination, judgment, 334

Family resemblance, and language game, 845

Family romance, 748

Fantasy, 225

Feelings, spontaneous overflow of, 484

Feminism, 6, 441, 624

Feudalism, 674, 938; and revolution, 609; theological-feudal tutelage, 1103

Fiction, 160, 358; advantage over real life, 359; form of discourse, 161; in scripture, 162; not lie, 161; problematic as literary feature, 1322

Figure, 163, 960; an abuse of language, 296; and sublime, 105, 106

Form, and matter, 503; consumes material, 470; *Formtrieb,* 460; Ideal form and beauty, 129; Platonic, 31, 48

Form and content, 1036; language and substance, 1074; neglect of in New Criticism, 1082

Formal criticism, 1145

Formal method, 868 ff.

Formal universals, 652

Formalism, 867; and metaphysics, 629; and Marxists, 1238; idea of literary evolution, 1247

Formalists, and Futurists, 871; and Symbolists, 869–70

Foundationalism, critique of, 1528 ff.

Free play, of cognitive powers, 424; of mind, 592

Functions, descriptive, 817

G

Gay, identities and heterosexual norms, 1495; professionalization of gayness, 1492

Gaze, skoptophilia, 753

Gender, 442 ff., and power, 1470–71; imitation with no original, 1494; transitivity, 1470

Genius, 396, 438 ff., 729; always above age, 619; and errors, 112, 454; and learning, 352; and taste, 400; cannot be bound, 455; compared to virtue, 351; grace beyond art, 299; not lawless, 496; repairs the decay of things, 575; Shakespeare above other writers, 362

Genocide, as absolute integration, 1114

Genre, 48; and intuition, 627; as contextual information, 1351; dynamism of, 882

Germany, fateful belongingness, 1062

Gestalt, 991; duck-rabbit, 849; switch, 849

God, 18; death of, 1064, 1263

Grammar, 63–64; and appropriateness conditions, 1350; and rhetoric, uncertain relation, 1324; as isotope of logic, 1323; construction of by child, 1173; describes, does not explain, 848

Grammatology, 1220 ff.; and semiology, 1229, 1233

Ground, requires concept of being, 657

Guilt, and compulsion to philosophize, 1115; of survivor after Auschwitz, 1114

H

Hegelism, and theological seminaries, 665; and totalization, 1178; from Marxist perspective, 1179; Peirce's rejection of, 666

Hegemony, 936; and orientalism, 1373; crisis of, 948; cultural, of Romantic thought, 1458; social and assent, 941

Heraclitus, flux, 46–47; here too gods present, 1066

Heresy, and fallacy, 1026; of paraphrase, 1036 ff.

Heteroglossia, polyglossia, monoglossia, 912, 917

Heterosexuality, as dependent term, 1474; compulsory, 1494, 1499

Hieroglyphic, 236

Historical materialism, and theology, 996

Historicism, and universal history, 1000; leads away from literature, 881

History, revolutionized by study of literature, 640

Hölderlin, and Heidegger, 1061; organic metaphor, de Man, 1309

Homelessness, essential, 1062

Homophobia, and heterosexuality as copy, 1495

Homosexuality, 967; and heterosexual definition, and effects, 1470, 1475

Humanism, and metaphysical ground, 1056; of Marx, Sartre, Christianity, 1055; Roman, 1056; why restore its meaning?, 1054

Humanitas, 1055

Humanities, and science, 633; crisis of, 1505

Hysteria, and Hamlet, 748

I

I (ego), formation of, 993

Ideal, 991

Ideal Form, 129

Idealism, and realism, 504; and violence, 1183; Kant's refutation of, 664–65; voluntarist, 1184

Ideality, and time, 1217; not fictitious, 1218

Ideas, 133, 514 n25; abstract, 285; aesthetical, 439; and social contract, 520; and theory, 518; and words, 282–83; as concrete unity, 555; as essences, 286; concept perfected to

point of irony, 478; construction of, 696; created by understanding, 286; current of, 598; distinguished from concept, 520; innate, 451; materials of creative power, 588; normal, rational, ideal, 430–31; of imagination, 308

Identification, heteromorphic, 992

Identity, categories as regulatory instruments, 1490; constituted by antagonism and exclusion, 1528; cultural, as "national origin validation," 1512; eternal, 454; of self, 562–63; pure, philosopheme of as death, 1114; thought of, 680

Ideology, and "ideologists," 1178; and bureaucracy, 1502; and expediency, 1108; and ideologies, 1298–99; and intellectual conquest, 940; and knowledge, 1303; and practices, 1302; and social formation, 1308; as socially necessary appearance, 1108; behavioral, 931; Christian religious, 1305; critique, 1107; has material existence, 1301 ff.; ideas and material conditions, 614; in general, no history, 1299; interpellation, calls or hails, 1303; morality, religion, metaphysics as, 614; religious, 938; representation of imaginary relation to real, 1299 ff.; structuring, 929; systems of, 930–31; transforms, recruits, individuals *as* subjects, 1304

Idolatry, 318

Idols, of the mind, 240; poetic, 219–21

Ignorance, understanding writer's, 501

Imaginary, and alienation, 1300; and symbolic, 990

Imagination, 66, 235, 604; and affection, 535; and eternal image, 459; and fancy, 308, 604–05; and genius, 438; and mind, 310; and reason as allies, 638; and sensibility, 409, 413; and sublime, 103, 436–37; and understanding, 437; creative power, 335; distinguished from fancy, 505; flow not freeze, 577; high sort of seeing, 575; imaginative *vs.* imaginary, 1139; metaphysical value of, 1024; must be guided by reason, 1022; pleasures of, 308 ff.; primary and secondary, 505–06; queen of faculties, 605; realm of opposed to reality, 524; required by all other faculties, 605; restrained by philosophy, 408; secondary pleasures, 309; the transmuter, 1008; theory of, 1001

Imitation, with no original, 1494

Imitation (*see also* Mimesis), 133; and emulation, 103, 257, 397; and original, 350; differ in poetry and painting, 379; ill effects of, 353; in painting, 394; life imitates art, 719; not end of poetry, 169; vulgar, 303

Immigration, and new cultural dominant, 1511

Immorality, of poetry, 541

Incest, love choice, 751; permitted to gods, 755

Incest dreams, typical, 754

Indication, 773; and motivation, 774

Individualism, 569–70; in Whitman, 674 ff.

Individuation, principle of, 688

Infection, as transfer of feeling, 759

Initiative, and method, 511

Inquiry, 242; do not block way of, 666

Inspiration, 11, 12, 172, 394, 451; and sublimity, 100; madness, 12–13, 36

Institutions, of criticism, 625

Intellect, being where and what it sees, 575; doubled on itself, 575

Intellectual, intuition, 629, 1205; native, and Western culture, 1192; power, as cause, 211; principle, 129

Intellectuals, colonized, must build own nation, 1202; ecclesiastical, 938; formation of, 937; negro in U.S., 945; organic and traditional, 937–38; social function of, 939; traditional: absent in U. S., 945; urban and rural, 941–42

Intention, 479; and expression, 776; and irony, 479; and meaning, 853; and poetry, 474; artistic, 1313; author's, 1027 ff.; not available as standard, 1027

Intentional fallacy, 1145; romantic, 1028

Interpellation, of individuals as subjects, 1302–03

Interpretant, requires correlate, 658

Interpretation, and community, 1402; and intention, 143; and method, 157; and seeing, 852; four fold, 151, 154; in anthropology, part of consultable record, 1342; interpretation of, 1215; mechanistic and hermeneutic, 1300; moral, 154–55; of scripture, 149; principles of faith, hope and charity, 143; read text as written, 300; resists conceptual articulation, 1339

Interpreters, and institutional community, 1402

Intimidation, as symbolic violence, 1409

Introspection, not required for logic, 657

Irony, 473; and context, 1044; and incomprehensibility, 480; and paradox, 1072; and pressures of context, 1048; and reflection, 320; and structure, 1043 ff.; dramatic, 967; in poetry, 1042; Socratic, 476

ISA, Ideological state apparatuses, 1298 ff.

Islam, and nationalism, 1190

J

Judaism, and Fascism, 1010

Judgment, by standards of past, 808; determinant and reflective, 419; faculty of, 419; rectitude of, 338; without prejudice, 327–28

Justice, 24, and literary heritage, 629; discourse of, 637; fragility of idea, 638; hope for under capitalism, 1512

K

Kant's Critical Philosophy, Peirce's critique of, 636

Knowledge, philosophical, turned back upon itself, 1316; pure and political, 1374

Koran (Qur'an), 323, 350

L

Labor, division of, 611; vulgar Marxist conception of, 998

Language, "original" never existed, 1236; "ordinary" and "poetic," 1349; a logically perfect, 741; acquisition of, 1170–71; aestheticizing of, 1439; and dead metaphor, 905; and dictatorship of private realm, 1054; and human nature, 532; and political unification, 1410; and speaking (parole), 531; as fossil poetry, 574; as immediate given, 526; as kind of wealth, 1404; as medium and practice, 1363; bipolar structure, 1133; contingency of, 1461; depth of, 531; devastation of, threat to humanity, 1054; differences without positive terms, 793; disguises thought, 830; foreign, changes world-view, 520; forms man, 528; house of Being, 1053; imperfection of, 741; materiality of, 1367; not a medium or entity, 1464, 1466; of *real* life, 505; official, and the state, 1405 ff.; origins of, 321; referential and emotive, 1085; totality of propositions, 829

Language game, 838 ff.; and rule, 845; form of life, 841

Langue and parole, 1121; brackets out other linguistic structures, 1345

Latency period, 753

Latent content, 748

Law, and idea, 520; as relation, 512

Leading thought, 511

Legislators, 41; lawgiver, 471; poets unacknowledged, 551

Legitimacy, cultural, 1190

Legitimation, and school system, 1407–08; cultural, 628; economic and social conditions, 1404–05; of criticism, 575; social, 1107

Lesbian, 1490 ff.

Letters, 29, 62; and knowledge, 45; invention of, 37; origin of, 321

Liar (*see also* Lying), art of framing lies in the right way, 66; basis of civilized society, 719; poet as, 16 ff., 163

Linguistic, community and linguistic domination, 1406; competence and performance, 1166; difference related to social and economic, 1412; differences, 528; system, created by social fact, 790; turn, 630, 1462; unification and the state, 1407; value, 789

Linguistic competence, as Saussure's *langue,* 1404

Linguistics, textual, 1240

Literacy, culture of, 628; transnational and graduate curriculum, 1520

Literariness, devices in literature common outside, 1345; not aesthetic response, 1321; not primarily mimetic, 1322; object of science of literature, 870

Literary history, and literary theory, 1238 ff.; as succession of systems, 1250; renewal of, 1239

Literary study, crisis of reconceptualizing object, 1508

Literary theory, and distinction between graduate and undergraduate, 1506; as application of Saussurian linguistics, 1321; inadequacy for novel, 915; language of self-resistance, 1327; linked to cultural theory, 1357; object of,

1320; separated from literary criticism and history, 1320; upsets rooted ideologies, 1322

Literature, "return" to, 628; a primary source of knowledge, 1317; and experiment, 700; and intellectual autonomy, 627; and nation, 651; and philosophy of value, 974; and society, 1250; as instruction in otherness, 1513; as linguistic category, 1346; as medicine, 1012; equipment for living, 1012 ff.; has never recognized the People, 676; historical conception of, 1357; hypothetical creation, 1148; informs only about its own language, 1322; reflects traits of civilization, 644; socially formative function of, 1254; sociology of, 1243; transcript of culture, 640

Logic, and fable, 318; and rhetoric inverted in Derrida, 1431; and validity of metaphysics, 980; as theory of science, 770; errors of Heidegger, 985; Heidegger on, 1064; limitation of traditional, 239; of classes, 286–87; of depiction, 830; poetic, 319 ff.

Logical Positivism, and Heidegger, 1051–52; and New Criticism, 1, 856, 978

Logocentrism, 1228

Lordship and Bondage, 561 ff.

Love, purest poetic theme, 584; universal agent, 363

Lying (see also Liar), 22; and plausibility, 121; and will to deceive, 142; decay of, 712 ff.; poets not liars, 163, 198

M

Madness, four kinds, 36

Magic, 18; view of world, 862

Man Thinking, and bookworm, 567

Marxism, and existentialism, 1176 ff.; going beyond, 1178; living, 1183; not taught, 1181; sclerosis of theory of, 1185

Master-Slave, see Lordship and Bondage, 561 ff.

Mathematics, 33; definition makes object, 517

Matter, and spirit, 471; held by Ideas, 136

Meaning, and connotation, 784; and fiction, 737; and internal image, 736; and mode of verification, 987; and objective reference, 781; and place in language game, 1466; and polysemy, 138; and reference, 781; and relation to tradition, 808; and syntax, 981; as criteria of application, 981; as synonymous with sense, 783; as truth-value, 738; core of, not paraphrase, 1037; determinate unavailable, 1396; direct and indirect, 736; five levels, 1163–64; four kinds of: sense, tone, feeling, intention, 863–64; hidden, 237; hide behind misleading sign, 1314; inseparable from context, 1045; internal and external evidence, 1030; inward, 1023; inward / outward, 1139, 1141; literal / descriptive, 1140; not a process, 855; not acquired through association, 981; of name, object itself, 736; of propositions lies in future, 672; pattern of resolved stresses, 1039; picture theory of, 636, 825 ff.

Meaningless expressions, 783

Mediation, 636–37; and language, 526; and objectivity, 634; mediating representation, 658

Memory, imagination and feeling, 462

Menippean satire, 923

Metaphor, 63, 72, 319; and figure an abuse of language, 296; and scripture, 159; and similarity, 145, 1133; and sublime, 111; and metonymy, 1132 ff.; commitment to, 1044; from body, 320; in scripture, 145, 150; instrument of thought, 637; sign of genius, 65; subdued, 906

Metaphysicians, musicians without musical ability, 989

Metaphysics, and attitude toward life, 988; and culture, 1115 ff.; and logic, 318, 661; in signified / signifier, 1207; inadequate substitute for art, 989; meaningless, 633; meditations on, 1114 ff.; modern and Hegel, 986; no language independent of its history, 1207; possibility of, 117; possible origin in mythology, 988; rejection of and empirical science, 979; sterile, 980; thinks the Being of beings, 1056

Method, and relations of things, 509; and self-development, 516; foreseeing the whole, 508; in fine arts, 513; not dead arrangement, 511; of traces, 208; philosophy and science, 513; progressive transition, 511; unity with progression, 516

Metonymy, 319; and contiguity, 1133

Mimesis (see also Imitation), 2, 121, 227; aesthetic pleasure, 53–54; and ideality, 524; and intentional fallacy, 1158; and making (poesis), 38; and names, 42; and Platonism, 1075; and pleasure, 53; and reality, 31; and truth, 30, 33; completing nature, 50; copy ancients, 299; eikastic / phantasic, 39–40, 199, 218; falsehood, 19–20; inferior, 34; means, object, manner, 52; mirror up to nature, 412, 1020, 1144; narration, 25; natural to man, 53, 179; objects of, 216; of action, 25; pleasant, 69; psychic, 1497 ff.; poetry not strictly imitative, 345; prohibited, 25; three removes from truth, 33

Mimetism, and loss, 1497

Mirror stage, 991 ff.

Modernism, 621; and the unpresentable, 1421

Multiculturalism, and universalism, 1256; liberal, 1510

Music, 16, 618; and method, 514; as bad art, 768; education in, 29; grammar of, 475; in tragedy, 55; sheer form, 470; spirit of, 690; type of all art, 722

Mystery, 131, 151, 731; and revelation, 158; and wonder in art, 146

Myth, 166; and education, 120; and thought, 1017; and truth, 89; gross constituent units, 1122; no unity or source, 1211; obstacle of origin and truth in, 1125; poets and legislators, 88; record and table, 1123

Mythology, 234; and machinery, 615; first science, 313–14

N

Name(s), 41; and definite descriptions, 815; and mixed modes, 289 ff.; and simple ideas, 293; designates its meaning,

737; expresses its sense, 737; limit of, 284; meaning as object, 778; proper, 735

Nameless, learning to exist in the, 1055

Nation, and national print language, 1428; and print culture, 1424–25; gentile nations, 315–16

Nation state, and literature, 627; and Platonic Republic, 628

National consciousness, 1424 ff.

National criticism, 578

National culture, and colonial domination, 1198; and fight for freedom, 1198 ff.; consciousness not nationalism, 1201; narratives of, 626

National origin validation, for cultural identity, 1512

Nationality, and epic past, 917; and language, 528

Native culture, error of revaluing in colonial frame, 1200

Native writers, addressing own people: national literature, 1199; evolution of, 1193; should use past to open future, 1196

Nature, 134; and culture: opposition, 1209; as dictionary, 606; follows landscape painters, 721; oracle of, 519; second, 574; Shakespeare as sport of, 495; too uncomfortable, 712; two senses of, 514 n25

Necessity, subjective, 432

Negation, and self-consciousness, 563

Negative Capability, 536

Negativity, truth of, 564

Negritude, poets of, 1190

Negroes, African and U.S., 945; in U.S. and Africa, different problems, 1190

Neo-Aristotelian critics, 1071

New Criticism, 5, 806, 856, 894, 953, 964, 1034; doubt about, 1072

New Historicism, 1478; and value judgment, 1480; renew marvelous, 1488

Nomadic thought, 1443 passim.

Nominalism, 661 ff., cf. 287; and positivism, trivial consciousness, 1115; incompatible with evolutionary systems, 662–63

Notation, complex, 1367; essence of, 829

Novel, and correspondence to real life, 892; and experimental method, 699 ff.; and Socratic dialogues, 922; as compendia of spiritual life, 475; as dominant genre, 914; as Socratic dialogues, 474; genre in the making, 916; no canon of its own, 913

Novelist, experimental, 709

O

Objective correlate, 780

Objective correlative, 806, 1148

Objective-subjective, 502 ff.; distinction difficult to maintain, 1019

Oedipus complex, 747 ff.; and morality, 754; and opposition to psychoanalysis, 753; backwards in the Trobriands, 1338;
described, 750; does not explain *Oedipus Rex,* 973; Freud's comments part of myth, 1126

Ontology, and ethics, 1066; and philosophy of Being, modes of reaction, 1113; and reproduction of social life, 1112; Heidegger's, political past no deterrent, 1110; ontological need, 1110 ff.

OPOYAZ group, 796, 870

Oppression, and class, 609–10; basis of society, 614

Orient, as Europe's Other, 1370

Orientalism, 1370 ff.; and area studies, 1370; and German scholarship, 1378–79; and political imperialism, 1376; as distribution of geopolitical awareness, 1375; as style of thought, 1370–71; *vs.* imitation, 718

Other, gendered, 1497; installed in self, 1497; installed in the self, 1497

Otherness, double sense of, 562

P

Painting, 39; and poetry, 79 (*see* Poetry)

Paradigm(s), and acquired similarity relations, 1288; and different worlds, 1289; and incommensurability, 1291; and logical positivism, 1280; and metaphysics, 1286; and scientific communities, 1283; and translation, 1293; as disciplinary matrix, 1285–86; as exemplary achievements, 1282; exemplars philosophically deeper, 1282; in teaching how to read, 1391; pre-paradigm competition for dominance, 1283; relation to theory, 1285; revolutions and relativism, 1294 ff.; shared examples (exemplars), 1287; two main senses, 1282; when applied to other disciplines, 1295

Paradox, 40–41, 625; and irony, 475; in poetry stems from language, 1077

Paraphrase, heresy of, 1036 ff.

Parmenides, *esti gar einai* unthought today, 1060

Parole, individual utterance, 932

Past, made present, 641; present moment of, 810; relation of poet to, 808

Perfection, and judgment of taste, 427

Peripetia (reversal), 57

Personality, escape from, 810; product of social inter-relations, 930; thick wall of, 619

Persuasion, 169; means of, 70

Perversity, polymorphous, 751

Philology, and Romanticism, 1244

Philosophy, and class consciousness, 1177; and literature, difference of genre, 1432–33, 1441; and *philosophies,* 1176; and poetics, 636; and praxis, 1177; clarification of thoughts, 831; critique of language, 830; dead or in crisis, 1178; not a natural science, 831; result of poetry and practice, 478; Scheme-content model, 1463; sets limits to natural science, 832; similarity to literary criticism, 1440

Philosophy and Poetry, ancient quarrel, 36, 147

Phoneme, the unimaginable itself, 1229

Photography, and the postmodern, 1419

Picture, a model of, form of reality, 826–27

Pity and fear (or terror), 59, 180, 231

Platonism, and modernist, 957; Nietzsche, Heidegger, Freud, last Platonist, 1208; Plato *vs.* Aristotle, 178

Play, and presence, 1214; definition of, 257; game of the world, 1232; of structure, 1206; *Spieltrieb,* 460

Pleasure, aesthetic, follows judgment, 424, 477; and pain, 335; grand elementary principle of, 487

Plot, in tragedy, 55–56; of Oedipus, 58; probable and necessary, 57; unity of, 56, 180

Plot and Story, 874, 876

Poem(s), as image of eternal truth, 541; as mental objects, 622; heroic, 231; long, contradiction in terms, 581; meter-making argument, 572; significance in structure, 1006

Poet, as catalyst, 809; as creator, 171, 317; as language maker, 574; as legislator, 32; as maker, 188; as man speaking to men, 486; as prophet (*vates*), 187; as sayer, 571; author of highest wisdom, 550; intention: the poem itself, 1146; no personality to express, 809; Plato as poet, 187; represents complete man, 570; Shakespeare, largest soul, 271; "strong," 1467

Poetic language, and image, 871; and practical language, 871; fallacy of, 1344 ff.

Poetic logic, in Cassirer, 1016

Poetic structure, resembles a play, 1040; structure of meanings, 1037

Poetic theory, impoverishment of, 1075

Poetics, and history of literature, 875; historical, 875; reduction to grammar, 1079

Poetry, and appearance, 32; and dream, 955; and education, 87, 89, 120; and history, 57, 190, 232; and language really used, 483; and legislators, 88; and liberation, 577; and logic: differ relative to will, 551; and music, 299; and ontology, 954 ff.; and oratory, 91; and painting, 35, 121, 191, 235, 411, 485, 1019; and philosophy, 123, 165, 191; and poem, 507; and poet, 507; and prophecy, 539; and prose, 532–33; and prose: linked to metaphor, metonymy, 1135; and revolution, 540; and science, 477, 478, 487, 958, 963; and science: ancient problem, 1085; and scripture, 158, 188; and solitude, 91, 92; and sophistic, 219–20; and Spinoza, 479; and theology, 158; and theology alike in method, 159; and wisdom, 314–15; as breath and finer spirit of knowledge, 487; as civic institution, 175, 179, 219; as concrete whole, 1084; as divine, 189; as form of reasoning, 634–35; as game, 221; as instituted, 626; as likeness to history, 177; as organism, 115; as overflow of powerful feelings, 484; as paradigmatic, 623; as philosophy, 87, 314; Coleridge's definition of, 1075; completing

nature, 189; connate with origin of man, 538; defense of, 186; differentiation of ends, 1076; differs from exact truth, 325; differs from painting, 379; disturbing moral life, 1020; emotion recollected in tranquility, 490; escape from emotion and personality, 810; final cause, 224; first rank, 440; highest learning, 360; immediate object pleasure, 506; knowledge, 31, 197; modern, 205; most spiritual art, 561; nature, poet and poem, 516; not strictly imitative, 345; only criticized by poetry, 477; origin of, 53; origins of, 318; physical, Platonic, metaphysical, 954 ff.; preparation for philosophy, 121; proceeds from God, 160; pure, 956; purged / exiled, 28, 36, 201, 223; record of best and happiest minds, 550; reject poetry, reject Old Testament, 162; rhythmic creation of beauty, 584; speaking picture, 479; supreme use of language, 972; teaches virtue, 195, 198; touchstones, 602; truth and seriousness, 603; unfair criticism of, 62; utility of, 548

Poets, as legislators, 539, 551; bards and liberating gods, 577; do not lie, never affirm, 198; exiled, 479; high mission of being unreliable, 718; like cooperating thoughts of one mind, 544

Political parties, and organic intellectual, 942

Political party, proletariat, 613

Polysemy, 154

Positionality, and orientalism, 1373

Position, of intellectuals, 943

Postmodern, 1418 ff.; a part of the modern, 1422; as critique of the Enlightenment, 1419; sublime and unpresentable in, 1423

Poststructuralism, 624

Power, absolute, 565; languages of, 1427; one, opposite manifestations, 518; theatricality of, 1477

Pragmatic maxim, 668, 671

Pragmatism / pragmaticism, 635, 668 ff.

Predicate, indefinite determinability of, 655

Prescind, 656

Presence, instituted via possibility of disappearance, 1218; metaphysics of, 1207

Privilege, and aesthetics, 627; politics of, 623

Production, forces and relations, 1180; industrial, 609; instruments and mode, 610–11; of things parallels ideas, 210; relations of, 615–16

Professionalism, 1501

Profit, as universal law of world, 1114

Property, 611 ff.

Proposition, and truth functions, 835; only one complete analysis, 828; picture of reality, 830; shows its sense, 830

Propositional function, 813; sign, 828

Prose and verse, 540; no essential difference, 485

Proverbs, 1012; as strategies, 1013

Pseudo-concept, 980

Pseudo-statement, 860, 980; and belief, 861; metaphysical, 984

Psyche, permanent failure of expression, 1498

Purposiveness, 417, 419, 425, 429 ff.

Q

Quotation, and repeatability: Derrida and Searle, 1434

Qur'an, *see* Koran, 323

R

Race, a source of moral state, 645

Radical politics, 936, 938 ff.

Rape, asymmetry of law, 1471

Reader, experience of, reception by, 1240

Reading, as contemporary theoretical problem, 1326; creative, 568; in original languages, 1523–24; not a half sleep, 685; same nature as writing, 568; systematically avoided today, 1324

Realism, and metonymy, 1135; failure as method, 717

Reason, 133; and imagination, 458, 538; as ratio, 457; subject centered critique of, 1430

Reasoning, in art as in conduct, 371; literature a form of, 634; practical, 668

Reception, aesthetics of, 1238; and aesthetic value, 1242; and genre, 1240; and historical unfolding of understanding, 1246; and horizon of expectation, 1241; and literary evolution, 1247; history of, 1238–39

Relations, and method, 509; materials of method, 512

Relativism, and paradigm(s), 1294–95; social and loss of substantiality, 1112

Religion, as unconscious poetry, 599; formal, economic, predatory, 1009; guide to progress, 765

Repetition, makes structure of myth apparent, 1131

Representation, and communication, 1216; and expression, 978–79; and imagination, 1215; and meaning, 1215 ff.; and signification: graphism, 1222; critique of, 636; expression and imagination, 1219

Repression, 748

Resonance, 1483 ff.

Revolution, and proletariat, 613; in linguistics, 1166; role of Bourgeois, 610

Revolutionary movements, 629

Rhetoric, and greed, 92; and sophistic, 125; and sublime, 102; dreary equation with psychology, not epistemology, 1327; politicized, 623; wisdom applied to discourse, 88

Rhetorical reading, and routinization effect, 1505; as disarticulation of *trivium,* 1327; as theory of impossibility of theory, 1327; symptom of unrationalized theory curriculum, 1508

Rhizome, 1443 ff.; and plateau, always in middle, 1454; connection and heterogeneity, 1445; not amenable to structural or generative model, 1448

Rigorismento, 947

Ritual, and dream, 1155–56; and magic, 1161

Romantic art, painting, music, poetry, 560–61

Romantic poetry, progressive and universal, 477

Romanticism, and subjectivism, 926; linked to metaphor, 1135; poem and poet, 481

Ruling class, and state, 946

S

Sacrifice, 17

School, and reproduction of social order, 1500

Science, and myth, 690; and poetry, 475, 1082; as paradigmatic human activity, 1458; division of, 238; foundations of, 240; incomplete without poetry, 599; strikingly different from other fields, 1296

Science of literature, 868

Scientific Revolution, 207; as metaphoric redescriptions, 1465

Scientific thought, and primitive mind, 1131

Screen memories, 749

Scripture, 141–46

Sculpture, 133, 559–60

Seeing, as interpreting, 849–50

Self-consciousness, duplication of, 562; in itself and for itself, 561–62

Self-reference, and myth, 1211; and speech, 1219

Self-trust, 568

Semantics, in poetry, 880

Semiology, as future science, 788

Semiotic(s), 140; and speculative grammar, 1231; Peirce as inventor of, 652; theory of culture, 1329

Sense, and meaning, 735 ff.; primary and secondary, 854; secondary not metaphorical, 854

Sense-giving, and sense-fulfilling acts, 777

Sensibility, 390; acquired and natural, 388; dissociation of, 460

Sentiment, 445; and morality, 323; of beauty, 326; system in, 643

Sexuality, and disclosure, 1491; and identity, truth, knowledge, 1471; and perversions, 752–53; in children, 751

Sibling rivalry, 749

Sign, and notation, 1365 ff.; arbitrary, 1229; arbitrary only from position of alienation, 1366; not an image, 1229; originally wrought by fiction, 1219; provisionality, a safeguard, 1493; thing itself a sign, 1232

Sign language, and translation, 829

Sign(s), and divine will, 317; and doctrine, 141; and expression not synonyms, 773; and first language, 319; and thing or concept, 525; arbitrary, 283, 788, 829; as motif, 1139; concept and sound image, 787; definite sense, 736; Icon, Index, Symbol, 659; literal and figurative, 146; natural and conventional, 140, 144; natural or arbitrary, 44; primitive, 828; signified, signifier, 787; universe storehouse of, 606; use=meaning, 829; word as, 282

Signification, 140; and difference, 792; infinite chain, 632; literal, historical, allegorical, 151, 154

Signifier, linear nature of, 789; overabundance of, 1213

Similarity, in difference (*see* Metaphor), 65

Similitude, 217; and dissimilitude, 490; of things, 286

Slavery, abolition of, 546

Social contract, and idea, 520

Social democracy, and conformism, 998

Social formation, 1307–08

Social justice, and Marxism, 608

Social situation, determines utterance, 928

Social sympathies, and imagination, 538–39

Sodomy, and law, 1472

Sokal affair, 634

Sophistic, and oratory, 126; first and second, 125

Sophists, 8, 38; and philosopher, 126; philosophical rhetoric, 125

Sophrosyny, 131

Soul, and form, 212; and matter, 130; faculty for Beauty, 129; universe externalization of, 573

Sound, syllable, not phoneme, 787

Spectacle, in tragedy, 59

Speech, and writing: natural order, 1223; representation of itself, 1219

Speech act, individual, a contradiction, 935

Speech act(s), and felicity conditions, 1350; and fiction, 1437; and fictivity, 1353; and gender, 1471; and literary discourse, 1344 ff.; classification, 1349; context dependent, 1351; debate between Searle and Derrida, 1434; illocutionary, perlocutionary, 1349; terms same in literature and other discourse, 1352

Speech functions, communicative and intimating, 776

Spirit, 448; and matter, 471; in aesthetic sense, 438; like voice, 214

Spiritual, perception, 455

State, 936; and civil society, 948 ff.

State apparatuses, coercive power, 941

Statement, in poetry, 1037

Stimulus-response, difficulties with, 1169–70

Story, 16; dangerous, 21

Structure, and center, 1207; rupture and redoubling, 1206

Structuralism, 5; and crisis, 629; and study of myth, 1120 ff.; as general methodology, 1311; method brings order, 1128

Style, 70; and character, 28; as literary category, 1250

Stylistic devices, 874

Subaltern, 936

Subaltern groups, 946–47; fragmented history, 947

Subject, and performance, 1496; class position, 1298; incapacitation of, 1113 ff.; other, God, 1305

Subject position, and New Historicism, 1480

Sublation, 552

Sublime, 305–06, 399; amplification, 102; and beautiful, 340–41, 418, 433, 458; and inspiration, 100; and pain, 437; and postmodern, 1420–22; defined, 434; echo of great soul, 98; in expression, 95; mathematical and dynamical, 434–38; source in pain and danger, 340; transport, 95; uniting contradictions, 101

Substance, and essence, 288; inapplicable to predicate, 656; phonic, reduction of, 1234; spiritual, 212

Suffrage, dangers of, 674

Superstructure, 939

Supplement, and signifier, 1213

Suppositions, idealizing, 1436

Symbol, 660; and allegory, 519; and linguistic sign, 788; as archetype, mythic phase, 1149; as image, formal phase, 1143; as monad, anagogic phase, 1159; develop out of signs, 1231; emblems, 573; Frye, theory of, 1136 ff.; literal-descriptive phase, 1139; nature as, 572–73; passage of world into soul, 574; symbolic art, 556

Symbolic form, 1018

Synecdoche, and metaphor, 320

Syntagmatic relations, and associative relations, 794–95

Syntax, and intelligibility, 732; and type confusion, 987

System, dangers in love of, 568; negation of by Kierkegaard, 1179; not scheme, 512

T

Tabula rasa, 281

Tacit knowledge, 1289 ff.

Taste, 400; and social affections, 372; belongs to imagination, 337; between intellect and moral sense, 583; corrupted by voluptuousness, 376; differences of, 323; faculty of, 334; grounded in common standard, 373–74; mental and bodily, 326; no disputing about, 372, 499; not an instinct, 339; not simple idea, 338; principles of, 405; standard same in all, 333; uniformity and morals, 375; uniformity of, 374–75; wrong, a defect of judgment, 338

Tautegorical, 519

Tautologies, and contradictions, 834; and truth conditions, 834

Teaching, of literature, transnational, 1510; scholarly, not intersubjective, 1318

Techné, 623, 1001, 1149

Technology, 940

Teleology, 48; and nature, 50

Text, as answer to question, 1245

Theology, pagan poets theologians, 166; poetic, natural, Christian, 315

Theoretician, changing conception of, 1319

Theories, and idea in electricity and magnetism, 518; and practice, 148, 623; as relation, 513; as social critique, 623; critical; orientation of, 1087 ff.; expressive, 1096; follows practice, 626; insufficiency in idea of, 622; interdependence of, 636; mimetic, 1088; objective, 1099; pragmatic, moral purpose, 1092; relation of poetry to, 623

Theorist, master, and charisma, 1503

Theory, choice and criteria, 1286; crisis of, 1503; impossibility of, and rhetorical readings, 1327; in interpretive science, 1340; passing, 1464; question distinction from politics, culture, media, 1490; resistance to trope in language, 1326; scientific, no algorithm for theory choice, 1292; undoing of, and rhetorical analysis, 1325

Thinking, and *techné,* 1054; and truth of Being, 1053; creates object, 528; technical interpretation of, 1054; to come, no longer philosophy, 1070

Thought, and word interdependent, 527; dependent on language, 527; logical picture of facts, 827; modeled on tree and root, 1451

Totality, wage war on, 1423

Totalization, and philosophy, 1177; and play, 1212; useless or impossible, 1212

Touchstone, of poetic quality, 602

Trace, difference cannot be thought without, 1236; instituted, 1230; map not trace, 1448; method of, 208–09

Tradition, and armed struggle, 1193; and epic past, 919; and individual talent, 807 ff.; and innovation, 80

Tragedy, and decay of social life, 543; and pseudotragic, 96; definition of, 55, 173; parts of, 55

Transcendence, a European disease, 1452; and concept of *Dasein,* 1065

Transcendental illusion, and terror, 1423

Treasure, metaphor of, 1404

Tree, as image of world, thought, 1444–45

Trinitarianism, 494

Tropes (*see* Figure); four types, 319–21

Truth, and mathematics, 456; as mobile army of metaphors, 694, 1465; cannot be "out there," 1459; made not found, 1458; no final, 667; no theory-independent access, 1295; property of sentences, 1460; "T" = God or world as His project, 1459

Truth tables, 833

Truth-value, 738

Two cultures, 634

Type confusion, and syntax, 987

U

Ugly, as primary evil, 131

Unconscious, 12; as infantile mental life, 752

Understanding, creates general and universal, 286

Unities, dramatic, 81, 180, 244, 258; ignored in Shakespeare, 366–68

Unity, of action, 245; of place, 250; of plot, 245; of time, 249; voice, 424

Universality, 479–80; and ruling, 1532 ff.

Universe, animated, 211; infinite, 213; storehouse of images and signs, 606

Utility, contrary to art, 711

V

Verification, 979

Verisimilitude, 177, 225

Vernacular, administrative and nationalism, 1426

Vienna Circle, 978

Virtue, and beauty, 128; and vice, 323

Vision, and allegory, 447; every eye sees differently, 449; of Last Judgment, 458

Vitalism, 516

Voice, self-present, 1220

Voyeuristic-sadistic, 993

Vulgarity, postulate of, 474

W

Wage labor, 614

Wit, and revenge, 475; erected, 189

Women, and fiction, 444–46; education of, 442 ff.; freedom of, 546; writers, 172; and loneliness, 888; way barred by men, 886; recovering lost works, 1383

Wonder, 69, 1486 ff.

Word, a two-sided act, 928; and meaning, 836; as shared territory, 928; complexity of, 525; once poem, 574

Words, abuse of, 295; affect without image, 343; aggregate, abstract, arbitrary, 341; and ideas, 310; as actions, 571; effects of, 342; general, 284–85; imperfect, 289; reasons for imperfection, 294; refer to reality of things, 283

Working class, as "trained gorilla," 939

World, totality of facts, 825; World Soul, 210

Worship, and poetic tales, 448

Writing, alphabetic, 1229; and archetypal violence, 1223; and interest, 474; as clothing, veil, 1223; as usurpation of origin, 1226; definition in Saussure, Plato, Aristotle, 1220; extends beyond "creative" and "discursive," 1358; inferior to living speech, 38; invention of, 37; judgment of, 298–99; systems of: Ideographic, Phonetic, 1222; tyranny of: Rousseau, 1227; want of skill in, 298